0   200 Miles

0   300 Kilometres

ENCYCLOPEDIA OF
PLANTS & FLOWERS

ENCYCLOPEDIA OF
PLANTS &
FLOWERS

EDITOR-IN-CHIEF
CHRISTOPHER BRICKELL

LONDON, NEW YORK, MUNICH, MELBOURNE, DELHI

DK LONDON
Senior Editor Helen Fewster
Project Editors Emma Callery, Joanna Chisholm, Chauney Dunford,
Caroline Reed, Becky Shackleton, Caroline West
Additional Editorial Assistance Monica Byles, May Corfield, Annelise
Evans, Diana Vowles, Fiona Wild
Senior Art Editors Joanne Doran, Elaine Hewson, Lucy Parissi
Designers Mark Latter, Laura Mingozzi, Vicky Read, Becky Tennant
Jacket Designer Mark Cavanagh
Database Manager David Roberts
Production Editor Joanna Byrne
Picture Researchers Mel Watson, Janet Johnson
DK Picture Library Jenny Baskaya
Managing Editor Esther Ripley
Managing Art Editor Alison Donovan
Associate Publisher Liz Wheeler
Art Director Peter Luff, Bryn Walls
Publisher Jonathan Metcalf

North American Editors Christine Heilman, Rebecca Warren
American Horticultural Society Editors David J. Ellis,
Caroline Bentley, Katherine Hoffman, Eileen Powell

DK INDIA
Editor Nidhilekha Mathur
Assistant Editors Archana Ramachandran, Suefa Lee,
Parameshwari Sircar
Designer Nitu Singh
Senior DTP Designer Tarun Sharma
Managing Editor Suchismita Banerjee
Managing Art Editor Romi Chakraborty
DTP Manager Sunil Sharma

FIRST EDITION
Senior Editor Jane Aspden
Editors Liza Bruml, Joanna Chisholm, Roger Smoothy, Jo Weeks
Additional editorial assistance from Jane Birdsell, Lynn Bresler,
Jenny Engelmann, Kate Grant, Shona Grimbly, Susanna Longley,
Andrew Mikolajski, Diana Miller, Celia Van Oss, Anthony Whitehorn
Senior Art Editor Ina Stradins
Designer Amanda Lunn

First edition published by Macmillan Publishing Company in 1989
Second edition published by DK Publishing in 2002
This fully revised and updated edition first published in 2011

Dorling Kindersley is represented in Canada by Tourmaline Editions Inc.
662 King Street West, Suite 304, Toronto, Ontario M5V 1M7

12 13 14 15 16   10 9 8 7 6 5 4 3 2 1
001—176672—October/2011
Copyright © 1989, 2002, 2011 Dorling Kindersley Limited
All rights reserved

Published in Great Britain by Dorling Kindersley Limited.

ISBN 978-1-55363-172-9

Color reproduction by Colourscan, Singapore
Printed and bound in China by L.Rex Printing Co Ltd

DK books are available at special discounts when purchased in bulk for corporate sales,
sales promotions, premiums, fund-raising, or educational use. For details, please contact
specialmarkets@tourmaline.ca

Discover more at
www.dk.com

PREFACE

North Americans enjoy many hobbies, but surveys continue to show that gardening is the single most popular leisure time activity. At the same time, given the fast-paced, multitasking, technology-driven lifestyle that seems to be the norm in the 21st century, most of us have less time for gardening than we might like.

In developing this revised and updated edition of the *Encyclopedia of Plants & Flowers*, our goal was to address this challenge by providing a wealth of practical and inspirational plant selection and design information in an easy-to-use format that is suited to both new gardeners and experienced ones.

Among the useful components is the Plant Selector section, which offers detailed lists of plants suited to particular garden sites—such as sun or shade, dry or moist soil, and containers—or plants with particular attributes, such as fragrant flowers or decorative fruits. Within each list, plants are subdivided by type and can be cross-referenced with the more detailed plant entries included in the Plant Catalog and Plant Dictionary sections.

The Plant Catalog is divided into plant groups such as annuals, perennials, bulbs, grasses, shrubs, vines, and trees. Under each broad category, special sections are devoted to popular or useful plant groups that include conifers, hollies, rhododendrons, hydrangeas, roses, clematis, hellebores, daylilies, and daffodils, to name but a few. New to this edition is a section for subtropical plants, orchids, and succulents, which have become very popular for use in containers or for summer color even in regions where they are not fully hardy. Each section of the catalog is further organized into useful categories such as season of bloom, mature size, and flower or foliage color so it is easy to locate plants that will provide exactly the features you want for any garden situation. Each entry includes a color photograph of the plant so you can see exactly what it looks like, and provides complete information on the plant's growing requirements.

In addition to the more than 4,000 plants illustrated in the catalog, another 4,000 are covered in the Plant Dictionary section, providing additional choices that are suitable for a wide range of gardens and regions, and supplementing the growing information provided in the catalog.

Whether you are a new gardener eager to begin designing your first yard or a veteran searching for the perfect plants to fill a few gaps, this encyclopedia allows you to quickly identify a variety of plants that will thrive in different sites in your garden. By enhancing your ability to select the best plants, we hope it will make your garden more enjoyable, successful, and productive—and allow you more time to relax and enjoy the fruits of your labor.

Happy gardening!

CONTRIBUTORS

FIFTH EDITION REVIEWED BY

Zia Allaway	*Bulbs*
Christopher Brickell	*Rock Plants, Climbers*
John R. L. Carter	*Water and Bog Plants*
Philip Clayton	*Perennials*
Philip Harkness	*Roses*
Graham Rice	*Annuals and Biennials, Perennials*
Tony Russell	*Trees, Shrubs*
Julian Shaw	*Tender and Exotics, Plant Dictionary*

FIRST EDITION CONTRIBUTORS

Susyn Andrews	*Hollies*
Larry Barlow with W. B. Wade	*Chrysanthemums*
Kenneth A. Beckett with David Pycraft	*Shrubs, Climbers, Bromeliads, Plant Selector*
John Brookes with Linden Hawthorne	*Introduction*
Eric Catterall with Richard Gilbert	*Begonias*
Allen J. Coombes	*Plant Origins, Trees, Shrubs, Glossary*
Philip Damp with Roger Aylett	*Dahlias*
Kate Donald	*Peonies, Daffodils*
Kath Dryden	*Rock Plants*
Raymond Evison	*Clematis*
Diana Grenfell	*Hostas*
Peter Harkness	*Roses*
Linden Hawthorne	*Chapter Introductions*
Terry Hewitt	*Cacti and Other Succulents*
David Hitchcock	*Carnations and Pinks*
Hazel Key	*Pelargoniums*
Sidney Linnegar	*Irises*
Brian Mathew	*Irises, Bulbs*
Victoria Matthews	*Climbers, Lilies, Tulips*
David McClintock	*Grasses, Bamboos, Rushes and Sedges*
Diana Miller with Richard Gilbert	*Perennials African Violets*
John Paton	*Perennials*
Charles Puddle	*Camellias*
Wilma Rittershausen with Sabina Knees	*Orchids*
Peter Q. Rose with Hazel Key	*Ivies*
Keith Rushforth	*Conifers*
A. D. Schilling	*Rhododendrons and Azaleas*
Arthur Smith	*Gladioli*
Philip Swindells with Peter Barnes with Kath Dryden and Jack Wemyss-Cooke with Peter Robinson	*Ferns Primulas Water Plants*
John Thirkell	*Delphiniums*
Alan Toogood	*Annuals and Biennials*
Major General Patrick Turpin with David Small	*Heathers*
Michael Upward	*Perennials*
John Wright with Nancy Darnley	*Fuchsias*

CONTENTS

HOW TO USE THIS BOOK

The core of this book is its two main sections—The Plant Catalog and the Plant Dictionary. Here you will find descriptions and cultivation advice for thousands of plants. Plant Names and Origins explains the system for classifying and naming plants, while the new introduction, Creating a Garden, offers advice on design, planting, and basic pruning.

The Plant Selector

The Plant Selector recommends plants for a variety of sites, soils, and purposes, making it easy to find one to suit your needs. The list is divided into 23 useful categories, including plants for groundcover in sun or shade, drought-tolerant plants, fragrant plants, and those suitable for hedges and windbreaks. Many are included in the Plant Catalog and are cross-referenced to a picture and full description.

Photographic reference
Garden themes and uses are illustrated, together with photographs of selected plants.

Top choices
Plants are arranged by group, then listed alphabetically.

The Plant Catalog

This section combines plant portraits and descriptions in a colorful catalog of 4,000 plants divided into groups: Trees (including conifers); Shrubs; Roses; Climbers and Wall Shrubs; Perennials (including grasses, bamboos, rushes, sedges, and ferns); Annuals, Biennials, and Bedding Plants; Rock Plants; Bulbs; Water and Bog Plants; and Tender and Exotic Plants. A short introduction to each group is followed by plants arranged by size, season of interest, and color and includes feature panels on plants with particular appeal.

Catalog page
If you know a plant but cannot recall its name, have a specimen that you want to identify, or simply wish to choose plants for your garden based on their size or coloring, the Plant Catalog is the place to start.

Page headings
The headings on each page reflect the way in which each plant group is subdivided—usually by size and main season of interest. (See also Size categories, left.)

Plant portraits
Color photographs assist in the identification and selection of plants.

Feature panels
Plant types or genera of special interest to the gardener are presented in separate feature panels within the appropriate group.

Key characteristics
The introduction describes the plants and gives guidance on cultivation and planting.

Plant portraits
Close-up photographs of individual flowers or plants allow quick identification or selection.

Plant names
The botanical name is given and the Group or classification where appropriate. Descriptions and cultivation advice appear in the Plant Dictionary.

Size categories

Within most groups in the Plant Catalog, plants are arranged by size (then subsequently by season of interest). Size categories range from large to small, but are defined differently from group to group. Sizes are based on plant heights. The specific height ranges for large, medium, and small can be found in the introductory section for the relevant plant group.

Color order

Within each group, plants are arranged by the color of their main feature. Colors are arranged in the same order: from white through reds, purples, and blues to greens, yellows, and oranges. Variegated plants are categorized by the color of their foliage variegation (e.g., white or yellow).

Key to symbols

- ☼ Prefers sun
- ☼ Prefers partial shade
- ☀ Tolerates full shade

- H Height (or length of trailing stems)
- S Spread

- ◊ Prefers well-drained soil
- ◐ Prefers moist soil
- ● Prefers wet soil

- pH Needs acidic soil
- ① Toxic plant

Rhododendron 'Percy Wiseman'
Evergreen rhododendron with a domed, compact habit. In late spring produces open funnel-shaped, peach-yellow flowers that fade to white.

☼ ◒ pH ① Z6–9 H9–6

10ft 3m
10ft 3m
0

Cultivation, cold-hardiness, and heat tolerance
Symbols show the plant's preferred growing conditions and tolerance of cold and heat. However, the climatic and soil conditions of your particular site should also be taken into account as they may affect a plant's growth. (See also key, left, and box, below.)

Toxic plants
This symbol indicates that the plant can be toxic. Details are given in the genus introductions in the Plant Dictionary.

Size and shape
For most plants the approximate height (H) and spread (S) are given at the end of each caption. (The "height" of a trailing plant is the length of its stems, either hanging or spreading.) For Trees, Conifers, and Shrubs, a scale drawing shows the size and shape of each plant at maturity.

SHRUBS

123

Plant names
The botanical name is given for each plant, and where appropriate, common names are listed in brackets.

Captions
Captions describe the plants in detail and draw attention to any special uses.

Color tabs
These indicate a change of color within the size group for each season.

Tabs
Color-coded tabs make it easy to find each plant group.

The Plant Dictionary

The Plant Dictionary contains entries for every genus in the Encyclopedia and includes another 4,000 recommended plants in addition to those featured in the Plant Catalog. It also functions as an index to the Plant Catalog.

Genus names
The genus name is followed by common names, where appropriate, and family names.

Genus entries
A concise introduction covers the distinctive characteristics and hardiness range of plants in the genus, as well as advice on siting, cultivation, propagation, and, if relevant, pruning, pests and diseases, and toxicity.

Plant names
Botanical names, synonyms, and common names are given as appropriate. The genus name is abbreviated; specific epithets (e.g., nobile) are abbreviated only if previously given in full.

Plant descriptions
Key characteristics of the plant are described. Hardiness and cultivation needs are included only if specific to the plant. Cultivar entries run on from the species entry, with the binomial omitted.

Hardiness and Heat zones
Indicate the zone(s) in which the plant can be expected to survive (see below).

Illustrated plants
Descriptions for illustrated plants appear in the Plant Catalog, unless part of a feature panel (see below left).

Cross-references
Synonym cross-references are listed alphabetically.

RHEUM
Rhubarb

POLYGONACEAE

Genus of perennials, grown for their foliage and overall appearance. Includes the edible rhubarb and various ornamental plants. Some species are extremely large and require plenty of space. Prefers sun or partial shade and deep, rich, well-drained soil. Propagate by division in spring or by seed in fall. ①Leaves may cause severe discomfort if ingested.

R. nobile, Clump-forming perennial. **H** 5ft (15m), **S** 3ft (1m). Has oblong to oval, leathery, basal, mid-green leaves, 2ft (60cm) long. In late summer produces long stems and conical spikes of large, overlapping, pale cream bracts that hide insignificant flowers. Z6–9 H9–6

R. palmatum (Chinese rhubarb), Clump-forming perennial. **H** and **S** 6ft (2m). Has rounded, 5-lobed, mid-green leaves, 2–2¹⁄₂ft (60–75cm) long. In early summer produces broad panicles of small, creamy-white flowers. Z5–9 H9–5

'Atrosanguineum' illus. p.439.

Rhipsalidopsis gaertneri. See *Hatiora gaertneri.*

Rhipsalidopsis rosea. See *Hatiora rosea.*

PLANT HARDINESS ZONES

A given plant's growth and survival is determined by its interaction with many soil and climatic factors over the life of the plant. Among the most important aspects of climate is temperature, and a plant's ability to withstand relative low and high temperatures is referred to as cold-hardiness and heat tolerance, respectively. To help gardeners select plants for their gardens based on these factors, the US Department of Agriculture and the American Horticultural Society have developed maps that divide Canada and the United States into recognizable zones. Based on information gathered at thousands of locations over many years, the maps and the individual cold-hardiness and heat-zone range codes that are based on them serve as a reliable guide for choosing plants for your garden. The zone maps appear on the endpapers of this book.

The individual codes for cold-hardiness and heat tolerance presented in this book are offered as approximate guides and should not be considered as absolute. Practicing horticultural techniques such as mulching and winter protection will alter a plant's interaction with its environment and may enable it to survive beyond the zones given in this or other publications.

Abbreviations

cv(s)	cultivar(s)	p(p).	page(s)	subsp.	subspecies
f.	forma	pl.	plural	syn.	synonym(s)
illus.	illustrated	sp.	species	var.	varietas
min.	minimum	spp.	species (pl.)		

PLANT NAMES AND ORIGINS

Plants have always been given local names, with the result that many of them were called by a different name in different regions and countries. To overcome this problem, a common naming system was devised and developed into the plant naming system that is now used worldwide.

The binomial system

Greek and Roman scholars laid the foundations of our plant-naming method, but the binomial system used today was largely established in the 18th century by Swedish botanist Carolus Linnaeus (1707–1778). Linnaeus classified each plant with two Latin words, rather than the descriptive phrases used previously. The first word describes the genus (e.g., *Ilex*) and the second the epithet (e.g., *aquifolium*). Together they provided a name for a particular plant species such as *Ilex aquifolium* (English holly). Other species in the same genus were given different epithets such as *Ilex crenata* and *Ilex serrata*. The system has been developed by scientists so that the entire plant kingdom is divided into a universally recognized "family tree" (see opposite).

The meaning of plant names

Plant names are derived from various sources. Some are commemorative—the *Fuchsia* is a tribute to German physician Leonhart Fuchs—while others indicate a plant's geographic origins, as with *Parrotia persica* (of Persia). A plant may be named after the collector who introduced it, such as *Primula forrestii*, cultivated by George Forrest. Alternatively, the name may describe the plant's characteristics—for example, *quinquefolia* in *Parthenocissus quinquefolia*, which means with foliage made up of five leaflets; it comes from the Latin *quinque* (five) and *folium* (leaf).

A plant name may change because the plant has been incorrectly identified; or because it has been given an earlier name; or because the name has been found to apply to two different plants; or because new knowledge changes the plant's classification. In this book, synonyms are included so renamed plants can be easily recognized.

Common names

Although many plants have familiar common names, botanical names are used because not all plants possess a common name, or they may share a name with other plants. In addition, a common name may be used in different regions to describe different plants. For example, in Scotland "plane" refers to *Acer pseudoplatanus* (sycamore); in England it refers to the London plane (*Platanus* x *hispanica*), and in the US both "plane" and "sycamore" are used for *Platanus occidentalis*. Common names may also refer to unrelated plants, as is the case with sea holly (*Eryngium*), hollyhock (*Alcea*), and summer holly (*Arctostaphylos diversifolia*), none of which is a true holly (*Ilex*). Another problem is that one plant may have several common names: heartsease, love-in-idleness, and Johnny-jump-up all refer to *Viola tricolor*.

Botanical divisions

Divided into a hierarchy, plants are classified according to the following groups, which help to identify them:

The family

Plants are grouped in families according to the structure of their flowers, fruits, and other organs. Families may consist of clearly related plants, such as orchids (family Orchidaceae), or embrace diverse plants as in the family Rosaceae: *Alchemilla, Cotoneaster, Crataegus, Malus, Geum, Prunus, Pyracantha, Sorbus* and *Spiraea*.

The genus and its species

A family may contain one genus (for example, *Eucryphia* is the only genus in the family Eucryphiaceae) or many—the daisy family Compositae has over 1,000 genera.

Each genus comprises related plants, such as oaks (genus *Quercus*) or lilies (genus *Lilium*), with several features in common, and a genus may contain one or many species. For example, a member of the genus *Lilium* could be any lily, but *Lilium candidum* denotes just one type.

A species is a group of plants that consistently and naturally reproduce themselves, often by seed or vegetatively, generating plant populations that share similar characteristics.

Subspecies, varieties, and forms

In the wild, even plants of the same species can exhibit slight differences, and these are split into three subdivisions. The subspecies (subsp.) is a distinct variant of the species; the variety (var.) differs slightly in its botanical structure; and the form (f.) has only minor variations, such as the habit or color of leaf, flower, or fruit.

ABOVE Wild origins
Many plant species that subsequently become garden plants are initially found in the wild. The North Cape Province of South Africa is home to many annuals and succulents, from which breeders have produced new cultivars and hybrids.

Cultivars

Plant breeders are constantly trying to improve a plant's performance, and produce new "cultivars" (a contraction of **culti**vated **var**ieties) that are more vigorous, produce more flowers, or possess other favorable characteristics that differentiate them from the wild form of the species Although many cultivars are bred by specialists, others are found in the wild or occur as mutations and are then introduced to cultivation. To reproduce cultivars that exhibit a consistent set of characteristics, many must be propagated vegetatively (cuttings, grafting, or division) or grown annually from specially selected seed.

Cultivars have vernacular names, which are printed in Roman type within single quotes (e.g., *Phygelius aequalis* 'Yellow Trumpet').When plant breeders raise a new cultivar, it is given a code name that may be different from the name under which the plant is sold. For example, the rose Casino also has the code name 'Macca'; in this book, both names are cited, and styled like this: *Rosa* casino ('Macca').

Hybrids

Sexual crosses between botanically distinct species or genera are known as hybrids and are indicated by a multiplication sign. If the cross is between species in different genera, the result is called an "intergeneric hybrid," and when two or more genera are crossed, the name given is a condensed form of the relevant genera; x *Cuprocyparis*, for example, covers hybrids between species of *Chamaecyparis* and *Cupressus*.

If more than three genera are involved, then the hybrids are named after a person and given the ending "-ara." Thus x *Potinara*, a hybrid of *Brassavola, Cattleya, Laelia,* and *Sophronitis,* commemorates M. Potin of the French orchid society. More common are "interspecific hybrids," which are crosses between species in the same genus. These have a collective name preceded by a multiplication sign: *Epimedium* x *rubrum* covers hybrids between *E. alpinum* and *E. grandiflorum.*

When a plant is grafted onto another, a new plant occasionally arises that contains tissues of both parents. These are named in the same way as sexual hybrids, but are denoted by a plus sign: + *Laburnocytisus adamii,* for example, is a graft hybrid between *Laburnum* and *Chamaecytisus.*

Cultivars of hybrids are listed under a botanical name, or if the parentage is complex, by giving the generic name followed solely by the cultivar name (e.g., *Rosa* 'Buff Beauty').

Visual Key to Plant Classification

In horticulture, plants are classified according to a hierarchical system and named primarily on the basis of Linnaeus's binomial approach (genus followed by species epithet). As an example, part of the family Rosaceae family is set out below, showing all levels of this system.

FAMILY
A group of several genera that share a set of underlying natural characteristics. Family names usually end in *-aceae.* Family limits are often controversial.

GENUS (PL. GENERA)
A group of one or more plants that share a range of distinctive characteristics. Several (rarely one) genera are classified into one family. Each genus contains one or more species and its name is printed in italic type with an initial capital letter.

SPECIES
A group of plants that breeds naturally to produce offspring with similar characteristics; these keep it distinct from other populations in nature. Each species has a two-part name printed in italic type.

SUBSPECIES
A naturally occurring, distinct variant of a species, differing in one or more characteristic. Indicated by "subsp." in Roman type and an epithet in italic type.

VARIETAS* AND *FORMA
A varietas (var.) is a minor species subdivision, differing slightly in botanical structure. A forma (f.) is a minor variant of a species, often differing in flower color or habit from others in the species.

CULTIVAR
Selected or artificially raised, distinct variant of a species, subspecies, *varietas, forma,* or hybrid. Indicated by a vernacular name printed in Roman type within single quotation marks.

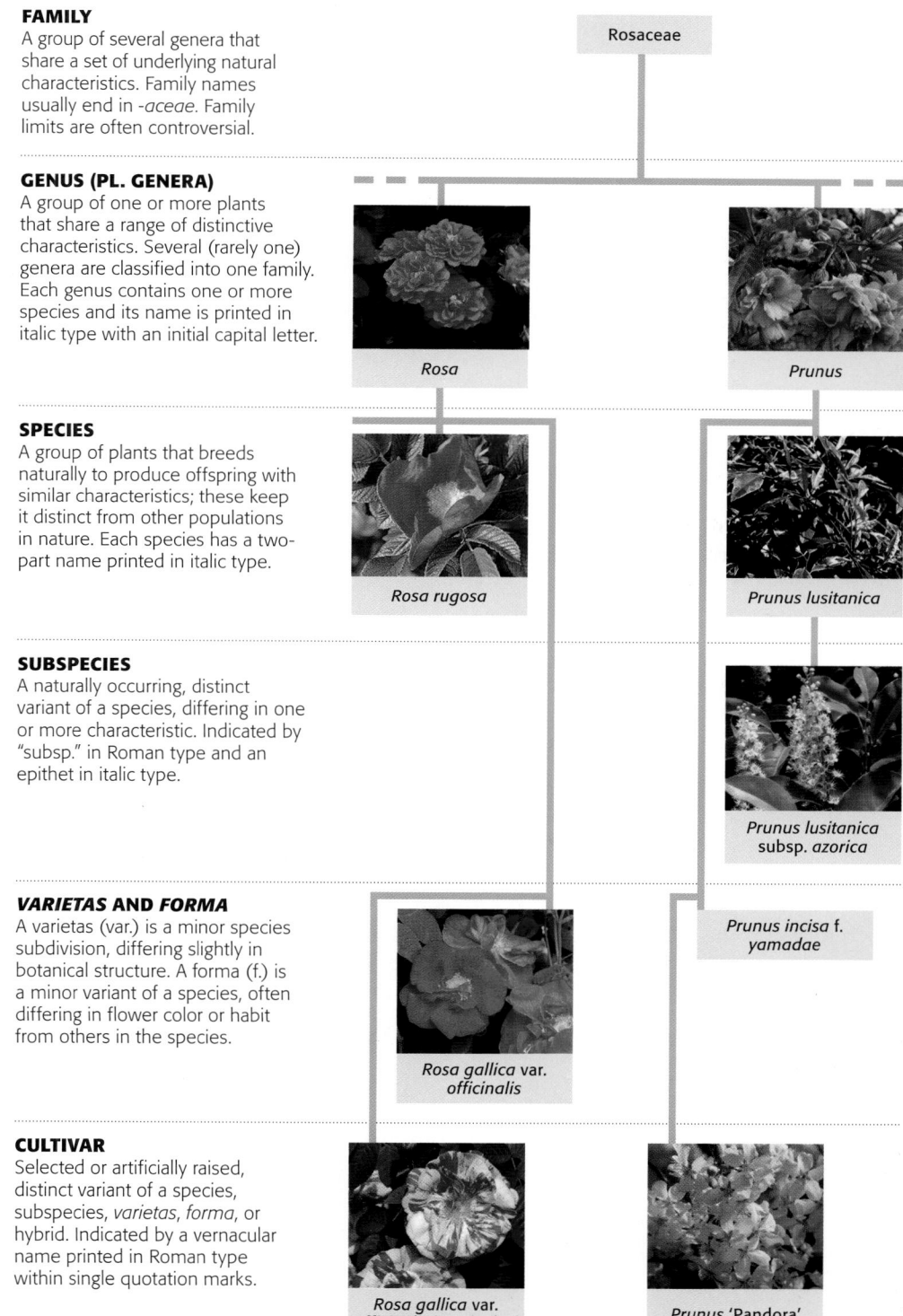

Rosaceae

Rosa

Prunus

Rosa rugosa

Prunus lusitanica

Prunus lusitanica subsp. *azorica*

Prunus incisa f. *yamadae*

Rosa gallica var. *officinalis*

Rosa gallica var. *officinalis* 'Versicolor'

Prunus 'Pandora'

CREATING A GARDEN

A beautiful garden is everyone's dream, and this chapter provides all the information you need to create stunning beds and borders. There is helpful advice on choosing color schemes, including dazzling hot beds, relaxing pastel designs, and elegant white displays, as well as ideas for using plant forms and textures to create arresting images throughout the year. There are also tips to help you select a garden style, whether you prefer the informality of a cottage garden or the ordered symmetry of a formal design. Practical advice on a range of gardening techniques, including preparing the soil, planting methods, and pruning basics, completes the picture.

INSPIRATIONAL STYLES

There are many different garden styles, and whether you yearn for neat, symmetrical formality, informal cottage-garden abundance, Japanese minimalism, or contemporary urban chic, it is important to select a look that suits both your home and lifestyle if you are to get the best from your outdoor space. Also think about how much time you have to maintain your design, as this will affect your range of choices.

The use of symmetry, clear simple geometric shapes, and clipped topiary and hedges are typical of the formal style. The reflective pool and rills bounce light into this primarily green planting scheme.

Formal gardens

A successful formal garden has a balanced design, achieved through symmetry and a clear ground plan. Essential characteristics are straight lines; order and geometry; and clearly delineated garden areas. Organized around a central axis or pathway, formal gardens often focus on a key view through the garden from the house. The geometry is clear, but generous scale and balanced proportions are key considerations.

Geometric shapes feature strongly, but any regular symmetrical shape can be used as long as it sits on at least one axis. Lawns and clipped hedges are important features, the latter defining spaces or views, while dwarf boxwood hedges can be used to edge borders, create decorative parterres, or form knot gardens. If space allows, avenues of trees may line paths to accentuate vistas and draw the eye to a distant focal point.

Balustrades, steps, terraces, and wide gravel pathways are all key features, with the range of hard-landscaping materials, such as gravel and regular paving stones, kept to a minimum. Decorative elements, such as cobble mosaics or brick designs, are also popular in formal gardens. Other features include classical ornaments, such as Versailles cases, urns and statuary, and topiary, which is often used as a focal point. Water is an important element, and pools with reflective surfaces or jets and fountains appear in many formal designs.

Although the rules of formality are simple and clear, it is still a remarkably flexible style. The overall layout can be completely symmetrical, or you can choose to adopt just a few formal elements in a more contemporary design. For example, one axis can be more dominant than another, or a series of balanced, rectangular beds can be veiled with soft, romantic planting. Another modern interpretation of the formal style is a paved courtyard garden with architectural planting, large-scale containers, and a small water feature.

Many formal designs also require very little maintenance, apart from annual hedge clipping and shrub pruning.

Informal gardens

Country gardens, cottage gardens, wildlife gardens, and prairie-style plantings are all informal designs. Unlike formal schemes, they allow a greater degree of flexibility in the design and planting plans.

Cottage gardens

Cottage gardens are traditionally simple in layout, often with a central path leading to the main door and planting beds filled with flowers, herbs, and vegetables on either side. If the garden is large enough, it may also include more naturalistic areas, such as orchards, meadows, and informal wildlife ponds.

The edges of flower beds are softened by a rich profusion of planting, with the flowers encouraged to flop over the path and self-seed at random. Typical cottage garden plants include hellebores, lungworts (*Pulmonaria*), grape hyacinths (*Muscari*), aquilegias, and species daffodils and tulips in spring, with hardy geraniums, lilies, lupines, poppies, campanulas, delphiniums, hollyhocks (*Alcea rosea*), and peonies in summer. Plants are often chosen for their range of flower forms, textures, and colors. Edible crops, such as herbs, vegetables, and fruit trees and bushes, are mixed with the ornamental plants, adding to the atmosphere of abundance and informality.

Natural stone, brick, cobbles, and slate are the best materials for hard landscaping, while simple post-and-rail or picket fences are ideal for boundaries and divisions.

Country gardens

Country gardens also have a relaxed style, with sweeping expanses of lawn and curved, flower-filled mixed beds and borders. Hedges are often used to divide the garden into a series of enclosed spaces with different planting designs and atmospheres in each.

Prairie and wildlife gardens

Prairie planting, championed by many contemporary designers, echoes the tightly woven density of cottage-garden planting by combining broad sweeps of ornamental grasses and sturdy perennials. Grasses such as stipas and calamagrostis are threaded through perennials, such as rudbeckias, echinaceas, heleniums, and asters. Prairie schemes suit large open sites in full sun where the bold swaths of planting produce the best effects.

Wildlife gardens are designed to provide habitats for birds, insects, and mammals. Domestic gardens can also be wildlife gardens, with naturalistic planting schemes comprising nectar-rich flowers, and trees for nesting and shelter. An informal pond is usually a feature, to provide homes for amphibians, reptiles, and insects.

Gardeners with more space may opt for a wildflower meadow. These require a sunny site and infertile soil for the rich profusion of native wild flowers and grasses to thrive.

RIGHT Prairie-style plantings
Prairie-style gardens combine the soft, feathery effects of grasses with the muted hues of perennials. Planted in informal drifts, this late summer scheme includes eupatorium, echinacea, and sedum.

BELOW Cottage-garden informality and abundance
The profuse pink flowers of a climbing rose clambering over an arbor echo the equally abundant planting of cottage-garden perennials in the beds below.

Mediterranean gardens

There are two types of gardens associated with the Mediterranean region: formal and informal. The formal gardens feature water and stone, as well as clipped hedges and specimen trees such as pencil cypresses. Decorative parterres are also common, with the plants selected for foliage rather than flower color. In some gardens in Spain, such as El Alhambra in Granada, there is a strong Moorish influence, with formal courtyards and water features.

However, the most attainable garden style has an informal structure and relaxed, Mediterranean atmosphere. Gravel is the main hard landscaping material, and it is used between areas of planting and to create pathways. Plants native to this region of Europe often have silvery, sage, gray-green, or blue-tinted foliage, which reflects the strong summer sun. Olive trees, citrus fruits, figs, vines, santolinas, and artemisias, as well as herbs like thyme, sage, lavender, and rosemary, are popular planting choices.

Another informal approach, often seen in urban areas, is to create a courtyard with walls that have been painted white, warm terra-cotta, or bold blues or pinks. Mosaic-tiled walls, cobbled floors, and terra-cotta pots planted with bright pelargoniums or white *Convolvulus cneorum* complete the Mediterranean theme. If you live in a cooler climate, a sun-drenched courtyard will also provide some shelter for tender plants. Hot, south-facing gardens call for a shady arbor or pergola festooned with flowering climbers, such as bougainvilleas or jasmine, to create a comfortable area for alfresco dining or relaxation.

ABOVE Mediterranean planting
Drought-tolerant plants, including spiky phormiums, rock roses, and artemisias, thrive in the gravel of a Mediterranean-style garden on a hot, sunny hillside.

Desert gardens

Dramatic, chic, and starkly beautiful, desert gardens have become very fashionable in hot, frost-free locations with low rainfall. Pale-colored walls, gravel, rocks, boulders, and driftwood are features, together with tough, drought-tolerant plants like cacti and succulents, such as agaves, aloes, and yuccas, which do not need extra irrigation in these hostile environments. In the right place, a desert garden is very eco-friendly, as it focuses on native plants that thrive with little water.

Japanese gardens

The Japanese garden style is designed to reflect the natural landscape using a limited planting palette to produce quiet, contemplative spaces. The key to creating a successful Japanese garden is to consider how the main elements, such as boulders, gravel, and plants, relate to one another, and how they are connected both symbolically and spiritually to the natural world.

In many instances, traditional Japanese spiritual beliefs are fundamental to the designs. The ancient religion of Shinto, and the Buddhist teachings that were introduced later, both celebrate nature, and all natural elements are regarded as sacred and worthy of respect. In Zen gardens, key elements are used to create representations of natural landscapes. For example, raked gravel is used to echo flowing water, with stones symbolizing islands, boats, or animals. The gravel is raked daily, a ritual viewed by Buddhists as an important aid to contemplation, and the gardens often include little or no planting, relying on moss and lichens rather than on large, dramatic plants.

The cultivation of beauty as a spiritual activity is also reflected in Japanese tea gardens in which a *roji* (dewy path) is lit by stone lanterns and leads the visitor on a journey past water basins, stone buddhas

ABOVE Cool Mediterranean courtyard
A Mediterranean courtyard, with gleaming white walls and floor that help reflect the heat of the sun, is perfect for growing sun-loving agapanthus.

ABOVE Japanese contemplative space
Natural materials, such as carefully positioned rocks and gravel, plants like acers and pines, and ornamental lanterns, are typical features of a Japanese garden.

and other spiritual symbols to the ceremonial tea house. These gardens are more heavily planted, and include maples (*Acer*), pines, azaleas, and camellias, which are subjected to a strict pruning regimen to restrict their size and create miniature forms of larger trees or shrubs. The planting does not focus solely on evergreens and there are splashes of color in the form of cherry blossom and camellias in the spring, elegant summer irises, and the fiery fall foliage of the maples contributing to the seasonal display.

Contemporary gardens

With many of us living increasingly urban lives, contemporary gardens have had to fulfill a number of different functions, providing a space for planting, relaxation, play, and entertaining. Modern urban gardens can differ in emphasis, and be treated either as purely functional spaces in which hard surfaces prevail along with furniture, lighting effects, and water features to create the ultimate outdoor room, or as green oases in which the planting dominates.

The layout of an urban garden is generally based on simple lines, often with an asymmetrical floor plan, and uses a combination of natural and man-made materials, such as concrete, glass, plastic, acrylic, and steel, to provide textural interest. Furniture often takes the form of integral benches, stylishly coordinated tables and chairs, and recliners, while sculpture provides a focal point, and can be combined with water. Jets or cascades are popular, but tanks of reflective water are becoming increasingly popular.

Contemporary planting designs

As space can be limited in today's urban gardens, the planting often focuses on a more limited choice of species, and those that provide architectural interest. Grasses, bamboos, and large-leaved foliage plants, such as the hardy banana (*Musa basjoo*), phormiums, and cordylines are popular in contemporary schemes.

Modernist designs employ large block plantings of boxwood (*Buxus*), or small festucas and ophiopogons. These may be used in conjunction with pleached trees planted along the boundaries to provide privacy in overlooked gardens. Dramatic containers made from clay, stone, or steel can be used as focal points or lined up in a row to add drama and rhythm to the design. Popular plants for containers include clipped topiary boxwood, bay or Japanese holly (*Ilex crenata*), bamboo, succulents like agaves, or bold grasses.

Tropical gardens

Although this style of garden is best suited to tropical and warm-temperate regions, where the native plants are naturally lush, a similar effect can be created in cooler climates with the careful selection of plants.

The design is informal, with man-made structures made from rough-hewn timber and unworked stone, reflecting the traditional crafts of people living in tropical environments. Water plays a large part in designs, mimicking the landscapes that inspired the style, with waterfalls, streams, and, occasionally, swimming pools adding to the lush picture.

A tropical garden is a celebration of foliage shapes, textures, and colors. Taller species such as eucalyptus, palms, bamboos, and cordylines provide height, with the space below filled with lower-growing shrubs, grasses, and flowering perennials, such as birds-of-paradise (*Strelitzia*) and streptocarpus.

This exciting look can be created in temperate areas with exotic architectural plants including tree ferns, bamboos, fatsias, ferns, phormiums, and hardy bananas (*Musa basjoo*). For shots of bright detail, use vibrant canna lilies, white arum lilies (*Zantedeschia*), dahlias, crocosmias, agapanthus, and lobelias.

ABOVE Contemporary urban chic
This urban, split-level garden with its integral benches shows how contemporary outdoor areas can function on many different levels—both as outdoor rooms and as areas for lawns and beautiful plants.

BELOW Tropical abundance
The striking leaves of elephant ears (*Alocasia*) provide a dramatic focal point in an exotic, junglelike garden. Bright sparks of color are provided by the vibrant red cannas that stand out amid the lush green foliage.

ASSESSING YOUR SITE AND SOIL

It is important to discover as much as possible about the conditions in your garden before you start planning and planting. Take note of the local environment and climate, as well as the topography and soil conditions, as your plant choices will be determined by these factors. Check the exposure, which influences the sun and shade in a garden, and the soil type, to discover its moisture and nutrient content.

Understanding exposure

Determining how much sun and shade your garden receives is of paramount importance when making plant selections. Some plants prefer full sun, for example, while others need partial or full shade to thrive. You can use a compass to work out which way areas or borders face. Those facing south will be in sun for most of the day, while those that face north will be shady. East-facing areas have morning sun and evening shade, while the opposite applies to those facing west.

Patterns of sun and shade also change throughout the day, and a garden that is in full sun at midday may have areas of shade in the morning and late afternoon. For this reason, it is wise to study your garden on a sunny day and make a note of the way shadows move around the yard. Remember, too, that the seasons can affect the level of sunlight in a garden; for example, an area that is in sun in the summer could be in constant shade during the winter, which may have an effect on evergreens that need a sunny site to thrive.

However much sun your garden receives, there are plenty of plants to choose from that will thrive in those conditions. As well as plants for sun or shade, there are many that are happy with a bit of both.

ABOVE Plants that thrive in sun
Alliums, with their dramatic globes of rich pinkish-purple flowers, thrive in open, sunny sites, and make great partners for other sun-lovers, like catmints and salvias.

Assessing microclimates

Variations in the conditions in different parts of a yard are described as "microclimates," and may include frost pockets at the bottom of a slope, sheltered hot spots by a warm wall, areas of wind turbulence, and exposed sites. Rather than limit your plant choice, microclimates actually allow you to grow a wider range of plants, so note the temperature, water levels, and air and wind circulation around your yard.

Types of soil

Knowing your soil type is key to growing healthy plants. It is always preferable to select those that thrive in the soil you have, rather than fighting it by trying to grow plants that are not adapted to your conditions, as they will inevitably suffer.

There are three main types of soil: sand, clay, and silt. They are categorized according to the size of the soil particles, which determines the amount of water and plant food they can hold. Most garden soils are a combination of sand and clay, with one type dominating the mix; the ideal soil is "loam," which contains almost equal measures of sand and clay.

Sandy soil Sandy soil particles are relatively large and water drains freely through the spaces between them. As a result, the soil is free-draining, but because plant nutrients are dissolved in water, it is also quite infertile. Sandy soil is ideal for Mediterranean plants.

Clay soils Clay particles are minute, and trap moisture in the gaps between them.

LEFT Growing shade-lovers
Shade-loving plants, such as the hart's-tongue fern (*Asplenium scolopendrium*), flourish under the light shade provided by silver birch trees (*Betula pendula*).

ABOVE **Plants that thrive in dry, sandy soil**
Dry, sandy soil and a sunny site provide the perfect conditions for many euphorbias, California poppies, bulbs like eremurus, and succulents such as agaves.

The particles are also porous, so these soils are very moisture-retentive and rich in nutrients. However, clay soils can become waterlogged in wet conditions and form impenetrable crusts when dry. They are ideal for "hungry" plants like fruit trees.

Silt soils Pure silt soils are rare, usually occurring on river plains. They have a high nutrient content, but can become compacted and waterlogged like clay.

Loam With almost equal proportions of sand and clay, loam offers the best of all worlds, retaining enough water for plant roots to absorb, but allowing excess moisture to drain away and preventing waterlogging. It also holds on to nutrients well, making it the perfect garden soil for most plants.

Improving your soil

Whether you have a dry, sandy soil or a sticky clay one, your plants will grow better if you improve its quality by applying plenty of organic matter, such as well-rotted farmyard manure, garden compost, or spent mushroom compost. Organic matter coats sandy soil particles, helping them to retain more water, while it also opens up the structure of clay soils, allowing water to drain more easily.

Either dig it into the soil when preparing for planting or lay a thick layer as a mulch.

Worms and microorganisms will then work it into the soil.

The structure and drainage of heavy clay soils can also be improved by the addition of horticultural grit. Simply dig the grit into the soil over a large area. In extreme circumstances, very heavy, waterlogged soils may require drains.

Understanding pH

The pH of a soil is a measure of its acidity or alkalinity, which also influences the types of plants you can grow successfully. It is measured on a scale from 1 to 14; neutral soil has a pH of 7, a number below this indicates acidic soil, and alkaline soils have a pH above 7. A precise measurement can be obtained by performing a simple soil test (*see right*). Although many plants are tolerant of a wide pH range, there are some that are adapted to particular soil type. Rhododendrons, azaleas, and heathers (*Erica*), for example, require acidic soil, while lilacs (*Syringa vulgaris*) and the pineapple broom (*Cytisus battandieri*) grow best in alkaline soil.

TESTING YOUR SOIL

An easy way to find out what type of soil you have is to dig up a small sample and roll it between your fingers to feel the texture. Soil with a high water content can be rolled into a ball. You can also use a simple kit to test the pH.

Sandy and silty soil
Soil rich in sand feels gritty between your fingers; silty soil feels silky. Both fall apart when rolled into a ball. Sandy soil is easy to dig, and warms up quickly in spring. You may also find that borderline hardy plants survive winters better in these dry soils.

Clay soil
Smooth, sticky, and dense, clay soil retains its shape when molded into a ball, and soil with a very high clay content remains intact even when rolled into a horseshoe. Clay soil is often described as "heavy" soil because it is difficult to dig.

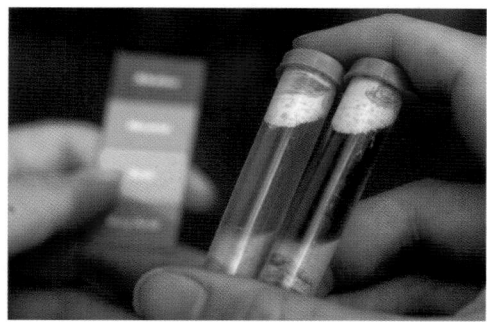

Using a pH test kit
You can buy pH test kits from garden centers. Place a small soil sample in the tube and add the solution provided with the kit. Wait until the solution changes color, and then match it to the chart. Take a few readings from different areas of the garden, as they may have different pH values.

DESIGNING WITH PLANTS

There is a plant for every situation, be it a tree, shrub, perennial, annual, or bulb. When designing with plants, you can include examples from all the plant groups to ensure year-round interest, or focus on just one or two groups for a contemporary look. The key to success is to vary shapes, textures, and colors, and consider how each plant will work with others in your border and in the garden as a whole.

Defining plant groups

Different plant groups fulfill different functions in a design, and understanding how each can be used to best effect will help you to create a balanced, coordinated display. Trees, large shrubs, and some climbers provide the framework for a planting scheme, offering permanent structure, height, and depth, as well as color and texture. Midrange plants include smaller shrubs, herbaceous perennials, some bulbs, and grasses. They help to define the style of your garden, and provide seasonal interest with their flowers and foliage. Focal plants offer eye-catching accents, drawing the eye to a border or vista, while groundcover plants create a low mat of leaves and blooms at a lower level. Annuals and biennials will put on a show from spring to early fall in containers, and fill the gaps between more permanent planting groups in borders.

Structural plants

Permanent structural plants, such as trees, shrubs, and hedges, make a vital contribution to the shape and form of the garden, and identifying these key plants, and deciding where to position them, is the first step in producing a coherent design.

Evergreens provide year-round interest, while deciduous trees and shrubs inject

dramatic displays of flowers in spring and colorful foliage in fall. Hedges not only define boundaries, but also offer shelter and create privacy. Evergreen hedges make colorful year-round screens and backdrops for other planting groups, while deciduous hedges allow in more light and offer seasonal color. Either type can be formal or informal in style, with leaf size, color, and flowers to consider. Leafy shrubs work in much the same way as hedges, providing

a green foliage backdrop for smaller midrange plants and groundcover.

You can also use structural plants to frame or block out views, and to lead the eye around the garden. In addition, trees and shrubs can help to create a visual link between the garden and the landscape beyond, extending the display. Repeated plants will also help to make connections between different areas of the garden and different planting areas.

Structural plants come in many different forms and shapes; for example, they may be rounded and neat, such as choisyas and photinias; spiky and textural, like mahonias, hollies, and yuccas; or looser in form, such as laburnums, weeping pears, or garryas. Many plants can be manipulated to create artificial structural effects, such as climbers clambering over arches, arbors, and pergolas, or along walls. Others can be clipped into topiary shapes; boxwood, yew, and holly are all good candidates for topiary balls, pyramids, and spirals.

LEFT Creating focal plants
In this beautiful country garden, naturalized tulips in vibrant shades create a carpet of spring color. The focal plant of this design is the light-reflecting white blossoms and architectural shape of a *Malus floribunda*.

Focal plants

These are key specimen plants that can be used to catch the eye in a bed or border, in the center of a lawn, or at the end of a pathway. Most focal plants are evergreen or have a distinctive shape or foliage form, but they can also include seasonal plants that perform for short periods of the year, providing an accent when it is needed most.

Use focal plants to direct the eye to key areas of interest, or as signposts to guide the visitor around the garden. Phormiums, acers, yuccas, cardoons, and white-stemmed birches will lead the eye to a particular area or distract attention away from unsightly features, like garbage cans.

Midrange plants

This group of plants are of medium height, and include the vast array of herbaceous perennials, bulbs like tulips, daffodils and alliums, deciduous grasses, and, to a lesser extent, small shrubs, including compact hebes and shrubby potentillas.

Some of the most effective midrange plants rely on their leaf shape and texture for interest more than their blooms, although seasonal flower color is an important feature of many and makes an exciting statement when plants are used *en masse* in a border. When grouped together, those with strong foliage forms, such as acanthus, hostas, ligularias, and rodgersias, also create bold plantings, or they can be used to separate plants with looser flowers or foliage forms.

Midrange plants contribute to the structure of the garden, but because many are perennial, dying down in late fall and appearing again in spring, they are not able to perform the same role as the more permanent woody plants.

Groundcover plants

Not only are groundcover plants highly ornamental, providing a tapestry of color, texture, and form, they also create a blanket over the soil, helping to suppress weeds. Groundcover plants are not restricted to low-growing types, however, and include a range of shapes and sizes, the only proviso being that they form a dense canopy.

A dry, sunny site makes an ideal home for drought-tolerant flowering plants, such as dwarf genistas, helianthemums, and sedums. Leafy groundcover plants include thyme and other mat-forming herbs, *Hebe pinguifolia*, *Santolina chamaecyparissus*, and catmint (*Nepeta*). A cool, shady site is perfect for groundcover plants such as *Cornus canadensis*, *Geranium macrorrhizum*, and epimediums under trees, and bergenias, hellebores, and ferns by a wall where the soil is reasonably moist.

Seasonal interest

By combining different plant groups and selecting those with a succession of seasonal highlights, you can easily create a garden with year-round appeal.

In spring, focus on flowering trees, such as cherries, crab apples, magnolias, and plums, as well as bulbs like hyacinths, muscari, crocus, daffodils, and tulips that provide color. Summer brings an explosion of flowering perennials, annuals, and bulbs, offering a range of colors, heights, and flower shapes. The fall stars are the trees and shrubs, with acers, cotoneasters, and cotinus all injecting foliage color. Team them with late-flowering perennials such as asters. The winter garden also provides seasonal interest, with witch hazels (*Hamamelis*), and sarcococcas offering fragrant flowers, and color provided by the stems of dogwoods (*Cornus*) and willow (*Salix*), and berries of hawthorns, hollies, and viburnums.

ABOVE Using midrange plants
Midrange plants like hostas are ideal feature plants for a mixed shady border. Repeating plants down the length of the border brings cohesion to the design.

BELOW Creating winter interest
The golden yellow flowers of *Mahonia* x *media* 'Lionel Fortescue' make a striking contrast with the flame red stems of *Cornus alba* 'Sibirica' in a winter border.

ABOVE Blanketing the ground with plants
Santolinas, with their buttonlike, yellow flowers, make excellent groundcover plants in a gravel planting in full sun, and associate beautifully with spiky eryngiums.

USING COLOR

Color choice is largely about personal preferences, but there are some useful theories on how to match and blend colors that will help you create pleasing combinations. Remember, too, that light and shade affect colors and that some visually leap forward, stealing the limelight, while others are more recessive. Color can also affect mood and tone, so choose carefully to create the desired atmosphere.

Combining colors

Before selecting colors for your beds and borders, it is a good idea to familiarize yourself with some of the principles of color theory, which will help you combine them more successfully.

Many designers use the color wheel to make their choices. The wheel is divided into primary, secondary, and tertiary colors. The primary colors are red, blue and yellow, and when mixed they create the secondary colors, green, orange, and purple. In this way, the primaries blue and red produce secondary purple; red and yellow produce secondary orange; and yellow and blue produce secondary green. Tertiary colors are produced by mixing adjacent primary and secondary colors.

The color wheel can help you create harmonious and contrasting schemes. For example, colors directly opposite one another on the wheel, such as yellow and purple or red and green, are considered to be "complementary." When placed next to each other, these contrasting colors create a sense of vibrancy and excitement.

Colors that sit next to each other on the wheel are known as "harmonious" or "analogous" colors and create a sense of order. Examples of harmonious colors are blue, purple, and pink, and green, yellow, and pale orange. Harmonious colors can create different moods, depending on whether you choose hot reds and oranges or cool blues and greens.

Triadic color schemes are created by selecting three colors that are spaced equally apart on the wheel. Green, orange, and purple is one example. The contrasting hues can create eye-catching combinations.

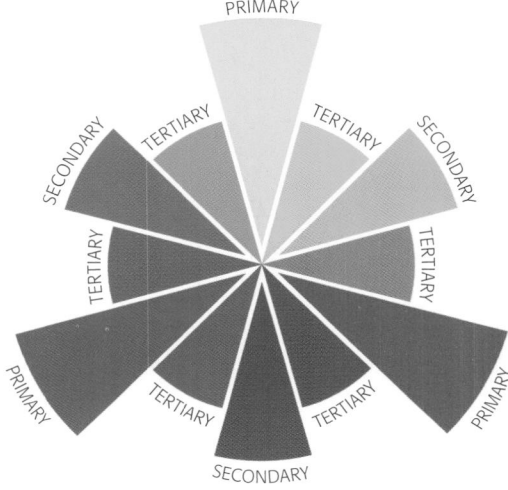

ABOVE The color wheel
Frequently employed by garden designers, the color wheel is a simple visual device that shows how to combine colors successfully, whether you want a vibrant scheme or a muted, harmonious grouping.

ABOVE Triadic colors
Green, orange, and purple are triadic colors. Using them together creates a sense of exuberance, as shown by the fall shades of this group of shrubs.

ABOVE Harmonious combination
This border combines adjoining colors: the pale pink *Dictamnus purpureus*, purple-pink *Allium* 'Purple Sensation', and a burgundy-red *Berberis* at the back.

ABOVE Tints and shades
This scheme of pale mauve campanulas, darker purple phlox, and deep pink geraniums uses tints of mauve together with pink to create a balanced scheme.

LEFT Complementary colors
The contrasting blue-purple veronicas and bright yellow inulas show how hues on opposite sides of the wheel produce an exciting contrast that draws the eye.

TEXTURE AND PATTERN

Mixing contrasting plant textures creates a lively effect in a border. Combine glossy and matt, or furry and rough foliage to make an impact. Look, too, at leaf patterns and match a variety of shapes and sizes to add to the interest.

Shiny and glossy
Many hollies (*Ilex*) have glossy leaves that reflect light. Their spiny leaves also add impact to a border, or they can be used as focal plants.

Soft and furry
Plants like lamb's ears (*Stachys byzantina*) and sages have a compelling tactile quality. Plant them at the front of a border where they are easy to reach and enjoy.

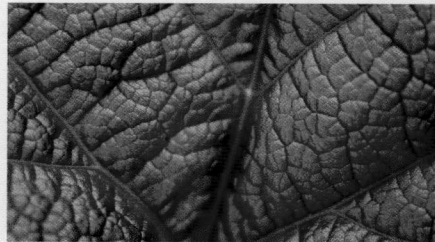

Rough and crinkled
The coarse-textured leaves of this decorative vine (*Vitis coignetiae*), are held on twisted, gnarled stems that wrap around its support.

Lacelike tracery
The soft, feathery foliage of an artemisia provides a foil for larger-leaved plants that like the same sunny conditions, such as sedums.

Tints and shades

As well as selecting colors from the color wheel, also consider the effects of tints, shades, and tones. As a rule, pure hues or saturated colors are more intense, while colors that have been mixed together are less vibrant. More subtle colors can be created by lightening colors using white to create a tint, or darkening them by adding black to create a shade. When gray is added to a hue, it creates a tone.

Tints and shades can be used as transitional colors between stronger hues and help to blend one color into another. However, too many muted shades can look a bit lifeless, so be sure to inject some stronger colors into your planting schemes to create highlights.

Creating moods and focal points with color

Color can convey a mood or message, and has a powerful effect on the atmosphere in a garden. For instance, vivid, hot colors, such as crimson, scarlet, magenta, golden yellow, and orange, generate a feeling of excitement, while cool colors like pale blue, pale pink, mauve, muted grays, and blue-greens create a tranquil feeling. Use these colors to produce different moods in your garden, perhaps creating a sizzling scheme of hot hues by the house and cooler tones

ABOVE Hot fiery border
Hot-hued plants in shades of red, orange, and yellow are guaranteed to brighten up a garden. This fiery border is perfect for a sunny spot.

BELOW Cool pastel shades
The purple flowers of *Salvia* x *sylvestris* 'Mainacht' and the deeper purple leaves of *Persicaria microcephala* 'Red Dragon' contrast with green grasses and green-flowered *Angelica archangelica*. The silvery leaves of *Heuchera* 'Beauty Color' are also veined with purple, thus continuing the silver-purple theme.

YEAR-ROUND INTEREST

When choosing plants for your garden, try to include a selection of feature trees and shrubs that have more than one season of interest. There is a wide range of trees and shrubs, both deciduous and evergreen, that perform for most of the year.

Cornus alba
A deciduous shrub with white flowers in late spring, as well as striking red shoots in winter. The leaves turn red or orange in fall.

Mahonia x media 'Charity'
Mahonias have shiny evergreen foliage, plus yellow flowers and purple or black fruits. 'Charity' has scented yellow flowers in winter.

Nandina domestica
The leaves of this evergreen shrub have red tints in spring and fall. Small white summer flowers are followed by bright red berries.

Prunus x subhirtella 'Autumnalis Rosea'
This cherry tree has tiny, pale pink flowers that appear in winter. The green leaves are bronze when young, turning golden-yellow in fall.

in a shady woodland area at the far end of the garden. Another option is to use the same bed or border to change in mood as the seasons progress, with bright daffodils and tulips in spring, followed by herbaceous summer plantings in blues, purples, pale pinks, and whites, and then fiery foliage color in the fall.

Single-color-themed borders, be they white and cream or varying shades of yellow, look highly sophisticated and produce a satisfying cohesion. The restricted plant choices can also make designing a little easier.

You can also use color to draw attention to a particular feature or planting area. To produce this effect, make sure your plants contrast with the surroundings to increase their visibility. For example, a single, bright orange plant against a recessive background color, such as green or blue, will create an effective accent. Planting schemes that combine swaths of warm and cool colors also work well, with the cooler colors providing a foil for the hot hues.

You can also exploit the way in which colors can alter perceptions of distance. For instance, bright reds and oranges planted at the end of a garden have a foreshortening effect, making the garden appear shorter, while pale colors can make the garden seem longer.

The effects of light and shade

The way that we perceive color is influenced by the amount of light it receives. Sunny borders will make colors appear bolder and brighter, while shady areas enhance more subtle colors and white. The colors of plants can therefore change depending on their location, the degree of shade cast on them, and the time of day. For example, pale colors that produce beautiful effects in the early morning or evening may be bleached out by strong midday sunlight. Bear this in mind if you tend to use your garden at a particular time of day. If you work and sit outside mainly in the evenings, choose white and pale flowers that take on a luminous quality in the fading light.

Choose colors that produce the best effects for different areas of the garden. Plant reds, oranges, bright pinks, and yellows in sunny spaces, as they will look muddy in the shade. Nature often makes this choice for you, as many hot-hued flowers need a sunny spot to thrive. Woodland plants, on the other hand, tend to produce flowers in whites, pastel shades of yellow, pink and purple, and blues, all of which show up better in shade.

Creating a succession of year-round color

When selecting plants, try to include a range that flower or are at their peak at different times of the year to sustain the interest. This is particularly important in small gardens, where the planting is on view year-round.

Consider the merits of each plant, including size, habit, leaf shape, texture and color, flowers, and fruit. For a prolonged display, focus on foliage, either evergreen for constant color, or deciduous, which in most cases endures from spring to fall. This leafy mix provides a backdrop for the succession of flowers that appear. When choosing flowering plants, remember that many have beautiful seedheads, including love-in-a-mist (*Nigella*), poppies, eryngiums, and sedums, that provide two seasons of interest. Also use containers to add an extra dimension to borders and deck displays; one large planter can be used for four different seasonal displays.

Spring

When spring makes a welcome appearance, the garden is soon awash with color. Some is provided by spring-flowering trees and shrubs, such as amelanchiers, ornamental cherries, apples, plums, and almonds (*Prunus*), magnolias, some viburnums, camellias, and forsythias, as well as a host of tough rock plants, including aubretias, saxifrages, and

Spring match
Create a balanced display in your borders with a mixture of tulips, such as 'Bleu Aimable', scented biennial wallflowers (*Erysimum*), and dainty violas providing color in the foreground.

violas. Add to these a selection of bulbs and corms, starting with snowdrops (*Galanthus*) in late winter or early spring, and followed by crocuses, grape hyacinths (*Muscari*), daffodils (*Narcissus*), and tulips (*Tulipa*). As the majority of these bold displays of bulbs die down, they are followed by spring-flowering azaleas and rhododendrons, which provide a wealth of colors, including magenta, pink, crimson, scarlet, golden yellow, and white. As the new leaves unfurl in late spring, blue ceanothus and the scented flowers of viburnums and lilacs enhance the spring garden further.

Summer

As temperatures rise and light levels increase, the garden is filled with a profusion of perennials, annuals, and biennials. Not many trees put on their best performance in summer, but shrubs are a key source of color. Roses start to bloom early in the season, many continuing well into fall. Other beautiful summer-flowering shrubs include sweetly scented mock oranges (*Philadelphus*), lavender, hibiscus, and the flowering dogwoods (*Cornus*). Even those that flowered in spring still play their part by providing a leafy backdrop to the flowers that offer the main show at this time of year.

Many climbers are also in full swing in summer. There are a vast number of clematis species and hybrids to choose from, providing color in the garden from early summer to late in the season, while jasmine, honeysuckle, and the frothy flat heads of climbing hydrangea (*Hydrangea petiolaris*) are other strong performers.

Perennials are the real stars of the summer border. There are thousands to choose from, including early summer-flowering aquilegias, and many geraniums and lupines, followed by campanulas, salvias, achilleas, and hemerocallis, with heleniums, rudbeckias, and echinaceas appearing later in the season. Biennials, such as foxgloves, make great partners for shade-loving perennials, while hardy and half hardy annuals produce an explosion of color in borders and container displays.

Hardy annuals, such as California poppies (*Eschscholzia californica*), annual mallows (*Malope*), and the shoo-fly plant (*Nicandra*) flower for months on end, offering great value for the money, and self-seeding to produce a repeat performance the following summer. Together with half-hardy annuals, like cosmos, impatiens, lobelia, and petunias, they provide color throughout the season, often only ceasing to flower when the frosts arrive in fall.

Fall

As summer fades, the foliage of many trees and shrubs flares into the fiery colors of fall. Some of the best choices for this seasonal display are maples, some cherries, amelanchiers, liquidambars, cotoneasters, sorbus, nyssa, and most forms of smoke tree (*Cotinus*).

Late-flowering perennials, such as Michaelmas daisies (*Aster*) and chrysanthemums, as well as dahlias with their rich variety of flower shapes and colors, brighten up the garden until the arrival of the first frosts. Grasses are also key features of these cooler months. Pampas grasses (*Cortaderia*), fountain grasses (*Pennisetum*), and *Stipa calamagrostis* produce feather- and brush-like seedheads at this time of the year.

Winter

During winter, flower interest is limited, but valuable sources include the scented blooms of winter box (*Sarcococca*) and witch hazels (*Hamamelis*). Bold sculptural shapes and foliage color provided by evergreens is of most importance now, with conifers, boxwood (*Buxus*), and ivy (*Hedera*) coming into their own.

Deciduous trees and shrubs also play an important role, their intricate skeletons of stems clearly visible at this time of year. Think, too, about bark color and texture; white-stemmed birches (*Betula*) and the polished coppery-brown stems of *Prunus serrula* are favorite trees, while brightly colored dogwood (*Cornus*) and willow (*Salix*) stems make exciting focal points. Enhance the winter scene further with berried shrubs, such as hollies (*Ilex*), pyracanthas, and sorbus.

Summer profusion
Perennials often lead the border chorus at this time of year. Crocosmias and veronicastrums provide color and form, with the pinky-purple domes of stately eupatoriums offering background color.

Fall brights
Most perennials are dying down at this time of year, but a few leave their best performance for last. Sedums and asters are key features of the fall border, here offset by buff grasses and red-leaved *Euonymus alata*.

Frosted features
Winter is a quiet time in the garden, but there is still beauty to be found in the form of stark borders filled with frost-encrusted grasses and the enduring seedheads of perennials such as sedums.

25

BASIC PLANTING TECHNIQUES

Once you have planned your garden, and assessed the exposure and soil, you can begin planting. Giving new plants a good start by improving soil will result in strong, healthy specimens that put on a display year after year. Choose a mild day when the soil is not frozen or waterlogged and, before starting, make sure the soil is free of weeds. Water all plants well in preparation, and water them again after planting.

Choosing healthy plants

Before going to the garden center or nursery, make a list of your chosen plants, and try to stick to it, to avoid making impulsive purchases. If some of the plants are not available, remember to check the eventual size and required growing conditions of any substitutes to make sure they will fulfill your needs.

Check each plant to ensure that you have chosen the healthiest specimen. Look at the leaves and stems for signs of pests and diseases, and reject any plant with wilted foliage. Then turn over the pot and check to see if there is a mass of roots growing through the drainage holes, a sign that the plant is "rootbound" and has been growing in the pot for too long. Finally, select plants with lots of leafy stems and plump buds.

Preparing the ground

It is always wise to take a few hours to prepare the soil well before you plant. Clear the site of any large stones and remove all weeds, ensuring that you dig out the whole root system of perennial weeds, like dandelions. Start by hand-weeding the site.

Remove the weeds
When weeding, try to remove the root systems completely to prevent the weeds from growing back. Pernicious weeds, such as ground elder and bindweed, may need to be treated with a weedkiller.

You can apply a weedkiller, if necessary, to tackle pernicious weeds such as bindweed, ground elder, Japanese knotweed, horsetail, nettles, and brambles. If weeds are really problematic, consider covering the site with some old carpet or plastic sheeting for a few seasons. This forms a physical barrier against settling weed seeds, and the lack of light and moisture prevents weed growth. When the site has been

Feed the soil
When making a new bed or border, enrich the soil by digging in well-rotted organic matter, such as manure or garden compost, before planting. Apply organic matter as a mulch around plants on existing beds.

cleared, enrich the soil with organic matter, such as well-rotted manure or garden compost. On a large plot, dig a series of trenches to the depth of a spade across the area and add manure to the base of each trench. Alternatively, spread a 3in (8cm) layer of organic matter over the border, and dig it into the top 6in (15cm) of soil. Dig some horticultural grit into heavy clay to improve drainage. Finally, rake the surface.

PLANTING A PERENNIAL OR SHRUB

Shrubs form the backbone of a garden, providing permanent structure, while most perennials die down in winter and emerge again in spring. Plants grown in containers can be planted at any time of year, but avoid times when the ground is frozen or excessively wet or dry. Also, prepare the soil well before you start (see above), so your plants establish quickly and produce healthy growth.

1 Make a planting hole
First, water the plants well. Dig out a planting hole for each plant, making sure that it is twice the diameter of the container and a little deeper. Fork the bottom and sides of the hole, and add some controlled-release fertilizer to the excavated soil.

2 Check planting depth
Remove the plant from its pot, teasing out the roots if they are congested. Use a cane to check that the plant will be at the same depth as it was in its pot. Put the plant in the hole and steadily trickle in water as you backfill with soil, firming as you go.

3 Water and mulch
Water the plant. Spread a mulch of organic matter around the plant, avoiding the stems, to conserve moisture and suppress weeds. Water plants in dry spells until fully established. Each spring, rake in a general-purpose fertilizer around the plant.

PLANTING DEPTHS

Most plants need to be planted at the same depth as they were in their pots or, if they are bare-root trees or shrubs, plant them at the depth they were growing at in the field, indicated by a dark soil mark on the stems. Among the exceptions are bearded irises (below); their rhizomes will rot if buried, so they should be planted with them exposed. Sun-loving shrubs and perennials, such as verbascums and sedums, also thrive when planted slightly above soil level. Moisture-loving plants like hostas prefer to be buried a little deeper than ground level.

Planting in containers

When choosing a container, look at the range of different materials and designs available to find those that suit both your garden style and the types of plants you plan to grow.

In late spring, after all danger of frost has passed, plant your summer bedding outside in containers, windowboxes, and hanging baskets. The method for planting containers and windowboxes differs slightly from that for hanging baskets (see below), and they require watering daily. If you have less time to spend watering and feeding, opt for pots of drought-tolerant shrubs, such as hebes, lavenders, and phormiums, or rock plants, like sedums and houseleeks (*Sempervivum*).

Trees and large shrubs in containers add height and stature to a design. Those suitable for growing in pots include boxwood (*Buxus*), many dwarf conifers, *Fatsia japonica, Hydrangea serrata,* and choisyas. These will need to be watered regularly in dry spells. In spring, remove the top few inches of potting mix and replace with fresh, together with some all-purpose controlled-release fertilizer.

Choosing pot sizes

When making your container selections, choose pots of several different sizes for a traditional grouping, or opt for a series of pots of the same size and line them up for a contemporary look.

The size of your pots will affect the amount of maintenance they require. Tiny pots dry out quickly and need watering on a daily basis in summer, unless you plant them with drought-tolerant rock plants. Larger pots hold more potting mix and

therefore more moisture and nutrients, reducing the need for such frequent watering and feeding.

Material options

The material a container is made from affects both the price and the maintenance needs of the plants. Clay is a beautiful natural material, but because it is porous, it dries out more rapidly than synthetic materials or natural stone. Choose glazed clay or plastic if you want colorful pots.

Terra-cotta elegance
Natural and the perfect foil for a shrub, such as a hebe, terra-cotta is porous and dries out quickly. To prevent moisture loss, line with bubble wrap before planting.

Size matters
Choose a pot size that balances your chosen plants. Opt for a tall, slim container for a fountain of foliage, or a small, wide pot for a rounded shrub or planting group.

PLANTING A SUMMER CONTAINER

You can create exciting displays in containers and windowboxes with easy summer flowers. Some grow quickly from seed, or you can buy plug plants via mail order or larger bedding plants from the garden center. When combining plants, try to balance the shapes, colors, and textures. This example includes red dahlias, French marigolds, and yellow bidens.

PLANTING A HANGING BASKET

Globes of flowers and foliage lend an exotic touch to patios and seating areas throughout summer. Plant a large hanging basket and hang it at about head height where you can see the colors and textures at close quarters. Hanging baskets filled with ivy, small evergreens, violas, and early bulbs also add a splash of color in fall and winter.

1 Add drainage material
Place a layer of broken clay pot pieces in the base of the pot to help ensure good drainage. For larger pots, you can reduce the amount of potting mix required and the weight of the container by filling the bottom third with pieces of polystyrene.

2 Plant the container
Fill the container to about 2in (5cm) from the rim with all-purpose potting mix. Work in some slow-release fertilizer granules. Water the plants about 30 minutes before planting. Tip them from their pots or trays and arrange on the soil surface.

Final effects
Plant the tallest plants at the back or in the middle of the container, and fill in around them with shorter or trailing types. Water the container well, and continue to water regularly. To extend the flowering period, remove the faded blooms with pruners at frequent intervals throughout summer.

1 Preparing the basket
Line the basket and add a circle of plastic to the bottom to create a water reservoir. Top with a layer of potting mix. Cut crosses around the sides of the liner. Protect the trailing plants with some plastic and thread them through the crosses, as shown.

2 Planting the top
Cover the roots of the trailing plants with more potting mix, and then start planting the top of the basket. Work from the center out, with the tallest plants (such as verbena) in the middle, with compact bedding and trailing types around the edges.

Finishing touches
Fill in around the plants with potting mix and work in some slow-release fertilizer granules. Water well and add a layer of gravel over the soil to help retain moisture. Water the basket daily, even if it has rained, and deadhead regularly to extend the flower display throughout the summer.

LOOKING AFTER YOUR GARDEN

To keep your garden in peak condition, you will need to perform regular maintenance tasks throughout the year. Watering is essential for young plants and those in containers, and to win the battle against weeds, you must be vigilant from spring to fall. It pays to give most plants fertilizer and mulch every year—usually in spring. Woody plants may also need to be pruned to keep them in good condition.

Weeding methods

You can limit the growth of weeds by top-dressing the soil with a thick mulch or a membrane, but you will never be completely free of them. The most useful tool for removing annual weeds over a large area is a hoe; as you move it back and forth, the blade slices through the necks of weeds where the stems meet the soil. Choose a dry, sunny day for hoeing, and leave the weeds on the soil surface to die—you can then gather them up and compost them.

Although hoeing kills annual weeds, such as chickweed and groundsel, perennial weeds, including brambles, dock, couch grass, and ground elder, will survive and regrow. Use a weeder to remove those with taproots, such as dandelions, and dig out perennials with fibrous root systems using a spade or trowel. If you have pernicious weeds that you cannot remove by hand, apply a glyphosate weedkiller.

Watering

In summer, watering is the main gardening task. Young plants in beds and borders and container displays are especially vulnerable to drought, and are best watered early in the morning or in the evening, when evaporation rates are low. A basic watering can is generally sufficient for small areas or

Dealing with dandelions
A weeder is the ideal tool for prying out perennial weeds with deep taproots, such as dandelions.

Slow-release watering
Drip hoses trickle water into the soil above the roots, exactly where it is most needed.

containers, and fits easily under a rain-barrel spigot. For seedlings and new plants, use a can with a fine spray, so that you do not wash soil away from the roots.

If you have a large new area to water, a garden hose is a more practical option. Attach a spray nozzle to give new plantings a gentle shower, and direct the hose at the soil, not the leaves or flowers. An even more efficient watering method is to lay perforated drip hoses around your plants; water gradually seeps out at soil level and penetrates deeply with little waste.

Fertilizing

Once established, most plants growing in reasonably good soil need an annual application of fertilizer in spring. The type of plant food you choose and how often you apply it will be determined by your soil and what you are trying to grow. Plants require a range of essential nutrients. The primary nutrients are nitrogen (N), which plants need for leaf growth; phosphorus (P) for healthy roots; and potassium (K) for good flower and fruit production. The secondary nutrients, calcium, magnesium, and sulfur, are required in smaller amounts, while the seven trace elements, such as iron, are needed in very small quantities.

Fertilizers are either organic (derived from plants and animals) or inorganic (chemically manufactured). Most are concentrated for convenience and available

FERTILIZER OPTIONS

Most plants benefit from an application of fertilizer once a year in spring. However, some may need extra nutrients to boost them at key times, such as flowering. Always follow the manufacturer's instructions carefully because too much fertilizer, or using the wrong type for a particular plant, may have a detrimental effect. Your local garden center or DIY store will stock a selection of organic and inorganic fertilizers.

Chemical fertilizer
A balanced chemical fertilizer is used to enrich the soil at sowing or planting time. It can also be applied as a top-dressing in the spring for all types of plants.

Organic matter
Well-rotted manure or garden compost is rich in trace elements and soil-conditioning substances. Dig it into the ground or apply it as a surface mulch.

Blood, fish and bonemeal
This organic, balanced fertilizer can be mixed into the soil when planting, and applied around plants in the spring or early summer.

Soluble food
Fast-acting soluble liquid fertilizer gives bedding and container plants the nutrients they need. They can also be used on plants that need a quick boost.

Slow-release granules
These granules are activated by warmth and moisture, and provide a steady supply of nutrients for many weeks in borders and containers.

MULCH OPTIONS

Mulches reduce weed growth and conserve water, which is why they should always be applied when the ground is moist. A gravel mulch helps to keep the leaves and stems of drought-loving plants dry, and prevents them from rotting. As well as being functional, many mulches are also attractive and produce a decorative surface for borders and containers. Recycled ground glass and dyed shells are colorful options.

Gravel
Gravel laid over landscape fabric creates a weed suppressant and a decorative foil for alpines and Mediterranean-style plantings. Plant through the fabric by cutting a cross and folding back the flaps. Apply the gravel on top after planting.

Bark chips
Available in different sizes, the smallest being the most attractive, bark breaks down slowly and makes a good weed suppressor. It also helps to conserve soil moisture, but does not supply many nutrients. Top off worn areas annually.

Garden compost
Rotted compost and manure lock moisture into the soil and help to suppress weed growth. As the mulch breaks down, it also releases plant foods and improves the structure of the soil.

Leaf mold
Although low in nutrients, rotted leaves help to improve the soil structure and trap moisture in. They are ideal for woodland and shade-loving plants, many of which would be mulched by leaves in their natural habitats.

as liquids, powders that you dilute in water, or granules. Organic fertilizers include pelleted chicken manure; blood, fish and bone meal; liquid seaweed fertilizer; and homemade plant foods, such as the diluted liquor from a worm bin or fertilizers made from soaking comfrey leaves. Inorganic fertilizers include potassium sulfate and granular rose fertilizers.

Fertilizers are grouped according to the quantities of N, P, and K they contain. For example, a balanced fertilizer for general use contains equal quantities of each primary nutrient, while a fertilizer for lawns has a higher concentration of nitrogen, and those for fruit bushes are rich in potassium.

Apply an all-purpose granular fertilizer to the soil when planting, and spread it around plants in spring. Containers, baskets, and some bedding annuals may need a regular liquid feeding during the growing season, or apply a controlled-release granular fertilizer when planting. Remember to follow the manufacturer's directions carefully.

Mulching

Mulches are materials that are spread on the soil surface, usually around plants. Some mulches serve a practical purpose— feeding the soil, suppressing weeds, retaining moisture, or insulating roots in winter—while others are primarily decorative. Decorative mulches include crushed glass or shells, and slate chips.

Mulches are applied at different times of the year, depending on their purpose and the plants' needs. For example, bark chips are spread over the soil surface after planting to suppress weeds, but may take nutrients from the soil as they decompose, so apply a nitrogen-rich fertilizer to compensate for this loss. Organic matter, such as farmyard manure or garden compost, helps to retain soil moisture while also fertilizing the ground. It must be laid over moist soil, either in spring (following fall and winter rains) or after watering. Apply organic mulches in a thick layer about 4in (10cm) deep, and replenish them annually as worms and soil microorganisms will break them down throughout the year.

Composting

Disposing of your organic kitchen waste and plant prunings by composting creates an excellent eco-friendly soil improver. There is a wide range of bins available, including standard plastic composters that hold plenty of waste, and more decorative types, such as wooden models that resemble beehives.

To produce good compost, you will need the right mix of ingredients. Too much soft green material, such as grass clippings and vegetable peelings, turns the pile into a slimy mess. On the other hand, if you include too much dry woody material, such as prunings, the pile will rot down too slowly. Aim for an equal measure of green and dry ingredients and add them in layers. Good air flow is also essential to the composting process, so turn over the contents regularly.

Leaf mold is one of the finest soil conditioners, and makes good use of fallen autumn leaves. It is very quick and easy to make, but takes at least a year to rot down and be ready for use in the garden.

1 Rake up the leaves
In fall, rake up the leaves in your yard and place them in large plastic garbage bags. If you chop them up first with a garden spade, they will decompose faster.

2 Water, tie, and leave
When the bags are half full, sprinkle the leaves with water. Continue to add leaves, and water again when full. Tie the bag and make a few holes with a fork to allow in some air. After a year or two, the leaf mold will be ready.

Good garden hygiene

By keeping your plants in good health and checking them regularly, you can keep many pests and diseases at bay. Aim to grow your plants in the right conditions because healthy specimens are more able to withstand attacks. Remember, too, that some plants are susceptible to certain diseases so, whenever possible, buy resistant varieties.

A few simple precautions will also pay dividends. Check new plants for signs of pests and diseases to ensure that they do not introduce them into your garden, and keep all tools and equipment clean to guard against the spread of diseases. Tools such as pruners and seed trays are best cleaned with household disinfectant. You can also put up physical barriers, such as cut-off plastic bottles to help protect your plants from pests such as slugs and snails.

If a plant does succumb to a disease, first try to identify the problem to gauge its seriousness, and remove and either burn or discard infected plant material. Minor pest attacks can usually be dealt with by removing the invaders by hand. Also, try to encourage natural predators, such as birds, frogs and toads, ladybugs, hoverflies, spiders, and lacewings into your garden, as together they will help to keep many pests under control. Pools, ponds, berried shrubs and trees, and nectar-rich open flowers will help to lure this pest army into your plot. If you have to resort to chemical pesticides and fungicides, use them sparingly and read the manufacturer's instructions carefully.

Pruning guidelines

It is not essential to prune any plant, but thinning and cutting back to varying degrees or selectively removing whole branches can be beneficial.

Pruning can rejuvenate old, congested specimens and help to extend the life of short-lived shrubs. It can also promote the growth of more flowering and fruiting wood, improve the shape of a plant, and reduce the incidence of disease.

Most pruning is performed annually, but if you spot dead, damaged, or diseased wood, or a sucker growing from a grafted plant, remove it immediately. A general tip is to prune plants that flower in spring just after they have bloomed, and prune those that flower in summer or fall in early spring before the buds break. Most evergreens are pruned in late spring.

It is important to use the right tools when pruning, as they will make the task easier. The tool you will require depends on the thickness of the material you need to remove. Use sharp pruners for stems the width of a pencil or smaller, and a pruning saw or loppers for larger branches. Never prune above head height, and call in a professional arborist for large jobs.

You can achieve many beautiful effects with careful pruning. Some plants are best trimmed lightly to create a natural look, while others can be clipped into elegant topiary. In addition, some pruning techniques encourage more flowering and fruiting stems to form.

Cutting out dead and diseased wood
Whenever you see dead or diseased wood on any woody plant, remove it immediately. If dead wood is left on a plant, disease can enter more easily and move down the stems.

Pruning for shape and form
Some plants need a gentle trim to retain their shape. This *Pittosporum tenuifolium* makes an attractive focal plant. The only pruning it requires is to retain the plant's symmetry by lightly trimming it in late spring.

Crossing and rubbing branches
Branches that rub each other can create open wounds that let in diseases. Remove one of the branches, choosing the weakest one or the stem that has suffered the most damage.

MAKING PRUNING CUTS

Trees, shrubs, and climbers grow in different ways, and their shoots, buds, and stems differ too. Before pruning, identify the type of buds and shoots on the plant and their position. Buds are found at the point where the leaves are about to grow, or where they have previously been attached to the stem. When pruning, cut just above a bud; this stimulates hormones that make the bud develop into a new stem.

Cutting opposite buds
The buds of some plants are opposite each other. Prune above a pair of buds with a flat, straight cut. When the buds grow, they will produce two shoots growing in opposite directions from one another.

Cutting alternate buds
Where the buds are positioned alternately along the stems, try to prune to one that is facing outward, away from the center of the plant. Make a sloping cut above the bud, so that water runs away from it.

Cutting to new growth
You can recognize new growth because it looks much fresher than old wood. When pruning, cut off old wood just above a new stem, using a sloping cut so that water runs away from the young growth.

PLANT
SELECTOR

The lists in this section suggest plants that are suitable

for growing in a range of situations, or that have special

uses or characteristics. Although the plants should thrive

in the conditions specified, bear in mind that they are

not always consistent and much of their success depends

on climate, location, exposure, and care. The list is

subdivided into plant groups for each category, following

the arrangement of the Plant Catalog on pages 56–496.

Plants that are featured in the Catalog are followed by

page numbers; refer to the Plant Directory for a whole

genus or for a plant not followed by a number.

Plants for sandy soil

Sandy soils are often termed "light" or "hungry." They are usually well-drained, but dry out rapidly and hold low reserves of plant nutrients. Many plants have adapted to such soils by developing deeply penetrating roots. Their leaves are modified to reduce moisture loss: small and reflexed, evergreen and glossy, or covered with fine gray or silver hairs. To improve moisture retention, incorporate some organic matter when planting in fall; little watering will then be needed and plants are able to establish well before summer.

TREES

Amelanchier lamarckii, p.110
Betula ermanii, p.78
Betula pendula 'Dalecarlica'
Castanea sativa
Celtis australis, p.62
Cercis siliquastrum, p.83
Crataegus laevigata 'Paul's Scarlet', p.84
Genista aetnensis, p.89
Nothofagus obliqua, p.63
Phoenix canariensis
Pinus bungeana, p.78
Pinus sylvestris, p.78
Quercus ilex

Conifers

Abies grandis, p.98
x *Cuprocyparis leylandii* and cvs
Juniperus
Larix decidua, p.97
Pinus pinaster, p.97

Pinus radiata, p.98
Pseudotsuga menziesii var. *glauca*, p.96
Thuja occidentalis and cvs

SHRUBS

Acacia dealbata, p.211
Artemisia arborescens 'Faith Raven'
Berberis empetrifolia, p.148
Brachyglottis 'Sunshine'
BUDDLEJAS, p.114
Calluna vulgaris and cvs, p.166
Caragana arborescens 'Lorbergii'
Ceanothus thyrsiflorus and forms
Cistus spp. and cvs, pp.150, 152, 153, 154
Convolvulus cneorum, p.149
Cotoneaster lacteus, p.117
Elaeagnus pungens 'Maculata', p.119
Enkianthus cernuus f. *rubens*, p.123
Erica spp. and cvs, p.166
Gaultheria mucronata 'Mulberry Wine', p.164

Gaultheria mucronata 'Wintertime', p.163
Genista tinctoria, p.148
Halimium 'Susan', p.160
Hippophae rhamnoides, p.142
Hypericum 'Hidcote', p.160
LAVENDERS, p.158
Olearia nummulariifolia, p.128
Perovskia 'Blue Spire', p.159
Phlomis fruticosa, p.160
Robinia hispida, p.133
Rosa spinosissima
Rosmarinus officinalis, p.157
SALVIAS, p.155
Santolina pinnata subsp. *neapolitana* 'Sulphurea', p.159
Spartium junceum, p.140
Tamarix ramosissima, p.114
Teucrium fruticans 'Azureum'
x *Halimiocistus sahucii*, p.149
Yucca gloriosa, p.132

CLIMBERS AND WALL SHRUBS

CLEMATIS, pp.198–200
Clianthus puniceus, p.193
Eccremocarpus scaber, p.208
Lapageria rosea, p.202
Vitis vinifera 'Purpurea', p.210

PERENNIALS

Acanthus spinosus, p.239
Achillea spp. and cvs, pp.235, 243, 247, 359, 360
Agapanthus 'Northern Star', p.241
Agapanthus 'Phantom'
Agapanthus 'Purple Cloud', p.241

Agapanthus inapertus subsp. *pendulus* 'Graskop', p.240
Agastache 'Black Adder', p.280
Artemisia ludoviciana 'Valerie Finnis', p.274
Artemisia absinthium 'Lambrook Silver'
Asphodeline
Aster divaricatus, p.249
Aster ericoides f. *prostratus* 'Snowflurry'
Aster species, selections and hybrids, pp.249, 250, 254, 367
Baptisia australis, p.240
Berkheya purpurea, p.269
Campanula persicifolia
Campanula punctata, *C. takesimana*, p.241
Campanula species, selections and hybrids, pp.241, 242, 342, 360, 367, 368, 369
CARNATIONS AND PINKS, pp.266–267
Centranthus ruber, p.248
Coreopsis 'Limerock Ruby', p.268
Delphinium grandiflorum 'Blue Butterfly', p.217
Diascia personata, p.223
Eremurus x *isabellinus* 'Cleopatra', p.220
Eryngium pandanifolium
Eryngium x *tripartitum*, p.250
Erysimum 'Bowles Mauve', p.261
Francoa sochifolia Rogerson's form

BELOW Hot and dry conditions
Acanthus spinosus and *Phlomis russeliana* make a perfect planting partnership on sandy soil.

Perovskia 'Blue Spire'

Antirrhinum majus

Helianthemum 'Wisley Primrose'

Eccremocarpus scaber

RIGHT A garden on sandy gravel
Alliums and lavenders thrive on light, sandy soils and are ideal for gravel gardens in dry areas.

Plants for clay soil

Clay soil is usually wet, sticky, and heavy in winter, and during drier summers it can shrink and crack, damaging plant roots. Whether establishing a new garden on clay or renovating an older one, always choose plants that will grow well in this type of soil. Prepare the planting area thoroughly, digging the soil in the fall, then leaving it over winter to allow the weathering effects of frost and winter rains to break down large clods. Dig in organic matter, and grit or sharp sand to increase drainage. Plant in early spring, at the beginning of the growing season, to avoid losses over winter.

Caltha palustris 'Plena'

Anemone hupehensis 'Hadspen Abundance'

Kalmia latifolia

Viburnum opulus

LEFT A waterside planting
The yellow skunk cabbage (*Lysichiton americanus*) and marsh marigolds (*Caltha palustris*) flourish together in the clay soil beside this stream.

TREES

Alnus glutinosa
Castanospermum australe
Drimys winteri, p.73
FLOWERING DOGWOODS, p.87
Fraxinus spp., pp.60, 66, 71, 74, 79
Juglans nigra, p.63
Magnolia virginiana
Melaleuca viridiflora var. *rubriflora*
Oxydendrum arboreum, p.76
Pinus sylvestris, p.78
Populus spp. and cvs, pp.60, 61, 62, 63, 74
Prunus maackii
Prunus serrula, p.78
Pterocarya fraxinifolia
Quercus palustris, p.66
Quercus robur
Quercus suber, p.78
Salix babylonica var. *pekinensis* 'Tortuosa', p.80
Salix x sepulcralis var. *chrysocoma*, p.69
SORBUS, p.91

Conifers

Cryptomeria japonica and cvs, p.104
Metasequoia glyptostroboides, p.96
Taxodium distichum, p.99

SHRUBS

Aronia arbutifolia, p.142
Berberis thunbergii 'Rose Glow', p.137
Berberis valdiviana, p.111
Calycanthus floridus
Chaenomeles cathayensis, p.142
Chaenomeles speciosa 'Snow', p.146
Choisya 'Aztec Pearl', p.122
Choisya ternata SUNDANCE ('Lich'), p.148
Clethra alnifolia
CORNUS, p.126
Cotoneaster conspicuus, p.142
Cotoneaster frigidus, p.142
Cotoneaster hupehensis
Cotoneaster salicifolius, p.142
Cotoneaster x watereri 'John Waterer', p.142
Disanthus cercidifolius, p.141
Elaeagnus umbellata, p.113
Euonymus europaeus 'Red Cascade', p.140
Euonymus spp., pp.117, 142
Fothergilla gardenii, p.163
Fothergilla major, p.117
Genista tenera 'Golden Shower', p.116
Kalmia latifolia, p.136
Ledum groenlandicum, p.145
Photinia serratifolia, p.111
Photinia x fraseri 'Red Robin', p.111
Ribes sanguineum 'Edward VII', p.146
Ruscus aculeatus, p.167
Salix caprea
Salix exigua, p.112
Salix purpurea
Sambucus racemosa 'Plumosa Aurea', p.139
Spiraea japonica 'Albiflora'
Symphoricarpos albus var. *laevigatus*, p.142
Tetrapanax papyrifer, p.120
Viburnum bitchiuense, p.122
Viburnum lentago
Viburnum opulus and cvs, pp.142, 162
Viburnum tinus 'Eve Price', p.143

CLIMBERS AND WALL SHRUBS

Celastrus scandens
Garrya elliptica 'James Roof', p.211
Humulus lupulus 'Aureus', p.194
Rosa filipes 'Kiftsgate', p.184
Vitis coignetiae, p.209

PERENNIALS

Acanthus mollis 'Hollard's Gold', p.219
Anemone hupehensis and cvs
Anemone tomentosa
Bergenia spp. and cvs, pp.255, 256, 280
Chrysosplenium macrophyllum, p.256
Doronicum orientale 'Magnificum', p.263
Eupatorium maculatum Atropurpureum Group 'Reisenschirm', p.221
Filipendula ulmaria 'Aurea', p.274
Geranium 'Orion', p.280
Geranium ROZANNE ('Gerwat'), p.271
Geum 'Bell Bank', p.268
Helianthus 'Lemon Queen', p.222
Helonias bullata
Houttuynia cordata 'Chameleon', p.444
Iris laevigata
JAPANESE ANEMONES, p.222
Leucanthemum x superbum 'Sonnenschein', p.231
Ligularia 'Britt Marie Crawford', p.445
Ligularia 'The Rocket', p.219
Lythrum salicaria 'Feuerkerze', p.234
Mimulus guttatus
Omphalodes cappadocia 'Cherry Ingram', p.261
Primula japonica
Rodgersia pinnata 'Fireworks', p.234
Scrophularia auriculata 'Variegata'
Trollius spp. and cvs, pp.358, 436, 445

Grasses and bamboos

Luzula sylvatica 'Hohe Tatra', p.288
Miscanthus sinensis and cvs, pp.284, 285, 286
Phyllostachys spp. and cvs, pp.286, 287, 288, 289

Ferns

Polystichum setiferum groups, p.291
Thelypteris palustris, p.291
Woodwardia radicans

BULBS, CORMS, AND TUBERS

Cardiocrinum giganteum, p.385
CANNA, p.394
Zantedeschia 'Cameo', p.395

WATER AND BOG PLANTS

Aruncus dioicus, p.436
Butomus umbellatus
Caltha palustris, p.444
Darmera peltata, p.438
Gunnera manicata, p.443
Lysichiton americanus, p.444
Matteuccia struthiopteris, p.443
Onoclea sensibilis, p.443
Osmunda regalis, p.443
Pontederia cordata, p.441
Primula florindae, p.445
Ranunculus lingua, p.444
Sagittaria latifolia, p.434
Thalia dealbata

TENDER AND EXOTIC PLANTS
Perennials

Cyperus papyrus, p.479

Plants for neutral to acidic soil

Some plants, notably camellias, rhododendrons, and most heathers, grow naturally in regions such as open woodlands, hillsides, or moorlands where the soil is neutral to acidic, and are intolerant of alkaline soils such as chalk or limestone. These are often termed "lime-haters" or "acid-lovers." Before planting, work in some acidic planting compost or humus. After planting, keep woody plants well mulched. In drier regions, check water needs regularly.

TREES

Acer davidii, p.78
Acer forrestii
Acer griseum, p.78
Acer grosseri, p.78
Acer palmatum and cvs, pp.78, 89, 90, 115, 117, 123, 138, 156
Acer pensylvanicum 'Erythrocladum', p.78
Arbutus menziesii
Arbutus unedo, p.93
Embothrium coccineum, p.86
Eucryphia (most), pp.85, 129
Michelia doltsopa, p.71
Nyssa sinensis, p.77
Nyssa sylvatica, p.66
Oxydendrum arboreum, p.76
Pinus densiflora
Pterostyrax hispida, p.73
Stewartia pseudocamellia, p.78
Stewartia sinensis, p.78
Styrax japonicus, p.72

Conifers

Abies spp. and cvs, pp.95, 96, 98, 100, 104, 105
Picea spp. and cvs, pp.98, 99, 100, 101, 103, 105
Pinus densiflora
Pinus pumila
Pseudolarix amabilis, p.102
Pseudotsuga menziesii var. *glauca*, p.96
Sciadopitys verticillata, p.101
Tsuga heterophylla

SHRUBS

Acer palmatum 'Shindeshojo', p.123
Amelanchier lamarckii, p.110
Andromeda polifolia 'Compacta', p.333
Arctostaphylos (some), pp.144, 147
CAMELLIAS, pp.120–121
Chamaedaphne calyculata
Cyrilla racemiflora
Enkianthus spp., pp.111, 120, 123
Fothergilla gardenii
Fothergilla major, p.117
Gaultheria spp., pp.145, 154, 163, 164
HEATHERS, p.166, most
Kalmia spp., pp.136, 156
Ledum groenlandicum, p.145
Leiophyllum buxifolium
Leptospermum scoparium 'Snow White', p.135
Leucothöe fontanesiana and cvs, p.167
Lyonia ligustrinum
Menziesia ciliicalyx var. *purpurea*, p.146
Myrica gale, p.162
Philesia magellanica
Pieris spp. and cvs, pp.110, 120, 137
RHODODENDRONS, pp.124–125, most
Styrax officinalis, p.112
Telopea speciosissima, p.137
Vaccinium (most), pp.150, 163, 165, 351
WITCH HAZELS, p.118
Zenobia pulverulenta, p.130

CLIMBERS AND WALL SHRUBS

Asteranthera ovata
Berberidopsis corallina, p.202
Crinodendron hookerianum, p.202
Desfontainia spinosa, p.203
Mitraria coccinea, p.193

PERENNIALS

Dianella tasmanica, p.239
Ourisia coccinea, p.269
Smilacina racemosa, p.223
Tolmiea menziesii
Trillium spp., pp.255, 260, 350
Uvularia grandiflora, p.262

Grasses and Bamboos

Deschampsisa cespitosa 'Gold Tau', p.289
Molinia caerulea subsp. *arundinacea* 'Transparent', p.286
Molinia caerulea subsp. *caerulea* 'Heidebraut', p.285

Ferns

Adiantum spp., pp.291, 292
Blechnum spp., pp.290, 292
Cryptogramma crispa, p.293

ANNUALS AND BIENNIALS

Calibrachoa cvs, pp.300, 306

ROCK PLANTS

Arctostaphylos spp. and cvs, pp.375, 376
Cassiope spp., pp.322, 349
Cornus canadensis, p.360
Corydalis cashmeriana
Cyananthus spp., pp.359, 369
Epigaea gaultherioides, p.351
Galax urceolata, p.336
Gaultheria spp., pp.346, 373
Gentiana sino-ornata, p.370
Linnaea borealis, p.363
Lithodora diffusa 'Heavenly Blue', p.343
Mitchella repens
Ourisia spp., pp.360, 362

Phlox adsurgens
Phlox stolonifera
Phyllodoce spp., pp.333, 334
Pieris nana
Shortia spp., pp.349, 352

BULBS, CORMS, AND TUBERS

Lilium speciosum var. *rubrum*
Lilium superbum, p.390

WATER AND BOG PLANTS

Sarracenia flava, p.445

TENDER AND EXOTIC PLANTS
Shrubs

Boronia megastigma, p.456
Epacris impressa, p.455
Gardenia augusta
Pimelea ferruginea, p.455
Protea spp., p.454

Climbers

Agapetes spp., p.461
Allamanda cathartica

Perennials

Aspidistra spp.
Calanthe striata, p.275
Caulokaempferia petelotii
Centropogon cordifolius
Cornukaempferia aurantiflora 'Jungle Gold', p.477
Cypripedium reginae, p.466
Drosera spp., p.473
Nepenthes x *hookeriana*, p.473
Peliosanthes arisanensis, p.472

BELOW A carpet of heather
Heathers (*Erica*) create dramatic sweeps of color in winter in this heather garden. The majority of heathers thrive in well-drained, acidic soil in full sun.

Gaultheria mucronata 'Wintertime'

Fothergilla major

Plants for limestone

Limestone regions are rich in wildflowers and wildlife, and where there is a reasonable depth of topsoil, a wide range of garden plants can be grown. However, often there are only a few inches of soil above bedrock, and here there is an increased risk of drought in summer. It may be necessary to excavate planting holes and incorporate organic matter to increase plants' chances of survival. On well-drained soil, plant in fall or spring; on wetter soil, defer planting until spring. Keep all young woody plants well mulched and watered until established.

TREES

Acer negundo 'Variegatum', p.74
Aesculus x *carnea* 'Briotii', p.60
Arbutus andrachne
Betula albo-sinensis, p.78
Betula ermanii, p.78
Betula nigra, p.78
Betula utilis var. *jacquemontii* cvs, p.78
Catalpa bignonioides, p.73
Cercis siliquastrum, p.83
Crataegus spp. and cvs, pp.80, 84, 90
Eucalyptus pauciflora subsp. *niphophila*, p.78
Fagus sylvatica, p.64
Fraxinus ornus, p.71
Gleditsia triacanthos 'Sunburst', p.72
HOLLIES, p.94
Laurus nobilis, p.80
Malus spp. and cvs, pp.71, 83, 90, 110
Morus nigra
Phillyrea latifolia

Prunus avium 'Plena', p.71
Prunus maackii
Prunus serrula, p.78
SORBUS (many), p.91
Tilia tomentosa

Conifers

Calocedrus decurrens, p.101
Cedrus libani, p.97
Chamaecyparis lawsoniana and cvs pp.96, 102, 103
Cupressus arizonica var. *glabra*
x *Cuprocyparis leylandii* and cvs
Ginkgo biloba, p.97
Juniperus spp and cvs, pp.100, 103, 105
Picea omorika, p.98
Pinus nigra
Platycladus orientalis and cvs
Taxus baccata and cvs, pp.101, 102, 105
Thuja plicata and cvs

SHRUBS

Abutilon 'Kentish Belle', p.162
Abutilon 'Ashford Red', p.137
Aucuba japonica 'Crotonifolia'
Azara microphylla, p.118
Berberis darwinii, p.111
Berberis valdiviana, p.111
BUDDLEJA, p.114
Ceanothus impressus, p.138

Ceratostigma griffithii
Chaenomeles cathayensis, p.142
Chaenomeles speciosa 'Snow', p.146
Chimonanthus praecox, p.144
Choisya 'Aztec Pearl', p.122
Choisya ternata, p.122
Choisya ternata SUNDANCE ('Lich'), p.148
Cistus spp, pp.150, 154
Colletia paradoxa, p.131
Cotinus coggygria 'Golden Spirit', p.116
Cotoneaster conspicuus, p.142
Cotoneaster frigidus, p.142
Cotoneaster hupehensis
Cotoneaster salicifolius, p.142
Cotoneaster x *watereri* 'John Waterer', p.142
Daphne bholua 'Jacqueline Postill', p.143
Deutzia spp. and cvs, pp.132, 149, 152
Edgeworthia chrysantha, p.126
Escallonia 'Donard Beauty', p.154
Euonymus europaeus 'Red Cascade', p.140
Euonymus hamiltonianus, p.142
Euonymus latifolius, p.140
Euonymus oxyphyllus, p.117
Genista tenera 'Golden Shower', p.116
HARDY FUCHSIAS, p.154
Hebe carnosula
Hebe 'Great Orme', p.153
Hypericum 'Hidcote', p.160
LAVENDERS, p.158
LILACS, p.115
Olearia ilicifolia, p.130
Olearia macrodonta, p.132
Philadelphus spp. and cvs, pp.127, 128, 131, 149
Phlomis fruticosa, p.160
Photinia serratifolia, p.111
Photinia x *fraseri* 'Red Robin', p.111
Potentilla fruticosa and cvs, pp.149, 160, 162
Ribes sanguineum 'Edward VII', p.146
ROSES (most), pp.172–187

Rosmarinus officinalis, p.157
Ruscus aculeatus, p.167
Salix exigua, p.112
SALVIA, p.155
Sambucus nigra 'Guincho Purple'
Sambucus racemosa 'Plumosa Aurea', p.139
Spartium junceum, p.140
Spiraea japonica 'Albiflora'
Spiraea nipponica 'Snowmound', p.131
Symphoricarpos albus var. *laevigatus*, p.142
Viburnum bitchiuense, p.122
Viburnum opulus
Viburnum tinus
Viburnum tinus 'Eve Price', p.143
Vitex agnus-castus
Weigela florida 'Variegata', p.152

CLIMBERS AND WALL SHRUBS

Actinidia kolomikta, p.201
Campsis radicans
Carpenteria californica, p.197
Celastrus orbiculatus
CLEMATIS, pp.198–200
Eccremocarpus scaber, p.208
Forsythia suspensa, p.195
Fremontodendron 'California Glory', p.206
Garrya elliptica 'James Roof', p.211
Hedera spp. and cvs, p.211
HONEYSUCKLE, p.207
Jasminum officinale f. *affine*, p.196
Parthenocissus henryana
Passiflora caerulea, p.204
Rosa 'Albéric Barbier', p.184

BELOW Early summer scent
A lilac, here combined with deutzia and peonies, grows in the shelter of a wall. Lilacs prefer alkaline soil, as long as it is well-drained.

BELOW Bright yellow display
Achillea 'Moonshine' is a perennial that thrives in alkaline soil and will withstand periods of drought. In summer, the flowers attract bees and butterflies.

Philadelphus 'Dame Blanche'

Lathyrus vernus

Rosa 'Albertine', p.185
Solanum crispum 'Glasnevin', p.204
Trachelospermum jasminoides, p.195
Wisteria sinensis

PERENNIALS
Acanthus spinosus, p.239
Anemone tomentosa
Anemone hupehensis
AQUILEGIA, p.226
ASTER, p.249
CAMPANULA, p.241
DELPHINIUMS, p.217
Doronicum spp., pp.227, 263
Eryngium spp., pp.240, 250, 271
Erysimum 'Bowles's Mauve', p.261
Eupatorium maculatum Atropurpureum Group 'Reisenscirm', p.221
Geranium ROZANNE ('Gerwat'), p.271
Geranium 'Orion', p.280
Geum 'Bell Bank', p.268
Gypsophila paniculata cvs, p.231
HELENIUM, p.248
Helianthus 'Lemon Queen', p.222
HEUCHERA, p.282
IRISES (most), pp.224–225
JAPANESE ANEMONES, p.222
Leucanthemum x superbum 'Sonnenschein', p.231
Nepeta 'Six Hills Giant', p.240
Omphalodes cappadocia 'Cherry Ingram', p.261
ORIENTAL POPPIES, p.238
PEONIES, p.229
Potentilla 'Arc-en-ciel', p.268
RUDBECKIA, p.251
SALVIA, p.250
Scabiosa caucasica 'Clive Greaves', p.270
Schizostylis 'Mrs Hegarty'
Sidalcea 'Oberon', p.233
Verbascum spp. and cvs, pp.243, 246
Veronicastrum virginicum 'Fascination', p.220
YARROW, p.247

Grasses and bamboos
Ampeldesmos mauritanica, p.287
Stipa tenuissima, p.288

Ferns
Asplenium scolopendrium, p.292
Asplenium trichomanes, p.291
Dryopteris filix-mas, p.292
Polypodium vulgare 'Cornubiense'

ANNUALS AND BIENNIALS
Ageratum houstonianum and cvs, pp.313, 314
Calendula officinalis and cvs, pp.321, 325, 326
Callistephus chinensis Series and cvs, pp.303, 304, 312
Calomeria amaranthoides
Erysimum cheiri 'Fire King', p.326
Gomphrena globosa, p.303
Lavatera trimestris 'Silver Cup', p.305
Limonium sinuatum
Lobularia maritima
Lunaria annua, p.310
Matthiola 'Giant Excelsior', p.303
Tagetes spp. and cvs, pp.308, 320, 322, 326
Ursinia anthemoides, p.322
Xeranthemum annuum, p.305
Zinnia spp. and cvs, pp.306, 316, 325,

ROCK PLANTS
Aethionema spp. and cvs, pp.338, 362, 364
Androsace lanuginosa, p.363
Aster alpinus, p.367
Campanula (most rock garden species), pp.342, 368, 342
Dianthus (most rock garden species), pp.363, 364, 366
Draba spp., pp.357, 358
Erysimum helveticum, p.358
Gypsophila repens
Helianthemum spp., pp.336, 337, 340, 345

Lathyrus vernus, p.260
Leontopodium alpinum, p.332
Linum arboreum, p.344
Lobularia maritima and cvs, pp.298, 304
Origanum dictamnus
Papaver burseri
Penstemon pinifolius, p.340
Rhodanthemum hosmariense, p.332
Saponaria ocymoides, p.364
Saxifraga, pp.332, 337, 348, 350, 358, 377
Thymus caespititius
Veronica austriaca subsp. teucrium, p.343
Veronica prostrata, p.343

BULBS, CORMS, AND TUBERS
Allium aflatunense, p.382
Allium atropurpureum, p.392
Allium 'Gladiator', p.392
Allium 'Globemaster', p.392
Allium 'Mount Everest', p.385
Allium neapolitanum Cowanii Group, p.409
Allium oreophilum, p.418
Allium 'Purple Sensation', p.392
Anemone blanda 'Violet Star', p.418
Anemone coronaria De Caen Group 'Mr Fokker', p.403
Anemone ranunculoides, p.263
Anomatheca laxa, p.423
Babiana rubrocyanea, p.418
Bellavalia romana, p.399
Calochortus superbus, p.409
Chionodoxa forbesii, p.419
Colchicum, pp.421, 424, 425
Crinum x powellii, p.385
CROCUSES, p.417
Cyclamen coum and cvs, pp.428, 429
Cyclamen hederifolium, p.426
DAFFODILS, pp.404–405
Fritillaria imperialis 'Lutea', p.382
Fritillaria persica 'Ivory Bells', p.382
GLADIOLI, p.384

Gladiolus murielae
Hermodactylus tuberosus, p.406
Hippeastrum 'Black Pearl'
Hyacinthus orientalis 'Blue Jacket', p.403
Hyacinthus orientalis 'White Pearl', p.415
Hymenocallis 'Sulphur Queen', p.412
Incarvillea delavayi, p.265
Iris reticulata and cvs
Lilium regale, p.388
Muscari spp. and cvs, pp.403, 415, 420, 421
Nerine bowdenii 'Nikita'
Ornithogalum nutans, p.399
Ornithogalum umbellatum, p.416
Pancratium illyricum, p.408
Polianthes tuberosa 'The Pearl', p.385
Scilla spp., pp.413, 416, 420, 423
Triteleia 'Queen Fabiola'
Tulbaghia simmleri, p.411
TULIPS, pp.400–401
Watsonia meriana, p.385
Zephyranthes spp., pp.413, 424

TENDER AND EXOTIC PLANTS
Shrubs
Nerium oleander, p.455

Cacti and succulents
Furcraea parmentieri

BELOW Colorful crevices
Naturally at home in cracks and crevices, these *Saxifraga* form neat mounds of color. They are ideal for sunny, well-drained rock and alpine gardens.

Plants for coastal sites

In coastal regions, salt from sea spray is carried a considerable distance inland on the wind, causing problems for many plants. However, some can tolerate high salt levels, and have hard-surfaced or glossy leaves with low absorbency levels, or foliage covered with fine hairs that prevent salt reaching the surface. Coastal gardens are often exposed, so protect plants with hedges or fences. Prepare sandy soil by incorporating organic matter and garden loam, to encourage deep root penetration, and use dense groundcover plants to stabilize the sand and keep root areas cool.

TREES

Acer pseudoplatanus and cvs, pp.65, 73, 84
Alnus incana, p.61
Arbutus andrachne
Arbutus unedo, p.93
Castanea sativa
Cordyline australis
Crataegus laevigata 'Paul's Scarlet', p.84
Eucalyptus coccifera, p.68
Eucalpytus gunnii, p.68
Fraxinus excelsior
Ilex aquifolium cvs, pp.92, 94
Laurus nobilis, p.80
Luma apiculata, p.78
Melaleuca viridiflora var. *rubriflora*
Melia azedarach, p.71
Populus alba, p.60
Quercus suber, p.78
Salix alba
Schinus molle
SORBUS, p.91

Conifers

Cupressus macrocarpa
Juniperus conferta
Pinus contorta var. *latifolia*, p.101
Pinus nigra subsp. *nigra*, p.98
Pinus radiata, p.98
x *Cuprocyparis leylandii*

SHRUBS

Acacia verticillata
Atriplex halimus
Baccharis halimifolia
Berberis darwinii, p.111
Brachyglottis Dunedin Group, p.161
Buddleja globosa, p.116
Bupleurum fruticosum, p.139
Cassinia leptophylla subsp. *fulvida*
Chamaerops humilis, p.165
Choisya ternata, p.122
Cistus ladanifer, p.150
Colutea arborescens, p.139
Corokia x *virgata*
Cotoneaster conspicuus, p.142
Cotoneaster salicifolius, p.142
Cotoneaster frigidus, p.142
Cytisus x *spachianus*
Elaeagnus pungens 'Maculata', p.119
Elaeagnus umbellata, p.113
Erica arborea var. *alpina*, p.166
Erica cinerea 'Eden Valley', p.166
Escallonia 'Donard Beauty', p.154
Escallonia rubra 'Crimson Spire'
Euonymus japonicus
Euphorbia characias subsp. *characias*, p.147
Fabiana imbricata
Felicia amelloides 'Santa Anita', p.157
Fuchsia magellanica, p.154
Fuchsia 'Riccartonii', p.154
Genista hispanica, p.160
Genista tenera 'Golden Shower', p.116
Griselinia littoralis
Halimium lasianthum subsp. *formosum*, p.161
Hebe 'White Gem', p.149
Helichrysum italicum
Hippophae rhamnoides, p.142
Hydrangea macrophylla and cvs, pp.134–135
Lavatera x *clementii* 'Rosea', p.136
LAVENDERS, p.158
Leptospermum scoparium 'Red Damask', p.123
Leycesteria formosa
Lonicera pileata, p.167
Lycium barbarum
Olearia ilicifolia, p.130
Olearia macrodonta, p.132
Ozothamnus ledifolius, p.151
Parahebe perfoliata, p.271
Phillyrea latifolia
Phlomis fruticosa, p.160
Pittosporum tobira
Pyracantha coccinea 'Lalandei'
Rhamnus alaternus 'Argenteovariegata'
Rosa rugosa, p.176
Rosmarinus officinalis, p.157
Sambucus racemosa and cvs
Spartium junceum, p.140

BELOW Coastal retreat
Dramatic agapanthus and architectural
phormiums are both ideal plants for
exposed coastal sites with mild winters.

Grasses and bamboos

ANNUALS AND BIENNIALS

ROCK PLANTS

BULBS, CORMS, AND TUBERS

TENDER AND EXOTIC PLANTS
Trees

Shrubs

Climbers

Perennials

Cacti and succulents

Euphorbia characias subsp. *characias*

Armeria maritima 'Vindictive'

Felicia amelloides 'Santa Anita'

Achillea filipendulina 'Parker's Variety'

Eryngium variifolium

Sedum spathulifolium 'Cape Blanco'

Trees and shrubs for exposed sites

In cold-climate gardens that are exposed to strong winter winds, only the hardiest plants thrive without the protection of a windbreak. Where providing one is not practical, it is essential to establish a basic framework of trees, shrubs, and conifers that are fully hardy. Carefully positioned within the garden, in groups, they provide sheltered situations where less hardy plants can be grown, while still retaining a degree of openness if desired.

Climbers and shrubs for shady walls

Against cold, north- or east-facing walls, it is essential to choose climbers that grow naturally in shade or semishade. These provide reliable and effective foliage cover, and some have attractive flowers. A few climbing roses flower reasonably well in partially shaded situations and, together with climbers and shrubs, add color to the backs of borders. Shade-tolerant plants prefer moist, woodland-type soils; when planting, dig in organic matter, such as leaf mold.

ABOVE Vibrant fall color
Cotinus species and hybrids make a dramatic statement in fall. They thrive in full sun or partial shade, and tolerate exposed sites.

TREES

Acer platanoides and cvs, pp.60, 67
Acer pseudoplatanus
Betula utilis var. *jacquemontii*
Crataegus laevigata 'Paul's Scarlet', p.84
Crataegus x lavallei 'Carrierei'
Fagus sylvatica and cvs, pp.61, 64, 79
Fraxinus excelsior 'Jaspidea', p.60
Fraxinus ornus, p.71
Laburnum x watereri 'Vossii', p.84
Populus tremula
SORBUS (many), p.91
Tilia cordata

Conifers

Chamaecyparis nootkatensis
Chamaecyparis obtusa and cvs, pp.104, 105
Chamaecyparis pisifera 'Filifera Aurea', p.105
Juniperus communis 'Hibernica'
Juniperus x pfitzeriana and cvs, p.105
Picea breweriana, p.99
Pinus nigra subsp. *nigra*, p.98
Pinus sylvestris, p.78
Taxus baccata and cvs, pp.101, 102, 105
Tsuga canadensis, p.102

SHRUBS

Arctostaphylos uva-ursi, p.376
Amorpha canescens
Berberis darwinii, p.111
Berberis 'Rubrostilla', p.162
Berberis x stenophylla, p.127
Buddleja davidii 'Royal Red'
Calluna vulgaris and cvs, p.166
Chaenomeles cathayensis, p.142
Cornus alba 'Sibirica', p.143

Corylus maxima 'Purpurea', p.115
Cotinus coggygria 'Golden Spirit', p.116
Cotinus 'Flame', p.117
Cotoneaster 'Gnom'
Cotoneaster lacteus, p.117
Cotoneaster salicifolius, p.142
Cotoneaster simonsii, p.143
Elaeagnus umbellata, p.113
Euonymus europaeus 'Red Cascade', p.140
Euonymus hamiltonianus, p.142
Euonymus hamiltonianus subsp. *sieboldianus*, p.142
Euonymus oxyphyllus, p.117
Ledum groenlandicum, p.145
LILACS, p.115
Lonicera pileata, p.167
Mahonia aquifolium, p.148
Philadelphus 'Beauclerk', p.127
Philadelphus 'Belle Etoile', p.128
Prunus laurocerasus 'Otto Luyken', p.145
Pyracantha x watereri, p.128
Ribes sanguineum 'Edward VII', p.146
Rubus thibetanus, p.143
Salix purpurea
Sambucus nigra 'Guincho Purple'
Spiraea japonica 'Albiflora'
Spiraea x vanhouttei, p.145
Symphoricarpos x chenaultii 'Hancock'
Ulex europaeus 'Flore Pleno'
Viburnum bitchiuense, p.122
Viburnum opulus 'Xanthocarpum'
Viburnum tinus 'Eve Price', p.143

SHRUBS

Azara microphylla, p.118
CAMELLIAS, pp.120–121
Chaenomeles speciosa 'Moerloosei', p.122
Chaenomeles x superba 'Rowallane', p.147
Choisya ternata, p.122
Cotoneaster lacteus, p.117
Cotoneaster salicifolius, p.142
Daphne bholua 'Jacqueline Postill', p.143
Drimys winteri, p.73
Eucryphia x nymansensis 'Nymansay', p.73
Fatsia japonica
Jasminum nudiflorum, p.144
Mahonia japonica, p.144
Mahonia x media 'Charity', p.118
Muehlenbeckia complexa
Osmanthus decorus
Pyracantha spp. and cvs, pp.118, 128, 141, 144
Ribes laurifolium, p.165
Rosa 'Albéric Barbier', p.184
Rosa 'Madame Alfred Carrière', p.184
Rosa 'Madame Grégoire Staechelin', p.185
Rosa 'Maigold', p.187
Rosa THE PRINCE'S TRUST ('Harholding'), p.186
Rosa WHITE STAR ('Harquill'), p.184

CLIMBERS AND WALL SHRUBS

Akebia quinata, p.193
Berberidopsis corallina, p.202
Celastrus scandens
Clematis 'Frances Rivis', p.200
Cotoneaster horizontalis, p.208
Crinodendron hookerianum, p.202
Ercilla volubilis, p.192
Euonymus fortunei 'Coloratus',
Euonymus fortunei 'Silver Queen', p.144
x *Fatshedera lizei*, p.211
Forsythia suspensa, p.195
Garrya elliptica 'James Roof', p.211
Hedera colchica 'Dentata Variegata'
Hedera colchica 'Sulphur Heart', p.211
Hedera helix cvs, p.211
HONEYSUCKLE, p.207
Hydrangea petiolaris, p.195
Itea ilicifolia, p.211
Lapageria rosea, p.202
Parthenocissus spp. and cvs, pp.209, 210
Pileostegia viburnoides, p.196
Schisandra rubriflora, p.202
Schizophragma hydrangeoides, p.197
Schizophragma integrifolium, p.197

BELOW Green-themed shade bed
Hostas and acers thrive in the shady conditions at the foot of sunless walls, providing attractive foliage patterns.

Drought-tolerant plants

Hot, sunny locations and free-draining, sandy soils demand plants that tolerate dry conditions. Drought-resistant plants will survive the increasing number of long, dry periods that some areas are now experiencing even in normally wet seasons. All the plants listed here have adapted to thrive in arid conditions, and will need little or no additional irrigation once established, but guard against waterlogged clay soils, in which they will quickly decline and die.

Agapanthus praecox subsp. *orientalis*

Miscanthus sinensis 'Cosmopolitan'

ABOVE Water-wise gardening
Perovskia and *Echinops* 'Veitch's Blue' can withstand periods of drought, while still providing a spectacular display.

Plants for hedges and windbreaks

Plants for hedging are often selected for their ornamental qualities, but there are other aspects to consider. Boundary hedges can provide visual privacy, or screen unsightly buildings; they may also be bushy or thorny to keep out animals or intruders. Make sure that plants for screening will grow to the required height, and select conifers or evergreen shrubs for year-round effect. In exposed sites, trees and deciduous shrubs can be used as windbreaks; two or three staggered rows are more effective than a single, closely planted one.

TREES

Arbutus unedo, p.93
Carpinus betulus
Carpinus betulus 'Fastigiata', p.93
Crataegus monogyna
Fagus sylvatica, p.64
HOLLIES, p.94
Laurus nobilis, p.80
Melaleuca viridiflora var. *rubriflora*
Nothofagus dombeyi, p.68
Nothofagus obliqua, p.63
Olea europaea
Populus x *canadensis* 'Robusta', p.62
Prunus lusitanica
Umbellularia californica, p.69

Conifers

Abies grandis, p.98
Cedrus deodara, p.96
Cephalotaxus harringtonii
Chamaecyparis lawsoniana
x *Cuprocyparis* 'Castlewellan', p.99
Cupressus macrocarpa
Juniperus communis
Larix decidua, p.97
Picea omorika, p.98
Pinus nigra
Pinus radiata, p.98
Pseudotsuga menziesii var. *glauca*, p.96
Taxus baccata
Thuja plicata
Tsuga canadensis, p.102

SHRUBS

Berberis darwinii, p.111
Berberis thunbergii 'Rose Glow', p.137
Buxus sempervirens 'Suffruticosa', p.167
Choisya ternata, p.122
Cotoneaster salicifolius, p.142
Cotoneaster simonsii, p.143
Elaeagnus umbellata, p.113
Elaeagnus ebbingei
Escallonia 'Langleyensis'
Escallonia 'Donard Beauty', p.154
Euonymus japonicus 'Macrophyllus'

Forsythia x *intermedia* cvs, p.127
Griselinia littoralis
Hippophäe rhamnoides, p.142
HYDRANGEAS, p.134
LAVENDERS, p.158
Leptospermum scoparium and cvs, pp.123, 130
Ligustrum ovalifolium, p.119
Lonicera nitida
Pittosporum tenuifolium, p.120
Prunus laurocerasus
Prunus lusitanica
Pyracantha x *watereri*, p.128
Rosa 'Céleste', p.173
Rosa 'Felicia', p.173
Rosa 'Frühlingsmorgen'
Rosa gallica var. *officinalis*
Rosa gallica var. *officinalis* 'Versicolor', p.174
Rosa glauca, p.176
Rosa GRAHAM THOMAS ('Ausmas'), p.176
Rosa 'Great Maiden's Blush', p.173
Rosa JACQUELINE DU PRÉ ('Harwanna'), p.172
Rosa 'Marguerite Hilling', p.173
Rosa moyesii 'Geranium', p.176
Rosa 'Nevada', p.173
Rosa 'Penelope', p.172
Rosa rugosa, p.176
Rosmarinus officinalis, p.157
Tamarix ramosissima, p.114
Viburnum tinus 'Eve Price', p.143

PERENNIALS

Eupatorium purpureum
Filipendula camtschatica
Phormium tenax

Grasses and bamboos

Arundo donax
Chimonobambusa timidissinoda, p.287
Cortaderia selloana 'Sunningdale Silver', p.284
Fargesia nitida
Miscanthus sinensis and cvs, pp.284, 285, 286
Phyllostachys spp. and cvs, pp.286, 287, 288, 289
Pseudosasa japonica, p.287
Semiarundinaria fastuosa, p.287

TENDER AND EXOTIC PLANTS

Trees

Codiaeum variegatum var. *pictum*, p.459
Metrosideros excelsa, p.450
Syzygium paniculatum, p.450

Shrubs

Dodonaea viscosa 'Purpurea', p.457
Hibiscus rosa-sinensis

Forsythia x *intermedia* 'Beatrix Farrand'

Rosa gallica var. *officinalis* 'Versicolor'

Lavandula angustifolia 'Hidcote'

RIGHT Formal definition
In this mature garden, yew hedges form green walls, providing shelter as well as excellent structure. Boxwood hedges give a formal edge to the flower beds.

Architectural plants

Plants that stand out and draw the eye with their strong, distinctive appearance are termed "architectural" plants. They give character and substance to a garden, and help to form the basic framework. Most are trees, conifers, and shrubs, which provide a permanent effect throughout the year, and they usually have a strong shape, such as vertical or conical forms of conifer, or bear striking foliage, such as giant-leaved gunneras and spiky phormiums.

Agave americana 'Marginata'

Yucca gloriosa

TREES
Acer griseum, p.78
Betula utilis var. *jacquemontii* and cvs, p.78
Cordyline australis 'Atropurpurea', p.451
CORNUS (many), p.126
Eucalyptus spp., pp.67, 68, 79
Kalopanax septemlobus, p.74
Luma apiculata, p.78
MAGNOLIAS, p.70
Paulownia tomentosa, p.72
Phoenix canariensis
Quercus suber, p.78
Trachycarpus fortunei, p.80
Trochodendron aralioides, p.79

Conifers
Abies spp., pp.95, 96, 100, 104
Araucaria araucana, p.98
Calocedrus decurrens, p.101
Cedrus spp., pp.95, 96, 97, 104
Juniperus x *pfitzeriana* 'William Pfitzer'
Metasequoia glyptostroboides, p.96
Picea glauca 'Coerulea', p.99
Picea pungens and cvs, pp.99, 105
Pinus bungeana, p.78
Pinus densiflora
Pinus sylvestris, p.78
Pseudolarix amabilis, p.102
Sciadopitys verticillata, p.101
Taxodium distichum, p.99
Tsuga heterophylla

SHRUBS
Aesculus parviflora, p.113
Acer palmatum 'Shindeshojo', p.123
Colletia paradoxa, p.131
FLOWERING DOGWOODS, p.87
Cotoneaster x *watereri* 'John Waterer', p.142
Daphniphyllum macropodum, p.111
Eriobotrya japonica, p.194
Fatsia japonica
Mahonia japonica, p.144
Mahonia x *media* and cvs, p.118
Olearia ilicifolia, p.130
Olearia macrodonta, p.132
Parkinsonia aculeata
Rhus typhina 'Dissecta', p.117
Yucca spp., pp.132, 151

CLIMBERS
Schizophragma spp., p.197
Vitis coignetiae, p.209
WISTERIA, p.205

PERENNIALS
Acanthus mollis 'Hollard's Gold', p.219
Acanthus spinosus, p.239
Angelica archangelica, p.219
Astelia chathamica, p.242
Begonia grandis subsp. *evansiana*, p.278
Berkheya macrocephala, p.243
Cynara cardunculus, p.216
Echinops bannaticus 'Taplow Blue', p.241
Eremurus x *isabellinus* 'Cleopatra', p.220
Eryngium pandanifolium

Euphorbia characias subsp. *characias*, p.147
Hedychium coccineum 'Tara', p.220
HOSTAS (many), pp.272–273
Kniphofia caulescens, p.254
Kniphofia northiae, p.254
Ligularia 'Britt Marie Crawford', p.445
Ligularia 'The Rocket', p.219
Mathiasella bupleroides 'Green Dream', p.242
Persicaria polymorpha, p.234
Phormium 'Dazzler', p.216
Rodgersia pinnata 'Fireworks'
Rudbeckia maxima, p.251
Verbascum olympicum, p.219

Grasses and bamboos
Ampeldesmos mauritanica, p.287
Chimonobambusa timidissinoda, p.287
Chusquea culeou, p.288
Cortadera richardii, p.284
Cortadera selloana and cvs, pp.284, 285
Elegia capensis, p.285
Miscanthus sinensis and cvs, pp.284, 285, 286
Molinia caerulea subsp. *arundinacea* 'Transparent', p.286
Phyllostachys spp. and cvs, pp.286, 287, 288, 289
Thamnocalamus crassinodus 'Kew Beauty', p.286

Ferns
Asplenium scolopendrium Marginatum Group, p.292
Blechnum tabulare
Dicksonia antarctica, p.290
Polystichum munitum, p.293
Woodwardia radicans

ANNUALS AND BIENNIALS
Alcea rosea
Amaranthus spp. and cvs, pp.307, 308
BEGONIAS, p.317
Calomeria amaranthoides
Onopordum acanthium, p.304
Silybum marianum, p.304

BULBS, CORMS, AND TUBERS
Arisaema consanguineum, p.393
Arum creticum, p.407
CANNAS, p.394
Cardiocrinum giganteum, p.385
CROCOSMIA, p.410
Dracunculus vulgaris, p.386
GLADIOLI, p.384
Sauromatum venosum, p.403
Zantedeschia aethiopica

WATER PLANTS
Darmera peltata, p.438
Eichhornia crassipes, p.441
Gunnera manicata, p.443
Ligularia spp., p.445
Lysichiton americanus, p.444
Matteuccia struthiopteris, p.443
Orontium aquaticum, p.444
Pontederia cordata, p.441

Rheum palmatum 'Atrosanguineum', p.439
Sagittaria latifolia, p.434
Thalia dealbata

TENDER AND EXOTIC PLANTS
Trees
Dracaena draco, p.451
Jacaranda mimosifolia, p.451
Washingtonia robusta, p.451

Shrubs
Cycas revoluta, p.457
Protea cynaroides, p.454

Climbers
Epipremnum aureum 'Marble Queen', p.460
Monstera deliciosa, p.463

Perennials
Cyathea australis, p.452
Ensete ventricosum, p.474

ABOVE Architectural beauty
A tropical effect is created by dramatic *Phoenix canariensis* and the vibrant leaves of *Imperata cylindrica* 'Rubra'.

GINGERS, p.477
Heliconia psittacorum, p.478
Platycerium bifurcatum, p.479
Puya chilensis, p.471
Strelitzia reginae, p.476

Cacti and succulents
Aeonium tabuliforme, p.491
AGAVES, p.482
ALOES (most), p.493
Carnegiea gigantea, p.492
Cereus spp., p.488
Cyphostemma juttae, p.487
Euphorbia candelabrum
Furcraea parmentieri
Opuntia spp., pp.481, 483, 486, 488, 494, 496

Plants for quick cover

In gardens with steep banks, large spaces that are impractical to sod or cultivate, or areas that have become neglected, or if there is little time for maintenance, plants that have good ground-covering qualities provide a practical solution. Their rapid, dense, leafy or twiggy growth helps to suppress weeds, while creating a decorative blanket of flowers and foliage. Old walls, fences, or screens masking utility areas that also need a quick disguise can be covered with vigorous climbers, such as ivy (*Hedera*). Always select plants that are suitable for the soil conditions.

CONIFERS
Juniperus conferta

SHRUBS
Ceanothus thyrsiflorus var. *repens*, p.159
Cotoneaster conspicuus, p.142
Cotoneaster 'Gnom'
Cotoneaster 'Skogholm'
Gaultheria shallon, p.154
Hypericum calycinum, p.161

BELOW A tapestry of green shades
The strappy leaves of gardener's garters (*Phalaris arundinacea* var. *picta*) provide excellent groundcover.

Rubus tricolor
Stephanandra incisa 'Crispa'
Symphoricarpos orbiculatus 'Follis Variegatis', p.160

CLIMBERS AND WALL SHRUBS
Hedera spp. and cvs, p.211
Hydrangea petiolaris, p.195
Lonicera japonica cvs, p.207
Trachelospermum jasminoides, p.195

PERENNIALS
Alchemilla mollis, p.275
Anemone tomentosa
Anthemis punctata subsp. *cupaniana*, p.264

Campanula punctata
Campanula takesimana, p.241
Chelidonium majus 'Flore Pleno', p.227
Chrysosplenium macrophyllum, p.256
Duchesnea indica
Euphorbia amygdaloides var. *robbiae*, p.262
Geranium 'Orion', p.280
Geranium macrorrhizum, p.269
Geranium x *oxonianum* 'Claridge Druce'
Glechoma hederacea 'Variegata', p.277
Lamium maculatum and cvs, pp.254, 255
LUNGWORTS, p.261
Nepeta 'Six Hills Giant', p.240
Osteospermum jucundum, p.265
PERSICARIA, p.234
Prunella grandiflora 'Pink Loveliness'
Stachys byzantina, p.274
Symphytum x *uplandicum* 'Variegatum', p.227

Grasses and Bamboos
Carex flagellifera, p.289
Chimonobambusa timidissinoda, p.287
Luzula sylvatica 'Hohe Tatra', p.288
Phalaris arundinacea var. *picta*

Ferns
Dryopteris dilatata
Polystichum aculeatum
Polystichum setiferum Groups, p.291

ANNUALS AND BIENNIALS
Petunia 'Wave Purple'
Portulaca grandiflora Series and cvs
Sanvitalia procumbens, p.322
Satureja douglasii
Tropaeolum majus Series and cvs, pp.307, 323, 327

ROCK PLANTS
Arabis alpina subsp. *caucasica* and cvs, pp.347, 352
Asarum europaeum, p.375
Aubrieta deltoidea 'Argenteovariegata', p.354
Campanula portenschlagiana, p.368
Cerastium tomentosum, p.350
Helianthemum spp. and cvs, pp.336, 337, 338, 340, 344, 345
Persicaria affinis 'Donald Lowndes', p.365
Persicaria vacciniifolia, p.373
Phlox douglasii and cvs, pp.365, 366
Phuopsis stylosa
Saxifraga stolonifera
Tiarella cordifolia, p.333
Waldsteinia ternata, p.372

TENDER AND EXOTIC PLANTS
Perennials
Heterocentron elegans

Pulmonaria 'Lewis Palmer'

Campanula poscharskyana

Geranium macrorrhizum

Anthemis punctata subsp. *cupaniana*

Alchemilla mollis

Persicaria affinis 'Donald Lowndes'

Groundcover plants for shade

An area that is shaded for some or most of the day may be regarded by some gardeners as a problem space, when in fact it should be viewed as an opportunity to experiment with a different, and often an equally exciting, range of plants. The following groundcover plants will provide a wealth of colorful flowers and foliage, and may be planted in even deep shade, provided the soil is reasonably fertile. Where the shade is caused by trees and large shrubs, the soil will also be very dry. Keep new plants well watered during their first year until established.

Astrantia maxima

Geranium sanguineum

Convallaria majalis

Epimedium 'Amber Queen'

SHRUBS
Cotoneaster conspicuus, p.142
Cotoneaster 'Gnom'
Cotoneaster 'Herbstfeuer'
Daphne laureola subsp. *philippi*, p.147
Epigaea asiatica
Euonymus fortunei 'Kewensis'
Gaultheria shallon, p.154
Hypericum calycinum, p.161
Leucothöe fontanesiana
Lonicera pileata, p.167
Mahonia aquifolium, p.148
Mahonia repens
Paxistima canbyi
Prunus laurocerasus 'Otto Luyken', p.145
Rubus tricolor
Ruscus hypoglossum, p.167
Sarcococca confusa, p.142
Sarcococca humilis, p.164
Vinca spp., pp.164, 165

CLIMBERS AND WALL SHRUBS
Hedera spp. and cvs, p.211

PERENNIALS
Acanthus spinosus, p.239
Ajuga pyramidalis
Ajuga reptans 'Atropurpurea'
Alchemilla mollis, p.275
Anemone apennina
Anemone tomentosa
Arisarum proboscideum
Asarum caudatum
Astrantia maxima, p.278
Brunnera macrophylla
Brunnera macrophylla 'Jack Frost', p.261
Chelidonium majus 'Flore Pleno', p.227
Chrysosplenium macrophyllum, p.256
Convallaria majalis, p.255
Dicentra formosa
Dicentra spectabilis, p.223
Duchesnea indica
Epimedium epsteinii, p.260
Epimedium 'Amber Queen', p.263
Epimedium davidii
Epimedium perralderianum
Euphorbia amygdaloides var. *robbiae*, p.262
Galium odoratum, p.263
Geranium macrorrhizum, p.269
Geranium renardii, p.264
Glechoma hederacea 'Variegata', p.277
HEUCHERA, p.282
HOSTAS (some), pp.272–273
Hypsela reniformis
Lamium maculatum and cvs, pp.254, 255
Liriope muscari, p.280
LUNGWORTS, p.261
Meehania urticifolia
Omphalodes cappadocica
Pachyphragma macrophyllum
Plectranthus oertendahlii
Symphytum grandiflorum
Tellima grandiflora Rubra Group, p.279

Tolmiea menziesii
Vancouveria hexandra

Grasses and bamboos
Chasmanthium latifolium, p.288
Luzula sylvatica 'Hohe Tatra', p.288
Phalaris arundinacea var. *picta*

Ferns
Adiantum venustum, p.292
Athyrium spp. and cvs, p.290
Blechnum penna-marina, p.290
Blechnum spicant
Polypodium cambricum 'Richard Kayse', p.293
Polypodium vulgare and cvs, p.291
Polystichum setiferum Groups, pp.291

ROCK PLANTS
Asarina procumbens, p.371
Asarum europaeum, p.375
Campanula portenschlagiana, p.368
Campanula poscharskyana, p.367
Cardamine trifolia, p.348
Ceratostigma plumbaginoides, p.346
Cornus canadensis, p.360
Galax urceolata, p.336
Geranium sanguineum, p.340
Homogyne alpina
Maianthemum bifolium, p.348
Mitchella repens
Pachysandra terminalis, p.375
Persicaria affinis 'Donald Lowndes', p.365
Prunella grandiflora, p.368
Saxifraga stolonifera
Saxifraga x *urbium*
Tiarella cordifolia, p.333
Viola riviniana Purpurea Group p.355
Waldsteinia ternata, p.372

TENDER AND EXOTIC PLANTS
Perennials
Elatostema repens
Fittonia albivenis

RIGHT A covering in shade
Ferns, hostas, and heucheras fill the space and offer interesting textures and contrasts in shady corners.

Groundcover plants for sun

Many plants grow naturally in dry, sunny conditions. Some have developed foliage characteristics to minimize moisture loss from their leaves; others are densely branched, keeping the soil surface shaded and cool. Most have extensive root systems that penetrate deeply to find moisture. These plants are adapted to well-drained soils; in poorly drained situations, they may not survive prolonged wet conditions. Although adapted to poorer, dry soils, young plants may have been grown in richer potting medium and well watered, so when planting, incorporate organic matter, such as leaf mold or coir, and water in dry weather until well established.

Centaurea montana

Osteospermum jucundum

CONIFERS
Juniperus communis 'Prostrata'
Juniperus horizontalis 'Wiltonii'
Juniperus squamata 'Blue Carpet', p.105
Microbiota decussata, p.105
Picea abies 'Inversa'

SHRUBS
Arctostaphylos nevadensis
Arctostaphylos uva-ursi, p.376
Berberis wilsoniae
Brachyglottis Dunedin Hybrids 'Sunshine'
Calluna vulgaris 'White Lawn'
Ceanothus thyrsiflorus var. *repens*, p.159
Cotoneaster cashmiriensis
Cotoneaster 'Skogholm'
Cytisus x *beanii*, p.335
Cytisus scoparius subsp. *maritimus*
Ephedra gerardiana
Erica carnea 'Springwood White', p.166
Euonymus fortunei 'Emerald Gaiety'
Euonymus fortunei 'Kewensis'
Gaultheria myrsinoides
Genista hispanica, p.160
x *Halimiocistus sahucii*, p.149
Hebe carnosula
Hebe pinguifolia 'Pagei', p.337
Hebe 'Youngii'
Hypericum calycinum, p.161
LAVENDERS, p.158
Leiophyllum buxifolium
Leptospermum rupestre, p.151
Potentilla fruticosa 'Abbotswood', p.149
Rosmarinus officinalis 'Prostratus'
Salix repens, p.147
Santolina spp., p.159
Stephanandra incisa 'Crispa'
Symphoricarpos x *chenaultii* 'Hancock'
Ulex europaeus 'Flore Pleno'
Vinca major 'Variegata'

CLIMBERS
Hedera colchica 'Dentata Variegata'
Hedera helix spp. and cvs, p.211
Lathyrus latifolius, p.201

PERENNIALS
Alchemilla mollis, p.275
Anthemis punctata subsp. *cupaniana*, p.264
Artemisia alba 'Canescens'
Aster ericoides f. *prostratus* 'Snowflurry'
Bergenia 'Beethoven', p.256
Bergenia 'Eric Smith'
Campanula takesimana, p.241
Centaurea montana, p.269
Euphorbia polychroma, p.262
Francoa sochifolia Rogerson's form
Geranium ROZANNE ('Gerwat'), p.271
Geranium 'Orion', p.280
Geranium sanguineum, p.340
Hypericum spp.
Lysimachia punctata, p.243
Nepeta 'Six Hills Giant', p.240
Nepeta x *faassenii*, p.270
Origanum vulgare 'Aureum', p.274

Osteospermum jucundum, p.265
Persicaria bisorta 'Superba', p.234
Phlomis russeliana, p.243
SEDUM, p.279
Stachys byzantina, p.274
Stachys officinalis 'Hummelo', p.268
Veronica prostrata and cvs, p.343
Waldsteinia ternata, p.372

Grasses and bamboos
Chionochloa rubra, p.285

ANNUALS AND BIENNIALS
Calibrachoa Cabaret Series CABARET APRICOT ('Balcabapt')
Calibrachoa Cabaret Series LIGHT PINK ('Balcablitpi'), p.300
Calibrachoa Million Bells Series MILLION BELLS CHERRY PINK ('Sunbelrichipi'), p.306
Dichondra argentea 'Silver Falls'
Dichondra repens 'Emerald Falls'
Lantana montevidensis, p.310
Tropaeolum spp. and cvs, pp.307, 323, 327

ROCK PLANTS
Acaena microphylla, p.374
Antennaria dioica var. *rosea*, p.351
Arabis alpina subsp. *caucasica* 'Variegata', p.347
Armeria maritima 'Vindictive', p.365
Aubrieta spp. and cvs, pp.353, 354, 355
Aurinia saxatilis and cvs, p.335
Campanula portenschlagiana, p.368
Campanula poscharskyana, p.367
Dianthus gratianopolitanus, p.363
Dryas octopetala, p.361
Helianthemum spp. and cvs, pp.336, 337, 338, 340, 344, 345,
Hypericum olympicum
Iberis sempervirens, p.332
Lithodora diffusa 'Heavenly Blue', p.343
Nierembergia repens, p.361
Phlox douglasii 'Crackerjack', p.365
Phuopsis stylosa, p.338
Thymus 'Bressingham', p.365
Thymus caespititus var. *cilicicus*, p.366
Veronica prostrata 'Kapitan'

BOG PLANTS
Rheum palmatum 'Atrosanguineum', p.439

TENDER AND EXOTIC PLANTS
Climbers
Kennedia rubicunda
Pyrostegia venusta

Perennials
Centropogon cordifolius
Heterocentron elegans

Tropaeolum majus Alaska Series

Santolina pinnata subsp. *neapolitana* 'Sulphurea'

RIGHT Purple and yellow display
Aubrietia deltoides and *Aurinia saxatilis* provide a bright display of ground-covering color in sun.

Plants for dry shade

Dry, shady conditions persist under evergreen trees throughout the year, and although very little moisture penetrates the soil beneath the leaf canopy of deciduous trees, except during prolonged rainfall, a few early-flowering bulbs, such as bluebells (*Hyacinthoides non-scripta*), and woodland plants grow naturally there, dying down as the trees resume growth in spring. In gardens, dry shade occurs under larger, low-branched trees or where eaves extend over borders. Plant in the fall so that roots are well established by the following spring, and fertilize regularly and water during dry weather until the plants are established.

TREES
HOLLIES, p.94

Conifers
Taxus baccata 'Adpressa'
Taxus cuspidata, p.104
Tsuga canadensis, p.102

SHRUBS
Berberis thunbergii 'Rose Glow', p.137
Berberis valdiviana, p.111
Buxus sempervirens
Choisya ternata, p.122
Cotoneaster salicifolius, p.142
Daphne laureola and forms
Elaeagnus x *ebbingei*
Euonymus fortunei 'Emerald Gaiety'
Euonymus japonicus
Fatsia japonica
Gaultheria shallon, p.154
Hypericum calycinum, p.161
Hypericum x *inodorum* 'Elstead', p.161
Hypericum x *moserianum*
Lonicera pileata, p.167
Mahonia aquifolium, p.148
Mahonia x *media* and cvs, p.118
Osmanthus decorus
Osmanthus delavayi, p.110
Pachysandra terminalis, p.375
Prunus laurocerasus 'Otto Luyken', p.145
Prunus laurocerasus 'Zabeliana', p.145
Prunus lusitanica
Rubus tricolor
Ruscus aculeatus, p.167
Ruscus hypoglossum, p.167
Sambucus nigra 'Guincho Purple'
Sarcococca humilis, p.164
Symphoricarpos albus var. *laevigatus*, p.142
Vaccinium angustifolium var. *laevifolium*, p.163
Viburnum rhytidophyllum, p.112
Viburnum tinus
Viburnum tinus 'Eve Price', p.143
Vinca major
Vinca minor, p.165

CLIMBERS AND WALL SHRUBS
Berberidopsis corallina, p.202
Celastrus orbiculatus
Cotoneaster horizontalis, p.208
Hedera canariensis
Hedera helix and cvs, p.211
Lapageria rosea, p.202
Lonicera japonica 'Halliana'
Lonicera periclymenum and cvs, p.207

PERENNIALS
Acanthus mollis 'Hollard's Gold', p.219
Acanthus spinosus, p.239
Ajuga reptans cvs

RIGHT Oceans of blue
English bluebells (*Hyacinthoides non-scripta*) are perfect plants for dry shade, producing a carpet of blue flowers.

Alchemilla mollis, p.275
Anemone tomentosa
Aster divaricatus, p.249
Campanula persicifolia
Chelidonium majus 'Flore Pleno', p.227
Corydalis lutea, p.344
Digitalis purpurea
Doronicum x *excelsum* 'Harpur Crewe'
Epimedium spp. and cvs, pp.254, 260, 262, 263
Euphorbia amygdaloides var. *robbiae*, p.262
Geranium macrorrhizum, pp.269, 223
Iris foetidissima, p.225
Lamium maculatum
Lunaria rediviva
LUNGWORTS, p.261
Pachysandra terminalis, p.375
Polygonatum x *hybridum*, p.223
Scopolia carniolica, p.260
Symphytum 'Goldsmith'
Symphytum ibericum
Tellima grandiflora
Tolmiea menziesii
Viola riviniana 'Purpurea'

Grasses and bamboos
Carex flagellifera, p.289
Luzula sylvatica 'Hohe Tatra', p.288

Ferns
Asplenium ceterach, p.293
Asplenium scolopendrium, p.292
Cyrtomium falcatum, p.291
Dryopteris filix-mas, p.293
Polypodium vulgare, p.291
Polystichum aculeatum

BULBS, CORMS, AND TUBERS
Camassia quamash, p.411
Colchicum autumnale, p.426
Cyclamen coum 'Maurice Dryden', p.428
Cyclamen coum Pewter Group, p.429
DAFFODILS, pp.404–405
Galanthus 'Hill Poe', p.427
Galanthus woronowii, p.428
Haemanthus albiflos
Hyacinthoides x *massartiana*, p.403
Hyacinthoides non-scripta, p.403
Incarvillea delavayi, p.265
Scilla siberica 'Alba', p.416

TENDER AND EXOTIC PLANTS
Climbers
Epipremnum aureum 'Marble Queen', p.460
Cissus striata

Perennials
Achimenes
Chirita
Clivia miniata, p.476
Nephrolepis exaltata
Pteris cretica
Tradescantia zebrina 'Quadricolor'

Cotoneaster horizontalis

Sarcococca hookeriana var. *digyna*

Geranium phaeum

Plants for moist shade

In areas with high rainfall, the soil in parts of the garden that receive little or no sun may be cool and moist throughout the year. Low-lying gardens with a high water table or drainage problems may also have shady, permanently damp areas. Similar conditions occur along the margins of natural streams, or when an artificial bog is created beside a garden pond. Take advantage of these situations to grow plants such as broad-leaved hostas, ferns, and taller moisture-loving primulas. Plant in spring, enriching lighter soils with well-rotted organic matter. Water during extended dry periods, if necessary.

TREES
Acer spp. and cvs, pp.60, 62, 65, 66, 67, 73, 74, 76, 77, 78, 79, 84, 85, 88, 89, 90, 91, 92, 115, 117, 123, 138, 156
Betula nigra, p.78
Stewartia pseudocamellia, p.78
Stewartia sinensis, p.78

SHRUBS
Anopterus glandulosus, p.110
Cassiope lycopodioides, p.349
Clethra arborea
Crataegus laevigata 'Punicea'
Cyathodes colensoi, p.346
Danäe racemosa

Disanthus cercidifolius, p.141
Gaultheria procumbens, p.373
Kalmia latifolia, p.136
Ledum groenlandicum, p.145
Leucothöe fontanesiana
Lindera benzoin, p.127
Lyonia ligustrina
Myrica gale, p.162
Neillia thibetica, p.133
Paeonia ludlowii, p.229
Paeonia rockii
Paxistima canbyi
Pieris formosa var. *forrestii* 'Wakehurst', p.137
Prunus laurocerasus

Galanthus elwesii

Passiflora coccinea

RHODODENDRONS, pp.124–125
Ruscus aculeatus, p.167
Salix exigua, p.112
Salix magnifica
Sarcococca spp. and cvs, pp.142, 164
Skimmia japonica, p.164
Spiraea japonica 'Albiflora'
Symphoricarpos albus var. *laevigatus*, p.142
Viburnum opulus and cvs, pp.142, 162
Viburnum 'Pragense', p.131
Viburnum tinus 'Eve Price', p.143

CLIMBERS AND WALL SHRUBS
Akebia quinata, p.193
Asteranthera ovata
Garrya elliptica 'James Roof', p.211
Humulus lupulus 'Aureus', p.194
Hydrangea petiolaris, p.195
Lonicera tragophylla, p.207
Pileostegia viburnoides, p.196
Schizophragma integrifolium, p.197

PERENNIALS
Aconitum 'Stainless Steel', p.241
Actaea pachypoda, p.246
Anemone x *hybrida* cvs, pp.220, 222
Anthurium scherzerianum
Asarum europaeum, p.375
Astelia chathamica, p.242
Astrantia major and cvs, pp.238, 278
Begonia grandis subsp. *evansiana*, p.278
Bergenia spp. and cvs, pp.255, 256, 280
Brunnera macrophylla and cvs, p.261
Calanthe striata, p.275
Cardamine pentaphyllos, p.260
Chrysosplenium macrophyllum, p.256
Cimicifuga racemosa
Convallaria majalis, p.255
Cortusa matthioli, p.341
Cyathodes colensoi, p.346
Deinanthe caerulea
Dianella caerulea CASSA BLUE ('Dbb03'), p.283
Digitalis x *mertonensis*
Epigaea gaultherioides, p.351
Hacquetia epipactis, p.356
Hedyotis michauxii, p.369
Helleborus x *hybridus*, p.281
HEUCHERA AND x HEUCHERELLA, p.282
HOSTAS, pp.272–273
Jeffersonia diphylla, p.333
Kirengeshoma palmata, p.251
Lamium maculatum
Lathraea clandestina, p.260
Ligularia 'The Rocket', p.219
Lithophragma parviflorum, p.332
Mitella breweri, p.371
Omphalodes cappadocica and cvs, pp.261, 334
Pachysandra terminalis, p.375
Polygonatum x *hybridum*, p.223
Pratia pedunculata, p.369
PRIMULAS (many), pp.257–259
Prunella grandiflora, p.368
Rodgersia pinnata 'Fireworks', p.234
Tiarella cordifolia, p.333
Trillium grandiflorum, p.255
Uvularia grandiflora, p.262
Vancouveria hexandra

LEFT Fresh, cool greens
Ferns and large-leaved hostas, seen here with blue *Corydalis flexuosa*, flourish in cool, moist shade.

Grasses and bamboos
Chasmanthium latifolium, p.288
Chimonobambusa timidissinoda, p.287
Imperata cylindrica 'Rubra', p.285
Phyllostachys spp. and cvs, pp.286, 287, 288, 289
Thamnocalamus crassinodus 'Kew Beauty', p.286

Ferns
Athyrium 'Ghost', p.290
Athyrium niponicum, p.290
Athyrium niponicum var. *pictum* 'Burgundy Lace', p.290
Blechnum tabulare
Cyathea medullaris
Dicksonia antarctica, p.290
Lygodium japonicum
Osmunda claytoniana
Polypodium cambricum 'Richard Kayse', p.293
Polystichum munitum, p.293
Woodwardia radicans

ANNUALS AND BIENNIALS
BEGONIAS, p.317
Impatiens walleriana and cvs, p.307
Satureja douglasii

BULBS, CORMS, AND TUBERS
Arisaema spp., p.393, 406, 408, 412, 422
Arisarum proboscideum
Arum italicum 'Marmoratum', p.421
Camassia leichtlinii, p.383
Cardiocrinum giganteum, p.385
Galanthus elwesii, p.427
Galanthus nivalis and cvs, pp.427, 428
Galanthus plicatus subsp. *plicatus*
Leucojum vernum, p.414

WATER AND BOG PLANTS
Aruncus dioicus, p.436
Darmera peltata, p.438
Leucojum aestivum, p.436
Ligularia 'Britt Marie Crawford', p.445
Matteuccia struthiopteris, p.443
Onoclea sensibilis, p.443

TENDER AND EXOTIC PLANTS
Climbers
Dioscorea discolor
Passiflora coccinea, p.462
Thunbergia mysorensis, p.464

Perennials
Alpinia hainanensis, p.477
Alpinia purpurata, p.477
Aspidistra spp. and cvs
Calathea zebrina, p.475
Caulokaempferia petelotii
Cornukaempferia aurantiflora 'Jungle Gold', p.477
Curcuma petiolata, p.477
Curcuma zedoaria, p.477
Cyathea australis, p.452
Dichorisandra reginae, p.473
Hemiorchis patlingii
Lysionotus pauciflorus
Maranta leuconeura 'Erythroneura', p.475
Peliosanthes arisanensis, p.472
Ponerorchis hybrids
Ruellia devosiana, p.465
Selaginella martensii, p.478
Streptocarpus spp. and cvs, pp.465, 469, 473
Xanthosoma sagittifolium, p.474
Zingiber mioga

Shrubs preferring wall protection

Walls can provide favorable growing conditions for shrubs, especially evergreens, that are borderline hardy for the region. Some winter-flowering shrubs also bloom more reliably and freely when given wall protection. The best wall-side situations are warm and sunny, and provide good shelter from cold winds in winter and early spring. The warmth from heat loss through house walls, and the well-drained conditions near the base of walls, also assist the survival of slightly tender shrubs that dislike damp soil.

SHRUBS
Abelia floribunda
Abutilon 'Ashford Red', p.137
Abutilon vitifolium 'Victoria Tennant', p.114
Acacia podalyriifolia
Acacia pravissima, p.92
Acca sellowiana, p.203
Aloysia triphylla, p.132
Artemisia spp. and cvs, pp.165, 216, 242, 274
Azara microphylla 'Variegata', p.119
Buddleja asiatica
Cantua buxifolia, p.146
Ceanothus impressus, p.138
Chaenomeles speciosa 'Moerloosei', p.122
Chimonanthus praecox, p.144
Cytisus x *spachianus*
Daphne odora 'Aureomarginata', p.164
Drimys winteri, p.73
Elsholtzia stauntonii
Escallonia 'Iveyi', p.112
Lagerstroemia indica
Leptospermum scoparium 'Red Damask', p.123
Leptospermum scoparium 'Snow White', p.130
Lonicera fragrantissima
Melianthus major, p.145
Myrtus communis, p.122

Olearia x *scilloniensis*
Osteomeles schweriniae, p.129
Robinia hispida, p.133
Rosa 'Mermaid', p.182
Rosmarinus officinalis, p.157
SALVIAS, p.155
Vestia foetida, p.194

CLIMBERS AND WALL SHRUBS
Abutilon megapotanicum, p.203
Azara serrata, p.195
Buddleja crispa, p.204
Callistemon citrinus 'Splendens', p.203
Carpenteria californica, p.197
Coronilla valentina subsp. *glauca*, p.195
Dendromecon rigida, p.206
Fabiana imbricata f. *violacea*, p.204
Fremontodendron 'California Glory', p.206
Garrya elliptica
Itea ilicifolia, p.211
Piptanthus nepalensis, p.206
Solanum crispum 'Glasnevin', p.204

TENDER AND EXOTIC PLANTS
Shrubs
Iochroma australe, p.138
Iochroma cyaneum, p.457
Tibouchina urvilleana, p.457

Leptospermum scoparium 'Red Damask'

Garrya eliptica

Melianthus major

Abutilon megapotamicum

Plants for paving and wall crevices

In mountainous regions, many alpine plants grow in deep cracks and crevices in the rock. Some are clump-forming or trailing in habit; others, such as saxifrages and sempervivums, grow as rosettes extending by means of runners. If laying paving, leave crevices for small plants, but restrict planting to little-used areas where they can survive. When building stone retaining walls, tilt slabs slightly backward to create deep pockets, and plant them as the wall is being constructed. Most wall plants thrive in sunny situations, but ramondas and most small ferns prefer moist shade.

PERENNIALS
AQUILEGIAS, p.226
Geum 'Bell Bank', p.268
Ourisia coccinea, p.269

Grasses and bamboos
Carex flagellifera, p.289
Imperata cylindrica 'Rubra', p.285
Stipa tenuissima, p.288

Ferns
Asplenium ceterach, p.293
Polypodium cambricum 'Richard Kayse', p.293

ANNUALS AND BIENNIALS (FOR PAVING)
Ageratum houstonianum
Limnanthes douglasii, p.321
Lobelia erinus cvs, pp.311, 314
Lobularia maritima
Malcolmia maritima, p.304
Nemophila maculata, p.299
Nemophila menziesii, p.314
Portulaca grandiflora Series and cvs, p.324

ROCK PLANTS
Acaena microphylla, p.374
Acantholimon glumaceum, p.363
Achillea x *kellereri*, p.360
Aethionema 'Warley Rose', p.362
Androsace sarmentosa
Antennaria dioica
Armeria maritima 'Vindictive', p.365
Artemisia schmidtiana 'Nana', p.374
Aubrieta spp. and cvs, pp.353, 354, 355

ABOVE A wall of bright color
Geranium 'Johnson's Blue' and *Helianthemum* 'Cerise Queen' tumble over a dry-stone wall.

Aurinia saxatilis and cvs, p.335
Campanula cochleariifolia, p.369
Campanula poscharskyana, p.367
Chamaemelum nobile
Chiastophyllum oppositifolium, p.335
Cyananthus microphyllus, p.369
Cymbalaria muralis
Dianthus deltoides 'Leuchtfunk', p.365
Draba aizoides
Dryas octopetala, p.361
Erigeron karvinskianus, p.363
Erinus alpinus, p.352
Gypsophila repens and cvs, p.362
Haberlea rhodopensis 'Virginalis', p.359
Helianthemum spp. and cvs, pp.336, 338, 337, 340, 344, 345
HOUSELEEKS, p.377
Hypericum olympicum
Lithodora diffusa 'Heavenly Blue', p.343
Mazus reptans, p.351
Mentha requienii
Nierembergia repens, p.361
Parahebe lyallii
Phlox douglasii 'Crackerjack', p.365
Physoplexis comosa (wall only), p.366
Ramonda myconi (wall only), p.369
Saxifraga cotyledon
Sedum spathulifolium 'Cape Blanco', p.375
Thymus 'Bressingham', p.365
Thymus caespititus var. *cilicicus*, p.366
Vitaliana primuliflora, p.358

Plants for containers

Containers packed with foliage and flowers can brighten patios, decks, and balconies. Large containers are best in sunny, sheltered sites, as they retain more moisture than small ones. Small trees, conifers, or shrubs, together with perennials, give long-term interest with their foliage and forms, and periods of flowering. For colorful displays, plant spring-flowering bulbs, followed by summer bedding, which will flower from late spring to the first frost.

BELOW Springtime tulips
Terra-cotta containers planted in late fall with single and double tulip bulbs make a colorful, elegant display the following spring.

TREES
Acer negundo
Crataegus laevigata and cvs, p.84
Eucalyptus (when young), pp.67, 68, 78, 79
HOLLIES, p.94
Laurus nobilis, p.80
Malus x *arnoldiana*, p.82
Malus x *magdeburgensis*, p.83
Melia azederach, p.71
Olea europaea

Conifers
DWARF CONIFERS, pp.104–105

SHRUBS
Buxus sempervirens and cvs, pp.144, 167
Choisya ternata, p.122
HARDY FUCHSIAS, p.154
Hebe cupressoides and cvs, pp.165, 347
HYDRANGEAS, pp.134–135
LAVENDERS, p.158
Myrtus communis, p.122
Pittosporum tenuifolium 'Tom Thumb', p.164
RHODODENDRONS (most), pp.124–125
ROSES (all patio varieties)
Santolina pinnata subsp. *neapolitana*, p.159
Viburnum tinus and cvs, p.143

CLIMBERS AND WALL SHRUBS
CLEMATIS (small cvs), pp.198–200
Cobaea scandens, p.204
Eccremocarpus scaber, p.208
Hedera helix and cvs, p.211
HONEYSUCKLE, p.207
Ipomoea hederacea, p.204
Ipomoea lobata, p.202
Ipomoea tricolor 'Heavenly Blue', p.205
Jasminum humile and cvs, pp.139, 206
Jasminum polyanthum, p.208
Lathyrus odoratus and cvs, pp.201, 202, 301
Passiflora caerulea, p.204
Tropaeolum speciosum, p.202

PERENNIALS
Agapanthus 'Northern Star', p.241
Agapanthus 'Purple Cloud', p.241
Agapanthus inapertus subsp. *pendulus* 'Graskop', p.240
Astelia chathamica, p.242
Bergenia spp. and cvs, pp.255, 256, 280
DAYLILIES, pp.244–245
Dianella caerulea CASSA BLUE ('Dbb03'), p.283
Geranium ROZANNE ('Gerwat'), p.271
HEUCHERA and x HEUCHERELLA, p.282
HOSTAS, pp.272–273
LUNGWORTS, p.261

Phormium 'Dazzler', p.216
PRIMULAS, pp.257–259
Rudbeckia fulgida var. *sullivantii* 'Goldsturm', p.251
SALVIA, p.250
Schizostylis 'Mrs Hegarty'
Sedum 'Bertram Anderson' and 'Ruby Glow', p.279
Stachys (some)
Verbena (some)

Grasses and bamboos
Carex flagellifera, p.289
Chionochloa rubra, p.285
Elegia capensis, p.285
Eragrostis curvula 'Totnes Burgundy', p.285
Imperata cylindrica 'Rubra', p.285
Miscanthus sinensis 'Yakushima Dwarf', p.285
Pennisetum 'Fairy Tails'
Pennisetum setaceum 'Rubrum'

Ferns
Adiantum (most)
Asplenium scolopendrium Marginatum Group, p.292
Polypodium vulgare 'Cornubiense', p.291
Polystichum setiferum Divisilobum Group, p.291

Ipomoea tricolor 'Heavenly Blue'

Phormium 'Dazzler'

Argyranthemum BUTTERFLY ('Ulyssis')

Pelargonium 'Bulls Eye Salmon'

Viola Joker Series

Tagetes 'Naughty Marietta'

ANNUALS AND BIENNIALS

Ageratum houstonianum and cvs
Antirrhinum spp. and cvs, pp.313, 314
Argyranthemum spp. and cvs, pp.298, 300, 319
Bassia scoparia f. *trichophylla*, p.316
BEGONIAS, p.317
Bidens 'Gold Star', p.319
Brachyscome 'Strawberry Mousse', p.300
Calendula officinalis series and cvs, pp.321, 322, 325, 326
Calibrachoa Series and cvs, pp.300, 306
Callistephus chinensis Series and cvs, pp.303, 304, 312
Catharanthus roseus and cvs, pp.298, 300, 306
Coreopsis 'Rum Punch', p.326
Cosmos atrosanguineus and cvs, pp.238, 306
Cuphea x *purpurea* 'Firecracker', p.306
Diascia LITTLE DANCER ('Pendan'), p.301
Dichondra argentea 'Silver Falls'
Dichondra repens 'Emerald Falls'
Duranta erecta 'Gold Edge', p.319
Erysimum cheiri 'Treasure Red'
FUCHSIAS, p.302
Glandularia x *hybrida* series, pp.303, 307
Helichrysum petiolare, p.165
HOUSELEEKS, p.377
Impatiens spp. and cvs, pp.300, 307, 325
Ipomoea batatas and cvs, pp.311, 318
Lantana camara Lucky Series, p.301
Lobelia erinus cvs
Lobularia maritima 'Snow Crystals'
Lysimachia congestiflora 'Outback Sunset', p.323
Mimulus 'Magic Yellow Blotch', p.320
Nemesia Amelie, p.301
Nemesia strumosa, p.307
Osteospermum ecklonis and cvs, pp.301, 311
Perilla 'Magilla Vanilla', p.318
x *Petchoa* Supercal Series, p.303
PELARGONIUMS, p.309
Petunia Series and cvs, pp.308, 311, 312, 316
Plecostachys serpyllifolia
Primula Belarina Series, pp.258, 303
Salpiglossis sinuata Series and cvs
Salvia farinacea 'Strata', p.314
Salvia splendens
Satureja douglasii 'Indian Mint'
Scaevola aemula 'Little Wonder'
Solenostemon scutellarioides Series and cvs, pp.310, 311
Sutera cordata Snowstorm Series GIANT SNOWFLAKE ('Danova906'), p.298
Tagetes Series and cvs, pp.308, 322, 324, 326
Tropaeolum majus and cvs, pp.307, 323, 327
Viola x *wittrockiana* hybrids and cvs, pp.308, 312, 313, 318, 323
Zinnia x *marylandica* Series, pp.298, 307

ROCK PLANTS

All are suitable, the following being particularly recommended:
Campanula portenschlagiana, p.368
Campanula poscharskyana, p.367
Dianthus gratianopolitanus, p.363
Geranium sanguineum, p.340
Hebe vernicosa p.337
Helianthemum spp. and cvs, pp.336, 337, 338, 340, 344, 345
Hypericum olympicum
Iberis sempervirens, p.332
Persicaria affinis 'Donald Lowndes', p.365

Phlox douglasii 'Crackerjack', p.365
Saponaria ocymoides, p.364
Saxifraga stolonifera
Saxifraga x *urbium*
Silene schafta, p.346
Thymus 'Bressingham', p.365
Thymus caespititus var. *cilicicus*, p.366

BULBS, CORMS, AND TUBERS

ALSTROEMERIAS, p.387
Anomatheca laxa, p.423
Bellavalia romana, p.399
Calochortus superbus, p.409
CANNAS, p.394
CROCOSMIA, p.410
CROCUSES, p.417
Cyclamen coum and cvs, pp.428, 429
DAFFODILS, pp.404–405
DAHLIAS, pp.396–398
Galanthus 'Hill Poe', p.427
Galanthus woronowii
GLADIOLI, p.428
Gladiolus murielae
Habenaria radiata, p.408
Hippeastrum 'Black Pearl'
Hyacinthus orientalis 'Blue Jacket', p.403
Hyacinthus orientalis 'White Pearl', p.415
Hymenocallis 'Sulphur Queen', p.412
Incarvillea delavayi, p.265
Iris reticulata and cvs, p.225
LILIES (most), pp.388–391
Muscari botryoides 'Album', p.415
Nerine bowdenii 'Nikita'
Polianthes tuberosa 'The Pearl', p.385
Triteleia ixioides 'Starlight', p.407
Triteleia 'Queen Fabiola'
Tulbaghia simmleri, p.411
TULIPS, pp.400–401
Watsonia meriana, p.385
Zantedeschia 'Cameo', p.395

WATER AND BOG PLANTS

Acorus calamus 'Argenteostriatus', p.435
Aponogeton distachyos, p.435
Eichhornia crassipes, p.441
Menyanthes trifoliata, p.434
Pontederia cordata, p.441
Thalia dealbata
WATER LILIES (small cvs), p.440
Zantedeschia aethiopica 'Crowborough', p.437

TENDER AND EXOTIC PLANTS

Trees
Cordyline australis 'Atropurpurea', p.451
Ficus spp., pp.450, 452, 458
Jacaranda mimosifolia, p.451
Washingtonia robusta, p.451

Shrubs
Plectranthus fructicosus 'James', p.454

Climbers
Cissus antarctica, p.463
Mandevilla spp., pp.460, 461
Stephanotis floribunda, p.460

Perennials
Browallia speciosa, p.472
Centropogon ferruginensis
Centropogon willdenowianus

Cacti and succulents
AGAVES, p.482
ALOES, p.493
Furcraea foetida 'Mediopicta', p.481

Trailing plants for walls or baskets

Many plants grow naturally in crevices, their trailing stems covering large areas of vertical rock. In gardens, they can be used at the top of retaining walls to soften the brickwork. Smaller trailing plants, including tender perennials and annuals, are ideal for hanging baskets. After planting, hang baskets on sturdy brackets on a wall or set them on large, inverted pots on a patio or old tree stump so that the plants form a conical mound of tumbling stems and flowers.

CONIFERS

Juniperus x *pfitzeriana* 'Old Gold', p.105
Juniperus squamata 'Blue Carpet', p.105
Microbiota decussata, p.105

SHRUBS

Arctostaphylos uva-ursi, p.376
Ceanothus thyrsiflorus var. *repens*, p.159
Leptospermum rupestre, p.151
Loiseleuria procumbens, p.364
Nematanthus strigillosus
Salix lindleyana
Salix repens, p.147

CLIMBERS AND WALL SHRUBS

Hedera (most), p.211

PERENNIALS

Campanula isophylla
Chrysosplenium macrophyllum, p.256
Glandularia 'Sissinghurst', p.268
Glechoma hederacea 'Variegata', p.277
Tropaeolum polyphyllum, p.276
Verbena peruviana

ANNUALS AND BIENNIALS

Bidens 'Gold Star', p.319
Calceolaria integrifolia
Calibrachoa hybrids and cvs, pp.300, 306
Diascia LITTLE DANCER ('Pendan'), p.301
Dichondra argentea 'Silver Falls'
Dichondra repens 'Emerald Falls'
Fuchsia procumbens
Helichrysum petiolare, p.165
Ipomoea batatas 'Blackie', p.311
Ipomoea batatas 'Margarita', p.318
Lantana montevidensis, p.310
Lathyrus odoratus 'Cupid Pink', p.301
Limnanthes douglasii, p.321
Lobelia erinus and cvs, pp.311, 314, 315
Lotus berthelotii, p.306
Lysimachia congestiflora 'Outback Sunset', p.323
Nemophila maculata, p.299
Nolana paradoxa
Pelargonium peltatum
x *Petchoa* Supercal Series, p.303
Petunia Surfinia Series, pp.311, 316
Petunia Tumbelina Series, p.311
Portulaca grandiflora Series and cvs
Sanvitalia procumbens, p.322
Scaevola aemula 'Little Wonder'
Solenostemon scutellarioides 'Inky Fingers', p.311
Sutera cordata GIANT SNOWFLAKE ('Danova906'), p.298
Tropaeolum majus Series and cvs, pp.307, 323, 327

ROCK PLANTS

Acaena saccaticupula 'Blue Haze'
Androsace lanuginosa, p.363
Arabis alpina subsp. *caucasica*
Campanula cochleariifolia, p.369
Convolvulus sabatius, p.342
Cymbalaria muralis
Cytisus x *beanii*, p.335
Euphorbia myrsinites, p.357
Genista lydia, p.345

Gypsophila repens
Iberis sempervirens, p.332
Lithodora diffusa cvs, p.343
Oenothera macrocarpa, p.372
Othonna cheirifolia, p.344
Parahebe catarractae, p.342
Parochetus communis, p.370
Persicaria vacciniifolia, p.373
Phlox subulata
Pterocephalus perennis, p.364
Saxifraga stolonifera

TENDER AND EXOTIC PLANTS

Shrubs
Chorizema ilicifolium

Perennials
Achimenes 'Peach Blossom', p.455
Aeschynanthus speciosus, p.478
Centropogon ferruginensis

Glandularia 'Sissinghurst'

Helichrysum petiolare

Petunia SURFINIA LIME ('Keiyeul')

Plants with aromatic foliage

The leaves of many plants contain essential aromatic oils, used in medicine or cooking. For gardeners, their value lies in the aromas released naturally or when leaves are bruised. Those of culinary value, such as rosemary, are often grown in herb gardens, or plant low-growing thymes next to paths or between paving stones, where they will emit their scent when stepped on. The fragrance from trees is best appreciated as it drifts through the garden on the wind.

TREES
Eucalyptus spp., pp.67, 68, 78, 79
Juglans regia, p.62
Laurus nobilis, p.80
Phellodendron chinense, p.75
Populus balsamifera
Populus trichocarpa
Sassafras albidum, p.64
Umbellularia californica, p.69

BELOW Scented seating
Create a relaxing resting place in the garden with a stylish wooden bench surrounded by aromatic herbs, such as lavender, thyme, and marjoram.

Conifers
Calocedrus decurrens, p.101
Chamaecyparis spp. and cvs, pp.96, 99, 101, 102, 103, 104, 105
Cupressus spp. and cvs, pp.95, 102, 104
Juniperus spp., pp.100, 103, 105
Pseudotsuga menziesii var. *glauca*, p.96
Thuja plicata 'Stoneham Gold', p.105

SHRUBS
Aloysia triphylla, p.132
Artemisia abrotanum, p.165
Caryopteris x *clandonensis* 'Arthur Simmonds', p.157

Choisya ternata and cvs, pp.122, 148
Cistus laurifolius
Elsholtzia stauntonii
Gaultheria procumbens, p.373
Helichrysum italicum
Hyssopus officinalis, p.157
LAVENDERS, p.158
Lindera benzoin, p.127
Myrtus communis, p.122
Perovskia 'Blue Spire', p.159
Phlomis fruticosa, p.160
Rhododendron rubiginosum
Rosa rubiginosa, p.176
Rosmarinus officinalis, p.157
Salvia officinalis and cvs, p.155
Santolina spp.

PERENNIALS
Achillea filipendulina
Agastache 'Black Adder', p.280
Artemisia spp. and cvs, pp.165, 216, 242, 274, 374
Chamaemelum nobile
Galium odoratum, p.263
Geranium macrorrhizum, p.269
Mentha suaveolens 'Variegata', p.274
Monarda didyma
Myrrhis odorata, p.230

Nepeta 'Six Hills Giant', p.240
Perovskia atriplicifolia
Tanacetum parthenium, p.300

ANNUALS AND BIENNIALS
PELARGONIUMS (scented-leaved forms), p.309
Satureja douglasii

ROCK PLANTS
Mentha requienii
Origanum laevigatum, p.340
Satureja montana,
Thymus spp. and cvs, pp.365, 366, 367

TENDER AND EXOTIC PLANTS
Trees
Agonis flexuosa, p.450

Shrubs
Boronia megastigma
Prostanthera ovalifolia, p.457

Perennials
Kaempferia pulchra, p.477

Phlomis fruticosa

Rosa rubiginosa

Nepeta 'Six Hills Giant'

Plants with fragrant flowers

Fragrance is a compelling feature of many plants. It can be strong, filling the garden with scent, or apparent only when you are close to individual blooms. Some plants release scent continuously, while the perfume of others is more noticeable at night. A sunny, sheltered patio or deck is an ideal spot for fragrant plants, or site them close to paths. Train fragrant climbers over arches and around doorways. Hyacinths provide early spring fragrance indoors.

TREES
Clethra arborea
Crataegus monogyna
Drimys winteri, p.73
Eucryphia lucida, p.85
Fraxinus ornus, p.71
Genista aetnensis, p.89
Laburnum x *watereri* 'Vossii', p.84
MAGNOLIAS, p.70
Malus coronaria 'Charlottae'
Malus hupehensis, p.69
Malus 'Profusion', p.71
Prunus mume 'Beni-chidori', p.123
Prunus padus 'Watereri', p.71
Prunus x *yedoensis*, p.82
Pterostyrax hispida, p.73
Robinia pseudoacacia
Styrax japonicus, p.72
Tilia 'Petiolaris', p.64

SHRUBS
Abelia x *grandiflora*, p.113
Acacia dealbata, p.211
Azara microphylla, p.118
Berberis x *stenophylla*, p.127
Brugmansia arborea
BUDDLEJAS, p.114
Chimonanthus praecox, p.144
Choisya ternata, p.122
Clerodendrum bungei, p.141
Clerodendrum trichotomum, p.142
Clethra delavayi, p.113
Colletia hystrix, p.130
Corylopsis pauciflora, p.126
Cytisus battandieri, p.116
Daphne odora and cvs
Deutzia x *elegantissima* cvs
Edgeworthia chrysantha, p.126
Elaeagnus x *ebbingei* 'Limelight', p.139
Erica lusitanica
Fothergilla major, p.117
LAVENDERS, p.158
Ligustrum lucidum
LILACS, p.115
Lupinus arboreus, p.159
MAGNOLIAS, p.70
Osmanthus spp. and cvs, pp.110, 119
Philadelphus spp. and cvs, pp.127, 128, 129, 131, 149
Pittosporum tenuifolium, p.120
ROSES (many), pp.168–187
Sarcococca spp., pp.142, 164
Viburnum spp. and cvs, pp.110, 111, 122, 143, 146
WITCH HAZELS, p.118

CLIMBERS AND WALL SHRUBS
Clematis montana 'Elizabeth'
Coronilla valentina subsp. *glauca*, p.195
HONEYSUCKLE, p.207
Itea ilicifolia, p.211
Jasminum humile and cvs, pp.139, 206
Jasminum officinale f. *affine*, p.196
Lathyrus odoratus and cvs, pp.201, 202, 203
Mandevilla laxa
ROSES (many)
Trachelospermum spp., pp.195, 196
WISTERIA, p.205

PERENNIALS
Anemone sylvestris, p.255
CARNATIONS AND PINKS, pp.266–267
Clematis heracleifolia 'Wyevale'
Convallaria majalis, p.255
Cosmos atrosanguineus, p.238
Crambe cordifolia, p.216
Galium odoratum, p.263
Hedychium coccineum 'Tara', p.220
Hemerocallis lilioasphodelus, p.245
Hesperis matronalis, p.230
Impatiens tinctoria, p.216
Iris graminea
Iris unguicularis
Mirabilis jalapa, p.233
Myrrhis odorata, p.230
PEONIES, pp.228–229
Persicaria polymorpha, p.234
Primula elatior, p.259
Primula veris, p.262

ANNUALS AND BIENNIALS
Amberboa moschata
Antirrhinum majus Series, p.303, 319, 320
Argemone mexicana, p.321
Dianthus barbatus and cvs
Erysimum cheiri Series and cvs
Exacum affine
Glandularia x *hybrida* Series, pp.303, 307, 312
Heliotropium arborescens, p.310
Iberis amara, p.299
Limnanthes douglasii, p.321
Lobularia maritima 'Snow Crystals', p.298
Matthiola incana
Nemesia 'Amelie', p.301
Nicotiana alata, p.231
Nicotiana sylvestris
Petunia 'Priscilla', p.311
Reseda odorata, p.300
Scabiosa atropurpurea

ROCK PLANTS
Dianthus gratianopolitanus, p.363
Erysimum helveticum, p.358
Papaver croceum
Primula auricula

BULBS, CORMS, AND TUBERS
Amaryllis belladonna, p.395
Arisaema candidissimum, p.422
Cardiocrinum giganteum, p.385
Chlidanthus fragrans, p.424
Crinum bulbispermum
Crinum x *powellii*, p.385
Crocus angustifolius
Crocus longiflorus
Cyclamen persicum, p.429
Eucharis amazonica, p.414
Gladiolus murielae, p.383
Habenaria radiata, p.408
Hyacinthus orientalis and cvs, pp.403, 407, 415

RIGHT Classic combination
Rosa 'Felicia' and *Lavandula angustifolia* provide pretty contrasts and a heady fragrance in a summer border.

Hymenocallis 'Sulphur Queen', p.412
LILIES (several), pp.388–391
Muscari armeniacum, p.420
Narcissus jonquilla and Div. 7 hybrids, pp.404–405
Narcissus tazetta and Div. 8 hybrids, pp.404, 405, 407
Ornithogalum arabicum, p.408
Polianthes tuberosa 'The Pearl', p.385

WATER AND BOG PLANTS
Aponogeton distachyos, p.435
Nymphaea 'Blue Beauty', p.440
Nymphaea 'James Brydon', p.440
Nymphaea odorata 'Sulphurea Grandiflora'

TENDER AND EXOTIC PLANTS
Trees
Bauhinia variegata
Plumeria rubra

Shrubs
Boronia megastigma
Gardenia augusta 'Veitchii'

Climbers
Hoya carnosa
Stephanotis floribunda

Perennials
Cattleya J.A.Carbone gx

Lilium regale

Lonicera etrusca 'Michael Rosse'

Wisteria sinensis 'Prolific'

Anemone sylvestris

Decorative fruit or seedheads

As winter approaches, dull corners or featureless borders can be brightened with the colorful fruits of barberries, cotoneasters, viburnums, and other ornamental berried shrubs. On pergolas and trellises, *Celastrus orbiculatus* and *Clematis orientalis* provide late-season interest with trailing skeins of yellow fruits and feathery seeds. Wall-trained pyracanthas will color drab winter walls with yellow, orange, or scarlet fruits, while hollies (*Ilex*) also sport berries for winter decoration. The dried seedheads of many plants produce beautiful effects for indoor and outdoor displays.

TREES
Arbutus unedo, p.93
Cornus kousa, p.85
Cotoneaster frigidus, p.142
Crataegus spp., pp.80, 84, 90
HOLLIES (most), p.94
Koelreuteria paniculata, p.89
MAGNOLIAS, p.70
Malus spp. (most), pp.82–110
Photinia davidiana, p.90
SORBUS, p.91

Conifers
Abies spp., pp.95, 96, 98, 100, 104, 105
Cedrus spp., pp.95, 96, 97, 104
Picea spp., pp.98, 99, 101, 103,105
Pinus spp., pp.78, 95, 96, 97, 98, 99, 100, 101, 102, 103, 104, 105

SHRUBS
Aucuba japonica
Berberis spp. and cvs, pp.111, 123, 127, 137, 141, 148, 160, 162
Callicarpa bodinieri var. *giraldii*, p.141
Cotoneaster spp. and cvs, pp.117, 122, 141, 142, 143, 208
Decaisnea fargesii, p.142
Euonymus europaeus 'Red Cascade', p.140
Euonymus latifolius, p.140
Euonymus myrianthus, p.117
Gaultheria mucronata and cvs, pp.163, 164

Hippophae rhamnoides, p.142
Hypericum x *inodorum* 'Elstead', p.161
Leycesteria formosa
Poncirus trifoliata, p.142
Pyracantha spp. and cvs, pp.118, 128, 141, 144, 209
ROSES (most), pp.168–187
Sambucus racemosa 'Plumosa Aurea', p.139
Sarcococca hookeriana var. *digyna*, p.164
Skimmia japonica, p.164
Symphoricarpos spp. and cvs, pp.148, 160
Symplocos paniculata, p.142
Viburnum davidii, p.165
Viburnum opulus and cvs, pp.142, 162
Viburnum tinus and cvs, p.143

CLIMBERS AND WALL SHRUBS
Actinidia deliciosa
Billardiera longiflora, p.210
Cardiospermum halicacabum
Celastrus orbiculatus
Clematis orientalis
Holboellia coriacea, p.194
ROSES (several), pp.168–187
Tropaeolum speciosum, p.202

PERENNIALS
Achillea filipendulina
Aconitum 'Stainless Steel', p.241
Actaea pachypoda, p.246
Agapanthus 'Northern Star', p.241

Agapanthus 'Phantom'
Agapanthus 'Purple Cloud', p.241
Clintonia borealis
Disporum hookeri
Duchesnea indica
Echinacea species and cvs, pp.221, 234
Eryngium pandanifolium
Eupatorium maculatum Atropurpureum Group 'Reisenschirm', p.221
Francoa sochifolia Rogerson's form
Iris foetidissima, p.225
Ligularia 'The Rocket', p.219
Ophiopogon spp., pp.280, 283
ORIENTAL POPPIES, p.238
PEONIES, pp.228–229
Persicaria polymorpha, p.234
Physalis alkekengi
Podophyllum hexandrum, p.255
Rudbeckia maxima, p.251
SEDUM, p.279
Smilacina racemosa, p.223
Veronicastrum virginicum 'Fascination', p.220

Grasses and bamboos
Ampeldesmos mauritanica, p.287
Briza maxima
Calamagrostis brachytricha, p.284
Chasmanthium latifolium, p.288
Cortaderia spp. and cvs, pp.284, 285
Deschampsisa cespitosa 'Gold Tau', p.289
Eragrostis curvula 'Totnes Burgundy', p.285
Miscanthus sinensis and cvs pp.284, 285, 286
Molinia caerulea subsp. *caerulea* 'Heidebraut', p.285
Molinia caerulea subsp. *arundinacea* 'Transparent', p.286
Panicum virgatum 'Northwind', p.289
Pennisetum spp. and cvs, pp.286, 311, 312
Stipa spp. and cvs, pp.286, 287, 288

ANNUALS AND BIENNIALS
Capsicum annuum 'Holiday Cheer'
Lagurus ovatus, p.284
Lunaria annua, p.310
Martynia annua, p.300

Nicandra physalodes
Nigella damascena and cvs, pp.314, 315
Solanum capsicastrum

ROCK PLANTS
Acaena microphylla, p.374
Cornus canadensis, p.360
Dryas octopetala, p.361
Gaultheria (most), pp.346, 373
Maianthemum bifolium, p.348
Nertera granadensis, p.373
Pulsatilla spp., pp.332, 334, 349
Vaccinium vitis-idaea subsp. *minus*, p.351

BULBS, CORMS, AND TUBERS
Allium aflatunense, p.382
Allium atropurpureum, p.392
Allium cowanii
Allium cristophii, p.411
Allium 'Gladiator', p.392
Allium 'Globemaster', p.392
Allium 'Mount Everest', p.385
Allium oreophilum, p.418
Allium 'Purple Sensation', p.392
Arisaema triphyllum, p.406
Arum italicum 'Marmoratum', p.421
Cardiocrinum giganteum, p.385

WATER AND BOG PLANTS
Ligularia 'Britt Marie Crawford', p.445
Nuphar lutea, p.444
Thalia dealbata

TENDER AND EXOTIC PLANTS
Trees
Cyphomandra betacea, p.456

Shrubs
x *Citrofortunella microcarpa*, p.458

BELOW Late-season sculpture
The seed heads of *Allium cristophii* complement the brown seed pods of *Nigella damascena*, adding texture to an herbaceous border as winter approaches.

Iris foetidissima

Rosa roxburghii

Symphoricarpus albus var. *laevigatus*

Ilex aquifolium 'Pyramidalis Aureomarginata'

Flowers for cutting

With careful selection, flowers can be cut from the garden at most times of the year, from the Christmas rose (*Helleborus niger*) in mid- or late winter to *Nerine bowdenii* in the fall. In small gardens, integrate plants for cutting into the general scheme, and leave some blooms for display, or plant away from the house so that the cutting is less noticeable. Fertilize regularly during the growing season, to counteract the weakening effects of cutting the plants.

SHRUBS

PERENNIALS

Grasses and bamboos

ANNUALS AND BIENNIALS

BULBS, CORMS, AND TUBERS

TENDER AND EXOTIC PLANTS
Shrubs

Perennials

RIGHT Late summer beauty
A selection of dahlias in shades of pink planted with vibrant blue agapanthus fill the late summer border and make excellent cut flowers.

Narcissus 'Tahiti'

Clarkia amoena 'Sybil Sherwood'

Allium aflatunense

Tulipa 'Spring Green'

Chrysanthemum 'Chelsea Physic Garden'

Alstroemeria 'Serenade'

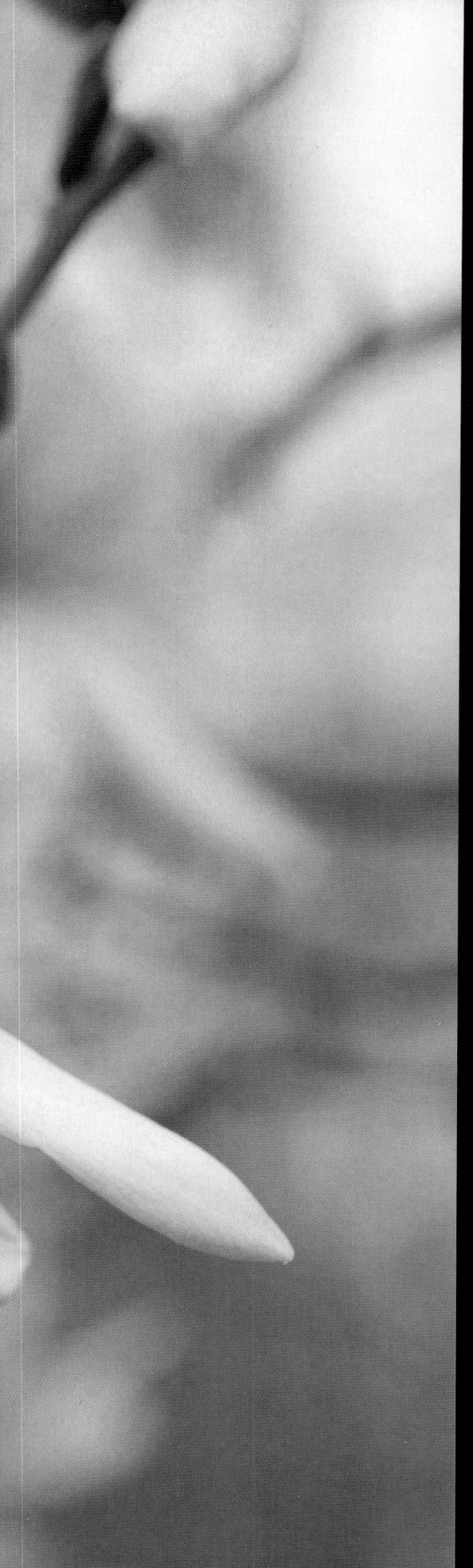

TREES

Trees are the most permanent elements in any planting
scheme, making a strong visual impact by virtue of their size
alone. There is a wealth of ornamental trees to choose from, with
a range to suit your climate and growing conditions, as well
as the size and style of your garden. Both deciduous and
evergreen trees provide year-round structure and beauty, but
they have many other benefits too, providing shade in summer,
shelter in winter, and nesting sites and food for birds, insects,
and other wildlife. Trees can also help reduce pollution and
combat climate change by absorbing carbon dioxide from the
atmosphere and replacing it with oxygen. They can
even help regulate groundwater, an important benefit
in areas at risk of flooding and soil erosion.

TREES

Dramatic and sculptural, trees are essential plants for gardens large and small. In design terms, they provide height, structure, and year-round interest, with flowers, foliage, fruit, and attractive bark, while also offering a home and source of food for birds and other wildlife.

SIZE CATEGORIES USED WITHIN THIS GROUP		
Large over 50ft (15m)	**Medium** 30–50ft (10–15m)	**Small** up to 30ft (10m)

What are trees?

Trees are woody plants, with life spans ranging from decades to several centuries. There are deciduous and evergreen trees, and most have a single stem with a crown of branches, although some produce multiple stems, either naturally or as a result of pruning. They range in size from conifers less than 3ft (1m) in height, to forest giants that soar up to 300ft (90m) or more. Trees also vary in shape. Some are narrowly conical or columnar, others are rounded or spreading, while some have an elegant arching, weeping habit. There is also a wide choice of leaf shape and color.

BELOW Letting in the light
Deciduous trees, such as *Acer shirasawanum* 'Aureum', can be used to make a wonderful garden centerpiece, underplanted with low plants to extend the interest before and after the main summer season.

Choosing trees

Before buying, match the needs of your chosen tree with the conditions in your garden. A tree is a long-term investment, so consider your site and soil carefully to be sure that it will thrive and that the size, shape, and style will suit your design scheme, since trees are difficult to move once established. Also calculate the amount of shade the tree will cast on your or your neighbor's garden when mature, and site large trees away from the house, and where their roots will not interfere with walls, pipes, sewers, or cables.

Designing with trees

Trees have many beautiful features and can be used in various ways to enhance a garden design. For example, several trees can be planted to form enclosures or define spaces; they can be used in pairs to frame a view, or in rows to form an avenue or tunnel. A line of trees also provides excellent wind protection, and those that tolerate clipping, such as beech (*Fagus sylvatica*), hornbeam (*Carpinus betulus*), and yew (*Taxus baccata*), make attractive hedges that diffuse wind and noise.

Many trees have eye-catching features that make beautiful focal points—those with colorful stems and bark or large sculptural leaves make good choices. The shape and form of a tree can also help to

REMOVING A TREE BRANCH

The best time to prune most trees is in late winter when the plants are dormant, but wait till mid- to late summer for hornbeam (*Carpinus*), pears (*Pyrus*), and plums and cherries (*Prunus*), which are susceptible to disease if cut earlier.

1 Make an undercut first
Shorten the branch first to reduce its weight and stop it from falling and tearing the bark. Cut halfway through the underside of the branch, then saw downward from the top, farther along the branch away from the trunk. Allow the branch to snap off.

2 Cut close to the trunk
Remove the final stump by cutting close to the trunk, but not flush with it. Make a smooth cut, angled away from the tree, just beyond the crease in the bark where the branch meets the trunk.

create a style. For example, the crisp outline of *Juniperus communis* 'Compressa', suits a formal design, while the shape, flowers, and fruit of many crab apples (*Malus* species) lend natural informality.

If you have space for several trees, you can create a small woodland, underplanted with shade-loving perennials. Many small trees, such as *Acer palmatum* and the corkscrew hazel (*Corylus avellana* 'Contorta'), and dwarf conifers are also suitable for growing in containers, and will add height and interest to patios, decks, and roof gardens.

Year-round interest

Broadleaf evergreens, such as hollies (*Ilex*) and bay laurel (*Laurus nobilis*), provide a valuable green backdrop throughout the year, while the needlelike foliage and candlelike cones of conifers offer a useful contrast in shape and texture. Against

this permanent display, plant deciduous trees for a seasonally changing palette of leaf colors, flowers, and fruit. Japanese cherries (*Prunus*), crab apples (*Malus*), and magnolias have vivid spring flowers, while many trees have large dramatic leaves or colorful foliage that brightens up the summer garden. A few trees, such as *Maackia amurensis* and *Arbutus unedo*, bear flowers in late summer and fall, but in the case of Japanese maples (*Acer*), the Chinese tupelo (*Nyssa sinensis*), and liquidambars, foliage color in fall is the main attraction; they produce luminous colors that set the garden ablaze.

Stem and bark color is a key feature of winter displays. The bleached white trunks of birches (*Betula*), glossy copper stems of *Prunus serrula*, and shaggy bark of *Acer griseum* provide focal points, while the dainty pink flowers of *Prunus* x *subhirtella* 'Autumnalis' lift late-winter days.

ABOVE Spring benefits
The profusion of large, double pink flowers of *Prunus serrulata* 'Kiku-shidare-sakura', makes a dramatic and colorful focal point in a spring garden.

PLANTING A CONTAINER-GROWN TREE

It is worth taking the time to prepare the site and plant your tree well, as this will increase its chances of survival and ensure that it thrives. Trees that have been grown in containers can be planted at most times of the year, but the warm, damp soil in fall provides ideal conditions. Bare-root trees are cheaper and available in fall or late winter. Plant them as soon as you get them home, unless the soil is frozen.

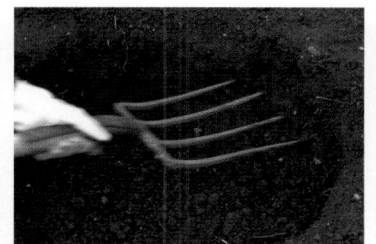

1 Break up the soil
Dig a hole twice the width of the pot and the same depth as the tree's rootball. Do not dig over the bottom of the hole as this may cause the tree to sink once planted. Instead, use a fork to puncture the base and sides.

2 Check planting depth
Remove the tree from its pot and put it in the hole. Use a cane to check that the top of the rootball is at the same level or slightly above the soil. Lift out the plant and cut away any roots that are circling the rootball.

3 Firm in
Tease out the roots, lower the tree back into the hole, and water it well. Then water again as you backfill the hole to ensure that there are no air pockets and the roots are in no danger of drying out. Firm the tree in gently.

4 Stake the tree
To prevent the tree from rocking in the wind, which can damage the roots, drive in a wooden tree stake with a mallet at an angle of 45 degrees. Make sure that the stake does not damage the rootball.

5 Fit the tree ties
Ensure that the top of the stake faces into the prevailing wind. Fit a tree tie with a spacer one-third of the way up the trunk from the base. Drive a nail through the tree tie into the stake to stop it from slipping down.

6 Continue to water in well
Water the tree well and apply a moisture-conserving bark mulch over the area around the tree, leaving space around the stem to prevent the bark from rotting it. Water the tree during dry spells for two years.

BARE-ROOT TREES

If the ground is still frozen when you receive your bare-root trees, or you are unable to plant them immediately for some other reason, fill a large pot with potting mix and heel them in. This simply means burying the roots to keep them moist. Plant the trees in the same way as shown here for container-grown plants, but take care to leave no air pockets when filling in around the roots with soil.

WHITE

Davidia involucrata
(Dove tree, handkerchief tree)
Deciduous, conical tree with heart-shaped, vivid green leaves, felted beneath. Large, white bracts appear on mature trees from late spring.

☼ ◊ Z6–8 H8–6  100ft 30m / 75ft 22.5m / 0

Populus x canescens (Gray poplar)
Vigorous, deciduous, spreading tree with slightly lobed leaves, gray when young, glossy, dark green in summer and yellow in fall. Usually bears grayish-red catkins in spring.

☼ ◊ Z4–9 H9–1  100ft 30m / 75ft 22.5m / 0

RED

Acer platanoides 'Crimson King'
Vigorous, deciduous, spreading tree. Leaves are large, lobed and deep reddish-purple, turning orange in fall. Tiny, red-tinged, deep yellow flowers are carried in midspring.

☼ ◊ Z3–7 H7–1  100ft 30m / 75ft 22.5m / 0

Aesculus x carnea 'Briotii'
Deciduous, round-headed tree. Leaves, consisting of 5 or 7 leaflets, are glossy, dark green. Panicles of red flowers are borne in late spring.

☼ ◊ ❗ Z7–8 H8–6  100ft 30m / 75ft 22.5m / 0

YELLOW

Fraxinus excelsior 'Jaspidea'
Vigorous, deciduous, spreading tree grown for its golden-yellow twigs and black buds, which are most evident in winter. Yellow leaves, with 9–11 oval leaflets, fade to light green and then gold, in fall.

☼ ◊ Z5–8 H8–5 ... 100ft 30m / 75ft 22.5m / 0

Acer macrophyllum (Oregon maple)
Deciduous, round-headed tree with large, deeply lobed, dark green leaves that turn yellow and orange in fall. Yellowish-green flowers in spring are followed by pale green fruits.

☼ ◊ Z3–8 H8–1  100ft 30m / 75ft 22.5m / 0

WHITE

Aesculus chinensis
(Chinese horse-chestnut)
Slow-growing, deciduous, spreading tree. Leaves are glossy, dark green with 7 leaflets. Slender spires of white flowers are produced in mid-summer.

☼ ◊ ❗ Z6–8 H8–6 100ft 30m / 75ft 22.5m / 0

Populus alba (White poplar)
Deciduous, spreading tree with wavy-margined or lobed leaves, dark green above, white beneath, turning yellow in fall.

☼ ◊ Z4–9 H9–1 100ft 30m / 75ft 22.5m / 0

Liriodendron tulipifera (Tulip tree)
Vigorous, deciduous, spreading tree. Deep green leaves, with a cut-off or notched tip and lobed sides, turn yellow in fall. In mid-summer, has tulip-shaped, orange-marked, greenish-white flowers.

☼ ◊ pH Z4–9 H9–2 100ft 30m / 75ft 22.5m / 0

Populus maximowiczii
Fast-growing, deciduous, conical tree. Oval, heart-shaped, bright green leaves have green-veined, white undersides and turn yellow in fall. Bears long, pendent seed heads surrounded by silky, white hairs in late summer.

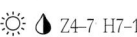 Z4–7 H7–1

Castanea sativa 'Albomarginata'
Deciduous, spreading tree. Has glossy, white-edged, dark green leaves that turn yellow in fall. Spikes of creamy-yellow flowers in summer are followed by edible fruits in fall.

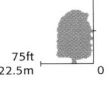 Z5–7 H7–5

Fagus sylvatica 'Rohanii'
Slow-growing, deciduous tree with oval, deeply cut, deep red-purple leaves, sometimes tinged with green or brown. Leaf margins are deeply cut into triangular teeth, which may bear serrations. Leaf veins and leaf stalk are prominently red.

 Z4–7 H9–4

Fagus sylvatica 'Riversii'
Fast-growing, deciduous, spreading tree with smooth, gray bark and elliptic, wavy-margined, dark purple leaves, which are larger than those of the species. New leaves on young shoots are wine-red and translucent.

 Z4–7 H9–4

Populus x canadensis 'Serotina de Selys'
Fast-growing, deciduous, upright tree. Has broadly oval, gray-green leaves, pale green when young, and red catkins in spring.

 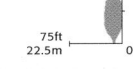 Z4–9 H9–1

Quercus macranthera (Caucasian oak)
Deciduous, spreading, sturdy-branched, handsome tree with large, deeply lobed, dark green leaves.

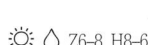 Z6–8 H8–6

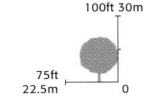

Alnus incana (Gray alder)
Deciduous, conical tree useful for cold, wet areas and poor soils. Yellow-brown catkins are carried in late winter and early spring, followed by oval, dark green leaves.

 Z2–6 H6–1

TREES

61

Populus x canadensis 'Robusta'
Fast-growing, deciduous, conical tree with upright branches. Broadly oval, bronze, young leaves mature to glossy, dark green. Bears long, red catkins in spring.

☀ ◊ Z4–9 H9–1   100ft 30m / 75ft 22.5m / 0

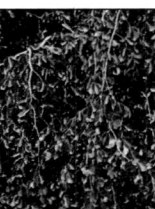

Fagus sylvatica f. pendula
(Weeping beech)
Deciduous, weeping tree with oval, wavy-edged, mid-green leaves that in fall take on rich hues of yellow and orange-brown.

☀ ◊ Z4–7 H9–4   100ft 30m / 75ft 22.5m / 0

Acer cappadocicum subsp. lobelii
(Lobel's maple)
Deciduous tree of narrow, upright habit, well-suited for growing in restricted space. Has wavy-edged, lobed leaves that turn yellow in fall.

☀ ◊ Z6–8 H8–6   100ft 30m / 75ft 22.5m / 0

Quercus robur f. fastigiata
Deciduous, upright, columnar tree of dense habit carrying lobed, dark green leaves.

☀ ◊ Z5–8 H8–3   100ft 30m / 75ft 22.5m / 0

Quercus canariensis
(Algerian oak, Mirbeck's oak)
Deciduous or semievergreen tree, narrow when young, broadening with age. Large, shallowly lobed, rich green leaves become yellowish-brown in fall, often persisting into late winter.

☀ ◊ Z7–9 H9–7   100ft 30m / 75ft 22.5m / 0

Quercus muehlenbergii
Deciduous, round-headed tree with sharply toothed, bright green leaves.

☀ ◊ Z4–8 H8–2   100ft 30m / 75ft 22.5m / 0

Celtis australis (European hackberry)
Deciduous, spreading tree. Has oval, pointed, sharply toothed, dark green leaves and small, purple-black fruits.

☀ ◊ Z6–8 H8–6   100ft 30m / 75ft 22.5m / 0

Juglans regia (English walnut)
Deciduous tree with a spreading head. Leaves, usually with 5 or 7 leaflets, are aromatic, bronze-purple when young, glossy, mid-green when mature. Produces edible nuts.

☀ ◊ Z3–7 H7–1   100ft 30m / 75ft 22.5m / 0

Acer saccharinum (Silver maple)
Fast-growing, deciduous, spreading tree, often with pendent branches. Deeply lobed, sharply toothed, mid-green leaves, with silver undersides, turn yellow in fall.

☼◑ ⬦ Z4–9 H8–1

Tilia oliveri
Deciduous, spreading, open tree with pointed, heart-shaped leaves, bright green above and silvery-white beneath. Produces small, fragrant, greenish-yellow flowers in summer, followed by winged fruits.

☼ ⬦ Z6–8 H9–6

Juglans nigra (Black walnut)
Fast-growing, deciduous, handsome, spreading tree with large, aromatic leaves of many pointed, glossy, dark green leaflets. Produces edible nuts in fall.

☼◑ ⬦ Z5–9 H9–5

Populus nigra 'Italica'
(Lombardy poplar)
Very fast-growing, deciduous, narrowly columnar tree with erect branches, diamond-shaped, bright green leaves and red catkins in midspring.

☼ ⬦ Z3–9 H9–1

Ailanthus altissima (Tree of heaven)
Fast-growing, deciduous, spreading tree with clusters of small, green flowers in mid-summer, followed by winged, green, then reddish-brown fruits. Large, dark green leaves are divided into paired, oval leaflets.

☼◑ ⬦ Z4–8 H8–1

Quercus petraea 'Columna'
Deciduous, upright, slender tree with large, wavy-edged, leathery, dark green leaves, tinged bronze when young.

☼ ⬦ Z5–8 H8–5

Tilia platyphyllos 'Rubra'
(Large-leaved linden)
Deciduous, spreading tree with red winter shoots and rounded, dark green leaves. Bears small, dull yellowish-white flowers in mid-summer.

☼◑ ⬦ Z5–8 H8–5

Platanus x hispanica (London plane)
Vigorous, deciduous, spreading tree with ornamental, flaking bark. Has large, sharply lobed, bright green leaves. Spherical fruit clusters hang from shoots in fall.

☼ ⬦ ❗ Z5–8 H8–5

Platanus orientalis (Oriental plane)
Vigorous, deciduous, spreading tree with flaking, gray, brown or cream bark and large, glossy, pale green leaves with 5 deep lobes. Green fruit clusters, later turning brown, persist in fall–winter.

☼ ⬦ Z3–8 H8–5

Nothofagus obliqua
(Roblé, Southern beech)
Fast-growing, deciduous, elegant tree with slender, arching branches. Has deep green leaves that turn orange and red in fall.

☼◑ ⬧ Z8–9 H9–8

Quercus nigra (Water oak)
Deciduous, spreading tree with glossy, bright green foliage retained until well into winter.

☼ ⬦ Z7–9 H9–7

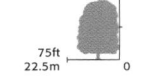
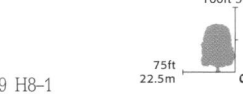

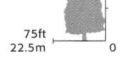

GREEN

Sassafras albidum
Deciduous, upright, later spreading tree. Aromatic, glossy, dark green leaves vary from oval to deeply lobed and turn yellow or red in fall. Has insignificant, yellowish-green flowers in spring.

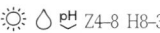 Z4–8 H8–3

Quercus castaneifolia
Deciduous, spreading tree with sharply toothed leaves, glossy, dark green above, gray beneath.

 Z7–9 H9–7

Fagus sylvatica (Common beech)
Deciduous, spreading tree with oval, wavy-edged leaves. These are pale green when young, mid- to dark green when mature, and turn rich yellow and orange-brown in fall, when nuts are produced.

 Z4–7 H9–4

Quercus frainetto (Hungarian oak)
Fast-growing, deciduous, spreading tree with a large, domed head and handsome, large, deeply lobed, dark green leaves.

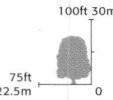 Z5–8 H8–1

Fagus sylvatica 'Aspleniifolia'
(Fern-leaved beech)
Fast-growing, deciduous, spreading tree. Has narrow, deeply cut, deep green leaves, which give a soft feathery outline to the tree. In fall, leaves turn golden-brown and persist well into winter.

Z4–7 H9–4

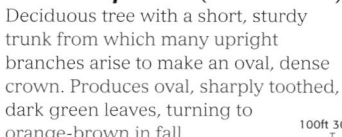

Zelkova carpinifolia (Caucasian elm)
Deciduous tree with a short, sturdy trunk from which many upright branches arise to make an oval, dense crown. Produces oval, sharply toothed, dark green leaves, turning to orange-brown in fall.

Quercus laurifolia
Deciduous, round-headed tree with narrow, glossy, bright green leaves, bronze-tinged when young, that are retained until late in the year.

 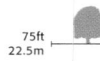 Z7–9 H9–7

Tilia 'Petiolaris'
(Weeping silver linden)
Deciduous, spreading tree with pendent branches. Pointed, heart-shaped leaves, dark green above, silver beneath, shimmer in the breeze. Has fragrant, creamy-yellow flowers in late summer.

 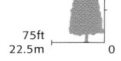 Z5–9 H9–5

  Z5–9 H9–5

Nothofagus x alpina
(Rauli, Southern beech)
Fast-growing, deciduous, conical tree. Leaves, with many impressed veins, are dark green, turning orange and red in fall.

 Z8–9 H9–8

YELLOW

RED

Liriodendron tulipifera 'Aureomarginatum'

Vigorous, deciduous tree. Deep green leaves have yellow margins, cut-off or notched tips and lobed sides. Bears cup-shaped, greenish-white flowers, splashed orange, in summer on mature trees.

☀ ◐ pH ⌣ Z4–9 H9–2   100ft 30m
75ft 22.5m / 0

Quercus rubra (Red oak)

Fast-growing, deciduous, spreading tree. Attractively lobed leaves, often large, are deep green becoming reddish- or yellowish-brown in fall.

☀ ◐ Z5–9 H9–5   100ft 30m
75ft 22.5m / 0

Acer pseudoplatanus f. erythrocarpum

Vigorous, deciduous, spreading tree with lobed, deep green leaves. Wings of young fall fruits are bright red.

☀ ◐ Z4–7 H7–1   100ft 30m
75ft 22.5m / 0

Quercus ellipsoidalis

Deciduous, spreading tree with deeply lobed, glossy, dark green leaves that turn dark purplish-red, then red in fall.

☀ ◐ Z4–7 H7–1   100ft 30m
75ft 22.5m / 0

Pterocarya x rehderiana

Very fast-growing, deciduous, spreading tree. Has glossy, bright green leaves consisting of narrow, paired leaflets that turn yellow in fall and long catkins of winged fruits in late summer and fall.

☀ ◐ Z6–9 H9–6   100ft 30m
75ft 22.5m / 0

Liquidambar styraciflua (Sweetgum)

Deciduous, conical to spreading tree. Shoots develop corky ridges. Lobed, glossy, dark green leaves turn brilliant orange, red and purple in fall.

☀ ◐ Z7–9 H9–7   100ft 30m
75ft 22.5m / 0

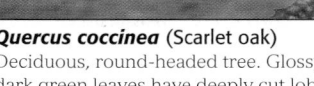

Quercus coccinea (Scarlet oak)

Deciduous, round-headed tree. Glossy, dark green leaves have deeply cut lobes ending in slender teeth. In fall, they turn bright red, usually persisting for several weeks on the tree.

☀ ◐ Z5–9 H9–4   100ft 30m
75ft 22.5m / 0

TREES

65

RED

Acer rubrum 'Scanlon'
Deciduous, upright tree. Has lobed, dark green foliage that in fall becomes bright red, particularly on acidic or neutral soil. Clusters of small, red flowers decorate bare branches in spring.

☀ ◊ Z3–9 H9–1 100ft 30m / 75ft 22.5m / 0

Nyssa sylvatica (Black gum, Tupelo)
Deciduous, broadly conical tree with oval, glossy, dark to mid-green leaves that turn brilliant yellow, orange and red in fall.

☀ ◖ Z5–9 H9–7 100ft 30m / 75ft 22.5m / 0

Acer rubrum 'Schlesingeri'
Deciduous, round-headed tree. In early fall, dark green leaves turn deep red. Tiny, red flowers appear on bare wood in spring.

☀ ◊ Z3–9 H9–1 100ft 30m / 75ft 22.5m / 0

Acer rubrum (Red maple)
Deciduous, round-headed tree. Dark green leaves turn bright red in fall, producing best color on acidic or neutral soil. In spring, bare branches are covered with tiny, red flowers.

☀ ◊ Z3–9 H9–1 100ft 30m / 75ft 22.5m / 0

Fraxinus angustifolia 'Raywood'
(Claret ash)
Vigorous, deciduous, spreading tree. Leaves have 5–7 narrowly oval, glossy, dark green leaflets that mature to bright reddish-purple in fall.

☀ ◊ Z6–9 H9–6 100ft 30m / 75ft 22.5m / 0

Quercus alba (White oak)
Deciduous, spreading tree. Deeply lobed, glossy, dark green leaves turn reddish-purple in fall.

☀ ◊ Z5–9 H8–1 100ft 30m / 75ft 22.5m / 0

Prunus serotina (Black cherry)
Deciduous, spreading tree. Spikes of fragrant, white flowers appear in early summer followed by red fruits that turn black in fall. Glossy, dark green leaves become yellow in fall.

☀ ◊ ❶ Z8–4 H8–1 100ft 30m / 75ft 22.5m / 0

Cercidiphyllum japonicum
(Katsura tree)
Fast-growing, deciduous, spreading tree. Leaves, bronze when young, turn rich green, then yellow to purple in fall, especially on acidic soil. Fallen leaves smell of burnt toffee.

☀ ◖ Z4–8 H8–1 100ft 30m / 75ft 22.5m / 0

Quercus palustris (Pin oak)
Fast-growing, deciduous, spreading tree with slender branches, pendulous at the tips. Deeply lobed, glossy, bright green leaves turn scarlet or red-brown in fall.

☀ ◊ Z5–8 H8–5 100ft 30m / 75ft 22.5m / 0

YELLOW

Acer platanoides 'Palmatifidum'
Vigorous, deciduous, spreading tree. Deeply divided, pale green leaves with slender lobes turn yellow or reddish-orange in fall. Tiny, yellow flowers appear in midspring.

 Z3–7 H7–1

Quercus phellos (Willow oak)
Deciduous, spreading tree of elegant habit. Narrow, willow-like, pale green leaves turn yellow then brown in fall.

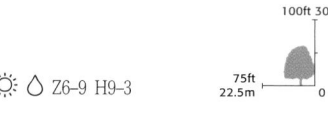 Z6–9 H9–3

Zelkova serrata
Deciduous, spreading tree with sharply toothed, finely pointed, dark green leaves that turn yellow or orange in fall.

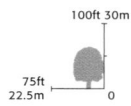 Z5–9 H9–5

Juglans ailantifolia var. cordiformis
Deciduous, spreading tree with large, aromatic leaves consisting of many glossy, bright green leaflets. Long, yellow-green, male catkins are borne in early summer. In fall has edible nuts.

 Z5–8 H8–5

Gymnocladus dioica
(Kentucky coffeetree)
Slow-growing, deciduous, spreading tree with small, star-shaped, white flowers borne in early summer. Large leaves, with 4–7 pairs of oval leaflets, are pinkish when young, green in summer, then yellow in fall.

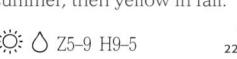 Z5–9 H9–5

Prunus avium (Mazzard, sweet cherry)
Deciduous, spreading tree with red-banded bark. Has sprays of white flowers in spring, deep red fruits and dark green leaves that turn red and yellow in fall.

 Z4–8 H8–1

Sophora japonica 'Violacea'
Fast-growing, deciduous, round-headed tree. Large sprays of pealike, white flowers, tinged with lilac-pink, appear in late summer and early fall.

Carya ovata (Shagbark hickory)
Deciduous tree with flaking, gray bark. Has dark green leaves, usually consisting of 5 slender leaflets, that turn golden-yellow in fall.

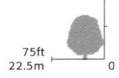 Z4–8 H8–1

WHITE

Betula papyrifera
(Canoe birch, Paper birch)
Vigorous, deciduous, open-branched, round-headed tree with peeling, shiny, white bark, yellowish catkins in spring and oval, coarsely serrated leaves that turn clear yellow in fall.

Z2–7 H7–1

Eucalyptus dalrympleana
(Mountain gum)
Vigorous, evergreen tree. Creamy-white, young bark becomes pinkish-gray, then peels. Leaves are long, narrow and pendent. Clusters of white flowers appear in late summer and fall.

Z9–10 H10–9

TREES

67

TREES

Eucalyptus gunnii (Cider gum)
Evergreen, conical tree with peeling, cream, pinkish and brown bark. Leaves are silver-blue when young, blue-green when mature. Clusters of white flowers, with numerous stamens, appear in mid-summer.

 ☼ ◊ Z8–10 H10–8   100ft 30m / 75ft 22.5m / 0

Quercus x turneri
Semievergreen, rounded, dense tree. Lobed, leathery, dark green leaves fall just before new foliage appears in spring.

☼ ◊ Z6–9 H9–6   100ft 30m / 75ft 22.5m / 0

Betula pendula 'Tristis' (Weeping birch)
Deciduous, slender, elegant tree with a strongly weeping habit and white bark. Oval, bright green leaves, with toothed margins, provide excellent golden color in fall.

 ☼ ◊ Z2–7 H7–1   100ft 30m / 75ft 22.5m / 0

Eucalyptus coccifera (Tasmanian snow gum, Mount Wellington peppermint)
Evergreen tree with peeling, blue-gray and white bark and aromatic, pointed, gray-green leaves. Bears clusters of white flowers, with numerous stamens, in summer.

 ☼ ◊ Z9–11 H11–10   100ft 30m / 75ft 22.5m / 0

Eucalyptus johnstonii
Fast-growing, evergreen tree with peeling, red to blue-green bark. Leaves are rounded and apple-green when young and spear-shaped, dark green and glossy when mature. Clusters of white flowers are followed by small, urn-shaped, seed capsules.

  ☼ ◊ Z9–10 H10–9   100ft 30m / 75ft 22.5m / 0

Nothofagus dombeyi
Evergreen, loosely conical tree of elegant habit with shoots that droop at the tips. Leaves are sharply toothed, glossy and dark green.

 ☼ ◖ Z8–9 H9–8   100ft 30m / 75ft 22.5m / 0

Quercus x hispanica 'Lucombeana' (Lucombe oak)
Semievergreen, spreading tree with toothed leaves, glossy, dark green above, gray beneath.

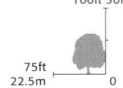 ☼ ◊ Z7–9 H9–7   100ft 30m / 75ft 22.5m / 0

GREEN/YELLOW

WHITE

Umbellularia californica (California laurel)

Evergreen, spreading tree with aromatic, leathery, glossy, dark green leaves and creamy-yellow flowers in late spring. Pungent leaves may cause nausea and headache when crushed.

☼ ◐ ! Z7–9 H9–7   75ft 22.5m / 100ft 30m / 0

Nothofagus betuloides

Evergreen, columnar tree with dense growth of oval, glossy, dark green leaves on bronze-red shoots.

☼ ◐ Z8–9 H9–8   75ft 22.5m / 100ft 30m / 0

Salix alba var. *vitellina* (Golden willow)

Deciduous, spreading tree, usually cut back hard to promote growth of strong, young shoots that are bright orange-yellow in winter. Lance-shaped, mid-green leaves appear in spring.

☼ ◐ Z4–9 H9–1   75ft 22.5m / 100ft 30m / 0

Malus baccata var. *mandschurica*

Vigorous, deciduous, spreading tree with dark green leaves and a profusion of white flowers in clusters in mid-spring, followed by long-lasting, small, red or yellow crab apples.

☼ ◐ Z3–7 H7–1   50ft 15m / 50ft 15m / 0

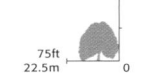

Nothofagus menziesii (Silver beech)

Evergreen, conical tree with silvery-white bark when young. Produces tiny, rounded, sharply toothed, glossy, dark green leaves.

◑ ◌ Z8–9 H9–8   75ft 22.5m / 100ft 30m / 0

Salix x sepulcralis var. *chrysocoma* (Golden weeping willow)

Deciduous tree with slender, yellow shoots falling to the ground as a curtain. Yellow-green, young leaves mature to mid-green.

☼ ◐ Z6–9 H9–6   75ft 22.5m / 100ft 30m / 0

Malus hupehensis (Tea crabapple)

Vigorous, deciduous, spreading tree. Has deep green leaves, large, fragrant, white flowers, pink in bud, from mid-to late spring, followed by small, red-tinged, yellow crab apples in late summer and fall.

☼ ◌ Z5–8 H8–5   50ft 15m / 50ft 15m / 0

Salix daphnoides (Violet willow)

Fast-growing, deciduous, spreading tree. Has lance-shaped, glossy, dark green leaves, silver, male catkins in spring and purple shoots with bluish-white bloom in winter.

☼ ◐ Z5–9 H9–5   50ft 15m / 50ft 15m / 0

TREES

69

MAGNOLIAS

A mature magnolia in full bloom makes a spectacular sight in spring. Most magnolias are elegant in habit and though slow-growing, eventually form imposing trees and shrubs. The flowers are generally saucer-, star-, or goblet-shaped and often have a subtle fragrance. Colors range from pure white, to white flushed or stained with pink or purple, to pink and rich red-purple. The genus includes some evergreen, summer-flowering species. These, and cultivars that are not fully hardy, are best planted against a sunny wall. Some magnolias prefer acidic or neutral soil, but most tolerate any soil provided it is humus-rich. Plenty of organic matter should be dug into the soil before planting. Avoid planting in exposed sites, as the flowers can be damaged by frost.

M. sprengeri var. *diva*

M. 'Vulcan'

Magnolia BLACK TULIP (**'Jurmag1'**)

M. 'Galaxy'

M. stellata '**Rosea**'

M. 'Ann'

M. grandiflora '**Exmouth**'

M. x loebneri '**Leonard Messel**'

M. x soulangeana '**Rustica Rubra**'

M. 'Elizabeth'

M. 'Pinkie'

M. stellata '**Waterlily**'

M. campbellii subsp. *mollicomata*

M. 'Butterflies'

WHITE

PINK

Prunus avium 'Plena'
Deciduous, spreading tree with reddish-brown bark and masses of double, pure white flowers in spring. Dark green foliage turns red in fall.

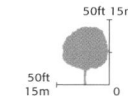  Z4–8 H8–1

Halesia monticola
(Mountain silverbell)
Fast-growing, deciduous, conical or spreading tree. Masses of pendent, bell-shaped, white flowers appear in late spring before leaves, followed by 4-winged fruits in fall.

 Z6–9 H9–6

Malus 'Profusion'
Deciduous, spreading tree. Dark green foliage is purple when young. Cup-shaped, deep purplish-pink flowers are freely borne in late spring, followed by small, reddish-purple crab apples in late summer and fall.

 Z4–8 H8–1

Prunus padus 'Watereri'
Deciduous, spreading tree with elliptic, matt, dark green leaves. Bears long, stiff racemes of cup-shaped, almond-scented, white flowers, to 8in (20cm) long, in late spring, followed by small, pea-shaped, black fruits, bitter to the taste.

Z4–8 H8–1

Michelia doltsopa
Evergreen, rounded tree with oval, glossy, dark green leaves, paler beneath. Strongly scented, magnolia-like flowers, with white to pale yellow petals, appear in winter–spring.

pH Z9–11 H11–1

Melia azedarach
(Chinaberry, bead tree)
Deciduous, spreading tree. Has dark green leaves with many leaflets and fragrant, star-shaped, pinkish-lilac flowers in spring, followed by pale orange-yellow fruits in fall.

H11–10

Fraxinus ornus (Manna ash)
Deciduous, round-headed tree. Has deep green leaves with 5–9 leaflets. Panicles of scented, creamy-white flowers appear in late spring and early summer.

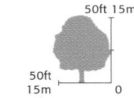 Z6–9 H9–4

Prunus mahaleb
Deciduous, round-headed, bushy tree that bears a profusion of fragrant, cup-shaped, white flowers from mid- to late spring. Rounded, glossy, dark green leaves turn yellow in fall.

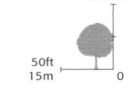 Z6–8 H8–6

Pyrus calleryana 'Chanticleer'
Deciduous, conical tree with glossy leaves that turn purplish in fall. Sprays of small, white flowers appear in spring. Resists fireblight.

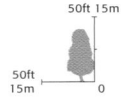 Z5–8 H8–3

Prunus jamasakura (Hill cherry)
Deciduous, spreading tree bearing cup-shaped, white or pink flowers from mid- to late spring. Oval leaves, bronze when young, mature to deep green.

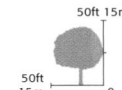 Z5–8 H8–5

TREES

Prunus 'Kanzan'

Deciduous, vase-shaped tree. Large, double, pink to purple flowers are borne profusely from mid- to late spring amid bronze, young leaves that mature to dark green.

☀ ◊ ❗ Z6–8 H8–6

Magnolia 'Heaven Scent'

Vigorous, deciduous tree or shrub with fragrant, vase-shaped flowers, each with usually 9 petals that are pink outside, white within, borne from mid-spring to early summer. Leaves are broadly elliptic and glossy green.

☀ ◊ Z6–9 H9–6

Aesculus x neglecta 'Erythroblastos'

Deciduous, spreading tree. Leaves with 5 leaflets emerge bright pink, turn yellow, then dark green, and finally orange and yellow in fall. May bear panicles of flowers in summer.

☀ ◊ ❗ Z5–8 H8–5

Paulownia tomentosa
(Empress tree, Princess tree)

Deciduous, spreading tree. Has large, lobed, mid-green leaves and terminal sprays of fragrant, foxglove-like, pinkish-lilac flowers in spring.

☀ ◊ Z5–8 H8–5

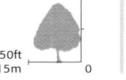

Prunus padus 'Colorata'

Deciduous, spreading tree, conical when young. Produces pendent racemes of fragrant, cup-shaped, pink flowers in late spring, followed by small, black fruits. Oval, purple young leaves mature to dark green and turn red or yellow in fall.

☀ ◊ ❗ Z4–8 H8–1

Quercus rubra 'Aurea'

Slow-growing, deciduous, spreading tree. Large, lobed leaves are clear yellow when young, becoming green by mid-summer. Produces best color in an open but sheltered position.

☀ ◊ Z5–9 H9–5

Gleditsia triacanthos 'Sunburst'

Deciduous, spreading tree with fernlike, glossy foliage that is golden-yellow when young, deep green in summer.

☀ ◊ Z3–7 H7–1

Styrax japonicus

Deciduous, spreading tree bearing in early summer a profusion of pendent, fragrant, bell-shaped, white flowers amid glossy, dark green foliage.

☀ ◊ pH Z6–8 H8–6

Ostrya virginiana
(American hop hornbeam, Ironwood)

Deciduous, conical tree with dark brown bark and deep green leaves, yellow in fall. Has yellowish catkins in spring, followed by greenish-white fruit clusters.

☀ ◊ Z5–9 H9–2

Catalpa speciosa

Deciduous, spreading tree. Heads of large, white flowers marked with yellow and purple are borne in mid-summer among glossy, mid-green leaves.

☀ ◊ Z4–8 H8–1

Eucryphia cordifolia (Ulmo)
Evergreen, columnar tree bearing oblong, wavy-edged, dull green leaves, with gray down beneath. Large, saucer-shaped, white flowers are produced in late summer and fall.

☀️◐ ⬤ Z8–11 H11–7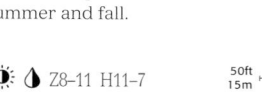

Pterostyrax hispida (Epaulette tree)
Deciduous, spreading tree or shrub with aromatic, gray bark and oblong to oval, mid-green leaves, 8in (20cm) long. Large, drooping panicles of small, bell-shaped, white flowers are borne from early to mid-summer.

☀️◐ ⬤ pH Z5–8 H8–5

Acer pseudoplatanus 'Simon Louis Frères'
Deciduous, spreading tree. Young leaves are marked with creamy-white and pink; older foliage is pale green with white markings.

☀️ ⬤ Z4–7 H7–1

Aesculus indica 'Sydney Pearce'
Deciduous, spreading tree with glossy, dark green leaves, bronze when young and orange or yellow in fall. Pinkish-white flowers, marked red and yellow, appear from early to mid-summer.

☀️ ⬤ ❗ Z7–8 H8–7

Catalpa bignonioides
(Indian bean tree)
Deciduous, spreading tree. Large, light green leaves are purplish when young. White flowers marked with yellow and purple appear in summer, followed by long, cylindrical, pendent pods.

☀️ ⬤ Z5–9 H9–5

Drimys winteri (Winter's bark)
Evergreen, conical, sometimes shrubby tree with long, glossy, pale or dark green leaves, usually bluish-white beneath. Bears clusters of fragrant, star-shaped, white flowers in early summer.

☀️ ⬤ Z8–11 H11–8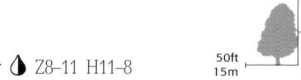

Toona sinensis
Deciduous, spreading tree with shaggy bark when old. Dark green leaves with many leaflets turn yellow in fall. Bears fragrant, white flowers in mid-summer. Shoots are onion-scented.

☀️ ⬤ Z5–8 H12–10

Catalpa fargesii f. duclouxii
Deciduous, broadly columnar tree grown for its bell-shaped, foxglove-like, delicate pink flowers, from early to mid-summer, followed by long, pendulous seed pods. Has large, heart-shaped, bright green leaves ending in a long point.

☀️ ⬤ Z6–8 H8–5

Quercus cerris 'Argenteovariegata'
Deciduous, spreading tree. Strongly toothed or lobed, glossy, dark green leaves are edged with creamy-white.

☀️ ⬤ Z7–9 H9–7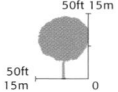

Eucryphia x nymansensis 'Nymansay'
Evergreen, columnar tree. Some of the leathery, glossy, dark green leaves are simple, others consist of 3 (rarely 5) leaflets. Clusters of large, white flowers open in late summer or early fall.

☀️◐ ⬤ Z8–9 H9–8

Sorbus pseudohupehensis
Deciduous, spreading tree with leaves of 4–8 pairs of blue-green leaflets turning orange-red in late fall. White flowers in spring are followed by long-lasting, pink fruits.

☀️ ⬤ ❗ Z4–7 H7–3

TREES

GREEN

Broussonetia papyrifera
(Paper mulberry)
Deciduous, round-headed tree.
Dull green leaves are large, broadly
oval, toothed and sometimes lobed.
In early summer, small globes
of purple flowers appear on
female plants.

  Z6–9 H9–6

Hovenia dulcis (Japanese raisintree)
Deciduous, spreading tree with large,
glossy, dark green leaves. In summer
it may bear small, greenish-yellow
flowers, the stalks of which become
red, fleshy and edible.

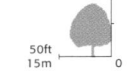 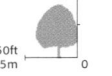 Z6–8 H8–5

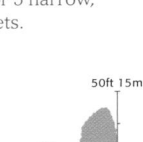

Fraxinus velutina (Arizona ash)
Deciduous, spreading tree. Leaves vary
but usually consist of 3 or 5 narrow,
velvety, gray-green leaflets.

 Z6–9 H9–6

Meliosma veitchiorum
Deciduous, spreading tree with stout,
gray shoots and large, dark green,
red-stalked leaves with 9 or 11 leaflets.
Small, fragrant, white flowers in
late spring are followed by
violet fruits in fall.

Z9–11 H11–10

Quercus garryana (Oregon oak)
Slow-growing, deciduous, spreading
tree with deeply lobed, glossy, bright
green leaves.

 Z7–9 H9–7

Populus tremula 'Pendula'
(European aspen)
Vigorous, deciduous, weeping
tree. Leaves, reddish when young,
gray-green in summer and yellow
in fall, tremble in the wind. Has
purplish catkins in late winter
and spring.

  Z2–8 H8–1

Acer negundo 'Variegatum'
Fast-growing, deciduous, spreading
tree. Has pinkish- then white-margined,
bright green leaves with 3 or 5 leaflets.
Inconspicuous, greenish-yellow flowers
appear in late spring.

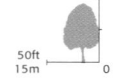 Z5–8 H8–3

Kalopanax septemlobus
Deciduous, spreading tree with spiny
stems, large, 5–7-lobed, glossy, dark
green leaves and umbels of small,
white flowers, then black fruits in fall.

 Z5–9 H9–4

TREES

74

Tilia cordata 'Rancho'
Deciduous, conical, dense tree,
spreading when young. Has small,
oval, glossy, dark green leaves, and
clusters of small, fragrant, cup-shaped,
yellowish flowers are borne in
mid-summer.

☼ ◊ Z3–8 H8–1

Phellodendron chinense
Deciduous, spreading tree.
Aromatic leaves, with 7–13 oblong
leaflets, are dark green, turning yellow
in fall. Pendent racemes of greenish
flowers in early summer are
followed on female trees by
berry-like, black fruits.

☼ ◊ Z5–8 H8–5

Idesia polycarpa
Deciduous, spreading tree with large,
heart-shaped, glossy, dark green
leaves on long stalks. Small, fragrant,
yellow-green flowers in mid-summer
are followed in fall, on female
plants, by red fruits hanging
in clusters.

☼ ◊ Z6–9 H9–6
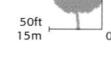

Quercus marilandica (Blackjack oak)
Deciduous, spreading tree. Large leaves,
3-lobed at the apex, are glossy, dark
green above, paler beneath, and turn
yellow, red or brown in fall.

☼ ◊ Z6–9 H9–6

Emmenopterys henryi
Deciduous, spreading tree. Large,
pointed, dark green leaves are bronze-
purple when young. Clusters of white
flowers (some bearing a large, white
bract) are rarely produced except
in hot summers.

☼ ◊ Z7–11 H11–7

Gleditsia japonica
Deciduous, conical tree with a trunk
armed with spines. Shoots are purplish
when young. Fernlike leaves consist
of many small, mid-green leaflets.

☼ ◊ Z8–11 H11–8
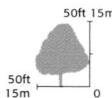

Quercus macrocarpa (Bur oak)
Slow-growing, deciduous, spreading
tree. Large, oblong-oval, lobed,
glossy, dark green leaves turn
yellow or brown in fall.

☼ ◊ Z3–9 H9–1
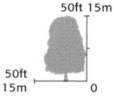

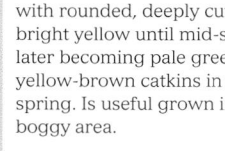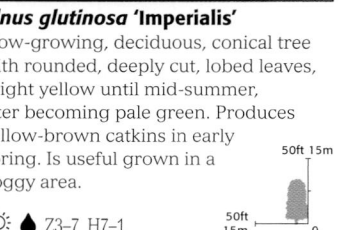

Alnus glutinosa 'Imperialis'
Slow-growing, deciduous, conical tree
with rounded, deeply cut, lobed leaves,
bright yellow until mid-summer,
later becoming pale green. Produces
yellow-brown catkins in early
spring. Is useful grown in a
boggy area.

☼ ● Z3–7 H7–1

**Quercus ithaburensis
subsp. macrolepis**
Deciduous or semievergreen,
spreading tree. Has gray-green
leaves with angular lobes.

☼ ◊ Z7–9 H9–6
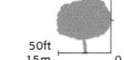

SUMMER

FALL

YELLOW

RED

Catalpa bignonioides 'Aurea'
Deciduous, spreading tree with broadly oval, bright yellow leaves, bronze when young. Bell-shaped, white flowers, marked with yellow and purple, borne in summer, are followed by long, pendent, cylindrical pods, often persisting after leaf fall.

 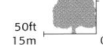 Z5–9 H9–5

Acer rufinerve (Snake-bark maple)
Deciduous tree with arching branches striped green and white. In fall, lobed, dark green leaves turn brilliant red and orange.

 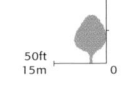 Z6–9 H9–6

Oxydendrum arboreum
(Sourwood, sorrel tree)
Deciduous, spreading tree with glossy, dark green foliage that turns bright red in fall. Sprays of white flowers appear in late summer and fall.

 Z5–9 H9–3

Ulmus minor 'Dicksonii'
(Dickson's golden elm)
Slow-growing, deciduous, conical tree of dense habit. Carries small, broadly oval, bright golden-yellow leaves.

 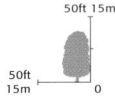 Z5–8 H8–5

Acer davidii 'Madeline Spitta'
Deciduous tree with upright branches that are striped green and white. Glossy, dark green foliage turns orange in fall after the appearance of winged, green fruits that ripen reddish-brown.

 Z5–7 H7–5

Stewartia monadelpha
Deciduous, spreading tree with peeling bark and glossy, dark green leaves that turn orange and red in fall. Small, violet-anthered, white flowers appear in mid-summer, followed by small fruits.

  Z6–9 H9–6

Robinia pseudoacacia 'Frisia'
Deciduous, spreading tree with luxuriant leaves divided into oval leaflets, golden-yellow when young, greenish-yellow in summer and orange-yellow in fall.

 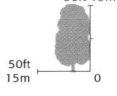  Z4–9 H9–3

Acer rubrum 'Columnare'
Deciduous, slender, upright tree with lobed, dark green foliage becoming a fiery column of red and yellow in fall.

 Z3–9 H9–1

Aesculus flava
(Sweet buckeye, Yellow buckeye)
Deciduous, spreading tree. Glossy, dark green leaves, with 5 or 7 oval leaflets, redden in fall. Has yellow flowers in late spring and early summer followed by round fruits (chestnuts).

  Z3–8 H8–1

Acer henryi
Deciduous, spreading tree. Dark green leaves with 3 oval, toothed leaflets turn bright orange and red in fall.

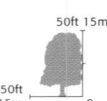 Z4–8 H8–1

TREES

Acer capillipes (Snake-bark maple)
Deciduous, spreading tree. Has lobed, bright green leaves that turn brilliant red and orange in fall. Older branches are striped green and white.

☀ ◊ Z5–7 H7–5

Malus tschonoskii
Deciduous, conical tree with broadly oval, glossy, mid-green leaves that turn brilliant shades of orange, red and purple in fall. Single, pink-tinged, white flowers, in late spring, are followed by red-flushed, yellowish-green crab apples.

☀ ◊ Z5–8 H8–5

Acer japonicum 'Vitifolium'
Vigorous, deciduous, bushy tree or large shrub with large, rounded, lobed, mid-green leaves that turn brilliant red, orange and purple in fall.

☀ ◊ Z5–7 H7–1

Prunus sargentii (Sargent cherry)
Deciduous, spreading tree. Oval, dark green leaves are red when young, turning brilliant orange-red in early fall. Clusters of blush-pink flowers appear in midspring.

☀ ◊ ① Z5–9 H9–5

Nyssa sinensis
Deciduous, spreading tree. Has long, narrow, pointed leaves that are purplish when young, dark green when mature and brilliant scarlet in fall.

☀ ◊ Z7–9 H9–7

Acer saccharum 'Temple's Upright'
Deciduous, columnar tree. In fall, large, lobed leaves turn brilliant orange and red.

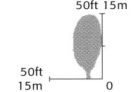

☀ ◊ Z4–9 H8–1

Quercus x heterophylla
(Bartram's oak)
Deciduous, spreading tree with toothed, glossy, bright green leaves that turn orange-red and yellow in fall.

☀ ◊ Z5–8 H8–5

Parrotia persica (Persian ironwood)
Deciduous, spreading, short-trunked tree with flaking, gray and fawn bark. Rich green leaves turn yellow, orange and red-purple in fall. Small, red flowers are borne on bare wood in early spring.

☀ ◖ Z4–7 H7–1

ORNAMENTAL BARK

Of the many ornamental features offered by trees, including flowers, fruit, and foliage, it is probably bark that makes the greatest impact in a garden. This is partly because bark is not transient and offers interest every day of the year and throughout the mature life of the tree. Chosen carefully, trees with ornamental bark can lighten up the darkest corner and provide superb contrast to other plants. While maple (*Acer*), birch (*Betula*), and cherry (*Prunus*) are obvious choices, there are many other species with stunning, textured or colored bark, such as the patterned stems of eucalyptus and *Stewartia*. Some trees display their colorful bark from an early age, others may take a few years to develop—but the end result is well worth waiting for.

Stewartia pseudocamellia

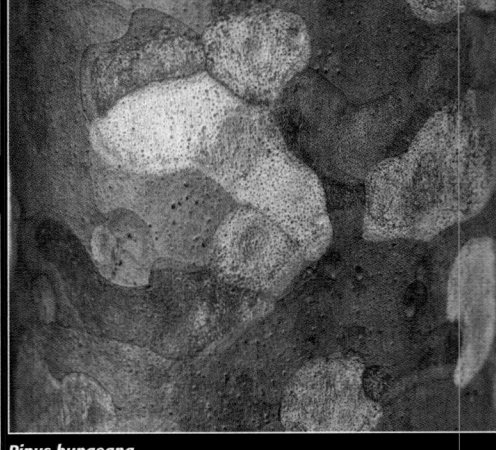

Pinus bungeana

Betula utilis var. *jacquemontii* 'Grayswood Ghost'

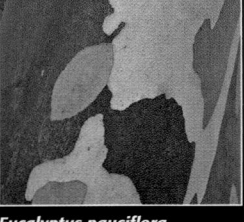

Eucalyptus pauciflora subsp. *niphophila*

Acer palmatum 'Sango-kaku'

Pinus sylvestris

Luma apiculata

Acer grosseri

Acer griseum

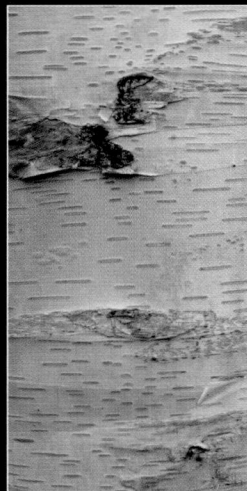

Betula utilis var. *jacquemontii* 'Jermyns'

Acer davidii

Betula albosinensis

Prunus serrula

Betula ermanii

Quercus suber

Betula nigra

Acer pensylvanicum 'Erythrocladum'

FALL

ALL YEAR

YELLOW

Betula lenta (Sweet birch, cherry birch)
Deciduous, broadly spreading tree that gives off a sweet fragrance when leaves, shoots or bark are crushed. Has dark red bark with purple flakes. Oval, mid-green leaves, to 5in (12cm) long, fleetingly turn vibrant gold in fall.

 ☼ ◊ Z3–7 H7–2

Cladrastis kentukea (Yellowwood)
Deciduous, round-headed tree. Leaves of 7 or 9 rounded-oval leaflets are dark green, turning yellow in fall. Clusters of fragrant, pealike, yellow-marked, white flowers appear in early summer.

 ☼ ◊ Z4–9 H9–1

Fagus sylvatica 'Dawyck'
Deciduous, narrowly columnar tree with upward-sweeping branches and oval, lime-green leaves, which darken as the season progresses, before turning a rich copper color in fall. The tree's form tends to "broaden out" in maturity.

 ☼ ◊ Z4–7 H9–4

Fraxinus excelsior 'Pendula'
Deciduous tree with long, slender, weeping branches, forming a spreading, umbrella-like canopy. Produces dull green leaves with 9–11 oval, shallowly toothed leaflets. Most trees are grafted onto *F. excelsior* at 10–16ft (3–5m) above the ground.

☼ ◊ Z5–8 H8–5

Acer pensylvanicum (Snake-bark maple)
Deciduous, upright tree. Shoots are boldly striped green and white. Large, lobed, mid-green leaves turn bright yellow in fall.

 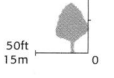 ☼ ◊ Z3–7 H7–1

GREEN

Arbutus x andrachnoides
Evergreen, bushy, spreading tree with peeling, reddish-brown bark and glossy, dark green foliage. Clusters of small, white flowers in fall to spring are followed by small, strawberry-like, orange or red fruits.

☼ ◊ Z8–9 H9–8

Eucalyptus pauciflora (Cabbage gum, Weeping gum, White sallee)
Evergreen, spreading tree with peeling, white, young bark and red, young shoots. In summer, white flower clusters appear amid glossy, bright gray-green foliage.

 ☼ ◊ Z9–11 H11–10

Trochodendron aralioides
Evergreen, broadly conical tree with glossy, dark green foliage. In late spring and early summer bears clusters of unusual, petal-less, wheel-like, green flowers.

 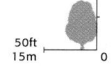 ☼ ◑ ◊ Z6–11 H12–10

TREES

79

GREEN

WHITE

TREES

Trachycarpus fortunei
(Chusan palm, Windmill palm)
Evergreen palm with unbranched stem and a head of large, deeply divided, fanlike, mid-green leaves. Sprays of fragrant, creamy-yellow flowers appear in early summer.

☼ ◊ Z8–11 H12–8

Quercus agrifolia
(California live oak)
Evergreen, spreading tree bearing rigid, spiny-toothed, glossy, dark green leaves.

☼ ◊ Z9–11 H11–9

Crataegus flava (Yellow hawthorn)
Deciduous, spreading tree. Has small, dark green leaves and white flowers in late spring and early summer, followed by greenish-yellow fruits.

☼ ◊ ❢ Z7–9 H9–7

Laurus nobilis (Bay laurel, Sweet bay)
Evergreen, broadly conical tree with narrowly oval, leathery, very aromatic, glossy, dark green leaves, used in cooking. Has small, star-shaped, pale yellow flowers in spring, followed by spherical to egg-shaped, green then black fruits.

☼ ◊ Z8–11 H11–1

Crataegus orientalis
Deciduous, spreading tree with deeply lobed, hairy, dark green leaves. A profusion of white flowers in late spring or early summer is followed by red fruits tinged with yellow.

☼ ◊ ❢ Z6–8 H8–6

Quercus myrsinifolia
Evergreen, rounded tree with narrow, pointed, glossy, dark green leaves, reddish-purple when young.

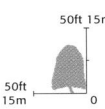

☼ ◊ Z7–9 H9–6

Jubaea chilensis
(Chilean wine palm, Coquito)
Slow-growing, evergreen palm with a massive trunk and large, silvery-green leaves. Has small, maroon and yellow flowers in spring and woody, yellow fruits in fall.

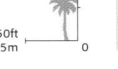

☼ ◊ Z8–11 H11–9

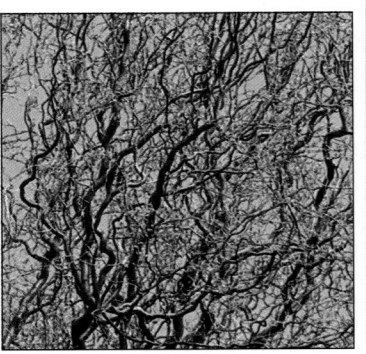

Salix babylonica var. pekinensis 'Tortuosa' (Dragon's-claw willow)
Fast-growing, deciduous, spreading tree with curiously twisted shoots and contorted, narrow, tapering, bright green leaves.

☼ ◐ Z6–9 H9–1

Mespilus germanica (Medlar)
Deciduous, spreading tree or shrub. Has dark green leaves that turn orange-brown in fall, white flowers in spring–summer and brown fruits in fall, edible when half rotten.

☼ ◊ Z6–9 H9–6

Prunus 'Shogetsu'
Deciduous, round-topped tree. In late spring, pink buds open to large, double, white flowers that hang in clusters from long stalks. Mid-green leaves turn orange and red in fall.

 ☼ ◊ ❗ Z6–8 H8–6

Malus 'Snowcloud'
Deciduous, compact tree of upright habit, with oval, bronze leaves that turn dark green. In spring, pink flower buds open to produce masses of semidouble to double, long-lasting, white flowers, followed in late summer by yellow fruits.

 ☼ ◊ Z4–7 H7–4

Aesculus californica
(California buckeye)
Deciduous, spreading, sometimes shrubby tree. Dense heads of fragrant, sometimes pink-tinged, white flowers appear in spring and early summer. Small, dark green leaves have 5–7 leaflets.

☼ ◊ ❗ Z7–8 H8–7

Prunus incisa (Fuji cherry)
Deciduous, spreading tree. White or pale pink flowers appear in early spring. Sharply toothed, dark green leaves are reddish when young, orange-red in fall.

 ☼ ◊ ❗ Z4–9 H9–1

Amelanchier laevis
Deciduous, spreading tree or large shrub. Oval, bronze, young leaves turn dark green in summer, red and orange in fall. Sprays of white flowers in spring are followed by rounded, fleshy, red fruits.

 ☼ ◊ Z5–9 H9–3

TREES

WHITE

Prunus 'Taihaku' (Great white cherry)
Vigorous, deciduous, spreading tree.
Very large, single, pure white flowers are
borne in mid-spring among bronze-red,
young leaves that mature to dark green.

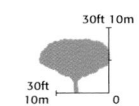 Z6–8 H8–6

Prunus 'Ukon'
Vigorous, deciduous, spreading tree.
Semidouble, pale greenish-white flowers
open from pink buds in mid-spring amid
pale bronze, young foliage that later
turns dark green.

 Z6–8 H8–6

Prunus 'Shirotae'
Deciduous, spreading tree with slightly
arching branches. Large, fragrant, single
or semidouble, pure white flowers
appear in mid-spring. Foliage turns
orange-red in fall.

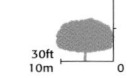 Z6–8 H8–6

PINK

Prunus x yedoensis (Yoshino cherry)
Deciduous, round-headed tree with
spreading, arching branches and
dark green foliage. Sprays of pink
buds open to white or pale pink
flowers in early spring.

 Z5–8 H8–3

Prunus 'Spire'
Deciduous, vase-shaped tree, conical
when young. Soft pink flowers appear
profusely from early to mid-spring.
Dark green leaves, bronze when
young, turn brilliant orange-red
in fall.

 Z6–8 H8–6

Prunus 'Hokusai'
Deciduous, spreading tree. Oval,
bronze, young leaves mature to dark
green, then turn orange and red in
fall. Semidouble, pale pink flowers
are borne in mid-spring.

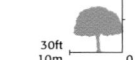 Z5–8 H8–5

Prunus 'Pandora'
Deciduous tree, upright when young,
later spreading. Massed, pale pink
flowers appear in early spring. Leaves
are bronze when young, dark green
in summer and often orange
and red in fall.

 Z6–8 H8–5

Malus x arnoldiana
Deciduous, low, spreading tree with
arching branches. In mid- to late spring
red buds open to fragrant, pink flowers
that fade to white. Bears small,
red-flushed, yellow crab apples
in fall. Leaves are oval.

Z4–7 H7–4

Prunus 'Yae-murasaki'
Deciduous, spreading tree with bright
green leaves, bronze when young,
orange-red in fall. Semidouble, deep
pink flowers are produced in mid-spring.

 Z6–8 H8–6

Prunus pendula 'Stellata'
Deciduous, spreading tree. Pink flowers
with narrow, pointed petals, red in bud,
open from early to mid-spring. Dark
green leaves turn yellow in fall.

☼ ◊ ❶ Z6–8 H8–6

Prunus 'Shirofugen'
Deciduous, spreading tree with bronze-
red leaves turning orange-red in fall.
Pale pink buds open to fragrant, double,
white blooms that turn pink before
they fade in late spring.

☼ ◊ ❶ Z6–8 H8–6

Prunus 'Pink Perfection'
Deciduous, upright tree that bears
double, pale pink flowers in late spring.
Oval leaves are bronze when young,
dark green in summer.

☼ ◊ ❶ Z6–8 H8–5

Prunus 'Accolade'
Deciduous, spreading tree with
clusters of deep pink buds opening
to semidouble, pale pink flowers
in early spring. Toothed, mid-green
leaves turn orange-red in fall.

☼ ◊ ❶ Z4–9 H9–1

Cercis siliquastrum (Judas tree)
Deciduous, spreading, bushy tree.
Clusters of pealike, bright pink
flowers appear in mid-spring, before
or with heart-shaped leaves, followed
by long, purplish-red pods in
late summer.

☼ ◊ Z6–9 H9–3

Malus x magdeburgensis
Deciduous, spreading tree with dark
green foliage. Dense clusters of large,
semidouble, deep pink flowers appear
in late spring, occasionally followed by
small, yellow crab apples in fall.

☼ ◊ Z4–7 H7–4

Prunus 'Kiku-shidare-zakura'
Deciduous, weeping tree. Has double,
bright pink flowers that cover pendent
branches from mid- to late spring.

☼ ◊ ❶ Z4–9 H9–1

Prunus x subhirtella 'Pendula Rubra'
Deciduous, weeping tree that bears
deep pink flowers in spring before oval,
dark green leaves appear; these turn
yellow in fall.

☼ ◊ ❶ Z6–8 H8–6

Prunus persica 'Prince Charming'
Deciduous, upright, bushy-headed
tree with narrow, bright green leaves.
Double, deep rose-pink flowers are
produced in mid-spring.

☼ ◊ Z4–8 H8–1

TREES

PINK

Malus floribunda
Deciduous, spreading, dense-headed tree with pale pink flowers, red in bud, appearing from mid- to late spring, followed by tiny, pea-shaped, yellow crab apples in fall.

☀ ○ Z4–8 H8–1

Prunus 'Pink Shell'
Deciduous, spreading tree with oval, bronze-colored leaves that turn bright green in early summer, then orange in fall. In mid-spring, a profusion of fragrant, 5-petaled, single, long-stalked, shell-pink flowers cover the branches.

☀ ○ Z5–8 H8–3

Acer pseudoplatanus 'Brilliantissimum'
Slow-growing, deciduous, spreading tree. Lobed leaves are salmon-pink when young, then turn yellow and finally dark green in summer.

☀ ○ Z4–7 H7–1

RED

Crataegus laevigata 'Paul's Scarlet'
Deciduous, spreading tree. Has toothed, glossy, dark green leaves and a profusion of double, red flowers in late spring and early summer.

☀ ○ ⚠ Z5–8 H8–3

Acacia baileyana 'Purpurea'
Evergreen, spreading tree with divided, fernlike, 2-pinnate, bronze-purple, young leaves that turn silver-gray later in spring. From late winter to early spring produces masses of spherical, golden-yellow flower heads in dense racemes. Is best grown against a wall.

☀ ○ pH Z10–11 H12–10

YELLOW

Malus 'Royalty'
Deciduous, spreading tree with glossy, purple foliage. Crimson-purple flowers appear from mid- to late spring, followed by dark red crab apples in fall.

☀ ○ Z4–8 H8–1

Malus 'Lemoinei'
Deciduous, spreading tree. Oval leaves are deep reddish-purple when young, later becoming tinged with bronze. Wine-red flowers in late spring are followed by dark reddish-purple crab apples in fall.

☀ ○ Z5–8 H8–5

Cercis canadensis 'Forest Pansy'
Deciduous, spreading tree or shrub. In mid-spring has flowers that are magenta in bud, opening to pale pink, before heart-shaped, reddish-purple leaves appear.

☀ ○ Z4–9 H9–2

Laburnum x watereri 'Vossii'
(Voss's laburnum)
Deciduous, spreading tree. Leaves, consisting of 3 leaflets, are glossy, deep green. Pendent chains of large, yellow flowers are borne in late spring and early summer.

☀ ○ ⚠ Z6–8 H8–3

Sophora tetraptera
Semievergreen, spreading tree or large shrub with dark green leaves composed of many tiny leaflets. Clusters of golden-yellow flowers appear in late spring.

☀ ○ ⚠ Z11–15 H12–10

WHITE

Eucryphia lucida

Evergreen, upright, bushy tree with narrow, glossy, dark green leaves and fragrant, white flowers in early or mid-summer.

 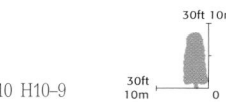 Z9–10 H10–9

Eucryphia glutinosa

Deciduous, upright or spreading tree. Glossy, dark green leaves, consisting of 3–5 leaflets, turn orange-red in fall. Large, fragrant, white flowers appear from mid- to late summer.

 Z8–11 H11–8

Hoheria lyallii

Deciduous, spreading tree with deeply toothed, gray-green leaves. Clusters of white flowers are borne in mid-summer.

 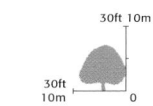 Z9–11 H11–10

Acer crataegifolium 'Veitchii'

Deciduous, bushy tree with branches streaked with green and white. Small, pointed, dark green leaves, blotched with white and paler green, turn deep pink and reddish-purple in fall.

 Z6–8 H8–6

Maackia amurensis

Deciduous, spreading tree with deep green leaves consisting of 7–11 leaflets. Dense, upright spikes of white flowers appear from mid- to late summer.

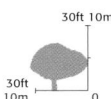 Z5–7 H7–5

Hoheria angustifolia

Evergreen, columnar tree with narrow, dark green leaves. Shallowly cup-shaped, white flowers are borne from mid- to late summer.

 Z9–11 H11–10

Cornus kousa

Deciduous, vase-shaped tree or shrub with oval, glossy, dark green leaves that turn bright red-purple in fall. Large, white bracts, surrounding insignificant flowers, in early summer, are followed by strawberry-like fruits.

  Z5–8 H8–5

TREES

PINK

Lagerstroemia indica 'Seminole'
Deciduous, compact, rounded tree
bearing trusses of mid-pink flowers,
with strongly waved petals, from
mid-summer to early fall. Narrowly
oval to oblong, dark green leaves
are bronze when young.

☀ ◊ Z7–9 H9–6

Robinia x slavinii 'Hilleri'
Deciduous, round-headed tree. Pinnate,
pea-green leaves, with 9 or 11 oval-
shaped leaflets, turn yellow in fall.
In early summer, pealike, lilac-
pink flowers are borne in loose
racemes. Branches are prone
to wind damage.

☀ ◊ Z5–9 H9–5

Albizia julibrissin (Silk tree)
Deciduous, spreading tree. Large
leaves are light to mid-green and
divided into many leaflets. Clusters
of brushlike, clear pink flowers
appear in late summer or fall.

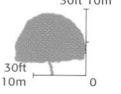

☀ ◊ Z6–9 H9–6

RED

Aesculus pavia 'Atrosanguinea'
Deciduous, round-headed, sometimes
shrubby tree. In summer, panicles
of deep red flowers appear among
glossy, dark green leaves, which
have 5 narrow leaflets.

☀ ◊ ❗ Z5–9 H9–5

Malus yunnanensis var. veitchii
Deciduous, upright tree with lobed,
heart-shaped leaves, covered with gray
down beneath. Bears white, sometimes
pink-tinged, flowers in late spring
and a mass of small, red-flushed,
brown crab apples in late
summer and fall.

☀ ◊ Z6–8 H8–7

Embothrium coccineum
(Chilean firebush, flameflower)
Evergreen or semievergreen, upright,
suckering tree with lance-shaped,
glossy, deep green leaves. Clusters
of brilliant orange-red flowers
are borne in late spring
and early summer.

◐ ◊ pH Z8–11 H11–8

Prunus cerasifera 'Nigra'
Deciduous, round-headed tree with
deep purple leaves, red when young.
Pink flowers are borne in profusion
from early to mid-spring.

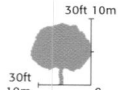

☀ ◊ ❗ Z5–9 H9–1

FLOWERING DOGWOODS

A genus of around 50 species of hardy plants, *Cornus* is perhaps best known for its shrubby dogwoods, such as *Cornus alba* 'Sibirica', which produce brightly colored winter stems. However, the flowering trees within this genus have much to offer, as they are highly ornamental, ideal for small gardens, and easy to grow—many accommodating a wide range of soil types. The majority flower in late spring or early summer. Their "flowers" consist of a rounded hub of tiny blooms, surrounded by showy petal-like bracts, up to 3 in (7.5 cm) across on some cultivars, which range in color from pure white, cream, and yellow to pink and red. In good summers, attractive, edible, strawberry-like fruits develop after flowering. Several species, such as *Cornus kousa*, also produce striking fall leaf color.

C. kousa 'National'

C. kousa 'Miss Satomi'

C. florida 'Cherokee Princess'

C. alternifolia

C. nuttallii 'Monarch'

C. florida 'Rainbow'

C. florida 'Cherokee Chief'

C. controversa

C. alternifolia 'Argentea' ①

C. 'Porlock' ①

C. mas

C. kousa var. chinensis 'China Girl'

C. capitata

GREEN

TREES

Pseudopanax ferox
Evergreen, upright tree with long, narrow, rigid, sharply toothed leaves that are dark bronze-green overlaid white or gray.

☀ ◊ Z8–11 H11–8

Ehretia dicksonii
Deciduous, spreading tree with sturdy, ridged branches and large, dark green leaves. Large, flattish heads of small, fragrant, white flowers are borne in mid-summer.

☀ ◊ Z7–11 H11–7

Cydonia oblonga 'Vranja'
(Common quince)
Deciduous, spreading tree. Pale green leaves, gray-felted beneath, mature to dark green and set off large, white or pale pink flowers in late spring and, later, very fragrant, golden-yellow fruits.

☀ ◊ Z5–9 H9–3

Juglans microcarpa
(Little walnut, Texas walnut)
Deciduous, bushy-headed tree with large, aromatic leaves of many narrow, pointed leaflets that turn yellow in fall.

☀ ◊ Z6–9 H9–6

Betula pendula 'Youngii'
(Young's weeping birch)
Deciduous, weeping tree forming a mushroom-shaped dome of thread-like branchlets. Has triangular, serrated leaves and smooth, white bark that is fissured black at maturity.

☀ ◊ Z2–7 H7–1

Pyrus salicifolia 'Pendula'
Deciduous, weeping, mound-shaped tree with white flowers in midspring and narrow, gray leaves.

☀ ◊ Z5–9 H9–5

Ulmus glabra 'Camperdownii'
Deciduous, strongly weeping tree with sinuous branches. Leaves are very large, rough and dull green.

☀ ◊ Z3–9 H8–2

Acer carpinifolium (Hornbeam maple)
Deciduous tree of elegant habit, often with several main stems. Prominent-veined, hornbeam-like leaves turn golden-brown in fall.

☀ ◊ Z4–7 H7–1

Morus alba 'Laciniata'
(White mulberry)
Deciduous, spreading tree. Has rounded, deeply lobed, glossy leaves that turn yellow in fall and bears edible, pink, red or purple fruits in summer.

☀ ◊ Z4–8 H8–1

YELLOW

Paraserianthes lophantha
Fast-growing, deciduous, spreading tree. Has fernlike, dark green leaves comprising many leaflets. Creamy-yellow flower spikes appear in spring–summer.

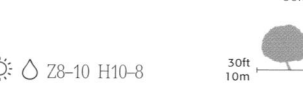 Z8–10 H10–8

Laburnum alpinum
(Scotch laburnum)
Deciduous, spreading tree. Leaves consist of 3 leaflets and are glossy, dark green. Long, slender chains of bright yellow flowers appear in late spring or early summer.

 Z4–7 H7–4

Koelreuteria paniculata
(Golden-rain tree, Pride of India)
Deciduous, spreading tree with mid-green leaves, turning yellow in fall. Bears sprays of yellow flowers in summer, followed by inflated, bronze-pink fruits.

 Z6–9 H9–1

Acer shirasawanum 'Aureum'
Deciduous, bushy tree or large shrub. Has rounded, many-lobed, pale yellow leaves.

Z5–7 H7–5

Genista aetnensis
(Mount Etna broom)
Almost leafless, rounded tree with many slender, bright green branches and a profusion of fragrant, pealike, golden-yellow flowers in mid-summer.

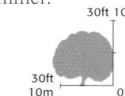 Z9–10 H10–9

RED

Cornus florida 'Welchii'
Deciduous, spreading tree. Bears white bracts, surrounding tiny flowers, in spring. Dark green leaves, edged with white and pink, turn red and purple in fall.

Z5–8 H8–3

Acer palmatum 'Atropurpureum'
Deciduous, bushy-headed shrub or small tree with lobed, reddish-purple foliage that turns brilliant red in fall. Small, reddish-purple flowers are borne in mid-spring.

 Z6–8 H8–2

Malus 'Veitch's Scarlet'
Deciduous, spreading tree with dark green foliage. Carries white flowers in late spring and crimson-flushed, scarlet crab apples in fall.

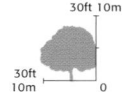 Z4–7 H7–4

TREES

89

RED

Photinia davidiana
Evergreen, spreading tree or large
shrub with narrow, glossy, dark green
leaves, older ones turning red in
fall. Sprays of white flowers in early
summer are followed by clusters
of bright red fruits in fall.

☼ ◊ Z7–9 H9–7   30ft
10m

Malus 'Cowichan'
Deciduous, spreading tree.
Has dark green foliage, reddish-
purple when young. Pink flowers
appear in mid-spring, followed
by reddish-purple crab apples.

☼ ◊ Z5–8 H8–5   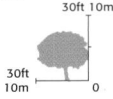 30ft
10m

Acer japonicum 'Aconitifolium'
Deciduous, bushy tree or large shrub.
Deeply divided, mid-green leaves
turn red in fall. Reddish-purple flowers
appear in mid-spring.

☼ ◊ Z5–7 H7–1   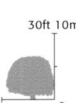 30ft
10m

Acer palmatum 'Osakazuki'
Deciduous, bushy-headed shrub
or tree with large, 7-lobed, mid-green
leaves that turn brilliant scarlet in fall.
Clusters of small, reddish-purple
flowers are borne in mid-spring.

☼ ◊ Z6–8 H8–2   30ft
10m

Acer tataricum subsp. *ginnala*
(Amur maple)
Deciduous, spreading tree or large
shrub. Clusters of fragrant, creamy-
white flowers are borne in early
summer amid dainty, bright
green leaves that turn red
in fall.

☼ ◊ Z3–7 H7–1   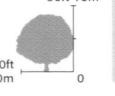 30ft
10m

Rhus trichocarpa
Deciduous, spreading tree. Large,
ashlike leaves with 13–17 leaflets are
pinkish when young, dark green in
summer and purple-red to orange
in fall. Bears pendent, bristly,
yellow fruits.

☼ ◊ Z7–9 H9–7   30ft
10m

Malus prunifolia
Deciduous, spreading tree. Has dark
green leaves and fragrant, white flowers
in mid-spring. In fall bears long-lasting,
small, red or occasionally yellowish
crab apples.

☼ ◊ Z4–8 H8–1   30ft
10m

Malus 'Marshall Oyama'
Deciduous, upright tree with
dark green leaves. Pink-flushed,
white flowers borne in late spring
are followed by a profusion of
large, rounded, crimson and
yellow crab apples in fall.

☼ ◊ Z4–8 H8–4   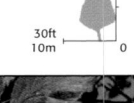 30ft
10m

Crataegus pedicellata
Deciduous, spreading tree with
sharply toothed, lobed, dark green
leaves that turn orange and red in
fall. White flowers with red anthers
in late spring are followed by
bright red fruits in fall.

☼ ◊ ❗ Z6–8 H8–6    30ft
10m

TREES

Acer triflorum
Slow-growing, deciduous, spreading tree with peeling, gray-brown bark. Leaves, composed of 3 leaflets, are dark green, turning brilliant orange-red in fall. Clusters of tiny, yellow-green flowers appear in late spring.

 ☼ ◊ Z5–7 H7–5

30ft 10m
30ft
10m 0

Malus 'Professor Sprenger'
Deciduous, rounded, dense tree. Dark green leaves turn yellow in late fall. White flowers, pink in bud, open from mid- to late spring and are followed by orange-red crab apples in fall.

 ☼ ◊ Z4–8 H8–1

30ft 10m
30ft
10m 0

Malus 'John Downie'
Deciduous tree, narrow and upright when young, conical when mature. White flowers, borne amid bright green foliage in late spring, are followed by large, edible, red-flushed, orange crab apples in fall.

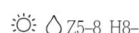 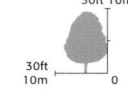 ☼ ◊ Z5–8 H8–5

30ft 10m
30ft
10m 0

SORBUS

Comprising more than 100 hardy species, the genus *Sorbus* includes a wide range of ornamental trees ideal for small to medium-sized gardens. They provide a year-round display of color and interest, with fragrant corymbs of cream flowers, attractive, divided foliage, vibrant fall color, and decorative berrylike fruits that last well into winter on some species. Most members of this genus fall into one of two categories: the Aucuparia group, which has pinnate leaves like rowan (*Sorbus aucuparia*), and the Aria group, which has rounded or oval leaves, such as whitebeam (*Sorbus aria*). Virtually all species are easy to grow and thrive in full sun or dappled shade, and in well-drained, fertile, acidic or alkaline soil , although species within the Aucuparia group are not long-lived on shallow alkaline soils.

S. scalaris

S. cashmiriana ⓘ

S. aucuparia ⓘ

S. forrestii

S. x kewensis

S. commixta ⓘ

S. thibetica 'John Mitchell' ⓘ

S. vilmorinii ⓘ

S. sargentiana

S. megalocarpa

S. intermedia

S. aria 'Lutescens' ⓘ

S. esserteauana

FALL

WINTER

YELLOW

YELLOW

Malus 'Golden Hornet'
Deciduous, spreading tree with dark
green foliage and open cup-shaped,
white flowers in late spring. In
fall, branches are weighed down
by a profusion of golden-yellow
crab apples.

☼ ◊ Z4–8 H7–4

Picrasma quassioides (Quassia)
Deciduous, spreading tree with glossy,
bright green leaves, composed of 9–13
leaflets, that turn brilliant yellow,
orange and red in fall.

☼ ◊ Z6–9 H9–6

Acer laxiflorum
Deciduous, spreading tree with arching
branches streaked with white and green.
In late summer has pale red, winged
fruits. Pointed, red-stalked, dark green
leaves turn orange in fall.

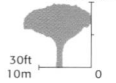

☼ ◊ Z6–7 H7–6

Acacia pravissima (Ovens wattle)
Evergreen, spreading, arching tree
or shrub. Has triangular, spine-tipped,
silver-gray phyllodes (flat, leaflike stalks)
and small heads of bright yellow flowers
in late winter or early spring.

☼ ◊ Z11 H11–10

Acacia baileyana
Evergreen, spreading tree with divided,
fernlike, 2-pinnate, silvery-gray or blue-
gray leaves. From late winter to early
spring produces masses of spherical,
golden-yellow flower heads
in dense, axillary racemes.
Is best grown against a wall.

☼ ◊ Z10–11 H11–10

Ilex aquifolium 'Amber'
Evergreen, much-branched, conical,
female tree with abundant, amber-
yellow berries. Mid-green stems
bear elliptic, usually entire, bright
green leaves.

 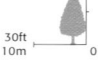

☼◑ ◊ Z7–9 H9–7

TREES

Carpinus betulus 'Fastigiata'
Deciduous, erect tree, with a very
distinctive flamelike outline that
becomes more open with age.
Oval, prominently veined, dark
green leaves turn yellow and
orange in fall.

☼ ◊ Z4–8 H8–1

Lithocarpus henryi
Slow-growing, evergreen, broadly
conical tree with glossy, pale green
leaves that are long, narrow and pointed.

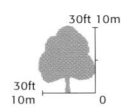

☼ ◊ Z8–10 H10–8

**Pittosporum eugenioides
'Variegatum'**
Evergreen, columnar tree. Wavy-edged,
glossy, dark green leaves have white
margins. Honey-scented, pale yellow
flowers are borne in spring.

 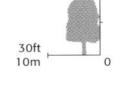

☼ ◊ Z9–11 H11–10

Aralia elata 'Variegata'
Deciduous tree or shrub with sparse,
sturdy, prickly stems. Large, dark green
leaves, with cream margins, are divided
into numerous oval, paired leaflets.
Billowing heads of tiny, white
flowers, forming large panicles,
are borne in late summer.

☼ ◊ Z4–9 H9–1

Arbutus unedo (Strawberry tree)
Evergreen, spreading tree or
shrub with rough, brown bark
and glossy, deep green leaves.
Pendent, urn-shaped, white flowers
appear in fall–winter as previous
season's strawberry-like, red
fruits ripen.

☼ ◊ Z8–9 H9–6

TREES

93

HOLLIES

The common holly, *Ilex aquifolium*, is one of the best-known evergreen trees, but many other *Ilex* cultivars make attractive garden plants. In size they range from tall specimen trees to small shrubs. Leaves may be smooth-edged or spiny and vary in color, several having gold, yellow, cream, white, or gray variegation. Small, often white, male and female flowers, borne on separate plants during summer, are followed by red, yellow, or black berries. In almost all cases, hollies are unisexual—that is, the berries are borne on female plants—so to obtain fruits it is usually necessary to grow plants of both sexes. When choosing, don't rely on variety names to sex plants; *I. aquifolium* 'Silver Queen' is male. Hollies respond well to pruning and many can be clipped to form hedges.

I. x altaclerensis 'Camelliifolia Variegata' ⓘ

I. pernyi ⓘ

I. x koehneana 'Chestnut Leaf'

I. crenata 'Convexa' ⓘ

I. aquifolium 'Argentea Marginata' ⓘ

I. aquifolium 'Silver Queen' ⓘ

I. aquifolium 'Madame Briot' ⓘ

I. aquifolium 'Silver Milkmaid' ⓘ

I. x altaclerensis 'Belgica Aurea' ⓘ

I. x altaclerensis 'Balearica' ⓘ

I. aquifolium 'Golden Milkboy' ⓘ

I. aquifolium 'Ferox Argentea'

I. x meserveae BLUE PRINCESS ('Conapri') ⓘ

I. aquifolium 'Pyramidalis Aureomarginata' ⓘ

I. x altaclerensis 'Golden King' ⓘ

I. aquifolium ⓘ

I. verticillata ⓘ

I. x altaclerensis 'Camelliifolia' ⓘ

I. aquifolium 'Bacciflava'

BLUE

SILVER

Cupressus cashmeriana
(Kashmir cypress)

Handsome, broadly conical conifer, spreading with age, with aromatic foliage borne in pendent, flat, glaucous blue sprays. Bears small, globose, dark brown, mature cones.

 Z6–9 H9–6

Cedrus atlantica f. glauca
(Blue Atlas cedar)

Conical conifer with silvery-blue foliage that is very bright, especially in spring. Erect, cylindrical cones are produced in fall. Is widely planted as a specimen tree.

 Z6–9 H9–6

Pinus ayacahuite
(Mexican white pine)

Spreading conifer with weeping leaves made up of lax, blue-green needles, to 6in (16cm) long, in bundles of 5. Pendent cones are generally covered with sticky, white resin and may grow 10in (25cm) or more long.

 Z7–9 H9–7

Abies procera (Noble fir)

Narrowly conical conifer with smooth, silvery-gray bark and gray-green or bright blue-gray leaves. Produces sturdy, cylindrical, green cones, 6–10in (15–25cm) long, that ripen to brown.

 Z5–6 H6–5

Abies concolor 'Argentea'

Conical conifer with silvery foliage that contrasts well with dark gray bark. Oblong to ovoid, pale blue or green cones are 3–5in (8–12cm) long.

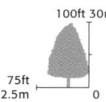 Z3–7 H7–1

Pinus x holfordiana (Holford pine)

Broadly conical, open conifer with large cones, brown when ripe. Pendent, glaucous blue-green leaves are held in clusters of 5.

 Z6–7 H7–6

x Cuprocyparis 'Haggerston Grey'

Vigorous, upright, columnar conifer, tapering at the apex. Has smooth bark, becoming stringy with age, flat sprays of pointed, gray-green leaves, and dark brown female cones. A popular screening plant.

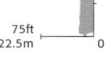 Z6–9 H12–9

Pinus peuce (Macedonian pine)

Upright conifer, forming a slender pyramid. Has dense, gray-green foliage and cylindrical, green cones with white resin that ripen brown in fall. Is an attractive tree that grows consistently well in all sites.

 Z5–9 H9–5

TREES

95

GREEN

TREES

Chamaecyparis lawsoniana 'Intertexta'

Elegant, weeping conifer with aromatic, gray-green foliage carried in lax, pendulous sprays. Old trees become columnar with some splayed branches.

 Z5–9 H9–5   75ft 22.5m

Wollemia nobilis (Wollemi pine)

Erect, bushy, conifer with narrowly oblong, pointed, needle-like, dark green leaves, and "bubbly," brown bark when mature. In winter, shoot tips are covered in a protective, white resin. Catkin-like female cones are borne on shoot tips.

 Z7–11 H11–1   75ft 22.5m

Pinus strobus (Eastern white pine)

Conifer with an open, sparse, whorled crown. Has gray-green foliage and cylindrical cones. Smooth, gray bark becomes fissured with age. Does not tolerate pollution.

 Z4–9 H9–1   75ft 22.5m   100ft 30m

Metasequoia glyptostroboides (Dawn redwood)

Fast-growing, deciduous, upright conifer with fibrous, reddish bark. Soft, blue-green leaves turn yellow, pink and red in fall. Cones are globose to ovoid, ¾in (2cm) long.

  Z5–10 H11–8   75ft 22.5m

Pseudotsuga menziesii var. glauca (Blue Douglas fir)

Fast-growing, conical conifer with thick, grooved, corky, gray-brown bark, aromatic, glaucous blue-green leaves, and sharply pointed buds. Cones have projecting, 3-pronged bracts.

 Z4–7 H7–1   75ft 22.5m   100ft 30m

Pinus coulteri (Big-cone pine, Coulter pine)

Fast-growing conifer with large, broadly ovoid, prickly cones, each 2–4½lb (1–2kg). Gray-green leaves in crowded clusters are sparsely set on branches. Grows in all soils, even heavy clays.

Z8–9 H9–8   75ft 22.5m   100ft 30m

Cedrus deodara (Deodar cedar)

Fast-growing conifer, densely conical with weeping tips when young, broader when mature. Has spirally arranged, needle-like, gray-green leaves and barrel-shaped, glaucous cones, 3–5in (8–12cm) long, ripening to brown.

Z6–9 H9–6   75ft 22.5m   100ft 30m

Abies veitchii (Veitch fir)

Upright conifer with dark green leaves, silvery beneath, and cylindrical, violet-blue cones.

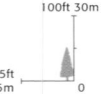 Z3–6 H6–1   75ft 22.5m   100ft 30m

Pinus ponderosa
(Ponderosa pine, western yellow pine)
Conical or upright conifer, grown for its distinctive, deeply fissured bark, with smooth, brown plates, and bold grayish-green foliage. Bears ovoid, purplish-brown cones.

 Z5–8 H8–5

Pinus muricata (Bishop pine)
Fast-growing, often flat-topped conifer. Leaves are blue- or gray-green and held in pairs. Ovoid cones, 3–3½in (7–9cm) long, rarely open. Does particularly well in a poor, sandy soil.

 Z7–9 H9–7

Pinus jeffreyi (Black pine, Jeffrey pine)
Upright, narrow-crowned conifer with sturdy, gray-green leaves, 5–10in (12–26cm) long. Bark is black with fine, deep fissures and shoots have an attractive, grayish bloom.

 Z6–8 H8–6

Larix decidua (European larch)
Fast-growing, deciduous conifer with a conical crown when young, broadening on maturity, and spaced branches. Shoots are yellow-brown in winter. Has light green leaves and small, erect, conical cones.

 Z3–6 H6–1

Ginkgo biloba (Maidenhair tree)
Long-lived, deciduous conifer, upright when young, spreading with age. Has fan-shaped, 5in (12cm) long, bright green leaves. Bears fruits with edible kernels in late summer and fall, if male and female plants are grown together.

 Z5–9 H9–3

Cedrus libani (Cedar of Lebanon)
Spreading conifer, usually with several arching stems. Branches carry flat layers of dark gray-green foliage and oblong to ovoid, grayish-pink cones, 3–6in (8–15cm) long.

 Z6–9 H9–3

Pinus patula (Mexican yellow pine)
Rounded to broadly spreading conifer with scaling, ocher-colored bark. Weeping shoots bear narrow, bright green leaves, to 30cm (12in) long, in clusters of 3–5. Long-conical, chestnut-brown cones have a prickle on each scale.

 Z8–9 H9–8

Sequoia sempervirens
(Coastal redwood)
Vigorous conical conifer with horizontal branches. Has soft, fibrous, red-brown bark and needle-like, flattened, pale green leaves, spirally arranged. Rounded to cylindrical cones, initially green, ripen to dark brown.

  Z8–9 H9–8

Pinus wallichiana
(Bhutan pine, Himalayan pine)
Conical conifer with long, drooping, blue-green leaves in 5s. Has smooth bark, gray-green on young trees, later fissured and dark, and cylindrical cones.

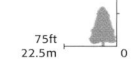 Z6–9 H9–5

Pinus pinaster
(Cluster pine, Maritime pine)
Vigorous, domed conifer with a long, branchless trunk. Has gray-green leaves and whorls of rich brown cones. Purple-brown bark is deeply fissured. Is well-suited to a dry, sandy soil.

 Z8–10 H10–7

TREES

Picea abies
(Common spruce, Norway spruce)
Fast-growing, pyramidal conifer with dark green leaves. Narrow, pendulous, glossy, brown cones are 4–8in (10–20cm) long. Much used as a Christmas tree but less useful as an ornamental.

  Z3–8 H8–1

Pinus nigra* subsp. *nigra
(Austrian pine)
Broadly crowned conifer, with well-spaced branches, often with several stems. Paired, dark green leaves are densely tufted. Tolerates an exposed site.

Z5–8 H8–4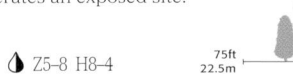

Araucaria araucana
(Chile pine, Monkey puzzle)
Open, spreading conifer with gray bark, wrinkled like elephant hide. Has flattened and sharp, glossy, dark green leaves and 6in (15cm) long cones. Makes a fine specimen tree.

 Z7–11 H11–6

Picea omorika (Serbian spruce)
Narrow, conical conifer, resembling a church spire, with dark green leaves that are white below. Branches are pendulous and arch out at tips. Violet-purple cones age to glossy brown. Grows steadily in all soils.

 Z4–8 H8–1

Pinus radiata (Monterey pine)
Very fast-growing conifer, conical when young, domed when mature. Black bark contrasts well with soft, bright green leaves. Makes an excellent windbreak.

Z7–9 H9–7

Abies grandis (Giant fir, Grand fir)
Very vigorous, narrow, conical conifer, with a neat habit. Mid-green leaves have an orange aroma when crushed. Cones, 3in (7–8cm) long, ripen red-brown. Makes a useful specimen tree.

 Z5–6 H6–5

Sequoiadendron giganteum
(Giant redwood, Wellingtonia)
Very fast growing, conical conifer. Has thick, fibrous, red-brown bark and sharp, bluish-green leaves. Is one of the world's largest trees when mature.

 Z6–9 H9–4

Pinus heldreichii (Bosnian pine)
Dense, conical conifer with scaly, ash-gray bark and dark green leaves held in pairs. Ovoid cones, 2–4in (5–10cm) long, are cobalt-blue in early summer, ripening to brown.

  Z4–8 H8–1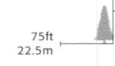

GREEN/YELLOW

x *Cuprocyparis* 'Castlewellan'
Upright, vigorous conifer, slightly slower growing than the species, grown for its bronze-yellow foliage.

☀ ◑ ❗ Z6–9 H12–9   100ft 30m / 75ft 22.5m / 0

Picea orientalis 'Skylands'
Dense, upright, graceful conifer with short, glossy leaves that retain their creamy-gold color throughout the year. Narrowly oblong cones are dark purple, males turning brick-red in spring.

◑ ◑ Z5–8 H8–5   100ft 30m / 75ft 22.5m / 0

**_Taxodium distichum_
(Bald cypress, Swamp cypress)**
Deciduous, broadly conical conifer with small, globose to ovoid cones. Yewlike, fresh green leaves turn rich brown in late fall. Grows in a very wet site, producing special breathing roots.

☀ ◑ Z5–11 H12–5   100ft 30m / 75ft 22.5m / 0

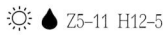

BLUE

**_Picea engelmannii_
(Engelmann spruce, Mountain spruce)**
Broadly conical conifer. Leaves encircle shoots and are prickly or soft, lush, glaucous or bluish-green. Bears small, cylindrical cones. Is good for a very poor site.

◑ ◑ Z3–8 H8–1   50ft 15m / 50ft 15m / 0

Picea glauca 'Coerulea'
Dense, upright, conical conifer with needle-like, blue-green to silver leaves and ovoid, light brown cones.

☀ ◑ Z2–6 H6–1   50ft 15m / 50ft 15m / 0

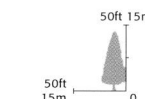

Picea breweriana (Brewer's spruce)
Upright conifer with level branches and completely pendulous branchlets, to 6ft (2m) long. Leaves are sturdy and blue-green. Bears oblong, purplish cones, 2½–3in (6–8cm) long.

☀ ◑ Z6–8 H8–6   50ft 15m / 50ft 15m / 0

Picea pungens 'Koster'
Upright conifer with whorled branches. Has scaly, gray bark and attractive, needle-like, silvery-blue leaves, which fade to green with age. Tends to suffer from aphid attack.

☀ ◑ Z2–8 H8–1   50ft 15m / 50ft 15m / 0

**_Chamaecyparis lawsoniana_
'Pembury Blue'**
Magnificent, conical conifer with aromatic, bright blue-gray foliage held in pendulous sprays.

☀ ◑ ❗ Z5–9 H9–5   50ft 15m / 50ft 15m / 0

Tsuga mertensiana 'Glauca'
Slow-growing, dwarf or medium-sized, columnar-conical conifer with red-brown shoots bearing spirally arranged, needle-like, flattened, glaucous, silver-gray leaves. Cones are yellow-green to purple, ripening to dark brown.

◑ ◑ Z6–8 H8–6   50ft 15m / 50ft 15m / 0

**_Pinus parviflora_
(Japanese white pine)**
Slow-growing, conical or spreading conifer with fine, bluish foliage and purplish-brown bark. Leaves are held in 5s. Bears ovoid cones, 2–4in (5–10cm) long.

☀ ◑ Z6–9 H9–6   50ft 15m / 50ft 15m / 0

TREES

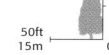

GREEN

Abies forrestii (Forrest fir)
Conical conifer with an open, whorled habit and smooth, silvery-gray bark. Shoots are red-brown, with spherical, white buds. Has dark green leaves, silvery-white beneath, and ovoid-cylindrical, violet-blue cones.

 Z5–6 H6–5

Juniperus chinensis 'Keteleeri'
Dense, regular, slender, columnar conifer with scalelike, aromatic, grayish-green leaves and peeling, brown bark. Makes a reliable, free-fruiting form for formal use.

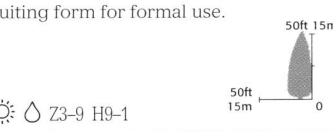 Z3–9 H9–1

Fitzroya cupressoides (Patagonian cypress)
Vase-shaped to sprawling conifer with red-brown bark that peels in long strips. White-lined, dark green leaves are held in open, pendulous, wiry sprays.

 Z7–9 H9–7

Picea likiangensis (Lijiang spruce)
Upright conifer with bluish-white leaves are well-spaced. Cones, 3–6in (8–15cm) long, are cylindrical, females bright red when young, ripening to purple; male cones are pink.

 Z4–8 H8–6

Pinus thunbergii (Japanese black pine)
Rounded conifer, conical when young, with dark green leaves and gray-brown cones, 1½–2½in (4–6cm) long. Buds are covered with a silky cobweb of white hairs. Tolerates sea spray well.

 Z5–8 H8–5

Pinus rigida (Northern pitch pine)
Conical conifer, often with sucker shoots from trunk. Twisted, dark green leaves are borne in 3s. Ovoid to globose, red-brown cones, 1¼–3in (3–8cm) long, persist, open, on the tree.

 Z4–7 H7–4

Podocarpus salignus
Upright conifer. Leaves are willow-like, 2–4in (5–11cm) long, and glossy above. Attractive, fibrous, red-brown bark peels in strips.

 Z8–11 H11–8

Juniperus recurva var. *coxii* (Coffin juniper)
Slow-growing, conical conifer with smooth bark flakes in thin sheets. Weeping sprays of long, needle-like, aromatic, incurved leaves are bright green. Globose or ovoid, fleshy berries are black.

 Z7–11 H11–7

Austrocedrus chilensis (Chilean incense cedar)
Conical conifer with flattened, feathery sprays of 4-ranked, small, dark green leaves, white beneath.

 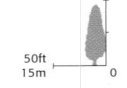 Z8–10 H11–8

Cunninghamia lanceolata (Chinese fir)
Upright conifer, mop-headed on a dry site, with distinctive, thick and deeply furrowed, red-brown bark. Glossy, green leaves are sharply pointed and lance-shaped.

 Z7–9 H9–7

Phyllocladus trichomanoides

Slow-growing conifer, conical when young, developing a more rounded top with age. Leaflike, deep green, modified shoots, 4–6in (10–15cm) long, have 5–10 lobed segments.

☼ ◗ H11–9

Sciadopitys verticillata (Japanese umbrella pine)

Conical conifer with reddish-brown bark. Deep green leaves, yellowish beneath, are whorled at the ends of shoots, like umbrella spokes. Ovoid cones ripen over 2 years.

☼ ◗ Z5–9 H9–4

Picea morrisonicola (Taiwan spruce)

Upright, conical conifer, becoming columnar with age. Needle-like, deep green leaves are pressed down on slender, pale brown shoots. Cones are cylindrical and 2–3in (5–7cm) long.

☼ ◗ Z7–9 H9–7

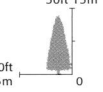

Calocedrus decurrens (Incense cedar)

Upright conifer with short, horizontal branches and flaky, gray bark, brown beneath. Has flat sprays of aromatic, dark green leaves. Resists honey fungus.

☼ ◗ Z5–8 H8–1

Pinus cembra (Arolla pine)

Dense, conical conifer with dark green or bluish-green leaves grouped in 5s. Ovoid, bluish or purplish cones, 2½–3in (6–8cm) long, ripen brown.

☼ ◗ Z3–7 H7–1

Taxus baccata 'Fastigiata' (Irish yew)

Slow-growing conifer with a broadly conical, later domed crown. Erect branches bear needle-like, flattened, dark green leaves that stand out all around shoots. Female plants bear cup-shaped, fleshy, bright red fruits.

◑ ◊ ⓘ Z7–8 H8–7

Pinus contorta var. *latifolia* (Lodgepole pine)

Conical conifer with bright green leaves, 2½–4in (6–9cm) long. Small, oval cones remain closed on the tree. Is suitable for a wet or coastal site.

☼ ◗ Z6–8 H8–6

Torreya californica (California nutmeg)

Upright conifer with very prickly, glossy, dark green leaves, yellowish-green beneath, similar to those of yew. Fruits are olive-like.

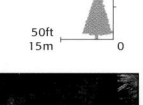

☼ ◗ Z7–11 H12–7

Chamaecyparis thyoides (White cypress)

Upright conifer with aromatic, green or blue-gray leaves in rather erratic, fan-shaped sprays on very fine shoots. Cones are small, round and glaucous blue-gray.

☼ ◗ ⓘ Z3–8 H8–1

TREES

GREEN

YELLOW

Pinus banksiana (Jack pine)
Slender, conical, scrubby-looking
conifer with fresh green leaves in
twisted, divergent pairs. Curved cones,
1¼–2½in (3–6cm) long, point forward
along shoots.

☼ ◊ Z3–8 H8–1   50ft 15m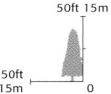

Tsuga canadensis
(Canada hemlock, Eastern hemlock)
Broadly conical conifer, often with
several stems. Gray shoots have
2-ranked, dark green leaves,
often inverted to show silver
lines beneath. Cones are ovoid
and light brown.

● ◊ Z4–8 H8–1   50ft 15m

Pinus contorta
(Beach pine, Shore pine)
Dense, conical or domed conifer.
Has paired, bright green leaves and
conical to ovoid cones, 1¼–3in (3–8cm)
long. Is well-suited to a windy,
barren site and tolerates
waterlogged ground.

☼ ◗ Z6–8 H8–6   50ft 15m

Pseudolarix amabilis (Golden larch)
Deciduous, open-crowned conifer,
slow-growing when young. Has clusters
of linear, fresh green leaves, 1–2½in
(2.5–6cm) long, which gradually turn
bright orange-gold in fall.

☼ ◗ Z5–9 H9–4   50ft 15m

Pinus halepensis (Aleppo pine)
Conical, open-crowned conifer with
an open growth of bright green leaves,
2½–4½in (6–11cm) long, and ovoid,
glossy, brown cones. Young trees
retain glaucous, juvenile needles
for several years.

☼ ◊ Z9–10 H10–9   50ft 15m

Cupressus sempervirens 'Stricta'
(Italian cypress)
Narrow, columnar conifer with upward
sweeping branches. Has fissured bark
and scalelike, deep green leaves. Bears
globular, prickly, woody, brown
cones, to 1¼in (3cm) across.

☼ ◊ Z7–9 H9–3   50ft 15m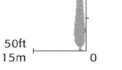

Chamaecyparis lawsoniana
'Green Pillar'
Conical conifer with upright branches.
Aromatic foliage is bright green
and becomes tinged with gold
in spring. Is suitable for hedging
as requires little clipping.

☼ ◊ ① Z5–9 H9–5   50ft 15m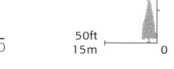

Chamaecyparis lawsoniana
'Lanei Aurea'
Upright conifer that forms a neat
column of aromatic, golden-yellow
tipped foliage.

☼ ◊ ① Z5–9 H9–5   50ft 15m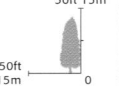

Taxus baccata 'Lutea'
(Yellow-berried yew)
Slow-growing conifer grown for its
fleshy, bright golden-yellow fruits.
These look particularly striking against
the needle-like, dark green
leaves and are often borne
in great profusion in fall.

☼ ◊ ① Z7–8 H8–7   50ft 15m

GREEN

Pinus aristata (Bristlecone pine)

Slow-growing, bushy conifer. Leaves are in bundles of 5, very dense and blue-white to gray-green, flecked with white resin. Ovoid cones, 1½–4in (4–10cm) long, have bristly prickles. Is the oldest known living plant, over 4,000 years old.

☼ ◊ Z2–10 H9–1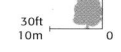

Chamaecyparis lawsoniana 'Columnaris'

Narrow, upright conifer that forms a neat column of aromatic, blue-gray foliage. Will tolerate poor soil and some clipping. Is an effective, small, specimen tree.

☼ ◊ ① Z5–9 H9–5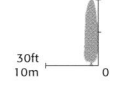

Picea mariana 'Doumetii'

Densely branched, globose or broadly conical conifer with short, needle-like, silvered, dark green leaves and pendulous, ovoid, purplish cones.

☼◑ ◊ Z2–6 H6–1

Juniperus recurva (Drooping juniper, Himalayan weeping juniper)

Slow-growing, conical conifer with aromatic, incurved, gray- or blue-green leaves and fleshy, black berries. Smooth bark flakes in thin sheets.

☼ ◊ Z7–11 H11–7

Juniperus chinensis 'Robusta Green'

Slow-growing, narrow, columnar conifer, making only 3in (7–8cm) a year, with aromatic, blue-green foliage and small, gray-green juniper berries.

☼ ◊ Z3–9 H9–1

Juniperus chinensis 'Obelisk'

Slender, irregularly columnar conifer. Has ascending branches and long, prickly, needle-like, aromatic, dark green leaves. Tolerates a wide range of soils and conditions but is particularly suited to a hot, dry site.

☼ ◊ Z3–9 H9–1

Pinus cembroides (Mexican stone pine, Pinyon)

Slow-growing, bushy conifer, rarely more than 20–22ft (6–7m) high. Scaly bark is a striking silver-gray or grayish-brown. Leaves, in clusters of 2 or 3, are sparse and dark green to gray-green.

☼ ◊ Z2–10 H9–1

TREES

103

TREES

Abies koreana (Korean fir)
Broadly conical conifer. Produces cylindrical, violet-blue cones when less than 3ft (1m) tall. Leaves are dark green above, silver beneath.

☀ ◌ Z5–7 H6–6

Cryptomeria japonica 'Cristata'
Conical conifer with twisted, curved shoots and soft, fibrous bark. Foliage is bright green, ageing brown.

☀ ◌ Z6–9 H9–4

Thujopsis dolabrata 'Variegata'
Slow-growing, broadly conical, bushy conifer. Sturdy, hatchet-shaped leaves have irregular, creamy patches above and are silvery beneath.

☀ ◌ Z5–7 H7–5

Taxus cuspidata (Japanese yew)
Evergreen, spreading conifer. Leaves are dark green above, yellowish-green beneath, sometimes becoming tinged red-brown in cold weather. Tolerates very dry and shady conditions.

☀ ◌ ❶ Z5–7 H7–1

Pinus pinea
(Stone pine, Umbrella pine)
Conifer with a rounded crown on a short trunk. Leaves are dark green, but blue-green, juvenile foliage is retained on young trees. Broadly ovoid cones ripen shiny brown; seeds are edible.

☀ ◌ Z9–11 H11–9

Cryptomeria japonica 'Pyramidata'
Narrowly columnar or obelisk-shaped conifer. Foliage is blue-green when young, maturing to dark green.

☀ ◌ Z6–9 H9–4

Pinus sylvestris 'Aurea'
Upright conifer that develops a rounded crown with age. Bark is flaking and red-brown on upper trunk, fissured and purple-gray at base. Golden-yellow leaves seen in winter–spring, otherwise blue-green. Green cones ripen to pale gray- or red-brown.

☀ ◌ Z3–7 H7–1

Cedrus deodara 'Aurea'
Slow-growing, upright conifer with pendent branch tips and golden-yellow leaves when young in spring–summer. Foliage matures to yellowish-green. Makes a dramatic, small-garden evergreen.

☀ ◌ Z6–9 H9–6

Chamaecyparis obtusa 'Crippsii'
Attractive, small-garden, conical conifer, grown for its flattened sprays of aromatic, bright golden foliage. Bark is stringy and red-brown. Cones are round, ½in (1cm) across, and brown.

☀ ◌ ❶ Z4–8 H8–1

Cupressus macrocarpa 'Goldcrest'
Fast-growing, conical conifer with aromatic, golden-yellow foliage held in plumelike sprays that are useful in flower arrangements. Dislikes clipping.

☀ ◌ Z7–11 H11–7

DWARF CONIFERS

Dwarf conifers are valuable plants, especially for the small garden, requiring little attention and providing year-round interest. They can be planted as features in their own right, for their varied shapes, habits, and often striking colors, or, in the rock garden, to provide scale or act as a foil for other plants such as bulbs. Several species and cultivars are spreaders and good for groundcover. Most conifers are suited to a wide range of growing conditions, although *Cedrus* and *Juniperus* do not tolerate shade, and *Juniperus* and *Pinus* are best for dry, sandy soils. Some species may be clipped to form a low hedge, but new growth seldom occurs from wood more than 3 or 4 years old. Dwarf conifers also make excellent container plants.

Thuja plicata 'Stoneham Gold'

Pinus heldreichii 'Smidtii'

Picea pungens 'Globosa'

Abies cephalonica 'Meyer's Dwarf'

Podocarpus nivalis

Picea abies 'Ohlendorffii'

Juniperus squamata 'Holger'

Juniperus squamata 'Blue Carpet'

Taxus baccata 'Dovastonii Aurea' ①

Juniperus scopulorum 'Skyrocket'

Microbiota decussata

Platycladus orientalis 'Aurea Nana' ①

Abies concolor 'Compacta'

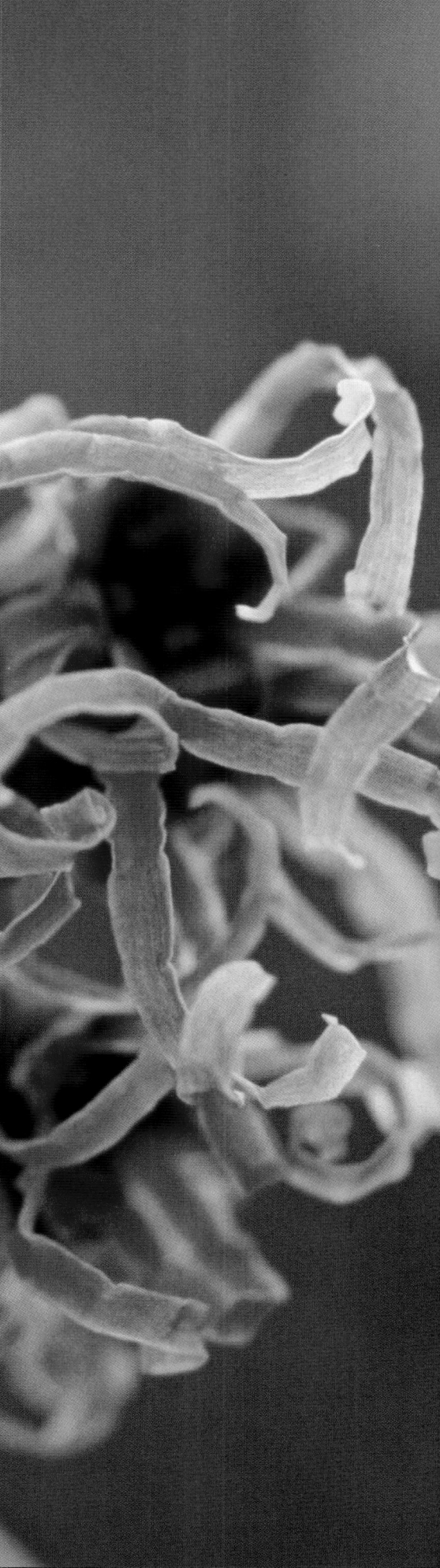

SHRUBS

Shrubs are key to any planting design, and provide color
and interest throughout the seasons with their wide variety
of foliage, flowers, fruits, and stems. Create a year-round
display with a selection of beautiful spring- and summer-
flowering shrubs, such as weigelas, buddlejas, and philadelphus,
together with those that sport brightly colored fall fruits, such as
pyracanthas and cotoneasters. You can then include witch hazels
and some species of honeysuckle to brighten bleak winter
months with their fragrant flowers. Whatever the size
or style of your garden, the permanent woody structure of
shrubs will form the framework, so make your selection and
plant them before the perennials. Some shrubs are also
ideal plants for hedges, enclosures, and screens.

SHRUBS

Star performers, shrubs form the backbone of many garden designs. They can be used together in shrub borders or with other plant groups in mixed displays. Providing color and interest with their foliage, flowers, and fruits, many also offer scented blooms and colorful stems.

SIZE CATEGORIES USED WITHIN THIS GROUP		
Large over 10ft (3m)	**Medium** 5–10ft (1.5–3m)	**Small** up to 5ft (1.5m)

ABOVE Spring color
The flowering stems of *Exochorda* x *macrantha* 'The Bride' arch gracefully above forget-me-nots (*Myosotis sylvatica*), daisies (*Bellis perennis*), and *Tulipa* 'Couleur Cardinal'.

What are shrubs?

Shrubs are woody-stemmed, deciduous or evergreen plants that branch out at or near ground level. Some can grow to more than 20ft (6m) in height, although most attain less than half this size. Leaves come in many forms, from large and glossy to gray and needlelike. There is sometimes an overlap between shrubs and trees because larger shrubs, such as flowering dogwoods (*Cornus* species), can be grown on a single stem. Subshrubs are another anomaly, with woody stems at the base, but softer top growth that may die back over winter in colder regions, like a perennial. Examples include ceratostigmas and fuchsias.

Choosing shrubs

When selecting shrubs, focus on those whose needs match your garden conditions. In general, shrubs with large, dark green leaves require shade; plants with gray foliage, such as lavender, require sun; and shrubs with colorful leaves need full sun or partial shade. Also consider the shrub's size and site it where it has space to mature, unless you are planning a topiary display.

Designing with shrubs

When creating a shrub display, try to combine plants with different shapes, habits, flower seasons, and foliage forms and patterns to create a visually balanced scheme and year-round interest. Knit them together in a shrub bed, or use them to provide a backdrop to more transient displays of bulbs, perennials, and annuals in a mixed border.

The shape and habit of shrubs provides a design with structure and form. Contrast low, spreading, prostrate or mat-forming shrubs, such as *Juniperus procumbens* and *Cotoneaster horizontalis*, with more upright forms, such as *Rosmarinus officinalis* 'Miss Jessopp's Upright', and the rounded shapes of bushy shrubs like hebes, skimmias, or boxwood topiary. Mix in shrubs with tiered branch structures, such as *Viburnum plicatum* 'Mariesii', which provide strong horizontal lines in a scheme. Graceful, arching shrubs, such as *Kolkwitzia amabilis*, *Buddleja alternifolia*, and *Genista tenera* 'Golden Shower' add an elegant note.

A wide range of shrubs are suitable for creating hedges, enclosures, or screens.

RENOVATING A SHRUB

When evergreens such as mahonias have outgrown their allotted space, many can be cut back hard from mid-winter to early spring after flowering. The plant may not flower for two years after such drastic pruning, but its overall appearance will be much improved. Other shrubs that respond well to this form of renovation include buddlejas, forsythias, kerrias, and smoke trees (*Cotinus*). Some, such as rosemary and lavender, do not.

New growth after pruning

1 Remove tall stems
Remove all dead and diseased wood, taking it back to healthy growth. Then prune back tall stems, removing them a little at a time so that they do not tear at the base. At this stage, cut the stems to about 24in (60cm) high, keeping in mind the plant's balanced shape as you prune.

2 Make final pruning cuts
Prune out any remaining crossing stems. Once you have cut back the tall growths, check where you can make your final pruning cuts. Cut out the old growths completely to leave five or six strong young stems.

3 Cut back remaining stems
Cut back the young healthy stems that are left, so that they are 12–16in (30–40cm) above the ground. The final cuts should be at an angle so rainwater can run off. Later in the year, a mass of young shoots will appear along these stems (see left).

ABOVE: Contrasting foliage
The golden leaves of *Choisya ternata* Sundance ('Lich') provide a glowing contrast with the adjacent rich pink-red *Berberis thunbergii* 'Rose Glow' and dark purple *Cotinus coggygria* 'Royal Purple'.

As well as evergreen staples like boxwood (*Buxus*), privet (*Ligustrum*), and shrubby honeysuckle (*Lonicera nitida*), which are commonly used, consider colorful deciduous shrubs, like the prickly *Berberis thunbergii* and its cultivars, or the evergreen *Photinia* x *fraseri* 'Red Robin', which produces fiery young foliage in spring and after clipping.

Certain shrubs are also ideal for topiary, their small leaves lending themselves to detailed shaping. Suitable shrubs include boxwood and shrubby honeysuckle.

Shrubs such as fuchsias, hebes, fatsias, and choisyas are ideal for containers. Pots also limit the size of larger shrubs.

Year-round interest

There is a shrub in flower almost every month of the year. Interest begins in spring with a range of colorful varieties, including flowering currants (*Ribes*), ceanothus, and rhododendrons. The display continues with an abundance of summer-flowering shrubs like fuchsias, hydrangeas, buddlejas, and spiraeas, followed in fall by a range of colorful berries offered by plants such as pyracanthas, cotoneasters, and *Skimmia japonica*. Many shrubs retain their fruits into winter, providing birds and wildlife with a much-needed supply of food.

As temperatures fall, the fragrant flowers of witch hazel (*Hamamelis*), mahonias, and winter box (*Sarcococca*) open, bringing new interest to the garden. Combine these with the vivid stems of coppiced dogwoods (*Cornus* species) and variegated evergreens for a dramatic winter scheme.

Spring pastels
Ceanothus flowers appear in late spring, decorating the garden with various shades of blue and white. These short-lived evergreens enjoy a warm, sunny site.

Feast of berries
The bright red berries of a female *Skimmia japonica*, produced where plants of both sexes are grown together, persist well into winter.

KEEPING SHRUBS IN SHAPE

Many young plants and shrubs, such as daphnes, produce long, leggy growths in spring or early summer after flowering. They do not require major pruning, but a light trim will produce a more compact, bushy shrub that will be covered in flowers the following year.

1 Assess your plant
In early summer, after daphnes have flowered, young leggy shoots sprout from the main stems. Before cutting them back, take a look at the shrub to see where to cut to produce a well-shaped plant.

2 Shorten leggy growths
Using a pair of pruners, shorten the leggy growths by 6–8in (15–20cm). It is important that you always prune immediately above a leaf bud with an angled, slanting cut, as shown above.

3 Work around the plant
Circle the plant, shortening each of the whippy stems, and checking that you are maintaining a good shape. The cut stems will then produce bushier growth and more flowers the following year.

WHITE

Osmanthus delavayi
Evergreen, rounded, bushy shrub with arching branches. Has small, glossy, dark green leaves and a profusion of very fragrant, tubular, white flowers from mid- to late spring.

☼ ◊ Z7–9 H9–7

Anopterus glandulosus
Evergreen, bushy shrub or, occasionally, small tree. Has narrow, glossy, dark green leaves, amid which clusters of cup-shaped, white or pink flowers appear from mid- to late spring.

☼ ◑ ◊ pH Z11 H11

Viburnum plicatum f. tomentosum 'Mariesii'
Deciduous, bushy, spreading shrub with tiered branches clothed in dark green leaves, which turn reddish-purple in fall. Large, rounded heads of flowers with white bracts appear in late spring and early summer.

☼ ◊ ❶ Z4–8 H8–1

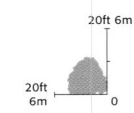

Osmanthus x burkwoodii
Evergreen, rounded, dense shrub. Glossy foliage is dark green and sets off a profusion of small, very fragrant, white flowers from mid- to late spring.

☼ ◊ Z7–9 H9–7

Pieris japonica
Evergreen, rounded, bushy, dense shrub with glossy, dark green foliage that is bronze when young. Produces drooping racemes of white flowers during spring.

☼ ◊ pH ❶ Z6–8 H8–6

Dipelta yunnanensis
Deciduous, arching shrub with peeling bark and glossy leaves. In late spring produces tubular, creamy-white flowers, marked orange inside.

☼ ◊ Z7–9 H9–1

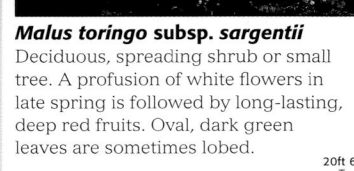

Amelanchier lamarckii
Deciduous, spreading shrub. Young leaves unfold bronze as abundant sprays of star-shaped, white flowers open from mid- to late spring. Foliage matures to dark green, then turns brilliant red and orange in fall.

☼ ◊ Z5–9 H9–5

Malus toringo subsp. sargentii
Deciduous, spreading shrub or small tree. A profusion of white flowers in late spring is followed by long-lasting, deep red fruits. Oval, dark green leaves are sometimes lobed.

☼ ◊ Z5–9 H9–5

Staphylea pinnata (Bladder nut)
Deciduous, upright shrub that in late spring carries clusters of white flowers, tinted pink with age, followed by bladder-like, green fruits. Foliage is divided and bright green.

☼ ◊ Z6–9 H9–6

Enkianthus campanulatus
Deciduous, bushy, spreading shrub
with red shoots and tufts of dull green
leaves that turn bright red in fall.
Small, bell-shaped, red-veined,
creamy-yellow flowers appear
in late spring.

☼ ◊ pH Z5–8 H8–4

Viburnum x carlcephalum
Deciduous, rounded, bushy shrub.
In late spring large, rounded heads
of pink buds open to fragrant, white
flowers. These are borne amid dark
green foliage that often turns
red in fall.

☼ ◊ ① Z6–8 H8–5

Dipelta floribunda
Vigorous, deciduous, upright, treelike
shrub with peeling, pale brown bark.
Fragrant, pale pink flowers, marked
yellow inside, open in late spring
and early summer. Has pointed,
mid-green leaves.

☼ ◊ Z6–9 H9–6

Staphylea holocarpa 'Rosea'
Deciduous, upright shrub or spreading,
small tree. From mid- to late spring
bears pink flowers, followed by
bladder-like, pale green fruits.
Bronze, young leaves mature
to blue-green.

☼ ◊ Z6–9 H9–6

Photinia serratifolia
Evergreen, upright shrub or bushy tree.
Oblong, often sharply toothed leaves
are red when young, maturing to glossy,
dark green. Small, 5-petaled flowers
from mid- to late spring are
sometimes followed by
spherical, red fruits.

☼ ◊ Z9–10 H10–9

Photinia x fraseri 'Red Robin'
Evergreen, upright, dense shrub.
Oblong, glossy, dark green leaves
are brilliant red when young. Bears
5-petaled flowers in late spring.
Has good resistance to damage
by late frosts.

☼ ◊ Z8–9 H9–8

Daphniphyllum macropodum
Evergreen, bushy, dense shrub
with sturdy shoots and dark green
leaves. Small flowers, green on
female plants, purplish on male
plants, appear in late spring.

☼ ◊ Z7–11 H11–7

Berberis valdiviana
Evergreen shrub with oval to ovate,
leathery leaves with 3-pronged spines.
Pendulous racemes, to 1½in (4cm) long,
of cup-shaped, fragrant, saffron-yellow
flowers, in late spring, are
followed by egg-shaped,
bloomed, purple fruits.

☼ ◊ Z8–10 H10–8

Corylopsis glabrescens
Deciduous, open shrub. Oval leaves,
with bristly teeth along margins,
are dark green above, blue-green
beneath. Drooping spikes of fragrant,
bell-shaped, pale yellow flowers
appear in mid-spring
on bare branches.

☼ ◊ pH Z6–9 H9–6

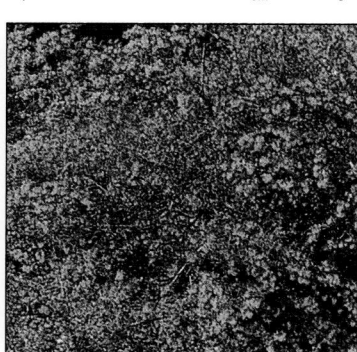

Berberis darwinii (Darwin's barberry)
Vigorous, evergreen, arching shrub.
Has small, glossy, dark green leaves and
a profusion of rounded, deep orange-
yellow flowers from mid- to late spring,
followed by bluish berries.

☼ ◊ ① Z7–9 H9–7

SHRUBS

WHITE

Salix exigua (Coyote Willow)
Deciduous, upright shrub with slender, green-gray branches and linear, finely toothed, silky, silvery-white leaves, which move in the breeze. Small, pale lemon catkins are produced in spring, at the same time as the leaves emerge from bud.
☼ ◊ Z4–6 H6–1

Ligustrum sinense
Deciduous or semievergreen, bushy, upright shrub with oval, pale green leaves. Large panicles of fragrant, tubular, white flowers are borne in mid-summer, followed by small, purplish-black fruits.
☼ ◊ ❶ Z7–9 H9–6

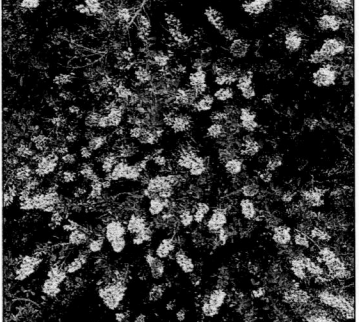

Escallonia leucantha
Evergreen, upright shrub. Narrow, oval, glossy, dark green leaves set off large racemes of small, shallowly cup-shaped, white flowers in mid-summer.
☼ ◊ Z8–9 H9–8

Olearia virgata
Evergreen, arching, graceful shrub with very narrow, dark gray-green leaves. Produces an abundance of small, star-shaped, white flower heads in early summer, arranged in small clusters along stems.
☼ ◊ Z7–11 H11–7

Styrax officinalis
Deciduous, loose to dense shrub or small tree. Fragrant, bell-shaped, white flowers appear in early summer among oval, dark green leaves with grayish-white undersides.
☼ ◖ pH Z14–15 H12–10

Escallonia 'Iveyi'
Evergreen, upright shrub. Glossy, dark green foliage sets off large racemes of fragrant, tubular, pure white flowers, with short lobes, borne from mid- to late summer.
☼ ◊ Z8–9 H9–8

Viburnum rhytidophyllum
Vigorous, evergreen, open shrub with long, narrow, deep green leaves. Dense heads of small, creamy-white flowers in late spring and early summer are succeeded by red fruits that mature to black.
☼ ◊ ❶ Z5–8 H8–5

Xanthoceras sorbifolium
Deciduous, upright shrub or small tree with bright green leaves divided into many slender leaflets. In late spring and early summer produces spikes of white flowers with red patches inside at the base of the petals.
☼ ◊ Z5–8 H8–5

Chionanthus virginicus (Fringe tree)
Deciduous, bushy shrub or small tree. Has large, glossy, dark green leaves that turn yellow in fall. Drooping sprays of fragrant, white flowers appear in early summer.
☼ ◖ Z4–9 H9–1

Elaeagnus umbellata

Vigorous, deciduous, bushy shrub with oblong, wavy-edged, bright green leaves, which are silvery when young. Has fragrant, bell-shaped, creamy-yellow flowers in late spring and early summer, followed by egg-shaped, red fruits.

☼ ◊ Z4–8 H8–1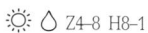

Abutilon vitifolium var. album

Fast-growing, deciduous, upright shrub. Large, bowl-shaped, white blooms, pink-tinged when young, are freely borne in late spring and early summer amid deeply lobed, sharply toothed, gray-green leaves.

☼ ◊ Z8–9 H9–8

Abelia triflora

Vigorous, deciduous, upright shrub with pointed, deep green leaves. Small, extremely fragrant, white flowers, tinged pale pink, appear in mid-summer.

☼ ◊ Z7–9 H9–7

Syringa vulgaris 'Madame Florent Stepman'

Deciduous, upright then spreading shrub with large panicles of fragrant, tubular, single, white flowers borne profusely in late spring. Has heart-shaped, dark green leaves.

☼ ◊ Z4–8 H8–1

Abelia x grandiflora

Vigorous, semievergreen, arching shrub. Has glossy, dark green foliage and an abundance of fragrant, pink-tinged, white flowers from mid-summer to mid fall.

☼ ◊ Z6–9 H9–6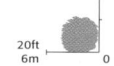

Holodiscus discolor

Fast-growing, deciduous, arching shrub. Has lobed, toothed, dark green leaves and large, pendent sprays of small, creamy-white flowers in mid-summer.

☼ ◊ Z6–9 H9–5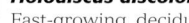

Crinodendron patagua

Vigorous, evergreen, upright shrub with slightly hairy, reddish young shoots and oval to ovate, coarsely toothed, leathery, dark green leaves. Bell-shaped, frilly-edged, white flowers in late summer are followed by angular, red seed pods.

◐ ◊ pH Z9–10 H10–9

Aesculus parviflora
(Bottlebrush buckeye)

Deciduous, open shrub. Leaves are bronze when young, dark green in summer and yellow in fall. Panicles of red-centered, white flowers appear from mid- to late summer.

☼ ◊ ❗ Z5–9 H9–4

Clethra delavayi

Deciduous, open shrub with lance-shaped, toothed, rich green leaves. Dense, spreading clusters of pink buds opening to scented, white flowers appear in mid-summer.

☼ ◊ pH Z7–9 H9–7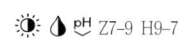

BUDDLEJAS

Buddleja is genus of approximately 100 species of highly ornamental evergreen and deciduous shrubs and small trees, originating predominantly in Asia, Africa, and the Americas. Buddlejas are often included in wildlife gardens as they encourage increased insect activity, which has earned one species the common name of butterfly bush, although they all also attract bees and hoverflies. They produce small, highly-scented, tubular flowers borne in either plume-shaped or globular clusters. Easy to grow, they thrive in almost any soil, and perform best in a warm, sunny position. They are particularly suitable for growing against a south-facing wall.

B. davidii 'White Profusion'

B. x weyeriana 'Moonlight'

B. colvilei 'Kewensis'

B. davidii 'Pink Delight'

B. salviifolia

B. alternifolia

B. davidii 'Black Knight'

B. davidii 'Dartmoor'

B. 'Lochinch'

B. x weyeriana 'Sungold'

PINK

Abutilon vitifolium 'Veronica Tennant'
Fast-growing, generally deciduous but sometimes semievergreen, upright shrub or small tree. Has rounded, toothed, gray-green leaves. In spring and early summer, large, saucer-shaped, purple-blue flowers are borne in profusion.

☼ ◊ Z8–9 H9–8

Kolkwitzia amabilis 'Pink Cloud'
Deciduous, arching shrub that bears a mass of bell-shaped, pink flowers amid small, oval, mid-green leaves in late spring and early summer.

☼ ◊ Z5–9 H9–5

Tamarix ramosissima
Deciduous, arching, graceful shrub or small tree with tiny, narrow, blue-green leaves. In late summer and early fall bears large, upright plumes of small, pink flowers.

☼ ◊ Z3–8 H8–1

Cotinus coggygria 'Notcutt's Variety'
Deciduous, bushy shrub with deep reddish-purple foliage. Long-lasting, purplish-pink plumes of massed, small flowers are produced in late summer.

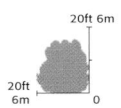

☼ ◊ Z5–9 H9–3

Acer palmatum var. heptalobum 'Rubrum'
Deciduous, bushy-headed shrub or small tree. Large leaves are red when young, bronze in summer and brilliant red, orange or yellow in fall. Has small, reddish-purple flowers in mid-spring.

☼ ◊ Z6–8 H8–2

Corylus maxima 'Purpurea'
Vigorous, deciduous, open shrub or small tree with deep purple leaves and purplish catkins, with yellow anthers, that hang from bare branches in late winter. Edible nuts mature in fall.

☼ ◊ Z4–9 H9–1

Prunus spinosa 'Purpurea'
Deciduous, dense, spiny shrub or small tree. Bright red, young leaves become deep reddish-purple. Bears saucer-shaped, pale pink flowers from early to mid-spring, followed by blue-bloomed, black fruits.

☼ ◊ Z5–8 H8–5

LILACS

The heady scent of the lilac (*Syringa*) epitomizes early summer. Apart from the classic lilacs and mauves, colors include white, pink, cream, and rich red-purple; double forms are also available. Most lilacs grown in gardens are vigorous shrubs derived from *S. vulgaris*. They may eventually become treelike and are best planted at the back of a shrub border. Spent flower heads should be removed, with care taken not to damage the new shoots. Otherwise, little pruning is required, though older plants may be rejuvenated by hard pruning in winter.

S. pubescens subsp. *patula* **'Miss Kim'**

S. pubescens subsp. *microphylla* **'Superba'**

S. x persica

S. vulgaris 'Katherine Havemeyer'

S. vulgaris 'Andenken an Ludwig Späth'

S. vulgaris 'Madame Lemoine'

S. meyeri 'Palibin'

115

SHRUBS

Genista tenera 'Golden Shower'

Vigorous, deciduous, arching shrub with narrowly oblong, gray-green leaves. Racemes of fragrant, pealike, golden-yellow flowers are produced in early to mid-summer.

☼ ◊ Z6–9 H9–6

Elaeagnus angustifolia
(Russian olive)

Deciduous, bushy shrub or spreading, small tree. Has narrow, silvery-gray leaves and small, fragrant, creamy-yellow flowers, with spreading lobes, in early summer, followed by small, oval, yellow fruits.

☼ ◊ Z2–8 H8–1

Genista cinerea

Deciduous, arching shrub that produces an abundance of fragrant, pealike, yellow blooms from early to mid-summer. Has silky, young shoots and narrow, gray-green leaves.

☼ ◊ Z7–9 H9–7

Cotinus coggygria GOLDEN SPIRIT ('Ancot') (Golden smokebush)

Deciduous, bushy shrub grown for its rounded, golden-yellow leaves, which turn orange in fall. In summer, tiny, fluffy, plumelike, gray flower clusters, on fine stalks, are borne above the leaves.

☼ ◊ Z5–9 H9–3

Cytisus battandieri
(Moroccan broom, Pineapple broom)

Semievergreen, open shrub. Leaves have 3 silver-gray leaflets. Pineapple-scented, yellow flowers appear in summer.

☼ ◊ ❢ Z7–9 H9–7

Buddleja globosa

Deciduous or semievergreen, open shrub with dark green foliage. Dense, rounded clusters of orange-yellow flowers are carried in early summer.

☼ ◊ Z7–9 H9–7

Caesalpinia gilliesii

Deciduous, open shrub or small tree. Has finely divided, dark green leaves and bears short racemes of yellow flowers with long, red stamens from mid- to late summer.

☼ ◊ H11–1

Paliurus spina-christi
(Christ's thorn, Jerusalem thorn)

Deciduous, bushy shrub with slender, thorny shoots. Has oval, glossy, bright green leaves, tiny, yellow flowers in summer and curious, woody, winged fruits in fall.

☼ ◊ Z7–9 H9–7

Cotoneaster 'Cornubia'
Vigorous, semievergreen, arching shrub. Clusters of white flowers, produced in early summer amid dark green foliage, are followed by large, pendent clusters of decorative, bright red fruits.

☀ ◊ ❗ Z6–8 H8–6

Rhus typhina 'Dissecta'
Deciduous, spreading, open shrub or small tree with velvety shoots. Fernlike, dark green leaves turn brilliant orange-red in fall, when deep red fruit clusters are also borne.

☀ ◊ Z3–8 H8–1

Cotinus 'Flame'
Deciduous, bushy, treelike shrub with dark green leaves that turn brilliant orange-red in fall. From late summer, showy, plumelike, purplish-pink flower heads appear above the foliage.

☀ ◊ Z5–8 H8–5

Acer palmatum var. heptalobum
Deciduous, bushy-headed shrub or small tree with large, lobed, mid-green leaves that turn brilliant red, orange or yellow in fall. Bears small, reddish-purple flowers in mid-spring.

☀ ◊ Z6–8 H8–2

Euonymus oxyphyllus
Deciduous, upright shrub or tree with oval, dull green leaves turning to purplish-red in fall. Produces tiny, greenish-white flowers in late spring, then globose, 4- or 5-lobed, deep red fruits with orange-scarlet seeds.

☀ ◊ ❗ Z6–9 H9–6

Fothergilla major
Deciduous, upright shrub with glossy, dark green leaves, slightly bluish-white beneath, that turn red, orange and yellow in fall. Tufts of fragrant, white flowers appear in late spring.

◑ ◊ pH Z5–8 H8–5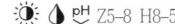

Euonymus myrianthus
Evergreen, bushy shrub with pointed, leathery, mid-green leaves. Dense clusters of small, greenish-yellow flowers in summer are followed by yellow fruits that open to show orange-red seeds.

☀ ◊ ❗ Z7–9 H9–7

Cotoneaster lacteus
Evergreen, arching shrub suitable for hedging. Oval, dark green leaves set off shallowly cup-shaped, white flowers from early to mid-summer. Long-lasting, red fruits are carried in large clusters in fall–winter.

☀ ◊ ❗ Z7–9 H9–4

WITCH HAZELS

Species of *Hamamelis* put on a beautiful show of fragrant flowers during the darkest, coldest months, securing their place in any winter planting scheme. The spiderlike blooms, ranging in color from deep red to sulfur yellow, appear on bare branches from late fall to early spring, the narrow, crepe-paper-like petals withstanding several degrees of frost and snow without damage. Witch hazels prefer moist but well-drained, fertile, acidic to neutral soil in full sun or partial shade. A spring dressing of lime-free potting mix or well-rotted leaf mold benefits young plants.

H. x *intermedia* 'Barmstedt Gold'

H. x *intermedia* 'Arnold Promise'

H. x *intermedia* 'Pallida'

H. x *intermedia* 'Jelena'

H. x *intermedia* 'Primavera'

H. x *intermedia* 'Aphrodite'

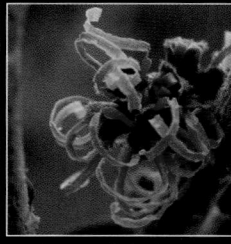

H. x *intermedia* 'Robert'

YELLOW

Pyracantha atalantioides 'Aurea'
Vigorous, evergreen, upright, spiny shrub, arching with age. Has narrowly oval, glossy, dark green leaves and white flowers in early summer, followed by large clusters of small, yellow berries in early fall.

☼ ◊ ⚠ Z6–9 H9–6

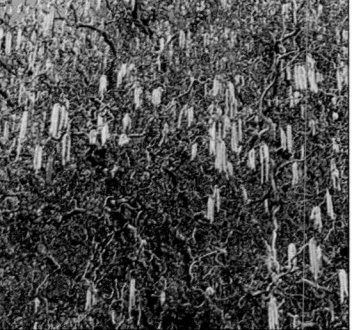

Corylus avellana 'Contorta'
(Harry Lauder's walking stick)
Deciduous, bushy shrub with curiously twisted shoots and broad, sharply toothed, mid-green leaves. In late winter, bare branches are covered with pendent, pale yellow catkins.

☼ ◊ Z3–9 H9–1

Mahonia x media 'Charity'
Evergreen, upright, dense shrub with large leaves composed of many spiny, dark green leaflets. Slender, upright, later spreading spikes of fragrant, yellow flowers are borne from early fall to early spring.

◐ ◊ Z8–9 H9–8

Hamamelis japonica 'Sulphurea'
Deciduous, upright, open shrub. In mid-winter, fragrant, spidery, pale yellow flowers with 4 narrow, crimped petals are borne on leafless branches. Broadly oval, dark green leaves turn yellow in fall.

☼ ◊ pH Z5–9 H9–5

Mahonia x media 'Buckland'
Evergreen, upright, dense shrub. Has large leaves with many spiny, dark green leaflets. Clustered, upright then spreading, long, branched spikes of fragrant, yellow flowers appear from late fall to early spring.

◐ ◊ Z8–9 H9–8

Azara microphylla
Elegant, evergreen shrub or small tree. Has tiny, glossy, dark green leaves and small clusters of vanilla-scented, deep yellow flowers in late winter and early spring.

☼ ◊ Z8–10 H11–10

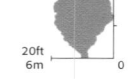

Prunus lusitanica 'Variegata'
Slow-growing, evergreen, bushy shrub with reddish-purple shoots. Has oval, glossy, dark green, white-edged leaves. Fragrant, shallowly cup-shaped, creamy-white flowers in summer are followed by purple fruits.

☀ ◊ ❶ Z7–9 H9–4

Ligustrum ovalifolium (Privet)
Vigorous, evergreen or semievergreen, upright, dense shrub with glossy, mid-green leaves. Dense racemes of small, rather unpleasantly scented, tubular, white flowers appear in mid-summer, followed by black fruits.

☀ ◊ ❶ Z6–8 H8–6

Azara microphylla 'Variegata'
Slow-growing, evergreen, compact shrub. Small, rounded, glossy, dark green leaves have margins of creamy-gold. In early spring bears rounded clusters of tiny, chocolate-scented, yellow-green flowers on the underside of the branches.

☀ ◊ Z8–10 H11–10

Griselinia littoralis 'Variegata'
Evergreen, upright shrub of dense, bushy habit. Leathery leaves are gray-green, marked with bright green and creamy-white. Bears inconspicuous, yellow-green flowers in late spring.

☀ ◊ Z7–9 H9–7

Pittosporum dallii
Evergreen, rounded, dense tree or shrub. Has purplish stems and sharply toothed, deep green leaves. Clusters of small, fragrant, shallowly cup-shaped, white flowers are borne in summer.

☀ ◊ Z9–11 H11–1

Elaeagnus pungens 'Maculata'
Evergreen, bushy, slightly spiny shrub. Glossy, dark green leaves are marked with a central, deep yellow patch. Very fragrant, urn-shaped, creamy-white flowers open from mid- to late fall.

☀ ◊ Z7–9 H9–7

Osmanthus heterophyllus 'Aureomarginatus'
Evergreen, upright shrub. Sharply toothed, holly-like, glossy, bright green leaves have yellow margins. Small, fragrant, white flowers are produced in fall.

☀ ◊ Z7–9 H9–7

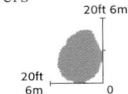

Pittosporum 'Garnettii'
Evergreen, columnar or conical shrub of dense, bushy habit. Rounded, gray-green leaves, irregularly edged creamy-white, become tinged with deep pink in cold areas. May bear small, greenish-purple flowers in spring–summer.

☀ ◊ Z9–11 H11–10

Prunus lusitanica subsp. azorica
Evergreen, bushy shrub with reddish-purple shoots and bright green leaves, red when young. Bears spikes of small, fragrant, white flowers in summer, followed by purple fruits.

☀ ◊ ❶ Z7–9 H9–4

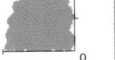

SHRUBS

119

SHRUBS

GREEN

WHITE

Pieris floribunda
(Japanese pieris, fetterbush)
Evergreen, bushy, dense, leafy shrub with oval, glossy, dark green leaves. Greenish-white flower buds appear in winter, opening to urn-shaped, white blooms from early to midspring.

☼ ◐ pH ① Z5–8 H8–5

10ft 3m

Tetrapanax papyrifer
(Rice-paper plant)
Evergreen, upright, suckering shrub. Long-stalked, circular leaves are deeply lobed. Has bold sprays of small, creamy-white flowers in summer and black berries in fall–winter.

☼ ◐ Z6–11 H12–6

20ft 6m

Enkianthus perulatus
Deciduous, bushy, dense shrub. Dark green leaves turn bright red in fall. A profusion of small, pendent, urn-shaped, white flowers is borne in midspring.

☼ ◐ pH Z6–8 H8–6

10ft 3m

Pittosporum tenuifolium
Evergreen, columnar, later rounded shrub or small tree with purple shoots and wavy-edged, oval, glossy, mid-green leaves. Bears honey-scented, purple flowers in late spring.

 ☼ ◐ Z9–11 H11–9

20ft 6m

Pieris japonica 'Scarlett O'Hara'
Evergreen, rounded, bushy, dense shrub. Young foliage and shoots are bronze-red, leaves becoming glossy, dark green. Produces sprays of white flowers in spring.

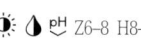 ☼ ◐ pH ① Z6–8 H8–6

10ft 3m

CAMELLIAS

These evergreen shrubs and small trees have long been valued for their luxuriant, rich green foliage and masses of showy flowers, in shades of white, pink, red, and yellow, borne mainly in winter and spring. Once thought suitable only for greenhouses, many camellias are hardy to Zone 6 if grown in sheltered positions, although blooms may suffer frost and rain damage. Ideal for shady gardens, they grow well against walls. Camellias require acidic soil but also make good container plants. The main flower forms are illustrated below.

Single—shallowly cup-shaped flowers each have not more than 8 petals, arranged in a single row, and a conspicuous, central boss of stamens.

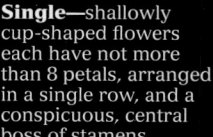

Semidouble—cup-shaped flowers each have 2 or more rows of 9–21 regular or irregular petals, and conspicuous stamens.

Anemone—rounded flowers each have one or more rows of large, outer petals lying flat or undulating; the domed centre has a mass of intermingled petaloids and stamens.

Peony-form—rounded, domed flowers have usually irregular petals intermingled with petaloids and stamens.

Rose-form—cup-shaped flowers each have several rows of overlapping petals and open to reveal stamens in the centre.

Formal double—rounded flowers have rows of regular, neatly overlapping petals that obscure stamens. **Irregular double forms** are similar but often have more loosely arranged, sometimes irregular, petals.

C. 'Cornish Snow' [single]

C. japonica 'Alba Plena' [formal double]

C. japonica 'Hagoromo' [semidouble]

C. japonica 'Janet Waterhouse' [semidouble]

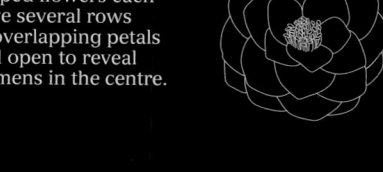

C. japonica 'Nobilissima' [peony]

C. japonica 'Lavinia Maggi'
[formal double]

C. x williamsii 'Donation'
[semidouble]

C. 'Freedom Bell' [semidouble]

C. x williamsii 'Debbie' [peony]

C. 'Spring Festival' [double]

C. japonica 'Margaret Davis'
[irregular double]

C. 'Inspiration' [semidouble]

C. x williamsii 'Water Lily'
[formal double]

C. japonica 'Adolphe Audusson'
[semidouble]

C. x williamsii 'J.C. Williams'
[single]

C. reticulata 'Captain Rawes'
[semidouble]

C. 'Leonard Messel'
[semidouble]

C. japonica 'Bob's Tinsie'
[anemone]

C. x williamsii 'Jury's Yellow'
[anemone]

C. japonica 'Tricolor' [semidouble]

C. 'Black Lace' [formal double]

C. japonica 'Brushfield's Yellow' [anemone]

SHRUBS

Chaenomeles speciosa 'Moerloosei'

Vigorous, deciduous, bushy shrub. Has glossy, dark green leaves and pink-flushed, white flowers in early spring, followed by greenish-yellow fruits.

☼ ◊ Z5–9 H9–1

Cotoneaster divaricatus

Deciduous, bushy, spreading shrub. Leaves are glossy, dark green, turning red in fall. Shallowly cup-shaped, pink-flushed, white flowers in late spring and early summer are followed by deep red fruits.

☼ ◊ ⚠ Z5–7 H7–5

Rhododendron 'Percy Wiseman'

Evergreen rhododendron with a domed, compact habit. In late spring produces open funnel-shaped, peach-yellow flowers that fade to white.

☼ ◊ pH ⚠ Z6–9 H9–6

Choisya 'Aztec Pearl'

Evergreen, compact shrub with aromatic, glossy, dark green leaves composed of 3–5 linear leaflets. Clusters of scented, white flowers, pink-flushed in bud, are produced in profusion in spring and then quite often again in early fall.

☼ ◊ Z8–10 H10–8

Choisya ternata (Mexican orange)

Evergreen, rounded, dense shrub with aromatic, glossy, bright green leaves composed of 3 leaflets. Clusters of fragrant, white blooms open in late spring and often again in fall.

☼ ◊ Z8–10 H10–8

Myrtus communis (Common myrtle)

Evergreen, bushy shrub with aromatic, glossy, dark green foliage. Fragrant, white flowers are borne from mid-spring to early summer, followed by purple-black berries.

☼ ◊ Z8–9 H9–8

Viburnum bitchiuense

Deciduous, bushy shrub with oval, dark green leaves. Rounded heads of fragrant, tubular, pale pink flowers, borne from mid- to late spring, are followed by egg-shaped, flattened, black fruits.

☼ ◊ ⚠ Z5–7 H7–5

Camellia x williamsii 'E.G. Waterhouse'

Evergreen, upright shrub with lance-shaped, pale green leaves. Formal double, pink flowers are freely produced in spring.

☼ ◊ pH ⚠ Z7–8 H8–7

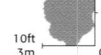

Ribes sanguineum 'Pulborough Scarlet' (Flowering currant)
Deciduous, upright shrub that in spring bears pendent, tubular, deep red flowers amid aromatic, dark green leaves, with 3–5 lobes, sometimes followed by black fruits with a white bloom.

 ☼ ◊ Z6–8 H8–6

Prunus mume 'Beni-chidori'
Deciduous, spreading shrub with fragrant, single, carmine flowers in early spring before pointed, dark green leaves appear.

 ☼ ◊ ① Z6–8 H8–6

Acer palmatum 'Corallinum'
Very slow-growing, deciduous, bushy-headed shrub or small tree. Lobed, bright reddish-pink, young foliage becomes mid-green, then brilliant red, orange or yellow in fall. Reddish-purple flowers appear in mid-spring.

 ☼ ◊ Z6–8 H8–2

Telopea truncata (Tasmanian waratah)
Evergreen, upright shrub, bushy with age. Has deep green leaves and dense, rounded heads of small, tubular, crimson flowers in late spring and summer.

 ◐ ◊ pH Z13–15 H12–10

Enkianthus cernuus f. rubens
Deciduous, bushy shrub with dense clusters of dull green leaves that turn deep reddish-purple in fall. Small, bell-shaped, deep red flowers appear in late spring.

 ◐ ◊ pH Z6–8 H8–6

Acer palmatum 'Shindeshojo'
Slow-growing, deciduous, rather twiggy shrub grown for its pink-red leaf coloring in spring. Palmate, deeply lobed leaves then turn bluish-green. Much used for bonsai. Hard frosts can scorch new growth.

☼ ◊ Z6–8 H8–2

Leptospermum scoparium 'Red Damask'
Evergreen, upright, bushy shrub. Narrow, aromatic, dark green leaves set off sprays of double, dark red flowers in late spring and summer.

 ☼ ◊ H11–3

Berberis thunbergii f. atropurpurea
Deciduous, arching, dense shrub. Reddish-purple foliage turns bright red in fall. Globose to cup-shaped, red-tinged, pale yellow flowers in mid-spring are followed by red fruits.

 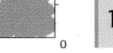 ☼ ◊ ① Z5–8 H8–5

SHRUBS

123

RHODODENDRONS

Rhododendrons and azaleas both belong to the huge genus *Rhododendron*, one of the largest in the plant kingdom. Azalea is the common name used for all the deciduous species and hybrids, and many of the dwarf, small-leaved evergreens. In stature the genus ranges from small alpine shrubs only a few inches high to tall, spreading trees, in the wild reaching 80ft (24m). Rhododendrons require well-drained, acidic soil rich in organic matter. Most prefer cool woodland conditions, although many dwarf forms thrive in more open sites. Many grow well in containers, in which it is often easier to provide suitable growing conditions. Once established, they require little attention apart from an annual mulch and occasional fertilizer, and provide a colorful display for years.

R. pachysanthum
[rhododendron]

R. 'Gomer Waterer'
[rhododendron]

R. decorum [rhododendron]

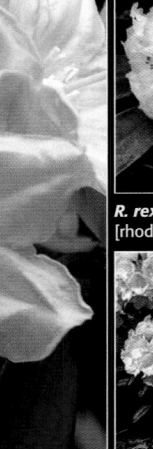

R. 'Polar Bear' ①
[rhododendron]

R. rex subsp. *fictolacteum* ①
[rhododendron]

R. yakushimanum ①
[rhododendron]

R. orbiculare ①
[rhododendron]

R. 'Loderi King George' ①
[rhododendron]

R. quinquefolium [azalea]

R. 'Fragrantissimum' ①
[rhododendron]

R. sinogrande ①
[rhododendron]

R. calophytum ① [rhododendron]

R. falconeri ① [rhododendron]

R. williamsianum ① [rhododendron]

R. 'Golden Torch' [rhododendron]

24

R. fulvum [rhododendron]

***R.* 'Purple Splendour'** [rhododendron]

***R.* 'Fastuosum Flore Pleno'** [rhododendron]

R. augustinii ! [rhododendron]

***R.* 'Mother's Day'** [azalea]

***R.* 'Goldkrone'** ! [rhododendron]

***R.* 'Blaauw's Pink'** [azalea]

***R.* 'Hotei'** [rhododendron]

***R.* 'Pink Pearl'** ! [rhododendron]

***R.* 'Seta'** ! [rhododendron]

***R.* 'Grace Seabrook'** [rhododendron]

***R.* 'Patty Bee'** [rhododendron]

***R.* 'Daviesii'** [azalea]

R. praecox [rhododendron]

***R.* 'Curlew'** ! [rhododendron]

R. luteum ! [azalea]

R. niveum [rhododendron]

R. cinnabarinum ! [rhododendron]

R. arboreum ! [rhododendron]

***R.* 'Blue Danube'** [azalea]

***R.* 'Gibraltar'** [azalea]

125

CORNUS

Shrubby members of the genus *Cornus* are justifiably popular among gardeners and landscape designers, admired for their highly ornamental brightly colored winter stems, ranging from lime green and yellow to orange and crimson, as well as their spring flowers, and, in some cultivars, variegated foliage. Extremely hardy, dogwoods tolerate extreme cold and exposure. They also grow well on most soils, and require little maintenance—simply cut back the stems to just above the ground every two years in late winter. This promotes young growth, which has the most vibrant color.

C. alba 'Elegantissima' ⚠

C. alba 'Spaethii' ⚠

C. sericea 'Kelseyi'

C. alba 'Aurea'

C. sericea 'Flaviramea'

C. alba 'Kesselringii' ⚠

C. sanguinea 'Winter Beauty'

C. sericea 'White Gold'

C. sanguinea 'Midwinter Fire'

YELLOW

Corylopsis pauciflora
Deciduous, bushy, dense shrub. Oval, bright green leaves, bronze when young, have bristly teeth. Bears fragrant, tubular to bell-shaped, pale yellow flowers from early to mid-spring.

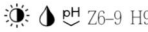 Z6–9 H9–6

Rhododendron 'Yellow Hammer'
Evergreen, erect, bushy rhododendron. Bears abundant clusters of tubular, bright yellow flowers in spring; frequently flowers again in fall.

Z5–8 H8–5

Edgeworthia chrysantha
Deciduous, rounded, open shrub with oval, dark green leaves. Very supple shoots produce terminal, rounded heads of fragrant, tubular, yellow flowers in late winter and early spring.

Z8–10 H10–8

ORANGE

WHITE

Berberis gagnepainii var. lanceifolia
Evergreen, bushy, dense shrub. Massed, globose to cup-shaped, yellow flowers appear among long, narrow, pointed, dark green leaves in late spring. Forms blue-bloomed, black berries.

 Z6–9 H9–6

Forsythia x intermedia 'Beatrix Farrand'
Vigorous, deciduous, bushy, arching shrub with sturdy shoots. A profusion of large, deep yellow flowers appears from early to mid-spring before oval, coarsely toothed, mid-green leaves emerge.

 Z6–9 H9–6

Berberis linearifolia 'Orange King'
Evergreen, upright, stiff-branched shrub with narrow, rigid, dark green leaves. Bears large, globose to cup-shaped, deep orange flowers in late spring.

Z6–9 H9–6

Forsythia x intermedia 'Spectabilis'
Vigorous, deciduous, spreading shrub with sturdy growth. A profusion of large, deep yellow flowers is borne from early to mid-spring before sharply toothed, dark green leaves appear.

 Z6–9 H9–6

Kerria japonica 'Pleniflora'
Vigorous, deciduous, graceful shrub. Double, golden-yellow flowers are borne along green shoots from mid- to late spring. Leaves are narrowly oval, sharply toothed and bright green.

Z4–9 H9–1

Berberis x lologensis 'Stapehill'
Vigorous, evergreen, arching shrub. Glossy, dark green foliage sets off profuse racemes of globose to cup-shaped, orange flowers from mid- to late spring.

Z6–9 H9–6

Philadelphus 'Beauclerk'
Deciduous, slightly arching shrub. Large, fragrant flowers, white with a small, central, pale purple blotch, are produced from early to mid-summer. Leaves are dark green.

Z5–8 H8–1

Lindera benzoin (Spicebush)
Deciduous, bushy shrub with aromatic, bright green leaves that turn yellow in fall. Tiny, greenish-yellow flowers in mid-spring are followed by red berries on female plants.

 pH Z4–9 H8–1

Berberis x stenophylla
Evergreen, arching shrub with slender shoots and narrow, spine-tipped, deep green leaves, blue-gray beneath. Massed, golden-yellow flowers appear from mid- to late spring followed by small, blue-black fruits.

 Z6–9 H9–6

Euphorbia mellifera (Honey spurge)
Evergreen, rounded shrub grown mainly for its long, narrowly oblong, rich green leaves with cream midribs. Small, honey-scented, brown flowers, surrounded by showy bracts, are produced in dome-shaped clusters in late spring.

Z9–10 H10–9

Deutzia scabra
Deciduous, upright shrub with narrowly oval, dark green leaves that, from early to mid-summer, set off dense, upright clusters of 5-petaled, white blooms.

Z6–8 H8–6

SHRUBS

127

WHITE

Philadelphus 'Belle Etoile'
Deciduous, arching shrub. Very fragrant, white flowers, each with a pale purple mark at the base, are borne profusely among mid-green foliage in late spring and early summer.

☀ ◌ Z5–8 H8–5

Pyracantha x watereri
Evergreen, upright, dense, spiny shrub with glossy, dark green foliage. Shallowly cup-shaped, white flowers in early summer are succeeded by bright red berries in fall.

☀ ◌ ❢ Z7–9 H9–7

Aronia melanocarpa
(Black chokeberry)
Deciduous, bushy shrub. White flowers appear in late spring and early summer, followed by black fruits. Has glossy, dark green leaves that turn red in fall.

☀ ◌ Z3–8 H8–1

Spiraea canescens
Deciduous shrub with upright shoots arching at the top. Small heads of white flowers are borne in profusion amid narrowly oval, gray-green leaves from early to mid-summer.

☀ ◌ Z7–9 H9–7

Olearia nummulariifolia
Evergreen, rounded shrub with stiff, upright shoots densely covered with small, very thick, mid- to dark green leaves. Small, fragrant, white flowers appear in mid-summer.

☀ ◌ Z7–10 H10–7

Rubus 'Benenden'
Deciduous, arching, thornless shrub with peeling bark. Large, roselike, pure white flowers are borne among lobed, deep green leaves in late spring and early summer.

☀ ◌ Z5–9 H9–5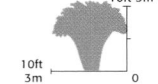

Fallugia paradoxa (Apache plume)
Deciduous, bushy shrub that bears white flowers in mid-summer, followed by silky, pink- and red-tinged, green fruits. Dark green leaves are finely cut and feathery.

☀ ◌ Z6–8 H8–5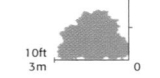

Sorbaria sorbifolia
Deciduous, upright shrub that forms thickets by suckering. Mid-green leaves consist of many sharply toothed leaflets. Large panicles of small, white flowers appear in summer.

☀ ◖ Z2–9 H9–1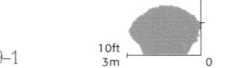

Philadelphus 'Boule d'Argent'
Deciduous, bushy, arching shrub with dark green foliage that sets off clusters of slightly fragrant, semidouble to double, pure white flowers from early to mid-summer.

☀ ◌ Z5–8 H8–5

Eucryphia milliganii

Evergreen, upright, narrow shrub. Has tiny, dark green leaves, bluish-white beneath, and small, white flowers, borne in mid-summer.

☼ ◐ ◊ pH Z8–9 H9–8

Philadelphus 'Lemoinei'
(Mock orange)

Deciduous, upright, slightly arching shrub that produces profuse racemes of small, extremely fragrant, white flowers from early to mid-summer.

☼ ◊ Z5–8 H8–3

Osteomeles schweriniae

Evergreen, arching shrub with long, slender shoots. Leaves, consisting of many small leaflets, are dark green. Clusters of small, white flowers in early summer are followed by red, later blue-black, fruits.

☼ ◊ Z7–11 H11–7

Prinsepia uniflora

Deciduous, arching, spiny shrub. From late spring to summer bears small, fragrant, white flowers amid narrow, glossy, dark green leaves followed by cherry-like, deep red fruits. Grows best in hot sun.

☼ ◊ Z3–6 H6–1

Styrax wilsonii

Deciduous, bushy shrub with slender shoots that produce an abundance of yellow-centered, white flowers in early summer. Leaves are small and deep green.

☼ ◐ ◊ pH Z7–9 H9–7

Clethra barbinervis

Deciduous, upright shrub with peeling bark. Has oval, toothed, dark green leaves that turn red and yellow in fall. Racemes of fragrant, white flowers are borne in late summer and early fall.

☼ ◐ ◊ pH Z5–8 H8–6

Ceanothus incanus

Evergreen, bushy shrub. Has spreading, spiny shoots, broad, gray-green leaves and large racemes of white flowers in late spring and early summer.

☼ ◊ Z8–11 H11–8

Philadelphus 'Dame Blanche'

Deciduous, bushy, compact shrub with dark, peeling bark. Dark green foliage sets off slightly fragrant, semidouble to loosely double, pure white flowers borne in profusion from early to mid-summer.

☼ ◊ Z5–8 H8–5

WHITE

Escallonia virgata
Deciduous, spreading, graceful shrub
with arching shoots and small, glossy,
dark green leaves. Bears racemes of
small, open cup-shaped, white flowers
from early to mid-summer.

☼ ◊ Z8–9 H9–8

Colletia hystrix
Almost leafless, arching, sturdy-
branched shrub armed with rigid, gray-
green spines. Pink flower buds open in
late summer to fragrant, tubular, white
blooms that last into fall.

☼ ◊ Z7–11 H11–7

Olearia* x *haastii (Daisy bush)
Evergreen, bushy, dense shrub, good
for hedging. Has small, oval, glossy, dark
green leaves and is covered with heads
of fragrant, daisylike, white flowers
from mid- to late summer.

☼ ◊ Z9–10 H10–9

***Viburnum dilatatum* 'Catskill'**
Deciduous, low, spreading shrub
with sharply toothed, dark green
leaves that turn yellow, orange and
red in fall. Flat heads of creamy-
white flowers in late spring and
early summer are followed
by bright red fruits.

☼ ◊ ⓘ Z5–8 H8–5

Olearia ilicifolia (Mountain holly)
Evergreen, bushy, dense shrub with
narrowly oblong, rigid, sharply
toothed, musk-scented, gray-
green leaves. Fragrant, white
flower heads are borne in
clusters in early summer.

☼ ◊ Z8–10 H10–8

***Leptospermum scoparium*
'Snow White'** (New Zealand tea-tree)
Evergreen, bushy shrub with small, oval,
sharply pointed, dark green leaves,
which are fragrant when bruised.
Produces masses of small,
5-petaled, white flowers from the
leaf axils in late spring.

☼ ◊ H11–3

Zenobia pulverulenta
Deciduous or semievergreen, slightly
arching shrub, often with bluish-white
bloomed shoots. Glossy leaves have
a bluish-white reverse when young.
Bears fragrant, bell-shaped,
white flowers from early to
mid-summer.

☼ ◊ pH Z5–8 H8–5

Colletia paradoxa
Deciduous, arching shrub with stiff
branches and stout, flattened, blue-green
spines. Fragrant, tubular, white flowers
are borne in late summer and early fall.

☀ ◊ Z7–11 H11–7

Spiraea nipponica 'Snowmound'
Deciduous, spreading shrub with sturdy,
arching, reddish branches. Small,
narrow, dark green leaves set off
profuse, dense clusters of small,
white flowers in early summer.

☀ ◊ Z4–8 H8–1

Philadelphus coronarius 'Variegatus'
Deciduous, bushy shrub with racemes
of very fragrant, creamy-white flowers
in late spring and early summer and
mid-green leaves broadly edged
with white.

☀ ◊ Z4–9 H9–4

Lonicera xylosteum (Fly honeysuckle)
Deciduous, upright, bushy, dense shrub.
Creamy-white flowers are produced
amid gray-green leaves in late spring
and early summer, and are followed
by red berries.

☀ ◊ ⓘ Z4–9 H9–1

Viburnum 'Pragense'
Evergreen, rounded, bushy shrub that
has dark green foliage and domed heads
of white flowers opening from pink buds
in late spring and early summer.

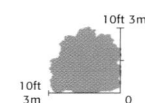

☀ ◊ ⓘ Z6–8 H8–6

Leptospermum polygalifolium
Evergreen, arching, graceful shrub with
small, glossy, bright green leaves. Bears
an abundance of small, pink-tinged,
white flowers in mid-summer.

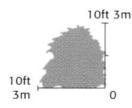

☀ ◊ H11–10

Philadelphus delavayi f. melanocalyx
Deciduous, upright shrub, grown for
its extremely fragrant flowers, with pure
white petals and deep purple sepals,
opening from early to mid-summer.
Leaves are dark green.

☀ ◊ Z6–9 H9–6

Escallonia 'Donard Seedling'
Vigorous, evergreen, arching shrub
with small, glossy, dark green leaves.
Masses of pink flower buds open to
white blooms, flushed with pale pink,
from early to mid-summer.

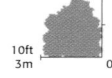

☀ ◊ Z8–9 H9–8

WHITE

Hibiscus syriacus 'Red Heart'
Deciduous, upright shrub that bears large, white flowers, with conspicuous red centers, from late summer to mid-fall. Oval leaves are lobed and deep green.

☀ ◊ Z5–9 H9–1

Deutzia x magnifica 'Staphyleoides'
Vigorous, deciduous, upright shrub. Large, 5-petaled, pure white blooms, borne in dense clusters in early summer, have recurved petals. Leaves are bright green.

☀ ◊ Z6–8 H8–6

Yucca gloriosa (Spanish dagger)
Evergreen shrub with a sturdy stem crowned with a tuft of long, pointed, deep green leaves, blue-green when young. Bears very long panicles of bell-shaped, white flowers in summer–fall.

☀ ◊ Z7–11 H12–7

SHRUBS

Olearia macrodonta (Arorangi)
Vigorous, evergreen, upright shrub, often treelike. Has holly-shaped, sharply toothed, gray-green leaves, silvery-white beneath. Large heads of fragrant, white flowers are produced in early summer.

☀ ◊ Z9–10 H10–9

Aloysia triphylla (Lemon verbena)
Deciduous, bushy shrub. Leaves are pale green and lemon-scented. Racemes of tiny, lilac-tinged, white flowers appear in early summer.

☀ ◊ Z8–11 H11–8

Stephanandra tanakae
Deciduous, arching shrub with orange-brown shoots and sharply toothed, mid-green leaves that turn orange and yellow in fall. Small, yellow-green buds open to white flowers from early to mid-summer.

☀ ◊ Z6–8 H8–6

Exochorda x macrantha 'The Bride'
Deciduous, arching, dense shrub that forms a mound of pendent branches. Large, white flowers are produced in abundance amid dark green foliage in late spring and early summer.

☀ ◊ Z5–9 H9–5

Escallonia 'Apple Blossom'

Evergreen, bushy, dense shrub. From early to mid-summer apple-blossom-pink flowers are borne in profusion amid glossy, dark green leaves.

☼ ◊ Z8–9 H9–8

Lonicera tatarica

Deciduous, bushy shrub. Tubular to trumpet-shaped, 5-lobed, white, pink or red flowers cover dark green foliage in late spring and early summer, and are succeeded by red fruits.

☼ ◊ ! Z3–9 H9–1

Deutzia longifolia 'Veitchii'

Deciduous, arching shrub with narrow, pointed leaves and large clusters of 5-petaled, deep pink flowers from early to mid-summer.

☼ ◊ Z7–8 H8–7

Lavatera assurgentiflora

Semievergreen shrub with twisted, gray stems. Clusters of hollyhock-like, darkly veined, deep cerise blooms open in mid-summer. Palmate, mid-green leaves are white-haired beneath.

☼ ◊ H11–9

Robinia hispida (Rose acacia)

Deciduous shrub of loose habit with brittle, bristly stems that carry dark green leaves composed of 7–13 leaflets. Pendent racemes of deep rose-pink blooms open in late spring and early summer.

☼ ◊ ! Z6–11 H12–6

Melaleuca nesophila
(Western tea-myrtle)

Evergreen, bushy shrub or small tree with oval, gray-green leaves. Flowers, consisting of a brush of lavender to rose-pink stamens, are borne in rounded, terminal heads in summer.

☼ ◊ H11–6

Indigofera heterantha

Deciduous, slightly arching shrub. Has grayish-green leaves consisting of many small leaflets and spikes of small, purplish-pink flowers from early summer to early fall.

☼ ◊ Z6–9 H9–6

Neillia thibetica

Deciduous, arching shrub. Slender spikes of rose-pink flowers are borne profusely in late spring and early summer. Leaves are sharply toothed.

☼ ◊ Z6–9 H9–6

Hydrangea aspera Villosa Group

Deciduous, upright shrub with peeling bark. From late summer to mid-fall, produces heads of small, blue or purple, central flowers and larger, white, sometimes flushed purplish-pink, outer ones.

☼◐ ◊ Z7–9 H9–7

HYDRANGEAS

Valued for their late summer flowers, hydrangeas are versatile shrubs that thrive in a variety of situations. Larger-growing species, some of which may become treelike with age, are suited to light woodland, while the range of cultivars, mostly of *H. macrophylla*, make excellent border plants. Some may also be grown in containers. Colors range from white through pink, red, and purple to blue. The truest blue is obtained only on acidic soil. Lacecap hydrangeas have a central corymb of small, fertile flowers surrounded by showy, colored bracts; mopheads (or hortensias) have domed heads of sterile bracts only. *H. paniculata* cultivars bear larger though fewer cone-shaped flower heads if pruned hard in spring.

H. serrata 'Diadem'   *H. paniculata* PINKY-WINKY ('Dvppinky')

H. heteromalla 'Snowcap'

H. arborescens 'Annabelle' ⓘ

 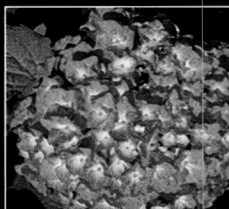

H. macrophylla 'Générale   *H. macrophylla* 'Altona' ⓘ
Vicomtesse de Vibraye' ⓘ

H. quercifolia 'Snowflake'

H. paniculata 'Big Ben'   *H. serrata* 'Kiyosumi'

H. macrophylla 'Madame Emile Mouillère'

H. macrophylla 'Hamburg' ⓘ

H. paniculata 'Phantom'

H. paniculata 'Silver Dollar'   *H. macrophylla* 'Lilacina' ⓘ

H. macrophylla 'Ami Pasquier'

H. macrophylla 'Ayesha'

H. macrophylla 'Europa'

H. macrophylla 'Möwe'

H. paniculata 'Dharuma'

H. serrata 'Bluebird' ⓘ

H. aspera 'Mauvette'

H. macrophylla 'Libelle'

H. macrophylla 'Blue Bonnet' ⓘ

H. serrata 'Grayswood'

H. paniculata PINK DIAMOND ('Interhydia') ⓘ

H. aspera subsp. *sargentiana*

H. paniculata 'Limelight'

PINK

Lavatera x clementii 'Rosea'
Semievergreen, erect shrub that produces abundant clusters of hollyhock-like, deep pink flowers throughout summer. Has lobed, sage-green leaves.

☀ ○ Z10–11 H12–3

Hibiscus syriacus 'Woodbridge'
Deciduous, upright shrub. From late summer to mid-fall large, reddish-pink flowers, with deeper-colored centers, appear amid lobed, dark green leaves.

☀ ○ Z5–9 H9–1

Kalmia latifolia
(Mountain laurel, calico bush)
Evergreen, bushy, dense shrub. In early summer large clusters of pink flowers open from distinctively crimped buds amid glossy, rich green foliage.

☀ ○ pH ① Z5–9 H9–5

RED

Paeonia delavayi (Tree peony)
Deciduous, upright, open, suckering shrub. Leaves are divided into pointed-oval leaflets, often with reddish stalks. Produces bowl-shaped, red, orange, yellow or white flowers, 2–2½in (5–6cm) across, with leafy bracts beneath, in late spring.

☀ ○ Z4–8 H8–1

Lonicera ledebourii
Deciduous, bushy shrub. Red-tinged, orange-yellow flowers are borne amid dark green foliage in late spring and early summer, and are followed by black fruits. As these ripen, deep red bracts enlarge around them.

☀ ○ ① Z5–9 H9–5

Erythrina x bidwillii
Deciduous, upright shrub with pale to mid-green leaves divided into 3 leaflets, up to 4in (10cm) long. Bright red flowers are carried in racemes in late summer or fall.

☀ ○ Z11 H11–6

SHRUBS

Pieris formosa var. forrestii 'Wakehurst'

Evergreen, bushy, dense shrub. Young leaves are brilliant red in early summer, becoming pink, creamy-yellow and finally dark green. Bears urn-shaped, white flowers in spring–summer.

   Z6–9 H9–6

Calycanthus occidentalis (California allspice)

Deciduous, bushy shrub. Leaves are large, aromatic and dark green. Fragrant, purplish-red flowers with many strap-shaped petals appear during summer.

 Z6–9 H9–6

Erythrina crista-galli (Cock's comb, Common coral tree)

Deciduous, mainly upright shrub or small tree. Leaves have 3 oval leaflets. Has leafy racemes of crimson flowers in summer–fall. Dies back to ground level in winter in cold areas.

  Z11 H11–8

Telopea speciosissima (Waratah)

Evergreen, erect, fairly bushy shrub with coarsely serrated leaves. Has tubular, red flowers in dense, globose heads, surrounded by bright red bracts, in spring–summer.

 Z10–15 H12–10

Melaleuca elliptica (Granite bottlebrush)

Evergreen, rounded shrub with long, leathery, usually grayish-green leaves. Flowers, consisting of a brush of red stamens, are borne in dense, terminal spikes in spring–summer.

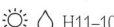 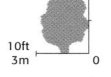 H11–10

Camellia japonica 'Mathotiana'

Evergreen, spreading shrub with lance-shaped to oval, slightly twisted, dark green leaves. Very large, formal double, velvety, dark crimson flowers become purplish with age and in warm climates often have rose-form centers.

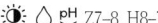 Z7–8 H8–7

Berberis thunbergii 'Rose Glow'

Vigorous, deciduous, dense shrub with spines. Broadly oval leaves are rich red-purple mottled with pink and cream, when young, maturing to burgundy-red in fall. Has small, red-tinged, yellow flowers in spring

 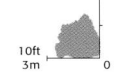 Z5–8 H8–5

Abutilon 'Ashford Red'

Strong-growing, evergreen, erect to spreading shrub with maple- to heart-shaped, serrated, pale to mid-green leaves. Pendent, bell-shaped, crimson flowers are borne from spring to fall.

 Z9–10 H10–1

Callistemon rigidus (Stiff bottlebrush)

Evergreen, bushy, slightly arching shrub with long, narrow, sharply pointed, dark green leaves and dense spikes of deep red flowers in late spring and early summer.

 Z10–11 H11–10

SHRUBS

Acer palmatum 'Bloodgood'
Deciduous, bushy-headed shrub or small tree with deep reddish-purple leaves that turn brilliant red in fall. Small, reddish-purple flowers in mid-spring are often followed by decorative, winged, red fruits.

☼ ◊ Z6–8 H8–2

Abutilon x suntense 'Violetta'
Fast-growing, deciduous, upright, arching shrub that carries an abundance of large, bowl-shaped, deep violet flowers in late spring and early summer. Vinelike leaves are sharply toothed and dark green.

☼ ◊ Z12–15 H12–6

Prostanthera rotundifolia
(Round-leaved mint-bush)
Evergreen, bushy, rounded shrub with tiny, sweetly aromatic, deep green leaves and short, leafy racemes of bell-shaped, lavender to purple-blue flowers in late spring or summer.

☼ ◊ Z11 H11–5

Ceanothus impressus
Evergreen, bushy shrub. Spreading growth is covered with small, crinkled, dark green leaves. Deep blue flowers appear in small clusters from mid-spring to early summer.

☼ ◊ Z8–11 H11–8

Hibiscus syriacus 'Oiseau Bleu'
Deciduous, upright shrub that carries large, red-centered, lilac-blue flowers from late summer to mid-fall. Has lobed, deep green leaves.

☼ ◊ Z5–9 H9–1

Iochroma australe
Deciduous, erect to spreading shrub with ovate, dark green leaves and bell-shaped, white to blue-purple flowers, ¾in (2cm) long, borne from short spurs in early summer, followed by spherical, yellow-orange fruits, ⅝in (1.5cm) across.

☼ ◊ ❗ Z10–11 H11–5

Sophora davidii
Deciduous, bushy shrub with arching shoots. Produces short racemes of small, pealike, purple and white flowers in late spring and early summer. Gray-green leaves have many leaflets.

☼ ◊ ❗ Z6–9 H9–6

Ceanothus 'Autumnal Blue'
Fast-growing, evergreen, bushy shrub. Has glossy, bright green foliage and large panicles of pale to mid-blue flowers from late spring to fall.

☼ ◊ Z9–10 H10–9

Eleutherococcus sieboldianus
Deciduous, bushy, elegant shrub. Has glossy, bright green leaves, divided into 5 leaflets, and is armed with spines. Clusters of small, greenish flowers appear in early summer.

☼ ◊ Z4–8 H9–3

Ptelea trifoliata 'Aurea'
Deciduous, bushy, dense shrub or low tree. Leaves, consisting of 3 leaflets, are bright yellow when young, maturing to pale green. Bears racemes of greenish flowers in summer, followed by winged, green fruits.

☼ ◊ Z5–9 H9–5

Callistemon pallidus
Evergreen, arching shrub. Gray-green foliage is pink-tinged when young and in early summer is covered with dense spikes of creamy-yellow flowers that resemble bottlebrushes.

 ☀ ◊ Z10–11 H11–10

Bupleurum fruticosum
(Shrubby hare's ear)
Evergreen, bushy shrub with slender shoots. From mid-summer to early fall rounded heads of small, yellow flowers are borne amid glossy, dark bluish-green foliage.

 ☀ ◊ Z7–11 H11–7

Sambucus racemosa 'Plumosa Aurea'
Slow-growing, deciduous, bushy shrub with leaves made up of 5 oval leaflets, each deeply cut. Leaves are bronze when young maturing to golden-yellow in early summer. Star-shaped, yellow flowers in spring are followed by scarlet fruits.

☀◑ ◊ Z3–7 H7–1

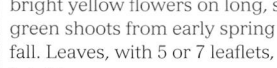

Jasminum humile (Yellow jasmine)
Evergreen, bushy shrub that bears bright yellow flowers on long, slender, green shoots from early spring to late fall. Leaves, with 5 or 7 leaflets, are bright green.

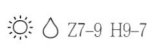 ☀ ◊ Z7–9 H9–7

Elaeagnus x ebbingei 'Limelight'
Evergreen, bushy, dense shrub with glossy, dark green leaves, silver beneath, centrally marked yellow and pale green. Bears small, fragrant, white flowers in fall.

 ☀ ◊ Z7–11 H11–1

Colutea arborescens (Bladder senna)
Fast-growing, deciduous, open shrub. Has pale green leaves with many leaflets, pealike, yellow flowers throughout summer, and bladder-like seed pods in late summer and fall.

 ☀ ◊ ❗ Z6–8 H8–6

SHRUBS

 139

SUMMER   **FALL**

YELLOW   **RED**

SHRUBS

Colutea x media
Vigorous, deciduous, open shrub. Gray-green leaves have many leaflets. Racemes of yellow flowers, tinged with copper-orange, appear in summer, followed by bladder-like, papery, red-tinged seed pods.

☀ ◊ ❗ Z6–8 H8–6

Ligustrum 'Vicaryi'
Semievergreen, bushy, dense shrub with broad, oval, golden-yellow leaves. Dense racemes of small, white flowers appear in mid-summer.

☀ ◊ ❗ Z4–8 H8–1

Spartium junceum (Spanish broom)
Deciduous, almost leafless, upright shrub that arches with age. Fragrant, pealike, golden-yellow flowers appear from early summer to early fall on dark green shoots.

☀ ◊ ❗ Z8–11 H12–8

Euonymus hamiltonianus subsp. sieboldianus 'Red Elf'
Deciduous, upright shrub with mid- to dark green foliage. Decorative, deep pink fruits, borne in profusion after tiny, green flowers in early summer, open in fall to reveal red seeds.

☀ ◊ ❗ Z6–8 H8–6

Euonymus europaeus 'Red Cascade'
Deciduous, bushy shrub or small tree with narrowly oval, mid-green leaves that redden in fall as red fruits open to show orange seeds. Has inconspicuous, greenish flowers in early summer.

☀ ◊ ❗ Z4–7 H7–1

Rhus glabra (Smooth sumac)
Deciduous, bushy shrub with bluish-white-bloomed, reddish-purple stems. Deep blue-green leaves turn red in fall. Bears panicles of greenish-red flower heads in summer followed by red fruits on female plants.

☀ ◊ Z2–8 H8–1

Euonymus latifolius
Deciduous, open shrub. Mid-green foliage turns brilliant red in late fall. At the same time large, deep red fruits with prominent wings open to reveal orange seeds.

☀ ◊ ❗ Z7–9 H9–7

Euonymus alatus
(Burning bush, winged spindle)
Deciduous, bushy, dense shrub with shoots that develop corky wings. Dark green leaves turn brilliant red in fall. Inconspicuous, greenish flowers in summer are followed by small, purple-red fruits.

☀ ◊ ❗ Z4–9 H9–1

Disanthus cercidifolius
Deciduous, rounded shrub with broadly
oval to almost circular, bluish-green
leaves that turn yellow, orange, red
or purple in fall. Has small, dark
red flowers in fall as the leaves
drop, or later.

 ☼◑ ◊ pH Z5–8 H8–5

Pyracantha 'Golden Charmer'
Evergreen, bushy, arching, spiny
shrub with glossy, bright green leaves.
Flattish clusters of white flowers in early
summer are succeeded by large, bright
orange berries in early fall.

 ☼ ◊ ! Z7–9 H9–7

Leonotis leonurus (Lion's ear)
Semievergreen, sparingly branched,
erect shrub. Has lance-shaped leaves
and whorls of tubular, bright orange
flowers in late fall and early winter.

 ☼ ◊ H11–6

Zanthoxylum simulans
Deciduous, bushy shrub or small tree
with sturdy spines. Aromatic, glossy,
bright green leaves consist of 5 leaflets.
Tiny, yellowish-green flowers in
late spring and early summer are
followed by orange-red fruits.

 ☼ ◊ Z6–9 H9–6

Clerodendrum bungei
Evergreen or deciduous, upright,
suckering shrub or subshrub with
heart-shaped, coarsely serrated leaves.
Has domed clusters of small, fragrant,
red-purple to deep pink flowers
in late summer and early fall.

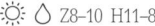 ☼ ◊ Z8–10 H11–8

Colquhounia coccinea
Evergreen or semievergreen, open
shrub. Has aromatic, sage-green leaves
and whorls of scarlet or orange flowers
in late summer and fall.

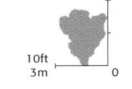 ☼ ◊ Z8–9 H9–8

Callicarpa bodinieri var. giraldii
(Beautyberry)
Deciduous, bushy shrub. Leaves
are pale green, often bronze-tinged
when young. Tiny, lilac flowers
in mid-summer are followed by
small, violet berries.

 ☼ ◊ Z5–8 H8–3

Berberis x carminea 'Barbarossa'
Semievergreen, arching shrub. Has
narrowly oval, dark green leaves and
racemes of rounded, yellow flowers in
late spring and early summer, followed
by globose, orange-scarlet fruits.

☼ ◊ ! Z6–9 H9–6

Cotoneaster sternianus
Evergreen or semievergreen, arching
shrub. Leaves are gray-green, white
beneath. Pink-tinged, white flowers
in early summer are followed
by orange-red fruits.

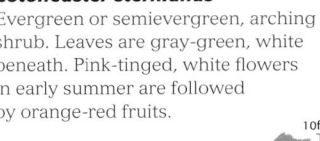
 ☼ ◊ ! Z7–9 H9–7

SHRUBS

141

SHRUBS FOR BERRIES

Most plants produce seeds in one form or another, but fruits and berries offer the best decorative value. Shrubs, in particular, offer a huge variety of berries in a range of colors, shapes, and sizes. Most appear from summer to late fall, with many enduring well into winter, brightening up the garden when color is in short supply, and providing an excellent source of nutrition for birds and wildlife. The most popular berried shrubs are cotoneaster, viburnum, and the snowberry (*Symphoricarpos*), with more unusual fruit produced by *Clerodendrum trichotomum* and *Decaisnea fargesii*, among others. Many of these plants are easy to grow, and will thrive in most soils, if given an annual application of all-purpose granular fertilizer in spring.

Cornus alba 'Sibirica Variegata'

Chaenomeles cathayensis

Poncirus trifoliata

Symphoricarpos albus var. *laevigatus* ①

Euonymus hamiltonianus subsp. *sieboldianus* ①

Cotoneaster frigidus

Daphne mezereum ①

Cotoneaster conspicuus

Cotoneaster salicifolius

Cotoneaster x watereri 'John Waterer'

Hippophae rhamnoides

Viburnum plicatum Pink Beauty' ①

Cornus sanguinea

Aronia arbutifolia

Viburnum betulifolium ①

Clerodendrum trichotomum

Euonymus hamiltonianus ①

Decaisnea fargesii

Symplocos paniculata

Sarcococca confusa

WHITE

Viburnum tinus 'Eve Price'
Evergreen, bushy, very compact shrub with oval, dark green leaves. In winter–spring, deep pink buds open into flattened heads of small, star-shaped, white flowers, which are followed by ovoid, blue fruits.

☼ ◊ ① Z8–10 H10–8

Viburnum farreri
Deciduous, upright shrub. In late fall and during mild periods in winter and early spring bears fragrant, white or pale pink flowers. Dark green foliage is bronze when young.

☼ ◊ ① Z6–8 H8–6

Rubus biflorus
Deciduous, upright shrub with chalky-white, young shoots in winter. Leaves, consisting of 5–7 oval leaflets, are dark green above, white beneath. White flowers in late spring and early summer are followed by edible, yellow fruits.

☼ ◊ Z6–9 H9–6

Rubus thibetanus
Deciduous, arching shrub with white-bloomed, brownish-purple, young shoots in winter and fernlike, glossy, dark green foliage, white beneath. Small, pink flowers from mid- to late summer are followed by black fruits.

☼ ◊ Z7–9 H9–7

Viburnum foetens
Deciduous, bushy shrub that has aromatic, dark green leaves. Dense clusters of pink buds open to very fragrant, white flowers from mid-winter to early spring.

☼ ◊ ① Z6–8 H8–6

PINK

Viburnum x bodnantense 'Dawn'
Deciduous, upright shrub with oval, bronze, young leaves that mature to dark green. Racemes of deep pink buds open to fragrant, pink flowers during mild periods from late fall to early spring.

☼ ◊ ① Z7–8 H8–7

Daphne bholua 'Jacqueline Postill'
Slow-growing, evergreen, upright, compact shrub with oval, leathery, deep green leaves. Masses of highly fragrant flowers, deep pink in bud opening to white, are borne in terminal clusters in late winter and early spring.

☼ ◊ ① Z7–9 H9–7

RED

Cornus alba 'Sibirica'
Deciduous, upright shrub with scarlet, young shoots in winter. Has dark green foliage and heads of creamy-white flowers in late spring and early summer, succeeded by rounded, white fruits.

☼ ◊ ① Z2–8 H8–1

Cotoneaster simonsii
Deciduous or semievergreen, upright shrub, suitable for hedging. Has oval, glossy, dark green leaves, shallowly cup-shaped, white flowers in early summer and long-lasting, orange-red fruits in fall.

☼ ◊ ① Z6–8 H8–6

Nandina domestica 'Fire Power'
Evergreen or semievergreen, elegant, bamboo-like, dwarf shrub. Leaves have dark green leaflets, purplish-red when young and in fall–winter. Bears small, white flowers in summer followed in warm areas by orange-red fruits.

☼ ◊ Z6–11 H11–4

SHRUBS

143

SHRUBS

YELLOW

Mahonia japonica
Evergreen, upright shrub with deep green leaves consisting of many spiny leaflets. Long, spreading sprays of fragrant, yellow flowers appear from late fall to spring, succeeded by purple-blue fruits.

☼ ◑ Z7–8 H8–7 10ft 3m

Jasminum nudiflorum
(Winter jasmine)
Deciduous, arching shrub with oval, dark green leaves. Bright yellow flowers appear on slender, leafless, green shoots in winter and early spring.

☼ ◑ Z6–9 H9–6 10ft 3m

Stachyurus praecox
Deciduous, spreading, open shrub with purplish-red shoots. Drooping spikes of pale greenish-yellow flowers open in late winter and early spring, before pointed, deep green leaves appear.

☼ ◑ pH Z6–8 H8–6 10ft 3m

Chimonanthus praecox (Wintersweet)
Deciduous, bushy shrub with oval, rough, glossy, dark green leaves. Bears very fragrant, many-petaled, cup-shaped, yellow flowers, with purple centers, on bare branches in mild periods during winter.

☼ ◑ Z7–9 H9–7 10ft 3m

Pyracantha 'Golden Dome'
Evergreen, rounded, very dense, spiny shrub. Dark green foliage sets off white flowers borne in early summer. These are followed by orange-yellow berries in early fall.

☼ ◑ ① Z7–9 H9–7 10ft 3m

WHITE

Euonymus japonicus 'Latifolius Albomarginatus'
Evergreen, upright, bushy and dense shrub with oval, dark green leaves broadly edged with white. Produces clusters of insignificant, greenish-white flowers in late spring.

☼ ◑ ① Z6–9 H9–1 10ft 3m

Euonymus fortunei 'Silver Queen'
Evergreen, bushy, sometimes scandent shrub with a dense growth of dark green leaves, broadly edged with white. Produces insignificant, greenish-white flowers in spring.

☼ ◑ ① Z5–9 H9–2 10ft 3m

Fatsia japonica 'Variegata'
Evergreen, rounded, bushy and dense shrub with palmate, glossy, dark green leaves, variegated marginally with creamy-white, and large sprays of small, white flowers in fall.

☼ ◑ Z8–10 H10–8 10ft 3m

GREEN

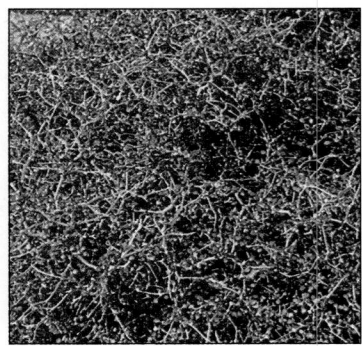

Corokia cotoneaster
(Wire-netting bush)
Evergreen, bushy, open shrub with interlacing shoots. Has small, spoon-shaped, dark green leaves, fragrant, yellow flowers in late spring and red fruits in fall.

☼ ◑ Z9–11 H11–10 10ft 3m

Arctostaphylos patula
Evergreen, rounded shrub with reddish-brown bark and bright gray-green foliage. Urn-shaped, white or pale pink flowers appear from mid- to late spring, followed by brown fruits.

☼ ◑ pH Z6–9 H9–6 10ft 3m

Buxus sempervirens 'Handsworthensis'
(Common boxwood)
Vigorous, evergreen, bushy, upright shrub or small tree. Has broad, very dark green leaves. A dense habit makes it ideal for hedging or screening.

☼ ◑ ① Z6–8 H8–6 10ft 3m

WHITE

Buxus balearica (Balearic boxwood)
Evergreen, treelike shrub suitable for hedging in mild areas. Has broadly oval, bright green leaves.

 ☼ ◊ ! Z7–9 H9–7

Melianthus major (Honeybush)
Evergreen, sprawling, shrub bearing blue-gray leaves, 25–45cm (10–18in) long, divided into 7–13 oval, toothed leaflets. Tubular, brownish-red flowers are produced in terminal spikes, 12in (30cm) long, in spring and summer.

 ☼ ◊ Z8–11 H11–8

Salix hastata 'Wehrhahnii'
Deciduous, upright-branched shrub with deep purple stems that contrast with silver-gray catkins borne in early spring before foliage appears. Stems later turn yellow. Has oval, bright green leaves.

 ☼ ◊ Z5–8 H8–5

Prunus glandulosa 'Alba Plena'
Deciduous, open shrub, with narrowly oval, mid-green leaves, bearing racemes of double, white flowers in late spring.

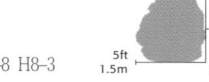 ☼ ◊ ! Z5–8 H8–3

Ledum groenlandicum (Labrador tea)
Evergreen, bushy shrub. Foliage is dark green and aromatic. Rounded heads of small, white flowers are carried from mid-spring to early summer.

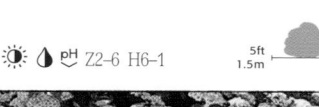 ☼ ◊ pH Z2–6 H6–1

Spiraea x vanhouttei (Bridal wreath)
Deciduous, compact shrub with slender, arching shoots. In late spring and early summer abundant, small, dense clusters of white flowers appear amid diamond-shaped, dark green leaves.

 ☼ ◊ Z4–8 H8–1

Deutzia gracilis
Deciduous, upright or spreading shrub. Massed, 5-petaled, pure white flowers are borne in upright clusters amid bright green foliage in late spring and early summer.

 ☼ ◊ Z5–8 H8–5

Prunus laurocerasus 'Zabeliana'
Evergreen, wide-spreading, open shrub. Leaves are very narrow and glossy, dark green. Spikes of white flowers in late spring are followed by cherry-like, red, then black, fruits.

 ☼ ◊ ! Z6–9 H9–6

Prunus laurocerasus 'Otto Luyken'
Evergreen, very dense shrub. Has upright, narrow, glossy, dark green leaves, spikes of white flowers in late spring, followed by cherry-like, red, then black, fruits.

 ☼ ◊ ! Z6–9 H9–6

Gaultheria x wisleyensis 'Wisley Pearl'
Evergreen, bushy, dense shrub with oval, deeply veined, dark green leaves. Bears small, white flowers in late spring and early summer, then purplish-red fruits.

 ☼ ◊ pH ! Z7–9 H9–7

SHRUBS

145

SHRUBS

WHITE

Viburnum x juddii
Deciduous, rounded, bushy shrub with dark green foliage. Rounded heads of very fragrant, pink-tinged, white flowers open from pink buds from mid- to late spring.

☀ ◊ ❗ Z5–9 H9–5

Viburnum carlesii
Deciduous, bushy, dense shrub with dark green leaves that redden in fall. Rounded heads of very fragrant, white and pink flowers, pink in bud, appear from mid- to late spring, followed by decorative, black fruits.

☀ ◊ ❗ Z5–8 H8–5

Chaenomeles speciosa 'Snow'
Slow-growing, deciduous shrub forming a dense framework of interlacing, spiny branches. Has oval, toothed, dark green leaves. Saucer-shaped, pure white flowers, 1½in (4cm) across, in spring are followed by spherical, edible, yellow fruits.

☀ ◊ Z5–9 H9–1

PINK

Deutzia x rosea
Deciduous, bushy, dense shrub. In late spring and early summer produces massed, broad clusters of 5-petaled, pale pink flowers. Leaves are oval and dark green.

☀ ◊ Z6–8 H8–6

Menziesia ciliicalyx var. purpurea
Deciduous, bushy shrub with bright green foliage and racemes of nodding, purplish-pink blooms in late spring and early summer.

☀ ◐ ◊ pH Z6–9 H9–6

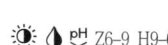

Daphne x burkwoodii 'Somerset'
Semievergreen, upright shrub that bears dense clusters of very fragrant, white and pink flowers in late spring, and sometimes again in fall. Leaves are lance-shaped and pale to mid-green.

☀ ◊ ❗ Z4–7 H7–1

RED

Daphne retusa
Evergreen, densely branched, rounded shrub clothed with leathery, glossy leaves notched at the tips. In late spring and early summer, deep purple buds open to very fragrant, pink-flushed, white flowers borne in terminal clusters.

☀ ◊ ❗ Z7–9 H9–7

Prunus tenella
Deciduous, bushy shrub with upright shoots and narrowly oval, glossy leaves. Shallowly cup-shaped, bright pink flowers appear from mid- to late spring.

☀ ◊ ❗ Z6–8 H8–6

Prunus x cistena
Slow-growing, deciduous, upright shrub with deep reddish-purple leaves, red when young. Small, pinkish-white flowers from mid- to late spring may be followed by purple fruits.

☀ ◊ ❗ Z3–8 H8–1

Cantua buxifolia
Evergreen, arching, bushy shrub. Has gray-green foliage and drooping clusters of bright red and magenta flowers from mid- to late spring.

☀ ◊ Z10–11 H11–10

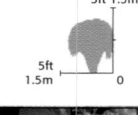

Ribes sanguineum 'Edward VII'
Deciduous, upright, compact shrub with rounded, 3–5-lobed, aromatic, dark green leaves. Small, tubular, reddish-pink flowers are borne, from mid- to late spring, and are sometimes followed by spherical, black fruits with a white bloom.

☀ ◊ Z6–8 H8–6

**Chaenomeles x superba
'Rowallane'** (Flowering quince)
Deciduous, low, spreading shrub.
Has glossy, dark green foliage and
bears a profusion of large, red flowers
during spring.

☼ ◊ Z5–9 H9–5

Salix lanata (Woolly willow)
Deciduous, bushy, dense shrub with
sturdy, woolly, gray shoots and broad,
silver-gray leaves. Large, yellowish-
green catkins appear in late spring
with foliage.

☼ ◊ Z3–5 H5–1

Salix repens (Creeping willow)
Deciduous, prostrate or semi-upright
and bushy shrub. Silky, gray catkins
become yellow from mid- to late spring,
before small, narrowly oval leaves,
which are gray-green above,
silvery beneath, appear.

☼ ◊ Z5–7 H7–5

**Chaenomeles x superba
'Nicoline'** (Flowering quince)
Deciduous, bushy, dense shrub.
Has glossy, dark green leaves and a
profusion of large, scarlet flowers in
spring, followed by yellow fruits.

☼ ◊ Z5–9 H9–5

**Euphorbia characias
subsp. _characias_**
Evergreen, upright shrub with clusters of
narrow, gray-green leaves. During spring
and early summer, bears dense spikes
of pale yellowish-green flowers
with deep purple centers.

☼ ◊ ! Z7–10 H10–7

Arctostaphylos 'Emerald Carpet'
Evergreen shrub that, with a low, dense
growth of oval, bright green leaves and
purple-red stems, makes excellent
groundcover. Bears small, urn-shaped,
white flowers in spring.

☼ ◊ pH Z6–9 H9–6

Daphne laureola subsp. **_philippi_**
Evergreen, dwarf shrub with oval, dark
green leaves. Slightly fragrant, tubular,
pale green flowers with short, spreading
lobes appear in late winter and early
spring, followed by black fruits.

☼ ◊ ! Z7–8 H8–7

Euphorbia characias subsp. _wulfenii_
Evergreen, upright shrub. Stems
are biennial, producing clustered,
gray-green leaves one year and
spikes of yellow-green blooms
the following spring.

☼ ◊ ! Z7–10 H10–7

SHRUBS

147

SHRUBS

YELLOW

Cytisus x praecox 'Warminster'
(Warminster broom)
Deciduous, densely branched shrub.
From mid- to late spring, pealike,
creamy-yellow flowers appear in
profusion amid tiny, silky, gray-
green leaves with 3 leaflets.

☀ ◊ ① Z6–9 H9–6

Mahonia aquifolium (Oregon grape)
Evergreen, open shrub. Leaves, with
glossy, bright green leaflets, often turn
red or purple in winter. Bunches of
small, yellow flowers in spring are
followed by blue-black berries.

☀ ◊ Z6–9 H9–6

Caragana arborescens 'Nana'
Deciduous, bushy, dwarf shrub with
mid-green leaves consisting of many
oval leaflets. Pealike, yellow flowers
are borne in late spring.

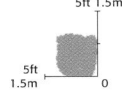

☀ ◊ Z2–8 H8–1

Cytisus x praecox 'Allgold'
(Allgold broom)
Deciduous, densely branched shrub
with silky, gray-green leaves, divided
into 3 leaflets, and a profusion of
pealike, yellow flowers from
mid- to late spring.

☀ ◊ ① Z6–9 H9–6

Ulex europaeus (Gorse)
Leafless or almost leafless, bushy shrub
with year-round, dark green shoots and
spines that make it appear evergreen.
Bears massed, fragrant, pealike,
yellow flowers in spring.

☀ ◊ pH ① Z6–8 H8–6

Berberis empetrifolia
Evergreen, arching, prickly shrub with
narrow, gray-green leaves, globose,
golden-yellow flowers in late spring
and black fruits in fall.

☀ ◊ ① Z7–9 H9–7

Genista tinctoria (Common woadwax,
Dyers' greenwood)
Deciduous, spreading, dwarf shrub
that bears dense spires of pealike,
golden-yellow flowers in spring
and summer. Leaves are narrow
and dark green.

☀ ◊ Z2–8 H8–1

Choisya ternata SUNDANCE **('Lich')**
Evergreen, rounded, dense shrub with
aromatic, glossy, bright yellow leaves
divided into 3 oblong leaflets. Fragrant,
star-shaped, white flowers are produced
in clusters in late spring and
often again in fall.

☀ ◊ Z8–10 H10–8

Deutzia monbeigii

Deciduous, arching, elegant shrub. Clusters of small, 5-petaled, white flowers appear in profusion among small, dark green leaves from early- to mid-summer.

☀ ◌ Z6–8 H8–6

Hebe 'White Gem'

Evergreen, rounded shrub that produces a dense mound of small, glossy leaves covered in early summer with tight racemes of small, white flowers.

☀ ◌ Z8–10 H10–8

Olearia phlogopappa var. subrepanda

Evergreen, upright, compact shrub. Heads of daisylike, white flowers are borne profusely from mid-spring to early summer amid narrow, toothed, gray-green leaves.

☀ ◌ H11–8

Rhodotypos scandens

Deciduous, upright or slightly arching shrub. In late spring and early summer, amid sharply toothed leaves, bears shallowly cupped, white flowers, followed by small, pea-shaped, black fruits.

☀ ◌ Z5–8 H8–5

Philadelphus 'Manteau d'Hermine'

Deciduous, bushy, compact shrub. Clusters of fragrant, double, creamy-white flowers appear amid small, pale to mid-green leaves from early to mid-summer.

☀ ◌ Z5–8 H8–5

Potentilla fruticosa 'Abbotswood'

Deciduous, bushy shrub. Large, pure white flowers are borne amid dark blue-green leaves, divided into 5 narrowly oval leaflets, throughout summer–fall.

☀ ◌ Z3–7 H7–1

Convolvulus cneorum

Evergreen, rounded, bushy, dense shrub. Pink-tinged buds opening to white flowers with yellow centers are borne from late spring to late summer among narrow, silky, silvery-green leaves.

☀ ◌ Z8–11 H11–8

Halimium umbellatum

Evergreen, upright shrub. Narrow, glossy, dark green leaves are white beneath. White flowers, centrally blotched with yellow, are produced in early summer from reddish buds.

☀ ◌ Z9–11 H11–9

Potentilla fruticosa 'Farrer's White'

Deciduous, bushy shrub with divided, gray-green leaves. Bears an abundance of white flowers during summer–fall.

☀ ◌ Z3–7 H7–1

x Halimiocistus sahucii

Evergreen, bushy, dense shrub with narrow, dark green leaves that set off an abundance of pure white flowers in late spring and early summer.

☀ ◌ Z7–9 H9–7

SHRUBS

149

SHRUBS

WHITE

Cistus salviifolius
Evergreen, bushy, dense shrub with slightly wrinkled, gray-green foliage. White flowers, with central, yellow blotches, appear in profusion during early summer.

☀ ◊ Z8–11 H11–8

Cistus x hybridus (Rock rose)
Evergreen, bushy, dense shrub. Has wrinkled, wavy-edged, dark green leaves and massed white flowers, with central, yellow blotches, carried in late spring and early summer.

☀ ◊ Z8–10 H8–1

Cistus x cyprius
Evergreen, bushy shrub with sticky shoots and narrow, glossy, dark green leaves. In early summer bears large, white flowers, with a red blotch at each petal base, that appear in succession for some weeks but last only a day.

☀ ◊ Z8–11 H11–8

Cassinia leptophylla subsp. *vauvilliersii*
Evergreen, upright shrub. Whitish shoots are covered with tiny, dark green leaves and heads of small, white flowers from mid- to late summer.

☀ ◊ Z8–9 H9–8

Cistus x aguilarii 'Maculatus'
Evergreen, bushy shrub with narrow, wavy-edged, slightly sticky, rich green leaves. Large, white flowers, with a central, deep red and yellow pattern, appear from early to mid-summer.

☀ ◊ Z9–11 H11–9

Cistus ladanifer
Evergreen, open, upright shrub. Leaves are narrow, dark green and sticky. Bears large, white flowers, with red markings around the central tuft of stamens, in profusion in early summer.

☀ ◊ Z7–10 H10–7

Rhaphiolepis umbellata
Evergreen, bushy shrub with rounded, leathery, dark green leaves and clusters of fragrant, white flowers in early summer.

☀ ◊ Z8–11 H11–8

Vaccinium corymbosum (Highbush blueberry)
Deciduous, upright, slightly arching shrub. Small, white or pinkish flowers in late spring and early summer are followed by sweet, edible, blue-black berries. Foliage turns red in fall.

☀ ◊ pH Z3–7 H7–1

Yucca whipplei
Evergreen, virtually stemless shrub that forms a dense tuft of slender, pointed, blue-green leaves. Very long panicles of fragrant, greenish-white flowers are produced in late spring and early summer.

 ☼ ○ Z7–9 H9–7

Viburnum acerifolium
Deciduous, upright-branched shrub with bright green leaves that turn orange, red and purple in fall. Decorative, red fruits, which turn purple-black, follow heads of creamy-white flowers in early summer.

 ☼ ○ ① Z4–8 H8–1

Yucca flaccida 'Ivory'
Evergreen, very short-stemmed shrub that produces tufts of narrow, dark green leaves and long panicles of bell-shaped, white flowers from mid- to late summer.

☼ ○ Z5–9 H9–5

Ozothamnus ledifolius
Evergreen, dense shrub. Yellow shoots are covered with small, aromatic leaves, glossy, dark green above, yellow beneath. Small, white flower heads are borne in early summer.

☼ ○ Z8–9 H9–8

Lomatia silaifolia
Evergreen, bushy shrub. Spikes of creamy-white flowers, each with 4 narrow, twisted petals, are borne amid deeply divided, dark green leaves from mid- to late summer.

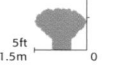 ☼ ○ pH Z11 H11–8

Hebe albicans
Evergreen shrub that forms a dense mound of blue-gray foliage covered with small, tight clusters of white flowers from early to mid-summer.

☼ ○ Z9–11 H11–9

Hebe recurva
Evergreen, open, spreading shrub. Leaves are narrow, curved and blue-gray. Small spikes of white flowers appear from mid- to late summer.

☼ ○ Z9–11 H11–9

Leptospermum rupestre
Evergreen, semiprostrate, widely arching shrub with reddish shoots and small, dark green leaves that turn bronze-purple in winter. Small, open cup-shaped, white flowers, red-flushed in bud, appear in early summer.

 ☼ ○ H11–10

SHRUBS

Deutzia 'Mont Rose'
Deciduous, bushy shrub that produces clusters of pink or pinkish-purple flowers, in early summer, with yellow anthers and occasionally white markings. Leaves are sharply toothed and dark green.

 Z6–8 H8–6

Weigela florida 'Variegata'
Deciduous, bushy, dense shrub. Carries a profusion of funnel-shaped, pink flowers in late spring and early summer, and has mid-green leaves broadly edged with creamy-white.

 Z5–8 H8–4

Fuchsia 'Lady Thumb'
Deciduous, upright, dwarf shrub bearing small, semidouble flowers with reddish-pink tubes and sepals, and pink-veined, white petals. May be trained as a miniature standard.

 Z9–11 H11–9

Indigofera dielsiana
Deciduous, upright, open shrub. Dark green leaves consist of 7–11 oval leaflets. Slender, erect spikes of pale pink flowers are borne from early summer to early fall.

 Z6–9 H9–6

Coprosma x kirkii 'Variegata'
Evergreen, densely branched shrub, prostrate when young, later semierect. White-margined leaves are borne singly or in small clusters. Tiny, translucent, white fruits appear in fall on female plants if both sexes are grown.

 Z8–10 H10–8

Hebe hulkeana 'Lilac Hint'
Evergreen, upright, open-branched shrub with toothed, glossy, pale green leaves. A profusion of small, pale lilac flowers appears in large racemes in late spring and early summer.

 Z9–11 H11–10

Cistus x skanbergii
Evergreen, bushy shrub. A profusion of pale pink flowers appears amid narrow, gray-green leaves from early to mid-summer.

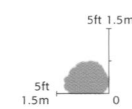 Z9–11 H11–9

Phlomis italica
Evergreen, upright shrub. In mid-summer, whorls of lilac-pink flowers are borne at the ends of shoots amid narrow, woolly, gray-green leaves.

 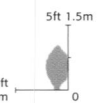 Z9–11 H11–9

Deutzia x elegantissima 'Rosealind'
Deciduous, rounded, bushy, dense shrub that produces clusters of 5-petaled, deep pink flowers from late spring to early summer.

☼ ◊ Z6–8 H8–6

Cistus x argenteus 'Peggy Sammons'
Evergreen, bushy shrub with oval, gray-green leaves. Saucer-shaped, pale purplish-pink flowers are produced freely during early summer.

☼ ◊ Z9–11 H11–9

Weigela florida 'Foliis Purpureis'
Deciduous, low, bushy shrub that bears funnel-shaped flowers, deep pink outside, pale pink to white inside, in late spring and early summer. Leaves are dull purple or purplish-green.

☼ ◊ Z5–8 H8–4

Penstemon isophyllus
Slightly untidy, deciduous shrub or subshrub that, from mid- to late summer, carries long sprays of large, white- and red-throated, deep pink flowers above spear-shaped, glossy, mid-green leaves.

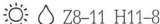
☼ ◊ Z8–11 H11–8

Hebe 'Great Orme'
Evergreen, rounded, open shrub. Has deep purplish shoots and glossy, dark green foliage. Slender spikes of deep pink flowers that fade to white are produced from mid-summer to mid-fall.

☼ ◊ Z9–11 H11–9

Spiraea japonica 'Little Princess'
Slow-growing, deciduous, mound-forming shrub that produces copious small heads of rose-pink blooms from mid- to late summer. Small, dark green leaves are bronze when young.

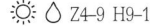
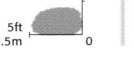
☼ ◊ Z4–9 H9–1

Ceanothus 'Perle Rose'
Deciduous, bushy shrub that from mid-summer to early fall bears dense racemes of bright carmine-pink flowers amid broad, oval, mid-green leaves.

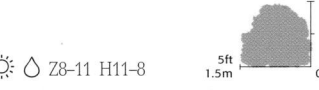
☼ ◊ Z8–11 H11–8

Abelia 'Edward Goucher'
Deciduous or semievergreen, arching shrub. Oval, bright green leaves are bronze when young. Bears a profusion of lilac-pink flowers from mid-summer to fall.

☼ ◊ Z7–9 H9–1

HARDY FUCHSIAS

With their vivid blooms and long flowering season, hardy fuchsias are outstanding garden shrubs. They flower throughout the summer months, producing an abundance of vibrant, pendent, single to double flowers, with flared or elegantly recurved sepals. These range in color from deep red and purple to soft pink and pure white, and are often bicolored. Unlike tender varieties (see p.302), hardy fuchsias can be grown outside down to Zone 7 in full sun or partial shade. They require moist, well-drained soil, and can be grown in large containers.

F. 'Madame Cornélissen'

F. magellanica

F. 'Riccartonii'

F. 'Rufus'

F. magellanica var. *gracilis*

F. 'Mrs Popple'

F. 'Corallina'

F. magellanica 'Thompsonii'

F. 'Howlett's Hardy'

F. 'Tom Thumb'

PINK

Abelia schumannii
Deciduous, arching shrub. Pointed, mid-green leaves are bronze when young. Yellow-blotched, rose-purple and white flowers appear from mid-summer to mid-fall.

☼ ◊ Z7–9 H9–1   5ft 1.5m / 5ft 1.5m / 0

Spiraea japonica 'Anthony Waterer'
Deciduous, upright, compact shrub. Red, young foliage matures to dark green. Heads of crimson-pink blooms appear from mid- to late summer.

☼ ◊ Z4–9 H9–1   5ft 1.5m / 5ft 1.5m / 0

Cistus creticus (Rock rose)
Evergreen, bushy shrub. Pink or purplish-pink flowers, each with a central, yellow blotch, appear amid gray-green leaves from early to mid-summer.

☼ ◊ Z9–10 H10–9   5ft 1.5m / 5ft 1.5m / 0

Escallonia 'Donard Beauty'
Evergreen, arching shrub with slender shoots. Deep pink flowers are produced from early to mid-summer among small, oval, dark green leaves.

☼ ◊ Z8–9 H9–8   5ft 1.5m / 5ft 1.5m / 0

Desmodium elegans
Deciduous, upright subshrub. Mid-green leaves consist of 3 large leaflets. Large racemes of pale lilac to deep pink flowers appear from late summer to mid-fall.

☼ ◊ Z8–11 H11–8    5ft 1.5m / 5ft 1.5m / 0

Gaultheria shallon (Shallon)
Evergreen, bushy shrub. Red shoots carry broad, sharply pointed, dark green leaves. Racemes of urn-shaped, pink flowers in late spring and early summer are followed by purple berries.

☼ ◑ pH ① Z6–8 H8–6    5ft 1.5m / 5ft 1.5m / 0

154

SALVIAS

Salvia is a vast genus of 900 species of mainly tender subshrubs or herbaceous perennials from North, Central, and South America and Africa. Most species have aromatic leaves and the foliage of common sage, *Salvia officinalis*, has been cultivated for centuries for culinary and medicinal use. The flowers of shrubby salvias, which are primarily white, pink, or red, are hooded and borne in whorls along the stems in summer and early fall. Most species are quite tender and need winter protection in frost-prone areas, although common sage and its cultivars are very hardy. *S. microphylla* will also withstand a few degrees of frost, but the others featured here are conservatory plants. Grow garden salvias in free-draining soil and full sun.

S. x *jamensis* 'Sierra San Antonio'

S. x *jamensis* 'La Luna'

S. *officinalis* 'Tricolor'

S. *officinalis* 'Berggarten'

S. *microphylla* 'Pink Blush'   **S. *microphylla* 'Newby Hall'**

S. *officinalis*

S. x *jamensis* 'Hot Lips'

S. *microphylla* 'La Foux'   **S. *greggii* 'Icing Sugar'**    **S. *officinalis* 'Purpurascens'**

S. *microphylla* 'Kew Red'

SHRUBS

RED

Kalmia angustifolia f. rubra
Evergreen, bushy, mound-forming shrub with oval, dark green leaves and clusters of small, deep red flowers in early summer.

☼ ◗ pH ❶ Z7–8 H8–7

Escallonia rubra 'Woodside'
Evergreen, bushy, dense shrub. Has small, glossy, dark green leaves and short racemes of small tubular, crimson flowers in summer–fall.

☼ ◗ Z8–9 H9–8

Phygelius aequalis
Evergreen or semievergreen, upright subshrub. Clusters of tubular, pale red flowers with yellow throats appear from mid-summer to early fall. Leaves are oval and dark green.

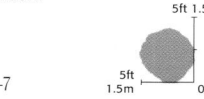

☼ ◗ Z7–9 H9–7

Potentilla fruticosa 'Red Ace'
Deciduous, spreading, bushy, dense shrub. Bright vermilion flowers, pale yellow on the backs of petals, are produced among mid-green leaves from late spring to mid-fall but fade quickly in full sun.

☼◑ ◗ Z3–7 H7–1

Salvia microphylla var. microphylla
Evergreen, well-branched, upright shrub with pale to mid-green leaves. Has tubular, bright red flowers from purple-tinted, green calyces in late summer and fall.

☼ ◗ Z12–15 H12–10

Spiraea japonica 'Goldflame'
Deciduous, upright, slightly arching shrub with orange-red, young leaves turning to bright yellow and finally pale green. Bears heads of deep rose-pink flowers from mid- to late summer.

☼ ◗ Z4–9 H9–1

Salvia fulgens
Evergreen, upright subshrub. Oval leaves are white and woolly beneath, hairy above. Racemes of tubular, 2-lipped, scarlet flowers appear in late summer.

☼ ◗ Z11–15 H12–9

Acer palmatum 'Dissectum Atropurpureum'
Deciduous shrub that forms a mound of deeply divided, bronze-red or purple foliage, which turns brilliant red, orange or yellow in fall. Has small, reddish-purple flowers in mid-spring.

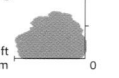

☼ ◗ Z6–8 H8–2

Hebe 'E.A. Bowles'
Evergreen, rounded, bushy shrub with narrow, glossy, pale green leaves and slender spikes of lilac flowers produced from mid-summer to late fall.

☼ ◊ Z10–11 H12–10

Hebe 'Autumn Glory'
Evergreen shrub that forms a mound of purplish-red shoots and rounded, deep green leaves, over which dense racemes of deep purple-blue flowers appear from mid-summer to early winter.

☼ ◊ Z9–10 H10–9

Hebe 'Purple Queen'
Evergreen, bushy, compact shrub with glossy, deep green leaves that are purple-tinged when young. Dense racemes of deep purple flowers appear from early summer to mid-fall.

☼ ◊ Z9–11 H11–9

Lavandula stoechas (French lavender)
Evergreen, bushy, dense shrub. Heads of tiny, fragrant, deep purple flowers, topped by rose-purple bracts, appear in late spring and summer. Mature leaves are silver-gray and aromatic.

☼ ◊ Z8–9 H9–8

Hebe 'Bowles's Variety'
Evergreen, rounded shrub with ovate-oblong, slightly glossy, mid-green leaves. In summer, bears mauve-blue flowers in compact, tapered, terminal racemes.

☼ ◊ Z10–11 H11–10

Caryopteris x *clandonensis* 'Arthur Simmonds'
Deciduous, bushy subshrub. Masses of blue to purplish-blue flowers appear amid narrowly oval, irregularly toothed, gray-green leaves from late summer to fall.

☼ ◊ Z6–9 H9–1

Hyssopus officinalis (Hyssop)
Semievergreen or deciduous, bushy shrub with aromatic, narrowly oval, deep green leaves. Small, blue flowers appear from mid-summer to early fall. Sometimes used as a culinary herb.

☼ ◊ Z6–9 H9–6

Felicia amelloides 'Santa Anita'
Evergreen, bushy, spreading shrub. Blue flower heads, with bright yellow centers, are borne on long stalks from late spring to fall among round to oval, bright green leaves.

☼ ◊ H11–9

Ceanothus 'Gloire de Versailles'
Vigorous, deciduous, bushy shrub. Has broad, oval, mid-green leaves and large racemes of pale blue flowers from mid-summer to early fall

☼ ◊ Z7–11 H11–7

Rosmarinus officinalis (Rosemary)
Evergreen, bushy, dense shrub with aromatic, narrow leaves. Small, purplish-blue to blue flowers appear from mid-spring to early summer and sometimes in fall. Used as a culinary herb.

☼ ◊ Z8–11 H12–8

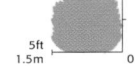

157

LAVENDERS

Lavandula is a popular genus of about 25 species of aromatic shrubs and herbs that originate predominantly from the Mediterranean region and northeast Africa, and thrive in hot, dry, sunny sites. Most have linear silver-gray foliage and produce erect spikes of fragrant flowers in shades of white, pink, blue, or purple, depending on the type. They are versatile plants, and can be used to edge borders, paths, and hard landscaping, or against a backdrop of stonework, as a dwarf hedge or informal divide, or in association with roses for a typical "English style" effect. They are also excellent plants for coastal areas, coping well with salt-laden maritime breezes, and thrive in well-drained soil; they will suffer if planted in shade or wet soil.

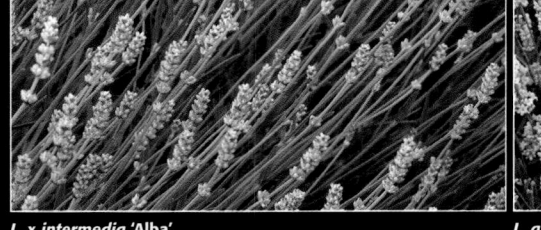

L. x intermedia 'Alba'

L. angustifolia LITTLE LOTTIE ('Clarmo')

L. stoechas 'Snowman'

L. angustifolia 'Miss Katherine'

L. 'Willow Vale'

L. angustifolia 'Wendy Carlile'

L. pedunculata subsp. *pedunculata* 'James Compton'

L. 'Fathead'

L. 'Regal Splendour'

L. stoechas f. *rosea* 'Kew Red'

L. 'Helmsdale'

L. angustifolia 'Little Lady'

L. angustifolia 'Imperial Gem'

L. x chaytorae 'Sawyers'

L. angustifolia 'Loddon Blue'

L. lanata

L. angustifolia 'Hidcote'

58

BLUE

Ceanothus thyrsiflorus var. repens
(Creeping blue blossom)

Evergreen, dense shrub that forms a mound of broad, glossy, dark green leaves. Racemes of blue flowers are borne in late spring and early summer.

 ☀ ◐ Z7–11 H10–3

Perovskia 'Blue Spire'

Deciduous, upright subshrub with gray-white stems. Profuse spikes of violet-blue flowers appear from late summer to mid fall above aromatic, deeply cut, gray-green leaves.

 ☀ ◐ Z6–8 H9–6

Ceratostigma willmottianum

Deciduous, open shrub. Has leaves that turn red in late fall and bright, rich blue flowers from late summer until well into fall.

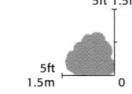 ☀ ◐ Z6–9 H9–6

YELLOW

Physocarpus opulifolius 'Dart's Gold'

Deciduous, compact shrub with peeling bark and oval, lobed, golden-yellow leaves. Produces clusters of shallowly cup-shaped, white or pale pink flowers in late spring.

☀ ◐ pH Z3–7 H7–1

Ruta graveolens 'Jackman's Blue'
(Common rue)

Evergreen, bushy, compact subshrub. Has aromatic, finely divided, blue foliage. In summer, clusters of small, mustard-yellow flowers are borne.

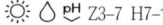 ☀ ◐ ① Z5–9 H9–5

Weigela middendorffiana

Deciduous, bushy, arching shrub. From mid-spring to early summer funnel-shaped, sulfur-yellow flowers, spotted with orange inside, are borne amid bright green foliage.

 ☀ ◐ Z5–7 H7–5

Potentilla fruticosa 'Vilmoriniana'

Deciduous, upright shrub that bears pale yellow or creamy-white flowers from late spring to mid fall. Leaves are silver-gray and divided into narrow leaflets.

☀ ◐ Z3–7 H7–1

Santolina pinnata
subsp. neapolitana 'Sulphurea'

Evergreen, rounded, bushy shrub with aromatic, deeply cut, feathery, gray-green foliage. Produces heads of pale primrose-yellow flowers in mid-summer.

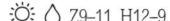 ☀ ◐ Z9–11 H12–9

Lupinus arboreus (Tree lupine)

Fast-growing, semievergreen, sprawling shrub that in early summer usually bears short spikes of fragrant, clear yellow flowers above hairy, pale green leaves composed of 6–9 leaflets.

  ☀ ◐ ① Z9–10 H10–9

SHRUBS

159

SHRUBS

Symphoricarpos orbiculatus 'Foliis Variegatis'

Deciduous, bushy, dense shrub with bright green leaves edged with yellow. Occasionally bears white or pink flowers in summer–fall.

☼ ◊ ① Z2–7 H7–1

Phygelius aequalis 'Yellow Trumpet'

Evergreen or semievergreen, upright subshrub. Bears clusters of pendent, tubular, pale creamy-yellow flowers from mid-summer to early fall.

☼ ◊ Z7–9 H9–7

Potentilla fruticosa 'Elizabeth'

Deciduous, bushy, dense shrub with small, deeply divided leaves and large, bright yellow flowers that appear from late spring to mid-fall.

☼ ◊ Z3–7 H7–1

Potentilla fruticosa 'Friedrichsenii'

Vigorous, deciduous, upright shrub. From late spring to mid fall pale yellow flowers are produced amid gray-green leaves.

☼ ◊ Z3–7 H7–1

Hypericum 'Hidcote'

Evergreen or semievergreen, bushy, dense shrub. Bears an abundance of large, golden-yellow flowers from mid-summer to early fall amid narrowly oval, dark green leaves.

☼ ◊ Z6–9 H9–6

Halimium 'Susan'

Evergreen, spreading shrub with narrow, oval, gray-green leaves. Numerous single or semidouble, bright yellow flowers with central, deep purple-red markings are borne in small clusters along branches in summer.

☼ ◊ Z9–11 H11–9

Phlomis fruticosa (Jerusalem sage)

Evergreen, spreading shrub with upright shoots. Whorls of deep golden-yellow flowers are produced amid sagelike, gray-green foliage from early to mid-summer.

☼ ◊ Z8–9 H9–8

Berberis thunbergii 'Aurea'

Deciduous, bushy, spiny shrub with small, golden-yellow leaves. Racemes of small, red-tinged, pale yellow flowers in mid-spring are followed by red berries in fall.

☼ ◊ ① Z5–8 H8–5

Cytisus nigricans

Deciduous, upright shrub with dark green leaves composed of 3 leaflets. Has a long-lasting display of tall, slender spires of yellow flowers during summer.

☼ ◊ ① Z6–8 H8–6

Genista hispanica (Spanish gorse)

Deciduous, bushy, very spiny shrub with few leaves. Bears dense clusters of golden-yellow flowers profusely in late spring and early summer.

☼ ◊ Z7–9 H9–7

Hypericum x inodorum 'Elstead'
Deciduous or semievergreen, upright shrub. Abundant, small, yellow flowers borne from mid-summer to early fall are followed by ornamental, orange-red fruits. Dark green leaves are aromatic when crushed.

☼ ◊ Z7–9 H9–7

Brachyglottis Dunedin Group
Evergreen, bushy shrub that forms a mound of silvery-gray, young leaves, later turning dark green. Bears bright yellow flower heads on felted shoots from early to mid-summer.

☼ ◊ Z9–10 H10–9

Hypericum calycinum (Aaron's beard)
Evergreen or semievergreen dwarf shrub that makes good groundcover. Has large, bright yellow flowers from mid-summer to mid-fall and dark green leaves.

☼ ◊ Z5–9 H9–4

Hypericum kouytchense
Deciduous or semievergreen, arching shrub. Golden-yellow flowers with conspicuous stamens are borne among foliage from mid-summer to early fall and followed by decorative, bronze-red fruit capsules.

☼ ◊ Z6–9 H9–6

Grindelia chiloensis
Mainly evergreen, bushy shrub with sticky stems. Sticky, lance-shaped, serrated leaves are up to 5in (12cm) long. Has large, daisylike, yellow flower heads in summer.

☼ ◊ Z11 H11–9

Brachyglottis monroi
Evergreen, bushy, dense shrub that makes an excellent windbreak in mild, coastal areas. Has small, wavy-edged, dark green leaves with white undersides. Bears heads of bright yellow flowers in mid-summer.

☼ ◊ Z9–10 H10–9

Coriaria terminalis var. xanthocarpa
Deciduous, arching subshrub. Leaves have oval leaflets and turn red in fall. Greenish flowers in late spring are followed by decorative, succulent, yellow fruits in late summer and fall.

☼ ◊ ❶ Z9–11 H11–1

Halimium lasianthum subsp. formosum
Evergreen, spreading, bushy shrub. Has gray-green foliage and golden-yellow flowers, with central, deep red blotches, borne in late spring and early summer.

☼ ◊ Z9–11 H11–9

SHRUBS

Cytisus scoparius f. *andreanus* (Scotch broom)

Deciduous, arching shrub with narrow, dark green leaves that are divided into 3 leaflets. Bears a profusion of bright yellow-and-red flowers along elegant, green branchlets in late spring and early summer.

 Z6–8 H8–6

Potentilla fruticosa 'Sunset'

Deciduous shrub, bushy at first, later arching. Deep orange flowers, fading in hot sun, appear from early summer to mid-fall. Mid-green leaves are divided into narrowly oval leaflets.

 Z3–7 H7–1

Abutilon 'Kentish Belle'

Semievergreen, arching shrub with purple shoots and deeply lobed, purple-veined, dark green leaves. Bears large, pendent, bell-shaped, orange-yellow and red flowers in summer–fall.

162    Z11 H11–9

Potentilla fruticosa 'Daydawn'

Deciduous, bushy, rather arching shrub. Creamy-yellow flowers, flushed with orange-pink, appear among divided, mid-green leaves from early summer to mid-fall.

Z3–7 H7–1

Cuphea cyanea

Evergreen, rounded subshrub with narrowly oval, sticky-haired leaves. Tubular flowers, orange-red, yellow and violet-blue, are carried in summer.

 H11–10

Mimulus aurantiacus

Evergreen, domed to rounded shrub with sticky, lance-shaped, glossy, rich green leaves. Has tubular, orange, yellow or red-purple flowers from late spring to fall.

Z7–11 H11–7

Myrica gale (Bog myrtle)

Deciduous, suckering shrub of dense habit. Produces narrowly oblong to rounded, highly aromatic, dark green leaves, with crinkled margins. Both male and female flowers, borne in mid- and late spring, are erect, golden brown catkins.

 Z1–6 H6–1

Berberis 'Rubrostilla'

Deciduous, arching shrub. Globose to cup-shaped, pale yellow flowers, appearing in early summer, are followed by a profusion of large, coral-red fruits. Gray-green leaves turn brilliant red in late fall.

Z7–9 H9–7

Viburnum opulus 'Compactum'

Deciduous, dense shrub. Has deep green leaves, red in fall, and profuse white flowers in spring and early summer, followed by bunches of bright red berries.

  Z3–8 H8–1

WHITE

Vaccinium parvifolium
Deciduous, upright shrub. Has small, dark green leaves that become bright red in fall. Edible, bright red fruits are produced after small, pinkish-white flowers borne in late spring and early summer.

☀ ◐ ◌ pH Z5–8 H8–5

Skimmia japonica 'Fructo Albo'
Evergreen, bushy, dense, dwarf shrub. Has aromatic, dark green leaves and dense clusters of small, white flowers from mid- to late spring, succeeded by white berries.

☀ ◐ ◌ (!) Z7–9 H9–7

SHRUBS

Vaccinium angustifolium var. laevifolium (Lowbush blueberry)
Deciduous, bushy shrub with bright green leaves that redden in fall. Edible, blue fruits follow white, sometimes pinkish, spring flowers.

☀ ◌ pH Z2–8 H8–1

Vaccinium corymbosum 'Pioneer'
Deciduous, upright, slightly arching shrub. Dark green leaves turn bright red in fall. Small, white or pinkish flowers in late spring are followed by sweet, edible, blue-black berries.

☀ ◌ pH Z3–7 H7–1

Fothergilla gardenii
Deciduous, bushy, dense shrub. Produces dense clusters of tiny, fragrant, white flowers from mid- to late spring, usually before broadly oval, dark blue-green leaves emerge. Leaves turn brilliant red in fall.

☀ ◌ pH Z4–8 H9–1

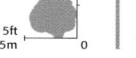

Gaultheria mucronata 'Wintertime'
Evergreen, bushy, dense shrub. Has prickly, glossy, dark green leaves and white flowers in late spring and early summer, followed by large, long-lasting, white berries.

☀ ◐ ◌ pH (!) Z8–9 H9–8

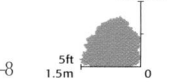

Lonicera x purpusii
Semievergreen, bushy, dense shrub with oval, dark green leaves. Small clusters of fragrant, short-tubed, white flowers, with spreading petal lobes and yellow anthers, appear in winter and early spring.

☀ ◌ (!) Z7–9 H9–7

SHRUBS

Sarcococca humilis
(Christmas box, sweet box)
Evergreen, low, clump-forming shrub. Tiny, fragrant, white flowers with pink anthers appear amid glossy, dark green foliage in late winter and are followed by spherical, black fruits.

☀ ◊ Z6–9 H9–6

Sarcococca hookeriana var. digyna
Evergreen, clump-forming, suckering, dense shrub with narrow, bright green leaves. Tiny, fragrant, white flowers, with pink anthers, open in winter and are followed by spherical, black fruits.

☀ ◊ Z6–9 H9–6

Vinca major 'Variegata'
(Greater periwinkle)
Evergreen, prostrate, arching, spreading subshrub. Has bright green leaves broadly edged with creamy-white and large, bright blue flowers borne from late spring to early fall.

☀ ◊ ! Z7–9 H9–7

Daphne odora 'Aureomarginata'
Evergreen, bushy shrub with glossy, dark green leaves narrowly edged with yellow. Clusters of very fragrant, deep purplish-pink and white flowers appear from mid-winter to early spring.

☀ ◊ ! Z7–9 H9–7

Gaultheria mucronata 'Mulberry Wine'
Evergreen, bushy, dense shrub with large, globose, magenta berries that mature to deep purple. These follow white flowers borne in spring–summer. Leaves are glossy, dark green.

☀ ◊ pH ! Z8–9 H9–8

Skimmia japonica 'Rubella'
Evergreen, upright, dense shrub with aromatic, red-rimmed, bright green foliage. Deep red flower buds in fall and winter open to dense clusters of small, white flowers in spring.

☀ ◊ ! Z7–9 H9–7

Correa pulchella
Evergreen, fairly bushy, slender-stemmed shrub with oval leaves. Small, pendent, tubular, rose-red flowers appear from summer to winter, and sometimes in other seasons.

☀ ◊ pH Z11 H11–10

Skimmia japonica subsp. reevesiana 'Robert Fortune'
Evergreen, bushy, rather weak-growing shrub with aromatic leaves. Small, white flowers in spring are followed by crimson berries.

☀ ◊ ! Z7–9 H9–7

Skimmia japonica
Evergreen, bushy, dense shrub. Has aromatic, mid- to dark green leaves and dense clusters of small, white flowers from mid- to late spring, followed on female plants by bright red fruits if plants of both sexes are grown.

☀ ◊ ! Z7–9 H9–7

Pittosporum tenuifolium 'Tom Thumb'
Evergreen, rounded, dense shrub with pale green, young leaves that contrast with deep reddish-brown, older foliage. Bears cup-shaped, purplish flowers in summer.

☀ ◊ Z9–11 H11–9

Ribes laurifolium

Evergreen, spreading shrub. Has leathery, deep green leaves and pendent racemes of greenish-yellow flowers in late winter and early spring. Produces edible, black berries on female plants if plants of both sexes are grown.

☀ ◊ Z7–9 H9–7

Vinca minor (Lesser periwinkle)

Evergreen, prostrate, spreading subshrub that forms extensive mats of small, glossy, dark green leaves. Bears small, purple, blue or white flowers, mainly from mid-spring to early summer.

◑ ◊ ⚠ Z4–9 H9–1

Artemisia abrotanum
(Southernwood, Old man)

Deciduous or semievergreen, moderately bushy shrub. Aromatic, gray-green leaves have many very slender lobes. Has clusters of small, yellowish flower heads in late summer.

☀ ◊ Z5–8 H8–5

Helichrysum petiolare 'Variegatum'

Evergreen shrub forming mounds of silver-green shoots and gray-felted leaves, variegated cream. Has creamy-yellow flower heads in summer. Often grown as an annual for groundcover and edging.

☀ ◊ Z10–11 H11–1

Viburnum davidii

Evergreen shrub that forms a dome of dark green foliage, over which heads of small, white flowers appear in late spring. If plants of both sexes are grown, female plants bear decorative, metallic-blue fruits.

☀ ◊ ⚠ Z7–9 H9–3

Chamaerops humilis
(Dwarf fan palm, European fan palm)

Slow-growing, evergreen palm, suckering with age. Fan-shaped leaves, 2–3ft (60–90cm) across, have green to gray-green lobes. Has tiny, yellow flowers in summer.

☀ ◊ H11–10

Hebe cupressoides

Evergreen, upright, dense shrub with cypress-like, gray-green foliage. On mature plants tiny, pale lilac flowers are borne from early to mid-summer.

☀ ◊ Z8–9 H9–8

Artemisia arborescens (Wormwood)

Evergreen, upright shrub, grown for its finely cut, silvery-white foliage. Heads of small, bright yellow flowers are borne in summer and early fall.

☀ ◊ Z5–9 H9–5

Ballota acetabulosa

Evergreen subshrub that forms a mound of rounded, gray-green leaves, felted beneath. Whorls of small, pink flowers open from mid- to late summer.

☀ ◊ Z8–9 H9–8

Vaccinium glaucoalbum

Evergreen shrub with deep green leaves that, when young, are pale green above, bluish-white beneath. Pink-tinged, white flowers in late spring and early summer are followed by white-bloomed, blue-black fruits.

◑ ◊ pH Z9–11 H12–10

Eurya emarginata

Slow-growing, evergreen, densely branched, rounded shrub with small, leathery, deep green leaves. Small, greenish-white flowers in late spring or summer are followed by tiny, purple-black berries.

☀ ◊ Z9–11 H11–10

SHRUBS

165

HEATHERS

As a group, heathers (or heaths) are remarkable in that species and cultivars are available to provide interest at all times of the year. Several are grown for their golden foliage, which often turns a deep burnt orange in winter, while others flower for a long period during summer, fall, or winter. Flowers come in a variety of hues, and are occasionally bicolored. In habit, heathers vary from tree-heaths of up to 20ft (6m) to dwarf, prostrate forms, many of which are excellent as groundcover. There are three genera: *Calluna*, *Daboecia*, and *Erica*. All *Calluna* and *Daboecia* cultivars and most *Erica* species must be grown in acidic soil, but otherwise heathers require little attention. Main seasons of interest are given for each plant.

E. arborea var. *alpina* [win–spr]

E. x *darleyensis* 'White Perfection' [win–spr]

E. ciliaris 'David McClintock' [sum]

E. carnea 'Springwood White' [win–spr]

E. carnea 'Challenger' [win–spr]

E. x *darleyensis* 'Furzey' [win–spr]

D. cantabrica 'Bicolor' [spr–fall]

E. erigena f. *alba* 'Brian Proudley' [win–spr]

E. vagans 'Birch Glow' [sum]

E. cinerea 'C.D. Eason' [sum]

E. vagans 'Mrs. D.F. Maxwell' [sum]

E. x *darleyensis* 'Arthur Johnson' [win–spr]

E. carnea 'Golden Starlet' [all year]

C. vulgaris 'Wickwar Flame' [all year]

E. vagans 'St. Keverne' [sum]

E. cinerea 'Eden Valley' [sum]

C. vulgaris 'Beoley Gold' [all year]

E. carnea 'Ann Sparkes' [win–spr]

E. erigena 'Irish Dusk' [win–spr]

C. vulgaris 'Dark Star' [sum–fall]

E. ciliaris 'Corfe Castle' [sum]

C. vulgaris 'Annemarie' [sum–fall]

C. vulgaris 'Peter Sparkes' [sum–fall]

C. vulgaris 'Tib' [sum]

Buxus microphylla 'Green Pillow'
Evergreen, compact, dwarf shrub, forming a dense, rounded mass of small, oval, dark green leaves. Bears insignificant flowers in late spring or early summer.

 Z6–9 H9–6

Buxus sempervirens 'Suffruticosa'
Evergreen, dwarf shrub that forms a tight, dense mass of oval, bright green leaves. Bears insignificant flowers in late spring or early summer. Trimmed to about 6in (15cm) is used for edging.

 Z6–8 H8–6

Leucothöe fontanesiana 'Rainbow'
Evergreen, arching shrub with sharply toothed, leathery, dark green leaves that age from pink- to cream-variegated. Racemes of white flowers open below shoots in spring.

 Z5–8 H8–3

Lonicera nitida 'Baggesen's Gold'
Evergreen, bushy shrub with long, arching shoots covered with tiny, bright yellow leaves. Insignificant, yellowish-green flowers in mid-spring are occasionally followed by mauve fruits.

 Z6–9 H9–5

Ruscus hypoglossum
Evergreen, clump-forming shrub with arching shoots. Pointed, glossy, bright green "leaves" are actually flattened shoots that bear tiny, yellow flowers in spring, followed by large, bright red berries.

 Z7–9 H9–7

Lonicera pileata
Evergreen, low, spreading, dense shrub with narrow, dark green leaves and tiny, short-tubed, creamy-white flowers in late spring, followed by violet-purple berries. Makes good groundcover.

 Z5–9 H9–5

Ruscus aculeatus (Butcher's broom)
Evergreen, erect, thicket-forming shrub with spine-tipped, glossy, dark green "leaves." Tiny, star-shaped, green flowers in spring are followed by large, spherical, bright red fruits.

 Z7–9 H9–7

Euonymus fortunei 'Emerald 'n' Gold'
Evergreen, bushy shrub with bright green leaves, margined with bright yellow and tinged with pink in winter.

 Z5–9 H9–2

SHRUBS

ROSES

These most romantic of flowers are unsurpassed in beauty and
fragrance, and many people consider them indispensable
features of the garden. With some 150 species and thousands
of cultivars, both ancient and modern, there is a rose to suit
almost any situation. They come from a wide range of habitats
throughout the Northern Hemisphere and, with a few exceptions,
most roses in cultivation are very hardy. They are also extremely
versatile, and can be grown among bulbs, perennials, and other
shrubs in a mixed border or in a more traditional formal rose
garden. Climbing and rambling roses can be trained over
arches, arbors, and pergolas, creating a blanket of scented
blooms and beautiful foliage; or, if you have a small garden,
you can plant a patio rose or two in a container.

ROSES

Prized for their beauty and fragrance, roses are considered the most romantic of flowers. They are indispensable in informal mixed planting schemes, and add an elegant note to formal parterres. With thousands of colors and forms to choose from, there is a rose for every garden.

Growing roses

With some 150 species and thousands of cultivars, both ancient and modern, there are members of the genus *Rosa* to suit an enormous number of garden situations. They come from a wide range of habitats throughout the Northern Hemisphere and, with few exceptions, most roses are very hardy. Many modern roses combine the best qualities of old roses, such as flower shape and scent, with disease resistance and extended flowering seasons.

When grown in a suitable site and soil, they will repay you with a profusion of blooms. All roses prefer an open, sunny site in fertile, humus-rich, moist but well-drained soil. However, avoid planting them in an area where roses have been grown before because the soil may be affected by "rose sickness," caused by a buildup of harmful soil organisms, and plants may fail to thrive. Roses also require a good supply of nutrients to perform well, and benefit from an annual application of all-purpose granular fertilizer in the spring.

Year-round interest

Although some roses, notably the climbers and species, bloom for a relatively short period, many hybrids are repeat-flowering, providing a colorful display throughout the summer. 'Frühlingsmorgen' offers the first flush of flowers in early summer, followed by the main flourish from mid-summer to the first frost. To help maintain this display, deadhead your roses regularly, as this redirects the plant's energy from seed formation to flower production. However, if you want attractive fruits (hips) in the fall, leave the blooms to fade. The best roses for hips include the Rugosa's tomato-like fruit, the flask-shaped, vibrant scarlet fruits of *R. moyesii*, and the rounded, black hips of *R. pimpinellifolia*.

Ornamental features

Roses embrace almost every color of the spectrum, apart from true blue, and some have a strong fragrance, such as the heady, sweet scent of the Damasks or musk and spicy fragrances of many modern roses. A few also have ornamental thorns, notably *R. sericea* subsp. *omeiensis* f. *pteracantha*, with large, triangular thorns that glow blood red when they are backlit.

Foliage can also provide interest. The soft gray-purple leaves of *R. glauca* and blue-green of the Alba roses provide attractive foils for crimson and purple flowers, while foliage textures, ranging from glossy to matt, and delicate fernlike to robustly wrinkled, as in *R. rugosa*, create beautiful contrasts.

Designing with roses

Roses have a diversity of habits, each of which can be used to create exciting designs. These include mound-forming groundcover roses, densely thorny Gallicas, and the arching Chinas and Damasks. A traditional rose garden laid out in a formal style with geometrically ordered beds is particularly suited to the upright growth of many bush roses.

ABOVE Container roses
Some roses have been bred specifically for containers, such as the patio rose REGENSBURG. Partner them with trailing annuals, such as *Sutera cordata* (syn. *Bacopa*).

LEFT Formal dressing
Here, a sturdy arch clothed with clematis and a vigorous, free-flowering rambler lends height to the scheme and forms a perfect frame to draw the eye to the sculpture used as a focal point.

Alliums, bearded irises, campanulas, and verbascums provide perfect companions to a profusion of scented roses in a pink-and-blue-themed summer border. Regular deadheading will prolong the show.

In contemporary schemes, shrub roses are often grown among bulbs, perennials, and other shrubs in a mixed border, but when designing these displays, make sure that neighboring plants do not compete directly for moisture and nutrients. Choose companions that are shallow-rooted, such as the many herbaceous geraniums and pinks (*Dianthus* cultivars), or space plants at a sufficient distance to allow for mulching and fertilizing around the rose's root zone.

Climbing and rambling roses can be trained on a wall as a colorful backdrop, or on a trellis to form a screen. In addition, they provide a cloak of flowers and foliage when grown on arches and over arbors, and make focal points on freestanding features like tripods and pyramids. Large rampant ramblers, such as *R.* 'Bobbie James' and *R.* 'Seagull', which both can achieve 30ft (10m) or more, will quickly scramble through a tree, offering a profusion of blooms just after most tree blossoms have faded.

Many climbing roses are available as weeping standards too. Tall cultivars of dense, thorny shrub roses, such as the Rugosa roses, also make decorative structural features. Use them to create large impenetrable boundary hedges that give privacy and security, or to divide up a garden into compartments. Vigorous groundcover roses are ideal for clothing sunny and inaccessible banks, since most require little regular pruning.

Not all roses will thrive in containers, but smaller patio roses such as *R.* ANNA FORD and *R.* REGENSBERG are a good choice, while dwarf trailing or spreading cultivars are suitable for hanging baskets.

PRUNING BUSH AND SHRUB ROSES

Modern hybrid tea and floribunda roses, which are commonly grown in gardens, need hard pruning in late winter or early spring to encourage the production of new flowering shoots. Shrub roses require a more gentle pruning regimen. Roses also benefit from a light pruning in fall to prevent stems from blowing in the wind and rocking the plant, which may result in root damage. Pruning in a methodical way has other horticultural advantages, helping to control attacks from fungal diseases such as black spot, to which roses are particularly susceptible, by removing infected wood. Before pruning, use a household disinfectant to clean your pruners, and apply it again before tackling each new plant to prevent the spread of disease. Also make sure your pruners are sharp, as clean cuts heal more quickly.

Pruning floribunda roses
Also known as cluster-flowered roses, floribundas produce flushes of blooms through summer and early fall. In early spring, remove dead, diseased, and crossing stems. Prune the other stems to outward-facing buds 8–12in (20–30cm) from the ground using sloping cuts. Aim to leave a framework of 8 to 10 strong, healthy stems.

Pruning hybrid tea roses
These are large-flowered roses, and include some varieties that repeat bloom, although they produce just one flower per stem. In late winter or early spring, cut the oldest stems to the ground, and shorten the remainder to 6in (15cm) from the base. Leave three to five strong young stems after pruning, and angle cuts to allow water to drain off the buds.

Pruning shrub and species roses
These usually flower once on wood made in previous years, so prune lightly in early spring. Remove dead, damaged, or diseased wood, and thin out congested growth to improve air flow. Also cut some of the oldest stems to the ground. Cut main stems back by a quarter and slightly reduce side shoots by an inch or two.

ROSES

ROSE CATEGORIES

Grown for the extraordinary beauty of their flowers, roses have been in cultivation for hundreds of years. They have been widely hybridized, producing a vast number of shrubs suitable for growing as specimen plants, in the border, as hedges, and as climbers for training on walls, arbors, and pillars. Roses are classified into three main groups:

SPECIES

Species, or wild, roses and **species hybrids**, which share most of the characteristics of the parent species, bear flowers generally in one flush in summer and hips in fall.

Old Garden roses

Alba—large, freely branching roses with clusters of flowers in mid-summer and abundant, grayish-green foliage.
Bourbon—open, remontant shrub roses that may be trained to climb. Flowers are borne, often 3 to a cluster, in summer–fall.
China—remontant shrubs with flowers borne singly or in clusters in summer–fall.
Damask—open shrubs bearing loose clusters of usually very fragrant flowers, mainly in summer.
Gallica—fairly dense shrubs producing richly colored flowers, often 3 to a cluster, in the summer months.
Hybrid Perpetual—vigorous, remontant shrubs with flowers borne singly or in 3s in summer–fall.
Moss—often lax shrubs with a furry, mosslike growth on stems and calyx, and flowers in summer.
Noisette—remontant climbing roses that bear large clusters of flowers, with a slight spicy fragrance, in summer–fall.
Portland—upright, rather dense, remontant shrubs bearing loose clusters of flowers in summer–fall.
Provence (Centifolia)—lax, thorny shrubs bearing scented flowers in summer.
Sempervirens—semievergreen climbing roses that bear numerous flowers in late summer.
Tea—remontant shrubs and climbers with elegant, pointed buds that open to loose flowers with a spicy fragrance.

Modern Garden roses

Shrub—a diverse group, illustrated here with the Old Garden roses because of their similar characteristics. Most are remontant and are larger than bush roses, with flowers borne singly or in sprays in summer and/or fall.
Large-flowered bush (Hybrid Tea)—remontant shrubs with large flowers borne in summer–fall.
Cluster-flowered bush (Floribunda)—remontant shrubs with usually large sprays of flowers in summer–fall.
Dwarf clustered-flowered bush (Patio)—neat, remontant shrubs with sprays of flowers borne in summer–fall.
Miniature bush—very small, remontant shrubs with sprays of tiny flowers in summer–fall.
Polyantha—tough, compact, remontant shrubs with many small flowers in summer–fall.
Groundcover—trailing and spreading roses, some flowering in summer only, others remontant, flowering in summer–fall.
Climbing—vigorous climbing roses, diverse in growth and flower, some flowering in summer only, others remontant, flowering in summer–fall.
Rambler—vigorous climbing roses with flexible stems that bear clusters of flowers mostly in summer.

FLOWER SHAPES

With the mass hybridization that has occurred in recent years, roses have been developed to produce plants with a wide variety of characteristics, in particular different forms of flowers, often with a strong fragrance. These flower types, illustrated below, give a general indication of the shape of the flower in its perfect state (which in some cases may be before it has opened fully). Growing conditions may affect the form of the flower. Flowers may be single (4–7 petals), semidouble (8–14 petals), double (15–30 petals), or fully double (over 30 petals).

Flat—open, usually single or semidouble flowers have petals that are almost flat.

Cupped—open, single to fully double flowers have petals curving outward gently from the center.

Pointed—elegant, "Hybrid Tea" shape; semidouble to fully double flowers have high, tight centers.

Urn-shaped—classic, curved, flat-topped, semidouble to fully double flowers are of "Hybrid Tea" type.

Rounded—usually double or fully double flowers have even-sized, overlapping petals that form a bowl-shaped or rounded outline.

Rosette—usually double or fully double flowers are rather flat with many confused, slightly overlapping petals of uneven size.

Quartered-rosette—rather flat, usually double or fully double flowers have confused petals of uneven size arranged in a quartered pattern.

Pompon—small, rounded, double or fully double flowers, usually borne in clusters, have masses of small petals.

R. 'Penelope'
Dense, bushy shrub rose with good disease resistance and plentiful, dark green foliage. Bears clusters of many scented, cupped, double, pink-cream flowers, 3in (8cm) across, in a single flush in summer. **H** and **S** 3ft (1m), more if lightly pruned.

☼ ◊ Z6–9 H9–6

R. 'Madame Hardy'
Vigorous, upright Damask rose with good disease resistance. Plentiful, leathery, matt leaves. Richly fragrant, quartered-rosette, fully double flowers, 4in (10cm) across, white with green eyes, are borne in a single flush in summer. **H** 5ft (1.5m), **S** 4ft (1.2m).

☼ ◊ Z4–9 H9–1

R. JACQUELINE DU PRE ('Harwanna')
Compact, bushy shrub rose with good disease resistance and repeat-flowering in summer–fall. Bears semidouble, red-stamened, white flowers, 10cm (4in) across, often with a pink blush and a strong musk perfume. Has glossy, dark green leaves. **H** 4ft (1.2m), **S** 3ft (1m).

☼ ◊ Z5–9 H9–5

R. 'Dupontii' (Snowbush rose)
Upright, bushy shrub rose with very good disease resistance and abundant, grayish foliage. Clusters of fragrant, flat, single, white flowers, tinged with blush-pink, 2½in (6cm) across, are borne in a single flush in summer. **H** and **S** 7ft (2.2m).

☼ ◊ Z5–9 H9–5

R. 'Nevada'
Dense, arching shrub rose with very good disease resistance and abundant, light green leaves. Scented, flat, semidouble, creamy-white flowers, 4in (10cm) across, are borne in a single flush in summer. **H** and **S** 7ft (2.2m).

☼ ◊ Z4–9 H9–1

R. 'Sally Holmes'
Bushy shrub rose with good disease resistance and prolific, glossy, deep green leaves. Substantial clusters of slightly scented, single, white flowers, 6in (15cm) across, with pink-peach buds, are borne in summer and again in fall. **H** 5ft (1.5m), **S** 4ft (1.2m).

☼ ◊ Z5–9 H9–3

R. 'Fantin-Latour'
Vigorous, shrubby Provence rose with good disease resistance. Flowers appear in a single flush in summer and are fragrant, cupped to flat, fully double, blush-pink, with neat, green button eyes, and 4in (10cm) across. Has broad, dark green leaves. **H** 5ft (1.5m), **S** 4ft (1.2m).

☼ ◊ Z4–9 H9–1

R. 'Great Maiden's Blush'
Vigorous, upright Alba rose with good disease resistance. Very fragrant, rosette, fully double, pinkish-white flowers, 3in (8cm) across, appear in a single flush in summer. **H** 6ft (2m), **S** 4½ft (1.3m).

☼ ◊ Z3–9 H9–1

R. 'Felicia'
Vigorous shrub rose with good disease resistance and abundant, healthy, grayish-green foliage. Scented, cupped, double flowers, 3in (8cm) across, are light pink, tinged with apricot, and are borne in a single flush in summer. **H** 5ft (1.5m), **S** 7ft (2.2m).

☼ ◊ Z6–9 H9–6

R. 'Céleste'
Vigorous, spreading, bushy Alba rose with good disease resistance. Fragrant, cupped, double, light pink flowers, 3in (8cm) across, appear in a single flush in summer. Makes a good hedge. **H** 5ft (1.5m), **S** 4ft (1.2m).

☼ ◊ Z3–9 H9–1

R. 'Marguerite Hilling'
Dense, arching shrub rose with good disease resistance. Many scented, flat, semidouble, rose-pink flowers, 4in (10cm) across, are borne in a single flush in summer. Has light green foliage. **H** and **S** 7ft (2.2m).

☼ ◊ Z4–9 H9–1

R. 'Reine Victoria'
Lax Bourbon rose with good disease resistance, slender stems and light green leaves. Sweetly scented, rosette, double flowers, 3in (8cm) across, in shades of pink, are borne in a single flush in summer. Grows well on a pillar. **H** 6ft (2m), **S** 4ft (1.2m).

☼ ◊ Z6–9 H9–6

PINK

R. ALISSAR PRINCESS OF PHOENICIA ('Harsidon')
Compact, upright, sturdy shrub rose with good disease resistance. Red leaves mature green. Slightly scented, flat, semidouble, dark-eyed, pink flowers, 4in (10cm) across, open summer and fall. **H** 4ft (1.2m), **S** 3ft (90cm).

☀ ◊ Z5–9 H9–5

R. x *odorata* 'Mutabilis'
Open species rose with coppery young foliage and good disease resistance. Bears shallowly cup-shaped, single, buff-yellow flowers, 2½in (6cm) across, in a single flush in summer, that age to coppery-pink or -crimson. **H** and **S** 3ft (1m), to 6ft (2m) against a wall.

☀ ◊ Z7–9 H9–7

R. 'Mrs. John Laing'
Bushy Hybrid Perpetual rose with good disease resistance and plentiful, light green foliage. Produces many richly fragrant, rounded, fully double, pink flowers, 5in (12cm) across, in a single flush in summer. **H** 3ft (1m), **S** 2½ft (80cm).

☀ ◊ Z5–9 H9–5

R. x *odorata* 'Pallida'
(Old blush china, Parson's pink china)
Bushy China rose with good disease resistance that may be trained as a climber on a sheltered wall. Cupped, double, pink flowers, 2½in (6cm) across, open in a single flush in summer. **H** 3ft (1m), **S** 2½ft (80cm) or more.

☀ ◊ Z7–9 H9–7

R. 'Complicata'
Very vigorous Gallica rose with good disease resistance and thorny, arching growth. Useful as a large hedge. Slightly fragrant, cupped, single flowers, 4½in (11cm) across, are pink with pale centers and appear in a single flush in summer. **H** 7ft (2.2m), **S** 8ft (2.5m).

☀ ◊ Z4–9 H9–1

R. CONSTANCE SPRY ('Austance')
Shrub rose of arching habit and good disease resistance that will climb if supported. Cupped, fully double, pink flowers, 5in (12cm) across, with a spicy scent, are borne in a single flush in summer. Leaves are large and plentiful. **H** 6ft (2m), **S** 5ft (1.5m).

☀ ◊ Z4–9 H9–1

R. STRAWBERRY HILL ('Ausrimini')
Bushy shrub rose with very good disease resistance. Has plentiful, glossy, mid-green leaves. Rosette, fully double, rich-pink flowers, 3in (7cm) across, with a strong myrrh scent, summer and fall. The flowers fade with age. **H** 5ft (1.5m), **S** 4ft (1.2m).

☀ ◊ Z5–9 H9–5

R. *gallica* var. *officinalis* 'Versicolor'
(Rosa mundi)
Neat, bushy Gallica rose with good disease resistance. In a single flush in summer produces striking, slightly scented, flat, semidouble flowers, 2in (5cm) across, very pale blush-pink with crimson stripes. **H** 2½ft (75cm), **S** 3ft (1m).

☀ ◊ Z3–9 H9–1

R. 'Madame Isaac Pereire'
Vigorous, arching Bourbon rose with good disease resistance. Fragrant, cupped to quartered-rosette, fully double flowers, 6in (15cm) across, are deep purplish-pink and are produced in a single flush in summer. **H** 7ft (2.2m), **S** 6ft (2m).

☀ ◊ Z6–9 H9–6

R. BENJAMIN BRITTEN ('Ausencart')
Willowy shrub rose with very good disease resistance, an open habit and large, matt-green leaves. Fully double, cupped, red flowers, 5in (12cm) across, with hints of scarlet and a strong fruity scent, open summer and fall. **H** 6ft (2m), **S** 5ft (1.5m).

☼ ◊ Z5–9 H9–5

R. CARDINAL HUME ('Harregale')
Bushy, spreading shrub rose with good disease resistance. Cupped, fully double, reddish-purple flowers, 3in (7.5cm) across, are borne in dense clusters in summer and again in fall, and have a musky scent. **H** and **S** 3ft (1m).

☼ ◊ Z5–9 H9–5

R. 'Cardinal de Richelieu'
Vigorous, compact Gallica rose with good disease resistance and plentiful, dark green foliage. Bears fragrant, rounded, fully double, deep burgundy-purple flowers, 3in (8cm) across, in a single flush in summer. **H** 4ft (1.2m), **S** 3ft (1m).

☼ ◊ Z3–9 H9–1

R. GERTRUDE JEKYLL ('Ausbord')
Upright shrub rose with good disease resistance and broad, matt, mid-green, well-spaced leaves. Plump, rounded buds open into rosette, fully double, deep pink flowers, 5in (12cm) across, with a rich sweet-myrrh scent, summer and fall. **H** 6ft (2m), **S** 4ft (1.2m).

☼ ◊ Z5–9 H9–1

R. RHAPSODY IN BLUE ('Frantasia')
Upright shrub rose with good disease resistance and large, light green leaves. Cupped, semidouble, purple flowers, 5in (12cm) across, with white eyes, yellow stamens and a pungent, spicy perfume, summer and fall. **H** 6ft (1.8m), **S** 4ft (1.2m).

☼ ◊ Z5–9 H9–5

R. 'Roseraie de l'Haÿ'
Vigorous, dense shrub rose with very good disease resistance. Bears many strongly scented, cupped to flat, double, reddish-purple flowers, 4½in (11cm) across, in summer and again in fall. Light green leaves are abundant. **H** 7ft (2.2m), **S** 6ft (2m).

☼ ◊ Z4–9 H9–1

R. 'Henri Martin'
Vigorous, upright Moss rose with good disease resistance. Rosette, double, purplish-crimson flowers, 3½in (9cm) across, appear in a single flush in summer and have a light scent and some furry, green "mossing" of the calyces underneath. **H** 5ft (1.5m), **S** 3ft (1m).

☼ ◊ Z4–9 H9–1

R. 'William Lobb'
Moss rose with good disease resistance and strong, arching, prickly stems. Will climb if supported. In a single flush in summer bears rosette, double, deep purplish-crimson flowers, 3½in (9cm) across, that fade to lilac-gray. **H** and **S** 6ft (2m).

☼ ◊ Z4–9 H9–1

HIPS AND THORNS

Roses have beautiful features that create interest for many months of the year. Although most are grown for their spectacular flowers, many also produce decorative hips that provide glowing fall and winter color, offer birds a valuable source of food, and paint a stunning picture in frost and snow. Fertilized flowers produce the hips, so avoid deadheading the blooms, as this will also remove the fruit. Thorns are another attractive feature on some species. For example, the winger thorn rose (*R. sericea* subsp. *omeiensis* f. *pteracantha*) has translucent thorns, while the fine prickly thorns of moss roses look furry, adding to their attraction. Prune these roses hard to ensure a supply of young, thorny wood.

R. roxburghii

R. multibracteata

R. sericea subsp. *omeiensis*
f. *pteracantha*

R. rubiginosa

R. glauca

R. rugosa

R. moyesii 'Geranium'

SHRUB AND OLD GARDEN ROSES

YELLOW

R. THE PILGRIM ('Auswalker')
Bushy shrub rose with very good disease resistance. Produces rosette, fully double, creamy-white flowers, 4in (10cm) across, with rich yellow centers and a strong, sweet perfume, in summer and again in fall. Has glossy, dark green leaves.
H 4ft (1.2m), **S** 3ft (1m).

☼ ◊ Z5–9 H9–5

R. TEASING GEORGIA ('Ausbaker')
Upright, lax, shrub rose with good disease resistance. Produces dark green leaves with a deep sheen. Slightly scented, rosette, fully double, pale yellow flowers, 5in (12cm) across, with deeper centers, open summer and fall.
H 6ft (1.8m), **S** 4ft (1.2m).

☼ ◊ Z5–9 H9–5

R. GRAHAM THOMAS ('Ausmas')
Vigorous, arching shrub rose with good disease resistance. Lax in habit, with glossy, bright green leaves. In summer, and again in fall, bears cupped, fully double, yellow flowers, 4½in (11cm) across, with some scent. **H** 4ft (1.2m), **S** 5ft (1.5m).

☼ ◊ Z5–9 H9–1

ORANGE

WHITE

R. 'Buff Beauty'
Dense, rounded Hybrid musk rose with good disease resistance. Masses of cupped, double, apricot-yellow to buff-yellow flowers, 3in (7cm) across, with a light musk scent, open in a single summer flush. Has glossy, mid-green leaves. **H** and **S** 4ft (1.2m).

☼ ◊ Z5–9 H10–6

R. EVELYN ('Aussaucer')
Slightly lax, arching shrub rose with good disease resistance and large, mid-green leaves. Bears strongly scented, rosette, fully double flowers, 5in (12cm) across, peach with hints of pastel pink and lemon, in summer and fall. **H** 5ft (1.5m). **S** 4ft (1.2m).

☼ ◊ Z5–9 H9–5

R. SUMMER SONG ('Austango')
Upright shrub rose with very good disease resistance and large, matt, mid-green leaves. Produces quartered-rosette, fully double, burnt-orange flowers, 4in (10cm) across, scented with traces of banana, summer and fall. **H** 5ft (1.5m), **S** 4ft (1.2m).

☼ ◊ Z5–9 H9–5

R. KENT ('Poulcov')
Dense groundcover rose with very good disease resistance and glossy, mid-green leaves. Produces large clusters of flat, semidouble, pure white flowers, 2in (5cm) across. Repeat-flowering, summer–fall. **H** 32in (80cm), **S** 36in (90cm).

☼ ◊ Z5–9 H9–5

R. ISN'T SHE LOVELY ('Diciluvit')
Upright Hybrid Tea rose with good disease resistance and semi-glossy, green leaves. Pointed, fully double, pale white-pink flowers, 4in (10cm) across, with creamy-peach centers and a fruity scent, are borne in summer and fall. **H** 3ft (1m), **S** 2ft (60cm).

☼ ◊ Z5–9 H9–5

R. CHAMPAGNE MOMENTS ('Korvanaber')
Vigorous Floribunda rose with very good disease resistance, repeat-flowering summer–fall. Produces clustered slightly scented, double flowers, 3in (7cm) across, cream to golden-amber. **H** 3ft (1m), **S** 32in (80cm).

☼ ◊ Z5–9 H9–5

R. ICEBERG ('Korbin')
Floribunda bush rose with moderate disease resistance, repeat-flowering summer–fall. Produces many sprays of cupped, fully double, white flowers, 3in (7cm) across. Has abundant, glossy leaves. **H** 30in (75cm), **S** 26in (65cm) or more.

☼ ◊ Z5–9 H9–5

R. MARGARET MERRIL ('Harkuly')
Upright, Floribunda bush rose with moderate disease resistance. Very fragrant, double, blush-white or white flowers, are well-formed, urn-shaped, 4in (10cm) across, and are borne singly or in clusters in summer and again in fall. **H** 3ft (1m), **S** 2ft (60cm).

☼ ◊ Z5–9 H9–5

R. SILVER ANNIVERSARY ('Poulari')
Vigorous Hybrid Tea rose with good disease resistance and slightly scented, pointed, double, almost pure white flowers, 5in (12cm) across, produced in summer and again in fall. Leaves are mid-green and semi-glossy. **H** 4ft (1.2m), **S** 32in (80cm).

☼ ◊ Z5–9 H9–5

ROSES

PINK

R. MAID OF HONOUR ('Jacwhink')
Bushy patio rose with very good
disease resistance. Produces dense,
small, glossy, leaves and abundant,
flat, single flowers, 1¼in (3cm) across,
with pink and white petals, and bright
yellow stamens. Repeat-flowering,
summer–fall. **H** and **S** 32in (80cm).

☼ ◊ Z5–9 H9–5

R. 'The Fairy'
Dense, cushion-forming, dwarf
cluster-flowered bush rose with good
disease resistance and abundant, small,
glossy leaves. Rosette, double, pink
flowers, 1in (2.5cm) across, are borne
freely in a single flush in summer.
H and **S** 24in (60cm).

☼ ◊ Z4–9 H9–5

R. PAUL SHIRVILLE ('Harqueterwife')
Spreading, Hybrid Tea bush rose with
moderate disease resistance. Bears
fragrant, pointed, fully double, rosy
salmon-pink flowers, 3½in (9cm) across,
in summer and again in fall. Leaves
are glossy, reddish and abundant.
H and **S** 30in (75cm).

☼ ◊ Z5–9 H9–5

R. 'Queen Elizabeth'
Upright, Floribunda bush rose with
moderate disease resistance. Bears
long-stemmed, fully double, pink
flowers, 4in (10cm) across, singly or
in clusters, summer and fall. Leaves
are large and leathery. **H** 5ft (1.5m),
S 2½ft (75cm) or more if not pruned hard.

☼ ◊ Z5–9 H9–5

R. MANY HAPPY RETURNS ('Harwanted')
Spreading Floribunda rose with good
disease resistance and semi-glossy,
light green leaves. In summer and fall
it bears big clusters of slightly fragrant,
cupped, semidouble, light pink flowers,
3in (7cm) across. **H** and **S** 32in (80cm).

☼ ◊ Z6–9 H9–1

R. APHRODITE ('Tanetidor')
Sturdy Floribunda rose with good
disease resistance and large, glossy,
dark green leaves. Slightly scented,
rounded, fully double, pale pink
flowers, 4in (10cm) across, with dense,
darker centers, open summer and fall.
H 3ft (1m), **S** 32in (80cm).

☼ ◊ Z5–9 H9–5

R. CHANDOS BEAUTY ('Harmisty')
Extremely vigorous Hybrid Tea rose
with good disease resistance. Produces
a strong, classic Tea-rose scent, from
pointed, fully double, light pink flowers,
5in (12cm) across. Has tough, glossy,
green leaves. Repeats summer–fall.
H 5ft (1.5m), **S** 3ft (1m).

☼ ◊ Z5–9 H9–5

R. SUSAN DANIEL ('Harlibra')
Vigorous Floribunda rose with very
good disease resistance and repeat-
flowering in summer–fall. Has glossy,
dark green leaves. Bears cupped, double,
apricot flowers, to 10cm (4in) across,
with creamy-white flashes. Scent is spicy
but mild. **H** 3ft (1m), **S** 32in (80cm).

☼ ◊ Z5–9 H9–5

R. SAVOY HOTEL ('Harvintage')
Spreading Hybrid Tea rose with good
disease resistance and matt, mid-green
leaves. Long-lasting, pointed, fully
double, pink flowers, 5in (12cm) across,
often with green on the outer petals,
open summer and fall. **H** 4ft (1.2m),
S 3ft (1m).

☼ ◊ Z5–9 H9–1

R. MEREDITH ('Wekmeredoc')
Sturdy Hybrid Tea rose with good
disease resistance. Pointed, double,
pale pink flowers, to 5in (12cm)
across, with a strong, sweet scent,
are produced summer and fall.
H 4ft (1.2m), **S** 32in (80cm).

☀ ◌ Z5–9 H9–5

R. GORDON'S COLLEGE ('Cocjabby')
Vigorous Floribunda rose with
good disease resistance and matt,
dark green leaves. Strongly scented,
urn-shaped, deep salmon-pink flowers,
4in (10cm) across, are borne in small
clusters in summer and again in fall.
H 4ft (1.2m), **S** 32in (80cm).

☀ ◌ Z5–9 H9–5

R. BELMONTE ('Harpearl')
Vigorous Floribunda rose with very
good resistance and large, semi-glossy,
mid-green leaves. Pointed, double,
pearl-pink flowers, darker in the center,
4in (10cm) across, with a strong, fruity
perfume, open summer and fall.
H 3½ft (1.1m), **S** 32in (80cm).

☀ ◌ Z5–9 H9–5

R. WARM WISHES ('Fryxotic')
Bushy Hybrid Tea rose with very good
disease resistance and matt, mid-green
leaves. Pointed, fully double, coral-pink
flowers, 4in (10cm) across, in summer
and again in fall, mature to rose-pink.
Floral scent is slight spice and myrrh.
H 3ft (1m), **S** 32in (80cm).

☀ ◌ Z5–9 H9–5

R. FLOWER CARPET ('Noatraum')
Spreading groundcover rose with
good disease resistance. Forms a dense,
prostrate mound of small, glossy, green
leaves. Cupped, semidouble, fuchsia-pink
flowers, 2in (5cm) across, are borne in
summer and again in fall. **H** 18in (45cm),
S 4ft (1.2m).

☀ ◌ Z5–9 H9–5

R. JOIE DE VIVRE ('Korfloci 01')
Compact, well-branched, bushy
Floribunda rose with very good disease
resistance and dense, mid-green leaves.
Scented, quartered-rosette, double, pink
to light apricot flowers, 4in (10cm) across,
open summer and fall. **H** 36in (90cm),
S 24in (60cm).

☀ ◌ Z5–9 H9–5

R. SWEET DREAM ('Fryminicot')
Bushy Patio rose with good disease
resistance. Produces slightly scented,
rounded, double flowers, 2in (5cm)
across, apricot-peach, summer and
fall. Has small, mid-green leaves.
Ideal in a pot or planter. **H** 18in (45cm),
S 12in (30cm).

☀ ◌ Z3–9 H9–1

R. NOSTALGIA ('Taneiglat')
Bushy Hybrid Tea rose with good
disease resistance and large, dark
green leaves. Pointed, fully double,
creamy-white flowers, 5in (12cm)
across, with pink-edged outer petals,
open summer and fall. The flowers
age to red. **H** 4ft (1.2m), **S** 32in (80cm).

☀ ◌ Z5–9 H9–5

R. CRAZY FOR YOU ('Wekroalt')
Sturdy, branching Floribunda rose with
good disease resistance and emerald
leaves. Summer and fall, produces
cupped, semidouble, cream flowers,
4in (10cm) across, splashed with cherry
flecks, and with a light, fruity perfume.
H 5ft (1.5m), **S** 3½ft (1.1m).

☀ ◌ Z5–9 H9–1

ROSES

R. DOUBLE DELIGHT ('Andeli')
Hybrid Tea bush rose of upright, uneven growth with good disease resistance. Fragrant, rounded, fully double flowers, 5in (12cm) across, are creamy-white, edged with red, and are borne in summer and again in fall.
H 3ft (1m), **S** 2ft (60cm).

☼ ◊ Z5–9 H9–5

R. ANNA FORD ('Harpiccolo')
Dwarf cluster-flowered bush rose with good disease resistance. Has urn-shaped (opening flat), double, orange-red flowers, 1½in (4cm) across, borne in summer and again in fall, and many small, dark green leaves.
H 18in (45cm), **S** 15in (38cm).

☼ ◊ Z5–9 H9–5

R. ROYAL WILLIAM ('Korzaun')
Vigorous, Hybrid Tea bush rose with good disease resistance and large, dark green leaves. Slightly scented, pointed, fully double, deep crimson flowers, 5in (12cm) across, are carried on long stems in summer and again in fall.
H 3ft (1m), **S** 2½ft (75cm).

☼ ◊ Z5–9 H9–5

R. SIMPLY SALLY ('Harpaint')
Rounded patio rose with very good disease resistance. Has numerous, small, matt, mid-green leaves. Slightly scented, flat, single flowers, 2in (5cm) across, open to pink with yellow centers. Repeat-flowering summer–fall.
H 32in (80cm), **S** 24in (60cm).

☼ ◊ Z5–9 H9–5

R. THE TIMES ROSE ('Korpeahn')
Spreading, Floribunda bush rose with good disease resistance. Slightly scented, cupped, double, deep crimson flowers, 3in (8cm) across, are borne in wide clusters in summer and again in fall. Foliage is dark green and plentiful.
H 24in (60cm), **S** 30in (75cm).

☼ ◊ Z5–9 H9–5

R. PINK PERFECTION ('Korpauvio')
Vigorous, bushy Hybrid Tea rose with very good disease resistance and glossy, mid-green leaves. Bears slightly scented, rounded, double, sugar-pink flowers, to 3in (7cm) across, with white veining and lighter reverses, in summer and again in fall. **H** 3ft (1m), **S** 32in (80cm).

☼ ◊ Z5–9 H9–5

R. ALEXANDER ('Harlex')
Vigorous, upright, Hybrid Tea bush rose with good disease resistance and abundant, dark green foliage. Slightly scented, pointed, double, bright red flowers, 5in (12cm) across, are borne on long stems in summer and again in fall. **H** 5ft (1.5m), **S** 2½ft (75cm).

☼ ◊ Z5–9 H9–5

R. CARRIS ('Harmanna')
Compact Hybrid Tea rose with very good disease resistance. Has a mass of glossy, mid-green leaves. Produces urn-shaped, bright scarlet flowers, to 5in (12cm) across, with a spicy myrrh scent. Repeat-flowering summer–fall.
H 3ft (1m), **S** 32in (80cm).

☼ ◊ Z5–9 H9–5

R. GEORGE BEST ('Dichimanher')
Bushy patio rose with very good disease resistance and small, matt, mid-green leaves. Slightly scented, urn-shaped, semidouble, deep red flowers, 2in (5cm) across, are borne in clusters in summer and fall. **H** and **S** 18in (45cm).

 ☼ ○ Z5–9 H9–5

R. RED FINESSE ('Korvillade')
Compact Floribunda rose with very good disease resistance and repeat-flowering in summer–fall. Produces abundant, glossy, dark green leaves and clusters of up to 15 cupped, double, dark red flowers, 3in (7cm) across. **H** 36in (90cm), **S** 24in (60cm).

☼ ○ Z5–9 H9–5

R. REMEMBRANCE ('Harxampton')
Well-branched Floribunda rose with good disease resistance and glossy leaves. Long-lasting, rounded, double, scarlet flowers, 3in (7cm) across, have darker outer petals, fading with age. Repeat-flowers summer–fall. **H** 32in (80cm), **S** 24in (60cm).

☼ ○ Z5–9 H9–5

R. GUY SAVOY ('Delstrimen')
Upright Floribunda rose with good disease resistance and glossy, dark green leaves. Produces cupped, semidouble white-striped, purple flowers, 3in (7cm) across, in large clusters. Repeat-flowering summer–fall. **H** 5ft (1.5m), **S** 3ft (1m).

☼ ○ Z5–9 H9–5

R. LOVING MEMORY ('Korgund')
Upright Hybrid Tea rose with good disease resistance and leathery, dark green leaves. Pointed, fully double, crimson flowers, 5in (12cm) across, are borne in summer and fall. Perfume is light but sweet. **H** 4ft (1.2m), **S** 32in (80cm).

 ☼ ○ Z5–9 H9–5

R. ALEC'S RED ('Cored')
Vigorous, Hybrid Tea bush rose with moderate disease resistance. Bears strongly fragrant, deep cherry-red flowers that are pointed and fully double, 6in (15cm) across, in summer and again in fall. **H** 36in (1m), **S** 24in (60cm).

☼ ○ Z5–9 H9–5

R. LANCASHIRE ('Korstesgli')
Ground-cover rose with good disease resistance and small, matt, dark green leaves. Cupped, semidouble, cherry-red flowers, 2in (5cm) across, fading to cerise, are produced in clusters of at least 7 in summer and again in fall. **H** 24in (60cm), **S** 36in (90cm).

☼ ○ Z5–9 H9–5

R. BURGUNDY ICE ('Prose')
Open Floribunda rose with good disease resistance and repeat-flowering in summer–fall. Has matt, light green leaves. Clusters of up to 7 cupped, double, mauve flowers, 3in (7cm) across, have pale mauve petal margins. **H** 4ft (1.2m), **S** 3ft (1m).

☼ ○ Z5–9 H9–5

ROSES

R. 'Arthur Bell'
Upright Floribunda rose with good disease resistance and large, glossy, mid-green leaves. Strongly scented, cupped, double, butter-yellow flowers, 3in (7cm) across, fading to creamy-white, are borne in summer and again in fall. **H** 3ft (1m), **S** 2ft (60cm).

☼ ◊ Z5–9 H9–1

R. EASY GOING ('Harglow')
Bushy Floribunda rose with good disease resistance and repeat-flowering in summer–fall. Has rich glossy, pale green leaves. Pointed buds open into cupped, double, deep amber flowers, 4in (10cm) across, with a moderately fruity scent. **H** 32in (80cm), **S** 24in (60cm).

☼ ◊ Z5–9 H9–5

R. GOLDEN BEAUTY ('Korberbeni')
Bushy Floribunda rose with very good disease resistance and glossy, mid-green leaves. In summer and in fall produces clusters of 3–5 slightly scented, rounded, fully double, golden-yellow flowers, 3in (8cm) across, deepening to amber-gold in centers. **H** 3ft (1m), **S** 30in (75cm).

☼ ◊ Z5–9 H9–5

R. GOLDEN MEMORIES ('Korholesea')
Bushy Floribunda rose with very good disease resistance and glossy, dark green leaves. In summer and fall, clusters of urn-shaped, fully double flowers, 3in (7.5cm) across, open wide to show stamens, deep yellow centers and paler yellow margins. **H** 3ft (1m), **S** 32in (80cm).

☼ ◊ Z5–9 H9–5

R. FREEDOM ('Dicjem')
Neat, large-flowered bush rose with good disease resistance, many shoots, and abundant, glossy foliage. Bears many lightly scented, rounded, double, bright yellow flowers, 3½in (9cm) across, in summer–fall. **H** 30in (75cm), **S** 24in (60cm).

☼ ◊ Z5–9 H9–5

R. MOUNTBATTEN ('Harmantelle')
Shrubby, cluster-flowered bush rose with good disease resistance. Bears scented, rounded, fully double, yellow flowers, 4in (10cm) across, singly or in clusters, in summer and again in fall. **H** 4ft (1.2m), **S** 30in (75cm).

☼ ◊ Z5–9 H9–5

R. PEACE ('Madame A. Meilland')
Vigorous, shrubby, large-flowered bush rose with moderate disease resistance. Scented, pointed to rounded, fully double flowers, 6in (15cm) across, are borne freely in clusters in summer and again in fall. Has abundant, large, glossy foliage. **H** 4ft (1.2m), **S** 3ft (1m).

☼ ◊ Z5–9 H9–5

R. JULIA CHILD ('Wekvossutono')
Vigorous Floribunda rose with very good disease resistance and repeat-flowering in summer–fall. Bears urn-shaped, yellow flowers, 4in (10cm) across, and glossy, green leaves. Scent has licorice overtones. **H** 3ft (1m), **S** 2ft (60cm).

☼ ◊ Z5–10 H9–5

R. GUY'S GOLD ('Harmatch')
Well-branched, bushy Hybrid Tea rose with very good disease resistance and repeat-flowering in summer–fall. Has glossy, mid-green leaves and masses of slightly scented, pointed, double, bright yellow flowers, 5in (12cm) across. **H** 32in (80cm), **S** 24in (60cm).

☼ ◊ Z5–9 H9–5

R. RACHEL ('Tangust')
Bushy Hybrid Tea rose with good disease resistance and large, mid-green leaves. Sweetly scented, rounded, fully double, orange-apricot flowers, 4in (10cm) across, in summer and again in fall, turn lighter with pink tones as they age. **H** 3ft (1m), **S** 24in (60cm).

☀ ◊ Z5–9 H9–5

R. 'Southampton'
Upright, cluster-flowered bush rose with very good disease resistance and glossy foliage. Bears fragrant, pointed, double, apricot flowers, 3in (8cm) across, singly or in clusters in summer and again in fall.
H 3ft (1m), **S** 24in (60cm).

☀ ◊ Z5–9 H9–5

R. SWEET MAGIC ('Dicmagic')
Branching, dwarf cluster-flowered bush rose with good disease resistance and repeat-flowering in summer–fall. Bears sprays of lightly fragrant, urn-shaped, double, pink-flushed, golden-orange flowers, 1½in (4cm) across. **H** 15in (38cm), **S** 12in (30cm).

☀ ◊ Z5–9 H9–5

R. REMEMBER ME ('Cocdestin')
Vigorous, dense, large-flowered bush rose with good disease resistance. Pointed, fully double, copper-orange flowers, 3½in (9cm) across, are borne freely in summer and again in fall. Leaves are abundant and glossy.
H 3ft (1m), **S** 2½ft (75cm).

☀ ◊ Z5–9 H9–5

R. EASY DOES IT ('Harpagent')
Compact Floribunda rose with very good disease resistance and repeat-flowering in summer–fall. Has matt, mid-green leaves. Produces spicy-scented, cupped, burnt-tangerine flowers, 4in (10cm) across, fading to pink. Many petals have wavy margins. **H** 3ft (1m), **S** 24in (60cm).

☀ ◊ Z5–9 H9–5

R. FELLOWSHIP ('Harwelcome')
Bushy Floribunda rose with good disease resistance and repeat-flowering in summer–fall. Has large, glossy, green leaves. Spicy-scented, cupped, double flowers, 4in (10cm) across, have orange outer petals, lightening inward to tangerine. **H** 30in (75cm), **S** 24in (60cm).

☀ ◊ Z5–9 H9–5

R. 'Just Joey'
Branching, open, large-flowered bush rose with good disease resistance and repeat-flowering in summer–fall. Bears rounded, fully double flowers, 5in (12cm) across, with waved, copper-pink petals and some scent. Has leathery, dark green leaves. **H** 30in (75cm), **S** 24in (60cm).

☀ ◊ Z5–7 H7–5

R. SIMPLY THE BEST ('Macamster')
Bushy Hybrid Tea rose with good disease resistance and dark green leaves. In summer and again in fall produces abundant, scented, urn-shaped, double, light orange flowers, 4in (10cm) across. Coloring lightens as it ages.
H 4ft (1.2m), **S** 32in (80cm).

☀ ◊ Z5–9 H9–5

R. SUPER TROOPER ('Fryleyeca')
Bushy Floribunda rose with very good disease resistance and lush, dark green leaves. Scented, pointed, double, bright orange flowers, flashed yellow beneath, open in small clusters, 4in (10cm) across, in summer and fall.
H 3ft (1m), **S** 32in (80cm).

☀ ◊ Z5–9 H9–5

ROSES

WHITE

R. 'Albéric Barbier'
Vigorous, semievergreen rambler
rose with very good disease resistance.
Clusters of slightly fragrant, rosette,
fully double, creamy-white flowers,
3in (8cm) across, appear in a single flush
in summer. Leaves are small and bright
green. **H** to 15ft (5m), **S** 10ft (3m).

☼ ◊ Z5–9 H9–7

R. 'Paul's Lemon Pillar'
Stiff, upright climbing rose with
good disease resistance and large,
dark green leaves. Scented, pointed
to rounded, fully double, lemon-white
flowers, 6in (15cm) across, appear in a
single flush in summer. Prefers a sunny,
sheltered wall. **H** 15ft (5m), **S** 10ft (3m).

☼ ◊ Z5–9 H9–5

R. filipes 'Kiftsgate'
Rampant climbing rose with very good
disease resistance and abundant, glossy,
light green foliage. Clusters of cupped
to flat, single, creamy-white flowers, 1in
(2.5cm) across, appear in a single flush
in summer. Use to grow up a tree or in a
wild garden. **H** and **S** 30ft (10m) or more.

☼ ◊ Z6–9 H9–6

R. 'Félicité Perpétue'
Sempervirens climbing rose with
long, slender stems. Clusters of rosette,
fully double, blush-pink to white
flowers, 1½in (4cm) across, appear
in mid-summer. Small leaves are
semievergreen. Prune spent wood
only. **H** 15ft (5m), **S** 12ft (4m).

☼ ◊ Z6–9 H9–6

R. 'Madame Alfred Carrière'
Noisette climbing rose with good
disease resistance and slender, smooth
stems. Very fragrant, rounded, double
flowers are creamy-white, tinged pink,
1½in (4cm) across, and are borne in a
single flush in summer. **H** to 18ft (5.5m),
S 10ft (3m).

☼ ◊ Z5–9 H9–5

R. 'Gloire de Dijon'
Stiffly branched Noisette or climbing
Tea rose with good disease resistance.
Fragrant, quartered-rosette, fully double,
creamy-buff flowers, 4in (10cm) across,
are borne in a single flush in summer.
H 12ft (4m), **S** 8ft (2.5m).

☼ ◊ Z5–9 H9–5

R. WHITE STAR ('Harquill')
Climber with very good disease
resistance and repeat-flowering in
summer–fall. Glossy, dark green leaves
are lighter when young. Slightly scented,
flat, semidouble, pure white flowers,
4in (10cm) across, have bright yellow
stamens. **H** 8ft (2.5m), **S** 6ft (1.8m).

☼ ◊ Z5–9 H9–5

R. 'Rambling Rector'
Rampant rambler rose with very good
disease resistance. Clusters of scented,
cupped to flat, semidouble, creamy-
white flowers, 1½in (4cm) across, with
golden stamens, appear in a single flush
in summer, followed by red hips. Has
grayish-green foliage. **H** and **S** 20ft (6m).

☼ ◊ Z5–9 H9–5

R. 'New Dawn'
Vigorous, very hardy climbing rose with good disease resistance. Fragrant, cupped, double, pale pearl-pink flowers, 3in (8cm) across, are borne in clusters in summer and again in fall. Tolerates a north-facing wall. **H** and **S** 15ft (5m).

☀ ◊ Z5–9 H9–5

R. 'Zéphirine Drouhin' (Climbing rose)
Lax, arching Bourbon rose that will climb if supported. Bears fragrant, cupped, double, deep pink flowers, 3in (8cm) across, in a single flush in summer. Is prone to mildew. May be grown as a hedge. **H** to 8ft (2.5m), **S** to 6ft (2m).

☀ ◊ Z5–9 H9–5

R. HIGH HOPES ('Haryup')
Vigorous, upright and arching, long-stemmed climbing rose with good disease resistance. Scented, urn-shaped to rounded, double, light pink flowers, 3in (8cm) across, are freely borne in summer–fall. Has purplish-green foliage. **H** 12ft (4m), **S** 7ft (2.2m).

☀ ◊ Z5–9 H9–5

R. 'Veilchenblau'
Vigorous rambler rose with good disease resistance. Rosette, double, violet flowers, streaked white, 1in (2.5cm) across, have a fruity scent and appear in clusters in a single flush in summer. **H** 12ft (4m), **S** 7ft (2.2m).

☀ ◊ Z5–9 H9–5

R. 'Albertine'
Vigorous rambler rose with good disease resistance and arching, thorny, reddish stems. Abundant clusters of scented, cup-shaped, fully double, salmon-pink flowers, 3in (8cm) across, are borne in a single flush in summer. Prone to mildew in a dry site. **H** to 15ft (5m), **S** 10ft (3m).

☀ ◊ Z5–9 H9–5

R. 'Aloha'
Strong-growing, bushy climbing rose with good disease resistance. Fragrant, cupped, fully double, rose- and salmon-pink flowers, 3½in (9cm) across, appear in summer and again in fall. Leaves are leathery and dark green. May be grown as a shrub. **H** and **S** 8ft (2.5m).

☀ ◊ Z5–9 H9–5

R. 'Madame Grégoire Staechelin'
Vigorous, arching climbing rose with good disease resistance. Bears large clusters of rounded to cupped, fully double flowers, 5in (13cm) across, with ruffled, clear pink petals, shaded carmine, in a single flush in summer. **H** to 20ft (6m), **S** to 12ft (4m).

☀ ◊ Z5–9 H9–5

R. 'Compassion'
Upright, free-branching climbing rose with good disease resistance. Fragrant, rounded, double, pink-tinted, salmon-apricot flowers, 4in (10cm) across, are borne in summer and again in fall. Has glossy, dark leaves on reddish stems. **H** 10ft (3m), **S** 8ft (2.5m).

☀ ◊ Z5–9 H9–5

R. 'Chaplin's Pink Companion'
Vigorous climbing rose with very good disease resistance and glossy, dark green foliage. Slightly scented, rounded, double, light pink flowers, 2in (5cm) across, are borne freely in large clusters in a single flush during summer. **H** and **S** 10ft (3m).

☀ ◊ Z5–9 H9–5

ROSES

185

ROSES

PINK

R. 'Cécile Brünner'
Vigorous climber with good disease resistance and light green leaves. Masses of sweetly-scented, pointed, double, blush-pink flowers, 1½in (4cm) across, fading to pearl, are borne in a single flush in summer. **H** 11½ft (3.5m), **S** 8ft (2.5m).

☼ ◊ Z5–9 H9–1

R. DANCING QUEEN ('Fryfestoon')
Climber with good disease resistance and large, mid-green leaves. Small clusters of slightly scented, rounded, double, rose-pink flowers, 4in (10cm) across, with a basal white flash on each outer petal, are produced in summer and again in fall. **H** 8ft (2.4m), **S** 6ft (1.8m).

☼ ◊ Z5–9 H9–5

R. PENNY LANE ('Hardwell')
Climber with very good disease resistance and glossy, mid-green leaves. Wide clusters of quartered-rosette, fully double flowers, 5in (12cm) across, in light pink with champagne, scented with myrrh and musk, are borne in summer and fall. **H** 8ft (2.5m), **S** 6ft (1.8m).

☼ ◊ Z5–9 H9–5

RED

R. 'Sympathie'
Vigorous, free-branching climbing rose with moderate disease resistance. Slightly scented, cupped, fully double, bright red flowers, 3in (8cm) across, are borne in summer and fall, usually in clusters. Has plentiful, glossy, dark green foliage. **H** 10ft (3m), **S** 8ft (2.5m).

☼ ◊ Z5–9 H9–5

R. DUBLIN BAY ('Macdub')
Dense, shrubby climbing rose with good disease resistance that may be pruned to grow as a shrub. Bears clusters of cupped, double, bright crimson flowers, 4in (10cm) across, in summer and again in fall. Foliage is glossy, dark green and plentiful. **H** and **S** 7ft (2.2m).

☼ ◊ Z5–9 H9–5

R. THE PRINCE'S TRUST ('Harholding')
Climber with good disease resistance and glossy, light to mid-green leaves. Produces dense clusters of slightly scented, cupped, double, bright red flowers, 4in (10cm) across, in summer and again in fall. **H** 10ft (3m), **S** 6ft (1.8m).

☼ ◊ Z5–9 H9–5

R. 'Dortmund'
Upright climbing rose with very good disease resistance that may be pruned to make a shrub. Flat, single, red flowers, 4in (10cm) across, with white eyes and a slight scent, are borne freely in clusters in summer and fall. Has dark green foliage. **H** 10ft (3m), **S** 6ft (1.8m).

☼ ◊ Z5–9 H9–5

R. 'Guinée'
Vigorous, stiffly branched climbing rose with moderate disease resistance. Fragrant, cupped, fully double, blackish-red to maroon flowers, 4½in (11cm) across, are borne in a single flush in summer. Leaves are large and leathery. **H** 15ft (5m), **S** 7ft (2.2m).

☼ ◊ Z5–9 H9–5

R. 'Mermaid'
Slow-growing climbing rose with good disease resistance and repeat-flowering in summer–fall. Produces flat, single, primrose-yellow flowers, 5in (12cm) across. Has stiff, reddish stems, large, hooked thorns and glossy, dark green leaves. **H** and **S** to 20ft (6m).

☼ ◊ Z5–9 H9–5

R. LAURA FORD ('Chewarvel')
Upright, stiffly branching climbing rose with good disease resistance. Sprays of scented, urn-shaped to flat, yellow flowers, 1¾in (4.5cm) across, appear in summer and again in fall. Has small, dark, glossy leaves. Good for pillars. **H** 7ft (2.2m), **S** 4ft (1.2m).

☼ ◊ Z5–9 H9–5

R. BRIDGE OF SIGHS ('Harglow')
Climber with good disease resistance and repeat-flowering in summer–fall. Has highly glossy, dark green leaves. Dense clusters of flat, semidouble, deep golden-amber flowers, 4in (10cm) across, have yellow stamens and a sweet spicy perfume. **H** 8ft (2.5m), **S** 6ft (1.8m).

☼ ◊ Z5–9 H9–5

R. GARDENERS GLORY ('Chewability')
Climber with very good disease resistance and light green leaves. Clusters of cupped, double, yellow flowers, 2in (5cm) across, fading to light yellow, are borne in summer and again in fall. **H** 7ft (2.2m), **S** 5ft (1.5m).

☼ ◊ Z5–9 H9–5

R. ALIBABA ('Chewalibaba')
Climber with very good disease resistance and repeat-flowering in summer–fall. Produces mid-green leaves and sweet-scented, cupped, double flowers, 3in (8cm) across, with ruffled petal edges, in shades of peach-salmon and red. **H** 7ft (2.2m), **S** 4ft (1.2m).

☼ ◊ Z5–9 H9–5

R. 'Emily Gray'
Semievergreen rambler rose with good disease resistance. Trusses of slightly fragrant, cupped, fully double, butter-yellow flowers, 2in (5cm) across, appear in a single flush in summer. Has long, lax stems and lustrous, dark green leaves. Is prone to mildew. **H** 15ft (5m), **S** 10ft (3m).

☼ ◊ Z5–9 H9–5

R. 'Maigold'
Vigorous climbing rose with very good disease resistance and prickly, arching stems. Fragrant, cupped, semidouble, bronze-yellow flowers, 4in (10cm) across, are borne freely in a single flush in summer. May be pruned to grow as shrub. **H** and **S** 8ft (2.5m).

☼ ◊ Z5–9 H9–5

R. SUMMER WINE ('Korizont')
Climber with good disease resistance and large, dark green leaves. Small clusters of flat, semidouble, salmon-pink flowers, to 4in (10cm) across, fading to pink, are produced in summer and again in fall. **H** 10ft (3m), **S** 6ft (1.8m).

☼ ◊ Z5–9 H9–5

ROSES

CLIMBERS AND WALL SHRUBS

Versatile and decorative, climbers offer great scope for imaginative garden design, their scrambling stems veiling other plants and structures with flowers and foliage. A few, such as ivy, will also trail across the ground, helping to suppress weeds. Climbers are often used as a backdrop to other plantings, or grown over arbors and gazebos to provide shade. You can also create focal points by weaving them through trees and pyramids and up pillars, or train them over a trellis to form boundary screens or dividers between different areas of the garden. The rigid stems of wall shrubs add another dimension to vertical schemes, covering walls and fences with foliage, blooms, and berries.

CLIMBERS AND WALL SHRUBS

One of the most versatile of plant groups, climbers bring height to the garden, adding interest to walls and fences, and clothing structures such as arches and arbors with flowers and foliage. A number of shrubs can also be trained against walls and fences to create textures, patterns, and backdrops to beds and borders.

What are climbers and wall shrubs?

Most climbers are woody, evergreen or deciduous plants, while a few are herbaceous perennials, or summer-flowering annuals. Climbers can be self-clinging or twining (with or without tendrils), or scandent—scrambling species that do not cling. It is important to identify the climbing method of your plant, since this dictates the method of support it needs. Self-clingers such as Virginia creeper (*Parthenocissus quinquefolia*) climb up their supports using adhesive pads, while ivies (*Hedera*) and the Swiss cheese plant (*Monstera deliciosa*) use aerial roots to attach themselves to vertical surfaces. Self-clinging climbers may initially need to be guided to their support with canes (see box below) but will then become self-supporting. By contrast, twiners coil

around the slim stems of a host plant; they will need wires, mesh, or a trellis to cling to if they are wall-trained. Clematis, passion flowers (*Passiflora*), hops (*Humulus lupulus*), sweet peas (*Lathyrus*), and morning glories (*Ipomoea*) fall into this group.

Scrambling plants like winter jasmine (*Jasminum nudiflorum*) attach themselves loosely by threading their flexible stems through host plants or over a framework of their old stems made in previous seasons. On smooth surfaces, such as walls and fences, their stems must be tied in to wires or trellis attached to the support, as they have no other means of clinging.

Wall shrubs such as chaenomeles, pyracanthas, and ceanothus are not natural climbers, but can be trained to decorate walls or fences. Some are best grown in this way, as they require the additional shelter and support a wall provides.

Ornamental features

Climbing plants have a range of attractive foliage forms, from the lobed leaves of *Tropaeolum speciosum* and palmate foliage of x *Fatshedera lizei*, to the heart-shaped leaves of *Actinidia deliciosa*. Leaf surfaces also offer textural contrasts, from the downy *Vitis vinifera* to glossy ivies (*Hedera*).

ABOVE Wisteria-clad wall
Vigorous climbers, such as *Wisteria sinensis*, need a sturdy trellis or wall for support to display their heavy flowers to perfection. When grown around a window, the subtle scent of its flowers can be appreciated indoors and out.

PLANTING A CLIMBER

Before planting, attach eye screws and horizontal wires, or a trellis, to the wall or fence. The lowest wire should be about 20in (50cm) above soil level, and the others 12–18in (30–45cm) apart. Work plenty of organic matter into the soil.

1 Dig a planting hole
Water the climber before planting. Dig a hole twice the diameter and deeper than the rootball, 18in (45cm) from the fence. Dig a slightly deeper hole for clematis, since they need to be planted 4in (10cm) deeper than the top of their rootball.

2 Plant the climber
Arrange a fan of canes in the hole. Place the climber in the hole and slant it toward the canes. Backfill with some soil enriched with rotted organic matter. Untie the stems from their original support and spread them out ready to attach to the canes.

3 Tie in the stems
Using soft garden twine, tie the stems to the canes using a figure-eight. Train the lower stems on to the lower wires and any tall stems at the center of the plant to cover the high wires.

4 Firm in the soil
Firm in the climber and create a shallow saucer shape around the base of the plant so that moisture runs into the area above the roots. Water, and apply a bark mulch, keeping it away from the plant stems.

Colors range from golden-hued *Humulus lupulus* 'Aureus' to the deep green of many jasmines, as well as the purple tints of plants such as *Vitis vinifera* 'Purpurea'. Others have bright, variegated foliage, such as *Actinidia kolomikta,* with its green leaves tipped with splashes of cream and pink. Some, most notably species of vitis and parthenocissus, produce their finest displays in fall, when both fire up with burning shades of red.

Climbers such as passion flowers (*Passiflora*) and clematis bear beautiful flowers, while some, especially wisteria, honeysuckles (*Lonicera*), and jasmines, are deliciously fragrant. The flower colors span the spectrum from the creamy whites of *Schizophragma integrifolium* and *Hydrangea petiolaris* to the magentas of bougainvillea, blues and purples of a whole range of clematis, and chocolate-maroon of *Rhodochiton atrosanguineus*. With many climbers, the season is further prolonged by silky seed heads, as in clematis, or striking berries, notably the oblong, purple fruits of *Billardiera longiflora* and the orange-yellow fruits of *Celastrus orbiculatus*.

Annual climbers such as sweet peas (*Lathyrus odoratus*) climb rapidly to the top of wigwams made from garden canes, producing a succession of scented flowers from mid- to late summer that are ideal for cutting. Morning glory (*Ipomoea tricolor* 'Heavenly Blue'), with its sky-blue trumpets,

and black-eyed Susan (*Thunbergia alata*), also offer a quick-fix solution, covering a trellis or adding height to containers on patios.

Wall shrubs are also valued for their attractive foliage and blooms. Ceanothus, for example, has both evergreen and deciduous forms, with flowers in varying shades of blue, white, and pink. The flowering quince (*Chaenomeles*) produces a profusion of cupped white, pink, orange, or scarlet-red flowers early in the year, followed by yellow fruits in the fall. Thorny pyracanthas make excellent security hedges, deterring intruders, and sport glossy evergreen foliage with an abundance of yellow, orange, or red berries in the fall.

Designing with climbers and wall shrubs

Growing climbers as a backdrop for other plants is one way of adding height to a border, but they can also be grown on freestanding supports to form screens or divisions between different parts of the garden. Grown through trees or on pillars and pyramids, they also create focal points.

Where a garden lacks shade, climbers allowed to ramble over arches and arbors offer a cool place to sit. You can also use climbers and wall shrubs to soften the lines of hard landscaping, while vigorous climbers will help to camouflage unsightly structures. Left unsupported, some climbers trail on the ground and, when pegged at the

ABOVE *Clematis* **'Bill MacKenzie'**
This small-flowered, late-blooming Group 3 clematis provides a natural, rambling backdrop of nodding yellow flowers and fluffy seedheads.

nodes, will root to form a carpet of groundcover. When growing climbers through other plants, make sure that you synchronize their flowering times for a dual effect, and match their pruning needs.

As well as growing shrubs such as pyracanthas and chaenomeles against walls, you can train them into fans and espaliers for a formal effect.

PRUNING CLEMATIS

Some clematis flower well if pruned lightly or not at all, while others bloom more effectively when cut back hard. They are divided into three groups, each with different pruning requirements. Group 1 clematis (including *C. montana* and *C. armandii*) are vigorous plants that flower in late spring on the previous year's growth. Group 2 clematis, such as *C.* 'Corona', and *C.* 'Henryi', flower in early summer on the previous year's growth. Group 3 clematis include small-flowered viticella and texensis types, such as *C.* 'Gravetye Beauty', and some large-flowered types including *C.* 'Perle d'Azur'. They bloom from mid-summer to fall on new growth formed earlier in the year.

Pruning Group 1 clematis
Plants in this group need little or no pruning once established, except to remove dead and damaged stems, or to keep them in check. After flowering, give them a light trim if necessary. Prune the leggy new season's growth, cutting above a pair of healthy buds, but do not cut them back hard.

Pruning Group 2 clematis
Prune this group in early spring when the buds are in growth and are clearly visible. Work from the top of the clematis, pruning each stem back to the first pair of healthy buds or shoots. Remove dead, diseased, or damaged wood; it will be brown and dry. The pruned stems will produce new growth and then flowers in early summer.

Pruning Group 3 clematis
Left unpruned, these clematis form flowers at the top of the plant, leaving bare, straggly stems at the bottom. In late winter, before the buds break, remove the tangle of shoots from their support and cut back all the stems hard to within 12in (30cm) of the ground. This encourages strong new shoots and flowers to form along their length.

WHITE

PINK

Holboellia latifolia [white form]

Variable, evergreen, twining climber with glossy, mid-green leaves divided into 3–9 ovate or oblong leaflets. Bears racemes of 3–7 sweetly scented, creamy-white, male flowers and greenish, female flowers in early summer, and sausage-shaped, purple fruit. **H** to 16ft (5m).

☼ ◊ Z10–11 H11–1

Stauntonia hexaphylla

Evergreen, woody-stemmed, twining climber. Leaves have 3–7 oval leaflets, 2–5in (5–13cm) long. In spring bears racemes of fragrant, cup-shaped, violet-tinged white flowers, followed by egg-shaped, edible, purple fruits, if plants of both sexes are grown. **H** to 30ft (10m).

☼ ◊ Z9–10 H10–9

Decumaria sinensis

Evergreen, woody-stemmed, root climber with oval, often toothed leaves, 1–3in (2.5–8cm) long. Conical clusters of small, honey-scented, cream flowers are produced in late spring and early summer. **H** to 6ft (2m) or more.

☼ ◊ Z7–9 H9–7

Prostanthera rotundifolia 'Rosea'

Evergreen, bushy, rounded shrub with tiny, sweetly aromatic, deep green leaves and short, leafy racemes of bell-shaped, purple-anthered, pale pink flowers in late spring or summer. **H** 6–13ft (2–4m), **S** 3–10ft (1–3m).

☼ ◊ Z11 H11–5

Clianthus puniceus f. albus

Evergreen or semievergreen, woody-stemmed, scrambling climber, grown for its drooping clusters of clawlike, creamy-white flowers that open in spring and early summer. Mid-green leaves consist of many small leaflets. **H** 12ft (4m).

☼ ◊ Z7–11 H11–7

Acradenia frankliniae

Evergreen, upright, stiffly branched shrub with aromatic, dark green leaves divided into 3 narrowly lance-shaped leaflets. From late spring to early summer bears small clusters of star-shaped, white flowers. **H** 10ft (3m), **S** 5ft (1.5m).

☼ ◊ Z10–11 H12–10

Ercilla volubilis

Evergreen, root climber with oval to heart-shaped, mid-green leaves, 1–2in (2.5–5cm) long. Spikes of petal-less flowers, each consisting of 5 greenish or purple sepals and 6–8 white stamens, are borne in spring. **H** to 30ft (10m) or more.

☼ ◊ Z10–11 H12–10

Campsis radicans 'Indian Summer'
Deciduous, woody-stemmed, root climber with leaves divided into 7–11 oval, toothed leaflets. Small clusters of trumpet-shaped, yellow-throated, orange-red flowers, 2½–3in (6–8cm) long, are produced in late summer and early fall. **H** 40ft (12m).

☼ ◊ Z5–9 H9–3

Mitraria coccinea
Evergreen, woody-stemmed, scrambling climber with oval, toothed leaves. Small, tubular, orange-red flowers are borne singly in leaf axils during late spring to summer. **H** to 6ft (2m).

☼ ◊ pH Z10–11 H11–10

Akebia quinata (Chocolate vine)
Woody-stemmed, twining climber, semievergreen in mild winters or warm areas, with leaves of 5 leaflets. Vanilla-scented, brownish-purple flowers appear in late spring, followed by sausage-shaped, purplish fruits. **H** 30ft (10m) or more.

☼ ◊ Z5–9 H9–5

Ribes speciosum
Deciduous, bushy, spiny shrub bearing slender, drooping, tubular, red flowers, with long, red stamens, in mid–late spring. Fruits are spherical and red. Has red, young shoots and oval, 3–5-lobed, glossy, bright green leaves. **H** and **S** 6ft (2m).

☼ ◊ Z7–9 H9–7

Chaenomeles x superba 'Crimson and Gold' (Flowering quince)
Deciduous, dense shrub with thorns and oval, glossy, green leaves. Bears masses of 5-petaled, deep red flowers, with conspicuous, golden-yellow anthers, in spring, followed by round, yellow fruits. **H** to 3ft (1m), **S** to 6ft (2m).

☼ ◊ Z5–9 H9–5

Clianthus puniceus (Parrot's bill)
Evergreen or semievergreen, woody-stemmed, scrambling climber with leaves composed of many leaflets. In spring and early summer bears drooping clusters of unusual, clawlike, brilliant red flowers. **H** 12ft (4m).

☼ ◊ Z7–11 H11–7

Jasminum beesianum
Evergreen, woody-stemmed, scrambling climber, deciduous in cool areas. Has lance-shaped leaves. Fragrant, tubular, usually 6-lobed, pinkish-red flowers, 1–3 together, borne in early summer, are followed by shiny, black berries. **H** to 15ft (5m).

☼ ◊ Z10–11 H11–1

PURPLE

Akebia x pentaphylla
Mainly deciduous, woody-stemmed, twining climber. Mid-green leaves, bronze-tinted when young, have 3 or 5 oval leaflets. Pendent racemes of small, 3-petaled, purple flowers (female at base, male at apex) are borne in spring. **H** to 30ft (10m).

☼ ◊ Z5–8 H8–5

Hardenbergia comptoniana
Evergreen, woody-stemmed, twining climber with leaves of 3 or 5 lance-shaped leaflets. Has racemes of pealike, deep purple-blue flowers in spring. **H** to 8ft (2.5m).

☼ ◊ Z11 H11–6

Holboellia latifolia [purple form]
Evergreen, twining climber with glossy, green leaves. Clusters of tiny, mauve, male flowers and, lower down stems, larger, purple-tinged, green-white female flowers are borne in spring, followed by sausage-shaped, purple fruits. **H** to 22ft (7m) or more.

◐ ◊ Z10–11 H11–1

BLUE

Ceanothus arboreus 'Trewithen Blue'
Vigorous, evergreen, bushy, spreading shrub with broadly oval to rounded, dark green leaves. In spring and early summer bears large, pyramidal clusters of rich blue flowers. **H** to 20ft (6m), **S** to 25ft (8m).

☼ ◊ Z9–10 H10–9

Sollya heterophylla
Evergreen, woody-based, twining climber with narrowly lance-shaped to oval leaves, ¾-2½in (2–6cm) long. Nodding clusters of 4–9 broadly bell-shaped, sky-blue flowers are carried from spring to fall. **H** to 10ft (3m).

☼ ◊ Z10–11 H12–6

YELLOW

Eriobotrya japonica (Loquat)
Evergreen, bushy shrub or spreading tree with stout shoots bearing large, oblong, prominently veined, glossy, dark green leaves. Fragrant, 5-petaled, white flowers borne in clusters in early fall are followed by pear-shaped, orange-yellow fruits. **H** and **S** 25ft (8m).

☼ ◊ Z8–11 H11–8

Humulus lupulus 'Aureus'
Herbaceous, twining climber with rough, hairy stems and toothed, yellowish leaves divided into 3 or 5 lobes. Greenish, female flower spikes are borne in pendent clusters in fall. **H** to 20ft (6m).

☼ ◊ Z4–8 H8–1

Vestia foetida
Evergreen, upright shrub with pendent, tubular, pale yellow flowers from midspring to mid-summer. Oblong, glossy, dark green leaves have an unpleasant scent. **H** 6ft (2m), **S** 5ft (1.5m).

☼ ◊ Z8–10 H10–8

WHITE

Azara serrata
Evergreen, upright shrub with glossy, bright green foliage and rounded bunches of fragrant, yellow flowers in late spring or early summer. **H** 12ft (4m), **S** 10ft (3m).

☼ ◊ Z9–10 H11–9

Gelsemium sempervirens
Moderately vigorous, evergreen, twining climber with pointed, lustrous leaves. Clusters of fragrant, funnel-shaped, pale to deep yellow flowers are borne from late spring to late summer. **H** to 20ft (6m).

☼ ◊ ⊘ Z7–9 H9–1

Trachelospermum jasminoides (Confederate jasmine, Star jasmine)
Evergreen, woody-stemmed, twining climber with oval leaves up to 6in (15cm) long. Has very fragrant, white flowers in summer, then pairs of pods, up to 6in (15cm) long. **H** to 28ft (9m).

☼ ◊ Z9–10 H10–9

Solanum laxum 'Album' (Potato vine)
Semievergreen, woody-stemmed, scrambling climber. Oval to lance-shaped leaves are sometimes lobed or divided into leaflets. Has star-shaped, white flowers, ¾–1in (2–2.5cm) across, in summer–fall. **H** to 20ft (6m).

☼ ◊ ⊘ Z10–11 H12–7

Coronilla valentina subsp. *glauca*
Evergreen, bushy, dense shrub. Has blue-gray leaves with 5 or 7 leaflets. Fragrant, pealike, yellow flowers are borne from midspring to early summer. **H** and **S** 5ft (1.5m).

☼ ◊ Z8–9 H9–8

Araujia sericifera (Cruel plant)
Evergreen, woody-stemmed, twining climber with leaves that are white-downy beneath. Has scented, white flowers, often striped pale maroon inside, from late summer to fall. **H** to 23ft (7m).

☼ ◊ Z10–11 H11–10

Forsythia suspensa
Deciduous, arching, graceful shrub with slender shoots. Nodding, narrow, trumpet-shaped, bright yellow flowers open from early to midspring, before mid-green leaves appear. **H** and **S** 10ft (3m).

☼ ◊ Z6–8 H8–6

Jasminum mesnyi (Primrose jasmine)
Evergreen or semievergreen, woody-stemmed, scrambling climber. Leaves are divided into 3 leaflets; semidouble, pale yellow flowers appear in spring. **H** to 10ft (3m).

☼ ◊ Z8–10 H10–8

Ampelopsis brevipedunculata var. *maximowiczii* 'Elegans'
Vigorous, deciduous, woody-stemmed, twining, tendril climber with hairy young stems. Has variable, densely white-mottled, pink-tinged leaves. Tiny flowers are produced in summer, followed by blue berries. **H** 16ft (5m).

☼ ◊ Z5–8 H8–2

Hydrangea petiolaris (Climbing hydrangea)
Deciduous, woody-stemmed, root climber. Has toothed leaves and lacy heads of small, white flowers in summer, only sparingly borne on young plants. **H** to 50ft (15m).

☼ ◊ ⊘ Z4–9 H9–1

195

CLIMBERS AND WALL SHRUBS

Pileostegia viburnoides
Slow-growing, evergreen, woody-stemmed, root climber. Tiny, white or cream flowers, with many prominent stamens, are borne in heads from late summer to fall. **H** to 20ft (6m).

☀ ◊ Z7–11 H11–7

Jasminum officinale f. affine
(Common jasmine)
Semievergreen or deciduous, woody-stemmed, twining climber with leaves comprising 7 or 9 leaflets. Clusters of fragrant, 4- or 5-lobed flowers, white inside and pink outside, are borne in summer–fall. **H** to 40ft (12m).

☀ ◊ Z9–10 H10–9

Wisteria floribunda 'Alba'
Deciduous, woody-stemmed, twining climber with leaves of 11–19 oval leaflets. Scented, pealike, white flowers are carried in drooping racemes, up to 2ft (60cm) long, in early summer. **H** to 28ft (9m).

☀ ◊ ❶ Z5–9 H9–3

Hydrangea serratifolia
Vigorous, evergreen, woody-stemmed climber with elliptic, sharply toothed, dark green leaves. In summer produces rounded clusters of small, white, fertile flowers opening from large, rounded buds. **H** 50–70ft (15–20m).

☽ ◊ Z8–10 H10–8

Hydrangea seemannii
Evergreen, woody-stemmed climber with elliptic to lance-shaped, leathery, mid-green leaves. In summer produces domed flower heads consisting of small, clustered, greenish-white, fertile flowers surrounded by larger, white, sterile flowers. **H** 50ft (15m).

☀ ◊ Z8–9 H9–8

Trachelospermum asiaticum
Evergreen, woody-stemmed, twining climber with oval, glossy, dark green leaves, 1in (2.5cm) long. Scented, tubular, cream flowers that age to yellow, are produced in summer. Pairs of long, slender pods, 5–9in (12–22cm) long, contain silky seeds. **H** to 20ft (6m).

☀ ◊ Z7–11 H12–7

196

Dregea sinensis
Evergreen, woody-stemmed, twining climber. Oval, green leaves, 1¼–4in (3–10cm) long, are grayish beneath. In summer produces clusters of 10–25 small, fragrant, star-shaped flowers, red-marked white or cream, followed by pairs of slender seed pods. **H** to 10ft (3m).

☼ ◊ Z8–10 H10–8

Schizophragma integrifolium
Deciduous, woody-stemmed, root climber with oval or heart-shaped leaves. In summer, white flowers are borne in flat heads up to 12in (30cm) across, marginal sterile flowers each having a large, white bract. **H** to 40ft (12m).

☼ ◊ Z5–9 H9–5

Anredera cordifolia
Fast-growing, evergreen, tuberous, twining climber with oval to lance-shaped, fleshy leaves. Tiny, fragrant, white flowers are borne in clusters from upper leaf axils in summer. **H** to 20ft (6m).

☼ ◊ Z10–11 H11–1

Prostanthera cuneata
Evergreen, bushy, erect to spreading shrub with small, aromatic, shiny, dark green leaves. In late spring and early summer produces dense racemes of shortly tubular, 2-lipped, white flowers, with purple and yellow markings in the throat. **H** and **S** 3ft (90cm).

☼ ◊ Z9–11 H11–9

Schizophragma hydrangeoides
Deciduous, woody-stemmed, climber with broadly oval leaves. Small white flowers, in flat heads 8–10in (20–25cm) across, are produced on pendent side-branches in summer; these are surrounded by marginal, sterile flowers, each with an oval, pale yellow sepal. **H** to 25–40ft (8–12m).

☼ ◊ Z6–9 H9–6

Drimys lanceolata
(Pepper tree, mountain pepper)
Evergreen, upright, dense shrub or tree with deep red shoots and oblong, dark green leaves. Produces clusters of star-shaped, white flowers in spring. **H** 12ft (4m), **S** 8ft (2.5m).

☼ ◊ Z9–10 H10–9

Carpenteria californica
Evergreen, bushy shrub. Glossy, dark green foliage sets off fragrant, yellow-centered, white flowers borne during summer. **H** 6ft (2m) or more, **S** 6ft (2m).

☼ ◊ Z8–9 H9–8

CLEMATIS

Among the climbers, clematis are unsurpassed in their long period of flowering (with species flowering in almost every month of the year), the variety of flower shapes and colors, and their tolerance of almost any exposure and climate. Some spring-flowering species and cultivars are vigorous and excellent for rapidly covering buildings, old trees, and pergolas. Other, less rampant cultivars display often large, exquisite blooms from early summer to fall in almost every color. Flower colors may vary according to your climatic conditions; generally speaking, the warmer the climate, the darker the flowers are likely to be.

Clematis look attractive when trained on walls or trellises and when grown in association with other climbers, trees, or shrubs, treating them as hosts. Less vigorous cultivars may also be left unsupported to scramble at ground level, where their flowers will be clearly visible.

The various types of clematis (see the Plant Dictionary) may be divided into 3 groups, each of which has different pruning requirements. Incorrect pruning may result in cutting out the stems that will produce flowers in the current season, so the following guidelines should be followed closely.

Group 1

Early-flowering species, Alpina, Macropetala, and Montana types

Flower stems are produced direct from the previous season's ripened stems. Prune after flowering to allow new growth to be produced and ripened for the next season. Remove dead or damaged stems and cut back other shoots that have outgrown their allotted space.

Flower stem direct from the previous season's ripened stems

Current season's stems have one flower and are 6–18 in (15–45 cm) long

Discarded previous season's old flower stem

Discarded previous season's leaves

Group 2

Early, large-flowered cultivars

Flowers are produced on short, current-season stems, so prune before new growth starts, in early spring. Remove dead or damaged stems and cut back all others to where strong, leaf-axil buds are visible. (These buds will produce the first crop of flowers.)

Group 3

Late, large-flowered cultivars, Late-flowering species, Small-flowered cultivars, and Herbaceous types

Flowers are produced on the current season's growth only, so prune before new growth starts, in early spring. Remove all of the previous season's stems down to a pair of strong, leaf-axil buds, 6–12 in (15-30 cm) above the soil.

Flower stems on current season's growth only

C. fasciculiflora [1, early small-fl.]

C. 'Andromeda' [2, early large-fl.]

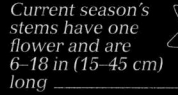
C. ARCTIC QUEEN ('Evitwo') [2, early large-fl.]

C. 'White Columbine' [1, early small-fl.]

C. armandii [1, early]

C. 'Guernsey Cream' [2, early large-fl.]

C. x cartmanii 'Avalanche' [1, early]

C. 'Early Sensation' [3, late]

C. x cartmanii 'Joe' [1, early]

C. 'Bella' [2, early large-fl.]

C. montana [1, Montana]

C. CHANTILLY ('Evipo021')
[2, early large-fl.]

C. florida PISTACHIO ('Evirida')
[3, late large-fl.]

C. montana var. rubens [1, Montana]

C. 'Alionushka' [3, early small-fl.]

C. 'Fireworks' [2, early large-fl.]

C. cirrhosa [1, early-fl.]

C. 'Jacqueline du Pré'
[1, early small-fl.]

**C. montana var. rubens
'Tetrarose'** [1, Montana]

C. 'Lincoln Star' [2, early large-fl.]

C. VIENNETTA ('Evipo006')
[3, large-fl.]

C. 'Sunrise' [1, early]

C. 'Jan Lindmark' [1, early small-fl.]

C. 'Henryi' [2, early large-fl.]

C. BLUE MOON ('Evirin')
[3, late large-fl.]

C. 'Corona' [2, early large-fl.]

C. 'Charissima' [2, late large-fl.]

C. 'Nelly Moser'
[2, early large-fl.]

C. florida var. sieboldiana
[3, small-fl.]

C. 'Huldine' [3, late large-fl.]

C. 'Barbara Jackman' [2, early large-fl.]

C. 'Barbara Dibley' [2, early lge-fl.]

C. 'Kakio' [2, early large-fl.]

199

C. 'Gravetye Beauty' [3, small-fl.]

C. 'Etoile Violette' [3, late-fl.]

C. 'Abundance' [3, late-fl.]

C. 'Madame Julia Correvon' [3, late-fl.]

C. 'Purpurea Plena Elegans' [3, late-fl.]

C. 'Rosy O'Grady' [1, early and late]

C. 'Jackmanii' [3, late large-fl.]

C. AVANT-GARDE ('Evipo033') 3, mid-season small-fl.]

C. ROSEMOOR ('Evipo002') [2, early large-fl.]

C. BOURBON ('Evipo018') [2, early large-fl.]

Clematis VINO ('Poulvo') [2, early large-fl.]

C. 'Polish Spirit' [3, late large-fl.]

C. 'Frankie' [1, early small-fl.]

C. 'Westerplatte' 2, early large-fl.]

C. ANNA LOUISE ('Evithree') [2, early large-fl.]

C. *cirrhosa* var. *purpurascens* 'Freckles' [1, early small-fl.]

C. 'Ernest Markham' [3, late large-fl.]

C. 'Perle d'Azur' [3, late large-fl.]

C. 'Frances Rivis' [1, early small-fl.]

C. 'Silver Moon' [2, early large-fl.]

C. *flammula* [3, late-fl.]

Lathyrus odoratus 'Mrs. Bernard Jones'

Vigorous, annual, tendril climber with mid-green leaves. Produces large, strongly scented, wavy-edged, sugar-pink flowers, suffused white at the margins, from summer to early fall. **H** 6ft (2m).

☼ ◊ ❶ Z9–10 H8–1

Lathyrus odoratus 'Charles Unwin'

Vigorous, annual, tendril climber with oval, mid-green leaves. Produces large, scented, wavy-margined, soft salmon-pink flowers with cream keels, paling to salmon-tinted cream at the margins in summer and early fall. **H** 6ft (2m).

☼ ◊ ❶ Z9–10 H8–1

Jasminum x stephanense

Vigorous, deciduous, twining climber with simple or pinnate, matt green leaves. Produces loose clusters of fragrant, 5-lobed, pale pink flowers, from early to mid-summer, sometimes producing a second flush later in the season. **H** 16–22ft (5–7m).

◐ ◊ Z7–11 H11–8

Lathyrus latifolius

(Everlasting pea, Perennial pea)

Herbaceous, tendril climber with winged stems. Leaves have broad stipules and a pair of leaflets. Has small racemes of pink-purple flowers in summer and early fall. **H** 6ft (2m) or more.

☼ ◊ ❶ Z5–9 H9–5

Actinidia kolomikta

Deciduous, woody-stemmed, twining climber with 3–6in (8–16cm) long leaves, the upper sections often creamy-white and pink. Has small, cup-shaped, white flowers in summer, male and female on separate plants. **H** 12ft (4m).

☼ ◊ Z5–8 H11–1

Lathyrus odoratus 'Lady Diana'

Moderately fast-growing, slender, annual, tendril climber with oval, mid-green leaves. Fragrant, pale violet-blue flowers are borne from summer to early fall. **H** 6ft (2m).

☼ ◊ ❶ Z9–10 H8–1

Grevillea 'Canberra Gem'

Vigorous, evergreen shrub with silky stems and linear, pointed, green leaves, to 1¼in (3cm) long. Late winter to mid-summer, and occasionally through the year, produces short racemes of small, tubular, white-tipped, pink-red flowers. **H** and **S** 6–13ft (2–4m).

☼ ◊ pH ❶ Z9–11 H11–9

Bomarea edulis

Deciduous, twining climber with lance-shaped, mid-green leaves. From early summer to fall bears umbel-like clusters of narrowly bell-shaped flowers, to 1½in (3.5cm) long, pink–light red, with yellow-flecked throats. **H** 6–10ft (2–3m).

☼ ◊ Z11 H12–10

CLIMBERS AND WALL SHRUBS

Lapageria rosea
(Chilean bellflower, Copihue)
Evergreen, woody-stemmed, twining
climber with oblong to oval, leathery
leaves. Has pendent, fleshy, pink to
red flowers, 2¾–3½in (7–9cm) long,
with paler flecks, from summer to
late fall. **H** to 15ft (5m).

☼ ◊ Z10–11 H11–10

Lathyrus odoratus 'Barry Dare'
Vigorous, annual, tendril climber
with ovate, mid-green leaves and
large, sweetly-scented, bright orange-
red, pea-flowers from summer to fall.
H 6ft (2m).

☼ ◊ ❗ Z9–10 H8–1

Cestrum elegans
Vigorous, evergreen, arching shrub.
Nodding shoots carry downy, deep
green foliage. Dense racemes of tubular,
purplish-red flowers in late spring and
summer are followed by deep red fruits.
H and **S** 10ft (3m).

☼ ◊ H11–10

Schisandra rubriflora
Deciduous, woody-stemmed, twining
climber with leathery, toothed leaves,
paler beneath. Has small, crimson
flowers in spring or early summer and
drooping, red fruits in late summer.
H to 20ft (6m).

☼ ◊ Z7–9 H9–7

Ipomoea lobata
Deciduous or semievergreen, twining
climber with 3-lobed leaves, usually
grown as an annual. One-sided racemes
of small, tubular, dark red flowers fade to
orange, then creamy-yellow, in summer.
H to 15ft (5m).

☼ ◊ ❗ H11–10

Berberidopsis corallina **(Coral plant)**
Evergreen, woody-stemmed, twining
climber with oval to heart-shaped,
leathery leaves edged with small spines.
Bears pendent clusters of globular, deep
red flowers in summer to early fall.
H 14ft (4.5m).

☼ ◊ pH Z8–9 H9–8

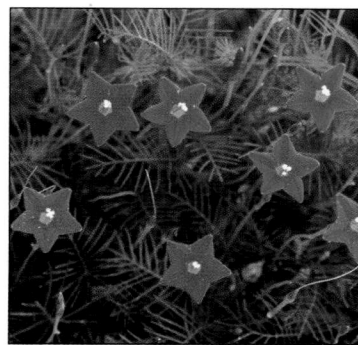

Ipomoea quamoclit **(Cypress vine)**
Annual, twining climber with oval,
bright green leaves cut into many
threadlike segments. Slender, tubular,
orange or scarlet flowers are carried
in summer–fall. **H** 6–12ft (2–4m).

☼ ◊ ❗ H11–6

Tropaeolum speciosum
(Flame creeper, Flame nasturtium)
Herbaceous, twining climber with a
creeping rhizome and lobed, blue-
green leaves. Bears scarlet flowers in
summer, followed by bright blue fruits
surrounded by deep red calyces. Roots
should be in shade. **H** to 10ft (3m).

☼ ◊ Z8–11 H12–8

Crinodendron hookerianum
(Lantern tree)
Evergreen, stiffly-branched shrub.
In late spring and early summer,
lantern-like, red flowers hang from
shoots clothed with narrow, dark
green leaves. **H** 20ft (6m), **S** 15ft (5m).

☼ ◊ pH Z9–11 H11–9

Desfontainia spinosa
Evergreen, bushy, dense shrub with spiny, holly-like, glossy, dark green leaves. Long, tubular, drooping, red flowers, tipped with yellow, are borne from mid-summer to late fall. **H** and **S** 6ft (2m).

☀ ◐ ◌ pH Z8–11 H11–8

Callistemon citrinus 'Splendens'
(Crimson bottlebrush)
Evergreen, arching shrub with broad, lemon-scented, gray-green leaves that are bronze-red when young. In early summer bright red flowers are borne in bottlebrush-like spikes. **H** 6–25ft (2–8m), **S** 5–20ft (1.5–6m).

☀ ◌ Z10–11 H11–10

Acca sellowiana (Pineapple guava)
Evergreen, bushy shrub or tree. Dark green leaves have white undersides. In mid-summer bears large, dark red flowers with white-edged petals, followed by edible, red-tinged, green fruits. **H** 6ft (2m), **S** 8ft (2.5m).

☀ ◌ Z8–11 H11–9

Grevillea rosmarinifolia
Evergreen, rounded, well-branched shrub. Dark green leaves are needle-shaped with reflexed margins, silky-haired beneath. Has short, dense clusters of tubular, red, occasionally pink or white flowers in summer. **H** 2–10ft (0.6–3m), **S** 3–15ft (1–5m).

☀ ◌ pH Z9–11 H11–6

Campsis grandiflora
Deciduous, woody-stemmed, root climber. Leaves have 7 or 9 oval, toothed leaflets. Drooping clusters of trumpet-shaped, orange or red flowers, 2–3in (5–8cm) long, are produced in late summer and fall, abundantly in warm areas. **H** 22–30ft (7–10m).

☀ ◌ Z7–9 H9–7

Callistemon subulatus
Evergreen, arching shrub with narrowly oblong, bright green leaves. Dense spikes of crimson flowers are produced in summer. **H** 5ft (1.5m), **S** 6ft (2m).

☀ ◌ Z8–11 H11–10

Cestrum 'Newellii'
Evergreen, arching shrub bearing clusters of tubular, crimson flowers in late spring and summer. Leaves are large, broadly lance-shaped and dark green. **H** and **S** 10ft (3m).

☀ ◌ Z8–11 H11–1

Abutilon megapotamicum
Evergreen shrub with long, slender branches normally trained against a wall. Pendent, bell-shaped, yellow-and-red flowers are produced from late spring to fall. Leaves are oval, with heart-shaped bases, and dark green. **H** and **S** 6ft (2m).

☀ ◌ Z8–10 H11–1

Rhodochiton atrosanguineus
Evergreen, leaf-stalk climber, usually grown as an annual, with toothed leaves. Has tubular, blackish-purple flowers, with bell-shaped, red-purple calyces, from late spring to late fall. **H** to 10ft (3m). Min. 41°F (5°C).

☀ ◌ H8–2

Lablab purpureus (Australian pea, Hyacinth bean, Lablab)
Deciduous, woody-stemmed, twining climber, often grown as an annual. Purple, pinkish or white flowers in summer are followed by long pods with edible seeds. **H** 30ft (10m). Min. 41°F (5°C).

☀ ◌ Z9–11 H11–9

CLIMBERS AND WALL SHRUBS

Ipomoea hederacea
Annual, twining climber with heart-shaped or 3-lobed, mid- to bright green leaves. Has funnel-shaped, red, purple, pink or blue flowers in summer to early fall. **H** 10–12ft (3–4m).

☼ ◊ ⚠ Z10–11 H11–10

Buddleja crispa
Deciduous, upright, bushy shrub that, from mid- to late summer, bears racemes of small, fragrant, lilac flowers with white eyes. Has woolly, white shoots and oval, grayish-green leaves. **H** and **S** 10ft (3m).

☼ ◊ Z8–9 H9–8

Fabiana imbricata f. violacea
Evergreen, upright shrub with shoots that are densely covered with tiny, heather-like, deep green leaves. Tubular, lilac flowers are borne profusely in early summer. **H** and **S** 8ft (2.5m).

☼ ◊ Z9–11 H11–10

Akebia trifoliata
Deciduous, woody-stemmed, twining climber. Mid-green leaves, bronze-tinted when young, have 3 oval leaflets. Drooping racemes of purple flowers in spring are followed by sausage-shaped, purplish fruits. **H** to 30ft (10m) or more.

☼ ◊ Z5–8 H8–5

Cobaea scandens
(Cup-and-saucer vine)
Evergreen or deciduous, woody-stemmed, tendril climber, grown as an annual. From late summer to first frosts has flowers that open yellow-green and age to purple. **H** 12–15ft (4–5m). Min. 39°F (4°C).

☼ ◊ Z11 H11–10

Aristolochia macrophylla
(Dutchman's pipe)
Vigorous, deciduous climber with heart-shaped, dark green leaves, to 12in (30cm) long. In summer produces malodorous, trumpet-shaped, cream-colored flowers, strongly mottled yellow, purple and brown. **H** 30ft (10m).

☼ ◊ Z5–8 H8–4

Passiflora caerulea (Blue passion flower, Common passion flower)
Fast-growing, evergreen or semievergreen, woody-stemmed, tendril climber. Has white flowers, sometimes pink-flushed, with blue- or purple-banded crowns, in summer–fall. **H** to 30ft (10m) or more.

☼ ◊ ⚠ Z6–9 H9–6

Aconitum hemsleyanum
Wiry, scandent, fibrous perennial with hooded, lilac flowers produced in drooping clusters in late summer. Leaves are divided and mid-green. Is best grown where it can scramble through a shrub or be supported. **H** 6–8ft (2–2.5m), **S** 3–4ft (1–1.2m).

◑ ◊ ⚠ Z5–8 H8–5

Solanum crispum 'Glasnevin'
(Chilean potato tree)
Vigorous, evergreen or semievergreen, woody-stemmed, scrambling climber with oval leaves. Has clusters of lilac to purple flowers, 1in (2.5cm) across, in summer. **H** to 20ft (6m).

☼ ◊ ⚠ Z9–15 H12–1

Codonopsis convolvulacea
Herbaceous, twining climber with 1–2in (5cm) long, oval or lance-shaped leaves. Widely bell- to saucer-shaped, bluish-violet flowers, 1–2in (5cm) across, are borne in summer. **H** to 6ft (2m).

☀ ◊ Z7–9 H9–7

***Ipomoea tricolor* 'Heavenly Blue'** (Morning glory)
Fast-growing, annual, twining climber with heart-shaped leaves and large, funnel-shaped, sky-blue flowers borne from summer to early fall. **H** to 10ft (3m).

☀ ◊ ① H11–1

Plumbago auriculata (Cape leadwort)
Fast-growing, evergreen, woody-stemmed, scrambling climber. Trusses of sky-blue flowers are carried from summer to early winter. **H** 10–20ft (3–6m).

☀ ◊ H11–10

***Ceanothus* 'Puget Blue'**
Vigorous, evergreen, spreading shrub with arching branches clothed with small, oval, wrinkled, dark green leaves. In mid-spring produces abundant clusters of small, deep blue flowers. Is best grown trained as a wall shrub. **H** and **S** 10–13ft (3–4m).

☀ ◊ Z8–11 H11–8

***Ceanothus* 'Burkwoodii'**
Evergreen, bushy, dense shrub producing dense panicles of bright blue flowers from mid-summer to mid fall. Has oval, glossy, dark green leaves, downy and gray beneath. **H** 5ft (1.5m), **S** 6ft (2m).

☀ ◊ Z9–10 H10–8

WISTERIA

Wisterias are large, vigorous, deciduous climbers that flower in late spring to early summer, producing pendent racemes 18in (45cm) long or more, of scented, pealike flowers. These open in shades of white through pale lilac-blue to dark purple, and are sweetly scented. Often seen growing on arches and arbors, wisterias need strong support, as they become heavy with age, and their roots may damage building foundations. They prefer fertile, moist, well-drained soil in full sun or partial shade. Unless the soil is very poor, don't fertilize them, as this encourages excess growth. Choosing wisteria can be confusing because many varieties are commonly mislabeled.

W. brachybotrys 'Shiro-kapitan' ①

W. floribunda 'Hon-beni' ①

W. brachybotrys 'White Silk' ①

W. frutescens ①

W. frutescens 'Longwood Purple' ①

W. sinensis 'Prolific' ①

W. floribunda 'Yae-kokuryu' ①

W. frutescens 'Amethyst Falls' ①

YELLOW

Thladiantha dubia
Fast-growing, herbaceous or deciduous, tendril climber. Oval to heart-shaped, mid-green leaves, 4in (10cm) long, are hairy beneath; bell-shaped, yellow flowers are carried in summer.
H 10ft (3m).

☼ ◊ Z8–11 H12–9

Grevillea juniperina f. sulphurea
Evergreen, rounded, bushy shrub with almost needle-like leaves, recurved and dark green above, silky-haired beneath. Has clusters of small, spidery, pale yellow flowers in spring–summer.
H 5–6ft (1.5–2m), **S** 6–10ft (2–3m).

☼ ◊ pH ❗ Z9–11 H11–10

Hypericum 'Rowallane'
Semievergreen, arching shrub with oval, rich green leaves. Bears large, bowl-shaped, deep golden-yellow flowers from mid-summer to mid- or late fall. Is cut to ground level in severe winters. **H** to 6ft (1.8m), **S** to 3ft (1m).

☼ ◊ Z7–9 H9–7

Dendromecon rigida
Vigorous, evergreen, upright shrub, best grown against a wall. Large, fragrant, golden-yellow flowers appear amid gray-green foliage from spring to fall. **H** and **S** 10ft (3m).

☼ ◊ Z9–11 H11–9

Fremontodendron 'California Glory'
Very vigorous, evergreen or semievergreen, upright shrub. Has rounded, lobed, dark green leaves and large, bright yellow flowers from late spring to mid-fall. **H** 20ft (6m), **S** 12ft (4m).

☼ ◊ ❗ Z8–10 H10–8

Lonicera x americana (Honeysuckle)
Very free-flowering, deciduous, woody-stemmed, twining climber. Leaves are oval, upper ones united and saucer-like. Has clusters of strongly fragrant, yellow flowers, flushed with red-purple, in summer. **H** to 23ft (7m).

☼ ◊ ❗ Z6–9 H9–6

Piptanthus nepalensis
Deciduous or semievergreen, open shrub with leaves consisting of 3 large, dark blue-green leaflets. Racemes of pealike, bright yellow flowers appear in spring–summer. **H** 8ft (2.5m), **S** 6ft (2m).

☼ ◊ Z11 H11–9

Jasminum humile 'Revolutum'
Evergreen, bushy shrub with glossy, bright green leaves divided into 3–7 oval leaflets. Bears large, fragrant, tubular, upright, bright yellow flowers, with 5 spreading lobes, on long, slender, green shoots from early spring to late fall.
H 8ft (2.5m), **S** 10ft (3m).

☼ ◊ Z7–9 H9–7

Campsis radicans f. flava
Deciduous, woody-stemmed, root climber with leaves divided into 7–11 oval, toothed leaflets, downy beneath. Small clusters of trumpet-shaped, yellow flowers, 2½–3in (6–8cm) long, are produced in late summer and early fall. **H** 40ft (12m).

☼ ◊ Z5–9 H9–3

Thunbergia alata
(Black-eyed Susan vine)
Moderately fast-growing, annual, twining climber. Has toothed, oval to heart-shaped leaves and rounded, rather flat, small flowers, orange-yellow with very dark brown centers, from early summer to early fall. **H** 10ft (3m).

☼ ◊ Z11–15 H12–10

**Tropaeolum tuberosum
var. lineamaculatum 'Ken Aslet'**
Herbaceous climber with yellowish, red-streaked tubers and blue-green leaves. From mid-summer to fall has flowers with red sepals and orange petals. In cool areas, lift and store tubers in winter. **H** to 8ft (2.5m).

☼ ◊ Z8–15 H12–8

Bomarea multiflora
Herbaceous, twining climber with rounded clusters of 5–40 tubular to funnel-shaped, orange-red flowers, spotted crimson within, in summer. **H** 10–12ft (3–4m).

☼ ◊ Z11 H12–10

HONEYSUCKLE

Fragrant, colorful, and easy to grow, honeysuckles (*Lonicera*) can illuminate a border, wall, or fence with their distinctive blooms. They are mainly cultivated for their flowers, which are tubular or funnel- to bell-shaped, and come in a range of colors, from the bright golden-yellow of *L. etrusca* 'Superba', to the deep pink of *L. periclymenum* 'Red Gables'. The genus includes deciduous, semievergreen, or evergreen shrubs and twining climbers, which have a sweet fragrance that intensifies at night. Honeysuckles need fertile, well-drained soil, in sun or partial shade. Prune back young growth soon after flowering. Most produce berries, which should not be eaten.

L. etrusca 'Superba'

L. etrusca 'Michael Rosse'

L. japonica 'Aureoreticulata'   *L. henryi*

L. sempervirens ①

L. periclymenum 'Serotina'   *L. periclymenum* 'Red Gables'

CLIMBERS AND WALL SHRUBS

Eccremocarpus scaber
(Chilean glory flower, Glory vine)
Evergreen, subshrubby, tendril climber,
often grown as an annual. In summer
has racemes of small, orange-red
flowers, followed by inflated fruit
pods containing many winged seeds.
H 6–10ft (2–3m).

☀ ◌ Z11 H11–10

Mutisia decurrens
Evergreen, tendril climber with narrowly
oblong leaves, 2¾–5in (7–13cm) long.
Flower heads, 4–5in (10–13cm) across
with red or orange ray flowers, are
produced in summer. Proves difficult
to establish, but is worthwhile.
H to 10ft (3m).

☀ ◌ Z8–9 H9–8

Campsis radicans 'Flamenco'
Deciduous, woody-stemmed, root
climber with leaves divided into 7–11
oval, toothed leaflets, downy beneath.
Small clusters of trumpet-shaped,
orange-red flowers, 2½–3in (6–8cm)
long, are produced in late summer
and early fall. **H** 40ft (12m).

☀ ◌ Z5–9 H9–3

Fallopia baldschuanica
(Mile-a-minute plant, Russian vine)
Vigorous, deciduous, woody-stemmed,
twining climber with drooping panicles
of pink or white flowers in summer–fall.
H 40ft (12m) or more.

☀ ◌ Z5–9 H9–5

Jasminum polyanthum
Evergreen, woody-stemmed, twining
climber. Dark green leaves have 5 or
7 leaflets. Large clusters of fragrant,
5-lobed, white flowers, sometimes
reddish on the outside, are carried
from late summer to winter.
H 10ft (3m) or more.

☀ ◌ Z9–10 H10–9

Campsis x tagliabuana
'Madame Galen'
Deciduous, woody-stemmed, root
climber with leaves of 7 or more
narrowly oval, toothed leaflets.
Trumpet-shaped, orange-red flowers
are borne in pendent clusters from
late summer to fall. **H** to 30ft (10m).

☀ ◌ Z5–9 H9–5

***Vitis* 'Brant'**
Deciduous, woody-stemmed, tendril
climber with lobed, toothed, green
leaves, 4–9in (10–22cm) long. In fall
leaves mature to brown-red, except
for the veins. Produces tiny flowers in
summer, followed by green or purple
fruits. **H** to 22ft (7m) or more.

☀ ◌ Z5–9 H9–5

Cotoneaster horizontalis (Rockspray)
Deciduous, stiff-branched, spreading
shrub. Glossy, dark green leaves redden
in late fall. Bears pinkish-white flowers
from late spring to early summer,
followed by red fruits. **H** 3ft (1m),
S 5ft (1.5m).

☀ ◌ ❗ Z4–7 H7–3

Pyracantha coccinea 'Mohave'
Evergreen, dense, bushy shrub with
oval, dark green leaves. Dense clusters
of small, 5-petaled, white flowers in
early summer are followed by spherical,
bright red fruits. **H** and **S** 12ft (4m).

☀ ◊ Z6–9 H9–6

Parthenocissus tricuspidata
(Boston ivy)
Vigorous, deciduous, woody-stemmed,
tendril climber. Has spectacular,
crimson, fall leaf color and dull blue
berries. Will cover large expanses
of wall. **H** to 70ft (20m).

☀ ◊ ① Z4–8 H8–1

Celastrus orbiculatus 'Diana'
Vigorous, deciduous, twining climber
with small, rounded, toothed leaves.
Clusters of 2–4 small, green flowers are
borne in summer. Tiny, long-lasting,
green fruit turns black in fall and finally
splits, showing yellow insides and red
seeds. **H** to 46ft (14m).

☀ ◊ Z4–8 H8–1

Vitis coignetiae (Crimson glory vine)
Vigorous, deciduous, woody-stemmed,
tendril climber. Large leaves, brown-
haired beneath, are brightly colored
in fall. Has tiny, pale green flowers in
summer, followed by purplish-bloomed,
black berries. **H** to 50ft (15m).

☀◑ ◊ Z5–9 H9–5

Cayratia thomsonii
Deciduous, woody-stemmed, tendril
climber. Has glossy, green leaves with
5 leaflets that turn red-purple in fall,
and black berries. Provide some shade
for best fall color. **H** to 30ft (10m).

☀ ◊ ① Z4–8 H8–1

Parthenocissus tricuspidata 'Lowii'
Vigorous, deciduous, woody-stemmed,
tendril climber with deeply cut and
crinkled, 3–7-lobed leaves that turn
crimson in fall. Has insignificant
flowers, followed by dull blue berries.
H to 70ft (20m).

☀◑ ◊ ① Z4–8 H8–1

CLIMBERS AND WALL SHRUBS

PURPLE

Billardiera longiflora
Evergreen, woody-stemmed, twining climber with narrow leaves. Small, bell-shaped, sometimes purple-tinged, green-yellow flowers are produced singly in leaf axils in summer, followed by purple-blue fruits in fall. **H** to 6ft (2m).

☀ ◊ Z8–9 H9–8

Ampelopsis megalophylla
Vigorous, deciduous climber with glaucous shoots and large, pinnate to 2-pinnate, dark green leaves, glaucous beneath. Axillary clusters of small, green flowers, in summer, are followed by small, top-shaped, purple fruits that later turn black. **H** 30ft (10m).

☀ ◊ Z5–8 H8–1

Ampelopsis brevipedunculata var. maximowiczii
Vigorous, deciduous, woody-stemmed, twining, tendril climber with dark green leaves that vary in size and shape. Bears inconspicuous, greenish flowers in summer, followed by pinkish-purple, later bright blue berries. **H** to 15ft (5m).

☀ ◐ ◊ Z5–8 H8–2

Vitis vinifera 'Purpurea'
Deciduous, woody-stemmed, tendril climber with toothed, 3- or 5-lobed, purplish leaves, white-haired when young. Has tiny, pale green flowers in summer and tiny, green or purple berries. **H** to 23ft (7m).

☀ ◊ Z6–9 H9–6

Parthenocissus tricuspidata 'Veitchii'
Vigorous, deciduous, woody-stemmed, tendril climber. Has spectacular, red-purple, fall leaf color and dull blue berries. Greenish flowers are insignificant. **H** to 70ft (20m).

☀ ◐ ◊ ❗ Z4–8 H8–1

Hedera helix 'Glacier'
Vigorous, evergreen, self-clinging climber or trailing perennial bearing 5-lobed, silvery-gray-green leaves.
H 10ft (3m).

 ☼ ◐ △ ❗ Z5–11 H11–6

x Fatshedera lizei (Tree ivy)
Evergreen, loose-branched shrub that forms a mound of deeply lobed, glossy, deep green leaves. May also be trained as a climber. Sprays of small, white flowers appear in fall.
H 4–6ft (1.2–2m), **S** 10ft (3m).

☼ △ Z8–11 H12–8

Acacia dealbata
(Mimosa, Silver wattle)
Fast-growing, evergreen, spreading tree. Has feathery, blue-green leaves with many leaflets. Racemes of globular, fragrant, bright yellow flower heads are borne in winter–spring. **H** 50ft (15m), **S** 50ft (15m).

☼ △ Z9–11 H11–1

Garrya elliptica 'James Roof'
Evergreen, bushy, dense shrub with oval, wavy-edged, leathery, dark green leaves. Very long, gray-green catkins, with yellow anthers, are borne from mid- or late winter to early spring.
H and **S** 12ft (4m).

☼ △ Z8–11 H11–8

Hedera colchica 'Sulphur Heart'
Evergreen, self-clinging climber or trailing perennial with large, oval, unlobed leaves variegated yellow and light green. Is suitable for growing against a wall. **H** 15ft (5m).

 ☼ ◐ △ ❗ Z6–11 H11–1

Hedera helix 'Oro di Bogliasco'
Vigorous, evergreen, self-clinging climber or trailing perennial bearing 5-lobed, dark green leaves with bright yellow centers. Is slow to establish, then grows rapidly; is not suitable for groundcover. **H** 20ft (6m).

 ☼ ◐ △ ❗ Z5–11 H12–6

Itea ilicifolia
Evergreen, bushy shrub with arching shoots and oval, sharply toothed, glossy, dark green leaves. Long, catkin-like racemes of small, greenish flowers appear in late summer and early fall.
H 10–15ft (3–5m), **S** 10ft (3m).

☼ △ Z7–9 H9–7

211

PERENNIALS

One of the largest plant groups, perennials offer seasonal color,

fragrance, form and texture, with a wealth of plants to suit

every size and style of garden. They are traditionally grown

in herbaceous borders, using a wall or hedge as the backdrop

for the main summer display, but since most gardens are not

large enough for long borders solely devoted to perennials, they

are usually grown in mixed borders, together with shrubs,

annuals, biennials, and bulbs that extend the seasons of interest.

Although some perennials are evergreen, most die back in fall

and emerge again in spring. While this can leave borders bare in

winter, the seedheads and dried stems of some perennials,

including rudbeckias, echinops, and sedums, provide

a beautiful display when others have disappeared.

PERENNIALS

One of the largest and most versatile plant groups, perennials offer a seasonally changing diversity of color, fragrance, form, and texture. The choice of perennials is vast, and there is a huge choice to suit any garden style, from traditional to modern.

SIZE CATEGORIES USED WITHIN THIS GROUP		
Large over 4ft (1.2m)	**Medium** 2–4ft (60cm–1.2m)	**Small** up to 2ft (60cm)

What are perennials?

Perennials are nonwoody plants that live for two or more years and, when mature, produce flowers annually. The term often includes grasses and ferns. Although some perennials are evergreen, most are herbaceous and will die back each fall, emerging again in spring.

Choosing perennials

When making your selections, first check that the plants suit the climate, exposure, soil type, and light levels in your garden. Plants struggling in unsuitable conditions will not fulfill their intended purpose if they fail to flower or grow to fill their allotted space. The best results are usually achieved by grouping plants with similar cultivation needs; you may also find inspiration for garden planting schemes by looking at natural landscapes for symbiotic planting groups. For example, a deciduous woodland may feature a range of shade-loving ferns that marry well together.

When perennials are massed together in borders, consider their eventual height and spread to ensure vigorous types do not overshadow or swamp more delicate plants.

Designing with perennials

Long herbaceous borders, often 10ft (3m) or more in depth, flanked by mowed lawn and backed by a wall or hedge, were traditionally planted with perennials that create a spectacular display in summer. Today, many people do not have space for such a scheme, and perennials are now more commonly used in smaller beds and borders with other plants, such as shrubs, bulbs, and annuals. However, the design ideas employed in these large borders can be used in more modest schemes, with tall plants sited at the back, midrange types in the middle, and compact perennials planted at the front, ensuring that all can be seen clearly and no plants are obscured by taller neighbors. Plants are grouped in swaths of three or more of the same species, which lends borders a visual unity and rhythm.

Groups of tall verbascums, eupatoriums, and delphiniums create a backdrop for the border plants in front, while low, ground-covering perennials such as *Cerastium tomentosum* and *Stachys byzantina* are ideal at the front. Superb effects can then be created by using large specimens as a focal points, especially those that have an architectural form, such as cardoons (*Cynara cardunculus*) and bear's breeches (*Acanthus*), or a tall grass such as a miscanthus or *Stipa gigantea*.

Introduce variety of shape and texture by combining the rounded forms of sedums and geraniums with the upright spires of *Kniphofia* or salvias, for instance, or finely-cut *Corydalis flexuosa* leaves with the

ABOVE Frosted seedheads
Most perennials die down in winter, leaving borders bare, but a few, such as *Echinacea purpurea* 'Kim's Knee High' form decorative seedheads that remain for many months in winter.

LEFT Contrasting colors and forms
This design focuses on matching the blues and yellows of delphiniums, echinops, salvias, *Thalictrum flavum* subsp. *glaucum*, nepetas, verbascums, and foxgloves. Contrasting flower forms intensify the effect.

bolder outlines of hostas in shady areas. Or use the stems of bleeding heart (*Dicentra spectabilis*) and *Polygonatum* x *hybridum* to gracefully arch over shorter plants, such as heucheras and *Alchemilla mollis*.

When making your selections, consider the foliage shape, form, and texture as well as flower colors. The boldly pleated foliage of veratrums and delicate, pinnate leaves of *Polemonium caeruleum* are worthy of consideration, while furry verbascums are seductively tactile.

The disadvantage of planting herbaceous perennials is that the garden looks bare in winter, unless you plant sturdy types with long-lasting seedheads, such as sedum,

ABOVE Contrasting foliage
In damp, dappled shade, elegant contrasts of foliage form and texture create an atmosphere of lush abundance. A selection of bergenias, hostas, ferns, and ligularias are included in this lush scheme.

rudbeckias, and many grasses. These can be left to stand and provide interest until new shoots appear in spring. Prairie-style schemes use these types of plants for year-round interest; rather than planting in long borders, perennials and grasses are used in large bold groups, with tall see-through plants in front of shorter ones. Just a few plant species are used, and repeated to mirror nature. The effects of prairie schemes are best seen in larger gardens.

STAKING BORDER PERENNIALS

Many tall perennials, such as delphiniums and achilleas, become top-heavy and require some form of support. If you provide plant supports early in the season, the plants will grow through and disguise them. Plants staked at a later date, especially once they have already flopped, always tend to look trussed up.

Using canes
Bamboo canes are ideal for supporting tall flowers such as delphiniums. Use soft twine to tie the stems to the supports.

Using twiggy sticks
Plants with moundlike growth will grow through and be supported by twiggy sticks placed around stems in spring.

Using metal spirals
Metal spirals provide good support for perennials such as this *Pimpinella* and also make decorative features.

DIVIDING PERENNIALS

This easy method of propagation can be used to propagate most herbaceous perennials as well as to rejuvenate large, tired clumps that are no longer flowering well. You can also divide newly bought perennials, provided they are large enough and have clearly divisible stems, to make the most of your purchases. Most perennials can be divided in fall or early spring just as the shoots appear.

1 Dig up the plant
In early spring, select a clump of plants and water them well. Cut back any old top growth to the ground. Using a fork, lift the clump of plants, taking great care to keep the whole rootball intact.

2 Divide with forks
Cut solid crowns into portions with a spade or old bread knife. If you cannot pry other pieces apart by hand, use two forks held back-to-back to split the clump into smaller sections.

3 Replant the divisions
Discard the dead central portions of overgrown clumps. Replant healthy, hand-sized pieces with strong buds in soil improved with well-rotted organic matter, such as manure. Water in well.

WHITE

Sanguisorba tenuifolia 'Alba'
Clump-forming, upright perennial
with branched, slender stems and
pinnate, toothed leaves. Pendent,
bottlebrush-like spikes of fluffy, white
flowers are borne in late summer.
H 6ft (1.8m), **S** 3ft (90cm).

☼ ◊ Z9–7 H7–1

Crambe cordifolia
Robust perennial with clouds of
small, fragrant, white flowers borne
in branching sprays in summer
above mounds of large, crinkled
and lobed, dark green leaves.
H to 6ft (2m), **S** 4ft (1.2m).

☼ ◊ Z6–9 H9–6

Artemisia lactiflora (White mugwort)
Vigorous, erect perennial. Many sprays
of creamy-white buds open to off-white
flowers in summer. Dark green leaves
are jagged-toothed. Needs staking
and is best as a foil to stronger colors.
H 4–5ft (1.2–1.5m), **S** 20in (50cm).

☼ ◊ Z5–8 H8–5

Romneya coulteri (Tree poppy)
Vigorous, bushy, subshrubby perennial,
grown for its large, fragrant, white
flowers, with prominent centers of
golden stamens, that appear in late
summer. Has deeply divided, gray
leaves. **H** and **S** 6ft (2m).

☼ ◊ Z8–10 H9–2

Epilobium angustifolium f. album
(White rosebay)
Vigorous, upright perennial bearing
sprays of pure white flowers along
wandlike stems in late summer.
Leaves are small and lance-shaped.
May spread rapidly. **H** 4–5ft (1.2–1.5m),
S 20in (50cm) or more.

☼ ◊ Z3–7 H7–1

Impatiens tinctoria
Vigorous, upright, tuberous perennial
with fleshy, branched stems and oval,
toothed, dark green leaves. In late
summer produces large, night-scented,
white-and-purple flowers. Needs shelter
and fertile soil. **H** 5ft (1.5m), **S** 3ft (90cm).

☼ ◊ H11–1

Eremurus robustus
Upright perennial with straplike leaves
that die back during summer as huge
racemes of cup-shaped, pink blooms
appear. Cover crowns in winter with
compost or straw. Needs staking.
H to 10ft (3m), **S** to 4ft (1.2m).

☼ ◊ Z5–8 H8–5

Macleaya microcarpa
'Kelway's Coral Plume'
Clump-forming perennial that in
summer produces branching spikes of
rich pink-buff flowers. Large, rounded,
lobed leaves are gray-green above,
gray-white beneath. **H** 6–8ft (2–2.5m),
S 3–4ft (1–1.2m).

☼ ◊ Z4–9 H9–1

Cynara cardunculus (Cardoon)
Stately perennial with large clumps
of arching, pointed, divided, silver-
gray leaves, above which rise large,
thistle-like, blue-purple flower heads
borne singly on sturdy, gray stems
in summer. Flower heads dry well.
H 6ft (2m), **S** 3ft (1m).

☼ ◊ Z7–10 H9–1

Veratrum nigrum
(Black false hellebore)
Erect, stately perennial that from late
summer onward bears long spikes of
chocolate-purple flowers at the ends
of sturdy, upright stems. Stems are
clothed with ribbed, oval to narrowly
oval leaves. **H** 6ft (2m), **S** 2ft (60cm).

☼ ◊ ① Z6–9 H9–6

Phormium 'Dazzler'
Evergreen, upright perennial with
tufts of bold, stiff, pointed leaves in
tones of yellow, salmon-pink, orange-red
and bronze. Bluish-purple stems carry
panicles of reddish flowers in summer.
H 6–8ft (2–2.5m) in flower, **S** 3ft (1m).

☼ ◊ Z9–11 H11–2

DELPHINIUMS

Delphiniums make a bold statement in summer gardens, with their elegant, showy spires of single or double flowers. Their classic color is blue, but hybrids are now available in a broad range of colors, from white and pastel shades of pink and lilac, to rich mauves, violet-purples, and new red selections. Grow tall delphiniums in a mixed border or island bed, and dwarf types in a rock garden. Plants thrive in full sun and well-drained soil, and apart from dwarf species and cultivars, all require staking to support their heavy flower spikes. In growth, water all plants freely, applying a balanced liquid fertilizer every 2–3 weeks. Deadhead by cutting spent flower spikes back to small, flowering side shoots. Protect plants from slugs and snails.

D. 'Gillian Dallas' ①

D. 'Can-Can' ①

D. 'Olive Poppleton' ①

D. 'Sandpiper' ①

D. 'Langdon's Royal Flush' ①

D. 'Min' ①

D. 'Cliveden Beauty' ①

D. 'Elizabeth Cook' ①

D. 'Spindrift' ①

D. 'Bruce' ①

D. grandiflorum 'Blue Butterfly' ①

D. 'Red Caroline' ①

D. 'Lucia Sahin' ①

D. 'Michael Ayres' ①

D. 'Alice Artindale' ①

D. 'Loch Leven' ①

PURPLE

Thalictrum 'Elin'
Clump-forming perennial with fernlike, blue-green leaves. Erect, sturdy, purplish-green stems bear billowing panicles of tiny, fluffy, creamy-yellow and purple flowers in summer.
H 8ft (2.5m), **S** 3ft (90cm) or more.

☀ ◊ Z5–8 H8–5

Galega x hartlandii 'Lady Wilson'
Vigorous, upright perennial with spikes of small, pealike, blue and pinkish-white flowers in summer above bold leaves divided into oval leaflets. Needs staking. **H** to 5ft (1.5m), **S** 3ft (1m).

☀ ◊ Z5–11 H11–5

BLUE

Meconopsis grandis
(Himalyan Blue poppy)
Erect perennial with oblong, slightly toothed, hairy, mid-green leaves produced in rosettes at the base. Sturdy stems bear slightly nodding, cup-shaped, deep blue flowers in early summer. Divide every 2–3 years. **H** 3–5ft (1–1.5m), **S** 12in (30cm).

☀ ◊ pH Z5–8 H8–5

HIMALAYAN POPPIES

With delicate flowers in a wide range of colors, including beautiful shades of sky blue, *Meconopsis* (Himalayan poppies) are striking garden plants. Some also have attractive rosettes of foliage that develop slowly before the first flowers appear. Many are suited to moist, woodland conditions in light or partial shade, and acidic, well-drained soil; others are best treated as alpines in raised beds or troughs. All prefer cooler conditions. Most of the big blue poppy cultivars are sterile and very long-lived. Other *Meconopsis* are monocarpic perennials, living for a few years before flowering, setting seed, and then dying.

M. x cookei 'Old Rose'

M. Infertile Blue Group 'Slieve Donard'

M. Infertile Blue Group 'Crewdson Hybrid'

Angelica archangelica (Angelica)
Upright perennial, usually grown as
a biennial, with deeply divided, bright
green leaves and white or green flowers
in late summer. Stems have culinary
usage and when crystallized may be
used for confectionery decoration.
H 6ft (2m), **S** 3ft (1m).

☀ ◊ Z4–9 H9–1

Musa basjoo (Japanese banana)
Evergreen, palmlike, suckering perennial
with arching leaves to 3ft (1m) long.
Has drooping, pale yellow flowers with
brownish bracts in summer followed
by green fruits. **H** 10–15ft (3–5m),
S 6–8ft (2–2.5m).

☀ ◊ Z8–11 H11–8

Acanthus mollis 'Hollard's Gold'
Semievergreen perennial with large,
oval, deeply cut, glossy leaves. New
leaves are golden-yellow, fading to
green. Spires of white and mauve
flowers are borne in summer.
H 5ft (1.5m), **S** 2ft (60cm) or more.

◐ ◊ Z7–11 H11–7

Verbascum olympicum
Semievergreen, rosette-forming
biennial or short-lived perennial.
Branching stems, arising from feltlike, gray foliage at the plant base,
bear sprays of 5-lobed, bright golden
flowers from mid-summer onward.
H 6ft (2m), **S** 3ft (1m).

☀ ◊ Z5–9 H9–5

Inula magnifica
Robust, clump-forming, upright
perennial with a mass of lance-shaped
to elliptic, rough leaves. Leafy stems
bear terminal heads of large, daisylike,
yellow flower heads in late summer.
Needs staking. **H** 6ft (1.8m), **S** 3ft (1m).

☀ ◊ Z5–8 H8–5

Ferula communis (Giant fennel)
Upright perennial. Large, cow-parsley-
like umbels of yellow flowers are borne
from late spring to summer on the
tops of stems that arise from a mound
of finely cut, mid-green foliage.
H 6–7ft (2–2.3m), **S** 3–4ft (1–1.2m).

☀ ◊ Z6–9 H9–6

Delphinium 'Sungleam'
Elatum Group herbaceous perennial
with spikes, 16–30in (40–75cm) long,
of semidouble, white flowers, 2–3in
(5–7cm) across, overlaid with pale
yellow and with yellow eyes, produced
in mid-summer. **H** 5½–6ft (1.7–2m),
S 24–36in (60–90cm).

☀ ◊ ❶ Z3–7 H8–3

Ligularia 'The Rocket'
Clump-forming perennial with
triangular, deeply toothed leaves
on tall stems. In summer produces
dark-stemmed racemes of daisylike,
bright yellow flower heads.
H 6ft (1.8m), **S** 3ft (1m).

☀ ◐ ◊ Z4–8 H8–1

PERENNIALS

219

SUMMER **FALL**

PERENNIALS

ORANGE

Heliopsis helianthoides var. scabra 'Light of Loddon'
Upright perennial bearing dahlia-like, double, bright orange flower heads on strong stems in late susmmer. Dark green leaves are coarse and serrated. **H** 4–5ft (1.2–1.5m), **S** 2ft (60cm).

☼ ◊ Z4–9 H9–1

Hedychium x moorei 'Tara'
Erect, rhizomatous perennial with stout, leafy stems bearing lance-shaped, gray-green leaves. Cylindrical racemes of tubular, spidery, scented, orange flowers, with prominent stamens, are borne in late summer. **H** 5ft (1.5m), **S** 2ft (60cm) or more.

☼ ◊ Z8–10 H10–8

Eremurus x isabellinus 'Cleopatra'
Clump-forming perennial with narrowly strap-shaped, soft green leaves. In summer produces stout, dense spikes of star-shaped, coppery-orange flowers. **H** 5ft (1.5m), **S** 20in (50cm).

☼ ◊ Z5–8 H8–5

WHITE

Cimicifuga simplex
Upright perennial with arching spikes of tiny, slightly fragrant, star-shaped, white flowers in fall. Leaves are glossy and divided. Needs staking. **H** 4–5ft (1.2–1.5m), **S** 24in (60cm).

☼◐ ◊ Z4–8 H11–1

Leucanthemella serotina
Erect perennial with lance-shaped, toothed, dark green leaves. Leafy stems produce sprays of large, green-centered, white flower heads in late fall. **H** 5ft (1.5m), **S** 3ft (90cm).

◐ ◊ Z4–9 H9–1

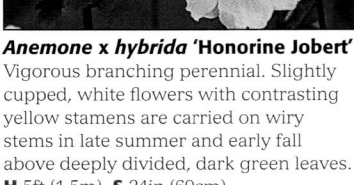

Anemone x hybrida 'Honorine Jobert'
Vigorous branching perennial. Slightly cupped, white flowers with contrasting yellow stamens are carried on wiry stems in late summer and early fall above deeply divided, dark green leaves. **H** 5ft (1.5m), **S** 24in (60cm).

☼◐ ◊ ① Z4–8 H8–5

PINK

Thalictrum delavayi 'Hewitt's Double'
Clump-forming perennial with fernlike, mid-green leaves. Bears large billowing panicles of tiny, double, lavender flowers from late summer to fall. **H** 5ft (1.5m), **S** 24in (60cm) or more.

☼ ◊ Z4–7 H7–1

Veronicastrum virginicum 'Fascination'
Upright perennial with stout stems bearing erect racemes of tiny, star-shaped, mauve flowers, which are darker at the tips, in mid- and late summer. Has lance-shaped, whorled, dark green leaves. **H** 5ft (1.5cm), **S** 16in (40cm).

☼ ◊ Z4–8 H8–3

Salvia involucrata 'Bethellii'
Subshrubby perennial that produces
long racemes of large, cerise-crimson
blooms, with pink bracts, in late summer
and fall. Leaves are oval to heart-shaped.
H 4–5ft (1.2–1.5m), **S** 3ft (1m).

☼ ◊ Z11–15 H12–10

Eupatorium maculatum 'Riesenschirm'
Upright, deciduous perennial with
rounded, fluffy, purple-pink flower heads
in late summer, which are attractive to
insects. Oval to lance-shaped, reddish-
green leaves are arranged in whorls up
purple stems. Is superb for the back of
a deep border. **H** 8ft (2.5m), **S** 5ft (1.5m).

☼ ◑ Z5–11 H9–1

Verbena bonariensis
Perennial with a basal clump of
dark green leaves. Upright, wiry
stems carry tufts of tiny, purplish-
blue flowers in summer–fall.
H 5ft (1.5m), **S** 24in (60cm).

☼ ◊ Z7–11 H12–7

ECHINACEA

Admired for their cone and daisylike
flowers, *Echinacea* cultivars have
expanded their repertoire; while once
they were restricted to purple, pink,
and white, a range of green, orange,
yellow, and red flowers are now
available, as well as double-flowered
forms. They create bold and beautiful
late summer and early fall displays,
and the faded flower heads also offer
structural interest into winter. Grow
plants in well-drained, humus-rich soil
in full sun, although they will tolerate
some shade. Protect young plants
from slug and snail damage.

E. angustifolia

E. 'Harvest Moon'

E. paradoxa

E. purpurea 'Doubledecker'

E. purpurea 'Razzmatazz'

E. purpurea 'Sundown'

JAPANESE ANEMONES

These useful plants fill the late summer and early fall garden with single or double flowers held on slender stems above handsome, divided, groundcovering foliage. The blooms are available in white and shades of pink and purple and are ideal for the middle to back of mixed borders, and in woodland gardens, injecting interest when many other flowers have faded. Border anemones are easy to grow, and thrive in a wide range of soil conditions and in sun or light shade. Once the plants are established, they develop into large clumps, which can be lifted and divided in fall or spring.

A. hupehensis var. *japonica* 'Bressingham Glow' ⓘ

A. x *hybrida* 'Robustissima'

A. hupehensis var. *japonica* 'Pamina'

A. x *hybrida* 'Königin Charlotte'

A. x *hybrida* 'September Charm' ⓘ

A. *hupehensis* 'Praecox'

YELLOW

Rudbeckia laciniata 'Goldquelle'
Erect perennial. In late summer and fall, daisylike, double, bright yellow flower heads with green centers are borne singly on stout stems. Has deeply divided, mid-green foliage. **H** 5–6ft (1.5–2m), **S** 2–2½ft (60–75cm).

☼ ◊ Z3–9 H9–1

Helianthus 'Lemon Queen'
Vigorous, upright, rhizomatous perennial with stout, branched stems bearing oval, rough, dark green leaves. Bears masses of large, daisylike, pale yellow flower heads in summer–fall. **H** 5ft (1.5m), **S** 24in (60cm) or more.

☼ ◊ Z4–9 H9–1

Helianthus x multiflorus 'Loddon Gold'
Upright perennial bearing showy, large, vivid deep yellow flower heads with rounded, double centers in late summer and early fall. Needs staking and may spread quickly. **H** 5ft (1.5m), **S** 2ft (60cm).

☼ ◊ ⓘ Z5–9 H9–5

Helianthus salicifolius
(Willow-leaved sunflower)
Upright, clump-forming perennial grown for its whorls of lance-shaped, dark green leaves. Clusters of daisylike, yellow flowers are borne on branching stems in fall. Is best at the back of a border. **H** 6ft (2m), **S** 2ft (60cm) or more.

☼ ◊ Z6–9 H9–6

WHITE

Smilacina racemosa
(False spikenard)
Arching perennial. Has oval, light green leaves terminating in feathery sprays of white flowers that appear from spring to mid-summer and are followed by fleshy, reddish fruits. **H** 30–36in (75–90cm), **S** 18in (45cm).

☼ ◊ ❗ Z4–9 H9–1

Ranunculus aconitifolius
Vigorous, clump-forming perennial with deeply divided, dark green leaves. Single, white flowers, about 1in (3cm) across, are borne in spring and early summer. **H** and **S** 3ft (1m).

☼ ◊ Z5–9 H9–5

Polygonatum x hybridum
(Solomon's seal)
Arching, leafy perennial with fleshy rhizomes. In late spring, clusters of small, pendent, tubular, greenish-white flowers are produced in axils of neat, oval leaves. **H** 4ft (1.2m), **S** 3ft (1m).

☼ ◊ ❗ Z6–9 H9–6

Dicentra spectabilis f. alba
Leafy perennial forming a hummock of fernlike, deeply cut, light green foliage with arching sprays of pendent, heart-shaped, pure white flowers in late spring and summer. **H** 24–30in (60–75cm), **S** 24in (60cm).

☼ ◊ ❗ Z3–9 H9–1

PINK

Dicentra spectabilis
(Bleeding heart, Dutchman's trousers)
Leafy perennial forming a hummock of fernlike, mid-green foliage, above which rise arching stems of pendent, heart-shaped, pinkish-red and white flowers in late spring and summer. **H** 30in (75cm), **S** 20in (50cm).

☽ ◊ ❗ Z3–9 H9–1

Diascia personata
Semievergreen, semi-erect perennial with masses of lobed, dusky-pink flowers held in spires from late spring to the first frosts. Small, narrowly ovate, mid-green leaves are borne on rather lax, brittle stems, which require support. **H** 4ft (1.2m), **S** 3ft (90cm).

☼ ◊ Z8–9 H9–7

PURPLE

Aquilegia vulgaris var. stellata 'Black Barlow'
Clump-forming, perennial with mid-green leaves divided into lobed leaflets. In later spring and early summer bears dark purple, bell-shaped flowers, with no spurs, and spreading petals in shades of blue or pink. **H** 3ft (1m), **S** 20in (50cm).

☼ ◊ Z3–8 H8–1

Geranium phaeum
(Mourning widow)
Clump-forming perennial with lobed, soft green leaves and maroon-purple flowers, with reflexed petals, borne on rather lax stems in late spring. **H** 30in (75cm), **S** 18in (45cm).

● ◊ Z4–8 H8–1

IRISES

Few other perennials show such diversity of flower color as irises; and you will find one for almost every position in the garden. They have a long flowering season, the earliest appearing in the first months of the year, the latest in early fall. Their flowers often have "beards" (short hairs) or crests that add to their appeal, while a few are grown for their foliage or seed heads. The genus is classified into many divisions. Of these, the easiest to grow are the bearded, crested, and Xiphium irises. Siberian and Japanese types are ideal for bog gardens or watersides, but they will tolerate drier sites. Juno, Oncocyclus, and Regelia irises are more difficult to grow, though their beautiful flowers are worth the effort. For more information, see the Plant Dictionary.

I. 'Ringo' [bearded]

I. ensata 'Rose Queen' ① [bearded]

I. japonica ① [Evansia]

I. 'Bold Print' ① [bearded]

I. 'Autumn Circus' ① [bearded]

I. 'Green Spot' ① [bearded]

I. hoogiana ① [Regelia]

I. x *robusta* 'Gerald Darby' ① [beardless]

confusa ① [crested]

I. ensata 'Moonlight Waves' ① [beardless]

I. 'Mountain Lake' ① [Siberian]

I. cristata ① [Evansia]

I. 'Dreaming Yellow' ① [Siberian]

I. 'Champagne Elegance' ① [bearded]

I. sanguinea 'Snow Queen' ① [beardless]

I. unguicularis subsp. *cretensis* ① [beardless]

I. 'Oriental Eyes' ① [beardless]

magnifica ① [Juno]

I. germanica 'Florentina' ① [bearded]

'Tropic Night' ⓘ [Siberian]

I. **'Joyce'** ⓘ [Reticulata]

I. **'Eyebright'** ⓘ [bearded]

I. variegata ⓘ [bearded]

I. winogradowii ⓘ [Reticulata]

I. **'Bumblebee Deelite'** ⓘ [bearded]

I. pseudacorus ⓘ [beardless]

versicolor **'Kermesina'** ⓘ [beardless]

I. **'Ola Kala'** ⓘ [bearded]

I. **'Berlin Tiger'** ⓘ [beardless]

I. **'Perry's Blue'** ⓘ [beardless]

sibirica **'Papillon'** ⓘ [Siberian]

I. sibirica **'Soft Blue'** ⓘ [Siberian]

I. **'Katharine Hodgkin'** ⓘ [Reticulata]

I. reticulata **'Cantab'** ⓘ [Reticulata]

I. **'Kent Pride'** ⓘ [bearded]

I. **'Holden Clough'** ⓘ [beardless]

AQUILEGIAS

Commonly known as columbines, *Aquilegia* are ideal cottage garden plants, well suited to growing in borders, rock gardens, and as fillers between summer-flowering shrubs. Most are graceful, elegant plants with divided basal foliage topped in late spring and summer by a succession of delicate, bell-shaped, usually spurred flowers, although some have rounded double blooms. They vary in color from light and dark blue, purple, almost black, dark red, and pink, to orange, yellow, and white; many are bicolored. *Aquilegia* thrive in moist but well-drained soil, and full sun or dappled shade. They are normally raised from seed, which is freely produced, and once established, they tend to self-seed, although most do not come true to type.

A. vulgaris var. *stellata* 'Ruby Port'   *A. flabellata* var. *pumila*

A. 'Dove' (Songbird Series)

A. 'Hensol Harebell'

A. vulgaris 'William Guiness'

A. 'Bluebird' (Songbird Series)

A. vulgaris 'Nivea'

A. 'Dragonfly'

A. coerulea

A. 'Bunting' (Songbird Series)

A. triternata

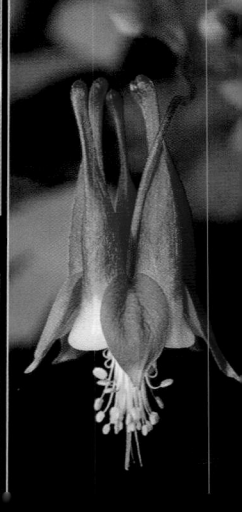

BLUE

YELLOW

Symphytum x uplandicum 'Variegatum'

Perennial with large, hairy, gray-green leaves that have broad, cream margins. In late spring and early summer, pink or blue buds open to tubular, blue or purplish-blue flowers. **H** 3ft (1m), **S** 24in (60cm).

☀ ◊ ❢ Z3–9 H9–1

Symphytum caucasicum

Clump-forming perennial carrying clusters of pendent, azure-blue flowers in spring above rough, hairy, mid-green foliage. Is best suited to a wild garden. **H** and **S** 24–36in (60–90cm).

☀ ◊ ❢ Z3–9 H9–1

Iris 'Butter and Sugar'

Rhizomatous, beardless Siberian iris with large, yellow and white flowers produced from late spring to early summer. **H** 3ft (1m), **S** indefinite.

☀ ◊ ❢ Z3–9 H9–1

Paeonia mlokosewitschii

Clump-forming perennial with soft bluish-green leaves, sometimes edged reddish-purple. Produces large, single, lemon-yellow flowers in late spring and early summer. **H** and **S** 30in (75cm).

☀ ◊ ❢ Z5–8 H8–5

Chelidonium majus 'Flore Pleno'

Upright perennial with divided, bright green leaves and many cup-shaped, double, yellow flowers borne on branching sprays in late spring and early summer. Seeds freely and is best in a wild garden. **H** 24–30in (60–90cm), **S** 12in (30cm).

☀ ◊ ❢ Z5–8 H8–5

Asphodeline lutea (Yellow asphodel)

Neat, clump-forming perennial that bears dense spikes of star-shaped, yellow flowers amid narrow, gray-green leaves in late spring. **H** 3–4ft (1–1.2m), **S** 2–3ft (60cm–1m).

☀ ◊ Z6–9 H9–6

Doronicum columnae 'Miss Mason'

Clump-forming, rhizomatous perennial with heart-shaped leaves. Slender stems bear daisylike, bright yellow flower heads, 3in (8cm) across, held well above the foliage, in mid- and late spring. **H** and **S** 24in (60cm).

☀ ◊ Z4–8 H8–1

Aciphylla aurea (Golden Spaniard)

Evergreen, rosette-forming perennial with long, bayonet-like, yellow-green leaves. Bears spikes of golden flowers up to 6ft (2m) tall from late spring to early summer. **H** and **S** in leaf 24–30in (60–75cm).

☀ ◊ Z8–11 H11–8

Euphorbia rigida

Mound-forming, evergreen perennial with semi-upright stems with whorls of lance-shaped, blue-green leaves. Terminal umbels of bright yellow-green flowers are borne in spring. **H** 24in (60cm), **S** 24in (60cm) or more.

☀ ◊ ❢ Z7–11 H11–7

PERENNIALS

227

PEONIES

Peonies (*Paeonia* species and cultivars) are valued for their showy blooms, filling borders with whites, pinks, yellows, and reds in late spring and early to mid-summer. Flowers include single, double, or anemone forms (with broad, outer petals and a mass of petaloids in the center); some are scented. They may need support when in full bloom and make good cut flowers. The foliage is striking, too, often tinged bronze when young and rich red in fall. As well as many attractive species and a wide range of herbaceous hybrids, there are several tree peonies (cultivars of *P. suffruticosa*), and intersectional hybrids, which are crosses between the latter two. Peonies prefer sun but will tolerate light shade, and need rich, well-drained soil. These long-lived plants resent transplanting and are best left undisturbed.

P. 'Sarah Bernhardt' ①
[double]

P. 'Kelway's Fairy Queen' [semidouble]

P. suffruticosa 'Hana-kisoi' ①
[tree peony]

P. suffruticosa 'Hakuo-jisi'
[tree peony]

P. 'White Wings' ① [single]

P. 'Whitleyi Major' ① [single]

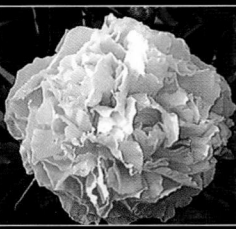

P. 'Shirley Temple' ① [double]

P. 'Bowl of Beauty' ①
[anemone]

P. cambessedesii ① [single]

P. 'Cheddar Gold' [semidouble]

P. 'Festiva Maxima' [double]

P. 'Lady Alexandra Duff'
[semidouble]

P. 'Pillow Talk' [double]

P. suffruticosa 'Yachiyo-tsubaki' [tree peony]

P. obovata var. *alba* ① [single]

P. japonica [single]

P. 'Jan van Leeuwen' [single]

P. emodi ① [single]

P. 'Coral Charm' [semidouble]

P. *suffrutixcosa* 'Rimpo' [tree peony]

P. 'Kelway's Gorgeous' ① [single]

P. 'Magic Orb' ① [double]

P. *suffruticosa* 'Cardinal Vaughan' ① [semidouble]

P. 'Bartzella' [double]

P. 'Paul M. Wild' [double]

P. 'America' ① [single]

P. 'Laura Dessert' ① [double]

P. 'Claire de Lune' [single]

P. 'Félix Crousse' [double]

P. 'Knighthood' ① [double]

P. *veitchii* ① [single]

P. 'Garden Treasure' [tree peony]

P. x *lemoinei* 'L'Espérance' ① [single]

P. x *lemoinei* 'High Noon' [tree peony]

P. *officinalis* 'Rubra Plena' ① [double]

P. *peregrina* 'Otto Froebel' ① [single]

P. 'Thunderbolt' [single]

P. *ludlowii* ① [single]

P. 'Buckeye Belle' [semidouble]

WHITE

**Ranunculus aconitifolius
'Flore Pleno'**
Clump-forming perennial with deeply
divided, dark green leaves. Double,
pure white flowers are borne on strong,
branched stems in spring–summer.
H 24–30in (60–75cm), **S** 20in (50cm).

☀ ○ Z5–9 H9–5

Libertia grandiflora
(New Zealand satin flower)
Loosely clump-forming, rhizomatous
perennial. In early summer produces
spikes of white flowers above grasslike,
dark green leaves that turn brown at
the tips. Has decorative seed pods
in fall. **H** 30in (75cm), **S** 24in (60cm).

☀ ○ Z8–11 H11–8

Leucanthemum x superbum 'Aglaia'
Robust perennial with large, daisylike,
semidouble, yellow-centered, pure
white flower heads, on stout, upright
stems, borne singly in early summer.
Has spoon-shaped, toothed, glossy,
dark green leaves. **H** 28in (70cm),
S 20in (50cm).

☀ ○ Z5–8 H8–1

Asphodelus albus (White asphodel)
Upright perennial with clusters
of star-shaped, white flowers borne
in late spring and early summer. Has
narrow, basal tufts of mid-green leaves.
H 3ft (1m), **S** 1½ft (45cm).

☀ ○ Z7–11 H11–7

Phlox paniculata 'Mount Fuji'
Upright perennial with star-shaped,
white flowers borne in conical heads in
late summer. Has oval, mid-green leaves.
H 4ft (1.2m), **S** 2ft (60cm).

☀ ○ Z4–8 H8–1

Dictamnus albus var. **albus**
(Dittany, gas plant)
Upright perennial bearing, in early
summer, spikes of fragrant, star-shaped,
white flowers with long stamens.
Light green leaves are divided into
oval leaflets. Dislikes disturbance.
H 3ft (1m), **S** 2ft (60cm).

☀ ○ ❗ Z3–8 H8–3

Selinum wallichianum
Upright, architectural perennial with
dainty, long-lasting, lacy umbels of
star-shaped, white flowers, borne
on leafy, branched stems, in mid-
and late summer. Has very finely
divided, fernlike, bright green leaves.
H 4ft (1.2m), **S** 16in (40cm).

☀ ○ Z4–7 H7–4

Hesperis matronalis
(Dame's rocket, sweet rocket)
Upright perennial with long spikes
of many 4-petaled, white or violet
flowers borne in summer. Flowers
have a strong fragrance in the evening.
Leaves are smooth and narrowly oval.
H 30in (75cm), **S** 24in (60cm).

☀ ○ Z4–9 H9–1

Myrrhis odorata (Sweet Cicely)
Graceful perennial that resembles
cow parsley. Has aromatic, fernlike,
mid-green foliage and fragrant, bright
creamy-white flowers in early summer.
H 24–36in (60–90cm), **S** 24in (60cm).

☀ ○ Z3–7 H7–1

Aruncus dioicus 'Kneiffii'

Hummock-forming perennial that has deeply cut, feathery leaves with lance-shaped leaflets on elegant stems and bears branching plumes of tiny, star-shaped, creamy-white flowers in mid-summer. **H** 3ft (90cm), **S** 20in (50cm).

☼ ◊ Z3–7 H7–1

Nicotiana alata

Rosette-forming perennial, often grown as an annual, that in late summer bears clusters of tubular, creamy-white flowers, pale brownish-violet externally, which are fragrant at night. Has oval, mid-green leaves. **H** 30in (75cm), **S** 12in (30cm).

☼ ◊ ❶ Z10–11 H11–1

Leucanthemum x superbum 'Sonnenschein'

Erect perennial with large, daisylike, single, creamy-yellow flower heads, each with a darker yellow center, borne from mid- to late summer. Has spoon-shaped, toothed, dark green leaves. May need staking. **H** 36in (90cm), **S** 20in (50cm).

☼ ◊ Z5–8 H8–1

Morina longifolia

Evergreen perennial that produces rosettes of large, spiny, thistle-like, rich green leaves. Whorls of hooded, tubular, white flowers, flushed pink within, are borne well above foliage in mid-summer. **H** 24–30in (60–75cm), **S** 12in (30cm).

☼ ◊ Z6–9 H9–6

Ageratina altissima (Hardy age, Mist flower, White snakeroot)

Erect perennial with nettle-like, gray-green leaves. In late summer bears dense, flat, white flower heads. **H** 4ft (1.2m), **S** 1½ft (45cm).

☼ ◊ Z4–8 H8–2

Anaphalis triplinervis 'Sommerschnee'

Variable, clump-forming perennial with obovate to elliptic, white-woolly leaves, prominently 3-veined. In mid- to late summer produces clusters of yellow-centered flower heads with bright silvery-white bracts. **H** 20in (50cm), **S** 18–24in (45–60cm).

☼ ◊ Z3–8 H8–3

Gillenia trifoliata

Upright perennial with many wiry, branching stems carrying clusters of dainty, white flowers with reddish-brown calyces in summer. Leaves are dark green and lance-shaped. Needs staking. Thrives in most situations. **H** 3–4ft (1–1.2m), **S** 24in (60cm).

☼ ◊ Z5–9 H9–5

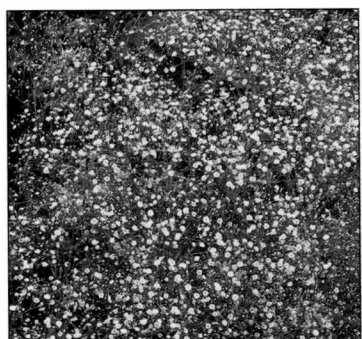

Gypsophila paniculata 'Bristol Fairy'

Perennial with small, dark green leaves and wiry, branching stems bearing panicles of tiny, double, white flowers in summer. **H** 2–2½ft (60–75cm), **S** 3ft (1m).

☼ ◊ Z5–9 H9–1

Anaphalis margaritacea (Pearly everlasting)

Bushy perennial that has lance-shaped, gray-green or silvery-gray leaves with white margins and many heads of small, white flowers on erect stems in late summer. Flower heads dry well. **H** 24–30in (60–75cm), **S** 24in (60cm).

☼ ◊ Z4–8 H8–1

Valeriana officinalis (Cat's valerian, Common valerian)

Clump-forming, fleshy perennial that bears spikes of white to deep pink flowers in summer. Leaves are deeply toothed and mid-green. Has the disadvantage of attracting cats. **H** 3–4ft (1–1.2m), **S** 3ft (1m).

☼ ◊ Z4–9 H9–1

Gaura lindheimeri

Bushy perennial with racemes of star-shaped, 4-petaled, butterfly-like, pink-tinged or white flowers, borne on wand-like stems, in summer. Leaves are lance-shaped and mid-green. Grows well with grasses and other dainty perennials. **H** 5ft (1.5m), **S** 36in (90cm).

☼ ◊ Z6–9 H9–6

ASTILBES

These elegant, colorful, tough perennials are useful plants for moist sites. Their feathery plumes open mainly in summer and are composed of hundreds, sometimes thousands, of tiny flowers that create diverse forms, from dense and upright to open and arching. Colors range from white through shades of pink to deep reds and purples. The blooms are set against neatly lobed or divided foliage, which, in some cultivars, has attractive metallic, bronze, or red tints. All prefer moist soil—they tolerate clay well—in sun or partial shade, and they make compact clumps in bog or waterside gardens. Watch out for signs of plant collapse as astilbes are susceptible to vine weevil attack.

A. 'Deutschland'   A. 'Sprite'   A. 'Straussenfeder'   A. x *crispa* 'Perkeo'

A. 'Europa'   A. 'Feuer'   A. 'Montgomery'

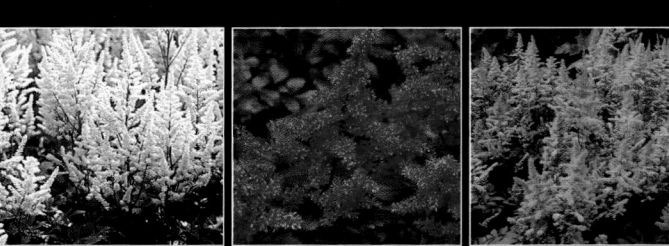

A. 'Irrlicht'   A. 'Granat'   A. 'Amethyst'

PINK

Linaria purpurea 'Canon J. Went'
Upright perennial bearing spikes of snapdragon-like, pink blooms with orange-tinged throats from mid- to late summer. Has narrow, gray-green leaves. **H** 2–3ft (60cm–1m), **S** 2ft (60cm).

☼ ◊ Z5–8 H8–5

Tanacetum coccineum 'Eileen May Robinson'
Upright perennial with slightly aromatic, feathery leaves. Daisylike, pink flowers with yellow centers are produced on strong stems in summer. **H** to 30in (75cm), **S** to 18in (45cm).

☼ ◊ ① Z5–9 H9–5

Malva moschata
Bushy, branching perennial producing successive spikes of saucer-shaped, rose-pink flowers during early summer. Narrow, lobed, divided leaves are slightly scented. **H** 2–3ft (60cm–1m), **S** 2ft (60cm).

☼ ◊ Z3–8 H8–1

Lupinus 'The Chatelaine'
Clump-forming perennial carrying spikes of pink-and-white flowers above divided, mid-green foliage in early summer. **H** 4ft (1.2m), **S** 18in (45cm).

☼ ◊ ① Z5–8 H8–5

Centaurea pulcherrima
Upright perennial with deeply cut, silvery leaves. Rose-pink flower heads, with thistle-like centers paler than surrounding star-shaped ray petals, are borne singly on slender stems in summer. **H** 2½ft (75cm), **S** 2ft (60cm).

☼ ◊ Z4–8 H8–1

Mirabilis jalapa
(Four o'clock flower, Marvel of Peru)
Bushy, tuberous perennial. Fragrant,
trumpet-shaped, crimson, pink, white
or yellow flowers, opening in evening,
cover mid-green foliage in summer.
H 2–4ft (60cm–1.2m), **S** 2–2½ft (60–75cm).

☼ ◊ ① Z10–11 H11–1

Physostegia virginiana 'Variegata'
Erect perennial. In late summer
produces spikes of tubular, purplish-
pink blooms that can be placed into
position. Toothed, mid-green leaves
are white-variegated. **H** 3–4ft (1–1.2m),
S 24in (60cm).

☼ ◗ Z2–8 H8–1

Penstemon 'Evelyn'
Semievergreen, bushy perennial with
racemes of small, tubular, pink flowers
produced from mid-summer to mid-
sfall. Broadly lance-shaped leaves
are mid-green. **H** and **S** 18in (45cm).

☼ ◊ Z7–10 H11–3

Thalictrum aquilegiifolium
'Thundercloud'
Clump-forming perennial with a
mass of fernlike, silvery-green leaves.
Bunched heads of fluffy, dark lilac
flowers, on sturdy stems, are borne
in summer. **H** 3ft (1m), **S** 12in (30cm).

☼ ◊ Z5–9 H9–5

Monarda 'Croftway Pink'
Clump-forming perennial carrying
whorls of hooded, soft pink blooms
throughout summer above neat
mounds of aromatic foliage.
H 3ft (1m), **S** 18in (45cm).

☼ ◗ Z4–9 H9–2

Geranium psilostemon
Clump-forming perennial that has
broad, deeply cut leaves with good
fall color and many cup-shaped, single,
black-centered, magenta flowers in
mid-summer. **H** and **S** 4ft (1.2m).

☼ ◊ Z5–8 H8–5

Sidalcea 'Oberon'
Upright perennial with rounded, deeply
cut leaves divided into narrowly oblong
segments. In summer, produces racemes
of shallowly cup-shaped, clear pink
flowers. **H** 24in (60cm), **S** 18in (45cm).

☼ ◊ Z5–7 H8–2

PERENNIALS

PINK

Astilbe 'Venus'
Leafy perennial bearing feathery, tapering plumes of tiny, pale pink flowers in summer. Foliage is broad and divided into leaflets; flowers remain on the plant, dried and brown, well into winter. Prefers rich soil. **H** and **S** to 3ft (1m).

 Z3–8 H8–2

Lythrum salicaria 'Feuerkerze'
Clump-forming perennial for a waterside or bog garden. Bears spikes of intense rose-red blooms from mid- to late summer. Small, lance-shaped leaves are borne on flower stems. **H** 3ft (1m), **S** 1½ft (45cm).

Z4–9 H9–1

Echinacea purpurea 'Robert Bloom'
Upright perennial. Has lance-shaped, dark green leaves and large, daisylike, deep crimson-pink flower heads, with conical, brown centers, borne singly on strong stems in summer. Needs rich soil. **H** 4ft (1.2m), **S** 20in (50cm).

Z3–9 H9–1

Rehmannia elata
Straggling perennial bearing foxglove-like, yellow-throated, rose-purple flowers in leaf axils of notched, stem-clasping, soft leaves from early to mid-summer. **H** 3ft (1m), **S** 1½ft (45cm). Min. 34°F (1°C).

H11–10

PERSICARIA

In recent years *Persicaria* have increased in popularity, as gardeners realize the value of these plants in a range of different situations. Most flower profusely for many weeks in summer, while those with handsome foliage are prized for the beauty of their leaves rather than their flowers. Taller selections are usually self-supporting, while lower-growing types form weed-suppressing groundcover. Grow *Persicaria* in moist soil in sun or partial shade; *P. bistorta* tolerates drier soil. A word of warning: some, such as *P.* 'Red Dragon', can be invasive and need to be kept under control.

P. **'Red Dragon'**

P. campanulata **'Rosenrot'**

P. affinis **'Superba'**

P. virginiana **'Lance Corporal'**

P. campanulata ①

234

Knautia macedonica
Upright perennial with deeply divided leaves and many rather lax, branching stems bearing double, almost globular, bright crimson flower heads in summer. Needs staking. **H** 30in (75cm), **S** 24in (60cm).

 ☼ ○ Z5–9 H9–5

Hedysarum coronarium
(French honeysuckle)
Spreading, shrubby perennial or biennial. Spikes of pealike, bright red flowers are produced in summer above divided, mid-green leaves. **H** and **S** 3ft (1m).

☼ ○ Z4–9 H9–1

Hemerocallis 'Red Precious'
Evergreen, clump-forming perennial bearing small, intensely red flowers, with a slim, greenish-yellow stripe on each petal and a golden throat, in late summer. **H** and **S** 20in (50cm).

☼ ◐ Z3–10 H11–2

Achillea 'Fanal'
Herbaceous perennial with slightly grayish-green, fernlike leaves that forms spreading, drought-resistant clumps. In early summer bears flat-topped, bold crimson flower heads that atttract bees and butterflies. **H** 30in (75cm), **S** 24in (60cm).

☼ ○ Z3–9 H9–1

Phlox paniculata 'Prince of Orange'
Upright perennial with tubular, 5-lobed, orange-red flowers borne in conical heads in late summer. Has oval, mid-green leaves. **H** 4ft (1.2m), **S** 2ft (60cm).

☼◑ ○ Z4–8 H8–1

Lychnis chalcedonica
(Jerusalem cross, Maltese cross)
Neat, clump-forming perennial that bears flat heads of small, vermilion flowers at the tips of sturdy stems in early summer. Foliage is mid-green. **H** 3–4ft (1–1.2m), **S** 12–18in (30–45cm).

☼ ○ Z3–8 H8–1

Monarda 'Cambridge Scarlet'
Clump-forming perennial that throughout summer bears whorls of hooded, rich red flowers above neat mounds of aromatic, hairy foliage. **H** 3ft (1m), **S** 18in (45cm).

 ☼ ◐ Z3–9 H9–1

Papaver orientale 'Beauty of Livermere'
Hairy-leaved perennial with deep, fleshy roots. Large, solitary, cup-shaped, crimson-scarlet flowers, with a black mark at the base of each petal, are borne from late spring to mid-summer. **H** 3–4ft (1–1.2m), **S** 3ft (1m).

☼ ○ Z3–9 H9–1

PERENNIALS

PENSTEMONS

Valued for their racemes of foxglovelike flowers, penstemons are elegant and reliable border perennials. Numerous cultivars are available, in colors that include white, pale and dark pink, warm cherry red, clear blue, and shades of purple. Many flowers have contrasting white throats or are streaked with other colors. Penstemons flower prolifically in summer and the display can be prolonged, provided the plants are regularly deadheaded. Some taller cultivars may need staking. All types thrive in well-drained soil, preferably in full sun. Some are not fully hardy, and where winters are severe, plants should be overwintered in a cold frame. Plants are more likely to survive frost if grown in a sheltered spot and mulched in fall. Penstemons are simple to propagate, and can easily be raised from cuttings.

P. **'Stromboli'**   *P.* **'Hidcote Pink'**   *P.* **'Stapleford Gem'**

P. fruticosus var. *scouleri* f. *albus*

P. **'White Bedder'**

P. **'Apple Blossom'**

P. **'Alice Hindley'**

P. **'Beech Park'**

P. **'Mother of Pearl'**

P. **'The Juggler'**

P. digitalis **'Husker Red'**

P. **'Margery Fish'**   *P.* **'Flamingo'**

P. **'Osprey'**

P. kunthii

P. 'Schoenholzeri'

P. 'Rubicundus'   P. glaber

P. 'Russian River'   P. 'Raven'

P. 'Sour Grapes'   P. 'King George V'   P. 'Andenken an Friedrich Hahn'   P. 'Papal Purple'   P. whippleanus

P. 'Burgundy'   P. 'Pensham Just Jayne'   P. 'Port Wine'   P. 'Hopleys Variegated'

P. 'Chester Scarlet'   P. barbatus   P. 'Cherry Ripe'   P. heterophyllus 'Heavenly Blue'

237

RED

***Astrantia major* 'Ruby Wedding'**
Clump-forming perennial producing ruby-red flower heads on tall, slender stems throughout summer above a mass of divided, purple-flushed, mid-green leaves. **H** and **S** 24in (60cm).

☼ ◊ Z4–7 H7–1

Cosmos atrosanguineus
(Chocolate cosmos)
Upright, tuberous perennial with chocolate-scented, maroon-crimson flower heads in late summer. In warm sites tubers may overwinter if protected. **H** 24in (60cm) or more, **S** 18in (45cm).

☼ ◊ Z7–11 H11–1

Filipendula purpurea
Upright perennial with deeply divided leaves. Produces large, terminal heads of masses of tiny, rich reddish-purple flowers in summer. Makes a good waterside plant. **H** 4ft (1.2m), **S** 24in (60cm).

◐ ◊ Z4–9 H9–1

PURPLE

Geranium palmatum
Evergreen perennial with large, palmate, bright, rather glossy, light green leaves held on sturdy stalks, growing from a central, rather woody stem. In early summer has tall, branched stems of 5-petaled, magenta flowers. **H** 3ft (1m), **S** 2ft (60cm).

☼◐ ◊ Z7–9 H9–7

ORIENTAL POPPIES

The large-flowered selections of *Papaver orientale* are stars of the early summer garden, their huge yet delicate blooms, some with fringed petals, appearing in profusion above mounds of hairy foliage. Numerous selections are available, with flowers in pastel shades of white, pink, and plum-purple, or red and orange for dramatic hot-hued borders. Large round seed heads keep the display going for a few more weeks after the flowers have faded. Poppies thrive in fertile soil in full sun, but plants die down in mid-summer; ensure that other later performers fill the gaps.

P. orientale 'Karine'

P. 'Medallion'

P. orientale 'Turkish Delight'

Acanthus spinosus
Stately perennial that has very large, arching, deeply cut and spiny-pointed, glossy, dark green leaves. Spires of funnel-shaped, soft mauve and white flowers are borne freely in summer. **H** 4ft (1.2m), **S** 24in (60cm) or more.

☼ ◊ Z5–9 H9–5

Linaria triornithophora
(Three birds toadflax)
Upright perennial that from early to late summer produces spikes of snapdragon-like, purple and yellow flowers above narrow, gray-green leaves. **H** 3ft (1m), **S** 2ft (60cm).

☼ ◊ Z7–9 H9–7

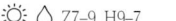

Dianella tasmanica
Upright perennial with nodding, star-shaped, bright blue or purple-blue flowers carried in branching sprays in summer, followed by deep blue berries in fall. Has untidy, evergreen, strap-shaped leaves. **H** 4ft (1.2m), **S** 20in (50cm).

☼ ◊ pH H11–10

Geranium pratense
'Mrs. Kendall Clark'
Clump-forming perennial with hairy stems and deeply divided leaves. In early and mid-summer, bears erect, saucer-shaped, pearl-gray or violet-blue flowers with white or pale pink veins. **H** 24–36in (60–90cm), **S** 24in (60cm).

☼ ◊ Z4–8 H8–1

Monarda fistulosa
Clump-forming perennial that produces small heads of lilac-purple flowers from mid- to late summer. **H** 4ft (1.2m), **S** 1½ft (45cm).

☼ ◊ Z3–9 H9–1

Geranium sylvaticum 'Mayflower'
Upright perennial with a basal clump of deeply lobed leaves, above which rise branching stems of cup-shaped, violet-blue flowers in early summer. **H** 3ft (1m), **S** 24in (60cm).

☼ ◊ Z8 H9–8

Thalictrum aquilegiifolium
Clump-forming perennial with a mass of finely divided, gray-green leaves, resembling those of maidenhair fern. Bunched heads of fluffy, lilac-purple flowers are borne on strong stems in summer. **H** 3–4ft (1–1.2m), **S** 1½ft (45cm).

☼ ◊ Z5–9 H9–5

Aconitum x cammarum 'Bicolor'
Compact, tuberous perennial with violet-blue and white flowers borne in summer along upright stems. Has deeply cut, divided, glossy, dark green leaves and poisonous roots. **H** 4ft (1.2m), **S** 20in (50cm).

☼ ◊ ❶ Z3–7 H8–3

Veronica spicata 'Romiley Purple'
Clump-forming perennial that in summer freely produces large spikes of purple flowers above whorled, mid-green leaves. **H** 3–4ft (1–1.2m), **S** 1–2ft (30–60cm).

☼ ◊ Z3–8 H8–1

Galega orientalis
Vigorous, upright but compact perennial that in summer bears spikes of pealike, blue-tinged, violet flowers above delicate leaves divided into oval leaflets. Needs staking. Spreads freely. **H** 4ft (1.2m), **S** 2ft (60cm).

☼ ◊ Z5–8 H8–5

PHLOX

Border phlox (cultivars of *P. maculata* and *P. paniculata*) are an elegant mainstay of the mid- to late summer border. Their dome-shaped or conical panicles of flowers, often delicately scented, are produced in white, pink, red, and purple, many with contrasting eyes. Some cultivars also have strikingly variegated foliage. Phlox thrive in sun or partial shade in fertile, well-drained soil; taller types may need staking. For larger flowers, reduce the number of stems in spring by pinching out the weakest shoots. To prolong flowering, deadhead regularly to encourage side shoots to bloom.

P. paniculata 'Fujiyama'
P. paniculata 'Eva Cullum'

P. paniculata 'Mia Ruys'
P. paniculata 'Brigadier'
P. paniculata 'Windsor'

P. paniculata 'Norah Leigh'
P. paniculata 'Amethyst'
P. paniculata 'Hampton Court'

PURPLE

Baptisia australis (False indigo)
Upright perennial bearing spikes of pealike, violet-blue flowers in summer. Bright green leaves are divided into oval leaflets. Dark gray seed pods may be used for winter decoration. **H** 30in (75cm), **S** 24in (60cm).

☼ ◊ Z3–9 H9–1

Erigeron 'Dunkelste Aller'
Clump-forming perennial with a mass of daisylike, deep purple flower heads, with yellow centers, in summer. Has narrowly oval, grayish-green leaves. **H** 32in (80cm), **S** 24in (60cm) or more.

☼ ◊ Z5–8 H8–5

BLUE

Eryngium alpinum
Upright perennial with basal rosettes of heart-shaped, deeply toothed, glossy foliage. In summer sturdy stems bear heads of conical, purplish-blue flower heads, surrounded by blue bracts and soft spines. **H** 2½–3ft (75cm–1m), **S** 2ft (60cm).

☼ ◊ Z6–9 H9–6

Agapanthus inapertus subsp. pendulus 'Graskop'
Clump-forming perennial with compact, rounded clusters of pendent, dark violet-blue flowers, in summer. Has narrowly strap-shaped, rich green leaves. **H** 36in (90cm), **S** 20in (50cm).

☼ ◊ Z9 H11–7

Nepeta 'Six Hills Giant'
Vigorous, clump-forming perennial with narrowly oval, toothed, hairy, aromatic, gray-green leaves. In summer bears loose spikes of tubular, 2-lipped, lavender-blue flowers. **H** 3ft (1m), **S** 4ft (1.2m).

☼ ◊ Z3–8 H8–1

Anchusa azurea 'Loddon Royalist'
Upright perennial that bears flat, single, deep blue flowers on branching spikes in early summer. Most of the lance-shaped, coarse, hairy leaves are at the base of plant. Needs staking. **H** 4ft (1.2m), **S** 24in (60cm).

 Z3–8 H8–1

Eryngium x oliverianum
Upright perennial that produces large, rounded heads of thistle-like, blue to lavender-blue flowers in late summer. Has heart-shaped, jagged-edged, basal, mid-green leaves. **H** 2–3ft (60cm–1m), **S** 1½–2ft (45–60cm).

 Z5–8 H8–5

Agapanthus 'Purple Cloud'
Compact, clump-forming perennial with large, rounded clusters of violet-blue flowers in summer followed by long-lasting seed heads. Has broadly strap-shaped, slightly silvery-gray leaves. **H** 4ft (1.2m), **S** 2ft (60cm) or more.

Z9–11 H12–7

Echinops bannaticus 'Taplow Blue'
Upright perennial with narrowly oval, divided, prickly, grayish-green leaves. Erect stems produce thistle-like, rounded heads of steely-blue flowers from mid- to late summer. Is suitable even for poor soils. Is attractive to insects. **H** 4ft (1.2m), **S** 3ft (90cm).

Z5–9 H9–5

Agapanthus 'Northern Star'
Clump-forming perennial bearing large, rounded clusters of inky-blue flowers, with reflexed petals, in summer, followed by long-lasting seed heads. Has narrowly strap-shaped, mid-green leaves stained purple at the bases. **H** 4ft (1.2m), **S** 2ft (60cm) or more.

Z8–11 H12–1

Aconitum 'Stainless Steel'
Erect, tuberous perennial with dense spikes of hooded, silvery-blue flowers in mid- to late summer, held above deeply divided, dark green leaves. **H** 3ft (1m), **S** 2ft (60cm).

Z4–8 H8–4

CAMPANULA
Archetypal cottage garden plants, tall campanulas are valued for their spires of pastel bell-shaped flowers, which appear from early- to mid-summer. They make good candidates for herbaceous borders, naturalistic planting schemes—perhaps at the edge of a woodland garden—or with shrubs such as roses. Developments using *C. punctata* have produced some superb, compact plants with dramatic drooping flowers suitable for the front of the border. *C. lactiflora* and tall types may need some support. Most are easily grown in sun or light shade in reasonably fertile, moist but well-drained soil.

C. alliariifolia   *C. punctata* 'Cherry Bells'   *C. trachelium* 'Bernice'

C. persicifolia 'Chettle Charm'

C. lactiflora 'Loddon Anna'   *C. glomerata* 'Superba'

C. takesimana   *C. lactiflora* 'Prichard's Variety'

PERENNIALS

BLUE

**Agapanthus praecox
subsp. orientalis**
Perennial with large, dense umbels of
sky-blue flowers borne on strong stems
in late summer over clumps of broad,
almost evergreen, dark green leaves.
Makes a good plant for pots. **H** 3ft (1m),
S 2ft (60cm).

☼ ◊ H11–7

Cichorium intybus (Chicory)
Clump-forming perennial with basal
rosettes of light green leaves and
daisylike, bright blue flower heads
borne along upper parts of willowy
stems in summer. Flowers are at
their best before noon. **H** 4ft (1.2m),
S 1½ft (45cm).

☼ ◊ ❢ Z4–8 H8–1

**Campanula persicifolia
'Telham Beauty'**
Perennial with basal rosettes of narrow,
bright green leaves. In summer, large,
nodding, cup-shaped, light blue flowers
are borne on slender spikes. **H** 3ft (1m),
S 12in (30cm).

☼ ◊ Z3–8 H8–1

SILVER

Artemisia 'Powis Castle'
Semievergreen, upright subshrub
with woody stems, usually grown as a
perennial, with fernlike, silvery-gray
leaves making an excellent foil for
other plants. If old growth is retained,
insignificant, yellow flowers are borne
in summer. **H** and **S** 3ft (1m).

☼ ◊ Z7–9 H11–8

Astelia chathamica
Evergreen, clump-forming perennial
with sword-shaped, erect, bright silvery-
gray leaves. Panicles of insignificant,
frothy, yellow flowers are borne in
summer. **H** and **S** 4ft (1.2m).

☼ ◊ Z8–9 H9–8

GREEN

Aciphylla squarrosa (Bayonet plant)
Evergreen, clump-forming perennial
with tufts of pointed, divided leaves.
In summer bears spiky, yellow
flowers in compound umbels with
male and female flowers often mixed.
H and **S** 3–4ft (1–1.2m).

☼ ◊ Z9–15 H12–1

**Mathiasella bupleuroides
'Green Dream'**
Upright, deciduous perennial with
divided, silvery-blue leaves. In early
summer has umbels of bell-shaped,
pendent, jade-green flowers, which turn
pinkish as they age. Needs good winter
drainage. **H** 3ft (1m), **S** 24in (60cm).

☼ ◊ Z8–11 H11–7

Euphorbia sikkimensis
Spreading, upright perennial
bearing yellow cyathia cupped by
pale to greenish-yellow involucres in
mid- to late summer. Young shoots are
bright pink and the leaves deep green.
H 4ft (1.2m), **S** 18in (45cm).

☼ ◊ ❢ Z6–9 H9–6

Verbascum 'Gainsborough'
Semievergreen, rosette-forming, short-lived perennial bearing branched racemes of 5-lobed, pale sulfur-yellow flowers throughout summer above oval, mid-green leaves borne on flower stems. **H** 2–4ft (60cm–1.2m), **S** 12–24in (30–60cm).

☼ ◊ Z5–9 H9–3

Inula hookeri
Clump-forming perennial with lance-shaped to elliptic, hairy leaves and a mass of slightly scented, daisylike, greenish-yellow flower heads borne in summer. **H** 30in (75cm), **S** 18in (45cm).

☼ ◊ Z4–8 H8–1

Aconitum lycoctonum subsp. **vulparia** (Wolf's bane)
Upright, fibrous perennial that has hooded, straw-yellow flowers in summer. Leaves are dark green and deeply divided. Needs staking. **H** 3–4ft (1–1.2m), **S** 1–2ft (30–60cm).

☼ ◊ ⓘ Z5–8 H8–5

Thermopsis rhombifolia
Upright perennial bearing spikes of bright yellow flowers above divided, mid-green leaves in summer. **H** 2–3ft (60cm–1m), **S** 2ft (60cm).

☼ ◊ Z3–8 H8–1

Gentiana lutea (Yellow gentian)
Erect, unbranched perennial with oval, stalkless leaves to 1ft (30cm) long. In summer has dense whorls of tubular, yellow flowers in axils of greenish bracts. **H** 3–4ft (1–1.2m), **S** 2ft (60cm).

☼ ◊ Z7–8 H8–7

Phlomis russeliana
Evergreen perennial, forming excellent groundcover, with large, rough, heart-shaped leaves. Sturdy flower stems bear whorls of hooded, butter-yellow flowers in summer. **H** 3ft (1m), **S** 2ft (60cm) or more.

☼ ◊ Z3–9 H9–1

Lysimachia punctata (Garden loosestrife)
Clump-forming perennial that in summer produces spikes of bright yellow flowers above mid-green leaves. **H** 24–30in (60–75cm), **S** 24in (60cm).

☼ ◖ Z4–8 H8–1

Anthemis tinctoria 'E.C. Buxton'
Clump-forming perennial with a mass of daisylike, lemon-yellow flower heads borne singly in summer on slim stems. Cut back hard after flowering to promote a good rosette of crinkled leaves for winter. **H** and **S** 3ft (1m).

☼ ◊ Z3–8 H8–3

Berkheya macrocephala
Upright perennial bearing large, daisylike, yellow flower heads on branched, spiny-leaved stems throughout summer. Prefers rich soil and a warm, sheltered position. **H** and **S** 3ft (1m).

☼ ◊ H11–10

Achillea filipendulina 'Gold Plate'
Upright perennial with stout, leafy stems carrying broad, flat, terminal heads of yellow flowers in summer, above filigree foliage. Flowers retain color if dried. Divide plants regularly. **H** 4ft (1.2m), **S** 2ft (60cm).

☼ ◊ ⓘ Z3–9 H9–1

DAYLILIES

Although they belong to the lily family (*Liliaceae*), daylilies (*Hemerocallis*) are not true lilies; their common name comes from their lilylike flowers that last just one day, but appear in succession for many weeks in summer. Daylilies range in size from compact plants that grow 12–15in (30–38cm) tall, to large plants that may reach 5ft (1.5m). They form clumps of arching, strappy foliage, and flower colors range from creamy white, yellow, orange, red, pink, and purple, to almost black; some also have bands of contrasting colors on the petals. The flower forms are classified as single, double, or spider, and some are fragrant. They thrive in most soils, except waterlogged, in sun or shade, but flower best when in sun for at least part of the day.

H. 'Pardon Me'

H. 'Neyron Rose'

H. 'Joan Senior'

H. 'Stoke Poges'

H. 'Always Afternoon'

H. 'Siloam Baby Talk'

H. 'Luxury Lace'

H. 'Pink Damask'

H. 'Summer Wine'

H. 'Canadian Border Patrol'

H. 'Cherry Cheeks'

H. 'Night Beacon'

H. 'Prairie Blue Eyes'

H. 'Green Flutter'

H. 'Whichford'

H. 'Bonanza'

H. 'Lemon Bells'

H. 'Little Wine Cup'

H. lilioasphodelus

H. dumortieri

H. fulva

H. 'Missenden'

H. citrina

H. 'Cream Drop'

H. 'Little Grapette'

H. 'Golden Chimes'

H. 'Cartwheels'

H. fulva 'Flore Pleno'

H. 'Mauna Loa'

H. 'Frans Hals'

H. 'Chicago Sunrise'

H. 'Stafford'

H. 'Burning Daylight'

H. 'Black Magic'

H. 'Cathy's Sunset'

ORANGE

WHITE

Euphorbia griffithii 'Fireglow'
Bushy perennial that bears orange-
red flowers in terminal umbels in early
summer. Leaves are lance-shaped,
mid-green and have pale red midribs.
H to 3ft (1m), **S** 20in (50cm).

☼ ◐ ◊ ! Z4–9 H9–2

Sphaeralcea ambigua
Branching, shrubby perennial. Broadly
funnel-shaped, orange-coral blooms
are produced singly in leaf axils from
summer until the onset of cold weather.
Leaves are soft, hairy and mid-green.
H and **S** 30–36in (75–90cm).

☼ ◊ Z6–9 H11–2

Asclepias tuberosa (Butterfly weed)
Erect, tuberous perennial with long,
lance-shaped leaves. Small, 5-horned,
bright orange-red flowers are borne
in summer and followed by narrow,
pointed pods, to 6in (15cm) long.
H to 30in (75cm), **S** 18in (45cm).

☼ ◊ ! Z4–9 H9–2

Verbascum 'Cotswold Beauty'
Rosette-forming perennial with
sometimes-branched spires of 5-petaled,
pale coppery-apricot flowers, each
with a soft purple center, in summer.
Has oval, gray-green leaves. May be
short-lived in rich soil. **H** 4ft (1.2m),
S 16in (40cm).

☼ ◊ Z5–9 H9–5

Actaea pachypoda
(Doll's eyes, White baneberry)
Compact, clump-forming perennial
with spikes of small, fluffy, white flowers
in summer and clusters of white berries,
borne on stiff, fleshy scarlet stalks, in fall.
H 3ft (1m), **S** 20in (50cm).

☀ ◊ ! Z4–9 H9–1

Leucanthemum x superbum
'Wirral Pride'
Robust, clump-forming perennial with
glossy, dark green, slightly toothed
leaves. Bears numerous, solitary, white
double flower heads with yellowish
anemone centers from early summer
to fall. **H** to 3ft (1m), **S** 24in (60cm).

☼ ◊ ! Z5–8 H8–1

PERENNIALS

Chrysanthemum 'Clara Curtis'
Bushy perennial producing many clusters of flat, daisylike, clear pink flower heads throughout summer and fall. Divide plants every other spring. **H** 30in (75cm), **S** 18in (45cm).

☀ ◌ ① Z4–8 H8–4

Tricyrtis formosana
Upright, rhizomatous perennial. In early fall bears spurred flowers, heavily spotted with purplish-pink and with yellow-tinged throats. Glossy, dark green leaves clasp stems. **H** 2–3ft (60cm–1m), **S** 18in (45cm).

☀ ◗ Z6–9 H9–6

Anemone hupehensis 'Hadspen Abundance'
Erect, branching perennial that bears pink flowers with rounded, dark reddish-pink outer tepals from summer to fall. Leaves are dark green and deeply divided, with toothed leaflets. **H** 2–4ft (60cm–1.2m), **S** 18in (45cm).

☀ ◗ ① Z5–7 H7–5

YARROW

Stalwarts of the summer garden, yarrow (*Achillea*) are easy-to-grow perennials for sunny sites and well-drained soils. Taller types are best planted toward the back of herbaceous borders, while shorter forms associate well with grasses in naturalistic planting schemes. Both selections also look at home in mixed beds and gravel gardens. Most have flattened flower heads, creating a horizontal plane that contrasts well with vertical flower spikes. Available in a range of colors, including white, yellow, pink, peach, and red, the flowers change color as they age, creating a two-tone effect. Many make good cut flowers; some can also be dried.

A. millefolium 'Red Velvet'

A. ptarmica 'The Pearl' ①

A. 'Heidi'

A. 'Belle Epoque'

A. millefolium 'Kelwayi'

A. filipendulina 'Parker's Variety'

A. 'Christine's Pink'

A. 'Terracotta'

A. 'Lachsschönheit'

HELENIUM

Of all late-summer, daisy-flowered perennials, *Helenium* are among the most colorful. They have become increasingly popular with the rise of naturalistic plantings, to which they are well suited, although they also add a dramatic note to herbaceous borders. The sturdy stems bear shuttlecock-shaped flowers in fiery tones of red, orange, and yellow that last for many weeks. Plants seldom need staking and form slowly spreading clumps if grown in sun and fertile soil. To lengthen the flowering season, select a variety of forms, and cut back some in early summer to promote later flowering.

H. 'Indianersommer'

H. 'Potter's Wheel'

H. 'Bruno' ①

H. 'Double Trouble'

H. 'Red Army'

H. 'Butterpat'

H. 'Feuersiegel'

'Rubinzwerg'

H. 'Waltraut'

Centranthus ruber (Red valerian)
Perennial forming spreading colonies of fleshy leaves. Branching heads of small, star-shaped, deep reddish-pink or white flowers are borne above foliage from late spring to fall. Thrives in poor, exposed sites. **H** 24–36in (60–90cm), **S** 18–24in (45–60cm) or more.

☼ ◊ Z5–8 H8–5

Lobelia cardinalis 'Queen Victoria'
Clump-forming perennial. From late summer to mid fall spikes of blazing red flowers on branching stems arise from basal, deep red-purple foliage. **H** 3ft (1m), **S** 12in (30cm).

☼ ◑ ① Z3–9 H9–1

MICHAELMAS DAISIES

Invaluable border plants, Michaelmas daisies (*Aster* species and cultivars; mostly *A. novae-angliae* and *A. novi-belgii*) flower later than many other perennials and continue the display until late fall. The smaller-flowered species and selections associate well with grasses and naturalistic planting schemes, while the larger flowers are excellent for cutting. The daisylike, single or double flowers range in color from white, pink, and red, to purple and blue. Michaelmas daisies thrive in sun or partial shade and well-drained soil, and tall cultivars may need staking. For large flowers, pinch out weaker shoots in spring; to produce bushier plants with a greater number of smaller flowers, pinch out the top 1–2in (2.5–5cm) of all shoots in late spring.

A. 'Coombe Fishacre'   A. 'Photograph'   A. novi-belgii 'Chequers'

A. divaricatus

A. novi-belgii 'Apple Blossom'

A. x frikartii 'Wunder von Stäfa'

A. novae-angliae 'Violetta'

A. novi-belgii 'Marie Ballard'

A. novae-angliae 'Harrington's Pink'

A. novae-angliae 'Rosa Sieger'

A. 'Little Carlow'

A. ericoides 'Golden Spray'

A. cordifolius 'Silver Spray'

A. novi-belgii 'Carnival '

A. 'Sunhelene'

A. ericoides 'White Heather'

A. novi-belgii 'Freda Ballard'

A. novi-belgii 'Orlando'

A. novi-belgii 'Professor Anton Kippenberg'

BLUE

PURPLE

Strobilanthes atropurpureus
Upright, branching perennial with
oval, toothed leaves. Spikes of
numerous, violet-blue to purple
flowers appear in summer–fall.
H to 4ft (1.2m), **S** to 2ft (60cm).

☀ ◊ Z5–9 H9–5

Aster amellus 'King George'
Bushy perennial with oval, rough leaves.
In fall produces many large, terminal,
daisylike, deep blue-violet flower heads
with yellow centers. **H** and **S** 20in (50cm).

◑ ◊ Z5–8 H8–1

Gentiana asclepiadea
(Willow gentian)
Arching perennial with narrow, oval
leaves to 3in (8cm) long. In late summer
to fall has arching sprays of trumpet-
shaped, deep blue flowers, spotted
and striped inside. **H** to 36in (90cm),
S to 24in (60cm).

◑ ◐ Z6–9 H9–6

Eryngium x tripartitum
Perennial with wiry stems above a
basal rosette of coarsely toothed,
gray-green leaves. Conical, metallic-
blue flower heads on blue stems are
borne in summer–fall and may be dried
for winter decoration. **H** 3–4ft (1–1.2m),
S 20in (50cm).

☀ ◊ Z5–8 H8–5

SALVIAS

Hardy perennial salvias are useful
plants, many flowering profusely in
late summer and lasting well into fall.
The genus is quite diverse, with plants
in a range of sizes and flower colors,
including white, true blue, purple, pink,
and red. A few, such as *S. argentea*, are
also grown for their foliage, which in
many species is aromatic. Salvias thrive
in hot, sunny sites and free-draining
soil, and grow quickly, many developing
into shrublike plants within a season. To
ensure that they survive cold winters, in
fall spread thick mulch over the plants
to protect the roots.

S. pratensis 'Pink Delight'

S. x sylvestris 'Mainacht'

S. nemorosa 'Caradonna'

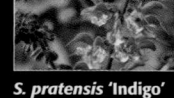

S. pratensis 'Indigo'

S. x sylvestris 'Blauhügel'

S. nemorosa 'Lubecca'

S. pratensis 'Swan Lake'

S. uliginosa

S. guaranitica 'Black and Blue'

S. argentea

S. nemorosa 'Amethyst'

S. nemorosa 'Ostfriesland'

S. verticillata 'Purple Rain'

S. patens

S. glutinosa

Kirengeshoma palmata
Upright perennial with rounded, lobed, bright green leaves, above which strong stems bearing clusters of narrowly funnel-shaped, creamy yellow flowers appear in late summer to fall. **H** 3ft (1m), **S** 24in (60cm).

☼ ◐ pH Z5–8 H8–5

Kniphofia 'Percy's Pride'
Upright perennial with large, terminal spikes of creamy flowers, tinged green and yellow, borne on erect stems in fall. Protect crowns with winter mulch. **H** 3ft (1m), **S** 20in (50cm).

☼ ◊ Z6–9 H9–6

Euphorbia schillingii
Robust, clump-forming perennial that produces long-lasting, yellow cyathia and rounded, greenish-yellow bracts from mid-summer to mid-fall. Stems are erect and leaves are dark green with pale green or white veins. **H** 3ft (1m), **S** 12in (30cm).

☼ ◐ ◊ ① Z7–9 H9–7

Solidago 'Goldenmosa'
Clump-forming perennial. Sprays of tufted, mimosa-like, yellow flower heads are carried in late summer and fall above lance-shaped, toothed, hairy, yellowish-green leaves. **H** 3ft (1m), **S** 24in (60cm).

☼ ◊ Z5–9 H9–5

RUDBECKIA

The golden daisy flowers of *Rudbeckia* illuminate late summer and early fall borders, perennial schemes, and gravel gardens. Most are just over knee height, but some forms of *R. hirta* are small and compact, ideal for the front of beds or containers, while others, like *R.* 'Herbstonne', tower above the rest, reaching up to 8ft (2.5m) in height. *R. maxima* also has attractive glaucous blue foliage. All types produce large flowers on sturdy stems that seldom need staking, and the blooms also attract beneficial insects. *Rudbeckia* thrive in an open, sunny situation, and moist but free-draining soil.

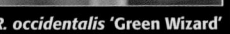

R. maxima   R. triloba

R. occidentalis 'Green Wizard'

R. fulgida var. **speciosa**

R. fulgida var. **sullivantii 'Goldsturm'**

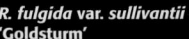

R. laciniata 'Herbstsonne'   **R. fulgida** var. **deamii**

CHRYSANTHEMUMS

Florist's chrysanthemums, as well as those that are grown as hardy garden plants, are grouped according to their differing flower forms, approximate flowering season (early, mid- or late fall), and habit. The best groups for garden decoration are the sprays, pompons, and semi-pompons, the hardy Korean, and early, reflexed chrysanthemums. The dwarf Charm-types, forming dense, domed masses of flowers, are most attractive displayed in pots for both indoor and outdoor use in fall. Most of the various flower forms are described below, with further details provided in the Plant Dictionary under Chrysanthemum.

Incurved—fully double, dense, spherical flowers have incurved petals arising from the base of the flower and closing tightly over the crown.

Fully reflexed—fully double flowers have curved, pointed petals reflexing outward and downward from the crown and back to touch the stem.

Reflexed—fully double flowers are similar to those of fully reflexed forms except that the petals are less strongly reflexed and form an umbrella-like or spiky outline.

Intermediate—fully double, roughly spherical flowers have loosely incurving petals, which may close at the crown or may reflex for the bottom half of each flower.

Anemone-centered—single flowers each have a central, dome-shaped disk, up to half the diameter of the bloom, and up to 5 rows of flat, or occasionally spoon-type, ray petals at right angles to the stem.

Single—flowers each have about 5 rows of flat petals, borne at right angles to the stem, that may incurve or reflex at the tips; the prominent central disk is golden throughout or has a small, green center.

Pompon—fully double, dense, spherical, or occasionally hemispherical, flowers have tubular petals with flat, rounded tips, growing outward from the crown.

Spoon-type—flowers are similar to those of single forms except that the ray petals are tubular and open out at their tips to form a spoon shape.

Spider-form—double flower heads with long, thin ray-florets; the outer ray-florets are more or less pendent, the inner ones curling upward.

Quill-shaped—double flower heads with tubular ray-florets that open out at their tips to form spoon shapes.

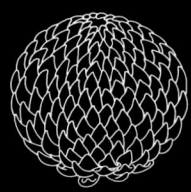

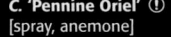

C. 'Innocence' ⓘ [single]

C. 'Pennine Oriel' ⓘ [spray, anemone]

C. 'Nell Gwynn' ⓘ [Korean Group]

C. 'Purleigh White' ⓘ [semi-pompon]

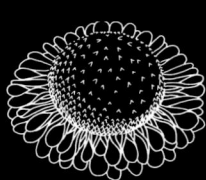
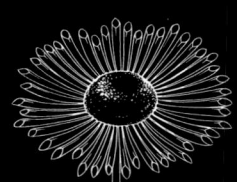

C. 'Emperor of China' ⓘ [double]

C. 'Enbee Wedding' ⓘ [spray, single]

C. 'Chesapeake' ⓘ [spray, quill]

C. 'Spartan Seagull' ⓘ [Korean Group]

C. 'Aunt Millicent' ⓘ [Korean Group]

'Anastasia' ⓘ
[semi-pompon]

C. 'Tapestry Rose' ⓘ
[Korean Group]

C. 'Ruby Mound' ⓘ [Korean Group]

C. 'Mary Stoker' ⓘ [single]

C. 'Nantyderry Sunshine' ⓘ
[semi-pompon]

'Carmine Blush' ⓘ [single]

C. 'Rumpelstilzchen' ⓘ [Korean Group]

C. 'Golden Chalice' ⓘ [charm]

C. 'Yellow John Hughes' ⓘ
[incurved]

'Grandchild' ⓘ [double]

C. 'Perry's Peach' ⓘ
[Korean Group]

C. 'Chelsea Physic Garden' ⓘ
[double]

C. 'Bronze Elegance' ⓘ
[semi-pompon]

C. 'Sea Urchin' ⓘ
[Korean Group]

C. 'George Griffiths' ⓘ
[reflexed]

C. 'Doctor Tom Parr' ⓘ
[semi-pompon]

C. 'Cottage Apricot' ⓘ [Korean Group]

. 'Mrs. Jessie Cooper' ⓘ [single]

RED-HOT POKERS

Red-hot pokers *(Kniphofia)* are dramatic hardy perennials, their upright forms providing focal points in borders, gravel gardens, and perennial schemes. Spires of tubular flowers in a range of fiery colors, or more muted shades of green, ivory, and pale yellow, rise from clumps of slender, often evergreen, foliage. Selections flower from mid-summer to late fall, and they enjoy an open site in full sun, with shelter from cold winds, and fertile, well-drained soil that does not dry out. Give them space to spread, as too much competition may limit their success. Protect plants over winter with a deep mulch.

K. 'Green Jade'   *K.* 'Wrexham Buttercup'   *K.* 'Royal Standard'   *K.* 'Atlanta'

K. 'Toffee Nosed'

K. caulescens

K. thomsonii var. *snowdenii*

K. 'Bees' Sunset'   *K.* 'Prince Igor'   *K. rooperi*

ORANGE

Helenium 'Moerheim Beauty'
Upright perennial with strong, branching stems bearing sprays of daisylike, rich reddish-orange flower heads in early fall above dark green foliage. Needs regular division in spring or fall. **H** 3ft (1m), **S** 24in (60cm).

☀ ◌ ⓘ Z4–8 H8–1

Aster linosyris (Goldilocks)
Upright, unbranched perennial with numerous small, dense, single, golden-yellow flower heads in late summer and fall. Leaves are narrowly lance-shaped. **H** 24in (60cm), **S** 12in (30cm).

☼ ◌ Z3–8 H8–1

WHITE

Epimedium x youngianum 'Niveum'
Compact, groundcover perennial with heart-shaped, serrated, bronze-tinted leaflets that turn green in late spring, when small, cup-shaped, snow-white flowers are borne. **H** 6–12in (15–30cm), **S** 12in (30cm).

☀ ◌ Z5–9 H9–5

Lamium maculatum 'White Nancy'
Semievergreen, mat-forming perennial with white-variegated, mid-green foliage and spikes of hooded, white flowers in late spring and summer. **H** to 6in (15cm), **S** to 3ft (1m).

☀ ◌ Z4–8 H8–1

Pulmonaria 'Sissinghurst White'
Semievergreen, clump-forming perennial that bears funnel-shaped, white flowers in spring above long, elliptic, mid-green, paler spotted leaves. **H** 12in (30cm), **S** 18–24in (45–60cm).

☀ ◌ Z6–8 H8–6

Anemone narcissiflora
Leafy perennial that in late spring and
early summer produces cup-shaped,
single, white flowers with a blue or
purplish-pink stain on reverse of petals.
Leaves are dark green and deeply
divided. **H** to 24in (60cm), **S** 20in (50cm).

☼ ◊ ! Z5–8 H8–5

Trillium grandiflorum (Wake-robin)
Clump-forming perennial. Large,
pure white flowers that turn pink
with age are borne singly in spring
just above large, 3-parted, dark green
leaves. **H** 15in (38cm), **S** 12in (30cm).

☼ ◊ Z4–7 H7–3

Lamium maculatum 'Album'
Semievergreen, mat-forming perennial
that has dark green leaves with central,
white stripes. Bears clusters of hooded,
white flowers in spring–summer.
H 8in (20cm), **S** 3ft (1m).

☼ ◊ Z4–8 H8–1

Bergenia 'Silberlicht'
Evergreen, clump-forming perennial
that has flat, oval, mid-green leaves
with toothed margins. Clusters of white
flowers, sometimes suffused with pink,
are borne on erect stems in spring.
H 12in (30cm), **S** 20in (50cm).

☼ ◊ Z3–8 H8–1

Convallaria majalis (Lily-of-the-valley)
Low-growing, rhizomatous perennial
with narrowly oval, mid- to dark green
leaves and sprays of small, very fragrant,
pendulous, bell-shaped, white flowers.
Likes rich soil. **H** 6in (15cm), **S** indefinite.

☼ ◊ ! Z2–7 H7–1

Sinopodophyllum hexandrum
(Himalayan Mayapple)
Perennial with pairs of 3-lobed, brown-
mottled leaves followed by white or
pink flowers in spring and fleshy, red
fruits in summer. **H** 12–18in (30–45cm),
S 12in (30cm).

☼ ◊ ! Z6–8 H8–5

Pachyphragma macrophyllum
Creeping, mat-forming perennial with
rosettes of rounded, long-stalked, glossy,
bright green leaves, each to 4in (10cm)
long. Bears many racemes of tiny, white
flowers in spring. **H** to 12in (30cm),
S indefinite.

☼ ◊ Z5–9 H9–5

Trillium ovatum
Clump-forming perennial with white
flowers, later turning pink, that are
carried singly in spring just above
red-stalked, 3-parted, dark green foliage.
H 10–15in (25–38cm), **S** 8in (20cm).

☼ ◊ Z5–8 H8–5

Trillium chloropetalum
Clump-forming perennial with reddish-
green stems carrying 3-parted, gray-
marbled, dark green leaves. Flowers
vary from purplish-pink to white
and appear above foliage in spring.
H and **S** 12–18in (30–45cm).

☼ ◊ Z6–9 H9–6

Anemone sylvestris
(Snowdrop windflower)
Carpeting perennial that may be
invasive. Fragrant, semi-pendent, white
flowers with yellow centers are borne in
spring and early summer. Has divided,
mid-green leaves. **H** and **S** 12in (30cm).

☼ ◊ ! Z3–9 H9–1

Helleborus x ericsmithii 'Bob's Best'
Evergreen, clump-forming perennial
with toothed, dark green leaves flushed
in pewter and divided into 3–5 leaflets.
From mid-winter to late spring bears
saucer-shaped, pink-tinted, white flowers,
often striped in green and with darker
petal backs. **H** 15in (38cm), **S** 18in (45cm).

☼ ◊ ! Z6–9 H9–6

WHITE

Chrysosplenium macrophyllum
Evergreen, groundcover perennial with large, rounded, fleshy, mid green leaves covered in silvery hairs. Lacy heads of flattish, pink-tinted, creamy flowers are borne in early spring. Spreads freely by runners. **H** 8in (20cm), **S** 36in (90cm).

☼ ◊ Z6–8 H8–5

Helleborus x ericsmithii
IVORY PRINCE ('Walhelivor')
Evergreen, clump-forming perennial with silver-veined, bluish-green leaves divided into 3–5 leaflets. From mid-winter to spring bears pink-tinted cream flowers, often striped in green and with darker petal backs. **H** 15in (38cm), **S** 18in (45cm).

☼ ◊ ① Z6–9 H9–6

Bergenia ciliata
Evergreen, clump-forming perennial with attractive, large, rounded, hairy leaves. In spring bears clusters of white flowers that age to pink. Leaves are often damaged by frost, although fresh ones will appear in spring. **H** 12in (30cm), **S** 20in (50cm).

☼ ◊ Z5–8 H8–1

PINK

Cypripedium Ulla Silkens gx
Deciduous, terrestrial orchid with 1–3 pouched, pastel white and pink flowers, 2–3in (5–7cm) long, borne in spring. Has broadly lance-shaped leaves, to 12in (30cm) long. **H** 12in (30cm), **S** 24in (60cm).

☼ ◊ Z3–7 H7–1

Dicentra 'Spring Morning'
Neat, leafy perennial with small, heart-shaped, pink flowers hanging in arching sprays in late spring and summer. Attractive, fernlike foliage is gray-green and finely cut. **H** and **S** 12in (30cm).

☼ ◊ ① Z3–9 H9–1

Bergenia 'Beethoven'
Evergreen, groundcovering perennial with masses of pink-tinged, white flowers, borne in branched panicles, in spring. Has spoon-shaped, leathery, mid-green leaves. Protect from spring frosts. **H** 16in (40cm), **S** 24in (60cm) or more.

☼ ◊ Z4–8 H8–1

Geranium macrorrhizum 'Ingwersen's Variety'
Compact, carpeting perennial, useful as weed-suppressing groundcover. Small, soft rose-pink flowers appear in late spring and early summer. Aromatic leaves turn bronze- and scarlet-tinted in fall. **H** 12in (30cm), **S** 24in (60cm).

☼ ◊ Z4–8 H8–1

Heloniopsis orientalis
Clump-forming perennial with basal rosettes of narrowly lance-shaped leaves, above which rise nodding, rose-pink flowers in spring. **H** and **S** 12in (30cm).

☼ ◊ Z7–9 H9–7

Helleborus thibetanus
Clump-forming perennial with palmate, mid-green leaves deeply divided into 7–9 toothed lobes. Bears deeply cup-shaped flowers, 4–6.5cm (1½–2¾in) across, in late winter–early spring that vary from white to white with pink veins, which darken with age. **H** and **S** 12in (30cm).

☼ ◊ ① Z5–8 H8–5

PRIMULAS

There are primulas to suit most garden situations, ranging from boggy areas and pond margins to woodlands, rock gardens, and containers. Of the various botanical groups, Candelabra, Auricula, and Primrose-Polyanthus primulas are the most widely grown. Auriculas are compact evergreen plants with leathery leaves and flowers with beautiful markings; they grow well in moist but well-drained soil. Candelabras prefer damp soil, and are taller and deciduous, with flowers arranged in rings up sturdy stems. The Primrose-Polyanthus group includes a diverse range of small winter-to spring-flowering plants, often sold as bedding or for containers, that thrive in moist soil. Most prefer some shade. For full cultivation details, see the Plant Dictionary.

P. 'Guinevere'

P. vialii

P. 'Lady Greer'

P. denticulata var. *alba*

P. allionii

P. frondosa

P. japonica 'Miller's Crimson'

P. 'Dawn Ansell'

P. Husky Series [white]

P. 'Woodland Walk'

P. Crescendo Series 'Crescendo Pink and Rose Shades'

P. sieboldii

P. vulgaris subsp. *sibthorpii*

P. 'Elizabeth Killelay'

P. 'Mark' [Auricula]

P. pulverulenta

P. 'Inverewe'

P. Barnhaven Blues Group

P. Charisma Series
'Charisma Blue'

P. Crescendo Series

P. Crescendo Series 'Crescendo Bright Red'

P. polyneura

P. beesiana

P. Belarina Series
'Belarina Cobalt Blue'

P. 'Fransisca'

P. sikkimensis

P. chungensis

P. palinuri

P. 'Margaret Martin' [Auricula]

P. 'Blairside Yellow' [Auricula]

P. forrestii

P. aureata

P. elatior

P. bulleyana

P. verticillata

P. kewensis

P. veris 'Katy McSparron'

P. Gold-laced Group

RED

PURPLE

Epimedium x rubrum
Carpeting perennial with dense, heart-shaped, divided leaves that are dark brownish-red in spring, when clusters of cup-shaped, crimson flowers with yellow spurs appear. **H** 12in (30cm), **S** 8in (20cm).

☀ ◊ Z4–8 H8–1

Glaucidium palmatum
Leafy perennial that has large, lobed leaves and, in spring, large, delicate, cup-shaped, lavender flowers. A woodland plant, it requires rich soil and a sheltered position. **H** and **S** 20in (50cm).

☀ ◊ Z6–9 H9–6

Helleborus purpurascens
Neat, clump-forming perennial with small, nodding, cup-shaped, pure deep purple or green flowers, splashed with deep purple on outside, in early spring. Dark green leaves are palmate and deeply divided into narrowly lance-shaped, toothed segments. **H** and **S** 12in (30cm).

☀ ◊ ① Z4–8 H8–3

Epimedium epsteinii
Rather compact, semievergreen, rhizomatous perennial with glossy green leaves divided into narrowly oval, toothed leaflets. Has clusters of pendent, long-spurred, white-and-purple flowers in spring. Good for groundcover. **H** 12in (30cm), **S** 16in (40cm).

☀ ◊ Z5–10 H9–4

Trillium erectum
(Birthroot, Squawroot)
Clump-forming perennial with 3-lobed, mid-green leaves and bright maroon-purple flowers in spring. **H** 12–18in (30–45cm), **S** 12in (30cm).

☀ ◊ Z4–7 H7–3

Cardamine pentaphyllos
Upright perennial spreading by fleshy, horizontal rootstocks. Produces clusters of large, white or pale purple flowers in spring. **H** 12–24in (30–60cm), **S** 18–24in (45–60cm).

☀ ◊ Z5–9 H9–5

Lathyrus vernus
Clump-forming perennial bearing in spring small, pealike, bright purple and blue flowers veined with red, several on each slender stem. Leaves are soft and fernlike. Proves difficult to transplant successfully. **H** and **S** 12in (30cm).

☀ ◊ ① Z5–7 H7–5

Trillium sessile
(Toadshade, Wake-robin)
Clump-forming perennial that in spring bears red-brown flowers, nestling in a collar of 3-lobed leaves, marked white, pale green or bronze. **H** 12–15in (30–38cm), **S** 12–18in (30–45cm).

☀ ◊ Z4–8 H8–1

Scopolia carniolica
Clump-forming perennial that carries spikes of nodding, purple-brown flowers, yellow inside, in early spring. **H** and **S** 24in (60cm).

☀ ◊ ① Z5–8 H8–5

Lathraea clandestina (Toothwort)
Spreading perennial that grows as a parasite on willow or poplar roots. Fleshy, underground stems have colorless scales instead of leaves. Bears bunches of hooded, purple flowers from late winter to early spring. **H** 4in (10cm), **S** indefinite.

☀ ◊ Z5–9 H9–5

Lamium orvala
Clump-forming perennial that forms a mound of mid-green leaves, sometimes with central white stripes. Clusters of pink or purple-pink flowers open in late spring to early summer. **H** and **S** 12in (30cm).

☀ ◊ Z4–8 H8–1

Erysimum 'Bowles's Mauve'
Shrubby, short-lived perennial with many clusters of purple flowers, each with 4 spreading petals, from early spring to early summer. Has narrowly lance-shaped, dark green leaves. Is best in poor soil. **H** 24in (60cm), **S** 16in (40cm).

☼ ◊ Z6–10 H10–3

Mertensia virginica
Elegant perennial with rich blue flowers, hanging in clusters in spring. Leaves are soft blue-green. Dies down in summer. Crowns are prone to slug damage. **H** 12–24in (30–60cm), **S** 12–18in (30–45cm).

☀ ◊ Z3–7 H7–1

Omphalodes cappadocica 'Cherry Ingram'
Clump-forming, rhizomatous perennial with oval, deeply veined, pointed, mid-green leaves. In spring bears loose racemes of 5-petaled, dark blue flowers. **H** 12in (30cm), **S** 24in (60cm).

☼ ◊ Z6–8 H8–6

Brunnera macrophylla 'Jack Frost'
Groundcover perennial with heart-shaped, silvery-gray leaves. Delicate sprays of small, star-shaped, forget-menot-like, blue flowers are produced in spring. Is ideal in the front of a border. **H** 24in (60cm), **S** 24in (60cm) or more.

☼ ◊ Z3–7 H7–1

LUNGWORTS

Invaluable shade-loving perennials, lungworts (*Pulmonaria*) produce clusters of bell-shaped spring flowers and hairy, groundcovering foliage. Selections are available in a range of colors, from white through to pink, blue, and purple; *P. rubra* has red blooms. Some cultivars have also been selected for the beauty of their foliage, which may be spotted or streaked with white or silver or variegated. Easy to grow, lungworts thrive in cool areas in soil that does not dry out. During summer, trim off the old foliage and fresh leaves, often more prominently marked, will soon appear.

P. rubra 'David Ward'

P. rubra

P. 'Lewis Palmer'

P. 'Excalibur'

P. OPAL ('Ocupol')

P. 'Margery Fish'

P. 'Mary Mottram'

P. 'Mawson's Blue'

GREEN

Helleborus argutifolius 'Pacific Frost'
Clump-forming perennial with pink shoot tips and evergreen, divided, spiny, dark green leaves densely speckled in cream. Produces large clusters of cup-shaped, pale green flowers in winter–spring. **H** 24in (60cm), **S** 18in (45cm).

☼ ◐ ◊ ① Z6–9 H9–6

Euphorbia cyparissias
Rounded, leafy perennial with a mass of slender, gray-green leaves and umbels of small, bright lime-green flowers in late spring. May be invasive. **H** and **S** 12in (30cm).

☼ ◊ ① Z4–9 H9–1

Euphorbia amygdaloides var. robbiae
Evergreen, spreading perennial with rosettes of dark green leaves, useful as groundcover even in poor, dry soil and semi-shade. Bears open, rounded heads of lime-green flowers in spring. **H** 18–24in (45–60cm), **S** 24in (60cm).

☼ ◐ ◊ ① Z6–9 H9–2

Helleborus x sternii
Evergreen, clump-forming perennial with divided leaves and cup-shaped, often pink-tinged, pale green flowers borne in terminal clusters in winter and early spring. **H** and **S** 18in (45cm).

☼ ◐ ◊ ① Z5–8 H8–5

Helleborus argutifolius 'Silver Lace'
Clump-forming perennial with evergreen, divided, spiny, bluish-green leaves and flared, cup-shaped, pale green flowers borne in large clusters in winter–spring. **H** 24in (60cm), **S** 18in (45cm).

☼ ◐ ◊ ① Z6–9 H9–6

YELLOW

Anemone x lipsiensis
Prostrate, carpeting perennial that in spring has many single, pale yellow flowers with bright yellow stamens. Leaves are deeply cut with long leaflets. **H** 6in (15cm), **S** 12in (30cm).

☼ ◐ ◊ ① Z5–8 H8–5

Epimedium x versicolor 'Neosulphureum'
Carpeting perennial with dense, heart-shaped, divided leaves, tinted reddish-purple in spring when it bears cup-shaped, pale yellow flowers in small, pendent clusters on wiry stems. **H** and **S** 12in (30cm).

☼ ◐ ◊ ① Z5–9 H9–4

Uvularia grandiflora
(Bellwort, Merrybells)
Clump-forming perennial. Clusters of long, bell-shaped, yellow flowers hang gracefully from slender stems in spring. **H** 18–24in (45–60cm), **S** 12in (30cm).

☼ ◐ ◊ Z3–7 H7–1

Valeriana phu 'Aurea'
Perennial with rosettes of lemon- to butter-yellow young foliage that turns mid-green by summer, when heads of insignificant, white flowers appear. **H** 15in (38cm), **S** 12–15in (30–38cm).

☼ ◊ ① Z5–9 H9–5

Adonis vernalis
Clump-forming perennial that in early spring produces buttercup-like, greenish-yellow blooms singly at the tips of stems. Mid-green leaves are delicately dissected. **H** and **S** 9–12in (23–30cm).

☼ ◊ ① Z4–7 H7–1

Euphorbia polychroma
Rounded, bushy perennial with mid-green leaves and heads of bright yellow flowers carried for several weeks in spring. **H** and **S** 20in (50cm).

☼ ◊ ◐ ① Z5–9 H9–5

PERENNIALS

ORANGE	WHITE

Primula veris (Cowslip)
Very variable, rosette-forming, evergreen or semievergreen perennial with tight clusters of fragrant, tubular, yellow flowers produced on sturdy stems in spring. Leaves are oval to lance-shaped, toothed and mid-green. **H** and **S** 10in (25cm).

☼ ◊ Z3–8 H8–1

Epimedium x warleyense
Carpeting perennial with heart-shaped, divided, light green leaves, tinged purple-red, and cup-shaped, rich orange flowers borne in clusters on wiry stems in spring. **H** and **S** 12in (30cm).

☼ ◊ Z5–9 H9–5

Anthericum liliago (St Bernard's lily)
Upright perennial that in early summer bears tall racemes of trumpet-shaped, white flowers above clumps of long, narrow, gray-green leaves. **H** 18–24in (45–60cm), **S** 12in (30cm).

☼ ◊ Z7–9 H9–7

Leucanthemum x superbum 'Esther Read'
Robust perennial with large, daisylike, double, white flower heads borne singly on strong stems in summer. **H** and **S** 18in (45cm).

☼ ◊ Z5–8 H8–1

Doronicum orientale 'Magnificum'
Clump-forming perennial with heart-shaped, lush, soft green leaves. Short stems bear daisylike, bright yellow flower heads in spring. Plants may die down by late summer. **H** 18in (45cm), **S** 16in (40cm).

☼ ◊ Z4–8 H8–1

Meconopsis cambrica (Welsh poppy)
Spreading perennial that in late spring carries lemon-yellow or rich orange blooms. Double forms are available. Has deeply divided, fernlike foliage. **H** 12–18in (30–45cm), **S** 12in (30cm).

☼ ◊ Z6–8 H8–6

Galium odoratum (Sweet woodruff)
Carpeting perennial that bears whorls of star-shaped, white flowers above neat, whorled leaves in summer. All parts of plant are aromatic. **H** 6in (15cm), **S** 12in (30cm) or more.

☼ ◊ Z5–8 H8–5

Anemone ranunculoides
Spreading perennial for damp woodland, bearing buttercup-like, single, deep yellow flowers in spring. Divided leaves have short stalks. **H** and **S** 8in (20cm).

☼ ◊ ① Z4–8 H8–1

Epimedium 'Amber Queen'
Evergreen, clump-forming perennial with clusters of spidery, pendent, long-spurred, orange flowers, held on wiry stems, in spring. Dark green leaves are mottled when young and divided into rounded heart-shaped, toothed leaflets. **H** 12in (30cm), **S** 16in (40cm).

☼ ◊ Z5–9 H9–5

Tradescantia Andersoniana Group **'Osprey'**
Clump-forming perennial with narrow, lance-shaped leaves, 6–12in (15–30cm) long. Has clusters of white flowers with purple-blue stamens, surrounded by 2 leaflike bracts, in summer. **H** to 24in (60cm), **S** 18in (45cm).

☼ ◊ ① Z5–9 H9–5

Geranium clarkei 'Kashmir White'
Carpeting, rhizomatous perennial with divided leaves and loose clusters of cup-shaped flowers, white with pale lilac-pink veins, borne for a long period in summer. **H** and **S** 18–24in (45–60cm).

☼ ◊ Z5–8 H8–5

PERENNIALS

263

PERENNILAS

Deinanthe bifida
Slow-growing, clump-forming
perennial with nodding, cup-shaped,
white flowers. Has oval, bristly,
soft green leaves on short stems.
H 16in (40cm), **S** 12in (30cm).

☼◑ ◊ Z4–8 H8–1

Diplarrhena moraea
Clump-forming perennial with fans
of long, strap-shaped leaves and
clusters of iris-like, white flowers,
with centers of yellow and purple,
borne on wiry stems in early summer.
H 18in (45cm), **S** 9in (23cm).

☼ ◊ Z9–10 H10–9

Anthemis punctata subsp. cupaniana
Evergreen, carpeting perennial with
dense, finely cut, silvery foliage that
turns green in winter. Small, daisylike,
white flower heads with yellow centers
are borne singly on short stems in early
summer. **H** and **S** 12in (30cm).

☼ ◊ Z6–9 H9–6

Geranium renardii
Compact, clump-forming perennial
with lobed, circular, sage-green leaves
and purple-veined, white flowers, borne
in early summer. **H** and **S** 12in (30cm).

☼ ◊ Z6–8 H8–6

Mimulus naiandinus
Spreading perennial, with hairy
leaves, that in summer bears
snapdragon-like, rose-pink flowers
tipped with creamy-yellow and spotted
deep pink. **H** 9in (23cm), **S** 10in (25cm).

☼ ◗ Z9–11 H11–8

Crambe maritima (Sea kale)
Robust perennial with a mound of
wide, curved, lobed, silvery-green
leaves. Bears large heads of small,
fragrant, white flowers, opening
into branching sprays in summer.
H and **S** 24in (60cm).

☼ ◊ Z6–9 H9–6

Melittis melissophyllum
(Bastard balm)
Erect perennial that in early summer
bears white flowers with purple lower
lips in axils of rough, oval, mid-green
leaves. **H** and **S** 12in (30cm).

☼◑ ◊ Z6–9 H9–6

Erigeron 'Charity'
Clump-forming perennial with a mass
of daisylike, light pink flower heads
with greenish-yellow centers borne
for a long period in summer. May need
some support. **H** and **S** to 24in (60cm).

☼ ◊ Z5–8 H8–5

x Heucherella tiarelloides
Evergreen, groundcover perennial that
has dense clusters of leaves and feathery
sprays of tiny, bell-shaped, pink flowers
in early summer. **H** and **S** 18in (45cm).

☼◑ ◊ Z5–8 H8–5

Geranium x oxonianum 'Wargrave Pink'
Semievergreen, carpeting perennial with dense, dainty, lobed, basal leaves acting as weed-suppressing groundcover. Cup-shaped, bright salmon-pink flowers are borne throughout summer. **H** 18in (45cm), **S** 24in (60cm).

☼ ◊ Z4–8 H8–1

Potentilla nepalensis 'Miss Willmott'
Clump-forming perennial with palmate, strawberry-like, bright green leaves. Numerous slender, branching stems carry cherry-red-centered, pink flowers throughout summer. **H** 20in (50cm), **S** 24in (60cm).

☼ ◊ Z4–7 H9–4

Erodium manescavii
Mound-forming perennial with divided, ferny, blue-green leaves. Produces loose clusters of single, deep pink, darker blotched flowers throughout summer. **H** 18in (45cm), **S** 24in (60cm).

☼ ◊ Z6–8 H8–6

Persicaria macrophylla
Compact perennial carrying neat spikes of rich rose-pink blooms above narrow, lance-shaped, glaucous leaves in late summer. **H** 18–24in (45–60cm), **S** 12in (30cm).

☼ ◊ ❗ Z5–9 H9–5

Centaurea hypoleuca 'John Coutts'
Upright perennial. Deep rose-red flower heads, with thistle-like centers encircled by star-shaped ray petals, are borne on slender stems in summer. Deeply divided leaves are white-gray beneath. **H** 24in (60cm), **S** 18in (45cm).

☼ ◊ Z3–9 H9–1

Incarvillea mairei
Compact, clump-forming perennial that has short stems bearing several trumpet-shaped, purplish-pink flowers in early summer. Leaves are divided into oval leaflets. Protect crowns with winter mulch. **H** and **S** 12in (30cm).

☼ ◊ Z4–8 H8–1

Lychnis flos-jovis
Clump-forming perennial with rounded clusters of deep rose-pink flowers, opening in mid-summer, that are set off by gray foliage. **H** and **S** 18in (45cm).

☼ ◊ Z4–8 H8–1

Dactylorhiza foliosa
Deciduous, terrestrial orchid with spikes of bright purple or pink flowers, ½–¾in (1–2cm) long, borne in spring-summer. Has lance-shaped or triangular leaves, 4–8in (10–20cm) long, arranged spirally on stem. **H** 24in (60cm), **S** 6in (15cm).

☼ ◊ Z7–8 H8–7

Osteospermum jucundum
Evergreen, neat, clump-forming perennial with mid-green leaves. In late summer, soft pink flower heads, mostly dark-eyed, are borne singly but in great abundance. **H** and **S** 12in (30cm).

☼ ◊ Z9–11 H6–1

Incarvillea delavayi
Clump-forming perennial with deeply divided leaves and erect stems bearing several trumpet-shaped, pinkish-red flowers in early summer. Has attractive seed pods. **H** 18–24in (45–60cm), **S** 12in (30cm).

☼ ◊ Z6–10 H9–3

Lychnis viscaria 'Splendens Plena'
Clump-forming perennial bearing spikes of double, magenta flowers in early summer. Stems and large, oval to lance-shaped, basal leaves are covered in sticky hairs. **H** 12–18in (30–45cm), **S** 9in (23cm) or more.

☼ ◊ Z3–7 H7–1

CARNATIONS AND PINKS

Although perhaps best known for providing excellent, long-lasting cut flowers, carnations and pinks (*Dianthus* cultivars) are highly ornamental border subjects, valued for their usually fragrant, clove-scented blooms, produced over a long period in summer, and their distinctive silvery- or gray-green foliage. Shorter-growing cultivars—the old-fashioned and modern pinks—make excellent edging plants. Many of the flowers are attractively marked or have fringed petals. Carnations and pinks need an open, sunny position, preferably in alkaline soil. All except the perpetual-flowering carnations are frost-hardy, and most can be easily propagated from cuttings. The myriad of carnation and pinks cultivars are divided into the following groups:

Border carnations—plants are of upright habit and flower prolifically in mid-summer in a single flush; each stem bears 5 or more flowers. Picotee-flowered forms, with petals outlined in a darker, contrasting color, are available.

Perpetual-flowering carnations—similar in habit to border carnations, they are usually grown for cut flowers and bloom year-round under glass. Plants are normally disbudded, leaving one flower per stem, but spray forms have up to 5 flowers per stem.

Malmaison carnations—these produce intensely fragrant flowers sporadically throughout the year under glass.

Old-fashioned pinks—these have a low, spreading habit and form neat cushions of foliage; masses of fragrant flowers are produced in mid-summer. Good for border edging and cutting.

Modern pinks—usually more vigorous than old-fashioned pinks, they are repeat-flowering and produce 2 or 3 main flushes of flowers in summer. Cut or deadhead to encourage further flowering.

Alpine pinks—in early summer, these plants form cushions of small, scented flowers. Good for edging, or in a rock garden, raised bed, trough, or alpine house.

D. 'Coquette'
[perpetual-flowering carnation]

Dianthus CANDY FLOSS ('Devon Flavia') [modern pink]

D. 'Milky Way'
[perpetual-flowering carnation]

D. 'White Ladies'
[old-fashioned pink]

D. 'Lady Madonna'
[modern pink]

D. 'Becky Robinson'
[modern pink]

D. 'Mrs. Sinkins'
[old-fashioned pink]

D. 'Musgrave's Pink'
[old-fashioned pink]

D. 'Gran's Favourite'
[old-fashioned pink]

D. 'Haytor White' [modern pink]

D. 'Doris' [modern pink]

D. 'Duchess of Westminster'
[Malmaison carnation]

D. 'Dad's Favourite'
[old-fashioned pink]

D. 'Brilliant Star' [modern pink]

D. 'Cranmere Pool' [modern pink]

D. 'Devon Dove' [modern pink]   *D.* 'Inchmery' [old-fashioned pink]

D. 'Evening Star' [modern pink]

D. 'Rose de Mai'
[old-fashioned pink]

***Dianthus* STARLIGHT ('Hilstar')**
[modern pink]

D. 'Tickled Pink' [modern pink]

D. 'Neon Star' [modern pink]

D. 'Fusilier' [modern pink]

D. *superbus* 'Crimsonia'
[old-fashioned pink]

D. 'Monica Wyatt' [modern pink]

D. 'Feuerhexe' [alpine pink]

D. 'Valda Wyatt' [modern pink]

D. 'Tayside Red'
[Malmaison carnation]

D. 'India Star' [modern pink]

D. 'Pixie Star' [modern pink]

D. 'Lily the Pink' [modern pink]

D. 'Moulin Rouge'
[modern pink]

D. 'Queen of Sheba'
[old-fashioned pink]

D. 'Prado Mint'
[perpetual-flowering carnation]

D. 'Devon Wizard' [modern pink] **D. 'Pink Jewel'** [alpine pink]

D. 'Passion' [modern pink]

D. 'Golden Cross' [border carnation]

267

PERENNIALS

Glandularia 'Sissinghurst'
Mat-forming perennial that throughout summer bears heads of brilliant pink flowers above mid-green foliage. Is excellent for edging a path or growing in a tub. **H** 6–8in (15–20cm), **S** 18in (45cm).

☀ ◌ Z7–11 H11–1

Stachys officinalis 'Hummelo'
Mat-forming perennial with oblong, round-toothed, hairy, dark green leaves. Upright, sturdy stems bear whorls of small, tubular, 2-lipped, pink flowers in summer. **H** and **S** 24in (60cm).

☀ ◌ Z5–8 H8–4

Dianthus 'Houndspool Ruby'
Modern pink with compact growth and an abundance of strongly scented, semidouble, ruby-pink flowers, each with a deeper eye. **H** 12–18in (30–45cm), **S** 9–12in (23–30cm).

☀ ◌ Z5–9 H8–1

Geum 'Bell Bank'
Clump-forming perennial with cup-shaped, nodding, semidouble, pink flowers, borne on slender, branching, hairy stems, in early summer. Has pinnate, lobed, mid-green leaves. Is easily grown in any soil that does not dry out. **H** 24in (60cm), **S** 12in (30cm).

☀ ◐ Z5–8 H8–5

Dicentra 'Stuart Boothman'
Tufted perennial with oval, finely cut, deep gray-green leaves. In spring–summer, produces arching sprays of heart-shaped, carmine flowers. **H** 12in (30cm), **S** 16in (40cm).

◑ ◌ ❗ Z3–9 H9–1

Potentilla 'Arc-en-ciel'
Clump-forming perennial with arching stems bearing loose sprays of large, saucer-shaped, double, yellow-centered, red flowers in late spring and summer. Has rounded, 3-lobed, toothed, mid-green basal leaves. **H** and **S** 12in (30cm).

☀ ◌ Z4–8 H8–1

Rhodiola heterodonta
Clump-forming perennial with heads of yellow or red, sometimes greenish flowers from spring to early summer. Stems bear toothed, blue-green leaves. **H** 18in (45cm), **S** 10in (25cm).

☀ ◌ Z5–9 H9–5

Lychnis coronaria
Clump-forming perennial, often grown as a biennial. From mid-to late summer, brilliant rose-crimson flowers are borne in panicles on branched, gray stems that rise from neat, gray leaves. **H** 18–24in (45–60cm), **S** 18in (45cm).

☀ ◌ Z3–8 H8–1

Crusea coccinea
Prostrate, creeping perennial with ovate, ribbed, light green leaves, 1¼–2in (3–5cm) long. Trumpet-shaped, bright red flowers, 1–1½in (2.5–4cm) long, in long-stalked, few-flowered, axillary clusters, are borne in summer–fall. **H** 6in (15cm), **S** 8–16in (20–40cm).

● ◌ Z10–11 H8–1

Coreopsis 'Limerock Ruby'
Upright perennial producing masses of daisylike, ruby-red flower heads, on branched, slender stems, throughout summer. Has small lance-shaped, dark green leaves. **H** 16in (40cm), **S** 18in (45cm).

☀ ◌ Z7–9 H9–1

Polemonium carneum
Clump-forming perennial that carries clusters of cup-shaped, pink or lilac-pink flowers in early summer. Foliage is finely divided. **H** and **S** 18in (45cm).

☼ ◊ Z4–8 H8–1

Geranium macrorrhizum
Semievergreen, carpeting perennial bearing magenta flowers in early summer. Rounded, divided, aromatic leaves make good, weed-proof groundcover and assume bright tints in fall. **H** 12–15in (30–38cm), **S** 24in (60cm).

◐ ◊ Z4–8 H8–1

Platycodon grandiflorus
(Balloon flower)
Neat, clump-forming perennial that in summer has clusters of large, balloon-like buds opening to bell-shaped, blue or purplish flowers. Stems are clothed with bluish-green leaves. **H** 18–24in (45–60cm), **S** 12–18in (30–45cm).

☼ ◊ Z4–9 H9–1

Ourisia coccinea
Mat-forming, evergreen perennial with rosettes of oval, toothed, strongly veined, bright green leaves. Loose racemes of tubular, nodding, rich red flowers are borne in mid- to late summer. **H** 8in (20cm), **S** 12in (30cm).

☀ ◊ Z7–9 H9–1

Verbena rigida
Neat, compact perennial bearing heads of pale violet flowers from mid-summer onward. Has lance-shaped, rough, mid-green leaves borne on flower stems. **H** 18–24in (45–60cm), **S** 12in (30cm).

☼ ◊ Z8–15 H12–1

Berkheya purpurea
Clump-forming perennial with large, daisylike, lavender flower heads in summer. Has oblong-lance-shaped, spiny, silvery-gray basal leaves. **H** 24in (60cm), **S** 12in (30cm).

◐ ◊ Z9–10 H10–9

Tradescantia Andersoniana Group 'Purple Dome'
Clump-forming perennial with narrow, lance-shaped leaves, 6–12in (15–30cm) long. Has clusters of rich purple flowers, surrounded by 2 leaflike bracts, in summer. **H** to 24in (60cm), **S** 18in (45cm).

☼ ◊ ! Z5–9 H9–5

Potentilla atrosanguinea
Clump-forming perennial with hairy, palmate, strawberry-like leaves. Loose clusters of dark red flowers are borne throughout summer. **H** 18in (45cm), **S** 24in (60cm).

☼ ◊ Z5–8 H8–5

Centaurea montana
Spreading perennial with many rather lax stems carrying, in early summer, one or more large, purple, blue, white or pink flower heads with thistle-like centers encircled by star-shaped ray petals. **H** 20in (50cm), **S** 24in (60cm).

☼ ◊ Z3–9 H9–1

Geranium x magnificum
Clump-forming perennial with hairy, deeply lobed leaves and cup-shaped, prominently veined, violet-blue flowers borne in small clusters in summer. **H** 18in (45cm), **S** 24in (60cm).

☼ ◊ Z4–8 H8–1

Stokesia laevis
Perennial with overwintering, evergreen rosettes. In summer, cornflower-like, lavender- or purple-blue flower heads are borne freely. Leaves are narrow and mid-green. **H** and **S** 12–18in (30–45cm).

☼ ◊ Z5–9 H9–5

PERENNIALS

Geranium 'Johnson's Blue'
Vigorous, clump-forming perennial with many divided leaves and cup-shaped, deep lavender-blue flowers borne throughout summer.
H 12in (30cm), **S** 24in (60cm).

☼ ◊ Z4–8 H8–1

Stachys macrantha 'Superba'
Clump-forming perennial with heart-shaped, soft, wrinkled, mid-green leaves, from which arise sturdy stems producing whorls of hooded, purple-violet flowers in summer. **H** 12–18in (30–45cm), **S** 12–24in (30–60cm).

☼ ◊ Z5–8 H8–4

Eryngium bourgatii
Clump-forming perennial that, from mid- to late summer, carries heads of thistle-like, blue-green, then lilac-blue, flowers on branched, wiry stems well above deeply cut, basal, gray-green leaves. **H** 18–24in (45–60cm), **S** 12in (30cm).

☼ ◊ Z5–9 H9–5

Polemonium caeruleum
(Jacob's ladder)
Clump-forming perennial. Clusters of cup-shaped, lavender-blue flowers with orange-yellow stamens open in summer amid finely divided foliage.
H and **S** 18–24in (45–60cm).

☼ ◊ Z4–9 H9–1

Nepeta x faassenii (Catmint)
Bushy, clump-forming perennial, useful for edging. Forms mounds of small, grayish-green leaves, from which loose spikes of tubular, soft lavender-blue flowers appear in early summer. **H** and **S** 18in (45cm).

☼ ◊ Z4–8 H8–1

Anemonopsis macrophylla
(False anemone)
Clump-forming perennial with waxy, nodding, purplish-blue flowers, borne on slender, branching stems in summer above fernlike leaves.
H 18–24in (45–60cm), **S** 20in (50cm).

☼ ◊ Z5–8 H8–5

Catananche caerulea 'Major'
Perennial forming clumps of grassy, gray-green leaves, above which rise wiry, branching stems each carrying a daisylike, lavender-blue flower head in summer. Propagate regularly by root cuttings. **H** 18–24in (45–60cm), **S** 24in (30cm).

☼ ◊ Z3–8 H8–1

Polemonium caeruleum
BRISE D'ANJOU ('Blanjou')
Clump-forming, short-lived perennial with clusters of cup-shaped, lavender-blue flowers in summer. Has finely divided, mid-green leaves with creamy-yellow margins, paler if grown in shade.
H 24in (60cm), **S** 10–12in (25–30cm).

☼ ◊ Z4–9 H9–1

Amsonia orientalis
Neat, clump-forming perennial. In summer, heads of small, star-shaped, gray-blue flowers open on tops of wiry stems clothed with green, sometimes grayish, leaves. **H** 18–24in (45–60cm), **S** 12–18in (30–45cm).

☼ ◊ ⓘ Z5–8 H8–5

Eryngium variifolium
Evergreen, rosette-forming perennial with stiff stems that, in late summer, bear heads of thistle-like, gray-blue flowers, each with a collar of white bracts. Jagged-edged leaves are mid-green, marbled with white. **H** 18in (45cm), **S** 10in (25cm).

☼ ◊ Z5–9 H9–5

Scabiosa caucasica 'Clive Greaves'
Clump-forming perennial that throughout summer has violet-blue flower heads with pincushion-like centers. Basal, mid-green leaves are lance-shaped and slightly lobed on the stems. **H** and **S** 18–24in (45–60cm).

☼ ◊ Z4–9 H9–1

Geranium ROZANNE **('Gerwat')**
Sprawling, deciduous perennial producing masses of large, shallowly cup-shaped, blue flowers during summer and into fall. Rounded, deeply divided basal leaves are mid-green with marbled, paler green markings. **H** and **S** 20in (50cm) or more.

◑ ◊ Z4–9 H10–2

Myosotidium hortensia
(Chatham Island forget-me-not)
Evergreen, clump-forming perennial bearing large clusters of forget-me-not-like, blue flowers in summer above a basal mound of large, ribbed, glossy leaves. **H** 18–24in (45–60cm), **S** 24in (60cm).

◑ ◊ H11–1

Parahebe perfoliata
(Digger's speedwell)
Evergreen subshrub with willowy stems clasped by leathery, glaucous leaves. Elegant, long, branching sprays of blue flowers are borne in summer. **H** 18–24in (45–60cm), **S** 18in (45cm).

☼ ◊ Z9–11 H11–3

Veronica peduncularis
Mat-forming perennial with ovate to lance-shaped, glossy, purple-tinged, mid-green leaves. Bears abundant, saucer-shaped, deep blue flowers, with small, white eyes, over a long period from early spring to summer. **H** to 4in (10cm), **S** 24in (60cm) or more.

☼ ◊ Z6–8 H8–6

Veronica gentianoides
Mat-forming perennial with spikes of very pale blue flowers opening in early summer on tops of stems that arise from glossy, basal leaves. **H** and **S** 18in (45cm).

☼ ◊ Z4–7 H7–1

Veronica spicata subsp. incana
Mat-forming perennial, densely covered with silver hairs, with linear to lance-shaped leaves. In summer, bears spikes of small, star-shaped, clear blue flowers. **H** and **S** 12in (30cm).

◑ ◊ Z3–8 H8–1

HOSTAS

Their luxuriant foliage and attractive habit have made hostas, or plantain lilies, increasingly sought after as garden plants. Native to Asia, they add an exotic touch to watersides or damp, shady corners, and large patio containers. Hostas vary in size from plants a few inches in height, to tall forms that make clumps up to 5ft (1.5m) across. Their elegant, deciduous leaves appear in mid-spring and are incredibly diverse in shape, texture, and color, with dramatic variegations and shadings. Many produce decorative flower spikes, which rise gracefully above the foliage in mid-summer and may be scented, according to variety. Although hostas are essentially shade- and moisture-loving plants, preferring rich, well-drained soil, they also tolerate drier soil. Protect the leaves from slug damage.

H. 'Cherry Berry'

H. 'Devon Green'

H. 'Antioch'

H. 'Regal Splendor'

H. 'Gold Edger'

H. 'Invincible'

H. nigrescens

H. sieboldiana

H. 'Night Before Christmas'

H. 'Hadspen Blue'

H. tokudama f. *flavocircinalis*

H. 'Ground Master'

H. 'Minuteman'

H. 'Halcyon'

H. 'June'

H. lancifolia

H. 'Fire and Ice'

H. 'Golden Prayers'

H. 'Fragrant Bouquet '

H. 'Golden Tiara'

H. 'August Moon '

H. 'Whirlwind '

H. 'Brim Cup'

H. 'Hydon Sunset'

H. 'Blue Wedgwood'

H. 'Allan P. McConnell '

H. 'Dream Weaver '

H. 'Revolution'

H. 'Birchwood Parky's Gold'

H. 'So Sweet'

H. 'Remember Me'

H. 'Sagae'

H. 'Ginko Craig'

H. 'Great Expectations '

H. 'Tattoo'

273

PERENNIALS

GRAY

Artemisia ludoviciana 'Valerie Finnis'
Semievergreen, upright then arching
perennial with silvery-gray leaves,
the lower ones are broad and lobed
while the upper ones are narrow
and spear-shaped. Bears spires of
insignificant, yellowish flowers in late
summer. **H** 2ft (60cm), **S** 3ft (90cm).

☼ ◊ Z4–9 H9–1

Stachys byzantina
(Lamb's ears, Woolly betony)
Evergreen, mat-forming perennial with
woolly, gray foliage that is excellent
for a border front or as groundcover.
Bears mauve-pink flowers in summer.
H 12–15in (30–38cm), **S** 24in (60cm).

☼ ◊ Z4–8 H8–1

GREEN

Mentha suaveolens 'Variegata'
(Variegated apple mint)
Spreading perennial with soft, woolly,
mid-green leaves, splashed with white
and cream, that smell of apples. Seldom
produces flowers. **H** 12–18in (30–45cm),
S 24in (60cm).

☼ ◊ Z6–9 H9–5

Filipendula ulmaria 'Aurea'
Leafy perennial, grown for its divided
foliage, which is bright golden-yellow
in spring and pale green in summer.
Clusters of creamy-white flowers are
carried in branching heads in mid-
summer. **H** and **S** 12in (30cm).

◑ ◊ Z5–9 H9–1

Hosta tokudama f. aureonebulosa
Very slow-growing, clump-forming
perennial bearing cup-shaped, puckered,
blue leaves with irregular, cloudy-yellow
centers. Racemes of trumpet-shaped, pale
lilac-gray flowers, on scapes 16in (40cm)
long, are produced just above foliage in
mid-summer. **H** 18in (45cm), **S** 30in (75cm).

☀ ◊ Z3–8 H8–3

YELLOW

Sisyrinchium striatum
Semievergreen perennial that forms
tufts of long, narrow, gray-green leaves.
Bears slender spikes of purple-striped,
straw-yellow flowers in summer.
Self-seeds freely. **H** 18–24in (45–60cm),
S 12in (30cm).

☼ ◊ Z7–8 H8–7

Origanum vulgare 'Aureum'
Woody-based perennial forming a
dense mat of aromatic, golden-yellow,
young leaves that turn pale yellow-
green in mid-summer. Occasionally
bears tiny, mauve flowers in summer.
H in leaf 3in (8cm), **S** indefinite.

☼ ◊ Z4–9 H10–2

Stachys byzantina 'Primrose Heron'
Evergreen, mat-forming perennial
with woolly, yellowish-gray leaves,
to 4in (10cm) long. Erect stems bear
interrupted spikes of pink-purple
flowers from early summer to early
fall. **H** 18in (45cm), **S** 24in (60cm).

☼ ◊ Z4–8 H8–1

Alchemilla mollis (Lady's mantle)
Clump-forming, groundcover
perennial that has rounded, pale green
leaves with crinkled edges. Bears small
sprays of tiny, bright greenish-yellow
flowers, with conspicuous outer calyces,
in mid-summer that may be dried.
H and **S** 20in (50cm).

☼◐ ◊ Z4–7 H7–1

Calanthe striata
Deciduous, terrestrial orchid with
erect spikes of fragrant, yellow or
yellow-and-brown flowers, each with
a 3-lobed lip, borne in late spring and
early summer, before the 2–3 long,
broadly oblong, ribbed leaves fully
expand. **H** 32in (80cm), **S** 20in (50cm).

☼◐ ◐ pH Z6–9 H9–6

Patrinia triloba
Clump-forming perennial with broad,
3- to 5-lobed, bright green leaves that
turn yellow in fall. In summer upright
stems bear panicles of small, fragrant,
5-petaled, bright yellow flowers.
H 20in (50cm), **S** 12in (30cm).

☼◐ ◊ Z5–8 H8–4

Oenothera fruticosa 'Fyrverkeri'
Clump-forming perennial that from
mid- to late summer bears spikes
of fragrant, cup-shaped flowers. Has
reddish stems and glossy, mid-green
foliage. **H** and **S** 12–15in (30–38cm).

☼ ◊ Z4–8 H8–1

Alchemilla conjuncta
Clump-forming perennial that has neat,
wavy, star-shaped leaves with pale
margins. In mid-summer, bears loose
clusters of tiny, greenish-yellow flowers,
with conspicuous, outer calyces, which
may be dried for winter decoration.
H and **S** 12in (30cm).

☼ ◊ Z3–7 H7–1

**Ranunculus constantinopolitanus
'Plenus'**
Clump-forming perennial with divided,
toothed leaves sometimes spotted gray
and white. Neat, pompon-like, double,
yellow flowers appear in early summer.
H 20in (50cm), **S** 12in (30cm).

☼ ◐ ⊘ Z7–9 H9–7

Helichrysum 'Schwefellicht'
Clump-forming perennial that
bears silver-gray leaves and a mass
of ever-lasting, fluffy, sulfur-yellow
flower heads from mid- to late summer.
H 16–24in (40–60cm), **S** 12in (30cm).

☼ ◊ Z10–11 H11–1

Solidago x luteus
Clump-forming perennial. From
mid-summer onward, slender stems
carry dense heads of bright creamy-
yellow flowers above narrow, mid-green
leaves. **H** 24in (60cm), **S** 30in (75cm).

☼ ◊ Z5–8 H8–5

YELLOW

Geum 'Lady Stratheden'
Clump-forming perennial with lobed leaves and cup-shaped, double, bright yellow flowers with prominent, green stamens borne on slender, branching stems for a long period in summer.
H 18–24in (45–60cm), **S** 18in (45cm).

 ☼ ◊ Z5–9 H9–5

Coreopsis verticillata
Bushy perennial with finely divided, dark green foliage and many tiny, star-shaped, golden flower heads borne throughout summer. Divide and replant in spring. **H** 16–24in (40–60cm), **S** 12in (30cm).

☼ ◊ Z4–9 H9–1

Potentilla megalantha
Clump-forming perennial with large, palmate, hairy, soft green leaves. Large, rich yellow flowers are produced in summer. **H** 8in (20cm), **S** 6in (15cm).

 ☼ ◊ Z5–8 H8–5

Eriophyllum lanatum
Perennial forming low cushions of divided, silvery leaves. Daisylike, yellow flower heads are produced freely in summer, usually singly, on gray stems. **H** and **S** 12in (30cm).

☼ ◊ Z5–8 H8–5

Ranunculus acris 'Flore Pleno' (Double meadow buttercup)
Clump-forming perennial. Wiry stems with lobed and cut leaves act as a foil for rosetted, double, golden-yellow flowers in late spring and early summer. **H** and **S** 18–24in (45–60cm).

☼ ◐ ① Z4–8 H8–1

Buphthalmum salicifolium (Yellow ox-eye)
Spreading perennial that carries daisylike, deep yellow flower heads singly on willowy stems throughout summer. May need staking. Divide regularly; spreads on rich soil.
H 24in (60cm), **S** 36in (90cm).

 ☼ ◊ Z5–8 H8–5

Tropaeolum polyphyllum
Prostrate perennial with spurred, short, trumpet-shaped, rich yellow flowers, borne singly in summer above trailing, gray-green leaves and stems. May spread widely once established but is good on a bank. **H** 2–3in (5–8cm), **S** 12in (30cm) or more.

 ☼ ◊ Z8–11 H12–1

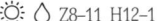

Coreopsis lanceolata
Bushy perennial that in summer freely produces daisylike, bright yellow flower heads on branching stems. Lance-shaped leaves are borne on flower stems. Propagate by seed or division.
H 18in (45cm), **S** 12in (30cm).

 ☼ ◊ Z4–9 H9–1

PERENNIALS

Hieracium lanatum
Clump-forming perennial that produces mounds of broad, downy, gray leaves, above which dandelion-like, yellow flower heads appear on wiry stems in summer. **H** 12–18in (30–45cm), **S** 12in (30cm).

☼ ◊ Z5–8 H8–5

Inula royleana
Upright, clump-forming perennial with dark green stems and ovate, hairy leaves. Bears solitary, orange-yellow flower heads, 4–5in (10–12cm) across, from mid-summer to early fall. **H** 18–24in (45–60cm), **S** 18in (45cm).

☼ ◊ Z4–8 H8–1

Libertia ixioides 'Goldfinger'
Evergreen, clump-forming rhizomatous perennial grown for its lance-shaped, golden-orange leaves, the color intensifying in winter. Has short panicles of saucer-shaped, white flowers in summer. **H** and **S** 24in (60cm).

☼ ◊ Z8–10 H10–8

Tricyrtis hirta var. alba
Upright, rhizomatous perennial that bears clusters of large, bell-shaped, spurred, white flowers, occasionally purple-spotted, in upper leaf axils of hairy, stem-clasping, dark green leaves during late summer and early fall. **H** 18–24in (45–60cm), **S** 18in (45cm).

☼ ◊ Z4–9 H9–8

Calceolaria 'John Innes'
Vigorous, evergreen, clump-forming perennial that in spring–summer produces large, pouchlike, reddish-brown-spotted, deep yellow flowers, several to each stem. Has broadly oval, basal, mid-green leaves. **H** 6–8in (15–20cm), **S** 10–12in (25–30cm).

☼ ◊ Z8–9 H6–1

Aspidistra elatior 'Variegata'
Evergreen, rhizomatous perennial with upright, narrow, glossy, dark green leaves that are longitudinally cream-striped. Occasionally has inconspicuous, cream to purple flowers near soil level. **H** 24in (60cm), **S** 18in (45cm).

◑ ◊ Z7–11 H11–4

Inula ensifolia
Clump-forming perennial with small, lance-shaped to elliptic leaves, bearing many daisylike, yellow flower heads, singly on wiry stalks, in late summer. **H** and **S** 12in (30cm).

☼ ◊ Z4–9 H9–1

Gaillardia 'Oranges and Lemons'
Upright, rather open perennial that produces daisylike, yellow-tipped, peachy-orange flower heads throughout summer. Has lance-shaped, toothed, hairy, mid-green leaves. Plants may be short-lived. Is excellent in a border. **H** and **S** 24in (60cm).

☼ ◊ Z6–9 H8–1

Glechoma hederacea 'Variegata'
(Variegated ground ivy)
Evergreen, carpeting perennial that has small, heart-shaped leaves, with white marbling, on trailing stems. Bears insignificant flowers in summer. Spreads rapidly but is useful for a container. **H** 6in (15cm), **S** indefinite.

☼ ◊ Z6–9 H9–6

PERENNIALS

277

PINK

Begonia grandis subsp. *evansiana*
Tuberous begonia with oval, toothed, often red- or bronze-tinged, olive-green leaves, up to 6in (15cm) long, and pendant fragrant, single, pink flowers, to 1¼in (3cm) across in late summer and fall. **H** 24in (60cm), **S** 12in (30cm).

☼ ◊ Z6–9 H9–5

Astrantia maxima
Clump-forming perennial that bears rose-pink flower heads during summer-fall. **H** 24in (60cm), **S** 12in (30cm).

☼ ◊ Z5–8 H8–1

Begonia taliensis
Erect, tuberous perennial with pointed, oval, light green leaves marbled silver and purple-brown. Produces many small, single, shell-pink flowers in late fall. **H** 20in (50cm), **S** 14in (35cm).

☼ ◊ H11–1

Astrantia major 'Roma'
Clump-forming perennial bearing masses of sterile, pink flower heads, which gradually fade to green, borne on slender stems from summer until the first frosts. **H** and **S** 24in (60cm).

☼ ◊ Z4–7 H7–1

Diascia barberae 'Blackthorn Apricot'
Mat-forming perennial with narrowly heart-shaped, tapering leaves. From summer to fall, produces loose racemes of apricot-pink flowers with small, narrow "windows" and almost straight, downward-pointing spurs. **H** 10in (25cm), **S** to 20in (50cm).

☼ ◊ Z8–9 H9–8

Schizostylis coccinea 'Sunrise'
Clump-forming, rhizomatous perennial that in early fall produces spikes of large, shallowly cup-shaped, pink flowers above grassy, mid-green foliage. **H** 24in (60cm), **S** 9–12in (23–30cm).

☼ ◊ Z7–9 H9–7

Sedum spectabile 'Brilliant'
(Ice-plant)
Clump-forming perennial that from late summer to fall produces flat heads of bright rose-pink flowers. These are borne over a mass of fleshy, gray-green leaves and attract butterflies. **H** and **S** 12–18in (30–45cm).

☼ ◊ ❶ Z4–9 H9–1

Senecio pulcher
Perennial with leathery, hairy, dark green leaves. In summer–fall produces handsome, daisylike, yellow-centered, bright purplish-pink flower heads. **H** 18–24in (45–60cm), **S** 20in (50cm).

☼ ◊ ❶ Z11–15 H12–6

Tellima grandiflora Rubra Group
Semievergreen, clump-forming perennial with a mass of hairy, basal, reddish-purple leaves, underlaid dark green. In late spring, erect stems bear spikes of bell-shaped, pinkish-cream flowers. **H** and **S** 24in (60cm).

☼◑ ◊ Z4–8 H8–1

Schizostylis coccinea 'Major'
Rhizomatous perennial with long, narrow, grasslike leaves. Gladiolus-like spikes of cup-shaped, bright crimson flowers appear in fall. **H** 24in (60cm) or more, **S** 12in (30cm) or more.

☼ ◉ Z7–9 H9–7

Cautleya spicata
Upright perennial that in summer and early fall bears spikes of light orange or soft yellow flowers in maroon-red bracts. Has handsome, long, mid-green leaves. Needs a sheltered site and rich, deep soil. **H** 24in (60cm), **S** 20in (50cm).

☼ ◉ Z7–9 H9–7

SEDUM

With fleshy, drought-resistant foliage and heads of tiny, star-shaped flowers from summer to fall, *Sedum* are useful perennials for herbaceous borders and gravel gardens, while their nectar-rich blooms also make them a good choice for wildlife and naturalistic schemes. The flowers of the taller herbaceous plants are mostly in shades of pink and red, although white and yellow blooms are also available. Many have purple-tinged or variegated foliage, which extends their season of interest; the faded flowers and seed heads also provide a colorful display in late fall and winter. Plants thrive in full sun and free-draining soil, and will bulk up quickly. Divide them regularly to prevent clumps from flopping open, and stake taller varieties. Protect young growth from slugs in spring and early summer.

S. telephium 'Purple Emperor'

S. erythrostictum 'Mediovariegatum'

S. 'Ruby Glow'

S. 'Red Cauli'

S. spectabile 'Iceberg'

S. 'Matrona'

S. telephium 'Gooseberry Fool'

S. telephium 'Strawberries and Cream'

S. aizoon 'Aurantiacum' ①

PERENNIALS

PURPLE

Tulbaghia violacea

Vigorous, semievergreen, clump-forming perennial that in summer–fall carries umbels of lilac-purple or lilac-pink flowers above a mass of narrow, glaucous, blue-gray leaves. **H** 18–24in (45–60cm), **S** 12in (30cm).

☼ ◊ Z7–10 H10–7

Liriope muscari

Evergreen, spreading perennial that in fall carries spikes of thickly clustered, rounded-bell-shaped, lavender or purple-blue flowers among narrow, glossy, dark green leaves. **H** 12in (30cm), **S** 18in (45cm).

☼ ◊ Z6–10 H11–1

Bergenia purpurascens

Evergreen, clump-forming perennial with oval to spoon-shaped, flat, dark green leaves turning to beet-red in late fall. In spring bears racemes of open cup-shaped rich red flowers. **H** 16in (40cm), **S** 42in (60cm) or more.

☼ ◊ Z3–8 H8–1

Physostegia virginiana 'Vivid' (Obedient plant)

Erect, compact perennial that in late summer and early fall bears spikes of tubular, dark lilac-pink flowers that can be placed in position. Has toothed, mid-green leaves. **H** and **S** 12–24in (30–60cm).

☼ ◖ Z2–8 H8–1

Ophiopogon planiscapus 'Nigrescens'

Evergreen, spreading, clump-forming perennial, grown for its distinctive, grasslike, black leaves. Racemes of lilac flowers in summer are followed by black fruits. **H** 9in (23cm), **S** 12in (30cm).

☼ ◊ Z6–11 H11–1

Agastache 'Black Adder'

Upright perennial with whorled spires of smoky, purple-blue flowers from early summer to mid fall, above oval, pointed, toothed, aromatic, mid-green leaves. Is good for attracting insects. **H** 24in (60cm), **S** 18in (45cm).

☼ ◊ Z8–11 H12–5

Geranium 'Orion'

Deciduous, clump-forming perennial producing masses of large, shallowly cup-shaped, violet-blue flowers from early summer until mid fall. Has deeply lobed, mid-green basal leaves, each divided to the base into 7 sections. **H** and **S** 20in (50cm).

☼ ◊ Z5–8 H8–5

Heuchera 'Plum Pudding'

Evergreen, clump-forming perennial with rounded, deeply lobed, silvery-purple leaves. Long sprays of tiny, bell-shaped, pinkish flowers are borne in summer. Rejuvenate regularly to keep it healthy. A good foil for other plants. **H** 20in (50cm), **S** 12in (30cm).

☼ ◊ Z3–8 H8–1

WHITE

Helleborus niger 'Potter's Wheel'
Evergreen, clump-forming perennial
with divided, deep green leaves and
cup-shaped, nodding, pure white
flowers, with overlapping petals
and green "eyes," borne in winter
or early spring. **H** and **S** 12in (30cm).

☀ ◐ ① Z4–8 H9–1

Helleborus niger 'HGC Josef Lemper'
Evergreen, clump-forming, upright
perennial with divided, rich, dark
green leaves. Slightly fragrant, rounded,
pure white flowers, with overlapping
petals, are borne on sturdy stems from
mid-fall to late winter. **H** to 12in (30cm),
S 18in (45cm).

☀ ◐ ① Z4–8 H9–1

Helleborus x nigercors
Evergreen, clump-forming perennial
with matt green leaves, 14in (35cm) long
with 3–5 broad, evenly toothed segments.
From mid-winter to early spring bears
branched clusters of 10–20 saucer-
shaped, green-tinted, cream or white
flowers. **H** 16in (40cm), **S** 20in (50cm).

☀ ◐ ① Z4–9 H9–1

LENTEN ROSES

Helleborus x hybridus (lenten roses) are
the hybrids between *H. orientalis* and
other species. They flower in winter and
spring, and are so varied that they're
often sold by description or collection,
rather than as named varieties. Their
single or double flowers last for a few
months and open in a range of whites,
yellows, pinks, and purples, often
spotted or with darker edges. Most are
evergreen, with large, toothed, divided
leaves, and prefer moist, neutral to
alkaline soil, but need protection from
strong, winter winds. They will naturally
hybridize and self-seed, and it's worth
allowing your own seedlings to develop.

Harvington hybrids
[single, white] ①

[single, red] ①

[double, slate] ①

Bradfield hybrids
[double, apricot with spots] ①

[double, plum] ①

Ashwood Garden hybrids
[double, black] ①

[single, green] ①

[double, white with spots] ①

Harvington hybrids
[double, apricot] ①

[single, yellow] ①

281

HEUCHERA AND X HEUCHERELLA

Once regarded as a useful cottage-garden groundcovering perennial, grown for its sprays of red flowers and evergreen foliage, the selections of *Heuchera* bred in recent years have transformed this humble plant into a horticultural superstar. The leaves come in many colors, from near black and purple to pink, peach, and yellow-green, and plants are ideal for containers as well as borders. Selections of x *Heucherella*, a cross between *Heuchera* and *Tiarella*, are smaller and more dainty. Plant all types in moist but well-drained soil and partial shade, but site brighter-leaved cultivars in a sunnier position. Most plants should be split and replanted every few years to prevent the crown from becoming woody and to keep them in good health.

Heuchera 'Black Beauty'   *Heuchera* 'Ginger Ale'

Heuchera 'Midnight Rose'   *Heuchera* 'Chocolate Ruffles'   *Heuchera* CRÈME BRÛLÉE ('Tnheu041')

Heuchera sanguinea 'Snow Storm'    *Heuchera* 'Pewter Moon' 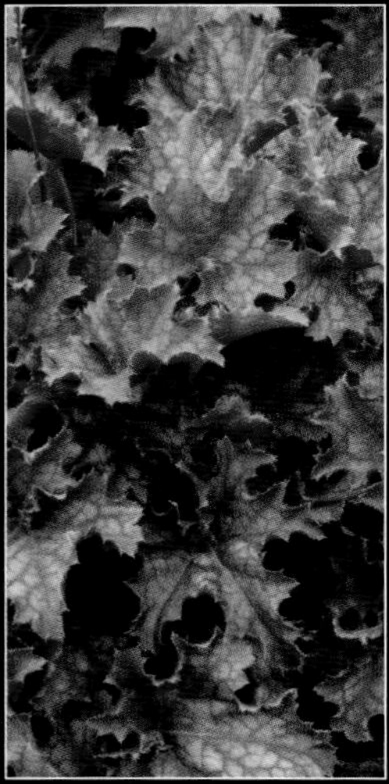   *Heuchera* 'Purple Petticoats'   *Heuchera* 'Southern Comfort'

Heuchera 'Silver Scrolls'   *Heuchera* 'Blackbird'   *Heuchera* 'Green Spice'

Heuchera 'Ebony and Ivory'   *Heuchera* 'Can-can'    *Heuchera* 'Beauty Colour'    x *Heucherella tiarelloides* 'Kimono'   *Heuchera* 'Tiramisu'   *Heuchera* 'Peach Flambé'

Heuchera 'Peppermint Spice'    *Heuchera* 'Lime Rickey'    x *Heucherella tiarelloides* 'Stoplight'

Heuchera 'Georgia Peach'

Heuchera 'Cinnabar Silver'    *Heuchera* 'Amber Waves'

Ophiopogon japonicus
Evergreen, clump or mat-forming perennial with grasslike, glossy, dark green foliage. Spikes of lilac flowers in late summer are followed by blue-black berries. **H** 12in (30cm) **S** indefinite.

☼ ◊ Z7–10 H11–1

Helleborus x sternii
'Boughton Beauty'
Evergreen, clump-forming perennial with purple-pink stems and divided, veined, mid-green leaves. Cup-shaped, pink-purple flowers, with green insides, are borne in terminal clusters in winter–early spring. **H** and **S** 20–24in (50–60cm).

☼ ◊ ! Z5–8 H8–5

Helleborus foetidus
(Stinking hellebore)
Evergreen, clump-forming perennial with deeply divided, dark green leaves and, in late winter and early spring, panicles of cup-shaped, red-margined, pale green flowers. **H** and **S** 18in (45cm).

☼ ◊ ! Z6–9 H9–6

Helleborus foetidus Wester Flisk Group
Evergreen, semiwoody perennial with small, cup-shaped, purple-rimmed pale green flowers, borne on floppy, red-green stems in winter and spring. Has red-stalked, dark gray-green leaves divided into slender, slightly toothed leaflets. **H** 24–36in (60–90cm), **S** 18in (45cm).

☼ ◊ ! Z6–9 H9–6

Dianella caerulea CASSA BLUE ('Dbb03')
Evergreen, tuft-forming perennial with narrowly lance-shaped, upright, dusky-blue leaves arising from a slowly creeping rootstock. Star-shaped, blue flowers in panicles in spring are followed by blue berries. **H** 20in (50cm), **S** 8in (20cm).

☼ ◊ Z9–10 H10–9

Helleborus odorus
Semievergreen, clump-forming perennial with deeply divided, deep green basal leaves, hairy beneath, with 5 central leaflets. From early winter–early spring bears clusters of 3–5 fragrant, saucer-shaped, bright green to yellow-green flowers. **H** and **S** to 12in (30cm).

☼ ◑ ! Z4–8 H8–1

Soleirolia soleirolii
(Baby's tears, Irish moss)
Usually evergreen, invasive, prostrate perennial with small, round, vivid green leaves that form a carpet. May choke other plants if not controlled. **H** 2in (5cm), **S** indefinite.

☼ ◊ Z10–15 H12–10

Helleborus cyclophyllus
Clump-forming perennial with palmate, deeply divided, bright green leaves. In early spring produces shallowly cup-shaped, yellow-green flowers with prominent, yellowish-white stamens. **H** 24in (60cm), **S** 18in (45cm).

☼ ◊ ! Z6–9 H9–6

PERENNIALS

Pleioblastus variegatus
(Dwarf white-stripe bamboo)
Evergreen, slow-spreading bamboo
with narrow, slightly downy, white-
striped leaves. Stems are branched near
the base. **H** 30in (80cm), **S** indefinite.

☼ ◊ Z6–11 H11–6

Sasa veitchii
Evergreen, slow-spreading bamboo.
Leaves, 10in (25cm) long, soon develop
white edges. Stems, often purple,
produce a single branch at each node.
White powder appears beneath nodes.
H to 5ft (1.5m), **S** indefinite.

☼ ◊ Z6–15 H12–1

Lagurus ovatus (Hare's-tail grass)
Tuft-forming, annual grass that in early
summer bears dense, egg-shaped,
soft panicles of white flower spikes,
with golden stamens, lasting well
into fall. Leaves are long, narrow and
flat. Self-seeds readily. **H** 18in (45cm),
S 6in (15cm).

284
☼ ◊ H11–1

**Cortaderia selloana
'Sunningdale Silver'**
Evergreen, clump-forming, perennial
grass with narrow, sharp-edged,
recurved leaves, 5ft (1.5m) long.
Bears long-lasting, feathery panicles
of creamy-white spikelets in late
summer. **H** 7ft (2.1m), **S** 4ft (1.2m).

☼ ◊ Z7–11 H11–7

Miscanthus sinensis 'Zebrinus'
Herbaceous, clump-forming, perennial
grass. Leaves, hairy beneath, have
transverse, yellowish-white ring
markings. May carry awned, hairy,
white spikelets in fan-shaped panicles
in fall. **H** 4ft (1.2m), **S** 18in (45cm).

☼ ◊ Z6–9 H9–1

Luzula nivea (Snowy woodrush)
Evergreen, slow-spreading, perennial
rush with fairly dense clusters of shining,
white flower spikes in early summer.
Leaves are edged with white hairs.
H 24in (60cm), **S** 18–24in (45–60cm).

◑ ◊ Z4–9 H9–1

Cortaderia richardii
Evergreen, clump-forming, perennial
grass with bladelike, sharply edged,
upright, olive-green leaves. In
summer has plumelike, 1-sided,
parchment-colored panicles on
tall stems. **H** 8ft (2.5m), **S** 3ft (1m).

☼ ◊ Z7–10 H10–7

Calamagrostis brachytricha
Herbaceous, clump-forming, perennial
grass with linear, arching, gray-green
leaves. In late summer has tall erect
stems bearing slender, gray-green
inflorescences in narrow panicles,
which last into winter, turning straw
colored. **H** 4½ft (1.4m), **S** 20in (50cm).

◑ ◐ Z4–9 H9–5

Miscanthus sinensis 'Yakushima Dwarf'
Compact, herbaceous, clump-forming, perennial grass with fine, arching, silvery-green leaves borne on short, upright stems. In late summer produces plumelike panicles of long-lasting, gray-white spikelets. **H** 3ft (1m), **S** 24in (60cm).

☀ ◊ Z6–9 H9–1

Cortaderia selloana 'Silver Comet'
Evergreen, clump-forming, perennial grass with very narrow, sharp-edged, recurved leaves, 3ft (1m) long, that have silver margins. Carries plumelike panicles of spikelets from late summer. **H** 4–5ft (1.2–1.5m), **S** 3ft (1m).

☀ ◊ Z7–11 H11–7

Miscanthus sinensis var. condensatus 'Cosmopolitan'
Herbaceous, clump-forming, perennial grass with white-striped leaves borne on upright, sturdy stems. Plumelike panicles of silvery-white spikelets appear from late summer. Dried stems remain attractive into winter. **H** 6ft (2m), **S** 32in (80cm).

☀ ◊ Z6–9 H9–1

Chionochloa rubra
Evergreen, tussock-forming, perennial grass with linear, arching, tightly inrolled, reddish-green leaves. In summer produces panicles of dainty, bronze-colored spikelets amid the leaves. Makes a superb potted specimen. **H** and **S** 28in (70cm).

☀ ◊ Z8–11 H12–7

Eragrostis curvula 'Totnes Burgundy'
Herbaceous, densely tufted, perennial grass with narrowly linear, arching, dark green leaves, which turn dark burgundy-red from the tips downward. Nodding panicles of brownish spikelets are borne in summer. **H** 36in (90cm), **S** 24in (60cm).

☀ ◊ Z9–11 H11–10

Imperata cylindrica 'Rubra'
Herbaceous, clump-forming, perennial grass. Linear, upright, bright green leaves turn bright red in late summer and fall, dying down in winter. Narrow, spikelike panicles of silvery-white spikelets are borne occasionally, in late summer. **H** and **S** 20in (50cm) or more.

☀ ◊ Z5–9 H9–3

Elegia capensis
Evergreen, clump-forming perennial with tall, horsetail-like, arching stems bearing whorls of soft, slender, dark green, needle-shaped, leaflike shoots. Stout, reddish-green shoots, with papery sheaths at each node, are produced from the base in spring. **H** 5ft (1.5m), **S** 3ft (1m).

☀ ◊ Z8–11 H11–7

Molinia caerulea subsp. caerulea 'Heidebraut'
Herbaceous, clump-forming, erect, perennial grass with linear, mid-green leaves that turn golden-yellow in fall. Has masses of tall, arching stems bearing purplish spikelets in late summer. **H** 5ft (1.5m), **S** 24in (60cm).

☀ ◊ pH Z5–9 H9–1

PERENNIALS

RED

Miscanthus sinensis 'Flamingo'
Herbaceous, clump-forming, perennial grass with narrow, arching, mid-green leaves borne on sturdy stems. In late summer has plumelike panicles of feathery, pinkish-red spikelets. These remain in good shape well into winter.
H 5ft (1.5m), **S** 24in (60cm).

☼ ◊ Z6–9 H9–1

Miscanthus sinensis 'Gracillimus'
Herbaceous, clump-forming, perennial grass with very narrow leaves, hairy beneath, often turning bronze. May bear fan-shaped panicles of awned, hairy, white spikelets in early fall.
H 4ft (1.2m), **S** 1½ft (45cm).

286 ☼ ◊ Z6–9 H9–1

PURPLE

Melica altissima 'Atropurpurea'
Evergreen, tuft-forming, perennial grass with broad leaves, short-haired beneath. Purple spikelets in narrow panicles, 4in (10cm) long, hang from the tops of stems during summer.
H and **S** 24in (60cm).

☼ ◊ Z5–8 H8–5

Phyllostachys nigra (Black bamboo)
Evergreen, clump-forming bamboo with grooved, greenish-brown stems that turn black in second season. Almost unmarked culm sheaths bear bristled auricles and mid-green leaves. Flowers are unimportant as they are so rarely produced. **H** 20–25ft (6–8m), **S** indefinite.

☼◐ ◊ Z7–11 H11–4

GREEN

Molinia caerulea subsp. **arundinacea 'Transparent'**
Herbaceous, clump-forming, erect, perennial grass with linear, mid-green leaves that turn straw-yellow in fall. Tall, supple stems bear open panicles of purplish-green spikelets in summer.
H 6ft (2m), **S** 24in (60cm).

☼ ◊ pH Z5–9 H9–1

Pennisetum villosum (Feather-top)
Herbaceous, tuft-forming, perennial grass with long-haired stems. In fall has panicles of creamy-pink spikelets, fading to pale brown, with very long, bearded bristles. **H** to 3ft (1m), **S** 20in (50cm).

☼ ◊ Z9–11 H11–1

Stipa calamagrostis
Herbaceous or semievergreen, perennial grass forming tufts of linear, inrolled, bluish-green leaves, turning yellowish in fall. In summer has feathery, arching panicles of silvery-white spikelets, which age to reddish brown. **H** and **S** 32in (80cm).

☼ ◊ Z7–10 H10–1

Hordeum jubatum
(Foxtail barley, Squirrel tail grass)
Tufted, short-lived perennial or annual grass. In summer to early fall has flat, arching, feathery, plume-like flower spikes with silky awns.
H 12–24in (30–60cm), **S** 12in (30cm).

☼ ◊ Z4–8 H8–1

Thamnocalamus crassinodus 'Kew Beauty'
Evergreen or semievergreen, clump-forming bamboo with small, lance-shaped, grayish-green leaves borne on arching, blue-gray stems that age gradually to reddish-brown. Needs a sheltered position. **H** 10ft (3m), **S** 5ft (1.5m).

☼◐ ◊ Z9–11 H12–8

Juncus effusus f. **spiralis**
(Corkscrew rush)
Evergreen, tuft-forming, perennial rush with leafless stems that twist and curl and are often prostrate. Fairly dense, greenish-brown flower panicles form in summer. **H** 3ft (1m), **S** 2ft (60cm).

☼ ◊ Z6–9 H9–6

Stipa gigantea (Golden oats)
Evergreen, tuft-forming, perennial grass with narrow leaves, 18in (45cm) or more long. In summer carries elegant, open panicles of silvery spikelets, with long awns and dangling, golden anthers, which persist well into winter. **H** 8ft (2.5m), **S** 3ft (1m).

☼ ◊ Z8–15 H12–1

Phyllostachys bambusoides
(Timber bamboo)
Evergreen, clump-forming bamboo with sturdy, erect, green stems. Bears leaf sheaths with prominent bristles, and large, broad leaves. **H** 20–25ft (6–8m), **S** indefinite.

☼ ◊ Z7–10 H10–7

Semiarundinaria fastuosa
(Narihira bamboo)
Evergreen, clump-forming bamboo with 6in (15cm) long leaves and short, tufted branches at each node. Culm sheaths open to reveal polished, purplish interiors. **H** 20ft (6m), **S** indefinite.

☼ ◊ Z6–9 H9–6

Pseudosasa japonica
(Arrow bamboo, Metake)
Evergreen, clump-forming bamboo that may run. Has long-persistent, roughly pubescent, brown sheaths and broad leaves, 14in (35cm) long. **H** 15ft (5m), **S** indefinite.

☼ ◊ Z7–10 H10–6

Ampelodesmos mauritanica
Dense, evergreen, clump-forming, perennial grass with linear, gray-green leaves, to 3ft (1m) long, with dark green undersides. In summer, long-lasting one-sided panicles of purplish-green flowers are borne on upright, lofty stems. **H** 8ft (2.5m), **S** 3ft (1m).

☼ ◊ Z8–10 H10–7

Phyllostachys nigra f. henonis
Evergreen, clump-forming bamboo with bristled auricles on culm sheaths and a profusion of leaves. **H** 30ft (10m), **S** 6–10ft (2–3m).

Phyllostachys viridiglaucescens
Evergreen, clump-forming bamboo with greenish-brown stems that arch at the base. Has white powder beneath nodes. **H** 20–25ft (6–8m), **S** indefinite.

Shibataea kumasasa
Evergreen, clump-forming bamboo with stubby, side branches on greenish-brown stems. Leaves are broad, 2–4in (5–10cm) long. **H** 3–5ft (1–1.5m), **S** 12in (30cm).

Chimonobambusa timidissinoda
Vigorous, evergreen, rhizomatous bamboo with curiously prominent, green stems, flared at each node. Lance-shaped, dark green leaves have a feathery look. May need restraining. **H** and **S** 16ft (5m) or more.

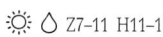
☼ ◊ Z7–11 H11–4

☼ ◊ Z7–11 H11–1

☼ ◊ Z6–15 H12–1

☼ ◊ Z9–11 H12–8

PERENNIALS

GREEN

Chasmanthium latifolium
Herbaceous, clump-forming, perennial
grass with broadly lance-shaped, short-
stemmed, light green leaves that turn
pale beige in winter. In summer has
open panicles of oatlike, arching, green
spikelets aging to beige. **H** 3ft (1m),
S 24in (60cm).

☼ ◊ Z5–9 H9–5

Helictotrichon sempervirens
(Blue oat grass)
Evergreen, tufted, perennial grass with
stiff, silvery-blue leaves up to 12in (30cm)
or more long. Produces erect panicles
of straw-colored flower spikes in
summer. **H** 3ft (1m), **S** 2ft (60cm).

☼ ◊ Z4–9 H9–1

***Yushania anceps* 'Pitt White'**
Very vigorous, evergreen, rhizomatous,
clump-forming bamboo with upright,
shiny, dark green stems that arch
with age. Produces almost weeping
branches of narrowly lance-shaped,
fresh green leaves, with purple-tinted
stalks. **H** 30ft (10m), **S** indefinite.

☼ ◊ Z8–13 H12–8

Chusquea culeou (Chilean bamboo)
Slow-growing, evergreen, clump-
forming bamboo. Bears long-lasting
culm sheaths, shining white when
young, at the swollen nodes of sturdy,
solid stems. **H** to 15ft (5m), **S** 8ft (2.5m)
or more.

☼ ◊ Z8–11 H8–10

***Luzula sylvatica* 'Hohe Tatra'**
Evergreen, mound-forming, perennial
sedge with broadly linear, bright
golden-yellow leaves turning yellowish-
green in summer. Short stems bear
open panicles of brown flowers in
summer. **H** 16in (40cm), **S** 12in (30cm).

● ◊ Z4–9 H9–4

YELLOW

Phyllostachys aurea
(Golden bamboo)
Vigorous, evergreen, clump-forming
bamboo with upright, grooved,
yellow-green stems and cup-shaped
swellings beneath each node. Has
narrowly lance-shaped, pointed, green
leaves. **H** 20ft (6m), **S** 13ft (4m) or more.

☼ ◊ Z7–11 H11–7

***Carex oshimensis* 'Evergold'**
Evergreen, tuft-forming, perennial
sedge with narrow, yellow-striped
leaves, 8in (20cm) long. Solid, triangular
stems may carry insignificant flower
spikes in summer. **H** 8in (20cm),
S 6–8in (15–20cm).

☼ ◊ Z6–9 H9–6

Stipa tenuissima
Deciduous, tuft-forming, perennial grass
with narrowly linear, upright, tightly
inrolled, bright green leaves. From
early summer has plumelike panicles
of silvery-green spikelets, turning to
pale beige as seeds form. **H** 24in (60cm),
S 16in (40cm).

☼ ◊ Z7–11 H12–7

Deschampsia cespitosa 'Goldtau'
Evergreen, tuft-forming, perennial grass with cloudlike panicles of tiny, golden-yellow spikelets in summer. Both spikelets and the linear, sharp-edged, dark green leaves turn golden in fall. **H** 28in (70cm), **S** 20in (50cm).

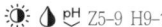 ☀ ◐ ᵖᴴ Z5–9 H9–1

Alopecurus pratensis 'Aureovariegatus' (Golden foxtail)
Herbaceous, tuft-forming, perennial grass with yellow or yellowish-green-streaked leaves and dense flower spikes in summer. **H** and **S** 9–12in (23–30cm).

 ☀ ◌ Z5–8 H8–5

Spartina pectinata 'Aureomarginata'
Herbaceous, spreading, rhizomatous grass with long, arching, yellow-striped leaves, which turn orange-brown in late fall to winter. **H** to 6ft (2m), **S** indefinite.

☀ ◌ Z8–11 H12–8

Panicum virgatum 'Northwind'
Herbaceous, clump-forming, erect, perennial grass with broad, dark bluish-green leaves turning golden-yellow in fall, when tall, narrow panicles of pinkish-green spikelets are borne and age to silvery-green. **H** 5ft (1.5m), **S** 36in (90cm).

 ☀ ◌ Z5–9 H9–1

Pleioblastus viridistriatus
Evergreen, slow-spreading bamboo with purple stems and broad, softly downy, bright yellow leaves with green stripes. **H** 5ft (1.5m), **S** indefinite.

☀ ◌ Z7–11 H11–1

Stipa lessoniana (Pheasant's-tail grass)
Evergreen/semievergreen, tuft-forming, perennial grass with linear, olive-green leaves tinted reddish-orange. In summer, arching, open panicles of tiny, purplish-green spikelets shimmer amid the leaves. Has good winter form and color. **H** 20in (50cm), **S** 32in (80cm).

☀ ◌ Z9–11 H12–7

Phyllostachys vivax f. aureocaulis
Evergreen, clump-forming, slow-growing bamboo with bright lemon-yellow stems. Narrowly lance-shaped, dark evergreen leaves make the perfect foil for the stems. **H** 20ft (6m), **S** 10ft (3m) or more.

☀ ◌ Z7–10 H10–7

Hakonechloa macra 'Aureola'
Slow-growing, herbaceous, shortly rhizomatous grass with purple stems and green-striped, yellow leaves that age to reddish-brown. Open panicles of reddish-brown flower spikes appear in early fall and last into winter. **H** 16in (40cm), **S** 18–24in (45–60cm).

☀ ◌ Z5–9 H9–5

Carex flagellifera
Evergreen, tuft-forming, perennial sedge with grasslike, reddish-brown leaves, upright, then arching, to the ground. Triangular stems bear insignificant, brown flower spikes in summer. Is good for winter color. **H** 32in (80cm), **S** 24in (60cm) or more.

☀ ◌ Z7–9 H9–7

PERENNIALS

Athyrium niponicum var. pictum 'Burgundy Lace'
Deciduous fern with a slow-creeping, reddish-brown rhizome and broadly triangular, divided, spreading fronds of metallic purplish-bronze with silvery-gray tips and bright pink-purple veins. **H** 20in (50cm), **S** 16in (40cm).

☼ ◊ Z5–8 H8–1

Athyrium 'Ghost'
Deciduous fern producing lance-shaped, rather upright, silvery-white fronds, with contrasting, purplish-green veins, in spring. Coloration is most pronounced in spring. **H** 24in (60cm), **S** 8in (20cm) or more.

☼ ◊ Z5–8 H8–1

Polystichum setiferum 'Pulcherrimum Bevis'
Evergreen or semievergreen fern with broadly lance-shaped, daintily cut, sharp-edged fronds that are yellowish-green in spring and mature to a glossy, rich dark green. **H** 24in (60cm), **S** 30in (75cm).

☼ ◊ Z6–9 H9–6

Blechnum penna-marina
Fast-growing, evergreen, carpeting fern. Has narrow, ladder-like, dark green fronds, red-tinged when young. Outer, sterile fronds are spreading; inner, fertile ones erect. **H** 6–12in (15–30cm), **S** 12–18in (30–45cm).

☼ ◊ pH Z10–11 H11–10

Dicksonia antarctica
(Australian tree fern)
Evergreen, treelike fern. Sturdy trunks are covered with brown fibers and crowned by spreading, somewhat arching, broadly lance-shaped, much-divided, palmlike fronds.
H 30ft (10m) or more, **S** 12ft (4m).

☼ ◊ H11–10

Asplenium trichomanes
(Maiden-hair spleenwort)
Semievergreen fern that has long,
slender, tapering fronds with glossy,
black, later brown, midribs bearing
many rounded-oblong, bright green
pinnae. Is suitable for limestone soils.
H 6in (15cm), **S** 6–12in (15–30cm).

☀ ◐ Z5–8 H8–3

Thelypteris palustris
(Marsh buckler fern, Marsh fern)
Deciduous fern. Has strong, erect,
lance-shaped, pale green fronds, with
widely separated, deeply cut pinnae,
produced from wiry, creeping, blackish
rhizomes. Grows well beside a pool or
stream. **H** 30in (75cm), **S** 12in (30cm).

☀ ◐ Z5–8 H8–5

Cyrtomium falcatum
(Japanese holly fern)
Evergreen fern. Fronds are lance-
shaped and have holly-like, glossy,
dark green pinnae; young fronds
are often covered with whitish or
brown scales. **H** 12–24in (30–60cm),
S 12–18in (30–45cm).

☀ ◐ Z6–11 H11–10

Polystichum setiferum
Divisilobum Group
Evergreen or semievergreen fern.
Broadly lance-shaped or oval, soft-
textured, much-divided, spreading
fronds are clothed with white scales as
they unfurl. **H** 24in (60cm), **S** 18in (45cm).

☀ ◐ Z6–9 H9–6

Adiantum aleuticum
Semievergreen fern with a short
rootstock. Has glossy, dark brown
or blackish stems and dainty, divided,
finger-like fronds, with blue-green
pinnae, that are more crowded than
those of *A. pedatum*. Grows well in
alkaline soils. **H** and **S** to 18in (45cm).

☀ ◐ Z3–8 H8–1

Polypodium interjectum
'Cornubiense'
Evergreen fern with narrow, lance-
shaped, divided, fresh green fronds;
segments are further subdivided
to give an overall lacy effect.
H and **S** 10–12in (25–30cm).

☀ ◐ Z5–9 H8–1

Adiantum pedatum
(Northern maidenhair fern)
Semievergreen fern with a sturdy,
creeping rootstock. Dainty, divided,
finger-like, mid-green fronds are
produced on glossy, dark brown or
blackish stems. **H** and **S** to 18in (45cm).

☀ ◐ pH Z3–8 H8–1

Polystichum setiferum
Plumosodivisilobum Group
Evergreen fern that produces a
"shuttlecock" of lance-shaped, divided
fronds with segments narrowed
toward the frond tips; lower pinnae
often overlap. **H** 4ft (1.2m), **S** 3ft (1m).

☀ ◐ Z6–9 H9–6

Polypodium vulgare
(Common polypody, Polypody)
Evergreen fern with narrow, lance-
shaped, divided, herringbone-like,
mid-green fronds, arising from
creeping rhizomes covered with
copper-brown scales. Suits a rock
garden. **H** and **S** 10–12in (25–30cm).

☀ ◐ Z6–8 H8–6

GREEN

Asplenium scolopendrium
(Hart's-tongue fern)
Evergreen fern with stocky rhizomes
and tongue-shaped, leathery, bright
green fronds. Is good in alkaline soils.
H 18–30in (45–75cm), **S** to 18in (45cm).

☀ ◊ Z6–8 H8–6

Asplenium scolopendrium
Marginatum Group
Evergreen fern with stocky, upright
rhizomes and lobed, slightly frilled,
tongue-shaped fronds that are leathery
and bright green. Is good in alkaline
soils. **H** and **S** 12in (30cm) or more.

☀ ◊ Z6–8 H8–6

Adiantum venustum
Deciduous fern. Bears delicate, pale
green fronds, tinged brown when
young, consisting of many small,
triangular pinnae, on glossy stems.
H 9in (23cm), **S** 12in (30cm).

☀ ◊ pH Z5–8 H8–5

Blechnum chilense
Splendid evergreen fern with
broadly lance-shaped, leathery,
dark green fronds on upright, scaly
brownish stems arise from a creeping
rootstock. Eventually forms a large
colony. **H** and **S** 3ft (1m).

☀ ◊ pH Z10–11 H11–10

Polystichum tsussimense
Evergreen fern bearing broadly lance-
shaped, rather leathery, dark green
fronds with narrowly oblong, spiny-
toothed, pointed pinnae. Is suitable
for a shaded rock garden or alpine
house. **H** 10in (25cm), **S** 8in (20cm).

☀ ◊ Z6–9 H9–5

Dryopteris wallichiana
(Wallich's wood fern)
Deciduous, clump-forming or often
solitary fern with an erect rhizome and
a "shuttlecock" of lance-shaped, divided,
bright yellow-green fronds, aging to
dark green with scaly, brownish-black
stems. **H** 3ft (90cm), **S** 12in (30cm).

☀ ◊ Z5–7 H11–10

Dryopteris erythrosora
(Japanese shield fern)
Usually evergreen, clump-forming fern
with broadly triangular, arching, shiny,
coppery-red flushed, pinkish-green
ageing to bronze then bright green.
H 16in (40cm), **S** 12in (30cm).

☀ ◊ Z5–9 H9–5

Asplenium ceterach (Rusty-back fern)
Semievergreen fern with lance-shaped,
leathery, dark green fronds divided into
alternate, bluntly rounded lobes. Backs
of young fronds are covered with silvery
scales that mature to reddish-brown.
H and **S** 6in (15cm).

☀ ◊ Z6–9 H9–7

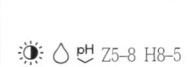

Cryptogramma crispa (Parsley fern)
Deciduous fern with broadly oval to
triangular, finely divided, bright pale
green fronds that resemble parsley. In
fall, fronds turn bright rusty-brown and
persist during winter. **H** 6–9in (15–23cm),
S 6–12in (15–30cm).

☀ ◊ pH Z5–8 H8–5

Dryopteris filix-mas (Male fern)
Deciduous or semievergreen fern
with "shuttlecocks" of elegantly arching,
upright, broadly lance-shaped, mid-
green fronds that arise from crowns
of large, upright, brown-scaled
rhizomes. **H** 4ft (1.2m), **S** 3ft (1m).

☀ ◊ Z4–8 H8–1

Polystichum munitum
(Giant holly fern)
Evergreen fern with erect, leathery,
lance-shaped, dark green fronds that
consist of small, spiny-margined
pinnae. **H** 4ft (1.2m), **S** 12in (30cm).

☀ ◊ Z3–8 H8–1

Polypodium cambricum
'Richard Kayse'
Evergreen fern with a slow-creeping
rhizome and lance-shaped to triangular-
oval, lacy, flat, bright green fronds. New
fronds appear in late summer and die
back in late spring. Sori are yellow in
winter. **H** 12in (30cm), **S** 8in (20cm).

☀ ◊ Z6–8 H8–6

ANNUALS, BIENNIALS, AND BEDDING

Invaluable for their rapid growth, instant color, and relatively
low cost, annuals and biennials are ideal gap fillers between
newly planted trees and shrubs, as well as in perennial displays
that might need reviving after the first flush of spring. They are
also useful as bedding in formal designs, such as parterres,
and in containers of all types. An important ingredient
in cottage gardens and wildflower meadows, they also
help to shape informal schemes.

ANNUALS, BIENNIALS, AND BEDDING

Indispensable in pots, containers, and borders, many of these colorful plants flower from early summer to early fall, and some also provide beautiful foliage. Combine them with plants that bloom in winter and spring to brighten up your garden all year.

What are annuals and biennials?

Annuals are plants that grow, bloom, set seed, and die in a single growing season. Biennials complete their life cycle in two seasons: most are sown in late spring or summer and produce leafy growth in the first year, then flower, set seed, and die in the next. Bedding plants usually refer to half-hardy or tender annuals that are traditionally used in summer flower schemes. Some plants in this category are technically perennials or even shrubs, but are referred to as annuals because they are used for just one season. Examples include pelargoniums, nemesias, and brachyscome, which are perennials, and marguerites (*Argyranthemum* species) and fuchsias, which are tender shrubs. Plants in this group are also sometimes described as "summer seasonals" and "spring seasonals."

BELOW Summer harmonies
Combine the shapes and colors of annuals for a balanced display. Begonias, heliotropes, silver-leaved senecio, and zinnias create a vibrant mix.

Growing annuals and biennials

Plants in this category can be grown from seed, bought as young seedlings known as "plug" plants, or purchased as mature specimens ready to plant.

Sowing seed is the most cost-effective option if you have a large space or lots of containers to fill; there are many half-hardy or frost-tender types that are very easy to grow in pots or trays on a windowsill or in a greenhouse, including petunias, French marigolds (*Tagetes*), and tobacco plants (*Nicotiana*). The seedlings should be hardened off for a few weeks in spring by placing them outside during the day and bringing them back under cover at night. Then plant them outside in late spring when all danger of frost has passed.

Hardy annuals are easier still, as they can be sown outside in spring where they are to flower. For earlier summer blooms, plants like love-in-a-mist (*Nigella*) and poppies (*Papaver rhoeas*) can be sown in early fall in free-draining soil. Sow your

ABOVE Shades of pink
Create an elegant basket using shades of pink. Dark cherry pink petunias, pale busy Lizzies, starry isotomas, and raspberry-colored diascias combine beautifully.

seeds in straight lines or curves, so that you can distinguish them from weed seedlings when they germinate.

For winter and spring color, most suitable plants, such as violas, are raised from seed sown in summer. Alternatively, buy young plants in the fall.

Biennials can be grown from seed or bought as plug plants in the summer before they bloom. Find a quiet corner of the garden to sow your seeds, as they will be there for many months, and may be swamped by other plants if sown directly into a summer bed or border.

Ornamental features

Annuals and biennials are available in a wide range of shapes and sizes, from low hummock-forming cultivars of *Ageratum houstonianum* and trailing petunias to the tall spires of foxgloves (*Digitalis purpurea*) and dramatic Scotch thistles (*Onopordum acanthium*) that shoot up to 6ft (1.8m).

Flowers offer a vast choice of colors and forms, including scented types such as heliotropes (*Heliotropium arborescens*), tobacco plants (*Nicotiana* species), and the chocolate-scented *Cosmos atrosanguineus*. Colors extend from the opalescent whites of *Lavatera trimestris* 'Mont Blanc' to the vibrant scarlets of pelargoniums, bright orange and yellow California poppies (*Eschscholzia californica*), and intense magentas and purples of petunias. For more subtle pastel schemes, opt for plants such as *Anoda cristata,* blue *Silene*

coeli-rosa, baby blue eyes (*Nemophila menziesii*), and pale green blooms of *Nicotiana langsdorffii*.

To provide a foil for the flowers, consider the wealth of foliage plants available. These include the vast variety of coleus (*Solenostemon*) with their multicolored leaves, the bright silver foliage of *Senecio cineraria*, and the dark purple-lobed leaves of *Ipomoea batatus* 'Blackie'.

Design options

Annuals and biennials provide an extended season of color in formal schemes, and are particularly useful for filling beds and gaps in borders. In addition, they can be used to edge flower beds and borders or to create Victorian-style bedding schemes, which are enjoying renewed popularity.

Hardy annuals like poppies, cornflowers (*Centaurea*), and California bluebell (*Phacelia campanularia*) are ideal for naturalistic or wildlife schemes. For mixed schemes, grow them in pots like half-hardy annuals or buy plug plants and set them between more permanent perennials and shrubs (many annual seeds will not germinate in these situations due to competition from neighboring plants).

Annuals and bedding plants make striking features in seasonal containers, windowboxes, and hanging baskets. Use feature plants, such as fuchsias, zinnias, and begonias in the center, together with trailers like *Helichrysum petiolatum* or trailing petunias to soften the edges of your pots. In fall and winter displays,

POTTING PLUG PLANTS

If you lack the space or time to sow seed, look for seedlings grown in cell packs, known as "plugs." Many popular plants, including busy Lizzies, begonias, lobelias, and fuchsias, are available in this form, with the largest choice available from mail-order specialists. Pot up small plugs and grow them on indoors until after the last frost.

 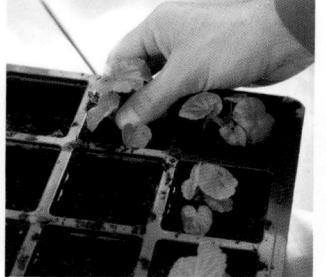 

1 Remove plugs
Water the plugs as soon as they arrive. Fill large cell trays or 3in (8cm) pots with good-quality potting mix designed for seedlings. Use the blunt end of a pencil to gently push them out of their original containers from the bottom.

2 Plant up modules
Make a hole in the potting mix with your finger or the pencil and insert a plug into each module or pot. Firm the soil around the plants with your fingers, ensuring that there are no air gaps and taking care not to compact the soil or damage the roots.

3 Water the plants
Using a watering can with a fine spray, water the plugs well. Set them in a cool, light, frost-free place and keep them well watered. Harden the young plants off before planting them outside after the risk of frost has passed.

combine dwarf conifers, such as *Juniperus communis* 'Compressa', with dainty violas.

Year-round color

The long flowering season of annuals and biennials provides months of color. Violas flower in winter but put on their best show in spring, when they are joined by forget-me-nots (*Myosotis*) and wallflowers (*Erysimum cheiri*), which look particularly

beautiful when combined with bulbs such as daffodils and tulips. Follow these with any of the summer annuals and biennials, such as foxgloves (*Digitalis*). Busy Lizzies (*Impatiens*) are particularly useful for shady sites. Fall stars include Chinese asters (*Callistephus chinensis*), and in warm climes, the fruits of *Solanum pseudocapsicum* will brighten a winter day. In cold areas, bring these bushy evergreens indoors.

SOWING SEED IN TRAYS

Growing summer bedding plants from seed can be very cost-effective, especially if you have several containers or beds to fill. Sowing seed in trays indoors is the ideal option for half-hardy or frost-tender plants, allowing you to start them off early in spring so that plants are mature and ready to flower when planted outside. Small seeds, such as petunias, are difficult to space evenly in trays; seedlings will need to be transplanted when they have a few leaves to larger trays, pots, or modules. Seed catalogs offer a huge variety of plants via mail order or online.

Pot of seed-sown annuals

1 Fill seed trays
Using good-quality seed-starting mix, fill some clean seed trays to within 1in (2cm) of the top. Gently press another seed tray on top to level out and firm the surface. Water the tray with a watering can with a fine spray and allow to drain.

2 Sow seeds
Pour some seeds into your hand and carefully space them out on the soil surface. Sprinkle sifted seed-starting mix over the seeds, and cover to the depth specified on the seed packet. Also check the seeds' required germination temperature.

3 Cover and keep moist
Label the seed tray, and cover with a lid or a clear plastic bag. Place in a light spot. Keep the soil moist, and remove the lid or plastic bag as soon as the seedlings emerge. Harden them off before planting them outside.

ANNUALS, BIENNIALS, AND BEDDING

Argyranthemum frutescens (Marguerite)
Evergreen, woody-based, bushy perennial that bears many daisylike, white, yellow or pink flower heads throughout summer. Attractive leaves are fresh green. **H** and **S** 28in (70cm).

☼ ◊ Z10–11 H11–1

Plectranthus forsteri 'Marginatus'
Evergreen, bushy perennial. Oval leaves, to 2½in (6cm) long, are grayish-green with scalloped, white margins. Irregularly has tubular, white to pale mauve flowers. **H** 10in (25cm), **S** to 3ft (1m). Min. 50°F (10°C).

☼ ◊ H11–1

Osteospermum 'Whirlygig'
Evergreen, clump-forming, semiwoody perennial of lax habit that bears bluish-white flower heads singly, but in great profusion, during summer. Leaves are gray-green. **H** and **S** 24in (60cm).

☼ ◊ Z10–11 H6–1

Catharanthus roseus
(Rose periwinkle)
Evergreen, spreading shrub, becoming untidy with age. Has white to rose-pink flowers in spring to fall, also in winter in warm areas. **H** and **S** 12–24in (30–60cm). Min. 41–5°F (5–7°C).

☼ ◊ H11–1

Sutera cordata Snowstorm Series
GIANT SNOWFLAKE ('Danova906')
Spreading or trailing annual with small, rounded, mid-green leaves and 5-lobed, bright white flowers throughout summer. Is excellent in a hanging basket or trailing from a tub. **H** 4–8in (10–20cm), **S** 8–12in (20–30cm).

☼ ◊ Z11–11 H12–1

Dahlia 'Gallery Art Fair'
Well-branched, small-flowered decorative dahlia, grown as an annual. Produces a prolific display of white flowers, 4in (10cm) across, with greenish-yellow centers, in summer–fall. Is ideal in a container. **H** 12–14in (30–35cm), **S** 10–12in (25–30cm).

☼ ◊ Z9–11 H11–1

Euphorbia hypericifolia
DIAMOND FROST ('Inneuphe')
Bushy perennial, grown as a summer annual, with slender, repeatedly branched stems bearing elliptical, grayish-green leaves. Small, white florets are produced in cloudlike flower heads in summer–fall. **H** 7in (18cm), **S** 16in (40cm).

☼ ◊ ❶ Z10–11 H11–1

Lobularia maritima 'Snow Crystals'
Ground-hugging, mound-forming annual with narrow, mid-green leaves and heads of unusually large, fragrant, 4-petaled, white flowers in summer–fall. Neater than older types. **H** 6–10in (15–25cm), **S** 12–14in (30–35cm).

☼ ◊ Z10–11 H11–1

Zinnia x marylandica Zahara Series
'Zahara Starlight Rose'
Mound-forming, disease-resistant annual with ovate, mid-green leaves and, in summer–fall, bears bright, double, daisylike, red-and-white, bicolored flower heads. Is drought-tolerant. **H** and **S** 12–18in (30–45cm).

☼ ◊ H12–1

Digitalis purpurea f. albiflora
Slow-growing, short-lived perennial, grown as a biennial. Has a rosette of large, pointed-oval leaves and erect stems carrying tubular, white flowers in summer. **H** 3–5ft (1–1.5m), **S** 12–18in (30–45cm).

☀◐ ◊ ❗ Z4–8 H9–1

Euphorbia marginata (Snow-in-summer, Snow-on-the-mountain)
Moderately fast-growing, upright, bushy annual. Has pointed-oval, bright green leaves; upper leaves are white-margined. Broad, petal-like, white bracts surround tiny flowers in summer. **H** 24in (60cm), **S** 12in (30cm).

☀ ◊ ❗ H11–1

Eustoma grandiflorum
Slow-growing, upright annual with lance-shaped, deep green leaves. Poppy-like, pink, purple, blue or white flowers, 2in (5cm) wide, are carried in summer. **H** 24in (60cm), **S** 12in (30cm). Min. 39–45°F (4–7°C).

☀ ◊ Z8–11 H11–1

Iberis amara
Fast-growing, erect, bushy annual with lance-shaped, mid-green leaves. Has flattish heads of small, scented, 4-petaled, white flowers in summer. **H** 12in (30cm), **S** 6in (15cm).

☀ ◊ Z11 H11–1

Lavatera trimestris 'Mont Blanc'
Moderately fast-growing, erect, branching annual with oval, lobed leaves. Shallowly trumpet-shaped, brilliant white flowers appear from summer to early fall. **H** to 24in (60cm), **S** 18in (45cm).

☀ ◊

Nicotiana x sanderae 'Saratoga Series' [white]
Slow-growing, bushy annual with ovate, mid-green leaves. In summer and early fall produces a long display of sparkling, white, long-tubed, salverform flowers. **H** and **S** 12in (30cm).

☀ ◊ ❗ Z10–11 H11–1

Dimorphotheca pluvialis (Rain daisy)
Branching annual with oval, hairy, deep green leaves. In summer has small, daisylike flower heads, the rays purple beneath and white above, with brownish-purple centers. **H** 8–12in (20–30cm), **S** 6in (15cm).

☀ ◊ Z9–11 H11–6

Gypsophila elegans
Fast-growing, erect, bushy annual. Has lance-shaped, grayish-green leaves and clouds of tiny, white flowers in branching heads from summer to early fall. **H** 24in (60cm), **S** 12in (30cm) or more.

☀ ◊ Z5–9 H9–1

Nemophila maculata (Five-spot)
Fast-growing, spreading annual with lobed leaves. Small, bowl-shaped, white flowers with purple-tipped petals are carried in summer. **H** and **S** 6in (15cm).

☀ ◊ Z9–10 H7–1

Omphalodes linifolia (Venus's navelwort)
Fairly fast-growing, slender, erect annual with lance-shaped, gray-green leaves. Tiny, slightly scented, rounded, white flowers, rarely tinged blue, are carried in summer. **H** 6–12in (15–30cm), **S** 6in (15cm).

☀ ◊

ANNUALS, BIENNIALS, AND BEDDING

Reseda odorata (Mignonette)
Moderately fast-growing, erect, branching annual with oval leaves. Conical heads of small, very fragrant, somewhat star-shaped, white flowers with orange-brown stamens are carried in summer and early fall.
H 12–24in (30–60cm), **S** 12in (30cm).

☼ ◊ ❢ Z10–11 H6–1

300

☼ ◊ ❢ Z4–9 H9–1

Hibiscus trionum (Flower-of-the-hour)
Fairly fast-growing, upright annual with oval, serrated leaves. Trumpet-shaped, creamy-white or pale yellow flowers, with purplish-brown centers, are borne from late summer to early fall.
H 24in (60cm), **S** 12in (30cm).

☼ ◊ Z10–11 H11–10

Impatiens balsamina (Balsam)
Fairly fast-growing, erect, compact, bushy annual with lance-shaped leaves. Small, cup-shaped, spurred, pink or white flowers are borne in summer and early fall. **H** to 30in (75cm), **S** 18in (45cm).

☼ ◊ H11–1

Tanacetum parthenium (Feverfew)
Moderately fast-growing, short-lived, bushy perennial, grown as an annual. Has aromatic leaves and small, white flower heads in summer and early fall.
H and **S** 8–18in (20–45cm).

Hypoestes phyllostachya
(Freckle face, Polka-dot plant)
Evergreen, bush perennial or subshrub. Dark green leaves are covered with irregular, pink spots. Bears small, tubular, lavender flowers intermittently.
H and **S** 30in (75cm). Min. 50°F (10°C).

☼ ◊ Z10–11 H11–9

Pentas lanceolata
(Egyptian star, Star-cluster)
Mainly evergreen, loosely rounded shrub with hairy, bright green leaves. In summer–fall produces dense clusters of pink, lilac, red or white flowers.
H 6ft (2m), **S** 3ft (1m). Min. 50–59°F (10–15°C).

☼ ◊ H11–1

Argyranthemum 'Summer Melody'
Evergreen, prolific shrub, grown as an annual, with daisylike, fully double, dark-centered, pale pink flower heads, 1¼in (3cm) across, from early summer and into fall. Has lobed, glossy, dull green leaves. **H** 11in (28cm), **S** 7in (17cm).

☼ ◊ Z7–11 H11–1

Brachyscome 'Strawberry Mousse'
Twiggy, semi-trailing, short-lived perennial, grown as an annual. Daisylike flower heads, 1¼–1½in (3–4cm) across, have slightly reflexed, deep pink ray petals and yellow eyes. Good for the edges of a raised bed or windowbox.
H 6in (15cm), **S** 14in (35cm).

☼ ◊ Z11 H12–1

Calibrachoa Caberet Series
LIGHT PINK ('Balcablitpi')
Mound-forming and trailing, prolific perennial, grown as an annual. In summer–fall, trumpet-shaped, vivid pink flowers, 1¼–1½in (3–4cm) across, are borne on twiggy stems with linear, dark green leaves. **H** 6in (15cm), **S** 18in (45cm).

☼ ◊ ᵖᴴ Z10–11 H11–1

Catharanthus roseus Boa Series
'Boa Peach'
Evergreen, semi-trailing, disease-tolerant shrub, grown as an annual. Flattish, rounded, very pale pink flowers, 2in (5cm) across, with a neat ring of reddish-pink around the tiny eye, are borne in summer.
H 6in (15cm), **S** 18–24in (45–60cm).

☼ ◊ H11–1

Martynia annua (Unicorn plant)
Fairly fast-growing, upright annual with long-stalked leaves. Has foxglove-like, lobed, creamy-white flowers marked red, pink and yellow in summer, followed by horned, green, then brown, fruits. **H** 24in (60cm), **S** 12in (30cm).

☼ ◊ H11–7

Diascia LITTLE DANCER ('Pendan')
Mound-forming or semi-trailing
perennial, usually grown as an annual.
Spikes of tubular, coral-pink flowers are
borne in clouds from late spring to fall.
Has heart-shaped, pale green leaves.
H 12in (30cm), **S** 18in (45cm).

 ☀ ◐ Z7–9 H9–6

Lathyrus odoratus Cupid Series
'Cupid Pink'
Neat, compact, annual with fragrant,
pink-and-white, bicolored flowers in
summer. Has pairs of mid-green, 1–2in
(2.5–5cm) leaves and no tendrils. Good at
the front of borders, as a potted specimen,
or in a basket. **H** 8in (20cm), **S** 12in (30cm).

 ☀ ◐ Z9–10 H8–1

Nemesia AMELIE ('Fleurame')
Mound-forming, twiggy perennial,
grown as an annual, with highly
fragrant, trumpet-shaped, 2-tone pink
flowers, 1½in (4cm) across, with yellow
lips, in summer. Has lance-shaped, neatly
toothed, dark green leaves. Good for a
container. **H** 5in (13cm), **S** 6in (15cm).

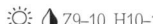 ☀ ◐ Z9–10 H10–1

Lantana camara Lucky Series
LUCKY HONEY BLUSH ('Baluclush')
Evergreen, mound-forming shrub, grown
as an annual. Clusters of tubular, 5-lobed,
yellow flowers, 1½in (4cm) across, maturing
to pink, with a spicy scent, are borne in late
spring–fall. Has oval, finely wrinkled, deep
green leaves. **H** 7in (18cm), **S** 12in (30cm).

 ☀ ◐ ❗ Z11 H11–1

Gaura lindheimeri 'Rosyjane'
Upright, woody-based perennial,
usually grown as an annual. Racemes
of tubular, white flowers, with bright
pink margins, are borne in summer–fall
on twiggy stems with lance-shaped
leaves. **H** 30in (75cm), **S** 18in (45cm).

 ☀ ◐ Z6–9 H9–6

Osteospermum Sunny Series
'Sunny Marina'
Evergreen, compact, slightly shrubby
perennial, grown as an annual. In
summer–fall, bears blue-eyed flowers, 3in
(7cm) across, with purple rays, shading to
white. Has narrow, slightly toothed, dark
green leaves. **H** and **S** 8–10in (20–25cm).

☀ ◐ Z10–11 H7–1

Fuchsia 'Leonora'
Vigorous, deciduous, upright shrub
bearing bell-shaped, single, pink
flowers with green-tipped sepals.
Is good for training as a standard.
H 5ft (1.5m), **S** 3ft (1m).

☀ ◐ Z9–11 H11–9

FUCHSIAS

Flowering freely all summer and throughout early fall until the first frost, fuchsias make excellent container and border plants. The single or double blooms vary from small and dainty to bold and frilly, their colorful outer sepals held above petals in similar or contrasting hues. A few also boast variegated foliage. Ranging in habit from strongly upright, through broad and bushy, to arching and trailing, there are fuchsias for many garden situations. Upright and bushy types inject summer color into permanent mixed border schemes or seasonal bedding displays, while larger types make good container specimens, combining well with other summer flowers. Trailing fuchsias are ideal for hanging baskets and windowboxes.

F. triphylla 'Firecracker'

F. Mojo Series 'Beebop'

F. 'Lye's Unique'

F. 'Celia Smedley'

F. 'Annabel'

F. 'Pink Galore'

F. 'Joanna Lumley'

F. 'Jack Shahan'

F. 'Dollar Prinzessin'

F. 'Mrs. Lovell Swisher'

F. Windchimes Series WINDCHIMES PINK AND WHITE ('Kiefuwind')

F. Shadowdancer Series PEGGY ('Goetzpeg')

F. 'Nellie Nuttall'

F. 'Golden Marinka'

F. California Dreamers Series 'Snowburner'

F. 'Bicentennial'

F. 'Swingtime'

F. 'Sunray'

F. 'Thalia'

F. 'Coralle'

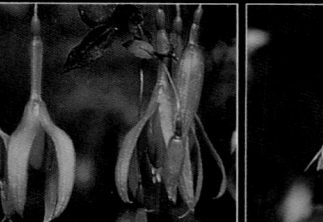

F. 'Red Spider'

F. fulgens

Primula Belarina Series
BELARINA PINK ICE ('Kerbelpice')
Rosette-forming, semievergreen,
Primrose Group primula. Double white
flowers, 1¾in (3cm) across, mature to
light pink-purple in late winter and
spring. Has oval, deeply veined, dark
green leaves. **H** 6in (16cm), **S** 12in (30cm).

☼ ◊ Z6–9 H8–6

Antirrhinum Luminaire Series
LUMINAIRE HOT PINK ('Balumhopi')
Semi-trailing subshrub, grown as an
annual with vibrant pink, 2-lipped
flowers, each with a yellow throat. Has
lance-shaped, dark green leaves. Is ideal
in a mixed basket or trailing over the
edge of a tub. **H** 6in (15cm), **S** 12in (30cm).

☼ ◊ Z9–11 H11–1

x Petchoa Supercal Series SUPERCAL
NEON ROSE ('Kakegawa S89')
Trailing evergreen perennial, grown
as an annual with abundant, flared,
trumpet-shaped yellow-eyed, vivid pink
flowers borne continuously all summer.
Is a Petunia/Calibrachoa hybrid.
H 10in (25cm), **S** 14in (35cm).

☼ ◊ Z10–11 H11–1

Glandularia x hybrida AZTEC DARK
PINK MAGIC ('Balazdapima')
Trailing or groundcover perennial, grown
as an annual. Stems bear oval, dark green
leaves divided into slender leaflets and
clusters of tubular, lobed, white-eyed,
rose pink flowers, 2½in (6cm) across, in
summer. **H** 5in (12cm), **S** 16in (40cm).

☼ ◊ Z9–11 H12–1

Matthiola 'Giant Excelsior'
Fast-growing, erect, bushy biennial,
grown as an annual. Lance-shaped
leaves are grayish-green; long spikes
of highly scented flowers in shades of
pink, red, pale blue or white appear in
summer. **H** to 30in (75cm), **S** 12in (30cm).

☼ ◊ Z5–8 H8–5

Gomphrena globosa
(Globe amaranth)
Moderately fast-growing, upright, bushy
annual with oval, hairy leaves. Has oval,
clover-like flower heads in pink, yellow,
orange, purple or white in summer and
early fall. **H** 12in (30cm), **S** 8in (20cm).

☼ ◊ Z11 H11–1

Callistephus chinensis
Ostrich Plume Series
Fast-growing, bushy annual with long,
branching stems. From late summer to
late fall, produces spreading, feathery,
reflexed, double flower heads, mainly
in pinks and crimsons. **H** to 24in (60cm),
S 12in (30cm).

☼ ◊ H9–1

Papaver somniferum
Paeoniiflorum Group
Fast-growing, erect annual with lobed,
pale grayish-green leaves. Has large,
rounded, often cup-shaped, double
flowers in a mixture of colors—red,
pink, purple or white—in summer.
H 30in (75cm), **S** 12in (30cm).

☼ ◊ ⓘ Z3–8 H8–1

Rhodanthe chlorocephala
subsp. rosea
Moderately fast-growing, erect annual.
Lance-shaped leaves are grayish-green;
small, daisylike, papery, semidouble,
pink flower heads appear in summer.
Flowers dry well. **H** 12in (30cm),
S 6in (15cm).

☼ ◊ H11–1

Silene coeli-rosa
Moderately fast-growing, erect annual
with lance-shaped, grayish-green
leaves. Has 5-petaled, pinkish-purple
flowers with white centers in summer.
H 18in (45cm), **S** 6in (15cm).

☼ ◊ H9–1

Agrostemma githago 'Milas'
Fast-growing, slender, upright, thin-stemmed annual. Has lance-shaped leaves and 5-petaled, purplish-pink flowers, 3in (8cm) wide, in summer. **H** 24–36in (60–90cm), **S** 12in (30cm).

☼ ◊ ⚠ H9–1

Lobularia maritima 'Rosie O'Day'
Fast-growing, compact annual with lance-shaped, mid-green leaves. In summer bears rounded, compact heads of small, sweet-scented flowers, which open white but become red-purple. **H** to 6in (15cm), **S** to 10in (25cm).

☼ ◊ Z10–11 H11–1

Schizanthus 'Dwarf Bouquet' [mixed]
Moderately fast-growing, erect annual with fernlike, mid-green leaves. Bears massed, 2-lipped, open-faced flowers in a range of colors from pink to red, purple, yellow or white in summer and fall. **H** and **S** 8–10in (20–25cm).

☼ ◊ Z12–15 H8–1

Malcolmia maritima (Virginian stock)
Fast-growing, slim, erect annual with oval, grayish-green leaves. Carries tiny, fragrant, 4-petaled, pink, red or white flowers from spring to fall. Sow in succession for a long flowering season. **H** 8in (20cm), **S** 2–3in (5–8cm).

☼ ◊ Z8–9 H9–1

Silybum marianum (Mary's thistle)
Biennial with a basal rosette of deeply lobed, very spiny, heavily white-marbled, deep green leaves. Has thistle-like, dark purplish-pink flower heads on erect stems in summer and early fall. **H** 4ft (1.2m), **S** 2ft (60cm).

☼ ◊ Z6–9 H6–1

Cleome hassleriana 'Colour Fountain'
Fast-growing, bushy annual with hairy stems and divided leaves. In summer has heads of narrow-petaled flowers, with long, protruding stamens, in shades of pink, purple or white. **H** 3–4ft (1–1.2m), **S** 1½–2ft (45–60cm).

☼ ◊ Z11 H11–1

Iberis umbellata Fairy Series
Fast-growing, upright, bushy annual with lance-shaped, mid-green leaves. Heads of small, 4-petaled flowers, in shades of pink, red, purple or white, are carried in summer and early fall. **H** and **S** 8in (20cm).

☼ ◊ H11–1

Onopordum acanthium (Scotch thistle)
Slow-growing, erect, branching biennial. Large, lobed, spiny leaves are hairy and bright silvery-gray; winged, branching flower stems bear deep purplish-pink flower heads in summer. **H** 6ft (1.8m), **S** 3ft (1m).

☼ ◊ Z6–8 H11–7

Callistephus chinensis Milady Super Series [rose]
Moderately fast-growing, erect, bushy annual with oval, toothed leaves. Has large, daisylike, double, rose-pink flower heads in summer and early fall. **H** 10–12in (25–30cm), **S** 12–18in (30–45cm).

☼ ◊ H9–1

Clarkia amoena 'Sybil Sherwood'
Erect annual with lance-shaped, sometimes toothed leaves. Single, fluted, salmon-pink flowers, fading to white at the margins, are borne at the tips of long, leafy shoots in summer. **H** to 18in (45cm), **S** 12in (30cm).

 ☀ ◊ H7–1

Clarkia 'Brilliant'
Fast-growing, erect, bushy annual with oval leaves. Large, rosette-like, double, bright reddish-pink flowers are carried in long spikes in summer and early fall. **H** to 24in (60cm), **S** 12in (30cm).

 ☀ ◊ H8–1

Dianthus chinensis Baby Doll Series
Neat, bushy annual or biennial, grown as an annual. Light or mid-green leaves are lance-shaped; small, single, zoned flowers in various colors are carried in summer and early fall. **H** 6in (15cm), **S** 6–12in (15–30cm).

 ☀ ◊ Z9–11 H11–1

Phlox drummondii 'Chanal'
Erect to spreading, but compact, bushy, hairy annual with very variable, stem-clasping leaves. In late spring, bears cymes of double, almost rose-like, pink flowers. **H** 4–18in (10–45cm), **S** to 10in (25cm) or more.

 ☀ ◊ H11–1

Cosmos bipinnatus Sensation Series
Moderately fast-growing, bushy, erect annual. Has feathery, mid-green leaves and daisylike flower heads, to 4in (10cm) wide, in shades of red, pink or white, from early summer to early fall. **H** to 36in (90cm), **S** 24in (60cm).

 ☀ ◊

Malope trifida
Moderately fast-growing, erect, branching annual with rounded, lobed leaves. Flared, trumpet-shaped, reddish-purple flowers, to 3in (8cm) wide and with deep pink veins, are carried in summer and early fall. **H** 36in (90cm), **S** 12in (30cm).

 ☀ ◊ H8–1

Lavatera trimestris 'Silver Cup'
Moderately fast-growing, erect, branching annual with oval, lobed leaves. Shallowly trumpet-shaped, rose-pink flowers are carried in summer and early fall. **H** 24in (60cm), **S** 18in (45cm).

 ☀ ◊

Xeranthemum annuum [double]
Erect annual with lance-shaped, silvery leaves and branching heads of daisylike, papery, double flower heads in shades of pink, mauve, purple or white, in summer. Produces good dried flowers. **H** 24in (60cm), **S** 18in (45cm).

 ☀ ◊ H12–1

Nicotiana x sanderae Saratoga Series [deep rose]
Slow-growing, bushy annual with ovate mid-green leaves. In summer and early fall produces a long display of sparkling, long-tubed, salverform, deep rose-colored flowers. **H** and **S** 12in (30cm).

 ☀ ◊ ⓘ Z10–11 H11–1

ANNUALS, BIENNIALS, AND BEDDING

Calibrachoa Million Bells Series CHERRY PINK ('Sunbelrichipi')
Semi-trailing, prolific perennial, grown as an annual. In summer–fall, trumpet-shaped, deep cherry-pink flowers, 1½in (4cm) across, are borne on twiggy stems with linear, dark green leaves. **H** 8in (20cm), **S** 22in (55cm).

☀ ○ pH Z10–11 H11–1

Lunaria annua 'Variegata'
Fast-growing, erect biennial with pointed-oval, serrated, white-variegated leaves. Heads of small, scented, 4-petaled, deep purplish-pink flowers are borne in spring and early summer followed by rounded, silvery seed pods. **H** 30in (75cm), **S** 12in (30cm).

☀ ○ Z3–9 H9–1

Brassica Northern Lights Series
Moderately fast-growing, evergreen biennial. Has compact heads of large, tightly packed, bluish green leaves, crinkled at the edges, opening purple, pink or creamy-white in the center. Is used for fall and winter color. **H** and **S** 12–16in (30–40cm).

☀ ○ Z7–11 H7–1

Lotus berthelotii (Coral gem)
Semievergreen, straggling perennial suitable for a hanging basket or large pan in an alpine house. Has hairy, silvery branches and leaves, and clusters of pealike, scarlet flowers in summer. **H** 12in (30cm) **S** indefinite. Min. 41°F (5°C).

☀ ○ H11–10

Gerbera jamesonii (Barberton daisy)
Evergreen, upright perennial with daisylike, variably colored flower heads, borne intermittently on long stems, and basal rosettes of large, jagged leaves. Flowers are excellent for cutting. **H** 24in (60cm), **S** 18in (45cm).

☀ ○ Z11 H11–6

Catharanthus roseus Cobra Series 'Cobra Burgundy'
Evergreen, well-branched, disease-resistant shrub, grown as an annual, with oval, glossy, dark green leaves. Produces flat, rounded, 5-petaled, deep burgundy-red flowers in summer. **H** 14–16in (35–40cm), **S** 22–26in (55–65cm).

☀ ○ H11–1

Zinnia elegans Dreamland Series [scarlet]
Moderately fast-growing, sturdy, erect annual with ovate, mid-green leaves. In summer and fall produces large, daisylike, semidouble, bright scarlet flower heads. **H** and **S** 12in (30cm).

☀ ○ H12–1

Antirrhinum majus 'Black Prince'
Erect, bushy perennial, grown as an annual. Lance-shaped, bronze leaves offset spikes of 2-lipped, deep crimson flowers produced in summer–fall. Dead-head regularly. **H** 18in (45cm), **S** 12in (30cm).

☀ ○ Z9–11 H11–1

Cosmos atrosanguineus CHOCAMOCHA ('Thomocha')
Bushy, tuberous perennial, grown as an annual, with slightly bowl-shaped, strongly chocolate-scented, deep red flower heads, 1½in (4cm) across, in summer–fall. Has pinnate, dark green leaves. **H** and **S** 14–15in (35–38cm).

☀ ○ Z7–11 H11–1

Cuphea x purpurea 'Firecracker'
Semi-trailing, subshrubby perennial, grown as an annual. Sticky stems bear lance-shaped, dark green leaves and, from late spring to fall, 2-lipped, bright red flowers. Is good in a mixed container. **H** 9in (23cm), **S** 16in (40cm).

☀ ○ Z10–11 H11–10

Dahlia HAPPY SINGLE ROMEO ('HS Romeo')
Bushy, single dahlia, grown as an annual, bearing deep purple leaves with oval leaflets. Produces dark-centered, deep red flowers, 4in (10cm) across, in summer and fall. **H** 22in (55cm), **S** 16in (40cm).

☀ ○ Z9–11 H11–1

ANNUALS, BIENNIALS, AND BEDDING

Glandularia x hybrida
Corsage Series 'Corsage Red'
Trailing perennial, grown as an annual.
Stems have oval, neatly lobed, dark
green leaves and, in summer, bear
clusters, 3in (7cm) across, of tubular,
lobed, double, vibrant red flowers.
H 14in (35cm), **S** 28in (70cm).

☀ ◊ Z9–11 H12–1

Nemesia strumosa Carnival Series
Fairly fast-growing, bushy annual with
serrated, pale green leaves. In summer
has small, somewhat trumpet-shaped
flowers in a range of colors, including
yellow, red, orange, purple and white.
H 8–12in (20–30cm), **S** 6in (15cm).

☀ ◊ H7–1

Impatiens walleriana
MASQUERADE ('Tuckmas')
Mound-forming, well-branched, prolific
perennial, grown as an annual. Oval,
fresh green leaves have yellow or cream
margins. In summer produces flattish,
5-petaled, spurred, single, bright orange-
red flowers. **H** and **S** 15–18in (38–45cm).

☀ ◊ Z11 H12–1

Tropaeolum majus
'Hermine Grashoff'
Trailing, short-lived perennial, grown as
an annual, with large, rounded, slightly
wavy-edged, pale green leaves. Produces
double, sterile, bright red flowers in
summer–fall. Is best in a large container.
H 18in (45cm), **S** 24in (60cm).

☀ ◊ Z11–12 H12–1

Pelargonium 'Happy Thought'
Fancy-leaved zonal pelargonium with
single, light crimson flowers in clusters
borne in summer. Rounded leaves
each have a greenish-yellow butterfly
marking in the center. **H** 16–18in
(40–45cm), **S** 8–10in (20–25cm).
Min. 36°F (2°C).

☀ ◊ H11–1

Amaranthus caudatus
(Love-lies-bleeding, Tassel flower)
Bushy annual with oval, pale green
leaves. Pendulous panicles of tassel-
like, red flowers, 18in (45cm) long, are
carried in summer–fall. **H** to 4ft (1.2m),
S 18in (45cm).

☀ ◊ Z10–11 H11–1

Zinnia x marylandica
Profusion Series 'Profusion Cherry'
Mound-forming, well-branched, disease-
resistant annual with ovate, mid-green
leaves. Has semidouble, rich cherry red
flower heads, 2–3in (5–7.5cm) across,
in summer–fall. **H** 12–18in (30–45cm),
S 16–24in (40–60cm).

☀ ◊ H12–1

Dianthus chinensis 'Fire Carpet'
Slow-growing, bushy annual or biennial,
grown as an annual. Lance-shaped
leaves are light or mid-green. Small,
rounded, single, bright red flowers
are carried in summer and early fall.
H 8in (20cm), **S** 6–12in (15–30cm).

☀ ◊ Z9–11 H11–1

Impatiens Expo Series
'Expo Pink' (Busy lizzie)
Fast-growing, evergreen, bushy
perennial usually grown as an annual.
Has pointed, ovate leaves and from late
spring to fall bears spurred, flat-faced,
red, pink or white flowers. **H** 4–6in
(10–15cm), **S** 6–12in (15–30cm).

☀ ◊ Z10–11 H11–1

ANNUALS, BIENNIALS, AND BEDDING

Linum grandiflorum 'Rubrum'
Fairly fast-growing, slim, erect annual.
Lance-shaped leaves are gray-green;
small, rounded, flattish, deep red flowers
are carried in summer. **H** 18in (45cm),
S 6in (15cm).

 ☼ ◊ H8–1

Petunia 'Mirage Velvet'
Branching, bushy perennial, grown as
an annual, with oval, dark green leaves.
Large, flared, trumpet-shaped, rich red
flowers, with almost black centers,
appear in summer–fall. **H** 10in (25m),
S 12in (30cm).

☼ ◊ Z11 H11–1

**_Viola_ x _wittrockiana_
Floral Dance Series**
Fairly fast-growing, bushy perennial,
grown as an annual or biennial. Has
oval, mid-green leaves and rounded,
5-petaled flowers in a wide range of
colors in winter. **H** 6–8in (15–20cm),
S 8in (20cm).

☼ ◊ Z8–11 H9–1

Salvia splendens Vista Series [red]
Slow-growing, bushy perennial grown
as an annual, with dark green, ovate,
toothed leaves. Produces long-tubed,
2-lipped, bright scarlet flowers in dense,
terminal spikes during summer and fall.
H and **S** 12in (30cm).

☼ ◊ Z11–12 H12–10

Tagetes 'Cinnabar'
Fast-growing, bushy annual with
aromatic, very feathery, deep green
leaves. Heads of rounded, daisylike,
single, rich rust-red flowers, yellow-red
beneath, are carried in summer and
early fall. **H** and **S** to 12in (30cm).

 ☼ ◊ ① H12–1

**_Amaranthus hypochondriacus_
(Prince's feather)**
Bushy annual with upright, sometimes
flattened panicles, 6in (15cm) long or
more, of dark red flowers in summer–
fall. Leaves are heavily suffused purple.
H to 4ft (1.2m), **S** 18in (45cm).

 ☼ ◊ H11–1

Ricinus communis 'Impala'
Fast-growing, evergreen, erect shrub,
usually grown as an annual. Has deeply
lobed, bronze leaves to 12in (30cm) wide,
and clusters of small, red flowers in
summer, followed by globular, prickly,
red seed heads. **H** 5ft (1.5m), **S** 3ft (1m).

☼ ◊ ① Z11–14 H12–1

Cuphea ignea (Cigar flower)
Evergreen, spreading, bushy subshrub
with bright green leaves. From spring
to fall has tubular, dark orange-red
flowers, each with a dark band and white
ring at the mouth. **H** 12–30in (30–75cm),
S 12–36in (30–90cm). Min. 36°F (2°C).

☼ ◊ Z10–11 H11–6

Alonsoa warscewiczii (Mask flower)
Perennial, grown as an annual, with
slender, branching, red stems carrying
oval, toothed, deep green leaves.
Spurred, bright scarlet flowers
are produced during summer–fall.
H 12–24in (30–60cm), **S** 12in (30cm).

☼ ◊ Z10–11 H11–10

PELARGONIUMS

Pelargoniums are perfect for containers and beds, and flower almost continuously in warm climates or under glass. Most fall into one of four main groups. Zonal geraniums have rounded leaves, clearly marked with a darker "zone," and single to double flowers. Regal types are shrubby with serrated leaves and delicate, trumpet-shaped flowers. Ivy-leaved pelargoniums are trailing plants with lobed leaves and single to double flowers—a good choice for hanging baskets. Scented-leaved types and species have small, star-shaped flowers and are grown principally for their fragrant foliage. Unique types are tall subshrubs with regal, brightly colored flowers; some also have scented leaves. To flower well, all types need sun and well-drained soil.

P. 'Alberta' ①
[zonal]

Pelargonium Fireworks Series FIREWORKS SCARLET ('Fiwoscarl') [scented-leaved]

P. 'Clorinda' ①
[scented-leaved]

P. 'Evka' [ivy-leaved]

P. Maverick Series 'Maverick Star' [zonal]

P. 'Fraiche Beauté' ①
[zonal]

P. 'Lady Plymouth' ①
[scented-leaved]

P. 'Voodoo' ①
[unique]

P. Regalia Series 'Regalia Chocolate'
[regal]

P. Horizon Deva Series 'Horizon Deva Raspberry Ripple' [zonal]

P. Decora Series 'Decora Dark Pink'
[ivy-leaved]

P. 'Lachskönigin' ①
[ivy-leaved]

P. 'Tip Top Duet' ①
[regal]

P. Bulls Eye Series
'Bulls Eye Salmon' [zonal]

P. 'Brookside Primrose' ①
[zonal]

P. Antik Series ANTIK SALMON ('Tiksal') [zonal]

P. BLUE WONDER ('Pacbla') [zonal]

P. Horizon Deva Series 'Horizon Deva Orange Ice' [zonal]

ANNUALS, BIENNIALS, AND BEDDING

Aeonium 'Zwartkop'
Bushy, perennial succulent with stems each crowned by a rosette, to 6in (15cm) across, of narrow, purple leaves. Bears golden pyramids of flowers in spring on 2–3-year-old stems, which then die. **H** 2ft (60cm), **S** 3ft (1m). Min. 41°F (5°C).

☼ ◑ Z9–11 H9–4

Lycianthes rantonnetii 'Royal Robe'
Evergreen, loosely rounded shrub with smooth, bright green leaves. In summer has clusters of rich purple-blue flowers that open almost flat. **H** and **S** 3–6ft (1–2m). Min. 45°F (7°C).

☼ ◑ ⓘ H11–6

Papaver rhoeas Shirley Group [single]
Fast-growing, slender, erect annual with lobed, light green leaves. Rounded, often cup-shaped, single flowers, in shades of red, pink, salmon or white, appear in summer. **H** 24in (60cm), **S** 12in (30cm).

☼ ◑ H11–1

Streptocarpus saxorum
(False African violet)
Evergreen, rounded, woody-based perennial with small, oval, hairy leaves in whorls. Lilac flowers with white tubes arise from leaf axils in summer–fall. **H** and **S** 12in (30cm) or more. Min. 50–59°F (10–15°C).

☼ ◑ Z14–15 H12–10

Lantana montevidensis
Evergreen, trailing or mat-forming shrub with serrated leaves. Has heads of rose-purple flowers, each with a yellow eye, intermittently all year but mainly in summer. **H** 8–39in (20–100cm), **S** 24–48in (60–120cm). Min. 50–55°F (10–13°C).

☼ ◑ ⓘ H11–9

Lunaria annua (Honesty)
Fast-growing, erect biennial with pointed-oval, serrated leaves. Heads of scented, 4-petaled, white to deep purple flowers in spring and early summer are followed by rounded, silvery seed pods. **H** 30in (75cm), **S** 12in (30cm).

☼ ◑ Z3–9 H9–1

Solenostemon scutellarioides Kong Series 'Kong Scarlet'
Fast-growing, large-leaved perennial, grown as an annual. Deepest crimson leaves are feathered to green at the margins and have a slender, central, cerise flash. Pinch out flower spikes. **H** and **S** 18–24in (45–60cm).

☼ ◐ Z11–12 H12–1

Tradescantia pallida 'Purpurea'
Evergreen, creeping perennial with dark purple stems and slightly fleshy leaves. Has pink or pink-and-white flowers in summer. **H** 12–16in (30–40cm), **S** 12in (30cm) or more. Min. 59°F (15°C).

☼ ◑ Z11–12 H12–1

Heliotropium arborescens
Evergreen, bushy shrub. Semi-glossy, dark green leaves are finely wrinkled. Purple to lavender flowers are borne in dense, flat clusters from late spring to winter. **H** 18in (45cm), **S** 12–18in (30–45cm). Min. 45°F (7°C).

☼ ◑ H11–9

**Alternanthera dentata
'Purple Knight'** (Joseph's coat)
Vigorous, evergreen perennial, grown
as an annual. Forms a spreading mound
of upright, purple stems clad in ovate,
slightly glossy, dark purple leaves.
H 2–3ft (60–90cm), **S** 3–4ft (90–120cm).
Min. 59–64°F (15–18°C).

☼ ◐ Z11 H12–1

**Angelonia angustifolia AngelMist
Series 'AngelMist Lavender Stripe'**
Evergreen, upright perennial, grown as
an annual, with lance-shaped, toothed
leaves. Slender racemes of 2-lipped
flowers, ¾in (2cm) across, purple above
and white below, are borne in summer.
H 12in (30cm), **S** 14in (35cm).

☼ ◐ Z9–10 H10–1

**Solenostemon scutellarioides
'Inky Fingers'**
Fast-growing, semi-trailing, bushy
perennial, grown as an annual. Rounded,
dark blackish-red leaves are cut into 5–11
mostly deep lobes and edged in green.
Pinch out once or twice when young.
H 12–24in (30–60cm), **S** 24–39in (60–100cm).

☼ ◐ Z11–12 H12–1

Solenostemon 'Chocolate Mint'
Fast-growing perennial, grown as an
annual, with broadly oval, chocolate-
brown leaves margined in fresh mint-
green. Pinch out any flower spikes.
H 14–20in (35–50cm), **S** 12–14in
(30–35cm).

☼◐ ◐ Z11–12 H12–1

Dahlia HAPPY SINGLE WINK ('HS Wink')
Bushy, single dahlia, grown as an
annual, bearing deep purple leaves with
oval leaflets. Pale purple flowers, 3in
(8cm) across, each have a dark purple
ring around the eye. Is good in a mixed
border. **H** 28in (70cm), **S** 18in (45cm).

☼ ◐ Z9–11 H11–1

Ipomoea batatas 'Blackie'
Evergreen, tuberous, trailing perennial
grown as an annual, with 3-lobed,
almost black leaves. In summer may
produce trumpet-shaped, purple-
throated, lavender flowers, 1in (2.5cm)
across. Is good in a mixed container.
H 6–10in (15–25cm), **S** 18–24in (45–60cm).

☼ ◐ ⚠ Z11 H11–1

**Lobelia erinus Waterfall Series
'Waterfall Light Lavender'**
Mound-forming, semi-trailing perennial,
grown as an annual, with narrowly oval
to lance-shaped, dark green leaves. Bears
2-lipped, lobed, pale violet flowers, ¾in
(2cm) across, with white eyes, in summer.
H 6–8in (15–20cm), **S** 8–12in (20–30cm).

☼◐ ◐ Z2–8 H8–1

**Petunia Surfinia Series
SURFINIA BLUE VEIN ('Sunsolos')**
Vigorous, trailing perennial, grown as an
annual. In summer, almost white flowers,
2in (5cm) across, developing mauve tints,
are borne with vivid purple-blue veins
and dark throats. Is good in a basket.
H 10in (25cm), **S** 24in (60cm).

☼ ◐ Z11 H11–1

**Pennisetum glaucum
'Purple Majesty'** (Pearl millet)
Tall, upright perennial, grown as an
annual, with long, straplike, arching
purple leaves. Bold, bristly, vertical
flower spikes, borne in summer, turn
from tan to purple. **H** 24–36in (60–90cm),
S 16–28in (40–70cm). Min. 36°F (2°C).

☼ ◐ H10–1

**Petunia Tumbelina Series
PRISCILLA ('Kerpril')**
Semi-trailing, well-branched perennial,
grown as an annual, with lance-shaped,
dark green leaves. Produces fragrant,
double, mauve flowers, veined in
dark purple, in summer and fall.
H 12in (30cm), **S** 20in (50cm).

☼ ◐ Z11 H11–1

Strobilanthes dyerianus
(Purple Shield)
Evergreen, relatively unbranched
subshrub, grown as an annual, with
elliptical, dark green, leaves, 6in (15cm)
long, almost fully flushed in silvery
purple, leaving only a pattern of dark
green veins. **H** and **S** 36in (90cm).

☼ ◐ Z11–12 H12–1

**Osteospermum Cape Daisy Series
NASINGA PURPLE ('Aksullo')**
Evergreen, slightly woody perennial,
grown as an annual, with lance-shaped,
slightly toothed leaves. In summer bears
blue-eyed flowers, 3in (7cm) across, with
fuchsia-purple rays, spooned at the tips.
H 12–15in (30–38cm), **S** 8–12in (20–30cm).

☼ ◐ Z10–11 H7–1

Viola x wittrockiana Imperial Series 'Imperial Frosty Rose'
Erect, bushy perennial, grown as an annual or biennial, with oval leaves. In summer, bears large, unusual, rose-purple flowers fading to pink and white. **H** 6–9in (16–23cm), **S** 9–12in (23–30cm).

☼ ◊ Z8–11 H9–1

Collinsia grandiflora
Moderately fast-growing, slender-stemmed annual. Upper leaves are lance-shaped; lower are oval. Whorls of pale purple flowers, with purplish-blue lips, are carried in spring–summer. **H** and **S** 6–12in (15–30cm).

◐ ◊ Z10–11 H11–1

Callistephus chinensis Milady Super Series [blue]
Moderately fast-growing, erect, bushy annual with oval, toothed leaves. Has large, daisylike, double, purplish-blue flower heads in summer and early fall. **H** 10–12in (25–30cm), **S** 12–18in (30–45cm).

☼ ◊ H9–1

Pennisetum setaceum 'Rubrum'
Clump-forming, herbaceous perennial grass, grown as an annual, with slender, upright, rather rough, dark purple leaves. In summer produces dense, cylindrical panicles of crimson spikelets, with bearded bristles, fading to green. **H** 36in (90cm), **S** 18in (45cm).

☼ ◊ Z8–11 H11–8

Nierembergia linariifolia 'Purple Robe'
Moderately fast-growing, rounded, branching perennial, grown as an annual, with narrow, lance-shaped leaves. Has cup-shaped, dark bluish-purple flowers in summer and early fall. **H** and **S** 6–8in (15–20cm).

☼ ◊ Z7–11 H11–7

Viola Joker Series
Bushy, spreading perennial, usually grown as an annual or biennial. Large, rounded, 5-petaled, purplish-blue flowers, with black and white "faces" and yellow eyes, appear in summer. **H** and **S** 6in (15cm).

☼ ◊ Z8–11 H9–1

Viola x wittrockiana Sorbet Series 'Sorbet Black Delight'
Neat, prolific perennial, grown as a biennial. Small, 5-petaled, deep black flowers, each with a small, gold eye, are borne in winter and spring over ovate, sparsely toothed, mid-green leaves. **H** and **S** 6–8in (15–20cm).

☼ ◊ Z8–11 H9–1

Cerinthe major 'Purpurascens'
Annual of lax habit with oval to spoon-shaped leaves, to 2½in (6cm) long. Bears terminal sprays of nodding, tubular, pale to mid-yellow flowers, with violet-tinged tips. Bracts around flowers are strongly suffused purple. **H** and **S** 24in (60cm).

☼ ◊ Z9–11 H12–5

Petunia Daddy Series 'Sugar Daddy'
Fairly fast-growing, branching, bushy, perennial, grown as an annual, with oval leaves. In early summer to fall, has large, purple flowers with dark veins. **H** to 14in (35cm), **S** 12–36in (30–90cm).

☼ ◊ Z11 H11–1

Salvia farinacea 'Victoria'
Moderately fast-growing perennial, grown as an annual, with many erect stems. Has oval or lance-shaped leaves and spikes of tubular, violet-blue flowers in summer. **H** 18in (45cm), **S** 12in (30cm).

☼ ◊ Z8–11 H12–1

Glandularia x hybrida AZTEC SILVER MAGIC ('Balazsilma')
Trailing or groundcover, mildew-tolerant perennial, grown as an annual, with small, finely lobed, green leaves. In summer, clusters, 2½in (6cm) across, of pale violet flowers are borne along the stems. **H** 3in (8cm), **S** 20in (50cm).

☼ ◊ Z9–11 H12–1

***Campanula medium*
'Bells of Holland'**
Slow-growing, evergreen, clump-forming, erect biennial with lance-shaped, toothed leaves. In spring and early summer has bell-shaped flowers in blue, lilac, pink or white. **H** to 24in (60cm), **S** 12in (30cm).

☼ ◊ Z5–8 H8–5

Salvia sclarea* var. *turkestanica
Moderately fast-growing, erect biennial, grown as an annual. Has aromatic, oval, hairy leaves and panicles of tubular, white and lavender-purple flowers with prominent, lavender-purple bracts in summer. **H** 30in (75cm), **S** 12in (30cm).

☼ ◊ Z5–9 H9–3

***Myosotis* Sylva Series**
Compact, bushy, early-flowering perennial, grown as a biennial. Has lance-shaped, hairy leaves and, from mid-spring to early summer, clustered spikes of small, 5-lobed flowers in blue, pink or white. **H** and **S** 9in (23cm).

◐ ◊ Z5–9 H8–1

***Viola* x *wittrockiana*
Ultima Radiance Series** [deep blue]
Spreading perennial, grown as a biennial. Produces large, neatly rounded, 5-petaled, deep blue flowers, with white faces, yellow lips and dark whiskers, in winter and spring. Leaves are oval and mid-green. **H** and **S** 6–8in (15–20cm).

☼ ◊ Z8–11 H9–1

Trachelium caeruleum (Throatwort)
Moderately fast-growing, erect perennial, grown as an annual. Has oval, serrated leaves and clustered heads of small, tubular, lilac-blue or white flowers in summer. **H** 24–36in (60–90cm), **S** 12in (30cm).

☼ ◊ Z9–13 H12–1

***Isotoma* Avant-Garde Series**
Neat, domed, woody-based perennial, grown as an annual. Rounded mounds of slender, lobed leaves are topped by star-shaped, 5-petaled flowers, in blue purple, pink and white, in summer. Is good in a container. **H** 6–12in (15–30cm), **S** 9–15in (23–38cm).

☼ ◊ Z10–11 H11–1

***Ageratum houstonianum*
'Blue Danube'**
Moderately fast-growing, hummock-forming annual with pointed-oval leaves. Has clusters of feathery, brushlike, lavender-blue flower heads in summer–fall. Makes a useful edging plant. **H** and **S** 6in (15cm).

☼ ◊ Z10–11 H11–1

Nigella damascena
Persian Jewels Series
Fast-growing, erect annual with feathery leaves. Small, semidouble flowers, in shades of blue, pink or white, appear in summer, followed by inflated seed pods that can be cut and dried.
H 18in (45cm), **S** 8in (20cm).

☼ ◊ H11–1

Nemophila menziesii
(Baby blue-eyes)
Fast-growing, spreading annual with serrated, gray-green leaves. Small, bowl-shaped, blue flowers with white centers are carried in summer.
H 8in (20cm), **S** 6in (15cm).

☼ ◊ H11–1

Phacelia campanularia
(California bluebell)
Moderately fast-growing, branching, bushy annual with oval, serrated, deep green leaves. Bell-shaped, pure blue flowers, 1in (2.5cm) wide, are carried in summer and early fall. **H** 8in (20cm), **S** 6in (15cm).

☼ ◊ ❗ Z5–10 H9–1

Salvia farinacea 'Strata'
Upright, slightly tuberous perennial, grown as an annual. White-mealy stems bear spikes of blue flowers, with broad lower lips, ¾in (2cm) long, each in a white calyx, in summer–fall. Has glossy, narrowly lance-shaped, gray-green leaves. **H** 24in (60cm), **S** 12in (30cm).

☼ ◊ Z8–11 H12–1

Gilia capitata
Erect, branching annual. Has very feathery, mid-green leaves and tiny, dense, rounded heads of soft lavender-blue flowers in summer and early fall. Is good for cut flowers. **H** 18in (45cm), **S** 8in (20cm).

☼ ◊ H11–1

Lobelia erinus Waterfall Series
'Waterfall Blue'
Mound-forming, semi-trailing perennial, grown as an annual, with narrowly oval to lance-shaped, toothed, green leaves. Racemes of 2-lipped, mid-blue flowers, ¾in (2cm) across, are borne in summer.
H 6–8in (15–20cm), **S** 8–12in (20–30cm).

☼ ◊ Z2–8 H8–1

Pericallis Senetti Series
SENETTI BLUE BICOLOR ('Sunseneribuba')
Mound-forming, bushy perennial, grown as an annual. Daisylike, white flower heads, 3in (7cm) across, with vivid blue tips and deep magenta eyes are borne in spring. Has oval, serrated, mid–deep green leaves. **H** 15–18in (38–45cm), **S** 12–15in (30–38cm).

☼ ◊ Z11 H11–5

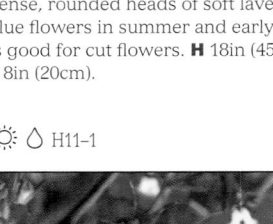

Lobelia erinus 'Sapphire'
Slow-growing, pendulous, spreading annual or occasionally perennial. Oval to lance-shaped leaves are pale green; small, sapphire-blue flowers with white centers are produced continuously in summer and early fall. **H** 8in (20cm), **S** 6in (15cm).

☼ ◊ Z2–8 H8–1

Convolvulus tricolor 'Blue Flash'
Moderately fast-growing, upright, bushy annual with oval to lance-shaped leaves. Has small, saucer-shaped, intense blue flowers with cream and yellow centers in summer. **H** 8–12in (20–30cm), **S** 8in (20cm).

☼ ◊ Z9–11 H11–10

Ageratum houstonianum 'Blue Mink'
Moderately fast-growing, hummock-forming. Has pointed-oval leaves and clusters of feathery, brushlike, pastel blue flower heads in summer–fall. Is a useful edging plant. **H** and **S** 8–12in (20–30cm).

☼ ◊ Z10–11 H11–1

Cynoglossum amabile 'Firmament'
Slow-growing, upright, bushy annual or biennial with lance-shaped, hairy, gray-green leaves. Pendulous, tubular, pure sky-blue flowers are carried in summer. **H** 18in (45cm), **S** 12in (30cm).

☼ ◊ Z5–8 H8–1

Commelina coelestis (Dayflower)
Fairly fast-growing, upright perennial, usually grown as an annual, with lance-shaped, mid-green leaves. Small, 3-petaled, bright pure blue flowers are freely produced from late summer to mid-fall. **H** to 18in (45cm), **S** 12in (30cm).

☼ ◊ Z9–10 H11–9

Myosotis sylvatica 'Blue Ball'
Slow-growing, bushy, compact perennial, often grown as a biennial. Has lance-shaped leaves and, in spring and early summer, spikes of tiny, 5-lobed, deep blue flowers. **H** to 8in (20cm), **S** 6in (15cm).

◑ ◊ Z5–9 H7–1

Senecio cineraria 'Silver Dust'
Moderately fast-growing, evergreen, bushy subshrub, usually grown as an annual, with deeply lobed, silver leaves. Small, daisylike, yellow flower heads appear in summer but are best removed. **H** and **S** 12in (30cm).

☼ ◊ Z8–11 H12–1

Anchusa capensis 'Blue Angel'
Bushy biennial, grown as an annual. Has lance-shaped, bristly leaves. Heads of shallowly bowl-shaped, brilliant blue flowers are borne in summer. **H** and **S** 8in (20cm).

☼ ◊ Z7–9 H9–7

Centaurea cyanus [tall, blue] (Cornflower)
Fast-growing, erect, branching annual. Has lance-shaped, gray-green leaves and branching heads of daisylike, blue flowers in summer and early fall. **H** to 36in (90cm), **S** 12in (30cm).

☼ ◊ H7–1

Borago officinalis (Borage)
Spreading, clump-forming, annual herb. Has oval, crinkled, rough-haired leaves and sprays of star-shaped, blue flowers in summer and early fall. Young leaves are sometimes used as a coolant in drinks. Self-seeds prolifically. **H** 36in (90cm), **S** 12in (30cm).

☼ ◊ H11–1

Senecio cineraria 'Silver Dust' continued

Nigella damascena 'Miss Jekyll'
Fast-growing, slender, erect annual. Feathery leaves are bright green; small, rounded, many-petaled, semidouble, blue flowers are carried in summer, followed by inflated seed pods that can be cut and dried. **H** 18in (45cm), **S** 8in (20cm).

☼ ◊ H11–1

Lobelia erinus 'Crystal Palace'
Slow-growing, spreading, compact, bushy annual or occasionally perennial. Bronzed leaves are oval to lance-shaped; small, deep blue flowers are produced continuously in summer and early fall. **H** 4–8in (10–20cm), **S** 4–6in (10–15cm).

☼ ◊ Z2–8 H8–1

Sedum caeruleum
Moderately fast-growing annual with branching flower stems. Oval, light green leaves become red-tinged when clusters of small, star-shaped, light blue flowers with white centers are borne in summer. **H** and **S** 4–6in (10–15cm).

☼ ◊ ❗ H9–1

Leucophyta brownii
Evergreen, intricately branched shrub with velvety, gray branches and tiny, scalelike leaves. Clusters of flower heads, silver in bud, yellowish when expanded, appear in summer. **H** 16–30in (40–75cm), **S** 16–36in (40–90cm). Min. 45–50°F (7–10°C).

☼ ◊ H11–10

315

Bassia scoparia* f. *trichophylla
(Burning bush, Summer cypress)
Moderately fast-growing, erect, very
bushy annual. Narrow, lance-shaped,
light green leaves, 2–3in (5–8cm) long,
turn red in fall. Has insignificant flowers.
H 36in (90cm), **S** 24in (60cm).

☼ ◊ Z9–11 H9–2

Nicotiana langsdorffii
Fairly slow-growing, erect, branching
perennial, grown as an annual, with
oval to lance-shaped leaves. Slightly
pendent, bell-shaped, pale green
to yellow-green flowers appear in
summer. **H** 3–5ft (1–1.5m), **S** 12in (30cm).

☼ ◊ ❗ Z10–11 H11–1

Moluccella laevis
(Bells of Ireland, Shell flower)
Fairly fast-growing, erect, branching
annual. Rounded leaves are pale green;
spikes of small, tubular, white flowers,
each surrounded by a conspicuous,
pale green calyx, appear in summer.
H 24in (60cm), **S** 8in (20cm).

☼ ◊ Z9–11 H9–1

***Zinnia elegans* 'Envy'**
Moderately fast-growing, sturdy,
erect annual. Has oval to lance-shaped,
pale or mid-green leaves and large,
daisylike, double, green flower heads
in summer and early fall. **H** 24in (60cm),
S 12in (30cm).

☼ ◊ H12–1

***Petunia* Surfinia Series**
SURFINIA LIME ('Keiyeul')
Vigorous, trailing perennial grown
as an annual, with slightly star-
shaped, white flowers, 2½in (6cm)
across, shading to lime-yellow in
the throats, in summer. Is good in a
basket. **H** 10in (25cm), **S** 24in (60cm).

☼ ◑ Z11 H11–1

BEGONIAS

The genus *Begonia* is one of the most versatile, providing interest throughout the year. Semperflorens begonias are excellent for summer bedding, while the *Rex-cultorum* group offers distinctive, handsome foliage in a huge variety of decorative shades and unusual textures. Other begonias, such as the *Tuberhybrida* cultivars with their large, showy blooms, are grown mostly for their flowers. Most begonias are not suitable for permanent outdoor cultivation in frost-prone areas as they are not hardy, but they make attractive houseplants and displays in summer containers. Begonias may be fibrous-rooted, rhizomatous, or tuberous, the tubers becoming dormant in winter. Grow them in a light position, shaded from direct sun.

B. serratipetala

B. boliviensis 'Bonfire'

B. x *tuberhybrida* Non Stop Series 'Non Stop White'

B. 'Ingramii'

B. x *tuberhybrida* Mocha Series 'Mocha Scarlet'

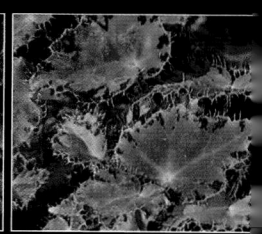

B. bowerae

B. 'Orpha C. Fox'

B. masoniana

B. dregei

B. albopicta

B. 'Merry Christmas'

B. DRAGON WING RED ('Bepared')

B. 'Tiger Paws'

B. prismatocarpa

ANNUALS, BIENNIALS, AND BEDDING

Ricinus communis (Castor bean)
Fast-growing, evergreen, erect shrub,
usually grown as an annual. Has large,
deeply lobed, mid-green leaves and
heads of green and red flowers in
summer, followed by globular, prickly
seed pods. **H** 5ft (1.5m), **S** 3ft (1m).

☀ ◊ ⚠ Z11–14 H12–1

***Ipomoea batatas* 'Margarita'**
Evergreen, tuberous, trailing perennial
grown as an annual, with 3-lobed, bright
lime green leaves. In summer, may
produce trumpet-shaped, purple-
throated, lavender flowers, 1in (2.5cm)
across. Is good in a mixed container.
H 6–12in (15–30cm), **S** 18–24in (45–60cm).

☀ ◊ ⚠ Z11 H11–1

***Viola* 'Green Goddess'**
Evergreen, clump-forming perennial,
often grown as an annual, with small,
oval, toothed, dark green leaves. Flattish,
5-petaled flowers, with whiskered,
yellow centers surrounded by hazy
green zones, are borne from spring
to fall. **H** 6in (15cm), **S** 10in (25cm).

☀ ◊ Z5–8 H8–5

***Perilla* 'Magilla Vanilla'**
Fast-growing perennial, grown as an
annual, with broadly oval, bright green
leaves brightly splashed in the centers
in rich cream. Spikes of tiny, bell-shaped
flowers are occasionally borne in late
summer; pinch them out. **H** 24–36in
(60–90cm), **S** 18–24in (45–60cm).

☀ ◊ H12–1

Setaria macrostachya (Italian millet)
Upright, clump-forming, perennial
grass, grown as an annual. Has long,
pointed, coarse, mid-green leaves each
with a pale central stripe. Erect spikes
of bristly, vivid green flower heads are
produced in summer. **H** 3ft (90cm),
S 2ft (60cm).

☀ ◊ Z9–11 H12–7

Argyranthemum 'Jamaica Primrose'
Evergreen, woody-based perennial with fernlike, pale green leaves. Daisylike, single, soft yellow flower heads are borne in summer. Take stem cuttings in early fall. **H** and **S** to 3ft (1m).

☼ ◊ Z7–11 H11–1

Osteospermum 'Buttermilk'
Evergreen, upright, semiwoody perennial. Daisylike, pale yellow flower heads, with dark eyes, are borne singly amid gray-green foliage from mid-summer to fall. **H** 24in (60cm), **S** 12in (30cm).

☼ ◊ H6–1

Brugmansia x candida 'Grand Marnier'
Evergreen, robust shrub with large, oval to elliptic leaves. Pendent, flared, trumpet-shaped, apricot flowers open from an inflated calyx in summer. **H** 10–15ft (3–5m), **S** 5–8ft (1.5–2.5m). Min. 45–50°F (7–10°C).

☼ ◊ ❗ Z11 H11–10

Iresine herbstii 'Aureoreticulata'
Evergreen, bushy perennial with red stems and inconspicuous flowers. Rounded, mid-green leaves, 4in (10cm) long, have yellow or red veins and notched tips. **H** to 24in (60cm), **S** 18in (45cm). Min. 50–59°F (10–15°C).

☼ ◊ Z11 H11–1

Euryops pectinatus
Evergreen, upright shrub. Deeply cut, gray-green leaves set off large heads of daisylike, bright yellow flowers, borne in late spring and early summer and often again in winter. **H** and **S** 3ft (1m). Min. 41–5°F (5–7°C).

☼ ◊ Z11 H11–9

Argyranthemum BUTTERFLY **('Ulyssis')**
Evergreen subshrub, grown as an annual, with finely divided, dark green leaves. Prolific, daisylike, single, bright yellow flower heads are produced in summer–fall. **H** 18–36in (45–90cm), **S** 15–18in (38–45cm).

☼ ◊ Z8–11 H11–1

Duranta erecta
(Pigeonberry, golden dewdrop)
Fast-growing, usually evergreen, bushy shrub. Has spikes of lilac-blue flowers, mainly in summer, followed by yellow fruits. **H** 10–20ft (3–6m), **S** 6–10ft (2–3m). Min. 50°F (10°C).

☼ ◊ Z11 H11–10

Bidens 'Gold Star'
Rather spreading, short-lived perennial, grown as an annual. Semi-trailing stems have divided leaves and bear star-shaped, golden-eyed, bright yellow flower heads in summer–fall. **H** 12in (30cm), **S** 18in (45cm).

☼ ◊ Z8–11 H11–7

Duranta erecta 'Gold Edge'
Evergreen, fast-growing, bushy shrub, grown as an annual, with oval, toothed, glossy, bright green leaves, 2–3in (5–7.5cm) long, irregularly margined in bright yellow. Rarely flowers. **H** and **S** 24in (60cm).

☼ ◊ Z11 H11–10

Antirrhinum majus Liberty Classic Series **'Liberty Yellow'**
Erect perennial, grown as an annual, branching from the base. Has lance-shaped, dull green leaves and in summer–fall bears spikes of tubular, 2-lipped, 2-tone yellow flowers. **H** 18–22in (45–55cm), **S** 12–14in (30–35cm).

☼ ◊ Z9–11 H11–1

Glaucium flavum (Horned poppy)
Slow-growing, erect biennial with oval, lobed, light grayish-green leaves. Poppy-like, vivid yellow flowers, 3in (8cm) wide, appear in summer and early fall. **H** 12–24in (30–60cm), **S** 18in (45cm).

☼ ◊ ❗ Z6–9 H9–6

Tagetes Gold Coins Series
Fast-growing, erect, bushy annual. Has aromatic, feathery, glossy, deep green leaves and large, daisylike, double flower heads in shades of yellow and orange in summer and early fall. **H** 36in (90cm), **S** 12–18in (30–45cm).

☼ ◊ ❗ H12–1

Sanvitalia procumbens (Creeping zinnia)
Moderately fast-growing, prostrate annual with pointed-oval leaves. Daisylike, yellow flower heads, 1in (2.5cm) wide, with black centers, are borne in summer. **H** 6in (15cm), **S** 12in (30cm).

☼ ◊ Z5–11 H12–1

Nemesia Sunsatia Series
SUNSATIA MANGO ('Inupyel')
Evergreen, semi-trailing, woody-based perennial, grown as an annual, with lance-shaped, mid-green leaves. Racemes of 2-lipped, yellow flowers, with golden lips and purple throats, are borne in summer. **H** 9in (23cm), **S** 18in (45cm).

☼ ◊ Z9–10 H10–1

Xerochrysum bracteatum Sundaze Series SUNDAZE GOLD ('Redbragol')
Bushy, rounded, short-lived perennial, grown as an annual, with lance-shaped, mid-green leaves. Produces small, papery, daisylike, yellow flower heads, with orange centers, in summer–fall. **H** 8–12in (20–30cm), **S** 12in (30cm).

☼ ◗ Z8–10 H10–7

Rudbeckia hirta 'Toto Gold'
Upright, strong-stemmed biennial or short-lived perennial, often grown as an annual, with ovate to lance-shaped, mid-green leaves. Has large, daisylike, bright yellow flower heads with very dark brown centers in summer and early fall. **H** and **S** to 18in (45cm).

☼ ◊ Z3–7 H7–1

Antirrhinum majus
Chimes Series [yellow]
Erect perennial usually grown as an annual, with branching shoots and mid- to dark green, lance-shaped leaves. During summer and fall produces racemes of bright yellow, 2-lipped flowers. **H** 12in (30cm), **S** 8in (20cm).

☼ ◊ Z9–11 H11–1

Platystemon californicus
(Cream cups)
Moderately fast-growing, upright, compact annual with lance-shaped, grayish-green leaves. Saucer-shaped, cream or pale yellow flowers, about 1in (2.5cm) across, appear in summer. **H** 12in (30cm), **S** 4in (10cm).

☼ ◊ H11–7

Argemone mexicana
(Devil's fig, Prickly poppy)
Spreading perennial, grown as an annual, with leaves divided into white-marked, grayish-green leaflets. In summer has fragrant, poppy-like, yellow or orange flowers, 3in (8cm) wide. **H** to 24in (60cm), **S** 12in (30cm).

☼ ◊ H11–1

Calendula officinalis 'Daisy May'
Fast-growing, bushy annual with aromatic, lance-shaped, mid-green leaves and numerous, semidouble, yellow flower heads from late spring to fall. **H** and **S** 12–16in (30–40cm).

☼ ◊ H6–1

Coreopsis grandiflora 'Sunray'
Spreading, clump-forming perennial, grown as an annual by sowing under glass in early spring. Has lance-shaped, serrated leaves and daisylike, double, bright yellow flower heads in summer. **H** 18in (45cm), **S** 12–18in (30–45cm).

☼ ◊ Z4–9 H11–1

Smyrnium perfoliatum
Slow-growing, upright biennial. Upper leaves, rounded and yellow-green, encircle stems that bear heads of yellowish-green flowers in summer. **H** 2–3ft (60cm–1m), **S** 2ft (60cm).

☼ ◊ Z6–10 H8–1

Cladanthus arabicus
Moderately fast-growing, hummock-forming annual with aromatic, feathery, light green leaves. Has fragrant, daisylike, single, deep yellow flower heads, 2in (5cm) wide, in summer and early fall. **H** 24in (60cm), **S** 12in (30cm).

☼ ◊ H12–1

Coreopsis tinctoria (Tickseed)
Fast-growing, erect, bushy annual with lance-shaped leaves. Large, daisylike, bright yellow flower heads with red centers are carried in summer and early fall. **H** 24–36in (60–90cm), **S** 8in (20cm).

☼ ◊ Z4–9 H12–1

Eschscholzia caespitosa
Fast-growing, slender, erect annual with feathery, bluish-green leaves. Cup-shaped, 4-petaled, yellow flowers, 1in (2.5cm) wide, appear in summer and early fall. **H** and **S** 6in (15cm).

☼ ◊ Z8–10 H9–2

Limnanthes douglasii
(Meadow foam, Poached-egg flower)
Fast-growing, slender, erect annual. Feathery leaves are glossy, light green; slightly fragrant, cup-shaped, white flowers with yellow centers are carried from early to late summer. **H** 6in (15cm), **S** 4in (10cm).

☼ ◊ H9–1

ANNUALS, BIENNIALS, AND BEDDING

Mimulus Magic Series 'Magic Yellow Blotch'

Erect, well-branched perennial, grown as an annual. Fleshy stems bear small, oval, toothed, mid-green leaves and in summer bear flared, tubular flowers in bright yellow heavily blotched in red. **H** and **S** 6–8in (15–20cm).

☼ ◊ Z9–10 H10–1

Xanthophthalmum segetum

Moderately fast-growing, erect annual with lance-shaped, gray-green leaves. Daisylike, single flower heads, to 3in (8cm) wide, in shades of yellow, are carried in summer and early fall. Is excellent for cut flowers. **H** 18in (45cm), **S** 12in (30cm).

☼ ◊ H9–1

Helianthus annuus 'Teddy Bear'

Fast-growing, compact, hairy-stemmed annual with toothed, roughly hairy leaves. Produces daisylike, double, deep yellow flower heads, to 5in (13cm) across, in summer. **H** 36in (90cm), **S** to 24in (60cm).

☼ ◊ ① H11–1

Calendula officinalis Pacific Beauty Series 'Lemon Queen'

Fast-growing, erect annual with softly hairy, aromatic leaves. Daisylike, double, lemon-yellow flower heads, with red-brown disc-florets, are borne from summer to fall. **H** to 18in (45cm), **S** 12–18in (30–45cm).

☼ ◊ H6–1

Tagetes 'Naughty Marietta'

Fast-growing, bushy annual with aromatic, deeply cut, deep green leaves. Heads of daisylike, bicolored flowers, deep yellow and maroon, are carried in summer and early fall. **H** and **S** 12in (30cm).

☼ ◊ ① H12–1

Ursinia anthemoides

Moderately fast-growing, bushy annual with feathery, pale green leaves. Small, daisylike, purple-centered flower heads with orange-yellow rays, purple beneath, appear in summer and early fall. **H** 12in (30cm), **S** 8in (20cm).

☼ ◊ H12–6

Helianthus annuus 'Music Box'

Fast-growing, free-flowering, many-branched, hairy-stemmed annual. Bears daisylike flower heads, 4–5in (10–12cm) across, with ray-florets ranging from creamy-yellow to dark red, and black disc-florets, in summer. **H** 28in (70cm), **S** to 24in (60cm).

☼ ◊ ① H11–1

Begonia 'Herzog von Sagan'

Upright Tuberhybrida begonia with few side shoots. Double, yellow flowers, 8in (20cm) across, with rough-edged, red petals, are borne in summer. **H** 3ft (1m), **S** 1½ft (45cm). Min. 41–45°F (5–7°C).

☼ ◐ ◊ H11–1

Gazania Daybreak Series 'Daybreak Bright Yellow'
Spreading perennial, grown as an annual, with narrowly lance-shaped, dark-green leaves. Daisylike, vivid yellow flower heads, 3in (7.5cm) across, with a dark ring round each golden eye, are borne all summer. **H** and **S** 8in (20cm).

☼ ◔ Z8–10 H10–8

Viola x wittrockiana Angel Series 'Tiger Eye'
Clump-forming, short-lived perennial, grown as a biennial or annual, with small, oval, toothed, dark leaves. 5-petaled, burnished-gold flowers, patterned with chestnut-brown whiskers, are borne in spring. **H** and **S** 8in (20cm).

☼ ◔ Z8–11 H9–1

Lysimachia congestiflora 'Outback Sunset'
Mat-forming or trailing perennial, grown as an annual. Lance-shaped, red-tinged, dark green leaves, 2in (5cm) long, are irregularly splashed in yellow. Has clusters of 5-lobed, trumpet-shaped, yellow flowers in summer. **H** 4in (10cm), **S** 12in (30cm).

☼ ◔ Z6–9 H9–6

Carthamus tinctorius
Moderately fast-growing, upright annual with coarse, spine-edged, linear foliage. Produces tufted, thistle-like flowers, surrounded by stiff green bracts, in summer. Suitable for drying. **H** and **S** 12–24in (30–60cm).

☼ ◔ H11–3

Tropaeolum majus Alaska Series
Fast-growing, bushy annual with rounded, variegated leaves. Spurred, trumpet-shaped flowers, in shades of red or yellow, appear in summer and early fall. **H** and **S** 12in (30cm).

☼ ◔ Z10–11 H9–1

Rudbeckia hirta 'Marmalade'
Moderately fast-growing, erect, branching perennial, grown as an annual, with lance-shaped leaves. In summer–fall bears daisylike, deep golden-orange flower heads, 3in (8cm) wide, with black centers. **H** 18in (45cm), **S** 12in (30cm).

☼ ◔ Z3–7 H7–1

ANNUALS, BIENNIALS, AND BEDDING

Erysimum x _allionii_ 'Orange Bedder'
Slow-growing, short-lived, evergreen, bushy perennial, grown as a biennial. Has lance-shaped, mid-green leaves. Heads of scented, 4-petaled, brilliant orange flowers appear in spring. **H** and **S** 12in (30cm).

☼ ◊ Z3–7 H7–1

Sanvitalia procumbens 'Mandarin Orange'
Moderately fast-growing, prostrate annual. Has pointed-oval, mid-green leaves and daisylike, orange flower heads, 1in (2.5cm) wide, in summer. **H** 6in (15cm), **S** 12in (30cm).

☼ ◊ Z5–11 H12–1

Portulaca Sundial Series 'Mango'
Spreading, slightly succulent perennial, grown as an annual, with lance-shaped, fleshy, red-tinted, dark green leaves. In summer bears bowl-shaped, semidouble, peach flowers, 2in (5cm) across. **H** 8–15in (20–38cm), **S** 10–12in (25–30cm).

☼ ◊ Z9–11 H9–1

Gazania Kiss Series 'Kiss Orange Flame'
Spreading perennial, grown as an annual, with long, narrowly lance-shaped, dark green leaves. All summer produces daisylike, orange flowers, 3in (7.5cm) across, with mahogany-striped petals. **H** and **S** 8in (20cm).

☼ ◊ Z10–11 H11–1

Tagetes Boy Series [orange]
Compact annual that bears double, crested flower heads in a range of colors, including shades of golden-yellow, yellow, orange or reddish-brown, with deep orange or yellow crests, in late spring and early summer. **H** to 6in (15cm), **S** to 12in (30cm).

☼ ◊ ❗ H12–1

Tithonia rotundifolia 'Torch'
Slow-growing, erect annual with rounded, lobed leaves. Has daisylike, bright orange or scarlet flower heads, 2–3in (5–7cm) wide, in summer and early fall. **H** 36in (90cm), **S** 12in (30cm).

☼ ◊ Z10–11 H12–1

Rudbeckia hirta 'Goldilocks'
Moderately fast-growing, erect, branching perennial, grown as an annual. Has lance-shaped leaves and daisylike, double or semidouble, golden-orange flower heads, 3in (8cm) across, in summer–fall. **H** 24in (60cm), **S** 12in (30cm).

☼ ◊ Z3–7 H7–1

Abutilon pictum 'Thompsonii'
Robust, evergreen, upright shrub with 3–5-lobed, serrated, rich green, heavily yellow-mottled leaves. Yellow-orange flowers with crimson veins are borne from summer to fall. **H** 15ft (5m), **S** 6–15ft (2–5m). Min. 41–5°F (5–7°C).

☼ ◊ Z8–10 H11–8

Calendula officinalis Fiesta Gitana Group
Fast-growing, bushy annual with strongly aromatic, lance-shaped, pale green leaves. Daisylike, double flower heads, ranging from cream to orange in color, are carried from spring to fall. **H** and **S** 12in (30cm).

☼ ◊ H6–1

Lantana 'Spreading Sunset'
Evergreen, rounded to spreading shrub with finely wrinkled, deep green leaves. Has tiny, tubular flowers in a range of colors, carried in dense, rounded heads from spring to fall. **H** and **S** 3–6ft (1–2m). Min. 50–55°F (10–13°C).

☼ ◊ ① Z11 H11–1

Zinnia haageana 'Orange Star'
Dwarf, bushy annual with daisylike, broad-petaled, orange flower heads, borne in summer. Is mildew-resistant and good for groundcover. **H** to 10in (25cm), **S** to 12in (30cm).

☼ ◊ H12–1

Impatiens Sunpatiens Series
SUNPATIENS COMPACT ORANGE ('Sakimp011')
Mound-forming, well-branched, prolific perennial, grown as an annual. Has flattish, 5-petaled, spurred, thick-petaled, vivid orange flowers, 2½in (6cm) across, in summer. **H** and **S** 24in (60cm).

☼ ◖ H10–1

Impatiens Fusion Series
FUSION PEACH FROST ('Balfuspeafro')
Evergreen, bushy perennial, grown as an annual, with elliptical, pale green leaves margined in cream. Tubular, 5-petaled, peach-pink flowers, ⅝in (1.5cm) across, with orange centers, are borne in summer. **H** and **S** 10–16in (25–40cm).

☼ ◖ H10–1

Tagetes 'Tangerine Gem'
Fast-growing, bushy annual with
aromatic, feathery leaves. Small, single,
deep orange flower heads appear in
summer and early fall. **H** 8in (20cm),
S 12in (30cm).

☼ ◊ ❶ H12–1

Coreopsis 'Rum Punch'
Bushy, rather spreading, prolific but
short-lived perennial, grown as an
annual. Slender stems have divided, dark
green leaves and in summer–fall bear
daisylike, coppery-pink flower heads,
1½in (3.5cm) across. **H** 18in (45cm),
S 24in (60cm).

☼ ◊ Z10–11 H10–1

Calendula officinalis 'Geisha Girl'
Fast-growing, bushy annual with
strongly aromatic, lance-shaped, pale
green leaves. Heads of double, orange
flowers with incurved petals are borne
from late spring to fall. **H** 24in (60cm),
S 12–24in (30–60cm).

☼ ◊ H6–1

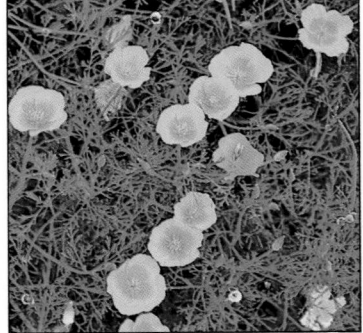

Eschscholzia californica
Fast-growing, slender, erect annual
with feathery, bluish-green leaves.
Cup-shaped, 4-petalled, vivid orange-
yellow flowers are borne in summer–fall.
H 12in (30cm), **S** 6in (15cm).

☼ ◊ Z11 H9–1

Erysimum cheiri 'Fire King'
Moderately fast-growing, evergreen,
bushy perennial, grown as a biennial.
Lance-shaped leaves are mid- to deep
green; heads of 4-petaled, reddish-
orange flowers are carried in spring.
H 15in (38cm), **S** 12–15in (30–38cm).

☼ ◊ Z3–7 H7–1

Emilia coccinea (Tassel flower)
Moderately fast-growing, upright annual with lance-shaped, grayish-green leaves and double, red or yellow flower heads in summer. **H** 12–24in (30–60cm), **S** 12in (30cm).

☼ ◊ H9–1

Solanum pseudocapsicum **'Red Giant'**
Fairly slow-growing, evergreen, bushy shrub, usually grown as an annual. Has lance-shaped, deep green leaves, small, white flowers in summer and large, round, orange-red fruits in winter. **H** and **S** 12in (30cm). Min. 41°F (5°C).

☼ ◊ ! Z11–12 H12–6

Tropaeolum **Jewel Series**
Fast-growing, bushy annual with rounded leaves. Spurred, trumpet-shaped flowers, in shades of red, yellow or orange, are held well above leaves from early summer to early fall. **H** and **S** 12in (30cm).

☼ ◊ Z11–12 H12–1

Dahlia **Dahlietta Series** **'Surprise Kelly'**
Compact, bushy, well-branched, tuberous perennial, grown as an annual. In summer has pointed-oval, toothed leaves and flat heads of daisylike, golden-yellow flowers, very heavy speckled in dark orange. **H** 10–12in (25–30cm), **S** 14–16in (35–40cm).

☼ ◊ Z9–11 H11–1

Eschscholzia californica **Thai Silk Series**
Fast-growing, compact, slender, erect annual with feathery, bluish-green leaves. In summer–fall, produces single or semidouble, fluted, bronze-tinged flowers in red, pink or orange. **H** 8–10in (20–25cm), **S** 6in (15cm).

☼ ◊

Gaillardia pulchella **'Lollipops'**
Moderately fast-growing, upright annual with lance-shaped, hairy, grayish-green leaves. Daisylike, double, red-and-yellow flower heads, 2in (5cm) wide, are carried in summer. **H** and **S** 12in (30cm).

☼ ◊ Z10–11 H11–1

Dahlia **'Dandy'**
Well-branched, erect, bushy, tuberous perennial, grown as an annual. Has pointed-oval, serrated leaves and heads of daisylike flowers, with contrasting central collars of quilled petals, in shades of red, yellow or orange in summer. **H** and **S** 24in (60cm).

☼ ◊ Z9–11 H11–1

Solanum pseudocapsicum **'Balloon'**
Evergreen, bushy shrub, grown as an annual. Has lance-shaped leaves and, in summer, small, star-shaped, white flowers. Large, cream fruits turn orange in winter. **H** 12in (30cm), **S** 12–18in (30–45cm). Min. 41°F (5°C).

☼ ◊ ! Z11–12 H12–6

ROCK PLANTS

Rock plants are prized for their natural charm, foliage forms, and, in many cases, masses of colorful flowers in spring and summer. Grow them in areas that mimic the conditions in which they thrive in the wild, which are usually exposed sites with stony, rapidly draining soils. As long as they have sharp drainage and protection from excessive winter moisture, you can grow rock plants in small gardens in a trough or container, or where there is more space, in a rock garden or scree bed. If the soil in your garden is unsuitable, you can also grow these ground-hugging plants in raised beds to create landscapes in miniature. Raised beds also have the advantage of bringing the small plants closer to eye level so that you can admire their tiny, delicate features in more detail.

ROCK PLANTS

The delicate flowers and foliage of many rock plants belies their tough nature, withstanding the burning sun and harsh winds typical of their alpine habitats. They make excellent plants for the garden, and are perfect for rock and scree gardens, wall crevices, troughs, and pots.

SIZE CATEGORIES USED WITHIN THIS GROUP		
Large over 6in (15cm)	**Medium** —	**Small** up to 6in (15cm)

What are rock plants?

The term rock plants includes bulbs and mat- and cushion-forming perennials— many of which are evergreen—as well as dwarf conifers and both evergreen and deciduous shrubs. Some are true alpines from mountain regions, while others are simply compact plants suitable for rock-garden planting schemes. While some alpines have specialized needs, many species and cultivars, including aubrietas and geraniums, are easy to grow and thrive in any well-drained soil and sunny site.

True alpines are found at high altitudes above the tree line on mountains, growing on scree slopes, in short sod, or finding protection from the wind by squeezing into rock crevices. Subalpine plants live below the tree line on rocky slopes or in high pastures or meadows. Most alpines are compact in habit and frequently deep-rooting, usually with small leaves that are leathery, fleshy, or covered in fine hair.

These adaptations help them survive the drying, high-velocity winds, brilliant, burning sun, and extreme temperature fluctuations of their natural habitats.

Most rock plants grow in areas that have stony soil with rapid drainage, which explains why few can cope with wet soil around the roots, which is experienced at lower altitudes. They also dislike warm, humid summers.

In the wild, high-growing species are insulated from winter cold by a blanket of snow, beneath which they remain dormant at temperatures around 32°F (0°C) until spring. Those environments that mimic conditions in the wild, such as rock gardens, scree and gravel beds, troughs, pots, raised beds, and open frames, are therefore ideal for growing rock plants. You can grow alpines successfully even in areas where the soil is unsuitable by filling raised beds, pots, and troughs with free-draining soil and horticultural grit.

Designing with rock plants

One of the major attractions of this group is their diminutive size, which allows you to grow a huge number of different plant types in a relatively confined space.

In a rock garden—as in larger-scale plantings—use small shrubs, such as the highly fragrant *Daphne cneorum* and *D. retusa* or the catkin-bearing *Salix bockii* and *S. apoda*, to form the structural framework of your design. Miniature conifers, such as *Juniperus communis* 'Compressa', provide vertical accents and year-round color, and work well in combination with the contrasting forms of rounded or domed plants, such as the evergreen *Hebe cupressoides* 'Boughton Dome' and *Cassiope lycopodioides*.

This structure can then be filled in with mat- and cushion-forming plants, such as sandworts (*Arenaria*) or *Dianthus deltoides*,

ABOVE Mediterranean mountains
Recreate a Mediterranean alpine scene with clay pots and pebbles decorating beds that include a range of sedums, saxifrages, thymes, and arabis, with clipped boxwood balls providing structure.

LEFT Colorful tapestry
Siting a rock garden on a gentle slope assists rapid drainage, while an open, sunny site is perfect for alpines. Choose plants with contrasting forms, such as teardrop-shaped, upright conifers and mats of colorful blooms.

ROCK PLANTS

PLANTING A GRAVEL OR SCREE GARDEN

Gravel gardens are ideal for alpines and rock plants. Stones can be worked into a scheme to create a rock garden, or a variety of rock and stone sizes used on a slope to form a natural scree. A gravel or slate chip mulch helps to keep the plant leaves and stems dry and prevents rotting, but lay weed-suppressing fabric over the soil first. This eliminates light and stops weed seeds from germinating but still allows moisture through to the plant.

A weed-free gravel garden

1 Lay the fabric
Measure your bed, and buy sufficient weed-suppressing fabric to cover it. Overlap the edges when joining two pieces together. Cut crosses where you plan to plant.

2 Plant up
Fold back the flaps, and dig a hole, putting the excavated soil on a plastic sheet. Insert the plant, water in, and backfill with soil. Firm in and replace the flaps around the plant stems.

3 Add gravel mulch
Trim the fabric around the stems and continue to plant in this way. When the bed is planted, spread a 2–3in (5–8cm) layer of gravel over the fabric and around each plant.

at the feet of slightly taller, feathery-leaved pulsatillas or the airy *Linum narbonense*. As well as shape and form, think about contrasting textures. Candidates include the almost beadlike foliage of certain sedums, spiky houseleek (*Sempervivum*) rosettes, and the pointy-tipped gray leaves of *Euphorbia myrsinites*, which would make eye-catching partners for the white-haired leaves of edelweiss (*Leontopodium*) or the silky, silver leaves of celmisias.

Most alpines like an open sunny site and will not thrive if they are shaded by overhanging trees or neighboring plants. Plant them with space to spread, and use a dry mulch, such as gravel, to keep the stems and leaves dry at all times. Mulches also act as a foil for the plants.

If you have limited space, plant a selection of alpines in small pots filled with gritty potting mix. Many plants in this group are drought-tolerant and thrive in containers, and when grouped together make colorful displays. Troughs can be given a modern makeover by planting alpines between slate chips (see box right), or using a ground glass or shell mulch.

Raised beds offer another design option for those with small gardens. They are also useful for people with reduced mobility, allowing them to access the plants more easily. Use raised beds to create miniature landscapes with plants spreading between rocks and pebbles. Dry-stone walls offer ideal sites for many crevice-lovers, such as aubretias and sedums, while cascading alpines, such as *Saxifraga* 'Tumbling Waters', are perfect for the tops of walls.

Year-round interest

Many alpines flower in spring and early summer, just after the snow melts and before the heat of mid-summer in their natural habitat. For color earlier in the year, plant spring bulbs, such as alpine narcissus or crocuses, among evergreen perennials, conifers, and small shrubs. The choice of flowers at the peak flowering times is vast, so coordinate your color schemes for a dramatic performance. Hot colors, such as the bright yellow sedums and wallflowers (*Erysimum*) and scarlet and orange helianthemums, create highlights against more subdued blues and purples. As the summer progresses, select later-flowering rock plants, including phlox, crepis, and diascias, followed by the pink *Silene schafta*, gentians, and berry-bearing gaultherias in the fall.

PLANTING A SLATE-FILLED TROUGH

Topped with slate chips, this decorative trough mirrors a natural mountain scree, and provides a long season of color in spring and summer. Plants included in this display are *Draba* species, erigerons, saxifrages, *Silene acaulis* and *Townsendia grandiflora*. However, any small alpines that have different leaf textures and flower colors will work equally well. Move your trough to its final position before you start, as it will be very heavy once planted.

1 Prepare the trough
Cover the drainage holes at the base of the trough with crocks. Add a 2in (5cm) layer of gravel. Fill up the trough with equal parts of soil-based potting mix and sand, to 2in (5cm) from the top.

2 Add slates and plants
Push the slate chips vertically into the medium, leaving spaces for the alpines. Water the plants, and plant them into the gaps, making sure the roots are covered with the sand and soil mix. Water well.

ROCK PLANTS

Leontopodium alpinum (Edelweiss)
Short-lived perennial with lance-shaped, woolly leaves. Small, silvery-white flower heads, in spring or early summer, are surrounded by petal-like, felted bracts in a star shape. Dislikes wet. **H** and **S** 6–8in (15–20cm).

☼ ◊ Z4–6 H6–1

Lithophragma parviflorum
Clump-forming, tuberous perennial that has small, open clusters of campion-like, white or pink flowers in spring above a basal cluster of deeply toothed, kidney-shaped leaves. Lies dormant in summer. **H** 6–8in (15–20cm), **S** to 8in (20cm).

☼ ◊ Z4–6 H6–1

Iberis sempervirens
Evergreen, spreading subshrub, with narrow, oblong, dark green leaves, bearing dense, rounded heads of white flowers in late spring and early summer. Trim after flowering. **H** 6–12in (15–30cm), **S** 18–24in (45–60cm).

☼ ◊ Z5–9 H9–3

Pulsatilla alpina (Alpine anemone)
Tufted perennial with feathery leaves. Has upright, or nodding, cup-shaped, white, sometimes blue- or pink-flushed flowers singly in spring and early summer, then feathery seed heads. **H** 6–12in (15–30cm), **S** to 4in (10cm).

☼ ◊ ① Z5–7 H7–5

Saxifraga granulata (Fair maids of France, Meadow saxifrage)
Clump-forming perennial that loses its kidney-shaped, crumpled, glossy leaves in summer. Sticky stems carry loose panicles of rounded, white flowers in late spring. **H** 9–15in (23–38cm), **S** to 6in (15cm) or more.

◑ ◊ Z7–8 H8–7

Rhodanthemum hosmariense
Evergreen, shrubby perennial with finely cut, bright silvery-green leaves that clothe lax, woody stems. From late spring to early fall, white flower heads are borne singly above foliage. **H** 6in (15cm) or more, **S** 12in (30cm).

☼ ◊ Z9–11 H11–7

Andromeda polifolia 'Alba'
Evergreen, open, twiggy shrub bearing terminal clusters of pitcher-shaped, white flowers in spring and early summer. Glossy, dark green leaves are leathery and lance-shaped. **H** 18in (45cm), **S** 24in (60cm).

☼ ◊ pH Z2–6 H6–1

Cassiope 'Muirhead'
Evergreen, loose, bushy shrub with scalelike, dark green leaves on upright branches. In spring, these bear tiny, virtually stemless, bell-shaped, white flowers along their length. **H** and **S** 8in (20cm).

◑ ◊ pH Z2–6 H6–1

Cassiope tetragona
Evergreen, upright shrub with dense, scalelike, dark green leaves concealing branched stems. In spring, leaf axils bear solitary pendent, bell-shaped, white flowers in red calyces. **H** 4–10in (10–25cm), **S** 4–6in (10–15cm).

☼ ◊ pH Z2–7 H7–1

Jeffersonia diphylla
Slow-growing, tufted perennial with distinctive, 2-lobed, light to mid-green leaves. Bears solitary cup-shaped, white flowers with prominent, yellow stamens in late spring. Do not disturb roots.
H 6–9in (15–23cm), **S** to 9in (23cm).

☀ ◊ Z5–7 H7–5

Daphne blagayana
Evergreen, prostrate shrub with trailing branches each bearing a terminal cluster of oval, leathery leaves and, in early spring, dense clusters of fragrant, tubular, white flowers. Likes rich soil. **H** 12–16in (30–40cm), **S** 24–32in (60–80cm) or more.

☀ ◊ ❗ Z7–9 H9–7

Tiarella cordifolia (Foamflower)
Vigorous, evergreen, spreading perennial. Lobed, pale green leaves sometimes have darker marks; veins turn bronze-red in winter. Bears many spikes of profuse white flowers in late spring and early summer. **H** 6–8in (15–20cm), **S** to 12in (30cm) or more.

☀ ◊ Z3–8 H7–1

Saxifraga 'Tumbling Waters'
Slow-growing, evergreen, mat-forming perennial with a tight rosette of narrow, lime-encrusted leaves. After several years produces arching sprays of white flowers in conical heads; main rosette then dies but small offsets survive.
H to 24in (60cm), **S** to 8in (20cm).

☀ ◊ Z6–7 H7–6

Daphne alpina
Compact and upright deciduous shrub with softly hairy, oval, gray-green leaves. In late spring produces terminal clusters of small, white flowers that are sweetly scented. These are followed by spherical, orange-red fruits. **H** and **S** to 24in (60cm).

☀ ◊ ❗ Z6–8 H8–6

Dodecatheon meadia f. album
Clump-forming perennial with basal rosettes of oval, pale green leaves. In spring, strong stems bear several white flowers with dark centers and reflexed petals. Lies dormant in summer. **H** 8in (20cm), **S** 6in (15cm).

☀ ◊ Z4–8 H8–1

Andromeda polifolia 'Compacta'
Evergreen, compact, twiggy shrub that bears delicate, terminal clusters of pitcher-shaped, coral-pink flowers, with white undertones, in spring and early summer. Leaves are lance-shaped and glossy, dark green. **H** 6–9in (15–23cm), **S** 12in (30cm).

☀ ◊ pH Z2–6 H6–1

Dodecatheon hendersonii
Clump-forming perennial with a flat rosette of kidney-shaped leaves, above which deep pink flowers with reflexed petals appear in late spring. Needs a dry, dormant summer period. **H** 12in (30cm), **S** 3in (8cm).

☀ ◊ Z5–7 H7–5

Phyllodoce x intermedia 'Drummondii'
Evergreen, bushy, dwarf shrub with narrow, heather-like, glossy leaves. From late spring to early summer bears terminal clusters of pitcher-shaped, rich pink flowers on slender, red stalks. **H** and **S** 9in (23cm).

☀ ◊ pH Z3–7 H7–1

Daphne cneorum
Evergreen, low-growing shrub with trailing branches clothed in small, oval, leathery, dark green leaves. Fragrant, deep rose pink flowers are borne in terminal clusters in late spring. Prefers rich soil. **H** 9in (23cm), **S** to 6ft (2m).

☀ ◊ ❗ Z5–7 H7–5

Dodecatheon pulchellum 'Red Wings'
Clump-forming perennial with a basal cluster of oblong, soft, pale green leaves. In late spring and early summer bears small, loose clusters of deep magenta flowers, with reflexed petals, on strong stems. Lies dormant in summer. **H** 8in (20cm), **S** 4in (10cm).

☀ ◊ Z4–7 H8–2

ROCK PLANTS

333

ROCK PLANTS

Phyllodoce empetriformis
Evergreen, mat-forming shrub with fine narrow, heather-like leaves and terminal clusters of bell-shaped, purplish-pink flowers in late spring and early summer. **H** 6–9in (15–23cm), **S** 8in (20cm).

☼ ◗ pH ⬡ Z3–6 H6–1

Phyllodoce caerulea
Evergreen, dwarf shrub with fine, narrow, heather-like leaves. Bears bell-shaped, purple to purplish-pink flowers, singly or in clusters, in late spring and summer. **H** and **S** to 12in (30cm).

☼ ◗ pH Z2–5 H5–1

Daphne x hendersonii 'Blackthorn Rose'
Evergreen, domed shrub with glossy, dark green leaves, to 1in (2.5cm) long. In spring produces numerous, rounded deep reddish-purple buds that open to very fragrant, pink flowers with spreading lobes. **H** 8–12in (20–30cm), **S** 18in (45cm).

☼ ◗ ❶ Z3–7 H7–3

Pulsatilla halleri
Tufted perennial, intensely hairy in all parts, that in spring bears nodding, later erect, cup-shaped flowers in shades of purple. Has feathery leaves and seed heads. **H** 6–15in (15–38cm), **S** 6–8in (15–20cm).

☼ ◗ ❶ Z5–7 H7–5

Pulsatilla vulgaris (Pasque flower)
Tufted perennial with feathery, light green leaves. In spring bears nodding, cup-shaped flowers, in shades of purple, red, pink or white, with bright yellow centers. Flower stems rapidly elongate as feathery seeds mature. **H** and **S** 6–9in (15–23cm).

☼ ◗ ❶ Z5–7 H7–5

Erinacea anthyllis (Hedgehog broom)
Slow-growing, evergreen subshrub with hard, blue-green spines. Pealike, soft lavender flowers appear in axils of spines in late spring to early summer. **H** and **S** 6–10in (15–25cm).

☼ ◗ Z7–8 H8–7

Aquilegia alpina (Alpine columbine)
Short-lived, upright perennial with spurred, clear blue or violet-blue flowers on slender stems in spring and early summer. Has basal rosettes of rounded, finely divided leaves. Needs rich soil. **H** to 18in (45cm), **S** to 12in (30cm).

☼ ◗ ❶ Z4–7 H7–1

Omphalodes verna
Semievergreen, clump-forming perennial that in spring bears long, loose sprays of flat, bright blue flowers with white eyes. Leaves are oval and mid-green. **H** and **S** 8in (20cm) or more.

☼ ◗ Z6–9 H9–6

Omphalodes cappadocica
Spreading perennial with creeping underground stems and many loose sprays of flat, bright blue flowers in spring–summer above tufts of oval, hairy, basal leaves. **H** 6–8in (15–20cm), **S** 10in (25cm) or more.

☼ ◗ Z6–8 H8–6

Corydalis cheilanthifolia
Evergreen perennial with fleshy roots. Produces spreading rosettes of fernlike, near-prostrate, sometimes bronze-tinted, mid-green leaves. Has dense spikes of short-spurred, yellow flowers in late spring and early summer. **H** 8–12in (20–30cm), **S** 6–8in (15–20cm).

☼ ◊ Z5–7 H7–3

Salix helvetica
Deciduous, spreading, much-branched, dwarf shrub that has small, oval, glossy leaves, white-haired beneath. In spring bears short-stalked, silky, gray, then yellow catkins. **H** 24in (60cm), **S** 12in (30cm).

☼ ◊ Z5–8 H8–5

Betula nana (Arctic birch)
Deciduous, bushy, dwarf shrub with small, toothed leaves that turn bright yellow in fall. Has tiny, yellowish-brown catkins in spring. **H** 12in (30cm), **S** 18in (45cm).

☼ ◊ pH Z2–5 H5–1

Aurinia saxatilis 'Citrina'
Evergreen, clump-forming perennial with oval, hairy, gray-green leaves. Bears racemes of many, small, pale lemon-yellow flowers in late spring and early summer. **H** 9in (23cm), **S** 12in (30cm).

☼ ◊ Z4–8 H8–1

Corydalis wilsonii
Evergreen perennial with a fleshy rootstock. Forms rosettes of near-prostrate, divided, bluish-green leaves. Loose racemes of spurred, green-tipped, yellow flowers are produced in spring. **H** and **S** 4–10in (10–25cm).

☼ ◊ Z6–7 H7–6

Chiastophyllum oppositifolium
Evergreen, trailing perennial with large, oblong, serrated, succulent leaves. In late spring and early summer bears many tiny, yellow flowers in arching sprays. **H** 6–8in (15–20cm), **S** 6in (15cm).

● ◊ Z6–9 H9–6

Cytisus x beanii
Deciduous, low-growing shrub with arching sprays of pealike, golden-yellow flowers that appear in late spring and early summer on previous year's wood. Leaves, divided into 3 leaflets, are small, linear and hairy. **H** 6–16in (15–40cm), **S** 12–30in (30–75cm).

☼ ◊ ① Z7–8 H8–7

Aurinia saxatilis 'Variegata'
Evergreen perennial that bears racemes of many small, yellow flowers in spring above a mat of large, oval, soft gray-green leaves with cream margins. **H** 9in (23cm), **S** 12in (30cm).

☼ ◊ Z4–8 H8–1

Hylomecon japonica
Vigorous, spreading perennial with large, cup-shaped, bright yellow flowers that are borne singly on slender stems in spring. Soft, dark green leaves are divided into 4 unequal lobes. **H** to 12in (30cm), **S** 8in (20cm).

◑ ◊ Z5–8 H8–5

Erysimum 'Moonlight'
Mat-forming, evergreen perennial with narrowly oval leaves. In early summer, produces clusters of pale, sulfur-yellow flowers on short, leafy stems. Prefers an open site and gritty soil. **H** 10in (25cm), **S** 18in (45cm).

☼ ◊ Z6–8 H8–6

Aurinia saxatilis (Gold dust)
Evergreen perennial forming low clumps of oval, hairy, gray-green leaves. Has substantial spikes of small, chrome-yellow flowers in spring. **H** 9in (23cm), **S** 12in (30cm).

☼ ◊ Z4–8 H8–1

SPRING **SUMMER**

ROCK PLANTS

***Erysimum* 'Bredon'**
Semievergreen, rounded, woody
perennial clothed in oval, dark green
leaves. In late spring bears dense spikes
of flat, bright mustard-yellow flowers.
H 12–18in (30–45cm), **S** 18in (45cm).

☼ ◊ Z5–8 H8–5

***Erysimum* x *kewense* 'Harpur Crewe'**
Evergreen, shrubby perennial with
stiff stems and narrow leaves. Fragrant,
double, deep yellow flowers open
in succession from late spring to
mid-summer. Grows best in poor soil
and a sheltered site. **H** and **S** 12in (30cm).

☼ ◊ Z5–8 H8–5

***Berberis* x *stenophylla*
'Corallina Compacta'**
Evergreen, neat, dwarf shrub with
spiny stems clothed in small, narrowly
oval leaves. In late spring bears many
tiny, bright orange flowers. Is slow-
growing and difficult to propagate.
H and **S** to 10in (25cm).

☼ ◊ ① Z6–9 H9–6

Parnassia palustris
(Grass of Parnassus)
Perennial with low, basal tufts of heart-
shaped, pale to mid-green leaves. Bears
saucer-shaped, white flowers, with dark
green or purplish-green veins, on erect
stems in late spring and early summer.
H 8in (20cm), **S** 2½in (6cm) or more.

☼ ● Z4–11 H11–1

Armeria pseudarmeria
Evergreen, clump-forming perennial
with large, spherical heads of white
flowers occasionally suffused pink;
these are borne in summer on stiff
stems above long, narrow, glaucous
leaves. **H** and **S** 12in (30cm).

☼ ◊ Z6–7 H7–6

Celmisia walkeri
Evergreen, loose, spreading perennial
with long, oval or lance-shaped leaves,
glossy, green above and hairy, white
beneath. Has large, daisylike, white
flower heads in summer. **H** 9in (23cm),
S to 6ft (2m).

☼ ◊ pH Z9–10 H10–9

Helianthemum apenninum
Evergreen, spreading, much-branched
shrub that bears saucer-shaped, pure
white flowers in mid-summer. Stems
and small, linear leaves are covered
in white down. **H** and **S** 18in (45cm).

☼ ◊ Z6–8 H8–5

Galax urceolata
Evergreen, clump-forming perennial.
Large, round, leathery, mid-green
leaves on slender stems turn bronze
in fall-winter. Has dense spikes of
small, white flowers in late spring
and early summer. **H** 6–8in (15–20cm),
S to 12in (30cm).

☼ ◊ pH Z5–8 H8–5

Helianthemum 'Wisley White'
Evergreen, spreading shrub, with
oblong, gray-green leaves, bearing
saucer-shaped, white flowers for a
long period in summer. **H** 9in (23cm),
S 12in (30cm) or more.

☼ ◊ Z6–8 H8–6

Chamaecytisus purpureus f. albus
Deciduous, low-growing shrub with
semi-erect stems clothed in leaves,
divided into 3 leaflets. A profusion of
pealike, white flowers appear in early
summer on previous year's wood.
H 18in (45cm), **S** 24in (60cm).

☼ ◊ Z6–9 H9–6

Saxifraga cuneifolia
Evergreen, carpeting perennial with
neat rosettes of rounded leaves. In late
spring and early summer bears panicles
of tiny, white flowers, frequently with
yellow, pink or red spots, on slender
stems. **H** 6–8in (15–20cm), **S** 12in (30cm)
or more.

☼ ◖ Z5–7 H7–5

Hebe pinguifolia 'Pagei'
Evergreen, semi-prostrate shrub with
small, oblong, slightly cupped, intensely
glaucous leaves. Bears short spikes of
small, white flowers in late spring or
early summer. Is excellent for ground
or rock cover. **H** 6–12in (15–30cm),
S 24in (60cm).

☼ ◊ Z8–10 H10–8

Hebe vernicosa
Evergreen, bushy, compact shrub with
small, oval, glossy, dark green leaves
densely packed on stems. In early and
mid-summer, spikes of small, 4-lobed,
white flowers are freely produced.
H 2ft (60cm), **S** 4ft (1.2m).

☼ ◊ Z9–10 H10–9

Diascia ICE CRACKER ('Hecrack')
Mat-forming perennial with narrowly
ovate, mid to dark green leaves. From
summer to fall produces upright
racemes of 2-lipped, hooded, shallowly
bell-shaped, spurred, white flowers,
touched pink at the base. **H** 12in (30cm),
S 6–8in (5–20cm).

☼ ◊ Z8–9 H9–7

Saxifraga callosa
Evergreen, tightly rosetted perennial
with long, linear, stiff, lime-encrusted
leaves and, in early summer, upright,
then arching panicles of star-shaped,
red-spotted white flowers. Rosettes
die after flowering. Suits a rock pocket.
H 10in (25cm), **S** to 8in (20cm).

☼ ◊ Z7–8 H8–7

Corydalis ochroleuca
Evergreen, clump-forming perennial
with fleshy, fibrous roots and much
divided, basal, gray-green leaves. Bears
slender, yellow-tipped, creamy-white
flowers in late spring and summer.
H and **S** 8–12in (20–30cm).

☼ ◊ Z6–8 H8–6

ROCK PLANTS

Aethionema grandiflorum
(Persian stone cress)
Short-lived, evergreen or semievergreen, lax shrub. Bears tiny, pale to deep rose-pink flowers in loose sprays in spring-summer. Blue-green leaves are narrow and lance-shaped.
H 12in (30cm), **S** 9in (23cm).

☀ ◊ Z5–7 H9–7

Rhodothamnus chamaecistus
Evergreen, low-growing, dwarf shrub with narrow, oval leaves, edged with bristles. In late spring and early summer bears cup-shaped, rose- to lilac-pink flowers, with dark stamens, in leaf axils.
H 6–8in (15–20cm), **S** to 10in (25cm).

☀ ◊ pH Z7–9 H9–7

Phuopsis stylosa
Low-growing perennial with whorls of pungent, pale green leaves and rounded heads of small, tubular, pink flowers in summer. Is good grown over a bank or large rock. **H** 12in (30cm), **S** 12in (30cm) or more.

☀ ◊ Z5–8 H8–5

Lewisia 'George Henley'
Evergreen, clump-forming perennial with rosettes of narrow, fleshy, dark green leaves. Bears dense sprays of open cup-shaped, deep pink flowers, with magenta veins, from late spring to late summer. **H** 6in (15cm) or more, **S** 4in (10cm).

◑ ◊ pH Z7–9 H9–6

Saxifraga 'Southside Seedling'
Evergreen, mat-forming perennial, with large, pale green rosettes of leaves, dying after flowering. In late spring and early summer bears arching panicles of open cup-shaped, white flowers, strongly red-banded within.
H to 12in (30cm), **S** to 8in (20cm).

☀ ◊ Z4–6 H6–1

Helianthemum 'Rhodanthe Carneum'
Evergreen, lax shrub with saucer-shaped, soft, pale pink flowers with orange centers borne for a long period in summer. Has oblong, gray-green leaves. **H** and **S** 12in (30cm) or more.

☀ ◊ Z6–8 H8–6

Onosma alborosea
Semievergreen, clump-forming perennial covered in fine hairs, which may irritate skin. Clusters of long, pendent, tubular flowers, borne for a long period in summer, open white and then turn pink.
H 6–12in (15–30cm), **S** 8in (20cm).

☀ ◊ Z7–9 H9–7

Anthyllis montana
Rounded, bushy or somewhat spreading perennial with loose branches and finely cut foliage. Heads of clover-like, pale pink flowers with red markings are borne in late spring and early summer.
H and **S** 12in (30cm).

☀ ◊ Z6–8 H8–6

Oxalis tetraphylla
Tuft-forming, tuberous perennial with brown-marked, basal leaves, usually divided into 4 leaflets. Produces loose sprays of widely funnel-shaped, deep pink flowers in late spring and summer. Needs a sheltered site.
H 6–12in (15–30cm), **S** 4–6in (10–15cm).

☀ ◊ Z8–9 H9–8

Origanum 'Kent Beauty'
Prostrate perennial with trailing stems
clothed in aromatic, rounded-oval
leaves. In summer bears short spikes
of tubular, pale pink flowers with darker
bracts. Is suitable for a wall or ledge.
H 6–8in (15–20cm), **S** 12in (30cm).

☼ ◊ Z5–8 H8–5

Astilbe x crispa 'Perkeo'
Erect, compact perennial bearing
small plumes of tiny, salmon-pink
flowers from mid- to late summer
on fine stems. Has stiff, deeply cut,
crinkled leaves. **H** 6–8in (15–20cm),
S 4in (10cm).

◐ ◊ Z4–9 H8–2

Diascia barberae 'Fisher's Flora'
Prostrate perennial with stems clothed
in heart-shaped, pale green leaves. Bears
terminal clusters of spurred, flat-faced,
bright pink flowers in summer and early
fall. **H** 6–8in (15–20cm), **S** 8in (20cm).

☼ ◊ Z8–9 H9–8

Crassula sarcocaulis
Evergreen or, in severe climates,
semievergreen, bushy subshrub
with tiny, oval, succulent leaves.
Bears terminal clusters of tiny, red
buds opening to pale pink flowers
in summer. **H** and **S** 12in (30cm).

☼ ◊ H9–1

Ononis fruticosa (Shrubby restharrow)
Deciduous shrub that in summer
bears pendent clusters of large, pealike,
purplish-pink blooms with darker
streaks. Leaves are divided into 3
serrated leaflets, which are hairy when
young. **H** and **S** 12–24in (30–60cm).

☼ ◊ Z7–10 H10–7

Diascia rigescens
Trailing perennial with semi-erect
stems covered in heart-shaped,
mid-green leaves. Spurred, flat-faced,
salmon-pink flowers are borne along
stem length in summer and early fall.
H 9in (23cm), **S** to 12in (30cm).

☼ ◊ Z7–9 H9–6

Geranium orientalitibeticum
Perennial spreading by tuberous,
underground runners. Has cup-shaped,
pink flowers, with white centers, in
summer. Leaves are deeply cut and
marbled in shades of green. May be
invasive. **H** in flower 6–10in (15–25cm),
S indefinite.

☼ ◊ Z5–7 H8–5

Dianthus carthusianorum
Evergreen perennial carrying rounded,
upward-facing, cherry-red or deep pink
flowers on slender stems in summer
above small tufts of grasslike leaves.
H 8in (20cm), **S** 3in (7cm).

☼ ◊ Z5–9 H9–5

PINK

RED

Lewisia Cotyledon Hybrids
Evergreen, clump-forming perennials with rosettes of large, thick, toothed leaves. In early summer bear clusters of flowers, in various shades of pink to purple, on erect stems. Is good for a rock crevice or an alpine house.
H to 12in (30cm), **S** 6in (15cm) or more.

☼ ◊ pH Z5–8 H8–1

Penstemon newberryi f. humilior
Evergreen, mat-forming shrub with arching branches clothed in small, leathery, dark green leaves. Bears short sprays of tubular, lipped, cherry-red to deep pink flowers in early summer. **H** 6–8in (15–20cm), **S** 12in (30cm).

☼ ◊ Z7–10 H10–7

Origanum laevigatum
Deciduous, mat-forming subshrub with small, aromatic, dark green leaves, branching, red stems and a profusion of tiny, tubular, cerise-pink flowers, surrounded by red-purple bracts, in summer. **H** 9–12in (23–30cm), **S** 8in (20cm) or more.

☼ ◊ Z7–10 H11–1

Delphinium nudicaule
Short-lived, upright perennial with erect stems bearing deeply divided, basal leaves and, in summer, spikes of hooded, red or occasionally yellow flowers, with contrasting stamens. **H** 8in (20cm), **S** 2–4in (5–10cm).

☼ ◊ ① Z5–7 H7–5

Zauschneria californica 'Dublin'
Clump-forming, woody-based perennial with lance-shaped, gray-green leaves. From late summer to early fall bears terminal clusters of tubular, deep orange-scarlet flowers. **H** 12in (30cm), **S** 18in (45cm).

☼ ◊ Z8–11 H12–8

Penstemon pinifolius
Evergreen, bushy shrub with branched stems clothed in fine, dark green leaves. In summer, very narrow, tubular, orange-red flowers are borne in loose, terminal spikes. **H** 4–8in (10–20cm), **S** 6in (15cm).

☼ ◊ Z4–10 H10–1

Punica granatum var. nana
(Dwarf pomegranate)
Slow-growing, deciduous, rounded shrub that, in summer, bears funnel-shaped, red flowers with somewhat crumpled petals, followed by small, rounded, orange-red fruits. **H** and **S** 12–36in (30–90cm).

☼ ◊ Z7–10 H11–1

Geranium sanguineum
(Bloody cranesbill)
Hummock-forming, spreading perennial with many cup-shaped, deep magenta-pink flowers borne in summer above round, deeply divided, dark green leaves. Makes good groundcover.
H to 10in (25cm), **S** 12in (30cm) or more.

☼ ◊ Z3–8 H8–1

Erigeron alpinus (Alpine fleabane)
Clump-forming perennial of variable size that bears daisylike, lilac-pink flower heads on erect stems in summer. Leaves are long, oval and hairy. Suits a sunny border, bank or large rock garden.
H 10in (25cm), **S** 8in (20cm).

☼ ◊ Z5–8 H8–5

Helianthemum 'Fire Dragon'
Evergreen, spreading shrub with saucer-shaped, orange-scarlet flowers in late spring and summer. Leaves are linear and gray-green.
H 9–12in (23–30cm), **S** 18in (45cm).

☼ ◊ Z6–8 H8–6

ROCK PLANTS

Cortusa matthioli
Clump-forming perennial with a basal rosette of rounded, dull green leaves and, in late spring and early summer, one-sided racemes of small, pendent, bell-shaped, reddish- or pinkish-purple flowers. **H** 6–8in (15–20cm), **S** 4in (10cm).

☀ ◌ Z5–8 H8–5

Erodium cheilanthifolium
Compact, mound-forming perennial with pink flowers, veined and marked with purple-red, borne on stiff stems in late spring and summer. Grayish-green leaves are crinkled and deeply cut. **H** 6–8in (15–20cm), **S** 8in (20cm) or more.

☀ ◌ Z5–8 H8–5

Scabiosa lucida
Clump-forming perennial with tufts of oval leaves and rounded heads of pale lilac to deep mauve flowers, borne on erect stems in summer. **H** 8in (20cm), **S** 6in (15cm).

☀ ◌ Z4–9 H9–1

Semiaquilegia ecalcarata
Short-lived, upright perennial with narrow, lobed leaves. In summer each slender stem bears several pendent, open bell-shaped, dusky-pink to purple flowers, with no spurs. **H** 8in (20cm), **S** 3in (7cm).

☀ ◌ Z6–8 H8–6

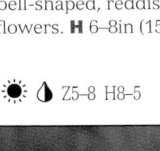

Penstemon serrulatus
Semievergreen subshrub, deciduous in severe climates, that has small, elliptic, dark green leaves and tubular, blue to purple flowers borne in loose spikes in summer. Soil should not be too dry. **H** 24in (60cm), **S** 12in (30cm).

☀ ◌ Z3–9 H9–1

Phlox divaricata subsp. laphamii 'Chattahoochee'
Short-lived, clump-forming perennial that has saucer-shaped, red-eyed, bright lavender flowers throughout summer–fall. Narrow, pointed leaves are dark reddish-purple when young. **H** 6–8in (15–20cm), **S** 12in (30cm).

☀ ◌ Z4–8 H8–1

Wulfenia amherstiana
Evergreen perennial with rosettes of narrowly spoon-shaped, toothed leaves. Erect stems bear loose clusters of small, tubular, purple or pinkish-purple flowers in summer. **H** 6–12in (15–30cm), **S** to 12in (30cm).

☀ ◌ Z5–9 H9–5

Phlox divaricata subsp. laphamii
Semievergreen, creeping perennial with oval leaves and upright stems bearing loose clusters of saucer-shaped, pale to deep violet-blue flowers in summer. **H** 12in (30cm), **S** 8in (20cm).

☀ ◌ Z4–8 H8–1

Calceolaria arachnoidea
Evergreen, clump-forming perennial with a basal rosette of wrinkled leaves, covered in white down. Upright stems carry spikes of many pouch-shaped, dull purple flowers in summer. Is best treated as a biennial. **H** 10in (25cm), **S** 5in (12cm).

☀ ◌ Z8–9 H6–1

341

ROCK PLANTS

PURPLE

BLUE

Parahebe catarractae
Evergreen subshrub with oval, toothed, mid-green leaves and, in summer, loose sprays of small, open funnel-shaped, white flowers, heavily zoned and veined pinkish-purple. **H** and **S** 12in (30cm).

☼ ◊ Z9–10 H10–9

Campanula barbata
(Bearded bellflower)
Evergreen perennial with a basal rosette of oval, hairy, gray-green leaves. In summer bears one-sided racemes of bell-shaped, white to lavender-blue flowers. Is short-lived but sets seed freely. **H** 8in (20cm), **S** 5in (12cm).

☼ ◊ Z5–8 H8–5

Linum perenne
Upright perennial with slender stems, clothed in grasslike leaves, that bear terminal clusters of open funnel-shaped, clear blue flowers in succession throughout summer. **H** 12in (30cm), **S** to 6in (15cm).

☼ ◊ Z7–9 H9–7

Convolvulus sabatius
Trailing perennial with slender stems clothed in small, oval leaves and open trumpet-shaped, vibrant blue-purple flowers in summer and early fall. Shelter in a rock crevice in a cold site. **H** 6–8in (15–20cm), **S** 12in (30cm).

☼ ◊ Z7–9 H9–7

Phyteuma scheuchzeri
Tufted perennial with narrow, dark green leaves and terminal heads of spiky, blue flowers that are borne in summer. Seeds freely; dislikes winter wet. **H** 6–8in (15–20cm), **S** 4in (10cm).

☼ ◊ Z5–8 H8–5

Sisyrinchium 'E.K. Balls'
Clump-forming, variable perennial with fans of narrowly sword-shaped, upright, mid-green leaves. In summer produces a succession of many star-shaped, bluish-mauve flowers. **H** 8in (20cm), **S** 6in (15cm).

☼ ◊ Z7–8 H8–7

Campanula wanneri
Clump-forming perennial with branching stems and hairy, oval leaves. In summer bears pendent, bell-shaped, blue to violet-blue flowers in loose, terminal spikes. **H** 6–9in (15–23cm), **S** 10in (25cm).

☼ ◊ Z7–9 H9–7

Lithodora oleifolia
Evergreen shrub with oval, pointed, silky, mid-green leaves. Curving stems carry loose sprays of several small, funnel-shaped, light blue flowers in early summer. **H** 6–8in (15–20cm), **S** to 3ft (1m).

☼ ◊ Z6–8 H8–6

Moltkia suffruticosa
Deciduous, upright subshrub. In summer bears clusters of funnel-shaped, bright blue flowers, pink in bud, on hairy stems. Leaves are long, pointed and hairy. **H** 6–16in (15–40cm), **S** 12in (30cm).

☼ ◊ Z7–9 H9–7

Veronica prostrata 'Trehane'
Dense, mat-forming perennial bearing
upright spikes of small, saucer-shaped,
deep violet-blue flowers in early summer
above narrow, toothed, yellow or
yellowish-green leaves. **H** in flower 6–8in
(15–20cm), **S** indefinite.

☼ ◊ Z5–8 H8–5

YELLOW

Erodium chrysanthum
Mound-forming perennial, grown
for its dense, silvery stems and finely
cut, fernlike leaves. Has small sprays
of cup-shaped, sulfur- or creamy-yellow
flowers in late spring and summer.
H and **S** 9in (23cm).

☼ ◊ Z7–8 H8–7

Veronica prostrata
(Prostrate speedwell)
Dense, mat-forming perennial that has
upright spikes of small, saucer-shaped,
brilliant blue flowers in early summer.
Foliage is narrow, oval and toothed.
H to 12in (30cm), **S** indefinite.

☼ ◊ Z5–8 H8–5

**Veronica austriaca
subsp. teucrium 'Kapitan'**
Dense, mat-forming perennial
bearing erect spikes of small,
saucer-shaped, bright deep blue
flowers in early summer. Foliage
is narrow, oval and toothed.
H to 12in (30cm), **S** indefinite.

☼ ◊ Z4–8 H8–3

**Hypericum olympicum
f. uniflorum 'Citrinum'**
Deciduous, dense, rounded subshrub
with tufts of upright stems, clothed
in small, oval, gray-green leaves.
Bears terminal clusters of lemon-
yellow flowers throughout summer.
H and **S** 6–12in (15–30cm).

☼ ◊ Z6–8 H8–6

Lithodora diffusa 'Heavenly Blue'
Evergreen, prostrate shrub with trailing
stems bearing pointed, oblong, hairy
leaves and, in summer, many open
funnel-shaped, deep blue flowers in leaf
axils. Trim stems hard after flowering.
H 6–12in (15–30cm), **S** to 18in (45cm).

☼ ◊ pH Z8–11 H11–10

Veronica austriaca subsp. teucrium
Spreading perennial with narrow spikes
of small, flat, outward-facing, bright
blue flowers in summer. Leaves are
small, divided, hairy and grayish-green.
H and **S** 10–24in (25–60cm).

☼ ◊ Z4–8 H8–3

Verbascum 'Letitia'
Evergreen, stiff-branched shrub with
toothed, gray leaves. Bears outward-
facing, 5-lobed, bright yellow flowers
with orange centers continuously
from late spring to mid-fall. Hates
winter wet; is good in an alpine house.
H and **S** 10in (25cm).

☼ ◊ Z5–9 H9–5

ROCK PLANTS

YELLOW

Linum arboreum
Evergreen, compact shrub with blue-green leaves. In summer has a succession of funnel-shaped, bright yellow flowers opening in sunny weather and borne in terminal clusters.
H to 12in (30cm), **S** 12in (30cm).

☼ ◊ Z6–9 H9–6

Corydalis lutea
Evergreen, clump-forming perennial with fleshy, fibrous roots, semierect, basal, gray-green leaves. Bears racemes of slender, yellow flowers, with short spurs, in late spring and summer.
H and **S** 8–12in (20–30cm).

☼ ◊ Z5–8 H8–4

Euryops acraeus
Evergreen, dome-shaped shrub with stems clothed in toothed, silvery-blue leaves. Bears solitary daisylike, bright yellow flower heads in late spring and early summer. **H** and **S** 12in (30cm).

☼ ◊ Z8–11 H11–9

Chrysogonum virginianum
Mat-forming perennial with daisylike, yellow flower heads borne on short stems in summer–fall and oval, toothed, mid-green leaves. Although plant spreads by underground runners, it is not invasive. **H** 6–8in (15–20cm), **S** 4–6in (10–15cm) or more.

◐ ◊ Z5–9 H9–2

Helianthemum 'Wisley Primrose'
Fast-growing, evergreen, compact shrub with saucer-shaped, soft pale yellow flowers in summer. Has oblong, gray-green leaves. **H** 9in (23cm), **S** 12in (30cm) or more.

☼ ◊ Z6–8 H8–6

Othonna cheirifolia
Evergreen shrub with narrow, somewhat fleshy, gray leaves. In early summer bears daisylike, yellow flower heads singly on upright stems. Needs a warm, sheltered site. **H** 8–12in (20–30cm), **S** 12in (30cm) or more.

☼ ◊ Z8–9 H9–8

Eriogonum umbellatum
Evergreen, prostrate to upright perennial with mats of green leaves, white and woolly beneath. In summer carries heads of tiny, yellow flowers that later turn copper. Dwarf forms are available. **H** 3–12in (8–30cm), **S** 6–12in (15–30cm).

☼ ◊ Z3–8 H8–1

Verbascum dumulosum
Evergreen, mat-forming, shrubby
perennial with hairy, gray or gray-green
leaves. In late spring and early summer
bears a succession of 5-lobed, bright
yellow flowers in short racemes. Dislikes
winter wet. **H** 6in (15cm) or more,
S 9–12in (23–30cm) or more.

☀ ◊ Z6–9 H9–6

Ranunculus gramineus
Erect, slender perennial with grasslike,
blue-green leaves. Bears several cup-
shaped, bright yellow flowers in late
spring and early summer. Prefers
rich soil. Seedlings will vary in height
and flower size. **H** 16–20in (40–50cm),
S 3–4in (8–10cm).

☀ ◊ ❗ Z6–8 H8–6

Sedum rupestre (Reflexed stonecrop)
Evergreen perennial with loose mats
of rooting stems bearing narrow,
fleshy leaves. Carries flat, terminal
heads of tiny, bright yellow flowers
in summer. Makes good groundcover.
H 6–8in (15–20cm), **S** indefinite.

☀ ◊ ❗ Z6–9 H9–6

Genista lydia
Deciduous, domed shrub with slender,
arching branches and blue-green leaves.
Massed terminal clusters of pealike,
bright yellow flowers appear in late
spring and early summer. Will trail
over a large rock or wall. **H** 18–24in
(45–60cm), **S** 24in (60cm) or more.

☀ ◊ Z6–9 H9–3

Ononis natrix
(Large yellow restharrow)
Deciduous, compact, erect shrub
with pealike, red-streaked, yellow
flowers in pendent clusters in summer.
Hairy leaves are divided into 3 leaflets.
H and **S** 12in (30cm) or more.

☀ ◊ Z7–9 H9–6

Diascia 'Salmon Supreme'
Mat-forming perennial with heart-
shaped leaves. Dense spikes of pretty,
pale-apricot flowers with very small,
deeply concave "windows" are
produced over a long period, from
summer through to fall. **H** 6in (15cm),
S to 20in (50cm).

☀ ◊ Z8–9 H9–8

Helianthemum 'Ben More'
Evergreen, spreading, twiggy shrub
that bears a succession of saucer-
shaped, reddish-orange flowers in
loose, terminal clusters in late spring
and summer. Has small, glossy,
dark green leaves. **H** 9–12in (23–30cm),
S 12in (30cm).

☀ ◊ Z6–8 H8–6

Crepis aurea
Clump-forming perennial with a basal
cluster of oblong, light green leaves.
In summer produces dandelion-like,
orange flower heads, singly, on stems
covered with black and white hairs.
H 4–12in (10–30cm), **S** 6in (15cm).

☀ ◊ Z5–7 H7–4

ROCK PLANTS

345

ROCK PLANTS

PINK

Sorbus reducta
Deciduous shrub forming a low
thicket of upright branches. Small,
gray-green leaves, divided into leaflets,
turn bronze-red in late fall. In early
summer bears loose clusters of flat,
white flowers, followed by pink berries.
H and **S** to 12in (30cm) or more.

☼ ◊ ❶ Z5–8 H8–4

Silene schafta
Spreading perennial with tufts of
narrow, oval leaves. Bears sprays
of 5-petaled, rose-magenta flowers
from late summer to late fall.
H 10in (25cm), **S** 12in (30cm).

☼ ◊ Z4–8 H9–3

BLUE

Ceratostigma plumbaginoides
Bushy perennial that bears small,
terminal clusters of single, brilliant
blue flowers on reddish, branched
stems in late summer and fall.
Oval leaves turn rich red in fall.
H 18in (45cm), **S** 12in (30cm).

☼ ◊ Z5–9 H9–4

Gentiana septemfida
Evergreen perennial with many upright,
then arching stems clothed with oval
leaves. Bears heads of trumpet-shaped,
mid-blue flowers in summer–fall.
Likes rich soil but tolerates reasonably
drained, heavy clay. **H** 6–8in (15–20cm),
S 12in (30cm).

☼ ◊ Z6–8 H8–6

WHITE

Gaultheria cuneata
Evergreen, compact shrub with stiff
stems clothed in leathery, oval leaves.
In summer bears nodding, urn-
shaped, white flowers, in leaf axils,
followed by white berries in fall.
H and **S** 12in (30cm).

☼ ◊ pH ❶ Z4–7 H7–1

Ranunculus calandrinioides
Clump-forming perennial that loses
its long, oval, blue-green leaves in
summer; in a reasonable winter will
bear a succession of cup-shaped,
pink-flushed, white flowers for many
weeks. Needs very sharp drainage.
H and **S** to 8in (20cm).

☼ ◊ ❶ Z7–8 H8–7

Leucopogon colensoi
Evergreen, low-growing shrub with
stiff stems clothed in tiny, gray-green
leaves. Bears clusters of small, tubular,
white flowers in spring at the ends of
new growth. Red or white berries in
late summer are rare in cultivation.
H and **S** 12in (30cm).

☀ ◊ Z8–9 H9–8

SILVER

Tanacetum argenteum
Mat-forming perennial, usually
evergreen, grown for its finely cut,
bright silver leaves. Has a profusion of
small, daisylike, white flower heads in
summer. **H** in flower 6–9in (15–23cm),
S 8in (20cm).

☼ ◊ ❶ Z5–7 H7–5

Celmisia semicordata
Evergreen perennial with swordlike,
silver leaves in large clumps and,
in summer, daisylike, white flower
heads borne singly on hairy stems.
H and **S** 12in (30cm).

☼ ◊ pH Z8–9 H9–8

GREEN

Hebe cupressoides 'Boughton Dome'
Slow-growing, evergreen, dome-shaped shrub with scalelike, stem-clasping, dark gray-green leaves. Has terminal clusters of small, 4-lobed, blue-tinged, white flowers in summer. **H** 12in (30cm), **S** to 24in (60cm).

☼ ◊ Z8–9 H9–8

Tanacetum densum subsp. amani
Clump-forming perennial retaining fernlike, hairy, gray leaves in winter in mild climates. Bears daisylike, yellow flower heads with woolly bracts in summer. Dislikes winter wet. **H** and **S** 8in (20cm).

☼ ◊ ① Z6–8 H8–6

WHITE

Androsace vandellii
Evergreen, dense, cushion-forming perennial with narrow, gray leaves and a profusion of stemless, white flowers in spring. Needs careful cultivation with a deep collar of grit under the cushion. **H** 1in (2.5cm), **S** to 4in (10cm).

☼ ◊ pH Z5–7 H7–5

Arabis alpina subsp. caucasica 'Variegata'
Evergreen, mat-forming perennial with rosettes of oval, cream-splashed, mid-green leaves. Bears bunches of single, sometimes pink-flushed, white flowers from early spring to summer. **H** and **S** 6in (15cm).

☼ ◊ Z4–8 H8–1

Ozothamnus coralloides
Evergreen, upright shrub with gray stems clothed in neat, dark green leaves, marked silver. Occasionally bears fluffy, yellow flower heads. Suits a cold frame or an alpine house. Hates winter wet. **H** 6–9in (15–23cm), **S** 6in (15cm).

☼ ◊ Z8–9 H9–8

Ozothamnus selago
Evergreen, upright shrub with stiff stems covered in scalelike leaves. Intermittently bears fluffy, creamy-white flower heads. Makes a good foil for spring bulbs. **H** and **S** 6–9in (15–23cm).

☼ ◊ Z9–10 H10–9

Salix x boydii
Very slow-growing, deciduous, upright shrub forming a gnarled, branched bush. Has oval, rough-textured leaves; catkins are rarely produced. Will tolerate light shade. **H** to 6–9in (15–23cm), **S** to 12in (30cm).

☼ ◊ Z4–7 H7–1

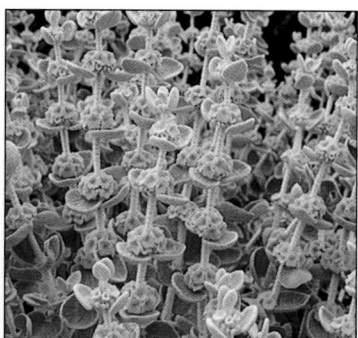

Ballota pseudodictamnus
Evergreen, mound-forming subshrub with rounded, gray-green leaves and stems covered with woolly, white hairs. In summer bears whorls of small, pink flowers with conspicuous, enlarged, pale green calyces. **H** 2ft (60cm), **S** 36in (90cm).

☼ ◊ Z7–9 H9–7

Arenaria balearica
Prostrate perennial that is evergreen in all but the most severe winters. Will form a green film over a wet, porous rock face. Minute, white flowers stud mats of foliage in late spring and early summer. **H** less than ½in (1cm), **S** indefinite.

☼ ◊ Z4–7 H7–1

ROCK PLANTS

ROCK PLANTS

WHITE

Saxifraga scardica
Slow-growing, evergreen perennial with hard cushions composed of blue-green rosettes of leaves. In spring bears small clusters of upward-facing, cup-shaped, white flowers. Does best in an alpine house or sheltered scree. **H** 1in (2.5cm), **S** 3in (8cm).

☀ ◑ ◊ Z7–8 H8–7

Saxifraga burseriana
Slow-growing, evergreen perennial with hard cushions of spiky, gray-green leaves. In spring bears open cup-shaped, white flowers on short stems. **H** 1–2in (2.5–5cm), **S** to 4in (10cm).

☀ ◊ Z6–8 H8–6

Sanguinaria canadensis (Bloodroot)
Rhizomatous perennial with fleshy, underground stems that exude red sap when cut. In spring bears white flowers, sometimes pink-flushed or slate-blue on reverses, as blue-gray leaves unfurl. **H** 4–6in (10–15cm), **S** 12in (30cm).

☀ ◊ Z3–9 H9–1

Maianthemum bifolium
Spreading, rhizomatous perennial with pairs of large, oval, glossy, dark green leaves arising direct from rhizomes. Stems produce a raceme of 4-petaled, white flowers in early summer, followed by small, spherical, red fruits. May be invasive. **H** 4in (10cm), **S** indefinite.

☀ ◊ pH Z4–5 H5–1

Cardamine trifolia
Groundcover perennial with creeping stems clothed in rounded, toothed, 3-parted leaves. In late spring and early summer bears loose heads of open cup-shaped, white flowers on bare stems. **H** 4–6in (10–15cm), **S** 12in (30cm).

☀ ◑ ◊ Z5–7 H7–5

Dicentra cucullaria
(Dutchman's breeches)
Compact perennial with fernlike foliage and arching stems each bearing a few small, yellow-tipped, white flowers, like tiny, inflated trousers, in spring. Lies dormant in summer. **H** 6in (15cm), **S** to 12in (30cm).

☀ ◊ ⚠ Z4–8 H8–1

Arenaria tetraquetra
Evergreen perennial that forms a gray-green cushion of small leaves. Stemless, star-shaped, white flowers appear in late spring. Is well-suited for a trough or an alpine house. **H** 1in (2.5cm), **S** 6in (15cm) or more.

☀ ◊ Z3–5 H5–1

Weldenia candida
Perennial with rosettes of strap-shaped, wavy-margined leaves, growing from tuberous roots. Bears a succession of upright, cup-shaped, pure white flowers in late spring and early summer. **H** and **S** 3–6in (8–15cm).

☀ ◊ Z9–10 H10–9

Pulsatilla vernalis
Tufted perennial with rosettes of feathery leaves. Densely hairy, brown flower buds appear in late winter and open in early spring to somewhat nodding, open cup-shaped, pearl-white flowers. Buds dislike winter wet. **H** 2–4in (5–10cm), **S** 4in (10cm).

☼ ◊ ① Z4–7 H7–1

Ranunculus alpestris
(Alpine buttercup)
Short-lived, evergreen, clump-forming perennial that bears cup-shaped, white flowers on erect stems from late spring to mid-summer. Glossy, dark green leaves are rounded and serrated. **H** 1–5in (2.5–12cm), **S** 4in (10cm).

☼ ◊ ① Z5–8 H8–5

Androsace villosa
Evergreen, mat-forming perennial with very hairy rosettes of tiny leaves. Bears umbels of small, white flowers, with yellow centers that turn red, in spring. **H** 1in (2.5cm), **S** 8in (20cm).

☼ ◊ Z5–7 H7–5

Ranunculus ficaria var. albus
Mat-forming perennial bearing in early spring cup-shaped, single, creamy-white flowers with glossy petals. Leaves are heart-shaped and dark green. Can spread rapidly; is good for a wild garden. **H** 2in (5cm), **S** 8in (20cm).

☼ ◊ ① Z4–8 H8–1

Cassiope lycopodioides
Evergreen, prostrate, mat-forming shrub with slender stems densely set with minute, scalelike, dark green leaves. In spring, short, reddish stems carry tiny, bell-shaped, white flowers, in red calyces, singly in leaf axils. **H** 3in (8cm), **S** 12in (30cm).

☼ ◊ pH Z7–8 H8–7

Corydalis popovii
Tuberous perennial with leaves divided into 3–6 bluish-green leaflets. In spring bears loose racemes of deep red-purple and white flowers, each with a long spur. Keep dry when dormant. **H** and **S** 4–6in (10–15cm).

☼ ◊ Z7–8 H8–7

Cassiope mertensiana
Evergreen, dwarf shrub with scalelike, dark green leaves tightly pressed to stems. In early spring carries bell-shaped, creamy-white flowers, with green or red calyces, in leaf axils. **H** 6in (15cm), **S** 8in (20cm).

☼ ◊ pH Z2–6 H6–1

Leptinella atrata subsp. luteola
Evergreen, mat-forming perennial that in late spring and early summer bears blackish-red flower heads with creamy-yellow stamens. Leaves are small, finely cut and dark green. Needs adequate moisture; best in an alpine house. **H** 1in (2.5cm), **S** to 10in (25cm).

☼ ◊ Z8–9 H9–8

Scoliopus bigelowii
Compact perennial with basal, veined leaves, sometimes marked brown. In early spring bears flowers with purple inner petals and greenish-white outer petals with deep purple lines. **H** 3–4in (8–10cm), **S** 4–6in (10–15cm).

☼ ◊ Z6–8 H8–6

Gypsophila cerastioides
Prostrate perennial with a profusion of small, saucer-shaped, purple-veined, white flowers borne in late spring and early summer above mats of rounded, velvety, mid-green foliage. **H** ¾in (2cm), **S** to 4in (10cm) or more.

☼ ◊ Z5–8 H8–5

Shortia galacifolia (Oconee bells)
Evergreen, clump-forming, dwarf perennial with round, toothed, leathery, glossy leaves. In late spring bears cup- to trumpet-shaped, often pink-flushed, white flowers with deeply serrated petals. **H** to 6in (15cm), **S** 6–9in (15–23cm).

☼ ◊ pH Z6–9 H9–6

ROCK PLANTS

Cerastium tomentosum
(Snow-in-summer)
Very vigorous, groundcover perennial, only suitable for a hot, dry bank, with prostrate stems covered by tiny, gray leaves. In late spring and summer bears star-shaped, white flowers above foliage.
H 3in (8cm), **S** indefinite.

☼ ◊ Z3–7 H7–1

Androsace pyrenaica
Evergreen perennial with small rosettes of tiny, hairy leaves, tightly packed to form hard cushions. Minute, stemless, single, white flowers appear in spring.
H 1½in (4cm), **S** to 4in (10cm).

☼ ◊ Z6–7 H7–6

Anemone trullifolia
Creeping, fibrous-rooted perennial with wedge-shaped, semi-erect, mid-green basal leaves, each with 3 deeply toothed lobes. Rounded flowers of 5 petals, varying from rich blue to near white, are borne in early summer and late summer.
H and **S** 8in (20cm).

☼ ◊ ! Z5–8 H8–5

Anemonella thalictroides
Perennial with delicate, fernlike leaves growing from a cluster of small tubers. From spring to early summer bears small, cup-shaped, white or pink flowers, singly on finely branched stems. Needs rich soil.
H 4in (10cm), **S** 1½in (4cm) or more.

☼ ◊ Z4–7 H7–1

Daphne jasminea
Evergreen, compact shrub. Bears small, white flowers, pink-flushed externally, in late spring and early summer and again in fall. Brittle stems are clothed in gray-green leaves. Suits an alpine house or a dry wall.
H 3–4in (8–10cm), **S** to 12in (30cm).

☼ ◊ ! Z7–9 H9–7

Paraquilegia anemonoides
Tufted perennial with fernlike, blue-green leaves. In spring, pale lavender-blue buds open to pendent, cup-shaped, almost white flowers borne singly on arching stems. May be difficult to establish. **H** and **S** 4–6in (10–15cm).

☼ ◊ Z5–8 H8–5

Trillium rivale
Perennial with oval leaves, divided into 3 leaflets. In spring bears open cup-shaped, white or pale pink flowers with dark-spotted, heart-shaped petals, singly on upright, later arching stems.
H to 6in (15cm), **S** 4in (10cm).

☼ ◊ Z5–8 H8–5

Saxifraga x irvingii 'Jenkinsiae'
Slow-growing perennial with very tight, gray-green cushions of foliage. Carries a profusion of open cup-shaped, lilac-pink flowers on slender stems in early spring.
H 3–4in (8–10cm), **S** to 6in (15cm).

☼ ◊ Z6–7 H7–6

Androsace carnea
Evergreen, cushion-forming perennial that has small rosettes of pointed leaves with hairy margins. In spring, 2 or more stems rise above each rosette, bearing tiny, single, pink flowers. Suits a trough.
H and **S** 2in (5cm).

☼ ◊ Z4–7 H7–1

Arenaria purpurascens
Evergreen, mat-forming perennial
with sharp-pointed, glossy leaves,
above which rise many small clusters
of star-shaped, pale to deep purplish-
pink flowers in early spring. **H** ½in (1cm),
S to 6in (15cm).

☀ ◊ Z4–7 H7–1

Antennaria rosea
Semievergreen perennial forming
a spreading mat of tiny, oval, woolly
leaves. Bears fluffy, rose-pink flower
heads in small, terminal clusters in
late spring and early summer. Is good
as groundcover with small bulbs.
H 1in (2.5cm), **S** to 16in (40cm).

☀ ◊ Z5–9 H9–4

Daphne arbuscula
Evergreen, prostrate shrub. In late
spring bears many very fragrant,
tubular, deep pink flowers in terminal
clusters. Narrow, leathery, dark green
leaves are crowded at the ends of
the branches. Likes rich soil. **H** 4–6in
(10–15cm), **S** 20in (50cm).

◑ ◊ ❶ Z5–7 H7–5

Daphne petraea 'Grandiflora'
Slow-growing, evergreen, compact
shrub that bears terminal clusters
of fragrant, rich pink flowers in late
spring and tiny, glossy leaves. Suits an
alpine house, a sheltered, humus-rich
rock garden or a trough. **H** to 6in (15cm),
S to 10in (25cm).

☀ ◊ ❶ Z5–7 H7–3

Vaccinium vitis-idaea subsp. minus
Evergreen, mat-forming subshrub with
tiny, oval, leathery leaves. In late spring
produces small, erect racemes of many
tiny, bell-shaped, deep pink or deep
pink-and-white flowers. **H** 2–3in (5–8cm),
S 4–6in (10–15cm).

◑ ◊ pH Z2–6 H6–1

Epigaea gaultherioides
Evergreen, prostrate subshrub
with cup-shaped, shell-pink flowers
borne in terminal clusters in spring.
Hairy stems carry heart-shaped,
dark green leaves. Is difficult to
grow and propagate. **H** to 4in (10cm),
S to 10in (25cm) or more.

☀ ◊ pH Z8–9 H9–8

Lewisia tweedyi
Evergreen, rosetted perennial with
large, fleshy leaves and stout, branched
stems that bear open cup-shaped,
many-petaled, white to pink flowers in
spring. Best grown in an alpine house.
H 6in (15cm), **S** 5–6in (12–15cm).

◑ ◊ pH Z4–7 H7–1

Claytonia megarhiza var. nivalis
Evergreen perennial with a rosette of
spoon-shaped, succulent leaves. Bears
small heads of tiny, deep pink flowers in
spring. Grows best in a deep pot of gritty
potting mix in an alpine house. **H** ½in
(1cm), **S** 3in (8cm).

☀ ◊ Z5–7 H7–5

Mazus reptans
Prostrate perennial that has tubular,
purple or purplish-pink flowers,
with protruding, white lips, spotted
red and yellow, borne singly on short
stems in spring. Narrow, toothed leaves
are in pairs along stem. **H** to 2in (5cm),
S 12in (30cm) or more.

☀ ◊ Z5–8 H8–5

ROCK PLANTS

Silene acaulis (Moss campion)
Evergreen, cushion-forming perennial
with minute, bright green leaves
studded with tiny, stemless, 5-petaled,
pink flowers in spring. May be difficult
to bring into flower; prefers a cool
climate. **H** to 1in (2.5cm), **S** 6in (15cm).

☼ ◊ Z3–5 H5–1

Oxalis adenophylla
Mat-forming, fibrous-rooted, tuberous
perennial with gray-green leaves divided
into narrow, wavy lobes. In spring bears
rounded, purplish-pink flowers, each
1–1½in (2.5–4cm) across, with darker
purple eyes. **H** to 2in (5cm), **S** 3–4in
(8–10cm).

☼ ◊ Z6–8 H8–6

Thlaspi cepaeifolium
subsp. rotundifolium
Clump-forming perennial with dense
tufts of round leaves and small, open
cup-shaped, pale to deep purplish- or
lilac-pink flowers in spring. Needs cool
conditions. May be short-lived. **H** 2–3in
(5–8cm), **S** 4in (10cm).

☼ ◊ Z6–9 H9–6

Armeria juniperifolia
Evergreen, cushion-forming perennial
composed of loose rosettes of sharp-
pointed, mid- to gray-green leaves.
Pale pink flowers are borne in spherical
umbels in late spring and early summer.
H 2–3in (5–8cm), **S** 6in (15cm).

☼ ◊ Z5–7 H8–4

Erinus alpinus
Semievergreen, short-lived perennial
with rosettes of soft, mid-green leaves
covered, in late spring and summer,
with small, purple, pink or white flowers.
Self-seeds freely. **H** and **S** 2–3in (5–8cm).

☼ ◊ Z4–7 H7–1

Oxalis acetosella
var. subpurpurascens
Creeping, rhizomatous perennial
forming mats of 3-lobed leaves.
Cup-shaped, soft pink flowers,
each ½ in (1cm) across, with 5
darker-veined petals, are produced
in spring.**H** 2in (5cm), **S** indefinite.

352 ◐ ◊ Z3–8 H8–1

Arabis alpina subsp. caucasica
'Douler Angevine'
Evergreen, mat-forming perennial
bearing loose rosettes of obovate,
toothed, mid-green leaves with irregular,
creamy-yellow margins. In spring
produces fragrant, 4-petaled, bright
pink flowers. **H** 6in (15cm), **S** 20in (50cm).

☼ ◊ Z4–8 H8–1

Shortia soldanelloides
Evergreen, mat-forming perennial with
rounded, toothed leaves and small,
pendent, bell-shaped and fringed, deep
pink flowers in late spring. **H** 2–4in
(5–10cm), **S** 4–6in (10–15cm).

◐ ◊ pH Z6–8 H8–5

Anagallis tenella 'Studland'
Short-lived perennial that forms
prostrate mats of tiny, bright
green leaves studded in spring
with honey-scented, star-shaped,
bright pink flowers. **H** ½in (1cm),
S 6in (15cm) or more.

☀ ◊ Z5–7 H7–5

Polygonatum hookeri
Slow-growing, dense, rhizomatous
perennial that bears loose spikes
of several small, bell-shaped, lilac-
pink flowers in late spring and early
summer. Leaves are tiny and lance-
shaped. Suits a peat bed. **H** to 2in (5cm),
S to 12in (30cm).

☀ ◊ ⏻ Z6–9 H9–6

Corydalis solida 'George Baker'
Tuberous perennial with fernlike, divided
leaves and dense racemes of spurred,
rich deep rose-red flowers in spring.
H to 10in (25cm), **S** to 8in (20cm).

☀ ◊ Z5–7 H7–3

Aubrieta 'Joy'
Vigorous, evergreen, trailing perennial
that forms mounds of soft green leaves.
In spring bears double, pale mauve-pink
flowers on short stems. **H** 4in (10cm),
S 8in (20cm).

☀ ◊ Z5–7 H7–5

**Saxifraga federici-augusti
subsp. grisebachii 'Wisley Variety'**
Evergreen perennial with rosettes of
lime-encrusted leaves. Crosier-shaped
stems with pale pink to bright red hairs,
bear dense racemes of dark red flowers
in spring. **H** 4in (10cm), **S** 6in (15cm).

☀ ◊ Z6–8 H8–6

Saxifraga oppositifolia
(Purple mountain saxifrage)
Evergreen, prostrate perennial with
clusters of tiny, white-flecked leaves.
Has open cup-shaped, dark purple,
purplish-pink or, rarely, white flowers
in early spring. Likes an open position.
H 1–2in (2.5–5cm), **S** 6in (15cm).

☀ ◊ Z1–7 H7–1

Androsace carnea subsp. laggeri
Evergreen, cushion-forming perennial
composed of small, tight rosettes of
pointed leaves. Cup-shaped, deep pink
flowers are borne in small clusters above
cushions in spring. **H** and **S** 2in (5cm).

☀ ◊ Z4–7 H7–1

**Arabis blepharophylla
'Frühlingszauber'**
Short-lived, evergreen, mat-forming
perennial bearing loose rosettes of
dark green leaves with gray margins.
Compact racemes of fragrant, 4-petaled,
dark purple-pink flowers are produced
in spring. **H** 5in (12cm), **S** 8in (20cm).

☀ ◊ Z5–8 H8–5

Saxifraga sempervivum
Evergreen, hummock-forming
perennial with tight rosettes of tufted,
silvery-green leaves. Crosier-shaped
flower stems, covered in silvery hairs
and emerging from rosettes, bear
racemes of dark red flowers in early
spring. **H** and **S** 4–6in (10–15cm).

☀ ◊ Z6–7 H7–6

ROCK PLANTS

ROCK PLANTS

**Aubrieta deltoidea
'Argenteovariegata'**
Evergreen, compact perennial, grown
for its trailing, green leaves which are
heavily splashed with creamy-white.
Produces pinkish-lavender flowers
in spring. **H** 2in (5cm), **S** 6in (15cm).

☼ ◊ Z5–7 H7–5

Saxifraga stribrnyi
Evergreen, mound-forming perennial
with small, lime-encrusted rosettes of
leaves. Crosier-shaped stems, covered in
pinkish-buff hairs, bear racemes of deep
maroon-red flowers above leaves in late
spring and early summer. **H** 3in (8cm),
S 4–5in (10–12cm).

◑ ◊ Z6–7 H7–6

Aubrieta 'J.S. Baker'
Evergreen perennial with single,
reddish-purple flowers with a white
eye borne in spring above mounds of
small, soft green leaves. **H** 4in (10cm),
S 8in (20cm).

☼ ◊ Z5–7 H7–5

Soldanella alpina (Alpine snowbell)
Evergreen, clump-forming perennial
with tufts of leaves and short, bell-
shaped, fringed, pinkish-lavender or
purplish-pink flowers in early spring.
Is difficult to flower well. **H** to 3in (8cm),
S 3–4in (8–10cm).

◑ ◊ Z4–7 H7–1

**Polygala chamaebuxus
var. grandiflora**
Evergreen, woody-based perennial with
terminal clusters of pealike, reddish-
purple and yellow flowers in late spring
and early summer. Leaves are small,
oval, leathery and dark green. **H** to 6in
(15cm), **S** to 12in (30cm).

☼ ◊ Z6–9 H9–6

Soldanella villosa
Evergreen, clump-forming perennial
with round, leathery, hairy-stalked
leaves and nodding, bell-shaped,
fringed, purplish-lavender flowers
borne on erect stems in early spring.
Dislikes winter wet. **H** 4in (10cm),
S 4–6in (10–15cm).

☼ ◊ Z4–7 H7–1

Aubrieta 'Greencourt Purple'
Evergreen, mat-forming perennial
with rosetted, mid-green leaves.
Produces masses of double, bright
purple flowers in spring. Is very good
on a dry wall. **H** 4–6in (10–15cm),
S 12in (30cm) or more.

☼ ◊ Z5–7 H7–5

Corydalis diphylla
Tuberous perennial with semi-erect,
basal leaves, divided into narrow
leaflets, and loose racemes of purple-
lipped flowers with white spurs in
spring. Protect tubers from excess
moisture in summer. **H** 4–6in (10–15cm),
S 3–4in (8–10cm).

☼ ◊ Z5–8 H8–5

Viola calcarata
Clump-forming perennial, with
oval leaves, that bears flat, outward-
facing, single, white, lavender or
purple flowers for a long period from
late spring to summer. Prefers rich soil.
H 4–6in (10–15cm), **S** to 8in (20cm).

☼ ◊ Z4–7 H7–1

Viola tricolor (Heartsease, Wild pansy)

Short-lived perennial or annual with neat, flat-faced flowers in combinations of white, yellow and shades of purple from spring to fall. Self-seeds profusely. **H** 2–6in (5–15cm), **S** 2–6in (5–15cm) or more.

 Z3–9 H12–1

Hepatica nobilis var. japonica

Slow-growing perennial with leathery, lobed leaves, semievergreen in all but very cold or arid climates. Bears slightly cupped, lilac-mauve, pink or white flowers in spring. **H** to 3in (8cm), **S** 5in (12cm).

 Z5–8 H8–4

Jeffersonia dubia

Tufted perennial with 2-lobed, blue-green leaves, sometimes flushed pink when unfolding. Bears cup-shaped, pale lilac to purplish blue flowers singly in spring. **H** 4–6in (10–15cm), **S** to 9in (23cm).

Z5–8 H8–5

Synthyris missurica var. stellata

Evergreen, mounded, rhizomatous perennial that bears dense spikes of small, violet-blue flowers in spring above rounded, deeply toothed leaves. Tolerates sun if soil remains moist. **H** 4–6in (10–15cm), **S** 6in (15cm).

Z2–6 H6–1

Aubrieta 'Purple Charm'

Evergreen, mat-forming perennial with rosetted, mid-green leaves. Produces masses of single, lavender-purple flowers, with yellow eyes, in spring. Is very good on a dry wall. **H** 4–6in (10–15cm), **S** 12in (30cm) or more.

Z5–7 H7–5

Viola riviniana Purpurea Group

Clump-forming perennial with tiny, flat-faced, purple flowers in spring-summer. Leaves are kidney-shaped and dark purple-green. Is invasive but suits a bank, woodland or wild garden. **H** 1–2in (2.5–5cm), **S** indefinite.

 Z5–8 H8–5

Jancaea heldreichii

Perennial with rosettes of thick, hairy, silver-green leaves, above which rise slender stems bearing clusters of tiny, lavender-blue flowers in late spring. Is rare and difficult to grow and is best in an alpine house. **H** and **S** to 3in (8cm).

Z5–7 H7–5

Viola pedata (Bird's-foot violet)

Clump-forming perennial with finely divided foliage and yellow-centered, pale violet, rarely white flowers borne singly on slender stems in late spring and early summer. Needs sharp drainage; grow in an alpine house. **H** 3in (5cm), **S** 3in (8cm).

Z4–8 H8–1

Viola 'Bowles's Black'

Clump-forming perennial with flat-faced, very dark violet, almost black, flowers, borne continuously from spring to fall. Oval leaves are sometimes lobed and toothed. Is short-lived; treat as biennial. **H** 2–6in (5–15cm), **S** 2–3in (5–8cm).

Z5–8 H8–1

ROCK PLANTS

BLUE

Myosotis alpestris
(Alpine forget-me-not)
Short-lived, clump-forming perennial
producing dense clusters of tiny, bright
blue flowers with creamy-yellow eyes in
late spring and early summer, just above
tufts of hairy leaves. Prefers gritty soil.
H and **S** 4–6in (10–15cm).

☼ ◊ Z4–8 H8–1

Anchusa cespitosa
Evergreen, mound-forming perennial
with rosettes of lance-shaped, dark
green leaves. In spring, stemless,
white-centered, blue flowers appear in
centers of rosettes. Old plants do not
flower well; take early summer cuttings.
H 1–2in (2.5–5cm), **S** to 9in (23cm).

☼ ◊ Z5–7 H7–5

Viola cornuta 'Minor'
Rhizomatous perennial with oval,
toothed leaves and flat-faced, rather
angular, spurred, lavender-blue,
occasionally white flowers in spring
and much of summer. **H** 3–4in (7–10cm),
S to 6in (15cm).

356   ☼ ◊ Z6–8 H8–6

Gentiana verna (Spring gentian)
Evergreen perennial, often short-
lived, with small rosettes of oval,
dark green leaves. In early spring,
tubular, bright blue flowers with
white throats are held upright on
short stems. **H** and **S** to 2in (5cm).

☼ ◊ Z4–7 H7–1

Mertensia maritima
Prostrate perennial with oval, fleshy,
bright silver-blue or silver-gray leaves.
Sturdy stems carry clusters of pendent,
funnel-shaped, sky-blue flowers in
spring. Is prone to slug damage. Needs
very sharp drainage. **H** 4–6in (10–15cm),
S 5in (12cm).

☼ ◊ Z3–7 H7–1

GRAY

Leucogenes grandiceps
Evergreen, dense, woody-based
perennial with neat rosettes of
downy, silver leaves. Yellow flower
heads, within woolly, white bracts,
are borne singly in spring or early
summer. **H** and **S** 4–6in (10–15cm).

☼ ◊ Z7–8 H8–7

Salix apoda
Slow-growing, deciduous, prostrate
shrub. In early spring, male forms
bear fat, silky, silver catkins with
orange to pale yellow stamens and
bracts. Oval, leathery leaves are hairy
when young, becoming dark green later.
H to 6in (15cm), **S** 12–24in (30–60cm).

☼ ◑ Z7–9 H9–1

YELLOW

Mandragora officinarum
Rosetted, fleshy-rooted perennial with
coarse, wavy-edged leaves. Bears
funnel-shaped, yellowish- or purplish-
white flowers in spring, followed by
large, tomato-like, shiny yellow fruits.
H 2in (5cm), **S** 12in (30cm).

☼ ◊ ❗ Z5–8 H8–5

Hacquetia epipactis
Clump-forming perennial spreading by
short rhizomes. In late winter and early
spring bears yellow or yellow-green
flower heads, encircled by apple-green
bracts, before rounded, 3-parted leaves
appear. **H** 2½in (6cm), **S** 6–9in (15–23cm).

☼ ◊ Z5–7 H7–5

Saxifraga x boydii
'Hindhead Seedling'
Evergreen perennial that forms a hard
dome of small, tufted, spiny, blue-green
leaves. In spring bears upward-facing,
open, cup-shaped, pale yellow flowers,
2 or 3 to each short stem. **H** 1in (2.5cm),
S 3in (8cm).

☼ ◊ Z6–8 H8–6

Euphorbia myrsinites
Evergreen, prostrate perennial with
terminal clusters of bright yellow-
green flowers in spring. Woody stems
are clothed in small, pointed, fleshy,
gray leaves. Is good on a wall or ledge.
H 2–3in (5–8cm), **S** to 8in (20cm).

 ☼ ◊ ① Z5–8 H8–5

Salix reticulata (Net-veined willow)
Deciduous, spreading, mat-forming
shrub. Carries plump, reddish-brown,
then yellow catkins on male plants
in spring and rounded, slightly
crinkled leaves. Likes cool, peaty soil.
H 2–3in (5–8cm), **S** 8in (20cm) or more.

 ☼ ◊ Z2–6 H6–1

**Saxifraga x apiculata
'Gregor Mendel'**
Evergreen perennial with a tight cushion
of bright green foliage. Bears clusters
of open, cup-shaped, pale yellow flowers
in early spring. **H** 4–6in (10–15cm),
S 6in (15cm) or more.

 ☼ ◊ Z6–8 H8–6

Saxifraga x elisabethae
Evergreen, cushion-forming perennial,
composed of densely packed, tiny
rosettes of spiny leaves. In spring, tight
upward-facing, bright yellow flowers
are carried on tops of red-based stems.
H 1in (2.5cm), **S** 4–6in (10–15cm).

 ☼ ◊ Z5–7 H7–5

Draba rigida
Evergreen perennial with tight
hummocks of minute, dark green
leaves. Tiny clusters of bright yellow
flowers on fine stems cover hummocks
in spring. Suits a rough, scree garden
or alpine house. Dislikes winter wet.
H 1½in (4cm), **S** 2½in (6cm).

 ☼ ◊ Z4–6 H6–1

Ranunculus ficaria Flore Pleno Group
Mat-forming perennial with heart-
shaped, dark green leaves and, in
early spring, double, bright yellow
flowers with glossy petals. May spread
rapidly. Is good for a wild garden.
H 1–2in (2.5–5cm), **S** 8in (20cm).

☼ ◊ ① Z4–8 H8–1

Draba longisiliqua
Semievergreen, cushion-forming
perennial composed of firm rosettes
of tiny, silver leaves. Bears sprays of
small, yellow flowers on long stalks
in spring. Needs plenty of water in
growth; is best grown in an alpine
house. **H** 2–3in (5–8cm), **S** 6in (15cm).

 ☼ ◊ Z4–6 H6–1

YELLOW

Vitaliana primuliflora
Evergreen, prostrate perennial with a mat of rosetted, mid-green leaves that are covered in spring with many small clusters of stemless, tubular, bright yellow flowers. **H** 1in (2.5cm), **S** 8in (20cm).

☼ ◊ Z5–8 H8–5

Morisia monanthos
Prostrate perennial with flat rosettes of divided, leathery, dark green leaves. Bears stemless, flat, bright yellow flowers in late spring and early summer. Needs very sharp drainage. **H** 1in (2.5cm), **S** 3in (8cm).

☼ ◊ Z7–9 H9–7

Trollius pumilus
Tufted perennial with leaves divided into 5 segments, each farther lobed. Carries solitary cup-shaped, bright yellow flowers in late spring and early summer. **H** 6in (15cm), **S** 6in (15cm) or more.

☼ ◐ Z4–6 H8–5

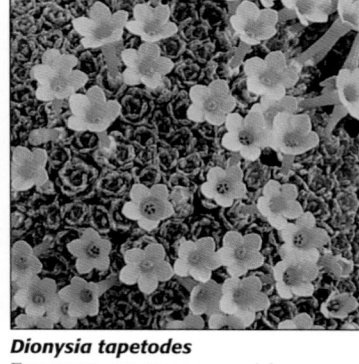

Dionysia tapetodes
Evergreen, prostrate perennial producing a tight mat of tiny, gray-green leaves. Bears small, upward-facing, yellow flowers in early spring. **H** ½in (1cm), **S** to 6in (15cm).

☼ ◊ Z5–7 H7–5

Erysimum helveticum
Semievergreen, clump-forming perennial with closely-packed tufts of long, narrow leaves and many fragrant, bright yellow flowers borne in flat heads in late spring and early summer. **H** 4in (10cm), **S** 6in (15cm).

☼ ◊ Z5–8 H8–5

Saxifraga sancta
Evergreen, mat-forming perennial with tufts of bright green leaves. Bears short racemes of upward-facing, open cup-shaped, bright yellow flowers in spring. **H** 2in (5cm), **S** 6in (15cm).

☼◐ ◊ Z7–8 H8–7

Draba mollissima
Semievergreen, cushion-forming perennial with clusters of tiny, yellow flowers on slender stems in spring. Minute leaves form a soft green dome, which should be packed beneath with small stones. Grow in an alpine house. **H** 1½in (4cm), **S** 6in (15cm) or more.

☼ ◊ Z4–6 H6–1

Dionysia aretioides
Evergreen perennial forming cushions of soft, hairy, grayish-green leaves that are covered in early spring by scented, stemless, round, bright yellow flowers. **H** 2–4in (5–10cm), **S** 6–12in (15–30cm).

☼ ◊ Z5–7 H7–5

Viola 'Jackanapes'
Clump-forming perennial with oval, toothed leaves. Produces flat-faced flowers with reddish-brown, upper petals and yellow, lower ones throughout late spring and summer. **H** 3–5in (8–12cm), **S** to 8in (20cm) or more.

☼ ◊ Z4–8 H8–1

Viola aetolica
Clump-forming perennial bearing flat-faced, yellow flowers singly on upright stems in late spring and early summer. Leaves are oval and mid-green. **H** 2–3in (5–8cm), **S** 6in (15cm).

☼ ◊ Z8–9 H9–8

Ranunculus ficaria var. aurantiacus
Mat-forming perennial bearing in early spring cup-shaped, single, orange flowers with glossy petals. Leaves are heart-shaped and mid-green. May spread rapidly. Is good for a wild garden. **H** 2in (5cm), **S** 8in (20cm).

☼ ◊ ❢ Z4–8 H8–1

WHITE

Silene alpestris
Perennial with branching stems and narrow leaves. Bears small, rounded, fringed, white, occasionally pink-flushed flowers in late spring and early summer. Self seeds freely. **H** 4–6in (10–15cm), **S** 8in (20cm).

☼ ◊ Z4–7 H7–1

Phlox stolonifera 'Ariane'
Evergreen, low-growing perennial with flowering sideshoots that bear heads of open, saucer-shaped, white blooms in early summer. Has oval, pale green leaves. Cut back flowered shoots by half after flowering. **H** to 6in (15cm), **S** 12in (30cm).

☼ ◊ pH Z4–8 H8–1

Achillea clavennae
Semievergreen, carpeting perennial that bears loose clusters of white flower heads with gold centers from summer to mid fall. Leaves are narrowly oval, many-lobed and covered with fine, white hairs. Dislikes winter wet. **H** 6in (15cm), **S** 9in (23cm) or more.

☼ ◊ ❢ Z3–8 H8–1

Haberlea rhodopensis 'Virginalis'
Evergreen perennial with small, arching sprays of funnel-shaped, pure white flowers borne in late spring and early summer above neat rosettes of oval, toothed, dark green leaves. **H** and **S** in flower 4–6in (10–15cm).

◐ ◊ Z5–7 H7–5

Potentilla alba
Vigorous mat-forming perennial bearing loose sprays of flat, single, white flowers in summer. Leaves are divided into oval leaflets and are silvery beneath. **H** 2–3in (5–8cm), **S** 3in (8cm).

☼ ◊ Z5–8 H8–3

Cyananthus lobatus f. albus
Prostrate perennial with branched stems clothed in small, wedge-shaped, dull green leaves. Bears funnel-shaped, single, white flowers with spreading lobes in late summer. **H** 3in (8cm), **S** 12in (30cm).

◐ ◊ Z6–7 H7–6

ROCK PLANTS

WHITE

Campanula carpatica 'Bressingham White'
Clump-forming perennial bearing open cup-shaped, white flowers, singly on unbranched stems, in summer. Has abundant, rounded, bright green leaves. **H** 4–6in (10–15cm), **S** 6in (15cm).

☼ ◊ Z4–7 H7–1

Arenaria montana
Prostrate perennial that forms loose mats of small, narrowly oval leaves and bears large, round, white flowers in summer. Suits a wall or rock crevice. Must have adequate moisture. **H** 2in (5cm), **S** 5in (12cm).

☼ ◊ Z3–5 H5–1

Cornus canadensis (Bunchberry)
Groundcover perennial with whorls of oval leaves. In late spring and early summer bears green, sometimes purple-tinged flowers, within white bracts, followed by red berries. **H** 4–6in (10–15cm), **S** 12in (30cm) or more.

☼ ◐ ◊ pH ① Z2–7 H7–1

Iberis saxatilis
Evergreen, dwarf subshrub that in late spring and early summer produces large heads of numerous small, white flowers, which become tinged violet with age. Glossy, dark leaves are linear and cylindrical. Trim after flowering. **H** 3–5in (8–12cm), **S** 12in (30cm).

☼ ◊ Z7–9 H9–7

Celmisia ramulosa
Evergreen, shrubby perennial with small, hairy, gray-green leaves. Daisylike, white flower heads are borne singly on short stems in late spring and early summer. **H** and **S** 4in (10cm).

☼ ◊ pH Z7–8 H8–7

Ourisia caespitosa
Evergreen, prostrate perennial with creeping rootstocks and stems bearing tiny, oval leaves and many outward-facing, open cup-shaped, white flowers in late spring and early summer. **H** 1in (2.5cm), **S** 4in (10cm).

☀ ◊ Z5–7 H7–5

Anacyclus pyrethrum var. depressus
Short-lived, prostrate perennial that has white flower heads, with red reverses to ray petals, in summer. Flowers close in dull light. Stems are clothed in fine leaves. Dislikes wet. **H** 1–2in (2.5–5cm) or more, **S** 4in (10cm).

☼ ◊ Z3–8 H8–1

Lewisia rediviva [white form] (Bitterroot)
Tufted, rosetted perennial with clusters of fine, narrow leaves that are summer-deciduous. Bears large, white flowers that open in bright weather in late spring and early summer. **H** ½–1½in (1–4cm), **S** to 2in (5cm).

☼ ◊ pH Z4–7 H7–1

Epilobium glabellum of gardens
Mat- or clump-forming, semievergreen perennial with elliptic to ovate, finely toothed, deep green leaves. Cup-shaped, creamy-white to pink flowers are borne on branching stems in summer. **H** and **S** 8in (20cm).

☼ ◐ ◊ Z5–8 H8–5

Achillea x kellereri
Semievergreen perennial that bears daisylike, white flower heads in loose clusters in summer. Leaves are feathery and gray-green. Is good for a wall or bank. Dislikes winter wet and must have perfect drainage. **H** 6in (15cm), **S** 9in (23cm) or more.

☼ ◊ ① Z5–7 H7–5

Nierembergia repens
Mat-forming perennial with upright, open bell-shaped, yellow-centered, white flowers, occasionally flushed pink with age, borne for a long period in summer. Leaves are small, oval and light green. Is useful for cracks in paving. **H** 2in (5cm), **S** 8in (20cm) or more.

☀ ◊ Z7–11 H11–7

Petrocosmea kerrii
Evergreen perennial with compact rosettes of oval, pointed, hairy, rich green leaves. In summer bears clusters of short, outward-facing, tubular, open-mouthed white flowers. Suits an alpine house. **H** to 3in (8cm), **S** 5–6in (12–15cm). Min. 36–41°F (2–5°C).

☀ ◊ Z10–11 H11–9

Penstemon hirsutus var. pygmaeus
Short-lived, evergreen, compact subshrub that bears tubular, lipped, hairy, purple- or blue-flushed, white flowers in summer. Has tightly packed, dark green leaves and is suitable for a trough. **H** and **S** 3in (8cm).

☀ ◊ Z3–9 H9–1

Dryas octopetala
Evergreen, prostrate perennial forming mats of oval, lobed, leathery, dark green leaves on sturdy stems. In late spring and early summer, cup-shaped, creamy-white flowers are borne just above foliage, followed by attractive, feathery seeds. **H** 2½in (6cm), **S** indefinite.

☀ ◊ Z3–6 H6–1

Carlina acaulis (Alpine thistle)
Clump-forming perennial that in summer–fall bears large, stemless, thistle-like, single, off-white or pale brown flower heads, with papery bracts, on rosettes of long, spiny-margined, deeply-cut leaves. **H** 3–4in (8–10cm), **S** 6–9in (15–23cm).

☀ ◊ Z5–7 H7–5

Alstroemeria hookeri
Tuberous perennial with narrow leaves and loose heads of widely flared, orange-suffused, pink flowers in summer; upper petals are spotted and blotched red and yellow. **H** 4–6in (10–15cm), **S** 18–24in (45–60cm).

☀ ◊ ❗ Z8–10 H10–8

Petrorhagia saxifraga (Tunic flower)
Mat-forming perennial with tufts of grasslike leaves. In summer bears a profusion of small, pale pink flowers, veined deeper pink, on slender stems. Grows best on poor soil and self-seeds easily. **H** 4in (10cm), **S** 6in (15cm).

☀ ◊ Z5–7 H7–5

361

ROCK PLANTS

Gypsophila repens 'Dorothy Teacher'
Semievergreen, prostrate perennial.
Sprays of small, rounded, white flowers,
which age to deep pink, cover mats of
narrow, bluish-green leaves in summer.
trim stems after flowering. **H** 1–2in
(2.5–5cm), **S** 12in (30cm) or more.

☼ ◊ Z4–7 H7–1

Convolvulus althaeoides
Vigorous perennial with long, trailing
stems clothed in heart-shaped, cut,
mid-green leaves, overlaid silver. Bears
large, open trumpet-shaped pink flowers
in summer. May be invasive in a mild
climate. **H** 2in (5cm), **S** indefinite.

☼ ◊ Z6–8 H8–1

Geranium sanguineum var. striatum
Hummock-forming, spreading perennial
that has cup-shaped, pink flowers, with
darker veins, borne singly in summer
above round, deeply divided, dark green
leaves. **H** 4–6in (10–15cm), **S** 12in (30cm)
or more.

☼ ◊ Z3–8 H8–1

Rhodohypoxis 'Margaret Rose'
Perennial with a tuber-like rootstock
and an erect, basal tuft of narrowly
lance-shaped, hairy leaves. Bears a
succession of upright, flattish, pale
pink flowers on slender stems in spring
and early summer. **H** 2–4in (5–10cm),
S 1–2in (2.5–5cm).

☼ ◊ Z9–10 H10–9

Ourisia microphylla
Semievergreen, mat-forming perennial,
with neat, scalelike, pale green leaves,
bearing a profusion of small, pink
flowers in late spring and early summer.
Is difficult to grow in an arid climate.
H 2–4in (5–10cm), **S** 6in (15cm).

◑ ◊ Z7–9 H9–7

Asperula suberosa
Clump-forming perennial with a
mound of loose stems bearing tiny,
hairy, gray leaves and, in early summer,
many tubular, pale pink flowers. Dislikes
winter wet but needs moist soil in
summer. Is best in an alpine house.
H 3in (8cm), **S** to 12in (30cm).

☼ ◊ Z5–7 H7–5

Erodium corsicum
Compact, clump-forming perennial that
has soft, gray-green leaves with wavy
margins. Bears flat-faced, pink flowers,
with darker veins, on stiff, slender stems
in late spring and summer. Is best in
an alpine house as it dislikes winter wet.
H 3in (8cm), **S** 6in (15cm).

☼ ◊ Z4–7 H7–1

Saponaria x olivana
Compact perennial with a firm cushion
of narrow leaves. Flowering stems,
produced around edges of the cushion,
bear flat, single, pale pink flowers in
summer. Needs very sharp drainage.
H 3in (8cm), **S** 4in (10cm).

☼ ◊ Z4–8 H8–1

Aethionema 'Warley Rose'
Short-lived, evergreen or
semievergreen, compact subshrub
with tiny, linear, bluish-green leaves.
Bears racemes of small, pink flowers
on short stems in profusion in
spring-summer. **H** and **S** 6in (15cm).

☼ ◊ Z6–8 H8–6

Phlox adsurgens 'Wagon Wheel'
Evergreen, prostrate perennial forming
wide mats of woody stems, clothed
in oval leaves. Bears heads of wheel-
shaped, pink flowers with narrow
petals in summer. Needs rich soil.
H 4in (10cm), **S** 12in (30cm).

☀◐ ◊ pH Z4–8 H8–1

Linnaea borealis (Twinflower)
Evergreen, mat-forming, subshrubby
perennial with rooting stems bearing
small, oval leaves, above which in
summer rise threadlike stems bearing
pairs of small, fragrant, tubular, pale
pink and white flowers. **H** ¾in (2cm),
S 12in (30cm) or more.

☀◐ ◊ pH Z6–9 H9–6

Geranium dalmaticum
Prostrate, spreading perennial with
outward-facing, almost flat, shell-pink
flowers borne in summer above divided,
dark green leaves. Will grow taller in
partial shade and is evergreen in all
but severest winters. **H** 3–4in (8–10cm)
or more, **S** 5–8in (12–20cm).

☀ ◊ Z5–7 H7–5

Acantholimon glumaceum
Evergreen, cushion-forming perennial
with hard, spiny, dark green leaves
and short spikes of small, star-shaped,
pink flowers in summer. **H** 4in (10cm),
S 8in (20cm).

☀ ◊ Z7–9 H9–7

Erigeron karvinskianus
Spreading perennial with lax stems
bearing narrow, lance-shaped, hairy
leaves and, in summer-fall, daisylike
flower heads that open white, turn pink
and fade to purple. **H** 4–6in (10–15cm),
S indefinite.

☀ ◊ Z5–7 H7–5

Dianthus pavonius
Evergreen, prostrate perennial with
comparatively large, rounded, pale
to deep pink flowers, buff on reverses,
borne on short stems in summer above
low mats of spiky leaves. **H** 2in (5cm),
S 3in (8cm).

☀ ◊ pH Z3–8 H8–1

Androsace lanuginosa
Evergreen, trailing perennial with loose
stems, covered in silky hairs, carrying
deep green leaves and, in summer,
clusters of small, flat, lilac-pink or pale
pink flowers with dark pink or yellow
eyes. **H** 1½in (4cm), **S** to 7in (18cm).

☀ ◊ Z5–7 H7–3

Dianthus 'Little Jock'
Evergreen, compact, clump-forming
perennial with spiky, silvery-green
foliage. In summer produces strongly
fragrant, rounded, semidouble, pink
flowers, with darker eyes, above foliage.
H and **S** 4in (10cm).

☀ ◊ Z5–9 H9–5

Dianthus gratianopolitanus
(Cheddar pink)
Evergreen perennial with loose
mats of narrow, gray-green leaves.
In summer, produces very fragrant,
flat, pale pink flowers on slender stems.
H to 6in (15cm), **S** to 12in (30cm).

☀ ◊ Z4–8 H8–1

ROCK PLANTS

PINK

Loiseleuria procumbens
(Alpine azalea, Trailing azalea)
Evergreen, prostrate shrub with small,
oval leaves, hairy and beige beneath.
Has terminal clusters of open funnel-
shaped, rose-pink to white flowers
in early summer. **H** to 3in (8cm),
S 4–6in (10–15cm).

☼ ◊ pH Z2–5 H5–1

Dianthus 'Pike's Pink'
Evergreen, compact, cushion-forming
perennial, with spiky, gray-green
foliage, that bears fragrant, rounded,
double, pink flowers in summer.
H and **S** 4in (10cm).

☼ ◊ Z5–8 H8–5

Aethionema armenum
Short-lived, evergreen or semievergreen,
dense subshrub with narrow, blue-green
leaves. Carries loose sprays of tiny, pale
to deep pink flowers in summer.
H and **S** 6in (15cm).

☼ ◊ Z7–9 H9–7

Saponaria caespitosa
Mat-forming perennial with small,
lance-shaped leaves. Tiny, flat, single,
pink to purple flowers are borne in small
heads in summer. Needs very sharp
drainage. **H** 3in (8cm), **S** 4in (10cm).

☼ ◊ Z4–8 H8–1

Pterocephalus perennis
Semievergreen, mat-forming perennial
with crinkled, hairy leaves. Bears tight,
rounded heads of tubular, pinkish-
lavender flowers, singly on short stems
in summer, followed by feathery seed
heads. **H** 2in (5cm), **S** 4in (10cm).

☼ ◊ Z5–7 H7–5

Saponaria ocymoides
(Rock soapwort)
Perennial with compact or loose,
sprawling mats of hairy, oval leaves,
above which a profusion of tiny, flat,
pale pink to crimson flowers is carried
in summer. Is excellent on a dry bank.
H 1–3in (2.5–8cm), **S** 16in (40cm).

☼ ◊ Z4–8 H8–1

Oxalis depressa
Tuberous perennial with 3-lobed leaves
and short-stemmed, widely funnel-
shaped, bright rose-pink flowers,
¾in (2cm) across, in summer. Needs
a sheltered site or cool greenhouse.
H 2in (5cm), **S** 3–4in (8–10cm).

☼ ◊ Z7–10 H10–7

Dianthus myrtinervius
Evergreen, spreading perennial
with numerous small, rounded, pink
flowers that appear in summer above
tiny, grasslike leaves. **H** 2in (5cm),
S 8in (20cm).

☼ ◊ Z4–9 H9–1

Dianthus alpinus (Alpine pink)
Evergreen, compact perennial that bears
comparatively large, rounded, rose-pink
to crimson flowers, singly in summer,
above mats of narrow, dark green
foliage. Likes rich soil. **H** 2in (5cm),
S 3in (8cm).

☼ ◊ Z4–8 H8–1

Dianthus 'Annabelle'
Evergreen, compact, clump-forming
perennial with spiky, gray-green foliage.
In summer bears fragrant, rounded,
semidouble, cerise-pink flowers, singly
on slender stems. **H** and **S** 4in (10cm).

☼ ◊ Z5–9 H8–1

Phlox 'Camla'
Evergreen mound-forming perennial
with wiry, arching stems and fine leaves.
Has a profusion of open saucer-shaped,
rich pink flowers in early summer.
Trim after flowering. Needs rich soil.
H 5in (12cm), **S** 12in (30cm).

☼ ◊ Z6–8 H8–6

Phlox subulata 'Marjorie'
Evergreen, mound-forming perennial
with fine leaves and a profusion of flat,
star-shaped, bright rose-pink flowers
in early summer. Trim after flowering.
H 4in (10cm), **S** 8in (20cm).

☼ ◊ Z3–8 H8–1

Dianthus 'La Bourboule'
Evergreen perennial with small clumps
of tufted, spiky foliage. Bears a profusion
of strongly fragrant, small, single,
pink flowers in summer. **H** 2in (5cm),
S 3in (8cm).

☼ ◊ Z5–9 H9–1

Persicaria affinis 'Donald Lowndes'
Evergreen, mat-forming perennial that
has sturdy, branching, spreading stems
clothed with pointed leaves. In summer
bears dense spikes of small, red flowers,
which become paler with age.**H** 3–6in
(8–15cm), **S** to 6in (15cm).

☼ ◊ ① Z3–8 H8–1

Phlox douglasii 'Crackerjack'
Evergreen, compact, mound-forming
perennial. Has a profusion of saucer-
shaped, bright crimson or magenta
flowers in early summer. Leaves are
lance-shaped and mid-green. Cut
back after flowering. **H** to 3in (8cm),
S 8in (20cm).

☼ ◊ Z5–7 H7–5

Armeria maritima 'Vindictive'
Evergreen, clump-forming perennial
with grasslike, dark blue-green leaves,
above which rise stiff stems bearing
spherical heads of small, deep rose-pink
flowers for a long period in summer.
H 4in (10cm), **S** 6in (15cm).

☼ ◊ Z3–9 H9–1

Lewisia rediviva [pink form]
(Bitterroot)
Tufted, rosetted perennial. Clusters of
narrow leaves are summer-deciduous.
Large, many-petaled, pink flowers
open on bright days in late spring and
early summer. Suits an alpine house.
H ½–1½in (1–4cm), **S** to 2in (5cm).

☼ ◊ pH Z4–7 H7–1

Rhodohypoxis 'Albrighton'
Perennial with tuber-like rootstock
and an erect, basal tuft of narrowly
lance-shaped, hairy leaves. Bears a
succession of erect, deep pink flowers
singly on slender stems in spring and
early summer. **H** 2–4in (5–10cm),
S 1–2in (2.5–5cm).

☼ ◊ Z9–10 H10–9

Dianthus deltoides 'Leuchtfunk'
Evergreen, mat-forming perennial.
Many small, flat, upward-facing,
brilliant cerise flowers are borne singly
above tiny, oblong, pointed leaves.
H 4–6in (10–15cm), **S** 8in (20cm).

☼ ◊ Z3–10 H10–1

Thymus 'Bressingham'
Evergreen, mat-forming, aromatic
subshrub with creeping stems and
elliptic, white-hairy, mid-green leaves.
Bears numerous, small, 2-lipped,
purple-pink flowers, splashed dark
crimson, in summer. **H** 1¼in (3cm),
S 5in (12cm).

☼ ◊ Z6–9 H9–6

ROCK PLANTS

PINK | **PURPLE**

Phlox bifida (Sand phlox)
Evergreen, mound-forming perennial with lance-shaped leaves. Bears a profusion of small heads of star-shaped, lilac or white flowers with deeply cleft petals in summer. Cut back stems by half after flowering. **H** 4–6in (10–15cm), **S** 6in (15cm).

☼ ◊ Z4–8 H8–1

Thymus caespititius
Compact, cushion-forming, aromatic subshrub with upright stems covered in small, prominently veined, dark-green leaves. In early summer, bears lilac or mauve flowers in dense rounded heads. **H** 6in (15cm), **S** 8in (20cm).

☼ ◊ Z4–9 H9–1

Androsace villosa var. **jacquemontii**
Evergreen, mat-forming perennial with small rosettes of hairy, gray-green leaves. Bears tiny, pinkish-purple flowers on red stems in late spring and early summer. Suits an alpine house. **H** ½–1½in (1–4cm), **S** 8in (20cm).

☼ ◊ Z5–7 H7–5

Teucrium polium
Deciduous, dome-shaped subshrub that has much-branched, woolly, white or yellowish stems and leaves with scalloped margins. Bears yellowish-white or pinkish-purple flowers in flat heads in summer. Requires very sharp drainage. **H** and **S** 6in (15cm).

☼ ◊ Z8–9 H9–8

Geranium cinereum 'Ballerina'
Spreading, rosetted perennial that bears cup-shaped, purplish-pink flowers, with deep purple veins, on lax stems in late spring and summer. Basal leaves are round, deeply divided and soft. **H** 4in (10cm), **S** 12in (30cm).

☼ ◊ Z5–9 H9–6

Phlox douglasii 'Boothman's Variety'
Evergreen, mound-forming perennial with lance-shaped leaves and masses of pale lavender-blue flowers, with violet-blue markings around eyes, in early summer. Cut back after flowering. **H** to 2in (5cm), **S** 8in (20cm).

☼ ◊ Z5–7 H7–5

Dianthus microlepis
Evergreen perennial with tiny tufts of minute, fine, grasslike leaves, above which rise numerous small, rounded, pink flowers in early summer. Is best suited to a trough. **H** 2in (5cm), **S** 8in (20cm).

☼ ◊ Z5–9 H8–1

Geranium subcaulescens
Spreading perennial with round, deeply divided, soft leaves. In summer bears brilliant purple-magenta flowers, with striking, black eyes and stamens, on lax stems. **H** 4in (10cm), **S** 12in (30cm).

☼ ◊ Z4–9 H9–3

Physoplexis comosa
Tufted perennial with deeply cut leaves and round heads of bottle-shaped, violet-blue, rarely white, flowers in summer. Suits crevices but dislikes winter wet. **H** 3in (8cm), **S** 4in (10cm).

☼ ◊ Z5–7 H7–5

Aster alpinus
Clump-forming, spreading perennial with lance-shaped, dark green leaves. Bears daisylike, purplish-blue or pinkish-purple flower heads, with yellow centers, from mid- to late summer. **H** 6in (15cm), **S** 12–18in (30–45cm).

 ☼ ◊ Z4–8 H8–1

Thymus 'Peter Davis'
Evergreen, aromatic, mound-forming subshrub with fine, twiggy stems and narrow leaves fringed with white hairs. Bears dense heads of small, pinkish-purple flowers with purple bracts in summer. **H** 4–5in (10–12cm), **S** 6in (15cm).

☼ ◊ Z6–9 H9–6

Phlox 'Emerald Cushion'
Evergreen perennial with emerald-green mounds of fine leaves, studded in late spring and early summer with large, saucer-shaped, bright violet-blue flowers. Trim after flowering. **H** 3in (8cm), **S** 6in (15cm).

 ☼ ◊ Z3–8 H8–1

Viola 'Nellie Britton'
Clump-forming perennial with small, oval, toothed leaves and flat-faced, lavender-pink flowers borne from late spring to late summer. Soil should not be too dry. **H** 3–6in (8–15cm), **S** to 8in (20cm).

Campanula poscharskyana
Rampant, spreading perennial with bell-shaped, violet flowers borne on leafy stems in summer. Leaves are round with serrated edges. Vigorous runners make it suitable for a bank or a wild garden. **H** 4–6in (10–15cm), **S** indefinite.

 ☼ ◊ Z3–9 H9–1

Globularia meridionalis
Evergreen, dome-shaped subshrub. In summer, globular, fluffy, lavender to lavender-purple flower heads are borne singly just above glossy leaves. **H** to 4in (10cm), **S** 8in (20cm).

☼ ◊ Z5–7 H7–5

Edraianthus serpyllifolius
Evergreen, prostrate perennial with tight mats of tiny leaves and small, bell-shaped, deep violet flowers, borne on short stems in early summer. Is uncommon and seldom sets seed in gardens. **H** ½in (1cm), **S** to 2in (5cm).

☼ ◊ Z7–9 H9–7

Campanula carpatica 'Jewel'
Low-growing, compact and clump-forming perennial with mid-green, toothed leaves on branching stems. Bright, purple-blue, upturned, bell-shaped flowers are produced over several months in summer. **H** and **S** 4–6in (10–15cm).

☼ ◊ Z4–7 H7–1

ROCK PLANTS

Viola 'Huntercombe Purple'
Perennial forming wide clumps of neat, oval, toothed leaves. Has a profusion of flat-faced, rich violet flowers from spring to late summer. Divide clumps every 3 years. **H** 4–6in (10–15cm), **S** 6–12in (15–30cm) or more.

☼ ◊ Z5–7 H7–5

Campanula portenschlagiana
Vigorous, evergreen, prostrate perennial with dense mats of small, ivy-shaped leaves and large clusters of erect, open bell-shaped, violet flowers in summer. **H** 6in (15cm), **S** indefinite.

☼ ◊ Z4–7 H7–1

Pinguicula grandiflora
Clump-forming perennial with a basal rosette of sticky, oval, pale green leaves. In summer bears spurred, open funnel-shaped, violet-blue to purple flowers singly on upright, slender stems. **H** 5–6in (12–15cm), **S** 2in (5cm).

☼ ● Z3–5 H5–3

Campanula 'G.F. Wilson'
Neat, mound-forming perennial with large, upturned, bell-shaped, violet flowers in summer. Has rounded, pale yellow-green leaves. **H** 3–4in (8–10cm), **S** 5–6in (12–15cm).

☼ ◊ Z4–7 H7–1

Aquilegia jonesii
Compact perennial that bears short-spurred, violet-blue flowers in summer, a few to each slender stem. Has small rosettes of finely divided, blue-gray or gray-green leaves. Is uncommon, suitable for an alpine house only. **H** 1in (2.5cm), **S** to 2in (5cm).

☼ ◊ ! Z4–8 H8–1

Prunella grandiflora (Large self-heal)
Semievergreen, spreading, mat-forming perennial with basal rosettes of leaves. In mid-summer bears short spikes of funnel-shaped, purple flowers in whorls. **H** 4–6in (10–15cm), **S** 12in (30cm).

☼ ◊ Z5–7 H8–5

Campanula 'Birch Hybrid'
Vigorous, evergreen perennial with tough, arching, prostrate stems and ivy-shaped, bright green leaves. Bears many open bell-shaped, deep violet flowers in summer. **H** 4in (10cm), **S** 12in (30cm) or more.

☼ ◊ Z4–7 H7–1

Edraianthus pumilio
Short-lived perennial with low tufts of fine, grasslike leaves. In early summer, upturned, bell-shaped, pale to deep lavender flowers, on very short stems, appear amid foliage. **H** 1in (2.5cm), **S** 3in (8cm).

☼ ◊ Z6–8 H8–6

Cyananthus microphyllus
Mat-forming perennial with very fine, red stems clothed in tiny leaves. Bears funnel-shaped, violet-blue flowers at the end of each stem in late summer. Likes rich soil. **H** ¾in (2cm), **S** 8in (20cm).

☀ ◊ Z5–7 H7–5

Ramonda myconi
Evergreen, rosette-forming perennial with hairy, crinkled leaves and, in late spring and early summer, flat, blue-mauve, pink or white flowers, borne on branched stems. **H** 3in (8cm), **S** to 4in (10cm).

☀ ◊ Z5–7 H7–5

Campanula cochleariifolia
(Fairy thimbles)
Spreading perennial. Runners produce mats of rosetted, tiny, round leaves. Bears small clusters of white, lavender or pale blue flowers in summer on many thin stems above foliage. **H** 3in (8cm), **S** indefinite.

☀ ◊ Z5–7 H7–1

Townsendia grandiflora
Short-lived, evergreen perennial with basal rosettes of small, spoon-shaped leaves. Upright stems carry solitary daisylike, violet or violet-blue flower heads in late spring and early summer. **H** to 6in (15cm), **S** 4in (10cm).

☀ ◊ Z4–7 H7–1

Sisyrinchium idahoense
Semievergreen, upright, clump-forming perennial that for a long period in summer and early fall has many flowering stems carrying tiny tufts of iris-like, blue to violet-blue flowers. Foliage is grasslike. Self seeds readily. **H** to 5in (12cm), **S** 4in (10cm).

☀ ◊ Z7–8 H8–7

Pratia pedunculata
Vigorous, evergreen, creeping perennial with small leaves and a profusion of star-shaped, pale to mid-blue or occasionally purplish-blue flowers borne in summer. Makes good groundcover in a moist site. **H** ½in (1cm), **S** indefinite.

☀ ◊ Z5–7 H7–5

Polygala calcarea 'Lillet'
Evergreen, prostrate, very compact perennial with rosettes of small, narrowly oval leaves and loose heads of bright blue flowers in spring and early summer. Likes rich soil. Suits a trough. **H** 1in (2.5cm), **S** 3–4in (8–10cm).

☀ ◊ Z7–9 H9–7

Hedyotis michauxii (Creeping bluets)
Vigorous perennial with rooting stems. Produces mats of mid-green foliage studded with star-shaped, violet-blue flowers in late spring and early summer. **H** 3in (8cm), **S** 12in (30cm).

☀ ◊ Z3–8 H8–1

Globularia cordifolia
Evergreen, mat-forming, dwarf shrub with creeping, woody stems clothed in tiny, oval leaves. Bears stemless, round, fluffy, blue to pale lavender-blue flower heads in summer. **H** 1–2in (2.5–5cm), **S** to 8in (20cm).

☀ ◊ Z5–7 H7–5

Trachelium asperuloides
Mat-forming perennial with threadlike stems clothed in minute, mid-green leaves, above which rise many tiny, upright, tubular, pale blue flowers in summer. Do not remove old stems in winter. **H** 3in (8cm), **S** to 6in (15cm).

☀ ◊ Z8–13 H12–6

GENTIANS

Although there are gentians large enough to hold their own in the herbaceous border, most are low-growing, deciduous or evergreen perennials, best suited to rock gardens, where they can form spreading mats. Flowering between spring and fall, they are renowned for their vivid blue trumpet-shaped flowers, which are produced in pale shades, such as *G.* 'Strathmore', to intensely dark, such as *G. acaulis,* although there are also white- and yellow-flowered forms. All require a cool position, sheltered from hot summer sun. Most need light, rich, moist but well-drained neutral soil; fall-flowering species and cultivars, such as *G. sino-ornata*, require acidic conditions to thrive. Protect from slugs and snails, particularly in spring.

G. saxosa

G. 'Ettrick'

G. 'Strathmore'

G. 'Soutra'

G. 'Eugen's Allerbester'

G. 'Blue Silk'

G. 'Shot Silk'

G. x macaulayi 'Wells's Variety'

G. 'Inverleith'

G. sino-ornata

G. acaulis

BLUE

Eritrichium nanum
Clump-forming perennial with tufts of hairy, gray-green leaves. Bears small, stemless, flat, pale blue flowers in late spring and early summer. Requires sharp drainage. Is only suitable for an alpine house. **H** ¾in (2cm), **S** 1in (2.5cm).

☀ ◊ Z5–7 H7–5

Parochetus communis
(Shamrock pea)
Evergreen, prostrate perennial with clover-like leaves and pealike, brilliant blue flowers that are borne almost continuously. Grows best in an alpine house. **H** 1–2in (2.5–5cm), **S** indefinite.

◑ ◊ Z8–11 H11–8

Polygala calcarea
Evergreen, prostrate, occasionally upright, perennial. Has small, narrowly oval leaves and pale to dark blue flowers in late spring and early summer. Likes rich soil. Suits a trough. May be difficult to establish. **H** 1in (2.5cm), **S** to 6in (15cm).

☀ ◊ Z7–9 H9–7

Polygala chamaebuxus
Evergreen, woody-based perennial
with tiny, hard, dark green leaves.
In late spring and early summer
bears many racemes of small, pealike,
white-and-yellow flowers, sometimes
marked brown. Needs rich soil.
H 2in (5cm), **S** 8in (20cm).

☀️◑ ○ Z6–9 H9–6

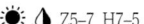

Mitella breweri
Neat, clump-forming, rhizomatous
perennial with slender, hairy stems
bearing small, pendent, tubular,
greenish-white flowers, with flared
mouths, in summer. Has lobed,
kidney-shaped, basal leaves.
H and **S** 6in (15cm).

☀️ ○ Z5–7 H7–5

Asarina procumbens
Semievergreen perennial with trailing
stems bearing soft, hairy leaves and
tubular, pale cream flowers, with
yellow palates, throughout summer.
Dislikes winter wet. Self-seeds freely.
H ½–1in (1–2.5cm), **S** 9–12in (23–30cm).

☀️ ○ Z6–9 H9–6

Sedum acre (Biting stonecrop,
Common stonecrop)
Evergreen, mat-forming perennial
with dense, spreading shoots and tiny,
fleshy, pale green leaves. Bears flat,
terminal heads of tiny, yellow summer
flowers. Is invasive but easily controlled.
H 1–2in (2.5–5cm), **S** indefinite.

☀️ ○ ① Z3–8 H8–1

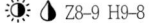

Gunnera magellanica
Mat-forming perennial, grown for its
rounded, toothed leaves, often bronze-
tinged when young, on short, creeping
stems. Small, green, unisexual flowers,
with reddish-bracts, are borne on male
and female plants. Likes peaty soil.
H 1in (2.5cm), **S** to 12in (30cm).

☀️◑ ○ Z8–9 H9–8

Sedum acre 'Aureum'
Evergreen, mat-forming perennial
with spreading shoots, yellow-tipped
in spring and early summer, clothed
in tiny, fleshy, yellow leaves. Has flat
heads of tiny, yellow flowers in
summer. Is invasive but easy to control.
H 1–2in (2.5–5cm), **S** to 9in (23cm).

☀️ ○ ① Z3–8 H8–1

Calceolaria tenella
Vigorous, evergreen, prostrate perennial
with creeping, reddish stems and oval,
mid-green leaves, above which rise
small spikes of pouch-shaped, red-
spotted, yellow flowers in summer.
H 4in (10cm), **S** indefinite.

☀️ ○ Z7–8 H6–1

Oxalis perdicaria
Clump-forming perennial with
woolly-coated tubers. Mid-green leaves
have up to 5 rounded lobes. Produces
racemes of widely funnel-shaped, bright
yellow flowers, ½–¾in (1–2cm) across,
in late summer and fall. **H** 2in (5cm),
S 3–4in (8–10cm).

☀️ ○ Z8–9 H9–8

YELLOW

Waldsteinia ternata
Semievergreen perennial with loose, spreading mats of toothed, 3-parted leaves. Bears saucer-shaped, yellow flowers in late spring and early summer. Is good on a bank. **H** 4in (10cm), **S** 8–12in (20–30cm).

☀ ◊ Z3–8 H8–1

Lysimachia nummularia 'Aurea'
(Golden creeping Jenny)
Prostrate perennial. Creeping, rooting stems bear pairs of round, soft yellow leaves, which later turn greenish-yellow or green in dense shade. Has bright yellow flowers in leaf axils in summer. **H** 1–2in (2.5–5cm), **S** indefinite.

☀ ◊ Z4–8 H8–1

Linum flavum 'Compactum'
Shrubby perennial with narrow leaves and terminal clusters of many upward-facing, open funnel-shaped, single, bright yellow flowers in summer. Provide a sunny, sheltered position and protection from winter wet. **H** and **S** 6in (15cm).

☀ ◊ Z5–7 H7–5

Potentilla aurea
Rounded perennial, with a woody base, that in late summer bears loose sprays of flat, single, yellow flowers with slightly darker eyes. Leaves are divided into oval, slightly silvered leaflets. **H** 4in (10cm), **S** 8in (20cm).

☀ ◊ Z5–8 H8–5

Oenothera macrocarpa
Spreading perennial with sturdy stems and oval leaves. Throughout summer bears a succession of wide, bell-shaped, yellow flowers, sometimes spotted red, that open at sundown. **H** to 4in (10cm), **S** to 16in (40cm) or more.

☀ ◊ Z5–8 H8–3

Scutellaria orientalis
Rhizomatous perennial with hairy, gray, rooting stems. Has terminal spikes of tubular, yellow flowers, with brownish-purple lips, in summer. Leaves are toothed and oval. May be invasive in a small space. **H** 2–4in (5–10cm), **S** to 9in (23cm).

☀ ◊ Z5–8 H8–5

Potentilla eriocarpa
Clump-forming perennial with tufts of oval, dark green leaves divided into leaflets. Flat, single, pale yellow flowers are borne throughout summer just above leaves. **H** 2–3in (5–8cm), **S** 4–6in (10–15cm).

☀ ◊ Z6–8 H8–1

Cytisus ardoinoi
Deciduous, hummock-forming, dwarf shrub with arching stems. In late spring and early summer, pealike, bright yellow flowers are produced in pairs in leaf axils. Leaves are divided into 3 leaflets. **H** 4in (10cm), **S** 6in (15cm).

☀ ◊ ❗ Z6–8 H8–6

Calceolaria 'Walter Shrimpton'
Evergreen, mound-forming perennial with glossy, dark green leaves. In early summer bears short spikes of many pouch-shaped, bronze-yellow flowers, spotted rich brown, with white bands across centers. **H** 4in (10cm), **S** 9in (23cm).

☀ ◊ Z8–9 H6–1

Hypericum empetrifolium subsp. tortuosum

Evergreen, prostrate shrub with angled branches and bright green leaves that have curled margins. Bears flat heads of small, bright yellow flowers in summer. Needs winter protection. **H** ¾in (2cm), **S** 12in (30cm).

☼ ◌ Z4–7 H7–1

Papaver fauriei

Short-lived, clump-forming perennial with basal rosettes of finely cut, hairy, soft gray leaves. Bears pendent, open cup-shaped, pale yellow flowers in summer. Dislikes winter wet. **H** and **S** 2–4in (5–10cm).

☼ ◌ Z5–7 H7–5

Hippocrepis comosa (Horseshoe vetch)

Vigorous perennial with prostrate, rooting stems bearing open spikes of pealike, yellow flowers in summer and leaves divided into leaflets. Self seeds freely and may spread rapidly. **H** 2–3in (5–8cm), **S** indefinite.

☼ ◌ Z5–7 H7–5

Persicaria vacciniifolia

Evergreen, perennial with woody, red stems. Leaves are tinged red in fall. Bears deep pink or rose-red flowers in late summer and fall. **H** 4–6in (10–15cm), **S** to 12in (30cm).

☼ ◌ ⊘ Z8–11 H11–3

Genista sagittalis

Deciduous, semi-prostrate shrub with winged stems bearing a few oval, dark green leaves. Pealike, yellow flowers appear in dense, terminal clusters in early summer, followed by hairy seed pods. **H** 3in (8cm), **S** 12in (30cm) or more.

☼ ◌ Z5–8 H8–5

Nertera granadensis (Bead plant)

Prostrate perennial with dense mats of tiny, bright green leaves. In early summer bears minute, greenish-white flowers, then many shiny, orange or red berries. Needs ample moisture in summer. **H** to ½in (1cm), **S** 4in (10cm).

◐ ◌ H6–1

Gaultheria procumbens

Vigorous, evergreen subshrub with prostrate stems carrying clusters of oval, leathery leaves that turn red in winter. In summer, solitary bell-shaped, pink-flushed, white flowers appear in leaf axils, followed by scarlet berries. **H** 2–6in (5–15cm), **S** indefinite.

◐ ◌ pH ⊘ Z3–8 H8–1

ROCK PLANTS

373

RED

Sedum lydium
Evergreen, mat-forming perennial with reddish stems and narrow, fleshy, often red-flushed leaves. Bears flat-topped, terminal clusters of tiny, white flowers in summer. **H** 2in (5cm), **S** to 6in (15cm).

☼ ◊ ❶ Z5–8 H8–5

Acaena microphylla
Compact, mat-forming perennial, usually evergreen, with leaves divided into tiny leaflets, bronze-tinged when young. Heads of small flowers with spiny, dull red bracts are borne in summer and develop into decorative burs. **H** 2in (5cm), **S** 6in (15cm).

☼ ◊ Z6–8 H8–6

GRAY

Artemisia schmidtiana 'Nana'
Prostrate perennial with fernlike, silver foliage. Has insignificant sprays of daisylike, yellow flowers in summer. Is suitable for a wall or bank. **H** 3in (8cm), **S** 8in (20cm).

☼ ◊ Z5–8 H8–5

Jovibarba hirta
Evergreen, mat-forming perennial with rosettes of hairy, mid-green leaves, often suffused red, and terminal clusters of star-shaped, pale yellow flowers in summer. Dislikes winter wet. **H** 3–6in (8–15cm), **S** 4in (10cm).

☼ ◊ Z5–8 H8–5

Sedum obtusatum
Evergreen, prostrate perennial with small, fat, succulent leaves that turn bronze-red in summer. Loose, flat sprays of tiny, bright yellow flowers are borne in summer. Dislikes summer wet. **H** 2in (5cm), **S** 4–6in (10–15cm).

☼ ◊ ❶ Z5–9 H9–5

Sedum spathulifolium
Evergreen, mat-forming perennial with rosettes of fleshy, green or silver leaves, usually strongly suffused bronze-red, and small clusters of tiny, yellow flowers borne just above foliage in summer. Tolerates shade. **H** 2in (5cm), **S** indefinite.

☼ ◊ ❶ Z5–9 H9–5

Raoulia hookeri var. *albosericea*
Evergreen, prostrate perennial with tiny rosettes of silver leaves. Flower heads appear briefly in summer as fragrant, yellow fluff. Is best in poor, gritty humus in an alpine house. Dislikes winter wet. **H** to ½in (1cm), **S** 10in (25cm).

☼ ◊ Z8–9 H9–8

Acaena caesiiglauca
Vigorous, groundcover perennial, usually evergreen. Has hairy, glaucous blue leaves divided into leaflets. Heads of small flowers with spiny, brownish-green bracts, borne in summer, develop into brownish-red burs. **H** 2in (5cm), **S** 30in (75cm) or more.

☼ ◊ Z6–9 H9–6

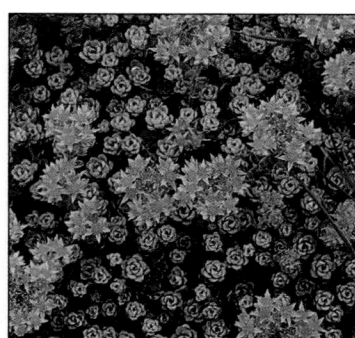

Arabis procurrens 'Variegata'
Evergreen, mat-forming perennial with small, oval, green leaves, splashed with cream. Bears small, white flowers in spring and early summer. May revert to type, with plain green leaves. **H** ¾in (2cm), **S** 12in (30cm).

☼ ◊ Z3–7 H8–1

Paronychia kapela
subsp. serpyllifolia
Evergreen, very compact, mat-forming perennial with minute, silver leaves. Inconspicuous flowers, borne in summer, are surrounded by papery, silver bracts. Is good for covering tufa. **H** to ½in (1cm), **S** 8in (20cm).

☼ ◊ ! Z8–10 H10–8

Asarum europaeum
(European wild ginger)
Vigorous, evergreen, prostrate, rhizomatous perennial with large, kidney-shaped, leathery, glossy leaves that hide tiny, brown flowers appearing in spring. **H** 6in (15cm), **S** indefinite.

◑ ◐ Z4–8 H8–1

Trifolium repens 'Purpurascens'
Vigorous, semievergreen, groundcover perennial, grown for its divided, bronze-green foliage, variably edged bright green. Produces heads of small, pealike, white blooms in summer. Suits a wild bank. **H** in flower 3–5in (8–12cm), **S** 8–12in (20–30cm) or more.

☼ ◊ Z4–8 H8–1

Arctostaphylos uva-ursi 'Point Reyes'
Evergreen, prostrate shrub with long shoots and glossy leaves. In late spring and early summer bears terminal clusters of urn-shaped, pale pink to white flowers, followed by red berries. **H** 4in (10cm), **S** 20in (50cm).

☼ ◊ pH Z2–6 H6–1

Sedum spathulifolium 'Cape Blanco'
Evergreen perennial with rosettes of fleshy leaves, frequently suffused purple. Tiny, yellow flowers appear above foliage in summer. Tolerates shade. **H** 2in (5cm), **S** indefinite.

☼ ◊ ! Z5–9 H9–5

Pachysandra terminalis
Evergreen, creeping perennial that has smooth leaves clustered at the ends of short stems. Bears spikes of tiny, white flowers, sometimes flushed purple, in early summer. Makes excellent groundcover in a moist or dry site. **H** 4in (10cm), **S** 8in (20cm).

◑ ◊ Z4–8 H8–1

Sempervivum ciliosum
Evergreen, mat-forming perennial with rosettes of hairy, gray-green leaves and, in summer, heads of small, star-shaped, yellow flowers. Dislikes winter wet; is best grown in an alpine house. **H** 3–4in (8–10cm), **S** 4in (10cm).

☼ ◊ Z7–11 H12–7

ROCK PLANTS

GREEN

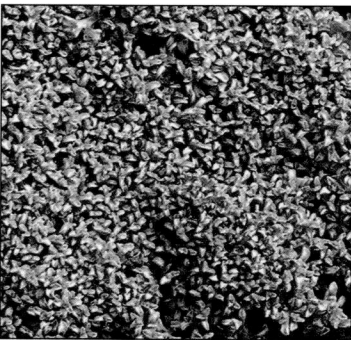

Raoulia australis
Evergreen, carpeting perennial forming a hard mat of gray-green leaves. Bears tiny, fluffy, sulfur-yellow flower heads in summer. **H** to ½in (1cm), **S** 10in (25cm).

☼ ◊ Z8–9 H9–8

Azorella trifurcata
Evergreen perennial forming tight, hard cushions of tiny, leathery, oval leaves in rosettes. Bears many small, stalkless umbels of yellow flowers in summer. **H** to 4in (10cm), **S** 6in (15cm).

☼ ◊ Z6–7 H11–1

Raoulia haastii
Evergreen perennial forming low, irregular hummocks of minute leaves that are apple-green in spring, dark green in fall and chocolate-brown in winter. Occasionally has small, fluffy, yellow flower heads in summer. **H** to ½in (1cm), **S** 10in (25cm).

☼ ◊ Z7–8 H8–7

Sagina boydii
Evergreen perennial with hard cushions of minute, stiff, bottle-green leaves in small rosettes. Bears insignificant flowers in summer. Is difficult and slow-growing. **H** ½in (1cm), **S** to 8in (20cm).

☼ ◊ Z5–7 H7–5

Arctostaphylos uva-ursi
Evergreen, low-growing shrub with arching, intertwining stems clothed in small, oval, bright green leaves. Bears urn-shaped, pinkish-white flowers in summer followed by scarlet berries. **H** 4in (10cm), **S** 20in (50cm).

☼ ◊ pH Z2–6 H6–1

Plantago nivalis
Evergreen perennial with neat rosettes of thick, silver-haired, green leaves. Bears spikes of insignificant, dull gray flowers in summer. Dislikes winter wet. **H** in leaf 1in (2.5cm), **S** 2in (5cm).

☼ ◊ Z6–7 H7–6

Bolax gummifer
Very slow-growing, evergreen perennial with neat rosettes of small, blue-green leaves forming extremely hard cushions. Insignificant, yellow flowers are rarely produced. Grows well on tufa. **H** 1in (2.5cm), **S** 4in (10cm).

☼ ◊ Z5–6 H6–5

Sedum kamtschaticum 'Variegatum'
Semievergreen, prostrate perennial
with fleshy, cream-edged leaves. Has
fleshy stems and leaf buds in winter
and loose, terminal clusters of orange-
flushed, yellow flowers in early fall.
H 2–3in (5–8cm), **S** 8in (20cm).

☀ ◊ ① Z3–8 H8–1

**Saxifraga exarata subsp. moschata
'Cloth of Gold'**
Evergreen hummock-forming
perennial with small, soft rosettes of
bright golden foliage; produces best
color in shade. Has star-shaped, white
flowers on slender stems in summer.
H 4–6in (10–15cm), **S** 6in (15cm).

☀ ◊ Z5–7 H7–5

HOUSELEEKS

The main attraction of houseleeks (*Sempervivum*) is their
colorful rosettes of leaves. These range from bright yellow,
through various shades of green, gray, pink, purple, red,
and orange, to almost black. The leaves may be dull or glossy,
or covered with soft down or longer hairs. Leaf shape can
also vary from short and succulent to long and tapering. The
rosettes are most striking in the spring and summer, but even
in the winter, many varieties remain attractively colored. It is
the endless range of different leaf shapes, shades, and textures
that make this group so interesting to enthusiasts. They do not
like damp or shady conditions, but thrive in well-drained soil
in full sun. Houseleeks are ideal for pots or sink gardens on
a south-facing patio, or can be planted out in rock gardens
or in the crevices of stone walls.

S. calcareum

S. 'Blood Tip'

S. 'Rosie'

S. calcareum 'Extra'

S. tectorum

S. arachnoideum

S. giuseppii

S. montanum

S. 'Gulle Dame'

S. 'Kappa'

S. 'Gallivarda'

BULBS

Bulbous plants are found throughout the world in habitats as diverse as woodland and scrub, meadows, river banks, the edges of streams, and rocky hills and mountains. There are bulbs to suit every garden site and design, from the tiny *Iris danfordiae* for a rock garden, to daffodils and tulips in beds and borders, and the carpeting erythroniums or statuesque *Cardiocrinum giganteum* for a woodland garden. Most have a distinct flowering season, yet with careful planning it is possible to extend or enhance this period of interest. Although most bloom in spring or early summer, producing splashes of color before many shrubs and perennials reach their peak, plant snowdrops for late winter color, and colchicums, cyclamen, and some crocuses to brighten a fall day.

BULBS

Embracing a wide range of decorative plants, bulbs provide exciting effects throughout the year, with large drifts of snowdrops in late winter, daffodils and tulips in spring, the exquisite perfume of lilies and vibrant dahlia colors in summer, and the spidery flowers of nerines in fall.

SIZE CATEGORIES USED WITHIN THIS GROUP		
Large over 30in (75cm)	**Medium** 9–30in (23–75cm)	**Small** up to 9in (23cm)

BULB DEFINITIONS

Bulbs are divided into smaller plant categories, including true bulbs, corms, and tubers. All of these swollen, underground, food-storage organs help the bulb to survive periods of drought.

Bulb
A true bulb is a storage organ made up of stems and fleshy leaves inside. Examples include daffodils, tulips, and eucomis (above).

Corm
Swollen stems that have adapted to store food are known as corms. They appear solid throughout, and include crocuses (above).

Tuber
Tuberous plants have swollen underground roots or stems. Examples include cyclamen, dahlias (above), and begonias.

What are bulbs?

The term "bulb" can be used to describe all swollen, underground, food-storage organs, and includes true bulbs as well as corms, rhizomes, and tubers. True bulbs have fleshy scales—modified leaves or leaf bases—that overlap and are often enclosed in a papery tunic, as in narcissi, or they may be naked and loosely arranged like lily bulbs.

Corms are compressed and enlarged stem bases, usually enclosed in a fibrous or papery tunic, as in the crocus. Each corm lasts one year, and is replaced by a new one after flowering. Tubers, such as cyclamen, are solid, underground sections of modified stem or root and seldom possess scales or tunics. Rhizomes are modified stems that creep at or just below soil level, and may be thin and wiry or swollen and fleshy.

A few bulbs are evergreen, but most grow and bloom during a short season, and then die back to below ground level. Their leaves produce the food store for

BELOW Carpets of spring color
A selection of daffodils has been naturalized in the grass beneath silver birches and spring-flowering trees, creating a sea of nodding yellow flowers.

the following year, which is why the foliage must not be cut down after flowering but allowed to wither naturally.

When below ground, bulbs are described as dormant, but they are, in fact, ripening and developing the following year's flowers, and must be planted in a suitable site to thrive. Bulbs that originate from dry, hot climates, such as nerines and watsonias, need warm, dry conditions when dormant to aid ripening and flower formation, while those from woodlands or other damp, shaded habitats, such as bluebells (*Hyacinthoides*) and snowdrops (*Galanthus*), require a cool, slightly moist spot.

Designing with bulbs

There are bulbs to suit all garden designs and planting styles. They range in size from the tiny *Iris danfordiae* and fall daffodil (*Sternbergia lutea*), both suitable for a scree or rock garden, to carpeting erythroniums for the dappled shade of a woodland garden, midrange alliums and tulips for a hot, sunny border, and tall, slender regal lilies that produce highly scented flowers on stems up to 6ft (1.8m) in height. The flower forms also lend themselves to certain garden styles. Tulips with sculptural cupped flowers planted *en masse,* and the sharp flower shapes of many dahlias, are ideal for formal schemes, while the looser flower forms of nectaroscordums and turkscap lilies, and arching spikes of crocosmias create an informal look. Sod spangled with crocuses or snake's-head fritillaries (*Fritillaria meleagris*) mimics their wild habitat and provides early color in naturalistic schemes.

Bulbs add seasonal color and interest to mixed borders with annuals, shrubs, and perennials. Daffodils (*Narcissus*), crown imperials (*Fritillaria imperialis*), alliums, and dahlias all blend well with other types of plantings. Unscented lilies make good partners for scented roses, while exotic-looking cannas and alstroemerias add spice to a tropical design. If you can't squeeze bulbs into your border, many are perfectly at home in containers and baskets.

Year-round interest

Choose carefully, and you can have a bulb in flower for most of the year. The first to appear in late winter are the snowdrops (*Galanthus*) and winter aconites (*Eranthis*), while early narcissus, muscari, crocuses, scillas, chionodoxas, dwarf iris, and *Anemone blanda* mark the onset of spring.

In mid-spring, fill your garden with vibrant yellow daffodils and bright tulips, or opt for the same plants in pastel shades—the choice is vast for both genera. Summer-

flowering bulbs, such as *Galtonia candicans,* most alliums, the Peruvian daffodil (*Hymenocallis narcissiflora*), and ornithogalums offer colorful highlights.

These are followed in late summer by gladioli, crinums, dahlias, and crocosmias, which may continue to bloom into the fall until the first frost. When the summer

spectacle is over, select fall-flowering nerines, crocuses, colchicums, and cyclamen, and to end the year, use *Cyclamen hederifolium,* whose marbled foliage often persists into winter.

For scented bulbs, choose hyacinths, bluebells, and scented daffodils for spring, and lilies and crinums for summer displays.

LAYERING BULBS IN CONTAINERS

Pots brimming with spring bulbs lift the spirits after a long winter, but you need to plan ahead to create the most spectacular displays. In fall, look for bulbs at garden centers or in mail-order catalogs, and check flowering times for a synchronized display of tulips, daffodils, and grape hyacinths (*Muscari*).

A multicolored display

1 Plant in layers
In fall, place crocks at the bottom of a large pot and add a 2in (5cm) layer of gravel. Then add a layer of good-quality potting mix. Place the largest bulbs—for example, daffodils—on the surface and cover with more potting mix so that the tips are just visible.

2 Cover the bulbs
Now place the next layer of bulbs, such as tulips, between the daffodil bulbs, and cover with more potting mix. Finally, add small bulbs, like grape hyacinths, on this top layer, and cover with potting mix. Press down lightly with your hands, and leave the pot in a sheltered sunny spot.

NATURALIZING BULBS

You can create spectacular effects by naturalizing bulbs in a lawn or under trees. Choose robust plants, such as snowdrops, daffodils, and crocuses, which are able to compete with tree roots and grass. To achieve a natural, random effect, toss the bulbs in the air and plant them individually where they fall. For each bulb, dig out a small plug of sod and soil, two to three times the depth of the bulb. After flowering, when the leaves have died, mow the grass.

BULB PLANTING PLANNER

Type of bulb	Planting time	Planting depth	Preferred conditions
Agapanthus	spring	4in (10cm)	Full sun in moist but well-drained soil
Allium	fall	2–6in (5–15cm)	Full sun in moist but well-drained soil
Colchicum	late summer	4in (10cm)	Full sun in well-drained soil
Crocus (spring)	fall	3in (8cm)	Full sun in well-drained soil
Crocus (fall)	late summer	3in (8cm)	Full sun in well-drained soil
Cyclamen	fall	4in (10cm)	Partial shade in well-drained soil
Galanthus	early fall	1–2in (2.5–5cm)	Full sun or partial shade in moist soil that does not dry out in summer
Hyacinthus	fall	4in (10cm)	Full sun or partial shade in moist, well-drained soil
Lilium	fall	4–6in (10–15cm)	Full sun or partial shade; most prefer acidic to neutral, well-drained soil.
Muscari	fall	2in (5cm)	Full sun in well-drained soil
Narcissus	fall	4–6in (10–15cm)	Sun or partial shade in any reasonable, well-drained garden soil
Tulipa	late fall	3–6in (8–15cm)	Full sun in well-drained soil

BULBS

Ornithogalum magnum
Late spring-flowering bulb with linear, gray-green basal leaves. Produces upright, pyramid-shaped racemes of small, star-shaped, white flowers, with a green stripe on the reverse. **H** 24–32in (60–80cm), **S** 4in (10cm).

☼ ◊ ❶ Z5–9 H10–5

Fritillaria verticillata
Spring-flowering bulb with slender leaves in whorls up the stem, which bears a loose spike of 1–15 bell-shaped, white flowers, ¾–1½in (2–4cm) long and checkered green or brown. **H** to 3ft (1m), **S** 3–4in (8–10cm).

◐ ◊ H8–6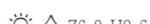

 (center-left bottom)

Fritillaria persica 'Ivory Bells'
Robust, late spring-flowering bulb with lance-shaped, glaucous, gray-green leaves on sturdy, upright stems. Produces a terminal raceme of 10–30 pendent, bell-shaped, creamy-white to greenish-white flowers. **H** 30–39in (75–100cm), **S** 4in (10cm).

☼ ◊ Z6–8 H8–6

Fritillaria persica
Spring-flowering bulb with narrow, lance-shaped, gray-green leaves along stem. Produces a spike of 10–20 or more narrow, bell-shaped, blackish- or brownish-purple flowers, ⅝–¾in (1.5–2cm) long. **H** to 5ft (1.5m), **S** 4in (10cm).

☼ ◊ Z6–8 H8–6

Allium aflatunense
Late spring-flowering bulb with strap-shaped, mid-green, basal leaves. Dense, spherical, terminal umbels of small, star-shaped, lilac-purple flowers are borne on sturdy stems. Seed heads may be dried for decorative use. **H** 32in (80cm), **S** 4–6in (10–15cm).

☼ ◊ Z4–8 H8–1

Fritillaria imperialis 'Lutea'
Spring-flowering bulb with whorls of lance-shaped, shiny, light green leaves and a head of up to 8 pendent, bell-shaped, bright yellow flowers, to 2in (6cm) long, crowned by a tuft of small, leaflike bracts. **H** 3ft (1m), **S** 10in (25cm).

☼ ◊ Z5–9 H9–4

Fritillaria raddeana
Robust, spring-flowering bulb with lance-shaped leaves in whorls on lower half of stem. Has a head of up to 20 widely conical, pale or greenish-yellow flowers, 1¼–1½in (3–4cm) long, topped by a "crown" of small leaves. **H** to 3ft (1m), **S** 6–9in (15–23cm).

☼ ◊ Z6–9 H9–6

ORANGE

WHITE

Fritillaria imperialis (Crown imperial)
Spring-flowering bulb with glossy, pale green leaves carried in whorls on leafy stems. Has up to 5 widely bell-shaped, orange flowers crowned by small, leaflike bracts. **H** to 5ft (1.5cm), **S** 9–12in (23–30cm).

☼ ◊ Z5–9 H9–4

Fritillaria recurva (Scarlet fritillary)
Spring-flowering bulb with whorls of narrow, lance-shaped, gray-green leaves. Bears a spike of up to 10 narrow, yellow-checkered, orange or red flowers with flared tips. **H** to 30in (1m), **S** 3–4in (8–10cm).

☼ ◊ Z6–9 H9–6

Crinum x powellii 'Album'
Late summer- or fall-flowering bulb, with a long neck, producing a group of semierect, strap-shaped leaves. Leafless flower stems carry heads of fragrant, widely funnel-shaped, white flowers. **H** to 3ft (1m), **S** 2ft (60cm).

☼ ◊ ① Z7–10 H11–8

Camassia leichtlinii
Tuft-forming bulb with long, narrow, erect, basal leaves. Each leafless stem bears a dense spike of 6-petaled, star-shaped, bluish-violet or white flowers, 1½–3in (4–8cm) across, in summer. **H** 3–5ft (1–1.5m), **S** 8–12in (20–30cm).

☼ ◗ Z4–11 H11–1

Crinum moorei
Summer-flowering bulb with a long neck, up to 3ft (1m) tall, and strap-shaped, semierect, gray-green leaves at neck top. Leafless flower stems bear heads of long-tubed, funnel-shaped, white to deep pink flowers. **H** 20–28in (50–70cm), **S** 24in (60cm).

☼ ◊ ① Z7–9 H12–7

Gladiolus murielae
Mid-summer-flowering corm with a loose spike of up to 10 sweetly scented, hooded, funnel-shaped, maroon-eyed, white flowers. Has linear, pleated leaves. Good for cutting. **H** 32in (80cm), **S** 2in (5cm).

☼ ◊ Z8–10 H10–8

Galtonia candicans (Summer hyacinth)
Late summer- or fall-flowering bulb with widely strap-shaped, fleshy, semierect, basal, gray-green leaves. Leafless stem has a spike of up to 30 pendent, short-tubed, white flowers. **H** 3–4ft (1–1.2m), **S** 7–9in (18–23cm).

☼ ◊ Z7–10 H10–7

BULBS

383

GLADIOLI

Comprising about 180 species, with over 10,000 hybrids and cultivars for garden cultivation, exhibiting, and cutting, gladioli are prized for their showy spikes of usually open, funnel-shaped flowers. *Gladiolus* hybrids are divided into the Grandiflorus Group, with long, densely packed flower spikes, categorized as miniature, small, medium-sized, large, or giant, according to the width of the lowest flowers, and the Primulinus and Nanus Groups, which have loose spikes of small flowers. Plant gladioli in borders or pots for late spring to early fall displays, and store corms in a frost-free place over winter. In cold areas, grow them by a sheltered, sunny wall; winter-flowering South African gladioli require a cool greenhouse. For more information, see the Plant Dictionary.

G. **'Purple Flora'**
[Grandiflorus Group]

G. **'Her Majesty'**
[Grandiflorus Group]

G. **'White Prosperity'**
[Grandiflorus Group]

G. **'Columbine'**

G. **'Velvet Eyes'**
[Grandiflorus Group]

G. **'Impressive'** [Nanus Group]

G. **'Blue Frost'**
[Grandiflorus Group]

G. **'Sancerre'**
[Grandiflorus Group]

G. **'Nova Lux'**
[Grandiflorus Group]

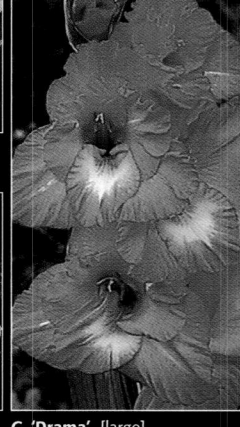

G. **'Morning Gold'**
[Grandiflorus Group]

G. **'Green Woodpecker'**
[medium]

G. **'Drama'** [large]

G. **x** *colvillii* **'The Bride'**
[Nanus Group]

G. **'White Ice'** [medium]

G. **'Wine and Roses'**
[Grandiflorus Group]

G. **'Nymph'** [Nanus Group]

G. **'Oscar'** [Grandiflorus Group]

G. **'Stella'** [Grandiflorus Group]

G. **'Peter Pears'** [large]

WHITE

Allium 'Mount Everest'
Late spring to early summer-flowering
bulb with sturdy stems bearing spherical
umbels, 5–6in (12–15cm) in diameter,
of tiny star-shaped, white flowers, with
green stamens. The basal strap-shaped,
semierect, leaves are grayish-green.
H 3½ft (1.1m), **S** 6in (15cm).

☼ ◊ Z4–9 H9–1

Cardiocrinum giganteum
(Giant lily)
Sturdy, leafy-stemmed bulb. In summer
has long spikes of fragrant, slightly
pendent, cream flowers, 6in (15cm)
long, with purple-red streaks inside,
then brown seed pods. **H** to 10ft (3m),
S 2½–3½ft (75cm–1.1m).

☼ ◊ Z7–9 H9–7

Nectaroscordum siculum
subsp. bulgaricum
Late spring- to early summer-flowering
bulb with pendent, bell-shaped, white
flowers, flushed purple-red and green.
In seed, stalks bend upward, holding
dry seed pods erect. **H** to 4ft (1.2m),
S 12–18in (30–45cm).

☼ ◊ Z6–10 H10–1

Polianthes tuberosa 'The Pearl'
Late summer-flowering, rhizomatous
perennial. Sweetly scented, flared,
funnel-shaped, double, white flowers are
borne in pairs above long, lance-shaped,
upright, basal leaves. Keep tuber dry
when dormant. **H** 3ft (1m), **S** 6in (15cm).

☼ ◊ Z7–11 H11–7

Nomocharis pardanthina
Summer-flowering bulb with stems
bearing whorls of lance-shaped leaves
and up to 15 outward-facing, white
or pale pink flowers, each with purple
blotches and a dark purple eye.
H to 3ft (1m), **S** 5–6in (12–15cm).

☼ ◊ Z7–9 H9–7

PINK

Crinum x powellii
Late summer- or fall-flowering bulb
with a long neck producing a group
of strap-shaped, semierect leaves.
Leafless flower stems bear heads of
fragrant, widely funnel-shaped, pink
flowers. **H** to 3ft (1m), **S** 2ft (60cm).

☼ ◊ ❗ Z7–10 H11–8

Watsonia meriana
Clump-forming, summer-flowering
corm with sword-shaped, erect leaves
at base, with smaller, sheathlike leaves
on the stem. Produces a loose spike of
trumpet-shaped flowers, 2–2½in (5–6cm)
long, in bright pink to vivid orange or
red. **H** 4ft (1.2m), **S** 6in (15cm).

☼ ◊ Z9–10 H10–9

BULBS

Dracunculus vulgaris
(Dragon's arum)
Spring- and summer-flowering tuber
with deeply divided leaves at apex of
thick, blotched stem. A blackish-maroon
spadix protrudes from a deep maroon
spathe, 14in (35cm) long. **H** to 3ft (1m),
S 1½–2ft (45–60cm).

☼ ◊ ① Z8–10 H10–8

Dierama pulcherrimum
Upright, summer-flowering corm
with long, narrow, straplike, evergreen
leaves, above which rise elegant,
arching, wiry stems bearing funnel-
shaped, deep pink flowers. Prefers deep,
rich soil. **H** to 5ft (1.5m), **S** to 24in (60cm).

☼ ◊ Z8–10 H10–8

Watsonia pillansii
Summer-flowering corm with long,
sword-shaped, erect leaves, some
basal and some on stem. Stem
carries a dense, branched spike of
tubular, orange-red flowers, each
2½–3in (6–8cm) long, with 6 short
lobes. **H** to 3ft (1m), **S** 1–1½ft (30–45cm).

☼ ◊ Z11–13 H12–6

Gloriosa superba 'Rothschildiana'
(Glory lily)
Deciduous, summer-flowering, tuberous,
tendril climber. Upper leaf axils each
bear a large flower that has 6 reflexed,
red petals with scalloped, yellow edges.
H to 6ft (2m), **S** 1–1½ft (30–45cm).
Min. 46°F (8°C).

☼ ◊ ① Z8–10 H11–7

Notholirion campanulatum
Early summer-flowering bulb with
long, narrow leaves in a basal tuft.
Leafy stem bears a spike of 10–40
pendent, funnel-shaped flowers, each
1½–2in (4–5cm) long, with green-tipped,
deep rose-purple petals. **H** to 3ft (1m),
S 3–4in (8–10cm).

☼ ◊ Z7–10 H10–7

Watsonia borbonica
Very robust, summer-flowering corm
with narrowly sword-shaped leaves
both at base and on stem. Produces
a loose, branched spike of rich pink
flowers, with 6 spreading, pointed,
rose-red lobes. **H** 3–5ft (1–1.5m),
S 1½–2ft (45–60cm).

☼ ◊ Z11–13 H12–6

Scadoxus multiflorus
subsp. *katherinae* (Blood lily)
Very robust, clump-forming bulb
with lance-shaped, wavy-edged
leaves. Bears an umbel of up to 200
red flowers in summer. **H** to 4ft (1.2m),
S 1–1½ft (30–45cm). Min. 50°F (10°C).

☼ ◊ Z14–15 H12–10

Dahlia 'Hillcrest Royal'
Medium-flowered cactus dahlia
producing rich purple flowers,
with incurving petals, held on
strong stems in summer–fall.
H 3½ft (1.1m), **S** 24in (60cm).

☼ ◊ Z9–11 H11–1

ALSTROEMERIAS

Commonly known as the Peruvian lily, lily of the Incas, or parrot lily, these South American tuberous perennials are prized for their delicate funnel-shaped blooms in yellow, orange, pink, red, white, or purple, with decorative markings in contrasting colors. They also have an exceptionally long flowering season, from mid-summer to the first frost, and make excellent cut flowers. Most suppliers offer plants, rather than tubers, which are best planted in spring after the last frost in a sunny site and free-draining soil, giving the roots time to establish before winter. Young plants are vulnerable to cold, wet conditions—protect them in winter with a thick mulch of well-rotted compost or manure.

A. PRINCESS JULIETA ('Zaprijul') ①   *A.* PRINCESS ARIANE ('Zapriari') ①

Elvira' ①

A. 'Apollo' ①

A. 'Polka' ①

A. 'Friendship' ①

A. 'Tara' ①

Blushing Bride' ①

A. 'Serenade' ①

A. 'Moulin Rouge' ①

A. 'Red Beauty' ①

A. aurea 'Orange King' ①

LILIES

Lilies (*Lilium* species and cultivars) make elegant additions to summer borders and containers. Their flamboyant flowers range from nodding, upright, and trumpet-shaped forms, to turkscaps with recurved petals. The blooms are often spotted with a darker or contrasting color, or have conspicuous stamens. Many lilies have a powerful, sweet fragrance, most notably the Oriental and Longiflorum hybrids, although a few species are unpleasantly scented. The hybrids thrive in sun and well-drained soil, and are available in a dazzling array of colors, from white, pink, and red, to shades of yellow and orange. Lily species prefer partially-shaded sites; some also require acidic soil. Leave plants undisturbed once established, as the bulbs are easily damaged. For more information, see the Plant Dictionary.

L. **'Casa Blanca'**

L. martagon var. *album*

L. TRIUMPHATOR (**'Zanlophator'**)

L. **'White Heaven'**

L. **'Sterling Star'**

L. **'Mona Lisa'**

L. **'Olivia'**

L. **'Nymph'**

L. **'Black Magic'**

L. **'Lady Alice'**

L. **'Arena'**

L. 'Tom Pouce'

L. 'Rosita'

L. 'Sumatra'

L. 'Elodie'

L. 'Miss Lucy'

L. 'Côte d'Azur'

L. 'Star Fighter'

L. rubellum

L. mackliniae

L. cernuum

L. 'Tiger Woods'

L. 'Sweet Lord'

L. 'Black Out'

L. martagon

L. lankongense

L. 'Journey's End'

L. 'Netty's Pride'

L. 'Conca d'Or'

L. canadense

L. leichtlinii

L. pyrenaicum

L. 'Bright Star'

L. 'Rosemary North'   L. superbum

L. rosthornii

L. 'Connecticut King'

L. medeoloides

L. pardalinum subsp. wigginsii

L. regale 'Royal Gold'   L. monadelphum

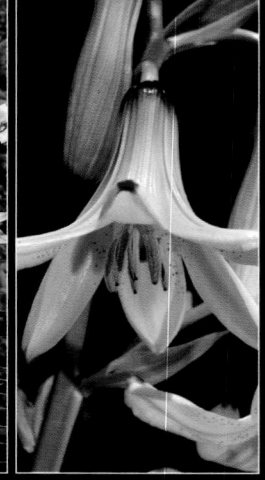
L. 'Limelight'

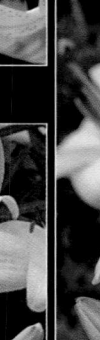

L. Citronella Group   L 'Roma'

L. 'Boogie Woogie'

L. 'Apollo'

L. hansonii

L. pyrenaicum f. *rubrum*

L. 'Crimson Pixie'

L. African Queen Group

L. bulbiferum var. *croceum*

L. henryi

L. 'Orange Pixie'

L. 'Grand Cru'

L. 'Red Carpet'

L. tsingtauense

L. 'Lady Bowes Lyon'

L. 'Enchantment'

L. lancifolium 'Splendens'

L. chalcedonicum

L. 'Orange Electric'

L. pomponium

L. 'Karen North'

L. pardalinum

L. 'Gran Paradiso'

BULBS

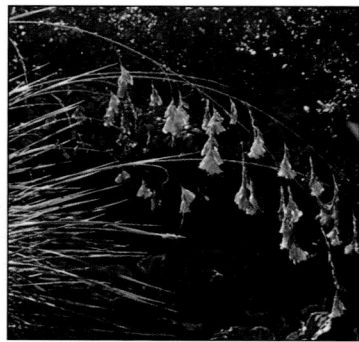

Dierama pendulum
(Angel's fishing rod, wand flower)
Clump-forming, late summer-flowering
corm with arching, basal leaves. Bears
pendulous, loose racemes of bell-
shaped, pinkish-purple flowers,
1in (2.5cm) long. **H** to 5ft (1.5m),
S 6–8in (15–20cm).

 ☼ ◊ Z7–9 H9–7

Allium giganteum
Robust, summer-flowering bulb with
long, wide, semierect, basal leaves.
Produces a sturdy stem with a dense,
spherical umbel, 5in (12cm) across, of
50 or more star-shaped, purple flowers.
H to 6ft (2m), **S** 12–14in (30–35cm).

 ☼ ◊ ① Z6–10 H9–5

***Allium* 'Globemaster'**
Summer-flowering bulb with dense
spherical umbels, 6–8in (15–20cm)
across, of small, star-shaped, deep violet
flowers. Has strap-shaped, semierect,
glossy, gray-green, basal leaves.
H 32in (80cm), **S** 8in (20cm).

☼ ◊ Z6–10 H8–1

Allium atropurpureum
Summer-flowering bulb with compact,
domed umbels, 3in (8cm) wide, of small,
star-shaped, deep red-purple flowers
borne from early to mid-summer. Basal
leaves are strap-shaped, semierect and
gray-green. **H** 32in (80cm), **S** 4in (10cm).

☼ ◊ Z4–7 H8–1

***Allium* 'Purple Sensation'**
Early summer-flowering bulb with
long, strap-shaped, semierect, gray-
green, basal leaves. Produces spherical
umbels of 50 or more star-shaped,
rich purple flowers on sturdy stems
in early summer. Is good for cut
flowers. **H** 32in (80cm), **S** 3in (7cm).

 ☼ ◊ Z4–9 H9–1

***Allium* 'Gladiator'**
Summer-flowering bulb with long,
strap-shaped, semierect, gray-green,
basal leaves. Produces large, densely
packed, spherical umbels of star-shaped,
lilac-purple flowers on sturdy stems in
summer. **H** 4ft (1.2m), **S** 8in (20cm).

 ☼ ◊ Z5–9 H9–1

Dichelostemma congestum
Early summer-flowering bulb with
semierect, basal leaves dying
away when a dense head of funnel-
shaped, purple flowers, each ⅝–¾in
(1.5–2cm) long, appears. **H** to 3ft (1m),
S 3–4in (8–10cm).

☼ ◊ Z6–10 H10–6

Aristea capitata
Robust, evergreen, clump-forming rhizome with sword-shaped, erect leaves, to 1in (2.5cm) across, and dense spikes of purple-blue flowers on short stalks in summer. **H** to 3ft (1m), **S** 1½–2ft (45–60cm).

☀ ○ 9–11 11–9

Neomarica caerulea
Summer-flowering rhizome with sword-shaped, semierect leaves in basal fans. Stems each bear a leaflike bract and a succession of iris-like, blue flowers, with white, yellow and brown central marks. **H** to 3ft (1m), **S** 3–5ft (1–1.5m). Min. 50°F (10°C).

☀ ○ H11–10

Arisaema consanguineum
Summer-flowering tuber with robust, spotted stems and erect, umbrella-like leaves with narrow leaflets. Produces purplish-white- or white-striped, green spathes, 6–8in (15–20cm) long, and bright red berries. **H** to 3ft (1m), **S** 1–1½ft (30–45cm).

☀ ○ ! Z5–9 H9–7

Galtonia viridiflora
Clump-forming, summer-flowering bulb with widely strap-shaped, fleshy, semi-erect, basal, gray-green leaves. Leafless stem bears a spike of up to 30 pendent, short-tubed, funnel-shaped, pale green flowers. **H** 3–4ft (1–1.2m), **S** 7–9in (18–23cm).

☀ ○ Z8–10 H10–8

Lilium Golden Splendor Group
Vigorous, variable Division 6a lilies. In mid-summer, strong, sturdy stems produce umbels of large, scented, shallowly trumpet-shaped, almost bowl-shaped flowers in shades of yellow with dark burgundy-red bands outside. **H** 4–6ft (1.2–2m), **S** 12in (30cm).

☀ ○ Z5–8 H8–1

Moraea huttonii
Summer-flowering corm with long, narrow, semierect, basal leaves. Tough stem bears a succession of iris-like, yellow flowers, 2–3in (5–7cm) across, with brown marks near the center. **H** 2½–3ft (75cm–1m), **S** 6–10in (15–25cm).

☀ ○ Z9–10 H10–9

Zantedeschia elliottiana
(Golden calla)
Summer-flowering tuber with heart-shaped, semierect, basal leaves with transparent marks. Bears a 6in (15cm) long, yellow spathe surrounding a yellow spadix. **H** 2–3ft (60cm–1m), **S** 1½–2ft (45–60cm). Min. 50°F (10°C).

☀ ○ ! Z8–10 H10–1

BULBS

393

CANNAS

Grown as much for their dramatic foliage as for their flamboyant flowers, cannas are ideal for lush tropical planting schemes, as an accent plant in a border, or as a bold addition to container displays. Large paddle- or broadly lance-shaped leaves are produced in a range of colors, from green to dark maroon, and many are striped or variegated, while the vibrant red, orange, or yellow flowers bloom for many months from summer to early fall. Plant these tender South American rhizomatic perennials after the last frost in spring in fertile soil and full sun—they require heat to flower well. In fall, cut down the stems and leaves when frost blackens the foliage, and store the rhizomes in a frost-free place over winter.

C. 'Striata'

C. 'Stuttgart'

C. 'Lucifer'

C. 'Ambassadour'

C. x *ehemanii*

C. 'Brillant'

C. 'Picasso'

C. 'Wyoming'

C. 'Richard Wallace'

C. 'Louis Cottin'

C. 'Königin Charlotte'

C. 'Durban'

ORANGE

WHITE

PINK

Canna iridiflora
Very robust, spring- or summer-flowering, rhizomatous perennial with broad, oblong leaves and spikes of pendent, long-tubed, reddish-pink or orange flowers, each 4–6in (10–15cm) long, with reflexed petals. **H** 10ft (3m), **S** 1½–2ft (45–60cm).

☀ ◊ Z8–11 H11–1

Littonia modesta
Deciduous, summer-flowering, tuberous, scandent climber with slender stems and lance-shaped leaves with tendrils at apex. Leaf axils bear bell-shaped, pendent, orange flowers, 1½–2in (4–5cm) across. **H** 3–6ft (1–2m), **S** 4–6in (10–15cm). Min. 61°F (16°C).

☀ ◊ H11–10

Amaryllis belladonna 'Hathor'
Fall-flowering bulb with a sturdy, purple stem bearing fragrant, pure white flowers, 4in (10cm) long, with yellow throats. Strap-shaped, semi-erect, basal leaves appear in late winter or spring. **H** 20–32in (50–80cm), **S** 12–18in (30–45cm).

☀ ◊ ① Z7–10 H11–7

x Amarcrinum memoria-corsii
Evergreen, clump-forming bulb with wide, semierect, basal leaves. Sturdy stems carry fragrant, rose-pink flowers in loose heads in late summer and fall. **H** and **S** to 3ft (1m).

☀ ◊ Z13–15 H12–9

Gladiolus papilio
Clump-forming, summer- or fall-flowering corm with stolons. Bears up to 10 yellow or white flowers, suffused violet, with hooded, upper petals and darker yellow patches on lower petals. **H** to 3ft (1m), **S** 6in (15cm).

☀ ◊ Z8–10 H10–8

x Amarygia parkeri
Early fall-flowering bulb. Sturdy stem carries a large head of funnel-shaped, deep rose flowers with yellow and white throats. Produces strap-shaped, semierect, basal leaves after flowering. **H** to 3ft (1m), **S** 2–3ft (60cm–1m).

☀ ◊ Z9–11 H12–9

Zantedeschia 'Cameo'
Summer-flowering, tuberous perennial with arrow-shaped, erect, white-spotted, mid-green leaves. Produces long-lasting, peach to salmon-orange spathes each with a dark maroon eye. **H** 28in (70cm), **S** 8in (20cm).

☀ ◊ ① Z8–10 H10–1

Dietes bicolor
Evergreen, tuft-forming, summer-flowering rhizome with tough, long and narrow, erect, basal leaves. Branching stems each bear a succession of flattish, iris-like, pale to mid-yellow flowers; each large petal has a brown patch. **H** to 3ft (1m), **S** 1–2ft (30–60cm).

☀ ◊ Z8–10 H10–8

Amaryllis belladonna
(Belladonna lily)
Fall-flowering bulb with a sturdy, purple stem bearing fragrant, funnel-shaped, pink flowers, 4in (10cm) long. Forms strap-shaped, semierect, basal leaves after flowering. **H** 20–32in (50–80cm), **S** 12–18in (30–45cm).

☀ ◊ ① Z7–10 H11–7

BULBS

DAHLIAS

The wide spectrum of dahlia hybrids offers a bold display of color and form from summer to the first frosts of fall. Flower colors range from deep red, crimson, purple, mauve, and vibrant pink, to white, apricot, orange, bronze, and bright scarlet, while the blooms range from tiny 2-in (5-cm) pompons to huge exhibition blooms more than 10in (25cm) across.

Dahlias flower prolifically—in the right conditions, a single plant may produce up to 100 blooms. They make beautiful border plants, compact types are ideal for containers, and all are good for cutting. In addition, no special skills are required to grow them, but protect the tubers from frost. The flower types below indicate the recognized groups.

D. **'Eveline'** [decorative]

Single—flowers usually have 8–10 broad petals surrounding an open, central disk.

Ball—spherical, fully double flowers, sometimes slightly flattened on top, with densely packed, almost tubular, petals.

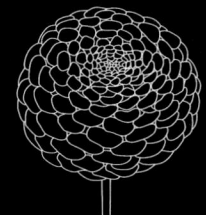

D. **'Trelyn Kiwi'** [semi-cactus]   D. **'White Moonlight'** [semi-cactus]

Anemone—fully double flowers each with one or more rings of flattened ray petals surrounding a dense group of shorter, tubular petals, usually longer than petals of single dahlias.

Pompon—a miniature form of ball flowers, but more spherical in shape, with fully double flowers no more than 2in (5cm) in diameter.

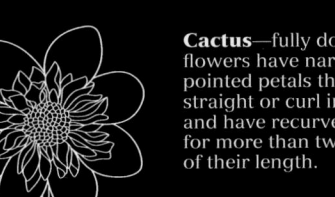

Collarette—single flowers with 8–10 broad, outer petals, and an inner "collar" of smaller petals surrounding an open, central disk.

Cactus—fully double flowers have narrow, pointed petals that can be straight or curl inward and have recurved edges for more than two-thirds of their length.

D. **'Café au Lait'** [decorative]

Water-lily—fully double flowers with large, generally sparse ray petals, which are flat or with slightly incurved or recurved margins, giving the flower a flat appearance.

Semi-cactus—fully double flowers similar to cactus types, but with broader-based petals, the edges of which are generally recurved toward their tips.

Decorative—fully double flowers with no visible central disk, and broad, flat petals, sometimes twisted, that incurve slightly at their margins.

Miscellaneous—flowers that fall into a wide range of unclassified types, including peony-like (shown right), single, and double forms.

D. **'Small World'** [pompon]

D. **'B.J. Beauty'** [decorative]   D. **'White Alva's'** [cactus]   D. **'White Klankstad'** [cactus]   D. **'White Ballet'** [collerette]   D. **'Jura'** [semi-cactus]

_D._ 'Brian's Dream' [decorative]

_D._ 'Roxy' [single]

D. coccinea [single]

_D._ 'Lilac Marston' [decorative]

_D._ 'Sorbet' [semi-cactus]

_D._ 'Tiptoe' [decorative]

_D._ 'Carolina Moon' [decorative]

_D._ 'Hillcrest Jessica' [decorative]

_D._ 'Gerrie Hoek' [water-lily]

_D._ 'Franz Kafka' [pompon]

_D._ 'New Dimension' [cactus]

_D._ 'Karma Choc' [decorative]

_D._ 'Bishop of Auckland' [single]

_D._ 'Ruskin Charlotte' [semi-cactus]

_D._ 'Ryecroft Gem' [decorative]

_D._ 'Berwick Wood' [decorative]

_D._ 'Sascha' [water-lily]

_D._ 'Mermaid of Zennor' [single]

_D._ 'Natal' [pompon]

D. 'Preston Park' [single]

D. 'Bishop of Llandaff' [miscellaneous]

D. 'Comet' [anemone]

D. 'Chimborazo' [collerette]

D. 'Akita' [miscellaneous]

D. 'Hamari Gold' [decorative]

D. 'Zorro' [decorative]

D. 'Black Narcissus' [semi-cactus.]

D. 'Alva's Supreme' [decorative]

D. 'Kenora Superb' [semi-cactus]

D. 'Biddenham Sunset' [decorative]

D. 'Charlie Dimmock' [water-lily]

D. 'Hamari Katrina' [semi-cactus]

D. 'Trengrove Millennium' [decorative]

D. 'Hexton Copper' [ball]

D. 'Hamari Accord' [semi-cactus]

D. 'Moonglow' [cactus]

D. 'Bishop of York' [single]

D. 'Ellen Huston' [miscellaneous]

D. 'Oosterbeck Remembered' [semi-cactus]

D. 'Yellow Hammer' [single]

D. 'Wootton Impact' [semi-cactus]

D. 'Onslow Renown' [semi-cactus]

D. HAPPY SINGLE FIRST LOVE [single]

D. 'So Dainty' [semi-cactus]

398

WHITE

Ornithogalum nutans
Late spring-flowering bulb with 1-sided racemes of semipendent, funnel-shaped, silvery-white flowers, with a broad pale green stripe down the center of each petal. Strap-shaped, semierect, mid-green leaves each have a central, silver stripe. **H** 10in (25cm). **S** 2in (5cm).

☀ ◊ ① Z4–9 H9–5

Erythronium californicum
'White Beauty'
Vigorous, clump-forming tuber with basal, mottled leaves. In spring has a loose spike of 1–10 reflexed, white flowers, each with a brown ring near the center. Spreads rapidly. **H** 8–12in (20–30cm), **S** 4–5in (10–12cm).

◑ ◊ Z3–9 H9–1

Pamianthe peruviana
Evergreen, spring-flowering bulb with a stemlike neck and semierect leaves with drooping tips. Stem has a head of 2–4 fragrant, white flowers, each with a bell-shaped cup and 6 spreading petals. **H** 20in (50cm), **S** 18–24in (45–60cm). Min. 54°F (12°C).

◑ ◊ H11–8

Allium neapolitanum
Spring-flowering bulb with narrow, semierect leaves on the lower quarter of flower stems. Stems each develop an umbel, 2–4in (5–10cm) across, of up to 40 white flowers. **H** 8–20in (20–50cm), **S** 4–5in (10–12cm).

☀ ◊ ① Z7–9 H9–7

Calochortus venustus
Late spring-flowering bulb with 1 or 2 narrow, erect leaves near the base of the branched stem. Bears 1–4 white, yellow, purple or red flowers, with a dark red, yellow-margined blotch on each large petal. **H** 8–24in (20–60cm), **S** 2–4in (5–10cm).

☀ ◊ Z6–10 H10–6

Bellevalia romana
Late spring-flowering bulb with loose conical racemes of bell-shaped, lightly fragrant, white flowers, ⅜in (8mm) long, aging to purplish-brown. Strap-shaped, basal leaves are erect and mid-green. **H** 12in (30cm), **S** 3in (8cm).

☀ ◊ ① Z7–9 H9–7

Erythronium oregonum
Clump-forming, spring-flowering tuber with 2 semierect, mottled, basal leaves. Has up to 3 pendent, white flowers, with yellow eyes and often brown rings near center; petals reflex as flowers open. Increases rapidly by offsets. **H** to 14in (35cm), **S** 5in (12cm).

◑ ◊ Z3–9 H9–1

BULBS

399

TULIPS

Tulips are excellent in the rock garden, in formal bedding, as elegant cut flowers, and for containers. Their bold flowers are generally simple in outline and held upright, often with bright, strong colors. Many of the species deserve to be more widely grown alongside the large variety of hybrids currently available. *Tulipa* is classified in 15 divisions, which are described below.

Div. 1 Single early—cup-shaped, single flowers, often opening wide in sun, are borne from early to mid-spring.

Div. 2 Double early—long-lasting, double flowers open wide in early and mid-spring.

Div. 3 Triumph—sturdy stems bear rather conical, single flowers, becoming more rounded, in mid- and late spring.

Div. 4 Darwin hybrids—large, single flowers are borne on strong stems from mid- to late spring.

Div. 5 Single late—single flowers, usually with pointed petals, are borne in late spring and very early summer.

Div. 6 Lily-flowered—strong stems bear narrow-waisted, single flowers, with long, pointed, often reflexed petals, in late spring.

Div. 7 Fringed—flowers are similar to those in Div. 6, but have fringed petals.

Div. 8 Viridiflora—variable, single flowers, with partly greenish petals, are borne in late spring.

Div. 9 Rembrandt—flowers are similar to those in Div. 6, but have striped or feathered patterns caused by viruses, and appear in late spring.

Div. 10 Parrot—has large, variable, single flowers, with frilled or fringed and usually twisted petals, in late spring.

Div. 11 Double late (peony-flowered—usually bowl-shaped, double flowers appear in late spring.

Div. 12 Kaufmanniana hybrids—single flowers are usually bicolored, open flat in sun and appear in early spring; leaves often mottled or striped.

Div. 13 Fosteriana hybrids—large, single flowers open wide in the sun from early to mid-spring. Leaves are often mottled or striped.

Div. 14 Greigii hybrids—large, single flowers appear in mid- and late spring. Mottled or striped leaves are often wavy-edged.

Div. 15 Miscellaneous—a diverse category of other species and their cultivars and hybrids. Flowers appear in spring and early summer.

T. 'White Dream' ⚠
[Div. 3]

T. 'White Triumphator' ⚠
[Div. 6]

T. 'Purissima' ⚠
[Div. 13]

T. 'Spring Green' ⚠
[Div. 8]

T. turkestanica ⚠
[Div. 15]

T. saxatilis ⚠
[Div. 15]

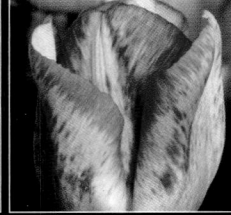

T. 'Shirley' ⚠
[Div. 3]

T. 'China Pink' ⚠
[Div. 6]

T. 'Albert Heijn' ⚠
[Div. 13]

T. 'Dreamland' ⚠
[Div. 5]

T. 'Carnaval de Nice' ⚠
[Div. 11]

T. 'Bird of Paradise' ⚠
[Div. 10]

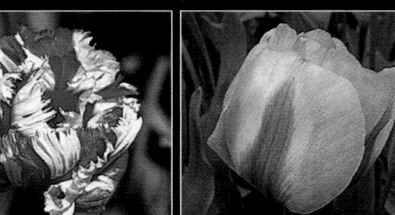

T. 'Ballade' ⚠ [Div. 6]   *T.* 'Estella Rijnveld' ⚠ [Div. 10]   *T.* 'Groenland' ⚠ [Div. 8]   *T.* 'Esperanto' ⚠ [Div. 8]

T. 'Red Riding Hood' ① [Div. 14]

T. 'Bellona' ① [Div. 1]

T. kaufmanniana ① [Div. 15]

T. clusiana var. chrysantha ① [Div. 15]

T. orphanidea ① [Div. 15]

Tulipa sprengeri ① [Div. 15]

T. 'Negrita' ① [Div. 3]

T. 'Maja' ① [Div. 7]

T. 'Apeldoorn's Elite' ① [Div. 4]

T. 'Candela' ① [Div. 13]

T. 'Madame Lefèber' ① [Div. 13]

Tulipa 'Uncle Tom' ① [Div. 11]

T. 'Queen of Night' ① [Div. 5]

T. 'Golden Apeldoorn' ① [Div. 4]

T. 'Prinses Irene' ① [Div. 1]

T. 'Glück' ① [Div. 12]

T. praestans 'Unicum' ① [Div. 15]

T. 'Blue Parrot' ① [Div. 10]

T. 'Dreaming Maid' ① [Div. 3]

T. sylvestris ① [Div. 15]

T. 'Menton' ① [Div. 5]

T. 'Artist' ① [Div. 8]

T. acuminata ① [Div. 15]

T. 'Abu Hassan' ① [Div. 3]

T. 'Black Hero' ① [Div. 11]

T. 'Ballerina' ① [Div. 6]

40

PINK

RED

Anemone pavonina
Leafy tuber with cup-shaped, single, dark-centered, scarlet, purple or blue flowers rising above divided, frilly leaves in early spring. **H** 16in (40cm), **S** 8in (20cm).

☼ ◊ ⊕ Z8–10 H10–8

Sprekelia formosissima
(Aztec lily, Jacobean lily)
Clump-forming, spring-flowering bulb with semierect, basal leaves. Stem bears a deep red flower, 5in (12cm) wide, that has 6 narrow petals with green-striped bases. **H** 6–14in (15–35cm), **S** 5–6in (12–15cm).

☼ ◊ Z13–15 H12–10

Erythronium hendersonii
Spring-flowering tuber with 2 semierect, basal, brown- and green-mottled leaves. Flower stem carries up to 10 lavender or lavender-pink flowers, with reflexed petals and deep purple, central eyes. **H** 8–12in (20–30cm), **S** 4–5in (10–12cm).

☼ ◊ Z3–9 H9–1

Allium unifolium
Late spring-flowering bulb with one semierect, basal, gray-green leaf. Each flower stem carries a domed umbel, 2in (5cm) across, of up to 30 purplish-pink flowers. **H** to 12in (30cm), **S** 3–4in (8–10cm).

Fritillaria meleagris
(Snake's-head fritillary)
Spring-flowering bulb with slender stems producing scattered, narrow, gray-green leaves. Has solitary bell-shaped, prominently checkered flowers, in shades of pinkish-purple or white. **H** to 12in (30cm), **S** 2–3in (5–8cm).

☼ ◊ ⊕ Z4–9 H9–1

☼ ◊ Z4–9 H8–2

Fritillaria camschatcensis
(Black sarana)
Spring-flowering bulb. Sturdy stems
carry lance-shaped, glossy leaves,
mostly in whorls. Bears up to 8 deep
blackish-purple or brown flowers.
Needs rich soil. **H** 6–24in (15–60cm),
S 3–4in (8–10cm).

☼ ◐ ◊ Z4–8 H8–2

Sauromatum venosum (Voodoo lily)
Early spring-flowering tuber. Bears
a large, acrid, purple-spotted spathe,
then a lobed leaf on a long, spotted
stalk. **H** 12–18in (30–45cm), **S** 12–14in
(30–35cm). Min. 41–45°F (5–7°C).

☼ ◐ ◊ Z7–10 H12–10

Fritillaria pyrenaica
Spring-flowering bulb with scattered,
lance-shaped leaves, often rather
narrow. Develops 1, or rarely 2,
broadly bell-shaped flowers with
flared-tipped, checkered, deep
brownish- or blackish-purple petals.
H 6–12in (15–30cm), **S** 2–3in (5–8cm).

☼ ◊ Z6–8 H8–6

Anemone coronaria De Caen Group
'Mister Fokker'
Spring-flowering perennial with
a knobby tuber. Bears shallowly
cup-shaped, single, violet-blue flowers,
with black stamens, above rounded,
divided, finely lobed, semierect, basal
leaves. **H** 10in (25cm), **S** 3in (8cm).

☼ ◊ Z8–11 H11–8

Muscari latifolium
Spring-flowering bulb with one strap-
shaped, semierect, basal, gray-green
leaf. Has a dense spike of tiny, bell-
shaped, blackish-violet to -blue flowers
with constricted mouths; upper ones are
paler and smaller. **H** to 10in (25cm),
S 2–3in (5–8cm).

☼ ◐ ◊ Z4–8 H8–1

Hyacinthoides x massartiana
(Spanish bluebell)
Spring-flowering bulb with strap-
shaped, glossy leaves and pendent,
bell-shaped, blue, white or pink flowers.
H to 12in (30cm), **S** 4–6in (10–15cm).

☼ ◐ ◊ ① Z4–10 H9–1

Hyacinthus orientalis 'Blue Jacket'
Mid-spring-flowering bulb with a dense,
cylindrical spike of highly fragrant,
bell-shaped, waxy, navy-blue flowers
with purple veining. Has lance-shaped,
channeled, erect, bright green, basal
leaves. **H** 10in (25cm), **S** 3in (8cm).

☼ ◐ ◊ ① Z5–9 H9–1

Hyacinthoides non-scripta
(English bluebell)
Tuft-forming, spring-flowering bulb
with strap-shaped leaves. An erect stem,
arching at the apex, bears fragrant, blue,
pink or white flowers. **H** to 16in (40cm),
S to 3in (8cm).

☼ ◐ ◊ ① Z4–10 H9–1

Ixiolirion tataricum
Spring- to early summer-flowering
bulb with long, narrow, semierect leaves
on the lower part of stem. Has
a loose cluster of blue flowers with
a darker, central line along each petal.
H to 16in (40cm), **S** 3–4in (8–10cm).

☼ ◊ Z10–11 H11–7

BULBS

403

DAFFODILS

Narcissus species and hybrids grace the garden from early to late spring with diverse flowers, ranging from the tiny Cyclamineus types, with their swept-back petals, to the stately trumpet daffodils. Some are also scented, including the Poeticus, Jonquilla, and many of the small-flowered forms. Daffodils can be naturalized to form a carpet in grass or a wild garden, or used to brighten up beds and borders, but dwarf forms are best in rock or gravel gardens, or planted in pots and troughs.

The genus is classified in 13 divisions. Their flower forms are illustrated below, with the exception of Div. 12, miscellaneous, and Div. 13, which comprise mostly wild species. Both have varying flowers, including hoop-petticoat forms, and are produced between fall and early summer.

N. 'Dove Wings' ⓘ [Div. 6]

N. 'Ice Follies' ⓘ [Div. 2]

N. 'Actaea' ⓘ [Div. 9]

N. 'Canaliculatus' ⓘ [Div. 8]

Div. 1 Trumpet—usually solitary flowers, each with a trumpet that is as long as, or longer than, the petals. Early to late spring-flowering.

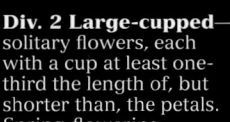

Div. 7 Jonquilla and Apodanthus—sweetly scented flowers, usually 1–5 per stem. Cups are short, sometimes flanged; petals are often flat, fairly broad, and rounded. Mid- to late spring-flowering.

Div. 2 Large-cupped—solitary flowers, each with a cup at least one-third the length of, but shorter than, the petals. Spring-flowering.

Div. 8 Tazetta—clusters of 12 or more small, fragrant flowers per stem, or 3 or 4 large ones. Cups are small and often straight-sided; petals are broad and mostly pointed. Late autumn- to mid-spring-flowering.

Div. 3 Small-cupped—flowers are often borne singly, each with a cup not more than one-third the length of the petals. Spring- or early summer-flowering.

Div. 9 Poeticus—1–2 flowers per stem, each with a small, colored cup and glistening white petals. Most are sweetly scented. Late spring- or early summer-flowering.

Div. 4 Double—most have solitary large, fully or semi-double flowers with the cup and petals, or just the cup, replaced by petaloid structures. Some have smaller flowers in clusters of 4 or more. Spring- or early summer-flowering.

Div. 10 Bulbocodium—flowers usually borne singly on very short stems, with insignificant petals and large, widely flaring cups. Winter- to spring-flowering.

N. 'Mount Hood' ⓘ [Div. 1]

Div. 5 Triandrus—2–6 nodding flowers per stem, each with a short, sometimes straight-sided cup and narrow, reflexed petals. Spring-flowering.

Div. 11 Split-cupped—usually solitary flowers with cups split along more than half their length. Spring-flowering.

(a) Collar—wide cup segments lie back on the petals.

(b) Papillon—narrower cup segments have tips arranged at the margin of the petals.

N. 'Cheerfulness' ⓘ [Div. 4]

N. 'Empress of Ireland' ⓘ [Div. 1]

Div. 6 Cyclamineus—usually 1 or 2 flowers per stem with cups that are sometimes flanged and often longer than those of Div. 5. Petals are narrow, pointed, and reflexed. Early to mid-spring flowering.

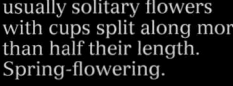

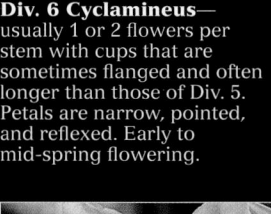
N. 'Thalia' ⓘ [Div. 5]

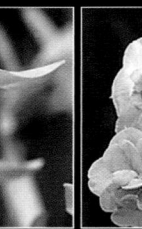
N. 'Bridal Crown' ⓘ [Div. 4]

N. 'Broadway Star' ⓘ [Div. 11b]

N. 'Fragrant Breeze' ⓘ [Div. 2]

N. 'Jack Snipe' ① [Div. 6] N. *bulbocodium* ① [Div. 13] N. 'Home Fires' ① [Div. 2]

N. 'Sir Winston Churchill' ① [Div. 8] N. 'Aircastle' ① [Div. 3] N. 'Stratosphere' ① [Div. 7]

N. 'Avalanche' ① [Div. 8] N. 'Charity May' ① [Div. 6] N. 'Pencrebar' ① [Div. 4] N. 'Pipit' ① [Div. 7] N. 'Bartley' ① [Div. 6]

N. 'Panache' ① [Div. 1] N. 'February Silver' ① [Div. 6] N. 'Liberty Bells' ① [Div. 5] N. 'Suzy' ① [Div. 7]

N. 'Hawera' ① [Div. 5]

N. 'Jenny' ① [Div. 6] N. 'Cassata' ① [Div. 11a] N. 'Binkie' ① [Div. 2] N. 'Tahiti' ① [Div. 4]

N. 'Passionale' ① [Div. 2] N. 'Irene Copeland' ① [Div. 4] N. 'Spellbinder' ① [Div. 1] N. 'Golden Ducat' ① [Div. 4] N. 'Ambergate' ① [Div. 2] N. 'Altruist' ① [Div. 3]

405

BULBS

GREEN

Fritillaria acmopetala
Spring-flowering bulb with slender stems that bear narrowly lance-shaped, scattered leaves, and 1 or 2 broadly bell-shaped, green flowers, with brown-stained petals flaring outward at the tips. **H** 6–16in (15–40cm), **S** 2–3in (5–8cm).

☼ ◊ Z6–8 H8–6

Fritillaria pontica
Spring-flowering bulb with stems carrying lance-shaped, gray-green leaves, the topmost in a whorl of 3. Has solitary broadly bell-shaped, green flowers, 1¼–1¾in (3–4.5cm) long, often suffused brown. **H** 6–18in (15–45cm), **S** 2–3in (5–8cm).

☼ ◊ Z7–8 H8–7

Fritillaria cirrhosa
Spring-flowering bulb with slender stems and narrow, whorled leaves; upper leaves have tendril-like tips. Produces up to 4 widely bell-shaped flowers, purple or yellowish-green with dark purple checkered patterns. **H** to 24in (60cm), **S** 2–3in (5–8cm).

☼ ◊ Z6–8 H8–6

Hermodactylus tuberosus
(Widow iris)
Spring-flowering perennial with finger-like tubers. Long, narrow, gray-green leaves are square in cross-section. Has a fragrant, yellowish-green flower with large, blackish-brown-tipped petals. **H** 8–16in (20–40cm), **S** 2–3in (5–8cm).

☼ ◊ Z7–9 H9–7

Arisaema triphyllum
(Jack-in-the-pulpit)
Summer-flowering tuber with 3-lobed, erect leaves. Produces green or purple spathes, hooded at tips, followed by bright red berries. **H** 16–20in (40–50cm), **S** 12–18in (30–45cm).

☼ ◊ ❗ Z4–9 H9–1

Ixia viridiflora
Spring- to early summer-flowering corm with very narrow, erect leaves mostly at stem base. Carries a spike of flattish, jade-green flowers, 1–2in (2.5–5cm) across, with purple-black eyes. **H** 12–24in (30–60cm), **S** 1–2in (2.5–5cm).

☼ ◊ Z10–11 H11–7

YELLOW

Calochortus luteus (Yellow mariposa)
Late spring-flowering bulb with long, narrow, erect leaves near the base of the loosely branched stem. Each branch bears a 3-petaled, yellow flower with central, brown blotches. **H** 8–18in (20–45cm), **S** 2–3in (5–10cm).

☼ ◊ Z5–10 H10–5

Erythronium 'Pagoda'
Robust, spring-flowering tuber with 2 semierect, basal, faintly mottled, glossy leaves. Flower stem produces up to 10 pendent, pale yellow flowers with reflexed petals. **H** 10–14in (25–35cm), **S** 6–8in (15–20cm).

☼ ◊ Z4–9 H9–1

Fritillaria pallidiflora
Robust, spring-flowering bulb with broadly lance-shaped, gray-green leaves, scattered or in pairs on stem. Has 1–5 widely bell-shaped, yellow to greenish-yellow flowers, usually faintly checkered brownish-red within. **H** 6–28in (15–70cm), **S** 3–4in (8–10cm).

☼ ◊ Z4–9 H8–2

Ferraria crispa
Spring-flowering corm with leafy stem bearing a succession of upward-facing, brown or yellowish-brown flowers, 1½–2in (4–5cm) across, with 6 wavy-edged, spreading petals that are conspicuously lined and blotched. **H** 8–16in (20–40cm), **S** 3–4in (8–10cm).

☼ ◊ Z10–11 H11–8

Stenomesson miniatum
Late spring-flowering bulb with strap-shaped, semierect, basal leaves. Bears a head of red or orange flowers, ¾–1½in (2–4cm) long, with yellow anthers. **H** 8–12in (20–30cm), **S** 4–6in (10–15cm). Min. 41°F (5°C).

☼ ◊ Z11–15 H12–10

Tulipa 'Giuseppe Verdi'
Mid-spring-flowering bulb (Div.12) with purple-marked leaves. Yellow-margined, carmine-red flowers are golden-yellow with small, red marks inside. **H** and **S** 8in (20cm).

☼ ◊ ① Z3–8 H8–1

Hyacinthus orientalis 'City of Haarlem'
Late spring-flowering bulb with lance-shaped, channeled, erect, bright green, basal leaves. Has a dense, cylindrical spike of fragrant, bell-shaped, primrose-yellow flowers. **H** 10in (25cm), **S** 3in (8cm).

☼◑ ◊ ① Z5–9 H9–1

Narcissus 'Silver Chimes'
Sturdy, mid- to late spring-flowering bulb (Div.8) with dark green leaves. Produces up to 10 fragrant flowers, each with broad, milk-white petals and a straight, shallow, creamy-primrose cup. Thrives in a warm site. **H** 13in (32cm).

☼ ◊ ① Z3–9 Z9–1
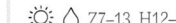

Triteleia ixioides 'Starlight'
Free-flowering, late spring-flowering corm with grasslike, semierect, basal leaves. Open umbels, to 5in (12cm) across, of star-shaped, creamy-yellow flowers have a central, green stripe on each petal. Is good for cut flowers. **H** 16in (40cm), **S** 3in (8cm).

☼ ◊ Z7–13 H12–7

Arum creticum
Spring-flowering tuber that bears white or yellow spathes, each bottle-shaped at the base, slightly reflexed at the apex and with a protruding, yellow spadix. Has arrow-shaped, semierect, deep green leaves in fall. **H** 12–20in (30–50cm), **S** 8–12in (20–30cm).

☼ ◊ ① Z8–10 H10–8

Stenomesson variegatum
Clump-forming bulb. Bears reddish-yellow, pink or white flowers, with 6 green lobes at the apex, in winter or spring. **H** 12–24in (30–60cm), **S** 12in (30cm). Min. 50°F (10°C).

☼ ◊ Z12–15 H12–10

BULBS

407

WHITE

Triteleia hyacinthina
Late spring- to early summer-flowering corm with long, narrow, semierect or spreading, basal leaves. Heads of white, sometimes purple-tinged flowers are borne on wiry stems. **H** 12–20in (30–45cm), **S** 3–4in (8–10cm).

☀ ◊ Z7–13 H12–7

Ornithogalum narbonense
Clump-forming, late spring- to summer-flowering bulb with long, narrow, semierect, basal, gray-green leaves. Leafless stem produces a spike of star-shaped, white flowers, ¾in (2cm) wide. **H** 12–16in (30–40cm), **S** 4–6in (10–15cm).

☀ ◊ ❶ Z7–10 H10–7

Pancratium illyricum
Summer-flowering bulb with strap-shaped, semierect, basal, grayish-green leaves. Leafless stem has a head of 5–12 fragrant, 6-petaled, white flowers, 3in (8cm) across. **H** to 18in (45cm), **S** 10–12in (25–30cm).

☀ ◊ Z8–11 H11–8

Zantedeschia aethiopica 'Green Goddess'
Robust, summer-flowering tuber with arrow-shaped, semierect, basal, deep green leaves. Bears a succession of green spathes each with a large, central, green-splashed, white area. **H** 1½–3ft (45cm–1m), **S** 1½–2ft (45–60cm).

☀ ◊ ❶ Z8–10 H10–4

Ismene narcissiflora (Peruvian daffodil)
Spring- or summer-flowering bulb with semierect, basal leaves, dying down in winter. Bears a loose head of 2–5 fragrant, white flowers. **H** to 24in (60cm), **S** 12–18in (30–45cm).

☀ ◊ H11–10

Arisaema sikokianum
Early summer-flowering tuber with erect leaves divided into 3–5 leaflets. Produces deep brownish-purple and white spathes, 6in (15cm) long, with clublike, white spadices protruding from the mouths. **H** 12–20in (30–50cm), **S** 12–18in (30–45cm).

☀ ◊ ❶ Z4–9 H9–3

Ornithogalum thyrsoides (Chincherinchee)
Summer-flowering bulb with strap-shaped, semierect, basal leaves. Bears a dense, conical spike of cup-shaped, white flowers, ¾–1¼in (2–3cm) across. **H** 12–18in (30–45cm), **S** 4–6in (10–15cm).

☀ ◊ ❶ Z7–10 H10–7

Habenaria radiata
Evergreen–deciduous, terrestrial orchid with fleshy tubers and linear, gray-green, basal leaves. In mid-summer, each slender flower stem bears 2 or 3 white flowers that resemble egret birds in flight. **H** 12in (30cm), **S** 4in (10cm).

☀ ◊ Z5–10 H10–5

Ornithogalum arabicum
Early summer-flowering bulb with strap-shaped, semierect leaves in a basal cluster. Has a flattish head of up to 15 scented, white or creamy-white flowers, 1½–2in (4–5cm) across, with black ovaries in centers. **H** 12–18in (30–45cm), **S** 4–6in (10–15cm).

☀ ◊ ❶ Z9–11 H11–9

Allium neapolitanum Cowanii Group
Late spring-flowering bulb with large umbels of up to 30 star-shaped, white flowers in late spring or early summer, after the lance-shaped, semierect, mid-green, basal leaves have withered. Is good for cut flowers. **H** 16in (40cm), **S** 2in (5cm).

☼ ◊ Z7–9 H9–7

Eucomis pallidiflora (Giant pineapple flower, Giant pineapple lily)
Summer-flowering bulb with sword-shaped, crinkly edged, semierect, basal leaves. Bears a dense spike of star-shaped, greenish-white flowers, topped with a cluster of leaflike bracts. **H** to 30in (75cm), **S** 12–24in (30–60cm).

☼ ◊ Z8–11 H11–8

Calochortus superbus
Bulb with linear, gray-green, basal leaves. In early summer, branched stems bear 1–3 upward-facing, cup-shaped, white, creamy-yellow or lavender-blue flowers, with purplish-brown markings at the base of each petal. **H** 16in (40cm), **S** 3in (8cm).

☼ ◊ Z5–10 H10–6

Eucomis comosa
Clump-forming bulb with strap-shaped, wavy-margined leaves, spotted purple beneath. Purple-spotted stem bears a spike of white or greenish-white, sometimes pink-tinted flowers, with purple ovaries. **H** to 28in (70cm), **S** 12–24in (30–60cm).

☼ ◊ Z8–11 H10–8

Tritonia disticha subsp. rubrolucens
Late summer-flowering corm with narrowly sword-shaped, erect leaves in a flattish, basal fan. Has pink flowers in a loose, one-sided spike. **H** 12–20in (30–50cm), **S** 3–4in (8–10cm).

☼ ◊ Z9–10 H10–9

Allium schubertii
Early summer-flowering bulb with widely strap-shaped, semierect, basal leaves. Bears large umbels of 40 or more star-shaped, pink or purple flowers on very unequal stalks, then brown seed capsules. **H** 12–24in (30–60cm), **S** 6–8in (15–20cm).

☼ ◊ ① Z4–10 H10–1

Allium senescens subsp. montanum
Vigorous, clump-forming, summer-flowering bulb with strap-shaped, often twisted, gray-green leaves. Has dense umbels, ¾in (2cm) across, of up to 30 long-lasting, cup-shaped, pink flowers. **H** 18in (45cm), **S** 24in (60cm).

☼ ◊ ① Z4–10 H10–1

Allium cernuum
Clump-forming, summer-flowering bulb with narrow, semierect, basal leaves. Each stem produces up to 30 cup-shaped, pink or white flowers in a loose, nodding umbel, ¾–1½in (2–4cm) across. **H** 12–28in (30–70cm), **S** 3–5in (8–12cm).

☼ ◊ ① Z3–9 H9–5

BULBS

409

CROCOSMIA

Cormous perennials with flowers in vibrant shades of yellow, orange, and red, and sword-shaped, pleated foliage, crocosmias are real crowd-pleasers. The flowers are held on elegant arching stems and bloom for many weeks between mid-summer and fall. Most are easy to grow, spreading quickly when conditions are right for them. Plants, rather than corms, are the best choice for beginners, and should be planted in spring in moist but well-drained fertile soil in sun or partial shade. Those that are borderline hardy will benefit from a warm site near a protective wall.

C. 'Lucifer'

C. 'Honey Angels'

C. 'Solfatare'

C. 'George Davison'   C. masoniorum   C. 'Severn Sunrise'

C. 'Star of the East'   C. 'Jackanapes'

RED

Lycoris radiata (Red spider lily)
Late summer-flowering bulb with a head of 5 or 6 bright rose-red flowers with narrow, wavy-margined, reflexed petals and conspicuous anthers. Has strap-shaped, semierect, basal leaves after flowering time. **H** 12–16in (30–40cm), **S** 4–6in (10–15cm).

☼ ◊ Z7–10 H10–7

Rhodophiala advena
Clump-forming, spring- to summer-flowering bulb with basal, gray-green leaves. Leafless stem carries a head of 2–8 narrowly funnel-shaped, red flowers, 2in (5cm) long. **H** to 16in (40cm), **S** 6–8in (15–20cm).

☼ ◊ Z9–10 H10–9

Phaedranassa carmioli
Spring- and summer-flowering bulb with upright, elliptic or lance-shaped, basal leaves. Bears a head of 6–10 pendent, pinkish-red flowers, with green bases and yellow-edged, green lobes at each apex. **H** 20–28in (50–70cm), **S** 12–18in (30–45cm).

☼ ◊ H11–9

Ranunculus asiaticus (Persian buttercup)
Early summer-flowering perennial with clawlike tubers and long-stalked leaves both at base and on stem. Has single or double flowers in red, white, pink, yellow or orange. **H** 18–22in (45–55cm), **S** 4in (10cm).

☼ ◊ ❶ Z7–11 H11–7

Gladiolus communis subsp. byzantinus
Early summer-flowering corm with a dense spike of up to 20 deep purplish-red or purplish-pink flowers, 1½–2½in (4–6cm) long. Produces a fan of sword-shaped, erect, basal leaves. **H** to 28in (70cm), **S** 4–6in (10–15cm).

☼ ◊ Z8–10 H10–8

BULBS

Tulbaghia simmleri
Semievergreen, bulbous perennial with clusters of narrow, grasslike, mid-green leaves. Produces terminal umbels of fragrant, tubular, light to deep purple flowers in early to mid-summer. **H** 24in (60cm), **S** 10in (25cm).

☼ ◊ Z7–9 H9–7

Allium cristophii
Summer-flowering bulb with semierect, hairy, gray leaves that droop at tips. Has a large, spherical umbel of 50 or more star-shaped, purplish-violet flowers, which dry well. **H** 6–16in (15–40cm), **S** 6–8in (15–20cm).

☼ ◊ ! Z5–8 H9–5

Camassia quamash
(Camass, Quamash)
Clump-forming bulb with racemes of shallowly cup-shaped, rich to pale blue or white flowers in late spring and early summer. Has long, linear, erect, basal leaves. **H** 12in (30cm), **S** 2in (5cm).

☼◑ ◊ Z4–11 H11–1

Allium caeruleum
Clump-forming, summer-flowering bulb with narrow, erect leaves on the lower third of slender flower stems, which bear 30–50 star-shaped, blue flowers in a dense, spherical umbel, 1¼–1½in (3–4cm) across. **H** 8–32in (20–80cm), **S** 4–6in (10–15cm).

☼ ◊ ! Z4–10 H10–1

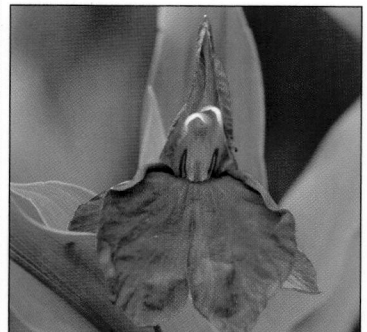

Roscoea auriculata
Early fall-flowering tuber with linear to broadly lance-shaped, semierect, dark green leaves. Orchid-like, rich purple flowers are borne from upper leaf axils from late summer to fall. **H** 18in (45cm), **S** 6in (15cm).

☀◑ ◊ Z6–9 H9–6

Triteleia laxa 'Koningin Fabiola'
Mid-summer-flowering corm with linear, semierect, basal leaves. These often die back before a loose umbel of funnel-shaped, deep violet-blue flowers, on long, slender stalks, is produced. Is good for cut flowers. **H** 12in (30cm), **S** 2in (5cm).

☼ ◊ Z6–10 H10–6

Triteleia laxa
Early summer-flowering corm with narrow, semierect, basal leaves. Stem carries a large, loose umbel of funnel-shaped, deep to pale purple-blue flowers, ¾–2in (2–5cm) long, mostly held upright. **H** 4–20in (10–50cm), **S** 3–4in (8–10cm).

☼ ◊ Z6–10 H10–6

BULBS

GREEN

Eucomis bicolor
Summer-flowering bulb with wavy-edged, semierect, basal leaves. Stem, often spotted purple, bears a spike of green or greenish-white flowers, with 6 purple-edged petals, topped by a cluster of leaflike bracts. **H** 12–20in (30–50cm), **S** 12–24in (30–60cm).

☀ ◊ Z8–10 H10–8

Arisaema jacquemontii
Summer-flowering tuber with 1 or 2 erect leaves, divided into wavy-edged leaflets. Produces slender, white-lined, green spathes that are hooded at tips and drawn out into long points. **H** 12–20in (30–50cm), **S** 12–15in (30–38cm).

☀ ◊ ❶ Z7–9 H9–7

Arisaema griffithii
Summer-flowering tuber with large, erect leaves above a green or purple spathe, 8–10in (20–25cm) long, strongly netted with paler veins and expanded like a cobra's hood. Protect in winter or lift for frost-free storage. **H** to 24in (60cm), **S** 18–24in (45–60cm).

☀ ◊ ❶ Z7–9 H9–7

YELLOW

Ranunculus asiaticus* var. *flavus
(Persian buttercup)
Early summer-flowering perennial with clawlike tubers and long-stalked, palmate leaves at base and on stem. Has single or double flowers in yellow, white, pink, red or orange. **H** 18–22in (45–55cm), **S** 3–4in (8–10cm).

☀ ◊ ❶ Z7–11 H11–7

Cypella herbertii
Summer-flowering bulb with a fan of narrow, sword-shaped, erect, basal leaves. Branched flower stem carries a succession of short-lived, iris-like, orange-yellow flowers, each spotted purple in the center. **H** 12–20in (30–50cm), **S** 3–4in (8–10cm).

☀ ◊ Z11 H11–1

Calochortus barbatus
Summer-flowering bulb with narrow, erect leaves near the base of the loosely branched stem. Each branch bears a pendent, yellow or greenish-yellow flower that is hairy inside. **H** 12–24in (30–60cm), **S** 2–4in (5–10cm).

☀ ◊ Z6–10 H10–6

Allium flavum
Clump-forming, summer-flowering bulb. Leaves are linear and semierect on lower half of slender flower stem. Produces a loose umbel of up to 60 small, bell-shaped, yellow flowers on thin, arching stalks. **H** 4–14in (10–35cm), **S** 2–3in (5–8cm).

☀ ◊ ❶ Z4–10 H9–1

Cyrtanthus mackenii* var. *cooperi
Clump-forming, summer-flowering bulb with long, narrow, semierect, basal leaves. Leafless stems each carry a head of up to 10 fragrant, tubular, cream or yellow flowers, 2in (5cm) long and slightly curved. **H** 12–16in (30–40cm), **S** 3–4in (8–10cm).

☀ ◊ Z11 H11–6

***Ismene* x *spofforthiae* 'Sulphur Queen'**
Summer-flowering bulb with strap-shaped, dark green, basal leaves. Bears terminal umbels of up to 6 large, fragrant, sulfur-yellow flowers, each with a frilly-edged, light yellow cup with green stripes and 6 spreading petals. **H** 24in (60cm), **S** 12in (30cm). Min. 59°F (15°C).

☀ ◊ Z10–11 H11–9

***Crocosmia* 'Golden Fleece'**
Clump-forming, late summer-flowering corm with sword-shaped, erect, basal, gray-green leaves. Flowers are funnel-shaped and clear golden-yellow. **H** 24–30in (60–75cm), **S** 6–8in (15–20cm).

☀ ◊ Z6–9 H10–9

ORANGE

Polianthes geminiflora
Summer-flowering tuber with narrowly strap-shaped, semierect leaves in a basal tuft. Stems each carry long spikes of downward-curving, tubular, red or orange flowers in pairs. **H** 8–16in (20–40cm), **S** 4–6in (10–15cm).

☼ ◊ H11–1

Alstroemeria Ligtu Hybrids
Summer-flowering tuber with narrow, twisted leaves and heads of widely flared flowers in shades of pink, yellow or orange, often spotted or streaked with contrasting colors. **H** 1½–2ft (45–60cm), **S** 2–3ft (60cm–1m).

☼ ◊ ① Z8–11 H11–7

Sandersonia aurantiaca
(Chinese-lantern lily)
Deciduous, summer-flowering, tuberous climber with a slender stem bearing scattered, lance-shaped leaves, some tendril-tipped. Orange flowers are produced in axils of upper leaves. **H** 24in (60cm), **S** 10–12in (25–30cm).

☼ ◊ Z11–14 H12–10

Tigridia pavonia
(Peacock flower, Tiger flower)
Summer-flowering bulb with sword-shaped, pleated, erect leaves near stem base. A succession of short-lived flowers vary from white to orange, red or yellow, often with contrasting spots. **H** to 18in (45cm), **S** 4–6in (12–15cm).

☼ ◊ Z8–10 H12–3

PINK

Zephyranthes carinata
Late summer- to early fall-flowering bulb with narrowly strap-shaped, semierect, basal leaves. Each stem bears a funnel-shaped, pink flower, held almost erect. **H** 8–12in (20–30cm), **S** 3–4in (8–10cm).

☼ ◊ Z8–11 H12–9

Nerine bowdenii
Fall-flowering bulb with a stout stem and strap-shaped, semierect, basal leaves. Carries a head of 5–10 glistening, pink flowers with petals that widen slightly toward wavy-margined, recurved tips. **H** 18–24in (45–60cm), **S** 5–6in (12–15cm).

☼ ◊ ① Z8–10 H10–8

Scilla scilloides
Late summer- and fall-flowering bulb with 2–4 narrowly strap-shaped, semierect, basal leaves. Stem bears a slender, dense spike of up to 30 flattish, pink flowers, ¼–½in (0.5–1cm) across. **H** to 12in (30cm), **S** 2in (5cm).

☼ ◊ ① Z4–8 H8–1

Nerine bowdenii f. alba
Fall-flowering bulb with a sturdy stem and strap-shaped, semierect, basal leaves. Produces a head of 5–10 white, often pink-flushed flowers; petals widen slightly toward wavy-margined, recurved tips. **H** 18–24in (45–60cm), **S** 5–6in (12–15cm).

☼ ◊ ① Z8–10 H10–8

(Nerine 'Orion' image)

Nerine 'Orion'
Fall-flowering bulb with strap-shaped, semierect, basal leaves. Sturdy, leafless stem bears a head of pale pink flowers with very wavy-margined petals that have recurved tips. **H** 12–20in (30–50cm), **S** 8–10in (20–25cm).

☼ ◊ ① Z8–10 H10–8

Nerine undulata
Fall-flowering bulb with narrowly strap-shaped, semierect, basal leaves. Flower stem carries a head of pink flowers with very narrow petals crinkled for their whole length. **H** 12–18in (30–45cm), **S** 4–5in (10–12cm).

☼ ◊ ① Z8–10 H10–8

BULBS

BULBS

ORANGE

Dahlia 'Harvest Inflammation'
Single dahlia bearing orange flowers, 2in (5cm) across, suffused orange-red, each with a central, orange-yellow disc, in summer–fall. **H** 22in (55cm), **S** 16in (40cm).

☼ ◊ Z9–11 H11–1

Nerine sarniensis (Guernsey lily)
Fall-flowering bulb with strap-shaped, semierect, basal leaves. Leafless stem carries a spherical head of up to 20 deep orange-pink flowers, 2½–3in (6–8cm) across, with wavy-margined petals. **H** 18–24in (45–60cm), **S** 5–6in (12–15cm).

☼ ◊ ! Z8–10 H10–8

WHITE

Eucharis amazonica
Evergreen, clump-forming bulb with strap-shaped, semierect, basal leaves. Bears a head of up to 6 fragrant, slightly pendent, white flowers at almost any season. **H** 16–24in (40–60cm), **S** 2–3ft (60cm–1m). Min. 59°F (15°C).

☼ ◊ H11–10

Hippeastrum 'Apple Blossom'
Winter- to spring-flowering bulb with strap-shaped, semierect, basal leaves produced as, or just after, flowers form. Sturdy stem has a head of 2–6 white flowers, becoming pink at petal tips. **H** 12–20in (30–50cm), **S** 12in (30cm). Min. 55°F (13°C).

☼ ◊ ! H11–1

Hippeastrum 'Striped'
Winter- to spring-flowering bulb with strap-shaped, semierect, basal leaves produced with or just after flowers. Sturdy stem has a head of 2–6 widely funnel-shaped flowers, striped white and red. **H** 20in (50cm), **S** 12in (30cm). Min. 55°F (13°C).

☼ ◊ ! H11–1

RED

Hippeastrum 'Red Lion'
Tuft-forming, winter- and spring-flowering bulb with a sturdy stem bearing a head of 2–6 dark red flowers with yellow anthers. Strap-shaped leaves appear with or just after flowers. **H** 12–20in (30–50cm), **S** 12in (30cm). Min. 55°F (13°C).

☼ ◊ ! H11–1

Hippeastrum aulicum
Winter- and spring-flowering bulb with a basal cluster of strap-shaped, semierect leaves. Sturdy stem bears two red flowers with green-striped petals and green throats. **H** 12–20in (30–50cm), **S** 12in (30cm). Min. 55–59°F (13–15°C).

☼ ◊ ! H11–10

Veltheimia bracteata
Clump-forming, winter-flowering bulb with semierect, strap-shaped, basal, glossy leaves and dense spikes of pendent, tubular, pink, red or yellowish-red flowers. **H** 12–18in (30–45cm), **S** 10–15in (25–38cm). Min. 50°F (10°C).

☼ ◊ Z13–15 H12–10

WHITE

Anemone blanda 'White Splendour'
Knobby tuber with semierect leaves that have 3 deeply toothed lobes. Bears upright, flattish, white flowers, 1½–2in (4–5cm) across, with 9–14 narrow petals, in early spring. **H** 2–4in (5–10cm), **S** 4–6in (10–15cm).

☼ ◊ ! Z4–8 H8–1

Leucojum vernum (Spring snowflake)
Spring-flowering bulb with strap-shaped, semierect, basal leaves. Leafless stem carries 1 or 2 pendent, bell-shaped flowers, ⅝–¾in (1.5–2cm) long, with 6 green-tipped, white petals. **H** 4–6in (10–15cm), **S** 3–4in (8–10cm).

☼ ◊ Z4–8 H9–3

Ornithogalum balansae
Spring-flowering bulb with 2 almost prostrate, inversely lance-shaped, mid-green basal leaves. Has a broad head of 2–5 flowers, glistening white inside, bright green outside, that open wide. **H** 2–6in (5–15cm), **S** 2–3in (5–8cm).

☼ ◊ ! Z7–10 H10–7

Sternbergia candida

Spring-flowering bulb. Strap-shaped, semierect, basal, grayish-green leaves appear together with a fragrant, funnel-shaped, white flower, 1½–2in (4–5cm) long, borne on a leafless stem. **H** 4–8in (10–20cm), **S** 3–4in (8–10cm).

:☼: ◊ Z8–10 H10–8

Muscari botryoides 'Album'

Late spring-flowering bulb with 3–4 narrow, semierect, basal leaves that widen slightly at the tips. Produces dense, cone-shaped racemes of tiny, fragrant, white flowers. **H** 6in (15cm), **S** 2in (5cm).

:☼: ◊ Z2–8 H8–1

Erythronium californicum

Clump-forming, spring-flowering tuber. Has 2 semierect, basal, mottled leaves. Up to 3 white or creamy-white flowers, sometimes red-brown externally, have reflexed petals, yellow eyes and often brown rings near centers. **H** 6–14in (15–35cm), **S** 4–5in (10–12cm).

:◐: ◊ Z3–9 H9–1

Iris 'Natascha'

Bulbous iris with solitary, slightly fragrant, very pale blue, almost white flowers, with a yellow spot on each petal, borne in early spring. Has linear, mid-green leaves. **H** 6in (15cm), **S** ¾in (2cm).

:☼: ◊ (!) Z5–8 H8–5

Puschkinia scilloides var. libanotica 'Alba'

Spring-flowering bulb with usually 2 strap-shaped, semierect, basal leaves. Produces a dense spike of star-shaped, white flowers, ⅝–¾in (1.5–2cm) across. **H** 6in (15cm), **S** 1–2in (2.5–5cm).

:☼: ◊ Z3–9 H9–1

Ornithogalum montanum

Clump-forming, spring-flowering bulb with strap-shaped, semierect, basal, gray-green leaves. Leafless stem produces a head of star-shaped, white flowers, 1¼–1½in (3–4cm) across, striped green outside. **H** and **S** 4–6in (10–15cm).

:☼: ◊ (!) Z6–10 H10–6

Ornithogalum lanceolatum

Spring-flowering, dwarf bulb with a rosette of prostrate, lance-shaped, basal leaves. Carries a head of flattish, star-shaped, white flowers, 1¼–1½in (3–4cm) across, broadly striped green outside. **H** 2–4in (5–10cm), **S** 4–6in (10–15cm).

:☼: ◊ (!) Z5–10 H10–1

Hyacinthus orientalis 'White Pearl'

Mid-spring-flowering bulb with linear to lance-shaped, channeled, erect, bright green, basal leaves. Produces a dense, cylindrical raceme of sweetly scented, tubular to bell-shaped, pure white flowers. **H** to 10in (25cm), **S** to 3in (8cm).

:◐: ◊ (!) Z5–9 H9–1

BULBS

WHITE

Ornithogalum umbellatum
Late spring-flowering bulb with linear, semierect, mid-green leaves with a whitish-green midrib. These fade as stems each bearing 6–20 star-shaped, white flowers, with green reverses, are produced in late spring and early summer. **H** 8in (20cm), **S** 4in (10cm).

☼ ◊ ① Z6–10 H10–1

Scilla siberica 'Alba'
Early to mid-spring-flowering bulb with 2–4 broadly linear, erect, basal leaves, widening toward the tips. Racemes of small, pendent, bowl-shaped, white flowers are produced at the same time as the leaves. **H** 6in (15cm), **S** 2in (5cm).

☼ ◊ ① Z5–8 H8–5

PINK

Allium akaka
Spring-flowering bulb with 1–3 broad, prostrate and basal, gray-green leaves and an almost stemless, spherical umbel, 2–3in (5–7cm) across of 30–40 star-shaped, white to pinkish-white flowers with red centers. **H** 6–8in (15–20cm), **S** 5–6in (12–15cm).

☼ ◊ ① Z4–9 H9–1

Anemone tschaernjaewii
Spring-flowering tuber with 3-palmate, oval, mid-green leaves, the leaflets shallowly lobed. Has 5-petaled, saucer-shaped, purple-centered, white or pink flowers, ¾–1¾in (2–4.5cm) across. Needs warm, dry, summer dormancy. **H** 2–4in (5–10cm), **S** 2–3in (5–8cm).

☼ ◊ ① Z5–8 H8–5

Chionodoxa 'Pink Giant'
Early spring-flowering bulb with 2 narrow, semierect, basal leaves. Leafless stem produces a spike of 5–10 flattish, white-eyed, pink flowers, ¾–1in (2–2.5cm) across. **H** 4–10in (10–25cm), **S** 1–2in (2.5–5cm).

☼ ◊ Z3–9 H9–1

Allium acuminatum
Spring-flowering bulb with 2–4 long, narrow, semierect, basal leaves. Stem bears an umbel, 2in (5cm) across, of up to 30 small, purplish-pink flowers. **H** 4–12in (10–30cm), **S** 2–3in (5–8cm).

☼ ◊ ① Z4–9 H9–1

Allium karataviense
Late spring-flowering bulb with narrowly elliptic to elliptic, prostrate, basal, grayish-purple leaves. Stem bears 50 or more star-shaped, pale purplish-pink flowers in a spherical umbel, 6in (15cm) or more across. **H** to 8in (20cm), **S** 10–12in (25–30cm).

☼ ◊ ① Z5–9 H9–5

CROCUSES

Crocus species and cultivars are versatile dwarf bulbous plants. Most flower in late winter or early spring; a few bloom in fall. Colors range from white, cream, and yellow to pinkish-lilac and purple, and many are attractively striped or feathered with other colors. The goblet-shaped flowers open wide in full sun, in some cases revealing contrasting centers or conspicuous stamens. Most crocuses are also fragrant. Plant in rock or gravel gardens with other early flowering dwarf bulbs or perennials, in drifts in grass, or beneath deciduous trees and shrubs, where they will rapidly spread. If naturalized in grass, delay mowing until the leaves have died down. Feed with an all-purpose granular fertilizer once the flowers have faded.

C. sieberi 'Hubert Edelsten'

C. vernus 'Remembrance'

C. goulimyi [Fall-flowering]

C. 'Eyecatcher'

C. vernus 'Pickwick'

C. 'E.P. Bowles'

C. 'Dorothy'

C. 'Snow Bunting'

C. 'Blue Bird'

C. etruscus 'Zwanenburg'

C. hadriaticus [Fall-flowering]

C. sieberi subsp. *sublimis* f. *tricolor*

C. tommasinianus 'Ruby Giant'

C. speciosus 'Conqueror' [Fall-flowering]

C. 'Zwanenberg Bronze'

BULBS

Bulbocodium vernum
Spring-flowering corm with stemless, widely funnel-shaped, reddish-purple flowers. Narrow, semierect, basal leaves appear with flowers but do not elongate until later. Dies down in summer.
H 1¼–1½in (3–4cm), **S** 1¼–2in (3–5cm).

☼ ◊ Z7–9 H9–7

Anemone x fulgens
Spring- or early summer-flowering tuber with deeply divided, semierect, basal leaves. Sturdy stems each carry an upright, bright red flower, 2–3in (5–7cm) across, with 10–15 petals.
H 4–12in (10–30cm), **S** 3–4in (8–10cm).

☼ ◊ ① Z8–11 H11–8

Iris 'Pixie'
Bulbous iris with solitary, slightly fragrant, rich deep purple-blue flowers, with yellow midribs and white stripes, borne in late winter and early spring. Has linear, mid-green leaves. **H** 6in (15cm), **S** ¾in (2cm).

☼ ◊ ① Z5–9 H9–4

Erythronium dens-canis
(Dog-tooth violet)
Spring-flowering tuber with 2 basal, mottled leaves. Stem has a pendent, pink, purple or white flower, with bands of brown, purple and yellow near the center and reflexed petals.
H 6–10in (15–25cm), **S** 3–4in (8–10cm).

☼ ◊ ① Z3–9 H9–1

Babiana rubrocyanea
(Baboon flower)
Spring-flowering corm with lance-shaped, erect, folded leaves in a basal fan. Carries short spikes of 5–10 flowers, each with 6 petals, purple-blue at the top and red at the base. **H** 6–8in (15–20cm), **S** 2–3in (5–8cm). Min. 50°F (10°C).

☼ ◊ H11–10

Allium oreophilum
Spring- and summer-flowering, dwarf bulb with 2 narrow, semierect, basal leaves. Has loose, domed umbels of up to 10 widely bell-shaped, deep rose-pink flowers, ⅝–¾in (1.5–2cm) across.
H 2–4in (5–10cm), **S** 3–4in (8–10cm).

☼ ◊ ① Z4–9 H9–1

Cyclamen libanoticum
Spring-flowering tuber with ivy-shaped, dull green leaves with lighter patterns and purplish-green undersides. Has musty-scented, clear pink flowers, each with deep carmine marks at the mouth. Grows best in an alpine house.
H to 4in (10cm), **S** 4–6in (10–15cm).

☼ ◊ ① Z11 H7–1

Anemone blanda var. rosea 'Radar'
Knobby tuber with semierect, deep green leaves with 3 deeply toothed lobes. In early spring, stems each bear an upright, flattish, white-centered, deep reddish-carmine flower with 9–14 narrow petals. **H** 2–4in (5–10cm), **S** 4–6in (10–15cm).

☼ ◊ ① Z4–8 H8–1

Sparaxis tricolor
Spring-flowering corm with erect, lance-shaped leaves in a basal fan. Stem produces a loose spike of up to 5 flattish, orange, red, purple, pink or white flowers, 2–2½in (5–6cm) across, with black or red centers. **H** 4–12in (10–30cm), **S** 3–5in (8–12cm).

☼ ◊ Z7–10 H10–7

Anemone blanda 'Violet Star'
Knobby tuber with rounded, semierect, dark green, basal leaves with divided, irregularly lobed leaves. In spring, stems each bear a saucer-shaped, white-centered, amethyst-violet flower that resembles a daisy. **H** and **S** 6in (15cm).

☼ ◊ Z4–8 H8–1

Ipheion uniflorum 'Froyle Mill'

Spring-flowering bulb with narrow, semierect, basal, pale green leaves that smell of onions if crushed. Each leafless stem carries a star-shaped, violet-blue flower, 1¼–1½in (3–4cm) across. **H** 4–6in (10–15cm), **S** 2–3in (5–8cm).

☼ ◊ Z5–9 H9–5

Bellevalia hyacinthoides

Spring-flowering bulb with prostrate, narrow leaves in a basal cluster. Bears a dense spike of up to 20 bell-shaped, pale lavender-blue, almost white flowers with darker, central veins. **H** 2–6in (5–15cm), **S** 2in (5cm).

☼ ◊ Z7–9 H9–7

Chionodoxa forbesii

Early spring-flowering bulb with 2 semierect, narrow, basal leaves. Bears a spike of 5–10 outward-facing, rich blue-lilac flowers with white eyes. **H** 4–10in (10–25cm), **S** 1–2in (2.5–5cm).

☼ ◊ Z3–9 H9–1

Anemone blanda 'Atrocaerulea'

Knobby tuber with semierect, dark green leaves that have 3 deeply toothed lobes. In early spring, stems each bear an upright, flattish, bright blue flower, 1½–2in (4–5cm) across, with 9–14 narrow petals. **H** 2–4in (5–10cm), **S** 4–6in (10–15cm).

☼ ◊ ! Z4–8 H8–1

Romulea bulbocodium

Spring-flowering corm with long, semierect, threadlike leaves in a basal tuft. Slender flower stems each carry 1–6 upward-facing flowers, usually pale lilac-purple with yellow or white centers. **H** 2–4in (5–10cm), **S** 1–2in (2.5–5cm).

☼ ◊ Z5–9 H9–5

x Chionoscilla allenii

Early spring-flowering bulb with 2 narrow, semierect, basal, dark green leaves and flattish, star-shaped, deep blue flowers, ½–¾in (1–2cm) across, in a loose spike. **H** 4–6in (10–15cm), **S** 1–2in (2.5–5cm).

☼ ◊ Z3–9 H9–1

Moraea sisyrinchium

Spring-flowering corm with 1 or 2 semierect, narrow, basal leaves. Wiry stems each carry a succession of lavender- to violet-blue flowers, 1¼–1½in (3–4cm) across, with white or orange patches on the 3 larger petals. **H** 4–8in (10–20cm), **S** 3–4in (8–10cm).

☼ ◊ Z9–10 H10–8

Muscari comosum 'Plumosum' (Feather grape hyacinth)

Spring-flowering bulb with up to 5 strap-shaped, semierect, basal, gray-green leaves. Sterile flowers are replaced by a fluffy mass of purple threads. **H** to 10in (25cm), **S** 4–5in (10–12cm).

☼ ◊ Z4–8 H8–1

Brimeura amethystina

Late spring-flowering bulb with very narrow, semierect, basal leaves. Each leafless stem bears a spike of up to 15 pendent, tubular, blue flowers. **H** 4–10in (10–25cm), **S** 1–2in (2.5–5cm).

◑ ◊ Z5–9 H9–5

BULBS

419

BLUE

BULBS

Chionodoxa luciliae

Early spring-flowering bulb with
2 somewhat curved, semierect,
basal leaves. Leafless stem bears
1–3 upward-facing, blue flowers
with white eyes. **H** 2–4in (5–10cm),
S 1–2in (2.5–5cm).

☼ ◊ Z3–9 H9–1

Scilla mischtschenkoana

Early spring-flowering bulb with
2 or 3 strap-shaped, semierect, basal,
mid-green leaves. Stems elongate
as cup-shaped or flattish, pale blue
flowers, with darker blue veins,
open. **H** 2–4in (5–10cm), **S** 2in (5cm).

☼ ◊ ① Z4–7 H9–6

Scilla siberica 'Atrocoerulea'

Early spring-flowering bulb with
2–4 strap-shaped, semierect, basal,
glossy leaves, widening toward tips.
Bell-shaped, deep rich blue flowers,
½–⅝in (1–1.5cm) long, are borne
in a short spike. **H** 4–6in (10–15cm),
S 2in (5cm).

☼ ◊ ① Z5–8 H8–5

Muscari neglectum

Spring-flowering bulb. Bears 4–6 often
prostrate leaves from fall to early
summer. Has small, ovoid, deep blue
or blackish-blue flowers with white-
rimmed mouths. Increases rapidly.
H 4–8in (10–20cm), **S** 3–4in (8–10cm).

☼ ◊ Z4–8 H8–1

Tecophilaea cyanocrocus
var. leichtlinii

Spring-flowering corm with 1 or 2
narrowly lance-shaped, semierect,
basal leaves and solitary upward-
facing, widely funnel-shaped, pale
blue flowers with large, white centers.
H 3–4in (8–10cm), **S** 2–3in (5–8cm).

☼ ◊ Z7–9 H9–7

Muscari aucheri

Spring-flowering bulb with 2 strap-
shaped, grayish-green leaves. Bears
small, almost spherical, bright blue
flowers with white-rimmed mouths;
upper flowers are often paler. **H** 2–6in
(5–15cm), **S** 2–3in (5–8cm).

☼ ◊ Z6–9 H9–5

Muscari armeniacum

Spring-flowering bulb with 3–6 long,
narrow, semierect, basal leaves.
Carries a dense spike of small, fragrant,
bell-shaped, deep blue flowers with
constricted mouths that have a rim
of small, paler blue or white "teeth."
H 6–8in (15–20cm), **S** 3–4in (8–10cm).

☼ ◊ Z4–8 H8–1

Tecophilaea cyanocrocus
(Chilean blue crocus)

Spring-flowering corm with 1 or 2
lance-shaped, semierect, basal leaves.
Carries upward-facing, funnel-shaped,
deep gentian-blue flowers, 1½–2in
(4–5cm) across, with white throats.
H 3–4in (8–10cm), **S** 2–3in (5–8cm).

☼ ◊ Z7–9 H9–7

Puschkinia scilloides var. libanotica
(Striped squill)
Spring-flowering bulb with usually
2 strap-shaped, semierect, basal
leaves. Carries a dense spike of
star-shaped, pale blue flowers with
a darker blue stripe down each petal
center. **H** 6in (15cm), **S** 1–2in (2.5–5cm).

☼ ◊ Z3–9 H9–1

Hyacinthella leucophaea
Spring-flowering bulb with 2 narrowly
strap-shaped, semierect, basal leaves
and a thin, wiry, leafless flower stem.
Carries a short spike of tiny, bell-shaped,
very pale blue, almost white flowers.
H 4in (10cm), **S** 1–2in (2.5–5cm).

☼ ◊ Z9–11 H10–7

Crocus 'Blue Pearl'
Early spring-flowering corm bearing
narrow, semierect, basal leaves, with
white lines along the centers. Fragrant,
long-tubed, funnel-shaped, soft
lavender-blue flowers, bluish-white
within, have golden-yellow throats.
H 3in (7cm), **S** 2in (5cm).

☼ ◊ Z3–8 H8–1

Ledebouria socialis
Evergreen, spring-flowering bulb
with lance-shaped, semierect,
basal, dark-spotted, gray or green
leaves. Produces a short spike of
bell-shaped, purplish-green flowers.
H 2–4in (5–10cm), **S** 3–4in (8–10cm).

☼ ◊ Z11 H11–6

Arum italicum 'Marmoratum'
Late spring-flowering tuber. Produces
semierect leaves, with cream or white
veins, in fall, followed by pale green or
creamy-white spathes, then red berries
in fall. Is good for flower arrangements.
H 6–10in (15–25cm), **S** 8–12in (20–30cm).

☼ ◊ ❶ Z7–9 H9–3

Colchicum luteum
Spring-flowering corm with wineglass-
shaped, yellow flowers—the only
known yellow Colchicum. Semierect,
basal leaves are short at flowering
time but later expand. **H** 2–4in (5–10cm),
S 2–3in (5–8cm).

☼ ◊ ❶ Z4–9 H9–1

Erythronium americanum
Spring-flowering tuber with 2 semierect, basal leaves, mottled green
and brown, and a pendent, yellow
flower, often bronze outside, with
petals reflexing in sunlight. Forms
clumps by stolons. **H** 2–10in (5–25cm),
S 2–3in (5–8cm).

☼ ◊ Z3–9 H9–2

Muscari macrocarpum
Spring-flowering bulb with 3–5 semi-
erect, basal, grayish-green leaves.
Carries a dense spike of fragrant,
brown-rimmed, bright yellow flowers.
Upper flowers may initially be
brownish-purple. **H** 4–8in (10–20cm),
S 4–6in (10–15cm).

☼ ◊ Z7–9 H9–7

BULBS

421

SPRING

SUMMER

BULBS

ORANGE

Dipcadi serotinum
Spring-flowering bulb with 2–5 very narrow, semierect, basal leaves. Leafless stem has a loose spike of nodding, tubular, brown or dull orange flowers, ½–⅝in (1–1.5cm) long. **H** 4–12in (10–30cm), **S** 2–3in (5–8cm).

☼ ◊ Z8–10 H10–8

Fritillaria pudica (Yellow fritillary)
Spring-flowering bulb with stems bearing scattered, narrowly lance-shaped, gray-green leaves. Has 1 or 2 deep yellow, sometimes red-tinged flowers, ½–1in (1–2.5cm) long. **H** 2–8in (5–20cm), **S** 2in (5cm).

422

☼ ◊ Z2–9 H9–1

WHITE

Arisaema candidissimum
Early summer-flowering tuber with large, cowl-like, pink-striped, white spathes, enclosing tiny, fragrant flowers on spadices, followed by broad, 3-palmate, semierect leaves, 12in (30cm) long. **H** 4–6in (10–15cm), **S** 12–18in (30–45cm).

☼ ◊ ① Z7–9 H9–7

Albuca humilis
Summer-flowering, dwarf bulb with very narrow, basal, dark green leaves. Carries a loose head of 1–3 cup-shaped, white flowers, ½in (1cm) long, striped green, later reddish, outside. **H** 2–4in (5–10cm), **S** 2–3in (5–8cm).

☼ ◊ Z10–11 H11–10

PINK

Allium schoenoprasum (Chives)
Clump-forming, summer-flowering bulb with narrow, hollow, erect, dark green leaves at base. Stems each carry up to 20 tiny, bell-shaped, pale purple or pink flowers in a dense umbel up to 2in (5cm) across. **H** 5–10in (12–25cm), **S** 2–4in (5–10cm).

☼ ◊ ① Z5–11 H11–1

Allium narcissiflorum
Clump-forming, summer-flowering bulb with very narrow, erect, gray-green leaves on the lower part of the flower stem. Has an umbel of up to 15 bell-shaped, pinkish-purple flowers. **H** 6–12in (15–30cm), **S** 3–4in (8–10cm).

☼ ◊ ① Z5–8 H8–5

Cyclamen purpurascens
Summer- and fall-flowering tuber with rounded, silver-patterned leaves. Bears very fragrant, lilac-pink to reddish-purple flowers. **H** to 4in (10cm), **S** 4–6in (10–15cm).

☼ ◊ ① Z5–9 H9–4

Cyrtanthus brachyscyphus

Clump-forming, summer-flowering bulb with strap-shaped, semierect, basal, bright green leaves. Leafless stem bears a head of 6–12 tubular, orange- or brilliant red flowers with 6 lobes. **H** 8–12in (20–30cm), **S** 4–6in (10–15cm).

☼ ◊ H11–10

Anomatheca laxa

Early summer-flowering corm with a loose spike of up to 6 small, long-tubed, funnel-shaped, red or orange-red flowers, with darker red marks on the lower petals, borne among narrowly sword-shaped, erect, mid-green leaves. **H** 8in (20cm), **S** 2in (5cm).

☼ ◊ Z8–10 H10–8

Roscoea humeana

Summer-flowering tuber. Erect, broadly lance-shaped, rich green leaves form a stemlike sheath at base. Has up to 10 long-tubed, purple flowers, each with a hooded, upper petal, a wide, pendent lip and 2 narrower petals. **H** 6–10in (15–25cm), **S** 6–8in (15–20cm).

☼ ◊ Z7–9 H9–7

BULBS

Haemanthus coccineus (Blood lily)

Summer-flowering bulb with 2 elliptic leaves, hairy beneath, that lie flat on the ground. Spotted stem, forming before leaves, bears a cluster of tiny, red flowers with prominent stamens, within fleshy, red or pink bracts. **H** to 12in (30cm), **S** 8–12in (20–30cm). Min. 50°F (10°C).

☼ ◊ ❗ H11–10

Allium cyathophorum var. farreri

Clump-forming, summer-flowering bulb with tufts of narrow, erect, basal leaves. Each stem bears a small, loose umbel, ⅝–1½in (1.5–4cm) wide, of up to 30 bell-shaped, dark reddish-purple flowers with sharply pointed petals. **H** 6–12in (15–30cm), **S** 4–6in (10–15cm).

☼ ◊ ❗ Z4–9 H9–1

Scilla peruviana

Early summer-flowering bulb with a basal cluster of up to 10 lance-shaped, semierect leaves. Stem bears a broadly conical head of up to 50 flattish, violet-blue flowers, ⅝–1¼in (1.5–3cm) across. **H** 4–10in (10–25cm), **S** 6–8in (15–20cm).

☼ ◊ ❗ Z8–9 H9–8

BULBS

YELLOW

Allium moly
Clump-forming, summer-flowering
bulb with 1–3 broad, semierect, basal,
gray-green leaves. Stems each bear
up to 40 star-shaped, yellow flowers
in a fairly dense umbel, 1½–3in
(4–8cm) across. **H** 4–14in (10–35cm),
S 4–5in (10–12cm).

☼ ◊ ❗ Z3–9 H9–5

Chlidanthus fragrans
Summer-flowering bulb with
narrow, semierect leaves in a basal
tuft. Leafless stem carries a head of
3–5 fragrant, funnel-shaped, yellow
flowers, 1½–2¾in (4–7cm) long.
H 4–12in (10–30cm), **S** 3–4in (8–10cm).

☼ ◊ H11–7

Roscoea cautleyoides
Summer-flowering tuber. Erect, lance-
shaped leaves form a stemlike sheath
at base. Has up to 5 long-tubed, yellow
flowers, each with a hooded, upper
petal, a broad, 2-lobed, lower lip and
2 narrower petals. **H** 6–10in (15–25cm),
S 4–6in (10–15cm).

☼ ◊ Z6–9 H9–6

WHITE

Colchicum speciosum 'Album'
Vigorous, fall-flowering corm with
large, semierect, basal leaves in late
winter or spring. Cup-shaped, white
flowers successfully withstand bad
weather. **H** and **S** 6–8in (15–20cm).

☼ ◊ ❗ Z4–9 H9–1

Acis autumnalis (Autumn snowflake)
Fall-flowering bulb with threadlike,
erect, basal leaves appearing with,
or just after, flowers. Slender stems
each produce a head of 14 bell-shaped,
white flowers, tinged pink at bases.
H 4–6in (10–15cm), **S** 1–2in (2.5–5cm).

☼ ◊ Z5–9 H9–1

Cyclamen hederifolium f. albiflorum
Fall-flowering tuber. Pure white flowers,
with reflexed petals, appear before or
with leaves, which vary but are often
ivy-shaped with silvery-green patterns.
H to 4in (10cm), **S** 4–6in (10–15cm).

◐ ◊ ❗ Z5–7 H9–7

Zephyranthes candida
Fall-flowering bulb with narrow, erect,
basal leaves forming rushlike tufts.
Each leafless stem carries crocus-like,
white flowers, to 2½in (6cm) across.
H 6–10in (15–25cm), **S** 2–3in (5–8cm).

☼ ◊ Z7–9 H9–6

Cyclamen africanum
Fall-flowering tuber with ivy-shaped,
deep green leaves with lighter patterns.
Bears pendent, white or pink flowers,
with reflexed petals and darker
stains around mouths, as or just
before leaves appear. **H** to 4in (10cm),
S 4–6in (10–15cm).

◐ ◊ ❗ Z8–9 H9–8

Colchicum bivonae
Fall-flowering corm with large, funnel-shaped, pinkish-purple flowers, strongly checkered darker purple and with purple anthers. Produces 8–10 erect leaves in spring. **H** 4–6in (10–15cm), **S** 6–8in (15–20cm).

☼ ◊ ① Z4–9 H9–1

Colchicum cilicicum
Fall-flowering corm with large, cup-shaped, pale pink to deep rose-purple flowers, sometimes slightly checkered. Very broad, semierect, basal leaves, ribbed lengthwise, appear soon after flowers have faded. **H** and **S** 6–8in (15–20cm).

☼ ◊ ① Z4–9 H9–1

Colchicum 'Waterlily'
Fall-flowering corm with rather broad, semierect, basal leaves in winter or spring. Tightly double flowers with 20–40 pinkish-lilac petals. **H** 4–6in (10–15cm), **S** 6–8in (15–20cm).

☼ ◊ ① Z4–9 H9–1

Colchicum agrippinum
Early fall-flowering corm. Narrow, slightly waved, semierect, basal leaves develop in spring. Bears erect, funnel-shaped, bright purplish-pink flowers with a darker checkered pattern and pointed petals. **H** 4–6in (10–15cm), **S** 3–4in (8–10cm).

☼ ◊ ① Z4–9 H9–1

Cyclamen graecum
Fall-flowering tuber with heart-shaped, toothed, velvety, dark green leaves, patterned silver or light green. Flowers are pink or white, with purple stains around mouths. Grows best in an alpine house. **H** to 4in (10cm), **S** 4–6in (10–15cm).

◐ ◊ ① Z5–9 H9–5

Cyclamen mirabile
Fall-flowering tuber with pale pink flowers with toothed petals and dark purple-stained mouths. Heart-shaped, patterned leaves, purplish-green beneath, are minutely toothed on margins. **H** to 4in (10cm), **S** 2–3in (5–8cm).

◐ ◊ ① Z8–9 H9–8

PINK

BULBS

Cyclamen hederifolium
Fall-flowering tuber. Pale to deep pink flowers, stained darker at mouths, appear before or with foliage. Leaves vary but are often ivy-shaped with silvery-green patterns. **H** 4in (10cm), **S** 4–6in (10–15cm).

☀ ◐ ◌ ❗ Z5–7 H9–7

Cyclamen rohlfsianum
Fall-flowering tuber with coarsely toothed leaves, zoned with light and dark green patterns, and pale pink-lilac flowers, stained darker at mouths. **H** to 4in (10cm), **S** 4–6in (10–15cm).

☀ ◌ ❗ Z8–9 H9–8

Colchicum x byzantinum
Robust, fall-flowering corm with up to 20 large, funnel-shaped, pale purplish-pink flowers, 4–6in (10–15cm) long. In spring produces very broad, semierect, basal leaves, ribbed lengthwise. **H** and **S** 6–8in (15–20cm).

☀ ◌ ❗ Z4–9 H9–1

Habranthus robustus
Late summer- to early fall-flowering bulb with narrowly strap-shaped, semi-erect, basal leaves. Leafless flower stems each bear a funnel-shaped, pink flower inclined at an angle. **H** 8–12in (20–30cm), **S** 3–4in (8–10cm).

☀ ◌ Z7–10 H10–7

Colchicum autumnale
(Autumn crocus, Meadow saffron)
Fall-flowering corm with up to 8 long-tubed, wineglass-shaped, purple, pink or white flowers, followed by 3–5 large, strap-shaped, semierect, basal, glossy leaves in spring. **H** and **S** 4–6in (10–15cm).

☀ ◌ ❗ Z4–9 H9–1

Cyclamen cilicium
Fall-flowering tuber with broadly heart-shaped leaves that have light and dark green zones. Has white or pink flowers, each with a dark purple stain at the mouth, just before or with leaves. **H** to 4in (10cm), **S** 2–4in (5–10cm).

☀ ◌ ❗ Z5–9 H9–3

WHITE

Galanthus 'Atkinsii'
Vigorous, late winter- and early spring-flowering bulb with strap-shaped, semierect, basal, gray-green leaves. Each stem carries a slender, white flower with a green mark at the apex of each inner petal. **H** 4–10in (10–25cm), **S** 2–3½in (5–9cm).

☀ ◊ ⓘ Z3–9 H9–1

Galanthus elwesii
Late winter- and early spring-flowering bulb with semierect, basal, gray-green leaves that widen gradually toward tips. Each inner petal of the white flowers bears green marks at the apex and base, which may merge. **H** 4–12in (10–30cm), **S** 2–3in (5–8cm).

☀ ◊ ⓘ Z3–9 H9–1

Crocus sieberi 'Albus'
Spring-flowering corm bearing narrow, semierect, basal leaves, with white lines along the centers. Scented, white flowers have large, deep yellow areas in throats and purple staining outside. **H** 1¼in–1¾in (3–4.5cm), **S** 2in (5cm).

☀ ◊ Z3–8 H8–1

Galanthus 'Hill Poë'
Early spring-flowering bulb with strap-shaped, semierect, gray-green leaves. Produces rosetted, double, white flowers, to 1¼in (3cm) long, with 4 larger outer petals and shorter, tightly packed, green-tipped inner petals. **H** 4–7in (10–18cm), **S** 2–3in (5–8cm).

☀ ◊ Z4–7 H7–4

Galanthus gracilis
Late winter- and early spring-flowering bulb with slightly twisted, strap-shaped, semierect, basal, gray-green leaves. Bears white flowers with 3 inner petals, each marked with a green blotch at the apex and base. **H** 4–6in (10–15cm), **S** 2–3in (5–8cm).

☀ ◊ ⓘ Z3–9 H9–1

Galanthus ikariae
Late winter- and early spring-flowering bulb with strap-shaped, semi-erect, basal, glossy, bright green leaves. Produces one white flower, ⅝–1in (1.5–2.5cm) long, marked with a green patch at the apex of each inner petal. **H** 4–10in (10–25cm), **S** 2–3in (5–8cm).

☀ ◊ ⓘ Z3–9 H9–1

Galanthus nivalis 'Flore Pleno'
(Double common snowdrop)
Late winter- and early spring-flowering bulb with semierect, basal, gray-green leaves. Bears rosetted, many-petaled, double, white flowers, some inner petals having a green mark at the apex. **H** 4–6in (10–15cm), **S** 2–3in (5–8cm).

☀ ◊ ⓘ Z3–8 H8–1

Galanthus nivalis 'Pusey Green Tip'
Late winter- and early spring-flowering bulb with narrowly strap-shaped, semierect, basal, gray-green leaves. Each stem bears a white flower with many mostly green-tipped petals. **H** 4–6in (10–15cm), **S** 2–3in (5–8cm).

☀ ◊ ⓘ Z3–8 H8–1

Galanthus plicatus subsp. byzantinus
Late winter- and early spring-flowering bulb. Semierect, basal, deep green leaves have a gray bloom and reflexed margins. White flowers have green marks at bases and tips of inner petals. **H** 4–8in (10–20cm), **S** 2–3in (5–8cm).

☀ ◊ ⓘ Z3–9 H9–1

WHITE

BULBS

Galanthus nivalis 'Sandersii'
Late winter- and early spring-flowering bulb with narrowly strap-shaped, semierect, basal, gray-green leaves. Flowers, ⅝–¾in (1.5–2cm) long, are white with yellow patches at the apex of each inner petal. **H** 4in (10cm), **S** 1–2in (2.5–5cm).

☀ ◊ ① Z3–8 H8–1

Galanthus woronowii
Late winter- to early spring-flowering bulb with inversely lance-shaped, semi-erect, basal, glossy to matt, dark to mid-green leaves. Produces white flowers, ¾–1in (2–2.5cm) long, with a green mark at the apex of each inner petal. **H** 4–6in (10–15cm), **S** 2–3in (5–8cm).

☀ ◊ Z4–7 H7–4

Galanthus rizehensis
Late winter- and early spring-flowering bulb with very narrow, strap-shaped, semierect, basal, dark green leaves. Produces white flowers, ⅝–¾in (1.5–2cm) long, with a green patch at the apex of each inner petal. **H** 4–8in (10–20cm), **S** 2in (5cm).

☀ ◊ Z3–9 H9–1

Cyclamen coum f. albissimum
Winter-flowering tuber with rounded, deep green leaves, sometimes silver-patterned. Carries white flowers, each with a maroon mark at the mouth. **H** to 4in (10cm), **S** 2–4in (5–10cm).

☀ ◊ ① Z5–9 H9–5

Galanthus nivalis 'Scharlockii'
Vigorous, late winter- and early spring-flowering bulb with semierect, basal, gray-green leaves. Has white flowers, with green marks at the apex of inner petals, overtopped by 2 narrow spathes that resemble donkeys' ears. **H** 4–6in (10–15cm), **S** 2–3in (5–8cm).

☀ ◊ ① Z3–8 H8–1

Cyclamen coum Pewter Group 'Maurice Dryden'
Winter- to early spring-flowering tuber with rounded, silver leaves edged dark green. Produces a succession of white flowers, occasionally pink-flushed, with dark purple-pink mouths. **H** and **S** 4–5in (10–12cm).

☀ ◊ ① Z5–9 H9–5

BULBS

***Cyclamen coum* Pewter Group**
Winter- to early spring-flowering tuber
with rounded, dark green-margined,
silvery-green leaves, each with a
variable-sized, dark green center.
Produces a succession of flowers in
shades of pink with dark purple-pink
mouths. **H** and **S** 4–5in (10–12cm).

☀ ◊ ! Z5–9 H9–5

***Eranthis hyemalis* (Winter aconite)**
Clump-forming tuber. Bears stalkless,
cup-shaped, yellow flowers, ¾–1in
(2–2.5cm) across, from late winter to
early spring. A dissected, leaflike bract
forms a ruff beneath each bloom.
H 2–4in (5–10cm), **S** 3–4in (8–10cm).

☀ ◊ ! Z4–9 H9–1

Cyclamen coum
Winter-flowering tuber with rounded
leaves, plain deep green or silver-
patterned. Produces bright carmine
flowers with dark stains at mouths.
H to 4in (10cm), **S** 2–4in (5–10cm).

☀ ◊ ! Z5–9 H9–5

Cyclamen persicum
Winter- or spring-flowering tuber with
heart-shaped leaves, marked light and
dark green and silver. Bears fragrant,
slender, white or pink flowers, 1¼–1½in
(3–4cm) long and stained carmine at
mouths. **H** 4–8in (10–20cm), **S** 4–6in
(10–15cm). Min. 41–45°F (5–7°C).

☀ ◊ ! H6–1

***Lachenalia aloides* 'Nelsonii'**
Winter- to spring-flowering bulb
with 2 strap-shaped, purple-spotted,
semierect, basal leaves. Has a spike of
10–20 pendent, tubular, green-tinged,
bright yellow flowers, 1¼in (3cm) long.
H 6–10in (15–25cm), **S** 2–3in (5–8cm).

☀ ◊ Z11 H11–10

Lachenalia aloides* var. *quadricolor
Winter- to spring-flowering bulb
with 2 strap-shaped, semierect, basal
leaves. Has a spike of 10–20 purplish-
red buds opening to greenish-yellow
or -orange flowers. **H** 6–10in (15–25cm),
S 2–3in (5–8cm).

☀ ◊ Z11 H11–10

WATER AND BOG PLANTS

The sound and reflective qualities of water have long been used to animate garden designs, and whether tiny or large, formal or informal, every garden has space for a water feature. A pond, pool, or container also greatly extends the range of plants that you can grow. They are classified according to the depth of water required for them to thrive, and include deep-water aquatics, marginal plants, and moisture-lovers or bog plants. Together, they offer a succession of interest, providing a diversity of foliage, form, and flower color. Informal ponds with sloping sides and richly planted banks will also attract a wide range of wildlife, including frogs, toads, and birds.

WATER AND BOG PLANTS

Still or moving water reflects light and adds a dynamic quality to garden designs. It also greatly extends the range of plants that you can grow, with aquatic and moisture-loving types injecting color, texture, and form into water features. They also provide excellent wildlife habitat.

What are water plants?

The broad definition of water plants includes all plants that grow rooted, submerged, or floating in water. They are further subdivided into deep-water aquatics, surface- or free-floating plants, marginals, and bog or moisture-loving plants, depending on the depth of water they require.

Water plants are grown for their beauty and ornamental value, but when a wide range of plants are grown together, they also create a healthy ecosystem that maintains the quality of the water in a feature or pond. A balanced range of plants will regulate the levels of light, oxygen, and nutrients, helping to keep the water clear.

Submerged plants like hornwort (*Ceratophyllum demersum*) are known as "oxygenators." These purify the water by using up nutrients and excluding light, which prevents algal growth. Surface-floaters, such as water hyacinths (*Eichhornia crassipes*), also absorb dissolved nutrients. Deep-water plants, including water lilies (*Nymphaea*), root at the bottom of ponds, while their flowers and leaves shade the surface, again helping to prevent the growth of algae. The roots of marginal plants are submerged, but their top growth is visible above the water, providing shelter for fish, amphibians, and other wildlife.

Ornamental planting

To maximize the planting potential of your pond, create areas at varying depths to accommodate different types. Begin planting at the center of your pond, using deep-water plants, such as Cape pondweed (*Aponogeton distachyos*) with its white flowers that pop up at the surface, and the floating water soldier (*Stratiotes aloides*), which has spiky leaves; both require a depth of about 24–36in (60–90cm). (See

ABOVE Patio feature
Tiny but perfectly formed, this patio water feature, fringed by ferns, supports flowering irises and arum lilies. Flow from a pump helps to oxygenate the water.

box below for details on plant depths.) Most water lilies need to root at depths of 12–36in (30–100cm), depending on the species or cultivar. Dwarf water lilies, such as *Nymphaea tetragona* or slender water irises (*Iris laevigata*) are good choices for

PLANTING DEPTHS

A pond with a range of planting depths allows you to grow a wide range of plants. Place plants at their appropriate depths, measured from the top of the soil in their containers to the water surface. Support young deep

water aquatics on bricks and lower them to their final depth as they grow. Fill the pool a few days before planting to allow the water to reach the air temperature and become populated with beneficial microorganisms.

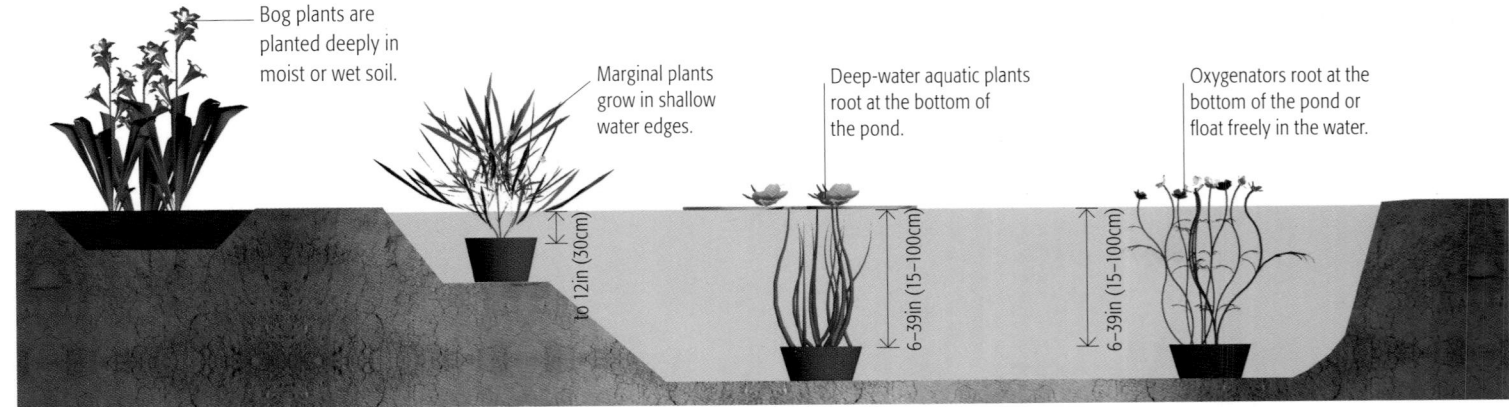

Bog plants are planted deeply in moist or wet soil.

Marginal plants grow in shallow water edges.

Deep-water aquatic plants root at the bottom of the pond.

Oxygenators root at the bottom of the pond or float freely in the water.

to 12in (30cm)

6–39in (15–100cm)

6–39in (15–100cm)

a small pond or water feature. Marginal plants thrive in shallow water. Many are planted just below the surface, while water irises prefer a depth of about 6in (15cm) and pickerel weeds (*Pontederia*) like their roots submerged to a depth of 12in (30cm).

Marginals help to disguise liners at the edges of ponds, create reflections, and provide wildlife cover. They have a range of habits, from the bog bean (*Menyanthes trifoliata*) with its clusters of white flowers in spring, to the flowering rush (*Butomus umbellatus*) with its umbels of small pink flowers, and the large, calla-like blooms of skunk cabbages (*Lysichiton*). Larger areas can be enhanced by bold clumps of cattails (*Typha latifolia*), while architectural plants such as *Pontederia cordata* provide focal points with their leaves and flower spikes.

The damp areas around the edges of a pond provide ideal conditions for bog natives and moisture-lovers. In very wet bogs, marginals will survive, but in drier conditions, opt for moisture-lovers. Bog gardens must have either drainage or water flowing through them to provide oxygen for the plant roots.

ABOVE Marginal planting
The curving edges of an informal pool offer ideal conditions for marginals such as *Pontederia cordata* and *Sagittaria latifolia*. Marginals disguise plastic liners and provide shelter for wildlife.

Designing with water plants

Every garden has space for a water feature and its associated plants, but match your plants to the size and design of your pond. Informal pools have sloping sides and boggy banks to attract birds, amphibians, and small mammals that prey on garden pests. In winter, water that is more than 24in (60cm) deep will help creatures survive freezing temperatures. The great advantage of an informal pool is that it offers versatility: its sinuous margins are longer than straight-sided ponds of a similar size, and the sloping banks provide a range of planting depths, increasing your choice of plants.

In small gardens, avoid vigorously spreading plants, such as the flag iris (*Iris pseudacorus*) or *Glyceria maxima*. For architectural plants for bogs, try *Filipendula camtschatica* and *Miscanthus sacchariflorus*. Astilbes, trollius, primulas, and ferns provide color around the edges.

Seasonal care

In fall, cut away dead foliage, trim over-sized plants, and remove weeds. It is also a good idea to place a net over ponds close to deciduous trees, as the fallen leaves can foul the water. Aim to reach a balance, so that rotting vegetation releases enough nutrition for next year's growth, but not so much as to encourage algae.

Water plants are best divided and repotted in spring as they start into growth. Keep planting baskets weeded, removing annual weed seedlings as they appear, as well as surplus water-plant seedlings. This task can be eased by deadheading the plants after flowering. Small ponds and water features will also need topping off in summer, using rainwater if possible.

PLANTING A POND

Submerged plants are planted in baskets rather than pots, using aquatic potting mix. Garden soil is unsuitable because it often contains nutrients that encourage the growth of algae. When choosing plants, look for healthy specimens that are free of algae and pond weeds. All submerged plants, such as water lilies and oxygenators, can be planted in the same way. Lift them from the pond for dividing and repotting every two or three years.

Established water lily pond

1 Use a pond basket
Choose a pond basket with small holes to prevent soil from leaking out into the water. Place a layer of aquatic potting mix in the bottom.

2 Position the plant
Remove the plant from its pot and put it in the center of the basket at the same level. Fill around the plant with more potting mix, firming as you go.

3 Mulch with gravel
Clean any algae or duckweed from the plant's leaves and stems. Wash some pea gravel and apply a thin layer to stabilize the soil surface.

WATER AND BOG PLANTS

Menyanthes trifoliata (Bog bean)
Deciduous, perennial, marginal water plant with 3-parted, green leaves on floating, spreading stems. To control, cut off extremities and replant. The fringed, white flowers open from cerise buds in early spring. **H** 9in (23cm), **S** indefinite.

 Z4–8 H8–1

Lysichiton camtschatcensis
Vigorous, deciduous, perennial, marginal water or bog plant. Pure white spathes, surrounding spikes of small, insignificant flowers, are borne in spring, before large, oblong to oval, bright green leaves emerge. **H** 30in (75cm), **S** 24in (60cm).

 Z5–9 H9–1

Hydrocharis morsus-ranae (Frogbit)
Deciduous, perennial, floating water plant with rosettes of kidney-shaped, olive-green leaves and small, white flowers during summer. Dormant buds can be eaten by fish in winter, so move a few plantlets to a protected place. **S** 4–39in (10–100cm).

 Z6–11 H11–7

Calla palustris (Bog arum)
Deciduous or semievergreen, perennial, spreading, marginal water plant with heart-shaped, glossy, mid- to dark green leaves. In spring produces large, white spathes usually followed by red or orange fruits. **H** 10in (25cm), **S** 12in (30cm).

 Z4–8 H8–1

Sagittaria latifolia (Broadleaf arrowhead, Duck potato, Wapato)
Deciduous, perennial, marginal water plant with curved, soft green leaves and sprays of white flowers in summer. It can be invasive, so confine it in a basket. **H** 5ft (1.5m), **S** 2ft (60cm).

 Z5–11 H12–5

Alisma plantago-aquatica (Water plantain)
Deciduous, perennial, marginal water plant with upright, oval, bright green leaves held well above water. Bears loose, conical panicles of small, pinkish to white flowers in summer. May be invasive. **H** 30in (75cm), **S** 18in (45cm).

 Z5–8 H8–5

Saururus cernuus (Lizard's tail)
Deciduous, perennial, marginal water
or bog plant. Has clumps of heart-
shaped, mid-green leaves and racemes
of creamy flowers in summer. It can
become invasive. In small ponds and
water features keep this confined in
a basket. **H** 9in (23cm), **S** 12in (30cm).

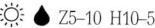 ☼ ◑ Z5–10 H10–5

Astilboides tabularis
Deciduous, clump-forming
perennial, bog plant with rounded,
mid-green leaves, 3ft (1m) across.
In mid-summer produces plumelike
panicles of numerous, tiny, white
flowers. **H** 4ft (1.2m), **S** 5ft (1.5m).

☼ ◑ Z5–7 H7–5

***Acorus calamus* 'Argenteostriatus'**
Semievergreen, perennial, marginal
water plant. Swordlike, tangerine-
scented, mid-green leaves have cream
variegation and are flushed rose-pink
in spring. Increase by division in mid-
spring. **H** 30in (75cm), **S** 24in (60cm).

☼ ◑ Z10–11 H11–2

Aponogeton distachyos
(Cape pondweed, Water hawthorn)
Deciduous, perennial, deep-water
plant with floating, oblong, mid- to dark
green leaves, often splashed with purple.
Very fragrant, "forked," white flowers
are borne throughout summer, often
into winter. **S** 4ft (1.2m).

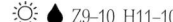 ☼ ◑ Z9–10 H11–10

Caltha leptosepala
Deciduous, perennial, marginal water
plant with heart-shaped, dark green
leaves and buttercup-like, white
flowers produced in late spring and
early summer. Increase by division
in mid-spring. **H** and **S** 12in (30cm).

 ☼ ◑ Z5–8 H8–5

Hottonia palustris (Water violet)
Deciduous, perennial, submerged water
plant. Dense whorls of much-divided,
light green leaves form a spreading
mass of foliage. Lilac or whitish flowers
appear above water surface in summer.
Helps to suppress algae. Increase by
division. **S** indefinite.

☼ ◑ Z5–11 H11–4

***Acorus gramineus* 'Variegatus'**
Semievergreen, perennial, marginal or
submerged water plant. Narrow, stiff,
grasslike leaves are dark green with
cream variegation. Other cultivars with
different colored foliage are available.
Useful for patio ponds. **H** 10in (25cm),
S 6in (15cm).

☼ ◑ Z10–11 H11–2

Stratiotes aloides (Water soldier)
Semievergreen, perennial, submerged,
free-floating water plant. Spiny,
olive-green leaves are arranged in
rosettes. Produces cup-shaped, white,
sometimes pink-tinged flowers in
summer. Increases by producing
small water buds. **S** 12in (30cm).

 ☼ ◑ Z5–11 H12–5

Aruncus dioicus (Goat's beard)
Hummock-forming perennial carrying large leaves with lance-shaped leaflets on tall stems and above them, in mid-summer, branching plumes of tiny, creamy-white flowers. **H** 6ft (2m), **S** 4ft (1.2m).

☼ ◊ Z3–7 H7–1

Schoenoplectus lacustris subsp. *tabernaemontani* 'Zebrinus'
Evergreen, spreading, perennial sedge with leafless stems, striped horizontally with white, and brown spikelets in summer. Withstands brackish water. **H** 5ft (1.5m), **S** indefinite.

☼ ● Z6–9 H9–6

Arundo donax var. versicolor
Herbaceous, rhizomatous, perennial grass with strong stems bearing broad, creamy-white-striped leaves. May bear dense, erect panicles of whitish-yellow spikelets in late summer. **H** 8–10ft (2.5–3m), **S** 2ft (60cm).

☼ ◊ Z7–9 H11–1

Glyceria maxima 'Variegata'
Herbaceous, spreading, perennial grass with cream-striped leaves, often tinged pink at the base. Bears open panicles of greenish spikelets in summer. **H** 30in (80cm), **S** indefinite.

☼ ◊ Z4–9 H10–3

Filipendula ulmaria (Meadowsweet)
Deciduous, perennial, bog plant with plumelike spikes of creamy-white flowers in mid-summer. Leafy stems bear divided, mid-green leaves. Self-seeds quite vigorously. **H** 3ft (1m), **S** 24in (60cm).

◑ ◊ Z5–9 H9–1

Leucojum aestivum
(Summer snowflake)
Spring-flowering bulb with long, strap-shaped, semi-erect, basal leaves. Bears heads of pendent, long-stalked, bell-shaped, green-tipped, white flowers on leafless stems. **H** 1½–3ft (50cm–1m), **S** 4–5in (10–12cm).

◑ ◊ Z3–9 H9–1

Rodgersia podophylla
Clump-forming, rhizomatous perennial with large, many-veined leaves that are bronze when young and later become mid-green, then copper-tinted. Panicles of creamy-white flowers are borne well above foliage in summer. **H** 4ft (1.2m), **S** 3ft (1m).

☼ ◊ Z5–8 H8–5

Trollius x cultorum 'Alabaster'
Clump-forming perennial producing rounded, yellowish-white flowers in spring. These emerge from a basal mass of rounded, deeply divided, mid-green leaves. **H** 24in (60cm), **S** 18in (45cm).

☼ ◊ Z5–8 H8–5

Zantedeschia aethiopica 'Crowborough'

Early to mid-summer-flowering tuber with arrow-shaped, semi-erect, basal, deep green leaves. Produces a succession of arum-like, white spathes, each with a yellow spadix. **H** 18–36in (45cm–90cm), **S** 14–18in (35–45cm).

☀ ◐ ❗ Z8–10 H10–4

Sanguisorba canadensis (Canadian burnet)

Clump-forming perennial. In late summer bears slightly pendent spikes of bottlebrush-like, white flowers on stems that arise from toothed, divided, mid-green leaves. **H** 4–6ft (1.2–2m), **S** 2ft (60cm).

☀ ◐ Z3–8 H8–1

Iris laevigata 'Rowden Starlight'

Deciduous, perennial, marginal water plant with single, white flowers in late spring and early summer. Leaves are linear, smooth and mid-green. **H** 30in (75cm), **S** 18in (45cm).

☀ ◐ ❗ Z3–9 H9–1

Rhynchospora colorata

Slow-growing, deciduous, spreading, perennial, marginal water plant or bog plant with pointed, green-tipped, white bracts surrounding an inconspicuous flower head in late summer. Has linear, slightly hairy, mid-green leaves. **H** 18in (45cm), **S** indefinite.

☀ ◐ Z7–10 H12–7

Rodgersia sambucifolia

Deciduous, clump-forming, perennial, bog plant with emerald-green leaves, sometimes bronze-tinged, divided into large, lobed leaflets. Bears broad spires of creamy-white flowers in summer. **H** 5ft (1.5m), **S** 3ft (1m).

☀ ◐ Z5–8 H8–5

Rodgersia aesculifolia

Clump-forming, rhizomatous perennial that is excellent for a bog garden or pond margin. In mid-summer, plumes of fragrant, pinkish-white flowers rise from crinkled, bronze foliage like that of a horse-chestnut tree. **H** and **S** 3ft (1m).

☀ ◐ Z5–8 H8–1

Lysimachia clethroides

Vigorous, clump-forming, spreading perennial carrying spikes of small, white flowers above mid-green foliage in late summer. **H** 3ft (1m), **S** 2–3ft (60cm–1m).

☀ ◐ Z4–9 H9–1

Anemone rivularis

Perennial with stiff, free-branching stems bearing delicate, cup-shaped, white flowers in summer above deeply divided, dark green leaves. **H** 24in (60cm), **S** 12in (30cm).

☀ ◐ ❗ Z6–8 H8–6

WATER AND BOG PLANTS

Nelumbo nucifera (Sacred lotus)
Vigorous, deciduous, perennial, marginal water plant. Sturdy stems carry very large, platelike, blue-green leaves and, in summer, large, vivid rose-pink flowers, maturing to flesh-pink. Grow under glass. **H** 3–5ft (1–1.5m) above water, **S** 4ft (1.2m). Min. 45°F (7°C).

☀ ● Z4–11 H11–3

Darmera peltata (Umbrella plant)
Spreading perennial with large, rounded leaves. Has clusters of white or pale pink flowers in spring on white-haired stems before foliage appears. **H** 3–4ft (1–1.2m), **S** 24in (60cm).

☀ ● Z5–9 H9–5

Cardamine raphanifolia
Deciduous, almost evergreen, perennial, bog plant with panicles of dark lilac flowers in late spring. Mid-green leaves are divided into oval to rounded leaflets. Self-seeds readily. **H** 20in (50cm), **S** 8in (20cm).

☀ ● Z3–9 H9–1

Iris versicolor 'Rowden Cadenza'
Deciduous, perennial, marginal water plant or bog plant with single, white flowers heavily veined cerise, borne in late spring and early summer. Has linear, erect to slightly arching, mid-green leaves. **H** 30in (75cm), **S** 18in (45cm).

☀ ● ❶ Z3–9 H9–1

Butomus umbellatus (Flowering rush)
Deciduous, perennial, rushlike, marginal water plant with narrow, twisted, mid-green leaves and umbels of pink to rose-red flowers in summer. **H** 3ft (1m), **S** 1½ft (45cm).

☀ ● Z3–11 H8–5

Filipendula rubra
(Queen of the prairie)
Vigorous, upright perennial with large, jagged leaves and feathery plumes of tiny, soft pink flowers on tall, branching stems in mid-summer. Will rapidly colonize a boggy site. **H** 6–8ft (2–2.5m), **S** 4ft (1.2m).

☀ ● Z3–9 H9–1

Chelone obliqua (Turtlehead)
Upright perennial that bears terminal spikes of hooded, lilac-pink flowers in late summer and fall. Leaves are dark green and lance-shaped. **H** 3ft (1m), **S** 20in (50cm).

◐ ● Z3–9 H9–3

Cardamine pratensis (Lady's smock)
Deciduous, clump-forming, perennial, marginal water plant or bog plant with dense panicles of single or double, lilac or white flowers in spring. Has rosettes of glossy, dark green leaves divided into rounded leaflets. **H** 18in (45cm), **S** 6in (15cm).

☀ ● Z5–8 H8–5

Liatris spicata
Clump-forming perennial. In late summer bears spikes of crowded, rose-purple flower heads on stiff stems that arise from basal tufts of grassy, mid-green foliage. **H** 24in (60cm), **S** 12in (30cm).

☀ ◌ Z4–9 H9–1

Rheum palmatum 'Atrosanguineum'
Clump-forming perennial with very
large, lobed, deeply cut leaves that are
deep red-purple when young. Bears
large, fluffy panicles of crimson flowers
in early summer. **H** and **S** 6ft (2m).

 Z5–9 H9–1

Lobelia cardinalis (Cardinal flower)
Deciduous, perennial, bog plant with
narrowly lance-shaped, fresh green
leaves. Produces spires of 2-lipped,
brilliant scarlet flowers in summer.
H 30in (75cm), **S** 9in (23in).

 Z2–8 H8–1

Astilbe 'Fanal'
Leafy perennial with strong stems. In
summer bears neat, tapering, feathery
panicles of tiny, crimson-red flowers
that turn brown and keep their shape
in winter. Broad leaves are divided into
leaflets. Prefers rich soil. **H** 24in (60cm),
S to 36in (90cm).

Z3–8 H8–2

Lobelia 'Cherry Ripe'
Clump-forming perennial bearing
spikes of cerise-scarlet flowers from
mid- to late summer. Leaves, usually
fresh green, are often tinged red-
bronze. **H** 3ft (1m), **S** 9in (23cm).

Z3–8 H8–1

Geum coccineum
Clump-forming perennial with
irregularly lobed leaves, above which
rise slender, branching, hairy stems
bearing single, orange flowers with
prominent, yellow stamens in summer.
H and **S** 12in (30cm).

 Z5–8 H8–5

Iris fulva
Rhizomatous, beardless iris. In late
spring or summer produces a slender,
slightly branched stem with 4–6
(occasionally more) copper- or
orange-red flowers, 2–3in (5–7cm)
across, with 2 flowers per leaf axil.
H 18–32in (45–80cm), **S** indefinite.

 Z6–9 Z9–6

Sarracenia purpurea (Common
pitcher plant, Huntsman's cup)
Evergreen, erect to semi-prostrate,
rosette-forming perennial. Inflated,
green pitchers are tinged purple-red.
In spring, 5-petaled, purple flowers
are borne above. **H** 12in (30cm),
S 12–16in (30–40cm). Min. 41°F (5°C).

 Z2–9 H9–1

WATER LILIES

These beautiful plants are often the focal point in a pond or water feature, be it naturalistic or formal. The leaves and flowers float on the surface, helping to control algae and providing cover for fish and wildlife. There are nearly 400 species and selections available, with flower colors in shades of white, yellow, pink, and red. Blue water lilies are not hardy in frost-prone climates. Lilies vary in size, and include miniature types that spread up to 24in (60cm) in diameter and need a water depth of just 8in (20cm); medium lilies, ranging from 3 to 5ft (1–1.5m); and large types that extend 5–12ft (1.5–4m) or more—these require a water depth of 24in (60cm) or more. All water lilies thrive in full sun and must be grown in still water. For more details, see the Plant Dictionary.

N. 'Froebelii' [medium]

N. Laydekeri Group 'Fulgens' [medium]

N. 'Blue Beauty' [tropical]

N. 'James Brydon' [medium]

N. odorata var. *minor* [medium]

N. 'American Star' [large]

N. 'Rose Arey' [medium]

N. 'Black Princess' [medium]

N. 'Helvola' [miniature]

N. Marliacea Group 'Chromatella' [large]

N. 'Gonnère' [large]

N. tetragona 'Alba' [miniature]

N. 'Attraction' [large]

N. 'Firecrest' [medium]

N. 'Lucidia' [medium]

N. 'Lemon Chiffon' [medium]

Iris ensata (Japanese iris)
Rhizomatous, beardless Japanese iris. Branched stem produces 3–15 purple or red-purple flowers, 3–6in (8–15cm) across, with a yellow blaze on each fall, from early to mid-summer. Many garden forms, including doubles and bicolors. **H** 2–3ft (60–90cm), **S** indefinite.

☼ ♦ ! Z3–9 H9–1

Iris setosa (Bristle-pointed iris)
Rhizomatous, beardless iris, very variable in stature. Bears 2–13 deep blue or purple-blue flowers, 2–3in (5–8cm) across, from each spathe in late spring and early summer. Falls have paler blue or white marks; each standard is reduced to a bristle. **H** 4–36in (10–90cm), **S** indefinite.

☼ ♦ ! Z3–8 H8–1

Pontederia cordata (Pickerel weed)
Deciduous, perennial, marginal water plant. In late summer, dense spikes of blue flowers emerge between lance-shaped, glossy, dark green leaves. **H** 30in (75cm), **S** 18in (45cm).

☼ ♦ Z3–11 H11–1

Mimulus ringens
Deciduous, perennial, marginal water plant or bog plant with snapdragon-like, mauve-blue flowers borne in the leaf axils on tall stems from early to mid-summer. Has lance-shaped to narrowly oblong, toothed, mid-green leaves. **H** 24in (60cm), **S** 6in (15cm).

☼ ♦ Z4–9 H9–4

Lobelia siphilitica
(Blue cardinal flower)
Clump-forming perennial with narrowly oval, green leaves. Racemes of 2-lipped, blue flowers are produced in late summer and fall. **H** 3ft (1m), **S** 9in (23cm).

☼ ♦ Z4–8 H8–1

Eichhornia crassipes (Water hyacinth)
Fully- or semievergreen, perennial water plant with glossy leaves and air-filled stalks. Bears spikes of blue-lilac flowers in summer in warmer climates but may be invasive. Ideal for indoor pools. **S** 9in (23cm). Min. 34ºF (1ºC).

☼ ♦ Z9–11 H11–1

Iris sibirica (Siberian iris)
Rhizomatous, beardless Siberian iris. From late spring to early summer, a branched stem bears 2 or 3 dark-veined, blue or blue-purple flowers, 2–4in (5–10cm) across, from each spathe. **H** 20–48in (50–120cm), **S** indefinite.

☼ ♦ ! Z3–8 H9–1

Myosotis scorpioides 'Mermaid'
(Water forget-me-not)
Deciduous, perennial, marginal water plant for mud or very shallow water. Narrow, mid-green leaves form sprawling mounds. Bears small, blue, forget-me-not flowers during summer. **H** 6in (15cm), **S** 12in (30cm).

☼ ♦ Z5–9 H9–5

441

BLUE

GREEN

Pistia stratiotes (Water lettuce)
Deciduous, perennial, floating water plant for a pool or aquarium, evergreen in tropical conditions. Hairy, soft green foliage is lettuce-like in arrangement. Does not survive outdoors in cooler climates. Replace annually. **H** and **S** 4in (10cm). Min. 50–59°F (10–15°C).

☀ ● Z9–11 H11–4

Iris versicolor (Blue flag, Wild iris)
Robust, rhizomatous, beardless iris. Branched stem produces 3–5 or more purple-blue, reddish-purple, lavender or slate-purple flowers, 2–4in (5–10cm) across, from early to mid-summer. Falls usually have a central white area veined purple. **H** 8–32in (20–80cm).

☀ ● ! Z3–9 H9–1

Typha latifolia (Cattail)
Deciduous, perennial, marginal water plant with large clumps of mid-green foliage. Produces spikes of beige flowers in late summer, followed by decorative, dark brown seed heads. Invasive. Smaller species available. **H** to 8ft (2.5m), **S** 2ft (60cm).

☀ ● Z2–12 H12–1

Trapa natans (Water chestnut)
Annual, floating water plant with diamond-shaped, mid-green leaves, often marked purple, arranged in rosettes. Bears white flowers in summer. In cooler climates it will not survive the winter. Replace annually. **S** 9in (23cm).

☀ ● Z14–15 H12–1

Veronica beccabunga (Brooklime)
Usually evergreen, marginal water plant with creeping, hollow, fleshy stems and rounded, mid-green leaves. Bears blue flowers with white centers from late spring to late summer. Grow in wet soil or water to 5in (12cm) deep. Invasive. **H** 4in (10cm) **S** indefinite.

  Z5–11 H12–5

***Iris laevigata* 'Weymouth Midnight'**
Deciduous, perennial, marginal water plant with double, deep blue flowers in late spring and early summer. Has linear, smooth, mid-green leaves. **H** 30in (75cm), **S** 18in (45cm).

☀ ● ! Z3–9 H9–1

Potamogeton crispus
(Curled pondweed)
Deciduous, perennial, submerged water plant that produces spreading colonies of seaweed-like, bronze-or mid-green foliage. Insignificant flowers are borne in summer. Prefers cool water. Helps to keep the water clear. **S** indefinite.

 Z7–11 H11–7

Sparganium erectum
(Branched bur reed)
Vigorous, deciduous or semievergreen, perennial, marginal water plant with narrow, mid-green leaves. Bears small, greenish-brown burs in summer. In small to medium ponds, control in a basket. **H** 3ft (1m), **S** 2ft (60cm).

 Z5–9 H9–5

Typha minima

Deciduous, perennial, marginal water plant with grasslike leaves. Spikes of rust-brown flowers in late summer are succeeded by decorative, black, cylindrical seed heads. Confine in a basket to keep under control.
H 18–24in (45–60cm), **S** 12in (30cm).

☀ ◐ Z3–11 H12–1

Gunnera manicata

Architectural perennial with rounded, prickly-edged leaves, to 5ft (1.5m) across. Has conical, light green flower spikes in early summer, followed by orange-brown seed pods. Needs mulch cover for crowns in winter and a sheltered site.
H 6ft (2m), **S** 7ft (2.2m).

☀ ◐ Z7–10 H11–7

Matteuccia struthiopteris
(Ostrich fern)

Deciduous, rhizomatous fern. Lance-shaped, erect, divided fronds are arranged like a shuttlecock; outermost, fresh green, sterile fronds surround denser, dark brown, fertile fronds.
H 3ft (1m), **S** 18in (45cm).

◐ ◐ Z2–8 H8–1

Myriophyllum verticillatum
(Whorled water milfoil)

Deciduous, perennial, spreading, submerged water plant, overwintering by club-shaped winter buds. Slender stems are covered with whorls of finely divided, olive-green leaves. An excellent water conditioner. **S** indefinite.

☀ ◐ Z3–11 H11–1

Peltandra virginica

Deciduous, perennial, marginal water plant with arrow-shaped, glossy, dark green leaves, 10in (25cm) long. Produces an inconspicuous, green spathe with a paler green spadix in late summer.
H and **S** 24in (60cm).

☀ ◐ Z5–9 H9–5

Onoclea sensibilis (Sensitive fern)

Deciduous, creeping fern with handsome, arching, almost triangular, divided, fresh pale green fronds, often suffused pinkish-brown in spring. In fall, fronds turn an attractive yellowish-brown. **H** and **S** 18in (45cm).

◐ ◐ Z4–9 H9–1

Osmunda regalis (Royal fern)

Deciduous fern with elegant, broadly oval to oblong, divided, bright green fronds, pinkish when young. Mature plants bear tassel-like, rust-brown fertile flower spikes at ends of taller fronds. **H** 6ft (2m), **S** 3ft (1m).

☀ ◐ Z2–10 H9–1

Houttuynia cordata 'Chameleon'
Vigorous, deciduous, perennial, groundcover, marginal water plant. Aromatic, leathery leaves are splashed yellow and red. Has small sprays of white flowers in summer. Needs some sun to enhance variegation. Potentially invasive. **H** 4in (10cm), **S** indefinite.

☼ ● Z5–11 H11–1

Lysichiton americanus
(Yellow skunk cabbage)
Vigorous, deciduous, perennial, marginal water or bog plant. In spring, before large, fresh green leaves appear, produces showy, bright yellow spathes. Avoid planting it near streams, as it spreads rapidly. **H** 3ft (1m), **S** 2.5ft (75cm).

☼ ● ① Z7–9 H9–7

Caltha palustris 'Plena'
Deciduous, perennial, marginal water plant with rounded, dark green leaves. Bears clusters of double, bright golden-yellow flowers in spring. Increase by division in March. **H** and **S** 10in (25cm).

☼ ● Z3–7 H7–1

Ranunculus lingua
Deciduous, perennial, marginal water plant with sturdy stems and lance-shaped, glaucous leaves. Clusters of yellow flowers are borne in late spring. Increase by division in March. Spreads rapidly. Confine to a basket in smaller ponds. **H** 3ft (90cm), **S** 1½ft (45cm).

☼ ● ① Z5–9 H9–1

Nymphoides peltata (Water fringe)
Deciduous, perennial, deep-water plant with floating, small, round, mid-green leaves, often spotted and splashed with brown. Produces small, fringed, yellow flowers throughout summer. In smaller ponds, keep under control in a basket. **S** 24in (60cm).

☼ ● Z6–11 H11–6

Caltha palustris (Marsh marigold)
Deciduous, perennial, marginal water plant that has rounded, dark green leaves and bears clusters of cup-shaped, bright golden-yellow flowers in spring. There are several varieties available. **H** 24in (60cm), **S** 18in (45cm).

☼ ● Z3–7 H7–1

Orontium aquaticum (Golden club)
Deciduous, perennial, deep-water plant or, less suitably, marginal water plant. In spring, pencil-like, gold-and-white flower spikes emerge from floating, oblong, blue-gray or blue-green leaves. Needs a large basket. Increase by division or seed. **S** 24in (60cm).

☼ ● Z6–10 H10–4

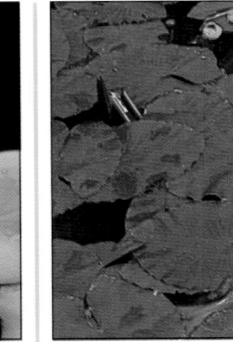

Nuphar lutea (Yellow water lily)
Vigorous, deciduous, perennial, deep-water plant for a large pool. Mid-green leaves are leathery. Small, sickly-smelling, bottle-shaped, yellow flowers open in summer, followed by decorative seed heads. Increase by division in early spring. **S** 5ft (1.5m).

☼ ● Z3–9 H9–1

Primula prolifera
Rosette-forming, evergreen,
Candelabra primula with bell-shaped,
yellow flowers borne in summer.
Leaves are oval, toothed and pale
green. **H** and **S** 24in (60cm).

 Z4–8 H8–1

Iris pseudacorus var. bastardii
Deciduous, perennial, marginal water
plant or bog plant with single, pale
lemon-yellow flowers in late spring
and early summer. Leaves are broadly
linear, ridged and mid-green. **H** 3ft (1m),
S 24in (60cm).

 Z5–8 H8–3

Primula florindae (Giant cowslip)
Bold, rosette-forming perennial
with broadly lance-shaped, toothed,
mid-green leaves. In summer produces
large heads of pendent, bell-shaped,
sulfur-yellow flowers. **H** 4ft (1.2m),
S 3ft (1m).

Z3–8 H8–1

Mimulus x hybridus (Monkey flower)
Deciduous, perennial, marginal water
plant or bog plant bearing snapdragon-
like, yellow flowers, with red spots
in the throat, from midspring to summer.
Bears toothed, mid- to dark green
leaves. Self-seeds freely. **H** 18in (45cm),
S 12in (30cm).

 Z9–10 H10–1

Ligularia 'Britt Marie Crawford'
Clump-forming perennial with
heart-shaped, dark purple leaves
and stems. In mid-summer has sturdy
racemes of large, daisylike, orange
flower heads. **H** 5ft (1.5m), **S** 3ft (1m).

 Z4–8 H8–1

Carex elata 'Aurea'
(Bowles' golden sedge)
Evergreen, tuft-forming, perennial
sedge with golden-yellow leaves.
Solid, triangular stems bear blackish-
brown flower spikes in summer.
H to 16in (40cm), **S** 6in (15cm).

 Z5–9 H9–3

Ligularia przewalskii
Loosely clump-forming perennial
with stems clothed in deeply cut, round,
dark green leaves. Narrow spires of
small, daisylike, yellow flower heads
appear from mid- to late summer.
H 4–6ft (1.2–2m), **S** 3ft (1m).

Z4–8 H8–1

Sarracenia flava (Yellow pitcher plant)
Erect perennial with red-marked,
yellow-green pitchers (modified leaves)
that have hooded tops. From late spring
to early summer bears nodding, yellow
or greenish-yellow flowers. **H** and **S** 18in
(45cm). Min. 41°F (5°C).

 Z7–10 H10–7

Trollius europaeus (Globeflower)
Clump-forming perennial that in spring
bears rounded, lemon- to mid-yellow
flowers above deeply divided, mid-green
leaves. **H** 24in (60cm), **S** 18in (45cm).

Z5–8 H8–5

TENDER AND EXOTIC PLANTS

Tropical and subtropical regions are home to a huge range
of plants, each thriving in varying growing conditions. If you live
in these areas, you can grow tender plants outside and create
dramatic planting schemes with architectural forms and exotic
flowers. In temperate regions, grow these exotic plants either
under glass or indoors as houseplants. There is a wealth of form,
color, and texture available, from plants with handsome foliage
to those with beautiful blooms, including bougainvilleas and
peace lilies. Unlike those grown outside, indoor plants are not
subject to seasonal extremes, and many need relatively little
attention, apart from watering, fertilizing, and annual repotting.

TENDER AND EXOTIC PLANTS

Gardeners have long been fascinated by tender and exotic plants that bring color and interest from all corners of the world. In warmer regions many of these can be grown in the garden, but in cooler areas they're best treated as houseplants, at least for part of the year.

What are tender and exotic plants?

This group of plants originate from many parts of the world, including tropical and subtropical areas, where they require temperatures no lower than 34–64°F (1–18°C), even in winter. Their specific cultural demands vary between plants and can be complex. In addition to warmth, many also require high light levels, long growing seasons, and often either very arid or humid growing conditions. A small few, including cacti and succulents, can tolerate frost if kept dry, but most cannot.

Where the climate allows, tender and exotic plants can be grown in the garden; where it doesn't, they must be grown indoors. The most tender plants require permanent protection and are commonly grown as houseplants, including flamingo flower, *Anthurium andraeanum*, peace lily, *Spathiphyllum wallisii*, and Madagascar jasmine, *Stephanotis floribunda*. Other plants are more robust and can spend the summer in sheltered positions in the garden, being brought back in before the first frost. These include *Banksia coccinea*, the Australian heath, *Epracris impressa*, and king protea, *Protea cynaroides*.

Designing with tender plants

The range of tender and exotic plants is vast, and includes many with bold flowers, attractive foliage, or an architectural habit. With such a diverse variety to grow, they are ideal for many different situations and planting styles. In areas where they can be grown outdoors all year, they can form the mainstay of beds and borders, even entire gardens, from jungle schemes to desert-style borders. In cooler areas, where they can only spend the warm summer months outside, they can still play a prominent role. Pot-grown plants like *Agave americana*, *Ensete ventricosum*, and even the bird of paradise, *Strelitzia reginae*, for example, will all give a dramatic but temporary display in the garden, or on a deck or roof terrace.

Indoors, tender and exotic plants can be put to many uses, from statement plants in grand reception rooms, and year-round greenery in conservatory planters, to lone windowsill potted plants for seasonal color.

BELOW Dramatic foliage
The Japanese sago palm (*Cycas revoluta*) is one of many tender shrubs that can be enjoyed indoors during winter, but can be put outside for summer. It is grown for its sculptural foliage and habit.

ABOVE Exotic flowers for indoors
Frangipani (*Plumeria rubra*) is famed for its rich scent and must be grown permanently in a large heated conservatory, where it can become very large. It needs a minimum winter temperature of 50°F (10°C).

ABOVE Conservatory climber
Bougainvillea is a vigorous shrubby climber in warmer climates. It needs a minimum temperature of 45°F (7°C), and must be treated as a large conservatory plant in cooler areas.

When choosing and positioning tender plants indoors, consider the conditions they require. Light levels may be poor, even near windows, and air-conditioning and central heating can create a dry atmosphere, which many plants dislike. Another consideration is how large the plants will become; many exotic plants commonly grown as houseplants, such as Swiss-cheese plant, *Monstera deliciosa*, and *Bougainvillea*, occupy considerable space over time, although they can be pruned and trained.

Caring for tender plants

Tender and exotic plants, like any other garden plant, all have their preferred growing conditions, so consider your site, soil, and exposure carefully when planting outdoors. This is even more important when growing them indoors as the plants are reliant on you for their care. The best approach is to try to mirror their natural conditions as closely as possible, providing the same degree of heat, light, shade, humidity, and ventilation. It is also very important to observe their natural growing seasons by fertilizing and watering them more frequently when they're in growth, less so, if at all, when they are dormant.

Heated conservatories and greenhouses provide the best indoor habitat for most tender plants, although many also thrive in houses. The care they require depends on the plant, but as a guide, position sun-loving plants near the windows, shade-lovers farther away, and maintain high humidity levels by standing your plants on trays of moist gravel and misting them regularly. Some plants, such as moth orchids, *Phalaenopsis*, require good light but not direct sunlight. This can be achieved by positioning them by a north-facing window, or on a shelf close to a bright window. Also watch out for pests, which can flourish in the favorable conditions you provide.

Finding areas that provide optimal growing conditions for houseplants indoors can be difficult, so it is worth making best use of them where they occur. A good approach is to plant "community planters" and grow plants that enjoy similar conditions together in a single container. This is ideal for sun-loving cacti, as well as epiphytic orchids and bromeliads that need high humidity, and insectivorous plants that prefer very moist soil.

MAKING AN ORCHID PLANTER

Orchids, such as *Colmanara* Masai gx 'Red', all require particular conditions to perform at their best. Where you have a suitable spot indoors, take full advantage of it and position two or more plants in the same container, at least while they're in flower. This will serve as a temporary community-planter, which will benefit the plants, and also create a more attractive display than growing them as individual specimens.

The completed planter

1 Make a base
Fill the base of a large, plastic-lined container with clay pebbles to hold the orchids in place, and to provide drainage and humidity. In a permanent community planter, you should use a suitable planting mix.

2 Position the plants
Place the orchids into the container, making sure the top of their pots sit just below the rim. Make sure the plants are upright and facing the right direction, before adding more pebbles to hold the plants in place.

3 Dress the top
Add a layer of moss or decorative material around the orchids to disguise the pots underneath. This will also help maintain humidity, although if you use natural moss, it will need to be sprayed regularly to keep it healthy.

TENDER AND EXOTIC PLANTS

WHITE

Agonis flexuosa
(Peppermint tree, Willow myrtle)
Evergreen, weeping tree. Aromatic, lance-shaped, leathery leaves are bronze-red when young. In spring–summer, mature trees bear masses of small, white flowers. **H** 20–40ft (6–12m), **S** 15–30ft (5–10m). Min. 50°F (10°C).

☼ ◊ Z10 H11–6

Syzygium paniculatum
(Australian brush cherry)
Evergreen tree with glossy leaves, coppery when young. Has creamy-white flowers, with reddish sepals, and fragrant, rose-purple fruits. **H** 30ft (10m) or more, **S** 10–30ft (3–10m). Min. 50°F (10°C).

☼ ◊ Z10–11 H12–1

***Ficus elastica* 'Doescheri'**
(Rubber plant)
Strong-growing, evergreen, upright then spreading tree with oblong to oval, leathery, lustrous, deep green leaves, patterned with gray-green, yellow and white. **H** 100–200ft (30–60m), **S** 70–200ft (20–60m). Min. 50°F (10°C).

☼ ◊ ❢ Z11 H11–10

***Ficus benjamina* 'Variegata'**
Evergreen, dense, round-headed, weeping tree, often with aerial roots. Has slender, pointed, lustrous leaves that are rich green with white variegation. **H** 100ft (30m) or more, **S** 50ft (15m) or more. Min. 59–64°F (15–18°C).

☼ ◊ ❢ Z10–11 H11–10

PINK

***Dombeya* x *cayeuxii* (Pink snowball)**
Evergreen, bushy tree with rounded, toothed, hairy leaves to 8in (20cm) long. Pink flowers appear in pendent, ball-like clusters in winter or spring. **H** 10–15ft (3–5m), **S** 6–10ft (2–3m). Min. 50–55°F (10–13°C).

☼ ◊ H11–10

***Chorisia speciosa* (Floss silk tree)**
Fast-growing, deciduous tree, the trunk and branches studded with thick, conical thorns. Pink to burgundy flowers appear as indented, light green leaves fall. **H** 50ft (15m), **S** 5ft (1.5m). Min. 59°F (15°C).

☼ ◊ H11–10

Bauhinia variegata
Deciduous, rounded tree with broadly oval, deeply notched leaves. Fragrant, magenta to lavender flowers, to 4in (10cm) across, appear in winter–spring, sometimes later. **H** 25–40ft (8–12m), **S** 10–25ft (3–8m). Min. 59–64°F (15–18°C).

☼ ◊ H11–10

RED

***Metrosideros excelsa* (New Zealand Christmas tree, Pohutukawa)**
Evergreen, wide-spreading tree. Oval, gray-green leaves are white felted beneath. Bears showy tufts of crimson stamens in winter. **H** to 70ft (20m), **S** 30–70ft (10–20m). Min. 41°F (5°C).

☼ ◊ Z11 H11–10

Brachychiton acerifolius
(Illawarra flame tree)
Deciduous tree with clusters of bright scarlet flowers in late winter, spring or summer before 3–7-lobed, lustrous leaves develop. **H** 50–120ft (15–35m), **S** 25–40ft (8–12m). Min. 45–50°F (7–10°C).

☼ ◊ pH H11–8

Grevillea banksii
Evergreen, loosely branched tree or tall shrub. Has leaves divided into 5–11 slender leaflets, silky-downy beneath. Spider-like, red flowers appear in dense heads intermittently throughout the year. **H** 3–30ft (1–10m), **S** 6–15ft (2–5m). Min. 50°F (10°C).

☼ ◊ pH ❢ Z10–11 H11–10

Cordyline australis 'Atropurpurea'
Slow-growing, evergreen tree with purple to purplish-green leaves. Has terminal sprays of white flowers in summer and small, globular, white fruits in fall. **H** 10–30ft (3–10m), **S** 3–12ft (1–4m). Min. 41°F (5°C).

☼ ◊ Z10–11 H11–10

Leucadendron argenteum (Silver tree)
Evergreen, conical to columnar tree, spreading with age. Leaves are covered with long, silky, white hairs. Has insignificant flowers set in silvery bracts in fall–winter. **H** 20–30ft (6–10m), **S** 6–12ft (2–4m). Min. 45°F (7°C).

☼ ◊ Z10–11 H11–10

Firmiana simplex
(Chinese parasol tree)
Robust, deciduous tree with large, lobed leaves, small, showy, lemon-yellow flowers and papery, leaflike fruits. **H** 50ft (15m), **S** 30ft (10m). Min. 36°F (2°C).

☼ ◊ Z7–11 H11–8

Beaucarnea recurvata
(Elephant's foot, Pony-tail)
Slow-growing, evergreen tree or shrub with a sparsely branched stem. Recurving leaves, 3ft (1m) long, persist after turning brown. **H** 12–25ft (4–8m), **S** 6–12ft (2–4m). Min. 45°F (7°C).

☼ ◊ H11–10

Jacaranda mimosifolia
Fast-growing, deciduous, rounded tree with fernlike leaves of many tiny, bright green leaflets. Has trusses of vivid blue to blue-purple flowers in spring and early summer. **H** 50ft (15m), **S** 22–30ft (7–10m). Min. 45°F (7°C).

☼ ◊ H11–10

Dracaena draco (Dragon tree)
Slow-growing, evergreen tree with a wide-branched head. Has stiff, lance-shaped, gray- or blue-green leaves. Mature trees bear clusters of orange fruits from mid- to late summer. **H** 10–30ft (3–10m) or more, **S** 6–25ft (2–8m) or more. Min. 55°F (13°C).

☼ ◊ Z11 H11–1

Meryta sinclairii (Puka, Pukanui)
Evergreen, round-headed tree with large, glossy, deep green leaves. Greenish flowers appear sporadically in spring to fall, followed by berry-like, black fruits. **H** 39ft (10m), **S** 15ft (5m). Min. 41°F (5°C).

☼ ◊ Z10–11 H12–9

Livistona chinensis (Chinese fan palm, Chinese fountain palm)
Slow-growing, evergreen palm with a sturdy trunk. Has fan-shaped, glossy leaves, 3–10ft (1–3m) across. Mature trees bear loose clusters of berry-like, black fruits in fall. **H** 40ft (12m), **S** 15ft (5m). Min. 45°F (7°C).

☼ ◊ Z11 H11–10

Corynocarpus laevigatus
Evergreen, upright tree, spreading with age. Has leathery leaves and clusters of small, greenish flowers in spring–summer. Plumlike, orange fruits appear in winter. **H** 30–50ft (10–15m), **S** 6–15ft (2–5m). Min. 45–50°F (7–10°C).

☼ ◊ Z11 H11–10

Washingtonia robusta
(Mexican fan palm)
Fast-growing, evergreen palm with large, fan-shaped leaves and, in summer, tiny, creamy-white flowers in large, long-stalked sprays. Black berries appear in winter–spring. **H** 80ft (25m), **S** 8–15ft (2.5–5m). Min. 50°F (10°C).

☼ ◊ Z13–15 H12–10

GREEN

Dracaena marginata 'Tricolor'
Slow-growing, evergreen, upright
tree or shrub with narrow, strap-
shaped, cream-striped, rich green
leaves, prominently edged with red.
H 6–15ft (2–5m), **S** 3–10ft (1–3m).
Min. 55°F (13°C).

☼ ◊ Z11 H11–1

Cyathea australis
(Australian tree fern)
Evergreen, upright tree fern with
a robust, almost black trunk. Finely
divided leaves, 6–12ft (2–4m) long,
are light green, bluish beneath.
H 3–10ft (1–3m). **S** 10–15ft (3–5m).
Min. 55°F (13°C).

☼ ◊ Z10–11 H11–7

Ficus benghalensis
(Banyan, Indian fig)
Evergreen, wide-spreading tree with
trunklike prop roots. Has oval, leathery
leaves, rich green with pale veins,
to 8in (20cm) long, and small, figlike,
brown fruits. **H** 70–100ft (20–30m),
S 700ft (200m). Min. 59–64°F (15–18°C).

☼ ◊ ❗ H11–10

YELLOW

Tecoma stans
(Yellow bells, Yellow elder)
Evergreen, rounded, upright tree or
large shrub. Leaves have 5–13 leaflets.
Has funnel-shaped, yellow flowers
from spring to fall. **H** 15–28ft (5–9m),
S 10–15ft (3–5m). Min. 55°F (13°C).

☼ ◊ Z11–15 H12–10

Archontophoenix alexandrae
(Alexandra palm,
Northern bungalow palm)
Evergreen palm with feather-shaped,
arching leaves. Mature trees bear
sprays of small, white or cream
flowers. **H** 80ft (25m), **S** 15–22ft (5–7m).
Min. 59°F (15°C).

☼ ◊ H11–10

Schefflera actinophylla
(Queensland umbrella tree)
Evergreen, upright tree with large,
spreading leaves of 5–16 leaflets. Has
large sprays of small, dull red flowers
in summer or fall. **H** 40ft (12m), **S** 20ft
(6m). Min. 61°F (16°C).

☼ ◊ ❗ Z14–15 H12–10

Dypsis lutescens
(Golden-feather palm, Yellow palm)
Evergreen, suckering palm, forming
clumps of robust, canelike stems.
Has long, arching leaves of slender,
yellowish-green leaflets. **H** 28ft (9m),
S 20ft (6m). Min. 61°F (16°C).

☼ ◊ Z14–15 H12–1

Tabebuia chrysotricha
(Golden trumpet tree)
Deciduous, round-headed tree with
dark green leaves, divided into 3–5
oval leaflets, and rich yellow flowers,
3in (7cm) long, borne in late winter or
early spring. **H** 80ft (25m), **S** 60ft (18m).
Min. 61–4°F (16–18°C).

☼ ◊ Z14–15 H12–10

ORANGE

WHITE

Chamelaucium uncinatum [white]
(Geraldton waxflower)
Evergreen, wiry-stemmed, bushy shrub.
Each needle-like leaf has a tiny, hooked
tip. Flowers ranging from deep rose-
purple to pink, lavender or white appear
in late winter or spring. **H** 6–15ft (2–5m),
S 6–12ft (2–4m). Min. 41°F (5°C).

☀ ◊ pH H11–10

Eriogonum arborescens
Evergreen, sparingly branched shrub.
Small leaves have recurved edges and
woolly, white undersides. Leafy umbels
of small, white or pink flowers appear
from spring to fall. **H** and **S** 2–5ft
(60cm–150cm). Min. 41°F (5°C).

☀ ◊ H11–9

***Carissa macrocarpa* 'Tuttlei'**
Evergreen, compact and spreading
shrub with thorny stems and leathery
leaves. Has fragrant flowers in spring–
summer and edible, plumlike, red
fruits in fall. **H** 6–10ft (2–3m) or more,
S 10ft (3m) or more. Min. 55°F (13°C).

☀ ◊ ① Z9–11 H11–9

Azorina vidalii
Evergreen subshrub with erect stems.
Has coarsely serrated, glossy, dark
green leaves and racemes of bell-
shaped, white or pink flowers in spring
and summer. **H** and **S** 16–24in (40–60cm).
Min. 41°F (5°C).

☀ ◊ H11–10

Sparrmannia africana (African hemp)
Evergreen, erect shrub or small tree.
Has large, shallowly lobed leaves
and clusters of white flowers, with
yellow and red-purple stamens, in late
spring and summer. **H** 10–20ft (3–6m),
S 6–12ft (2–4m). Min. 45°F (7°C).

☀ ◊ Z12–15 H12–10

Dracaena sanderiana (Ribbon plant)
Evergreen, upright shrub with seldom
branching, canelike stems. Lance-
shaped leaves, 6–10in (15–25cm) long,
are pale to gray-green, with bold,
creamy-white edges. **H** 5ft (1.5m),
S 16–32in (40–80cm). Min. 55°F (13°C).

☀ ◊ H11–10

Plumeria rubra (Frangipani)
Deciduous, spreading tree or large
shrub, sparingly branched. Has fragrant
flowers, in shades of yellow, orange,
pink, red and white, in summer–fall.
H 22ft (7m), **S** 15ft (5m). Min. 55°F (13°C).

☀ ◊ ① H11–10

Spathodea campanulata
(African tulip tree, Flame-of-the-forest)
Evergreen, showy tree. Leaves
have 9–19 deep green leaflets. Clusters
of tulip-shaped, scarlet or orange-
red flowers appear intermittently.
H 60–80ft (18–25m), **S** 30–60ft (10–18m).
Min. 61–64°F (16–18°C).

☀ ◊ Z13–14 H12–10

Westringia fruticosa
(Australian rosemary)
Evergreen, rounded, compact shrub.
Crowded leaves, in whorls of 4,
are white-felted beneath. White to
palest blue flowers open in spring–
summer. **H** and **S** 3–5ft (1–1.5m).
Min. 41–45°F (5–7°C).

☀ ◊ Z13–15 H12–9

Acokanthera oblongifolia
(Wintersweet)
Evergreen, rounded shrub. Has fragrant,
white or pinkish flowers in late winter
and spring and poisonous, black fruits in
fall. **H** 10–20ft (3–6m), **S** 5–12ft (1.5–4m).
Min. 50°F (10°C).

☀ ◊ ① H11–10

Calliandra eriophylla (Fairy duster)
Evergreen, stiff, dense shrub. Leaves
have numerous tiny leaflets. From late
spring to fall has pompons of tiny,
pink-anthered, white florets, followed
by brown seed pods. **H** 3ft (1m),
S 32in (80cm). Min. 55°F (13°C).

☀ ◊ H11–10

WHITE

PINK

Pandanus tectorius 'Veitchii'
(Veitch's screw pine)
Evergreen, upright, arching shrub
with rosettes of long, light green leaves
that have spiny, white to cream margins.
H 10–20ft (3–6m), **S** 6–12ft (2–4m).
Min. 55–61°F (13–16°C).

☀ ◊ H11–10

Gardenia jasminoides 'Veitchii'
Fairly slow-growing, evergreen, leafy
shrub with oval, glossy leaves up to
4in (10cm) long and fragrant, double,
white flowers from summer to winter.
H 6–40ft (2–12m), **S** 3–10ft (1–3m).
Min. 59°F (15°C).

☀◑ ◊ pH H11–10

Dracaena fragrans Deremensis
Group 'Warneckei'
Slow-growing, evergreen shrub.
Erect to arching, lance-shaped leaves
are banded gray-green and cream.
H 15–50ft (5–15m), **S** 3–10ft (1–3m).
Min. 59–64°F (15–18°C).

☀◑ ◊ H11–1

Myoporum parvifolium
Evergreen, spreading to prostrate shrub
with semi-succulent leaves. In summer
has clusters of small, honey-scented
flowers, white or pink with purple
spots, and tiny, purple fruits in fall.
H 24in (60cm), **S** 24–36in (60–90cm).
Min. 36–41°F (2–5°C).

☀ ◊ Z11 H11–10

Plectranthus fructicosus 'James'
Evergreen, erect, shrub. Purple stems
bear broadly ovate, coarsely toothed,
fleshy, purple-veined, mid-green leaves.
Bears terminal panicles of tubular pink
flowers, with darker spots, to 12in (30cm)
long, in late summer. **H** and **S** 5ft (1.5m).
Min. 41°F (5°C).

☀ ◊ Z9–10 H10–5

Chamelaucium uncinatum [pink]
(Geraldton waxflower)
Evergreen, wiry-stemmed, bushy shrub.
Each needle-like leaf has a tiny, hooked
tip. Flowers ranging from deep rose-
purple to pink, lavender or white appear
in late winter or spring. **H** 6–15ft (2–5m),
S 6–12ft (2–4m). Min. 41°F (5°C).

☀ ◊ pH H11–10

Protea cynaroides (King protea)
Evergreen, bushy, rounded shrub.
Water lily-shaped flower heads,
5–8in (13–20cm) wide, with silky-haired,
petal-like, pink to red bracts, appear
in spring–summer. Leaves are oval and
mid- to dark green. **H** and **S** 3–6ft (1–2m).
Min. 41–45°F (5–7°C).

☀ ◊ pH H11–9

Protea neriifolia
Evergreen, bushy, upright shrub with
narrow leaves. Flower heads, about
5in (13cm) long, are red, pink or white,
the bracts tipped with tufts of black
hair, and appear in spring–summer.
H and **S** 10ft (3m). Min. 41–45°F (5–7°C).

☀ ◊ pH Z11 H12–10

Calliandra haematocephala
[pink form]
Evergreen, spreading shrub. Leaves
have 16–24 narrowly oval leaflets.
Flower heads consist of many pink-
stamened florets from late fall to spring.
H 10–20ft (3–6m), **S** 6–12ft (2–4m).
Min. 45°F (7°C).

☀ ◊ H11–10

Pimelea ferruginea
Evergreen, dense, rounded shrub
with tiny, recurved, deep green leaves.
Small, tubular, rich pink flowers appear
in dense heads in spring or early
summer. **H** 3–6ft (1–2m), **S** 3–5ft (1–1.5m).
Min. 45°F (7°C).

☀ ◊ pH H11–10

Chorizema ilicifolium
(Holly flame pea)
Evergreen, sprawling or upright shrub,
with spiny-toothed, leathery leaves.
Has spikes of bicolored, orange and
pinkish-red flowers in spring–summer.
H and **S** 3–10ft (1–3m). Min. 45°F (7°C).

☀ ◊ pH H11–10

Nerium oleander (Oleander)
Evergreen, upright, bushy shrub with leathery, deep green leaves. Clusters of salver-form, pink, white, red, apricot or yellow flowers appear from spring to fall, often on dark red stalks. **H** 6–20ft (2–6m), **S** 3–10ft (1–3m). Min. 50°F (10°C).

 H11-1

Justicia carnea (King's crown)
Evergreen, sparingly branched shrub with velvety-haired leaves. Has spikes of pink to rose-purple flowers in summer–fall. **H** 6ft (2m), **S** 3ft (1m). Min. 50–59°F (10–15°C).

 H11-10

Justicia brandegeeana (Shrimp plant)
Evergreen, rounded shrub intermittently, but mainly in summer, producing white flowers surrounded by shrimp-pink bracts. **H** 3ft (1m), **S** 24–36in (60–90cm). Min. 50–59°F (10–15°C).

 H11-10

Hibiscus rosa-sinensis 'The President'
Evergreen, bushy shrub with toothed, oval, glossy, dark green leaves. In summer bears large, magenta-centered, bright pink flowers with prominent, yellow anthers. **H** 8–15ft (2.5–5m), **S** 5–10ft (1.5–3m). Min. 59°F (15°C).

 H11-1

Euphorbia pulcherrima (Poinsettia)
Evergreen, sparingly branched shrub. Has small, greenish-red flowers surrounded by bright red, pink, yellow or white bracts from late fall to spring. **H** 6–12ft (2–4m), **S** 3–8ft (1–2.5m). Min. 59°F (15°C).

 H11-10

Medinilla magnifica
Evergreen, upright shrub, with sparingly produced, 4-angled, robust stems and boldly veined leaves. Pink to coral-red flowers hang in long trusses beneath large, pink bracts in spring–summer. **H** 3–6ft (1–2m), **S** 2–5ft (60cm–150cm). Min. 61–64°F (16–18°C).

 H11-10

Epacris impressa (Australian heath)
Evergreen, usually erect, fairly open, heather-like shrub with short, red-tipped leaves. Tubular, pink or red flowers appear in late winter and spring. **H** 12–48in (30–120cm), **S** 12–36in (30–90cm). Min. 41°F (5°C).

 pH Z11 H12-10

Greyia sutherlandii
Deciduous or semievergreen, rounded shrub. Coarsely serrated, leathery leaves turn red in fall. Spikes of small, bright red flowers appear in spring with new foliage. **H** 6–15ft (2–5m), **S** 5–10ft (1.5–3m). Min. 45–50°F (7–10°C).

 H11-10

455

RED

Nymania capensis
Evergreen, more or less rounded, rigidly branched shrub or small tree. In spring has flowers with upright, pink to rose-purple petals. Bears papery, inflated, red fruits in fall. **H** 6–10ft (2–3m) or more, **S** 3–6ft (1–2m). Min. 45–50°F (7–10°C).

☀ ◊ H11–10

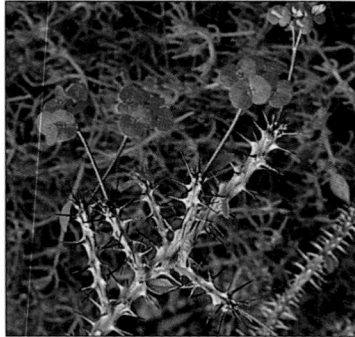

Euphorbia milii (Crown of thorns)
Fairly slow-growing, mainly evergreen, spiny, semi-succulent shrub. Clusters of tiny, yellowish flowers, enclosed by 2 bright red bracts, open intermittently during the year. **H** 3ft (1m) or more, **S** 18in (45cm). Min. 46°F (8°C).

☀ ◊ ① Z11 H11–1

Solanum betaceum (Tree tomato)
Evergreen, sparingly branched shrub or small tree, upright when young, with large, heart-shaped, rich green leaves. Has edible, tomato-like, red fruits from summer to winter. **H** 6–10ft (2–3m), **S** 3–6ft (1–2m). Min. 50°F (10°C).

☀ ◊ Z11 H12–7

Sutherlandia frutescens
Evergreen, upright shrub. Has leaves of 13–21 gray-haired, deep green leaflets; bright red flowers in late spring and summer are followed by pale green, later red-flushed, inflated seed pods. **H** 2–6ft (0.6–2m), **S** 3–5ft (1–1.5m). Min. 50°F (10°C).

☀ ◊ Z13–15 H12–9

Bouvardia ternifolia
(Scarlet trompetilla)
Mainly evergreen, bushy, upright shrub with leaves in whorls of 3. Has tubular, bright scarlet flowers from summer to early winter. **H** 24–36in (60–90cm), **S** 12–24in (30–60cm). Min. 45–50°F (7–10°C).

☀ ◊ H11–10

Leucospermum reflexum
Evergreen, erect shrub with ascending branchlets. Has small, blue-gray or gray-green leaves. Slender, tubular, crimson flowers with long styles are carried in tight, rounded heads in spring–summer. **H** 10ft (3m), **S** 6–12ft (2–4m). Min. 50°F (10°C).

☀ ◊ H11–10

Ixora coccinea
Evergreen, rounded shrub with glossy, dark green leaves to 4in (10cm) long. Small, tubular, red, pink, orange or yellow flowers appear in dense heads in summer. **H** 8ft (2.5m), **S** 5–6ft (1.5–2m). Min. 55–61°F (13–16°C).

☀ ◊ H11–10

Boronia megastigma
Evergreen, well branched, wiry-stemmed shrub. Small leaves have 3–5 narrow leaflets. Fragrant, bowl-shaped, brownish-purple and yellow flowers hang from leaf axils in late winter and spring. **H** 3–10ft (1–3m), **S** 3–6ft (1–2m). Min. 45–50°F (7–10°C).

☀ ◊ pH H11–10

Banksia coccinea
Evergreen, dense shrub with toothed, dark green leaves, gray-green beneath. Flower heads comprising clusters of bright red flowers with prominent styles and stigmas are borne in late winter and spring. **H** 12–25ft (4–8m), **S** 5–12ft (1.5–4m). Min. 50°F (10°C).

☀ ◊ H11–10

Ardisia crenata
(Coralberry, Spiceberry)
Evergreen, upright, open shrub. Has fragrant, star-shaped, white flowers in early summer, followed by long-lasting, bright red fruits. **H** to 6ft (2m), **S** 24in (60cm). Min. 50°F (10°C).

☀ ◐ Z8–11 H12–7

Acalypha wilkesiana
(Copperleaf, Jacob's coat)
Evergreen, bushy shrub. Oval, serrated leaves are 4in (10cm) or more long, rich copper-green, variably splashed with shades of red. **H** 6ft (2m), **S** 3–6ft (1–2m). Min. 61°F (16°C).

☀ ◊ ① H11–1

Prostanthera ovalifolia
Evergreen, bushy, rounded shrub with tiny, sweetly aromatic, oval, thick-textured leaves. Cup-shaped, 2-lipped, purple flowers appear in short, leafy racemes in spring–summer. **H** 8–12ft (2.5–4m), **S** 5–8ft (1.5–2.5m). Min. 41°F (5°C).

☼ ◊ H11–5

Dodonaea viscosa 'Purpurea'
Evergreen, bushy shrub or tree. Firm-textured leaves are flushed copper-purple. Has clusters of small, reddish or purplish seed capsules in late summer or fall. Makes a good hedge in a windy site. **H** 3–15ft (1–5m), **S** 3–10ft (1–3m). Min. 41°F (5°C).

☼ ◊ H11–10

Tibouchina urvilleana (Glory bush)
Evergreen, slender-branched shrub. Velvet-haired leaves are prominently veined. Has satiny, blue-purple flowers in clusters from summer to early winter. **H** 10–20ft (3–6m), **S** 6–10ft (2–3m). Min. 45°F (7°C).

☼ ◊ ᵖᴴ Z13–15 H12–10

Polygala x dalmaisiana
Evergreen, erect shrub with small, grayish-green leaves. White-veined, rich purple flowers appear from late spring to fall. **H** and **S** 3–8ft (1–2.5m). Min. 45°F (7°C).

☼ ◊ H11–9

Iochroma cyaneum
Evergreen, semi-upright, slender-branched shrub. Tubular, deep purple-blue flowers, with flared mouths, appear in dense clusters from late fall to early summer. **H** 10ft (3m), **S** 5–6ft (1.5–2m). Min. 45–50°F (7–10°C).

☼ ◊ H11–10

Brunfelsia pauciflora 'Macrantha'
Evergreen, spreading shrub with leathery leaves. Blue-purple flowers, aging to white in about 3 days, appear from winter to summer. **H** 3–10ft (1–3m), **S** 2–5ft (0.6–1.5m). Min. 50–55°F (10–13°C).

☼ ◊ ① H11–10

Sabal minor (Dwarf palmetto)
Evergreen, suckering fan palm with stems mainly underground. Has leaves of 20–30 green or gray-green lobes. Erect sprays of small, white flowers are followed by shiny, black fruits. **H** 3–6ft (1–2m), **S** 10ft (3m). Min. 41°F (5°C).

☼ ◊ Z12–15 H12–10

Portulacaria afra (Elephant bush)
Semievergreen, upright shrub with horizontal branches and tiny, fleshy, bright green leaves. Clusters of pale pink flowers appear in late spring and summer. **H** 6–10ft (2–3m), **S** 5ft (1.5m). Min. 45–50°F (7–10°C).

☼ ◊ H11–10

Encephalartos ferox
Slow-growing, evergreen, palmlike plant, almost trunkless for many years. Feather-shaped leaves, 2–6ft (60–180cm) long, have many serrated and spine-tipped, leathery, grayish leaflets. **H** 3ft (1m), **S** 6–10ft (2–3m). Min. 50–55°F (10–13°C).

☼ ◊ H11–10

Schefflera elegantissima (False aralia)
Evergreen, upright, open shrub. Large leaves have 7–10 coarsely toothed, lustrous, gray-green, sometimes bronze-tinted, leaflets. **H** 25–50ft (8–15m), **S** 6–10ft (2–3m). Min. 55°F (13°C).

☼ ◊ ① Z14–15 H12–1

Cycas revoluta (Japanese sago palm)
Slow-growing, evergreen, palmlike plant that may produce several trunks. Leaves have spine-tipped leaflets with rolled margins. Bears tight clusters of reddish fruits in fall. **H** and **S** 3–6ft (1–2m). Min. 55°F (13°C).

☼ ◊ H11–6

Mimosa pudica
(Humble plant, Sensitive plant)
Short-lived, evergreen shrub with prickly stems; needs support. Fernlike leaves fold when touched. Has minute, pale mauve-pink flowers in summer–fall. **H** 12–30in (30–75cm), **S** 16–36in (40–90cm). Min. 55–61°F (13–16°C).

☼ ◊ H11–10

GREEN

Rhapis excelsa (Miniature fan palm)
Evergreen fan palm, eventually forming clumps. Leaves are 8–12in (20–30cm) long, composed of 20 or more narrow, glossy, deep green lobes in fan formation. **H** and **S** 5–15ft (1.5–5m). Min. 59°F (15°C).

☼ ◊ H11–10

Ficus deltoidea (Mistletoe fig)
Slow-growing, evergreen, bushy shrub with bright green leaves, red-brown-tinted beneath. Bears small, greenish-white fruits that mature to dull yellow. **H** 15–22ft (5–7m), **S** 3–10ft (1–3m). Min. 59–64°F (15–18°C).

☼ ◊ ❶ H11–1

***Polyscias guilfoylei* 'Victoriae'**
(Lace aralia)
Slow-growing, evergreen, rounded shrub or small tree with leaves that are divided into several oval to rounded, serrated, white-margined, deep green leaflets. **H** 5ft (1.5m), **S** 32in (80cm). Min. 59–64°F (15–18°C).

☼ ◊ ❶ H11–1

Philodendron bipinnatifidum
Evergreen, unbranched shrub. Glossy leaves, to 2ft (60cm) or more long, are divided into many finger-like lobes. Occasionally produces greenish-white spathes. **H** and **S** 15ft (5m). Min. 59–64°F (15–18°C).

☼ ◊ ❶ H11–4

Polyscias filicifolia (Fernleaf aralia)
Evergreen, erect, sparingly branched shrub. Leaves are 12in (30cm) long and are divided into many small, serrated, bright green leaflets. **H** 6–8ft (2–2.5m), **S** 3ft (1m). Min. 59–64°F (15–18°C).

☼ ◊ ❶ H11–1

Chamaedorea elegans
(Dwarf mountain palm, Parlor palm)
Evergreen, slender palm, suckering with age. Feather-shaped leaves of many glossy leaflets are 2–3ft (60–100cm) long. **H** 6–10ft (2–3m), **S** 3–6ft (1–2m). Min. 64°F (18°C).

☼ ◊ H11–1

YELLOW

x *Citrofortunella microcarpa*
(Calamondin)
Evergreen, bushy shrub with leathery, leaves. Intermittently has tiny, fragrant flowers followed by orange-yellow fruits. **H** 10–20ft (3–6m), **S** 6–10ft (2–3m). Min. 41–50°F (5–10°C).

☼ ◊ Z13–15 H12–10

Hibbertia cuneiformis
Evergreen, upright, bushy shrub with small, oval leaves, serrated at tips. Has small clusters of bright yellow flowers, with spreading petals, in spring–summer. **H** 3–6ft (1–2m), **S** 3–5ft (1–1.5m). Min. 41–45°F (5–7°C).

☼ ◊ H11–10

Acacia pulchella
(Western prickly Moses)
Semievergreen or deciduous shrub of diffuse habit, with spiny twigs and rich green foliage. Tiny, deep yellow flowers appear in dense, globular heads in spring. **H** 2–5ft (0.6–1.5m), **S** 3–6ft (1–2m). Min. 41–45°F (5–7°C).

☼ ◊ Z11 H11–10

Senna corymbosa
Vigorous, evergreen or semievergreen shrub. Leaves have 4–6 oval, bright green leaflets; sprays of bowl-shaped, rich yellow flowers appear in late summer. **H** 6–12ft (2–4m), **S** 5–10ft (1.5m–3m). Min. 45°F (7°C).

☼ ◊ Z12–15 H12–8

Reinwardtia indica (Yellow flax)
Evergreen, upright subshrub, branching from the base. Has grayish-green leaves and small clusters of yellow flowers mainly in summer but also during the year. **H** and **S** 24–36in (60–90cm). Min. 50°F (10°C).

☼ ◊ H11–10

Senna didymobotrya
(Golden wonder)
Evergreen, rounded, sometimes spreading shrub with leaves of several leaflets. Spikes of rich yellow flowers open from glossy, blackish-brown buds throughout the year. **H** 8ft (2.5m), **S** 5–10ft (1.5–3m). Min. 55°F (13°C).

☼ ◊ Z14–15 H12–10

Pachystachys lutea (Lollipop plant)
Evergreen, loose, more or less rounded shrub, often grown annually from cuttings. Has tubular, white flowers in tight, golden-bracted spikes in spring–summer. **H** 3ft (1m), **S** 18–30in (45–75cm). Min. 55°F (13°C).

☼ ◊ Z11 H11–10

Crotalaria agatiflora
(Canary-bird bush)
Evergreen, loose, somewhat spreading shrub with gray-green leaves. Racemes of greenish-yellow flowers appear in summer and also intermittently during the year. **H** 6–10ft (2–3m), **S** 3–6ft (1–2m). Min. 59°F (15°C).

☼ ◊ H11–10

Codiaeum variegatum var. pictum
(Croton)
Evergreen, erect, sparingly branched shrub. Leathery, glossy leaves vary greatly in size and shape, and are variegated with red, pink, orange or yellow. **H** 3–6ft (1–2m), **S** 2–5ft (0.6–1.5m). Min. 50–55°F (10–13°C).

◑ ◊ ① H11–10

Nematanthus gregarius
Evergreen, prostrate or slightly ascending shrub with fleshy, glossy leaves. Inflated, orange and yellow flowers appear mainly from spring to fall. **H** 32in (80cm), **S** 36in (90cm) or more. Min. 55–59°F (13–15°C).

◑ ◊ H11–9

Isoplexis canariensis
Evergreen, rounded, sparingly branched shrub. Bears foxglove-like, yellow to red- or brownish-orange flowers in dense, upright spikes, to 12in (30cm) tall, in summer. **H** 5ft (1.5m), **S** 3ft (1m). Min. 45°F (7°C).

☼ ◊ H11–9

Pandorea jasminoides (Bower vine)
Evergreen, woody-stemmed, twining climber with leaves of 5–9 leaflets. Has clusters of funnel-shaped, white flowers, with pink-flushed throats, from late winter to summer. **H** 15ft (5m). Min. 41°F (5°C).

☼ ◊ Z11 H11–8

Dioscorea dodecaneura
(Ornamental yam)
Evergreen, woody-stemmed, twining climber. Heart-shaped, olive-green leaves are 5–6in (12–15cm) long, marbled silver, paler green and brown, and are red beneath. **H** to 6ft (2m). Min. 41°F (5°C).

☼ ◊ Z11 H12–10

Beaumontia grandiflora
(Herald's trumpet)
Vigorous, evergreen, woody-stemmed, twining climber with rich green leaves that are hairy beneath. Has large, fragrant, white flowers from late spring to summer. **H** 25ft (8m). Min. 45–50°F (7–10°C).

☼ ◊ H11–10

TENDER AND EXOTIC PLANTS

TENDER AND EXOTIC PLANTS

WHITE

Bougainvillea glabra 'Snow White'
Vigorous, evergreen or semievergreen, woody-stemmed, scrambling climber with rounded-oval leaves. In summer has clusters of white floral bracts with green veins. **H** to 15ft (5m). Min. 45–50°F (7–10°C).

☼ ◊ H11–1

Epipremnum aureum 'Marble Queen'
Fairly fast-growing, evergreen, woody-stemmed, root climber. Leaves are streaked and marbled with white. Is less robust than the species. **H** 10–30ft (3–10m). Min. 59–64°F (15–18°C).

◐ ◊ ① H11–1

Hoya lanceolata subsp. bella
Evergreen, woody-stemmed, trailing shrub with narrowly oval, pointed leaves. In summer bears tiny, star-shaped, white flowers, with red centers, in pendulous, flattened clusters. **H** 18in (45cm). Min. 50–54°F (10–12°C).

◐ ◊ H11–1

Clerodendrum thomsoniae
Vigorous, evergreen, woody-stemmed, scandent shrub with oval, rich green leaves. Flowers with crimson petals and bell-shaped, pure white calyces appear in clusters in summer. **H** 10ft (3m) or more. Min. 61°F (16°C).

◐ ◊ H11–1

Stephanotis floribunda
(Madagascar jasmine, Wax flower)
Moderately vigorous, evergreen, woody-stemmed, twining climber with leathery, glossy leaves. Scented, waxy, white flowers appear in small clusters from spring to fall. **H** 15ft (5m) or more. Min. 55–61°F (13–16°C).

☼ ◊ Z14–15 H12–10

Syngonium podophyllum 'Trileaf Wonder'
Evergreen, woody-stemmed, root climber with tufted stems and arrow-head-shaped leaves when young. Mature leaves have 3 glossy leaflets with pale green or silvery-gray veins. **H** 6ft (2m) or more. Min. 64°F (18°C).

☼ ◊ ① Z14–15 H12–10

PINK

Lophospermum erubescens
Evergreen, soft-stemmed, scandent, perennial climber, sometimes woody-stemmed, often grown as an annual. Stems and leaves are downy. Rose-pink flowers, 2¾in (7cm) long, are borne in summer–fall. **H** to 10ft (3m) or more. Min. 41°F (5°C).

☼ ◊ H11–10

Hoya carnosa (Wax plant)
Fairly vigorous, evergreen, woody-stemmed, twining, root climber. Scented, star-shaped flowers, white, fading to pink, with deep pink centers, are borne in dense trusses in summer–fall. **H** to 15ft (5m) or more. Min. 41–45°F (5–7°C).

◐ ◊ H11–8

Mandevilla splendens
Evergreen, woody-stemmed, twining climber. Has lustrous leaves and trumpet-shaped, rose-pink flowers, with yellow centers, appearing in late spring or early summer. **H** 10ft (3m). Min. 45–50°F (7–10°C).

◐ ◊ ① H11–10

***Mandevilla* x *amabilis* 'Alice du Pont'**
Vigorous, evergreen, woody-stemmed, twining climber with oval, impressed leaves. Has large clusters of trumpet-shaped, glowing pink flowers in summer. **H** 10ft (3m). Min. 45–50°F (7–10°C).

☀ ◊ ❗ H11–1

Distictis buccinatoria
(Mexican blood flower)
Vigorous, evergreen, woody-stemmed, tendril climber. Has trumpet-shaped, rose-crimson flowers, orange-yellow within, from early spring to summer. **H** to 15ft (5m) or more. Min. 41°F (5°C).

☀ ◊ Z9–11 H11–9

Clytostoma callistegioides
Fast-growing, evergreen, woody-stemmed, tendril climber. Each leaf has 2 oval leaflets and a tendril. Small, nodding clusters of purple-veined, lavender flowers, fading to pale pink, are borne in spring–summer. **H** to 15ft (5m). Min. 50–55°F (10–13°C).

☀ ◊ H11–9

Agapetes variegata* var. *macrantha
Evergreen or semievergreen, loose, scandent shrub that may be trained against supports. Has lance-shaped leaves and narrowly urn-shaped, white or pinkish-white flowers, patterned in red, in winter. **H** 3–6ft (1–2m). Min. 59–64°F (15–18°C).

☀ ◊ pH H11–10

Tropaeolum tricolorum
Herbaceous climber with delicate stems, small tubers and 5–7-lobed leaves. Small, orange or yellow flowers with black-tipped, reddish-orange calyces are borne from early spring to early summer. **H** to 3ft (1m). Min. 41°F (5°C).

☀ ◊ Z12–15 H12–10

Agapetes serpens
Evergreen, arching to pendulous, scandent shrub, best grown with support as a perennial climber. Has small, lance-shaped, lustrous leaves and pendent flowers, rose-red with darker veins, in spring. **H** 6–10ft (2–3m). Min. 41°F (5°C).

☀ ◊ pH H11–10

TENDER AND EXOTIC PLANTS

461

RED

Kennedia rubicunda
(Dusky coral pea)
Fast-growing, evergreen, woody-stemmed, twining climber with leaves divided into 3 leaflets. Coral-red flowers are borne in small trusses in spring–summer. **H** to 10ft (3m). Min. 41–45°F (5–7°C).

☼ ◊ H11–10

Quisqualis indica (Rangoon creeper)
Fairly fast-growing, deciduous or semievergreen, scandent shrub, often grown as an annual. From late spring to late summer has fragrant flowers, varying from orange to red, sometimes pink. **H** 10–15ft (3–5m). Min. 50°F (10°C).

◐ ◊ H11–10

Passiflora coccinea
(Red passion flower)
Vigorous, evergreen, woody-stemmed, tendril climber with rounded, oblong leaves. Has bright deep scarlet flowers, with red, pink and white crowns, from spring to fall. **H** 10–12ft (3–4m). Min. 59°F (15°C).

☼ ◊ H11–10

PURPLE

Hoya macgillivrayi
Strong-growing, twining climber with thick stems and lustrous, dark green leaves. From spring to summer, bears large, cup-shaped, red-purple, purple or brownish-red flowers, with dark red, occasionally white-centered coronas. **H** 15–25ft (5–8m). Min. 45°F (7°C).

◐ ◊ H11–10

Ipomoea indica (Blue dawn flower)
Vigorous, perennial climber with evergreen, mid-green leaves. From late spring to fall bears abundant, funnel-shaped, rich purple-blue to blue flowers, often maturing to purplish-red. **H** 20ft (6m) or more. Min. 45°F (7°C).

☼ ◊ ❗ H11–9

Hardenbergia violacea
'Happy Wanderer'
Evergreen, woody-stemmed, twining climber. In spring, bears pendent panicles of deep mauve-purple flowers, with yellow marks on upper petals. **H** to 10ft (3m). Min. 45°F (7°C).

☼ ◊ H11–10

***Bougainvillea glabra* 'Sanderiana'**
Vigorous, mainly evergreen, woody-stemmed, scrambling climber. Rounded-oval, dark green leaves are edged with creamy-white. Has many bright purple floral bracts in summer. **H** to 15ft (5m). Min. 45–50°F (7–10°C).

☼ ◊ H11–1

Bougainvillea glabra
Vigorous, evergreen or semievergreen, woody-stemmed, scrambling climber with rounded-oval leaves. Clusters of floral bracts, in shades of cyclamen-purple, appear in summer. **H** to 15ft (5m). Min. 45–50°F (7–10°C).

☼ ◊ H11–1

Passiflora quadrangularis
(Giant granadilla)
Strong-growing, evergreen, woody-stemmed climber with angled, winged stems. White, pink, red or pale violet flowers, the crowns banded white and deep purple, appear mainly in summer. **H** 15–25ft (5–8m). Min. 50°F (10°C).

☼ ◊ H11–10

Aristolochia littoralis (Calico flower)
Fast-growing, evergreen, woody-stemmed, twining climber with heart- to kidney-shaped leaves. Heart-shaped, 5in (12cm) wide flowers, maroon with white marbling, are carried in summer. **H** to 22ft (7m). Min. 55°F (13°C).

☼ ◊ H11–10

Gynura aurantiaca
(Purple velvet plant)
Evergreen, woody-based, soft-stemmed, semi-scrambling climber or lax shrub with purple-haired stems and leaves. Clusters of daisylike, orange-yellow flower heads are borne in winter. **H** 6–10ft (2–3m), less as a shrub. Min. 61°F (16°C).

☼ ◊ H11–10

Solanum seaforthianum
(Italian jasmine, St. Vincent lilac)
Evergreen, scrambling climber with nodding clusters of star-shaped, blue, purple, pink, or white flowers, with yellow stamens, from spring to fall, followed by scarlet fruits. **H** 6–10ft (2–3m). Min. 45°F (7°C).

☼ ◊ ① Z12–15 H12–10

Solanum wendlandii
Robust, mainly evergreen, prickly-stemmed, scrambling climber with oblong, variably lobed leaves. Lavender flowers appear in late summer and fall. **H** 10–20ft (3–6m). Min. 50°F (10°C).

☼ ◊ ① Z13–15 H12–10

Petrea volubilis
Strong-growing, evergreen, woody-stemmed, twining climber with elliptic, rough-textured leaves and deep violet and lilac-blue flowers carried in simple or branched spikes from late winter to late summer. **H** 20ft (6m) or more. Min. 55–59°F (13–15°C).

☼ ◊ H11–6

Cissus antarctica (Kangaroo vine)
Moderately vigorous, evergreen, woody-stemmed, tendril climber. Oval, pointed, coarsely serrated leaves are lustrous, rich green. **H** to 15ft (5m). Min. 45°F (7°C).

☼ ◊ H11–10

Asparagus scandens
Evergreen, scrambling climber with lax stems and short, curved, leaflike shoots in whorls of 3. Tiny, nodding, white flowers appear in clusters of 2–3 in summer, followed by red fruits. **H** 3ft (1m) or more. Min. 50°F (10°C).

☼ ◊ ① H11–10

Tetrastigma voinierianum
(Chestnut vine)
Strong-growing, evergreen, woody-stemmed, tendril climber. Young stems and leaves are rust-colored and hairy; mature leaves turn lustrous, deep green above. **H** 30ft (10m) or more. Min. 59–64°F (15–18°C).

☼ ◊ Z14–15 H12–10

Monstera deliciosa
(Swiss-cheese plant)
Robust, evergreen, woody-stemmed, root climber with large-lobed, holed leaves, 16–36in (40–90cm) long. Mature plants bear cream spathes, followed by scented, edible fruits. **H** to 20ft (6m). Min. 59–64°F (15–18°C).

☼ ◊ ① H11–10

Syngonium podophyllum
Evergreen, woody-stemmed, root climber with tufted stems and arrowhead-shaped leaves when young. Mature plants have leaves of 7–9 glossy leaflets up to 12in (30cm) long. **H** 6ft (2m). Min. 61–64°F (16–18°C).

◑ ◊ ① Z14–15 H12–10

Philodendron scandens (Heartleaf)
Fairly fast-growing, evergreen, woody-based, root climber. Rich green leaves are 4–6in (10–15cm) long when young, to 12in (30cm) long on mature plants. **H** 12ft (4m) or more. Min. 59–64°F (15–18°C).

◑ ◊ ① H11–10

YELLOW

***Tecoma capensis* 'Aurea'**
Erect, scrambling, evergreen shrub or climber with lustrous, mid- to dark green leaves. Racemes, to 6in (15cm) long, of slender, tubular, yellow flowers, to 2in (5cm) long, are borne mainly in summer. **H** 12ft (4m). **S** 6ft (2m). Min. 41°F (5°C).

☀ ◊ Z12–15 H12–10

Solandra maxima
(Cup of gold, Golden-chalice vine)
Strong-growing, evergreen, woody-stemmed, scrambling climber with glossy leaves. In spring–summer bears fragrant, pale yellow, later golden flowers. **H** 23–30ft (7–10m) or more. Min. 55–61°F (13–16°C).

☀ ◊ ❶ Z11–1 H12–6

Thunbergia mysorensis
Evergreen, woody-stemmed, twining climber. Has narrow leaves and pendent spikes of flowers with yellow tubes and recurved, reddish-brown lobes from spring to fall. **H** 20ft (6m). Min. 59°F (15°C).

☀ ◊ Z14–15 H12–6

Canarina canariensis
(Canary Island bellflower)
Herbaceous, tuberous, scrambling climber with triangular, serrated leaves. Has waxy, orange flowers with red veins from late fall to spring. **H** 6–10ft (2–3m). Min. 45°F (7°C).

☀ ◊ H11–10

***Senecio macroglossus* 'Variegatus'**
Evergreen, woody-stemmed, twining climber with triangular, fleshy leaves, bordered in white to cream, and, mainly in winter, daisylike, cream flower heads. **H** 10ft (3m). Min. 45°F (7°C).

☀ ◊ ❶ Z12–15 H12–10

Streptosolen jamesonii
(Marmalade bush)
Evergreen or semievergreen, loosely scrambling shrub. Has oval, finely corrugated leaves and, mainly in spring–summer, many bright orange flowers. **H** 6–10ft (2–3m). Min. 45°F (7°C).

☀ ◊ Z12–15 H12–10

Stigmaphyllon ciliatum
Fast-growing, evergreen, woody-stemmed, twining climber with heart-shaped, pale green leaves fringed with hairs. Bright yellow flowers with ruffled petals appear in spring–summer. **H** 15ft (5m) or more. Min. 59–64°F (15–18°C).

☀ ◊ Z14–15 H12–10

Pyrostegia venusta **(Flame flower, Flame vine, Golden shower)**
Fast-growing, evergreen, woody-stemmed, tendril climber with clusters of tubular, golden-orange flowers from fall to spring. **H** 30ft (10m) or more. Min. 55–59°F (13–15°C).

☀ ◊ H11–10

***Allamanda cathartica* 'Hendersonii'**
Fast-growing, evergreen, woody-stemmed, scrambling climber. Has lance-shaped leaves in whorls and trumpet-shaped, rich bright yellow flowers in summer–fall. **H** to 15ft (5m). Min. 55–59°F (13–15°C).

◑ ◊ ❶ H11–10

Streptocarpus 'Crystal Ice'
Herbaceous, stemless, basal-rosetted perennial with long, narrowly strap-shaped, wrinkled, lightly hairy, green leaves. Produces clusters of 7–13 funnel-shaped, white flowers, with blue veins, in winter. **H** 16in (40cm), **S** 12in (30cm). Min. 41°F (5°C).

☀ ◑ Z11 H12–10

Coelogyne cristata
Evergreen, epiphytic orchid for a cool greenhouse. In winter produces crisp, white flowers, 2in (5cm) across, and marked orange on each lip. Narrowly oval leaves are 3–4in (8–10cm) long. Needs good light in summer. **H** 12in (30cm), **S** 24in (60cm). Min. 50°F (10°C).

☀ ◐ H11–6

Chlorophytum comosum 'Vittatum'
Evergreen, tufted, rosette-forming perennial. Long, narrow, lance-shaped, creamy-white leaves have green stripes and margins. Irregularly has small, star-shaped, white flowers on thin stems. **H** and **S** 12in (30cm). Min. 41°F (5°C).

◐ ◐ H11–10

Pilea cadierei (Aluminium plant)
Evergreen, bushy perennial with broadly oval leaves, each with a sharply pointed tip and raised, silvery patches that appear quilted. Has insignificant, greenish flowers. **H** and **S** 12in (30cm). Min. 50°F (10°C).

◐ ◐ H11–1

Peperomia caperata (Emerald ripple)
Evergreen, bushy perennial with pinkish leaf stalks. Has oval, fleshy, wrinkled, dark green leaves, to 2in (5cm) long, with sunken veins; spikes of white flowers appear irregularly. **H** and **S** to 6in (15cm). Min. 50°F (10°C).

◐ ◐ H11–1

Ctenanthe oppenheimiana 'Tricolor'
Robust, evergreen, bushy perennial. Has leathery, lance-shaped leaves, over 12in (30cm) long, splashed with large, cream blotches, and, intermittently, spikes of 3-petaled, white flowers. **H** and **S** 3ft (1m). Min. 59°F (15°C).

◐ ◐ H11–10

Dieffenbachia seguine 'Exotica'
Evergreen, tufted perennial, sometimes woody at the base. Broadly lance-shaped leaves, to 18in (45cm) long, are blotched with creamy-white. **H** and **S** 3ft (1m) or more. Min. 59°F (15°C).

◐ ◐ ⚠ H11–1

Anthurium crystallinum
(Crystal anthurium)
Evergreen, erect, tufted perennial. Long, velvety, dark green leaves are distinctively pale green- to white-veined. Has long-lasting, red-tinged, green spathes. **H** to 30in (75cm), **S** to 24in (60cm). Min. 59°F (15°C).

◐ ◐ ⚠ H11–10

Ruellia devosiana
Evergreen, bushy subshrub with spreading, purplish branches. Leaves are broadly lance-shaped, dark green with paler veins above and purple below. Has mauve-tinged, white flowers in spring–summer. **H** and **S** to 18in (45cm) or more. Min. 59°F (15°C).

◐ ◐ Z14–15 H12–10

Episcia dianthiflora (Laceflower)
Evergreen perennial with creeping prostrate stems. Has thick, velvety leaves with brownish midribs and, intermittently, pure white flowers with fringed petals. **H** 6in (15cm), **S** 12in (30cm). Min. 59°F (15°C).

☀ ◐ H11–6

ORCHIDS

Elegant and exotic, orchids are prized for their unusual flowers. There are two main groups. Terrestrials [t] grow in a wide range of habitats in the wild; many are at least frost hardy. Epiphytes [e], the more showy of the two and mostly native to the tropics, cling to tree branches or rocks, obtaining nourishment through their leaves and aerial roots. An aura of mystique surrounds these plants, but their cultivation is not always difficult and some thrive indoors as houseplants. They need special growing medium and in cool climates must be grown under glass. An orchid hybrid is called a grex [gx], from the Latin for a flock. A grex name applies to all the individual seedlings from any given cross, the individual plants of which may also be given cultivar names. Several cultivars may also be given a Group name within a grex. See also the Plant Dictionary.

Calanthe vestita [t]

Paphiopedilum Freckles gx ① [t]

Rhynchostele rossii [e]

Cymbidium Portelet Bay gx ① [e]

Spiranthes cernua [t]

Brassavola nodosa [e]

Masdevallia tovarensis [e]

Oncidium alexandrae [e]

Cypripedium reginae [t]

Coelogyne flaccida [e]

Ophrys tenthredinifera [t]

Laelia anceps [e]

Miltoniopsis Robert Strauss gx 'Ardingly' [e]

Dendrobium infundibulum [e]

Coelogyne nitida [e]

Rhyncholaeliocattleya Mount Adams gx [e]

Pleione bulbocodioides [t]

Dendrobium nobile [e]

Vanda Rothschildiana gx [e]

Anacamptis morio [t]

Oncidium sotoanum [e]

Platilla striata [t]

Oncidium Hambühren Stern gx 'Cheam' [e]

Phaius tankervilleae [t]

Miltoniopsis Anjou gx 'St. Patrick' [e]

Ada aurantiaca [e]

Cymbidium Caithness Ice gx 'Trinity' ① [e]

x **Oncidopsis** Cambria gx 'Lensing's Favorite' [e]

Cymbidium Strathkanaid gx ① [e]

x **Cattlianthe** Rojo gx 'Mont Millais' [e]

Oncidium Tigersun gx 'Orbec' [e]

Masdevallia wagneriana [e]

Oncidium Artur Elle gx 'Colombien' [e]

Paphiopedilum bellatulum ① [t]

Oncidium Memoria Commander Wiggs gx 'Kay' [e]

Phalaenopsis Lundy gx [e]

Paphiopedilum Buckhurst gx 'Mont Millais' ① [t]

Paphiopedilum Lyric gx 'Glendora' ① [t]

Paphiopedilum Maudiae gx ① [t]

Paphiopedilum fairrieanum ① [t]

Paphiopedilum armeniacum

Rossioglossum grande [e]

Oncidium Eric Young gx [e]

Paphiopedilum rothschildianum

Gomesa flexuosa [e]

Brasiliorchis porphyrostele [e]

Oncidium Julie Barbara Good gx [e]

Lycaste cruenta [e]

x **Cattlianthe** Hazel Boyd gx 'Apricot Glow' [e]

Cymbidium elegans ① [e]

Oncidium tigrinum [e]

Ophrys lutea [t]

Phragmipedilum besseae

Psychopsis papilio [e]

467

WHITE

Spathiphyllum 'Mauna Loa'
Robust, evergreen, tufted perennial with rhizomes. Has long, lance-shaped, glossy leaves. Irregularly bears fleshy, white spadices of fragrant flowers enclosed in large, oval, white spathes. **H** and **S** 18–24in (45–60cm). Min. 59°F (15°C).

☀ ◊ ① Z14–15 H12–6

Fittonia albivenis Argyroneura Group (Silver net-leaf)
Evergreen, creeping perennial with small, oval, white-veined, olive-green leaves. Remove flowers if they form. **H** to 6in (15cm), **S** indefinite. Min. 59°F (15°C).

☀ ◊ H11–1

Aglaonema commutatum 'Treubii'
Evergreen, erect, tufted perennial. Lance-shaped leaves, to 12in (30cm) long, are marked with pale green or silver. Occasionally has greenish-white spathes. **H** and **S** to 18in (45cm). Min. 59°F (15°C).

☀ ◊ ① H11–1

Tradescantia fluminensis 'Albovittata'
Strong-growing, evergreen perennial with trailing, rooting stems. Bluish-green leaves have broad, white stripes. Bears small, white flowers. **H** 12in (30cm), **S** indefinite. Min. 59°F (15°C).

☀ ◊ ① Z13–15 H12–1

Spathiphyllum wallisii (Peace lily, White sails)
Evergreen, tufted, rhizomatous perennial. Has clusters of long, lance-shaped leaves. Fleshy, white spadices of fragrant flowers in white spathes are irregularly produced. **H** and **S** 12in (30cm) or more. Min. 59°F (15°C).

☀ ◊ ① Z14–15 H12–1

Angraecum sesquipedale
Evergreen, epiphytic orchid. Waxy, white flowers, 3in (8cm) across, with a 12in (30cm) long spur, are borne, usually 2 to a stem, in winter. Has narrow, semi-rigid, horizontal leaves, 6in (15cm) long. Needs shade in summer but full light in winter. **H** and **S** 12in (30cm) or more. Min. 55°F (13°C).

☀ ◊ H11–10

Achimenes 'Little Beauty'
Bushy perennial with oval, toothed
leaves. Large, funnel-shaped, deep pink
flowers with yellow eyes are carried in
summer. **H** 10in (25cm), **S** 12in (30cm).
Min. 50°F (10°C).

 H11–1

Streptocarpus 'Nicola'
Evergreen, stemless perennial with a
rosette of strap-shaped, wrinkled leaves.
Funnel-shaped, rose-pink flowers are
produced intermittently in small clusters.
H 10in (25cm), **S** 20in (50cm). Min.
50–59°F (10–15°C).

 Z13–15 H12–10

Saintpaulia 'Colorado'
Evergreen, rosette-forming perennial
(Standard Group saintpaulia) with
broadly ovate to oval, dark green leaves.
Produces star-shaped, frilled, single,
magenta flowers throughout the year.
H 6–8in (15–20cm). Min. 59°F (15°C).

H12–10

Tradescantia sillamontana
Evergreen, erect perennial. Oval, stem-
clasping leaves are densely covered
with white, woolly hairs. Has clusters
of small, bright purplish-pink flowers
in summer. **H** and **S** to 12in (30cm).
Min. 50–59°F (10–15°C).

 Z14–15 H12–10

Oplismenus africanus 'Variegatus'
Evergreen, creeping, perennial grass
with wiry, rooting stems. White-striped
leaves, with wavy margins, are often
tinged pink. Bears inconspicuous
flowers intermittently. **H** 8in (20cm)
or more, **S** indefinite. Min. 54°F (12°C).

 H11–1

Kohleria digitaliflora
Erect, bushy, rhizomatous perennial
with white-haired stems. Has scalloped,
hairy leaves and clusters of tubular,
hairy, pink-and-white flowers, with
purple-spotted, green lobes, in
summer–fall. **H** 24in (60cm) or more,
S 18in (45cm). Min. 59°F (15°C).

H11–10

Tradescantia zebrina
(Silver inch plant, wandering Jew)
Evergreen, trailing or mat-forming
perennial. Bluish-green leaves, purple-
tinged beneath, have 2 broad, silver
bands. Has pink or violet-blue flowers
intermittently during the year. **H** 6in
(15cm), **S** indefinite. Min. 59°F (15°C).

Z14–15 H12–1

469

TENDER AND EXOTIC PLANTS

Anigozanthos manglesii
(Red-and-green kangaroo paw)
Vigorous, bushy perennial that bears
racemes of large, tubular, woolly,
red-and-green flowers in spring
and early summer. Has long, narrow,
gray-green leaves. May suffer from
ink disease. **H** 3ft (1m), **S** 1½ft (45cm).

☼ ◊ pH Z10–11 H11–10

Columnea x banksii
Evergreen, trailing perennial with
oval, fleshy leaves, glossy above,
purplish-red below. Tubular, hooded,
brilliant red flowers, to 3in (8cm) long,
appear from spring to winter. Makes
a useful plant for a hanging basket.
H 3ft (1m), **S** indefinite. Min. 59°F (15°C).

☼ ◊ H11–10

Anthurium andraeanum
(Flamingo flower)
Evergreen, erect perennial. Long-
stalked, oval leaves, with a heart-
shaped base, are 8in (20cm) long. Has
long-lasting, bright red spathes with
yellow spadices. **H** 24–30in (60–75cm),
S 20in (50cm). Min. 59°F (15°C).

☼ ◊ ❢ H11–10

Musa ornata (Flowering banana)
Evergreen, palmlike, suckering perennial
with oblong, waxy, bluish-green leaves
to 6ft (2m) long. In summer has erect,
yellow-orange flowers with pinkish
bracts and greenish-yellow fruits. **H** to
10ft (3m), **S** 7ft (2.2m). Min. 64°F (18°C).

☼ ◊ H11–10

Doryanthes palmeri
Evergreen perennial with a rosette of
arching, ribbed leaves, to 6ft (2m) long.
Intermittently bears panicles of small,
red-bracted, orange-red flowers, white
within. Flowers are often replaced by
bulbils. **H** 6–8ft (2–2.5m), **S** 8ft (2.5m).
Min. 50°F (10°C).

☼ ◊ H11–10

Russelia equisetiformis (Coral plant)
Evergreen, branching, bushy subshrub
with rushlike stems and tiny leaves.
Showy, pendent clusters of tubular,
scarlet flowers appear in summer–fall.
H to 3ft (1m) or more, **S** 2ft (60cm).
Min. 59°F (15°C).

☼ ◊ Z11–12 H12–1

Sinningia 'Switzerland'
Short-stemmed, tuberous perennial
with rosettes of oval, velvety leaves,
to 8in (20cm) long. In summer has large,
fleshy, trumpet-shaped, bright scarlet
flowers with ruffled, white borders.
H to 12in (30cm), **S** 18in (45cm).
Min. 59°F (15°C).

☼ ◊ Z14–15 H12–10

Caladium bicolor 'Pink Beauty'
Tufted, tuberous perennial. Has
long-stalked, triangular, pink-mottled,
green leaves, to 18in (45cm) long,
with darker pink veins. White spathes
appear in summer. **H** and **S** 36in (90cm).
Min. 66°F (19°C).

☼ ◊ ❢ H11–4

Bromelia balansae (Heart of flame)
Evergreen, clump-forming, basal-rosetted
perennial bearing strap-shaped, arching,
gray-green leaves with hooked spines.
Club-shaped panicles of tubular, red or
purple flowers, with long, bright red
bracts, are borne in spring–summer. **H** 3ft
(1m), **S** 5ft (1.5m). Min. 41–45°F (5–7°C).

☼ ◊ H11–1

Kohleria eriantha
Robust, bushy, rhizomatous perennial
with reddish-haired stems. Oval leaves,
to 5in (13cm) long, are edged with
red hairs. Has tubular, red flowers,
with yellow-spotted lobes, in nodding
clusters in summer. **H** and **S** 3ft (1m)
or more. Min. 59°F (15°C).

☼ ◊ H11–10

Columnea crassifolia
Evergreen, shrubby perennial with
fleshy, lance-shaped leaves. Erect,
tubular, hairy, scarlet flowers, about
3in (8cm) long, each with a yellow throat,
are carried from spring to fall. **H** and
S to 18in (45cm). Min. 59°F (15°C).

☼ ◊ H11–10

Smithiantha 'Orange King'
Strong-growing, erect, rhizomatous
perennial. Large, scalloped, velvety
leaves are emerald-green with dark
red-marked veins. In summer–fall
has tubular, orange-red flowers,
red-spotted within and with yellow lips.
H and **S** to 24in (60cm). Min. 59°F (15°C).

☀ ◊ Z14–15 H12–10

Episcia cupreata (Flame violet)
Evergreen, creeping perennial.
Has small, downy, wrinkled leaves,
usually silver-veined or -banded, and,
intermittently, scarlet flowers marked
yellow within. **H** 4in (10cm), **S** indefinite.
Min. 59°F (15°C).

☀ ◊ H11–7

Nautilocalyx lynchii
Robust, evergreen, erect, bushy
perennial. Broadly lance-shaped, slightly
wrinkled leaves are glossy, greenish-red
above, reddish beneath. In summer has
tubular, red-haired, pale yellow flowers
with red calyces. **H** and **S** to 24in (60cm).
Min. 59°F (15°C).

☀ ◊ H11–1

BROMELIADS

Bromeliads, or plants that belong to the family *Bromeliaceae*
are distinguished by their bold, usually rosetted foliage
and showy flowers in shades of white, red, or purple, borne
in dense, cylindrical or conical inflorescences in summer.
The flowers are followed by ovoid yellow fruits containing
large brown seeds. Many bromeliads are epiphytes, or
air plants (absorbing their food through moisture in the
atmosphere), and will grow outdoors only in tropical
regions. In cooler climates, bromeliads make attractive
houseplants or will thrive in a warm greenhouse. Follow
watering instructions with care.

Tillandsia argentea

Ananas bracteatus
var. tricolor

Aechmea fasciata

Cryptanthus bivittatus
'Pink Starlight'

Aechmea recurvata

Neoregelia concentrica

Vriesea splendens

Tillandsia stricta

Tillandsia lindenii

Puya chilensis

AFRICAN VIOLETS

African violet is the common name for the genus *Saintpaulia*, although it is often applied to the numerous cultivars derived from *S. ionantha*. These low-growing, rosetted, evergreen perennials have a wide range of attractive flower colors, varying from white, pink, blue, and violet, to bi- or multicolored. Their petal edges can be ruffled, rounded, frilled, or fringed, and leaves are somewhat succulent, usually hairy, and, in some cases, variegated. They may be grown as summer bedding in warm, humid climates but also make attractive houseplants, flowering freely throughout the year if kept in a suitable draft-free, light, humid location.

'Garden News'

S. 'Powder Keg'

'Starry Trail'

S. 'Pip Squeek'

S. 'Ice Maiden'

S. 'Porcelain'

S. 'Falling Raindrops'

S. 'Zoja'

S. 'Bright Eyes'

PURPLE

Peliosanthes arisanensis
Evergreen perennial with slow-spreading rhizomes. Stems have oblong, pleated, thin-textured, light green leaves, 8-12in (20-30cm) long, and in spring bear spikes of up to 20, 6-petaled, nodding, purple-centered, yellow flowers. **H** 12in (30cm). **S** 16in (40cm). Min. 32°F (0°C).

☀ ◊ ⚑ Z10–11 H11–9

Heterocentron elegans
Evergreen, mat-forming perennial with dense, creeping, mid-green foliage. Massed, bright deep purple flowers open in summer–fall and, under glass, in winter. **H** 2in (5cm), **S** indefinite. Min. 41°F (5°C).

☀ ◊ H11–1

Browallia speciosa (Bush violet)
Bushy perennial, usually grown as an annual, propagated by seed each year. Has oval leaves to 4in (10cm) long and showy, violet-blue flowers with white eyes, the season depending when sown. **H** 24–30in (60–75cm), **S** 18in (45cm). Min. 50–59°F (10–15°C).

☀ ◊ Z10–11 H8–1

Tetranema roseum
(Mexican foxglove, Mexican violet)
Short-stemmed perennial with crowded, stalkless leaves, bluish-green beneath. Intermittently, has nodding, purple flowers with paler throats. **H** to 8in (20cm), **S** 12in (30cm). Min. 55°F (13°C).

☀ ◊ Z10–15 H12–10

Calathea sanderiana
Evergreen, clump-forming perennial. Broadly oval, leathery, glossy leaves, to 2ft (60cm) long, are dark green with pink to white lines above, and purple beneath. Intermittently has short spikes of white to mauve flowers. **H** 4–5ft (1.2–1.5m), **S** 3ft (1m). Min. 59°F (15°C).

☀ ◊ H11

Alocasia cuprea
Evergreen, tufted perennial. Oval leaves are 12in (30cm) long, with a metallic sheen and darker, impressed veins above, purple below; leaf stalks arise from the lower surface. Purplish spathes appear intermittently. **H** and **S** to 3ft (1m). Min. 59°F (15°C).

☀ ◊ ! H11–10

Chirita lavandulacea

Evergreen, erect perennial with downy, pale green leaves to 8in (20cm) long. In leaf axils has clusters of lavender-blue flowers with white tubes. May be sown in succession to flower from spring to fall. **H** and **S** 24in (60cm). Min. 59°F (15°C).

☀ ◑ ◊ H11–10

Hemigraphis repanda

Evergreen, prostrate perennial with spreading, rooting stems. Lance-shaped, toothed, purple-tinged leaves, 2in (5cm) long, are darker purple below. Has tiny, tubular, white flowers intermittently. **H** to 6in (15cm). Min. 59°F (15°C).

☀ ◊ H11–1

Elatostema repens
(Watermelon begonia)

Evergreen, creeping perennial with rooting stems. Broadly oval, olive-green leaves have purplish-brown edges and paler green centers. Flowers are insignificant. **H** 4in (10cm), **S** indefinite. Min. 59°F (15°C).

☀ ◑ ◊ Z8–10 H10–8

Nepenthes x hookeriana

Evergreen, epiphytic, insectivorous perennial with oval, leathery leaves to 12in (30cm) lonsg and pendent, pale green pitchers, with reddish-purple markings and a spurred lid, to 5in (13cm) long. **H** 24–30in (60–75cm). Min. 64°F (18°C).

☀ ◑ ◊ H11–10

Dichorisandra reginae

Evergreen, erect, clump-forming perennial. Glossy, often silver-banded and flecked leaves are purple-red beneath. Has small spikes of densely set, purple-blue flowers in summer–fall. **H** 24–30in (60–75cm), **S** to 12in (30cm). Min. 68°F (20°C).

☀ ◑ ◊ H11–10

Streptocarpus 'Amanda'

Evergreen, stemless perennial with a few, long, strap-shaped, wrinkled, finely hairy, mid-green leaves. Funnel-shaped, rich blue flowers, with darker veining and white throat, are produced in tight clusters in spring. **H** 12in (30cm), **S** 8in (20cm). Min. 41°F (5°C).

☀ ◑ ◊ Z11 H12–10

Pycnostachys dawei

Strong-growing, bushy perennial with toothed, oblong leaves, 5–12in (12–30cm) long, that are reddish below. Has compact spikes of tubular, 2-lipped, bright blue flowers in winter–spring. **H** 4–5ft (1.2–1.5m), **S** 1–3ft (30–90cm). Min. 59°F (15°C).

☀ ◊ H11–10

Dionaea muscipula (Venus flytrap)

Evergreen, insectivorous perennial with rosettes of 6 or more spreading, hinged leaves, pink-flushed inside, edged with stiff bristles. Clusters of tiny, white flowers are carried in summer. **H** 4in (10cm), **S** 12in (30cm). Min. 41°F (5°C).

☀ ◊ H11–1

Drosera spatulata

Evergreen, insectivorous perennial with rosettes of spoon-shaped leaves that have sensitive, red, glandular hairs. Has many small, pink or white flowers on leafless stems in summer. **H** and **S** to 3in (8cm). Min. 41–50°F (5–10°C).

☀ ◊ Z11 H12–1

Drosera capensis (Cape sundew)

Evergreen, insectivorous perennial. Rosettes of narrow leaves have sensitive, red, glandular hairs. Many small, purple flowers are borne on leafless stems in summer. **H** and **S** to 6in (15cm). Min. 41–50°F (5–10°C).

☀ ◊ Z8–10 H10–8

TENDER AND EXOTIC PLANTS

Ensete ventricosum
Evergreen, palmlike perennial
with small, banana-like fruits. Has
20ft (6m) long leaves with reddish
midribs and, intermittently, reddish-
green flowers with dark red bracts.
H 20ft (6m), **S** 10ft (3m). Min. 50°F (10°C).

☼ ◊ Z10–11 H11–1

Asparagus densiflorus
Evergreen, trailing perennial with
clusters of narrow, bright green, leaflike
stems. In summer has pink-tinged,
white flowers, followed by red fruits.
Suits a hanging basket. **H** to 3ft (1m),
S 20in (50cm). Min. 50°F (10°C).

☼ ◊ ① H11–1

Asparagus densiflorus 'Myersii'
(Foxtail fern)
Evergreen, erect perennial with spikes
of tight, feathery clusters of leaflike
stems and pinkish-white flowers in
summer, then red fruits. **H** to 3ft (1m),
S 20in (50cm). Min. 50°F (10°C).

☼ ◊ ① H11–1

Peperomia marmorata
(Sweetheart peperomia, silver heart)
Evergreen, bushy perennial with
insignificant flowers. Has oval,
long-pointed, fleshy, dull green
leaves, marked with grayish-white
and quilted above, reddish below.
H and **S** to 8in (20cm). Min. 50°F (10°C).

☼ ◊ H11–1

Peperomia glabella (Wax privet)
Evergreen perennial with wide-
spreading, red stems. Has broadly
oval, fleshy, glossy, bright green leaves,
to 2in (5cm) long, and insignificant
flowers. **H** to 6in (15cm), **S** 12in (30cm).
Min. 50°F (10°C).

☼ ◊ H11–1

Peperomia obtusifolia 'Variegata'
Evergreen, bushy perennial with
spade-shaped, fleshy leaves, to
8in (20cm) long, that have irregular,
yellowish-green to creamy-white
margins and usually grayish centers.
Flowers are insignificant. **H** and
S to 6in (15cm). Min. 50°F (10°C).

☼ ◊ H11–10

Pilea nummulariifolia
(Creeping Charlie)
Evergreen, mat-forming perennial
with creeping, rooting, reddish stems.
Rounded, pale green leaves, ¾in (2cm)
wide, have a ridged surface. Flowers
are insignificant. **H** to 2in (5cm),
S 12in (30cm). Min. 50°F (10°C).

☼ ◊ H11–1

Xanthosoma sagittifolium
Spreading, tufted perennial with thick
stems. Broadly arrow-shaped leaves,
2ft (60cm) or more long, on long leaf
stalks, are green with a grayish bloom.
Has green spathes intermittently
during the year. **H** to 6ft (2m) in flower,
S 6ft (2m) or more. Min. 59°F (15°C).

☼ ◊ ① Z14–15 H12–10

**Dieffenbachia seguine
'Rudolph Roehrs'**
Evergreen, tufted perennial, sometimes
woody at the base. Leaves, to 18in
(45cm) long, are yellowish-green or
white with green midribs and margins.
H and **S** 3ft (1m). Min. 59°F (15°C).

☼ ◊ ① H11–1

Aglaonema pictum
Evergreen, erect, tufted perennial. Oval leaves, to 6in (15cm) long, are irregularly marked with grayish-white or gray-green. Has creamy-white spathes in summer. **H** and **S** to 24in (60cm). Min. 59°F (15°C).

☀ ◌ ⓘ H11–1

Columnea microphylla 'Variegata'
Evergreen, trailing perennial. Has rounded leaves narrowly bordered with cream and tubular, hooded, scarlet flowers, with yellow throats, in winter–spring. **H** 3ft (1m) or more, **S** indefinite. Min. 59°F (15°C).

☀ ◌ H11–10

Calathea zebrina (Zebra plant)
Robust, evergreen, clump-forming perennial with long-stalked, velvety, dark green leaves, to 2ft (60cm) long (less if pot-grown), with paler veins, margins and midribs. Has short spikes of white to pale purple flowers. **H** and **S** to 3ft (90cm). Min. 59°F (15°C).

☀ ◌ Z11 H11–1

Aglaonema 'Silver King'
Evergreen, erect, tufted perennial. Broadly lance-shaped, mid-green leaves, to 12in (30cm), are marked with dark and light green. Has greenish-white spathes in summer. **H** and **S** to 18in (45cm). Min. 59°F (15°C).

☀ ◌ ⓘ Z11 H11–1

Maranta leuconeura 'Erythroneura' (Herringbone plant)
Evergreen perennial. Oblong leaves have veins marked red, with paler yellowish-green midribs, and are upright at night, flat by day. **H** and **S** to 12in (30cm). Min. 59°F (15°C).

☀ ◌ H11–1

Sansevieria trifasciata 'Hahnii'
Evergreen, stemless perennial with a rosette of about 5 stiff, erect, broadly lance-shaped and pointed leaves, banded horizontally with pale green or white. Occasionally has small, pale green flowers. **H** 6–12in (15–30cm), **S** 4in (10cm). Min. 59°F (15°C).

☀ ◌ Z14–15 H12–1

Calathea makoyana (Peacock plant)
Evergreen, clump-forming perennial. Horizontal leaves, 12in (30cm) long, are dark and light green above, reddish-purple below. Has short spikes of white flowers intermittently. **H** to 2ft (60cm), **S** to 4ft (1.2m). Min. 59°F (15°C).

☀ ◌ H11–1

Maranta leuconeura 'Kerchoveana' (Rabbit tracks)
Evergreen perennial that intermittently bears white to mauve flowers. Oblong leaves with dark brown blotches become greener with age and are upright at night, flat by day. **H** and **S** to 12in (30cm). Min. 59°F (15°C).

☀ ◌ H11–1

YELLOW

ORANGE

Arctotheca calendula
(Cape dandelion)
Carpeting perennial. Leaves are
woolly below, rough-haired above.
Heads of daisylike, bright yellow flowers,
with darker yellow centers, appear
from late spring to fall. **H** 12in (30cm),
S indefinite. Min. 41°F (5°C).

☀ ◊ H11–10

Sansevieria trifasciata 'Laurentii'
Evergreen, stemless perennial with
a rosette of about 5 stiff, erect, lance-
shaped and pointed leaves with yellow
margins. Occasionally has pale green
flowers. Propagate by division to avoid
reversion. **H** 1½–4ft (45cm–1.2m),
S 4in (10cm). Min. 50–59°F (10–15°C).

☀ ◊ Z14–15 H12–1

Strelitzia reginae
(Bird-of-paradise flower)
Evergreen, clump-forming perennial
with long-stalked, bluish-green leaves.
Has beaklike, orange-and-blue flowers
in boat-shaped, red-edged bracts
mainly in spring. **H** over 3ft (1m),
S 2½ft (75cm). Min. 41–50°F (5–10°C).

☽ ◊ Z13–15 H12–1

Hedychium gardnerianum
Upright, rhizomatous perennial. In late
summer and early fall has many spikes
of short-lived, fragrant, lemon-yellow
and red flowers. Lance-shaped leaves
are grayish-green, most markedly when
young. **H** 5–6ft (1.5–2m), **S** 2½ft (75cm).
Min. 41°F (5°C).

☀ ◕ Z8–10 H11–9

Aphelandra squarrosa 'Louisae'
Evergreen, erect perennial. Long, oval,
glossy, slightly wrinkled, dark green
leaves have white veins and midribs.
Bears dense spikes of golden-yellow
flowers from axils of yellow bracts
in late summer to fall. **H** to 3ft (1m),
S 2ft (60cm). Min. 55°F (13°C).

☀ ◊ H11–10

**Sansevieria trifasciata
'Golden Hahnii'**
Evergreen, stemless perennial with
a rosette of about 5 stiff, erect, broadly
lance-shaped leaves with wide, yellow
borders. Sometimes bears small, pale
green flowers. **H** 6–12in (15–30cm),
S 4in (10cm). Min. 59°F (15°C).

☽ ◊ Z14–15 H12–1

Impatiens repens
Evergreen, creeping perennial
with rooting stems. Has small, oval
to rounded leaves and, in summer,
yellow flowers, each with a large,
hairy spur. **H** to 2in (5cm), **S** indefinite.
Min. 50°F (10°C).

☀ ◕ H11–4

**Peristrophe hyssopifolia
'Aureovariegata'**
Evergreen, bushy perennial. Small
leaves are broadly lance-shaped with
long, pointed tips and central, creamy-
yellow blotches. Has tubular, rose-pink
flowers in winter. **H** to 2ft (60cm) or
more, **S** 4ft (1.2m). Min. 59°F (15°C).

☀ ◊ Z10–11 H12–7

Anigozanthos flavidus
(Yellow kangaroo paw)
Bushy perennial with racemes of large,
woolly, tubular, yellowish-green flowers,
with reddish anthers, borne in spring–
summer. Narrow leaves, to 2ft (60cm)
long, are mid-green. **H** 4ft (1.2m),
S 1½ft (45cm). Min. 32°F (0°C).

☀ ◊ pH H11–10

Clivia miniata
Evergreen, tuft-forming rhizome with
strap-shaped, semi-erect, basal, dark
green leaves, 16–24in (40–60cm) long.
Stems each produce a head of 10–20
orange or red flowers in spring or
summer. **H** 16in (40cm), **S** 12–24in
(30–60cm). Min. 50°F (10°C).

☽ ◊ ❶ Z9–11 H11–1

GINGERS

Gingers have been cultivated in Europe for over 100 years and bring colorful, intricate flowers, tropical foliage, and, quite literally, spice to the garden. Evergreen types need to be overwintered under glass or gradually dried off in fall to induce artificial dormancy, whereas many deciduous types such as *Roscoea* and *Cautleya* will die off naturally and, being frost-hardy, can remain in the ground with a protective mulch. Most gingers do not tolerate wet winter conditions and benefit from some shade. A brighter location encourages flowering, whereas shade encourages better foliage, so site accordingly. They should not be allowed to dry out while in growth, and are heavy feeders, so give them frequent applications of liquid fertilizer.

Alpinia zerumbet

Hedychium thyrsiforme

Hedychium stenopetalum

Hedychium yunnanense

Alpinia hainanensis

Costus speciosus

Curcuma petiolata

Roscoea scillifolia

Alpinia purpurata

Curcuma zedoaria

Hedychium maximum

Curcuma petiolata 'Jungle Gold'

Hedychium densiflorum

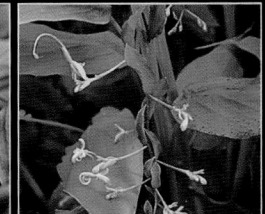

Globba winitii

TENDER AND EXOTIC PLANTS

ORANGE

Heliconia psittacorum
(Parrot's flower, Parrot's plantain)
Tufted perennial with long-stalked, lance-shaped leaves. In summer, mature plants carry green-tipped, orange flowers with narrow, glossy, orange-red bracts. **H** to 6ft (2m), **S** 3ft (1m). Min. 64°F (18°C).

☀ ◐ H11–10

Aeschynanthus speciosus
Evergreen, trailing perennial with waxy, narrowly oval leaves usually carried in whorls. Erect, tubular, bright orange-red flowers are borne in large clusters in summer. **H** and **S** 12–24in (30–60cm). Min. 64°F (18°C).

☀ ◐ H11–1

GREEN

Cyperus involucratus
Evergreen, tuft-forming, perennial sedge with leaflike bracts forming a whorl beneath the clustered flower spikes in summer. **H** to 3ft (1m), **S** 12in (30cm). Min. 39–45°F (4–7°C).

☀ ◐ H11–10

Cyperus papyrus
(Paper reed, Papyrus)
Evergreen, clump-forming, perennial sedge with sturdy, triangular, leafless stems, carrying in summer huge umbels of spikelets with up to 100 rays. Grows in water. **H** to 10–15ft (3–5m), **S** 3ft (1m). Min. 45–50°F (7–10°C).

☀ ● H11–6

Microlepia speluncae
Large, terrestrial fern with a spreading rhizome and triangular, divided, softly hairy fronds, consisting of triangular to lance-shaped pinnae. **H** to 4ft (1.2m), **S** to 6ft (2m). Min. 41–50°F (5–10°C).

☀ ◐ H11–10

Selaginella martensii
Evergreen, mosslike perennial with dense, much-branched, frondlike sprays of glossy, rich green foliage. **H** and **S** 9in (23cm). Min. 41°F (5°C).

☀ ◌ Z12–15 H12–1

Pteris cretica 'Wimsettii'
Evergreen or semievergreen fern with broadly ovate fronds divided into narrow pinnae, each with an incised margin and crested tip. **H** 18in (45cm), **S** 12in (30cm). Min. 41°F (5°C).

☀ ◐ H11–10

Phlebodium aureum
Evergreen fern with creeping, golden-scaled rhizomes. Has arching, deeply lobed, mid-green or glaucous fronds with attractive, orange-yellow sporangia on reverses. **H** 3–5ft (90cm–1.5m), **S** 2ft (60cm). Min. 41°F (5°C).

☀ ◌ H11–10

Nephrolepis exaltata (Sword fern)
Evergreen fern. Has erect, sometimes spreading, lance-shaped, divided, pale green fronds borne on wiry stems. **H** and **S** 36in (90cm) or more. Min. 41°F (5°C).

☀ ◐ H11–1

Selaginella kraussiana
Evergreen, trailing, more or less prostrate, mosslike perennial with bright green foliage. **H** ½in (1cm), **S** indefinite. Min. 41°F (5°C).

☀ ◌ Z7–10 H12–1

WHITE

Asplenium nidus (Bird's-nest fern)
Evergreen fern. Produces broadly
lance-shaped, glossy, bright green
fronds in a shuttlecock-like arrangement.
H 2–4ft (60cm–1.2m), **S** 1–2ft (30–60cm).
Min. 41°F (5°C).

☀ ◐ H11–3

***Phlebodium aureum* 'Mandaianum'**
Evergreen fern with creeping rhizomes.
Has arching, deeply lobed, glaucous
fronds with attractive, orange-yellow
sporangia on reverses; pinnae are
deeply cut and wavy. **H** 3–5ft (1–1.5m),
S 2ft (60cm). Min. 41°F (5°C).

☀ ◐ H11–10

Platycerium bifurcatum
(Common stag's-horn fern)
Evergreen, epiphytic fern with broad,
platelike sterile fronds and long, arching
or pendent, forked, gray-green fertile
fronds bearing velvety, brownish spore
patches beneath. **H** and **S** 3ft (1m).
Min. 41°F (5°C).

☀ ◐ H11–10

Selenicereus grandiflorus
(Queen-of-the-night)
Climbing, perennial cactus. Has
7-ribbed, ½–¾in (1–2cm) wide, green
stems with yellow spines. White
flowers, 7–12in (18–30cm) across,
open at night in summer. **H** 10ft (3m),
S indefinite. Min. 41°F (5°C).

☀ ◐ Z12–15 H12–7

Pereskia aculeata
(Barbados gooseberry, Lemon vine)
Fast-growing, deciduous, climbing
cactus with broad, glossy leaves.
Orange-centered, creamy-white flowers
appear in fall, only on plants over 3ft
(1m) high. **H** to 30ft (10m), **S** 15ft (5m).
Min. 41°F (5°C).

☀ ◐ H11–10

Cephalocereus senilis
(Old-man cactus)
Very slow-growing, columnar,
perennial cactus with a green stem
covered in long, white hairs, masking
short, white spines. Is unlikely to flower
in cultivation. **H** 50ft (15m), **S** 6in (15cm).
Min. 41°F (5°C).

☀ ◐ H11–10

Cleistocactus strausii (Silver torch)
Fast-growing, columnar, perennial
cactus with 3in (8cm) wide stems and
short, dense, white spines. Tubular,
red flowers appear in spring on plants
over 2ft (60cm) high. **H** 10ft (30cm),
S 3–6ft (1–2m). Min. 41°F (5°C).

☀ ◐ H11–10

Mammillaria hahniana
(Old-lady cactus, Old-woman cactus)
Spherical to columnar, perennial cactus
with a green stem bearing long, woolly,
white hairs. Carries cerise flowers
in spring and spherical, red fruits in
fall. **H** 16in (40cm), **S** 6in (15cm). Min.
41°F (5°C).

☀ ◐ H11–10

479

TENDER AND EXOTIC PLANTS

Coryphantha cornifera
Spherical to columnar, perennial cactus with angular tubercles, each bearing a curved, dark, central spine and shorter, radial spines. Has funnel-shaped, yellow flowers in summer. **H** 6in (15cm), **S** 4in (10cm). Min. 41°F (5°C).

 H11–10

Gasteria bicolor* var. *liliputana
Perennial succulent that forms rosettes of dark green leaves blotched with white. Flower stems, to 6in (15cm) long, bear spikes of bell-shaped, orange-green flowers in spring. **H** 3in (7cm), **S** 4in (10cm). Min. 41°F (5°C).

H11–10

Crassula socialis
Spreading, perennial succulent with short, dense rosettes of fleshy, triangular, green leaves, to ½in (1cm) across. Produces clusters of star-shaped, white flowers on 1¼in (3cm) tall stems in spring. **H** 2in (5cm), **S** indefinite. Min. 41°F (5°C).

H11–10

Haworthia attenuata
Clump-forming, perennial succulent with a basal rosette of triangular, 1¼in (3cm) long, dark green leaves, that have pronounced white dots. Has tubular, white flowers, with spreading petals, from spring to fall. **H** 3in (7cm), **S** 10in (25cm). Min. 41°F (5°C).

H11–10

Mammillaria geminispina
Clump-forming, perennial cactus. Has a spherical, green stem densely covered with short, white, radial spines and very long, white, central spines. Has red flowers, ½–¾in (1–2cm) across, in spring. **H** 10in (25cm), **S** 20in (50cm). Min. 41°F (5°C).

H11–10

Escobaria vivipara
Spherical, perennial cactus with a green stem densely covered with gray spines. Bears funnel-shaped, pink flowers, 1½in (3.5cm) across, in summer. Is much more difficult to grow than many other species in this genus. **H** and **S** 2in (5cm). Min. 41°F (5°C).

H11–10

Gasteria carinata* var. *verrucosa
Clump-forming, perennial succulent with stiff, dark green leaves, with raised, white dots and incurved edges. Has spikes of bell-shaped, orange-green flowers in spring. **H** 4in (10cm), **S** 12in (30cm). Min. 41°F (5°C).

H11–10

Mammillaria bocasana
(Powder-puff cactus)
Clump-forming, perennial cactus. Long, white hairs cover a hemispherical stem. Has cream or rose-pink flowers in summer and red seed pods the following spring–summer. **H** 4in (10cm), **S** 12in (30cm). Min. 41°F (5°C).

H11–10

Senecio rowleyanus (String-of-beads)
Pendent, perennial succulent. Very slender, green stems bear cylindrical, green leaves. Has heads of fragrant, tubular, white flowers from spring to fall. Suits a hanging pot. **H** 3ft (1m), **S** indefinite. Min. 41°F (5°C).

☀ ◊ Z12–15 H12–10

Opuntia polyacantha
Bushy, perennial cactus with a green stem of 6in (15cm) long, flattened segments. Areoles bear 6–15 flattened, 8in (20cm) long, hairlike spines. Has masses of saucer-shaped, red or yellow flowers in summer. **H** 20in (50cm), **S** 6ft (2m). Min. 41°F (5°C).

☀ ◊ ① Z7–10 H11–7

Lithops karasmontana
Egg-shaped, perennial succulent, divided into 2 unequal-sized, gray leaves that have pink, upper surfaces with sunken, darker pink marks. Bears a white flower in late summer or early fall. **H** to 1½in (4cm), **S** 2in (5cm). Min. 41°F (5°C).

☀ ◊ H11–10

Crassula ovata
(Friendship tree, Jade tree, Money tree)
Perennial succulent with a swollen stem crowned by glossy, green leaves, at times red-edged. Bears 5-petaled, white flowers in fall–winter. **H** 12ft (4m), **S** 6ft (2m). Min. 41°F (5°C).

☀ ◊ Z11 H11–1

Echinopsis oxygona
Spherical to columnar, perennial cactus with a 13–15-ribbed, green stem and long spines. Has 4in (10cm) wide, tubular, white to lavender flowers, to 8in (20cm) long, in spring–summer. **H** and **S** 12in (30cm). Min. 41°F (5°C).

☀ ◊ H11–10

Strombocactus disciformis
Very slow-growing, hemispherical, perennial cactus with a gray-green to brown stem set with a spiral of blunt tubercles. Woolly crown has bristly spines, which soon fall off, and cream flowers in summer. **H** 1¼in (3cm), **S** 4in (10cm). Min. 41°F (5°C).

☀ ◊ Z12–15 H12–10

Trichodiadema mirabile
Bushy to prostrate, perennial succulent with cylindrical, dark green leaves tipped with dark brown bristles and covered in papillae. Stem tip bears white flowers, 1½in (4cm) across, from spring to fall. **H** 6in (15cm), **S** 12in (30cm). Min. 41°F (5°C).

☀ ◊ Z12–15 H12–10

Agave americana 'Striata'
Basal-rosetted, perennial succulent. Has sharply pointed, sword-shaped, blue-green leaves with yellow edges. Stem carries white flowers, each 3½in (9cm) long, in spring–summer. Offsets freely. **H** and **S** 6ft (2m). Min. 32°F (0°C).

☀ ◊ Z9–11 H11–5

Gibbaeum velutinum
Clump-forming, perennial succulent with paired, finger-like, velvety, bluish gray-green leaves, to 2½in (6cm) long. Produces daisylike, pink, lilac or white flowers, 2in (5cm) across, in spring. **H** 3in (8cm), **S** 12in (30cm). Min. 41°F (5°C).

☀ ◊ H11–10

Gymnocalycium gibbosum
Spherical to columnar, perennial cactus that has a dark green stem with 12–19 rounded ribs, pale yellow spines, darkening with age, and white flowers, to 3in (7cm) long, in summer. **H** 12in (30cm), **S** 8in (20cm). Min. 41°F (5°C).

☀ ◊ H11–10

Furcraea foetida 'Mediopicta'
Basal-rosetted, perennial succulent with broad, sword-shaped, green leaves, striped with creamy-white, to 8ft (2.5m) long. Has bell-shaped, green flowers, with white interiors, in summer. **H** 10ft (3m), **S** 15ft (5m). Min. 43°F (6°C).

☀ ◊ H11–10

AGAVES

Tough plants originating from the Americas, agaves are able to withstand drought, heat, and full sun. Some species are frost-hardy too. Agaves arrest attention with bold rosettes of thick sculptured leaves, often of great architectural value. The rosette slowly increases in size over several years before producing a flower spike, sometimes of treelike proportions, so site carefully. Some species die after flowering, but may produce seed, bulbils among the flowers, and offsets around the base of the old rosette. Care should be taken when planting due to sharp thorns at the end of the leaves.

A. parrasana

A. potatorum

A. macroacantha

A. polianthiflora

A. parviflora

A. americana 'Marginata'

A. victoriae-reginae

A. filifera

WHITE

Kalanchoe blossfeldiana 'Calandiva'
Bushy, perennial succulent with oval to oblong, toothed, glossy, dark green leaves. Clusters of tubular, double, red, orange, pink, purple or white flowers, ¼in (0.5cm) across, of any combination of these colors, appear year-round. **H** and **S** 12in (30cm). Min. 50°F (10°C).

☀ ◊ Z11 H11–1

Echinocereus leucanthus
Clump-forming, tuberous cactus with spined, 6- or 7-ribbed, prostrate stems. In spring bears often terminal, dark-throated, white flowers, softly streaked purple, with green stigmas. **H** 8in (20cm), **S** 12in (30cm). Min. 46°F (8°C).

☀ ◊ H11–10

Epiphyllum laui
Bushy, perennial cactus, usually with strap-shaped, red-tinged, glossy stems, which may also be spiny, cylindrical or 4-angled. Has fragrant, white flowers, with brown sepals, in spring–summer. **H** 12in (30cm), **S** 20in (50cm). Min. 50°F (10°C).

☀ ◊ H11–1

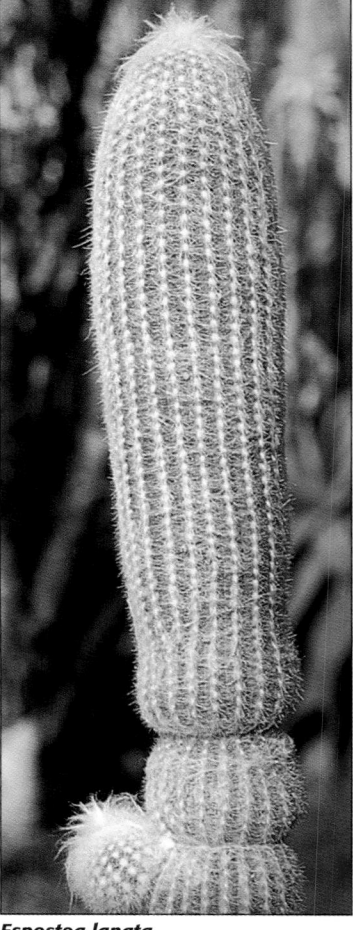

Espostoa lanata
(Cotton ball, Peruvian old-man cactus)
Very slow-growing, columnar, perennial cactus with a branching, woolly, green stem. Foul-smelling, white flowers appear in summer, only on plants over 3ft (1m) high. **H** to 12ft (4m), **S** 6ft (2m). Min. 50°F (10°C).

☀ ◊ H11–10

Kalanchoe fedtschenkoi 'Variegata'
Bushy, perennial succulent. Blue-green and cream leaves also color red. Bears a new plantlet in each leaf notch. Has brownish-pink flowers in late winter. **H** and **S** to 3ft (1m). Min. 50°F (10°C).

☀ ◊ Z11 H11–10

Mammillaria plumosa
Clump-forming, perennial cactus.
Has a spherical, green stem completely
covered with feathery, white spines.
Carries cream flowers in mid-winter.
Is difficult to grow. Add calcium
to soil. **H** 5in (12cm), **S** 16in (40cm).
Min. 50°F (10°C).

☼ ◊ ❢ H11–10

Neolloydia conoidea
Clump-forming, perennial cactus.
Has a columnar, blue-green stem
densely covered with white, radial
spines and longer, black, central spines.
Bears funnel-shaped, purple-violet
flowers in summer. **H** 4in (10cm),
S 6in (15cm). Min. 50°F (10°C).

☼ ◊ H11–10

Pachycereus pringlei
Slow-growing, columnar, perennial
cactus with a branched, bluish-green
stem that has 10–15 ribs. Large
areoles each have 15–25 black-tipped,
white spines. Is unlikely to flower in
cultivation. **H** 35ft (11m), **S** 10ft (3m).
Min. 50°F (10°C).

☼ ◊ Z11 H11–10

Opuntia microdasys var. albispina
Bushy, perennial cactus with green,
flattened, oval segments. Spineless
areoles, with slender, barbed, white
hairs, are set in diagonal rows. Funnel-
shaped, yellow flowers appear in
summer. **H** 24in (60cm), **S** 12in (30cm).
Min. 50°F (10°C).

☼ ◊ ❢ Z11 H11–9

Euphorbia tithymaloides 'Variegata'
(Redbird flower)
Bushy, perennial succulent with stems
angled at each node. Leaves have white
or pink marks. Stem tips carry small,
greenish flowers in red to yellowish-
green bracts in summer. **H** to 10ft (3m),
S 12in (30cm). Min. 50°F (10°C).

◑ ◊ ❢ Z11 H12–1

Rhipsalis cereuscula (Coral cactus)
Pendent, perennial cactus with 4- or
5-angled or cylindrical, green stems and
branches, to 1¼in (3cm) long in whorls.
Bell-shaped, white flowers on stem tips
in winter–spring. **H** 24in (60cm), **S** 20in
(50cm). Min. 50°F (10°C).

◑ ◊ H11–10

Pilosocereus leucocephalus
Columnar, perennial cactus with a
10–12-ribbed stem and white-haired
crown. Bears tubular, pink flowers, with
cream anthers, at night in summer, on
plants over 5ft (1.5m) tall. **H** to 20ft (6m),
S 3ft (1m). Min. 52°F (11°C).

☼ ◊ H11–10

Aporocactus flagelliformis
(Rat's-tail cactus)
Pendent, perennial cactus with pencil-
thick, green stems bearing short, golden
spines. Has double, cerise flowers along
stems in spring. Is good for a hanging
basket. **H** 3ft (1m), **S** indefinite.
Min. 32°F (0°C).

☼ ◊ H11–10

Rebutia 'Carnival'
Clump-forming, spherical, perennial
cactus with low, tuberculate ribs bearing
areoles of white hairs and thin spines. In
spring produces masses of funnel-shape
flowers around the stem base; in white,
pink, salmon, orange or orange-red.
H 2in (5cm), **S** 6in (15cm). Min. 41°F (5°C).

☼ ◊ Z11 H12–1

PINK

Rebutia 'Jenny'
Clump-forming, perennial cactus with low, tuberculate ribs bearing areoles with short, white spines. In spring produces funnel-shaped flowers, the outer sepals dark pink shading to off-white toward the center of each flower. **H** 2in (5cm), **S** 6in (15cm). Min. 41°F (5°C).

☼ ◊ Z11 H12–1

Echinocereus pentalophus
Clump-forming, perennial cactus with spined, green stems, 1¼–1½in (3–4cm) wide, that have 4–8 ribs, later rounded. Has trumpet-shaped, bright pink flowers, paler at base, to 5in (12cm) across, in spring. **H** 2ft (60cm), **S** 3ft (1m). Min. 41°F (5°C).

☼ ◊ H11–10

Echeveria elegans
Clump-forming, perennial succulent with a basal rosette of broad, fleshy, pale silvery-blue leaves, edged with red, and yellow-tipped, pink flowers in summer. Keep dry in winter. Makes a good bedding plant. **H** 2in (5cm), **S** 20in (50cm). Min. 41°F (5°C).

☼ ◊ H11–10

Stenocactus obvallatus
Spherical, perennial cactus with wavy-margined ribs. White areoles each bear 5–12 grayish-brown spines. In spring, has pale yellow to pale pink flowers, with a purplish-red stripe on each petal. **H** and **S** 3in (8cm). Min. 45°F (7°C).

☼ ◊ Z12–15 H12–10

Hesperaloe parviflora
Basal-rosetted, perennial succulent, often with peeling, white fibers at leaf edges. Flower stems each bear a raceme of bell-shaped, pink to red flowers in summer–fall. **H** 3ft (1m) or more, **S** 6ft (2m). Min. 37°F (3°C).

☼ ◊ Z6–11 H8–6

Mammillaria sempervivi
Slow-growing, spherical, perennial cactus. Has a dark green stem with short, white spines. Has white wool between short, angular tubercles on plants over 1½in (4cm) high. Bears cerise flowers in spring. **H** and **S** 3in (7cm). Min. 41°F (5°C).

☼ ◊ H11–10

Aptenia cordifolia
Fast-growing, prostrate, perennial succulent with oval, glossy, green leaves and, in summer, daisylike, bright pink flowers. Is ideal for groundcover. **H** 2in (5cm), **S** indefinite. Min. 45°F (7°C).

☼ ◊ Z11 H12–10

Thelocactus bicolor
Spherical to columnar, perennial cactus with an 8–13-ribbed stem. Areoles each have 4 usually flattened, yellow, central spines, or bicolored yellow and red, and numerous shorter, radial spines. Flowers are purple-pink. **H** and **S** 8in (20cm). Min. 45°F (7°C).

☼ ◊ Z12–15 H12–10

Conophytum concordans
Clump-forming, perennial succulent with 2 fleshy, gray-green leaves that are broad, erect and united for most of their length but have distinctly divided, upper lobes. Pale pink flowers appear in late summer. **H** 1in (2.5cm), **S** ½in (1cm). Min. 41°F (5°C).

☼ ◊ Z11 H12–10

Lampranthus spectabilis
Spreading, perennial succulent with erect stems and narrow, cylindrical, gray-green leaves. In summer produces daisylike flowers, cerise with yellow centers or golden-yellow throughout. **H** 12in (30cm), **S** indefinite. Min. 41°F (5°C).

☼ ◊ H11–10

Echinocereus reichenbachii var. baileyi
Columnar, perennial cactus with a slightly branched stem bearing 12–23 ribs and yellowish-white, 1¼in (3cm) long spines. Produces pink flowers with darker bases in spring. **H** 12in (30cm), **S** 8in (20cm). Min. 45°F (7°C).

☼ ◊ H11–10

Crassula multicava
Bushy, perennial succulent with oval, gray-green leaves, 3in (8cm) across. Carries numerous clusters of small, star-shaped, pink flowers on elongated stems in spring, followed by small plantlets. **H** 6in (15cm), **S** 3ft (1m). Min. 45°F (7°C).

☼ ◊ H11–10

Crassula schmidtii

Carpeting, perennial succulent with dense rosettes of linear, dark green leaves, pitted and marked, each 1¼–1½in (3–4cm) long. Bears masses of star-shaped, bright pinkish-red flowers in clusters in winter. **H** 4in (10cm), **S** 12in (30cm). Min. 45°F (7°C).

☼ ◊ H11–10

Oscularia deltoides

Spreading, perennial succulent. Has chunky, triangular, blue-green leaves, to ½in (1cm) long, with small-toothed, often reddened leaf margins. Fragrant, pink flowers, ½–¾in (1–2cm) wide, appear in early summer. **H** 6in (15cm), **S** 3ft (1m). Min. 45°F (7°C).

☼ ◊ H11–10

Eriosyce napina

Flattened spherical, perennial cactus with very short, gray spines pressed flat against a greenish-brown stem. Produces white, pink, carmine or brown flowers, 2in (5cm) across, from the crown in summer. **H** ¾in (2cm), **S** 1½in (3.5cm). Min. 46°F (8°C).

☼ ◊ Z11 H12–10

Disocactus 'Gloria'

Erect, then pendent, perennial cactus. Strap-shaped, flattened, green stems have toothed edges. Produces pinkish-red flowers, 4in (10cm) across, in spring. **H** 12in (30cm), **S** 3ft (1m). Min. 50°F (10°C).

☼ ◊ Z11 H12–10

Frithia pulchra

Basal-rosetted, perennial succulent with erect, rough, gray leaves, cylindrical with flattened tips. Produces masses of stemless, daisylike, bright pink flowers, with paler centers, in summer. **H** 1¼in (3cm), **S** 2½in (6cm). Min. 50°F (10°C).

☼ ◊ Z8–10 H10–7

Disocactus 'M.A. Jeans'

Erect, then pendent, perennial cactus. Strap-shaped, flattened, green stems have shallowly toothed edges. In spring has deep pink flowers, 3in (8cm) across, with white anthers. **H** 12in (30cm), **S** 20in (50cm). Min. 50°F (10°C).

☼ ◊ Z11 H12–10

Kalanchoe 'Wendy'

Semi-erect, perennial succulent with narrowly oval, glossy, green leaves, 3in (7cm) long. In late winter bears bell-shaped, pinkish-red flowers, ¾in (2cm) long, with yellow tips. Is ideal for a hanging basket. **H** and **S** 12in (30cm). Min. 50°F (10°C).

☼ ◊ H11–10

Hatiora rosea

Bushy, perennial cactus with slender, 3- or 4-angled, bristly, green stem segments, usually tinged purple, to 2in (5cm) long. Has masses of bell-shaped, pink flowers, to 1½in (4cm) across, in spring. **H** and **S** 4in (10cm). Min. 50°F (10°C).

☼ ◊ H11–10

Graptopetalum bellum

Basal-rosetted, perennial succulent with triangular to oval, gray leaves, 2in (5cm) long. Has clusters of deep pink to red flowers, ¾in (2cm) across, in spring–summer. **H** 1¼in (3cm), **S** 6in (15cm). Min. 50°F (10°C).

☼ ◊ H11–10

Disocactus phyllanthoides 'Deutsche Kaiserin'

Pendent, epiphytic, perennial cactus with flattened, toothed, glossy, green stems, each 2in (5cm) across. Stem margins each bear pink flowers, to 4in (10cm) across, in spring. **H** 2ft (60cm), **S** 3ft (1m). Min. 50°F (10°C).

☼ ◊ Z11 H12–10

Pereskia grandifolia (Rose cactus)

Deciduous, bushy, perennial cactus with black spines. Single roselike, pink flowers form in summer–fall only on plants over 1ft (30cm) high. **H** 15ft (5m), **S** 10ft (3m). Min. 50°F (10°C).

☼ ◊ H11–10

PINK

Mammillaria zeilmanniana
(Rose pincushion)
Clump-forming, perennial cactus with a spherical, green stem that has hooked spines and bears a ring of deep pink to purple flowers in spring. **H** 6in (15cm), **S** 12in (30cm). Min. 50°F (10°C).

☼ ◊ H11–10

Oroya peruviana
Spherical, perennial cactus with a much-ribbed stem covered in yellow spines, ⅝in (1.5cm) long, with darker bases. Pink flowers, with yellow bases, open in spring–summer. **H** 10in (25cm), **S** 8in (20cm). Min. 50°F (10°C).

☼ ◊ Z9–11 H12–7

Senecio articulatus 'Variegatus'
Deciduous, spreading, perennial succulent with gray-marked stems. Has cream- and pink-marked, blue-green leaves in summer and yellow flower heads from fall to spring. **H** 24in (60cm), **S** indefinite. Min. 50°F (10°C).

☼ ◊ ! Z13–15 H12–10

Parodia mueller-melchersii
Columnar, perennial cactus. Areoles each have about 15 radial spines and 2 upward- or downward-pointing, central spines. Has cream-centered, pink flowers in summer. **H** 4in (10cm), **S** 2in (5cm). Min. 50°F (10°C).

◑ ◊ Z9–11 H12–7

Schlumbergera 'Gold Charm'
Erect, then pendent, perennial cactus. Has flattened, oblong, green stem segments with toothed margins. Yellow flowers in early fall turn pinkish-orange in winter. **H** 6in (15cm), **S** 12in (30cm). Min. 50°F (10°C).

◑ ◊ Z13–15 H12–10

Adenium obesum
Treelike, perennial succulent with a fleshy, tapering, green trunk and stems crowned by oval, glossy, green leaves, dull green beneath. Carries funnel-shaped, pink to pinkish-red flowers, white inside, in summer. **H** 6ft (2m), **S** 20in (50cm). Min. 59°F (15°C).

◑ ◊ ! Z11 H11–10

RED

Echinopsis chamaecereus
(Peanut cactus)
Clump-forming, perennial cactus with spined stems, initially erect, then prostrate. Has funnel-shaped, orange-red flowers in late spring. **H** 4in (10cm), **S** indefinite. Min. 37°F (3°C).

☼ ◊ Z11 H12–7

Opuntia verschaffeltii
Clump-forming, perennial cactus with cylindrical, usually spineless stems, to 10in (25cm) long. Stem tips each bear short-lived, cylindrical leaves from spring to fall. Has orange-red flowers in spring. **H** 6in (15cm), **S** 3–6ft (1–2m). Min. 41°F (5°C).

☼ ◊ ! Z11 H11–9

Rebutia deminuta
Clump-forming, perennial cactus with a spherical, spined, green stem, to 1½in (4cm) across, becoming columnar with age. Bears masses of slender-tubed, orange-red flowers at base in late spring. **H** 4in (10cm), **S** 8in (20cm). Min. 41°F (5°C).

☼ ◊ Z11 H12–1

Rebutia minuscula [red]
Clump-forming, perennial cactus with a tuberculate, dark green stem. Bears prominent, white areoles with very short, white spines. Trumpet-shaped, bright red flowers, to 2in (5cm) across, appear at stem base in spring. **H** 2in (5cm), **S** 8in (20cm). Min. 41°F (5°C).

☼ ◊ H11–10

Ferocactus hamatacanthus
Slow-growing, spherical to columnar, perennial cactus with a 13-ribbed stem that bears hooked, red spines, to 5in (12cm) long. Has yellow blooms in summer, then spherical, red fruits. **H** and **S** 24in (60cm). Min. 41°F (5°C).

☼ ◊ H11–10

Echeveria secunda
Clump-forming, perennial succulent
with short stems each crowned by a
rosette of broad, fleshy, light green to
gray leaves, reddened near tips. Bears
cup-shaped, red-and-yellow flowers
in spring–summer. **H** 1½in (4cm),
S 12in (30cm). Min. 41°F (5°C).

☼ ◊ H11–10

Stenocactus coptonogonus
Spherical, perennial cactus. White
areoles each have 3–5 flat, upward-
curving, pale brownish-red spines.
Bears purple to white flowers, with
pink-purple or violet-purple stripes,
in spring. **H** 4in (10cm), **S** 6in (16cm).
Min. 45°F (7°C).

☼ ◊ Z12–15 H12–10

Kalanchoe blossfeldiana
Bushy, perennial succulent with oval
to oblong, toothed, glossy, green leaves.
Produces clusters of yellow, orange,
pink, red or purple flowers, year-round.
Makes an excellent houseplant. **H** and
S 12in (30cm). Min. 50°F (10°C).

☼ ◊ Z11 H11–1

Parodia haselbergii
subsp. *haselbergii* (Scarlet ball cactus)
Slow-growing, perennial cactus with a
stem covered in white spines. Slightly
sunken crown bears red flowers, with
yellow stigmas, in spring. **H** 4in (10cm),
S 10in (25cm). Min. 50°F (10°C).

◐ ◊ H11–10

Parodia microsperma
Clump-forming, perennial cactus.
Has a much-ribbed, green stem densely
covered with brown, radial spines and
red, central spines, some of which are
hooked. Bears blood-red, occasionally
yellow flowers in spring. **H** 3in (8cm),
S 12in (30cm). Min. 50°F (10°C).

◐ ◊ H11–10

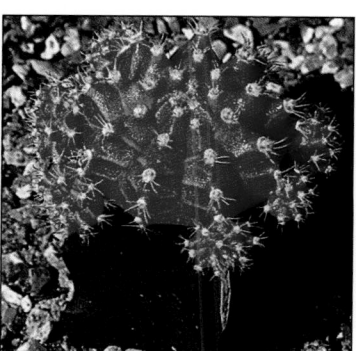

Gymnocalycium mihanovichii
'Red Head'
Perennial cactus with a red stem,
8 angular ribs and curved spines. Must
be grafted onto any fast-growing stock
as it contains no chlorophyll. Has pink
flowers in spring–summer. **H** and **S** as
per graft stock. Min. 50°F (10°C).

☼ ◊ H11–10

Parodia nivosa
Ovoid, perennial cactus that has a
much-ribbed, green stem with stiff,
white spines, each ½–¾in (1–2cm) long.
Has a white, woolly crown and bright
red flowers, to 2in (5cm) across, in
summer. **H** to 6in (15cm), **S** 4in (10cm).
Min. 50°F (10°C).

☼ ◊ H11–10

Kalanchoe 'Tessa'
Prostrate to pendent, perennial
succulent with narrowly oval, green
leaves, 1¼in (3cm) long. Bears tubular,
orange-red flowers, ¾in (2cm) long, in
late winter. **H** 12in (30cm), **S** 24in (60cm).
Min. 50°F (10°C).

◐ ◊ H11–10

Rebutia steinbachii
subsp. *tiraquensis*
Variable, perennial cactus with a green
stem. Elongated areoles bear spines
of gold or bicolored red and white.
Has dark pink- or orange-red flowers
in spring. **H** 6in (15cm), **S** 4in (10cm).
Min. 50°F (10°C).

☼ ◊ H11–10

Cyphostemma juttae
Perennial succulent. Swollen stem has
peeling bark and deciduous, scandent
branches with broad leaves. Bears
inconspicuous, yellow-green flowers
in summer. Green fruits turn yellow or
red. **H** and **S** 6ft (2m). Min. 50°F (10°C).

☼ ◊ H11–10

Schlumbergera truncata
(Crab cactus, Lobster cactus)
Erect, then pendent, perennial cactus.
Oblong stem segments have toothed
margins. Bears purple-red flowers
in early fall and winter. **H** 6in (15cm),
S 12in (30cm). Min. 50°F (10°C).

◐ ◊ Z13–15 H12–10

Hatiora gaertneri (Easter cactus)
Bushy, perennial cactus with flat,
oblong, glossy, green stem segments,
each to 2in (5cm) long, often tinged
red at edges. Segment ends each bear
orange-red flowers in spring. **H** 6in
(15cm), **S** 13in (20cm). Min. 55°F (13°C).

☼ ◊ Z11 H11–1

TENDER AND EXOTIC PLANTS

TENDER AND EXOTIC PLANTS

Schlumbergera 'Bristol Beauty'
Erect, then pendent, perennial cactus with flattened, green stem segments with toothed margins. Bears reddish-purple flowers, with silvery-white tubes, in early fall and winter. **H** 6in (15cm), **S** 12in (30cm). Min. 50°F (10°C).

☀◐ ◊ Z13–15 H12–10

Orbea variegata (Star flower)
Clump-forming, branching, perennial succulent with 4-angled, indented stems. Flowers, variable in color and blotched yellow, purple- or red-brown, appear in summer–fall. **H** to 4in (10cm), **S** indefinite. Min. 52°F (11°C).

☀ ◊ Z11 H11–9

Crassula deceptor
Slow-growing, clump-forming, perennial succulent with branching stems surrounded by fleshy, gray leaves set in 4 rows. Each leaf has minute lines around raised dots. Bears insignificant flowers in spring. **H** and **S** 4in (10cm). Min. 41°F (5°C).

☀ ◊ H11–10

Browningia hertlingiana
Slow-growing, columnar, perennial cactus with a silvery-blue stem, golden spines and tufted areoles. Nocturnal, white flowers appear in summer, only on plants over 3ft (1m) high. **H** 25ft (8m), **S** 12ft (4m). Min. 45°F (7°C).

☀ ◊ H11–10

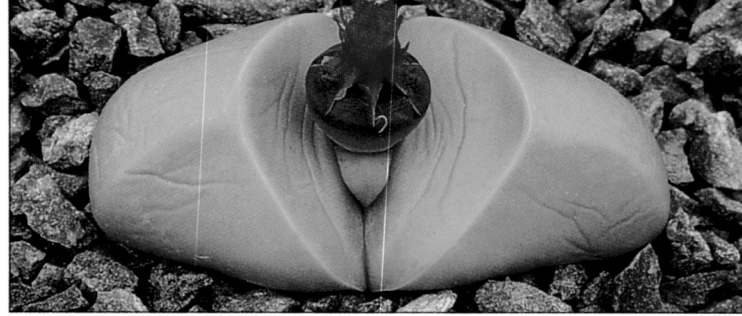

Argyroderma delaetii
Prostrate, egg-shaped, perennial succulent with 2 very fleshy, silvery-green leaves between which daisylike, pink-purple flowers, 2in (5cm) across, appear in late summer. **H** 1½in (3cm), **S** 2in (5cm). Min. 41°F (5°C).

☀ ◊ H11–10

Opuntia robusta
Bushy, perennial cactus. Silvery-blue stem has flattened, oval segments with either no spines or 8–12 white ones, to 2in (5cm) long, per areole. Saucer-shaped, yellow flowers, 3in (7cm) across, appear in spring–summer. **H** and **S** 15ft (5m). Min. 41°F (5°C).

☀ ◊ ① H11–1

Cereus hildmannianus
Columnar, perennial cactus. Has a branching, silvery-blue stem and golden spines on 4–8 indented ribs. Bears cup-shaped, white flowers, 4in (10cm) across, at night in summer, and pear-shaped, red fruits. **H** 15ft (5m), **S** 12ft (4m). Min. 45°F (7°C).

☀ ◊ Z11 H12–10

Huernia macrocarpa
Clump-forming, perennial succulent with finger-shaped, 4- or 5-sided, green stems. Produces short-lived, deciduous leaves and, in fall, bell-shaped, white-haired, dark purple flowers with recurved petal tips. **H** and **S** 4in (10cm). Min. 46°F (8°C).

☀◐ ◊ H11–10

Stapelia grandiflora
Clump-forming, perennial succulent with 4-angled, hairy, toothed, green stems. In summer–fall carries star-shaped, purple-brown flowers, to 4in (10cm) across, ridged with white or purple hairs. **H** to 8in (20cm), **S** indefinite. Min. 52°F (11°C).

☀◐ ◊ Z13–15 H12–10

Aloinopsis schooneesii
Dwarf, mounded, perennial succulent with tuberous roots and fleshy, almost spherical, blue-green leaves arranged tightly in tufts. Produces flattish, yellow flowers in winter–spring. **H** 1½in (3cm), **S** to 3in (7cm). Min. 45°F (7°C).

☀ ◊ Z10–11 H11–10

Cereus hankeanus
Columnar, perennial cactus with a branching, blue-green stem bearing dark spines on 4–7 prominent ribs. Has 10in (25cm) long, cup-shaped, white flowers at night in summer, followed by red fruits. **H** 22ft (7m), **S** 10ft (3m). Min. 45°F (7°C).

☀ ◊ Z11 H12–10

Copiapoa cinerea
Very slow-growing, clump-forming, perennial cactus. Blue-green stem bears up to 25 ribs and black spines. Has a woolly, white-gray crown and, on plants over 4in (10cm) across, yellow flowers in spring–summer. **H** 20in (50cm), **S** 6ft (2m). Min. 50°F (10°C).

 H11–10

Echinopsis lageniformis
Columnar, perennial cactus with 4–8-ribbed stems branching at base. Areoles each produce up to 6 spines. Scented, funnel-shaped, white flowers open at night in summer. **H** to 15ft (5m), **S** 3ft (1m). Min. 50°F (10°C).

 H11–10

Myrtillocactus geometrizans (Blue candle)
Columnar, perennial cactus with a branched, 5- or 6-ribbed, blue-green stem. Bears short, black spines, on plants over 1ft (30cm) tall, and white flowers at night in summer. **H** to 12ft (4m), **S** 6ft (2m). Min. 54°F (12°C).

 H11–10

Aeonium haworthii (Pinwheel)
Bushy, perennial succulent. Freely branching stems bear rosettes, 5in (12cm) across, of blue-green leaves, often with red margins. Has a terminal spike of star-shaped, pink-tinged, pale yellow flowers in spring. **H** 2ft (60cm), **S** 3ft (1m). Min. 41°F (5°C).

 H11–1

Agave parryi
Basal-rosetted, perennial succulent with stiff, broad, gray-green leaves, each to 12in (30cm) long with a solitary dark spine at its pointed tip. Flower stem, to 12ft (4m) long, bears creamy-yellow flowers in summer. **H** 20in (50cm), **S** 3ft (1m). Min. 41°F (5°C).

 Z9–11 H11–5

Graptopetalum paraguayense (Mother-of-pearl plant)
Clump-forming, perennial succulent with a basal rosette, 6in (15cm) across, of gray-green leaves, often tinged pink. Bears star-shaped, yellow-and-red flowers in summer. **H** 4in (10cm), **S** 3ft (1m). Min. 41°F (5°C).

 H11–10

Agave attenuata
Perennial succulent with a thick stem crowned by a rosette of sword-shaped, spineless, pale green leaves. Arching flower stem, to 5ft (1.5m) long, is densely covered with yellow flowers in spring–summer. **H** 3ft (1m), **S** 6ft (2m). Min. 41°F (5°C).

Z9–11 H11–5

Crassula perfoliata var. falcata (Aeroplane propeller)
Bushy, perennial succulent that branches freely. Long leaves each twist like a propeller. Has large clusters of fragrant, red flowers in late summer. **H** and **S** 3ft (1m). Min. 45°F (7°C).

H11–10

Lithops marmorata
Egg-shaped, perennial succulent, divided into 2 unequal-sized, swollen, pale gray leaves with dark gray marks on convex, upper surfaces. Bears a white flower in late summer or early fall. **H** ¾–1¼in (2–3cm), **S** 2in (5cm). Min. 41°F (5°C).

H11–10

TENDER AND EXOTIC PLANTS

489

GRAY

GREEN

Leuchtenbergia principis
Basal-rosetted, perennial cactus with narrow, angular, dull gray-green tubercles, each 4in (10cm) long and crowned by papery spines to 4in (10cm) long. Crown bears yellow flowers, to 3in (7cm) across, in summer. **H** and **S** 12in (30cm). Min. 43°F (6°C).

☀ ◊ H11–10

Dudleya pulverulenta
Basal-rosetted, perennial succulent with strap-shaped, pointed, silvery-gray leaves. Bears masses of star-shaped, red flowers in spring–summer. **H** 24in (60cm), **S** 12in (30cm). Min. 45°F (7°C).

☀ ◊ H11–10

Eriosyce villosa
Clump-forming, perennial cactus with a branched, green to dark gray-green stem. Has dense, sometimes curved, gray spines, 1¼in (3cm) long. Produces tubular, pink or white flowers in spring or fall. **H** 6in (15cm), **S** 4in (10cm). Min. 46°F (8°C).

☀ ◊ Z11 H12–10

Beschorneria yuccoides
Clump-forming, perennial succulent with a basal rosette of up to 20 rough, grayish-green leaves, to 3ft (1m) long and 2in (5cm) across. Produces pendent, tubular, bright red flowers in summer in spikes over 6ft (2m) tall. **H** 3ft (1m), **S** 10ft (3m). Min. 32°F (0°C).

☀ ◊ H11–10

Crassula arborescens
(Silver jade plant)
Perennial succulent with a thick, robust stem crowned by branches bearing rounded, silvery-blue leaves, often with red edges. Has 5-petaled, pink flowers in fall–winter. **H** 12ft (4m), **S** 6ft (2m). Min. 45°F (7°C).

☀ ◊ Z11 H11–1

x Pachyveria glauca
Clump-forming, perennial succulent with a dense, basal rosette of fleshy, incurved, oval, silvery-blue leaves, to 2½in (6cm) long, with darker marks. Bears star-shaped, yellow flowers, each with a red tip, in spring. **H** and **S** 12in (30cm). Min. 45°F (7°C).

☀ ◊ Z10–11 H12–3

Pachyphytum oviferum (Moonstones, Sugared-almond plum)
Clump-forming, perennial succulent with a basal rosette of oval, pinkish-blue leaves. Stem bears 10–15 bell-shaped flowers, with powder-blue calyces and orange-red petals, in spring. **H** 4in (10cm), **S** 12in (30cm). Min. 50°F (10°C).

☀ ◊ H11–10

Maihuenia poeppigii
Slow-growing, clump-forming, perennial cactus. Has a cylindrical, branched, spiny, green-brown stem. Most branches produce a spike of cylindrical, green leaves at the tip, with a funnel-shaped, yellow flower in summer. **H** 2½in (6cm), **S** 12in (30cm). Min. 5°F (-15°C).

☀ ◊ Z11 H11–6

Ceropegia linearis (Heart vine, Rosary vine, String-of-hearts)
Semievergreen, trailing, succulent subshrub with tuberous roots. Leaves redden in sun. Has hairy, pinkish-green flowers from spring to fall. **H** 3ft (1m), **S** indefinite. Min. 45°F (7°C).

◐ ◊ H11–10

Kalanchoe tomentosa
(Panda plant, Pussy ears)
Bushy, perennial succulent with thick, oval, gray leaves, covered with velvety bristles and often edged with brown at tips. Has yellowish-purple flowers in winter. **H** 20in (50cm), **S** 12in (30cm). Min. 50°F (10°C).

☀ ◊ Z11 H11–1

Frailea pygmaea
Columnar, perennial cactus with a much-ribbed, dark green stem bearing white to light brown spines. Buds, which rarely open to flattish, yellow flowers in summer, become tufts of spherical, spiny seed pods. **H** to 2in (5cm), **S** ¾in (2cm). Min. 41°F (5°C).

◐ ◊ H11–10

Aeonium tabuliforme
Prostrate, almost stemless, short-lived, perennial succulent with a basal rosette, to 12in (30cm) across, like a flat, bright green plate. Has star-shaped, yellow flowers in spring, then dies. Propagate from seed. **H** 2in (5cm), **S** 12in (30cm). Min. 41°F (5°C).

☀ ◊ Z9–11 H9–4

Mammillaria microhelia
Columnar, perennial cactus with a ⅝in (5cm) wide, green stem bearing cream or brown spines, discoloring with age. Has ⅝in (5cm) wide, yellow or pink flowers in spring. Offsets slowly with age. **H** 8in (20cm), **S** 16in (40cm). Min. 41°F (5°C).

☀ ◊ H11–10

Argyroderma pearsonii
Prostrate, egg-shaped, perennial succulent. A united pair of very fleshy, silvery-gray leaves has a deep fissure in which a red flower, 1¼in (3cm) across, appears in summer. **H** 1¼in (3cm), **S** 2in (5cm). Min. 41°F (5°C).

☀ ◊ H11–10

Lithops lesliei var. albinica
Egg-shaped, perennial succulent, divided into 2 unequal-sized leaves; convex, pale green, upper surfaces have dark green and yellow marks. Bears a white flower in late summer or early fall. **H** ¾–1¼in (2–3cm), **S** 2in (5cm). Min. 41°F (5°C).

☀ ◊ H11–10

Schwantesia ruedebuschii
Mat-forming, perennial succulent with cylindrical, bluish-green leaves, 1–2in (3–5cm) long, with expanded tips. Leaf edges each produce 3–7 minute, blue teeth with brown tips. Has yellow flowers in summer. **H** 2in (5cm), **S** 8in (20cm). Min. 41°F (5°C).

☀ ◊ Z12–15 H12–10

Echinopsis marsoneri
Columnar, perennial cactus with a 20–25-ribbed, bluish- to dark green stem that has yellow, radial spines with longer, darker, central ones. In summer produces yellow flowers, 3in (7cm) across, with red throats. **H** 12in (30cm), **S** 6in (15cm). Min. 41°F (5°C).

☀ ◊ Z11 H12–6

Echinopsis pentlandii
Clump-forming or solitary, variable, perennial cactus with a 10–20-ribbed stem and 6–20 spined aeroles. Has white, pink, purple or orange flowers, with paler throats, in summer. **H** 3in (8cm), **S** 4in (10cm). Min. 41°F (5°C).

☀ ◊ H11–10

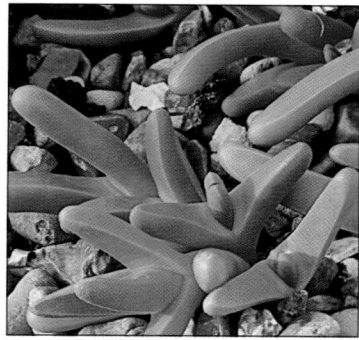

Argyroderma fissum
Clump-forming, perennial succulent with finger-shaped, fleshy leaves, 2–4in (5–10cm) long and often reddish at the tip. Has light red flowers between leaves in summer. **H** 6in (15cm), **S** 4in (10cm). Min. 41°F (5°C).

☀ ◊ H11–10

Lithops dorotheae
Egg-shaped, perennial succulent, divided into 2 unequal-sized leaves, pale pink-yellow to green with darker areas and red marks on upper surfaces. Produces a daisylike, yellow flower in summer or fall. **H** ¾–1¼in (2–3cm), **S** 2in (5cm). Min. 41°F (5°C).

☀ ◊ H11–10

Pachyphytum compactum
Clump-forming, perennial succulent with a basal rosette of green leaves, each narrowing to a blunt point, with angular, paler edges. Stems each bear 3–10 flowers with green to pink calyces and orange petals in spring. **H** 6in (15cm), **S** indefinite. Min. 41°F (5°C).

☀ ◊ H11–10

Echinopsis backebergii
Clump-forming, almost spherical, perennial cactus with a 10–15-ribbed, spined, dark green stem. Has funnel-shaped, pink, red or purple flowers, with paler throats, in summer. **H** 4in (10cm), **S** 6in (15cm). Min. 41°F (5°C).

☀ ◊ H11–10

Haworthia arachnoidea
Slow-growing, clump-forming, perennial succulent with a basal rosette of triangular leaves. Bears soft, white teeth along leaf margins. Has white flowers from spring to fall. **H** 2in (5cm), **S** 4in (10cm). Min. 43°F (6°C).

◑ ◊ H11–10

TENDER AND EXOTIC PLANTS

Carnegiea gigantea (Saguaro)
Very slow-growing, perennial cactus with a thick, 12–24-ribbed, spiny, green stem. Tends to branch and bears short, funnel-shaped, fleshy, white flowers at stem tips in summer, only when over 12ft (4m) high. **H** to 40ft (12m), **S** 10ft (3m). Min. 45°F (7°C).

☀ ◊ H11–10

Kalanchoe daigremontiana (Mexican hat plant)
Erect, perennial succulent with a stem bearing fleshy, boat-shaped, toothed leaves. Produces a plantlet in each leaf notch. Umbels of pink flowers appear at stem tops in winter. **H** to 3ft (1m), **S** 12in (30cm). Min. 45°F (7°C).

☀ ◊ Z11 H11–1

Adromischus maculatus
Clump-forming, perennial succulent with rounded, glossy, green leaves with purple marks. Leaf tips are often wavy. Carries tubular, purplish-white flowers, on a 12in (30cm) tall stem, in summer. **H** 2½in (6cm), **S** 4–6in (10–15cm). Min. 45°F (7°C).

☀◑ ◊ H11–10

Echinopsis spachiana (Torch cactus)
Clump-forming, perennial cactus with glossy, green stems bearing 10–15 ribs and pale golden spines. Fragrant, funnel-shaped, white flowers open at night in summer. **H** and **S** 6ft (2m). Min. 46°F (8°C).

☀ ◊ H11–10

Echinopsis candicans
Clump-forming, branching, perennial cactus with up to 11 ribs. Areoles each have 10–15 radial spines and 4 central ones. Fragrant, funnel-shaped, white flowers open at night in summer. **H** 3ft (1m), **S** indefinite. Min. 46°F (8°C).

☀ ◊ H11–10

Echinocereus schmollii (Lamb's-tail cactus)
Erect to prostrate, tuberous cactus with 8–10-ribbed, purplish-green stems and mostly white spines. Has pinkish-purple flowers in spring-summer. **H** and **S** 12in (30cm). Min. 46°F (8°C).

☀ ◊ Z11 H12–10

Aloe vera
Clump-forming, perennial succulent with basal rosettes of tapering, thick leaves, mottled green, later gray-green. Flower stems carry bell-shaped, yellow flowers in summer. Propagate by offsets as plant is sterile. **H** 24in (60cm), **S** indefinite. Min. 50°F (10°C).

☀ ◊ ❶ Z10–11 H11–10

Haworthia truncata
Clump-forming, perennial succulent with a basal fan of broad, erect, rough, blue-gray leaves with pale gray lines and flat ends. Produces small, tubular, white flowers, with spreading petals, from spring to fall. **H** ¾in (2cm), **S** 4in (10cm). Min. 50°F (10°C).

☀◑ ◊ H11–10

Dioscorea elephantipes (Elephant's foot)
Very slow-growing, deciduous, perennial succulent with a domed, woody trunk, annual, climbing stems and yellow flowers in fall. **H** 20in (50cm), **S** 3ft (1m). Min. 50°F (10°C).

☀ ◊ Z8–10 H11–10

Lophophora williamsii (Dumpling cactus, Mescal button)
Very slow-growing, clump-forming, perennial cactus with an 8-ribbed, blue-green stem. Masses of pink flowers appear in summer on plants over 1¼in (3cm) high. **H** 2in (5cm), **S** 3in (8cm). Min. 50°F (10°C).

☀ ◊ Z9–11 H12–7

Pachycereus schottii
Columnar, perennial cactus, branching with age. Olive- to dark green stem, covered with small, white spines, bears 4–15 ribs. Funnel-shaped, pink flowers are produced at night in summer.
H 22ft (7m), **S** 6ft (2m). Min. 50ºF (10ºC).

☀ ◊ H11–10

Rhipsalis floccosa
Pendent, perennial cactus with cylindrical, green stems, to ½in (1cm) across, branching less than many other *Rhipsalis* species. Has masses of very pale pink flowers in early summer, then pinkish-white fruits. **H** 3ft (1m), **S** 20in (50cm). Min. 50ºF (10ºC).

◑ ◊ H11–10

Oreocereus celsianus
(Old man of the Andes)
Slow-growing, perennial cactus. Has heavy and wispy spines. Mature plants bear pink flowers in summer.
H 3ft (1m), **S** 12in (30cm). Min. 50ºF (10ºC).

☀ ◊ H11–1

Epithelantha micromeris
Slow-growing, spherical, perennial cactus with a green stem completely obscured by close-set areoles bearing tiny, white spines. Bears funnel-shaped, pale pinkish-red flowers, ¼in (0.5cm) across, on a woolly crown in summer. **H** and **S** 1½in (4cm). Min. 50ºF (10ºC).

☀ ◊ H11–10

Duvalia corderoyi
Clump-forming, perennial succulent. Has a prostrate, leafless stem with 6 often purple, indistinct ribs. Bears star-shaped, dull green flowers, ½in (1cm) across and covered in purple hairs, in summer–fall. **H** 2in (5cm), **S** 24in (60cm). Min. 50ºF (10ºC).

◑ ◊ H11–10

Euphorbia obesa (Living baseball)
Spherical, perennial succulent. Spineless, dark green stem, often checkered light green, has 8 low ribs. Crown bears rounded heads of cupped, yellow flowers in summer. **H** 5in (12cm), **S** 6in (15cm). Min. 50ºF (10ºC).

☀ ◊ ! H11–10

ALOES
Aloes are abundant in Mediterranean and African gardens. There is a huge range of species and hybrids providing a kaleidoscope of growth forms, flowers, and leaf variegation. Unlike agaves, aloes do not die after flowering, but gradually produce a trunk, becoming shrubs or small trees. Aloes typically produce their leaves singly, and the center of the rosette is usually hollow, reminiscent of a bromeliad. A few species, such as *A. aristata*, are frost-hardy, and can be grown in rock gardens or at the base of a south-facing wall in mild areas.

A. arborescens 'Variegata' ①

A. striata ①   A. variegata ①

A. ferox ①   A. aristata ①

A. ciliaris ①   A. hemmingii ①

TENDER AND EXOTIC PLANTS

GREEN

Pachypodium lamerei
Treelike, perennial succulent with a
spiny, pale green stem crowned by linear
leaves. Has fragrant, trumpet-shaped,
creamy-white flowers in summer, on
plants over 5ft (1.5m) tall. Stems branch
after flowering. **H** 20ft (6m), **S** 6ft (2m).
Min. 52°F (Min.11°C).

☼ ○ H11–6

Pachycereus marginatus
(Organ-pipe cactus)
Columnar, perennial cactus with a 5-
or 6-ribbed, branching, shiny stem.
Areoles bear minute spines. Produces
funnel-shaped, white flowers in summer.
H 22ft (7m), **S** 10ft (3m). Min. 52°F (11°C).

☼ ○ H11–10

Caralluma joannis
Clump-forming, perennial succulent
with blue-gray stems and rudimentary
leaves on stem angles. Bears clusters of
star-shaped, purple flowers, with short,
fine hairs on petal tips, in late summer
near stem tips. **H** 8in (20cm), **S** 3ft (1m).
Min. 52°F (11°C).

☼ ○ H11–10

Epiphyllum anguliger
(Fishbone cactus)
Erect, then pendent, perennial cactus.
Has strap-shaped, flattened, green stems
with indented margins. Produces
tubular, 4in (10cm) wide, white flowers
in summer. **H** 3ft (1m), **S** 16in (40cm).
Min. 52°F (11°C).

☼ ○ Z11 H11–1

Neobuxbaumia euphorbioides
Columnar, perennial cactus. Has
gray-green to dark green stems,
4in (10cm) across, with 8–10 ribs and
1 or 2 black spines per areole. Funnel-
shaped, wine-red flowers appear in
summer. **H** to 10ft (3m), **S** 3ft (1m).
Min. 59°F (15°C).

☼ ○ H11–10

Melocactus intortus (Melon cactus)
Flattened spherical, perennial cactus.
Has an 18–20-ribbed stem with yellow-
brown spines. Crown matures to a
white column with brown spines. Bears
pink flowers in summer. **H** 8in (20cm),
S 10in (25cm). Min. 59°F (15°C).

☼ ○ H11–10

YELLOW

Opuntia humifusa
Prostrate, perennial cactus. Each areole
bears up to 3 spines, 1¼in (3cm) long.
Has flat, rounded to oval, purple-tinged,
dark green stem segments, 3–7in
(7–18cm) long. Bears 3in (8cm) wide,
yellow flowers in spring–summer. Keep
dry in winter. **H** 6in (15cm), **S** 3ft (1m).

☼ ○ ❗ Z11 H11–9

Conophytum bilobum
Slow-growing, clump-forming,
perennial succulent with 2-lobed,
fleshy, green leaves, each 1½in (4cm)
long and ¾in (2cm) wide. Has a flared,
yellow flower, 1¼in (3cm) across,
in fall. **H** 1½in (4cm), **S** 6in (15cm).
Min. 39°F (4°C).

☼ ○ H11–10

Mammillaria elongata (Lace cactus)
Clump-forming, perennial cactus. Has
a columnar, green stem, 1¼in (3cm)
across, densely covered with yellow,
golden or brown spines. Bears
cream flowers in summer. Offsets
freely. **H** 6in (15cm), **S** 12in (30cm).
Min. 41°F (5°C).

☼ ○ H11–10

Astrophytum myriostigma
(Bishop's cap, Bishop's mitre)
Slow-growing, spherical to slightly
elongated, perennial cactus. A fleshy
stem has 4–6 ribs and is flecked with
tiny tufts of white spines. Bears yellow
flowers in summer. **H** 12in (30cm),
S 8in (20cm). Min. 41°F (5°C).

☼ ○ H11–10

Ferocactus cylindraceus
Slow-growing, columnar, perennial
cactus, spherical when young. Green,
10–20-ribbed stem has large, hooked,
red or yellow spines. Funnel-shaped,
yellow flowers form in summer on plants
over 10in (25cm) across. **H** 10ft (3m),
S 32in (80cm). Min. 41°F (5°C).

☼ ○ H11–10

Rhombophyllum rhomboideum
Clump-forming, perennial succulent.
Linear, glossy, gray-green leaves have
expanded middles and white margins.
Stems, ¾–2in (2–5cm) long, bear 3–7
yellow flowers, to 1½in (4cm) across,
in summer. **H** 2in (5cm), **S** 6in (15cm).
Min. 41°F (5°C).

☼ ○ H11–10

Astrophytum ornatum
Elongated, spherical, perennial cactus with a very fleshy, 8-ribbed stem. Crown of each rib bears 2–4½in (5–11cm) long spines on each raised areole. Has yellow flowers, 3in (8cm) across, in summer. **H** 6in (15cm), **S** 5in (12cm). Min. 41°F (5°C).

☼ ◊ H11–10

Lithops pseudotruncatella subsp. dendritica
Egg-shaped, perennial succulent, divided into 2 unequal-sized, gray leaves with dark green and red marks on upper surfaces. Has a yellow flower in summer or fall. **H** ¾–1¼in (2–3cm), **S** 1½in (4cm). Min. 41°F (5°C).

☼ ◊ H11–10

Pleiospilos bolusii
(Living rock, Mimicry plant)
Clump-forming, perennial succulent with 1 or 2 pairs of gray leaves, often wider than long and narrowing at incurved tips. Has golden-yellow flowers in early fall. **H** 4in (10cm), **S** 8in (20cm). Min. 41°F (5°C).

☼ ◊ H11–10

Echinopsis aurea
Columnar, perennial cactus. Has narrow, much-ribbed, green stems covered with pale, radial spines often surrounded by 1–3 very sturdy, central spines, to 1in (2.5cm) long. Produces yellow flowers in summer. **H** and **S** 4in (10cm). Min. 41°F (5°C).

☼ ◊ Z11 H12–10

Glottiphyllum nelii
Clump-forming, perennial succulent with semicylindrical, fleshy, green leaves, to 1½in (5cm) long. Carries daisylike, golden-yellow flowers, 1½in (5cm) across, in spring–summer. **H** 2in (5cm), **S** 12in (30cm). Min. 41°F (5°C).

☼ ◊ H11–10

Pleiospilos compactus
Clump-forming, perennial succulent with 1 or 2 pairs of thick, gray leaves, to 3in (8cm) long. Bears coconut-scented, yellow flowers in early fall. **H** 4in (10cm), **S** 12in (30cm). Min. 41°F (5°C).

☼ ◊ Z10–11 H12–6

Lithops schwantesii
Egg-shaped, perennial succulent, divided into 2 unequal-sized leaves with blue or red marks on upper surface. Has a yellow flower in late summer or fall. **H** ¾–1¼in (2–3cm), **S** 1¼in (3cm). Min. 41°F (5°C).

☼ ◊ H11–10

Aichryson x aizoides var. domesticum 'Variegatum'
Prostrate, perennial succulent with stems crowned by rosettes of hairy, cream-marked, green leaves, sometimes pure cream. Has star-shaped, yellow flowers in spring. **H** 6in (15cm), **S** 16in (40cm). Min. 41°F (5°C).

☼ ◊ H11–10

Fenestraria rhopalophylla subsp. aurantiaca (Baby's toes)
Clump-forming, perennial succulent with a basal rosette of glossy leaves. Has yellow flowers in late summer and fall. **H** 2in (5cm), **S** 12in (30cm). Min. 43°F (6°C).

☼ ◊ H11–10

Faucaria tigrina (Tiger-jaws)
Clump-forming, stemless, perennial succulent. Fleshy, green leaves, 2in (5cm) long, have 9 or 10 teeth along each margin. Bears daisylike, yellow flowers, 2in (5cm) across, in fall. **H** 4in (10cm), **S** 20in (50cm). Min. 43°F (6°C).

☼ ◊ H11–10

Thelocactus setispinus
Slow-growing, perennial cactus with a 13-ribbed stem and yellow or white spines. Fragrant, yellow flowers with red throats appear in summer, only on plants over 2in (5cm) across. **H** and **S** 12in (30cm). Min. 45°F (7°C).

☼ ◊ Z12–15 H12–10

Sclerocactus scheeri
Spherical to columnar, perennial cactus. Stem bears spines and, in spring, funnel-shaped, straw-colored flowers. Lowest and longest spines are darker and hooked. **H** 4in (10cm), **S** 2½in (6cm). Min. 45–50°F (7–10°C).

☼ ◊ Z13–15 H12–10

TENDER AND EXOTIC PLANTS

YELLOW

Titanopsis calcarea
Clump-forming, perennial succulent
with a basal rosette of very fleshy,
triangular, blue-gray leaves covered
in wartlike, gray-white and beige
tubercles. Has yellow flowers from
fall to spring. **H** 1¼in (3cm), **S** 4in (10cm).
Min. 46°F (8°C).

☀ ◊ Z13–15 H12–10

Rebutia arenacea
Spherical, perennial cactus. Has a
brown-green stem with white spines
on spirally arranged tubercles. Has
golden-yellow blooms, to 1¼in (3cm)
across, in spring. **H** 2in (5cm),
S 2½in (6cm). Min. 50°F (10°C).

☀ ◊ Z11 H12–1

Parodia chrysacanthion
Spherical, perennial cactus with a
much-ribbed, green stem densely
covered with bristlelike, golden spines,
each ½–¾in (1–2cm) long. Crown bears
yellow flowers in spring and, often,
pale yellow wool. **H** and **S** 12in (30cm).
Min. 50°F (10°C).

☀ ◊ H11–10

Disocactus 'Jennifer Ann'
Erect, then pendent, perennial cactus.
Has strap-shaped, flattened, green
stems with toothed margins. Bears
yellow flowers, 6in (15cm) across,
in spring. **H** 12in (30cm), **S** 20in (50cm).
Min. 50°F (10°C).

☀ ◊ Z11 H12–10

Opuntia tunicata
Mounded, perennial cactus. Cylindrical,
green stem segments are covered
with 2in (5cm) long, golden spines,
enclosed in a silver papery sheath.
Bears shallowly saucer-shaped, yellow
flowers in spring–summer. **H** 2ft (60cm),
S 3ft (1m). Min. 50°F (10°C).

☀ ◊ ⚠ H11–1

Stapelia gigantea
Clump-forming, perennial succulent.
In summer–fall bears star-shaped,
red-marked, yellow-brown flowers,
12in (30cm) across, with white-haired,
recurved edges. **H** to 8in (20cm),
S indefinite. Min. 52°F (11°C).

☀ ◊ Z13–15 H12–10

ORANGE

Echinocereus triglochidiatus
var. paucispinus
Clump-forming, perennial cactus with
a 4in (10cm) wide, dark green stem that
has 6 or 7 ribs, and 4–6 spines, 1¼–1½in
(3–4cm) long, per areole. Has orange-
red flowers in spring. **H** 8in (20cm),
S 20in (50cm). Min. 41°F (5°C).

☀ ◊ Z11 H11–9

Conophytum frutescens
Slow-growing, spherical, perennial
succulent forming clumps of 2-lobed,
very fleshy, gray-green leaves, often
with a red spot on edge of fissure
between the lobes. Carries copper-
orange flowers in fall. **H** 1¼in (3cm),
S indefinite. Min. 39°F (4°C).

☀ ◊ Z11 H12–10

Rebutia fiebrigii
Clump-forming, perennial cactus.
Has a dark green stem densely covered
with soft, white spines, to ¼in (0.5cm)
long. Bears bright orange flowers,
¾–1¼in (2–3cm) across, in late
spring. **H** 4in (10cm), **S** 6in (15cm).
Min. 41°F (5°C).

☀ ◊ H11–10

Lampranthus aurantiacus
Erect, then prostrate, sparse-branching
perennial succulent with short,
cylindrical, tapering, gray-green
leaves. Masses of daisylike, bright
orange flowers, 2in (5cm) wide,
open in summer sun. **H** 20in (50cm),
S 28in (70cm). Min. 41°F (5°C).

☀ ◊ H11–10

Malephora crocea
Erect or spreading, perennial succulent
with semi-cylindrical, blue-green
leaves on short shoots. Carries solitary
daisylike, orange-yellow flowers,
reddened on outsides, in spring–
summer. **H** 8in (20cm), **S** 3ft (1m).
Min. 41°F (5°C).

☀ ◊ H11–10

Kalanchoe delagoensis
Erect, perennial succulent with long,
almost cylindrical, gray-green leaves
with reddish-brown mottling and
flattened, notched tips that form plantlets.
Bears an umbel of orange-yellow flowers
in late winter. **H** to 3ft (1m), **S** 12in (30cm).
Min. 46°F (8°C).

☀ ◊ H11–10

PLANT DICTIONARY

A complete listing of more than 8,000 plants, suitable for growing in temperate gardens worldwide. Includes full descriptions of the characteristics and cultivation of over 4,000 plants not already described in the Plant Catalog.

ABELIA
CAPRIFOLIACEAE

Genus of deciduous, semievergreen or evergreen shrubs, grown for their foliage and freely borne flowers. Does best against a south- or west-facing wall at the limits of hardiness. Requires a sheltered, sunny position and fertile, well-drained soil. Remove dead wood in late spring and prune out older branches after flowering to restrict growth, if required. Propagate by softwood cuttings in summer.

A.'Edward Goucher', illus. p.153.
A. floribunda (Mexican abelia). Evergreen, arching shrub. **H** 10ft (3m), **S** 12ft (4m). Has oval, glossy, dark green leaves and, in early summer, drooping, tubular, bright red flowers. Z8–11 H11–8.
A. x grandiflora, illus. p.113. **'Francis Mason'** is a vigorous, semievergreen, arching shrub. **H** 6ft (2m), **S** 10ft (3m). Has coppery-yellow young shoots and oval, yellowish-green leaves, darker in centers. Bears a profusion of fragrant, bell-shaped, white flowers, tinged with pink, from mid-summer to mid-fall. Z6–9 H9–6.
A. schumannii, illus. p.154.
A. triflora, illus. p.113.

ABELIOPHYLLUM
OLEACEAE

Genus of one species of deciduous shrub, grown for its winter flowers. In cold regions grow against a south- or west-facing wall. Requires plenty of sun and fertile, well-drained soil. Thin out excess older shoots after flowering each year to encourage vigorous, young growth. Propagate by softwood cuttings in summer.

A. distichum (Korean abelialeaf). Deciduous, open shrub. **H** and **S** 4ft (1.2m). In late winter produces fragrant, star-shaped, white flowers, tinged with pink, on bare stems; flowers may be damaged by hard frosts. Leaves are oval and dark green. Z5–9 H9–1.

ABIES
Silver fir
PINACEAE

Genus of tall conifers with whorled branches. Spirally arranged leaves are needlelike, flattened, usually soft and often have silvery bands beneath. Bears erect cones that ripen in their first fall to release seeds and scales. See also CONIFERS.

A. alba (European silver fir). Fast-growing, conical conifer. **H** 50–80ft (15–25m), **S** 15–25ft (5–8m). Has silvery-gray bark and dull green leaves, silvery beneath. Cylindrical cones, 4–6in (10–15cm) long, ripen to red-brown. Z5–8 H8–5.
A. amabilis (Pacific fir). Conical conifer. **H** 50ft (15m), **S** 12–15ft (4–5m). Dense, notched, square-tipped, glossy, dark green leaves, banded with white beneath, are borne on hairy, gray shoots. Oblong, violet-blue cones are 3½–6in (9–15cm) long. Z6–8 H8–6. **'Spreading Star'**, **H** 20in (50cm), **S** 12–15ft (4–5m), is a procumbent form suitable for use as a groundcover.
A. balsamea (Balsam fir). **f. hudsonia**, syn. *A. balsamea* Hudsonia Group is a dense, dwarf conifer of flattened to globose habit. **H** and **S** 2–3ft (60cm–1m). Has smooth, gray bark and gray-green leaves that are semi-spirally arranged. Z3–6 H6–1. **Hudsonia Group.** See *A. balsamea* f. *hudsonia*. **'Nana'** is another dwarf form that makes a dense, globose mound with leaves that are spirally arranged.
A. cephalonica (Greek fir). Upright conifer with a conical crown; old trees have massive, spreading, erect branches. **H** 70–100ft (20–30m), **S** 15–30ft (5–10m). Sharp, stiff, glossy, deep green leaves are whitish-green beneath. Cylindrical, tapered cones, 4–6in (10–15cm) long, are brown when ripe. Z5–6 H6–5. **'Meyer's Dwarf'** (illus. p.105), **H** 20in (50cm), **S** 5ft (1.5m), has short leaves and forms a spreading, flat topped-mound.
A. concolor (White fir). Upright conifer. **H** 50–100ft (15–30m), **S** 15–25ft (5–8m). Has widely spreading, blue-green or gray leaves and cylindrical, green or pale blue cones, 3–5in (8–12cm) long. Z3–7 H7–1. **'Argentea'**, illus. p.95. **'Compacta'**, syn. *A. concolor* 'Glauca Compacta' (illus. p.105), **H** 6ft (2m), **S** 6–10ft (2–3m), is a cultivar with steel-blue foliage. **'Glauca Compacta'**. See *A. concolor* 'Compacta'.
A. delavayi (Delavay's fir). Upright conifer producing tiered, spreading branches. **H** 30–50ft (10–15m), **S** 12–20ft (4–6m). Has maroon shoots and curved, bright deep green leaves, spirally arranged, with vivid silver bands beneath and rolled margins. Cones are narrowly cylindrical, 2½–6in (6–15cm) long, and violet-blue. Z8–9 H9–8.
A. forrestii, illus. p.100.

A. grandis, illus. p.98.
A. homolepis (Nikko fir). Conifer that is conical when young, later columnar. **H** 50ft (15m), **S** 20ft (6m). Pink-gray bark peels in fine flakes. Has pale green leaves, silver beneath, and cylindrical, violet-blue cones, 3–5in (8–12cm) long. Tolerates urban conditions. Z4–6 H6–4.
A. koreana, illus. p.104.
A. lasiocarpa (Subalpine fir). Narrowly conical conifer. **H** 30–50ft (10–15m), **S** 10–12ft (3–4m). Has gray or blue-green leaves and cylindrical, violet-blue cones, 2½–4in (6–10cm) long. Z5–6 H6–5. **var. arizonica 'Compacta'**, **H** 12–15ft (4–5m), **S** 5–6ft (1.5–2m), is a slow-growing, ovoid to conical tree with corky bark and blue foliage. **'Roger Watson'**, **H** and **S** 2½ft (75cm), is dwarf and conical, with silvery-gray leaves.
A. nordmanniana (Caucasian fir). Columnar, dense conifer. **H** 50–80ft (15–25m), **S** 15ft (5m). Luxuriant foliage is rich green. Cylindrical cones, 4–6in (10–15cm) long, are green-brown, ripening to brown. Z4–6 H6–4. **'Golden Spreader'**, **H** and **S** 3ft (1m), is a dwarf form with a spreading habit and bright golden-yellow leaves.
A. procera, illus. p.95.
A. veitchii, illus. p.96.

ABUTILON
Flowering maple
MALVACEAE

Genus of evergreen, semievergreen or deciduous shrubs, perennials and annuals, grown for their flowers and foliage. Needs full sun or partial shade and fertile, well-drained soil. Water containerized specimens freely when in full growth, less at other times. In the growing season, young plants may need tip pruning to promote bushy growth. Mature specimens may have previous season's stems cut back hard annually in early spring. Tie lax-growing species to a support if necessary. Propagate by seed in spring or by softwood, greenwood or semiripe cuttings in summer. Whitefly and red spider mite may be troublesome.

A. 'Ashford Red', illus. p.137.
A. 'Golden Fleece'. Strong-growing, evergreen, rounded shrub. **H** and **S** 6–10ft (2–3m). Has maple- to heart-shaped, serrated, rich green leaves. Pendent, bell-shaped, yellow flowers are borne from spring to fall. Z12–11 H10–1.
A. 'Kentish Belle', illus. p.162.
A. megapotamicum, illus. p.203.
A. pictum of gardens, syn. *A. striatum*.

'Thompsonii', illus. p.325.
A. striatum. See *A. pictum* of gardens.
A. x suntense. Fast-growing, deciduous, upright, arching shrub. **H** 15ft (5m), **S** 10ft (30m) Has oval, lobed, toothed, dark green leaves. Produces an abundance of large, bowl-shaped, pale to deep purple, occasionally white, flowers from late spring to early summer. Z13–14 H11–6. **'Violetta'**, illus. p.138.
A. vitifolium. Fast-growing, deciduous, upright shrub. **H** 12ft (4m), **S** 8ft (2.5m). Masses of large, bowl-shaped, purplish-blue flowers are produced in late spring and early summer. Has oval, lobed, sharply toothed, gray-green leaves. Z8–9 H9–8. **var. album**, illus. p.113. **'Veronica Tennant'**, illus. p.114.

ACACIA
Wattle
LEGUMINOSAE/MIMOSACEAE

Genus of evergreen, semievergreen or deciduous trees and shrubs, grown for their tiny flowers, composed of massed stamens, and for their foliage. Many species have phyllodes instead of true leaves. Requires full sun and well-drained soil. Propagate by seed in spring. Red spider mite and mealy bug may be problematic.

A. baileyana, illus. p.92. **'Purpurea'**, illus. p.84.
A. dealbata, illus. p.211.
A. juniperina. See *A. ulicifolia*.
A. longifolia (Sydney golden wattle). Evergreen, spreading tree. **H** and **S** 20ft (6m). Has narrowly oblong, dark green phyllodes. Bears cylindrical clusters of golden-yellow flowers in early spring. Z9–11 H12–1.
A. podalyriifolia (Mount Morgan wattle, Queensland silver wattle). Evergreen, arching shrub. **H** 10–15ft (3–5m), **S** 10–12ft (3–4m). Has blue-green phyllodes and produces racemes of bright yellow flowers in spring. Z11 H11–10.
A. pravissima, illus. p.92.
A. pulchella, illus. p.458.
A. ulicifolia, syn. *A. juniperina*. Evergreen, bushy shrub. **H** 3ft (1m), **S** 5ft (1.5m). Has very narrow, cylindrical, spine-like, rich green phyllodes and, in mid-spring, globular clusters of pale yellow flowers. Z11–15 H12–10.
A. verticillata (Prickly Moses). Evergreen, spreading tree or bushy shrub. **H** and **S** 28ft (9m). Has needlelike, dark green phyllodes and, in spring, dense, bottle brushlike spikes of bright yellow flowers. Z11 H11–10.

ACAENA

New Zealand burr

ROSACEAE

Genus of mainly summer-flowering subshrubs and perennials, evergreen in all but the severest winters, grown for their leaves and colored burs and as groundcover. Has tight, rounded heads of small flowers. Is good for a rock garden. Some species may be invasive. Needs sun or partial shade and well-drained soil. Propagate by division in early spring or by seed in fall.

A. anserinifolia. See *A. novae-zelandiae*.
A. buchananii. Vigorous, evergreen, prostrate perennial. **H** ³/₄in (2cm), **S** 30in (75cm) or more. Bears glaucous leaves composed of 11–17 oval, toothed leaflets. Globose, green flower heads are borne in summer and develop into spiny, yellow-green burs. Z6–8 H8–6.
A. caerulea. See *A. caesiiglauca*.
A. caesiiglauca, syn. *A. caerulea*, illus. p.374.
A. microphylla, illus. p.374.
A. novae-zelandiae, syn. *A. anserinifolia* of gardens. Vigorous, evergreen, prostrate subshrub. **H** 4in (10cm), **S** 30in (75cm) or more. Has brown-green leaves, divided into 9–13 oval, toothed leaflets. In summer, red-spined, brownish burs develop from spherical heads of greenish-brown flowers. Z6–8 H8–6.
A. 'Pewter'. See *A. saccaticupula* 'Blue Haze'.
A. saccaticupula 'Blue Haze', syn. *A.* 'Pewter'. Vigorous, evergreen, prostrate perennial. **H** 4in (10cm), **S** 30in (75cm) or more. Leaves are divided into 9–15 oval, toothed, steel-blue leaflets. Produces spherical, brownish-red flower heads that develop in fall to dark red burs with pinkish-red spines. Z7–9 H9–7.

ACALYPHA

EUPHORBIACEAE

Genus of evergreen shrubs and perennials, grown for their flowers and foliage. Needs partial shade and rich, well-drained soil. Water container plants freely when in full growth, much less at other times and in low temperatures. Stem tips of young plants may be removed in growing season to promote branching. Propagate by softwood, greenwood or semiripe cuttings in summer. Red spider mite, whitefly and mealy bug may be troublesome.
A. hispida (Chenille plant). Evergreen, upright, soft-stemmed shrub. **H** 6ft (2m) or more, **S** 3–6ft (1–2m). Has oval, toothed, lustrous, deep green leaves. Tiny, crimson flowers hang in long, dense, catkin-like spikes, intermittently year-round. May be grown as a short-lived cordon. Z11 H11–6.
A. wilkesiana, illus. p.456.

ACANTHOLIMON

Prickly thrift

PLUMBAGINACEAE

Genus of evergreen perennials, grown for their flowers and tight cushions of spiny leaves. Is suitable for rock gardens and walls. Prefers sun and well-drained soil. Dislikes damp winters. Seed is rarely set in cultivation. Propagate by softwood cuttings in late spring.
A. glumaceum, illus. p.363.

A. venustum. Evergreen, cushion-forming perennial. **H** and **S** 4in (10cm). Small spikes of star-shaped, pink flowers, on 1¼in (3cm) stems, are produced from late spring to early summer amid rosetted, spear-shaped, spiny, blue-green leaves that are edged with silver. Needs a very hot, well-drained site. Makes an excellent alpine house plant. Z7–9 H9–7.

Acanthopanax. See *Eleutherococcus*, except for **A. ricinifolius**, for which see *Kalopanax septemlobus*.

ACANTHUS

Bear's breeches

ACANTHACEAE

Genus of perennials, some of which are semievergreen, grown for their large, deeply cut leaves and their spikes of flowers. Prefers full sun, warm conditions and well-drained soil, but will tolerate shade. Protect crowns in first winter after planting. Long, thong-like roots make plants difficult to eradicate if wrongly placed. Propagate by seed or division in early fall or spring, or by root cuttings in winter.
A. balcanicus. See *A. hungaricus*.
A. dioscoridis. Upright, architectural perennial. **H** to 3ft (1m), **S** 18in (45cm). Has oval, deeply cut, rigid, basal leaves and hairy stems. Dense spikes of small, funnel-shaped, purple-and-white flowers are produced in summer. Z6–9 H9–6.
A. hungaricus, syn. *A. balcanicus*, *A. longifolius* (Balkan bear's breeches). Upright perennial. **H** 2–3ft (60cm–1m), **S** 3ft (1m). Has long, deeply cut, basal, dark green leaves. Spikes of white or pink-flushed flowers, set in spiny, red-purple bracts, are borne in summer. Z6–9 H9–5.
A. longifolius. See *A. hungaricus*.
A. mollis (Common bear's breeches). Semievergreen, stately, upright perennial. **H** 4ft (1.2m), **S** 18in (45cm). Has long, oval, deeply cut, bright green leaves and, in summer, produces many spikes of funnel-shaped, mauve-and-white flowers. Z7–11 H11–7. **'Hollard's Gold',** illus. p.219.
A. spinosus (Spiny bear's breeches), illus. p.239.

ACCA

syn. FEIJOA

MYRTACEAE

Genus of evergreen, opposite-leaved shrubs, grown for their shallowly cup-shaped flowers. Needs a sheltered, sunny site and light, well-drained soil. Propagate by seed sown as soon as ripe or by semiripe cuttings in summer.
A. sellowiana, illus. p.203.

ACER

Maple

ACERACEAE/SAPINDACEAE

Genus of deciduous or evergreen trees and shrubs, grown for their foliage, which often colors brilliantly in fall and, in some cases, for their ornamental bark or stems. Small, but often attractive flowers are followed by 2-winged fruits. Requires sun or semi-shade and fertile, moist but well-drained soil. Many acers produce their best fall color on neutral to acid soil. Propagate species by seed as soon as ripe or in fall;

cultivars by various grafting methods in late winter or early spring, or by budding in summer. Leaf-eating caterpillars or aphids sometimes infest plants, and maple tar spot may affect *A. platanoides* and *A. pseudoplatanus*.
A. buergerianum (Trident maple). Deciduous, spreading tree. **H** 30ft (10m) or more, **S** 25ft (8m). Has 3-lobed, glossy, dark green leaves, usually providing long-lasting display of red, orange and purple in fall. Z5–9 H9–5.
A. capillipes, illus. p.77.
A. cappadocicum (Cappadocian maple). Deciduous, spreading tree. **H** 70ft (20m), **S** 50ft (15m). Has 5-lobed, bright green leaves that turn yellow in fall. Z5–7 H7–5. **'Aureum'** has bright yellow young leaves that turn light green in summer and assume yellow fall tints. Z5–7 H7–5. **subsp. lobelii,** syn. *A. lobelii* (Lobel's maple) illus. p.62.
A. carpinifolium, illus. p.88.
A. circinatum (Vine maple). Deciduous, spreading, bushy tree or shrub. **H** 15ft (5m) or more, **S** 20ft (6m). Rounded, 7–9-lobed, mid-green leaves turn brilliant orange and red in fall. Bears clusters of small, purple-and-white flowers in spring. Z6–9 H9–4.
A. cissifolium (Ivy-leaved maple). Deciduous, spreading tree. **H** 25ft (8m), **S** 40ft (12m). Leaves consist of 3 oval, toothed leaflets, bronze-tinged when young, dark green in summer, turning red and yellow in fall. Prefers partial shade and neutral to acid soil. Z4–8 H8–1. **subsp. henryi.** See *A. henryi*.
A. crataegifolium (Hawthorn maple). Deciduous, arching tree. **H** and **S** 30ft (10m). Branches are streaked green and white. Small, oval, mid-green leaves turn orange in fall. Z6–8 H8–6. **'Veitchii'** illus. p.85.
A. davidii (David's maple, Snakebark maple), illus. p.78. Deciduous tree with upright branches. **H** and **S** 50ft (15m). Branches are striped green and white. Oval, glossy, dark green leaves often turn yellow or orange in fall. Z5–7 H7–5. **subsp. grosseri.** See *A. grosseri*. **'Madeline Spitta',** illus. p.76.
A. ginnala. See *A. tataricum* subsp. *ginnala*.
A. giraldii. Deciduous, spreading tree. **H** and **S** 30ft (10m). Shoots have blue-gray bloom. Large, sycamore-like, shallowly lobed leaves, with long, pink stalks, are dark green above, blue-white beneath. Z7–9 H9–7.
A. grandidentatum. See *A. saccharum* subsp. *grandidentatum*.
A. griseum (Paperbark maple), illus. p.78. Deciduous, spreading tree. **H** and **S** 30ft (10m). Has peeling, orange-brown bark. Dark green leaves have 3 leaflets and turn red and orange in fall. Z4–8 H8–1.
A. grosseri, syn. *A. davidii* subsp. *grosseri* (Snakebark maple), illus. p.78. Deciduous, upright and spreading tree. **H** and **S** 30ft (10m). Has white-striped trunk and branches. Broadly oval, deeply lobed, bright green leaves turn red in fall. Z5–7 H7–5.
A. henryi, syn. *A. cissifolium* subsp. *henryi*, illus. p.76.
A. japonicum (Fullmoon maple, Japanese maple). Deciduous, bushy tree or shrub. **H** and **S** 30ft (10m). Rounded, lobed leaves are mid-green, turning red in fall. Clusters of small, reddish-purple flowers open in mid-spring. Shelter from strong winds. Z5–7 H7–1. **'Aconitifolium',** illus. p.90.

'Aureum'. See *A. shirasawanum* 'Aureum'. **'Vitifolium',** illus. p.77.
A. laxiflorum. See *A. pectinatum* subsp. *laxiflorum*, illus. p.92.
A. lobelii. See *A. cappadocicum* subsp. *lobelii*.
A. macrophyllum, illus. p.60.
A. maximowiczianum, syn. *A. nikoense* (Nikko maple). Slow-growing, deciduous, round-headed tree. **H** and **S** 40ft (12m). Leaves have 3 oval, bluish-green leaflets that turn brilliant red and yellow in fall. Z6–9 H9–6.
A. monspessulanum (Montpelier maple). Deciduous, usually compact, round-headed tree or shrub. **H** and **S** 40ft (12m). Small, 3-lobed, glossy, dark green leaves remain on tree until late fall. Z7–9 H9–7.
A. negundo (Ash-leaved maple, Box elder). Fast-growing, deciduous, spreading tree. **H** 50ft (15m), **S** 25ft (8m). Bright green leaves have 3–5 oval leaflets. Clusters of inconspicuous, greenish-yellow flowers are borne in late spring. Z5–8 H8–3. **'Variegatum',** illus. p.74. **var. violaceum** has purplish branchlets covered in a glaucous bloom and prominent clusters of tassel-like, purplish-pink flowers.
A. nikoense. See *A. maximowiczianum*.
A. opalus (Italian maple). Deciduous, round-headed tree. **H** and **S** 50ft (15m). Clusters of small, yellow flowers emerge from early to mid-spring, before foliage. Leaves are broad, 5-lobed and dark green, turning yellow in fall. Z5–8 H8–5.
A. palmatum (Japanese maple). Deciduous, bushy-headed shrub or tree. **H** and **S** 20ft (6m) or more. Palmate, deeply lobed, mid-green leaves turn brilliant orange, red or yellow in fall. Clusters of small, reddish-purple flowers are borne in mid-spring. Z6–8 H8–2. **'Atropurpureum',** illus. p.89. **'Bloodgood',** illus. p.138. **'Butterfly'** has gray-green leaves edged with cream and pink. **'Chitose-yama'** has mid-green foliage that gradually turns brilliant red from late summer to fall. **'Corallinum',** illus. p.123. **var. coreanum** has mid-green leaves turning brilliant red in fall. **'Dissectum Atropurpureum',** syn. *A. palmatum* 'Ornatum' illus. p.156. **var. heptalobum,** illus. p.117. **var. heptalobum 'Lutescens'** has large leaves that become clear yellow in fall. Winged fruits follow flowers. **var. heptalobum 'Rubrum',** illus. p.115. **'Lorbergii'.** See *A. platanoides* 'Palmatifidum'. **'Ornatum'.** See *A. palmatum* 'Dissectum Atropurpureum'. **'Osakazuki',** illus. p.90. **'Sango-kaku',** syn. *A. palmatum* 'Senkaki' (Coralbark maple), illus. p.78. Young winter shoots are coral-pink; the orange-yellow leaves turn green, becoming pink and finally yellow in fall. Z6–8 H8–2. **'Senkaki'.** See *A. palmatum* 'Sango-kaku'. **'Shindeshojo',** illus. p.123.
A. pectinatum subsp. laxiflorum. See *A. laxiflorum*.
A. pensylvanicum, illus. p.79. **'Erythrocladum'** (illus. p.78), is a deciduous, upright tree. **H** 30ft (10m), **S** 20ft (6m). Has brilliant candy-pink, young shoots in winter and large, boldly lobed, mid-green leaves that turn bright yellow in fall. Z3–7 H7–1.
A. platanoides (Norway maple). Vigorous, deciduous, spreading tree. **H** 80ft (25m), **S** 50ft (15m). Has large, broad, sharply lobed, bright green leaves that

turn yellow or orange in fall and clusters of yellow flowers borne in mid-spring before the leaves appear. Considered invasive in northeastern North America. Z3–7 H7–1. **'Columnare'**, **H** 40ft (12m), **S** 25ft (8m), is dense and columnar. **'Crimson King'**, illus. p.60. **'Drummondii'** has leaves broadly edged with creamy-white. **'Emerald Queen'** is upright when young. **'Globosum'**, **H** 25ft (8m), **S** 30ft (10m), has a dense, round crown. **'Palmatifidum'**, syn. *A. palmatum* 'Lorbergii' illus. p.67. **'Royal Red'** has deep reddish-purple leaves. Those of **'Schwedleri'** are bright red when young, maturing to purplish-green in summer and turn orange-red in fall. **'Summershade'** has dark green leaves.

A. pseudoplatanus (Sycamore). Fast-growing, deciduous, spreading tree. **H** 100ft (30m), **S** 50ft (15m). Has broadly 5-lobed, dark green leaves. Makes a fine specimen tree and is good for an exposed position. Z4–7 H7–1. **'Brilliantissimum'**, illus. p.84. **f. erythrocarpum**, illus. p.65. **'Simon-Louis Frères'**, illus. p.73.

A. rubrum, illus. p.66. **'Columnare'**, illus. p.76. **'October Glory'** is a deciduous, spreading tree. **H** 70ft (20m), **S** 40ft (12m). Has 3- or 5-lobed, glossy, dark green leaves that become intense red in fall, particularly on neutral to acid soil. In spring, bare branches are covered with clusters of tiny, red flowers. Z3–9 H9–1. **Red Sunset ('Franksred')** has dense growth that also turns brilliant red in fall. Z3–9 H9–1. **'Scanlon'**, illus. p.66. **'Schlesingeri'**, illus. p.66.

A. rufinerve, illus. p.76. **f. albolimbatum**. See *A. rufinerve* 'Hatsuyuki'. **'Hatsuyuki'**, syn. *A. rufinerve* f. *albolimbatum* is a deciduous, arching tree. **H** 30ft (10m), **S** 25ft (8m). Branches are striped green and white. Has 3-lobed, mid-green leaves, mottled and edged with white, that turn orange and red in fall. Z6–9 H9–6.

A. saccharinum, illus. p.63. **f. laciniatum 'Wieri'** is a fast-growing, deciduous, spreading tree with pendent, lower branches. **H** 80ft (25m), **S** 50ft (15m). Deeply lobed, mid-green leaves, with silver undersides, turn yellow in fall. Z4–8 H8–1.

A. saccharum (Sugar maple). **subsp. grandidentatum**, syn. *A. grandidentatum* (Sugar maple) is a deciduous, spreading tree. **H** and **S** 30ft (10m) or more. Broad 3- or 5-lobed, bright green leaves turn bright orange-red in early fall. Z4–8 H8–1. **'Green Mountain'**, **H** 70ft (20m), **S** 40ft (12m), is upright. Large, 5-lobed leaves turn brilliant scarlet in fall. **'Temple's Upright'**, illus. p.77.

A. shirasawanum **'Aureum'**, syn. *A. japonicum* 'Aureum', illus. p.89.

A. tataricum **subsp. ginnala**, syn. *A. ginnala*, illus. p.90.

A. triflorum, illus. p.91.

A. velutinum (Persian maple). Deciduous, spreading tree. **H** 70ft (20m), **S** 50ft (15m). Produces large, sycamore-like, lobed, dark green leaves, with undersides covered with pale brown down. Z7–9 H9–7. **var. vanvolxemii** (Van Volxem's maple) has even larger leaves, slightly glaucous and smooth beneath.

ACHILLEA
Yarrow
ASTERACEAE/COMPOSITAE

Genus of mainly upright perennials, some of which are semievergreen, suitable for borders and rock gardens. Has fernlike foliage and large, usually platelike, flower heads mainly in summer. Flower heads may be dried for winter decoration. Tolerates most soils but does best in a sunny, well-drained site. Tall species and cultivars need staking. Propagate by division in early spring or fall or by softwood cuttings in early summer.
① Contact with foliage may aggravate skin allergies.

A. aegyptica. See *A.* 'Taygetea'.
A. argentea. See *Tanacetum argenteum*.
A. argentea of gardens. See *A. clavennae*.
A. 'Belle Epoque', illus. p.247. Semievergreen, upright perennial. **H** 3ft (1m), **S** 16in (40cm). Has feathery, dark green, basal leaves and bears flat heads of rose-red flowers, maturing to lemon-yellow, in summer. Z3–9 H9–1.
A. 'Christine's Pink', illus. p.247. Semievergreen, upright perennial. **H** 3ft (90cm), **S** 16in (40cm). Has feathery, dark green, basal leaves. In summer produces flat heads of pale pink flowers, which fade as they age. Z3–9 H9–1.
A. clavennae, syn. *A. argentea*, illus. p.359.
A. clypeolata. Semievergreen, upright perennial. **H** 18in (45cm), **S** 12in (30cm). Has divided, hairy, silver leaves and dense, flat heads of small, yellow flowers in summer. Divide plants regularly in spring. Z3–9 H9–1.
A. 'Coronation Gold'. Upright perennial. **H** 3ft (1m), **S** 2ft (60cm). Has feathery, silvery leaves. Produces large, flat heads of small, golden flower heads in summer that dry well for winter decoration. Divide and replant every third year. Z3–9 H9–1.
A. 'Fanal', syn. *A.* 'The Beacon', illus. p.235.
A. filipendulina (Fernleaf yarrow). Upright perennial. **H** 3–4ft (1–1.2m), **S** 2ft (60cm). Has deeply divided, pale green, basal leaves. In summer, erect flowering stems bear dense, domed heads of tiny, daisylike, bright yellow flowers. Is good for cut flowers and drying them. Z3–9 H9–1. **'Gold Plate'**, illus. p.243. **'Parker's Variety'** (illus. p.247), **H** to 4½ft (1.4m), has rather rounded flower heads.
A. 'Heidi', illus. p.247. Semievergreen, upright perennial. **H** 24in (60cm) or more, **S** 16in (40cm). Has feathery, dark green, basal leaves. Bears flat heads of pink flowers, maturing to near white, in summer. Z3–9 H9–1.
A. x kellereri, illus. p.360.
A. 'Lachsschönheit', illus. p.247. Semievergreen, upright perennial. **H** 3ft (1m) or more, **S** 16in (40cm). Has feathery, dark green, basal leaves. Bears flat heads of pinkish-orange flowers, maturing to pinkish-cream, in summer. Z3–9 H9–1.
A. x lewisii **'King Edward'**. Semievergreen, rounded, compact, woody-based perennial. **H** 4in (10cm), **S** 9in (23cm) or more. Has feathery, soft, gray-green leaves. Bears compact heads of minute, buff-yellow flower heads in summer. Is suitable for a rock garden, wall or bank. Z3–8 H8–1.
A. 'Lucky Break'. Semievergreen, upright perennial. **H** 32in (80cm) or more, **S** 20in (50cm). Has feathery, silvery-green,

basal leaves. Bears flat heads of pale yellow flowers, maturing to creamy-white, in summer. Z3–9 H9–1.
A. millefolium (Yarrow). Variable, spreading, sometimes invasive perennial. **H** to 4ft (1.2m), **S** 2ft (60cm) or more. Has long, narrow, divided, dark green basal leaves. From late spring to late summer, erect flowering stems bear flattened heads of tiny, daisylike, white or sometimes pink flowers. Thrives on poor soil. Z3–9 H9–1. **'Fire King'** has dark green leaves and rich red flowers in summer. **'Kelwayi'** (illus. p.247), **H** 2ft (60cm), produces heads of rich red flower heads. **'Red Velvet'** (illus. p.247), **H** 24in (60cm), bears rich rose-red flowers. **'Tickled Pink'**, **H** 32–39in (80–100cm), is variable and produces flower heads from rich red-pink to softer, pastel shades.
A. 'Moonshine'. Upright perennial. **H** 24in (60cm), **S** 20in (50cm). Has flat heads of bright yellow flowers throughout summer above a mass of small, feathery, gray-green leaves. Divide plants regularly in spring. Z3–8 H8–1.
A. 'Paprika'. Semievergreen, upright perennial. **H** 32in (80cm) or more, **S** 16in (40cm). Has feathery, silvery-green, basal leaves. Bears flat heads of rich rusty-red flowers in summer. Z3–9 H9–1.
A. 'Pretty Belinda'. Semievergreen, upright perennial. **H** 20in (50cm), **S** 16in (40cm) or more. Has feathery, dark green, basal leaves. In summer bears a succession of rounded, deep pink flower heads, fading gradually to a softer color, creating a 2-tone effect. Z3–9 H9–1.
A. ptarmica **'The Pearl'**, illus. p.247. Upright perennial. **H** and **S** 30in (75cm). Has large heads of small, pompon-like, white flowers in summer and tapering, glossy, dark green leaves. May spread rapidly. Z3–8 H8–1.
A. 'Schwellenburg'. Spreading perennial. **H** 18in (45cm), **S** 24in (60cm). Has branched stems and gray-green leaves. Silvery buds are followed by lemon-yellow flower heads from early summer to early fall. Z3–9 H9–1.
A. 'Summerwine'. Semievergreen, upright perennial. **H** 32in (80cm) or more, **S** 16in (40cm) or more. Has feathery, dark-green, basal leaves. In summer bears flat heads of deep red flowers maturing to soft purplish-brown. Z4–9 H9–2.
A. 'Taygetea', syn. *A. aegyptica*. Upright perennial. **H** and **S** 20in (50cm). Has lemon-yellow flowers above clumps of feathery, gray leaves. Divide and replant every third year. Z3–8 H8–1.
A. 'Terracotta', illus. p.247. Semievergreen, upright perennial. **H** 3ft (1m), **S** 2ft (60cm). Has feathery, gray-green, basal leaves. Bears flat heads of burnt-orange flowers, maturing to cream, in summer. Z3–9 H9–1.
A. 'The Beacon'. See *A.* 'Fanal'.

ACHIMENES
Hot-water plant
GESNERIACEAE

Genus of erect or trailing perennials with small rhizomes and showy flowers. Prefers bright light, but not direct sunlight, and well-drained soil. Use tepid water for watering pot-grown plants. Allow plants to dry out after flowering and store rhizomes

in a frost-free place over winter. Propagate by division of rhizomes or by seed, if available, in spring or by stem cuttings in summer.
A. antirrhina. Erect perennial. **H** and **S** 14in (35cm) or more. Has oval, toothed leaves, to 2in (5cm) or more long and of unequal size in each opposite pair. In summer bears funnel-shaped, red-orange flowers, to 1½in (4cm) long, with yellow throats. Z15 H11–1.
A. 'Brilliant'. Erect, compact perennial. **H** and **S** 12in (30cm). Has oval, toothed leaves and, in summer, large, funnel-shaped, scarlet flowers. Z15 H11–1.
A. coccinea. See *A. erecta*.
A. erecta, syn. *A. coccinea*, *A. pulchella*. Erect, bushy, branching perennial. **H** and **S** 18in (45cm). Has narrowly oval, toothed leaves, often arranged in whorls of 3. Tubular, scarlet flowers with yellow eyes are produced in summer. Z15 H11–1.
A. grandiflora. Erect perennial. **H** and **S** to 24in (60cm). Oval, toothed leaves are often reddish below. In summer has tubular, dark pink to purple flowers with white eyes. Z15 H11–1.
A. 'Little Beauty', illus. p.469.
A. 'Paul Arnold'. Erect, compact, free-flowering perennial. **H** and **S** 12in (30cm). Has oval, toothed leaves. Bears large, funnel-shaped, purple flowers in summer. Z15 H11–1.
A. 'Peach Blossom'. Trailing perennial. **H** and **S** to 10in (25cm). Has oval, toothed leaves, and large, funnel-shaped, peach-colored flowers in summer. Z15 H11–1.
A. pulchella. See *A. erecta*.

Achnatherum calamagrostis. See *Stipa calamagrostis*.
Acidanthera bicolor **var. murielae**. See *Gladiolus murielae*.
Acidanthera murielae. See *Gladiolus murielae*.

ACIPHYLLA
Bayonet plant, Speargrass
UMBELLIFERAE/APIACEAE

Genus of evergreen perennials, grown mainly for the architectural value of their spiky foliage but also for their flowers, which are produced more freely on male plants. Requires sun and well-drained soil. Protect neck of plant from winter wet with a deep layer of stone chippings. Propagate by seed when fresh, in late summer, or in early spring.
A. aurea, illus. p.227.
A. scott-thomsonii (Giant Spaniard). Evergreen, rosette-forming perennial. **H** to 14ft (4.5m), **S** 2–3ft (60cm–1m). Much-dissected, spiny foliage is bronze when young, maturing to silver-gray. Prickly spikes of tiny, creamy-yellow flowers are rarely produced. Prefers moist but well-drained soil. Z8–11 H11–8.
A. squarrosa, illus. p.242.

ACIS
AMARYLLIDACEAE

Genus of bulbs, grown for their pendent, bell-shaped, white or pink flowers in fall or spring. Some species prefer a moist, partially shaded site; others do best in sun and well-drained soil. Propagate by division in spring or early fall or by seed in fall.

A. autumnalis, syn. *Leucojum autumnale* (Autumn snowflake), illus. p.424.

A. rosea, syn. *Leucojum roseum.* Early fall-flowering bulb. **H** to 4in (10cm), **S** 1–2in (2.5–5cm). Slender stems bear usually solitary, pale pink flowers, ¹/₂in (1cm) long. Threadlike, erect, basal leaves appear with, or just after, flowers. Prefers sun and well-drained soil. Z3–9 H9–1.

Acnistus australis. See *Iochroma australe.*

ACOKANTHERA
APOCYNACEAE

Genus of evergreen shrubs and trees, grown for their flowers and overall appearance. Requires full light and good drainage. Water container plants moderately, less when not in full growth. Propagate by division in spring or fall or by semiripe cuttings in summer. ① The sap and small, plum-like fruits that follow the flowers are highly toxic if ingested.
A. oblongifolia, syn. *A. spectabilis, Carissa spectabilis* (Wintersweet), illus. p.453.
A. spectabilis. See *A. oblongifolia.*

ACONITUM
Aconite, Monkshood, Wolf's bane
RANUNCULACEAE

Genus of perennials with poisonous, tuberous or fibrous roots and upright, sometimes scandent, stems, bearing curious, hooded flowers in summer. Leaves are mostly rounded in outline. Is good when grown in rock gardens and borders. Prefers a position in sun, but tolerates some shade and this may enhance flower color. Requires fertile, well-drained soil. Propagate by division in fall, every 2–3 years, or by seed in fall. ① Contact with the foliage may irritate skin; all parts are highly toxic if ingested.
A. anthora. Compact, tuberous perennial. **H** 24in (60cm), **S** 20in (50cm). Has erect, leafy stems that bear several hooded, yellow flowers in summer. Leaves are divided and dark green. Z5–8 H8–5.
A. x bicolor. See *A. x cammarum* 'Bicolor'.
A. 'Bressingham Spire'. Compact, upright, tuberous perennial. **H** 3ft (1m), **S** 20in (50cm). Very erect spikes of hooded, violet-blue flowers are produced in summer. Bears deeply divided leaves that are glossy and dark green. Z3–7 H8–3.
A. x cammarum 'Bicolor', syn. *A. x bicolor,* illus. p.239.
A. carmichaelii 'Arends', syn. *A. carmichaelii* 'Arendsii'. Erect, tuberous perennial. **H** 5ft (1.5m), **S** 1ft (30cm). Has divided, rich green leaves and, in fall, spikes of hooded, rich deep blue flowers. Upright stems may need staking, particularly if planted in a shady site. Z3–8 H8–3. **'Arendsii'.** See *A. carmichaelii* 'Arends'.
A. hemsleyanum, syn. *A. volubile,* illus. p.204.
A. 'Ivorine'. Upright, tuberous perennial. **H** 5ft (1.5m), **S** 20in (50cm). Bears hooded, creamy-white flowers in erect spikes in early summer. Strong stems bear deeply divided, glossy, green leaves. Z3–8 H8–3.
A. lycoctonum subsp. vulparia, syn. *A. orientale, A. vulparia,* illus. p.243.

A. napellus (Helmet flower, Monkshood). Upright, tuberous perennial. **H** 5ft (1.5m), **S** 1ft (30cm). Bears tall, slender spires of hooded, light indigo-blue flowers in late summer and deeply cut, mid-green leaves. Z3–8 H8–3. **'Albiflorus'.** See *A. napellus* subsp. *vulgare* 'Albidum'.
subsp. vulgare 'Albidum', syn. *A. napellus* 'Albiflorus' has white flowers. Z3–8 H8–3.
A. 'Newry Blue'. Upright, tuberous perennial. **H** 4ft (1.2m), **S** 20in (50cm). Produces hooded, dark blue flowers on erect stems in summer and has deeply divided, glossy, dark green leaves. Z5–8 H8–5.
A. orientale. See *A. lycoctonum* subsp. *vulparia.*
A. 'Spark's Variety'. Upright, tuberous perennial. **H** 4ft (1.2m), **S** 20in (50cm). Bears violet-blue flowers on branching stems in summer and has deeply divided, glossy, dark green leaves. Z5–8 H8–5.
A. 'Stainless Steel', illus. p.241.
A. volubile. See *A. hemsleyanum.*
A. vulparia. See *A. lycoctonum* subsp. *vulparia.*

ACORUS
Sweet flag
ACORACEAE

Genus of semievergreen, perennial, marginal and submerged water plants, grown for their frequently aromatic foliage. Needs an open, sunny position. *A. calamus* requires up to 10in (25cm) depth of water. Tidy up fading foliage in fall and lift and divide plants every 3 or 4 years, in spring, as clumps become congested.
A. calamus 'Argenteostriatus', illus. p.435.
A. gramineus var. pusillus (Dwarf Japanese rush). Semievergreen, perennial, marginal water plant or submerged aquarium plant. **H** and **S** 4in (10cm). Has narrow, grasslike, stiff leaves. Rarely, insignificant, greenish flower spikes are produced in summer. Z10–11 H11–2. **'Variegatus'** (Variegated Japanese rush), illus. p.435.

ACRADENIA
RUTACEAE

Genus of evergreen shrubs, grown for their foliage and flowers. Requires a sheltered position in sun or semi-shade and fertile, well-drained soil. Does best planted against a south- or west-facing wall. Propagate by semiripe cuttings in summer.
A. frankliniae, illus. p.192.

Acroclinium. See *Rhodanthe.*
Acroclinium roseum. See *Rhodanthe chlorocephala* subsp. *rosea.*

ACTAEA
Baneberry
RANUNCULACEAE

Genus of clump-forming perennials, grown for their colorful, poisonous berries. Likes woodland conditions—moist, peaty soil and shade. Propagate by division in spring or by seed in fall. ① The berries are highly toxic if ingested.

A. alba. See *A. pachypoda.*
A. alba of gardens. See *A. rubra* f. *neglecta.*
A. erythrocarpa. See *A. rubra.*
A. pachypoda, syn. *A. alba* (Doll's eyes, White baneberry), illus. p.246.
A. racemosa. See *Cimicifuga racemosa.*
A. rubra, syn. *A. erythrocarpa* (Red baneberry). Clump-forming perennial. **H** 20in (50cm), **S** 12in (30cm). Small, fluffy, white flowers are followed in fall by clusters of poisonous, rounded, scarlet berries, borne above oval, divided, bright green leaves. Z4–8 H8–1. **f. neglecta,** syn. *A. alba* has white berries.
A. simplex. See *Cimicifuga simplex.*

ACTINIDIA
ACTINIDIACEAE

Genus of mainly deciduous, woody-stemmed, twining climbers. Grows in partial shade but needs sun for fruit to form and ripen. Grows in any well-drained soil that does not dry out. Prune in winter if necessary. Propagate by seed in spring or fall, by semiripe cuttings in mid-summer or by layering in winter.
A. arguta (Hardy kiwi). Deciduous, woody-stemmed, twining climber. **H** 22–30ft (7–10m). Has ovate to oblong–ovate, bristle-toothed, dark green leaves, to 5in (12cm) long. In early summer produces clusters of fragrant, cup-shaped, white, unisexual flowers which in male plants have purple anthers. Oblong, smooth-skinned, edible, yellow-green fruits, to 1in (2.5cm) long, are produced on female plants. Z3–8 H8–1. **'Issai'** is self-fertile.
A. chinensis. See *A. deliciosa.*
A. deliciosa, syn. *A. chinensis* (Chinese gooseberry, Kiwi fruit). Vigorous, mainly deciduous, woody-stemmed, twining climber. **H** 28–30ft (9–10m). Heart-shaped leaves are 5–8in (13–20cm) long. In summer bears clusters of cup-shaped, white flowers that later turn yellowish, followed by edible, hairy, brown fruits. To obtain fruits, both male and female plants must usually be grown. Z7–9 H9–7.
A. kolomikta, illus. p.201.
A. pilosula. Vigorous, deciduous, woody-stemmed, twining climber. **H** 16–22ft (5–7m). Has lance-shaped, pointed, bristle-margined, dark green leaves with silvery-white markings at the leaf tips that often also cover half the leaf surface. Clusters of cup-shaped, pink, unisexual flowers are borne singly or in small clusters in the leaf axils in spring. Egg-shaped, edible, yellow-green fruits may be produced on female plants. Z7–9 H9–1.
A. polygama (Silver vine). Mainly deciduous, woody-stemmed, twining climber. **H** 12–20ft (4–6m). Heart-shaped leaves, 3–5in (7–13cm) long, are bronze when young and sometimes have creamy upper sections. In summer has scented, cup-shaped, white flowers, usually arranged in groups of 3 male, female or bisexual, followed by edible but not very palatable, egg-shaped, bright yellow fruits. Z4–9 H9–7.

ADA
ORCHIDACEAE

See also ORCHIDS.
A. aurantiaca, illus. p.467. Evergreen, epiphytic orchid for a cool greenhouse. **H** 9in (23cm). Bears sprays of tubular, orange flowers, 1in (2.5cm) long, in early spring. Has narrowly oval leaves, 4in (10cm) long. Needs shade in summer. H11–6.

ADANSONIA
Baobab
BOMBACACEAE/MALVACEAE

Genus of deciduous or semievergreen, mainly spring-flowering trees, grown for their characteristically swollen trunks, their foliage and for shade. Has flowers only on large, mature specimens. Requires full light and sharply drained soil. Allow soil of container specimens almost to dry out between waterings. Propagate by seed sown in spring. Pot specimens under glass are susceptible to red spider mite.
A. digitata (Baobab). Slow-growing, semievergreen, rounded tree. **H** and **S** 50ft (15m) or more. Has palmate leaves of 5–7 lustrous, green leaflets. Produces fragrant, pendent, long-stalked, white flowers, with 5 reflexed petals, in spring, followed by edible, sausage-shaped, brown fruits. Z11 H11–10.

ADENIUM
Desert rose
APOCYNACEAE

Genus of perennial succulents with fleshy, swollen trunks. Needs sun or partial shade and well-drained soil; plants are very prone to rotting. Propagate by seed sown in spring or summer. ① The milky sap that exudes from broken stems may irritate skin and cause severe discomfort if ingested.
A. obesum, illus. p.486.

ADENOCARPUS
LEGUMINOSAE/PAPILIONACEAE

Genus of deciduous or semievergreen shrubs, grown for their profuse, broom-like, yellow flowers, which are produced in spring or early summer. Requires a site in full sun and well-drained soil. Does best grown against a south-or west-facing wall. Propagate by seed sown in fall.
A. viscosus. Semievergreen, arching shrub. **H** and **S** 3ft (1m). Gray-green leaves with 3 narrowly lance-shaped leaflets densely cover shoots. Produces dense, terminal racemes of orange-yellow flowers in late spring. Z10–11 H12–9.

ADENOPHORA
Gland bellflower
CAMPANULACEAE

Genus of summer-flowering, fleshy-rooted perennials. Requires a site in full sun and rich, well-drained but not over-dry soil. May sometimes become invasive but resents disturbance. Propagate by basal cuttings taken in early spring or by seed sown in fall.
A. potaninii. Rosette-forming perennial. **H** 18in (45cm) or more, **S** 24in (60cm). Arching sprays of bell-shaped, pale bluish-

lavender flowers are produced in late summer. Has oval to lance-shaped, basal, mid-green leaves. Z4–8 H8–1.

Adhatoda duvernoia. See *Justicia adhatoda*.

ADIANTUM
Maidenhair fern
ADIANTACEAE/PTERIDACEAE

Genus of deciduous, semievergreen or evergreen ferns. Prefers semi-shade and moist, neutral to acid soil (*A. aleuticum* prefers alkaline soil). Remove fading fronds regularly. Propagate by spores in summer.
A. aleuticum, syn. *A. pedatum* var. *aleuticum*, illus. p.291.
A. capillus-veneris (Maidenhair fern). Semievergreen or evergreen fern. **H** and **S** 12in (30cm). Has dainty, triangular to oval, segmented, arching, light green fronds borne on black stems. Z8–11 H11–8.
A. cuneatum. See *A. raddianum*.
A. pedatum, illus. p.291. **var. aleuticum.** See *A. aleuticum*.
A. raddianum, syn. *A. cuneatum* (Delta maidenhair). Semievergreen or evergreen fern. **H** and **S** 12in (30cm). Triangular, divided, pale green segments are borne on finely dissected fronds that have purplish-black stems. Z11 H11–10.
'Fritz Lüthi' has bright green fronds.
'Grandiceps' (Tassel maidenhair) has elegant, tasselled fronds.
A. tenerum (Brittle maidenhair fern). Semievergreen or evergreen fern. **H** 1–3ft (30cm–1m), **S** 2–3ft (60cm–1m). Broadly lance-shaped, much-divided, spreading, mid-green fronds consist of rounded or diamond-shaped pinnae. Z9–11 H11–9.
A. venustum, illus. p.292.

ADLUMIA
PAPAVERACEAE/FUMARIACEAE

Genus of one species of herbaceous, biennial, leaf-stalk climber, grown for its leaves and flowers. Grows in semi-shade in any soil. Propagate by seed in spring.
A. cirrhosa. See *A. fungosa*.
A. fungosa, syn. *A. cirrhosa* (Allegheny vine, Climbing fumitory). Herbaceous, biennial, leaf-stalk climber. **H** 10–12ft (3–4m). Delicate leaves have numerous leaflets. Tiny, tubular, spurred, white or purplish flowers are borne in drooping panicles in summer. Z3–7 H7–1.

ADONIS
RANUNCULACEAE

Genus of spring-flowering perennials, grown for their foliage and flowers. Some thrive in semi-shade; others require an open, well-drained site. Propagate by seed when fresh, in late summer, or by division after flowering.
A. amurensis (Amur adonis). Clump-forming perennial. **H** 12in (30cm), **S** 9–12in (23–30cm). Mid-green leaves are finely cut. Bears cup-shaped, golden flowers singly at the tips of stems in late winter and early spring. Z4–7 H7–1.
A. brevistyla. Clump-forming perennial. **H** and **S** 6–9in (15–23cm). Mid-green leaves are finely cut. Has cup-shaped, white flowers, tinged blue outside and borne singly at the tips of stems in early spring. Z4–9 H9–1.
A. vernalis, illus. p.262.

ADROMISCHUS
CRASSULACEAE

Genus of perennial succulents and evergreen subshrubs with rounded, thin or fat leaves. Needs partial shade and very well-drained soil. Propagate by leaf or stem cuttings in spring or summer.
A. cooperi, syn. *Cotyledon cooperi*, *Echeveria cooperi* (Plover eggs). Freely branching perennial succulent. **H** 4in (10cm), **S** to 6in (15cm). Has grayish-brown stems and inversely lance-shaped, glossy, gray-green leaves, to 2in (5cm) long, often purple-marked above. In summer produces tubular, green-and-red flowers, with white-margined, pink or purple lobes, on a stem 10in (25cm) or more long. Z14–15 H11–10.
A. maculatus, illus. p.492.

AECHMEA
BROMELIACEAE

Genus of evergreen, rosette-forming, epiphytic perennials, cultivated for their foliage, flowers, and fruits. May be grown in full light or a semi-shaded site. Provide a rooting medium of equal parts rich soil and either sphagnum moss or bark or plastic chips used for orchid culture. Using soft water, water moderately in summer, sparingly at all other times, and keep cup-like, rosette centers filled with water from spring through to fall. Propagate by offsets in late spring.
A. distichantha. Evergreen, basal-rosetted, epiphytic perennial. **H** and **S** to 3ft (1m). Forms dense rosettes of narrowly oblong, round-tipped, arching leaves that are dull green above, gray and scaly beneath. Has panicles of small, tubular, purple or blue flowers among white-felted, pink bracts, usually in summer. Z15 H11–1.
A. fasciata, syn. *Billbergia rhodocyanea* (Silver vase plant, Urn plant), illus. p.471. Evergreen, tubular-rosetted, epiphytic perennial. **H** 16–24in (40–60cm), **S** 12–20in (30–50cm). Has loose rosettes of broadly oblong, round-tipped, incurved, arching leaves with dense, gray scales and silver cross-banding. Bears dense, pyramidal panicles of tubular, blue-purple flowers among pink bracts, just above foliage, from spring to fall. H11–1.
A. Foster's Favorite Group (Lacquered wine-cup). Evergreen, basal-rosetted, epiphytic perennial. **H** and **S** 12–24in (30–60cm). Has loose rosettes of strap-shaped, arching, lustrous, wine-red leaves. Drooping spikes of small, tubular, deep purple-blue flowers are borne in summer, followed by pear-shaped, red fruits. Z15 H11–1.
A. fulgens (Coral berry). Evergreen, basal-rosetted, epiphytic perennial. **H** and **S** 16–30in (40–75cm). Forms loose rosettes of broadly oblong, arching, glossy, mid-green leaves with gray scales beneath and rounded or pointed tips. In summer produces, above foliage, erect panicles of small, tubular, violet-purple flowers that turn red with age. These are succeeded by small, rounded to ovoid, red fruits on red stalks. Z15 H11–1.
A. nudicaulis. Evergreen, basal-rosetted, epiphytic perennial. **H** and **S** 16–30in (40–75cm). Produces loose rosettes of a few broadly strap-shaped, arching, olive-green leaves with spiny edges and usually banded with gray scales beneath. Spikes of small, tubular, yellow flowers open above large, red bracts in summer. Z9–11 H11–1.
A. recurvata, illus. p.471. Evergreen, basal-rosetted, epiphytic perennial. **H** and **S** 6–8in (15–20cm). Narrowly triangular, tapered, spiny-edged, arching, red-flushed, mid-green leaves are produced in dense rosettes. In summer bears a short, dense spike of tubular, red-and-white flowers, with red bracts, just above leaves. Z9–11 H11–1.

AEGOPODIUM
Bishop's weed, Goutweed
UMBELLIFERAE/APIACEAE

Genus of invasive, rhizomatous perennials, most of which are weeds although *A. podagraria* 'Variegatum' provides excellent groundcover. Tolerates sun or shade and any well-drained soil. Propagate by division of rhizomes in spring or fall.
A. podagraria 'Variegatum'. Vigorous, spreading perennial. **H** 4in (10cm), **S** indefinite. Has lobed, creamy-white-variegated leaves. Insignificant, white flowers, borne in summer, are best removed. Z4–9 H9–1.

AEONIUM
CRASSULACEAE

Genus of perennial succulents, some of which are short-lived, and evergreen, succulent shrubs, grown for their rosettes of bright green or blue-green, occasionally purple, leaves. Prefers partial shade and very well-drained soil. Most species grow from fall to spring and are semi-dormant in mid-summer. Propagate by seed in summer or, for branching species, by stem cuttings in spring or summer.
A. arboreum. Bushy, perennial succulent. **H** to 2ft (60cm), **S** 3ft (1m). Branched stems are each crowned by a rosette, up to 6in (15cm) across, of broadly lance-shaped, glossy, bright green leaves. In spring produces cones of small, star-shaped, golden flowers on 2–3-year-old stems, which then die back. Z9–11 H9–4.
'Schwarzkopf'. See *A.* 'Zwartkop'.
A. haworthii, illus. p.489.
A. tabuliforme, illus. p.491.
A. 'Zwartkop', syn. *A. arboreum* 'Schwarzkopf', illus. p.310.

AESCHYNANTHUS
GESNERIACEAE

Genus of evergreen, climbing, trailing or creeping perennials, useful for growing in hanging baskets. Needs a fairly humid atmosphere and a position out of direct sun. Water sparingly in low temperatures. Propagate by tip cuttings in spring or summer.
A. 'Black Pagoda'. Semi-trailing perennial. **H** 24in (60cm), **S** to 18in (45cm). Has elliptic leaves, to 4in (10cm) long, pale green with dark brown marbling above, and purple beneath. Bears terminal clusters of deep burnt-orange flowers, with green calyces, from summer to winter. Z15 H11–10.
A. longicaulis, syn. *A. marmoratus*, *A. zebrinus*. Evergreen, trailing perennial. **H** and **S** to 24in (60cm). Oval, waxy leaves are dark green, veined yellowish-green above, purplish below. Produces tubular, greenish flowers, with dark brown markings, borne in terminal clusters in summer. Z15 H11–10.
A. marmoratus. See *A. longicaulis*.
A. pulcher (Lipstick plant, Royal red bugler). Evergreen, climbing or trailing perennial. **H** and **S** indefinite. Produces thick, oval leaves and small, tubular, hooded, bright red flowers, with yellow throats, borne in terminal clusters from summer to winter. Z14–15 H11–10.
A. speciosus, syn. *A. splendens*, illus. p.478.
A. splendens. See *A. speciosus*.
A. zebrinus. See *A. longicaulis*.

AESCULUS
Buckeye, Horse chestnut
HIPPOCASTANACEAE/SAPINDACEAE

Genus of deciduous trees and shrubs, grown for their bold, divided leaves and conspicuous, upright panicles or clusters of flowers, followed by fruits (horse-chestnuts) sometimes with spiny outer casings. Requires sun or semi-shade and fertile, well-drained soil. Propagate species by sowing seed in fall, cultivars by budding in late summer or by grafting in late winter. Leaf spot may affect young foliage, and coral spot fungus may attack damaged wood. ① All parts of these plants may cause mild stomach upset if ingested.
A. californica, illus. p.81.
A. x carnea (Red horse-chestnut). **'Briotii',** illus. p.60.
A. chinensis, illus. p.60.
A. flava, syn. *A. octandra*, illus. p.76.
A. glabra (Ohio buckeye). Deciduous, round-headed, sometimes shrubby tree. **H** and **S** 30ft (10m). Leaves, usually composed of 5 narrowly oval leaflets, are dark green. Bears 4-petaled, greenish-yellow flowers in upright clusters in late spring and early summer. Z3–7 H7–1.
A. hippocastanum (Common horse chestnut). Vigorous, deciduous, spreading tree. **H** 60ft (18m), **S** 50ft (15m). Has large leaves with 5 or 7 leaflets and spires of white flowers, flushed pink and yellow in centers in spring. Spiny fruits contain glossy, brown nuts in fall. Z3–8 H8–1. **'Baumannii', H** 100ft (30m), has dark green leaves turning to yellow in fall and double, yellow- or red-marked, white flowers.
A. indica (Indian horse-chestnut). Deciduous, spreading tree. **H** 70ft (20m), **S** 40ft (12m). Glossy, dark green leaves with usually 7 narrowly oval leaflets are bronze when young, orange or yellow in fall. Upright panicles of 4-petaled, pink-tinged, white flowers, marked with red or yellow, appear in mid-summer. Z7–8 H8–7.
'Sydney Pearce', illus. p.73.
A. x neglecta (Sunrise horse-chestnut). **'Erythroblastos',** illus. p.72.
A. octandra. See *A. flava*.
A. parviflora, illus. p.113.
A. pavia (Red buckeye). Deciduous, round-headed, sometimes shrubby tree. **H** 15ft (5m), **S** 10ft (3m). Glossy, dark green leaves consist of 5 narrowly oval leaflets. Has panicles of 4-petaled, red flowers in early summer. Z5–9 H9–5. **'Atrosanguinea',** illus. p.86.
A. turbinata (Japanese horse-chestnut). Deciduous, spreading, sturdy-branched tree. **H** 70ft (20m), **S** 40ft (12m). Large, dark

A

green leaves consist of 5 or 7 narrowly oval leaflets. Panicles of creamy-white flowers appear in late spring and early summer. Z6–8 H8–6.

AETHIONEMA
Stonecress
BRASSICACEAE/CRUCIFERAE

Genus of short-lived, evergreen or semievergreen shrubs, subshrubs and perennials, grown for their prolific flowers. Needs sun and well-drained soil. Propagate by softwood cuttings in spring or by seed in fall. Most species self-seed readily.

A. armenum, illus. p.364.

A. grandiflorum, syn. *A. pulchellum*, illus. p.338.

A. iberideum (Iberis stonecress). Evergreen or semievergreen, rounded, compact shrub. **H** and **S** 6in (15cm). Bears small, lance-shaped, gray-green leaves and, in summer, $^3/_4$in (2cm) stems each bear a raceme of small, saucer-shaped, white flowers. Z6–8 H8–6.

A. pulchellum. See *A. grandiflorum*.

A. 'Warley Rose', illus. p.362.

A. 'Warley Ruber'. Evergreen or semievergreen, rounded, compact subshrub. **H** and **S** 6in (15cm). Has tiny, linear, bluish-green leaves. Racemes of small, deep rose-pink flowers are produced on $^3/_4$–$1^1/_4$in (2–3cm) stems in spring–summer. Z6–8 H8–6.

AGAPANTHUS
African blue lily
AGAPANTHACEAE

Genus of clump-forming perennials, some of which are evergreen, with erect stems that carry large umbels of bell- to tubular-bell-shaped or trumpet-shaped flowers, usually blue and often fading to purple with age. Leaves are strap-shaped. Grows in full sun and in moist, well-drained soil. Protect crowns in winter with ash or mulch. Plants increase slowly but may be propagated by division in spring; may also be raised from seed in fall or spring. Named cultivars will not come true from seed.

A. africanus (African lily). Evergreen, clump-forming perennial. **H** 3ft (1m), **S** 20in (50cm). In late summer has rounded umbels of deep blue flowers on upright stems, above broad, dark green leaves. Z9–10 H11–1.

A. 'Alice Gloucester'. Clump-forming perennial. **H** 3ft (1m), **S** 20in (50cm). Produces large, dense, rounded umbels of white flowers in summer, above narrow, mid-green leaves. Z7–11 H10–7.

A. 'Ben Hope'. Clump-forming perennial. **H** 3–4ft (1–1.2m), **S** 20in (50cm). Erect stems support dense, rounded umbels of deep blue flowers in late summer and early fall, borne over narrow, grayish-green leaves. Z7–10 H10–7.

A. 'Blue Giant'. Clump-forming perennial. **H** 4ft (1.2m), **S** 24in (60cm). Has rounded heads of open, bell-shaped, rich blue flowers in mid- to late summer. Z8–11 H11–1.

A. campanulatus. Clump-forming perennial. **H** 2–4ft (60cm–1.2m), **S** 20in (50cm). Rounded umbels of blue flowers

are borne on strong stems in summer, above narrow, grayish-green leaves. Z7–11 H11–7.

A. 'Cherry Holley'. Clump-forming perennial. **H** 3ft (1m), **S** 20in (50cm). Rounded umbels of dark blue flowers, borne in summer above narrow leaves, do not fade to purple with age. Z7–10 H10–7.

A. 'Dorothy Palmer'. Clump-forming perennial. **H** 3ft (1m), **S** 20in (50cm). Rounded umbels of rich blue flowers, fading to reddish-mauve, are borne on erect stems above narrow, grayish-green leaves in late summer. Z9–11 H12–7.

A. inapertus. Clump-forming perennial. **H** 5ft (1.5m), **S** 2ft (60cm). Pendent, narrowly tubular, blue flowers are borne on very erect stems, above narrow, bluish-green leaves, in late summer and fall. Z9–11 H11–7. **subsp. pendulus 'Graskop'**, illus. p.240.

A. 'Lilliput'. Compact, clump-forming perennial. **H** 32in (80cm), **S** 20in (50cm). Has small, rounded umbels of dark blue flowers in summer. Leaves are narrow and mid-green. Z6–9 H9–4.

A. 'Loch Hope'. Clump-forming perennial. **H** 3–4ft (1–1.2m), **S** 20in (50cm). Bears large, rounded umbels of deep blue flowers in late summer and early fall, above narrow, grayish-green leaves. Z8–11 H12–1.

A. 'Northern Star', illus. p.241.

A. orientalis. See *A. praecox* subsp. *orientalis*.

A. 'Phantom'. Evergreen, clump-forming perennial. **H** 4ft (1.2m), **S** 2ft (60cm) or more. Large, rounded clusters of white flowers, flushed pale blue at the edges, are borne on sturdy stems in mid- to late summer. Has broadly strap-shaped, bright green leaves. Z9–11 H12–1.

A. praecox subsp. orientalis, syn. *A. orientalis*, illus. p.242.

A. 'Purple Cloud', illus. p.241.

AGAPETES
SYN. PENTAPTERYGIUM
ERICACEAE

Genus of evergreen or deciduous, scandent shrubs and semi-scrambling climbers, grown for their flowers. Needs full light or partial shade and a rich, well-drained but not dry, neutral to acid soil. Water potted specimens freely when in full growth, but moderately at other times. Overlong stems may be cut back to promote branching, but they are best tied to supports. Propagate by seed sown in spring or by semiripe cuttings taken in late summer.

A. incurvata, syn. *A. rugosa* var. *rugosa*. Evergreen, loose shrub with arching or spreading stems. **H** and **S** to 10ft (3m). Leaves are lance-shaped, wrinkled and bright green. In spring, clusters of pendent, urn-shaped, white flowers, patterned with purple-red, are borne from leaf axils. Z12–13 H11–10.

A. 'Ludgvan Cross'. Evergreen, scandent shrub with arching or pendulous stems. **H** and **S** 6–10ft (2–3m). Lance-shaped leaves are dark green. Urn-shaped, red flowers with darker patterns are produced in spring. Z10–11 H11–7.

A. macrantha. See *A. variegata* var. *macrantha*.

A. rugosa var. **rugosa.** See *A. incurvata*.

A. serpens, illus. p.461.

A. variegata var. **macrantha,** syn. *A. macrantha*, illus. p.461.

AGASTACHE
Mexican giant hyssop
LABIATAE/LAMIACEAE

Genus of summer-flowering perennials with aromatic leaves. Requires full sun and fertile, well-drained soil. Plants are short-lived and should be propagated each year by softwood or semiripe cuttings taken in late summer.

A. 'Black Adder', illus. p.280.

A. mexicana, syn. *Brittonastrum mexicanum*, *Cedronella mexicana* (Mexican giant hyssop). Upright perennial with aromatic leaves. **H** to 3ft (1m), **S** to 1ft (30cm). In summer bears clusters of small, tubular flowers in shades of pink to crimson. Leaves are oval, pointed, toothed and mid-green. Z7–11 H11–7.

Agathaea. See *Felicia*.

AGATHOSMA
RUTACEAE

Genus of evergreen shrubs, grown for their flowers and overall appearance. Needs full light and well-drained, acid soil. Water container specimens moderately, less when not in full growth. Propagate by semiripe cuttings in late summer.

A. pulchella, syn. *Barosma pulchella*. Evergreen, rounded, wiry, aromatic shrub. **H** and **S** to 3ft (1m). Has a dense mass of small, oval, leathery leaves. Small, 5-petaled, purple flowers are freely produced in terminal clusters in spring–summer. Z9–10 H11–9.

AGAVE
AGAVACEAE/ASPARAGACEAE

Genus of rosetted, perennial succulents with sword-shaped, sharp-toothed leaves. Small species, to 1ft (30cm) high, flower only after 5–10 years; tall species, to 15ft (5m) high, may take 20–40 years to flower. Requires full sun and well-drained soil. Propagate by seed or offsets in spring or summer.

A. americana (Century plant). Basal-rosetted, perennial succulent. **H** 3–6ft (1–2m), **S** 6–10ft (2–3m) or more. Has sharply pointed, toothed leaves, to 5–6ft (1.5–2m) long. Branched flower stem, to 25ft (8m) long, bears dense, tapering spikes of bell-shaped, white to pale creamy-yellow flowers, each $3^1/_2$in (9cm) long, in spring–summer. Offsets freely. Z8–11 H12–5. **'Marginata'**, (illus. p.482), **H** and **S** 6ft (2m), has yellow margins and a central green zone to each leaf. Z9–11 H11–5. **'Mediopicta'**, **H** and **S** 6ft (2m), has central, yellow stripes along leaves. Z8–11 H12–5. **'Striata'**, illus. p.481.

A. attenuata, illus. p.489.

A. duplicata. See *Polianthes geminiflora*.

A. filifera (Thread agave), illus. p.482. Basal-rosetted, perennial succulent. **H** 3ft (1m), **S** 6ft (2m). Has narrow, green leaves, each spined at the tip. White leaf margins gradually break away, leaving long, white fibers. Produces yellow-green flowers on a 8ft (2.5m) tall stem in summer. Offsets freely. H11–5.

A. flexispina. Basal-rosetted, perennial succulent. **H** 14in (35cm), **S** 30in (75cm). Sword-shaped, glaucous to yellowish-green leaves have wavy margins and flexible, brown spines. Flower stem, to $11^1/_2$ft (3.5m) long, bears a rather open panicle of cylindrical, red-tinged, greenish-yellow flowers, $^3/_4$in (2cm) long, in summer. Z8–10 H11–8.

A. macroacantha, illus. p.482. Basal-rosetted, perennial succulent. **H** 12–16in (30–40cm), **S** 10–16in (25–40cm). Has narrowly sword-shaped, toothed, bluish-gray leaves with dark brown spines. Flower stem, to 6ft (2m) long, bears slender panicles of tubular, purple-tinged, green flowers, 2in (5cm) long, and sometimes bulbils, in summer. Z8–11 H11–4.

A. maculosa, syn. *Manfreda maculosa*. Basal-rosetted, perennial succulent. **H** 24–72in (20–60cm), **S** 12–36in (30–90cm). Lance-shaped, grooved, dark green leaves, with small, distantly spaced teeth, sometimes have dark green- or brown-spotted patterns. Flower stem, to 6ft (1.8m) long, bears narrow spikes of bell-shaped, white to yellowish-white flowers, $^5/_8$in (1.5cm) long, in summer. Z8–11 H12–5.

A. parrasana, illus. p.482. Basal-rosetted, compact, perennial succulent. **H** 12–16in (30–40cm), **S** 12–18in (30–45cm). Ovate, closely packed and overlapping, thick, rigid, light gray leaves have toothed margins with short, grayish-brown spines. Flower stem, 10–13ft (3–4m) long, produces ellipsoidal panicles of bell-shaped, pale yellow flowers, 2in (5cm) long, flushed red or purple, in summer. Z9–11 H12–4.

A. parryi, illus. p.489.

A. parviflora, illus. p.482. Basal-rosetted, perennial succulent. **H** 5in (1.5m), **S** 20in (50cm). Has narrow, white-marked, dark green leaves with white fibers peeling from edges. Produces white flowers in summer. H11–10.

A. polianthes. See *Polianthes tuberosa*.

A. polianthiflora, illus. p.482. Basal-rosetted, perennial succulent. **H** 4–8in (10–20cm), **S** 4–12in (10–30cm). Lance-shaped, white-marked, mid-green leaves have wispy, white filaments on the margins; minute teeth are borne only towards leaf bases. Red flower stem, 3–6ft (1–2m) long, bears narrow spikes of tubular, pink and red flowers, $1^1/_2$in (4cm) long, in summer. Z10–11 H12–5.

A. potatorum (Butterfly agave), illus. p.482. Basal-rosetted, compact, perennial succulent. **H** 12in (30cm), **S** 12–18in (30–45cm). Broadly sword-shaped, glaucous-white to green leaves have wavy to notched margins and sharp, sinuous, chestnut-brown spines. Red to purple flower stem, 10–13ft (3–4m) long, produces egg-shaped panicles of bell-shaped, red-tinged, light green to yellowish flowers, 2–3in (5–8cm) long, in summer. Z10–11 H12–9.

A. schottii. Basal-rosetted, perennial succulent. **H** 8–16in (20–40cm), **S** 12–18in (30–45cm). Narrowly linear, yellowish-green to green leaves have margins bearing brittle threads. Often crooked flower stem, to 6ft (2m) long, produces slender spike of tubular, yellow flowers, $1^1/_4$–$1^1/_2$in (3–4cm) long, in summer. Z8–11 H12–7.

A. utahensis. Basal-rosetted, perennial succulent. **H** 9in (23cm) or more, **S** 6ft (2m). Has rigid, blue-gray leaves, each with spines up margins and a long, dark spine at tip. Flower stem, to 5ft (1.5m) long, bears yellow flowers in summer. Z11 H12–6.

A. victoriae-reginae, illus. p.482. Very slow-growing, domed, perennial succulent with a basal rosette of spineless white-striped and -edged leaves. Has cream flowers on 12ft (4m) tall stem in spring-summer after 20-30 years. Z9–11 H12–5. **'Compacta', H** 12in (30cm), **S** 18in (45cm), has tight fitting, tapered, deep green leaves, each with a small, terminal spine and smooth, spineless, white margins. Flower stem, to 16ft (5m) long, bears a narrow, dense spike of funnel-shaped, purple- or red-tinged, cream flowers, ³⁄₄–1¹⁄₄in (2–3cm) long, in summer.

A. zebra. Basal-rosetted, perennial succulent. **H** 4ft (1m), **S** 1¹⁄₂–3ft (45–60cm). Lance-shaped, thick, rigid, rough, wavy-margined, patterned, light gray leaves have curved, gray spines. Flower stem, 20–25ft (6–8m) long, produces narrow, panicle of bell-shaped, yellow flowers, 1³⁄₄in (4.5cm) long, in summer. Z11.

AGERATINA

COMPOSITAE/ASTERACEAE

Genus of perennials, subshrubs and shrubs, many of which are evergreen, grown mainly for their flowers, some also for their architectural foliage. Requires full light or partial shade. Tolerates any conditions, although most species prefer moist but well-drained soil. Water container plants freely when in full growth, moderately at other times. Propagate by seed in spring, shrubs and subshrubs by softwood or greenwood cuttings in summer, perennials by division in early spring or fall. Red spider mite and whitefly may be troublesome.

A. altissima, syn. *Eupatorium ageratoides, Eupatorium rugosum, Eupatorium urticifolium,* illus. p.231. Erect perennial. **H** 4ft (1.2m), **S** 1¹⁄₂ft (45cm). Has nettle-like, gray-green leaves. In late summer bears dense, flat, white flower heads. Z4–8 H8–2

A. ligustrina, syn. *Eupatorium ligustrinum, Eupatorium micranthum, Eupatorium weinmannianum.* Evergreen, rounded shrub. **H** and **S** 6–12ft (2–4m). Has elliptic to lance-shaped, bright green leaves and, in fall, fragrant, groundsel-like, white or pink flowers produced in flattened clusters, 4–8in (10–20cm) across. Z13–15 H11–1.

AGERATUM

Floss flower

COMPOSITAE/ASTERACEAE

Genus of annuals and biennials. Grow in sun and in fertile, well-drained soil, which should not be allowed to dry out otherwise growth and flowering will be poor. Dead-head regularly to ensure continuous flowering. Propagate by seed sown outdoors in late spring.

A. houstonianum. Moderately fast-growing, hummock-forming annual. Tall

cultivars, **H** and **S** 12in (30cm); medium, **H** and **S** 8in (20cm); dwarf, **H** and **S** 6in (15cm). All have oval, mid-green leaves and clusters of feathery, brushlike flower heads throughout summer and into fall. Is useful for bedding. Z10–11 H11–1. **'Blue Danube'** (dwarf), illus. p.313. **'Blue Mink'** (tall), illus. p.314. **Hawaii Series** includes uniform, compact plants, with deep to pale blue or white flower heads. **'Pacific'** (medium) is neat, with tight clusters of deep violet-blue flower heads. **'Swing Pink'** (dwarf) has pink flower heads.

AGLAONEMA

Chinese evergreen

ARACEAE

Genus of evergreen, erect, tufted perennials, grown mainly for their foliage. Tolerates shade, although the variegated forms need more light, and prefers moist but well-drained soil. Water moderately when in full growth, less in winter. Propagate by division or stem cuttings in summer. Mealy bug may be a problem.

A. commutatum. Evergreen, erect, tufted perennial. **H** and **S** to 18in (45cm) or more. Broadly lance-shaped leaves are 12in (30cm) long and dark green with irregular, grayish-white patches along lateral veins. Has greenish-white spathes produced in summer. Z14–15 H11–1. **'Malay Beauty',** syn. *A. commutatum* 'Pewter' bears very dark green leaves mottled greenish-white and cream. Z15 H11–1. **'Pewter'.** See *A. commutatum* 'Malay Beauty'. **'Treubii',** illus. p.468.

A. pictum, illus. p.475.

A. 'Silver King', illus. p.475.

AGONIS

Willow myrtle

MYRTACEAE

Genus of evergreen, mainly spring-flowering shrubs and trees, grown for their foliage, flowers and graceful appearance. Needs full light and well-drained but moisture-retentive soil. Water container specimens moderately, scarcely at all in winter. Pruning is tolerated when necessary. Propagate by seed in spring or by semiripe cuttings in summer.

A. flexuosa, illus. p.450.

AGROSTEMMA

Corn cockle

CARYOPHYLLACEAE

Genus of summer-flowering annuals. Grow in sun; flowers best in very well-drained soil that is not very fertile. Support with sticks and deadhead to prolong flowering. Propagate by seed sown *in situ* in spring or early fall. *A. githago* escapes cultivation readily and is considered invasive in parts of North America. ⓘ Seeds may cause severe discomfort if ingested.

A. coeli-rosa. See *Silene coeli-rosa.*

A. githago. Fast-growing, erect annual with thin stems. **H** 2–3ft (60cm–1m), **S** 1ft (30cm). Has lance-shaped, mid-green leaves and, in summer, produces 5-petaled, open trumpet-shaped, pink flowers, 3in (8cm) wide. Seeds are tiny, rounded, dark brown and poisonous. H9–1. **'Milas',** illus. p.304.

AICHRYSON

CRASSULACEAE

Genus of annual and perennial succulents, often shrub-like, grown for their fleshy, spoon-shaped to rounded, hairy leaves. Most species are short-lived, dying after flowering. Requires a position in full sun or partial shade and very well-drained soil. Propagate by seed or stem cuttings in spring or summer.

A. x aizoides. var. domesticum 'Variegatum', syn. *A. x domesticum* 'Variegatum' illus. p.495.

A. x domesticum 'Variegatum'. See *A. x aizoides* var. *domesticum* 'Variegatum'.

AILANTHUS

SIMAROUBACEAE

Genus of deciduous trees, grown for their foliage and 3–5-winged fruits. They are very tolerant of urban pollution, drought, and poor soil, but because of their tendency to escape cultivation they are considered noxious weeds in parts of the northeastern United States. Needs sun or semi-shade. To grow as shrubs, cut back hard in spring, after which vigorous shoots bearing very large leaves are produced. Propagate by seed sown in fall or by suckers or root cuttings taken in winter. May be invasive in parts of North America. ⓘ Male flowers are unpleasantly scented; the pollen may cause an allergic reaction.

A. altissima, syn. *A. glandulosa,* illus. p.63.

A. glandulosa. See *A. altissima.*

AJUGA

Bugleweed

LABIATAE/LAMIACEAE

Genus of annuals and perennials, some of which are semievergreen or evergreen and excellent as groundcover. Tolerates sun or shade and any soil, but grows more vigorously in moist conditions. Propagate by division in spring.

A. pyramidalis (Pyramidal bugle). Semievergreen perennial. **H** 6in (15cm), **S** 18in (45cm). Forms a creeping carpet of oblong to spoon-shaped, deep green leaves, above which are borne spikes of whorled, 2-lipped, blue flowers in spring. Z3–9 H9–1. **'Metallica Crispa'** has crisp, curled leaves, with a metallic-bronze lustre, and dark blue flowers.

A. reptans 'Atropurpurea'. Evergreen, groundcover perennial, spreading freely by runners. **H** 6in (15cm), **S** 36in (90cm). Has small rosettes of ovate to oblong-spoon-shaped, toothed or slightly lobed, glossy, deep bronze-purple leaves. Short spikes of 2-lipped, blue flowers are borne in spring. Z3–9 H9–1. **'Jungle Beauty', H** 15in (38cm), **S** 24in (60cm), is semievergreen and has large, dark green leaves, sometimes suffused purple. **'Multicolor',** syn. *A. reptans* 'Rainbow', **H** 5in (12cm), **S** 18in (45cm), has dark green leaves, marked with cream and pink. **'Rainbow'.** See *A. reptans* 'Multicolor'.

AKEBIA

Chocolate vine

LARDIZABALACEAE

Genus of deciduous or semievergreen, woody-stemmed, twining climbers, grown for their leaves and flowers. Individual plants seldom produce fruits; cross-pollination between 2 individuals is required for fruit formation. Prefers a position in full sun and any good, well-drained soil. Tolerates an east- or north-facing position. Dislikes disturbance. May be propagated in a number of ways: by seed sown in fall or spring; by semiripe cuttings taken in summer; or by layering in winter.

A. lobata. See *A. trifoliata.*

A. x pentaphylla, illus. p.194.

A. quinata, illus. p.193.

A. trifoliata, syn. *A. lobata,* illus. p.204.

ALANGIUM

ALANGIACEAE/CORNACEAE

Genus of deciduous or evergreen trees and shrubs, grown for their foliage and flowers. Needs full sun and any fertile, well-drained soil. Propagate by sowing seed in spring or by taking softwood cuttings in summer.

A. platanifolium. Deciduous, upright, treelike shrub. **H** 10ft (3m), **S** 6ft (2m). Produces maple-like, 3-lobed, mid-green leaves. Fragrant, tubular, white flowers are borne from early to mid-summer. Z7–8 H8–7.

ALBIZIA

LEGUMINOSAE/MIMOSACEAE

Genus of deciduous or semievergreen trees, grown for their feathery foliage and unusual flower heads, composed of numerous stamens and resembling bottlebrushes. Requires full sun and well-drained soil. May be short-lived, and its seedlings may become a nuisance. *A. julibrissin* may be grown as a summer bedding plant for its foliage. Propagate by seed in fall. Susceptible to fungal disease verticillum.

A. distachya. See *Paraserianthes lophantha.*

A. julibrissin, illus. p.86.

A. lophantha. See *Paraserianthes lophantha.*

ALBUCA

HYACINTHACEAE/ASPARAGACEAE

Genus of spring- or summer-flowering bulbs. Needs an open, sunny position and well-drained soil. Dies down in spring or late summer after flowering. Propagate by seed in spring or by offsets when dormant.

A. canadensis, syn. *A. major, A. minor.* Spring-flowering bulb. **H** 6in (15cm), **S** 3–4in (8–10cm). Has 3–6 narrowly lance-shaped, erect, basal leaves. Produces a loose spike of tubular, yellow flowers, ⁵⁄₈–³⁄₄in (1.5–2cm) long, with a green stripe on each petal. Z11 H11–7.

A. humilis, illus. p.422.

A. major. See *A. canadensis.*

A. minor. See *A. canadensis.*

ALCEA
Hollyhock
MALVACEAE

Genus of biennials and short-lived perennials, grown for their tall spikes of flowers. Needs full sun and well-drained soil. Propagate by seed in late summer or spring. Rust may be a problem.

A. rosea, syn. *Althaea rosea* (Hollyhock). Erect biennial. **H** 5–6ft (1.5–2m), **S** to 2ft (60cm). Has rounded, lobed, rough-textured leaves. Spikes of single flowers, in a range of colors including pink, yellow and cream, are borne in summer and early fall. Z3–9 H10–3. **Chater's Double Group, H** 6–8ft (1.8–2.4m), bears double flowers in several different colors in summer and early fall. **'Majorette', H** 24in (60cm), **S** to 12in (30cm), produces double flowers, in several different colors, in summer and early fall. **'Summer Carnival'** (annual or biennial), **H** 6–8ft (1.8–2.4m), **S** to 2ft (60cm), has double flowers in mixed colors.

ALCHEMILLA
Lady's mantle
ROSACEAE

Genus of perennials that produce sprays of tiny, greenish-yellow flowers, with conspicuous outer calyces, in summer. Some are good for groundcover. Grow in sun or partial shade, in all but boggy soils. Propagate by seed or division in spring or fall.

A. alpina (Alpine lady's mantle). Mound-forming perennial. **H** 6in (15cm), **S** 24in (60cm) or more. Rounded, lobed, pale green leaves are covered in silky hairs. Bears upright spikes of tiny, greenish-yellow flowers, with conspicuous, green, outer calyces, in summer. Is suitable for groundcover and a dry bank. Z3–7 H8–1.
A. conjuncta, illus. p.275.
A. mollis, illus. p.275.

x ALICEARA
ORCHIDACEAE

See also ORCHIDS.

x A. Dark Warrior gx (Dark Warrior). Evergreen, epiphytic orchid for a cool greenhouse. **H** 10in (25cm). Produces sprays of wispy, mauve-brown, cream-yellow or green flowers, 1½in (4cm) across; flowering season varies. Leaves, 4in (10cm) long, are narrowly oval. Grow in partial shade in summer. Z15 H11–6.

x A. Eurostar gx, syn. x *Beallara* Eurostar gx. Evergreen, epiphytic orchid for a cool greenhouse. **H** 24in (60cm), **S** 16in (40cm). In spring bears star-shaped, maroon sepals and petals, each with white or cream tips and a large, spade-shaped, weakly 3-lobed lip, which is white in lower half and pink, maroon or speckled in upper half. Large, elliptic, compressed pseudobulb produces 1–3 strap-shaped leaves. Needs shade in summer. Z15 H11–6.

ALISMA
Water plantain
ALISMATACEAE

Genus of deciduous, perennial, marginal water plants, grown for their foliage and flowers. Requires an open, sunny position

in mud or up to 10in (25cm) depth of water. Tidy up fading foliage in fall and remove dying flower spikes before ripening seeds are dispersed. Propagate by division in spring or by seed in late summer. ! Contact with sap may irritate skin; all parts may cause mild stomach upset if ingested.

A. natans. See *Luronium natans*.
A. plantago-aquatica, illus. p.434.
A. ranunculoides. See *Baldellia ranunculoides*.

ALLAMANDA
APOCYNACEAE

Genus of evergreen, woody-stemmed, scrambling climbers, grown for their trumpet-shaped flowers. Prefers partial shade in summer and rich, well-drained, neutral to acid soil. Water regularly, less when not in full growth. Stems must be tied to supports. Prune previous season's growth back to 1 or 2 nodes in spring. Propagate by softwood cuttings in spring or summer. Whitefly and red spider mite may be troublesome. ! Contact with sap may irritate skin; all parts may cause mild stomach upset if ingested.

A. cathartica (Golden trumpet). **'Hendersonii'** illus. p.464.

ALLIUM
Ornamental onion
LILIACEAE/ALLIACEAE

Genus of perennials, some of which are edible, with bulbs, rhizomes or fibrous rootstocks. Nearly all have narrow, basal leaves smelling of onions when crushed, and most have small flowers packed together in a dense, spherical or shuttlecock-shaped umbel. Dried umbels of tall border species are good for winter decoration. Requires an open, sunny situation and well-drained soil; is best left undisturbed to form clumps. Plant in fall. Propagate by seed in fall or by division of clumps—spring-flowering varieties in late summer and summer-flowering ones in spring. ! Contact with the bulbs may irritate skin or aggravate skin allergies.

A. acuminatum, syn. *A. murrayanum,* illus. p.416.
A. aflatunense, illus. p.382.
A. aflatunense of gardens. See *A. hollandicum.*
A. akaka, illus. p.416.
A. albopilosum. See *A. cristophii.*
A. atropurpureum, illus. p.392.
A. azureum. See *A. caeruleum.*
A. beesianum. Clump-forming, late summer-flowering bulb. **H** 8–12in (20–30cm), **S** 2–4in (5–10cm). Has linear, gray-green leaves and, in late summer, pendent heads of bell-shaped, blue flowers. Z6–10 H10–6.
A. caeruleum, syn. *A. azureum,* illus. p.411.
A. campanulatum. Clump-forming, summer-flowering bulb. **H** 4–12in (10–30cm), **S** 2–4in (5–10cm). Linear, semierect, basal leaves die away before flowering time. Bears a domed umbel, 1–3in (2.5–7cm) wide, of up to 30 small, star-shaped, pale pink or white flowers. Z9–10 H10–9.
A. carinatum subsp. pulchellum, syn. *A. pulchellum.* Clump-forming, summer-

flowering bulb. **H** 12–24in (30–60cm), **S** 3–4in (8–10cm). Linear, semierect leaves sheathe lower two-thirds of stem. Has an umbel of pendent, cup-shaped, purple flowers. Z6–9 H9–6.
A. cernuum, illus. p.409.
A. cowanii. See *A. neapolitanum.*
A. cristophii, syn. *A. albopilosum,* illus. p.411.
A. cyaneum. Tuft-forming, summer-flowering bulb. **H** 4–12in (10–30cm), **S** 2–3in (5–8cm). Leaves are threadlike and erect. Stems each bear a small, dense umbel of 5 or more pendent, cup-shaped, blue or violet-blue flowers, ¼in (0.5cm) long. Z5–9 H9–5.
A. cyathophorum var. farreri, illus. p.423.
A. flavum, illus. p.412.
A. giganteum, illus. p.392.
A. 'Gladiator', illus. p.392.
A. 'Globemaster', illus. p.392.
A. hollandicum, syn. *A. aflatunense* of gardens. Tuft-forming, summer-flowering bulb. **H** 3ft (1m), **S** 4in (10cm). Has mid-green, basal leaves dying away by flowering time. Carries numerous star-shaped, purplish-pink flowers in a dense, spherical umbel, 4in (10cm) across. Z4–11 H11–1.
A. kansuense. See *A. sikkimense.*
A. karataviense, illus. p.416.
A. macranthum. Tuft-forming, summer-flowering bulb. **H** 8–12in (20–30cm), **S** 4–5in (10–12cm). Has linear leaves on lower part of flower stem, which bears a loose umbel of up to 20 bell-shaped, deep purple flowers, each ½in (1cm) long, on slender stalks. Z4–10 H10–4.
A. mairei. Clump-forming, late summer-to fall-flowering bulb. **H** 4–8in (10–20cm), **S** 4–5in (10–12cm). Leaves are erect, threadlike and basal. Wiry stems each bear a small, shuttlecock-shaped umbel of up to 20 upright, bell-shaped, pink flowers, ½in (1cm) long. Z4–10 H10–4.
A. moly, illus. p.424.
A. 'Mount Everest', illus. p.385.
A. murrayanum. See *A. acuminatum.*
A. murrayanum of gardens. See *A. unifolium.*
A. narcissiflorum, syn. *A. pedemontanum,* illus. p.422.
A. neapolitanum, syn. *A. cowanii,* illus. p.399. **Cowanii Group,** illus. p.409.
A. oreophilum, syn. *A. ostrowskianum,* illus. p.418.
A. ostrowskianum. See *A. oreophilum.*
A. pedemontanum. See *A. narcissiflorum.*
A. pulchellum. See *A. carinatum* subsp. *pulchellum.*
A. 'Purple Sensation', illus. p.392.
A. rosenbachianum. Tuft-forming, summer-flowering bulb. **H** 3ft (1m), **S** 4in (10cm). Has ridged stems and straplike, gray-green, basal leaves. Produces 50 or more star-shaped, deep purple flowers in a spherical umbel, 4in (10cm) across. Z6–9 H9–1.
A. schoenoprasum, illus. p.422.
A. schubertii, illus. p.409.
A. senescens var. calcareum. See *A. senescens* subsp. *montanum.* **subsp. montanum,** syn. *A. senescens* var. *calcareum,* illus. p.409.
A. sikkimense, syn. *A. kansuense.* Tuft-forming, summer-flowering bulb. **H** 4–10in (10–25cm), **S** 2–4in (5–10cm). Leaves are linear, erect and basal. Up to 15 bell-

shaped, blue flowers, ¼–½in (0.5–1cm) long, are borne in a small, pendent umbel. Z6–10 H10–6.
A. sphaerocephalon (Drumstick allium, Round-headed garlic). Clump-forming, summer-flowering bulb. **H** to 24in (60cm), **S** 3–4in (8–10cm). Has linear, semierect leaves on basal third of slender, wiry stems and a very dense umbel, ¾–1½in (2–4cm) across, of up to 40 small, bell-shaped, pinkish-purple flowers. Z4–11 H11–1.
A. stipitatum. Summer-flowering bulb. **H** 3–4ft (1–1.5m), **S** 6–8in (15–20cm). Sturdy stems with straplike, semierect, basal leaves carry 50 or more star-shaped, purplish-pink flowers in a spherical umbel, 3–5in (8–12cm) across. Z4–9 H9–1.
A. unifolium, syn. *A. murrayanum* of gardens, illus. p.402.

ALNUS
Alder
BETULACEAE

Genus of deciduous trees and shrubs, grown mainly for their ability to thrive in wet situations. Flowers are borne in catkins in late winter or early spring, the males conspicuous and attractive, the females forming persistent, woody, cone-like fruits. Most do best in sun and any moist or even waterlogged soil, but *A. cordata* will also grow well on poor, dry soils. Propagate species by seed sown in fall, cultivars by budding in late summer or by hardwood cuttings taken in early winter.

A. cordata (Italian alder). Fast-growing, deciduous, conical tree. **H** 60ft (18m), **S** 30ft (9m). Yellow, male catkins are borne in late winter and early spring, followed by heart-shaped, glossy, deep green leaves. Has persistent, round, woody fruits in fall. Z5–7 H7–5.
A. glutinosa (Black alder, Common alder). **'Aurea'** is a slow-growing, deciduous, conical tree. **H** to 80ft (25m), **S** 30ft (10m). Has rounded leaves, bright yellow until mid-summer, later becoming pale green. Produces yellow-brown catkins in early spring. Is useful grown in a boggy area. Z3–7 H7–1. **'Imperialis'** illus. p.75.
A. incana, illus. p.61. **'Aurea'** is a deciduous, conical tree. **H** 70ft (20m), **S** 25ft (8m). Has reddish-yellow or orange shoots in winter and broadly oval, yellow leaves. Reddish-yellow or orange catkins are borne in late winter and early spring. Is useful for cold, wet areas and poor soils. Z2–6 H6–1. **'Ramulis Coccineis'** has red winter shoots and buds, and orange catkins.

ALOCASIA
Elephant's ear
ARACEAE

Genus of evergreen perennials with underground rhizomes, grown for their attractive foliage. Produces tiny flowers on a spadix enclosed in a leaflike spathe. Needs high humidity, partial shade and well-drained soil. Propagate by seed, stem cuttings or division of rhizomes in spring. ! Contact with sap may irritate skin; all parts may cause mild stomach upset if ingested.

A. cuprea, illus. p.472.
A. longiloba, syn. *A. lowii* var. *picta,*

A. *lowii* var. *veitchii*, A. *veitchii*. Evergreen, tufted perennial. **H** 3ft (1m) or more, **S** 30in (75cm). Narrow leaves, triangular with arrow-shaped bases, are 18in (45cm) long and green with grayish midribs, veins and margins, purple below. Produces greenish spathes. Z14–15 H12–10.

A. *lowii* var. *picta*. See A. *longiloba*.
var. *veitchii*. See A. *longiloba*.

A. *macrorrhiza* (Giant elephant's ear, Taro). Evergreen, tufted perennial with a thick, trunklike stem. **H** to 10ft (3m) or more, **S** 6ft (2m). Broadly arrow-shaped, glossy, green leaves, to 3ft (1m) long, are borne on stalks 3ft (1m) long. Has yellowish-green spathes to 8in (20cm) high. Z11 H11–8.

A. *veitchii*. See A. *longiloba*.

ALOE
LILIACEAE/ASPHODELACEAE

Genus of evergreen, rosetted trees, shrubs, perennials and scandent climbers with succulent foliage and tubular to bell-shaped flowers. Tree aloes and shrubs with a spread more than 1ft (30cm) prefer full sun; most smaller species prefer partial shade. Needs very well-drained soil. Propagate by seed, stem cuttings or offsets in spring or summer.

A. *arborescens* (Candelabra plant). Evergreen, bushy, succulent-leaved shrub. **H** and **S** 6ft (2m). Stems are crowned by rosettes of widely spreading, long, slender, curved, dull blue-green leaves with toothed margins. Long flower stems produce masses of tubular to bell-shaped, red flowers, 1½in (4cm) long, in late winter and spring. Z11 H11–10. '**Variegata**' (illus. p.493) has numerous spikes of red flowers in late winter and spring.

A. *aristata* (Lace aloe, Torch plant), illus. p.493. Clump-forming, perennial succulent. **H** 4in (10cm), **S** 12in (30cm). Has a basal rosette of pointed, dark green leaves with white spots and soft-toothed edges. Produces orange flowers in spring. Offsets freely. H11–10.

A. *barbadensis*. See A. *vera*.
A. *brevifolia*. Basal-rosetted, perennial succulent, producing many offsets. **H** 6in (15cm), **S** 12in (30cm). Has broadly sword-shaped, fleshy, blue-green leaves with a few teeth along edges. In spring, flower stems, 20in (50cm) long, bear narrowly bell-shaped, bright red flowers, 1¼–1½in (3–4cm) long. Z10–11 H11–3.

A. *broomii*. Basal-rosetted, perennial succulent. **H** 4in (10cm), **S** 12in (30cm). Ovate to lance-shaped, mid-green leaves have minutely-toothed, red-brown margins and sharp, terminal spines. In summer unbranched flower stems, to 3ft (1m) long, bear dense spikes of tubular, pale lemon flowers, ¾in (2cm) long. Z10–11 H12–8.

A. *ciliaris*, illus. p.493. Climbing, perennial succulent. **H** 15ft (5m), **S** 1ft (30cm). Has a slender stem crowned by a rosette of narrow, green leaves and white teeth where leaf base joins stem. Bears bell-shaped, scarlet flowers, with yellow and green mouths, in spring. Z10–11 H12–10.

A. *concinna*. See A. *squarrosa*.
A. *descoingsii*. Clump-forming, basal-rosetted, perennial succulent. **H** 4in (10cm),

S 6in (15cm). Triangular, dull green leaves have white-toothed margins and many raised, white spots. In summer, unbranched flower stems, 6in (15cm) long, produce urn-shaped, red-orange flowers, ¼in (7mm) long. Z13–15 H11–10.

A. *erinacea*. See A. *melanacantha* var. *erinacea*.

A. *ferox* (Cape aloe), illus. p.493. Evergreen, succulent tree. **H** to 10ft (3m), **S** 5–6ft (1.5–2m). Has a woody stem crowned by a dense rosette of sword-shaped, blue-green leaves that have spined margins. Produces an erect spike of bell-shaped, orange-scarlet flowers in spring. Z10–11 H11–10.

A. *haworthioides*. Stemless, perennial succulent suckering to form clumps. **H** 8in (20cm), **S** 4in (10cm). Has dense rosettes of lance-shaped, dark green leaves, with many raised, white bristles and margins with small, white teeth set close together. Unbranched flower stems, 8–12in (15–30cm) long, bear bell-shaped, white to pale pink flowers, 3in (8cm) long, in summer. Z13–15 H11–10.

A. *hemmingii*, illus. p.493. Basal-rosetted, perennial succulent. **H** 6in (15cm), **S** 10in (25cm). Ovate to lance-shaped, olive-green leaves, with dull, white streaks, have short, sharp teeth at the margins. Produces unbranched flower stems, 12in (30cm) long, with tubular, minutely spotted, flamingo-pink to pale rose flowers, 1in (2.5cm) long, in summer. Z11 H12–9.

A. *humilis*. Rosetted, perennial succulent. **H** 4in (10cm), **S** 12in (30cm). Has a dense, basal rosette of narrowly sword-shaped, spine-edged, fleshy, blue-green leaves, often erect, with incurving tips. Flower stems, 12in (30cm) long, each bear a spike of narrowly bell-shaped, orange flowers, 1½–1¾in (3.5–4.5cm) long, in spring. Offsets freely. Z10–11 H12–10.

A. *mcloughlinii*. Solitary or sometimes clump-forming, perennial succulent. **H** 20in (50cm), **S** to 39in (100cm). Has dense rosettes of lance-shaped, smooth, glossy, dark green leaves with many small, pale green spots and margins bearing firm, reddish-brown teeth. In summer produces branched flower spikes, to 4ft (1.2m) long, of tubular, strawberry-red to pink flowers, 1in (2.5cm) long. Z11 H12–9.

A. *melanacantha* var. *erinacea*, syn. A. *erinacea*. Slow-growing, clump-forming, perennial succulent. **H** 6in (15cm), **S** 12in (30cm). Compact rosettes of triangular to lance-shaped, dull-green leaves have sharp, black spines at the margins and a black spine at each tip. Unbranched flower stems, to 3ft (1m) long, produce dense, cylindrical clusters of bell-shaped, scarlet flowers, 1in (3cm) long, fading to yellow, in summer. Z10–11 H11–8.

A. *microstigma*. Basal-rosetted, perennial succulent. **H** 12in (30cm), **S** 10–24in (25–60cm). Lance-shaped to triangular, red-tinged, mid-green leaves, often white spotted, especially beneath, have reddish-brown margins with small, reddish-brown teeth. Unbranched flower stems, 24in (60cm) long, bear conical racemes of bell-shaped, orange flowers, 10in (25cm) long, fading to greenish-yellow, in summer. Z10–11 H12–8.

A. *plicatilis*. Perennial succulent with leaves in opposite pairs up the stem. **H** and **S** to 24in (60cm). Has strap-shaped, smooth, dull to glaucous green leaves with margins almost without teeth. In summer, unbranched flower stems, to 20in (50cm) long, produce cylindrical spikes of bell-shaped, scarlet flowers, 2in (5cm) long. Z11 H12–9.

A. *punctata*. See A. *variegata*.
A. *rauhii*. Basal-rosetted, perennial succulent eventually forming dense clumps. **H** to 4in (10cm), **S** 8in (20cm). Unbranched flower stems, to 10in (25cm) long, of tubular, scarlet flowers, 1in (2.5cm) long, pale red to greenish towards mouths, are borne throughout the year. Lance-shaped, grayish or bright green leaves have many elongated, white spots and small, white teeth at the margins. In some forms, the leaves have raised dots or are almost white with green dots. Z11 H11–10.

A. *somaliensis*. Basal-rosetted, perennial succulent. **H** 12in (30cm), **S** 10in (25cm). Lance-shaped, glossy olive-green leaves, with dull, white streaks, have short, sharp teeth at the margins. Branched flower stems, 12–24in (30–60cm) long, with tubular, minutely spotted, flamingo-pink to pale rose flowers, 1in (2.5cm) long, are borne in summer. Z11 H12–9.

A. *squarrosa*, syn. A. *concinna*. Prostrate, perennial succulent. **H** 12in (30cm), **S** 8in (20cm). Has lance-shaped, strongly recurved, toothed, white-speckled, mid-green leaves borne along short stems. Unbranched, pendulous flower stems, 4–10in (10–25cm) long, of tubular, red flowers, 1in (2.5cm) long, are produced in summer. Z11 H12–9.

A. *striata* (Coral aloe), illus. p.493. Basal-rosetted, perennial succulent. **H** and **S** 3ft (1m). Has broad, blue-green leaves, with white margins and marks, that become suffused red in full sun. Produces reddish-orange flowers in spring. Makes a good house plant. Z10–11 H11–10.

A. *variegata*, syn. A. *punctata* (Partridge-breasted aloe), illus. p.493. Humped, perennial succulent. **H** 12in (30cm), **S** 4in (10cm). Has triangular, white-marked, dark green leaves with pronounced keels beneath. Bears a spike of pinkish-red flowers in spring. Makes a good house plant. Z10–11 H11–10.

A. *vera*, syn. A. *barbadensis*, illus. p.492.
A. *zebrina*. Basal-rosetted, perennial succulent. **H** 8in (20cm), **S** 16in (40cm). Lance-shaped, dull green leaves, with white chevrons, have sharp, brown teeth at the margins. Branched flower stems, 3ft (1m) long, of tubular, coral-red to dull red flowers, 1¼in (3cm) long, are produced in summer Z10–11 H11–10.

ALOINOPSIS
AIZOACEAE

Genus of dwarf, tuberous, perennial succulents with daisylike flowers from late summer to early spring. Requires a sunny site and very well-drained soil. Is very susceptible to overwatering. Propagate by seed in summer.

A. *schooneesii*, illus. p.488.

ALONSOA
Mask flower
SCROPHULARIACEAE

Genus of perennials, grown as annuals. May be used for cut flowers. Grow in sun and in rich, well-drained soil. Flowering may be poor outdoors in a wet summer. Young plants should have growing shoots pinched out to encourage bushy growth. Propagate by seed sown outdoors in late spring. Aphids may be troublesome, particularly when grown in greenhouses.

A. *warscewiczii*, illus. p.308.

ALOPECURUS
Foxtail grass
GRAMINEAE/POACEAE

See also GRASSES, BAMBOOS, RUSHES and SEDGES.

A. *pratensis* 'Aureomarginatus'. See A. *pratensis* 'Aureovariegatus'.
'**Aureovariegatus**', syn. A. *pratensis* 'Aureomarginatus', illus. p.289.

ALOYSIA
VERBENACEAE

Genus of deciduous or evergreen, summer-flowering shrubs, grown for their aromatic foliage and sprays of tiny flowers. Needs full sun and well-drained soil. Cut out any dead wood in early summer. Propagate by softwood cuttings in summer.

A. *triphylla*, syn. *Lippia citriodora*, illus. p.132.

ALPINIA
Ginger lily
ZINGIBERACEAE

Genus of mainly evergreen perennials with fleshy rhizomes, grown for their flowers. Needs well-drained soil with plenty of humus, partial shade and a moist atmosphere. Is not easy to grow successfully in containers. Propagate by division in late spring or early summer. Red spider mite may be a problem.

A. *calcarata* (Indian ginger). Evergreen, upright, clump-forming perennial. **H** and **S** to 3ft (1m). Has stalkless, aromatic, lance-shaped leaves, to 1ft (30cm) long. At any time of year may bear horizontal spikes of whitish flowers, with yellow lips, 1in (2.5cm) long, marked reddish-purple. Z14–15 H11–10.

A. *hainanensis*, illus. p.477. Evergreen, clump-forming perennial. **H** and **S** 36–48in (90–120cm). Has short stalked, lance-shaped, slightly hairy, mid-green leaves, to 16in (40cm) long. In spring-summer, honey-scented, white flowers, with red-lined lips, 1in (4.5cm) long, are borne on old stems. Z13–15 H12–1.

A. *nutans*. See A. *zerumbet*.
A. *purpurata* (Cone ginger), illus. p.477. Vigorous, evergreen, upright perennial. **H** 10ft (to 3m), **S** 3ft (1m). In summer produces cone-like spires, 14in (35cm) long, of many small, white flowers, to 1in (2.5cm) long, in the axils of persistent, red or pink bracts. Has stalked, oblong, hairless, mid-green leaves, to 36in (90cm) long. Is good for cut flowers. Z11 H11–10.

A. speciosa. See *A. zerumbet.*

A. zerumbet, syn. *A. nutans, A. speciosa* (Shell flower, Shell ginger), illus. p.477. Evergreen, clump-forming perennial. **H** 10ft (3m), **S** 3ft (1m). Has racemes of white flowers, with yellow lips and pink- or red-marked throats, mainly in summer. H11–10.

Alsobia dianthiflora. See *Episcia dianthiflora.*
Alsophila. See *Cyathea.*
Alsophila australis. See *Cyathea australis.*

ALSTROEMERIA
Peruvian lily
ALSTROEMERIACEAE

Genus of mostly summer- to fall-flowering, tuberous perennials with showy, funnel-shaped, multicolored flowers. Flowers are good for cutting as they last well. Produces erect stems with alternate or scattered, linear to lance-shaped, mid- to gray-green leaves, usually 3–5in (7–12cm) long, held on twisted leaf stalks. Where marginally hardy, protect by covering dormant tubers with a loose, dry mulch. Needs sun and well-drained soil. Propagate by seed or division in early spring. ① Contact with foliage may aggravate skin allergies.
A. 'Apollo', illus. p.387. Mid-summer to fall-flowering, tuberous perennial. **H** 3ft (1m), **S** 2¹/₂ft (75cm). Bears large, open, white flowers with brown markings and yellow throats. Z7–10 H10–7.
A. aurantica. See *A. aurea.*
A. aurea, syn. *A. aurantica.* Summer-flowering, tuberous perennial. **H** to 3ft (1m), **S** 2–3ft (60cm–1m). Produces orange flowers, tipped with green and streaked dark red. Z7–10 H10–7. 'Orange King' (illus. p.387) has bright orange flowers, with brown-speckled throats, from mid-summer to fall.
A. 'Blushing Bride', illus. p.387. Mid-summer to fall-flowering, tuberous perennial. **H** and **S** 2ft (60cm). Produces cream flowers with brown-speckled, pink and pale yellow throats. Z7–10 H10–7.
A. 'Charm'. Mid-summer-flowering, tuberous perennial. **H** 2¹/₂ft (75cm), **S** 2ft (60cm). Produces pale peach flowers with brown speckles and primrose-yellow throats. Z7–10 H10–7.
A. 'Elvira', illus. p.387. Mid-summer to fall-flowering, tuberous perennial. **H** 2¹/₂ft (75cm), **S** 2ft (60cm). Produces cream flowers with bold, pink flecks on outer edges of petals and at the throats. Z7–10 H10–7.
A. 'Friendship', illus. p.387. Mid-summer to fall-flowering, tuberous perennial. **H** 3ft (1m), **S** 2¹/₂ft (75cm). Produces pale lime-yellow flowers with brown-red speckled, yellow throats. Z7–10 H10–7.
A. hookeri, illus. p.361.
A. **Inca Ice** ('Koice'), illus. p.387. Late spring to fall-flowering, tuberous perennial. **H** and **S** to 3ft (1m). Produces cream and pale yellow flowers with pink throats and purple-brown speckling on the upper and lower petals. Z7–10 H10–7.
A. **Inca Tropic** ('Kotrop'), illus. p.387. Mid-summer to fall-flowering, tuberous perennial. **H** and **S** 18in (45cm). Produces orange flowers with yellow throats flecked with brown markings. Young leaves are brown tinged.

A. 'Koice'. See *A.* **Inca Ice.**
A. 'Kotrop'. See *A.* **Inca Tropic.**
A. **Ligtu Hybrids,** illus. p.413.
A. 'Little Miss Tara'. Mid-summer to fall-flowering, tuberous perennial. **H** and **S** 6in (15cm). Produces relatively large, reddish-pink flowers with brown markings and yellow throats. Z7–10 H10–7.
A. **Margaret** ('Stacova'). Mid- to late summer-flowering tuberous perennial. **H** 3ft (1m), **S** 2–3ft (60cm–1m). Produces widely flared, funnel-shaped, deep red flowers. Z8–11 H12–7.
A. 'Moulin Rouge', illus. p.387. Mid-summer to fall-flowering, tuberous perennial. **H** and **S** 18in (45cm). Produces soft red flowers with dark brown-speckled, yellow throats. Z7–10 H10–7.
A. 'Parigo Charm'. Summer-flowering, tuberous perennial. **H** 3ft (1m), **S** 24in (60cm). Produces salmon-pink flowers with primrose-yellow inner tepals, marked carmine-red. Z8–10 H11–7.
A. pelegrina. Summer-flowering, tuberous perennial. **H** 1–2ft (30–60cm), **S** 2–3ft (60cm–1m). Each leafy stem has 1–3 white flowers, stained pinkish-mauve and spotted yellow and brownish-purple. Z8–10 H10–8.
A. 'Polka', illus. p.387. Mid-summer to fall-flowering, tuberous perennial. **H** 2¹/₂ft (75cm), **S** 2ft (60cm). Produces bright magenta-blushed, pale pink flowers with dark brown-speckled, yellow throats. Z7–10 H10–7.
A. **Princess Ariane** ('Zapriari'), illus. p.387. Mid-summer to fall-flowering, tuberous perennial. **H** 8in (20cm), **S** 6in (15cm). Produces yellow flowers with purple-marked petal tips and dark brown speckled throats. Z7–10 H10–7.
A. **Princess Julieta** ('Zaprijul'), illus. p.387. Mid-summer to fall-flowering, tuberous perennial. **H** and **S** 12in (30cm). Produces pale purple flowers with darker purple markings and white throats. Z7–10 H10–7.
A. **Princess Paola** ('Stapripal'). Mid-summer to fall-flowering, tuberous perennial. **H** 10in (25cm), **S** 8in (20cm). Produces pale pink flowers with dark pink markings and dark brown-speckled, yellow throats. Z7–10 H10–7.
A. psittacina, syn. *A. pulchella* (Parrot lily), illus. p.387. Summer-flowering, tuberous perennial. **H** 3ft (1m), **S** 1¹/₂ft (45cm). Mauve-spotted stems bear open umbels of red-marked, green flowers. Z8–10 H11–8.
A. pulchella. See *A. psittacina.*
A. 'Red Beauty', illus. p.387. Mid-summer to fall-flowering, tuberous perennial. **H** 3ft (1m), **S** 2¹/₂ft (75cm). Produces bright scarlet flowers with dark brownish-black-speckled, yellow throats. Z7–10 H10–7.
A. 'Serenade', illus. p.387. Mid-summer to fall-flowering, tuberous perennial. **H** 2¹/₂ft (75cm), **S** 2ft (60cm). Produces pale pink flowers with deep magenta markings and black-speckled, yellow throats. Z7–10 H10–7.
A. 'Stacova'. See *A.* **Margaret.**
A. 'Stapripal'. See *A.* **Princess Paola.**
A. 'Tara', illus. p.387. Late spring to fall-flowering, tuberous perennial. **H** 4–12in (10–30cm), **S** 12in (30cm). Produces dark brownish-black-speckled, red flowers with yellow throats. Z7–10 H10–7.
A. 'Walter Fleming'. Summer-flowering, tuberous perennial. **H** to 3ft (1m), **S** 2–3ft

(60cm–1m). Each leafy stem produces narrowly lance-shaped, twisted leaves and widely funnel-shaped, deep yellow flowers flushed purple with reddish-purple spots. Z8–11 H11–7.
A. 'Zapriari'. See *A.* **Princess Ariane.**
A. 'Zaprijul'. See *A.* **Princess Julieta.**

ALTERNANTHERA
AMARANTHACEAE

Genus of bushy perennials, grown for their attractive, colored foliage. Is useful for carpeting or bedding. Needs sun or partial shade and moist but well-drained soil. Propagate by tip cuttings or division in spring.
A. amoena. See *A. ficoidea* var. *amoena.*
A. dentata 'Purple Knight', illus. p.311.
A. ficoidea (Parrot leaf). **var. amoena**, syn. *A. amoena* is a mat-forming perennial. **H** 2in (5cm), **S** indefinite. Has narrowly oval, green leaves, marked red, yellow and orange, with wavy margins. Z11 H11–1. **'Versicolor'**, syn. *A. versicolor* is an erect form, **H** and **S** to 12in (30cm), with rounded to spoon-shaped leaves shaded brown, red and yellow.
A. versicolor. See *A. ficoidea* 'Versicolor'.

Althaea rosea. See *Alcea rosea.*

ALYSSOIDES
CRUCIFERAE/BRASSICACEAE

Genus of one species of short-lived, evergreen subshrub, grown for its flowers and swollen fruits. Is particularly suitable for dry banks and rock gardens. Needs sun and well-drained soil. Propagate by seed sown in fall.
A. utriculata. Evergreen, rounded subshrub. **H** and **S** 12in (30cm). Has oval, glossy, dark green leaves. Loose sprays of small, bright yellow flowers, in spring, are followed by balloon-like, buff seed pods. Z6–9 H9–6.

ALYSSUM
CRUCIFERAE/BRASSICACEAE

Genus of perennials, some of which are evergreen, and annuals, grown for their flowers. Requires a sunny site and well-drained soil. Cut back lightly after flowering. Propagate either by softwood cuttings taken in late spring or by seed sown in fall.
A. maritimum. See *Lobularia maritima.*
A. montanum. Evergreen, prostrate perennial. **H** and **S** 6in (15cm). Leaves are small, oval, hairy and gray. Flower stems, 6in (15cm) long, each bear an open, spherical raceme of small, highly fragrant, soft yellow flowers in summer. Is a good plant for a rock garden. Z4–9 H9–1.
A. saxatile. See *Aurinia saxatilis.*
A. spinosum, syn. *Ptilotrichum spinosum.* Semievergreen, rounded, compact shrub. **H** 8in (20cm) or more, **S** 12in (30cm). Intricate branches bear spines and narrowly oval to linear, silver leaves. Spherical heads of tiny, 4-petaled, white to purple-pink flowers are borne in early summer. Z5–9 H9–5.
A. wulfenianum. Prostrate perennial. **H** ³/₄in (2cm), **S** 8in (20cm). Loose heads of small, bright yellow flowers are produced in summer above small, oval, gray leaves. Z6–9 H9–6.

AMARANTHUS
AMARANTHACEAE

Genus of annuals, grown for their dense panicles of tiny flowers or their colorful foliage. Grow in a sunny position in rich or fertile, well-drained soil. Propagate from seed sown outdoors in late spring. Aphids may be a problem.
A. caudatus, illus. p.307.
A. hypochondriacus, illus. p.308.
A. tricolor (Chinese spinach, Tampala). 'Joseph's Coat' Bushy annual. **H** to 3ft (1m), **S** 1¹/₂ft (45cm) or more. Has oval, scarlet, green and yellow leaves, to 8in (20cm) long, and produces small panicles of tiny, red flowers in summer. H11–1. 'Molten Fire' has crimson, bronze and purple leaves.

x AMARCRINUM
AMARYLLIDACEAE

Hybrid genus (*Amaryllis* x *Crinum*) of one robust, evergreen bulb, grown for its large, funnel-shaped flowers. Needs a sunny position and well-drained soil. Plant with neck just covered by soil. Propagate by division in spring.
x *A. memoria-corsii,* syn. x *Crinodonna corsii,* illus. p.395. Evergreen, clump-forming bulb. **H** and **S** to 3ft (1m). Has wide, semierect, basal leaves. Sturdy stems bear fragrant, rose-pink flowers in loose heads in late summer and fall.

x AMARYGIA
AMARYLLIDACEAE

Hybrid genus (*Amaryllis* x *Brunsvigia*) of sturdy, fall-flowering bulbs, which are cultivated for their large, showy flowers. Needs full sun and, preferably, the shelter of a wall. Plant bulbs just beneath the surface of well-drained soil. Propagate by division in spring.
x *A. parkeri,* syn. x *Brunsdonna parkeri,* illus. p.395. Early fall-flowering bulb. **H** to 3ft (1m), **S** 2–3ft (60–100cm). Sturdy stem bears a large head of funnel-shaped, deep rose flowers with yellow and white throats. Produces strap-shaped, semierect, basal leaves after flowering.

AMARYLLIS
AMARYLLIDACEAE

Genus of fall-flowering bulbs, grown for their funnel-shaped flowers. Requires a sheltered, sunny situation and well-drained soil. Plant bulbs in at least 3in (8cm) of soil. Propagate by division in late spring, as leaves die down, or in late summer, before growth recommences.
A. belladonna, illus. p.395. 'Hathor', illus. p.395.

AMBERBOA
Sweet sultan
COMPOSITAE/ASTERACEAE

Genus of erect annuals or biennials, grown for their cornflower-like flower heads, which are borne from spring to fall. Needs full sun and moderately fertile, well-drained soil. Deadhead to prolong flowering. Propagate by seed in spring or fall.
A. moschata, syn. *Centaurea moschata* (Sweet sultan). Fast-growing, upright,

slender-stemmed annual. **H** 18in (45cm), **S** 8in (20cm). Has lance-shaped, grayish-green leaves and large, fragrant flower heads, in a range of colors, in summer and early fall. H11–1.

AMELANCHIER
Juneberry, Serviceberry, Shadbush
ROSACEAE

Genus of deciduous, spring-flowering trees and shrubs, grown primarily for their profuse flowers and their foliage, which is frequently brightly colored in fall, and their edible fruit. Requires sun or semi-shade and well-drained but not too dry, preferably neutral to acid soil. Propagate in fall by seed, in late fall to early spring by layering or, in the case of suckering species, by division. Fireblight may sometimes be troublesome.

A. alnifolia (Alder-leaved serviceberry, Saskatoon). Deciduous, upright, suckering shrub. **H** 12ft (4m) or more, **S** 10ft (3m) or more. Leaves are oval to rounded and dark green. Erect spikes of star-shaped, creamy-white flowers are borne in late spring, followed by small, edible, juicy, rounded, purple-black fruits. Z4–9 H8–3.

A. arborea (Downy serviceberry). Deciduous, spreading, sometimes shrubby, tree. **H** 30ft (10m), **S** 40ft (12m). Clusters of star-shaped, white flowers appear in mid-spring as oval, white-haired, young leaves unfold. Foliage matures to dark green, turning to red or yellow in fall. Rounded fruits are small, dry and reddish-purple. Z4–9 H9–4.

A. asiatica (Asian serviceberry). Deciduous, spreading tree or shrub. **H** 25ft (8m), **S** 30ft (10m). Leaves are oval and dark green, usually woolly when young and turning yellow or red in fall. Star-shaped, white flowers are borne profusely in late spring, followed by edible, juicy, rounded, blackcurrant-like fruits. Z5–7 H7–5.

A. canadensis (Shadblow, Shadbush). Deciduous, upright, dense shrub. **H** 20ft (6m), **S** 10ft (3m). Star-shaped, white flowers are borne from mid- to late spring amid unfolding, oval, white-haired leaves that mature to dark green and turn orange-red in fall. Fruits are edible, rounded, blackish-purple, sweet and juicy. Z3–7 H7–1.

A. laevis, illus. p.81.
A. lamarckii, illus. p.110.

Amomyrtus luma. See *Luma apiculata.*

AMORPHA
LEGUMINOSAE/PAPILIONACEAE

Genus of deciduous shrubs and subshrubs, grown for their flowers and foliage. Is a useful plant for cold, dry, exposed positions. Requires full sun and well-drained soil. May be propagated by softwood cuttings taken in summer or by seed sown in fall.

A. canescens (Lead plant). Deciduous, open subshrub. **H** 3ft (1m), **S** 5ft (1.5m). Dense spikes of tiny, pealike, purple flowers, with orange anthers, are produced in late summer and early fall, amid oval, gray-haired leaves divided into 21–41 narrowly oval leaflets. Z2–8 H8–1.

AMORPHOPHALLUS
Devil's tongue, Snake palm
ARACEAE

Genus of tuberous perennials, cultivated for their huge and dramatic, but foul-smelling, spathes, which surround tiny flowers on sturdy spadices. Requires partial shade and rich soil kept continuously moist during the growing season. Keep tubers dry in winter. Propagate by seed sown in spring or by offsets in spring or summer.

A. konjac, syn. *A. rivieri* (Devil's tongue, Snake palm, Umbrella arum). Summer-flowering, tuberous perennial. **H** to 16in (40cm), **S** 2–3ft (60cm–1m). Produces a flattish, wavy-edged, dark reddish-brown spathe, to 16in (40cm) long, from which protrudes an erect, dark brown spadix. Brownish-green-mottled, pale green stem, 3ft (1m) long, bears one large, deeply lobed leaf after flowering. Z13–15 H11–10.
A. rivieri. See *A. konjac.*

AMPELODESMOS
GRAMINEAE/POACEAE

See also GRASSES, BAMBOOS, RUSHES AND SEDGES.
A. mauritanica, illus. p.287.

AMPELOPSIS
VITACEAE

Genus of deciduous, woody-stemmed, tendril climbers, some of which are twining, grown for their leaves. Grow in a sheltered position, in sun or partial shade in any soil. Needs plenty of room as grows quickly and can cover a large area. Propagate by greenwood or semiripe cuttings in mid-summer.

A. aconitifolia, syn. *Vitis aconitifolia* (Monkshood vine). Fast-growing, deciduous, woody-stemmed, twining, tendril climber. **H** to 40ft (12m). Rounded leaves have 3 or 5 toothed, lobed, dark green leaflets. Inconspicuous, greenish flowers, in late summer, are followed by orange berries. Z5–8 H8–1.

A. brevipedunculata var. maximowiczii, syn. *A. glandulosa* var. *brevipedunculata, A. heterophylla, Vitis heterophylla,* illus. p.210.
var. maximowiczii 'Elegans', syn. *A. brevipedunculata* 'Tricolor', *A. brevipedunculata* 'Variegata', illus. p.195. **'Tricolor'.** See *A. brevipedunculata* var. *maximowiczii* 'Elegans'. **'Variegata'.** See *A. brevipedunculata* var. *maximowiczii* 'Elegans'.
A. glandulosa var. brevipedunculata. See *A. brevipedunculata* var. *maximowiczii.*
A. heterophylla. See *A. brevipedunculata* var. *maximowiczii.*
A. megalophylla, illus. p.210.
A. sempervirens. See *Cissus striata.*
A. veitchii. See *Parthenocissus tricuspidata* 'Veitchii'.

AMSONIA
Bluestar
APOCYNACEAE

Genus of slow-growing, clump-forming, summer-flowering perennials. Needs full sun and well-drained soil. Is best left undisturbed for some years. Propagate

by division in spring, by softwood cuttings in summer or by seed in fall.
① Contact with the milky sap may irritate skin.
A. orientalis, syn. *Rhazya orientalis,* illus. p.271.
A. tabernaemontana (Willow bluestar). Clump-forming perennial. **H** 18–24in (45–60cm), **S** 12in (30cm). Leaves are small and narrow. Willowy stems bear drooping clusters of small, tubular, pale blue flowers in summer. Z3–9 H9–1.

ANACAMPTIS
ORCHIDACEAE

See also ORCHIDS.
A. morio, syn. *Orchis morio* (Gandergoose, Green-veined orchid), illus. p.466. Deciduous, terrestrial orchid. **H** 16in (40cm). Reddish-purple, mauve or rarely white flowers, $^1\!/_2$in (1cm) long, with green veins on the cupped sepals, open along stems in spring. Has a basal cluster of lance-shaped or broadly oblong, pale to mid-green leaves, 4–6in (10–16cm) long. Requires sun or partial shade. Z12–15 H12–6.

Anacharis densa. See *Egeria densa.*

ANACYCLUS
COMPOSITAE/ASTERACEAE

Genus of summer-flowering, prostrate perennials with stems radiating from a central rootstock. Needs full sun and well-drained soil. Propagate by softwood cuttings in spring or by seed in fall.
A. depressus. See *A. pyrethrum* var. *depressus.*
A. pyrethrum var. depressus, syn. *A. depressus,* illus. p.360.

ANAGALLIS
Pimpernel
PRIMULACEAE

Genus of annuals and creeping perennials, grown for their flowers. Plant in an open, sunny site in fertile, moist soil. Propagate by seed or division in spring. Raise *A. tenella* by soft-tip cuttings in spring or early summer.
A. tenella. 'Studland' illus. p.353.

ANANAS
Pineapple
BROMELIACEAE

Genus of evergreen, rosette-forming perennials, grown for their foliage and edible fruits (pineapples). Prefers full light, but tolerates some shade. Needs fertile, well-drained soil. Water moderately during growing season, sparingly at other times. Propagate by suckers or cuttings of 'leafy' fruit tops in spring or summer.
A. bracteatus (Red pineapple, Wild pineapple). **var. tricolor,** syn. *A. bracteatus* 'Striata', *A. bracteatus* 'Tricolor' (illus. p.471) is an evergreen, basal-rosetted perennial. **H** and **S** 3ft (1m). Forms dense rosettes of strap-shaped, spiny-edged, arching, deep green leaves, longitudinally yellow-striped and often with marginal, red spines. Dense spikes of small, tubular, lavender-violet flowers, with prominent, reddish-pink bracts, are borne

usually in summer. These are followed by brownish-orange-red fruits that are 6in (15cm) or more long. Z15 H11–1. **'Striata'.** See *A. bracteatus* var. *tricolor.* **'Tricolor'.** See *A. bracteatus* var. *tricolor.*
A. comosus 'Variegatus'. Evergreen, basal-rosetted perennial. **H** and **S** 24in (60cm) or more. Very narrowly strap-shaped, channeled, rigid, gray-green leaves are suffused pink, have cream margins, are gray-scaled beneath and sometimes have spiny edges. Produces tubular, purple-blue flowers with inconspicuous, green bracts; fruits are the edible pineapples grown commercially, but are much smaller on pot-grown plants. Z11 H11–1.

ANAPHALIOIDES
Pearly everlasting
ASTERACEAE/COMPOSITAE

Genus of summer flowering perennials and dwarf shrubs grown for silver foliage and "everlasting" flower heads. Requires full sun and very well-drained soil. Propagate by heel or semiripe cuttings in summer.
A. bellidioides, syn. *Helichrysum bellidioides.* Evergreen, prostrate shrub. **H** 2in (5cm), **S** 9in (23cm). Has small, rounded, fleshy, dark green leaves and, in early summer, terminal clusters of daisylike, white flower heads.

ANAPHALIS
Pearly everlasting
ASTERACEAE/COMPOSITAE

Genus of perennials with heads of small, papery flowers, used dried for winter decoration. Prefers sun but will grow in semi-shade. Soil should be well-drained but not too dry. Propagate by seed in fall or by division in winter or spring.
A. margaritacea, illus. p.231.
A. nepalensis var. monocephala, syn. *A. nubigena.* Dwarf, leafy perennial. **H** 8–12in (20–30cm), **S** 6in (15cm). Woolly, silvery stems bear lance-shaped leaves. Bears dense, terminal clusters of white flower heads in late summer. Z5–8 H8–5.
A. nubigena. See *A. nepalensis* var. *monocephala.*
A. triplinervis. Variable, clump-forming perennial. **H** 32–36in (80–90cm), **S** 18–24in (45–60cm). Has obovate to elliptic, white-woolly leaves, prominently 3-veined. In mid- to late summer produces clusters of white-bracted, yellow-centered flower heads. Z5–8 H8–5. **'Sommerschnee',** syn. *A. triplinervis* 'Summer Snow' illus. p.231. **'Summer Snow'.** See *A. triplinervis* 'Sommerschnee'.

ANCHUSA
Alkanet
BORAGINACEAE

Genus of annuals, biennials and perennials, some of which are evergreen, with usually blue flowers. Needs sun and well-drained soil; resents too much winter wet. Tall, perennial species may need to be staked and allowed room to spread. Propagate perennials by root cuttings in winter, annuals and biennials by seed in fall or spring.

A. azurea, syn. *A. italica.* **'Little John'** is a clump-forming perennial. **H** 20in (50cm), **S** 24in (60cm). Mainly basal leaves are narrowly oval and hairy. Bears branching racemes of large, open cup-shaped, dark blue flowers in early summer. Z3–8 H8–1. **'Loddon Royalist',** illus. p.241. **'Opal',** **H** 4ft (1.2m), has paler blue flowers.
A. caespitosa. See *A. cespitosa.*
A. capensis. 'Blue Angel', illus. p.315. **'Blue Bird'** is a bushy biennial, grown as an annual. **H** to 18in (45cm), **S** 8in (20cm). Has lance-shaped, bristly, mid-green leaves and, in summer, heads of shallowly bowl-shaped, sky-blue flowers. Z7–9 H9–7.
A. cespitosa, syn. *A. caespitosa,* illus. p.356.
A. italica. See *A. azurea.*

Ancistrocactus megarhizus. See *Sclerocactus scheeri.*
Ancistrocactus scheeri. See *Sclerocactus scheeri.*
Ancistrocactus uncinatus. See *Sclerocactus uncinatus.*

ANDROMEDA
Bog rosemary
ERICACEAE

Genus of evergreen shrubs with an open, twiggy habit. Needs full light and rich, moist, acid soil. Propagate by semiripe cuttings taken in late summer or by seed sown in spring.
A. polifolia. Evergreen, open, twiggy shrub. **H** 12–18in (30–45cm), **S** 24in (60cm). Has narrow, leathery, glossy, mid-green leaves. Bears terminal clusters of pitcher-shaped, pink flowers in spring and early summer. Z2–6 H6–1. **'Alba'** illus. p.332. **'Compacta'** illus. p.333.

ANDROSACE
Rock jasmine
PRIMULACEAE

Genus of annuals and evergreen perennials, usually compact cushion-forming and often with soft, hairy leaves. Many species are suitable for cold greenhouses and troughs with winter cover. Needs sun and very well-drained soil; some species prefer acid soil. Resents wet foliage in winter. Propagate by tip cuttings in summer or by seed in fall. Is prone to botrytis and attack by aphids.
A. carnea, illus. p.350. **subsp.** *laggeri* illus. p.353.
A. chamaejasme. Evergreen, basal-rosetted, variable perennial with easily rooted stolons. **H** 1¼–2½in (3–6cm), **S** to 6in (15cm). Has open, hairy rosettes of oval leaves. In spring bears clusters of 2–8 flattish, white flowers, each with a yellow eye that sometimes turns red with age. Z4–7 H7–1.
A. cylindrica. Evergreen, basal-rosetted perennial. **H** ½–¾in (1–2cm), **S** 4in (10cm). Leaves are linear and glossy. Flower stems each bear up to 10 small, flattish, white flowers, each with a yellow-green eye, in early spring. Is suitable for a cold greenhouse. Z6–7 H7–6.
A. hedraeantha. Evergreen, tight cushion-forming perennial. **H** ½–¾in (1–2cm), **S** to 4in (10cm). Bears loose rosettes of narrowly oval, glossy leaves. Umbels of 5–10 flattish, yellow-throated, pink flowers are produced in spring. Is best in a cold greenhouse. Z6–7 H7–6.
A. hirtella. Evergreen, tight cushion-

forming perennial. **H** ½in (1cm), **S** to 4in (10cm). Produces rosettes of small, thick, linear to oblong, hairy leaves. Almond-scented, flattish, white flowers are borne in spring on very short stems, 1 or 2 per rosette. Z6–8 H8–6.
A. imbricata. See *A. vandellii.*
A. lanuginosa, illus. p.363.
A. pyrenaica, illus. p.350.
A. sarmentosa. Evergreen, mat-forming perennial, spreading by runners. **H** 1½–4in (4–10cm), **S** 12in (30cm). Has open rosettes of small, narrowly elliptic, hairy leaves. Large clusters of flattish, yellow-eyed, bright pink flowers open in spring. Is a good rock plant in all but extremely wet areas. Z5–7 H7–5.
A. sempervivoides. Evergreen, mat-forming, rosetted perennial with stolons. **H** ½–3in (1–7cm), **S** 12in (30cm). Has leathery, oblong or spoon-shaped leaves. In spring produces small heads of 4–10 flattish, pink flowers, with yellow, then red, eyes. Is a good rock plant. Z5–7 H7–5.
A. vandellii, syn. *A. imbricata,* illus. p.347.
A. villosa, illus. p.349. **var.** *jacquemontii* illus. p.366.

Anemanthele lessioniana. See *Stipa lessoniana.*

ANEMONE
Windflower
RANUNCULACEAE

Genus of spring-, summer- and fall-flowering perennials, sometimes tuberous or rhizomatous, with mainly rounded, shallowly cup-shaped flowers. Leaves are rounded to oval, often divided into 3–15 leaflets. Most thrive in full light or semi-shade in rich, well-drained soil. Propagate by division in spring, by seed sown in late summer, when fresh, or by root cuttings in winter. ① Contact with the sap may irritate skin.
A. apennina (Apennine anemone). Spreading, spring-flowering, rhizomatous perennial. **H** and **S** 6–8in (15–20cm). Fernlike leaves have 3 deeply toothed lobes. Each stem bears a large, upright, flattish, blue, white or pink flower, with 10–20 narrow petals. Z5–9 H9–3.
A. blanda. Spreading, early spring-flowering perennial with a knobby tuber. **H** 2–4in (5–10cm), **S** 4–6in (10–15cm). Leaves are broadly oval and semierect, with 3 deeply toothed lobes. Each stem bears an upright, flattish, blue, white or pink flower, 1½–2in (4–5cm) across, with 9–14 narrow petals. Z4–8 H8–1. **'Atrocaerulea',** illus. p.419. **'Ingramii'** bears purple-backed, deep blue flowers. **'Radar'.** See *A. blanda* var. *rosea* 'Radar'. **var.** *rosea* **'Radar',** syn. *A. blanda* 'Radar', illus. p.418. **'Violet Star',** illus. p.418. **'White Splendour'** illus. p.414.
A. coronaria. Spring-flowering perennial with a misshapen tuber. **H** 2–10in (5–25cm), **S** 4–6in (10–15cm). Produces parsley-like, divided, semierect leaves. Each stiff stem bears a large, 5–8-petaled, shallowly cup-shaped flower in shades of red, pink, blue or purple. Garden groups include **De Caen Group** and **Saint Bridgid Group**, which have larger flowers varying in color from white through red to blue. Z8–11 H11–8. **De Caen Group 'Mister Fokker'** illus. p.403.
A. x fulgens, illus. p.418.
A. hepatica. See *Hepatica nobilis.*
A. hupehensis (Chinese anemone,

Japanese anemone). Erect perennial with a creeping, woody-based rootstock. **H** 36in (100cm), **S** 36in (100cm) or more. Large, rounded, dark green leaves have 3-toothed lobes. In late summer, flower stems bear smaller leaves and 5-petaled, slightly cupped, pale pink or white flowers, 2–2½in (5–6cm) across, with yellow stamens. Z5–7 H7–5. **'Bowles's Pink'** (illus. p.222) bears rich pink-purple flowers. **'Hadspen Abundance'** illus. p.247. **var.** *japonica* **'Bressingham Glow',** syn. *A. x hybrida* 'Bressingham Glow', illus. p.222, **H** 4–5ft (1.2–1.5m), **S** 60cm (2ft), has semidouble, rose-purple flowers on wiry stems. **var.** *japonica* **'Pamina',** illus. p.222, **H** 32in (80cm), bears masses of rather small, semidouble, reddish-purple flowers. Z4–8 H8–5. **var.** *japonica* **'Prinz Heinrich',** syn. *A. x hybrida* 'Prince Henry' has single, deep pink flowers on slender stems. **'Praecox'** (illus. p.222), **H** 32in (80cm), bears single, pink flowers in mid-summer. **'September Charm'.** See *A. x hybrida* 'September Charm'.
A. x hybrida, syn. *A. japonica* (Japanese anemone). Group of vigorous, branching perennials. **H** 5ft (1.5m), **S** 2ft (60cm). Bears shallowly cup-shaped, single, semidouble or double flowers in late summer and early fall. Leaves are deeply divided and dark green. Z4–8 H8–5. **'Bressingham Glow'.** See *A. hupehensis* var. *japonica* 'Bressingham Glow'. **'Elegans',** syn. *A. x hybrida* 'Max Vogel' has semidouble, pinkish-mauve flowers on wiry stems. **'Honorine Jobert',** illus. p.220. **'Königin Charlotte'** (illus. p.222), **H** 4ft (1.2m), has large, semidouble, bright pink flowers. **'Lady Gilmour',** **H** 3ft (1m), produces crested leaves and pink flowers with often uneven, twisted petals. **'Max Vogel'.** See *A. x hybrida* 'Elegans'. **'Montrosa',** **H** 4ft (1.2m), has large, double, soft reddish-pink flowers with rather twisted petals. **'Prince Henry'.** See *A. hupehensis* var. *japonica* 'Prinz Heinrich'. **'Richard Ahrens',** **H** 4ft (1.2m), bears large, single, soft pink flowers in mid-summer. **'Robustissima'** (illus. p.222), **H** 4ft (1.2m), has single, dark pink flowers borne on reddish stems. **'September Charm',** syn. *A. hupehensis* 'September Charm' (illus. p.222), **H** 30in (75cm), **S** 20in (50cm), has single, clear pink flowers on wiry stems. Z5–7 H7–5. **'Whirlwind',** syn. *A. x hybrida* 'Wirbelwind' (illus. p.222), **H** 32–39in (80–100cm), bears irregularly formed double, white flowers, with some petals green flushed. **'Wirbelwind'.** See *A. x hybrida* 'Whirlwind'.
A. x intermedia. See *A. x lipsiensis.*
A. japonica. See *A. x hybrida.*
A. x lipsiensis, syn. *A. x intermedia, A. x seemannii,* illus. p.262.
A. narcissiflora, illus. p.255.
A. nemorosa (Wood anemone). Vigorous, carpeting, rhizomatous perennial. **H** 6in (15cm), **S** 12in (30cm). Produces masses of star-shaped, single, white flowers, with prominent, yellow stamens, in spring and early summer, above deeply cut, mid-green leaves. Likes woodland conditions. Z4–8 H8–1. **'Allenii'** produces many large, cup-shaped, single, rich lavender-blue flowers in spring. **'Robinsoniana'** has lavender-blue flowers, pale creamy-gray beneath, on maroon stems. **'Vestal'** has anemone-centered, double, white flowers. **'Wilks'

Giant',** syn. *A. nemorosa* 'Wilk's Giant' has larger, single, white flowers.
A. pavonina, illus. p.402.
A. ranunculoides, illus. p.263. **'Flore Pleno'.** See *A. ranunculoides* 'Pleniflora'. **'Pleniflora',** syn. *A. ranunculoides* 'Flore Pleno' is a spreading, rhizomatous perennial. **H** and **S** 8in (20cm). Bears buttercup-like, double, yellow flowers in spring. Leaves are divided. Likes damp, woodland conditions. Z4–8 H8–1.
A. rivularis, illus. p.437.
A. x seemannii. See *A. x lipsiensis.*
A. sylvestris, illus. p.255. **'Macrantha'** is a clump-forming perennial that can be invasive. **H** and **S** 12in (30cm). Large, fragrant, semi-pendent, shallowly cup-shaped, white flowers are produced in spring and early summer. Leaves are divided and mid-green. Z3–9 H9–1.
A. thalictroides 'Schoaf's Double'. See *Anemonella thalictroides* 'Oscar Schoaf'.
A. tomentosa, syn. *A. vitifolia.* Vigorous, clump-forming perennial with a creeping rootstock. **H** 4ft (1.2m), **S** 5ft (1.5m) or more. Large, 3–7 lobed mid-green leaves with toothed margins have white-hairy undersides. In summer, flower stems bear 5-petaled, slightly cupped, pale pink flowers, with yellow stamens. Z5–9 H9–3.
A. trullifolia, illus. p.350.
A. tschaernjaewii, illus. p.416.
A. vitifolia (Grape-leaved anemone). Branching, clump-forming perennial. **H** 4ft (1.2m), **S** 20in (50cm). In summer bears open cup-shaped, occasionally pink-flushed, white flowers with yellow stamens. Vine-like leaves are woolly beneath. Z5–8 H8–3.
A. vitifolia of gardens. See *A. tomentosa.*

ANEMONELLA
RANUNCULACEAE

Genus of one species of tuberous perennial, grown for its flowers. Needs shade and rich, moist soil. Propagate by seed when fresh or by division every 3–5 years in fall.
A. thalictroides, illus. p.350. **'Oscar Schoaf',** syn. *Anemone thalictroides* 'Schoaf's Double' is a slow-growing, tuberous perennial. **H** 4in (10cm), **S** 1½in (4cm) or more. Has delicate, fernlike leaves. From spring to early summer bears small, cup-shaped, double, strawberry-pink flowers, singly on finely branched, slender stems. Z4–7 H7–1.

ANEMONOPSIS
False anemone
RANUNCULACEAE

Genus of one species of perennial, related to *Anemone.* Likes a sheltered, semi-shaded position and rich, moist but well-drained soil. Propagate by division in spring or by seed sown in late summer, when fresh.
A. macrophylla (False anemone), illus. p.270.

ANEMOPAEGMA
BIGNONIACEAE

Genus of evergreen, tendril climbers, grown for their flowers. Needs partial shade in summer and rich, well-drained soil. Water regularly and freely when in

A

full growth, less at other times. Provide support and in summer thin out stems at intervals; shorten all growths by half in spring. Propagate by softwood or semiripe cuttings in spring or summer.

A. chamberlaynei. Fast-growing, evergreen, tendril climber. **H** to 20ft (6m). Leaves have 2 pointed, oval leaflets and a 3-hooked tendril. Foxglove-like, primrose-yellow flowers are borne in pairs from upper leaf axils in summer. Z12–15 H11–10.

ANGELICA
UMBELLIFERAE/APIACEAE

Genus of summer-flowering, often short-lived perennials, some of which have culinary and medicinal uses. Grows in sun or shade and in any well-drained soil. Remove seed heads when produced, otherwise plants may die. Propagate by seed when ripe.

A. archangelica, illus. p.219.

ANGELONIA
SCROPHULARIACEAE/ PLANTAGINACEAE

Genus of evergreen subshrubs and soft-stemmed perennials, grown for their shallowly cup-shaped, summer flowers. Makes good bedding plants in containers and borders. Needs sun and fertile, moist but well-drained soil. Propagate by seed or softwood cuttings in spring.

A. angustifolia AngelMist Series 'AngelMist Lavender Stripe', illus. p.311.

ANGRAECUM
ORCHIDACEAE

See also ORCHIDS.
A. sesquipedale, illus. p.468.

ANGULOA
Cradle orchid, Tulip orchid
ORCHIDACEAE

See also ORCHIDS.
A. clowesii (Cradle orchid). Deciduous, epiphytic orchid for a cool greenhouse. **H** 24in (60cm). Fragrant, erect, cup-shaped, lemon-yellow flowers, 4in (10cm) long, each with a loosely hinged, yellow lip, are produced singly in early summer. Broadly oval, ribbed leaves are 18in (45cm) long. Grow in partial shade in summer. Z13–15 H11–10.

ANIGOZANTHOS
Kangaroo paw
HAEMODORACEAE

Genus of perennials with thick rootstocks and fans of sword-shaped leaves, grown for their curious flowers. Needs an open, sunny position and does best in well-drained, peaty or leafy, acid soil. Propagate by division in spring or by seed when fresh, in late summer.

A. flavidus, illus. p.476.
A. manglesii, illus. p.470.
A. rufus. Tufted perennial. **H** 3ft (1m), **S** 2ft (60cm). Panicles of 2-lipped, rich burgundy flowers, covered with purple hairs, are produced in spring. Has long, sword-shaped, stiff, mid-green leaves. Z10–11 H11–10.

ANISODONTEA
MALVACEAE

Genus of evergreen shrubs and perennials, grown for their flowers. Needs full light and well-drained soil. Water container plants freely when in full growth, very little at other times. In growing season, young plants may need tip pruning to promote a bushy habit. Propagate by seed in spring or by greenwood or semiripe cuttings in late summer.

A. capensis, syn. *Malvastrum capensis.* Evergreen, erect, bushy shrub. **H** to 3ft (1m), **S** 2ft (60cm) or more. Each oval leaf has 3–5 deep lobes. Bowl-shaped, 5-petaled, rose-magenta flowers, with darker veins, are borne from spring to fall. Z8–9 H9–8.

ANNONA
Cherimoya, Custard apple, Sweet sop
ANNONACEAE

Genus of deciduous or evergreen shrubs and trees, grown for their edible fruits and ornamental appearance. Needs full light or partial shade and fertile, moisture-retentive but well-drained soil. Water container specimens moderately when in full growth, sparingly in winter. Propagate by seed in spring or by semiripe cuttings in late summer. Red spider mite may be a nuisance.

A. reticulata (Bullock's heart, Custard apple). Mainly deciduous, rounded tree. **H** 20ft (6m) or more, **S** 10–15ft (3–5m). Has oblong to lance-shaped leaves, 5–10in (13–25cm) long. Cup-shaped, olive-green flowers, often flushed purple, are borne in summer, followed by edible, heart-shaped, red-flushed, greenish-brown fruits, 5in (13cm) long. Z14–15 H12–10.

Anoiganthus breviflorus. See *Cyrtanthus breviflorus.*
Anoiganthus luteus. See *Cyrtanthus breviflorus.*

ANOMATHECA
IRIDACEAE

Genus of upright, summer-flowering corms, grown for their trumpet- to funnel-shaped, red flowers, followed by egg-shaped seed pods that split to reveal red seeds. Plant 2in (5cm) deep in an open, sunny situation and in well-drained soil. In cold areas, lift corms and store dry for winter. Propagate by seed in spring.

A. cruenta. See *A. laxa.*
A. laxa, syn. *A. cruenta, Lapeirousia cruenta, Freesia laxa, Lapeirousia laxa,* illus. p.423.

ANOPTERUS
ESCALLONIACEAE

Genus of evergreen shrubs or small trees, grown for their foliage and flowers. Needs full or semi-shade and moist but well-drained, lime-free soil. Propagate by semiripe cuttings in summer.

A. glandulosus, illus. p.110.

ANREDERA
Madeira vine, Mignonette vine
BASELLACEAE

Genus of evergreen, tuberous, twining climbers, grown for their luxuriant foliage and small, scented flowers. If grown

in cool areas will die down in winter. Requires a position in full light and well-drained soil. Water moderately in growing season, but sparingly at other times. Provide support. Cut back the previous season's growth by half or to just above ground level in spring. Propagate by tubers, produced at stem bases, in spring or by softwood cuttings in summer.

A. cordifolia, syn. *Boussingaultia basilloides* (Madeira vine, Mignonette vine), illus. p.197.

ANTENNARIA
Cat's ears
COMPOSITAE/ASTERACEAE

Genus of evergreen or semievergreen perennials, grown for their almost stemless flower heads and mats of often woolly leaves. Makes good groundcover. Needs sun and well-drained soil. Propagate by seed or division in spring.

A. dioica (Common pussy-toes). Semievergreen, mat-forming, dense perennial. **H** 1in (2.5cm), **S** 10in (25cm). Leaves are tiny, oval, usually woolly and greenish-white. Short stems bear fluffy, white or pale pink flower heads in late spring and early summer. Is good when grown in a rock garden. Z5–9 H9–4.
'Nyewoods' a compact plant with very deep rose-pink flowers. **var. rosea.** See *A. rosea.*
A. rosea, syn. *A. dioica* var. *rosea,* illus. p.351.

ANTHEMIS
COMPOSITAE/ASTERACEAE

Genus of carpeting and clump-forming perennials, some of which are evergreen, grown for their daisylike flower heads and fernlike foliage. Prefers a position in sun and well-drained soil. May need staking for support. Cut to ground level after flowering to produce good leaf rosettes in winter. Propagate by division in spring or, for some species, by basal cuttings in late summer, fall or spring.

A. nobilis. See *Chamaemelum nobile.*
A. punctata subsp. **cupaniana,** illus. p.264.
A. sancti-johannis. Evergreen, spreading, bushy perennial. **H** and **S** 24in (60cm). In summer bears many daisylike, bright orange flower heads among fernlike, shaggy, mid-green leaves. Z3–8 H8–3.
A. tinctoria (Golden marguerite, Ox-eye chamomile). Evergreen, clump-forming perennial. **H** and **S** 3ft (1m). Produces a mass of daisylike, yellow flower heads in mid-summer, borne singly above a basal clump of fernlike, crinkled, mid-green leaves. Propagate by basal cuttings in spring or late summer. Z3–8 H8–3.
'E.C. Buxton' illus. p.243.

ANTHERICUM
Spider plant
LILIACEAE/ASPARAGACEAE

Genus of upright perennials with saucer- or trumpet-shaped flowers rising in spike-like racemes from clumps of leaves. Prefers a sunny site and fertile, well-drained soil that does not dry out in summer. Propagate by division in spring or by seed in fall.

A. graminifolium. See *A. ramosum.*
A. liliago, illus. p.263.
A. ramosum, syn. *A. graminifolium.* Upright perennial. **H** 3ft (1m), **S** 1ft (30cm). Erect racemes of small, saucer-shaped, white flowers are borne in summer above a clump of grasslike, grayish-green leaves. Z5–8 H8–5.

Antholyza paniculata. See *Crocosmia paniculata.*

ANTHURIUM
Flamingo flower, Tail flower
ARACEAE

Genus of evergreen, erect, climbing or trailing perennials, some grown for their foliage and others for their bright flower spathes. Prefers bright light in winter and indirect sun in summer; needs a fairly moist atmosphere and moist, but not waterlogged, peaty soil. Propagate by division in spring. ① All parts may cause mild stomach disorder if digested; contact with sap may irritate skin.

A. andraeanum, illus. p.470.
A. crystallinum, illus. p.465.
A. scherzerianum (Flamingo flower). Evergreen, erect, tufted perennial. **H** and **S** 12–24in (30–60cm). Has oblong, leathery, dark green leaves, to 8in (20cm) long. Produces large, long-lasting, bright red spathes and fleshy, orange to yellow spadices. Z11 H11–10.
'Rothschildianum', H and **S** 12in (30cm), bears white-spotted, red spathes and yellow spadices.
A. veitchii (Queen anthurium). Evergreen, erect, short-stemmed perennial. **H** 3ft (1m) or more, **S** to 3ft (1m). Glossy, corrugated leaves, to 3ft (1m) long, are oval, with heart-shaped bases on leaf stalks, 2–3ft (60cm–1m) long. Intermittently bears a long-lasting, leathery, green to white spathe that surrounds a cream spadix. Z11 H12–10.

ANTHYLLIS
LEGUMINOSAE/PAPILIONACEAE

Genus of rounded, bushy perennials, grown for their flowers and finely divided leaves. Needs sun and well-drained soil. Propagate by softwood cuttings in summer or by seed in fall.

A. hermanniae. Rounded, bushy perennial. **H** and **S** to 24in (60cm). Spiny, tangled stems bear simple or 3-parted, bright green leaves. Has small, pealike, yellow flowers in summer. Is good for a rock garden. Z6–8 H8–6.
A. montana, illus. p.338. **'Rubra'** is a rounded or spreading, woody-based perennial. **H** and **S** 12in (30cm). Divided leaves consist of 17–41 narrowly oval leaflets. Heads of clover-like, bright pink flowers are borne in late spring and early summer. Is good for a rock garden. Z6–8 H8–6.

ANTIGONON
Coral vine
POLYGONACEAE

Genus of evergreen, woody-stemmed, tendril climbers, grown for their foliage and profuse clusters of small flowers. Grow in full light and any fertile, well-drained soil. Water freely in growing season, sparingly at other times. Needs tropical conditions to flower well. Provide support. Thin out congested growth in early spring. Propagate by seed in spring or by softwood cuttings in summer.

A. leptopus (Confederate vine, Mexican creeper). Fast-growing, evergreen, woody-stemmed, tendril climber. **H** 20ft (6m). Has crinkly, pale green leaves. Dense trusses of bright pink, sometimes red or white, flowers grow mainly in summer, but all year in tropical conditions. Z15 H11–10.

ANTIRRHINUM
Snapdragon
SCROPHULARIACEAE/PLANTAGINACEAE

Genus of perennials and semievergreen subshrubs, usually grown as annuals, flowering from spring to fall, or as winter annuals in warm regions. Needs sun and rich, well-drained soil. Deadhead to prolong flowering season. Propagate by seed sown outdoors in late spring or by stem cuttings in early fall or spring. Rust disease may be a problem with *A. majus*, but rust-resistant cultivars are available.

A. asarina. See *Asarina procumbens*.
A. Balumhopi'. See *A. Luminaire Series* LUMINAIRE HOT PINK.
A. Luminaire Series LUMINAIRE HOT PINK (**'Balumhopi'**), illus. p.303.
A. majus. Erect perennial that branches from the base. Cultivars are grown as annuals and are grouped according to size and flower type: tall, **H** 2–3ft (60cm–1m), **S** 12–18in (30–45cm); intermediate, **H** and **S** 18in (45cm); dwarf, **H** 8–12in (20–30cm), **S** 12in (30cm); regular tubular-shaped (hyacinth-like) flowers; penstemon, trumpet-shaped flowers; double; and irregular tubular-shaped flowers. All have lance-shaped leaves and, from spring to fall, bear spikes of usually 2-lipped, sometimes double, flowers in a variety of colors, including white, pink, red, purple, yellow and orange. Z9–11 H11–1. **Bells Series** (dwarf, regular) is early-flowering, with long-lasting flowers in purple, purple and white, red, rose-pink, pink, bronze, yellow, or white. **'Black Prince'** illus. p.306. **Chimes Series** (dwarf, regular) is very compact, producing flowers in a wide color range including several bicolors. **Chimes Series** (yellow), illus. p.320. **Coronette Series** (tall, regular) is compact with tubular, 2-lipped flowers in a wide range of colors. **'Floral Showers'** (dwarf, regular) is early-flowering, bearing flowers in up to 10 colors, including some bicolors; tolerates wet weather. **Kim Series** (intermediate, regular) has flowers in scarlet, deep rose, deep orange, primrose-yellow and white as well as orange bicolor. **Liberty Classic Series 'Liberty Yellow'**, illus. p.319. **Madame Butterfly Series** (tall, peloric) is available in a mixture of colors. **Rocket Series** (tall, regular) is vigorous, with flowers in a broad color range; they are excellent for cut flowers. **Sonnet Series** (intermediate, regular) is bushy and has flowers in a variety of colors. **'Trumpet Serenade'** (dwarf, penstemon) has bicolored flowers in a mixture of pastel shades.

APHELANDRA
ACANTHACEAE

Genus of evergreen shrubs and perennials, grown for their showy flowers. Prefers bright light but keep out of direct sun in summer. Use soft water and keep soil moist but not waterlogged. Benefits from feeding when flower spikes are forming. Propagate by seed or tip cuttings from young stems in spring.

A. squarrosa (Zebra plant). **'Dania'** is an evergreen, compact perennial. **H** 3ft (1m), **S** 2ft (60cm). Oval, glossy, dark green leaves, to 1ft (30cm) long, have white veins and mid-ribs. Produces dense, 4-sided spikes, to 6in (15cm) long, of 2-lipped, bright yellow flowers in axils of yellow bracts in fall. Z14–15 H11–10. **'Louisae'**, illus. p.476.

APHYLLANTHES
LILIACEAE/ASPARAGACEAE

Genus of one species of summer-flowering perennial. Grow in a sunny, warm, sheltered corner, preferably in an alpine house, and in well-drained, sandy, peaty soil. Resents disturbance. Propagate by seed in fall or spring.

A. monspeliensis. Tuft-forming perennial. **H** 6–8in (15–20cm), **S** 2in (5cm). Star-shaped, pale to deep blue flowers are borne singly or in small groups at tops of wiry, glaucous green stems from early to mid-summer. Leaves are reduced to red-brown sheathers surrounding stems. Z9–10 H11–10.

APONOGETON
APONOGETONACEAE

Genus of deciduous, perennial, deep-water plants, grown for their floating foliage and often heavily scented flowers. Requires an open, sunny position. Tidy fading foliage in fall. Propagate by division in spring or by seed when fresh.

A. distachyos, illus. p.435.

APOROCACTUS
Rat's tail cactus
CACTACEAE

Genus of perennial cacti, grown for their pendent, slender, fleshy stems and bright flowers. Is suitable for hanging baskets. Needs partial shade and very well-drained soil. Occasional light watering in winter will stop stems dying back from the tips. Propagate by stem cuttings in spring or summer.

A. flagelliformis, syn. *Disocactus flagelliformis*, illus. p.483.

APTENIA
AIZOACEAE

Genus of fast-growing, perennial succulents, with trailing, freely branching stems, that make good groundcover. Requires full sun and very well-drained soil. Keep dry in winter. Propagate by seed or stem cuttings in spring or summer.

A. cordifolia, syn. *Mesembryanthemum cordifolium*, illus. p.484. **'Variegata'** is a fast-growing, prostrate, perennial succulent. **H** 2in (5cm), **S** indefinite. Has oval, glossy, bright green leaves,

with creamy-white margins, and small, daisylike, bright pink flowers in summer. Z12–15 H12–10.

AQUILEGIA
Columbine
RANUNCULACEAE

Genus of clump-forming, short-lived perennials, grown for their mainly bell-shaped, spurred flowers in spring and summer. Is suitable for rock gardens and woodland gardens. Prefers an open, sunny site and well-drained soil. Propagate species by seed in fall or spring. Selected forms, such as *A. vulgaris* var. *stellata* 'Nora Barlow', only occasionally come true from seed as they cross freely. Is prone to aphid attack. ① Contact with sap may irritate skin.

A. akitensis. See *A. flabellata* var. *pumila*.
A. alpina, illus. p.334.
A. atrata (Black columbine). Clump-forming perennial **H** 24–28in (60–70cm), **S** 12in (30cm). Bell-shaped, fluted, deep purple-violet flowers with spreading sepals and strongly hooked spurs, ¼in (1cm) long, are borne in early summer above mid-green, glaucous-backed leaves divided into 9 segments. Z4–8 H7–1.
A. bertolonii, syn. *A. reuteri*. Clump-forming, compact perennial. **H** 4–12in (10–30cm), **S** 3–8in (8–20cm). Bell-shaped, blue-violet flowers with spreading sepals and curved spurs, ¼in (1cm) long, are borne in late spring and early summer above dark green leaves divided into 9 segments. Z4–7 H7–1.
A. Biedermeier Group. Short-stemmed, compact perennials. **H** 12–14in (30–35cm), **S** 8–12in (20–30cm). More or less upward-facing, open-bell-shaped flowers in colors varying from purple-blue to lilac, red, pink or white are produced from late spring to mid-summer above divided, bluish-green foliage. Z4–7 H7–1.
A. 'Bluebird' (Songbird Series), illus. p.226. Clump-forming, compact perennial. **H** 24–28in (60–70cm), **S** 14–16in (35–40cm). Very large, open bell-shaped, fluted flowers with white petals, soft pale violet-blue sepals and long, slightly curved spurs are borne in late spring and early summer above fernlike, divided, mid-green leaves. Z4–9 H9–1.
A. 'Bunting' (Songbird Series), illus. p.226. Clump-forming, compact perennial. **H** 24in (60cm), **S** 12–14in (30–35cm). Open bell-shaped, fluted flowers with blue-flushed, white petals, violet-blue sepals and long spurs are produced in late spring and early summer above fernlike, divided, mid-green leaves. Z4–9 H9–1.
A. canadensis (Canadian columbine), illus. p.226. Clump-forming, leafy perennial. **H** 24in (60cm), **S** 12in (30cm). In early summer bears semi-pendent, bell-shaped flowers, with yellow sepals and red spurs, several per slender stem, above fernlike, dark green foliage. Z3–8 H8–1.
A. 'Cardinal' (Songbird Series). Clump-forming, compact perennial. **H** 20in (50cm), **S** 12–14in (30–35cm). Open bell-shaped, fluted flowers with white petals, deep red-pink at the base, dark red sepals and long, curved spurs are produced in late spring and early summer above fernlike, divided, mid-green leaves. Z4–8 H8–1.
A. chrysantha (Yellow columbine), illus.

p.226. Vigorous, clump-forming perennial. **H** 4ft (1.2m), **S** 2ft (60cm). Bears semi-pendent, bell-shaped, pale to bright yellow flowers, with long spurs, several per stem, in early summer. Has fernlike, divided, mid-green leaves. Z3–8 H8–1. **'Yellow Queen'** has golden-yellow flowers.
A. coerulea (Rocky mountain columbine), illus. p.226. Upright perennial. **H** 24–32in (60–80cm), **S** 12–16in (30–40cm). More or less upward-facing flowers, with open-spreading, white sepals, pale to deep sky-blue petals and long spurs are borne from late spring to mid-summer above divided, mid-green leaves. Z4–7 H7–1.
A. 'Dove' (Songbird Series), illus. p.226. Clump-forming, compact perennial. **H** 30in (75cm), **S** 14–16in (35–40cm). Large, open bell-shaped, fluted flowers, with white petals, sepals and long spurs, are produced in late spring and early summer above fernlike, divided, light green leaves. Z4–9 H9–1.
A. 'Dragonfly', illus. p.226. Upright perennial. **H** 24in (60cm), **S** 12in (30cm). Large, upright to semierect, bell-shaped, fluted, yellow flowers, with basally red-flushed petals and purplish-red sepals and spurs, are produced from late spring to mid-summer above fernlike, divided, mid-green leaves. Z4–7 H7–1.
A. flabellata (Fan columbine). Clump-forming perennial. **H** 10in (25cm), **S** 4in (10cm). Bell-shaped, soft blue flowers, each with fluted petals and a short spur, are produced in summer. Rounded, finely divided leaves form an open, basal rosette. Needs partial shade and moist soil. Z4–9 H9–1. **var. alba 'White Jewel'** has white flowers. **Jewel Series,** flowers vary from blue to pink or white. **'Ministar'** has slightly nodding blooms with purple-blue, spreading sepals and blue-based, white petals. **'Nana Alba'.** See *A. flabellata* var. *pumila* f. *alba*. **var. pumila,** syn. *A. akitensis* (illus. p.226) grows to 4in (10cm) and has deep blue and white petals. **var. pumila f. alba,** syn. *A. flabellata* 'Nana Alba', **H** 4in (10cm), is compact and has white flowers.
A. 'Florida' (State Series). Clump-forming, upright perennial. **H** 24in (60cm), **S** 12in (30cm). Open bell-shaped, fluted, mid-yellow flowers, with creamy-yellow, spreading sepals and long spurs, are produced in late spring and early summer above fernlike, divided, light green leaves. Z4–8 H8–1.
A. fragrans. Upright perennial. **H** 6–16in (15–40cm), **S** 6–8in (15–20cm). Nodding, bell-shaped, fragrant flowers, with creamy-white petals and bluish- or pinkish-white sepals, are borne in mid-summer above finely divided, bluish-green leaves. Z4–8 H8–1.
A. 'Goldfinch' (Songbird Series). Clump-forming, compact perennial. **H** 24–28in (60–70cm), **S** 14in (35cm). Open bell-shaped, fluted, bright yellow flowers are borne in late spring and early summer above fernlike, divided, mid-green leaves. Z4–8 H8–1.
A. 'Hensol Harebell', illus. p.226. Clump-forming, compact perennial. **H** 2ft (60cm), **S** 1ft (30cm). Has fernlike, divided, pale green leaves. In late spring, tall, slender stems bear pendent, bell-shaped, short-spurred, soft blue flowers. Z4–7 H7–1.
A. jonesii, illus. p.368.

A

A. karelinii. Clump-forming perennial. **H** 8–32in (20–80cm), **S** 5–12in (12–30cm). Nodding, bell-shaped, violet to wine-purple flowers, with spreading sepals and short, hooked spurs, are produced in early summer above slightly glaucous, light green leaves. Z3–9 H8–1.

A. longissima (Longspur columbine), illus. p.226. Clump-forming, leafy perennial. **H** 24in (60cm), **S** 20in (50cm). Bell-shaped, pale yellow flowers, with very long, bright yellow spurs, are borne, several per stem, in early summer, above fernlike, divided, mid-green leaves. Z4–9 H9–1.

A. 'Mrs. Scott Elliott'. See *A.* Mrs. Scott Elliott Hybrids.

A. Mrs. Scott Elliott Hybrids, syn. *A.* 'Mrs. Scott Elliott'. Clump-forming, leafy perennial. **H** 3ft (1m), **S** 20in (50cm). Bell-shaped flowers of various colors, often bicolored, have long spurs and are borne in early summer on branching, wiry stems. Has fernlike, divided, bluish-green leaves. Z4–7 H7–1.

A. 'Nuthatch' (Songbird Series). Clump-forming, compact perennial. **H** 24–28in (60–70cm), **S** 12in (30cm). Open bell-shaped, fluted, pink-based, white flowers, with deep pink sepals and long spurs, are produced in late spring and early summer above fernlike divided, mid-green leaves. Z4–8 H8–1.

A. reuteri. See *A. bertolonii*.

A. 'Robin' (Songbird Series). Clump-forming, compact perennial. **H** 24in (60cm), **S** 12in (30cm). Open bell-shaped, fluted, white flowers, pink-flushed at the base, with spreading, dusky pink sepals and long spurs, are produced in late spring and early summer above fernlike, divided, pale to mid-green leaves. Z4–8 H8–1.

A. rockii. Upright perennial. **H** 20–32in (50–80cm), **S** 12–14in (30–35cm). Nodding to semierect, narrowly bell-shaped, deep purple flowers, with spreading sepals and curved spurs, are borne in late spring and early summer above divided, mid-green leaves, glaucous beneath. Z6–8 H7–1.

A. scopulorum. Clump-forming perennial. **H** 2¹⁄₂in (6cm), **S** 3¹⁄₂in (9cm). In summer produces bell-shaped, fluted, pale blue, or rarely pink, flowers, each with a cream center and very long spurs. Leaves are divided into 9 oval, glaucous leaflets. Z4–8 H8–1.

A. 'Sunburst Ruby'. Clump-forming perennial. **H** 24in (60cm), **S** 12in (30cm). Semi-upright, semidouble to double, deep ruby-red flowers are borne in late spring and early summer above fernlike, divided, golden leaves. Z4–8 H8–1.

A. triternata, illus. p.226. Upright perennial. **H** 8–24in (20–60cm), **S** 8–12in (20–30cm). Nodding, narrowly bell-shaped, short-petaled, yellow flowers, sometimes red-flushed, with red sepals, are produced in early summer above 3-parted, mid-green leaves. Z3–9 H8–1.

A. viridiflora, illus. p.226. Upright, short-lived perennial. **H** 8–20in (20–50cm), **S** 4–8in (10–20cm). In late spring and early summer produces fragrant, nodding, bell-shaped, purple, chocolate-brown, or sometimes yellow-green, flowers, with green sepals, above 3-parted, mid-green leaves. Z4–8 H8–1.

A. vulgaris (Granny's bonnets). Clump-forming, leafy perennial. **H** 3ft (1m), **S** 20in (50cm). Many funnel-shaped, short-spurred

flowers, in shades of pink, crimson, purple and white, are borne, several per long stem, in early summer. Leaves are gray-green, rounded and divided into leaflets. Z3–8 H8–1. **var. alba** produces white flowers. **'Magpie'.** See *A. vulgaris* 'William Guiness'. **'Munstead White'.** See *A. vulgaris* 'Nivea'. **'Nivea',** syn. *A. vulgaris* 'Munstead White' (illus. p.226) has gray-green leaves and glistening white flowers. **var. stellata 'Black Barlow',** illus. p.223. bears spurless, double, deep purple-black flowers. **var. stellata 'Nora Barlow'** (illus. p.226) produces double red flowers, pale green at the tips. **var. stellata 'Ruby Port'** (illus. p.226) has spurless, deep ruby-red double flowers. **'William Guiness',** syn. *A. vulgaris* 'Magpie' (illus. p.226) has nodding, deep blue-purple flowers with white-tipped petals.

A. 'Winky Red-White' (Winky Series). Clump-forming, compact perennial. **H** 14–20in (35–50cm), **S** 12in (30cm). Double or semidouble, red-and-white flowers are produced in late spring and early summer above fernlike, divided, pale to mid-green leaves. Z4–8 H8–1.

ARABIS
Rock cres
CRUCIFERAE/BRASSICACEAE
Genus of robust, evergreen perennials. Makes excellent groundcover in a rock garden. Needs sun and well-drained soil. Propagate by softwood cuttings in summer or by seed in fall.

A. albida. See *A. alpina* subsp. *caucasica*.

A. alpina subsp. caucasica, syn. *A. albida, A. caucasica* (Wall rock cress). Evergreen, mat-forming perennial. **H** 6in (15cm), **S** 20in (50cm). Bears loose rosettes of obovate, toothed, mid-green leaves and, in late spring and summer, fragrant, 4-petaled, white, occasionally pink, flowers. Is excellent on a dry bank. Trim back after flowering. Z4–8 H8–1. **'Douler Angevine',** illus. p.352. **'Flore Pleno',** syn. *A. caucasica* 'Plena' has double, white flowers. Z4–8 H8–1. **'Variegata',** syn. *A. caucasica* 'Variegata', illus. p.347.

A. x arendsii 'Rosabella', syn. *A. caucasica* 'Rosabella'. Evergreen, mat-forming perennial. **H** 6in (15cm), **S** 12in (30cm). Has large rosettes of small, oval, soft green leaves and a profusion of single, deep pink flowers in spring and early summer. Z5–8 H8–5.

A. blepharophylla (California rock cress, Rose cress, Fringed rock cress). Short-lived, evergreen, mat-forming perennial. **H** 5in (12cm), **S** 8in (20cm). Dislikes winter wet. Has oval, toothed, dark green leaves, with hairy, gray margins, borne in loose rosettes. Fragrant, 4-petaled, bright pink to white flowers are produced in spring. Z5–8 H8–5. **'Frühlingszauber',** syn. *A. blepharophylla* 'Spring Charm', illus. p.353. **'Spring Charm'.** See *A. blepharophylla* 'Frühlingszauber'.

A. caucasica. See *A. alpina* subsp. *caucasica*. **'Plena'.** See *A. alpina* subsp. *caucasica* 'Flore Pleno'. **'Rosabella'.** See *A.* x *arendsii* 'Rosabella'. **'Variegata'.** See *A. alpina* subsp. *caucasica* 'Variegata'.

A. ferdinandi-coburgi 'Variegata'. See *A. procurrens* 'Variegata'.

A. procurrens 'Variegata', syn. *A. ferdinandi-coburgi* 'Variegata', illus. p.375.

ARALIA
ARALIACEAE
Genus of deciduous trees, shrubs and perennials, grown for their bold leaves and small, but profusely borne, flowers. Requires sun or semi-shade, some shelter and fertile, well-drained soil. Propagate those listed below by seed in fall or by suckers or root cuttings in late winter.

A. elata (Japanese aralia tree). Deciduous tree or suckering shrub with sparse, sturdy, prickly stems. **H** and **S** 30ft (10m). Has large, dark green leaves with numerous oval, paired leaflets. Billowing heads of tiny, white flowers, forming a large panicle, 12–24in (30–60cm) long, are borne in late summer and fall. Z4–9 H9–1. **'Albomarginata'.** See *A. elata* 'Variegata'. **'Aureovariegata'** has leaflets broadly edged with yellow. **'Variegata',** syn. *A. elata* 'Albomarginata' illus. p.93.

A. elegantissima. See *Schefflera elegantissima*.

A. japonica. See *Fatsia japonica*.

A. sieboldii. See *Fatsia japonica*.

ARAUCARIA
ARAUCARIACEAE
See also CONIFERS.

A. araucana, illus. p.98.

A. excelsa. See *A. heterophylla*.

A. heterophylla, syn. *A. excelsa* (Norfolk Island pine). Upright conifer. **H** 100ft (30m), **S** 15–25ft (5–8m). Has spirally set, needlelike, incurved, fresh green leaves. Cones are seldom produced in cultivation. Is often grown as a shade-tolerant house plant. Z9–11 H11–9.

ARAUJIA
ASCLEPIADACEAE/APOCYNACEAE
Genus of evergreen, twining climbers with woody stems that exude milky juice when cut. Needs sun and fertile, well-drained soil. Propagate by seed in spring or by stem cuttings in late summer or early fall.

A. sericifera, illus. p.195.

ARBUTUS
Manzanita, Strawberry tree
ERICACEAE
Genus of evergreen trees and shrubs, grown for their leaves, clusters of small, urn-shaped flowers, ornamental bark and strawberry-like fruits, which are edible but insipid. Must be protected from strong, cold winds when young. Prefers full sun and needs fertile, well-drained soil; *A. menziesii* requires acid soil. Propagate by semiripe cuttings in late summer or by seed in fall.

A. andrachne (Grecian strawberry tree). Evergreen, spreading tree or shrub. **H** and **S** 20ft (6m). Has oval, glossy, dark green leaves and peeling, reddish-brown bark. Panicles of urn-shaped, white flowers in late spring are followed by orange-red fruits. Prefers a sheltered position. Z7–9 H9–7.

A. x andrachnoides, illus. p.79.

A. menziesii (Madroña, Madroñe). Evergreen, spreading tree. **H** and **S** 50ft (15m). Has smooth, peeling, reddish bark and oval, dark green leaves. Large, upright, terminal panicles of urn-shaped, white

flowers in early summer are followed by orange or red fruits. Z7–9 H9–7. **A. unedo,** illus. p.93.

ARCHONTOPHOENIX
King palm
PALMAE/ARECACEAE
Genus of evergreen palms, grown for their majestic appearance. Needs full light or partial shade and rich, well-drained soil. Water container specimens moderately, less when temperatures are low. Propagate by seed in spring at not less than 75°F (24°C). Red spider mite may be troublesome.

A. alexandrae, illus. p.452.

A. cunninghamiana (Illawarra palm, Piccabeen palm). Evergreen palm. **H** 50–70ft (15–20m), **S** 6–15ft (2–5m). Has long, arching, feather-shaped leaves. Mature trees produce large clusters of small, lavender or lilac flowers in summer followed by large, egg-shaped, red fruits. Z10–11 H11–9.

Arcterica nana. See *Pieris nana*.

ARCTOSTAPHYLOS
Manzanita
ERICACEAE
Genus of evergreen shrubs and trees, grown for their foliage, flowers and fruits. Some species are also grown for their bark, others as groundcovers. Provide shelter from strong winds. Does best in full sun and well-drained, acid soil. Propagate by semiripe cuttings in summer or by seed in fall.

A. alpina, syn. *Arctous alpinus* (Alpine bearberry). Deciduous, creeping shrub. **H** 2in (5cm), **S** to 5in (12cm). Produces drooping, terminal clusters of tiny, urn-shaped, pink-flushed, white flowers in late spring. These are followed by rounded, purple-black berries. Leaves are oval, toothed, glossy and bright green. Z2–7 H7–1.

A. diversifolia, syn. *Comarostaphylis diversifolia* (Summer holly). Evergreen, upright shrub or tree. **H** 15ft (5m), **S** 10ft (3m). Leaves are oblong, glossy and dark green. Terminal racemes of fragrant, urn-shaped, white flowers are borne from early to mid-spring, followed by spherical, red fruits. Z7–9 H9–7.

A. 'Emerald Carpet', illus. p.147.

A. hookeri 'Monterey Carpet', syn. *A. uva-ursi* subsp. *hookeri* 'Monterey Carpet'. Evergreen, open shrub. **H** 4–6in (10–15cm), **S** 16in (40cm) or more. Has hairy branchlets bearing glossy, pale green leaves and, in early summer, urn-shaped, white flowers, sometimes flushed pink, which are followed by globose, red fruits. Z8–9 H9–8.

A. manzanita (Manzanita, Parry manzanita). Evergreen, upright shrub. **H** and **S** 6ft (2m) or more. Has peeling, reddish-brown bark and oval, leathery, gray-green leaves. From early to mid-spring produces small, urn-shaped, deep pink flowers. Z8–10 H9–8.

A. nevadensis (Pine-mat manzanita). Evergreen, prostrate shrub. **H** 4in (10cm), **S** 3ft (1m). Has small, oval leaves. In summer, pendent, urn-shaped, white flowers are borne in clusters in leaf axils, followed by globose, brownish-red fruits.

A

Is useful as groundcover. Z7–9 H9–7.

A. nummularia (Fort Bragg manzanita). Evergreen, erect to prostrate shrub. **H** 1ft (30cm) or more, **S** 3ft (1m). Leaves are small, rounded, leathery and toothed. Pendent, urn-shaped, white flowers are borne in clusters from leaf axils in summer, followed by globose, green fruits. Makes good groundcover. Z7–9 H9–7.

A. patula, illus. p.144.

A. stanfordiana (Stanford manzanita). Evergreen, erect shrub. **H** and **S** 5ft (1.5m). Bark is smooth and reddish-brown. Has narrowly oval, glossy, bright green leaves. Drooping clusters of urn-shaped, pink flowers are borne from early to mid-spring. Z6–9 H9–6.

A. uva-ursi, illus. p.376. **'Point Reyes'** illus. p.375. **'Vancouver Jade'** is an evergreen, trailing, sometimes arching shrub. **H** 4in (10cm), **S** 20in (50cm). Has small, oval, bright green leaves and bears urn-shaped, white flowers in summer. Z2–6 H6–1.

A. uva-ursi subsp. hookeri 'Monterey Carpet'. See *A. hookeri* 'Monterey Carpet'.

ARCTOTHECA
COMPOSITAE/ASTERACEAE

Genus of creeping perennials. Requires a position in bright light and fertile, well-drained soil; dislikes humid conditions. Propagate by seed or division in spring.

A. calendula, syn. *Cryptostemma calendulaceum* (Cape dandelion), illus. p.476.

ARCTOTIS
SYN. **x VENIDIOARCTOTIS**
African daisy
COMPOSITAE/ASTERACEAE

Genus of annuals and perennials, grown for their flower heads and foliage. Requires full sun and leafy loam with sharp sand added. Propagate by seed in fall or spring or by stem cuttings year-round.

A. Harlequin Hybrids, syn. *A. x hybrida*. Fairly slow-growing, upright, branching perennial, usually grown as an annual. **H** and **S** 18in (45cm). Lance-shaped, lobed leaves are grayish-green above, white below. In summer has large, daisylike flower heads in many shades, including yellow, orange, bronze, purple, pink, cream and red. **'Bacchus'**. has purple flower heads; **'China Rose'** deep pink; **'Sunshine'** yellow; **'Tangerine'** orange-yellow; and **'Torch'** bronze. Z13–15 H11–10.

A. x hybrida. See A. Harlequin Hybrids.

A. stoechadifolia. See A. venusta.

A. venusta, syn. *A. stoechadifolia* (African daisy). Compact perennial, often grown as an annual. **H** 20in (50cm) or more, **S** 16in (40cm). Daisylike, creamy-white flower heads with blue centers are borne singly throughout summer and into fall. Chrysanthemum-like leaves are dark green above, gray beneath. Z13–15 H11–10.

Arctous alpinus. See *Arctostaphylos alpina*.

ARDISIA
MYRSINACEAE/PRIMULACEAE

Genus of evergreen shrubs and trees, grown for their fruits and foliage. Needs partial shade and rich, well-drained but not dry soil. Water potted plants freely when in full growth, moderately at other times. Cut back old plants in early spring if required. Propagate by seed in spring or by semiripe cuttings in summer.

A. crenata, syn. *A. crenulata*, illus. p.456.

A. crenulata. See *A. crenata*.

Areca lutescens. See *Dypsis lutescens*.
Arecastrum romanozoffianum. See *Syagrus romanozoffianum*.
Aregelia carolinae. See *Neoregelia carolinae*.

ARENARIA
Sandwort
CARYOPHYLLACEAE

Genus of spring- and summer-flowering annuals and perennials, some of which are evergreen. Most need sun and well-drained, sandy soil. Propagate by division or softwood cuttings in early summer or by seed in fall or spring.

A. balearica, illus. p.347.

A. montana, illus. p.360.

A. purpurascens, illus. p.351.

A. tetraquetra, illus. p.348.

ARGEMONE
Prickly poppy
PAPAVERACEAE

Genus of robust perennials, most of which are best treated as annuals. Grow in sun and in very well-drained soil without supports. Deadhead to prolong the flowering season. Propagate by seed sown outdoors in late spring.

A. mexicana, illus. p.321.

ARGYRANTHEMUM
COMPOSITAE/ASTERACEAE

Genus of evergreen subshrubs, grown for their daisylike flowers. Needs full sun and moderately fertile, well-drained soil. Propagate by semiripe cuttings in summer or root greenwood cuttings in spring.

A. BUTTERFLY ('Ulysiss'), illus. p.319.

A. frutescens, syn. *Chrysanthemum frutescens* (Marguerite), illus. p.298.

A. 'Jamaica Primrose', syn. *Chrysanthemum frutescens* 'Jamaica Primrose', illus. p.319.

A. 'Mary Wootton', syn. *Chrysanthemum frutescens* 'Mary Wootton'. Evergreen, woody-based, bushy perennial. **H** and **S** to 3ft (1m). Has fernlike, divided, pale green foliage and bears daisylike, pink flower heads throughout summer. Z10–11 H11–1.

A. 'Summer Melody', illus. p.300.

ARGYREIA
CONVOLVULACEAE

Genus of evergreen, twining climbers, closely allied to *Ipomoea* and grown for their showy flowers. Needs full light and fertile, well-drained soil. Water freely when in full growth, sparingly at other times. Support is needed. Thin out previous season's growth in spring. Propagate by seed in spring or by softwood or greenwood cuttings in summer. Red spider mite and whitefly may be troublesome.

A. nervosa, syn. *A. speciosa* (Woolly morning glory). Evergreen, twining climber. **H** 25–30ft (8–10m). Has oval, silver-backed leaves, 7–11in (18–27cm) long. Clusters of funnel-shaped, lavender-blue flowers, with darker bases and white downy in bud, are produced in summer–fall. Z13–15 H11–1.

A. speciosa. See *A. nervosa*.

Argyrocytisus battandieri. See *Cytisus battandieri*.

ARGYRODERMA
AIZOACEAE

Genus of perennial succulents, grown for their very fleshy, gray-green leaves united in a prostrate, egg shape. In summer, daisylike flowers appear in central split between leaves. Needs full sun and extremely well-drained soil. Propagate by seed in summer.

A. aureum. See A. delaetii.

A. blandum. See A. delaetii.

A. brevipes. See A. fissum.

A. delaetii, syn. *A. aureum, A. blandum*, illus. p.488.

A. fissum, syn. *A. brevipes*, illus. p.491.

A. pearsonii, syn. *A. schlechteri*, illus. p.491.

A. schlechteri. See A. pearsonii.

ARIOCARPUS
Living rock
CACTACEAE

Genus of very slow-growing, perennial cacti with large, swollen roots. Has flattened, spherical, green stems with angular tubercles and tufts of wool. Prefers full sun and extremely well-drained, lime-rich soil. Is very prone to rotting. Propagate by seed in spring or summer.

A. fissuratus (Living rock). Very slow-growing, flattened spherical, perennial cactus. **H** 4in (10cm), **S** 6in (15cm). Gray stem is covered with rough, triangular tubercles each producing a tuft of wool. Bears pink-red flowers, 1½in (4cm) across, in fall. Z12–15 H11–10.

ARISAEMA
ARACEAE

Genus of tuberous perennials, grown for their large, curious, hooded spathes, each enclosing a pencil-shaped spadix. Forms spikes of fleshy, red fruits in fall, before dying down. Needs sun or partial shade and moist but well-drained rich soil. Plant tubers 6in (15cm) deep in spring. Propagate by seed in fall or spring or by offsets in spring.

A. atrorubens. See A. triphyllum.

A. candidissimum, illus. p.422.

A. consanguineum, illus. p.393.

A. griffithii, illus. p.412.

A. jacquemontii, illus. p.412.

A. ringens (Cobra jack). Early spring-flowering, tuberous perennial. **H** 10–12in (25–30cm), **S** 12–18in (30–45cm). Bears 2 erect leaves, each with 3 long-pointed lobes, and a widely hooded, green spathe, enclosing the spadix, that has paler green stripes and is edged with dark brown-purple. Z6–9 H9–6.

A. sikokianum, illus. p.408.

A. tortuosum. Summer-flowering, tuberous perennial. **H** 1–3ft (30cm–1m), **S** 1–1½ft (30–45cm). Each dark green-mottled, pale green stem bears 2–3 erect leaves, divided into several oval leaflets. A hooded, green or purple spathe, with a protruding, S-shaped spadix, overtops leaves. Produces spikes of fleshy, red fruits in fall. Z8–9 H9–7.

A. triphyllum, syn. *A. atrorubens*, illus. p.406.

ARISARUM
ARACEAE

Genus of tuberous perennials, grown mainly for their curious, hooded spathes enclosing spadices with minute flowers. Needs partial shade and rich, well-drained soil. Propagate in fall by dividing established clumps of tubers, which produce offsets freely.

A. proboscideum (Mouse plant). Clump-forming, spring-flowering, tuberous perennial. **H** to 4in (10cm), **S** 8–12in (20–30cm). Leaves are arrow-shaped and prostrate. Produces a spadix of minute flowers concealed in a hooded, dark brown spathe that is drawn out into a tail up to 6in (15cm) long, creating a mouse-like effect. Z7–9 H9–7.

ARISTEA
IRIDACEAE

Genus of evergreen, clump-forming, rhizomatous perennials, grown for their spikes of blue flowers in spring or summer. Prefers a sunny position and well-drained soil. Established plants cannot be moved satisfactorily. Propagate by seed in fall or spring.

A. capitata, syn. *A. major, A. thyrsiflora*, illus. p.393.

A. ecklonii. Evergreen, clump-forming, rhizomatous perennial. **H** 12–24in (30–60cm), **S** 8–16in (20–40cm). Has long, sword-shaped, tough leaves, overtopped in summer by loosely branched spikes of saucer-shaped, blue flowers, produced in long succession. Z9–10 H10–9.

A. major. See A. capitata.

A. thyrsiflora. See A. capitata.

ARISTOLOCHIA
Birthwort
ARISTOLOCHIACEAE

Genus of evergreen or deciduous, woody-stemmed, twining and scrambling climbers, grown for their foliage and flowers. Requires partial shade in summer and well-drained soil. Water regularly, less when not in full growth. Provide support. Cut back previous season's growth to 2 or 3 nodes in spring. Propagate by seed in spring or by semiripe cuttings in summer. Red spider mite and whitefly may be a nuisance.

A. durior. See A. macrophylla.

A. elegans. See A. littoralis.

A. gigas. See A. grandiflora.

A. grandiflora, syn. *A. gigas* (Pelican flower, Swan flower). Fast-growing, evergreen, woody-stemmed, twining climber. **H** 22ft (7m) or more. Leaves are broadly oval, 6–10in (15–25cm) long. In summer bears large, unpleasant-smelling, tubular, purple-veined, white flowers, each with a long tail and expanding at the mouth into a heart-shaped lip. Z13–15 H11–10.

A. griffithii, syn. *Isotrema griffithii*. Moderately vigorous, evergreen, woody-stemmed, twining climber. **H** 15–20ft

A

(5–6m). Deciduous in cold winters. Has heart-shaped leaves and tubular, dark red flowers, each with an expanded, spreading lip, in summer. Z10–11 H11–7.
A. littoralis, syn. *A. elegans* , illus. p.462.
A. macrophylla, syn. *A. durior*, *A. sipho*, illus. p.204.
A. sipho. See *A. macrophylla*.

ARISTOTELIA
ELAEOCARPACEAE

Genus of evergreen shrubs and deciduous trees, grown for their foliage. Needs separate male and female plants in order to obtain fruits. Needs sun or semi-shade and fertile, well-drained soil. Propagate by semiripe cuttings in summer.
A. chilensis, syn. *A. macqui*. Evergreen, spreading shrub. **H** 10ft (3m), **S** 15ft (5m). Leaves are oval, glossy and deep green. Tiny, star-shaped, green flowers are borne in summer, followed by small, spherical, black fruits. Z9–11 H11–7.
A. macqui. See *A. chilensis*.

ARMERIA
Sea pink, Thrift
PLUMBAGINACEAE

Genus of evergreen perennials and, occasionally, subshrubs, grown for their tuftlike clumps or rosettes of leaves and their flower heads. Needs sun and well-drained soil. Propagate by semiripe cuttings in summer or by seed in fall.
A. 'Bees Ruby', syn. *A. pseudarmeria* 'Bees Ruby'. Evergreen, clump-forming subshrub. **H** and **S** 12in (30cm). Round heads of many small, ruby-red flowers are produced in summer on stiff stems above narrow, grasslike, dark green leaves. Z5–7 H9–4.
A. caespitosa. See *A. juniperifolia*.
A. juniperifolia, syn. *A. caespitosa*, illus. p.352. **'Bevans Variety'** is an evergreen, densely cushioned subshrub. **H** 2–3in (5–8cm), **S** 6in (15cm). Has narrow, pointed, mid- to gray-green leaves in loose rosettes. Round heads of small, deep pink flowers are borne in late spring and early summer. Z5–7 H9–4.
A. latifolia. See *A. pseudarmeria*.
A. maritima. Evergreen, clump-forming perennial or subshrub. **H** 4in (10cm), **S** 6in (15cm). Leaves are narrow, grasslike and dark green. Stiff stems bear round heads of many small, white to pink flowers in summer. Makes a good edging plant. Z3–9 H9–1. **'Vindictive'** illus. p.365.
A. pseudarmeria, syn. *A. latifolia*, illus. p.336. **'Bees Ruby'**. See *A. 'Bees Ruby'*.

ARNEBIA
BORAGINACEAE

Genus of perennials with hairy leaves, suitable for rock gardens and banks. Needs sun and gritty, well-drained soil. Propagate by seed in fall, by root cuttings in winter or by division in spring.
A. echioides. See *A. pulchra*.
A. pulchra, syn. *A. echioides*, *Macrotomia echioides*, *Echioides longiflorum* (Prophet flower). Clump-forming perennial. **H** 9–12in (23–30cm), **S** 10in (25cm). Leaves are lance-shaped to narrowly oval, hairy and light green. In summer produces loose racemes of

tubular, bright yellow flowers, each with 5 spreading lobes and fading dark spots at petal bases. Z6–8 H8–6.

ARNICA
COMPOSITAE/ASTERACEAE

Genus of rhizomatous perennials, grown for their large, daisylike flower heads. Is suitable for large rock gardens. Prefers sun and rich, well-drained soil. Propagate by division or seed in spring. ① All parts may cause severe discomfort if ingested, and contact with sap may aggravate skin allergies.
A. montana. Tufted, rhizomatous perennial. **H** 12in (30cm), **S** 6in (15cm). Bears narrowly oval to oval, hairy, gray-green leaves and, in summer, solitary daisylike, golden flower heads, 2in (5cm) wide. Prefers acid soil. Z5–8 H8–5.

ARONIA
Chokeberry
ROSACEAE

Genus of deciduous shrubs, grown for their flowers, fruits and colorful fall foliage. Needs sun (for fall color at its best) or semi-shade and fertile, well-drained soil. Propagate by softwood or semiripe cuttings in summer, by seed sown in fall or by division from early fall to spring.
A. arbutifolia (Red chokeberry), illus. p.142. Deciduous shrub, upright when young, later arching. **H** 10ft (3m), **S** 5ft (1.5m). Clusters of small, white flowers, with red anthers, in late spring, are followed by red berries. Dark green leaves turn red in fall. Z5–9 H8–4.
A. melanocarpa, illus. p.128.
A. x prunifolia (Purple chokeberry). Deciduous, upright shrub. **H** 10ft (3m), **S** 8ft (2.5m). Oval, glossy, dark green leaves redden in fall. Produces star-shaped, white flowers in late spring and early summer, followed by spherical, purplish-black fruits. Z5–9 H9–5.

ARRHENATHERUM
Oat grass
GRAMINEAE/POACEAE

See also GRASSES, BAMBOOS, RUSHES and SEDGES.
A. elatius (False oat grass). **subsp. bulbosum 'Variegatum'** (False oat grass) is a loosely tuft-forming, herbaceous, perennial grass. **H** 20in (50cm), **S** 8in (20cm). Has a basal stem swelling, hairless, gray-green leaves, with white margins, and open panicles of brownish spikelets in summer. Z5–8 H8–5.

ARTEMISIA
Wormwood
COMPOSITAE/ASTERACEAE

Genus of perennials and spreading, dwarf subshrubs and shrubs, some of which are evergreen or semievergreen, grown mainly for their fernlike, silvery foliage, which is sometimes aromatic. Prefers an open, sunny, well-drained site; dwarf types benefit from a winter protection of sharp grit or gravel. Trim lightly in spring. Propagate by division in spring or fall or by softwood or semiripe cuttings in summer.
A. abrotanum, illus. p.165.
A. absinthium 'Lambrook Silver'.

Evergreen, bushy perennial, woody at base. **H** 32in (80cm), **S** 20in (50cm). Has a mass of finely divided, aromatic, silvery-gray leaves. Produces tiny, insignificant, gray flower heads, borne in long panicles, in summer. Needs protection in an exposed site. Z4–8 H9–1.
A. alba 'Canescens', syn. *A. canescens*, *A. splendens*. Semievergreen, bushy perennial. **H** 20in (50cm), **S** 12in (30cm). Has delicate, finely cut, curling, silvery-gray leaves. In summer, insignificant, yellow flower heads are borne on erect, silver stems. Makes good groundcover. Z4–8 H8–1.
A. arborescens, illus. p.165. **'Brass Band'**. See *A. 'Powis Castle'*. **'Faith Raven'** is an evergreen, upright shrub. **H** 4ft (1.2m), **S** 3ft (1m). Differs from the species only in that it is hardier. Has finely cut, aromatic, silvery-white foliage and, in summer and early fall, rounded heads of small, bright yellow flowers. Z5–9 H9–5.
A. assoana. See *A. caucasica*.
A. canescens. See *A. alba 'Canescens'*.
A. caucasica, syn. *A. assoana*, *A. lanata*, *A. pedemontana*. Evergreen or semievergreen, prostrate perennial. **H** and **S** 12in (30cm). Fernlike foliage is densely covered with silvery-white hairs. Small clusters of small, rounded, yellow flower heads are borne in summer. Suits a rock garden or wall. Z5–9 H9–1.
A. frigida. Semievergreen, mat-forming perennial with a woody base. **H** 12in (30cm) in flower, **S** 12in (30cm) or more. Bears small, fernlike, aromatic, silky, gray-white leaves, divided into many linear lobes. In summer produces narrow panicles of small, rounded, yellow flower heads. Z3–8 H8–3.
A. lactiflora, illus. p.216.
A. lanata. See *A. caucasica*.
A. ludoviciana (Western mugwort, White sage). Semievergreen, rhizomatous, clump-forming perennial. **H** 4ft (1.2m), **S** 2ft (60cm). Has aromatic, lance-shaped, woolly, silvery-gray leaves with jagged margins. Bears slender plumes of tiny, grayish-white flower heads in summer. Z4–9 H9–1. **'Silver Queen', H** 30in (75cm), has densely white-woolly panicles of brownish-yellow flower heads from mid-summer to fall. Z4–9 H9–1. **'Valerie Finnis'** illus. p.274.
A. pedemontana. See *A. caucasica*.
A. pontica (Roman wormwood). Vigorous, upright perennial. **H** 24in (60cm), **S** 8in (20cm). Has aromatic, feathery, silver-green foliage and tall spikes of small, grayish flower heads in summer. May spread. Z4–8 H8–1.
A. 'Powis Castle', syn. *A. arborescens* 'Brass Band', illus. p.242.
A. schmidtiana (Silvermound). Semievergreen, hummock-forming perennial with creeping stems. **H** 3–12in (8–30cm), **S** 24in (60cm). Has fernlike, very finely and deeply cut, silver leaves and, in summer, produces short racemes of small, rounded, pale yellow flower heads. Is good for a large rock garden, wall or bank. Needs sandy, peaty soil. Z5–8 H8–5. **'Nana'** illus. p.374.
A. splendens. See *A. alba 'Canescens'*.
A. stelleriana (Beach wormwood). Evergreen, rounded, rhizomatous perennial with a woody base. **H** 1–2ft (30–60cm), **S** 2–3ft (60cm–1m). White-haired, silver leaves are deeply lobed or toothed. Bears slender sprays of small, yellow flower

heads in summer. Needs light soil. Z3–7 H7–1. **'Boughton Silver'**, syn. *A. stelleriana* 'Mori', *A. stelleriana* 'Silver Brocade', **S** 3ft (1m), is vigorous and arching in habit. Z3–7 H7–1. **'Mori'**. See *A. stelleriana* 'Boughton Silver'. **'Silver Brocade'**. See *A. stelleriana* 'Boughton Silver'.

ARTHROPODIUM
LILIACEAE/ASPARAGACEAE

Genus of tufted perennials, grown for their flowers. Prefers a position against a sunny, sheltered wall in fertile soil. Propagate by division in spring or by seed in spring or fall.
A. cirratum, syn. *A. cirrhatum* (Rienga lily, Rock lily). Branching perennial. **H** 3ft (1m), **S** 1ft (30cm). Bears sprays of nodding, shallowly cup-shaped, white flowers on wiry stems in early summer. Has a basal tuft of narrowly sword-shaped leaves and fleshy roots. Z8–9 H9–8.
A. cirrhatum. See *A. cirratum*.

ARUM
ARACEAE

Genus of tuberous perennials, grown for their leaves and spathes, each enclosing a pencil-shaped spadix of tiny flowers. Requires sun or partial shade and moist but well-drained soil. Propagate by seed in fall or by division in early fall.
A. creticum, illus. p.407.
A. dioscoridis. Spring-flowering, tuberous perennial. **H** 8–14in (20–35cm), **S** 12–18in (30–45cm). Has a sail-like, green or purple spathe, blotched dark purple, surrounding a blackish-purple spadix. Arrow-shaped, semierect leaves are produced in fall. Needs a sheltered, sunny site. Z7–9 H9–7.
A. dracunculus. See *Dracunculus vulgaris*.
A. italicum 'Marmoratum', syn. *A. italicum* 'Pictum', illus. p.421. **'Pictum'**. See *A. italicum* 'Marmoratum'.
A. pictum. Fall-flowering, tuberous perennial. **H** 6–10in (15–25cm), **S** 6–8in (15–20cm). Arrow-shaped, semierect, glossy leaves, with cream veins, appear at same time as cowl-like, deep purple-brown spathe and dark purple spadix. Z6–9 H9–6.

ARUNCUS
ROSACEAE

Genus of perennials, grown for their hummocks of broad, fernlike leaves and their plumes of white flowers in summer. Thrives in full light and any well-drained soil. Propagate by seed in fall or by division in spring or fall.
A. dioicus, syn. *A. sylvester*, *Spiraea aruncus* (Goat's beard), illus. p.436.
'Kneiffii' illus. p.231.
A. sylvester. See *A. dioicus*.

Arundinaria anceps. See *Yushania anceps*.
Arundinaria auricoma. See *Pleioblastus viridistriatus*.
Arundinaria falconeri. See *Himalayacalamus falconeri*.
Arundinaria fastuosa. See *Semiarundinaria fastuosa*.
Arundinaria fortunei. See *Pleioblastus variegatus*.

Arundinaria japonica. See *Pseudosasa japonica.*

Arundinaria jaunsarensis. See *Yushania anceps.*

Arundinaria murieliae. See *Fargesia murieliae.*

Arundinaria nitida. See *Fargesia nitida.*

Arundinaria variegata. See *Pleioblastus variegatus.*

ARUNDO
GRAMINEAE/POACEAE

See also GRASSES, BAMBOOS, RUSHES and SEDGES.

A. donax (Giant reed). Herbaceous, rhizomatous, perennial grass. **H** to 20ft (6m), **S** 3ft (1m). Has thick stems that bear broad, floppy, blue-green leaves. Produces dense, erect panicles of whitish-yellow spikelets in summer. Can be grown in moist soil. Z6–9 H11–1. **var. versicolor,** syn. *A. donax* 'Variegata' illus. p.436. **'Variegata'.** See *A. donax* var. *versicolor.*

ASARINA
SCROPHULARIACEAE/PLANTAGINACEAE

Genus of evergreen climbers and perennials, often with scandent stems, grown for their flowers. Is herbaceous in cold climates. Needs full light and well-drained soil. Propagate by seed in spring.

A. barclayana. See *Maurandya barclayana.*

A. erubescens. See *Lophospermum erubescens.*

A. procumbens, syn. *Antirrhinum asarina,* illus. p.371.

ASARUM
SYN. HEXASTYLIS
Wild ginger
ARISTOLOCHIACEAE

Genus of rhizomatous perennials, some of which are evergreen, with pitcher-shaped flowers carried under kidney- or heart-shaped leaves. Makes good groundcover, although leaves may become damaged in severe weather. Prefers shade and rich, moist but well-drained soil. Propagate by division in spring. Self-seeds readily.

A. caudatum. Evergreen, prostrate, rhizomatous perennial. **H** 3in (8cm), **S** 10in (25cm) or more. Heart-shaped, leathery, glossy, dark green leaves, 2–4in (5–10cm) across, conceal small, pitcher-shaped, reddish-brown or brownish-purple flowers, with tail-like lobes, in early summer. Z7–9 Z9–7.

A. europaeum, illus. p.375.

A. hartwegii (Sierra wild ginger). Evergreen, prostrate, rhizomatous perennial. **H** 3in (8cm), **S** 10in (25cm) or more. Pitcher-shaped, very dark brown, almost black, flowers, with tail-like lobes, are produced in early summer beneath heart-shaped, silver-marked, mid-green leaves, 2–4in (5–10cm) wide. Z2–8 H8–1.

A. shuttleworthii (Shuttleworth ginger). Evergreen, prostrate, rhizomatous perennial. **H** 3in (8cm), **S** 10in (25cm) or more. Has broadly heart-shaped, usually silver-marked, mid-green leaves, 3in (8cm) across. Bears pitcher-shaped, dark brown flowers, mottled violet inside, in early summer. Z5–9 H9–1.

ASCLEPIAS
Milkweed
ASCLEPIADACEAE/APOCYNACEAE

Genus of tuberous perennials or subshrubs, some of which are evergreen, grown for their flowers which attract poll. Stems exude milky, white latex when cut. Hardy species prefer a position in sun and rich, well-drained soil. Propagate by division or seed in spring. Tender species require sun and a moist atmosphere; cut back during periods of growth. Water very sparingly in low temperatures. Propagate by tip cuttings or seed in spring.
ⓘ Contact with the milky sap may irritate skin.

A. curassavica (Bloodflower). Evergreen, bushy, tuberous subshrub. **H** and **S** 3ft (1m). Has narrowly oval leaves, to 6in (15cm) long. Umbels of small but showy, 5-horned, orange-red flowers, with yellow centers, are produced in summer–fall and are followed by narrowly ovoid, pointed fruits, 3in (8cm) long, with silky seeds. Z9–11 H11–6.

A. hallii. Upright, tuberous perennial. **H** to 3ft (1m), **S** 2ft (60cm). Has oblong leaves, to 5in (13cm) long. Umbels of small, 5-horned, dark pink flowers are borne in summer; tightly packed silky seeds are enclosed in narrowly ovoid fruits, to 6in (15cm) long. Z9–11 H11–10.

A. physocarpa. See *Gomphocarpus physocarpus.*

A. syriaca (Common milkweed). Upright, tuberous perennial. **H** and **S** 3ft (1m) or more. Bears oval leaves, to 8in (20cm) long. Produces umbels of small, 5-horned, purplish-pink flowers borne on drooping flower stalks in summer, are followed by narrowly ovoid fruits, to 6in (15cm) long and filled with silky seeds. Z3–9 H9–2.

A. tuberosa (Butterflyweed), illus. p.246.

ASIMINA
ANNONACEAE

Genus of deciduous or evergreen shrubs and trees, grown for their foliage and flowers. Prefers full sun and fertile, deep, moist but well-drained soil. Propagate by seed in fall or by layering or root cuttings in winter.

A. triloba (Pawpaw). Deciduous, open shrub or small tree. **H** and **S** 12–25ft (4–8m). Large, oval, mid-green leaves emerge in late spring or early summer, just after, or at the same time as, 6-petaled, purplish-brown flowers. Edible fruits are small, globular and pale green. Leaves turn yellow in fall. Z6–8 H8–6.

ASPARAGUS
LILIACEAE/ASPARAGACEAE

Genus of perennials and scrambling climbers and shrubs, some of which are evergreen, grown for their foliage. Grow in partial shade or bright light, but not direct sun, in any fertile, well-drained soil. Propagate by seed or division in spring.

A. densiflorus, illus. p.474. **'Myersii'**, syn. *A. meyeri, A.* 'Myers' (Foxtail fern), illus. p.474.

A. meyeri. See *A. densiflorus* 'Myersii'.

A. 'Myers'. See *A. densiflorus* 'Myersii'.

A. scandens, illus. p.463.

ASPERULA
Woodruff
RUBIACEAE

Genus of annuals and perennials; some species make good alpine houseplants. Most species need sun and well-drained soil with moisture at roots. Dislikes winter wet on crown. Propagate by softwood cuttings or seed in early summer.

A. athoa. See *A. suberosa.*

A. odorata. See *Galium odoratum.*

A. suberosa, syn. *A. athoa,* illus. p.362.

ASPHODELINE
Jacob's rod
LILIACEAE/ASPHODELACEAE

Genus of perennials with thick, fleshy roots. Requires sun and not over-rich soil. Propagate by division in early spring, taking care not to damage roots, or by seed in fall or spring.

A. liburnica. Neat, clump-forming perennial. **H** 10–24in (25–60cm), **S** 12in (30cm). In spring produces racemes of shallowly cup-shaped, yellow flowers on slender stems above linear, gray-green leaves. Z6–9 H9–6.

A. lutea, illus. p.227.

ASPHODELUS
Asphodel
LILIACEAE/ASPHODELACEAE

Genus of spring- or summer-flowering annuals and perennials. Requires sun; most prefer fertile, well-drained soil. *A. albus* prefers light, well-drained soil. Propagate by division in spring or by seed in fall.

A. acaulis. Prostrate perennial. **H** 2in (5cm), **S** 9in (23cm). In spring or early summer, stemless, funnel-shaped, flesh-pink flowers are produced in the center of each cluster of grasslike, mid-green leaves. Is suitable for an alpine house. Z9–10 H10–9.

A. aestivus, syn. *A. microcarpus* (Asphodel). Upright perennial. **H** 3ft (1m), **S** 1ft (30cm). Dense panicles of star-shaped, white flowers are borne in late spring. Has basal rosettes of upright, then spreading, grasslike, channeled, leathery, mid-green leaves. Z7–10 H10–7.

A. albus, illus. p.230.

A. microcarpus. See *A. aestivus.*

ASPIDISTRA
LILIACEAE/ASPARAGACEAE

Genus of evergreen, rhizomatous perennials that spread slowly, grown mainly for their glossy foliage. Although very tolerant, is best grown in a cool, shady position away from direct sunlight and in well-drained soil. Water frequently when in full growth, less at other times. Propagate by division of rhizomes in spring.

A. attenuata. Evergreen, rhizomatous perennial. **H** 36in (100cm), **S** 20in (50cm) or more. Has long-stalked, pointed, elliptic, yellow-spotted, glossy, deep green leaves, 18–20in (45–50cm) long. Small, urn-shaped red and yellow flowers are produced at ground level in spring or fall. Z10–13 H12–1.

A. daibuensis. Evergreen, rhizomatous perennial. **H** 36in (100cm), **S** 20in (50cm) or more. Produces lance-shaped, yellow-spotted, glossy, deep green leaves, 16–24in (40–60cm) long. Cup-shaped, yellow flowers are borne near ground level, in summer–fall. Z10–13 H12–1.

A. elatior (Cast-iron plant). Evergreen, rhizomatous perennial. **H** 24in (60cm), **S** 18in (45cm). Has upright, narrow, pointed-oval leaves, to 24in (60cm) long. Inconspicuous, cream to purple flowers are occasionally produced on short stalks near soil level. Z7–11 H11–4. **'Asahi'** has variegated leaves each with a narrow, inverted wedge-shaped, white zone extending down the leaf from the apex. Z7–11 H11–4. **'Variegata',** illus. p.277.

A. zongbayi 'Uan Fat Lady'. Evergreen, rhizomatous perennial. **H** 20in (50cm), **S** 12in (30cm) or more. Slender leaf stalks bear broadly oval, wavy-margined, bright green leaves, 8in (20cm) long, speckled with greenish-yellow and with a central, broad, pale stripe. Cup-shaped, purple flowers are produced near ground level from late summer to fall. Z11–14 H12–1.

ASPLENIUM
ASPLENIACEAE

Genus of evergreen or semievergreen ferns. Plants described prefer partial shade, but *A. trichomanes* tolerates full sun. Grow in any moist soil, although container plants should be cultivated in a compost that includes chopped sphagnum moss or coarse peat. Regularly remove any fronds that are fading. Propagate by spores or bulbils, if produced, in late summer.

A. bulbiferum (Hen-and-chicken fern, Mother spleenwort). Semievergreen or evergreen fern. **H** 6–12in (15–30cm), **S** 12in (30cm). Lance-shaped, finely divided, dark green fronds produce bulbils from which young plants develop. Z9–11 H11–8.

A. ceterach, syn. *Ceterach officinarum,* illus. p.293.

A. nidus, illus. p.479.

A. scolopendrium, syn. *Phyllitis scolopendrium, Scolopendrium vulgare,* illus. p.292. **Marginatum Group,** syn. *Phyllitis scolopendrium* 'Marginatum', illus. p.292.

A. trichomanes, illus. p.291.

ASTELIA
ASTELIACEAE

Genus of clump-forming perennials, grown mainly for their foliage. Prefers full sun or semi-shade and fertile soil that does not dry out readily. Propagate by division in spring.

A. chathamica, illus. p.242.

A. nervosa. Clump-forming perennial. **H** 2ft (60cm), **S** 5ft (1.5m). Has long, sword-shaped, arching, silvery-gray leaves, above which, in summer, rise branching panicles of small, star-shaped, pale brown flowers. Z8–9 H9–8.

ASTER
Michaelmas daisy
COMPOSITAE/ASTERACEAE

Genus of perennials and deciduous or evergreen subshrubs with daisylike flower heads borne in summer–fall. Prefers sun or

A

partial shade and fertile, well-drained soil, with adequate moisture all summer. Tall asters require staking. Propagate by softwood cuttings in spring or by division in spring or fall. Some species may suffer from powdery mildew. See also feature panel p.249.

A. acris. See *A. sedifolius.*

A. albescens, syn. *Microglossa albescens.* Deciduous, upright, slender-stemmed subshrub. **H** 3ft (1m), **S** 5ft (1.5m). Has narrowly lance-shaped, gray-green leaves and flattish sprays of lavender-blue flower heads, with yellow centers, in mid-summer. Z7–10 H10–7.

A. alpinus, illus. p.367. **'Dark Beauty'.** See *A. alpinus* 'Dunkle Schöne'. **'Dunkle Schöne',** syn. *A. alpinus* 'Dark Beauty' is a clump-forming perennial. **H** 10in (25cm), **S** 18in (45cm). Leaves are lance-shaped and dark green. Deep purple flower heads are borne from mid- to late summer. Is suitable for a rock garden. Z4–8 H8–1.

A. amellus (Italian aster). **'King George'** illus. p.250. **'Mauve Beauty'** is a bushy perennial. **H** and **S** 20in (50cm). In fall bears clusters of large, terminal, daisylike, violet flower heads with yellow centers. Leaves are lance-shaped, coarse and mid-green. Z5–8 H8–1. **'Nocturne',** **H** 30in (75cm), has deep lilac flower heads with yellow centers. Z5–8 H8–1. **'Rudolph Goethe'** with large, violet-blue flower heads, Z5–8 H8–1. **'Sonia'** with pink flower heads and Z5–8 H8–1. **'Veilchenkönigin',** syn. *A. amellus* 'Violet Queen' with deep violet flower heads are other good cultivars. Z5–8 H8–1. **'Violet Queen'.** See *A. amellus* 'Veilchenkönigin'.

A. capensis. See *Felicia amelloides.*

***A.* 'Coombe Fishacre',** illus. p.249. Clump-forming, upright perennial. **H** to 36in (90cm), **S** 14in (35cm). Has lance-shaped, mid-green leaves. In late summer, erect stems bear masses of daisylike, pinkish-mauve flower heads with yellow centers that age to red. Z4–8 H8–1.

***A. cordifolius* 'Silver Spray',** illus. p.249. Bushy perennial. **H** 4ft (1.2m), **S** 3ft (1m). Dense, arching stems bear sprays of small, pink-tinged, white flower heads in fall. Mid-green leaves are lance-shaped. Needs staking. Z5–8 H8–1.

A. diffusus. See *A. lateriflorus.*

A. divaricatus (White wood aster), illus. p.249. Spreading, upright perennial. **H** 16in (40cm), **S** 12in (30cm). Has pointed, oval, toothed, glossy, dark green leaves. In late summer, purplish-black, wiry, branching, arching stems bear daisylike, white flower heads. Is best in shade, where it makes good groundcover. Z4–8 H9–1.

A. ericoides (Heath aster). Clump-forming, bushy perennial. **H** 3ft (1m), **S** 12in (30cm). From late summer to late fall produces daisylike, yellow-centered, white flower heads, sometimes shaded pink or blue, in lax panicles. Has small, lance-shaped, mid-green leaves and slender, freely branched stems. Z5–8 H8–1. **'Blue Star',** **H** 32in (80cm), has soft mauve-blue ray florets. Z5–8 H8–1. **'Golden Spray'** (illus. p.249) produces pink-tinged, white flower heads, with golden-yellow centers. Z5–8 H8–1. **'Pink Cloud',** **H** 32in (80cm), is vigorous, with arching sprays of pale pink flower heads. Z5–8 H8–1. **f. *prostratus,*** **H** to 8in (20cm), **S** 24in (60cm), makes good groundcover and has tiny, needlelike leaves and white or pale mauve flower heads. Z5–8 H8–1. **f. *prostratus* 'Snow Flurry'** has pure white flowers; is good in gravel or in a rock garden. Z5–8 H8–1. **'White Heather'** (illus. p.249) produces long-lasting, neat, white flower heads in late fall and wire stems that may need support. Z5–8 H8–1.

***A. x frikartii* 'Mönch'.** Bushy perennial. **H** 30in (75cm), **S** 18in (45cm). Bears daisylike, single, soft lavender-blue flower heads with yellowish-green centers continuously from mid-summer to late fall. Leaves are oval and rough. May need staking. Z5–8 H8–1. **'Wunder von Stäfa'** (illus. p.249) has lavender flowers. Z5–8 H8–1.

***A.* 'Kylie'.** Clump-forming, upright perennial. **H** 36in (100cm), **S** 18in (45cm). Has lance-shaped, mildew-resistant, deep-green leaves. In late summer, upright then arching sprays of small, daisylike, clear pastel-pink flower heads are borne in profusion. Z4–8 H8–1.

A. laevis (Smooth aster). Variable, clump-forming perennial. **H** 48in (120cm), **S** 20in (50cm). Has long, lance-shaped, mildew-resistant, mid-green leaves. In late summer, upright purplish stems bear abundant sprays of daisylike, pale purple flowers. Z4–8 H8–1. **'Bluebird'** has violet-blue flowers. Z4–8 H8–1.

A. lateriflorus, syn. *A. diffusus* (Calico aster). Branching perennial. **H** 24in (60cm), **S** 20in (50cm). Bears sprays of tiny, mauve flower heads, with pinkish-brown centers, in fall. Lance-shaped leaves are small and dark green. Z4–8 H8–1. **var. *horizontalis*** has flower heads that are sometimes tinged pink, with darker pink centers. Z4–8 H8–1. **'Lady in Black',** **H** 4ft (1.2m), has bronze-purple leaves and yellow-centered, white flower heads and retains its leaf coloring well during growing season. Z4–8 H8–1. **'Prince',** **H** 20in (50cm), has bronze-purple leaves, which fade to dark green, and small, pink-centered, white flower heads. Z4–8 H8–1.

A. linosyris, illus. p.254.

***A.* 'Little Carlow',** illus. p.249. Clump-forming, upright perennial. **H** 48in (120cm), **S** 18in (45cm). Has lance-shaped, mildew-resistant, deep-green leaves. In fall, upright sprays bear masses of daisylike, bright mauve-blue flower heads. Z4–9 H9–1.

A. novae-angliae (New England aster). Z4–8 H8–1. **'Andenken an Alma Pötschke'** Vigorous, upright perennial. **H** 30in (75cm), **S** to 24in (60cm). In fall produces clusters of single, pink flower heads on stiff stems. Has lance-shaped, rough leaves. May need staking. **'Autumn Snow'.** See *A. novae-angliae* 'Herbstschnee'. **'Barr's Pink'** bears semidouble, bright rose-pink flower heads in summer–fall. **'Harrington's Pink',** (illus. p.249), **H** 4–5ft (1.2–1.5m), has single, clear pink flower heads with yellow centers. **'Herbstschnee',** syn. *A. novae-angliae* 'Autumn Snow', **H** 2½–3½ft (75cm–1.1m), are white with yellow centers. **'Rosa Sieger'** (illus. p.249), **H** 4ft (1.2m), has pink flower heads. **'Violetta'** (illus. p.249), **H** 5ft (1.5m), produces yellow-centered, bright violet-purple flower heads.

A. novi-belgii (New York aster). Z4–8 H8–1. **'Apple Blossom'** (illus. p.249) Vigorous, spreading perennial. **H** 36in (90cm), **S** 24–30in (60–75cm). Panicles of single, pale soft pink flowers are borne in fall amid lance-shaped, mid-green leaves. **'Carnival '** (illus. p.249), **H** 30in (75cm), **S** to 18in (45cm), bears double, cerise-red flower heads with yellow centers. Leaves are dark green. Is prone to mildew. **'Chequers'** (illus. p.249), **H** 36in (90cm), **S** 24–30in (60–75cm), has single, purple flowers. **'Climax',** **H** 5ft (1.5m), **S** 2ft (60cm), bears single, light blue flowers. Is mildew-resistant. The flower heads of **'Fellowship',** **H** 4ft (1.2m), **S** 20in (50cm), are large, double, and clear, deep pink; those of **'Freda Ballard'** (illus. p.249) are semidouble and rich rose-red. **'Kristina',** **H** 12in (30cm), **S** 18in (45cm), has large, semidouble, white flower heads with yellow centers. **'Lassie',** **H** 4ft (1.2m), **S** 30in (75cm), produces large, single, clear pink flowers. **'Little Pink Beauty',** **H** 18in (45cm), **S** 20in (50cm), is a good dwarf semidouble, pink cultivar. **'Marie Ballard'** (illus. p.249), **H** to 3ft (1m), **S** to 18in (45cm), has double, mid-blue flowers. Is prone to mildew. **'Orlando'** (illus. p.249), **H** 3ft (1m), **S** to 18in (45cm), has large, single, bright pink flower heads with golden centers. Leaves are bright green. Mildew may be a problem. **'Patricia Ballard',** **H** 4ft (1.2m), **S** 30in (75cm), produces semidouble, pink flowers. The large, single flowers of **'Peace'** are mauve; those of **'Professor Anton Kippenberg'** (illus. p.249), **H** 12in (30cm), **S** to 18in (45cm), are clear blue with yellow centers; and those of **'Raspberry Ripple'** **H** 30in (75cm), **S** 24in (60cm), are smaller and reddish-violet. **'Royal Ruby',** **H** and **S** to 18in (45cm), bears semidouble, rich red flower heads with yellow centers. Is prone to mildew. **'Royal Velvet',** **H** 4ft (1.2m), **S** 30in (75cm), has single, deep violet flowers. **'Sandford White Swan',** **H** 36in (90cm), **S** 24in (60cm), bears white flower heads.

***A.* 'Photograph',** illus. p.249. Clump-forming, upright, compact perennial. **H** 3ft (1m), **S** 1ft (30cm). Has heart-shaped, mid-green leaves. In fall, upright then arching, branched sprays bear masses of daisylike, glowing violet-blue flower heads. Z4–8 H8–1.

A. pilosus* var. *demotus, syn. *A. tradescantii.* Erect perennial. **H** 4ft (1.2m), **S** 20in (50cm). Has lance-shaped, mid-green leaves. In fall, clusters of small, white flower heads appear on wiry, leafy stems and provide a good foil to bright, fall leaf colors. Z5–9 H9–1.

***A.* 'Ringdove'.** Clump-forming, upright, compact perennial. **H** 3ft (1m), **S** 1ft (30cm). Has narrowly lance-shaped, mid-green leaves. In fall, upright then arching, branched sprays bear masses of small, daisylike, yellow-centered, soft lilac flower heads. Z4–8 H8–1.

A. sedifolius, syn. *A. acris.* Bushy perennial. **H** 3ft (1m), **S** 2ft (60cm). Produces clusters of almost star-shaped, lavender-blue flower heads, with yellow centers, in fall. Has small, narrowly oval, bright green leaves. Z4–7 H8–1. **'Nanus',** **H** and **S** 20in (50cm), makes a compact dome of blooms. Z4–7 H8–1.

***A.* 'Sunhelene',** illus. p.249. Clump-forming, upright, compact perennial. **H** 36in (100cm), **S** 16in (40cm). Has lance-shaped, mildew-resistant, mid-green leaves. In late summer and fall, upright, branched sprays bear masses of daisylike, double, blue-mauve flower heads. Z4–7 H8–1.

A. thomsonii. Upright perennial. **H** 3ft (1m), **S** 20in (50cm). Produces long-petaled, pale lilac flower heads, freely in fall. Leaves are slightly heart-shaped. Z4–8 H8–1. **'Nanus'** is more compact, **H** 18in (45cm), **S** 9in (23cm). Z4–8 H8–1.

A. tongolensis (East Indies aster). Mat-forming perennial. **H** 20in (50cm), **S** 12in (30cm). Large, lavender-blue flower heads, with orange centers, are borne singly in early summer. Has lance-shaped, hairy, dark green leaves. Z4–8 H8–1.

A. tradescantii. See *A. pilosus* var. *demotus.*

A. turbinellus. Clump-forming perennial. **H** 5ft (1.5m), **S** 3ft (1m). Has lance-shaped, dark green leaves. In late summer and fall, upright, wiry, purplish-green stems bear panicles of daisylike, yellow-centered, pale violet flowers. Z4–8 H8–1.

ASTERANTHERA

GESNERIACEAE

Genus of one species of evergreen, root climber. May be grown up mossy tree-trunks, trained against walls or used as groundcover. Needs a dampish, semi-shaded position and neutral to slightly acid soil. Propagate by tip cuttings in summer or by stem cuttings in late summer or early fall.

A. ovata. Evergreen, root climber with stems covered in white hairs. **H** to 12ft (4m). Has small, oblong, toothed leaves. Tubular, reddish-pink flowers, 2–2½in (5–6cm) long, often with yellow-striped, lower lips, are borne singly or in pairs in leaf axils in summer. Z8–9 H9–8.

ASTILBE

SAXIFRAGACEAE

Genus of summer-flowering perennials, grown for their panicles of flowers that remain handsome even when dried brown in winter. Is suitable for borders and rock gardens. Needs partial shade for most species, and rich, moist soil. Leave undisturbed if possible, and give a spring mulch of well-rotted compost. Propagate species by seed sown in fall; others by division in spring or fall.

***A.* 'Amethyst'** (x *arendsii* hybrid)**,** illus. p.232. Clump-forming perennial. **H** and **S** 3ft (1m). Tiny, star-shaped, vivid purple flowers are borne in long, rather open, slightly arching panicles in mid-summer above sharply divided, matt, dark green leaves. Is good towards the back of a border. Z4–8 H8–2.

***A.* 'Beauty of Ernst'** (x *arendsii* hybrid)**.** Clump-forming perennial. **H** 10–12in (25–30cm), **S** 18in (45cm). Compact, oval,

A

sharply divided, vivid green leaves become increasingly tinted wine-red and purple, then develop fiery fall colors. Tiny, star-shaped, pale pink flowers, maturing to apricot, are borne in open sprays in early summer. Z4–8 H8–1.

A. 'Brautschleier' (x *arendsii* hybrid), syn. *A*. 'Bridal Veil'. Clump-forming perennial. **H** and **S** 30in (75cm). Conical plumes of tiny, star-shaped, white flowers open in mid-summer from bright green buds then fade to cream. Oval, sharply divided leaves are glossy and bright green. Is less vigorous than many taller cultivars. Z3–8 H8–2.

A. 'Bressingham Beauty'. Leafy, clump-forming perennial. **H** and **S** to 3ft (1m). In summer bears feathery, tapering panicles of small, star-shaped, rich pink flowers on strong stems. Broad leaves are divided into oblong to oval, toothed leaflets. Z3–8 H8–2.

A. 'Bridal Veil'. See *A*. 'Brautschleier'.

A. 'Bronce Elegans' (*simplicifolia* hybrid). Compact, clump-forming perennial. **H** 12in (30cm), **S** 10in (25cm). Pyramidal, slightly drooping panicles of tiny, star-shaped, purplish-pink flowers are borne in late summer on reddish stems. Oval, sharply divided, dark green leaves slowly turn to reddish-purple. Z4–8 H8–2.

A. 'Bumalda' (x *arendsii* hybrid). Clump-forming perennial. **H** and **S** 30in (75cm). Tiny, star-shaped, bright white flowers are borne in open panicles in mid-summer. Has more or less oval, jaggedly toothed, red-tinted, bronze leaves. Z4–8 H8–1.

A. chinensis var. pumila Clump-forming perennial. **H** 12in (30cm), **S** 8in (20cm). Lower two-thirds of flower stem bears deeply dissected, coarse, toothed, hairy, dark green leaves. Dense, fluffy spikes of tiny, star-shaped, deep raspberry-red flowers appear in summer. Is good for a shaded, moist rock garden. Z4–8 H8–2. **var. taquetii 'Superba', H** and **S** 4¹⁄₂ft (1.3m), is vigorous and has narrow, upright spikes of vivid magenta-purple flowers. **'Vision in Red', H** 28in (70cm), **S** 26in (65cm), has a vigorous, upright habit, very dark, slightly metallic green leaves and strong, dark purple stems and leaf stalks bearing purple flowers.

A. x crispa 'Perkeo', syn. *A*. 'Perkeo', illus. p.339.

A. 'Deutschland' (*japonica* hybrid), illus. p.232. Early-flowering, slow-spreading, clump-forming, robust perennial. **H** 20in (50cm), **S** 12in (30cm). Has oval, sharply divided, bright green leaves. Slightly arching panicles of tiny, star-shaped, white flowers are produced in late spring. Z4–9 H8–2.

A. 'Dusseldorf' (*japonica* hybrid). Tightly clump-forming perennial. **H** 24in (60cm), **S** 18in (45cm). Produces neat, regular panicles of tiny, star-shaped, salmon-pink flowers in mid-summer above oval, sharply divided, slightly bronze- or deep-red tinted, dark green leaves. Z4–8 H8–2.

A. Elizabeth Bloom ('Eliblo') (x *arendsii* hybrid). Vigorous, clump-forming perennial. **H** 32in (80cm), **S** 24in (60cm).

Oval, densely packed panicles of tiny, star-shaped, pale purplish pink flowers are borne in mid-summer. Has oval, sharply divided, glossy, very dark green leaves. Z4–8 H8–2.

A. 'Europa' (*japonica* hybrid), illus. p.232. Early-flowering, clump-forming perennial. **H** 24in (60cm), **S** 18in (45cm). In early summer produces tiny, star-shaped, unusually broad-petaled, pale purplish-pink flowers in dense panicles. Has oval, sharply divided, glossy, mid-green leaves. Z3–8 H8–1.

A. 'Fanal', illus. p.439.

A. 'Feuer' (x *arendsii* hybrid), syn. *A*. 'Fire', illus. p.232. Clump-forming perennial. **H** and **S** 3ft (1m). Conical plumes of tiny, star-shaped, rich purplish-red flowers are borne in early summer above oval, sharply divided, glossy, bright green leaves. Z3–8 H8–1.

A. 'Fire'. See *A*. 'Feuer'.

A. glaberrima var. saxatilis. Mound-forming perennial. **H** 4in (10cm), **S** 6in (15cm). In summer produces tiny, star-shaped, white-tipped, mauve flowers in short spikes. Oval, sharply divided, glossy, deeply toothed, dark green leaves are tinted red underneath. Thrives in consistently moist soil. Z3–8 H8–1.

A. 'Gnom', syn. *A. simplicifolia* 'Gnom'. Arching, clump-forming, slender-stemmed perennial. **H** 6in (15cm), **S** 4in (10cm). Has oval, deeply lobed or cut, crimped, reddish-green leaves in a basal rosette. Produces dense racemes of tiny, star-shaped, pink flowers in summer. Is good for a shaded, moist rock garden or peat bed. Self-seeds in damp places but will not come true. Z4–8 H8–2.

A. 'Granat', illus. p.232. Clump-forming, leafy perennial. **H** 2ft (60cm), **S** to 3ft (1m). Produces pyramidal trusses of tiny, star-shaped, deep red flowers in summer above broad, bronze-flushed, rich green leaves, which are divided into oblong to oval, toothed leaflets. Z4–8 H8–2.

A. 'Irrlicht', illus. p.232. Leafy perennial. **H** 1¹⁄₂–2ft (45–60cm), **S** to 3ft (1m). Bears tapering, feathery plumes of tiny, white flowers in summer. Foliage is dark green and flowers remain on the plant, dried and brown, well into winter. Z4–8 H8–2.

A. 'Koln' (*japonica* hybrid). Clump-forming perennial. **H** 24in (60cm), **S** 18in (45cm). Panicles of tiny, star-shaped, deep pink flowers are borne in mid-summer. Oval, sharply divided, dark green leaves are tinted bronze or deep red. Z4–8 H8–2.

A. 'Montgomery', illus. p.232. Leafy perennial. **H** 2¹⁄₂ft (75cm), **S** to 3ft (1m). Bears tapering, feathery plumes of tiny, deep salmon-red flowers in summer. Foliage is broad and divided into leaflets; flowers, brown when dried, remain on the plant well into winter. Z3–8 H8–2.

A. 'Ostrich Plume'. See *A*. 'Straussenfeder'.

A. 'Perkeo'. See *A*. x *crispa* 'Perkeo'.

A. 'Professor van der Wielen' (*thunbergii* hybrid). Clump-forming perennial. **H** 4ft (1.2m), **S** 3ft (1m). Arching sprays of tiny, star-shaped, pure white flowers are borne in early summer above oval, sharply divided, fresh green leaves. Z4–8 H8–2.

A. 'Rheinland' (*japonica* hybrid). Clump-forming perennial. **H** 20in (50cm), **S** 18in (45cm). Compact, conical, upright panicles of tiny, star-shaped, deep pink flowers are produced in early and mid-summer above conspicuously divided, mid-green leaves. Z4–8 H8–2.

A. simplicifolia 'Gnom'. See *A*. 'Gnom'.

A. 'Sprite', illus. p.232. Clump-forming, dwarf, leafy perennial. **H** 20in (50cm), **S** to 3ft (1m). Has feathery, tapering panicles of tiny, star-shaped, shell-pink flowers in summer, borne above broad leaves divided into narrowly oval, toothed leaflets. Z4–8 H8–1.

A. 'Straussenfeder', syn. *A*. 'Ostrich Plume', illus. p.232. Leafy perennial. **H** and **S** to 3ft (1m). Has divided leaves. Arching, feathery, tapering plumes of tiny, coral-pink flowers are produced in summer; dry, brown flowers remain on plant well into winter. Z3–8 H8–2.

A. 'Venus', illus. p.234.

A. 'Willie Buchanan' (*simplicifolia* hybrid). Clump-forming perennial. **H** 8–12in (20–30cm), **S** 8in (20cm). Produces neat clumps of divided, red- or bronze-tinted, green leaves. Loose, conical sprays of tiny, star-shaped, pale pink flowers, with white petals, are borne in mid- and late summer. Z4–8 H8–1.

ASTILBOIDES
SAXIFRAGACEAE

Genus of one species of hardy perennial, grown for its foliage, which turns reddish in fall. Needs partial shade and moist but well-drained soil. Propagate by division or seed in fall.

A. tabularis, syn. *Rodgersia tabularis*, illus. p.435.

ASTRANTIA
Masterwort
UMBELLIFERAE/APIACEAE

Genus of perennials, widely used in flower arrangements. Requires sun or semi-shade and well-drained soil. Propagate by division in spring or by seed when fresh, in late summer.

A. major (Masterwort). Clump-forming perennial. **H** 24in (60cm), **S** 18in (45cm). Produces greenish-white, sometimes pink-tinged flower heads throughout summer–fall above a dense mass of divided, mid-green leaves. Z4–7 H7–1. **subsp. carinthiaca.** See *A. major* subsp. *involucrata* **'Hadspen Blood'** has red bracts and flowers. **subsp. involucrata**, syn. *A. major* subsp. *carinthiaca* has pink-tinged flowerheads with long bracts through summer. **'Roma'**, illus. p.278. **'Ruby Wedding'**, illus. p.238.

A. maxima, illus. p.278.

ASTROPHYTUM
CACTACEAE

Genus of slow-growing, perennial cacti, grown for their freely produced, flattish, yellow flowers, some with red centers. Frost tender, min. 41°F (5°C). Prefers sun and very well-drained, lime-rich soil. Allow to dry completely in winter. Is prone to rot if wet. Propagate by seed sown in spring or summer.

A. asterias, syn. *Echinocactus asterias* (Sea urchin, Silver dollar cactus). Slow-growing, slightly domed, perennial cactus. **H** 3–4in (8–10cm), **S** 4in (10cm). Spineless stem has about 8 low ribs bearing small, tufted areoles. Produces bright yellow flowers, to 2¹⁄₂in (6cm) across, in summer. Z13–15 H11–10.

A. myriostigma, syn. *Echinocactus myriostigma*, illus. p.494.

A. ornatum, syn. *Echinocactus ornatum*, illus. p.495.

Asystasia bella. See *Mackaya bella*.

ATHEROSPERMA
ATHEROSPERMATACEAE/MONIMIACEAE

Genus of evergreen trees, grown for their foliage and flowers in summer. Needs full light or partial shade and well-drained soil. Water container specimens moderately, less in winter. Pruning is tolerated if necessary. Propagate by seed in spring or by semiripe cuttings in summer.

A. moschatum (Australian sassafras, Tasmanian sassafras). Evergreen, spreading tree, conical when young. **H** 50–80ft (15–25m), **S** 15–30ft (5–10m). Has lance-shaped, nutmeg-scented, glossy leaves, slightly toothed and covered with white down beneath. Produces small, saucer-shaped, creamy-white flowers in summer. Z9–11 H11–9.

ATHROTAXIS
Tasmanian cedar
TAXODIACEAE/CUPRESSACEAE

Genus of conifers with awl-shaped leaves that clasp stems. See also CONIFERS.

A. selaginoides (King William pine). Irregularly conical conifer. **H** 50ft (15m) or more, **S** 15ft (5m). Has tiny, thick-textured, loosely overlapping, dark green leaves and insignificant, globular cones. Z8–9 H9–8.

ATHYRIUM
ATHYRIACEAE/WOODSIACEAE

Genus of deciduous or, occasionally, semievergreen ferns. Needs shade and rich, moist soil. Remove fading fronds regularly. Propagate by spores in late summer or by division in fall or winter.

A. filix-femina (Lady fern). Deciduous fern. **H** 2–4ft (60cm–1.2m), **S** 1–3ft (30cm–1m). Dainty, lance-shaped, much-divided, arching fronds are pale green. Has very variable frond dissection. Z4–9 H9–1.

A. 'Ghost', illus. p.290.

A. goeringianum. See *A. niponicum*.

A. niponicum, syn. *A. goeringianum*, *A. nipponicum* (Japanese painted fern). **var. pictum 'Burgundy Lace'** illus. p.290.

A. nipponicum. See *A. niponicum*.

A. otophorum. Semievergreen fern. **H** and **S** to 30in (75cm). Has arching, broadly ovate, divided, mid-green or purple-tinged fronds, 18–30in (45–75cm) long. Stalk and midrib are deep wine-purple. Z5–8 H8–2.

ATRIPLEX

CHENOPODIACEAE/AMARANTHACEAE

Genus of annuals, perennials and evergreen or semievergreen shrubs, grown for their foliage. Grows well by the coast. Needs full sun and well-drained soil. Propagate by softwood cuttings in summer or by seed in fall.

A. halimus (Tree purslane). Semievergreen, bushy shrub. **H** 6ft (2m), **S** 10ft (3m). Oval leaves are silvery-gray. Produces flowers very rarely. Z7–9 H9–7.

A. hortensis var. rubra (Red mountain spinach, Red orach). Fast-growing, erect annual. **H** 4ft (1.2m), **S** 1ft (30cm). Triangular, deep red leaves, to 6in (15cm) long, are edible. Bears insignificant flowers in summer. Z7–9 H9–7.

AUBRIETA

Aubretia

CRUCIFERAE/BRASSICACEAE

Genus of evergreen, trailing and mound-forming perennials. Is useful on dry banks, walls and in rock gardens. Thrives in a sunny position and in any well-drained soil. To maintain a compact shape, cut back hard after flowering. Propagate by greenwood cuttings in summer or by semiripe cuttings in late summer or fall.

A. 'Carnival'. See *A.* 'Hartswood Purple'.
A. 'Cobalt Violet'. Evergreen, mound-forming perennial. **H** 4in (10cm), **S** 8in (20cm). Has small, soft green leaves. Single, blue-violet flowers are borne in short, terminal spikes in spring. Z5–7 H7–5.
A. deltoidea 'Argenteovariegata', illus. p.354.
A. 'Doctor Mules'. Vigorous, evergreen, mound-forming perennial. **H** 2–3in (5–8cm), **S** 12in (30cm). Has rounded, toothed, soft green leaves and, in spring, large, single, rich purple flowers on short spikes. Z5–7 H7–5.
A. 'Greencourt Purple', illus. p.354.
A. 'Gurgedyke'. Evergreen, mound-forming perennial. **H** 4in (10cm), **S** 8in (20cm). Bears rounded, toothed, soft green leaves. Produces 4-petaled, deep purple flowers in spring. Z5–7 H7–5.
A. 'Hartswood Purple', syn. *A.* 'Carnival'. Vigorous, evergreen, mound-forming perennial. **H** 4in (10cm), **S** 12in (30cm). Has small, soft green leaves and many short spikes of large, single, violet-purple flowers borne in spring. Z5–7 H7–5.
A. 'J.S. Baker', illus. p.354.
A. 'Joy', illus. p.353.
A. 'Purple Charm', illus. p.355.

AUCUBA

CORNACEAE/GARRYACEAE

Genus of evergreen shrubs, grown for their foliage and fruits. To obtain fruits, grow both male and female plants. Makes good houseplants when kept in a cool, shaded position. Tolerates full sun through to dense shade. Grow in any but waterlogged soil. To restrict growth, cut old shoots back hard in spring. Propagate by semiripe cuttings taken in summer.

A. japonica (Japanese aucuba). Evergreen, dense, bushy shrub. **H** and

S 8ft (2.5m). Has sturdy, green shoots and glossy, dark green leaves. Small, purplish flowers in mid-spring are followed on female plants by rounded to egg-shaped, bright red berries. Z6–10 H11–6.
'Crotonifolia', H 6ft (2m), **S** 6ft (2m), has leaves heavily mottled yellow. **'Gold Dust'** has gold-speckled, dark green leaves.
'Picturata' the bright green leaves (male) each have a central, golden blotch. Some plants of 'Crotonifolia' and 'Picturata' are known to be female and have produced fruits.

AURINIA

BRASSICACEAE/CRUCIFERAE

Genus of evergreen perennials, grown for their gray-green foliage and showy flower sprays. Is suitable for rock gardens, walls and banks. Needs sun and well-drained soil. Propagate by softwood or greenwood cuttings in early summer or by seed in fall.

A. saxatilis, syn. *Alyssum saxatile*, illus. p.335. **'Citrina'** illus. p.335. **'Dudley Nevill'** is an evergreen, clump-forming perennial. **H** 9in (23cm), **S** 12in (30cm). Has oval, hairy, gray-green leaves and, in late spring and early summer, produces racemes of many small, 4-petaled, buff-yellow flowers. Z4–8 H8–1. **'Variegata'** illus. p.335.

AUSTROCEDRUS

CUPRESSACEAE

Genus of conifers with flattish sprays of scalelike leaves. See also CONIFERS.
A. chilensis, syn. *Libocedrus chilensis*, illus. p.100.

Austrocylindropuntia cylindrica. See *Opuntia cylindrica*.
Austrocylindropuntia verschaffeltii. See *Opuntia verschaffeltii*.
Avena candida. See *Helictotrichon sempervirens*.
Avena sempervirens. See *Helictotrichon sempervirens*.

AZARA

FLACOURTIACEAE/SALICACEAE

Genus of evergreen shrubs and trees, grown for their foliage and for their yellow flowers, which are composed of a mass of stamens. Where marginally hardy, plants are best grown against a south- or west-facing wall for added protection. Grows in sun or shade and in fertile, well-drained soil. Propagate by semiripe cuttings in summer.

A. lanceolata. Evergreen, bushy shrub or spreading tree. **H** and **S** 20ft (6m). Has narrowly oval, sharply toothed, bright green leaves. Has small, rounded clusters of pale yellow flowers in late spring or early summer. Z8–10 H11–10.
A. microphylla, illus. p.118. **'Variegata'** illus. p.119.
A. serrata, illus. p.195.

AZOLLA

AZOLLACEAE

Genus of deciduous, perennial, floating water ferns, grown for their foliage and also to control algal growth by

reducing light in water beneath. Grows in sun or shade. If not kept in check, may be invasive; reduce spread by removing portions with a net. Propagate by redistributing clusters of plantlets when they appear.
A. caroliniana. See *A. filiculoides*.
A. filiculoides, syn. *A. caroliniana* (Fairy moss, Water fern). Deciduous, perennial, floating water fern. **S** indefinite. Divided fronds vary from red to purple in full sun and from pale green to blue-green in shade. Z7–11 H11–1.

AZORELLA

UMBELLIFERAE/APIACEAE

Genus of evergreen, tufted or spreading perennials, grown for their flowers and neat, rosetted foliage. Is useful as an alpine house plant. Thrives in full light and well-drained soil. Propagate by division in spring.
A. nivalis. See *A. trifurcata*.
A. trifurcata, syn. *A. nivalis*, illus. p.376.

AZORINA

CAMPANULACEAE

Genus of one species of erect, evergreen shrub with bell-shaped flowers. Needs full light and fertile, moist but well-drained soil. Propagate by seed in spring or by softwood or semiripe cuttings in summer.
A. vidalii, syn. *Campanula vidalii*, illus. p.453.

Azureocereus. See *Browningia*.
Azureocereus hertlingianus. See *Browningia hertlingiana*.

B

BABIANA

Baboon flower

IRIDACEAE

Genus of spring- and early summer-flowering corms, grown for their brightly colored flowers, which are somewhat like freesias. Requires a position in sun and well-drained soil. Propagate in fall by seed or natural division of corms.
B. disticha. See *B. fragrans*.
B. fragrans, syn. *B. disticha, B. plicata*. Spring-flowering corm. **H** 4–8in (10–20cm), **S** 2–3in (5–8cm). Has a fan of lance-shaped, erect, basal leaves and short spikes of funnel-shaped, violet-blue flowers, 1½–2in (4–5cm) long, with yellow-patched petals. Z13–15 H12–10.
B. plicata. See *B. fragrans*.
B. rubrocyanea (Winecups), illus. p.418.
B. stricta. Spring-flowering corm. **H** 4–8in (10–20cm), **S** 2–3in (5–8cm). Produces a fan of narrowly lance-shaped, erect, basal leaves and short spikes of up to 10 funnel-shaped, purple, blue, cream or pale yellow flowers, 1–1½in (2.5–4cm) long and sometimes red-centered. Z13–15 H11–10.

BACCHARIS

COMPOSITAE/ASTERACEAE

Genus of evergreen or deciduous, mainly fall-flowering shrubs, grown for their foliage and fruits. Is useful for exposed, coastal gardens and dry soil. Requires a position in full sun and well-drained soil. Propagate by softwood cuttings in summer.
B. halimifolia (Bush groundsel). Vigorous, deciduous, bushy shrub. **H** and **S** 12ft (4m). Has oval, sharply toothed, gray-green leaves. Large clusters of tiny, white flower heads in mid-fall are followed by fluffy, white heads of tiny fruits. Z3–7 H7–1.

Bahia lanata. See *Eriophyllum lanatum*.

BALDELLIA

ALISMATACEAE

Genus of deciduous or evergreen, perennial, bog plants and submerged water plants, grown for their foliage. Prefers a position in sun, but tolerates shade. Remove fading foliage and excess growth as required. Propagate by division in spring or summer.
B. ranunculoides, syn. *Alisma ranunculoides, Echinodorus ranunculoides*. Deciduous, perennial, bog plant or submerged water plant. **H** 9in (23cm), **S** 6in (15cm). Has lance-shaped, mid-green leaves and, in summer, umbels of small, 3-parted, pink or white flowers with basal, yellow marks. Z5–8 H8–5.

BALLOTA

LABIATEA/LAMIACEAE

Genus of perennials and evergreen or deciduous subshrubs, grown for their foliage and flowers. Requires very well-drained soil and full sun. Cut back in spring before growth starts. Propagate

B

by semiripe cuttings in summer.
B. acetabulosa, illus. p.165.
B. pseudodictamnus (False dittany), illus. p.347.

BAMBUSA

GRAMINEAE/POACEAE

See also GRASSES, BAMBOOS, RUSHES and SEDGES.
B. glaucescens. See *B. multiplex*.
B. multiplex, syn. *B. glaucescens* (Hedge bamboo). Evergreen, clump-forming bamboo. **H** to 50ft (15m), **S** indefinite. Has narrow leaves, 4–6in (10–15cm) long. Is useful for a hedge or windbreak. Z8–11 H11–1.

BANKSIA

PROTEACEAE

Genus of evergreen shrubs and trees, grown for their flowers and foliage. Requires full light and sharply drained, sandy soil that contains little phosphate or nitrate. Water container plants moderately when in full growth, sparingly at other times. Freely ventilate plants grown under glass. Propagate by seed in spring.
B. baxteri. Evergreen, spreading, open shrub. **H** and **S** 6–10ft (2–3m). Leathery, mid-green leaves are strap-shaped, cut from the midrib into triangular, sharply pointed lobes. Produces dense, spherical heads of small, tubular, yellow flowers in summer. Z10–11 H11–10.
B. coccinea, illus. p.456.
B. ericifolia (Heath banksia). Evergreen, irregularly rounded, wiry, freely branching shrub. **H** and **S** to 10ft (3m). Has small, needlelike leaves and dense, upright, bottlebrush-like spikes, 4–6in (10–15cm) long, of small, tubular, bronze-red or yellow flowers in late winter and spring. Z10–11 H11–10.
B. serrata. Evergreen, bushy, upright shrub or tree. **H** 10–30ft (3–10m), **S** 5–10ft (1.5–3m). Oblong to lance-shaped, saw-toothed, leathery leaves are mid- to deep green. Small, tubular, reddish-budded, cream flowers are borne in dense, upright, bottlebrush-like spikes, 4–6in (10–15cm) long, from spring to late summer. Z10–11 H11–10.

BAPTISIA

False indigo

LEGUMINOSAE/PAPILIONACEAE

Genus of summer-flowering perennials, grown for their flowers. Requires full sun and deep, well-drained, preferably neutral to acidic soil. Is best not disturbed once planted. Propagate by division in early spring or by seed in fall.
B. australis, illus. p.240.

Barbacenia elegans. See *Vellozia elegans*.

BARBAREA

CRUCIFERAE/BRASSICACEAE

Genus of summer-flowering perennials, biennials and annuals. Most species are weeds or winter salad plants, but the variegated form of *B. vulgaris* is grown for decorative purposes. Grows in a sunny or shady position and in any well-drained

but not very dry soil. Propagate by seed or division in spring. May be invasive in parts of North America.
B. vulgaris (Winter Cress, Yellow rocket). Z4–9 H9–1. **'Variegata'** is a rosette-forming perennial. **H** 10–18in (25–45cm), **S** 9in (23cm). Has long, toothed, glossy leaves, blotched with cream. Produces heads of small, silvery-yellow flowers in early summer. Z4–9 H9–1.

BARLERIA

ACANTHACEAE

Genus of evergreen shrubs and perennials, grown for their flowers. Needs full light or partial shade and fertile soil. Water container plants well when in full growth, moderately at other times. In the growing season, prune tips of young plants to encourage branching. For a more compact habit, shorten long stems after flowering. May be propagated by seed in spring or by greenwood or semiripe cuttings in summer.
B. cristata (Philippine violet). Evergreen, semierect shrub. **H** and **S** 2–4ft (60cm–1.2m). Has elliptic, coarsely haired leaves. Tubular, light violet flowers, sometimes pale pink or white, are produced from upper leaf axils in summer. Z10–11 H11–10.
B. obtusa. Evergreen, erect, spreading shrub. **H** and **S** to 3ft (1m). Leaves are elliptic. Tubular, mauve flowers are produced from upper leaf axils in winter–spring. Z9–12 H12–9.

Barosma pulchella. See *Agathosma pulchella*.

BARTLETTINA

COMPOSITAE/ASTERACEAE

Genus of perennials, subshrubs and shrubs, many of which are evergreen, grown mainly for their flowers, some also for their architectural foliage. Requires full light or partial shade. Will grow in any conditions, although most species prefer moist but well-drained soil. Water container plants freely when in full growth, moderately at other times. Prune shrubs lightly after flowering or in spring. Propagate by seed in spring; shrubs and subshrubs may also be propagated by softwood or greenwood cuttings in summer, perennials by division in early spring or fall. Red spider mite and whitefly may be troublesome.
B. sordida, syn. *Eupatorium ianthinum, Eupatorium sordidum*. Evergreen, rounded, robust stemmed shrub. **H** and **S** 3–6ft (1–2m). Oval, serrated, deep green leaves are red haired. Produces fragrant, pomponlike, violet-purple flower heads in flattened clusters, 4in (10cm) wide, mainly in winter. Z13–15 H12–1.

Bartonia aurea. See *Mentzelia lindleyi*.

BASSIA

SYN. KOCHIA

CHENOPODIACEAE

Genus of annuals and perennials, grown for their habit, the feathery effect of their leaves and their fall tints. Does best in sun and in fertile, well-drained soil. May require support in very windy areas. Propagate by seed sown under glass in early to mid-spring, or outdoors in late spring.
B. scoparia f. trichophylla, illus. p.316.

BAUERA

CUNONIACEAE

Genus of evergreen shrubs, grown mainly for their flowers. Needs full sun and rich, well-drained, neutral to acidic soil. Water container plants moderately, less when not in full growth. Remove straggly stems after flowering. Propagate by seed in spring or by semiripe cuttings in late summer.
B. rubioides. Evergreen, bushy, wiry-stemmed shrub, usually of spreading habit. **H** and **S** 1–2ft (30–60cm). Leaves each have 3 oval to lance-shaped, glossy leaflets. Bowl-shaped, pink or white flowers are borne in early spring and summer. Z13–15 H11–1.

BAUHINIA

Orchid tree

LEGUMINOSAE/CAESALPINIACEAE

Genus of evergreen, semievergreen or deciduous trees, shrubs and scandent climbers, grown for their flowers. Requires full light and fertile, well-drained soil. Water container specimens freely when in full growth, less in winter. Thin out congested growth after flowering. Propagate by seed in spring.
B. galpinii, syn. *B. punctata* (Red bauhinia). Semievergreen or evergreen, spreading shrub, occasionally semi-climbing. **H** 10ft (3m), **S** 8ft (2m). Has 2-lobed leaves and, in summer, fragrant, bright brick-red flowers. Z13–15 H11–10.
B. punctata. See *B. galpinii*.
B. variegata, illus. p.450. **'Candida'** is a deciduous tree, rounded when young, spreading with age. **H** 8ft (2m), **S** 10ft (3m). Has broadly oval, deeply notched leaves and fragrant, pure white flowers, 4in (10cm) across, in winter–spring or sometimes later. Z13–15 H11–10.

x Beallara Eurostar gx. See x *Aliceara* Eurostar gx.

BEAUCARNEA

AGAVACEAE/ASPARAGACEAE

Genus of evergreen shrubs and trees, grown mainly for their intriguing overall appearance. Needs full light and sharply drained, fertile soil; drought conditions are tolerated. Water container specimens moderately; allow potting mix almost to dry out between waterings. Propagate by seed or suckers in spring or by stem-tip cuttings in summer.
B. recurvata, syn. *Nolina recurvata, Nolina tuberculata*, illus. p.451.

BEAUMONTIA

APOCYNACEAE

Genus of evergreen, woody-stemmed, twining climbers, grown for their large, fragrant flowers and handsome leaves. Requires fertile, well-drained soil and full light. Water freely in growing season, sparingly at other times. Provide support. Thin out previous season's growth after flowering. Propagate by semiripe cuttings in late summer.
B. grandiflora, illus. p.459.

BEGONIA

BEGONIACEAE

Genus of evergreen or deciduous shrubs and small, treelike plants, perennials and annuals, grown for their colorful flowers and/or ornamental leaves. Prefers slightly acidic soil. Is susceptible to powdery mildew and botrytis from late spring to early fall. Commonly cultivated begonias are divided into the following groupings, each with varying cultivation requirements. See also feature panel p.317.

Cane-stemmed begonias
Evergreen, woody perennials, many known as "Angelwings," with usually erect, cane-like stems bearing regularly spaced, swollen nodes and flowers in large, pendulous panicles. Encourage branching by pinching out growing tips. New growth develops from base of plant. Grow under glass in good light but not direct sun (poor light reduces quantity of flowers) and in free-draining, soil-based potting mix. Stake tall plants. Propagate in spring by seed or tip cuttings.

Rex-cultorum begonias
Mostly evergreen, rhizomatous perennials of variable habit derived from crosses of *B. rex* and related species. They are grown for their brilliantly colored, oval to lance-shaped leaves, 3–12in (8–30cm) long, that are sometimes spirally twisted. Prefer 40–75% relative humidity. Grow under glass in cool climates, in partial shade and well-drained soil; water only sparingly. Do not allow water to remain on the leaves, otherwise they become susceptible to botrytis. Propagate in spring by seed, leaf cuttings or division of rhizomes.

Rhizomatous begonias
Variable, mostly evergreen, rhizomatous perennials, grown for their foliage and small, single flowers. Smooth, crested or puckered, green or brown leaves, 3–12in (8–30cm) long, often marked silver, are sometimes spirally twisted. Creeping cultivars are more freely branched than erect ones and are useful for hanging baskets. Prefer 40–75% relative humidity. Grow under glass in cool climates, in partial shade and well-drained soil; water only sparingly. Do not allow water to remain on the leaves, otherwise they become susceptible to botrytis. Propagate in spring by seed, leaf cuttings or division of rhizomes.

Semperflorens begonias
Evergreen, bushy perennials, derived from *B. cucullata* var. *hookeri*, *B. schmidtiana* and other species, often grown as half-hardy bedding annuals. Stems are soft, succulent and branch freely, bearing generally rounded, green, bronze or variegated leaves, 2in (5cm) long. Flowers are single or double. Pinch out growing tips to produce bushy plants. Needs sun or partial shade and well-drained soil. Propagate in spring by seed or stem cuttings.

Shrublike begonias
Evergreen, multistemmed, bushy perennials, usually freely branched with flexible, erect or pendent stems, often hairy. Leaves may be hairy or glabrous and up to 6in (15cm) across, 4–12in (10–30cm) long. Single flowers are pink, cream or white. Prefer 55% relative humidity. Grow under

B

glass in good light and moist but well-drained soil. Propagate in spring by seed or stem cuttings.

Tuberous begonias (including the Tuberhybrida, Multiflora and Pendula begonias)
Mostly upright, bushy, tuberous, winter-dormant perennials grown for their foliage and flowers. Tuberhybrida begonias, **H** and **S** 30in (75cm), vary from pendent to erect, with sparsely branched, succulent stems and oval, pointed, glossy, bright to dark green leaves, 8in (20cm) long. Most are summer flowering and mainly double-flowered. Multiflora cultivars, **H** and **S** 12in (30cm), are more bushy and have 3in (8cm) long leaves and single, semidouble or double flowers, each $1^1/_2$–2in (4–5cm) across, in summer; tolerates full sun. Pendula cultivars, **H** to 3ft (1m), have long, thin, trailing stems; leaves are $2^1/_2$–3in (6–8cm) long. Masses of single or double flowers are borne in summer. Outdoors, grow in dappled shade and moist conditions; under glass, plant in cool shade with 65–70% relative humidity. Tubers are dormant in winter. Start into growth in spring for mid-summer to early fall flowering. Remove all flower buds until stems show at least 3 pairs of leaves; with large-flowered types allow only central male bud to flower, so remove flanking buds. Plants may require staking. Propagate in spring by seed, stem or basal cuttings or division of tubers.

Winter-flowering begonias
Evergreen, low-growing, very compact perennials, with succulent, thin stems, that are often included in the tuberous group. Two main groups are recognized: the single-flowered, usually pink or white, Lorraine, Cheimantha or Christmas begonias; and the single, semidouble or double, Elatior and Rieger begonias, which occur in a wide range of colors. Leaves are green or bronze, 2in (5cm) long. Flowers are borne mainly from late fall to mid-spring. Prefer 40% relative humidity. Prefers indirect sun and moist soil. Cut back old stems to 4in (10cm) after flowering. Propagate in spring by seed or stem cuttings.

B. albopicta**,** illus. p.317. Fast-growing, evergreen, cane-stemmed begonia. **H** to 3ft (1m), **S** 1ft (30cm). Freely branched, green stems turn brown-green when mature. Narrowly oval to lance-shaped, wavy-edged, green leaves are silver-spotted. Has clusters of single, green-white flowers in summer–fall. H11–1.
B. angularis**,** syn. *B. compta, B. stipulacea, B. zebrina*. Evergreen, cane-stemmed begonia. **H** 2–4ft (60cm–1.2m), **S** 1ft (30cm). Bears well-branched, angular stems and oval, wavy-edged, gray-green leaves, 8in (20cm) long, with silver-gray veins, pale green beneath. Single, white flowers are produced in winter–spring. Z13–15 H11–1.
***B.* 'Apricot Cascade'.** Pendent Tuberhybrida begonia. **H** and **S** 2ft (60cm). Has emerald-green leaves and, from early summer to mid-fall, double, orange-apricot flowers. Other cascades are **'Bridal Cascade'** (pink-edged, white petals), **'Crimson Cascade', 'Gold Cascade', 'Orange Cascade'.** Z13–15 H11–1.
***B.* 'Beatrice Haddrell'.** Evergreen, creeping, rhizomatous begonia. **H** 8–12in (20–30cm), **S** 10–12in (25–30cm). Oval leaves are deeply cleft, 3–6in (8–15cm) long and dark green with paler veins. Produces single, pink flowers, above foliage, in winter and early spring. Z13–15 H11–1.
***B.* 'Bethlehem Star'.** Evergreen, creeping, rhizomatous begonia. **H** 8–12in (20–30cm), **S** 10–12in (25–30cm). Oval, slightly indented, almost black leaves, less than 3in (8cm) long, each have a central, creamy-green star. Bears masses of single, pale pink flowers, with darker pink spots, from late winter to early spring. Z13–15 H11–1.
***B.* 'Billie Langdon'.** Upright Tuberhybrida begonia. **H** 2ft (60cm), **S** 18in (45cm). In summer has masses of heavily veined, double, white flowers, 7in (18cm) across, each with a perfect rose-bud center. Z13–15 H11–1.
***B.* 'Bokit'.** Evergreen, erect, rhizomatous begonia. **H** 8–12in (20–30cm), **S** 10–14in (25–35cm). Has oval, spirally twisted, yellow-green leaves with brown tiger stripes. Bears masses of single, white flowers, flecked with pink, in winter. Z13–15 H11–1.
***B. boliviensis* 'Bonfire',** illus. p.317. Semi-trailing begonia.**H** 30in (75cm), **S** 36in (100cm). Succulent stems bear lance-shaped, slightly hairy leaves, 5in (12cm) long, with narrow, toothed, red edges. Produces abundant, pendulous, single, orange-red flowers from late spring to fall. H11–1.
B. bowerae (Eyelash begonia), illus. p.317. Evergreen, creeping, rhizomatous begonia. **H** 10–12in (25–30cm), **S** 8–10in (20–25cm). Has oval, bright green leaves, 1in (2.5cm) long, with chocolate marks and bristles around edges. Bears single, pink-tinted, white flowers freely in winter. H11–1.
***B.* 'Can-can'.** See *B.* 'Herzog von Sagan'.
***B.* 'City of Ballarat'.** Vigorous, upright Tuberhybrida begonia. **H** 2ft (60cm), **S** 18in (45cm). Leaves are rich dark green. Produces double, glowing orange flowers, 7in (18cm) across, with broad petals and formal centers, in summer. Z13–15 H11–1.
B. coccinea (Angelwing begonia). Evergreen, cane-stemmed begonia. **H** 4ft (1.2m), **S** 1ft (30cm). Produces narrowly oval, glossy, green leaves, buff-colored beneath, and, in spring, many single, pink or coral-red flowers. Z13–15 H11–1.
***B.* 'Cocktail Series'.** Semperflorens begonia. **H** and **S** 8–12in (20–30cm). Produces rounded, wavy, green-bronze leaves and pink, red or white flowers from summer until fall frosts. Z13–15 H11–1.
B. compta**.** See *B. angularis.*
***B.* 'Corallina de Lucerna'.** See *B.* 'Lucerna'.
***B.* 'Curly Merry Christmas'.** Rex-cultorum begonia. **H** 10in (25cm), **S** 12in (30cm). Is a sport of *B.* 'Merry Christmas' with spirally twisted leaves. Z13–15 H11–1.
B. dichroa**.** Evergreen, cane-stemmed begonia. **H** 14in (35cm), **S** 10in (25cm). Oval, mid-green leaves are 5in (12cm) long; occasionally new leaves bear silver spots. Produces small, single, orange flowers, each with a white ovary, in summer. Z13–15 H11–1.
***B.* Dragon Wing Red ('Bepared') (Dragon Wing Series),** illus. p.317. Vigorous, Semperflorens begonia. **H** and **S** 18in (45cm). Semi-trailing, succulent stems bear oval, slightly waxy, mid-green leaves, 2–3in (5–7.5cm). Produces clusters of single, scarlet flowers from late summer to fall. H11–1.
B. dregei (Mapleleaf begonia), illus. p.317. Semi-tuberous begonia. **H** 30in (75cm), **S** 14in (35cm). Has small, maple-like, lobed, purple-veined, bronze leaves, red beneath and at times silver-speckled when young. Profuse, pendent, single, white flowers are borne in summer. Needs winter rest. H11–1.
***B.* 'Duartei'.** Rex-cultorum begonia. **H** and **S** 18–24in (45–60cm). Has spirally twisted, red-haired, very dark green leaves, more than 6in (15cm) long, with silver-gray streaks and almost black edges. Is difficult to grow to maturity. Z13–15 H11–1.
B.* x *erythrophylla**.** See *B.* 'Erythrophylla'.
***B.* 'Erythrophylla',** syn. *B.* x *erythrophylla, B.* 'Feastii'. Evergreen, creeping, rhizomatous begonia. **H** 8in (20cm), **S** 9–12in (23–30cm). Thick, mid-green leaves, 3–6in (8–15cm) long, are almost rounded, with leaf stalks attached to center of red undersides; slightly wavy margins have white hairs. Produces single, light pink flowers well above foliage, in early spring. Z13–15 H11–1.
***B.* 'Feastii'.** See *B.* 'Erythrophylla'.
***B.* 'Flamboyant'.** Upright Tuberhybrida begonia. **H** 7in (17cm), **S** 6in (15cm). Leaves are slender and bright green. Has single, scarlet flowers in profusion in summer. Z13–15 H11–1.
B. foliosa**.** Evergreen, shrublike begonia. **H** 12–20in (30–50cm), **S** 12–14in (30–35cm). Bears erect, then arching stems and oval, toothed, dark green leaves, $^1/_2$in (1cm) long. Has very small, single, white flowers in spring and fall. Is susceptible to whitefly. Z13–15 H11–1. **var. *miniata*,** syn. *B. fuchsiioides* (Fuchsia begonia), **H** to 4ft (1.2m), **S** 1ft (30cm), has leaves $1^1/_2$in (4cm) long and pendent, single, bright red flowers borne in winter. Z13–15 H11–1.
B. fuchsiioides**.** See *B. foliosa* var. *miniata.*
***B.* 'Gloire de Lorraine'** (Christmas begonia, Lorraine begonia). Evergreen, winter-flowering, Cheimantha begonia. **H** 12in (30cm), **S** 12–14in (30–35cm). Is well-branched with rounded, bright green leaves and single, white to pale pink flowers. Male flowers are sterile, female ones highly infertile. Z13–15 H11–1.
***B. gracilis* var. *martiana*,** syn. *B. martiana*. Tuberous begonia. **H** 24–30in (60–75cm), **S** 16in (40cm). Has small, oval to lance-shaped, lobed, pale green or brown-green leaves with tapering tips and large, fragrant, single, pink flowers, 1in (2.5cm) across, in summer. Z13–15 H11–1.
***B. grandis* subsp. *evansiana*,** illus. p.278.
B. haageana**.** See *B. scharffii.*
***B.* 'Helen Lewis'.** Rex-cultorum begonia. **H** and **S** 18–24in (45–60cm). Has an erect rhizome and silky, deep royal purple leaves, 6–8in (15–20cm) long, with silver bands. Slightly hairy, single, cream flowers are produced in early summer. Z13–15 H11–1.
***B.* 'Herzog von Sagan',** syn. *B.* 'Can-can', illus. p.322.
***B.* 'Ikon White Blush',** illus. p.317. Semperflorens begonia. **H** and **S** to 6in (15cm). Has broadly oval, pointed, slightly bronzed, mid-green leaves. Produces clusters of single, pink and white flowers in summer–fall. H11–1.
***B.* Illumination Series.** Double and semidouble Pendula begonia. **H** 24in (60cm), **S** 12in (30cm). Has oval, toothed, brightly veined, mid- to dark green leaves. Bears prolific, double flowers, 3in (7.5cm) across, in red, pink, orange and yellow shades and white including bicolors. Z13–15 H11–1. **'Illumination Salmon Pink'** (illus. p.317) is pale salmon-pink. H11–1.
B. imperialis**.** Rhizomatous begonia. **H** 5in (13cm), **S** 9in (23cm). Ovate, toothed, light green leaves, 4in (10cm) long, have puckered edges and silver-green splashes on the main veins. Has sprays of sparse white flowers, to $^1/_2$in (1.5cm) wide, in winter. Z13–15 H11–1.
***B.* 'Ingramii',** illus. p.317. Evergreen, shrublike begonia. **H** 28in (70cm), **S** 18in (45cm). Produces elliptic, toothed, bright green leaves, 3in (8cm) long, and, intermittently from spring to fall, masses of single, pink flowers on spreading branches. H11–1.
***B.* 'Iron Cross'.** See *B. masoniana.*
***B.* 'Krefeld'.** Evergreen, winter-flowering, Rieger begonia. **H** 10in (25cm), **S** 12in (30cm). Is semi-tuberous with succulent stems, oval, mid-green leaves and masses of single, vivid orange or bright crimson flowers. Is very susceptible to botrytis and mildew at base of stems, so water by pot immersion. Z13–15 H11–1.
***B.* 'Lucerna',** syn. *B.* 'Corallina de Lucerna'. Vigorous, evergreen, cane-stemmed begonia. **H** 6–7ft (2–2.2m), **S** $1^1/_2$–2ft (45–60cm). Has oval, silver-spotted, bronze-green leaves, 10–14in (25–35cm) long, with tapered tips and, year-round, large panicles of single, deep pink flowers; male flowers remain almost closed. Z13–15 H11–1.
***B.* 'Mac's Gold'.** Evergreen, creeping, rhizomatous begonia. **H** and **S** 8–10in (20–25cm). Star-shaped, lobed, yellow leaves, 3–6in (8–15cm) long, have chocolate-brown marks. Has single, pink flowers intermittently in spring–summer but in moderate quantity. Z13–15 H11–1.
***B.* 'Madame Richard Galle'.** Upright Tuberhybrida begonia. **H** 10in (25cm), **S** 8in (20cm). Has masses of small, double, soft apricot flowers in summer. Z13–15 H11–1.
B. manicata**.** Evergreen, erect, rhizomatous begonia. **H** 24in (60cm), **S** 12–16in (30–40cm). Bears large, oval, brown-mottled, green leaves and, below each leaf base, a collar of stiff, red hairs around leaf stalk. Produces single, pale pink flowers in very early spring. Propagate by plantlets during growing season. Z13–15 H11–1. **'Crispa',** syn. *B. manicata* 'Cristata' has deeper pink flowers and light green leaves with crested margins. **'Cristata'.** See *B. manicata* 'Crispa'.
B. martiana**.** See *B. gracilis* var. *martiana.*
B. masoniana**,** syn. *B.* 'Iron Cross' (Iron cross begonia), illus. p.317. Evergreen, creeping, rhizomatous begonia. **H** 18–24in (45–60cm), **S** 12–18in (30–45cm). Bears oval, toothed, rough, bright green leaves, 6in (15cm) long, with tapering tips and cross-shaped, black or dark brown centers. Has single, pink-flushed, white flowers in summer. H11–1.

B

B. mazae. Evergreen, trailing, rhizomatous begonia. **H** to 9in (23cm), **S** indefinite. Bears rounded, red-veined, bronze-green leaves and, in early spring, fragrant, single, red-spotted, pink flowers. Is good for a hanging basket. Z13–15 H11–1.

B. 'Merry Christmas', syn. B. 'Ruhrtal', illus. p.317. Rex-cultorum begonia. **H** and **S** 10–12in (25–30cm). Has satiny, red leaves, 6–8in (15–20cm) long, each with an outer, broad band of emerald-green and a deep velvet-red center, sometimes edged with gray. H11–1.

B. metallica (Metal-leaf begonia). Evergreen, shrublike begonia. **H** 20in–4ft (50cm–1.2m), **S** 18in (45cm). Bears white-haired stems and oval, toothed, silver-haired, bronze-green leaves, 7in (18cm) long, with dark green veins, red beneath. Has single, pink flowers, with red bristles, in summer–fall. Z13–15 H11–1.

B. 'Oliver Twist'. Evergreen, creeping, rhizomatous begonia. **H** 18–24in (45–60cm), **S** 10–18in (25–45cm). Oval, pale to mid-green leaves, to 12in (30cm) long, have heavily crested edges. Bears single, pink flowers in early spring. Z13–15 H11–1.

B. olsoniae. Evergreen, compact, shrub-like begonia. **H** 9–12in (23–30cm), **S** 12in (30cm). Rounded, satiny, bronze-green leaves have cream veins. Bears single, very pale pink flowers, year-round, on arching stems, 12in (30cm) long. Z13–15 H11–1.

B. 'Orange Rubra', illus. p.317. Slow-growing, evergreen, cane-stemmed begonia. **H** 20in (50cm), **S** 18in (45cm). Oval leaves are light green. Produces abundant clusters of single, orange flowers year-round. H11–1.

B. 'Organdy'. Weather-resistant Semperflorens begonia. **H** and **S** 6in (15cm). Has rounded, waxy, green-bronze leaves and pink, red or white flowers throughout summer until fall frosts. Z13–15 H11–1.

B. 'Orpha C. Fox', illus. p.317. Evergreen, cane-stemmed begonia. **H** 3ft (1m), **S** 1ft (30cm). Oval, silver-spotted, olive-green leaves, 6in (15cm) long, are maroon beneath. Produces large clusters of single, bright pink flowers year-round. H11–1.

B. paulensis. Evergreen, creeping, rhizomatous begonia. **H** and **S** 10–12in (25–30cm). Erect stems produce rounded, mid-green leaves, 6in (15cm) long, with "seersucker" surfaces crisscrossed with a spider web of veins. Produces single, cream-white flowers, with wine-colored hairs, in late spring. Z13–15 H11–1.

B. 'Président Carnot'. Vigorous, evergreen, cane-stemmed begonia. **H** to 7ft (2.2m), **S** 1^1/$_2$ft (45cm). Erect stems bear 11in (28cm) long, "angelwing," green leaves, with lighter spots. Produces large panicles of single, pink flowers, 1^1/$_2$in (4cm) across, year-round. Z13–15 H11–1.

B. 'Princess of Hanover'. Rex-cultorum begonia. **H** and **S** 10–12in (25–30cm). Has spirally twisted, deep green leaves, 8in (20cm) long, with bands of silver edged with ruby-red; entire leaf surfaces are covered with fine, pink hairs. Z13–15 H11–1.

B. prismatocarpa, illus. p.317. Evergreen, creeping, rhizomatous begonia. **H** 6–8in (15–20cm), **S** 8–10in (20–25cm). Leaves are oval, lobed, light green and less than 3in (8cm) long. Produces single, bright yellow flowers year-round. Needs 60–65% relative humidity. H11–1.

B. pustulata. Evergreen, creeping, rhizomatous begonia. **H** 6–8in (15–20cm), **S** 8–10in (20–25cm). Bears oval, fine-haired, dark green leaves, with small blisters or pustules, and single, rose-pink flowers in summer. Prefers 70–75% relative humidity. Z13-15 H11–1. **'Argentea',** syn. B. 'Silver' has silver-splashed leaves and creamy-white flowers.

B. 'Red Ascot'. Semperflorens begonia. **H** and **S** 6in (15cm). Has rounded, emerald-green leaves and masses of crimson-red flowers in summer. Z13–15 H11–1.

B. rex. Rhizomatous begonia, the parent of the Rex-cultorum begonias. **H** 10in (25cm), **S** 12in (30cm). Has heart-shaped, deep green leaves, 8–10in (20–25cm) long, with a metallic sheen, zoned silvery-white above. Produces pink flowers in winter. Z13–15 H11–1.

B. 'Roy Hartley'. Upright Tuberhybrida begonia. **H** 2ft (60cm), **S** 18in (45cm). In summer bears double, salmon-colored flowers, with soft pink tinge. Color depth depends on light intensity. Has few side shoots. Z12–15 H11–1.

B. 'Ruhrtal'. See B. 'Merry Christmas'.

B. scharffii, syn. B. haageana, illus. p.317. Evergreen, shrublike begonia. **H** 2–4ft (60cm–1.2m), **S** 2ft (60cm). Stems are often covered with white hairs. Has oval, fine-haired, dark metallic-green leaves, 11in (28cm) long, with tapered tips and reddish-green undersides. Produces single, pinkish-white flowers, each with a pink beard, from fall to summer. H11–1.

B. 'Scherzo'. Evergreen, creeping, rhizomatous begonia. **H** 10–12in (25–30cm), **S** 12–14in (30–35cm). Oval leaves are small, highly serrated and yellow with black marks. Bears single, white flowers in early spring. Z13–15 H11–1.

B. serratipetala, illus. p.317. Evergreen, trailing, shrublike begonia. **H** and **S** 18in (45cm). Obliquely oval leaves are highly serrated and bronze-green, with raised, deep pink spots. Produces mostly female, single, deep pink flowers intermittently throughout the year. Prefers 60% relative humidity, but with fairly dry roots. H11–1.

B. 'Silver'. See B. pustulata 'Argentea'.

B. 'Silver Helen Teupel'. Rex-cultorum begonia. **H** and **S** 12–14in (30–35cm). Has long, deeply cut, silver leaves, each with a glowing pink center, giving a feathered effect. Z13–15 H11–1.

B. stipulacea. See B. angularis.

B. 'Sugar Candy'. Tuberhybrida begonia. **H** 24in (60cm), **S** 18in (45cm). Leaves are mid-green. Produces double, clear pink flowers in summer. Z13–15 H11–1.

B. sutherlandii, illus. p.317. Trailing, tuberous begonia. **H** 3ft (1m), **S** indefinite. Slender stems bear small, lance-shaped, lobed, bright green leaves, with red veins, and, in summer, loose clusters of single, orange flowers in profusion. In late fall, leaves and stems collapse prior to winter dormancy. Makes an excellent hanging-basket plant. Is particularly susceptible to mildew. H11–1.

B. taliensis, illus. p.278.

B. 'Thurstonii'. Evergreen, shrublike begonia. **H** to 4ft (1.2m), **S** 1^1/$_2$ft (45cm). Has rounded to oval, smooth, glossy, bronze-green leaves, with dark red veins, and, in summer, bears single, pink flowers. Z13–15 H11–1.

B. 'Tiger Paws', illus. p.317. Evergreen, creeping, rhizomatous begonia. **H** 6in (15cm), **S** 10–12in (25–30cm). Small, rounded, bright green leaves, with yellow and brown splashes, have bristly, white hairs on margins. Many clusters of small, white flowers are borne well above foliage in spring. H11–1.

B. x tuberhybrida Mocha Series. Bushy, dark-leaved, Tuberhybrida begonia. **H** and **S** 12in (30cm). Has green-veined, chocolate-brown leaves, and, held tightly above the foliage, double flowers, 3–4in (7.5–10cm) across, in about 6 varied, individual colors. Z13–15 H11–1. **'Mocha Scarlet'** (illus. p.317) is deep red with very dark leaves. H11–1.

B. x tuberhybrida Non Stop Series. Bushy Tuberhybrida begonia. **H** and **S** 12in (30cm). Has double flowers, 3–4in (7.5–10cm) across, in about 12 varied individual colors and mixtures held close to heart-shaped, mid-green leaves. Z13–15 H11–1. **'Non Stop White'** (illus. p.317) has creamy-centered, white flowers opening from pink buds. H11–1.

B. versicolor. Evergreen, creeping, rhizomatous begonia. **H** 6in (15cm), **S** 6–12in (15–30cm). Produces broadly oval or oblong, velvety leaves, 3in (8cm) long, in shades of mahogany, apple-green and maroon, and, in spring–summer, single, salmon-pink flowers. Provide 65–70% relative humidity. Z13–15 H11–1.

B. x weltoniensis. See B. 'Weltoniensis'.

B. 'Weltoniensis', syn. B. x weltoniensis (Mapleleaf begonia). Semi-tuberous begonia with a shrublike habit. **H** 12–20in (30–50cm), **S** 12in (30cm). Has small, oval, long-pointed, toothed, dark green leaves. Heads of 5–8 single, pink or white flowers are produced from leaf axils in summer. Z13–15 H11–1.

B. xanthina. Evergreen, bushy, creeping, rhizomatous begonia. **H** 10–12in (25–30cm), **S** 12–14in (30–35cm). Bears oval, dark green leaves, 6–9in (15–23cm) long, with yellow veins, purple and hairy beneath. Pendent, single, orange-yellow flowers are borne in summer. Provide 75% relative humidity. Z13–15 H11–1.

B. zebrina. See B. angularis.

BELAMCANDA

IRIDACEAE

Genus of summer-flowering bulbs, grown for their iris-like flowers. Requires sun and well-drained, rich soil. Propagate by seed in spring.

B. chinensis, syn. *Iris domestica* (Blackberry lily). Summer-flowering bulb. **H** 1^1/$_2$–3ft (45cm–1m), **S** 6–10in (15–25cm). Produces a fan of sword-shaped, semierect leaves. A loosely branched stem bears a succession of flattish, orange-red flowers, 1^1/$_2$–2in (4–5cm) across, with darker blotches. Seeds are shiny and black. Z5–9 H9–5.

BELLEVALIA

LILIACEAE/ASPARAGACEAE

Genus of spring-flowering bulbs, similar to *Muscari*, but with longer, more tubular flowers. Some species have ornamental value, but most are uninteresting horticulturally. Needs an open, sunny position and well-drained soil that dries out in summer. Propagate by seed, preferably in fall.

B. hyacinthoides, syn. *Strangweja spicata*, illus. p.419.

B. paradoxa. See B. pycnantha.

B. pycnantha, syn. B. paradoxa, Muscari pycnantha. Spring-flowering bulb. **H** to 16in (40cm), **S** 2–3in (5–8cm). Has strap-shaped, semierect, basal, grayish-green leaves. Tubular, deep dusky-blue flowers, ^{1}/$_4$in (0.5cm) long and with yellow tips, are produced in a dense, conical spike. Z7–9 H9–7.

B. romana, illus. p.399.

BELLIS

Daisy

COMPOSITAE/ASTERACEAE

Genus of perennials, some grown as biennials for spring bedding. Grow in sun or semi-shade and in fertile, very well-drained soil. Deadhead regularly. Propagate by seed in early summer or by division after flowering.

B. perennis (Common daisy). Stoloniferous, carpeting perennial. Cultivars are grown as biennials. **H** and **S** 6–8in (15–20cm). All have inversely lance-shaped to spoon-shaped, mid-green leaves and semidouble to fully double flower heads in spring. Large-flowered (flower heads to 3in (8cm) wide) and miniature-flowered (flower heads to 1in (2^1/$_2$cm) wide) cultivars are available. **Habanera Series** cultivars bear long-petaled, pink, white or red flower heads, to 2^1/$_2$in (6cm) across, in early summer. **Pomponette Series** cultivars bear double, pink, white or red flower heads, to 11_2in (4cm) across, with quilled petals. **Roggli Series** cultivars flower early and prolifically, with semidouble, red, rose-pink, salmon-pink or white flower heads, to 1^1/$_4$in (3cm) across. **Tasso Series** cultivars have double, pink, white or red flower heads, to 2^1/$_2$in (6cm) across, with quilled petals.

Beloperone guttata. See *Justicia brandegeeana*.

BERBERIDOPSIS

FLACOURTIACEAE/BERBERIDOPSIACEAE

Genus of one species of evergreen, woody-stemmed, twining climber. Dislikes strong winds and strong sun and is best grown in a north- or west-facing site. Needs moist but well-drained, preferably lime-free soil. Cut out dead growth in spring; train to required shape. Propagate by seed in spring or by stem cuttings or layering in late summer or fall.

B. corallina, illus. p.202.

BERBERIS

Barberry

BERBERIDACEAE

Genus of deciduous, semievergreen or evergreen, spiny shrubs, grown mainly for their rounded to cup-shaped flowers, with usually yellow sepals and petals, and for their fruits. The evergreens are also cultivated for their leaves, the deciduous shrubs for their colorful fall foliage. Requires sun or semi-shade and any but waterlogged soil. Propagate species by seed in fall, deciduous hybrids and cultivars

B

by softwood or semiripe cuttings in summer, evergreen hybrids and cultivars by semiripe cuttings in summer. *B. thunbergii* has escaped cultivation in northeastern North America. ① All parts may cause mild stomach upset if ingested; contact with the spines may irritate skin.

B. aggregata. Deciduous, bushy shrub. **H** and **S** 5ft (1.5m). Oblong to oval, mid-green leaves redden in fall. Dense clusters of pale yellow flowers, borne in late spring or early summer, are followed by egg-shaped, white-bloomed, red fruits. Z6–9 H9–6.

B. buxifolia. Semievergreen or deciduous, arching shrub. **H** 8ft (2.5m), **S** 10ft (3m). Has oblong to oval, spine-tipped, leathery, dark green leaves. Deep orange-yellow flowers, borne from early to mid-spring, are followed by spherical, black fruits with a white bloom. Z6–9 H9–6.

B. calliantha. Evergreen, bushy shrub. **H** and **S** 3–5ft (1–1.5m). Has oblong, sharply spiny, glossy, green leaves, white beneath, and large, pale yellow flowers in late spring, followed by egg-shaped, black fruits with a white bloom. Z7–9 H9–7.

B. candidula (Paleleaf barberry). Evergreen, bushy, compact shrub. **H** and **S** 3ft (1m). Leaves are narrowly oblong, glossy, dark green, white beneath. Has bright yellow flowers in late spring, then egg-shaped, blue-purple fruits. Z6–9 H9–6.

B. x carminea. 'Pirate King' is a deciduous, arching shrub. **H** 6ft (2m), **S** 10ft (3m). Has oblong, dark green leaves. In late spring and early summer produces clusters of yellow flowers, followed by spherical, pale red fruits. Z6–9 H9–6. **'Barbarossa',** illus. p.141.

B. 'Chenault'. See *B.* 'Chenaultii'.
B. 'Chenaultii', syn. *B.* 'Chenault'. Evergreen, bushy shrub. **H** 5ft (1.5m), **S** 6ft (2m). Narrowly oblong, wavy-edged, glossy, dark green leaves set off golden-yellow flowers in late spring and early summer. Bears egg-shaped, blue-black fruits. Z6–9 H9–6.

B. coxii. Evergreen, bushy, dense shrub. **H** 6ft (2m), **S** 10ft (3m). Produces narrowly oval, glossy, dark green leaves with white undersides and, in late spring, yellow flowers. Egg-shaped, blue-black fruits have a gray-blue bloom. Z6–9 H9–6.

B. darwinii (Darwin's barberry), illus. p.111.

B. empetrifolia, illus. p.148.

B. gagnepainii var. lanceifolia, illus. p.127.

B. jamesiana. Vigorous, deciduous, arching shrub. **H** and **S** 12ft (4m). Yellow flowers in late spring are followed by pendent racemes of spherical, red berries. Oval, dark green leaves redden in fall. Z7–9 H9–7.

B. julianae (Wintergreen barberry). Dense, bushy, evergreen shrub. **H** 8ft (2.5m), **S** 10ft (3m). Has glossy, dark green leaves, yellow flowers in late spring–early summer, and egg-shaped, blue-black fruits in fall. Z6–9 H9–4.

B. linearifolia 'Orange King', illus. p.127.

B. x lologensis. Vigorous, evergreen, arching shrub. **H** 10ft (3m), **S** 15ft (5m). Has broadly oblong, glossy, dark green leaves. Profuse clusters of orange flowers are borne from mid- to late spring. Z6–9 H9–6. **'Stapehill',** illus. p.127.

B. x ottawensis f. purpurea 'Superba', syn. *B. x ottawensis* 'Purpurea'. is a deciduous, arching shrub. **H** and **S** 8ft (2.5m). Produces rounded to oval, deep reddish-purple leaves. Bears small, red-tinged, yellow flowers in late spring, then egg-shaped, red fruits in fall. Z4–8 H8–3. **'Purpurea'.** See *B. x ottawensis f. purpurea* 'Superba'.
B. 'Park Jewel'. See *B.* 'Parkjuweel'.
B. 'Parkjuweel', syn. *B.* 'Park Jewel'. Semievergreen, bushy, rounded shrub. **H** and **S** 3ft (1m). Leaves are oval, glossy and bright green; some turn red in fall. Flowers are of little value. Z6–9 H9–6.
B. polyantha. See *B. prattii*.
B. prattii, syn. *B. polyantha*. Deciduous, bushy shrub. **H** and **S** 10ft (3m). Produces oblong, glossy, dark green leaves. Large clusters of small, yellow flowers in late summer are followed by a profusion of long-lasting, egg-shaped, coral-pink fruits. Z6–9 H9–6.
B. x rubrostilla. See *B.* 'Rubrostilla'.
B. 'Rubrostilla', syn. *B. x rubrostilla*, illus. p.162.
B. sargentiana. Evergreen, bushy shrub. **H** and **S** 6ft (2m). Leaves are oblong, glossy, bright green. Yellow flowers produced in late spring and early summer are succeeded by egg-shaped, blue-black fruits. Z5–8 H8–5.
B. x stenophylla, illus. p.127. **'Corallina Compacta'** illus. p.336.
B. thunbergii (Japanese barberry). Deciduous, arching, dense shrub. **H** 6ft (2m), **S** 10ft (3m). Broadly oval, pale to mid-green leaves turn brilliant orange-red in fall. Small, red-tinged, pale yellow flowers are produced in mid-spring, followed by egg-shaped, bright red fruits. Z5–8 H8–5. **f. atropurpurea,** illus. p.123. **'Atropurpurea Nana',** syn. *B. thunbergii* 'Crimson Pygmy', **H** and **S** 24in (60cm), bears reddish-purple foliage. Z5–8 H8–5. **'Aurea',** illus. p.160. **'Crimson Pygmy'.** See *B. thunbergii* 'Atropurpurea Nana'. **'Erecta'** upright branches spread with age. **'Golden Ring'** has purple leaves narrowly margined with golden-yellow, turning red in fall, and produces red fruit. Z5–8 H8–5.
'Rose Glow', illus. p.137.
B. valdiviana, illus. p.111.
B. verruculosa (Warty barberry). Slow-growing, evergreen, bushy shrub. **H** and **S** 5ft (1.5m). Glossy, dark green leaves have blue-white undersides. Clusters of small, cup-shaped, bright yellow flowers in late spring and early summer are followed by blue-black fruits. Z6–9 H9–4.
B. wilsoniae. Deciduous or semievergreen, bushy shrub. **H** 3ft (1m), **S** 5ft (1.5m). Narrowly oblong, gray-green leaves turn bright orange-red in fall. In late spring and early summer produces yellow flowers, then showy, spherical, coral-red fruits. Z6–9 H9–6.

BERCHEMIA

RHAMNACEAE

Genus of deciduous, twining climbers, grown for their leaves and fruit. Is useful for covering walls, fences and tree stumps. Grow in sun or shade, in any well-drained soil. Propagate by seed in fall or spring, by semiripe cuttings in summer or by layering

or root cuttings in winter. May be invasive in parts of North America.
B. racemosa 'Variegata'. Deciduous, twining climber. **H** 15ft (5m) or more. Produces heart-shaped, green leaves, 1¼–3in (3–8cm) long and paler beneath, that are variegated creamy-white. Small, bell-shaped, greenish-white flowers in summer are followed by rounded, green fruits that turn red, then black. Z6–9 H9–6.

BERGENIA

SYN. MEGASEA
Bergenia

SAXIFRAGACEAE

Genus of evergreen perennials with thick, usually large, rounded to oval or spoon-shaped, leathery leaves, with indented veins, that make ideal groundcover. Tolerates sun or shade and any well-drained soil, but leaf color is best on poor soil and in full sun. Propagate by division in spring after flowering.

B. 'Abendglut', syn. *B.* 'Evening Glow'. Evergreen, clump-forming perennial. **H** 9in (23cm), **S** 12in (30cm). Bears rosettes of oval, crinkled, short-stemmed, maroon leaves, from which arise racemes of open cup-shaped, semidouble, deep magenta flowers in spring. Z6–9 H9–6.

B. 'Ballawley'. Evergreen, clump-forming perennial. **H** and **S** 24in (60cm). Large, rounded to oval, flat, deep green leaves turn red in winter. Racemes of cup-shaped, bright crimson flowers are borne on red stems in spring. Shelter from cold winds. Z6–9 H9–6.

B. beesiana. See *B. purpurascens*.
B. 'Beethoven', illus. p.256.
B. ciliata, illus. p.256.
B. cordifolia (Heartleaf bergenia). Evergreen, clump-forming perennial. **H** 18in (45cm), **S** 24in (60cm). Leaves are rounded, puckered and crinkle-edged. Produces racemes of open cup-shaped, light pink flowers in spring. Z3–8 H8–1. **'Purpurea', H** and **S** 20in (50cm). Has large, rounded, purple-tinged, deep green leaves. Clusters of bell-shaped, rose-pink flowers are borne on red stems from late winter to early spring.
B. crassifolia (Winter-blooming bergenia). Evergreen, clump-forming perennial. **H** 12in (30cm), **S** 18in (45cm). Has oval- or spoon-shaped, fleshy, flat leaves that turn mahogany in fall. Bears spikes of open cup-shaped, lavender-pink flowers in spring. Z3–8 H8–1.
B. 'Eric Smith'. Evergreen, groundcover perennial. **H** 16in (40cm), **S** 24in (60cm) or more. Large, rounded, rather upright, leathery, mid-green leaves, which in winter are reddish tinted. Rich pink flowers are borne on sturdy stalks in spring. Z4–8 H8–1.
B. 'Evening Glow'. See *B.* 'Abendglut'.
B. 'Morgenröte', syn. *B.* 'Morning Red'. Evergreen, clump-forming perennial. **H** 18in (45cm), **S** 12in (30cm). Leaves are rounded, crinkled and deep green. Spikes of open cup-shaped, deep carmine flowers in spring are often followed by a second crop in summer. Z4–9 H9–2.
B. 'Morning Red'. See *B.* 'Morgenröte'.
B. purpurascens, syn. *B. beesiana*, illus. p.280.

B. x schmidtii. Evergreen, clump-forming perennial. **H** 12in (30cm), **S** 24in (60cm). Oval, flat leaves have toothed margins. Sprays of open cup-shaped, soft pink flowers are borne in early spring on short stems. Z4–8 H8–1.
B. 'Silberlicht', syn. *B.* 'Silver Light', illus. p.255.
B. 'Silver Light'. See *B.* 'Silberlicht'.
B. stracheyi. Evergreen, clump-forming perennial. **H** 9in (23cm), **S** 12in (30cm). Small, rounded, flat leaves form neat rosettes, among which nestle heads of open cup-shaped, white or pink flowers in spring. Z4–8 H8–1.
B. 'Sunningdale'. Evergreen, clump-forming perennial. **H** 24in (60cm), **S** 12in (30cm). Rounded, slightly crinkled, deep green leaves are mahogany beneath. Bears racemes of open cup-shaped, lilac-carmine flowers on red stalks in spring. Z3–8 H8–1.

BERKHEYA

COMPOSITAE/ASTERACEAE

Genus of summer-flowering perennials. Where marginally hardy, grow most species against a south- or west-facing wall. Needs full sun and fertile, well-drained soil. Sow seed in fall or divide in spring.
B. macrocephala, illus. p.243.
B. purpurea, illus. p.269.

BERTOLONIA

MELASTOMATACEAE

Genus of evergreen perennials, grown for their foliage. Requires a fairly shaded position and high humidity, although soil should not be waterlogged. Propagate by tip or leaf cuttings in spring or summer.
B. marmorata. Evergreen, rosette-forming perennial. **H** 6in (15cm) or more in flower, **S** 18in (45cm). Broadly oval, slightly fleshy leaves have heart-shaped bases, silvery midribs and puckered surfaces, and are reddish-purple below, velvety green above. Intermittently produces spikes of saucer-shaped, pinkish-purple flowers. Z14–15 H11–10.

BERZELIA

BRUNIACEAE

Genus of evergreen, heather-like, summer-flowering shrubs, grown for their flowers. Requires full sun and well-drained, neutral to acidic soil. Water container plants moderately, less when not in full growth. Plants may be cut back lightly after flowering. Propagate by seed in spring or by semiripe cuttings in late summer.
B. lanuginosa. Evergreen, erect shrub with soft-haired, young shoots. **H** and **S** to 3ft (1m). Has small, heather-like leaves. Compact, spherical heads of tiny, creamy-white flowers are borne in dense, terminal clusters in summer. Z14–15 H12–10.

BESCHORNERIA

AGAVACEAE/ASPARAGACEAE

Genus of perennial succulents with narrowly lance-shaped leaves forming erect, almost stemless, basal rosettes. Needs full sun and very well-drained soil. Propagate by seed or division in spring or summer.
B. yuccoides, illus. p.490.

B

BESSERA

LILIACEAE/ASPARAGACEAE

Genus of summer-flowering bulbs, grown for their brightly colored flowers. Needs an open, sunny situation and well-drained soil. Propagate by seed in spring. May be invasive in parts of North America.

B. elegans (Coral drops). Summer-flowering bulb. **H** to 24in (60cm), **S** 3–4in (8–10cm). Has long, narrow, erect, basal leaves. Each leafless stem bears pendent, bell-shaped, bright red flowers on long, slender stalks. Z13–15 H11–10.

Betonica officinalis. See *Stachys officinalis.*

BETULA
Birch

BETULACEAE

Genus of deciduous trees and shrubs, grown for their bark and fall color. Needs sun and moist but well-drained soil; some species prefer acidic soil. Transplant young trees in fall. Propagate by grafting in late winter or by softwood cuttings in early summer.

B. albosinensis (White Chinese birch), illus. p.78. Deciduous, open-branched tree. **H** 80ft (25m), **S** 30ft (10m). Has oval to lance-shaped, serrated, pale green leaves. Peeling bark is honey-colored or reddish-maroon with a gray bloom. Z5–8 H8–5.

B. alleghaniensis, syn. *B. lutea* (Yellow birch). Deciduous, upright, open tree, often multi-stemmed. **H** 40ft (12m) or more, **S** 10ft (3m). Smooth, glossy, golden-brown bark peels in thin shreds. Oval, mid- to pale green leaves rapidly turn gold in fall. Bears yellow-green catkins in spring. Z4–7 H7–1.

B. ermanii (Erman birch), illus. p.78. Deciduous, open-branched tree. **H** 70ft (20m), **S** 40ft (12m). Oval, glossy, green leaves turn yellow in fall. Has peeling, pinkish-white bark, distinctively marked with large lenticels. Z5–8 H8–5.

B. jacquemontii. See *B. utilis* var. *jacquemontii.*

B. 'Jermyns'. See *B. utilis* var. *jacquemontii* 'Jermyns'.

B. lenta, illus. p.79.

B. lutea. See *B. alleghaniensis.*

B. maximowicziana (Monarch birch). Fast-growing, deciduous, broad-headed tree with orange-brown or pink bark. **H** 60ft (18m), **S** 10ft (3m). Has racemes of yellowish catkins in spring. Large, oval, mid-green leaves turn bright butter-yellow in fall. Z6–8 H8–6.

B. nana, illus. p.335.

B. nigra (River birch), illus. p.78. Deciduous, conical then spreading tree with peeling, pink-orange bark, which becomes fissured with age. **H** 50ft (15m), **S** 30ft (10m). Diamond-shaped, glossy, mid-green leaves turn golden-orange in fall. Bears yellow, male catkins in spring. Can be coppiced to encourage multiple, brightly colored stems. Grows well in damp soil. Z4–9 H9–1. Many excellent cultivars are available, including **'Heritage',** which has larger, glossier leaves.

B. papyrifera, illus. p.67.

B. pendula (Silver birch). Deciduous, broadly columnar or conical tree. **H** 80ft (25m) or more, **S** 30ft (10m). Has slender, drooping shoots and silver-white bark that

becomes black and rugged at base of trunk with age. Yellow-brown catkins appear in spring. Oval, bright green leaves turn yellow in fall. Unfortunately very susceptible to bronze birch borer, which reduces the lifespan of this species. Z2–7 H7–1. **'Dalecarlica'** has a more upright habit, with pendent, shorter shoots at the end of the branches, and has much more deeply cut leaves. Z2–7 H7–1. **'Laciniata'** develops a narrow crown. Z2–7 H7–1. **'Tristis',** illus. p.68. **'Youngii',** illus. p.88.

B. platyphylla var. szechuanica. See *B. szechuanica.*

B. szechuanica, syn. *B. platyphylla* var. *szechuanica* (Szechuan birch). Vigorous, deciduous, open tree with stiff branches. **H** 46ft (14m), **S** 8ft (2.5m). Bark is chalky-white when mature. Has triangular to oval, serrated, leathery, deep green leaves that turn brilliant gold in fall. Produces yellow-green catkins in spring. Z5–7 H7–5.

B. utilis (Himalayan birch). Deciduous, upright, open tree. **H** 60ft (18m), **S** 30ft (10m). Paper-thin, peeling bark varies from creamy-white to dark copper-brown. Yellow-brown catkins are borne in spring. Oval, mid-green leaves, hairy beneath when young, turn golden-yellow in fall. Z5–7 H7–5. **var. jacquemontii,** syn. *B. jacquemontii* has bright white bark and oval, serrated, mid-green leaves that turn clear yellow in fall. **var. jacquemontii 'Grayswood Ghost',** illus. p.78. has bright, white bark, slightly pendent branchlets and dark green leaves. **var. jacquemontii 'Jermyns',** syn. *B. 'Jermyns'* (illus. p.78), **H** 50ft (15m), **S** 30ft (10m), produces bright white bark and very long, elegant, yellow, male catkins.

BIARUM

ARACEAE

Genus of mainly fall-flowering, tuberous perennials with tiny flowers carried on a pencil-shaped spadix, enclosed within a tubular spathe. Upper part of spathe is hooded or flattened out and showy. In winter protect in a cold frame or greenhouse. Needs a sunny position and well-drained soil. Dry out tubers when dormant in summer. Propagate in fall by seed or offsets.

B. eximium. Early fall-flowering, tuberous perennial. **H** and **S** 3–4in (8–10cm). Lance-shaped, semierect, basal leaves follow stemless, tubular, velvety, blackish-maroon spathe, up to 6in (15cm) long and often lying flat on ground. Upper part is flattened out. Spadix is upright and black. Z7–9 H9–7.

B. tenuifolium. Late summer- or fall-flowering tuberous perennial. **H** to 8in (20cm), **S** 3–4in (8–10cm). Produces clusters of acrid, narrow, erect, basal leaves after which stemless, upright and often twisted, blackish-purple spathes appear. Z7–9 H9–7.

BIDENS

COMPOSITAE/ASTERACEAE

Genus of annuals and perennials, grown for their large, yellow flowers and finely dissected leaves. A few perennials, usually treated as annuals, are grown as creeping hanging basket and container plants. Grow in full sun and reasonably

fertile, moist but well-drained soil. Propagate by seed in spring or divide perennials in spring.

B. atrosanguinea. See *Cosmos atrosanguineus.*

B. 'Gold Star', illus. p.319.

BIGNONIA
Cross vine

BIGNONIACEAE

Genus of one species of evergreen, tendril climber. In colder areas may lose its leaves in winter. Requires sun and fertile soil to flower well. If necessary, prune in spring. Propagate by stem cuttings in summer or fall or by layering in winter.

B. capensis. See *Tecoma capensis.*

B. capreolata, syn. *Doxantha capreolata* (Cross vine, Trumpet flower). Evergreen, tendril climber. **H** 30ft (10m) or more. Each leaf has 2 narrowly oblong leaflets and a branched tendril. In summer, funnel-shaped, reddish-orange flowers are borne in clusters in leaf axils. Pea-pod-shaped fruits, to 6in (15cm) long, are produced in fall. Z6–9 H9–5.

B. grandiflora. See *Campsis grandiflora.*

B. jasminoides. See *Pandorea jasminoides.*

B. pandorana. See *Pandorea pandorana.*

B. radicans. See *Campsis radicans.*

B. stans. See *Tecoma stans.*

B. unguis-cati. See *Macfadyena unguis-cati.*

Bilderdykia. See *Fallopia.*

BILLARDIERA

PITTOSPORACEAE

Genus of evergreen, woody-stemmed, twining climbers, grown mainly for their fruits. Grow in any well-drained soil, in a sheltered position and partial shade. Propagate by seed in spring or stem cuttings in summer or fall.

B. longiflora, illus. p.210.

BILLBERGIA

BROMELIACEAE

Genus of evergreen, rosette-forming perennials, grown for their flowers and foliage. Requires semi-shade and well-drained soil, ideally adding sphagnum moss or plastic chips used for orchid culture. Water moderately when in full growth, sparingly at other times. Propagate by division or offsets after flowering or in late spring.

B. nutans (Queen's tears). Evergreen, clump-forming, tubular-rosetted perennial. **H** and **S** to 16in (40cm). Strap-shaped leaves are usually dark green. In spring, pendent clusters of tubular, purple-blue-edged, lime-green flowers emerge from pink bracts. Z9–11 H11–1.

B. rhodocyanea. See *Aechmea fasciata.*

B. x windii (Angel's tears). Evergreen, clump-forming, tubular-rosetted perennial. **H** and **S** to 16in (40cm). Is similar to *B. nutans*, but produces broader, spreading, gray-green leaves and larger bracts. Flowers intermittently from spring to fall. Z9–15 H12–10.

Biota orientalis. See *Platycladus orientalis.*

BLECHNUM
Hard fern

BLECHNACEAE

Genus of evergreen or semievergreen ferns. Most species prefer semi-shade. Requires moist, neutral to acidic soil. Remove fading fronds regularly. Propagate *B. penna-marina* by division in spring, other species by spores in late summer.

B. alpinum. See *B. penna-marina.*

B. chilense, syn. *B. tabulare*, illus. p.292.

B. penna-marina, syn. *B. alpinum*, illus. p.290.

B. spicant (Hard fern). Evergreen fern. **H** 12–30in (30–75cm), **S** 12–18in (30–45cm). Bears narrowly lance-shaped, indented, leathery, spreading, dark green fronds. Prefers shade and peaty or leafy soil. Z10–11 H11–10.

B. tabulare. See *B. chilense.*

BLETILLA

ORCHIDACEAE

See also ORCHIDS.

B. hyacinthina. See *B. striata.*

B. striata, syn. *B. hyacinthina* (Chinese ground orchid), illus. p.466. Deciduous, terrestrial orchid. **H** to 24in (60cm). In late spring or early summer produces magenta or white flowers, 1¼in (3cm) long, and broadly lance-shaped leaves, 20in (50cm) long. Needs shade in summer. Z5–8 H8–5.

BLOOMERIA

LILIACEAE/ASPARAGACEAE

Genus of onion-like, spring-flowering bulbs, with spherical flower heads on leafless stems, which die down in summer. Requires a sheltered, sunny situation and well-drained soil. Propagate by seed in fall or by division in late summer or fall.

B. crocea. Late spring-flowering bulb. **H** to 12in (30cm), **S** to 4in (10cm). Long, narrow, semierect, basal leaves die at flowering time. Each leafless stem bears a loose, spherical head, 4–6in (10–15cm) across, of star-shaped, dark-striped, yellow flowers. Z8–9 H9–8.

Bocconia cordata. See *Macleaya cordata.*

BOENNINGHAUSENIA

RUTACEAE

Genus of one species of deciduous subshrub, usually with soft, herbaceous stems, grown for its foliage and flowers. Needs full sun and fertile, well-drained but not too dry soil. Propagate by softwood cuttings in summer or by seed in fall.

B. albiflora. Deciduous, bushy subshrub. **H** and **S** 3ft (1m). Has pungent, mid-green leaves, divided into oval leaflets. Bears loose panicles of small, cup-shaped, white flowers from mid-summer to early fall. Z6–10 H10–6.

BOLAX

UMBELLIFERAE/APIACEAE

Genus of evergreen, hummock- and cushion-forming perennials, often included in *Azorella*. Is grown for its symmetrical rosettes of small, thick, tough leaves. Flowers only rarely in cultivation. Is

suitable for gritty screes, troughs and alpine houses. Needs sun and rich, well-drained soil. Propagate by rooting rosettes in summer.
B. gummifer, illus. p.376.

BOMAREA
ALSTROEMERIACEAE

Genus of herbaceous or evergreen, tuberous-rooted, scrambling and twining climbers, grown for tubular or bell-shaped flowers. Needs full light and well-drained soil. Water regularly in growth, sparingly when dormant. Provide support. Some species grow well out of doors planted beneath shrubs through which they can climb; mulch to protect tubers before winter. Cut out old flowering stems at ground level when leaves yellow. Propagate by seed or division in early spring.
B. andimarcana, syn. *B. pubigera.* Deciduous, scrambling climber with straight, slender stems. **H** 6–10ft (2–3m). Has lance-shaped leaves, white and hairy beneath. Bears nodding, tubular, green-tipped, pale yellow flowers, suffused pink, from early summer to fall. Z9–10 H10–9.
B. caldasii. See *B. multiflora.*
B. edulis, illus. p.201.
B. hirsuta. Herbaceous, twining climber. **H** 3–6ft (1–2m). Has narrowly ovate, mid-green leaves, softly hairy beneath. Bears tight clusters of pendent, bell-shaped, reddish-orange flowers, with yellow-orange interiors, from mid-summer to fall. Z9–11 H12–9.
B. kalbreyeri of gardens. See *B. multiflora.*
B. multiflora, syn. *B. caldasii, B. kalbreyeri* of gardens, illus. p.207.
B. pubigera of gardens. See *B. andimarcana.*
B. salsilla. Herbaceous, twining climber. **H** 3–5ft (1–1.5m). Ovate leaves are grayish-green. Produces open clusters of pendent, bell-shaped, green-tipped, cerise flowers in summer. Z9–11 H12–9.

BORAGO
Borage
BORAGINACEAE

Genus of annuals and perennials, grown for culinary use as well as for their flowers. Requires sun and fertile, well-drained soil. For culinary use gather only young leaves. Propagate by seed sown outdoors in spring. Some species will self-seed prolifically and may become invasive.
B. officinalis (Borage), illus. p.315.

BORONIA
RUTACEAE

Genus of evergreen shrubs, grown mainly for their flowers. Requires full light and sandy, neutral to acidic soil. Water container specimens moderately, less when they are not in full growth. For a compact habit, shorten long stems after flowering. Propagate by seed in spring or by semiripe cuttings in late summer. Red spider mite may be a problem.
B. megastigma, illus. p.456.

Borzicactus. See *Cleistocactus.*

BOUGAINVILLEA
Bougainvillea
NYCTAGINACEAE

Genus of deciduous or evergreen, woody-stemmed, scrambling climbers, grown for their showy, floral bracts. Grow in fertile, well-drained soil in full light. Water moderately in the growing season; keep container plants almost dry when dormant. Tie to a support. Cut back previous season's lateral growths in spring, leaving ³⁄₄–1¹⁄₄in (2–3cm) long spurs. Propagate by semiripe cuttings in summer or by hardwood cuttings when dormant. Whitefly and mealy bug may attack.
B. x buttiana. Vigorous, evergreen, woody-stemmed, scrambling climber. **H** 25–40ft (8–12m). Has ovate, mid-green leaves, to 3in (8cm) long, lighter below. Bears large clusters of strongly waved, golden-yellow, purple or red floral bracts from summer to fall. Z13–15 H11–1. **'Enid Lancaster',** syn. *B.* x *buttiana* 'California Gold', *B.* x *buttiana* 'Golden Glow' floral bracts are orange-yellow. Z13–15 H11–1. **'Miss Manila',** syn. *B.* 'Miss Manila', *B.* 'Tango' has pink floral bracts. **'Mrs. Butt',** syn. *B.* x *buttiana* 'Crimson Lake' has crimson-magenta floral bracts; **'Scarlet Queen'** are scarlet.
B. x buttiana 'California Gold'. See *B.* x *buttiana* 'Enid Lancaster'.
B. x buttiana 'Crimson Lake'. See *B.* x *buttiana* 'Mrs. Butt'.
B. x buttiana 'Golden Glow'. See *B.* x *buttiana* 'Enid Lancaster'.
B. 'Dania'. Vigorous, mainly evergreen, woody-stemmed, scrambling climber. **H** 15ft (to 5m). Has rounded-oval, mid-green leaves and bears clusters of deep pink floral bracts in summer. Z12–15 H11–1.
B. glabra, illus. p.462. **'Sanderiana'**, illus. p.462. **'Snow White',** illus. p.460.
B. 'Miss Manila'. See *B.* x *buttiana* 'Miss Manila'.
B. spectabilis. Strong-growing, mainly evergreen, woody-stemmed, scrambling climber; stems usually have a few spines. **H** to 22ft (7m). Has elliptic to oval leaves and, in summer, large trusses of red-purple floral bracts. Z9–11 H11–1.
B. 'Tango'. See *B.* x *buttiana* 'Miss Manila'.

Boussingaultia basellaoides of gardens. See *Anredera cordifolia.*

BOUTELOUA
Grama grass
GRAMINEAE/POACEAE

See also GRASSES, BAMBOOS, RUSHES and SEDGES.
B. gracilis, syn. *B. oligostachya* (Blue grama, Mosquito grass). Semievergreen, tuft-forming, narrow-leaved, perennial grass. **H** 20in (50cm), **S** 8in (20cm). In summer bears comblike flower spikes, 1¹⁄₂in (4cm) long, held at right-angles to stems. Z5–9 H9–5.
B. oligostachya. See *B. gracilis.*

BOUVARDIA
RUBIACEAE

Genus of deciduous, semievergreen or evergreen shrubs and perennials, grown for their flowers. Prefers full light and fertile, well-drained soil. Water freely when in full growth, moderately at other times. Cut back stems by half to three-quarters after flowering. Propagate by softwood cuttings in spring or by greenwood or semiripe cuttings in summer. Whitefly and mealy bug may be troublesome.
B. humboldtii. See *B. longiflora.*
B. longiflora, syn. *B. humboldtii.* Semievergreen, spreading shrub. **H** and **S** 3ft (1m) or more. Has lance-shaped leaves, and terminal clusters of fragrant, white flowers, with slender tubes and 4 petal lobes, from summer to early winter. Z13–15 H11–10.
B. ternifolia, syn. *B. triphylla* (Scarlet trompetilla), illus. p.456.
B. triphylla. See *B. ternifolia.*

BOWIEA
LILIACEAE/ASPARAGACEAE

Genus of summer-flowering, bulbous succulents with scrambling, branched, green stems that produce no proper leaves. Needs sun and well-drained soil; plant with half of bulb above soil level. Support with sticks or canes. Propagate by seed, sown under glass in winter or spring. May produce offsets.
B. volubilis. Bulbous summer-flowering succulent. **H** 3–6ft (1–2m), **S** 1¹⁄₂–2ft (45–60cm). Has climbing, much-branched, slender stems and no proper leaves. Produces small, star-shaped, green flowers at tips of stems. Provide support. Z14–15 H11–10.

BOYKINIA
SAXIFRAGACEAE

Genus of mound-forming perennials. Most species require shade and rich, moist but well-drained, acidic soil. Propagate by division in spring or by seed in fall.
B. aconitifolia. Mound-forming perennial. **H** 3ft (1m), **S** 6in (15cm). Has rounded to kidney-shaped, lobed leaves. In summer, flower stems carry very small, bell-shaped, white flowers. Z5–9 H9–5.
B. jamesii. Mound-forming, rhizomatous perennial. **H** and **S** 6in (15cm). Each woody stem bears a rosette of kidney-shaped leaves with lacerated edges. In early summer bears open bell-shaped, frilled, pink flowers with green centers. Z5–9 H9–6.

Brachychilum horsfieldii. See *Hedychium horsfieldii.*

BRACHYCHITON
STERCULIACEAE/MALVACEAE

Genus of evergreen or deciduous, mainly spring- and summer-flowering trees, grown for their flowers and overall appearance. Needs full light and rich, well-drained, preferably acidic soil. Water container plants moderately, much less in winter. Prune if needed. Propagate by seed in spring at min. 75°F (24°C). Red spider mite may be a nuisance.
B. acerifolius, syn. *Sterculia acerifolia* (Illawarra flame tree), illus. p.450.
B. populneus, syn. *Sterculia diversifolia* (Kurrajong). Evergreen, conical tree, pyramidal when young. **H** and **S** 50–70ft (15–20m). Pointed or 3–5 lobed, glossy, deep green leaves are chartreuse when young. In spring–summer has panicles of saucer-shaped, cream or greenish-white flowers with red, purple or yellow throats. Z9–11 H11–10.

BRACHYGLOTTIS
COMPOSITAE/ASTERACEAE

Genus of evergreen shrubs and trees, grown for their bold foliage and daisylike flower heads. Needs full light or partial shade and well-drained soil. Water container plants freely in summer, moderately at other times. Take semiripe cuttings in late summer.
B. compacta, syn. *Senecio compactus.* Evergreen, bushy, dense shrub. **H** 3ft (1m), **S** 6ft (2m). Feltlike, white hairs cover the shoots. Bears small, oval, white-edged, dark green leaves, white below, and daisylike, bright yellow flowers in clustered heads from mid- to late summer. Z9–10 H10–9.
B. Dunedin Group, syn. *Senecio* Dunedin Hybrids, *Senecio greyi, Senecio laxifolius,* illus. p.161.
B. laxifolia, syn. *Senecio laxifolius.* Evergreen, bushy, spreading shrub. **H** 3ft (1m), **S** 6ft (2m). Oval, gray-white leaves become dark green. Has large clusters of daisylike, golden-yellow flower heads in summer. Z8–10 H10–8.
B. monroi, syn. *Senecio monroi,* illus. p.161.
B. repanda (Pukapuka, Rangiora). Evergreen, bushy shrub or tree, upright when young. **H** 10ft (3m), **S** 10ft (3m) or more. Has robust, downy, white stems and veined leaves that are white beneath. Produces fragrant, white flower heads in summer. Z12–15 H11–10.
B. rotundifolia, syn. *Senecio reinholdii, Senecio rotundifolius.* Evergreen, rounded, dense shrub. **H** and **S** 3ft (1m). Has rounded, leathery, glossy leaves, dark green above, white-felted below, and tiny, yellow flower heads from early to mid-summer. Withstands salt winds in mild coastal areas. Z9–10 H10–9.

BRACHYSCOME
COMPOSITAE/ASTERACEAE

Genus of annuals and perennials, grown for their daisylike flower heads and very variable, often finely divided foliage. Requires sun, a sheltered position and rich, well-drained soil. Pinch out growing shoots of young plants to encourage a bushy habit. Propagate by seed sown under glass in spring or outdoors in late spring.
B. iberidifolia (Swan River daisy). Moderately fast-growing, thin-stemmed, bushy annual. **H** and **S** to 18in (45cm). Has deeply cut leaves and small, fragrant, daisylike flowers, usually blue but also pink, mauve, purple or white, in summer and early fall. H11–1.
B. 'Strawberry Mousse', illus. p.300.

Bracteantha bracteata. See *Xerochrysum bracteatum.*
Brasiliopuntia brasiliensis. See *Opuntia brasiliensis.*

B

B

BRASILIORCHIS
ORCHIDACEAE

See also ORCHIDS.

B. picta, syn. *Maxillaria picta.* Evergreen, epiphytic orchid for a cool greenhouse. **H** 9in (23cm). Fragrant, deep yellow to white flowers, 1in (2.5cm) across, marked purple to dark reddish-brown outside, are produced singly beneath foliage in winter. Has narrowly oval leaves, 6–9in (15–23cm) long. Requires partial shade in summer. Z14–15 H12–6.

B. porphyrostele, syn. *Maxillaria porphyrostele,* illus. p.467. Evergreen, epiphytic orchid for a cool greenhouse. **H** 3in (8cm). White- and red-lipped, yellow flowers, ½in (1cm) across, are borne singly in summer–fall. Narrowly oval leaves are 3in (8cm) long. Needs good light in summer. Z14–15 H12–10.

Brassaia. See *Schefflera.*

BRASSAVOLA
ORCHIDACEAE

See also ORCHIDS.

B. nodosa (Lady-of-the-night), illus. p.466. Evergreen, epiphytic orchid for an intermediate greenhouse. **H** 9in (23cm). Narrow-petaled, pale green flowers, 2in (5cm) across and each with a white lip, are produced, 1–3 to a stem, in spring; they are fragrant at night. Leaves, 3–4in (8–10cm) long, are thick and cylindrical. Is best grown on a bark slab. Provide good light in summer. H11–10.

BRASSICA
CRUCIFERAE/BRASSICACEAE

Genus of annuals and evergreen biennials and perennials. Most are edible vegetables, e.g. cabbages and kales, but forms of *B. oleracea* are grown for ornamental foliage. Grow in sun and fertile, well-drained soil. Lime-rich soil is preferable, though not essential. Propagate by seed sown outdoors in spring or under glass in early spring. Is susceptible to club root.

B. Northern Lights Series, illus. p.306.

B. oleracea forms (Ornamental cabbage). Moderately fast-growing, evergreen, rounded biennial, grown as an annual. **H** and **S** 12–18in (30–45cm). Has heads of large, often crinkled leaves, in combinations of red/green, white/pink, pink/green. Do not allow to flower. Z7–11 H6–1.

x **Brassocattleya Mount Adams gx.** See x *Rhyncholaeliocattleya* Mount Adams gx.

x **Brassolaeliocattleya Hetherington Horace gx 'Coronation'.** See x *Rhyncholaeliocattleya* Hetherington Horace gx 'Coronation'.

x **Brassolaeliocattleya St. Helier gx.** See x *Rhyncholaeliocattleya* St. Helier gx.

Bravoa geminiflora. See *Polianthes geminiflora.*

BREYNIA
EUPHORBIACEAE/PHYLLANTHACEAE

Genus of evergreen shrubs and trees, grown for their foliage. Requires full light or partial shade and fertile, well-drained

soil. Water container plants freely when in full growth, moderately at other times. Large bushes should be cut back hard after flowering. Propagate by greenwood or semiripe cuttings in summer. Whitefly, red spider mite and mealy bug may be troublesome.

B. disticha, syn. *B. nivosa, Phyllanthus nivosus* (Snow bush). Evergreen, well-branched shrub with slender stems. **H** 3ft (1m) or more, **S** 24–39in (60–100cm). Ovate, dark green leaves have white marbling. Tiny, greenish flowers, borne intermittently, have no petals. Z14–15 H11–10. **'Roseopicta', H** and **S** to 3ft (1m), has green leaves variably bordered and splashed with white and flushed pink.

B. nivosa. See *B. disticha.*

Bridgesia. See *Ercilla.*

BRIGGSIA
GESNERIACEAE

Genus of evergreen perennials, grown for their rosettes of hairy leaves. Needs shade and peaty soil with plenty of moisture in summer and good air circulation in winter. Protect against damp in winter. Propagate by seed in spring.

B. muscicola. Evergreen, basal-rosetted perennial. **H** 3–4in (8–10cm), **S** 9in (23cm). Leaves are oval, silver-haired and pale green. Arching flower stems bear loose clusters of tubular, pale yellow flowers, with protruding tips, in early summer. Is best grown in an alpine house. Z12–15 H11–10.

BRIMEURA
LILIACEAE/ASPARAGACEAE

Genus of spring-flowering bulbs, similar to miniature bluebells, cultivated for their flowers. Is suitable for rock gardens and shrub borders. Requires partial shade and prefers rich, well-drained soil. Propagate by seed in fall or by division in late summer.

B. amethystina, syn. *Hyacinthus amethystinus,* illus. p.419.

Brittonastrum mexicanum. See *Agastache mexicana.*

BRIZA
Quaking grass
GRAMINEAE/POACEAE

See also GRASSES, BAMBOOS, RUSHES and SEDGES.

B. maxima (Greater quaking grass). Robust, tuft-forming, annual grass. **H** to 20in (50cm), **S** 3–4in (8–10cm). Mid-green leaves are mainly basal. Produces loose panicles of up to 10 pendent, purplish-green spikelets, in early summer, that dry particularly well for winter decoration. Self-seeds readily. H11–1.

B. media (Common quaking grass). Evergreen, tuft-forming, rhizomatous, perennial grass. **H** 12–24in (30–60cm), **S** 3–4in (8–10cm). Mid-green leaves are mainly basal. In summer produces open panicles of up to 30 pendent, purplish-brown spikelets that dry well for winter decoration. Z4–11 H11–1.

BRODIAEA
LILIACEAE/ASPARAGACEAE

Genus of mainly spring-flowering bulbs with colorful flowers produced in loose heads on leafless stems. Needs a sheltered, sunny situation and light, well-drained soil. Dies down in summer. Propagate in fall by seed or in late summer and fall by freely produced offsets.

B. capitata. See *Dichelostemma pulchellum.*

B. congesta. See *Dichelostemma congestum.*

B. coronaria, syn. *B. grandiflora* (Harvest brodiaea). Late spring- to early summer-flowering bulb. **H** 4–10in (10–25cm), **S** 3–4in (8–10cm). Long, narrow, semierect, basal leaves die down by flowering time. Leafless stems each carry a loose head of erect, funnel-shaped, violet-blue flowers on long, slender stalks. Z8–10 H10–8.

B. grandiflora. See *B. coronaria.*

B. hyacinthina. See *Triteleia hyacinthina.*

B. ida-maia. See *Dichelostemma ida-maia.*

B. ixioides. See *Triteleia ixioides.*

B. lactea. See *Triteleia hyacinthina.*

B. laxa. See *Triteleia laxa.* **'Queen Fabiola'.** See *Triteleia laxa* 'Koningin Fabiola'.

B. lutea. See *Triteleia ixioides.*

B. peduncularis. See *Triteleia peduncularis.*

B. pulchella. See *Dichelostemma pulchellum.*

BROMELIA
BROMELIACEAE

Genus of evergreen, rosette-forming perennials, grown for their overall appearance. Needs full light and well-drained soil. Water moderately in summer, sparingly at other times. Propagate by suckers in spring.

B. balansae, illus. p.470.

BROMUS
Brome
GRAMINEAE/POACEAE

See also GRASSES, BAMBOOS, RUSHES and SEDGES.

B. ramosus (Hairy brome grass). Evergreen, tuft-forming, perennial grass. **H** to 6ft (2m), **S** 1ft (30cm). Mid-green leaves are lax and hairy. Produces long, arching panicles of nodding, gray-green spikelets in summer. Prefers shade. H12–1.

BROUSSONETIA
MORACEAE

Genus of deciduous trees and shrubs, grown for their foliage and unusual flowers. Male and female flowers are produced on different plants. Requires full sun and well-drained soil. Propagate by softwood cuttings in summer or by seed in fall.

B. papyrifera, illus. p.74.

BROWALLIA
Amethyst flower
SOLANACEAE

Genus of shrubby perennials, usually grown as annuals, with showy, open trumpet-shaped flowers. Grows best in

sun or partial shade and in fertile, well-drained soil that should not dry out completely. Feed when flowering if container-grown and pinch out young shoots to encourage bushiness. Propagate by seed in spring; for winter flowers, sow in late summer.

B. americana, syn. *B. elata.* Moderately fast-growing, bushy perennial, usually grown as an annual. **H** 12in (30cm), **S** 6in (15cm). Produces oval, mid-green leaves and, in summer, trumpet-shaped, blue flowers, 1½in (4cm) wide. Z10–11 H8–1.

B. elata. See *B. americana.*

B. speciosa, illus. p.472.

BROWNINGIA
SYN. AZUREOCEREUS
CACTACEAE

Genus of slow-growing, eventually treelike, perennial cacti. Spiny, silvery- or green-blue stems, with up to 20 or more ribs, are crowned by stiff, erect, green-blue branches. Requires full sun and very well-drained soil. Propagate by seed in spring or summer.

B. hertlingiana, syn. *Azureocereus hertlingianus,* illus. p.488.

Bruckenthalia spiculifolia. See *Erica spiculifolia.*

BRUGMANSIA
Angels' trumpets
SOLANACEAE

Genus of evergreen or semievergreen shrubs, trees and annuals, grown for their flowers borne mainly in summer–fall. Prefers full light and fertile, well-drained soil. Water container specimens freely in full growth, moderately at other times. May be pruned hard in early spring. Propagate by seed in spring or by greenwood or semiripe cuttings in early summer or later. Whitefly and red spider mite may be troublesome. ① All parts are highly toxic if ingested.

B. arborea, syn. *B. versicolor* (Common angels' trumpet). Evergreen or semievergreen, rounded, robust shrub. **H** and **S** to 10ft (3m). Bears narrowly oval leaves, 8in (20cm) or more long. Produces strongly fragrant, pendent, trumpet-shaped, white flowers, 6–8in (16–20cm) long with a spathe-like calyx, in summer–fall. Z11 H11–10.

B. aurea. Evergreen, rounded shrub or tree. **H** and **S** 20–35ft (6–11m). Has oval leaves, 6in (15cm) long. In summer–fall produces pendent, trumpet-shaped, white or yellow flowers, 6–10in (15–25cm) long. Z11 H11–10.

B. x candida. Semievergreen, rounded shrub or small tree. **H** 10–15ft (3–5m), **S** 5–8ft (1.5–2.5m). Has oval, downy leaves and strongly scented, pendulous, white flowers, sometimes cream or pinkish, in summer–fall. Z11 H11–10. **'Grand Marnier',** syn. *B.* 'Grand Marnier' illus. p.319.

B. 'Grand Marnier'. See *B. x candida* 'Grand Marnier'.

B. rosei. See *B. sanguinea.*

B. sanguinea, syn. *B. rosei* (Red angels' trumpet). Semievergreen, erect to rounded shrub or small tree. **H** 10–15ft (3–5m), **S** 6–10ft (2–3m). Has lobed, young leaves and large, trumpet-shaped, yellow and

orange-red flowers from late summer to winter. Z11 H11–10.
B. versicolor. See *B. arborea*.

BRUNFELSIA
SOLANACEAE

Genus of evergreen shrubs, grown for their flowers. Needs semi-shade and rich, well-drained soil. Water container plants moderately, much less in low temperatures. Remove stem tips to promote branching in growing season. Propagate by semiripe cuttings in summer. Mealy bug and whitefly may be a problem.
B. calycina. See *B. pauciflora*.
B. eximia. See *B. pauciflora*.
B. pauciflora, syn. *B. calycina, B. eximia* (Yesterday-today-and-tomorrow). Evergreen, spreading shrub. **H** and **S** 2ft (60cm) or more. Bears oblong to lance-shaped, leathery, glossy leaves. Blue-purple flowers, each with a tubular base and 5 overlapping, wavy-edged petals, are produced from winter to summer. Z12–15 H11–10. **'Macrantha',** illus. p.457.

BRUNNERA
BORAGINACEAE

Genus of spring-flowering perennials. Prefers light shade and moist soil. Propagate by division in spring or fall or by seed in fall.
B. macrophylla (Siberian bugloss). Clump-forming perennial. **H** 18in (45cm), **S** 24in (60cm). Delicate sprays of small, star-shaped, forget-me-not-like, bright blue flowers in early spring are followed by heart-shaped, rough, long-stalked leaves. Makes good groundcover. Z3–7 H7–1. **'Dawson's White'** has delicate sprays of small, bright blue flowers in spring. Shelter from wind to prevent leaf damage. Z3–7 H7–1. **'Jack Frost'** illus. p.261.

x Brunsdonna parkeri. See x *Amarygia parkeri*.

BRUNSVIGIA
AMARYLLIDACEAE

Genus of fall-flowering bulbs with heads of showy flowers. Requires sun and well-drained soil. Water in fall to encourage bulbs into growth and continue watering until summer, when the leaves will die away; dormant bulbs should be kept fairly dry and warm. Propagate by seed sown in fall or by offsets in late summer.
B. josephinae (Josephine's lily). Fall-flowering bulb. **H** to 18in (45cm), **S** 18–24in (45–60cm). Bears a sturdy, leafless stem with a spherical head of 20–30 funnel-shaped, red flowers, 3–3¹⁄₂in (7–9cm) long, with recurved petal tips. Semierect, oblong leaves are produced after flowering. Z12–15 H12–10.

Bryophyllum. See *Kalanchoe*.

BUDDLEJA
Butterfly bush
BUDDLEJACEAE/SCROPHULARIACEAE

Genus of deciduous, semievergreen or evergreen shrubs and trees, grown for their clusters of small, often fragrant flowers. Requires full sun and fertile,

well-drained soil. *B. crispa, B. davidii, B. fallowiana,* B. 'Lochinch' and B. x *weyeriana* should be cut back hard in spring. Prune *B. alternifolia* by removing shoots that have flowered. Other species may be cut back lightly after flowering. Propagate by semiripe cuttings in summer.
B. agathosma. Deciduous, upright shrub. **H** and **S** 10ft (3m). Large, triangular-shaped, feltlike, silvery-green leaves have wavy margins. Fragrant, tubular, lilac flowers, with orange centers, are borne in late spring. Z5–7 H7–4.
B. alternifolia (Fountain butterfly bush), illus. p.114. Deciduous, arching shrub that can be trained as a weeping tree. **H** and **S** 12ft (4m). Has slender, pendent shoots and narrow, gray-green leaves. Neat clusters of fragrant, lilac-purple flowers are borne in early summer. Z6–9 H10–1.
B. asiatica. Evergreen, arching shrub. **H** and **S** 10ft (3m). Long plumes of very fragrant, tubular, white flowers appear amid long, narrow, dark green leaves in late winter and early spring. Grow against a south- or west-facing wall. Z8–9 H9–8.
B. colvilei. Deciduous, arching shrub, often treelike with age. **H** and **S** 20ft (6m). Has lance-shaped, dark green foliage among which large, tubular, white-throated, deep pink to purplish-red flowers are borne in drooping racemes in early summer. Z8–9 H9–8. **'Kewensis'** (illus. p.114), **H** and **S** 15ft (5m), has white-throated, deep red flowers. Z8–9 H9–8.
B. crispa, illus. p.204.
B. davidii (Butterfly bush). Variable, fast-growing, deciduous shrub. **H** 10–16ft (3–5m), **S** to 16ft (5m). Long, arching branches bear lance-shaped, pointed, mid- to gray-green leaves, to 10in (25cm) long. Bears dense, semi-pendent panicles, to 8in (20cm) or more, of small, very fragrant, tubular, lilac to purple or white flowers from mid-summer to fall. Is tolerant of dry conditions. Z6–9 H9–1. **'Black Knight'** (illus. p.114) has dark green leaves with white-felted undersides and dark violet-purple flowers. **'Dartmoor'** (illus. p.114) has deeply cut leaf margins and produces large, branched panicles of deep rich lilac-purple flowers. **'Empire Blue'** has rich violet-blue flowers. **'Harlequin'** has red-purple flowers. **'Peace'** bears long plumes of white flowers. **'Pink Delight'** (illus. p.114) has panicles, 12in (30cm) long, of orange-eyed, bright pink flowers. **'Pink Pearl'** produces pale lilac-pink flowers. **'Royal Red'** has rich purple-red flowers. **'White Profusion'** (illus. p.114) bears masses of snow-white flowers, each with a yellow eye. Z6–9 H9–1.
B. fallowiana. Deciduous, arching shrub. **H** 6ft (2m), **S** 10ft (3m). Shoots and lance-shaped leaves, when young, are covered with white hairs; foliage then becomes dark gray-green. Has fragrant, tubular, lavender-purple flowers in late summer and early fall. Is often damaged in very severe winters; grow against a wall in cold areas. Z6–9 H9–6. **var. alba** has white flowers.
B. globosa, illus. p.116.
B. 'Lochinch', illus. p.114. Deciduous,

arching shrub. **H** and **S** 10ft (3m). Long plumes of fragrant, tubular, lilac-blue flowers are borne above lance-shaped, gray-green leaves in late summer and fall. Z6–9 H9–6.
B. madagascariensis, syn. *Nicodemia madagascariensis*. Evergreen, arching shrub. **H** and **S** 12ft (4m) or more. Has narrowly lance-shaped, dark green leaves, white beneath, and, in late winter and spring, long clusters of tubular, orange-yellow flowers. Grow against a south- or west-facing wall. Z12–15 H11–1.
B. salviifolia (South African sage wood), illus. p.114. Semievergreen, arching shrub. **H** 13ft (4m), **S** 10ft (3m). Has sage-like, lance-shaped, wrinkled, blue-green leaves, covered in fine hairs. Fragrant, tubular, white to pale lilac flowers are produced in early summer. Z8–11 H11–8.
B. x weyeriana. Deciduous, arching shrub. **H** and **S** 12ft (4m). Bears lance-shaped, dark green leaves, and loose, rounded clusters of tubular, orange-yellow flowers, often tinged purple, from mid-summer to fall. Z5–9 H9–2. **'Moonlight'** (illus. p.114) bears pale cream flowers with deep orange-yellow throats. **'Sungold'** (illus. p.114) has dense clusters of dark orange-yellow flowers.

BULBOCODIUM
LILIACEAE/COLCHICACEAE

Genus of spring-flowering corms, related to *Colchicum* and with funnel-shaped flowers. Is particularly suitable for rock gardens and cool greenhouses. Requires an open, sunny site and well-drained soil. Propagate by seed in fall or by division in late summer and early fall.
B. vernum, illus. p.418.

BULBOPHYLLUM
ORCHIDACEAE

See also ORCHIDS.
B. careyanum. Evergreen, epiphytic orchid for an intermediate greenhouse. **H** 3in (8cm). Oval leaves are 3–4in (8–10cm) long. In spring produces tight sprays of many slightly fragrant, brown flowers, ¼in (0.5cm) across. Grows best in a hanging basket. Needs partial shade in summer. Z13–15 H11–10.

BUPHTHALMUM
COMPOSITAE/ASTERACEAE

Genus of summer-flowering perennials. Requires full sun; grows well in any but rich soil. Propagate by seed in spring or fall or by division in fall. Needs frequent division to curb invasiveness.
B. salicifolium, illus. p.276.
B. speciosum. See *Telekia speciosa*.

BUPLEURUM
UMBELLIFERAE/APIACEAE

Genus of perennials and evergreen shrubs, grown for their foliage and flowers. Grows well in coastal gardens. Needs full sun and well-drained soil. Propagate by semiripe cuttings in summer.
B. fruticosum, illus. p.139.

BUTIA
Yatay palm
ARECACEAE/PALMAE

Genus of evergreen palms, grown for their overall appearance. Grow in fertile, well-drained soil and in full light or partial shade. Water regularly, less in winter. Red spider mite may be a problem.
B. capitata, syn. *Cocos capitata* (Jelly palm). Slow-growing, evergreen palm. **H** 12–20ft (4–6m), **S** 10–15ft (3–5m). Feather-shaped leaves, 6ft (2m) or more long and composed of many leathery leaflets, are strongly arching to recurved. Z11 H11–10.

BUTOMUS
BUTOMACEAE

Genus of one species of deciduous, perennial, rushlike, marginal water plant, grown for its fragrant, cup-shaped flowers. Requires an open, sunny situation in up to 10in (25cm) depth of water. Propagate by division in spring or by seed in spring or late summer.
B. umbellatus, illus. p.438.

BUXUS
Boxwood, box
BUXACEAE

Genus of evergreen shrubs and trees, grown for their foliage and habit. Is excellent for edging, hedging and topiary work. Flowers are insignificant. Requires sun or semi-shade and any but waterlogged soil. Trim hedges in summer. Promote new growth by cutting back stems to 12in (30cm) or less in late spring. Propagate by semiripe cuttings in summer. ① Contact with boxwood sap may irritate skin.
B. balearica (Balearic boxwood), illus. p.145.
B. microphylla (Small-leaved boxwood). Evergreen, bushy shrub. **H** 3ft (1m), **S** 5ft (1.5m). Forms a dense, rounded mass of small, oblong, dark green leaves. Z6–9 H9–6. **'Green Pillow',** illus. p.167.
B. sempervirens (Common boxwood). Evergreen, bushy shrub or tree. **H** and **S** 15ft (5m). Produces leaves that are oblong, glossy and dark green. Is useful for hedging and screening. Z6–8 H8–6. **'Handsworthensis',** illus. p.144. **'Suffruticosa',** illus. p.167.
B. wallichiana (Himalayan boxwood). Slow-growing, evergreen, bushy shrub with open habit. **H** and **S** 6ft (2m). Produces long, narrow, glossy, bright green leaves. Z9–10 H10–8.

C

CABOMBA

CABOMBACEAE

Genus of deciduous or semievergreen, perennial, submerged water plants with finely divided foliage. Is suitable for aquariums. Prefers partial shade. Propagate by stem cuttings in spring or summer.

C. caroliniana (Fanwort, Fish grass, Washington grass). Deciduous or semievergreen, perennial, submerged water plant. **S** indefinite. Forms dense, spreading hummocks of fan-shaped, coarsely cut, bright green leaves. Is used as an oxygenating plant in aquariums or ponds. Z6–11 H11–6.

Cacalia. See *Emilia*.

CAESALPINIA

LEGUMINOSAE/CAESALPINIACEAE

Genus of deciduous or evergreen shrubs, trees and scrambling climbers, grown for their foliage and flowers. Needs full sun and fertile, well-drained soil. Propagate by softwood cuttings in summer or by seed in fall or spring.

C. gilliesii, syn. *Poinciana gilliesii*, illus. p.116.

C. pulcherrima, syn. *Poinciana pulcherrima* (Barbados pride). Evergreen, erect to spreading shrub or tree. **H** and **S** 10–20ft (3–6m). Has fernlike leaves composed of many small, mid-green leaflets. In summer bears cup-shaped, yellow flowers, 1¼in (3cm) wide, with very long, red anthers, in short, dense, erect racemes. Z9–11 H11–9.

CALADIUM

ARACEAE

Genus of perennials with tubers from which arise long-stalked, ornamental leaves. Requires partial shade and moist, rich soil. After leaves have died down, store tubers in a frost-free, dark place. Propagate by separating small tubers when planting in spring. ① Contact with all parts may irritate skin, and may cause mild stomach upset if ingested.

C. bicolor (fancy-leaf caladium). Z15 H11–4. **'Candidum'** is a tufted perennial. **H** and **S** to 36in (90cm). Triangular, green-veined, white leaves, to 18in (45cm) long, have arrow-shaped bases and long leaf stalks. Intermittently bears white spathes; small flowers clustered on spadix sometimes produce whitish berries. **'John Peed'** has purple stems and waxy, green leaves with metallic orange-red centers and scarlet veins. **'Pink Beauty'** illus. p.470. **'Pink Cloud'** has large, dark green leaves with mottled pink centers, and pink to white areas along the veins.

CALAMAGROSTIS

GRAMINEAE/POACEAE

See also GRASSES, BAMBOOS, RUSHES and SEDGES.

C. brachytricha, illus. p.284.

Calandrinia megarhiza of gardens. See *Claytonia megarhiza*.

CALANTHE

ORCHIDACEAE

See also ORCHIDS.

C. sieboldii. See *C. striata*.

C. striata, syn. *C. sieboldii*, illus. p.275.

C. vestita, illus. p.466. Deciduous, terrestrial orchid. **H** 24in (60cm). In winter bears sprays of many white flowers, 1½in (4cm) across, each with a large, red-marked lip. Has broadly oval, ribbed, soft leaves, 12in (30cm) long. In summer requires partial shade and regular feeding. H11–10.

CALATHEA

MARANTACEAE

Genus of frost-sensitive evergreen perennials, grown for their brightly colored and patterned leaves. Prefers a shaded, humid position, without fluctuations of temperature, in rich, well-drained soil. Water with rain- or filtered water, sparingly in low temperatures, but do not allow to dry out completely. Propagate by division in spring.

C. lindeniana. Evergreen, clump-forming perennial. **H** 3ft (1m), **S** 2ft (60cm). Lance-shaped, long-stalked, more or less upright leaves, 1ft (30cm) or more long, are dark green, with paler green, feathered midribs above and marked reddish-purple below. Intermittently bears short, erect spikes of 3-petaled, pale yellow flowers. Z14–15 H11–10.

C. majestica 'Roseolineata', syn. *C. ornata* 'Roseolineata'. Evergreen, clump-forming, stemless perennial. **H** to 6ft (2m), **S** to 5ft (1.5m). Narrowly oval, leathery leaves, to 2ft (60cm) long, are dark green, with close-set, fine, pink stripes along the lateral veins and reddish-purple below. Intermittently bears short, erect spikes of 3-petaled, white to mauve flowers. Z14–15 H11–1. **'Sanderiana'.** See *C. sanderiana*.

C. makoyana, illus. p.475.

C. oppenheimiana. See *Ctenanthe oppenheimiana*.

C. ornata 'Roseolineata'. See *C. majestica* 'Roseolineata'.

C. sanderiana, syn. *C. majestica* 'Sanderiana', illus. p.472.

C. zebrina, illus. p.475.

CALCEOLARIA

Pouch flower, Slipper flower

SCROPHULARIACEAE

Genus of annuals, biennials and evergreen perennials, subshrubs and scandent climbers, some of which are grown as annuals. Most prefer sun but some like a shady, cool site and moist but well-drained soil, incorporating sharp sand and compost, and dislike wet conditions in winter. Propagate by softwood cuttings in late spring or summer or by seed in fall.

C. acutifolia. See *C. polyrrhiza*.

C. Anytime Series. Compact, bushy annuals or biennials. **H** 8in (20cm), **S** 6in (15cm). Has oval, slightly hairy, mid-green leaves and, in spring–summer, heads of rounded, pouch-shaped flowers, 2in (5cm) long, in red and yellow shades, including bicolors. Z8–9 H6–1.

C. arachnoidea, illus. p.341.

C. 'Bright Bikinis'. Compact, bushy annual or biennial. **H** and **S** 8in (20cm). Has oval, slightly hairy, mid-green leaves, and

heads of small, rounded, pouch-shaped flowers in shades of yellow, orange or red in summer. Z8–9 H6–1.

C. darwinii. See *C. uniflora* var. *darwinii*.

C. fothergillii. Evergreen, clump-forming, short-lived perennial. **H** and **S** 5in (12cm). Has a rosette of rounded, light green leaves with hairy edges and, in summer, solitary pouch-shaped, sulfur-yellow flowers with crimson spots. Is good for a sheltered rock ledge or trough or in an alpine house. Needs gritty, rich, acidic soil. Is prone to aphid attack. Z8–9 H6–1.

C. integrifolia. Evergreen, upright subshrub, usually grown as an annual. **H** to 4ft (1.2m), **S** 2ft (60cm). In summer bears crowded clusters of pouch-shaped, yellow to red-brown flowers above oblong to elliptic, mid-green leaves, sometimes rust-colored beneath. Z8–9 H6–1. **'Sunshine'**, **H** and **S** 8in (20cm), is compact and bushy with bright golden-yellow flowers in late spring and summer.

C. 'John Innes', illus. p.277.

C. 'Monarch'. Group of bushy annuals or biennials. **H** and **S** 12in (30cm). Has oval, lightly hairy, mid-green leaves and, in spring–summer, bears heads of large, rounded, pouch-shaped flowers, 2in (5cm) long, in a wide range of colors. Z8–9 H6–1.

C. pavonii. Robust, evergreen, scandent climber. **H** 6ft (2m) or more. Has oval, serrated, soft-haired leaves with winged stalks. Pouch-shaped, yellow flowers with brown marks are produced in large trusses from late summer to winter. Z8–9 H6–1.

C. polyrrhiza, syn. *C. acutifolia*. Evergreen, prostrate perennial. **H** 1in (2.5cm), **S** 6in (15cm). Has rounded, hairy, mid-green leaves along flower stem, which bears pouch-shaped, purple-spotted, yellow flowers in summer. Is good for a shady rock garden. May also be propagated by division in fall or spring. Z8–9 H6–1.

C. tenella, illus. p.371.

C. uniflora var. darwinii, syn. *C. darwinii*. Evergreen, clump-forming, short-lived perennial. **H** 3in (8cm), **S** 4in (10cm). Bears rounded, wrinkled, glossy, dark green leaves. In late spring, flower stems carry pendent, pouch-shaped, yellow flowers with dark brown spots on lower lips and central, white bands. Is difficult to grow. Needs a sheltered, sunny site in moist, gritty, rich acidic soil. Is prone to attack by aphids. Z8–9 H6–1.

C. 'Walter Shrimpton', illus. p.372.

CALENDULA

Marigold

COMPOSITAE/ASTERACEAE

Genus of annuals and evergreen shrubs. Grow in sun or partial shade and in any well-drained soil. Dead-head regularly to prolong flowering. Propagate annuals by seed sown outdoors in spring or fall, shrubs by stem cuttings in summer. Annuals may self-seed. Cucumber mosaic virus and powdery mildew may cause problems.

C. officinalis (English marigold). Fast-growing, bushy annual. Tall cultivars, **H** and **S** 24in (60cm); dwarf forms, **H** and **S** 12in (30cm). All have lance-shaped, strongly aromatic, pale green leaves. Daisylike, single or double flower heads in a wide range of yellow and orange shades are produced from spring to fall. Z8–9 H6–1. **'Daisy May' (dwarf)** illus. p.321.

'Fiesta Gitana' Fiesta Gitana Group (dwarf), syn. *C. officinalis* 'Fiesta Gitana' illus. p.325. **'Geisha Girl' (tall)** illus. p.326. **Pacific Beauty Series 'Lemon Queen' (dwarf)** illus. p.322. See *C. officinalis* Fiesta Gitana Group.

CALIBRACHOA

SOLANACEAE

Genus of shrubby perennials, once included in *Petunia*, grown for their showy flowers. Is good as a hanging basket or container plant. Needs full sun and well-drained soil. Propagate by semiripe cuttings in summer or by seed in spring.

C. Cabaret Series CABARET APRICOT **('Balcabapt')** Mound-forming and trailing, prolific tender perennial, grown as an annual. **H** 5in (13cm), **S** 18in (45cm). Has twiggy stems with narrowly ovate, dark green leaves. Trumpet-shaped flowers, 1¼–1½in (3–4cm) across, flecked in apricot, cream and yellow, are borne in summer–fall. CABERET LIGHT PINK **('Balcablitpi')** illus. p.300.

C. Million Bells Series MILLION BELLS CHERRY PINK **('Sunbelrichipi'),** illus. p.306.

CALLA

ARACEAE

Genus of one species of deciduous or semievergreen, perennial, spreading, marginal water plant, grown for its foliage and showy spathes that surround insignificant flower clusters. Requires a sunny position, in mud or in shallow water to 10in (25cm) deep. Propagate by division in spring or by seed in late summer. ① Contact with the foliage may aggravate skin allergies.

C. palustris, illus. p.434.

CALLIANDRA

LEGUMINOSAE/MIMOSACEAE

Genus of evergreen trees, shrubs and scandent semi-climbers, grown for their flowers and overall appearance. Requires full sun or partial shade and well-drained soil. Water container plants freely when in full growth, much less when temperatures are low. To restrict growth, cut back stems by one-half to two-thirds after flowering. Propagate by seed sown indoors in spring. Whiteflies and mealy bug may be troublesome.

C. eriophylla, illus. p.453.

C. haematocephala (Red powder puff) is an evergreen, spreading shrub. **H** 10–20ft (3–6m), **S** 6–12ft (2–4m). Leaves have 16–24 leaflets. Flower heads comprising many white-stamened florets appear from late fall to spring. illus. p.454. Z12–15 H11–10.

CALLIANTHEMUM

RANUNCULACEAE

Genus of perennials, grown for their daisylike flowers and thick, dissected leaves. Is excellent for rock gardens and alpine houses. Needs sun and moist but well-drained soil. Propagate by seed when fresh.

C. coriandrifolium, syn. *C. rutifolium*. Prostrate perennial with upright flower stems. **H** 3in (8cm), **S** 8in (20cm). Leaves,

forming open rosettes, are long-stalked, very dissected and blue-green. In spring has short-stemmed, many-petaled, white flowers with yellow centers. Is susceptible to slugs. Z4–7 H7–1.
C. rutifolium. See *C. coriandrifolium.*

CALLICARPA
Beautyberry
VERBENACEAE/LAMIACEAE

Genus of deciduous, summer-flowering shrubs, grown for their small but striking, clustered fruits. Does best in full sun and fertile, well-drained soil. Propagate by softwood cuttings in summer.
C. bodinieri (Bodinier beautyberry). Deciduous, bushy shrub. **H** 10ft (3m), **S** 8ft (2.5m). Has oval, dark green leaves. Tiny, star-shaped, lilac flowers in mid-summer are followed by dense clusters of spherical, violet fruits. Z5–8 H8–3. **var. giraldii** illus. p.141.

CALLISIA
COMMELINACEAE

Genus of evergreen, prostrate perennials, grown for their ornamental foliage and trailing habit. Grow in full light, but out of direct sunlight, in fertile, well-drained soil. Propagate by tip cuttings in spring, either annually or when plants become straggly.
C. navicularis, syn. *Tradescantia navicularis.* Evergreen, low-growing perennial with creeping, rooting shoots. **H** 2–3in (5–8cm), **S** indefinite. Has 2 rows of oval, keeled leaves, 1in (2.5cm) long, sheathing the stem, and stalkless clusters of small, 3-petaled, pinkish-purple flowers in leaf axils in summer–fall. Z6–8 H8–6.
C. repens. Evergreen, creeping perennial with rooting stems. **H** 4in (10cm), **S** indefinite. Has densely packed leaves, sometimes white-banded and often purplish beneath. Rarely, has inconspicuous, white flowers in winter. Z14–15 H11–10.

CALLISTEMON
Bottlebrush
MYRTACEAE

Genus of evergreen shrubs, usually with narrow, pointed leaves, grown for their clustered flowers, which, with their profusion of long stamens, resemble bottlebrushes. Where marginally hardy, grow against a south- or west-facing wall or in a cool greenhouse. Requires full sun and fertile, well-drained soil. Propagate by semiripe cuttings in summer or by seed in fall or spring.
C. citrinus 'Splendens', illus. p.203.
C. pallidus, illus. p.139.
C. paludosus. See *C. sieberi.*
C. pityoides. Evergreen, compact, upright shrub. **H** 5ft (1.5m), **S** 3ft (1m). Fully hardy. Is densely covered with sharply pointed dark green leaves, and has short spikes of yellow flowers in mid- and late summer. Z12–15 H11–10.
C. rigidus, illus. p.137.
C. sieberi, syn. *C. paludosus.* Evergreen, bushy, dense shrub. **H** 5ft (1.5m), **S** 3ft (1m). Has short, narrowly lance-shaped, rigid, mid-green leaves and, from mid- to late summer, small clusters of pale yellow flowers. Z10–11 H11–10.

C. speciosus (Albany bottlebrush). Evergreen, bushy shrub. **H** and **S** 10ft (3m). Produces long, narrow, gray-green leaves. Cylindrical clusters of bright red flowers are produced in late spring and early summer. Z10–11 H11–10.
C. subulatus, illus. p.203.
C. viminalis (Weeping bottlebrush). Evergreen, arching shrub. **H** and **S** 15ft (5m). Narrowly oblong, bronze, young leaves mature to dark green. Bears clusters of bright red flowers in summer. Z9–11 H11–10.

CALLISTEPHUS
China aster
COMPOSITAE/ASTERACEAE

Genus of one species of annual. Requires sun, a sheltered position and fertile, well-drained soil. Tall cultivars need support; all should be dead-headed. Propagate by seed sown in a cold frame in spring; seed may also be sown outdoors in mid-spring. Wilt disease, viruses, root rot and aphids may be a problem.
C. chinensis. Moderately fast-growing, erect, bushy annual. Tall cultivars, **H** 24in (60cm), **S** 18in (45cm); intermediate, **H** 18in (45cm), **S** 12in (30cm); dwarf, **H** 10–12in (25–30cm), **S** 12–18in (30–45cm); very dwarf, **H** 8in (20cm), **S** 12in (30cm). All have oval, toothed, mid-green leaves and flower in summer and early fall. Different forms are available in a wide color range, including pink, red, blue and white. H9–1. **Duchesse Series (tall)** has incurved, chrysanthemum-like flower heads. **Milady Super Series (dwarf)** has incurved, fully double flower heads available either in mixed or single colors, illus. p.304, p.312. **Ostrich Plume Series (tall)** illus. p.303. **Pompon Series (tall)** has small, double flower heads. **Princess Series (tall)** has double flower heads with quilled petals.

CALLUNA
ERICACEAE

See also HEATHERS.
C. vulgaris. Evergreen, bushy shrub. **H** to 24in (60cm), **S** 18in (45cm). Slightly fleshy, linear leaves, in opposite and overlapping pairs, may range in color from bright green to many shades of gray, yellow, orange and red. Spikes of bell- to urn-shaped, single or double flowers are produced from mid-summer to late fall. Unlike *Erica,* most of the flower color derives from the sepals. The following cultivars are **H** 18in (45cm), have mid-green leaves and bear single flowers in late summer and early fall, unless otherwise stated. Z5–7 H7–5. **'Alba Plena',** **H** 12–18in (30–45cm), bears double, white flowers. **'Alexandra',** **H** 12in (30cm), **S** 16in (40cm), has an upright habit, dark green foliage, and deep crimson buds until early winter. **'Alicia',** **H** 12in (30cm), **S** 16in (40cm), has white buds until early winter, and a neat, compact habit. **'Allegro',** **H** 24in (60cm), is compact in habit and produces purple-red flowers. **'Alportii',** **H** 24–36in (60–90cm), has purple-red flowers. **'Anette',** **H** 14in (35cm), **S** 16in (40cm), has clear pink buds until early winter. **'Annemarie'** (illus. p.166), **H** 20in (50cm), **S** 24in (60cm), has double, rose-pink flowers, ideal for cutting. **'Anthony Davis'** has gray leaves

and white flowers. **'Beoley Gold'** (illus. p.166), **S** 20in (50cm), has golden foliage and white flowers. **'Beoley Silver',** **H** 16in (40cm), has silver foliage and white flowers. **'Blazeaway',** **H** 14in (35cm), **S** 24in (60cm), has gold foliage in summer that turns orange, then fiery red in winter. **'Bonfire Brilliance',** **H** 12in (30cm), has bright, flame-colored foliage and mauve-pink flowers. **'Boskoop',** **H** 12in (30cm), is compact with golden foliage that turns deep orange in winter and lilac-pink flowers. **'County Wicklow',** **H** 12in (30cm), **S** 14in (35cm), is compact with double, shell-pink flowers. **'Dark Beauty',** **H** 8in (20cm), **S** 14in (35cm), is neat and compact, and bears bright, semidouble, crimson flowers. **'Darkness',** **H** 16in (40cm), **S** 14in (35cm), is compact with crimson flowers. **'Dark Star'** (illus. p.166), **H** 8in (20cm), **S** 14in (35cm), has short racemes of semidouble, deep crimson flowers. **'Elsie Purnell'** is a spreading cultivar with grayish-green leaves and double, pale pink flowers. **'Finale'** bears dark pink flowers from late fall to early winter. **'Firefly',** **H** 20in (50cm), with deep mauve flowers, has foliage that is terra-cotta in summer, brick-red in winter. **'Foxii Nana',** **H** 6in (15cm), forms low mounds of bright green foliage and produces a few mauve-pink flowers. **'Fred J. Chapple'** has bright pink- and coral-tipped foliage in spring; mauve-pink flowers are borne on long stems. **'Golden Feather'** has bright yellow foliage, turning orange in winter, and mauve-pink flowers. **'Gold Haze'** has bright golden foliage and white flowers. **'Hammondii Aureifolia',** **H** 12in (30cm), **S** 16in (40cm), has white flowers. Foliage is light green, tipped yellow in spring and early summer. **'H.E. Beale',** **H** 20in (50cm), is one of the best double-flowered heathers, with pale pink flowers on long stems. **'J.H. Hamilton',** **H** 8in (20cm), **S** 16in (40cm), is compact with double, salmon-pink flowers. **'Joy Vanstone'** has golden foliage, turning orange and bronze, and mauve-pink flowers. **'Kerstin',** **H** 12in (30cm), produces mauve flowers and has downy, deep lilac-gray foliage in winter, tipped pale yellow and red in spring. **'Kinlochruel',** **H** 12in (30cm), **S** 14in (35cm), bears an abundance of large, double, white flowers. **'Loch Turret',** **H** 12in (30cm), has emerald-green foliage and produces white flowers in early summer. **'Mair's Variety',** an old cultivar, has white flowers on long spikes. **'Marleen'** is unusual in that its long-lasting, dark mauve flower buds, borne from early to late fall, do not open fully. **'Mullion',** **H** 10in (25cm), **S** 20in (50cm), is a spreading cultivar with rich mauve-pink flowers. **'Multicolor',** **H** 8in (20cm 8in), is compact with foliage in shades of yellow, orange, red and green year-round; flowers are mauve-pink. **'My Dream',** syn. *C. vulgaris* 'Snowball', **H** 20in (50cm), produces double, white flowers that are borne on long, tapering stems. **'Peter Sparkes'** (illus. p.166), **H** 20in (50cm), **S** 22in (55cm), bears double, deep pink flowers. **'Robert Chapman'** is a spreading cultivar and grown mainly for its foliage, which is golden-yellow in summer, turning orange and brilliant red in winter; flowers are mauve-pink. **'Ruth Sparkes',**

H 10in (25cm), has golden foliage and white flowers. **'Silver Knight',** **H** 12in (30cm), is of upright habit with gray leaves and mauve-pink flowers. **'Silver Queen',** **H** 16in (40cm), **S** 22in (55cm), is a spreading cultivar with dark mauve-pink flowers. **'Sir John Charrington'** has bright-colored foliage, varying from golden-yellow in summer to orange and red in winter, and dark mauve-pink flowers. **'Sister Anne',** **H** 6in (15cm), has gray leaves and pale mauve-pink flowers. **'Snowball'.** See *C. vulgaris* 'My Dream'. **'Spring Cream'** has bright green leaves, which have cream tips in spring, and white flowers. **'Spring Torch',** **H** 16in (40cm), **S** 24in (60cm), has mauve flowers with cream, orange and red tips in spring. **'Sunset',** **H** 10in (25cm), has brightly colored foliage, changing from golden-yellow in spring to orange in summer and fiery red in winter; flowers are mauve-pink. **'Tib'** (illus. p.166), **H** 12in (30cm), **S** 16in (40cm), is the earliest flowering double cultivar, producing small, double, deep pink flowers in early summer. **'White Lawn',** **H** 4in (10cm), is a creeping cultivar with bright green foliage and white flowers on long stems; is suitable for a rock garden. **'Wickwar Flame'** (illus. p.166) is primarily a foliage plant with leaves in shades of yellow, orange and flame that are particularly effective in winter; flowers are mauve-pink.

CALOCEDRUS
CUPRESSACEAE

See also CONIFERS.
C. decurrens, syn. *Libocedrus decurrens,* illus. p.101.

Calocephalus brownii. See *Leucophyta brownii.*

CALOCHONE
RUBIACEAE

Genus of evergreen, scrambling climbers, grown for their flowers. Needs full light and rich, well-drained soil. Water regularly, less in cold weather. Needs tying to a support. Thin out stems after flowering. Propagate by semiripe cuttings in summer.
C. redingii. Moderately vigorous, evergreen, scrambling climber. **H** 10–15ft (3–5m). Has oval, pointed, hairy leaves, 3–5in (7–12cm) long. Trusses of primrose-shaped, red to orange-pink flowers are produced in winter. Z14–15 H11–10.

CALOCHORTUS
Cat's ears, Fairy lanterns, Mariposa lilies
LILIACEAE

Genus of bulbs, grown for their spring and summer flowers. Needs a sheltered, sunny site and well-drained soil. In cold, damp climates, cover or lift spring-flowering species when dormant, or grow in cold frames or cool greenhouses. After flowering, remove bulbils for propagation. Propagate by seed or bulbils: spring-flowering species in fall, summer-flowering species in spring.
C. albus (Fairy lantern). Spring-flowering bulb. **H** 8–20in (20–50cm), **S** 2–4in (5–10cm). Has long, narrow, erect, gray-green leaves near the base of the loosely branched stem. Each branch bears a pendent, globose, white or pink flower. Z6–10 H10–6.

C

CALODENDRUM

C. **barbatus**, syn. *Cyclobothra lutea*, illus. p.412.

C. **luteus**, illus. p.406.

C. **monophyllus.** Summer-flowering bulb. **H** 3–8in (8–20cm), **S** 2in (5cm). Has an erect, branched stem with 1–3 slender leaves and 1 long, narrow basal leaf. Bears cup-shaped, deep yellow flowers, often with a reddish mark on the claws. Petals are fringed and densely bearded. Z7–10 H9–6.

C. **splendens.** Late spring-flowering bulb. **H** 8–24in (20–60cm), **S** 2–4in (5–10cm). Bears 1 or 2 linear, erect leaves near base of branched stem and 1–4 upward-facing, saucer-shaped, pale purple flowers, 2–3in (5–7cm) across, with a darker blotch at the base of each of the 3 large petals. Z8–10 H9–6.

C. **superbus**, illus. p.409.

C. **venustus**, illus. p.399.

C. **vestae.** Late spring-flowering bulb. **H** 8–24in (20–60cm), **S** 2–4in (5–10cm). Is similar to *C. splendens*, but flowers are white or purple, with a rust-brown mark near the base of each of the 3 large petals. Z5–10 H10–5.

C. **weedii.** Summer-flowering bulb. **H** 12–24in (30–60cm), **S** 2–4in (5–10cm). Has a linear, erect leaf near base of stem. Produces usually 2 upright, saucer-shaped, orange-yellow flowers, 1½–2in (4–5cm) across, with brown lines and flecks and hairy inside. Z7–10 H9–6.

CALODENDRUM

RUTACEAE

Genus of evergreen trees, grown for their flowers, which are produced mainly in spring-summer. Needs full light and fertile, moist but well-drained soil. Water container specimens freely when in full growth, less at other times. Tolerates some pruning. Propagate by seed in spring or by semiripe cuttings in summer.

C. **capense** (Cape chestnut). Fairly fast-growing, evergreen, rounded tree. **H** and **S** to 50ft (15m) or more. Has oval leaves patterned with translucent dots. Terminal panicles of 5-petaled, light pink to deep mauve flowers are produced from spring to early summer. Z12–15 H12–10.

CALOMERIA

SYN. HUMEA

COMPOSITAE/ASTERACEAE

Genus of perennials and evergreen shrubs. Only *C. amaranthoides* is cultivated, usually as a biennial. Needs sun and fertile, well-drained soil. Propagate by seed sown in a cold frame in mid-summer.

C. **amaranthoides**, syn. *C. elegans* (Incense plant). Erect, branching biennial. **H** to 6ft (1.8m), **S** 3ft (90cm). Has lance-shaped leaves and heads of tiny, pink, brownish-red or crimson flowers, with a strong fragrance of incense, in summer–fall. Z12–15 H11–10.

C. **elegans.** See *C. amaranthoides*.

Calonyction aculeatum. See *Ipomoea alba*.

CALOSCORDUM

LILIACEAE/ALLIACEAE

Genus of one species of summer-flowering bulb, related and similar to *Allium*. Is suitable for rock gardens. Needs an open, sunny situation and well-drained soil. Lies dormant in winter. Propagate in early spring by seed or division before growth starts.

C. **neriniflorum**, syn. *Nothoscordum neriniflorum*. Clump-forming bulb. **H** 4–10in (10–25cm), **S** 3–4in (8–10cm). Threadlike, semierect, basal leaves die down at flowering time. Each leafless stem produces a loose head of 10–20 small, funnel-shaped, pinkish-red flowers in late summer. Z5–10 H10–5.

CALOTHAMNUS

MYRTACEAE

Genus of evergreen, summer-flowering shrubs, grown for their flowers and overall appearance. Thrives in a dryish, airy environment. Requires full sun and well-drained, sandy soil. Water container plants moderately when in full growth, less at other times. Propagate by seed or semiripe cuttings in summer.

C. **quadrifidus** (Common net bush). Erect to spreading, evergreen shrub. **H** 6–12ft (2–4m), **S** 6–15ft (2–5m). Has linear, grayish to dark green or gray leaves. Irregular, axillary, one-sided spikes of rich red, feathery flowers, 1in (2.5cm) long, are produced from late spring to fall, often forming clusters, 8in (20cm) or more across, around the stems. Z12–15 H11–10.

CALTHA

RANUNCULACEAE

Genus of deciduous, perennial, marginal water plants, bog plants and rock garden plants, grown for their flowers. Most prefer an open, sunny position. Smaller-growing species are suitable for rock gardens, troughs and alpine houses and require moist but well-drained soil; larger species are best in marginal conditions. Propagate species by seed in fall or by division in fall or early spring, selected forms by division in fall or early spring.

C. **leptosepala**, illus. p.435.

C. **palustris**, illus. p.444. **var. alba**, syn. *C. palustris* 'Alba' is a compact, deciduous, perennial, marginal water plant. **H** 9in (22cm), **S** 12in (30cm). Has rounded, glossy, dark green leaves, and bears solitary, white flowers, with yellow stamens, in early spring, often before the foliage develops. **'Alba'.** See *C. palustris* var. *alba*. **'Flore Pleno'.** See *C. palustris* 'Plena'. **'Plena'**, syn. *C. palustris* 'Flore Pleno', illus. p.444.

CALYCANTHUS

CALYCANTHACEAE

Genus of deciduous, summer-flowering shrubs, grown for their purplish- or brownish-red flowers with strap-shaped petals. Requires sun or light shade and fertile, deep, moist but well-drained soil. Propagate by softwood cuttings in summer or by seed in fall.

C. **floridus** (Allspice, Sweetshrub). Deciduous, bushy shrub. **H** and **S** 6ft (2m). Has oval, aromatic, dark green leaves and, from early to mid-summer, fragrant, brown-red flowers with masses of spreading petals. Z5–9 H9–1.

C. **occidentalis**, illus. p.137.

CALYPSO

ORCHIDACEAE

See also ORCHIDS.

C. **bulbosa.** Deciduous, terrestrial orchid. **H** 2–8in (5–20cm). Cormlike stem produces a single, oval, pleated leaf, 1¼–4in (3–10cm) long. Purplish-pink flowers, ⅝–¾in (1.5–2cm) long, with hairy, purple-blotched, white or pale pink lips, are produced singly in late spring or early summer. Requires a damp, partially shaded position with a mulch of leaf mold. Z6–9 H9–6.

CAMASSIA

Camass

LILIACEAE/ASPARAGACEAE

Genus of summer-flowering bulbs, suitable for borders and pond margins. Requires sun or partial shade and deep, moist soil. Plant bulbs in fall, 4in (10cm) deep. Lies dormant in fall–winter. Propagate by seed in fall or by division in late summer. If seed is not required, cut off stems after flowering.

C. **esculenta.** See *C. quamash*.

C. **leichtlinii**, illus. p.383. **'Semiplena'** is a tuft-forming, summer-flowering bulb. **H** 3–5ft (1–1.5m), **S** 8–12in (20–30cm). Has long, narrow, erect, basal leaves. Each leafless stem bears a dense spike of narrow-petaled, double, creamy-white flowers, 1½–3in (4–8cm) across.

C. **quamash**, syn. *C. esculenta*, illus. p.411.

CAMELLIA

THEACEAE

Genus of evergreen shrubs and trees, grown for their flowers and foliage. Flowers are classified according to the following types: single, semidouble, anemone-form, peony-form, rose-form, formal double and irregular double. See feature panel pp.124–5 for illustrations and descriptions. Grows well against walls and in containers. Most forms prefer a sheltered position and semi-shade. Well-drained, neutral to acidic soil is essential. Prune to shape after flowering. Propagate by semiripe or hardwood cuttings from mid-summer to early winter or by grafting in late winter or early spring. Aphids, thrips and scale insects may cause problems under glass.

C. **'Black Lace'**, illus. p.121. Slow-growing, dense, upright shrub. **H** 5–8ft (1.5–2.5m), **S** 3–8ft (1–2.5m). Has ovate, dark green leaves, 3in (8cm) long, and large, formal double, deep velvet-red flowers from early to late spring. Z7–8 H8–7.

C. **chrysantha.** See *C. nitidissima*.

C. **'Cornish Snow'**, illus. p.120. Fast-growing, evergreen, upright, bushy shrub. **H** 10ft (3m), **S** 5ft (1.5m). Has lance-shaped leaves, bronze when young, maturing to dark green. In early spring bears a profusion of small, cup-shaped, single, white flowers. Z7–8 H8–7.

C. **cuspidata.** Evergreen, upright shrub becoming bushy with age. **H** 10ft (3m), **S** 5ft (1.5m). Has small, lance-shaped leaves, bronze when young, maturing to purplish-green. Small, cup-shaped, single, pure white flowers are freely produced from leaf axils in early spring. Z7–8 H8–7.

C. **'Dr. Clifford Parks'.** Evergreen, spreading shrub. **H** 12ft (4m), **S** 8ft (2.5m).

In mid-spring has large, flame-red flowers, often semidouble, peony- and anemone-form on the same plant. Leaves are large, oval and dark green. Z7–8 H8–7.

C. **'Francie L.'.** Vigorous shrub with long, fan-shaped branches. **H** 15ft (5m), **S** 20ft (6m). Leaves are lance-shaped and dark green, 2½–4in (6–10cm) long. Has large, semidouble, salmon-red to deep rose-red flowers from late winter to late spring. Z7–8 H8–7.

C. **'Freedom Bell'**, illus. p.121. Evergreen, dense, rounded shrub. **H** and **S** 7ft (2.2m). Has masses of semidouble, bright red flowers, from late winter to early spring, and ovate, glossy, rich green leaves. Z7–8 H8–7.

C. **granthamiana.** Evergreen, open shrub. **H** to 10ft (3m), **S** 6ft (2m). Oval, leathery leaves are crinkly and glossy, deep green. In late fall bears large, saucer-shaped, single, white flowers, to 7in (18cm) across, with up to 8 broad petals. Z7–8 H8–7.

C. **hiemalis.** Evergreen, upright, bushy shrub. **H** 6–10ft (2–3m), **S** 5ft (1.5m). Has small, lance-shaped leaves and fragrant, single, cup-shaped, semi- or irregular double, white, pink or red flowers borne in late fall and winter. Is good for hedging. Z7–8 H8–7.

C. **hongkongensis.** Evergreen, bushy shrub or tree. **H** to 10ft (3m), **S** 6ft (2m). Lance-shaped leaves, 4in (10cm) long, are dark red when young, maturing to dark green. Bears cup-shaped, single, deep crimson flowers, velvety beneath, in late spring. Z7–8 H8–7.

C. **'Innovation'.** Evergreen, open, spreading shrub. **H** 15ft (5m), **S** 10ft (3m). Has large, oval, leathery leaves and, in spring, produces large, peony-form, lavender-shaded, wine-red flowers with twisted petals. Z7–8 H8–7.

C. **'Inspiration'**, illus. p.121. Evergreen, upright shrub. **H** 12ft (4m), **S** 6ft (2m). Leaves are oval and leathery. Saucer-shaped, semidouble, phlox-pink flowers are freely produced in spring. Z7–8 H8–7.

C. **japonica** (Japanese camellia). Evergreen shrub or small tree that is very variable in habit, foliage and floral form. **H** 30ft (10m), **S** 25ft (8m). Numerous cultivars are available; they are spring-flowering unless otherwise stated. Z7–8 H8–7. **'Adolphe Audusson'** (illus. p.121) is a very reliable, old cultivar that is suitable for all areas and will withstand lower temperatures than most other variants. Produces large, saucer-shaped, semidouble, dark red flowers with prominent, yellow stamens. Leaves are broadly lance-shaped and dark green. **'Alba Plena'** (illus. p.120) has an erect habit with elliptic, mid-green leaves and large, formal double, white flowers. **'Alba Simplex'** is bushy in habit with broadly lance-shaped, mid-to yellow-green leaves and cup-shaped, single, white flowers in early spring. **'Alexander Hunter'**, an upright, compact shrub, has flattish, single, deep crimson flowers, with some petaloids, and lance-shaped, dark green leaves. **'Althaeiflora'** has a vigorous, bushy habit, large, peony-form, dark red flowers and broadly oval, very dark green leaves. **'Apollo'**, syn. *C. japonica* 'Paul's Apollo' is a vigorous, branching shrub that produces semidouble, red flowers sometimes blotched with white.

C

Leaves are glossy, dark green. **'Berenice Boddy'** is a vigorous shrub that bears semidouble, light pink flowers amid lance-shaped, dark green leaves. **'Betty Sheffield Supreme'** is upright in habit with lance-shaped, mid-green leaves. Irregular double flowers have white petals bordered with shades of rose-pink. **'Bob's Tinsie'** (illus. p.121) has a dense, upright habit, and bears miniature, anemone-form, brilliant red flowers from early to late spring. **'Brushfield's Yellow'** (illus. p.121) has an erect, compact habit, elliptic, dark green leaves and anemone-form, cream flowers, each with a pale yellow center. **'Coquettii',** syn. *C. japonica* 'Glen 40' is a slow-growing, erect shrub. In early and mid-spring bears profuse, medium to large, deep red flowers, sometimes formal double, sometimes peony-form. Z7–9 H9–7. **'Donckelaeri'.** See *C. japonica* 'Masayoshi'. **'Elegans'** has a spreading habit and anemone-form, deep rose-pink flowers with central petaloids often variegated white. Leaves are broadly lance-shaped and dark green. **'Glen 40'.** See *C. japonica* 'Coquettii'. **'Gloire de Nantes'** is an upright shrub, becoming bushy with age, that bears flattish to cup-shaped, semidouble, bright rose-pink flowers over a long period. Has oval to lance-shaped, glossy, dark green leaves. **'Guilio Nuccio'** is an upright, free-flowering cultivar that spreads with age. Produces large, cup-shaped, semidouble, rose-red flowers with wavy petals and often a confused center of petaloids and golden stamens. Dark green leaves are lance-shaped and occasionally have "fishtail" tips. **'Hagoromo',** syn. *C. japonica* 'Magnoliiflora' (illus. p.120) has a bushy habit and flattish to cup-shaped, semidouble, blush-pink flowers. Twisted, light green leaves point downward. **'Janet Waterhouse'** (illus. p.120) is strong-growing and has semidouble, white flowers with golden anthers borne amid dark green foliage. **'Julia Drayton'** has an upright habit and large, crimson flowers varying from formal double to rose-form. Dark green leaves are oval to lance-shaped and slightly twisted. **'Jupiter'** is an upright shrub that bears lance-shaped, dark green leaves and large, saucer-shaped, single, pinkish-red flowers with golden stamens. **'Kumasaka',** syn. *C. japonica* 'Lady Marion' has an upright habit with narrowly lance-shaped, mid-green leaves. Produces formal double, or occasionally peony-form, deep rose-pink flowers. **'Lady Marion'.** See *C. japonica* 'Kumasaka'. **'Lady Vansittart'** is upright, with unusual, holly-like, twisted, mid-green foliage. Saucer-shaped, semidouble, white flowers are flushed rose-pink; flower color is variable and often self-colored mutations appear. **'Lavinia Maggi'** (illus. p.121) has an upright habit and formal double, white flowers striped with pink and carmine. Sometimes sports red flowers. **'Magnoliiflora'.** See *C. japonica* 'Hagoromo'. **'Margaret Davis'** (illus. p.121) is a spreading cultivar, with oval to lance-shaped, dark green leaves. Has irregular double blooms with ruffled, creamy-white petals, often lined with pink. Edges of each petal are bright rose-red. **'Masayoshi',** syn. *C. japonica* 'Donckelaeri' is slow-growing, bushy and pendulous with saucer-shaped, semidouble, red flowers, often white-marbled. Has lance-shaped, dark green leaves. **'Mathotiana'** illus. p.137. **'Mrs. D.W. Davis'** is a dense, spreading cultivar that bears very large, pendulous, cup-shaped, semidouble, delicate pink flowers that are backed by oval to lance-shaped, dark green leaves. **'Nobilissima'** (illus. p.120) has a semierect habit, elliptic, dark green leaves and peony-form, lemon-tinted, white flowers in late winter and early spring. **'Paul's Apollo'.** See *C. japonica* 'Apollo'. **'R.L. Wheeler'** has robust, upright growth; large, broadly oval, leathery, very dark green leaves and very large, flattish, anemone-form to semidouble, rose-pink flowers, with distinctive rings of golden stamens, often including some petaloids. **'Rubescens Major'** is an upright cultivar, becoming bushy with age, with oval to lance-shaped, dark green leaves. Bears formal double, crimson-veined, rose-red flowers. Z7–9 H9–7. **'Sieboldii'.** See *C. japonica* 'Tricolor'. **'Tomorrow's Dawn'** is similar to 'Tomorrow Park Hill', but produces pale pink flowers, each with a white border and frequently red-streaked. **'Tomorrow Park Hill',** one of the best of many mutations of 'Tomorrow', is of vigorous, upright habit. Has lance-shaped, mid-green leaves and bears irregular double flowers with deep pink, outer petals gradually fading to soft pink centers that are often variegated with white. **'Tricolor',** syn. *C. japonica* 'Sieboldii' (illus. p.121) has bright green, crinkled, holly-like leaves, and bears medium, single or semidouble, red flowers, striped pink and white, in early spring.

***C.* 'Leonard Messel',** illus. p.121. Evergreen, open shrub. **H** 12ft (4m), **S** 8ft (2.5m). Has large, oval, leathery, dark green leaves. In spring bears a profusion of large, flattish to cup-shaped, semidouble, rose-pink flowers. Z7–8 H8–7.

***C.* x *maliflora*.** Evergreen, upright, bushy shrub. **H** 6ft (2m), **S** 3ft (1m). Has small, lance-shaped, thin-textured, light green leaves and, in spring, produces flattish to cup-shaped, semidouble, pale pink- or white-centered flowers with rose-pink margins. Z7–8 H8–7.

***C. nitidissima*,** syn. *C. chrysantha*. Fast-growing, evergreen, open shrub or tree. **H** 20ft (6m) or more, **S** 10ft (3m). Has large, oval, leathery, veined leaves. Small, stalked, cup-shaped, single, clear yellow flowers are produced from leaf axils in spring. Z7–8 H8–7.

C. oleifera (Tea-oil camellia). Evergreen, bushy shrub. **H** 6ft (2m), **S** 5ft (1.5m). Leaves are oval and dull green. Has cup-shaped, single, sometimes pinkish, white flowers in early spring. Z6–9 H9–5.

***C. reticulata*.** Evergreen, open, treelike shrub. **H** 30ft (10m) or more, **S** 15ft (5m). Has large, oval, leathery leaves; large, saucer-shaped, single, rose-pink and salmon-red flowers are borne in spring. Needs shelter. Z7–8 H8–7. **'Arch of Triumph'** bears very large, loose peony-form, orange-tinted, crimson-pink flowers. **'Butterfly Wings'.** See *C. reticulata* 'Houye Diechi'. **'Captain Rawes'** (illus. p.121) has a profusion of large, semidouble, carmine-rose blooms. **'Houye Diechi',** syn. *C. reticulata* 'Butterfly Wings' produces very large, flattish to cup-shaped, semidouble, rose-pink flowers with wavy, central petals. **'Mandalay Queen'** has large, semidouble, deep rose-pink flowers. **'Robert Fortune'.** See *C. reticulata* 'Songzilin'. **'Songzilin',** syn. *C. reticulata* 'Robert Fortune' is upright and has large, formal double, deep red flowers.

***C. rosiflora*.** Evergreen, spreading shrub. **H** and **S** 3ft (1m). Leaves are oval and dark green. In spring bears small, saucer-shaped, single, rose-pink flowers. Z7–8 H8–7.

***C. saluenensis*.** Fast-growing, evergreen, bushy shrub. **H** to 12ft (4m), **S** to 8ft (2.5m). Has lance-shaped, stiff, dull green leaves. Cup-shaped, single, white to rose-red flowers are freely produced in early spring. Some forms may withstand lower temperatures. Z7–8 H8–7.

C. sasanqua (Sasanqua camellia). Fast-growing, evergreen, dense, upright shrub. **H** 10ft (3m), **S** 5ft (1.5m). Has lance-shaped, glossy, bright green leaves. In fall bears a profusion of fragrant, flattish to cup-shaped, single, rarely semidouble, white flowers; they may occasionally be pink or red. Does best in a hot, sunny site. Z7–8 H8–7. **'Hugh Evans'** is vigorous and has an upright habit, so can be trained against a wall, and bears single, pale pink flowers in winter. **'Jean May'** produces large, peony-form to double, pale pink flowers, from winter to early spring. **'Narumigata'** has large, cup-shaped, single, white flowers, sometimes pink-flushed. **'Shishigashira'** has small, semidouble to rose-form, double, pinkish-red flowers.

***C.* 'Satan's Robe'.** Vigorous, erect shrub. **H** 10–15ft (3–5m), **S** 6–10ft (2–3m). Leaves are broadly elliptic, glossy and dark green, 5–6in (12–16cm) long. From early to late spring produces large, semidouble, bright carmine-red flowers, with yellow stamens. Z7–8 H8–7.

***C.* 'Shiro-wabisuke'.** Slow-growing, compact shrub. **H** 8ft (2.5m), **S** 5ft (1.5m). Has narrow, mid-green leaves. From mid-winter to early spring produces small, single, bell-shaped, white flowers. Z7–8 H8–7.

***C.* 'Spring Festival',** illus. p.121. Evergreen, upright shrub. **H** 6–13ft (2–4m), **S** 2–6ft (0.6–2m). Has elliptic, dark green leaves. Miniature, formal double, pink flowers, maturing to pale pink, are produced in mid-spring. Z7–8 H8–7.

***C. tsaii*.** Evergreen, bushy shrub. **H** 12ft (4m), **S** 10ft (3m). Small, lance-shaped, light green leaves turn bronze with age. Small, cup-shaped, single, white flowers are freely produced in spring. Z7–8 H8–7.

***C.* x *vernalis*.** Fast-growing, evergreen, upright shrub. **H** to 10ft (3m), **S** 5ft (1.5m). Has lance-shaped, bright green leaves and, in late winter, fragrant, flattish to cup-shaped, single, white, pink or red flowers. Some forms produce irregular double flowers. Z7–8 H8–7.

***C.* 'William Hertrich'.** Strong-growing, evergreen, open shrub. **H** 15ft (5m), **S** 10ft (3m). Is free-flowering with large, flattish to cup-shaped, semidouble blooms of a bright cherry-red in spring. Petal formation is very irregular, and petals often form a confused center with only a few golden stamens. Leaves are large, oval and deep green. Z7–8 H8–7.

***C.* x *williamsii*. 'Anticipation'** Robust, evergreen, upright shrub. **H** 10ft (3m), **S** 5ft (1.5m). Has lance-shaped, dark green leaves. Large, peony-form, deep rose-pink blooms are freely produced in spring. Z7–9 H9–7. **'Bow Bells', H** 12ft (4m), **S** 8ft (2.5m), has a spreading habit with small, mid-green leaves and, in early spring, masses of cup-shaped, single, rose-pink flowers with deeper pink centers and veins. **'Brigadoon'** is a bushy shrub, bearing semidouble, rose-pink flowers with broad, down-curving petals. **'Debbie'** (illus. p.121) bears large, peony-form, rose-pink flowers. Z7–8 H8–7. **'Donation'** (illus. p.121) is a compact, upright plant that is very floriferous, with large, cup-shaped, semidouble, pink flowers. Z7–8 H8–7. **'Dream Boat'** has a spreading habit, and bears medium, formal double, pale purplish-pink flowers, with incurved petals, in mid-spring. **'E.G. Waterhouse'** (illus. p.122) is an upright, free-flowering cultivar bearing formal double, pink flowers among pale green foliage. **'Elizabeth de Rothschild'** is vigorous and upright; cup-shaped, semidouble, rose-pink flowers are produced among glossy foliage. **'Elsie Jury'** has glossy, deep green leaves and large, full peony-form, clear pink flowers. **'Francis Hanger'** has an upright habit and bears single, white flowers with gold stamens. **'George Blandford'** is spreading and bears semidouble, bright crimson-pink flowers in early spring. **'Golden Spangles'** is a cup-shaped, single, deep pink cultivar with unusual, variegated foliage, yellowish in centers of leaves with dark green margins. **'J.C. Williams'** (illus. p.121) is of pendulous habit when mature and bears cup-shaped, single, pink flowers from early winter to late spring. Z7–8 H8–7. **'Joan Trehane'** has strong, upright growth and large, rose-form, double, rose-pink flowers. **'Jury's Yellow'** (illus. p.121) is narrow and erect, bearing medium, anemone-form, white flowers, with centers of yellow petaloids. Z7–8 H8–7. **'Ruby Wedding'** produces anemone to peony-form, vivid red flowers, which are sometimes specked white in the center. **'Saint Ewe'** has glossy, light green foliage and funnel-shaped, single, deep pink flowers. **'Water Lily'** (illus. p.121) is an upright, compact cultivar with dark green leaves and bears formal double, mid-pink flowers with incurving petals in mid- to late spring. Z7–8 H8–7. **'Wilber Foss'** is rounded with dark green foliage and large, broad, peony-form, brilliant pink-red flowers.

CAMPANULA

Bellflower

CAMPANULACEAE

Genus of spring- and summer-flowering annuals, biennials and perennials, some of which are evergreen. Grows in sun or shade, but delicate flower colors are preserved best in shade. Most forms thrive in moist but well-drained soil. Propagate by softwood or basal cuttings in summer or by seed or division in fall or spring. Is prone to slug attack, and rust may be a problem in fall.

***C. alliariifolia*,** illus. p.241. Mound-forming perennial. **H** 24in (60cm), **S** 20in (50cm). Has heart-shaped leaves, above which rise nodding, bell-shaped, creamy-white flowers borne along arching, wiry stems throughout summer. Z3–7 H7–1.

C. armena, syn. *Symphyandra armena.* Upright or spreading perennial. **H** 1–2ft (30–60cm), **S** 1ft (30cm). Produces panicles of upright, bell-shaped, blue or white flowers in summer. Leaves are oval, irregularly toothed, hairy and mid-green. Z7–9 H9–7.
C. barbata, illus. p.342.
C. betulifolia. Prostrate, slender-stemmed perennial. **H** 3/4in (2cm), **S** 12in (30cm). In summer, long, branching flower stems each bear a cluster of open bell-shaped, single, white to pink flowers, deep pink outside. Leaves are wedge-shaped. Z5–8 H8–5.
***C.* 'Birch Hybrid',** illus. p.368.
C. x burghaltii. See *C.* 'Burghaltii'.
***C.* 'Burghaltii',** syn. *C. x burghaltii.* Mound-forming perennial. **H** 24in (60cm), **S** 12in (30cm). Leaves are oval, soft and leathery. Produces long, pendent, funnel-shaped, pale lavender flowers on erect, wiry stems in summer. May need staking. Z4–8 H8–1.
C. carpatica (Carpathian harebell). Clump-forming perennial. **H** 3–4in (8–10cm), **S** to 12in (30cm). Leafy, branching stems bear rounded to oval, toothed leaves and, in summer, broadly bell-shaped, blue or white flowers. Z4–7 H7–1. **'Bressingham White'** illus. p.360. **'Jewel'** illus. p.367. **'Turbinata',** syn. *C. carpatica* var. *turbinata* has pale lavender flowers. **var. *turbinata.*** See *C. carpatica* 'Turbinata'.
C. cochleariifolia, syn. *C. pusilla,* illus. p.369.
***C.* 'G.F. Wilson',** illus. p.368.
C. garganica. Spreading perennial. **H** 2in (5cm), **S** 12in (30cm). Has small, ivy-shaped leaves along stems. Bears clusters of star-shaped, single, pale lavender flowers from leaf axils in summer. Makes an excellent plant for a wall or slope. Z4–7 H7–1. **'W.H. Paine'** has bright lavender-blue flowers, each with a white eye.
***C. glomerata* 'Superba',** illus. p.241. Vigorous, clump-forming perennial. **H** 2 1/2ft (75cm), **S** 3ft (1m) or more. Has dense, rounded heads of large, bell-shaped, purple flowers borne in summer. Bears oval leaves in basal rosettes and on flower stems. Must be divided and replanted regularly. Z3–8 H8–1.
C. x haylodgensis. See *C. x haylodgensis* 'Plena'. **'Plena',** syn. *C. x haylodgensis.* is a spreading perennial. **H** 2in (5cm), **S** 8in (20cm). Has small, heart-shaped leaves and, in summer, pomponlike, double, deep lavender-blue flowers. Is suitable for a rock garden or wall. Z5–8 H8–5.
C. isophylla (Italian bellflower). Evergreen, dwarf, trailing perennial. **H** 4in (10cm), **S** 12in (30cm). In summer, star-shaped, blue or white flowers are borne above small, heart-shaped, toothed leaves. Is ideal for a hanging basket. Z13–15 H9–1. **Kristal Hybrids 'Stella Blue',** **H** 6–8in (15–20cm), **S** to 12in (30cm), is compact and free-flowering; large, upright, saucer-shaped, pale blue flowers are produced in mid-summer.
***C.* 'Joe Elliott'.** Mound-forming perennial. **H** 3in (8cm), **S** 5in (12cm). In summer, large, funnel-shaped, mid-lavender-blue flowers almost obscure small, heart-shaped, downy, gray-green leaves. Is good for an alpine house, trough or rock garden. Needs well-drained, alkaline soil. Protect from winter moisture. Is prone to slug attack. Z5–8 H8–5.
***C.* 'Kent Belle'.** Sturdy, spreading but clump-forming perennial. **H** 28in (70cm), **S** 18in (45cm) or more. Has rounded, toothed, glossy, mid-green leaves. In summer produces large, pendent, bell-shaped, violet-blue flowers. Z5–9 H9–5.
C. lactiflora (Milky bellflower). Upright, branching perennial. **H** 4ft (1.2m), **S** 2ft (60cm). In summer, slender stems bear racemes of large, nodding, bell-shaped, blue, occasionally pink or white flowers. Leaves are narrowly oval. Needs staking on a windy site. Z5–7 H7–5. **'Loddon Anna'** (illus. p.241) has soft dusty-pink flowers. **'Prichard's Variety'** (illus. p.241) has violet-blue flowers from early summer to late fall
C. latifolia (Great bellflower). **'Amethyst'** Clump-forming, spreading perennial. **H** 36–39in (90–100cm), **S** 24in (60cm). Strong stems are clothed with large, open bell-shaped, pastel amethyst-blue flowers in summer. Oval, toothed leaves are rough-textured. **'Brantwood'** has violet-purple flowers.
C. latiloba. Rosette-forming perennial. **H** 3ft (1m), **S** 1 1/2ft (45cm). Leaves are oval. Widely cup-shaped flowers, in shades of blue, occasionally white, are borne in summer. Z5–7 H7–5. **'Hidcote Amethyst'** has large, vivid violet-blue flowers with purple highlights. **'Percy Piper'** has lavender flowers.
C. medium (Canterbury bell). Slow-growing, evergreen, erect, clump-forming biennial. Tall cultivars, **H** 3ft (1m), **S** 1ft (30cm); dwarf, **H** 2ft (60cm), **S** 1ft (30cm). All have lance-shaped, toothed, fresh green leaves. Bell-shaped, single or double flowers, white or in shades of blue and pink, are produced in spring and early summer. Z5–8 H8–5. **'Bells of Holland'** illus. p.313.
C. morettiana. Tuft-forming perennial. **H** 1in (2.5cm), **S** 3in (7cm). Leaves are ivy-shaped with fine hairs. Arching flower stems each bear a solitary, erect, bell-shaped, violet-blue flower in late spring and early summer. Needs gritty, alkaline soil and a dry but not arid winter climate. Red spider mite may be troublesome. Z5–7 H7–5.
C. pendula, syn. *Symphyandra pendula.* Arching perennial. **H** 1–2ft (30–60cm), **S** 1ft (30cm). Produces panicles of pendent, bell-shaped, cream flowers in summer. Has oval, hairy, pale green leaves. Becomes woody at base with age. Z5–8 H8–5.
C. persicifolia (Peachleaf bellflower). Rosette-forming, spreading perennial. **H** 3ft (1m), **S** 1ft (30cm). In summer, nodding, bell-shaped, papery, white or blue flowers are borne above narrowly lance-shaped, bright green leaves. Z3–8 H8–1. **'Chettle Charm'** (illus. p.241), H 60cm (2ft), bears large, white flowers with violet-blue margins. **'Fleur de Neige'** has double, white flowers. **'Pride of Exmouth'** bears double, powder-blue flowers. **'Telham Beauty'** illus. p.242.
C. portenschlagiana, illus. p.368.
C. poscharskyana, illus. p.367.
C. pulla. Often short-lived perennial that spreads by underground runners. **H** 1in (2.5cm), **S** 4in (10cm). Tiny, rounded leaves form rosettes, 1/2in (1cm) wide, each bearing a flower stem with a solitary, pendent, bell-shaped, deep violet flower from late spring to early summer. Is good for a scree or rock garden. Needs gritty, alkaline soil that is not too dry. Slugs may prove troublesome. Z5–7 H7–5.
C. punctata (Spotted bellflower). Vigorous, clump-forming but spreading perennial. **H** 16in (40cm), **S** 24in (60cm) or more. Has heart-shaped, light green, basal leaves. In summer, tall flowering stems bear sprays of pendent, tubular, dusky-pink flushed, creamy-white flowers. Z4–8 H8–1. **'Alina's Double',** **H** 12in (30cm), has large, hose-in-hose, double, rich pink flowers. **'Cherry Bells'** (illus. p.241), **H** 20in (50cm), bears cream-tipped, rose-pink flowers. **'Wine 'n' Rubies',** **H** 12in (30cm), has dark green leaves and bears large, rich purple-red flowers, with heavily speckled interiors, in mid-summer.
***C.* 'Purple Sensation'.** Clump-forming perennial. **H** 16in (40cm), **S** 12in (30cm) or more. Has oval, dark green leaves. Pendent, tubular, deep violet-black flowers are produced in summer. Z5–9 H8–1.
C. pusilla. See *C. cochleariifolia.*
C. pyramidalis (Chimney bellflower). Erect, branching biennial. **H** 6ft (2m), **S** 2ft (60cm). Produces long racemes of star-shaped, blue or white flowers in summer. Leaves are heart-shaped. Needs staking. Z6–8 H8–6.
C. raineri. Perennial that spreads by underground runners. **H** 1 1/2in (4cm), **S** 3in (8cm). Leaves are oval, toothed and gray-green. Flower stems each bear a large, upturned, bell-shaped, pale lavender flower in summer. Is suitable for an alpine house or trough that is protected from winter moisture. Requires partial shade. Z5–7 H7–5.
C. takesimana (Korean bellflower), illus. p.241. Vigorous, spreading perennial. **H** 30in (75cm), **S** 39in (100cm). Forms rosettes of heart-shaped, glossy, mid-green leaves. In summer and fall, flowering stems bear pendent, tubular to bell-shaped, ivory-white flowers with red speckled interiors. Is best in sun. Z5–7 H7–5.
C. trachelium (Nettle-leaved bellflower). Upright perennial. **H** 2–3ft (60cm–1m), **S** 1ft (30cm). Has oval, pointed, rough, serrated, basal leaves. Widely bell-shaped, blue or purple-blue flowers are borne along erect stems in summer. Z5–8 H8–5. **'Bernice'** (illus. p.241) has double purple-violet flowers.
C. vidalii. See *Azorina vidalii.*
C. wanneri, syn. *Symphyandra wanneri,* illus. p.342.
C. zoysii. Tuft-forming perennial. **H** 2in (5cm), **S** 4in (10cm). Has tiny, rounded, glossy green leaves. In summer, flower stems each bear a bottle-shaped, lavender flower held horizontally. Needs gritty, alkaline soil. Is difficult to grow and encourage to flower, dislikes winter wet and is prone to slug attack. Z5–7 H7–5.

CAMPSIS

Trumpet vine

BIGNONIACEAE

Genus of deciduous, woody-stemmed, root climbers, grown for their flowers. Needs sun and fertile, well-drained soil. Water regularly in summer. Prune in spring. Propagate by semiripe cuttings in summer or by layering in winter.
C. chinensis. See *C. grandiflora.*
C. grandiflora, syn. *C. chinensis, Bignonia grandiflora, Tecoma grandiflora,* illus. p.203.
C. radicans, syn. *Bignonia radicans.* Vigorous, deciduous, woody-stemmed, root climber. **H** to 40ft (12m). Leaves of 7–11 oval, toothed leaflets are downy beneath. Small clusters of trumpet-shaped, orange, scarlet or yellow flowers, 2 1/2–3in (6–8cm) long, are borne in late summer and early fall. Z5–9 H9–3. **'Flamenco'** illus. p.208. **f. *flava,*** syn. *C. radicans* 'Yellow Trumpet' illus. p.206. **'Indian Summer'** illus. p.193. **'Yellow Trumpet'.** See *C. radicans* f. *flava.*
***C. x tagliabuana* 'Madame Galen',** illus. p.208.

CANARINA

CAMPANULACEAE

Genus of herbaceous, tuberous, scrambling climbers, grown for their flowers. Grow in full light and in any fertile, well-drained soil. Water moderately from early fall to late spring, then keep dry. Needs tying to a support. Remove dead stems when dormant. Propagate by basal cuttings or seed sown in spring or fall.
C. campanula. See *C. canariensis.*
C. canariensis, syn. *C. campanula,* illus. p.464.

Candollea. See *Hibbertia.*

CANNA

CANNACEAE

Genus of robust, showy, rhizomatous perennials, grown for their striking flowers and ornamental foliage. Is generally used for summer-bedding displays and in containers. Requires a warm, sunny position and rich, moist soil. If grown for summer bedding, encourage into growth in spring at 61°F (16°C) and store rhizomes in slightly damp soil in winter. Most cannas survive in the ground if mulched. Propagate in spring by division or in winter by seed sown at 68°F (20°C) or more.
***C.* 'Ambassadour',** illus. p.394. Rhizomatous perennial. **H** to 6ft (2m), **S** 24–36in (60–90cm). Has broadly lance-shaped, slightly glaucous, mid-green leaves. From mid-summer to fall produces large, creamy-white flowers flushed orange-yellow within at the bases. Z8–11 H11–1.
***C.* 'Assault'.** See *C.* 'Assaut'.
***C.* 'Assaut',** syn. *C.* 'Assault'. Summer-flowering, rhizomatous perennial. **H** to 4ft (1.2m), **S** 1 1/2–2ft (45–60cm). Has sturdy, leafy stems bearing wide, purple-green leaves with a spike of scarlet flowers surrounded by purple bracts. Z8–11 H11–1.
***C.* 'Bengal Tiger'.** See *C.* 'Striata'.
***C.* 'Black Knight'.** Rhizomatous perennial. **H** 6ft (1.8m), **S** 1 1/2–2ft (45–60cm). Sturdy stems bear broadly lance-shaped, bronze-green leaves. From mid-summer to early fall has large racemes of gladiolus-like, very dark red flowers, 3in (7cm) across, with wavy petals. Z8–11 H11–1.
***C.* 'Brillant',** illus. p.394. Mid-summer to early-fall-flowering, rhizomatous perennial. **H** 3ft (1m), **S** 20in (50cm). Produces iris-like, bright red flowers and broadly lance-shaped, mid-green leaves. Z8–11 H11–1.
***C.* 'Durban',** illus. p.394. Mid-summer to early-fall-flowering, rhizomatous perennial. **H** 5 1/2ft (1.6m), **S** 20in (50cm). Produces gladiolus-like, dark orange-red flowers above broadly elliptical, pink-veined, purple leaves fading to orange. Z8–11 H11–1.

C

C. x ehemanii, syn. *C. iridiflora* 'Ehemanii', illus. p.394. Mid-summer to early-fall-flowering, rhizomatous perennial. **H** 6ft (2m), **S** 2ft (60cm). Broadly elliptical, dark bluish-green leaves have red margins. Produces trumpet-shaped, bright pinkish-red flowers. Z8–11 H11–1.

C. 'Ermine'. Clump-forming, mid-summer to early-fall-flowering, rhizomatous perennial. **H** 36in (100cm), **S** 20in (50cm). Has broadly lance-shaped, mid-green leaves. Very large, gladiolus-like, creamy-white flowers are pale yellow flushed toward the centers. Z8–11 H11–1.

C. 'Gnom'. Mid-summer to early-fall-flowering, rhizomatous perennial. **H** 24in (60cm), **S** 18in (45cm). Produces gladiolus-like, salmon-pink flowers, with overlapping petals, and broadly elliptical, mid-green leaves. Z8–11 H11–1.

C. iridiflora, illus. p.395. **'Ehemanii'.** See *C.* x *ehemanii.*

C. 'King Midas'. See *C.* 'Richard Wallace'.

C. 'Königin Charlotte', syn. *C.* 'Queen Charlotte', illus. p.394. Mid-summer to early-fall-flowering, rhizomatous perennial. **H** 3–4ft (1–1.2m), **S** 20in (50cm). Has broadly lance-shaped, mid-green leaves. From mid-summer to early fall produces velvety, blood-red flowers, with canary-yellow-margined petals. Z8–11 H11–1.

C. 'Louis Cottin', illus. p.394. Mid-summer to early-fall-flowering, rhizomatous perennial. **H** 4ft (1.2m), **S** 1½ft (50cm). Produces trumpet-shaped, apricot flowers and broadly lance-shaped, dark blackish-green leaves. Z8–11 H11–1.

C. 'Lucifer', illus. p.394. Compact, mid-summer to early-fall-flowering, rhizomatous perennial. **H** 24in (60cm), **S** 20in (50cm). Produces relatively small, iris-like, red and yellow flowers and elliptic, mid-green leaves. Z8–11 H11–1.

C. 'Musifolia'. Mid-summer to early-fall-flowering, rhizomatous perennial. **H** 10ft (3m), **S** 5ft (1.5m). Bears small, iris-like, orange flowers. Very long, oval, mid-green leaves have dark margins and red-tinted midribs. Z8–11 H11–1.

C. 'Picasso', illus. p.394. Mid-summer to early-fall-flowering, rhizomatous perennial. **H** 4ft (1.2m), **S** 20in (50cm). Produces gladiolus-like, yellow flowers with orange and red spots. Has large, broadly ovate, mid-green leaves. Z8–11 H11–1.

C. 'Pretoria'. See *C.* 'Striata'.

C. 'Queen Charlotte'. See *C.* 'Königin Charlotte'.

C. 'Richard Wallace', syn. *C.* 'King Midas', illus. p.394. Mid-summer to early-fall-flowering, rhizomatous perennial. **H** 5ft (1.5m), **S** 1½ft (50cm). Produces gladiolus-like, bright yellow flowers, with spotted throats and frilly-edged petals, and elliptical, apple-green leaves. Z8–11 H11–1.

C. 'Striata', syn. *C.* 'Bengal Tiger', *C.* 'Pretoria', illus. p.394. Mid-summer to early-fall-flowering, rhizomatous perennial. **H** 5ft (1.5m), **S** 1½ft (50cm). Gladiolus-like, bright orange flowers are produced above ovate, light green to yellow-green leaves, with bright yellow veins. Z8–11 H11–1.

C. 'Stuttgart', illus. p.394. Mid-summer to early-fall-flowering, rhizomatous perennial. **H** 7ft (2.1m), **S** 2ft (60cm). Produces small, iris-like, pale apricot flowers, fading to pink. Broadly lance-shaped, white-and-green leaves require some shade to prevent burning. Z8–11 H11–1.

C. 'Whithelm Pride'. Mid-summer to early-fall-flowering, rhizomatous perennial. **H** 3ft (1m), **S** 1½ft (50cm). Produces large, gladiolus-like, pink flowers and ovate, bronze leaves. Z8–11 H11–1.

C. 'Wyoming', illus. p.394. Mid-summer to early-fall-flowering, rhizomatous perennial. **H** 6ft (1.8m), **S** 20in (50cm). Produces gladiolus-like, soft orange flowers and large, ovate, purple-bronze leaves, with darker purple veins. Z8–11 H11–1.

CANTUA
POLEMONIACEAE

Genus of evergreen shrubs, grown for their showy flowers in spring. Only one species is in general cultivation. Often benefits from being grown against a south- or west-facing wall. Requires full sun and fertile, well-drained soil. Propagate by semiripe cuttings in summer.

C. buxifolia, syn. *C. dependens,* illus. p.146.
C. dependens. See *C. buxifolia.*

CAPSICUM
SOLANACEAE

Genus of evergreen shrubs, subshrubs and short-lived perennials, usually grown as annuals. Some species produce edible fruits (e.g. sweet peppers), others small, ornamental ones. Needs sun and fertile, well-drained soil. Spray flowers with water to encourage fruit to set. Propagate by seed sown under glass in spring. Red spider mite may cause problems.

C. annuum (Ornamental pepper). Z9–11 H11–1. **'Holiday Cheer'** is a moderately fast-growing, evergreen, bushy perennial, grown as an annual. **H** and **S** 8–12in (20–30cm). Has oval, mid-green leaves. Bears small, star-shaped, white flowers in summer and, in fall–winter, spherical, green fruits maturing to red.

CARAGANA
Peashrub
LEGUMINOSAE/PAPILIONACEAE

Genus of deciduous shrubs, grown for their foliage and flowers. Requires full sun and fertile but not over-rich, well-drained soil. Propagate species by softwood cuttings in summer or by seed in fall, cultivars by softwood or semiripe cuttings or budding in summer or by grafting during winter.

C. arborescens (Siberian peashrub). Fast-growing, deciduous, upright shrub. **H** 20ft (6m), **S** 12ft (4m). Has spine-tipped, dark green leaves, each composed of 8–12 oblong leaflets. Produces clusters of pealike, yellow flowers in late spring. Z2–8 H8–1. Arching **'Lorbergii', H** 10ft (3m), **S** 8 ft (2.5m) has very narrow leaflets and smaller flowers and is often grown as a tree by top-grafting. **'Nana'** illus. p.148. **'Walker', H** 1ft (30cm), **S** 6–10ft (2–3m), is prostrate but is usually top-grafted to form a weeping tree, **H** 6ft (2m), **S** 2½ft (75cm).

C. frutex 'Globosa'. Slow-growing, deciduous, upright shrub. **H** and **S** 1ft (30cm). Mid-green leaves each have 4 oblong leaflets. Pealike, bright yellow flowers are borne only rarely in late spring. Z2–8 H8–1.

CARALLUMA
ASCLEPIADACEAE

Genus of perennial succulents with 4–6-ribbed, finger-like, blue-gray or blue-green to purple stems. Needs sun and extremely well-drained soil. Water sparingly, only in the growing season. May be difficult to grow. Propagate by seed or stem cuttings in summer.

C. europaea, syn. *Stapelia europaea.* Clump-forming, perennial succulent. **H** 8in (20cm), **S** 3ft (1m). Rough, 4-angled, erect to procumbent, gray stems often arch over and root. Has clusters of small, star-shaped, yellow and brownish-purple flowers near stem crown from mid- to late summer, then twin-horned, gray seed pods. Flowers smell faintly of rotten meat. Is one of the easier species to grow. Z13–15 H10–1.

C. joannis, illus. p.494.

CARDAMINE
Bitter cress
CRUCIFERAE/BRASSICACEAE

Genus of spring-flowering annuals and perennials. Some are weeds, but others are suitable for informal and woodland gardens. Requires sun or semi-shade and moist soil. Propagate by seed or division in fall.

C. enneaphyllos, syn. *Dentaria enneaphyllos.* Lax perennial spreading by fleshy, horizontal rootstocks. **H** 12–24in (30–60cm), **S** 18–24in (45–60cm). In spring, nodding, pale yellow or white flowers are produced at the ends of shoots arising from deeply divided leaves. Z5–8 H8–5.

C. latifolia. See *C. raphanifolia.*

C. pentaphyllos, syn. *Dentaria pentaphyllos,* illus. p.260.

C. pratensis, illus. p.438. **'Flore Pleno'** is a neat, clump-forming perennial. **H** 18in (45cm), **S** 12in (30cm). Bears dense sheaves of double, lilac flowers in spring. Mid-green leaves are divided into rounded leaflets. May also be propagated by leaf-tip cuttings in mid-summer. Prefers a moist or wet site.

C. raphanifolia, syn. *C. latifolia,* illus. p.438.

C. trifolia, illus. p.348.

CARDIOCRINUM
LILIACEAE

Genus of summer-flowering, lily-like bulbs, grown for their spectacular flowers. Needs partial shade and deep, rich, moist soil. Plant bulbs just below soil surface, in fall. Water well in summer and mulch with humus. Provide a deep mulch in winter. After flowering, main bulb dies, but produces offsets. To produce flowers in up to 5 years, propagate by offsets in fall; may also be propagated by seed in fall or winter and will then flower in 7 years.

C. giganteum, illus. p.385. **var. yunnanense** is a sturdy, leafy-stemmed bulb. **H** 5–6ft (1.5–2m), **S** 2½–3ft (75cm–1m). Has bold, heart-shaped, bronze-green leaves. Fragrant, pendent, trumpet-shaped, cream flowers, 6in (15cm) long, with purple-red streaks inside, are borne in long spikes in summer and are followed by decorative seed heads.

CARDIOSPERMUM
SAPINDACEAE

Genus of herbaceous or deciduous, shrubby climbers, grown mainly for their attractive fruits. Is useful for covering bushes or trellises. Grow in full light and any soil. Propagate by seed in spring.

C. halicacabum (Balloon vine). Deciduous, shrubby, scandent, perennial climber, usually grown as an annual or biennial. **H** to 10ft (3m). Has toothed leaves of 2 oblong leaflets. Inconspicuous, whitish flowers are produced in summer, followed by downy, spherical, inflated, 3-angled, straw-colored fruits containing black seeds, each with a heart-shaped, white spot. Z10–11 H11–1.

CAREX
Sedge
CYPERACEAE

See also GRASSES, BAMBOOS, RUSHES and SEDGES.

C. buchananii (Leatherleaf sedge). Evergreen, tuft-forming, perennial sedge. **H** to 24in (60cm), **S** 8in (20cm). Very narrow, copper-colored leaves turn red toward base. Solid, triangular stems bear insignificant, brown spikelets in summer. Z6–9 H9–5.

C. elata, syn. *C. stricta* (Tufted sedge). Evergreen, tuft-forming, perennial sedge. **H** to 3ft (1m), **S** 6in (15cm). Leaves are somewhat glaucous. Solid, triangular stems bear blackish-brown spikelets in summer. Z5–9 H9–3. **'Aurea'** illus. p.445.

C. flagellifera, illus. p.289.

C. grayi (Gray's sedge). Evergreen, tuft-forming, perennial sedge. **H** to 24in (60cm), **S** 8in (20cm). Has bright green leaves. Large, female spikelets, borne in summer, mature to pointed, knobby, greenish-brown fruits. Z3–8 H8–1.

C. hachijoensis 'Evergold'. See *C. oshimensis* 'Evergold'.

C. morrowii of gardens. See *C. oshimensis.*

C. oshimensis, syn. *C. morrowii.* Evergreen, tuft-forming, perennial sedge. **H** 8–20in (20–50cm), **S** 8–10in (20–25cm). Has narrow, mid-green leaves. Solid, triangular stems bear insignificant spikelets in summer. Z6–9 H9–6. **'Evergold',** syn. *C. hachijoensis* 'Evergold' illus. p.288.

C. pendula (Pendulous sedge). Evergreen, tuft-forming perennial. **H** 3ft (1m), **S** 1ft (30cm). Has narrow, green leaves. Solid, triangular stems freely produce pendent, greenish-brown flower spikes in summer. Z5–9 H9–5.

C. riparia (Greater pond sedge). **'Variegata'** is a vigorous, evergreen, perennial sedge. **H** 2–3ft (60cm–1m), **S** indefinite. Has broad, white-striped, mid-green leaves and solid, triangular stems that bear narrow, bristle-tipped, dark brown spikelets in summer.

C. stricta. See *C. elata.*

CARISSA
APOCYNACEAE

Genus of evergreen, spring- to summer-flowering shrubs, grown for their flowers and overall appearance. Needs partial shade and well-drained soil. Water container specimens moderately, less when temperatures are low. Propagate by seed when ripe or in spring or by semiripe cuttings in summer. ① The seeds are poisonous.

C. grandiflora. See *C. macrocarpa*.
C. macrocarpa, syn. *C. grandiflora* (Natal plum). Z9–11 H11–9. **'Tuttlei'** illus. p.453.
C. spectabilis. See *Acokanthera oblongifolia*.

CARLINA
Carline thistle
COMPOSITAE/ASTERACEAE

Genus of annuals, biennials and perennials, grown for their ornamental flower heads. Requires a sunny position and well-drained soil. Propagate by seed: annuals in spring, perennials in fall.
C. acaulis, illus. p.361.

CARMICHAELIA
LEGUMINOSAE/PAPILIONACEAE

Genus of deciduous, usually leafless shrubs, grown for their profusion of tiny flowers in summer. Flattened, green shoots assume function of leaves. Needs full sun and well-drained soil. Cut out dead wood in spring. Propagate by semiripe cuttings in summer or by seed in fall or spring.
C. arborea. Deciduous, upright shrub. **H** 6ft (2m), **S** 5ft (1.5m). Small clusters of pealike, pale lilac flowers are borne from early to mid-summer. May need staking when mature. Z9–10 H9–7.
C. carmichaeliae, syn. *Notospartium carmichaeliae* (Pink broom). Leafless, arching shrub. **H** 6ft (2m), **S** 5ft (1.5m). Short, dense spikes of pealike, purple-blotched, pink flowers are produced in mid-summer on slender, drooping, green shoots. Z8–10 H9–7.
C. enysii. Deciduous, mound-forming, dense shrub. **H** and **S** 1ft (30cm). Shoots are rigid. Pealike, violet flowers are borne in mid-summer. Is best grown in a rock garden. Z9–10 H10–8.
C. stevensonii, syn. *Chordospartium stevensonii*. Deciduous, almost leafless, arching shrub. **H** 10ft (3m), **S** 6ft (2m). Produces small, pealike, purplish-pink flowers in cylindrical racemes in mid-summer. Z8–10 H10–7.

CARNEGIEA
CACTACEAE

Genus of one species of very slow-growing, perennial cactus with thick, 12–24-ribbed, spiny stems. Is unlikely to flower or branch at less than 12ft (4m) high. Requires full sun and very well-drained soil. Propagate by seed in spring or summer.
C. gigantea, illus. p.492.

CARPENTERIA
HYDRANGEACEAE

Genus of one species of evergreen, summer-flowering shrub, cultivated for its flowers and foliage. Grows well against a south- or west-facing wall. Prefers full sun and fairly moist but well-drained soil. Propagate by softwood cuttings in summer or by seed in fall.
C. californica, illus. p.197.

CARPINUS
Hornbeam
CORYLACEAE/BETULACEAE

Genus of deciduous trees, grown for their foliage, fall color and clusters of small, winged nuts. Needs sun or semi-shade and fertile, well-drained soil. Propagate species by seed in fall, cultivars by budding in late summer.
C. betulus (European hornbeam). Deciduous, round-headed tree. **H** 80ft (25m), **S** 70ft (20m). Has a fluted trunk and oval, prominently veined, dark green leaves that turn yellow and orange in fall. Bears green catkins from late spring to fall, when clusters of winged nuts develop. Z4–8 H8–1. **'Fastigiata',** syn. *C. betulus* 'Pyramidalis' illus. p.93.
'Pyramidalis'. See *C. betulus* 'Fastigiata'.
C. caroliniana (American hornbeam). Deciduous, spreading tree with branches that droop at tips. **H** and **S** 30ft (10m). Has a fluted, gray trunk, green catkins in spring and oval, bright green leaves that turn orange and red in fall, when clusters of winged nuts develop. Z3–9 H9–1.
C. tschonoskii (Yeddo hornbeam). Deciduous, rounded tree with branches drooping at tips. **H** and **S** 40ft (12m). Has oval, sharply toothed, glossy, dark green leaves. Green catkins are produced in spring and clusters of small, winged nuts develop in fall. Z6–9 H9–1.
C. turczaninowii. Deciduous, spreading tree. **H** 40ft (12m), **S** 30ft (10m). Green catkins are borne in spring. Produces clusters of small, winged nuts in fall, when small, oval, glossy, deep green leaves turn orange. Z6–9 H9–1.

CARPOBROTUS
Ice plant
AIZOACEAE

Genus of mat-forming, perennial succulents with triangular, fleshy, dark green leaves and daisylike flowers. Is excellent for binding sandy soils. Needs full sun and well-drained soil. Propagate by seed or stem cuttings in spring or summer.
C. edulis (Hottentot fig). Carpeting, perennial succulent. **H** 6in (15cm), **S** indefinite. Prostrate, rooting branches bear leaves ⁵⁄₈in (1.5cm) thick and 5in (12cm) long. Yellow, purple or pink flowers, 5in (12cm) across, open in spring–summer from about noon in sun. Bears edible, figlike, brownish fruits in late summer and fall. Z12–14 H11–10.

CARRIEREA
FLACOURTIACEAE/SALICACEAE

Genus of deciduous trees. Only *C. calycina*, grown for its flowers, is in general cultivation. Requires full sun and fertile, well-drained soil. Propagate by softwood cuttings in summer.
C. calycina. Deciduous, spreading tree. **H** 25ft (8m), **S** 30ft (10m). Oval, glossy, mid-green leaves set off upright clusters of cup-shaped, creamy-white or greenish-white flowers borne in early summer. Z13–15 H12–10.

CARTHAMUS
COMPOSITAE/ASTERACEAE

Genus of annuals and herbaceous perennials, grown for their flowers, foliage and medicinal properties. Needs full sun and light, well-drained soil. Propagate by seed in spring.
C. tinctorius, illus. p.323.

CARYA
Hickory
JUGLANDACEAE

Genus of deciduous trees, grown for their stately habit, divided leaves, fall color and, in some cases, edible nuts. Has insignificant flowers in spring. Requires sun or semi-shade and deep, fertile soil. Plant young seedlings in a permanent position during their first year since older plants resent transplanting. Propagate by seed in fall.
C. cordiformis (Bitternut hickory, Swamp hickory). Vigorous, deciduous, spreading tree. **H** 80ft (25m), **S** 50ft (15m). Bark is smooth at first, later fissured. Bright yellow, winter leaf buds develop into large, dark green leaves, with usually 7 oval to oblong leaflets; these turn yellow in fall. Nuts are pear-shaped or rounded, ³⁄₄–1¹⁄₂in (2–4cm) long, each with a bitter kernel. Z4–9 H9–1.
C. glabra (Pignut, Pignut hickory). Deciduous, spreading tree. **H** 80ft (25m), **S** 70ft (20m). Dark green leaves, with usually 5 narrowly oval leaflets, turn bright yellow and orange in fall. Pear-shaped or rounded nuts, ³⁄₄–1¹⁄₂in (2–4cm) long, each have a bitter kernel. Z5–8 H8–1.
C. ovata, illus. p.67.

CARYOPTERIS
Bluebeard
VERBENACEAE/LAMIACEAE

Genus of deciduous subshrubs, grown for their foliage and small, but freely produced, blue flowers. Prefers full sun and light, well-drained soil. Cut back hard in spring. Propagate species by greenwood or semiripe cuttings in summer or by seed in fall; increase cultivars by cuttings only, in summer.
C. x clandonensis (Blue mist shrub, Bluebeard). Z6–9 H9–1. **'Arthur Simmonds'** illus. p.157. **'Heavenly Blue'** is a deciduous, bushy subshrub. **H** and **S** 3ft (1m). Forms an upright, compact mass of lance-shaped, gray-green leaves. Dense clusters of tubular, blue to purplish-blue flowers, with prominent stamens, are borne from late summer to fall.
C. incana, syn. *C. mastacanthus* (Common bluebeard). Deciduous, bushy subshrub. **H** and **S** 4ft (1.2m). Bears tubular, violet-blue flowers, with prominent stamens, amid lance-shaped, gray-green leaves from late summer to early fall. Z6–9 H9–1.
C. mastacanthus. See *C. incana*.

CASSIA
Senna
LEGUMINOSAE/CAESALPINIACEAE

Genus of annuals, perennials and evergreen or deciduous trees and shrubs, grown for their flowers mainly produced from winter to summer. Needs full light and fertile, well-drained soil. Water container specimens freely when in full

growth, moderately to sparingly in winter. Pruning is tolerated, severe if need be, but trees are best left to grow naturally. Propagate by seed in spring.
C. artemisioides. See *Senna artemisioides*.
C. corymbosa. See *Senna corymbosa*. **var. plurijuga** of gardens. See *Senna x floribunda*. Z12–15 H12–10.
C. didymobotrya. See *Senna didymobotrya*.
C. fistula (Golden shower, Indian laburnum, Pudding pipe-tree). Fast-growing, almost deciduous, ovoid tree. **H** 25–30ft (8–10m), **S** 12–20ft (4–6m). Leaves, each with 4–8 pairs of oval leaflets, are coppery when young. In spring produces racemes of small, fragrant, 5-petaled, cup-shaped, bright yellow flowers. Cylindrical, dark brown pods, to 24in (60cm) long, yield cassia pulp. Z11 H11–10.
C. x floribunda. See *Senna x floribunda*.
C. siamea. See *Senna siamea*.

CASSINIA
COMPOSITAE/ASTERACEAE

Genus of evergreen shrubs, grown for their foliage and flowers. Needs full sun and fertile, well-drained soil. Propagate by softwood cuttings in summer.
C. fulvida. See *C. leptophylla* subsp. *fulvida*.
C. leptophylla subsp. fulvida, syn. *C. fulvida*. Evergreen, bushy shrub. **H** and **S** 6ft (2m). Has yellow shoots, small, oblong, dark green leaves and, in mid-summer, clustered heads of minute, white flowers. Z8–9 H9–8. **subsp. vauvilliersii,** syn. *C. vauvilliersii* illus. p.150.
C. vauvilliersii. See *C. leptophylla* subsp. *vauvilliersii*.

CASSIOPE
ERICACEAE

Genus of evergreen, spring-flowering shrubs, suitable for peat beds and walls and for rock gardens. Needs a sheltered, shaded or semi-shaded site and moist, peaty, acidic soil. Propagate by semiripe or greenwood cuttings in summer or by seed in fall or spring.
C. 'Edinburgh'. Evergreen, dwarf shrub. **H** and **S** 8in (20cm). Has tiny, dark green leaves tightly pressed to upright stems. In spring, many small, bell-shaped, white flowers are borne singly in leaf axils. Z2–6 H6–1.
C. fastigiata. Evergreen, upright, loose shrub. **H** 12in (30cm), **S** 6–8in (15–20cm). In spring, bell-shaped, creamy-white flowers, resting in green or red calyces, are borne on short stalks in leaf axils. Leaves are tiny and scalelike. Needs partial shade. Z2–6 H6–1.
C. lycopodioides, illus. p.349.
C. mertensiana, illus. p.349.
C. 'Muirhead', illus. p.332.
C. selaginoides. Evergreen, spreading shrub. **H** 10in (25cm), **S** 6in (15cm). Stem is hidden by dense, scalelike, mid-green leaves. Bears solitary, relatively large, pendent, bell-shaped, white flowers in spring. Needs a shaded site. Z7–8 H8–7.
C. tetragona, illus. p.332.
C. wardii. Evergreen, upright to spreading, loose shrub. **H** 6in (15cm), **S** 8in (20cm). Semi-upright stems are

C

densely clothed with scalelike, dark green leaves that give them a squared appearance. Bell-shaped, white flowers, set close to stems, are produced in spring. Needs shade in all but cool areas. May also be propagated by division of runners in spring. Z4–6 H6–1.

CASTANEA
Chestnut
FAGACEAE

Genus of deciduous, summer-flowering trees and shrubs, grown for their foliage, stately habit, flowers and edible fruits (chestnuts). Requires sun or semi-shade; does particularly well in hot, dry areas. Needs fertile, well-drained soil; grows poorly on shallow, chalky soil. Propagate species by seed in fall, cultivars by budding in summer or by grafting in late winter.
C. dentata (American chestnut). Deciduous, spreading tree with rough bark. **H** 100ft (30m), **S** 50ft (15m). Oblong, toothed, dull green leaves turn orange-yellow in fall. Has catkins of greenish-white flowers in summer, then typical spiny "chestnut" fruits. Z5–8 H8–5.
C. sativa (Spanish chestnut, Sweet chestnut). Deciduous, spreading tree. **H** 100ft (30m), **S** 50ft (15m). Bark becomes spirally ridged with age. Oblong, glossy, dark green leaves turn yellow in fall. Produces spikes of small, creamy-yellow flowers in summer, followed by edible fruits in rounded, spiny husks. Z5–7 H7–5. **'Albomarginata'** illus. p.61.

CASTANOPSIS
FAGACEAE

Genus of evergreen shrubs and trees, grown for their habit and foliage. Flowers are insignificant. Needs a sheltered position in sun or semi-shade and fertile, well-drained but not too dry, acidic soil. Propagate by seed when ripe, in fall.
C. cuspidata. Evergreen, bushy, spreading shrub or tree with drooping shoots. **H** and **S** 25ft (8m) or more. Bears long, oval, slender-tipped, leathery leaves, glossy, dark green above, bronze beneath. Z9–11 H11–10.

CASTANOSPERMUM
Black bean tree, Moreton Bay chestnut
LEGUMINOSAE/PAPILIONACEAE

Genus of one species of evergreen tree, grown for its overall appearance and for shade. Requires full light and fertile, moist but well-drained soil. Water container specimens freely when in full growth, moderately at other times. Propagate by seed in spring.
C. australe. Strong-growing, evergreen, rounded tree. **H** 50ft (15m) or more, **S** 25ft (8m) or more. Leaves have 8–17 oval leaflets. Racemes of large, pealike, yellow flowers, that age to orange and red, are produced in fall, but only on mature trees, and are followed by cylindrical, reddish-brown pods, 10in (25cm) long, containing large, chestnut-like seeds. Z11 H11–10.

CATALPA
BIGNONIACEAE

Genus of deciduous, summer-flowering trees and shrubs, extremely resistant to urban pollution, grown for their foliage and bell- or trumpet-shaped flowers with frilly lobes. Trees are best grown as isolated specimens. Prefers full sun and does best in hot summers. Needs deep, fertile, well-drained but not too dry soil. Propagate species by seed in fall, cultivars by softwood cuttings in summer or by budding in late summer.
C. bignonioides, illus. p.73. **'Aurea'** illus. p.76.
C. x erubescens 'Purpurea'. Deciduous, spreading tree. **H** and **S** 50ft (15m). Broadly oval or 3-lobed, very dark purple, young leaves age to dark green. Fragrant, bell-shaped, white flowers, marked with yellow and purple, are produced from mid- to late summer. Z5–9 H9–5.
C. fargesii f. duclouxii, illus. p.73.
C. ovata (Northern catalpa). Deciduous, spreading tree. **H** and **S** 30ft (10m). Bears 3-lobed, purplish leaves when young, maturing to pale green. Has large clusters of bell-shaped, white flowers, spotted with red and yellow, from mid- to late summer. Z4–8 H8–1.
C. speciosa, illus. p.72.

CATANANCHE
Cupid's dart
COMPOSITAE/ASTERACEAE

Genus of perennials with daisylike flower heads that may be successfully dried for winter flower arrangements. Needs sun and light, well-drained soil. Propagate by seed in spring or by root cuttings in winter.
C. caerulea 'Major', illus. p.270.

CATHARANTHUS
APOCYNACEAE

Genus of evergreen shrubs, grown for their flowers. *C. roseus* is often grown annually from seed or cuttings and used as a summer bedding plant in cool climates. Needs full light and well-drained soil. Water container specimens moderately, less when temperatures are low. Prune long or straggly stems in early spring to promote a more bushy habit. Propagate by seed in spring or by greenwood or semiripe cuttings in summer.
C. roseus, syn. *Vinca rosea,* illus. p.298.
Boa Series 'Boa Peach' illus. p.300.
Cobra Series 'Cobra Burgundy' illus. p.306.

CATTLEYA
ORCHIDACEAE

See also ORCHIDS.
C. bowringiana. See *Guarianthe bowringiana.*
C. cinnabarina, syn. *Laelia cinnabarina.* Evergreen, epiphytic orchid for an intermediate greenhouse. **H** 6in (15cm). Produces sprays of slender, orange flowers, 2in (5cm) or more across, usually in winter. Has narrowly oval, rigid leaves, 3–4in (8–10cm) long. Needs full light in summer. Z14–15 H12–6.
C. J.A. Carbone gx. Evergreen, epiphytic orchid for an intermediate greenhouse.

H 18in (45cm). Large heads of fragrant, pinkish-mauve flowers, 4in (10cm) across and each with a yellow-marked, deep pink lip, are borne in early summer. Has oval, stiff leaves, 4–6in (10–15cm) long. Avoid spraying from overhead. Z12–14 H11–6.
C. Trizac gx 'Purple Emperor', syn. x *Sophrolaeliocattleya* Trizac gx 'Purple Emperor'. Evergreen, epiphytic orchid for an intermediate greenhouse. **H** 4in (10cm). In spring bears crimson-lipped, pinkish-purple flowers, 2½in (6cm) across, in small heads. Has oval, rigid leaves, 4in (10cm) long. Provide full light in summer. Z12–14 H11–6.

x CATTLIANTHE
ORCHIDACEAE

See also ORCHIDS.
x C. Hazel Boyd gx 'Apricot Glow', syn. x *Sophrolaeliocattleya* Hazel Boyd gx 'Apricot Glow', illus. p.467. Evergreen, epiphytic orchid for an intermediate greenhouse. **H** 4in (10cm). In spring and early summer produces small heads of apricot-orange flowers, 3½in (9cm) across, with crimson marks on lips. Has oval, rigid leaves, 4in (10cm) long. Grow in full light in summer. Z14–15 H12–6.
x C. Rojo gx 'Mont Millais', syn. x *Laeliocattleya* Rojo gx 'Mont Millais', illus. p.467. Evergreen, epiphytic orchid for an intermediate greenhouse. **H** 12in (30cm). In winter–spring bears arching heads of slender, reddish-orange flowers, ¾in (2cm) across. Oval leaves are up to 6in (15cm) long. Provide full light in summer. Z14–15 H12–6.

CAULOKAEMPFERIA
ZINGIBERACEAE

Genus of herbaceous, rhizomatous perennials, grown for their small but numerous, bright flowers, from late spring to fall, produced from the same stem as the leaves. Requires a shady, sheltered position and moist, rich soil. Propagate by division or seed in early spring.
C. petelotii. Herbaceous, rhizomatous perennial. **H** and **S** 8in (20cm). Has 6–8 narrowly lance-shaped, mid-green leaves. Clusters of broad-lipped, bright canary-yellow flowers, surrounded by long, narrow, green bracts, are borne from spring into fall.

CAUTLEYA
ZINGIBERACEAE

Genus of summer- and fall-flowering perennials. Needs a sunny, sheltered position and deep, rich, moist but well-drained soil. Propagate by seed or division in spring.
C. spicata, illus. p.279.

CAYRATIA
VITACEAE

Genus of deciduous, woody-stemmed, tendril climbers, grown for their leaves and fall color. Tendril tips have sucker-like pads that cling to supports. Insignificant greenish flowers appear in summer. Grow in shade or semi-shade and well-drained soil. Propagate by softwood or greenwood cuttings in summer or by hardwood

cuttings in early spring. ⓘ The berries may cause mild stomach upset if ingested.
C. thomsonii, syn. *Parthenocissus thomsonii,* illus. p.209.

CEANOTHUS
RHAMNACEAE

Genus of evergreen or deciduous shrubs and small trees, grown for their small but densely clustered, mainly blue flowers. At the limits of hardiness, plant against a south- or west-facing wall. Needs a sheltered site in full sun and light, well-drained soil. Cut dead wood from evergreens in spring and trim their sideshoots after flowering. Cut back shoots of deciduous species to basal framework in early spring. Propagate by semiripe cuttings in summer.
C. arboreus 'Trewithen Blue', illus. p.194.
C. 'Autumnal Blue', illus. p.138.
C. 'Blue Mound'. Evergreen, bushy, dense shrub. **H** 5ft (1.5m), **S** 6ft (2m). Forms a mound of oblong, glossy, dark green leaves, covered, in late spring, with rounded clusters of deep blue flowers. Z9–10 H10–8.
C. 'Burkwoodii', illus. p.205.
C. 'Burtonensis'. Evergreen, bushy, spreading shrub. **H** 6ft (2m) or more, **S** 12ft (4m) Has small, rounded, almost spherical, crinkled leaves that are lustrous and dark green. Small, deep blue flowers are produced in clusters, ¾in (2cm) wide, from mid- spring to early summer. Z9–10 H10–8.
C. 'Cascade'. Vigorous, evergreen, arching shrub. **H** and **S** 12ft (4m). Leaves are narrowly oblong, glossy and dark green. Large panicles of powder-blue flowers are borne in late spring and early summer. Z9–11 H11–9.
C. 'Delight'. Fast-growing, evergreen, bushy shrub. **H** 10ft (3m), **S** 15ft (5m). Bears oblong, glossy, deep green leaves. Long clusters of rich blue flowers are borne in late spring. Z9–10 H10–9.
C. x delileanus 'Glore de Versailles'. See *C.* 'Gloire de Versailles'.
C. dentatus (Point Reyes ceanothus). Evergreen, bushy, dense shrub. **H** 5ft (1.5m), **S** 6ft (2m). Produces small, oblong, glossy, dark green leaves and is covered, in late spring, with rounded clusters of bright blue flowers. Z9–10 H10–9.
C. dentatus of gardens. See *C.* x *lobbianus.*
C. 'Gloire de Versailles', syn. *C.* x *delileanus* 'Glore de Versailles', illus. p.157.
C. gloriosus. Evergreen, prostrate shrub. **H** 1ft (30cm), **S** 6ft (2m). Leaves are oval and dark green. Rounded clusters of deep blue or purplish-blue flowers are produced from mid- to late spring. May suffer from chlorosis on chalky soil. Z7–9 H9–7.
C. impressus, illus. p.138. **'Puget Blue'.** See *C.* 'Puget Blue'.
C. incanus, illus. p.129.
C. 'Italian Skies'. Evergreen, bushy, spreading shrub. **H** 5ft (1.5m), **S** 10ft (3m). Has small, oval, glossy, dark green leaves. Produces dense, conical clusters of bright blue flowers in late spring. Z9–10 H10–9.
C. x lobbianus, syn. *C. dentatus* of gardens. Evergreen, bushy, dense shrub. **H** and **S** 6ft (2m). Rounded clusters of bright, deep blue flowers are borne in late spring and early summer amid oval, dark green leaves. Z8–10 H10–7.

C

C. 'Marie Simon'. Deciduous, bushy shrub. **H** and **S** 5ft (1.5m). Has broadly oval, mid-green leaves. Conical clusters of soft pink flowers are produced in profusion from mid-summer to early fall. Z8–10 H10–8.

C. papillosus. Evergreen, arching shrub. **H** 10ft (3m), **S** 15ft (5m). Leaves are narrowly oblong, glossy, dark green and sticky. Produces dense racemes of blue or purplish-blue flowers in late spring. Z9–10 H10–9.

C. 'Perle Rose', illus. p.153.

C. 'Puget Blue', syn. *C. impressus* 'Puget Blue', illus. p.205.

C. rigidus. See *C. rigidus* var. *rigidus*. **var. rigidus,** syn. *C. rigidus* (Monterey ceanothus). Evergreen, bushy shrub of dense, spreading habit. **H** 4ft (1.2m), **S** 8ft (2.5m). Bears oblong to rounded, glossy, dark green leaves and, from mid-spring to early summer, produces rounded clusters of deep purplish-blue flowers. Z9–10 H10–9.

C. 'Southmead' (Santa Barbara ceanothus). Evergreen, bushy, dense shrub. **H** and **S** 5ft (1.5m). Has small, oblong, glossy, dark green leaves. Deep blue flowers are produced in rounded clusters in late spring and early summer. Z9–10 H10–9.

C. thyrsiflorus (Blueblossom). Evergreen, bushy shrub or spreading tree. **H** and **S** 20ft (6m). Has broadly oval, glossy, mid-green leaves and, in late spring and early summer, rounded clusters of pale blue flowers. Z7–11 H10–3. **var. repens** illus. p.159.

C. x veitchianus. Vigorous, evergreen, bushy shrub. **H** and **S** 10ft (3m). Dense, oblong clusters of deep blue flowers are borne in late spring and early summer amid oblong, glossy, dark green leaves. Z9–10 H10–9.

Cedrela sinensis. See *Toona sinensis.*
Cedronella mexicana. See *Agastache mexicana.*

CEDRUS
Cedar
PINACEAE

See also CONIFERS.

C. atlantica, syn. *C. libani* subsp. *atlantica* (Atlas cedar). Conifer that is conical when young, broadening with age. **H** 50–80ft (15–25m), **S** 15–30ft (5–10m). Leaves are spirally arranged, needlelike, dull green or bright blue-gray. Has ovoid cones, males pale brown, females pale green, ripening to brown. Z6–9 H9–6. **f. fastigiata,** syn. *C. atlantica* Fastigiata Group, **S** 12–15ft (4–5m), has a narrower, more upright habit. **Fastigiata Group.** See *C. atlantica* f. *fastigiata*. **f. glauca,** syn. *C. atlantica* Glauca Group, illus. p.95. **Glauca Group.** See *C. atlantica* f. *glauca*.

C. deodara, illus. p.96. **'Aurea',** illus. p.104.

C. libani, illus. p.97. **subsp. atlantica.** See *C. atlantica*. **'Comte de Dijon',** **H** 3–6ft (1–2m), **S** 2–4ft (60cm–1.2m), is a dwarf form that grows only 2in (5cm) a year. **'Sargentii', H** and **S** 3–5ft (1–1.5m), has horizontal, then weeping branches and makes a bush that is rounded in shape.

CEIBA
BOMBACACEAE

Genus of evergreen, semievergreen or deciduous trees, grown for their overall appearance and for shade. Requires full sun or partial shade and fertile, moist but well-drained soil. Water container specimens freely while in full growth, less at other times. Pruning is tolerated if necessary. Propagate by seed in spring or by semiripe cuttings in summer.

C. pentandra (Kapok, Silk cotton tree). Fast-growing, semievergreen tree with a spine-covered trunk. **H** and **S** 80ft (25m) or more. Hand-shaped leaves have 5–9 elliptic leaflets, red when young, becoming mid-green. Bears clusters of 5-petaled, white, yellow or pink flowers in summer, followed by woody, brownish seed pods containing silky kapok fiber. Z13–15 H11–10.

C. speciosa. See *Chorisia speciosa.*

CELASTRUS
Bittersweet
CELASTRACEAE

Genus of deciduous shrubs and twining climbers, grown for their fruits. Most species bear male and female flowers on separate plants, so both sexes must be grown to obtain fruits; hermaphrodite forms of *C. orbiculatus* are available. Grow in any soil and in full or partial shade. Likes regular feeding. Prune in spring to cut out old wood and maintain shape. Propagate by seed in fall or spring or by semiripe cuttings in summer.

C. articulatus. See *C. orbiculatus.*

C. orbiculatus, syn. *C. articulatus* (Asian bittersweet). Vigorous, deciduous, twining climber. **H** to 46ft (14m). Has small, rounded, toothed leaves. Clusters of 2–4 small, green flowers are produced in summer; tiny, long-lasting, spherical fruits begin green, turn black in fall, and finally split and show yellow insides and red seeds. Tends to self-seed and is considered invasive in some regions. Z4–8 H8–1. **'Diana'** illus. p.209.

C. scandens. Deciduous, twining climber. **H** to 30ft (10m). Oval leaves are 2–4in (5–10cm) long. Tiny, greenish flowers are borne in small clusters in leaf axils in summer. Long-lasting, spherical fruits are produced in bunches, 2–3in (5–8cm) long; each fruit splits to show an orange interior and scarlet seeds. Z3–8 H8–1.

CELMISIA
COMPOSITAE/ASTERACEAE

Genus of evergreen, late spring- and summer-flowering perennials, grown for their foliage and daisylike flower heads. Is suitable for rock gardens and peat beds, but may be difficult to grow in hot, dry climates. Needs a sheltered, sunny site and rich, moist but well-drained, sandy, acidic soil. Propagate by division in early summer or by seed when fresh.

C. bellidioides. Evergreen, mat-forming perennial. **H** $^3/_4$in (2cm), **S** to 6in (15cm). Has rounded, leathery, dark green leaves. Bears almost stemless, white flower heads, $^1/_2$in (1cm) across, in early summer. Z8–9 H9–8.

C. coriacea of gardens. See *C. semicordata.*

C. ramulosa, illus. p.360.

C. semicordata, syn. *C. coriacea*, illus. p.346.

C. traversii. Slow-growing, evergreen, clump-forming perennial. **H** 6in (15cm), **S** 8in (20cm). Sword-shaped, dark green leaves have reddish-brown margins and cream undersides. In summer bears white flower heads, 2$^1/_2$–3in (6–7cm) across. Is difficult to establish.

C. walkeri, syn. *C. webbiana*, illus. p.336.

C. webbiana. See *C. walkeri.*

CELOSIA
Cockscomb
AMARANTHACEAE

Genus of erect perennials, grown as annuals. Prefers a sunny, sheltered position and fertile, well-drained soil. Propagate by seed sown under glass in spring.

C. argentea. Moderately fast-growing, erect, bushy perennial, grown as an annual. **H** 12–24in (30–60cm), **S** to 18in (45cm). Has oval to lance-shaped, pale to mid-green leaves and, in summer, pyramid-shaped, feathery, silvery-white flower heads, to 4in (10cm) long. Cultivars are available in red, orange, yellow and cream. H9–2. Dwarf cultivars, **H** 12in (30cm), include **'Fairy Fountains',** which has flower heads, to 6in (15cm) long, in a wide range of colors in summer–fall, and **Olympia Series** (Yunnan hackberry), which has crested, coral-like heads of tightly clustered flower heads, 3–5in (8–12cm) across, in colors such as golden-yellow, scarlet, light red, deep cerise and purple.

CELTIS
Hackberry
ULMACEAE/CANNABACEAE

Genus of deciduous trees, with inconspicuous flowers in spring, grown for their foliage and small fruits. Needs full sun (doing best in hot summers) and fertile, well-drained soil. Propagate by seed in fall.

C. australis, illus. p.62.

C. occidentalis (Common hackberry). Deciduous, spreading tree. **H** and **S** 70ft (20m). Oval, sharply toothed, glossy, bright green leaves turn yellow in fall, when they are accompanied by globose, yellowish-red, then red-purple fruits. Z2–9 H9–1.

C. sinensis (Chinese hackberry). Deciduous, rounded tree. **H** and **S** 30ft (10m). Has oval, glossy, dark green leaves, with fine teeth, and small, globose, orange fruits. Z7–9 H9–7.

CENTAUREA
COMPOSITAE/ASTERACEAE

Genus of annuals and perennials, grown for their flower heads that each have a thistle-like center surrounded by a ring of slender ray petals. Requires sun; grows in any well-drained soil, even poor soil. Propagate by seed or division in fall or spring.

C. cyanus, illus. p.315. Fast-growing, upright, branching annual. **H** 1–3ft (30cm–1m), **S** 1ft (30cm). Has lance-shaped, gray-green leaves and, in summer and early fall, branching stems with usually double, daisylike flower heads in shades of blue, pink, red, purple or white. Flowers are excellent for cutting. Tall (blue, illus. p.315) and dwarf cultivars are available. **Baby Series** (Persian cornflower) (dwarf), **H** to 1ft (30cm), has blue, white or pink flower heads.

C. dealbata. Erect perennial. **H** 3ft (1m), **S** 2ft (60cm). Lilac-purple flower heads are borne freely in summer, one or more to each stem. Has narrowly oval, finely cut, light green leaves. Z3–9 H9–1. **'Steenbergii',** **H** 2ft (60cm), has carmine-lilac flowers.

C. hypoleuca 'John Coutts', illus. p.265.

C. macrocephala (Mountain bluet). Robust, clump-forming perennial. **H** 3ft (1m), **S** 2ft (60cm). In summer, sturdy stems bear large, yellow flower heads, within papery, silvery-brown bracts. Mid-green leaves are narrowly oval and deeply cut. Z3–7 H7–1.

C. montana, illus. p.269.

C. moschata. See *Amberboa moschata.*

C. pulcherrima, illus. p.232.

CENTRADENIA
MELASTOMATACEAE

Genus of evergreen perennials and shrubs, grown for their flowers and foliage. Needs partial shade and fertile, well-drained soil. Water container plants freely when in full growth, moderately at other times. Tip prune young plants to promote a bushy habit; old plants become straggly unless trimmed each spring. Propagate from early spring to early summer by seed or by softwood or greenwood cuttings. If grown as container plants, propagate annually.

C. floribunda. Evergreen, loosely rounded, soft-stemmed shrub. **H** and **S** to 24in (60cm). Lance-shaped leaves are prominently veined, glossy, green above, bluish-green beneath. Large, terminal clusters of 4-petaled, pink or white flowers develop from pink buds in late winter and spring. Z13–15 H11–10.

CENTRANTHUS
VALERIANACEAE/CAPRIFOLIACEAE

Genus of late spring- to fall-flowering perennials. Requires sun. Thrives in an exposed position and in poor, alkaline soil. Propagate by seed in fall or spring.

C. ruber, illus. p.248.

CENTROPOGON
CAMPANULACEAE

Genus of herbaceous or subshrubby, upright, scrambling or climbing, deciduous or evergreen perennials, grown for their tubular flowers and uppermost leaves, which are sometimes patterned or variegated. Needs sun or partial shade and rich, moist but well-drained soil. Propagate by seed in spring.

C. ayavacensis, syn. *C. willdenowianus.* Deciduous, trailing perennial. **H** and **S** 3ft (1m). Flexuous, purple stems have rounded to broadly elliptic, mid-green leaves, to 2in (5cm) long. Bears tubular, cerise flowers, 2–2$^1/_2$in (5–6cm) long, with reflexed petals, from early spring to summer. Needs a sunny position. Protect roots from frost.

C. cordifolius. Herbaceous, weakly climbing or trailing perennial. **H** 1$^1/_2$ft (0.5m), **S** 3–6ft (1–2m). Red stems have heart-shaped, toothed, gray-green leaves, to 3in (7.5cm) long, and bear flared, tubular, cerise flowers, 1$^1/_2$in (4cm) long, from late spring to summer. Requires a sunny position. Protect roots from frost.

C. ferrugineus. Herbaceous, trailing perennial. **H** 1$^1/_2$–6ft (0.5–2m), **S** 3–6ft (1–2m). Long, wiry, pendent stems bear narrowly ovate, silver-marked, mid-green leaves, 2$^1/_2$–6in (6–13cm) long, with narrowly toothed margins. Flared, tubular, bright pink flowers, 1$^1/_2$–2in (4–5cm) long,

from summer into fall, are followed by spherical fruits. Is best in a container.
C. willldenowianus. See *C. ayavacensis*.

CEPHALARIA
DIPSACACEAE/CAPRIFOLIACEAE

Genus of coarse, summer-flowering perennials, suitable for large borders and wild gardens. Prefers sun and well-drained soil. Propagate by division in spring or by seed in fall.
C. gigantea, syn. *C. tatarica* (Giant scabious, Yellow scabious). Robust, branching perennial. **H** 6ft (2m), **S** 4ft (1.2m). In early summer, wiry stems bear pincushionlike heads of primrose-yellow flowers above lance-shaped, deeply cut, dark green leaves. Z3–7 H7–1.
C. tatarica. See *C. gigantea*.

CEPHALOCEREUS
CACTACEAE

Genus of slow-growing, columnar, perennial cacti with 20–30-ribbed, green stems. Prefers full sun and extremely well-drained, lime-rich soil. Is prone to rot if overwatered. Propagate by seed in spring or summer.
C. senilis, illus. p.479.

CEPHALOPHYLLUM
AIZOACEAE

Genus of clump-forming, bushy, perennial succulents with semicylindrical to cylindrical, green leaves. Flowers are borne after 1 or 2 years. Needs sun and well-drained soil. Propagate by seed in spring or summer.
C. alstonii (Red spike). Prostrate, perennial succulent. **H** 4in (10cm), **S** 3ft (1m). Has cylindrical, gray-green leaves, to 3in (7cm) long. Produces daisylike, dark red flowers, 3in (8cm) across, in summer. Z12–14 H11–10.
C. pillansii (Griffith's leadwort). Clump-forming, perennial succulent. **H** 3in (8cm), **S** 24in (60cm). Leaves are cylindrical, 2¹⁄₂in (6cm) long, dark green and covered in darker dots. Short flower stems produce daisylike, red-centered, yellow flowers, 2¹⁄₂in (6cm) across, from spring to fall. Z13–15 H12–10.

CEPHALOTAXUS
Plum yew
CEPHALOTAXACEAE/TAXACEAE

See also CONIFERS.
C. harringtonii (Plum yew). Bushy, spreading conifer. **H** 15ft (5m), **S** 10ft (3m). Needlelike, flattened leaves are glossy, dark green, grayish beneath, radiating around erect shoots. Bears ovoid, fleshy, green fruits that ripen to brown. Z6–9 H9–3.

CERASTIUM
CAROPHYLLACEAE

Genus of annuals and perennials, grown for their star-shaped flowers. Some species are useful as groundcover. Needs sun and well-drained soil. Propagate by division in spring.
C. alpinum (Alpine chickweed). Prostrate perennial. **H** 3in (8cm), **S** 16in (40cm). Tiny, oval, gray leaves cover stems. Flower stems bear solitary, star-shaped, white flowers, ¹⁄₂in (1cm) wide, throughout summer. Z3–7 H7–1.
C. tomentosum, illus. p.350.

CERATOPHYLLUM
CERATOPHYLLACEAE

Genus of deciduous, perennial, submerged water plants, grown for their foliage. Is suitable for ponds and cold-water aquariums. Prefers an open, sunny position, but tolerates shade better than most submerged plants. Propagation occurs naturally when scaly young shoots or winter buds separate from main plants. Take stem cuttings in growing season.
C. demersum (Hornwort). Deciduous, perennial, spreading, submerged water plant that occasionally floats. **S** indefinite. Has small, dark green leaves with 3 linear lobes. Is best suited to a cool-water pool. Z6–9 H9–6.

CERATOPTERIS
PARKERIACEAE

Genus of deciduous or semievergreen, perennial, floating water ferns, grown for their foliage. Is suitable for aquariums. Prefers a sunny position. Remove fading fronds regularly. Propagate in summer by division or by buds that develop on the leaves.
C. thalictroides (Water fern). Semievergreen, perennial, spreading, floating water fern that sometimes roots and becomes submerged. **S** indefinite. Lance-or heart-shaped, soft green fronds are wavy-edged. Z13–15 H11–10.

CERATOSTIGMA
PLUMBAGINACEAE

Genus of deciduous, semievergreen or evergreen shrubs and perennials, grown for their blue flowers and fall color. Requires a sunny position and well-drained soil. Cut out dead wood from shrubs in spring. Propagate shrubs by softwood cuttings in summer, perennials by division in spring.
C. griffithii (Leadwort). Evergreen or semievergreen, bushy, dense shrub. **H** 3ft (1m), **S** 5ft (1.5m). Spoon-shaped, bristly, purple-edged, dull green leaves redden in fall. Clusters of tubular, bright blue flowers, with spreading petal lobes, are borne in late summer and fall. Z7–10 H10–7.
C. plumbaginoides, illus. p.346.
C. willmottianum, illus. p.159.

CERCIDIPHYLLUM
CERCIDIPHYLLACEAE

Genus of deciduous trees, grown for their foliage and often spectacular fall color. Late frosts may damage young foliage, but do not usually cause lasting harm. Requires sun or partial shade and fertile, moist but well-drained soil. Propagate by seed in fall.
C. japonicum, illus. p.66.

CERCIS
Redbud
LEGUMINOSAE/CAESALPINIACEAE

Genus of deciduous shrubs and trees with sometimes shrubby growth, grown for their foliage and small, pealike flowers,
borne profusely in spring. Requires full sun and deep, fertile, well-drained soil. Plant out as young specimens. Resents transplanting. Propagate species by seed in fall, cultivars by budding in summer.
C. canadensis (Eastern redbud). Deciduous, spreading tree or shrub. **H** and **S** 30ft (10m). Heart-shaped, dark green leaves turn yellow in fall. Pealike flowers are magenta in bud, opening to pale pink in mid-spring before leaves emerge. Z4–9 H9–2. **'Forest Pansy'** illus. p.84.
C. siliquastrum, illus. p.83.

CEREUS
CACTACEAE

Genus of columnar, perennial cacti with spiny stems, most having 4–10 pronounced ribs. Cup-shaped flowers usually open at night. Needs full sun and very well-drained soil. Propagate in spring by seed or, for branching species, by stem cuttings.
C. forbesii. See *C. hankeanus*.
C. hankeanus, syn. *C. forbesii*, illus. p.488.
C. hildmannianus, syn. *C. peruvianus*, illus. p.488. **'Monstrosus'** (Honeywort) is a columnar, perennial cactus. **H** 15ft (5m), **S** 12ft (4m). Swollen, occasionally fan-shaped, silvery-blue stems bear golden spines on 4–8 (or more) uneven ribs. Is unlikely to flower in cultivation. Z11 H12–10.
C. peruvianus of gardens. See *C. hildmannianus*.
C. spachianus. See *Echinopsis spachiana*.

CERINTHE
BORAGINACEAE

Genus of annuals, biennials and perennials with somewhat fleshy stems and leaves. Requires full sun, and dry to moist but well-drained soil. Propagate by seed in fall or spring.
C. major 'Purpurascens', illus. p.312.

CEROPEGIA
ASCLEPIADACEAE/APOCYNACEAE

Genus of semievergreen, succulent shrubs and subshrubs, most with slender, climbing or pendent stems, grown for their unusual flowers. Needs partial shade and very well-drained soil. Propagate by seed or stem cuttings in spring or summer. *C. linearis* subsp. *woodii* is often used as grafting stock for difficult asclepiads.
C. distincta subsp. haygarthii. See *C. haygarthii*.
C. haygarthii, syn. *C. distincta* subsp. *haygarthii* (Orange cestrum). Semievergreen, climbing, succulent subshrub. **H** 6ft (2m) or more, **S** indefinite. Bears oval or rounded, dark green leaves, ¹⁄₂–³⁄₄in (1–2cm) long. In summer produces masses of small, white or pinkish-white flowers, each with a pitcher-shaped tube, widening towards the top and then united at the tip by purplish-spotted petals that form a short stem ending in 5 "knobs" edged with fine hairs. The whole resembles an insect hovering over a flower. Z12–15 H12–10.
C. linearis, syn. *C. linearis* subsp. *woodii*, *C. woodii*, illus. p.490. **subsp. woodii.** See *C. linearis*.
C. sandersoniae. See *C. sandersonii*.
C. sandersonii, syn. *C. sandersoniae* (Fountain flower, Parachute plant).
Semievergreen, scrambling, succulent subshrub. **H** 6ft (2m), **S** indefinite. Leaves are triangular to oval, fleshy and ³⁄₄in (2cm) long. In summer–fall has tubular, green flowers, 2in (5cm) long, with paler green to white marks; the petals are flared widely at tips to form "parachutes". Z12–14 H11–10.
C. woodii. See *C. linearis*.

CESTRUM
SOLANACEAE

Genus of deciduous or evergreen shrubs and semi-scrambling climbers, grown for their showy flowers. Foliage has an unpleasant scent. Requires a sheltered, sunny position and fertile, well-drained soil. Water container specimens freely when in full growth, moderately at other times. Support is needed for scrambling species. Propagate frost-hardy species by softwood cuttings in summer, tender species by seed in spring or by semiripe cuttings in summer.
C. aurantiacum (Red cestrum). Mainly evergreen semi-scrambler that remains a rounded shrub if cut back annually. **H** and **S** to 6ft (2m). Deciduous at low temperatures. Bears oval, bright green leaves. Tubular, bright orange flowers are borne in large, terminal trusses in summer and may be followed by spherical, white fruits. Prune annually, cutting out old stems to near base after flowering. Z11 H11–10.
C. elegans, syn. *C. purpureum* of gardens, illus. p.202.
C. 'Newellii', illus. p.203.
C. parqui. Deciduous, open shrub. **H** and **S** 6ft (2m). Large clusters of tubular, yellowish-green flowers, fragrant at night, are borne in profusion in summer amid narrowly lance-shaped, mid-green leaves. Z8–11 H11–8.
C. purpureum of gardens. See *C. elegans*.

Ceterach officinarum. See *Asplenium ceterach*.

CHAENOMELES
Flowering quince
ROSACEAE

Genus of deciduous, usually thorny, spring-flowering shrubs, grown for their showy flowers and fragrant fruits, produced in fall and used for preserves. Prefers sun and well-drained soil. On wall-trained shrubs cut back sideshoots after flowering to 2 or 3 buds and shorten shoots growing away from wall during growing season. Propagate species by softwood or greenwood cuttings in summer or by seed in fall, cultivars by cuttings only in summer. Fireblight and, on alkaline soil, chlorosis are common problems.
C. cathayensis (Common flowering quince), illus. p.142. Deciduous, spreading, open shrub with thorns. **H** and **S** 10ft (3m) or more. Produces long, narrow, pointed, mid-green leaves. Small, 5-petaled, pink-flushed, white flowers are produced from early to mid-spring, followed by large, egg-shaped, yellow-green fruits. Z7–9 H9–7.
C. japonica (Japanese flowering quince). Deciduous, bushy, spreading shrub with thorns. **H** 3ft (1m), **S** 6ft (2m). Has oval, mid-green leaves and, in spring, a profusion of 5-petaled, red or orange-red flowers, then spherical, yellow fruits. Z5–9 H9–1.
C. speciosa. Vigorous, deciduous, bushy

535

shrub with thorns. **H** 8ft (2.5m), **S** 15ft (5m). Leaves are oval, glossy and dark green. Clustered, 5-petaled, red flowers are borne from early to mid-spring, and are followed by spherical, greenish-yellow fruits. Z5–9 H9–1. **'Moerloosei'** illus. p.122. **'Nivalis'** has pure white flowers. **'Simonii'**, **H** 3ft (1m), **S** 6ft (2m), bears masses of semidouble, deep red flowers. **'Snow'** illus. p.146.
C. x **superba 'Etna'**. is a deciduous, bushy, dense shrub with thorns. **H** 5ft (1.5m), **S** 10ft (3m). Has oval, glossy, dark green leaves. Bears masses of 5-petaled, scarlet flowers, with conspicuous, golden-yellow anthers, in spring, followed by round, yellow fruits. Z5–9 H9–5. **'Crimson and Gold'** illus. p.193. **'Knap Hill Scarlet'** (Fernbush), **H** 5ft (1.5m), **S** 10ft (3m), produces large, brilliant red flowers. **'Nicoline'** illus. p.147. **'Rowallane'** illus. p.147.

CHAMAEBATIARIA
ROSACEAE

Genus of one species of deciduous shrub, grown for its foliage and summer flowers. Needs a sheltered, sunny position and well-drained soil. Propagate by semiripe cuttings in summer.

C. millefolium. Deciduous, upright, open shrub. **H** and **S** 3ft (1m). Has finely divided, aromatic, gray-green leaves. Shallowly cup-shaped, white flowers, with yellow stamens, are borne in terminal, branching panicles from mid- to late summer. Z4–7 H7–4.

Chamaecereus silvestrii. See *Echinopsis chamaecereus.*

CHAMAECYPARIS
False cypress
CUPRESSACEAE

① Contact with the foliage may aggravate skin allergies. See also CONIFERS.
C. lawsoniana (Lawson false cypress). Upright, columnar conifer with branches drooping at tips. **H** 50–80ft (15–25m), **S** 10–12ft (3–4m). Bears flattened sprays of scalelike, aromatic, dark green leaves and globular cones, the males brick-red, the females insignificant and green. Z5–9 H9–5. **'Columnaris'** illus. p.103. **'Ellwoodii'**, **H** 10ft (3m), **S** 5ft (1.5m), is erect with incurved, blue-gray leaves. **'Fletcheri'**, **H** 15–40ft (5–12m), **S** 6–10ft (2–3m), has gray leaves that are incurved. **'Gnome'**, **H** and **S** 20in (50cm), is a dwarf, bun-shaped form with blue foliage. **'Green Pillar'** illus. p.102. **'Intertexta'** illus. p.96. **'Kilmacurragh'**, **H** 30–50ft (10–15m), **S** 3ft (1m), has very bright green foliage. **'Lanei Aurea'**, illus. p.102. **'Minima'**, **H** and **S** 3ft (1m), is dwarf and globular, and has light green foliage. **'Pembury Blue'** illus. p.99. **'Tamariscifolia'**, syn. *C. lawsoniana* Tamariscifolia Group, **H** 10ft (3m), **S** 12ft (4m), is a dwarf, spreading form. **Tamariscifolia Group.** See *C. lawsoniana* 'Tamariscifolia'. **'Triomf van Boskoop'**, **H** 70ft (20m), is broadly columnar, with gray-blue foliage. **'Wisselii'**, **H** 50ft (15m), **S** 6–10ft (2–3m), is fast-growing, with erect branches and blue-green leaves.
C. nootkatensis (Alaska cedar, Nootka false cypress). Almost geometrically conical conifer. **H** 50ft (15m), **S** 20ft (6m). Bears long, pendent sprays of scalelike, aromatic, gray-green leaves and globular, hooked,

dark blue and green cones that ripen to brown. Z4–7 H9–1. **'Pendula'** has a gaunt crown of arching, weeping foliage.
C. obtusa (Hinoki false cypress). Conical conifer. **H** 50–70ft (15–20m), **S** 15ft (5m). Has stringy, red-brown bark and scalelike, aromatic, dark green leaves with bright silver lines at sides and incurving tips. Small, rounded cones ripen to yellow-brown. Z4–8 H8–1. **'Coralliformis'**, **H** to 20in (50cm), **S** 3ft (1m), is dwarf, with threadlike shoots. **'Crippsii'** illus. p.104. **'Intermedia'**, **H** to 12in (30cm), **S** 16in (40cm), is a globular, open, dwarf shrub with downward-spreading, light green foliage. **'Kosteri'**, **H** 3–6ft (1–2m), **S** 6–10ft (2–3m), forms a sprawling bush with twisted, lustrous foliage. Is extremely slow-growing. **'Nana'** eventual **H** 3ft (1m), **S** 5–6ft (1.5–2m), makes a flat-topped bush. **'Nana Aurea'**, **H** and **S** 6ft (2m), has golden-yellow leaves. **'Nana Gracilis'** (illus. p.105), **H** 6ft (2m), **S** 5–6ft (1.5–2m), has glossy foliage. **'Tetragona Aurea'**, **H** 30ft (10m), **S** 6–10ft (2–3m), produces golden- or bronze-yellow leaves.
C. pisifera (Sawara false cypress). Conical conifer with horizontal branches. **H** 50ft (15m), **S** 15ft (5m). Has ridged, peeling, red-brown bark, scalelike, aromatic, fresh green leaves, white at sides and beneath, and angular, yellow-brown cones. Z4–8 H8–1. **'Boulevard'** has silver-blue foliage. **'Filifera'** has whiplike, hanging shoots and dark green foliage. **'Filifera Aurea'** (illus. p.105), **H** 40ft (12m), **S** 10–15ft (3–5m), also has whiplike shoots, but with golden-yellow leaves. **'Filifera Nana'**, **H** 2ft (60cm), **S** 3ft (1m), is a dwarf form with whiplike branches. **'Nana'**, **H** and **S** 20in (50cm), is also dwarf, with dark bluish-green foliage. **'Plumosa'** is broadly conical to columnar, with yellowish-gray-green leaves. **'Plumosa Rogersii'**, **H** 6ft (2m), **S** 3ft (1m), has yellow foliage. Slow-growing **'Squarrosa'**, **H** to 70ft (20m), has a broad crown and soft, blue-gray foliage.
C. thyoides, illus. p.101. **'Andelyensis'** is a slow-growing, conical, dwarf conifer. **H** 10ft (3m), **S** 3ft (1m). Has wedge-shaped tufts of scalelike, aromatic, blue-green leaves. Globular cones are glaucous blue-gray.

CHAMAECYTISUS
LEGUMINOSAE/PAPILIONACEAE

Genus of evergreen and deciduous trees, shrubs and subshrubs, grown for pealike flowers. Best in full sun and moderately fertile, well-drained soil. Propagate by seed in fall or spring or by semiripe cuttings in summer.

C. albus, syn. *Cytisus albua, Cytisus leucanthus*. Deciduous, spreading shrub. **H** 1ft (30cm), **S** 3ft (1m). Has oval leaves, each with 3 tiny leaflets and, from early to mid-summer, creamy-white flowers borne in dense clusters. Z6–9 H9–6.
C. demissus, syn. *C. hirsutus* var. *demissus, Cytisus demissus*. Slow-growing, deciduous, prostrate shrub. **H** 3in (8cm), **S** 8–12in (20–30cm). Densely hairy stems bear tiny, bright green leaves with 3-palmate, obovate leaflets. Produces axillary clusters of 2–4 bright yellow flowers, each with a brown keel, in early summer. Is good for a rock garden or trough. Z6–9 H9–6.

C. hirsutus var. *demissus*. See *C. demissus.*
C. purpureus, syn. *Cytisus purpureus* (Purple broom). Deciduous, arching shrub. **H** 18in (45cm), **S** 24in (60cm). Semierect stems are clothed with leaves of 3-palmate, obovate leaflets. Clusters of 2–3 pale lilac to purple flowers are produced in early summer on previous year's wood. Is suitable for a bank or sunny border. Z6–9 H9–6. **f. albus** illus. p.337.
C. supinus, syn. *Cytisus supinus*. Deciduous, bushy, rounded shrub. **H** and **S** 3ft (1m). Dense, terminal heads of large, yellow flowers are borne from mid-summer to fall amid gray-green leaves with 3-palmate, oblong-elliptic leaflets. Z5–9 H9–5.

CHAMAEDAPHNE
ERICACEAE

Genus of one species of evergreen shrub, grown for its white flowers. Needs sun or partial shade and moist, peaty, acidic soil. Propagate by semiripe cuttings in summer.
C. calyculata (Leatherleaf). Evergreen, arching, open shrub. **H** 2$\frac{1}{2}$ft (75cm), **S** 3ft (1m). Leaves are small, oblong, leathery and dark green. Leafy racemes of small, urn-shaped flowers are borne on slender branches in mid- to late spring. Z3–6 H6–1.

CHAMAEDOREA
ARECACEAE/PALMAE

Genus of evergreen palms, grown for their overall appearance. Needs full or partial shade and rich, well-drained soil. Water container plants moderately, less when temperatures are low. Propagate by seed in spring at not less than 77°F (25°C). Red spider mite may be troublesome.
C. elegans, syn. *Neanthe bella*, illus. p.458.

CHAMAEMELUM
COMPOSITAE/ASTERACEAE

Genus of evergreen perennials, suitable as groundcover or for a lawn. Flowers may be used to make tea. Needs sun and well-drained soil. Propagate by division in spring or by seed in fall.
C. nobile, syn. *Anthemis nobilis* (Chamomile). Evergreen, mat-forming, invasive perennial. **H** 4in (10cm), **S** 18in (45cm). Has finely divided, aromatic leaves and daisylike, white flower heads, with yellow centers, borne in late spring or summer. Z6–9 H9–6. **'Treneague'** is a non-flowering, less invasive cultivar that, requiring less mowing, is better for a lawn.

Chamaenerion. See *Epilobium.*
Chamaepericlymenum canadense. See *Cornus canadensis.*

CHAMAEROPS
ARECACEAE/PALMAE

Genus of evergreen palms, cultivated for their overall appearance. Needs full sun and fertile, well-drained soil. Water container plants moderately, less when not in full growth. Propagate by seed in spring at not less than 72°F (22°C) or by suckers in late spring. Red spider mite may be a nuisance.
C. humilis, illus. p.165.

Chamaespartium sagittale. See *Genista sagittalis.*
Chamaespartium sagittale subsp. *delphinense.* See *Genista delphinensis.*

CHAMELAUCIUM
MYRTACEAE

Genus of evergreen shrubs, grown for their flowers and overall appearance. Requires full sun and well-drained, sandy, neutral to acidic soil. Water container specimens moderately when in growth, sparingly at other times. To maintain a more compact habit, cut back flowered stems by half when the last bloom falls. Propagate by seed in spring or by semiripe cuttings in summer.
C. uncinatum [white], illus. p.453; [pink], illus. p.454.

CHASMANTHE
IRIDACEAE

Genus of corms, grown for their showy flowers. Needs a site in full sun or partial shade and well-drained soil, with plenty of water in late winter and early spring. Reduce watering in summer–fall. Propagate by division in fall.
C. aethiopica. Spring- and early summer-flowering corm. **H** to 32in (80cm), **S** 5–7in (12–18cm). Has narrowly sword-shaped, erect, basal leaves in a flat fan. Produces a spike of scarlet flowers, all facing one way, with yellow tubes, 2–2$\frac{1}{2}$in (5–6cm) long, and hooded, upper lips. Z8–10 H10–8.
C. floribunda (Wild oats). Summer-flowering corm. **H** to 32in (80cm), **S** 5–7in (12–18cm). Is similar to *C. aethiopica*, but the leaves are much wider, and the longer, orange or scarlet flowers do not all face the same way. Z9–10 H10–9.

CHASMANTHIUM
GRAMINAE/POACEAE

See also GRASSES, BAMBOOS, RUSHES and SEDGES.
C. latifolium, illus. p.288.

CHEILANTHES
ADIANTACEAE/PTERIDACEAE

Genus of evergreen ferns. Needs full sun and rich, well-drained soil. Do not overwater container plants or splash water on fronds. Remove fading foliage regularly. Propagate by spores in summer.
C. lanosa of gardens. See *C. tomentosa.*
C. tomentosa, syn. *C. lanosa.* Evergreen fern. **H** and **S** 6–9in (15–23cm). Leaves are triangular or lance-shaped and have much divided, soft green fronds on hairy, black stems. Z6–9 H9–6.

Cheiranthus **'Bowles' Mauve'.** See *Erysimum* 'Bowles's Mauve'.
Cheiranthus **'Bredon'.** See *Erysimum* 'Bredon'.
Cheiranthus cheiri. See *Erysimum cheiri.*
Cheiranthus cheiri **'Harpur Crewe'.** See *Erysimum* x *kewense* 'Harpur Crewe'.
Cheiranthus **'Moonlight'.** See *Erysimum* 'Moonlight'.

C

CHEIRIDOPSIS

AIZOACEAE

Genus of clump-forming, perennial succulents with pairs of semicylindrical leaves. Needs sun and well-drained soil. Water in fall to encourage flowers. Propagate by seed or stem cuttings in spring or summer.

C. candidissima. See *C. denticulata*.
C. denticulata, syn. *C. candidissima*. Clump-forming, perennial succulent. **H** 4in (10cm), **S** 8in (20cm). Has semicylindrical, slender, fleshy, blue-gray leaves, each with a flat top, joined in pairs for almost half their length. Bears daisylike, shiny, white flowers, to 2¹/₂in (6cm) across, in spring. Z9–11 H11–10.
C. purpurata. See *C. purpurea*.
C. purpurea, syn. *C. purpurata*. Carpeting, perennial succulent. **H** 4in (10cm), **S** 12in (30cm). Has semicylindrical, thick, short, glaucous green leaves, each with a flat top. In early spring produces daisylike, purple-pink flowers, 1¹/₂in (4cm) across. Z13–15 H11–10.

CHELIDONIUM

Greater celandine

PAPAVERACEAE

Genus of one species of perennial that rapidly forms groundcover. Grows in sun or shade and in any but very wet soil. Propagate by seed or division in fall.
ⓘ Contact with the sap may cause skin blisters.

C. majus 'Flore Pleno', illus. p.227.

CHELONE

Turtlehead

SCROPHULARIACEAE/PLANTAGINACEAE

Genus of summer- and fall-flowering perennials. Needs partial shade and moist soil. Propagate by soft-tip cuttings in summer or by division or seed in fall or spring.

C. barbata. See *Penstemon barbatus*.
C. obliqua, illus. p.438.

CHIASTOPHYLLUM

CRASSULACEAE

Genus of one species of evergreen perennial, grown for its succulent leaves and sprays of small, yellow flowers. Thrives in rock crevices. Needs shade and well-drained soil that is not too dry. Propagate by sideshoot cuttings in early summer or by seed in fall.

C. oppositifolium, syn. *Cotyledon simplicifolia,* illus. p.335.

CHIMONANTHUS

CALYCANTHACEAE

Genus of deciduous or evergreen, winter-flowering shrubs, grown for their flowers. At limits of hardiness reduce susceptibility of flowers to frost by training plants against a south- or west-facing wall. Needs full sun and fertile, well-drained soil. Propagate species by seed when ripe, in late spring and early summer, cultivars by softwood cuttings in summer.

C. fragrans. See *C. praecox*. **var. luteus.** See *C. praecox* 'Luteus'.
C. praecox, syn. *C. fragrans,* illus. p.144.

var. concolor. See *C. praecox* 'Luteus'.
'Luteus', syn. *C.* var. *luteus, C. praecox* var. *concolor, C. praecox* 'Concolor' has pure yellow flowers.

CHIMONOBAMBUSA

GRAMINEAE/POACEAE

See also GRASSES, BAMBOOS, RUSHES and SEDGES.

C. timidissinoda, illus. p.287.

CHIONANTHUS

Fringetree

OLEACEAE

Genus of deciduous shrubs, grown for their profuse, white flowers. Flowers more freely in areas with hot summers. Prefers full sun and fertile, well-drained but not too dry soil. Propagate by seed in fall.

C. retusus (Chinese fringe tree). Deciduous, often treelike, arching shrub. **H** and **S** 10ft (3m). From early to mid-summer, star-shaped, pure white flowers are produced in large clusters amid oval, bright green leaves. Z5–9 H9–3.
C. virginicus, illus. p.112.

CHIONOCHLOA

GRAMINEAE/POACEAE

See also GRASSES, BAMBOOS, RUSHES and SEDGES.

C. conspicua (Hunangemoho grass). Evergreen, tussock-forming, perennial grass. **H** 4–5ft (1.2–1.5m), **S** 3ft (1m). Very long, mid-green leaves are tinged reddish-brown. Has sturdy, arching stems with long, loose, open panicles of cream spikelets in summer. Z7–10 H10–7.
C. rubra, illus. p.285.

CHIONODOXA

Glory-of-the-snow

LILIACEAE/ASPARAGACEAE

Genus of spring-flowering bulbs, related to *Scilla*. Is suitable for rock gardens and for naturalizing under shrubs, in sun or partial shade. Requires well-drained soil, top-dressed with leaf mold or mature garden compost in fall. Propagate by seed in fall or by division in late summer or fall.

C. forbesii, syn. *C. luciliae, C. siehei, C. tmolusii,* illus. p.419.
C. gigantea. See *C. luciliae*.
C. luciliae, syn. *C. gigantea,* illus. p.420.
C. luciliae of gardens. See *C. forbesii*.
C. 'Pink Giant', illus. p.416.
C. sardensis. Early spring-flowering bulb. **H** 4–8in (10–20cm), **S** 1–2in (2.5–5cm). Has 2 narrowly lance-shaped, semierect, basal leaves. Leafless stem has 4–15 flattish, slightly pendent or outward-facing, deep rich blue flowers, ⁵/₈–³/₄in (1.5–2cm) across and with, or without an indistinct, white eye. Z3–9 H9–1.
C. siehei. See *C. forbesii*.
C. tmolusii. See *C. forbesii*.

x CHIONOSCILLA

LILIACEAE/ASPARAGACEAE

Hybrid genus (*Chionodoxa* x *Scilla*) of spring-flowering bulbs, suitable for rock gardens. Needs full sun or partial shade

and rich, well-drained soil. Propagate by division in late summer or fall.

x C. allenii, illus. p.419.

CHIRITA

GESNERIACEAE

Genus of evergreen perennials or subshrubs, grown for their flowers. Requires well-drained soil, a fairly humid atmosphere and a light position out of direct sunlight. Propagate by tip cuttings in summer or, if available, seed in late winter or spring.

C. lavandulacea, illus. p.473.
C. sinensis. Evergreen, stemless, rosetted perennial. **H** to 6in (15cm), **S** 10in (25cm) or more. Has oval, almost fleshy leaves, the corrugated, hairy surfaces usually patterned with silver marks. In spring–summer, clusters of tubular, lavender flowers are held above leaves. Z14–15 H11–10.

CHLIDANTHUS

AMARYLLIDACEAE

Genus of one species of summer-flowering bulb, grown for its showy, funnel-shaped flowers. Needs a sunny site and well-drained soil. Plant in the open in spring. After flowering, if necessary, lift and dry off for winter. Propagate by offsets in spring.

C. fragrans, illus. p.424.

CHLOROGALUM

LILIACEAE/HYACINTHACEAE

Genus of summer-flowering bulbs, grown more for botanical interest than for floral display. Requires sun and well-drained soil. Propagate by seed in fall or spring.

C. pomeridianum. Summer-flowering bulb. **H** to 8ft (2.5m), **S** 6–8in (15–20cm). Semierect, basal leaves are long, narrow and gray-green, with wavy margins. Produces a large, loosely branched head of small, saucer-shaped, white flowers, with a central, green or purple stripe on each petal, that open after midday.

CHLOROPHYTUM

LILIACEAE/ASPARAGACEAE

Genus of evergreen, stemless perennials with short rhizomes, grown for their foliage. Grow in a light position, away from direct sun, in fertile, well-drained soil. Water freely in growing season but sparingly at other times if container-grown. Propagate by seed, division or plantlets (produced on flower stems of some species) at any time except winter.

C. capense. Evergreen, tufted perennial. **H** 12in (30cm), **S** indefinite. Forms rosettes of lance- or strap-shaped, bright green leaves, to 24in (60cm) long. Tiny, white flowers in racemes, to 24in (60cm) long, are borne in summer. Does not produce plantlets. Z13–15 H11–10.
C. capense of gardens. See *C. comosum*.
C. comosum, syn. *C. capense* (Spider plant). Evergreen, tufted perennial. **H** 12in (30cm), **S** indefinite. Very narrow leaves, to 18in (45cm) long, spread from a rosette. Racemes of many small, star-shaped, white flowers are produced on thin stems, 24in (60cm) or more long, at

any time. Small rosettes of leaves may appear on flower stems, forming plantlets. Z13–15 H11–10.
'Vittatum' illus. p.465.

CHOISYA

RUTACEAE

Genus of evergreen shrubs, grown for their foliage and flowers. Requires full sun and fertile, well-drained soil. Propagate by semiripe cuttings in late summer.

C. 'Aztec Pearl', illus. p.122.
C. ternata, illus. p.122. SUNDANCE ('Lich') illus. p.148.

Chordospartium stevensonii. See *Carmichaelia stevensonii.*

CHORISIA

Floss silk tree

BOMBACACEAE/MALVACEAE

Genus of deciduous trees, usually with spine-covered trunks, grown mainly for their flowers in fall and winter and their overall appearance. Needs full light and well-drained soil. Water container specimens freely when in full growth, very little when leafless. Pruning is tolerated if necessary. Propagate by seed in spring. Red spider mite may be troublesome.

C. speciosa, syn. *Ceiba speciosa,* illus. p.450.

CHORIZEMA

LEGUMINOSAE/PAPILIONACEAE

Genus of evergreen subshrubs, shrubs and scandent climbers, grown mainly for their flowers. Requires full light and rich, well-drained, sandy soil, preferably neutral to acidic. Water container plants moderately, less when not in full growth. Tie climbers to supports, or grow in hanging baskets. Propagate by seed in spring or by semiripe cuttings in summer.

C. ilicifolium, illus. p.454.

Chrysalidocarpus lutescens. See *Dypsis lutescens.*

CHRYSANTHEMUM

COMPOSITAE/ASTERACEAE

Genus of annuals, perennials, some of which are evergreen, and evergreen subshrubs, grown for their flowers. Each flower head is referred to horticulturally as a flower, even though it does in fact comprise a large number of individual flowers or florets; this horticultural usage has been followed in the descriptions below. Leaves are usually deeply lobed or cut, often feathery, oval to lance-shaped. Florists' chrysanthemums (nowadays considered to belong to the genus *Dendranthema*) comprise the vast majority of chrysanthemums now cultivated and are perennials grown for garden decoration, cutting and exhibition. Florists' chrysanthemums (and the other chrysanthemums treated here) generally perform well in Z5–9 H9–5; for extra protection, crowns should be lifted and stored in a frost-free place over winter. Needs a sunny site and reasonably fertile, well-drained soil. If grown for exhibition, requires regular feeding. Pinch out growing tips to encourage lateral growths on which flowers will be borne, and stake tall plants with canes. Propagate annuals by seed sown in position in spring; thin out, but do not transplant. Propagate hardy perennials by division in fall, after flowering, or in early spring. Florists' chrysanthemums should be propagated from basal softwood cuttings in spring. Spray regularly to control aphids, capsids, froghoppers, earwigs, mildew and white rust.

Florists' chrysanthemums
Florists' chrysanthemums are grouped according to their widely varying flower forms, approximate flowering season (early, mid- or late fall) and habit. They are divided into disbudded and non-disbudded types. For descriptions and illustrations of flower forms, see feature panel pp.252–3.
Disbudded types—single, anemone-centered, incurved, intermediate and reflexed—are so called because all buds, except the one that is to flower, are removed from each stem. To produce exhibition flowers, incurved, intermediate and reflexed chrysanthemums may be restricted to only 2 blooms per plant by removing all except the 2 most vigorous lateral growths. In gardens, allow 4 or 5 blooms per plant to develop. Single and anemone-centered flowers should be reduced to 4–8 blooms per plant for exhibition, according to their vigor, and 10 or more for garden decoration or cutting.
Non-disbudded types—charm, pompom and spray chrysanthemums—have several flowers per stem.
Charm chrysanthemums are dwarf plants that produce hundreds of star-shaped, single flowers, 1in (2.5cm) across, densely covering each plant to form a hemispherical to almost spherical head. For exhibition, finish growing in at least 12in (30cm) pots. Plants for indoor decoration are grown in smaller pots and have correspondingly smaller, though equally dense, heads of blooms.
Pompom chrysanthemums are also dwarf. Each plant has 50 or more dense, spherical or occasionally hemispherical, fully double flowers that have tubular petals (for illustrations see p.252). They are excellent for growing in borders.
Semi-pompom chrysanthemums, sometimes called Japanese pompom, have similar flowers to those of the pompom but as they mature the yellow centers are revealed.
Spray chrysanthemums have a variety of flower forms: single, anemone-centered, intermediate, reflexed, pompom, spoon-shaped (in which each straight, tubular floret opens out like a spoon at its tip), quill-shaped and spider-form. Each plant should be allowed to develop 4 or 5 stems with at least 5 flowers per stem. Grow l ate-flowering sprays on up to 3 stems per plant. With controlled day length, to regulate flowering dates for exhibition purposes, late sprays should be allowed to develop at least 12 flowers per stem; without day length control, 6 or 7 flowers per stem.

Korean Group chrysanthemums
Korean Group chrysanthemums have a variety of flower forms: anemone-centered, pompom, reflexed, single, intermediate, spider, quill and spoon. All are derived from plants originally developed in Connecticut in the 1930s and the prime quality, which they all have in common, is their dependable hardiness: they can be left in the ground all winter without protection. They are ideal for general garden use, in fact they require little special treatment other than good winter drainage; their hardiness can be compromised if grown in poorly drained soil. Some are usefully late in coming into flower; some need support while others are short and bushy. The taller types make good cut flowers.
Those most suitable for garden decoration are sprays, pompoms and early reflexed chrysanthemums. All are suitable for cutting, except for charms. Late-flowering chrysanthemums are suitable for growing only under glass as flowers need protection from poor weather; they should be grown in pots and placed in a greenhouse in early fall, when the flower buds have developed. Intermediate cultivars are also less suitable for garden decoration as florets may collect and retain rain and thus become damaged. Those cultivars suitable for exhibition are noted below. Measurements of flowers given are the greatest normally achieved and may vary considerably depending on growing conditions.

C. 'Alison Kirk'. Incurved florists' chrysanthemum. **H** 4ft (1.2m), **S** 1–2ft (30–60cm). Produces white flowers, to 5–6in (12–15cm) across, in early fall. Is more suitable for exhibition than for garden use.
C. alpinum. See *Leucanthemopsis alpina.*
C. 'Amber Yvonne Arnaud'. Reflexed florists' chrysanthemum. **H** 4ft (1.2m), **S** 2–2½ft (60–75cm). Is a sport of *C.* 'Yvonne Arnaud' with fully reflexed, amber flowers in early fall.
C. 'Anastasia', illus. p.253. Semi-pompom chrysanthemum. **H** 24in (60cm), **S** 20in (50cm). Has flat-topped, dark purplish-pink flowers, 1¼in (3cm) across, with yellow centers, in mid-fall.
C. 'Apollo', illus. p.253. Korean Group chrysanthemum. **H** 36in (90cm), **S** 30in (75cm). Single, bronze-red flowers, 2in (5cm) across, with petals of uneven length, open from dark red buds in late fall.
C. 'Aunt Millicent', illus. p.252. Korean Group chrysanthemum. **H** 30in (75cm), **S** 24in (60cm). Produces abundant, single, silvery-pink flowers, 1½in (4cm) across, each with a pale zone around the yellow center, in mid-fall. Has rather large leaves.
C. 'Autumn Days'. Intermediate florists' chrysanthemum. **H** 3½–4ft (1.1–1.2m), **S** to 2½ft (75cm). Bears loosely incurving, bronze flowers, 5in (12cm) across, in early fall.
C. 'Beacon'. Intermediate florists' chrysanthemum. **H** 4ft (1.2m), **S** 2ft (60cm). Bears red, sometimes bronze, flowers, to 7in (18cm) wide, in late fall. Is good for exhibition.
C. 'Bill Wade'. Intermediate florists' chrysanthemum. **H** 4½ft (1.35m), **S** 2ft (60cm). Loosely incurving, white flowers, 7–8in (18–20cm) across, are borne in early fall. Is more suitable for exhibition than for garden use.
C. 'Brietner'. Reflexed florists' chrysanthemum. **H** 3½–4ft (1.1–1.2m), **S** 2½ft (75cm). Fully reflexed, pink flowers, to 5in (12cm) wide, are borne in early fall.
C. 'Bronze Elegance', illus. p.253. Semi-pompon chrysanthemum. **H** 24in (60cm), **S** 20in (50cm). Light bronze flowers, 1in (2.5cm) across, with yellow centers, are borne on small-leaved plants in mid-fall.
C. 'Bronze Fairie'. Pompon florists' chrysanthemum. **H** 1–2ft (30–60cm), **S** 2ft (60cm). Has bronze flowers, 1½in (4cm) across, in early fall.
C. 'Bronze Hedgerow'. Single florists' chrysanthemum. **H** 5ft (1.5m), **S** 2½–3ft (75cm–1m). Produces bronze flowers, 5in (12cm) across, in late fall.
C. 'Bronze Yvonne Arnaud'. Reflexed florists' chrysanthemum. **H** 4ft (1.2m), **S** 2–2½ft (60–75cm). Is a sport of *C.* 'Yvonne Arnaud' with fully reflexed, bronze flowers in early fall.
C. 'Buff Margaret'. Spray florists' chrysanthemum. **H** 4ft (1.2m), **S** to 2½ft (75cm). Has reflexed, pale bronze flowers, to 3½in (9cm) wide, in early fall.
C. carinatum. See *Ismelia carinata.*
C. 'Carmine Blush', illus. p.253. Rubellum Group chrysanthemum. **H** 24in (60cm), **S** 18in (45cm). Produces single, clear rose-pink flowers, 1½in (4cm) across, each with a greenish-yellow center, from mid-fall to early winter.
C. 'Chelsea Physic Garden', illus. p.253. Rubellum Group chrysanthemum. **H** 45in (115cm), **S** 36in (90cm). In late fall bears double, bronze flowers, 2½in (6cm) across, with yellow-petaled undersides.
C. 'Chesapeake', illus. p.252. Spider-form florists' chrysanthemum. **H** 48in (1.2m), **S** 20in (50cm). Quill-shaped, white flowers, to 8in (20cm) across, are borne in fall when disbudded.
C. 'Chessington'. Intermediate florists' chrysanthemum. **H** 6–7ft (2–2.2m), **S** 2½ft (75cm). Produces fairly tightly incurving, white flowers, 7–8in (18–20cm) across, in early fall. Is more suitable for exhibition than for garden use.
C. 'Christina'. Intermediate florists' chrysanthemum. **H** 4½–5ft (1.35–1.5m), **S** 2–2½ft (60–75cm). Bears loosely incurving, white flowers, to 5½in (14cm) wide, in early fall. Is suitable for exhibition.
C. 'Claire Louise'. Reflexed florists' chrysanthemum. **H** 4–4½ft (1.2–1.35m), **S** 2½ft (75cm). Produces fully reflexed, bronze flowers, to 6in (15cm) across, in early fall. Is ideal for exhibition.
C. 'Clara Curtis', illus. p.247.
C. coccineum. See *Tanacetum coccineum.*
C. coronarium. See *Xanthophthalmum coronarium.*
C. 'Cottage Apricot', illus. p.253. Korean Group chrysanthemum. **H** 30in (75cm), **S** 24in (60cm). Single, bright orange flowers, 2½in (6cm) across, each with a narrow yellow ring around the yellow center, are borne in mid-fall.
C. densum. See *Tanacetum densum* subsp. *amani.*
C. 'Doctor Tom Parr', illus. p.253. Semi-pompon chrysanthemum. **H** and **S** 18in (45cm). Rather flat, rose-madder flowers, 1¼in (3cm) across, with gold flashes fading to beige, are produced in mid-fall. Is a darker sport of *C.* 'Anastasia'.
C. 'Duchess of Edinburgh', illus. p.253. Korean Group chrysanthemum. **H** and **S** 24in (60cm). In early and mid-fall bears semidouble, rich coppery-red flowers, 2in (5cm) across, with yellow centers, some with tufts of petals in the center. Z4–8 H8–4.
C. 'Elsie Prosser'. Fully reflexed florists' chrysanthemum. **H** 4½–5ft (1.3–1.5m), **S** 1ft (30cm). Bears pink flowers, 10in (25cm) wide, in late fall. Is good for exhibition.
C. 'Emperor of China', illus. p.252. Rubellum Group chrysanthemum. **H** 4ft (1.2m), **S** 2ft (60cm). Double, silvery pink flowers, 2in (5cm) across, with quilled petals, are borne in late fall above red-tinted leaves.
C. 'Enbee Wedding', illus. p.252. Spray florists' chrysanthemum. **H** 4ft (1.2m), **S** 2½ft (75cm). Has single, light pink flowers, to 3in (8cm) wide, in early fall. Is good for exhibition.
C. 'Fairweather'. Incurved florists' chrysanthemum. **H** 3½ft (1.1m), **S** 2ft (60cm). Bears pale purplish-pink flowers, 5½in (14cm) wide, in late fall. Is good for exhibition.
C. 'Fiona Lynn'. Reflexed florists' chrysanthemum. **H** 5ft (1.5m), **S** 2½ft (75cm). Fully reflexed, pink flowers, to 7–8in (18–20cm) across, are produced in early fall. Is ideal for exhibition.
C. frutescens. See *Argyranthemum frutescens.* **'Jamaica Primrose'.** See *Argyranthemum* 'Jamaica Primrose'. **'Mary Wootton'.** See *Argyranthemum* 'Mary Wootton'.
C. 'George Griffiths', illus. p.253. Reflexed florists' chrysanthemum. **H** 4–4½ft (1.2–1.35m), **S** 2½ft (75cm). Produces fully reflexed, deep red flowers, to 5½in (14cm) wide, in early fall. Is excellent for exhibition.
C. 'Gigantic'. Tightly incurved or loosely reflexed florists' chrysanthemum, its form depending on the amount of warmth provided. **H** 4½ft (1.3m), **S** 1ft (30cm). Has salmon-pink flowers, 10–11in (25–27cm) wide, in late fall. Is good for exhibition.
C. 'Ginger Nut'. Intermediate florists' chrysanthemum. **H** 4ft (1.2m), **S** 2–2½ft (60–75cm). Bears tightly incurving, light bronze flowers, to 5½in (14cm) across, occasionally closing at top to form a true incurved flower, in early fall. Is good for exhibition.
C. 'Golden Chalice', illus. p.253. Charm florists' chrysanthemum. **H** and **S** 3ft (1m). Bears single, yellow flowers, 1in (2.5cm) wide, in late fall. Is good for exhibition.
C. 'Golden Gigantic'. Tightly incurved or loosely reflexed florists' chrysanthemum. **H** 4½ft (1.3m), **S** 1ft (30cm). Produces large, gold flowers, 10–11in (25–27cm) wide, in late fall. Is good for exhibition.
C. 'Golden Woolman's Glory'. Single florists' chrysanthemum. **H** 5ft (1.5m), **S** 3ft (1m). Golden flowers, to 7in (18cm) across, are borne in late fall. Is excellent for exhibition.
C. 'Grandchild', illus. p.253. Korean Group chrysanthemum. **H** 18in (45cm), **S** 16in (40cm). Has double, bright mauve flowers, 2in (5cm) across, in early fall.
C. 'Green Satin'. Intermediate florists' chrysanthemum. **H** 4ft (1.2m), **S** 2ft (60cm). Produces loosely incurving, green flowers, to 5in (12cm) wide, in late fall.
C. haradjanii. See *Tanacetum haradjanii.*
C. hosmariense. See *Rhodanthemum hosmariense.*
C. 'Idris'. Incurved florists' chrysanthemum. **H** 4½ft (1.3m), **S** 1½ft (45cm). Has salmon-pink flowers, 8–10in (21–25cm) wide, in late fall.
C. 'Innocence', illus. p.252. Rubellum Group chrysanthemum. **H** 32in (80cm), **S** 20in (50cm). Single, palest pink flowers,

2½in (6cm) across, with several layers of petals and a narrow, white ring round the green-centered, yellow disc, are produced in mid- and late fall over red-tinted leaves.
***C.* 'John Wingfield'.** Reflexed florists' chrysanthemum. **H** 5ft (1.5m), **S** 1½–2ft (45–60cm). Produces white, often pink-flushed, flowers, 5in (12cm) wide, in late fall. Is good for exhibition.
***C.* 'Keith Luxford'.** Incurved florists' chrysanthemum. **H** 5ft (1.5m), **S** 1½ft (45cm). Bears pink flowers, 8–10in (21–25cm) wide, in late fall. Is good for exhibition.
***C.* 'Lemon Rynoon'.** Spray florists' chrysanthemum. **H** 5ft (1.5m), **S** 30–39in (75–100cm). Has single, yellow-centered flower heads, 3in (8cm) across, in pale lemon-yellow fading to white, in late fall.
***C.* 'Lundy'.** Fully reflexed florists' chrysanthemum. **H** 5ft (1.5m), **S** 1½ft (45cm). Bears white flowers, 8–10in (21–25cm) wide, often broader than they are deep, in late fall. Is good for exhibition.
***C.* 'Madeleine'.** Spray florists' chrysanthemum. **H** 4ft (1.2m), **S** 2½ft (75cm). Has reflexed, pink flowers, to 3in (8cm) across, in early fall. Is good for exhibition.
***C.* 'Majestic'.** Fully reflexed florists' chrysanthemum. **H** 4½ft (1.3m), **S** 1½ft (45cm). Has light bronze flowers, 8–10in (21–25cm) wide, in late fall. Is good for exhibition.
***C.* 'Maria'.** Pompom florists' chrysanthemum. **H** 1½ft (45cm), **S** 1–2ft (30–60cm). Bears masses of pink flowers, to 1½in (4cm) across, in early fall.
***C.* 'Marian Gosling'.** Reflexed florists' chrysanthemum. **H** 4–4½ft (1.2–1.35m), **S** 2ft (60cm). Fully reflexed, pale pink flowers, to 5½in (14cm) wide, are produced in early fall. Is good for exhibition.
***C.* 'Marion'.** Spray florists' chrysanthemum. **H** 4ft (1.2m), **S** 2½ft (75cm). Produces reflexed, pale yellow flowers, to 3in (8cm) wide, from late summer.
***C.* 'Mary Stoker',** illus. p.253. Rubellum Group chrysanthemum. **H** 39in (100cm), **S** 36in (90cm). Bears slightly ragged-looking, single, creamy-apricot flowers, 2in (5cm) across, each with a domed, yellow center, in mid-fall. Tends to run at the roots. Z4–8 H8–4.
***C.* 'Mason's Bronze'.** Single florists' chrysanthemum. **H** 4½–5ft (1.35–1.5m), **S** to 3ft (1m). Has bronze flowers, to 5in (12cm) wide, in late fall. Is excellent for exhibition.
C. maximum **of gardens.** See *Leucanthemum* x *superbum.*
***C.* 'Mei-kyo'.** Semi-pompom chrysanthemum. **H** and **S** 20in (50cm). In mid- and late fall produces pale mauve flowers, 1in (2.5cm) across, each with a small, yellow center and with new petals in the center a darker shade. Has small leaves.
***C.* 'Mrs. Jessie Cooper',** illus. p.253. Rubellum Group chrysanthemum. **H** 36in (90cm), **S** 24in (60cm). Single, vivid cerise-pink, flowers, 2in (5cm) across, each with a slender, white ring around the domed, yellow center, are borne in mid- and late fall above broad, dark green leaves.
***C.* 'Myss Saffron'.** Spray chrysanthemum. **H** 34in (85cm), **S** 30in (75cm). In late summer and early fall bears erect sprays of double, yellow flowers, 2½in (6cm) across, fading to cream.
***C.* 'Nancye Furneaux'.** Reflexed florists' chrysanthemum. **H** 5ft (1.5m), **S** 1½ft (45cm). Has yellow flowers, 8–10in (21–25cm) wide, in late fall. Is good for exhibition.
***C.* 'Nantyderry Sunshine',** illus. p.253. Semi-pompom chrysanthemum. **H** and **S** 20in (50cm). Bright yellow flowers, 1in (2.5cm) across, each with a small, yellow center, are borne in mid- to late fall. May occasionally revert to the pink of *C.* 'Mei-kyo'.
***C.* 'Nell Gwynn',** illus. p.252. Korean Group chrysanthemum. **H** 30in (75cm), **S** 24in (60cm). Single, rose-pink flowers, 2¾in (6.5cm) across, each with a primrose-yellow ring around the yellow center, are produced in late summer and early fall above broad, mid-green leaves.
***C.* 'Oracle'.** Intermediate florists' chrysanthemum. **H** 4ft (1.2m), **S** 2–2½ft (60–75cm). Produces loosely incurving, pale bronze flowers, to 5in (12cm) wide, in early fall. Is useful for exhibition.
C. parthenium. See *Tanacetum parthenium.*
***C.* 'Paul Boissier',** illus. p.253. Rubellum Group chrysanthemum. **H** 39in (1m), **S** 30in (75cm). Has semidouble, orange-bronze flowers, 2in (5cm) across, with sharp-pointed petals, in mid- to late fall.
***C.* 'Peach Brietner'.** Reflexed florists' chrysanthemum. **H** 3½–4ft (1.1–1.2m), **S** 2½ft (75cm). Is a sport of *C.* 'Brietner' with fully reflexed, peach-colored flowers.
***C.* 'Pennine Alfie'.** Spray florists' chrysanthemum. **H** 4ft (1.2m), **S** 2–2½ft (60–75cm). Spoon-shaped, pale bronze flowers, to 2½–3in (6–8cm) wide, are borne in early fall. Is suitable for exhibition. Z4–9 H9–1.
***C.* 'Pennine Flute'.** Quill-shaped florists' chrysanthemum. **H** 4ft (1.2m), **S** 2–2½ft (60–75cm). Is similar to *C.* 'Pennine Alfie', but has pink flowers.
***C.* 'Pennine Oriel',** illus. p.252. Spray florists' chrysanthemum. **H** 4ft (1.2m), **S** 2–2½ft (60–75cm). Anemone-centered, white flowers, to 9cm (3½in) across, are produced in early fall. Is very good for exhibition.
***C.* 'Perry's Peach',** illus. p.253. Korean Group chrysanthemum. **H** 20in (50cm), **S** 16in (40cm). Single, peach-pink flowers, 2in (5cm) across, each with a narrow, cream band round the golden-yellow center, are produced in mid-fall over red-tinted leaves.
***C.* 'Peterkin'.** Semi-pompom chrysanthemum. **H** and **S** 20in (50cm). In mid- and late fall bears golden-yellow flowers, 1in (2.5cm) across, with each petal tipped in rusty-orange, becoming paler with age, and with a small, yellow center. Has small leaves.
***C.* 'Peter Rowe'.** Incurved florists' chrysanthemum. **H** 4½ft (1.35m), **S** 2–2½ft (60–75cm). Produces yellow flowers, to 5½in (14cm) across, in early fall. Is ideal for exhibition.
***C.* 'Primrose Fairweather'.** Incurved florists' chrysanthemum. **H** 3–3½ft (1–1.1m), **S** to 2½ft (75cm). Produces pale yellow flowers, to 5½–6in (14–15cm) wide, in late fall. Is good for exhibition.
***C.* 'Primrose John Hughes'.** Perfectly incurved florists' chrysanthemum. **H** 4ft (1.2m), **S** 2–2½ft (60–75cm). Bears primrose-yellow flowers, 5–5½in (12–14cm) wide, in late fall. Is good for exhibition.
***C.* 'Primrose West Bromwich'.** Reflexed florists' chrysanthemum. **H** 7ft (2.2m), **S** 1½–2ft (45–60cm). Fully reflexed, pale yellow flowers, to 7in (18cm) or more wide, are borne in mid-fall. Use only for exhibition.
***C.* 'Purleigh White',** illus. p.252. Semi-pompom chrysanthemum. **H** and **S** 20in (50cm). In mid- and late fall bears white flowers, 1in (2.5cm) across, slightly blushed in pink, each with a small, yellow center. Has small leaves.
***C.* 'Purple Pennine Wine'.** Spray florists' chrysanthemum. **H** 4ft (1.2m), **S** 2–2½ft (60–75cm). Bears reflexed, purplish-red flowers, to 3in (8cm) wide, in early fall. Is very good for exhibition.
***C.* 'Ringdove'.** Charm florists' chrysanthemum. **H** and **S** 3ft (1m). Has masses of pink flowers, 1in (2.5cm) across, in late fall. Is excellent for exhibition.
***C.* 'Robeam'.** Spray florists' chrysanthemum. **H** 5ft (1.5m), **S** 2½–3ft (75–100cm). Produces reflexed, yellow flowers, to 3in (8cm) wide, in late fall. Is good for exhibition.
***C.* 'Rose Yvonne Arnaud'.** Reflexed florists' chrysanthemum. **H** 4ft (1.2m), **S** 2–2½ft (60–75cm). Is a sport of *C.* 'Yvonne Arnaud', producing fully reflexed, red flowers in early fall. Z4–9 H9–1.
***C.* 'Roy Coopland'.** Intermediate to loosely incurved florists' chrysanthemum. **H** 4½ft (1.3m), **S** 2ft (60cm). Produces bronze flowers, 6in (15cm) wide, in late fall. Is good for exhibition.
***C.* 'Ruby Mound',** illus. p.253. Korean Group chrysanthemum. **H** 36in (90cm), **S** 32in (80cm). Prolific, fully double, rich deep maroon flowers, 2½in (6cm) across, are borne in mid- and late fall.
***C.* 'Rumpelstilzchen',** illus. p.253. Korean Group chrysanthemum. **H** 24in (60cm), **S** 20in (50cm). Single, rich red flowers, 1½in (4cm) across, with several layers of petals and a narrow, yellow ring around the yellow center, are produced in early fall. Dislikes wet soil in winter.
***C.* 'Rytorch'.** Spray florists' chrysanthemum. **H** 5ft (1.5m), **S** 30–39in (75–100cm). Produces single, light bronze, yellow-centered flower heads, to 3in (8cm) across, in late fall.
***C.* 'Salmon Fairie'.** Pompom florists' chrysanthemum. **H** 1–2ft (30–60cm), **S** 2ft (60cm). Is similar to *C.* 'Bronze Fairie', but has salmon flowers.
***C.* 'Salmon Margaret'.** Spray florists' chrysanthemum. **H** 4ft (1.2m), **S** to 2½ft (75cm). Is similar to *C.* 'Buff Margaret', but has salmon flowers.
***C.* 'Sea Urchin',** illus. p.253. Korean Group chrysanthemum. **H** 24in (60cm), **S** 20in (50cm). Produces spider-form, fully double, lemon-yellow flowers, 3in (7cm) across, in early and mid-fall. Dislikes winter wet.
C. segetum. See *Xanthophthalmum segetum.*
***C.* 'Senkyo Emiaki'.** Spider-form florists' chrysanthemum. **H** 1–2ft (30–60cm), **S** to 2ft (60cm). Bears light pink flowers, 6in (15cm) wide, in early fall. Is good for exhibition.
C. serotinum. See *Leucanthemella serotina.*
***C.* 'Spartan Seagull',** illus. p.252. Korean Group chrysanthemum. **H** 28in (70cm), **S** 20in (50cm). Slightly ruffled, single, white flowers, 3in (7cm) across, are borne in early fall. Has dark green leaves.
***C.* x *superbum*.** See *Leucanthemum* x *superbum.*
***C.* 'Talbot Jo'.** Spray florists' chrysanthemum. **H** 4½ft (1.3m), **S** 30in (75cm). Bears single, yellow-centered, pink flower heads, 3in (8cm) across, in early fall. Is good for exhibition.
***C.* 'Tapestry Rose',** illus. p.253. Korean Group chrysanthemum. **H** 36in (90cm), **S** 24in (60cm). Slightly messy, rich rose-pink flowers, 1½in (4cm) across, with green-centered, yellow discs, are produced in mid-fall.
C. tricolor. See *Ismelia carinata.*
C. ulignosum. See *Leucanthemella serotina.*
***C.* 'Venice'.** Reflexed florists' chrysanthemum. **H** 4ft (1.2m), **S** 2–2½ft (60–75cm). Reflexed, pink flowers, to 6in (15cm) wide, are produced in early fall. Is good for exhibition.
***C.* 'Wendy'.** Spray florists' chrysanthemum. **H** 4ft (1.2m), **S** 2–2½ft (60–75cm). Produces reflexed, pale bronze flowers, to 3in (8cm) wide, in early fall. Is excellent for exhibition. Z4–9 H9–1.
C. weyrichii. Mat-forming, rhizomatous perennial. **H** 12in (30cm), **S** 18in (45cm). In fall bears single, yellow-centered, pink or white flowers, 5cm (2in) across. Z5–9 H9–5.
***C.* 'Woking Rose'.** Intermediate florists' chrysanthemum. **H** 5ft (1.5m), **S** 1½ft (45cm). Has rose-pink flowers, to 8in (21cm) wide, in late fall. Is good for exhibition.
***C.* 'Yellow Brietner'.** Reflexed florists' chrysanthemum. **H** 3½–4ft (1.1–1.2m), **S** 2½ft (75cm). Is a sport of *C.* 'Brietner' with fully reflexed, yellow flowers in early fall.
***C.* 'Yellow John Hughes',** illus. p.253. Incurved florists' chrysanthemum. **H** 4ft (1.2m), **S** 2–2½ft (60–75cm). Yellow flowers, to 5–5½in (12–14cm) wide, are produced in late fall. Is excellent for exhibition.
***C.* 'Yvonne Arnaud'.** Reflexed florists' chrysanthemum. **H** 4ft (1.2m), **S** 2–2½ft (60–75cm). Fully reflexed, purple flowers, to 5in (12cm) wide, are produced in early fall.

CHRYSOGONUM

COMPOSITAE/ASTERACEAE

Genus of one species of summer- to fall-flowering perennial. Is suitable for rock gardens. Needs partial shade and moist but well-drained, peaty, sandy soil. Propagate by division in spring or by seed when fresh.
C. virginianum, illus. p.344.

CHRYSOSPLENIUM

SAXIFRAGACEAE

Genus of creeping hardy perennials, grown for their foliage and early spring flowers. Requires a shady position and moist, poor to moderately fertile, rich soil. Propagate by division or soft-tip cuttings in spring or by seed in fall.
C. macrophyllum, illus. p.256.

CHUSQUEA

GRAMINEAE/POACEAE

See also GRASSES, BAMBOOS, RUSHES and SEDGES.
C. culeou, illus. p.288.

CICERBITA

SYN. MULGEDIUM

COMPOSITAE/ASTERACEAE

Genus of perennials, grown for their flower heads. Needs shade and damp but well-drained soil. Propagate by division in spring or by seed in fall. Some species may be invasive.

C. alpina, syn. *Lactuca alpina* (Mountain sow thistle). Branching, upright perennial. **H** to 6ft (2m), **S** 2ft (60cm). Mid-green leaves are lobed, with a large, terminal lobe. Bears elongated panicles of thistle-like, pale blue flower heads in summer. Z5–9 H9–5.

C. bourgaei, syn. *Lactuca bourgaei.* Rampant, erect perennial. **H** to 6ft (2m), **S** 2ft (60cm). Leaves are oblong to lance-shaped, toothed and light green. Many-branched panicles of thistle-like, mauve-blue or purplish-blue flower heads appear in summer. Z5–9 H9–5.

CICHORIUM

Chicory

COMPOSITAE/ASTERACEAE

Genus of annuals, biennials and perennials, grown mainly in herb or kitchen gardens (*C. intybus* has edible leaves). Needs full sun and well-drained soil. Propagate by seed in fall or spring. ① Contact with all parts of the plants may irritate skin or aggravate skin allergies.

C. intybus, illus. p.242.

CIMICIFUGA

Black cohosh, Bugbane

RANUNCULACEAE

Genus of perennials, grown for their flowers, which have an unusual, slightly unpleasant smell. Requires partial shade and moist soil. Needs staking. Propagate by seed when fresh or by division in spring. Sometimes included in the closely related genus *Actaea*, which has fleshy, berry-like fruits, whereas the pods of *Cimicifuga* are dry and not fleshy.

C. cordifolia, syn. *C. racemosa* var. *cordifolia, C. rubifolia* (Black snakeroot). Clump-forming perennial. **H** 5ft (1.5m), **S** 2ft (60cm). Feathery plumes of star-shaped, creamy-white flowers are produced in mid-summer above broadly oval to lance-shaped, dissected, light green leaves. Z6–8 H8–5.

C. racemosa, syn. *Actaea racemosa* (Kamchatka bugbane). Clump-forming perennial. **H** 1–5ft (30–150cm), **S** 2ft (60cm). Spikes of bottlebrush-like, pure white flowers are borne in mid-summer above broadly oval, divided, fresh green leaves. Z3–8 H9–1.

var. cordifolia. See *C. cordifolia.*

C. rubifolia. See *C. cordifolia.*

C. simplex, syn. *Actaea simplex,* illus. p.220. **'Elstead'** is an upright perennial. **H** 4ft (1.2m), **S** 2ft (60cm). Purple stems bear arching racemes of fragrant, bottlebrush-like, white flowers in fall. Has broadly oval to lance-shaped, divided, glossy leaves. Z4–8 H9–1. **'Prichard's Giant'** (Camphor tree), **H** 7ft (2.2m), has large, much-divided leaves and produces white flowers on arching panicles. Z4–8 H9–1.

Cineraria cruentus of gardens. See *Pericallis x hybrida.*

Cineraria x hybridus. See *Pericallis x hybrida.*

CINNAMOMUM

LAURACEAE

Genus of evergreen trees, grown for their foliage and to provide shade. Requires full light or partial shade and fertile, moist but well-drained soil. Water container specimens freely when in full growth, less at other times. May be pruned if necessary. Propagate by seed in spring or by semiripe cuttings in summer.

C. camphora. Moderately fast-growing, evergreen, rounded tree. **H** and **S** 40ft (12m) or more. Oval, lustrous, rich green leaves, tinted blue-gray beneath, reddish or coppery when young, are camphor-scented when bruised. Produces insignificant flowers in spring. Z8–10 H10–8.

CIONURA

ASCLEPIADACEAE/APOCYNACEAE

Genus of one species of deciduous, twining climber, grown for its flowers. Grow in any soil and in full sun. Prune after flowering. Propagate by seed in spring or by stem cuttings in late summer or early fall. ① Contact with the latex exuded by cut leaves and stems may irritate skin or cause blisters, and may cause severe discomfort if ingested.

C. erecta, syn. *Marsdenia erecta.* Deciduous, twining climber. **H** 10ft (3m) or more. Heart-shaped, grayish-green leaves are 1¼–2¼in (3–6cm) long. In summer, clusters of fragrant, white flowers, with 5 spreading petals, are borne in leaf axils, followed by fruits, 3in (7cm) long, containing many silky seeds, in fall. Z9–10 H11–10.

CIRSIUM

COMPOSITAE/ASTERACEAE

Genus of annuals, biennials and perennials. Most species are not cultivated—indeed, some are pernicious weeds—but *C. rivulare* has decorative flower heads. Tolerates sun or shade and any but wet soil. Propagate by division in spring or by seed in fall.

C. rivulare 'Atropurpureum'. Erect perennial. **H** 4ft (1.2m), **S** 2ft (60cm). Heads of pincushionlike, deep crimson flowers are borne on erect stems in summer. Leaves are narrowly oval to oblong or lance-shaped and deeply cut, with weakly spiny margins. Z4–8 H8–1.

CISSUS

VITACEAE

Genus of evergreen, woody-stemmed, mainly tendril climbers, grown for their foliage. Bears insignificant, greenish flowers, mainly in summer. Needs fertile, well-drained soil, and partial shade in summer. Water regularly, less in cold weather. Needs tying to supports. Thin out crowded stems in spring. Propagate by semiripe cuttings in summer.

C. antarctica, illus. p.463.

C. bainesii. See *Cyphostemma bainesii.*

C. discolor (Rex begonia vine). Moderately vigorous, evergreen, tendril climber with slender, woody stems. **H** to 10ft (3m). Oval, pointed leaves, 4–6in (10–15cm) long, are deep green with silver bands above, maroon beneath. Z11 H11–10.

C. hypoglauca. Evergreen, woody-stemmed, scrambling climber. **H** 6–10ft (2–3m). Leaves are divided into 4 or 5 oval leaflets that are pale green above and blue-gray beneath. Z13–15 H11–10.

C. juttae. See *Cyphostemma juttae.*

C. rhombifolia, syn. *Rhoicissus rhombifolia, Rhoicissus rhomboidea* (Grape ivy). Moderately vigorous, evergreen, woody-stemmed, tendril climber. **H** 10ft (3m) or more. Has lustrous leaves divided into 3 coarsely toothed leaflets. Z12–14 H11–10.

C. striata, syn. *Ampelopsis sempervirens, Parthenocissus striata, Vitis striata* (Ivy of Uruguay, Miniature grape ivy). Fast-growing, evergreen, woody-stemmed, tendril climber. **H** 30ft (10m) or more. Has leaves of 3–5 oval, serrated, lustrous, green leaflets. Mature plants may produce pea-shaped, glossy, black fruits in fall. Z12–14 H11–10.

C. voinieriana. See *Tetrastigma voinierianum.*

Cistanthe tweedyi. See *Lewisia tweedyi.*

CISTUS

Rock rose

CISTACEAE

Genus of evergreen shrubs, grown for their succession of freely borne, short-lived, showy flowers. Is good in coastal areas, withstanding sea winds well. Prefers full sun and light, well-drained soil. Resents being transplanted. Cut out any dead wood in spring, but do not prune hard. Propagate species by softwood or greenwood cuttings in summer or by seed in fall, hybrids and cultivars by cuttings only in summer.

C. x aguilari 'Maculatus', illus. p.150.

C. albidus (Crimson-spot rockrose). Evergreen, bushy shrub. **H** and **S** 3ft (1m). Leaves are oblong and white-felted. Saucer-shaped, pale rose-pink flowers, each with a central, yellow blotch, are produced in early summer. Z8–10 H10–8.

C. algarvensis. See *Halimium ocymoides.*

C. x argenteus 'Peggy Sammons', illus. p.153.

C. x corbariensis. See *C. x hybridus.*

C. creticus, syn. *C. incanus* subsp. *creticus,* illus. p.154.

C. x cyprius, illus. p.150.

C. x dansereaui, syn. *C. x lusitanicus* of gardens. Evergreen, bushy, compact shrub. **H** and **S** 3ft (1m). Leaves are narrowly oblong and dark green. Saucer-shaped, white flowers, each with a central, deep red blotch, are borne from early to mid-summer. Z8–10 H10–8.

C. x hybridus, syn. *C. x corbariensis,* illus. p.150.

C. incanus subsp. creticus. See *C. creticus.*

C. ladanifer, syn. *C. ladaniferus,* illus. p.150.

C. ladaniferus. See *C. ladanifer.*

C. laurifolius. Evergreen, bushy, dense shrub. **H** and **S** 6ft (2m). Has oval, aromatic, dark green leaves and, in summer, saucer-shaped, white flowers, each with a central, yellow blotch. Z8–10 H10–8.

C. x lenis 'Grayswood Pink', syn. *C. 'Silver Pink'.* Evergreen, bushy shrub. **H** 2ft (60cm), **S** 3ft (1m). Oval, dark green leaves set off large, saucer-shaped, clear pink flowers, each with conspicuous, yellow stamens, from early to mid-summer. Z8–10 H10–8.

C. x lusitanicus of gardens. See *C. x dansereaui.*

C. monspeliensis. Evergreen, bushy shrub. **H** 3ft (1m), **S** 5ft (1.5m). Has narrow, wrinkled, dark green leaves and small, white flowers freely borne from early to mid-summer. Z8–11 H11–8.

C. parviflorus (Sageleaf rockrose). Evergreen, bushy, dense shrub. **H** and **S** 3ft (1m). Small, saucer-shaped, pale pink flowers are produced among oval, gray-green leaves in early summer. Z8–10 H10–8.

C. x purpureus. Evergreen, bushy, rounded shrub. **H** and **S** 3ft (1m). Produces saucer-shaped, deep purplish-pink flowers, each blotched with deep red, from early to mid-summer. Leaves are narrowly lance-shaped and gray-green. Z9–10 H10–8.

C. revolii of gardens. See *Halimiocistus sahucii.*

C. salviifolius, illus. p.150.

C. 'Silver Pink'. See *C. x lenis* 'Grayswood Pink'.

C. x skanbergii, illus. p.152.

x CITROFORTUNELLA

RUTACEAE

Hybrid genus (*Citrus x Fortunella*) of evergreen shrubs and trees, grown for their flowers, fruits and overall appearance. Needs full light and fertile, well-drained but not dry soil. Water container specimens freely when in full growth, moderately at other times. Propagate by seed when ripe or by greenwood or semiripe cuttings in summer. Whitefly, red spider mite, mealy bug, lime-induced and magnesium-deficiency chlorosis may be troublesome.

x C. microcarpa, syn. x *C. mitis, Citrus mitis,* illus. p.458.

x C. mitis. See x *C. microcarpa.*

Citrus mitis. See *Citrofortunella microcarpa.*

CLADANTHUS

COMPOSITAE/ASTERACEAE

Genus of one species of annual, grown for its fragrant foliage and daisylike flower heads. Grow in sun and in reasonably fertile, very well-drained soil. Dead-head to prolong flowering. Propagate by seed sown outdoors in mid-spring.

C. arabicus, illus. p.321.

Cladastris lutea. See *Cladrastis kentukea.*

CLADRASTIS

LEGUMINOSAE/PAPILIONACEAE

Genus of deciduous, summer-flowering trees, grown for their pendent, wisteria-like flower clusters and fall foliage. Requires full sun and fertile, well-drained soil. Propagate by seed in fall or by root cuttings in late winter. The wood is brittle: old trees are prone to damage by strong winds.

C. kentukea, syn. *Cladastris lutea,* illus. p.79.

CLARKIA

SYN. GODETIA

ONAGRACEAE

Genus of annuals, grown for their flowers, which are good for cutting. Needs sun and reasonably fertile, well-drained soil. Avoid rich soil as this encourages vegetative growth at the expense of flowers. Propagate by seed sown outdoors in spring, or in early fall in mild areas. Botrytis may be troublesome.

C. amoena. Fast-growing annual with upright, thin stems. **H** to 24in (60cm), **S** 12in (30cm). Has lance-shaped, mid-green leaves. Spikes of 5-petaled, single or double flowers, in shades of lilac to pink, are produced in summer. Tall forms, **H** 24in (60cm), have double flowers in shades of pink or red. H7–1. **Grace Series** (intermediate), **H** to 20in (50cm), has single, lavender-pink, red, salmon-pink or pink flowers with contrasting centers. **Princess Series** (dwarf), **H** 12in (30cm), has frilled flowers in shades of pink. **Satin Series** (dwarf), **H** to 8in (20cm), has single flowers in various colors, many with white margins or contrasting centers. **'Sybil Sherwood'** illus. p.305.

***C.* 'Brilliant',** illus. p.305.

CLAYTONIA

PORTULACACEAE

Genus of mainly evergreen perennials with succulent leaves; is related to *Lewisia*. Grows best in alpine houses. Fully hardy. Tolerates sun or shade and prefers well-drained soil. Propagate by seed or division in fall. May be difficult to grow.

C. megarhiza, syn. *Calandrinia megarhiza*. Evergreen, basal-rosetted perennial with a long taproot. **H** ½in (1cm), **S** 3in (8cm). Leaves are spoon-shaped and fleshy. Bears small heads of tiny, bowl-shaped, white flowers in spring. Prefers sun and gritty soil. Is prone to aphid attack. Z5–7 H7–5. **var. *nivalis*** illus. p.351.

C. virginica (Spring beauty). Clump-forming perennial with flat, black tubers. **H** 4in (10cm), **S** 8in (20cm) or more. Narrowly spoon-shaped leaves, reddish when young, later turn green and glossy. Branched stems bear cup-shaped, white or pink flowers, striped deep pink, in early spring. Needs shade. Z4–9 H6–1.

CLEISTOCACTUS

SYN. BORZICACTUS

CACTACEAE

Genus of columnar, perennial cacti with branched, cylindrical, much-ribbed stems with spines. Is one of the faster-growing cacti, some reaching 6ft (2m) in 5 years or less. Tubular flowers contain plenty of nectar and are pollinated by hummingbirds. Needs full sun and very well-drained soil. Propagate by seed or stem cuttings in spring or summer.

C. baumannii. Erect, then prostrate, perennial cactus. **H** 3ft (1m) or more, **S** 15ft (5m). Thick stems produce long, uneven, variable-colored spines. Has S-shaped, tubular, bright orange-red flowers in spring–summer. Z13–15 H12–10.

C. celsianus. See *Oreocereus celsianus.*

C. smaragdiflorus. Erect, then prostrate, perennial cactus. **H** 5ft (1.5m), **S** 20ft (6m). Is similar to *C. baumannii*, but has straight, tubular flowers with green-tipped petals. Z13–15 H11–10.

C. strausii, illus. p.479.

C. trollii. See *Oreocereus trollii.*

CLEMATIS

RANUNCULACEAE

Genus of evergreen or deciduous, mainly twining climbers and herbaceous perennials, cultivated for their mass of flowers, often followed by decorative seed heads, and grown on walls and trellises and together with trees, shrubs and other host plants. Only early-flowering species are evergreen, although some later-flowering species are semievergreen. Most species have nodding, bell-shaped flowers, with 4 petals (botanically known as perianth segments), or flattish flowers, each usually with 4–6 generally pointed petals. Large-flowered cultivars also bear flattish flowers, but with 4–10 petals. Flower color may vary according to climatic conditions: in general, the warmer the climate, the darker the flower color. May be grown in partial shade or full sun, but prefers rich, well-drained soil with roots shaded. Propagate cultivars in early summer by softwood or semiripe cuttings or layering, species from seed in fall. Aphids, mildew and clematis wilt may cause problems.

Clematis may be divided into groups according to their flowering seasons, habit and pruning needs. See also feature panel pp.198–200.

Group 1

Early-flowering species prefers a sheltered, sunny site with well-drained soil. Small, single flowers, either bell-shaped or open-bell-shaped, ½–2in (2–5cm) long, or saucer-shaped, 1¼–2in (4–5cm) across, are borne on the previous season's ripened shoots in spring or, occasionally, in late winter. Leaves are evergreen and glossy, or deciduous, and usually divided into 3 lance-shaped, 5in (12cm) long leaflets or into 3 fernlike, 2in (5cm) long leaflets.

***C. alpina, C. macropetala* and their cultivars** tolerate cold, exposed positions. Small, bell-shaped to open bell-shaped, single, semidouble or double flowers, 2in (5cm) across, are borne on the previous season's ripened shoots in spring, occasionally also on the current season's shoots in summer. Deciduous, pale to mid-green leaves are divided into 3–5 lance-shaped to broadly oblong, toothed leaflets, 1¼in (3cm) long.

***C. montana* and its cultivars** are vigorous, deciduous climbers, suitable for growing over large buildings and trees. Small, flat to saucer-shaped, usually single flowers, 2–3in (5–7cm) across, are borne on the previous season's ripened shoots in late spring. Leaves are mid- to purplish-green and divided into 3 lance-shaped to broadly oval, serrated leaflets, 3in (8cm) long with pointed tips.

Prune all group 1 clematis after flowering to allow new growth to be produced and ripened for the following season. Remove dead or damaged stems and cut back other shoots that have outgrown their allotted space. This will encourage new growth to bear flowers in the following season.

Group 2

Early- to mid-season, large-flowered cultivars bearing mostly saucer-shaped, single, semidouble or fully double flowers, 4–8in (10–20cm) across, that are borne on the previous season's ripened shoots, in late spring and early summer, and on new shoots in mid- and late summer. Generally the second flush of flowers on semidouble and double forms produces single flowers. Deciduous, pale to mid-green leaves are usually 4–6in (10–15cm) long and divided into 3 ovate or lance-shaped leaflets, or are simple and ovate, and to 4in (10cm) long.

Prune before new growth starts, in early spring. Remove any dead or damaged stems and cut back all remaining shoots to where strong buds are visible. These buds provide a framework of second-year shoots which, in turn, produce sideshoots that flower in late spring and early summer. The flowers may then be removed. Young shoots bear more flowers later in the summer.

Group 3

Late, large-flowered cultivars producing outward-facing, usually saucer-shaped, single flowers, 3–6in (7–15cm) across, borne on new shoots in summer or early fall. Leaves are deciduous and similar to those of early cultivars (group 2), described above.

Late-flowering species and small-flowered cultivars that bear small, single or double flowers on the current season's shoots in summer–fall. Flowers vary in shape and may be star-shaped, tubular, bell-shaped, flattish or resembling nodding lanterns; they vary in size from ½in (1cm) to 4in (10cm) across. Have generally deciduous, pale to dark green or gray-green leaves divided into 3 lance-shaped to broadly oval leaflets, each ½in (1cm) long, or hairy and/or toothed leaves divided into 5 or more lance-shaped to broadly oval leaflets, each ½–4in (1–10cm) long.

Herbaceous species and cultivars producing single flowers that are either saucer-shaped, ½–¾in (1–2cm) wide, or bell-shaped or tubular, ½–1½in (1–4cm) long, and are produced on the current season's shoots in summer. Mid- to dark green or gray-green leaves are simple and lance-shaped to elliptic, 1–6in (2.5–15cm) long, or are divided into 3–5 lance-shaped to ovate, serrated leaflets, each 4–6in (10–15cm) long with a pointed tip. Prune all group 3 clematis before new growth begins, in early spring. Cut back all the previous season's stems to a pair of strong buds, 6–8in (15–20cm) above soil level.

***C.* 'Abundance',** syn. *C. viticella*, illus. p.200. Late-flowering clematis (group 3). **H** 6–10ft (2–3m), **S** 3ft (1m). Produces flattish, deep purplish-red flowers, 2in (5cm) across, with cream anthers, in summer. Z4–11 H9–1.

***C.* Alabast ('Poulala')** (Alpine clematis). Vigorous, large-flowered clematis (group 2). **H** 10ft (3m), **S** 3ft (1m). Freely produces large, rounded, creamy-green flowers, 5–6in (12–15cm) across, with creamy-yellow anthers, in late spring and again from mid- to late summer.

***C.* 'Alionushka',** illus. p.199. Semi-herbaceous, non-clinging clematis (group 3). **H** 3–4ft (1–1.2m), **S** 3ft (1m). In mid-summer to early fall produces single, rich mauvish-pink flowers, 2½–3in (6–8cm) across, with a satin sheen when young, with deep ridges on the reverse and crumpled edges; the petal tips recurve and twist as they age.

C. alpina. Alpina clematis (group 1). **H** 6–10ft (2–3m), **S** 5ft (1.5m). Has lantern-shaped, single, blue flowers, 1½–3in (4–7cm) long, in spring and, occasionally, summer. Forms fluffy, silvery seed heads in summer. Is ideal for a north-facing or very exposed site. Z4–9 H9–6. **'Columbine'.** See *C.* 'Columbine'. **'Constance'.** See *C.* 'Constance'. **'Frances Rivis'.** See *C.* 'Frances Rivis'. **'Frankie'.** See *C.* 'Frankie'.

***C.* 'Andromeda',** illus. p.198. Early, large-flowered clematis (group 2). **H** 6–10ft (2–3m), **S** 3ft (1m). Semidouble, white flowers, with bright pink stripes in the center of each sepal, are produced in spring and again later in the year when they are single.

***C.* Angelique ('Evipo017').** Compact, mid- to late season clematis (group 2). **H** 3–4ft (90cm–1.2m), **S** 3ft (1m). Produces an abundance of lilac-blue, brown-anthered flowers, 4in (10cm) across, from early summer to late fall. Z5–9 H9–5.

***C.* Anna Louise ('Evithree'),** illus. p.200. Compact, early, large-flowered clematis (group 2). **H** 3–4ft (1–1.2m), **S** 3ft (1m). Freely produces single flowers with violet petals with a red-purple central bar, and striking brown anthers, in late spring to early summer, and again in late summer to early fall. Z4–9 H9–1.

***C.* Arctic Queen ('Evitwo'),** illus. p.198. Early, large-flowered clematis (group 2). **H** 10ft (3m), **S** 3ft (1m). From early summer to early fall freely produces double, clear creamy-white flowers, 4–7in (10–18cm) across, with yellow anthers. Z7–9 H9–7.

C. armandii (Evergreen clematis), illus. p.198. Strong-growing, evergreen, early-flowering clematis (group 1). **H** 10–15ft (3–5m), **S** 6–10ft (2–3m). Bears scented, flattish, single, white flowers, 1½in (4cm) across, in early spring. Needs a sheltered, south- or south-west-facing site. Z7–11 H9–7.

***C.* 'Ascotiensis'.** Vigorous, late, large-flowered clematis (group 3). **H** 10–12ft (3–4m), **S** 3ft (1m). Single, bright violet-blue flowers, 3½–5in (9–12cm) across, with pointed petals and brownish-green anthers, are produced in summer. Z4–11 H9–1.

***C.* Avant-Garde ('Evipo033'),** illus. p.200. Vigorous, mid-season clematis (group 3). **H** 10ft (3m), **S** 3ft (1m). Freely produces deep red flowers, to 2in (5cm) across, with central pompoms of pink, petaloid stamens, from mid-summer to fall. Z5–9 H9–5.

***C.* 'Barbara Dibley',** illus. p.199. Early, large-flowered clematis (group 2). **H** 8ft (2.5m), **S** 3ft (1m). In late spring produces single, petunia-red flowers, to 9in (23cm) across, with carmine-red to red-purple stripes along each sepal and red-purple stamens.

***C.* 'Barbara Jackman',** illus. p.199. Early, large-flowered clematis (group 2). **H** to 10ft (3m), **S** 3ft (1m). In early summer produces single, bluish-mauve flowers, with crimson stripes and creamy-white stamens, followed in late summer by a further flush. Grow in partial shade as flowers fade in full sun. Z4–11 H9–1.

***C.* 'Bees Jubilee'.** Compact, early, large-flowered clematis (group 2). **H** 8ft (2.5m),

S 3ft (1m). In early summer bears a profusion of single, deep pink flowers, 4–5in (10–12cm) across, with brown anthers and a central, rose-madder stripe on each petal. Prefers partial shade. Z4–11 H9–1.
C. 'Bella', illus. p.198. Early, large-flowered clematis (group 2). H to 3m (10ft), S 1m (3ft). Single, white flowers, with white anthers and purple-red filaments, are produced in spring and again in late summer. Z6–11 H9–6.
C. 'Betty Corning', illus. p.200. Late, small-flowered clematis (group 3). **H** to 13ft (4m), **S** 3ft (1m). Slightly scented, bell-shaped, lilac to pinkish-mauve flowers, 1½– 2½in (4–6cm) across, are borne from early summer to early fall. Z4–11 H9–1.
C. 'Bill MacKenzie'. Vigorous, late-flowering clematis (group 3). **H** 22ft (7m), **S** 10–12ft (3–4m). Has dark green leaves. From mid-summer to late fall produces open bell-shaped, yellow flowers, 2½–3in (6–7cm) across. Is best pruned with shears. Z6–11 H9–6.
C. 'Black Prince', illus. p.200. Late, small-flowered clematis (group 3). **H** to 13ft (4m), **S** 3ft (1m). In mid-summer produces bell-shaped, semi-nodding, very dark blackish-claret-red flowers, to 3½in (9cm) across, with maroon stamens.
C. Blue Moon ('Evirin'), illus. p.199. Compact, free-flowering, early, large-flowered clematis (group 2). **H** 8–10ft (2.5–3m), **S** 3ft (1m). In late spring to early summer bears single, white flowers, 6–7in (15–18cm) across, suffused with pale lilac becoming darker at the wavy petal edges. In late summer to early fall, flowers are slightly smaller and darker. Z7–9 H9–7.
C. Bonanza ('Evipo031'). Vigorous, mid-season clematis (group 3). **H** 10ft (3m), **S** 3ft (1m). Freely produces blue-purple flowers, to 3in (7cm) across, with pale yellow anthers, from mid-summer to fall. Z5–9 H9–5.
C. Bourbon ('Evipo018'), illus. p.200. Compact, mid-season clematis (group 2). **H** 4–6ft (1.2–2m), **S** 3ft (1m). Produces an abundance of vibrant, yellow-centered, red flowers, 3in (8cm) across, from early to mid-summer. Z5–9 H9–5.
C. 'Broughton Star', syn. *C. montana* 'Broughton Star'. Vigorous Montana clematis (group 1). **H** 12–15ft (4–5m), **S** 6–13ft (2–4m). Bears semidouble to fully double, cup-shaped, dusty pink flowers, with slightly darker veins, from spring to early summer.
C. calycina. See *C. cirrhosa*.
C. 'Carnaby'. Compact, early, large-flowered clematis (group 2). **H** 8ft (2.5m), **S** 3ft (1m). In early summer has a profusion of single, deep pink flowers, 3–4in (8–10cm) across, with a darker stripe on each petal and red anthers. Prefers partial shade. Z4–11 H9–5.
C. x cartmanii (*C. marmorata* x *C. paniculata*)**.** Evergreen, clump-forming, bushy shrub (group 1) with some procumbent stems. **H** 8–10in (20–25cm), **S** 20in (50cm). Has dissected, leathery, shiny, dark green leaves varying in shape. Leafy panicles of shallowly cup-shaped, pure white flowers, ¾–1½in (2–4cm) across, with white anthers, are freely produced in early spring. Z7–9 H9–6. **'Avalanche'** (illus. p.198), **H** and **S** 10–16ft (3–5m), has roughly ovate, deeply toothed leaves and white flowers flushed pale green at the base. **'Joe'** (illus. p.198), **H** to 6ft (2m), has 3-parted, toothed leaves; procumbent stems can be trained upward.
C. Cassis ('Evipo020'). Vigorous, late, large-flowered clematis (group 3). **H** and **S** 6–10ft (2–3m). Freely produces rosetted, fully double, plum-red flowers, 3in (8cm) across, from early summer to early fall. Z5–9 H9–5.
C. Cezanne ('Evipo023'). Compact, large-flowered clematis (group 2). **H** 3–4ft (90cm–1.2m), **S** 3ft (1m). Freely produces sky-blue flowers, 4in (10cm) across, with broad overlapping sepals and yellow anthers, from early summer to late fall. Z5–9 H9–5.
C. Chantilly ('Evipo021'), illus. p.199. Compact, early, large-flowered clematis (group 2). **H** 3–4ft (90cm–1.2m), **S** 3ft (1m). Freely produces single, occasionally semidouble, pale pink flowers, to 4in (10cm) across, the sepals with a pronounced, deeper pink central bar, from early summer to late fall. Z5–9 H9–5.
C. 'Charissima', illus. p.199. Free-flowering, early, large-flowered clematis (group 2). **H** 8–10ft (2.5–3m), **S** 3ft (1m). In late spring to early summer produces single flowers, 6–7in (15–18cm) across, with pointed, cerise-pink petals, a deeper pink bar and veins throughout the flower, and dark maroon anthers. Z7–9 H9–7.
C. Chinook ('Evipo013'). Scandent, non-clinging clematis (group 3). **H** 3ft (1m), **S** 2ft (60cm). Produces numerous, nodding, mid-violet-blue flowers, 5in (12cm) across, with twisted sepals, each with a prominent, central boss of yellow stamens, from mid-summer to early fall. Z5–9 H9–5.
C. cirrhosa, syn. *C. calycina*, illus. p.199. Evergreen, early-flowering clematis (group 1). **H** 6–10ft (2–3m), **S** 3–6ft (1–2m). Produces bell-shaped, cream flowers, 1¼in (3cm) across and spotted red inside, in late winter and early spring during frost-free weather. Z7–11 H9–7. **var. *balearica*** has fragrant, pale cream flowers, speckled reddish-brown. Z7–11 H10–7. **var. *purpurascens* 'Freckles'** (illus. p.200) has creamy-pink flowers, **H** 2–3in (5–8cm) across, heavily speckled red within.
C. Clair de Lune ('Evirin'). Vigorous, large-flowered clematis (group 2). **H** 8–10ft (2.5–3m), **S** 3–5ft (1–1.5m). Produces an abundance of large, blue-purple flowers, to 5in (12cm) across, with paler central bands on the sepals and dark anthers, from late spring to early summer and again from late summer to early fall.
C. 'Columbine', syn. *C. alpina* 'Columbine' (Atragene Group) (Atragene Group). Deciduous, early-flowering clematis (group 1). **H** 6–12ft (2–4m), **S** 3ft (1m). In early and mid-spring produces nodding, bell-shaped, soft lavender-blue flowers, 1½–2in (4–5cm) across, with creamy-white or green staminodes; sometimes blooms again in summer.
C. 'Columella' (Atragene Group), illus. p.200. Deciduous, early-flowering clematis (group 1). **H** 10ft (3m), **S** 3ft (1m). From mid-to late spring produces strongly scented, pendent, broadly bell-shaped, purplish-violet to deep rosy-pink flowers, to 2¾in (6.5cm) across, with yellow staminodes.
C. 'Comtesse de Bouchaud'. Strong-growing, late, large-flowered clematis (group 3). **H** 6–10ft (2–3m), **S** 3ft (1m). In summer has masses of single, bright mauve-pink flowers, 3–4in (8–10cm) across, with yellow anthers. Z4–11 H9–1.
C. Confetti ('Evipo036'). Vigorous, small-flowered clematis (group 3). **H** 10ft (3m), **S** 3ft (1m). Nodding, open bell-shaped, pink flowers, 1½in (4cm) across, are produced freely from mid-summer to fall. Z5–9 H9–5.
C. 'Constance', syn. *C. alpina* 'Constance' (Atragene Group) (Atragene Group). Deciduous, early-flowering clematis (group 1). **H** 6–12ft (2–4m), **S** 3ft (1m). Nodding, bell-shaped, semidouble, rich purple-pink or reddish-pink flowers, 1–2½in (2.5–6cm) across, with purple or creamy-white staminodes, are produced from early to mid-spring and occasionally again in summer. Z4–9 H9–6.
C. 'Corona', illus. p.199. Moderately vigorous, early, large-flowered clematis (group 2). **H** to 11½ft (3.5m), **S** 3ft (1m). Bears numerous single, rich velvety-crimson flowers, 6in (15cm) across, with red and white stamens, in late spring and early summer, followed in late summer by a further flush of slightly smaller, paler flowers. Z4–11 H9–1.
C. Crystal Fountain ('Evipo038'). Compact, large-flowered clematis (group 2). **H** 4–6ft (1.5–2m), **S** 3ft (1m). Produces an abundance of double, deep lilac-blue flowers, to 4in (10cm) across, with a central boss of narrow staminodes, from late spring to early summer and again in early fall. Z5–9 H9–5.
C. 'Daniel Deronda'. Vigorous, early, large-flowered clematis (group 2). **H** 10ft (3m), **S** 3ft (1m). Has double and semidouble, deep purple- blue flowers, 4–5½in (10–14cm) across, with cream anthers, then single flowers in late summer. Z7–9 H9–7.
C. 'Doctor Ruppel'. Early, large-flowered clematis (group 2). **H** 8ft (2.5m), **S** 3ft (1m). Single flowers, 4–6in (10–15cm) across, with deep rose-pink petals with darker central bands and light chocolate anthers, are freely produced throughout summer. Z4–11 H8–1.
C. 'Duchess of Albany'. Vigorous, small-flowered clematis (group 3). **H** 8ft (2.5m), **S** 3ft (1m). In summer and early fall has masses of small, tulip-like, single, soft pink flowers, 2½in (6cm) long, with brown anthers and a deeper pink stripe inside each petal. Z4–11 H9–1.
C. 'Duchess of Edinburgh'. Early, large-flowered clematis (group 2). **H** 6–10ft (2–3m), **S** 3ft (1m). In summer produces double, white flowers, 3–4in (8–10cm) across, with yellow anthers and green, outer petals. May be weak-growing. Z4–11 H9–1.
C. x durandii. Semi-herbaceous, late-flowering clematis (group 3). **H** 3–6ft (1–2m), **S** 1½–5ft (45cm–1.5m). In summer has flattish, single, deep blue flowers, 2½–3in (6–8cm) across, with 4 petals and yellow anthers. Leaves are elliptic. Z5–11 H9–5.
C. 'Early Sensation' (Forsteri Group), illus. p.198. Evergreen, late-flowering clematis (group 1). **H** 6ft (2m), **S** 3ft (1m). Dark green leaves are bronzed when young. From early to mid-spring bears scented, bell- to cup-shaped, white flowers, 2–3in (5–7.5cm) across, with yellow anthers often tinged purple.
C. 'Elizabeth', syn. *C. montana* 'Elizabeth'. Vigorous Montana clematis (group 1). **H** 30–40ft (10–12m), **S** 6–10ft (2–3m). Has scented, single, soft pink flowers, 2–2½in (5–6cm) across, with widely spaced petals, in late spring. Z6–9 H9–6.
C. 'Elsa Spath'. Early, large-flowered clematis (group 2). **H** 6–10ft (2–3m), **S** 3ft (1m). Bears masses of single, rich mauve-blue flowers, 5in (12cm) wide, with overlapping petals and red anthers, throughout summer. Z4–11 H9–1.
C. 'Ernest Markham', illus. p.200. Vigorous, late, large-flowered clematis (group 3). **H** 10–12ft (3–4m), **S** 3ft (1m). In summer bears single, vivid magenta flowers, 4in (10cm) wide, with blunt-tipped petals and chocolate anthers. Thrives in full sun. Z4–11 H9–1.
C. 'Etoile Violette', syn. *C. viticella* 'Etoile Violette', illus. p.200. Vigorous, late-flowering clematis (group 3). **H** 10–15ft (3–5m), **S** 5ft (1.5m). Produces masses of flattish, single, violet-purple flowers, 1½–2½in (4–6cm) wide, with yellow anthers, in summer. Z4–11 H9–1.
C. 'Evifour'. See *C.* Royal Velvet.
C. Evijohill. See *C.* 'Josephine'.
C. 'Evione'. See *C.* Sugar Candy.
C. 'Evipo001'. See *C.* Wisley.
C. 'Evipo002'. See *C.* Rosemoor.
C. 'Evipo003'. See *C.* Ice Blue.
C. 'Evipo004'. See *C.* Harlow Carr.
C. 'Evipo005'. See *C.* Peppermint.
C. 'Evipo006. See *C.* Vienetta.
C. 'Evipo007'. See *C.* Victor Hugo.
C. 'Evipo008'. See *C.* Franziska Maria.
C. 'Evipo009'. See *C.* Hyde Hall.
C. 'Evipo012'. See *C.* Parisienne.
C. 'Evipo013'. See *C.* Chinook.
C. 'Evipo014'. See *C.* Gazelle.
C. 'Evipo015'. See *C.* Savannah.
C. 'Evipo017'. See *C.* Avant-Garde.
C. 'Evipo018'. See *C.* Bourbon.
C. 'Evipo019'. See *C.* Medley.
C. 'Evipo020'. See *C.* Cassis.
C. 'Evipo021'. See *C.* Chantilly.
C. 'Evipo023'. See *C.* Cezanne.
C. 'Evipo031'. See *C.* Bonanza.
C. 'Evipo032'. See *C.* Galore.
C. 'Evipo033'. See *C.* Angelique.
C. 'Evipo036'. See *C.* Confetti.
C. 'Evipo038'. See *C.* Crystal Fountain.
C. 'Evirida'. See *C.* Florida Pistachio.
C. 'Evirin'. See *C.* Clair De Lune.
C. 'Evirin'. See *C.* Blue Moon.
C. 'Evisix'. See *C.* Petit Faucon.
C. 'Evithree'. See *C.* Anna Louise.
C. 'Evitwo'. See *C.* Arctic Queen.
C. fasciculiflora, illus. p.198. Evergreen, early-flowering species (group 1). **H** and **S** 20ft (6m) or more. Dark green leaves have silver midribs. From late winter to mid-spring produces solitary or clustered, fragrant, bell-shaped, nodding, creamy-white to yellowish-white flowers, ½–¾in (1.5–2cm) across. Needs a warm, sunny position. Z7–9 H9–6.
C. 'Fireworks', illus. p.199. Early, large-flowered clematis (group 2). **H** 13ft (4m), **S** 3ft (1m). In late spring and early summer produces single, blue-mauve flowers, 4–6in (10–15cm) across, with wine-red and white stamens and a central, bright cerise-purple stripe on each sepal. Late summer flowers are slightly smaller.
C. flammula, illus. p.200. Vigorous, late-flowering clematis; may be semievergreen (group 3). **H** 10–15ft (3–5m), **S** 6ft (2m). Produces masses of almond-scented,

C

flattish, single, white flowers, 3/4in (2cm) across, in summer and early fall. Z4–11 H9–7.
C. florida. 'Bicolor'. See *C. florida* var. *sieboldiana*. **PISTACHIO ('Evirida'),** illus. p.199. is a vigorous, small-flowered clematis (group 3). **H** 10ft (3m), **S** 3ft (1m). From early summer to late fall produces an abundance of rounded, creamy-white flowers, 2½–3½in (6–9cm) across, each with a central cluster of pinkish-gray anthers and green styles. Z7–11 H10–6. **var. *sieboldiana*,** syn. *C. florida* 'Bicolor', *C. florida* 'Sieboldii', illus. p.199. **H** 6–10ft (2–3m), is weaker growing and produces creamy-white flowers each with a domed boss of petal-like, rich purple stamens; needs a sheltered site. Z7–11 H10–6. **'Sieboldii'.** See *C. florida* var. *sieboldiana*.
C. 'Frances Rivis', syn. *C. alpina* 'Frances Rivis' (Atragene Group), illus. p.200. Deciduous, early-flowering clematis (group 1). **H** 6–12ft (2–4m), **S** 3ft (1m). In early and mid-spring produces an abundance of nodding, bell-shaped, deep blue flowers, 2–3in (5–8cm) across, with white staminodes. Z4–9 H9–6.
C. 'Frankie', syn. *C. alpina* 'Frankie' (Atragene Group), illus. p.200. Deciduous, early-flowering clematis (group 1). **H** 7–12ft (2.2–4m), **S** 3ft (1m). In early and mid-spring produces nodding, bell-shaped, mid-blue to deep mauve-blue flowers, 1–2½in (2.5–6cm) across, with blue-tipped, creamy-white staminodes.
C. FRANZISKA MARIA ('Evipo008'). Compact, early, large-flowered clematis (group 2). **H** 5–10ft (1.5–3m), **S** 3–6ft (1–2m). Produces masses of fully double, deep blue-purple flowers, 4–6in (10–15cm) across, with yellow anthers, from early summer to early fall. Z5–9 H9–5.
C. GALORE ('Evipo032'). Vigorous, mid-season, small-flowered clematis (group 3). **H** 10ft (3m), **S** 3ft (1m). From mid-summer to fall has numerous, deep purple flowers, to 3in (7cm) across, with yellow anthers. Z5–9 H9–5.
C. GAZELLE ('Evipo014'). Scandent, non-clinging clematis (group 3). **H** 3ft (1m), **S** 2ft (60cm). Produces numerous slightly scented, nodding, white flowers, to 2½in (6cm) across, with twisted sepals and yellow stamens, from mid-summer to early fall. Z5–9 H9–5.
C. 'Général Sikorski'. Early, large-flowered clematis (group 2). **H** 10ft (3m), **S** 3ft (1m). Has numerous single, blue flowers, 4in (10cm) wide, with large, overlapping petals and cream anthers, in summer. Z4–11 H9–1.
C. 'Gipsy Queen'. Vigorous, late, large-flowered clematis (group 3). **H** 10ft (3m), **S** 3ft (1m). Bears single, velvety, violet-purple flowers, 4in (10cm) wide, with red anthers, in summer. Z4–11 H9–1.
C. 'Gravetye Beauty', illus. p.200. Vigorous, small-flowered clematis (group 3). **H** 8ft (2.5m), **S** 3ft (1m). In summer and early fall has masses of small, tulip-like, single, bright red flowers, 2½in (6cm) long, with brown anthers. Is similar to *C.* 'Duchess of Albany', but flowers are more open. Z4–11 H9–5.
C. 'Guernsey Cream', illus. p.198. Early, large-flowered clematis (group 2). **H** 8ft (2.5m), **S** 3ft (1m). Bears single flowers, 5in (12cm) across, with creamy yellow petals and anthers, in early summer. Flowers are smaller and creamy white in late summer. Fades in full sun. Z5–9 H9–5.
C. 'Hagley Hybrid'. Vigorous, late, large-flowered clematis (group 3). **H** 8ft (2.5m), **S** 3ft (1m). Produces single, rose-mauve flowers, 3–4in (8–10cm) wide, with red anthers, in summer. Prefers partial shade. Z4–11 H9–1.
C. HARLOW CARR ('Evipo004'). Scandent, herbaceous clematis (group 3). **H** 6–10ft (2–3m), **S** 3ft (1m). From early to late summer produces semi-pendent, dark violet-blue flowers, to 3in (7cm) across, each with 4 twisted petals, dark brown anthers and white filaments. Z5–9 H9–5.
C. 'Henryi', illus. p.199. Vigorous, early, large-flowered clematis (group 2). **H** 10ft (3m), **S** 3ft (1m). Has single, white flowers, 5in (12cm) wide, with dark chocolate anthers, in summer. Z4–11 H9–1.
C. heracleifolia var. davidiana. See *C. tubulosa*.
C. heracleifolia of gardens**.** See *C. tubulosa*.
C. 'H.F. Young'. Compact, early, large-flowered clematis (group 2). **H** 8ft (2.5m), **S** 3ft (1m). Bears single, violet-tinged, blue flowers, 4in (10cm) wide, with cream anthers, in summer. Is ideal for a container or patio garden. Z4–11 H9–1.
C. 'Huldine', illus. p.199. Very vigorous, late, large-flowered clematis (group 3). **H** 10–12ft (3–4m), **S** 6ft (2m). In summer has single, white flowers, 2½in (6cm) wide, mauve beneath and with cream anthers. Is ideal for an archway or pergola. Z4–11 H9–1.
C. HYDE HALL ('Evipo009'). Vigorous, large-flowered clematis (group 2). **H** 6–8ft (2–2.5m), **S** 3ft (1m). Flowers prolifically from early to mid-summer producing single, creamy-white flowers, 5–7in (12–18cm) across, sometimes tinged pink or green, with chocolate-brown anthers. Z5–9 H9–5.
C. ICE BLUE ('Evipo003'). Early, large-flowered clematis (group 2). **H** 6–8ft (2–2.5m), **S** 3ft (1m). In late spring and early summer produces an abundance of single, ice-blue flowers, 6–8in (15–20cm) across, repeat-flowering during late summer and early fall. Z5–9 H9–5.
C. integrifolia. Herbaceous clematis (group 3). **H** and **S** 30in (75cm). Leaves are narrowly lance-shaped. In summer bears bell-shaped, single, deep blue flowers, 1¼in (3cm) long, with cream anthers, followed by gray-brown seed heads. Z4–11 H7–1.
C. 'Jackmanii', illus. p.200. Vigorous, late, large-flowered clematis (group 3). **H** 10ft (3m), **S** 3ft (1m). Bears masses of velvety, single, dark purple flowers, 3–4in (8–10cm) across, fading to violet, with light brown anthers, in mid-summer. Z4–11 H9–1.
C. 'Jackmanii Superba'. Vigorous, late, large-flowered clematis (group 3). **H** 10ft (3m), **S** 3ft (1m). Is similar to *C.* 'Jackmanii', but has more rounded, darker flowers. Z4–9 H9–1.
C. 'Jacqueline du Pré' (Atragene Group), illus. p.199. Deciduous, early-flowering clematis (group 1). **H** 8–13ft (2.5–4m), **S** 5ft (1.5m). Has nodding, bell-shaped, rosy-mauve flowers, 2–21/2 in (5–6cm) across, with silvery-pink petal margins and pink-flushed, white staminodes, in spring.
C. 'Jan Lindmark' (Atragene Group), illus. p.199. Deciduous, early-flowering clematis (group 1). **H** to 13ft (4m), **S** 3ft (1m). In spring produces pendent, bell-shaped, purple-mauve flowers, 1½–3in (4–8cm) across, with purple, outer stamens and shorter, white, inner staminodes. Z4–9 H9–3.
C. 'John Huxtable'. Late, large-flowered clematis (group 3). **H** 6–10ft (2–3m), **S** 3ft (1m). Bears masses of single, white flowers, 3in (8cm) wide, with cream anthers, in mid-summer. Z7–9 H9–1.
C. JOSEPHINE ('Evijohill'). Early, large-flowered clematis (group 2). **H** 8ft (2.5m), **S** 3ft (1m). From early summer to early fall bears double flowers, 5in (12cm) across, with almost bronze, green-tinged petals with a darker central bar; the petals become lilac in mid-summer, with a pink bar. Colors best in sun. Z4–9 H9–1.
C. x jouiniana (Spider flower). Sprawling, subshrubby, late-flowering clematis (group 3). **H** 3ft (1m), **S** 10ft (3m). Has coarse foliage and, in summer, masses of tubular, single, soft lavender or off-white flowers, 3/4in (2cm) wide, with reflexed petal tips. Is non-clinging. H3–8 H8–1. **'Praecox'.** See *C.* 'Praecox'.
C. 'Kakio', syn. *C.* PINK CHAMPAGNE, illus. p.199. Early, large-flowered clematis (group 2). **H** 10ft (3m), **S** 3ft (1m). In late spring and early summer produces single, vivid purple-red to deep pink flowers, with central, white stripes on each petal. Z4–11 H9–1.
C. 'Kardynal Wyszyński', illus. p.200. Early, large-flowered clematis (group 2). **H** 10ft (3m), **S** 3ft (1m). Produces single, bright crimson flowers, with pale violet filaments and dark brown anthers, from early to late summer.
C. 'Kathleen Wheeler'. Early, large-flowered clematis (group 2). **H** 8–10ft (2.5–3m), **S** 3ft (1m). Has single, plum-mauve flowers, 5–5½in (12–14cm) across with yellow anthers, in early summer. Z4–9 H9–1.
C. 'Lasurstern'. Vigorous, early, large-flowered clematis (group 2). **H** 6–10ft (2–3m), **S** 3ft (1m). In summer bears single, blue flowers, 4–5in (10–12cm) across, with overlapping, wavy-edged petals and cream anthers. Z4–9 H9–1.
C. 'Lincoln Star', illus. p.199. Early, large-flowered clematis (group 2). **H** 6–10ft (2–3m), **S** 3ft (1m). Has single, raspberry-pink flowers, 4–5in (10–12cm) wide, with red anthers, in early summer. Early flowers are darker than late ones, which have very pale pink petal edges. Prefers partial shade. Z4–11 H9–1.
C. macropetala (Downy clematis). Macropetala clematis (group 1). **H** 10ft (3m), **S** 5ft (1.5m). In late spring and summer has masses of semidouble, mauve-blue flowers, 2in (5cm) long, lightening in color toward the center, then fluffy, silvery seed heads. Z4–9 H9–3. **'Markham's Pink'** has pink flowers.
C. 'Madame Edouard André'. Late, large-flowered clematis (group 3). **H** 8ft (2.5m), **S** 3ft (1m). Freely produces single, deep red flowers, 3–4in (8–10cm) across, with silver undersides, pointed petals and yellow anthers, in mid-summer. Z4–11 H9–1.
C. 'Madame Julia Correvon', syn. *C. viticella* 'Madame Julia Correvon', illus. p.200. Late-flowering clematis (group 3). **H** 8–11ft (2.5–3.5m), **S** 3ft (1m). Has flattish, single, wine-red flowers, 2–3in (5–7cm) wide, with twisted petals, in summer. Z4–11 H9–1.
C. 'Madame Le Coultre'. See *C.* 'Marie Boisselot'.
C. 'Marie Boisselot', syn. *C.* 'Madame Le Coultre'. Vigorous, early, large-flowered clematis (group 2). **H** 10ft (3m), **S** 3ft (1m). Bears single, white flowers, 5in (12cm) across, with overlapping petals and cream anthers, in summer. Z4–11 H9–1.
C. MEDLEY ('Evipo019'). Scandent, non-clinging clematis (group 3). **H** 3ft (1m), **S** 2ft (60cm). From mid-summer to fall produces slightly scented, nodding, light pink flowers, 1½–2in (4–5cm) across, with twisted sepals that open to reveal a boss of yellow stamens in the center. Z5–9 H9–5.
C. 'Miss Bateman'. Compact, early, large-flowered clematis (group 2). **H** 8ft (2.5m), **S** 3ft (1m). Masses of single, white flowers, 3–4in (8–10cm) across, with red anthers, are produced in summer. Is good for a container or patio garden. Z4–11 H9–1.
C. montana (Anemone clematis), illus. p.198. Vigorous, Montana clematis (group 1). **H** 22–40ft (7–12m), **S** 6–10ft (2–3m). In late spring bears masses of single, white flowers, 1½–2in (4–5cm) across, with yellow anthers. Z6–9 H9–6. **'Broughton Star'.** See *C.* 'Broughton Star'.**'Elizabeth'.** See *C.* 'Elizabeth'. **var. *rubens*,** illus. p.199. **var. *rubens* 'Tetrarose'** (illus. p.199), **H** 22–25ft (7–8m), has coarse leaflets, 3in (8cm) long, and deep satin pink flowers, 2½–3in (6–7cm) across.
C. 'Mrs. Cholmondeley'. Early, large-flowered clematis (group 2). **H** 6–10ft (2–3m), **S** 3ft (1m). In summer has single, light bluish-lavender flowers, 4–5in (10–12cm) across, with widely spaced petals and light chocolate anthers. Z4–9 H9–1.
C. 'Mrs. George Jackman'. Early, large-flowered clematis (group 2). **H** 6–10ft (2–3m), **S** 3ft (1m). Bears semidouble, creamy-white flowers, 4in (10cm) wide, with light brown anthers, in early summer. Z4–9 H9–1.
C. 'Mrs. N. Thompson'. Compact, early, large-flowered clematis (group 2). **H** 8ft (2.5m), **S** 3ft (1m). In summer produces masses of single, magenta flowers, 3–4in (8–10cm) wide, with a central, slightly darker stripe on each bluish-purple-edged petal and red anthers. Is good for a container or patio garden. Z4–11 H9–1.
C. 'Nelly Moser', illus. p.199. Early, large-flowered clematis (group 2). **H** 11ft (3.5m), **S** 3ft (1m). In early summer has single, rose-mauve flowers, 5–6½in (12–16cm) wide, with reddish-purple anthers and, on each petal, a carmine stripe that fades in strong sun. Prefers a shaded, east-, west- or north-facing site. Z4–11 H9–1.
C. 'Niobe'. Early, large-flowered clematis (group 2). **H** 6–10ft (2–3m), **S** 3ft (1m). Throughout summer produces masses of single, rich deep red flowers, 4–5½in (10–14cm) across, with yellow anthers. Z4–11 H9–1.
C. orientalis. Late-flowering clematis (group 3). **H** 10–12ft (3–4m), **S** 5ft (1.5m). Leaves are gray- to dark green. In summer, lantern-shaped, single, greenish-yellow

C

flowers, $1^1/_4$in (3cm) wide, with recurved petal tips, are followed by feathery seed heads. Z6–9 H9–6.
C. Parisienne ('Evipo012'). Compact, large-flowered clematis (group 2). **H** 3–4ft (90–120cm), **S** 2ft (60cm). Produces an abundance of single, pale violet flowers, 3–4in (7–10cm) across, with wavy-edged sepals and red anthers, from early summer to late fall. Z5–9 H9–5.
C. Peppermint ('Evipo005'). Vigorous, large-flowered clematis (group 3). **H** 6–10ft (2–3m), **S** 3ft (1m). From early summer to late fall has numerous rosetted, creamy-white flowers, 3–4in (7–10cm) across, with 6 large, outer sepals, which drop as the tight, inner rosette of smaller sepals expand. The late season's flowers are greenish-white. Z5–9 H9–5.
C. 'Perle d'Azur', illus. p.200. Late, large-flowered clematis (group 3). **H** 10ft (3m), **S** 3ft (1m). Single, azure-blue flowers, 3in (8cm) across, with recurved petal tips and creamy-green anthers, are borne in summer. Z4–11 H9–1.
C. Petit Faucon ('Evisix'). Vigorous, scandent, non-clinging clematis (group 3). **H** 3–5ft (1–1.5m), **S** 2ft (60cm). From summer to early fall produces nodding to semi-pendent, broadly bell-shaped, deep blue-violet flowers, 2–3in (5–8cm) across, with violet filaments and orange-yellow anthers. Z4–9 H9–1.
C. Pink Champagne. See *C.* 'Kakio'.
C. 'Polish Spirit', illus. p.200. Strong-growing, late, large-flowered clematis (group 3). **H** to 13ft (4m), **S** 3ft (1m). Single, velvety, deep purple flowers, with dark purple-red and greenish-white stamens, are produced from early summer to early fall. Z4–11 H9–5.
C. 'Praecox', syn. *C. x jouiniana* 'Praecox'. Sprawling, subshrubby, non-clinging, late-flowering clematis (group 3). **H** 3ft (1m), **S** 10ft (3m). Has coarse foliage and, in summer, masses of tubular, single, soft lavender or off-white flowers, $^3/_4$in (2cm) wide, with reflexed petal tips.
C. 'Purpurea Plena Elegans', syn. *C. viticella* 'Purpurea Plena Elegans', illus. p.200. Late-flowering clematis (group 3). **H** 6–10ft (2–3m), **S** 3ft (1m). Bears abundant, double, purplish-mauve flowers, $1^1/_2$in (3.5cm) long, occasionally with green outer petals, and no anthers, from mid-summer to late fall. Z4–11 H9–1.
C. 'Ramona'. Early, large-flowered clematis (group 2). **H** 10ft (3m), **S** 3ft (1m). Has coarse, dark green leaves offset, in summer, by single, pale blue flowers, 4–5in (10–12cm) across, with red anthers. Prefers a south-or south-west-facing position. Z4–11 H9–1.
C. recta. Clump-forming, herbaceous clematis (group 3). **H** 3–6ft (1–2m), **S** 20in (50cm). Leaves are dark or gray-green. Bears masses of sweetly scented, flattish, single, white flowers, $^3/_4$in (2cm) across, in mid-summer. Z4–11 H7–1.
C. rehderiana, illus. p.200. Vigorous, late-flowering clematis (group 3). **H** 20–22ft (6–7m), **S** 6–10ft (2–3m). Bears loose clusters of fragrant, tubular, single, yellow flowers, $^1/_2$–$^3/_4$in (1–2cm) long, in late summer and early fall. Leaves are coarse-textured. Z6–9 H9–6.
C. 'Rhapsody'. Compact, early, large-flowered clematis (group 2). **H** 8ft (2.5m), **S** 3ft (1m). From early summer to early fall bears single, sapphire-blue flowers, 4–5in (10–13cm) across, with splayed, creamy-yellow anthers. Color deepens with age. Z4–9 H9–1.
C. 'Richard Pennell'. Early, large-flowered clematis (group 2). **H** 6–10ft (2–3m), **S** 3ft (1m). Produces single, rich purple-blue flowers, 4–5in (10–12cm) wide, with golden-yellow anthers, in summer. Z4–11 H9–1.
C. Rosemoor ('Evipo002'), illus. p.200. Vigorous, large-flowered clematis (group 2). **H** 6–8ft (2–2.5m), **S** 3ft (1m). From early summer to fall, single, deep red flowers, 5–6in (12–15cm) across, with yellow anthers, are produced in abundance. Z5–9 H9–5.
C. 'Rosy O'Grady' (Atragene Group), illus. p.200. Deciduous, early-flowering clematis (group 1). **H** 10–13ft (3–4m), **S** 3ft (1m). Open bell-shaped, semidouble, deep pink to mauve-pink flowers, $2^1/_2$–5in (6–12cm) across, with creamy-white staminodes, are produced from late spring to early summer and again in fall. Z4–9 H9–3.
C. 'Rouge Cardinal'. Early, large-flowered clematis (group 3). **H** 6–10ft (2–3m), **S** 3ft (1m). In summer has single, velvety, crimson flowers, 3–4in (8–10cm) across, with red anthers. Z4–11 H9–1.
C. Royal Velvet ('Evifour'). Early, large-flowered clematis (group 2). **H** 6–8ft (2–2.5m), **S** 3ft (1m). In early and mid-summer bears single, bluish, rich velvet-purple flowers, 4–6in (10–15cm) wide, with darker central bands on petals, and red anthers. Z4–9 H9–1.
C. Savannah ('Evipo015'). Scandent, non-clinging clematis (group 3). **H** 3ft (1m), **S** 2ft (60cm). From mid-summer to fall produces nodding, single, dark pink flowers, to $2^1/_2$in (6cm) across, with twisted sepals that open to reveal clusters of yellow stamens in the center. Z5–9 H9–5.
C. 'Silver Moon', illus. p.200. Early, large-flowered clematis (group 2). **H** to 13ft (4m), **S** 3ft (1m). Produces single, silvery-mauve flowers, 4–6in (10–15cm) across, from late spring to early fall. Z4–11 H9–1.
C. 'Souvenir du Capitaine Thuilleaux'. Compact, early, large-flowered clematis (group 2). **H** 8ft (2.5m), **S** 3ft (1m). In early summer bears single, deep pink-striped, cream-pink flowers, 3–4in (8–10cm) wide, with red anthers. Is ideal for a container or patio garden. Z4–9 H9–1.
C. 'Star of India'. Vigorous, late, large-flowered clematis (group 3). **H** 10ft (3m), **S** 3ft (1m). Bears masses of single, deep purple-blue flowers, 3–4in (8–10cm) wide, with light brown anthers, in mid-summer; each petal has a deep carmine-red stripe. Z4–11 H9–1.
C. Sugar Candy ('Evione') (Golden clematis). Vigorous, early, large-flowered clematis (group 2). **H** 10ft (3m), **S** 3ft (1m). Has masses of pinkish-mauve to light purple flowers, 4–6in (10–18cm) across, with darker, central bars on the petals and yellow anthers. Z5–9 H9–5.
C. 'Sunrise', illus. p.199. Vigorous, Montana clematis (group 1). **H** and **S** 25–30ft (8–10m). Leaves are reddish-purple when young. Slightly scented, semidouble or double, deep pink flowers, 2in (5cm) across, are borne in spring.
C. tangutica. Vigorous, late-flowering clematis (group 3). **H** 15–20ft (5–6m), **S** 6–10ft (2–3m). Has lantern-shaped, single, yellow flowers, $1^1/_2$in (4cm) long, throughout summer and early fall; these are followed by fluffy, silvery seed heads. Z5–11 H9–6.
C. 'The President'. Early, large-flowered clematis (group 2). **H** 6–10ft (2–3m), **S** 3ft (1m). In early summer bears masses of single, rich purple flowers, 4in (10cm) wide, silver beneath, with red anthers. Z4–11 H9–1.
C. tubulosa, syn. *C. heracleifolia* var. *davidiana*, *C. heracleifolia*. Herbaceous clematis (group 3). **H** 3ft (1m), **S** $2^1/_2$ft (75cm). In summer, thick stems bear axillary clusters of scented, tubular, single, pale blue flowers, $^3/_4$–$1^1/_4$in (2–3cm) long, with reflexed petal tips. Z4–8 H8–3. **'Wyevale'** has strongly scented, dark blue flowers.
C. Victor Hugo ('Evipo007'). Vigorous, scandent, non-clinging clematis (group 3). **H** 8–10ft (2.5–3m), **S** 3ft (1m). Produces an abundance of red-violet flowers, 3in (8cm) across, with dark, violet-tipped stamens, from early summer to fall. Z5–9 H9–5.
C. Viennetta ('Evipo006'), illus. p.199. Vigorous, large-flowered clematis (group 3). **H** 6–10ft (2–3m), **S** 3ft (1m). From early summer to fall produces passion-flower-like, creamy-white flowers, with purple, modified stamens and a dark center. In fall, the outer petals develop a greenish hue. Z5–9 H9–5.
C. 'Ville de Lyon'. Late, large-flowered clematis (group 3). **H** 6–10ft (2–3m), **S** 3ft (1m). In mid-summer has single, bright carmine-red flowers, 3–4in (8–10cm) across, with darker petal edges and yellow anthers. Lower foliage tends to become scorched by late summer. Z4–11 H9–1.
C. Vino ('Poulvo') illus. p.200. (Italian clematis), Vigorous, early, large-flowered clematis (group 2). **H** 10ft (3m), **S** 3ft (1m). Produces numerous, single, deep petunia-red flowers, 4–7in (10–18cm) across, with white to cream filaments and yellow anthers, in late spring and again in late summer and early fall. Z4–11 H9–1.
C. viticella. Late-flowering clematis (group 3). **H** 6–10ft (2–3m), **S** 3ft (1m). Produces nodding, open bell-shaped, single, purple-mauve flowers, $1^1/_2$in (3.5cm) long, in summer. Z4–11 H9–1. See *C.* 'Abundance'. **'Etoile Violette'.** See *C.* 'Etoile Violette'. **'Madame Julia Correvon'.** See *C.* 'Madame Julia Correvon'. **'Purpurea Plena Elegans'.** See *C.* 'Purpurea Plena Elegans'.
C. 'Vyvyan Pennell'. Early, large-flowered clematis (group 2). **H** 6–10ft (2–3m), **S** 3ft (1m). Has double, lilac flowers, 4–5in (10–12cm) wide, with a central, lavender-blue rosette of petals and golden-yellow anthers, in early summer, then single, blue-mauve flowers. Z4–11 H9–1.
C. 'W.E. Gladstone'. Vigorous, early, large-flowered clematis (group 2). **H** 10–12ft (3–4m), **S** 3ft (1m). Produces single, lavender flowers, 6in (15cm) wide, with red anthers, in summer. Z4–11 H9–1.
C. 'Westerplatte', illus. p.200. Early, large-flowered clematis (group 2). **H** 8ft (2.5m), **S** 3ft (1m). From late spring to early summer, and again from late summer to early fall, produces single, dark velvet-red flowers, with white filaments and deep red anthers. Z4–11 H9–1.
C. 'White Columbine' (Atragene Group), illus. p.198. Deciduous, early-flowering clematis (group 1). **H** and **S** 6–10ft (2–3m). In spring produces purple-tinted buds that open into nodding, bell-shaped, single, creamy-white flowers, $1^1/_2$–2in (4–5cm) across, maturing to pure white, with petal-like, greenish-white staminodes.
C. 'William Kennett'. Early, large-flowered clematis (group 2). **H** 6–10ft (2–3m), **S** 3ft (1m). In summer has masses of single, lavender-blue flowers, 4–5in (10–12cm) across, with red anthers and tough petals, each bearing a central, darker stripe that fades as the flower matures. Z4–11 H9–1.
C. Wisley ('Evipo001'). Strong-growing, large-flowered clematis (group 3). **H** 8–10ft (2.5–3m), **S** 3ft (1m). From mid-summer to early fall produces numerous, slightly nodding, violet-blue flowers, 4–5in (10–12cm) across, with yellow anthers. Z5–9 H9–5.

CLEOME

Spider flower

CAPPARACEAE/CLEOMACEAE

Genus of annuals and a few evergreen shrubs, grown for their unusual, spidery flowers. Needs sun and fertile, well-drained soil. Remove dead flowers. Propagate by seed sown outdoors in late spring. Aphids may be a problem.
C. hassleriana, syn. *C. spinosa*. Fast-growing, bushy annual. **H** to 4ft (1.2m), **S** $1^1/_2$ft (45cm). Has hairy, spiny stems and mid-green leaves divided into lance-shaped leaflets. Large, rounded heads of narrow-petaled, pink-flushed, white flowers, with long, protruding stamens, are produced in summer. Z11 H11–1. **'Colour Fountain'** illus. p.304. **'Rose Queen'** (Cashmere bouquet) has rose-pink flowers.
C. spinosa of gardens. See *C. hassleriana*.

CLERODENDRUM

Glorybower

VERBENACEAE/LAMIACEAE

Genus of evergreen or deciduous, small trees, shrubs, subshrubs and woody-stemmed, twining climbers, grown for their showy flowers. Needs rich, well-drained soil and full sun, with partial shade in summer. Water freely in growing season, less at other times. Stems require support. Thin out crowded growth in spring. Propagate by seed in spring, by softwood cuttings in late spring or by semiripe cuttings in summer. Whitefly, red spider mite and mealy bug may be a problem.
C. bungei, illus. p.141.
***C. chinense* var. *chinense*,** syn. *C. chinense* 'Pleniflorum', *C. fragrans* 'Pleniflorum', *C. philippinum*. Evergreen or deciduous, bushy shrub. **H** and **S** to 8ft (2.5m). Leaves are broadly oval, coarsely and shallowly toothed and downy. Fragrant, double, pink or white flowers are borne in domed, terminal clusters in summer. Z11 H11–1.
C. fallax. See *C. speciosissimum*.
***C. fragrans* 'Pleniflorum'.** See *C. chinense* var. *chinense*.
C. philippinum. See *C. chinense* var. *chinense*.
C. speciosissimum, syn. *C. fallax*. Evergreen, erect to spreading, sparingly

C

branched shrub. **H** and **S** to 10ft (3m). Bears broadly heart-shaped, wavy-edged leaves, to 1ft (30cm) across, on long stalks and, from late spring to fall, tubular, scarlet flowers, with spreading petal lobes, in terminal clusters 1ft (30cm) long. Makes a good container plant. Z12–14 H11–10.

C. splendens (Bleeding heart glorybower). Vigorous, evergreen, woody-stemmed, twining climber. **H** 10ft (3m) or more. Has oval to elliptic, rich green leaves. Clusters of 5-petaled, tubular, scarlet flowers, 1in (2.5cm) wide, are produced in summer. Z11 H11–10.

C. thomsoniae, illus. p.460.

C. trichotomum (Japanese clethra), illus. p.142. Deciduous, upright, bushy-headed, treelike shrub. **H** and **S** 15–20ft (5–6m). Clusters of deep pink and greenish-white buds open to fragrant, white flowers above large leaves from late summer to mid-fall, followed by blue fruits. Z7–9 H9–7.

CLETHRA
CLETHRACEAE

Genus of deciduous or evergreen shrubs and trees, grown for their fragrant, white flowers. Needs partial shade and moist, peaty, acidic soil. Propagate by softwood cuttings in summer or by seed in fall.

C. alnifolia (Summersweet, Sweet pepper-bush). Deciduous, bushy shrub. **H** and **S** 8ft (2.5m). Has oval, toothed, mid-green leaves and, in late summer and early fall, slender spires of small, bell-shaped flowers. Z3–9 H9–1.

C. arborea (Lily-of-the-valley tree). Evergreen, bushy, dense shrub or tree. **H** 25ft (8m), **S** 20ft (6m). Bears long, nodding clusters of small, strongly fragrant, bell-shaped, white flowers among oval, toothed, rich green leaves from late summer to mid-fall. Z8–9 H9–8.

C. barbinervis, illus. p.129.

C. delavayi, illus. p.113.

CLEYERA
THEACEAE/PENTAPHYLACEAE

Genus of evergreen, summer-flowering shrubs and trees, grown for their foliage and flowers. Requires a sheltered position in sun or partial shade and moist, acidic soil. Propagate by semiripe cuttings in summer.

C. fortunei 'Variegata'. See *C. japonica* 'Fortunei'

C. japonica. Evergreen, bushy shrub. **H** and **S** 10ft (3m). Small, fragrant, bowl-shaped, creamy-white flowers are borne in summer amid narrowly oblong to oval-oblong, glossy, dark green leaves. Occasionally has small, spherical, red fruits, ripening to black. Z8–11 H11–7.

'Fortunei', syn. *C. fortunei* 'Variegata', *Eurya japonica* 'Variegata', **H** and **S** 6ft (2m), produces pink-flushed, young leaves, later green edged with creamy-white.

CLIANTHUS
LEGUMINOSAE/PAPILIONACEAE

Genus of evergreen or semievergreen, woody-stemmed, scrambling climbers, grown for their flowers. Grow outdoors in warm areas in well-drained soil and full sun. In cooler areas needs to be under glass. In spring, prune out growing tips to

give a bushier habit and cut out any dead wood. Propagate by seed in spring or by stem cuttings in late summer.

C. puniceus, illus. p.193. **f. albus,** illus. p.192.

CLINTONIA
LILIACEAE/CONVALLARIACEAE

Genus of late spring- or summer-flowering, rhizomatous perennials. Prefers shade and moist but well-drained, peaty, neutral to acidic soil. Propagate by division in spring or by seed in fall.

C. andrewsiana (Bluebead). Clump-forming, rhizomatous perennial. **H** 24in (60cm), **S** 12in (30cm). In early summer produces clusters of small, bell-shaped, pinkish-purple flowers at tops of stems, above sparse, broadly oval, glossy, rich green leaves. Bears globose, blue fruits in fall. Z8–9 H9–1.

C. borealis. Clump-forming, rhizomatous perennial. **H** and **S** 12in (30cm). In early summer produces small, nodding, bell-shaped, yellowish-green flowers, followed by small, globose, blackish fruits. Has sparse, broadly oval, glossy, rich green leaves. Z2–7 H8–1.

C. uniflora (Bride's bonnet). Spreading, rhizomatous perennial. **H** 6in (15cm), **S** 12in (30cm). Has oval, glossy, green leaves. Slender stems bear solitary star-shaped, white flowers in late spring, then large, globose, blue-black fruits. Z4–8 H8–1.

CLITORIA
LEGUMINOSAE/PAPILIONACEAE

Genus of perennials and evergreen shrubs and twining climbers, grown for their large, pealike flowers. Grow in full light and in any fertile, well-drained soil. Water moderately, less when not in full growth. Provide support for stems. Thin out crowded stems in spring. Propagate by seed in spring or by softwood cuttings in summer. Whitefly and red spider mite may be a problem.

C. ternatea. Evergreen, twining climber with slender stems. **H** 10–15ft (3–5m). Leaves are divided into 3 or 5 oval leaflets. Clear bright blue flowers, 3–5in (7–12cm) wide, are borne in summer. Z11 H11–10.

CLIVIA
AMARYLLIDACEAE

Genus of robust, evergreen, rhizomatous perennials, grown for their funnel-shaped flowers. Is suitable for borders and large containers. Needs partial shade and well-drained soil. Water well in summer, less in winter. Propagate by seed in winter or spring or by division in spring or summer after flowering. Mealy bugs may cause problems. ① All parts of *C. miniata* may cause mild stomach upset if ingested, and the sap may irritate skin.

C. miniata, illus. p.476.

C. nobilis (Violet trumpet vine). Evergreen, spring- or summer-flowering, rhizomatous perennial. **H** 12–16in (30–40cm), **S** 12–24in (30–60cm). Has strap-shaped, semierect, basal leaves, 16–24in (40–60cm) long. Each leafless stem bears a dense, semi-pendent head of more than 20 narrowly funnel-shaped, red flowers, with green tips and yellow margins to petals. Z12–14 H11–10.

CLUSIA
CLUSIACEAE

Genus of evergreen, mainly summer-flowering climbers, shrubs and trees, grown for their foliage and flowers. Needs partial shade and well-drained soil. Water container specimens moderately, very little when temperatures are low. Pruning is tolerated if necessary. Propagate by layering in spring or by semiripe cuttings in summer. Whitefly and red spider mite may be a problem.

C. major. See *C. rosea*.

C. rosea, syn. *C. major* (Autograph tree, Copey, Fat pork tree, Pitch apple). Slow-growing, evergreen, rounded tree or shrub. **H** and **S** to 50ft (15m). Bears oval, lustrous, deep green leaves. Cup-shaped, pink flowers, 2in (5cm) wide, are produced in summer, followed by globose, greenish fruits that yield a sticky resin. Z14–15 H12–10.

CLYTOSTOMA
BIGNONIACEAE

Genus of evergreen, woody-stemmed, tendril climbers, grown for their flowers. Grow in well-drained soil, with partial shade in summer. Water freely in summer, less at other times. Provide support for stems. Thin out congested growth after flowering or in spring. Propagate by semiripe cuttings in summer.

C. callistegioides, syn. *Pandorea lindleyana,* illus. p.461.

COBAEA
COBAEACEAE/POLEMONIACEAE

Genus of evergreen or deciduous, woody-stemmed, tendril climbers. Only one species, *C. scandens*, is generally cultivated. Grow outdoors in warm areas in full sun and well-drained soil. In cool regions may be grown under glass or treated as an annual. Propagate by seed in spring.

C. scandens, illus. p.204. **f. alba** (Asian bellflower) is an evergreen, woody-stemmed, tendril climber. **H** 12–15ft (4–5m). Has long-stalked, bell-shaped, green, then white flowers from late summer until first frosts. Leaves have 4 or 6 oval leaflets. Z11–13 H12–10.

Cocos capitata. See *Butia capitata.*

CODIAEUM
EUPHORBIACEAE

Genus of evergreen shrubs, grown for their foliage. Prefers partial shade and fertile, moist but well-drained soil. Remove tips from young plants to promote a branched habit. Propagate by greenwood cuttings from firm stem tips in spring or summer. Mealy bug and soft scale may be a nuisance. ① Contact with the foliage may aggravate skin allergies.

C. variegatum var. pictum, illus. p.459.

CODONOPSIS
CAMPANULACEAE

Genus of perennials and mostly herbaceous, twining climbers, grown for their bell- or saucer-shaped flowers. Needs partial shade and light, well-drained soil. Train over supports or leave to

scramble through other, larger plants. Propagate by seed in fall or spring.

C. clematidea. Herbaceous, twining climber. **H** to 5ft (1.5m). Has small, oval, mid-green leaves. In summer produces nodding, bell-shaped, blue-tinged, white flowers, 1in (2.5cm) long, marked inside with darker veining and 2 purple rings. Z7–9 H9–7.

C. convolvulacea, illus. p.205.

C. ovata. Upright perennial with scarcely twining stems. **H** and **S** to 12in (30cm). Has small, oval leaves and, in summer, small, bell-shaped, pale blue flowers, often with darker veins. Z7–9 H9–7.

COELOGYNE
ORCHIDACEAE

See also ORCHIDS.

C. cristata, illus. p.465.

C. flaccida, illus. p.466. Evergreen, epiphytic orchid for a cool greenhouse. **H** 6in (15cm). In spring bears drooping spikes of fragrant, star-shaped, light buff flowers, 1½in (4cm) across, with yellow and brown marks on each lip. Has narrowly oval, semi-rigid leaves, 3–4in (8–10cm) long. Needs partial shade in summer. H11–6.

C. nitida, syn. *C. ochracea,* illus. p.466. Evergreen, epiphytic orchid for a cool greenhouse. **H** 5in (12cm). In spring produces sprays of very fragrant, white flowers, 1in (2.5cm) across and with a yellow mark on each lip. Narrowly oval, semi-rigid leaves are 3–4in (8–10cm) long. Requires partial shade in summer. H11–6.

C. ochracea. See *C. nitida.*

C. speciosa. Vigorous, evergreen, epiphytic orchid for an intermediate greenhouse. **H** 10in (25cm). In summer produces pendent, light green flowers, 2½in (6cm) across, with brown- and white-marked lips, that open in succession along stems. Has broadly oval leaves, 9–10in (23–25cm) long. Z14–15 H11–6.

COIX
GRAMINEAE/POACEAE

See also GRASSES, BAMBOOS, RUSHES and SEDGES.

C. lacryma-jobi (Job's tears). Tuft-forming, annual grass. **H** 18–36in (45–90cm), **S** 4–6in (10–15cm). Has broad leaves and insignificant spikelets followed by hard, beadlike, green fruits turning shiny, grayish-mauve in fall. Z7–11 H11–1.

COLCHICUM
Autumn crocus, Meadow saffron
LILIACEAE/COLCHICACEAE

Genus of spring- and fall-flowering corms, grown for their mainly goblet-shaped blooms, up to 8in (20cm) long, most of which emerge before leaves. Each corm bears 2–7 narrowly strap-shaped to broadly elliptic, basal leaves. Needs an open, sunny situation and well-drained soil. Propagate by seed or division in fall. ① All parts are highly toxic if ingested and, if in contact with skin, may cause irritation.

C. agrippinum, illus. p.425.

C. autumnale, illus. p.426. **'Alboplenum'** is an fall-flowering corm. **H** and **S** 4–6in (10–15cm). In spring has 3–5 large,

C

semierect, basal, glossy, green leaves. Produces a bunch of up to 8 long-tubed, rounded, double, white flowers with 15–30 narrow petals. Z4–9 H9–1.

C. 'Beaconsfield'. Robust, fall-flowering corm. **H** and **S** 6–8in (15–20cm). Bears large, goblet-shaped, rich pinkish-purple flowers, faintly checkered and white in centers. Large, semierect, basal leaves are borne in spring. Z4–9 H9–1.

C. bivonae, syn. *C. bowlesianum, C. sibthorpii,* illus. p.425.

C. bowlesianum. See *C. bivonae.*

C. x byzantinum, illus. p.426.

C. cilicicum, illus. p.425.

C. 'Lilac Wonder'. Vigorous, fall-flowering corm. **H** and **S** 6–8in (15–20cm). Has goblet-shaped, deep lilac-pink flowers, 6–8in (15–20cm) long. Broad, semierect, basal leaves are produced in spring. Z4–9 H9–1.

C. luteum, illus. p.421.

C. sibthorpii. See *C. bivonae.*

C. speciosum. Vigorous, fall-flowering corm. **H** and **S** 6–8in (15–20cm). Bears goblet-shaped, pale to deep pinkish-purple flowers, 6–8in (15–20cm) long, often with white throats. Large, semierect, basal leaves develop in winter or spring. Z4–9 H9–1. **'Album',** illus. p.424.

C. 'The Giant'. Robust, fall-flowering corm. **H** and **S** 6–8in (15–20cm). Produces up to 5 funnel-shaped, deep mauve-pink flowers, 6–8in (15–20cm) long, fading to white in the center. Broad, semierect, basal leaves are produced in winter or spring. Z4–9 H9–1.

C. variegatum. Fall-flowering corm. **H** 4–6in (10–15cm), **S** 3–4in (8–10cm). Bears widely funnel-shaped, reddish-purple flowers with strong checkered patterns. More or less horizontal, basal leaves with wavy margins are produced in spring. Needs a hot, sunny site. Z4–9 H9–1.

C. 'Waterlily', illus. p.425.

COLEONEMA

RUTACEAE

Genus of evergreen, heather-like shrubs, grown for their flowers and overall appearance. Requires full sun and well-drained, neutral to acidic soil. Water container plants moderately when in full growth, sparingly at other times. For a more compact habit, clip after flowering. Propagate by seed in spring or by semiripe cuttings in late summer.

C. pulchrum. Evergreen, spreading to domed shrub with wiry stems. **H** 2–4ft (60cm–1.2m), **S** 3–5ft (1–1.5m). Has soft, needlelike, bright green leaves. Produces 5-petaled, pale pink to red flowers in spring–summer. Z8–11 H11–8.

Coleus blumei var. verschaffeltii. See *Solenostemon scutellarioides.*
Coleus thyrsoideus. See *Plectranthus thyrsoideus.*

COLLETIA

RHAMNACEAE

Genus of deciduous, usually leafless shrubs, grown for their curious, spiny shoots and profuse, small flowers. Shoots assume function of leaves. Requires a sheltered, sunny site and well-drained soil. Propagate by semiripe cuttings in late summer.

C. armata. See *C. hystrix.*
C. cruciata. See *C. paradoxa.*
C. hystrix, syn. *C. armata,* illus. p.130. **'Rosea'** is a deciduous, sturdily branched shrub. **H** 8ft (2.5m), **S** 15ft (5m). Shoots have rigid, gray-green spines. Bears fragrant, tubular, pink flowers in late summer and early fall. Z7–11 H12–7.
C. paradoxa, syn. *C. cruciata,* illus. p.131.

COLLINSIA

SCROPHULARIACEAE

Genus of spring- to summer-flowering annuals. Needs partial shade and fertile, well-drained soil. Support with thin sticks. Propagate by seed sown outdoors in spring or early fall.
C. grandiflora, illus. p.312.

COLOCASIA

ARACEAE

Genus of deciduous or evergreen, perennial, marginal water plants, grown for their foliage. Has edible tubers, known as "taros," for which it is widely cultivated. Is suitable for the edges of frost-free ponds; may also be grown in wet soil in pots. Grows in sun or light shade and in mud or shallow water. Propagate by division in spring. ① All parts may cause mild stomach upset if ingested without cooking, and contact with the sap may irritate the skin.

C. antiquorum. See *C. esculenta.*
C. esculenta, syn. *C. antiquorum.* **'Fontanesii'** is a deciduous, perennial, marginal water plant. **H** 3^1/$_2$ft (1.1m), **S** 2ft (60cm). Has large, bold, oval, mid-green leaves with dark green veins and margins and blackish-violet leaf stalks and spathe tubes. Z9–11 H12–8. **'Illustris'** has brownish-purple leaf stalks and dark green leaf blades with purple spots.

COLQUHOUNIA

LABIATAE/LAMIACEAE

Genus of evergreen or semievergreen shrubs, grown for their flowers in late summer and fall. Needs a sheltered, sunny position and well-drained soil. Propagate by softwood cuttings in summer.
C. coccinea, illus. p.141.

COLUMNEA

GESNERIACEAE

Genus of evergreen, creeping or trailing perennials or subshrubs, grown for their showy flowers. Trailing species are useful for hanging baskets. Needs bright but indirect light, a fairly humid atmosphere and moist soil, except in winter. Propagate by tip cuttings after flowering.
C. x banksii, illus. p.470.
C. crassifolia, illus. p.470.
C. gloriosa (Goldfish plant). Evergreen, trailing perennial with more or less unbranched stems. **H** and **S** to 3ft (90cm). Oval leaves have reddish hairs. Has tubular, hooded, scarlet flowers, to 3in (8cm) long, with yellow throats, in winter–spring. Z13–15 H11–10.
C. microphylla. Evergreen perennial, sparsely branched on each trailing stem. **H** and **S** 3ft (1m) or more. Has small, rounded leaves with brown hairs. Hooded,

tubular, scarlet flowers, to 3in (8cm) long, with yellow throats, are produced in winter–spring. Z14–15 H11–10. **'Variegata',** illus. p.475.

COLUTEA

LEGUMINOSAE/PAPILIONACEAE

Genus of deciduous, summer-flowering shrubs, grown for their foliage, pealike flowers and bladder-shaped seed pods. Grow in full sun and any but waterlogged soil. Propagate by softwood cuttings in summer or by seed in fall. ① The seeds may cause mild stomach upset if ingested.
C. arborescens, illus. p.139.
C. x media, illus. p.140.
C. orientalis. Deciduous, bushy shrub. **H** and **S** 6ft (2m). Has blue-gray leaves consisting of 7 or 9 oval leaflets. Clusters of yellow-marked, coppery-red flowers produced in summer are followed by inflated, green, then pale brown seed pods. Z6–9 H9–6.

Comarostaphylis diversifolia. See *Arctostaphylos diversifolia.*

COMBRETUM

COMBRETACEAE

Genus of evergreen trees, shrubs and scandent to twining climbers, grown for their small, showy flowers. Provide rich, well-drained soil, with partial shade in summer. Water freely in summer, less at other times. Support for stems is necessary. Thin out and spur back congested growth after flowering. Propagate by semiripe cuttings in summer. Red spider mite may be a problem.
C. grandiflorum. Moderately vigorous, evergreen, scandent to twining climber. **H** to 20ft (6m). Has oblong to elliptic, pointed leaves, 4–8in (10–20cm) long. Tubular, bright red flowers with long stamens are borne in summer in one-sided spikes, 4–5in (10–13cm) long. Z11 H11–10.
C. indicum. See *Quisqualis indica.*

COMMELINA

Day flower

COMMELINACEAE

Genus of perennials, usually grown as annuals. Needs a sunny, sheltered position and fertile, well-drained soil. Crowns should be lifted before the frosts and overwintered in slightly moist, frost-free conditions. Propagate by seed sown under glass or by division of the crown in spring.
C. coelestis, syn. *C. tuberosa* Coelestis Group, illus. p.315.
C. tuberosa Coelestis Group. See *C. coelestis.*

CONANDRON

GESNERIACEAE

Genus of one species of tuberous perennial, grown for its fleshy leaves and drooping flower clusters. Grow in alpine houses. Needs shade and rich, well-drained soil. Keep container plants moist in summer, dry when dormant in winter. Propagate by division or seed in spring.
C. ramondioides. Hummock-forming, tuberous perennial. **H** 12in (30cm), **S** 8in (20cm). Produces broadly oval, fleshy, wrinkled, mid-green leaves with toothed

edges. In mid-summer, each flower stem bears 5–25 tubular flowers, usually lilac, but white, purple or pink forms also occur. Z7–8 H8–7.

CONIFERS

Group of trees and shrubs, distinguished botanically from others by producing seeds exposed or uncovered on the scales of fruits. Most conifers are evergreen, have needlelike leaves and bear woody fruits (cones). All genera in the Cupressaceae family, however, have needlelike juvenile leaves and, excepting many junipers and some other selected forms, scalelike adult leaves. Conifers described in this book are evergreen unless otherwise stated.

Conifers are excellent garden plants. Most provide year-round foliage, which may be green, blue, gray, bronze, gold or silver. They range in height from trees 130ft (40m) or more tall to dwarf shrubs that grow less than 2in (5cm) every 10 years. Tall conifers may be planted as specimen trees or to provide shelter, screening or hedging. Dwarf conifers make good features in their own right as well as in groups; they also associate well with heathers, add variety to rock gardens and provide excellent groundcover. They may also be grown in containers.

Position and soil

Cupressus, x *Cuprocyparis, Larix* and *Pinus* need full sun. *Cedrus, Juniperus* and *Pseudolarix* do not tolerate shade. All other conifers will thrive in sun or shade, and most *Abies* and all *Cephalotaxus, Podocarpus, Taxus, Thuja, Torreya* and *Tsuga* will grow in deep shade once established. *Wollemia* prefers a sheltered location out of full sun.

Conifers grow well on most soils, but certain genera and species will not do well on soils over chalk or limestone. In this book, such conifers are: *Abies, Pseudolarix, Pseudotsuga* and *Tsuga;* also *Picea,* except *P. likiangensis, P. omorika* and *P. pungens;* and *Pinus,* except *P. aristata, P. armandii, P. cembroides, P. halepensis, P. heldreichii, P. nigra, P. peuce* and *P. wallichiana.* Certain conifers tolerate extreme conditions. *Abies alba, A. homolepis, A. nordmanniana, Cryptomeria, Cunninghamia, Metasequoia, Pinus coulteri, P. peuce, P. ponderosa, Sciadopitys, Sequoia, Sequoiadendron* and *Taxodium* will grow on heavy clay soils. *Picea omorika, P. sitchensis, Pinus contorta, Sciadopitys verticillata* and *Thuja plicata* are all happy on wet soil, and *Metasequoia* and *Taxodium* thrive in waterlogged conditions. *Cupressus, Juniperus* and *Pinus* grow well on dry, sandy soil.

Pruning

If a conifer produces more than one leader, remove all but one. Bear in mind when trimming hedges that most conifers will not make new growth when cut back into old wood or from branches that have turned brown. This does not, however, apply to *Cephalotaxus, Cryptomeria, Cunninghamia, Sequoia, Taxus, Torreya* and *Wollemia,* and these conifers may be kept to a reasonable size in the garden by cutting back the main stem, which will later coppice (make new growth). Young specimens of *Araucaria, Ginkgo, Metasequoia* and *Taxodium* will sometimes do the same.

Propagation

Seed is the easiest method of propagation, but forms selected for leaf color (other than blue in some species) do not come true. Sow in fall or spring. All genera apart from *Abies*, *Cedrus*, *Picea* (except young plants or dwarf forms), *Pinus*, *Pseudolarix*, *Pseudotsuga* and *Tsuga* (except young plants or dwarf forms) may be raised fairly easily from cuttings: current growth from fall to spring for evergreens, softwood cuttings in summer for deciduous conifers. Tall-growing forms of Pinaceae (*Abies*, *Cedrus*, *Picea*, *Pinus*, *Pseudolarix*, *Pseudotsuga* and *Tsuga*) are usually propagated by grafting in late summer, winter or early spring. Layering may be possible for some dwarf conifers. It is illegal to propagate *Wollemia nobilis*.

Pests and diseases

Honey fungus attacks many conifers, especially young plants. Most resistant to the disease are *Abies*, *Calocedrus*, *Larix*, *Pseudotsuga* and *Taxus*. Green spruce aphid may be a problem on *Picea*, and conifer spinning mite may defoliate *Abies*, *Picea* and some *Pinus*.

Conifers are illustrated on pp.95–105, dwarf forms on pp.105. See also *Abies*, *Araucaria*, *Athrotaxis*, *Austrocedrus*, *Calocedrus*, *Cedrus*, *Cephalotaxus*, *Chamaecyparis*, *Cryptomeria*, *Cunninghamia*, *Cupressus*, x *Cuprocyparis*, *Fitzroya*, *Ginkgo*, *Juniperus*, *Larix*, *Metasequoia*, *Microbiota*, *Phyllocladus*, *Picea*, *Pinus*, *Platycladus*, *Podocarpus*, *Prumnopitys*, *Pseudolarix*, *Pseudotsuga*, *Saxegothaea*, *Sciadopitys*, *Sequoia*, *Sequoiadendron*, *Taxodium*, *Taxus*, *Thuja*, *Thujopsis*, *Torreya*, *Tsuga* and *Wollemia*.

CONOPHYTUM

AIZOACEAE

Genus of slow-growing, clump-forming, perennial succulents with spherical or 2-eared leaves that grow for only 2 months each year, after flowering. In early summer, old leaves gradually shrivel to papery sheaths from which new leaves and flowers emerge in late summer. Needs full sun and well-drained soil. Keep dry in winter. Propagate by seed from spring to fall or by division in late summer.

C. bilobum, illus. p.494.
C. concordans, syn. *Ophthalmophyllum villetii*, illus. p.484.
C. frutescens, syn. *C. notabile*, illus. p.496.
C. longum, syn. *Ophthalmophyllum herri*, *Ophthalmophyllum longum*. Clump-forming, perennial succulent. **H** 1¼in (3cm), **S** ⅝in (1.5cm). Has 2 almost united, erect, cylindrical, very fleshy, gray-green to brown leaves. In late summer bears daisylike, white to pink flowers, ¾in (2cm) across. Z12–14 H11–10.
C. notabile. See *C. frutescens*.
C. truncatum (Larkspur). Slow-growing, clump-forming, perennial succulent. **H** ⅝in (1.5cm), **S** 6in (15cm). Has pea-shaped, dark-spotted, blue-green leaves, each with a sunken fissure at the tip. Produces daisylike, cream flowers, ⅝in (1.5cm) across, in fall. Z12–15 H11–10.

CONSOLIDA

Larkspur

RANUNCULACEAE

Genus of annuals, providing excellent cut flowers. Needs sun and fertile, well-drained soil. Support stems of tall-growing plants with sticks. Propagate by seed sown outdoors in spring, or in early fall in mild areas. Protect young plants from slugs and snails. ① The seeds are poisonous.
C. ajacis, syn. *C. ambigua*, *Delphinium consolida*. Fast-growing, upright, branching annual. Giant forms, **H** to 4ft (1.2m), **S** 1ft (30cm); dwarf, **H** and **S** 1ft (30cm). All have feathery, mid-green leaves and, throughout summer, spikes of rounded, spurred flowers. H9–1. **Dwarf Hyacinth Series** has spikes of tubular flowers in shades of pink, mauve, blue or white. **Giant Imperial Series** (Giant larkspur) has spikes of rounded, spurred, double flowers in pink, blue or white.
C. ambigua. See *C. ajacis*.

CONVALLARIA

Lily-of-the-valley

LILIACEAE/ASPARAGACEAE

Genus of spring-flowering, rhizomatous perennials. Prefers partial shade and rich, moist soil. Propagate by division after flowering or in fall. ① The seeds of *C. majalis* may cause mild stomach upset if ingested.
C. majalis, illus. p.255. Z2–7 H7–1. **'Flore Pleno'** is a low-growing, rhizomatous perennial. **H** 9–12in (23–30cm), **S** indefinite. Sprays of small, very fragrant, pendent, bell-shaped flowers that are double and white are produced in spring. Narrowly oval leaves are mid- to dark green. **'Fortin's Giant'**, **H** 18in (45cm), has larger flowers and leaves that appear a little earlier.

CONVOLVULUS

CONVOLVULACEAE

Genus of dwarf, bushy and climbing annuals, perennials and evergreen shrubs and subshrubs. Grow in sun and in poor to fertile, well-drained soil. Deadhead to prolong flowering. Propagate by seed sown outdoors in mid-spring for hardy plants or under glass in spring for tender plants; increase perennials and subshrubs by softwood cuttings in late spring or summer.
C. althaeoides, illus. p.362.
C. cneorum, illus. p.149.
C. mauritanicus. See *C. sabatius*.
C. minor. See *C. tricolor*.
C. purpureus. See *Ipomoea purpurea*.
C. sabatius, syn. *C. mauritanicus*, illus. p.342.
C. tricolor, syn. *C. minor*. Moderately fast-growing, upright, bushy or climbing annual. **H** 8–12in (20–30cm), **S** 8in (20cm). Has oval to lance-shaped, mid-green leaves. In summer bears saucer-shaped, blue or white flowers, 1in (2.5cm) wide, with yellowish-white throats. Tall, climbing forms, **H** to 10ft (3m), are half-hardy and have flowers to 4in (10cm) wide. Z9–11 H11–10. **'Blue Flash'** (bushy) illus. p.314. **'Flying Saucers'** (climber) has blue-and-white-striped flowers.

COPIAPOA

CACTACEAE

Genus of slow-growing, perennial cacti with funnel-shaped, yellow flowers. Many species have large taproots. Needs partial shade and very well-drained soil. Propagate by seed or grafting in spring or summer.
C. cinerea, illus. p.489.
C. coquimbana. Clump-forming, spherical, then columnar, perennial cactus. **H** to 1ft (30cm), **S** 3ft (1m). Dark gray-green stem has 10–17 ribs. Areoles each bear 8–10 dark brown radial spines and 1 or 2 sturdier central spines. Yellow flowers, 1¼in (3cm) across, are borne in summer. Is slow to form clumps. Z13–15 H12–10.
C. echinoides. Flattened spherical, perennial cactus, ribbed like a sea urchin. **H** 6in (15cm), **S** 4in (10cm). Solitary gray-green stem bears dark brown spines, 1¼in (3cm) long, which soon fade to gray. In summer produces pale yellow flowers, 1½in (4cm) across. Z13–15 H12–10.
C. marginata. Clump-forming, perennial cactus. **H** 2ft (60cm), **S** 1ft (30cm). Gray-green stem bears very close-set areoles with dark-tipped, pale brown spines, to 1¼in (3cm) long. Has yellow flowers, ¾–2in (2–5cm) across, in spring–summer. Z13–15 H12–10.

COPROSMA

RUBIACEAE

Genus of evergreen shrubs and trees, grown for their foliage and fruits. Separate male and female plants are needed to obtain fruits. Prefers full light and well-drained soil. Water container specimens freely in summer, moderately at other times. Propagate by seed in spring or by semiripe cuttings in late summer.
C. baueriana. See *C. repens*.
C. baueri of gardens. See *C. repens*.
C. x kirkii. Evergreen, prostrate, then semierect, densely branched shrub. **H** to 3ft (1m), **S** 4–6ft (1.2–2m). Narrowly oblong to lance-shaped, leathery, glossy leaves are borne singly or in small clusters. In late spring has insignificant flowers, followed on female plants by tiny, egg-shaped, translucent, white fruits with red speckles. Z8–10 H10–8. **'Variegata'**, illus. p.152.
C. repens, syn. *C. baueriana*, *C. baueri*. Evergreen, spreading, then erect shrub. **H** and **S** to 6ft (2m). Has broadly oval, leathery, lustrous, rich green leaves. Produces insignificant flowers in late spring, followed on female plants by egg-shaped, orange-red fruits from late summer to fall. Z8–10 H10–8. Leaves of **'Picturata'** each have a central, cream blotch.

CORDYLINE

AGAVACEAE/ASPARAGACEAE

Genus of evergreen shrubs and trees, grown mainly for their foliage, although some also have decorative flowers. Provide fertile, well-drained soil and full light or partial shade. Water container plants moderately, less in winter. Propagate by seed or suckers in spring or by stem cuttings in summer. Red spider mite may be a nuisance.
C. australis, syn. *Dracaena australis* (New Zealand cabbage palm). Slow-growing, evergreen, sparsely branched tree. **H** 50ft (15m) or more, **S** 15ft (5m) or more. Each stem is crowned by a rosette of strap-shaped leaves, 1–3ft (30cm–1m) long. Has small, scented, white flowers in large, open panicles in summer and, in fall, globose, white fruits. Z10–11 H11–10. **'Atropurpurea'**, illus. p.451. Long, sword-shaped leaves of **'Veitchii'** have red bases and midribs.
C. fruticosa, syn. *C. terminalis* (Ti plant). Slow-growing, evergreen, upright shrub, sparingly branched and suckering. **H** 6–12ft (2–4m), **S** 3–6ft (1–2m). Broadly lance-shaped, glossy, deep green leaves are 1–2ft (30–60cm) long. Produces branched panicles of small, white, purplish or reddish flowers in summer. Z11 H11–7. Foliage of **'Baptistii'** is deep green with pink and yellow stripes and spots. **'Imperialis'** has red- or pink-marked, deep green leaves.
C. indivisa, syn. *Dracaena indivisa*. Slow-growing, evergreen, erect tree or shrub. **H** 10ft (3m) or more, **S** 6ft (2m). Bears lance-shaped, green leaves, 2–6ft (60cm–2m) long, orange-brown veined above, blue-gray tinted beneath. In summer, tiny, star-shaped, white flowers in dense clusters, 2ft (60cm) or more long, are followed by tiny, spherical, blue-purple fruits. Z9–10 H11–10.
C. terminalis. See *C. fruticosa*.

COREOPSIS

Tickseed

COMPOSITAE/ASTERACEAE

Genus of annuals and perennials, grown for their daisylike flower heads. Needs full sun and fertile, well-drained soil. Propagate annuals by seed in spring; *C. lanceolata* by seed or division in spring; *C. auriculata* 'Superba' and *C. grandiflora* 'Badengold' by softwood cuttings or division in spring or summer; and *C. verticillata* by division in spring.
C. auriculata 'Superba' (Tickseed). Bushy perennial. **H** and **S** 18in (45cm). Daisylike, rich yellow flower heads, with central, purple blotches, are borne in summer. Oval to lance-shaped leaves are lobed and light green. Some plants grown as *C. auriculata* are the closely related annual *C. basalis*. Z4–9 H9–1.
C. Coloropsis Series 'Jive'. Bushy, well-branched, prolific perennial grown as an annual. **H** 12–18in (30–45cm), **S** 18–24in (45–60cm). Has narrowly lance-shaped, dark green leaves. Daisylike, deep crimson flower heads, 2in (5cm) across, margined in pure white, are borne in summer–fall.
C. 'Goldfink'. See *C. lanceolata* 'Goldfink'.
C. grandiflora. Z4–9 H11–1. **'Badengold'** Short-lived, erect perennial with lax stems. **H** 30in (75cm), **S** 24in (60cm). Bears large, daisylike, rich buttercup-yellow flower heads in summer and broadly lance-shaped, divided, bright green leaves. **'Sunray'**, syn. *C.* 'Sunray' illus. p.321.
C. lanceolata, illus. p.276. **'Goldfink'**, syn. *C.* 'Goldfink' is a short-lived, dwarf, bushy perennial. **H** and **S** 12in (30cm). Sprays of daisylike, deep yellow flower heads are held in summer above narrowly oval, deep green leaves. Z4–9 H9–1.
C. 'Limerock Ruby', illus. p.268.
C. rosea 'American Dream'. Upright perennial. **H** 14in (35cm), **S** 12in (30cm). Has

small, lance-shaped, dark green leaves. Produces masses of daisylike, yellow-centered, pink flower heads, borne on self-supporting, branched stems, in mid-summer. Z4–8 H8–1.
***C.* 'Rum Punch',** illus. p.326.
***C.* 'Sunray'.** See *C. grandiflora* 'Sunray'.
C. tinctoria, illus. p.321. **'Golden Crown'** (Threadleaf coreopsis) is a fast-growing, upright, bushy annual. **H** 24in (60cm), **S** 8in (20cm). Has lance-shaped, deep green leaves and, in summer and early fall, large, daisylike, deep yellow flower heads with brown centers. Z4–9 H12–1.
C. verticillata, illus. p.276.

CORIARIA

CORIARIACEAE

Genus of deciduous, spring- or summer-flowering shrubs and subshrubs, grown for their habit, foliage and fruits. Needs full sun and fertile, well-drained soil. Propagate by softwood cuttings in summer or by seed in fall. ⓘ The leaves and fruits of some species may cause severe stomach upset if ingested; in other species, the fruits are edible, although the seeds are thought to be poisonous.
C. terminalis. Deciduous, arching subshrub. **H** 3ft (1m), **S** 6ft (2m). Broadly lance-shaped, fernlike, mid-green leaves turn red in fall. Minute, green flowers in late spring are followed by small, spherical, black fruits. Z9–11 H11–1. **var. *xanthocarpa,*** illus. p.161.

CORNUKAEMPFERIA

ZINGIBERACEAE

Genus of one species of herbaceous perennial with underground rhizomes, grown for its large, colorful leaves and flowers. Grow in moist but well-drained soil in partial or full shade. Keep dry when dormant. Propagate by division in spring or by seed in spring.
C. aurantiflora. Herbaceous, rhizomatous perennial. **H** 28in (70cm), **S** 20in (50cm). Has ovate, ribbed, dark green and silver leaves, to 10in (25cm) long, with purple undersides, borne close to the ground. Tubular, orange flowers, 2in (5cm) long, are borne, in summer, from short stalks in the leaf axils. Requires full shade. **'Jungle Gold'** (illus. p.477) has largely silver leaves and deep orange-red buds that open into orange-gold flowers, with red lines.

CORNUS

Dogwood

CORNACEAE

Genus of deciduous shrubs and deciduous or evergreen trees, grown for their flowers, foliage or brightly colored winter stems. Needs sun or partial shade and fertile, well-drained soil. Those grown for winter stem color do best in full sun. *C. florida, C. kousa* and *C. nuttallii* dislike shallow, chalky soil. *C. canadensis* prefers acidic soil. Plants grown for their stems should be cut back almost to ground level each year in early spring. Propagate *C. alba* and *C. sericea* 'Flaviramea' by softwood cuttings in summer or by hardwood cuttings in fall or winter; variegated forms of *C. alternifolia* and *C. controversa* by grafting in winter; *C. canadensis* by division in spring or fall; *C. capitata, C. florida* and *C. kousa* by seed in fall or by softwood cuttings in summer; *C. nuttallii* by seed in fall; all others described here by softwood cuttings in summer.
ⓘ The fruits of some species may cause mild stomach upset if ingested; contact with the leaf hairs may irritate skin.
C. alba (Tatarian dogwood). Vigorous, deciduous, upright, then spreading shrub. **H** and **S** 10ft (3m). Young shoots are bright red in winter. Has oval, dark green leaves, often red or orange in fall. Bears flattened heads of star-shaped, creamy-white flowers in late spring and early summer, followed by spherical, sometimes blue-tinted, white fruits. Z2–8 H8–1. **'Aurea'** (illus. p.126) has pale greenish-yellow leaves in summer. **'Elegantissima'** (illus. p.126) has white-edged, gray-green leaves. **'Gouchaultii'** has pink-flushed leaves broadly edged with yellow. **'Kesselringii'** (illus. p.126) has dark green leaves flushed reddish-purple in fall. **'Sibirica'** illus. p.143. **'Sibirica Variegata'** (illus. p.142) has gray-green leaves with creamy-white margins. **'Spaethii'** (Pagoda dogwood) (illus. p.126) has bright green leaves with yellow edges.
C. alternifolia, illus. p.87. Deciduous, spreading tree or bushy shrub, with tiered branches. **H** and **S** 20ft (6m). Oval, bright green leaves, which each taper to a point, often turn red in fall. Clusters of tiny, star-shaped, creamy-white flowers in early summer are followed by small, rounded, blue-black fruits. Z4–8 H8–1. **'Argentea'** (Giant dogwood), illus. p.87 has narrowly oval, white-variegated leaves.
C. canadensis, syn. *Chamaepericlymenum canadense*, illus. p.360.
C. capitata, syn. *Dendrobenthamia capitata* (Evergreen dogwood), illus. p.87. Evergreen or semievergreen, spreading tree. **H** and **S** to 40ft (12m). Pale yellow bracts, surrounding insignificant flowers, are produced in early summer, followed by large, strawberry-like, red fruits. Has oval, gray-green leaves. Is good for a mild coastal area. Z8–9 H9–8.
C. controversa (Flowering dogwood), illus. p.87. Deciduous tree with layered branches. **H** and **S** 50ft (15m). Leaves are oval, pointed and bright green, turning purple in fall. Clusters of small, star-shaped, white flowers are borne in summer. Z6–9 H9–6. **'Variegata'** (Giant dogwood), **H** and **S** 25ft (8m), leaves are bright green with broad, creamy-white margins and turn yellow in fall.
***C.* 'Eddie's White Wonder',** illus. p.87. Deciduous, spreading tree or shrub. **H** 20ft (6m), **S** 15ft (5m). Large, white bracts, surrounding insignificant flowers, are produced in late spring. Oval leaves are mid-green, turning red and purple in fall. Z5–8 H8–5.
C. florida (Flowering dogwood). Deciduous, spreading tree. **H** 20ft (6m), **S** 25ft (8m). In late spring bears white or pinkish-white bracts surrounding tiny, insignificant flowers. Oval, pointed, dark green leaves turn red and purple in fall. Z5–8 H8–3. **'Apple Blossom'** has pale pink bracts. **'Cherokee Chief'** (illus. p.87) bears pink-red bracts, fading to white close to each flower. **'Cherokee Princess'** (illus. p.87) has bronze-colored leaves that mature to dark green. **'Rainbow'** (illus. p.87) has a compact, erect habit, white bracts and yellow-edged leaves turning purple-red in fall. **f. *rubra*** bears pink or red bracts. **'Spring Song'** has pink bracts. **'Welchii',** illus. p.89. **'White Cloud'** has large white bracts.
C. kousa, illus. p.85. **var. *chinensis*** (illus. p.87) has larger flower heads and more narrowly pointed bracts. **var. *chinensis* 'China Girl'** (Bigleaf dogwood) (illus. p.87) bears creamy-white bracts and mid-green leaves turning orange-red in fall. **'Miss Satomi'** (illus. p.87) has deep pink bracts and bright green leaves turning orange and red in fall. **'National'** (illus. p.87) is vigorous, has bright green leaves turning to orange and red in fall, and bears large, white bracts that mature to pink.
C. macrophylla. Deciduous, spreading tree. **H** 40ft (12m), **S** 25ft (8m). Glossy, bright green leaves are large, pointed and oval. Clusters of small, creamy-white flowers are produced in summer. Z7–8 H8–7.
C. mas (Cornelian cherry), illus. p.87. Deciduous, spreading, open shrub or tree. **H** and **S** 15ft (5m). Oval, dark green leaves change to reddish-purple in fall. Produces small, star-shaped, yellow flowers on bare shoots in late winter and early spring, then edible, oblong, bright red fruits. Z5–8 H8–5. **'Aureoelegantissima',** syn. *C. mas* 'Elegantissima' (illus. p.87), **H** 6ft (2m), **S** 10ft (3m), has pink-tinged leaves edged with yellow. **'Elegantissima'.** See *C. mas* 'Aureoelegantissima'. **'Variegata'** is bushy and dense and produces white-edged, dark green leaves.
***C.* 'Norman Hadden'.** Deciduous, spreading tree. **H** and **S** 25ft (8m). Creamy-white bracts around tiny flowers turn to deep pink in summer. These are often followed by strawberry-like fruits in fall. Z5–8 H8–5.
C. nuttallii (Western dogwood). Deciduous, conical tree. **H** 40ft (12m), **S** 25ft (8m). Has oval, dark green leaves and large, white bracts, surrounding tiny flowers, borne in late spring. Z7–8 H8–7. **'Monarch'** (illus. p.87) is a vigorous, spreading tree with rounded, white bracts in mid-spring and purple-blushed shoots bearing mid-green leaves.
***C.* 'Porlock'** (Kousa dogwood), illus. p.87. Deciduous, spreading tree. **H** 30ft (10m), **S** 15ft (5m). Creamy-white bracts around tiny flowers turn to deep pink in summer. These are often followed by heavy crops of strawberry-like fruits in fall. Z5–9 H9–5.
C. sanguinea (Bloodtwig dogwood), illus. p.142. Deciduous, upright shrub. **H** to 10ft (3m), **S** 3ft (1m). Reddish-green, sometimes entirely green, winter shoots are a deep red color when young. Ovate, mid-green leaves turn reddish-purple in fall. Flattened heads of star-shaped, white flowers, in late spring, are followed by egg-shaped, blue-black fruits. Thrives in damp soil. Z4–7 H7–1. **'Midwinter Fire'** (illus. p.126) produces flame-colored stems—yellow at the bases rising to scarlet-red on younger growth. **'Winter Beauty'** (illus. p.126) has orange-yellow winter stems, tipped with crimson, and yellow-red fall leaf color.
C. sericea, syn. *C. stolonifera* (Red osier dogwood). Z3–8 H8–1. **'Flaviramea'** (illus. p.126) is a vigorous, deciduous shrub. **H** 6ft (2m), **S** 13ft (4m). Has olive-green to yellow, young shoots in winter and ovate, mid-green leaves. Flattened heads of small, star-shaped cream flowers, in late spring and early summer, are followed by ovoid, creamy-white fruits. **'Kelseyi'** (illus. p.126), **H** 2½ft (75cm), **S** 5ft (1.5m), is compact and has yellow-green winter stems tipped with orange-red. **'White Gold',** syn. *C. sericea* 'White Spot' (illus. p.126) has mid-green leaves margined and mottled with white. **'White Spot'.** See *C. sericea* 'White Gold'.
C. stolonifera. See *C. sericea.*

COROKIA

ESCALLONIACEAE/ARGOPHYLLACEAE

Genus of evergreen shrubs, grown for their habit, foliage, flowers and fruits. Is good in mild, coastal areas, where it is very wind-tolerant. Protect from strong winds at limits of hardiness. Needs full sun and fertile, well-drained soil. Propagate by softwood cuttings in summer.
C. buddlejoides. Evergreen, upright shrub. **H** 10ft (3m), **S** 6ft (2m). Has slender, gray shoots and narrowly oblong, glossy, dark green leaves. Bears panicles of star-shaped, yellow flowers in late spring, followed by spherical, blackish-red fruits. Z9–10 H10–9.
C. cotoneaster, illus. p.144.
C.* x *virgata. Evergreen, upright, dense shrub. **H** and **S** 10ft (3m). Leaves are oblong and glossy, dark green above, white beneath. Produces star-shaped, yellow flowers in mid-spring, then egg-shaped, bright orange fruits. Makes a good hedge, especially in coastal areas. Z8–10 H10–8.

CORONILLA

LEGUMINOSAE/PAPILIONACEAE

Genus of deciduous or evergreen shrubs and perennials, grown for their foliage and flowers. Requires full sun and light, well-drained soil. Propagate by softwood cuttings in summer.
C. glauca. See *C. valentina* subsp. *glauca.*
C. valentina* subsp. *glauca, syn. *C. glauca*, illus. p.195.

CORREA

RUTACEAE

Genus of evergreen shrubs, grown for their flowers. Prefers full light or partial shade and fertile, well-drained, neutral to acidic soil. Water container specimens moderately, less when not in flower. Propagate by seed in spring or by semiripe cuttings in late summer.
C. backhouseana. Evergreen, rounded, well-branched shrub. **H** and **S** 6ft (2m). Leaves are oval to elliptic and dark green, with dense, pale buff down beneath. Tubular, pale yellow-green to white flowers are produced in spring and intermittently until fall. Z9–10 H10–8.
C.* x *harrisii. See *C.* 'Mannii'.
***C.* 'Mannii',** syn. *C.* x *harrisii, C.* 'Harrisii'. Evergreen, bushy, slender-stemmed shrub. **H** and **S** 6ft (2m). Has narrowly oval leaves with short hairs beneath. Tubular, scarlet flowers are borne in summer–fall, sometimes in other seasons. Z9–10 H10–9.
C. pulchella, illus. p.164.
C. reflexa, syn. *C. speciosa*. Evergreen, bushy, slender-stemmed shrub. **H** and **S** to 6ft (2m). Oval leaves have thick down beneath. Bears tubular, greenish-yellow to crimson or rose flowers, with greenish-

white petal tips, in summer–fall, sometimes in other seasons. Z9–10 H10–9.
C. speciosa. See *C. reflexa.*

CORTADERIA
GRAMINEAE/POACEAE

See also GRASSES, BAMBOOS, RUSHES and SEDGES.
C. richardii, illus. p.284.
C. selloana (Pampas grass). Evergreen, clump-forming, stately, perennial grass. **H** to 8ft (2.5m), **S** 4ft (1.2m). Has narrow, very sharp-edged, outward-curving leaves, 5ft (1.5m) long. In late summer, erect, plumelike, silvery racemes, up to 2ft (60cm) long, are borne above mid-green leaves. Male and female flowers are produced on separate plants; females, with long, silky hairs, are more decorative. Z7–11 H11–7.
'Aureolineata', syn. *C. selloana* 'Gold Band', **H** to 7ft (2.2m), is compact, and has leaves with rich yellow margins aging to dark golden-yellow. **'Gold Band'.** See *C. selloana* 'Aureolineata'. **'Silver Comet'** illus. p.285. **'Sunningdale Silver',** illus. p.284.

CORTUSA
PRIMULACEAE

Genus of clump-forming, spring- and summer-flowering perennials, related to *Primula*, with one-sided racemes of bell-shaped flowers. Is not suitable for hot, dry climates as needs shade and rich, moist soil. Propagate by seed when fresh or by division in fall.
C. matthioli, illus. p.341.

CORYDALIS
PAPAVERACEAE/FUMARIACEAE

Genus of spring- and summer-flowering annuals and tuberous or fibrous-rooted perennials, some of which are evergreen, grown for their tubular, spurred, 2-lipped flowers or for their fernlike leaves. Needs full sun or partial shade and well-drained soil; some require rich soil and cool growing conditions. Propagate by seed in fall or by division when dormant: fall for spring-flowering species, spring for summer-flowering species.
C. ambigua of gardens. See *C. fumariifolia.*
C. bulbosa of gardens. See *C. cava.*
C. cashmeriana. Tuft-forming, fibrous-rooted perennial. **H** 4–10in (10–25cm), **S** 3–4in (8–10cm). Has divided, semierect, basal leaves and, in summer, dense spikes of 2-lipped, brilliant blue flowers. Needs cool, partially shaded, rich, neutral to acidic soil. Is good for a rock garden. Dies down in winter. Z6–8 H8–6.
C. cava, syn. *C. bulbosa.* Spring-flowering, tuberous perennial. **H** 4–8in (10–20cm), **S** 3–4in (8–10cm). Leaves are semierect, basal and much divided. Produces dense spikes of tubular, dull purple flowers. Dies down in summer. Z6–8 H8–6.
C. cheilanthifolia, illus. p.335.
C. diphylla, illus. p.354.
C. fumariifolia, syn. *C. ambigua.* Tuberous perennial. **H** to 6in (15cm), **S** to 4in (10cm). Stem bears much-divided leaves and a short spike of 2-lipped, azure-blue or purplish-blue flowers, with

flattened, triangular spurs, from spring to early summer. Dies down in summer. Z5–8 H8–5.
C. halleri. See *C. solida.*
C. lutea, syn. *Pseudofumaria lutea,* illus. p.344.
C. nobilis. Perennial with long, fleshy, fibrous roots. **H** and **S** 8–14in (20–35cm). Bears much-divided leaves on lower part of flower stems, each of which bears a dense spike of long-spurred, pale yellow flowers, with lips tipped green or brown, in early summer. Z5–8 H8–5.
C. ochroleuca of gardens, syn. *Pseudofumaria alba, Pseudofumaria ochroleuca,* illus. p.337.
C. popovii, illus. p.349.
C. solida, syn. *C. halleri.* Tuft-forming, tuberous perennial. **H** 4–8in (10–20cm), **S** 3–5in (8–12cm). Leaves alternate on flower stems, each of which bears a dense spike of dull purplish-red flowers in spring. Dies down in summer. Z5–7 H7–3. **'George Baker',** syn. *C. solida* 'G.P. Baker', illus. p.353. **'G.P. Baker'.** See *C. solida* 'George Baker'.
C. wilsonii, illus. p.335.

CORYLOPSIS
Winterhazel
HAMAMELIDACEAE

Genus of deciduous shrubs and trees, grown for their fragrant, yellow flowers, which are produced before hazel-like leaves emerge. Late frosts may damage flowers. Prefers partial shade and fertile, moist but well-drained, acidic soil. Propagate by softwood cuttings in summer or by seed in fall.
C. glabrescens, illus. p.111.
C. pauciflora, illus. p.126.
C. sinensis, syn. *C. willmottiae.* Vigorous, deciduous, spreading, open shrub. **H** and **S** 12ft (4m). Leaves are bright green above, blue-green beneath. Clusters of bell-shaped, pale yellow flowers are produced from early to mid-spring. Z5–9 H9–2.
'Spring Purple' (Spike winter hazel) has deep plum-purple, young leaves.
C. spicata. Deciduous, spreading, open shrub. **H** 6ft (2m), **S** 10ft (3m). Bristle-toothed leaves are dull, pale green above, blue-green beneath. Drooping clusters of bell-shaped, pale yellow flowers are borne in mid-spring. Z5–8 H8–5.
C. willmottiae. See *C. sinensis.*

CORYLUS
Hazel
CORYLACEAE/BETULACEAE

Genus of deciduous trees and shrubs, grown for their habit, catkins and often edible fruits (nuts). Prefers sun or partial shade and fertile, well-drained soil. Cut out suckers as they arise. Propagate species by seed in fall, cultivars by grafting in late summer or by suckers or layering in late fall to early spring. Mildew may cause defoliation; other fungi and insects may spoil nuts.
C. avellana (European filbert). **'Contorta'** illus. p.118.
C. colurna (Turkish hazel). Deciduous, conical tree. **H** 70ft (20m), **S** 22ft (7m). Has broadly oval, strongly toothed, almost lobed, dark green leaves. Long, yellow catkins are borne in late winter. Clusters

of nuts are set in fringed husks. Z5–7 H7–5.
C. maxima (Giant filbert). Vigorous, deciduous, bushy, open shrub or tree. **H** 20ft (6m), **S** 15ft (5m). Bears oval, toothed, mid-green leaves, long, yellow catkins in late winter and edible, egg-shaped, brown nuts. Z4–9 H9–1. **'Purpurea'** illus. p.115.

CORYNOCARPUS
CORYNOCARPACEAE

Genus of evergreen trees, grown for their foliage and overall appearance. Needs full light or partial shade and fertile, moist but well-drained soil. Water container specimens moderately, less when temperatures are low. Pruning is tolerated if necessary. Propagate by seed when ripe or by semiripe cuttings in summer.
C. laevigatus, illus. p.451.

CORYPHANTHA
CACTACEAE

Genus of perennial cacti with roughly spherical, spiny, green stems. Stems have elongated areoles in grooves running along upper sides of tubercles; many species show this groove only on very old plants. Funnel-shaped flowers are produced in summer, followed by cylindrical, green seed pods. Needs full sun and very well-drained soil. Propagate by seed in spring or summer.
C. cornifera, syn. *C. radians,* illus. p.480.
C. radians. See *C. cornifera.*
C. vivipara. See *Escobaria vivipara.*

COSMOS
COMPOSITAE/ASTERACEAE

Genus of summer- and early fall-flowering annuals and tuberous perennials. Needs sun and does best in moist but well-drained soil. In mild areas, tubers of half-hardy *C. atrosanguineus* may be overwintered in ground if protected with a deep mulch. Propagate half-hardy species by basal cuttings in spring, annuals by seed in fall or spring.
C. atrosanguineus, syn. *Bidens atrosanguineus,* illus. p.238. **CHOCAMOCHA ('Thomocha')** illus. p.306.
C. bipinnatus. Upright, bushy annual. **H** to 5ft (1.5m), **S** 1 1/2ft (45cm). Has feathery, mid-green leaves, and, throughout summer, produces solitary, bowl- or saucer-shaped flower heads in white, pink, or crimson, with yellow centers. H12–1.
'Candy Stripe', **H** to 3ft (90cm), has white flower heads, edged and flecked with crimson. **'Sea Shells',** **H** to 3ft (90cm), produces carmine-red, pink, or white flower heads with tubular florets.
Sensation Series illus. p.305.
C. sulphureus Ladybird Series. Group of upright, bushy annuals. **H** 12–16in (30–40cm), **S** 8in (20cm). Has feathery, mid-green leaves, and in summer produces clusters of bowl-shaped, semidouble flower heads in yellow, orange, or scarlet, with black centers. H12–1.

COSTUS
Ginger lily, Spiral flag
ZINGIBERACEAE

Genus of mostly clump-forming, rhizomatous perennials, grown for their showy, solitary or paired, tubular flowers

with basal bracts. Grow in a humid atmosphere, out of direct sunlight, in rich soil. Propagate by division in spring. Container-grown plants may be attacked by red spider mite.
C. speciosus (Malay ginger), illus. p.477. Clump-forming, rhizomatous perennial. **H** 6ft (2m) or more, **S** 3ft (1m). Has narrowly oval, downy leaves, to 10in (25cm) long. Reddish bracts are spine-tipped, each surrounding a white or pink-flushed flower, to 4in (10cm) wide, with a broad, yellow-centered lip; flowers are produced intermittently throughout the year. H11–9.

COTINUS
ANACARDIACEAE

Genus of deciduous shrubs and trees, grown for their foliage, flower heads and fall color. Individual flowers are inconspicuous. Requires a position in full sun or partial shade, with fertile but not over-rich soil. Purple-leaved forms need full sun to bring out their best colors. Propagate species by softwood or greenwood cuttings in summer or by seed in fall, cultivars by cuttings only in summer.
C. americanus. See *C. obovatus.*
C. coggygria, syn. *Rhus cotinus* (Smoke bush). Deciduous, bushy shrub. **H** and **S** 15ft (5m). Leaves are rounded or oval and light green, becoming yellow or red in fall. From late summer, as insignificant fruits develop, masses of tiny flower stalks form plumelike, pale fawn, later gray clusters. Z5–9 H9–3. **'Flame'.** See *C.* 'Flame'. **GOLDEN SPIRIT ('Ancot')** illus. p.116. **'Notcutt's Variety'** illus. p.115. **'Royal Purple'** has deep pink plumes and deep purplish-red leaves.
C. 'Flame', syn. *C. coggyria* 'Flame', illus. p.117.
C. obovatus, syn. *C. americanus, Rhus cotinoides* (Creeping cotoneaster). Vigorous, deciduous, bushy shrub or tree. **H** 30ft (10m), **S** 25ft (8m). Has large, oval leaves that are bronze-pink when young, maturing to mid-green and turning orange, red and purple in fall. Z4–8 H8–1.

COTONEASTER
ROSACEAE

Genus of deciduous, semievergreen or evergreen shrubs and trees, grown for their foliage, flowers and fruits. Some species make fine specimen plants; others may be used for hedging or groundcover. Deciduous species and cultivars prefer full sun, but evergreens do well in either sun or partial shade. All resent waterlogged soil and are particularly useful for dry sites. Propagate species by cuttings in summer or by seed in fall, hybrids and cultivars by cuttings only, in summer. Take semiripe cuttings for evergreens and semievergreens, softwood cuttings for deciduous plants. Fireblight is a common problem. ① The seeds may cause mild stomach upset if ingested.
C. adpressus. Deciduous, arching shrub. **H** 1ft (30cm), **S** 6ft (2m). Rounded, wavy-edged, dark green leaves redden in fall. Produces small, 5-petaled, pink flowers in early summer, then spherical, red fruits. Z5–7 H7–1.
C. 'Autumn Fire'. See *C.* 'Herbstfeuer'.
C. bullatus 'Firebird', syn. *C.* 'Firebird'.

C

Deciduous, bushy, open shrub. **H** and **S** 10ft (3m). Large, oval, deeply veined, dark green leaves redden in fall. Small, 5-petaled, white flowers in early summer are followed by masses of spherical, bright red fruits. Z6–8 H8–6. **var. macrophyllus.** See *C. rehderi*.

C. cashmiriensis, syn. *C. cochleatus*, *C. microphyllus* var. *cochleatus* of gardens (Pyrenees cotoneaster). Evergreen, prostrate shrub. **H** to 1½ft (45cm), **S** 6ft (2m). Has small, oval, notched, dark green leaves. Small, white flowers are produced in late spring, followed by spherical, red fruits. Z6–8 H8–6.

C. cochleatus of gardens. See *C. cashmiriensis*.

C. congestus (Wintergreen cotoneaster). Evergreen, prostrate shrub. **H** 8in (20cm), **S** 6ft (2m). Forms dense mounds of oval, dull green leaves. Produces small, 5-petaled, pinkish-white flowers in early summer, followed by spherical, bright red fruits. Is excellent for a rock garden. Z7–8 H8–7.

C. conspicuus, syn. *C. conspicuus* var. *decorus*, illus. p.142. Evergreen, prostrate, arching shrub. **H** 1ft (30cm), **S** 6–10ft (2–3m). Has oblong, glossy, very dark green leaves. Small, 5-petaled, white flowers in late spring are succeeded by large, spherical, scarlet or orange-red fruits. Z6–8 H8–6. **var. decorus.** See *C. conspicuus*.

C. 'Coral Beauty'. Evergreen, arching, dense shrub. **H** 3ft (1m), **S** 6ft (2m). Has small, oval, glossy, dark green leaves and, in early summer, produces small, 5-petaled, white flowers. Fruits are spherical and bright orange-red. Z7–8 H8–7.

C. 'Cornubia', illus. p.117.

C. dielsianus (Spreading cotoneaster). Deciduous, arching shrub. **H** and **S** 8ft (2.5m). Slender shoots are clothed in oval, dark green leaves. Produces small, 5-petaled, pink flowers in early summer, followed by spherical, glossy, red fruits. Z6–8 H8–6.

C. divaricatus, illus. p.122.

C. 'Exburiensis'. Evergreen or semievergreen, arching shrub. **H** and **S** 15ft (5m). Has narrowly lance-shaped, bright green leaves, small, 5-petaled, white flowers, in early summer, and spherical, yellow fruits, sometimes tinged pink later. Z6–8 H8–6.

C. 'Firebird'. See *C. bullatus* 'Firebird'.

C. franchetii. Evergreen or semievergreen, arching shrub. **H** and **S** 10ft (3m). Oval, gray-green leaves are white beneath. Bears small, 5-petaled, pink-tinged, white flowers in early summer, then a profusion of oblong, bright orange-red fruits. Z7–9 H9–7. **var. sternianus.** See *C. sternianus*.

C. frigidus (Tree cotoneaster), illus. p.142. Vigorous, deciduous tree, upright when young, arching when mature. **H** and **S** 30ft (10m). Has large, broadly oval, wavy-edged, dull green leaves and broad heads of small, 5-petaled, white flowers borne in early summer, followed by large clusters of small, long-lasting, spherical, bright red fruits. Z7–8 H8–7.

C. glaucophyllus. Evergreen, arching, open shrub. **H** and **S** 10ft (3m). Leaves are oval, dark green, bluish-white beneath. Produces small, white flowers in mid-summer, followed by small, spherical, deep red fruits in fall. Z7–8 H8–7. **var.**

serotinus. See *C. serotinus*.

C. 'Gnom', syn. *C.* 'Gnome', *C. salicifolius* 'Gnom'. Evergreen, prostrate shrub. **H** 8in (20cm), **S** 6ft (2m). Bears narrowly lance-shaped, dark green leaves, small, 5-petaled, white flowers, in early summer, and clusters of small, spherical, red fruits. Makes good groundcover. Z7–8 H8–7.

C. 'Gnome'. See *C. 'Gnom'*.

C. 'Herbstfeuer', syn. *C.* 'Autumn Fire'. Evergreen, prostrate or arching shrub. **H** 1ft (30cm), **S** 6ft (2m). Has lance-shaped, bright green leaves. Small, 5-petaled, white flowers in early summer are followed by spherical, bright red fruits. May be grown as groundcover or as a weeping standard. Z5–8 H8–5.

C. horizontalis, illus. p.208.

C. hupehensis. Deciduous, arching shrub. **H** 6ft (2m), **S** 10ft (3m). Oval, bright green leaves turn yellow in fall. Masses of small, 5-petaled, white flowers in late spring are succeeded by large, spherical, bright red fruits. Z5–8 H8–5.

C. 'Hybridus Pendulus'. Evergreen, prostrate shrub, almost always grown as a weeping standard. **H** 6ft (2m), **S** 5ft (1.5m). Has oblong, dark green leaves. Small, 5-petaled, white flowers in early summer are followed by spherical, deep red fruits. Z6–8 H8–6.

C. integrifolius, syn. *C. microphyllus* of gardens. Evergreen, spreading, dense shrub. **H** 3ft (1m), **S** 6ft (2m). Rigid shoots are clothed in small, oval, dark green leaves. Small, 5-petaled, white flowers in late spring are followed by spherical, red fruits. Z6–8 H8–6.

C. lacteus, illus. p.117.

C. linearifolius, syn. *C. microphyllus* var. *thymifolius* of gardens. Evergreen, prostrate shrub. **H** 2ft (60cm), **S** 6ft (2m). Rigid branches bear tiny, narrow, blunt-ended, glossy leaves. Produces small, white flowers in late spring, followed by spherical, red fruits. Z6–8 H8–6.

C. microphyllus of gardens. See *C. integrifolius*. **var. cochleatus** of gardens. See *C. cashmiriensis*. **var. thymifolius** of gardens. See *C. linearifolius*.

C. prostratus of gardens. See *C. rotundifolius*.

C. rehderi, syn. *C. bullatus* var. *macrophyllus*. Deciduous, bushy, open shrub. **H** 15ft (5m), **S** 10ft (3m). Very large, oval, deeply veined, dark green leaves turn red in fall. Clusters of small, 5-petaled, pink flowers, borne in late spring and early summer, are succeeded by spherical, bright red fruits. Z6–8 H8–6.

C. 'Rothschildianus'. Evergreen or semievergreen, arching shrub. **H** and **S** 15ft (5m). Has narrowly oval, bright green leaves, small, 5-petaled, white flowers, in early summer, and large clusters of spherical, golden-yellow fruits. Z6–8 H8–6.

C. rotundifolius, syn. *C. prostratus* (Willowleaf cotoneaster). Evergreen, arching shrub. **H** 5ft (1.5m), **S** 8ft (2.5m). Has small, oval, glossy, dark green leaves. Produces small, 5-petaled, white flowers in early summer, followed by spherical, deep red fruits. Z7–8 H8–7.

C. salicifolius, illus. p.142. Vigorous, evergreen, arching shrub. **H** and **S** 15ft (5m). Has narrowly lance-shaped, dark green leaves. Small, 5-petaled, white flowers, in early summer, are followed by

clusters of small, spherical, red fruits. Z6–8 H8–3. **'Gnom'.** See *C. 'Gnom'*.

C. serotinus, syn. *C. glaucophyllus* var. *serotinus*. Evergreen, arching, open shrub. **H** and **S** 20ft (6m). Has oval, dark green leaves. Small, white flowers are borne from mid- to late summer and the egg-shaped to almost spherical, bright red fruits last until spring. Z7–8 H8–7.

C. simonsii, illus. p.143.

C. 'Skogsholmen'. See *C. x suecicus* 'Skogholm'.

C. sternianus, syn. *C. franchetii* var. *sternianus*, illus. p.141.

C. x suecicus 'Skogholm', syn. *C.* 'Skogsholmen'. Evergreen, arching, wide-spreading shrub. **H** 2ft (60cm), **S** 10ft (3m). Leaves are small, oval and glossy, dark green. Bears small, 5-petaled, white flowers in early summer, then rather sparse, spherical, red fruits. Makes good groundcover. Z6–8 H8–6.

C. x watereri 'John Waterer', illus. p.142. Vigorous, evergreen or semievergreen, arching shrub. **H** and **S** 15ft (5m). Has lance-shaped, dark green leaves. Bears small, 5-petaled, white flowers, in early summer, followed by a profusion of spherical, red fruits in large clusters. Z6–8 H8–6.

COTULA
COMPOSITAE/ASTERACEAE

Genus of perennials and a few marginal water plants, most of which are evergreen, grown for their neat foliage and button-like flower heads. Many species are useful for cracks in paving stones, but may be invasive. Most need a position in full sun, with well-drained soil that is not too dry. Propagate by division in spring.

C. atrata. See *Leptinella atrata*.

C. coronopifolia (Brass buttons). Short-lived, deciduous, perennial, marginal water plant. **H** 6in (15cm), **S** 12in (30cm). Has fleshy stems, small, lance-shaped, mid-green leaves and, in summer, button-like, yellow flower heads. Z7–9 H9–7.

COTYLEDON
CRASSULACEAE

Genus of evergreen, succulent shrubs and subshrubs, grown for their diverse foliage that ranges from large, oval, gray leaves to small, cylindrical, mid-green leaves. Prefers a sunny or partially shaded site and very well-drained soil. Propagate by seed or stem cuttings in spring or summer.

C. cooperi. See *Adromischus cooperi*.

C. orbiculata. Evergreen, upright, succulent shrub. **H** and **S** 20in (50cm) or more. Swollen stem bears thin, oval, mid-green leaves, densely coated in white wax and sometimes red-edged. Flower stems, to 28in (70cm) long, have pendent, tubular, orange flowers in fall. Z12–15 H12–10. **var. oblonga,** syn. *C. undulata* has flat, wavy tips to the leaves and bell-shaped, orange flowers.

C. paniculata. See *Tylecodon paniculatus*.

C. reticulata. See *Tylecodon reticulatus*.

C. simplicifolia. See *Chiastophyllum oppositifolium*.

C. tomentosa subsp. ladismithensis. Evergreen, freely branching, later prostrate, succulent subshrub. **H** and **S** 8in (20cm). Has fleshy, green leaves, swollen

and blunt at tips and covered with short, golden-brown hairs. Clusters of tubular, brownish-red flowers are borne in fall. Z12 H11–10.

C. undulata. See *C. orbiculata* var. *oblonga*.

C. wallichii. See *Tylecodon wallichii*.

CRAMBE
BRASSICACEAE/CRUCIFERAE

Genus of annuals and perennials, grown for their bold leaves and large sprays of white flowers in summer. Leaf shoots of *C. maritima* are eaten as a spring vegetable. Grow in any well-drained soil; prefers an open position in full sun but tolerates some shade. Propagate by division in spring or by seed in fall or spring.

C. cordifolia, illus. p.216.

C. maritima, illus. p.264.

CRASPEDIA
COMPOSITAE/ASTERACEAE

Genus of basal-rosetted, summer-flowering perennials, some of which are best treated as annuals. Needs sun and well-drained soil. Propagate by seed when very fresh, in summer.

C. incana. Basal-rosetted perennial. **H** 8–12in (20–30cm), **S** 4in (10cm). Has narrowly oval, basal leaves, with dense, woolly, white hairs beneath, and smaller leaves on flower stem. In summer, many domed heads of 3–10 tiny, tubular, yellow flowers are produced in large, terminal clusters. Z9–10 H10–9.

CRASSULA
CRASSULACEAE

Genus of perennial succulents and evergreen, succulent shrubs and subshrubs, ranging from ¾in (2cm) high, very succulent-leaved species to 15ft (5m) shrubby types. Most are easy to grow. Most prefer full sun; others like partial shade. Needs very well-drained soil and a little water in winter. Propagate by seed or stem cuttings in spring or fall.

C. arborescens, illus. p.490.

C. argentea of gardens. See *C. ovata*.

C. coccinea, syn. *Rochea coccinea*. Evergreen, erect, succulent shrub. **H** to 24in (60cm), **S** 12in (30cm) or more. Alternate pairs of fleshy, oval to oblong-oval, hairy-margined, dull green leaves, each united at the base, are arranged at right angles in 4 rows up woody, green stems. Produces umbels of tubular, bright red flowers in summer or fall. Z12–15 H12–10.

C. cooperi. See *C. exilis* subsp. *cooperi*.

C. deceptor, syn. *C. deceptrix*, illus. p.488.

C. deceptrix. See *C. deceptor*.

C. exilis subsp. cooperi, syn. *C. cooperi*. Carpeting, perennial succulent. **H** ¾in (2cm), **S** 12in (30cm). Has small, spoon- to lance-shaped, light green leaves, pitted with darker green or blackish-green marks. Produces clusters of minute, 5-petaled, white to pale pink flowers in winter. Z12–15 H12–10.

C. falcata. See *C. perfoliata* var. *falcata*.

C. lactea. Prostrate to semierect, perennial succulent. **H** 8in (20cm), **S** 3ft (1m). Leaves are triangular-oval, glossy and dark green. In winter produces masses of small,

C

5-petaled, white flowers in terminal clusters. Likes partial shade. Z12–15 H12–10.

C. lycopodioides. See *C. muscosa*.

C. multicava, illus. p.484.

C. muscosa, syn. *C. lycopodioides*. Dense, bushy, woody-based, perennial succulent. **H** 6in (15cm), **S** 12in (30cm). Bears small, scalelike, neatly overlapping, mid-green leaves arranged in 4 rows around erect stems. In spring produces tiny, 5-petaled, greenish-yellow flowers. Likes partial shade. Z12–15 H12–10.

C. ovata, syn. *C. argentea, C. portulacea*, illus. p.481.

C. perfoliata var. falcata, syn. *C. falcata*, illus. p.489.

C. portulacea. See *C. ovata*.

C. sarcocaulis, illus. p.339.

C. schmidtii, illus. p.485.

C. socialis, illus. p.480.

+ CRATAEGOMESPILUS

ROSACEAE

Group of grafted, hybrid, deciduous trees (*Crataegus* and *Mespilus*), grown for their flowers, foliage and fruits. Requires sun or partial shade and fertile, well-drained soil. Propagate by grafting in late summer.

+ C. dardarii (Bronvaux medlar). **'Jules d'Asnières'** is a deciduous, spreading tree. **H** and **S** 20ft (6m). Has drooping branches and spiny shoots. Variable, oval or deeply lobed, dark green leaves, gray when young, turn orange and yellow in fall. Clusters of saucer-shaped, sometimes rose-tinted, white flowers in late spring or early summer are followed by small, rounded, red-brown fruits. Z7–9 H9–7.

CRATAEGUS

Hawthorn

ROSACEAE

Genus of deciduous, or more rarely semievergreen, spiny, often spreading trees and shrubs, grown for their clustered, 5-petaled, occasionally double flowers in spring–summer, ornamental fruits and, in some cases, fall color. Prefers full sun but is suitable for most sites and may be grown in any but very wet soil. Is useful for growing in polluted urban areas, exposed sites and coastal gardens. Propagate species by seed in fall, cultivars by budding in late summer. Fireblight is sometimes a problem. ① The seeds may cause mild stomach upset if ingested.

C. cordata. See *C. phaenopyrum*.

C. crus-galli (Cockspur hawthorn). Deciduous, flat-topped tree. **H** 25ft (8m), **S** 30ft (10m). Has shoots armed with long, curved thorns and oval, glossy, dark green leaves that turn bright crimson in fall. Clusters of white flowers, with pink anthers, in late spring are followed by long-lasting, rounded, bright red fruits. Z4–7 H7–1.

C. crus-galli of gardens. See *C. x persimilis* 'Prunifolia'.

C. ellwangeriana. Deciduous, spreading tree. **H** and **S** 20ft (6m). Broadly oval, dark green leaves are shallowly toothed and lobed. Bears clusters of white flowers, with pink anthers, in late spring, followed by rounded, glossy, crimson fruits. Z5–7 H7–5.

C. flava, illus. p.80.

C. laciniata of gardens. See *C. orientalis*.

C. laevigata, syn. *C. oxyacantha* (English hawthorn). **'Paul's Scarlet'**, illus. p.84. **'Punicea'** is a deciduous, spreading tree. **H** and **S** 20ft (6m). In late spring and early summer, oval, lobed, toothed, glossy, dark green leaves set off clusters of crimson flowers, which are followed by rounded, red fruits. Z5–8 H8–3.

C. x lavallei 'Carrierei'. Vigorous, deciduous, spreading tree. **H** 22ft (7m), **S** 30ft (10m). Oval, glossy, dark green leaves turn red in late fall. Has clusters of white flowers in late spring, followed by long-lasting, rounded, orange-red fruits. Z5–7 H7–4.

C. macrosperma var. acutiloba (Downy hawthorn). Deciduous, spreading tree. **H** 20ft (6m), **S** 25ft (8m). Has broad, sharply toothed, dark green leaves. White flowers with red anthers in late spring are followed by bright red fruits in fall. Z4–8 H8–1.

C. mollis. Deciduous, spreading tree. **H** 30ft (10m), **S** 40ft (12m). Large, broadly oval, lobed, dark green leaves have white-haired undersides when young. Bears heads of large, white flowers in late spring, followed by short-lived, rounded, red fruits. Z3–6 H6–1.

C. monogyna (Singleseed hawthorn). Deciduous, round-headed tree. **H** 30ft (10m), **S** 25ft (8m). Has broadly oval, deeply lobed, glossy, dark green leaves. Clusters of fragrant, white flowers are borne from late spring to early summer, followed by rounded, red fruits. Makes a dense hedge. Z5–7 H7–4. **'Biflora'** (Glastonbury thorn) has flowers and leaves in mild winters as well as in spring.

C. orientalis, syn. *C. laciniata*, illus. p.80.

C. oxyacantha of gardens. See *C. laevigata*.

C. pedicellata, illus. p.90.

C. x persimilis 'Prunifolia', syn. *C. crus-galli, C. x prunifolia*. Deciduous, spreading, thorny tree. **H** 25ft (8m), **S** 30ft (10m). Oval, glossy, dark green leaves turn red or orange in fall. Has clusters of white flowers, with pink anthers, in early summer, then rounded, dark red fruits. Z6–7 H7–6.

C. phaenopyrum, syn. *C. cordata* (Washington thorn). Deciduous, round-headed tree. **H** and **S** 30ft (10m). Broadly oval leaves are sharply lobed, glossy and dark green. Clusters of white flowers, with pink anthers, are produced from early to mid-summer, followed by rounded, glossy, red fruits that last through winter. Z4–8 H8–1.

C. x prunifolia. See *C. x persimilis* 'Prunifolia'.

C. tanacetifolia (Tansy-leaved hawthorn). Deciduous, upright, usually thornless tree. **H** 30ft (10m), **S** 25ft (8m). Has oval to diamond-shaped, deeply cut, gray-green leaves, clusters of fragrant, white flowers, with red anthers, in mid-summer and small, apple-shaped, yellow fruits. Z6–7 H7–6.

CREMANTHODIUM

COMPOSITAE/ASTERACEAE

Genus of basal-rosetted perennials, grown for their pendent, half-closed, daisylike flower heads. Is often very difficult to grow in all but very cool areas with snow cover. Dislikes winter wet. Needs shade and rich, moist but well-drained soil. Propagate by seed when fresh.

C. reniforme. Basal-rosetted perennial. **H** and **S** 8in (20cm). Leaves are large and kidney-shaped. Sturdy stems each bear a large, daisylike, yellow flower head in summer.

CREPIS

Hawk's beard

COMPOSITAE/ASTERACEAE

Genus of summer-flowering annuals, biennials and perennials, some of which are evergreen, with long taproots and leaves in flat rosettes. Many species are persistent weeds, but some are grown for their many-petaled, dandelion-like flower heads. Tolerates sun or shade and prefers well-drained soil. Propagate annuals and biennials by seed in fall, perennials by root cuttings (not from taproot) in late winter, although most species self-seed freely.

C. aurea, illus. p.345.

C. incana (Pink dandelion). Basal-rosetted perennial. **H** 8in (20cm), **S** 4in (10cm). Bears oblong, divided, hairy, grayish-green leaves. Uneven discs of ragged, pink flower heads are produced on stiff stems in summer. Is good for a sunny rock garden or border. Z5–7 H7–4.

C. rubra. Fairly fast-growing, rosette-forming annual. **H** 12in (30cm), **S** 6in (15cm). Has lance-shaped, serrated leaves. In summer bears dandelion-like, pink, occasionally red or white flower heads. Z5–7 H7–4.

CRINODENDRON

ELAEOCARPACEAE

Genus of evergreen shrubs and trees, grown for their flowers and foliage. Requires full or partial shade, with plant base in cool shade. Soil should be fertile, moist but well-drained, and acidic. Propagate by softwood cuttings in summer or by seed in fall.

C. hookerianum, syn. *Tricuspidaria lanceolata*, illus. p.202.

C. patagua, illus. p.113.

x Crinodonna corsii. See *x Amarcrinum memoria-corsii*.

CRINUM

AMARYLLIDACEAE

Genus of robust bulbs, grown for their often fragrant, funnel-shaped flowers. Needs full sun, shelter and rich, well-drained soil. Propagate by offsets in spring or by seed when fresh or in spring. ① All parts may cause severe discomfort if ingested; contact with the sap may irritate skin.

C. americanum. Tuft-forming, spring- and summer-flowering bulb. **H** 16–30in (40–75cm), **S** 24in (60cm). Has 6–10 strap-shaped, semierect, basal leaves. Leafless stem bears a head of up to 6 fragrant, long-tubed, white flowers with narrow petals. Z8–11 H11–8.

C. asiaticum. Clump-forming bulb. **H** 1½–2ft (45–60cm), **S** 2–3ft (60cm–1m). Has strap-shaped, semierect, basal, dark green leaves, 3ft (1m) long. Leafless flower stems produce heads of long-tubed, white flowers, with narrow petals, in spring or summer. Z8–11 H11–8.

C. bulbispermum, syn. *C. longifolium*. Summer-flowering bulb. **H** to 3ft (1m), **S** 2ft (60cm). Leafless flower stem has a head of fragrant, long-tubed, white or pinkish-red flowers with darker red stripes. Bears long, strap-shaped, semierect leaves grouped in a tuft on a short stalk. Z7–11 H12–8.

C. longifolium. See *C. bulbispermum*.

C. macowanii. Fall-flowering bulb. **H** and **S** 2ft (60cm) or more. Is similar to *C. bulbispermum*, but leaves are wavy-edged. Z10–11 H11–10.

C. moorei, illus. p.383.

C. x powellii, illus. p.385. **'Album'** illus. p.383.

CROCOSMIA

Montbretia

IRIDACEAE

Genus of corms, grown for their brightly colored flowers produced mainly in summer. Forms dense clumps of sword-shaped, erect leaves. Requires well-drained soil and an open, sunny site. In very cold areas, plant in a sheltered position or lift and store corms over winter. Propagate by division as growth starts in spring.

C. aurea. Tuft-forming, summer-flowering corm. **H** 20–30in (50–75cm), **S** 6–8in (15–20cm). Erect, basal leaves are long, narrow and sword-shaped. Produces a loosely branched spike of tubular, orange or yellow flowers, 1–2in (3–5cm) long, each with 6 spreading petals. Z6–9 H9–6.

C. 'Bressingham Blaze'. Clump-forming, late summer-flowering corm. **H** 30in (75cm), **S** 6–8in (15–20cm). Has erect, sword-shaped, pleated, basal leaves. Branched stem bears widely funnel-shaped, fiery-red flowers. Z6–9 H9–6.

C. 'Citronella' of gardens. See *C. 'Golden Fleece'*.

C. x crocosmiiflora. Robust, sometimes invasive, variable, late summer-flowering corm. **H** 24in (60cm), **S** 3in (8cm). Has erect, sword-shaped, pale green, basal leaves. Produces thin, slightly arching, sometimes branched spikes of funnel-shaped, orange or yellow flowers in summer. Z6–9 H9–3.

'George Davison' See *C. 'George Davison'*. **'Honey Angels'** See *C. 'Honey Angels'*. **'Solfatare'** See *C. 'Solfatare'*.

C. 'Emily McKenzie'. Compact, late summer-flowering corm. **H** to 24in (60cm), **S** 6–8in (15–20cm). Leaves are erect, basal and sword-shaped. Bears a dense spike of widely funnel-shaped, deep orange flowers, each with a dark mahogany throat. Z6–9 H9–2.

C. 'George Davison', syn. *C. x crocosmiiflora* 'George Davison' (illus. p.410). Mid- to late summer-flowering corm. **H** 3–4ft (90cm–1.2m), **S** 6in (15cm). Has erect, sword-shaped, pleated, mid-green, basal leaves. Produces branched stems bearing large, trumpet-shaped, pale orange-yellow flowers, tinted deeper orange externally. Z6–9 H10–9.

C. 'Golden Dew'. Late summer-flowering corm. **H** 30in (75cm), **S** 3in (8cm). Has erect, sword-shaped, mid-green, basal leaves. Produces large, funnel-shaped, yellow and gold flowers on wiry, dark reddish stems. Z6–9 H9–6.

C. 'Golden Fleece', syn. *C. 'Citronella'*, illus. p.412.

C. 'Harlequin'. Late summer-flowering corm. **H** 36in (90cm), **S** 3in (8cm). Has erect, sword-shaped, mid-green, basal leaves. Well-branched, upright stems bear funnel-

C

shaped, bright yellow flowers with alternate, red and orange outer petals. Z6–9 H9–6.

C. 'Honey Angels', syn. *C. x crocosmiiflora* 'Honey Angels' (illus. p.410). Summer-flowering corm. **H** 30in (75cm), **S** 6in (15cm). Has erect, sword-shaped, pleated, bronzed-green leaves and trumpet-shaped, pale yellow flowers. Z6–9 H9–6.

C. 'Jackanapes', illus. p.410. Clump-forming, late summer-flowering corm. **H** 16–24in (40–60cm), **S** 6–8in (15–20cm). Has erect, sword-shaped, basal leaves. Produces bicolored, yellow and orange-red flowers. Z8–10 H11–3.

C. 'John Boots'. Mid- to late summer-flowering corm. **H** 18in (45cm), **S** 3in (8cm). Has erect, sword-shaped, mid-green, basal leaves. Bears funnel-shaped, golden-yellow flowers. Z6–9 H9–6.

C. 'Lucifer', illus. p.410. Robust, clump-forming corm. **H** to 3ft (1m), **S** 8–10in (20–25cm). Has erect, sword-shaped, basal, bright green leaves. Bears funnel-shaped, deep rich red flowers in dense, branching spikes in mid-summer. Z6–9 H9–6.

C. masoniorum, syn. *C. masonorum*, illus. p.410. Robust, clump-forming corm. **H** to 5ft (1.5m), **S** 1–1¹⁄₂ft (30–45cm). Has erect, deep green, basal leaves, pleated lengthways. Erect, branched stem has a horizontal, upper part, which bears upward-facing, funnel-shaped, reddish-orange flowers in summer–fall. Z6–9 H9–2. **'Rowallane Yellow'**, **H** 3ft (1m), **S** 3in (8cm), has warm yellow flowers.

C. masonorum. See *C. masoniorum*.
C. paniculata, syn. *Antholyza paniculata*, *Curtonus paniculatus*. Summer-flowering corm. **H** to 5ft (1.5m), **S** 1–1¹⁄₂ft (30–45cm). Has erect, sword-shaped, basal leaves, pleated lengthwise. Produces long-tubed, orange flowers on branched stems, which are strongly zigzag in shape. Z6–9 H9–2.

C. 'Severn Sunrise', illus. p.410. Late summer-flowering corm. **H** 36in (90cm), **S** 3in (8cm). Has erect, sword-shaped, mid-green, basal leaves. Produces tightly clustered, funnel-shaped flowers in shades of salmon, apricot and yellow. Z6–9 H9–6.

C. 'Solfatare', syn. *C. x crocosmiiflora* 'Solfatare' (illus. p.410). Mid- to late summer-flowering corm. **H** 26–28in (65–70cm), **S** 6in (15cm). Bears erect, sword-shaped, pleated, bronzed-green leaves and trumpet-shaped, pale to mid-yellow flowers. Z6–9 H9–6.

C. 'Star of the East', illus. p.410. Late summer-flowering corm. **H** 28in (70cm), **S** 8in (3in). Has erect, sword-shaped, mid-green, basal leaves. Bears horizontal-facing, funnel-shaped, clear orange flowers, with a paler orange center, on branched stems. Z6–9 H9–6.

CROCUS

IRIDACEAE

Genus of mainly spring- or fall-flowering corms with funnel-shaped to rounded, long-tubed flowers. Has long, very narrow, semierect, basal leaves, each with a white line along center, usually 1–5 per corm. Some fall-flowering species have no leaves at flowering time, these appearing in winter or spring. Most species are less than 4in (10cm) tall when in flower and have a spread

of 1–3in (2.5–8cm). Is ideal for rock gardens and for forcing in bowls for an early indoor display. Most require well-drained soil and a sunny situation; *C. banaticus* prefers moist soil and partial shade. Plant 2–2¹⁄₂in (5–6cm) deep, in late summer or early fall. Propagate in early fall by seed or division of corm clumps. See also feature panel p.417.

C. 'Advance'. Late winter- to mid-spring-flowering corm. Funnel-shaped flowers are buttercup-yellow inside and paler yellow outside, suffused violet-bronze. Z3–8 H8–1.

C. aerius of gardens. See *C. biflorus* subsp. *pulchricolor*.

C. ancyrensis. Spring-flowering corm. Produces up to 7 fragrant, bright orange-yellow flowers. Z3–8 H8–1.

C. angustifolius, syn. *C. susianus* (Cloth-of-gold crocus). Spring-flowering corm. Fragrant flowers are bright golden-yellow, striped or stained bronze outside. Z3–8 H8–1.

C. aureus. See *C. flavus*.

C. balansae. See *C. olivieri* subsp. *balansae*.

C. banaticus, syn. *C. iridiflorus*. Fall-flowering corm. Usually has solitary, long-tubed, pale violet flower; outer 3 petals are much larger than inner 3. Very narrow, semierect, basal leaves, each with a paler line along the center, are produced in spring. Z3–8 H8–1.

C. baytopiorum. Spring-flowering corm. Each corm bears 1 or 2 rounded, clear turquoise-blue flowers with slightly darker veins. Z3–8 H8–1.

C. biflorus. Early spring-flowering corm. Has semierect, narrow, basal leaves, each with a white line along the center. Bears fragrant, white or purplish-white flowers, with yellow throats, vertically striped purple outside. Z3–8 H8–1. **subsp. alexandri** has fragrant, deep violet flowers, with white insides. **subsp. pulchricolor**, syn. *C. aerius* has rich deep blue flowers, with golden-yellow centers.

C. 'Blue Bird', illus. p.417. Late winter- to mid-spring-flowering corm. Funnel-shaped flowers are white inside with deep yellow throats and violet margined with white outside. Z3–8 H8–1.

C. 'Blue Pearl', illus. p.421.

C. boryi. Fall-flowering corm. Flowers are ivory-white, sometimes veined or flushed with mauve outside. Z4–8 H8–1.

C. cancellatus. Fall-flowering corm. Slender flowers are pale blue, slightly striped outside. Leaves form after flowering, in spring. Z5–8 H8–5.

C. cartwrightianus. Fall-flowering corm. Produces leaves at same time as strongly veined, violet or white flowers, **H** 1¹⁄₂–2¹⁄₂in (4–6cm) across, each with 3 long, bright red stigmas, similar to those of *C. sativus*. Z6–8 H8–6.

C. chrysanthus. Spring-flowering corm. Scented flowers are orange-yellow throughout with deeper orange-red stigmas. Z3–8 H10–1. **'Zwanenberg Bronze'**. See *C.* 'Zwanenberg Bronze'.

C. 'Cream Beauty', illus. p.417. Spring-flowering corm. Scented, rich cream flowers, with deep yellow throats, are stained purplish-brown outside at base. Bears semierect, very narrow, dark green, basal leaves, each with a white, central line. Z3–8 H8–1.

C. cvijicii. Spring-flowering corm. Usually has solitary funnel-shaped, yellow flower.

Produces semierect, very narrow, basal leaves, each with a white line along the center, which scarcely show at flowering time. Z3–8 H8–1.

C. dalmaticus. Spring-flowering corm. Semierect, very narrow leaves have central, white lines. Bears 1–3 purple-veined, pale violet flowers, with yellow centers, overlaid with silver or yellow outside. Z3–8 H8–1.

C. 'Dorothy', illus. p.417. Spring-flowering corm. Scented flowers are pale lemon-yellow. Z3–8 H8–1.

C. 'Dutch Yellow'. See *C.* 'Golden Yellow'.

C. 'E.P. Bowles', illus. p.417. Early spring-flowering corm. Has scented, funnel-shaped, deep yellow flowers, stained bronze near base on outside. Has semierect, narrow leaves, each with a central white line. Increases well by offsets. Z3–8 H8–1.

C. etruscus. Spring-flowering corm. Has semierect, very narrow, dark green, basal leaves with central, white lines. Bears long-tubed, funnel-shaped, pale purple-blue flowers, washed silver outside, with violet veining. Z3–8 H8–1. **'Zwanenburg'** (illus. p.417) has pale purple-blue flowers, washed with biscuit-brown and flecked violet outside.

C. 'Eyecatcher', illus. p.417. Late winter- to mid-spring-flowering corm. Funnel-shaped, yellow-throated, gray-white flowers have white-edged, deep purple outer segments. Z3–8 H8–1.

C. flavus, syn. *C. aureus*. Spring-flowering corm. Fragrant flowers are bright yellow or orange-yellow throughout; often several flowers are produced together or in quick succession. Z5–8 H8–5.

C. gargaricus. Spring-flowering corm. Bears yellow flowers. Increases by stolons. Tolerates slightly damper conditions than most crocuses. Z5–8 H8–5.

C. 'Golden Yellow', syn. *C.* 'Dutch Yellow', *C. x luteus* 'Golden Yellow'. Very vigorous, clump-forming, spring-flowering corm. Bears yellow flowers faintly striped outside at bases. Naturalizes well in grass. Z3–8 H8–1.

C. goulimyi, illus. p.417. Fall-flowering corm. Usually has solitary, long-tubed, pale lilac to pinkish-lilac flower, with a white throat and 3 inner petals usually paler than the 3 outer ones. Leaves and flowers are produced together. Needs a warm site. Z3–8 H8–1.

C. hadriaticus, illus. p.417. Fall-flowering corm. Leaves are produced at same time as white flowers, which usually have yellow throats and may be lilac-feathered at the base. Z3–8 H8–1.

C. imperati. Bicolored, spring-flowering corm. Develops 1 or 2 scented, purple flowers, fawn with purple striping outside and with yellow throats. Z3–8 H8–1. In **'De Jager'** flowers are rich violet-purple inside and biscuit-colored with violet feathering outside.

C. iridiflorus. See *C. banaticus*.

C. korolkowii (Celandine crocus). Spring-flowering corm. Produces up to 20 narrow leaves. Produces fragrant, yellow flowers that are speckled or stained brown or purple outside. When open in sun, petals have glossy surfaces. Z3–8 H8–1.

C. kotschyanus, syn. *C. zonatus*, illus. p.417. Fall-flowering corm. Pinkish-lilac or purplish-blue flowers have yellow centers

and white anthers. Semierect, narrow, basal leaves, with white lines along centers, are produced in winter–spring. Z3–8 H8–1.

var. leucopharynx has pale lilac-blue flowers with white centers and white anthers.

C. 'Ladykiller'. Late winter- to mid-spring-flowering corm. Has funnel-shaped flowers, white or pale lilac within and deep violet-purple with white margins outside. Z3–8 H8–1.

C. laevigatus. Very variable corm, flowering intermittently for a month or more in fall or winter depending on the form. Fragrant flowers are produced with leaves and are usually lilac-purple with bold stripes on outside; inside each has a yellow eye and cream-white anthers. Z3–8 H8–1.

C. longiflorus. Fall-flowering corm. Produces fragrant, slender, purple flowers, which are striped darker purple outside, at the same time as leaves. Flowers have yellow centers and anthers and red stigmas. Z5–8 H8–5.

C. x luteus 'Golden Yellow'. See *C.* 'Golden Yellow'.

C. malyi. Spring-flowering corm. Has 1 or 2 funnel-shaped, white flowers with yellow throats, brown or purple tubes and bright orange stigmas. Leaves are semierect, very narrow and basal with central, white lines. Z3–8 H8–1.

C. medius. Fall-flowering corm. Has 1 or 2 funnel-shaped, uniform rich purple flowers, with yellow anthers and red stigmas cut into many threadlike branches. Linear, basal leaves are produced in winter–spring, after flowering. Z3–8 H8–1.

C. minimus. Late spring-flowering corm. Has semierect, very narrow, dark green, basal leaves that have central, white lines. Bears 1 or 2 flowers, purple inside and stained darker violet or sometimes darker striped on outside. Z3–8 H8–1.

C. niveus. Fall-flowering corm. Produces 1 or 2 white or pale lavender flowers, with yellow throats. Leaves are produced at same time as flowers or just afterward. Needs a warm, sunny site. Z3–8 H8–1.

C. nudiflorus (Autumn-flowering crocus). Fall-flowering corm. Has linear, basal leaves in winter–spring. Usually bears solitary, slender, long-tubed, rich purple flower, with a frilly, bright orange or yellow stigma. Naturalizes in grass. Z3–8 H8–1.

C. olivieri. Spring-flowering corm. Bears rounded, bright orange flowers. Z5–8 H8–5. Flowers of **subsp. balansae**, syn. *C. balansae* are stained or striped bronze-brown outside.

C. pulchellus. Fall-flowering corm. Bears long-tubed, pale lilac-blue flowers with darker veins, conspicuous, yellow throats and white anthers. Leaves are semierect, very narrow and basal, with white lines along centers. Z3–8 H8–1.

C. salzmannii. See *C. serotinus* subsp. *salzmannii*.

C. sativus, syn. *C. sativus* var. *cashmirianus* (Saffron crocus). Fall-flowering corm. Leaves are produced with saucer-shaped, dark-veined, purple flowers, each with 3 long, bright red stigmas that yield saffron. Z5–8 H8–1.

var. cashmirianus. See *C. sativus*.

C. serotinus subsp. salzmannii, syn. *C. salzmannii*. Fall-flowering corm. Lilac-blue flowers, sometimes with yellow throats, are produced at the same time as leaves. Z5–8 H8–1.

C. sieberi. Spring-flowering corm. Fully hardy. Has scented, white flowers with yellow throats and purple staining outside, either in horizontal bands or vertical stripes. Z3–8 H8–1. **'Albus'**, syn. *C. sieberi* 'Bowles' White' illus. p.427. **subsp. atticus** has pale lilac to violet-blue flowers with frilly, orange stigmas. **'Bowles' White'.** See *C. sieberi* 'Albus'. **'Hubert Edelsten'** (illus. p.417) has yellow-throated, pale lilac flowers, the outer segments of which are white-tipped, centrally marked and feathered with rich purple. **subsp. sublimis f. tricolor** (illus. p.417) has unusual flowers, divided into 3 distinct bands of lilac, white and golden yellow.

C. 'Snow Bunting', illus. p.417. Spring-flowering corm. Fragrant, long-tubed, funnel-shaped, white flowers have mustard-yellow centers and orange stigmas. Semierect, very narrow, basal leaves are dark green with white, central lines. Z3–8 H8–1.

C. speciosus, illus. p.417. Fall-flowering corm. Produces lilac-blue to deep purple-blue flowers, usually with a network of darker veins and a much-divided, orange stigma. Leaves are produced in winter–spring. Z3–8 H8–1. **'Conqueror'** (illus. p.417) has large, deep sky-blue flowers. **'Oxonian'** produces dark violet-blue flowers with prominent, darker veining externally.

C. susianus. See *C. angustifolius*.

C. tommasinianus. Spring-flowering corm. **H** to 4in (10cm), **S** 1–3in (2.5–8cm). Bears slender, long-tubed, funnel-shaped flowers, varying in color from lilac or purple to violet, sometimes with darker tips to petals and occasionally silver outside. Naturalizes well. Z3–8 H8–1. **f. albus** has white flowers. **'Ruby Giant'** (illus. p.417) bears clusters of large, rich reddish-purple flowers. **'Whitewell Purple'** has slender, reddish-purple flowers.

C. tournefortii. Fall-flowering corm. Leaves appear at same time as 1 or 2 pale lilac-blue flowers that open flattish to reveal a much-divided, orange stigma and white anthers. Requires a warm, sunny site. Z5–8 H8–1.

C. vernus (Dutch crocus, Spring crocus). Spring-flowering corm. **H** to 4in (10cm), **S** 1–3in (2.5–8cm). Variable in color from white to purple or violet and often striped and feathered. Stigmas are large, frilly and orange or yellow. Is suitable for naturalizing. Z3–8 H8–1. **subsp. albiflorus** has small, white flowers, sometimes slightly marked or striped purple. **'Jeanne d'Arc'** has white flowers with a deep purple base. **'Pickwick'** (illus. p.417) has pale, grayish-white flowers, with dark violet stripes and purplish bases. **'Prinses Juliana'** has mid-purple flowers with darker veins. **'Purpureus Grandiflorus'** has shiny, violet-purple flowers. **'Queen of the Blues'** (illus. p.417) has rich blue flowers that have higher margins and a darker base. **'Remembrance'** (illus. p.417) has shiny, violet flowers. **'Vanguard'**, a very early cultivar, has bluish-lilac flowers, paler and silvered outside.

C. 'Zephyr'. Fall-flowering corm. Bears very pale silver-blue flowers, veined darker, each with a yellow throat and white anthers. Z3–8 H8–1.

C. zonatus. See *C. kotschyanus*.

C. 'Zwanenberg Bronze', syn. *C. chrysanthus* 'Zwanenberg Bronze', illus. p.417. Spring-flowering corm. **H** to 4in (10cm), **S** 1–3in (2.5–8cm). Has bicolored flowers, rich yellow inside, stained bronze outside. Z3–8 H8–1.

CROSSANDRA
ACANTHACEAE

Genus of evergreen perennials, subshrubs and shrubs, grown mainly for their flowers. Needs partial shade or full light and rich, well-drained soil. Water container plants freely when in full growth, moderately at other times. For a strong branch system, cut back flowered growth by at least half in late winter. Propagate by seed in spring or by greenwood cuttings in late spring or summer. Whitefly may be troublesome.

C. infundibuliformis, syn. *C. undulifolia*. Evergreen, erect to spreading, soft-stemmed shrub or subshrub. **H** to 3ft (1m), **S** 2ft (60cm). Has oval to lance-shaped, glossy, deep green leaves and, in summer–fall or earlier, fan-shaped, salmon-red flowers in conical spikes, 4in (10cm) long. Z14–15 H12–1.

C. nilotica. Evergreen, upright to spreading, leafy shrub. **H** 12–24in (30–60cm), **S** to 14in (35cm). Has oval, pointed, rich green leaves. Small, tubular, apricot to pale brick-red flowers, with spreading petals, are borne in short spikes from spring to fall. Z14–15 H12–9.

C. undulifolia. See *C. infundibuliformis*.

CROTALARIA
LEGUMINOSAE/PAPILIONACEAE

Genus of evergreen shrubs, perennials and annuals, grown mainly for their flowers. Requires full light and well-drained soil. Water container specimens freely when in full growth, less at other times. For a more compact habit, cut back old stems by half after flowering. Propagate by seed in spring or by semiripe cuttings in summer. Red spider mite may be troublesome.

C. agatiflora, illus. p.459.

Crucianella stylosa. See *Phuopsis stylosa*.

CRUSEA
RUBIACEAE

Genus of annuals and perennials, grown for their showy flowers. Needs partial to full shade in moist but well-drained, rich soil. Propagate by seed in spring, by division in spring or summer or by cuttings in summer.

C. coccinea, illus. p.268.

CRYPTANTHUS
BROMELIACEAE

Genus of evergreen, rosette-forming perennials, grown for their foliage. Needs partial shade and well-drained soil, preferably mixed with sphagnum moss. Water moderately in the growing season, sparingly at other times. Propagate by offsets or suckers in late spring.

C. acaulis (Green earth star). Evergreen, clump-forming, basal-rosetted perennial. **H** to 4in (10cm), **S** 6–12in (15–30cm). Loose, flat rosettes of lance-shaped to narrowly triangular, wavy, mid-green leaves have serrated edges. A cluster of fragrant, tubular, white flowers is produced from each rosette center, usually in summer. Z15 H12–10. **'Ruber'** has red-flushed foliage. Z15 H11–10.

C. bivittatus. Evergreen, clump-forming, basal-rosetted perennial. **H** to 6in (15cm), **S** 10–15in (25–38cm). Loose, flat rosettes of broadly lance-shaped, wavy, mid- to yellowish-green leaves have finely toothed margins and are striped lengthwise with 2 coppery-fawn to buff bands. Small clusters of tubular, white flowers are produced from center of each rosette, usually in summer. Z15 H12–10. **'Pink Starlight'** (illus. p.471), **H** 8in (20cm) or more, **S** 14in (35cm) or more, has green leaves striped yellowish-green, and heavily suffused deep pink. H11–10.

C. bromelioides (Rainbow star). Evergreen, spreading, basal-rosetted perennial. **H** 8in (20cm) or more, **S** 14in (35cm) or more. Strap-shaped, wavy, finely toothed, arching, mid- to bright green leaves are produced in dense rosettes. Occasionally bears clusters of tubular, white flowers in center of each rosette, usually in summer. Z15 H12–10. **'Tricolor'** has carmine-suffused, white-striped foliage.

C. zonatus. Evergreen, basal-rosetted perennial. **H** 4–6in (10–15cm), **S** 12–16in (30–40cm). Forms loose, flat rosettes of strap-shaped, wavy, finely toothed, sepia-green leaves, cross-banded with gray-buff and with grayish-white scales beneath. A cluster of tubular, white flowers is produced in each rosette, usually in summer. Z15 H12–10. **'Zebrinus'** produces silver-banded foliage. Z15 H11–10.

x CRYPTBERGIA
BROMELIACEAE

Hybrid genus (*Cryptanthus* x *Billbergia*) of evergreen, rosette-forming perennials, grown for their foliage. Needs partial shade and fertile, well-drained soil. Water moderately during the growing season, sparingly in winter. Propagate by suckers or offsets in spring.

x C. 'Rubra'. Evergreen, clump-forming, basal-rosetted perennial. **H** and **S** 6–12in (15–30cm). Loose rosettes comprise strap-shaped, pointed, bronze-red leaves. Rarely, small, tubular, white flowers are produced in rosette centers in summer. Z15 H12–10.

CRYPTOCORYNE
ARACEAE

Genus of semievergreen, perennial, submerged water plants and marsh plants, grown for their foliage. Is suitable for tropical aquariums. Needs sun and rich soil. Remove fading foliage, and divide plants periodically. Propagate by division in spring or summer.

C. beckettii var. ciliata. See *C. ciliata*.

C. ciliata, syn. *C. beckettii* var. *ciliata*. Semievergreen, perennial, submerged water plant. S6in (15cm). Lance-shaped, deep green leaves have paler midribs. Small, hooded, fringed, purplish spathes are produced intermittently at base of plant. Z10–11 H12–10.

C. spiralis. Semievergreen, perennial, submerged water plant. S6in (15cm). Small, hooded, purplish spathes are produced intermittently among lance-shaped, purplish-green leaves. Z10–11 H11–10.

CRYPTOGRAMMA
ADIANTACEAE/PTERIDACEAE

Genus of deciduous or semievergreen ferns. Needs partial shade and moist but well-drained, neutral or acidic soil. Remove fading fronds. Propagate by spores in late summer.

C. crispa, illus. p.293.

CRYPTOMERIA
TAXODIACEAE/CUPRESSACEAE

See also CONIFERS.

C. japonica (Japanese cryptomeria). Fast-growing, columnar to conical, open conifer. **H** 50–70ft (15–20m), **S** 15–25ft (5–8m). Has soft, fibrous, red-brown bark, needlelike, incurved, mid- to dark green leaves, spirally arranged, and globular, brown cones. Z6–9 H9–4. **'Bandai-sugi'**, **H** and **S** 6ft (2m), makes an irregularly rounded shrub with foliage that turns bronze in winter. **'Cristata'** illus. p.104. **'Elegans Compacta'**, **H** 6–15ft (2–5m), **S** 6ft (2m), is a dwarf form. **'Pyramidata'** illus. p.104. **'Sekkan-sugi'**, **H** 30ft (10m), **S** 10–12ft (3–4m), has semi-pendulous branches and light golden-cream foliage. **'Spiralis'**, **H** and **S** 6–10ft (2–3m), forms a tree or dense shrub with spirally twisted foliage and is very slow-growing. **'Vilmoriniana'**, **H** and **S** 3ft (1m), forms a globular mound of yellow-green foliage that turns bronze in winter.

CRYPTOSTEGIA
ASCLEPIADACEAE/APOCYNACEAE

Genus of evergreen, twining climbers, grown for their flowers. Needs fertile, well-drained soil and full light. Water regularly when in growth, less at other times. Stems require support. Spur back previous season's old flowering stems in spring. Propagate by seed in spring or by softwood cuttings in summer.

C. grandiflora (Rubber vine). Strong-growing, evergreen, twining climber. **H** 30ft (10m) or more. Has oval, thick-textured, glossy leaves. Funnel-shaped, reddish to lilac-purple flowers are borne in summer. ⓘ Stems yield a poisonous latex that may cause severe discomfort if ingested. Z11 H12–10.

Cryptostemma calendulaceum. See *Arctotheca calendula*.

CTENANTHE
MARANTACEAE

Genus of evergreen, bushy perennials, grown for their ornamental foliage. Requires a humid atmosphere, even temperature and partial shade. Prefers moist but well-drained soil and soft water; do not allow to dry completely. Propagate by division in spring.

C. lubbersiana. Evergreen, clump-forming, bushy perennial. **H** and **S** to 30in (75cm) or more. Long-stalked, lance-shaped, sharply pointed leaves are 10in (25cm) long, green above, irregularly marked and striped with pale yellowish-green, and pale greenish-yellow below.

C

Intermittently bears dense, one-sided spikes of many small, 3-petaled, white flowers. Z15 H12–10.

C. oppenheimiana, syn. *Calathea oppenheimiana*. Robust, evergreen, bushy perennial. **H** and **S** 3ft (1m) or more. Lance-shaped, leathery leaves are 1ft (30cm) or more long, red below, dark green above with pale green or white bands along veins on either side of midribs. Dense, one-sided spikes of many small, 3-petaled, white flowers are borne intermittently. Z14–15 H12–10. **'Tricolor'** illus. p.465.

Cudrania tricuspidata. See *Maclura tricuspidata*.

CUNNINGHAMIA
TAXODIACEAE/CUPRESSACEAE

See also CONIFERS.
C. lanceolata, illus. p.100.

CUNONIA
CUNONIACEAE

Genus of evergreen, summer-flowering trees, grown for their foliage, flowers and overall appearance. Requires full light and well-drained soil. Water container plants moderately, less in winter. Pruning is tolerated. Propagate by seed in spring or by semiripe cuttings in summer.

C. capensis (African red alder). Moderately fast-growing, evergreen, rounded tree. **H** and **S** 30–50ft (10–15m), more in rich soil. Has lustrous, dark green leaves, divided into pairs of lance-shaped, serrated leaflets. Tiny, long-stamened, white flowers are produced in dense, bottlebrush-like spikes, 4–5in (10–13cm) long, in late summer. Z10–11 H11–10.

CUPHEA
LYTHRACEAE

Genus of annuals, perennials and evergreen shrubs and subshrubs, grown for their flowers. Prefers full sun and fertile, well-drained soil. Water freely when in full growth, moderately at other times. Remove flowered shoots after flowering to maintain a bushy habit. Propagate by seed in spring or by greenwood cuttings in spring or summer. Red spider mite may be troublesome.

C. cyanea, illus. p.162.
C. ignea, syn. *C. platycentra*, illus. p.308.
C. platycentra. See *C. ignea*.
C. x purpurea 'Firecracker', illus. p.306.

x Cupressocyparis leylandii. See x *Cuprocyparis leylandii* .

CUPRESSUS
Cypress
CUPRESSACEAE

See also CONIFERS.
C. arizonica var. glabra, syn. *C. glabra* (Arizona cypress, Smooth cypress). Conical conifer. **H** 30–50ft (10–15m), **S** 10–15ft (3–5m). Has smooth, flaking, reddish-purple bark and upright, spirally arranged sprays of scalelike, aromatic, glaucous blue-gray leaves that are flecked with white resin. Globular cones are chocolate-brown. Z6–9 H9–2.

C. cashmeriana, syn. *C. torulosa* 'Cashmeriana', illus. p.95.

C. glabra. See *C. arizonica* var. *glabra*.
C. lusitanica (Cedar of Goa, Mexican cypress). Conical conifer. **H** 70ft (20m), **S** 15–25ft (5–8m). Has fissured bark and spreading, spirally arranged sprays of scalelike, aromatic, gray-green leaves. Bears small, globular cones that are glaucous blue when young, ripening to glossy brown. Z9–10 H10–8.
C. macrocarpa (Monterey cypress). Fast-growing, evergreen conifer, columnar when young, often wide-spreading with age. **H** 70ft (20m), **S** 20–80ft (6–25m). Bark is shallowly fissured. Scalelike, aromatic, bright to dark green leaves are borne in plumelike sprays. Globular cones are glossy and brown. Z7–11 H11–7.
'Goldcrest' illus. p.104.
C. sempervirens 'Stricta', illus. p.102.
C. torulosa 'Cashmeriana'. See *C. cashmeriana*.

x CUPROCYPARIS
CUPRESSACEAE

⚠ Contact with the foliage may aggravate skin allergies. See also CONIFERS.
x C. leylandii, syn. x *Cupressocyparis leylandii*. **'Harlequin'** is a very fast-growing, columnar conifer with a conical tip. **H** 80–120ft (25–35m), **S** 12–15ft (4–5m). Gray-green foliage, with patches of clear ivory-white, is held in plumelike sprays. **'Leighton Green'** bears flattened sprays of paired, scalelike, rich green leaves and globular, glossy, dark brown cones. **'Robinson's Gold',** **H** 50–70ft (15–20m), has bright golden leaves. **'Castlewellan',** illus. p.99. **'Haggerston Grey',** illus. p.95.

CURCUMA
ZINGIBERACEAE

Genus of herbaceous perennials, grown for their patterned leaves and showy bracts atop the flower spikes. The lower bracts form pouches from which the flowers emerge; the upper bracts are without flowers, but are larger and brightly colored or white. Needs partial shade and rich, moist but well-drained soil. Keep completely dry in winter. Propagate by division of rhizome in spring.

C. cordata. See *C. zedoaria*.
C. petiolata, illus. p.477. Herbaceous, clump-forming perennial. **H** 48in (120cm), **S** 20in (50cm). Has narrowly ovate, strongly ribbed, mid-green leaves, 24in (60cm) long. In summer produces a spike, to 14in (35cm) long, of lemon-yellow flowers and bright pink upper bracts. H11–10.
C. zedoaria, syn. *C. cordata* (Zedoary), illus. p.477. Herbaceous, clump-forming perennial. **H** 60in (150cm), **S** 20in (50cm). Has ovate, ribbed, mid-green leaves, to 36in (90cm) long, with dark red stripes on upper sides. In mid- to late spring bears a spike, 2–3in (5–8cm) long, of yellow flowers and pink to purple-red upper bracts.

Curtonus paniculatus. See *Crocosmia paniculata*.

CYANANTHUS
CAMPANULACEAE

Genus of late summer-flowering perennials, suitable for rock gardens, walls and troughs. Needs partial shade and rich,

moist but well-drained soil. Propagate by softwood cuttings in spring or by seed in fall.

C. lobatus. Prostrate perennial. **H** ³⁄₄in (2cm), **S** 8in (20cm). Branched stems are clothed in small, wedge-shaped, dull green leaves. In late summer, each stem bears a funnel-shaped, blue flower. Z6–7 H7–6.
f. albus illus. p.359.
C. microphyllus, illus. p.369.

CYANOTIS
COMMELINACEAE

Genus of evergreen, creeping perennials, grown for their foliage. Prefers a position in sun or partial shade, with rich, well-drained soil. Propagate by tip cuttings from spring to fall.

C. kewensis (Teddy-bear vine). Evergreen perennial forming rosettes with trailing stems. **H** 2in (5cm), **S** 12in (30cm). Clasping the stem are 2 rows of overlapping, oval leaves, to 2in (5cm) long, dark green above, purple with velvety, brown hairs below. Stalkless clusters of 3-petaled, purplish-pink flowers are produced in axils of leaflike bracts almost all year round. Z13–15 H12–10.
C. somaliensis (Pussy ears) Evergreen, creeping perennial. **H** 2in (5cm), **S** indefinite. Small, narrow, glossy, dark green leaves, with white hairs, surround stems. Has purplish-blue flowers in leaf axils in winter–spring. Z13–15 H12–10.

CYATHEA
SYN. ALSOPHILA, SPHAEROPTERIS
CYATHEACEAE

Genus of evergreen tree ferns, grown for their foliage and overall appearance. Needs a humid atmosphere, sun or partial shade and rich, moisture-retentive but well-drained soil. Water container plants freely in summer, moderately at other times. Propagate by spores in spring.

C. australis, syn. *Alsophila australis*, illus. p.452.
C. medullaris (Black tree fern, Mamaku). Evergreen, upright tree fern with a slender, black trunk. **H** 22–52ft (7–16m), **S** 20–40ft (6–12m). Has arching fronds, to 22ft (7m) long, divided into small, oblong, glossy, dark green leaflets, paler beneath. Z10–11 H11–10.

Cyathodes colensoi. See *Leucopogon colensoi*.

CYBISTAX
BIGNONIACEAE

Genus of deciduous trees, grown for their spring flowers and for shade. Needs full light and fertile, moist but well-drained soil. Will not bloom when confined to a container. Young plants may be pruned to shape when leafless; otherwise pruning is not required. Propagate by seed or air-layering in spring or by semiripe cuttings in summer.

C. donnell-smithii, syn. *Tabebuia donnell-smithii*. Fairly fast-growing, deciduous, rounded tree. **H** and **S** 30ft (10m) or more. Leaves have 5–7 oval leaflets, 2–8in (5–20cm) long. Bell-shaped, 5-lobed, bright yellow flowers are produced, often in great profusion, in spring before the leaves. Z14–15 H12–10.

CYCAS
CYCADACEAE

Genus of slow-growing, evergreen, woody-stemmed perennials, grown for their palm-like appearance. Prefers a position in full light and rich, well-drained soil. Water container specimens moderately when in full growth, less at other times. Propagate in spring by seed or suckers taken from mature plants.

C. revoluta, illus. p.457.

CYCLAMEN
PRIMULACEAE

Genus of tuberous perennials, some of which are occasionally evergreen, grown for their pendent flowers, each with 5 reflexed petals and a mouth often stained with a darker color. Needs sun or partial shade and rich, well-drained soil. If grown in containers, in summer dry off tubers of all except *C. purpurascens* (which is evergreen and flowers in summer); repot in fall and water to restart growth. Propagate by seed in late summer or fall. *C. persicum* and its cultivars are susceptible to black root rot. ⚠ All parts may cause severe discomfort if ingested.

C. africanum, illus. p.424.
C. alpinum, syn. *C. trochopteranthum*. Spring-flowering, tuberous perennial. **H** 4in (10cm), **S** 2–4in (5–10cm). Bears rounded or heart-shaped leaves, zoned with silver. Produces musty-scented, pale carmine or white flowers, stained dark carmine at mouths; petals are twisted and propeller-shaped. Z8–9 H9–8.
C. caucasicum. See *C. coum* subsp. *caucasicum*.
C. cilicium, illus. p.426.
C. coum, illus. p.429. **f. albissimum,** syn. *C. coum* 'Album' illus. p.428. **'Album'.** See *C. coum* f. *albissimum*. **subsp. caucasicum,** syn. *C. caucasicum* is a winter-flowering, tuberous perennial. **H** to 4in (10cm), **S** 2–4in (5–10cm). Has heart-shaped, silver-patterned leaves and produces a succession of bright carmine flowers, each with a dark stain at the mouth. **Pewter Group** illus. p.429. **Pewter Group 'Maurice Dryden'** illus. p.428.
C. creticum. Spring-flowering, tuberous perennial. **H** to 4in (10cm), **S** 2–4in (5–10cm). Produces heart-shaped, dark green leaves, sometimes silver-patterned, and fragrant, white flowers. Z6–9 H9–7.
C. cyprium. Fall-flowering, tuberous perennial. **H** to 4in (10cm), **S** 2–4in (5–10cm). Heart-shaped, toothed, dark green leaves, patterned with lighter green, are produced with or just after fragrant, white flowers, each with carmine marks around the mouth. Z7–9 H9–7.
C. europaeum. See *C. purpurascens*.
C. fatrense. See *C. purpurascens*.
C. graecum, illus. p.425.
C. hederifolium, syn. *C. neapolitanum*, illus. p.426. **f. albiflorum** illus. p.424.
C. libanoticum, illus. p.418.
C. mirabile, illus. p.425.
C. neapolitanum. See *C. hederifolium*.
C. persicum, illus. p.429. **'Esmeralda'** is a winter-flowering tuberous perennial. **H** 4–8in (10–20cm), **S** 6–8in (15–20cm). Has heart-shaped, silver-patterned leaves and fragrant, broad-petaled, carmine-red

flowers. Z13–15 H6–1. **Halios Series,** **H** 12in (30cm), **S** 7in (18cm), has blunt-toothed, dark green leaves with silver marbling and produces a succession of white, pink, scarlet, lilac or purple flowers in late summer or fall. Z13–15 H6–1. **Kaori Series** produces flowers in a wide range of colors in winter. Z13–15 H6–1. **'Pearl Wave'**, **S**4–6in (10–15cm), has leaves marked light and dark green and silver and in winter and spring produces slender, deep pink flowers, with frilly-edged petals. Z13–15 H6–1. **'Renown'**, **S**4–6in (10–15cm), has silver-green leaves, each with a central, dark green mark, and produces slender, scarlet flowers in winter–spring. Z13–15 H6–1. **'Scentsation'**, **H** 6in (15cm), bears strongly scented flowers in pink, carmine-red or crimson from early winter to early spring. Z13–15 H6–1.

C. pseudibericum. Spring-flowering, tuberous perennial. **H** to 4in (10cm), **S** 4–6in (10–15cm). Has heart-shaped, toothed leaves patterned with silvery- and dark green zones. Flowers are deep carmine-purple with darker, basal stains and white-rimmed mouths. Z8–9 H9–8.

C. purpurascens, syn. *C. europaeum, C. fatrense,* illus. p.422.

C. repandum. Spring-flowering, tuberous perennial. **H** to 4in (10cm), **S** 4–6in (10–15cm). Has heart-shaped, jagged-toothed, dark green leaves with lighter patterns. Bears fragrant, slender, reddish-purple flowers. Z7–9 H9–7.

C. rohlfsianum, illus. p.426.

C. trochopteranthum. See *C. alpinum.*

Cyclobothra lutea. See *Calochortus barbatus.*

CYDONIA
ROSACEAE

Genus of one species of deciduous, spring-flowering tree, grown for its flowers and fruits, which are used as a flavoring and for preserves. Grow against a south- or west-facing wall at the limits of hardiness. Requires sun and fertile, well-drained soil. Propagate species by seed in fall, cultivars by softwood cuttings in summer. Mildew, brown rot and fireblight are sometimes a problem.

C. oblonga (Common quince). Z5–9 H9–3. **'Lusitanica'** is a deciduous, spreading tree. **H** and **S** 15ft (5m). Broadly oval, dark green leaves are gray-felted beneath. Has a profusion of large, 5-petaled, pale pink flowers in late spring, followed by fragrant, pear-shaped, deep yellow fruits. **'Vranja'** illus. p.88.

C. sinensis. See *Pseudocydonia sinensis.*

Cylindropuntia tunicata. See *Opuntia tunicata.*

CYMBALARIA
SCROPHULARIACEAE/PLANTAGINACEAE

Genus of annuals, biennials and short-lived perennials, related to *Linaria,* grown for their tiny flowers on slender stems. Is good for rock gardens, walls and banks, but may be invasive. Needs shade and moist soil. Propagate by seed in fall. Self-seeds readily.

C. muralis (Ivy-leaved toadflax, Kenilworth ivy). Spreading perennial. **H** 2in (5cm), **S** 5in (12cm). Bears small, ivy-shaped, pale green leaves and, in summer, masses of tiny, tubular, spurred, sometimes purple-tinted, white flowers. Z4–8 H8–1.

CYMBIDIUM
ORCHIDACEAE

ⓘ Contact with the foliage may aggravate skin allergies. See also ORCHIDS.

C. Caithness Ice gx 'Trinity', illus. p.467. Evergreen, epiphytic orchid for a cool greenhouse. **H** 30in (75cm). Sprays of green flowers, 4in (10cm) across, each with a red-marked, white lip, are borne in early spring. Has narrowly oval leaves, to 24in (60cm) long. Needs a position in partial shade in summer. Z12–15 H12–6.

C. Christmas Angel gx 'Cooksbridge Sunburst'. Evergreen, epiphytic orchid for a cool greenhouse. **H** 30in (75cm). In winter produces sprays of yellow flowers, 4in (10cm) across and with red-spotted lips. Narrowly oval leaves are up to 24in (60cm) long. Grow in partial shade in summer. Z12–15 H12–6.

C. devonianum. Evergreen, epiphytic orchid for a cool greenhouse. **H** 24in (60cm). In early summer bears pendent spikes of olive-green flowers, 1in (2.5cm) wide, overlaid with purple and with purple lips. Has semi-rigid, broadly oval leaves, to 12in (30cm) long. Needs partial shade in summer. Z12–15 H12–6.

C. elegans, syn. *Cyperorchis elegans,* illus. p.467. Evergreen, epiphytic orchid for a cool greenhouse. **H** 30in (75cm). Dense, pendent sprays of fragrant, tubular, yellow flowers, 1¹⁄₂in (4cm) across, are produced in early summer. Has narrowly oval leaves, to 24in (60cm) long. Requires partial shade in summer. Z12–15 H12–6.

C. grandiflorum. See *C. hookerianum.*
C. hookerianum, syn. *C. grandiflorum.* Evergreen, epiphytic orchid for a cool greenhouse. **H** 30in (75cm). In winter produces sprays of deep green flowers, 3in (8cm) across, each with a hairy, brown-spotted, creamy-white lip. Narrowly oval leaves are up to 24in (60cm) long. Grow in partial shade in summer. Z14–15 H12–6.

C. King's Loch gx 'Cooksbridge'. Evergreen, epiphytic orchid for a cool greenhouse. **H** 24in (60cm). Sprays of green flowers, 2in (5cm) across and each with a purple-marked, white lip, open in spring. Leaves are narrowly oval and up to 24in (60cm) long. Provide partial shade in summer. Z12–15 H12–6.

C. Pontac gx 'Mont Millais'. Evergreen, epiphytic orchid for a cool greenhouse. **H** 30in (75cm). In spring bears sprays of rich deep red flowers, 3in (8cm) across, edged and marked with white. Has narrowly oval leaves, to 24in (60cm) long. Needs partial shade in summer. Z14–15 H12–6.

C. Portelet Bay gx, illus. p.466. Evergreen, epiphytic orchid for a cool greenhouse. **H** 30in (75cm). Red-lipped, white flowers, 4in (10cm) across, are borne in sprays in spring. Has narrowly oval leaves, to 24in (60cm) long. Provide partial shade in summer. H11–6.

C. Strathbraan gx. Evergreen, epiphytic orchid for a cool greenhouse. **H** 24in (60cm). In spring produces slightly arching spikes of off-white flowers, 2in (5cm) across, with red marks on each lip. Leaves are narrowly oval, to 24in (60cm) long. Requires partial shade in summer. Z14–15 H12–6.

C. Strathdon gx 'Cooksbridge Noel'. Evergreen, epiphytic orchid for a cool greenhouse. **H** 3ft (1m). Sprays of rich pink flowers, 2in (5cm) across, with red-spotted, yellow-tinged lips, are produced in winter. Has narrowly oval leaves, to 24in (60cm) long. Needs partial shade in summer. Z14–15 H12–6.

C. Strathkanaid gx, illus. p.467. Evergreen, epiphytic orchid for a cool greenhouse. **H** 24in (60cm). In spring bears arching spikes of deep red flowers, 2in (5cm) across. Lips are white, marked deep red. Has narrowly oval leaves, to 24in (60cm) long. Requires partial shade in summer. H11–1.

C. tracyanum. Evergreen, epiphytic orchid for a cool greenhouse. **H** 30in (75cm). In fall produces long spikes of fragrant, olive-green flowers, 3in (8cm) across, overlaid with reddish dots and dashes. Has narrowly oval leaves, to 24in (60cm) long. Needs partial shade in summer. Z14–15 H12–6.

CYNARA
COMPOSITAE/ASTERACEAE

Genus of architectural perennials, grown for their large heads of flowers. The plant described is grown both as a vegetable and as a decorative border plant. Requires sun and fertile, well-drained soil. Propagate by seed or division in spring.

C. cardunculus, illus. p.216.

CYNOGLOSSUM
Hound's tongue
BORAGINACEAE

Genus of annuals, biennials and perennials, grown for their long flowering period from late spring to early fall. Needs sun and fertile but not over-rich soil. Propagate by division in spring or by seed in fall or spring.

C. amabile 'Firmament', illus. p.315.

CYPELLA
IRIDACEAE

Genus of summer-flowering bulbs, grown for their short-lived, iris-like flowers that have 3 large, spreading outer petals and 3 small, incurved inner ones. May survive outdoors in marginal areas if planted near a sunny wall. Needs full sun and well-drained soil. Lift bulbs when dormant; partially dry off in winter. Propagate by seed in spring.

C. herbertii, illus. p.412.

Cyperorchis elegans. See *Cymbidium elegans.*

CYPERUS
CYPERACEAE

See also GRASSES, BAMBOOS, RUSHES and SEDGES.

C. albostriatus, syn. *C. diffusus, C. elegans.* Evergreen, perennial sedge. **H** 24in (60cm), **S** indefinite. Stem has prominently veined, mid-green leaves and, in summer, up to 8 leaflike, green bracts surrounding a well-branched umbel of brown spikelets. Z10–11 H11–4. **'Variegatus'** has white-striped leaves and bracts.

C. alternifolius of gardens. See *C. involucratus.*
C. diffusus of gardens. See *C. albostriatus.*
C. elegans of gardens. See *C. albostriatus.*
C. flabelliformis. See *C. involucratus.*
C. involucratus, syn. *C. alternifolius, C. flabelliformis,* illus. p.478.
C. isocladus of gardens. See *C. papyrus 'Nanus'.*
C. longus (Galingale). Deciduous, spreading, perennial sedge. **H** 5ft (1.5m), **S** indefinite. Bears rough-edged, glossy, dark green leaves and, in summer, umbels of narrow, flattened, milk-chocolate-colored spikelets that keep their color well. Tolerates its roots in water. Z3–11 H11–1.
C. papyrus, illus. p.478. **'Nanus',** syn. *C. isocladus* is an evergreen, spreading, perennial sedge with a red rhizome; it is a dwarf variant of the species, sometimes considered distinct, and is often grown under misapplied names. **H** 32in (80cm), **S** indefinite. Triangular, leafless stems bear umbels of brown spikelets, on stalks 3–4in (8–10cm) long, in summer. Z13–15 H12–6.

Cyphomandra betacea. See *Solanum betaceum.*
Cyphomandra crassicaulis. See *Solanum betaceum.*

CYPHOSTEMMA
VITACEAE

Genus of deciduous, perennial succulents with very thick, fleshy, almost woody caudices and branches. Leaf undersides often exude droplets of resin. Needs full sun and very well-drained soil. Keep dry in winter. Is difficult to grow. Propagate by seed in spring.

C. bainesii, syn. *Cissus bainesii.* Deciduous, perennial succulent. **H** and **S** 24in (60cm). Has a thick, swollen, bottle-shaped trunk, often unbranched, covered in peeling, papery, yellow bark. Fleshy, silvery-green leaves, with deeply serrated edges, are divided into 3 oval leaflets, silver-haired when young. Bears tiny, cup-shaped, yellow-green flowers in summer, then grapelike, red fruits. Z13–15 H12–10.
C. juttae, syn. *Cissus juttae,* illus. p.487.

CYPRIPEDIUM
Lady's slipper
ORCHIDACEAE

See also ORCHIDS.

C. acaule (Pink lady's-slipper). Deciduous, terrestrial orchid. **H** to 16in (40cm). Yellowish-green or purple flowers, 1¹⁄₂–2¹⁄₂in (4–6cm) long, each with a pouched, pink or white lip, are borne singly in spring–summer. Has broadly lance-shaped, pleated leaves, 4–12in (10–30cm) long. Prefers partial shade. Z3–7 H7–1.

C. calceolus. Deciduous, terrestrial orchid. **H** 30in (75cm). In spring–summer bears paired or solitary yellow-pouched, purple flowers, 1¹⁄₄–3in (3–7cm) long. Broadly lance-shaped leaves, 2–8in (5–20cm) long, are arranged in a spiral up stem. Stems and leaves are slightly hairy. Prefers partial shade. Z3–7 H7–1. **var. pubescens.** See *C. pubescens.*

C. macranthon. See *C. macranthos.*
C. macranthos, syn. *C. macranthon.* Deciduous, terrestrial orchid. **H** 20in (50cm). Pouched, violet or purplish-red flowers, 1¹⁄₂–2¹⁄₂in (4–6cm) long, usually

borne singly, are produced in spring–summer. Stems and oval leaves, 1½–3in (4–7cm) long, are slightly hairy. Prefers partial shade. Z3–7 H7–1.

C. pubescens, syn. *C. calceolus* var. *pubescens.* Deciduous, terrestrial orchid. **H** 30in (75cm). Has large, purple-marked, greenish-yellow flowers, 3–4in (8–10cm) long, in spring–summer. Large, broadly lance-shaped leaves, 6–8in (15–20cm) long, are arranged in a spiral up stem. Stems and leaves are hairy. Prefers partial shade. Z3–7 H7–1.

C. reginae, illus. p.466. Deciduous, terrestrial orchid. **H** to 3ft (1m). In spring–summer, white flowers, ¾–2in (2–5cm) long, each with a pouched, white-streaked, pink lip, are borne singly or in groups of 2 or 3. Stem and oval leaves, 4–10in (10–25cm) long, are hairy. Prefers partial shade. Z2–7 H7–1.

C. Ulla Silkens gx, illus. p.256.

CYRILLA
CYRILLACEAE

Genus of one very variable species of deciduous or evergreen shrub, grown for its flowers in late summer and fall. Prefers full sun and needs peaty, acidic soil. Propagate by semiripe cuttings in summer.

C. racemiflora (Leatherwood). Deciduous or evergreen, bushy shrub. **H** and **S** 4ft (1.2m). Oblong, glossy, dark green leaves redden in fall. Slender spires of small, 5-petaled, white flowers are borne in late summer and fall. Z6–9 H9–5.

CYRTANTHUS
AMARYLLIDACEAE

Genus of bulbs with brightly colored flowers, usually in summer. Requires full sun and free-draining, light soil. In frost-free areas, may flower for much of the year. Plant in spring. Water freely in the growing season. Propagate by seed or offsets in spring.

C. brachyscyphus, syn. *C. parviflorus,* illus. p.423.

C. breviflorus, syn. *Anoiganthus breviflorus, Anoiganthus luteus.* Clump-forming, summer-flowering bulb. **H** 8–12in (20–30cm), **S** 3–4in (8–10cm). Has semierect, narrowly strap-shaped, basal leaves. Leafless flower stem bears up to 6 funnel-shaped, yellow flowers, ¾–1¼in (2–3cm) long. Prefers a warm, sheltered situation. Z10–11 H11–10.

C. elatus, syn. *C. purpureus, Vallota speciosa.* Clump-forming, summer-flowering bulb. **H** 12–20in (30–50cm), **S** 5–6in (12–15cm). Bears semierect, widely strap-shaped, bright green, basal leaves. Sturdy stem produces a head of up to 5 widely funnel-shaped, scarlet flowers, 3–4in (8–10cm) long. Makes an excellent house plant. Z8–10 H10–8.

C. mackenii. Clump-forming, summer-flowering bulb. **H** 12–16in (30–40cm), **S** 3–4in (8–10cm). Bears semierect, strap-shaped, basal leaves. Leafless stems each bear an umbel of up to 10 fragrant, tubular, white flowers, 2in (5cm) long and slightly curved. Z11 H11–6. **var. cooperi** illus. p.412. illus. p.412

C. obliquus. Clump-forming, summer-flowering bulb. **H** 8–24in (20–60cm), **S** 5–6in (12–15cm). Bears semierect, widely strap-

shaped, grayish-green, basal leaves, twisted lengthwise. Produces a head of up to 12 pendent, tubular, red-and-yellow flowers, 3in (7cm) long. Z10–11 H11–10.

C. parviflorus. See *C. brachyscyphus.*

C. purpureus. See *C. elatus.*

C. sanguineus. Clump-forming, summer-flowering bulb. **H** 12–20in (30–50cm), **S** 5–6in (12–15cm). Has semierect, strap-shaped, bright green, basal leaves. Sturdy stem bears 1 or 2 long-tubed, scarlet flowers, 3–4in (8–10cm) long. Z10–11 H11–10.

CYRTOMIUM
DRYOPTERIDACEAE

Genus of evergreen ferns. Does best in partial shade and rich, moist soil. Remove fading fronds. Propagate by division in spring or summer or by spores in summer.

C. falcatum, illus. p.291.

C. fortunei, syn. *Phanerophlebia fortunei.* Evergreen fern. **H** 24in (60cm), **S** 16in (40cm). Has erect, dull, pale green fronds, 12–24in (30–60cm) long, with broadly sickle-shaped pinnae, 1–2in (2.5–5cm) long. Z7–10 H10–7.

CYSTOPTERIS
WOODSIACEAE

Genus of deciduous ferns, suitable for rock gardens. Prefers partial shade and soil that never dries out. Remove fronds as they fade. Propagate by division in spring, by spores in summer or by bulbils when available.

C. bulbifera (Bulblet bladder fern). Deciduous fern. **H** 6in (15cm), **S** 9in (23cm). Broadly lance-shaped, much-divided, dainty, pale green fronds produce tiny bulbils along their length. Propagate by bulbils as soon as mature. Z4–8 H8–1.

C. dickieana. Deciduous fern. **H** 6in (15cm), **S** 9in (23cm). Has broadly lance-shaped, divided, delicate, pale green fronds, with oblong, blunt, indented pinnae, that arch downward. Z2–7 H7–1.

C. fragilis (Brittle bladder fern). Deciduous fern. **H** 6in (15cm), **S** 9in (23cm). Broadly lance-shaped, pale green fronds are delicate and much divided into oblong, pointed, indented pinnae. Z4–8 H8–1.

CYTISUS
Broom
LEGUMINOSAE/PAPILIONACEAE

Genus of deciduous or evergreen shrubs, grown for their abundant, pealike flowers. Prefers full sun and fertile, but not over-rich, well-drained soil. Resents being transplanted. Propagate species by semiripe cuttings in summer or by seed in fall, hybrids and cultivars by semiripe cuttings in late summer. Some species are considered invasive; check with local experts before planting. ① All parts, especially the seeds, may cause mild stomach upset if ingested.

C. albua. See *Chamaecytisus albus.*

C. ardoinii. See *C. ardoinoi.*

C. ardoinoi, syn. *C. ardoinii,* illus. p.372.

C. battandieri, syn. *Argyrocytisus battandieri,* illus. p.116.

C. x beanii, illus. p.335.

C. canariensis of gardens. See *Genista x spachiana.*

C. demissus. See *Chamaecytisus demissus.*

C. 'Firefly'. Deciduous, bushy shrub with slender, arching shoots. **H** and **S** 5–6ft (1.5–2m). Small, mid-green leaves are oblong and have 3 tiny leaflets. Produces masses of yellow flowers, marked with red, from late spring to early summer. Z6–9 H9–6.

C. x kewensis. Deciduous, arching shrub. **H** 1ft (30cm), **S** to 6ft (2m). Has leaves, each composed of 3 leaflets, along downy stems. In late spring bears creamy-white flowers. Is good for a bank or large rock garden. Z6–8 H8–6.

C. leucanthus. See *Chamaecytisus albus.*

C. nigricans, syn. *Lembotropis nigricans,* illus. p.160.

C. x praecox (Broom). **'Allgold'** illus. p.148. **'Warminster'** illus. p.148.

C. purpureus. See *Chamaecytisus purpureus.*

C. racemosus of gardens. See *Genista x spachiana.*

C. scoparius (Scotch broom). **f. andreanus,** illus. p.162. **subsp. maritimus,** syn. *C. scoparius* var. *prostratus* is a decidous, prostrate shrub forming dense mounds of interlocking shoots. **H** 8in (20cm) **S** 4–6ft (1.2–2m). Small gray-green leaves usually have 3 oblong leaflets, but may be reduced to a single leaflet. Has masses of golden-yellow flowers in late spring and early summer. Z6–8 H8–6. **var. prostratus.** See *C. scoparius* subsp. *maritimus.*

C. supinus. See *Chamaecytisus supinus.*

C. 'Windlesham Ruby'. Deciduous, bushy shrub with slender, arching shoots. **H** and **S** 5–6ft (1.5–2m). Small, mid-green leaves have 3 oblong leaflets. Large, rich red flowers are borne in profusion in late spring and early summer. Z7–9 H9–7.

C. 'Zeelandia'. Deciduous, bushy shrub with slender, arching shoots. **H** and **S** 5–6ft (1.5–2m). Small, mid-green leaves have 3 oblong leaflets. Has masses of bicolored, creamy-white and lilac-pink flowers from late spring to early summer. Z6–9 H9–6.

D

DABOECIA
Irish heath
ERICACEAE

See also HEATHERS.

D. azorica (Azores heath). Evergreen, compact shrub. **H** to 6in (15cm), **S** to 24in (60cm). Lance-shaped leaves are dark green above, silver-gray beneath. Urn- to bell-shaped, vivid red flowers are borne in late spring or early summer. Z6–8 H8–6.

D. cantabrica (Cantabrian heath, Irish heath, St. Dabeoc's heath). Evergreen, straggling shrub. **H** to 18in (45cm), **S** 24in (60cm). Top growth may be damaged by frost and cold winds, but plants respond well to hard pruning and produce new growth from base. Leaves are lance-shaped to oval, dark green above, silver-gray beneath. Bears bell- to urn-shaped, single or double, white, purple or mauve flowers from late spring to mid-fall. Z6–8 H8–6. **'Bicolor'** (illus. p.166) bears white, purple and striped flowers on the same plant. **'Praegerae',** **H** 14in (35cm), has glowing, deep pink flowers. **subsp. scotia.** See *D. x scotica.* **'Snowdrift'** has bright green foliage and long racemes of large, white flowers.

D. x scotica, syn. *D. cantabrica* subsp. *scotia.* Evergreen, compact shrub. **H** to 6in (15cm), **S** to 2ft (60cm). Lance-shaped to oval leaves are dark green above, silver-gray beneath. Bears bell- to urn-shaped, white, purple or mauve flowers from late spring to mid-fall. Z6–8 H8–6. **'Jack Drake',** **H** 8in (20cm), has small, dark green leaves and ruby-colored flowers. **'Silverwells'** has small, bright green leaves and large, white flowers. **'William Buchanan',** **H** 18in (45cm), is a vigorous cultivar with dark green leaves and deep purple flowers.

DACTYLIS
GRAMINEAE/POACEAE

See also GRASSES, BAMBOOS, RUSHES and SEDGES.

D. glomerata. **'Variegata'** is an evergreen, tuft-forming, perennial grass. **H** 3ft (1m), **S** 8–10in (20–25cm). Silver-striped, red-green leaves arise from tufted rootstock. In summer bears panicles of densely clustered, awned, purplish-green spikelets. Z5–9 H9–5.

DACTYLORHIZA
ORCHIDACEAE

See also ORCHIDS.

D. elata, syn. *Orchis elata* (Marsh orchid). Deciduous, terrestrial orchid. **H** 3½ft (1.1m). Spikes of pink or purple flowers, ½–¾in (1–2cm) long, are borne in spring–summer. Lance-shaped leaves, 6–10in (15–25cm) long, are spotted with brownish-purple and arranged spirally on stem. Requires shade outdoors; keep pot plants partially shaded in summer. Z6–8 H8–6.

D. foliosa, syn. *D. maderensis, Orchis maderensis,* illus. p.265.

D. maderensis. See *D. foliosa.*

C

DAHLIA
COMPOSITAE/ASTERACEAE

Genus of bushy, summer- and fall-flowering, tuberous perennials, grown as bedding plants or for their flower heads, which are good for cutting or exhibition. Dwarf forms are used for mass-planting and are also suitable for containers. Needs a sunny position and well-drained soil. All apart from dwarf forms require staking. After flowering, lift tubers and store in a frost-free place; replant once all frost danger has passed. In frost-free areas, plants may be left in ground as normal herbaceous perennials, but they benefit from regular propagation to maintain vigor. Propagate dwarf forms by seed sown under glass in late winter, others in spring by seed, basal shoot cuttings or division of tubers. Dahlias may be subject to attack by aphids, red spider mite and thrips. In recent years, powdery mildew has become a problem in certain areas, and spraying is essential. Dahlias also succumb quickly to virus infection. See also feature panel pp.396–98.

Border dahlias
Prolific and long-flowering, various species of *Dahlia* have been hybridized and, with constant breeding and selection, have developed into many forms and have a wide color range (although there is no blue). Shoots may be stopped, or pinched out, to promote vigorous growth and a bushy shape. Spread measurements depend on the amount of stopping carried out and the time at which it is done: early stopping encourages a broader shape, stopping later in the growing season results in a taller plant with much less spread, even in the same cultivar. Leaves are generally mid-green and divided into oval leaflets, some with rounded tips and some with toothed margins. Each flower head is referred to horticulturally as a flower, even though it does in fact comprise a large number of individual flowers. This horticultural usage has been followed in the descriptions below. All forms with flower heads to 6in (15cm) across are suitable for cutting; those suitable for exhibition are so noted.

Groups and flower sizes
Dahlias are divided into groups, according to the size and type of their flower heads, although the latter may vary in color and shape depending on soil and weather conditions. The groups are: (1) single; (2) anemone; (3) collerette; (4) water-lily; (5) decorative; (6) ball; (7) pompon; (8) cactus; (9) semi-cactus; (10) miscellaneous; (11) fimbriated; (12) single orchid; (13) double orchid. For illustrations and descriptions see p.396. Certain groups have been subdivided; flower sizes are as follows:

Groups 4, 5, 8 and 9
A—giant-flowered; usually over 10in (25cm) in diameter. B—large-flowered; usually 8–10in (20–25cm) in diameter. C—medium-flowered; usually 6–8in (15–20cm) in diameter. D—small-flowered; usually 4–6in (10–15cm) in diameter. E—miniature-flowered; usually not exceeding 4in (10cm) in diameter.

Group 6
A—small ball dahlias; usually 4–6in (10–15cm) in diameter. B—miniature ball dahlias; usually 2–4in (5–10cm) in diameter.

Group 7
Pompon dahlias; not exceeding 2in (5cm) in diameter.

D. **'Akita'** (illus. p. 398). Miscellaneous dahlia. **H** 4ft (1.2m), **S** 2ft (60cm). In summer and fall produces dark crimson to red flowers, to 5in (13cm) across, with yellow centers. The reverses of the petals are tipped white. Z9–11 H11–1.

D. **'Alva's Supreme'** (illus. p.398). Giant-flowered decorative dahlia. **H** 4ft (1.2m), **S** 2ft (60cm). Produces yellow flowers in summer–fall. Is suitable for exhibition. Z9–11 H11–1.

D. **'Anniversary Ball'**, syn. *D.* 'Brookfield Enid'. Miniature ball dahlia. **H** 3ft (1m), **S** 2ft (60cm). Produces lilac and pink flowers in summer–fall. Z9–11 H12–1.

D. **'Appetiser'**. Small-flowered semi-cactus dahlia. **H** 4ft (1.2m), **S** 2ft (60cm). Produces yellow-and-pink flowers in summer–fall. Z9–11 H12–1.

D. **'Arabian Night'** (illus. p.397). Small-flowered decorative dahlia. **H** 4ft (1.2m), **S** 1½ft (50cm). Has dark green leaves. Double, dark burgundy-red flowers are borne in summer–fall. Z9–11 H11–1.

D. **'Aranka'**. Collerette dahlia. **H** 4ft (1.2m), **S** 2ft (60cm). Produces flowers, with white-tipped, dark pink outer petals, white inner petals and yellow centers, in summer–fall. Z9–11 H12–1.

D. **'Autumn Fairy'**. Miniature-flowered semi-cactus dahlia. **H** 16in (40cm), **S** 12in (30cm). Soft orange flowers, with darker centers, are produced from mid-summer to fall. Z9–11 H12–1.

D. **'Avoca Cree'**. Small-flowered semi-cactus dahlia. **H** 5ft (1.5m), **S** 2ft (60cm). Produces masses of bright orange flowers in summer–fall. Is good for cutting. Z9–11 H12–1.

D. **'Avoca Kiowa'**. Small-flowered semi-cactus dahlia. **H** 4ft (1.2m), **S** 2ft (60cm). Produces masses of lavender-tipped, pale yellow flowers in summer–fall. Is good for cutting. Z9–11 H12–1.

D. **'Barry Williams'**. Medium-flowered decorative dahlia. **H** 4ft (1.2m), **S** 2ft (60cm). Bears pink-and-yellow flowers in summer–fall. Z9–11 H12–1.

D. **'Berwick Wood'** (illus. p.397). Medium-flowered decorative dahlia. **H** 4½ft (1.3m), **S** 2ft (60cm). In summer–fall produces dark-centered, purple flowers on strong stems. Z9–11 H11–1.

D. **'Bicentenary'**. Medium-flowered decorative dahlia. **H** 4ft (1.2m), **S** 2ft (60cm). In summer–fall produces dark orange flowers, fading to pale orange at the tips. Is good for cutting. Z9–11 H12–1.

D. **'Biddenham Sunset'** (illus. p. 398). Small-flowered decorative dahlia. **H** 3½ft (1.1m), **S** 2ft (60cm). Orange-red flowers are borne in mid-summer and fall. Z9–11 H11–1.

D. **'Bishop of Auckland'** (illus. p.397). Single dahlia. **H** 32in (80cm), **S** 18in (45cm). Produces matt, blackish-green leaves and open-centered, single, dusky-red flowers from mid-summer to fall. Z9–11 H11–1.

D. **'Bishop of Llandaff'** (illus. p.398). Miscellaneous dahlia. **H** 3ft (1m), **S** 18in (45cm). Has bronze-green leaves and open-centered, semidouble, dark red flowers in summer–fall. Is excellent as a bedding plant. Z9–11 H11–1.

D. **'Bishop of York'** (illus. p.398). Single dahlia. **H** 32in (80cm), **S** 18in (45cm).

Produces dark purple leaves and open-centered, single, orange-blushed, golden flowers from mid-summer to fall. Z9–11 H11–1.

D. **'B.J. Beauty'** (illus. p.396). Medium-flowered decorative dahlia. **H** 4ft (1.2m), **S** 2ft (60cm). Double, white flowers are borne on strong stems in summer–fall. Z9–11 H11–1.

D. **'Black Narcissus'** (illus. p. 398). Medium-flowered semi-cactus dahlia. **H** 5ft (1.5m), **S** 2ft (60cm). Produces intensely dark red blooms in summer–fall. Z9–11 H11–1.

D. **'Brian's Dream'** (illus. p.397). Miniature-flowered decorative dahlia. **H** 3–4ft (1–1.2m), **S** 2ft (60cm). Produces creamy-white flowers with the tips of the petals suffused purplish-pink, in summer–fall. Z9–11 H11–1.

D. **'Brookfield Enid'**. See *D.* 'Anniversary Ball'.

D. **'Butterball'**. Miniature-flowered decorative dahlia. **H** 2ft (60cm), **S** 1ft (30cm). Produces bright yellow flowers in early summer. Z9–11 H12–1.

D. **'Café au Lait'** (illus. p.396). Giant-flowered decorative dahlia. **H** 36in (90cm), **S** 24in (60cm). Cream flowers that merge into pale peach in centers are borne from mid-summer to fall. Z9–11 H11–1.

D. **'Cameo'**. Small-flowered water-lily dahlia. **H** 30in (75cm), **S** 18in (45cm). Cream flowers, with yellow bases, are produced from mid-summer to fall. Z9–11 H12–1.

D. **'Candy Cupid'**. Miniature ball dahlia. **H** 3½ft (1.1m), **S** 2ft (60cm). In summer and fall bears lavender-pink flowers that are good for exhibition. Z9–11 H12–1.

D. **'Carolina Moon'** (illus. p.397). Small-flowered decorative dahlia. **H** 4ft (1.2m), **S** 2ft (60cm). Lilac-edged, white flowers are produced from mid-summer to fall. Z9–11 H11–1.

D. **'Charlie Dimmock'** (illus. p. 398). Small-flowered water-lily dahlia. **H** 5½ft (1.6m), **S** 2ft (60cm). Produces apricot flowers on a pale yellow ground, in summer–fall. Z9–11 H11–1.

D. **'Chat Noir'**. Medium-flowered semi-cactus dahlia. **H** 3ft (1m), **S** 2ft (60cm). Produces deep reddish-black flowers from mid-summer to fall. Z9–11 H12–1.

D. **'Cherokee Beauty'**. Giant-flowered decorative dahlia. **H** 4½ft (1.3m), **S** 24–32in (60–80cm). In summer–fall has pink flowers. Z9–11 H12–1.

D. **'Cherwell Skylark'**. Small-flowered semi-cactus dahlia. **H** 3ft (1m), **S** 20–24in (50–60cm). Bears orange-flushed, salmon-pink blooms in summer–fall. Z9–11 H12–1.

D. **'Chimborazo'** (illus. p. 398). Collerette dahlia. **H** 3½ft (1.1m), **S** 2ft (60cm). Leaves are glossy, dark green. Flowers have red, outer petals and yellow, inner petals, in summer–fall. Is good for exhibition. Z9–11 H11–1.

D. **'Clair de Lune'**. Collerette dahlia. **H** 3½ft (1.1m), **S** 2ft (60cm). Flowers have lemon-yellow, outer petals and paler yellow, inner petals, in summer–fall. Is good for exhibition. Z9–11 H12–1.

D. coccinea (illus. p.397). Tuberous-rooted herbaceous perennial. **H** 6–10ft (2–3m), **S** 3–6ft (1–2m). From summer to late fall produces sprays of single, yellow, orange-red, maroon or purple-red flowers, 2–3in (5–8cm) across. Is a parent of many garden dahlias. Z9–11 H11–1.

D. **'Coltness Gem'**. Well-branched, erect, bushy, tuberous perennial, grown as an annual. **H** and **S** 18in (45cm). Has deeply lobed leaves and daisylike, single flower heads in many colors throughout summer until fall frosts. Z9–11 H12–1.

D. **'Comet'** (illus. p. 398). Anemone dahlia. **H** 3½ft (1.1m), **S** 2ft (60cm). Leaves are glossy, dark green. Dark red flowers are produced in summer–fall. Z9–11 H11–1.

D. **'Cornel'** (illus. p.397). Small-flowered ball dahlia. **H** 4ft (1.2m), **S** 2ft (60cm). Deep maroon-red flowers are produced from mid-summer to fall. Z9–11 H11–1.

D. **'Cottesmore'**. Medium-flowered water-lily dahlia. **H** 3½ft (1.1m), **S** 2ft (60cm). Produces purplish-pink flowers, with yellow shading at the petal bases, in summer–fall. Z9–11 H12–1.

D. **'Currant Cream'**. Small ball dahlia. **H** 4ft (1.2m), **S** 2ft (60cm). In summer–fall produces dark pink flowers with the pink-and-white petal bases. Is good for cutting. Z9–11 H12–1.

D. **Dahlietta Series 'Surprise Kelly'**, illus. p.327.

D. **'Dancing Queen'**. Small-flowered semi-cactus dahlia. **H** 3½ft (1.1m), **S** 2ft (60cm). In summer–fall produces pink flowers, with deeper pink centers. Petals are primrose-yellow at the bases. Z9–11 H12–1.

D. **'Dandy'**, illus. p.327.

D. **'Davenport Sunlight'**. Medium-flowered semi-cactus dahlia. **H** 4ft (1.2m), **S** 2ft (60cm). Has bright yellow flowers in summer–fall. Is good for exhibition. Z9–11 H12–1.

D. **'Deborah's Kiwi'**. Small-flowered cactus dahlia. **H** 3½ft (1.1m), **S** 2ft (60cm). Produces pink flowers, with white bases to the petals, in summer–fall. Z9–11 H12–1.

D. **'Demi Schneider'**. Collerette dahlia. **H** 5ft (1.5m), **S** 2ft (60cm). In summer–fall produces single, red flowers with yellow centers. Z9–11 H12–1.

D. **'Downham Royal'**. Miniature-flowered ball dahlia. **H** 4ft (1.2m), **S** 2ft (60cm). Produces deep claret-red flowers from mid-summer to fall. Z9–11 H12–1.

D. **'Dutch Triumph'**. Large-flowered water-lily dahlia. **H** 3½ft (1.1m), **S** 2ft (60cm). Bears yellow-pink flowers in summer–fall. Z9–11 H12–1.

D. **'East Anglian'**. Small-flowered decorative dahlia. **H** 3ft (1m), **S** 2ft (60cm). Has orange-yellow flowers in summer–fall. Z9–11 H12–1.

D. **'Easter Sunday'**. Collerette dahlia. **H** 3ft (1m), **S** 2ft (60cm). Leaves are glossy, dark green. Flowers have white, inner and outer petals and dark yellow centers, in summer–fall. Is good for exhibition. Z9–11 H12–1.

D. **'Ellen Huston'** (illus. p. 398). Dwarf bedding dahlia. **H** 16in (40cm), **S** 18in (45cm). Has dark bronzed leaves and produces rich orange flowers from mid-summer to fall. Z9–11 H11–1.

D. **'Embrace'**. Small-flowered cactus dahlia. **H** 3½ft (1.1m), **S** 2ft (60cm). Pale orange flowers are borne from mid-summer to fall. Z9–11 H12–1.

D. **'Eveline'** (illus. p.396). Small-flowered decorative dahlia. **H** 3ft (1m), **S** 2ft (60cm). White flowers, with a touch of purple at the centers and petal tips, are produced from mid-summer to fall. Z9–11 H11–1.

D. **'Fascination'**. Dwarf miscellaneous

dahlia. **H** 18in (45cm), **S** 12in (30cm). Has light purple flowers in summer–fall. Is useful for bedding. Z9–11 H12–1.

D. 'Franz Kafka' (illus. p.397). Miniature-flowered pompon dahlia. **H** 32in (80cm), **S** 22in (55cm). Produces lilac flowers from mid-summer to fall. Z9–11 H11–1.

D. 'Fusion'. Small-flowered decorative dahlia. **H** 3ft (1m), **S** 2ft (60cm). In summer–fall produces white flowers, the outer petals flushed pale pink, the inner petals veined purple-violet. Has bronze-tinged, dark green foliage. Z9–11 H12–1.

D. 'Gallery Art Deco'. Miniature-flowered decorative dahlia. **H** 12–18in (30–45cm), **S** 8in (20cm). Produces dark green leaves and bears double, red-centered, deep orange flowers from mid-summer to fall. Z9–11 H12–1.

D. 'Gallery Art Fair', illus. p.298.

D. 'Gallery Art Nouveau' (illus. p.397). Miniature-flowered decorative dahlia. **H** 12–18in (30–45cm), **S** 8in (20cm). From mid-summer to fall produces double, pink and purple flowers above dark green foliage. Z9–11 H11–1.

D. 'Gateshead Festival'. See *D.* 'Peach Melba'.

D. 'Gay Princess'. Small-flowered decorative dahlia. **H** 4ft (1.2m), **S** 2ft (60cm). Produces lilac-lavender flowers in summer–fall. Z9–11 H12–1.

D. 'Geerling's Moonlight'. Medium-flowered semi-cactus dahlia. **H** 4¹⁄₂ft (1.3m), **S** 2ft (60cm). Produces brilliant yellow flowers in summer–fall. Z9–11 H12–1.

D. 'Gerrie Hoek' (illus. p.397). Small-flowered water-lily dahlia. **H** 3ft (1m), **S** 2ft (60cm). Abundant, rose-pink flowers are borne on sturdy stems from mid-summer to fall. Z9–11 H11–1.

D. 'Gilwood Terry G'. Small-flowered semi-cactus dahlia. **H** 4¹⁄₂ft (1.3m), **S** 3–4ft (1–1.2m). Flowers have bronze-tinted, orange outer petals and yellow inner petals, borne in summer–fall. Is excellent for cutting. Z9–11 H12–1.

D. 'Giraffe'. Double orchid dahlia. **H** 3ft (1m), **S** 2ft (60cm). In summer–fall has spotted, yellow-bronze flowers. Is good for cutting. Z9–11 H12–1.

D. 'Glorie van Heemstede'. Small-flowered water-lily dahlia. **H** 4¹⁄₂ft (1.35m), **S** 2ft (60cm). Clear yellow flowers are produced on sturdy stems from mid-summer to fall. Z9–11 H12–1.

D. 'Grenidor Pastelle'. Medium-flowered semi-cactus dahlia. **H** 4¹⁄₂ft (1.3m), **S** 2ft (60cm). Bears salmon-pink flowers, with cream petal bases, in summer–fall. Is good for exhibition. Z9–11 H12–1.

D. 'Gwyneth'. Small-flowered water-lily dahlia. **H** 6ft (1.8m), **S** 2ft (60cm). Bears bronze-tinted, orange flowers in summer–fall. Is good for cutting. Z9–11 H12–1.

D. 'Hamari Accord' (illus. p. 398). Large-flowered semi-cactus dahlia. **H** 4ft (1.2m), **S** 2ft (60cm). Has clear yellow flowers held on strong stems in summer–fall. Is good for exhibition. Z9–11 H11–1.

D. 'Hamari Gold' (illus. p. 398). Giant-flowered decorative dahlia. **H** 3¹⁄₂ft (1.1m), **S** 2ft (60cm). Has golden orange-bronze flowers in summer–fall. Is suitable for exhibition. Z9–11 H11–1.

D. 'Hamari Katrina' (illus. p. 398). Large-flowered semi-cactus dahlia. **H** 4ft (1.2m), **S** 2ft (60cm). Bears deep butter-yellow

flowers in summer–fall. Is good for exhibition. Z9–11 H11–1.

D. Happy Single First Love ('HS First Love'), illus. p. 398. Single dahlia. **H** 24in (60cm), **S** 18in (45cm). Produces dark purple leaves. Peach flowers, with a central red ring, are produced from mid-summer to fall. Z9–11 H11–1.

D. Happy Single Juliet ('HS Juliet'). Single dahlia. **H** 24in (60cm), **S** 18in (45cm). Produces fuchsia-pink flowers, from mid-summer to fall, and dark purple leaves. Z9–11 H12–1.

D. Happy Single Kiss ('HS Kiss'). Single dahlia. **H** 24in (60cm), **S** 18in (45cm). Flowers with salmon-pink petals that blend into yellow at the center with a dark brown eye are produced from mid-summer to fall above dark purple foliage. Z9–11 H12–1.

D. Happy Single Romeo ('HS Romeo'), illus. p.306.

D. Happy Single Wink ('HS Wink'), illus. p.311. Single dahlia. **H** 24in (60cm), **S** 18in (45cm). Produces lilac-pink flowers, each with a central, red ring around a dark eye, from mid-summer to fall. Leaves are dark purple.

D. 'Harvest Inflammation', illus. p.414.

D. 'Hayley Jayne'. Small-flowered semi-cactus dahlia. **H** 3¹⁄₂ft (1.1m), **S** 2ft (60cm). Produces flowers that are white at base with purple-red tips, in summer–fall. Is good for exhibition. Z9–11 H12–1.

D. 'Hexton Copper' (illus. p. 398). Small ball dahlia. **H** 3¹⁄₂ft (1.1m), **S** 2ft (60cm). In summer–fall has orange flowers. Z9–11 H11–1.

D. 'Hillcrest Jessica' (illus. p.397). Large-flowered decorative dahlia. **H** 4ft (1.25m), **S** 2ft (60cm). Bears red-purple flowers in summer–fall. Z9–11 H11–1.

D. 'Hillcrest Royal' (illus. p.386). Medium-flowered cactus dahlia. **H** 3¹⁄₂ft (1.1m), **S** 2ft (60cm). In summer–fall has rich purple flowers, with incurving petals, held on strong stems.

D. 'Hillcrest Ultra'. Small-flowered decorative dahlia. **H** 4ft (1.2m), **S** 2ft (60cm). Produces flowers, with pink outer petals and lemon-yellow inner petals, in summer–fall. Z9–11 H12–1.

D. 'Honka'. Single orchid dahlia. **H** 3–4ft (1–1.2m), **S** 2ft (60cm). Has masses of star-shaped, bright yellow flowers, with darker yellow centers, in summer–fall. Is good for cutting. Z9–11 H12–1.

D. 'HS First Love'. See *D.* Happy Single First Love.

D. 'HS Juliet'. See *D.* Happy Single Juliet.

D. 'HS Kiss'. See *D.* Happy Single Kiss.

D. 'HS Romeo'. See *D.* Happy Single Romeo.

D. 'HS Wink'. See *D.* Happy Single Wink.

D. 'Jaldec Joker'. Small-flowered semi-cactus dahlia. **H** 3¹⁄₂ft (1.1m), **S** 2ft (60cm). In summer–fall has bright orange-red flowers, shading to yellow at the bases. Petals are tipped white. Z9–11 H12–1.

D. 'Jeanette Carter'. Miniature-flowered decorative dahlia. **H** 3¹⁄₂ft (1.1m), **S** 2ft (60cm). Bears yellow flowers, sometimes flushed pink in the centers, in summer–fall. Z9–11 H12–1.

D. 'Jean Fairs'. Miscellaneous dahlia. **H** 4¹⁄₂ft (1.3m), **S** 2ft (60cm). In summer–fall produces semidouble, orange-yellow flowers, the yellow outer petals strongly flushed orange, the inner petals orange-red. Z9–11 H12–1.

D. 'Jescot Julie'. Double orchid dahlia. **H** 24in (60cm), **S** 18in (45cm). Has sparse, mid-green foliage and orange-purple flowers, with purple-backed petals, in summer–fall. Z9–11 H12–1.

D. 'Jim Branigan'. Large-flowered semi-cactus dahlia. **H** 4¹⁄₂ft (1.3m), **S** 2ft (60cm). Bright red flowers are held well above the foliage in summer–fall. Is good for exhibition. Z9–11 H12–1.

D. 'Julie One'. Double orchid dahlia. **H** 4ft (1.2m), **S** 2ft (60cm). In summer–fall produces bronze-purple flowers. Is good for cutting. Z9–11 H12–1.

D. 'Jura' (illus. p.396). Small-flowered semi-cactus dahlia. **H** 4ft (1.2m), **S** 2ft (60cm). In summer–fall produces purple-tipped, white flowers. Z9–11 H11–1.

D. 'Kaiser Waltzer'. See *D.* 'Kaiserwalzer'.

D. 'Kaiserwalzer', syn. *D.* 'Kaiser Waltzer'. Collerette dahlia. **H** 3¹⁄₂ft (1.1m), **S** 2ft (60cm). Produces flowers, with large, red outer petals and narrower, yellow inner petals, in summer–fall. Is good as a border plant. Z9–11 H12–1.

D. 'Karma Amanda'. Small-flowered decorative dahlia. **H** 34in (85cm), **S** 24in (60cm). From mid-summer to fall produces white flowers with lilac petal tips and darker lilac coloring extending towards the base. Z9–11 H12–1.

D. 'Karma Choc' (illus. p.397). Small-flowered decorative dahlia. **H** 4ft (1.2m), **S** 2ft (60cm). Has black-green leaves. Velvety, dark maroon flowers are produced from mid-summer to fall. Z9–11 H11–1.

D. 'Kathryn's Cupid'. Miniature ball dahlia. **H** 4ft (1.2m), **S** 2ft (60cm). In summer–fall produces peach flowers that are good for exhibition. Z9–11 H12–1.

D. 'Kenora Sunset'. Medium-flowered semi-cactus dahlia. **H** 4ft (1.2m), **S** 2ft (60cm). Bears bicolored, brilliant red and yellow blooms in summer–fall. Z9–11 H12–1.

D. 'Kenora Superb' (illus. p.398). Giant-flowered semi-cactus dahlia. **H** 4ft (1.2m), **S** 2ft (60cm). Produces bright orange-and-yellow flowers in summer–fall. Z9–11 H11–1.

D. 'Klondike', syn. *D.* 'Klondyke'. Large-flowered semi-cactus dahlia. **H** 4ft (1.2m), **S** 2ft (60cm). Produces white flowers in summer–fall. Z9–11 H12–1.

D. 'Klondyke'. See *D.* 'Klondike'.

D. 'Lakeland Sunset'. Small-flowered cactus dahlia. **H** 5¹⁄₂ft (1.65m), **S** 2ft (60cm). Bears yellow-orange flowers, with brighter yellow centers, in late summer–fall. Is good for cutting. Z9–11 H12–1.

D. 'Lavender Athalie'. Small-flowered cactus dahlia. **H** 4ft (1.2m), **S** 2ft (60cm). Has glossy, dark green leaves and bears soft lilac-lavender flowers in summer–fall. Is good for exhibition. Z9–11 H12–1.

D. 'Lilac Marston' (illus. p.397). Miniature-flowered decorative dahlia. **H** 4ft (1.2m), **S** 2ft (60cm). Bears warm lilac flowers from mid-summer to fall. Z9–11 H11–1.

D. 'Lilac Time'. Medium-flowered decorative dahlia. **H** 4ft (1.2m), **S** 2ft (60cm). Produces white-edged, lilac flowers from mid-summer to fall. Z9–11 H12–1.

D. 'Mabel Ann'. Giant-flowered decorative dahlia. **H** 3ft (1m), **S** 2ft (60cm). Apricot flowers, with pale yellow centers, are produced from mid-summer to fall. Z9–11 H12–1.

D. 'Marie Schnugg'. Single orchid dahlia. **H** 3¹⁄₂ft (1.1m), **S** 2ft (60cm). Bears star-like, red flowers in summer–fall. Is good as a border plant as well as for cutting. Z9–11 H12–1.

D. 'Mark Hardwick'. Giant-flowered decorative dahlia. **H** 3¹⁄₂ft (1.1m), **S** 2ft (60cm). Bears bright, deep yellow flowers, on strong stems, in summer–fall. Is good for exhibition. Z9–11 H12–1.

D. 'Mary Richards'. Small-flowered decorative dahlia. **H** 4ft (1.2m), **S** 2ft (60cm). In summer–fall produces white flowers strongly suffused lavender-pink. Z9–11 H12–1.

D. 'Mermaid of Zennor' (illus. p.397). Single dahlia. **H** 30in (75cm), **S** 2ft (60cm). In summer–fall produces lavender flowers above delicate foliage. Is good as a border plant. Z9–11 H11–1.

D. 'Minley Carol'. Pompon dahlia. **H** 3ft (1m), **S** 2ft (60cm). Pale orange flowers, with a hint of red at the petal tips, are produced from mid-summer to fall. Z9–11 H12–1.

D. 'Mi Wong'. Pompon dahlia. **H** 3¹⁄₂ft (1.1m), **S** 2ft (60cm). Bears white flowers, suffused pink, in summer–fall. Is good for exhibition. Z9–11 H12–1.

D. 'Moonfire'. Dwarf, single dahlia. **H** 18in (45cm), **S** 12in (30cm). Produces dark foliage before yellow-red flowers are produced in summer–fall. Is very good as a container plant and in a border. Z9–11 H12–1.

D. 'Moonglow' (illus. p. 398). Large-flowered semi-cactus dahlia. **H** 3ft (1m), **S** 2ft (60cm). Pale creamy-yellow flowers are produced from mid-summer to fall. Z9–11 H11–1.

D. 'Moor Place'. Pompon dahlia. **H** 3ft (1m), **S** 2ft (60cm). Leaves are glossy, dark green. Has red-purple flowers in summer–fall. Is a good exhibition cultivar. Z9–11 H12–1.

D. 'Mum's Lipstick'. Fimbriated cactus dahlia. **H** 3–4ft (1–1.2m), **S** 2ft (60cm). Bears red-tipped, yellow flowers in summer–fall. Z9–11 H12–1.

D. 'Nargold'. Medium-flowered semi-cactus dahlia. **H** 3ft (90cm), **S** 2ft (60cm). Produces rich orange flowers, with fringed petals, from summer to fall. Z9–11 H12–1.

D. 'Natal' (illus. p.397). Pompon dahlia. **H** 3ft (90cm), **S** 2ft (60cm). Dark red flowers are produced from mid-summer to fall. Z9–11 H11–1.

D. 'New Dimension' (illus. p.397). Small-flowered semi-cactus dahlia. **H** 30in (75cm), **S** 16in (40cm). Produces light rose-pink flowers, with pale yellow centers, from mid-summer to fall. Z9–11 H11–1.

D. 'Noreen'. Pompon dahlia. **H** 3ft (1m), **S** 2ft (60cm). In summer–fall produces dark pinkish-purple flowers. Is good for exhibition. Z9–11 H12–1.

D. 'NZ's Robert'. Miniature water-lily dahlia. **H** 20in (50cm), **S** 12in (30cm). Produces red-pink flowers, with greeny-yellow centers, in summer–fall. Is a good container plant. Z9–11 H12–1.

D. 'Onesta'. Small-flowered water-lily dahlia. **H** 4ft (1.2m), **S** 2ft (60cm). Produces masses of flowers, with dark pink inner petals fading to pale pink outer petals, in summer–fall. Is good for cutting. Z9–11 H12–1.

D. 'Onslow Renown' (illus. p.398). Large-flowered semi-cactus dahlia. **H** 4ft (1.2m),

S 2ft (60cm). Bears yellowish-orange flowers in summer–fall. Z9–11 H11–1.
***D.* 'Oosterbeck Remembered'** (illus. p. 398). Small-flowered semi-cactus dahlia. **H** 4ft (1.2m), **S** 2ft (60cm). Bears dark orange flowers, with bright yellow inner petals, in summer–fall. Is good for cutting. Z9–11 H11–1.
***D.* 'Orange Berger's Record'.** Medium-flowered semi-cactus dahlia. **H** 4ft (1.2m), **S** 2ft (60cm). Bears yellowish-orange flowers in summer–fall. Z9–11 H12–1.
***D.* 'Park Princess'.** Small-flowered cactus dahlia. **H** 24in (60cm), **S** 18in (45cm). Pink flowers are borne in profusion from mid-summer to fall. Z9–11 H12–1.
***D.* 'Peach Melba',** syn. *D.* 'Gateshead Festival'. Small-flowered decorative dahlia. **H** 4ft (1.2m), **S** 2ft (60cm). In summer–fall bears peach to orange flowers with lemon-yellow petal bases. Is good for exhibition. Z9–11 H12–1.
***D.* 'Pearl of Heemstede'.** Small-flowered water-lily dahlia. **H** 3ft (1m), **S** 18in (45cm). Produces pale silvery-pink flowers on long, thin stems in summer–fall. Is extremely free-flowering. Z9–11 H12–1.
***D.* 'Pink Jupiter'.** Giant-flowered semi-cactus dahlia. **H** 4½ft (1.3m), **S** 2ft (60cm). In summer–fall produces deep pinkish-mauve flowers. Is good for exhibition. Z9–11 H12–1.
***D.* 'Pink Shirley Alliance'.** Small-flowered cactus dahlia. **H** 4ft (1.2m), **S** 2ft (60cm). Has soft lilac-pink flowers in summer–fall. Z9–11 H12–1.
***D.* 'Pink Symbol'.** Medium-flowered semi-cactus dahlia. **H** 3–4ft (1–1.2m), **S** 2ft (60cm). Bears pink flowers in summer–fall. Is good for exhibition. Z9–11 H12–1.
***D.* 'Pontiac'.** Small-flowered cactus dahlia. **H** 3ft (1m), **S** 2ft (60cm). Leaves are glossy, dark green. Bears dark pinkish-purple flowers in summer–fall. Z9–11 H12–1.
***D.* 'Pooh'.** Collerette dahlia. **H** 3ft (1m), **S** 2ft (60cm). Produces yellow-tipped, scarlet flowers, with central, yellow collars, from mid-summer to fall. Z9–11 H12–1.
***D.* 'Preston Park'** (illus. p.398). Dwarf single dahlia. **H** 18in (45cm), **S** 12in (30cm). Bedding plant with nearly black foliage. In summer–fall bears bright scarlet flowers, with prominent yellow anthers, on short stems. Z9–11 H11–1.
***D.* 'Rhonda'.** Pompon dahlia. **H** 3ft (1m), **S** 2ft (60cm). In summer–fall produces whitish-lilac flowers. Good for exhibition. Z9–11 H12–1.
***D.* 'Rip City'.** Small-flowered semi-cactus dahlia. **H** 3ft (1m), **S** 2ft (60cm). Produces maroon flowers, with darker maroon-black centers, from mid-summer to fall. Z9–11 H12–1.
***D.* 'Roxy'** (illus. p.397). Single dahlia. **H** 18in (45cm), **S** 16in (40cm). Bedding plant with magenta-purple flowers, borne from mid-summer to fall, and dark green-black leaves. Z9–11 H11–1.
***D.* 'Ruskin Charlotte'** (illus. p.397). Large-flowered semi-cactus dahlia. **H** 3ft (1m), **S** 2ft (60cm). Lavender-pink flowers, with white bases, are produced from mid-summer to fall. Z9–11 H11–1.
***D.* 'Ryecroft Gem'** (illus. p.397). Miniature-flowered decorative dahlia. **H** 3ft (90cm), **S** 2ft (60cm). In summer–fall produces violet-margined, lavender-pink flowers. Is good for exhibition. Z9–11 H11–1.
***D.* 'Sascha'** (illus. p.397). Small-flowered water-lily dahlia. **H** 6ft (1.8m), **S** 2ft (60cm). Bears bright purple-pink flowers, fading to paler purple-pink towards the margins, in summer–fall. Z9–11 H11–1.
***D.* 'Shandy'.** Small-flowered semi-cactus dahlia. **H** 3½ft (1.1m), **S** 2ft (60cm). Produces pale orange-brown flowers in summer–fall. Z9–11 H12–1.
***D.* 'Shirley Alliance'.** Small-flowered cactus dahlia. **H** 4½ft (1.3m), **S** 2ft (60cm). In summer–fall bears soft orange flowers with a gold base to each petal. Is good for exhibition. Z9–11 H12–1.
***D.* 'Sir Alf Ramsey'.** Giant-flowered decorative dahlia. **H** 3½ft (1.1m), **S** 2ft (60cm). In summer–fall produces lavender-pink flowers, with white petal bases. Z9–11 H12–1.
***D.* 'Small World'** (illus. p.396). Pompon dahlia. **H** 3ft (1m), **S** 2ft (60cm). Leaves are glossy, dark green. Has white flowers in summer–fall. Is suitable for exhibition. Z9–11 H11–1.
***D.* 'Smokey O'.** Medium-flowered semi-cactus dahlia. **H** 3–4ft (1–1.2m), **S** 2ft (60cm). Produces dark pink flowers in summer–fall. Z9–11 H12–1.
***D.* 'So Dainty'** (illus. p. 398). Miniature-flowered semi-cactus dahlia. **H** 3½ft (1.1m), **S** 2ft (60cm). Produces bronze-colored flowers in summer–fall that are suitable for exhibition. Z9–11 H11–1.
***D.* 'Sorbet'** (illus. p.397). Medium-flowered semi-cactus dahlia. **H** 4ft (1.2m), **S** 2ft (60cm). Produces white flowers, with dark purple-red tips, from mid-summer to fall. Z9–11 H11–1.
***D.* 'Swanvale'.** Small-flowered decorative dahlia. **H** 3½ft (1.1m), **S** 2ft (60cm). Bears yellow flowers in summer–fall. Z9–11 H12–1.
***D.* 'Tiptoe'** (illus. p.397). Miniature-flowered decorative dahlia. **H** 3ft (90cm), **S** 2ft (60cm). Wine-red flowers, with white-tipped petals, are borne from mid-summer to fall. Z9–11 H11–1.
***D.* 'Trelyn Kiwi'** (illus. p.396). Small-flowered semi-cactus dahlia. **H** 4ft (1.2m), **S** 2ft (60cm). Produces pink-flushed, white flowers, with darker pink central petals, in summer–fall. Z9–11 H11–1.
***D.* 'Trengrove Millennium'** (illus. p. 398). Medium-flowered decorative dahlia. **H** 4ft (1.2m), **S** 2ft (60cm). Produces yellow flowers in summer–fall. Is suitable for exhibition. Z9–11 H11–1.
***D.* 'Tui Ruth'.** Small-flowered semi-cactus dahlia. **H** 3½ft (1.1m), **S** 2ft (60cm). Produces pink-yellow flowers in summer–fall. Z9–11 H12–1.
***D.* 'Vicky Crutchfield'.** Small-flowered water-lily dahlia. **H** 3ft (1m), **S** 2ft (60cm). Bears pink flowers in summer–fall. Is suitable for exhibition. Z9–11 H12–1.
***D.* 'Vulkan'.** Large-flowered semi-cactus dahlia. **H** 3ft (1m), **S** 2ft (60cm). Scarlet-striped, yellow flowers are borne from mid-summer to fall. Z9–11 H12–1.
***D.* 'Wanda's Capella'.** Giant-flowered decorative dahlia. **H** 4ft (1.2m), **S** 2ft (60cm). Has bright yellow flowers in summer–fall. Is suitable for exhibition. Z9–11 H12–1.
***D.* 'Weston Pirate'.** Miniature-flowered cactus dahlia. **H** 4½ft (1.3m), **S** 20–24in (50–60cm). Produces prolific, semidouble, dark red flowers in summer–fall. Is good for cutting. Z9–11 H12–1.
***D.* 'Weston Spanish Dancer'.** Miniature-flowered cactus dahlia. **H** 3ft (1m), **S** 2ft (60cm). Bright scarlet flowers, with yellow bases, are produced from mid-summer to fall. Is good for exhibition. Z9–11 H12–1.
***D.* 'Whale's Rhonda'.** Pompon dahlia. **H** 3ft (1m), **S** 2ft (60cm). Leaves are glossy, very dark green. In summer–fall has bright purple flowers. Is good for exhibition. Z9–11 H12–1.
***D.* 'White Alva's'** (illus. p.396). Giant-flowered decorative dahlia. **H** 4ft (1.2m), **S** 2ft (60cm). Produces pure white flowers, held well above the foliage on strong stems, in summer–fall. Is good for exhibition. Z9–11 H11–1.
***D.* 'White Ballet'** (illus. p.396). Small-flowered water-lily dahlia. **H** 3ft (1m), **S** 2ft (60cm). Produces pure white flowers in summer–fall. Z9–11 H11–1.
***D.* 'White Klankstad'** (illus. p.396). Small-flowered cactus dahlia. **H** 3½–4ft (1.1–1.2m), **S** 2ft (60cm). Has glossy, dark green leaves and white flowers in summer–fall. Is good for exhibition. Z9–11 H11–1.
***D.* 'White Moonlight'** (illus. p.396). Medium-flowered semi-cactus dahlia. **H** 4ft (1.2m), **S** 2ft (60cm). White flowers are produced on sturdy stems from mid-summer to fall. Z9–11 H11–1.
***D.* 'Wootton Cupid'** (illus. p.397). Miniature ball dahlia. **H** 3½–4ft (1.1–1.2m), **S** 2ft (60cm). Has pink flowers in summer–fall. Is good for exhibition. Z9–11 H11–1.
***D.* 'Wootton Impact',** (illus. p. 398). Medium-flowered semi-cactus dahlia. **H** 4ft (1.2m), **S** 2ft (60cm). Has flowers in shades of bronze, held well above the foliage on strong stems, in summer–fall. Is good for exhibition. Z9–11 H11–1.
***D.* 'Yellow Hammer'** (illus. p. 398). Dwarf, single dahlia. **H** 18in (45cm), **S** 12in (30cm). Has rich yellow flowers in summer–fall. Z9–11 H11–1.
***D.* 'Yelno Enchanted'.** See *D.* 'Yelno Enchantment'.
***D.* 'Yelno Enchantment',** syn. *D.* 'Yelno Enchanted'. Small-flowered water-lily dahlia. **H** 4ft (1.2m), **S** 2ft (60cm). Bears pale pink flowers in summer–fall. Is good for cutting. Z9–11 H12–1.
***D.* 'Yelno Firelight'.** Small-flowered water-lily dahlia. **H** 4ft (1.2m), **S** 2ft (60cm). In summer–fall has red and yellow flowers, with a neat petal formation, held on strong stems. Z9–11 H12–1.
***D.* 'Zorro'** (illus. p. 398). Giant-flowered decorative dahlia. **H** 4ft (1.2m), **S** 2ft (60cm). Bears bright blood-red flowers in summer–fall. Is good for exhibition. Z9–11 H11–1.

DAIS

THYMELAEACEAE

Genus of deciduous, summer-flowering shrubs, grown for their flowers and overall appearance. Requires full sun and well-drained soil. Water container plants well when in full growth, less when leafless. Propagate by seed in spring or by semiripe cuttings in summer.
D. cotinifolia. Deciduous, bushy, neat shrub. **H** and **S** 6–10ft (2–3m). Has small, oval to oblong, lustrous leaves. In summer bears scented, star-shaped, rose-lilac flowers in flattened clusters, 3in (8cm) across. Bark yields fibers strong enough to be used as thread. Z10–11 H12–10.

Daiswa polyphylla. See *Paris polyphylla.*

DANÄE

LILIACEAE/ASPARAGACEAE

Genus of one species of evergreen shrub, with inconspicuous flowers, grown for its flattened, leaflike shoots. Grows in sun or shade and in moist soil. Propagate by seed in fall or by division from fall to spring.
D. racemosa (Alexandrian laurel). Evergreen, arching, dense shrub. **H** and **S** 3ft (1m). Has slender stems, lance-shaped, leaflike, glossy, green shoots and pointed, glossy, bright green "leaves." Occasionally bears spherical, red berries. Z6–9 H9–2.

DAPHNE

THYMELAEACEAE

Genus of evergreen, semievergreen or deciduous shrubs, grown for their usually fragrant, tubular flowers, each with 4 spreading lobes, and, in some species, for their foliage or fruits (seeds are poisonous). Dwarf species and cultivars are good for rock gardens. Most need full sun (although *D. alpina, D. arbuscula* and *D. blagayana* may be grown in partial shade and *D. laureola* tolerates deep shade) and fertile, well-drained but not over-dry soil. Resents being transplanted. Propagate species by seed when fresh or by semiripe cuttings in summer, cultivars by cuttings only. Is susceptible to viruses that cause leaf mottling. ⓘ All parts, including the seed, are highly toxic if ingested, and contact with the sap may irritate skin.
D. alpina (illus. p.333). Deciduous, erect shrub. **H** 20in (50cm), **S** 16in (40cm). Leaves are oval, downy and gray-green. Produces terminal clusters of fragrant, white flowers in late spring. Is suitable for a rock garden.
D. arbuscula, illus. p.351.
D. bholua. Evergreen, occasionally deciduous, upright shrub. **H** 6–12ft (2–4m), **S** 5ft (1.5m). Has leathery, dark green foliage. Terminal clusters of richly fragrant, purplish-pink and white flowers are borne in winter. Z7–9 H9–7. **'Jacqueline Postill',** illus. p.143.
D. blagayana, illus. p.333.
***D. x burkwoodii* 'Somerset',** illus. p.146. **'Somerset Variegated'** is a semievergreen, upright shrub. **H** 5ft (1.5m), **S** 3ft (1m). Bears dense clusters of very fragrant, white-throated, pink flowers in late spring, sometimes again in fall. Narrowly oblong, gray-green leaves are edged with creamy-white or pale yellow. Z4–7 H7–1.
D. cneorum, illus. p.333. **'Eximia'** is an evergreen, prostrate shrub. **H** 4in (10cm), **S** 20in (50cm) or more. Has small, oval, leathery, dark green leaves and, in late spring, terminal clusters of fragrant, white flowers, crimson outside and often pink-flushed within.
D. collina. Evergreen, domed, compact shrub. **H** and **S** 20in (50cm). Oval, dark green leaves densely cover upright branches. Has terminal clusters of small, fragrant, purple-rose flowers in late spring. Is good for a rock garden or shrubbery. Z7–8 H8–7.
D. genkwa (Lilac daphne). Deciduous, upright, open shrub. **H** and **S** 5ft (1.5m). Oval, dark green leaves are bronze when young. Large, faintly scented, lilac flowers are borne from mid- to late spring. Z6–9 H9–6.
D. giraldii. Deciduous, upright shrub. **H** and **S** 2ft (60cm). Clusters of fragrant,

golden-yellow flowers are produced amid oblong, pale blue-green leaves in late spring and early summer and are followed by egg-shaped, red fruits. Z4–8 H8–1.

D. x hendersonii 'Blackthorn Rose', illus. p.334.

D. jasminea, illus. p.350.

D. laureola (Spurge laurel). Evergreen, bushy shrub. **H** 3ft (1m), **S** 5ft (1.5m). Has oblong, dark green leaves. Slightly fragrant, pale green flowers are borne from late winter to early spring, followed by spherical, black fruits. Z7–8 H8–7.

subsp. philippi, illus. p.147.

D. mezereum (February daphne, Mezereon), illus. p.142. Deciduous, upright shrub. **H** 4ft (1.2m), **S** 3ft (1m). Very fragrant, purple and pink flowers clothe the bare stems in late winter and early spring, followed by red fruits. Mature leaves are narrowly oval and dull gray-green. Z5–8 H8–5. **f. alba** (February daphne) has white or creamy-white flowers and yellow fruits.

D. odora (February daphne). Evergreen, bushy shrub. **H** and **S** 5ft (1.5m). Has oval, glossy, dark green leaves and, from mid-winter to early spring, very fragrant, deep purplish-pink-and-white flowers. Z7–9 H9–7. **'Aureomarginata',** illus. p.164.

D. petraea 'Grandiflora', illus. p.351.

D. retusa. See *D. tangutica* Retusa Group.

D. tangutica, syn. *D. retusa.* Evergreen, bushy shrub with sturdy shoots. **H** and **S** 3ft (1m). Narrowly oval, leathery leaves are dark green. Bears clusters of fragrant, white-flushed, purple-pink flowers from mid- to late spring. Z7–9 H9–7. **Retusa Group,** illus. p.146.

DAPHNIPHYLLUM
DAPHNIPHYLLACEAE

Genus of evergreen trees and shrubs, grown for their habit and foliage. Male and female flowers are borne on separate plants. Needs a sheltered position in sun or partial shade and deep, fertile, well-drained but not too dry soil. Propagate by semiripe cuttings in summer.

D. himalaense subsp. macropodum. See *D. macropodum.*

D. macropodum, syn. *D. himalaense* subsp. *macropodum,* illus. p.111.

DARMERA
SYN. PELTIPHYLLUM
SAXIFRAGACEAE

Genus of one species of perennial, grown for its unusual foliage. Makes fine marginal water plants. Grows in sun or shade and requires moist soil. Propagate by division in spring or by seed in fall or spring.

D. peltata, illus. p.438.

DARWINIA
Scent myrtle
MYRTACEAE

Genus of evergreen, spring-flowering shrubs, grown for their flowers and overall appearance. Needs full light and moist, neutral to acid soil, not rich in nitrogen. Water moderately when in full growth, sparingly at other times. Propagate by seed in spring or by semiripe cuttings in late summer. Is difficult to root and to grow in a greenhouse.

D. citriodora. Evergreen, rounded, well-branched shrub. **H** and **S** 2–4ft (60cm–1.2m). Oblong to broadly lance-shaped, blue-green leaves are lemon-scented when bruised. In spring produces pendent, terminal heads of usually 4 small, tubular, yellow or red flowers, each surrounded by 2 red or yellowish bracts. Z9–11 H12–9.

DASYLIRION
DRACAENACEAE/ASPARAGACEAE

Genus of evergreen, palm-like perennials, grown for their foliage and flowers. Male and female flowers are produced on separate plants. Requires well-drained soil and a sunny position. Water freely when in full growth, sparingly at other times. Propagate by seed in spring.

D. texanum (Green Texas spoon, Texas sotol). Evergreen, palm-like, woody-stemmed perennial. **H** 3ft (1m) or more, **S** 10ft (3m). Has a rosette of narrow, drooping, green leaves, 2–3ft (60–90cm) long, with yellowish prickles along margins. Stems, 15ft (5m) long, emerge from center of plant carrying dense, narrow panicles of small, bell-shaped, whitish flowers in summer. Dry, 3-winged fruits develop in fall. Z9–11 H12–1.

DAVALLIA
DAVALLIACEAE

Genus of evergreen or semievergreen, often epiphytic ferns, suitable for pots and baskets. Needs partial shade and fibrous, moist, peaty soil. Cut off fading fronds regularly. Propagate by division in spring or summer or by spores in summer.

D. canariensis (Deer's foot fern, Hare's foot fern). Semievergreen fern. **H** and **S** 12in (30cm). Broadly lance-shaped, mid-green fronds, with triangular pinnae, are produced from a scaly, brown rootstock. Z10–11 H12–10.

D. mariesii. Evergreen fern. **H** 6in (15cm), **S** 9in (23cm). Broadly triangular, delicately divided, leathery, mid-green fronds are produced from a creeping, scaly, brown rootstock. Z9–11 H12–9.

DAVIDIA
CORNACEAE/NYSSACEAE

Genus of one species of deciduous, spring- and summer-flowering tree, grown for its habit and showy, white bracts surrounding insignificant flowers. Needs shelter from strong winds. Requires sun or partial shade and fertile, moist but well-drained soil. Propagate by semiripe cuttings in spring or by seed when ripe in fall.

D. involucrata, illus. p.60.

DECAISNEA
LARDIZABALACEAE

Genus of deciduous, summer-flowering shrubs, grown for their foliage, flowers and sausage-shaped fruits. Requires a sheltered, sunny situation and fertile soil that is not too dry. Propagate by seed in fall.

D. fargesii (illus. p.142). Deciduous, semi-arching, open shrub. **H** and **S** 20ft (6m). Has blue-bloomed shoots and large, deep green leaves of paired leaflets. Racemes of greenish flowers in early summer are followed by pendent, sausage-shaped, bluish fruits. Z7–9 H9–7.

DECUMARIA
HYDRANGEACEAE

Genus of evergreen or deciduous, woody-stemmed, root climbers. Prefers sun and loamy, well-drained soil that does not dry out. Prune, if necessary, after flowering. Propagate by stem cuttings in late summer or early fall.

D. barbara (Wood vamp). Deciduous climber. **H** to 30ft (10m). Has ovate to ovate-oblong, glossy, dark green leaves. In summer produces rounded, terminal clusters, ⅝in (1.5cm) across, of small, white flowers each with a central "brush" of white or creamy-white stamens. Z6–9 H9–6.

D. sinensis, illus. p.192.

DEINANTHE
HYDRANGEACEAE

Genus of slow-growing perennials with creeping, underground rootstocks. Is useful for rock gardens and peat beds. Needs shaded, moist soil. Propagate by division in spring or by seed when fresh.

D. bifida, illus. p.264.

D. caerulea. Slow-growing, mound-forming perennial. **H** 8in (20cm), **S** to 6in (15cm). Stems, each bearing a cluster of nodding, bowl-shaped, pale violet-blue flowers, rise above 3–4 oval, toothed leaves in summer. Z5–9 H9–5.

Delairea odorata. See *Senecio mikanioides.*

DELOSPERMA
Ice plant
AIZOACEAE

Genus of densely branched, trailing, perennial, sometimes shrubby succulents, some with tuberous roots. Requires full sun and very well-drained soil. Propagate by seed or stem cuttings in spring or summer.

D. cooperi. Spreading, mat-forming, perennial succulent. **H** 2in (5cm), **S** indefinite. Has cylindrical, fleshy, light green leaves, 2in (5cm) long, and, in mid- to late summer, solitary, daisylike, magenta flowers. Z8–10 H10–8.

DELPHINIUM
RANUNCULACEAE

Genus of perennials, biennials and annuals, grown for their spikes of irregularly cup-shaped, sometimes hooded, spurred flowers. Needs an open, sunny position and fertile or rich, well-drained soil. Tall cultivars need staking and ample feeding and watering in spring and early summer. In spring, remove thin growths from well-established plants, leaving 5–7 strong shoots. If flower spikes are removed after they fade, a second flush may be produced in late summer, provided plants are fed and watered well. Propagate species by seed in fall or spring; Belladonna Group cultivars by division or basal cuttings of young shoots in spring; Elatum Group cultivars by cuttings only. ⓘ All parts may cause severe discomfort if ingested, and contact with foliage may irritate skin. See also feature panel p.217.

For ease of reference, delphinium cultivars have been grouped as follows:

Belladonna Group. Upright, branched perennials with palmately lobed leaves.

H 3–4ft (1–1.2m), **S** to 18in (45cm). Wiry stems bear loose, branched spikes, 12in (30cm) long, of elf cap-shaped, single flowers, ¾in (2cm) or more across, with spurs up to 1¼in (3cm) long, in early and late summer.

Elatum Group. Erect perennials with large, palmate leaves. **H** 5–6ft (1.5–2m), **S** 24–36in (60–90cm). In summer, produce closely packed spikes, 16in–4ft (40cm–1.2m) long, of regularly spaced, semidouble, rarely fully double flowers, 3–4in (8–10cm) wide, in a range of colors from white to blue and purple, sometimes red-pink, usually with contrasting eyes.

Pacific Hybrids. Similar to Elatum Group cultivars, but grown as annuals or biennials. They produce short-lived, large, semidouble flowers on spikes in early and mid-summer.

University Hybrids. Erect, branched herbaceous perennials with palmately lobed, mid-green leaves. **H** 3–4ft (1–1.2m), **S** to 18in (45cm). In summer, stems bear loose, branched spikes of large, semidouble or double flowers in a range of colors in shades of red, orange or pink. Plants need careful cultivation to succeed.

D. 'Ailsa'. Elatum Group herbaceous perennial. **H** 5½ft (1.7m). In early to mid-summer produces semidouble, off-white or very pale grayish-white flowers, 2½–3in (6–7.5cm) across, with white eyes, on spikes 28–36in (70–90cm) long. Z3–8 H7–1.

D. 'Alice Artindale' (illus. p.217). Elatum Group herbaceous perennial. **H** 5ft (1.5m). Produces neat, button-like, fully double, bicolor, rosy-mauve and sky-blue flowers, to 1¼in (3cm) across, on narrow spikes, 20–24in (50–60cm) or more long, in early to mid-summer. Z3–7 H8–3.

D. 'Anne Kenrick'. Elatum Group herbaceous perennial. **H** 5ft (1.5m). In mid-summer produces semidouble, pale blue flowers, to 3in (8cm) across, with a pink suffusion towards the central white eye, borne on tapering spikes, to 3ft (1m) long. Z3–8 H7–1.

D. 'Ann Woodfield'. Elatum Group herbaceous perennial. **H** 5ft (1.5m). In mid-summer produces semidouble, pale blue flowers, to 4in (10cm) across, suffused pale mauve, on tapering spikes, to 3ft (1m) long. Z3–8 H7–1.

D. 'Atlantis'. Vigorous, Belladonna Group herbaceous perennial. **H** 4½ft (1.4m), **S** 20in (50cm). Produces spikes of mauve-flushed, deep blue flowers, 1¼in (3cm) across, in mid-summer. Has dark green leaves. Z3–8 H7–1.

D. Black Knight Group. Short-lived, Pacific Hybrids herbaceous perennial. **H** 5–5½ft (1.5–1.7m). Produces semidouble, black-eyed, purple to deep purple flowers, to 3in (8cm) across, on spikes, 2–3ft (60–100cm), in early to mid-summer. Z3–8 H7–1.

D. 'Blue Dawn'. Elatum Group herbaceous perennial. **H** 8ft (2.5m). In mid-summer, spikes, to 4ft (1.2m) long, bear pale blue flowers, to 3in (7cm) wide, with dark brown eyes. Z3–7 H7–1.

D. Blue Fountains Group. Short-lived, Pacific Hybrids herbaceous perennial. **H** 5ft (1.5m). In early to mid-summer has variable, white-eyed, mid-blue flowers, to 3in (7cm) across, on spikes 2–3ft (70–100cm) long. Z3–8 H7–1.

***D.* 'Blue Lagoon'.** See *D.* 'Langdon's Blue Lagoon'.
***D.* 'Blue Nile'.** Elatum Group herbaceous perennial. **H** 5–6ft (1.5–1.8m). In mid-summer has rich blue flowers, 2½–3in (6–7cm) across, with lightly blue-streaked, white eyes, on spikes to 34in (85cm) long. Z3–8 H7–1.
***D.* 'Bruce'** (illus. p.217). Elatum Group herbaceous perennial. **H** 5½–7ft (1.7–2.2m). In mid-summer, spikes to 4ft (1.2m) long bear deep violet-purple flowers, to 3in (8cm) across, silver-flushed towards centers and with dark brown eyes. Z3–7 H8–3.
***D. brunonianum*.** Upright herbaceous perennial. **H** and **S** to 8in (20cm). Hairy stems bear rounded, 3- or 5-lobed leaves. In early summer, flower stems each produce a spike, to 6in (15cm) long, of hooded, single, pale blue to purple flowers, 1½in (4cm) wide, with short, black spurs. Is good for a rock garden. Z3–7 H7–1.
***D.* 'Butterball'.** Elatum Group herbaceous perennial. **H** 5–5½ft (1.5–1.7m). In mid-summer bears cream-eyed, white flowers, to 3in (8cm) across, overlaid with very pale greenish-yellow, on spikes to 20in (50cm) long. Z3–7 H7–1.
***D.* 'Can-Can'** (illus. p.217). Elatum Group herbaceous perennial. **H** 6ft (1.9m). In mid-summer, spikes to 30in (75cm) long bear fully double flowers, to 3½in (9cm) across, the outer sepals margined dark blue, the inner sepals purple-mauve with darker veining. Z3–7 H8–3.
***D. cardinale*.** Short-lived, upright herbaceous perennial. **H** 3–6ft (1–2m), **S** 2ft (60cm). In summer has single, scarlet flowers, 1½in (4cm) wide, with yellow eyes, on spikes, 12–18in (30–45cm) long, above palmate, finely divided leaves. Z3–7 H7–1.
***D.* 'Chelsea Star'.** Elatum Group herbaceous perennial. **H** 6ft (2m). Has rich deep violet flowers, 2½–3in (6–8cm) across, with white eyes, on spikes to 3½ft (1.1m) long in mid-summer. Z3–7 H7–1.
***D. chinense*.** See *D. grandiflorum.*
***D.* 'Claire'.** Elatum Group herbaceous perennial. **H** 4½ft (1.4m). In mid-summer, semidouble, pale mauve-pink flowers, to 2in (5cm) across, with cream to pale brown eyes, are borne on spikes to 22in (55cm) long. Z3–8 H7–1.
***D.* 'Clifford Lass'.** Elatum Group herbaceous perennial. **H** 4½ft (1.3m). In mid-summer, spikes 32–36in (80–100cm) long bear semidouble, dusky-pink flowers, to 3in (7.5cm) across, with white-tipped, dark brown eyes. Z3–8 H7–1.
***D.* 'Clifford Sky'.** Elatum Group herbaceous perennial. **H** 6ft (2m). In mid-summer bears semidouble, white-eyed, sky-blue flowers, to 3in (7.5cm) across, on spikes to 3ft (1m) long. Z3–8 H7–1.
***D.* 'Cliveden Beauty'** (illus. p.217). Belladonna Group herbaceous perennial. **H** 3–4ft (1–1.2m). Produces sky-blue flowers, ¾–1in (2–3cm) across, on spikes 12in (30cm) long from early to mid-summer. Z3–7 H8–3.
***D. consolida*.** See *Consolida ajacis.*
***D.* 'Conspicuous'.** Elatum Group herbaceous perennial. **H** 5ft (1.5m). In mid-summer produces semidouble, pale mauve and blue flowers, 2–2½in (5–6cm) across, with prominent dark eyes, in dense spikes to 2ft (60cm) long. Z3–7 H7–1.
***D.* 'Crown Jewel'.** Elatum Group herbaceous perennial. **H** 5ft (1.5m). Spikes, to 34in (85cm) long, bear semidouble, pale blue and mauve flowers, to 2in (5cm) across, with deep brown eyes, in summer. Z3–8 H7–1.
***D.* 'Dora Larkan'.** Elatum Group herbaceous perennial. **H** 6ft (2m). In mid-summer produces spikes, 2ft (60cm) long, of deep mid-blue flowers, to 2½in (6cm) across, with white eyes. Z3–8 H7–1.
***D.* 'Dunsden Green'.** Elatum Group herbaceous perennial. **H** 41_2ft (1.3m). Spikes, 2ft (60cm) long, of semidouble, lime-green-suffused, white flowers, to 2in (5cm) across, with small, green eyes, are produced in mid-summer. Z3–8 H7–1.
***D.* 'Elizabeth Cook'** (illus. p.217). Elatum Group herbaceous perennial. **H** 5–5½ft (1.5–1.7m), **S** 1½ft (50cm). In mid-summer bears white flowers, 2½in (6cm) across, held in spires that gradually taper towards the tips. Z3–7 H8–3.
***D.* 'Emily Hawkins'.** Elatum Group herbaceous perennial. **H** 6–7ft (2–2.2m). Semidouble, purple-mauve flowers, to 2½in (6cm) across, with light yellowish-brown eyes, are borne in mid-summer on spikes to 32in (80cm) long. Z3–7 H7–1.
***D.* 'Fanfare'.** Elatum Group herbaceous perennial. **H** 6–7ft (2–2.2m). In mid-summer bears pale blue to silvery-mauve flowers, 2½–3in (6–7cm) across, with white-and-violet eyes, on spikes 2–2½ft (60–75cm) long. Z3–7 H7–1.
***D.* 'Fenella'.** Elatum Group herbaceous perennial. **H** 3–5½ft (1–1.65m). Bears purple-flushed, gentian-blue blooms, 2–2½in (5–6cm) across, with black eyes, on spikes to 3ft (1m) long in mid-summer. Z3–7 H7–1.
***D.* 'Foxhill Nina'.** Elatum Group herbaceous perennial. **H** 4ft (1.2m). Bears semidouble, white-eyed, pale pink flowers, 2–2½in (5–6cm) across, on spikes, to 2ft (60cm) long, in mid-summer. Z3–7 H7–1.
***D.* 'Franjo Sahin'.** Elatum Group herbaceous perennial. **H** 6ft (2m). In mid-summer, tapering spikes, to 3½ft (1.1m) long, produce semidouble, purplish–mauve flowers, to 4in (10cm) across, with black eyes. Z3–7 H7–1.
***D.* 'Galileo'.** Elatum Group herbaceous perennial. **H** 6ft (1.8m). In early and mid-summer, tapering spikes, to 32in (80cm) long, bear semidouble, violet-blue blooms, 3in (7cm) wide, paling slightly towards the center, with brownish-black eyes. Z3–7 H7–1.
***D.* 'Gemini'.** Elatum Group herbaceous perennial. **H** 6ft (1.8m). In mid-summer, spikes to 34in (85cm) long bear semidouble, pale violet flowers, to 3in (7.5cm) across, edged reddish-violet with dark black-brown eyes, white near the center. Z3–7 H7–1.
***D.* 'Gemma'.** Elatum Group herbaceous perennial. **H** 6ft (2m). Semidouble, pale lavender flowers, to 3in (7.5cm) across, with white eyes, are borne in mid-summer on spikes to 3ft (1m) long. Z3–8 H7–1.
***D.* 'Gertrude Sahin'.** Elatum Group herbaceous perennial. **H** 5½–6ft (1.7–1.9m). In mid-summer produces mid- to light blue flowers, 3–3½in (7.5–9.5cm) across, with prominent, white eyes, on spikes to 3ft (1m) long. Z3–8 H7–1.
***D.* 'Gillian Dallas'** (illus. p.217). Elatum Group herbaceous perennial. **H** 5ft (1.5m). In mid-summer has spikes, to 3ft (90cm) long, of blue-violet flowers, to 3in (8cm) across, with white eyes and violet flecks. Z3–7 H8–3.
***D.* 'Giotto'.** Elatum Group herbaceous perennial. **H** 5½–6ft (1.7–2m). In mid-summer, spikes to 32in (80cm) long bear semidouble flowers, to 3in (7.5cm) wide, with deep purple inner sepals, dark blue outer sepals and light yellow-brown eyes. Z3–8 H7–1.
***D.* 'Gordon Forsyth'.** Elatum Group herbaceous perennial. **H** 6ft (2m). In mid-summer produces semidouble, amethyst-purple blooms, 2½–3in (6–7cm) across, with violet-flecked, black eyes, on spikes 24–28in (60–70cm) long. Z3–7 H7–1.
***D. grandiflorum*,** syn. *D. chinense.* Z3–8 H7–1. **'Blue Butterfly'** (illus. p.217) is a short-lived, erect herbaceous perennial, usually grown as an annual. **H** 1½ft (45cm), **S** 1ft (30cm). Has palmate, divided leaves. In summer produces loose, branching spikes, to 6in (15cm) long, of single, deep blue flowers, 1½in (3.5cm) wide. Is useful as a bedding plant. Z3–8 H8–1.
***D.* 'Holly Cookland Wilkins'.** Elatum Group herbaceous perennial. **H** 5ft (1.5m). Produces tapering spikes, 3ft (1m) long, of semidouble, black-eyed, lavender flowers, to 3in (7.5cm) across, in mid-summer. Z3–8 H7–1.
***D.* 'Joan Edwards'.** Elatum Group herbaceous perennial. **H** 5ft (1.5m). In mid-summer, tapering spikes, 32–36in (80–90cm) long, bear semidouble, vivid purplish-blue flowers, 2¼–3in (5.5–7.5cm) across, becoming paler and purple striated towards the central, white eye. Z3–8 H7–1.
***D.* 'Kennington Classic'.** Elatum Group herbaceous perennial. **H** 5ft (1.5m). Semidouble, rich cream flowers, to 3in (8cm) across, with well-formed, yellow eyes, are borne in mid-summer on spikes to 3ft (90cm) long. Z3–7 H7–1.
***D.* 'Langdon's Blue Lagoon',** syn. *D.* 'Blue Lagoon'. Elatum Group herbaceous perennial. **H** 6ft (2m). Tapering spikes, to 36in (90cm) long, bear semidouble, pale to mid-blue flowers, to 3in (7cm) across, which are paler towards the center, with blue-specked, white eyes. Z3–7 H7–1.
***D.* 'Langdon's Royal Flush'** (illus. p.217). Elatum Group herbaceous perennial. **H** 6ft (2m). In mid-summer has semidouble, magenta-pink flowers, 2–2½in (5–6cm) across, on spikes to 34in (85cm) long; upper petals are a darker shade than lower ones. Z3–7 H7–1.
***D.* 'Loch Leven'** (illus. p.217). Elatum Group herbaceous perennial. **H** to 5ft (1.5m). Bears semidouble, mid-blue flowers, to 3in (7.5cm) across, with white eyes, on 3ft (1m) spikes in early to mid-summer. Z3–7 H8–3.
***D.* 'Lord Butler'.** Elatum Group herbaceous perennial. **H** 5–5½ft (1.5–1.7m). Produces semidouble, mid-blue flowers, to 3in (7.5cm) across, lightly flushed with pale lilac and with blue-marked, white eyes, on spikes to 30in (75cm) long. Z3–7 H9–1.
***D.* 'Lucia Sahin'** (illus. p.217). Elatum Group herbaceous perennial. **H** 6ft (2m). In mid-summer, spikes to 36in (90cm) long bear semidouble, deep purple-pink flowers, to 3in (7.5cm) across, with dark brown eyes. Z3–7 H8–3.
***D.* 'Michael Ayres'** (illus. p.217). Elatum Group herbaceous perennial. **H** 6ft (1.8m). In early and mid-summer, semidouble, deep purple-blue flowers, to 2½in (6cm) across, with black-brown eyes, are borne on spikes to 32in (80cm) long. Z3–7 H8–3.
***D.* 'Mighty Atom'.** Elatum Group herbaceous perennial. **H** 5–6ft (1.5–2m). In mid-summer has semidouble, mid-violet flowers, to 2½in (6cm) across, with violet-marked, yellowish-brown eyes, on spikes to 2½ft (75cm) long. Z3–7 H7–1.
***D.* 'Min'** (illus. p.217). Elatum Group herbaceous perennial. **H** 5½–6ft (1.7–2m). In mid-summer, tapering spikes, to 3ft (1m) long, bear semidouble, pale lavender flowers, to 3¾in (9.5cm) across, with deep lavender suffusions and veining, as well as dark brown eyes. Z3–7 H8–3.
***D.* 'Nobility'.** Elatum Group herbaceous perennial. **H** 5½ft (1.7m). Semidouble, deep purple and dark mauve flowers, to 3in (7.5cm) across, with prominent, white eyes, are borne in mid-summer on spikes to 3ft (1m) long. Z3–8 H7–1.
***D. nudicaule*,** illus. p.340.
***D.* 'Olive Poppleton'** (illus. p.217). Elatum Group herbaceous perennial. **H** 6–8ft (2–2.5m). Off-white flowers, 2–2½in (5–6cm) across, sometimes very faintly flushed pink and with fawn eyes, are borne on spikes to 3ft (1m) long in mid-summer. Z3–7 H8–3.
***D.* 'Pink Ruffles'.** Elatum Group herbaceous perennial. **H** 5ft (1.5m). Fully double, shell-pink flowers, to 3in (7.5cm) across, are borne in mid-summer on spikes to 32in (80cm) long. Z3–8 H7–1.
***D.* 'Red Caroline'** (illus. p.217). University Hybrids herbaceous perennial. **H** 3ft (1m), **S** 1ft (30cm). Has large, palmate, soft green, basal leaves. In summer produces spikes of flattish, bright red flowers. Z3–7 H8–3.
D.* x *ruysii (Elatum Group delphinium and *D. nudicale*)**.** University Hybrids herbaceous perennial. **H** 32–39in (80–100cm), **S** 16in (40cm). Has palmate, mid-green, basal leaves. In early summer produces loose branched spikes of cup-shaped flowers in shades of red and pink. Z3–7 H7–1. **'Pink Sensation'** has slightly mauve-tinged, salmon-pink flowers.
***D.* 'Sandpiper'** (illus. p.217). Elatum Group herbaceous perennial. **H** 3–5ft (1–1.5m). In mid-summer has semidouble, white flowers, to 2½in (6cm) across, with dark creamy-brown eyes, on spikes to 2½ft (75cm) long. Z3–7 H8–3.
***D.* 'Shimmer'.** Elatum Group herbaceous perennial. **H** 6ft (1.8m). In mid-summer produces semidouble, bright blue flowers, 2–3in (5–7cm) across, with prominent, white eyes, on spikes to 32in (80cm) long. Z3–8 H7–1.
***D.* 'Spindrift'** (illus. p.217). Elatum Group herbaceous perennial. **H** 5½–6ft (1.7–2m). In early and mid-summer produces spikes, to 3ft (1m) long, of semidouble, pinkish-purple flowers, 2–3in (5–7cm) across, overlaid with pale blue and with creamy-white eyes; towards centers, the pinkish-purple becomes paler and the blue darker. Flower color varies according to different types of soil; on acid soil, flowers are greenish. Z3–7 H8–3.
***D.* 'Strawberry Fair'.** Elatum Group herbaceous perennial. **H** 5½ft (1.7m). Has semidouble, white-eyed, mulberry-pink flowers, 2–3in (5–7cm) across, on spikes to 31in (78cm) long in mid-summer. Z3–7 H7–1.
***D.* 'Sungleam',** illus. p.219.
***D.* 'Sunkissed'.** Elatum Group herbaceous perennial. **H** 5½ft (1.7m). In mid-summer, spikes to 32in (80cm) long

bear semidouble, cream flowers, to 2³/₄in (6.5cm) across, with canary-yellow eyes. Z3–8 H7–1.

D. tatsienense. Short-lived, upright herbaceous perennial. **H** 12in (30cm), **S** 2–4in (5–10cm). Loose spikes, to 6in (15cm) long, of small-spurred, single, bright blue flowers, 1in (2.5cm) long, are borne in summer. Leaves are rounded to oval and deeply cut. Is suitable for a rock garden. Requires gritty soil. Z3–7 H7–1.

D. 'Tiddles'. Elatum Group herbaceous perennial. **H** 6ft (1.8m). In mid-summer, semidouble to almost double, grayish-violet flowers, 2–2¹/₂in (5–6cm) across, with brown eyes, are borne on spikes to 3ft (90cm) long. Z3–8 H7–1.

D. 'Tiger Eye'. Elatum Group herbaceous perennial. **H** 5¹/₂ft (1.7m). In mid-summer, spikes 24–28in (60–70cm) long bear semidouble, light violet flowers, 2–2¹/₂in (5–6cm) across, with yellow-edged, brown eyes. Z3–7 H7–1.

Dendrathema. See Chrysanthemum.
Dendrobenthamia capitata. See *Cornus capitata*.

DENDROBIUM
ORCHIDACEAE

See also ORCHIDS.

D. aphyllum, syn. *D. pierardii*. Deciduous, epiphytic orchid for an intermediate greenhouse. **H** to 24in (60cm). In early spring produces pairs of soft pink flowers, 1¹/₂in (4cm) across, with large, cream lips. Has oval leaves, 2–3in (5–8cm) long. Requires partial shade in summer. Is best grown hanging from a bark slab. Z12–15 H12–10.

D. chrysotoxum. Deciduous, epiphytic orchid for an intermediate greenhouse. **H** 24in (60cm). Trusses of cup-shaped, deep yellow flowers, ³/₄in (2cm) across and with hairy, red-marked lips, are borne in spring. Oval leaves are 2–3in (5–8cm) long. Provide full light in summer. Z14–15 H12–6.

D. infundibulum (illus. p.466). Evergreen, epiphytic orchid for a cool greenhouse. **H** 12in (30cm). In spring, stems each produce up to 6 pure white flowers, 3in (8cm) wide, with yellow-marked lips. Has oval leaves, 2–3in (5–8cm) long. Needs partial shade in summer. H11–1.

D. Momozono gx 'Princess'. Evergreen, epiphytic orchid for an intermediate greenhouse. **H** 24in (60cm) **S** 12in (30cm). In spring, produces pairs of dark pink flowers, 3in (7cm) across, fading to white in the centers, and with white and pink marks on lips. Oblong leaves are 4in (10cm) long. Requires partial shade in summer. Z13–15 H12–10.

D. nobile (illus. p.466). Deciduous, epiphytic orchid (often evergreen in cultivation) for a cool greenhouse. **H** 12in (30cm). Trusses of delicate, rose-pink flowers, 2in (5cm) across, with prominent, maroon lips, are borne in spring. Oval leaves are 2–3in (5–8cm) long. Requires partial shade in summer. H11–1.

D. 'Oriental Paradise'. Evergreen, epiphytic orchid. **H** 24in (60cm). White flowers, 3in (7cm) across, with dark pink notches on petals and yellow-marked lips, are borne in pairs in spring. Oblong leaves are 4in (10cm) long. Requires partial shade in summer. Z12–15 H12–10.

D. pierardii. See *D. aphyllum*.

DENDROCHILUM
ORCHIDACEAE

See also ORCHIDS.

D. glumaceum (Hay-scented orchid). Evergreen, epiphytic orchid for a cool greenhouse. **H** 4in (10cm). Pendent sprays of fragrant, pointed, orange-lipped, creamy-white flowers, ¹/₂in (1cm) long, are produced in fall. Narrowly oval leaves are 6in (15cm) long. Requires partial shade in summer. Z14–15 H12–10.

DENDROMECON
PAPAVERACEAE

Genus of evergreen shrubs, grown for their foliage and showy flowers. Plant against a sunny wall in cold areas. Requires full sun and very well-drained soil. Propagate by softwood cuttings in summer, by seed in fall or spring or by root cuttings in winter.

D. rigida, illus. p.206.

Dentaria enneaphyllos. See *Cardamine enneaphyllos*.
Dentaria pentaphyllos. See *Cardamine pentaphyllos*.

DESCHAMPSIA
Hair grass
GRAMINEAE/POACEAE

See also GRASSES, BAMBOOS, RUSHES and SEDGES.

D. cespitosa (Tufted hair grass, Tussock grass). Evergreen, tuft-forming, perennial grass. **H** to 3ft (1m), **S** 10–12in (25–30cm). Has narrow, rough-edged, dark green leaves. In summer produces dainty, open panicles of tiny, pale brown spikelets that last well into winter. Tolerates sun and shade. Z4–8 H8–1. **'Goldtau',** illus. p.289.

DESFONTAINIA
DESFONTAINIACEAE/LOGANIACEAE

Genus of evergreen shrubs, grown for their foliage and tubular flowers. Provide shelter in cold areas. Needs some shade, particularly in dry areas, and moist, peaty, preferably acid soil. Propagate by semiripe cuttings in summer.

D. spinosa, illus. p.203.

DESMODIUM
LEGUMINOSAE/PAPILIONACEAE

Genus of perennials and deciduous shrubs and subshrubs, grown for their flowers. Needs full sun and well-drained soil. Propagate by softwood cuttings in late spring or by seed in fall. May also be divided in spring.

D. elegans, syn. *D. tiliifolium*, illus. p.154.
D. tiliifolium. See *D. elegans*.

DEUTZIA
HYDRANGEACEAE

Genus of deciduous shrubs, grown for their profuse, 5-petaled flowers. Needs full sun and fertile, well-drained soil. Plants benefit from regular thinning out of old shoots after flowering. Propagate by softwood cuttings in summer.

D. x elegantissima 'Fasciculata'
Deciduous, upright shrub. **H** 6ft (2m), **S** 5ft (1.5m). From late spring to early summer

produces large clusters of 5-petaled, pale pink flowers. Leaves are oval, toothed and mid-green. **'Rosealind',** illus. p.153.
D. gracilis, illus. p.145.
D. 'Joconde'. Deciduous, upright shrub. **H** and **S** 5ft (1.5m). Bears 5-petaled, white flowers, striped purple outside, in early summer. Oval, mid-green leaves have long points. Z6–8 H8–6.
D. longifolia. Deciduous, arching shrub. **H** 6ft (2m), **S** 10ft (3m). Large clusters of 5-petaled, deep pink flowers are produced from early to mid-summer. Narrowly lance-shaped leaves are gray-green. Z7–8 H8–7. **'Veitchii',** illus. p.133.
D. x magnifica. Vigorous, deciduous, upright shrub. **H** 8ft (2.5m), **S** 6ft (2m). Fully hardy. Produces dense clusters of 5-petaled, pure white flowers in early summer. Leaves are narrowly oval and bright green. Z6–8 H8–5. **'Staphyleoides',** illus. p.132.
D. monbeigii, illus. p.149.
D. 'Mont Rose', illus. p.152.
D. pulchra. Vigorous, deciduous, upright shrub. **H** 8ft (2.5m), **S** 6ft (2m). Has peeling, orange-brown bark and lance-shaped, dark green leaves. Slender, pendulous panicles of 5-petaled, pink-tinged, white flowers are borne in late spring and early summer. Z7–8 H8–7.
D. x rosea, illus. p.146.
D. scabra, illus. p.127. **'Flore Pleno'.** See *D. scabra* 'Plena'. **'Plena',** syn. *D. scabra* 'Flore Pleno' is a deciduous, upright shrub. **H** 10ft (3m), **S** 6ft (2m). Narrowly oval, dark green leaves set off dense, upright clusters of double, white flowers, purplish-pink outside, from early to mid-summer.
D. setchuenensis var. corymbiflora. Deciduous, upright shrub with peeling, pale brown bark when mature. **H** 6ft (2m), **S** 5ft (1.5m). Small, 5-petaled, white flowers are borne in broad clusters in early and mid-summer. Produces lance-shaped, long-pointed, gray-green leaves. Z6–8 H8–6.

DIANELLA
Flax lily
LILIACEAE/PHORMIACEAE

Genus of evergreen, summer-flowering perennials. Is suitable outdoors only in mild areas and elsewhere requires a cold greenhouse or frame. Needs sun and well-drained, neutral to acid soil. Propagate by division or seed in spring.

D. caerulea. Evergreen, tuft-forming perennial. **H** 30in (75cm), **S** 12in (30cm). In summer has panicles of small, star-shaped, blue flowers, above grasslike leaves, followed by blue berries. Z9–10 H10–9. Cassa Blue ('Dbb03'), illus. p.283.
D. tasmanica, illus. p.239.

DIANTHUS
Carnation, Pink
CARYOPHYLLACEAE

Genus of evergreen or semievergreen, mainly summer-flowering perennials, annuals and biennials, grown for their mass of flowers, often scented, some of which are excellent for cutting. Carnations and pinks (see below) are excellent for cut flowers and border decoration, the biennial *D. barbatus* is suitable for bedding and smaller, tuft-forming species and cultivars are good for rock gardens. Needs an open,

sunny position and well-drained, slightly alkaline soil, except for *D. pavonius*, which prefers acid soil. Dead-heading of repeat-flowering types is beneficial. Tall forms of carnations and pinks have a loose habit and need staking. Propagate border carnations by layering in late summer, other named forms by softwood cuttings in early to mid-summer and species by seed at any time. Is susceptible to rust, red spider mite and virus infection through aphids, but many cultivars are available from virus-free stock.

Carnations and pinks have narrowly lance-shaped, silvery- or gray-green leaves, scattered up flower stems, which may coil outwards on carnations. They are divided into the following groups, all with self-colored and bicolored cultivars. See also feature panel pp.266–67.

Carnations
Border carnations are annuals or evergreen perennials that flower prolifically once in mid-summer and are good for border decoration and cutting. Each stem bears 5 or more often scented, semidouble or double flowers, to 3in (8cm) across; picotee forms (with petals outlined in a darker color) are available. **H** 2½–3½ft (75cm–1.1m), **S** to 1ft (30cm).

Perpetual-flowering carnations are evergreen perennials that flower year-round if grown in a greenhouse, but more prolifically in summer. They are normally grown for cut flowers: flower stems should be disbudded, leaving one terminal bud per stem. Fully double flowers, to 4in (10cm) across, are usually unscented and are often flecked or streaked. **H** 3–5ft (1–1.5m), **S** 1ft (30cm) or more.

Spray forms are not disbudded so have 5 or more flowers per stem, each 2–2½in (5–6cm) across. **H** 2–3ft (60cm–1m), **S** to 1ft (30cm).

Malmaison carnations are evergreen perennials, derived from *D.* 'Souvenir de la Malmaison'. Grown under glass, they bear large, double, scented flowers sporadically during the year. The flowers can reach up to 5in (13cm) across. They are mostly self-colored, and tend to split their calyces. **H** 20–28in (50–70cm), **S** 16in (40cm).

Pinks
Evergreen, clump-forming perennials, grown for border decoration and cutting, that in summer produce a succession of basal shoots, each bearing 4–6 fragrant, single to fully double flowers, 1½–2½in (3.5–6cm) across. **H** 12–18in (30–45cm), **S** 9–12in (23–30cm) or more.

Old-fashioned pinks have a low, spreading habit and produce masses of flowers in one flowering period in mid-summer. Mule types (a border carnation crossed with a Sweet William) and laced types (in which the central color extends as a loop around each petal) are available.

Modern pinks, obtained by crossing an old-fashioned pink with a perpetual-flowering carnation, are more vigorous than old-fashioned pinks, and are repeat-flowering with 2 or 3 main flushes of flowers in summer.

Alpine pinks are evergreen species and cultivars forming neat mat or cushion plants. They will grow at the edge of borders or in rock gardens, troughs or

D

alpine houses. In early summer, they bear single, semidouble or double, often scented flowers. Foliage is gray-green. **H** 3–4in (8–10cm), **S** 8in (20cm).

***D.* 'A. J. Macself'**. See *D.* 'Dad's Favourite'.
***D.* 'Albisola'.** Perpetual-flowering carnation. Fully double flowers are clear tangerine-orange. Z5–9 H8–1.
***D.* 'Aldridge Yellow'.** Border carnation. Semidouble flowers are clear yellow. Z5–9 H8–1.
***D.* 'Alice'.** Modern pink. Has clove-scented, semidouble, ivory-white flowers, each with a bold, crimson eye. Z5–9 H8–1.
***D. alpinus*,** illus. p.364.
***D.* 'Annabelle',** illus. p.364.
D. armeria (Deptford pink). Evergreen, tuft-forming perennial, sometimes grown as an annual. **H** 12in (30cm), **S** 18in (45cm). Has narrowly lance-shaped, dark green leaves. In summer, tall stems each bear small, 5-petaled, cerise-pink flowers in small bunches. Is good for a rock garden or bank. Z3–9 H9–1.
D. barbatus (Sweet William). **Roundabout Series** (dwarf). Slow-growing, upright, bushy biennial. **H** 6in (15cm), **S** 8–12in (20–30cm). Has lance-shaped leaves. In early summer bears flat heads of single and bicolored flowers in shades of pink, red and white. Z3–9 H9–1.
***D.* 'Becky Robinson'** (illus. p.266). Modern pink. Has strongly clove-scented, double, rose-pink flowers laced and flecked with crimson. Z5–9 H9–5.
***D.* 'Bombardier'.** Evergreen, tuft-forming perennial. **H** and **S** 4in (10cm). Has a basal tuft of linear, gray-green leaves and, in summer, small, double, scarlet flowers. Is good for a rock garden. Z5–9 H8–1.
***D.* 'Bookham Fancy'.** Border carnation. Produces bright yellow flowers, margined and flecked carmine-purple, on short, stiff stems. Z5–9 H8–1.
***D.* 'Bookham Perfume'.** Perennial border carnation. Has scented, semidouble, crimson flowers. Z5–9 H8–1.
***D.* 'Bovey Belle'.** Modern pink. Has clove-scented, fully double, bright purple flowers that are excellent for cutting. Z5–9 H8–1.
***D.* 'Brilliant Star'.** See *D.* Star Series 'Brilliant Star'.
***D.* 'Brympton Red'.** Old-fashioned pink. Flowers are single, bright crimson with deeper shading. Z5–9 H8–1.
***D. caesius*.** See *D. gratianopolitanus.*
***D. carthusianorum*,** illus. p.339.
***D.* Candy Floss 'Devon Flavia',** See D. Scent First Series Candy Floss.
***D.* 'Charles Musgrave'.** See *D.* 'Musgrave's Pink'.
D. chinensis (China pink, Indian pink). Slow-growing, bushy annual. **H** and **S** 6–12in (15–30cm). Lance-shaped leaves are pale or mid-green. Tubular, single or double flowers, 1in (2.5cm) or more wide and with open, spreading petals, in shades of pink, red or white, are produced in summer and early fall. Z9–11 H12–1. **Baby Doll Series,** illus. p.305. **'Fire Carpet',** illus. p.307. **Heddewigii Group, H** 12in (30cm), has flowers in mixed colors. Z5–9 H8–1.
***D.* 'Christine Hough'.** Perennial border carnation. Semidouble, apricot flowers are overlaid and streaked with rose-pink. Z5–9 H8–1.
***D.* 'Christopher'.** Modern pink. Produces lightly scented, fully double, bright salmon-red flowers. Z5–9 H8–1.
***D.* 'Clara'.** Perpetual-flowering carnation. Fully double flowers are yellow with salmon flecks. Z5–9 H8–1.
***D.* 'Constance Finnis'.** See *D.* 'Fair Folly'.
***D.* 'Coquette',** illus. p.266. Perpetual-flowering, spray carnation. Double, slightly purplish-red flowers have toothed, almost white margins. Z5–9 H8–1.
***D.* 'Cranmere Pool',** illus. p.266. Modern pink. Double, pink-tinted, white flowers have crimson centers and a light fragrance. Z4–8 H8–1.
***D.* 'Cream Sue'.** Perpetual-flowering carnation. Flowers are cream colored. Z5–9 H8–1.
***D.* 'Crompton Princess'.** Perpetual-flowering carnation. Flowers are white. Z5–9 H8–1.
***D.* 'Dad's Favourite',** syn. *D.* 'A.J. Macself' (illus. p.266). Old-fashioned pink. Bears scented, semidouble, white flowers with chocolate-brown lacing. Z5–9 H8–1.
***D. deltoides*.** Evergreen, mat-forming, basal-tufted perennial. **H** 6in (15cm), **S** 12in (30cm). In summer, small, 5-petaled, white, pink or cerise flowers are borne singly above tiny, lance-shaped leaves. Is good for a rock garden or bank. Trim back after flowering. Z3–10 H10–1. **'Flashing Light'.** See *D. deltoides* 'Leuchtfunk'. **'Leuchtfunk',** syn. *D. deltoides* 'Flashing Light', illus. p.365.
***D.* 'Denis'.** Modern pink. Strongly clove-scented, fully double, magenta flowers. Z5–9 H8–1.
***D.* Devon Series.** Modern pink. Prolific, double-flowered, long-flowering, medium to tall plants raised in Devon. Z5–9 H9–5. **'Devon Dove'** (illus. p.266) produces well-scented, pure white flowers with lacy tips. **'Devon Wizard'** (illus. p.267) is vigorous, and bears vibrant, well-scented, cerise-purple flowers with deep red centers.
***D.* 'Doris'** (illus. p.266). Modern pink. Has compact growth and an abundance of fragrant, semidouble, pale pink flowers, each with a salmon-red ring towards base of flower. Is good for cutting. Z5–9 H8–1.
***D.* 'Duchess of Westminster'** (illus. p.266). Vigorous Malmaison carnation. Bears salmon-pink flowers with stronger calyces than most Malmaison carnations. Z5–9 H8–1.
***D.* 'Emile Paré'.** Old-fashioned, mule pink. Has clusters of semidouble, salmon-pink flowers and, unusually for a pink, mid-green foliage. Z5–9 H8–1.
***D.* 'Eva Humphries'.** Perennial border carnation. Has fragrant, semidouble flowers with white petals, each outlined in purple. Z5–9 H8–1.
***D.* 'Fair Folly'.** syn. *D.* 'Constance Finnis'. Modern pink. Flowers are single and usually dusky-pink to dusky-purple with 2 white splashes on each petal. Z5–9 H8–1.
***D.* 'Feuerhexe'** (illus. p.267). Alpine pink. Strongly scented, fringed, single, magenta flowers are produced throughout summer. Has silvery-blue leaves. Z3–10 H10–1.
***D.* 'Forest Treasure'.** Perennial border carnation. Has double, white flowers with reddish-purple splashes on each petal. Z5–9 H8–1.
***D.* 'Freckles'.** Compact modern pink. Has fully double flowers that are red-speckled and dusky-pink. Z5–9 H8–1.
***D.* 'Fusilier'** (illus. p.267). Dwarf, modern pink. **H** 6in (15cm). Fragrant, single, rose-red flowers have blood-red eyes. Z4–8 H8–1.
***D.* 'Golden Cross'** (illus. p.267). Border carnation. Produces bright yellow flowers on short, stiff stems. Z5–9 H8–1.
***D.* 'Gran's Favourite'** (illus. p.266). Old-fashioned pink. Bears fragrant, semidouble, white flowers with deep raspberry lacing. Z5–9 H8–1.
***D. gratianopolitanus*,** syn. *D. caesius,* illus. p.363.
***D.* 'Green Eyes'.** See *D.* 'Musgrave's Pink'.
***D. haematocalyx*.** Evergreen, tuft-forming perennial. **H** 5in (12cm), **S** 4in (10cm). Leaves are lance-shaped and usually glaucous. Bears 5-petaled, toothed, beige-backed, deep pink flowers on slender stems in summer. Is suitable for a rock garden or scree. Z5–9 H9–5.
***D.* 'Happiness'.** Perennial border carnation. Semidouble flowers are yellow, striped scarlet-orange. Z5–9 H8–1.
***D.* 'Haytor'.** See *D.* 'Haytor White'.
***D.* 'Haytor White',** syn. *D.* 'Haytor' (illus. p.266). Modern pink. Fully double, white flowers, borne on strong stems, have a good scent. Is widely grown, especially to provide cut flowers. Z5–9 H8–1.
***D.* 'Hidcote'.** Evergreen, tufted, compact perennial. **H** and **S** 4in (10cm). Bears a basal tuft of linear, spiky, gray-green leaves and, in summer, double, red flowers. Is suitable for a rock garden. Z5–9 H8–1.
***D.* 'Houndspool Ruby',** syn. *D.* 'Ruby', *D.* 'Ruby Doris', illus. p.268.
***D.* 'Ibiza'.** Perpetual-flowering, spray carnation. Fully double flowers are shell-pink. Z5–9 H8–1.
***D.* 'Iceberg'.** Modern pink. Fragrant flowers are semidouble and pure white. Has a somewhat looser habit than *D.* 'Haytor White'. Z5–9 H8–1.
***D.* 'Inchmery'** (illus. p.266). Old-fashioned, mule pink. Highly scented, double, pale pink flowers are borne above blue-green leaves. Does well on heavy soil. Z4–9 H9–1.
***D.* 'India Star'** See *D.* Star Series 'India Star'.
***D.* 'Joy'.** Modern pink. Bears semidouble, pink flowers that are strongly scented and good for cutting. Z5–9 H8–1.
***D.* 'Kobusa'.** See *D.* Pierrot.
***D.* 'La Bourbille'.** See *D.* 'La Bourboule'.
***D.* 'La Bourboule',** syn. *D.* 'La Bourbille', illus. p.365.
***D.* 'Laced Monarch'.** Modern pink. Double flowers are pink, laced with maroon-red. Z5–9 H8–1.
***D.* 'Laced Prudence'.** See *D.* 'Prudence'.
***D.* 'Lady Madonna'** (illus. p.266). Modern pink. Double, white flowers have fringed petals, bright ruby centers and a powerful clove fragrance. Z4–8 H8–1.
***D.* 'Lavender Clove'.** Vigorous border carnation. Bears lavender-gray flowers on long stems. Z5–9 H8–1.
***D.* Lily the Pink ('WP05 Idare'),** illus. p.267. Modern pink. Fringed, double, vivid lavender-pink flowers have redder centers and a sweet, spicy fragrance. Is unusually vigorous. Z4–8 H8–1.
***D.* 'Little Jock',** illus. p.363.
***D.* 'London Brocade'.** Modern pink. Has clove-scented, crimson-laced, pink flowers. Z5–9 H8–1.
***D.* 'London Delight'.** Old-fashioned pink. Fragrant flowers are semidouble and lavender, laced with purple. Z5–9 H8–1.
***D.* 'Manon'.** Perpetual-flowering carnation. Is one of the best deep pink cultivars with fully double flowers. Z5–9 H8–1.
***D.* 'Mars'.** Evergreen, tuft-forming perennial. **H** and **S** 4in (10cm). Has small, double, cherry-red flowers in summer. Bears a basal tuft of linear, gray-green leaves. Is good in a rock garden. Z5–9 H8–1.
***D.* 'Master Stuart'.** Perennial border carnation. Has semidouble, white flowers with scarlet stripes. Z5–9 H8–1.
***D. microlepis*,** illus. p.366.
***D.* 'Milky Way'** (illus. p.266). Perpetual-flowering, spray carnation. Shallowly toothed, double, white flowers may be slightly cream in the centers. Z4–8 H8–1.
***D.* Miss Pinky.** See *D.* 'Valda Wyatt'.
***D.* 'Monica Wyatt'** (illus. p.267). Modern pink. Fragrant, fringed, double, deep pink flowers, with crimson centers, are borne over an unusually long season. Z5–9 H8–1.
***D. monspessulanus*.** Evergreen, mat-forming perennial. **H** 12in (30cm), **S** 4–6in (10–15cm). In summer, masses of strongly fragrant, 5-petaled, deeply fringed, pale lavender flowers rise on slender stems above short tufts of fine, grasslike leaves. Is good for a rock garden. Needs gritty soil. Z5–9 H8–1.
***D.* 'Moulin Rouge'** (illus. p.267). Modern pink. Has double, pink flowers with burgundy lacing, rich burgundy centers and a strong clove scent. Z5–9 H8–1.
***D.* 'Mrs. Sinkins'** (illus. p.266). Old-fashioned pink. Flowers are heavily scented, fringed, fully double and white. Z5–9 H8–1.
***D.* 'Murcia'.** Perpetual-flowering carnation. Has fully double, deep golden-yellow flowers. Z5–9 H8–1.
***D.* 'Musgrave's Pink',** syn. *D.* 'Charles Musgrave', *D.* 'Green Eyes' (illus. p.266). Old-fashioned pink. Bears single, white flowers with green eyes. Z5–9 H8–1.
***D. myrtinervius*,** illus. p.364.
***D. neglectus*.** See *D. pavonius.*
***D.* 'Neon Star'** See *D.* Star Series 'Neon Star'.
***D.* 'Nina'.** Perpetual-flowering carnation. Is one of the best crimson cultivars. Fully double flowers have smooth-edged petals. Z5–9 H8–1.
***D.* Passion ('WP Passion'),** See *D.* Scent First series 'Passion'.
***D. pavonius*,** syn. *D. neglectus*, illus. p.363.
***D.* Pierrot ('Kobusa').** Perpetual-flowering carnation. Bears fully double, light rose-lavender flowers with purple-edged petals. Z5–9 H8–1.
***D.* 'Pike's Pink',** illus. p.364.
***D.* 'Pink Calypso'.** See *D.* 'Truly Yours'.
***D.* 'Pink Jewel'** (illus. p.267). Alpine pink. Has strongly scented, semidouble, pink flowers. Z5–9 H8–1.
***D.* 'Pixie Star',** illus. p.267.
***D. pavonius*,** syn. *D. neglectus*, illus. p.363.
***D.* 'Prado Mint'** (illus. p.267). Perpetual-flowering carnation. Double, pale yellowish-green flowers have shallowly toothed margins. Z4–8 H8–1.
***D.* 'Prudence',** syn. *D.* 'Laced Prudence'. Old-fashioned pink. Fragrant flowers are semidouble and pinkish-white with purple lacing. Has a spreading habit. Z5–9 H8–1.
***D.* 'Queen of Sheba'** (illus. p.267). Old-fashioned pink. Has clove-scented, single, white flowers laced and flaked with magenta-purple. Z5–8 H8–5.
***D.* 'Raggio di Sole'.** Perpetual-flowering carnation. Fully double flowers are bright orange. Z5–9 H8–1.

D

D

D. 'Red Barrow'. Perpetual-flowering, spray carnation. Fully double, bright scarlet flowers are borne in abundance. Z5–9 H8–1.

D. 'Rose de Mai' (illus. p.267). Old-fashioned, mule pink. Double, mauve-pink flowers have darker centers. Z4–9 H9–1.

D. 'Ruby'. See D. 'Houndspool Ruby'.

D. 'Ruby Doris'. See D. 'Houndspool Ruby'.

D. 'Sam Barlow'. Old-fashioned pink. Bears very fragrant, frilly, fully double, white flowers with brown centers. Z5–9 H8–1.

D. 'Sandra Neal'. Border carnation. Fully double, golden-apricot flowers are flaked deep rose-pink. Z5–9 H8–1.

D. Scent First Series. Modern pink. Compact, repeat-flowering, strongly scented plants that tolerate extreme weather conditions. Z5–9 H8–1. CANDY FLOSS ('Devon Flavia'), illus. p.266, has highly scented, double, bright sugar-pink flowers, with lacy tips and richer pink centers. Z5–9 H9–5. PASSION ('WP Passion'), illus. p.267, produces rounded, fragrant, double, bright red flowers over an unusually long season. Z4–8 H8–1. TICKLED PINK ('Devon PP 11'), illus. p.267, bears rounded, semidouble, fringed, deep lavender flowers, with a strong spicy scent, over a long season.

D. 'Show Ideal'. Modern pink. Flat-petaled, semidouble flowers are white and are strongly scented. Is excellent for exhibition. Z5–9 H8–1.

D. 'Sops-in-wine'. Old-fashioned pink. Bears fragrant, single, maroon flowers with white markings. Z5–9 H8–1.

D. STARLIGHT ('Hilstar'), illus. p.267. Modern pink. Strongly scented, single, rose-lavender flowers turn to lilac, then mature to almost white. Z5–9 H8–1.

D. Star Series. Prolific Modern pink with single or semidouble flowers over mounded foliage. Z5–9 H8–1. 'Brilliant Star' (illus. p.266) has fragrant, semidouble, glistening white flowers, with rich velvet-red centers. 'Evening Star' (illus. p.266) bears single or semidouble, rounded, bright deep pink flowers with gently rippled edges and crimson eyes. 'India Star' (illus. p.267) produces single, rich rose-pink flowers with bold, deep red eyes and a fine fragrance. 'Neon Star' (illus. p.267) has silvery-green leaves and single, vivid magenta flowers over a very long season. Z4–9 H8–1. 'Pixie Star' (illus. p.267) bears single, rose-lavender flowers with slightly wavy petals and deep pink eyes. Z4–8 H8–1.

D. superbus. Evergreen, mat-forming perennial. H to 8in (20cm), S 6in (15cm). Has narrowly lance-shaped, pale green leaves. In summer, slender stems bear very fragrant, 5-petaled, deeply fringed, pink flowers with darker centers. Is suitable for a rock garden. Z3–8 H8–1. 'Crimsonia' (illus. p.267) has slender, rather floppy stems bearing fragrant, well-dissected, single, scarlet flowers. Z3–8 H8–1.

D. 'Tayside Red', illus. p.267. Malmaison carnation. Produces brick-red flowers through summer and into fall. Does best in a cool glasshouse or conservatory. Z4–8 H8–1.

D. 'Tickled Pink'. See D. Scent First Series TICKLED PINK.

D. 'Tigré'. Perpetual-flowering carnation. Has fully double, yellow flowers with a uniform, pinkish-purple stripe and edging to each petal. Z5–9 H8–1.

D. 'Tony'. Perpetual-flowering, spray carnation. Fully double flowers are yellow with red stripes. Z5–9 H8–1.

D. 'Truly Yours', syn. D. 'Pink Calypso'. Perpetual-flowering carnation. Fully double flowers are a good pink. Z5–9 H8–1.

D. 'Valda Wyatt', syn. D. MISS PINKY, illus. p.267. Modern pink. Very fragrant flowers are fully double and rose-lavender. Z5–9 H8–1.

D. 'Valencia'. Perpetual-flowering carnation. Has fully double, orange blooms. Z5–9 H8–1.

D. 'Whatfield Magenta'. Alpine pink. Fragrant, single, brilliant magenta flowers have paler throats. Has deep blue leaves. Z3–8 H8–1.

D. 'White Ladies' (illus. p.266). Old-fashioned pink. Produces very fragrant, fully double, white flowers with greenish centers. Z5–9 H8–1.

D. 'Widecombe Fair'. Modern pink. Semidouble flowers, borne on strong stems, are of unusual coloring—peach-apricot, opening to blush-pink. Z5–9 H8–1.

D. 'WP05 Idare'. See D. LILY THE PINK.

D. 'WP Passion'. See D. Scent First Series PASSION.

DIAPENSIA

DIAPENSIACEAE

Genus of evergreen, spreading subshrubs, suitable for rock gardens and troughs. Needs partial shade and peaty, sandy, acid soil. Is very difficult to grow in hot, dry climates at low altitudes. Propagate by seed in spring or by semiripe cuttings in summer.

D. lapponica. Evergreen, spreading subshrub. H and S 3in (7cm). Has tufts of small, rounded, leathery leaves. Bears solitary, tiny, bowl-shaped, white flowers in early summer. Z1–5 H5–1.

DIASCIA

SCROPHULARIACEAE

Genus of summer- and fall-flowering annuals and perennials, some of which are semievergreen, grown for their tubular, pink flowers. Is suitable for banks and borders. Needs sun and rich, well-drained soil that is not too dry. Cut back old stems in spring. Propagate by softwood cuttings in late spring, by semiripe cuttings in summer or by seed in fall.

D. barberae (Twinspur). 'Blackthorn Apricot', syn. D. 'Blackthorn Apricot', illus. p.278. 'Fisher's Flora', syn. D. cordata of gardens, illus. p.339. 'Ruby Field' is a mat-forming perennial. H 3in (8cm), S 6in (15cm). Heart-shaped, pale green leaves clothe short, wiry stems. Produces tubular, wide-lipped, salmon-pink flowers throughout summer.

D. 'Blackthorn Apricot'. See D. barberae 'Blackthorn Apricot'.

D. cordata of gardens. See D. barberae 'Fisher's Flora'.

D. ICE CRACKER ('Hecrack'), illus. p.337.

D. LITTLE DANCER ('Pendan'), illus. p.301.

D. personata, illus. p.223.

D. rigescens, illus. p.339.

D. 'Salmon Supreme', illus. p.345.

D. vigilis. Prostrate perennial. H 12–16in (30–40cm), S 24in (60cm). Pale green leaves are small, rounded and toothed. Upright branchlets bear loose spikes of flattish, outward-facing, pale pink flowers in summer. Z7–9 H9–7.

DICENTRA
Bleeding heart

PAPAVERACEAE/FUMARIACEAE

Genus of perennials, grown for their sprays of pendent flowers. Most do best in partial shade and rich, moist but well-drained soil. Propagate by division when dormant in late winter, species also by seed in fall. ⚠ Contact with the foliage may aggravate skin allergies.

D. 'Adrian Bloom'. Spreading, tuft-forming perennial. H 18in (45cm), S 12in (30cm). Has sprays of pendent, heart-shaped, rich carmine-pink flowers above oval, gray-green leaves. Z4–8 H10–1.

D. cucullaria, illus. p.348.

D. eximia of gardens. See D. formosa.

D. formosa, syn. D. eximia of gardens (Western bleeding heart). Spreading, tufted perennial. H 18in (45cm), S 12in (30cm). In spring–summer bears slender, arching sprays of pendent, heart-shaped, pink or dull red flowers above oval, finely cut, gray-green leaves. Z4–8 H8–1.

D. peregrina. Tuft-forming perennial. H 3in (8cm), S to 2in (5cm). Locket-shaped, pink flowers are borne in spring–summer above fernlike, blue-green leaves. Needs gritty soil. Is suitable for an alpine house. Z4–8 H8–1.

D. spectabilis, syn. Lamprocapnos spectabilis, illus. p.223. f. alba, syn. Lamprocapnos spectabilis f. alba, illus. p.223.

D. 'Spring Morning', illus. p.256.

D. 'Stuart Boothman', illus. p.268.

DICHELOSTEMMA

LILIACEAE/ASPARAGACEAE

Genus of summer-flowering bulbs, grown for their dense flower heads on leafless stems. Is related to Brodiaea and is similar to Allium in appearance. Needs sunny and well-drained soil. Water freely in spring, but dry out after flowering. Propagate by seed in fall or spring or by offsets in fall before growth commences.

D. congestum, syn. Brodiaea congesta, illus. p.392.

D. ida-maia, syn. Brodiaea ida-maia. Early summer-flowering bulb. H to 3ft (1m), S 3–4in (8–10cm). Long, narrow leaves are semierect and basal. Leafless stem bears a dense head of flowers, 3/4–1in (2–2.5cm) long, each with a red tube and 6 green petals. Z5–8 H8–5.

D. pulchellum, syn. Brodiaea capitata, Brodiaea pulchella. Early summer-flowering bulb. H 12–24in (30–60cm), S 3–4in (8–10cm). Long, narrow leaves are semierect and basal. Leafless stem bears a dense head of narrowly funnel-shaped, pale to deep violet flowers, 1/2–3/4in (1–2cm) long, with violet bracts. Z6–10 H10–6.

DICHORISANDRA

COMMELINACEAE

Genus of erect, clump-forming, evergreen perennials, grown for their ornamental foliage. Prefers fertile, moist but well-drained soil, humid conditions and partial shade. Propagate by division in spring or by stem cuttings in summer.

D. reginae, illus. p.473.

Dichromena colorata. See Rhynchospora colorata.

DICKSONIA

DICKSONIACEAE

Genus of evergreen or semievergreen, treelike ferns that resemble palms and that are sometimes used to provide height in fern plantings. Needs partial shade and rich, moist soil. Remove faded fronds regularly. Propagate by spores in summer.

D. antarctica, illus. p.290.

D. fibrosa. Evergreen, treelike fern (deciduous in cold climates). H to 20ft (6m), S to 12ft (4m). Sturdy trunks are crowned by a rosette of spreading, divided, lance-shaped, dark green fronds, to 6ft (2m) long. Z9–10 H10–9.

D. squarrosa. Evergreen, treelike fern (deciduous in cold climates). H to 20ft (6m), S to 12ft (4m). Slender trunks are crowned by a rosette of spreading, divided, lance-shaped, mid-green fronds, to 6ft (2m) long, with blackish stalks and midribs. Z9–10 H10–9.

DICTAMNUS

RUTACEAE

Genus of summer-flowering perennials. Requires full sun and fertile, well-drained soil. Resents disturbance. Propagate by seed sown in late summer when fresh. ⚠ The foliage, roots and seeds of D. albus may cause mild stomach upset if ingested, and contact with the foliage may cause photodermatitis.

D. albus (Burning bush, Dittany, Gas plant). var. albus, illus. p.230. var. purpureus, syn. D. fraxinella. Upright perennial. H 3ft (1m), S 2ft (60cm). Has light green leaves divided into oval leaflets. In early summer bears spikes of fragrant, star-shaped, purplish-pink flowers with long stamens. Z3–8 H8–3.

D. fraxinella. See D. albus var. purpureus.

Didiscus coeruleus. See Trachymene coerulea.

DIDYMOCHLAENA

DRYOPTERIDACEAE/ASPIDIACEAE

Genus of one species of evergreen fern. Has tufts of glossy, mid-green fronds, tinged with rose-pink or red when young. Requires partial shade, high humidity and moist, rich soil. Propagate by spores as soon as ripe, or divide in spring.

D. lunulata. See D. truncatula.

D. truncatula, syn. D. lunulata. Evergreen fern. H and S to 3ft (1m). Has erect rhizomes and triangular, divided fronds, 2–5ft (60cm–1.5m) long, with simple diamond-shaped segments. Z9–11 H12–9.

DIEFFENBACHIA
Dumb cane, Mother-in-law's tongue

ARACEAE

Genus of evergreen, tufted perennials, grown for their foliage. Needs fertile, well-drained soil and partial shade. Propagate in spring or summer by stem cuttings or pieces of leafless stem placed horizontally in compost. Scale insect or red spider mite may be troublesome. ① All parts may cause severe discomfort if ingested, and contact with sap may irritate skin.

D. amoena of gardens. See *D. seguine* 'Amoena'.

D. 'Exotica'. See *D. seguine* 'Exotica'.

D. maculata 'Exotica'. See *D. seguine* 'Exotica'. **'Rudolph Roehrs'.** See *D. seguine* 'Rudolph Roehrs'.

D. 'Memoria'. See *D. seguine* 'Memoria Corsii'.

D. seguine. Evergreen, tufted perennial. **H** and **S** 3ft (1m) or more. Broadly lance-shaped leaves, to 18in (45cm) long, are glossy and dark green. Insignificant, tiny, greenish-white flowers, clustered on the spadix, are surrounded by a narrow, leaflike spathe that is produced intermittently. Z14–15 H12–1. **'Amoena'**, syn. *D. amoena* of gardens, **H** to 6ft (2m), is robust and has creamy-white bars along lateral veins on leaves. **'Exotica'**, syn. *D.* 'Exotica', *D. maculata* 'Exotica', illus. p.465. **'Memoria Corsii'**, syn. *D.* 'Memoria' has gray-green leaves, marked dark green and spotted white. **'Rudolph Roehrs'**, syn. *D. maculata* 'Rudolph Roehrs', *D. seguine* 'Roehrs', illus. p.474. **'Roehrs'.** See *D. seguine* 'Rudolph Roehrs'.

DIERAMA

Angel's fishing rod, Wandflower

IRIDACEAE

Genus of evergreen, clump-forming, summer-flowering corms, grown for their pendent, funnel- or bell-shaped flowers on long, arching, wiry stems. Flourishes near pools. Prefers a warm, sheltered, sunny site and well-drained soil that should be kept moist in summer when in growth. Dies down partially in winter. Propagate by division of corms in spring or by seed in fall or spring. Resents disturbance, and divisions take a year or more to settle and start flowering again.

D. 'Blackbird'. Evergreen, upright perennial. **H** 5ft (1.5m), **S** 1ft (30cm). Produces cascades of nodding, funnel-shaped, violet-mauve flowers on wiry, pendulous stems, in summer, above grasslike leaves. Z7–9 H9–7.

D. dracomontanum, syn. *D. pumilum*. Vigorous, evergreen, upright perennial. **H** 30in (75cm), **S** 12in (30cm). In summer freely produces nodding, funnel-shaped flowers, in shades of pink and violet, on wiry stems. Leaves are grasslike. Z8–9 H9–7.

D. ensifolium. See *D. pendulum*.
D. pendulum, syn. *D. ensifolium*, illus. p.392.
D. pulcherrimum, illus. p.386.
D. pumilum. See *D. dracomontanum*.

DIERVILLA

CAPRIFOLIACEAE

Genus of deciduous, summer-flowering shrubs. Is similar to *Weigela*. Needs partial shade or full sun and moderately fertile, well-drained soil. To keep the shrub neat, remove 2- and 3-year-old stems in winter or after flowering. Propagate by semiripe cuttings in late summer or by hardwood cuttings in fall.

D. sessilifolia (Southern bush honeysuckle). Deciduous, spreading shrub. **H** and **S** 3–5ft (1–1.5m). Narrowly oval, pointed, serrated, green leaves are often copper-tinted when young. Has terminal and lateral clusters of tubular, pale yellow flowers in summer. To treat as an herbaceous perennial, cut back to ground level each spring and apply mulch and fertilizer. Z4–8 H8–1.

DIETES

IRIDACEAE

Genus of evergreen, iris-like, rhizomatous perennials, grown for their flowers in spring or summer. Needs sun or partial shade and rich, well-drained soil that does not dry out excessively. Propagate by seed in fall or spring or by division in spring (although divisions do not become re-established very readily).

D. bicolor, illus. p.395.
D. iridioides, syn. *D. vegeta* of gardens. Evergreen, spring- and summer-flowering, rhizomatous perennial. **H** to 2ft (60cm), **S** 1–2ft (30–60cm). Bears semierect, sword-shaped, basal leaves in a spreading fan. Branching, wiry stems bear iris-like, white flowers, 2½–3in (6–8cm) across; each of the 3 large petals has a central, yellow mark. Z8–11 H12–8.
D. vegeta of gardens. See *D. iridioides*.

DIGITALIS

Foxglove

SCROPHULARIACEAE/PLANTAGINACEAE

Genus of biennials and perennials, some are evergreen, grown for their summer flower spikes. Species mentioned below grow in most conditions, even dry, exposed sites, but do best in partial shade and moist but well-drained soil. Propagate by seed in fall. ① All parts may cause severe discomfort if ingested. Contact with foliage may irritate skin.

D. ambigua. See *D. grandiflora*.
D. canariensis. See *Isoplexis canariensis*.
D. eriostachya. See *D. lutea*.
D. ferruginea (Rusty foxglove). Perennial best treated as a biennial. **H** 3–4ft (1–1.2m), **S** 1ft (30cm). Long, slender spikes bear funnel-shaped, orange-br own and white flowers in mid-summer above basal rosettes of oval, rough leaves. Z4–9 H9–1.
D. grandiflora, syn. *D. ambigua* (Yellow foxglove). Evergreen, clump-forming perennial. **H** 30in (75cm), **S** 12in (30cm). Racemes of downward-pointing, tubular, creamy-yellow flowers are borne in summer above a rosette of oval to oblong, smooth, strongly veined leaves. Z3–8 H8–1.
D. lutea, syn. *D. eriostachya*. Upright perennial. **H** 30in (75cm), **S** 12in (30cm). In summer, delicate spires of downward-pointing, narrowly tubular, creamy-yellow flowers are borne above a rosette of oval, smooth, mid-green leaves. Z3–8 H8–1.
D. x mertonensis. Clump-forming perennial. **H** 30in (75cm), **S** 12in (30cm). Produces spikes of downward-pointing, tubular, rose-mauve to coppery flowers in summer, above a rosette of oval, hairy, soft leaves. Divide after flowering. Z3–8 H8–1.
D. purpurea (Common foxglove). Upright, short-lived perennial, grown as a biennial. **H** 3–5ft (1–1.5m), **S** 2ft (60cm). Has a rosette of oval, rough, deep green

leaves and, in summer, tall spikes of tubular flowers in shades of pink, red, purple or white. Z4–8 H9–1. **f. albiflora**, syn. *D. purpurea* f. *alba*, illus. p.299. **f. alba**. See *D. purpurea* f. *albiflora*.

DILLENIA

DILLENIACEAE

Genus of evergreen or briefly deciduous, spring-flowering trees, grown for their flowers and foliage and for shade. Needs moist, fertile soil and full light. Water container plants freely while in full growth, less in winter. Propagate by seed in spring.

D. indica (Chulta). Briefly deciduous, spreading tree. **H** and **S** 25–40ft (8–12m). Has oval, serrated, boldly parallel-veined, glossy leaves, 1ft (30cm) long. Nodding, cup-shaped, white flowers, 6–8in (15–20cm) wide, are produced in spring, followed by edible, globular, greenish fruits. Z14–15 H12–1.

DIMORPHOTHECA

African daisy, Cape marigold

COMPOSITAE/ASTERACEAE

Genus of annuals, perennials and evergreen subshrubs. Requires sun and fertile, very well-drained soil. Dead-head to prolong flowering. Propagate annuals by seed sown under glass in mid-spring, perennials by semiripe cuttings in summer. Is susceptible to botrytis in wet summers.

D. annua. See *D. pluvialis*.
D. barberae of gardens. See *Osteospermum jucundum*.
D. pluvialis, syn. *D. annua*, illus. p.299.

DIONAEA

DROSERACEAE

Genus of evergreen, insectivorous, rosette-forming perennials. Needs partial shade and a humid atmosphere; grow in a mixture of peat and moss, kept constantly moist. Propagate by seed or division in spring.

D. muscipula, illus. p.473.

DIONYSIA

PRIMULACEAE

Genus of evergreen, cushion-forming perennials. Grow in an alpine house in sun and very gritty, well-drained soil. Position deep collar of grit under cushion and ensure good ventilation at all times. Dislikes winter wet. Propagate by softwood cuttings in summer. Plants are susceptible to botrytis.

D. aretioides, illus. p.358.
D. microphylla. Evergreen perennial. **H** 2in (5cm), **S** 6in (15cm). Rosettes of oval to rounded, often sharply pointed, gray-green leaves, with mealy, yellow coating beneath, form tight cushions. Small, short-stemmed, 5-petaled, white-eyed, pale to deep violet-yellow flowers, with darker petal bases, are produced in early spring. Z5–7 H7–5.
D. tapetodes, illus. p.358.

DIOON

ZAMIACEAE

Genus of evergreen shrubs, grown for their palm-like appearance. Requires full sun and fertile, well-drained soil. Water container

specimens moderately when in full growth, less at other times. Propagate by seed in spring.

D. edule (Chestnut dioon, Mexican fern palm). Slow-growing, evergreen, palm-like shrub, eventually with a thick, upright trunk. **H** 6–12ft (2–4m), **S** 5–10ft (1.5–3m). Feather-like leaves, 2–4ft (60cm–1.2m) long, have spine-tipped, blue-green leaflets. Z8–11 H12–5.

DIOSCOREA

DIOSCOREACEAE

Genus of tuberous perennials, some of which are succulent, and herbaceous or evergreen, twining climbers, grown mainly for their leaves. Insignificant flowers are generally yellow. Prefers full sun or partial shade and fertile, well-drained soil. Propagate by division, or by cutting off sections of tuber in spring or fall or by seed in spring.

D. discolor. See *D. dodecaneura*.
D. dodecaneura, syn. *D. discolor*, illus. p.459.
D. elephantipes, syn. *Testudinaria elephantipes*, illus. p.492.

DIOSMA

RUTACEAE

Genus of evergreen, wiry-stemmed shrubs, grown for their flowers and overall appearance. Needs full light and well-drained, neutral to acid soil. Water container specimens moderately when in full growth, less at other times. To create a compact habit, shorten flowered stems after flowering. Propagate by seed in spring or by semiripe cuttings in late summer.

D. ericoides (Breath of heaven). Fast-growing, evergreen, loosely rounded shrub. **H** and **S** 1–2ft (30–60cm). Aromatic, needlelike leaves are crowded on stems. In winter–spring produces a profusion of small, fragrant, 5-petaled, white flowers, sometimes tinted red. Z13–15 H12–10.

Diosphaera. See *Trachelium*.
Diosphaera asperuloides. See *Trachelium asperuloides*.

DIOSPYROS

EBENACEAE

Genus of deciduous or evergreen trees and shrubs, grown for their foliage and fruits. To obtain fruits, plants of both sexes should be grown. Needs full sun and does best in hot summers. Requires fertile, well-drained soil. Propagate by seed in fall.

D. kaki (Chinese persimmon, Japanese persimmon, Kaki). Deciduous, spreading tree. **H** 30ft (10m), **S** 22ft (7m). Oval, glossy, dark green leaves turn orange, red and purple in fall. Tiny, yellowish-white flowers in summer are followed on female trees by large, edible, rounded, yellow or orange fruits. Z7–10 H10–7.
D. lotus (Date plum). Deciduous, spreading tree. **H** 30ft (10m), **S** 20ft (6m). Has oval, glossy, dark green leaves, tiny, red-tinged, green flowers from mid- to late summer and, on female trees, unpalatable, rounded, purple or yellow fruits. Z6–10 H10–6.

D

DIPCADI

LILIACEAE/ASPARAGACEAE

Genus of spring-flowering bulbs, grown mainly for botanical interest. Will not tolerate cold, wet winters, so is best grown in a cold frame or alpine house. Needs a warm, sunny situation and light, well-drained soil. Is dormant in summer. Propagate by seed in fall.
D. serotinum, illus. p.422.

DIPELTA

CAPRIFOLIACEAE

Genus of deciduous shrubs, with bold, long-pointed leaves, grown for their tubular flowers and peeling bark. After flowering, bracts beneath flowers enlarge and become papery and brown, surrounding the fruits. Requires sun or partial shade and fertile, well-drained soil. Benefits from the occasional removal of old shoots after flowering. Propagate by softwood cuttings in summer.
D. floribunda, illus. p.111.
D. yunnanensis, illus. p.110.

DIPHYLLEIA

BERBERIDACEAE

Genus of perennials with creeping rootstocks and umbrella-like leaves. Is best suited to woodland gardens. Needs partial shade and moist soil. Propagate by division in spring or by seed in fall.
D. cymosa (Umbrella leaf). Rounded perennial. **H** 24in (60cm), **S** 12in (30cm). Has large, rounded, 2-lobed leaves. In spring bears loose heads of inconspicuous, white flowers followed by indigo-blue berries on red stalks. Z7–10 H10–7.

Dipidax. See Onixotis.
Dipidax triquetrum. See Onixotis triquetra.
Diplacus glutinosus. See Mimulus aurantiacus.
Dipladenia. See Mandevilla.
Dipladenia boliviensis. See Mandevilla boliviensis.
Dipladenia splendens. See Mandevilla splendens.

DIPLARRHENA

IRIDACEAE

Genus of one species of summer-flowering perennial. Needs sun and well-drained soil. Propagate by seed or division in spring.
D. moraea, illus. p.264.

DIPSACUS

Teasel

DIPSACACEAE/CAPRIFOLIACEAE

Genus of biennials or short-lived perennials, grown for their flower heads, which are good for drying. Requires sun or partial shade and fertile soil. Sow seed in fall or spring.
D. fullonum (Teasel). Prickly biennial. **H** 5–6ft (1.5–2m), **S** 12–32in (30–80cm). In the first year produces basal rosette of toothed, dark green leaves covered in spiny pustules. Thistle-like, pinkish-purple or white flower heads, with stiff, prickly bracts, are borne terminally on upright stems with paired leaves in

mid- and late summer of the second year. Self-seeds readily and can escape cultivation. Z5–8 H8–5.

DIPTERONIA

ACERACEAE/SAPINDACEAE

Genus of deciduous trees, grown for their foliage and fruits. Needs full sun and fertile, well-drained soil. Propagate by softwood cuttings in summer or by seed in fall.
D. sinensis. Deciduous, spreading, sometimes shrubby tree. **H** 30ft (10m), **S** 20ft (6m). Large, mid-green leaves have 7–11 oval to lance-shaped leaflets. Inconspicuous, greenish-white flowers in summer are followed by large clusters of winged, red fruits. Z8–10 H10–8.

DISA

ORCHIDACEAE

See also ORCHIDS.
D. uniflora. Deciduous, terrestrial orchid. **H** 1½–2ft (45–60cm). Has narrowly lance-shaped, glossy, dark green leaves, 9in (22cm) long. In early summer each stem bears up to 7 hooded, scarlet flowers, 3–4in (8–10 cm) long, that have darker veins and are suffused yellow. Needs partial shade and continually moist soil. Grow from seed or propagate by division of offsets when dormant. Z13–15 H12–10.

DISANTHUS

HAMAMELIDACEAE

Genus of one species of deciduous, fall-flowering shrub, grown for its overall appearance and fall color. Needs partial shade and rich, moist but not wet, neutral to acid soil. Propagate by layering in spring or by seed when ripe or in spring.
D. cercidifolius, illus. p.141.

DISCARIA

RHAMNACEAE

Genus of deciduous or almost leafless shrubs and trees, grown for their habit and flowers. Spiny, green shoots assume function of leaves. Needs a sheltered, sunny site and fertile, well-drained soil. Propagate by softwood cuttings in summer.
D. toumatou (Wild Irishman). Deciduous or almost leafless, bushy shrub. **H** and **S** 6ft (2m). Shoots have sharp, rigid spines. Tiny, star-shaped, greenish-white flowers are borne in dense clusters in late spring. Z8–9 H9–8.

DISOCACTUS

CACTACEAE

Genus of epiphytic, perennial cacti with flattened, strap-shaped stems. Is closely related to Epiphyllum, with which it hybridizes. Spines are insignificant. Stems may die back after flowering. Needs partial shade and rich, well-drained soil. Propagate by stem cuttings in spring or summer.
D. ackermannii, syn. Epiphyllum ackermannii, Nopalxochia ackermannii (Red orchid cactus). Erect, then pendent, epiphytic, perennial cactus. **H** 1ft (30cm), **S** 2ft (60cm). Has fleshy, toothed, green stems, to 3in (7cm) across and 16in (40cm) long. Bears funnel-shaped, red flowers, 6in

(15cm) wide, in spring–summer along indented edges of stems. Z11–14 H12–5.
D. flagelliformis. See Aporocactus flagelliformis.
D. 'Gloria', illus. p.485.
D. 'Jennifer Ann', illus. p.496.
D. 'M.A. Jeans', illus. p.485.
D. phyllanthoides 'Deutsche Kaiserin', illus. p.485.

DISPORUM

Fairy bells

LILIACEAE/COLCHICACEAE

Genus of spring- and early summer-flowering perennials. Is suitable for woodland gardens. Requires partial shade and rich soil. Propagate by division in spring or by seed in fall.
D. hookeri. Clump-forming perennial. **H** 30in (75cm), **S** 12in (30cm). Leaves are narrow, oval and mid-green. Orange-red berries in fall follow clusters of drooping, open bell-shaped, greenish-white flowers in spring. Z4–9 H9–1.
D. sessile 'Variegatum'. Rapidly spreading, clump-forming perennial. **H** 18in (45cm), **S** 12in (30cm). Solitary, tubular-bell-shaped to bell-shaped, creamy-white flowers are produced in spring. Has narrowly oval, pleated leaves irregularly striped with white. Z4–9 H9–1.

DISTICTIS

BIGNONIACEAE

Genus of evergreen, woody-stemmed, tendril climbers, grown for their colorful, trumpet-shaped flowers. Needs well-drained soil and full light. Water freely in summer, less at other times. Support for stems is necessary. Thin out congested growth in spring. Propagate by softwood cuttings in early summer or by semiripe cuttings in late summer.
D. buccinatoria, syn. Phaedranthus buccinatorius, illus. p.461.

DISTYLIUM

HAMAMELIDACEAE

Genus of evergreen shrubs and trees, grown for their foliage and flowers. Prefers a sheltered, partially shaded position and moist, peaty soil. Propagate by semiripe cuttings in summer.
D. racemosum. Evergreen, arching shrub. **H** 6ft (2m), **S** 10ft (3m). Leaves are oblong, leathery, glossy and dark green. Bears small flowers, with red calyces and purple anthers, from late spring to early summer. Z11 H12–10.

Dizygotheca elegantissima. See Schefflera elegantissima.

DOCYNIA

ROSACEAE

Genus of evergreen or semievergreen, spring-flowering trees, grown for their flowers and foliage; is related to Cydonia. Requires full sun and well-drained soil. Other than shaping while young, pruning is not necessary. Propagate by seed in spring or fall, by budding in summer or by grafting in winter. Caterpillars may be troublesome.
D. delavayi. Evergreen or semievergreen, spreading tree. **H** and **S** 25ft (8m) or more. Oval to lance-shaped leaves are white-

felted beneath. In spring has fragrant, white flowers, pink in bud; ovoid, downy, yellow fruits follow in fall. Z8–10 H10–8.

DODECATHEON

Shooting stars

PRIMULACEAE

Genus of spring- and summer-flowering perennials, grown for their flowers, with reflexed petals and prominent stamens. Once fertilized, flowers turn skywards—hence their common name. Is dormant after flowering. Prefers sun or partial shade and moist but well-drained soil. Propagate by seed in fall or by division in winter.
D. dentatum (White shooting star). Clump-forming perennial. **H** 3in (7cm), **S** 10in (25cm). Leaves are long, oval and toothed. In late spring bears white flowers, with dark stamens and reflexed petals. Prefers partial shade. Z4–8 H8–2.
D. hendersonii, illus. p.333.
D. meadia (Eastern shooting star). Clump-forming perennial. **H** 8in (20cm), **S** 6in (15cm). Leaves are oval and pale green. In spring bears pale pink flowers, with reflexed petals, above foliage. Prefers partial shade. Z4–8 H8–1. **f. album,** illus. p.333.
D. pauciflorum. See D. pulchellum.
D. pulchellum, syn. D. pauciflorum. Clump-forming perennial. **H** 6in (15cm), **S** 4in (10cm). Is similar to D. meadia but flowers are usually deep cerise. Z4–7 H8–2. **'Red Wings',** illus. p.333.

DODONAEA

SAPINDACEAE

Genus of evergreen trees and shrubs, grown mainly for their foliage and overall appearance. Prefers full sun and well-drained soil. Water container plants freely when in full growth, less at other times. Cut back in late summer and in spring if needed, to maintain a balanced shape. Propagate by seed in spring or by semiripe cuttings in late summer.
D. viscosa 'Purpurea', illus. p.457.

Dolichos lablab. See Lablab purpureus.
Dolichos purpureus. See Lablab purpureus.

DOMBEYA

STERCULIACEAE/MALVACEAE

Genus of evergreen shrubs and trees, grown for their flowers. Needs full sun or partial shade and fertile, well-drained soil. Water container plants freely when in full growth, less when temperatures fall. Cut back after flowering. Propagate by seed in spring or by semiripe cuttings in summer. Whitefly and red spider mite may be a nuisance.
D. burgessiae, syn. D. mastersii. Evergreen shrub. **H** 6–12ft (2–4m), **S** 5–10ft (1.5–3m). Has rounded, 3-lobed, downy leaves and dense clusters of fragrant, white flowers, with pink to red veins, in fall–winter. Z12–15 H12–10.
D. x cayeuxii, illus. p.450.
D. mastersii. See D. burgessiae.

Dondia. See Hacquetia.

DORONICUM

Leopard's bane

COMPOSITAE/ASTERACEAE

Genus of perennials, grown for their daisylike flowers, which are good for cutting. Most prefer full sun or partial shade and moist but well-drained soil. Propagate by division in fall.

D. austriacum. Clump-forming perennial. **H** 18in (45cm), **S** 12in (30cm). Bears daisylike, pure yellow flower heads on slender stems in spring. Heart-shaped, wavy-edged bright green leaves are hairy. Z5–8 H8–5.

D. x excelsum 'Harpur Crewe', syn. *D. plantagineum* 'Excelsum'. Clump-forming perennial. **H** 3ft (1m), **S** 2ft (60cm). Large, daisylike, buttercup-yellow flower heads are borne, 3 or 4 to a stem, in spring. Leaves are heart-shaped and bright green. Is good for a dry, shaded site. Z4–8 H8–1.

D. 'Frühlingspracht'. Clump-forming perennial. **H** 18in (45cm), **S** 12in (30cm). Produces daisylike, double, bright yellow flower heads in spring. Has heart-shaped, bright green leaves. Z5–8 H8–5.

D. 'Miss Mason', illus. p.227.

D. orientale 'Magnificum', illus. p.263.

D. plantagineum 'Excelsum'. See *D. x excelsum* 'Harpur Crewe'.

DOROTHEANTHUS

AIZOACEAE

Genus of succulent annuals, suitable for hot, dry places such as rock gardens, screes and gaps in paving. Needs sun and grows well in poor, very well-drained soil. Dead-head to prolong flowering. Propagate by seed sown under glass in early spring, or outdoors in mid-spring. Protect from slugs and snails.

D. bellidiformis, syn. *Mesembryanthemum criniflorum* (Livingstone daisy). Z11 H9–1. **'Magic Carpet'** is a carpeting annual. **H** 6in (15cm), **S** 12in (30cm). Has lance-shaped, pale green leaves. Daisylike flowers, in bright shades of red, pink, yellow or white, open in sun.

DORYANTHES

LILIACEAE/DORYANTHACEAE

Genus of evergreen, rosette-forming perennials, grown for their flowers. Needs a sunny position and rich, well-drained soil. Propagate by mature bulbils, by seed in spring or by suckers after flowering.

D. palmeri, illus. p.470.

Dorycnium hirsutum. See *Lotus hirsutus*.

Douglasia vitaliana. See *Vitaliana primuliflora*.

Doxantha capreolata. See *Bignonia capreolata*.

Doxantha unguis-cati. See *Macfadyena unguis-cati*.

DRABA

CRUCIFERAE/BRASSICACEAE

Genus of spring-flowering annuals and evergreen or semievergreen, cushion- or mat-forming perennials. Some species form soft, green cushions that in winter turn brown except at the tips, appearing dead. Is suitable for alpine houses. Needs sun and gritty, well-drained soil. Dislikes winter wet. Propagate by softwood cuttings of the rosettes in late spring or by seed in fall.

D. aizoides (Yellow whitlow grass). Semievergreen, mat-forming perennial. **H** 1in (2.5cm), **S** 6in (15cm). Has lance-shaped, stiff-bristled leaves in rosettes and, in spring, 4-petaled, bright yellow flowers. Is suitable for a gravel garden. Z4–6 H6–1.

D. bryoides. See *D. rigida* var. *bryoides*.

D. hispanica. Semievergreen, cushion-forming perennial. **H** 2in (5cm), **S** 4in (10cm). Pale green leaves are oval and soft. Clusters of flat, 4-petaled, pale yellow flowers are borne in spring. Z4–6 H6–1.

D. longisiliqua, illus. p.357.

D. mollissima, illus. p.358.

D. polytricha. Semievergreen, cushion-forming perennial. **H** 2^{1}/$_{2}$in (6cm), **S** 6in (15cm). Forms rosettes of tiny round leaves. Bears flat, 4-petaled, golden-yellow flowers in spring. Is difficult to grow. Keep stones under cushion at all times. Remove dead rosettes at once. Z4–6 H6–1.

D. rigida, illus. p.357. **var. bryoides,** syn. *D. bryoides* is an evergreen, hummock-forming perennial. **H** 1^{1}/$_{2}$in (4cm), **S** 2^{1}/$_{2}$ft (6cm). Has tiny, round, dark green leaves. Produces small clusters of almost stemless, 4-petaled, bright yellow flowers that cover hummocks in spring.

DRACAENA

AGAVACEAE/ASPARAGACEAE

Genus of evergreen trees and shrubs, grown for their foliage. Needs full sun or partial shade and well-drained soil. Water container plants moderately, much less in low temperatures. Rejuvenate leggy plants by cutting back to near soil level in spring. Propagate by seed or air-layering in spring or by tip or stem cuttings in summer. Mealy bug may be a nuisance.

D. australis. See *Cordyline australis*.

D. deremensis. See *D. fragrans* Deremensis Group. **'Souvenir de Schrijver'.** See *D. fragrans* Deremensis Group 'Warneckei'. **'Warneckei'.** See *D. fragrans* Deremensis Group 'Warneckei'.

D. draco, illus. p.451.

D. fragrans (Corn plant). Z14–15 H12–1. **Deremensis Group,** syn. *D. deremensis* is a slow-growing, evergreen, sparsely branched shrub. **H** 6ft (2m) or more, **S** 3ft (1m) or more. Has erect to arching, lance-shaped, glossy, deep green leaves, to 18in (45cm) long. Mature plants may bear large panicles of small, red-and-white flowers in summer. **'Warneckei',** syn. *D. deremensis* 'Souvenir de Schrijver', *D. deremensis* 'Warneckei', illus. p.454. **'Massangeana'** has broad longitudinally banded leaves of yellow and pale green interspersed with narrow, gray-green stripes. Z13–15 H12–10.

D. indivisa. See *Cordyline indivisa*.

D. marginata. Slow-growing, evergreen, erect shrub or tree. **H** 10ft (3m) or more, **S** 3–6ft (1–2m) or more. Leaves are narrowly strap-shaped and rich green with red margins. Flowers are rarely produced. Z11–12 H12–1. **'Tricolor',** illus. p.452.

D. sanderiana, illus. p.453.

DRACOCEPHALUM

Dragon's head

LABIATAE/LAMIACEAE

Genus of summer-flowering annuals and perennials, suitable for rock gardens and borders. Prefers sun and fertile, well-drained soil. Propagate by seed or division in spring or fall or by basal cuttings of young growth in spring.

D. ruyschiana. Erect perennial. **H** 18–24in (45–60cm), **S** 12in (30cm). Freely bears whorled spikes of 2-lipped, violet-blue flowers from early to mid-summer. Mid-green leaves are linear to lance-shaped. Z3–7 H7–1.

D. sibiricum. See *Nepeta sibirica*.

DRACUNCULUS

ARACEAE

Genus of robust, tuberous perennials that produce roughly triangular, foul-smelling spathes. Where marginally hardy protect dormant tubers with a heavy mulch. Needs sun and well-drained soil that dries out in summer. Propagate by offsets in late summer or by seed in fall.

D. vulgaris, syn. *Arum dracunculus*, illus. p.386.

DREGEA

ASCLEPIADACEAE/APOCYNACEAE

Genus of evergreen, woody-stemmed, twining climbers, grown for botanical interest. Needs sun and well-drained soil. Propagate by seed in spring or by stem cuttings in summer or fall.

D. corrugata. See *D. sinensis*.

D. sinensis, syn. *D. corrugata, Wattakaka sinensis*, illus. p.197.

Drejerella guttata. See *Justicia brandegeeana*.

Drepanostachyum falconeri. See *Himalayacalamus falconeri*.

DRIMIA

LILIACEAE/HYACINTHACEAE

Genus of late summer- or early fall-flowering bulbs, growing on or near soil surface, with spear-shaped flower spikes up to 5ft (1.5m) high. Needs sun and well-drained soil that dries out while bulbs are dormant in summer. Plant in mid- to late summer. Water until leaves die down. Propagate by seed in fall or by offsets in late summer.

D. maritima, syn. *Urginea maritima*. Late summer- or early fall-flowering bulb. Bears broadly sword-shaped, erect, basal leaves in fall after long spikes of small star-shaped, white flowers.

DRIMYS

WINTERACEAE

Genus of evergreen trees and shrubs, grown for their foliage and star-shaped flowers. Where marginally hardy, grow against a sunny wall. Needs sun or partial shade and fertile, moist but well-drained soil. Propagate by semiripe cuttings in summer or by seed in fall.

D. aromatica. See *D. lanceolata*.

D. axillaris. See *Pseudowintera axillaris*.

D. colorata. See *Pseudowintera colorata*.

D. lanceolata, syn. *D. aromatica*, illus. p.197.

D. winteri, syn. *Wintera aromatica*, illus. p.73.

DROSANTHEMUM

AIZOACEAE

Genus of erect or prostrate, succulent shrubs with slender stems and summer flowers. Needs full sun and very well-drained soil. Propagate by seed or stem cuttings in spring or summer.

D. hispidum. Shrub with arching or spreading branches that root down. **H** 2ft (60cm), **S** 3ft (1m). Has cylindrical, light green leaves, ^{5}/$_{8}$–1in (1.5–2.5cm) long. In summer bears masses of daisylike, purple flowers, to 1^{1}/$_{4}$in (3cm) across. Z10–13 H12–9.

D. speciosum. Erect, shrubby succulent. **H** 2ft (60cm), **S** 3ft (1m). Has semicylindrical leaves, ^{1}/$_{2}$–^{3}/$_{4}$in (1–2cm) long. Masses of daisylike, green-centered, orange-red flowers, to 2in (5cm) across, are produced in summer. Z9–13 H12–9.

DROSERA

Sundew

DROSERACEAE

Genus of evergreen, insectivorous perennials. Grow in sun, in a mixture of peat and moss that is not allowed to dry out. Propagate by seed or division in spring.

D. capensis, illus. p.473.

D. spatulata, illus. p.473.

DRYANDRA

PROTEACEAE

Genus of evergreen, spring- to summer-flowering shrubs and trees, grown for their flowers, foliage and overall appearance. Needs full light and well-drained, sandy soil that is low in nutrients. Is difficult to grow. Water container plants moderately, less in low temperatures. Plants under glass must be freely ventilated. Propagate by seed in spring.

D. formosa. Evergreen, bushy shrub. **H** 6–15ft (2–5m), **S** 5–10ft (1.5–3m). Strap-shaped leaves are divided into triangular, closely set lobes, creating a saw-blade effect. In spring produces small, scented, tubular, orange-yellow flowers in domed, terminal heads. Z10–11 H12–10.

DRYAS

Mountain avens

ROSACEAE

Genus of evergreen, prostrate, woody-based perennials, grown for their oak-like leaves and cup-shaped flowers. Is useful on banks and walls, in rock gardens and as groundcover. Prefers sun and gritty, well-drained, peaty soil. Propagate by seed or by semiripe cuttings in summer.

D. drummondii. Evergreen, prostrate, woody-based perennial. **H** 2in (5cm), **S** indefinite. Sturdy stems are clothed in small, oval, lobed, leathery, dark green

D

leaves. In early summer bears nodding, cream flowers that never fully open. Z2–6 H6–1.
D. octopetala, illus. p.361.
D. x suendermannii. Evergreen, prostrate, woody-based perennial. **H** 2in (5cm), **S** indefinite. Is similar to *D. drummondii*, but has slightly nodding, pale cream flowers that open horizontally. Z3–6 H6–1.

DRYOPTERIS
Wood fern
DRYOPTERIDACEAE/ASPIDIACEAE

Genus of deciduous or semievergreen ferns, many of which form regular, shuttlecock-like crowns. Requires shade and moist soil. Regularly remove fading fronds. Propagate by spores in summer or by division in fall or winter.
D. affinis, syn. *D. borreri*, *D. pseudomas* (Golden male fern). Virtually evergreen fern. **H** and **S** to 3ft (1m). Has a "shuttlecock" of lance-shaped, divided fronds, 8–32in (20–80cm) tall, from an erect rhizome. Fronds are pale green as they unfurl in spring, in contrast to the scaly, golden brown midribs; they mature to dark green and often remain green through winter. Is distinguished from *D. filix-mas* by a dark spot where each pinna joins the midrib. Z6–8 H8–6.
D. atrata. See *D. cycadina*.
D. austriaca. See *D. dilatata*.
D. borreri. See *D. affinis*.
D. carthusiana (Spinulose wood fern, Toothed wood fern). Deciduous or semievergreen, creeping, rhizomatous fern. **H** 3ft (1m), **S** 18in (45cm). Produces lance-shaped, much-divided, mid-green fronds with triangular to oval pinnae. Z6–8 H8–6.
D. cycadina, syn. *D. atrata*, *D. hirtipes*. Deciduous fern. **H** 24in (60cm), **S** 18in (45cm). Has an erect rhizome producing a "shuttlecock" of lance-shaped, divided, bright green fronds, 18in (45cm) long, with green midribs. Z6–9 H9–6.
D. dilatata, syn. *D. austriaca* (Broad buckler fern). Deciduous or semievergreen fern. **H** 3ft (1m), **S** 18in (45cm). Has much-divided, arching, mid-green fronds, with triangular to oval pinnae, on sturdy, dark brown stems. Z6–8 H8–5.
D. erythrosora, illus. p.293.
D. filix-mas, illus. p.293. **'Grandiceps Wills'** is a deciduous fern. **H** and **S** 3ft (90m). Has "shuttlecocks" of broadly lance-shaped, tasselled, arching, mid-green fronds, arising from crowns of large, upright, brown-scaled rhizomes. Tip of each frond has a heavy crest, and pinnae are also finely crested.
D. goldieana (Giant wood fern, Goldie's fern). Deciduous fern. **H** 3ft (1m), **S** 2ft (60cm). Has broadly oval, light green fronds divided into numerous oblong, indented pinnae. Z6–8 H8–5.
D. hirtipes. See *D. cycadina*.
D. marginalis (Marginal wood fern). Deciduous fern. **H** 24in (60cm), **S** 12in (30cm). Fronds are lance-shaped, dark green and divided into numerous oblong, slightly indented pinnae. Z3–8 H8–1.
D. pseudomas. See *D. affinis*.
D. sieboldii. Semievergreen, tufted fern. **H** and **S** 1–2ft (30–60cm). Produces erect or arching, long-stalked, yellowish-green

fronds, 8–20in (20–50cm) long, with up to 6 pairs of narrowly lance-shaped pinnae, 6–12in (15–30cm) long. Z6–8 H8–6.
D. wallichiana, illus. p.292.

DUCHESNEA
ROSACEAE

Genus of perennials, some of which are semievergreen, grown as groundcover as well as for their flowers. Is suitable for hanging baskets. Needs well-drained soil and sun or partial shade. Propagate by division in spring, by rooting plantlets formed at ends of runners in summer or by seed in fall.
D. indica, syn. *Fragaria indica* (Indian strawberry). Semievergreen, trailing perennial. **H** to 4in (10cm), **S** indefinite. Dark green leaves have 3 toothed leaflets like those of strawberries. Solitary, 5-petaled, bright yellow flowers, to 1in (2.5cm) wide, with leafy, green frills of sepals, are borne from spring to early summer. Strawberry-like, tasteless, red fruits develop in late summer. Z6–8 H8–6.

DUDLEYA
CRASSULACEAE

Genus of basal-rosetted, perennial succulents, closely related to *Echeveria*. Requires full sun and very well-drained soil. Water sparingly when plants are semi-dormant in mid-summer. Propagate by seed or division in spring or summer.
D. brittonii. Basal-rosetted, perennial succulent. **H** 8–24in (20–60cm) or more when in flower, **S** 20in (50cm). Has narrowly lance-shaped, tapering, fleshy, silvery-white leaves. Masses of star-shaped, pale yellow flowers are produced in spring–summer. Z13–15 H12–10.
D. pulverulenta, illus. p.490.

DURANTA
VERBENACEAE

Genus of fast-growing, evergreen or partially deciduous trees and shrubs, grown for their flowers and overall appearance. Needs full light and fertile, well-drained soil. Water container plants freely when in full growth, moderately at other times. Prune as necessary to curb vigor. Propagate by seed in spring or by semiripe cuttings in summer. Whitefly may be troublesome.
D. erecta, syn. *D. plumieri*, *D. repens*, illus. p.319. **'Gold Edge',** illus. p.319.
D. plumieri. See *D. erecta*.
D. repens. See *D. erecta*.

DUVALIA
ASCLEPIADACEAE

Genus of clump-forming or carpeting, perennial succulents with short, thick, leafless stems; is closely related to *Stapelia*. Star-shaped flowers have thick, fleshy petals recurved at tips. Requires partial shade and very well-drained soil. Propagate by seed or stem cuttings in spring or summer.
D. corderoyi, illus. p.493.

Duvernoia adhatodoides. See *Justicia adhatoda*.

DYCKIA
BROMELIACEAE

Genus of evergreen, rosette-forming perennials. Requires full light and well-drained soil containing sharp sand or grit. Water moderately in summer, scarcely or not at all in winter. Propagate by offsets or division in spring.
D. remotiflora. Evergreen, basal-rosetted perennial. **H** and **S** 12–20in (30–50cm). Has dense rosettes of arching, very narrowly triangular, pointed, thick-textured, dull green leaves with hooked spines and gray scales beneath. Woolly spikes of tubular, orange-yellow flowers are produced above the foliage in summer–fall. Z13–15 H12–10.

DYPSIS
PALMAE/ARECACEAE

Genus of evergreen palms, grown for their elegant appearance. Needs full light or partial shade and fertile, well-drained soil. Water container specimens moderately, much less when temperatures are low. Propagate by seed in spring at not less than 79°F (26°C). Red spider mite may sometimes be a nuisance.
D. lutescens, syn. *Areca lutescens*, *Chrysalidocarpus lutescens*, illus. p.452. (Azores heath)

ECCREMOCARPUS
BIGNONIACEAE

Genus of evergreen, subshrubby, tendril climbers, grown for their flowers, which appear over a long period. One species only is commonly grown. Usually treated as an annual. Needs full sun and well-drained soil. Propagate by seed in early spring.
E. scaber, illus. p.208.

ECHEVERIA
CRASSULACEAE

Genus of rosetted, perennial succulents with long-lasting flowers. Leaves take on their brightest colors from fall to spring. Needs sun, good ventilation and very well-drained soil. Propagate by seed, stem or leaf cuttings, division or offsets in spring or summer.
E. agavoides. Basal-rosetted, perennial succulent. **H** 6in (15cm), **S** 12in (30cm). Has tapering, light green leaves, often red-margined. Bears cup-shaped, red flowers, ¹⁄₂in (1cm) long, in summer. Z10–11 H12–1.
E. cooperi. See *Adromischus cooperi*.
E. derenbergii. Clump-forming, perennial succulent. **H** 1¹⁄₂in (4cm), **S** 12in (30cm). Produces short-stemmed rosette of rounded, gray-green leaves. Flower stem, 3in (8cm) long, produces cup-shaped, yellow-and-red or orange flowers in spring. Offsets freely. Is often used as a parent in breeding. Z13–15 H12–10.
E. elegans, illus. p.484.
E. gibbiflora. Rosetted, perennial succulent. **H** 4–10in (10–25cm), **S** 12in (30cm). Rosettes of spoon-shaped, pointed, gray-green leaves, often tinged red-brown, are stemless or borne on short stems. Cup-shaped, red flowers, yellow within, are borne on stems, 3ft (90cm) long, in fall–winter. Z13–15 H12–10. **var. metallica,** syn. *E. gibbiflora* 'Metallica' has white- or red-margined, purple-green leaves that mature to green-bronze. **'Metallica'.** See *E. gibbiflora* var. *metallica*.
E. harmsii, syn. *Oliveranthus elegans*. Bushy, perennial succulent. **H** 8in (20cm), **S** 12in (30cm). Erect stems are each crowned by rosette, 2¹⁄₂in (6cm) wide, of short, narrowly lance-shaped, pale green leaves covered in short hairs. In spring bears cup-shaped, orange-tipped, red flowers, yellow within. Z13–15 H12–10.
E. montana. Rosetted, perennial succulent. **H** 12in (30cm), **S** 4in (10cm). Spoon-shaped, pointed, waxy-bloomed, light green leaves are produced in a small, short-stemmed, clustered rosette. Slender flower stem, 12–16in (30–40cm) long, bears cup-shaped, yellow to orange flowers in summer. Z13–15 H12–10.
E. pulvinata (Plush plant). Bushy, perennial succulent. **H** 12in (30cm), **S** 20in (50cm). Has brown-haired stems topped by rosette of thick, rounded, green leaves that become red-edged in fall. Leaves have short, white hairs. Bears red flowers in spring. Z12–15 H12–10.
E. secunda, illus. p.487.
E. setosa (Mexican firecracker). Basal-rosetted, perennial succulent. **H** 1¹⁄₂in (4cm),

S 12in (30cm). Has long, narrow, mid-green leaves covered in short, thick, white hairs. Bears cup-shaped, red-and-yellow flowers in spring. Is prone to rotting: do not water foliage. Z13–15 H12–10.

ECHINACEA
Coneflower
COMPOSITAE/ASTERACEAE

Genus of summer-flowering perennials. Prefers sun and rich, moist but well-drained soil. Propagate by division or root cuttings in spring.

E. angustifolia, illus. p.221. Clump-forming perennial. **H** 32in (80cm), **S** 18in (45cm). Has narrowly lance-shaped, hairy, dark green leaves. In summer, upright stems bear solitary, daisylike flower heads with narrow, reflexed, pale pinkish-purple ray florets and a central, orange-brown cone. Needs an open position. Z4–9 H9–1.

E. 'Green Envy'. Clump-forming, erect perennial. **H** 36in (100cm), **S** 12in (30cm). Has lance-shaped, dark green leaves. In summer, upright stems bear solitary, daisylike, lime-green flower heads with a central, greenish-purple cone and rather broad, overlapping ray florets, which are pinkish-purple at bases. Z4–9 H9–1.

E. 'Green Jewel'. Clump-forming, erect perennial. **H** 20–24in (50–60cm), **S** 12in (30cm). Has lance-shaped, dark green leaves. In summer, upright stems bear solitary, daisylike, soft-green flower heads with rather short, overlapping ray florets and a central, bright green cone. Z4–9 H9–1.

E. 'Harvest Moon', illus. p.221. Clump-forming, erect perennial. **H** to 24in (60cm), **S** 12in (30cm). Has lance-shaped, dark green leaves. In summer, upright often branched stems bear daisylike flower heads with rather reflexed, orange-tinged, soft yellow ray florets and a central, greenish-yellow cone. Z4–9 H9–1.

E. paradoxa, illus. p.221. Clump-forming perennial. **H** 3ft (1m), **S** 12in (30cm) or more. Has narrowly lance-shaped, dark green leaves. In summer, upright stems bear solitary, daisylike, bright yellow flower heads with drooping, long, slender ray florets and a central, dark brown cone. Needs an open position. Z4–8 H8–1.

E. Pixie Meadowbrite ('CBG Cone 2'). Compact perennial. **H** 20in (50cm), **S** 12in (30cm). Has lance-shaped, dark green leaves. In summer, sturdy, well-branched stems bear solitary, daisylike, bright pink flower heads with horizontal ray florets and a central, greenish-pink cone, which matures to crimson. Z4–9 H9–1.

E. purpurea, syn. Rudbeckia purpurea (Purple coneflower). Erect perennial. **H** 4ft (1.2m) or more, **S** 1½ft (45cm) or more. Has oval, hairy, dark green, basal leaves. From summer to mid-fall, branching stems bear solitary, daisylike, pinkish-purple or white flower heads with horizontal or reflexed ray florets and a central, orange-brown cone. Is best in an open position. Z3–9 H9–1. **'Coconut Lime'** (illus. p.221), **H** to 2ft (60cm), has reflexed, white ray florets and a central cone that develops into a rounded pompom of shorter, green florets forming a shuttlecock-shaped head. **'Doppelganger'.** See E. purpurea 'Doubledecker'. **'Doubledecker'**, syn. E. purpurea 'Doppelganger' (illus. p.221), **H** 3ft (1m), has reflexed, magenta-pink ray florets and a central, dark brown cone, out of which develop further, smaller ray florets. **Elton Knight ('Elbrook')**, **H** 2ft (60cm) has a compact, bushy habit and produces numerous flower heads with horizontal, bright pink ray florets and a central, purplish-red cone. **'Fragrant Angel'** (illus. p.221), **H** 3ft (1m), bears fragrant flower heads with overlapping, horizontal, white ray florets, sometimes green tinged, and a central, orange cone. **'Kim's Knee High'**, **H** 2ft (60cm) has a compact habit and produces masses of small, warm pink flower heads with reflexed ray florets and a central, orange cone. **'Kim's Mop Head'**, **H** 20–24in (50–60cm), has a compact habit and produces near-horizontal, white ray florets and a central, greenish-orange cone. **'Magnus'** (illus. p.221), **H** 3ft (1m), produces large, red-pink flower heads with rather broad, overlapping, horizontal ray florets. **'Razzmatazz'** (illus. p.221), **H** 36in (90cm), has soft pink flower heads, the central cone of which develops into a rounded pompom of shorter, reddish-pink ray florets. May need staking. **'Robert Bloom'** illus. p.234. **'Rubinstern'**, **H** 32in (80cm), bears large, reddish-pink flowers with horizontal ray florets and a central, brownish-red cone. **'Ruby Giant'**, **H** 32in (80cm), produces sturdy stems bearing rich pink flower heads with a second row of ray florets; these are held horizontally, giving flowers an impression of greater size than selections with drooping ray florets. **'Sundown'** (illus. p.221), **H** 32in (80cm), has a variable form and flower color, and bears usually overlapping, near-horizontal, warm orange ray florets and a central, dark orange cone. **'White Lustre'**, **H** 4ft (1.2m), has lance-shaped leaves and produces strong stems bearing white flower heads with a prominent, central, orange-brown cone. Z3–9 H12–1. **'White Swan'**, **H** 28in (70cm), bears rather reflexed, warm white ray florets and a central, orange-brown cone.

E. 'Tiki Torch'. Clump-forming, erect perennial. **H** 28in (70cm), **S** 12in (30cm). Has lance-shaped, dark green leaves. In summer, upright stems bear solitary, daisylike, bright orange flower heads with a central, reddish-brown cone and rather reflexed ray florets, which are darkest at bases. Z4–9 H9–1.

E. 'Tomato Soup'. Clump-forming, erect perennial. **H** 32in (80cm), **S** 12in (30cm). Has lance-shaped, dark green leaves. In summer, upright stems bear daisylike, fiery orange-red flower heads with ray florets held more or less horizontally and a central, greenish-brown cone. Z4–9 H9–1.

ECHINOCACTUS
Barrel cactus
CACTACEAE

Genus of slow-growing, hemispherical, perennial cacti. Cold temperatures cause yellow patches on E. grusonii. Requires full sun and very well-drained soil. Yellow-flowered species are easy to grow. Propagate by seed in spring.

E. asterias. See Astrophytum asterias.
E. chilensis. See Eriosyce chilensis.
E. eyriesii. See Echinopsis oxygona.
E. grusonii (Golden barrel cactus). Slow-growing, hemispherical, perennial cactus. **H** to 24in (60cm), **S** to 32in (80cm). Spined, green stem has 30 ribs. Woolly crown bears a ring of straw-colored flowers in summer, only on stems more than 15in (38cm) wide. Z9–10 H10–8.
E. ingens. See E. platyacanthus.
E. myriostigma. See Astrophytum myriostigma.
E. ornatus. See Astrophytum ornatum.
E. platyacanthus, syn. E. ingens. Slow-growing, hemispherical, perennial cactus. **H** 10ft (3m), **S** 6ft (2m). Gray-blue stem has a woolly crown and up to 50 ribs. Funnel-shaped, yellow flowers, 1¼in (3cm) across, are produced in summer only on plants more than 16in (40cm) in diameter. Z12–15 H12–10.
E. scheeri. See Sclerocactus scheeri.
E. uncinatus. See Sclerocactus uncinatus.

ECHINOCEREUS
Hedgehog cactus
CACTACEAE

Genus of spherical to columnar, perennial cacti, freely branching with age, some with tuberous rootstocks. Buds, formed inside spiny stem, burst through skin, producing long-lasting flowers, with reflexed petal tips and prominent, green stigmas, followed by pear-shaped, spiny seed pods. Some species tolerate light frost if dry. Needs full sun and very well-drained soil. Propagate by seed or stem cuttings in spring or summer.

E. baileyi. See E. reichenbachii var. baileyi.
E. cinerascens. Clump-forming, perennial cactus. **H** 1ft (30cm), **S** 3ft (1m). Has stems 3in (7cm) wide, each with 5–12 ribs. Areoles each bear 8–15 yellowish-white spines. Mature plants produce masses of trumpet-shaped, bright pink or purple flowers, 5in (12cm) across and with paler petal bases, in spring. Z12–15 H12–10.
E. leucanthus, syn. Wilcoxia albiflora, illus. p.482.
E. pectinatus. Columnar cactus. **H** 14in (35cm), **S** 8in (20cm). Has sparsely branched, green stems with 12–23 ribs and short, comblike spines, often variably colored. In spring bears trumpet-shaped, purple, pink or yellow flowers, 5in (12cm) across, with paler bases. Z12–15 H12–10.
E. pentalophus, syn. E. procumbens, illus. p.484.
E. procumbens. See E. pentalophus.
E. reichenbachii. Columnar cactus. **H** 14in (35cm), **S** 8in (20cm). Slightly branched, multicolored stem with 12–23 ribs has comblike spines, ⅝in (1.5cm) long. Trumpet-shaped, pink or purple flowers, 5in (12cm) across, with darker petal bases, are produced in spring. Z13–15 H12–10. **var. baileyi**, syn. E. baileyi, illus. p.484. **E. schmollii**, syn. Wilcoxia schmollii, illus. p.492.
E. triglochidiatus. Clump-forming, perennial cactus. **H** 12in (30cm), **S** 6in (15cm). Has a short, thick, dark green stem with 3–5 spines, to 1in (2.5cm) long, per areole. In spring bears funnel-shaped, bright red flowers, 3in (7cm) across, with red stamens and green stigmas. Z11–12 H12–9. **var. paucispinus** illus. p.496.

Echinodorus ranunculoides. See Baldellia ranunculoides.
Echinofossulocactus. See Stenocactus.
Echinomastus macdowellii. See Thelocactus macdowellii.

ECHINOPS
Globe thistle
COMPOSITAE/ASTERACEAE

Genus of summer-flowering perennials, grown for their globelike, spiky flower heads. Does best in full sun and in poor soil. Propagate by division or seed in fall or by root cuttings in winter. Flower heads dry well.

E. bannaticus. Upright perennial. **H** 4–5ft (1.2–1.5m), **S** 2½ft (75cm). Has narrow, deeply cut leaves and pale to mid-blue heads of spherical flowers, borne on branching stems in late summer. Z5–9 H9–5. **'Taplow Blue'**, illus. p.241.
E. ritro 'Veitch's Blue'. Upright perennial. **H** 4ft (1.2m), **S** 2½ft (75cm). Sharply divided, dark green leaves are covered in down beneath. Has round, thistle-like, purplish-blue heads of flowers borne in late summer on silvery stems. Z3–9 H11–1.
E. sphaerocephalus. Massive, bushy perennial. **H** 6ft (2m), **S** 3ft (1m). Has deeply cut, mid-green leaves, pale gray beneath, and gray stems bearing round, grayish-white flower heads in late summer. Z3–9 H9–1.

ECHINOPSIS
Easter lily cactus, Sea urchin cactus
CACTACEAE

Genus of spherical to columnar, perennial cacti, mostly freely branching; it is sometimes held to include Trichocereus. Requires full sun and well-drained soil. Propagate by seed or offsets in spring or summer.

E. aurea, syn. Lobivia aurea, Pseudolobivia aurea, Lobivia cylindrica, illus. p.495.
E. backebergii, syn. E. backerbergii subsp. backebergii, Lobivia backebergii, illus. p.491. **subsp. backebergii.** See E. backebergii.
E. bridgesii. See E. lageniformis.
E. candicans, syn. Trichocereus candicans, illus. p.492.
E. chamaecereus, syn. Chamaecereus silvestrii, Lobivia silvestrii, illus. p.486.
E. cinnabarina, syn. Lobivia cinnabarina. Spherical, perennial cactus. **H** and **S** 6in (15cm). Glossy, dark green stem has about 20 warty ribs and mostly curved, dark spines. In summer bears funnel-shaped to flattish, carmine-red flowers, 3in (8cm) across. Z13–15 H12–10.
E. eyriesii. See E. oxygona.
E. lageniformis, syn. E. bridgesii, Trichocereus bridgesii, illus. p.489.
E. marsoneri, syn. Lobivia haageana, illus. p.491.
E. multiplex. See E. oxygona.
E. oxygona, syn. E. eyriesii, E. multiplex, Echinocactus eyriesii, illus. p.481.
E. pentlandii, syn. Lobivia pentlandii, illus. p.491.
E. rhodotricha. Spherical to columnar, perennial cactus. **H** 2ft (60cm), **S** 8in (20cm). Produces branching, dark green stems, 3½in (9cm) across, with 8–13 ribs. Curved, dark spines, ¾in (2cm) long, later turn pale. Has tubular, white to pink flowers in spring–summer. Z13–15 H12–10.
E. spachiana, syn. Cereus spachianus, Trichocereus spachianus, illus. p.492.

Echioides longiflorum. See Arnebia pulchra.

ECHIUM

BORAGINACEAE

Genus of annuals and evergreen shrubs, biennials and perennials, grown for their flowers. Needs full sun and fertile, well-drained soil. Water container specimens freely in summer, moderately at other times. Propagate by seed in spring or by greenwood or semiripe cuttings in summer. Whitefly may sometimes be troublesome. ① All parts may cause mild stomach upset if ingested; contact with the foliage may irritate skin.

E. bourgaeanum. See *E. wildpretii*.

E. vulgare (Blueweed, Viper's bugloss) (dwarf). Moderately fast-growing, erect, bushy annual or biennial. **H** 12in (30cm), **S** 8in (20cm). Has lance-shaped, dark green leaves. Spikes of tubular flowers, in white, pink, blue or purple, are borne in summer. Z3–8 H8–1.

E. wildpretii, syn. *E. bourgaeanum*. Evergreen, erect, unbranched biennial that dies after fruiting. **H** 8ft (2.5m) or more, **S** 2ft (60cm). Narrowly lance-shaped, silver-haired leaves, 1ft (30cm) long, form a dense rosette. Has compact spires, 3–5ft (1–1.5m) long, of small, funnel-shaped, red flowers in late spring and early summer. Z9–10 H10–8.

EDGEWORTHIA

THYMELAEACEAE

Genus of deciduous shrubs, grown for their flowers in late winter and early spring. Is best grown against a south- or west-facing wall where marginally hardy. Requires full sun and well-drained soil. Dislikes being transplanted. Propagate by semiripe cuttings in summer or by seed in fall.

E. chrysantha, syn. *E. papyrifera*, illus. p.126.

E. papyrifera. See *E. chrysantha*.

EDRAIANTHUS

CAMPANULACEAE

Genus of short-lived perennials, some of which are evergreen, usually growing from central rootstocks. In winter, a small bud is just visible from each rootstock. In spring, prostrate stems radiate to carry leaves and flowers. Is suitable for rock gardens, screes and troughs. Needs sun and well-drained soil. Propagate by softwood cuttings from sideshoots in early summer or by seed in fall.

E. dalmaticus. Upright, then arching perennial. **H** 4in (10cm), **S** 6in (15cm). Bears narrowly lance-shaped, pale green leaves and, in early summer, terminal clusters of bell-shaped, violet-blue flowers, 1in (2.5cm) across. Z8–9 H9–8.

E. pumilio, illus. p.368.

E. serpyllifolius, syn. *Wahlenbergia serpyllifolia*, illus. p.367. **'Major'** is an evergreen, prostrate perennial. **H** ½in (1cm), **S** to 2in (5cm). Has tight mats of tiny, oval, dark green leaves. In early summer, bell-shaped, deep violet flowers, ⅝in (1.5cm) wide, are borne on very short stems. Needs a sheltered site. Seldom sets seed.

Edwardsia microphylla. See *Sophora microphylla*.

EGERIA

HYDROCHARITACEAE/RESTIONACEAE

Genus of semievergreen or evergreen, perennial, floating or submerged water plants, grown for their foliage. Is similar to *Elodea*, but has more conspicuous flowers, borne above water surface. Plants are useful for oxygenating water in aquariums and provide a suitable depository for fish spawn. Needs a sunny position. Thin regularly to keep under control. Some species are invasive if allowed to escape cultivation. Propagate by stem cuttings in spring or summer.

E. densa, syn. *Anacharis densa*, *Elodea densa*. Semievergreen perennial, spreading, submerged water plant. for aquariums. **S** indefinite. Forms a mass of small, lance-shaped, whorled, dark green leaves borne on long, wiry stems. Small, 3-parted, white flowers are produced in summer. *E. densa* is considered a noxious weed in many regions of North America, and should be restricted to aquarium plantings. Z6–15 H12–6.

EHRETIA

BORAGINACEAE

Genus of deciduous, summer-flowering trees, grown for their foliage and star-shaped flowers. May suffer cold damage when young. Requires sun or partial shade and fertile, well-drained soil. Propagate by softwood cuttings in summer.

E. dicksonii, illus. p.88.

EICHHORNIA

PONTEDERIACEAE

Genus of evergreen or semievergreen, perennial, floating and marginal water plants. Needs an open, sunny position in warm water. Considered a noxious weed in the southern United States, it grows prolifically and requires regular thinning year-round. Propagate by detaching young plants as required.

E. crassipes, syn. *E. speciosa*, illus. p.441.

E. speciosa. See *E. crassipes*.

ELAEAGNUS

ELAEAGNACEAE

Genus of deciduous or evergreen shrubs and trees, grown for their foliage and small, usually fragrant flowers, and ornamental fruits. Evergreens make good shelter belts or hedging, particularly in coastal areas. Most evergreen species thrive in sun or shade, but silver-leaved and deciduous species prefer full sun. Requires fertile, well-drained soil. Trim hedges in late summer. Propagate by seed in fall, evergreen forms also by semiripe cuttings in summer, deciduous forms by softwood or semiripe cuttings in summer.

E. angustifolia, illus. p.116.

E. x ebbingei. Evergreen, bushy, dense shrub. **H** and **S** 15ft (5m). Has oblong to oval, glossy, dark green leaves, silvery beneath. Fragrant, bell-shaped, silvery-white flowers are borne from mid- to late fall. Z7–11 H12–7. **'Gilt Edge'** have golden-yellow margins. Z7–10 H10–7. **'Limelight',** illus. p.139.

E. macrophylla. Evergreen, bushy, dense shrub. **H** and **S** 10ft (3m). Broadly oval leaves are silvery-gray when young, becoming glossy and dark green above, but remaining silvery-gray beneath, when mature. Fragrant, bell-shaped, creamy-yellow flowers, silvery outside, are produced from mid- to late fall, followed by egg-shaped, red fruits. Z7–9 H9–7. **'Aureovariegata'.** See *E. pungens* 'Maculata'.

E. pungens 'Maculata', syn. *E. pungens* 'Aureovariegata', illus. p.119.

E. umbellata, illus. p.113.

ELAEOCARPUS

ELAEOCARPACEAE

Genus of evergreen, spring- and summer-flowering shrubs and trees, grown for their flowers and foliage. Requires full sun or partial shade and fertile, well-drained but not dry soil. Water container plants freely when in growth, less in winter. Current season's growth may be cut back in winter. Propagate by seed in spring or by semiripe cuttings in summer. Red spider mite and whitefly may cause problems.

E. cyaneus, syn. *E. reticulatus* (Blueberry ash). Evergreen, rounded shrub or tree. **H** and **S** 10ft (3m). Bears elliptic to lance-shaped, toothed, lustrous leaves and, in summer, bell-shaped, fringed, white flowers, and globular, blue fruits in fall. Z14–15 H12–10.

E. reticulatus. See *E. cyaneus*.

ELATOSTEMA

SYN. PELLIONIA

URTICACEAE

Genus of evergreen, creeping perennials and subshrubs that make useful groundcover. Requires humid conditions, indirect light and moist soil. Propagate from stem cuttings in spring or summer.

E. pulchra, syn. *E. repens* var. *pulchra*. Evergreen, slightly fleshy perennial with rooting, creeping stems. **H** 3–4in (8–10cm), **S** 2ft (60cm) or more. Broadly oval leaves, 2in (5cm) long, are blackish-green with dark green veins above, purple below. Flowers are insignificant. Z13–15 H12–10.

E. repens, syn. *Pellionia daveauana*, *Pellionia repens*, illus. p.473. **var. pulchra.** See *E. pulchra*.

ELEGIA

RESTIONACEAE

See also GRASSES, BAMBOOS, RUSHES and SEDGES.

E. capensis, illus. p.285.

ELEOCHARIS

CYPERACEAE

See also GRASSES, BAMBOOS, RUSHES and SEDGES.

E. acicularis (Needle spike-rush). Evergreen, rhizomatous, perennial sedge. **H** to 4in (10cm), **S** indefinite. Basal, mid-green leaves are very narrow. Hairless, unbranched, square stems produce solitary, tiny, brown spikelets in summer. Z9–11 H12–9.

ELEUTHEROCOCCUS

SYN. ACANTHOPANAX

ARALIACEAE

Genus of deciduous shrubs and trees, grown for their foliage and fruits. Produces tiny, usually greenish-white flowers. Prefers full sun and needs well-drained soil. Propagate by seed in spring or by root cuttings in late winter.

E. sieboldianus, illus. p.138.

Elliottia paniculata. See *Tripetaleia paniculata*.

Elodea crispa of gardens. See *Lagarosiphon major*.

Elodea densa. See *Egeria densa*.

ELSHOLTZIA

LABIATAE/LAMIACEAE

Genus of perennials and deciduous shrubs and subshrubs, grown for their flowers. Needs full sun and fertile, well-drained soil. Cut back old shoots hard in early spring. Propagate by softwood cuttings in summer.

E. stauntonii. Deciduous, open subshrub. **H** and **S** 5in (1.5m). Sharply toothed, mint-scented, dark green leaves turn red in fall. Slender spires of pale purple blooms are produced in late summer–fall. Z5–8 H8–5.

Elymus arenarius. See *Leymus arenarius*.

EMBOTHRIUM

PROTEACEAE

Genus of evergreen or semievergreen trees, grown for their flowers. Provide shelter from cold winds. Needs partial shade and moist but well-drained, acidic soil. Propagate by suckers in spring or fall or by seed in fall.

E. coccineum, illus. p.86.

EMILIA

SYN. CACALIA

COMPOSITAE/ASTERACEAE

Genus of annuals and perennials with flowers that are good for cutting. Is ideal for hot, dry areas and coastal soils. Requires sun and very well-drained soil. Propagate by seed sown under glass in spring, or outdoors in late spring.

E. coccinea, syn. *E. flammea*, *E. javanica*, illus. p.327.

E. flammea. See *E. coccinea*.

E. javanica of gardens. See *E. coccinea*.

EMMENOPTERYS

RUBIACEAE

Genus of deciduous trees, grown for their foliage; flowers only appear in hot summers. Even where reliably hardy, young growths may be damaged by late frosts. Needs full sun and deep, fertile, well-drained soil. Propagate by softwood cuttings in summer.

E. henryi, illus. p.75.

ENCEPHALARTOS

ZAMIACEAE

Genus of evergreen shrubs and trees, grown for their palmlike leaves. Needs full sun and well-drained soil. Water container

E

plants moderately when in full growth, less at other times. Propagate by seed in spring.
E. ferox, illus. p.457.
E. longifolius. Slow-growing, evergreen tree, sometimes branched with age. **H** 10ft (3m) or more, **S** 5–8ft (1.5–2.5m). Has feather-shaped leaves, 2–5ft (60cm–1.5m) long, divided into narrowly lance-shaped to oval, blue-green leaflets, usually with hook-tipped teeth. Conelike, brown flower heads are produced intermittently. Z11 H12–10.

ENCYCLIA

ORCHIDACEAE

See also ORCHIDS.
E. cochleata. Evergreen, epiphytic orchid for a cool greenhouse. **H** 12in (30cm). Upright spikes of green flowers, 2in (5cm) long, with dark purple lips at the top and ribbon-like sepals and petals, are produced in summer and, on mature plants, intermittently throughout the year. Has narrowly oval leaves, 6in (15cm) long. Requires partial shade in summer. Z14–15 H12–10.
E. radiata. Evergreen, epiphytic orchid for a cool greenhouse. **H** 10in (25cm). Bears upright spikes of very fragrant, rounded, creamy-white flowers, $\frac{1}{2}$in (1cm) across, with red-lined, white lips, in summer. Narrowly oval leaves are 4–6in (10–15cm) long. Z14–15 H12–10.

Endymion. See *Hyacinthoides.*

ENKIANTHUS

ERICACEAE

Genus of deciduous or semievergreen, spring-flowering shrubs and trees, grown for their mass of small, bell- or urn-shaped flowers and their fall color. Needs sun or partial shade and moist, peaty, acidic soil. Propagate by semiripe cuttings in summer or by seed in fall.
E. campanulatus, illus. p.111.
E. cernuus f. rubens, illus. p.123.
E. perulatus, illus. p.120.

ENSETE

MUSACEAE

Genus of evergreen perennials, grown for their foliage, which resembles that of bananas, and fruits. Has false stems made of overlapping leaf sheaths that die after flowering. Needs sun or partial shade and rich soil. Propagate by seed in spring or by division year-round.
E. ventricosum, syn. *Musa arnoldiana, Musa ensete,* illus. p.474.

EOMECON

PAPAVERACEAE

Genus of one species of perennial. Is suitable for large rock gardens. Needs sun and well-drained soil. Propagate by seed or runners in spring.
E. chionantha (Snow poppy). Vigorous, spreading perennial. **H** to 16in (40cm), **S** indefinite. Leaves are large, palmate and gray. Erect stems bear long panicles of small, poppy-like, white flowers in summer. Z7–9 H9–7.

EPACRIS

ERICACEAE/EPACRIDACEAE

Genus of evergreen, heather-like shrubs, grown for their flowers. Needs full sun and rich, well-drained, neutral to acidic soil. Water container plants moderately when in full growth, less at other times. Cut back flowered stems after flowering to maintain a neat habit. Propagate by seed in spring or semiripe cuttings in late summer.
E. impressa, illus. p.455.

EPHEDRA

EPHEDRACEAE

Genus of evergreen shrubs, grown for their habit and green shoots. Makes good groundcover in dry soil. Grow male and female plants together in order to obtain fruits. Requires full sun and well-drained soil. Propagate by seed in fall or by division in fall or spring.
E. gerardiana. Evergreen, spreading shrub with slender, erect, rushlike, green shoots. **H** 2ft (60cm), **S** 6ft (2m). Leaves and flowers are inconspicuous. Bears small, spherical, red fruits. Z5–9 H9–5.

EPIDENDRUM

ORCHIDACEAE

See also ORCHIDS.
E. difforme. Evergreen, epiphytic orchid for an intermediate greenhouse. **H** 9in (23cm). Large heads of semitranslucent, green flowers, $\frac{1}{4}$in (0.5cm) across, are produced in fall. Has oval, rigid leaves, 1–2in (2.5–5cm) long. Requires shade in summer. Avoid spraying, which can cause spotting of leaves. Propagate by division in spring. Z14–15 H12–10.
E. ibaguense, syn. *E. radicans.* Evergreen, epiphytic orchid for a cool greenhouse. **H** 6ft (2m) or more. Produces a succession of feathery-lipped, deep red flowers, $\frac{1}{4}$in (0.5cm) across. Leaves, 1–2in (2.5–5cm) long, are oval and rigid. Grow in partial shade in summer. Propagate by tip cuttings in spring. Z14 H12–6.
E. radicans. See *E. ibaguense.*

EPIGAEA

ERICACEAE

Genus of evergreen, prostrate, spring-flowering subshrubs. Needs shade and rich, moist, acidic soil. Most are difficult to cultivate. Propagate by seed in spring or by softwood cuttings in early summer.
E. asiatica. Evergreen, creeping subshrub. **H** to 4in (10cm), **S** to 8in (20cm). Stems and heart-shaped, deep green leaves are covered with brown hairs. Bears terminal clusters of 3–6 tiny, slightly fragrant, urn-shaped, white or pink flowers in spring. Z5–7 H7–5.
E. gaultherioides, syn. *Orphanidesia gaultherioides,* illus. p.351.
E. repens (Mayflower, Trailing arbutus). Evergreen, creeping subshrub. **H** 4in (10cm), **S** 12in (30cm). Hairy stems, bearing heart-shaped, leathery leaves, root at intervals. In spring produces terminal clusters of 4–6 cup-shaped, white flowers, sometimes flushed pink. Is relatively easy to grow. Z3–9 H9–1.

EPILOBIUM

syn. CHAMAENERION, CHAMERION
Willow herb

ONAGRACEAE

Genus of annuals, biennials, semievergreen and deciduous perennials and subshrubs, grown for their deep pink to white flowers in summer. Is useful on dry banks; many species are invasive. Tolerates sun or shade and prefers moist but well-drained soil. Propagate species by seed in fall, selected forms by softwood cuttings from sideshoots in spring.
E. angustifolium f. album, illus. p.216.
E. californicum. See *Zauschneria californica.*
E. canum. See *Zauschneria californica* subsp. *cana.*
E. chlorifolium var. kaikourense. Clump-forming, deciduous, woody-based perennial. **H** 12in (30cm), **S** 6in (15cm). Has persistent, oval, hairy, bronze and dark green leaves. Produces short spikes of funnel-shaped, white to pink flowers in summer. Z4–6 H6–1.
E. glabellum of gardens, illus. p.360.
E. obcordatum. Clump-forming perennial. **H** 6in (15cm), **S** 4in (10cm). Oval leaves are glossy green. Spikes of open cup-shaped, deep rose-pink flowers are borne in summer. Is good for a rock garden or alpine house. Requires a sheltered position and full sun. In cultivation may not retain character, especially in mild climates. Z5–8 H8–5.
E. septentrionale. See *Zauschneria septentrionalis.*

EPIMEDIUM

Barrenwort

BERBERIDACEAE

Genus of spring-flowering perennials, some of which are evergreen. Flowers are cup-shaped with long or short spurs. Makes good groundcover. Fully hardy. Does best in partial shade and rich, moist but well-drained soil. Cut back just before new growth appears in spring. Propagate by division in spring or fall.
E. alpinum. Evergreen, clump-forming perennial. **H** 9in (23cm), **S** to 12in (30cm). Racemes of pendent, short-spurred flowers, with crimson sepals and yellow petals, are produced in spring. Has finely toothed, glossy leaves divided into oval, angled, mid-green leaflets, bronze when young. Z4–9 H9–4.
E. 'Amber Queen', illus. p.263.
E. davidii. Vigorous, evergreen, groundcover perennial. **H** 12in (30cm), **S** 16in (40cm). Dainty, mid-green leaves are tinged bronze when young and divided into rounded heart-shaped, toothed leaflets. Produces clusters of pendent, long-spurred, butter-yellow flowers in spring. Z5–9 H9–4.
E. epsteinii, illus. p.260.
E. grandiflorum 'Crimson Beauty' Clump-forming perennial. **H** and **S** 12in (30cm). Racemes of pendent, long-spurred, copper-crimson flowers are produced in spring at the same time as heart-shaped, copper-marked, light green leaves, divided into oval leaflets, which mature to mid-green. **'Rose Queen'** has wiry stems bearing clusters of cup-shaped, deep pink flowers with white-tipped spurs in spring.

Z4–8 H8–2. **f. violaceum** has young leaves that are flushed bronze and produces purple-and-white flowers.
E. x perralchicum. Evergreen, carpeting perennial. **H** 18in (45cm), **S** 12in (30cm). Short spires of pendent, yellow flowers, with short spurs, are borne in spring. Leaves, divided into rounded to oval leaflets, are dark green. Z5–8 H8–5.
E. perralderianum. Semievergreen, carpeting perennial. **H** 12in (30cm), **S** 18in (45cm). Clusters of small, pendent, short-spurred, bright yellow flowers are borne in spring. Has large, toothed, glossy, deep green leaves, divided into rounded to oval leaflets. Z5–8 H8–5.
E. pinnatum subsp. colchicum. Evergreen, carpeting perennial. **H** and **S** 12in (30cm). In spring, clusters of small, pendent, bright yellow flowers, with short spurs, are produced above dark green leaves, hairy when young, divided into oval leaflets. Z5–9 H9–4.
E. pubigerum. Evergreen, carpeting perennial. **H** and **S** 18in (45cm). Has heart-shaped, divided, smooth, dense foliage and clusters of cup-shaped, creamy-white or pink flowers in spring. Z5–9 H9–4.
E. x rubrum, illus. p.260.
E. x versicolor. Clump-forming perennial. **H** and **S** 12in (30cm). Small, pendent clusters of yellow flowers, with long, red-tinged spurs, are produced in spring. Heart-shaped, fresh green leaves are divided into oval leaflets that are tinted reddish-purple. Z5–9 H9–4. **'Neosulphureum',** illus. p.262.
E. x warleyense, illus. p.263.
E. x youngianum 'Niveum', illus. p.254.

EPIPHYLLUM

Orchid cactus

CACTACEAE

Genus of perennial cacti with strap-shaped, flattened, green stems that have notched edges. Flowers are produced at notches. Needs sun or partial shade and rich, well-drained soil. Propagate by stem cuttings in spring or summer.
E. ackermannii. See *Disocactus ackermannii.*
E. anguliger, illus. p.494.
E. crenatum. Erect, then pendent, perennial cactus. **H** and **S** 10ft (3m). Has a flattened stem. Bears lightly perfumed, funnel-shaped, broad-petaled, white flowers, 8in (20cm) across, in spring–summer. Is often used as a parent for breeding. Z11–12 H12–1.
E. laui, illus. p.482.
E. oxypetalum. Erect, then pendent, perennial cactus. **H** 10ft (3m), **S** 3ft (1m). Produces freely branching, flattened stems, 5in (12cm) across. In spring–summer bears nocturnal, tubular, white flowers, 10in (25cm) long. Makes a good house plant. Z11–12 H12–1.

EPIPREMNUM

syn. POTHOS

ARACEAE

Genus of evergreen, woody-stemmed, root climbers, including *Pothos,* grown for their foliage. Grow in light shade away from direct sun; any well-drained, moisture-retentive soil is suitable. Water regularly, less in cold weather. Stems need good supports. Remove shoot tips

E

to induce branching at any time. Propagate by leaf-bud or stem-tip cuttings in late spring or by layering in summer. ① All parts may cause severe discomfort if ingested, and contact with the sap of *E. aureum* may irritate skin.

E. aureum 'Marble Queen', syn. *Scindapsus aureus* 'Marble Queen', illus. p.460.

E. pictum 'Argyraeum'. See *Scindapsus pictus* 'Argyraeus'.

EPISCIA
Flame violet
GESNERIACEAE

Genus of evergreen, low-growing and creeping perennials, grown for their ornamental leaves and colorful flowers. Is useful as groundcover or in hanging baskets. Requires high humidity, a shaded site and rich, well-drained soil. Keep well watered, but avoid waterlogging. Propagate in summer by stem cuttings, division or removing rooted runners.

E. cupreata, illus. p.471. **'Metallica'** is an evergreen, creeping perennial. **H** 4in (10cm), **S** indefinite. Has oval, downy, wrinkled leaves, tinged pink to copper and with broad, silvery bands along midribs. Funnel-shaped, orange-red flowers, marked yellow within, are borne intermittently. Z14–15 H9–1. **'Tropical Topaz'** has yellow flowers.

E. dianthiflora, syn. *Alsobia dianthiflora*, illus. p.465.

E. lilacina. Evergreen, low-growing perennial, with runners bearing plantlets. **H** 4in (10cm), **S** indefinite. Has oval, hairy, pale green leaves, to 3in (8cm) long. Funnel-shaped, white flowers, tinged mauve and with yellow eyes, are produced in small clusters from fall to spring. Z11–12 H12–1. Leaves of **'Cuprea'** are bronze-tinged.

EPITHELANTHA
CACTACEAE

Genus of very slow-growing, spherical, perennial cacti densely covered with very short spines. Needs full sun and well-drained soil; prone to rotting if overwatered. Propagate by grafting, seed or stem cuttings in spring or summer.

E. micromeris, illus. p.493.

ERAGROSTIS
Love grass
GRAMINEAE/POACEAE

See also GRASSES, BAMBOOS, RUSHES and SEDGES.

E. curvula 'Totnes Burgundy', illus. p.285.

ERANTHEMUM
ACANTHACEAE

Genus of perennials and evergreen shrubs, grown for their flowers. Requires full light or partial shade and fertile, well-drained soil. Water container plants freely when in full growth, moderately at other times. In spring or after flowering, remove at least half of each spent flowering stem to encourage a bushier habit. Propagate by softwood cuttings in late spring. Whitefly may be a nuisance.

E. atropurpureum. See *Pseuderanthemum atropurpureum*.

E. nervosum. See *E. pulchellum*.

E. pulchellum, syn. *E. nervosum*. Evergreen, erect shrub. **H** 3–4ft (1–1.2m), **S** 2ft (60cm) or more. Produces elliptic to oval, prominently veined, deep green leaves. Blue flowers, each with a tube 1¼in (3cm) long and rounded petal lobes, are produced in winter–spring. Z13–15 H12–10.

ERANTHIS
RANUNCULACEAE

Genus of clump-forming perennials, with knobby tubers, grown for their cup-shaped flowers surrounded by leaflike ruffs of bracts. Prefers partial shade and rich soil, well-drained but not drying out excessively. Dies down in summer. Propagate by seed in fall or by division of clumps immediately after flowering while still in leaf. ① All parts may cause mild stomach upset if ingested, and contact with the sap may irritate skin.

E. hyemalis, illus. p.429.

E. x tubergenii 'Guinea Gold'. Late winter- or early spring-flowering, tuberous perennial. **H** 3–4in (8–10cm), **S** 1½–2½in (4–6cm). Stems each bear a stalkless, deep golden-yellow flower, 1¼–1½in (3–4cm) across, surrounded by a bronze-green bract, cut into narrow lobes. Rounded leaves are divided into finger-shaped lobes. Z4–9 H9–1.

ERCILLA
SYN. BRIDGESIA
PHYTOLACCACEAE

Genus of evergreen, root climbers, grown for their neat, green leaves and green and purple flower spikes. Needs sun or partial shade and well-drained soil. Prune after flowering, if required. Propagate by stem cuttings in late summer or fall.

E. spicata. See *E. volubilis*.

E. volubilis, syn. *E. spicata*, illus. p.192.

EREMURUS
Desert candle, Foxtail lily
LILIACEAE/ASPHODELACEAE

Genus of perennials, with fleshy, finger-like roots, grown for their stately spires of shallowly cup-shaped flowers in summer. Requires a sunny, warm position and well-drained soil. Tends to come into growth very early, and young shoots may be frosted. Provide a covering of dry bracken in late winter to protect the crowns when shoots are first developing. Stake tall species and hybrids. Propagate by division in spring or early fall or by seed in fall.

E. himalaicus. Upright perennial. **H** 6–8ft (2–2.5m), **S** 3ft (1m). Has strap-shaped, bright green basal leaves. In early summer, tall stems bear dense racemes of open cup-shaped, pure white flowers, with long stamens. Z5–8 H8–5.

E. x isabellinus 'Cleopatra', illus. p.220.

E. robustus, illus. p.216.

E. Shelford Hybrids. Perennials of varying habit and flower color. **H** 5ft (1.5m), **S** 2ft (60cm). Long racemes of orange, buff, pink or white flowers are borne freely in mid-summer. Leaves are strap-shaped, in basal rosettes. Z6–9 H9–4.

E. spectabilis. Erect perennial. **H** 4ft (1.2m), **S** 2ft (60cm). Bears long racemes of pale yellow flowers, with brick-red anthers, in early summer. Leaves are strap-shaped, in basal rosettes. Z7–9 H9–7.

ERIA
ORCHIDACEAE

See also ORCHIDS.

E. coronaria, syn. *Trichosma suavis*. Evergreen, epiphytic orchid for a cool greenhouse. **H** 9in (23cm). Sprays of fragrant, rounded, creamy-white flowers, ½in (1cm) across, with red- and yellow-marked lips, are produced in fall. Has broadly oval, glossy leaves, 4in (10cm) long. Needs partial shade in summer and moist compost year-round. Z6–8 H8–6.

ERICA
Heath
ERICACEAE

See also HEATHERS.

E. arborea (Tree heath). Evergreen, upright, shrublike tree heather. **H** 20ft (6m), **S** 5ft (1.5m). Liable to damage from frost and cold winds. Has needlelike, bright green leaves in whorls of 3 or 4 and bears scented, bell-shaped, white flowers from late winter to late spring. May tolerate slightly alkaline soil. Z9–10 H10–9.

'Albert's Gold', **H** 6ft (2m), retains its golden foliage year-round. **var. alpina** (illus. p.166) has vivid green foliage and compact racemes of white flowers. May be pruned hard to keep its shape and to encourage new growth.

E. australis (Spanish heath, Spanish tree heath). Evergreen, shrublike tree heather. **H** to 7ft (2.2m), **S** 3ft (1m). Stems may be damaged by snow and frost. Has needlelike leaves in whorls of 4 and tubular to bell-shaped, white or purplish-pink flowers in spring. May tolerate slightly alkaline soil. Z9–10 H10–9. **f. albiflora 'Mr. Robert'** has white flowers. **'Riverslea'** has bright purple-pink flowers, mostly in clusters of 4.

E. canaliculata (Channeled heath). Evergreen, erect shrub. **H** to 10ft (3m), **S** 3ft (1m). Produces whorls of 3 dark green narrow, needlelike leaves. Cup-shaped, pearl-white flowers, sometimes rose-tinted, with dark brown, almost black anthers, are borne in winter (in a greenhouse) or early spring (in the open). Requires acidic soil. Z9–10 H10–9.

E. carnea, syn. *E. herbacea* (Alpine heath, Winter heath). Evergreen, spreading shrub. **H** to 12in (30cm), **S** to 18in (45cm) or more. Produces whorls of needlelike, mid- to dark green leaves and bears tubular to bell-shaped flowers that are in shades of pink and red, occasionally white, from early winter to late spring. Tolerates limestone and some shade. Makes good groundcover. Z5–7 H7–5. **'Altadena'** has golden foliage and pale pink flowers. **'Ann Sparkes'** (illus. p.166), **H** 6in (15cm), has golden foliage, turning to bronze in winter, and rose-pink flowers. **'Bell's Extra Special'**, **H** 6in (15cm), **S** 16in (40cm), has a neat habit, with crimson flowers borne on whiskey-colored foliage, flecked with tints of orange and gold. **'Cecilia M. Beale'**, **H** 6in (15cm), bears an abundance of white flowers from mid-winter to early spring. **'Challenger'** (illus. p.166) has magenta

flowers, with deep pink sepals, set against dark green leaves. **'December Red'** has a spreading habit, vigorous growth and deep rose-pink flowers borne in winter. **'Foxhollow'**, a vigorous, spreading cultivar, has foliage that is golden-yellow in summer, with orange tips in spring, and a few pale pink flowers. **'Golden Starlet'** (illus. p.166), **H** 6in (15cm), **S** 16in (40cm), bears white flowers set on lime-green foliage that turns a glowing yellow in summer. **'Ice Princess'**, **H** 6in (15cm), **S** 14in (35cm), has white flowers held erect on bright green foliage. **'Isabell'**, **H** 6in (15cm), **S** 14in (35cm), has large, white flowers on bright green foliage, and an erect but spreading habit. **'King George'**, **H** 8in (20cm), has dark green foliage and deep rose-pink flowers from early winter to mid-spring. **'Loughrigg'**, **H** 6in (15cm), produces dark purplish-red flowers from late winter to spring. **'March Seedling'** has a spreading habit, dark green foliage and rich, rose-purple flowers. **'Myretoun Ruby'**, **H** 8in (20cm), is vigorous but compact with brilliant deep purple-red flowers in late winter and early spring. **'Nathalie'**, **H** 6in (15cm), **S** 16in (40cm), the deepest and brightest of the *E. carnea* cultivars, has purple flowers, neat, dark green foliage and a compact, upright habit. **'Pink Spangles'**, **H** 6in (15cm), is vigorous with flowers that have shell-pink sepals and deeper pink corollas. **'Pirbright Rose'** is very floriferous with bright pink flowers from early winter to early spring. **'R.B. Cooke'**, **H** 8in (20cm), bears clear pink flowers from early winter to early spring. **'Rosalie'**, **H** 6in (15cm), **S** 14in (35cm), has bright pink flowers, bronze-green foliage and a low, upright but spreading habit. **'Springwood White'** (illus. p.166), **H** 6in (15cm), the most vigorous white cultivar, is excellent as groundcover and bears large, white flowers, with brown anthers, from late winter to spring. **'Vivellii'**, **H** 6in (15cm), has dark bronze-green foliage and deep purple-pink flowers from late winter to spring. **'Westwood Yellow'** is compact with golden-yellow foliage and deep pink flowers. **'Wintersonne'**, **H** 6in (15cm), **S** 14in (35cm), has magenta flowers and red-brown foliage.

E. ciliaris (Dorset heath). Evergreen, loose shrub. **H** to 12in (30cm), **S** 16in (40cm). May be damaged in severe weather. Has needlelike, dark green leaves in whorls of 3. Bears long racemes of bell-shaped, bright pink flowers in tiers of 3 or 4 in summer. Requires acidic soil and prefers warm, moist conditions. Z8–9 H9–8. **'Aurea'** has somewhat straggly growth with golden foliage and clear pink flowers. **'Corfe Castle'** (illus. p.166) produces salmon-pink flowers from summer to early fall. **'David McClintock'** (illus. p.166) has light gray-green foliage and bears white flowers, with deep pink tips, from summer to early fall. **'Mrs. C.H. Gill'** has dark gray-green foliage and clear red flowers. **'White Wings'**, a sport of 'Mrs. C.H. Gill', has dark gray-green foliage and white flowers.

E. cinerea (Bell heather). Evergreen, compact shrub. **H** 12in (30cm), **S** 18–24in (45–60cm). Has needlelike, mid- to deep green leaves and bears bell-shaped flowers that are in shades of pink and dark red, occasionally white, from early summer to early fall. Prefers a warm, dry position. Requires acidic

E

soil. Z6–8 H8–6. **'Atropurpurea'** has deep purple flowers in long racemes. **'C.D. Eason'** (illus. p.166) has dark green foliage and bright red flowers. **'Cevennes'** is upright in habit and bears a profusion of mauve flowers. **'C.G. Best'** has mid-green foliage and rose-pink flowers. **'Domino'** produces white flowers that contrast with dark brown stems and sepals and almost black stigmas. **'Eden Valley'** (illus. p.166), **H** 8in (20cm), bears white flowers with lavender-mauve tips. **'Fiddler's Gold'**, **H** 10in (25cm), has golden-yellow foliage, deepening to red in winter, and lilac-pink flowers. **'Golden Hue'**, **H** 14in (35cm), has amethyst flowers set on pale yellow foliage, tipped orange in winter. **'Hookstone White'**, **H** 14in (35cm), has bright green foliage and bears long racemes of large, white flowers. **'Lime Soda'**, **H** 14in (35cm), bears soft lavender flowers in profusion on lime-green foliage. **'Pentreath'** has rich purple flowers. **'Pink Ice'**, **H** 8in (20cm), is compact with soft pink flowers. **'P.S. Patrick'** is a vigorous cultivar with purple flowers and dark green foliage. **'Purple Beauty'** has purple flowers and dark foliage. **'Stephen Davis'**, **H** 10in (25cm), has brilliant, almost fluorescent, red flowers. **'Velvet Night'**, **H** 10in (25cm), produces very dark purple, almost black flowers. **'Windlebrooke'**, **H** 10in (25cm), is vigorous, with golden foliage, turning bright orange-red in winter, and mauve flowers.

***E.* x *darleyensis*.** Evergreen, bushy shrub. **H** 18in (45cm), **S** 3ft (1m) or more. Has needlelike, mid-green foliage, with cream, pink or red, young growth in late spring. Bell-shaped, white, pink or purple flowers are borne in racemes from early winter to late spring. Tolerates limestone. Z7–8 H8–7. **'Archie Graham'**, **H** 20in (50cm), is vigorous with mauve-pink flowers. **'Arthur Johnson'** (illus. p.166), **H** 3ft (1m), has young foliage with cream and pink tips in spring and long racemes of mauve-pink flowers from mid-winter to spring. **'Darley Dale'** bears pale mauve flowers from mid-winter to spring. **'Furzey'** (illus. p.166) has a compact, vigorous habit and bears deep pink flowers and dark green leaves. **'George Rendall'** produces deep pink flowers from early winter to early spring. **'Ghost Hills'** has cream-tipped foliage in spring and a profusion of pink flowers from mid-winter to spring. **'Jack H. Brummage'**, **H** 12in (30cm), has golden foliage, with yellow and orange tints, and mauve flowers. **'J.W. Porter'**, **H** 12in (30cm), has reddish young shoots in spring and mauve-pink flowers from mid-winter to late spring. **'Kramer's Red'**. See *E.* x *darleyensis* 'Kramer's Rote'. **'Kramer's Rote'**, syn. *E.* x *darleyensis* 'Kramer's Red' has dark bronze-green foliage with deep purple-red flowers from late fall to late spring. Spring foliage does not have cream or red tips. **'Molten Silver'**. See *E.* x *darleyensis* 'Silberschmelze'. **'Silberschmelze'**, syn. *E.* x *darleyensis* 'Molten Silver' is vigorous and produces young shoots with creamy-pink tips in spring and white flowers. **'White Glow'**, **H** 12in (30cm), bears white flowers. **'White Perfection'** (illus. p.166) has bright green foliage and white flowers.

***E. erigena*,** syn. *E. hibernica*, *E. mediterranea*. Evergreen, upright shrub. **H** to 8ft (2.5m), **S** to 3ft (1m). Top growth may be damaged in severe weather, but plant recovers well from the base. Has needlelike, mid-green leaves and, usually, bell-shaped, mauve-pink flowers from early winter to late spring. Tolerates limestone. Flowers of some cultivars have a pronounced scent of honey. Z8–9 H9–8. **f. *alba* 'Brian Proudley'** (illus. p.166), **H** 36in (90cm), **S** 16in (40cm), is a vigorous, erect cultivar with bright green leaves and long racemes of white flowers borne from late fall to mid-spring. **'Brightness'**, **H** 18in (45cm), has bronze-green foliage and mauve-pink flowers in spring. **'Golden Lady'**, **H** 12in (30cm), has a neat, compact habit with year-round, golden foliage and white flowers in late spring. **'Irish Dusk'** (illus. p.166), H 45cm (18in), has dark green foliage and salmon-pink flowers from mid-winter to early spring. **'Superba'**, **H** 6ft (2m), bears strongly scented, rose-pink flowers in spring. **'W.T. Rackliff'**, **H** 2ft (60cm), has dark green foliage and produces thick clusters of white flowers from late winter to late spring.

***E. gracilis*.** Evergreen, compact shrub. **H** and **S** to 12in (30cm). Has needlelike, mid-green leaves and clusters of small, bell-shaped, cerise flowers from early fall to early spring. Is usually grown as a container plant; may be planted outdoors in summer in a sheltered site. Z10–11 H12–10.

***E. herbacea*.** See *E. carnea*.

***E. hibernica*.** See *E. erigena*.

***E.* x *hiemalis*.** Evergreen, bushy shrub. **H** and **S** 12in (30cm). Has needlelike, mid-green foliage and racemes of tubular to bell-shaped, pink-tinged, white flowers from late fall to mid-winter. Z7–8 H8–7.

E. lusitanica (Portuguese heath). Evergreen, upright, bushy tree heather. **H** to 10ft (3m), **S** 3ft (1m). Has feathery, bright green leaves and, from late fall to late spring, bears tubular to bell-shaped flowers that are pink in bud but pure white when fully open. Z8–10 H10–8. **'George Hunt'** has golden foliage; needs a sheltered position.

***E. mackaiana*.** See *E. mackayana*.

***E. mackayana*,** syn. *E. mackaiana* (Mackay's heath). Evergreen, spreading shrub. **H** to 10in (25cm), **S** 16in (40cm). Has needlelike, mid-green leaves and bears umbels of rounded, pink, mauve-pink or white flowers from mid-summer to early fall. Likes damp, acidic soil. Z5–7 H7–5. **'Dr Ronald Gray'**, **H** 6in (15cm), has dark green foliage and pure white flowers. **'Plena'**, **H** 6in (15cm), has double, deep-pink flowers, shading to white in centers.

***E. mediterranea*.** See *E. erigena*.

***E. pageana*.** Evergreen, bushy shrub. **H** to 2ft (60cm), **S** 1ft (30cm). Has needlelike, mid-green leaves and, from late spring to early summer, bell-shaped, rich yellow flowers. Z10 H12–10.

E. perspicua (Prince of Wales heath). Variable, evergreen shrub. **H** to 6ft (2m), **S** 3ft (1m). Has overlapping, needlelike, gray-green leaves and, mainly from early fall to winter, tubular flowers in white, pink-and-white, red-and-white, purple-and-white or red. Needs damp soil.

***E.* x *praegeri*.** See *E.* x *stuartii*.

E. scoparia (Besom heath). Evergreen, bushy shrub. **H** to 10ft (3m), **S** 3ft (1m). Has needlelike, dark green leaves. Clusters of rounded, bell-shaped, greenish-brown flowers are produced in late spring and early summer. Requires acidic soil. Z8–9 H9–8. **'Minima'**, **H** 12in (30cm), has bright green foliage.

***E. spiculifolia*,** syn. *Bruckenthalia spiculifolia* (Spike heath). Evergreen, heather-like shrub. **H** and **S** 6in (15cm). Needlelike, glossy, dark green leaves clothe stiff stems. Terminal clusters of tiny, pink flowers are borne in summer. Z5–7 H7–5.

***E. stricta*.** See *E. terminalis*.

***E.* x *stuartii*,** syn. *E.* x *praegeri*. Evergreen, compact shrub. **H** 6in (15cm), **S** 12in (30cm). Has needlelike, dark green leaves. Numerous umbels of bell-shaped, pink flowers are produced in late spring and summer. Prefers moist, acidic soil. Z5–7 H7–5. **'Irish Lemon'** produces young foliage with lemon-yellow tips in spring and bright pink flowers. **'Irish Orange'** has orange-tipped young foliage and dark pink flowers.

***E. terminalis*,** syn. *E. stricta* (Corsican heath). Evergreen, shrublike tree heather with stiff, upright growth. **H** and **S** to 8ft (2.5m). Has needlelike, mid-green foliage. Bell-shaped, mauve-pink flowers, borne from early summer to early fall, turn russet as they fade in winter. Tolerates limestone. Z5–7 H7–5.

E. tetralix (Cross-leaved heath). Evergreen, spreading shrub. **H** to 12in (30cm), **S** 18in (45cm). Has needlelike, gray-green leaves in whorls of 4. Umbels of bell-shaped, pink flowers are produced from summer to early fall. Requires acidic, preferably moist soil. Z5–7 H7–5. **'Alba Mollis'** has silver-gray foliage and bears white flowers from early summer to late fall. **'Con Underwood'** has dark red flowers. **'Hookstone Pink'** has silver-gray foliage and bears rose-pink flowers from late spring to early fall. **f. *stellata* 'Pink Star'** produces pink flowers held upright in a starlike pattern.

***E. umbellata*.** Evergreen, bushy shrub. **H** and **S** 2ft (60cm). Has needlelike, mid-green foliage and bell-shaped, mauve flowers, with chocolate-brown anthers, in late spring.

E. vagans (Cornish heath). Vigorous, evergreen, bushy shrub. **H** and **S** 30in (75cm). Leaves are needlelike and mid-green. Rounded, bell-shaped, pink, mauve or white flowers are borne from mid-summer to late fall. Tolerates some limestone. Responds well to hard pruning. Z5–7 H7–5. **f. *aureifolia* 'Valerie Proudley'**, **H** 18in (45cm), has golden evergreen foliage when grown in full light, and bears sparse white flowers in late summer and fall. **'Birch Glow'** (illus. p.166), **H** 18in (45cm), has bright green foliage and glowing rose-pink flowers. **'Lyonesse'**, **H** 18in (45cm), has dark green foliage and long, tapering spikes of white flowers with brown anthers. **'Mrs. D.F. Maxwell'** (illus. p.166), **H** 18in (45cm), has dark green foliage and glowing deep pink flowers. **'St. Keverne'** (illus. p.166), **H** 18in (45cm), is a neat, bushy shrub with rose-pink flowers; may be used for a low hedge.

***E.* x *veitchii*.** Evergreen, bushy, shrublike tree heather. **H** to 6ft (2m), **S** 3ft (1m). Has needlelike, mid-green leaves. Scented, tubular to bell-shaped, white flowers are produced in dense clusters from mid-winter to spring. Z8–9 H9–8. **'Exeter'** has a profusion of white flowers, almost obscuring the foliage. **'Gold Tips'** is similar to 'Exeter', but young foliage has golden tips in spring. **'Pink Joy'** has pink flower buds that open to clear white.

***E. verticillata*.** Evergreen, erect shrub. **H** to 2ft (60cm), **S** 1ft (30cm). Has an unusual arrangement of flowers tightly packed in whorls at intervals along an otherwise almost bare stem. Tubular, pale mauve-pink flowers, ½in (1.5cm) long, are produced intermittently throughout the year.

***E.* x *watsonii*.** Evergreen, compact shrub. **H** 12in (30cm), **S** 15in (38cm). Needlelike, mid-green leaves often have bright-colored tips in spring. Bears rounded, bell-shaped, pink flowers from mid- to late summer. Z5–7 H7–5. **'Cherry Turpin'** has long racemes of pale pink flowers from mid-summer to mid-fall. **'Dawn'** produces young foliage with orange-yellow tips and bears deep mauve-pink flowers in compact clusters all summer.

***E.* x *williamsii*.** Evergreen, spreading shrub. **H** 12in (30cm), **S** 24in (60cm). Has needlelike, dark green leaves, with bright yellow tips when young in spring. Bears bell-shaped, mauve or pink flowers in mid-summer. Prefers acidic soil. Z5–7 H7–5. **'Gwavas'** has pale pink flowers on a neat, compact plant from mid-summer to fall. **'P.D. Williams'**, **H** 18in (45cm), has dark mauve-pink flowers; sometimes keeps its golden foliage tips all summer.

ERIGERON

Fleabane

COMPOSITAE/ASTERACEAE

Genus of mainly spring- and summer-flowering annuals, biennials and perennials, grown for their daisylike flower heads. Is good for rock gardens or herbaceous borders. Prefers sun and well-drained soil but should not be allowed to dry out during growing season. Resents winter damp. Propagate by division in spring or early fall or by seed in fall, selected forms by softwood cuttings in early summer.

***E. alpinus*,** illus. p.340.

***E. aurantiacus*.** Clump-forming perennial. **H** 6in (15cm), **S** 12in (30cm). Has long, oval, gray-green leaves and produces daisylike, brilliant orange flower heads in summer. Propagate by seed or division in spring. Z5–8 H8–5.

***E. aureus*.** Short-lived, clump-forming perennial. **H** 2–4in (5–10cm), **S** 6in (15cm). Bears small, spoon-shaped to oval, hairy leaves. Slender stems each bear a relatively large, daisylike, golden-yellow flower head in summer. Dislikes winter wet with no snow cover. Is excellent for a scree, trough or alpine house; is prone to aphid attack. Z5–8 H8–5. **'Canary Bird'**, **H** to 4in (10cm), is longer lived, and bears bright canary-yellow flower heads.

***E.* 'Charity',** illus. p.264.

***E.* 'Darkest of All'.** See *E.* 'Dunkelste Aller'.

***E.* 'Dunkelste Aller',** syn. *E.* 'Darkest of All', illus. p.240.

***E.* 'Foersters Liebling'.** Clump-forming perennial. **H** 32in (80cm), **S** 24in (60cm). In summer, daisylike, semidouble, pink flower heads, with yellow centers, are borne above narrowly oval, grayish-green leaves. Z5–8 H8–5.

E

E. glaucus 'Elstead Pink'. Tufted perennial. **H** 12in (30cm), **S** 6in (15cm). Daisylike, dark lilac-pink flower heads are produced throughout summer above oval, gray-green leaves. Z5–8 H8–5.
E. karvinskianus, syn. *E. mucronatus,* illus. p.363.
E. mucronatus. See *E. karvinskianus.*
E. 'Quakeress'. Clump-forming perennial. **H** 32in (80cm), **S** 24in (60cm). Produces a mass of daisylike, delicate lilac-pink flower heads, with yellow centers, in summer. Narrowly oval leaves are grayish-green. Z5–8 H8–5.
E. 'Serenity'. Clump-forming perennial. **H** and **S** to 24in (60cm). Daisylike, violet-mauve flower heads, with yellow centers, are borne from early to mid-summer. Z5–8 H8–5.

ERINACEA
LEGUMINOSAE/PAPILIONACEAE

Genus of one species of slow-growing, evergreen subshrub, grown for its hard, sharp, blue-green spines and pealike flowers. In spring, produces short-lived, soft leaves. Needs a sheltered position with full sun and deep, gritty, well-drained soil. Propagate by seed when available or by softwood cuttings in late spring or summer.
E. anthyllis, syn. *E. pungens,* illus. p.334.
E. pungens. See *E. anthyllis.*

ERINUS
Fairy foxglove
SCROPHULARIACEAE/PLANTAGINACEAE

Genus of short-lived, semievergreen perennials, suitable for rock gardens, walls and troughs. Needs sun and well-drained soil. Propagate species by seed in fall (but seedlings will vary considerably), selected forms by softwood cuttings in early summer. Self-seeds freely.
E. alpinus, illus. p.352. **'Dr. Haenele'.** See *E. alpinus* 'Dr. Hähnle'. **'Dr. Hähnle',** syn. *E. alpinus* 'Dr. Haenele' is a semievergreen, basal-rosetted perennial. **H** and **S** 2–3in (5–8cm). Small, flat, 2-lipped, deep pink flowers are produced in late spring and summer. Leaves are small, oval and mid-green.

ERIOBOTRYA
Loquat
ROSACEAE

Genus of evergreen, fall-flowering trees and shrubs, grown for their foliage, flowers and edible fruits. Where marginally hardy, it is best grown against a south- or west-facing wall. Fruits, which ripen in spring, may be damaged by hard, winter frosts. Requires sunny, fertile, well-drained soil. Propagate by seed in fall or spring.
E. japonica, illus. p.194.

ERIOGONUM
St. Catherine's lace, Wild buckwheat
POLYGONACEAE

Genus of annuals, biennials and evergreen perennials, subshrubs and shrubs, grown for their rosetted, hairy, often silver or white leaves. Needs full sun and well-drained, even poor soil. In cool, wet-winter areas, protect shrubby species and hairy-leaved perennials. Water container plants

moderately in summer, less in spring and fall, very little in winter. Remove flower heads after flowering unless seed is required. Propagate by seed in spring or fall or by semiripe cuttings in summer. Divide perennial root clumps in spring.
E. arborescens, illus. p.453.
E. crocatum. Evergreen, subshrubby perennial. **H** to 8in (20cm), **S** 6in (15cm). Oval, hairy leaves have woolly, white undersides. Heads of minute, sulfur-yellow flowers are borne in summer. Is a good alpine house plant. Z9–10 H10.
E. giganteum (St. Catherine's lace). Evergreen, rounded shrub. **H** and **S** 3–6ft (1–2m). Has oblong to oval, gray leaves, white-downy beneath. In summer, small, white flowers are produced in branching clusters to 12in (30cm) long. Z11–15 H12–10.
E. ovalifolium. Evergreen, domed perennial. **H** 12in (30cm), **S** 4in (10cm). In summer bears tiny, bright yellow flowers in umbels above branched stems. Has tiny, spoon-shaped, hairy, gray leaves. Is excellent for an alpine house. Z4–8 H8–1.
E. umbellatum, illus. p.344.

ERIOPHYLLUM
COMPOSITAE/ASTERACEAE

Genus of summer-flowering perennials and evergreen subshrubs, grown for their silvery foliage and daisylike flowers. Is suitable for rock gardens and front of borders. Needs sun and well-drained soil. Propagate by division in spring or by seed in fall.
E. lanatum, syn. *Bahia lanata,* illus. p.276.

ERIOSYCE
CACTACEAE

Genus of spherical to columnar, perennial cacti, grown for their egg-shaped, red, brown or green seed pods, which are similar to those of *Wigginsia.* Requires full sun and very well-drained soil. Propagate by seed in spring or summer.
E. chilensis, syn. *Echinocactus chilensis, Neoporteria chilensis.* Spherical, then columnar, perennial cactus. **H** 12in (30cm), **S** 4in (10cm). Pale green stem has a dense covering of sturdy, golden spines. Crown bears flattish, pink-orange or white flowers, to 2in (5cm) across, in summer. Z9–11 H11–8.
E. kunzei, syn. *Neoporteria nidus.* Spherical to columnar, perennial cactus. **H** 4in (10cm), **S** 3in (8cm). Long, soft, gray spines completely encircle dark greenish-brown stem. In spring or fall produces tubular, pink to cerise flowers, 1¼–2in (3–5cm) long, with paler bases; they open only at the tips. Z9–11 H11–8.
E. napina, syn. *Neoporteria mitis, Neochilenia mitis, Neoporteria napina,* illus. p.485.
E. subgibbosa, syn. *Neoporteria litoralis, Neoporteria subgibbosa.* Spherical to columnar, perennial cactus. **H** 12in (30cm), **S** 4in (10cm). Light green to dark gray-green stem bears large, woolly areoles and sturdy, amber spines. In late summer bears flattish, carmine-pink flowers, 1½in (4cm) across. Z9–11 H11–8.
E. villosa, syn. *Neoporteria villosa,* illus. p.490.

ERITRICHIUM
BORAGINACEAE

Genus of short-lived perennials, grown for their soft, gray-green leaves and forget-me-not-like flowers. Is suitable for rock gardens and alpine houses. Needs sun and well-drained, peaty, sandy soil with a deep collar of grit; dislikes damp conditions. Is extremely difficult to grow. Propagate by seed when available or by softwood cuttings in summer.
E. elongatum. Tuft-forming perennial. **H** ¾in (2cm), **S** 1¼in (3cm). Leaves are oval, hairy and gray-green. Short flower stems each bear small, rounded, flattish, blue flowers in early summer. Z5–7 H7–5.
E. nanum, illus. p.370.

ERODIUM
GERANIACEAE

Genus of mound-forming perennials, suitable for rock gardens. Needs sun and well-drained soil. Propagate by semiripe cuttings in summer or by seed when available.
E. chamaedryoides. See *E. reichardii.*
E. cheilanthifolium, syn. *E. petraeum* subsp. *crispum,* illus. p.341.
E. chrysanthum, illus. p.343.
E. corsicum, illus. p.362.
E. foetidum, syn. *E. petraeum.* Compact, mound-forming perennial. **H** 6–8in (15–20cm), **S** 8in (20cm). Produces saucer-shaped, single, red-veined, pink flowers in summer. Oval, gray leaves have deeply cut edges. Z6–8 H8–6.
E. manescaui, syn. *E. manescavii,* illus. p.265.
E. manescavii. See *E. manescaui.*
E. petraeum. See *E. foetidum.*
E. petraeum subsp. crispum. See *E. cheilanthifolium.*
E. reichardii, syn. *E. chamaedryoides* (Cranesbill). Mound-forming perennial. **H** 1in (2.5cm), **S** 2½–3in (6–8cm). In summer, saucer-shaped, single flowers, either white or pink with darker veins, are borne above tiny, oaklike leaves. Is good for a rock garden or trough. Z8–9 H9–8.
E. x variabile 'Flore Pleno' Variable, cushion-forming or spreading perennial. **H** 4in (10cm), **S** 12in (30cm). Has oval to narrowly oval, dark to gray-green leaves with scalloped edges and long stalks. From spring to fall, flower stems each bear 1 or 2 rounded, double, pink flowers with darker veins; outer petals are rounded, inner petals narrower. **'Ken Aslet'** has single, deep pink flowers.

Erpetion reniforme. See *Viola hederacea.*

ERYNGIUM
Sea holly
UMBELLIFERAE/APIACEAE

Genus of biennials and perennials, some of which are evergreen, grown for their flowers, foliage and habit. Needs sun and fertile, well-drained soil. Propagate species by seed in fall, selected forms by division in spring or root cuttings in winter.
E. agavifolium, syn. *E. bromeliifolium.* Evergreen, clump-forming perennial. **H** 5ft (1.5m), **S** 2ft (60cm). Forms rosettes of sword-shaped, sharply toothed, rich green

leaves. Thistle-like, greenish-white flower heads are produced on branched stems in summer. Z6–9 H9–6.
E. alpinum, illus. p.240.
E. amethystinum. Rosette-forming perennial. **H** and **S** 24in (60cm). Oval, mid-green leaves are divided and spiny. In summer bears branched stems of small, thistle-like, blue flowers surrounded by spiky, darker blue bracts. Z3–8 H8–1.
E. bourgatii, illus. p.270.
E. bromeliifolium of gardens. See *E. agavifolium.*
E. eburneum, syn. *E. paniculatum.* Evergreen perennial. **H** 5–6ft (1.5–2m), **S** 2ft (60cm). Has spiny, linear, mid-green leaves. Bears heads of thistle-like, green flowers with white stamens on branched arching stems in late summer. Z9–11 H12–10.
E. giganteum. Clump-forming biennial or short-lived perennial that dies after flowering. **H** 3–4ft (1–1.2m), **S** 2½ft (75cm). Heart-shaped, basal leaves are mid-green. Has large, rounded heads of thistle-like, blue flowers, surrounded by spiny, silvery bracts, in late summer. Z4–9 H11–1.
E. x oliverianum, illus. p.241.
E. pandanifolium. Clump-forming, evergreen perennial. **H** 8ft (2.5m), **S** 5ft (1.5m). Has narrowly sword-shaped, arching, slightly toothed, pale green basal leaves. Bears towering umbels of small, thistle-like, greenish-purple flower heads in summer. Z9–10 H12–9.
E. paniculatum. See *E. eburneum.*
E. x tripartitum, illus. p.250.
E. variifolium, illus. p.271.
E. x zabelii 'Violetta'. Upright perennial. **H** 30in (75cm), **S** 24in (60cm). Has rounded, divided, mid-green leaves. Loose heads of thistle-like, deep violet flowers, surrounded by narrow, spiny, silvery-blue bracts, are produced in late summer. Z5–8 H8–5.

ERYSIMUM
Wallflower
CRUCIFERAE/BRASSICACEAE

Genus of annuals, biennials, evergreen or semievergreen, short-lived perennials and subshrubs, grown for their flowers. Is closely related to *Cheiranthus* and is suitable for borders, banks and rock gardens. Requires sun and well-drained soil. Propagate by seed in spring or fall or by softwood cuttings in summer.
E. x allionii, syn. *E. x marshallii* (Siberian wallflower). **'Orange Bedder',** illus. p.324.
E. 'Bowles's Mauve', syn. *E.* 'E.A. Bowles', *Cheiranthus* 'Bowles' Mauve', illus. p.261.
E. 'Bredon', syn. *Cheiranthus* 'Bredon', illus. p.336.
E. cheiri, syn. *Cheiranthus cheiri* (English wallflower). Evergreen, bushy perennial, grown as a biennial. **H** 10–32in (25–80cm), **S** 12–16in (30–40cm). Has lance-shaped, mid- to deep green leaves. Heads of fragrant, 4-petaled flowers in red, yellow, bronze, white and orange, are borne in spring. Z3–7 H7–1. **Bedder Series** is dwarf and has golden-yellow, primrose-yellow, orange or scarlet-red flowers. **Fair Lady Series** produces flowers in pale pink, yellow and creamy white, with some reds. **'Fire King',** illus. p.326. Flowers of **'Ivory White'** are creamy white. **Treasure Series 'Treasure Red'** has red flowers.

E. 'E.A. Bowles'. See *E.* 'Bowles's Mauve'.
E. helveticum, syn. *E. pumilum,* illus. p.358.
E. x kewense 'Harpur Crewe', syn. *Cheiranthus cheiri* 'Harpur Crewe', illus. p.336.
E. linifolium. Short-lived, semievergreen, open, dome-shaped subshrub. **H** to 12in (30cm), **S** 8in (20cm) or more. Leaves are narrowly lance-shaped and blue-gray. Tight heads of small, 4-petaled, pale violet flowers are produced in early summer. Z7–9 H9–7.
E. x marshallii. See *E.* x *allionii.*
E. 'Moonlight', syn. *Cheiranthus* 'Moonlight', illus. p.335.
E. pumilum. See *E. helveticum.*

ERYTHRINA
Coral tree
LEGUMINOSAE/PAPILIONACEAE

Genus of deciduous or semievergreen trees, shrubs and perennials, grown for their flowers. Requires full sun and well-drained soil. Water container plants moderately, very little in winter or when leafless. Propagate by seed in spring or semiripe cuttings in summer. Red spider mite may be a problem.
E. americana. See *E. coralloides.*
E. x bidwillii, illus. p.136.
E. coralloides, syn. *E. americana* (Flame coral tree, Naked coral tree). Deciduous, untidily rounded shrub or tree with somewhat prickly stems. **H** and **S** 10–20ft (3–6m). Has leaves of 3 triangular leaflets, the largest central one 4¹/₂in (11cm) long. Racemes of pealike, red flowers are borne on leafless stems in early spring and summer. Z9–11 H12–1.
E. crista-galli, illus. p.137.

ERYTHRONIUM
LILIACEAE

Genus of spring-flowering, tuberous perennials, grown for their pendent flowers and, in some cases, mottled leaves. Requires partial shade and rich, well-drained soil, where tubers will not dry out in summer while dormant. Propagate by seed in fall. Some species increase by offsets, which can be divided in late summer. Do not allow tubers to dry out before replanting, 6in (15cm) deep.
E. americanum, illus. p.421.
E. californicum, illus. p.415. **'White Beauty',** illus. p.399.
E. dens-canis, illus. p.418.
E. grandiflorum. Spring-flowering, tuberous perennial. **H** 4–12in (10–30cm), **S** 2–3in (5–8cm). Has 2 lance-shaped, semierect, basal, plain bright green leaves. Stem bears 1–3 pendent, bright yellow flowers, with reflexed petals. Z4–9 H9–1.
E. hendersonii, illus. p.402.
E. oregonum, illus. p.399.
E. 'Pagoda', illus. p.406.
E. revolutum. Tuberous perennial. **H** 8–12in (20–30cm), **S** 6in (15cm). Has lance-shaped, semierect, basal, brown-mottled, green leaves and a loose spike of 1–4 pendent, pale to deep pink flowers, with reflexed petals, in spring. Z5–8 H8–5.
E. tuolumnense. Tuberous perennial. **H** to 12in (30cm), **S** 5–6in (12–15cm). Has 2 lance-shaped, semierect, basal, glossy,

plain green leaves. Produces a spike of up to 10 pendent, bright yellow flowers, with reflexed petals. Z3–9 H9–1.

ESCALLONIA
ESCALLONIACEAE

Genus of evergreen, semievergreen or deciduous shrubs and trees, grown for their 5-petaled flowers and glossy foliage. Thrives in mild areas, where *Escallonia* is wind-resistant and ideal for hedging in coastal gardens. At the limits of hardiness, protect from strong winds and grow against a south- or west-facing wall. Requires full sun and fertile, well-drained soil. Trim hedges and wall-trained plants after flowering. Propagate by softwood cuttings in summer.
E. 'Apple Blossom', illus. p.133.
E. 'Donard Beauty', illus. p.154.
E. 'Donard Seedling', illus. p.131.
E. 'Edinensis'. Vigorous, evergreen, arching shrub. **H** 6ft (2m), **S** 10ft (3m). Bears small, oblong, bright green leaves. Small, pink flowers are produced from early to mid-summer. Is one of the hardier escallonias. Z8–9 H9–8.
E. 'Iveyi', illus. p.112.
E. 'Langleyensis'. Evergreen or semievergreen, arching shrub. **H** 6ft (2m), **S** 10ft (3m). Has small, glossy, bright green leaves and an abundance of rose-red flowers from early to mid-summer. Z8–9 H9–8.
E. leucantha, illus. p.112.
E. rubra. 'Crimson Spire' Very vigorous, evergreen, upright shrub. **H** and **S** 10ft (3m). Has oval, rich green leaves and, throughout summer, tubular, deep red flowers. **'Woodside',** illus. p.156.
E. virgata, illus. p.130.

ESCHSCHOLZIA
California poppy
PAPAVERACEAE

Genus of annuals, grown for their bright, poppy-like flowers. Is suitable for rock gardens and gaps in paving. Requires sun and poor, very well-drained soil. Dead-head regularly to ensure a long flowering period. Propagate by seed sown outdoors in spring or early fall.
E. caespitosa, illus. p.321.
E. californica, illus. p.326. (mixed) Fast-growing, slender, erect annual. **H** 12in (30cm), **S** 6in (15cm). Feathery leaves are bluish-green. Cup-shaped, 4-petaled, single flowers, in shades of red, orange, yellow or cream, are borne in summer–fall. Z11 H9–1. **Ballerina Series** has flowers in shades of red, orange, yellow or cream. **Thai Silk Series,** illus. p.327.

ESCOBARIA
CACTACEAE

Genus of mainly spherical to columnar, perennial cacti. The stems are studded with tubercles (each with a furrow immediately above it) and very spiny, generally white areoles. Needs full sun and poor to moderately fertile, well-drained soil. Propagate by seed in spring or by offsets in summer.
E. vivipara, syn. *Coryphantha vivipara,* illus. p.480.

ESPOSTOA
CACTACEAE

Genus of columnar, perennial cacti, each with a 10–30-ribbed stem, eventually becoming bushy or treelike with age. Most species are densely covered in woolly, white hairs masking short, sharp spines. Bears cup-shaped flowers, as well as extra wool down the side of stems facing the sun, only after about 30 years. Needs full sun and very well-drained soil. Propagate by seed in spring or summer.
E. lanata, illus. p.482.

EUCALYPTUS
Gum
MYRTACEAE

Genus of evergreen trees and shrubs, grown for their bark, flowers and aromatic foliage. Needs full sun, shelter from cold winds, and fertile, well-drained soil. Plant smallest obtainable trees. Water container plants moderately, less in winter. Attractive, young foliage of some species, normally lost with age, may be retained by cutting growth back hard in spring. Propagate by seed in spring or fall.
E. camaldulensis (Red gum, River red gum). Fast-growing, drought-resistant, evergreen, rounded tree. **H** 100ft (30m) or more, **S** 70ft (20m) or more. Young bark is gray, brown and cream; leaves are lance-shaped, slender, green or blue-green. Has umbels of small, cream flowers in summer. Z9–10 H10–9.
E. coccifera, illus. p.68.
E. dalrympleana, illus. p.67.
E. ficifolia (Red-flowering gum). Moderately fast-growing, evergreen, rounded tree. **H** and **S** to 25ft (8m). Has broadly lance-shaped, glossy, deep green leaves and, in spring–summer, large panicles of many-stamened, pale to deep red flowers. Prefers acidic soil. Z9–10 H10–9.
E. glaucescens (Tingiringi gum). Evergreen, spreading tree. **H** 40ft (12m), **S** 25ft (8m). Young bark is white. Leaves are silvery-blue and rounded when young; long, narrow and blue-gray when mature. In fall bears clusters of many-stamened, white flowers. Z9–10 H10–9.
E. globulus (Blue gum, Tasmanian blue gum). Very fast-growing, evergreen, spreading tree. **H** 100ft (30m), **S** 40ft (12m). Bark peels in ribbons. Large, oval to oblong, silvery-blue leaves are long, narrow and glossy, mid-green when mature. White flowers, consisting of tufts of stamens, are borne in summer–fall, often year-round. Z9–10 H10–9.
E. gunnii, illus. p.68.
E. johnstonii, illus. p.68.
E. niphophila. See *E. pauciflora* subsp. *niphophila.*
E. pauciflora, illus. p.79. **subsp. niphophila,** syn. *E. niphophila* (Snow gum), illus. p.78, is an evergreen, spreading tree. **H** 25ft (8m), **S** 20–50ft (6–15m). Flaking bark reveals yellow, bronze, or greenish patches. Lance-shaped foliage is blue-green, gray-green when young. Bears whitish-cream flowers in summer. Z9–10 H10–9.
E. perriniana (Spinning gum). Fast-growing, evergreen, spreading tree. **H** 12–30ft (4–10m), **S** 10–25ft (3–8m). Has

rounded, gray-blue, young leaves joined around stems. Leaves on mature trees are long and pendulous. White flowers are borne in late summer. Z8–10 H10–8.
E. viminalis (Manna gum, Ribbon gum). Vigorous, evergreen, spreading tree. **H** 100ft (30m), **S** 50ft (15m). Bark peels on upper trunk. Lance-shaped, dark green leaves become very long, narrow and pale green when mature. Bears clusters of stamened, white flowers in summer. Z8–10 H10–8.

EUCHARIS
AMARYLLIDACEAE

Genus of evergreen bulbs, grown for their fragrant, white flowers that resemble large, white daffodils, with a cup and 6 spreading petals. Prefers at least 50% relative humidity. Needs partial shade and rich soil. Water freely in summer. Propagate by seed when ripe or by offsets in spring.
E. amazonica, syn. *E. grandiflora,* illus. p.414.
E. grandiflora of gardens. See *E. amazonica.*

EUCOMIS
Pineapple flower, Pineapple lily
LILIACEAE/ASPARAGACEAE

Genus of summer- and fall-flowering bulbs, grown for their dense spikes of flowers, which are overtopped by a tuft of small, leaflike bracts, as in a pineapple. Where not hardy, lift in fall and overwinter indoors. Needs full sun and well-drained soil. Plant in spring and water freely in summer. Propagate by seed or division of clumps in spring.
E. autumnalis, syn. *E. undulata.* Late summer- to fall-flowering bulb. **H** 8–12in (20–30cm), **S** 24–30in (60–75cm). Has strap-shaped, wavy-edged leaves in a semierect, basal tuft. Leafless stem bears small, star-shaped, pale green or white flowers in a dense spike, with cluster of leaflike bracts at apex. Z7–10 .
E. bicolor, illus. p.412.
E. comosa, illus. p.409.
E. pallidiflora, illus. p.409.
E. undulata. See *E. autumnalis.*

EUCOMMIA
EUCOMMIACEAE

Genus of one species of deciduous tree, grown for its unusual foliage. Needs full sun and fertile, well-drained soil. Propagate by softwood cuttings in summer.
E. ulmoides (Hardy rubber tree). Deciduous, spreading tree. **H** 40ft (12m), **S** 25ft (8m). Drooping, oval leaves are pointed and glossy, dark green; when pulled apart, leaf pieces stay joined by rubbery threads. Inconspicuous flowers are produced in late spring before leaves. Z4–7 H7–1.

EUCRYPHIA
EUCRYPHIACEAE/CUNONIACEAE

Genus of evergreen, semievergreen or deciduous trees and shrubs, grown for their foliage and often fragrant, white flowers. Needs a sheltered, semi-shaded position in all but mild, wet areas, where it will withstand more exposure. Does best with roots in a cool, moist, shaded site and crown in sun. Needs fertile, well-drained, lime-free soil, except for *E. cordifolia* and *E. x nymansensis*. Propagate by semiripe cuttings in late summer.

E. cordifolia, illus. p.73.
E. glutinosa, illus. p.85.
E. lucida, illus. p.85.
E. milliganii, illus. p.129.
E. x nymansensis 'Nymansay', illus. p.73.

Eugenia australis of gardens. See *Syzygium paniculatum*.
Eugenia paniculata. See *Syzygium paniculatum*.
Eugenia ugni. See *Ugni molinae*.
Euodia. See *Tetradium*.
Euodia hupehensis. See *Tetradium daniellii*.

EUONYMUS
CELASTRACEAE

Genus of evergreen or deciduous shrubs and trees, sometimes climbing, grown for their foliage, fall color and fruits. Needs sun or semi-shade and well-drained soil, although, for evergreen species in full sun, soil should not be very dry. Propagate by semiripe cuttings in summer or by seed in fall. *E. europaeus* and *E. japonicus* may be attacked by caterpillars; *E. japonicus* is susceptible to mildew. ① All parts may cause mild stomach upset if ingested.

E. alatus, illus. p.140. **'Compactus'** is a deciduous, bushy, dense shrub. **H** 3ft (1m), **S** 10ft (3m). Shoots have corky wings. Oval, dark green leaves turn brilliant red in fall. Bears inconspicuous, greenish-white flowers in summer, followed by small, 4-lobed, purple or red fruits. Z3–9 H9–1.
E. cornutus var. quinquecornutus. Deciduous, spreading, open shrub. **H** 6ft (2m), **S** 10ft (3m). Has narrowly lance-shaped, dark green leaves. Small, purplish-green flowers in summer are followed by 5-horned, pink fruits that open to reveal orange-red seeds. Z9–10 H10–8.
E. europaeus (Spindle tree). **'Red Cascade'**, illus. p.140.
E. fortunei. Evergreen shrub, grown only as **var. radicans** and its cultivars, which are climbing or prostrate. **H** 15ft (5m) if supported, **S** indefinite. Bears oval, dark green leaves and inconspicuous, greenish-white flowers from early to mid-summer. Makes good groundcover. Z5–9 H9–2. Foliage of **'Coloratus'** turns reddish-purple in fall–winter. **'Emerald 'n' Gold'** illus. p.167. **'Emerald Gaiety'**, **H** 3ft (1m), **S** 5ft (1.5m), is bushy, with rounded, white-edged, deep green leaves. Young, rounded leaves of **'Golden Prince'**, syn. *E. fortunei* 'Gold Tip' are edged bright yellow, aging to creamy-white. **'Gold Tip'**. See *E. fortunei* 'Golden Prince'. **'Kewensis'**, **H** 4in (10cm) or more, has slender stems and tiny leaves, and forms dense mats of growth. **'Sarcoxie'**, **H** and **S** 4ft (1.2m), is vigorous, upright and bushy, with glossy, dark green leaves. **'Silver Queen'**, illus. p.144. **'Sunspot'** bears deep green leaves, each marked in center with golden-yellow.
E. hamiltonianus, illus. p.142.

Deciduous, treelike shrub or small tree, sometimes semievergreen. **H** and **S** 25ft (8m). Oval, mid-green leaves often turn pink and red in fall. Tiny, green flowers in late spring and early summer are followed by 4-lobed, rose-pink fruits enclosed in a bright red casing. Z6–8 H8–6. **subsp. sieboldianus**, syn. *E. yedoensis* (illus. p.142), **H** and **S** 20ft (6m) or more, has pink fruits. **subsp. sieboldianus 'Red Elf'**, illus. p.140.
E. japonicus (Japanese spindle). **'Latifolius Albomarginatus'**, syn. *E. japonicus* 'Macrophyllus Albus' illus. p.144. **'Macrophyllus'** is an evergreen, upright, dense shrub. **H** 12ft (4m), **S** 6ft (2m). Has large, oval, glossy, dark green leaves and, in summer, small, star-shaped, green flowers, followed by spherical, pink fruits with orange seeds. Is good for hedging, particularly in coastal areas. Z6–8 H8–6. **'Macrophyllus Albus'**. See *E. japonicus* 'Latifolius Albomarginatus'. Leaves of **'Ovatus Aureus'** are broadly edged with golden-yellow.
E. latifolius, illus. p.140.
E. myrianthus, illus. p.117.
E. oxyphyllus, illus. p.117.
E. planipes, syn. *E. sachalinensis*. Deciduous, upright, shrub. **H** and **S** 10ft (3m). Bears oval, mid-green leaves that turn to brilliant red in fall, as large, 4- or 5-lobed, red fruits open to reveal bright orange seeds. Star-shaped, green flowers are produced in late spring. Z5–9 H9–5.
E. sachalinensis of gardens. See *E. planipes*.
E. yedoensis. See *E. hamiltonianus* subsp. *sieboldianus*.

EUPATORIUM
COMPOSITAE/ASTERACEAE

Genus of perennials, subshrubs and shrubs, many of which are evergreen, grown mainly for their flowers, some also for their architectural foliage. Requires full light or partial shade. Will grow in any conditions, although most species prefer moist but well-drained soil. Water container plants freely when in full growth, moderately at other times. Prune shrubs lightly after flowering or in spring. Propagate by seed in spring; shrubs and subshrubs may also be propagated by softwood or greenwood cuttings in summer, perennials by division in early spring or fall. Red spider mite and whitefly may be troublesome.

E. ageratoides. See *Ageratina altissima*.
E. ianthinum. See *Bartlettina sordida*.
E. ligustrinum. See *Ageratina ligustrina*.
E. maculatum 'Riesenschirm', illus. p.221.
E. micranthum. See *Ageratina ligustrina*.
E. purpureum (Joe Pye weed). Stately, upright perennial. **H** to 7ft (2.2m), **S** to 3ft (1m). Oval leaves are arranged in whorls along purplish stems. Terminal heads of tubular, pinkish-purple flowers are borne in late summer–early fall. Z3–9 H9–1.
E. rugosum. See *Ageratina altissima*.
E. sordidum. See *Bartlettina sordida*.
E. urticifolium. See *Ageratina altissima*.
E. weinmannianum. See *Ageratina ligustrina*.

EUPHORBIA
Milkweed, Spurge
EUPHORBIACEAE

Genus of shrubs, succulents and perennials, some of which are semievergreen or evergreen, and annuals. Flower heads consist of cup-shaped bracts, in various colors and usually each containing several flowers lacking typical sepals and petals. Prefers sun or partial shade and moist but well-drained soil. Propagate by basal cuttings in spring or summer, by division in spring or early fall or by seed in fall or spring. ① All parts may cause severe discomfort if ingested; contact with their milky sap may irritate skin.

E. amygdaloides (Wood spurge). **'Purpurea'** is a semievergreen, erect perennial. **H** and **S** 1ft (30cm). Stems and narrowly oval leaves are green, heavily suffused purple-red. Has flower heads of cup-shaped, yellow bracts in spring. Is susceptible to mildew. Z6–10 H10–2. **var. robbiae**, syn. *E. robbiae* illus. p.262.
E. bicompacta var. rubra, syn. *Synadenium compactum* var. *rubrum*, *Synadenium grantii* 'Rubrum'. Evergreen, erect, robust-stemmed shrub. **H** 10–12ft (3–4m), **S** 6ft (2m) or more. Has very small, red flowers in fall, largely concealed by lance-shaped to oval, glossy, purplish-green leaves, red-purple beneath. Z10–11 H12–9. **'Rubrum'** Evergreen, erect, robust-stemmed shrub. **H** 10–12ft (3–4m), **S** 6ft (2m) or more. Has very small, red flowers in fall, largely concealed by lance-shaped to oval, glossy, purplish-green leaves, red-purple beneath.
E. biglandulosa. See *E. rigida*.
E. candelabrum. Deciduous, treelike, perennial succulent. **H** 30ft (10m), **S** 15ft (5m). Erect, 3–5-angled, deeply indented, glossy, dark green stems, often marbled white, branch and rebranch candelabra-like. Has short-lived, spear-shaped leaves. Rounded heads of small flowers, with cup-shaped, yellow bracts, are produced in spring. Z10–11 H12–10.
E. characias subsp. characias, illus. p.147. **subsp. wulfenii**, illus. p.147.
E. cyparissias, illus. p.262.
E. epithymoides. See *E. polychroma*.
E. fulgens (Scarlet plume). Evergreen, erect, arching shrub. **H** 3–5ft (1–1.5m), **S** 2–3ft (60cm–1m). Has elliptic to lance-shaped, mid- to deep green leaves, to 4in (10cm) long. From winter to spring bears leafy, wandlike sprays of small flowers, each cluster surrounded by 5 petal-like, scarlet bracts, $^3/_4$–1$^1/_4$in (2–3cm) across. Z14–15 H12–10.
E. gorgonis (Gorgon's head). Deciduous, hemispherical, perennial succulent. **H** 3in (8cm), **S** 4in (10cm). Has a much-ribbed, green main stem crowned by 3–5 rows of prostrate stems, $^1/_2$in (1cm) wide, that are gradually shed. In spring, crown also bears rounded heads of small, fragrant flowers with cup-shaped, yellow bracts. Z14–15 H12–10.
E. griffithii 'Fireglow', illus. p.246.
E. hypericifolia DIAMOND FROST ('Inneuphe'), illus. p.298.
E. marginata, illus. p.299.
E. mellifera, illus. p.127.

E. milii, illus. p.456. **var. splendens**, syn. *E. splendens* is a slow-growing, mainly evergreen, spreading, spiny, semi-succulent shrub. **H** to 6ft (2m), **S** to 3ft (1m). Has oblong to oval leaves and, intermittently year-round but especially in spring, clusters of tiny flowers enclosed in large, petal-like, red bracts. Z11–12 H12–1.
E. myrsinites, illus. p.357.
E. nicaeensis. Clump-forming perennial with a woody base. **H** 30in (75cm), **S** 18in (45cm). Has narrowly oval, fleshy, gray-green leaves. Umbels of greenish-yellow flower heads with cup-shaped bracts are borne throughout summer. Z5–8 H8–5.
E. obesa, illus. p.493.
E. palustris. Bushy perennial. **H** and **S** 3ft (1m). Clusters of yellow-green flower heads, with cup-shaped bracts, are produced in spring above oblong to lance-shaped, yellowish-green leaves. Z7–9 H7–6.
E. polychroma, syn. *E. epithymoides*, illus. p.262.
E. pulcherrima, illus. p.455. **'Paul Mikkelson'** is a mainly evergreen, erect, freely branching shrub. **H** and **S** 10–12ft (3–4m). Bears oval to lance-shaped, shallowly lobed leaves. From late fall to spring has flattened heads of small, greenish-white flowers with large, leaflike, bright red bracts. Z13–15 H12–1.
E. rigida, syn. *E. biglandulosa*, illus. p.227.
E. robbiae. See *E. amygdaloides* var. *robbiae*.
E. schillingii, illus. p.251.
E. seguieriana. Clump-forming, semievergreen perennial. **H** and **S** 18in (45cm). Has narrowly lance-shaped, glaucous leaves on slender stems. Bears large, terminal clusters of yellowish-green flowers in late spring. Z8–11 H12–8.
E. sikkimensis, illus. p.242.
E. splendens. See *E. milii* var. *splendens*.
E. tithymaloides, syn. *Pedilanthus tithymaloides*. Bushy, perennial succulent. **H** 10ft (3m), **S** 1ft (30cm). Has thin, erect stems zigzagging at each node. Leaves are mid-green and boat-shaped, with prominent ribs beneath. Red to yellowish-green bracts are produced at each of the stem tips in summer. Prefers partial shade. Z10–11 H12–10. **'Variegata'**, illus. p.483.

EUPTELEA
EUPTELEACEAE

Genus of deciduous trees, grown for their foliage. Prefers full sun and fertile, well-drained soil. Propagate by seed in fall.

E. polyandra. Deciduous, bushy-headed tree. **H** 25ft (8m), **S** 20ft (6m). Long-stalked, narrowly oval, pointed, sharply toothed leaves are glossy and bright green, turning red and yellow in fall. Has inconspicuous flowers in spring before leaves emerge. Z6–14 H12–1.

EURYA
THEACEAE/PENTAPHYLACACEAE

Genus of evergreen shrubs and trees, grown for their foliage. Insignificant flowers are produced from spring to summer. Tolerates partial shade or full light and needs fertile, well-drained soil. Water container specimens freely when in full growth, less at other times. Propagate by seed when ripe or in spring or by semiripe cuttings in late summer.

E. emarginata, illus. p.165.

E. japonica. Evergreen, bushy shrub or small tree. **H** and **S** 30ft (10m). Has elliptic to lance-shaped, bluntly toothed, leathery, dark green leaves. Inconspicuous, green flowers, borne from spring to summer, are followed on female plants by tiny, spherical, purple-black fruits. Z8–10 H10–8.

'**Variegata**' of gardens. See *Cleyera japonica* 'Fortunei'.

EURYALE
NYMPHAEACEAE

Genus of one species of annual, deep-water plant, grown for its floating foliage; is suitable only for tropical pools. Needs full light, constant warmth and heavy feeding. Propagate by seed in spring.

E. ferox. Annual, deep-water plant. **S** 5ft (1.5m). Has floating, rounded, spiny, olive-green leaves, with rich purple undersides. Bears small, shuttlecock-like, red or violet-purple flowers in summer. Z12–15 H12–6.

EURYOPS
COMPOSITAE/ASTERACEAE

Genus of evergreen shrubs and subshrubs, grown for their foliage and daisylike flower heads. Is suitable for borders and rock gardens. Needs sun and moist but well-drained soil. May not tolerate root disturbance. Propagate by softwood cuttings in summer.

E. acraeus, syn. *E. evansii*, illus. p.344.

E. evansii of gardens. See *E. acraeus*.

E. pectinatus, illus. p.319.

EUSTOMA
GENTIANACEAE

Genus of annuals and perennials, grown for their poppy-like flowers that are good for cutting. Makes a good container-grown plant. Needs sun and well-drained soil. Propagate by seed sown under glass in late winter.

E. grandiflorum, syn. *E. russellianum*, *Lisianthus russellianus*, illus. p.299. **Heidi Series** produces flowers in shades of rose-pink, blue, white and bicolors. Z8–11 H12–1.

E. russellianum. See *E. grandiflorum*.

EXACUM
GENTIANACEAE

Genus of annuals, biennials and perennials, grown for their profusion of flowers, that are excellent as pot plants. Needs sun and well-drained soil. Propagate by seed sown in early spring for flowering the same year or in late summer for the following year.

E. affine (Persian violet). Evergreen, bushy perennial, usually grown as an annual. **H** and **S** 8–12in (20–30cm). Has oval, glossy leaves and masses of tiny, scented, saucer-shaped, purple, rose-pink or white flowers, with yellow stamens, in summer and early fall. H7–1.

EXOCHORDA
Pearl bush
ROSACEAE

Genus of deciduous shrubs, grown for their abundant, showy, white flowers. Prefers full sun and fertile, well-drained soil. Improve vigor and flowering by thinning out old shoots after flowering. Propagate by softwood cuttings in summer or by seed in fall. Chlorosis may be a problem on shallow, chalky soil.

E. giraldii. Deciduous, widely arching shrub. **H** and **S** 10ft (3m). Has pinkish-green, young growths and oblong leaves. Bears upright racemes of large, 5-petaled, white flowers in late spring. Z6–9 H9–6.

E. x macrantha '**The Bride**', illus. p.132.

E. racemosa (Common pearl bush). Deciduous, arching shrub. **H** and **S** 12ft (4m). Has upright clusters of 5-petaled, white flowers in late spring. Leaves are oblong and deep blue-green. Prefers acidic soil. Z5–9 H9–5.

F

FABIANA
SOLANACEAE

Genus of evergreen shrubs, grown for their foliage and flowers. Requires full sun and fertile, well-drained soil. Propagate by softwood cuttings in summer.

F. imbricata '**Prostrata**'. Evergreen, mound-forming, very dense shrub. **H** 3ft (1m), **S** 6ft (2m). Shoots are densely covered with tiny, heather-like, deep green leaves. Bears a profusion of tubular, white flowers in early summer. Z9–11 H12–10.

f. *violacea*, syn. *F. imbricata* 'Violacea', illus. p.204. '**Violacea**'. See *F. imbricata* f. *violacea*.

FAGUS
Beech
FAGACEAE

Genus of deciduous trees, grown for their habit, foliage and fall color. Insignificant flowers appear in late spring and hairy fruits ripen in fall to release edible, triangular nuts. Requires sun or semi-shade; purple-leaved forms prefer full sun, yellow-leaved forms a little shade. Grows well in any but waterlogged soil. *F. sylvatica*, when used as hedging, should be trimmed in summer. Propagate species by seed in fall, and selected forms by budding in late summer. Problems may be caused by bracket fungi, canker-causing fungi, aphids and beech coccus.

F. americana. See *F. grandifolia*.

F. grandifolia (American beech), syn. *F. americana*. Deciduous, spreading tree. **H** and **S** 30ft (10m). Oval, silky, pale green young leaves mature to dark green in summer, then turn golden-brown in fall. Z3–9 H9–1.

F. orientalis. (Oriental beech) Deciduous, spreading tree. **H** 70ft (20m), **S** 50ft (15m). Has large, oval, wavy-edged, dark green leaves that turn yellow in fall. Z4–7 H7–1.

F. sylvatica (European beech), illus. p.64. '**Aspleniifolia**', illus. p.64.

f. *atropunicea*, syn. *F. sylvatica* Atropurpureum Group, *F. sylvatica* f. *purpurea* (Copper beech, Purple beech) is a deciduous, round-headed tree. **H** 80ft (25m), **S** 50ft (15m). Has oval, wavy-margined, purple leaves that turn a rich coppery color in fall. Z5–7 H7–5.

Atropurpureum Group. See *F. sylvatica* f. *atropunicea*. **Aurea Pendula**', **H** 100ft (30m), **S** 80ft (25m), is a slender tree with pendulous branches and bright yellow leaves that become rich yellow and orange-brown in fall. '**Dawyck**', illus. p.79.

'**Dawyck Purple**' is similar, but has deep purple foliage. Leaves of **f. laciniata** (Cutleaf beech) are deeply cut. **f. pendula**, syn. *F. sylvatica* 'Pendula', illus. p.62.

'**Pendula**'. See *F. sylvatica* f. *pendula*.

f. *purpurea*. See *F. sylvatica* f. *atropunicea*.

'**Purpurea Pendula**', **H** and **S** 10ft (3m), has stiff, weeping branches and blackish-purple foliage. '**Riversii**', illus. p.61.

'**Rohanii**' illus. p.61. '**Zlatia**' produces yellow young foliage that later becomes mid- to dark green.

FALLOPIA
SYN. BILDERDYKIA, REYNOUTRIA
POLYGONACEAE

Genus of rhizomatous, climbing or scrambling, woody-based perennials that are good for training on pergolas and deciduous trees or for covering unsightly structures. Needs full sun or partial shade and moist but well-drained soil. Propagate by seed sown as soon as ripe or in spring or by semi-ripe cuttings in summer or hardwood cuttings in fall.

F. aubertii, syn. *Polygonum aubertii* (Silver flea vine, Silver lace vine). Vigorous, deciduous, woody-stemmed, twining climber. **H** to 40ft (12m) or more. Leaves are broadly heart-shaped. Panicles of small, white or greenish flowers, aging to pink, are borne in summer–fall and are followed by angled, pinkish-white fruits. Is often confused with *F. baldschuanica*. Z5–9 H9–3.

F. aubertii of gardens. (Silver flea vine, Silver lace vine) See *F. baldschuanica*.

F. baldschuanica, syn. *F. aubertii* of gardens, *Polygonum baldschuanicum*, illus. p.208.

FALLUGIA
ROSACEAE

Genus of one species of deciduous shrub, grown for its flowers and showy fruit clusters. Requires a hot, sunny position and well-drained soil. Propagate by softwood cuttings in summer or by seed in fall.

F. paradoxa, illus. p.128.

FARFUGIUM
COMPOSITAE/ASTERACEAE

Genus of perennials, grown for their foliage and daisy-like flower heads. Needs sun or semi-shade and moist but well-drained soil. Propagate by division in spring or by seed in fall or spring.

F. japonicum, syn. *Ligularia tussilaginea* (Leopard plant). Loosely clump-forming perennial. **H** and **S** 24in (60cm). Has large, rounded, toothed, mid-green, basal leaves, above which rise woolly, branched stems bearing clusters of daisy-like, pale yellow flower heads in late summer. Z7–9 H9–7.

'**Aureomaculatum**' has variegated, gold-and-white leaves.

FARGESIA
GRAMINEAE/POACEAE

See also GRASSES, BAMBOOS, RUSHES and SEDGES.

F. murieliae, syn. *Arundinaria murieliae*, *F. spathacea* of gardens, *Sinarundinaria murieliae*, *Thamnocalamus murieliae*, *Thamnocalamus spathaceus* of gardens (Umbrella bamboo). Evergreen, clump-forming bamboo. **H** 12ft (4m), **S** indefinite. Has gray young culms with loose, light brown sheaths and broad, apple-green leaves, each very long- drawn-out at its tip. Flower spikes are unimportant. Z5–9 H9–4.

F. nitida (Fountain bamboo), syn. *Arundinaria nitida*, *Sinarundinaria nitida*. Evergreen, clump-forming bamboo. **H** 15ft (5m), **S** indefinite. Has small, pointed, mid-green leaves on dark purple stalks and several branches at each node. Stems are often purple with close sheaths. Z5–9 H9–5.

F. spathacea of gardens. See *F. murieliae*.

F

F

FASCICULARIA
BROMELIACEAE

Genus of evergreen, rosette-forming perennials, grown for their overall appearance. Prefers full light; any well-drained soil is suitable. Water moderately from spring to fall, sparingly in winter. Propagate by offsets or division in spring.

F. andina. See *F. bicolor*.

F. bicolor, syn. *F. andina*. Evergreen, rosetted perennial forming congested hummocks. **H** to 18in (45cm), **S** to 24in (60cm). Has dense rosettes of linear, tapered, arching, mid- to deep green leaves. In summer produces a cluster of tubular, pale blue flowers, surrounded by bright red bracts, at the heart of each mature rosette. Z10–13 H12–7.

x FATSHEDERA
ARALIACEAE

Hybrid genus (*Fatsia japonica* 'Moseri' x *Hedera helix* 'Hibernica') of one evergreen, fall-flowering shrub, grown for its foliage. Is good trained against a wall or pillar or, if supported by canes, cultivated as a house plant. Prefers a sunny or shaded position and fertile, well-drained soil. Propagate by semi-ripe cuttings in summer.

x F. lizei, (Aralia ivy, Botanical wonder) illus. p.211. **'Variegata'** is an evergreen, mound-forming, loose-branched shrub. **H** 5ft (1.5m) or more if trained as a climber, **S** 10ft (3m). Has rounded, deeply lobed, glossy, deep green leaves, narrowly edged with creamy-white. From mid- to late fall bears sprays of small, white flowers. Z8–11 H12–8.

FATSIA
ARALIACEAE

Genus of one species of evergreen, fall-flowering shrub, grown for its foliage, flowers and fruits. Is excellent for conservatories. At limits of hardiness, provide shelter from strong winds. Tolerates sun or shade and requires fertile, well-drained soil. Propagate by semi-ripe cuttings in summer or by seed in fall or spring.

F. japonica, syn. *Aralia japonica, Aralia sieboldii* (Japanese fatsia). Evergreen, rounded, dense shrub. **H** and **S** 10ft (3m). Has sturdy shoots and very large, rounded, deeply lobed, glossy, dark green leaves. Dense clusters of tiny, white flowers, produced in mid-fall, are followed by rounded, black fruits. Z8–10 H10–8. **'Variegata'** illus. p.144.

F. papyrifera. See *Tetrapanax papyrifer*.

FAUCARIA
Tiger jaws
AIZOACEAE

Genus of clump-forming, stemless, perennial succulents, grown for their semi-cylindrical or 3-angled, fleshy, bright green leaves and yellow flowers that open in late afternoons in fall. Buds and dead flowers may appear orange or red. Requires full sun and well-drained soil. Keep dry in winter and water sparingly in spring. Propagate by seed or stem cuttings in spring or summer.

F. tigrina, illus. p.495.

Feijoa. See *Acca*.

FELICIA
syn. AGATHAEA
Blue daisy
COMPOSITAE/ASTERACEAE

Genus of annuals, evergreen subshrubs and (rarely) shrubs, grown for their daisy-like, mainly blue flower heads. Requires full sun and well-drained soil. Water container plants moderately when in full growth, less at other times; dislikes wet conditions, particularly in low temperatures. Cut off dead flowering stems and cut back straggly shoots regularly. Propagate by seed in spring or by greenwood cuttings in summer or early fall.

F. amelloides, syn. *Aster capensis* (Blue daisy). Bushy sub-shrub, grown as an annual. **H** and **S** 12–24in (30–60cm). Bears deep green leaves, to 1¼in (3cm) long, and light to deep blue flowers from summer to fall. Z8–11 H12–8. **'Santa Anita',** illus. p.157.

F. bergeriana (Kingfisher daisy). Fairly fast-growing, mat-forming annual. **H** and **S** 6in (15cm). Has lance-shaped, hairy, gray-green leaves. Small, daisy-like, blue flower heads, with yellow centers, open only in sunshine in summer and early fall. Z11 H11–1.

FENESTRARIA
AIZOACEAE

Genus of clump-forming, perennial succulents, grown for their basal rosettes of fleshy leaves that have gray 'windows' in their flattened tips. Needs sun and very well-drained soil. Keep bone dry in winter. Propagate by seed in spring or summer.

F. aurantica. See *F. rhopalophylla* subsp. *aurantiaca*.

F. rhopalophylla. Clump-forming, perennial succulent. **H** 2in (5cm), **S** 8in (20cm). Forms open cushions of erect, club-shaped, glossy, glaucous to mid-green leaves, each with a flattened tip. Bears daisy-like, white flowers, on long stems, in late summer and fall. Z13–15 H12–10. **subsp. aurantiaca,** syn. *F. aurantica* illus. p.495.

FEROCACTUS
Barrel cactus
CACTACEAE

Genus of slow-growing, spherical, perennial cacti, becoming columnar after many years. Needs full sun and very well-drained soil. Propagate by seed in spring or summer. Treat blackened areoles with systemic fungicide and ensure plants have good ventilation.

F. acanthodes. See *F. cylindraceus*.

F. chrysacanthus. Slow-growing, spherical, perennial cactus. **H** 3ft (1m), **S** 2ft (60cm). Green stem, with 15–20 ribs, is fairly densely covered with curved, yellow-white spines. In summer bears funnel-shaped, yellow, rarely red, flowers, 2in (5cm) across, only on plants 10in (25cm) or more in diameter. Z12–15 H12–10.

F. cylindraceus, syn. *F. acanthodes,* illus. p.494.

F. hamatacanthus, syn. *Hamatocactus hamatacanthus,* illus. p.486.

F. latispinus (Devil's tongue). Slow-growing, flattened spherical, perennial cactus. **H** 8in (20cm), **S** 16in (40cm). Green stem, with 15–20 ribs, bears broad, hooked, red or yellow spines. Funnel-shaped, pale yellow or red flowers are produced in summer on plants more than 4in (10cm) wide. Z13–15 H12–10.

F. setispinus. See *Thelocactus setispinus*.

F. wislizenii (Fishhook cactus). Slow-growing, spherical, perennial cactus. **H** 6ft (2m), **S** 3ft (1m). Green stem, with up to 25 ribs, is covered in flattened, fish-hook, usually reddish-brown spines, to 5cm (2in) long. Funnel-shaped, orange or yellow flowers, 6cm (2½in) across, are produced in late summer, on plants more than 10in (25cm) wide, which should attain this size 10–15 years after raising from seed. Z13–15 H12–10.

FERRARIA
IRIDACEAE

Genus of spring-flowering corms, grown for their curious flowers with 3 large, outer petals and 3 small, inner ones, with very wavy edges. Is unpleasant-smelling to attract flies, which pollinate flowers. Requires full sun and well-drained soil. Plant in fall, water during winter and dry off after flowering. Dies down in summer. Propagate by division in late summer or by seed in fall.

F. crispa, syn. *F. undulata,* illus. p.407.

F. undulata. See *F. crispa*.

FERULA
Giant fennel
UMBELLIFERAE/APIACEAE

Genus of mainly summer-flowering perennials, grown for their bold, architectural form. Should not be confused with culinary fennel, *Foeniculum*. Needs sun and well-drained soil. Propagate by seed when fresh, in late summer.

F. communis, illus. p.219.

FESTUCA
Fescue
GRAMINEAE/POACEAE

See also GRASSES, BAMBOOS, RUSHES and SEDGES.

F. glauca, syn. *F. ovina* var. *glauca* (Gray fescue). Group of evergreen, tuft-forming, perennial grasses. **H** and **S** 4in (10cm). Bears narrow leaves in various shades of blue-green to silvery-white. Produces unimportant panicles of spikelets in summer. Is good for bed edging. Divide every 2–3 years in spring. Z4–8 H8–1.

F. ovina var. **glauca.** See *F. glauca*.

Ficaria verna. See *Ranunculus ficaria*.

FICUS
Fig
MORACEAE

Genus of evergreen or deciduous trees, shrubs and scrambling or root climbers, grown for their foliage and for shade; a few species also for fruit. All bear insignificant clusters of flowers in spring or summer. Prefers full light or partial shade and fertile, well-drained soil. Water container specimens moderately, very little when temperatures are low. Propagate by seed in spring or by leaf-bud or stem-tip cuttings or air-layering in summer. Red spider mite may be a nuisance. ① The foliage may cause mild stomach upset if ingested; the sap may irritate skin or aggravate allergies.

F. benghalensis, illus. p.452.

F. benjamina (Weeping fig). Evergreen, weeping tree, often with aerial roots. **H** and **S** 60–70ft (18–20m). Has slender, oval leaves, 3–5in (7–13cm) long, in lustrous, rich green. Z10–11 H12–10. **'Variegata'** illus. p.450.

F. deltoidea, illus. p.458.

F. elastica (India rubber fig). **'Decora'** is a strong-growing, evergreen, irregularly ovoid tree. **H** to 100ft (30m), **S** 50–70ft (15–20m). Has broadly oval, leathery, lustrous, deep green leaves, pinkish-bronze when young. Z11 H12–10. **'Doescheri',** illus. p.450. Leaves of **'Variegata'** are cream-edged, mottled with gray-green. Z14–15 H12–10.

F. lyrata (Banjo fig). Evergreen, ovoid, robust-stemmed tree. **H** 50ft (15m) or more, **S** to 30ft (10m). Fiddle-shaped leaves, 1ft (30cm) or more long, are lustrous, deep green. Z11–12 H12–7.

F. macrophylla (Australian banyan, Moreton Bay fig). Evergreen, wide-spreading, dense tree with a buttressed trunk when mature. **H** 70–100ft (20–30m), **S** 100–130ft (30–40m). Oval leaves, to 8in (20cm) long, are leathery, glossy, deep green. Z11–12 H12–7.

F. pumila, syn. *F. repens* (Climbing fig, Creeping fig). Evergreen, root climber. **H** 25ft (8m), 5ft (1.5m) as a container plant. Bright green leaves are heart-shaped when young; 1¼–3in (3–8cm) long, leathery and oval when mature. Unpalatable fruits are 6cm (2½in) long, orange at first, then flushed red-purple. Only reaches adult stage in very warm regions or under glass. Pinch out branch tips to encourage branching. Z9–11 H12–1. The young leaves of **'Minima'** are shorter and narrower.

F. religiosa (Bo tree, Peepul, Sacred fig). Mainly evergreen, rounded to wide-spreading tree with prop roots from branches. **H** and **S** 70–100ft (20–30m). Leaves, 4–6in (10–15cm) long, are broadly oval to almost triangular with long, thread-like tips, pink-flushed when expanding. Z14–15 H12–10.

F. repens. See *F. pumila*.

F. rubiginosa (Port Jackson fig, Rusty-leaved fig). Evergreen, dense-headed tree with a buttressed trunk. **H** and **S** 70–100ft (20–30m) or more. Elliptic, blunt-pointed leaves, to 4in (10cm) long, are glossy, dark green above, usually with rust-colored down beneath. Z14–15 H12–10.

FILIPENDULA
ROSACEAE

Genus of spring- and summer-flowering perennials. Most grow in full sun or partial shade, in moist but well-drained, leafy soil; some species, e.g. *F. rubra*, will thrive in boggy sites. *F. vulgaris* needs a drier site, in full sun. Propagate by seed in fall or by division in fall or winter.

F. camtschatica, syn. *F. kamtschatica*. Clump-forming perennial. **H** to 5ft (1.5m), **S** 3ft (1m). In mid-summer produces frothy, flat heads of scented, star-shaped, white or pale pink flowers above large, lance-shaped, divided and cut leaves. Z3–9 H9–1.

F. hexapetala. See *F. vulgaris.* **'Flore Pleno'.** See *F. vulgaris* 'Multiplex'.
F. kamtschatica. See *F. camtschatica.*
F. purpurea, illus. p.238.
F. rubra, illus. p.438.
F. ulmaria, syn. *Spiraea ulmaria,* illus. p.436. **'Aurea',** illus. p.274.
F. vulgaris, syn. *F. hexapetala* (Dropwort). **'Multiplex',** syn. *F. hexapetala* 'Flore Pleno' is an upright, rosette-forming perennial with fleshy, swollen roots. **H** 3ft (1m), **S** 1¹/₂ft (45cm). In summer produces flat panicles of rounded, double, white flowers, sometimes flushed pink, above fern-like, finely divided, toothed, hairless, dark green leaves. Z4–7 H8–1.

FIRMIANA
STERCULIACEAE/MALVACEAE

Genus of mainly deciduous trees and shrubs, grown for their foliage and to provide shade. Requires fertile, moist but well-drained soil and full light or partial shade. Water container specimens freely when in full growth, less in winter. Pruning is tolerated if necessary. Propagate by seed when ripe or in spring.
F. platanifolia. See *F. simplex.*
F. simplex, syn. *F. platanifolia, Sterculia x platanifolia,* illus. p.451.

FITTONIA
Nerve plant, Painted net leaf
ACANTHACEAE

Genus of evergreen, creeping perennials, grown mainly for their foliage. Is useful as ground cover. Needs a fairly humid atmosphere. Needs shade and well-drained soil; keep well watered but avoid waterlogging, especially in winter. If it becomes too straggly, cut back in spring. Propagate in spring or summer, with extra heat, by division or stem cuttings.
F. albivenis Argyroneura Group, syn. *F. argyroneura, F. verschaffeltii* var. *argyroneura,* illus. p.468. **Verschaffeltii Group,** syn. *F. verschaffeltii* (Painted net-leaf) is an evergreen, creeping perennial. **H** to 6in (15cm), **S** indefinite. Produces small, oval, red-veined, olive-green leaves. Flowers are best removed if they form. Z14–15 H11–1.
F. argyroneura. See *F. albivenis* Argyroneura Group.
F. verschaffeltii. See *F. albivenis* Verschaffeltii Group. **var. *argyroneura.*** See *F. albivenis* Argyroneura Group.

FITZROYA
CUPRESSACEAE

See also CONIFERS.
F. cupressoides, syn. *F. patagonica,* illus. p.100.
F. patagonica. See *F. cupressoides.*

FOENICULUM
Fennel
UMBELLIFERAE/APIACEAE

Genus of summer-flowering biennials and perennials, some of which are grown for their umbels of yellow flowers. Is also grown for its leaves, which are both decorative in borders and used for culinary flavoring. Needs an open, sunny position and fertile, well-drained soil. Remove flower heads after fading to prevent self-seeding. Propagate by seed in fall.
F. vulgare (Common fennel). Z6–9 H9–6. **'Purpureum'** is an erect, branching perennial. **H** 6ft (2m), **S** 1¹/₂ft (45cm). Has very finely divided, hair-like, bronze leaves and, in summer, large, flat umbels of small, yellow flowers.

FONTINALIS
Water moss
SPHAGNACEAE/FONTINALACEAE

Genus of evergreen, perennial, submerged water plants, grown for their foliage, which provides dense cover for fish and a good site for the deposit of spawn. Grows in sun or partial shade in streams and other running water; tolerates still water if cool, but then does not grow to full size. Propagate by division in spring.
F. antipyretica (Water moss, Willow moss). Evergreen, perennial, submerged water plant. **H** 1in (2.5cm), **S** indefinite. Forms spreading colonies of moss-like, dark olive-green leaves. Z4–8.

FORSYTHIA
OLEACEAE

Genus of deciduous, spring-flowering shrubs, grown for their usually profuse, yellow flowers, which are produced before the leaves emerge. *F.* 'Beatrix Farrand' and *F. x intermedia* 'Lynwood Variety' make attractive, flowering hedges. Prefers full sun and fertile, well-drained soil. Thin out old shoots and trim hedges immediately after flowering. Propagate by softwood cuttings in summer or by hardwood cuttings in fall or winter.
F. **'Flo Jar'.** See *F. x intermedia* MINIGOLD.
F. x intermedia **'Arnold Giant'** Deciduous, bushy shrub. **H** 5ft (1.5m), **S** 8ft (2.5m). Has sturdy shoots and oblong, sharply toothed, mid-green leaves. Large, 4-lobed, deep yellow flowers are produced sparsely from early to mid-spring. Z6–9 H9–5. **'Beatrix Farrand',** illus. p.127. **'Karl Sax',** **H** 8ft (2.5m), is dense-growing, with an abundance of flowers. Some leaves turn red or purple in fall. **'Lynwood',** **H** 10ft (3m), is very free-flowering, vigorous and upright. MINIGOLD **('Flo Jar'), H** and **S** 6ft (2m), has oblong, mid-green leaves, produces masses of small, yellow flowers. **'Spectabilis',** illus. p.127. **'Spring Glory', H** 6ft (2m), **S** 5ft (1.5m), has clusters of large, 4-lobed, pale yellow flowers borne in mid-spring and bright green leaves.
F. ovata (Early forsythia, Korean forsythia). Deciduous, bushy shrub. **H** and **S** 5ft (1.5m). Bears broadly oval, toothed, dark green leaves. Produces small, 4-lobed, bright yellow flowers in early spring. Z5–7 H7–5. **'Tetragold'** has larger flowers. Z4–7 H7–3.
F. suspensa, illus. p.195.

FOTHERGILLA
HAMAMELIDACEAE

Genus of deciduous, spring-flowering shrubs, grown for their fall color and fragrant flowers, each with a dense, bottlebrushlike cluster of stamens, which open before or as leaves emerge. Grows in sun or partial shade, but colors best in full sun. Requires moist, peaty, acidic soil. Propagate by softwood cuttings in summer.

F. gardenii, illus. p.163.
F. major, syn. *F. monticola,* illus. p.117.
F. monticola. See *F. major.*

Fragaria indica. See *Duchesnea indica.*

FRAILEA
CACTACEAE

Genus of spherical to columnar, perennial cacti with tuberculate ribs. Bears short spines, mostly bristly. In summer produces masses of buds, most of which develop into small, spherical, shiny pods without opening. Needs partial shade and very well-drained soil. Is not well-adapted to long periods of drought. Propagate by seed in spring or summer.
F. pulcherrima. See *F. pygmaea.*
F. pygmaea, syn. *F. pulcherrima,* illus. p.490.

FRANCOA
Bridal wreath
SAXIFRAGACEAE/FRANCOACEAE

Genus of summer- and early fall-flowering perennials. Needs full sun and fertile, well-drained soil. Propagate by seed or division in spring.
F. appendiculata. Clump-forming perennial. **H** 24in (60cm), **S** 18in (45cm). Racemes of small, bell-shaped, pale pink flowers, spotted with deep pink at base, are borne on erect stems from summer to early fall, above oblong to oval, lobed, hairy, crinkled, dark green leaves. Z6–9 H9–6.
F. sonchifolia. Clump-forming perennial. **H** 30in (75cm), **S** 18in (45cm). Bears racemes of cup-shaped, red-marked, pink flowers from summer to early fall. Lobed leaves each have a large, terminal lobe. Z7–9 H9–7. Rogerson's form, **H** 24in (60cm), **S** 24in (60cm) or more, has lance-shaped, lobed, dark green leaves and slender, wandlike racemes of star-shaped, rich pink and red flowers in summer. Is good for groundcover.

FRANKLINIA
Franklin tree
THEACEAE

Genus of one species of deciduous tree or shrub, grown for its flowers and fall color. Requires full sun and moist but well-drained, neutral to acidic soil. Propagate by softwood cuttings in summer, by seed in fall or by hardwood cuttings in early winter.
F. alatamaha. Deciduous, upright tree or shrub. **H** and **S** 15ft (5m) or more. Large, shallowly cup-shaped, white flowers, with yellow stamens, are borne in late summer and early fall. Oblong, glossy, bright green leaves turn red in fall. Z6–9 H9–6.

FRAXINUS
Ash
OLEACEAE

Genus of deciduous trees and shrubs, grown mainly for their foliage of paired leaflets; flowers are usually insignificant. Requires sun and fertile, well-drained but not too dry soil. Propagate species by seed in fall, selected forms by budding in summer. ⚠ Contact with lichens on the bark may aggravate skin allergies.

F. americana (White ash). Fast-growing, deciduous, spreading tree. **H** 80ft (25m), **S** 50ft (15m). Leaves are dark green, with 5–9 oval to lance-shaped leaflets, sometimes turning yellow or purple in fall. Z6–9 H9–6.
F. angustifolia. **subsp. *oxycarpa*,** syn. *F. oxycarpa* Deciduous, spreading tree. **H** 80ft (25m), **S** 40ft (12m). Leaves usually consist of 9–11 slender, lance-shaped, glossy, dark green leaflets that turn golden-yellow in fall. Z6–9 H9–6.
F. excelsior (European ash). Vigorous, deciduous, spreading tree. **H** 100ft (30m), **S** 70ft (20m). Dark green leaves, with usually 9–11 oval leaflets, sometimes become yellow in fall. Black leaf buds are conspicuous in winter. Z5–8 H8–5. **f. *diversifolia*** has leaves that are simple or with only 3 leaflets. **'Jaspidea',** illus. p.60. **'Pendula',** illus. p.79. **'Raywood',** illus. p.66.
F. mariesii. See *F. sieboldiana.*
F. ornus, illus. p.71.
F. oxycarpa (Narrow-leaved ash). See *F. angustifolia* subsp. *oxycarpa.*
F. pennsylvanica (Green ash, Red ash). Fast-growing, deciduous, spreading tree. **H** and **S** 70ft (20m). Leaves of usually 7 or 9 narrowly oval, dull green leaflets are often velvety beneath, like the shoots, and turn yellow in fall. Z3–9 H9–4. **'Patmore'** is disease-resistant, with long-lasting, glossy leaves, but does not bear fruit.
F. sieboldiana, syn. *F. mariesii.* Slow-growing, deciduous, compact-headed tree. **H** 20ft (6m), **S** 15ft (5m). Leaves consist of 3–5 oval, dark green leaflets, each on a purple stalk. Produces clusters of small, fragrant, star-shaped, creamy-white flowers in early summer, followed by narrowly oblong, purple fruits. Z7–10 H10–7.
F. velutina, illus. p.74.

FREESIA
IRIDACEAE

Genus of winter- and spring-flowering corms, grown for their usually fragrant, funnel-shaped flowers, which are popular for cutting. Requires full sun and well-drained soil. Plant in fall and water throughout winter. Support with twigs or small canes. Dry off corms after flowering. Plant specially prepared corms outdoors in spring for flowering in summer. Propagate by offsets in fall or by seed in spring.
F. alba, syn. *F. refracta* var. *alba.* Late winter- and spring-flowering corm. **H** 8–12in (20–30cm), **S** 1¹/₂ –2¹/₂in (4–6cm). Has narrowly sword-shaped, erect leaves in a basal fan. Leafless stems bear loose spikes of very fragrant, white flowers, sometimes with a yellow blotch on the lowest petal, 2–3in (5–8cm) long. Z10–11 H12–6.
F. alba of gardens. See *F. caryophyllacea.*
F. armstrongii. See *F. corymbosa.*
F. caryophyllacea, syn. *F. alba* of gardens, *F. lactea, F. xanthospila.* Late winter- and spring-flowering corm. **H** to 6in (15cm), **S** 1¹/₂ –2¹/₂in (4–6cm). Has narrowly sword-shaped leaves growing at an angle. Short, leafless stems bear spikes of white, narrowly tubular flowers, 1¹/₄–2in (3–5cm) long, with the lower 3 petals usually marked with yellow. Z11 H12–6.
F. corymbosa, syn. *F. armstrongii.* Late winter- and spring-flowering corm. **H** to 12in (30cm), **S** 1¹/₂ –2¹/₂in (4–6cm). Has narrowly sword-shaped, erect, basal leaves.

Flower stem bends horizontally near the top and bears a spike of unscented, upright, pink flowers, $1\frac{1}{4}$–$1\frac{1}{2}$in (3–3.5cm) long, with yellow bases. Z10–11 H12–6.
***F.* 'Golden Melody'.** Winter- and spring-flowering corm. **H** to 12in (30cm), **S** $1\frac{1}{2}$–$2\frac{1}{2}$in (4–6cm). Is similar to *F. corymbosa*, but has larger, fragrant flowers, yellow throughout. Z10–11 H12–6.
F. lactea. See *F. caryophyllacea.*
F. laxa. See *Anomatheca laxa.*
***F.* 'Oberon'.** Winter- and spring-flowering corm. **H** to 16in (40cm), **S** $1\frac{1}{2}$–$2\frac{1}{2}$in (4–6cm). Has narrowly sword-shaped, erect, basal leaves and yellow flowers, $1\frac{1}{2}$–2in (4–5cm) long, light blood-red inside; the throats are lemon-yellow with small, red veins. Z10–11 H12–6.
***F. refracta* var. *alba*.** See *F. caryophyllacea.*
***F.* 'Romany'.** Winter- and spring-flowering corm. **H** to 12in (30cm), **S** $1\frac{1}{2}$–$2\frac{1}{2}$in (4–6cm). Is similar to *F. corymbosa*, but has fragrant, double, pale mauve flowers. Z10–11 H12–6.
***F.* 'White Swan'.** Winter- and spring-flowering corm. **H** to 12in (30cm), **S** $1\frac{1}{2}$–$2\frac{1}{2}$in (4–6cm). Is similar to *F. corymbosa* but has very fragrant, white flowers with cream throats. Z10–11 H12–6.
F. xanthospila. See *F. caryophyllacea.*

Fremontia. See *Fremontodendron.*

FREMONTODENDRON

SYN. FREMONTIA
Flannel bush

STERCULIACEAE/MALVACEAE

Genus of vigorous, evergreen or semi-evergreen shrubs, grown for their large, very showy flowers. At the limits of hardiness, plant against a south- or west-facing wall. Needs full sun and light, not too rich, well-drained soil. In mild areas, may be grown as a spreading shrub, but needs firm staking when young. Resents being transplanted. Propagate by semi-ripe cuttings in summer or by seed in fall or spring. ⓘ Contact with the foliage and shoots may irritate the skin.
***F.* 'California Glory',** illus. p.206.
F. californicum (California flannel bush). Vigorous, evergreen or semi-evergreen, upright shrub. **H** 20ft (6m), **S** 12ft (4m) when grown against a wall. Large, saucer-shaped, bright yellow flowers are borne amid dark green leaves, each with 3 rounded lobes, from late spring to mid-fall. Z8–10 H10–8.
F. mexicanum (Mexican flannel bush). Vigorous, evergreen or semi-evergreen, upright shrub. **H** 20ft (6m), **S** 12ft (4m) when grown against a wall. Dark green leaves have 5 deep, rounded lobes. Bears masses of large, saucer-shaped, deep golden-yellow flowers from late spring to mid-fall. Z9–10 H10–9.
***F.* 'Pacific Sunset'.** Upright, evergreen shrub. **H** 15ft (5m), **S** 10–12ft (3–4m). Rounded, strongly lobed leaves are dark green. In summer produces saucer-shaped, bright yellow flowers, to $2\frac{1}{2}$in (6cm) across, with long, slender-pointed lobes. Z9–10 H10–9.

FRITHIA

AIZOACEAE

Genus of one species of rosette-forming, perennial succulent. Needs sun and well-drained soil. Propagate by seed in spring or summer.
F. pulchra, illus. p.485.

FRITILLARIA

Fritillary

LILIACEAE

Genus of spring-flowering bulbs, grown for their pendent, mainly bell-shaped flowers on leafy stems. Protect smaller, 2–6in (5–15cm) high species in cold frames or cold greenhouses. Needs full sun or partial shade and well-drained soil that dries out slightly in summer when bulbs are dormant but that does not become sunbaked. Grow *F. meleagris*, which is good for naturalizing in grass, in moist soil. Propagate by offsets in summer or by seed in fall or winter.
F. acmopetala, illus. p.406.
F. bucharica. Spring-flowering bulb. **H** 4–14in (10–35cm), **S** 2in (5cm). Stems each bear scattered, lance-shaped, gray-green leaves and a raceme of up to 10 cup-shaped, green-tinged, white flowers, $\frac{5}{8}$–$\frac{3}{4}$in (1.5–2cm) long. Z8–10
F. camschatcensis, illus. p.403.
F. chitralensis. Spring- to early summer-flowering bulb. **H** 20–32in (50–80cm), **S** 4in (10cm). Has ovate, mid- to light green leaves and open umbels of 4 or 5 pendent, conical, bright yellow flowers. Is similar to *F. imperialis.* Z6–8 H8–6.
F. cirrhosa, illus. p.406.
F. crassifolia. Spring-flowering bulb. **H** 4–8in (10–20cm), **S** 2in (5cm). Has scattered, lance-shaped, gray leaves. Stems each produce 1–3 bell-shaped, green flowers, $\frac{3}{4}$–1in (2–2.5cm) long and checkered with brown. Z6–8 H6–8.
F. delphinensis. See *F. tubiformis.*
F. imperialis, illus. p.383. **'Lutea'** illus. p.382. **'Rubra Maximia'** is a very robust, spring-flowering bulb. **H** to 5ft (1.5m), **S** 9–12in (23–30cm). Leafy stems each bear lance-shaped, light green leaves in whorls and a head of up to 5 widely bell-shaped, red flowers, 2in (5cm) long, crowned by small, leaf-like bracts.
F. meleagris, illus. p.402.
F. michailovskyi. Spring-flowering bulb. **H** 4–8in (10–20cm), **S** 2in (5cm). Has lance-shaped, gray leaves scattered on stem. Bears 1–4 bell-shaped, purplish-brown flowers, $\frac{3}{4}$–$1\frac{1}{4}$in (2–3cm) long, with upper third of petals bright yellow. Z5–8 H8–5.
F. pallidiflora, illus. p.406.
F. persica, illus. p.382. **'Adiyaman'** is a spring-flowering bulb. **H** to 5ft (1.5m), **S** 4in (10cm). Has narrowly lance-shaped, gray leaves along stem. Produces a spike of 10–20 or more narrowly bell-shaped, deep blackish-purple flowers, $\frac{5}{8}$–$\frac{3}{4}$in (1.5–2cm) long. **'Ivory Bells'** illus. p.382.
F. pontica, illus. p.406.
F. pudica, illus. p.422.
F. pyrenaica, illus. p.403.
F. raddeana, illus. p.382.
F. recurva, illus. p.383.
F. sewerzowii, syn. *Korolkowia sewerzowii.* Spring-flowering bulb. **H** 6–10in (15–25cm), **S** 3–4in (8–10cm). Stems bear scattered, broadly lance-shaped leaves. Produces a spike of up to 10 narrowly bell-shaped, green or metallic purplish-blue flowers, 1–$1\frac{1}{2}$in (2.5–3.5cm) long, with flared mouths. Z6–8 H8–6.
F. tubiformis, syn. *F. delphinensis.* Spring-flowering bulb. **H** 6–14in (15–35cm), **S** 2–3in (5–8cm). Stems bear scattered, narrowly lance-shaped, gray leaves and a solitary, broadly bell-shaped, purplish-pink flower, $1\frac{1}{2}$–2in (3.5–5cm) long, conspicuously checkered and suffused gray outside. Z7–9 H9–7.
F. verticillata, illus. p.382.

FUCHSIA

ONAGRACEAE

Genus of deciduous or evergreen shrubs and trees, grown for their flowers, usually borne from early summer to early fall. If temperature remains above 39°F (4°C), deciduous plants are evergreen, but temperatures above 90°F (32°C) should be avoided. Prolonged low temperatures cause loss of top growth. If top growth dies in winter, cut back to ground level in spring. Needs a sheltered, partially shaded position, except where stated otherwise, and fertile, moist but well-drained soil. When grown as container plants in a greenhouse, fuchsias also need high-nitrogen feeds and, when flowering, plenty of potash. Propagate by softwood cuttings in any season.

Tubular flowers are almost always pendulous and often bicolored, with petals of one hue, and a tube and 4 sepals of another. Leaves are oval and mid-green unless otherwise stated. Spherical to cylindrical, usually blackish-purple fruits are edible, but mostly poor-flavored. Upright types may be trained as compact bushes or standards or, with more difficulty, as pyramids. Lax or trailing plants are good for hanging baskets, but may be trained on trellises; if they are used for summer bedding, they require staking. Heights given in descriptions below are of plants grown in frost-free conditions. See also feature panels, p.154 (hardy fuchsias) and p.302 (tender fuchsias).
***F.* 'Alice Hoffman'.** Deciduous, compact shrub. **H** and **S** $2\frac{1}{2}$ft (75cm). Has bronze foliage and small, semi-double flowers with rose-red tubes and sepals and rose-veined, white petals. Z9–11 H12–9.
***F.* 'Annabel'** (illus. p.302). Deciduous, upright shrub. **H** 3ft (1m), **S** $2\frac{1}{2}$ft (75cm). Produces large, double, pink-tinged, creamy-white flowers amid pale green leaves. Makes an excellent standard. Z9–11 H11–9.
***F.* 'Applause'.** Deciduous, lax, upright shrub. **H** 12–18in (30–40cm), **S** 18–24in (45–60cm). Bears very large, double flowers with short, thick, pale carmine tubes, very broad, carmine sepals with a pale central streak, and many, spreading, deep orange-red petals. Produces best color in shade. Needs staking as a bush, but will trail with weights. Z9–11 H12–9.
F. arborea. See *F. arborescens.*
F. arborescens, syn. *F. arborea* (Lilac fuchsia). Evergreen, upright tree. **H** 25ft (8m), **S** 8ft (2.5m). Foliage is mid- to dark green. Erect heads of tiny, pale mauve to pink flowers, borne year-round, are followed by black fruits with gray-blue bloom. May also be grown as a container plant. Z9–11 H12–9.
***F.* 'Auntie Jinks'.** Deciduous, trailing shrub. **H** 6–8in (15–20cm), **S** 8–16in (20–40cm). Bears small, single flowers with pink-red tubes, cerise-margined, white sepals and white-shaded, purple petals. Z9–11 H12–9.
***F.* 'Autumnale',** syn. *F.* 'Burning Bush'. Deciduous, lax shrub, grown mainly for its foliage. **H** 6ft (2m), **S** 20in (50cm). Bears variegated red, gold and bronze leaves. Flowers have red tubes and sepals with reddish-purple petals. Is suitable for a hanging basket or for training as a weeping standard. Z9–11 H12–9.
F. x bacillaris, syn. *F. parviflora* of gardens. Group of deciduous, lax shrubs. **H** and **S** $2\frac{1}{2}$ft (75cm). Small leaves are mid- to dark green. Bears minute, white, pink or crimson flowers (color varying according to sun), sometimes followed by glossy, black fruits. Is suitable for a rock garden or hanging basket. Z9–11 H12–9.
***F.* 'Ballet Girl'.** Deciduous, upright shrub. **H** 12–18in (30–45cm), **S** 18–30in (45–75cm). Produces large, double flowers with bright cerise tubes and sepals, and white petals with cerise veins at the base. Z9–11 H12–9.
***F.* 'Bicentennial',** illus. p.302. Deciduous, lax shrub. **H** 12–18in (30–45cm), **S** 18–24in (45–60cm). Bears medium, double flowers with thin, white tubes, orange sepals and double corollas with magenta centers surrounded by orange petals. Z9–11 H11–9.
F. boliviana. Fast-growing, deciduous, upright shrub. **H** 10ft (3m), **S** 3ft (1m). Has large, soft, gray-green leaves with reddish midribs. Long-tubed, scarlet flowers, bunched at ends of branches, are followed by edible, black fruits. Needs a large pot and plenty of space to grow well. Resents being pinched back. Is very susceptible to whitefly. Z13–15 H12–9. **var. *alba*** (syn. *F. boliviana* var. *luxurians* 'Alba', *F. corymbiflora* 'Alba') has flowers with white tubes and sepals and scarlet petals, followed by green fruits. **var. *luxurians* 'Alba'.** See *F. boliviana* var. *alba.*
***F.* 'Bon Accorde'.** Vigorous, deciduous, upright shrub. **H** 5ft (1.5m), **S** 20in (50cm). Small, erect flowers have white tubes and sepals and pale purple petals. Z9–11 H12–9.
***F.* 'Brookwood Belle'.** Deciduous, lax, bushy shrub with strong, short-jointed stems. **H** and **S** 18–24in (45–60cm). Medium, double flowers have deep cerise tubes and sepals, and white petals flushed pink and veined deep rose-pink. Z9–11 H12–9.
***F.* 'Brutus'.** Vigorous, deciduous, upright shrub. **H** 5ft (1.5m), **S** 3ft (1m). Single or semi-double flowers have crimson-red tubes and sepals and deep purple petals. Z9–11 H12–9.
***F.* 'Burning Bush'.** See *F.* 'Autumnale'.
***F.* California Dreamer Series.** Deciduous, semi-trailing shrub. **H** and **S** 18in (45cm). Produces very large, blowsy, fully double flowers. Is ideal in a large container. Z9–11 H12–9. **'Snowburner'** (illus. p.302) has wavy, horizontal, red sepals and ruffled, white petals delicately patterned with red veins. Z9–11 H11–9.
***F.* 'Cascade'.** Deciduous, trailing shrub. **H** 6ft (2m), **S** indefinite. Bears red-tinged, white tubes and sepals and deep carmine petals. Is excellent in a hanging basket. Z9–11 H12–9.
***F.* 'Celia Smedley'** (illus. p.302). Vigorous, deciduous, upright shrub. **H** 5ft (1.5m), **S** 3ft (1m). Large, single or semi-double flowers have greenish-white tubes, pale pinkish-white sepals and currant-red petals. Is best when trained as a standard. Z9–11 H11–9.
***F.* 'Checkerboard'.** Vigorous, deciduous, upright shrub with strong stems. **H** 30–36in (75–90cm), **S** 18–30in (45–75cm). Produces medium, single flowers with slightly recurved, long red tubes, red sepals turning white and white-based, dark red petals. Z9–11 H12–9.

F

F. 'Cloverdale Pearl'. Deciduous, upright shrub. **H** 3ft (1m), **S** 2½ft (75cm). Foliage is mid-green with crimson midribs. Flowers have pinkish-white tubes, pink-veined, white petals and green-tipped, pink sepals. Is readily trained as a standard. Z9–11 H12–9.

F. 'Coquet Bell'. Vigorous, deciduous, upright shrub. **H** 5ft (1.5m), **S** 3ft (1m). Has a profusion of single or semi-double flowers with pinkish-red tubes and sepals and red-veined, pale mauve petals. Z9–11 H12–9.

F. 'Coralle', syn. *F.* 'Koralle' (illus. p.302). Deciduous, upright shrub. **H** and **S** 3ft (1m). Foliage is velvety and deep green. Salmon-orange flowers, with long, narrow tubes and small sepals and petals, are bunched at branch ends. Is useful for summer bedding and as a specimen plant. Prefers sun. H11–9.

F. 'Corallina' (illus. p.154). Deciduous, spreading shrub. **H** 16in (40cm), **S** 60in (1.5m). Has burgundy-red stems and mid-green leaves flushed pink at the bases. Pendent, medium flowers have narrow, spreading, scarlet sepals and broader, shorter, purple petals tinted red at the bases. Z9–11 H12–9.

***F. corymbiflora* 'Alba'.** See *F. boliviana* var. *alba*.

F. 'Dancing Flame'. Deciduous, lax shrub. **H** and **S** 18in (45cm). Strong stems bear small, oval, deep green leaves. Double, purple and blue flowers have bright pink sepals. Z9–11 H12–9.

F. 'Dark Eyes'. Deciduous, bushy, upright shrub. **H** 18–24in (45–60cm), **S** 24–30in (60–75cm). Bears medium, double flowers that hold their shape for a long period. Tubes and upturned sepals are deep red, and petals deep violet-blue. Z9–11 H12–9.

F. denticulata. Deciduous, straggling shrub. **H** 12ft (4m), **S** indefinite. Leaves are glossy, dark green above and reddish-green beneath. Flowers have long, crimson tubes, green-tipped, pale pink sepals and vermilion petals. With good cultivation under glass, flowers are borne in fall–winter. Z9–11 H12–9.

F. 'Display'. Deciduous, upright shrub. **H** 3ft (1m), **S** 2½ft (75cm). Bears saucer-shaped flowers in shades of pink. Z9–11 H12–9.

F. 'Dollar Princess'. See *F.* 'Dollar Prinzessin'.

F. 'Dollar Prinzessin', syn. *F.* 'Dollar Princess', illus. p.302. Deciduous, upright shrub. **H** 3ft (1m), **S** 2½ft (75cm). Small, double flowers have cerise-red tubes and sepals and purple petals. Z9–11 H11–9.

F. 'Estelle Marie'. Deciduous, upright shrub. **H** 3ft (1m), **S** 20in (50cm). Flowers with white tubes, green-tipped, white sepals and mauve petals are borne above foliage. Is excellent for summer bedding. Z9–11 H12–9.

F. 'Flash'. Fast-growing, deciduous, stiffly erect shrub. **H** 8ft (2.5m), **S** 20in (50cm). Produces small, red flowers amid small leaves. Z9–11 H12–9.

F. 'Flirtation Waltz'. Vigorous, deciduous, upright shrub. **H** 3ft (1m), **S** 2½ft (75cm). Produces large, double flowers with petals in shades of pink, and white tubes and sepals. Z9–11 H12–9.

F. fulgens, (illus. p.302). Deciduous, upright shrub with tubers. **H** 6ft (2m), **S** 3ft (1m). Long-tubed, orange flowers hang in short clusters amid large, pale green leaves and are followed by edible but acidic, green fruits. Tubers may be stored dry for winter. May also be propagated by division of tubers in spring. Is highly susceptible to whitefly. H11–9.

F. 'Garden News'. Deciduous, upright shrub with strong stems. **H** and **S** 18–24in (45–60cm). Medium, double flowers have short, thick, pink tubes, frost-pink sepals and magenta-rose petals becoming rose-pink at the base. Z9–11 H12–9.

F. 'Genii'. Deciduous, erect shrub. **H** 5ft (1.5m), **S** 2½ft (75cm). Has golden-green foliage. Produces small flowers with cerise-red tubes and sepals and reddish-purple petals. Makes a good standard. Z9–11 H12–9.

F. 'Golden Dawn'. Deciduous, upright shrub. **H** 5ft (1.5m), **S** 2½ft (75cm). Flowers are salmon-pink. Is good for training as a standard. Z9–11 H12–9.

F. 'Golden Marinka' (illus. p.302). Deciduous, trailing shrub. **H** 6ft (2m), **S** indefinite. Has red flowers and variegated golden-yellow leaves with red veins. Is excellent for a hanging basket. Z9–11 H11–9.

F. 'Gruss aus dem Bodethal'. Deciduous, upright shrub. **H** 3ft (1m), **S** 2½ft (75cm). Small, single or semi-double, crimson flowers open almost black, becoming larger and paler with age. Z9–11 H12–9.

F. 'Harry Gray'. Deciduous, lax shrub. **H** 6ft (2m), **S** indefinite. Bears a profusion of double flowers with pale pink tubes, green-tipped, white sepals and white to pale pink petals. Is excellent in a hanging basket. Z9–11 H12–9.

F. 'Heidi Weiss', syn. *F.* 'White Ann' of gardens, *F.* 'White Heidi Ann' of gardens. Deciduous, upright shrub. **H** 3ft (1m), **S** 2½ft (75cm). Has double flowers with red tubes and sepals and cerise-veined, white petals. Is good for training as a standard. Z9–11 H12–9.

F. 'Howlett's Hardy', (illus. p.154). Deciduous, mound-forming shrub. **H** 16in (40cm), **S** 24in (60cm). Dark red-purple stems bear slightly bronzed, mid-green leaves. Throughout summer produces numerous, pendent, medium flowers with spreading to reflexed, scarlet sepals and bright purple petals veined red at the bases. Z9–11 H12–9.

F. 'Hula Girl'. Deciduous, trailing shrub. **H** 6ft (2m), **S** indefinite. Bears large, double flowers with deep rose-pink tubes and sepals and pink-flushed, white petals. Thrives in a large hanging basket or when trained against a trellis. Z9–11 H12–9.

F. 'Jack Shahan', (illus. p.302). Vigorous, deciduous, trailing shrub. **H** 6ft (2m), **S** indefinite. Has large, pale to deep pink flowers. Is excellent for a hanging basket or for training into a weeping standard or upright against a trellis. Z9–11 H11–9.

F. 'Joanna Lumley' (illus. p.302). Deciduous, semi-trailing shrub. **H** and **S** 12–15in (30–38cm). Has large, double flowers with rather upright, blushed white sepals and lilac petals stained pink at the bases. Z9–11 H12–9.

F. 'Joy Patmore'. Vigorous, deciduous, upright shrub. **H** 5ft (1.5m), **S** 3ft (1m). Flowers have white tubes, green-tipped, white sepals and cerise petals with white bases. Makes a good standard. Z9–11 H12–9.

F. 'Koralle'. See *F.* 'Coralle'.

F. 'La Campanella'. Deciduous, trailing shrub. **H** 5ft (1.5m), **S** indefinite. Has small, semi-double flowers with white tubes, pink-flushed, white sepals and cerise-purple petals. Thrives in a hanging basket or trained against a trellis. Z9–11 H12–9.

F. 'Lady Thumb', illus. p.152.

F. 'Lena'. Deciduous, lax shrub. **H** and **S** 3ft (1m). Bears double flowers with pale pink sepals and tubes and pink-flushed, purple petals. Makes a good standard. Z9–11 H12–9.

F. 'Leonora', illus. p.301.

F. 'Love's Reward'. Deciduous, upright, short-jointed shrub. **H** and **S** 12–18in (30–45cm). Small to medium, single flowers have white to pale pink tubes and sepals and violet-blue petals. Z9–11 H12–9.

F. 'Lye's Unique' (illus. p.302). Vigorous, deciduous, upright shrub. **H** 5ft (1.5m), **S** 3ft (1m). Has small flowers with long, white tubes and sepals and orange-red petals. Is excellent for training as a large pyramid. Z9–11 H11–9.

F. 'Madame Cornélissen' (illus. p.154). Deciduous, arching shrub. **H** and **S** to 3ft (1m). Has long, white tubes and mauve-red sepals. Z9–11 H12–9.

F. magellanica (illus. p.154). Deciduous, upright shrub. **H** 10ft (3m), **S** 6ft (2m). Small flowers with red tubes, long, red sepals and purple petals are followed by black fruits. Z6–9 H9–6. **'Alba'** see *F. magellanica* var. *molinae*. **var. *gracilis*** (illus. p.154), **H** 32in (80cm) **S** 1.2m (48in), is a compact, mound-forming shrub with rich red stems and pendent, medium flowers with narrow, slightly spreading, scarlet sepals and shorter, deep purple petals. **var. *molinae*** (syn. *F. magellanica* 'Alba') has very pale pink flowers. **var. *molinae* 'Enstone'** has gold and green, variegated foliage. **var. *molinae* 'Sharpitor'** produces cream and pale green, variegated leaves. **'Thompsonii'** (illus. p.154), **H** 5ft (1.5m), **S** 3ft (1m), has bright red sepals and purple petals, red-tinted at the bases.

F. 'Margaret Brown'. Deciduous, free-flowering, upright shrub. **H** and **S** 2–3ft (60–90cm). Has strong stems and light green foliage, and bears small, single, 2-tone pink flowers in summer. Z9–11 H12–9.

F. 'Marinka'. Deciduous, trailing shrub. **H** 6ft (2m), **S** indefinite. Red flowers with darker petals that are folded at outer edges are produced amid dark green leaves with crimson midribs. Foliage becomes discolored in full sun or cold winds. Is excellent in a hanging basket. Z9–11 H12–9.

F. 'Micky Goult'. Vigorous, deciduous, upright shrub. **H** 3ft (1m), **S** 2½ft (75cm). Small flowers, with white tubes, pink-tinged, white sepals and pale purple petals, are produced amid pale green foliage. Z9–11 H12–9.

F. 'Mieke Meursing'. Deciduous, upright shrub. **H** 3ft (1m), **S** 2½ft (75cm). Single to semi-double flowers have red tubes and sepals and pale pink petals with cerise veins. Z9–11 H12–9.

F. Mojo Series. Deciduous, bushy, well-branched shrub. **H** 10–14in (25–35cm), **S** 12–16in (30–40cm). Produces small, nodding or slightly outward-facing, bicolored flowers from mid-spring to fall in a range of color combinations. Z9–11 H12–9. **'Beebop'** (illus. p.302) has slightly upturned, pale pink sepals and magenta petals, paler at the bases.

F. 'Mrs. Lovell Swisher' (illus. p.302). Deciduous, upright shrub. **H** 18–24in (45–60cm), **S** 12–24in (30–60cm). Produces masses of small, single flowers with flesh-pink tubes, pinkish-white sepals and deep rose-pink petals. Z9–11 H11–9.

F. 'Mrs. Popple' (illus. p.154). Vigorous, deciduous, upright shrub. **H** 5ft (1.5m), **S** 2½ft (75cm). Has flowers with red tubes, overhanging, red sepals and purple petals. In a sheltered area may be grown as a hedge. Z9–11 H11–9.

F. 'Mrs. Rundle'. Vigorous, deciduous, lax shrub. **H** and **S** 2½ft (75cm). Produces large flowers with long, pink tubes, green-tipped, pink sepals and vermilion petals. Is good for training as a standard or growing in a large hanging basket. Z9–11 H12–9.

F. 'Nancy Lou'. Vigorous, deciduous, upright shrub. **H** and **S** 3ft (1m). Large, double flowers have pink tubes, upright, green-tipped, pink sepals and bright white petals. Z9–11 H12–9.

F. 'Nellie Nuttall' (illus. p.302). Vigorous, deciduous, upright shrub. **H** 3ft (1m), **S** 2½ft (75cm). Flowers, with rose-red tubes and sepals and white petals, are borne well above foliage. Is especially suitable for summer bedding; is also good as a standard. Z9–11 H11–9.

F. 'Other Fellow'. Deciduous, upright shrub. **H** 5ft (1.5m), **S** 2½ft (75cm). Has small flowers with white tubes and sepals and pink petals. Z9–11 H12–9.

F. 'Pacquesa'. Vigorous, deciduous, upright shrub. **H** 3ft (1m), **S** 2½ft (75cm). Has flowers with deep red tubes and sepals and red-veined, white petals. Is good for training as a standard. Z9–11 H12–9.

F. parviflora of gardens. See *F.* x *bacillaris*.

F. 'Peppermint Stick'. Deciduous, upright shrub. **H** and **S** 3ft (1m). Double, carmine-red flowers have a central, white stripe and royal purple sepals. Z9–11 H12–9.

F. 'Phyllis'. Deciduous, upright shrub. **H** 6ft (2m), **S** 3ft (1m). Single to semi-double flowers, with rose-red tubes and sepals and crimson petals, are followed by masses of black fruits. In a sheltered area may be grown as a hedge. Z9–11 H12–9.

F. 'Pink Fantasia'. Deciduous, stiff, upright shrub. **H** 12–18in (30–40cm), **S** 18–24in (45–60cm). Bears single, upward-looking flowers, in profusion, with white tubes and sepals blushed dark pink, and dark purple petals, veined pink, with white bases. Is excellent for a border or pot. Z9–11 H12–9.

F. 'Pink Galore' (illus. p.302). Deciduous, trailing shrub. **H** 5ft (1.5m), **S** indefinite. Has large, double, pale pink flowers. Thrives in a large hanging basket or when trained against a trellis. Z9–11 H12–9.

F. procumbens (Trailing fuchsia). Deciduous, prostrate shrub. **H** 4in (10cm), **S** indefinite. Produces tiny, erect, petalless, yellow-tubed flowers with purple sepals and bright blue pollen. Has small, dark green leaves and large, red fruits. Is suitable for a rock garden as well as a hanging basket. Encourage flowering by root restriction or growing in poor, sandy soil. Z9–11 H12–9.

F. 'Red Spider' (illus. p.302). Deciduous, trailing shrub. **H** 5ft (1.5m), **S** indefinite. Has long, red flowers with long, narrow, spreading sepals and darker petals. Is best in a large hanging basket or when trained against a trellis. Z9–11 H11–9.

F. **'Riccartonii'** (illus. p.154). Deciduous, stiff, upright shrub. **H** 6ft (2m), **S** 5ft (1.5m). Has small flowers with red tubes, broad, overhanging, red sepals and purple petals. In a sheltered area may be grown as a hedge. Many plants sold under name of *F.* 'Riccartoni' are lax hybrids of *F. magellanica.* Z9–11 H11–9.

F. **'Rose Fantasia'.** Deciduous, stiff, upright shrub. **H** 12–18in (30–40cm), **S** 18–24in (45–60cm). Produces single, upward-looking flowers, in profusion, with rose-pink tubes, dark rose-pink sepals with green tips and red-purple petals, veined rose-pink. Is excellent in a border or pot. Z9–11 H12–9.

F. **'Rose of Castile'.** Vigorous, deciduous, upright shrub. **H** 5ft (1.5m), **S** 3ft (1m). Produces small flowers with white tubes, green-tipped, white sepals and purple-flushed, pink petals. Makes a good standard. Z9–11 H12–9.

F. **'Rough Silk'.** Vigorous, deciduous, trailing shrub. **H** 6ft (2m), **S** indefinite. Bears large flowers with pink tubes, long, spreading, pink sepals and wine-red petals. Thrives in a large hanging basket or when trained against a trellis. Z9–11 H12–9.

F. **'Royal Velvet'.** Vigorous, deciduous, upright shrub. **H** 5ft (1.5m), **S** 2¹/₂ft (75cm). Has large, double flowers with red tubes and sepals and deep purple petals, splashed deep pink. Makes an excellent standard. Z9–11 H12–9.

F. **'Rufus'** (illus. p.154). Vigorous, deciduous, upright shrub. **H** 5ft (1.5m), **S** 2¹/₂ft (75cm). Has a profusion of small, bright red flowers. Is easily trained as a standard. Z9–11 H11–9.

F. **Shadowdancer Series.** Deciduous, bushy, well-branched shrubs. **H** and **S** 8–12in (20–30cm). Produce small single flowers and bloom continuously from spring to late summer or fall. Is ideal in a small container or as edging. Z9–11 H12–9. Pᴇɢɢʏ **('Goetzpeg'),** (illus. p.302) has pale pink sepals and rich pink petals tinted in vivid orange.

F. **'Shelford'.** Deciduous, upright, short-jointed shrub. **H** 14–20in (35–50cm), **S** 18–24in (45–60cm). Bears masses of medium-sized, single flowers with slightly fluted, baby-pink tubes, long, narrow, baby-pink sepals and white petals with slight pink veining at the base. Is suitable for all forms of training. Z9–11 H12–9.

F. **splendens.** Deciduous, upright shrub. **H** 6ft (2m), **S** 3ft (1m). Small flowers, with broad, orange tubes, pinched in their middles, and short, green sepals and petals, are produced in spring amid pale green foliage. Is extremely susceptible to whitefly. Z9–11 H12–9.

F. **'Strawberry Delight'.** Deciduous, lax shrub. **H** and **S** 3ft (1m). Leaves are yellowish-green and slightly bronzed. Produces large, double flowers with red tubes and sepals and pink-flushed, white petals. Is excellent as a standard or in a hanging basket. Z9–11 H12–9.

F. **'Sunray'** (illus. p.302). Deciduous, upright shrub. **H** and **S** to 28in (70cm). White-edged, light green leaves are sometimes pink flushed. Red-violet flowers, with deep pink sepals, are borne freely in summer–fall. Z9–11 H12–9.

F. **'Swingtime'** (illus. p.302). Vigorous, deciduous, lax shrub. **H** and **S** 3ft (1m). Has large, double flowers with red tubes and

sepals and red-veined, creamy-white petals. Makes a good standard or hanging basket plant. Z9–11 H11–9.

F. **'Texas Longhorn'.** Deciduous, lax shrub. **H** and **S** 2¹/₂ft (75cm). Produces very large, double flowers with red tubes, long, spreading, red sepals and cerise-veined, white petals. Grow as a standard or in a hanging basket. Z9–11 H12–9.

F. **'Thalia'** (illus. p.302). Deciduous, upright shrub. **H** and **S** 3ft (1m). Foliage is dark maroon and velvety. Long, slender flowers, with long, red tubes, small, red sepals and small, orange-red petals, are bunched at ends of branches. Makes an excellent specimen plant in summer bedding schemes. Prefers a position in full sun. Z9–11 H11–9.

F. **thymifolia.** Deciduous, lax shrub. **H** and **S** 3ft (1m). Has pale green foliage and a few minute, greenish-white flowers that age to purplish-pink. Bears black fruits on female plants if pollen-bearing plants of this species or of *F.* x *bacillaris* are also grown. Z9–11 H12–9.

F. **'Tom Thumb'** (illus. p.154). Deciduous, upright shrub. **H** and **S** 20in (50cm). Bears small flowers with red tubes and sepals and mauve-purple petals. May be trained as a miniature standard. Z9–11 H11–9.

F. **'Tom West'.** Deciduous, upright, lax shrub. **H** and **S** 12–24in (30–60cm). Has green and cream variegated foliage and small, single flowers with red tubes and sepals and purple petals. Z9–11 H12–9.

F. **triphylla.** Deciduous, upright shrub, sometimes confused with *F.* 'Thalia'. **H** and **S** 20in (50cm). Spikes of narrow, long-tubed, bright reddish-orange flowers, with small petals and sepals, are borne above dark bronze-green leaves that are purple beneath. Is very difficult to grow. Z9–11 H12–9. **'Firecracker'** (illus. p.302) has pink-veined, olive-green leaves edged in cream and bears bright orange flowers.

F. **'Waveny Gem'.** Deciduous, trailing shrub. **H** and **S** 12–18in (30–45cm). Produces medium, single, white and mauve-pink flowers from early summer. Z9–11 H12–9.

F. **'White Ann'** of gardens. See *F.* 'Heidi Weiss'.

F. **'White Heidi Ann'** of gardens. See *F.* 'Heidi Weiss'.

F. **'Whiteknights Pearl'.** Deciduous, upright shrub. **H** and **S** 3ft (1m) or more. In summer–fall freely produces small, single flowers with long, thin, white tubes, pale pink sepals with small green tips and clear pink corollas with rounded petals. Z9–11 H12–9.

F. **Windchimes Series.** Deciduous, semi-trailing, slightly mound-forming shrubs. **H** and **S** 18in (45cm). Produces single flowers continuously from spring to late summer or early fall. Is suitable for a hanging basket or at the edge of a large container, as well as in a border. Z9–11 H12–9. Wɪɴᴅᴄʜɪᴍᴇs Pɪɴᴋ ᴀɴᴅ Wʜɪᴛᴇ **('Kiefuwind'),** illus. p.302, has narrow, salmon-pink sepals and white petals.

F. **'Winston Churchill'.** Deciduous, bushy, upright, extremely free-flowering shrub. **H** and **S** 18–30in (45–75cm). Produces medium, fully double flowers with green-tipped, pink tubes, broad, reflexed sepals and lavender-blue corollas, maturing purple. Is good for summer bedding, or when trained as a standard in a container. Z9–11 H12–9.

FURCRAEA
AGAVACEAE/ASPARAGACEAE

Genus of perennial succulents, grown for their dense clusters of sword-shaped, fleshy, toothed leaves in terminal or basal rosettes; rosettes die after flowering. Resembles *Agave,* but has short-tubed flowers. Requires full sun and well-drained soil. Protect from winter wet. Propagate by bulbils, borne on lower stems, when developed.

F. **bedinghausii.** See *F. parmentieri.*
F. **foetida,** syn. *F. gigantea.* Basal-rosetted, perennial succulent. **H** 10ft (3m), **S** 15ft (5m). Has broadly sword-shaped, fleshy, mid-green leaves, to 8ft (2.5m) long, with edges toothed only at the base. Flower stems, to 25ft (8m), produce scented, bell-shaped, green flowers, which are white within, in summer. Z10–15 H12–10. **var. mediopicta.** See *F. foetida* 'Mediopicta'. **'Mediopicta',** (syn. *F. foetida* var. *mediopicta, F. foetida* 'Variegata') illus. p.481. **'Variegata'.** See *F. foetida* 'Mediopicta'.
F. **gigantea.** See *F. foetida.*
F. **parmentieri,** syn. *F. bedinghausii.* Basal-rosetted, perennial succulent. **H** 24in (60cm), **S** 3ft (1m). Has sword-shaped, minutely toothed, glaucous, mid-green leaves. In summer produces a pyramidal, erect spike, to 6ft (2m) long, with drooping branches and clusters of 2–4 creamy flowers, 1¹/₄–1¹/₂in (3–4cm), followed by numerous bulbils. Often incorrectly labelled *F. longaeva.* Z10–12 H12–9.

G

GAGEA
LILIACEAE

Genus of spring-flowering bulbs, grown for their clusters of funnel- or star-shaped, white or yellow flowers. Is suitable for rock gardens. Prefers full sun and well-drained soil that does not become too hot and dry. Dies down in summer. Propagate by division in spring or fall or by seed in fall.

G. **graeca,** syn. *Lloydia graeca.* Spring-flowering bulb. **H** 2–4in (5–10cm), **S** 1¹/₄–2in (3–5cm). Threadlike, semierect leaves form at ground level and on wiry stems. Bears up to 5 widely funnel-shaped, purple-veined, white flowers, ¹/₂–³/₄in (1–1.5cm) long. Z7–9 H9–7.
G. **peduncularis.** Spring-flowering bulb. **H** 2–6in (5–15cm), **S** 1–2in (2.5–5cm). Has threadlike, semierect leaves at base and on stem. Produces a loose head of flat, star-shaped, yellow flowers, ⁵/₈–1¹/₄in (1.5–3cm) across, with green stripes outside. Z6–9 H9–6.

GAILLARDIA
Blanket flower
COMPOSITAE/ASTERACEAE

Genus of summer-flowering annuals and perennials that tend to be short-lived. Requires sun and prefers well-drained soil. May need staking. Propagate species by seed in fall or spring, selected forms by root cuttings in winter.

G. **aristata.** Upright, rather open perennial. **H** 24in (60cm), **S** 20in (50cm). Has large, terminal, daisylike, single flower heads, yellow with red centers, in summer, and aromatic, divided leaves. Z3–8 H8–1.
G. x **grandiflora 'Dazzler'** Upright, rather open perennial. **H** 24in (60cm), **S** 20in (50cm). Bears large, terminal, daisylike, yellow-tipped, red flower heads for a long period in summer. Leaves are soft and divided. **'Wirral Flame'** is a clump-forming, short-lived perennial with deep cardinal-red flower heads in summer. Leaves are lance-shaped, lobed and soft green.
G. **'Oranges and Lemons',** illus. p.277.
G. **pulchella** (Blanket flower, Indian blanket). Moderately fast-growing, upright annual or short-lived perennial. **H** 18in (45cm), **S** 12in (30cm). Has lance-shaped, hairy, grayish-green leaves and, in summer, daisylike, double, crimson-zoned, yellow, pink, or red flower heads. Z10–11 H12–1. **'Lollipops',** illus. p.327.

GALANTHUS
Snowdrop
AMARYLLIDACEAE

Genus of bulbs, grown for their pendent, white flowers, one on each slender stem between 2 basal leaves. Is easily recognized by its 3 large, outer petals and 3 small, inner ones forming a cup, which is green-marked. Needs a cool, partially shaded position and rich, moist soil. Do not allow bulbs to dry out excessively. Propagate by division in spring after flowering or during late summer or fall when bulbs are dormant. ⓘ All parts may cause mild stomach upset if ingested; contact with the bulbs may irritate skin.

G. 'Atkinsii', illus. p.427.
G. elwesii, illus. p.427.
G. gracilis, syn. *G. graecus,* illus. p.427.
G. graecus. See *G. gracilis.*
G. 'Hill Poë', illus. p.427.
G. ikariae, illus. p.427.
G. nivalis. Late winter- and early spring-flowering bulb. **H** 4–6in (10–15cm), **S** 2–3in (5–8cm). Produces narrowly strap-shaped, semierect, gray-green, basal leaves. Flowers, ³/₄–1in (2–2.5cm) long, have a green mark at the tip of each inner petal. Z3–8 H8–1. **'Flore Pleno',** illus. p.427. **'Lutescens'.** See *G. nivalis* 'Sandersii'. **'Pusey Green Tip',** illus. p.427. **'Sandersii',** syn. *G. nivalis* 'Lutescens', illus. p.428. **'Scharlockii',** illus. p.428. **'Viridapicicis'** has a very long spathe, sometimes split in 2, and green marks on the outer tepals.
G. plicatus subsp. byzantinus, illus. p.427. **subsp. plicatus** is a late winter- and early spring-flowering bulb. **H** 4–8in (10–20cm), **S** 2–3in (5–8cm). Bears broadly strap-shaped, semierect, deep green, basal leaves that have gray bands along the centers and reflexed margins. White flowers, ³/₄–1¹/₄in (2–3cm) long, have a green patch at the tip of each inner petal.
G. rizehensis, illus. p.428.
G. woronowii, illus. p.428.

GALAX
Wandflower
DIAPENSIACEAE

Genus of one species of evergreen perennial, grown for its foliage and flowers, borne in late spring and summer. Is useful for underplanting shrubs. Requires shade and moist, peaty, acidic soil. Propagate by division of rooted runners in spring.
G. aphylla. See *G. urceolata.*
G. urceolata, syn. *G. aphylla,* illus. p.336.

GALEGA
Goat's rue
LEGUMINOSAE/PAPILIONACEAE

Genus of summer-flowering perennials. Grow in an open, sunny position and well-drained soil. Requires staking. Propagate by seed in fall or by division in winter.
G. x hartlandii 'Lady Wilson', illus. p.218.
G. 'Her Majesty'. See *G.* 'His Majesty'.
G. 'His Majesty', syn. *G.* 'Her Majesty'. Vigorous, upright perennial. **H** to 5ft (1.5m), **S** 3ft (1m). In summer produces spikes of small, pealike, clear lilac-mauve and white flowers. Bold, oblong to lance-shaped leaves are divided into oval leaflets. Z5–11 H12–5.
G. orientalis, illus. p.239.

GALIUM
Bedstraw
RUBIACEAE

Genus of spring- and summer-flowering perennials, many of which are weeds; *G. odoratum* is cultivated as groundcover.

Prefers partial shade, but tolerates sun, and thrives in well-drained soil. Propagate by division in early spring or fall.
G. odoratum, syn. *Asperula odorata,* illus. p.263.

GALTONIA
LILIACEAE/ASPARAGACEAE

Genus of summer- and fall-flowering bulbs, grown for their spikes of pendent, funnel-shaped, white or green flowers. Needs a sheltered, sunny site and fertile, well-drained soil that does not dry out in summer. Dies down in winter. May be lifted for replanting in spring. Propagate by seed in spring or by offsets in fall or spring.
G. candicans, illus. p.383.
G. viridiflora, illus. p.393.

GARDENIA
RUBIACEAE

Genus of evergreen shrubs and trees, grown for their flowers and foliage. Prefers partial shade and rich, well-drained, neutral to acidic soil. Water container specimens freely when in full growth, moderately at other times. After flowering, shorten strong shoots to maintain a shapely habit. Propagate by greenwood cuttings in spring or by semiripe cuttings in summer. Whitefly and mealy bug may cause problems.
G. augusta. See *G. jasminoides.*
G. capensis. See *Rothmannia capensis.*
G. florida. See *G. jasminoides.*
G. grandiflora. See *G. jasminoides.*
G. jasminoides, syn. *G. augusta, G. florida, G. grandiflora.* Z8–11 H12–7. **'Veitchii',** illus. p.454.
G. rothmannia. See *Rothmannia capensis.*
G. thunbergia. Evergreen, bushy shrub with white stems. **H** and **S** to 6ft (2m) or more. Has elliptic, glossy, deep green leaves. Fragrant, 7–9-petaled, white flowers, 2¹/₂–4in (6–10cm) wide, are borne in winter–spring. Z8–11 H12–8.

GARRYA
GARRYACEAE

Genus of evergreen shrubs and trees, grown for their catkins in winter and spring, which are longer and more attractive on male plants. Hard frosts may damage catkins. Requires a sheltered, sunny site and tolerates any poor soil. Is suitable for a south- or west-facing wall. Dislikes being transplanted. Propagate by semiripe cuttings in summer.
G. elliptica. Bushy, dense shrub. **H** and **S** 12ft (4m). Has leathery, wavy-edged, dark green leaves. Gray-green catkins are borne from mid-winter to early spring. Z8–11 H11–8. **'James Roof',** illus. p.211. has very long, gray-green catkins with yellow anthers.

GASTERIA
LILIACEAE/ASPHODELACEAE

Genus of perennial succulents, grown for their thick, fleshy leaves, usually arranged in a fan, later becoming a tight rosette. Needs sun or partial shade and very well-drained soil. Propagate by seed, leaf cuttings or division in spring or summer.

G. bicolor var. bicolor, syn. *G. caespitosa* Fan-shaped, perennial succulent. **H** 6in (15cm), **S** 12in (30cm). Produces triangular, thick, dark green leaves, 6in (15cm) long, with horny borders. Upper leaf surfaces have numerous white or pale green dots, usually in diagonal rows. Bears spikes of bell-shaped, orange-green flowers in spring. **var. liliputana,** syn. *G. liliputana,* illus. p.480.
G. caespitosa. See *G. bicolor* var. *bicolor.*
G. carinata var. verrucosa, syn. *G. verrucosa,* illus. p.480.
G. liliputana. See *G. bicolor* var. *liliputana.*
G. verrucosa. See *G. carinata* var. *verrucosa.*

x Gaulnettya 'Pink Pixie'. See *Gaultheria* 'Pink Pixie'.
x Gaulnettya 'Wisley Pearl'. See *Gaultheria* 'Wisley Pearl'.

GAULTHERIA
ERICACEAE

Genus of evergreen shrubs and subshrubs, grown for their foliage, flowers and fruits. Prefers shade or semi-shade and requires moist, peaty, acidic soil. Tolerates sun provided the soil is permanently moist. Propagate by semiripe cuttings in summer or by seed in fall; increase *G. shallon* and *G. trichophylla* by division in fall or spring. ⓘ All parts may cause mild stomach upset if ingested, except the fruits, which are edible.
G. cuneata, illus. p.346.
G. forrestii. Evergreen, rounded shrub. **H** and **S** 5ft (1.5m). Has oblong, glossy, dark green leaves and racemes of small, fragrant, rounded, white flowers, in spring, followed by rounded, blue fruits. Z7–8 H8–7.
G. miqueliana. Evergreen, compact shrub. **H** and **S** 10in (25cm). Has oval, leathery leaves clothing stiff stems. In late spring produces bell-shaped, pink-tinged, white flowers, up to 6 per stem, followed by rounded, white or pink fruits. Z6–8 H8–6.
G. mucronata, syn. *Pernettya mucronata.* Evergreen, bushy, dense shrub, spreading by underground stems. **H** and **S** 4ft (1.2m). Oval, prickly, glossy, dark green leaves set off tiny, urn-shaped, white flowers in late spring and early summer. Spherical, fleshy fruit are produced and these vary in color between cultivars. Sprays of fruit are good for indoor display. Z8–9 H9–8. Fruits of **'Cherry Ripe'** (female) are large and bright cherry-red. **'Edward Balls'** (male) produces sturdy, upright, red shoots and sharply spined, bright green leaves. **'Mulberry Wine'** (female), illus. p.164. **'Wintertime'** (female), illus. p.163.
G. myrsinoides, syn. *G. prostrata, Pernettya prostrata.* Evergreen, spreading shrub. **H** 6–12in (15–30cm), **S** 12in (30cm) or more. Bears oval, leathery, dark green leaves. Urn-shaped, white flowers are produced in early summer and are followed by large, rounded, blue-purple fruits. Is suitable for a rock garden or peat bed. Z7–8 H8–7.
G. nummarioides. Evergreen, compact shrub. **H** 4–6in (10–15cm), **S** 8in (20cm). Leaves are oval to heart-shaped and leathery. Egg-shaped, pink-flushed, white flowers are produced from the upper leaf

axils in late spring or summer. Produces rounded, blue-black fruits, but only rarely. Z7–8 H8–7.
G. procumbens, illus. p.373.
G. prostrata. See *G. myrsinoides.*
G. pumila, syn. *Pernettya pumila.* Evergreen, mat-forming, creeping shrub. **H** 2in (5cm), **S** 12–24in (30–60cm). Prostrate branches bear tiny, bell-shaped, white flowers in early summer among tiny, rounded, leathery leaves. Rounded fruits are pink or white. Is good for a rock garden or peat bed. Z7–8 H8–7.
G. shallon, illus. p.154.
G. tasmanica, syn. *Pernettya tasmanica.* Evergreen, mat-forming shrub. **H** 2–3in (5–8cm), **S** 8in (20cm). Has oval, toothed, leathery leaves with wavy edges. Bell-shaped, white flowers in early summer are followed by rounded, red fruits. Is good for a rock garden or peat bed. Z8–9 H9–8.
G. trichophylla. Evergreen, compact shrub with creeping, underground stems. **H** 3–6in (7–15cm), **S** 8in (20cm). Bell-shaped, pink flowers in early summer are followed by egg-shaped, blue fruits produced from leaf axils. Leaves are small and oval. Z6–8 H8–6.
G. x wisleyensis. Evergreen, dense, bushy shrub. **H** and **S** 3ft (1m). Bears broadly oval, deeply veined, dark green leaves. Small, urn-shaped, pale pink flowers, produced in late spring and early summer, are followed by spherical, purplish-red fruits. Z7–9 H9–7. **'Pink Pixie',** syn. x *Gaulnettya* 'Pink Pixie' **'Wisley Pearl',** syn. x *Gaulnettya* 'Wisley Pearl', illus. p.145.

GAURA
ONAGRACEAE

Genus of summer-flowering annuals and perennials that are sometimes short-lived. Prefers full sun and light, well-drained soil. Propagate by softwood or semiripe cuttings in summer or by seed in fall or spring.
G. lindheimeri, illus. p.231. Bushy perennial. **H** 36in (90cm), **S** 24in (60cm). In summer produces racemes of star-shaped, pink-suffused, white flowers. Leaves are lance-shaped and mid-green. **'Rosyjane',** illus. p.301.

GAYLUSSACIA
Huckleberry
ERICACEAE

Genus of deciduous, occasionally evergreen shrubs, grown for their flowers, fruits and fall color. Needs sun or partial shade and moist, peaty, acidic soil. Propagate by softwood cuttings in summer or by seed in fall.
G. baccata. Deciduous, bushy shrub. **H** and **S** 3ft (1m). Oval, sticky, dark green leaves redden in fall. Produces clusters of small, urn-shaped, dull red flowers in late spring, then edible, spherical, black fruits. Z3–7 H7–1.

GAZANIA
COMPOSITAE/ASTERACEAE

Genus of evergreen perennials, often grown as annuals and useful for summer bedding, pots and tubs. Requires sun and

G

sandy soil. Propagate by seed in spring or by heel cuttings in spring or summer.

G. Daybreak Series. Carpeting perennials, grown as annuals. **H** and **S** 8in (20cm). Have lance-shaped leaves and, in summer, large, daisylike flower heads in a mixture of orange, yellow, pink, bronze and white. Flowers remain open in dull weather. Z8–10 H10–8. **'Daybreak Bright Yellow'**, illus. p.323.

G. Kiss Series 'Kiss Orange Flame', illus. p.324.

G. pinnata. Mat-forming perennial. **H** 6in (15cm), **S** 12in (30cm). Daisylike, orange-red flower heads, with central, black rings, are borne singly in early summer above oval, finely cut, hairy, bluish-gray leaves. Z8–10 H10–8.

G. rigens var. uniflora, syn. *G. uniflora.* Mat-forming perennial, grown as an annual in all except mildest areas. **H** 9in (23cm), **S** 8–12in (20–30cm). Yellow or orange-yellow flower heads, sometimes with central white spots, are borne singly in early summer above rosettes of narrow, silver-backed leaves. Z8–10 H10–6.

G. Talent Series. Vigorous perennials. **H** and **S** to 10in (25cm). Have highly ornamental, mid-green leaves, to 6in (15cm) long, gray-felted on both surfaces. In summer produce solitary, yellow, orange, pink or brown flower heads on short stems just above the leaves. Z8–10 H10–8.

G. uniflora. See *G. rigens* var. *uniflora.*

GELSEMIUM

ASTERACEAE/GELSEMIACEAE

Genus of evergreen, twining climbers, grown for their fragrant, jasmine-like flowers. In cool climates, is best grown under glass. Needs full sun and fertile, well-drained soil. Water regularly, less in cold weather. Support stems and thin them out after flowering or during spring. Propagate by seed in spring or by semiripe cuttings in summer.

G. sempervirens, (Carolina jasmine, Carolina sweet jessamine), illus. p.195.

GENISTA
Broom

LEGUMINOSAE/PAPILIONACEAE

Genus of deciduous, sometimes almost leafless, shrubs and trees, grown for their mass of small, pealike flowers. Does best in full sun and not over-rich, well-drained soil. Resents being transplanted. Propagate species by softwood or semiripe cuttings in summer or by seed in fall, selected forms by softwood cuttings only in summer.

G. aetnensis, illus. p.89.

G. cinerea, illus. p.116.

G. delphinensis, syn. *G. sagittalis* subsp. *delphinensis, Chamaespartium sagittale* subsp. *delphinense.* Deciduous, prostrate shrub. **H** 1/2in (1cm), **S** 8in (20cm). Has tangled, winged branches, covered with minute, oval, dark green leaves. Masses of golden-yellow flowers are produced along stems in early summer. Is suitable for a rock garden or wall. Z5–8 H8–5.

G. fragrans. See *G. x spachiana.*

G. hispanica, illus. p.160.

G. lydia, illus. p.345.

G. pilosa. Deciduous, domed shrub. **H** and **S** 12in (30cm). Narrowly oval leaves

are silky-haired beneath. Bright yellow flowers on short stalks are borne in leaf axils in summer. Is useful on a bank or as groundcover. Propagate by semiripe cuttings in summer. Z9–11 H12–9.

G. sagittalis, syn. *Chamaespartium sagittale,* illus. p.373. **subsp. delphinensis.** See *G. delphinensis.*

G. x spachiana, syn. *G. fragrans, Cytisus canariensis, Cytisus racemosus.* Vigorous, evergreen, arching shrub. **H** and **S** 10ft (3m). Has dark green leaves with 3 oval leaflets. Produces long, slender clusters of fragrant, golden-yellow flowers in winter and early spring. Is often grown as a houseplant. Z9–11 H12–9.

G. tenera 'Golden Shower', illus. p.116.

G. tinctoria, illus. p.148. **'Royal Gold'** is a deciduous, upright shrub. **H** and **S** 3ft (1m). Produces long, conical panicles of golden-yellow flowers, in spring–summer, and narrowly lance-shaped, dark green leaves. Z4–8 H8–1.

GENTIANA
Gentian

GENTIANACEAE

Genus of annuals, biennials, and perennials, some of which are semievergreen or evergreen, grown for their usually blue flowers. Is excellent for rock gardens and peat beds. Prefers sun or partial shade and rich, moist but well-drained, neutral to acidic soil. Some species grow naturally on limestone soils. Propagate by division or offshoots in spring or by seed in fall. Divide fall-flowering species and *G. clusii* every 3 years in early spring and replant in fresh soil. See also feature panel p.370.

G. acaulis, syn. *G. excisa, G. kochiana,* illus. p.370. Evergreen, clump-forming perennial. **H** in leaf 3/4in (2cm), **S** to 4in (10cm) or more. Has narrowly oval, glossy leaves and trumpet-shaped, deep blue flowers, with green-spotted throats, on short stems in spring and often in fall. Tolerates alkaline soil. Z5–8 H8–5.

G. angustifolia. Evergreen, clump-forming perennial. **H** 4in (10cm), **S** 8in (20cm). Has rosettes of oblong, dull green leaves and, in summer, solitary, tubular, sky-blue flowers on 3in (7cm) stems. Tolerates alkaline soils. Z6–8 H8–6.

G. asclepiadea, illus. p.250.

G. 'Blue Silk', illus. p.370. Evergreen, procumbent perennial. **H** 2in (5cm), **S** to 5in (12cm) or more. Has basal rosettes of lance-shaped, mid-green leaves. In late summer and fall produces upright, trumpet-shaped, deep blue flowers, banded white and dark blue on the outer surfaces. Requires acidic soil. Z4–7 H7–4.

G. clusii. Evergreen, clump-forming perennial. **H** 2in (5cm), **S** 6–9in (15–23cm). Has rosettes of oval, glossy, dark green leaves. Trumpet-shaped, azure-blue flowers, with green-spotted, paler throats, are borne on 1–4in (2.5–10cm) stems in early summer. Tolerates alkaline soil. Z7–9 H9–7.

G. 'Ettrick', illus. p.370. Evergreen, procumbent, perennial. **H** 2in (5cm), **S** to 5in (12cm) or more. Has basal rosettes of linear to lance-shaped, mid-green leaves. In late summer and fall produces upright, trumpet-shaped, clear white flowers, flecked with blue spots on the inner surfaces. Requires acidic soil. Z5–7 H7–5.

G. 'Eugen's Allerbester', illus. p.370. Vigorous, evergreen, procumbent perennial. **H** 2in (5cm), **S** to 8in (20cm) or more. Has basal rosettes of linear, mid-green leaves. In late summer and fall produces upright, trumpet-shaped, double, deep blue flowers, banded white on the outer surfaces. Requires acidic soil. Z5–7 H7–5.

G. excisa. See *G. acaulis.*

G. gracilipes. Semievergreen, tufted perennial with arching stems. **H** 6in (15cm), **S** 8in (20cm). Forms a central rosette of long, strap-shaped, dark green leaves from which lax flower stems bearing tubular, dark purplish-blue flowers, greenish within, are produced in summer. Tolerates some shade. Z6–8 H8–6.

G. 'Inverleith', illus. p.370. Vigorous, evergreen, procumbent perennial. **H** 2in (5cm), **S** to 5in (12cm) or more. Has basal rosettes of linear to lance-shaped, mid-green leaves. In late summer produces upright, trumpet-shaped, bright blue flowers, banded green on the outer surfaces. Requires acidic soil. Z5–7 H7–5.

G. kochiana. See *G. acaulis.*

G. lutea, illus. p.243.

G. x macaulayi 'Wells's Variety', syn. *G.* 'Wellsii', illus. p.370. Evergreen, prostrate perennial. **H** in flower 2in (5cm), **S** 8in (20cm). Has trumpet-shaped, mid-blue flowers in late summer and fall. Spreading stems are clothed in narrow, mid-green leaves. Requires moist, acidic soil. Z5–7 H7–5.

G. ornata. Semievergreen, clump-forming perennial with small, overwintering rosettes. **H** 2in (5cm), **S** 4in (10cm). Forms a central rosette of grasslike leaves. In fall, each stem tip carries an upright, bell-shaped, mid-blue flower, with a white throat and deep blue stripes shading to creamy-white outside. Requires acidic soil and a moist atmosphere. Z5–7 H7–5.

G. saxosa, illus. p.370. Evergreen, hummock-forming perennial. **H** 2in (5cm), **S** 6in (15cm). Is clothed in small, spoon-shaped, fleshy, dark green leaves. Produces small, upturned, bell-shaped, white flowers in early summer. Is a short-lived scree plant. Tolerates alkaline soil. Z4–8 H8–1.

G. scabra. Deciduous, upright perennial. **H** 12in (30cm), **S** 8–12in (20–30cm). Has long, ovate to lance-shaped, deep green leaves borne in opposite pairs on herbaceous stems. Narrowly bell-shaped, deep blue flowers are borne in terminal clusters and also in pairs in upper leaf axils in mid-fall. Requires acidic soil. Z4–8 H8–4.

G. septemfida, illus. p.346.

G. 'Shot Silk', illus. p.370. Evergreen, procumbent perennial. **H** 2in (5cm), **S** to 5in (12cm) or more. Has basal rosettes of linear to lance-shaped, deep green leaves. In late summer and fall produces upright, trumpet-shaped, silky, deep purple-blue flowers, banded green and purple on the outer surfaces. Requires acidic soil. Z5–7 H7–5.

G. sino-ornata, illus. p.370. Evergreen, prostrate, spreading perennial. **H** in flower 2in (5cm), **S** to 12in (30cm). In fall bears trumpet-shaped, rich blue flowers singly at the ends of stems. Leaves are narrow. Requires acidic soil. Z5–7 H7–5.

G. 'Soutra', illus. p.370. Evergreen, procumbent, perennial. **H** 2in (5cm), **S** to

5in (12cm) or more. Has basal rosettes of linear to lance-shaped, mid-green leaves. In late summer and fall produces upright, trumpet-like, white flowers, suffused pale green on the outer surfaces. Requires acidic soil. Z5–7 H7–5.

G. 'Strathmore', illus. p.370. Evergreen, procumbent perennial. **H** 2in (5cm), **S** to 5in (12cm) or more. Has basal rosettes of linear to lance-shaped, pale green leaves. In late summer and fall produces upright, trumpet-shaped, blue-mauve flowers, with vertical, greenish-white stripes on the outer surfaces. Requires acidic soil. Z5–7 H7–5.

G. 'Susan Jane'. Vigorous, semievergreen, spreading perennial with small, overwintering rosettes. **H** 2in (5cm), **S** 12in (30cm). Prostrate stems bear grasslike leaves. Large, trumpet-shaped, white-throated, deep blue flowers, greenish within, are produced in fall. Requires acidic soil. Z5–7 H7–5.

G. verna, illus. p.356.

G. 'Wellsii'. See *G. x macaulayi* 'Wells's Variety'.

GERANIUM
Cranesbill

GERANIACEAE

Genus of perennials, some of which are semievergreen, grown for their flowers and often as groundcover. Compact species are suitable for rock gardens. Most species prefer sun, but some do better in shade. Tolerates all but waterlogged soils. Propagate species by semiripe cuttings in summer or by seed or division in fall or spring, cultivars by division or cuttings only.

G. anemonifolium. See *G. palmatum.*

G. 'Ann Folkard'. Spreading perennial. **H** 20in (50cm), **S** 36in (1m). Has rounded, deeply cut, yellowish-green leaves and, in summer–fall, masses of shallowly cup-shaped, rich magenta flowers with black veins. Z5–9 H9–3.

G. armenum. See *G. psilostemon.*

G. cinereum (Grayleaf cranesbill). Semievergreen, rosetted perennial with spreading flowering stems. **H** 6in (15cm), **S** 12in (30cm). Has cup-shaped flowers, either white to pale pink, strongly veined with purple, or pure white, on lax stems in late spring and summer. Basal leaves are rounded, deeply divided, soft and gray-green. Is good for a large rock garden. Z5–9 H9–5. **'Ballerina'**, illus. p.366. **var. subcaulescens.** See *G. subcaulescens.*

G. clarkei 'Kashmir Purple', syn. *G. pratense* 'Kashmir Purple' Carpeting, rhizomatous perennial. **H** and **S** 18–24in (45–60cm). Bears loose clusters of cup-shaped, deep purple flowers in summer. Rounded leaves are deeply divided and finely veined. Z5–8 H8–5. **'Kashmir White'**, syn. *G. pratense* 'Kashmir White' illus. p.263.

G. dalmaticum, illus. p.363.

G. endressii. Semievergreen, compact, carpeting perennial. **H** 18in (45cm), **S** 24in (60cm). Has small, lobed leaves and cup-shaped, rose-pink flowers borne throughout summer. Z5–9 H9–1. **'Wargrave Pink'.** See *G. x oxonianum* 'Wargrave Pink'.

G. farreri. Rosetted perennial with a taproot. **H** 4in (10cm), **S** 4–6in (10–15cm)

or more. Outward-facing, flattish, very pale mauve-pink flowers set off blue-black anthers in early summer. Has kidney-shaped, matt green leaves. Both flower and leaf stems are red. Z4–7 H7–1.

G. grandiflorum. See *G. himalayense*.

G. himalayense, syn. *G. grandiflorum*, *G. meeboldii* (Lilac geranium). Clump-forming perennial. **H** 12in (30cm), **S** 24in (60cm). Has large, cup-shaped, violet-blue flowers borne on long stalks in summer over dense tufts of neatly cut leaves. Z4–7 H7–1.

G. ibericum. Clump-forming perennial. **H** and **S** 24in (60cm). In summer produces sprays of 5-petaled, saucer-shaped, violet-blue flowers. Has heart-shaped, lobed or cut, hairy leaves. Z5–8 H8–5.

G. incanum. Semievergreen, spreading, mounded perennial. **H** 12–15in (30–38cm), **S** 24–36in (60cm–90cm). Shallowly cup-shaped flowers are variable, but usually deep pink, and borne singly in summer above aromatic, deeply divided, gray-green leaves with linear segments. Z5–8 H8–5.

G. 'Johnson's Blue', illus. p.270.

G. macrorrhizum, illus. p.269.

'Ingwersen's Variety', illus. p.256.

G. maculatum (Spotted geranium). Clump-forming perennial. **H** 30in (75cm), **S** 18in (45cm). In spring bears heads of flattish, pinkish-lilac flowers above rounded, lobed or scalloped, mid-green leaves that turn fawn and red in fall. Z4–8 H8–1.

G. maderense. Vigorous, semievergreen, bushy perennial with a woody base. **H** and **S** 3ft (1m). Produces large sprays of shallowly cup-shaped, deep magenta flowers in summer above palmate, finely cut, dark green leaves. Z8–9 H9–8.

G. x magnificum, illus. p.269.

G. meeboldii. See *G. himalayense*.

G. nodosum. Clump-forming perennial. **H** and **S** 18in (45cm). Has lobed, glossy leaves and delicate, cup-shaped, lilac or lilac-pink flowers borne in spring–summer. Tolerates deep shade. Z4–8 H8–1.

G. orientalitibeticum, syn. *G. stapfianum* var. *roseum*, illus. p.339.

G. 'Orion', illus. p.280.

G. oxonianum 'Claridge Druce'. Vigorous, semievergreen, carpeting perennial. **H** and **S** 24–30in (60–75cm). Bears clusters of cup-shaped, darker-veined, mauve-pink flowers throughout summer. Has dainty, rounded, lobed leaves.

'Wargrave Pink', syn. *G. endressii* 'Wargrave Pink', illus. p.265.

'Winscombe', **S** 18in (45cm), has deep pink flowers that fade to pale pink.

G. palmatum, syn. *G. anemonifolium*, illus. p.238. Vigorous, semievergreen, bushy perennial with a woody base. **H** 18in (45cm), **S** 24in (60cm). Has palmate, deeply lobed, dark green leaves and, in late summer, large sprays of shallowly cup-shaped, purplish-red flowers. Z7–9 H9–7

G. phaeum, illus. p.223.

G. pratense (Meadow cranesbill). Clump-forming perennial. **H** 30in (75cm), **S** 24in (60cm). Bears 5-petaled, saucer-shaped, violet-blue flowers on branching stems in summer. Rounded, lobed to deeply divided, mid-green leaves become bronze in fall. Z4–8 H8–1. **'Plenum Violaceum'** is more compact than the species with

double, deep violet flowers. Z5–7 H8–1.

Kashmir Purple'. See *G. clarkei* 'Kashmir Purple'. **'Kashmir White'.** See *G. clarkei* 'Kashmir White'.

'Mrs. Kendall Clark', illus. p.239.

G. procurrens. Carpeting perennial. **H** 12in (30cm), **S** 24in (60cm). Has rounded, lobed, glossy leaves and, in summer, clusters of saucer-shaped, deep rose-purple flowers. Z7–9 H9–1.

G. psilostemon, syn. *G. armenum*, illus. p.233.

G. pylzowianum. Spreading perennial with underground runners and tiny tubers. **H** 5–10in (12–25cm), **S** 10in (25cm) or more. Bears semicircular, deeply cut, dark green leaves and, in late spring and summer, trumpet-shaped, green-centered, deep rose-pink flowers. May be invasive. Z5–8 H8–5.

G. renardii, illus. p.264.

G. x riversleaianum 'Russell Prichard'. Semievergreen, clump-forming perennial. **H** 1ft (30cm), **S** 3ft (1m). Saucer-shaped, clear pink flowers are borne singly or in small clusters from early summer to fall. Rounded leaves are lobed and gray-green. Z6–8 H8–6.

G. ROZANNE ('Gerwat'), illus. p.271.

G. sanguineum, illus. p.340.

var. striatum, illus. p.362.

G. stapfianum var. roseum. See *G. orientalitibeticum*.

G. subcaulescens, syn. *G. cinereum* var. *subcaulescens*, illus. p.366.

G. sylvaticum 'Mayflower', illus. p.239.

G. traversii var. elegans. Semievergreen, rosetted perennial with spreading stems. **H** 4in (10cm), **S** 10in (25cm). Large, upward-facing, saucer-shaped, pale pink flowers, with darker veins, rise above rounded, lobed, gray-green leaves in summer. Is suitable for a sheltered ledge or rock garden. Protect from winter wet. Requires gritty soil. Z8–9 H9–8. **'Buxton's Blue'.** See *G. wallichianum* 'Buxton's Variety'.

G. wallichianum 'Buxton's Variety', syn. *G. wallichianum* 'Buxton's Blue'. Spreading perennial. **H** 12–18in (30–45cm), **S** 36in (90cm). Has luxuriant, white-flecked leaves and large, white-centered, blue or blue-purple flowers from mid-summer to fall. Prefers partial shade. Z4–8 H8–1.

G. wlassovianum. Clump-forming perennial. **H** and **S** 24in (60cm). Has velvety stems and rounded, lobed, dark green leaves. Saucer-shaped, deep purple flowers are borne singly or in small clusters in summer. Z4–8 H8–1.

GERBERA
COMPOSITAE/ASTERACEAE

Genus of perennials, flowering from summer to winter depending on growing conditions. Needs full sun and light, sandy soil. Propagate by heel cuttings from sideshoots in summer or by seed in fall or early spring.

G. 'Amgerbpink'. See *G.* EVERLAST PINK.

G. EVERLAST PINK ('Amgerbpink'). Clump-forming perennial. **H** 14in (35cm), **S** 12in (30cm). Has oval, irregularly lobed leaves. Large, daisylike, soft pink flower heads are borne on tall, slender stems in mid- and late summer. Z11 H12–5.

G. jamesonii, (Barberton daisy, Transvaal daisy) illus. p.306.

GEUM
Avens
ROSACEAE

Genus of summer-flowering perennials. Prefers sun and moist but well-drained soil. Propagate by division or seed in fall.

G. 'Bell Bank', illus. p.268.

G. x borisii. See *G. coccineum*.

G. chiloense, syn. *G. coccineum*. Clump-forming perennial. **H** 16–24in (40–60cm), **S** 24in (60cm). Saucer-shaped, scarlet flowers are produced from early to late summer. Pinnate leaves are deeply lobed and toothed. Z5–9 H9–5.

G. coccineum, syn. *G. x borisii*, illus. p.439.

G. coccineum of gardens. See *G. chiloense*.

G. 'Fire Opal'. Clump-forming perennial. **H** 32in (80cm), **S** 18in (45cm). Rounded, double, bronze-scarlet flowers are borne in small clusters in summer above oblong to lance-shaped, lobed, fresh green leaves. Z5–9 H9–5.

G. 'Goldball'. See *G.* 'Lady Stratheden'.

G. 'Lady Stratheden', syn. *G.* 'Goldball', illus. p.276.

G. 'Lionel Cox'. Clump-forming perennial. **H** and **S** 12in (30cm). In early summer produces small clusters of 5-petaled, cup-shaped, shrimp-red flowers above oblong to lance-shaped, lobed, fresh green leaves. Z3–7 H7–1.

G. montanum. Dense, clump-forming, rhizomatous perennial that spreads slowly. **H** 4in (10cm), **S** 9in (23cm). Shallowly cup-shaped, golden-yellow flowers in early summer are followed by fluffy, buff-colored seed heads. Leaves are pinnate, each with a large, rounded, terminal lobe. Is suitable for a rock garden. Z4–8 H8–1.

G. 'Mrs. J.Bradshaw'. Clump-forming perennial. **H** 32in (80cm), **S** 18in (45cm). Rounded, double, crimson flowers are borne in small sprays in summer. Fresh green leaves are oblong to lance-shaped and lobed. Z5–9 H9–5.

GEVUINA
PROTEACEAE

Genus of evergreen trees, grown for their foliage and flowers in summer. Requires partial shade and fertile, moist but well-drained soil. Propagate by semiripe cuttings in late summer or by seed in fall.

G. avellana (Chile nut, Chilean hazel). Evergreen, conical tree. **H** and **S** 30ft (10m). Has large, glossy, dark green leaves divided into numerous oval, toothed leaflets. Slender spires of spidery, white flowers in late summer are followed by cherry-like, red then black fruits. Z9–10 H10–9.

GIBBAEUM
AIZOACEAE

Genus of clump-forming, perennial succulents, grown for their pairs of small, swollen leaves, often of unequal size. Needs full sun and very well-drained soil. Water very lightly in early winter. Propagate by seed or stem cuttings in spring or summer.

G. petrense. Carpeting, perennial succulent. **H** 1½in (3cm), **S** 12in (30cm)

or more. Each branch bears 1 or 2 pairs of thick, triangular, pale gray-green leaves, ½in (1cm) long. Bears daisylike, pink-red flowers, ⅝in (1.5cm) across, in spring. Z12–15 H12–10.

G. velutinum, illus. p.481.

GILIA
POLEMONIACEAE

Genus of summer- and fall-flowering annuals. Prefers sun and fertile, very well-drained soil. Stems may need support, especially on windy sites. Propagate by seed sown outdoors in spring, or in early fall for early flowering the following year.

G. achilleifolia. Fast-growing, upright, bushy annual. **H** 24in (60cm), **S** 8in (20cm). Finely divided, mid-green leaves are hairy and sticky. Heads of funnel-shaped, blue flowers, 1in (2.5cm) wide, are produced in summer. H12–1.

G. capitata, illus. p.314.

GILLENIA
ROSACEAE

Genus of summer-flowering perennials. Grow in sun or shade and any well-drained soil. Needs staking. Propagate by seed in fall or spring.

G. trifoliata, (Bowman's root, Indian physic) illus. p.231.

GINKGO
Maidenhair tree
GINKGOACEAE

See also CONIFERS.

G. biloba, illus. p.97.

GLADIOLUS
IRIDACEAE

Genus of corms, each producing a spike of funnel-shaped flowers and a fan of erect, sword-shaped leaves on basal part of flower stem. Is suitable for cutting or for planting in mixed borders; most hybrids are also good for exhibition. Needs sun and fertile, well-drained soil. Plant 4–6in (10–15cm) deep and the same distance apart in spring. Water well in summer and support tall cultivars with canes. Lift half-hardy types in fall, cut off stems and dry corms in a frost-free but cool place. Pot up spring-flowering species and cultivars in fall and place in a cool greenhouse; after flowering, dry off corms during summer months and repot in fall.

Propagate by seed or by removal of young cormlets from parent. Seed sown in early spring in a cool greenhouse will take 2–3 years to flower and may not breed true to type. Cormlets, removed after lifting, should be stored in frost-free conditions and then be planted out 2in (5cm) deep in spring; lift in winter as for mature corms. They will flower in 1–2 years.

While in storage, corms may be attacked by various rots. Protect sound, healthy corms by dusting with a fungicide or soaking in a fungicide solution before drying; store in an airy, cool, frost-free place. Gladiolus scab causes blotches on leaves; gladiolus yellows shows as yellowing stripes on leaves, which then die; in both cases, destroy affected corms. As a preventative measure, always plant healthy corms in a new site each year. See also feature panel p.384.

Gladiolus hybrids
Most hybrids are derived from *G. x hortulanus*. All have stiff leaves, 8–20in (20–50cm) long, ranging from pale willow-green or steely blue-green to almost bottle-green. All are good for flower arranging. They are divided into Grandiflorus, Primulinus, and Nanus Groups.

Grandiflorus Group
Produces long, densely packed spikes of funnel-shaped flowers, with ruffled, thick-textured petals or plain-edged, thin-textured ones. Giant-flowered hybrids have a bottom flower of over 5½in (14cm) across (flower head is 26–32in (65–80cm) long); large-flowered 4½–5½in (11–14cm) across (flower head 24–36in (60cm–1m) long); medium-flowered 3½–4½in (9–11cm) across (flower head 24–32in (60–80cm) long); small-flowered 2½–3½in (6–9cm) across (flower head 20–28in (50–70cm) long); and miniature-flowered 1½–2½in (3.5–6cm) across (flower head 16–24in (40–60cm) long).

Primulinus Group
Has fairly loose spikes of plain-edged, funnel-shaped flowers, 2½–3in (6–8cm) across, each with a strongly hooded, upper petal over the stigma and anthers. Flower heads are 12in (30cm) long.

Nanus Group
Produces 2 or 3 slender spikes, with loosely arranged flowers, 1½–2in (4–5cm) across. Flower heads are 9–14in (22–35cm) long.

G

G. 'Amanda Mahy'. Nanus Group gladiolus. **H** 32in (80cm), **S** 3–4in (8–10cm). Produces spikes of up to 7 salmon-pink flowers, with lip petals flecked violet and white, in early summer. Z8–10 H9–1.
G. 'Amsterdam'. Grandiflorus Group, giant-flowered gladiolus. **H** 5½ft (1.7m), **S** 1ft (30cm). Spikes of up to 27 slightly upward-facing, finely ruffled, white flowers are produced in late summer. Is good for exhibition. Z8–10 H9–1.
G. 'Amy Beth'. Grandiflorus Group, small-flowered gladiolus. **H** 4ft (1.2m), **S** 8–10in (20–25cm). Produces spikes of up to 22 heavily ruffled, lavender flowers, with thick, waxy, cream-lipped petals, in late summer. Z8–10 H9–1.
G. 'Anna Leorah'. Grandiflorus Group, large-flowered gladiolus. **H** 5½ft (1.6m), **S** 6in (15cm). In mid-summer bears spikes of up to 25 strongly ruffled, mid-pink flowers with large, white throats. Is good for exhibition. Z8–10 H9–1.
G. 'Atlantis'. Grandiflorus Group, medium-flowered gladiolus. **H** 5ft (1.5m), **S** 8–10in (20–25cm). Produces spikes of up to 20 lightly ruffled, deep violet-blue flowers, with small, white throats, in late summer. Z8–10 H9–1.
G. 'Beau Rivage'. Grandiflorus Group, large-flowered gladiolus. **H** to 4ft (1.2m), **S** 1ft (30cm). Spikes of up to 15 ruffled, deep coral-pink flowers are produced in summer. Is good for exhibition. Z8–10 H9–1.
G. 'Beauty of Holland'. Grandiflorus Group, large-flowered gladiolus. **H** 5½ft (1.7m), **S** 6in (15cm). Produces spikes of up to 27 ruffled, pink-margined, white flowers in mid-summer. Is good for exhibition. Z8–10 H9–1.
G. 'Black Jack'. Grandiflorus Group, medium-flowered gladiolus. **H** 36in (90cm), **S** 3in (8cm). Bears spikes of black-edged, dark maroon flowers in summer. Z8–10 H9–1.
G. 'Black Lash'. Grandiflorus Group, small-flowered gladiolus. **H** 4½ft (1.35m), **S** 6–8in (15–20cm). Bears spikes of up to 25 lightly ruffled, deep black-rose flowers, with pointed, slightly reflexed petals, from late summer to early fall. Z8–10 H9–1.
G. blandus. See *G. carneus*.
G. 'Blue Frost', illus. p.384. Grandiflorus Group, large-flowered gladiolus. **H** 4ft (1.2m), **S** 6in (15cm). In mid-summer produces spikes of white flowers with ruffled, lilac edges and darker purple eyes. Z8–10 H10–8.
G. Butterfly Group. Small-flowered gladiolus. **H** 32in (80cm), **S** 3in (8cm). From mid- to late summer produces spikes of wavy, ruffled, bicolored flowers with petals that resemble the wings of a butterfly. They are produced in a range of colors, including red, orange, pink and yellow, and have contrasting colors at the throat. Z8–10 H9–1.
G. byzantinus. See *G. communis* subsp. *byzantinus*.
G. callianthus. See *G. murielae*.
G. cardinalis. Summer-flowering corm. **H** to 4ft (1.2m), **S** 4–6in (10–15cm). Arching stem bears a spike of up to 12 widely funnel-shaped, bright red flowers, 3in (8cm) long, with spear-shaped, white marks on lower 3 petals. Z8–10 H9–1.
G. carneus, syn. *G. blandus*. Spring-flowering corm. **H** 8–16in (20–40cm), **S** 3–4in (8–10cm). Stem bears a loose spike of 3–12 widely funnel-shaped, white or pink flowers, 1½–2½in (4–6cm) long, marked on lower petals with darker red or yellow blotches. Z8–10 H9–1.
G. 'Charmer'. Grandiflorus Group, large-flowered gladiolus. **H** 5½ft (1.7m), **S** 6in (15cm). In early and mid-summer produces spikes of up to 27 strongly ruffled, almost translucent, light pink flowers. Is good for exhibition. Z8–10 H9–1.
G. 'Charming Lady'. Nanus Group gladiolus. **H** 28in (70cm), **S** 3in (8cm). Produces spikes of pink flowers, with pale lilac throats, from early to mid-summer. Z8–10 H9–1.
G. 'Christabel'. Spring-flowering corm (a hybrid of *G. tristis*). **H** to 18in (45cm), **S** 3–4in (8–10cm). Loose spikes of up to 10 fragrant, widely funnel-shaped, primrose-yellow flowers, 2½–3in (6–8cm) across, with purple-brown-veined, upper petals, are produced in spring. Z8–10 H9–1.
G. 'Columbine', illus. p.384. Grandiflorus Group, small-flowered gladiolus. **H** 36in (90cm), **S** 3in (8cm). In early summer produces spikes of light carmine-rose flowers with creamy-white throats. Z8–10 H10–8.
***G. x colvillii* 'The Bride',** illus. p.384. Nanus Group gladiolus. **H** 32in (80cm), **S** 3–4in (8–10cm). Produces spikes of up to 7 white flowers, with green-marked throats, in early summer. Z8–10 H9–1.
***G. communis* subsp. *byzantinus*,** syn. *G. byzantinus*, illus. p.410.
G. 'Côte d'Azur'. Grandiflorus Group, giant-flowered gladiolus. **H** 5½ft (1.7m), **S** 6in (15cm). Bears spikes of up to 23 ruffled, mid-blue flowers, with pale blue throats, in early summer. Is good for exhibition. Z8–10 H9–1.
G. dalenii, syn. *G. natalensis, G. primulinus, G. psittacinus*. Vigorous, summer-flowering corm. **H** to 5ft (1.5m), **S** 4–6in (10–15cm). Produces up to 14 red, yellow-orange, yellow or greenish-yellow flowers, 3–5in (8–12cm) long, each with a hooded, upper petal and often flecked or streaked red. Z8–10 H9–1.
G. 'Dancing Queen'. Grandiflorus Group, large-flowered gladiolus. **H** 5ft (1.5m), **S** 5–6in (12–15cm). In mid- to late summer produces spikes of up to 20 white flowers, with feathered, dark red markings at the base of the lower petals. Z8–10 H9–1.
G. 'Deliverance'. Grandiflorus Group, large-flowered gladiolus. **H** 5½ft (.1.7m), **S** 5–6in (12–15cm). In mid- to late summer produces spikes of 20 or more ruffled, coral-pink flowers, deeper peach-pink at the margins, with yellow-tinted, white throats. Z8–10 H9–1.
G. 'Drama', illus. p.384. Grandiflorus Group, large-flowered gladiolus. **H** 5½ft (1.7m), **S** 10–12in (25–30cm). In late summer produces spikes of up to 26 lightly ruffled, deep watermelon-pink flowers with red-marked, yellow throats. Is superb for exhibition. Z8–10 H10–8.
G. 'Dutch Mountain'. Grandiflorus Group, large-flowered gladiolus. **H** 5½ft (1.7m), **S** 6in (15cm). In mid-summer produces spikes of up to 25 slightly ruffled, white flowers with small green marks in the throats. Is good for exhibition. Z8–10 H9–1.
G. 'Esta Bonita'. Grandiflorus Group, giant-flowered gladiolus. **H** 5½ft (1.7m), **S** 1ft (30cm). Produces spikes of up to 24 apricot-orange flowers, slightly darker toward petal edges, in late summer. Is good for exhibition. Z8–10 H9–1.
G. 'Firestorm'. Grandiflorus Group, miniature-flowered gladiolus. **H** 3½ft (1.1m), **S** 3–4in (8–10cm). Spikes of up to 22 loosely spaced, ruffled, vivid scarlet flowers, with yellowish-white flecks on the outer tepals, are produced in early summer. Is good for exhibition. Z8–10 H9–1.
G. 'Flevo Bambino'. Grandiflorus Group, medium-flowered gladiolus. **H** 2ft (60cm), **S** 3in (8cm). From late summer to early fall produces spikes of pale yellow flowers with purple throats. Z8–10 H9–1.
G. 'Florence C'. Grandiflorus Group, large-flowered gladiolus. **H** 5½ft (1.7m), **S** 6in (15cm). In late summer produces spikes of up to 26 strongly ruffled, white flowers. Z8–10 H9–1.
G. 'Georgette'. Grandiflorus Group, small-flowered gladiolus. **H** 4ft (1.2m), **S** 3–4in (8–10cm). Produces spikes of up to 22 slightly ruffled, yellow-suffused, orange flowers, with large lemon-yellow throats, in mid-summer. Is good for exhibition. Z8–10 H9–1.
G. 'Green Isle'. Grandiflorus Group, medium-flowered gladiolus. **H** 4½ft (1.35m), **S** 8–10in (20–25cm). Spikes of up to 22 slightly informal, lime-green flowers, with chiseled ruffling, are produced in late summer. Z8–10 H9–1.
G. 'Green Woodpecker', illus. p.384. Grandiflorus Group, medium-flowered gladiolus. **H** 5ft (1.5m), **S** 1ft (30cm). Has spikes of up to 25 lime-green flowers, with wine-red throats, in late summer. Is very good for exhibition. Z8–10 H10–8.
G. 'Halley'. Nanus Group gladiolus. **H** 3ft (1m), **S** 3–4in (8–10cm). In early summer produces spikes of up to 7 white-flushed, pale yellow flowers, with bright red marks in throats. Z8–10 H9–1.
G. 'Her Majesty', illus. p.384. Grandiflorus Group, large-flowered gladiolus. **H** 46in (115cm), **S** 6in (5cm). Produces spikes of sky-blue flowers, with much paler throats, in mid-summer. Z8–10 H10–8.
G. 'Ice Cap'. Grandiflorus Group, large-flowered gladiolus. **H** 5½ft (1.7m), **S** 10–12in (25–30cm). Produces spikes of up to 27 heavily ruffled, ice-white flowers from late summer to early fall. Z8–10 H9–1.
G. 'Impressive', illus. p.384. Nanus Group gladiolus. **H** 28in (70cm), **S** 3in (8cm). Spikes of pale pink flowers, with hot pink markings, are borne in early summer. Z8–10 H10–8.
G. 'Inca Queen'. Grandiflorus Group, large-flowered gladiolus. **H** 5ft (1.5m), **S** 8–10in (20–25cm). Bears spikes of up to 25 heavily ruffled, waxy, deep salmon-pink flowers, with lemon-yellow lip petals and throats, in late summer. Z8–10 H9–1.
G. italicus, syn. *G. segetum*. Early summer-flowering corm. **H** to 3ft (1m), **S** 4–6in (10–15cm). Produces a loose spike of up to 20 pinkish-purple flowers, 1½–2in (4–5cm) long, and has a fan of erect, sword-shaped leaves from the basal part of stem. Z8–10 H9–1.
G. 'Little Darling'. Primulinus Group gladiolus. **H** 3½ft (1.1m), **S** 3–4in (8–10cm). Bears spikes of up to 16 loosely spaced, salmon- to rose-pink flowers, with lemon lip petals, in mid-summer. Is good for exhibition. Z8–10 H9–1.
G. 'Magistral'. Grandiflorus Group, large-flowered gladiolus. **H** 6ft (1.8m), **S** 6in (15cm). Produces spikes of up to 24 ruffled, oyster-white flowers, with magenta lines, in mid-summer. Is good for exhibition. Z8–10 H9–1.
G. 'Melodie'. Grandiflorus Group, small-flowered gladiolus. **H** 4ft (1.2m), **S** 6–8in (15–20cm). Produces spikes of up to 17 salmon-rose flowers, with longitudinal, spearlike, red-orange marks in throats, in late summer. Z8–10 H9–1.
G. 'Mi Mi'. Grandiflorus Group, small-flowered gladiolus. **H** 4½ft (1.3m), **S** 3–4in (8–10cm). In mid-summer bears spikes of up to 24 strongly ruffled, deep lavender-pink flowers with white throats. Is good for exhibition. Z8–10 H9–1.
G. 'Miss America'. Grandiflorus Group, medium-flowered gladiolus. **H** 5ft (1.5m), **S** 1ft (30cm). In late summer produces spikes of up to 24 deep pink flowers that are heavily ruffled. Is excellent for exhibition. Z8–10 H9–1.
G. 'Morning Gold', illus. p.384. Grandiflorus Group, large-flowered gladiolus. **H** 39in (100cm), **S** 4in (10cm). Spikes of green-tinted, golden-yellow flowers are produced from mid-summer to early fall. Z8–10 H10–8.
G. murielae, syn. *G. callianthus, Acidanthera bicolor* var. *murielae, Acidanthera murielae*, illus. p.383. Late summer-flowering corm. **H** to 3ft (1m), **S** 4–6in (10–15cm). Has a loose spike of up

to 10 fragrant flowers, each with a curved tube, 4in (10cm) long, and 6 white petals, with a deep purple blotch at each base.
G. natalensis. See *G. dalenii*.
G. 'Nova Lux', illus. p.384. Grandiflorus Group, giant-flowered gladiolus. **H** 39in (100cm), **S** 6in (15cm). Spikes of clear yellow flowers are borne in mid-summer. Z8–10 H10–8.
G. 'Nymph', illus. p.384. Nanus Group gladiolus. **H** 28in (70cm), **S** 3in (8cm). In early summer produces spikes of creamy-white flowers, with teardrop-shaped, pink-edged markings on the lower petals. Z8–10 H10–8.
G. 'Oscar', illus. p.384. Grandiflorus Group, large-flowered gladiolus. **H** 39in (100cm), **S** 6in (15cm). Produces spikes of velvety-red flowers in mid-summer. Z8–10 H10–8.
G. papilio, syn. *G. purpureoauratus*, illus. p.395.
G. 'Parade'. Grandiflorus Group, giant-flowered gladiolus. **H** 5¹/₂ft (1.7m), **S** 10–14in (25–35cm). Produces spikes of up to 27 finely ruffled, salmon-pink flowers, with small, cream throats, in early fall. Is superb for exhibition. Z8–10 H9–1.
G. 'Passos'. Grandiflorous Group, large-flowered gladiolus. **H** 4ft (1.2m), **S** 6in (15cm). Spikes of purple-flecked, pale lilac to white flowers, with dark purple throats, are produced in mid-summer. Z8–10 H9–1.
G. 'Peace'. Grandiflorus Group, giant-flowered gladiolus. **H** 5¹/₂ft (1.7m), **S** 6in (15cm). Bears spikes of up to 26 strongly ruffled, cream flowers, with pale lemon throats and pale pink margins, in mid-summer. Is good for exhibition. Z8–10 H9–1.
G. 'Peter Pears', illus. p.384. Grandiflorus Group, large-flowered gladiolus. **H** 5¹/₂ft (1.7m), **S** 14in (35cm). In late summer has spikes of up to 26 apricot-salmon flowers with red throat marks. Is excellent for exhibition. Z8–10 H10–8.
G. 'Pink Flare'. Grandiflorus Group, small-flowered gladiolus. **H** 4¹/₂ft (1.3m), **S** 3–4in (8–10cm). Spikes of up to 25 ruffled, mid-pink flowers, each with a small, white throat, are produced in mid-summer. Is good for exhibition. Z8–10 H9–1.
G. 'Pink Lady'. Grandiflorus Group, large-flowered gladiolus. **H** 5ft (1.5m), **S** 10–12in (25–30cm). Has spikes of up to 25 lightly ruffled, deep rose-pink flowers, with large, white throats, in late summer and early fall. Z8–10 H9–1.
G. primulinus. See *G. dalenii*.
G. psittacinus. See *G. dalenii*.
G. 'Pulchritude'. Grandiflorus Group, medium-flowered gladiolus. **H** 4¹/₂ft (1.3m), **S** 5in (12cm). Produces spikes of up to 27 ruffled, light lavender-pink flowers, deepening at the petal margins, and with a magenta-red mark on each lip petal, in mid-summer. Is good for exhibition. Z8–10 H9–1.
G. 'Purple Flora', illus. p.384. Grandiflorus Group, large-flowered gladiolus. **H** 39in (100cm), **S** 6in (15cm). Produces spikes of rich deep purple flowers, with paler lilac markings, in mid-summer. Z8–10 H10–8.
G. purpureoauratus. See *G. papilio*.
G. 'Renegade'. Grandiflorus Group, large-flowered gladiolus. **H** 5ft (1.5m),

S 5–6in (12–15cm). In mid- to late summer produces spikes of 15–20 ruffled, deep red flowers. Z8–10 H9–1.
G. 'Rose Supreme'. Grandiflorus Group, giant-flowered gladiolus. **H** 5¹/₂ft (1.7m), **S** 10–12in (25–30cm). Spikes of up to 24 rose-pink flowers, flecked and streaked darker pink toward petal tips, and with cream throats, are produced in late summer. Z8–10 H11–1.
G. 'Royal Dutch'. Grandiflorus Group, large-flowered gladiolus. **H** 5¹/₂ft (1.7m), **S** 10–12in (25–30cm). Produces spikes of up to 27 flowers, pale lavender blending into a white throat, from late summer to early fall. Is very good for exhibition. Z8–10 H9–1.
G. 'Sancerre', illus. p.384. Grandiflorus Group, large-flowered gladiolus. **H** 4ft (1.2m), **S** 6in (15cm). Spikes of pure white flowers are borne in mid-summer. Z8–10 H10–8.
G. segetum. See *G. italicus*.
G. 'Stardust'. Grandiflorus Group, miniature-flowered gladiolus. **H** 4ft (1.2m), **S** 3–4in (8–10cm). Has spikes of up to 21 ruffled, pale yellow flowers, with lighter yellow throats, in mid-summer. Is good for exhibition. Z8–10 H9–1.
G. 'Stella', illus. p.384. Grandiflorus Group, medium-flowered gladiolus. **H** 24in (60cm), **S** 3in (8cm). Spikes of yellow flowers, with a star-shaped, dark red mark at the throat, are produced in mid-summer. Z8–10 H10–8.
G. 'Tendresse'. Grandiflorus Group, medium-flowered gladiolus. **H** 5ft (1.5m), **S** 8–10in (20–25cm). In late summer has spikes of up to 28 slightly ruffled, dark pink flowers, with small, cream throats marked with longitudinal, faint rose-pink "spears." Z8–10 H9–1.
G. 'Tesoro'. Grandiflorus Group, medium-flowered gladiolus. **H** 5ft (1.5m), **S** 8–10in (20–25cm). Bears spikes of up to 26 silky flowers, slightly ruffled and glistening yellow, in early fall. Is among the top exhibition gladioli. Z8–10 H9–1.
G. 'The Bride'. See *G. colvillii* 'The Bride'.
G. 'Trader Horn'. Grandiflorus Group, large-flowered gladiolus. **H** 4ft (1.2m), **S** 6in (15cm). Tall spikes of scarlet flowers, with a white mark on throat, are produced in mid-summer. Z8–10 H9–1.
G. 'Vaucluse'. Grandiflorus Group, giant-flowered gladiolus. **H** 6ft (1.9m), **S** 6in (15cm). In late summer bears spikes of up to 27 slightly ruffled, vermilion-red flowers with small, creamy-white throats. Is good for exhibition. Z8–10 H9–1.
G. 'Velvet Eyes', illus. p.384. Grandiflorus Group, large-flowered gladiolus. **H** 4ft (1.2m), **S** 6in (15cm). Produces spikes of dark bluish-purple flowers, with reddish-purple throats, in mid-summer. Z8–10 H10–8.
G. 'Victor Borge'. Grandiflorus Group, large-flowered gladiolus. **H** 5¹/₂ft (1.7m), **S** 14in (35cm). Spikes of up to 22 vermilion-orange flowers, with pale cream throat marks, are produced in late summer. Z8–10 H9–1.
G. 'White Ice', illus. p.384. Grandiflorus Group, medium-flowered gladiolus. **H** 5ft (1.5m), **S** 5in (12cm). Produces spikes of up to 25 ruffled, white flowers in late summer. Is good for exhibition. Z8–10 H10–8.
G. 'White Prosperity', illus. p.384. Grandiflorus Group, large-flowered gladiolus. **H** 4ft (1.2m), **S** 6in (15cm). Spikes

of pure white flowers, with ruffled petals, are borne in mid-summer. Z8–10 H10–8.
G. 'Wine and Roses', illus. p.384. Grandiflorus Group, large-flowered gladiolus. **H** 4ft (1.2m), **S** 6in (15cm). Spikes of soft pink flowers, with burgundy-red throats, are produced in mid-summer. Z8–10 H10–8.
G. 'Zephyr'. Grandiflorus Group, large-flowered gladiolus. **H** 5¹/₂ft (1.7m), **S** 6in (5cm). In mid-summer has spikes of up to 26 light lavender-pink flowers with small, ivory throats. Is good for exhibition. Z8–10 H9–1.

GLANDULARIA

VERBENACEAE

Genus of summer- and fall-flowering evergreen perennials, often treated as annuals. Needs sun and well-drained soil. Propagate by stem cuttings in late summer and fall or by layering or seed in fall or spring.
G. 'Balazdapima'. See *G.* x *hybrida* AZTEC DARK PINK MAGIC.
G. 'Balazsilma'. See *G.* x *hybrida* AZTEC SILVER MAGIC.
G. x hybrida, syn. *Verbena* x *hortensis*, *Verbena* x *hybrida*. **AZTEC DARK PINK MAGIC ('Balazdapima')**, illus. p.303. **AZTEC SILVER MAGIC ('Balazsilma')**, illus. p.312. **Corsage Series 'Corsage Red'**, illus. p.307. **Derby Series** are erect, bushy perennials, grown as annuals. **H** 10in (25cm), **S** 12in (30cm). Have oval, serrated, mid- to deep green leaves. Clusters of small, tubular, lobed flowers, in a wide color range, including red, pink, blue, mauve and white, are borne in summer and early fall. Z9–15 H12–1. Cultivars of **Novalis Series** are erect and bushy, with flowers in rose-pink, deep blue, pinkish-red and scarlet, as well as single colors of bright scarlet, white, or rose-pink. **'Peaches and Cream'** is spreading and branching, and produces pastel orange-pink flowers, maturing to apricot-yellow, and eventually creamy-yellow. Cultivars of **'Quartz Mix'** are compact and bushy with lance-shaped leaves and rounded heads of pink, red, maroon, or purple flowers with white "eyes." **Romance Series** cultivars are erect and bushy, and have flowers in deep wine-red, intense scarlet, carmine-rose-red and blue-purple, as well as single colors of white, bright scarlet, dark rose or lavender-pink.
G. x maonettii, syn. *Verbena alpina*, *Verbena tenera*. Spreading perennial with a slightly woody base. **H** 3in (8cm), **S** 6in (15cm). Half-hardy. Has oblong to oval leaves, deeply cut into linear, toothed, mid-green segments and, in summer, terminal clusters of small, tubular, reddish-violet flowers, with white-edged lobes. Z7–9 H9–6.
G. peruviana, syn. *Verbena chamaedrifolia*, *Verbena chamaedrioides*. Semievergreen, prostrate perennial. **H** to 3in (8cm), **S** 3ft (1m). Heads of small, tubular, brilliant scarlet flowers, with spreading petal lobes, are produced from early summer to early fall. Oval, toothed leaves are mid-green. Prefers to grow in dry soil that is not too rich. Z9–11 H12–9.
G. 'Sissinghurst', syn. *Verbena* 'Sissinghurst', illus. p.268.

Glandulicactus uncinatus. See *Sclerocactus uncinatus*.

GLAUCIDIUM

GLAUCIDIACEAE/RANUNCULACEAE

Genus of one species of spring-flowering perennial. Is excellent in woodland gardens. Needs a partially shaded, sheltered position and moist, peaty soil. Propagate by seed in fall.
G. palmatum, illus. p.260.

GLAUCIUM

Horned poppy

PAPAVERACEAE

Genus of annuals, biennials and perennials, grown for their bright, poppy-like flowers. Requires sun and fertile, well-drained soil. Propagate annuals by seed sown outdoors in spring, perennials by seed sown outdoors in spring or fall, biennials by seed sown under glass in late spring or early summer. ① Roots are toxic if ingested.
G. flavum, illus. p.320.

GLECHOMA

LABIATAE/LAMIACEAE

Genus of evergreen, summer-flowering perennials. Makes good groundcover, but may be invasive. Tolerates sun or shade. Prefers moist but well-drained soil. Propagate by division in spring or fall or by softwood cuttings in spring.
G. hederacea 'Variegata', illus. p.277.

GLEDITSIA

Honeylocust

LEGUMINOSAE/CAESALPINIACEAE

Genus of deciduous, usually spiny trees, grown for their foliage. Has inconspicuous flowers, often followed by large seed pods after hot summers. Young plants may suffer frost damage. Requires plenty of sun and fertile, well-drained soil. Propagate species by seed in fall, selected forms by budding in late summer.
G. caspica (Caspianlocust). Deciduous, spreading tree. **H** 40ft (12m), **S** 30ft (10m). Trunk is armed with long, branched spines. Has fernlike, glossy, mid-green leaves. Z7–10 H10–7.
G. japonica, illus. p.75.
G. triacanthos (Honeylocust). Deciduous, spreading tree. **H** 70ft (20m), **S** 50ft (15m). Trunk is very thorny. Fernlike, glossy, dark green leaves turn yellow in fall. Z3–7 H7–1. **f. inermis** (Thornless honey locust) is thornless. **'Shademaster'** is vigorous, with long-lasting leaves. **'Skyline'** is thornless, broadly conical and has golden-yellow foliage in fall. **'Sunburst'**, illus. p.72.

GLOBBA

ZINGIBERACEAE

Genus of evergreen or herbaceous, clump-forming perennials, grown for their flowers. Needs partial shade, high humidity and rich, well-drained soil. Keep plants dry when dormant in winter. Propagate by division or seed in spring or by mature bulbils that fall off plants. See also feature panel p.477.
G. platystachya. Herbaceous, clump-forming perennial. **H** and **S** 3ft (1m).

GLOBULARIA

Has lance-shaped, silver-patterned, mid-green leaves, to 12in (30cm) long. Pendent racemes of small, tubular, golden-yellow flowers are borne at the shoot tips along with bulbils in late summer. Z13–15 H12–8.

G. winitii, illus. p.477. Evergreen, clump-forming perennial. **H** 3ft (1m), **S** 1ft (30cm). Has lance-shaped leaves, to 8in (20cm) long. Intermittently produces pendent racemes of tubular, yellow flowers with large, reddish-purple, reflexed bracts. H11–8.

GLOBULARIA
Globe daisy

GLOBULARIACEAE/PLANTAGINACEAE

Genus of mainly evergreen, summer-flowering shrubs and subshrubs, grown for their dome-shaped hummocks and usually blue or purple flower heads. Needs full sun and well-drained soil. Propagate by division in spring, by softwood or semiripe cuttings in summer or by seed in fall.

G. bellidifolia. See *G. meridionalis.*
G. cordifolia, illus. p.369. **subsp. bellidifolia.** See *G. meridionalis.*
G. meridionalis, syn. *G. bellidifolia, G. cordifolia, G. pygmaea,* illus. p.367.
G. pygmaea. See *G. meridionalis.*

GLORIOSA

LILIACEAE/COLCHICACEAE

Genus of deciduous, summer-flowering, tendril climbers with finger-like tubers. Needs full sun and rich, well-drained soil. Water freely in summer and liquid feed every 2 weeks. Provide support. Dry off tubers in winter and keep cool but frost-free. Propagate by seed or division in spring. ① Highly toxic if ingested; handling tubers may irritate the skin.

G. rothschildiana. See *G. superba* 'Rothschildiana'.
G. superba. Deciduous, tendril climber with tubers. **H** to 6ft (2m), **S** 1–1¹/₂ft (30–45cm). Slender stems bear scattered, broadly lance-shaped leaves. In summer, upper leaf axils bear large, yellow or red flowers, with 6 sharply reflexed, wavy-edged petals, changing to dark orange or deep red. Stamens are prominent. Z8–10 H12–7. **'Rothschildiana',** syn. *G. rothschildiana* illus. p.386.

GLOTTIPHYLLUM

AIZOACEAE

Genus of clump-forming, perennial succulents, grown for their semicylindrical leaves often broader at tips. Needs full sun and poor, well-drained soil. Propagate by seed or stem cuttings in spring or summer.

G. difforme, syn. *G. semicylindricum.* Clump-forming, perennial succulent. **H** 3in (8cm), **S** 12in (30cm) or more. Has semicylindrical, bright green leaves, 2¹/₂in (6cm) long, with a tooth halfway along each margin. Short-stemmed, daisylike, golden-yellow flowers, 1¹/₂in (4cm) across, are produced in spring–summer. Z10–11 H12–9.

G. nelii, illus. p.495.
G. semicylindricum. See *G. difforme.*

588

GLOXINIA

GESNERIACEAE

Genus of late summer- to fall-flowering, rhizomatous perennials. Needs partial shade and rich, well-drained soil. Dies down in late fall or winter; then keep rhizomes nearly dry. Propagate by division or seed in spring or by stem or leaf cuttings in summer.

G. perennis. Late summer- to fall-flowering rhizome. **H** to 24in (60cm), **S** 12–14in (30–35cm). Has heart-shaped, toothed, hairy leaves on spotted stems and bell-shaped, lavender-blue flowers, with rounded lobes and purple-blotched throats. Z13–15 H12–10.
G. speciosa. See *Sinningia speciosa.*

GLYCERIA
Manna grass

GRAMINEAE/POACEAE

See also GRASSES, BAMBOOS, RUSHES and SEDGES.

G. aquatica 'Variegata'. See *G. maxima* 'Variegata'.
G. maxima 'Variegata', syn. *G. aquatica* 'Variegata', illus. p.436.

GLYCYRRHIZA

LEGUMINOSAE/PAPILIONACEAE

Genus of summer-flowering perennials. Needs sun and deep, rich, well-drained soil. Propagate by division in spring or seed in fall or spring.

G. glabra. Upright perennial. **H** 4ft (1.2m), **S** 3ft (1m). Has pealike, purple- blue and white flowers, borne in short spikes on erect stems in late summer, and large leaves divided into oval leaflets. Is grown commercially for production of licorice. Z9–11 H12–10.

Godetia. See *Clarkia.*

GOMESA

ORCHIDACEAE

See also ORCHIDS.

G. flexuosum, syn. *Oncidium flexuosum* (Dancing-doll orchid, Glory Lily), illus. p.467. Evergreen, epiphytic orchid for a cool or intermediate greenhouse. **H** 9in (23cm). In fall produces terminal sprays of many small, large-lipped, bright yellow flowers, ¹/₄in (0.5cm) across, with red-brown markings on sepals and petals. Bears narrowly oval leaves, 4in (10cm) long. Is best grown on a bark slab. Keep in partial shade in summer. Z13–15 H12–1.
G. planifolia. Evergreen, epiphytic orchid for a cool greenhouse. **H** 9in (23cm). Sprays of star-shaped, pea-green flowers, ¹/₄in (0.5cm) across, are produced in fall. Narrowly oval leaves are 6in (15cm) long. Grow in partial shade in summer. Z14–15 H12–6.

GOMPHOCARPUS

ASCLEPIADACEAE/APOCYNACEAE

Genus of evergreen and deciduous subshrubs and perennials. Hooded, cup-shaped flowers are followed by seed pods that are usually inflated. Needs sun or partial shade and well-drained soil.

Propagate by seed or softwood cuttings in spring. ① Some species exude a milky sap, which may aggravate skin allergies.
G. physocarpus, syn. *Asclepias physocarpa.* Deciduous, erect, hairy subshrub. **H** to 6ft (2m), **S** 2ft (60cm). Has lance-shaped leaves, 10cm (4in) long, and umbels of 5-horned, creamy-white flowers in summer, followed by large, inflated, globose seed pods with soft bristles. Z12–15 H12–10.

GOMPHRENA

AMARANTHACEAE

Genus of annuals, biennials and perennials. Only one species, *G. globosa,* is usually cultivated; its flower heads are good for cutting and drying. Prefers sun and fertile, well-drained soil. Propagate by seed sown under glass in spring.
G. globosa, illus. p.303.

GONGORA

ORCHIDACEAE

See also ORCHIDS.
G. quinquenervis. Evergreen, epiphytic orchid for an intermediate greenhouse. **H** 10in (25cm). In summer, fragrant, brown, orange and yellow flowers, ¹/₂in (1cm) across, which resemble birds in flight, are produced in long, pendent spikes. Has oval, ribbed leaves, 5–6in (12–15cm) long. Is best grown in a hanging basket. Requires partial shade in summer. Z14–15 H12–6.

GRAPTOPETALUM

CRASSULACEAE

Genus of rosetted, perennial succulents very similar to *Echeveria,* with which it hybridizes. Needs sun or partial shade and very well-drained soil. Propagate by seed or by stem or leaf cuttings in spring or summer.

G. amethystinum. Clump-forming, prostrate, perennial succulent. **H** 16in (40cm), **S** 36in (90cm). Produces thick, rounded, blue-gray to red leaves, 3in (7cm) long, in terminal rosettes and star-shaped, yellow-and-red flowers, ¹/₂–³/₄in (1–2cm) across, in spring–summer. Z13–15 H12–10.
G. bellum, syn. *Tacitus bellus,* illus. p.485.
G. paraguayense, illus. p.489.

GRAPTOPHYLLUM

ACANTHACEAE

Genus of evergreen shrubs, grown mainly for their foliage. Needs partial shade and fertile, well-drained soil. Water container plants freely when in full growth, much less when temperatures are low. Young plants need tip-pruning after flowering to promote branching; leggy specimens may be cut back hard after flowering or in spring. Propagate by greenwood or semiripe cuttings in spring or summer.

G. pictum (Caricature plant). Evergreen, erect, loose shrub. **H** to 6ft (2m), **S** 2ft (60cm) or more. Has oval, pointed, glossy, green leaves with central, yellow blotches. Bears short, terminal spikes of tubular, red to purple flowers in spring and early summer. Z13–15 H12–10.

GRASSES, BAMBOOS, RUSHES AND SEDGES

Group of evergreen or herbaceous, perennial and annual grasses or grasslike plants belonging to the Gramineae (including Bambusoideae), Juncaceae and Cyperaceae families. They are grown mainly as foliage plants, adding grace and contrast to borders and rock gardens, although several grasses have attractive flower heads in summer that may be dried for winter decoration. Dead foliage may be cut back on herbaceous perennials when dormant. Propagate species by seed in spring or fall or by division in spring, selected forms by division only. Pests and diseases usually give little trouble. Grasses, bamboos, rushes and sedges are illustrated on pp.284–49.

Grasses (Gramineae)
Family of evergreen, semievergreen or herbaceous, sometimes creeping perennials, annuals and marginal water plants, usually with rhizomes or stolons, that form tufts, clumps or carpets. All have basal leaves and rounded flower stems that bear alternate, long, narrow leaves. Flowers are bisexual (males and females in same spikelet) and are arranged in panicles, racemes or spikes. Each flower head comprises spikelets, with one or more florets, that are covered with glumes (scales) from which awns (long, slender bristles) may grow. Unless otherwise stated, grasses will tolerate a range of light conditions and flourish in any well-drained soil. Many genera, such as *Briza,* self-seed readily. See also *Alopecurus, Anemanthele, Arrhenatherum, Arundo, Bouteloua, Briza, Bromus, Chionochloa, Coix, Cortaderia, Dactylis, Deschampsia, Festuca, Glyceria, Hakonechloa, Helictotrichon, Holcus, Hordeum, Lagurus, Lamarckia, Leymus, Melica, Melinis, Milium, Miscanthus, Molinia, Oplismenus, Panicum, Pennisetum, Phalaris, Sesleria, Setaria, Spartina, Stenotaphrum, Stipa, Zea* and *Zizania.*

Bamboos (Bambusoideae)
Sub-family of Gramineae, comprising evergreen, rhizomatous perennials, sometimes grown as hedging as well as for ornamentation. Most bamboos differ from other perennial grasses in that they have woody stems (culms). These are hollow (except in *Chusquea*), mostly greenish-brown and, due to their silica content, very strong, with a circumference of up to 6in (15cm) in some tropical species. Leaves are lance-shaped with cross veins that give a tessellated appearance, which may be obscured in the more tender species. Flowers are produced at varying intervals but are not decorative. After flowering, stems die down but few plants die completely. Bamboos thrive in a sheltered, not too dry situation in sun or shade, unless otherwise stated. See also *Bambusa, Chusquea, Fargesia, Himalayacalamus, Phyllostachys, Pleioblastus, Pseudosasa, Sasa, Semiarundinaria, Shibataea* and *Yushania.*

Rushes (Juncaceae)
Family of evergreen, tuft-forming or creeping, mostly rhizomatous annuals and perennials. All have either rounded,

leafless stems or stems bearing long, narrow, basal leaves that are flat and hairless except *Luzula* (woodrushes) which has flat leaves, edged with white hairs. Rounded flower heads are generally unimportant. Most rushes prefer sun or partial shade and a moist or wet situation, but *Luzula* prefers drier conditions. See also *Isolepis, Juncus* and *Luzula*.

Sedges (Cyperaceae)
Family of evergreen, rhizomatous perennials that form dense tufts. Stems are triangular and bear long, narrow leaves, sometimes reduced to scales. Spikes or panicles of florets covered with glumes are produced and contain both male and female flowers, although some species of *Carex* have separate male and female flower heads on the same stem. Grow in sun or partial shade. Some sedges grow naturally in water, but many may be grown in any well-drained soil. See also *Carex, Cyperus, Eleocharis, Schoenoplectus* and *Scirpoides*.

GREVILLEA
PROTEACEAE

Genus of evergreen shrubs and trees, grown for their flowers and foliage. Grow in full sun and well-drained, preferably acidic soil. Water container specimens moderately, very little in winter. Pruning is tolerated if necessary. Propagate by seed in spring or by semiripe cuttings in summer. ① All parts may aggravate skin allergies.

G. alpestris. See *G. alpina*.
G. alpina, syn. *G. alpestris*. Evergreen, rounded, wiry-stemmed shrub. **H** and **S** 1–2ft (30–60cm). Has narrowly oblong or oval leaves, dark green above, silky-haired beneath. Bears tubular, red flowers in small clusters in spring–summer. Z9–10 H10–9.
G. banksii, illus. p.450.
G. 'Canberra Gem', illus. p.201.
G. juniperina f. sulphurea, syn. *G. sulphurea*, illus. p.206.
G. 'Poorinda Constance'. Evergreen, bushy, rounded shrub. **H** and **S** to 6ft (2m). Has small, lance-shaped, mid- to deep green leaves with prickly toothed margins. Tubular, bright red flowers, in conspicuous clusters, are borne from spring to fall, sometimes longer. Z10–11 H12–10.
G. robusta (Silk oak). Fast-growing, evergreen, upright to conical tree. **H** 100ft (30m), **S** to 50ft (15m). Fernlike leaves are 6–10in (15–25cm) long. Mature specimens bear upturned bell-shaped, bright yellow or orange flowers in dense, one-sided spikes, 4in (10cm) or more long, in spring–summer. Z10–11 H12–3.
G. 'Robyn Gordon'. Evergreen, sprawling shrub. **H** 3–5ft (1–1.5m), **S** 20–60in (50–150cm). Has leathery, dark green leaves and arching stems that bear racemes of crimson flowers, with protruding, recurved styles, from early spring to late summer. Z13–15 H12–9.
G. rosmarinifolia, illus. p.203. Evergreen, rounded, well-branched shrub. **H** and **S** to 6ft (2m). Dark green leaves are needle-shaped with reflexed margins, silky-haired beneath. Has

short, dense clusters of tubular, red, occasionally pink or white flowers in summer.
G. sulphurea. See *G. juniperina* f. *sulphurea*.

GREYIA
GREYIACEAE/MELANTHIACEAE

Genus of evergreen, semievergreen or deciduous, spring-flowering shrubs and trees, grown for their flowers and overall appearance. Needs full light and well-drained soil. Water container specimens moderately when in full growth, less at other times. Remove or shorten flowered stems after flowering. Propagate by seed in spring or by semiripe cuttings in summer. Plants grown under glass need plenty of ventilation.
G. sutherlandii, illus. p.455.

GRINDELIA
Gum plant, Rosinweed
COMPOSITAE/ASTERACEAE

Genus of annuals, biennials, evergreen perennials and subshrubs, grown for their flower heads. Needs a warm, sheltered site. Requires sun and well-drained soil. Water container specimens moderately when in full growth, less at other times. Remove spent flowering stems either as they die or in following spring. Propagate by seed in spring or by semiripe cuttings in late summer.
G. chiloensis, syn. *G. speciosa*, illus. p.161.
G. speciosa. See *G. chiloensis*.

GRISELINIA
Tarweed
CORNACEAE/GRISELINIACEAE

Genus of evergreen shrubs and trees, with inconspicuous flowers, grown for their foliage. Thrives in mild, coastal areas where it is effective as a hedge or windbreak as it is very wind- and salt-resistant. In colder areas, provide shelter. Requires sun and fertile, well-drained soil. Restrict growth and trim hedges in early summer. Propagate by semiripe cuttings in summer.
G. littoralis (Broadleaf). Fast-growing, evergreen, upright shrub of dense habit. **H** 20ft (6m), **S** 15ft (5m). Bears oval, leathery leaves that are bright apple-green. Tiny, inconspicuous, yellow-green flowers are borne in late spring. Z7–9 H9–7. **'Dixon's Cream', H** 10ft (3m), **S** 6ft (2m), is slower-growing and has central, creamy-white leaf variegation. **'Variegata',** illus. p.119.
G. lucida. Fast-growing, evergreen, upright shrub. **H** 20ft (6m), **S** 15ft (5m). Is similar to *G. littoralis*, but has larger, glossy, dark green leaves. Z7–9 H9–7.

GUARIANTHE
ORCHIDACEAE

See also ORCHIDS.
G. bowringiana, syn. *Cattleya bowringiana*, illus. p.466. Evergreen, epiphytic orchid for a cool greenhouse. **H** 18in (45cm). In fall bears large heads of rose-purple-lipped, magenta flowers, 3in (8cm) across. Has oval, stiff leaves, 3–4in (8–10cm) long. Grow in partial shade in summer and do not spray from overhead. Z12–15 H12–9.

GUNNERA
GUNNERACEAE/HALORAGIDACEAE

Genus of summer-flowering perennials, grown mainly for their foliage. Some are clump-forming with very large leaves; others are mat-forming with smaller leaves. Shelter from wind in summer and cover with hay or compost in winter. Some require sun while others do best in partial shade; all need moist soil. Propagate by seed in fall or spring; small species by division in spring.
G. chilensis. See *G. tinctoria*.
G. magellanica, illus. p.371.
G. manicata, illus. p.443.
G. scabra. See *G. tinctoria*.
G. tinctoria, syn. *G. chilensis, G. scabra*. Robust, rounded, clump-forming perennial. **H** and **S** 5ft (1.5m) or more. Has very large, rounded, puckered and lobed leaves, 1½–2ft (45–60cm) across. In early summer produces dense, conical clusters of tiny, dull reddish-green flowers. Z9–10 H10–9.

GUZMANIA
BROMELIACEAE

Genus of evergreen, rosette-forming, epiphytic perennials, grown for their overall appearance. Needs semi-shade and a rooting medium of equal parts rich soil and either sphagnum moss, or bark or plastic chips used for orchid culture. Using soft water, water moderately during growing season, sparingly at other times, and keep rosette centers filled with water from spring to fall. Propagate by offsets in spring or summer.
G. lingulata. Evergreen, basal-rosetted, epiphytic perennial. **H** and **S** 12–18in (30–45cm). Forms loose rosettes of broadly strap-shaped, arching, mid-green leaves. Bears a cluster of tubular, white to yellow flowers, surrounded by a rosette of bright red bracts, usually in summer. Z14–15 H12–1. **var. minor, H** and **S** 6in (15cm), has yellow-green leaves and red or yellow bracts.
G. monostachia, syn. *G. monostachya, G. tricolor*. Evergreen, basal-rosetted, epiphytic perennial. **H** and **S** 12–16in (30–40cm). Has dense rosettes of strap-shaped, erect to arching, pale to yellowish-green leaves. In summer, elongated spikes of tubular, white flowers emerge from axils of oval bracts, the upper ones red, the lower ones green with purple-brown stripes. Z14–15 H12–1.
G. monostachya. See *G. monostachia*.
G. sanguinea. Evergreen, basal-rosetted, epiphytic perennial. **H** 8in (20cm), **S** 12–14in (30–35cm). Has dense, slightly flat rosettes of broadly strap-shaped, arching, mid- to deep green leaves. In summer, a compact cluster of tubular, yellow flowers, surrounded by red bracts, is produced at the heart of each mature rosette. Z14–15 H12–1.
G. tricolor. See *G. monostachia*.
G. vittata. Evergreen, basal-rosetted, epiphytic perennial. **H** and **S** 14–24in (35–60cm). Produces fairly loose rosettes of strap-shaped, erect, dark green leaves with pale green cross-bands and recurved tips. Stem bears a compact, egg-shaped head of small, tubular, white flowers in summer. Z14–15 H12–1.

GYMNOCALYCIUM
CACTACEAE

Genus of perennial cacti, grown for their masses of funnel-shaped flowers in spring–summer. Crowns generally bear smooth, scaly buds. Needs full sun or partial shade and very well-drained soil. Propagate by seed or offsets in spring or summer.
G. andreae. Clump-forming, spherical, perennial cactus. **H** 2½in (6cm), **S** 4in (10cm). Has a glossy, dark green stem bearing 8 rounded ribs and up to 8 pale yellow-white spines per areole. Yellow flowers, 2in (5cm) wide, are produced in spring–summer. Z11–12 H12–10.
G. gibbosum, illus. p.481.
G. mihanovichii 'Red Head', syn. *G. mihanovichii* 'Hibotan', *G. mihanovichii* 'Red Cap', illus. p.487.
G. quehlianum. Flattened spherical, perennial cactus. **H** 2in (5cm), **S** 3in (7cm). Gray-blue to brown stem has 11 or so rounded ribs. Areoles each produce 5 curved spines. Produces white flowers, 2in (5cm) across, with red throats, in spring–summer. Is easy to flower. Z13–15 H12–10.
G. schickendantzii. Spherical, perennial cactus. **H** and **S** 4in (10cm). Dark green stem has 7–14 deeply indented ribs and long, red-tipped, gray-brown spines. Bears greenish-white to pale pink flowers, 2in (5cm) across, in summer. Z13–15 H12–10.

GYMNOCARPIUM
DRYOPTERIDACEAE/WOODSIACEAE

Genus of deciduous, rhizomatous, terrestrial ferns with triangular fronds, ideal for groundcover. Needs deep shade and prefers leafy, moist, neutral to acidic soil. Propagate from spores when ripe, or divide in spring.
G. dryopteris (Oak fern). Deciduous fern. **H** 8in (20cm), **S** indefinite. Bears divided fronds, each with a leaf blade 4–7in (10–18cm) long and across, on stem 4in (10cm) long. Pinnae are triangular, with oblong to ovate, toothed and scalloped segments. Pale yellowish green, young fronds darken to vivid rich green as they mature. Z4–8 H0.

GYMNOCLADUS
LEGUMINOSAE/CAESALPINIACEAE

Genus of deciduous trees, grown for their foliage. Needs full sun and deep, fertile, well-drained soil. Propagate by seed in fall.
G. dioica, illus. p.67.

Gynandiris sisyrinchium. See *Moraea sisyrinchium*.

GYNURA
COMPOSITAE/ASTERACEAE

Genus of evergreen perennials, shrubs and semi-scrambling climbers, grown for their ornamental foliage or flower heads. Requires a lightly shaded position in summer and any fertile, well-drained soil. Water moderately throughout the year, less in cool conditions; do not overwater. Provide support for stems. Remove stem tips to encourage branching. Propagate by softwood or semiripe cuttings in spring or summer.

G. aurantiaca, illus. p.462. **'Purple Passion',** syn. *G. sarmentosa* is an evergreen, erect, woody-based, soft-stemmed shrub or semi-scrambling climber. **H** 2ft (60cm) or more. Stems and lance-shaped, lobed, serrated leaves are covered with velvety, purple hairs. Leaves are purple-green above, deep red-purple beneath. In winter, clusters of daisylike, orange-yellow flower heads are produced and these become purplish as they mature. Z14–15 H12–10.

G. sarmentosa. See *G. aurantiaca* 'Purple Passion'.

GYPSOPHILA
CARYOPHYLLACEAE

Genus of spring- to fall-flowering annuals and perennials, some of which are semievergreen. Needs sun. Prefers deep, well-drained soil but tolerates dry, sandy and stony soils. Resents being disturbed. Cut back after flowering for a second flush of flowers. Propagate *G. paniculata* cultivars by grafting in winter, others by softwood cuttings in summer or by seed in fall or spring.

G. cerastioides, illus. p.349.

G. elegans, illus. p.299.

G. paniculata (Baby's breath). **'Bristol Fairy',** illus. p.231. **'Flamingo'** is a spreading, short-lived perennial. **H** 2–2$\frac{1}{2}$ft (60–75cm), **S** 3ft (1m). In summer bears panicles of numerous, small, rounded, double, pale pink flowers on wiry, branching stems. Has small, linear, mid-green leaves.

G. repens. Semievergreen, prostrate perennial with much-branched rhizomes. **H** 1–2in (2.5–5cm) or more, **S** 12in (30cm) or more. In summer produces sprays of small, rounded, white, lilac or pink flowers on slender stems on which are borne narrowly oval, bluish-green leaves. Is excellent for a rock garden, wall or dry bank. May also be propagated by division in spring. Z4–7 H7–1. **'Dorothy Teacher',** illus. p.362.

HAAGEOCEREUS
CACTACEAE

Genus of perennial cacti, grown for their ribbed, densely spiny, columnar, green stems branching from the base. Requires full sun and very well-drained soil. Propagate by seed or stem cuttings in spring or summer.

H. ambiguus. See *H. decumbens*.

H. chosicensis. See *H. pseudomelanostele*.

H. decumbens, syn. *H. ambiguus*, *H. litoralis*. Prostrate, perennial cactus. **H** 1ft (30cm), **S** 3ft (1m). Stems, 2$\frac{1}{2}$in (6cm) across, with 20 or so ribs, have dark brown, central spines, 2in (5cm) long, and shorter, dense, golden, radial spines. Tubular, white flowers, 3in (8cm) across, are produced in summer near crowns, only on mature plants. Z13–15 H12–10.

H. litoralis. See *H. decumbens*.

H. pseudomelanostele, syn. *H. chosicensis*. Upright, perennial cactus. **H** 5ft (1.5m), **S** 3ft (1m). Green stem, 4in (10cm) across, with 19 or so ribs, bears white, golden or red, central spines and shorter, dense, bristly, white, radial ones. Has tubular, white, lilac-white or pinkish-red flowers, 3in (7cm) long, near crown in summer. Z13–15 H12–10.

H. versicolor. Columnar, perennial cactus. **H** to 6ft (2m), **S** 3ft (1m). Dense, golden, red or brown, radial spines at times form colored bands around a longer, central spine up the green stem. Long-tubed, white flowers are borne near crown of plant in summer. Z13–15 H12–10.

HABENARIA
ORCHIDACEAE

See also ORCHIDS.

H. radiata, illus. p.408.

HABERLEA
GESNERIACEAE

Genus of evergreen, rosetted perennials, grown for their sprays of flowers. Is useful on walls. Needs partial shade and moist soil. Resents disturbance to roots. Propagate by seed in spring or by leaf cuttings or offsets in early summer.

H. ferdinandi-coburgii. Evergreen, dense, basal-rosetted perennial. **H** 4–6in (10–15cm), **S** 12in (30cm). Has oblong, toothed, dark green leaves, hairy below, almost glabrous above. Sprays of funnel-shaped, blue-violet flowers, each with a white throat, are borne on long stems in late spring and early summer. Z5–8 H8–5.

H. rhodopensis. Evergreen, dense, basal-rosetted perennial. **H** 4in (10cm), **S** 6in (15cm) or more. Is similar to *H. ferdinandi-coburgii*, but leaves are hairy on both surfaces. Z5–7 H7–5. **'Virginalis'** illus. p.359.

HABRANTHUS
AMARYLLIDACEAE

Genus of summer- and fall-flowering bulbs, grown for their funnel-shaped flowers. Needs a sheltered, sunny site and fertile soil, which is well supplied with moisture in growing season. Propagate by seed or offsets in spring.

H. andersonii. See *H. tubispathus*.

H. brachyandrus. Summer-flowering bulb. **H** to 12in (30cm), **S** 2–3in (5–8cm). Long, linear, semierect, narrow leaves form a basal cluster. Each flower stem bears a semierect, widely funnel-shaped, pinkish-red flower, 3–4in (7–10cm) long. Z10–11 H12–10.

H. robustus, syn. *Zephyranthes robusta*, illus. p.426.

H. tubispathus, syn. *H. andersonii*. Summer-flowering bulb. **H** to 6in (15cm), **S** 2in (5cm). Has linear, semierect, basal leaves and a succession of flower stems each bearing solitary, funnel-shaped flowers, 1–1$\frac{1}{2}$in (2.5–3.5cm) long, yellow inside, copper-red outside. Z10–11 H12–10.

HACQUETIA
SYN. DONDIA
UMBELLIFERAE/APIACEAE

Genus of one species of clump-forming, rhizomatous perennial that creeps slowly, grown for its yellow or yellow-green flower heads borne on leafless plants in late winter and early spring. Is good in rock gardens. Prefers shade and rich, moist soil. Resents disturbance to roots. Propagate by division in spring, by seed when fresh in fall or by root cuttings in winter.

H. epipactis, illus. p.356.

HAEMANTHUS
AMARYLLIDACEAE

Genus of summer-flowering bulbs, grown for their dense heads of small, star-shaped flowers, often brightly colored. Prefers full sun or partial shade and well-drained soil or sandy compost. Liquid feed in the growing season. Leave undisturbed as long as possible before replanting. Propagate by offsets or seed before growth commences in early spring. ① All parts may cause mild stomach upset if ingested; contact with the sap may irritate skin.

H. albiflos (Shaving brush plant, White paintbrush). Summer-flowering bulb. **H** 2–12in (5–30cm), **S** 8–12in (20–30cm). Has 2–6 almost prostrate, broadly elliptic leaves with hairy edges. Flower stem, produced between leaves, bears a brushlike head of up to 50 white flowers with very narrow petals and protruding stamens. Z13–15 H12–10.

H. coccineus, illus. p.423.

H. katherinae. See *Scadoxus multiflorus* subsp. *katherinae*.

H. magnificus. See *Scadoxus puniceus*.

H. multiflorus. See *Scadoxus multiflorus*.

H. natalensis. See *Scadoxus puniceus*.

H. puniceus. See *Scadoxus puniceus*.

H. sanguineus. Summer-flowering bulb. **H** to 12in (30cm), **S** 8–12in (20–30cm). Bears 2 prostrate, elliptic, rough, dark green leaves, hairy beneath. Brownish-purple-spotted, green flower stem, forming before leaves, produces a dense head of small, narrow-petaled, red flowers, surrounded by whorls of narrow, leaflike, red or pink bracts. Z13–15 H12–10.

HAKEA
PROTEACEAE

Genus of evergreen shrubs and trees, grown for their often needlelike leaves and their flowers. Is very wind-resistant, except in cold areas. Requires full sun and fertile, well-drained soil. Water container specimens moderately in growing season, but only sparingly in winter. Propagate by semiripe cuttings in summer or by seed in fall.

H. drupacea, syn. *H. suaveolens*. Evergreen, rounded shrub. **H** and **S** 6ft (2m) or more. Leaves are divided into cylindrical, needlelike leaflets or occasionally are undivided and lance-shaped. Small, fragrant, tubular, white flowers, in short, dense clusters, are produced from summer to winter. Z10–11 H12–9.

H. lissosperma, syn. *H. sericea* (Mountain hakea). Evergreen, upright, densely branched shrub of pine-like appearance. **H** 15ft (5m), **S** 10ft (3m). Bears long, slender, sharply pointed, gray-green leaves and, in late spring and early summer, produces clusters of small, spidery, white flowers. Z10–11 H12–10.

H. sericea of gardens. See *H. lissosperma*.

H. suaveolens. See *H. drupacea*.

HAKONECHLOA
Hakone grass
GRAMINEAE/POACEAE

See also GRASSES, BAMBOOS, RUSHES and SEDGES.

H. macra 'Aureola', illus. p.289.

HALESIA
Silverbell, Snowdrop tree
STYRACACEAE

Genus of deciduous, spring-flowering trees and shrubs, grown for their showy, pendent, bell-shaped flowers and their curious, winged fruits. Needs a sunny, sheltered position. Prefers moist but well-drained, neutral to acid soil. Propagate by softwood cuttings in summer or by seed in fall.

H. carolina, syn. *H. tetraptera* (Carolina silverbell). Deciduous, spreading tree or shrub. **H** 25ft (8m), **S** 30ft (10m). Oval leaves are mid-green. Masses of bell-shaped, white flowers, hanging from bare shoots, produced in late spring, are followed by 4-winged, green fruits. Z5–8 H8–4.

H. monticola, illus. p.71.

H. tetraptera. See *H. carolina*.

x HALIMIOCISTUS
CISTACEAE

Hybrid genus (*Cistus* x *Halimium*) of evergreen shrubs, grown for their flowers. Requires full sun and well-drained soil. Propagate by semiripe cuttings in summer.

x H. sahucii, syn. *Cistus revolii*, illus. p.149.

x H. wintonensis, syn. *Halimium wintonense*. Evergreen, bushy shrub. **H** 2ft (60cm), **S** 3ft (1m). Saucer-shaped, white flowers, each with deep red bands and a yellow center, are produced amid lance-shaped, gray-green leaves in late spring and early summer. Z7–9 H9–7.

G

HALIMIUM

CISTACEAE

Genus of evergreen shrubs, grown for their flowers. Is good for coastal gardens. Prefers full sun and light, well-drained soil. Propagate by semiripe cuttings in summer.

H. formosum. See *H. lasianthum* subsp. *formosum*.

H. lasianthum. Evergreen, bushy, spreading shrub. **H** 3ft (1m), **S** 5ft (1.5m). Leaves are oval and gray-green. In late spring and early summer bears saucer-shaped, golden-yellow flowers, sometimes with small, central, red blotches. Z9–11 H12–9. **subsp. formosum,** syn. *H. formosum,* illus. p.161.

H. ocymoides, syn. *Cistus algarvensis.* Evergreen, bushy shrub. **H** 2ft (60cm), **S** 3ft (1m). Narrowly oval leaves, covered in white hairs when young, mature to dark green. In early summer has upright clusters of saucer-shaped, golden-yellow flowers, conspicuously blotched with black or purple. Z9–11 H12–9. **'Susan'.** See *H.* 'Susan'.

H. 'Susan', syn. *H. ocymoides* 'Susan', illus. p.160.

H. umbellatum, syn. *Helianthemum umbellatum,* illus. p.149.

H. wintonense. See *Halimiocistus wintonensis.*

HAMAMELIS

Witch hazel

HAMAMELIDACEAE

Genus of deciduous, fall- to early spring-flowering shrubs, grown for their fall color and fragrant, frost-resistant flowers, each with 4 narrowly strap-shaped petals. Needs sun or partial shade and prefers fertile, well-drained, peaty, acid soil, although tolerates good, deep soil over chalk. Propagate species by seed in fall, selected forms by softwood cuttings in summer, by budding in late summer or by grafting in winter. See also feature panel p.118.

H. x intermedia 'Aphrodite' (illus. p.118) Deciduous, upright shrub. **H** and **S** 12ft (4m) or more. Has oval, bright green leaves. Bears masses of large, fragrant, spidery, golden-orange flowers, along bare branches, in winter. **'Arnold Promise'** (illus. p.118) has a spreading habit, bright green leaves that turn to yellow in fall and yellow flowers in mid- and late winter. **'Barmstedt Gold'** (illus. p.118) has deep golden-yellow flowers, with red-tinted bases, and leaves that turn to yellow in fall. **'Diane'** has deep red flowers from mid- to late winter. Leaves turn yellow and red in fall. Z5–9 H9–1. **'Jelena'** (illus. p.118) has coppery-orange flowers from early to mid-winter and bright orange or red leaves in fall. **'Pallida',** syn. *H. mollis* 'Pallida' (illus. p.118), **S** 10ft (3m), bears dense clusters of large, sulfur-yellow flowers. **'Primavera'** (illus. p.118) has yellow flowers in late winter and early spring. **'Robert'** (illus. p.118) has orange-red flowers. **'Vesna'** produces golden-yellow flowers flushed with red. Z5–9 H9–1.

H. japonica (Japanese witch hazel). Deciduous, upright, open shrub. **H** and **S** 12ft (4m). Broadly oval, mid-green leaves turn yellow in fall. Fragrant, yellow flowers, with crinkled petals, are produced on bare branches from mid- to late winter.

Z5–9 H9–5. **'Sulphurea',** illus. p.118. **'Zuccariniana'** bears paler, lemon-yellow flowers in early spring and mid-green leaves turn orange-yellow in fall.

H. mollis (Chinese witch hazel). Deciduous, upright, open shrub. **H** and **S** 12ft (4m) or more. Broadly oval, mid-green leaves turn yellow in fall. Produces extremely fragrant, spidery, yellow flowers, along bare branches, in mid- and late winter. Z5–9 H9–5. **'Coombe Wood'** has golden-yellow flowers. Z5–9 H9–1. **'Jermyn's Gold'** bears large clusters of broad-petaled, bright yellow flowers. **'Pallida'.** See *H. x intermedia* 'Pallida'.

H. vernalis 'Sandra'. Deciduous, upright, open shrub. **H** and **S** 15ft (5m). Bears small, fragrant, spidery, deep yellow flowers in late winter and early spring. Oval leaves are purple when young, mid-green in summer and purple, red, orange and yellow in fall. Z4–8 H9–5.

H. virginiana (Common witch hazel). Deciduous, open, upright shrub. **H** and **S** 15ft (5m). Small, fragrant, spidery, yellow flowers, with 4 narrow petals, are produced in fall as leaves fall. Broadly oval leaves turn yellow in fall. Z3–8 H8–1.

Hamatocactus hamatacanthus. See *Ferocactus hamatacanthus.*
Hamatocactus uncinatus. See *Sclerocactus uncinatus.*

HARDENBERGIA

Coral pea

LEGUMINOSAE/PAPILIONACEAE

Genus of evergreen, woody-stemmed, twining climbers or subshrubs, grown for their curtains of leaves and racemes of pealike flowers. Prefers sun and well-drained soil that does not dry out. Propagate by stem cuttings in late summer or fall or by seed (soaked before sowing) in spring.

H. comptoniana, illus. p.194.
H. monophylla. See *H. violacea.*
H. violacea, syn. *H. monophylla* (Purple coral pea). Evergreen, woody-stemmed, twining climber. **H** to 10ft (3m). Narrowly oval leaves are 1–5in (2.5–12cm) long. Violet, occasionally pink or white, flowers, with yellow blotches on upper petals, are borne in spring. Brownish pods, 1¼–1½in (3–4cm) long, are produced in fall. Z12–15 H12–10. **'Happy Wanderer'** illus. p.462.

HATIORA

CACTACEAE

Genus of perennial, epiphytic cacti, grown for their short, jointed, cylindrical stems, each swollen at one end like a bottle. Requires partial shade and very well-drained soil. Keep damp in summer; water a little in winter. Propagate by stem cuttings in spring or summer.

H. clavata. See *Rhipsalis gaertneri.*
H. gaertneri, syn. *Rhipsalidopsis gaertneri,* illus. p.487.
H. rosea, syn. *Rhipsalidopsis rosea,* illus. p.485.
H. salicornioides, syn. *Rhipsalis salicornioides* (Drunkard's dream). Bushy, perennial, epiphytic cactus. **H** and **S** 1ft (30cm). Has freely branching stems, 1¼in (3cm) long, joints with expanded tips and, in spring, terminal, bell-shaped, golden-yellow flowers. Z13–15 H12–10.

HAWORTHIA

LILIACEAE/ASPHODELACEAE

Genus of basal-rosetted, clump-forming, perennial succulents, grown for their triangular to rounded, green leaves. Roots tend to wither in winter or during long periods of drought. Needs partial shade to stay green and grow quickly; if planted in full sun turns red or orange and grows slowly. Requires very well-drained soil. Keep dry in winter. Propagate by seed or division from spring to fall.

H. arachnoidea, syn. *H. setata,* illus. p.491.
H. attenuata, illus. p.480.
H. x cuspidata. Clump-forming, perennial succulent. **H** 2in (5cm), **S** 10in (25cm). Produces a basal rosette of smooth, rounded, fleshy, light green leaves covered with translucent marks. Tubular to bell-shaped, white flowers are produced from spring to fall on long, slender stems. Z13–15 H12–10.

H. fasciata. Slow-growing, clump-forming, perennial succulent. **H** 6in (15cm), **S** 12in (30cm). Has raised, white dots, mostly in bands, on undersides of triangular, slightly incurved leaves, to 3in (8cm) long, which are arranged in a basal rosette. Bears tubular to bell-shaped, white flowers, on long, slender stems, from spring to fall. Z12–15 H12–10.

H. setata. See *H. arachnoidea.*
H. truncata, illus. p.492.

HEATHERS

ERICACEAE

Heathers (otherwise known as heaths) are evergreen, woody-stemmed shrubs, grown for their flowers and foliage, both of which may provide color in the garden all year round. There are 3 genera: *Calluna*, *Daboecia* and *Erica*. *Calluna* has only one species, *C. vulgaris*, but it contains a large number of cultivars that flower mainly from mid-summer to late fall. *Daboecia* has 2 species, both of which are summer-flowering. The largest genus is *Erica*, which, although broadly divided into 2 groups—winter- and summer-flowering species—has some species also flowering in spring and fall. They vary in height from tree heaths, which may grow to 20ft (6m), to dwarf, prostrate plants that, if planted apart, soon spread to form a thick mat of groundcover.

Heathers prefer an open, sunny position and require rich, well-drained soil. *Calluna* and *Daboecia* dislike limestone and must be grown in acid soil; some species of *Erica* tolerate slightly alkaline soil but all are better grown in acid soils. Prune lightly after flowering each year to keep plants bushy and compact. Propagate species by seed in spring or by softwood cuttings, division or layering in summer. Seed cannot be relied onto come true. All cultivars should be vegetatively propagated. Heathers are illustrated on p.166.

HEBE

SCROPHULARIACEAE/PLANTAGINACEAE

Genus of evergreen shrubs, grown for their often dense spikes, panicles or racemes of flowers and for their foliage. Grows well in coastal areas. Smaller species and cultivars

are suitable for rock gardens. Requires full sun and well-drained soil. Growth may be restricted, or leggy plants tidied, by cutting back in spring. Propagate by semiripe cuttings in summer.

H. albicans, illus. p.151. **'Cranleigh Gem'** is an evergreen, rounded shrub. **H** 2ft (60cm), **S** 3ft (1m). Has dense spikes of small, 4-lobed, white flowers, with conspicuous, black anthers, amid narrowly oval, gray-green leaves in early summer. Z9–10 H10–9.

H. 'Alicia Amherst'. Fast-growing, evergreen, upright shrub. **H** and **S** 4ft (1.2m). Has large, oblong, glossy, dark green leaves and, in late summer–fall, large spikes of small, 4-lobed, deep violet-purple flowers. Z9–10 H10–9.

H. x andersonii 'Variegata', syn. *H.* 'Andersonii Variegata'. Evergreen, bushy shrub. **H** and **S** 6ft (2m). Leaves are oblong and dark green, each with a gray-green center and creamy-white margins. Has dense spikes of small, 4-lobed, lilac flowers from mid-summer to fall. Z10–11 H12–10.

H. 'Autumn Glory', illus. p.157.
H. 'Bowles's Variety', illus. p.157.
H. brachysiphon. Evergreen, bushy, dense shrub. **H** and **S** 6ft (2m). Has oblong, dark green leaves. Produces dense spikes of small, 4-lobed, white flowers in mid-summer. Z8–10 H10–8. **'White Gem'.** See *H.* 'White Gem'.

H. buchananii. Evergreen, dome-shaped shrub. **H** and **S** 6in (15cm) or more. Very dark stems bear oval, bluish-green leaves. In summer produces clusters of small, 4-lobed, white flowers at stem tips. Z8–10 H10–8. **'Minor',** **H** 2–4in (5–10cm), has smaller leaves.

H. canterburiensis, syn. *H.* 'Tom Marshall'. Evergreen, spreading shrub. **H** and **S** 1–3ft (30–90cm). Small, oval, glossy, dark green leaves are densely packed on stems. In early summer, short racemes of small, white flowers are freely produced in leaf axils. Z8–10 H10–8.

H. 'Carl Teschner'. See *H.* 'Youngii'.
H. carnosula. Evergreen, prostrate shrub. **H** 6–12in (15–30cm), **S** 12in (30cm) or more. Has small, oblong to oval, slightly convex, fleshy, glaucous leaves. Terminal clusters of many small, white flowers, with 4 pointed lobes, are borne in late spring or early summer. Z9–10 H10–8.

H. cupressoides, illus. p.165. **'Boughton Dome',** illus. p.347.
H. 'E.A. Bowles', illus. p.157.
H. 'Eveline', syn. *H.* 'Gauntlettii'. Evergreen, upright shrub. **H** and **S** 3ft (1m). Has long spikes of small, 4-lobed, pink flowers, each with a purplish tube, amid rich green, oblong leaves from late summer to late fall. Z10–11 H11–9.

H. 'Fairfieldii'. Evergreen, upright shrub. **H** and **S** 2ft (60cm). Oval, toothed, glossy, bright green leaves are red-margined. Large, open panicles of small, 4-lobed, pale lilac flowers are produced in late spring and early summer. Z9–10 H10–9.

H. x franciscana 'Blue Gem'. Evergreen, spreading shrub. **H** 2ft (60cm), **S** 4ft (1.2m). Has oblong, densely arranged, mid-green leaves. Dense spikes of small, 4-lobed, violet-blue flowers are borne from mid-summer until early winter. Z9–10 H10–9.

H. 'Gauntlettii'. See *H.* 'Eveline'.
H. 'Great Orme', illus. p.153.

H. hulkeana. Evergreen, upright, open shrub. **H** and **S** 3ft (1m). Oval, toothed, glossy, dark green leaves have red margins. Has masses of small, 4-lobed, pale lilac flowers in large, open panicles in late spring and early summer. Z9–11 H12–10. **'Lilac Hint',** illus. p.152.
***H.* 'La Séduisante',** syn. *H.* 'Ruddigore', *H. speciosa* 'Ruddigore'. Evergreen, upright shrub. **H** and **S** 3ft (1m). Oval, glossy, deep green leaves are purple beneath. Produces small, 4-lobed, deep purplish-red flowers in large spikes from late summer to late fall. Z9–11 H12–9.
H. macrantha. Evergreen, bushy shrub. **H** 2ft (60cm), **S** 3ft (1m). Has oval, toothed, fleshy, bright green leaves and produces racemes of large, 4-lobed, pure white flowers in early summer. May become bare at base. Z9–11 H12–9.
***H.* 'Midsummer Beauty'.** Evergreen, rounded, open shrub. **H** 6ft (2m), **S** 5ft (1.5m). Long, narrow, glossy, bright green leaves are reddish-purple beneath. Long spikes of small, 4-lobed, lilac flowers that fade to white are borne from mid-summer to late fall. Z9–11 H12–9.
H. ochracea. Evergreen, bushy, dense shrub. **H** and **S** 3ft (1m). Slender shoots are densely covered with tiny, scalelike, ocher-tinged, olive-green leaves. Clusters of small, 4-lobed, white flowers are borne in late spring and early summer. Z8–10 H10–8.
H. pinguifolia (Disk-leaved hebe). Z8–10 H10–8. **'Pagei'** illus. p.337.
***H.* 'Purple Queen',** illus. p.157.
H. rakaiensis. Evergreen, rounded, compact shrub. **H** 3ft (1m), **S** 4ft (1.2m). Produces small, dense spikes of 4-lobed, white flowers amid small, oblong, mid-green leaves from early to mid-summer. Z8–10 H10–8.
H. recurva, illus. p.151.
***H.* 'Ruddigore'.** See *H.* 'La Séduisante'.
H. salicifolia. Evergreen, upright shrub. **H** and **S** 8ft (2.5m). Has long, narrow, pointed, pale green leaves and, in summer, produces slender spikes of small, 4-lobed, white or pale lilac flowers. Z8–10 H10–8.
***H. speciosa* 'Ruddigore'.** See *H.* 'La Séduisante'.
***H.* 'Tom Marshall'.** See *H. canterburiensis.*
H. vernicosa, illus. p.337.
***H.* 'White Gem',** syn. *H. brachysiphon* 'White Gem', illus. p.149.
***H.* 'Youngii',** syn. *H.* 'Carl Teschner'. Evergreen, prostrate, becoming dome-shaped, shrub. **H** 6in (15cm), **S** 12in (30cm) or more. Blackish-brown stems are covered in small, oval, glossy, dark green leaves. Bears short racemes of tiny, 4-lobed, white-throated, purple flowers in summer. Is excellent as a border plant. Z8–9 H9–8.

HEDERA

Ivy

ARALIACEAE

Genus of evergreen, woody-stemmed, trailing perennials and self-clinging climbers with adventitious rootlets, used for covering walls and fences and as groundcover. Takes a year or so to become established, but thereafter growth is rapid. On the ground and while climbing, mostly bears roughly triangular, usually lobed leaves. Given extra height and access to light, leaves become less lobed and, in fall, umbels of small, yellowish-green flowers are produced, followed by globose, black, occasionally yellow, fruits. Ivies with green leaves are very shade tolerant and do well against a north-facing wall. Those with variegated or yellow leaves prefer more light, are usually less hardy and may sustain frost and wind damage in severe winters. All prefer well-drained, alkaline soil. Prune in spring to control height and spread, and to remove any damaged growth. Propagate in late summer by softwood cuttings or rooted layers. Red spider mite may be a problem when plants are grown against a south-facing wall or in dry conditions. ⓘ All parts of ivy may cause severe discomfort if ingested; contact with the sap may aggravate skin allergies or irritate skin.
H. algeriensis, syn. *H. canariensis*. Fast-growing, evergreen, self-clinging climber. **H** to 20ft (6m), **S** 15ft (5m). May be damaged in severe winters but soon recovers. Has oval to triangular, unlobed, glossy, mid-green leaves and reddish-purple stems. Is suitable for growing against a wall in a sheltered area. Z6–11 H12–6. **'Gloire de Marengo'** has silver-variegated leaves. **'Ravensholst'** is vigorous with large leaves; makes good groundcover.
H. canariensis of gardens. See *H. algeriensis.*
H. colchica (Colchis ivy, Persian ivy). Evergreen, self-clinging climber or trailing perennial. **H** 30ft (10m), **S** 15ft (5m). Has large, oval, unlobed, dark green leaves. Is suitable for growing against a wall. Z6–11 H12–1. **'Dentata'** is more vigorous and has large, light green leaves that droop, hence its common name. Is good when grown against a wall or for groundcover. **'Dentata Variegata',** **H** 15ft (5m), has variegated, cream-yellow leaves; is useful to brighten a shady corner. **'Paddy's Pride'.** See *H. colchica* 'Sulphur Heart'. **'Sulphur Heart',** syn. *H. colchica* 'Paddy's Pride' illus. p.211.
H. cypria, syn. *H. pastuchovii* var. *cypria*. Vigorous, evergreen, self-clinging climber. **H** 10ft (3m), **S** 6ft (2m). Has shield-shaped, glossy, dark green leaves with prominent, gray-green veins. Should be grown only against a wall. Z5–11 H12–6.
H. helix (English ivy). Vigorous, evergreen, self-clinging climber or trailing perennial. **H** 30ft (10m), **S** 15ft (5m). Has 5-lobed, dark green leaves. Makes good wall cover, but can be invasive if used for groundcover. For a small garden, the more decorative cultivars are preferable. Z5–11 H12–6. **'Adam',** **H** 4ft (1.2m), **S** 3ft (1m), has small, light green leaves variegated-yellow; may suffer leaf damage in winter, but will recover. **'Angularis Aurea',** **H** 12ft (4m), **S** 8ft (2.5m), has glossy, light green leaves, with bright yellow variegation; is not suitable as groundcover. **'Anna Marie',** **H** 4ft (1.2m), **S** 3ft (1m), has light green leaves with cream variegation, mostly at margins; may suffer leaf damage in winter. **'Atropurpurea',** syn. *H. helix* 'Purpurea', **H** 12ft (4m), **S** 8ft (2.5m), has dark green leaves that turn deep purple in winter. **var. *baltica*,** syn. *H. helix* 'Baltica', an exceptionally hardy cultivar, has small leaves and makes good groundcover in an exposed area. **'Baltica'.** See *H. helix* var. *baltica*. **'Buttercup',** **H** 6ft (2m), **S** 8ft (2.5m), has light green leaves that turn rich butter-yellow in full sun. Z5–11 H11–6. **'Caenwoodiana'.** See *H. helix* 'Pedata'. **'Congesta',** **H** 1½ft (45cm), **S** 2ft (60cm), is a non-climbing, erect cultivar with spire-like shoots and small leaves; is suitable for a rock garden. **'Conglomerata',** **H** and **S** 3ft (1m), has small, curly, unlobed leaves; will clamber over a low wall or grow in a rock garden. **'Cristata'.** See *H. helix* 'Parsley Crested'. **'Curylocks'.** See *H. helix* 'Manda's Crested'. **'Deltoidea'.** See *H. hibernica* 'Deltoidea'. **'Digitata'.** See *H. hibernica* 'Digitata'. **'Erecta',** **H** 3ft (1m), **S** 4ft (1.2m), is a non-climbing, erect cultivar similar to *H.helix* 'Congesta'. Z5–11 H11–6. **'Eva',** **H** 4ft (1.2m), **S** 3ft (1m), has small, gray-green leaves with cream variegation; may suffer leaf damage in winter. **'Glacier',** illus. p.211. **'Glymii',** **H** 8ft (2.5m), **S** 6ft (2m), has glossy, dark green leaves that turn deep purple in winter; is not suitable for groundcover. **'Goldchild',** syn. *H. helix* 'Gold Harald', **H** 3ft (1m), has small, 3–5-lobed, gray-green leaves with broad, yellow margins. **'Gold Harald'.** See *H. helix* 'Goldchild'. **'Goldheart'.** See *H. helix* 'Oro di Bogliasco'. **'Gracilis'.** See *H. hibernica* 'Gracilis'. **'Green Ripple',** **H** and **S** 4ft (1.2m), has mid-green leaves with prominent, light green veins; is good for groundcover or for growing against a low wall. **'Hahn's Self-branching'.** See *H. helix* 'Pittsburgh'. **'Heise',** **H** 1ft (30cm), **S** 2ft (60cm), has small, gray-green leaves with cream variegation; is suitable as groundcover for a small, sheltered area. **var. *hibernica*.** See *H. hibernica*. **'Ivalace',** **H** 3ft (1m), **S** 4ft (1.2m), has curled and crimped, glossy leaves; is good for groundcover and for growing against a low wall. **'Jubiläum Goldherz'.** See *H. helix* 'Oro di Bogliasco'. **'Jubilee Goldheart'.** See *H. helix* 'Oro di Bogliasco'. **'Königers Auslese',** syn. *H. helix* 'Sagittifolia', **H** 4ft (1.2m), **S** 3ft (1m), has finger-like, deeply cut leaves; is not suitable for groundcover. **'Little Diamond',** is slow-growing and has entire, diamond-shaped, gray-green leaves, variegated creamy-white. **'Lobata Major'.** See *H. hibernica* 'Lobata Major'. **'Manda's Crested',** syn. *H. helix* 'Curylocks', **H** and **S** 6ft (2m), has wavy-edged, mid-green leaves that turn a coppery shade in winter. **'Merion Beauty',** **H** 4ft (1.2m), **S** 3ft (1m), delicately lobed leaves; is not suitable for groundcover. **'Nigra',** **H** and **S** 4ft (1.2m), has small, very dark green leaves that turn purple-black in winter. **'Oro di Bogliasco',** syn. *H. helix* 'Goldheart', *H. helix* 'Jubiläum Goldherz', *H. helix* 'Jubilee Goldheart', illus. p.211. **'Parsley Crested',** syn. *H. helix* 'Cristata', **H** 6ft (2m), **S** 4ft (1.2m), has light green leaves, crested at margins; is not suitable for groundcover. **'Pedata',** syn. *H. helix* 'Caenwoodiana' (Bird's-foot ivy), **H** 12ft (4m), **S** 10ft (3m), has gray-green leaves shaped like a bird's foot; is not suitable for groundcover. **'Pittsburgh',** syn. *H. helix* 'Hahn's Self-branching', **H** 3ft (1m), **S** 4ft (1.2m), has mid-green leaves; is suitable for growing against a low wall and for groundcover. **f. *poetarum*,** syn. *H. helix* 'Poetica', *H. helix* 'Poetica Arborea' (Italian ivy, Poet's ivy), **H** 10ft (3m), is slow-growing with large, 5-lobed, shiny, mid-green leaves. Is often grown as a "bush ivy", as it bears distinctive, orange-yellow fruit, even on comparatively young plants. **'Poetica'.** See *H. helix* f. *poetarum*. **'Poetica Arborea'.** See *H. helix* f. *poetarum*. **'Purpurea'.** See *H. helix* 'Atropurpurea'. **'Sagittifolia'** of gardens. See *H. helix* 'Königers Auslese'. **'Telecurl',** **H** and **S** 3ft (1m), has twisted, light green leaves. **'Triton',** **H** 1½ft (45cm), **S** 3ft (1m), is a non-climbing cultivar that has leaves with deeply incised lobes that resemble whips; makes good groundcover. **'Woeneri',** **H** 12ft (4m), **S** 10ft (3m), is a vigorous cultivar that has bluntly lobed, gray-green leaves, with lighter colored veins, that turn purple in winter.
H. hibernica, syn. *H. helix* var. *hibernica* (Irish ivy). Vigorous, evergreen climber. **H** 15ft (5m), **S** 20ft (6m). Has large, mid-green leaves. Tends to escape cultivation in temperate regions. Z6–11 H12–6. **'Deltoidea',** syn. *H. helix* 'Deltoidea' (Sweetheart ivy), **H** 15ft (5m), **S** 10ft (3m), has heart-shaped leaves; is suitable only for growing against a wall. **'Digitata',** syn. *H. helix* 'Digitata' (Finger-leaved ivy), **H** 20ft (6m), has large leaves; is not suitable for groundcover. **'Gracilis',** syn. *H. helix* 'Gracilis', **H** 15ft (5m), has sharply lobed, dark green leaves that turn bronze-purple in winter; is not suitable for groundcover. **'Lobata Major',** syn. *H. helix* 'Lobata Major', **H** 15ft (5m), is vigorous with large, 3-lobed leaves. **'Sulphurea',** **H** and **S** 10ft (3m), has medium-sized leaves with sulfur-yellow variegation; is suitable for growing against a wall or for groundcover, and as a foil for brightly colored plants.
H. nepalensis (Nepalese ivy). Evergreen, self-clinging climber. **H** 12ft (4m), **S** 8ft (2.5m). Young growth may suffer damage from late frosts. Has oval to triangular, toothed, olive-green leaves and is suitable only for growing against a sheltered wall. Z8–11 H12–1. **'Suzanne',** **H** 6ft (2m), has 5-lobed leaves with backward-pointing basal lobes.
H. pastuchovii. Moderately vigorous, evergreen, self-clinging climber. **H** 8ft (2.5m), **S** 6ft (2m). Has shield-shaped, glossy, dark green leaves. Should be grown only against a wall. Z6–11 H12–6. **var. *cypria*.** See *H. cypria.*
H. rhombea (Japanese ivy). Evergreen, self-clinging climber. **H** and **S** 4ft (1.2m). Has small, fairly thick, diamond-shaped, unlobed, mid-green leaves. Is suitable for growing only against a low wall. Z6–11 H12–6. **'Variegata'** has leaves with narrow, white margins.

HEDYCHIUM

Garland flower, Ginger lily

ZINGIBERACEAE

Genus of perennials with sturdy, fleshy rhizomes. Fragrant, showy flowers are short-lived, but borne profusely. Grow in sheltered borders and conservatories. Requires sun and rich, moist soil. Propagate by division in spring; should not be divided when dormant. See also feature panel p.477.
H. coccineum (Red ginger lily, Scarlet ginger lily). Upright, rhizomatous perennial. **H** and **S** to 6ft (2m). Has long-

stalked, narrowly lance-shaped, grayish-green leaves. Bears spikes of short-lived, orange to red flowers, each with a 2-lobed lip, in summer. Is very variable, with many named forms, some of which are frost hardy. Z8–10 H10–8.

H. coronarium (Garland flower, White ginger lily). Upright, rhizomatous perennial. **H** 5ft (1.5m), **S** 2–3ft (60cm–1m). Produces dense spikes of very fragrant, butterfly-like, white flowers with basal, yellow blotches in mid-summer. Lance-shaped, mid-green leaves are downy beneath. Z7–11 H12–6.

H. densiflorum, illus. p.477. Clump-forming, rhizomatous perennial. **H** 4–6ft (1.2–2m), **S** 2ft (60cm). Bears a profusion of short-lived, fragrant, orange or yellow flowers in dense spikes in late summer. Broadly lance-shaped leaves are glossy, mid-green. Z8–11 H11–8.

H. flavescens. Upright, rhizomatous perennial. **H** 3–6ft (1–2m), **S** 3ft (1m). Lance-shaped, mid-green leaves are softly hairy. Produces spikes of short-lived, very fragrant, pale to lemon-yellow flowers, each with a 2-lobed lip, in late fall. Is good in a tub. Z9–11 H12–8.

H. gardnerianum, illus. p.476.

H. gracile. Arching, rhizomatous perennial. **H** 48in (120cm), **S** 20in (50cm). In summer, thin stems bear short-lived, sometimes fragrant, white flowers, each with a narrow, 2-lobed lip, narrow sepals and red stamens. Has lance-shaped, mid-green leaves. Requires staking. Is good in a raised container or on a bank. Z8–10 H10–7.

H. horsfieldii, syn. *Brachychilum horsfieldii*. Clump-forming, tufted perennial. **H** and **S** to 3ft (1m). Has short-stalked, lance-shaped, leathery leaves. Produces showy, tubular, yellow-and-white flowers, in summer, followed by orange fruits that open to reveal red seeds. Z10–12 H12–9.

H. maximum, illus. p.477. Upright, rhizomatous perennial. **H** 6–10ft (2–3m), **S** 3ft (1m). Has large, thick stems bearing lance-shaped, mid-green leaves. Short-lived, fragrant, pale yellow flowers, with golden centers and 2-lobed lip, are produced in fall. Z8–11 H11–8.

H. x moorei 'Tara', illus. p.220.

H. stenopetalum, illus. p.477. Upright, rhizomatous perennial. **H** 10–13ft (3–4m), **S** 3ft (1m) or more. Has very large, thick stems bearing lance-shaped, deep green leaves that are hairy beneath. Short-lived, white flowers, each with a 2-lobed lip, are borne in a spike in late summer and fall. Is prone to wind damage. Z9–11 H11–8.

H. thyrsiforme, illus. p.477. Upright, rhizomatous perennial. **H** 3–6ft (1–2m), **S** 20in (50cm). Broadly lance-shaped leaves are dark green. Small, short-lived, white flowers, each with a 2-lobed lip and very long stamens, are borne in fall–winter. Flower spike is wider than tall, which distinguishes it from other species. Z8–11 H11–7.

H. yunnanense, illus. p.477. Upright, rhizomatous perennial. **H** 20–32in (50–80cm), **S** 12in (30cm). Has broadly lance-shaped, mid-green leaves. Short-lived, fragrant, cream and white flowers, each with a 2-lobed lip, are produced in summer. Z9–11 H11–8.

HEDYOTIS
Bluets

RUBIACEAE

Genus of mat-forming, summer-flowering perennials. Prefers shade and moist, sandy leaf mold. Propagate by division in spring or by seed in fall.

H. michauxii, syn. *Houstonia serpyllifolia*, illus. p.369.

HEDYSARUM

LEGUMINOSAE/PAPILIONACEAE

Genus of perennials, biennials and deciduous subshrubs. Prefers sun and well-drained soil. Roots resent being disturbed. Propagate by seed in fall or spring.

H. coronarium, illus. p.235.

Heeria. See *Heterocentron*.
Heimerliodendron brunonianum. See *Pisonia umbellifera*.

HELENIUM
Sneezeweed

COMPOSITAE/ASTERACEAE

Genus of late summer- and fall-flowering perennials, grown for their daisylike flower heads, each with a prominent, central disc. Needs full sun and well-drained soil. Propagate by division in spring or fall.

① All parts may cause severe discomfort if ingested; contact with foliage may aggravate skin allergies. See also feature panel p.248.

H. 'Biedermeier'. Clump-forming, erect, bushy perennial. **H** 48in (120cm), **S** 18in (45cm). Has lance-shaped, mid-green leaves. In late summer, erect stems bear sprays of yellow-tipped, red flower heads with a central, dark brown disc. The ray florets become reflexed with age. Z4–8 H8–1.

H. 'Blopip'. See *H.* Pipsqueak.

H. 'Bressingham Gold'. Erect, bushy perennial. **H** 3ft (1m), **S** 2ft (60cm). Sturdy stems are clothed in lance-shaped, mid-green leaves. Produces sprays of bright yellow flower heads in late summer–fall. Z4–8 H8–1.

H. 'Bruno', illus. p.248. Erect, bushy perennial. **H** 4ft (1.2m), **S** 2½ft (75cm). Sprays of deep bronze-red flower heads are borne in late summer–fall. Sturdy stems are clothed in lance-shaped leaves. Z4–8 H8–1.

H. 'Butterpat', illus. p.248. Compact perennial. **H** 3ft (1m), **S** 2ft (60cm). Has sturdy stems clothed in lance-shaped leaves. Bears sprays of rich deep yellow flower heads in late summer–fall. Z4–8 H8–1.

H. 'Coppelia'. Clump-forming, erect, bushy perennial. **H** to 32in (80cm), **S** 18in (45cm). Has lance-shaped, mid-green leaves. In mid– to late summer bears sprays of deep reddish-orange flower heads, which fade with age, with central, brown discs. Z4–8 H8–1.

H. 'Double Trouble', illus. p.248. Clump-forming, erect, bushy perennial. **H** to 32in (80cm), **S** 18in (45cm). Has lance-shaped, mid-green leaves. In mid- to late summer produces sprays of double, bright yellow flower heads with twin layers of ray florets, held horizontally. Z4–8 H8–1.

H. 'Dunkelpracht'. Clump-forming, erect, bushy perennial. **H** to 3ft (1m), **S** 18in (45cm). Has lance-shaped, mid-green

leaves. In late summer bears sprays of dark brown-red flower heads. Z4–8 H8–1.

H. 'Feuersiegel', illus. p.248. Clump-forming, erect, bushy perennial. **H** to 36in (100cm) or more, **S** 18in (45cm). Has lance-shaped, mid-green leaves. In mid- to late summer produces sprays of rich yellow flower heads with horizontally held ray florets, marked with an irregular, orange-red band, and central, soft brown discs. Z4–8 H8–1.

H. 'Indianersommer', illus. p.248. Clump-forming, erect, bushy perennial. **H** to 36in (100cm) or more, **S** 18in (45cm). Has lance-shaped, mid-green leaves. In mid- to late summer bears sprays of dark brownish-red flower heads, aging to orange and yellow, and central, greenish-brown discs. Z4–8 H8–1.

H. 'Moerheim Beauty', illus. p.254.

H. Pipsqueak ('Blopip'). Clump-forming, compact, bushy perennial. **H** to 2ft (60cm), **S** 1ft (30cm). Has lance-shaped, mid-green leaves. In mid- to late summer produces sprays of shuttlecock-shaped, yellow flower heads with short, reflexed ray florets and large, central, rich brown discs. Z4–8 H8–1.

H. 'Potter's Wheel', illus. p.248. Clump-forming, erect, bushy perennial. **H** to 32in (80cm), **S** 18in (45cm). Has lance-shaped, mid-green leaves. From mid-summer to fall bears sprays of dark red flower heads with gold-edged ray florets and central, brown discs. Z4–8 H8–1.

H. 'Red Army', illus. p.248. Clump-forming, erect, bushy perennial. **H** to 36in (90cm), **S** 18in (45cm). Has lance-shaped, mid-green leaves. From mid-summer to mid-fall produces sprays of reddish-orange flower heads, intensifying in color as they age to dark red, with central, dark brown discs. Z4–8 H8–1.

H. 'Riverton Gem'. Erect, bushy perennial. **H** 4½ft (1.4m), **S** 3ft (1m). Has sprays of red-and-gold flower heads in late summer–fall. Stems are clothed in lance-shaped leaves. Z4–8 H8–1.

H. 'Rubinzwerg', illus. p.248. Clump-forming, erect, bushy perennial. **H** to 39in (100cm), **S** 18in (45cm). Has lance-shaped, mid-green leaves. From mid-summer to fall bears sprays of rich red flower heads with reflexed ray florets and central, dark brown discs. Z4–8 H8–1.

H. 'Sahin's Early Flowerer'. Clump-forming, erect, bushy perennial. **H** to 36in (90cm), **S** 18in (45cm). Has lance-shaped, mid-green leaves. From mid-summer until the first frosts produces large, bright reddish-orange flower heads with long ray florets, aging to orange and warm yellow, and central, brown discs. Z4–8 H8–1.

H. 'The Bishop'. Clump-forming, erect, bushy perennial. **H** to 36in (90cm), **S** 18in (45cm). Has lance-shaped, mid-green leaves. From mid-summer to fall produces sprays of yellow flower heads with reflexed ray florets and large, central, brown discs. Z4–8 H8–1.

H. 'Waltraut', illus. p.248. Clump-forming, erect, bushy perennial. **H** to 36in (90cm), **S** 18in (45cm). Has lance-shaped, mid-green leaves. From late summer produces sprays of copper-orange and yellow flower heads that intensify in color as they age; the central disc is brown. Z4–8 H8–1.

H. 'Wyndley'. Bushy perennial with branching stems. **H** 30in (80cm), **S** 20in

(50cm). Bears sprays of daisylike, orange-yellow flower heads in late summer–fall. Foliage is dark green. Needs regular division in spring or fall. Z4–8 H8–1.

HELIANTHEMUM
Rock rose, Sun rose

CISTACEAE

Genus of evergreen, spring- to fall-flowering shrubs and subshrubs, grown for their flowers. Is useful for rock gardens and dry banks. Needs full sun and well-drained soil. Cut back lightly after flowering. Propagate by semiripe cuttings in early summer.

H. 'Amy Baring'. Evergreen, spreading shrub. **H** 4–6in (10–15cm), **S** 24in (60cm). Small, oblong, light gray leaves are hairy beneath. In summer bears a succession of saucer-shaped, orange-centered, deep yellow flowers in loose, terminal clusters. Z6–8 H8–6.

H. apenninum, illus. p.336.

H. 'Ben Hope'. Evergreen, domed shrub. **H** 9–12in (23–30cm), **S** 18in (45cm). Bears small, linear, gray-green leaves and saucer-shaped, carmine-red flowers in mid-summer. Z6–8 H8–6.

H. 'Ben More', illus. p.345.

H. 'Ben Nevis'. Evergreen, hummock-forming, compact shrub. **H** and **S** 6–9in (15–23cm). Has small, linear, dark green leaves and, in mid-summer, saucer-shaped, orange flowers with bronze centers. Z6–8 H8–6.

H. 'Fire Dragon', illus. p.340.

H. 'Golden Queen'. Evergreen, domed, compact shrub. **H** 9in (23cm), **S** 12in (30cm). Saucer-shaped, golden-yellow flowers are produced amid small, linear, dark green leaves in mid-summer. Z6–8 H8–6.

H. guttatum. See *Tuberaria guttata*.

H. 'Jubilee'. Evergreen, domed, compact shrub. **H** 6–9in (15–23cm), **S** 9–12in (23–30cm). Has small, linear, dark green leaves. Bears saucer-shaped, double, pale yellow flowers from spring to late summer. Z6–8 H8–6.

H. oelandicum subsp. alpestre. Evergreen, open, twiggy shrub. **H** 3–5in (7–12cm), **S** 6in (15cm) or more. Produces terminal clusters of 3–6 saucer-shaped, bright yellow flowers from early to mid-summer. Leaves are tiny, oblong and mid-green. Is suitable for growing in a trough. Z6–8 H8–6.

H. 'Raspberry Ripple'. Evergreen, spreading shrub. **H** 6–9in (15–23cm), **S** 9–12in (23–30cm). Saucer-shaped, red-centered, white flowers are borne in mid-summer. Has small, linear, gray-green leaves. Z6–8 H8–6.

H. 'Rhodanthe Carneum', syn. *H.* 'Wisley Pink', illus. p.338.

H. umbellatum. See *Halimium umbellatum*.

H. 'Wisley Pink'. See *H.* 'Rhodanthe Carneum'.

H. 'Wisley Primrose', illus. p.344.

H. 'Wisley White', illus. p.337.

HELIANTHUS
Sunflower

COMPOSITAE/ASTERACEAE

Genus of summer- and fall-flowering annuals and perennials, grown for their large, daisylike, usually yellow flower

heads. May be invasive. All need sun and well-drained soil; some prefer moist conditions. Needs staking. Propagate by seed or division in fall or spring.
① Contact with the foliage may aggravate skin allergies.

H. annuus (Sunflower). Fast-growing, erect annual. **H** 3–10ft (1–3m) or more, **S** 12–18in (30–45cm). Has oval, serrated, mid-green leaves. Daisylike, brown- or purplish-centered, yellow flower heads, 12in (30cm) or more wide, are produced in summer. Tall, intermediate and dwarf cultivars are available. H12–1. **'Music Box'**, illus. p.322. **'Russian Giant'** (tall), **H** 10ft (3m) or more, produces yellow flower heads with green-brown centers. **'Teddy Bear'**, illus. p.322.

H. debilis subsp. cucumerifolius 'Italian White'. Erect perennial. **H** 4ft (1.2m), **S** 1½–2ft (45–60cm). In summer has large, black-centered, creamy-white flower heads. Purple-mottled stems bear coarsely hairy, sharply toothed, glossy, mid-green leaves. H12–1.

H. 'Lemon Queen', illus. p.222.

H. 'Monarch'. Erect perennial. **H** 7ft (2.2m), **S** 3ft (1m). Bears terminal, daisylike, semidouble, golden-yellow flower heads on branching stems in late summer. Has lance-shaped, coarse, mid-green leaves. Replant each spring to keep in check. Z5–9 H9–3.

H. x multiflorus. Upright perennial. **H** 5ft (1.5m), **S** 2ft (60cm). Has large, yellow flower heads, with double centers surrounded by larger, rayed segments, in late summer and early fall. Leaves are lance-shaped, coarse and mid-green. Z5–9 H9–5. **'Capenoch Star'**, **H** 4ft (1.2m), has lemon-yellow flower heads. **'Loddon Gold'** illus. p.222.

H. orgyalis. See *H. salicifolius*.
H. salicifolius, syn. *H. orgyalis*, illus. p.222.

HELICHRYSUM
COMPOSITAE/ASTERACEAE

Genus of summer- and fall-flowering perennials, annuals and evergreen subshrubs and shrubs. When dried, flower heads are "everlasting". Needs sun and well-drained soil. Propagate shrubs and subshrubs by heel or semiripe cuttings in summer, perennials by division or seed in spring, annuals by seed in spring.

H. angustifolium. See *H. italicum*.
H. bellidioides. See *Anaphalioides bellidioides*.
H. coralloides. See *Ozothamnus coralloides*.

H. italicum, syn. *H. angustifolium* (Curry plant). Evergreen, bushy subshrub. **H** 2ft (60cm), **S** 3ft (1m). Has linear, aromatic, silvery-gray leaves. Broad clusters of small, oblong, bright yellow flower heads are produced on long, upright, white shoots in summer. Dislikes winter wet and cold climates. Z7–11 H12–1. **subsp. serotinum**, syn. *H. serotinum* (Curry plant) is dome-shaped; stems and oval leaves are densely felted with white hairs. Z7–10 H10–7.

H. ledifolium. See *Ozothamnus ledifolius*.
H. marginatum of gardens. See *H. milfordiae*.
H. milfordiae, syn. *H. marginatum*. Evergreen, mat-forming, dense subshrub. **H** 2in (5cm), **S** 9in (23cm). On sunny days in early summer, large, conical, red buds

open into daisylike, white flower heads with red-backed petals; they close in dull or wet weather. Has basal rosettes of oval, hairy, silver leaves. Prefers very gritty soil. Dislikes winter wet. Propagate in spring by rooting single rosettes. Z7–10 H10–7.

H. petiolare, syn. *H. petiolatum* (Licorice plant). Evergreen shrub. **H** 20in (50cm), **S** 6ft (2m). Forms mounds of silver-green shoots and oval to heart-shaped, gray-felted leaves. Has daisylike, creamy-yellow flower heads in summer. Is often grown as an annual for groundcover and edging. Z11–15 H12–10. **'Limelight'** has lime-yellow leaves. Z10–11 H12–1. **'Variegatum'** illus. p.165.

H. petiolatum of gardens. See *H. petiolare*.
H. rosmarinifolium. See *Ozothamnus rosmarinifolius*.
H. 'Schwefellicht', syn. *H.* 'Sulphur Light', illus. p.275.
H. selago. See *Ozothamnus selago*.
H. serotinum. See *H. italicum* subsp. *serotinum*.

H. splendidum. Evergreen, bushy, dense shrub. **H** and **S** 4ft (1.2m). Woolly, white shoots are clothed in small, oblong, silvery-gray leaves. Small, oblong, bright yellow flower heads are produced in clusters from mid-summer to fall or sometimes into winter. Z9–11 H12–9.

H. 'Sulphur Light'. See *H.* 'Schwefellicht'.

HELICONIA
HELICONIACEAE/MUSACEAE

Genus of tufted perennials, evergreen in warm climates, grown for their spikes of colorful flowers and for the attractive foliage on younger plants. Needs partial shade and rich, well-drained soil. Water generously in growing season, very sparingly when plants die down in winter. Propagate by seed or division of rootstock in spring.

H. metallica. Tufted perennial. **H** to 10ft (3m), **S** 3ft (1m). Oblong, long-stalked leaves, to 2ft (60cm) long, are velvety-green above with paler veins, sometimes purple below. In summer, mature plants bear erect stems with tubular, glossy, greenish-white-tipped, red flowers enclosed in narrow, boat-shaped, green bracts. Z12–14 H12–10.

H. psittacorum, illus. p.478.

HELICTOTRICHON
Blue oat grass
GRAMINEAE/POACEAE

See also GRASSES, BAMBOOS, RUSHES and SEDGES.

H. sempervirens, syn. *Avena candida*, *Avena sempervirens*, illus. p.288.

HELIOPSIS
COMPOSITAE/ASTERACEAE

Genus of summer-flowering perennials. Requires sun and well-drained soil. Propagate by seed or division in fall or spring.

H. 'Ballet Dancer'. Upright perennial. **H** 3–4ft (1–1.2m), **S** 2ft (60cm). Flowers freely in late summer, bearing double, yellow flower heads with frilled petals. Dark green leaves are coarse and serrated. Z4–9 H9–1.

H. helianthoides 'Incomparabilis' Upright perennial. **H** to 5ft (1.5m), **S** 2ft (60cm). Bears daisylike, single, orange flower heads in late summer. Leaves are narrowly oval, coarsely toothed and mid-green. Z4–9 H9–1. **'Patula'** bears flattish, semidouble, orange-yellow flower heads. Z4–9 H9–1. **subsp. scabra**, syn. *H. scabra* has very rough stems and leaves and double, orange-yellow flower heads. **subsp. scabra 'Light of Loddon'**, syn. *H.* 'Light of Loddon' illus. p.220. **H. 'Light of Loddon'.** See *H. helianthoides* subsp. *scabra*' Light of Loddon'.
H. scabra. See *H. helianthoides* subsp. *scabra*.

Heliosperma alpestre. See *Silene alpestris*.

HELIOTROPIUM
Heliotrope
BORAGINACEAE

Genus of annuals, evergreen subshrubs and shrubs, grown for their fragrant flowers. Needs full sun and fertile, well-drained soil. Water container plants freely when in full growth, moderately at other times. In spring, tip prune young plants to promote a bushy habit and cut leggy, older plants back hard. Propagate by seed in spring, by greenwood cuttings in summer or by semiripe cuttings in early fall.

H. arborescens, syn. *H. peruvianum*, illus. p.310.
H. peruvianum. See *H. arborescens*.

Helipterum manglesii. See *Rhodanthe manglesii*.
Helipterum roseum. See *Rhodanthe chlorocephala* subsp. *rosea*.

HELLEBORUS
Hellebore
RANUNCULACEAE

Genus of perennials, some of which are evergreen, grown for their winter and spring flowers. Most deciduous species retain their old leaves over winter. These should be cut off in early spring as flower buds develop. Is excellent in woodlands. Prefers partial shade and moist but well-drained soil. Propagate by seed when fresh or by division in fall or very early spring. Is prone to aphid attack in early summer. ① All parts may cause severe discomfort if ingested, and the sap may irritate skin on contact. See also feature panel p.281.

H. argutifolius, syn. *H. corsicus*, *H. lividus* subsp. *corsicus* (Corsican hellebore). Evergreen, clump-forming perennial. **H** 24in (60cm), **S** 18in (45cm). Has divided, spiny, dark green leaves. Cup-shaped, pale green flowers are borne in large clusters in winter–spring. Z6–9 H9–6. **'Pacific Frost'**, illus. p.262. **'Silver Lace'**, illus. p.262.
H. atrorubens of gardens. See *H. orientalis* subsp. *abchasicus* Early Purple Group.
H. x ballardiae 'December Dawn'. Clump-forming perennial with deep bluish-green leaves. **H** to 14in (35cm), **S** 12in (30cm). From mid-winter to early spring bears saucer-shaped, white flowers, flushed pinkish-purple, maturing to a dull metallic purple. Z6–9 H9–6.

H. corsicus. See *H. argutifolius*.
H. cyclophyllus, illus. p.283.
H. x ericsmithii. 'Bob's Best' illus. p.255. **Ivory Prince ('Walhelivor')** illus. p.256.
H. foetidus, illus. p.283. **Wester Flisk Group** illus. p.283.
H. x hybridus (Lenten rose). Evergreen, clump-forming perennial. **H** and **S** 18in (45cm). Has dense, divided foliage, above which rise nodding, cup-shaped, white, pink or purple flowers, sometimes darker spotted, in winter or early spring. Z6–9 H9–6. There is a range of single and double-flowered cultivars available in various colors, including the following: double, plum; double, slate; double, white; double, white with spots; single, apricot; single, green; single, red; single, white with spots; single, yellow; single, yellow with spots (all illus. p.281).
Ashwood Garden hybrids (double, black; double, pink; both illus. p.281).
Bradfield hybrids (double, apricot with spots, illus. p. 281). **Harvington hybrids** (double, apricot; single, white; both illus. p.281).
H. lividus. Evergreen, clump-forming perennial. **H** and **S** 18in (45cm). Has 3-parted, mid-green leaves, marbled pale green, purplish-green below, with obliquely oval, slightly toothed or entire leaflets. Produces large clusters of cup-shaped, purple-suffused, yellow-green flowers in late winter. Z8–9 H9–8. **subsp. corsicus.** See *H. argutifolius*.
H. niger (Christmas rose). Evergreen, clump-forming perennial. **H** and **S** 12in (30cm). Has divided, deep green leaves and cup-shaped, nodding, white flowers, with golden stamens, borne in winter or early spring. Z4–8 H9–1. **'HGC Josef Lemper'** illus. p.281. **'Potter's Wheel'** illus. p.281.
H. x nigercors, illus. p.281.
H. odorus, illus. p.283.
H. orientalis subsp. abchasicus Early Purple Group, syn. *H. atrorubens*. Clump-forming perennial. **H** and **S** 1ft (30cm). Shallowly cup-shaped, deep purple flowers are borne in late winter. Has palmate, deeply divided, toothed, glossy, dark green leaves. Z4–8 H8–3.
H. purpurascens, illus. p.260.
H. x sternii, illus. p.262. **'Boughton Beauty'** illus. p.283.
H. thibetanus, illus. p.256.
H. viridis (Green hellebore). Deciduous, clump-forming perennial. **H** and **S** 12in (30cm). Has divided, dark green leaves and cup-shaped, green flowers in late winter or early spring. Z6–9 H9–6.

HELONIAS
LILIACEAE/MELANTHACEAE

Genus of one species of spring-flowering perennial. Is excellent when grown in bog gardens. Requires an open, sunny position and moist to wet soil. Propagate by division in spring or by seed in fall.

H. bullata (Swamp pink). Rosetted, clump-forming perennial. **H** 15–18in (38–45cm), **S** 12in (30cm). Produces rosettes of strap-shaped, fresh green leaves, above which dense racemes of small, fragrant, star-shaped, pinkish-purple flowers are borne in spring. Z5–9 H9–5.

HELONIOPSIS

LILIACEAE/MELANTHIACEAE

Genus of spring-flowering, rosette-forming perennials. Needs partial shade and moist soil. Propagate by division in fall or by seed in fall or spring.

H. orientalis, illus. p.256.

HELWINGIA

HELWINGIACEAE

Genus of deciduous shrubs, bearing flowers and showy fruits directly on leaf surfaces, grown mainly for botanical interest. Requires separate male and female plants in order to produce fruits. Needs sun or partial shade and moist soil. Propagate by softwood cuttings in summer.

H. japonica. Deciduous, bushy, open shrub. **H** and **S** 5ft (1.5m). Oval, bright green leaves have bristly teeth. In early summer has tiny, star-shaped, green flowers at center of each leaf, followed by spherical, black fruits. Z4–9 H9–4.

Helxine soleirolii. See *Soleirolia soleirolii.*

HEMEROCALLIS

Daylily

LILIACEAE/HEMEROCALLIDACEAE

Genus of perennials, some of which are semievergreen or evergreen. Flowers, borne in succession, each last for only a day. Prefers full sun and fertile, moist soil. Propagate by division in fall or spring. Cultivars raised from seed will not come true to type; species may come true if grown in isolation from other daylilies. Slug and snail control is essential in early spring when young foliage appears. See also feature panel pp.244–5.

H. 'Always Afternoon', illus. p.244. Robust, semievergreen, clump-forming perennial. **H** 22in (55cm), **S** to 30in (75cm). In summer and again in fall produces rounded, slightly ruffled, lavender-mauve flowers, each with a dark purple band above yellow-green throat. Z3–10 H11–2.

H. 'Arctic Snow'. Deciduous, clump-forming perennial. **H** 22in (55cm), **S** 20in (50cm). Produces huge, funnel-shaped, ivory-white flowers, with green throats and black anthers, from mid-summer to early fall. Z3–10 H12–2.

H. aurantiaca. Robust, semievergreen perennial, spreading freely from underground runners. **H** 3ft (90cm), **S** 3ft (1m) or more. Produces numerous funnel-shaped, burnt-orange flowers, with yellowish midribs, over a long period in summer. Z3–10 H12–2.

H. 'Berlin Red'. Vigorous, deciduous or semievergreen, clump-forming perennial. **H** 28–36in (70–90cm), **S** 24in (60cm). In mid-summer produces open, rounded, rich velvety-red flowers with a blackish-red bloom at the margins and yellow midribs and throats. Z3–10 H12–2.

H. 'Betty Woods'. Robust, evergreen, clump-forming perennial. **H** 26in (65cm), **S** 24in (60cm). Large, peony-like, yellow flowers are borne in mid- and late summer. Z3–10 H12–2.

H. 'Black Magic', illus. p.245. Deciduous, clump-forming perennial. **H** and **S** 36in (90cm). Has star-shaped, pale-edged, dark

reddish-black flowers, with green throats, from mid-summer to early fall. Z3–10 H11–2.

H. 'Bonanza', illus. p.245. Vigorous, deciduous or semievergreen, clump-forming perennial. **H** 3ft (1m), **S** 28in (70cm). Produces open, star-like, bright yellow flowers, with strongly red-marked centers, in mid-summer. Z3–10 H11–2.

H. 'Brocaded Gown'. Semievergreen, clump-forming perennial. **H** and **S** to 2ft (60cm). In summer has rounded, ruffled, creamy-yellow flowers. Z3–10 H12–2.

H. 'Burning Daylight', illus. p.245. Robust, deciduous or semievergreen, clump-forming perennial. **H** 2¹/₂ft (75cm), **S** 2ft (60cm). Produces orange-brown flowers, with paler midribs and red marks around throat bases, over a long period in summer. Z3–10 H11–2.

H. 'Canadian Border Patrol', illus. p.244. Vigorous, semievergreen, clump-forming perennial. **H** 26in (65cm), **S** 24in (60cm). Produces masses of funnel-shaped, cream flowers, with purple throats, from mid-summer to early fall. Z3–10 H11–2.

H. 'Cartwheels', illus. p.245. Deciduous, clump-forming perennial. **H** 30in (75cm), **S** 24in (60cm). In mid-summer has trumpet-shaped, broad, deep yellow to orange flowers, with small, green throats and widely spreading petals. Z3–10 H11–2.

H. 'Cathy's Sunset', illus. p.245. Deciduous, clump-forming perennial. **H** 24in (60cm), **S** 20in (50cm). From mid-summer to early fall bears small, funnel-shaped flowers each with 3 yellow-striped, brick-red, inner petals and 3 yellow, outer petals. Z3–10 H11–2.

H. 'Cat's Cradle'. Semievergreen, clump-forming perennial. **H** 3ft (1m), **S** 2¹/₂ft (75cm). In summer produces large, spider-shaped, bright yellow flowers. Z3–10 H12–2.

H. 'Cherry Cheeks', illus. p.244. Vigorous, deciduous or semievergreen, clump-forming perennial. **H** 32in (80cm), **S** 20in (50cm). Produces bright cherry-red flowers, with white midribs, over a long period in summer. Z3–10 H11–2.

H. 'Chicago Apache'. Very vigorous, deciduous, clump-forming perennial. **H** 26in (65cm), **S** 20in (50cm). Funnel-shaped, ruffled, rich scarlet flowers, with white midribs, lemon-green throats and black anthers, are borne above prolific leaves in summer. Is very adaptable. Z3–10 H12–2.

H. 'Chicago Sunrise', illus. p.245. Vigorous, clump-forming perennial. **H** 28in (70cm), **S** 34in (85cm). Very rounded, slightly ruffled, rich yellow flowers, with faint bronze bands and darker throats, are borne in summer. Z3–10 H11–2.

H. 'Children's Festival'. Deciduous, clump-forming perennial. **H** 22in (55cm), **S** 20in (50cm). Unusually thick petals form funnel-shaped flowers, with rosy tints and apricot throats, from mid-summer to early fall. Z3–10 H12–2.

H. 'Chorus Line'. Extended-blooming, semievergreen, clump-forming perennial. **H** 20in (50cm), **S** 24in (60cm). Produces remontant, triangular, slightly fragrant, bright pink flowers, with pink- and yellow-marked petals and dark green throats, from early to mid-summer. Z3–10 H12–2.

H. 'Christmas Is'. Vigorous, deciduous, clump-forming perennial. **H** and **S** 24in

(60cm). Funnel-shaped flowers, with green throats, are produced from mid-summer to early fall.

H. 'Citrina', illus. p.245. Vigorous, coarse-leaved, clump-forming perennial. **H** and **S** 2¹/₂ft (75cm). Many large, very fragrant, trumpet-shaped, rich lemon-yellow flowers are produced at night in mid-summer; each lasts one day. Z3–10 H11–2.

H. 'Corky'. Clump-forming perennial. **H** and **S** 18in (45cm). Bears trumpet-shaped, lemon-yellow flowers, brown on outsides, in late spring and early summer. Flowers, borne prolifically, last only a day. Z3–10 H11–2.

H. 'Cream Drop', illus. p.245. Robust, deciduous or semievergreen, clump-forming perennial. **H** 24in (60cm), **S** 18in (45cm). In mid-summer produces numerous, scented, well-formed, creamy-yellow flowers, with slightly ruffled margins. Z3–10 H11–2.

H. 'Crimson Pirate'. Vigorous, deciduous, clump-forming perennial. **H** 30in (75cm), **S** 20in (50cm). Produces open, star-shaped, bright crimson-red flowers, with paler midribs, in mid- and late summer. Z3–10 H12–2.

H. 'Custard Candy'. Vigorous, deciduous, clump-forming perennial. **H** 24in (60cm), **S** 16in (40cm). In early and mid-summer produces an abundance of rounded, creamy-yellow flowers, each with a feathered band around greenish-yellow eye. Z3–10 H12–2.

H. dumortieri, illus. p.245. Compact, clump-forming perennial. **H** 1¹/₂ft (45cm), **S** 2ft (60cm). In early summer produces fragrant, trumpet-shaped, brown-backed, golden-yellow flowers. Mid-green leaves are strap-shaped, stiff and coarse. Z3–10 H11–2.

H. 'Ed Murray'. Vigorous, free-flowering, deciduous or semievergreen, clump-forming perennial. **H** 26–28in (65–70cm), **S** 20in (50cm). Has rounded, ruffled, deep maroon-red flowers, with yellowish-green throats, in early and mid-summer. Z3–10 H12–2.

H. 'Eenie Weenie'. Clump-forming perennial. **H** and **S** 1ft (30cm). Has masses of clear yellow flowers in early summer. Z3–10 H12–2.

H. flava. See *H. lilioasphodelus.*

H. 'Frans Hals', illus. p.245. Strong-growing, free-flowering, deciduous, clump-forming perennial. **H** 24in (60cm), **S** 16in (40cm). In mid- and late summer bears open, star-shaped flowers, with yellow outer petals and three cinnamon-red inner petals with yellow midribs. Z3–10 H11–2.

H. fulva (Tawny daylily), illus. p.245. Vigorous, clump-forming perennial. **H** 3ft (1m), **S** 2¹/₂ft (75cm). Trumpet-shaped, tawny-orange flowers are produced from mid- to late summer above a mound of strap-shaped, light green leaves. Z3–10 H11–2. **'Flore Pleno'** (illus. p.245), **H** 30in (75cm), has double flowers with dark red eyes. **'Kwanzo Variegated'** has leaves variably marked with white. Z3–10 H12–2.

H. 'Gentle Shepherd'. Semievergreen, clump-forming perennial. **H** 28in (70cm), **S** 24in (60cm). In early and mid-summer has ruffled, white flowers, with green throats. Z3–10 H12–2.

H. 'Golden Chimes', illus. p.245. Clump-forming perennial. **H** 2¹/₂ft (75cm), **S** 2ft (60cm). Bears small, delicate, trumpet-

shaped, golden-yellow flowers, with a brown reverse, lasting only a day, from early to mid-summer. Z3–10 H11–2.

H. 'Golden Prize'. Vigorous, deciduous, clump-forming perennial. **H** 26–28in (65–70cm), **S** 16–20in (40–50cm). Produces large, rounded, golden-yellow flowers in mid- and late summer. Z3–10 H12–2.

H. 'Grape Velvet'. Deciduous, clump-forming perennial. **H** 20in (50cm), **S** 24in (60cm). From early to late summer produces funnel-shaped flowers, each with rather pointed, deep wine-red petals, a central, paler stripe and a yellow-green throat. Z3–10 H12–2.

H. 'Green Flutter', illus. p.245. Semievergreen, clump-forming perennial. **H** 20in (50cm), **S** 16in (40cm). Produces masses of star-shaped, ruffled, canary-yellow flowers, with bright green throats, in late summer and early fall. Z3–10 H11–2.

H. 'Happy Returns'. Deciduous, clump-forming perennial. **H** 16in (40cm), **S** 24in (60cm). Bears small, fragrant, rounded flowers from early to late summer. Z3–10 H12–2.

H. 'Helle Berlinerin'. Evergreen, clump-forming perennial. **H** 30in (75cm), **S** 32in (80cm). Has rounded flowers, with a faint apricot blush and yellow throats, borne on unusually strong stems in mid-summer. Z3–10 H12–2.

H. 'Hyperion'. Clump-forming perennial. **H** and **S** 3ft (90cm). In mid-summer has very fragrant, lily-like, pale lemon-yellow flowers. Z3–10 H12–2.

H. 'Joan Senior', illus. p.244. Vigorous, semievergreen, clump-forming perennial. **H** 25in (63cm), **S** 3ft (1m). Open trumpet-shaped, almost pure white flowers are produced on well-branched stems from mid- to late summer. Z3–10 H11–2.

H. 'Jolyene Nichole'. Semievergreen, clump-forming perennial. **H** and **S** 20in (50cm). Bears rounded, ruffled, rose-pink flowers amid lush, blue-green leaves. Z3–10 H11–2.

H. 'Lady Fingers'. Semievergreen, clump-forming perennial with narrow leaves. **H** 32in (80cm), **S** 30in (75cm). In mid-summer bears spider-shaped, pale yellow-green flowers with green throats and spoon-shaped petals. Z3–10 H12–2.

H. 'Lark Song'. Vigorous, deciduous, clump-forming perennial. **H** 32–36in (80–90cm), **S** 24in (60cm). Has fragrant, open bowl-shaped, bright pale yellow flowers, on blackish stems, in mid- and late summer. Z3–10 H12–2.

H. 'Lemon Bells', illus. p.245. Evergreen, clump-forming perennial. **H** 34in (85cm), **S** 24in (60cm). Produces prolific sprays of small, orange-yellow flowers, with green-tinted throats, in mid-summer. Z3–10 H11–2.

H. lilioasphodelus, syn. *H. flava,* illus. p.245. Robust, clump-forming, spreading perennial. **H** and **S** 2ft (60cm) or more. Very fragrant, delicate, lemon- to chrome-yellow flowers, lasting only 1 or 2 days, are borne in late spring and early summer. Strap-shaped leaves are mid-green. Z3–10 H11–2.

H. 'Little Grapette', illus. p.245. Free-flowering, deciduous, clump-forming perennial. **H** 18in (45cm), **S** 12in (30cm). Has lightly ruffled, wine-purple flowers, with yellow throats, in mid- and late summer. Z3–10 H11–2.

H. **'Little Wine Cup'**, illus. p.245. Vigorous, deciduous, clump-forming perennial. **H** 18in (45cm), **S** 12in (30cm). Produces masses of lightly ruffled, wine-red flowers, with paler midribs and yellow-green throats, in early and mid-summer. Z3–10 H11–2.

H. **'Luxury Lace'**, illus. p.244. Vigorous, deciduous, clump-forming perennial. **H** 30in (75cm), **S** 16in (40cm). Has fragrant, funnel-shaped, vibrant orange flowers, with dark green throats, from mid-summer to early fall. Z3–10 H11–2.

H. **'Mallard'**. Deciduous, clump-forming perennial. **H** and **S** 24in (60cm). Produces funnel-shaped flowers, with a slender, central, pale stripe on each petal, from mid-summer to early fall. Z3–10 H12–2.

H. **'Marion Vaughn'**. Clump-forming perennial. **H** 3ft (1m), **S** 2ft (60cm). Produces fragrant, trumpet-shaped, green-throated, pale lemon-yellow flowers, in late summer, each lasting only a day. Each petal has a raised, near-white midrib. Z3–10 H12–2.

H. **'Mauna Loa'**, illus. p.245. Vigorous, free-flowering, evergreen, clump-forming perennial. **H** 22in (55cm), **S** 3ft (1m). Produces rounded, bright tangerine-orange flowers, with chartreuse throats and black anthers, in mid- to late summer. Z3–10 H11–2.

H. **'Michele Coe'**. Vigorous, evergreen or semievergreen, clump-forming perennial. **H** 28in (70cm), **S** 34in (85cm). In mid-summer has rounded, pale apricot flowers with light lavender-pink midribs. Z3–10 H12–2.

H. **'Millie Schlumpf'**. Vigorous, free-flowering, evergreen, clump-forming perennial. **H** 20in (50cm), **S** 24in (60cm). Triangular to rounded, pale pink flowers, with deeper pink bands and green throats, are borne from early to mid-summer. Z3–10 H12–2.

H. **minor** (Grass-leaved daylily). Compact, clump-forming perennial. **H** 16in (40cm), **S** 18in (45cm). In early summer bears fragrant, trumpet-shaped, lemon-yellow flowers, with tawny-backed, outer petals. Has narrowly strap-shaped, mid-green leaves that die back in early fall. Z3–10 H12–2.

H. **'Missenden'**, illus. p.245. Vigorous, deciduous, clump-forming perennial. **H** 3¹/₂ft (1.1m), **S** 24–28in (60–70cm). In mid-summer has large, funnel-shaped, rich velvety-red flowers with a velvety, black sheen and yellow midribs. Z3–10 H11–2.

H. **'Neyron Rose'**, illus. p.244. Vigorous, deciduous, clump-forming perennial. **H** 3ft (1m), **S** 24–28in (60–70cm). In early and mid-summer has pink-suffused, orange-brown flowers, with white midribs. Z3–10 H11–2.

H. **'Night Beacon'**, illus. p.244. Evergreen, clump-forming perennial. **H** 28in (70cm), **S** 30in (75cm). In early and mid-summer produces rounded, very dark burgundy-black flowers, with black-purple bands, lemon-green throats and pearl-white midribs. Z3–10 H11–2.

H. **'Pardon Me'**, illus. p.244. Deciduous, clump-forming perennial. **H** 18in (45cm), **S** 24in (60cm). Small, fragrant, funnel-shaped, bright burgundy-red flowers, with greenish-yellow throats, are borne from mid-summer to early fall. Z3–10 H11–2.

H. **'Pink Damask'**, illus. p.244. Vigorous, deciduous, free-flowering, clump-forming

perennial. **H** 3ft (1m), **S** 24–28in (60–70cm). Produces masses of rich salmon-pink flowers in summer. Z3–10 H11–2.

H. **'Prairie Blue Eyes'**, illus. p.244. Semievergreen, clump-forming perennial. **H** 32in (80cm), **S** 36in (90cm). In mid-summer produces lavender flowers, banded with blue-purple, that have green throats. Z3–10 H11–2.

H. **'Real Wind'**. Vigorous, free-flowering, evergreen, clump-forming perennial with dense foliage. **H** 26in (65cm), **S** 3ft (1m). Produces triangular to rounded, pale buff to salmon-pink flowers, with bold rose-pink eyes, from mid- to late summer. Z3–10 H12–2.

H. **'Red Precious'**, illus. p.235.

H. **'Rose Emily'**. Semievergreen, clump-forming perennial. **H** and **S** 18in (45cm). In mid-summer bears rounded, rose-pink flowers with ruffled margined petals and pale green throats. Z3–10 H12–2.

H. **'Ruffled Apricot'**. Slow-growing, clump-forming perennial. In mid-summer produces large, deep apricot flowers with lavender-pink midribs and ruffled petal margins. Z3–10 H12–2.

H. **'Scarlet Oak'**. Vigorous, semievergreen, clump-forming perennial. **H** 3¹/₂ft (1.1m), **S** 24–28in (60–70cm). In mid- and late summer has open rounded, scarlet flowers, with white midribs. Z3–10.

H. **'Scarlet Orbit'**. Semievergreen, clump-forming perennial. **H** 20in (50cm), **S** 26in (65cm). Scarlet flowers, with green throats, open flat in mid-summer. Z3–10 H12–2.

H. **'Siloam Baby Talk'**, illus. p.244. Vigorous, free-flowering, deciduous, clump-forming perennial. **H** 14–16in (35–40cm), **S** 8–10in (20–25cm). Has rounded, ruffled-margined, creamy-pink flowers, with pale purple bands above bright green throats, in mid-summer. Z3–10 H11–2.

H. **'Siloam Ethel Smith'**. Evergreen, clump-forming perennial. **H** 20in (50cm), **S** 18in (45cm). In mid-summer bears masses of rounded, creamy-beige flowers, with triangular, red, yellow and olive-green eyes. Z3–10

H. **'Siloam Virginia Henson'**. Clump-forming perennial. **H** 18in (45cm), **S** 26in (65cm). In early summer bears rounded, ruffled, creamy-pink flowers banded with rose-pink and with green throats. Z3–10 H12–2.

H. **'Solano Bulls Eye'**. Vigorous, free-flowering, evergreen, clump-forming perennial. **H** 20in (50cm), **S** 30in (75cm). Produces rounded, bright yellow flowers, with deep brownish-purple eyes, over a long period from early to late summer. Z3–10 H12–2.

H. **'Stafford'**, illus. p.245. Vigorous, evergreen, clump-forming perennial. **H** 28in (70cm), **S** 3ft (1m). In mid-summer bears masses of star-shaped, scarlet flowers with yellow midribs and throats. Z3–10 H11–2.

H. **'Stoke Poges'**, illus. p.244. Deciduous, clump-forming perennial. **H** 28in (70cm), **S** 20in (50cm). In mid-summer has fragrant, funnel-shaped, salmon-pink flowers, with reflexed petal tips and a deep pink zone around each golden throat. Z3–10 H11–2.

H. **'Strawberry Candy'**. Robust, deciduous or semievergreen, clump-forming perennial. **H** 30in (75cm), **S** 20in

(50cm). In early and mid-summer bears bright apricot-pink flowers, with red picotee margins and ruby-red marks around yellowish throats. Z3–10 H12–2.

H. **'Strutter's Ball'**. Deciduous, clump-forming perennial. **H** and **S** 24in (60cm). Has funnel-shaped, rich deep, blue-purple flowers, each with a silvery zone above small, lemon-yellow throat, from mid-summer to early fall. Z3–10 H12–2.

H. **'Summer Wine'**, illus. p.244. Strong-growing, deciduous, clump-forming perennial. **H** 24in (60cm), **S** 18in (45cm). In early and mid-summer bears open, soft purple flowers, with yellowish-green throats and very pale purple to white midribs. Broad inner petals are slightly ruffled. Z3–10 H11–2.

H. **'Super Purple'**. Clump-forming perennial. **H** 27in (68cm), **S** 26in (65cm). Bears rounded, ruffled, velvety, red-purple flowers, with lime-green throats, in mid-summer. Z3–10 H12–2.

H. **'Whichford'**, illus. p.245. Deciduous, clump-forming perennial. **H** 28in (70cm), **S** 20in (50cm). Fragrant, slightly star-shaped, green-budded, clear lemon-yellow flowers, with green throats, are borne on sturdy stems from mid-summer. Z3–10 H11–2.

H. **'White Temptation'**. Semievergreen, clump-forming perennial. **H** 30in (75cm), **S** 26in (65cm). Funnel-shaped, white flowers, with slightly crinkled edges and green throats, are produced from mid-summer to early fall. Z3–10 H12–2.

HEMIGRAPHIS

ACANTHACEAE

Genus of annuals and evergreen perennials, usually grown for their foliage. Prefers bright but not direct sunlight and moist but well-drained soil. Water frequently in growing season, less in winter. Regularly cut back straggly stems to tidy. Propagate by stem cuttings in spring or summer.

H. **repanda**, illus. p.473.

HEMIORCHIS

ZINGIBERACEAE

Genus of herbaceous, rhizomatous perennials, grown for their orchid-like flowers, which emerge above ground before the leaves. Needs shade and rich, moist but well-drained soil. Is more tolerant of winter wet than most gingers, so water occasionally during dormancy. Propagate by division of the rhizome in early spring.

H. **patlingii**. Herbaceous, rhizomatous perennial. **H** and **S** 12in (30cm). Stem, 4–6in (10–15cm) long, produces up to 20 flowers, opening in succession in spring, each with 3 pale brown outer lobes surrounding a deep red-veined, golden-yellow inner lobe. Has broadly lance-shaped, glossy, mid-green leaves, to 6in (15cm) long. Z3–10 H12–2.

HEPATICA

RANUNCULACEAE

Genus of very variable perennials, some of which are semievergreen. Flowers are produced in early spring before new leaves are properly formed. Needs partial shade

and deep, rich, moist soil. Sturdy, much-branched rootstock resents disturbance. Propagate by seed when fresh or by division or removing sideshoots in spring.

H. **angulosa**. See *H. transsilvanica.*

H. **x media 'Ballardii'**. Slow-growing, dome-shaped perennial. **H** 4in (10cm), **S** 12in (30cm). Has rounded, 3-lobed, stalked, soft green leaves and, in early spring, shallowly cup-shaped, many-petaled, intense blue flowers. Fully double, colored forms are also known. Propagate only by division. Z3–8 H8–1.

H. **nobilis**, syn. *H. triloba, Anemone hepatica*. Slow-growing, semievergreen, dome-shaped perennial. **H** 3in (8cm), **S** 4–5in (10–12cm). Bears rounded, 3-lobed, fleshy, mid-green leaves. Shallowly cup-shaped, many-petaled flowers—white through pink to carmine, pale to deep blue or purple—are produced in early spring. Fully double, colored forms are also known. Is excellent in a woodland or rock garden. Z5–8 H8–4. **var. japonica** illus. p.355.

H. **transsilvanica**, syn. *H. angulosa.* Semievergreen, spreading perennial. **H** 3in (8cm), **S** 8in (20cm). Shallowly cup-shaped, many-petaled flowers, varying from blue to white or pink, are produced in early spring amid rounded, 3-lobed, hairy, green leaves. Fully double, colored forms are also known. Z5–8 H8–5.

H. **triloba**. See *H. nobilis.*

HERBERTIA

IRIDACEAE

Genus of spring-flowering bulbs, grown mainly for their iris-like flowers. Requires full sun and well-drained soil. Reduce watering when bulb dies down after flowering. Propagate by seed in fall.

H. **pulchella**. Spring-flowering bulb. **H** 4–6in (10–15cm), **S** 1¹/₄ –2in (3–5cm). Leaves are narrowly lance-shaped, pleated, erect and basal. Bears a succession of upward-facing, violet-blue flowers, 2–2¹/₂in (5–6cm) wide and usually with dark-spotted centers. Z10–11 H12–10.

HERMANNIA

STERCULIACEAE/MALVACEAE

Genus of evergreen subshrubs and shrubs, grown mainly for their flowers. Prefers full light and fertile, well-drained soil. Water container plants freely when in full growth, moderately at other times. Tip prune young plants to produce well-branched specimens. Propagate by softwood or greenwood cuttings in late spring or summer.

H. **candicans**. See *H. incana.*

H. **incana**, syn. *H. candicans.* Evergreen, bushy subshrub. **H** and **S** 24in (60cm) or more. Oval to oblong leaves are covered with white down beneath. Produces small, nodding, bell-shaped, bright yellow flowers, in terminal clusters, to 6in (15cm) long, in spring–summer. Z12–15 H12–10.

HERMODACTYLUS

IRIDACEAE

Genus of one species of spring-flowering tubers, with elongated, finger-like rootstock, grown mainly for its iris-like flowers. Requires a hot, sunny site, where tubers will ripen well in summer, and well-drained soil. Grows particularly successfully on hot, chalky soils. Propagate by division in late summer.

H. tuberosus, syn. *Iris tuberosa*, illus. p.406.

HESPERALOE

AGAVACEAE/ASPARAGACEAE

Genus of basal-rosetted, perennial succulents, grown for their very narrow, strap-shaped, grooved, dark green leaves, which often have peeling, white fibers at their margins. Is closely related to *Agave* and *Yucca*. Prefers sun and very well-drained soil. Propagate by seed or division in spring or summer, or from offsets, freely produced at base.

H. parviflora, syn. *Yucca parviflora*, illus. p.484.

HESPERANTHA

IRIDACEAE

Genus of spring-flowering corms, grown for their spikes of small, funnel- or cup-shaped flowers. Needs full sun and well-drained soil. Plant in fall, water through winter and dry off corms after flowering. Propagate by seed in fall or spring.

H. buhrii. See *H. cucullata*.

H. coccinea. See *Schizostylis coccinea*.

H. cucullata, syn. *H. buhrii*. Spring-flowering corm. **H** 8–12in (20–30cm), **S** 1¼–2in (3–5cm). Has linear, erect leaves on lower part of branched stems, each of which produces a spike of up to 7 cup-shaped, white flowers, flushed pink or purple outside, that open only at evening. Z10–11 H12–10.

HESPERIS

CRUCIFERAE/BRASSICACEAE

Genus of late spring- or summer-flowering annuals and perennials. Requires sun and well-drained soil. *H. matronalis* tolerates poor soil. Tends to become woody at base, so raise new stock from seed every few years. Propagate by basal cuttings in spring or by seed in fall or spring.

H. matronalis, illus. p.230.

HESPEROCALLIS

LILIACEAE/HYACINTHACEAE

Genus of spring- to summer-flowering bulbs. Needs a sunny, well-drained site. Is difficult to cultivate in all but warm, dry areas; in cool, damp climates, protect in a cool greenhouse. Requires ample water in spring, followed by a hot, dry period during its summer dormancy. Propagate by seed in fall.

H. undulata. Spring- to summer-flowering bulb. **H** 8–20in (20–50cm), **S** 4–6in (10–15cm). Has a basal cluster of long, narrow, wavy-margined, semierect or prostrate leaves. Sturdy stems each bear a spike of upward-facing, funnel-shaped, white flowers, with a central, green stripe along each of the 6 petals. Z9–10 H10–9.

Hesperoyucca. See *Yucca*.

HETEROCENTRON

SYN. HEERIA

MELASTOMATACEAE

Genus of evergreen, summer- and fall-flowering perennials and shrubs. Requires sun and well-drained soil. Propagate by softwood or stem-tip cuttings in late winter or early spring.

H. elegans, syn. *Schizocentron elegans*, illus. p.472.

HETEROMELES

ROSACEA

Genus of one species of evergreen tree or large shrub, grown mainly for its showy clusters of holly-like fruits. Requires fertile, well-drained soil in full sun, with protection from cold, drying winds in winter. Propagate by seed in fall or by semiripe cuttings in summer.

H. arbutifolia. See *H. salicifolia*.

H. salicifolia, syn. *H. arbutifolia*, *Photinia arbutifolia*. Evergreen, bushy, spreading shrub or tree. **H** 20ft (6m), **S** 25ft (8m). Has oblong, sharply toothed, leathery, glossy, dark green leaves. Broad, flat heads of small, 5-petaled, white flowers, produced in late summer, are succeeded by large clusters of rounded, red fruits.

HEUCHERA

Coral flower

SAXIFRAGACEAE

Genus of evergreen, summer-flowering perennials forming large clumps of leaves, that are often tinted bronze or purple. Makes good groundcover. Prefers partial shade and moist but well-drained soil. Propagate species by seed in fall or by division in fall or spring, cultivars by division only, using young, outer portions of crown. See also feature panel p.282.

H. 'Amber Waves', illus. p.282. Evergreen, clump-forming perennial. **H** 8–12in (20–30cm), **S** to 20in (50cm). Rounded, lobed, lightly ruffled, orange-yellow leaves are pale burgundy underneath. In summer produces loose sprays of small, pendent, bell-shaped, light-rose flowers. Z3–8 H8–1.

H. americana 'Harry Hay'. Vigorous, evergreen, clump-forming perennial. **H** 20–39in (50–100cm), **S** 32in (80cm) or more. Has large, rounded, lobed, purplish-brown leaves. In summer produces tall spires of pendent, bell-shaped, white flowers. Z4–8 H8–1.

H. 'Beauty Colour', illus. p.282. Evergreen, clump-forming perennial. **H** 8–12in (20–30cm), **S** to 20in (50cm). Rounded, lobed, burgundy-veined leaves are marbled with silver and bordered with green. Leaf color intensifies in cold periods. In summer produces loose, arching sprays of small, pendent, bell-shaped, ivory flowers. Z3–8 H8–1.

H. 'Black Beauty', illus. p.282. Evergreen, clump-forming, rather compact perennial. **H** 8–10in (20–25cm), **S** to 10in (25cm). Rounded, lobed, ruffled, glossy, dark purple-black leaves are held rather upright. In summer produces loose sprays of small, pendent, bell-shaped, white flowers. Z3–8 H8–1.

H. 'Blackbird', illus. p.282. Evergreen, clump-forming perennial. **H** 10–12in

(25–30cm), **S** to 12in (30cm). Has rounded, lobed, rather ruffled, maroon-brown leaves. In summer produces loose sprays of small, pendent, bell-shaped, rose-pink flowers. Z3–8 H8–1.

H. 'Can-can', illus. p.282. Vigorous, evergreen, clump-forming perennial. **H** and **S** 20in (50cm). Rounded, lobed, ruffled, dark-veined, silver-gray leaves are rich wine-red beneath; leaves turn pinkish with cooler conditions. In summer produces loose sprays of small, pendent, bell-shaped, ivory flowers. Z3–8 H8–1.

H. 'Chocolate Ruffles', illus. p.282. Evergreen, clump-forming perennial. **H** and **S** 12in (30cm). Rounded, lobed, ruffled, chocolate-brown leaves have burgundy undersides. In summer produces loose sprays of small, pendent, bell-shaped, white flowers. Z3–8 H8–1.

H. 'Cinnabar Silver', illus. p.282. Evergreen, clump-forming perennial. **H** 12in (30cm), **S** 20in (50cm). Forms a mound of rounded, lobed, purple-flushed, silver leaves; the purple color intensifies in cool conditions. In summer produces loose sprays of small, pendent, bell-shaped, red flowers. Z3–8 H8–1.

H. 'Citronelle'. Evergreen, clump-forming perennial. **H** and **S** 20in (50cm). Has rounded, lobed, lime-green leaves. In summer produces loose sprays of small, pendent, bell-shaped, white flowers. Z4–8 H8–1.

H. 'Coral Cloud'. Evergreen, clump-forming perennial. **H** 18–30in (45–75cm), **S** 12–18in (30–45cm). In early summer bears long, feathery sprays of small, pendent, bell-shaped, coral-red flowers. Leaves are rounded, lobed, toothed, glistening and dark green. Z4–8 H8–1.

H. Crème Brûlée ('Tnheu041'), illus. p.282. Evergreen, clump-forming perennial. **H** 16–20in (40–50cm), **S** 16in (40cm). Rounded, lobed, glowing caramel, bronze and gold leaves fade in intensity as they age. In summer produces loose sprays of small, pendent, bell-shaped, white flowers. Z3–8 H8–1.

H. cylindrica 'Greenfinch'. Evergreen, clump-forming perennial. **H** 18–24in (45–60cm), **S** 20in (50cm). Has rosettes of lobed, heart-shaped leaves and, in summer, spikes of small, bell-shaped, pale green or greenish-white flowers. Z4–8 H8–1.

H. Ebony and Ivory ('E and I'), illus. p.282. Evergreen, clump-forming, rather compact perennial. **H** and **S** 12in (30cm). Has rounded, lobed, rather ruffled, ebony-black leaves. In summer produces numerous loose sprays of small, pendent, bell-shaped, ivory-white flowers. Z3–8 H8–1.

H. 'Firebird'. Evergreen, compact perennial. **H** 2ft (60cm), **S** 1ft (30cm). In early summer bears long, feathery sprays of small, pendent, bell-shaped, crimson-scarlet flowers. Leaves are rounded, lobed, toothed and dark green. Z4–8 H8–1.

H. 'Georgia Peach', illus. p.282. Evergreen, clump-forming perennial. **H** 12in (30cm), **S** 20in (50cm). Large, rounded, lobed, silvery pinkish-peach leaves are most vibrant when young. In summer produces loose sprays of small, pendent, bell-shaped, white flowers. Z3–8 H8–1.

H. 'Ginger Ale', illus. p.282. Evergreen, clump-forming perennial. **H** 12–16in

(30–40cm), **S** 12in (30cm). Has rounded, lobed, silvery-white-marbled, pale orange leaves. In summer produces loose sprays of small, pendent, bell-shaped, creamy-pink flowers. Z3–8 H8–1.

H. 'Green Spice', illus. p.282. Evergreen, clump-forming perennial. **H** 8–12in (20–30cm), **S** 12in (30cm). Rounded, lobed, silvery-green leaves have dark purple veins and dark gray edges. In summer produces loose sprays of small, pendent, bell-shaped, greenish-white flowers. Z3–8 H8–1.

H. Key Lime Pie ('Tnheu042'). Evergreen, clump-forming perennial. **H** and **S** 16in (40cm). Has rounded, lobed, lime-green leaves. In summer produces loose sprays of small, pendent, bell-shaped, pinkish-white flowers. Z4–8 H8–1.

H. 'Lime Rickey', illus. p.282. Strong-growing, evergreen, clump-forming perennial. **H** 16–20in (40–50cm), **S** 20in (50cm). Rounded, lobed, ruffled, lime-green leaves are brightest in spring. In summer produces loose sprays of small, pendent, bell-shaped, white flowers. Z3–8 H8–1.

H. 'Midnight Rose', illus. p.282. Evergreen, clump-forming perennial. **H** and **S** 20in (50cm). Rounded, lobed, dark purple leaves have pink speckles that get larger as the season progresses and may fade to cream. In summer produces loose sprays of small, pendent, bell-shaped, cream flowers. Z3–8 H8–1.

H. 'Obsidian'. Evergreen, clump-forming perennial. **H** and **S** 20in (50cm). Has rounded, lobed, smooth, glossy, dark purple-black leaves. In summer produces loose sprays of small, pendent, bell-shaped, ivory flowers on red stems. Z4–8 H8–1.

H. 'Palace Purple'. Clump-forming perennial. **H** and **S** 18in (45cm). Has persistent, heart-shaped, deep purple leaves and sprays of small, white flowers in summer. Cut leaves last well in water. Z3–8 H8–1.

H. 'Peach Flambé', illus. p.282. Evergreen, clump-forming perennial. **H** and **S** 20in (50cm). Large, rounded, lobed, smooth, rich peach leaves develop purplish hues in winter. In summer produces loose sprays of small, pendent, bell-shaped, white flowers. Z3–8 H8–1.

H. 'Pearl Drops'. Evergreen, clump-forming perennial. **H** 2ft (60cm), **S** 1ft (30cm). In early summer bears small, pendent, bell-shaped, white flowers tinged pink. Leaves are rounded, lobed, toothed and dark green. Z3–8 H8–1.

H. 'Peppermint Spice', illus. p.282. Evergreen, clump-forming, rather compact perennial. **H** 16in (40cm), **S** 12–16in (30–40cm). Has rounded, lobed, purple-veined, silver green leaves. In summer produces loose sprays of small, pendent, bell-shaped, soft pink flowers. Z3–8 H8–1.

H. 'Pewter Moon', illus. p.282. Evergreen, clump-forming perennial. **H** 16in (40cm), **S** 12–20in (30–50cm). Rounded, lobed, veined, silvery-green leaves have deep maroon undersides. In summer produces loose sprays of small, pendent, bell-shaped, soft pink flowers on maroon stems. Z3–8 H8–1.

H. 'Plum Pudding', illus. p.280.

H. 'Purple Petticoats', illus. p.282. Evergreen, clump-forming perennial. **H** 16in (40cm), **S** 12–20in (30–50cm). Rounded, lobed, ruffled, rich purple leaves are a brighter reddish-purple beneath. In summer produces loose sprays of small, pendent, bell-shaped, cream flowers. Z3–8 H8–1.

H. 'Red Spangles'. Evergreen, clump-forming perennial. **H** and **S** 12in (30cm). Has heart-shaped, purplish-green leaves and spikes of small, bell-shaped, crimson-scarlet flowers in summer. Z3–8 H8–1.

H. sanguinea 'Snow Storm', illus. p.282. Slow-growing, evergreen, clump-forming perennial. **H** 16in (40cm), **S** 12–16in (30–40cm). Rather small, rounded, lobed, green leaves each have a large, creamy-white center. In summer produces loose sprays of small, pendent, bell-shaped, coral-pink flowers. May be short-lived. Z3–8 H8–1.

H. 'Scintillation'. Evergreen, clump-forming perennial. **H** 18–30in (45–75cm), **S** 12–18in (30–45cm). In early summer produces long, feathery sprays of small, pendent, bell-shaped, deep pink flowers, each rimmed with coral-pink. Bears rounded, lobed, toothed, dark green leaves. Z3–8 H8–1.

H. 'Silver Scrolls', illus. p.282. Evergreen, clump-forming perennial. **H** 20in (50cm), **S** 16–20in (40–50cm). Rounded, lobed, silver and burgundy leaves are at their most vibrant when young. In summer produces loose sprays of small, pendent, bell-shaped, pinkish-white flowers. Z3–8 H8–1.

H. 'Southern Comfort', illus. p.282. Strong-growing, evergreen, clump-forming perennial. **H** 20–24in (50–60cm), **S** 24–28in (60–70cm). Large, rounded, lobed, rather hairy, brownish-peach leaves age to burnt-copper. In summer produces loose sprays of small, pendent, bell-shaped, white flowers. Z3–8 H8–1.

H. 'Stormy Seas'. Evergreen, clump-forming perennial. **H** 16in (40cm), **S** 16–20in (40–50cm). Rounded, lobed, gray-silver-mottled, glossy, maroon-purple leaves, aging to bronze-green, have vivid purple undersides. In summer produces loose sprays of small, pendent, bell-shaped, cream flowers. Z4–8 H8–1.

H. 'Tiramisu', illus. p.282. Evergreen, clump-forming perennial. **H** 12–16in (30–40cm), **S** 12in (30cm). Has rounded, lobed, red-flushed, copper-yellow leaves. In summer produces loose sprays of small, pendent, bell-shaped, pinkish-cream flowers. Z3–8 H8–1.

H. 'Tnheu041'. See *H.* CRÈME BRÛLÉE.
H. 'Tnheu042'. See *H.* KEY LIME PIE.

x HEUCHERELLA

SAXIFRAGACEAE

Hybrid genus (*Heuchera* x *Tiarella*) of evergreen, mainly late spring- and summer-flowering perennials. Prefers partial shade and needs fertile, well-drained soil. Propagate by basal cuttings in spring or by division in spring or fall. See also feature panel p.282.

x H. alba 'Bridget Bloom'. Evergreen, clump-forming perennial. **H** 18in (45cm), **S** 12in (30cm). Has dense, bright green leaves and, in early summer, many feathery sprays of tiny, bell-shaped, rose-pink flowers, which continue intermittently until fall. Z5–8 H8–5.

x H. tiarelloides, illus. p.264. **'Alabama Sunrise'** is an evergreen, groundcover perennial. **H** and **S** 12in (30cm). Rounded,

deeply lobed, red-veined, golden-yellow young leaves fade to bright green and develop orange tints in fall. In early summer produces feathery sprays of small, bell-shaped, pendent, white flowers. **'Dayglow Pink'**, **H** and **S** 12–16in (30–40cm), has dark-veined, rich green leaves and numerous feathery sprays of bright pink flowers. **'Heart of Darkness'**, **H** and **S** 16in (40cm), has green leaves, each with a large dark purple central zone surrounded by silver-gray, and produces white flowers. **'Kimono'** (illus. p.282), **H** and **S** 16in (40cm), is vigorous and has very deeply lobed, purple-veined, silvery-purple and green leaves and loose sprays of cream flowers. **'Stoplight'** (illus. p.282), **H** and **S** 16in (40cm), has red-veined, bright yellow leaves and white flowers.

Hexastylis. See *Asarum.*

HIBBERTIA

SYN. CANDOLLEA

DILLENIACEAE

Genus of evergreen shrubs and twining climbers, grown for their flowers. Needs full light or partial shade and well-drained soil. Water freely in summer, less at other times. Provide stems with support. Thin out congested growth in spring. Propagate by semiripe cuttings in summer.

H. cuneiformis, illus. p.458.
H. scandens, syn. *H. volubilis.* Vigorous, evergreen, twining climber. **H** 20ft (6m). Has oblong to lance-shaped, glossy, deep green leaves, 1½–3½in (4–9cm) long. Saucer-shaped, bright yellow flowers, 1½in (4cm) across, are produced mainly in summer. Z12–15 H12–10.
H. volubilis. See *H. scandens.*

HIBISCUS

MALVACEAE

Genus of evergreen or deciduous shrubs, trees, perennials and annuals, grown for their flowers. Needs full sun and rich, well-drained soil. Water container specimens freely when in full growth, moderately at other times. Tip prune young plants to promote bushiness; cut old plants back hard in spring. Propagate by seed in spring, shrubs and trees by greenwood cuttings in late spring or by semiripe cuttings in summer, perennials by division in fall or spring. Whitefly may cause problems.

H. mutabilis (Confederate rose, Cotton rose). Evergreen, erect to spreading shrub or tree. **H** and **S** 10–15ft (3–5m). Rounded leaves have 5–7 shallow lobes. In summer–fall bears funnel-shaped, sometimes double, white or pink flowers, 3–4in (7–10cm) wide, that age from pink to deep red. In light frost dies back to ground level. Z10–11 H12–8.

H. rosa-sinensis (Chinese hibiscus, Hawaiian hibiscus, Rose of China). Evergreen, rounded, leafy shrub. **H** and **S** 5–10ft (1.5–3m) or more. Oval, glossy leaves are coarsely serrated. Produces funnel-shaped, bright crimson flowers, 4in (10cm) wide, mainly in summer but also in spring and fall. Z14–15 H12–1. Many color selections are grown including **'The President'**, illus. p.455.

H. schizopetalus (Japanese lantern). Evergreen, upright, spreading, loose shrub. **H** to 10ft (3m), **S** 6ft (2m) or more. Has oval,

serrated leaves and, in summer, pendent, long-stalked flowers, 2½in (6cm) wide, with deeply fringed, reflexed, pink or red petals. May be trained as a climber. Z13–15 H12–10.

H. syriacus (Rose of Sharon). **'Blue Bird'.** See *H. syriacus* 'Oiseau Bleu'. **'Diana'** is a deciduous, upright shrub. **H** 10ft (3m). **S** 6ft (2m). Has oval, lobed, deep green leaves and very large, trumpet-shaped, pure white flowers, with wavy-edged petals, from late summer to mid-fall. Z5–9 H9–1. **'Oiseau Bleu'**, syn. *H. syriacus* 'Blue Bird', illus. p.138. **'Red Heart'**, illus. p.132. **'Woodbridge'**, illus. p.136.

H. trionum, illus. p.300.

HIDALGOA

Climbing dahlia

COMPOSITAE/ASTERACEAE

Genus of evergreen, leaf stalk climbers, grown for their single, dahlia-like flower heads. Requires full light and rich, well-drained soil. Water freely when in full growth, less at other times. Needs support. In spring, thin out crowded stems or cut back all growth to ground level. Propagate by softwood cuttings in spring. Aphids, red spider mite and whitefly may be troublesome.

H. wercklei. Moderately vigorous, evergreen, leaf stalk climber. **H** 15ft (5m) or more. Oval leaves are divided into 3, 5, or more, coarsely serrated leaflets. In summer bears dahlia-like, scarlet flower heads, yellowish in bud. Z11–13 H12–10.

HIERACIUM

Hawkweed

COMPOSITAE/ASTERACEAE

Genus of perennials; most are weeds, but the species described below is grown for its foliage. Needs sun and poor, well-drained soil. Propagate by seed or division in fall or spring.

H. lanatum, illus. p.277.

HIMALAYACALAMUS

GRAMINEAE/POACEAE

See also GRASSES, BAMBOOS, RUSHES and SEDGES.

H. falconeri, syn. *Arundinaria falconeri, Drepanostachyum falconeri, Thamnocalamus falconeri.* Evergreen, clump-forming bamboo. **H** 15–30ft (5–10m), **S** 3ft (1m). Greenish-brown stems have a dark purple ring beneath each node. Has yellowish-green leaves, 4–6in (10–15cm) long, without visible tessellation, and unimportant flower spikes. Z9–11 H12–8.

HIPPEASTRUM

Amaryllis

AMARYLLIDACEAE

Genus of bulbs, grown for their huge, funnel-shaped flowers. Is often incorrectly cultivated as *Amaryllis.* Requires full sun or partial shade and well-drained soil. Plant large-flowered hybrids in fall, half burying bulb; after the leaves die away, dry off bulb until following fall. Smaller, summer-flowering species should be kept dry while dormant in winter. Propagate by seed in spring or by offsets in spring (summer-

flowering species) or fall (large-flowered hybrids). ① All parts may cause mild stomach upset if ingested.

H. advenum. See *Rhodophiala advena.*
H. 'Apple Blossom', illus. p.414.
H. aulicum, syn. *H. morelianum*, illus. p.414.
H. 'Belinda'. Winter- and spring-flowering bulb with a basal leaf cluster. **H** 12–20in (30–50cm), **S** 12in (30cm). Is similar to *H. aulicum*, but flowers are deep velvety-red throughout, stained darker towards centers. Z14–15 H12–1.
H. 'Black Pearl'. Winter-flowering bulb. **H** 20in (50cm), **S** 12in (30cm). Has a sturdy stem bearing 4–5 large, funnel-shaped, dark maroon flowers and strap-shaped, semierect, basal leaves that develop with or after the flowers. Z14–15 H12–1.
H. 'Bouquet'. Winter- and spring-flowering bulb with a basal leaf cluster. **H** 12–20in (30–50cm), **S** 12in (30cm). Is similar to *H. aulicum*, but has very wide, salmon-pink flowers, with deep red veins and red centers. Z14–15 H12–1.
H. morelianum. See *H. aulicum.*
H. 'Orange Sovereign'. Winter- to spring-flowering bulb. **H** 12–20in (30–50cm), **S** 12in (30cm). Has strap-shaped, semierect, gray-green, basal leaves produced as, or just after, flowers form. Sturdy stem bears head of 2–6 rich orange-red flowers. Z14–15 H12–10.
H. procerum. See *Worsleya rayneri.*
H. 'Red Lion', illus. p.414.
H. reginae (Mexican lily). Summer-flowering bulb. **H** to 20in (50cm), **S** 8–10in (20–25cm). Flower stem produces a head of 2–4 scarlet flowers, 4–6in (10–15cm) across, with star-shaped, green mark in throat. Long, strap-shaped, semierect leaves develop at base after flowering has finished. Z11–12 H12–1.
H. rutilum. See *H. striatum.*
H. striatum, syn. *H. rutilum.* Spring- and summer-flowering bulb. **H** 12in (30cm), **S** 8–10in (20–25cm). Has strap-shaped, semierect, bright green, basal leaves. Funnel-shaped flowers have pointed, scarlet petals with central, green stripes. Z14–15 H12–10.
H. 'Striped', illus. p.414.
H. vittatum (St. Joseph's lily). Vigorous, spring-flowering bulb. **H** 3ft (1m), **S** 1ft (30cm). Leaves are broadly strap-shaped, semierect and basal. Sturdy, leafless stem precedes leaves and terminates in a head of 2–6 red-striped, white flowers, 5–8in (12–20cm) across. Z13–15 H12–10.
H. 'White Dazzler'. Winter- and spring-flowering bulb with a basal leaf cluster. **H** 12–20in (30–50cm), **S** 12in (30cm). Is similar to *H. aulicum*, but has pure white flowers. Z14–15 H12–1.

HIPPOCREPIS

Horseshoe vetch, Vetch

LEGUMINOSAE/PAPILIONACEAE

Genus of annuals and perennials, grown for their pealike flowers. Requires full sun and well-drained soil. Propagate by seed in spring or fall. Self-seeds readily. May be invasive.

H. comosa, illus. p.373. **'E.R. Janes'** is a vigorous, prostrate, woody-based perennial. **H** 2–3in (5–8cm), **S** 6in (15cm) or more. Rooting stems bear small, loose spikes of pealike, yellow flowers from late spring to late summer. Leaves are divided, with 3–8 pairs of narrowly oval leaflets.

HIPPOPHAE

ELAEAGNACEAE

Genus of deciduous shrubs and trees, with inconspicuous flowers, grown for their foliage and showy fruits. Separate male and female plants are required in order to obtain fruits. Is suitable for coastal areas, where it is wind-resistant and excellent when grown as hedging. Needs sun and is especially useful for poor, dry or very sandy soil. Propagate by softwood cuttings in summer or by seed in fall. See also feature panel p.142.

H. rhamnoides (Sea buckthorn), illus. p.142. Deciduous, bushy, arching shrub or small tree. **H** and **S** 20ft (6m). Has narrow, silvery leaves. Tiny, yellow flowers borne in mid-spring are followed in fall by bright orange berries on female plants. Z3–8 H8–1.

HOHERIA

MALVACEAE

Genus of deciduous, semievergreen or evergreen trees and shrubs, grown for their flowers produced mainly in summer. Requires sun or semi-shade and fertile, well-drained soil. Propagate by semiripe cuttings in summer or by seed in fall.

H. angustifolia, illus. p.85.

H. 'Glory of Amlwch'. Semievergreen, spreading tree: **H** 22ft (7m), **S** 20ft (6m). Has long, narrowly oval, glossy, bright green leaves and a profusion of large, 5-petaled, white flowers from mid- to late summer. Z9–10 H10–9.

H. lyallii, illus. p.85.

H. populnea (Lacebark). Evergreen, spreading tree. **H** 40ft (12m), **S** 30ft (10m). Bears narrowly oval, glossy, dark green leaves. Produces dense clusters of 5-petaled, white flowers in late summer and early fall. Bark on mature trees is pale brown and white and often flaky. Z9–10 H10–9.

H. sexstylosa (Ribbonwood). Fast-growing, evergreen, upright tree or shrub. **H** 25ft (8m), **S** 20ft (6m). Glossy, pale green leaves are narrowly oval and sharply toothed. Star-shaped, 5-petaled, white flowers are borne in clusters from mid- to late summer. Z9–10 H10–9.

HOLBOELLIA

LARDIZABALACEAE

Genus of evergreen, twining climbers, grown mainly for their fine foliage. Both male and female flowers are borne on the same plant. Needs partial shade or full sun and well-drained soil. Propagate by stem cuttings in late summer or fall.

H. brachyandra. Evergreen, twining climber. **H** to 30ft (10m). Has mid-green leaves, to 5in (12cm) long, divided into 3 ovate to elliptic leaflets. In summer produces racemes of 4–8 large, fragrant, white flowers.

H. coriacea. Evergreen, twining climber. **H** 16ft (to 5m). Has glossy, mid- to dark green leaves divided into 3 ovate to elliptic leaflets. In early summer

produces racemes of 5–8 fragrant, bell-shaped flowers with sepals of female flowers reddish-purple; white, male flowers have purple lines at bases. Flowers are sometimes followed by ovoid, light purple fruits. Z10–11 H12–10.

H. latifolia [purple form] illus. p.194; [white form] illus. p.192.

HOLCUS

GRAMINEAE/POACEAE

See also GRASSES, BAMBOOS, RUSHES and SEDGES.

H. mollis (Creeping soft grass). **'Albovariegatus'**, syn. *H. mollis* 'Variegatus' Evergreen, spreading, variegated, perennial grass. **H** 12–18in (30–45cm), **S** indefinite. Has white-striped leaves and hairy nodes. In summer produces purplish-white flower spikes. Z5–9 H9–5. **'Variegatus'**. See *H. mollis* 'Albovariegatus'.

HOLMSKIOLDIA

VERBENACEAE/LAMIACEAE

Genus of evergreen shrubs or scrambling climbers. Needs full light and fertile, well-drained soil. Water freely in growing season, less at other times. Requires tying to supports. Thin out crowded growth in spring or after flowering has finished. Propagate by seed in spring or by softwood or semiripe cuttings in summer. Whitefly and red spider mite may be troublesome.

H. sanguinea (Chinese hat plant). Evergreen, straggly shrub. **H** to 15ft (5m), **S** 6ft (2m). Has oval, serrated leaves, 2–4in (5–10cm) long. Produces showy, red or orange flowers, with saucer-shaped calyces and central, 5-lobed tubes, in fall–winter. Z10–11 H12–10.

HOLODISCUS

ROSACEAE

Genus of deciduous shrubs, grown for their flowers in summer. Needs sun or partial shade and any but very dry soil. Propagate by softwood cuttings in summer.

H. discolor, illus. p.113.

HOMERIA

IRIDACEAE

Genus of spring- or summer-flowering corms, grown for their widely funnel-shaped, cup-shaped or flattish flowers. Needs sun and well-drained soil. To produce flowers in spring, pot in fall in a cool greenhouse, water until after flowering, then dry off for summer. To produce flowers in summer, plant in the open in spring. Propagate by seed, division or offsets in fall. ⚠ *H. collina* is toxic to livestock.

H. ochroleuca. Spring- or summer-flowering corm. **H** to 22in (55cm), **S** 2–3in (5–8cm). Slender, wiry stems each bear 1 or 2 long, narrow, semierect leaves on lower part of stem. Produces a succession of upright, cup-shaped to flattish, yellow flowers, each sometimes with a central, orange stain. Z9–10 H10–9.

HOMOGYNE

COMPOSITAE/ASTERACEAE

Genus of evergreen perennials, useful for groundcover in rock gardens and woodland. Needs shade and moist soil. Propagate by division in spring or by seed when fresh.

H. alpina (Alpine coltsfoot). Mat-forming, rhizomatous perennial. **H** 3–6in (8–15cm), **S** 6in (15cm) or more. Has kidney-shaped, toothed, glossy leaves and, in summer, stems, 3–6in (8–15cm) or more long, each bear a daisylike, rose-purple flower head.

HOODIA

ASCLEPIADACEAE/APOCYNACEAE

Genus of branching, perennial succulents, grown for their firm, erect, green stems, generally branching from the base. Needs full sun and very well-drained soil. Is difficult to cultivate. Water sparingly at all times. Propagate by seed or grafting in spring or summer.

H. bainii. See *H. gordonii*.

H. gordonii, syn. *H. bainii*. Variable, erect, clump-forming, perennial succulent. **H** 32in (80cm), **S** 12in (30cm). Green stem is covered with short, spine-tipped tubercles in distorted rows. Often branches into clumps. Produces 5-lobed, flesh-colored to brownish flowers in late summer. Z13–15 H12–10.

HORDEUM

GRAMINEAE/POACEAE

See also GRASSES, BAMBOOS, RUSHES and SEDGES.

H. jubatum, illus. p.286.

HORMINUM

LABIATAE/LAMIACEAE

Genus of one species of basal-rosetted perennial, suitable for rock gardens. Requires sun and well-drained soil. Propagate by division in spring or by seed in fall.

H. pyrenaicum (Dragon's mouth, Pyrenean dead nettle). Basal-rosetted perennial. **H** and **S** 8in (20cm). In summer produces whorls of nodding, short-stalked, funnel-shaped, blue-purple or white flowers above oval, leathery, dark green leaves, 3–4in (8–10cm) long. Z6–8 H8–6.

HOSTA
Plantain lily

LILIACEAE/ASPARAGACEAE

Genus of perennials, grown mainly for their decorative foliage. Forms large clumps that are excellent for groundcover (heights given are those of foliage). Most species prefer shade and rich, moist but well-drained, neutral soil. Propagate by division in early spring. Seed-raised plants (except *H. ventricosa*) very rarely come true to type. Slug and snail control is essential. See also feature panel pp.272–3.

H. albomarginata. See *H. sieboldii* 'Paxton's Original'.

H. 'Allan P. McConnell ', illus. p.273. Clump-forming perennial. **H** 6–8in (15–20cm), **S** 12–18in (30–45cm). Has broadly to narrowly ovate, olive-green leaves with narrow, white margins. In mid-

summer produces bell-shaped, purple flowers on scapes 14–16in (35–40cm) long. Z3–9 H9–2.

H. 'American Halo'. Robust, densely mounded, clump-forming perennial. **H** 22in (55cm), **S** 5ft (1.5m). Has large, broadly ovate, strongly veined, dark blue-green leaves, with heart-shaped bases and wide, irregular, yellow margins becoming ivory-white as they mature. In early and mid-summer produces broadly funnel-shaped, pure white flowers on scapes 2ft (60cm) long. Z3–8 H8–1.

H. 'Antioch', illus. p.272. Robust, clump-forming perennial. **H** 20in (50cm), **S** 36in (90cm). Has broadly ovate, matt, dark green leaves irregularly margined gray-green and creamy-yellow, fading to white. In mid-summer bears funnel-shaped, lavender-blue flowers on scapes 36in (90cm) long. Z3–9 H9–2.

H. 'August Moon ', illus. p.273. Vigorous, clump-forming perennial. **H** 20in (50cm), **S** 30in (75cm). Has rounded to heart-shaped, cupped, puckered, pale green leaves becoming golden-yellow with a faint glaucous bloom. In summer bears bell-shaped, grayish-white flowers on scapes 36in (90cm) long. Z3–9 H9–2.

H. 'Big Daddy'. Clump-forming perennial. **H** 2ft (60cm), **S** 3ft (1m). Has rounded to heart-shaped, cupped, deeply puckered, glaucous, gray-blue leaves. In early summer bears bell-shaped, grayish-white flowers on scapes 32in (80cm) long. Z3–8 H8–1.

H. 'Birchwood Parky's Gold', syn. *H.* 'Golden', *H.* 'Golden Nakaiana', illus. p.273. Vigorous, clump-forming perennial. **H** 14–16in (35–40cm), **S** . Has heart-shaped, matt, yellow-green leaves becoming rich yellow with age. In mid-summer bears bell-shaped, pale lavender-blue flowers on scapes 28in (70cm) long. Z3–9 H9–2.

H. 'Blue Angel'. Slow-growing, clump-forming perennial. **H** 14in (35cm), **S** 24in (60cm). Has ovate to heart-shaped, wavy, glaucous, bluish-gray leaves. In mid-summer bears bell-shaped, grayish- or mauvish-white flowers on scapes 3ft (1m) long. Z3–8 H8–1.

H. 'Blue Cadet'. Clump-forming perennial. **H** 14–16in (35–40cm), **S** 30in (75cm). Has small, broadly ovate leaves, blue-green above and glaucous beneath, with heart-shaped bases. Produces funnel-shaped, rich lavender flowers in long, dense racemes, 22in (55cm) long, from mid- to late summer. Z3–8 H8–1.

H. 'Blue Moon'. Slow-growing, compact, clump-forming perennial. **H** 5in (12cm), **S** 12in (30cm). Oval to rounded, grayish-blue leaves taper to a point. In mid-summer, dense clusters of trumpet-shaped, mauve flowers, on scapes 8–10in (20–25cm) long, are borne just above leaves. Is suitable for a rock garden. Prefers partial shade. Z3–9 H9–1.

H. 'Blue Mouse Ears'. Slow-growing, clump-forming perennial. **H** 6in (15cm), **S** 12in (30cm). Has very small, shallowly cupped, ovate, rich blue-green leaves, which in mature plants are almost round in shape. Produces clusters of bell-shaped, lavender-striped, rich violet flowers, on scapes 8in (20cm) long, in mid- and late summer. Z3–8 H8–1.

H. 'Blue Wedgwood', illus. p.273. Slow-growing, clump-forming perennial. **H** 1ft

H

(30cm), **S** 1½ft (45cm). Has wedge-shaped, deeply quilted, blue leaves and, in summer, produces lavender flowers on scapes 16in (40cm) long. Z3–9 H9–2.
***H.* 'Brim Cup',** illus. p.273. Slow-growing, clump-forming perennial. **H** 12in (30cm), **S** 14–16in (35–40cm). Erect, heart-shaped, slightly cupped and puckered, thick, dark green leaves are irregularly margined with cream fading to white. Bears pale lavender-blue flowers, on scapes 18in (45cm) long, in summer. Z3–9 H9–2.
***H.* 'Buckshaw Blue'.** Slow-growing, clump-forming perennial. **H** 14in (35cm), **S** 24in (60cm). Has ovate to heart-shaped, concave, puckered, glaucous, deep blue-green leaves. In early summer bears bell-shaped, grayish-white flowers on scapes to 18in (45cm) long. Z3–8 H8–1.
***H.* 'Candy Hearts'.** Vigorous, clump-forming perennial. **H** 14–16in (35–40cm), **S** 22in (55cm). Has heart-shaped, pointed, greenish-gray-blue leaves. In summer bears bell-shaped, pale lavender-blue to off-white flowers on scapes to 20in (50cm) long. Z3–8 H8–1.
***H.* 'Cherry Berry',** illus. p.272. Mounded, clump-forming perennial. **H** 12in (30cm), **S** 24in (60cm). Has broadly lance-shaped, creamy-yellow leaves, becoming ivory-white, with broad, irregular, green margins. In mid- to late summer produces funnel-shaped, deep purple flowers on red scapes 18in (45cm) long. Z3–9 H9–2.
H. decorata. Stoloniferous perennial. **H** 12in (30cm), **S** 18in (45cm). Oval to rounded, dark green leaves have white margins. Dense racemes of trumpet-shaped, deep violet or sometimes white flowers, on scapes to 20in (50cm) long, are borne in mid-summer. Z3–9 H9–1. **f. *normalis*** has plain green leaves.
***H.* 'Devon Green',** illus. p.272. Clump-forming perennial. **H** 18in (45cm), **S** 16in (40cm). Red-spotted leaf stalks bear lance-shaped, glossy, dark green leaves maturing to broadly ovate to heart-shaped. In mid-summer bears bell-shaped, grayish-lavender-blue flowers on scapes to 18in (45cm) long. Z3–9 H9–2.
***H.* 'Dream Weaver',** illus. p.273. Vigorous, clump-forming perennial. **H** 18in (45cm), **S** 36in (90cm). Has large, broadly ovate, strongly ribbed, chartreuse-green leaves, later ivory-white in the center, with very broad, dark blue-green margins, glaucous beneath. Produces funnel-shaped, lavender-striped, white flowers, on scapes to 28in (70cm) long, in mid- and late summer. Z3–9 H9–2.
***H.* 'Fire and Ice',** illus. p.273. Vigorous, clump-forming perennial. **H** 14–16in (35–40cm), **S** indefinite. Has heart-shaped, matt, yellow-green leaves becoming rich yellow with age. In mid-summer bears bell-shaped, pale lavender-blue flowers on scapes 28in (70cm) long. Z3–9 H9–2.
***H.* 'Fire Island'.** Clump-forming perennial. **H** 10in (25cm), **S** 18in (45cm). Bright red stems bear ovate, puckered, bright yellow leaves becoming more green as the season progress, the red stem coloring seeping into the leaf blade. In mid-summer has bell-shaped, lavender flowers on scapes 20in (50cm) long. Z3–8 H8–1.
***H. fluctuans* 'Variegata'.** See *H.* 'Sagae'.
H. fortunei. Group of vigorous, clump-forming, hybrid perennials. **H** 2½–3ft (75cm–1m), **S** 3ft (1m) or more. Leaves are oval to heart-shaped. Z3–9 H9–1. **var. *albopicta,*** syn. *H. fortunei* 'Albopicta' has pale green leaves, with creamy-yellow centers, fading to dull green from mid-summer. Racemes of trumpet-shaped, pale violet flowers, on scapes, 30in (75cm) long, are produced in early summer. **var. *aureomarginata,*** syn. *H. fortunei* 'Aureomarginata', *H. fortunei* 'Yellow Edge' has mid-green leaves, with irregular, creamy-yellow edges, and violet flowers. Mass planting looks very effective. Tolerates full sun. **'Yellow Edge'.** See *H. fortunei* var. *aureomarginata.*
***H.* 'Fragrant Bouquet',** illus. p.273. Mounded, clump-forming perennial. **H** 18in (45cm), **S** 26in (65cm). Produces heart-shaped, slightly puckered, slightly wavy, chartreuse leaves edged in cream. In late summer, large, fragrant, flared, very pale lavender flowers are borne on scapes 36in (90cm) long. Z3–9 H9–2.
***H.* 'Francee'.** Vigorous, clump-forming perennial. **H** 22in (55cm), **S** 3ft (1m). Has oval to heart-shaped, slightly cupped and puckered, olive-green leaves with irregular, white margins. In summer produces arching, leafy scapes, 28in (70cm) long, bearing funnel-shaped, lavender-blue flowers. Is late to emerge. Z3–9 H9–1.
***H.* 'Ginko Craig',** illus. p.273. Clump-forming perennial. **H** and **S** 1ft (30cm). Has small, narrow, dark green leaves irregularly margined white. In summer produces spikes of bell-shaped, deep mauve flowers on scapes, 22in (55cm) long. Is a good edging plant. Z3–9 H9–2.
***H.* 'Gold Edger',** illus. p.272. Densely mounded, clump-forming perennial. **H** to 12in (30cm), **S** 12in (30cm) or more. Has heart-shaped, matt, golden-yellow leaves that fade to chartreuse with age. In late summer produces bell-shaped, lavender flowers on scapes to 12in (30cm) long. Z3–9 H9–2.
***H.* 'Golden'.** See *H.* 'Birchwood Parky's Gold'.
***H.* 'Golden Nakaiana'.** See *H.* 'Birchwood Parky's Gold'.
***H.* 'Golden Prayers',** illus. p.273. Upright, clump-forming perennial. **H** 6in (15cm), **S** 12in (30cm). Cupped leaves are puckered and bright golden-green. Produces white flowers suffused with pale lavender on scapes 18in (45cm) long. Is suitable for a rock garden. Z3–9 H9–2.
***H.* 'Golden Tiara',** illus. p.273. Clump-forming perennial. **H** 6in (15cm), **S** 12in (30cm). Neat, broadly heart-shaped, dark green leaves have well-defined, chartreuse-yellow margins. In summer produces long spikes of lavender-purple flowers on scapes 24in (60cm) long. Z3–9 H9–2.
***H.* 'Gold Standard'.** Vigorous, clump-forming perennial. **H** 2½ft (75cm), **S** 3ft (1m). Oval to heart-shaped leaves are pale green, turning to gold from mid-summer, with narrow, regular, dark green margins. Racemes of trumpet-shaped, violet flowers, on scapes, 3½ft (1.1m) long, are produced in mid-summer. Prefers partial shade. Z3–9 H9–1.
H. gracillima. Clump-forming perennial. **H** 2in (5cm), **S** 7in (18cm). Has lance-shaped, wavy-margined, glossy, deep green leaves, paler beneath. In summer–fall produces purple-dotted scapes, 10in (25cm) long, of widely funnel-shaped, lavender-blue flowers, purple striped within. Z3–8 H8–1.
***H.* 'Grand Tiara'.** Vigorous perennial forming a compact mound. **H** 12in (30cm), **S** 20in (50cm). Has ovate to heart-shaped, mid-green leaves with irregular, wide, yellow margins. In summer produces bell-shaped, sometimes remontant, deep purple flowers, striped lavender-blue within, on scapes 32in (80cm) long. Z3–9 H9–1.
***H.* 'Great Expectations',** illus. p.273. Clump-forming perennial. **H** 22in (55cm), **S** 34in (85cm). Green-margined, white leaf stalks bear heart-shaped, stiff, puckered, thick leaves that are glaucous, blue-green and irregularly but widely splashed with yellow, fading to white in centers. In early summer, bell-shaped, grayish-white flowers are borne on leafy scapes, 28in (70cm) long,. Z3–9 H9–2.
***H.* 'Green Fountain'.** Clump-forming perennial. **H** 24in (60cm), **S** 18in (45cm). Red-dotted leaf stalks bear arching, lance-shaped, wavy-margined, glossy, mid- green leaves. Funnel-shaped, pale mauve flowers are borne in summer, on scapes 24in (60cm) long. Z3–8 H8–1.
***H.* 'Ground Master',** illus. p.272. Vigorous, stoloniferous, prostrate perennial. **H** 10in (25cm), **S** 22in (55cm). Has ovate to lance-shaped, matt, olive-green leaves, with wavy, irregular, creamy margins, fading to white. In summer bears straight, leafy scapes, 24in (60cm) long, of funnel-shaped, purple flowers,. Z3–9 H9–2.
***H.* 'Guacamole'.** Vigorous, clump-forming perennial. **H** 18in (45cm), **S** 26in (65cm). Bold, heart-shaped, slightly wavy, soft gold leaves are irregularly edged in green. In mid-summer has flared, very pale lavender flowers on scapes 34in (85cm) long. Leaves color best in good light. Z3–8 H8–1.
***H.* 'Hadspen Blue',** illus. p.272. Slow-growing, clump-forming perennial. **H** and **S** 12in (30cm). Smooth leaves are heart-shaped and deep glaucous blue. Produces short spikes of lavender flowers, on scapes 14in (35cm) long, in summer. Z3–9 H9–2.
***H.* 'Halcyon',** illus. p.272. Robust, clump-forming perennial. **H** 1ft (30cm), **S** 3ft (1m). Has heart-shaped, tapering, grayish-blue leaves that fade to muddy-green in full sun; texture may be spoiled by heavy rain. Heavy clusters of trumpet-shaped, violet-mauve flowers, on scapes 18in (45cm) long, open just above foliage in mid-summer. Z3–9 H9–2.
***H.* 'Honeybells'.** Clump-forming perennial. **H** 3ft (1m), **S** 2ft (60cm). Light green leaves are blunt at the tips and have wavy margins. In late summer bears fragrant, pale lilac flowers on scapes 3½ft (1.1m) long. Z3–9 H9–1.
***H.* 'Hydon Sunset',** illus. p.273. Densely mounded, clump-forming perennial. **H** and **S** to 24in (60cm). Has heart-shaped leaves, bright gold in spring and mid-green by late summer. In late summer produces bell-shaped, purple flowers on scapes to 24in (60cm) long. Z3–9 H9–2.
H. hypoleuca. Clump-forming perennial. **H** 1½ft (45cm), **S** 3ft (1m). Broadly oval leaves have widely spaced veins and are pale green above, striking white beneath. In late summer bears drooping racemes of trumpet-shaped, milky-violet flowers, on scapes 14in (35cm) long, with mauve-flecked, pale green bracts. Tolerates full sun. Z3–8 H8–1.
***H.* 'Inniswood'.** Densely mounding, clump-forming perennial. **H** 24in (60cm), **S** 36in (90cm). Has large, broadly ovate to rounded, heart-shaped, seersuckered, rich golden-yellow leaves, with dark green margins and glaucous beneath. In mid-summer produces funnel-shaped, pale lavender flowers on scapes 30in (75cm) long. Z3–8 H8–1.
***H.* 'Invincible',** illus. p.272. Densely mounded, clump-forming perennial. **H** and **S** to 24in (60cm). Has heart-shaped, long-tipped, leathery, glossy, olive-green leaves. In late summer produces slightly fragrant, funnel-shaped, pale lavender flowers on scapes to 24in (60cm) long. Z3–9 H9–2.
***H.* 'June',** illus. p.272. Dense, clump-forming perennial. **H** 15in (38cm), **S** 28in (70cm). Has heart-shaped, smooth, gray-blue leaves irregularly splashed in centers with yellow and yellowish green. Bell-shaped, lavender-gray flowers, on scapes 18in (45cm) long, are borne in late summer. Is a sport of *H.* 'Halcyon'. Z3–9 H9–2.
***H.* 'Kabitan'.** See *H. sieboldii* f. *kabitan.*
H. kikutii. Clump-forming perennial. **H** 16in (40cm), **S** 2ft (60cm). Has oval to lance-shaped, deeply veined, dark green leaves. Racemes of bell-shaped, near-white flowers are borne in a tight bunch at the top of raceme on conspicuously leaning scapes, 24in (60cm) long, in mid-summer. Z3–9 H9–1. **var. *caput-avis*** is smaller, and flower bud resembles a bird's head. **'Kifukurin'** has larger leaves margined with cream.
***H.* 'Krossa Regal'.** Vase-shaped, clump-forming perennial. **H** and **S** 3ft (1m). Arching, deeply ribbed leaves are grayish-blue. Produces long spikes of pale lilac flowers, on scapes 4½ft (1.4m) long, in summer. Tolerates sun. Z3–9 H9–1.
H. lancifolia, illus. p.273. Clump-forming perennial. **H** 18in (45cm), **S** 30in (75cm). Arching, narrowly lance-shaped, glossy, dark green leaves overlap neatly into a dense mound. Bell-shaped, lavender flowers, on scapes 26in (65cm) long, are produced in late summer. Z3–9 H9–2.
***H.* 'Love Pat'.** Vigorous, clump-forming perennial. **H** and **S** to 2ft (60cm). Produces rounded, deeply puckered, deep glaucous blue leaves. Bears racemes of pale lilac flowers, on scapes 22in (55cm) long, in summer. Z3–9 H9–1.
***H.* 'Minuteman',** illus. p.272. Clump-forming perennial. **H** 30in (75cm), **S** 24in (60cm). Has oval, slightly wavy-rimmed, white-margined, dark green leaves. In mid- and late summer produces funnel-shaped, lavender flowers on scapes 30in (75cm) long. Z3–9 H9–2.
H. montana. Vigorous, clump-forming perennial. **H** 3½ft (1.1m), **S** 3ft (1m). Has oval, prominently veined, glossy, dark green leaves. Racemes of trumpet-shaped, pale violet flowers, on scapes 36in (90cm) long, are produced in mid-summer. Z3–9 H9–1. **'Aureomarginata'** has leaves irregularly edged with golden-yellow. Is always the first hosta to appear in spring.
***H.* 'Moonlight'.** Clump-forming perennial. **H** 20in (50cm), **S** 28in (70cm). Has pale yellow leaves that emerge olive-green, narrowly margined white. Produces funnel-shaped, violet-budded, pinkish-lavender flowers, on scapes 28in (70cm) long, in mid-summer. Requires full shade. Z3–9 H9–1.

***H.* 'Morning Light'.** Clump-forming perennial forming upright mounds of foliage. **H** 18in (45cm), **S** 28in (70cm). Has ovate, long-pointed, rich ivory-yellow leaves, with irregular, dark green margins. Produces narrowly funnel-shaped, lavender flowers, on scapes to 28in (70cm) long, in mid-summer. Z3–9 H9–1.

***H.* 'Night Before Christmas',** illus. p.272. Clump-forming perennial. **H** 2ft (60cm), **S** 5ft (1.5m). Large, oval, slightly wavy, rich dark green leaves are boldly splashed with a central, bright white flash. Has narrowly funnel-shaped, lavender flowers, on scapes 36in (90cm) long, in mid-summer. Z3–9 H9–2.

H. nigrescens, illus. p.272. Vigorous, clump-forming perennial. **H** 28in (70cm), **S** 26in (65cm). In late summer has oval to heart-shaped, concave, puckered, glaucous gray-green leaves, and racemes of funnel-shaped, pearl-gray to white flowers, on undulating scapes 4½ft (1.4m) long. Z3–9 H9–2.

***H.* 'Paxton's Original'.** See *H. sieboldii* 'Paxton's Original'.

***H.* 'Piedmont Gold'.** Slow-growing, clump-forming perennial. **H** 2ft (60cm), **S** 2½ft (75cm). Smooth leaves are bright yellowish-green with fluted margins. Racemes of white flowers, on scapes to 26in (65cm) long, are produced in summer. Is best in partial shade. Z3–9 H9–1.

H. plantaginea. Lax, clump-forming perennial. **H** 2ft (60cm), **S** 4ft (1.2m). Leaves are oval and glossy, pale green. Rising well above these are scapes, 26–30in (65–75cm) long, crowned in late summer and early fall with fragrant, trumpet-shaped, white flowers that open in the evening. Prefers sunny conditions. Z3–9 H9–1. **var. *japonica*,** syn. *H. plantaginea* 'Grandiflora' has larger, longer-tubed flowers, to 5in (13cm) long. Z3–9 H9–2. **'Grandiflora'.** See *H. plantaginea* var. *japonica*.

H. rectifolia. Upright, clump-forming perennial. **H** 3ft (1m), **S** 2½ft (75cm). Produces oval to lance-shaped, dark green leaves and racemes of large, trumpet-shaped, violet flowers, to 24–30in (60–75cm) long, from mid- to late summer. Z3–9 H9–1.

***H.* 'Regal Splendor',** illus. p.272. Clump-forming perennial. **H** and **S** 3ft (1m). Arching, grayish-blue leaves are suffused white or yellow at margins. Lilac flowers, on scapes 4½ft (1.4m) long, are produced in summer. Z3–9 H9–2.

***H.* 'Remember Me',** illus. p.273. Densely mounded, clump-forming perennial. **H** 16in (40cm), **S** 12in (30cm). Has narrowly oval, bright ivory-white to creamy-yellow leaves with irregular, green-margins. Tubular, lavender flowers, on scapes 16in (40cm) long, are produced in mid-summer. Z3–9 H9–2.

***H.* 'Revolution',** illus. p.273. Clump-forming perennial. **H** 20in (50cm), **S** 3½ft (1.1m). Ivory-white leaf stalks, finely outlined dark green, bear broadly ovate, wavy, lustrous, green-flecked, ivory-cream leaves, margined and splashed dark green and overlaid with light olive-green. In mid-summer has narrowly funnel-shaped, lavender-blue flowers on scapes 20in (50cm) long. Z3–9 H9–2.

***H.* 'Royal Standard'.** Upright, clump-forming perennial. **H** 2ft (60cm), **S** 4ft (1.2m). Broadly oval leaves are glossy, pale green. Pure white, slightly fragrant, trumpet-shaped flowers, to 3ft (1m) long, are produced well above foliage and open in the evening. Prefers sun. Z3–9 H9–1.

***H.* 'Sagae',** syn. *H. fluctuans* 'Variegata', illus. p.273. Semierect, clump-forming perennial. **H** 2½ft (75cm), **S** 5ft (1.5m). Very large, roughly triangular, dark green leaves have gold edges which fade to cream or white. Flared, lavender flowers are borne, on scapes 4ft (1.2m) long, in mid-summer. Z3–9 H9–2.

***H.* 'Sea Thunder'.** Vigorous, dense-mounding, clump-forming perennial. **H** 16–20in (40–50cm), **S** 3ft (1m). Has narrowly ovate to ovate, ivory-cream leaves, irregularly margined dark olive-green, often with intrusions of olive-green towards center. Produces broadly funnel-shaped, purple flowers, on scapes 36in (90cm) long, in late summer. Z3–8 H8–1.

***H.* 'Shade Fanfare'.** Vigorous, clump-forming perennial. **H** 1½ft (45cm), **S** 2½ft (75cm). Heart-shaped leaves are pale green with cream margins. In summer has an abundance of lavender flowers on scapes 24in (60cm) long. Z3–8 H8–1.

H. sieboldiana, illus. p.272. Robust, clump-forming perennial. **H** 3ft (1m) or more, **S** 5ft (1.5m). Large, heart-shaped, deeply ribbed, puckered leaves are bluish-gray. Racemes of trumpet-shaped, very pale lilac flowers, on scapes 24in (60cm) long, are produced in early summer, just above foliage. Makes good groundcover. Tolerates sun, but leaves may then turn dull green. Z3–9 H9–2. **var. *elegans*** has larger, bluer leaves and scapes 28in (70cm) long. **'Frances Williams'** has yellow-margined leaves, scapes 28in (70cm) long, is slower-growing and should not be grown in full sun. Z3–9 H9–1.

***H. sieboldii* f. *kabitan*,** syn. *H.* 'Kabitan' Clump-forming perennial, spreading by short runners. **H** to 1ft (30cm), **S** 2ft (60cm). Lance-shaped, thin-textured, glossy leaves are yellow-centered and have narrow, undulating, dark green margins. In early summer produces small, trumpet-shaped, pale violet flowers on scapes 12–16in (30–40cm) long. Is suitable for a shaded rock garden. Needs establishing in a pot for first few years. Z3–8 H8–1. **'Paxton's Original',** syn. *H. albomarginata*, *H.* 'Paxton's Original', **H** 1½ft (45cm), is vigorous, and has round-tipped, mid- to dark green leaves with irregular, white margins. Violet flowers are produced in late summer and are followed by ovoid, glossy, dark green, then brown seed heads, which are useful for flower arrangements.

***H.* 'Snowden'.** Clump-forming perennial. **H** and **S** 3ft (1m) or more. Has large, pointed, glaucous, blue leaves that mature to sage-green. Long stems produce white flowers tinged with green, on thick scapes 3ft (1m) long, in summer. Z3–9 H9–1.

***H.* 'So Sweet',** illus. p.273. Clump-forming perennial. **H** 14in (35cm), **S** 22in (55cm). Has ovate to lance-shaped, glossy, mid-green leaves margined creamy-white. In mid- and late summer, lavender-blue buds open to fragrant, funnel-shaped, purple-striped, white flowers on scapes 24in (60cm) long. Z3–9 H9–2.

***H.* 'Stiletto'.** Vigorous, clump-forming perennial. **H** 6in (15cm), **S** 8in (20cm). Has lance-shaped, rippled, mid-green leaves margined creamy-white. In summer produces funnel-shaped, purple-striped, lavender-blue flowers on scapes 12in (30cm) long. Z3–8 H8–1.

***H.* 'Striptease'.** Densely mounding, clump-forming perennial. **H** 20in (50cm), **S** 4ft (1.2m). Has narrowly ovate to ovate leaves, dark green leaves, glaucous beneath, with chartreuse-green centers, sometimes white-flecked, later becoming ivory-yellow. Produces funnel-shaped, violet then lavender flowers on scapes, 28in (70cm) long, in mid-summer. Z3–8 H8–1.

***H.* 'Sum and Substance'.** Vigorous, clump-forming perennial. **H** and **S** to 3ft (1m). Produces large, greenish-gold leaves that are thick in texture and, in mid-summer, pale lavender flowers on scapes 3ft (1m) long. Tolerates full sun. Z3–8 H8–1.

***H.* 'Tall Boy'.** Clump-forming perennial. **H** and **S** 2ft (60cm). Has large, bright green leaves ending in long points. In summer produces masses of rich lilac flowers on scapes 4ft (1.2m) or more long. Z3–9 H9–1.

H. tardiflora. Slow-growing, clump-forming perennial. **H** 1ft (30cm), **S** 2½ft (75cm). Has narrowly lance-shaped, thick-textured, dark green leaves. Dense racemes of trumpet-shaped, lilac-purple flowers, on scapes 14in (35cm) long, are borne from late summer to early fall. Z3–9 H9–1.

***H.* 'Tattoo',** illus. p.273. Clump-forming perennial. **H** 12in (30cm), **S** 18in (45cm). Broadly ovate, slightly puckered, pale green leaves have a maple-leaf-shaped, gold centers edged in darker green. Bears bell-shaped, lavender flowers, on scapes 18in (45cm) long, in mid-summer. Z3–9 H9–2.

***H.* 'Thomas Hogg'.** See *H. undulata* var. *albomarginata*.

H. tokudama, syn. *H.* 'Tokudama'. Very slow-growing, clump-forming perennial. **H** 1½ft (45cm), **S** 2½ft (75cm). Produces cup-shaped, puckered, blue leaves. Racemes of trumpet-shaped, pale lilac-gray flowers, on scapes 16in (40cm) long, are produced in mid-summer. Z3–9 H9–1. **f. *aureonebulosa*,** syn. *H. tokudama* 'Aureonebulosa', *H. tokudama* 'Variegata', illus. p.274. **'Aureonebulosa'.** See *H. tokudama* f. *aureonebulosa*. **f. *flavocircinalis*** (illus. p.272), often mistaken for a juvenile *H. sieboldiana* 'Frances Williams', has heart-shaped leaves with wide, irregular, creamy-yellow margins. Z3–9 H9–2. **'Variegata'.** See *H. tokudama* f. *aureonebulosa*.

***H.* 'Tokudama'.** See *H. tokudama*.

***H.* 'Torchlight'.** Clump-forming perennial. **H** 14in (35cm), **S** 34in (85cm). Strongly red-streaked leaf stalks bear ovate, slightly folded, wavy, smooth, dark olive-green leaves lightly streaked chartreuse, with irregular, ivory margins. Bears funnel-shaped, rich lavender-blue flowers, on scapes 30in (75cm) long, in late summer. Z3–9 H9–1.

***H. undulata* var. *undulata*,** syn. *H.* 'Undulata'. Clump-forming perennial. **H** to 3ft (1m), **S** 18in (45cm). Has lance-shaped to elliptic or narrowly ovate, slightly pointed, twisted, deeply channeled, mid-green leaves that are thin but leathery and strongly wavy-margined, with central, white or pale yellow-white markings. Funnel-shaped, mauve flowers, on arching leaf scapes 20–32in (50–80cm) long, are produced in early and mid-summer. Z3–9 H9–1. **var. *albomarginata*,** syn. *H.* 'Thomas Hogg', *H.* 'Undulata Albomarginata'. **H** 22in (55cm), **S** 24in (60cm), has broadly oval, flat or slightly wavy-margined, dark green leaves, with irregular, cream or pale yellow margins. Z3–9 H9–2. **var. *erromena*,** syn. *H.* 'Undulata Erromena'. **H** 1½ft (45cm), **S** 2ft (60cm), is robust and bears broadly oval, tapering, matt, mid-green leaves. **var. *univittata*,** syn. *H.* 'Undulata Univittata'. **H** 1½ft (45cm), **S** 28in (70cm), has oval, twisted, matt, olive-green leaves that have narrow, cream centers.

***H.* 'Undulata'.** See *H. undulata* var. *undulata*.

***H.* 'Undulata Albomarginata'.** See *H. undulata* var. *albomarginata*.

***H.* 'Undulata Erromena'.** See *H. undulata* var. *erromena*.

***H.* 'Undulata Univittata'.** See *H. undulata* var. *univittata*.

H. ventricosa. Clump-forming perennial. **H** 28in (70cm), **S** 3ft (1m) or more. Has heart-shaped to oval, slightly wavy-margined, glossy, dark green leaves. Racemes of bell-shaped, deep purple flowers, on scapes 32–36in (80–100cm) long, are produced above foliage in late summer. Z3–9 H9–1. **'Aureomarginata'.** See *H. ventricosa* 'Variegata'.**'Variegata',** syn. *H. ventricosa* 'Aureomarginata' produces leaves with irregular, cream margins.

H. venusta. Vigorous, mat-forming perennial. **H** 1in (2.5cm), **S** to 12in (30cm). Has oval to lance-shaped, mid- to dark green leaves. Abundant racemes of trumpet-shaped, purple flowers, on scapes 10–14in (25–35cm) long, are borne well above foliage in mid-summer. Is suitable for a rock garden. Z3–9 H9–1. **'Suzuki Thumbnail'** produces small leaves, 2in (5cm) long. Z3–8 H8–1.

***H.* 'Whirlwind ',** illus. p.273. Clump-forming perennial. **H** 17in (43cm), **S** 34in (85cm). Has ovate to heart-shaped, folded, twisted and pointed, white to yellowish-green leaves, with wide, dark green margins. Funnel-shaped, lavender-blue flowers, on scapes 24in (60cm) long, are produced in mid- and late summer. Z3–9 H9–2.

***H.* 'Wide Brim'.** Vigorous, clump-forming perennial. **H** and **S** to 2½ft (75cm). Leaves are heavily puckered and dark blue-green, with wide, irregular, creamy-white margins. Produces white or very pale lavender flowers, on scapes 22in (55cm) long, in summer. Z3–9 H9–1.

***H.* 'Yellow River'.** Clump-forming perennial. **H** 22in (55cm), **S** 3ft (1m). Has ovate to heart-shaped, pointed, thick, dark green leaves with irregular, yellow margins. Leafy scapes, 3ft (1m) long, of funnel-shaped, very pale lavender-blue flowers are produced in early summer. Z3–9 H9–1.

***H.* 'Zounds'.** Slow-growing, clump-forming perennial. **H** and **S** to 3ft (1m). Large, bright gold leaves are corrugated and have metallic sheen. White or pale lavender flowers, on scapes 24in (60cm) long, are produced in early summer. Z3–9 H9–1.

HOTTONIA
PRIMULACEAE

Genus of deciduous, perennial, submerged water plants, grown for their foliage and delicate, primula-like flowers. Needs sun and clear, cool water, still or running. Periodically, thin overcrowded growth. Propagate by stem cuttings in spring or summer.

H. palustris, illus. p.435.

Houstonia serpyllifolia. See *Hedyotis michauxii.*

HOUTTUYNIA
SAURURACEAE

Genus of one species of perennial or deciduous marginal water plant, with far-spreading rhizomes. Is sometimes used for groundcover, but can be quite invasive. Prefers partial shade and moist soil or shallow water, beside streams and ponds. Propagate by runners in spring.

H. cordata. Chameleon', syn. *H. cordata* 'Variegata' illus. p.444. **'Flore Pleno',** syn. *H. cordata* 'Plena' is a spreading perennial. **H** 6–24in (15–60cm), **S** indefinite. Spikes of insignificant flowers, surrounded by 8 or more oval, white bracts, are produced above aromatic, fleshy, leathery, heart-shaped, pointed leaves, in spring. Z6–11 H12–2. **'Plena'.** See *H. cordata* 'Flore Pleno'. **'Variegata'.** See *H. cordata* 'Chameleon'.

HOVENIA
RHAMNACEAE

Genus of one species of deciduous, summer-flowering tree, grown for its foliage. Young, immature growth is susceptible to frost damage. Prefers full sun and requires fertile, well-drained soil. Propagate by softwood cuttings in summer or by seed in fall.

H. dulcis, illus. p.74.

HOWEA
SYN. HOWEIA, KENTIA
Sentry palm
PALMAE/ARECACEAE

Genus of evergreen palms, grown for their ornamental appearance. Needs partial shade and rich, well-drained soil. Water container specimens freely in summer, minimally in winter and moderately at other times. Propagate by seed in spring at not less than 79°F (26°C). Is prone to red spider mite.

H. forsteriana, syn. *Kentia fosteriana* (Kentia palm, Thatch-leaf palm). Evergreen, upright palm with a slender stem. **H** 30ft (10m), **S** 10–12ft (3–4m). Has spreading, feather-shaped leaves, 5–8ft (1.5–2.5m) long, made up of strap-shaped leaflets. Branching clusters of several spikes of small, greenish-brown flowers are produced in winter. Z11–12 H12–1.

Howeia. See *Howea.*

HOYA
Wax flower
ASCLEPIADACEAE/APOCYNACEAE

Genus of evergreen, woody-stemmed, twining and/or root climbers and loose shrubs, grown for their flowers and foliage.

Grow in rich, well-drained soil with partial shade in summer. Water moderately when in full growth, sparingly at other times. Stems require support. Cut back and thin out crowded stems after flowering or in spring. Propagate by semiripe cuttings in summer.

H. australis, syn. *H. darwinii.* Moderately vigorous, evergreen, woody-stemmed, twining, root climber. **H** to 15ft (5m). Has fleshy, rich green leaves. In summer produces trusses of 20–50 fragrant, star-shaped, white flowers, with red-purple markings. Z14–15 H12–8.
H. bella. See *H. lanceolata* subsp. *bella.*
H. carnosa, illus. p.460.
H. coronaria. Slow-growing, evergreen, woody-stemmed, twining and root climber. **H** 6–10ft (2–3m). Bears thick, leathery, oblong to oval leaves. In summer, bell-shaped, yellow to white flowers are borne, each spotted with red. Z13–15 H12–9.
H. darwinii of gardens**.** See *H. australis.*
H. imperialis. Vigorous, evergreen, woody-stemmed, twining and root climber. **H** to 20ft (6m). Oval, leathery, fleshy, mid-green leaves, 4–9in (10–23cm) long, are covered with down. In summer produces large, star-shaped, brown-purple to deep magenta flowers, each with a cream center. Z12–15 H12–9.
H. lanceolata subsp. bella, syn. *H. bella,* illus. p.460.
H. macgillivrayi, illus. p.462.

HUERNIA
ASCLEPIADACEAE/APOCYNACEAE

Genus of clump-forming, perennial succulents, grown for their finger-like, usually 4-angled stems. Has minute, short-lived, deciduous leaves on new growth. Needs sun or partial shade and very well-drained soil. Is one of easiest stapeliads to grow. Propagate by seed or stem cuttings in spring or summer.

H. macrocarpa, syn. *H. macrocarpa* var. *arabica,* illus. p.488. **var. arabica.** See *H. macrocarpa.*
H. pillansii. Deciduous, clump-forming, perennial succulent. **H** 2in (5cm), **S** 4in (10cm). Has a finger-like, light green stem that is densely covered with short tubercles with hairlike tips. Produces bell-shaped, creamy-red flowers, with red spots, at base of new growth, in summer–fall. Z13–15 H12–10.
H. primulina. See *H. thuretii* var. *primulina.*
H. thuretii var. primulina, syn. *H. primulina.* Deciduous, clump-forming, perennial succulent. **H** 4in (10cm), **S** 6in (15cm). Stems are short, thick and gray-green. In summer–fall, bell-shaped, dull yellow flowers, 3/4in (2cm) across, with reflexed, blackish tips, are produced at base of new growth. Z13–15 H12–10.
H. zebrina (Owl's eyes). Deciduous, clump-forming, perennial succulent. **H** 4in (10cm), **S** 6in (15cm). Is similar to *H. thuretii* var. *primulina,* but has pale yellow-green flowers with bands of red-brown. Z13–15 H12–10.

Humea. See *Calomeria.*

HUMULUS
Hops
CANNABACEAE

Genus of herbaceous, twining climbers. Is useful for concealing unsightly garden sheds or tree-stumps. Male and female

flowers are borne on separate plants; female flower spikes become drooping clusters known as "hops". Needs sun or partial shade and well-drained soil. Propagate by tip cuttings in spring.
H. lupulus (Hops). Z4–8 H8–1. **'Aureus'** illus. p.194.

HUNNEMANNIA
PAPAVERACEAE

Genus of poppy-like perennials, usually grown as annuals. Needs sun and very well-drained soil. Dead-head plants regularly. Provide support, especially in windy areas. Propagate by seed sown under glass in early spring, or outdoors in mid-spring.
H. fumariifolia (Mexican tulip poppy). Z10–11 H12–9. **'Sunlite'** is a fast-growing, upright perennial, grown as an annual. **H** 24in (60cm), **S** 8in (20cm). Has oblong, very divided, bluish-green leaves and, in summer and early fall, poppy-like, semidouble, bright yellow flowers, to 3in (8cm) wide.

HYACINTHELLA
LILIACEAE/ASPARAGACEAE

Genus of spring-flowering bulbs, grown for their short spikes of small, bell-shaped flowers. Is suitable for rock gardens and cold greenhouses. Requires an open, sunny situation and well-drained soil, which partially dries out while bulbs are dormant in summer. Propagate by seed in fall.
H. leucophaea, illus. p.421.

HYACINTHOIDES
SYN. ENDYMION
Bluebell
LILIACEAE/ASPARAGACEAE

Genus of spring-flowering bulbs, grown for their bluebell flowers. Is suitable for growing in borders and for naturalizing in grass beneath trees and shrubs. Requires partial shade and plenty of moisture. Prefers heavy soil. Plant bulbs in fall 4–6in (10–15cm) deep. Propagate by division in late summer or by seed in fall. ① All parts may irritate skin on contact, and may cause severe discomfort if ingested.
H. hispanica of gardens**.** See *H. x massartiana.*
H. italica, syn. *Scilla italica.* Spring-flowering bulb. **H** 6–8in (15–20cm), **S** 2–3in (5–8cm). Produces a basal cluster of narrowly strap-shaped, semierect leaves. Leafless stem produces a conical spike of many flattish, star-shaped, blue flowers, 1/2in (1cm) across. Z4–9 H9–1.
H. x massartiana (*H. hispanica* x *H. non-scripta*), syn. *H. hispanica, Scilla campanulata, Scilla hispanica,* illus. p.403.
H. non-scripta, syn. *Scilla non-scripta, Scilla nutans,* illus. p.403.

HYACINTHUS
Hyacinth
LILIACEAE/ASPARAGACEAE

Genus of bulbs, grown for their dense spikes of fragrant, tubular flowers. Is ideal for spring bedding displays and for pot cultivation indoors. Needs an open, sunny situation or partial shade and well-drained soil. Plant in fall. For winter flowers, force

large-size, specially "treated" bulbs of *H. orientalis* cultivars by potting in early fall, then keep cool and damp for several weeks to ensure adequate root systems develop. When shoot tips are visible, move into max. 50°F (10°C) at first, raising temperature as more shoot appears and giving as much light as possible. After forcing, keep in a cool place to finish growth, then plant out to recover. Propagate by offsets in late summer or early fall. ① All parts may cause stomach upset if ingested; contact with the bulbs may aggravate skin allergies.
H. amethystinus. See *Brimeura amethystina.*
H. azureus. See *Muscari azureum.*
H. orientalis (Common hyacinth). **'Amsterdam'** Winter- or spring-flowering bulb. **H** 4–8in (10–20cm), **S** 2 1/2 –4in (6–10cm). Has strap-shaped, channeled, semierect, glossy, basal leaves that develop fully only after flowering. Flower stem bears a dense, cylindrical spike of fragrant, tubular, bright rose-red flowers, each with 6 recurving petals. **'Blue Jacket',** illus. p.403. **'City of Haarlem',** illus. p.407. **'Delft Blue'** has violet-flushed, soft blue flowers. **'Distinction'** produces slender, open spikes of reddish-purple flowers; those of **'Jan Bos'** are crimson. **'Lady Derby'** bears rose-pink flowers. **'L' Innocence'** has ivory-white flowers. **'Ostara'** has a large spike of blue flowers, with a dark stripe along each petal center. **'Pink Pearl'** has a dense spike of carmine-pink flowers. Flowers of **'Princess Maria Christina'** are salmon-pink; those of **'Queen of the Pinks'** are soft pink. **'Violet Pearl'** produces spikes of violet flowers. **'White Pearl',** illus. p.415. Z5–9 H9–1.

HYDRANGEA
HYDRANGEACEAE

Genus of deciduous shrubs and deciduous or evergreen, root climbers, grown for their mainly domed or flattened flower heads. Each head usually consists of masses of small, inconspicuous, fertile flowers, surrounded by or mixed with much larger, sterile flowers bearing showy, petal-like sepals. However, in some forms, all or most of the flowers are sterile. Prefers full sun or partial shade and fertile, moist but well-drained soil. Needs more shade in dry areas. Propagate by softwood cuttings in summer. ① All parts of hydrangeas may cause mild stomach upset if ingested; contact with the foliage may aggravate skin allergies. See also feature panel pp.134–135.
H. anomala subsp. petiolaris. See *H. petiolaris.*
H. arborescens (Smooth hydrangea). **'Annabelle'** (illus. p.134) Deciduous, open shrub. **H** and **S** 8ft (2.5m). Long-stalked, broadly oval leaves are glossy, dark green above, paler beneath. Very large, rounded heads of mainly sterile, white flowers are borne in summer. Z4–9 H9–1. **'Grandiflora'** has smaller flower heads but larger sterile flowers. Z4–9 H9–1.
H. aspera. Deciduous, upright shrub with arching branches. **H** and **S** to 13ft (4m). Young stems are finely haired. Has lance-shaped to ovate, dark green leaves, downy beneath. Pale blue, inner flowers, surrounded by lilac-pink to white, outer

H

ones, are borne in summer. Z6–9 H9–5. **'Mauvette'** (illus. p.135) has slightly deeper purple-mauve flowers. **subsp. *sargentiana*,** syn. *H. sargentiana* (illus. p.135), **S** 6ft (2m), is a gaunt shrub with peeling bark, sturdy shoots and very large, narrowly oval, bristly, dull green leaves, gray down beneath. In late summer to mid-fall bears broad heads of flowers, the inner ones small and blue or deep purple, the outer ones larger and white, sometimes flushed purplish-pink. Z7–8 H8–7. **Villosa Group,** syn. *H. villosa* illus. p.133.

H. bretschneideri. See *H. heteromalla* 'Bretschneideri'.

H. heteromalla. Deciduous, arching shrub. **H** 15ft (5m), **S** 10ft (3m). Narrowly oval, dark green leaves turn yellow in fall. Broad, flat, open heads of white flowers, 7in (17cm) across, are borne in mid- and late summer. Z4–9 H9–1. **'Bretschneideri',** syn. *H. bretschneideri* has peeling, chestnut-brown bark and large leaves, to 5in (12cm) long and half as much wide. Z5–8 H8–5. **'Snowcap'** (illus. p.134) has large, flat, white flower heads, to10in (25cm) across. Z5–8 H8–5.

H. integerrima. See *H. serratifolia.*

H. involucrata. Deciduous, spreading, open shrub. **H** 3ft (1m), **S** 6ft (2m). Has broadly heart-shaped, bristly, mid-green leaves. In late summer–fall bears heads of small, blue, inner flowers surrounded by large, pale blue to white, outer ones. Z7–9 H9–7. **'Hortensis'** is smaller and has clusters of cream, pink and green flowers.

H. longipes. Deciduous shrub with lax, spreading habit. **H** and **S** to 10ft (3m). Rounded to ovate, toothed, rough, gray-green leaves are produced on long leaf stalks. Has flat, white flower heads in mid-summer.

H. macrophylla (Bigleaf hydrangea, Florist's hydrangea). Deciduous, bushy shrub. **H** 5–6ft (1.5–2m), **S** 6–8ft (2–2.5m). Has oval, toothed, glossy, light green leaves. In mid- to late summer, blue or purple flowers are produced in acid soils with a pH of up to about 5.5. In neutral or alkaline soils above this level, flowers are pink or red. White flowers are not affected by pH. Prune older shoots back to base in spring. Trim back winter-damaged shoots to new growth and remove spent flower heads in spring. Is divided into 2 groups: Hortensias, which have domed, dense heads of mainly sterile flowers; and Lacecaps, which have flat, open heads, each with fertile flowers in center and larger, sterile flowers on outside that are green in bud. Z6–9 H9–6. **'Altona'** (Hortensia), illus. p.134, **H** 3ft (1m), **S** 5ft (1.5m), has large heads of rich pink to deep purple-blue flowers. **'Ami Pasquier'** (Hortensia), illus. p.135, **H** 2ft (60cm), **S** 3ft (1m), is compact, with deep crimson or blue-purple flowers. **'Ayesha'** (Hortensia), illus. p.135, **H** and **S** 3ft (1m), has flattened heads of pink to lilac flowers and deep green leaves. **'Blue Bonnet'** (Hortensia), illus. p.135, **H** 6ft (2m), **S** 8ft (2.5m), produces heads of rich blue or lilac to pink flowers. **'Blue Wave'.** See *H. macrophylla* 'Mariesii Perfecta'.**'Europa'** (Hortensia), illus. p.135, **H** 5ft (1.5m), **S** 3ft (1m), produces large florets of rich pink flowers. Flower heads of **'Générale Vicomtesse de Vibraye'** (Hortensia), illus. p.134, **H** and **S** 5ft (1.5m), are rounded and pale blue or pink. Foliage is light green. **'Goliath'** (Hortensia), **H** and **S** 3ft (1m), has dark green leaves and produces very large florets of soft pink to pale blue flowers in small heads. **'Hamburg'** (Hortensia), illus. p.134, **H** 3ft (1m), **S** 5ft (1.5m), is vigorous and has large, deep pink to deep blue flowers with serrated sepals. **'Lanarth White'** (Lacecap) , **H** and **S** 5ft (1.5m), has pink or blue fertile flowers edged with pure white sterile flowers. **'Libelle'** (Lacecap), illus. p.135, **H** and **S** 5ft (1.5m), produces very pale blue flowers, fading to creamy-white, over a long period. **'Lilacina',** syn. *H. macrophylla* 'Mariesii Lilacina' (Lacecap), illus. p.134, **H** and **S** 6ft (2m), has deep lilac central flowers and pinkish-purple outer flowers. **'Madame Emile Mouillère'** (Hortensia), illus. p.134 has white flowers, becoming pale pink, and prefers partial shade. **'Mariesii Lilacina'.** See *H. macrophylla* 'Lilacina'. **'Mariesii Perfecta',** syn. *H. macrophylla* 'Blue Wave' (Lacecap) , **H** 6ft (2m), **S** to 8ft (2.5m), produces heads of rich blue or lilac to pink flowers. **'Möwe'** (Lacecap), illus. p.135, **H** and **S** 3ft (1m), has broad, flat flower heads ranging in color from purple-red to deep pink. **'Nigra'** (Hortensia), **H** and **S** 3ft (1m), has almost black stems bearing pink or occasionally blue flowers. **'Preziosa'.** See *H.* 'Preziosa'. **subsp. *serrata*.** See *H. serrata.* **'Tokyo Delight'** (Lacecap), **H** and **S** 3ft (1m), produces pink or white flowers maturing to red-wine. **'Tricolor'** (Lacecap), **H** 6ft (2m), **S** 5ft (1.5m), has variegated, gray-green and yellow leaves and bears pale pink to white in late summer. **'Veitchii'** (Lacecap) has lilac-blue flowers. **'Westfallen'** (Hortensia) , **H** and **S** 3ft (1m), bears bright red to purple flowers.

H. paniculata (Panicle hydrangea). Vigorous, deciduous, spreading to upright shrub. **H** 6–10ft (2–3m), **S** 8–10ft (2.5–3m). Has ovate, pointed, toothed, mid- to dark green leaves. In summer and early fall produces large, usually conical panicles of tiny, sometimes rose-tinted, creamy-white, fertile flowers surrounded by large, petal-like, white, sterile flowers (florets) that usually mature to varying shades of pink. Prune moderately to hard annually to promote vigorous growth and large inflorescences. Z4–8 H8–1. **'Big Ben'** (illus. p.134), **H** and **S** 5½ft (1.7m), has an upright habit, red stems and, in mid-summer, produces masses of large, conical panicles of pale green, sterile florets that turn white and then mature to deep pink in mid-fall. Needs moderate to hard pruning. **'Brussels Lace'** has dark green leaves and white flowers in late summer and early fall. Needs moderate pruning. **'Dharuma'** (illus. p.135), **H** and **S** 4ft (1.2m), is a compact, relatively slow-growing cultivar with mahogany-red stems, dark green leaves and rounded panicles of white, sterile florets in mid-summer; these mature to deep pink by mid-fall. Is best left unpruned or given only light pruning annually. Is good in a small garden. **'Floribunda'** has dense conical heads of small, fertile, central flowers surrounded by large, white ray flowers. **'Grandiflora'** has large, oval and dark green leaves. Large, conical panicles of mostly sterile, white flowers turn pink or red from late summer. Prune back hard in spring to obtain largest panicles. **'Limelight'** (illus. p.135), **H** 5½ft (1.7m), **S** 7ft (2.2m), is robust and produces very dense, broadly conical panicles of lime-green, sterile florets in mid-summer gradually maturing to a mixture of lime-green and warm pink by mid-fall. Needs moderate pruning. **'Phantom'** (illus. p.134), **H** 5ft (1.5m), **S** 7ft (2.2m), is a robust, upright cultivar producing dense, conical, rounded panicles of sterile, white florets, flushed yellow-green at tips, in mid-summer; these mature to warm, deep pink by early fall. Needs moderate to hard pruning. Flower heads of **Pink Diamond ('Interhydia'),** illus. p.135 turn pink with age. **Pinky-Winky ('Dvppinky'),** illus. p.134, **H** 4½ft (1.4m), **S** 5½ft (1.6m), has a compact, upright, slightly spreading habit with dark red stems, yellowish-green leaves and dense, tapered, conical panicles of lime-green, sterile florets in mid-summer; these mature to deep pink by early fall. Responds well to moderate pruning. Is good in a small garden. **'Praecox'** flowers from mid-summer. **'Silver Dollar'** (illus. p.134), **H** 4ft (1.2m), **S** 5½ft (1.7m), is compact with strong stems supporting very dense, rounded panicles of white, sterile florets, tipped pale yellow-green, produced in mid-summer and maturing to pink in mid-fall. Responds well to hard pruning. Is very good in a small garden. **'Tardiva'** has both fertile and sterile flowers from early to mid-fall. **'Unique'** is similar to *H.p.* 'Grandiflora', but is more vigorous and has larger flowers.

H. petiolaris, syn. *H. anomala* subsp. *petiolaris*, illus. p.195.

***H.* 'Preziosa',** syn. *H. macrophylla* subsp. *serrata* 'Preziosa', *H. serrata* 'Preziosa'. Deciduous, bushy shrub. **H** 5–6ft (1.5–2m), **S** 6–8ft (2–2.5m). Has oval, toothed, light green leaves. Pink flowers turn to deep crimson. Z6–9 H9–6.

H. quercifolia (Oakleaf hydrangea). Deciduous, bushy, mound-forming shrub. **H** and **S** 6ft (2m). Deeply lobed, dark green leaves turn red and purple in fall. Has white flower heads from mid-summer to mid-fall. Z5–9 H9–5. **Snowflake ('Brido'),** illus. p.134 produces pure white fertile flower bracts surrounded by a double rank of white sterile flower bracts.

H. sargentiana, syn. *H. aspera* subsp. *sargentiana*. Deciduous, upright, gaunt shrub. **H** 8ft (2.5m), **S** 6ft (2m). Has peeling bark, sturdy shoots and very large, narrowly oval, bristly, dull green leaves with gray down beneath. In late summer to mid-fall bears broad heads of flowers, the inner ones small and blue or deep purple, the outer ones larger and white, sometimes flushed purplish-pink. Z7–8 H8–7.

***H. scandens* subsp. *chinensis*.** Deciduous, woody-stemmed, scandent shrub. **H** and **S** to 10ft (3m). Has spreading, often pendent, branchlets and lance-shaped, slightly leathery, toothed, mid-green leaves. In summer produces numerous, flattened flower heads with central clusters of small, white, sterile flowers and several blue to white, sterile flowers along the margins. Is suitable for training along a low wall. Z7–9 H9–7.

H. seemannii, illus. p.196.

H. serrata, syn. *H. macrophylla* subsp. *serrata* (Mountain hydrangea). Deciduous, bushy, dense shrub. **H** and **S** 4ft (1.2m). Has slender stems and light green leaves. From mid- to late summer bears flat heads of pink, lilac or white inner and pink or blue outer flowers. Z6–9 H9–6. **'Bluebird'** (illus. p.135) has pale pink, pale purple or blue flowers. **'Diadem'** (illus. p.134) has a compact habit and bright blue—sometimes pink—flowers. **'Grayswood'** (illus. p.135), **H** and **S** 5ft (1.5m), is slow-growing and bears blue fertile flowers surrounded by white to pink, sterile flowers. **'Kiyosumi'** (illus. p.134) produces purple, young leaves and pink to white fertile flowers surrounded by red-edged, white sterile flowers. **'Preziosa'.** See *H.* 'Preziosa'.

H. serratifolia, syn. *H. integerrima*, illus. p.196.

H. villosa. See *H. aspera* Villosa Group.

HYDROCHARIS

Frogbit

HYDROCHARITACEAE

Genus of one species of deciduous, perennial, floating water plant, grown for its foliage and flowers. Requires an open, sunny position in still water. Propagate by detaching young plantlets as required.

H. morsus-ranae, illus. p.434.

Hydrocleis. See *Hydrocleys.*

HYDROCLEYS

SYN. HYDROCLEIS

LIMNOCHARITACEAE/ALISMATACEAE

Genus of deciduous or evergreen, annual or perennial, water plants, grown for their floating foliage and flowers. Is best grown in large aquariums and tropical pools with good light. Propagate by seed when ripe or by tip cuttings year-round.

H. nymphoides (Water poppy). Deciduous, perennial, deep-water plant, evergreen in tropical conditions. **S** to 2ft (60cm). Has floating, oval, mid-green leaves and poppy-like, yellow flowers held above foliage in summer. Considered invasive in subtropical regions of North America. Z9–10 H10–7.

HYGROPHILA

ACANTHACEAE

Genus of deciduous or evergreen, perennial, submerged water plants and marsh plants, grown for their foliage. Remove fading leaves regularly. Propagate by stem cuttings in spring or summer.

H. corymbosa 'Stricta'. Deciduous, erect perennial suited to pond margins. **H** and **S** 12in (30cm). Long, slender leaves are purple in spring and fall. Clusters of blue flowers bloom on the main stem in summer. Z9-11, H12-8.

HYLOCEREUS

CACTACEAE

Genus of fast-growing, perennial cacti, grown for their erect, slender, climbing stems that are jointed into sections, and many aerial roots. Makes successful grafting stock, except in northern Europe. Needs sun or partial shade and very well-drained soil. Propagate by stem cuttings in spring or summer.

H. undatus (Night-blooming cereus, Queen-of-the-night). Fast-growing, climbing, perennial cactus. **H** 3ft (1m),

S indefinite. Has freely branching, 3-angled, weakly spined, dark green stems, 3in (7cm) wide and jointed into sections. In summer bears flattish, white flowers, 12in (30cm) across, that last only one night. Z11 H12–10.

HYLOMECON
PAPAVERACEAE

Genus of one species of vigorous perennial, grown for its large, cup-shaped flowers. Is good for rock gardens, borders and woodlands but may be invasive. Prefers partial shade and rich, moist soil. Propagate by division in spring or by seed in fall.

H. japonica, illus. p.335.

Hylotelephium anacampseros. See *Sedum anacampseros.*
Hylotelephium cauticola. See *Sedum cauticola.*
Hylotelephium ewersii. See *Sedum ewersii.*
Hylotelephium populifolium. See *Sedum populifolium.*
Hylotelephium sieboldii. See *Sedum sieboldii.*
Hylotelephium spectabile. See *Sedum spectabile.*
Hylotelephium tatarinowii. See *Sedum tatarinowii.*
Hymenanthera crassifolia. See *Melicytus crassifolius.*
Hymenanthera. See *Melicytus.*

HYMENOCALLIS
Spider lily
AMARYLLIDACEAE

Genus of bulbs, some of which are evergreen, grown for their fragrant flowers, somewhat like those of large daffodils. Needs a sheltered site, full sun or partial shade and well-drained soil. Plant in early summer, lifting for winter in cold districts. Alternatively, grow in a heated greenhouse; reduce water in winter, without drying out completely, then repot in spring. Propagate by offsets in spring or early summer.

H. calathina. See *Ismene narcissiflora.*
H. festalis. See *Ismene* x *deflexa.*
H. x macrostephana. See *Ismene* x *macrostephana.*
H. narcissiflora. See *Ismene narcissiflora.*
H. speciosa. Evergreen, winter-flowering bulb. **H** and **S** 12–18in (30–45cm). Has broadly elliptic, semierect, basal leaves. Produces a head of 5–10 fragrant, white or green-white flowers, 8–12in (20–30cm) wide, with a funnel-shaped cup and 6 long, narrow petals. Z14–15 H12–10.
H. x spofforthiae 'Sulphur Queen'. See *Ismene* x *spofforthiae* 'Sulphur Queen'.

HYMENOSPORUM
Australian frangipani
PITTOSPORACEAE

Genus of one species of evergreen shrub or tree, grown for its flowers and overall appearance. Prefers full sun, though some shade is tolerated. Requires rich, well-drained soil, ideally neutral to acid. Water container specimens freely when in full growth, less at other times. Propagate by seed when ripe, in fall, or in spring or by semiripe cuttings in late summer.

H. flavum (Australian frangipani). Evergreen, erect shrub or tree, gradually spreading with age. **H** 30ft (10m) or more, **S** 15ft (5m) or more. Has oval to oblong, lustrous, rich green leaves. In spring–summer bears terminal panicles of very fragrant, tubular, 5-petaled, cream flowers that age to deep sulfur-yellow. Z9–11 H12–9.

HYPERICUM
St. John's-wort
HYPERICACEAE/CLUSIACEAE

Genus of perennials and deciduous, semievergreen or evergreen subshrubs and shrubs, grown for their conspicuous yellow flowers with prominent stamens. Large species and cultivars need sun or partial shade and fertile, not too dry soil. Smaller types, which are good in rock gardens, do best in full sun and well-drained soil. Propagate species subshrubs and shrubs by softwood cuttings in summer or by seed in fall, cultivars by softwood cuttings only in summer, perennials by seed or division in fall or spring. Is generally trouble-free but *H.* x *inodorum* 'Elstead' is susceptible to rust, which produces orange spots on leaves, *H.* 'Hidcote' to a virus that makes leaves narrow and variegated.

H. balearicum. Evergreen, compact shrub. **H** and **S** to 2ft (60cm). Small, oval, green leaves have wavy edges and rounded tips. Solitary, large, fragrant, shallowly cup-shaped, yellow flowers are produced at stem tips above foliage from early summer to fall. Z6–9 H9–6.
H. beanii 'Gold Cup'. See *H.* x *cyathiflorum* 'Gold Cup'.
H. bellum. Semievergreen, arching shrub. **H** 3ft (1m), **S** 5ft (1.5m). Cup-shaped, golden-yellow flowers are borne from mid-summer to early fall. Shoots are red. Oval, wavy-edged, mid-green leaves redden in fall. Z5–9 H9–5.
H. calycinum, illus. p.161.
H. cerastioides, syn. *H. rhodoppeum.* Vigorous, evergreen subshrub with upright and arching branches. **H** 6in (15cm) or more, **S** 16–20in (40–50cm). Leaves are oval, hairy and soft grayish-green. In late spring and early summer produces masses of saucer-shaped, bright yellow flowers in terminal clusters. Cut back hard after flowering. Is suitable for a large rock garden. Z6–9 H9–6.
H. coris. Evergreen, open, dome-shaped, occasionally prostrate, subshrub. **H** 6–12in (15–30cm), **S** 8in (20cm) or more. Bears long-stemmed whorls of 3 or 4 pointed, oval leaves. Produces panicles of shallowly cup-shaped, bright yellow flowers, streaked red, in summer. Is suitable for a sheltered rock garden. Z7–9 H9–7.
H. x cyathiflorum 'Gold Cup', syn. *H. beanii* 'Gold Cup'. Semievergreen, arching shrub. **H** and **S** 3ft (1m). Produces pinkish-brown shoots, oval, dark green leaves and, from mid-summer to early fall, large, cup-shaped, golden-yellow flowers. Z8–9 H9–8.
H. empetrifolium subsp. oliganthum. See *H. empetrifolium* var. *prostratum* of gardens. **var. prostratum** of gardens, syn. *H. empetrifolium* subsp. *oliganthum* illus. p.373.
H. 'Hidcote', illus. p.160.
H. x inodorum 'Elstead', illus. p.161.
H. kouytchense, syn. *H. patulum* var. *grandiflorum,* illus. p.161.

H. x moserianum. Deciduous, arching shrub. **H** 12in (30cm), **S** 24in (60cm). Small, bowl-shaped, yellow flowers are produced above oval, dark green leaves from mid-summer to mid-fall. Z7–9 H9–7. **'Tricolor'** has leaves margined white and pink. Prefers a sheltered position.
H. olympicum. Deciduous, upright, slightly spreading, dense subshrub. **H** 6–12in (15–30cm), **S** to 6in (15cm). Tufts of upright stems are covered in small, oval, gray-green leaves. Produces terminal clusters of up to 5 cup-shaped, bright yellow flowers in summer. Z5–8 H8–5.
'Sulphureum'. See *H. olympicum* f. *uniflorum* 'Citrinum'. **f. uniflorum 'Citrinum',** syn. *H. olympicum* 'Sulphureum' illus. p.343.
H. patulum. Evergreen or semievergreen, upright shrub. **H** and **S** 3ft (1m). Large, cup-shaped, golden-yellow flowers are produced above oval, dark green leaves from mid-summer to mid-fall. Z7–9 H9–7.
H. patulum var. grandiflorum. See *H. kouytchense.*
H. reptans. Deciduous, mat-forming shrub. **H** 2in (5cm), **S** 8in (20cm). Oval, green leaves turn yellow or bright red in fall. In summer produces flattish, golden-yellow flowers, crimson-flushed outside. Is suitable for a rock garden. Z7–9 H9–7.
H. rhodoppeum. See *H. cerastioides.*
H. 'Rowallane', illus. p.206.

Hypocyrta radicans. See *Nematanthus gregarius.*
Hypocyrta strigillosa. See *Nematanthus strigillosus.*

HYPOESTES
Polka-dot plant
ACANTHACEAE

Genus of mainly evergreen perennials, shrubs and subshrubs, grown for their flowers and foliage. Needs bright light and well-drained soil. Water often in growing season, less in winter. Cut back straggly stems. Propagate by stem cuttings in spring or summer. *H. phyllostachya* may be grown as an annual using seed sown in spring.

H. aristata (Ribbon bush). Evergreen, bushy perennial or subshrub. **H** to 3ft (1m), **S** 2ft (60cm). Has oval, mid-green leaves, to 3in (8cm) long. Small, tubular, deep pink to purple flowers are produced in terminal spikes in late winter. Z14–15 H12–10.
H. phyllostachya, syn. *H. sanguinolenta,* illus. p.300.
H. sanguinolenta of gardens. See *H. phyllostachya.*

HYPOXIS
Starflower
HYPOXIDACEAE

Genus of spring- or summer-flowering corms, grown for their flat, star-shaped flowers. Is suitable for rock gardens. Requires full sun and light, well-drained soil. Propagate by seed in fall or spring.

H. angustifolia. Summer-flowering corm. **H** 4–8in (10–20cm), **S** 2–3in (5–8cm). Has slender, hairy, semierect, basal leaves. Stems each bear 3–7 star-shaped, yellow flowers. Z11–14 H12–8.
H. capensis, syn. *H. stellata, Spiloxene capensis.* Spring-flowering corm with a basal leaf cluster. **H** 4–8in (10–20cm),

S 2–3in (5–8cm). Has very slender, narrowly lance-shaped, erect leaves. Stems each produce an upward-facing flower with pointed, white or yellow petals and purple eye. Z9–10 H10–9.
H. stellata. See *H. capensis.*

HYPSELA
CAMPANULACEAE

Genus of vigorous, creeping perennials, grown for their flowers and heart-shaped leaves. Is good as groundcover, especially in rock gardens. Needs shade and moist soil. Propagate by division in spring.

H. longiflora. See *H. reniformis.*
H. reniformis, syn. *H. longiflora.* Vigorous, creeping, stemless perennial. **H** 3/4in (2cm), **S** indefinite. Has tiny, heart-shaped, fleshy leaves and, in spring–summer, small, star-shaped, pink-and-white flowers. Z7–9 H9–7.

HYSSOPUS
Hyssop
LABIATAE/LAMIACEAE

Genus of perennials and semievergreen or deciduous shrubs, grown for their flowers, which attract bees and butterflies, and for their aromatic foliage, which has culinary and medicinal uses. May be grown as a low hedge. Requires full sun and fertile, well-drained soil. Cut back hard or, if grown as a hedge, trim lightly, in spring. Propagate by softwood cuttings in summer or by seed in fall.

H. officinalis, illus. p.157. **subsp. aristatus** is a semievergreen or deciduous, upright, dense shrub. **H** 2ft (60cm), **S** 3ft (1m). Aromatic, narrowly lance-shaped leaves are bright green. Densely clustered, small, 2-lipped, dark blue flowers are produced from mid-summer to early fall. Z6–8 H9–2.

I

IBERIS

Candytuft

CRUCIFERAE/BRASSICACEAE

Genus of annuals, perennials, evergreen subshrubs and shrubs, grown for their flowers and excellent for rock gardens. Some species are short-lived, flowering themselves to death. Requires sun and well-drained soil. Propagate by seed in spring, subshrubs and shrubs by semiripe cuttings in summer.

I. amara, illus. p.299. **'Giant Hyacinth-flowered'** is a group of fast-growing, upright, bushy annuals. **H** 12in (30cm), **S** 6in (15cm). Has lance-shaped, mid-green leaves and, in summer, flattish heads of large, scented, 4-petaled flowers in a variety of colors. Z11 H10–1.

I. commutata. See *I. sempervirens* .

I. saxatilis, illus. p.360.

I. sempervirens, syn. *I. commutata*, illus. p.332. **'Schneeflocke'.** See *I. sempervirens* 'Snowflake'. **'Snowflake',** syn. *I. sempervirens* 'Schneeflocke' is an evergreen, spreading subshrub. **H** 6–12in (15–30cm), **S** 18–24in (45–60cm). Leaves are narrowly oblong, glossy and dark green. Dense, semi-spherical heads of 4-petaled, white flowers are produced in late spring and early summer. Trim after flowering. Z5–9 H9–5.

I. umbellata (Globe candytuft). Fast-growing, upright, bushy annual. **H** 6–12in (15–30cm), **S** 8in (20cm). Has lance-shaped, mid-green leaves. Heads of small, 4-petaled, white or pale purple flowers, sometimes bicolored, are produced in summer and early fall. H12–1. **Fairy Series,** illus. p.304.

IDESIA

FLACOURTIACEAE/SALICACEAE

Genus of one species of deciduous, summer-flowering tree, grown for its foliage and fruits. Both male and female plants are required to obtain fruits. Needs sun or partial shade and fertile, moist but well-drained soil, preferably neutral to acidic. Propagate by softwood cuttings in summer or by seed in fall.

I. polycarpa, illus. p.75.

ILEX

Holly

AQUIFOLIACEAE

Genus of evergreen or deciduous trees and shrubs, grown for their foliage and fruits Mainly spherical berries, ranging in color from red through yellow to black, are produced in fall, following insignificant, usually white, flowers borne in spring. Almost all plants are unisexual, and to obtain fruits on a female plant a male also needs to be grown. All prefer well-drained soil. Grow in sun or shade, but deciduous plants and those with variegated foliage do best in sun or partial shade. Hollies resent being transplanted, but respond well to hard pruning which should be done in late spring. Propagate by seed in spring or by semiripe cuttings from late summer to early winter. Holly leaf miners and holly aphids may cause problems. ⓘ Berries may cause mild stomach upset if ingested. See also feature panel p.94.

I. x altaclerensis. Group of vigorous, evergreen shrubs and trees. Is resistant to pollution and coastal exposure. Z7–9 H9–7. **'Balearica'** (illus. p.94) is an erect, female tree. **H** 40ft (12m), **S** 15ft (5m). Has green to olive-green young branches and large, broadly oval, spiny- or smooth-edged, glossy, dark green leaves. Freely produces large, bright red berries. **'Belgica',** **H** 40ft (12m), **S** 15ft (5m), is an erect, dense, female tree. Young branches are green to yellowish-green. Has large, lance-shaped to oblong, spiny- or smooth-edged, glossy, mid-green leaves. Large, orange-red fruits are freely produced. **'Belgica Aurea',** syn. *I.* x *altaclerensis* 'Silver Sentinel', *I. perado* 'Aurea' (illus. p.94), **H** 25ft (8m), **S** 10ft (3m), is an upright, female tree. Young branches are green with yellow streaks. Has large, lance-shaped, mainly spineless, dark green leaves, mottled with gray-green and irregularly edged with yellow. Red berries are produced only rarely. **'Camelliifolia'** (illus. p.94), **H** 46ft (14m), **S** 10ft (3m), is a narrow, pyramidal, female tree with purple young branches and large, oblong, mainly smooth-edged, glossy, dark green leaves. Reliably produces large, scarlet fruits; is an excellent specimen tree. **'Camelliifolia Variegata'** (illus. p.94), **H** 25ft (8m), **S** 10ft (3m), is similar to *I.* x *a.* 'Camelliifolia', but leaves have broad, yellow margins. **'Golden King'** (illus. p.94), **H** 20ft (6m), **S** 15ft (5m), is a bushy, female shrub. Young branches are green with a purplish flush. Has large, oblong to oval, sometimes slightly spiny, dark green leaves, splashed with gray-green in center and with bright yellow margin that turns to cream on older leaves. Is not a good fruiter, bearing only a few reddish-brown berries, but is excellent as a hedge or a specimen plant. **'Hodginsii',** **H** 46ft (14m), **S** 30ft (10m), is a vigorous, dense, male tree. Shoots are purple; leaves are broadly oval, sparsely spiny and glossy, blackish-green. **'Lawsoniana',** **H** 20ft (6m), **S** 15ft (5m), is a bushy, female shrub. Is similar to *I.* x *a.* 'Golden King', but has leaves splashed irregularly in center with gold and lighter green. Foliage tends to revert to plain green. **'N.F. Barnes',** **H** 18ft (5.5m), **S** 12ft (4m), is a dense, female shrub with purple shoots, oval, mainly entire but spine-tipped, glossy, dark green leaves and red berries. **'Silver Sentinel'.** See *I.* x *altaclerensis* 'Belgica Aurea'.**'Wilsonii',** **H** 25ft (8m), **S** 15ft (5m), is a vigorous, female tree with purplish-green young branches and large, oblong to oval, glossy, mid-green leaves with prominent veins and large spines. Freely produces large, scarlet fruits and makes a good hedging or specimen plant.

I. aquifolium (English holly), illus. p.94. Evergreen, much-branched, erect shrub or tree. **H** 70ft (20m), **S** 20ft (6m). Has variably shaped, wavy, sharply spined, glossy, dark green leaves and bright red berries. Z7–9 H9–7. **'Amber',** illus. p.92. **'Argentea Marginata'** (illus. p.94), **H** 46ft (14m), **S** 15ft (5m), is a columnar, female tree with green young branches streaked with cream. Broadly oval, spiny, dark green leaves, with wide, cream margins, are shrimp-pink when young. Bears an abundance of bright red berries. Is good for hedging. **'Argentea Marginata Pendula',** **H** 20ft (6m), **S** 15ft (5m), is a slow-growing, weeping, female tree with purple young branches and broadly oval, spiny, dark green leaves, mottled with gray-green and broadly edged with cream. Bears red fruits. Is good as a specimen plant in a small garden. **'Atlas',** **H** 15ft (5m), **S** 10ft (3m), is an erect, male shrub with green young branches and oval, spiny, glossy, dark green leaves. Is useful for landscaping and hedging. **'Aurea Regina'.** See *I. aquifolium* 'Golden Queen'. **'Aurifodina',** **H** 20ft (6m), **S** 10ft (3m), is an erect, dense, female shrub with purplish young branches. Oval, spiny leaves are olive-green with golden margins that turn tawny-yellow in winter. Produces a good crop of deep scarlet fruits. **f. *bacciflava.*** See *I. a.* 'Bacciflava'. **'Bacciflava',** syn. *I. a. bacciflava* (illus. p.94), **H** 70ft (20m), **S** 20ft (6m), is a much-branched, usually erect shrub or tree with variably shaped, wavy, sharply spined, glossy, dark green leaves and yellow fruits. **'Crispa Aureopicta',** **H** 30ft (10m), **S** 20ft (6m), is a male tree of open habit. Narrowly oval, twisted, sparsely spiny, blackish-green leaves are centrally blotched with golden-yellow. Foliage tends to revert to plain green. **'Ferox'** (Hedgehog holly), **H** 20ft (6m), **S** 12ft (4m), is an open, male shrub with purple young branches and oval, dark green leaves with spines over the entire leaf surface. **'Ferox Argentea'** (illus. p.94) is similar to *I.a.* 'Ferox', but has leaves with cream margins. **'Flavescens'** (Moonlight holly), **H** 20ft (6m), **S** 15ft (5m), is a columnar, female shrub with purplish-red young branches. Variably shaped leaves are dark green, with yellowish flush when young that will last year-round when grown in good light. Produces plentiful, red berries. **'Golden Milkboy'** (illus. p.94), **H** 20ft (6m), **S** 12ft (4m), is a dense, male shrub with purplish-green young branches and oval, very spiny, bright green leaves with heavily blotched, bright yellow centers. Leaves tend to revert to plain green. **'Golden Queen',** syn. *I. aquifolium* 'Aurea Regina', **H** 30ft (10m), **S** 20ft (6m), is a dense tree that, despite its name, is male. Broadly oval, very spiny, mid-green leaves are edged with golden-yellow. **'Golden van Tol',** **H** 12ft (4m), **S** 10ft (3m), a sport of *I.a.* 'J.C. van Tol', is an upright, female shrub with purple young branches. Oval, puckered, slightly spiny, dark green leaves have irregular, clear yellow margins. Produces a sparse crop of red fruits. Is good for hedging or as a specimen plant. **'Handsworth New Silver',** **H** 25ft (8m), **S** 15ft (5m), is a dense, columnar, female shrub with purple branches. Oblong to oval, spiny, dark green leaves have broad, cream margins. Bears a profusion of bright red fruits. Is excellent as a hedge or specimen plant and is good for a small garden. **'Hascombensis',** **H** 5ft (1.5m), **S** 3–4ft (1–1.2m), is a slow-growing, dense shrub of unknown sex with purplish-green young branches and small, oval, spiny, dark green leaves. Does not produce berries. Is suitable for a rock garden. **'J.C. van Tol',** **H** 20ft (6m), **S** 12ft (4m), is an open, female shrub that does not require cross-fertilization to produce fruits. Branches are dark purple when young. Oval, puckered, slightly spiny leaves are dark green. Produces a good crop of red berries. Is useful as a hedge or for a tub. **'Madame Briot'** (illus. p.94), **H** 30ft (10m), **S** 15ft (5m), is a vigorous, bushy, female tree with purplish-green young branches. Leaves are large, broadly oval, spiny and dark green with bright golden borders. Bears scarlet berries. **'Ovata Aurea',** **H** 15ft (5m), **S** 12ft (4m), is a dense, male shrub with reddish-brown young branches and oval, regularly spiny, dark green leaves with bright golden margins. **'Pyramidalis',** **H** 20ft (6m), **S** 15ft (5m), is a dense, female tree that does not require cross-fertilization to produce fruits. Has green young branches and narrowly elliptic, slightly spiny, mid-green leaves. Produces masses of scarlet fruits. Is suitable for a small garden. **'Pyramidalis Aureomarginata'** (illus. p.94), **H** 20ft (6m), **S** 15ft (5m), is an upright, female shrub with green young branches and narrowly elliptic, mid-green leaves with prominent, golden margins and spines on upper half. Bears a large crop of red berries. **'Pyramidalis Fructu Luteo',** **H** 20ft (6m), **S** 12ft (4m), is a conical, female shrub that broadens with age. Branches are green when young. Has oval, often spineless, dark green leaves and bears yellow berries. Is excellent for a small garden. **'Scotica',** **H** 20ft (6m), **S** 12ft (4m), is a large, stiff, compact, female shrub with oval, usually spineless, slightly twisted, glossy, very dark green leaves and red fruits. **'Silver King'.** See *I. aquifolium* 'Silver Queen'. **'Silver Milkboy'.** See *I. aquifolium* 'Silver Milkmaid'. **'Silver Milkmaid',** syn. *I. aquifolium* 'Silver Milkboy' (illus. p.94), **H** 18ft (5.5m), **S** 12ft (4m), is a dense, female shrub. Oval, wavy-edged, very spiny leaves are bronze when young, maturing to bright green, each with a central, creamy-white blotch, but tend to revert to plain green. Produces an abundance of scarlet berries. Makes an excellent specimen plant. **'Silver Queen',** syn. *I. aquifolium* 'Silver King' (illus. p.94), **H** 15ft (5m), **S** 12ft (4m), is a dense shrub that, despite its name, is male. Has purple young branches. Oval, spiny leaves, pink when young, mature to very dark green, almost black, with broad, cream edging. **'Watereriana',** syn. *I. aquifolium* 'Waterer's Gold', **H** and **S** 15ft (5m), is a dense, male bush with green young branches streaked yellow. Oval, spiny- or smooth-edged, grayish-green leaves have broad, golden margins. Is best grown as a specimen plant. **'Waterer's Gold'.** See *I. aquifolium* 'Watereriana'.

I. x aquipernyi. Evergreen, upright shrub. **H** 15ft (5m), **S** 10ft (3m). Has small, oval, spiny, glossy, dark green leaves with long tips. Berries are large and red. Z6–8 H8–6.

I. chinensis. See *I. purpurea* .

I. ciliospinosa. Evergreen, upright shrub or tree. **H** 20ft (6m), **S** 12ft (4m). Has small, oval, weak-spined, dull green leaves and red berries. Z6–9 H9–6.

I. cornuta (Chinese holly). Evergreen, dense, rounded shrub. **H** 12ft (4m), **S** 15ft (5m). Rectangular, dull green leaves are spiny except on older bushes. Produces large, red berries. Z7–9 H9–7. **'Burfordii',** **S** 8ft (2.5m), is female, has glossy leaves with only a terminal spine and bears a profusion of fruits. Z6–9 H9–1. **'Rotunda',**

H 6ft (2m), **S** 4ft (1.2m), is also female and produces a small crop of fruits; is useful for a tub or small garden.
I. crenata (Japanese holly). Evergreen, spreading shrub or tree. **H** 15ft (5m), **S** 10ft (3m). Has very small, oval, dark green leaves with rounded teeth. Bears glossy, black fruits. Is useful for landscaping or as hedging. Z5–7 H7–5. **'Bullata'.** See *I. crenata* 'Convexa'. **'Convexa'**, syn. *I. crenata* 'Bullata' (illus. p.94), **H** 8ft (2.5m), **S** 4–5ft (1.2–1.5m), is a dense, female shrub with purplish-green young branches and oval, puckered, glossy leaves. Bears glossy, black fruits. **'Helleri'**, **H** 4ft (1.2m), **S** 3–4ft (1–1.2m), is a spreading, female shrub with green young branches, oval leaves with few spines and glossy, black fruits. Is much used for landscaping. **f. latifolia**, syn. *I. crenata* 'Latifolia', **H** 20ft (6m), **S** 10ft (3m), is a spreading to erect, female shrub or tree with green young branches and broadly oval leaves with tiny teeth. Produces glossy, black berries. **'Latifolia'.** See *I. crenata* f. *latifolia*. **var. paludosa**, **H** 6–12in (15–30cm), **S** indefinite, is a prostrate shrub or tree with very small, oval, dark green leaves with rounded teeth. Bears glossy, black fruits. **'Variegata'**, **H** 12ft (4m), **S** 8ft (2.5m), is an open, male shrub. Oval leaves are spotted or blotched with yellow, but tend to revert to plain green.
I. dipyrena (Himalayan holly). Evergreen, dense, upright tree. **H** 40ft (12m), **S** 25ft (8m). Elliptic, dull green leaves are spiny when young, later smooth-edged. Bears large, red fruits. Z7–9 H9–7.
I. fargesii. Evergreen, broadly conical tree or shrub. **H** 20ft (6m), **S** 15ft (5m). Has green or purple shoots and oval, small-toothed, mid- to dark green leaves. Produces red berries. Z6–9 H9–6. **var. brevifolia**, **H** 12ft (4m), is dense and rounded.
I. georgei. Evergreen, compact shrub. **H** 15ft (5m), **S** 12ft (4m). Has small, lance-shaped or oval, weak-spined, glossy, dark green leaves with long tips. Berries are red. Z5–8 H8–5.
I. glabra (Inkberry). Evergreen, dense, upright shrub. **H** 8ft (2.5m), **S** 6ft (2m). Small, oblong to oval, dark green leaves are smooth-edged or may have slight teeth near tips. Produces black fruits. Z5–9 H9–3.
I. insignis. See *I. kingiana*.
I. integra. Evergreen, dense, bushy shrub or tree. **H** 20ft (6m), **S** 15ft (5m). Has oval, blunt-tipped, bright green leaves with smooth edges. Bears large, deep red berries. Z7–11 H10–7.
I. 'Jermyns Dwarf'. See *I. pernyi* 'Jermyns Dwarf'.
I. kingiana, syn. *I. insignis*. Evergreen, upright tree. **H** 20ft (6m), **S** 12ft (4m). Very large, oblong, leathery, dark green leaves have small spines. Berries are bright red. Z7–9 H9–7.
I. x koehneana. Evergreen, conical shrub. **H** 20ft (6m), **S** 15ft (5m). Young branches are green. Has very large, oblong, spiny, mid-green leaves and red fruits. Z7–9 H9–7.
'Chestnut Leaf' (illus. p.94) has elliptic, regularly spined, yellow-green leaves reminiscent of sweet chestnut.
I. latifolia. Evergreen, upright shrub. **H** 20ft (6m), **S** 15ft (5m). Half hardy. Has sturdy, olive-green young branches, very large, oblong, dark green leaves with short spines and plentiful, red fruits. Z7–9 H9–6.

I. macrocarpa. Deciduous, upright tree. **H** 30ft (10m), **S** 20ft (6m). Has large, oval, saw-toothed, mid-green leaves and very large, black berries. Z7–9 H9–7.
I. x meserveae (Blue holly). Group of vigorous, evergreen, dense shrubs. Does not thrive in a maritime climate. Has oval, glossy, greenish-blue leaves. Z5–9 H9–5. **BLUE PRINCESS ('Conapri')**, illus. p.94, **H** 10ft (3m), **S** 4ft (1.2m), is female and has purplish-green young branches, small, oval, wavy, spiny leaves and an abundance of red fruits.
I. opaca (American holly). Evergreen, erect tree. **H** 46ft (14m), **S** 4ft (1.2m). Does not thrive in a maritime climate. Oval leaves are dull green above, yellow-green beneath and spiny- or smooth-edged. Has red fruits. Z5–9 H9–5.
I. pedunculosa (Longstalk holly). Evergreen, upright shrub or tree. **H** 30ft (10m), **S** 20ft (6m). Oval, dark green leaves are smooth-edged. Bright red berries are borne on very long stalks. Z6–9 H9–6.
I. perado 'Aurea'. See *I. x altaclerensis* 'Belgica Aurea'.
I. pernyi, illus. p.94. Slow-growing, evergreen, stiff shrub. **H** 25ft (8m), **S** 12ft (4m). Has pale green young branches and small, oblong, spiny, dark green leaves. Produces red berries. Z6–9 H9–6. **'Jermyns Dwarf'**, syn. *I.* 'Jermyns Dwarf', **H** 2ft (60cm), **S** 4ft (1.2m), is low-growing and female, with glossy, very spiny leaves.
I. purpurea, syn. *I. chinensis*. Evergreen, upright tree. **H** 40ft (12m), **S** 20ft (6m). Oval, thin-textured, glossy, dark green leaves have rounded teeth. Lavender flowers are followed by egg-shaped, glossy, scarlet fruits. Z7–9 H9–7.
I. serrata (Japanese winterberry). Deciduous, bushy shrub. **H** 12ft (4m), **S** 8ft (2.5m). Small, oval, finely toothed, bright green leaves are downy when young. Pink flowers are followed by small, red fruits. Z5–7 H7–5. **f. leucocarpa** bears white berries.
I. verticillata (Winterberry), illus. p.94. Deciduous, dense, suckering shrub. **H** 6ft (2m), **S** 4–5ft (1.2–1.5m). Young branches are purplish-green. Produces oval or lance-shaped, saw-toothed, bright green leaves. Bears masses of long-lasting, red berries that remain on bare branches in winter. Z5–8 H8–5.
I. yunnanensis. Evergreen, spreading to erect shrub. **H** 12ft (4m), **S** 8ft (2.5m). Branches are downy. Small, oval leaves, with rounded teeth, are brownish-green when young, glossy, dark green in maturity. Produces red berries. Z5–8 H8–5.

ILLICIUM

ILLICIACEAE/SCHISANDRACEAE

Genus of evergreen, spring- to early summer-flowering trees and shrubs, grown for their foliage and unusual flowers. Does best in partial or full shade and moist, neutral to acidic soil. Propagate by semiripe cuttings in summer.
I. anisatum (Chinese anise). Slow-growing, evergreen, conical tree or shrub. **H** and **S** 20ft (6m). Produces oval, aromatic, glossy, dark green leaves. Star-shaped, greenish-yellow flowers, with numerous narrow petals, are borne in mid-spring. Z7–9 H9–7.

I. floridanum (Purple anise). Evergreen, bushy shrub. **H** and **S** 6ft (2m). Lance-shaped, leathery, deep green leaves are very aromatic. Star-shaped, red or purplish-red flowers, with numerous narrow petals, are produced in late spring and early summer. Z7–9 H9–4.

IMPATIENS
Balsam, Busy Lizzie

BALSAMINACEAE

Genus of annuals and mainly evergreen perennials and subshrubs, often with succulent but brittle stems. In cold climates, some may be herbaceous. Prefers sun or partial shade and moist but not waterlogged soil. Propagate by seed or by stem cuttings in spring or summer. Red spider mite, aphids and whitefly may cause problems under glass.
I. balsamina, illus. p.300. **'Blackberry Ice'** is a fast-growing, upright, bushy annual. **H** 28in (70cm), **S** 18in (45cm). Half hardy. Has lance-shaped, pale green leaves and, in summer and early fall, large, double, purple flowers, splashed with white. H12–1. **Tom Thumb Series**, **H** to 12in (30cm), **S** 18in (45cm), is a dwarf, sparsely branched, slightly hairy annual with toothed leaves. From summer to early fall produces double, pink, scarlet, violet or white flowers. H12–1.
I. **Expo Series 'Expo Pink'**, illus. p.307.
I. **Fusion Series FUSION PEACH FROST ('Balfuspeafro')**, illus. p.325.
I. **New Guinea Group 'Mimas'.** Subshrubby hybrid perennial, grown as an annual. **H** 12in (30cm), **S** 14–16in (35–40cm). Opposite or whorled, toothed, mid-green leaves often have central yellowish-green marks. Bears large, red open-faced flowers in spring–fall. Z9–15 H7–1.
I. niamniamensis. Evergreen, bushy perennial. **H** to 3ft (90cm), **S** 1ft (30cm). Has reddish-green stems and oval, toothed leaves. Showy, 5-petaled, hooded, yellowish-green flowers, each with a long, orange, red, crimson or purple spur, are produced in summer–fall. Z13–15 H12–1. **'Congo Cockatoo'** has red, green and yellow flowers.
I. oliveri. See *I. sodenii*.
I. repens, illus. p.476.
I. sodenii, syn. *I. oliveri*. Evergreen, strong-growing, bushy perennial. **H** 4ft (1.2m) or more, **S** 2ft (60cm). Narrowly oval, toothed leaves are in whorls of 4–10. Almost flat, white or pale pink to mauve flowers are produced mainly in summer. Z10–15 H12–1.
I. **Sunpatiens Series SUNPATIENS COMPACT ORANGE ('Sakimp011')**, illus. p.325.
I. tinctoria, illus. p.216.
I. walleriana (Busy lizzie, Patience plant). Fast-growing, evergreen, bushy perennial, usually grown as an annual. **H** and **S** to 2ft (60cm). Has oval, fresh green leaves. Flattish, 5-petaled, spurred, bright red, pink, purple, violet or white flowers are produced in spring–fall. Z10–15 H12–1. **Accent Series 'Accent Pink'**, **H** 8–10in (20–25cm), **S** 10–12in (25–30cm), is compact and has blush-pink flowers, with dark centers, in summer–fall. Hates drought. **Confection Series**, **H** and **S** 8–12in (20–30cm) have fresh green leaves and

small, double or semidouble flowers, in shades of red or pink. **Fiesta Series 'Fiesta Apple Blossom'**, **H** 10–16in (25–40cm), **S** 10–14in (25–35cm), is a mound-forming, well branched and prolific. Produces fully double, dark-centered, blush-pink flowers in summer–fall. Is good in a hanging basket or other container or in a border. Hates drought. **Masquerade ('Tuckmas')**, illus. p.307. **Super Elfin Series**, **H** and **S** 8in (20cm), has flowers in mixed colors. **Swirl Series** plants, **H** 6–8in (15–20cm), **S** to 24in (60cm), have light green to red-flushed stems and leaves. In summer bear pink- and orange flowers margined in rose-red. **Tempo Series**, **H** to 9in (23cm), include shades of violet, orange, pink and red, as well as bicolors and picotees.

IMPERATA

GRAMINEAE/POACEAE

See also GRASSES, BAMBOOS, RUSHES and SEDGES.
I. cylindrica **'Rubra'**, illus. p.285.

INCARVILLEA

BIGNONIACEAE

Genus of late spring- or summer-flowering perennials, suitable for rock gardens and borders. Protect crowns with straw or compost in winter. Requires sun and fertile, well-drained soil. Propagate by seed in fall or spring.
I. delavayi, illus. p.265.
I. mairei, illus. p.265.

INDIGOFERA

LEGUMINOSAE/PAPILIONACEAE

Genus of perennials and deciduous shrubs, grown for their foliage and small, pealike flowers. Cold weather often cuts plants to ground, but they usually regrow from the base in spring. Needs full sun and fertile, well-drained soil. Cut out dead wood in spring. Propagate by softwood cuttings in summer or by seed in fall.
I. decora. Deciduous, bushy shrub. **H** 1½ft (45cm), **S** 3ft (1m). Glossy, dark green leaves each have 7–13 oval leaflets. Long spikes of pink or white flowers are borne from mid- to late summer. Z7–9 H9–7.
I. dielsiana, illus. p.152.
I. gerardiana. See *I. heterantha*.
I. heterantha, syn. *I. gerardiana*, illus. p.133.
I. pseudotinctoria. Deciduous, arching shrub. **H** 3ft (1m) or more, **S** 6ft (2m). Each dark green leaf has usually 7–9 oval leaflets. Long, dense racemes of small, pale pink flowers are borne in mid-summer to early fall. Z7–9 H9–7.

INULA

COMPOSITAE/ASTERACEAE

Genus of summer-flowering, clump-forming, sometimes rhizomatous perennials. Most need sun and moist but well-drained soil. Propagate by seed or division in spring or fall.
I. acaulis. Tuft-forming, rhizomatous perennial. **H** 2–4in (5–10cm), **S** 6in (15cm). Has lance-shaped to elliptic, hairy leaves. Solitary, almost stemless, daisylike, golden-yellow flower heads are produced in

summer. Is good for a rock garden. Z4–9 H8–1.

I. ensifolia, illus. p.277.

I. hookeri, illus. p.243.

I. macrocephala. See *I. royleana*.

I. magnifica, illus. p.219.

I. oculis-christi. Spreading, rhizomatous perennial. **H** 18in (45cm), **S** 24in (60cm). Stems each bear 2 or 3 daisylike, yellow flower heads in summer. Has lance-shaped to elliptic, hairy, mid-green leaves. Z4–8 H8–4.

I. royleana, syn. *I. macrocephala*, illus. p.277.

IOCHROMA
SOLANACEAE

Genus of evergreen, semievergreen and deciduous shrubs and small trees, grown for their flowers. Needs full light or partial shade and fertile, well-drained soil. Water container plants freely when in full growth, moderately at other times. Tip-prune young plants to stimulate a bushy habit. Cut back flowered stems by half in late winter. Propagate by greenwood or semiripe cuttings in summer. Whitefly and red spider mite are sometimes troublesome.

I. australe, syn. *Acnistus australis*, illus. p.138.

I. cyaneum, syn. *I. tubulosum*, illus. p.457.

I. tubulosum. See *I. cyaneum* .

IONOPSIDIUM
CRUCIFERAE/BRASSICACEAE

Genus of annuals. Only one species is usually cultivated, for rock gardens and as edging. Needs partial shade and fertile, well-drained soil. Propagate by seed sown outdoors in spring, early summer or early fall.

I. acaule (Violet cress). Fast-growing, upright annual. **H** 2–3in (5–8cm), **S** 1in (2.5cm). Rounded leaves are mid-green. Tiny, 4-petaled, lilac or white flowers, flushed with deep blue, are produced in summer and early fall. H8–1.

IPHEION
LILIACEAE/ALLIACEAE

Genus of bulbs, grown for their freely produced, star-shaped, blue, white or yellow flowers in spring. Makes excellent container plants in cold greenhouses. Prefers a sheltered situation in dappled sunlight and well-drained soil. Plant in fall; after flowering, dies down for summer. Propagate by offsets in late summer or early fall.

I. uniflorum (Spring starflower). **'Froyle Mill',** illus. p.419. **'Wisley Blue'** is a spring-flowering bulb. **H** 4–6in (10–15cm), **S** 2–3in (5–8cm). Bears linear, semierect, pale green, basal leaves, which smell of onions if damaged. Leafless stems each produce an upward-facing, pale blue flower, 1¼–1½ in (3–4cm) across. Z6–9 H9–6.

IPOMOEA
SYN. MINA, PHARBITIS
Morning glory
CONVOLVULACEAE

Genus of mainly evergreen shrubs, perennials, annuals and soft- or woody-stemmed, twining climbers. Needs full light and rich, well-drained soil. Water freely when in full growth, less at other times. Support is needed. Thin out or cut back congested growth in spring. Propagate by seed in spring or by softwood or semiripe cuttings in summer. Whitefly and red spider mite may cause problems. ① Seeds are highly toxic if ingested.

I. acuminata. See *I. indica* .

I. alba, syn. *I. bona-nox, Calonyction aculeatum* (Belle de nuit, Moonflower). Evergreen, soft-stemmed, twining climber with prickly stems that exude milky juice when cut. **H** 22ft (7m) or more. Has oval or sometimes 3-lobed leaves. Fragrant, tubular, white flowers, with expanded mouths, open at night in summer. Z12–15 H12–10.

I. batatas (Sweet potato). **'Blackie',** illus. p.311. **'Margarita',** illus. p.318.

I. bona-nox. See *I. alba* .

I. coccinea, syn. *Quamoclit coccinea* (Red morning glory, Star morning glory). Annual, twining climber. **H** to 10ft (3m). Arrow- or heart-shaped leaves are long-pointed and often toothed. Fragrant, tubular, scarlet flowers, with yellow throats and expanded mouths, are produced in late summer and fall. H12–1.

I. hederacea, illus. p.204.

I. horsfalliae. Strong-growing, evergreen, woody-stemmed, twining climber. **H** 6–10ft (2–3m). Leaves have 5–7 radiating lobes or leaflets; stalked clusters of funnel-shaped, deep rose-pink or rose-purple flowers are borne in summer–winter. Z13–15 H12–6. The flowers of **'Briggsii'** are larger and more richly colored than those of the species.

I. imperialis. See *I. nil*.

I. indica, syn. *I. acuminata, I. learii*, illus. p.462.

I. learii. See *I. indica* .

I. lobata, syn. *I. versicolor, Quamoclit lobata*, illus. p.202.

I. x multifida, syn. *I. x sloteri* (Cardinal climber). Annual, twining climber. **H** 10ft (3m). Triangular-oval leaves are divided into 7–15 segments. Tubular, wide-mouthed, crimson flowers, with white eyes, are produced in summer. H12–1.

I. nil, syn. *I. imperialis*. **'Early Call'** is a short-lived, soft-stemmed, perennial, twining climber with hairy stems, best grown as an annual. **H** to 12ft (4m). Leaves are heart-shaped or 3-lobed. From summer to early fall bears large, funnel-shaped flowers in a range of colors, with white tubes. H12–1. **'Scarlett O'Hara'** has deep red flowers.

I. purpurea, syn. *Convolvulus purpureus* (Common morning glory). Short-lived, soft-stemmed, perennial, twining climber, best grown as an annual. **H** to 15ft (5m). Has hairy stems and heart-shaped or 3-lobed leaves. From summer to early fall bears funnel-shaped, deep purple to bluish-purple or reddish flowers, with white throats and bristly sepals. H12–1.

I. quamoclit, syn. *Quamoclit pennata*, illus. p.202.

I. rubrocaerulea 'Heavenly Blue'. See *I. tricolor* 'Heavenly Blue'.

I. x sloteri. See *I. x multifida*.

I. tricolor 'Heavenly Blue', syn. *I. rubrocaerulea* 'Heavenly Blue', illus. p.205.

I. tuberosa. See *Merremia tuberosa*.

I. versicolor. See *I. lobata*.

IPOMOPSIS
POLEMONIACEAE

Genus of perennials and biennials, often grown as container plants for greenhouses and conservatories. Needs cool, airy conditions with bright light and fertile, well-drained soil. Propagate by seed sown under glass in early spring or early summer.

I. aggregata. Slow-growing biennial with upright, slender, hairy stems. **H** to 3ft (1m), **S** 1ft (30cm). Mid-green leaves are divided into linear leaflets. Fragrant, trumpet-shaped flowers, borne in summer, are usually brilliant red, sometimes spotted yellow, but may be rose, yellow or white. Z6–9 H9–6.

IRESINE
AMARANTHACEAE

Genus of perennials, grown for their colorful leaves. Requires bright light to retain leaf color and a good-quality, loamy, well-drained soil. Pinch out tips in growing season to obtain bushy plants. Propagate by stem cuttings in spring.

I. herbstii (Beefsteak plant). Bushy perennial. **H** to 24in (60cm), **S** 18in (45cm). Has red stems and rounded, purplish-red leaves, notched at their tips and 4in (10cm) long, with paler or yellowish-red veins. Flowers are insignificant. Z11–12 H12–1. **'Aureoreticulata',** illus. p.319.

I. lindenii (Blood leaf). Bushy perennial. **H** 24in (60cm), **S** 18in (45cm). Has lance-shaped, dark red leaves, 2–4in (5–10cm) long. Flowers are insignificant. Z11–12 H12–1.

IRIS
IRIDACEAE

Genus of upright, rhizomatous or bulbous (occasionally fleshy-rooted) perennials, some of which are evergreen, grown for their distinctive and colorful flowers. Each flower has 3 usually large "falls" (pendent or semi-pendent petals), which in a number of species have conspicuous beards or crests; 3 generally smaller "standards" (erect, horizontal or, occasionally, pendent petals); and a 3-branched style. In many irises, the style branches are petal-like. Unless otherwise stated below, flower stems are unbranched. Green, then brown seed pods are ellipsoid to cylindrical and often ribbed. Irises are suitable for borders, rock gardens, woodlands, watersides, bog gardens, alpine houses, cold frames and containers. Some groups thrive only in the specific growing conditions mentioned below. Propagate species by division of rhizomes or offsets in late summer or by seed in fall, named cultivars by division only.

Botanically, irises are divided into a number of sub-genera and sections, and it is convenient, for horticultural purposes, to use some of these botanical names for groups of irises with similar characteristics and requiring comparable cultural treatment. ① All parts may cause severe discomfort if ingested; contact with the sap may irritate skin. See also feature panel pp.224–25.

Rhizomatous These irises have rhizomes as rootstocks; leaves are sword-shaped and usually in a basal fan.

Bearded irises are rhizomatous and have "beards," consisting of numerous often colored hairs, along the center of each fall. In some irises, the end of the beard is enlarged into the shape of a horn. The group covers the vast majority of irises, including many named cultivars, grown in gardens; all are derived from *I. pallida* and related species. Bearded irises thrive in full sun in fairly rich, well-drained, preferably slightly alkaline soil. Some are very tolerant and will grow and flower reasonably in partial shade in poorer soil. For horticultural purposes, various groupings of hybrid bearded irises are recognized, based mainly on the height of the plants in flower. These include **Miniature Dwarf, H** to 8in (20cm); **Standard Dwarf, H** 8–16in (20–40cm); **Intermediate, H** 16–28in (40–70cm); and **Tall, H** 28in (70cm) or more (this last category may be further subdivided). In general, the shorter the iris, the earlier the flowering season (from early spring to early summer). **Oncocyclus** irises are rhizomatous, with very large and often bizarrely colored flowers, one to each stem, which have bearded falls. They require full sun, sharply drained but fairly rich soil and, after flowering, a dry period of dormancy in summer and early fall. Difficult to cultivate successfully, they are best grown in an alpine house or covered frame in climates subject to summer rains.

Regelia irises are closely related to Oncocyclus irises, differing in having bearded standards as well as falls and in having 2 flowers to each stem. They require similar conditions of cultivation, although a few species, such as *I. hoogiana*, have proved easier to grow than Oncocyclus irises. Hybrids between the 2 groups have been raised and are known as **Regeliocyclus** irises.

Beardless irises, also rhizomatous, lack hairs on the falls; most have very similar cultural requirements to bearded irises but some prefer heavier soil. Various groupings are recognized, of which the following are the most widely known. **Pacific Coast** irises, a group of Californian species and their hybrids, prefer acidic to neutral soil and grow well in sun or partial shade, appreciating some humus in the soil; they are best grown from seed as they resent being moved. **Spuria** irises (*I. spuria* and its relatives) grow in sun or partial shade and well-drained but moist soil. A number of species and hybrids prefers moist, waterside conditions; these include the well-known Siberian irises (*I. sibirica* and its relatives) and the **Japanese** water irises, such as *I. ensata* and *I. laevigata*, which may also be grown as border plants, but succeed best in open, sunny, rich, moist positions. **Crested** irises, also rhizomatous, have ridges, or cockscomb-like crests, instead of beards. They include the **Evansia** irises, with often widely spreading, creeping stolons. Most have very similar cultivation requirements to bearded irises but some prefer damp, rich conditions.

Bulbous These irises are distinguished by having bulbs as storage organs, sometimes with thickened, fleshy roots, and leaves that are lance-shaped and channeled; 4-sided (more or less square in cross section); or almost cylindrical—unlike the flat and usually sword-shaped leaves of the rhizomatous irises. **Xiphium** irises include the commonly grown Spanish, English and Dutch irises, which are excellent both for garden decoration and as cut flowers. All are easy to cultivate in sunny, well-drained sites, preferring slightly alkaline conditions, but also growing well on acidic soil. **Spanish** irises are derived from *I. xiphium*, which is variable in flower color, from blue and violet to yellow and white, and produces its channeled leaves in fall. **English** irises have been produced from *I. latifolia*, which varies from blue to violet (occasionally white) and produces its channeled leaves in spring. **Dutch** irises are hybrids of *I. xiphium* and the related pale to deep blue *I. latifolia*. They are extremely variable in flower color. **Juno** irises have bulbs with thickened, fleshy roots, channeled leaves and very small standards that are sometimes only bristly and usually horizontally placed. Although very beautiful in flower, they are mostly difficult to grow successfully, requiring the same cultivation conditions as Oncocyclus irises to thrive. Care must be taken not to damage the fleshy roots when transplanting or dividing clumps.

Reticulata irises include the dwarf, bulbous irises valuable for flowering early in the year. Unlike other bulbous irises, they have netlike bulb tunics and leaves that are 4-sided, or occasionally cylindrical. With few exceptions (not described here), Reticulata irises grow well in open, sunny, well-drained sites.

I. **'About Town'.** Vigorous, rhizomatous, bearded iris (Tall). **H** 39in (1m), **S** indefinite. Very frilly flowers with soft mauve-lilac standards and deep violet falls, edged with soft mauve-lilac, are borne from early to mid-summer. Beards are orange. Z11–13 H12–1.
I. **acutiloba.** Rhizomatous Oncocyclus iris. **H** 3–10in (8–25cm), **S** 12–15in (30–38cm). Has narrowly sickle-shaped, mid-green leaves. In late spring produces solitary, strongly purple-violet- or brownish-purple-veined, white flowers, 2–3in (5–7cm) across, with a dark brown blaze around the beard of each fall. Z13–15 H12–1.
I. **'Alida'.** Bulbous Reticulata iris. **H** 4–6in (10–15cm), **S** 1½–2½in (4–6cm). In early spring bears a solitary, fragrant, long-tubed, light blue flower, 1½–2½in (4–6cm) wide, with a yellow ridge down each fall center. Z13–15 H12–1.
I. **'Alizes'.** Vigorous, rhizomatous, bearded iris (Tall). **H** 32in (80cm), **S** indefinite. In summer, large, frilly white flowers are produced with violet-blue falls that pale to white in center of petals. Beards are yellow. Z13–15 H12–1.
I. **'Amethyst Dancer'.** Rhizomatous, bearded iris (Tall). **H** 34in (85cm), **S** indefinite. Scented flowers with peach-buff standards, crinkled around edges, are produced in summer. Wine-purple falls are faded around edges, and white veins sit around orange-tipped beards. Z13–15 H12–1.
I. **'Annabel Jane'.** Vigorous, rhizomatous, bearded iris (Tall). **H** 4ft (1.2m), **S** indefinite. In summer, well-branched stem bears 8–12 flowers, 6–10in (15–25cm) across, with pale lilac falls and paler standards. Z4–9 H9–1.

I. **'Anniversary'.** Rhizomatous, beardless Siberian iris. **H** 2½ft (75cm), **S** indefinite. In mid- and late spring bears 1–4 white flowers, 2–4in (5–10cm) across, with a yellow stripe in throat of each fall. Grows well in moist soil or a bog garden. Z4–9 H9–1.
I. **aphylla.** Rhizomatous, bearded iris. **H** 6–12in (15–30cm), **S** indefinite. Branched stem produces up to 5 pale to dark purple or blue-violet flowers, 2½–3in (6–7cm) across, in late spring and sometimes again in fall if conditions are suitable. Z3–9 H9–1.
I. **aucheri.** Bulbous Juno iris. **H** 6–10in (15–25cm), **S** 6in (15cm). Has channeled, mid-green leaves packed closely together on stem, looking somewhat leek-like. In late spring bears up to 6 blue to white flowers, 2½–3in (6–7cm) across, with yellow-ridged falls, in leaf axils. Z3–9 H9–1.
I. **aurea.** See *I. crocea* .
I. **'Autumn Circus'**, illus. p.224. Vigorous, rhizomatous, bearded iris (Tall). **H** 32in (80cm), **S** indefinite. Well-branched stems bear scented, gently ruffled, white flowers, with violet-blue margins and violet-blue feathering and penciling on standards and falls, in late spring. Often blooms again in summer. Z3–9 H9–1.
I. **'Autumn Leaves'.** Vigorous, rhizomatous, bearded iris (Tall). **H** 32in (80cm), **S** indefinite. In mid-spring produces branched sprays of sweetly scented, caramel-colored flowers, a blend of brown and purple, with orange-yellow beards. Z3–9 H9–1.
I. **'Badlands'.** Rhizomatous, bearded iris (Tall). **H** 38in (95cm), **S** indefinite. In early to mid-summer, branched stem produces large, ruffled, black, well-proportioned flowers. Z3–9 H9–1.
I. **bakeriana.** Bulbous Reticulata iris. **H** 4in (10cm), **S** 2–2½in (5–6cm). In early spring bears a solitary, long-tubed, pale blue flower, 2–2½in (5–6cm) across, with each fall having a dark blue blotch at tip and a spotted, deep blue center. Has narrow, almost cylindrical leaves that are very short at flowering time but elongate later. Z3–9 H9–1.
I. **'Ballyhoo'.** Robust, rhizomatous, bearded iris (Tall). **H** 36–39in (90–100cm), **S** indefinite. In mid- to late spring produces large blooms with ruffled, lemon-white standards and veined, rosy-purple falls with yellow-tipped, white beards. Z3–9 H9–1.
I. **'Banbury Beauty'.** Rhizomatous, beardless Pacific Coast iris. **H** 18in (45cm), **S** indefinite. In late spring and early summer, branched stem produces 2–10 light lavender flowers, 4–6in (10–15cm) across, with purple zone on each fall. Z3–9 H9–1.
I. **'Berlin Tiger'**, illus. p.225. Rhizomatous, beardless Japanese iris. **H** 4ft (1.2m), **S** indefinite. In early summer, branched stems bear 3–5 small, dark yellow flowers, 2in (5cm) across, strongly netted with deep brownish-purple veins. Grow in rich, moist soil. Z3–9 H9–1.
I. **'Bibury'.** Rhizomatous, bearded iris (Standard Dwarf). **H** 12in (30cm), **S** indefinite. Has 2–4 cream flowers, 4in (10cm) wide, on a branched stem in late spring. Z3–9 H9–1.
I. **'Blenheim Royal'.** Vigorous, rhizomatous, bearded iris (Tall). **H** 3ft (1m), **S** indefinite. Produces lightly scented,

ruffled, rich blue flowers in summer. Z3–9 H9–1.
I. **'Blue Eyed Brunette'.** Rhizomatous, bearded iris (Tall). **H** 3ft (1m), **S** indefinite. Well-branched stem produces 7–10 brown flowers, 4–6in (10–15cm) wide, with blue blaze and golden beard on each fall, in early summer. Z3–9 H9–1.
I. **'Blue Notes Blue'.** Rhizomatous, bearded iris (Tall). **H** 36in (90cm), **S** indefinite. Scented, ruffled, mid-blue flowers, paler around edges, are produced in summer. White beards are tipped with orange toward back. Z3–9 H9–1.
I. **'Blue Rhythm'**, illus. p.225. Vigorous, rhizomatous, bearded iris (Tall). **H** 3½ft (1.1m), **S** indefinite. In early and mid-summer produces lemon-scented, well-formed, violet-blue flowers, the veins on standards slightly paler than those on the broad falls, with their yellow-tipped, white beards. Z3–9 H9–1.
I. **'Bold Print'**, illus. p.224. Rhizomatous, bearded iris (Intermediate). **H** 22in (55cm), **S** indefinite. In late spring or early summer, branched stem bears up to 6 flowers, 5in (13cm) wide, with purple-edged, white standards and white falls that are each purple-stitched at edge and have bronze-tipped, white beard. Z3–9 H9–1.
I. **'Bronze Queen'.** Bulbous Xiphium iris (Dutch). **H** to 32in (80cm), **S** 6in (15cm). In spring and early summer produces 1 or 2 golden-brown flowers, 3–4in (8–10cm) wide, flushed bronze and purple. Lance-shaped, channeled, mid-green leaves are scattered up flower stem. Z3–9 H9–1.
I. **'Brown Lasso'.** Rhizomatous, bearded iris (Intermediate). **H** 22in (55cm), **S** indefinite. In early summer, sturdy, well-branched stem bears 6–10 flowers, 4–5in (10–13cm) across, with deep butterscotch standards and brown-edged, light violet falls. Z3–9 H9–1.
I. **bucharica**, illus. p.224. Vigorous, bulbous Juno iris. **H** 8–16in (20–40cm), **S** 5in (12cm). In late spring produces 2–6 flowers, 2½in (6cm) across, golden-yellow to white with yellow falls, from leaf axils. Has narrowly lance-shaped, channeled, glossy, mid-green leaves scattered up flower stem. Is easier to grow than most Juno irises. Z5–9 H9–5.
I. **'Bumblebee Deelite'**, illus. p.225. Rhizomatous, bearded iris (Miniature Tall). **H** 18in (45cm), **S** indefinite. In late spring and early summer has flowers with yellow standards, yellow-margined, maroon falls and orange beards. Z3–9 H9–1.
I. **'Butter and Sugar'**, illus. p.227.
I. **'Carnaby'**, illus. p.225. Rhizomatous, bearded iris (Tall). **H** to 3ft (1m), **S** indefinite. Well-branched stem bears 6–8 flowers, 6–7in (15–18cm) wide, with pale pink standards and deep rose-pink falls with orange beards, in early summer. Z4–9 H9–1.
I. **chamaeiris.** See *I. lutescens* .
I. **'Champagne Elegance'**, illus. p.224. Vigorous, rhizomatous, bearded iris (Tall). **H** 34in (85cm), **S** indefinite. In early to mid-spring and again in summer produces scented, strongly ruffled flowers, with pink-washed, white standards and flaring, apricot-pink falls with darker veining and pale orange beards. Z4–9 H9–1.
I. **'Change of Pace'.** Vigorous, rhizomatous, bearded iris (Tall). **H** 36in (90cm), **S** indefinite. Large, scented flowers

are produced from early to late spring, the ruffled, veined, delicate pink standards contrasting with the brilliant white falls, which are broadly margined and flecked deep rosy-violet. Z4–9 H9–1.
I. **'Chasing Rainbows'.** Rhizomatous, bearded iris (Tall). **H** 32in (80cm), **S** indefinite. In summer produces strongly scented flowers with buff-peach standards, flushed with lilac. Falls are pale violet, fading to buff-peach at edges, with orange beards. Z4–9 H9–1.
I. **'Chief Moses'.** Rhizomatous, bearded iris (Tall). **H** 38in (95cm), **S** indefinite. From early to mid-summer produces large, scented, ruffled, brown flowers, with falls flushed with yellow, and orange beards. Z4–9 H9–1.
I. **chrysographes**, illus. p.225. Rhizomatous, beardless Siberian iris. **H** 16in (40cm), **S** indefinite. From late spring to early summer, branched stem bears 1–4 deep red-purple or purple-black flowers, 2–4in (5–10cm) across, with gold etching down falls. Prefers a moist site. Z3–9 H9–1.
I. **'Clairette'**, syn. *I. reticulata* 'Clairette'. Bulbous Reticulata iris. **H** 4–6in (10–15cm), **S** 1½–2½in (4–6cm). In early spring bears a solitary, fragrant, long-tubed, pale blue flower, 1½–2½in (4–6cm) wide, with white-flecked, deep violet falls. Narrow, squared leaves elongate after flowering time. Z5–9 H8–4.
I. **clarkei.** Rhizomatous, beardless Siberian iris. **H** 2ft (60cm), **S** indefinite. From late spring to early summer, solid stem produces 2–3 branches each with 2 blue to red-purple flowers, 2–4in (5–10cm) across, with violet-veined, white blaze on each fall. Prefers moist conditions. Z4–9 H9–1.
I. **colchica.** See *I. graminea*.
I. **confusa**, illus. p.224. Evergreen or semievergreen, rhizomatous Crested iris. **H** 3ft (1m) or more, **S** indefinite. Bamboo-like, erect stem is crowned by a fan of broad leaves. In mid-spring, widely branched flower stem produces a long succession of up to 30 short-lived, white flowers, 1½–2in (4–5cm) across, with yellow or purple spots around yellow crests. Prefers well-drained soil and protection of south-facing wall. Z4–10 H11–9.
I. **'Conjuration'.** Rhizomatous, bearded iris (Tall). **H** 3ft (90cm), **S** indefinite. In early summer bears 6–11 flowers with standards that are white at margins, suffusing inward to pale violet-blue, and white falls suffusing to deep amethyst-violet at margins. White horned beard is yellow-tipped. Z4–9 H9–1.
I. **cretensis.** See *I. unguicularis* subsp. *cretensis*.
I. **cristata**, illus. p.224. Evansia iris with much-branched rhizomes. **H** 4in (10cm), **S** indefinite. Has neat fans of lance-shaped leaves. In early summer produces 1 or 2 virtually stemless, long-tubed, lilac, blue, lavender or white flowers, 1¼–1½in (3–4cm) across, with white patch and orange crest on each fall. Prefers partial shade and moist soil; is ideal for a peat bank. Z4–10 H10–1.
I. **crocea**, syn. *I. aurea.* Rhizomatous, beardless Spuria iris. **H** 3–4ft (1–1.2m), **S** indefinite. Has long leaves. Strong, erect, sparsely branched stem produces terminal clusters of 2–10 golden-yellow flowers, 5–7in (12–18cm) across, with wavy-

margined falls, in early summer. Resents being disturbed. Z5–8 H8–4.

I. cuprea. See *I. fulva*.

***I.* 'Custom Design'.** Rhizomatous, beardless Spuria iris. **H** 3ft (1m), **S** indefinite. Strong, erect-branched stem produces 2–10 deep maroon-brown flowers, 2–5in (5–12cm) wide, with heavily veined, bright yellow blaze on each fall, from early to mid-summer. Z4–8 H8–1.

I. danfordiae. Bulbous Reticulata iris. **H** 2–4in (5–10cm), **S** 2in (5cm). In early spring bears usually solitary, yellow flower, 1¹/₄–2in (3–5cm) across, with green spots on each fall. Standards are reduced to short bristles. Narrow, squared leaves are very short at flowering time but elongate later. Tends to produce masses of small bulblets and requires deeper planting than other Reticulata irises to maintain bulbs at flowering size. Z5–8 H8–4.

***I.* 'Deep Black',** illus. p.224. Rhizomatous, bearded iris (Tall). **H** 34in (85cm), **S** indefinite. In early summer, branched stem produces unruffled flowers, 3–4in (7–10cm) across, with deep purple standards and dark indigo falls, each with orange-tipped beard. Z5–8 H8–4.

***I.* 'Desert Song'.** Rhizomatous, bearded iris (Tall). **H** 36in (90cm), **S** indefinite. In summer produces pale yellow flowers with slightly crinkled petals and long, white flash in front of bright yellow beards. Z5–8 H8–4.

I. domestica. See *Belamcanda chinensis*.

I. douglasiana. Evergreen, rhizomatous, beardless Pacific Coast iris. **H** 10–28in (25–70cm), **S** indefinite. Leathery, dark green leaves are stained red-purple at base. Branched stem produces 1–3 lavender to purple, occasionally white, flowers, 3–5in (7–12cm) wide, with variable, central, yellowish zones on falls, in late spring and early summer. Z7–9 H9–7.

***I.* 'Dreaming Spires'.** Rhizomatous, beardless Siberian iris. **H** 3ft (1m), **S** indefinite. From late spring to early summer, branched stem produces 1–4 flowers, 2–4in (5–10cm) wide, with lavender standards and royal-blue falls. Prefers moist soil. Z5–9 H9–5.

***I.* 'Dreaming Yellow',** illus. p.224. Rhizomatous, beardless Siberian iris. **H** 3ft (1m), **S** indefinite. From late spring to early summer, branched stem produces 1–4 flowers, 2–4in (5–10cm) across. Standards are white; falls creamy-yellow fading to white with age. Prefers moist soil. Z4–9 H9–1.

***I.* 'Early Light'.** Rhizomatous, bearded iris (Tall). **H** 3ft (1m), **S** indefinite. In early summer, well-branched stem bears 8–10 ruffled, white flowers, 6–7in (15–18cm) wide, heavily flushed lemon-yellow on standards; yellow-veined falls have broad margins flushed slightly deeper lemon-yellow and yellow beard. Z3–9 H9–1.

***I.* 'Electric Rays'.** Strong-growing, rhizomatous Japanese iris. **H** 3ft (1m), **S** indefinite. Ruffled, double, rich violet flowers, with white and intense, deep blue veining, are borne freely in early summer. Z3–9 H9–1.

***I.* 'Elmohr'.** Rhizomatous, bearded iris. **H** 3ft (1m), **S** indefinite. In early summer, well-branched stem produces 2–5 strongly veined, red-purple flowers, 6–8in (15–20cm) across. Z7–9 H9–7.

***I.* 'English Charm'.** Rhizomatous, bearded iris (Tall). **H** 34in (85cm), **S** indefinite. Gently ruffled flowers with cream standards, heavily veined with soft apricot-yellow, are borne in summer. Soft apricot falls are paler along edges; beards are reddish-orange. Z3–9 H9–1.

***I.* 'English Cottage',** illus. p.224. Robust, rhizomatous, bearded iris (Tall). **H** 36–39in (90–100cm), **S** indefinite. In mid- to late spring and again in summer or early fall produces large, white flowers with margins of both standards and falls washed pale blue-violet. Has deeper veining at base of falls and yellow-tipped, white beards. Z3–9 H9–1.

I. ensata, syn. *I. kaempferi*, illus. p.464. Rhizomatous, beardless Japanese iris. **H** 2–3ft (60cm–1m), **S** indefinite. Branched stem produces 3–15 purple or red-purple flowers, 3–6in (8–15cm) across, with yellow blaze on each fall, from early to mid-summer. May be distinguished from the related, smooth-leaved *I. laevigata* by the prominent midrib on leaves. Has produced many hundreds of garden forms, some with double flowers, in shades of purple, pink, lavender and white, sometimes bicolored. Prefers partial shade and thrives in a water or bog garden. **'Caprician Butterfly', H** 36in (90cm), has dark purple standards with fringed, white margins; falls are white with dark purple veins and gold patches. **'Galathea',** syn. *I.* 'Galatea', **H** 32in (80cm), has blue-purple flowers with yellow blaze on each fall. **'Moonlight Waves'** (illus. p.224), **H** 36in (90cm), is strong-growing and produces large, open, spreading, white flowers, with lime-green blazes at base of each petal. **'Rose Queen',** syn. *I. laevigata* 'Rose Queen' (illus. p.224), **H** 36–39in (90–100cm), is strong-growing and produces large, soft pink flowers, with deeper pink veining and yellow blaze at base of each fall. **'Variegata', H** 30in (75cm), has narrow foliage, brightly edged in white.

I. extremorientalis. See *I. sanguinea*.

***I.* 'Eyebright',** illus. p.225. Rhizomatous, bearded iris (Standard Dwarf). **H** 12in (30cm), **S** indefinite. In late spring produces 2–4 bright yellow flowers, 3–4in (7–10cm) wide, each with brown zone on falls surrounding beard, on usually unbranched stem. Z3–9 H9–1.

***I.* 'Feminine Charm'.** Rhizomatous, bearded iris (Tall). **H** 36in (90cm), **S** indefinite. Scented, soft pinkish-apricot flowers, with a hint of yellow, are produced in summer. Apricot falls are white edged. Z3–9 H9–1.

***I.* 'Filibuster'.** Rhizomatous, bearded iris (Tall). **H** 36in (90cm), **S** indefinite. Heavily scented, frilly flowers with rosy-purple standards are produced in summer. Pale peach falls are stained with rosy-purple, and beards are burnt orange. Z3–9 H9–1.

***I.* 'Flamenco'.** Rhizomatous, bearded iris (Tall). **H** 3ft (1m), **S** indefinite. In early summer, well-branched stem produces 6–9 flowers, 6in (15cm) wide, with gold standards, infused red, and white to yellow falls with red borders. Z4–9 H9–1.

***I.* 'Flight of Butterflies'.** Rhizomatous, beardless Siberian iris. **H** 36in (90cm), **S** indefinite. From early to mid-summer produces delicate flowers with violet-blue standards and white falls veined deep violet-blue. Z4–9 H9–1.

***I.* 'Florentina'.** See *I. germanica* 'Florentina'.

I. foetidissima (Stinking gladwin, Stinking iris), illus. p.225. Evergreen, rhizomatous, beardless iris. **H** 1–3ft (30cm–1m), **S** indefinite. Branched stem bears up to 9 yellow-tinged, dull purple or occasionally pure yellow flowers, 2–4in (5–10cm) wide, from early to mid-summer. Cylindrical seed pods open to reveal rounded, bright scarlet fruits throughout winter. Thrives in a bog or water garden, although tolerates drier conditions. Z4–9 H9–2.

I. forrestii. Rhizomatous, beardless Siberian iris. **H** 6–16in (15–40cm), **S** indefinite. From late spring to early summer, unbranched stem produces 1 or 2 fragrant, yellow flowers, 2–2¹/₂in (5–6cm) across, with black lines on each fall and occasionally brownish-flushing on standards. Has linear, glossy, mid-green leaves, gray-green below. Prefers moist, lime-free soil. Z6–9 H9–6.

***I.* 'Fortunate Son'.** Rhizomatous, bearded iris (Tall). **H** 36in (90cm), **S** indefinite. Branches of scented, velvety, rich burgundy flowers, with purple beards, are produced from early to mid-summer. Z6–9 H9–6.

I. fosteriana. Bulbous Juno iris. **H** 4–6in (10–15cm), **S** 2¹/₂in (6cm). In spring produces 1 or 2 long-tubed flowers, 1¹/₂–2in (4–5cm) wide, with downward-turned, rich purple standards, which are larger than those of most Juno irises, and creamy-yellow falls. Has narrowly lance-shaped, channeled, silver-edged, mid-green leaves scattered on flower stem. Is difficult to grow and is best in an alpine house or cold frame. Z6–9 H9–6.

***I.* 'Frank Elder'.** Bulbous Reticulata iris. **H** 2¹/₂–4in (6–10cm), **S** 2–3in (5–7cm). Has a solitary, very pale blue flower, 2¹/₂–3in (6–7cm) wide, suffused pale yellow and veined and spotted darker blue, in early spring. Narrow, squared leaves are very short at flowering time but elongate later. Z3–9 H9–1.

***I.* 'Frost and Flame',** illus. p.224. Strong-growing, rhizomatous, bearded iris (Tall). **H** 36in (90cm), **S** indefinite. In early to mid-spring produces fragrant, glistening, white flowers with gently ruffled standards, rounded falls and bright orange beards. Z3–9 H9–1.

I. fulva, syn. *I. cuprea*, illus. p.439.

***I.* 'Fulvala'.** See *I.* x *fulvala*.

***I.* x *fulvala*,** syn. *I.* 'Fulvala'. Rhizomatous, beardless iris. **H** 18in (45cm), **S** indefinite. In summer, zigzag stem produces 4–6 (occasionally more) velvety, deep red-purple flowers, 2–5in (5–12cm) across, with 2 flowers per leaf axil. Has yellow blaze on each fall. Thrives in a bog or water garden. Z6–9 H9–6.

***I.* 'Galatea'.** See *I. ensata* 'Galathea'.

***I.* 'Geisha Gown'.** Robust, rhizomatous, beardless Japanese iris. **H** 36in (90cm), **S** indefinite. In mid- and late spring produces large, delicate, double, white ruffled flowers with dark violet-blue veining and deep purple-violet center. Z3–9 H9–1.

I. germanica (Common German flag). Rhizomatous, bearded iris. **H** to 2–4ft (60cm–1.2m), **S** indefinite. Sparsely branched stem produces up to 6 yellow-bearded, blue-purple or blue-violet flowers, 4–6in (10–15cm) wide, in late spring and early summer. Z3–8 **'Florentina',** syn. *I.* 'Florentina' (Orris root), illus. p.224, has strongly scented, white flowers .

***I.* 'Golden Harvest'.** Bulbous Xiphium iris (Dutch). **H** to 32in (80cm), **S** 6in (15cm). Bears 1 or 2 deep rich yellow flowers, 2¹/₂–3in (6–8cm) wide, in spring and early summer. Has scattered, narrowly lance-shaped, channeled, mid-green leaves. Z3–9 H9–1.

I. gracilipes. Clump-forming, rhizomatous Evansia iris with short stolons. **H** 6–8in (15–20cm), **S** indefinite. In late spring and early summer, slender, branched stem produces a succession of 4 or 5 lilac-blue flowers, 1¹/₄–1¹/₂in (3–4cm) across, with violet-veined, white zone surrounding yellow-and-white crest. Has narrow, grasslike leaves. Prefers partial shade and peaty soil. Z5–8 H8–5.

I. graeberiana. Bulbous Juno iris. **H** 6–14in (15–35cm), **S** 2¹/₂ –3in (6–8cm). In late spring produces 4–6 bluish-lavender flowers, 2¹/₂–3in (6–8cm) across, with white crest on each fall, from leaf axils. Lance-shaped, channeled leaves are white-margined, glossy, mid-green above, grayish-green below, and scattered up flower stem. Is easier to grow than most Juno irises. Z6–9 H9–6.

I. graminea, syn. *I. colchica*. Rhizomatous, beardless Spuria iris. **H** 8–16in (20–40cm), **S** indefinite. In late spring, narrowly lance-shaped leaves partially hide up to 10 plum-scented flowers, 2–5in (5–12cm) wide, with wine-purple standards and heavily veined, violet-blue falls, borne on flattened, angled stem. Resents being disturbed. Z6–9 H9–5.

***I.* 'Green Spot',** illus. p.224. Rhizomatous, bearded iris (Standard Dwarf). **H** 12in (30cm), **S** indefinite. In late spring, branched stems bear 2–4 ivory-white flowers, 4in (10cm) across, with olive-green mark and yellow throat on each fall. Z6–9 H9–5.

***I.* 'Harmony'.** Bulbous Reticulata iris. **H** 2¹/₂–4in (6–10cm), **S** 2¹/₂–3in (6–7cm). In early spring bears solitary, fragrant, long-tubed, clear pale blue flower, 2–2¹/₂in (5–6cm) across, with white marks and yellow ridge down each fall center. Narrow, squared leaves are very short at flowering time but elongate later. Z5–8 H8–5.

I. histrioides. Bulbous Reticulata iris. **H** 2¹/₂ –4in (6–10cm), **S** 2¹/₂ –3in (6–7cm). In early spring produces solitary flowers, 2¹/₂–3in (6–7cm) across, which vary from light to deep violet-blue. Each fall is lightly to strongly spotted with dark blue and has white marks and yellow ridge down center. Narrow, squared leaves are very short at flowering time but elongate later. Z5–8 H8–4. **'Lady Beatrix Stanley'** has light blue flowers and heavily spotted falls. **'Major'** has darker blue-violet flowers.

***I.* 'Holden Clough',** illus. p.225. Rhizomatous, beardless iris. **H** 20–28in (50–70cm), **S** indefinite. In early summer, branched stem bears 6–12 yellow flowers, 2in (5cm) wide, with very heavy, burnt-sienna veining. Is excellent in a bog or water garden, but also grows well in rich, well-drained soil. Z5–8 H8–5.

I. hoogiana, illus. p.224. Regelia iris with sturdy rhizomes. **H** 16–24in (40–60cm), **S** indefinite. Produces 2 or 3 scented, delicately veined, lilac-blue flowers, 3–4in (7–10cm) across, in late spring and early summer. Is relatively easy to cultivate. Z7–9 H9–7.

I. iberica. Rhizomatous Oncocyclus iris. **H** 6–8in (15–20cm), **S** indefinite. Has narrow, strongly curved, gray-green leaves. Bears solitary, bicolored flowers, 4–5in (10–12cm) across, in late spring. Standards are white, pale yellow, or pale blue with slight brownish-purple veining; spoon-shaped falls are white or pale lilac, spotted and strongly veined brownish-purple. Grows best in a frame or alpine house. Z7–9 H9–7.

I. innominata. Evergreen or semievergreen, rhizomatous, beardless Pacific Coast iris. **H** 6–10in (16–25cm), **S** indefinite. Stem bears 1 or 2 flowers, 2½–3in (6.5–7.5cm) across, from late spring to early summer. Varies greatly in color from cream to yellow or orange and from lilac-pink to blue or purple; falls are often veined with maroon or brown. Z7–9 H9–7.

I. japonica, illus. p.224. Vigorous, rhizomatous Evansia iris with slender stolons. **H** 18–32in (45–80cm), **S** indefinite. Has fans of broadly lance-shaped, glossy leaves. In late spring produces branched flower stem with a long succession of flattish, frilled or ruffled, pale lavender or white flowers, ½–3in (1–8cm) across, marked violet around orange crest on each fall. Prefers the protection of a sheltered, sunny wall. Z7–9 H9–7. **'Variegata',** **H** 28in (70cm), has mid-green leaves boldly striped with white.

***I.* 'Jesse's Song'.** Vigorous, rhizomatous, bearded iris (Tall). **H** 36in (90cm), **S** indefinite. In early to mid-spring produces scented, ruffled, white flowers, the standards heavily suffused violet, the falls irregularly margined and speckled violet and the white beard tipped pale violet. Z7–9 H9–7.

***I.* 'Joette'.** Rhizomatous, bearded iris (Intermediate). **H** 18in (45cm), **S** indefinite. In late spring or early summer, branched stems bear uniformly lavender-blue flowers with yellow beards. Is excellent for cut flowers. Z3–9 H9–1.

***I.* 'Joyce',** illus. p.225. Bulbous Reticulata iris. **H** 2½–4in (6–10cm), **S** 2½–3in (6–7cm). In early spring bears a solitary, fragrant, long-tubed, clear blue flower, 2–2½in (5–6cm) across, with white marks and yellow ridge down each fall center. Narrow, squared leaves are very short at flowering time but elongate later. Z5–8 H8–5.

***I.* 'June Prom'.** Vigorous, rhizomatous, bearded iris (Intermediate). **H** 20in (50cm), **S** indefinite. In late spring or early summer, branched stem bears up to 6 pale blue flowers, 3–4in (8–10cm) wide, with green tinge on each fall. Z6–9 H9–6.

I. kaempferi. See *I. ensata* .

***I.* 'Katharine Hodgkin',** illus. p.225. Bulbous Reticulata iris. **H** 2½–4in (6–10cm), **S** 2–3in (5–7cm). Is similar to *I.* 'Frank Elder', but has yellower flowers suffused pale blue, lined and dotted with dark blue. Z5–8 H8–5.

***I.* 'Kent Pride',** illus. p.225. Strong-growing, rhizomatous, bearded iris (Tall). **H** 36in (90cm), **S** indefinite. In mid-spring produces deep chestnut-brown and white flowers; standards are faintly suffused yellow and falls have white central patch, yellow beards and yellow and brown veining, surrounded by chestnut-brown margins.

I. kerneriana. Rhizomatous, beardless Spuria iris. **H** 10in (25cm), **S** indefinite. Has very narrow, grasslike leaves. Strong, erect-branched stem bears 2–4 soft lemon- or creamy-yellow flowers, 2–5in (5–12cm) across, from each pair of bracts, in early summer. Resents being disturbed. Z6–9 H9–6.

I. korolkowii. Regelia iris with sturdy rhizomes. **H** 16–24in (40–60cm), **S** indefinite. From late spring to early summer, each spathe encloses 2 or 3 delicately blackish-maroon- or olive-green-veined, creamy-white or light purple flowers, 2½–3in (6–8cm) across. Is best grown in a bulb frame. Z8–9 H9–8.

***I.* 'Krasnia'.** Rhizomatous, bearded iris (Tall). **H** 3ft (1m), **S** indefinite. In early summer, well-branched stem produces 8–12 flowers, 5–7in (13–18cm) wide, with purple standards and purple-margined, white falls. Z3–9 H9–1.

***I.* 'Lady Mohr'.** Rhizomatous, bearded Arilbred iris. **H** 30in (75cm), **S** indefinite. In early spring produces flowers with pearly-white standards and pale yellow falls veined and spotted brownish-purple around chrome-yellow beards.

***I.* 'Lady of Quality'.** Rhizomatous, beardless Siberian iris. **H** to 3ft (1m), **S** indefinite. In mid- and late spring produces flowers with light blue-violet standards and lighter blue falls. Z3–9 H9–1.

I. laevigata. Rhizomatous, beardless Japanese iris. **H** 2–3ft (60–90cm) or more, **S** indefinite. Sparsely branched stem produces 2–4 blue, blue-purple or white flowers, 2–5in (5–12cm) across, from early to mid-summer. Is related to *I. ensata* but has smooth, not ridged leaves. Grows well in sun or partial shade in moist conditions or in shallow water. Z3–9 H9–1. **'Regal'** bears single, cyclamen-red flowers. **'Rose Queen'.** See *I. ensata* 'Rose Queen'. **'Rowden Starlight',** illus. p.437. **'Snowdrift'** has single, white flowers marked yellow at bases of falls. **'Variegata',** **H** 10in (25cm), has white-and-green-striped leaves and often flowers a second time, in early fall. Z5–9 H9–1. **'Weymouth Midnight',** illus. p.442.

***I.* 'Langport Storm'.** Strong-growing, rhizomatous, bearded iris (Intermediate). **H** 18in (45cm), **S** indefinite. In mid-spring produces smoky-chartreuse flowers, the falls overlaid with deep red-brown patches suffused and veined yellow, with cream beards. Z5–9 H9–1.

I. latifolia, syn. *I. xiphioides* (English iris). Bulbous Xiphium iris (English). **H** 32in (80cm), **S** 6in (15cm). In late spring and summer, 1 or 2 blue to deep violet flowers, 3–4in (8–10cm) wide, with yellow stripe down center of each very broad fall, are produced from the bracts. Lance-shaped, channeled, mid-green leaves are scattered up flower stem. Z5–8 H8–5. **'Duchess of York'** bears purple flowers. Flowers of **'Mont Blanc'** are pure white. **'Queen of the Blues'** has blue standards and purple-blue falls.

***I.* 'Lavender Royal'.** Rhizomatous, beardless Pacific Coast iris. **H** 18in (45cm), **S** indefinite. In late spring to early summer, branched stems bear lavender flowers with darker flushes. Z5–8 H8–5.

I. lazica. Evergreen, rhizomatous, beardless iris. **H** 6–10in (15–25cm), **S** indefinite. Has arching fans of broad, bright green leaves. In early spring produces stemless, long-tubed, lavender-blue flowers. Falls are white in lower halves, spotted and veined lavender, each with central yellow stripe. Thrives in partial shade in moist soil. Z8–10 H10–7.

I. lutescens, syn. *I. chamaeiris*. Fast-growing, very variable, rhizomatous, bearded iris. **H** 2–12in (5–30cm), **S** indefinite. Branched stem produces 1 or 2 yellow-bearded, violet, purple, yellow, white or bicolored flowers, 2½–3in (6–8cm) across, in early summer. Z7–9 H9–7. **'Nancy Lindsay'** has scented, yellow flowers.

***I.* 'Magic Man'.** Rhizomatous, bearded iris (Tall). **H** 3ft (1m), **S** indefinite. In early summer, branched stems produce flowers that have light blue standards and velvety purple falls with light blue margins; beards are orange. Z3–9 H9–1.

I. magnifica, illus. p.224. Bulbous Juno iris. **H** 12–24in (30–60cm), **S** 6in (15cm). In late spring produces 3–7 very pale lilac flowers, 2½–3in (6–8cm) across, with central, yellow area on each fall, from leaf axils. Bears scattered, lance-shaped, channeled, glossy, mid-green leaves. Z6–8 H8–6.

***I.* 'Making Eyes'.** Rhizomatous, bearded iris (Standard Dwarf). **H** 12–14in (30–35cm), **S** indefinite. In early spring produces neat flowers with pale lemon-white standards, narrow, white-margined, dark purple-violet falls and yellowish-white beards. Z3–8 H9–1.

***I.* 'Margot Holmes'.** Rhizomatous, beardless Siberian iris. **H** 10in (25cm), **S** indefinite. In early summer produces 2 or 3 purple-red flowers, 4–6in (10–15cm) across, with yellow veining on each fall. Z6–8 H7–9.

***I.* 'Marhaba'.** Rhizomatous, bearded iris (Miniature Dwarf). **H** 6in (15cm), **S** indefinite. Bears 1, rarely 2 deep blue flowers, 2–3in (5–8cm) wide, in mid-spring. Z6–8 H8–6.

***I.* 'Mary Frances'.** Rhizomatous, bearded iris (Tall). **H** 3ft (1m), **S** indefinite. In early summer, well-branched stem bears 6–9, occasionally to 12 pink-lavender flowers, 6in (15cm) wide. Z3–9 H9–1.

***I.* 'Mary McIlroy'.** Rhizomatous, bearded iris (Intermediate). **H** 16–20in (40–50cm), **S** indefinite. In early to mid-spring produces bright yellow flowers, the standards veined slightly deeper yellow, with darker veins on falls and lemon-yellow beards. Z3–8 H9–1.

***I.* 'Matinata'.** Rhizomatous, bearded iris (Tall). **H** 3ft (1m), **S** indefinite. In early summer, well-branched stem produces 6–9, occasionally to 12 flowers, 6in (15cm) wide, that are dark purple-blue throughout. Z3–9 H9–1.

I. missouriensis, syn. *I. tolmeiana*. Very variable, rhizomatous, beardless Pacific Coast iris. **H** to 2½ft (75cm), **S** indefinite. Branched stem produces 2 or 3 pale blue, lavender, lilac, blue or white flowers, 2–3in (5–8cm) wide, in each spathe, in late spring or early summer. Falls are veined and usually have yellow blaze. Z3–9 H9–1.

***I.* 'Morwenna'.** Robust, rhizomatous, bearded iris (Tall). **H** 28–32in (70–80cm), **S** indefinite. In mid- to late spring bears ruffled, pale blue flowers, with both standards and falls feathered a slightly deeper blue, and with white beards. Z3–9 H9–1.

***I.* 'Mountain Lake',** illus. p.224. Rhizomatous, beardless Siberian iris. **H** 3ft (1m), **S** indefinite. From late spring to early summer, branched stem produces 1–4 mid-blue flowers, 2–4in (5–10cm) across, with darker veining on falls. Prefers moist soil. Z3–8 H8–1.

***I.* 'Natascha',** illus. p.415.

I. ochroleuca. See *I. orientalis* .

***I.* 'Ola Kala',** illus. p.225. Robust, rhizomatous, bearded iris (Tall). **H** 3ft (1m), **S** indefinite. Produces neat, scented, rich deep yellow flowers; falls have darker yellow bases and yellow beards. Z3–9 H9–1.

***I.* 'Oriental Eyes',** illus. p.224. Vigorous, rhizomatous, beardless Japanese iris. **H** 3ft (1m), **S** indefinite. In early summer produces large, ruffled, strongly veined, purple violet flowers, with bright golden-yellow flares at base of each petal. Z3–8 H9–1.

I. orientalis, syn. *I. ochroleuca*, illus. p.224. Rhizomatous, beardless Spuria iris. **H** to 3ft (90cm), **S** indefinite. In late spring each stem, usually with one branch, bears 3–5 white flowers, 3–4in (8–10cm) wide. Falls are white with yellow centers. Leaves are often present over winter. Z6–9 H9–5.

I. orientalis of gardens. See *I. sanguinea*.

I. pallida. Rhizomatous, bearded iris. **H** 28–36in (70–90cm) or more, **S** indefinite. In late spring and early summer produces 2–6 scented, lilac-blue flowers, 3–5in (8–12cm) across, with yellow beards, from silvery spathes on strong, branched stems. Z4–9 H9–1. Leaves of **'Variegata',** syn. *I. pallida* 'Aurea Variegata' are striped green and yellow. **'Aurea Variegata'.** See *I. pallida* 'Variegata'.

***I.* 'Paradise Bird'.** Rhizomatous, bearded iris (Tall). **H** 34in (85cm), **S** indefinite. In early summer, well-branched stem produces 8–10 flowers, 5½–6in (14–15cm) wide, with magenta falls and paler standards. Z3–9 H9–1.

***I.* 'Peach Frost'.** Rhizomatous, bearded iris (Tall). **H** 3ft (1m), **S** indefinite. Well-branched stem bears 6–10 flowers, 6in (15cm) wide, in early summer. Standards are peach-pink, falls white with peach-pink margins and tangerine beards. Z4–9 H9–1.

***I.* 'Perry's Blue',** illus. p.225. Robust, rhizomatous, beardless Siberian iris. **H** 3ft (1m), **S** indefinite. In late spring and early summer produces pale purplish-blue flowers, with deeper blue veins. Slightly twisted standards and broad, rounded falls are white margined and creamy-white near bases, and have dark yellow markings in throats. Z3–8 H9–1.

***I.* 'Piona'.** Rhizomatous, bearded iris (Intermediate). **H** 18in (45cm), **S** indefinite. In late spring and early summer, branched stem bears up to 6 deep violet flowers, 3–4in (8–10cm) wide, with golden beards. Mid-green leaves have purple bases. Z3–9 H9–1.

***I.* 'Pixie',** illus. p.418.

***I.* 'Professor Blaauw'.** Bulbous Xiphium iris (Dutch). **H** 32in (80cm), **S** 6in (15cm). From spring to early summer produces 1 or 2 rich violet-blue flowers, 2½–3in (6–8cm) across. Narrowly lance-shaped, channeled, mid-green leaves are scattered up flower stem. Z3–9 H9–1.

I. pseudacorus (Yellow flag), illus. p.225. Robust, rhizomatous, beardless iris. **H** to 6ft (2m), **S** indefinite. Branched stem produces 4–12 golden-yellow flowers, 2–5in (5–12cm) wide, usually with brown or violet veining and darker yellow patch on falls, from early to mid-summer. Leaves are broad, ridged and grayish-green. Prefers partial shade and thrives in a water garden. Z5–8 H8–3. **var. *bastardii*,** syn. *I. pseudacorus* 'Sulphur Queen', illus. p.445. **'Variegata'** has yellow-and-green-striped foliage in spring, often turning green before flowering. **'Sulphur Queen'.** See *I. pseudacorus* var. *bastardii*.

I. pumila. Rhizomatous, bearded iris. **H** 4–6in (10–15cm), **S** indefinite. In mid-spring, flower stem bears 2 or 3 long-tubed flowers, 1–2in (2.5–5cm) wide, varying from violet-purple to white, yellow or blue, with yellow or blue beards on falls. Prefers very well-drained, slightly alkaline soil. Z4–9 H9–1.

***I.* 'Rare Treat'.** Robust, rhizomatous, bearded iris (Tall). **H** 36in (90cm), **S** indefinite. In mid- to late spring produces ruffled, snow-white flowers, with both standards and falls margined deep purple-blue, and bases of falls and beards similarly colored. Z4–9 H9–1.

***I.* 'Raspberry Candy'.** Vigorous, rhizomatous, beardless Japanese iris. **H** 32–36in (80–90cm), **S** indefinite. In late spring and early summer produces large, open, white flowers strongly veined red-violet, with bright yellow blazes at bases of falls. Z4–9 H9–1.

I. reticulata (Reticulated iris). Bulbous Reticulata iris. **H** 4–6in (10–15cm), **S** 1½–2½in (4–6cm). In early spring bears solitary, fragrant, long-tubed, deep violet-purple flower, 1½–2½in (4–6cm) wide, with yellow ridge down each fall center. Narrow, squared leaves elongate after flowering time. Z5–8 H8–5. **'Cantab'** (illus. p.225) has clear pale blue flowers with a deep yellow ridge on each fall. **'Clairette'.** See *I.* 'Clairette'. **'Edward',** **H** 6in (15cm), **S** ¾in (2cm), has solitary, slightly fragrant, orange-striped, blue-purple flowers from late winter to early spring. Leaves are linear and mid-green. Flowers of **'J.S. Dijt'** are reddish-purple with orange ridge on each fall. **'Violet Beauty'.** See *I.* 'Violet Beauty'.

***I.* 'Ringo',** illus. p.224. Vigorous, rhizomatous, bearded iris (Tall). **H** 36in (90cm), **S** indefinite. In late spring and early summer, lightly ruffled flowers have white standards touched purple on midribs and dark reddish-purple falls with narrow, white margins and orange beards. Z5–8 H8–5.

***I.* 'Rippling Rose'.** Rhizomatous, bearded iris (Tall). **H** 3ft (1m), **S** indefinite. In early summer, well-branched stem has 6–10 white flowers, 6in (15cm) wide, with purple marks and lemon-yellow beards. Z4–9 H9–1.

***I.* x *robusta* 'Gerald Darby',** illus. p.224. Rhizomatous, beardless Species Hybrid iris. **H** 32in (80cm), **S** indefinite. In late spring and early summer, unbranched purplish-green stems bear up to 4 violet-blue flowers, with deep yellow signals on falls. Leaves are stained purple at bases. Prefers wet conditions. Z4–9 H9–3.

I. rosenbachiana. Bulbous Juno iris. **H** 4–6in (10–15cm), **S** 2½in (6cm). In spring produces 1 or 2 long-tubed flowers, 1½–2in (4–5cm) wide, with small, downward-turned, rich purple standards and reddish-purple falls, each with yellow ridge in center. Has lance-shaped, channeled, mid-green leaves in basal tuft. Is difficult to grow and is best in an alpine house or cold frame. Z4–9 H9–1.

***I.* 'Ruban Bleu'.** Strong-growing, rhizomatous, bearded iris (Tall). **H** 32–36in (85–90cm), **S** indefinite. In late spring and early summer has scented flowers with snow-white standards and slightly ruffled, dark blue-violet falls each with large, white basal patch and orange beard. Z3–8 H9–1.

***I.* 'Ruffled Velvet'.** Rhizomatous, beardless Siberian iris. **H** to 3ft (1m), **S** indefinite. In early summer produces 2 or 3 red-purple flowers marked with yellow. Z4–9 H9–1.

***I.* 'Saffron Jewel'.** Rhizomatous, bearded iris (Intermediate). **H** 30in (75cm), **S** indefinite. In early summer, branched stem produces 2–5 flowers, 2–4in (5–10cm) across, with oyster falls, veined chartreuse, and paler standards. Falls each have blue blaze and beard. Z3–9 H9–1.

I. sanguinea, syn. *I. extremorientalis*, *I. orientalis* of gardens. Rhizomatous, beardless Siberian iris. **H** to 3ft (1m), **S** indefinite. From late spring to early summer, branched stem produces 2 or 3 deep purple or red-purple flowers, 2–4in (5–10cm) wide, from each set of bracts. Falls are red-purple with white throats finely veined purple. Z3–9 H9–1. **'Snow Queen'** (illus. p.224) has pure white flowers with yellow-green marks at base of falls.

***I.* 'Sapphire Star'.** Rhizomatous, beardless Japanese iris. **H** 4ft (1.2m), **S** indefinite. In summer, branched stem bears 3–5 white-veined, lavender flowers, 6–12in (15–30cm) wide, penciled with white halo around yellow blaze on each fall. Prefers moist soil. Z3–8 H8–1.

***I.* 'Saturday Night Live'.** Vigorous, rhizomatous, bearded iris (Tall). **H** 36–38in (90–95cm), **S** indefinite. Has mildly scented, deep red-brown to burgundy-red flowers, with bronze-yellow beards and faint, light yellow veining near bases of falls, from mid-spring to early summer. Z3–8 H8–1.

I. setosa, illus. p.441.

***I.* 'Shepherd's Delight'.** Rhizomatous, bearded iris (Tall). **H** 3ft (1m), **S** indefinite. In early summer, well-branched stem produces 6–10 clear pink flowers, 6–7in (15–18cm) wide, with yellow cast. Z3–8 H8–1.

I. sibirica, illus. p.441. Rhizomatous, beardless Siberian iris. **H** 20–48in (50–120cm), **S** indefinite. From late spring to early summer, branched stem bears 2 or 3 dark-veined, blue or blue-purple flowers, 5–10cm (2–4in) across, from each spathe. Prefers moist or boggy conditions. Z3–8 H9–1. **'Papillon'** (illus. p.225), **H** 36in (90cm), produces a prolific display of soft blue flowers, veined in white on falls. **'Shirley Pope'** (illus. p.225), **H** 34in (85cm), has velvety, dark, almost blue-back flowers, with white zone veined in purple at base of horizontal falls. **'Soft Blue'** (illus. p.225). **H** 30in (75cm), **S** indefinite. In early to mid-spring produces pale blue flowers; the long, arching falls have yellow basal markings and darker blue veins.

I. sintenisii. Rhizomatous, beardless Spuria iris. **H** 12in (30cm), **S** indefinite. Has linear, dark green leaves. In late spring produces 2 white flowers, densely veined blue-purple. Z6–8 H8–6.

***I.* 'Soft Blue'.** See *I. sibirica* 'Soft Blue'.

***I.* 'Splash Down'.** Rhizomatous, beardless Siberian iris. **H** 3ft (1m), **S** indefinite. From late spring to early summer, branched stem produces 1–4 flowers, 2–4in (5–10cm) across. Standards are pale blue and falls speckled blue on pale ground. Prefers moist soil. Z3–9 H9–1.

I. spuria. Very variable, rhizomatous, beardless Spuria iris. **H** 20–36in (50–90cm), **S** indefinite. Strong, erect-branched stem produces 2–5 pale blue-purple, sky-blue, violet-blue, white or yellow flowers, 2–5in (5–12cm) across, in early summer. Prefers moist soil. Z6–9 H9–5.

***I.* 'Stepping Out'.** Rhizomatous, bearded iris (Tall). **H** 3ft (1m), **S** indefinite. Well-branched stem produces 8–11 white flowers, 5½–6in (14–15cm) wide, with deep blue-purple marks, in early summer. Z3–9 H9–1.

I. stylosa. See *I. unguicularis*.

***I.* 'Sun Miracle'.** Rhizomatous, bearded iris (Tall). **H** 3ft (1m), **S** indefinite. Well-branched stem produces 7–10 pure yellow flowers, 6–7in (15–18cm) wide, in early summer. Z3–9 H9–1.

***I.* 'Supreme Sultan'.** Vigorous, rhizomatous, bearded iris (Tall). **H** 3ft (1m), **S** indefinite. In late spring and early summer bears large, ruffled flowers, with deep golden-yellow standards, rich dark red-brown falls that are paler at margins, and deep yellow beards. Z3–8 H9–1.

I. susiana (Mourning iris). Rhizomatous Oncocyclus iris. **H** 14–16in (35–40cm), **S** indefinite. In late spring produces solitary, grayish-white flower, 3–6in (8–15cm) wide, heavily veined deep purple. Standards appear larger than incurved falls, which each have black blaze and deep purple beard. Grows best in a frame or alpine house. Z7–9 H9–1.

***I.* 'Sweet Musette'.** Vigorous, rhizomatous, bearded iris (Tall). **H** 36–38in (90–95cm), **S** indefinite. In mid- and late spring produces large, ruffled, frilly flowers, with lavender-flushed, peach-pink standards, purplish-pink falls and orange beards. Z3–8 H9–1.

I. tectorum (Roof iris). Evansia iris with sturdy rhizomes. **H** 10–14in (25–35cm), **S** indefinite. Has fans of broadly lance-shaped, ribbed leaves. In early summer, sparsely branched stem produces 2–3 darker-veined, bright lilac flowers, ½–3in (1–8cm) across, with white crest on each fall, from each spathe. Prefers a sheltered, sunny site near a south- or west-facing wall. Z5–9 H9–3.

I. tenax. Rhizomatous, beardless Pacific Coast iris. **H** 6–12in (15–30cm), **S** indefinite. From late spring to early summer produces 1 or 2 deep purple to lavender-blue flowers, 3–5in (8–12cm) across, often with yellow-and-white marking on falls. White, cream and yellow variants also occur. Narrow, dark green leaves are stained pink at base. Z5–9 H9–5.

***I.* 'Theseus'.** Rhizomatous Regeliocyclus iris. **H** 18in (45cm), **S** indefinite. From late spring to early summer produces usually 2 flowers, 4–6in (10–15cm) across, with violet standards and violet-veined, cream falls. Is best in a frame or alpine house. Z7–9 H9–7.

***I.* 'Thornbird'.** Rhizomatous, bearded iris (Tall). **H** 3ft (90cm), **S** indefinite. In early summer produces up to 7 flowers, with pale greenish-white standards and greenish-brown falls overlaid with deep violet lines. Long, horned beard is violet, tipped with mustard-yellow. Z3–9 H9–1.

***I.* 'Titan's Glory'.** Robust, rhizomatous, well-branched, bearded iris (Tall). **H** 36–38in (90–100cm), **S** indefinite. Produces very large, deep purple-blue flowers, with almost silken texture, in mid-spring. Z3–8 H9–1.

I. tolmeiana. See *I. missouriensis*.

***I.* 'Tropic Night',** illus. p.225. Strong-growing, rhizomatous, beardless Siberian iris. **H** 36in (90cm), **S** indefinite. In late spring and early summer produces deep violet-blue flowers; upright standards and rounded falls have strong, white feathering and veining near bases and are touched yellow around throats. Z3–8 H9–1.

I. tuberosa. See *Hermodactylus tuberosus*.

I. unguicularis, syn. *I. stylosa* (Algerian iris, Winter iris). Evergreen, rhizomatous, beardless iris. **H** to 8in (20cm), **S** indefinite. Has narrow, tough leaves. Almost stemless, primrose-scented, lilac flowers, 2–3in (5–8cm) across with yellow centers to falls and with very long tubes, are produced from late fall to early spring. Buds are prone to slug attack. Is excellent for cut flowers. Prefers a sheltered site against a south- or west-facing wall. Z7–9 H9–7. **'Mary Barnard'** has deep violet-blue flowers. **subsp. *cretensis*,** syn. *I. cretensis* (illus. p.224), **H** 4in (10cm), has violet or lavender-blue standards and white or yellow falls with violet veining at bases and clear violet tips. Flowers of **'Walter Butt'** are pale silvery-lavender.

I. variegata (Variegated iris), illus. p.225. Rhizomatous, bearded iris. **H** 12–20in (30–50cm), **S** indefinite. In early summer, branched stem produces 3–6 flowers, 2–3in (5–8cm) across, with bright yellow standards and white or pale yellow falls, heavily veined red-brown and appearing striped. Z5–9 H9–5.

I. verna (Vernal iris). Rhizomatous, beardless iris. **H** 2in (5cm), **S** indefinite. In mid-spring bears 1, occasionally 2, lilac-blue flowers, 1–2in (2.5–5cm) across, with narrow, orange stripe in center of each fall. Prefers partial shade and moist but well-drained soil. Z5–9 H9–5.

I. versicolor, illus. p.442. **'Kermesina'** (illus. p.225) is a robust, rhizomatous, beardless iris. **H** 2ft (60cm), **S** indefinite. Branched stem produces 3–5 or more red-purple flowers, 2–4in (5–10cm) across, with dense, white feathering at bases of falls, from early to mid-summer. Prefers partial shade and thrives in moist soil or in shallow water. **'Rowden Cadenza',** illus. p.438.

***I.* 'Violet Beauty',** syn. *I. reticulata* 'Violet Beauty'. Bulbous Reticulata iris. **H** 4–6in (10–15cm), **S** 1½–2½in (4–6cm). In early spring bears solitary, fragrant, long-tubed, deep violet-purple flower, 1½–2½in (4–6cm) wide, with orange ridge down center of each fall. Narrow, squared leaves elongate after flowering time. Z5–9 H8–4.

I. warleyensis. Bulbous Juno iris. **H** 8–18in (20–45cm), **S** 3in (8cm). In spring produces up to 5 pale lilac or violet-blue flowers, 2–3in (5–7cm) across, in leaf axils. Each fall has darker blue apex and yellow stain in center. Bears scattered, lance-shaped, channeled, mid-green leaves. Is best in an unheated greenhouse. Z6–8 H8–6.

I. 'White Excelsior'. Bulbous Xiphium iris (Dutch). **H** to 32in (80cm), **S** 6in (15cm). From spring to early summer bears 1 or 2 white flowers, 2½–3in (6–8cm) wide, with yellow stripe down each fall center. Narrowly lance-shaped, channeled, mid-green leaves are scattered on flower stem. Z6–8 H8–6.

I. winogradowii, illus. p.225. Bulbous Reticulata iris. **H** 2½–4in (6–10cm), **S** 2½–3in (6–7cm). Solitary, pale primrose-yellow flower, 2½–3in (6–7cm) wide, spotted green on falls, is produced in early spring. Narrow, squared leaves are very short at flowering time but elongate later. Z6–8 H8–6.

I. 'Wisley White'. Rhizomatous, beardless Siberian iris. **H** to 3ft (1m), **S** indefinite. Each stem has 2 or 3 white flowers, held well above foliage, in early summer. Z6–8 H8–6.

I. xiphioides. See I. latifolia.

I. xiphium. Bulbous Xiphium iris (Spanish). **H** to 32in (80cm), **S** 6in (15cm). Has 1 or 2 blue or violet, occasionally yellow or white, flowers, 2½–3in (6–8cm) across, with central orange or yellow marks on falls, in spring and early summer. Narrowly lance-shaped, channeled, mid-green leaves are scattered on flower stem. Z5–9 H9–5. **'Blue Angel'** bears bright mid-blue flowers with yellow mark in center of each fall. Z4–9 H9–3. Flowers of **'Lusitanica'** are pure yellow. Z4–9 H9–3. **'Queen Wilhelmina'** produces white flowers in spring. Z4–9 H9–3. **'Wedgwood'** has bright blue flowers. Z4–9 H9–3.

ISATIS
CRUCIFERAE/BRASSICACEAE

Genus of summer-flowering annuals, biennials and perennials. Needs sun and fertile, well-drained soil. Propagate by seed in fall or spring.

I. tinctoria (Woad). Vigorous, upright biennial. **H** to 4ft (1.2m), **S** 1½ft (45cm). Has oblong to lance-shaped, glaucous leaves and, in summer, large, terminal panicles of 4-petaled, yellow flowers. Z4–8 H8–1.

ISMELIA
COMPOSITAE/ASTERACEAE

Genus of one species of annuals, grown for its daisylike flower heads. Needs full sun and well-drained soil. Propagate by seed in spring.

I. carinata, syn. Chrysanthemum carinatum, Chrysanthemum tricolor. **'Monarch Court Jesters'** is a fast-growing, erect, branching annual. **H** 24in (60cm), **S** 12in (30cm). Has feathery, gray-green leaves and, in summer, daisylike, zoned flower heads, to 3in (8cm) wide, in various color combinations. H9–1. **Tricolor Series** is a group of fast-growing, upright, branching annuals. Tall cultivars, **H** 24in (60cm), **S** 12in (30cm); dwarf, **H** and **S** 12in (30cm). In summer produces single or double flower heads in many color combinations.

ISMENE
AMARYLLIDACEAE

Genus of bulbs, grown for their large, white, scented flowers. Is similar to Hymenocallis and Pancratium. Requires a sheltered site in sun or partial shade and rich, well-drained soil. Plant in early summer, lifting before the first frosts in cold areas, or grow under glass, reduce watering in winter, repot in spring. Propagate by offsets in spring or by seed when ripe.

I. calanthina. See I. narcissiflora.

I. x deflexa, syn. Hymenocallis festalis. Spring- or summer-flowering bulb with a basal leaf cluster. **H** to 32in (80cm), **S** 12–18in (30–45cm). Bears strap-shaped, semierect leaves. Produces a head of 2–5 scented, white flowers, 8in (20cm) across, each with a deep, central cup and 6 narrow, reflexed petals. Z8–10 H10–6.

I. x macrostephana, syn. Hymenocallis x macrostephana. Evergreen, spring- or summer-flowering bulb. **H** 32in (80cm), **S** 12–18in (30–45cm). Has strap-shaped, semierect, basal leaves and fragrant, white or cream- to greenish-yellow flowers, 6–8in (15–20cm) wide. Z8–10 H10–7.

I. narcissiflora syn. I. calanthina, Hymenocallis calathina, Hymenocallis narcissiflora, (Peruvian daffodil) illus. p.408.

I. x spofforthiae 'Sulphur Queen', syn. Hymenocallis x spofforthiae 'Sulphur Queen', illus. p.412.

ISOLEPIS
CYPERACEAE

See also GRASSES, BAMBOOS, RUSHES and SEDGES.

I. setaceus syn. Scirpus setaceus, (Bristle club-rush). Tuft-forming, annual or short-lived, perennial rush. **H** 4–6in (10–15cm), **S** 3in (8cm). Has very slender, lax, basal leaves. Very slender, unbranched stems each bear 1–3 minute, egg-shaped, green spikelets in summer. Z12–15 H12–10.

ISOPLEXIS
SCROPHULARIACEAE/PLANTAGINACEAE

Genus of evergreen, mainly summer-flowering shrubs, grown for their flowers. Is closely related to Digitalis. Tolerates full light or partial shade and prefers well-drained soil. Water container specimens freely when in full growth, moderately at other times. Remove spent flower spikes. Propagate by seed in spring or by semiripe cuttings in late summer.

I. canariensis, syn. Digitalis canariensis, illus. p.459.

ISOPYRUM
False rue anemone
RANUNCULACEAE

Genus of spring-flowering perennials, grown for their small flowers and delicate foliage. Is suitable for peat beds, woodlands and rock gardens. Requires shade and rich, moist soil. Propagate by seed when fresh or by division in fall. Self-seeds readily.

I. thalictroides. Dainty, clump-forming perennial. **H** and **S** 10in (25cm). Central

stalk bears fernlike, 3-parted leaves, each leaflet being divided into 3. Produces small, nodding, cup-shaped, white flowers in spring. Z5–8 H8–5.

ISOTOMA
CAMPANULACEAE

Genus of perennials, often cultivated as annuals, grown for their long, tubular flowers. Is suitable for containers and summer bedding. Needs sun and moist but well-drained soil. Propagate by seed in spring, by tip cuttings in spring or softwood cuttings in summer or by division.

I. Avant-Garde Series, illus. p.313.

Isotrema griffithii. See Aristolochia griffithii.

ITEA
ESCALLONIACEAE/ITEACEAE

Genus of deciduous or evergreen trees and shrubs, grown for their foliage and flowers. Needs sun or partial shade and fertile, well-drained but not too dry soil. Propagate by softwood cuttings in summer.

I. ilicifolia, illus. p.211.

IXIA
Corn lily
IRIDACEAE

Genus of spring- and summer-flowering corms with wiry stems, grown for their spikes of flattish flowers. Needs an open, sunny situation and well-drained soil. Plant in fall for spring and early summer flowers; plant in spring for later summer display. Dry off after flowering. Propagate in fall by seed or by offsets at replanting time.

I. 'Mabel'. Spring- to early summer-flowering corm. **H** 16in (40cm), **S** 1–2in (2.5–5cm). Has linear, mid-green, basal leaves and spikes of deep pink flowers. Z10–11 H12–10.

I. maculata. Spring- to early summer-flowering corm. **H** 16in (40cm), **S** 1–2in (2.5–5cm). Leaves are linear, erect and mostly basal. Wiry stem bears a spike of flattish, orange or yellow flowers, 1–2in (2.5–5cm) across, with brown or black centers. Z10–11 H12–10.

I. monadelpha. Spring- to early summer-flowering corm. **H** 12in (30cm), **S** 1–2in (2.5–5cm). Linear, erect leaves are mostly basal. Stem produces a dense spike of 5–10 flattish, white, pink, purple or blue flowers, 1¼–1½in (3–4cm) across, often with differently colored eyes. Z10–11 H12–10.

I. viridiflora, illus. p.406.

IXIOLIRION
AMARYLLIDACEAE/IXIOLIRIACEAE

Genus of bulbs, grown for their funnel-shaped flowers mainly in spring. Needs a sheltered, sunny site and well-drained soil that becomes hot and dry in summer to ripen the bulb. Propagate by seed or offsets in fall.

I. montanum. See I. tataricum.

I. tataricum, syn. I. montanum (Tatar lily), illus. p.403.

IXORA
RUBIACEAE

Genus of evergreen, summer-flowering shrubs, grown mainly for their flowers, some also for their foliage. Prefers full sun and rich, well-drained soil. Water container specimens freely when in full growth, moderately at other times. Propagate by seed in spring or by semiripe cuttings in summer.

I. coccinea (Flame of the woods, Jungle flame, Jungle geranium), illus. p.456.

I

J K

JACARANDA
BIGNONIACEAE

Genus of deciduous or evergreen trees, grown for their flowers in spring–summer and their foliage. Needs full light and well-drained soil. Water container specimens freely when in full growth, sparingly at other times. Potted plants grown for their foliage only may be cut back hard in late winter. Propagate by seed in spring or by semiripe cuttings in summer.
J. acutifolia. See *J. mimosifolia.*
J. mimosifolia, syn. *J. acutifolia, J. ovalifolia,* illus. p.451.
J. ovalifolia. See *J. mimosifolia.*

Jacobinia carnea. See *Justicia carnea.*
Jacobinia coccinea. See *Pachystachys coccinea.*
Jacobinia pohliana. See *Justicia carnea.*
Jacobinia spicigera. See *Justicia spicigera.*

JACQUEMONTIA
CONVOLVULACEAE

Genus of evergreen, twining climbers, grown for their flowers. Needs full light and well-drained soil. Water freely except in cold weather. Provide support. Thin out by cutting old stems to ground level in spring. Propagate by seed in spring or by semiripe cuttings in summer. Red spider mite and whitefly may cause problems.
J. pentantha, syn. *J. violacea.* Fast-growing, evergreen, twining climber. **H** 6–10ft (2–3m). Has heart-shaped, pointed leaves and funnel-shaped, rich violet-blue or pure blue flowers, 1in (2.5cm) wide, in long-stalked clusters in summer–fall. Z12–15 H12–10.
J. violacea. See *J. pentantha.*

JAMESBRITTENIA
SCROPHULARIACEAE

Genus of annuals, perennials and evergreen shrubs. Needs a position in sun and in moist but well-drained soil. Propagate by seed or division in spring or by softwood cuttings in spring or summer.
J. grandiflora, syn. *Sutera grandiflora.* Much-branched, subshrubby perennial, used for summer bedding. **H** 3ft (1m), **S** 12–18in (30–45cm). Has oval to oblong round toothed leaves. Tubular, 5-lobed, frilled deep purple flowers are produced from mid-summer to fall. Z12–15 H12–10.

JAMESIA
SCROPHULARIACEAE/HYDRANGEACEAE

Genus of one species of deciduous shrub, grown for its flowers. Needs full sun and fertile, well-drained soil. Propagate by softwood cuttings in summer.
J. americana (Cliffbush, Waxflower). Deciduous, bushy shrub. **H** 5ft (1.5m), **S** 8ft (2.5m). Rounded, gray-green leaves are gray-white beneath. Clusters of small, slightly fragrant, star-shaped, white flowers are produced in late spring. Z5–9 H12–10.

JANCAEA
syn. JANKAEA
GESNERIACEAE

Genus of one species of evergreen, rosetted perennial, grown for its flowers and silver-green leaves. Makes a good alpine house plant. Is difficult to grow, as needs shade from mid-day sun in high summer, a rich, gritty, moist, alkaline soil and a gritty collar. Dislikes winter wet. Propagate by seed in spring or by leaf cuttings in mid-summer.
J. heldreichii, illus. p.355.

Jankaea. See *Jancaea.*

JASIONE
Sheep's bit
CAMPANULACEAE

Genus of summer-flowering annuals, biennials and perennials, grown for their flower heads. Needs sun and sandy soil. Remove old stems in fall. Propagate by seed in fall or by division in spring.
J. laevis, syn. *J. perennis* (Sheep's bit scabious, Shepherd's scabious). Tufted perennial. **H** 2–12in (5–30cm), **S** 4–8in (10–20cm). Has narrowly oblong, very hairy or glabrous, gray-green leaves and, in summer, spiky, spherical, blue flower heads borne on erect stems. Is good for a rock garden. Z6–8 H8–6.
J. perennis. See *J. laevis.*

JASMINUM
Jasmine
OLEACEAE

Genus of deciduous or evergreen shrubs and woody-stemmed, scrambling or twining climbers, grown for their star-shaped, often fragrant flowers and their foliage. Needs full sun and fertile, well-drained soil. *J. nudiflorum,* which needs support, benefits from having its old shoots thinned out after flowering, when others may be pruned. Propagate by semiripe cuttings in summer.
J. angulare, syn. *J. capense.* Evergreen, woody-stemmed, scrambling climber. **H** 6ft (2m) or more. Dark green leaves have 3 oval leaflets. Small clusters of fragrant, tubular, 5-lobed, white flowers are borne in late summer. Z10–11 H12–9.
J. beesianum, illus. p.193.
J. capense. See *J. angulare.*
J. grandiflorum. See *J. officinale* f. *affine.*
J. humile, illus. p.139. **'Revolutum'** illus. p.206. **f. wallichianum** has semi-pendent flowers and 7–13 leaflets.
J. mesnyi, syn. *J. primulinum,* illus. p.195.
J. nobile subsp. rex, syn. *J. rex.* Evergreen, woody-stemmed, twining climber. **H** 10ft (3m). Has broadly oval, leathery, deep green leaves. Scentless, tubular, 5-lobed, pure white flowers are pink-tinged in bud and are produced intermittently all year if warm enough. Z13–15 H12–10.
J. nudiflorum, illus. p.144.
J. officinale (Common jasmine, Poet's jasmines). Semievergreen or deciduous, woody-stemmed, twining climber. **H** to 40ft (12m). Leaves comprise 7 or 9 leaflets. Has clusters of fragrant, 4- or 5-lobed, white flowers in summer–fall. Z8–11 H12–8. **f. affine,** syn. *J. grandiflorum* illus. p.196.
J. parkeri. Evergreen, domed shrub.

H 6in (15cm), **S** 15in (38cm) or more. Produces a tangled mass of fine stems and twigs bearing minute, oval leaves. Masses of tiny, tubular, 5-lobed, yellow flowers are produced from leaf axils in early summer. Z7–11 H12–7.
J. polyanthum, illus. p.208.
J. primulinum. See *J. mesnyi.*
J. rex. See *J. nobile* subsp. *rex.*
J. x stephanense, illus. p.201.

JEFFERSONIA
Twinleaf
BERBERIDACEAE

Genus of spring-flowering perennials. Needs shade or partial shade and rich, moist soil. Extensive root systems resent disturbance. Top-dress crown in late fall. Propagate by seed as soon as ripe.
J. diphylla, illus. p.333.
J. dubia, syn. *Plagiorhegma dubia,* illus. p.355.

JOVIBARBA
CRASSULACEAE

Genus of evergreen perennials that spread by short stolons and are grown for their symmetrical rosettes of oval to strap-shaped, pointed, fleshy leaves. Makes ground-hugging mats, suitable for rock gardens, screes, walls, banks and alpine houses. Needs sun and gritty soil. Takes several years to reach flowering size. Rosettes die after plants have flowered, but leave numerous offsets. Propagate by offsets in summer.
J. hirta, syn. *Sempervivum globiferum* subsp. *hirtum,* illus. p.374.
J. sobolifera, syn. *Sempervivum globiferum* subsp. *globiferum.* Vigorous, evergreen, mat-forming perennial. **H** 4in (10cm), **S** 8in (20cm). Rounded, grayish-green or olive-green rosettes are often red-tinged. Flower stems bear terminal clusters of small, cup-shaped, 6-petaled (rarely 5 or 7), pale yellow flowers in summer. Z5–8 H8–5.

JUANULLOA
SOLANACEAE

Genus of evergreen, summer-flowering shrubs, grown for their flowers. Low temperatures cause leaf drop. Prefers full light and fertile, well-drained soil. Water container specimens moderately when in full growth, less at other times. To encourage a branching habit, tip prune young plants. Propagate by semiripe cuttings in summer. Whitefly, red spider mite and mealy bug may be troublesome.
J. aurantica. See *J. mexicana.*
J. mexicana, syn. *J. aurantica.* Evergreen, upright, sparingly branched shrub. **H** 6ft (2m) or more, **S** 2–3ft (60–100cm). Leaves are felted beneath. Has orange flowers, each with a ribbed calyx, in short, nodding clusters in summer. Z13–15 H12–9.

JUBAEA
Chilean wine palm
PALMAE/ARECACEAE

Genus of one species of evergreen palm, grown for its overall appearance. Needs full light and fertile, well-drained soil. Water container specimens moderately,

less frequently in winter. Propagate by seed in spring at not less than 77°F (25°C). Red spider mite may be a nuisance.
J. chilensis, syn. *J. spectabilis,* illus. p.80.
J. spectabilis. See *J. chilensis.*

JUGLANS
Walnut
JUGLANDACEAE

Genus of deciduous trees, with aromatic leaves, grown for their foliage, stately habit and, in some species, edible nuts (walnuts). Produces greenish-yellow catkins in spring and early summer. Young plants are prone to frost damage. Requires full sun and deep, fertile, well-drained soil. Propagate by seed, when ripe, in fall.
J. ailantifolia, syn. *J. sieboldiana* (Japanese walnut). Deciduous, spreading tree with sturdy shoots. **H** and **S** 50ft (15m). Very large leaves consist of 11–17 oblong, glossy, bright green leaflets. Bears edible walnuts in fall. Z5–8 H8–5. **var. cordiformis,** syn. *J. cordiformis* illus. p.67.
J. cathayensis (Chinese walnut). Deciduous, spreading tree. **H** and **S** 70ft (20m). Has very large leaves, consisting of 11–17 oval to oblong, dark green leaflets. Bears edible walnuts in fall. Z5–8 H8–5.
J. cinerea (Butternut). Fast-growing, deciduous, spreading tree. **H** 80ft (25m), **S** 70ft (20m). Leaves are large and very aromatic, with 7–19 oval to oblong, pointed, bright green leaflets. Bears dense clusters of large, rounded nuts in fall. Z3–9 H9–1.
J. cordiformis. See *J. ailantifolia* var. *cordiformis.*
J. microcarpa, syn. *J. rupestris,* illus. p.88.
J. nigra, illus. p.63.
J. regia, illus. p.62.
J. rupestris. See *J. microcarpa.*
J. sieboldiana. See *J. ailantifolia.*

JUNCUS
Rush
JUNCACEAE

See also GRASSES, BAMBOOS, RUSHES and SEDGES.
J. effusus f. spiralis, syn. *J. effusus* 'Spiralis', illus. p.286. **'Spiralis'.** See *J. effusus* f. *spiralis.*

JUNIPERUS
Juniper
CUPRESSACEAE

See also CONIFERS.
J. chinensis (Chinese juniper). Conical conifer, making a tree. **H** 50ft (15m), **S** 6–10ft (2–3m), or a spreading shrub **H** 3–15ft (1–5m), **S** 10–15ft (3–5m). Has peeling bark. Both scale- and needlelike, aromatic, dark green leaves, paired or in 3s, are borne on same shoot. Globose, fleshy, berry-like fruits are glaucous white. Many cultivars commonly listed under *J. chinensis* are forms of *J. x pfitzeriana.* Z3–9 H9–1. **'Aurea',** **H** 30–50ft (10–15m), **S** 10–12ft (3–4m), is a slow-growing, oval or conical form with gold foliage and abundant yellow, male cones. **'Blaauw',** syn. *J. x media* 'Blaauw', **H** and **S** 6ft (2m), is a spreading shrub with blue-green foliage. **'Expansa Variegata',** syn. *J. davurica* 'Expansa Variegata', **H** 30in (75cm), **S** 5–6ft (1.5–2m), has trailing or ascending

branchlets and yellow-variegated, bluish-green leaves. **'Kaizuka', H** 15ft (5m), **S** 10–15ft (3–5m), forms a sprawling, irregular bush and has a profusion of cones. **'Keteleeri'**, illus. p.100. **'Obelisk'**, illus. p.103. **'Plumosa Aurea'**, syn. *J.* x *media* 'Plumosa Aurea' is more erect, with green-gold foliage, turning bronze in winter. **'Pyramidalis', H** 30ft (10m), **S** 3–6ft (1–2m), is a columnar, dense form with ascending branches bearing needlelike, blue-green leaves. **'Robusta Green'**, syn. *J. virginiana* 'Robusta Green', illus. p.103. **'Stricta', H** to 15ft (5m), **S** to 3ft (1m), is conical, with soft, blue-green, young foliage.

J. communis (Common juniper). Conifer, ranging from a spreading shrub to a narrow, upright tree. **H** 1–25ft (30cm–8m), **S** 3–12ft (1–4m). Has needlelike, aromatic, glossy, mid- or yellow-green leaves in 3s and bears globular to ovoid, fleshy, greenish berries that become glaucous blue, then ripen to black in their third year. Z2–6 H6–1. **'Compressa', H** 30in (75cm), **S** 6in (15cm), is a dwarf, erect form. **'Hibernica', H** 10–15ft (3–5m), **S** 12in (30cm), is columnar. **'Hornibrookii', H** 20in (50cm), **S** 6ft (2m), and **'Prostrata', H** 8–12in (20–30cm), **S** 3–6ft (1–2m), are carpeting plants.

J. conferta, syn. *J. rigida* subsp. *conferta* (Shore juniper). Prostrate, shrubby conifer. **H** 6in (15cm), **S** 3–6ft (1–2m). Spreading branches bear dense, needlelike, aromatic, glossy, bright green leaves, glaucous beneath. Produces glaucous black berries. Tolerates salty, coastal air.

***J. davurica* 'Expansa Variegata'**. See *J. chinensis* 'Expansa Variegata'.

J. drupacea (Syrian juniper). Columnar conifer. **H** 30–50ft (10–15m), **S** 3–6ft (1–2m). Has needlelike, aromatic, light green leaves, in 3s, and ovoid or almost globose, fleshy, brown berries. Z7–10 H10–7

J. horizontalis (Creeping juniper). Prostrate, wide-spreading, mat-forming, shrubby conifer. **H** 20in (50cm), **S** indefinite. Has scale- or needlelike, aromatic, blue-green or blue-gray leaves and pale blue-gray berries. Z3–9 H9–1. Leaves of **'Andorra Compact'**, syn. *J. horizontalis* 'Plumosa Compacta' turn bronze-purple in winter. **'Douglasii'** has glaucous blue foliage that turns plum-purple in winter. **'Plumosa'** is less dense than *J.h.* 'Andorra Compact' and has gray-green leaves, becoming purple in winter. **'Plumosa Compacta'.** See *J. horizontalis* 'Andorra Compact'. **'Prince of Wales'** has bright green foliage, tinged blue when young and turning purple-brown in winter. **'Turquoise Spreader'** has turquoise-green foliage. **'Wiltonii'** has bluish-gray leaves that retain their color over winter.

J. x media. See *J.* x *pfitzeriana*. **'Blaauw'.** See *J. chinensis* 'Blaauw'. **'Blue and Gold'.** See *J.* x *pfitzeriana* 'Blue and Gold'.**'Hetzii'.** See *J. virginiana* 'Hetzii'. **'Pfitzeriana'.** See *J.* x *pfitzeriana* 'William Pfitzer'. **'Pfitzeriana Aurea'.** See *J.* x *pfitzeriana* 'Aurea'. **'Pfitzeriana Glauca'.** See *J.* x *pfitzeriana* 'Glauca'. **'Plumosa Aurea'.** See *J. chinensis* 'Plumosa Aurea'.

J. x pfitzeriana, syn. *J.* x *media*. Group of spreading to conical conifers. **H** 50ft (15m), **S** 6–10ft (2–3m). Has peeling bark. Mainly scalelike, dark green leaves exude a fetid smell when crushed. Fruits are globose to rounded, white or blue-black. Cultivars are suitable as groundcover or as specimen plants in a small garden. Some forms are commonly listed under *J. chinensis*. Z4–9 H9–1. **'Aurea'**, syn. *J.* x *media* 'Pfitzeriana Aurea' has golden foliage. **'Blue and Gold'**, syn. *J.* x *media* 'Blue and Gold', **H** to 3ft (1m), **S** 3ft (1m), is a spreading form with leaves variegated sky-blue and gold. **'Glauca'**, syn. *J.* x *media* 'Pfitzeriana Glauca' produces gray-blue leaves. **'Old Gold'** (illus. p.105), **H** 3ft (1m), **S** 8ft (2.5m), has a compact, spreading, flat-topped habit and bronze-yellow leaves. **'Pfitzeriana Compacta', H** and **S** 5ft (1.5m), has a dense, compact habit and a tendency to produce more juvenile leaves. **'William Pfitzer'**, syn. *J.* x *media* 'Pfitzeriana', **H** 10ft (3m), **S** 10–15ft (3–5m), is a spreading, flat-topped shrub and produces grayish-green leaves.

J. procumbens (Bonin Isles juniper). Spreading, prostrate, shrubby conifer. **H** 30in (75cm), **S** 6ft (2m). Has red-brown bark. Thick branches bear needlelike, aromatic, light green or yellow-green leaves and globose, fleshy, brown or black berries. Z3–9 H9–1. **'Nana', H** 6–8in (15–20cm), **S** 30in (75cm), is less vigorous and is mat-forming.

J. recurva, illus. p.103. **var. *coxii***, illus. p.100. **'Densa'**, syn. *J. recurva* 'Nana' is a spreading conifer. **H** 1ft (30cm), **S** 3ft (1m). Shaggy bark flakes in thin sheets. Sprays of long, needlelike, aromatic, dark green leaves are erect at tips. Ovoid, fleshy berries are black. Z7–11 H12–7. **'Nana'.** See *J. recurva* 'Densa'.

J. rigida (Needle juniper). Sprawling, shrubby conifer. **H** and **S** 25ft (8m). Gray or brown bark peels in strips. Very sharp, needlelike, aromatic, bright green leaves, in 3s, are borne in nodding sprays. Globose, fleshy fruits are purplish-black. Z6–9 H9–6 **subsp. *conferta*.** See *J. conferta*.

J. sabina (Savin juniper). Spreading, shrubby conifer. **H** to 12ft (4m), **S** 10–15ft (3–5m). Has flaking, red-brown bark. Slender shoots bear mainly scalelike, aromatic, dark green leaves that give off a fetid smell when crushed. Produces rounded, blue-black berries. Z4–7 H7–1. **'Blaue Donau'**, syn. *J. sabina* 'Blue Danube', **H** 6ft (2m), **S** 6–12ft (2–4m), is a spreading form with branch tips curved upward and gray-blue foliage. **'Blue Danube'.** See *J. sabina* 'Blaue Donau' **'Cupressifolia', H** 6ft (2m), **S** 12ft (4m), is a free-fruiting, female form with horizontal or ascending branches and blue-green leaves. **'Mas'** has ascending branches. Leaves are blue above, green below, purplish in winter. **var. *tamariscifolia*** (Tamarisk juniper), **H** 3ft (1m), **S** 6ft (2m), produces tiered layers of mainly needlelike, bright green or blue-green leaves.

J. scopulorum (Rocky Mountain juniper). Slow-growing, round-crowned conifer. **H** 30ft (10m), **S** 12ft (4m). Reddish-brown bark is furrowed into strips or squares and peels on branches. Scalelike, aromatic leaves are gray-green to dark green. Bears globose, fleshy, blue berries. Z3–7 H7–1. **'Skyrocket'**, syn. *J. virginiana* 'Skyrocket' (illus. p.105), **H** 26ft (8m), **S** 2½ft (75cm), is very narrow in habit with glaucous blue foliage. **'Springbank'** is narrowly conical with drooping branch tips and intense silvery-blue foliage. **'Tabletop', H** 6ft (2m), **S** 15ft (5m), has a flat-topped habit and silvery-blue leaves.

J. squamata (Singleseed juniper). Prostrate to sprawling, shrubby conifer. **H** 1–12ft (30cm–4m), **S** 3–15ft (1–5m). Bark is red-brown and flaking. Needlelike, aromatic, fresh green or bluish-green leaves spread at tips of shoots. Produces ovoid, fleshy, black berries. Z4–9 H9–1. **'Blue Carpet'** (illus. p.105), **H** 1ft (30cm), **S** 6–10ft (2–3m), is vigorous and prostrate, with glaucous blue foliage. **'Blue Star', H** 20in (50cm), **S** 24in (60cm), forms a dense, rounded bush and has blue foliage. **'Chinese Silver', H** and **S** 10–12ft (3–4m), has branches with nodding tips and bluish leaves with bright silver undersides. **'Holger'** (illus. p.105), **H** and **S** 6ft (2m), produces sulfur-yellow young leaves that contrast with steel-blue old foliage. **'Meyeri', H** and **S** 15ft (5m), has a sprawling habit and produces steel-blue foliage.

J. virginiana (Eastern juniper, Eastern red cedar). Slow-growing, conical or broadly columnar conifer. **H** 50–70ft (15–20m), **S** 20–25ft (6–8m). Both scale- and needlelike, aromatic, gray-green leaves are borne on same shoot. Ovoid, fleshy berries are brownish-violet and extremely glaucous. Z3–9 H9–1. **'Burkii', H** to 20ft (6m), **S** 3ft (1m), has blue-gray leaves that become purple-tinged over winter. **'Grey Owl', H** 10ft (3m), **S** 10–15ft (3–5m), is a low, spreading cultivar with ascending branches and silvery-gray foliage. **'Hetzii'**, syn. *J.* x *media* 'Hetzii', **H** 10–12ft (3–4m), **S** 12ft (4m), produces tiers of gray-green foliage.

***J. virginiana* 'Robusta Green'.** See *J. chinensis* 'Robusta Green'.

***J. virginiana* 'Skyrocket'.** See *J. scopulorum* 'Skyrocket'.

JUSTICIA

ACANTHACEAE

Genus of evergreen perennials, subshrubs and shrubs, grown mainly for their flowers. Requires full light or partial shade and fertile, well-drained soil. Water container specimens freely when in full growth, moderately at other times. Some species need regular pruning. Propagate by softwood or greenwood cuttings in spring or early summer. Whitefly may cause problems.

J. adhatoda, syn. *Duvernoia adhatodoides, Adhatoda duvernoia* (Snake bush). Evergreen, erect shrub. **H** 6–10ft (2–3m), **S** 3–6ft (1–2m). Has elliptic, dark green leaves. Fragrant, tubular, white or mauve flowers, with pink, red or purple marks, are produced in summer–fall. Z12–15 H12–1

J. brandegeeana, syn. *Beloperone guttata, Drejerella guttata*, illus. p.455. **'Chartreuse'** is an evergreen, arching shrub. **H** to 3ft (1m), **S** 2–3ft (60–90cm). Has white flowers surrounded by pale yellow-green bracts mainly in summer but also intermittently during the year. Z14–15 H12–9.

J. carnea, syn. *J. pohliana, Jacobinia carnea*, illus. p.455.

***J. coccinea*.** See *Pachystachys coccinea*.

***J. floribunda*.** See *J. rizzinii*.

***J. ghiesbreghtiana*.** See *J. spicigera*.

***J. pauciflora*.** See *J. rizzinii*.

***J. pohliana*.** See *J. carnea*.

J. rizzinii, syn. *J. floribunda, J. pauciflora, Libonia floribunda*. Evergreen, rounded, freely branching shrub. **H** and **S** 1–2ft (30–60cm). Leaves are oval and mid-green. Bears nodding clusters of tubular, yellow-tipped, scarlet flowers mainly fall–spring. Divide every few years.

J. spicigera, syn. *J. ghiesbreghtiana, Jacobinia spicigera*. Evergreen, well-branched shrub. **H** 3–6ft (1–1.8m), **S** 2½–4ft (75–120cm). Has spikes of tubular, orange or red flowers in summer and occasionally other seasons. Z14–15 H12–10.

KADSURA

SCHISANDRACEAE

Genus of evergreen, twining climbers, grown for their foliage and fruits. Male and female flowers are borne on separate plants, so plants of both sexes must be grown to obtain fruits. Needs partial shade and tolerates any soil. Propagate by stem cuttings in late summer.

***K. japonica*.** Evergreen, twining climber. **H** 10–12ft (3–4m). Has oval or lance-shaped, mid-green leaves. Solitary, small, fragrant, cream flowers are produced in leaf axils in summer, followed by bright red berries. Prefers well-drained soil.

KAEMPFERIA

ZINGIBERACEAE

Genus of tufted, rhizomatous perennials, grown for their aromatic leaves and their flowers. Needs a moist atmosphere, partial shade and moist, rich soil. Allow to dry out when plants become dormant. Propagate by division in late spring. See also feature panel p.477.

K. pulchra, illus. p.477. Tufted, rhizomatous perennial. **H** 6in (15cm), **S** 12in (30cm). Has horizontal, aromatic, dark green leaves, variegated with paler green above. Short spikes of lilac-pink flowers are produced from center of tufts in summer. H11–10.

K. roscoeana (Dwarf ginger lily, Peacock lily). Rhizomatous perennial without an obvious stem. **H** 2–4in (5–10cm), **S** 8–10in (20–25cm). Usually has only 2 almost rounded, aromatic leaves, to 4in (10cm) long, dark green with pale green marks above, reddish-green below, that are held horizontally. Short spike of pure white flowers, each with a deeply lobed lip, are produced from center of leaf tuft in fall. Z11–12 H12–10.

K. rotunda (Resurrection lily). Herbacous, rhizomatous perennial. **H** 2ft (60cm), **S** 1ft (30cm). Has 2–4 broadly lance-shaped leaves, 8–10in (20–25cm) long, patterned silver and deep green, with red undersides. White flowers, with pink to purple lips, borne on a separate stem before leafy stem emerges, open in succession from late spring to summer. A number of cultivars are grown for their patterned foliage.

KALANCHOE

SYN. BRYOPHYLLUM

CRASSULACEAE

Genus of perennial succulents or shrubs, grown for their very fleshy, mainly cylindrical, oval or linear leaves and bell-shaped to tubular flowers. Many species produce new plantlets from indented leaf margins. Requires sun or partial shade and well-drained soil. Keep moist from spring to fall. Water lightly and only occasionally in winter. Propagate by seed, offsets or stem cuttings in spring or summer.

K. beharensis (Felt bush, Velvet leaf). Bushy, perennial succulent. **H** and **S** to 12ft (4m). Has triangular to lance-shaped, olive-green leaves covered with fine, brown hairs. Bell-shaped, yellow flowers are produced in late winter, only on plants more than 6ft (2m) high. Z11–12 H12–1.

K. blossfeldiana, illus. p.487. **'Calandiva'**, illus. p.482.

K. daigremontiana, illus. p.492.

K. delagoensis, syn. *K. tubiflora*, illus. p.496.

K. fedtschenkoi. Bushy, perennial succulent. **H** and **S** 3ft (1m). Produces oval, indented, blue-gray leaves with new plantlets in each notch. Bell-shaped, brownish-pink flowers, ³⁄₄in (2cm) long, are borne in late winter. Prefers a sunny position. Z11 H12–10. **'Variegata'**, illus. p.482.

K. laetivirens. Evergreen, perennial succulent. **H** 10in (25cm), **S** 6in (15cm). Oblong to elliptic, glaucous, mid-green leaves, turning pink in strong light, produce small plantlets from notches along margins. Bears clusters of tubular, greenish-white to purplish flowers, ⁵⁄₈in (1.5cm) long, in winter.

K. pumila. Creeping, perennial succulent. **H** 4in (10cm), **S** indefinite. Has oval, powdery gray-white leaves with indented margins. Tubular, pink flowers, ¹⁄₂in (1cm) long, are produced in spring. Is suitable for a hanging basket in a sunny position. Z11 H12–1.

K. 'Tessa', illus. p.487.

K. tomentosa, illus. p.490.

K. tubiflora. See *K. delagoensis*.

K. uniflora, syn. *Kitchingia uniflora*. Creeping, perennial succulent. **H** 2¹⁄₂in (6cm), **S** indefinite. Produces rounded, mid-green leaves, ¹⁄₄–1¹⁄₄in (0.5–3cm) long, and bell-shaped, yellow-flushed, reddish-purple flowers, ¹⁄₂in (1cm) long, in late winter. Prefers partial shade. Z11-15 H12–1.

K. 'Wendy', illus. p.485.

KALMIA
ERICACEAE

Genus of evergreen, summer-flowering shrubs, grown for their clusters of distinctive, usually cup-shaped flowers. Needs sun or partial shade and moist, peaty, acid soil. Propagate species by softwood cuttings in summer or by seed in fall, selected forms by softwood cuttings in summer. ① All parts may cause severe discomfort if ingested.

K. angustifolia. f. rubra, syn. *K. angustifolia* 'Rubra' (Lambkill kalmia, Sheep laurel), illus. p.156. **'Rubra'**. See *K. angustifolia* f. *rubra*.

K. latifolia, illus. p.136. **'Ostbo Red'** is an evergreen, bushy, dense shrub. **H** and **S** 10ft (3m). Has oval, glossy, rich green leaves. Large, showy clusters of deep pink flowers open in early summer from distinctively crimped, deep red buds. Prefers full sun. Z5–9 H9–5.

KALMIOPSIS
ERICACEAE

Genus of one species of evergreen, spring-flowering shrub, grown for its flowers. Is suitable for peat gardens. Requires partial shade and moist, peaty, acidic soil. Propagate by softwood or semiripe cuttings in summer.

K. leachiana 'La Piniec', syn. *K. leachiana* 'M. le Piniec'. Evergreen, bushy shrub. **H** and **S** 12in (30cm). Terminal clusters of small, widely bell-shaped, purplish-pink flowers are produced from early to late spring. Has small, oval, glossy, dark green leaves. Z7–9 H9–7. **'M. le Piniec'**. See *K. leachiana* 'La Piniec'.

KALOPANAX
ARALIACEAE

Genus of one species of deciduous, fall-flowering tree, grown for its foliage and fruits. Unripened wood on young plants is susceptible to cold damage. Prefers sun or partial shade and fertile, moist but well-drained soil. Propagate by softwood cuttings in summer.

K. pictus. See *K. septemlobus*.

K. ricinifolius. See *K. septemlobus*.

K. septemlobus, syn. *K. pictus, K. ricinifolius, Acanthopanax ricinifolius*, illus. p.74.

KELSEYA
ROSACEAE

Genus of one species of extremely small, evergreen subshrub. Is difficult to grow and is best in an alpine house as foliage deeply resents both summer and winter wet. Requires full sun and moist, alkaline soil. Propagate by soft-tip cuttings in late spring or by seed in fall. Is susceptible to molds, so remove any dead rosettes at once.

K. uniflora. Slow-growing, evergreen, rosetted subshrub. **H** ¹⁄₂in (1cm), **S** to 8in (20cm). Forms a hard mat of closely packed, small rosettes of tiny, oval, dark green leaves. In early spring produces stemless, star-shaped, occasionally pink-flushed, white flowers. Z5–7 H7–5.

KENNEDIA
SYN. KENNEDYA
LEGUMINOSAE/PAPILIONACEAE

Genus of evergreen, woody-stemmed, trailing and twining climbers, grown for their pealike flowers. Needs full light and moderately fertile, sandy soil. Water regularly when in full growth, sparingly in cold weather. Requires support. Thin out congested growth after flowering or in spring. Propagate by seed in spring or by semiripe cuttings in summer.

K. nigricans (Black coral pea). Vigorous, evergreen, woody-stemmed, twining climber. **H** to 6ft (2m). Leaves are divided into 3 leaflets with notched tips. Has small trusses of pealike, velvety, black-purple flowers, with yellow blazes, in spring–summer. Z13–15 H12–10.

K. rubicunda (Dusky coral pea), illus. p.462.

Kennedya. See *Kennedia*.
Kentia fosteriana. See *Howea forsteriana*.

KERRIA
ROSACEAE

Genus of one species of deciduous shrub, grown for its showy, yellow flowers. Needs sun or partial shade and fertile, well-drained soil. Thin out old shoots after flowering. Propagate by softwood cuttings in summer or by division in fall.

K. japonica 'Pleniflora', illus. p.127. **var. simplex**. is a deciduous, arching shrub. **H** and **S** 6ft (2m). Has bright green foliage. Single, buttercup-like, golden-yellow flowers are borne from mid- to late spring. Z5–9 H9–3.

KIGELIA
Sausage tree
BIGNONIACEAE

Genus of one species of evergreen tree, grown for its flowers, curious, sausage-like fruits and for shade. Requires full light and rich, well-drained soil. Water container specimens moderately, very little when temperatures low. Propagate by seed in spring at not less than 73°F (23°C).

K. africana, syn. *K. pinnata* (Sausage tree). Evergreen, spreading, fairly bushy tree. **H** and **S** 25ft (8m) or more. Leaves have 7–11 oblong to oval leaflets. Scented, bell-shaped, purplish-red flowers open at night in fall–spring. Bears inedible, cylindrical, hard-shelled, brown fruits, 12–18in (30–45cm) long. Z10–11 H12–10.

K. pinnata. See *K. africana*.

KIRENGESHOMA
HYDRANGEACEAE

Genus of late summer- and fall-flowering perennials. Needs partial shade and deep, moist, lime-free soil. Propagate by seed or division in fall or spring.

K. palmata (Yellow waxbells), illus. p.251.

KITAIBELA
SYN. KITAIBELIA
MALVACEAE

Genus of one species of summer-flowering perennial. Needs full sun and fertile, preferably dry soil. Propagate by seed in fall or spring.

K. vitifolia. Bushy, upright perennial. **H** to 5ft (1.5m), **S** 2ft (60cm). In summer bears small clusters of open cup-shaped, white or rose-pink flowers. Has palmately lobed, coarsely toothed leaves. Z6–8 H8–6.

Kitaibelia. See *Kitaibela*.
Kitchingia uniflora. See *Kalanchoe uniflora*.
Kleinia articulata. See *Senecio articulatus*.
Kleinia rowleyana. See *Senecio rowleyanus*.

KNAUTIA
DIPSACACEAE/CAPROFOLIACEAE

Genus of summer-flowering annuals and perennials. Needs sun and well-drained soil. Requires staking. Propagate by basal cuttings in spring or by seed in fall.

K. arvensis, syn. *Scabiosa arvensis* (Blue buttons). Erect perennial. **H** 4ft (1.2m), **S** 1¹⁄₂ft (45cm). Produces heads of pincushion-like, bluish-lilac flowers in summer. Stems are clothed in narrowly oval to lyre-shaped, deeply divided leaves. Z5–9 H9–5.

K. macedonica, syn. *Scabiosa rumelica*, illus. p.235.

KNIGHTIA
PROTEACEAE

Genus of evergreen, summer-flowering trees, grown for their flowers, foliage and overall appearance. Needs sun or partial shade and reasonably fertile, well-drained soil. Water container specimens moderately, less in winter. Propagate by seed in spring.

K. excelsa (New Zealand honeysuckle, Rewarewa). Evergreen, upright tree. **H** 70ft (20m) or more, **S** 6–12ft (2–4m). Has oblong to lance-shaped, coarsely serrated, leathery, glossy, deep green leaves. Dense racemes of slender, tubular, deep red flowers are produced in summer. Z10–11 H12–10.

KNIPHOFIA
Red-hot poker, Torch lily
LILIACEAE/ASPHODELACEAE

Genus of perennials, some of which are evergreen. Needs full sun and well-drained conditions, with constantly moist soil in summer. Propagate species by seed or division in spring, cultivars by division only in spring. See also feature panel p.254.

K. 'Ada'. Semievergreen, clump-forming perennial. **H** 36in (100m), **S** 18in (45cm). Has long, lance-shaped, mid-green, basal leaves. In summer, upright, dark green stems bear racemes of tubular, orange-yellow flowers, the buds rather darker in color.

K. 'Alcazar'. Semievergreen, clump-forming perennial. **H** 36in (100cm), **S** 18in (45cm). Has long, lance-shaped, mid-green, basal leaves. In summer, upright, dark green stems bear racemes of reddish-orange buds opening to tubular, golden-yellow flowers.

K. 'Atlanta', illus. p.254. Evergreen, upright perennial. **H** to 3ft (1m), **S** 1¹⁄₂ft (45cm). In summer, sturdy stems bear dense, terminal racemes of tubular, bright orange-yellow flowers. Has thick, grasslike, chaneled leaves. Does well in a coastal area. Z6–9 H9–4.

K. 'Bee's Lemon'. Upright perennial. **H** 3ft (1m), **S** 1¹⁄₂ft (45cm). Has dense, terminal racemes of tubular, green-tinged, citron-yellow flowers on sturdy stems in late summer and fall. Grasslike, deep green leaves have serrated edges. Z6–9 H9–6.

K. 'Bees' Sunset', illus. p.254. Semievergreen, clump-forming perennial. **H** 48in (120cm), **S** 18in (45cm). Has long, grasslike, mid-green, basal leaves. In summer, upright, purplish-green stems bear slender racemes of tubular, warm orange-flushed, yellow flowers. Z6–9 H9–6.

K. 'Brimstone'. Semievergreen, clump-forming perennial. **H** 36in (100cm), **S** 18in (45cm). Has long, narrowly lance-shaped, mid-green, basal leaves. In summer, upright stems bear slender racemes of tubular, soft greenish-yellow flowers.

J
K

K. 'C.M. Prichard'. See *K. rooperi*.
K. caulescens, illus. p.254. Evergreen, upright perennial. **H** 4ft (1.2m), **S** 2ft (60cm). Has basal tufts of narrow, blue-green leaves and smooth, sturdy stems bearing terminal spikes of reddish-salmon flowers in fall. Z6–9 H9–4.
K. 'Cobra'. Semievergreen, clump-forming perennial. **H** 36in (100cm) or more, **S** 18in (45cm). Has long, lance-shaped, mid-green, basal leaves. In summer, upright stems bear sturdy, broad, dense racemes of tubular, brown-tinged, orange flowers that age to yellowish-white.
K. 'Green Jade', illus. p.254. Semievergreen, clump-forming perennial. **H** 48in (120cm), **S** 22in (55cm). Has long, lance-shaped, mid-green, basal leaves. In summer, upright stems bear rather slender racemes of tubular, pale green flowers, fading to warm ivory-white. Z6–9 H9–4.
K. linearifolia. Semievergreen, clump-forming perennial. **H** 60in (1.5m), **S** 32in (80cm). Has very long, rather lax, grasslike, mid-green leaves. In summer, upright stems bear dense racemes of orange-red buds opening to tubular, bright yellow flowers.
K. 'Little Maid'. Semievergreen, clump-forming perennial. **H** 2ft (60cm), **S** 1ft (30cm). Has long, grasslike, mid-green, basal leaves. In summer, upright stems bear dainty racemes of tubular, greenish yellow flowers that fade to creamy-white. Z6–9 H9–6.
K. 'Maid of Orleans'. Upright perennial. **H** 4ft (1.2m), **S** 1½ft (45cm). In summer, slender stems are each crowned with a dense raceme of yellow buds that open to tubular, creamy-white flowers. Leaves are fresh green, basal and strap-shaped. Z6–9 H9–6.
K. northiae. Evergreen, rosette-forming perennial. **H** 5ft (1.5m), **S** 3ft (1m) or more. Has rather lax, broadly strap-shaped, pointed, pale green leaves. In summer produces dense racemes of tubular, greenish-yellow flowers.
K. 'Percy's Pride', illus. p.251.
K. 'Prince Igor', illus. p.254. Semievergreen, clump-forming perennial. **H** 6ft (2m) or more, **S** 3ft (1m). Has long, lance-shaped, mid-green, basal leaves. In summer, upright stems bear racemes of tubular, yellow-tinged, reddish-orange flowers. Z6–9 H9–4.
K. rooperi, syn. *K.* 'C. M. Prichard', illus. p.254. Robust, evergreen perennial. **H** 4ft (1.2m), **S** 2ft (60cm). Has arching, linear, dark green leaves. From early to late fall produces racemes of tubular, orange-red flowers, becoming orange-yellow. Z6–9 H9–4.
K. 'Royal Standard', illus. p.254. Semievergreen, clump-forming perennial. **H** 36in (100cm) or more, **S** 22in (55cm). Bears long, lance-shaped, mid-green, basal leaves. In summer, upright stems bear 2-toned racemes of bright red buds opening to tubular, yellow flowers. Z6–9 H9–6.
K. 'Samuel's Sensation'. Semievergreen, clump-forming perennial. **H** 66in (165cm) or more, **S** 32in (80cm). Bears long, lance-shaped, mid-green, basal leaves. In summer, upright stems bear racemes of tubular, pinkish-red flowers aging to orange-yellow. Z6–9 H9–6.
K. snowdenii. See *K. thomsonii* var. *snowdenii*.

K. 'Star of Baden-Baden'. Semievergreen, clump-forming perennial. **H** 72in (180m), **S** 32in (80cm). Has long, lance-shaped, mid-green, basal leaves. In summer, upright stems bear racemes of tubular, greenish-golden-yellow flowers.
K. 'Strawberries and Cream'. Largely herbaceous, rather compact, clump-forming perennial. **H** 24in (60cm), **S** 14in (35cm). Has lance-shaped, mid-green, basal leaves. In summer bears upright racemes of tubular, pinkish-ivory flowers, opening from darker buds.
K. 'Tetbury Torch'. Semievergreen, clump-forming perennial. **H** 36in (100cm), **S** 18in (45cm). Bears lance-shaped, mid-green, basal leaves. In early summer and often in later summer produces upright racemes of tubular, orange flowers that fade to warm yellow.
K. thomsonii var. snowdenii, syn. *K. snowdenii*, illus. p.254. Upright perennial. **H** 3ft (1m), **S** 20in (50cm). Has grasslike, basal leaves. In summer bears coral-pink flowers, with yellowish interiors, spaced widely along terminal spikes. Z7–9 H9–7.
K. 'Timothy'. Semievergreen, clump-forming perennial. **H** 36in (100cm), **S** 18in (45cm). Has long, lance-shaped, mid-green, basal leaves. In summer, upright, purplish-green stems bear racemes of tubular, warm peachy-pink flowers.
K. 'Toffee Nosed', illus. p.254. Semievergreen, clump-forming perennial. **H** 36in (100cm), **S** 18in (45cm). Has long, lance-shaped, mid-green, basal leaves. In summer, upright stems bear racemes of tubular, brown-orange flowers that fade to warm cream.
K. uvaria (Red-hot poker). Z5–9 H9–1. **'Nobilis'** is an upright perennial with erect, then spreading leaves. **H** 6ft (2m), **S** 3ft (1m). In late summer and fall, sturdy stems each bear a dense, terminal raceme of tubular, bright red flowers. Has strap-shaped, chaneled, dark green leaves.
K. 'Wrexham Buttercup', illus. p.254. Semievergreen, clump-forming perennial. **H** 48in (120cm), **S** 22in (55cm). Has long, lance-shaped, mid-green, basal leaves. In summer, upright stems bear broad racemes of tubular, bright yellow flowers, opening from greenish buds. Z6–9 H9–6.

Kochia. See *Bassia*.

KOELREUTERIA

SAPINDACEAE

Genus of deciduous, summer-flowering trees, grown for their foliage, flowers and fruits. Requires full sun, doing best in hot summers, and fertile, well-drained soil. Propagate by seed in fall or by root cuttings in late winter.
K. paniculata, illus. p.89.

KOHLERIA

GESNERIACEAE

Genus of erect perennials with scaly rhizomes, grown for their showy, tubular flowers borne mainly in summer. Needs full sun or partial shade and moist but well-drained soil. Water sparingly in winter; overwatering will cause rhizomes to rot. Propagate in spring by division of rhizomes or by seed if available.

K. amabilis (Beautybush). Rhizomatous perennial. **H** 3–6in (8–16cm), **S** 2ft (60cm). Oval, hairy leaves, to 3in (8cm) long, are often marked with silver and brown above. Small, nodding, tubular, deep pink flowers, with red-marked lobes, are borne in summer. Is useful for a hanging basket. Z14–15 H12–10.
K. bogotensis. Erect, rhizomatous perennial. **H** and **S** 18in (45cm) or more. Oval, velvety, green leaves, to 3in (8cm) long, are sometimes marked with paler green above. In summer has small, tubular flowers, red with a yellow base outside, red-dotted, yellow within. Z14–15 H12–10.
K. digitaliflora, illus. p.469.
K. eriantha, illus. p.470.
K. warscewiczii. Erect, rhizomatous perennial. **H** 3ft (1m), **S** 2ft (60cm). Oval, dark green leaves have scalloped margins. In summer and fall produces tubular, hairy, yellow-based, scarlet flowers, with red- or brown-spotted, greenish-yellow or bright yellow lobes. Z14–15 H12–10.

KOLKWITZIA

Beautybush

CAPRIFOLIACEAE

Genus of one species of deciduous shrub, grown for its abundant flowers. Prefers full sun and fertile, well-drained soil. Cut out old shoots after flowering. Propagate by softwood cuttings in summer.
K. amabilis. Deciduous, arching shrub. **H** and **S** 10ft (3m). Has peeling bark and oval, dark green leaves. Bell-shaped, yellow-throated, white or pink flowers are borne in late spring and early summer. Z5–9 H9–5. **'Pink Cloud'**, illus. p.114.

Korolkowia sewerzowii. See *Fritillaria sewerzowii*.

KUNZEA

MYRTACEAE

Genus of evergreen shrubs and trees, grown for their flowers and overall appearance. Prefers full light and sandy, well-drained, neutral to acidic soil. Water container specimens moderately when in full growth, less at other times. Propagate by semiripe cuttings in late summer or by seed in spring.
K. baxteri. Evergreen, rounded, wiry-stemmed shrub. **H** and **S** to 6ft (2m). Has narrow, cylindrical, pointed leaves and, in early summer, deep red flowers, each with a brush of stamens, in spikes 2in (5cm) long.

L

LABLAB

LEGUMINOSAE/PAPILIONACEAE

Genus of one species of deciduous, woody-stemmed, twining climber, grown for its pealike flowers (in tropics is grown for green manure and animal feed, and for its edible pods and seeds). Is often raised as an annual. Needs sun and well-drained soil. Propagate by seed in spring.
L. purpureus, syn. *Dolichos lablab*, *Dolichos purpureus*, illus. p.203.

+ LABURNOCYTISUS

LEGUMINOSAE/PAPILIONACEAE

Deciduous tree, grown for its flowers. Is a graft hybrid between *Laburnum anagyroides* and *Chamaecytisus purpureus*. Requires full sun and tolerates any but waterlogged soil. Propagate by grafting on laburnum in late summer.
+ L. 'Adamii'. Deciduous, spreading tree. **H** 25ft (8m), **S** 20ft (6m). In late spring and early summer bears 3 types of blooms: yellow, laburnum flowers; purple, cytisus flowers; and laburnum-like, yellow and pinkish-purple flowers. Leaves, divided into 3 oval leaflets, are dark green. Z6–8 H8–6.

LABURNUM

LEGUMINOSAE/PAPILIONACEAE

Genus of deciduous trees, grown for their profuse, pendent flower clusters in spring and summer. Prefers full sun and tolerates any but waterlogged soil. Propagate species by seed in fall, hybrids by budding in summer. ① All parts, including seeds, are highly toxic if ingested.
L. alpinum, illus. p.89.
L. anagyroides syn. *L. vulgare* (Common laburnum). Deciduous, spreading tree. **H** and **S** 22ft (7m). Gray-green leaves are divided into 3 oval leaflets. Short, pendent, dense clusters of large, pealike, yellow flowers are borne in late spring and early summer. Z6–8 H8–5.
L. vulgare. See *L. anagyroides*.
L. x watereri 'Vossii', illus. p.84.

LACHENALIA

Cape cowslip

LILIACEAE/ASPARAGACEAE

Genus of winter- and spring-flowering bulbs, grown for their tubular or bell-shaped flowers; some also have attractively mottled leaves. Is useful as pot plants and in open borders. Requires sun and light, well-drained soil. Plant in early fall; dry off in summer when foliage has died down. Propagate in fall by seed or freely produced offsets.
L. aloides, syn. *L. tricolor*, *L.* 'Tricolor'. Winter- and spring-flowering bulb. **H** 6–10in (15–25cm), **S** 2–3in (5–8cm). Has 2 strap-shaped, semierect, purple-spotted, green, basal leaves. Produces spike of 10–20 pendent flowers, 1¼in (3cm) long, with yellow tube shading to red at apex and with flared, green tips. Z11 H12–10. **'Nelsonii'**, syn. *L.* 'Nelsonii', illus. p.429.

var. **quadricolor,** illus. p.429.
L. angustifolia. See *L. contaminata.*
L. contaminata, syn. *L. angustifolia.*
Winter- and spring-flowering bulb.
H to 8in (20cm), **S** 2–3in (5–8cm). Has
narrowly strap-shaped, semierect leaves
in basal cluster. Bears spike of bell-
shaped, white flowers, ¼in (0.5cm) long,
suffused and tipped with red and green.
Z11 H12–10.
L. glaucina. See *L. orchioides* var.
glaucina.
L. mutabilis. Winter- and spring-
flowering bulb. **H** to 12in (30cm), **S** 2–3in
(5–8cm). Has 2 strap-shaped, semierect,
basal leaves. Stem bears loose spike of up
to 25 tubular flowers, ½in (1cm) long, that
are purple or lilac in bud and open to
reddish-brown-tipped petals with green
tube base.
L. 'Nelsonii'. See *L. aloides* 'Nelsonii'.
L. orchioides. Winter- and spring-
flowering bulb. **H** 6–12in (15–30cm), **S** 2–3in
(5–8cm). Has 2 strap-shaped, semierect,
green, basal leaves, sometimes spotted
blackish- or purple-brown. Stem produces
a dense spike of fragrant, semierect,
tubular, white flowers, ½in (1cm) long,
blue-tinged and tipped with green. Z11–14
H12–6. **var. glaucina,** syn. *L. glaucina* has
leaves usually spotted purple and whitish-
blue or pale lilac flowers.
L. rubida. Winter-flowering bulb. **H** to
10in (25cm), **S** 2–3in (5–8cm). Bears 2 strap-
shaped, semierect, purple-spotted, green,
basal leaves and a loose spike of pendent,
tubular, red flowers, ¾–1¼in (2–3cm) long,
shading to yellow at tips.
L. tricolor. See *L. aloides.*

Lactuca alpina. See *Cicerbita alpina.*
Lactuca bourgaei. See *Cicerbita bourgaei.*

LAELIA
ORCHIDACEAE
See also ORCHIDS.
L. anceps, illus. p.466. Evergreen,
epiphytic orchid for a cool greenhouse.
H 10in (25cm). Lilac-pink flowers, 2½in
(6cm) wide, each with a deep mauve lip,
are borne in tall spikes in fall. Has oval,
rigid leaves, 4–6in (10–15cm) long. Needs
partial shade in summer. H11–6.
L. cinnabarina. See *Cattleya cinnabarina.*

x **Laeliocattleya Rojo gx 'Mont Millais'.** See x *Cattlianthe* Rojo gx 'Mont Millais'.

LAGAROSIPHON
Curly water thyme
HYDROCHARITACEAE
Genus of semievergreen, perennial,
spreading, submerged water plants, grown
for their foliage. Oxygenates water. Needs
full sun. Thin regularly to keep under
control. Propagate by stem cuttings in
spring or summer.
L. major, syn. *Elodea crispa.*
Semievergreen, perennial, spreading,
submerged water plant. **S** indefinite. Forms
dense, underwater swards of foliage.
Ascending stems are covered in narrow,
reflexed, dark green leaves. Bears
insignificant flowers in summer. Z8–11
H12–6.

LAGERSTROEMIA
LYTHRACEAE
Genus of deciduous or evergreen, summer-
flowering shrubs and trees, grown for their
flowers. Prefers full light and fertile, well-
drained soil. Water container specimens
freely when in full growth, less at other
times. To maintain as shrubs, cut back hard
the previous season's stems each spring.
Propagate by seed in spring or by semiripe
cuttings in summer.
L. indica (Crape myrtle). Deciduous,
rounded tree or large shrub. **H** and
S 25ft (8m). Has trusses of flowers with
strongly waved, pink, white or purple
petals in summer and early fall. Z7–9
H9–7. **'Seminale',** illus. p.86.
L. speciosa (Giant crape myrtle, Pride of
India). Deciduous, rounded tree. **H** 50–70ft
(15–20m), **S** 30–50ft (10–15m). Has narrowly
oval, mid- to deep green leaves, 3–7in
(8–18cm) long. Produces panicles of funnel-
shaped, rose-pink to rose-purple flowers in
summer–fall, often when leafless. Z9–10
H10–9.

LAGUNARIA
Norfolk Island hibiscus
MALVACEAE
Genus of one species of evergreen tree,
grown for its flowers in summer–fall and its
overall appearance. Prefers full light and
fertile, well-drained soil. Water container
plants freely when in full summer growth,
moderately at other times. Pruning is
tolerated, if required. Propagate by seed in
spring or by semiripe cuttings in summer.
Under cover, red spider mite may be
troublesome. ① Contact with the seeds
may irritate skin.
L. patersonii (Cow itch tree, Queensland
pyramidal tree). Fast-growing, evergreen,
upright tree, pyramidal when young.
H 30–46ft (10–14m), **S** 15–22ft (5–7m). Oval,
rough-textured leaves are matt-green
above, whitish-green beneath. Bears
hibiscus-like, rose-pink flowers, 2in (5cm)
wide, in summer. Z12–15 H12–10.

LAGURUS
Hare's tail
GRAMINEAE/POACEAE
See also GRASSES, BAMBOOS, RUSHES
and SEDGES.
L. ovatus (Hare's-tail grass), illus. p.284.

LAMARCKIA
GRAMINEAE/POACEAE
See also GRASSES, BAMBOOS, RUSHES
and SEDGES.
L. aurea (Golden top, Toothbrush grass).
Tuft-forming, annual grass. **H** and **S** 8in
(20cm). Wiry stems bear scattered, pale
green leaves and, in summer, erect, dense,
one-sided, golden panicles. Needs sun.
H7–1.

LAMIUM
Deadnettle
LABIATAE/LAMIACEAE
Genus of spring- or summer-flowering
perennials, most of which are
semievergreen, including a number of
weeds; some species make useful
groundcover. Prefers full or partial shade
and moist but well-drained soil. Resents
excessive winter wet. Propagate by stem-
tip cuttings of non-flowering shoots in mid-
summer or by division in fall or early
spring.
**L. galeobdolon subsp. montanum
'Florentinum',** syn. *L. galeobdolon*
'Variegatum'. Semievergreen, carpeting
perennial. **H** to 12in (30cm), **S** indefinite.
Oval, mid-green leaves are marked with
silver. Has racemes of tubular, 2-lipped,
lemon-yellow flowers in summer. Z4–8
H8–1. **'Variegatum'.** See *L. galeobdolon*
subsp. *montanum* 'Florentinum'.
L. maculatum (Spotted deadnettle).
Semievergreen, mat-forming perennial.
H 6in (15cm), **S** 36in (90cm). Has mauve-
tinged, often pink-flushed, mid-green
leaves with central, silvery stripes. Clusters
of hooded, mauve-pink flowers are borne
in mid-spring. Z4–8 H8–1. **'Album',** illus.
p.255. **'Aureum',** syn. *L. maculatum*
'Gold Leaf', **H** 8in (20cm), **S** 24in (60cm),
produces oval, yellow leaves with paler
white centers. Whorls of hooded, pink
flowers are borne on short stems in
summer. **'Beacon Silver'** bears mauve-
tinged, silver leaves, sometimes with
narrow, green margins, and clear pale pink
flowers. **'Gold Leaf'.** See *L. maculatum*
'Aureum'. **'White Nancy',** illus. p.254.
L. orvala, illus. p.260.

LAMPRANTHUS
AIZOACEAE
Genus of creeping, bushy, perennial
succulents and subshrubs, grown for their
daisylike flowers. Becomes woody after
several years, when is best replenished. Is
good for summer bedding, particularly in
arid conditions. Leaves redden in strong
sun. Requires full sun and very well-
drained soil. Propagate by seed or stem
cuttings in spring or fall. ① Contact with the seeds
may irritate skin.
L. aurantiacus, syn. *L. glaucoides*, illus.
p.496.
L. deltoides. See *Oscularia deltoides.*
L. glaucoides. See *L. aurantiacus.*
L. haworthii. Erect to creeping, perennial
succulent. **H** 20in (50cm), **S** indefinite. Has
cylindrical, blue-gray leaves, 2in (5cm)
long. In spring bears masses of daisylike,
cerise flowers, 3in (7cm) across, that only
open in sun. Z12–15 H12–10.
L. roseus, syn. *Mesembryanthemum
multiradiatum.* Creeping, perennial
succulent. **H** 6in (15cm), **S** indefinite.
Produces solid, 3-angled, mid- to glaucous
green leaves, 2in (5cm) long. Daisylike,
dark rose-red flowers, 1½in (4cm) across,
open only in sun from spring to fall.
Z12–15 H12–10.
L. spectabilis, illus. p.484.

Lamprocapnos spectabilis. See
Dicentra spectabilis.
Lamprocapnos spectabilis f. alba. See
Dicentra spectabilis f. alba.

LANTANA
Shrub verbena
VERBENACEAE
Genus of evergreen perennials and shrubs,
grown for their flowers. Needs full light
and fertile, well-drained soil. Water
container specimens freely when in full
growth, moderately at other times. Tip-
prune young plants to promote a bushy
habit and more flowering stems. Propagate
by seed in spring or by semiripe cuttings in
summer. Red spider mite and whitefly may
be troublesome. ① All parts may cause
severe discomfort if ingested, and contact
with foliage may irritate skin.
L. camara. Evergreen, rounded to
spreading shrub. **H** and **S** 3–6ft (1–2m).
Bears oval, finely wrinkled, deep green
leaves. From spring to fall, tiny, tubular,
5-lobed flowers, in dense, domed heads,
open yellow, then turn red. Many color
forms have been selected. Z11 H12–1.
**Lucky Series LUCKY HONEY BLUSH
('Baluclush'),** illus. p.301.
L. delicatissima. See *L. montevidensis.*
L. montevidensis, syn. *L. delicatissima,
L. sellowiana* (Weeping lantana) illus. p.310.
L. sellowiana. See *L. montevidensis.*
L. 'Spreading Sunset', illus. p.325.

LAPAGERIA
PHILESIACEAE/LILIACEAE
Genus of one species of evergreen, woody-
stemmed, twining climber, grown for its
large, waxy blooms. Requires partial shade
and rich, well-drained soil. Water
moderately when in full growth, scarcely at
all at other times. Provide support. Thin out
congested growth in spring. Propagate in
spring by seed, soaked for 2 days before
sowing, or in spring or fall by layering.
L. rosea (Chilean bellflower), illus. p.202.
var. albiflora is an evergreen, woody-
stemmed, twining climber. **H** to 15ft (5m).
Has oblong to oval, leathery, dark green
leaves. From summer to late fall bears
pendent, fleshy, narrowly bell-shaped,
white flowers. Z10–11 H12–10.

Lapeirousia cruenta. See *Anomatheca
laxa.*
Lapeirousia laxa. See *Anomatheca laxa.*

LARDIZABALA
LARDIZABALACEAE
Genus of evergreen, woody-stemmed,
twining climbers, grown for their foliage.
Male and female flowers are produced
on the same plant in late fall to winter. Is
useful for growing on trellises or pergolas.
Needs sun or partial shade and well-
drained soil. Propagate by seed in spring
or by stem cuttings in late summer or fall.
L. biternata. See *L. funaria.*
L. funaria, syn. *L. biternata.* Evergreen,
woody-stemmed, twining climber. **H** 10–12ft
(3–4m). Rounded leaves have broadly oval,
leathery, dark green leaflets. In winter
produces brown flowers with tiny, whitish
petals, the males in drooping spikes, the
females solitary. In winter–spring bears
many-seeded, berry-like, purple fruits,
2–3in (5–8cm) long.

LARIX
Larch
PINACEAE
See also CONIFERS.
L. decidua (European larch), syn.
L. europaea, illus. p.97.
L. europaea. See *L. decidua.*
L. kaempferi (Japanese larch), syn.
L. leptolepis. Fast-growing, deciduous,
columnar conifer with a conical tip.
H 80–100ft (25–30m), **S** 15–25ft (5–8m).

L

Shoots are purplish-red and leaves are needlelike, flattened, grayish-green or bluish. Small cones have reflexed scales. Z5–7 H7–4.

L. leptolepis. See *L. kaempferi*.

LATHRAEA

SCROPHULARIACEAE

Genus of spreading perennials that grow as parasites on the roots of trees, in the case of *L. clandestina* on willow or poplar. True leaves are not produced. Needs partial shade cast by host tree and prefers moist conditions. Roots resent being disturbed. Propagate by seed when fresh, in late summer.

L. clandestina (Toothwort), illus. p.260.

LATHYRUS

LEGUMINOSAE/PAPILIONACEAE

Genus of annuals and perennials, many of them tendril climbers, grown for their racemes of flowers. Flowers are followed by long, thin seed pods. Needs full light and rich, fertile, well-drained soil. Provide support and remove dead flowers regularly. Cut down perennials in late fall. Propagate annuals by seed (soaked before sowing) in early spring or early fall, perennials by seed in fall or by division in spring. Botrytis and mildew may cause problems. ① Seeds may cause mild stomach upset if ingested.

L. grandiflorus (Everlasting pea). Herbaceous, tendril climber. **H** to 5ft (1.5m). Has unwinged stems, and neat racemes of pink-purple and red flowers in summer. Z6–9 H9–5.

L. latifolius (Everlasting pea, Perennial pea), illus. p.201.

L. magellanicus. See *L. nervosus*.

L. nervosus, syn. *L. magellanicus* (Blue pea). Herbaceous, tendril climber. **H** to 15ft (5m). Gray-green leaves each have a pair of leaflets, a 3-branched tendril and large stipules. Fragrant, purplish-blue flowers are borne in long-stalked racemes in summer. Z3–10 H10–1.

L. odoratus (Sweet pea). Moderately fast-growing, annual, tendril climber. **H** to 10ft (3m). Has oval, mid-green leaves with tendrils. Scented flowers are produced in shades of pink, blue, purple or white, from summer to early fall. Dwarf, non-climbing cultivars are available. Z9–10 H8–1. **'Barry Dare'**, illus. p.202. **'Bijou'**, **H** and **S** 18in (45cm), has large flowers in shades of pink, red or blue. **'Charles Unwin'**, illus. p.201. **Cupid Series 'Cupid Pink'**, illus. p.301. **'Jayne Amanda'** bears racemes of usually 4, rarely 5, rose-pink flowers, and may be grown as a cordon or bush. **'Knee Hi'**, **H** and **S** 3ft (90cm), has large flowers in shades of pink, red, blue or white. **'Lady Diana'**, illus. p.201. **'Mrs. Bernard Jones'**, illus. p.201.

L. rotundifolius (Persian everlasting pea). Herbaceous, tendril climber with winged stems. **H** to 3ft (1m). Leaves each have narrow stipules, a pair of leaflets and a 3-branched tendril. Has small racemes of 3–8 pink to purplish flowers in summer. Z5–10 H10–1.

L. sylvestris (Perennial pea). Herbaceous, tendril climber with winged stems. **H** to 6ft (2m). Leaves each have narrow stipules, a pair of leaflets and a terminal, branched

tendril. In summer and early fall bears racemes of 4–10 rose-pink flowers, marked with green and purple. Z6–9 H9–6.

L. vernus, syn. *Orobus vernus* (Spring vetchling), illus. p.260. **'Alboroseus'** is a clump-forming perennial. **H** and **S** 12in (30cm). In spring, slender stems each bear 3–5 white-and-deep-pink flowers. Has fernlike, much-divided, soft leaves.

LAURELIA

MONIMIACEAE/ATHEROSPERMATACEAE

Genus of evergreen trees and shrubs, grown for their aromatic foliage. Requires sun or partial shade amd tolerates any but very dry soil. Propagate by semiripe cuttings in summer.

L. sempervirens, syn. *L. serrata*. Evergreen, broadly conical tree or shrub. **H** and **S** to 50ft (15m). Oval, leathery leaves are glossy, dark green and very aromatic. In summer bears small, inconspicuous flowers. Z9–10 H10–9.

L. serrata. See *L. sempervirens*.

LAURUS

LAURACEAE

Genus of evergreen trees, grown for their foliage. Needs a sheltered position in sun or partial shade and fertile, well-drained soil. In tubs may be grown well as standards, which should be trimmed during summer. Propagate by semiripe cuttings in summer or by seed in fall.

L. nobilis (Bay laurel, Sweet bay), illus. p.80.

LAVANDULA
Lavender

LABIATAE/LAMIACEAE

Genus of evergreen, mainly summer-flowering shrubs, with entire or divided, often gray-green leaves, grown for their aromatic foliage and flowers. Makes an effective, low hedge. Needs full sun and fertile, well-drained soil. Trim hedges lightly in spring to maintain a compact habit. New growth is rarely produced from old wood. Propagate by semiripe cuttings in summer. See also feature panel p.158.

L. angustifolia (English lavender). Evergreen, bushy shrub. **H** 16–32in (40–80cm), **S** 16–24in (40–60cm). Has linear to narrowly ovate, aromatic, gray-felted leaves. In mid-summer produces small, fragrant, compact, violet-blue, sometimes pink or white flower spikes, on stalks 4–12in (10–30cm) long. Z5–8 H8–5. **'Batlad'** see L.a. LITTLE LADY. **'Clarmo'** see *L.a.* LITTLE LOTTIE. **'Hidcote'**, syn. *L.* 'Hidcote' (illus. p.158), **H** 24in (60cm), **S** 30in (75cm), has dense spikes of deep purple flowers from mid- to late summer and silvery-gray leaves. **'Imperial Gem'** (illus. p.158), **H** and **S** 2ft (60cm). has narrowly oblong, silvery-gray leaves and produces dense spikes of tiny, deep purple flowers from mid- to late summer. **LITTLE LADY ('Batlad')**, illus. p.158, **H** 26in (65cm), **S** 32in (80cm), has a compact, erect habit, gray- to sage-green leaves and bears abundant spikes of white-centered, dark violet flowers from summer to early fall. **LITTLE LOTTIE ('Clarmo')**, illus. p.158, **H** 16in (40cm), **S** 26in (65cm), is a neat, domed shrub, spreading with age, with bright gray-green leaves and dense spikes

of pale mauve-pink flowers with bluish stripes down center of each corolla lobe. **'Lodden Blue'** (illus. p.158), **H** 16in (40cm), bears lilac-blue flowers. **'Lodden Pink'**, **H** to 30in (75cm), has pale pink flowers. **'Miss Katherine'** (illus. p.158) bears deep pink flowers. **'Munstead'**, **H** and **S** 24in (60cm), has gray-green leaves and blue flowers from mid- to late summer. Z5–8 H8–3. **'Nana Alba'**, **H** to 12in (30cm), produces white flowers. **'Old English Lavender'**, **H** to 20in (50cm), has purple flowers borne on long, erect stems. **'Wendy Carlile'** (illus. p.158), **H** 12in (30cm), is similar to *L.a.* 'Nana Alba', but has a more erect, uniform habit.

L. x chaytoriae 'Richard Gray' Evergreen, bushy, compact shrub. **H** and **S** 20in (50cm). Has linear, aromatic, silvery-gray leaves. Cylindrical spikes of deep purple flowers are borne in summer. **'Sawyers'** (illus. p.158), **H** 24in (60cm), has large, more pointed, deep purple flower spikes.

L. dentata (Fringed lavender). Evergreen, bushy shrub. **H** and **S** 3ft (1m). Aromatic leaves are fernlike, toothed and gray-green. Dense spikes of small, slightly fragrant, tubular, lavender-blue flowers and purple bracts are borne from mid- to late summer. Z5–9 H9–4.

L. 'Fathead', illus. p.158. Evergreen, robust, rounded, bushy shrub. **H** 20in (50cm), **S** 24in (60cm). Has linear, aromatic, mid- to dark green leaves and dark violet flower spikes, with large, petal-like, reddish-purple, terminal bracts, borne on dark green stalks to 5in (12cm) long. Flowers from late spring through summer if deadheaded regularly.

L. 'Grappenhall'. See *L. x intermedia* 'Pale Pretender'.

L. 'Helmsdale', illus. p.158. Evergreen, robust, rounded shrub. **H** 28in (70cm), **S** 43in (110cm). Has linear, aromatic, mid-to dark leaves. Bright green stalks, to 5in (12cm) long, bear dark violet flower spikes with reddish-purple bracts. Flowers from mid-spring through summer if deadheaded regularly.

L. 'Hidcote'. See *L. angustifolia* 'Hidcote'.

L. x intermedia (*L. angustifolia* x *L. latifolia*; Lavandin). Evergreen, spreading shrub. **H** 32–56in (80–140cm), **S** 28–36in (70–90cm). Has narrowly elliptic to obovate, very aromatic, silver- to greenish-gray leaves, covered in fine, silvery-gray hairs. From mid-summer to early fall, long, sometimes branched, stalks, 8–28in (20–70cm) long, bear spikes of fragrant, tubular, violet-blue to white flowers, with green to dark violet calyces. Is the main source of commercial lavender, lavandine. Z5–8 H8–5. **'Alba'** (illus. p.158) is a vigorous, erect shrub with white flowers, occasionally tinted pale purple. **'Grappenhall'.** See *L. x intermedia* 'Pale Pretender'.**'Hidcote Giant'**, **H** to 4ft (1.2m), has dense spikes of deep lavender-blue flowers. **'Pale Pretender'**, syn. *L.* 'Grappenhall', *L. x intermedia* 'Grappenhall', **H** to 4ft (1.2m), **S** 5ft (1.5m), produces blue-purple flowers.

L. lanata, illus. p.158. Evergreen, bushy shrub. **H** and **S** 20in (50cm). Young shoots and linear leaves are covered with whitish "wool." Produces strongly fragrant, tubular, bright violet flowers on erect spikes in summer. Z8–9 H8–1.

L. pedunculata subsp. pedunculata.

Evergreen, clump-forming shrub. **H** and **S** 20–32in (50–80cm). Ascending branches bear linear, aromatic, gray-green leaves covered with greenish-gray hairs. In spring and summer, compact, deep purple flower spikes, with dark purple apical terminal bracts, are borne on stalks 12in (30cm) long. **subsp. pedunculata 'James Compton'** (illus. p.158), **H** 28in (70cm), **S** 20in (50cm), has purple-margined, green stalks, to 8in (20cm) long, bearing dark purple flower spikes with dark purplish-mauve, apical bracts. Flowers from mid-spring to summer if regularly deadheaded.

L. 'Regal Splendour', illus. p.158. Evergreen, erect shrub. **H** 28in (70cm), **S** 20in (50cm). Has linear, aromatic, bright green leaves. Dark violet-blue flower spikes, with dark purple, apical terminal bracts, are produced on stems to 5in (12cm) long. Flowers from mid-spring to summer if regularly deadheaded.

L. stoechas (French lavender), illus. p.157. Evergreen, spreading shrub. **H** and **S** 8–28in (20–70cm). Has linear, gray-green leaves, with soft, white hairs. From mid-spring to fall (if regularly deadheaded) produces fragrant, dark violet-purple flower spikes, with purplish-violet apical terminal bracts, on stalks to 1¼in (3cm) long. **f. rosea** produces pink to rose-red flowers and reddish-purple bracts. **f. rosea 'Kew Red'** (illus. p.158), **H** and **S** 18in (45cm), is a compact, upright cultivar with mid- to gray-green leaves and pale green, purple-flushed stalks, 1¼–2in (3–5cm) long, bearing rounded, cerise-crimson flower spikes with soft pink bracts. **subsp. stoechas f. leucantha** has white flowers. **subsp. stoechas f. leucantha 'Snowman'** (illus. p.158), **H** and **S** 20in (50cm), is a compact shrub with numerous short, dense spikes of small, white flowers, topped by white bracts, in summer. Leaves are strongly aromatic.

L. 'Willow Vale', illus. p.158. Evergreen, compact shrub. **H** and **S** 20–28in (50–70cm). Has linear, aromatic, gray-green leaves and bears long spikes of purple flowers, with wavy or crinkly flower bracts, in summer.

LAVATERA
Mallow

MALVACEAE

Genus of mainly summer-flowering annuals, biennials, perennials and semievergreen subshrubs and shrubs. Needs sun and well-drained soil. Propagate perennials, subshrubs and shrubs by softwood cuttings in early spring or summer, annuals and biennials by seed in spring or early fall.

L. assurgentiflora, illus. p.133.

L. cachemiriana, syn. *L. cachemirica*. Semievergreen, woody-based perennial or subshrub. **H** 5–6ft (1.5–2m), **S** 3ft (1m). Wiry stems bear panicles of trumpet-shaped, silky, clear pink flowers in summer and ivy-shaped, downy, mid-green leaves. Z4–9 H9–1.

L. cachemirica. See *L. cachemiriana*.

L. x clementii. 'Barnsley' Vigorous, semievergreen subshrub. **H** and **S** 6ft (2m). Mid-green, palmate leaves have 3–5 lobes. Throughout summer bears profuse clusters of open funnel-shaped, red-eyed, white flowers, aging to soft pink, with deeply notched petals. Z6–9 H9–5. **'Rosea'**, syn. *L. olbia* 'Rosea', illus. p.136.

L. olbia 'Rosea'. See *L. x clementii* 'Rosea'.
L. trimestris 'Mont Blanc', illus. p.299. **'Silver Cup',** illus. p.305.

LAYIA

COMPOSITAE/ASTERACEAE

Genus of annuals, useful for hot, dry places. Needs sun and very well-drained soil. Propagate by seed in spring or early fall.
L. elegans. See *L. platyglossa*.
L. platyglossa, syn. *L. elegans* (Tidy tips). Fast-growing, upright, bushy annual. **H** 18in (45cm), **S** 12in (30cm). Has lance-shaped, grayish-green leaves. Daisylike flower heads, 2in (5cm) wide, with white-tipped, yellow ray petals and yellow centers, are produced from early summer to early fall. Is suitable for cut flowers. H12–6.

Lechenaultia. See *Leschenaultia*.

LEDEBOURIA

LILIACEAE/ASPARAGACEAE

Genus of bulbs, some of which are evergreen, with ornamental, narrowly lance-shaped leaves. Produces very small flowers with reflexed tips. Makes good pot plants in cool greenhouses. Needs full light, to allow leaf marks to develop well, and loose, open soil. Propagate by offsets in spring.
L. cooperi, syn. *Scilla adlamii, Scilla cooperi*. Summer-flowering bulb. **H** 2–4in (5–10cm), **S** 1–2in (2.5–5cm). Semierect, green, basal leaves, with brownish-purple stripes, die away in winter. Stem bears short spike of small, bell-shaped, greenish-purple flowers. Z9–10 H10–9.
L. socialis, syn. *Scilla socialis, Scilla violacea*, illus. p.421.

LEDUM

ERICACEAE

Genus of evergreen shrubs, grown for their aromatic foliage and small, white flowers. Needs full or partial shade and moist, peaty, acid soil. Benefits from dead-heading. Propagate by semiripe cuttings in summer or by seed in fall.
L. groenlandicum (Labrador tea), illus. p.145.

LEIOPHYLLUM

ERICACEAE

Genus of one species of evergreen shrub with an extensive, spreading root system. Prefers partial shade and well-drained, peaty, acid soil. Top-dress regularly with peaty soil. Propagate by seed in spring or by semiripe cuttings in summer.
L. buxifolium (Sand myrtle). Evergreen, dome-shaped shrub. **H** 10in (25cm), **S** 18in (45cm). Stems are covered with tiny, oval, leathery, dark green leaves. In late spring, terminal clusters of deep pink buds develop into small, star-shaped, white flowers, with prominent stamens. Z6–8 H8–6.

Lemairocereus euphorbioides. See *Neobuxbaumia euphorbioides*.
Lemairocereus marginatus. See *Pachycereus marginatus*.
Lemairocereus thurberi. See *Stenocereus thurberi*.

Lemboglossum bictoniense. See *Rhynchostele bictoniensis*.
Lemboglossum cervantesii. See *Rhynchostele cervantesii*.
Lemboglossum cordatum. See *Rhynchostele cordatum*.
Lemboglossum rossii. See *Rhynchostele rossii*.
Lembotropis nigricans. See *Cytisus nigricans*.

LEONOTIS

LABIATAE/LAMIACEAE

Genus of annuals, evergreen and semievergreen perennials, subshrubs and shrubs, grown for their flowers and overall appearance. Needs full sun and rich, well-drained soil. Water container specimens freely when in full growth, much less at other times of year. Cut back perennials, subshrubs and shrubs to within 6in (15cm) of the ground in early spring. Propagate by seed in spring or by greenwood cuttings in early summer.
L. leonurus (Lion's ear), illus. p.141.

LEONTOPODIUM

Edelweiss

COMPOSITAE/ASTERACEAE

Genus of short-lived, spring-flowering, woolly perennials, grown for their distinctive flower heads. Is suitable for rock gardens, containers and alpine troughs. Requires sun, gritty, well-drained soil and a deep collar of grit to improve surface drainage. Shelter from prevailing, rain-bearing winds, because crowns are extremely intolerant of winter wet and may rot off. Propagate by division in spring or by seed when fresh. Many seeds are not viable.
L. alpinum (Edelweiss), illus. p.332.
L. stracheyi. Mound-forming, spreading, woolly perennial. **H** and **S** 4in (10cm). Star-shaped, glistening, white flower heads are produced among thick, oval, silver leaves in spring. Makes a good alpine house plant. Z5–7 H7–5.

Leopoldia comosa. See *Muscari comosum*.

LEPISMIUM

CACTACEAE

Genus of epiphytic and lithophytic (growing on rocks) perennial cacti often pendulous in habit, grown for their cylindrical, ribbed, angled or flat, usually segmented stems. Small, funnel- to disc-shaped flowers are followed by spherical, often purple or red berries. Needs partial shade and rich, well-drained soil. Prefers 80% relative humidity—higher than for most cacti. Give only occasional, very light watering in winter. Propagate by seed or stem cuttings in spring or summer.
L. warmingianum, syn. *Rhipsalis warmingiana*. Erect, then pendent, perennial cactus. **H** 3ft (1m), **S** 20in (50cm). Has slender, notched, cylindrical, green branches, sometimes tinged red or brown, with 2–4 angles, and green-white flowers in winter–spring, followed by violet berries. Z13–15 H12–10.

LEPTINELLA

COMPOSITAE/ASTERACEAE

Genus of annuals and creeping perennials that are effective as low groundcover. Needs full sun and moderately fertile, sharply drained soil. Propagate by seed as soon as ripe or by division in spring.
L. atrata, syn. *Cotula atrata*. Evergreen, mat-forming perennial. **H** 1in (2.5cm), **S** to 10in (25cm). Has small, finely cut, grayish-green leaves and blackish-red flower heads in late spring and early summer. Is not easy to grow successfully. Z8–9 H9–8. **subsp. luteola,** illus. p.349.

LEPTOSPERMUM

Tea tree

MYRTACEAE

Genus of evergreen trees and shrubs, grown for their foliage and small, often profuse flowers. Grows well in coastal areas if not too exposed. Needs full sun and fertile, well-drained soil. Propagate by semiripe cuttings in summer.
L. flavescens. See *L. polygalifolium*.
L. humifusum. See *L. rupestre*.
L. polygalifolium, syn. *L. flavescens*, illus. p.131.
L. rupestre, syn. *L. humifusum*, illus. p.151.
L. scoparium (Manuka, New Zealand tea-tree). **var. incanum 'Keatleyi'** is an evergreen, rounded shrub. **H** and **S** 10ft (3m). Narrowly lance-shaped, aromatic, gray-green leaves set off a profusion of large, star-shaped, pale pink flowers in late spring–summer. **'Nicholsii'** produces bronze-purple leaves and smaller, crimson flowers. Z12–15 H12–10. **'Red Damask',** illus. p.123. **'Snow White'** (New Zealand tea-tree), illus. p.130.

LESCHENAULTIA

SYN. LECHENAULTIA

GOODENIACEAE

Genus of evergreen shrubs, grown for their flowers. Needs full light and peaty, well-drained soil with few phosphates and nitrates. Water container plants moderately during growing season, sparingly at other times. Shorten over-long stems after flowering. Propagate by seed in spring or by semiripe cuttings in summer. Most species are not easy to grow under glass; good ventilation is essential.
L. floribunda. Evergreen, domed, wiry-stemmed shrub. **H** and **S** 12–24in (30–60cm). Has narrow, cylindrical, pointed leaves and, in spring-summer, short, tubular, pale blue flowers, with 5 angular petals, in terminal clusters. Z12–15 H12–10.

LEUCADENDRON

PROTEACEAE

Genus of evergreen shrubs and trees, grown for their flower heads from fall to spring and for their foliage. Needs full light and sharply drained soil, mainly of sand and peat, ideally with very little nitrogen and phosphates. Water container specimens moderately while in growth, sparingly at other times. Propagate by seed in spring.
L. argenteum, illus. p.451.

LEUCANTHEMELLA

COMPOSITAE/ASTERACEAE

Genus of hairy perennials, grown for their daisylike flower heads in fall. Needs full sun or partial shade and reliably moist soil. Propagate by division or basal cuttings in spring.
L. serotina, syn. *Chrysanthemum serotinum, Chrysanthemum uliginosum*, illus. p.220.

LEUCANTHEMOPSIS

COMPOSITAE/ASTERACEAE

Genus of dwarf, tufted, clump- or mat-forming perennials, grown for their solitary, daisylike flower heads in summer. Needs full sun and sharply drained soil. Propagate by seed as soon as ripe or by division or basal cuttings in spring.
L. alpina, syn. *Chrysanthemum alpinum* (Alpine chrysanthemum). Tuft-forming, short-lived perennial. **H** 4in (10cm), **S** 8in (20cm). Small tufts of deeply cut leaves are produced from short, rhizomatous roots. Has large, white flower heads, with yellow centers, in summer. Is good for a rock or scree garden, or an alpine planter. Z6–9 H9–6.

LEUCANTHEMUM

COMPOSITAE/ASTERACEAE

Genus of annuals and perennials, grown for their flowers. Cultivars of *L. x superbum* are valued for their profusion of large, daisylike summer flowers. Some species are suitable for rock gardens. Needs full sun and well-drained soil. Taller cultivars require staking. Propagate species by seed in spring or fall or by division in early spring or late summer, cultivars by division only.
L. x superbum, syn. *Chrysanthemum maximum, C. x superbum* (Shasta daisy). Robust perennial. **H** 3ft (1m), **S** 2ft (60cm). Lift, divide and replant plants every 2 years to maintain vigor. Z5–8 H8–5. **'Aglaia',** illus. p.230. **'Elizabeth'** has large, solitary, daisylike, pure white flower heads borne in summer. **'Esther Read',** illus. p.263. **'Sonnenschein',** illus. p.231. **'Wirral Pride',** illus. p.246. **'Wirral Supreme'** is double with short, central florets. Z5–8 H8–1.

LEUCHTENBERGIA

CACTACEAE

Genus of one species of perennial cactus. Looks like *Agave* in foliage, but its flowers, seed pods and seeds are similar to *Ferocactus*. Tubercles eventually form on short, rough, woody stems. Needs full sun and very well-drained soil. Keep completely dry in winter; water sparingly from spring to fall. Propagate by seed in spring or summer.
L. principis, illus. p.490.

LEUCOCORYNE

LILIACEAE/ALLIACEAE

Genus of spring-flowering bulbs, grown for their loose heads of flattish flowers. Needs sun and well-drained soil. Plant in fall, water well during their growing season and keep almost dry when dormant in summer. Propagate by seed or offsets in fall.

L

L. ixioides (Glory of the sun). Spring-flowering bulb. **H** 12–16in (30–40cm), **S** 3–4in (8–10cm). Has long, narrow, semierect, basal leaves that are withered by flowering time. Wiry, slender flower stem has a loose head of up to 10 lilac-blue flowers. Z12–14 H8–1.

LEUCOGENES
New Zealand edelweiss

COMPOSITAE/ASTERACEAE

Genus of evergreen, woody-based perennials, grown mainly for their foliage. Is excellent for alpine houses in areas where summers are cool. Needs sun and gritty, well-drained, peaty soil. Resents winter wet and may be difficult to grow. Propagate by seed when fresh or by softwood cuttings in late spring or early summer.
L. grandiceps, illus. p.356.
L. leontopodium, syn. *Raoulia leontopodium* (North Island edelweiss). Evergreen, rosetted perennial. **H** and **S** 5in (12cm). Has oblong to oval, overlapping, silvery-white to yellowish leaves. In early summer produces up to 15 small, star-shaped, woolly, silvery-white flower heads surrounded by thick, felted, white bracts. Z7–8 H8–7.

LEUCOJUM
Snowflake

AMARYLLIDACEAE

Genus of bulbs, grown for their pendent, bell-shaped, white or pink flowers in fall or spring. Some species prefer a moist, partially shaded site, others do best in sun and well-drained soil. Propagate by division in spring or early fall or by seed in fall.
L. aestivum, illus. p.436.
L. autumnale. See *Acis autumnalis*.
L. roseum. See *Acis rosea*.
L. vernum, illus. p.414.

LEUCOPHYTA
Cushion bush

COMPOSITAE/ASTERACEAE

Genus of annuals, evergreen perennials and small shrubs, often used as summer bedding. Requires full light and well-drained soil. Water container plants moderately when in full growth, sparingly at other times. Remove tips to promote a bushy habit. Propagate by semiripe cuttings in late summer. Botrytis may be troublesome if plants are kept too cool and damp in winter.
L. brownii, syn. *Calocephalus brownii*, illus. p.315.

LEUCOPOGON

ERICACEAE

Genus of evergreen, heather-like shrubs, suitable for rock gardens and peat beds. Needs a sheltered, shaded site and gritty, moist, peaty soil. Propagate in summer by seed or semiripe cuttings.
L. colensoi, syn. *Cyathodes colensoi*, illus. p.346.

LEUCOSPERMUM
Pincushion

PROTEACEAE

Genus of evergreen shrubs, grown for their flower heads. Requires full light and sandy, well-drained soil with few phosphates and nitrates. Water container specimens moderately when in growth, sparingly at other times. Propagate by seed in spring. Is not easy to cultivate long term under glass; good ventilation is essential.
L. cordifolium, syn. *L. nutans*. Evergreen, rounded to spreading, well-branched shrub. **H** and **S** 4ft (1.2m). Elongated, heart-shaped, blue-gray leaves each have a 3-toothed tip. In summer, very slender, tubular, brick-red to orange flowers, each with a long style, are borne in tight heads that resemble single blooms. Z12–15 H12–10.
L. nutans. See *L. cordifolium*.
L. reflexum, illus. p.456.

LEUCOTHÖE

ERICACEAE

Genus of evergreen, semievergreen or deciduous shrubs, grown for their white flowers and their foliage. Needs full or partial shade and moist, peaty, acid soil. Propagate by semiripe cuttings in summer.
L. catesbaei. See *L. fontanesiana*.
L. fontanesiana, syn. *L. catesbaei*, *L. walteri* (Drooping leucothoe, Fetterbush). Evergreen, arching shrub. **H** 5ft (1.5m), **S** 10ft (3m). Lance-shaped, leathery, glossy, dark green leaves have long points and sharp teeth. Short racemes of small, urn-shaped, white flowers are borne beneath shoots from mid- to late spring. Z5–8 H8–5. **'Rainbow'**, illus. p.167. **SCARLETTA** **('Zeblid')** has dark red-purple young foliage, which turns dark green, then bronze in winter. Z5–8 H8–3. **'Zeblid'** See *L.f.* **SCARLETTA**.
L. keiskei. Evergreen shrub with erect or semiprocumbent stems. **H** 6–24in (15–60cm), **S** 12–24in (30–60cm). Oval, thin-textured, glossy, dark green leaves have a red flush when young and leathery appearance. Bears pendent, urn-shaped, white flowers from leaf axils in summer. Is good for a rock garden, peat bed or alpine house. Prefers mild, damp climates. Z6–8 H8–6.
L. walteri. See *L. fontanesiana*.

LEWISIA

PORTULACACEAE

Genus of perennials, some of which are evergreen, with rosettes of succulent leaves and deep tap roots. Most species are good in alpine houses, troughs and rock gardens. Evergreen species need partial shade and rich, moist or well-drained, neutral to acid soil and resent water in their rosettes at all times. Herbaceous species shed their leaves in summer and require sun and well-drained, neutral to acid soil; dry off after flowering. Propagate herbaceous species by seed in spring or fall, evergreen species by seed in spring or by offsets in summer. Seed of *L.* Cotyledon Hybrids may not come true.
L. columbiana. Evergreen, basal-rosetted perennial. **H** 6in (15cm) or more, **S** 4–6in (10–15cm). Bears thick, narrowly oblong, flat, glossy, green leaves and, in early summer, terminal sprays of small, cup-shaped, deeply veined, white to deep pink flowers. Prefers moist soil. Z4–8 H8–3.
L. Cotyledon Hybrids, illus. p.340.
L. 'George Henley', illus. p.338.
L. nevadensis. Loose, basal-rosetted perennial. **H** 1½–2½in (4–6cm), **S** 3in (8cm). In summer, large, almost stemless, cup-shaped, white flowers are borne above small clusters of strap-shaped, dark green leaves. Z3–4 H4–1.
L. rediviva, [pink form] illus. p.365; [white form] illus. p.360.
L. tweedyi, syn. *Lewisiopsis tweedi*, *Cistanthe tweedyi*, illus. p.351.

Lewisiopsis tweedi. See *Lewisia tweedyi*.

LEYCESTERIA

CAPRIFOLIACEAE

Genus of deciduous shrubs, grown for their showy flower clusters. Needs full sun and fertile, well-drained soil. Propagate by softwood cuttings in summer or by seed or division in fall.
L. formosa (Himalayan honeysuckle). Deciduous, upright shrub. **H** and **S** 6ft (2m). Has blue-green shoots and slender, oval, dark green leaves. In summer and early fall, small, funnel-shaped, white flowers are produced at tip of each pendent cluster of purplish-red bracts and are followed by spherical, reddish-purple fruits. Cut weak shoots to ground level in early spring. Z7–9 H9–6.

LEYMUS

GRAMINEAE/POACEAE

See also GRASSES, BAMBOOS, RUSHES, and SEDGES.
L. arenarius, syn. *Elymus arenarius*. Vigorous, spreading, herbaceous, rhizomatous, perennial grass. **H** to 5ft (1.5m), **S** indefinite. Has broad, glaucous leaves. Produces sturdy, terminal spikes of grayish-green flowers on erect stems in late summer. Is useful for binding coastal dunes. Z4–10 H10–1.

LIATRIS
Blazing star, Gayfeather

COMPOSITAE/ASTERACEAE

Genus of summer-flowering perennials with thickened, corm-like rootstocks, grown for their flowers. Prefers sun and well-drained soil. Propagate by division in spring.
L. callilepis of gardens. See *L. spicata*.
L. pycnostachya (Kansas gayfeather). Clump-forming perennial. **H** 4ft (1.2m), **S** 1ft (30cm). In summer bears tall spikes of clustered, feathery, mauve-pink flower heads. Grasslike, dark green leaves form basal tufts. Z3–9 H9–2.
L. spicata, syn. *L. callilepis* (Gayfeather, Spike blazing star), illus. p.438.

LIBERTIA

IRIDACEAE

Genus of rhizomatous perennials, grown for their foliage, decorative seed pods and flowers. Needs a sheltered, sunny or partially shaded site and well-drained soil. Propagate by division in spring or by seed in fall or spring.
L. grandiflora, illus. p.230.
L. ixioides. Clump-forming, rhizomatous perennial. **H** and **S** 24in (60cm). Produces panicles of saucer-shaped, white flowers in summer. Grasslike, dark green leaves turn orange-brown in winter. **'Goldfinger'**, illus. p.277.

Libocedrus chilensis. See *Austrocedrus chilensis*.
Libocedrus decurrens. See *Calocedrus decurrens*.
Libonia floribunda. See *Justicia rizzinii*.

LIGULARIA

COMPOSITAE/ASTERACEAE

Genus of perennials, grown for their foliage and large, daisylike flower heads. Needs sun or partial shade and moist but well-drained soil. Propagate by division in spring or by seed in fall or spring. Is prone to damage by slugs and snails.
L. 'Britt Marie Crawford', illus. p.445.
L. clivorum 'Desdemona'. See *L. dentata* 'Desdemona'.
L. dentata 'Desdemona', syn. *L. clivorum* 'Desdemona'. Compact, clump-forming perennial. **H** 4ft (1.2m), **S** 2ft (60cm). Has heart-shaped, long-stalked, leathery, basal, dark brownish-green leaves, almost mahogany beneath. Bears terminal clusters of large, daisylike, vivid orange flower heads on branching stems from mid- to late summer. Z4–8 H8–1.
L. 'Gregynog Gold'. Clump-forming perennial. **H** 6ft (2m), **S** 2ft (60cm). Leaves are large, heart-shaped and deep green. Conical panicles of daisylike, orange-yellow flower heads are borne from mid- to late summer. Z6–9 H9–6.
L. przewalskii, syn. *Senecio przewalskii*, illus. p.445.
L. stenocephala. Loosely clump-forming perennial. **H** 4ft (1.2m) or more, **S** 2ft (60cm). Has rounded, jagged-edged, mid-green leaves. Large heads of daisylike, yellow-orange flowers are borne on purplish stems from mid- to late summer. Z4–8 H8–1.
L. 'The Rocket', illus. p.219.
L. tussilaginea. See *Farfugium japonicum*.

LIGUSTRUM
Privet

OLEACEAE

Genus of deciduous, semievergreen or evergreen shrubs and trees, grown for their foliage and, in some species, flowers. Requires sun or partial shade, the variegated forms doing best in full sun. Thrives on any well-drained soil, including chalky soil. All except *L. lucidum* occasionally need cutting back in mid-spring to restrict growth. Propagate by semiripe cuttings in summer. ① All parts may cause severe discomfort if ingested.
L. japonicum (Japanese privet). Evergreen, bushy, dense shrub. **H** 10ft (3m), **S** 8ft (2.5m). Has oval, glossy, very dark green leaves and, from mid-summer to early fall, large, conical panicles of small, tubular, white flowers with lobes. Z7–10 H10–7. **'Coriaceum'**. See *L. japonicum* 'Rotundifolium'. **'Rotundifolium'**, syn. *L. japonicum* 'Coriaceum' is slow-growing, and produces a dense mass of rounded, leathery leaves.
L. lucidum (Chinese privet). Evergreen, upright shrub or tree. **H** 30ft (10m), **S** 25ft (8m). Bears large, oval, glossy, dark green leaves. Produces large panicles of small, tubular, white flowers, with 4 lobes, in late summer and early fall. Z8–10 H10–8.

L

'**Excelsum Superbum**' has bright green leaves, marked with pale green and yellow-edged. Z8–11 H12–8.

L. ovalifolium (Privet), illus. p.119.
'**Aureum**' is a vigorous, evergreen or semievergreen, upright, dense shrub. **H** 12ft (4m), **S** 10ft (3m). Oval, glossy, mid-green leaves are broadly edged bright yellow. Dense panicles of small, rather unpleasantly scented, tubular, white flowers, with 4 lobes, in mid-summer are followed by spherical, black fruits. Cut back hedges to 1ft (30cm) after planting and prune hard for first 2 years; then trim as necessary in growing season. Z6–10 H10–9.

L. sinense, illus. p.112.
L. x vicaryi. See *L.* 'Vicaryi'.
L. '**Vicaryi**', syn. *L. x vicaryi*, illus. p.140.
L. vulgare (Common privet). Deciduous or semievergreen, bushy shrub. **H** and **S** 10ft (3m). Has narrowly lance-shaped, dark green leaves. Produces panicles of small, strongly scented, tubular, white flowers, with 4 lobes, from early to mid-summer, then spherical, black fruits. Cut back hedges to 1ft (30cm) after planting and prune hard for first 2 years; then trim as necessary in growing season. Z5–8 H8–5. '**Aureum**', **H** and **S** 6ft (2m), has golden-yellow foliage.

LILIUM
Lily

LILIACEAE

Genus of mainly summer-flowering bulbs, grown for their often fragrant, brightly colored flowers. Each fleshy-scaled bulb produces one unbranched, leafy stem, in some cases with annual roots in lower part. Mostly lance-shaped or linear leaves, to 9in (22cm) long, are scattered or in whorls, sometimes with bulbils in axils. Flowers, usually several per stem, are mainly trumpet- to bowl-shaped or with the 6 petals strongly reflexed to form a turkscap shape. (Petals of *Lilium* are known botanically as perianth segments.) Three categories of flower size—small, medium and large—are used in the descriptions below. For turkscap, bowl-, cup-, and star-shaped flowers: small is up to 2in (5cm) across; medium is 2–3in (5–7cm) across; large is over 3in (7cm) across. For trumpet- and funnel-shaped flowers: small is up to 3in (7cm) long; medium is 3–4in (7–10cm) long; large is over 4in (10cm) long. Each plant has a spread of up to 12in (30cm). Needs sun and well-drained soil, unless otherwise stated. Propagate by seed in fall or spring, by bulb scales in summer or by stem bulbils in fall. Virus, fungal diseases, and lily beetle may cause problems. Lilies are classified into 9 divisions. See feature panel pp.388–91.

Division 1 (Asiatic hybrids)
These lilies are derived from various Asiatic species, including *L. bulbiferum*, *L. cernuum*, *L. concolor*, *L. davidii*, *L. lancifolium* and *L. x maculatum*. The flowers are borne in racemes or umbels, and are usually unscented. The leaves are narrowly ovate and arranged alternatively. There are 3 subdivisions: **1a**) upward-facing flowers; **1b**) outward-facing flowers; **1c**) pendent flowers.

Division 2 (Martagon hybrids)
Derived primarily from *L. hansonii* and *L. martagon*, these lilies produce racemes of turkscap, sometimes scented flowers, and have whorls of elliptic leaves.

Division 3 (Candidum hybrids)
Derived from *L. candicum* and other European species, except *L. martagon*, these lilies produce sometimes scented, mostly turkscap flowers, singly or in umbels or racemes. Leaves are elliptic, and spirally arranged or scattered.

Division 4 (American hybrids)
Derived from American species, these lilies bear racemes of sometimes scented, mostly turkscap, but occasionally funnel-shaped flowers, and have whorls of lance-shaped to elliptic leaves.

Division 5 (Longiflorum hybrids)
Derived from *L. formosanum* and *L. longiflorum*, these lilies bear racemes or umbels of large, often sweetly scented, trumpet- or funnel-shaped flowers, sometimes only 2 or 3 per stem. Leaves are linear to narrowly lance-shaped, and scattered.

Division 6 (Trumpet and Aurelian hybrids)
Derived from Asiatic species, including *L. regale*, *L. henryi* and *L. sargentiae*, these lilies bear racemes or umbels of usually scented flowers. Leaves are elliptic to linear, and alternate or spirally arranged. There are 4 subdivisions: **6a**) trumpet-shaped flowers; **6b**) bowl-shaped flowers; **6c**) very shallowly bowl-shaped flowers, some almost flat; **6d**) distinctly recurved flowers.

Division 7 (Oriental hybrids)
Derived from E. Asian species, such as *L. auratum*, *L. japonicum* and *L. speciosum*, as well as their hybrids with *L. henryi*, these lilies have flowers borne in racemes or panicles, and are often scented. Leaves are lance-shaped and alternate. There are 4 subdivisions: **7a**) trumpet-shaped flowers; **7b**) bowl-shaped flowers; **7c**) flat or very shallowly bowl-shaped flowers; **7d**) turkscap or various recurved flowers.

Division 8. Other hybrids

Division 9. All true species.

L. **African Queen Group**, illus. p.391. Summer-flowering Division 6 lily. **H** 3ft (1m). Produces 3 large, fragrant flowers, brownish-purple outside and apricot-orange on the inside, with recurved petals. Z5–8 H8–5.
L. '**Altari**', illus. p.388. Summer-flowering Division 5 and 7 crossbred lily. **H** 3ft (1m). Highly scented, white flowers have cranberry-red inner throats.
L. amabile. Summer-flowering Division 9 lily with stem roots. **H** 1–3ft (30cm–1m). Scattered leaves are lance-shaped. Has up to 10 unpleasant-smelling, nodding, turkscap, black-spotted, red flowers; each petal is 2–2¹⁄₄in (5–5.5cm) long. Z3–8 H8–1.
L. '**Amber Gold**'. Summer-flowering Division 1c lily. **H** 4–5ft (1.2–1.5m). Has medium-sized, nodding, turkscap, deep yellow flowers, each with maroon spots in throat. Z3–8 H8–1.
L. '**Angela North**'. Mid-summer-flowering Division 1c lily. **H** to 3ft (1m). Has medium-sized, slightly fragrant, dark red flowers, spotted darker red, that have strongly recurved petals. Z3–8 H8–1.
L. '**Apollo**', illus. p.391. Summer-flowering Division 1a lily. **H** 4ft (1.2m). Has downward-facing, turkscap, pale orange flowers with strongly reflexed petals. Z3–8 H8–1.

L. '**Arena**', illus. p.388. Vigorous, summer-flowering Division 7b lily. **H** 4ft (1.2m). Large, outward-facing, bowl-shaped to slightly trumpet-shaped, recurving, greenish- to yellowish-white flowers have deep red central veining on the insides and yellow-green throats with deep red spots.
L. auratum (Golden-rayed lily of Japan). Summer- and fall-flowering Division 9 lily with stem roots. **H** 2–5ft (60cm–1.5m). Has long, scattered, lance-shaped leaves. Produces up to 10, sometimes more, fragrant, outward-facing, widely bowl-shaped, white flowers; each petal is 5–7in (12–18cm) long with a central, red or yellow band and often red or yellow spots. Requires partial shade and neutral to acid soil. Z3–8 H8–1. var. *platyphyllum* (illus. p.388) has broader leaves; petals have a central, yellow band and fewer spots. Z5–8 H8–1.
L. '**Black Beauty**'. Summer-flowering Division 7d lily. **H** 5–6ft (1.5–2m). Has medium-sized, outward-facing, flattish, green-centered, very deep red flowers with recurved, white-margined petals. Z3–8 H8–1.
L. '**Black Dragon**'. Summer-flowering Division 6a lily. **H** 5ft (1.5m). Has large, outward-facing, trumpet-shaped flowers with dark purplish-red outsides and white insides. Z3–8 H8–1.
L. '**Black Magic**', illus. p.388. Summer-flowering Division 6a lily. **H** 4–6ft (1.2–2m). Scented, outward-facing, trumpet-shaped flowers are purplish-brown outside and white inside. Z3–8 H8–1.
L. '**Black Out**', illus. p.389. Summer-flowering Division 1b lily. **H** 4ft (1.2m). Glossy, dark red flowers have black-red throats, with tiny, black spots.
L. '**Black Pearl**'. Summer-flowering Division 1a lily. **H** 3ft (1m). Bears deep purple-red flowers.
L. '**Bonfire**'. Late summer-flowering Division 7b lily. **H** 4–5ft (1.2–1.5m). Produces outward-facing, bowl-shaped flowers with broad petals, white outside flushed with pink, and dark crimson inside, spotted paler crimson. Z3–8 H8–1.
L. '**Boogie Woogie**', illus. p.390. Summer-flowering Division 5 and 6 crossbred Orienpet lily. **H** 3ft (1m). Bears large, fragrant flowers with recurved, pink-edged, yellow petals.
L. '**Bright Star**', illus. p.390. Summer-flowering Division 6b lily. **H** 3–5ft (1–1.5m). Has large, flattish, white flowers; petals have recurved tips and central, orange streak inside. Z5–8 H8–1.
L. '**Brocade**'. Early summer-flowering Division 2 lily. **H** 5ft (1.5m). Produces nodding, turkscap, orange-yellow flowers, suffused rosy-pink, with purple-red spots on insides of recurved petals.
L. '**Bronwen North**'. Mid-summer-flowering Division 1c lily. **H** to 3ft (1m). Each stem bears 7 or more medium-sized, slightly fragrant flowers with strongly recurving, pale mauve-pink petals, paler at the tips, and pale pink throats with dark spots and lines; nectaries are reddish-black. Z3–8 H8–1.
L. '**Brushmarks**'. Early summer-flowering Division 1a lily. **H** 4¹⁄₂ft (1.35m). Large, upward-facing, cup-shaped, orange flowers are green-throated. Petals have deep red blotches and sometimes spots. Z3–8 H8–1.

L. bulbiferum (Fire lily, Orange lily). Summer-flowering Division 9 lily with stem roots. **H** 16in–5ft (40cm–1.5m). Stem bears scattered, lance-shaped leaves and, usually, bulbils in leaf axils. Bears 1–5 or more upward-facing, shallowly cup-shaped, orange-red flowers. Each petal is 2¹⁄₂–3¹⁄₄in (6–8.5cm) long and spotted black or deep red. Z3–8 H8–1. var. *croceum* (illus. p.391) has orange flowers and does not normally bear bulbils.
L. '**California Gold**'. Vigorous, summer-flowering Division 6a lily. **H** 3–4ft (1–1.2m). Produces sprays of outward-facing, trumpet- to bowl-shaped, deep lemon-yellow flowers, with the reverses of the gently recurving petals bronze-green.
L. canadense (Canada lily, Meadow lily, Wild yellow lily), illus. p.390. Summer-flowering Division 9 lily with stem roots. **H** to 5ft (1.5m). Narrowly to broadly lance-shaped leaves are mainly in whorls. Bears about 10 nodding, bell-shaped, yellow or red flowers; each petal is 2–3in (5–8cm) long, with dark red or purple spots in lower part. Z3–8 H8–1.
L. candidum (Madonna lily). Summer-flowering Division 9 lily. **H** 3–6ft (1–2m). Flower stem bears scattered, lance-shaped leaves and 5–20 fragrant, outward-facing, broadly funnel-shaped, white flowers. Each petal is 2–3in (5–8cm) long with yellow base and slightly recurved tip. In fall bears basal leaves, which remain throughout winter but die off as flowering stems mature. Prefers lime-rich soil. Z6–9 H9–6.
L. carniolicum. See *L. pyrenaicum* subsp. *carniolicum*.
L. '**Casa Blanca**', illus. p.388. Late summer-flowering Division 7b lily. **H** 3ft (90cm). Large, waxy, white flowers have yellowish-white midribs and violet-red nectaries. Z6–9 H9–6.
L. cernuum (Nodding lily), illus. p.389. Summer-flowering Division 9 lily with stem roots. **H** to 2ft (60cm). Long, linear leaves are scattered. Produces 7–15 fragrant, nodding, turkscap flowers, usually pinkish-purple with purple spots. Each petal is 1¹⁄₂–2in (3.5–5cm) long. Z2–6 H6–1.
L. chalcedonicum, syn. *L. heldreichii* (Scarlet turkscap lily) illus. p.391. Summer-flowering Division 9 lily with stem roots. **H** 20in–5ft (50cm–1.5m). Leaves are scattered and mostly lance-shaped; lower ones are spreading, upper ones smaller and closer to stem. Bears up to 12 slightly scented, nodding, turkscap flowers with red or reddish-orange petals, 2–3in (5–7cm) long. Z7–9 H8–1.
L. **Citronella Group**, illus. p.390. Mid-summer-flowering Division 1 lily. **H** 3ft (1m). Produces nodding heads of large, scented flowers with recurved, black-spotted, bright yellow petals. Z3–8 H8–1.
L. '**Conca d'Or**', illus. p.390. Summer-flowering Division 5 and 6 crossbred Orienpet lily. **H** 4ft (1.2m). Produces to 3 large, spicy-scented, creamy-yellow flowers with lemon-yellow throats.
L. '**Connecticut King**', illus. p.390. Early to mid-summer-flowering Division 1a lily. **H** 3ft (1m). Flowers are medium-sized, upward-facing, cup-shaped and bright yellow. Z5–8 H8–1.
L. '**Corsage**'. Summer-flowering Division 1b lily. **H** 4ft (1.2m). Bears outward-facing,

bowl-shaped flowers with recurved petals, pink-flushed outside and pink inside with white centers and maroon spots. Z3–8 H8–1.

L. 'Côte d'Azur', illus. p.389. Summer-flowering Division 1a lily. **H** 16in (40cm). Strong stems bear deep rose-pink flowers with darker-spotted throats. Z3–8 H8–1.

L. 'Cover Girl'. Summer- to early fall-flowering Division 7c lily. **H** 5–6ft (1.5–1.9m). Has very large, outward- or slightly downward-facing, soft pink flowers, with white at tips of gently recurved petals which are centrally banded deep pink and strongly red-spotted.

L. 'Crimson Pixie', illus. p.391. Early summer-flowering Division 1a lily. **H** 16in (40cm). Has umbels of upright, open bowl-shaped, unspotted, deep warm red-orange flowers. Is good as a pot plant.

L. x *dalhansonii*. Variable, summer-flowering Division 9 lily. **H** 5–6ft (1.5–2m). Has unpleasant-smelling, turkscap, chestnut-brown or dark maroon flowers with gold spots. Z3–8 H8–1.

L. x *dalhansonii* 'Marhan'. See *L.* 'Marhan'.

L. *davidii*. Summer-flowering Division 9 lily with stem roots. **H** 3–4½ft (1–1.4m). Linear leaves are scattered. Produces 5–20 nodding, turkscap, red or reddish-orange flowers; each petal is 2–3in (5–8cm) long with dark purple spots. Z3–8 H8–1. **var. *willmottiae*** has slender, arching stems to 6ft (2m) and pendent flower stalks.

L. 'Destiny'. Early summer-flowering Division 1a lily. **H** 3–4ft (1–1.2m). Flowers are medium-sized, upward-facing, cup-shaped and yellow with brown spots. Z3–8 H8–1.

L. *duchartrei*. Summer-flowering Division 9 lily. **H** 2–3ft (60cm–1m). Lance-shaped leaves are scattered up stems. Has up to 12 fragrant, nodding, turkscap, white flowers that are flushed purple outside and spotted deep purple inside. Z7–8 H8–7.

L. 'Ed', syn. *L.* 'Mr. Ed'. Summer- to early fall-flowering Division 7 lily. **H** 16in (40cm). Has large, outward-facing, bowl-shaped, greenish-white flowers, with the petals centrally banded pale yellow and flushed pale red, and dark red spots on one-third of each petal.

L. 'Elodie', illus. p.389. Summer-flowering Division 1a lily. **H** 4ft (1.2m). Semidouble, pale pink flowers have dark pink-freckled centers.

L. 'Enchantment', illus. p.391. Early summer-flowering Division 1a lily. **H** 3ft (1m). Produces medium-sized, upward-facing, cup-shaped, orange-red flowers with black-spotted throats. Z3–8 H8–1.

L. 'Eros'. Mid-summer-flowering Division 1c lily. **H** 3–3½ft (90cm–1.1m). Has small, unscented, turkscap, buff flowers.

L. 'Garden Party'. Summer-flowering Division 7 lily. **H** 20in (50cm) Produces large, fragrant, outward-facing, red-speckled, white flowers with gold and red or pink stripes in center of each petal.

L. Golden Clarion Group. Late spring- to early summer-flowering bulb. **H** 3–6ft (1–2m). Produces outward-facing, trumpet-shaped, pale to deep yellow flowers that may be flushed with reddish-purple on outside. Z5–7 H7–5.

L. Golden Splendor Group, illus. p.393.

L. 'Grand Cru', illus. p.391. Early summer-flowering Division 1a lily. **H** 4ft (1.2m). Has upright, open bowl-shaped, vivid-yellow flowers, strongly red-suffused in throats for about half petal lengths, and with a few red spots at base internally. Is good as a pot plant.

L. 'Gran Paradiso', illus. p.391. Mid-summer-flowering Division 1a lily. **H** 3ft (1m). Produces medium-sized, unscented, bowl-shaped, red flowers with slightly recurved petals.

L. *hansonii*, illus. p.391. Summer-flowering Division 9 lily with stem roots. **H** 3–5ft (1–1.5m). Long leaves in whorls are lance-shaped to oval. Has 3–12 scented, nodding, turkscap, orange-yellow flowers. Each thick petal, 1¼–1½in (3–4cm) long, has brown-purple spots towards base. Z2–7 H7–1.

L. 'Harmony'. Summer-flowering Division 1a lily. **H** 1½–3ft (50cm–1m). Orange flowers are upward-facing, cup-shaped and spotted with maroon. Z3–8 H8–1.

L. *heldreichii*. See *L. chalcedonicum.*

L. *henryi*, illus. p.391. Late summer-flowering Division 9 lily with stem roots. **H** 3–10ft (1–3m). Has scattered, lance-shaped leaves. Produces 5–20, sometimes up to 70, nodding, turkscap, orange flowers; petals, 2½–3in (6–8cm) long, have dark spots and prominent warts towards bases. Prefers lime-rich soil. Z2–7 H7–1.

L. 'Holebibi'. See *L.* LOLLYPOP.

L. Imperial Crimson Group. Late summer-flowering Division 7c lily. **H** 5ft (1.5m). Large, fragrant, flattish, deep crimson flowers have white throats and white-margined petals. Z5–8 H8–5.

L. Imperial Gold Group. Summer-flowering Division 7c lily. **H** 6ft (2m). Bears large, fragrant, flattish, white flowers, spotted maroon, and with yellow stripe up each petal center. Z5–8 H8–5.

L. 'Journey's End', illus. p.389. Late summer-flowering Division 7d lily. **H** 6ft (2m). Large, outward-facing, bowl-shaped, maroon-spotted, deep pink flowers have recurved petals, white at tips and edges. Z5–8 H8–1.

L. 'Karen North', illus. p.391. Summer-flowering Division 1c lily. **H** to 4½ft (1.4m). Turkscap flowers are medium-sized, downward-facing, with orange-pink petals sparsely spotted with deep pink. Z4–8 H8–1.

L. 'Lady Alice', illus. p.388. Summer-flowering Divison 8 lily. **H** 4ft (1.2m). Pendent, turkscap flowers have recurved, brown-speckled, cream petals with apricot-orange centers.

L. 'Lady Bowes Lyon', illus. p.391. Summer-flowering Division 1c lily. **H** 3–4ft (1–1.2m). Downward-facing, black-spotted, red flowers have reflexed petals. Z3–8 H8–1.

L. *lancifolium*, syn. *L. tigrinum* (Tiger lily). Summer- to early fall-flowering Division 9 lily with stem roots. **H** 2–5ft (60cm–1.5m). Has long, scattered, narrowly lance-shaped leaves. Produces 5–10, sometimes up to 40, nodding, turkscap, pink- to red-orange flowers; each petal, 3–4in (7–10cm) long is purple spotted. Z2–7 H7–1. **var. *flaviflorum*** has yellow flowers. Z3–8 H8–1. Vigorous **'Splendens'** (illus. p.391) bears larger, brighter red-orange flowers. Z2–7 H8–1.

L. *lankongense*, illus. p.389. Summer-flowering Division 9 lily with stem roots. **H** to 4ft (1.2m). Leaves are scattered and lance-shaped. Has up to 15 scented, nodding, turkscap, pink flowers. Petals, 1½–2½in (4–6.5cm) long with central, green stripe and red-purple spots mainly on edges, are often mauve-flushed. Needs partial shade in warm areas. Z3–8 H8–1.

L. *leichtlinii*, illus. p.390. Summer-flowering Division 9 lily with stem roots. **H** to 4ft (1.2m). Scattered leaves are linear to narrowly lance-shaped. Produces 1–6 nodding, turkscap, yellow flowers; each petal, 2½–3¼in (6–8.5cm) long, has dark reddish-purple spots. Needs partial shade. Z2–7 H7–1.

L. 'Limelight', illus. p.390. Moderately robust, mid-summer-flowering Division 9 lily. **H** 3–6ft (1–2m). Large, fragrant, slightly pendent, trumpet-shaped, lime-yellow flowers are flushed green, especially outside. Z3–8 H8–1.

L. 'Lime Star'. Vigorous, summer-flowering Division 7a/b lily. **H** 4ft (1.2m). Has outward-facing, bowl-shaped to flat flowers, with recurving, white petals. Each petal is strongly banded bright greenish-yellow and has slightly ruffled margins.

L. LOLLYPOP ('Holebibi'), syn. *L.* 'Lollypop'. Early summer-flowering Division 1a lily. **H** 2ft (60cm). Has upright, open bowl-shaped, white flowers, with the upper parts of gently recurving petals strongly suffused deep red.

L. *longiflorum* (Bermuda lily, Easter lily, White trumpet lily), illus. p.388. Summer-flowering Division 9 lily with stem roots. **H** 1–3ft (30cm–1m). Leaves are scattered and lance-shaped. Produces 1–6 fragrant, outward-facing, funnel-shaped, white flowers. Each petal, 5–8in (13–20cm) long, has slightly recurved tip. Z7–9 H9–7. **'White American',** **H** 3ft (1m), is a Division 5 lily and produces white flowers with green tips and deep yellow anthers. Is often grown for cut flowers. **'White Heaven'** (illus. p.388), **H** 4ft (1.2m), is a Division 5 lily with delicately scented, pure white flowers.

L. 'Luxor'. Vigorous, summer-flowering Division 1b lily. **H** 3–5ft (90cm–1.5m). Produces large, outward-facing, bowl-shaped, bright yellow flowers, slightly darker yellow and speckled with dark red spots on lower half of each petal.

L. *mackliniae* (Manipur lily), illus. p.389. Late spring- to summer-flowering Division 9 lily with stem roots. **H** to 16in (40cm). Small, narrowly lance-shaped to narrowly oval leaves are scattered or whorled near top of stem. Has 1–6 usually nodding, broadly bell-shaped, purplish-pink flowers; each petal is 1¾–2in (4.5–5cm) long. Needs partial shade. Z7–8 H8–7.

L. *maculatum*, syn. *L. thunbergianum.* Summer-flowering Division 9 lily with stem roots. **H** to 2ft (60cm). Scattered leaves are lance-shaped or oval. Has 1–6 upward-facing, cup-shaped, yellow, orange or red flowers with darker spots; each petal is 3–4in (8–10cm) long. Z3–8 H8–1.

L. 'Magic Pink'. Early summer-flowering Division 7b lily. **H** 3–4ft (1–1.2m). Large flowers are pink with darker pink spots. Z3–8 H8–1.

L. 'Marhan', syn. *L.* x *dalhansonii* 'Marhan'. Early summer-flowering Division 2 lily. **H** 4–6ft (1.2–2m). Medium-sized, nodding, turkscap, deep orange flowers are spotted red-brown. Z3–8 H8–1.

L. *martagon* (Martagon lily), illus. p.389. Summer-flowering Division 9 lily with stem roots. **H** 3–6ft (1–2m). Has lance-shaped to oval leaves in whorls and up to 50 scented, nodding, turkscap flowers. Petals are 1¼–1¾in (3–4.5cm) long and pink or purple, often with darker spots. Z3–7 H7–1. **var. *album*** (illus. p.388) has pure white flowers.

L. *medeoloides*, illus. p.390. Summer-flowering Division 9 lily. **H** to 2½ft (75cm). Has lance-shaped leaves and up to 10 turkscap, apricot to orange-red flowers, usually with darker spots. Z3–7 H7–1.

L. 'Miss Lucy', illus. p.389. Summer-flowering Division 7 lily. **H** 4ft (1.2m). Produces highly fragrant, double, pinkish-white flowers with 18 petals.

L. *monadelphum*, syn. *L. szovitsianum,* illus. p.390. Summer-flowering Division 9 lily with stem roots. **H** 1½–6ft (50cm–2m). Has scattered, lance-shaped to oval leaves. Produces usually 1–5, sometimes up to 30, scented, nodding, turkscap, yellow flowers, usually with deep red or purple spots inside. Petals are 2½–4in (6–10cm) long. Z5–8 H8–5.

L. 'Mona Lisa', illus. p.388. Summer-flowering Division 7b/c lily. **H** 18in (45cm). Has large, shallowly bowl-shaped to flat, light reddish-purple flowers, with ivory-white margins suffused red, greenish petal tips, dark red spots on lower half of each petal and light green throats.

L. 'Mont Blanc'. Summer-flowering Division 1a lily. **H** 3ft (90cm). Has large, upward-facing, creamy-white flowers, spotted with brown. Z5–8 H8–5.

L. 'Montreux'. Mid-summer-flowering Division 1a lily. **H** 3ft (1m). Bears about 8 medium-sized, pink flowers with darker pink midribs; orange-pink throats are spotted with brown. Z3–8 H8–1.

L. 'Mr. Ed'. See *L.* 'Ed'.

L. 'Muscadet'. Summer-flowering Division 7 lily. **H** 3ft (1m). Large, fragrant, white flowers have pink markings and maroon spots.

L. *nanum*, syn. *Nomocharis nana.* Late spring- or summer-flowering Division 9 lily. **H** 2½–18in (6–45cm). Scattered leaves are linear. Bears usually nodding, broadly bell-shaped, purplish-pink flower, with petals 1¾–2in (4.5–5cm) long. Needs partial shade. Z3–8 H8–1. **var. *flavidum*** has pale yellow flowers.

L. *nepalense*. Summer-flowering Division 9 lily with stem roots. **H** 28–36in (70cm–1m). Has scattered, lance-shaped leaves. Produces often unpleasant-smelling, nodding, funnel-shaped, greenish-white or greenish-yellow flowers, each with dark reddish-purple base inside and petals to 6in (15cm) long. Z7–8 H8–7.

L. 'Netty's Pride', illus. p.389. Summer-flowering Division 1b lily. **H** 2ft (60cm). Bears dark maroon flowers with ivory-tipped petals.

L. 'New Wave'. Early to mid-summer-flowering Division 1a lily. **H** 2ft (60cm). Produces large, pure white flowers with scattered, maroon spots.

L. 'Nymph', illus. p.388. Summer-flowering Division 7 lily. **H** 4ft (1.2m). Produces large, scented, white flowers with deep pink stripes along center of each petal.

L. 'Olivia', illus. p.388. Late summer-flowering Division 7b lily. H 2½–3ft (75cm–1m). Has medium-sized, scented, slightly reflexed, bowl-shaped, white flowers.

L. Olympic Group. Vigorous, summer-flowering Division 6a lily. H 4–6ft (1.2–2m). Produces racemes of up to 15 large, sweetly scented, trumpet-shaped flowers ranging from white, greenish-white, cream and yellow to pink and purple, often yellow in throats. Petals are flushed pink or purplish-red on outside.

L. 'Orange Electric', illus. p.391. Summer-flowering Division 1a lily. H 4ft (1.2m). Bears white flowers with orange and yellow stripes and brown spots.

L. 'Orange Pixie', illus. p.391. Early summer-flowering Division 1a lily. H 10–12in (25–30cm). Has upright umbels of open bowl-shaped, deep golden-orange flowers. Is good as a pot plant.

L. pardalinum (Leopard lily, Panther lily), illus. p.391. Summer-flowering Division 9 lily. H 6–10ft (2–3m). Long, narrowly elliptic leaves are mainly in whorls. Has up to 10 often scented, nodding, turkscap flowers. Each petal, 2–3½in (5–9cm) long, has red upper part. Orange lower parts have maroon spots, some of which are encircled with yellow. Z5–8 H8–5. **subsp. wigginsii**, illus. p.390. H 3–4ft (90–120cm). Linear-lance-shaped, deep green leaves are scattered and in 2–4 whorls roughly halfway up hairless stems. Produces few-flowered racemes of unscented, pendent, turkscap, deep yellow flowers, with purple spots. Needs moist acid soil, and partial or dappled shade.

L. Pink Perfection Group. Summer-flowering Division 6a lily with sturdy stems. H 5–6ft (1.5–2m). Produces large, scented, slightly nodding, trumpet-shaped flowers, deep purplish-red or purple-pink flowers, with bright orange anthers. Z3–8 H8–1.

L. 'Pink Tiger'. Vigorous, late summer-flowering Division 1b lily. H 4ft (1.2m). Produces medium-sized, unscented, turkscap, pink flowers.

L. pomponium, illus. p.391. Slender, stem-rooting, summer-flowering Division 9 lily. H 3ft (1m). Green stems are spotted purple on lower halves. Has scattered, linear, mid-green leaves with silver-hairy margins. Produces racemes of up to 6 (rarely up to 10) pungently scented, pendent, turkscap, sealing-wax-red flowers, generally with black spots and streaks in throats. Prefers alkaline soil in full sun or partial shade. Z5–8 H8–5.

L. ponticum. See *L. pyrenaicum* subsp. *ponticum*.

L. pumilum, syn. *L. tenuifolium*. Summer-flowering Division 9 lily with stem roots. H 6–36in (15cm–1m). Small, scattered leaves are linear. Produces usually up to 7 but occasionally up to 30 slightly scented, nodding, turkscap flowers; each petal, 1¼–1½in (3–3.5cm) long, is scarlet with or without black, basal spots. Z3–8 H8–1.

L. pyrenaicum (Yellow turkscap lily), illus. p.390. Late spring to early summer-flowering Division 9 lily, often with stem roots. H 1–4½ft (30cm–1.35m). Has scattered, linear to narrowly elliptic, hairless leaves. Produces up to 12 unpleasant-smelling, nodding, turkscap flowers. Each petal, 1½–2½in (4–6.5cm)

long, is yellow or green-yellow with prominent, dark purple spots and lines. Z3–8 H8–1. **subsp. carniolicum**, syn. *L. carniolicum* has red- or orange-spotted flowers. Leaves may be hairless or downy. **subsp. ponticum**, syn. *L. ponticum* bears deep yellow flowers, densely lined and spotted with red-brown or purple; leaves are downy beneath. **f. rubrum** (illus. p.391) has orange-red or dark red flowers.

L. 'Red Carpet', illus. p.391. Early summer-flowering Division 1a lily. H 1ft (30cm). Has upright umbels of open bowl-shaped, unspotted, deep red flowers. Is good as a pot plant.

L. regale (Regal lily), illus. p.388. Summer-flowering Division 9 lily with stem roots. H 20in–6ft (50cm–2m). Linear leaves are scattered. Produces up to 25 fragrant, outward-facing, funnel-shaped flowers. Petals, 5–6in (12–15cm) long, are white inside with yellow base and pinkish-purple outside. Z4–7 H8–5. **'Royal Gold'**, syn. *L. 'Royal Gold'* (illus. p.390), H 4–5ft (1.2–1.5m), is vigorous and produces clusters of large flowers, mid-yellow inside and purple-brown outside.

L. 'Roma', illus. p.390. Early summer-flowering Division 1a lily. H 5ft (1.5m). Green buds open to cream flowers that sometimes age to pale greenish-yellow. Z3–8 H8–1.

L. 'Rosemary North', illus. p.390. Mid- to late summer-flowering Division 1c lily. H to 3ft (1m). Produces 12 or more medium-sized, slightly fragrant, rich orange flowers that sometimes have darker spots. Z3–8 H8–1.

L. 'Rosita', illus. p.389. Early summer-flowering Division 1a lily. H 2½ft (75cm). Has umbels of upright, open bowl-shaped, green-centered, blush-pink flowers, with slightly recurving petals.

L. rosthornii, illus. p.390. Vigorous, stem-rooting, clump-forming, summer-flowering Division 9 lily. H 16–39in (40–100cm). Has long, scattered, lance-shaped leaves on lower part of stem; upper stem leaves are much shorter and oval in shape. Produces up to 9 nodding, turkscap, orange or orange-yellow flowers. Strongly recurved, channeled petals have green central bands and purple-red, basal spots.

L. 'Royal Gold'. See *L. regale* 'Royal Gold'.

L. rubellum, illus. p.389. Early summer-flowering Division 9 lily with stem roots. H 12–32in (30–80cm). Has scattered, narrowly oval leaves and up to 9 scented, outward-facing, broadly funnel-shaped, pink flowers with dark red spots at bases; each petal is 2½–3in (6–8cm) long. Z4–7 H8–1.

L. 'Shuksan'. Summer-flowering Division 4 lily. H 4–6ft (1.2–2m). Medium-sized, nodding, turkscap, yellowish-orange flowers are flushed red at petal tips and sparsely spotted with black. Z3–8 H8–1.

L. 'Sixth Sense'. Summer-flowering Division 1b lily. H 28in (70cm). Produces white-edged, dark burgundy-red flowers with dark purple-brown spots.

L. speciosum. Late summer-flowering Division 9 lily with stem roots. H 3–5½ft (1–1.7m). Has long, scattered, broadly lance-shaped leaves. Produces up to 12 scented, nodding, turkscap, white or pink flowers; each petal, to 4in (10cm) long, has pink or crimson spots. Requires neutral to

acid soil. Z3–8 H8–1. **var. album** has white flowers and purple stems. Flowers of **var. rubrum** are carmine, stems are purple. Z5–7 H10–8.

L. 'Star Fighter', illus. p.389. Summer-flowering Division 7 lily. H 20in (50cm). Bears spicy-scented, maroon-speckled, deep pinkish-purple flowers with prominent, white edges.

L. 'Star Gazer'. Late summer-flowering Division 7c lily. H 3ft (90cm). Large, highly fragrant, rich crimson flowers are spotted maroon, with white edges. Z3–8 H8–1.

L. 'Sterling Star', illus. p.388. Summer-flowering Division 1a lily. H 3–4ft (1–1.2m). Has large, upward-facing, cup-shaped, white flowers with tiny, brown spots. Z5–7 H8–1.

L. 'Sumatra', illus. p.389. Summer-flowering Division 7 lily. H 36in (90cm). Produces large, scented, dark wine-red flowers with hint of white at tips of petals.

L. superbum (Swamp lily, Turkscap lily), illus. p.390. Late summer- to early fall-flowering Division 9 lily with stem roots. H 5–10ft (1.5–3m). Lance-shaped to elliptic leaves are mainly in whorls. Bears up to 40 nodding, turkscap, orange flowers. Each petal, 2½–4in (6–10cm) long, is green base inside and usually flushed red and spotted maroon. Requires neutral to acid soil. Z4–7 H8–1.

L. 'Sweet Lord', illus. p.389. Early to mid-summer-flowering Division 1a lily. H 20in (50cm). Produces purple- red flowers.

L. szovitsianum. See *L. monadelphum*.

L. tenuifolium. See *L. pumilum*.

L. x testaceum (Nankeen lily). Summer-flowering Division 9 lily. H 3–5ft (1–1.5m). Has scattered, linear, often twisted leaves. Produces 6–12 fragrant, nodding, turkscap, light orange to brownish-yellow flowers; each petal, 3in (8cm) long, usually has reddish spots inside. Z3–8 H8–1.

L. thunbergianum. See *L. maculatum*.

L. 'Tiger Woods', illus. p.389. Summer-flowering Division 7 lily. H 3ft (1m). Bears very large, scented, white flowers with rich crimson stripe down center of each petal surrounded by crimson spots.

L. tigrinum. See *L. lancifolium*.

L. 'Tom Pouce', illus. p.389. Summer-flowering Division 7 lily. H 36in (90cm). Bears large, highly scented, pink flowers with pale yellow stripe down center of each petal and pale yellow freckles. Z5–8 H8–1.

L. TRIUMPHATOR ('Zanlophator'), illus. p.388. Summer-flowering Division 6 lily. H 3ft (1m). Produces large, fragrant, outward-facing, white flowers with rich rose-pink centers.

L. tsingtauense, illus. p.391. Summer-flowering Division 9 lily with stem roots. H 3ft (1m). Lance-shaped leaves are mainly in whorls. Produces 1–5 upward-facing, cup-shaped, orange to orange-red flowers; petals, to 2in (5cm) long are maroon spotted. Z3–7 H8–1.

L. wallichianum. Late summer- to fall-flowering Division 9 lily with stem roots. H to 6ft (2m). Long, scattered leaves are linear or lance-shaped. Bears 1–4 fragrant, outward-facing, funnel-shaped, white or cream flowers that are green or yellow towards bases. Each petal is 6–12in (15–30cm) long. Z3–8 H8–1.

L. 'White Heaven', illus p.388. Summer-flowering Division 5 lily. H 4ft (1.2m). Bears fragrant, long, trumpet-shaped, pure white flowers.

L. 'Zanlophator'. See *L. TRIUMPHATOR*.

L. wigginsii. See *L. pardalinum* subsp. *wigginsii*.

Limnanthemum nymphoides. See *Nymphoides peltata*.

LIMNANTHES
Poached-egg plant
LIMNANTHACEAE

Genus of annuals, useful for rock gardens, containers and for edging borders. Prefers sun and fertile, well-drained soil. Propagate by seed in spring or early fall. Self-seeds very freely, although easy to control.

L. douglasii, illus. p.321.

LIMONIUM
Sea lavender, Statice
PLUMBAGINACEAE

Genus of summer- and fall-flowering perennials, sometimes grown as annuals, and subshrubs, some of which are evergreen. Needs full sun and well-drained soil. Propagate by division in spring, by seed in fall or early spring or by root cuttings in winter.

L. bellidifolium, syn. *L. reticulatum*. Evergreen, dome-shaped perennial with a woody base. H 6–8in (15–20cm), S 4in (10cm). Has basal rosettes of rounded, dark green leaves. Much-branched flower stems produce masses of small, "everlasting", trumpet-shaped, blue flowers in summer–fall. Is excellent for a rock garden. Z7–9 H9–7.

L. latifolium 'Blue Cloud'. Clump-forming perennial. H 12in (30cm), S 18in (45cm). In late summer produces diffuse clusters of bluish-mauve flowers that can be dried for indoor decoration. Has large, leathery, dark green leaves. Z4–9 H9–1.

L. perezii. Evergreen, rounded subshrub. H and S 3ft (1m) or more. Has long-stalked, oval to diamond-shaped, deep green leaves. Dense clusters, 8in (20cm) wide, of tiny, tubular, deep mauve-blue flowers are borne well above leaves in fall. Needs good ventilation if grown under glass. Z10–11 H12–1.

L. reticulatum. See *L. bellidifolium*.

L. sinuatum (Statice). Fairly slow-growing, bushy, upright perennial, grown as an annual. H 18in (45cm), S 12in (30cm). Has lance-shaped, lobed, deep green leaves and, in summer and early fall, tiny, blue, pink or white flowers borne in clusters on winged stems. H9–3. **Fortress Series** have small, tubular flowers in a mixture of shades such as pink, yellow or blue. Leaves are often wavy-margined.

L. suworowii. See *Psylliostachys suworowii*.

LINARIA
Toadflax
SCROPHULARIACEAE/PLANTAGINACEAE

Genus of spring-, summer- or fall-flowering annuals, biennials and perennials, useful for rock gardens and borders. Prefers sun or partial shade and well-drained soil. Propagate by seed in fall or spring. Self-seeds freely.

L. alpina (Alpine toadflax). Tuft-forming, compact, annual, biennial or short-lived perennial with a sparse root system. H 6in (15cm), S 4–6in (10–15cm). Has whorls of linear to lance-shaped, fleshy, gray-green leaves. A succession of snapdragon-like, yellow-centered, purple-violet flowers is borne in loose racemes in summer. Z4–9 H9–1.

L. dalmatica (Dalmation toadflax). Upright perennial. **H** 3–4ft (1–1.2m), **S** 2ft (60cm). Is similar to *L. genistifolia*, but has much larger, golden-yellow flowers and broader, more glaucous leaves. Z5–8 H8–5.

L. genistifolia. Upright perennial. **H** 2–4ft (60cm–1.2m), **S** 9in (23cm). From mid-summer to fall produces racemes of small, snapdragon-like, orange-marked, yellow flowers. Lance-shaped, glossy, mid-green leaves clasp the stems. Z5–8 H8–5.

L. maroccana 'Fairy Lights'. Fast-growing, erect, bushy annual. **H** 8in (20cm), **S** 6in (15cm). Has lance-shaped, pale green leaves. Tiny, snapdragon-like flowers, in shades of red, pink, purple, yellow or white, are borne throughout summer. H9–1.

L. purpurea. Upright perennial. **H** 2–3ft (60cm–1m), **S** 2ft (60cm). From mid- to late summer, racemes of snapdragon-like, purplish-blue flowers, touched with white at throats, are produced above narrowly oval, gray-green leaves. Z5–8 H8–5. **'Canon J. Went',** illus. p.232.

L. triornithophora, illus. p.239.

LINDERA

LAURACEAE

Genus of deciduous or evergreen shrubs and trees, grown for their foliage, which is often aromatic, and their fall color. Fruits are produced on female plants if male plants are also grown. Needs partial shade and moist, acid soil. Propagate by softwood cuttings in summer or by seed in fall.

L. benzoin, illus. p.127.

L. obtusiloba (Japanese spicebush). Deciduous, bushy shrub. **H** and **S** 20ft (6m). Has 3-lobed, aromatic, glossy, dark green leaves, becoming butter-yellow in fall. Clusters of small, star-shaped, deep yellow flowers, borne on bare shoots from early to mid-spring, are followed by small, spherical, black fruits. Z6–9 H9–6.

LINDHEIMERA

Star daisy

COMPOSITAE/ASTERACEAE

Genus of late summer- and early fall-flowering annuals. Needs sun and fertile, well-drained soil. Propagate by seed sown under glass in early spring or outdoors in late spring.

L. texana (Star daisy). Moderately fast-growing, erect, branching annual. **H** 12–24in (30–60cm), **S** 12in (30cm). Has hairy stems and oval, serrated, hairy leaves. Daisylike, yellow flower heads are produced in late summer and early fall. H12–7.

LINNAEA

Twinflower

CAPRIFOLIACEAE

Genus of one species of evergreen, creeping, summer-flowering, subshrubby perennial that makes an extensive, twiggy mat. Is useful as groundcover on peat beds and rock gardens. Requires partial shade and moist, peaty, acid soil. Propagate by rooted runners in spring, by softwood cuttings in summer or by seed in fall.

L. borealis, illus. p.363.

LINUM

Flax

LINACEAE

Genus of annuals, biennials, perennials, subshrubs and shrubs, some of which are evergreen or semievergreen, grown for their flowers. Is suitable for rock gardens. Prefers sun and rich, well-drained, peaty soil. Propagate subshrubs and shrubs by semiripe cuttings in summer or by seed in fall, annuals, biennials and perennials by seed in fall.

L. arboreum, illus. p.344.

L. flavum (Golden flax, Yellow flax). Bushy perennial with a woody rootstock. **H** 12in (30cm), **S** 6in (15cm). Has narrowly oval, green leaves and, in summer, upward-facing, funnel-shaped, yellow flowers in terminal clusters. Z5–7 H7–5. **'Compactum',** illus. p.372.

L. 'Gemmell's Hybrid'. Semievergreen, domed perennial with a woody rootstock. **H** 6in (15cm), **S** 8in (20cm). Leaves are oval and gray-green. In summer, short-stalked, bushy funnel-shaped, bright chrome-yellow flowers are produced in terminal clusters. Prefers alkaline soil. Z6–9 H9–5.

L. grandiflorum 'Rubrum', illus. p.308.

L. narbonense. Clump-forming, short-lived perennial, best renewed frequently from seed. **H** 12–24in (30–60cm), **S** 12in (30cm). Has lance-shaped, grayish-green leaves and heads of somewhat cup-shaped, pale to deep blue flowers in spring–summer. Z7–9 H9–7.

L. perenne, illus. p.342.

L. salsoloides. See *L. suffruticosum* subsp. *salsoloides*.

L. suffruticosum subsp. salsoloides, syn. *L. salsoloides*. Perennial with spreading, sometimes woody-based stems. **H** 2–8in (5–20cm), **S** 3in (8cm). Slender stems produce fine, heather-like, gray-green leaves and, in summer, a succession of short-lived, saucer-shaped, pearl-white flowers, flushed blue or pink, in terminal clusters. Z5–8 H8–5.

Lippia citriodora. See *Aloysia triphylla*.

LIQUIDAMBAR

Sweetgum

HAMAMELIDACEAE/ALTINGIACEAE

Genus of deciduous trees, with inconspicuous flowers, grown for their maple-like foliage and fall color. Requires sun or partial shade and fertile, moist but well-drained soil; grows poorly on shallow, chalky soil. Propagate by softwood cuttings in summer or by seed in fall.

L. formosana, syn. *L. monticola*. Deciduous, broadly conical tree. **H** 40ft (12m), **S** 30ft (10m). Has large, 3-lobed, toothed leaves, purple when young, dark green in summer and turning orange, red and purple in fall. Z7–9 H9–7.

L. monticola. See *L. formosana*.

L. orientalis (Oriental sweetgum). Slow-growing, deciduous, bushy tree. **H** 20ft (6m), **S** 12ft (4m). Small, 5-lobed, mid-green leaves turn vivid orange in fall. Z7–9 H9–7.

L. styraciflua (Sweet gum), illus. p.65. **'Lane Roberts'** is a deciduous, broadly conical to spreading tree. **H** 80ft (25m), **S** 40ft (12m). Shoots usually bear corky ridges. Glossy, green leaves, each with 5 lobes, turn deep reddish-purple in fall. Z6–9 H9–6.

LIRIODENDRON

Tulip tree

MAGNOLIACEAE

Genus of deciduous trees, grown for their foliage and flowers in summer. Flowers are almost hidden by unusual leaves and are not produced on young trees. Requires sun or partial shade and deep, fertile, well-drained, preferably slightly acid, soil. Propagate species from seed in fall, and selected forms by budding in late summer.

L. chinense (Chinese tulip tree). Fast-growing, deciduous, spreading tree. **H** 80ft (25m), **S** 40ft (12m). Bears large, deep green leaves, cut off at tips and with deep lobe on each side; leaves become yellow in fall. Cup-shaped, orange-based, greenish-white flowers are borne in mid-summer. Z4–9 H9–2.

L. tulipifera (Tulip tree), illus. p.60. **'Aureomarginatum',** illus. p.65.

LIRIOPE

Lilyturf

LILIACEAE/ASPARAGACEAE

Genus of evergreen perennials with swollen, fleshy rhizomes. Some are grown as groundcover. Requires sun and well-drained soil. Propagate by division in spring or by seed in fall.

L. graminifolia var. densiflora. See *L. muscari*.

L. muscari, syn. *L. graminifolia* var. *densiflora*, *L. platyphylla*, illus. p.280. **'Majestic'** is an evergreen, spreading, rhizomatous perennial. **H** 12in (30cm), **S** 18in (45cm). In late fall produces spikes of thickly clustered, rounded-bell-shaped, violet flowers among linear, glossy, green leaves. Z6–10 H12–1.

L. platyphylla. See *L. muscari*.

L. spicata. Evergreen, spreading, rhizomatous perennial. **H** 12in (30cm), **S** 12–16in (30–40cm). Grasslike, glossy, dark green leaves make good groundcover. Produces spikes of rounded-bell-shaped, pale lavender flowers in late summer. Z6–11 H12–1.

Lisianthus russellianus. See *Eustoma grandiflorum*.

LITHOCARPUS

FAGACEAE

Genus of evergreen trees, grown for their foliage. Needs sun or partial shade and prefers well-drained, neutral to acid soil. Shelter from strong winds. Propagate by seed, when ripe, in fall.

L. densiflorus (Tanbark oak). Evergreen, spreading tree. **H** and **S** 30ft (10m). Has sweet chestnut-like, leathery, glossy, dark green leaves and upright, pale yellow flower spikes borne in spring and often again in fall. Z8–10 H10–8.

L. henryi, illus. p.93.

LITHODORA

BORAGINACEAE

Genus of evergreen subshrubs and shrubs, grown for their flowers. Is excellent in rock gardens. Needs full sun and moist, well-drained soil; some species are limestone haters and require acid conditions. Resents root disturbance. Propagate by semiripe

cuttings in mid-summer or by seed in fall.

L. diffusa, syn. *Lithospermum diffusum*. **'Grace Ward'** is an evergreen, compact, semiprostrate shrub. **H** 6–12in (15–30cm), **S** to 12in (30cm). Trailing stems bear lance-shaped, hairy, dull green leaves. In early summer produces masses of funnel-shaped, deep blue flowers in terminal clusters. Needs acid soil. Trim back plants after flowering. Z6–8 H8–6. **'Heavenly Blue',** illus. p.343.

L. oleifolia, syn. *Lithospermum oleifolium*, illus. p.342.

L. zahnii, syn. *Lithospermum zahnii*. Evergreen, much-branched, upright shrub. **H** and **S** 12in (30cm) or more. Stems are covered in oval, hairy, dark green or grayish-green leaves. Funnel-shaped, azure-blue flowers, with spreading lobes, open in succession from early spring to mid-summer. Sets buds and flowers intermittently until mid-fall. Prefers alkaline soil. Z8–10 H10–8.

LITHOPHRAGMA

Woodland star

SAXIFRAGACEAE

Genus of tuberous perennials, grown for their campion-like flowers. Is dormant in summer. Tolerates all but deepest shade and prefers rich, moist soil. Propagate by seed or division in spring or fall.

L. parviflorum, illus. p.332.

LITHOPS

Living stones, Stone plant

AIZOACEAE

Genus of prostrate, egg-shaped, perennial succulents, grown for their almost united pairs of swollen, erect leaves that are separated on upper surface by a fissure from which a solitary, daisylike flower emerges. Each pair of old leaves splits and dries away to papery skin in spring to reveal a pair of new leaves growing at right angles to old ones. Slowly forms clumps after 3–5 years. Needs full sun and extremely well-drained soil or gritty compost. Water regularly in growing season (mid-summer to early fall), not at all in winter. Propagate by seed in spring or summer.

L. aucampiae. Egg-shaped, perennial succulent. **H** 1/2in (1cm), **S** 1 1/4in (3cm). Pairs of brown leaves have flat, upper surfaces bearing darker marks. Produces solitary, yellow flower in late summer or early fall. Z12–15 H12–10.

L. 'Bella'. See *L. karasmontana* subsp. *bella*.

L. bromfieldii. Egg-shaped, perennial succulent. **H** 3/4–1 1/4in (2–3cm), **S** 3/4in (2cm). Slightly convex, upper surfaces of paired, brown leaves have dark green windows and red dots and lines. Produces solitary, yellow flower in late summer or early fall.

L. dorotheae, illus. p.491.

L. fulleri. Egg-shaped, perennial succulent. **H** and **S** 3/4in (2cm). Pairs of leaves are dove-gray to brown-yellow. Convex, upper surfaces have sunken, darker marks. In late summer or early fall bears solitary, white flower. Z12–15 H12–10.

L. hookeri. See *L. turbiniformis*.

L. julii. Egg-shaped, perennial succulent. **H** 3/4–1 1/4in (2–3cm), **S** 2in (5cm). Has paired, pearl- to pink-gray leaves, each with a slightly convex, darker-marked, upper surface. In late summer or fall produces solitary, white flower. Z12–15 H12–10.

L. karasmontana, illus. p.481. **subsp. bella**, syn. L. 'Bella' is an egg-shaped, perennial succulent. **H** ¾–1¼in (2–3cm), **S** 5⁄8in (1.5cm). Has pairs of brown to brown-yellow leaves with darker marks on convex, upper surfaces. Produces solitary, white flower in late summer or early fall. Z12–15 H12–10.

L. lesliei. Egg-shaped, perennial succulent. **H** ½in (1cm), **S** ¾in (2cm). Is similar to L. aucampiae, but upper leaf surfaces are convex. Z12–15 H12–10. **var. albinica**, illus. p.491.

L. marmorata, illus. p.489.

L. olivacea. Egg-shaped, perennial succulent. **H** and **S** ¾in (2cm). Paired, dark olive-green leaves have darker windows on convex, upper surfaces. Yellow flower is borne in late summer or early fall. Z12–15 H12–10.

L. otzeniana. Egg-shaped, perennial succulent. **H** 1¼in (3cm), **S** ¾in (2cm). Paired, gray-violet leaves each have a convex, upper surface with a light border and large, semitranslucent windows. In late summer or early fall bears solitary, yellow flower. Z12–15 H12–10.

L. pseudotruncatella. Egg-shaped, perennial succulent. **H** 1¼ (3cm), **S** 1½in (4cm). Bears pairs of pale gray or blue to lilac leaves with darker marks on convex, upper surfaces. Fissure reaches from side to side only on mature plants. Has solitary, yellow flower in late summer or early fall. Z12–15 H12–10. **subsp. dendritica**, illus. p.495.

L. schwantesii, illus. p.495.

L. turbiniformis, syn. L. hookeri. Egg-shaped, perennial succulent. **H** 1½in (4cm), **S** ¾in (2cm). Has a flattish, upper surface with, usually, sunken, dark brown marks on paired, brown leaves. Has solitary, yellow flower in late summer or early fall. Z12–15 H12–10.

Lithospermum diffusum. See Lithodora diffusa.
Lithospermum oleifolium. See Lithodora oleifolia.
Lithospermum zahnii. See Lithodora zahnii.
Litsea glauca. See Neolitsea sericea.

LITTONIA
COLCHICACEAE

Genus of deciduous, perennial, scandent, tuberous climbers, grown for their pendent, bell-shaped flowers in summer. Requires full sun and rich, well-drained soil. Provide support. Dies down in winter; lift and dry off tubers and store in a frost-free place. Propagate by seed in spring; tubers sometimes will divide naturally.
L. modesta, illus. p.395.

LIVISTONA
ARECACEAE

Genus of evergreen palms, grown for their overall appearance. Has clusters of insignificant flowers in summer. Needs full light or partial shade and fertile, well-drained soil, ideally neutral to acid. Water container specimens moderately, less in winter. Propagate by seed in spring at not

less than 73°F (23°C). Red spider mite may be a nuisance on container plants.
L. australis (Australian fan palm, Cabbage palm). Slow-growing, evergreen palm with a fairly slender trunk. **H** 50–70ft (15–20m), **S** 10–20ft (3–6m). Has fan-shaped leaves, 4–8ft (1.2–2.5m) wide, divided into narrow, slender-pointed, glossy, green leaflets. Leaf stalks are spiny. Z11–10 H12–10.
L. chinensis, illus. p.451.

LLOYDIA
LILIACEAE

Genus of summer-flowering bulbs, grown for their small, graceful, bell-shaped flowers. Is not easy to grow. Requires partial shade and well-drained, peaty soil; provide plenty of moisture in summer but, preferably, keep fairly dry in winter. Propagate by seed in spring.
L. graeca. See Gagea graeca.
L. serotina (Alp lily). Early summer-flowering bulb. **H** 2–6in (5–15cm), **S** 1–2in (2.5–5cm). Has wiry stems bearing scattered, threadlike, semierect leaves near stem base. Bears 1 or 2 bell-shaped, white flowers, ½–5⁄8in (1–1.5cm) long, with purple or purple-red veins. Z6–9 H9–6.

LOBELIA
CAMPANULACEAE

Genus of annuals, perennials and deciduous or evergreen shrubs, grown for their flowers. Some are suitable for wild gardens or by the waterside. Prefers sun and moist but well-drained soil. Resents wet conditions in winter; in cold areas, some perennials and shrubs are therefore best lifted in fall and placed in well-drained compost in frames. Propagate annuals by seed in spring, perennial species by seed or division in spring, perennial cultivars by division only, and shrubs by semiripe cuttings in summer. ① Contact with the milky sap of some species may irritate skin.
L. angulata, syn. Pratia angulata. Evergreen, creeping perennial. **H** ½in (1cm), **S** indefinite. Bears small, broadly oval, dark green leaves. Star-shaped, white flowers, with 5 unevenly spaced petals, are borne in leaf axils in late spring and are followed by globose, purplish-red fruits in fall. Z6–10 H10–6.
L. cardinalis, syn. L. fulgens, L. splendens, illus. p.439. **'Queen Victoria'**, illus. p.248.
L. 'Cherry Ripe', illus. p.439.
L. 'Dark Crusader'. Clump-forming perennial. **H** 3ft (1m), **S** 9in (23cm). From mid- to late summer bears racemes of 2-lipped, dark red flowers above lance-shaped, fresh green or red-bronze leaves. Z4–8 H8–1.
L. erinus. 'Blue Ball', illus. p.315. **'Blue Cascade'** Slow-growing, pendulous, spreading annual, occasionally perennial. **H** 4–8in (10–20cm), **S** 4–6in (10–15cm). Oval to lance-shaped leaves are pale green. Small, 2-lipped, pale blue flowers are produced continuously in summer and early fall. **'Cambridge Blue'** is compact and has blue flowers. **'Colour Cascade'** has flowers in a mixture of colors, such as blue, red, pink, mauve or white. **'Crystal Palace'**, illus. p.315. **'Red Cascade'** produces white-eyed, purple-red flowers. **'Sapphire'**, illus. p.314. **Waterfall Series 'Waterfall Blue'**, illus. p.314; **Waterfall**

Series 'Waterfall Light Lavender', illus. p.311.
L. fulgens. See L. cardinalis.
L. x gerardii 'Vedrariensis'. See L. x speciosa 'Vedrariensis'.
L. pedunculata, syn. Pratia pedunculata. **'County Park'** is a vigorous, evergreen, creeping perennial. **H** ½in (1cm), **S** indefinite. Has small, rounded to oval leaves and, in summer, a profusion of star-shaped, rich violet-blue flowers. Makes good groundcover.
L. siphilitica, illus. p.441.
L. x speciosa 'Vedrariensis', syn. L. x gerardii 'Vedrariensis', L. 'Vedrariensis'. Clump-forming perennial. **H** 3ft (1m), **S** 1ft (30cm). In late summer produces racemes of 2-lipped, purple flowers. Has lance-shaped, dark green leaves. Z5–8 H8–5.
L. splendens. See L. cardinalis.
L. tupa. Clump-forming perennial. **H** 5–6ft (1.5–2m), **S** 3ft (1m). Bears large spikes of 2-lipped, vivid brick-red flowers, in late summer, above narrowly oval, hairy, light green leaves. Performs best in a sheltered, sunny site with well-drained soil. Z8–10 H10–8.
L. 'Vedrariensis'. See L. x speciosa 'Vedrariensis'.
L. 'Will Scarlet'. Clump-forming perennial. **H** 3ft (1m), **S** 1ft (30cm). Racemes of 2-lipped, bright red flowers are borne in summer. Lance-shaped leaves are coppery-green. Z4–8 H8–1.

Lobivia aurea. See Echinopsis aurea.
Lobivia backebergii. See Echinopsis backebergii.
Lobivia cinnabarina. See Echinopsis cinnabarina.
Lobivia cylindrica. See Echinopsis aurea.
Lobivia haageana. See Echinopsis marsoneri.
Lobivia pentlandii. See Echinopsis pentlandii.
Lobivia pygmaea. See Rebutia pygmaea.
Lobivia silvestrii. See Echinopsis chamaecereus.

LOBULARIA
Sweet alyssum
CRUCIFERAE/BRASSICACEAE

Genus of summer- and early fall-flowering annuals. Is ideal for containers and edging. Needs sun and fertile, well-drained soil. Deadhead to encourage continuous flowering. Propagate by seed sown under glass in spring, or outdoors in late spring. May self-seed.
L. Maritima, syn. Alyssum maritimum (Sweet alyssum). Fast-growing, spreading annual. **H** 3–6in (8–15cm), **S** 8–12in (20–30cm). Has lance-shaped, grayish-green leaves. Rounded heads of tiny, scented, 4-petaled, white flowers are produced in summer and early fall. Z10–11 H12–1. **'Carpet of Snow'**, **H** to 4in (10cm), is a ground-hugging, loosely branched and has white flowers. **'Rosie O'Day'**, illus. p.304. **'Snow Crystals'**, illus. p.298.

LOISELEURIA
Alpine azalea, Trailing azalea
ERICACEAE

Genus of one species of evergreen, creeping, prostrate shrub, grown for its flowers. Requires full light and rich, well-drained, acid soil. Is difficult to grow.

Propagate by seed in spring or by softwood or semiripe cuttings in summer.
L. procumbens, illus. p.364.

LOMATIA
PROTEACEAE

Genus of evergreen shrubs and trees, grown for their foliage and flowers, which have 4 narrow, twisted petals. Often best in a cool greenhouse. Requires sun or partial shade and moist but well-drained, acid soil. Propagate by softwood or semiripe cuttings in summer.
L. ferruginea. Evergreen, upright shrub or tree. **H** 30ft (10m), **S** 15ft (5m). Sturdy, brown-felted shoots bear oblong to oval, dark green leaves, deeply cut into 6–15 oblong lobes. Racemes of yellow-and-red flowers are borne in mid-summer. Thrives outside only in mild, moist areas. Z11 H12–8.
L. silaifolia, illus. p.151.

LONICERA
Honeysuckle
CAPRIFOLIACEAE

Genus of deciduous, semievergreen or evergreen shrubs and woody-stemmed, twining climbers, grown mainly for their flowers, which are often fragrant. Flowers are tubular, with spreading, 2-lipped petal lobes. Climbers may be trained into large shrubs. Needs sun or partial shade and fertile, well-drained soil. Prune out flowered wood of climbers after flowering. Prune shrubs only to remove dead shoots or restrain growth. Propagate by seed in fall or spring, by semiripe cuttings in summer or by hardwood cuttings in late fall. Aphids may be a problem. ① The berries may cause mild stomach upset if ingested. See also feature panel p.207.
L. x americana, syn. L. x italica, illus. p.206.
L. x brownii (Scarlet trumpet honeysuckle). Z3–9 H9–1. **'Dropmore Scarlet'** is a deciduous, woody-stemmed, twining climber. **H** to 12ft (4m). Has oval, blue-green leaves. Small, fragrant, red flowers, with orange throats, are borne throughout summer.
L. etrusca (Etruscan honeysuckle). Deciduous or semievergreen, woody-stemmed, twining climber. **H** to 12ft (4m). Oval, mid-green leaves are blue-green beneath, the upper ones united into cups. Fragrant, long-tubed, pale yellow flowers, borne in summer–fall, turn deeper yellow and become red-flushed with age. Needs sun. **'Michael Rosse'** (illus. p.207) has glaucous leaves and pale yellow flowers that deepen in color as they mature. Z7–9 H9–4. **'Superba'** (illus. p.207) is very vigorous and has red-flushed young shoots and bright red and white flowers that turn orange-yellow as they age. Z7–9 H9–4.
L. fragrantissima (Winter honeysuckle). Deciduous or semievergreen, bushy, spreading shrub. **H** 6ft (2m), **S** 12ft (4m). Bears oval, dark green leaves. Fragrant, short-tubed, creamy-white flowers are produced in winter and early spring. Z4–8 H8–3.
L. 'Gold Flame'. See L. x heckrottii 'Gold Flame'.
L. x heckrottii. Deciduous or semievergreen, twining climber. **H** 15ft

L

(5m). Oval, dark green leaves are blue-green beneath, the upper pairs united. Bears terminal whorls of fragrant, pink flowers, orange-yellow inside, in summer, sometimes followed by red berries. Z6–9 H9–6. **'Gold Flame'**, syn. *L.* 'Gold Flame' is deciduous, and requires support. Has oblong or oval leaves, bluish beneath, upper ones joined into shallow cups. Produces orange-throated, pink flowers.

L. henryi, illus. p.207. Evergreen or semievergreen, woody-stemmed, twining climber. **H** to 30ft (10m). Narrowly oval, dark green leaves are paler beneath. Terminal clusters of long-tubed, red-purple flowers are produced in summer–fall, followed by black berries. Z3–8 H8–1.

L. hildebrandiana (Giant Burmese honeysuckle). Evergreen or semievergreen, woody-stemmed, twining climber. **H** to 70ft (20m). Oval or rounded, mid-green leaves are paler beneath. Long-tubed, white or cream flowers, aging to creamy-orange or brownish-yellow, are produced in pairs in leaf axils or at shoot tips in summer. Needs full sun. Z6–8 H8–6.

L. x *italica* of gardens. See *L.* x *americana*.

L. japonica (Japanese honeysuckle). Vigorous, evergreen or semievergreen, twining climber. **H** to 30ft (10m). Has soft-hairy, woody stems and ovate, sometimes lobed, dark green leaves. In summer and early fall produces fragrant, long-tubed, 2-lipped, white flowers that turn yellow as they mature. Is ideal for hiding an unsightly fence, shed or wall and also good as groundcover although requires control if space is limited. **'Aureoreticulata'** (illus. p.207) has bright green leaves with bright yellow veining. Z4–10 H10–1. **'Halliana'** has very fragrant, white flowers, aging to pale yellow. Z4–11 H12–1.

L. ledebourii, illus. p.136.

L. maackii (Amur honeysuckle). Vigorous, deciduous, bushy shrub. **H** and **S** 15ft (5m). Leaves are oval and dark green. Fragrant, short-tubed, white, later yellow flowers, are followed by spherical, bright red fruits. Z2–8 H9–4.

L. morrowii. Deciduous, spreading shrub with arching branches. **H** 6ft (2m), **S** 10ft (3m). Has oval, dark green leaves and, in late spring and early summer, small, short-tubed, creamy-white flowers that age to yellow. Z4–9 H9–4.

L. nitida (Boxleaf honeysuckle). Evergreen, bushy, dense shrub. **H** 6ft (2m), **S** 10ft (3m). Leaves are small, oval, glossy and dark green. Tiny, fragrant, short-tubed, creamy-white flowers, in late spring, are followed by small, spherical, purple fruits. Is good for hedging. Z6–9 H9–5. **'Baggesen's Gold'**, illus. p.167. **'Yunnan'** is more upright, has sturdier shoots and larger leaves and flowers more freely.

L. periclymenum (Common honeysuckle, Woodbine). Vigorous, deciduous, twining or scrambling climber. **H** 20–22ft (6–7m). Has ovate to oblong, mid-green leaves, grayish-green beneath. From early summer to early fall produces terminal clusters of very fragrant, long-tubed, 2-lipped, purple-red and/or yellow flowers, with creamy-white to white insides. Z5–9 H9–5. **'Graham Thomas'** has mid-green leaves that are bluish beneath and white flowers, which age to yellow. (illus. p.207) **'Serotina'** (Late Dutch honeysuckle), illus. p.207, has rich red-purple flowers,

white inside. **'Sweet Sue'** bears very fragrant, creamy-white flowers that mature to yellow.

L. pileata, illus. p.167.

L. x *purpusii*, illus. p.163. **'Winter Beauty'** is a semievergreen, bushy, dense shrub. **H** 6ft (2m), **S** 8ft (2.5m). Has red-purple shoots and oval, dark green leaves. Freely bears very fragrant, white flowers on bare, leafless stems in winter and early spring. Z7–9 H9–7.

L. sempervirens (Coral honeysuckle, Trumpet honeysuckle), illus. p.207. Evergreen or deciduous, woody-stemmed, twining climber. **H** to 12ft (4m). Has oval leaves, upper ones united and saucer-like, and salmon-red to orange flowers, yellow inside, in whorls on shoot tips in summer. Z4–9 H9–1.

L. standishii. Evergreen, bushy shrub. **H** and **S** 6ft (2m). Has peeling bark, oblong, bristly, dark green leaves and, in winter, fragrant, short-tubed, creamy-white flowers. Z5–8 H8–4.

L. tatarica (Tatarian honeysuckle), illus. p.133. **'Hack's Red'** is a deciduous, bushy shrub. **H** and **S** 8ft (2.5m). Produces short-tubed, deep pink flowers in late spring and early summer, followed by spherical, red fruits. Leaves are oval and dark green. Z3–9 H9–1.

L. x *tellmanniana*. Deciduous, woody-stemmed, twining climber. **H** to 15ft (5m). Has oval leaves; the upper ones are joined and resemble saucers. Bright yellow-orange flowers are produced in clusters from late spring to mid-summer. Z7–9 H9–7.

L. tragophylla. Deciduous, woody-stemmed, twining climber. **H** 15–20ft (5–6m). Oval leaves are bluish-green, the uppermost pair united into a cup. Produces clusters of up to 20 long-tubed, bright yellow flowers in early summer. Z6–9 H9–6.

L. x *xylosteoides* **'Clavey's Dwarf'**. Deciduous, upright, dense shrub. **H** 6ft (2m), **S** 3ft (1m). Leaves are oval and gray-green. Bears short-tubed, pink flowers in late spring, then spherical, red fruits. Z4–9 H9–1.

L. xylosteum, illus. p.131.

Lophocereus schottii. See *Pachycereus schottii*.

LOPHOMYRTUS
MYRTACEAE

Genus of evergreen shrubs or small trees, grown for their flowers, foliage and fruit. Needs partial shade and fertile, rich, moist but well-drained soil. Propagate by seed sown as soon as ripe or by semiripe cuttings in summer.

L. bullata, syn. *Myrtus bullata*. Evergreen, upright shrub. **H** 15ft (5m), **S** 10ft (3m). Rounded, puckered leaves, bronze-purple when young, mature to glossy dark green. Produces saucer-shaped, white flowers in late spring and early summer, then egg-shaped, black-red fruits. Z10–15 H 12–10.

LOPHOPHORA
Peyote
CACTACEAE

Genus of very slow-growing, perennial cacti that resemble small, blue dumplings, with up to 10 ribs, each separated by an indented line. Has long tap roots. Flowering areoles each produce tufts of short, white hairs. Needs sun and well-

drained soil. Is very prone to rotting, so water lightly from spring to fall. Propagate by seed in spring or summer.

L. echinata. See *L. williamsii*.

L. lutea. See *L. williamsii*.

L. williamsii, syn. *L. echinata*, *L. lutea*, illus. p.492.

LOPHOSPERMUM
SCROPHULARIACEAE/PLANTAGINACEAE

Genus of deciduous and evergreen, perennial climbers and shrubs, grown for their tubular to funnel-shaped flowers and triangular to rounded leaves. Needs sun and moist but well-drained soil. Propagate by seed in spring or semiripe cuttings in late summer.

L. erubescens, syn. *Asarina erubescens*, *Maurandya erubescens*, illus. p.460.

LOPHOSTEMON
MYRTACEAE

Genus of evergreen trees and shrubs, grown for their overall appearance when mature and for shade. Is related to *Tristania* and *Eucalyptus*. Needs sun or partial shade and fertile, well-drained soil. Other than shaping plants in winter, pruning is seldom necessary. Propagate by seed in spring or by semiripe cuttings in summer.

L. confertus, syn. *Tristania conferta* (Brush box). Fast-growing, evergreen, round-headed tree. **H** and **S** 50–130ft (15–40m). Produces lance-shaped, leathery, lustrous leaves. In spring bears white flowers with prominent, feathery stamen bundles. **'Perth Gold'** has bright green leaves strongly variegated yellow.

LOROPETALUM
HAMAMELIDACEAE

Genus of evergreen shrubs, grown for their flowers. Requires full light or partial shade and rich, well-drained, neutral to acid soil. Water container plants freely when in full growth, moderately at other times. Propagate by layering or seed in spring or by semiripe cuttings in late summer.

L. chinense. Evergreen, rounded, well-branched shrub. **H** and **S** 4ft (1.2m). Asymmetrically oval leaves are deep green. White flowers, each with 4 strap-shaped petals, are borne in tufted, terminal clusters, mainly in winter–spring. Z8–9 H9–8.

LOTUS
LEGUMINOSAE/PAPILIONACEAE

Genus of summer-flowering perennials, some of which are semievergreen, and evergreen subshrubs, grown for their foliage and flowers. Prefers sun and well-drained soil. Propagate by softwood cuttings from early to mid-summer or by seed in fall or spring.

L. berthelotii (Coral gem), illus. p.306.

L. hirsutus syn. *Dorycnium hirsutum* (Hairy canary clover). Deciduous, upright subshrub. **H** and **S** 24in (60cm). Bears silvery-gray leaves divided into 3 oval leaflets. Dense clusters of pealike, pink-tinged, white flowers in summer and early fall are followed by oblong to ovoid, reddish-brown seed pods. Z6–9 H9–6.

LUCULIA
RUBIACEAE

Genus of evergreen shrubs, grown for their flowers and foliage. Needs full light or partial shade and fertile, well-drained soil. Water container specimens freely when in full growth, moderately at other times. Cut back flowered stems hard in spring, if container-grown. Propagate by seed in spring or by semiripe cuttings in summer.

L. grandifolia. Evergreen, rounded to upright, robust shrub. **H** and **S** 10–20ft (3–6m). Oval, green leaves have red veins and stalks. Fragrant, tubular, white flowers, 2½in (6cm) long, with 5 rounded petal lobes, are borne in terminal clusters in summer. Z7–9 H9–7.

LUETKEA
ROSACEAE

Genus of one species of deciduous subshrub, grown for its fluffy flower heads. Is suitable for banks and rock gardens. Requires shade and well-drained but not too dry soil. Propagate by division or seed in spring.

L. pectinata. Deciduous, spreading, decumbent subshrub. **H** to 12in (30cm), **S** 8in (20cm). Stems are clothed in finely dissected, very dark green leaves. In summer has terminal racemes of small, fluffy, off-white flower heads.

LUMA
MYRTACEAE

Genus of evergreen shrubs and small trees, grown for their aromatic leaves and cup-shaped, white flowers. Needs sun or partial shade and fertile, ideally rich, well-drained soil. Propagate by seed in spring or by semiripe cuttings in late summer. See also feature panel p.78.

L. apiculata, syn. *Myrceugenia apiculata*, *Myrtus apiculata*, *Amomyrtus luma*, *Myrtus luma*, illus. p.78. Strong-growing, evergreen shrub. **H** and **S** 30–50ft (10–15m). Has peeling, golden-brown and gray-white bark and cup-shaped, white flowers amid broadly elliptic, aromatic, glossy, dark green leaves from mid-summer to mid-fall. Z9–11 H11–10. **'Glanleam Gold'**, **H** and **S** 30ft (10m), has sturdy stems, peeling, brown-and-white bark and bright green leaves edged with creamy-yellow. Z9–10 H10–9.

L. chequen, syn. *Myrtus chequen*. Strong-growing, evergreen, upright shrub or small tree. **H** 20ft (6m), **S** 15ft (5m). Has broadly ovate, wavy-margined, aromatic, dark green leaves. In late summer and early fall bears cup-shaped, white flowers singly or in small clusters followed by black berries. Z9–10 H10–9.

LUNARIA
Honesty
CRUCIFERAE/BRASSIACEAE

Genus of biennials and perennials, grown for their flowers and silvery seed pods. Prefers partial shade and well-drained soil. Propagate perennials by seed in fall or spring or by division in spring, biennials by seed only. Self-seeds prolifically.

L. annua , syn. *L. biennis*, illus. p.310.

'Variegata', illus. p.306.

L. biennis. See *L. annua*.

L

L. rediviva (Perennial honesty). Rosette-forming perennial. **H** 24–30in (60–75cm), **S** 12in (30cm). Produces racemes of 4-petaled, lilac or white flowers in spring, followed by elliptical, silvery seed pods that are useful for indoor decoration. Has oval, coarse, often maroon-tinted, mid-green leaves. Z6–9 H9–6.

LUPINUS
Lupine
LEGUMINOSAE/PAPILIONACEAE

Genus of annuals, perennials and semievergreen shrubs, grown for their large, imposing racemes of pealike flowers. Prefers sun and well-drained soil. Remove seed heads of most varieties to prevent self-seeding. Propagate species by seed when fresh in fall; selected forms by cuttings from non-flowering sideshoots in spring or early summer. Aphids can be a problem. ① The seeds may cause severe discomfort if ingested.

L. arboreus, illus. p.159.
L. Band of Nobles Series. Clump-forming perennial. **H** to 5ft (1.5m), **S** 2½ft (75cm). In early and mid-summer, racemes of flowers in white, yellow, pink, red, blue, or bicolors (usually white or yellow in combination with another color) arise above palmate, deeply divided, mid-green leaves. Z5–8 H8–5.
L. 'My Castle'. Clump-forming perennial. **H** 3ft (90cm), **S** 2½ft (75cm). Bears racemes of deep rose-pink flowers above palmate, deeply divided, mid-green leaves in early and mid-summer. Z4–7 H7–1.
L. 'Noble Maiden'. Clump-forming perennial. **H** 3ft (90cm), **S** 2½ft (75cm). In early and mid-summer, racemes of creamy-white flowers are produced above deeply divided, palmate, mid-green leaves. Z4–7 H7–1.
L. 'The Chatelaine', illus. p.232.
L. 'The Page'. Clump-forming perennial. **H** 36–39in (90–100cm), **S** 30in (75cm). Bears spikes of intense, deep red flowers above palmate, divided, mid-green, basal leaves from early to mid-summer.

LURONIUM
ALISMATACEAE

Genus of deciduous, perennial, marginal water plants and marsh plants, grown for their foliage and flowers. Requires full sun and shallow water. Thin plants when overcrowded. Propagate in spring by seed or division.

L. natans, syn. *Alisma natans* (Floating water plantain). Deciduous, perennial, marginal water plant. **H** 1–2in (2.5–5cm), **S** 12in (30cm). Produces small, elliptic to lance-shaped, mid-green leaves and, in summer, small, 3-lobed, yellow-spotted, white flowers. Z5–8 H8–5.

LUZULA
Woodrush
JUNCACEAE

See also GRASSES, BAMBOOS, RUSHES, and SEDGES.
L. maxima. See *L. sylvatica*.
L. nivea, illus. p.284.
L. sylvatica, syn. *L. maxima* (Greater woodrush). **'Aureomarginata'.** See *L. sylvatica* 'Marginata'. **'Hohe Tatra'**, illus. p.288. **'Marginata'**, syn. *L. sylvatica* 'Aureomarginata' is a slow-growing, evergreen, spreading, rhizomatous, perennial grass. **H** to 12in (30cm), **S** indefinite. Produces thick tufts of broad, hairy-edged, mid-green leaves, with white margins. Leafy stems bear terminal, open, brown flower spikes in summer. Tolerates shade; is suitable for a woodland garden. Z4–9 H9–4.

LYCASTE
ORCHIDACEAE

See also ORCHIDS.
L. cruenta, illus. p.467. Vigorous, deciduous, epiphytic orchid for a cool greenhouse. **H** 12in (30cm). Fragrant, triangular, green-and-yellow flowers, 2in (5cm) across, are produced singly in spring. Has broadly oval, ribbed, soft leaves, to 12in (30cm) long. Grow in partial shade in summer and avoid spraying, which can mark leaves. H11–6.

LYCHNIS
Campion, Catchfly
CARYOPHYLLACEAE

Genus of summer-flowering annuals, biennials and perennials. Requires sun or partial shade and well-drained soil. Propagate by division or seed in fall or spring.

L. 'Abbotswood Rose'. See *L.* x *walkeri* 'Abbotswood Rose'.
L. alpina, syn. *Viscaria alpina* (Alpine campion, Alpine catchfly). Tuft-forming perennial. **H** 2–6in (5–15cm), **S** 4–6in (10–15cm). Has dense tufts of thick, linear, deep green leaves. In summer, sticky stems each bear rounded head of pale to deep pink or, rarely, white flowers with spreading, frilled petals. Is suitable for a rock garden. Z4–7 H7–1.
L. chalcedonica, illus. p.235.
L. coeli-rosa. See *Silene coeli-rosa*.
L. coronaria, illus. p.268.
L. flos-jovis (Flower of Jove, Flower of Jupiter), illus. p.265.
L. x haageana, syn. *L.* x *haagena*. Short-lived, clump-forming perennial. **H** 18in (45cm), **S** 12in (30cm). Produces clusters of large, 5-petaled, white, orange or red flowers in summer. Oval leaves are mid-green. Is best raised regularly from seed.
L. x haagena. See *L.* x *haageana*. Z6–8 H8–6.
L. viscaria. Clump-forming perennial. **H** 12in (30cm), **S** 12–18in (30–45cm). From early to mid-summer, rather sticky, star-shaped, reddish-purple flowers are borne in dense clusters above narrowly oval to oblong, dark green leaves. Is suitable for the front of a border or a rock garden. Z3–7 H3–1. **'Splendens Plena'**, illus. p.265.
L. x walkeri 'Abbotswood Rose', syn. *L.* 'Abbotswood Rose'. Neat, clump-forming perennial. **H** 12–15in (30–38cm), **S** 9in (23cm). Has oval, gray leaves and gray, branching stems that, from mid- to late summer, bear sprays of rounded, 5-petaled, bright rose-pink flowers.

LYCIANTHES
SOLANACEAE

Genus of perennials and deciduous, semievergreen or evergreen shrubs, grown for their flowers, and sometimes also for their colored or variegated foliage. Is good in containers for summer bedding and in borders. Needs sun and moist but well-drained, neutral to slightly alkaline soil. Propagate by seed in spring or by semiripe cuttings in summer or early fall.

L. rantonnetii, syn. *Solanum rantonnei*, *Solanum rantonnetii* (Blue potato bush). **'Royal Robe'**, illus. p.310.

LYCIUM
SOLANACEAE

Genus of deciduous shrubs, sometimes with long, scandent branches, grown for their habit, flowers and fruits. Is useful for poor, dry soil and coastal gardens. May be grown as a hedge. Prefers full sun and not too rich, well-drained soil. Remove dead wood in winter and cut back to restrict growth if necessary. Cut back hedges hard in spring. Propagate by softwood cuttings in summer, by seed in fall or by hardwood cuttings in winter.

L. barbarum, syn. *L. halimifolium* (Chinese box thorn). Deciduous, arching, often spiny shrub. **H** 8ft (2.5m), **S** 15ft (5m). Funnel-shaped, purple or pink flowers, in late spring and summer, are followed by spherical, orange-red berries. Leaves are lance-shaped, bright green or gray-green. Z6–9 H9–5.
L. halimifolium. See *L. barbarum*.

LYCORIS
AMARYLLIDACEAE

Genus of late summer- and early fall-flowering bulbs, grown for their showy flower heads on leafless stems. In colder areas is best grown in pots. Needs sun, well-drained soil and a warm period in summer to ripen bulbs so they flower. Provide regular liquid feed while in growth. After summer dormancy, water from early fall until following summer, when foliage dies away. Propagate by seed when ripe or in spring or summer or by offsets in late summer.

L. aurea (Golden spider lily). Late summer- and early fall-flowering bulb. **H** 12–16in (30–40cm), **S** 4–6in (10–15cm). Produces a head of 5 or 6 bright yellow flowers that have narrow, reflexed petals, with very wavy margins, and conspicuous stamens. Strap-shaped, semierect, basal leaves are produced after flowering. Z8–10 H10–8.
L. radiata (Red spider lily), illus. p.410.
L. squamigera (Resurrection lily). Late summer- or early fall-flowering bulb. **H** 18–24in (45–60cm), **S** 4–6in (10–15cm). Bears a head of 6–8 fragrant, funnel-shaped, rose-pink flowers, 4in (10cm) long, with reflexed petal tips. Strap-shaped, semierect, basal leaves are produced after flowers. Z6–11 H12–6.

LYGODIUM
Climbing fern
SCHIZAEACEAE/LYGODIACEAE

Genus of deciduous or semievergreen, climbing ferns, usually with two kinds of fronds: vegetative and fertile. Needs full or partial shade and rich, moist, peaty soil. Is best grown among shrubby plants that can provide support. Plants grown under glass in pots need support. Remove faded fronds regularly. Propagate by division in spring or by fresh spores in summer.

L. japonicum (Japanese climbing fern). Deciduous, climbing fern. **H** 6ft (2m), **S** indefinite. Mid-green, vegetative fronds consist of delicate, finger-shaped pinnae; fertile fronds are broader and 3–5 lobed, with a longer, terminal lobe. Z10–11 H12–9.

LYONIA
ERICACEAE

Genus of deciduous, semievergreen or evergreen shrubs and trees, grown for their racemes of urn-shaped flowers. Needs full or partial shade and moist, peaty, acid soil. Propagate by semiripe cuttings in summer.

L. ligustrina. Deciduous, bushy shrub. **H** and **S** 6ft (2m). Oval, dark green leaves set off dense racemes of white flowers from mid- to late summer. Z5–9 H9–5.
L. ovalifolia. Deciduous or semievergreen, bushy shrub. **H** and **S** 6ft (2m). Produces red shoots and oval, dark green leaves. Racemes of white flowers are borne in late spring and early summer. Z5–9 H9–5.

LYONOTHAMNUS
ROSACEAE

Genus of one species of evergreen tree, grown for its foliage and flowers. Needs sun or partial shade, a warm, sheltered position and fertile, well-drained soil. Propagate by softwood cuttings in summer or by seed in fall.

L. floribundus (Catalina ironwood). Evergreen tree grown only in the form **subsp. aspleniifolius**. This is a slender tree. **H** 40ft (12m), **S** 20ft (6m). Has rather stringy, reddish-brown bark and much divided, fernlike, dark green leaves. Large, flattened heads of 5-petaled, star-shaped white flowers are produced in early summer. Z9–10 H10–9.

LYSICHITON
Skunk cabbage
ARACEAE

Genus of deciduous, perennial, marginal water plants and bog plants, grown for their spathes and very large, glossy foliage. Prefers full sun, but tolerates partial shade. Tolerates still and running water. Propagate by seed when fresh, in late summer.

L. americanum. See *L. americanus*.
L. americanus, syn. *L. americanum*, illus. p.444.
L. camtschatcensis, illus. p.434.

LYSIMACHIA
Loosestrife
PRIMULACEAE

Genus of summer-flowering annuals and perennials, suitable for the border or rock gardens. Prefers sun or partial shade and moist but well-drained soil. Propagate by division in spring or by seed in fall.

L. clethroides, illus. p.437.
L. congestiflora 'Outback Sunset', illus. p.323.
L. ephemerum. Neat, clump-forming perennial. **H** 3ft (1m), **S** 1ft (30cm). Erect, terminal racemes of star-shaped, grayish-white flowers are borne on slender stems in summer, followed by light green seed

L

heads. Lance-shaped leaves are leathery and glaucous.

L. nummularia (Creeping Jenny). **'Aurea'**, illus. p.372.

L. punctata, illus. p.243.

LYSIONOTUS

GESNERIACEAE

Genus of evergreen, creeping, shrubby perennials, grown for their relatively large, tubular, inflated, white to pink flowers. Requires partial or full shade and rich, moist but well-drained soil. Propagate by cuttings in summer or by seed in spring.

L. pauciflorus. Evergreen, suckering, shrubby perennial. **H** 8–12in (20–30cm), **S** 20in (50cm). Erect, woody stems have ovate, toothed, rigid, leathery, dark green leaves, 3/4–11/4in (2–3cm) long, and bear tubular, purple-striped, pale lilac flowers in summer–fall.

LYTHRUM

Loosestrife

LYTHRACEAE

Genus of summer-flowering perennials that thrive by the waterside and in bog gardens. Needs sun or partial shade and moist or wet soil. Propagate cultivars by division in spring, species by seed or division in spring or fall. Some species have become noxious weeds in the USA.

L. salicaria (Purple loosestrife). **'Feuerkerze'**, syn. *L. salicaria* 'Fire Candle', illus. p.234. **'Fire Candle'.** See *L. salicaria* 'Feuerkerze'. **'Robert'** is a clump-forming perennial. **H** 30in (75cm), **S** 18in (45cm). Produces racemes of 4-petaled, clear pink flowers from mid- to late summer. Leaves are mid-green and lance-shaped. Z3–9 H9–1.

L. virgatum (Purple loosestrife). **'Rose Queen'** Clump-forming perennial. **H** 3ft (1m), **S** 2ft (60cm). Racemes of 4-petaled, star-shaped, light pink flowers are produced from mid- to late summer above lance-shaped, hairless, mid-green leaves. Z4–9 H9–1. **'The Rocket', S** 11/2ft (45cm), has slender spikes of rose-red flowers. Is good for a waterside or bog garden. Z4–9 H9–1.

M

MAACKIA

LEGUMINOSAE/PAPILIONACEAE

Genus of deciduous, summer-flowering trees, grown for their foliage and flowers. Requires full sun and fertile, well-drained soil. Propagate by seed in fall.

M. amurensis, illus. p.85.

MACADAMIA

LEGUMINOSAE/PAPILIONACEAE

Genus of evergreen trees, grown for their foliage and fruits. Prefers full light, though some shade is tolerated. Needs rich, moist but well-drained soil. Water freely while in full growth, moderately at other times. Pruning is not usually necessary, but is tolerated in fall. Propagate by seed when ripe, in fall, or in spring.

M. integrifolia (Macadamia nut, Queensland nut). Spreading tree. **H** and **S** 50ft (15m). Has whorls of leathery, semi-glossy leaves and edible, brown nuts in fall. Produces panicles of small, creamy-yellow flowers in spring. Z13–15 H12–11.

MACFADYENA

SYN. DOXANTHA

Cat's claw vine

BIGNONIACEAE

Genus of evergreen, woody-stemmed, tendril climbers, grown for their foxglove-like flowers. Needs full light and fertile, well-drained soil. Water regularly when in full growth, less at other times. Provide support for stems. Thin out crowded shoots after flowering or in spring. Propagate by semiripe cuttings in summer.

M. unguis-cati, syn. *Bignonia unguis-cati, Doxantha unguis-cati* (Common cat's claw vine). Fast-growing, evergreen, woody-stemmed, tendril climber. **H** 25–30ft (8–10m). Leaves have 2 leaflets and a tendril. Has yellow flowers, 4in (10cm) long, in late spring or early summer. Z11–15 H12–10.

MACKAYA

ACANTHACEAE

Genus of one species of evergreen shrub, grown for its flowers and overall appearance. Requires full light or partial shade and fertile, well-drained soil. Water container plants freely when in full growth, moderately at other times. Pruning is tolerated in winter if necessary. Propagate by greenwood cuttings in spring or by semiripe cuttings in summer.

M. bella, syn. *Asystasia bella*. Evergreen, erect, then spreading, well-branched shrub. **H** to 5ft (1.5m), **S** 4–5ft (1.2–1.5m). Leaves are oval, pointed, glossy and mid- to deep green. Has spikes of tubular, dark-veined, lavender flowers, each with 5 large, flared petal lobes, from spring to fall. In warm conditions, above 55°F (13°C), will flower into winter. Z9–11 H12–9.

MACLEANIA

ERICACEAE

Genus of evergreen, spring- to summer-flowering shrubs and scrambling climbers, grown mainly for their flowers. Needs partial shade and rich, well-drained, neutral to acidic soil. Water container specimens moderately when in full growth, less at other times. Long shoots may be shortened in winter or after flowering. Propagate by seed in spring, by semiripe cuttings in summer or by layering in fall.

M. insignis. Evergreen, scrambling climber with erect, sparingly branched, wandlike stems. **H** 10ft (3m), **S** 3–10ft (1–3m). Has oval, leathery, deep green leaves, red-flushed when young. Tubular, waxy, scarlet flowers, with white tips, hang in clusters in summer. Needs support.

MACLEAYA

Plume poppy

PAPAVERACEAE

Genus of summer-flowering perennials, grown for their overall appearance. Requires sun and well-drained soil. May spread rapidly. Propagate by division in early spring or by root cuttings in winter.

M. cordata, syn. *Bocconia cordata* (Plume poppy). Spreading, clump-forming perennial. **H** 5ft (1.5m) or more, **S** 2ft (60cm) or more. Large, rounded, lobed, gray-green leaves, gray-white beneath, are produced at base of plant and up lower parts of stems. Large, feathery panicles of creamy-white flowers are produced in summer. Z4–8 H8–1.

M. microcarpa 'Kelway's Coral Plume', illus. p.216.

MACLURA

MORACEAE

Genus of 15 species of evergreen or deciduous trees, shrubs and climbers, grown for their foliage and unusual fruits. Both male and female trees need to be planted to obtain fruits. Young plants are susceptible to cold damage. Requires full sun and needs hot summers to thrive in cold areas. Grows in any but waterlogged soil. Propagate by softwood cuttings in summer, by seed in fall or by root cuttings in late winter.

M. aurantiaca. See *M. pomifera*.

M. pomifera, syn. *M. aurantiaca* (Osage orange). Deciduous, rounded, spreading tree. **H** 50ft (15m), **S** 40ft (12m). Has spiny shoots and oval, dark green leaves that turn yellow in fall. Tiny, cup-shaped, yellow flowers in summer are followed on female trees by large, rounded, wrinkled, pale green fruits. Z5–9 H9–5.

M. tricuspidata, syn. *Cudrania tricuspidata*. Deciduous, spreading tree. **H** 22ft (7m), **S** 20ft (6m). Bears oval, dark green leaves that are sometimes 3-lobed. Produces small, rounded clusters of tiny, green flowers in mid-summer. Z5–9 H9–5.

Macrotomia echioides. See *Arnebia pulchra*.

MACROZAMIA

ZAMIACEAE

Genus of slow-growing, evergreen shrubs and small trees, with or without trunks, grown for their palmlike appearance. Mature plants may produce conical, green flower spikes. Needs full light or partial shade and well-drained soil. Water container plants moderately when in full growth, less at other times. Propagate by seed in spring.

M. corallipes. See *M. spiralis*.

M. spiralis, syn. *M. corallipes*. Evergreen, palmlike shrub with a very short, mainly underground trunk. **H** and **S** 2–3ft (60cm–1m). Has a rosette of deep green leaves, each with a spirally twisted midrib and very narrow, leathery leaflets. Z10–13 H12–10.

MAGNOLIA

Magnolia

MAGNOLIACEAE

Genus of deciduous, semievergreen or evergreen trees and shrubs, grown for their showy, usually fragrant flowers. Leaves are mainly oval. Flowers and buds of early-flowering magnolias may be damaged by late frosts. Needs sun or partial shade and shelter from strong winds. Prefers fertile, well-drained soil. *M. delavayi, M. kobus, M. sieboldii* and *M. wilsonii* grow on chalky soil. Other species prefer neutral to acidic soil, but will tolerate alkaline soil if deep and rich. Dry, sandy soils should be generously enriched with manure and leaf mold before planting. Propagate species by semiripe cuttings in summer or by seed, when ripe, in fall, selected forms by semiripe cuttings in summer or by grafting in winter. See also feature pp.70–71.

M. acuminata (Cucumber tree magnolia). Vigorous, deciduous tree, conical when young, later spreading. **H** 70ft (20m), **S** 30ft (10m). Has fragrant, cup-shaped, bluish-green flowers from early to mid-summer amid large, oval, pale green leaves, followed by small, egg-shaped, green, later red fruits. Z4–8 H8–2.

M. 'Ann', illus. p.70. Deciduous, erect, multi-stemmed tree. **H** and **S** to 20ft (6m). Has oval, deep green leaves. In spring produces an abundance of fragrant, narrowly goblet-shaped, rich pinkish-red flowers. Z3–8 H8–1.

M. BLACK TULIP ('Jurmag1'), illus. p.70. Deciduous, densely branched tree. **H** to 40ft (12m), **S** 20ft (6m). Has large, goblet-shaped, deep wine-red flowers borne in early spring before the large, oval, mid-green leaves unfold.

M. x brooklynensis 'Yellow Bird', illus. p.70. Deciduous, upright, slightly pyramidal tree. **H** 40ft (12m), **S** 20ft (6m). Has oval, mid-green leaves. Goblet-shaped, dark yellow flowers, sometimes tinted green, are borne in spring. Z4–8 H8–1.

M. 'Butterflies', illus. p.70. Deciduous, upright tree. **H** and **S** 10ft (3m). Has oval, mid-green leaves. Goblet- to tulip-shaped, bright deep yellow flowers, in mid-spring, open wide as they mature to reveal orange-red stamens. Z4–9 H9–1.

M. campbellii. Deciduous tree, upright when young, later spreading. **H** 50ft (15m), **S** 30ft (10m). Large, slightly fragrant, cup-and-saucer-shaped, pale to deep pink

flowers are borne on leafless branches from late winter to mid-spring on trees 15–20 years old or more. Leaves are large, oval and mid-green. Z7–9 H9–7. **'Charles Raffill'** bears purplish-pink flowers. **'Darjeeling'** has very deep pink flowers. **'Kew's Surprise'** produces deep purplish-pink flowers. **subsp. *mollicomata*** (illus. p.70) has lilac-pink flowers slightly earlier in year.
***M.* 'Charles Coates'.** Deciduous, rounded, open, spreading tree. **H** 70ft (19m), **S** 25ft (8m). Extremely fragrant, saucer-shaped, creamy-white flowers, with conspicuous, red stamens, are produced in late spring and early summer amid large, light green leaves. Z6–9 H9–8.
M. cylindrica. Deciduous, spreading tree or large shrub. **H** and **S** 15ft (5m). Fragrant, goblet- to cup-shaped, creamy-white flowers are produced in mid-spring, after which young leaves turn dark green. Z6–9 H9–6.
M. cylindrica of gardens. See *M.* 'Pegasus'.
M. dawsoniana. Deciduous tree or shrub, with a broadly oval head. **H** 50ft (15m), **S** 30ft (10m). In early spring, large, fragrant, pendent, open cup-shaped, pale lilac-pink flowers are borne profusely on older plants (20 years from seed, 10 years from grafting). Leaves are oval, leathery and deep green. Z7–9 H9–7.
M. delavayi. Evergreen, rounded, dense shrub or tree. **H** and **S** 30ft (10m). Large, slightly fragrant, bowl-shaped, parchment-white flowers are short-lived and open intermittently from mid-summer to early fall. Large, oval leaves are deep blue-green above and bluish-white beneath. Z8–9 H9–8.
M. denudata, syn. *M. heptapeta* (Lily tree, Yulan). Deciduous, rounded, bushy shrub or spreading tree. **H** and **S** 30ft (10m). Has masses of fragrant, cup-shaped, white flowers, from mid- to late spring, before oval, mid-green leaves are produced. Z6–9 H9–6.
M. doltsopa. See *Michelia doltsopa.*
***M.* 'Elizabeth',** illus. p.70. Deciduous, multi-stemmed, conical tree. **H** to 25ft (8m), **S** to 20ft (6m). In spring produces fragrant, cup-shaped, primrose-yellow flowers, with 6–9 petals and red stamens. Obovate, dark green leaves are coppery in color when they unfold in spring. Z6–9 H9–5.
M. figo. See *Michelia figo.*
M. fraseri (Fraser magnolia). Deciduous, spreading, open tree. **H** 30ft (10m), **S** 25ft (8m). Fragrant, narrowly goblet-shaped, white or pale yellow flowers are borne in late spring and early summer amid large, pale green leaves. Z6–9 H9–6.
***M.* 'Galaxy',** illus. p.70. Deciduous, conical to upright tree. **H** 20ft (6m), **S** 10ft (3m). Large, slightly fragrant, narrowly goblet-shaped, pinkish-purple flowers, purple-red outside, open from deep purple buds in early spring before elliptic, mid-green leaves emerge. Z6–9 H9–6.
M. globosa. Deciduous, bushy shrub. **H** and **S** 15ft (5m). In early summer, large, oval, glossy, dark green leaves set off fragrant, cup-shaped, creamy-white flowers with red anthers.
M. grandiflora (Southern magnolia). Evergreen, broadly conical or rounded, dense tree. **H** and **S** 30ft (10m). Bears large, very fragrant, bowl-shaped, white flowers intermittently from mid-summer to early fall. Has oblong, glossy, mid- to dark green leaves. Z7–9 H9–1. **'Exmouth'** (illus. p.70) produces creamy-white flowers and narrow, leathery leaves. **'Ferruginea'** produces dark green leaves that are rust-brown beneath. Z8–9 H9–8.
***M.* 'Heaven Scent',** illus. p.72.
M. heptapeta. See *M. denudata.*
M. hypoleuca. See *M. obovata.*
M. insignis. See *Manglietia insignis.*
***M.* x *kewensis* 'Wada's Memory'.** See *M. salicifolia* 'Wada's Memory'.
M. kobus. Deciduous, broadly conical tree. **H** 30ft (10m), **S** 25ft (8m). Bears a profusion of fragrant, cup-and-saucer-shaped, pure white flowers, in mid-spring, before small, slightly aromatic, dark green leaves are produced. Z5–9 H9–5.
M. liliiflora, syn. *M. quinquepeta* (Lily-flowered magnolia). Deciduous, bushy shrub. **H** 10ft (3m), **S** 12ft (4m). Fragrant, upright, goblet-shaped, purplish-pink flowers are borne amid oval, very dark green leaves from mid-spring to mid-summer. Z4–9 H9–1. **'Nigra'** (illus. p.70) has large, deep purple flowers.
***M.* x *loebneri.* 'Merrill'** has funnel-shaped, white flowers. **'Leonard Messel'** (illus. p.70) Deciduous, upright shrub or small tree. **H** 25ft (8m), **S** 20ft (6m). In mid-spring, fragrant, star-shaped flowers with many pale lilac-pink petals are produced before and after oval, deep green leaves emerge. Z5–9 H9–5.
M. macrophylla (Bigleaf magnolia). Deciduous, broadly upright tree, becoming rounded with age. **H** and **S** 30ft (10m). Produces sturdy, blue-gray shoots and very large, oval, bright green leaves. Large, fragrant, bowl-shaped, parchment-white flowers are borne in early summer. Z6–9 H9–6.
***M.* 'Manchu Fan'.** Vigorous, deciduous shrub or tree. **H** 20ft (6m), **S** 15ft (5m). In late spring has large, goblet-shaped, creamy-white flowers with usually 9 petals, the inner ones flushed purple-pink at base. Leaves are ovate. Z6–9 H9–6.
***M.* 'Norman Gould'.** Deciduous, spreading tree or bushy shrub. **H** and **S** 15ft (5m). Silky buds open into fragrant, star-shaped, white flowers in mid-spring. Leaves are oblong and dark green. Z6–9 H9–6.
M. obovata, syn. *M. hypoleuca* (Japanese bigleaf magnolia, Whitebark magnolia). Vigorous, deciduous, upright tree. **H** 50ft (15m), **S** 30ft (10m). Large, fragrant, cup-shaped, pink-flushed, white or pale cream flowers, with crimson stamens, are produced in early summer. Z5–9 H9–5.
***M.* 'Pegasus',** syn. *M. cylindrica.* Deciduous shrub or multi-stemmed tree, initially vase-shaped, later spreading. **H** and **S** 20ft (6m). Has elliptic, dark green leaves, pale green beneath. In spring, before and with the young leaves, produces cup-shaped, creamy-white or yellowish-white flowers, suffused purplish-pink at bases.
***M.* 'Pinkie',** illus. p.70. Deciduous, upright shrub. **H** and **S** to 12ft (4m). In spring produces cup-shaped, pale pinkish-purple flowers, with white inner surfaces, followed by ovate to elliptic, mid-green leaves.
M. quinquepeta. See *M. liliiflora.*
***M.* 'Ricki'.** Deciduous, upright shrub. **H** and **S** 12ft (4m). Goblet-shaped flowers, each with 15 twisted petals that are pink to dark purple-pink at bases, are produced from dark purple-pink buds in mid-spring. Leaves are broadly oval and mid-green. Z6–9 H9–6.
M. salicifolia (Anise magnolia, Willow-leaved magnolia). Deciduous, conical tree. **H** 30ft (10m), **S** 15ft (5m). Has aromatic, oval leaves, mid-green above, gray-white beneath. Fragrant, star-shaped, pure white flowers are produced in mid-spring before foliage emerges. Z6–9 H9–6. **'Wada's Memory',** syn. *M.* x *kewensis* 'Wada's Memory' has dark green foliage and a profusion of large flowers borne from mid- to late spring.
M. sargentiana. Deciduous, broadly conical tree. **H** 50ft (15m), **S** 30ft (10m). Large, fragrant, narrowly bowl-shaped, many-petaled flowers, white inside, purplish-pink outside, are borne from mid- to late spring, before oval, dark green leaves emerge. Z7–9 H9–7.
M. sieboldii (Oyama magnolia). Deciduous, arching shrub or wide-spreading tree. **H** 25ft (8m), **S** 40ft (12m). Fragrant, cup-shaped, white flowers, with crimson anthers, are produced above oval, dark green leaves from late spring to late summer. Z6–9 H9–6. **subsp. *sinensis,*** syn. *M. sinensis* has slightly larger, fully pendent flowers and more rounded, oval leaves.
M. sinensis. See *M. sieboldii* subsp. *sinensis.*
M.* x *soulangeana (Saucer magnolia). Z5–9 H8–7. **'Alba'.** See *M.* x *soulangeana* 'Alba Superba'. **'Alba Superba',** syn. *M.* x *soulangeana* 'Alba' is a deciduous, rounded, spreading shrub or small tree. **H** and **S** 20ft (6m). Bears large, fragrant, tulip-like, white flowers, faintly flushed with pink at bases, from mid- to early spring, the first before mid- to dark green leaves emerge. Z6–9 H9–6. **'Brozzonii',** **H** 25ft (8m), is treelike, with large, purple-flushed, white flowers. Z6–9 H9–6. **'Etienne Soulange-Bodin'** bears purple-flushed, white flowers. Flowers of **'Lennei'** are large, goblet-shaped and deep rose-purple. **'Lennei Alba'** has ivory-white flowers. **'Picture',** **H** 25ft (8m), is vigorous, compact and upright, with large, erect, deep reddish-purple flowers. **'Rubra'** of gardens. See *M.* x *soulangeana* 'Rustica Rubra'. **'Rustica Rubra',** syn. *M.* x *soulangeana* 'Rubra' (illus. p.70) has purplish-red flowers suffused pink.
M. sprengeri. Deciduous, spreading tree. **H** 50ft (15m), **S** 30ft (10m). In mid-spring has fragrant, bowl-shaped, white flowers, sometimes fringed with red or pale pink, before oval, dark green leaves are produced. Z7–9 H9–7. **var. *diva*** (illus. p.70) bears rich deep pink flowers, paler inside. **'Wakehurst'** has deep purplish-pink flowers.
M. stellata (Star magnolia, Swamp magnolia). Deciduous, bushy, dense shrub. **H** 10ft (3m), **S** 12ft (4m). Fragrant, star-shaped, pure white flowers, with many narrow petals sometimes faintly pink flushed, open from silky buds from early to mid-spring. Leaves are narrow and deep green. Z5–9 H9–5. **'Rosea'** (illus. p.70) has warm pink buds that open pale pink. **'Waterlily'** (illus. p.70) has large, white flowers with many petals.
M. tripetala (Umbrella tree magnolia). Deciduous, spreading, open tree, conical when young. **H** 30ft (10m), **S** 25ft (8m). Has large, dark green leaves, clustered around shoot tips, and rather unpleasantly scented, cup-shaped, creamy-white flowers, with narrow petals, in late spring and early summer. Z5–9 H9–5.
***M.* x *veitchii* 'Peter Veitch'.** Fast-growing, deciduous, spreading tree. **H** 60ft (20m), **S** 50ft (15m). Produces large, fragrant, goblet-shaped, pale pink and white flowers in mid-spring, before dark green leaves emerge. Usually flowers within 10 years of planting. Z7–9 H9–7.
M. virginiana (Sweetbay magnolia). Deciduous or semievergreen, conical shrub or tree. **H** 28ft (9m), **S** 20ft (6m). Has very fragrant, cup-shaped, creamy-white flowers from early summer to early fall. Oblong, glossy, mid- to dark green leaves are bluish-white beneath. Z6–9 H9–6.
***M.* 'Vulcan',** illus. p.70. Deciduous, open-branched tree. **H** 20ft (6m), **S** 13ft (4m). Has oval, mid-green leaves. In spring bears large, cup- to goblet-shaped, erect, deep wine-red flowers, with outward curved petals. Flowers from a young age.
M.* x *watsonii. See *M.* x *wieseneri.*
M.* x *wieseneri, syn. *M.* x *watsonii,* illus. p.70. Deciduous, spreading, open tree or shrub. **H** 25ft (8m), **S** 15ft (5m). Rounded, white buds open in late spring to early summer to fragrant, bowl-shaped, creamy-white flowers, flushed pink outside and with crimson stamens. Z7–9 H9–7.
M. wilsonii, illus. p.70. Deciduous, spreading tree or shrub. **H** 25ft (8m), **S** 22ft (7m). In late spring and early summer, fragrant, cup-shaped, white flowers, with crimson stamens, hang from arching branches amid narrow, dark green leaves. Z7–9 H9–7.

x MAHOBERBERIS

BERBERIDACEAE

Hybrid genus (*Berberis* x *Mahonia*) of evergreen shrubs, grown for their foliage, flowers and botanical interest. Needs sun or partial shade and fertile, well-drained soil. Propagate by semiripe cuttings in summer.
x *M. aquisargentii.* Evergreen, upright, densely leaved shrub. **H** and **S** 6ft (2m). Leaves are bright green, often with 3 leaflets, some oblong and finely toothed, others holly-shaped. Terminal clusters of berberis-like, yellow flowers are sparsely produced in late spring. Z6–8 H8–6.

MAHONIA

BERBERIDACEAE

Genus of evergreen shrubs, grown for their foliage, their usually short racemes of often fragrant, rounded, bell-shaped, yellow flowers and, with tall species and cultivars, for their deeply fissured bark. Large mahonias make good specimen plants; low-growing ones are excellent for groundcover. Prefers full or partial shade and fertile, well-drained but not too dry soil. Propagate species by leaf-bud or semiripe cuttings in summer or by seed in fall, selected forms by leaf-bud or semiripe cuttings only.
M. acanthifolia. See *M. napaulensis.*
M. aquifolium, illus. p.148.
M. bealei. See *M. japonica* Bealei Group.
***M.* 'Heterophylla'.** Evergreen, upright shrub. **H** 3ft (1m), **S** 5ft (1.5m). Has reddish-purple shoots and glossy, bright green leaves, divided into 5 or 7 narrowly lance-shaped, wavy-edged or curled leaflets

that turn reddish-purple in winter. Small clusters of yellow flowers are produced in spring. Z9–10 H10–9.

M. japonica, illus. p.144. **Bealei Group,** syn. *M. bealei* (Leatherleaf mahonia) is an evergreen, upright shrub. **H** 6ft (2m), **S** 10ft (3m). Has blue-green leaves divided into broad, spiny leaflets. Long, spreading sprays of fragrant, pale yellow flowers, in short, upright racemes, are borne from late fall to spring and followed by purple-blue fruits. Z7–8 H8–7.

M. lomariifolia. Evergreen, very upright shrub. **H** 10ft (3m), **S** 6ft (2m). Large, dark green leaves each have 19–37 narrow, holly-like, spiny leaflets. Fragrant, bright yellow flowers are produced in dense, upright racemes in late fall and winter. Z8–9 H9–5.

***M. x media* 'Buckland',** illus. p.118. **'Charity',** illus. p.118.

M. napaulensis, syn. *M. acanthifolia.* Evergreen, upright, open shrub. **H** 8ft (2.5m), **S** 10ft (3m). Leaves are composed of up to 15 holly-like, spiny, dark green leaflets. Produces long, slender racemes of yellow flowers in early and mid-spring. Z8–9 H9–8.

M. repens (Creeping mahonia). Evergreen, upright shrub that spreads by underground stems. **H** 1ft (30cm), **S** 6ft (2m). Blue-green leaves each consist of 3–7 oval leaflets, with bristly teeth. Dense clusters of deep yellow flowers are borne from mid- to late spring. Z5–8 H8–3.

***M. x wagneri* 'Undulata'.** Evergreen, upright shrub. **H** and **S** 6ft (2m). Glossy, dark green leaves each have 5–9 holly-like, wavy-edged leaflets that become bronzed in winter. Bears dense clusters of deep yellow flowers in mid- and late spring. Z5–8 H8–5.

MAIANTHEMUM
May lily

LILIACEAE/ASPARAGACEAE

Genus of perennials with extensive, spreading rhizomes. Is useful as groundcover in woodlands and wild areas. Prefers full or partial shade and rich, moist, sandy, neutral to acidic soil. Propagate by seed in fall or by division in any season.

M. bifolium, illus. p.348.

M. canadense. Vigorous, groundcover, rhizomatous perennial. **H** 4in (10cm), **S** indefinite. Has large, upright, oval, wavy-edged, glossy leaves. Slender stems bear sprays of small, white flowers in late spring and early summer followed by red berries. Z4–7 H7–1.

M. racemosum. See *Smilacina racemosa.*

MAIHUENIA

CACTACEAE

Genus of slow-growing, summer-flowering, alpine cacti, clump-forming with age, with cylindrical stems. Requires sun and well-drained soil. Protect from winter rain. Propagate by seed or stem cuttings in spring or summer.

M. poeppigii, illus. p.490.

MALCOLMIA

CRUCIFERAE/BRASSICACEAE

Genus of spring- to fall-flowering annuals. Needs sun and fertile, well-drained soil. Propagate by seed in spring, summer or early fall. Self-seeds freely.

M. Maritima, illus. p.304.

MALEPHORA

AIZOACEAE

Genus of erect or spreading, perennial succulents with semicylindrical leaves. Needs sun and very well-drained soil. Propagate by seed or stem cuttings in spring or summer.

M. crocea, illus. p.496.

MALOPE

MALVACEAE

Genus of annuals, grown for their showy flowers that are ideal for cutting. Needs sun and fertile, well-drained soil. Propagate by seed in spring. Self-seeds freely.

M. trifida, illus. p.305.

MALUS
Apple, Flowering crabapple

ROSACEAE

Genus of deciduous, mainly spring-flowering trees and shrubs, grown for their shallowly cup-shaped flowers, fruits, foliage or fall color. Crab apples may be used to make preserves. Prefers full sun, but tolerates partial shade; grows in any but waterlogged soil. In winter, cut out dead or diseased wood and prune to maintain a balanced branch system. Propagate by budding in late summer or by grafting in mid-winter. Trees are sometimes attacked by aphids, caterpillars and red spider mite, and are susceptible to fireblight and apple scab.

M. 'Almey'. Deciduous, rounded tree. **H** and **S** 25ft (8m). Oval leaves are reddish-purple when young, maturing to dark green. Single, deep pink flowers, with paler pink, almost white centers, in late spring are followed by long-lasting, rounded, orange-red crab apples, which are subject to apple scab.

M. x arnoldiana, illus. p.82.

M. x atrosanguinea. Deciduous, spreading tree. **H** and **S** 20ft (6m). Produces oval, glossy, dark green leaves. Red flower buds open to single, rich pink flowers in late spring. Bears small, rounded, red-flushed, yellow crab apples. Z4–8 H8–1.

M. baccata (Siberian crabapple). Deciduous, spreading tree. **H** and **S** 50ft (15m). Has oval, dark green leaves and a profusion of single, white flowers from mid- to late spring followed by tiny, rounded, red or yellow crab apples in fall. Z3–7 H7–1. **var.** ***mandschurica*** illus. p.69.

M. 'Chilko'. Deciduous, spreading tree. **H** and **S** 25ft (8m). Oval, dark green leaves are reddish-purple when young. Has single, rose-pink flowers in mid-spring, followed by large, rounded, bright crimson crab apples. Z5–8 H8–5.

***M. coronaria* 'Charlottae'.** Deciduous, spreading tree. **H** and **S** 28ft (9m). Broadly oval, lobed or deeply toothed leaves are dark green, turning red in fall. Semidouble, pale pink flowers are borne in late spring and early summer. Z4–8 H8–1.

M. 'Cowichan', illus. p.90.

M. 'Dorothea'. Deciduous, spreading tree. **H** and **S** 25ft (8m). Semidouble, silvery-pink flowers, red in bud, are borne in late spring, followed by rounded, yellow crab apples. Oval leaves are mid-green. Is prone to apple scab.

M. 'Eleyi', syn. *M. x purpurea* 'Eleyi'. Deciduous, spreading tree. **H** and **S** 25ft (8m). Oval leaves are dark reddish-purple when young, dark green when mature. Bears single, deep purplish-red flowers from mid- to late spring, followed by rounded, purplish-red crab apples.

M. floribunda, illus. p.84.

M. 'Frettingham's Victoria'. Deciduous, upright tree. **H** 25ft (8m), **S** 12ft (4m). Single, white flowers, borne amid oval, dark green leaves in late spring, are followed by rounded, red-flushed, yellow crab apples.

M. 'Golden Hornet', syn. *M. x zumi* 'Golden Hornet', illus. p.92.

***M. x hartwigii* 'Katherine'.** See *M.* 'Katherine'.

M. 'Hopa'. Deciduous, spreading tree. **H** and **S** 30ft (10m). Oval, dark green leaves are reddish-purple when young. Single, deep pink flowers in mid-spring are followed by rounded, orange-and-red crab apples.

M. hupehensis, illus. p.69.

M. 'John Downie', illus. p.91.

M. 'Katherine', syn. *M. x hartwigii* 'Katherine'. Deciduous, round-headed tree. **H** and **S** 20ft (6m). Has oval, mid-green leaves. Large, double, pale pink flowers, fading to white, from mid- to late spring, are followed by tiny, rounded, yellow-flushed, red crab apples. Z3–9 H9–1.

M. 'Lemoinei', syn. *M. x purpurea* 'Lemoinei', illus. p.84.

M. x magdeburgensis, illus. p.83.

M. 'Marshall Oyama', illus. p.90.

***M. x moerlandsii* 'Profusion'.** See *M.* 'Profusion'.

M. 'Neville Copeman', syn. *M. x purpurea* 'Neville Copeman'. Deciduous, spreading tree. **H** and **S** 28ft (9m). Oval, dark green leaves are purplish-red when young. Single, dark purplish-pink flowers, borne from mid- to late spring, are followed by rounded, orange-red to carmine crab apples.

M. niedzwetskyana, syn. *M. pumila* var. *niedzwetskyana.* Deciduous, spreading tree. **H** 20ft (6m), **S** 25ft (8m). Oval leaves are red when young, maturing to purple. Produces clusters of single, deep reddish-purple flowers in late spring, followed by very large, conical, reddish-purple crab apples.

M. prattii. Deciduous tree, upright when young, later spreading. **H** and **S** 30ft (10m). Oval, red-stalked, glossy, mid-green leaves become orange and red in fall. Single, white flowers in late spring are followed by small, rounded or egg-shaped, white-flecked, red crab apples. Z5–8 H8–5.

M. 'Professor Sprenger', illus. p.91.

M. 'Profusion', syn. *M. x moerlandsii* 'Profusion', illus. p.71.

M. prunifolia, illus. p.90.

M. pumila* var. *niedzwetskyana. See *M. niedzwetskyana.*

M. x purpurea. Deciduous, spreading tree. **H** 25ft (8m), **S** 30ft (10m). Oval, young leaves are reddish, maturing to green. Single, deep ruby-red flowers, becoming paler with age, are produced in late spring and are followed by rounded, reddish-purple crab apples. Z5–8 H8–5. **'Eleyi'.** See *M.* 'Eleyi'. **'Lemoinei'.** See *M.* 'Lemoinei'. **'Neville Copeman'.** See *M.* 'Neville Copeman'.

M. x robusta. Vigorous, deciduous, spreading tree. **H** 40ft (12m), **S** 30ft (10m). Bears masses of single, white or pink flowers above oval, dark green leaves in late spring. These are followed by long-lasting, rounded, yellow or red crab apples. Z4–8 H8–1. **'Yellow Siberian'** produces white flowers, which are sometimes pink-tinged, and yellow crab apples. Z4–8 H8–4.

M. 'Royalty', illus. p.84.

M. sargentii, illus. p.110. Deciduous, spreading shrub with arching branches. **H** 12ft (4m), **S** 15ft (5m). Dark green leaves, often lobed, turn red or yellow in fall. Bears white or pale to deep pink flowers in mid-spring followed by small, red or yellow fruits.

***M. x scheidekeri* 'Red Jade'.** Deciduous, weeping tree. **H** 12ft (4m), **S** 20ft (6m). In late spring has single, white flowers, sometimes pale pink-flushed, followed by long-lasting, rounded to egg-shaped, red crab apples. Leaves are dark green and oval. Z5–8 H8–5.

M. 'Snowcloud', illus. p.81.

M. spectabilis (Chinese flowering crabapple). Deciduous, round-headed tree. **H** and **S** 30ft (10m). Has oval, dark green leaves. Single, blush-pink flowers, rose-red in bud, from mid- to late spring, are followed by large, rounded, yellow crab apples. Z5–8 H8–5.

M. toringoides. Deciduous, spreading tree. **H** 25ft (8m), **S** 30ft (10m). Oval, deeply lobed, glossy, bright green leaves turn yellow in fall. Bears single, white flowers in late spring followed by rounded or egg-shaped, red-flushed, yellow crab apples in fall. Z5–8 H8–5.

M. transitoria. Deciduous, spreading tree. **H** 25ft (8m), **S** 30ft (10m). Oval, deeply lobed, mid-green leaves turn yellow in fall. Has masses of single, white flowers, in late spring, followed by small, rounded, pale yellow crab apples. Z5–8 H8–5.

M. trilobata. Deciduous, conical tree. **H** 50ft (15m), **S** 22ft (7m). Has maple-like, lobed, glossy, bright green leaves that often become brightly colored in fall. Bears single, white flowers, in early summer, followed by small, rounded or pear-shaped, red or yellow crab apples. Z5–8 H8–5.

M. tschonoskii, illus. p.77.

M. 'Van Eseltine'. Deciduous, upright tree. **H** 20ft (6m), **S** 12ft (4m). Bears double, pink flowers, in late spring, followed by rounded, yellow crab apples in fall. Has oval, dark green leaves. Z4–8 H8–1.

M. 'Veitch's Scarlet', illus. p.89.

M. yunnanensis* var. *veitchii, illus. p.86.

M. x zumi* var. *calocarpa. Deciduous, spreading tree. **H** 9m (28ft), **S** 8m (25ft). Dark green leaves are sometimes deeply lobed. White flowers in late spring are followed by dense clusters of long-lasting, rounded, red crab apples in fall. Z4–8 H8–1. **'Golden Hornet'.** See *M.* 'Golden Hornet'.

MALVA
Mallow

MALVACEAE

Genus of annuals, biennials and free-flowering, short-lived perennials. Requires sun and fertile, well-drained soil. Propagate species by seed in fall, selected forms by cuttings from firm, basal shoots in late spring or summer. These shoots may be encouraged by cutting plant back after first flowers have faded.

M. moschata, illus. p.232.

Malvastrum capensis. See *Anisodontea capensis.*

M

MALVAVISCUS
MALVACEAE

Genus of evergreen shrubs and trees, grown for their flowers. Requires full light and fertile, well-drained soil. Water container plants freely in growing season, moderately at other times. To maintain shape, flowered stems may be cut back hard in late winter. Propagate by seed in spring or by semiripe cuttings in summer. Whitefly and red spider mite may be troublesome.

M. arboreus (Wax mallow). Vigorous, evergreen, rounded shrub. **H** to 12ft (4m) or more, **S** 5–10ft (1.5–3m). Ovate to heart-shaped, toothed, bright green leaves are soft-haired. Has bright red flowers, with protruding stamens, in summer–fall. Z14–15 H12–6.

MAMMILLARIA
CACTACEAE

Genus of hemispherical, spherical or columnar cacti, grown for their rings of funnel-shaped flowers that develop near crowns. Flowers, offsets and long, slender to spherical seed pods grow between tubercles on a spiny, green stem with extended areoles. Requires full sun and very well-drained soil. Keep completely dry in winter, otherwise plants rot easily. Propagate by seed in spring or summer.

M. bocasana, illus. p.480.
M. candida. See *Mammilloydia candida.*
M. centricirrha. See *M. magnimamma.*
M. conoidea. See *Neolloydia conoidea.*
M. crinita. See *M. zeilmanniana.*
M. densispina. Slow-growing, spherical, perennial cactus. **H** 4in (10cm), **S** 8in (20cm). Has green stem densely covered with sturdy, golden spines and, in spring, yellow flowers, $^1/_2$–$^3/_4$in (1–2cm) wide. Z12–15 H12–10.
M. elegans of gardens. See *M. haageana.*
M. elongata, illus. p.494.
M. geminispina, illus. p.480.
M. gracilis. See *M. vetula* subsp. *gracilis.*
M. haageana, syn. *M. elegans.* Spherical to columnar, perennial cactus. **H** 12in (30cm), **S** 8in (20cm). Bears green stem densely covered with short, bristly spines and bright red flowers, $^1/_2$ in (1cm) across, in spring. Offsets occasionally. Z12–15 H12–10.
M. hahniana, illus. p.479.
M. magnimamma, syn. *M. centricirrha.* Clump-forming, perennial cactus. **H** 1ft (30cm), **S** 2ft (60cm). Green stem has very pronounced, angular, dark green tubercles with white spines of variable length. Bears cream, pink or red flowers, $^1/_2$–$^3/_4$in (1–2cm) wide, in spring and possibly again in late summer. Z12–15 H12–10.
M. microhelia, illus. p.491.
M. plumosa, illus. p.483.
M. prolifera (Strawberry cactus). Clump-forming, perennial cactus. **H** 4in (10cm), **S** 12in (30cm). Green stem bears dense, golden-yellow to white spines. Produces masses of cream or yellow flowers, $^1/_2$–$^3/_4$in (1–2cm) wide, in summer, followed by edible red berries that taste like strawberries. Z12–15 H12–10.
M. rhodantha. Spherical to columnar, perennial cactus. **H** and **S** 2ft (60cm). Green stem, branching from crown with age, is densely covered with brown to yellow

spines, often curved. In late summer produces bright red flowers, $^1/_2$–$^3/_4$in (1–2cm) across. Z12–15 H12–10.
M. schiedeana. Clump-forming, perennial cactus. **H** 4in (10cm), **S** 12in (30cm). Green stem is covered with short, feathery, yellow spines that turn white. Produces cream flowers, $^3/_4$in (2cm) long, and narrow, red seed pods in late summer. Z13–15 H12–10.
M. sempervivi, illus. p.484.
M. vetula subsp. gracilis, syn. *M. gracilis.* Clump-forming, perennial cactus. **H** 2in (5cm), **S** 8in (20cm). Produces columnar, green stem densely covered with pure white spines. In early summer produces pale cream flowers, $^1/_2$–$^3/_4$in (1–2cm) across. Stem is shallow-rooted and reroots readily. Z12–15 H12–10.
M. zeilmanniana, syn. *M. crinita,* illus. p.486.

MAMMILLOYDIA
CATACEAE

Genus of a single species of clump-forming cactus grown for ornamental spines and rings of small flowers. Grow in well-drained soil in full sun. Keep dry in winter. Propagate by seed sown in spring.
M. candida, syn. *Mammilloydia candida.* Slow-growing, clump-forming, perennial cactus. **H** and **S** 6in (15cm). Columnar, green stem is densely covered with short, stiff, white spines. Produces cream to rose flowers, $^1/_2$–$^3/_4$in (1–2cm) across, in spring. Water sparingly in summer.

MANDEVILLA
SYN. DIPLADENIA
APOCYNACEAE

Genus of evergreen, semievergreen or deciduous, woody-stemmed, twining climbers, grown for their large, trumpet-shaped flowers. Needs light shade in summer and well-drained soil. Water freely when in full growth, sparingly at other times. Provide support and thin out and spur back congested growth in early spring. Propagate by seed in spring or by semiripe cuttings in summer. Whitefly and red spider mite may cause problems.
① Contact with the sap may cause skin irritation, and all parts may cause mild stomach upset if ingested.
M. x amabilis 'Alice du Pont'. See *M. x amoena* 'Alice du Pont'.
M. x amoena 'Alice du Pont', syn. *M. x amabilis* 'Alice du Pont', illus. p.461.
M. boliviensis, syn. *Dipladenia boliviensis.* Vigorous, evergreen, woody-stemmed, twining climber. **H** to 12ft (4m). Oblong, pointed leaves are lustrous green. Has small clusters of large, trumpet-shaped, white flowers, with gold eyes, in summer. Z13–15 H12–1.
M. laxa, syn. *M. suaveolens, M. tweediana* (Chilean jasmine). Fast-growing, deciduous or semievergreen, woody-stemmed, twining climber. **H** 15ft (5m) or more. Oval leaves have heart-shaped bases. Clusters of fragrant, white flowers are borne in summer. Z12–15 H12–1.
M. splendens, syn. *Dipladenia splendens,* illus. p.460.
M. suaveolens. See *M. laxa.*
M. tweediana. See *M. laxa.*

MANDRAGORA
Mandrake
SOLANACEAE

Genus of rosetted perennials with large, deep, fleshy roots. Needs sun or partial shade and deep, rich, well-drained soil. Resents being transplanted. Propagate by seed in fall. ① Alkaloids in the plant may be harmful if ingested.
M. officinarum, illus. p.356.

MANETTIA
RUBIACEAE

Genus of evergreen, soft- or semiwoody-stemmed, twining climbers, grown for their small but showy flowers. Needs partial shade in summer and rich, well-drained soil. Water regularly, sparingly when temperatures are low. Stems need support. Cut back if required in spring. Propagate by softwood or semiripe cuttings in summer. Whitefly is sometimes a problem.
M. bicolor. See *M. luteorubra.*
M. cordifolia (Firecracker vine). Fast-growing, evergreen, soft-stemmed, twining climber. **H** 6ft (2m) or more. Has narrowly heart-shaped, glossy leaves. Funnel-shaped, red flowers, sometimes yellow flushed on lobes, are produced in small clusters in summer. Z12–15 H12–10.
M. inflata. See *M. luteorubra.*
M. luteorubra, syn. *M. bicolor, M. inflata* (Brazilian firecracker). Fast-growing, evergreen, semiwoody-stemmed, twining climber. **H** 6ft (2m). Has glossy leaves and small, funnel-shaped, red flowers, with yellow tips, in spring–summer. Z12–15 H12–10.

Manfreda maculosa. See *Agave maculosa.*

MANGLIETIA
MAGNOLIACEAE

Genus of evergreen trees, grown for their foliage and flowers. Needs full light or partial shade and rich, moist but well-drained, acidic soil. Water container plants freely when in full growth, less at other times. Pruning is tolerated if necessary. Propagate by seed in spring.
M. insignis, syn. *Magnolia insignis.* Evergreen, broadly conical tree. **H** 25–40ft (8–12m) or more, **S** 10–15ft (3–5m) or more. Leaves are narrowly oval, lustrous, dark green above, bluish-green beneath. In early summer produces solitary, magnolia-like, pink to carmine flowers that are cream-flushed. Z11 H12–10.

MARANTA
MARANTACEAE

Genus of evergreen perennials, grown for their distinctively patterned, colored foliage. Needs constant, high humidity, a shaded position away from drafts or wind and rich, well-drained soil. Propagate by division in spring or summer or by stem cuttings in summer.
M. leuconeura (Prayer plant). Z14–15 H12–1. **'Erythroneura',** syn. *M. leuconeura* 'Erythrophylla' illus. p.475.

'Erythrophylla'. See *M. leuconeura* 'Erythroneura'. **'Kerchoveana',** illus. p.475. **'Massangeana'** is an evergreen, short-stemmed perennial, branching at base. **H** and **S** 1ft (30cm). Each oblong, velvety, dark green leaf, 6in (15cm) long, has a wide, irregular, pale midrib, white, lateral veins and is often purplish-green below. Leaves stand upright at night but lie flat during the day. Bears small, 3-petaled, white to mauve flowers in slender, upright spikes year-round.

Marginatocereus marginatus. See *Pachycereus marginatus.*

MARGYRICARPUS
ROSACEAE

Genus of evergreen shrubs, grown for their fruits. Is good for rock gardens. Needs a sheltered, sunny position and well-drained soil. Propagate by softwood cuttings in early summer or by seed in fall.
M. pinnatus, syn. *M. setosus* (Pearl fruit). Evergreen, prostrate shrub. **H** 9–12in (23–30cm), **S** 3ft (1m). Has dark green leaves divided into linear, silky leaflets. Has tiny, inconspicuous, green flowers, in early summer, followed by small, globose, glossy, white fruits. Z8–10 H10–8.
M. setosus. See *M. pinnatus.*

Marsdenia erecta. See *Cionura erecta.*

MARTYNIA
PEDALIACEAE

Genus of annuals, grown for their flowers and horned fruits. Requires a sunny, sheltered site and fertile, well-drained soil. Propagate by seed sown under glass in early spring.
M. annua, illus. p.300.
M. louisianica. See *Proboscidea louisianica.*

MASDEVALLIA
ORCHIDACEAE

See also ORCHIDS.
M. coccinea, illus. p.466. Evergreen, epiphytic orchid for a cool greenhouse. **H** 6in (15cm). Narrowly oval leaves are 4in (10cm) long. Bears rich cerise flowers, 3in (8cm) long, in summer. Needs shade in summer. H11–6.
M. infracta. Evergreen, epiphytic orchid for a cool greenhouse. **H** 6in (15cm). Narrowly oval leaves are 4in (10cm) long. Bears rounded, red-and-white flowers, 2in (5cm) long, with tail-like, greenish sepals, in summer. Needs shade from hot summer sun. Z14–15 H12–6.
M. tovarensis, illus. p.466. Evergreen, epiphytic orchid for a cool greenhouse. **H** 6in (15cm). Has oval leaves, 4in (10cm) long, and in fall milky-white flowers, 1$^1/_2$in (4cm) long, with short-tailed sepals, singly or up to 3 to a stem. Needs shade in summer. H11–6.
M. wagneriana, illus. p.467. Evergreen, epiphytic orchid for a cool greenhouse. **H** 3in (8cm). Narrowly oval leaves are 4in (10cm) long. Bears pale yellow flowers, 1$^1/_2$in (4cm)) long, with long, tail-like sepals, singly or in pairs in summer. Needs summer shade. Z14–15 H12–6.

M

MATHIASELLA
APIACEAE/UMBELLIFERAE

Genus of one species of perennial, grown for its umbels of bell-shaped, green flowers and silvery-blue leaves. Needs sun and well-drained soil. Needs good winter drainage.

M. bupleuroides **'Green Dream'**, illus. p.242.

MATTEUCCIA
DRYOPTERIDACEAE/ONOCLEACEAE

Genus of deciduous, rhizomatous ferns. Prefers partial shade and wet soil. Remove faded fronds regularly and divide plants when crowded. Propagate by division in fall or winter.

M. orientalis. Deciduous, rhizomatous fern. **H** and **S** to 3ft (1m). Produces "shuttlecock" of sterile, arching, broadly ovate, divided fronds, to 32in (80cm) long, light green when young, becoming darker. Fertile, erect, blackish-green fronds are produced from center of plant in summer. Z3–8 H8–1.

M. struthiopteris, illus. p.443.

MATTHIOLA
Stock
CRUCIFERAE/BRASSICACEAE

Genus of annuals, biennials, perennials and evergreen subshrubs. Flowers of most annual or biennial stocks are highly scented and excellent for cutting. Needs sun or partial shade and fertile, well-drained, ideally lime-rich soil. Tall cultivars may need support. If grown as biennials outdoors, provide cloche protection in winter. To produce flowers outdoors the same summer, sow seed of annuals under glass in early spring, or outdoors in mid-spring. Sow seed of perennials under glass in spring. Propagate subshrubs by semiripe cuttings in summer. Is prone to aphids, flea beetle, club root, downy mildew and botrytis.

M. **Brompton Group.** Fast-growing, erect, bushy biennial, grown as an annual. **H** 18in (45cm), **S** 12in (30cm). Lance-shaped leaves are grayish-green; long spikes of highly scented flowers, in shades of pink, red, purple, yellow or white, are borne in summer. Z8–9 H9–1.

M. **East Lothian Group.** Group of fast-growing, upright, bushy biennials and short-lived perennials, grown as annuals. **H** and **S** 1ft (30cm). Has lance-shaped, grayish-green leaves and, in summer, spikes, 6in (15cm) or more long, of scented, 4-petaled, single or double flowers, in shades of pink, red, purple, yellow or white. Z8–9 H9–1.

M. **'Giant Excelsior'**, illus. p.303.
M. **'Giant Imperial'.** Fast-growing, erect, bushy biennial, grown as an annual. **H** to 24in (60cm), **S** 12in (30cm). Has lance-shaped, grayish-green leaves and long spikes of highly scented, white to creamy-yellow flowers in summer. Z8–9 H9–1.

M. incana (Stock). Fast-growing, upright, bushy biennial or short-lived perennial, grown as an annual. **H** 1–2ft (30–60cm), **S** 1ft (30cm). Has lance-shaped, grayish-green leaves and, in summer, scented, 4-petaled, light purple flowers borne in spikes, 3–6in (7–15cm) long. Z5–8 H8–5.

M. **'Mammoth Column'.** Fast-growing, upright, bushy biennial or short-lived perennial, grown as an annual. **H** to 2½ft (75cm), **S** 1ft (30cm). Has lance-shaped, grayish-green leaves and, in summer, scented, 4-petaled flowers, available in mixed or single colors, in spikes 12–15in (30–38cm) long. Is excellent for cut flowers. Z8–9 H9–1.

M. **Park Series.** Group of fast-growing, upright, bushy biennials and short-lived perennials, grown as annuals. **H** and **S** to 1ft (30cm). Lance-shaped leaves are grayish-green. In summer, spikes, 6in (15cm) or more long, of scented, 4-petaled flowers are borne in a wide range of colors. Z8–9 H9–1.

M. **Ten-week Group.** Group of fast-growing, upright, bushy biennials and short-lived perennials, grown as annuals. **H** and **S** to 1ft (30cm). Has lance-shaped, grayish-green leaves. Scented, 4-petaled flowers, in spikes 6in (15cm) or more long, are produced in a wide range of colors in summer. Dwarf and "selectable" cultivars have double flowers. Z8–9 H9–1.

M. **'Trysomic'.** Fast-growing, upright, bushy biennial or short-lived perennial, grown as an annual. **H** and **S** to 1ft (30cm). Lance-shaped leaves are grayish-green. Spikes, 6in (15cm) or more long, of scented, mostly double flowers are produced in a wide range of colors in summer. Z8–9 H9–1.

MATUCANA
CACTACEAE

Genus of low-growing, spherical to shortly cylindrical, solitary to clustering perennial cacti, with thick, ribbed stems, often with some spines, usually branching from the base. Solitary, narrowly funnel-shaped yellow, orange or red flowers are produced around the stem tips in summer. Needs full sun and very well-drained, slightly alkaline soil. Propagate by seed in spring or summer.

M. aurantiaca, syn. *Oreocereus aurantiacus.* Spherical, perennial cactus. **H** 5in (12cm), **S** 16in (40cm). Has 15–17-ribbed stem and elongated areoles each bearing up to 30 spines. Produces orange-yellow flowers in summer.

M. haynei. Slow-growing, spherical to columnar, perennial cactus. **H** 24in (60cm), **S** 4in (10cm). Has cylindrical, much-ribbed, grass-green stem densely covered with short, white or yellow spines. Produces red, orange-brown or purple-crimson flowers in summer on plants more than 6in (15cm) high.

MAURANDYA
SCROPHULARIACEAE/PLANTAGINACEAE

Genus of twining, woody-based, perennial climbers, suitable for growing against a wall or for clothing a trellis. Needs full sun and moderately fertile, moist but well-drained soil. Propagate by seed in spring or by softwood cuttings in late spring.

M. barclayana, syn. *Asarina barclayana.* Evergreen, soft-stemmed, scandent climber, herbaceous in cold climates. **H** to 6ft (2m). Has angular, heart-shaped, hairless leaves. Trumpet-shaped, white, pink or purple flowers, each with a green or whitish throat, 2½–3in (6–7cm) long, are produced in summer–fall. Z9–10 H10–9.

M. erubescens. See *Lophospermum erubescens.*

Maxillaria picta. See *Brasiliorchis picta.*
Maxillaria porphyrostele. See *Brasiliorchis porphyrostele.*
Maxillaria tenuifolia. See *Maxillariella tenuifolia.*

MAXILLARIELLA
ORCHIDACEAE

See also ORCHIDS.

M. tenuifolia, syn. *Maxillaria tenuifolia.* Evergreen, epiphytic orchid for a cool greenhouse. **H** 6in (15cm). Fragrant, yellow flowers, 1in (2.5cm) across, heavily overlaid with red and with white lips, are borne singly throughout summer. Has narrowly oval leaves, 6in (15cm) long. Needs good light in summer. Z14–15 H12–6.

MAYTENUS
CELASTRACEAE

Genus of evergreen trees, grown for their neat foliage. Requires sun or partial shade and fertile, well-drained soil. Propagate by semiripe cuttings in summer or by suckers in fall or spring.

M. boaria, syn. *M. chilensis* (Mayten). Evergreen, bushy-headed tree. **H** 30ft (10m), **S** 25ft (8m). Bears narrowly oval, glossy, dark green leaves on slender shoots, and tiny, star-shaped, green flowers in late spring. Z9–10 H10–9.

M. chilensis. See *M. boaria.*

MAZUS
SCROPHULARIACEAE/PHRYMACEAE

Genus of creeping, spring-flowering perennials. Is useful for rock gardens and in paving. Needs a sheltered, sunny site and moist soil. Propagate by division in spring or by seed in fall.

M. reptans, illus. p.351.

MECONOPSIS
PAPAVERACEAE

Genus of perennials, some long-lived, some short-lived and others monocarpic (die after flowering), grown for their flowers. Needs partial shade and, in warm areas, a cool position. Most prefer rich, moist, neutral to acidic soil. *M. baileyi* and *M.* Infertile Blue Group 'Crewdson Hybrid' tolerate more alkaline soil. Propagate sterile perennial hybrids and perennial species by division in late summer or early spring, fertile species and hybrids (that set viable seed) by seed in late summer or winter. Division of perennial species and cultivars is advisable every 3 years.

M. baileyi, syn. *M. betonicifolia* (Blue poppy). Clump-forming perennial. **H** 3–4ft (1–1.2m), **S** 1½ft (45cm). Bears clusters of cup-shaped, blue flowers in late spring and early summer. Oblong, hairy, mid-green leaves, with heart-shaped bases, are produced in basal rosettes and in decreasing size up flowering stems. Z7–8 H8–5. **'Alba'** (illus. p.218), **H** 4–5ft (1.2–1.5m), **S** 1½–2ft (45–60cm), has pure white flowers in early summer.

M. betonicifolia of gardens. See *M. baileyi.*

M. cambrica, illus. p.263.
M. x cookei **'Old Rose'**, illus. p.218. Clump forming, long-lived perennial. **H** 18in (45cm), **S** 12in (30cm). Produces numerous pendent, cup-shaped, deep pink flowers in late spring and early summer. Has basal rosettes of oval–oblong, bristly, mid-green leaves. Does not produce viable seed.

M. **Fertile Blue Group 'Lingholm'**, illus. p.218. Clump-forming perennial. **H** 4–5ft (1.2–1.5m), **S** 1½–2ft (45–60cm). In early summer bears clusters of shallow cup-shaped, sky-blue flowers. Has rosettes of oblong to oval–lance-shaped, slightly toothed, hairy, mid-green leaves. Divide every 3 years to maintain vigor.

M. grandis, illus. p.218.
M. **Infertile Blue Group 'Crewdson Hybrid'**, illus. p.218. Clump forming, long-lived perennial. **H** 3–4ft (1–1.2m), **S** 1½–2ft (45–60cm). In early summer bears clusters of funnel- to cup-shaped, clear deep blue flowers. Has rosettes of oblong, hairy, mid-green leaves, with brownish tinge and scalloped edges. **'Slieve Donard'**, illus. p.218. Clump-forming, long-lived perennial. **H** 4–5ft (1.2–1.5m), **S** 1½–2ft (45–60cm). In early summer bears clusters of shallow cup-shaped, sky-blue flowers. Has rosettes of oblong to oval, hairy, mid-green leaves, with marginal teeth absent or very few and tiny. Fertile seed is not produced. Z7–8 H8–7.

M. integrifolia (Yellow Chinese poppy). Rosette-forming biennial or short-lived perennial. **H** 18–24in (45–60cm), **S** 24in (60cm). Produces spikes of large, cup-shaped, pale yellow flowers in late spring and early summer. Has large, oval–oblong, hairy, pale green leaves. Z7–8 H8–7.

M. **'Jimmy Bayne' (George Sherriff Group)**, illus. p.218. Rhizomatous, long-lived perennial. **H** 4–5ft (1.2–1.5m), **S** 1½–2ft (45–60cm). In early summer bears clusters of shallowly bowl-shaped flowers, deep blue or with a purplish tinge. Has rosettes of oval–lance-shaped, hairy, mid-green leaves edged with rounded teeth.

M. **'Marit'**, illus. p.218. Clump forming, long-lived perennial. **H** 4–5ft (1.2–1.5m), **S** 1½–2ft (45–60cm)). In early summer bears clusters of cup-shaped, white to pale creamy-white flowers. Has rosettes of oblong to lance-shaped, hairy, mid-green leaves with regular and neatly toothed edges. Divide every 3 years to maintain vigor. Seed is not produced.

M. napaulensis of gardens (Satin poppy), illus. p.218. Clump-forming, short-lived perennial that dies after flowering. **H** 5ft (1.5m), **S** 2ft (60cm). Produces racemes of nodding, shallowly cup-shaped, yellow, pink, red or white flowers in late spring or early summer. Bears large rosettes of oblong to lance-shaped, deeply lobed and cut, hairy, yellowish-green leaves. Z8–9 H9–8.

M. quintuplinervia (Harebell poppy). Mat-forming perennial. **H** 12–18in (30–45cm), **S** 12in (30cm). Cup-shaped, nodding, lavender-blue flowers, deepening to purple at bases, are borne singly on hairy stems in late spring and early summer above dense mat of large, oblong to lance-shaped, mid-green leaves. Seed is notoriously difficult to germinate. Z7–8 H8–7.

MEDICAGO

Alfafa, Medick

LEGUMINOSAE/PAPILIONACEAE

Genus of annuals, perennials and evergreen shrubs, grown for their flowers. Is good in mild, coastal areas as is very wind-resistant. Requires sun and well-drained soil. Cut out dead wood in spring. Propagate shrubs by semiripe or softwood cuttings in summer or by seed in fall or spring, annuals and perennials by seed in fall or spring.

M. arborea. Evergreen, bushy, dense shrub. **H** and **S** 6ft (2m). Bears clusters of small, pealike, yellow flowers from mid-spring to late fall or winter, followed by curious, flattened, snail-like, green, then brown seed pods. Dark green leaves, divided into 3 narrowly triangular leaflets, are silky-haired when young. Z7–9 H9–7.

MEDINILLA

MELASTOMATACEAE

Genus of evergreen shrubs and scrambling climbers, grown for their flowers and foliage. Needs partial shade and rich, well-drained soil. Water container plants freely when in full growth, moderately at other times. Propagate by greenwood cuttings in spring or summer.

M. magnifica, illus. p.455.

MEEHANIA

LABIATAE/LAMIACEAE

Genus of perennials often with creeping stems, grown mainly as groundcover. Prefers full or partial shade and well-drained but not dry, rich soil. Propagate by seed, division or stem cuttings in spring.

M. urticifolia. Trailing, hairy perennial with long, creeping, leafy stems and erect flowering stems. **H** to 1ft (30cm), **S** indefinite. Oval to triangular, toothed leaves, 4in (10cm) or more long, are on creeping stems—smaller on flowering stems. Whorls of fragrant, 2-lipped, purplish-blue flowers, to 2in (5cm) long, are borne in erect spikes in late spring. Z5–8 H8–5.

Megasea. See *Bergenia.*

MELALEUCA

MYRTACEAE

Genus of evergreen, spring- and summer-flowering trees and shrubs, grown for their flowers and overall appearance. Needs full light and well-drained soil, preferably without much nitrogen. Some species tolerate waterlogged soils. Water container specimens moderately, less in low temperatures. Propagate by seed in spring or by semiripe cuttings in summer.

M. armillaris (Bracelet honey myrtle). Evergreen, rounded, wiry-stemmed shrub or tree. **H** 10–20ft (3–6m), **S** 4–10ft (1.2–3m). Has needlelike, deep green leaves and, in summer, dense, bottlebrush-like clusters, 1¼–2½in (3–6cm) long, each flower consisting of a small brush of white stamens. Z12–15 H12–10.

M. elliptica, illus. p.137.

M. hypericifolia. Evergreen, rounded shrub. **H** and **S** 6–15ft (2–5m). Leaves are oblong to elliptic and mid- to deep green above, paler beneath. Small, red flowers, with crimson stamens, ¾–1in (2–2.5cm)

long, are produced in summer, mainly in bottlebrush-like spikes, 1½–3in (4–8cm) long. Z12–15 H12–10.

M. nesophila, syn. *M. nesophylla,* illus. p.133.

M. nesophylla. See *M. nesophila.*

M. quinquenervia. See *M. viridiflora* var. *rubriflora.*

M. squarrosa (Scented paper-bark). Evergreen, erect, wiry-stemmed shrub or tree. **H** 10–20ft (3–6m), **S** 6–12ft (2–4m). Has tiny, oval, deep green leaves. Bears spikes, 1½in (4cm) long, of scented flowers, with cream stamens, in late spring and summer.

M. viridiflora var. **rubriflora,** syn. *M. quinquenervia* (Paper-bark tree). Strong-growing, evergreen, rounded tree. **H** 20–40ft (6–12m), **S** 10–20ft (3–6m). Leaves are elliptic and lustrous. Has peeling, papery, tan-colored bark and, in spring, small, white or creamy-pink flowers in bottlebrush-like clusters. Tolerates waterlogged soil. Z12–15 H12–10.

MELASPHAERULA

IRIDACEAE

Genus of one species of spring-flowering corm, grown mainly for botanical interest. Needs sun and well-drained soil. Plant in fall and keep watered until after flowering, then dry off. Propagate by seed or offsets in fall.

M. graminea. See *M. ramosa.*

M. ramosa, syn. *M. graminea.* Spring-flowering corm. **H** to 24in (60cm), **S** 4–6in (10–15cm). Has narrowly sword-shaped, semi-erect leaves in basal fan. Wiry, branched stem bears loose sprays of small, pendent, funnel-shaped, yellowish-green flowers, with pointed petals.

MELASTOMA

MELASTOMATACEAE

Genus of evergreen, mainly summer-flowering shrubs and trees, grown for their flowers and foliage. Requires full light or partial shade and fertile, well-drained soil. Water container specimens freely when in full growth, moderately at other times. Pruning is tolerated in late winter, if necessary. Propagate by softwood or greenwood cuttings in spring or summer. Red spider mite and whitefly may cause problems.

M. candidum. Evergreen, rounded, bristly-stemmed shrub. **H** and **S** 3–6ft (1–2m). Bears oval, leathery, bristly leaves. Small, terminal clusters of fragrant, 5–7-petaled, white or pink flowers are produced profusely in summer. Z9–10 H10–9.

MELIA

MELIACEAE

Genus of deciduous, spring-flowering trees, grown for their foliage, flowers and fruits. Is useful for very dry soil and does well in coastal gardens in mild areas. Requires full sun and well-drained soil. Propagate by seed in fall.

M. azedarach, illus. p.71.

MELIANTHUS

MELIANTHACEAE

Genus of evergreen perennials and shrubs, grown mainly for their foliage. Requires sun and fertile, well-drained soil. Water

container specimens freely in summer, moderately at other times. Long stems may be shortened in early spring. Propagate by seed in spring or by greenwood cuttings in summer. Red spider mite may be troublesome.

M. major, illus. p.145.

MELICA

GRAMINEAE/POACEAE

See also GRASSES, BAMBOOS, RUSHES and SEDGES,.

M. altissima (Siberian melick). Evergreen, tuft-forming, perennial grass. **H** 24in (60cm), **S** 8in (20cm). Slender stems bear broad, mid-green leaves, rough beneath. In summer produces pendent, tawny spikelets in narrow panicles. Z5–8 H8–5. **'Atropurpurea'** illus. p.286.

MELICYTUS

SYN. HYMENANTHERA

VIOLACEAE

Genus of evergreen shrubs and trees, grown for their overall appearance and ornamental fruits. Requires sun or partial shade and well-drained soil. Water container plants moderately, less in winter. Pruning is tolerated, if required. Propagate by seed when ripe, in fall, or in spring.

M. crassifolius, syn. *Hymenanthera crassifolia.* Evergreen, densely twiggy shrub of irregular outline. **H** and **S** to 4ft (1.2m). Bears narrowly oval to oblong, leathery, mid-green leaves. Tiny, bell-shaped, 5-petaled, yellow flowers, in spring–summer, are followed by egg-shaped, purple fruits. Z9–10 H10–9.

M. ramiflorus (Mahoe, Whiteywood). Evergreen, spreading shrub or tree. **H** and **S** 20–30ft (6–10m). Bark is gray-white. Bears lance-shaped, bluntly toothed, bright green leaves. Small, rounded, greenish flowers are produced in axillary clusters in summer, followed by tiny, violet to purple-blue berries. Z5–8 H8–5.

MELINIS

GRAMINEAE/POACEAE

see also GRASSES, BAMBOOS, RUSHES AND SEDGES.

M. repens, syn. *Rhynchelytrum repens, Rhynchelytrum roseum.* Tuft-forming, annual or short-lived, perennial grass. **H** 4–6ft (1.2–2m), **S** 2–3ft (60cm–1m). Leaves are mid-green, flat and finely pointed. Produces loose panicles of awned, pink spikelets in summer. Z9–10 H10–9.

MELIOSMA

MELIOSMACEAE/SABIACEAE

Genus of deciduous trees and shrubs, grown for their habit, foliage and flowers, which, however, do not appear reliably. Prefers full sun and deep, fertile, well-drained soil. Propagate by seed in fall.

M. oldhamii. See *M. pinnata* var. *oldhamii.*

M. pinnata var. **oldhamii,** syn. *M. oldhamii.* Deciduous, sturdy-branched tree, upright when young, spreading when mature. **H** 30ft (10m), **S** 20ft (6m). Has very large, dark green leaves divided into 5–13 oval leaflets. Bears large clusters of small, fragrant, star-shaped, white flowers in early summer. Z9–10 H10–9.

M. veitchiorum, illus. p.74.

MELITTIS

Bastard balm

LABIATAE/LAMIACEAE

Genus of one species of summer-flowering perennial. Prefers partial shade and requires fertile, well-drained soil. Propagate by seed in fall or by division in spring or fall.

M. melissophyllum, illus. p.264.

MELOCACTUS

Turk's cap cactus

CACTACEAE

Genus of spherical, ribbed, perennial cacti. On reaching flowering size, usually 6in (15cm) high, stems produce woolly crowns; then stems appear to stop growing while woolly crowns develop into columns. Has funnel-shaped flowers in summer, followed by elongated or rounded, red, pink or white seed pods. Requires full sun and extremely well-drained soil. Propagate by seed in spring or summer.

M. actinacanthus. See *M. matanzanus.*

M. bahiensis. Spherical, perennial cactus. **H** and **S** 6in (15cm). Dull green stem bears 10–15 ribs. Produces sturdy, slightly curved, dark brown spines that become paler with age. Crown bears brown bristles and pink flowers, ½–¾in (1–2cm) across, in summer. Z14–15 H12–10.

M. communis. See *M. intortus.*

M. curvispinus, syn. *M. oaxacensis.* Spherical to columnar, perennial cactus. **H** 8in (20cm), **S** 6in (15cm). Green stem has 15 rounded ribs. Areoles each bear a straight central spine and curved radial spines. Flat, woolly crown bears deep pink flowers, ½in (1cm) across, in summer. Z14–15 H12–10.

M. intortus, syn. *M. communis,* illus. p.494.

M. matanzanus, syn. *M. actinacanthus.* Spherical, perennial cactus. **H** and **S** 4in (10cm). Dark green stem has short spines and develops a woolly crown about 5 years from seed. In summer produces pink flowers, ½in (1cm) across. Z14–15 H12–10.

M. oaxacensis. See *M. curvispinus.*

MENISPERMUM

Moonseed

MENISPERMACEAE

Genus of deciduous, woody or semiwoody, twining climbers, grown for their fruits that each contain a crescent-shaped seed—hence the common name. Separate male and female plants are required in order to obtain fruits. Needs sun and well-drained soil. Propagate by seed or suckers in spring. ① The fruits may cause severe discomfort if ingested.

M. canadense (Canada moonseed, Yellow parilla). Vigorous, deciduous, woody-stemmed, twining climber spreading by underground suckers. **H** to 15ft (5m). Produces dense tangle of stems. Oval to heart-shaped, rounded leaves are usually 3–7-lobed. Has small, cup-shaped, greenish-yellow flowers in summer, followed by poisonous, spherical, glossy, blackish fruits. Z5–8 H8–5.

M

MENTHA
Mint

LABIATAE/LAMIACEAE

Genus of perennials, some of which are semievergreen, grown for their aromatic foliage, which is both decorative and used as a culinary herb. Plants are invasive, however, and should be used with caution. Needs sun or partial shade and well-drained soil. Propagate by division in spring or fall.

M. corsica. See *M. requienii*.

M. x gentilis 'Variegata'. See *M. x gracilis* 'Variegata'. Z6–9 H9–6.

M. x gracilis 'Variegata', syn. *M. x gentilis* 'Variegata' (Ginger mint, Red mint). Spreading perennial. **H** 18in (45cm), **S** 24in (60cm). Forms a mat of oval, dark green leaves that are speckled and striped with yellow, most conspicuously in full sun. Produces stems that carry whorls of small, 2-lipped, pale mauve flowers in summer.

M. x piperita f. citrata (Eau de Cologne mint, Lemon mint). Vigorous, spreading perennial. **H** 12–24in (30–60cm), **S** 24in (60cm). Reddish-green stems, bearing terminal spikes of small, 2-lipped, purple flowers in summer, arise from a carpet of oval, slightly toothed, mid-green leaves that have a scent which is similar to *eau de Cologne*. Z3–7 H7–1.

M. requienii, syn. *M. corsica* (Corsican mint). Semievergreen, mat-forming, creeping perennial. **H** to ½in (1cm), **S** indefinite. Rounded, bright apple-green leaves exude strong peppermint fragrance when crushed. Produces tiny, stemless, lavender-purple flowers in summer. Is suitable for a rock garden. Needs shade and moist soil. Z6–9 H9–6.

M. rotundifolia of gardens. See *M. suaveolens*. Z6–9 H9–5.

M. suaveolens, syn. *M. rotundifolia* (Apple mint). **'Variegata',** illus. p.274.

MENTZELIA
Starflower

LOASACEAE

Genus of annuals, perennials and evergreen shrubs. Requires sun and fertile, very well-drained soil. Tender species are best grown in pots under glass. Propagate by seed in spring, shrubs also by semiripe cuttings in summer.

M. lindleyi, syn. *Bartonia aurea* (Blazing star). Fairly fast-growing, bushy annual. **H** 18in (45cm), **S** 8in (20cm). Has fleshy stems and lance-shaped, toothed leaves. In summer has fragrant, cup-shaped, deep yellow flowers, with conspicuous stamens. H9–1.

MENYANTHES

MENYANTHACEAE

Genus of deciduous, perennial, marginal water plants, grown for their foliage and flowers. Prefers an open, sunny position. Remove fading flower heads and foliage, and divide overcrowded clumps in spring. Propagate by stem cuttings in spring.

M. trifoliata, illus. p.434.

MENZIESIA

ERICACEAE

Genus of deciduous shrubs, grown for their small, urn-shaped flowers. Needs partial shade and fertile, moist, peaty,

acidic soil. Propagate by softwood cuttings in summer or by seed in fall.

M. ciliicalyx var. lasiophylla. See *M. ciliicalyx* var. *purpurea*. **var. purpurea,** syn. *M. ciliicalyx* var. *lasiophylla*, illus. p.146.

MERENDERA

COLCHICACEAE

Genus of corms similar to *Colchicum* but with less showy flowers. Needs sun and well-drained soil. In cool, damp areas, grow in an unheated greenhouse or frame where corms can dry out in summer. Plant in fall and keep watered through winter and spring. Propagate by seed or offsets in fall.

M. bulbocodium. See *M. montana*.

M. montana, syn. *M. bulbocodium*. Fall-flowering corm. **H** to 2in (5cm), **S** 2–3in (5–8cm). Has narrowly strap-shaped, semierect, basal leaves, produced just after upright, broad-petaled, funnel-shaped, rose- or purple-lilac flowers emerge. Z6–9 H9–6.

M. robusta. Spring-flowering corm. **H** 3in (8cm), **S** 2–3in (5–8cm). Narrowly lance-shaped, semi-erect, basal leaves are produced at same time as upright, funnel-shaped, pale purplish-pink or white flowers, 2–2½in (5–6cm) wide, with narrow petals. Z7–9 H9–7.

MERREMIA

CONVOLVULACEAE

Genus of evergreen, twining climbers, grown for their flowers and fruits. Prefers full light and fertile, well-drained soil. Water moderately when in full growth, much less at other times. Provide support. Thin out congested stems in spring. Propagate by seed in spring. Red spider mite may be a problem.

M. tuberosa, syn. *Ipomoea tuberosa*, *Operculina tuberosa* (Spanish morning glory). Fast-growing, evergreen, twining climber. **H** 20ft (6m) or more. Leaves have 7 radiating lobes. In summer bears funnel-shaped, yellow flowers, followed by semiwoody, globose, ivory-brown fruits. Z13–15 H12–10.

MERTENSIA

BORAGINACEAE

Genus of perennials, grown for their funnel-shaped flowers. Requires sun or partial shade and deep, well-drained soil. Propagate by division in spring or by seed in fall.

M. echioides. Clump-forming perennial. **H** 6–9in (15–23cm), **S** 6in (15cm). Has basal rosettes of long, oval, hairy, blue-green leaves. Slender stems bear many open funnel-shaped, dark blue flowers in summer. Z6–9 H9–6.

M. maritima, illus. p.356.

M. pulmonarioides. See *M. virginica*.

M. virginica, syn. *M. pulmonarioides*, illus. p.261.

MERWILLA

HYACINTHACEAE/LILIACEAE

Genus of 3 bulbs grown for their spikes of blue flowers in summer. Grows in well-drained soil in full sun or semi-shade. Propagate by division when dormant or by seed in fall.

M. plumbea, syn. *Scilla natalensis*. Clump-forming summer-flowering bulb **H** 12–18in (30–45cm) **S** 6–8in (15–20cm). Has lance-shaped, semierect, finely hairy basal leaves with a long spike of up to 100 flatish blue flowers, each one 5/8–3/4in (1.5–2cm) across. Z9–10 H10–9.

MERYTA

ARALIACEAE

Genus of evergreen trees, grown for their foliage. Requires full light or partial shade and rich, moist but moderately drained soil. Water container plants freely when in full growth, less at other times. Propagate by semiripe cuttings in summer or by seed when ripe, in late summer.

M. sinclairii, illus. p.451.

Mesembryanthemum cordifolium. See *Aptenia cordifolia*.

Mesembryanthemum criniflorum. See *Dorotheanthus bellidiformis*.

Mesembryanthemum multiradiatum. See *Lampranthus roseus*.

MESPILUS

ROSACEAE

Genus of one species of deciduous tree or shrub, grown for its habit, flowers, foliage and edible fruits. Requires sun or partial shade and fertile, well-drained soil. Propagate species by seed in fall, named forms (for fruit) by budding in late summer.

M. germanica, illus. p.80.

METASEQUOIA

TAXODIACEAE/CUPRESSACEAE

See also CONIFERS.

M. glyptostroboides, illus. p.96.

METROSIDEROS
Pohutakawa, Rata

MYRTACEAE

Genus of evergreen, winter-flowering shrubs, trees and scrambling climbers, grown for their flowers, the trees also for their overall appearance and for shade. Needs full light and fertile, well-drained soil. Water container specimens freely when in full growth, moderately at other times. Pruning is tolerated, if necessary. Propagate by seed in spring or by semiripe cuttings in summer.

M. excelsa, syn. *M. tomentosa*, illus. p.450.

M. robusta (New Zealand Christmas tree, Northern rata). Robust, evergreen, rounded tree. **H** 70–80ft (20–25m) or more, **S** 30–50ft (10–15m). Oblong to elliptic, leathery leaves are dark green and lustrous. Has large clusters of flowers, which are mostly composed of long, dark red stamens, in winter.

M. tomentosa. See *M. excelsa*.

MEUM

UMBELLIFERAE/APIACEAE

Genus of summer-flowering perennials, grown for their aromatic leaves. Is useful on banks and in wild gardens. Needs sun and well-drained soil. Propagate by seed when fresh, in fall.

M. athamanticum (Baldmoney, Spignel). Upright, clump-forming perennial.

H 6–18in (15–45cm), **S** 4–6in (10–15cm). Mainly basal and deeply dissected leaves have narrowly linear leaflets. In summer produces flattish flower heads consisting of clusters of tiny, white or purplish-white flowers. Z10–15 H12–10.

MICHELIA

MAGNOLIACEAE

Genus of evergreen, winter- to summer-flowering shrubs and trees, grown for their flowers and foliage. Needs full light or partial shade and rich, well-drained, neutral to acidic soil. Water container specimens freely when in full growth, less in winter. Pruning is seldom necessary. Propagate by semiripe cuttings in summer or by seed when ripe, in fall, or in spring.

M. doltsopa, syn. *Magnolia doltsopa*, illus. p.71.

M. figo, syn. *Magnolia figo* (Banana shrub). Evergreen tree or rounded shrub. **H** 10–20ft (3–6m), **S** 11ft (1.5–3.5m) Has oval, glossy, rich green leaves and banana-scented, maroon-edged, creamy-yellow flowers in spring–summer. Z12–15 H12–10.

MICROBIOTA

CUPRESSACEAE

See also CONIFERS.

M. decussata, illus. p.105. Spreading, shrubby conifer. **H** 20in (50cm), **S** 6–10ft (2–3m). Flat sprays of scalelike, yellow-green leaves turn bronze in winter. Globose, yellow-brown cones have only one seed. Z3–7 H7–1.

Microglossa albescens. See *Aster albescens*.

MICROLEPIA

DENNSTAEDTIACEAE

Genus of deciduous, semievergreen or evergreen ferns, best grown in pans and hanging baskets. Requires full or partial shade and moist soil. Remove faded fronds regularly. Propagate by division in spring or by spores in summer.

M. speluncae, illus. p.478.

MICROMERIA

LABIATAE/LAMIACEAE

Genus of evergreen or semievergreen shrubs, subshrubs and perennials, suitable for rock gardens and banks. Needs sun and well-drained soil. Propagate by seed in spring or by softwood cuttings in early summer.

M. juliana. Evergreen or semievergreen, bushy shrub or subshrub. **H** and **S** 12in (30cm). Produces small, oval, aromatic, green leaves pressed close to stems. In summer, minute, tubular, bright deep pink flowers are borne in whorls on upper parts of stems. Z7–10 H10–7.

MIKANIA

COMPOSITAE/ASTERACEAE

Genus of evergreen or herbaceous, scrambling or twining climbers, shrubs and erect perennials, grown for their foliage and flower heads. Needs partial shade and fertile, well-drained soil. Water

M

regularly when in full growth, less at other times. Stem support is needed. Thin out congested growth in spring. Propagate by semiripe or softwood cuttings in summer. Aphids may be a problem.
M. scandens (Hemp vine). Herbaceous, twining climber. **H** 10–15ft (3–5m). Oval to triangular, mid-green leaves have 2 basal lobes. Tiny, groundsel-like, pink to purple flower heads are produced in compact clusters in summer–fall. Z12–15 H12–10.

MILIUM
GRAMINEAE/POACEAE

See also GRASSES, BAMBOOS, RUSHES and SEDGES.

M. effusum (Wood millet). Z6–9 H9–6. **'Aureum'** is an evergreen, tuft-forming, perennial grass. **H** 3ft (1m), **S** 1ft (30cm). Has flat, golden-yellow leaves. Produces open, tiered panicles of greenish-yellow spikelets in summer. Self-seeds readily in a shady site.

MILLA
LILIACEAE/ALLIACEAE

Genus of summer-flowering bulbs, grown for their fragrant flowers, each comprising a slender tube with 6 spreading, star-shaped petals at the tip. Needs a sheltered, sunny position and well-drained soil. Plant in spring. After flowering, lift bulbs and partially dry off for winter. Propagate by seed or offsets in spring.
M. biflora. Summer-flowering bulb. **H** 12–18in (30–45cm), **S** 3–4in (8–10cm). Has long, narrow, semi-erect, basal leaves. Stem bears loose head of 2–6 erect, white flowers, 1¼–2½in (3–6cm) across, each on a slender stalk to 8in (20cm) long. Z9–10 H10–9.

MILTONIA
ORCHIDACEAE

See also ORCHIDS.
M. candida. Evergreen, epiphytic orchid for a cool or intermediate greenhouse. **H** 8in (20cm). Cream-lipped, green-patterned, brown flowers, 2in (5cm) across, are borne in spikes in fall. Has narrowly oval leaves, 4–5in (10–12cm) long. Needs partial shade in summer. Z14–15 H12–6.
M. clowesii. Evergreen, epiphytic orchid for an intermediate greenhouse. **H** 8in (20cm). In early summer produces large spikes of yellow flowers, 1½in (4cm) wide, barred with reddish-brown and with white-and-mauve lips. Has broadly oval leaves, 12in (30cm) long. Needs partial shade in summer. Z14–15 H12–6.

MILTONIOPSIS
Pansy orchid
ORCHIDACEAE

See also ORCHIDS.
M. Anjou gx 'St. Patrick', illus. p.467. Evergreen, epiphytic orchid for a cool greenhouse. **H** 6in (15cm). Has sprays of deep crimson flowers, 4in (10cm) across, with red and yellow patterns on each lip, mainly in summer. Narrowly oval, soft leaves are 4–5in (10–12cm) long. Needs shade in summer. H11–6.
M. Robert Strauss gx 'Ardingly', illus. p.466. Evergreen, epiphytic orchid for a

cool greenhouse. **H** 6in (15cm). Bears sprays of white flowers, 4in (10cm) across, marked reddish-brown and purple; flowering season varies. Narrowly oval, soft leaves are 4–5in (10–12cm) long. Requires shade in summer. H11–6.

MIMOSA
LEGUMINOSAE/MIMOSACEAE

Genus of annuals, evergreen perennials, shrubs, trees and scrambling climbers, grown for their flowers and foliage. *M. pudica* is usually grown as an annual. Needs partial shade and fertile, well-drained soil. Water container specimens freely when in full growth, moderately at other times. Propagate by seed in spring, shrubs also by semiripe cuttings in summer. Red spider mite may be a nuisance.
M. pudica, illus. p.457.

MIMULUS
Monkey musk
SCROPHULARIACEAE/PHRYMACEAE

Genus of annuals, perennials and evergreen shrubs. Small species are suitable for damp pockets in rock gardens. Most prefer full sun and wet or moist soil; some such as *M. aurantiacus* need a dry site. Propagate perennials by division in spring, subshrubs by softwood cuttings in late summer, annuals and all species by seed in fall or early spring.
M. 'Andean Nymph'. See *M. naiandinus*.
M. aurantiacus, syn. *M. glutinosus, Diplacus glutinosus,* illus. p.162.
M. cupreus 'Whitecroft Scarlet'. Short-lived, spreading perennial. **H** 8–12in (20–30cm), **S** 12in (30cm). Bears snapdragon-like, scarlet flowers freely from early to late summer. Has oval, toothed, mid-green leaves. Z8–9 H9–8.
M. glutinosus. See *M. aurantiacus*.
M. guttatus, syn. *M. langsdorffii* (Common large monkey flower). Spreading, mat-forming perennial. **H** and **S** 24in (60cm). Snapdragon-like, bright yellow flowers, spotted with reddish-brown on lower lobes, are borne in succession in summer and early fall. Oval, mid-green leaves are coarsely or sometimes deeply toothed. Z6–9 H9–6.
M. x hybridus, illus. p.445.
M. langsdorffii. See *M. guttatus*.
M. lewisii. Upright perennial. **H** 24in (60cm), **S** 18in (45cm). Has downy, sticky, gray leaves that provide an excellent foil for snapdragon-like, deep rose-pink flowers borne singly in summer. Z5–8 H8–5.
M. luteus (Monkey musk, Yellow monkey flower). Spreading perennial. **H** and **S** 12in (30cm). Throughout summer, snapdragon-like, occasionally red-spotted, yellow flowers are freely produced above hairy, mid-green leaves. Z7–9 H9–7.
M. Magic Series. Early-flowering perennial. **H** 6–8in (15–20cm). In summer produces small, snapdragon-like flowers, ranging from bright orange, yellow, and red to more usual pastel shades and bicolors. Z9–10 H10–9. **'Magic Yellow Blotch'** illus. p.322.
M. moschatus (Musk). Deciduous, prostrate, perennial, bog plant. **H** 4in (10cm), **S** 6in (15cm). Has oval, hairy, pale green leaves. Small, pale yellow flowers,

lightly speckled with brown, are borne in late summer. Z7–10 H10–7.
M. naiandinus, syn. *M. 'Andean Nymph',* illus. p.264.
M. ringens, illus. p.441.
M. 'Royal Velvet'. Compact perennial, often grown as an annual. **H** 12in (30cm), **S** 9in (23cm). Leaves are mid-green. Produces many large, snapdragon-like, mahogany-red flowers, with mahogany-speckled, gold throats, throughout summer. Z6–9 H9–6.

Mina. See *Ipomoea*.

MIRABILIS
NYCTAGINACEAE

Genus of summer-flowering annuals and tuberous perennials. Prefers a sheltered, sunny position and fertile, well-drained soil. Lift tubers and store over winter in frost-free conditions. Propagate by seed or division of tubers in early spring.
M. jalapa, illus. p.233.

MISCANTHUS
GRAMINEAE/POACEAE

See also GRASSES, BAMBOOS, RUSHES and SEDGES.
M. sacchariflorus (Silver banner grass). Vigorous, herbaceous, slow-spreading, rhizomatous, perennial grass. **H** 10ft (3m), **S** indefinite. Hairless, mid-green leaves last into winter, often turning bronze. Produces open, branched panicles of hairy, purplish-brown spikelets in summer. Z8–9 H9–8.
M. sinensis (Eulalia grass, Japanese silver grass). **var. condensatus** 'Cosmopolitan' illus. p.285. **'Flamingo'** illus. p.286. **'Gracillimus'** illus. p.286. **'Yakushima Dwarf'** illus. p.285. **'Zebrinus'** illus. p.284.

MITCHELLA
Partridgeberry
RUBIACEAE

Genus of evergreen, trailing subshrubs, grown for their foliage and fruits. Makes excellent groundcover, especially in woodlands, although is sometimes difficult to establish. Prefers partial shade and rich, neutral to acidic soil. Propagate by division of rooted runners in spring or by seed in fall.
M. repens (Partridgeberry). Evergreen, trailing, mat-forming subshrub. **H** 2in (5cm), **S** indefinite. Bears small, oval, white-striped, green leaves with heart-shaped bases. In early summer has pairs of tiny, fragrant, tubular, white flowers, sometimes purple-tinged, followed by spherical, bright red fruits. Is suitable for a rock garden or peat bed. Z4–9 H9–1.

MITELLA
Bishop's cap, Miterwort
SAXIFRAGACEAE

Genus of clump-forming, summer-flowering, slender-stemmed, rhizomatous perennials. Requires partial shade and rich, moist soil. Propagate by division in spring or by seed in fall.
M. breweri, illus. p.371.

MITRARIA
GESNERIACEAE

Genus of one species of evergreen, woody-stemmed, scrambling climber. Requires partial shade and peaty, acidic soil. Propagate by seed in spring or by stem cuttings in summer.
M. coccinea, illus. p.193.

MOLINIA
GRAMINEAE/POACEAE

See also GRASSES, BAMBOOS, RUSHES and SEDGES.
M. altissima. See *M. caerulea* subsp. *arundinacea.*
M. caerulea (Purple moor grass). Z5–9 H9–1. **subsp. arundinacea,** syn. *M. altissima* is a tuft-forming, herbaceous, perennial grass. **H** 8ft (2.5m), **S** 2ft (60cm). Has broad, flat, gray-green leaves and spreading panicles of purple spikelets on stiff, erect stems in summer. Needs a dry, sunny position and acidic soil. **subsp. arundinacea 'Transparent',** illus. p.286. **subsp. caerulea 'Heidebraut',** illus. p.285. **subsp. caerulea 'Variegata'** (Variegated purple moor grass), **H** 2ft (60cm), has yellow-striped, mid-green leaves and, in late summer, panicles of purplish spikelets.

MOLTKIA
BORAGINACEAE

Genus of deciduous, semievergreen or evergreen subshrubs and perennials, grown for their funnel-shaped flowers in summer. Prefers sun and well-drained, neutral to acidic soil. Propagate by semiripe cuttings in summer or by seed in fall.
M. x intermedia. Evergreen, open, dome-shaped subshrub. **H** 12in (30cm), **S** 20in (50cm). Stems are clothed in narrowly linear, dark green leaves. Masses of loose spikes of small, open funnel-shaped, bright blue flowers are borne in summer. Z7–9 H9–7.
M. petraea. Semievergreen, bushy shrub. **H** 12in (30cm), **S** 24in (60cm). Fully hardy. Has long, narrow, hairy leaves. Clusters of pinkish-purple buds open into funnel-shaped, violet-blue flowers in summer. Z7–9 H9–7.
M. suffruticosa, illus. p.342.

MOLUCCELLA
LABIATAE/LAMIACEAE

Genus of annuals and perennials, grown for their flowers, which may be dried successfully. Needs sun and rich, very well-drained soil. Propagate by seed sown under glass in spring, or outdoors in late spring.
M. laevis, illus. p.316.

MONARDA
Bee balm
LABIATAE/LAMIACEAE

Genus of annuals and perennials, grown for their aromatic foliage as well as their flowers. Requires sun and moist soil. Propagate species and cultivars by division in spring, species only by seed in spring.
M. 'Adam'. Clump-forming perennial. **H** 30in (75cm), **S** 18in (45cm). Bears dense whorls of 2-lipped, cerise flowers throughout summer. Oval, usually toothed, mid-green leaves are aromatic and hairy. Z4–9 H9–1.

M

635

M. **'Cambridge Scarlet'**, illus. p.235.
M. **'Croftway Pink'**, illus. p.233.
M. fistulosa, illus. p.239.
M. **'Prairie Night'**. See *M.* 'Prärienacht'.
M. **'Prärienacht'**, syn. *M.* 'Prairie Night'. Clump-forming perennial. **H** 4ft (1.2m), **S** 1^1/$_2$ft (45cm). Produces dense whorls of 2-lipped, rich violet-purple flowers from mid- to late summer. Oval, toothed leaves are mid-green. Z4–9 H9–1.
M. spathacea. See *Moraea spathulata*.

MONSTERA

ARACEAE

Genus of evergreen, woody-stemmed, root climbers, grown for their large leaves. Bears insignificant, creamy-white flowers with hooded spathes intermittently. Needs partial shade and rich, well-drained soil. Water moderately, less when temperatures are low. Provide support. If necessary, shorten long stems in spring. Propagate by leaf-bud or stem-tip cuttings in summer. ① All parts except the fruit may cause mild stomach upset when ingested, and contact with the fruit may irritate skin.
M. acuminata (Shingle plant). Evergreen, woody-stemmed, root climber with robust stems. **H** 10ft (3m) or more. Has lopsided, oval, pointed, rich green leaves with heart-shaped base, sometimes cleft into a few large lobes, to 10in (25cm) long. Z14–15 H12–10.
M. deliciosa, illus. p.463.

MORAEA

IRIDACEAE

Genus of corms, grown for their short-lived, iris-like flowers. Divides into two groups: winter- and summer-growing species. Winter-growing species need full sun and well-drained soil; keep dry in summer during dormancy and start into growth by watering in fall. Summer-growers are dormant in winter; grow in a sheltered, sunny site and well-drained soil. Propagate winter growers by seed in fall, summer growers by seed in spring.
M. huttonii, illus. p.393.
M. polystachya. Winter-growing corm. **H** to 12in (30cm), **S** 2–3in (5–8cm). Bears long, narrow, semi-erect, basal leaves. Stem has a succession of erect, flattish, blue or lilac flowers, 3in (8cm) wide, in winter–spring. Outer petals each have central, yellow mark. Z9–10 H10–9.
M. ramosissima. Late spring- to early summer-flowering corm. **H** 20–48in (50–120cm), **S** 4in (10cm). Has numerous, semierect, narrowly linear, channeled, basal leaves. Bears yellow flowers, with deeper yellow marks on inner petals, on many-branched stems. Z11–13 H12–6.
M. sisyrinchium, syn. *Gynandiris sisyrinchium,* illus. p.419.
M. spathulata, syn. *Monarda spathacea.* Summer-flowering corm. **H** to 3ft (1m), **S** 4–6in (10–15cm). Has solitary, long, narrow, semi-erect, basal leaf. Tough flower stem bears a succession of up to 5 upward-facing, yellow flowers, 2–3in (5–7cm) wide, with reflexed, outer petals, in summer. Z8–10 H10–8.

MORINA

MORINACEAE/CAPRIFOLIACEAE

Genus of evergreen perennials, only one species of which is in general cultivation: this is grown for its thistle-like foliage and its flowers. Protect from drying spring winds. Needs full sun and well-drained, preferably sandy soil. Propagate by division directly after flowering or by seed when fresh, in late summer.
M. longifolia, illus. p.231.

MORISIA

CRUCIFERAE/BRASSICACEAE

Genus of one species of rosetted perennial with a long taproot. Is good for rock gardens and alpine houses. Needs sun and gritty, well-drained soil. Propagate by seed in fall or by root cuttings in winter.
M. hypogaea. See *M. monanthos*.
M. monanthos, syn. *M. hypogaea,* illus. p.358.

MORUS

Mulberry

MORACEAE

Genus of deciduous trees, grown for their foliage and edible fruits. Tiny flowers are produced in spring. Requires full sun and fertile, well-drained soil. Propagate by softwood cuttings in summer or by seed in fall.
M. alba (White mulberry). Z4–8 H8–1. **'Laciniata'** illus. p.88. **'Pendula'** is a deciduous, weeping tree. **H** 10ft (3m), **S** 15ft (5m). Rounded, sometimes lobed, glossy, deep green leaves turn yellow in fall. Edible, oval, fleshy, pink, red or purple fruits ripen in summer.
M. nigra (Black mulberry). Deciduous, round-headed tree. **H** 40ft (12m), **S** 50ft (15m). Heart-shaped, dark green leaves turn yellow in fall. Bears edible, oval, succulent, dark purplish-red fruits in late summer or early fall. Z5–9 H9–5.

MUCUNA

LEGUMINOSAE/PAPILIONACEAE

Genus of vigorous, evergreen, twining climbers, grown for their large, pealike flowers. Needs partial shade and rich, moist but well-drained soil. Water freely when in full growth, less at other times. Needs plenty of space to climb; provide support. Thin out crowded stems in spring. Propagate by seed in spring or by layering in late summer. Whitefly and red spider mite may cause problems.
M. bennettii (New Guinea creeper). Fast-growing, evergreen, twining climber. **H** 50–80ft (15–25m). Leaves are divided into 3 oval leaflets. In summer has pendent clusters of pealike, orange-scarlet flowers. Z5–9 H9–5.
M. deeringiana. See *M. pruriens* var. *utilis*.
M. pruriens var. utilis, syn. *M. deeringiana.* Vigorous, evergreen, twining climber. **H** 50ft (15m) or more. Has pealike, both green- and red-purple flowers in long, pendent clusters in summer–fall. Leaves, divided into 3 oval leaflets, are used for fodder and green manure. May be short-lived. Z14–15 H12–10.

MUEHLENBECKIA

POLYGONACEAE

Genus of deciduous or evergreen, slender-stemmed, summer-flowering shrubs and woody-stemmed, scrambling climbers, grown for their foliage. Needs sun or partial shade and well-drained soil. Propagate by semiripe cuttings in summer.
M. axillaris of gardens. See *M. complexa*.
M. complexa, syn. *M. axillaris* of gardens. (Maidenhair vine). Deciduous, mound-forming shrub or twining climber. **H** 2–3ft (60cm–1m), **S** 3ft (1m). Slender, wiry stems bear variably shaped (oval to fiddle-shaped), dark green leaves. Tiny, star-shaped, greenish-white flowers, in mid-summer, are followed by small, spherical, waxy, white fruits. Z8–10 H10–8.

Mulgedium. See *Cicerbita*.

MURRAYA

RUTACEAE

Genus of evergreen trees and shrubs, grown for their overall appearance. Requires full light or partial shade and rich, well-drained soil. Water container plants freely when in full growth, moderately at other times. Pruning is tolerated in late winter, if necessary. Propagate by seed in spring or by semiripe cuttings in summer. Whitefly may be troublesome.
M. exotica. See *M. paniculata*.
M. paniculata, syn. *M. exotica* (Orange jasmine). Evergreen, rounded shrub or tree. **H** and **S** 6–12ft (2–4m). Pungently aromatic, edible, glossy, rich green leaves are divided into 9 or more oval leaflets. Fragrant, 5-petaled, white flowers, in terminal clusters year-round, are followed by tiny, egg-shaped, red fruits. Z9–11 H12–9.

MUSA

Banana

MUSACEAE

Genus of evergreen, palmlike, suckering perennials, with false stems formed from overlapping leaf sheaths, grown for their foliage, flowers and fruits (bananas), not all of which are edible. Needs sun or partial shade and rich, well-drained soil. Propagate by division year-round, by offsets in summer or by suckers after flowering.
M. arnoldiana. See *Ensete ventricosum*.
M. basjoo, syn. *M. japonica,* illus. p.219.
M. coccinea, syn. *M. uranoscopus* of garden (Scarlet banana). Evergreen, palmlike perennial. **H** to 3ft (1m), **S** 5ft (1.5m). Bears oblong to oval, dark green leaves, to 3ft (1m) long, that are paler below. In summer produces erect spirals of tubular, yellow flowers, enclosed in red bracts, followed by banana-like, orange-yellow fruits, 2in (5cm) long. Z11–12 H12–5.
M. ensete. See *Ensete ventricosum*.
M. japonica. See *M. basjoo*.
M. ornata, illus. p.470.
M. uranoscopus of gardens. See *M. coccinea*.

MUSCARI

Grape hyacinth

HYACINTHACEAE/LILIACEAE.

Genus of spring-flowering bulbs, each with a cluster of narrowly strap-shaped, basal leaves, usually appearing in spring just before flowers. Leafless flower stems bear dense spikes of small flowers, most of which have constricted mouths. Needs sun and fairly well-drained soil. Plant in fall. Propagate by division in late summer or by seed in fall.
M. armeniacum, illus. p.420. **'Blue Spike'** is a spring-flowering bulb. **H** 6–8in (15–20cm), **S** 3–4in (8–10cm). Produces 3–6 long, narrow, semi-erect, basal leaves. Bears dense spikes of fragrant, bell-shaped, deep blue flowers; constricted mouths have rims of paler blue or white "teeth".
M. aucheri, syn. *M. lingulatum,* illus. p.420.
M. azureum, syn. *Pseudomuscari azureum, Hyacinthus azureus.* Spring-flowering bulb. **H** 4–6in (10–15cm), **S** 2–3in (5–8cm). Bears 2 or 3 narrow, semi-erect, grayish-green, basal leaves, slightly wider towards tips. Produces very dense spike of bell-shaped, pale clear blue flowers; mouths have small "teeth" with central, dark blue stripes. May self-seed freely. Z5–9 H9–1.
M. botryoides (Common grape hyacinth). Spring-flowering bulb. **H** 6–8in (15–20cm), **S** 2–3in (5–8cm). Bears 2–4 narrow, semierect, basal leaves that widen slightly at tips. Each minute, nearly spherical, bright blue flower has a constricted mouth and white-toothed rim. Z2–8 H8–1. **'Album'** illus. p.415.
M. comosum, syn. *Leopoldia comosa* (Tassel grape hyacinth). Late spring-flowering bulb. **H** 8–12in (20–30cm), **S** 4–5in (10–12cm). Has up to 5 strap-shaped, semierect, gray-green, basal leaves. Bears loose spike of bell-shaped, fertile, brownish-yellow flowers, with tuft of threadlike, sterile, purplish-blue flowers at tip. Z4–8 H8–1. **'Monstrosum'.** See *M. comosum* 'Plumosum'. **'Plumosum'**, syn. *M. comosum* 'Monstrosum' illus. p.419.
M. latifolium, illus. p.403.
M. lingulatum. See *M. aucheri*.
M. macrocarpum, illus. p.421.
M. neglectum, syn. *M. racemosum,* illus. p.420.
M. pycnantha. See *Bellevalia pycnantha*.
M. racemosum. See *M. neglectum*.

MUSSAENDA

RUBIACEAE

Genus of evergreen shrubs and scrambling climbers, grown for their flowers. Requires full light and fertile, well-drained soil. Water freely when in full growth, less at other times. Provide support and thin out crowded stems in spring. Propagate by seed in spring or by air-layering in summer. Whitefly and red spider mite may cause problems.
M. erythrophylla. Moderately vigorous, evergreen, scrambling climber. **H** 20–30ft (6–10m). Has broadly oval, bright green leaves and flowers in summer–fall. Each flower has greatly enlarged, oval, bract-like, red sepal, a red tube and yellow petal lobes. Z11 H12–7.

M

MUTISIA

COMPOSITAE/ASTERACEAE

Genus of evergreen, tendril climbers, grown for their long-lasting flower heads. Plant with roots in shade and leafy parts in sun, in well-drained soil. Propagate by seed in spring, by stem cuttings in summer or by layering in fall.

M. decurrens, illus. p.208.
M. oligodon. Evergreen, tendril climber. **H** to 5ft (1.5m). Oblong, glossy, green leaves, 1–1$\frac{1}{2}$in (2.5–3.5cm) long, have sharply toothed margins. In summer–fall produces long-stalked, daisylike, pink flower heads, with yellow centers. Grow against a low wall or through a shrub. Z9–10 H10–9.

MYOPORUM

MYOPORACEAE/SCROPHULARIACEAE

Genus of evergreen shrubs and trees, grown for their overall appearance and as hedges and windbreaks. Prefers full light and well-drained soil; will tolerate poor soil. Water container specimens moderately. Propagate by seed when ripe or in spring or by semiripe cuttings in late summer.

M. laetum (Ngaio). Evergreen, rounded to upright shrub or tree. **H** 10–30ft (3–10m), **S** 6–15ft (2–5m). Has fleshy, oval, lustrous, bright green leaves. Axillary clusters of small, bell-shaped, white flowers, dotted with purple, in spring–summer, are followed by tiny, narrowly ovoid, pale to deep red-purple fruits. Z11–15 H12–10.
M. parvifolium, illus. p.454.

MYOSOTIDIUM

BORAGINACEAE

Genus of one species of evergreen perennial that is suitable for mild, coastal areas. Prefers partial shade and moist soil. Seaweed is often recommended as a mulch. Is not easy to cultivate, and once established should not be disturbed. Propagate by division in spring or by seed when ripe, in summer or fall.

M. hortensia, syn. *Myosotidium nobile*, illus. p.271.

Myosotidium nobile. See *Myosotidium hortensia.*

MYOSOTIS

Forget-me-not

BORAGINACEAE

Genus of annuals, biennials and perennials, grown for their flowers. Most species are good for rock gardens and screes; *M. scorpioides* is best grown as a marginal water plant. Most prefer sun or partial shade and fertile, well-drained soil. Propagate by seed in fall.

M. alpestris, syn. *M. rupicola*, illus. p.356.
M. australis. Short-lived, tuft-forming perennial. **H** 5in (12cm), **S** 3in (8cm). Has oval, rough-textured leaves and, in summer, tight sprays of open funnel-shaped, yellow or white flowers. Is good for a scree. Z4–8 H8–1.
M. caespitosa. See *M. laxa* subsp. *caespitosa.*
M. laxa subsp. *caespitosa*, syn. *M. caespitosa.* Clump-forming annual

or short-lived perennial. **H** 5in (12cm), **S** 6in (15cm). Lance-shaped, leathery leaves are dark green. Bears rounded, bright blue flowers in summer. Z4–8 H8–1.
M. palustris. See *M. scorpioides.*
M. rupicola. See *M. alpestris.*
M. scorpioides, syn. *M. palustris* (Water forget-me-not). Z5–9 H9–5. **'Mermaid'** illus. p.441.
M. Sylva Series, illus. p.313.
M. sylvatica **'White Ball'** is a slow-growing, short-lived, bushy, compact perennial, grown as a biennial. **H** to 8in (20cm), **S** 6in (15cm). Leaves are lance-shaped. Sprays of tiny, 5-lobed, pure white flowers are produced in early summer.

Myrceugenia apiculata. See *Luma apiculata.*

MYRICA

MYRICACEAE

Genus of deciduous and evergreen, usually suckering shrubs and trees, suitable as screening plants. *M. gale* is a useful bog garden plant. Requires full sun or partial shade and rich, moist soil. Propagate by layering in spring, by greenwood cuttings in summer or by seed as soon as ripe.
M. gale, illus. p.162.

MYRIOPHYLLUM

Milfoil

HALORAGACEAE

Genus of deciduous, perennial, submerged water plants, grown for their foliage. Most species are ideal as depositories for fish spawn. Requires full sun. Spreads widely; keep in check by removing excess growth as required. Propagate by stem cuttings in spring or summer.

M. aquaticum, syn. *M. proserpinacoides* (Diamond milfoil). Deciduous, perennial, partially or completely submerged water plant. **S** indefinite. Spreading, finely divided, blue-green leaves turn reddish in fall if they surface. Z6–11 H12–6.
M. hippuroides (Western milfoil). Deciduous, perennial, spreading, submerged water plant with thin stems. **S** indefinite. Produces dense mass of small, feathery, pale green leaves. Inconspicuous, greenish-cream flowers are borne from axils of emergent leaves in summer. Is suitable for a cold-water aquarium. Z9–11 H12–10.
M. proserpinacoides. See *M. aquaticum.*
M. verticillatum, illus. p.443.

MYRRHIS

Sweet Cicely

UMBELLIFERAE/APIACEAE

Genus of one species of summer-flowering perennial. Requires sun or partial shade and well-drained soil. Propagate by seed in fall or spring.
M. odorata, illus. p.230.

MYRSINE

MYRSINACEAE/PRIMULACEAE

Genus of evergreen shrubs and trees, with inconspicuous flowers, grown mainly for their foliage. Also bears decorative fruits, to obtain which plants of both sexes must be grown. Is suitable for rock

gardens. Needs sun or partial shade and any fertile, well-drained soil other than a shallow, chalky one. Propagate by semiripe cuttings in summer.

M. africana (African boxwood). Very slow-growing, evergreen, bushy, dense shrub. **H** and **S** 30in (75cm). Small, glossy, dark green leaves are aromatic and rounded. Tiny, yellowish-brown flowers in late spring are followed by spherical, pale blue fruits. Z9–10 H10–9.

MYRTILLOCACTUS

CACTACEAE

Genus of branching, perennial cacti, grown for their ribbed, spiny, blue-green stems. Bears star-shaped flowers that open at night. Needs sun and well-drained soil. Propagate by seed or stem cuttings in spring or summer.
M. geometrizans, illus. p.489.

MYRTUS

Myrtle

MYRTACEAE

Genus of evergreen shrubs, sometimes treelike, grown for their flowers, fruits and aromatic foliage. At limits of hardiness, plant against a south- or west-facing wall. Requires full sun and fertile, well-drained soil. May be pruned in spring. Propagate by semiripe cuttings in late summer.

M. apiculata. See *Luma apiculata.*
M. bullata. See *Lophomyrtus bullata.*
M. chequen. See *Luma chequen.*
M. communis, illus. p.122. **subsp. tarentina** (Dwarf myrtle) is an evergreen, bushy shrub. **H** and **S** 6ft (2m). Bears small leaves that are narrowly oval, glossy and dark green. Produces fragrant, saucer-shaped, white flowers, each with dense cluster of stamens, from mid-spring to early summer, followed by spherical, white fruits. Is very wind-resistant and good for hedging in a mild area. Z8–9 H9–8.
M. luma. See *Luma apiculata.*
M. ugni. See *Ugni molinae.*

N

NANDINA

BERBERIDACEAE

Genus of one species of evergreen or semievergreen, summer-flowering shrub, grown for its foliage and flowers. Prefers a sheltered, sunny site and fertile, well-drained but not too dry soil. On established plants, prune untidy, old stems to base in spring. Propagate by semiripe cuttings in summer.

N. domestica. Evergreen or semievergreen, upright shrub. **H** and **S** 6ft (2m). Leaves have narrowly lance-shaped, dark green leaflets, purplish-red when young and in fall–winter. Large panicles of small, star-shaped, white flowers, with large yellow anthers, in mid-summer are followed in warm climates by spherical, red fruits. Z6–11 H12–4. **'Fire Power'**, illus. p.143.

NARCISSUS

Daffodil

AMARYLLIDACEAE

Genus of bulbs, grown for their flowers. Daffodils have usually linear, basal leaves and a spread of up to 8in (20cm). Each flower has a trumpet or cup and petals (botanically known as perianth segments). Prefers sun or partial shade and well-drained soil, but Div.8 cultivars (see below) prefer a sunny site and tolerate lighter soils. Deadhead flowers and remove the faded foliage in mid-summer. Most cultivars increase naturally by offsets; dense clumps should be divided no sooner than 6 weeks after flowering every 3–5 years. Propagate species by seed when fresh, in late summer or fall. Narcissus yellow stripe virus, basal rot, slugs, large narcissus fly and bulb and stem eelworm may cause problems. ① Contact with the sap of daffodils may irritate skin or aggravate skin allergies. Horticulturally, *Narcissus* is split into the following divisions (see also feature panel pp.404–05).

Div.1 Trumpet—usually solitary flowers each have a trumpet that is as long as, or longer than, the petals. Early to late spring-flowering.

Div.2 Large cupped—solitary flowers each have a cup at least one-third the length of, but shorter than, the petals. Spring-flowering.

Div.3 Small-cupped—flowers are often borne singly; each has a cup not more than one-third the length of the petals. Spring- or early summer-flowering.

Div.4 Double—most have solitary, large, fully or semidouble flowers, sometimes scented, with both cup and petals or cup alone replaced by petaloid structures. Some have smaller flowers, produced in clusters of 4 or more, which are often sweetly fragrant. Spring- or early summer-flowering.

Div.5 Triandrus—nodding flowers, with short, sometimes straight-sided cups and narrow, reflexed petals, are borne 2–6 per stem. Flowers are produced in spring.

Div.6 Cyclamineus—flowers are borne usually 1 or 2 per stem, each with a cup sometimes flanged and often longer than those of Div.5. Petals are narrow, pointed and reflexed. Early to mid-spring-flowering.

Div.7 Jonquil and Apodanthus—sweetly scented flowers are borne usually 2 or more per stem. Cup is short, sometimes flanged; petals are often flat, fairly broad and rounded. Spring-flowering.

Div.8 Tazetta—sweetly fragrant flowers of small-flowered cultivars are borne in clusters of 12 or more per stem; large-flowered cultivars have 3 or 4 flowers per stem. All have a small, often straight-sided cup and broad, mostly pointed petals. Late fall- to mid-spring-flowering. Fall-flowering hybrids provide valuable cut flowers; "prepared" bulbs may be grown in pots for mid-winter flowering.

Div.9 Poeticus—flowers, sometimes borne 2 per stem, may be sweetly fragrant. Each has a small, colored cup and glistening white petals. Some *N. poeticus* hybrids are categorized as Div.3 or 8. Late spring- or early summer-flowering.

Div.10 Bulbocodium—flowers usually borne singly on very short stems, showing all the hallmarks of hoop-petticoat daffodils (*N. bulbocodium* subsp. *bulbocodium*), with insignificant petals and a disproportionately large, widely flaring cup. Winter- to spring-flowering.

Div.11 Split-corona—usually solitary flowers that have cups split for more than half their length. In (**a**), Collar daffodils, the overlapping segments of the cup lie against the petals, but in (**b**), Papillon daffodils, the segments of the cup tend to be narrower, with their tips arranged at the margin of the petals. Most flowers fall into category (a). Spring-flowering.

Div.12 Miscellaneous—a miscellaneous category containing hybrids with varying, intermediate flower shapes that cannot be satisfactorily classified elsewhere. Fall- to spring-flowering.

Div.13 Daffodils distinguished solely by botanical name—a wide variety of flowers showing the huge range of floral characteristics of wild daffodils, from the tiny *N. cyclamineus* and the sweetly scented, many-flowered *N. tazetta* to the stately trumpet species. Flower in early fall to early summer.

Narcissus generally grow well in Z3–9 H9–1.

***N.* 'Acropolis',** Div.4. Mid- to late spring-flowering bulb. **H** 17in (42cm). Large, double flowers have white, outer petals and petaloids; white, inner petals are interspersed with shorter, orange-red petaloids. Is suitable for exhibition. Z3–9 H9–1.

***N.* 'Actaea',** Div.9 (illus. p.404). Late spring-flowering bulb. **H** 16in (40cm). Fragrant flowers have glistening white petals and shallow, flanged, rich lemon cups with narrow, orange-red rims. Z3–9 H9–1.

***N.* 'Aircastle',** Div.3 (illus. p.405). Mid-spring-flowering bulb. **H** 16in (40cm). Flowers have white petals that age greenish; shallow, flat, lemon-yellow cups deepen in color at rim. Z3–9 H9–1.

***N.* 'Albus Plenus Odoratus'.** See *N. poeticus* 'Plenus'.

***N.* 'Altruist',** Div.3 (illus. p.405). Mid-spring-flowering bulb. **H** 18in (45cm). Flowers have smooth, pale orange petals and neat, ribbed, shallow, orange-red cup. Z3–9 H9–1.

***N.* 'Ambergate',** Div.2 (illus. p.405). Mid-spring-flowering bulb. **H** 18in (45cm). Flowers each have shallow, widely expanded, fiery scarlet cup and soft tangerine petals. Z3–9 H9–1.

***N.* 'Arctic Gold',** Div.1. Mid-spring-flowering bulb. **H** 16in (40cm). Rich golden-yellow flowers have broad petals and well-proportioned, flanged trumpets with neatly serrated rims. Is suitable for exhibition. Z3–9 H9–1.

***N. assoanus*,** syn. *N. juncifolius*, *N. requienii* Div.13. Mid-spring-flowering bulb. **H** 6in (15cm). Is similar to *N. jonquilla*, but has thin, cylindrical leaves and rounded, bright clear yellow flowers with a sweet, slightly lemony fragrance. Thrives in sunny, gritty soil. Z3–9 H9–1.

***N. asturiensis*,** syn. *N. minimus* of gardens, Div.13. Late winter- or early spring-flowering bulb. **H** 3in (8cm). Small, pale yellow flowers have waisted trumpets and slender petals. Prefers full sun. Z3–9 H9–1.

***N.* 'Avalanche',** Div.8 (illus. p.405). Early spring-flowering bulb. **H** 14in (35cm). Produces 8 or more sweetly fragrant flowers, with white petals and primrose-yellow cup that scarcely fades. May be forced for mid-winter flowering. Z3–9 H9–1.

***N.* 'Avalon',** Div.2. Mid-spring-flowering bulb. **H** 14in (35cm). Rounded, bright lemon-yellow flowers have wide, fluted cups that become white with age.

***N.* 'Barrett Browning',** Div.3. Early to mid-spring-flowering bulb. **H** 16in (40cm). Flowers have pure white petals and short, frilled, orange-red cups.

***N.* 'Bartley',** Div.6 (illus. p.405). Early spring-flowering bulb. **H** 14in (35cm). Long, slender, golden flowers have reflexed petals and narrow, angled trumpets. Flowers are long-lasting. Z3–9 H9–1.

***N.* 'Belcanto',** Div.11a. Late spring-flowering bulb. **H** 18in (45cm). Flowers have rounded petals, almost obscured by flattened, pale yellow cups. Z3–9 H9–1.

***N.* x *biflorus*.** See *N.* x *medioluteus*.

***N.* 'Binkie',** Div.2 (illus. p.405). Early spring-flowering bulb. **H** 12in (30cm). Flowers open pale lemon and cups turn sulfur-white with ruffled, lemon rims. Z3–9 H9–1.

***N.* 'Birma',** Div.3. Mid-spring-flowering bulb. **H** 18in (45cm). Flowers have soft yellow petals and fiery orange cups with heavily ruffled rims. Z3–9 H9–1.

***N.* 'Bravoure',** Div.1. Early to mid-spring-flowering bulb. **H** 15in (38cm). Large flowers have overlapping, white petals and unusually slender, only slightly flared, lemon-yellow trumpets, with entire rims. Z3–9 H9–1.

***N.* 'Bridal Crown',** Div.4 (illus. p.404). Late spring-flowering bulb. **H** 16in (40cm). Long-lasting, small, sweetly scented flowers are semidouble, with rounded, milk-white petals and white petaloids interspersed with shorter, saffron-orange ones toward center. Z3–9 H9–1.

***N.* 'Broadway Star',** Div.11b (illus. p.404). Mid-spring-flowering bulb. **H** 16in (40cm). Has white flowers. Expanded segments of split cups are flattened against petals; each has narrow, orange mid-stripe running lengthwise. Z3–9 H9–1.

***N.* 'Brunswick',** Div.2. Early spring-flowering bulb. **H** 16in (40cm). Long-lasting flowers have white petals and long, flared, primrose cups, which fade to lemon, with darker rims. Foliage is bluish-green. Is suitable for cut flowers. Z3–9 H9–1.

N. bulbocodium (Hoop-petticoat daffodil) Div.13 (illus. p.405). Vigorous, spring-flowering bulb. **H** 3–6in (8–15cm). Flowers are golden-yellow with conical cups and narrow, pointed petals. Thrives in moist sod in full sun. Z3–9 H9–1. **var. *citrinus*,** **H** 6in (15cm), has slender, dark green leaves and clear pale lemon flowers. Hybrids of this species are in Div.10.

***N. campernelli*.** See *N.* x *odorus*.

***N.* 'Canaliculatus',** Div.8 (illus. p.404). Mid-spring-flowering bulb. **H** 9in (23cm). Each stem produces cluster of 4 or more small, fragrant flowers, with reflexed, white petals and shallow, straight-sided, yellow cup. Z6–10 H10–3.

***N.* 'Canisp',** Div.2. Robust, mid-spring-flowering bulb. **H** 16in (40cm). Bears large, milky-white flowers, with broad, overlapping petals, lightly reflexed at apex, and slightly darker, flanged, trumpet-like cup, with rolled, crenate mouth. Z3–9 H9–1.

***N.* 'Cantabile',** Div.9. Late spring-flowering bulb. **H** 10in (25cm). Stiff stems bear neat, well-rounded, glistening white flowers, with tiny, red-rimmed, yellow cups and prominent, green eyes. Z3–9 H9–1.

N. cantabricus (White hoop-petticoat daffodil) Div.13. Winter-flowering bulb. **H** 6–8in (15–20cm). Milky- or ice-white flowers have conical trumpets and tiny, pointed petals. Thrives in an alpine house or greenhouse. Z8–9 H9–8.

***N.* 'Cantatrice',** Div.1. Mid-spring-flowering bulb. **H** 16in (40cm). Flowers have pure white petals and slender, milky-white trumpets. Z3–9 H9–1.

***N.* 'Capax Plenus'.** See *N.* 'Eystettensis'.

***N.* 'Cassata',** Div.11a (illus. p.405). Mid-spring-flowering bulb. **H** 16in (40cm). Cups are soft primrose and distinctly split into segments with ruffled margins, while petals are broad and milky-white. Z3–9 H9–1.

***N.* 'Charity May'** Div.6 (illus. p.405). Early to mid-spring-flowering bulb. **H** 12in (30cm). Small, pale lemon flowers have broad, reflexed petals and slightly darker cups. Z3–9 H9–1.

***N.* 'Cheerfulness'** Div.4 (illus. p.404). Mid-spring-flowering bulb. **H** 16in (40cm). Long-lasting, small, sweetly scented, fully double flowers are borne several to a stem, with milky-white petals and petaloids interspersed with shorter, orange-yellow ones at center. Is excellent for cut flowers. Z3–9 H9–1.

***N.* 'Cool Crystal',** Div.3. Mid-spring-flowering bulb. **H** 20in (50cm). Has white flowers with bowl-shaped, green-eyed cups.

***N. cyclamineus*,** Div.13. Late winter- to early spring-flowering bulb. **H** 6in (15cm). Slender, nodding, clear gold flowers have narrow, reflexed petals and long, slender, flanged, waisted trumpets. Z3–9 H9–1.

***N.* 'Daydream',** Div.2. Mid-spring-flowering bulb. **H** 14in (35cm). Flowers have green-yellow petals and pale trumpets that fade to white as they age.

***N.* 'Diversity',** Div.11a. Free-flowering, mid-spring-flowering bulb. **H** 16in (40cm). Flowers have pure white petals and large, shallow bowl-shaped, pink-tinted cups. Is suitable for cut flowers.

***N.* 'Dove Wings',** Div.6 (illus. p.404). Mid-spring-flowering bulb. **H** 12in (30cm). Has small flowers with milky-white petals and fairly long, soft primrose cups. Z3–9 H9–1.

***N.* 'Dutch Delight',** Div.2. Vigorous, early- or mid-spring-flowering bulb. **H** 18in (45cm). Has large flowers with bright yellow petals and deep, orange-red trumpets.

***N.* 'Electrus',** Div.11a. Mid-spring-flowering bulb. **H** 16in (40cm). Bears large flowers with white petals and flattened, green-eyed, pink-orange cups.

***N.* 'Empress of Ireland',** Div.1 (illus. p.404). Mid-spring-flowering bulb. **H** 16in (40cm). Large, robust, milk-white flowers have broad, overlapping petals, reflexed at the apex, and a slightly darker, flanged trumpet with a rolled, crenate mouth. Z3–9 H9–1.

***N.* 'Eystettensis',** syn. *N.* 'Capax Plenus' (Queen Anne's double daffodil) Div.4. Mid-spring-flowering bulb. **H** 8in (20cm). Dainty, double flowers are composed of pointed, soft pale primrose petaloids neatly arranged in whorls. Z3–9 H9–1.

***N.* 'February Gold',** Div.6. Early spring-flowering bulb. **H** 13in (32cm). Solitary, long-lasting flowers have clear golden petals and long, flanged, slightly darker trumpets. Is useful for a border and for naturalizing. Z3–9 H9–1.

***N.* 'February Silver',** Div.6 (illus. p.405). Robust, early spring-flowering bulb. **H** 13in (32cm). Long-lasting flowers with milky-white petals and long, sturdy, nodding trumpets open rich lemon and age to creamy-yellow. Z3–9 H9–1.

***N.* 'Fortune',** Div.2. Early to mid-spring-flowering bulb. **H** 16in (40cm). Flowers have ribbed, dark lemon petals and bold, flared, copper-orange cups. Is very good for cut flowers. Z3–9 H9–1.

***N.* 'Foxfire',** Div.2. Mid-spring-flowering bulb. **H** 14in (35cm). Has very rounded flowers with white petals. Small, greenish-cream cups have small, green eye zone and coral-orange outer rim. Z3–9 H9–1.

***N.* 'Fragrant Breeze',** Div.2 (illus. p.404). Early to mid-spring-flowering bulb. **H** 17in (43cm). Fragrant flowers have pure white petals and vase-shaped, apricot-yellow cups. Z3–9 H9–1.

***N.* 'Fragrant Rose',** Div.2. Late-spring-flowering bulb. **H** 18in (45cm). Flowers have white petals, which become pink tinted with age, and conical, green-eyed, red-pink cups.

***N.* 'Gay Kybo',** Div.4. Mid-spring-flowering bulb. **H** 18in (45cm). Bears large, double flowers with multiple layers of creamy-white petals and shorter, orange trumpets.

***N.* 'Geranium',** Div.8. Mid- to late-spring-flowering bulb. **H** 14in (35cm). Stems bear up to 6 scented flowers, with white petals and flattened, flared, orange-red cups. Is excellent for cut flowers, and can be grown for indoor pots.

***N.* 'Gold Convention',** Div.2. Mid-spring-flowering bulb. **H** 20in (50cm). Large flowers have rich golden petals and deep trumpets in same color.

***N.* 'Golden Ducat'** Div.4 (illus. p.405). Mid-spring-flowering bulb. **H** 15in (38cm). Produces variable, sometimes poorly formed, double, rich golden flowers. Is suitable for cut flowers. Z3–9 H9–1.

***N.* 'Golden Vale',** Div.1. Mid-spring-flowering bulb. **H** 18in (45cm). Flowers have rich golden-yellow petals and

N

matching, flared trumpets. Is suitable for cut flowers.
N. 'Grand Primo Citronère', Div.8. Late fall- to early spring-flowering bulb. **H** 13in (32cm). Bears 8 or more fragrant flowers, with milky-white petals and clear lemon cups, which fade to cream. Treated bulbs may be forced for mid-winter flowering. Is good for cut flowers. Z3–9 H9–1.
N. 'Grand Soleil d'Or', Div.8. Late fall- to early spring-flowering bulb. **H** 14in (35cm). Flowers are sweetly scented with dash of lemon. Each has rich golden-yellow petals and clear tangerine cups. May be forced for mid-winter flowering, but staking is needed. Is excellent for cut flowers. Z7–9 H9–7.
N. 'Hawera', Div.5 (illus. p.405). Mid-spring-flowering bulb. **H** 8in (20cm). Nodding flowers are delicate lemon-yellow. Requires a sunny position. Is suitable for a rock garden or alpine bed; also makes a good indoor container plant. Z3–9 H9–1.
N. 'Highfield Beauty', Div.8. Mid-spring-flowering bulb. **H** 20in (50cm). Stem bears up to 3 slightly scented flowers, with butter-yellow petals and slightly darker trumpets.
N. 'Home Fires', Div.2 (illus. p.405). Early spring-flowering bulb. **H** 18in (45cm). Flowers have pointed, rich lemon petals and orange-scarlet cups with lobed and frilled rim. Z3–9 H9–1.
N. 'Honeybird', Div.1. Mid-spring-flowering bulb. **H** 20in (50cm). Large, well-proportioned flowers open greenish-yellow. Trumpets gradually fade almost to pure white as they age. Z3–9 H9–1.
N. 'Ice Follies', Div.2 (illus. p.404). Early spring-flowering bulb. **H** 16in (40cm). Flowers have milky-white petals and very wide, almost flat, primrose-yellow cups, fading to cream. Is excellent for cut flowers. Z3–9 H9–1.
N. 'Irene Copeland', Div.4 (illus. p.405). Mid-spring-flowering bulb. **H** 14in (35cm). Bears large, fully double flowers of neatly arranged, milky-white petaloids interspersed with shorter, pale creamy-yellow ones. Is excellent for cut flowers. Z3–9 H9–1.
N. 'Jack Snipe', Div.6 (illus. p.405). Sturdy, early to mid-spring-flowering bulb. **H** 9in (23cm). Long-lasting, milky-white flowers are similar to those of *N.* 'Dove Wings', but have narrower petals with incurved margins and medium-length cups of rich dark lemon-yellow. Z3–9 H9–1.
N. 'Jenny', Div. 6 (illus. p.405). Early to mid- spring-flowering bulb. **H** 12in (30cm). Bears long-lasting flowers with milky-white petals and medium-length, flanged, soft lemon trumpets that turn creamy-white. Z3–9 H9–1.
N. 'Jetfire', Div.6. Free-flowering, early spring-flowering bulb. **H** 9in (23cm). Flowers have overlapping, reflexed, clear golden-yellow petals and cylindrical, ribbed, vibrant orange cups, slightly waisted before crenate rim. Z3–9 H9–1.
N. jonquilla (Wild jonquil) Div.13. Mid-spring-flowering bulb. **H** 12in (30cm). Richly fragrant flowers are borne in cluster of 6 or more; each has tapering, yellow petals and shallow, dark gold cup. Has semicylindrical, grooved, glossy, dark green leaves. Z3–9 H9–1. **'Flore Pleno'** (Queen Anne's jonquil) has loosely double flowers; broad, incurved, yellow petals are interspersed with short, darker ones.
N. 'Jumblie', Div.12. Early spring-flowering bulb. **H** 8in (20cm). Bears 2 or 3 long-lasting flowers, with broad, golden petals and sturdy, flanged, orange-yellow cups. Is ideal as a container plant. Z3–9 H9–1.
N. juncifolius. See *N. assoanus.*
N. 'Kilworth', Div.2. Vigorous, late spring-flowering bulb. **H** 15in (38cm). Flowers have pointed, milky-white petals and green-eyed, dark reddish-orange cups. Is effective in large groups. Z3–9 H9–1.
N. 'Kingscourt', Div.1. Sturdy, mid-spring-flowering bulb. **H** 17in (42cm). Flowers have broad, rounded, golden-yellow petals and flanged, flared, richer golden-yellow trumpets. Z3–9 H9–1.
N. 'Liberty Bells', Div.5 (illus. p.405). Sturdy, mid-spring-flowering bulb. **H** 13in (32cm). Paired, nodding flowers are slightly fragrant and clear lemon yellow. Z3–9 H9–1.
N. 'Little Beauty', Div.1. Early-spring-flowering bulb. **H** 5½in (14cm). Small flowers have creamy-white petals and yellow trumpets. Is suitable for a rock garden or container.
N. 'Little Witch', Div.6. Early to mid-spring-flowering bulb. **H** 9in (23cm). Produces golden-yellow flowers with reflexed petals and trumpet-shaped cups.
N. 'Manley', Div.4. Early- to mid-spring-flowering bulb. **H** 18in (45cm). Produces double flowers with whorls of greenish-yellow petals, interspersed with bright orange trumpets.
N. x medioluteus, syn. *N. x biflorus,* Div.13. Mid- to late-spring-flowering bulb. **H** 16in (40cm). Produces medium-sized, sweetly scented flowers of rounded outline, with overlapping, almost pure white petals and small, shallow bowl-shaped, primrose-yellow cups. Is usually twin-headed. Z3–9 H9–1.
N. 'Merlin', Div.3. Mid-spring-flowering bulb. **H** 14in (35cm). Flowers have broad, rounded, glistening white petals and relatively large, almost flat, rich gold cups, with small, green eye and broad, lightly ruffled, orange-red rim. Is excellent for exhibition. Z3–9 H9–1.
N. minimus of gardens. See *N. asturiensis.*
N. 'Minnow', Div.8. Robust, early to mid-spring-flowering bulb. **H** 7in (18cm). Each stem bears cluster of 4 or more fragrant flowers, with rounded, creamy-yellow petals and lemon-yellow cups. Increases freely and will naturalize in grass. Is suitable for a rock garden and can be grown indoors as a container plant. Z3–9 H9–1.
N. minor, syn. *N. nanus* of gardens, Div.13. Early spring-flowering bulb. **H** 8in (20cm). Flowers have slightly overlapping, soft yellow petals and almost straight, darker yellow trumpets with frilled rims. Z3–9 H9–1. **subsp. pumilus.** See *N. pumilus.*
N. minor of gardens. See *N. pumilus.*
N. 'Mission Bells', Div.5. Mid-spring-flowering bulb. **H** 10in (25cm). Stems bear 1–3 flowers with white petals, and matching trumpets with greenish centers.
N. 'Mount Hood', Div.1 (illus. p.404). Vigorous, mid-spring-flowering bulb. **H** 16in (40cm). Trumpet-shaped, creamy-yellow flowers soon fade to white. Z3–9 H9–1.
N. nanus, Div.13. Early spring-flowering bulb. **H** 5in (12cm). Flowers have twisted, creamy petals and sturdy, straight, dull yellow trumpets with frilled rim. Leaves are particularly broad. Is suitable for naturalizing. Z3–9 H9–1.
N. nanus of gardens. See *N. minor.*
N. obvallaris, syn. *N. pseudonarcissus* subsp. *obvallaris* (Tenby daffodil), Div.13. Sturdy, early spring-flowering bulb. **H** 12in (30cm). Golden-yellow flowers have short petals and broad trumpets, and are borne on stiff stems. Z3–9 H9–1.
N. x odorus, syn. *N. campernelli* (Campernelle jonquil), Div.13. Robust, mid-spring-flowering bulb. **H** 8–12in (20–30cm). Has usually 2 richly fragrant, dark golden-yellow flowers. Z3–9 H9–1. **'Rugulosus',** Div.7, **H** 11in (28cm), is more vigorous and produces up to 4 small-cupped, rich golden-yellow flowers.
N. 'Panache', Div.1 (illus. p.405). Mid-spring-flowering bulb. **H** 16in (40cm). Produces very large, pure white flowers with well-balanced trumpets tinged green at bases and broad, overlapping petals. Z3–9 H9–1.
N. 'Paper White Grandiflorus', syn. *N.* 'Paper White Snowflake', *N. papyraceus* 'Grandiflorus', Div.8. Winter- to mid-spring-flowering bulb. **H** 14in (35cm). Has 10 or more long-lived, heavily fragrant, star-shaped, glistening white flowers, with long, spreading petals and small, flanged cups containing conspicuous, saffron-yellow stamens. Produces flowers continuously through winter indoors. Z7–9 H9–7.
N. 'Paper White Snowflake'. See *N.* 'Paper White Grandiflorus'.
N. papyraceus 'Grandiflorus'. See *N.* 'Paper White Grandiflorus'.
N. 'Passionale', Div.2 (illus. p.405). Mid-spring-flowering bulb. **H** 16in (40cm). Each flower has milky-white petals and long, flanged, apricot-tinged, pink cups. Z3–9 H9–1.
N. 'Pencrebar', Div.4 (illus. p.405). Mid-spring-flowering bulb. **H** 7in (18cm). Fragrant flowers are small, rounded and fully double, often in pairs. Outer petaloids and large, inner ones are pale gold and are evenly interspersed with darker ones. Z3–9 H9–1.
N. 'Pipit', Div.7 (illus. p.405). Mid-spring-flowering bulb. **H** 10in (25cm). Bears up to 3 scented flowers per stem, slightly greenish sulfur-yellow on opening. Ruffled, flared cups and base of overlapping petals become almost white at maturity. Z3–9 H9–1.
N. poeticus (Poet's narcissus), Div.13. Variable, late spring-flowering bulb. **H** 9–17in (22–42cm). Fragrant flowers have glistening white petals and small, shallow, red-rimmed, yellow or orange cups. Is ideal for naturalizing in moist sod although slow to establish. Z3–9 H9–1. **'Flore Pleno'.** See *N. poeticus* 'Plenus'. **'Plenus',** syn. *N.* 'Albus Plenus Odoratus', *N. poeticus* 'Flore Pleno' Div.13 , **H** 16in (40cm), has loosely double, pure white flowers, with inconspicuous, greenish-yellow or orange centers, in late spring or early summer. Is good for cut flowers. **var. recurvus** (Pheasant's eye), Div.13, **H** 17in (42cm), bears larger, long-lasting flowers with strongly swept-back petals and very shallow, crimson-rimmed, greenish-yellow cups, in early summer.
N. 'Portrush', Div.3. Late spring- to early summer-flowering bulb. **H** 14in (35cm). Produces small flowers with green-tinged, glistening milky-white petals and small, shallow, flanged, creamy-white cups with bright green eye. Z3–9 H9–1.
N. 'Pride of Cornwall', Div.8. Mid-spring-flowering bulb. **H** 15in (38cm). Bears several large, fragrant flowers, with milky-white petals and arich yellow cups shading to orange-red rim outside. Is excellent for cut flowers. *N.* 'Martha Washington' and *N.* 'Geranium' are similar in appearance. Z3–9 H9–1.
N. pseudonarcissus (Lent lily, Wild daffodil), Div.13. Extremely variable, early spring-flowering bulb. **H** 6–12in (15–30cm). Nodding flowers have overlapping, straw-yellow petals and large, darker yellow trumpets. Is ideal for naturalizing. Z3–9 H9–1. **subsp. obvallaris.** See *N. obvallaris.*
N. pumilus, syn. *N. minor, N. minor* subsp. *pumilus,* Div.13. Early spring-flowering bulb. **H** 6–9in (15–22cm). Bears bright gold flowers with separated, slightly paler petals and large trumpets with lobed and frilled rims. Z3–9 H9–1. **'Plenus'.** See *N.* 'Rip van Winkle'.
N. 'Rainbow', Div.2. Vigorous, mid-spring-flowering bulb. **H** 18in (45cm). White flowers have cups that are broadly banded with coppery-pink at rim. Z3–9 H9–1.
N. 'Replete', Div.4. Mid-spring-flowering bulb. **H** 16in (40cm). Produces double flowers with white petals, interspersed with reddish-orange trumpet fragments.
N. requienii. See *N. assoanus.*
N. 'Rip van Winkle', syn. *N. pumilus* 'Plenus' Div.4. Early spring-flowering bulb. **H** 6in (15cm). Shaggy, double flowers have densely arranged, flat, tapering, greenish-lemon petals with incurving tips. Z3–9 H9–1.
N. 'Rockall', Div.3. Mid-spring-flowering bulb. **H** 20in (50cm). Produces neat flowers with overlapping, white petals and shallow, ribbed, intense orange-red, bowl-shaped cups. Z3–9 H9–1.
N. romieuxii, Div.13. Early spring-flowering bulb. **H** 4in (10cm). Best grown in a frame or an alpine house. Is similar to *N. bulbocodium,* but has fragrant flowers with large, almost flat, flanged cups of pale primrose. Z3–9 H9–1.
N. rupicola, Div.13. Mid-spring-flowering bulb. **H** 3in (8cm). Has thin, cylindrical, keeled, erect, gray-green leaves and solitary, golden-yellow flowers, with shallow, 6-lobed cups. Z3–9 H9–1. **subsp. watieri,** Div.13, **H** 4in (10cm), produces relatively large, fragrant, crystalline-textured, white flowers.
N. 'Saint Keverne', Div.11b. Sturdy, early to mid-spring-flowering bulb. **H** 17in (42cm). Solitary flowers have clear rich golden-yellow petals and slightly darker cups of almost trumpet proportions. Z3–9 H9–1.
N. 'Saint Patrick's Day', Div.2. Early spring-flowering bulb. **H** 16in (40cm). Flowers have broad, flattish, greenish-yellow petals and large cups with dark yellow margins.

N. 'Salome', Div.2. Early to mid-spring-flowering bulb. **H** 14in (35cm). Flowers have white petals and long, trumpet-shaped, pink cups, which are slightly frilled with hint of warm gold at edge. Is excellent for cut flowers.

N. 'Satin Pink', Div.2. Mid-spring-flowering bulb. **H** 17in (42cm). Each flower has broad, ribbed, milk-white petals and long, barely flared, flanged, soft buff-pink cup of almost trumpet proportions. Z3–9 H9–1.

N. 'Scarlet Gem', Div.8. Mid-spring-flowering bulb. **H** 14in (35cm). Produces 7–8 scented flowers with golden petals and scarlet or deep orange-red cups. Z3–9 H9–1.

N. 'Segova', Div.3. Mid-spring-flowering bulb. **H** 16in (40cm). Flowers have pure white petals and small, lemon-yellow cups.

N. 'Sempre Avanti', Div.2. Early to mid-spring-flowering bulb. **H** 16in (40cm). Flowers have creamy-white petals and yellow cups. Is good for naturalizing in grass.

N. 'Shepherds Hey', Div.7. Mid-spring-flowering bulb. **H** 10in (25cm). Produces 2 or more fragrant flowers per stem, with overlapping, golden-yellow petals and small, fluted cups.

N. 'Shining Light', Div.2. Mid-spring-flowering bulb. **H** 17in (42cm). Well-balanced flowers have smooth, overlapping, clear, pale golden-yellow petals and slightly ribbed, rich orange-red cups. Lightly toothed rim is slightly darker. Is excellent for exhibition. Z3–9 H9–1.

N. 'Silver Chimes', Div.8 (illus. p.407).

N. 'Sinopel', Div.3. Mid-spring-flowering bulb. **H** 18in (45cm). Flowers have pure white petals and shallow-bowled, green cups edged with deep yellow.

N. 'Sir Winston Churchill', Div.4 (illus. p.405). Mid-spring-flowering bulb. **H** 14in (35cm). Produces fragrant, double, white flowers with orange-yellow segments in centers. Z3–9 H9–1.

N. 'Slim Whitman', Div.2. Early to mid-spring-flowering bulb. **H** 16in (40cm). Flowers have ivory-white petals and orange cups with sulfur-yellow rim.

N. 'Spellbinder', Div.1 (illus. p.405). Early spring-flowering bulb. **H** 17in (42cm). Long-lasting, bright sulfur-yellow flowers have slender, flanged trumpets, reversing to palest sulfur-white inside, except for lobed, rolled-back rim, which is tinged with lemon. Z3–9 H9–1.

N. 'Spring Pride', Div.2. Early to mid-spring-flowering bulb. **H** 16in (40cm). Flowers have ivory-white petals and yellow cups edged with apricot.

N. 'Stint', Div.5. Mid-spring-flowering bulb. **H** 12in (30cm). Produces 2 or more pendent, bright yellow flowers with pale lemon-yellow cups.

N. 'Stratosphere', Div.7 (illus. p.405). Mid-spring-flowering bulb. **H** 16in (40cm). Bears usually 3 fragrant flowers, with yellow petals and darker golden-yellow cups. Is excellent for exhibition. Z3–9 H9–1.

N. 'Sun Disc', Div.7. Mid-spring-flowering bulb. **H** 6in (15cm). Produces 2 or more rounded, sweetly scented flowers per stem, with yellow petals and small, flat cups.

N. 'Suzy', Div.7 (illus. p.405). Robust, mid-spring-flowering bulb. **H** 15in (38cm).

Produces 3 or 4 long-lasting, large, fragrant flowers, with clear golden-yellow petals and large, flanged, rich tangerine cups. Is suitable for cut flowers. Z3–9 H9–1.

N. 'Sweetness', Div.7. Early spring-flowering bulb. **H** 15in (38cm). Sweetly fragrant flowers, occasionally borne in pairs, have intense golden-yellow petals and darker, wavy-edged cups of strong substance. Is good for cut flowers. Z3–9 H9–1.

N. 'Tahiti', Div.4 (illus. p.405). Robust, mid-spring-flowering bulb. **H** 15in (38cm). Solitary, loosely double flowers have golden petals and petaloids, interspersed with short, fiery orange, inner petaloids. Z3–9 H9–1.

N. tazetta, Div.13. Extremely variable, late fall- to mid-spring-flowering bulb. **H** 12–16in (30–40cm). Bears usually 12 or more fragrant flowers, generally with slender, white or yellow petals and shallow, white or yellow cups. Z7–9 H9–1.

N. 'Tête-à-Tête', Div.12. Early spring-flowering bulb. **H** 6–12in (15–30cm). Long-lasting flowers have reflexed, rich golden-yellow petals and square, flanged, warm yellowish-orange cups. Should be twin-flowered. Is very susceptible to viruses. Z3–9 H9–1.

N. 'Thalia', Div.5 (illus. p.404). Vigorous, mid-spring-flowering bulb. **H** 15in (38cm). Each stem has 3 or more long-lived, milky-white flowers, with irregularly formed, often propeller-shaped petals and flanged, bold cups. Z3–9 H9–1.

N. 'Tresamble', Div.5. Sturdy, early spring-flowering bulb. **H** 16in (40cm). Each stem bears up to 6 flowers, with milky-white petals and flanged, creamy-white cups that are paler at rim. Z3–9 H9–1.

N. 'Trevithian', Div.7. Vigorous, early to mid-spring-flowering bulb. **H** 18in (45cm). Produces 2 or 3 large, fragrant, rounded, soft primrose flowers, with broad petals and short cups. Z3–9 H9–1.

N. triandrus (Angel's tears), Div.13. Early spring-flowering bulb. **H** 5in (12cm). Bears nodding, milky-white flowers, with narrow, reflexed petals and fairly long, straight-sided cups. Is suitable for a rock garden or as a container plant. Z3–9 H9–1.

N. 'Tripartite', Div.11. Mid-spring-flowering bulb. **H** 10in (25cm). Each stem produces 2–3 lemon and golden-yellow flowers, with split trumpets that sit flat against petals.

N. 'Trousseau', Div.1. Early spring-flowering bulb. **H** 17in (42cm). Flowers have milky-white petals and straight, flanged, soft lemon trumpets, with flared, lobed rim turning rich creamy-buff tinged with pale pink. Z3–9 H9–1.

N. 'Tudor Minstrel', Div.2. Mid-spring-flowering bulb. **H** 17in (42cm). Produces flowers with pointed, white petals. Chrome-yellow cups are slender and flanged outward. Z3–9 H9–1.

N. 'Verger', Div.3. Mid-spring flowering bulb. **H** 16in (40cm). Flowers have pure white petals and small, shallow, deep orange-red cups.

N. 'W.P. Milner', Div.1. Early spring-flowering bulb. **H** 9in (23cm). Nodding flowers have slender, twisted, light creamy-

yellow petals and flared, pale lemon-yellow trumpets, which fade to palest sulfur. Z3–9 H9–1.

N. 'Waterperry', Div.7. Mid-spring-flowering bulb. **H** 10in (25cm). Flowers have dull creamy-white petals. Lightly flanged, spreading, primrose cups turn rich buff-yellow, shading to pinkish-apricot rims. Z3–9 H9–1.

N. 'White Lady', Div.3. Vigorous, mid- to late-spring-flowering bulb. **H** 18in (45cm). Large, scented flowers have spreading, slightly overlapping, pure white petals. Small, shallow, heavily frilled cups are strong primrose-yellow on opening, becoming more creamy-yellow with maturity. Z3–9 H9–1.

N. 'White Lion', Div.4. Mid-spring-flowering bulb. **H** 14in (35cm). Produces double, white flowers interspersed with bright yellow.

N. 'White Marvel', Div.5. Mid-spring-flowering bulb. **H** 14in (35cm). Produces 2 or more pendent, fragrant, double, white flowers per stem.

N. 'Woodland Star', Div.3. Mid-spring-flowering bulb. **H** 20in (50cm). Large flowers have white petals and small, bowl-shaped, deep red cups. Z3–9 H9–1.

N. 'Yellow Cheerfulness', Div.8. Mid-spring-flowering bulb. **H** 14in (35cm). Produces multiheaded stems of fragrant, pale yellow flowers.

NAUTILOCALYX

GESNERIACEAE

Genus of evergreen, erect, bushy perennials, grown for their flowers and foliage. Requires high humidity, partial shade and well-drained soil; avoid waterlogging. Propagate by stem cuttings in summer or by seed, if available, in spring.

N. bullatus, syn. N. tessellatus. Evergreen, erect, bushy perennial. **H** and **S** 2ft (60cm). Narrowly oval, wrinkled leaves, to 9in (23cm) long, are dark green with bronze sheen above, reddish-green beneath. Clusters of small, tubular, white-haired, pale yellow flowers are produced in leaf axils mainly in summer. Z14–15 H12–10.

N. lynchii, illus. p.471.

N. tessellatus. See N. bullatus.

Neanthe bella. See Chamaedorea elegans.

NECTAROSCORDUM

LILIACEAE/ALLIACEAE

Genus of summer-flowering bulbs, related to Allium and Lilium, grown for their umbels of bell-shaped flowers and for their seed heads when dried. Exudes a very strong, onion-like smell when bruised. Stems with erect, shuttlecock-like seed heads may be dried for winter decoration. Needs partial shade and tolerates any soil that is neither too dry nor waterlogged. Plant in rough grass or borders. Propagate by freely produced offsets in late summer or by seed in fall.

N. dioscoridis. See N. siculum subsp. bulgaricum.

N. siculum subsp. bulgaricum, syn. N. dioscoridis, illus. p.385.

NEILLIA

ROSACEAE

Genus of deciduous shrubs, grown for their graceful habit and profuse clusters of small flowers. Requires sun or partial shade and fertile, well-drained soil. Established plants benefit from having some older shoots cut to base after flowering. Propagate by softwood cuttings in summer or by suckers in fall.

N. longiracemosa. See N. thibetica.

N. sinensis. Deciduous, arching shrub. **H** and **S** 6ft (2m). Has peeling, brown bark and oval, sharply toothed, mid-green leaves. Bears nodding racemes of small, tubular, pinkish-white flowers in late spring and early summer. Z5–7 H7–5.

N. thibetica, syn. N. longiracemosa, illus. p.133.

NELUMBO

Lotus

NYMPHAEACEAE/NELUMBONACEAE

Genus of deciduous, perennial, marginal water plants, grown for their foliage, flowers and seed pods. Needs an open, sunny position and 24in (60cm) depth of water. Remove fading foliage; flowers may be left to develop into decorative seed pods. Divide overgrown plants in spring. Propagate species by seed in spring, selected forms by division in spring.

N. lutea (American lotus, Water chinquapin). Vigorous, deciduous, perennial, marginal water plant. **H** and **S** 3ft (1m). Rounded, blue-green leaves, prominently veined beneath, develop on sturdy stems, 1–2ft (30–60cm) long. Large, chalice-shaped, yellow flowers are produced in summer. Z4–11 H12–1.

N. nucifera, illus. p.438. **'Alba Grandiflora'** is a vigorous, deciduous, perennial, marginal water plant. **H** 4–6ft (1.2–1.8m), **S** 4ft (1.2m). Has very large, rounded, wavy-margined, dark green leaves, on sturdy stems, with large, fragrant, chalice-shaped, white flowers, 9–10in (22–25cm) across, in summer. Z4–11 H12–3. **'Alba Striata'** bears white flowers, 6in (15cm) across, with jagged, red margins. Z4–11 H12–3. **'Rosea Plena'** produces double, soft pink flowers, to 12in (30cm) across. Z4–11 H12–3.

NEMATANTHUS

GESNERIACEAE

Genus of perennials and soft-stemmed, evergreen shrubs, grown for their flowers and foliage. Requires partial shade and rich, moist but well-drained soil. Water container specimens moderately, allowing soil almost to dry out between applications. Tip prune young plants to stimulate branching. Propagate by softwood or greenwood cuttings in summer.

N. gregarius, syn. N. radicans, Hypocyrta radicans, illus. p.459.

N. radicans. See N. gregarius.

N. strigillosus, syn. Hypocyrta strigillosa. Evergreen, prostrate shrub. **H** 6–12in (15–30cm), **S** 2–3ft (60cm–1m). Elliptic, slightly cupped leaves are clothed in dense down. Small, tubular, orange or orange-red flowers are produced in leaf axils mainly from spring to fall.

NEMESIA
SCROPHULARIACEAE

Genus of annuals, perennials and evergreen subshrubs, commonly grown for summer bedding and as greenhouse plants. Prefers sun and fertile, well-drained soil. Cut back stems after flowering to encourage new buds. Pinch out growing shoots of young plants to ensure a bushy habit. Propagate by seed sown under glass in early spring, or outdoors in late spring.

N. Amelie ('Fleurame'), illus. p.301.
N. Maritana Series Maritana Blue Lagoon ('Pengoon'). Rather upright, twiggy perennial, grown as an annual. **H** 14in (35cm), **S** 24in (60cm). Slightly fragrant, 2-lipped, blue-purple flowers, $^3/_4$in (2cm) across, are borne in dense spikes in summer and fall above lance-shaped, slightly scalloped, mid-green leaves. Prefers moist soil.
N. strumosa. Fast-growing, bushy annual. **H** 8–18in (20–45cm), **S** 6in (15cm). Has lance-shaped, serrated, pale green leaves and, in summer, trumpet-shaped, yellow, white or purple flowers, 1in (2.5cm) across. Is good for cut flowers. H7–1. **Carnival Series,** illus. p.307.
N. Sunsatia Series Sunsatia Mango ('Inupyel'), illus. p.320.

NEMOPHILA
HYDROPHYLLACEAE/BORAGINACEAE

Genus of annuals, useful for rock gardens and for edging. Needs sun or partial shade and fertile, well-drained soil. Propagate by seed in spring or early fall. Is prone to aphids.

N. insignis. See *N. menziesii*.
N. maculata, illus. p.299.
N. menziesii, syn. *N. insignis*, illus. p.314.

NEOBUXBAUMIA
CACTACEAE

Genus of columnar or treelike perennial cacti with cylindrical stems and usually low-set ribs. Nocturnal flowers, produced in summer, are followed by angular fruits, which open like stars when ripe. Requires sun and poor to moderately fertile, sharply drained, gritty soil. Propagate by seed in spring.

N. euphorbioides, syn. *Lemaireocereus euphorbioides, Rooksbya euphorbioides*, illus. p.494.

Neochilenia mitis of gardens. See *Eriosyce napina*.

NEOLITSEA
LAURACEAE

Genus of evergreen trees and shrubs, grown for their foliage. In cold areas, needs shelter from strong winds; does best against a south- or west-facing wall. Requires sun or partial shade and fertile, well-drained soil. Propagate by semiripe cuttings in late summer.

N. sericea, syn. *Litsea glauca, Neolitsia glauca*. Evergreen, broadly conical, dense tree or shrub. **H** and **S** 20ft (6m). Narrowly oval, pointed leaves are glossy, mid-green above, white beneath and, when young, are densely covered with silky, brown hairs. Small, star-shaped, yellow flowers are borne in fall. Z8–11 H12–8.

Neolitsia glauca. See *Neolitsea sericea*.

NEOLLOYDIA
CACTACEAE

Genus of spherical to columnar, perennial cacti with dense spines and short tubercles in spirals. Most species are exceptionally difficult to cultivate unless grafted. Needs full sun and well-drained soil. Water sparingly from spring to fall; keep dry in winter. Propagate by seed in spring or summer.

N. conoidea, syn. *Mammillaria conoidea*, illus. p.483.

NEOMARICA
IRIDACEAE

Genus of evergreen, summer-flowering, iris-like, rhizomatous perennials, grown for their clusters of short-lived flowers. Needs partial shade and fertile, moist, preferably rich soil. Water freely in summer; reduce water in winter but do not allow plants to dry out. Propagate by seed in spring or by division in spring or summer.
N. caerulea, illus. p.393.

NEOPANAX
ARALIACEAE

Small genus of evergreen shrubs, grown for their foliage. Grow in sun or semi-shade in a good, well-drained soil. Propagate by semiripe cuttings in summer or by seed in fall.
N. arboreus (Five fingers). Evergreen, round-headed, sturdy-branched tree. **H** 20ft (6m), **S** 12ft (4m). Large, glossy, dark green leaves are divided into 5 or 7 oblong leaflets. Produces tiny, honey-scented, green flowers in summer, followed by rounded, purplish-black fruits on female plants.
N. laetus. Evergreen, round-headed, sturdy-branched tree or shrub. **H** and **S** 10ft (3m). Has large, long-stalked, leathery, dark green leaves divided into 5 or 7 oblong leaflets. Bears tiny, greenish-purple flowers, in summer, followed by rounded, purplish-black fruits on female plants in fall.

Neoporteria chilensis. See *Eriosyce chilensis*.
Neoporteria litoralis. See *Eriosyce subgibbosa*.
Neoporteria mitis. See *Eriosyce napina*.
Neoporteria napina. See *Eriosyce napina*.
Neoporteria nidus. See *Eriosyce kunzei*.
Neoporteria subgibbosa. See *Eriosyce subgibbosa*.
Neoporteria villosa. See *Eriosyce villosa*.

NEOREGELIA
BROMELIACEAE

Genus of evergreen, rosette-forming, epiphytic perennials, grown for their overall appearance. Requires partial shade and a rooting medium of equal parts rich soil and sphagnum moss or bark or plastic chips used for orchid culture. Using soft water, water moderately in growing season, sparingly at other times, and keep rosette centers filled with water from spring to fall. Propagate by offsets in spring or summer.
N. carolinae, syn. *Aregelia carolinae, Nidularium carolinae* (Blushing bromeliad). Evergreen, spreading, basal-rosetted, epiphytic perennial. **H** 8–12in (20–30cm), **S** 16–24in (40–60cm). Strap-shaped, finely spine-toothed, lustrous, bright green leaves are produced in dense rosettes. Compact cluster of tubular, blue-purple flowers, surrounded by red bracts, is borne at center of each mature rosette, usually in summer. Z13–15 H12–1. **f. tricolor,** syn. *N. carolinae* 'Tricolor' has leaves striped with ivory-white, that flush pink with age. **'Tricolor'.** See *N. carolinae* f. *tricolor*.
N. concentrica, illus. p.471. Evergreen, spreading, basal-rosetted, epiphytic perennial. **H** 8–12in (20–30cm), **S** to 28in (70cm). Very broadly strap-shaped to oval, glossy, dark green leaves, with spiny, black teeth and usually with dark blotches, are borne in dense rosettes. In summer, compact cluster of tubular, pale blue flowers, surrounded by pinkish-lilac bracts, is produced at center of each mature rosette. **var. plutonis,** syn. *N. concentrica* 'Plutonis' has bracts flushed with red. H11–1. **'Plutonis'.** See *N. concentrica* var. *plutonis*.

NEPENTHES
Monkey cup, Tropical pitcher plant
NEPENTHACEAE

Genus of evergreen, insectivorous, mostly epiphytic perennials, with leaves adapted to form pendulous, lidded, colored pitchers that trap and digest insects. Is suitable for hanging baskets. Requires a humid atmosphere, partial shade and moist, fertile soil with added peat and moss. Propagate by seed in spring or by stem cuttings in spring or summer.
N. x hookeriana, illus. p.473.
N. rafflesiana. Evergreen, epiphytic, insectivorous perennial. **H** 10ft (3m), **S** 3–4ft (1–1.2m). Has lance-shaped, dark green leaves. Greenish-yellow pitchers, to 10in (25cm) long, are mottled purple and brown and have spurred lids. Inconspicuous, green flowers in racemes are produced intermittently. Z15 H12–10.

NEPETA
Catmint
LABIATAE/LAMIACEAE

Genus of summer-flowering perennials, useful for edging, particularly where they can tumble over paving. Needs sun or partial shade and well-drained soil. Propagate by division in spring or by stem-tip or softwood cuttings in spring or summer, species only by seed in fall. Cats may be attracted to this plant, rolling on it and crushing it. Leaves can be dried and used in cat toys.
N. 'Blue Beauty'. See *N.* 'Souvenir d'André Chaudron'.
N. x faassenii, illus. p.270.
N. grandiflora. Neat, erect perennial. **H** 16–32in (40–80cm), **S** 18–24in (45–60cm). Has slightly hairy stems, oval, round-toothed, light green leaves, with heart-shaped bases, and, in summer, racemes of small, hooded, blue flowers. Z3–8 H8–1.
N. macrantha. See *N. sibirica*.

N. nervosa. Clump-forming perennial. **H** 14in (35cm), **S** 12in (30cm). Forms mound of narrowly oblong to lance-shaped, pointed, prominently veined, mid-green leaves. Dense racemes of small, tubular, pale blue flowers are produced from early to mid-summer. Z5–7 H7–5.
N. sibirica, syn. *N. macrantha, Dracocephalum sibiricum*. Erect, leafy perennial. **H** 36in (90cm), **S** 18in (45cm). Bears long, whorled cymes of blue to lavender-blue flowers in mid- and late summer. Leaves are dark green and aromatic. Z3–8 H8–1. **'Souvenir d'André Chaudron'.** See *N.* 'Souvenir d'André Chaudron'.
N. 'Six Hills Giant', illus. p.240.
N. 'Souvenir d'André Chaudron', syn. *N.* 'Blue Beauty', *N. sibirica* 'Souvenir d'André Chaudron'. Spreading, clump-forming perennial. **H** and **S** 18in (45cm). Tubular, blue flowers are borne throughout summer above oval to lance-shaped, toothed, gray leaves. Z3–8 H8–1.

NEPHROLEPIS
NEPHROLEPIDACEAE/LOMARIOPSIDACEAE

Genus of evergreen or semievergreen ferns. Needs partial shade and prefers moist soil, but is extremely tolerant of both drought and waterlogging. Remove fading fronds and divide regularly. Propagate by division in summer or early fall.
N. cordifolia (Ladder fern, Sword fern). Semievergreen fern. **H** 18in (45cm), **S** 12in (30cm). Has narrowly lance-shaped, arching, dark green fronds with rounded, finely serrated pinnae. Z9–11 H12–1.
N. exaltata, illus. p.478.

NEPHTHYTIS
ARACEAE

Genus of evergreen, tufted perennials, with horizontal, creeping rhizomes, grown for their foliage. Requires a humid atmosphere, partial shade and moist, rich soil. Propagate by division in spring or summer.
N. afzelii. Evergreen, creeping, rhizomatous perennial. **H** to 30in (75cm), **S** indefinite. Has tufts of arrow-shaped, lobed, dark green leaves, to 10in (25cm) long. Intermittently bears hooded, greenish spathe, enclosing green spadix, followed by spherical, orange fruits. Z14–15 H12–10.
N. triphylla of gardens. See *Syngonium podophyllum*.

NERINE
AMARYLLIDACEAE

Genus of bulbs, some of which are semievergreen, grown for their spherical heads of wavy-petaled, pink to red, occasionally white, flowers. Most flower in fall before leaves appear. Needs full sun and light, sandy soil. Plant in early fall. Dislikes being disturbed. Water until leaves die down, then dry off. Propagate by seed when fresh or divide offsets in fall or when leaves have died down. ① All parts may cause mild stomach upset if ingested.
N. 'Baghdad'. Fall-flowering bulb. **H** 24in (60cm), **S** 6–8in (15–20cm). Leaves are strap-shaped, semierect and basal. Has crimson flowers, paler toward centers;

long, narrow petals have recurved tips and crisped margins. Z8–10 H10–8.

N. 'Blanchefleur'. Fall-flowering bulb. **H** 12–20in (30–50cm), **S** 6–8in (15–20cm). Produces strap-shaped, semierect, basal leaves and tight head of 5–10 pure white flowers. Upper parts of petals are twisted. Z8–10 H10–8.

N. bowdenii, illus. p.413. **f. alba,** illus. p.413. **'Rowie'** is a fall-flowering bulb. **H** 24in (60cm), **S** 3in (8cm). Bears umbels of soft apricot-pink flowers with recurved petal tips. Strap-shaped, semierect, basal leaves persist throughout winter and die down in spring.

N. 'Brian Doe'. Fall-flowering bulb. **H** 12–20in (30–50cm), **S** 8–10in (20–25cm). Has strap-shaped, semierect, basal leaves. Sturdy, leafless stem bears head of salmon-pink flowers with reflexed, wavy-margined petals. Z8–10 H10–8.

N. 'Corusca Major', syn. *N. sarniensis* var. *corusca* 'Major'. Fall-flowering bulb. **H** 24in (60cm), **S** 5–6in (12–15cm). Forms strap-shaped, semierect, basal leaves. Sturdy stem bears 10–15 scarlet-red flowers with narrow petals. Is good for cut flowers. Z8–10 H10–8.

N. crispa. See *N. undulata.*

N. filifolia. Fall-flowering bulb. **H** to 10in (25cm), **S** 3–4in (8–10cm). Has threadlike, semierect leaves in basal tuft. Slender stem has pale pink flowers with narrow petals. Z8–10 H10–8.

N. flexuosa, syn. *N. undulata* Flexuosa Group. Semievergreen, fall-flowering bulb. **H** 16–20in (40–50cm), **S** 5–6in (12–15cm). Bears strap-shaped, semierect, basal leaves and 10–15 pink flowers; each petal has deeper pink mid-vein and recurved, wavy upper half. Z8–10 H10–8. **'Alba'** has white flowers.

N. 'Fothergillii Major'. Late summer- to early fall-flowering bulb. **H** 18–24in (45–60cm), **S** 5–6in (12–15cm). Leaves are strap-shaped, semierect and basal. Very strong stem has about 10 bright scarlet-salmon flowers with recurved petals. Z8–10 H10–8.

N. masoniorum. Fall-flowering bulb. **H** 6–8in (15–20cm), **S** 3–4in (8–10cm). Produces threadlike, semierect leaves in basal tuft. Stem bears pink flowers with very crisped petal margins. Z8–10 H10–8.

N. 'Nikita'. Fall-flowering bulb. **H** 18in (45cm), **S** 3in (8cm). Has broadly strap-shaped, semierect, basal leaves. Sturdy stem bears loose umbels of funnel-shaped, pale pink flowers with wavy-margined, recurved petal tips.

N. 'Orion', illus. p.413.

N. sarniensis, illus. p.414. **var. corusca 'Major'.** See *N.* 'Corusca Major'.

N. undulata, syn. *N. crispa,* illus. p.413. **Flexuosa Group.** See *N. flexuosa.*

NERIUM
Oleander
APOCYNACEAE

Genus of evergreen shrubs, grown for their flowers. Needs full sun and well-drained soil. Water container plants freely when in full growth, sparingly at other times. Tip-prune young plants to promote branching. Propagate by seed in spring or by softwood cuttings in summer. ⓘ All parts are highly toxic if ingested; contact with foliage may irritate skin.

N. oleander, illus. p.455.

NERTERA
RUBIACEAE

Genus of creeping perennials, grown for their mass of spherical, beadlike fruits in fall. Makes excellent alpine houseplants. Requires a sheltered, semi-shaded position and moist but well-drained, gritty, sandy soil. Resents winter wet. Propagate in spring by seed, division or tip cuttings.

N. depressa. See *N. granadensis.*

N. granadensis, syn. *N. depressa,* illus. p.373.

NICANDRA
SOLANACEAE

Genus of one species of annual, grown for its short-lived flowers. Needs sun and rich, well-drained soil. Propagate by seed in spring.

N. physalodes (Apple of Peru, Shoo-fly). Fast-growing, upright, branching annual. **H** 3ft (1m), **S** 1ft (30cm) or more. Has oval, serrated, mid-green leaves. In summer to early fall produces bell-shaped, white-throated, light violet-blue flowers, 1in (2.5cm) or more wide, that last one day. Spherical, green fruits, 2in (5cm) wide, are surrounded by purple and green calyces. Is thought to repel flies, hence its name. H9–1.

Nicodemia madagascariensis. See *Buddleja madagascariensis.*

NICOTIANA
Tobacco plant
SOLANACEAE

Genus of annuals, perennials that are usually grown as annuals, and semievergreen shrubs. Needs sun or partial shade and fertile, well-drained soil. Propagate annuals and perennials by seed in early spring, shrubs by semiripe cuttings in summer. ⓘ Contact with the foliage may irritate skin.

N. affinis. See *N. alata.*

N. alata, syn. *N. affinis,* illus. p.231.

N. glauca. Semievergreen, upright shrub. **H** and **S** 8–10ft (2.5–3m). Sturdy, blue-gray shoots bear narrowly oval, fleshy, blue-gray leaves. Showy, tubular, bright yellow flowers are produced in summer and early fall. Z10–11 H12–1.

N. langsdorffii, illus. p.316.

N. 'Lime Green'. Upright annual. **H** 24in (60cm), **S** 10in (25cm). Mid-green leaves are spoon-shaped. In late summer and fall produces racemes of open trumpet-shaped, greenish-yellow flowers that are fragrant at night. Z10–11 H12–1.

N. x sanderae. Nicki Series, H 15in (38cm), produces fragrant flowers in an extensive color range that includes white, pink, red and purple. **'Crimson Rock'** Fairly slow-growing, bushy annual. **H** 2ft (60cm), **S** 1ft (30cm). Oval leaves are mid-green. Evening-scented, trumpet-shaped, bright crimson flowers, to 3in (8cm) long, are produced throughout summer and early fall. **Saratoga Series** (rose), illus. p.305; (white), illus. p.299.

N. sylvestris (Flowering tobacco). Branching perennial, often grown as an annual. **H** 5ft (1.5m), **S** 2½ft (75cm). Produces panicles of fragrant, tubular, white flowers at ends of stems in late

summer. Sweet flower scent is strongest at night. Has long, rough, mid-green leaves that are sticky to touch. Prefers sun. Z10–11 H11–1.

NIDULARIUM
Bird's-nest bromeliad
BROMELIACEAE

Genus of evergreen, rosette-forming, epiphytic perennials, grown for their overall appearance. Requires partial shade and a rooting medium of equal parts rich soil and sphagnum moss or bark or plastic chips generally used for orchid culture. Using soft water, water moderately in growing season, sparingly at other times, and keep centers of rosettes filled with water from spring to fall. Propagate by offsets in spring or summer.

N. carolinae. See *Neoregelia carolinae.*

N. fulgens (Blushing bromeliad). Evergreen, spreading, basal-rosetted, epiphytic perennial. **H** 8in (20cm) or more, **S** 16–20in (40–50cm). Has dense rosettes of strap-shaped, spiny-toothed, arching, glossy, rich green leaves. Tubular, white-and-purple flowers, almost hidden in rosette of bright scarlet bracts, are produced mainly in summer. Z14–15 H12–10.

N. innocentii. Evergreen, spreading, basal-rosetted, epiphytic perennial. **H** 8–12in (20–30cm), **S** 24in (60cm). Has dense rosettes of strap-shaped, prickle-toothed, arching, dark green, sometimes reddish-green leaves, with reddish-purple undersides. Tubular, white flowers, partially hidden in rosette of bright red bracts, are produced mainly in summer. Z14–15 H12–10.

N. procerum. Evergreen, spreading, basal-rosetted, epiphytic perennial. **H** 8–12in (20–30cm), **S** 20–30in (50–75cm). Strap-shaped, spiny-toothed, bright green leaves are produced in dense rosettes. Clusters of small, tubular, blue flowers are borne in summer. Z14–15 H12–10.

NIEREMBERGIA
Cup flower
SOLANACEAE

Genus of summer-flowering perennials, sometimes grown as annuals, and deciduous or semievergreen subshrubs. Prefers sun and moist but well-drained soil. Propagate by division in spring, by semiripe cuttings in summer or by seed in fall.

N. caerulea. See *N. linariifolia.*

N. hippomanica. See *N. linariifolia.*

N. linariifolia, syn. *N. caerulea, N. hippomanica.* **'Purple Robe'** illus. p.312.

N. repens, syn. *N. rivularis,* illus. p.361.

N. rivularis. See *N. repens.*

NIGELLA
RANUNCULACEAE

Genus of annuals, grown for their flowers, which are suitable for cutting, and their ornamental seed pods. Prefers sun and fertile, well-drained soil. Deadhead plants to prolong flowering if seed heads are not required. Propagate by seed in spring or early fall.

N. damascena (Love-in-a-mist). Fast-growing, upright annual. **H** 24in (60cm), **S** 8in (20cm). Has feathery, bright green leaves. Spurred, many-petaled, blue or

white flowers are produced in summer, followed by inflated, rounded, green, then brown seed pods that may be cut and dried. H12–1. **'Miss Jekyll',** illus. p.315. **Persian Jewels Series,** illus. p.314.

NOLANA
SOLANACEAE

Genus of annuals, useful for growing in hot, dry sites and rock gardens and as edging. Needs sun and fertile, well-drained soil. Propagate by seed in spring.

N. atriplicifolia. See *N. paradoxa.*

N. grandiflora. See *N. paradoxa.*

N. paradoxa, syn. *N. atriplicifolia, N. grandiflora.* Moderately fast-growing, prostrate annual. **H** 3in (8cm), **S** 6in (15cm). Has oval, mid-green leaves and, in summer, funnel-shaped, purplish-blue flowers, to 2in (5cm) wide, with white-zoned, yellow throats. Z9–11 H12–1.

Nolina recurvata. See *Beaucarnea recurvata.*

Nolina tuberculata. See *Beaucarnea recurvata.*

NOMOCHARIS
LILIACEAE

Genus of bulbs, grown for their lily-like habit and, in summer, loose spikes of flattish flowers, often conspicuously spotted. Requires partial shade and rich, well-drained soil. In summer, keep soil moist but not waterlogged. Remains dormant throughout winter. Propagate by seed in winter or spring.

N. mairei. See *N. pardanthina.*

N. nana. See *Lilium nanum.*

N. pardanthina, syn. *N. mairei,* illus. p.385.

N. saluenensis. Summer-flowering bulb. **H** 34in (85cm), **S** 5–6in (12–15cm). Leafy stems bear lance-shaped, scattered leaves. Has loose spike of 2–6 saucer-shaped, white or pink flowers, with dark purple eyes and purple spots. Z7–9 H9–7.

Nopalxochia ackermannii. See *Disocactus ackermannii.*

NOTHOFAGUS
Southern beech
FAGACEAE/NOTHOFAGACEAE

Genus of deciduous or evergreen trees, grown for their habit, foliage and, in the case of deciduous species, fall color. Has inconspicuous flowers in late spring. Requires sun or partial shade and, because it is not very resistant to strong winds, should have the shelter of other trees. Prefers deep, fertile, moist but well-drained soil; is not suitable for shallow, chalky soil. Propagate by seed in fall.

N. x alpina, syn. *N. procera,* illus. p.64.

N. antarctica (Antarctic beech, Nirre). Deciduous, broadly conical tree, sometimes with several main stems. **H** 50ft (15m), **S** 30ft (10m). Small, oval, crinkly-edged, glossy, dark green leaves turn yellow in fall. Z7–10 H10–7.

N. betuloides, illus. p.69.

N. dombeyi, illus. p.68.

N. menziesii, illus. p.69.

N. obliqua, illus. p.63.

N. procera. See *N. x alpina.*

NOTHOLIRION
LILIACEAE

Genus of summer-flowering bulbs, related to *Lilium*, grown for their funnel-shaped flowers. Often produces early leaves, which may be damaged by spring frosts, so grow in a cool greenhouse in areas subject to alternating mild and cold periods in spring. Prefers partial shade or sun and rich, well-drained soil. Bulb dies after flowering. Propagate in spring or fall by offsets, which take 2–3 years to reach flowering size, or in winter or spring by seed.

N. campanulatum, illus. p.386.

Nothopanax. See *Pseudopanax*.
Nothoscordum neriniflorum. See *Caloscordum neriniflorum*.
Notocactus apricus. See *Parodia concinna*.
Notocactus haselbergii. See *Parodia haselbergii* subsp. *haselbergii*.
Notocactus leninghausii. See *Parodia leninghausii*.
Notocactus mammulosus. See *Parodia mammulosa*.
Notocactus ottonis. See *Parodia ottonis*.
Notocactus rutilans. See *Parodia mueller-melchersii*.
Notocactus scopa. See *Parodia scopa*.
Notospartium carmichaeliae. See *Carmichaelia carmichaeliae*.

NUPHAR
Spatterdock, Yellow pond lily
NYMPHAEACEAE

Genus of deciduous, perennial, deep-water plants, grown for their floating foliage and spherical flowers. Needs sun and running or still water; is often grown for a water-lily effect in conditions where true water lilies would not thrive. Remove fading foliage and flowers, and divide crowded plants. Propagate by division in spring.

N. advena (Common spatterdock). Deciduous, perennial, deep-water plant. **S** 4ft (1.2m). Has broadly oval, floating, mid-green leaves; central ones are occasionally erect. Small, purple-tinged, yellow flowers in summer are followed by ovoid to flask-shaped fruits. Z6–11 H12–6.
N. lutea, illus. p.444.

Nuttallia. See *Oemleria*.

NYMANIA
AITONIACEAE/MELIACEAE

Genus of one species of evergreen, spring-flowering shrub, grown for its flowers and fruits. Needs full light and fertile, well-drained soil. Water container specimens moderately when in full growth, less at other times. Propagate by seed in spring or by semiripe cuttings in summer.
N. capensis, illus. p.456.

NYMPHAEA
Waterlily
NYMPHAEACEAE

Genus of deciduous, summer-flowering, perennial water plants, grown for their floating, usually rounded leaves and brightly colored flowers. Needs an open, sunny position and still water; they are not suitable for streams, or positions close to

fountains. Remove fading foliage to prevent it polluting water. Plants have tuber-like rhizomes and require dividing and replanting in spring or early summer every 3 or 4 years. Most frost-tender plants may be treated as annuals. May also be propagated by seed or by separating plantlets in spring or early summer. Water lily beetle and China mark moth eat the foliage and can be problems. See also feature panel p.440.

N. 'Amabilis'. Deciduous, perennial water plant with floating leaves. **S** 5–7ft (1.5–2.2m). Rounded leaves, reddish-purple when young, mature to dark green with red-margined, light green undersides. In summer has star-shaped, pink flowers, 6–7in (15–19cm) across, with light pink tips and dark yellow stamens. Z3–11 H12–1.
N. 'American Star', illus. p.440. Deciduous, perennial water plant with floating leaves. **S** to 4ft (1.2m). Young leaves are purplish-green or bronze, maturing to bright green. Star-shaped flowers, 4in (10cm) across, are deep pink and are held above water throughout summer. Z3–11 H11–1.
N. 'Attraction', illus. p.440. Deciduous, perennial water plant with floating leaves. **S** to 6ft (2m). Has dark green leaves. In summer bears cup-shaped, white-flecked, garnet-red flowers, 6in (15cm) across. Z3–11 H11–1.
N. 'Aurora'. Deciduous, perennial water plant with floating leaves. **S** to 30in (75cm). Olive-green leaves are mottled with purple. In summer has star-shaped flowers, 2in (5cm) across, cream in bud, opening to yellow, then passing through orange to blood-red. Is suitable for a small- to medium-sized pool. Z10–11 H12–7.
N. 'Black Princess', illus. p.440. Deciduous, perennial water plant with floating leaves. **S** 4ft (1.2m). Rounded, red-bronze leaves mature to dark green. In summer produces cup-shaped, very dark blackish-purple flowers, 3in (8cm) across, with dark orange stamens.
N. 'Blue Beauty', illus. p.440. Deciduous, perennial water plant with floating leaves. **S** to 8ft (2.5m). Leaves are brown-freckled, dark green above, purplish-green beneath. Fragrant, rounded, deep blue flowers, to 12in (30cm) across, are produced in summer. Z10–11 H11–7.
N. capensis (Cape blue waterlily). Deciduous, perennial water plant with floating leaves. **S** to 6ft (2m). Large, mid-green leaves are often splashed with purple beneath. Star-shaped, bright blue flowers, 6–8in (15–20cm) across, are borne in summer. Z10–11 H12–7.
N. 'Emily Grant Hutchings'. Deciduous, perennial water plant with floating leaves. **S** to 4ft (1.2m). Has small, green leaves overlaid with bronze-crimson. Cup-shaped, pinkish-red flowers, 6–8in (15–20cm) across, open during night in summer. Z10–11 H12–7.
N. 'Escarboucle', illus. p.440. Deciduous, perennial water plant with floating leaves. **S** to 10ft (3m). Leaves are dark green. In summer has cup-shaped, deep crimson flowers, 4–6in (10–15cm) across, with bright golden-yellow centers. Z3–11 H12–1.
N. 'Fabiola'. Deciduous, perennial water plant with floating leaves. **S** to 5ft (1.5m). In summer produces fragrant, peony-shaped flowers, 6–7in (15–18cm) across, with

strongly flecked, pink petals, above mid-green leaves. Z10–11 H12–7.
N. 'Firecrest', illus. p.440. Deciduous, perennial water plant with floating leaves. **S** to 4ft (1.2m). Dark green leaves are suffused with purple. In summer bears star-shaped, deep pink flowers, 6–8in (15–20cm) across, with bold, red-tipped stamens. Z3–11 H11–1.
N. 'Froebelii', illus. p.440. Deciduous, perennial water plant with floating leaves. **S** 3ft (90cm). Has rounded, pale green leaves, bronzed when young. In summer produces cup-shaped, later star-shaped, burgundy-red flowers, 4–5in (10–12cm) across, with red stamens. Z3–11 H11–1.
N. 'General Pershing'. Deciduous, perennial water plant with floating leaves. **S** 5–6ft (1.5–1.8m). Leaves are rounded, wavy-margined, olive-green and marked with purple. In summer bears highly fragrant, cup-shaped, later flat, lavender-pink flowers, 8–11in (20–27cm) across, with yellow stamens. Z10–11 H12–7.
N. 'Gladstoneana'. Deciduous, perennial water plant with floating leaves. **S** to 10ft (3m). Leaves are mid-green. Star-shaped, white flowers, 6–12in (15–30cm) across, are produced in summer. Z3–11 H12–1.
N. 'Gonnère', illus. p.440. Deciduous, perennial water plant with floating leaves. **S** to 5ft (1.5m). Has bright pea-green leaves and, in summer, rounded, white flowers, 6–8in (15–20cm) across. Z3–11 H12–1.
N. 'Green Smoke'. Deciduous, perennial water plant with floating leaves. **S** to 6ft (2m). Bronze-green leaves have bronze speckling. Star-shaped flowers, 4–8in (10–20cm) across, are chartreuse, shading to blue. Z10–11 H12–7.
N. 'Helvola', syn. *N. pygmaea* 'Helvola', *N. tetragona* 'Helvola', illus. p.440. Deciduous, perennial water plant with floating leaves. **S** to 18in (45cm). Has small, olive-green leaves with heavy purple or brown mottling. Produces star-shaped, yellow flowers, $3/4$–$1^1/4$in (2–4cm) across, in summer.
N. 'James Brydon', illus. p.440. Deciduous, perennial water plant with floating leaves. **S** to 8ft (2.5m). Fragrant, peony-shaped, orange-suffused, crimson flowers, 6–8in (15–20cm) across, are borne in summer above glossy, dark green leaves. Z3–11 H11–1.
N. 'Laydekeri Fulgens'. See *N.* 'Fulgens' Laydekeri Group.
N. Laydekeri Group 'Fulgens', syn. *N.* 'Laydekeri Fulgens', illus. p.440. Deciduous, perennial water plant with floating leaves. **S** to 3ft (1m). Dark green leaves have purplish-green undersides. Star-shaped, bright crimson flowers, 2–4in (5–10cm) across, are borne in summer. Z3–11 H11–1.
N. 'Lemon Chiffon', illus. p.440. Deciduous, perennial water plant with floating leaves. **S** 6ft (2m). Rounded, mid-green leaves, red spotted underneath, are strongly splashed with bronze. Produces spherical, pale lemon flowers, 6in (15cm) across, in summer.
N. 'Lucida', illus. p.440. Deciduous, perennial water plant with floating leaves. **S** 5–6ft (1.5–1.8m). Has broadly ovate, mid-green leaves. Star-shaped flowers, 5–6in (12–15cm) across, with red inner petals, pink-veined, whitish- pink outer petals and yellow stamens, are produced in summer. Z3–11 H11–1.

N. 'Madame Wilfon Gonnère'. Deciduous, perennial water plant with floating leaves. **S** to 5ft (1.5m). Has mid-green leaves and, in summer, cup-shaped, white flowers, 6in (15cm) across, spotted with deep rose-pink. Z10–11 H12–7.
N. Marliacea Group 'Albida' (illus. p.440) Deciduous, perennial water plant with floating leaves. **S** to 6ft (2m). Deep green leaves have red or purplish-green undersides. Bears fragrant, cup-shaped, pure white flowers, 6–8in (15–20cm) across, in summer. Z3–11 H11–1. **'Chromatella'** (illus. p.440), has olive-green leaves, heavily mottled with maroon and bronze, and canary-yellow flowers. Z3–11 H11–1.
N. odorata var. minor (illus. p.440), Deciduous, perennial water plant with floating leaves. **S** 3ft (1m). Small, rounded, soft green leaves have dark red undersides. Produces fragrant, star-shaped, white flowers, 3in (8cm) across, in summer. Z3–11 H11–1. **'Sulphurea Grandiflora'**, syn. *N.* 'Odorata Sulphurea Grandiflora' has dark green leaves, heavily mottled with maroon, and star-shaped, yellow flowers, 4–6in (10–15cm) across. Z2–10 H12–1.
N. 'Odorata Sulphurea Grandiflora'. See *N. odorata* 'Sulphurea Grandiflora'.
N. 'Pink Sensation'. Deciduous, perennial water plant with floating leaves. **S** 4ft (1.2m). In summer bears cup-shaped, later star-shaped, pink flowers, 5–6in (12–15cm) across, with yellow inner stamens and pink outer stamens. Has rounded, mid-green leaves, purple-green when young. Z3–11 H12–1.
N. pygmaea. See *N. tetragona*. **'Helvola'**. See *N.* 'Helvola'.
N. 'Pygmaea Rubra'. Deciduous, perennial water plant with floating leaves. **S** 2ft (60cm). Small, reddish-green young leaves mature to purplish-green. Produces cup-shaped, blood-red flowers, 2in (5cm) across, in summer.
N. 'Ray Davies'. Deciduous, perennial water plant with floating leaves. **S** to 5ft (1.5m). In summer produces peony-shaped, light pink flowers, 6–7in (15–18cm) across, slightly yellow in center, above rounded, deep green leaves. Z10–11 H12–7.
N. 'Red Flare'. Deciduous, perennial water plant with floating leaves. **S** 5–6ft (1.5–1.8m). Leaves are rounded, strongly toothed and reddish-green. In summer bears night-blooming, flat, dark red flowers, 7–10in (17–25cm) across, with light pink or yellowish stamens. Z10–11 H12–7.
N. 'Rose Arey', illus. p.440. Deciduous, perennial water plant with floating leaves. **S** to 5ft (1.5m). Leaves are purple when young, maturing to reddish-green. In summer bears star-shaped, deep rose-pink flowers, 4–6in (10–15cm) across, that pale with age and have strong aniseed fragrance. Z3–11 H11–1.
N. 'Saint Louis'. Deciduous, perennial water plant with floating leaves. **S** to 6ft (2m). Bright green leaves are spotted with brown when young. Produces open, star-shaped, bright yellow flowers, 6–10in (15–25cm) across, in summer. Z10–11 H12–7.
N. 'Sunrise', illus. p.440. Deciduous, perennial water plant with floating leaves. **S** to 6ft (2m). Mid-green leaves have downy stalks and undersides. Bears star-shaped, yellow flowers, 4–6in (10–15cm) across, in summer. Z3–11 H11–1.

N

N. tetragona, syn. *N. pygmaea.* Z3–11 H12–1. **'Alba'** (illus. p.440) is a deciduous, perennial water plant with floating leaves. **S** to 12in (30cm). Has small, dark green leaves, purplish-green beneath, and, in summer, star-shaped, white flowers, ¾–1¼in (2–3cm) across. Z3–11 H11–1. **'Helvola'.** See *N.* 'Helvola'.

N. 'Virginia'. Deciduous, perennial water plant with floating leaves. **S** to 5ft (1.5m). Produces purplish-green leaves and, in summer, star-shaped, white flowers, 4–6in (10–15cm) across. Z3–11 H12–1.

N. 'Wood's White Knight'. Deciduous, perennial water plant with floating leaves. **S** to 6ft (2m). Leaves are mid-green, dappled with darker green beneath. In summer produces star-shaped, creamy-white flowers, 4–8in (10–20cm) across, with prominent, gold stamens, which open at night. Z10–11 H12–7.

NYMPHOIDES
Floating heart
MENYANTHACEAE

Genus of deciduous, perennial, deep-water plants, with floating foliage, grown for their flowers. Requires an open, sunny position. Propagate by division in spring or summer.

N. peltata, syn. *Limnanthemum nymphoides, Villarsia nymphoides,* illus. p.444.

NYSSA
Tupelo
NYSSACEAE

Genus of deciduous trees, grown for their foliage and fall color. Needs sun or partial shade and moist, neutral to acidic soil. Does best in hot summers. Resents being transplanted. Propagate by softwood cuttings in summer or by seed in fall.

N. sinensis, illus. p.77.

N. sylvatica, illus. p.66.

OCHNA
Bird's eye bush
OCHNACEAE

Genus of mainly evergreen trees and shrubs, grown mostly for their flowers and fruits. Prefers full light and well-drained soil. Water container specimens moderately, less when not in full growth. Prune, if necessary, in early spring. Propagate by seed in spring or by semiripe cuttings in summer.

O. multiflora. See *O. serrulata.*

O. serratifolia of gardens. See *O. serrulata.*

O. serrulata, syn. *O. multiflora, O. serratifolia* of gardens (Mickey Mouse plant). Evergreen, irregularly rounded, twiggy shrub that is semievergreen in low temperatures. **H** to 6ft (2m), **S** 3–6ft (1–2m) or more. Leaves are narrowly elliptic, toothed and glossy. Has 5-petaled, bright yellow flowers in spring–summer, followed by shuttlecock-shaped, red fruits, each with 1–5 berry-like seeds clustered on top. Z11 H12–9.

x ODONTIODA
ORCHIDACEAE

See also ORCHIDS.

O. **Mount Bingham gx.** See *Oncidium* Mount Bingham.

x *O.* Pacific Gold gx. See x *Oncostele* Pacific Mystery gx.

O. **Petit Port gx.** See *Oncidium* Petit Port.

x *Odontocidium* Artur Elle gx 'Columbian'. See *Oncidium* Artur Elle gx 'Colombien'.

x *Odontocidium* Tiger Hambuhren gx. See *Oncidium* Tiger Hambuhren.

x *Odontocidium* Tigersun gx 'Orbec'. See *Oncidium* Tigersun gx 'Orbec'.

Odontoglossum bictoniense. See *Rhynchostele bictoniensis.*

Odontoglossum **Buttercrisp gx.** See *Oncidium* Julie Barbara Good gx.

Odontoglossum cervantesii. See *Rhynchostele cervantesii.*

Odontoglossum cordatum. See *Rhynchostele cordatum.*

Odontoglossum crispum. See *Oncidium alexandrae.*

Odontoglossum **Eric Young gx.** See *Oncidium* Eric Young gx.

Odontoglossum grande. See *Rossioglossum grande.*

Odontoglossum **Le Nez Point gx.** See *Oncidium* Le Nez Point gx.

Odontoglossum rossii. See *Rhynchostele rossii.*

Odontoglossum **Royal Occasion gx.** See *Oncidium* Royal Occasion.

OEMLERIA
syn. NUTTALLIA, OSMARONIA
ROSACEAE

Genus of one species of deciduous, early spring-flowering shrub, grown for its fragrant flowers and decorative fruits. Separate male and female plants are needed in order to obtain fruits. Prefers sun or partial shade and moist soil. To restrict growth, remove suckers and cut old shoots back or down to base in late winter. Propagate by suckers in fall.

O. cerasiformis (Indian plum, Oregon plum, Oso berry). Deciduous, upright, then arching shrub that forms dense thickets. **H** 8ft (2.5m), **S** 12ft (4m). Leaves are narrowly oval and dark blue-green. Has nodding clusters of small, fragrant, bell-shaped, white flowers in early spring, followed by small, plum-shaped, purple fruits. Z6–10 H10–6.

OENOTHERA
Evening primrose, Sundrops
ONAGRACEAE

Genus of annuals, biennials and perennials, grown for their profuse but short-lived flowers in summer. Needs full sun and well-drained, sandy soil. Propagate by seed or division in fall or spring or by softwood cuttings in late spring.

O. acaulis. Tuft-forming perennial. **H** 6in (15cm), **S** 8in (20cm). Has oblong to oval, deeply toothed or lobed leaves. Cup-shaped, white flowers, turning pink, open at sunset in summer. Z5–9 H9–5.

O. caespitosa. Clump-forming, stemless perennial. **H** 5in (12cm), **S** 8in (20cm). Has narrowly oval, entire or toothed, mid-green leaves. Flowers, opening at sunset in summer, are fragrant, cup-shaped and white, becoming pink with age. Is suitable for a rock garden. Z4–8 H8–1.

O. fraseri. See *O. fruticosa* subsp. *glauca.*

O. fruticosa (Sundrops). **subsp. *glauca,*** syn. *O. fraseri, O. glauca, O. tetragona* is a clump-forming perennial. **H** 18–24in (45–60cm), **S** 18in (45cm). Dense spikes of fragrant, cup-shaped, bright yellow flowers are produced from mid- to late summer. Leaves, borne on reddish-green stems, are narrowly oval to lance-shaped and glossy, mid-green. **'Fyrverkeri',** syn. *O. fruticosa* 'Fireworks' illus. p.275. **'Fireworks'.** See *O. fruticosa* 'Fyrverkeri'.

O. glauca. See *O. fruticosa* subsp. *glauca.*

O. macrocarpa, syn. *O. missouriensis,* illus. p.372.

O. missouriensis. See *O. macrocarpa.*

O. perennis, syn. *O. pumila* (Sundrops). Clump-forming perennial. **H** 6–24in (15–60cm), **S** 12in (30cm). In summer, loose spikes of nodding buds open to fragrant, funnel-shaped, yellow flowers above spoon-shaped, mid-green leaves. Z3–8 H8–1.

O. pumila. See *O. perennis.*

O. speciosa (White evening primrose). Often short-lived, clump-forming perennial with running rhizomes. **H** 18in (45cm), **S** 12in (30cm) or more. In summer bears spikes of fragrant, saucer-shaped, green-centered, pure white flowers that age to pink and open flat. Leaves are narrowly spoon-shaped, deeply cut and mid-green. Z5–8 H8–1.

O. tetragona. See *O. fruticosa* subsp. *glauca.*

OLEA
Olive
OLEACEAE

Genus of evergreen trees, grown for their foliage and edible fruits. Needs full sun and deep, fertile, very well-drained soil. Propagate by semiripe cuttings in summer or by seed in fall.

O. europaea (Olive). Slow-growing, evergreen, spreading tree. **H** and **S** 30ft (10m). Is very long-lived. Narrowly oblong leaves are gray-green above, silvery beneath. Tiny, fragrant, white flowers, borne in short racemes in late summer, are followed by edible, oval, green, later purple fruits. Z8–10 H10–8.

OLEARIA
Daisy bush
COMPOSITAE/ASTERACEAE

Genus of evergreen shrubs and trees, grown for their foliage and daisylike flower heads. In mild, coastal areas, provides good, very wind-resistant shelter. Needs full sun and well-drained soil. Cut out dead wood in spring. Propagate by semiripe cuttings in summer.

O. albida of gardens. See *O.* 'Talbot de Malahide'.

O. avicenniifolia. Evergreen, rounded, dense shrub. **H** 10ft (3m), **S** 15ft (5m). Oval to lance-shaped, dark gray-green leaves are white beneath. Bears wide heads of fragrant, white flowers in late summer and early fall.

O. x haastii, illus. p.130.

O. 'Henry Travers', syn. *O. semidentata.* Evergreen, rounded, compact shrub. **H** and **S** 10ft (3m). Has white shoots and narrowly lance-shaped, leathery, gray-green leaves. Large heads of purple-centered, lilac flowers are borne from early to mid-summer.

O. ilicifolia, illus. p.130. Evergreen, bushy, dense shrub. **H** and **S** 10ft (3m). Narrowly oblong, rigid leaves are sharply toothed, gray-green and musk-scented. Fragrant, white flower heads are borne in clusters in early summer.

O. lacunosa. Evergreen, upright, dense shrub. **H** and **S** 10ft (3m). Narrowly oblong, pointed, rigid leaves have rust-brown hairs when young and mature to glossy, dark green with central, white veins. Produces white flower heads only rarely.

O. macrodonta, illus. p.132. Vigorous, evergreen, upright shrub, often treelike. **H** 20ft (6m), **S** 15ft (5m). Has holly-shaped, sharply toothed, gray-green leaves, silvery-white beneath. Large heads of fragrant, white flowers are borne in early summer.

O. x mollis. Evergreen, rounded, dense shrub. **H** 3ft (1m), **S** 5ft (1.5m). Has oval, wavy-edged, silvery-gray leaves. Large heads of small, white flowers are borne profusely in late spring. **'Zennorensis',** **H** and **S** 6ft (2m), has narrowly oblong leaves.

O. nummulariifolia, illus. p.128.

O. phlogopappa. Evergreen, upright, compact shrub. **H** and **S** 6ft (2m). Has oblong, wavy-edged, gray-green leaves. Massed, white flower heads are produced in late spring. Z12–15 H12–8. **var. subrepanda,** illus. p.149.

O. x scilloniensis. Evergreen, upright, then rounded, dense shrub. **H** and **S** 6ft (2m). Narrowly oblong, wavy-edged, gray-green leaves set off masses of white flower heads in late spring.

O. semidentata of gardens. See *O.* 'Henry Travers'.

O. 'Talbot de Malahide', syn. *O. albida.* Evergreen, bushy, dense shrub. **H** 10ft (3m),

N

S 15ft (5m). Oval, dark green leaves are silvery beneath. Bears broad heads of fragrant, white flowers in late summer. Is excellent for an exposed, coastal garden. Z9–10 H10–9.

O. virgata, illus. p.112.

Oliveranthus elegans. See *Echeveria harmsii.*

OLSYNIUM
IRIDACEAE

Genus of fibrous-rooted, clump-forming perennials, grown for their nodding, trumpet- to bell-shaped flowers in spring. Requires partial shade and rich, moderately fertile, moist soil. Propagate by seed in fall. Young plants take 2 or 3 years to flower.

O. biflorum, syn. *Phaiophleps biflora, Sisyrinchium odoratissimum.* Clump-forming, spring- to summer-flowering, rhizomatous perennial. **H** 10–14in (25–35cm), **S** 2–3in (5–8cm). Has cylindrical, rush-like, erect, basal leaves. Bears small head of pendent, white flowers that are striped and veined red. Z9–10 H10–9.

O. douglasii, syn. *Sisyrinchium douglasi, Sisyrinchium grandiflorum.* Stiff, upright, summer-deciduous perennial. **H** 10in (25cm), **S** 6in (15cm). Has grasslike leaves sheathing very short, threadlike flowering stems and, in early spring, a succession of pendent, bell-shaped, violet to red-purple, or sometimes white, flowers. Is suitable for a rock garden or alpine house. Z4–9 H9–3.

OMPHALODES
Navelwort
BORAGINACEAE

Genus of annuals and perennials, some of which are evergreen or semievergreen. Makes good groundcover, especially in rock gardens. Needs full or partial shade and moist but well-drained soil, except for *O. linifolia* and *O. luciliae,* which prefer sun. Propagate by seed or division in spring.

O. cappadocica, illus. p.334. **'Cherry Ingram'** illus. p.261.

O. linifolia, illus. p.299.

O. luciliae. Semievergreen, mound-forming perennial. **H** 3in (7cm), **S** 6in (15cm). Has oval, blue-gray leaves. In spring–summer, loose sprays of pink buds develop into flattish, sky-blue flowers. Resents winter wet, so plant in a sheltered site or alpine house. Prefers sun and very gritty soil. Z7–9 H9–7.

O. verna, illus. p.334.

OMPHALOGRAMMA
PRIMULACEAE

Genus of perennials, closely related to *Primula,* grown for their flowers. Makes good rock garden plants, but is difficult to grow, especially in hot, dry areas. Needs shade and moist but well-drained, gritty, peaty soil. Propagate by seed in spring.

O. vinciflorum. Basal-rosetted perennial. **H** 6in (15cm), **S** 4in (10cm). Has oval, hairy, mid-green leaves. In spring produces nodding, funnel-shaped, violet flowers, each with deeper violet throat and flat, flared mouth.

ONCIDIUM
ORCHIDACEAE

See also ORCHIDS.

O. alexandrae, syn. *Odontoglossum crispum,* illus. p.466. Evergreen, epiphytic orchid for a cool greenhouse or conservatory. **H** 6in (15cm). Bears long sprays of rounded flowers, 3in (8cm) across, white or spotted or flushed with pink, each with red-and-yellow-marked lip; flowering season varies. Has narrowly oval leaves, 4–6in (10–15cm) long. Requires shade in summer. Z13–15 H12–6.

O. Artur Elle gx 'Colombien', syn. x *Odontocidium* Artur Elle gx 'Columbian', illus. p.467. Evergreen, epiphytic orchid for a cool greenhouse. **H** 9in (23cm). Produces tall spikes of pale yellow flowers, 2½in (6cm) across, with intricate, brown patterns; flowering season varies. Has narrowly oval leaves, 4–6in (10–15cm) long. Requires shade in summer. Z14–15 H12–6.

O. Eric Young gx, syn. *Odontoglossum* Eric Young gx, illus. p.467. Evergreen, epiphytic orchid for a cool greenhouse. **H** 6in (15cm). Has spikes of white-lipped, pale yellow flowers, 3in (8cm) across, spotted with rich yellow; flowering season varies. Bears narrowly oval leaves, 4–6in (10–15cm) long. Grow in shade in summer. Z13–15 H12–6.

O. flexuosum. See *Gomesa flexuosum.*

O. Hambühren Stern gx 'Cheam', syn. x *Wilsonara* Hambühren Stern gx 'Cheam', illus. p.467. Evergreen, epiphytic orchid for a cool greenhouse. **H** 9in (23cm). Narrowly oval leaves are 4in (10cm) long. Bears spikes of deep reddish-brown flowers, 4in (10cm) across, each with yellow lip; flowering season varies. Requires shade in summer. Z14–15 H12–6.

O. Julie Barbara Good gx, syn. x *Odontoglossum* Buttercrisp gx, illus. p.467. Evergreen, epiphytic orchid for a cool greenhouse. **H** 9in (23cm). Produces arching spikes of intricately patterned, red, tan, orange and yellow flowers, 3in (8cm) across; flowering season varies. Has narrowly oval leaves, 4–6in (10–15cm) long. Needs shade in summer. Z14–15 H12–6.

O. Le Nez Point gx, syn. *Odontoglossum* Le Nez Point gx. Evergreen, epiphytic orchid for a cool greenhouse. **H** 6in (15cm). Crimson flowers, 2½in (6cm) across, are borne in spikes; flowering season varies. Has narrowly oval leaves, 4–6in (10–15cm) long. Needs shade in summer. Z13–15 H12–6.

O. Memoria Commander Wiggs gx 'Kay', (x *Odontocidium* Tiger Butter gx, x *Wilsonara* Wigg's gx 'Kay'), illus. p.467. Evergreen, epiphytic orchid for a cool greenhouse. **H** 9in (23cm). Bears spikes of mottled, deep reddish-brown flowers, 2in (5cm) across, with rich golden-yellow lip; flowering season varies. Narrowly oval leaves are 4–6in (10–15cm) long. Grow in shade in summer. Z14–15 H12–6.

O. Mount Bingham, syn. x *Odontioda* Mount Bingham gx. Evergreen, epiphytic orchid for a cool greenhouse. **H** 9in (23cm). Bears pink-edged, red flowers, 3½in (9cm) across, in spikes; flowering season varies. Has narrowly oval leaves, 4–6in (10–15cm) long. Needs shade in summer. Z14–15 H12–6.

O. papilio. See *Psychopsis papilio.*

O. Petit Port, syn. x *Odontioda* Petit Port gx. Evergreen, epiphytic orchid for a cool greenhouse. **H** 9in (23cm). Bears spikes of rich red flowers, 3in (8cm) across, with pink-and-yellow-marked lip; flowering season varies. Narrowly oval leaves are 4–6in (10–15cm) long. Needs shade in summer. Z14–15 H12–6.

O. Royal Occasion, syn. *Odontoglossum* Royal Occasion gx. Evergreen, epiphytic orchid for a cool greenhouse. **H** 6in (15cm). Has spikes of white flowers, 3in (8cm) across, with deep yellow markings in centers of lips, in fall–winter. Leaves are narrowly oval and 4–6in (10–15cm) long. Needs shade in summer. Z13–15 H12–6.

O. sotoanum, illus. p.466. Evergreen, epiphytic orchid for a cool greenhouse. **H** 6in (15cm). Dense, arching sprays of very fragrant, rose-lilac flowers, ¼in (0.5cm) across, with yellow highlight, are borne freely in fall. Has narrowly oval leaves, 4in (10cm) long. Requires partial shade in summer. Z14–15 H12–6.

O. Tiger Hambuhren gx, syn. x *Odontocidium* Tiger Hambuhren gx. Evergreen, epiphytic orchid for a cool greenhouse. **H** 9in (23cm). Deep yellow flowers, 3in (8cm) across and heavily patterned with chestnut-brown, are borne in tall spikes; flowering season varies. Has narrowly oval leaves, 4–6in (10–15cm) long. Needs shade in summer. Z14–15 H12–6.

O. Tigersun gx 'Orbec', syn. x *Odontocidium* Tigersun gx 'Orbec', illus. p.467. Evergreen, epiphytic orchid for a cool greenhouse. Is very similar to x *O.* Tiger Hambuhren, but the flowers are slightly smaller, with lighter patterning. Z14–15 H12–6.

O. tigrinum, illus. p.467. Evergreen, epiphytic orchid for a cool or intermediate greenhouse. **H** 9in (23cm). Branching spikes of fragrant, yellow-marked, brown flowers, 2in (5cm) across, with large, yellow lip, are borne in fall. Has oval leaves, 6in (15cm) long. Requires partial shade in summer. H11–6.

x ONCIDOPSIS
ORCHIDACEAE

See also ORCHIDS.

x O. Cambrica gx 'Lensing's Favorite', syn. x *Vuylstekeara* Cambrica gx 'Lensing's Favorite', illus. p.467. Evergreen, epiphytic orchid for a cool greenhouse. **H** 9in (23cm). Has narrowly oval leaves, 4–6in (10–15cm) long. Bears long sprays of wine-red flowers, 4in (10cm) across, heavily marked with white; flowering season varies. Needs shade in summer.

x O. Olga gx. Evergreen, epiphytic orchid for a cool greenhouse. **H** 6in (15cm). Pure white flowers, 4in (10cm) across, with large, reddish-brown-blotched lips, are borne in tall, arching racemes, mainly in fall. Produces ovoid pseudobulbs and narrowly oval leaves, 5in (12cm) long. Is best grown in shade in summer.

x ONCOSTELE
ORCHIDACEAE

See also ORCHIDS.

x O. Pacific Mystery gx (*Odontoglossum* cordatum, x *Odontioda* Pacific Gold gx). Evergreen, epiphytic orchid for a cool greenhouse. **H** 9in (23cm). Bears long

spikes of yellow-striped and -marked, rich chocolate-brown flowers, 3in (7cm) across; flowering season varies. Leaves are narrowly oval and 4–6in (10–15cm) long. Grow in shade in summer. Z14–15 H12–6.

ONIXOTIS
SYN. DIPIDAX
LILIACEAE/COLCHICACEAE

Genus of spring-flowering corms, cultivated mainly for botanical interest. Requires sun and well-drained soil. Plant corms in early fall and keep them watered until after flowering. Dry off in summer. Propagate by seed in fall.

O. triquetra, syn. *Dipidax triquetrum.* Spring-flowering corm. **H** 8–12in (20–30cm), **S** 2–3in (5–8cm). Long, narrow leaves are semierect and basal. Produces a spike of flattish, star-shaped, white flowers, each narrow petal having basal, red mark.

ONOCLEA
WOODSIACEAE/ONOCLEACEAE

Genus of one species of deciduous fern that rapidly colonizes wet areas via spreading, underground rhizomes. Needs partial shade and wet soil. Remove fronds as they fade. Propagate by division in fall or winter.

O. sensibilis, illus. p.443.

ONONIS
Restharrow
LEGUMINOSAE/PAPILIONACEAE

Genus of summer-flowering annuals, perennials and deciduous or semievergreen shrubs and subshrubs, grown for their pealike flowers. Is good for rock gardens, walls and banks. Needs sun and well-drained soil. Propagate by seed in fall or spring, shrubs also by softwood cuttings in summer.

O. fruticosa, illus. p.339.

O. natrix, illus. p.345.

O. rotundifolia. Deciduous or semievergreen, glandular, upright subshrub. **H** 8–24in (20–60cm), **S** 8–12in (20–30cm) or more. Bears small, rounded, 3-parted, toothed, hairy, green leaves, with terminal leaflet long-stalked. Relatively large, red-streaked, rose-pink flowers are produced in small clusters in summer. Z7–10 H10–7.

Onopordon. See *Onopordum.*

ONOPORDUM
SYN. ONOPORDON
Cotton thistle, Scotch thistle
COMPOSITAE/ASTERACEAE

Genus of annuals, biennials and perennials, ranging from stemless to tall, branching plants. Needs sun or partial shade and rich, well-drained soil. To prevent self-seeding, remove dead flower heads. Propagate by seed in fall or spring. Leaves are prone to slug and snail damage.

O. acanthium, illus. p.304.

ONOSMA
BORAGINACEAE

Genus of summer-flowering annuals, semievergreen biennials, perennials and subshrubs, grown for their long, pendent, tubular flowers. Is suitable for rock

O

gardens. Needs full sun and well-drained soil. Dislikes wet summers. Propagate by softwood cuttings in summer or by seed in fall.

O. alborosea, illus. p.338.

O. stellulata. Semievergreen, upright subshrub. **H** and **S** 6in (15cm). Leaves are oblong and covered in hairs which may irritate the skin. Clusters of yellow flowers are produced in late spring and summer. Z8–9 H9–8.

OOPHYTUM
AIZOACEAE

Genus of clump-forming, egg-shaped, perennial succulents with two united, very fleshy leaves. These are covered in dry, papery sheaths, except in spring when sheaths split open, revealing a new pair of leaves. Flowers are produced from a slight central fissure on upper surface. Is difficult to grow. Requires sun and well-drained soil. Propagate by seed or stem cuttings in spring or summer.

O. nanus. Clump-forming, perennial succulent. **H** ³/₄in (2cm), **S** ¹/₂in (1cm). Has 2 united, fleshy, green leaves and daisylike, white flowers, ¹/₂in (1cm) wide, in fall.

Operculina tuberosa. See *Merremia tuberosa.*

OPHIOPOGON
Lilyturf
LILIACEAE/ASPARAGACEAE

Genus of evergreen perennials, grown mainly for their grasslike foliage. Needs sun or partial shade and fertile, well-drained soil. Propagate by division in spring or by seed in fall.

O. jaburan (Jaburan lily, White lilyturf). Evergreen, clump-forming perennial. **H** 6in (15cm), **S** 12in (30cm). Has dark green leaves. In early summer produces racemes of bell-shaped, white flowers, followed by deep blue berries. Z7–10 H10–7. **'Vittatus',** syn. *O. jaburan* 'Variegatus' has white- or yellow-striped leaves and is much less robust. **'Variegatus'.** See *O. jaburan* 'Vittatus'.

O. japonicus, illus. p.283.

O. planiscapus 'Nigrescens', illus. p.280.

OPHRYS
ORCHIDACEAE

See also ORCHIDS.

O. aranifera. See *O. sphegodes.*

O. fuciflora of gardens, syn. *O. holoserica.* Deciduous, terrestrial orchid. **H** 6–22in (15–55cm). Spikes of flowers, ¹/₂in (1cm) long, from white through pink to blue and green, are borne in spring–summer. Leaves are oval to oblong, 2–4in (5–10cm) long. Z7–9 H9–7.

O. fusca (Somber bee orchid). Deciduous, terrestrial orchid. **H** 4–16in (10–40cm). Spikes of greenish, yellow or brown flowers, ¹/₄in (5cm) long, with yellow-edged, bluish, brown or purple lip, are produced in spring. Has oval or lance-shaped leaves, 3–5in (8–12cm) long. Z12–15 H12–6.

O. holoserica of gardens. See *O. fuciflora* of gardens.

O. lutea, illus. p.467. Deciduous, terrestrial orchid. **H** 3–12in (8–30cm). In spring bears short spikes of flowers, ¹/₂in (1cm) long,

with greenish sepals, yellow petals and brown-centered, bright yellow lips. Has oval, basal leaves, 2–4in (5–10cm) long. Z8–9 H9–8.

O. speculum, syn. *O. vernixia.* Deciduous, terrestrial orchid. **H** 3–12in (8–30cm). In spring produces dense spikes of flowers, ¹/₂in (1cm) long, with greenish or yellow sepals, purple petals and 3-centered, brown lips. Has oblong to lance-shaped leaves, 1¹/₂–3in (4–7cm) long. Z7–9 H9–7.

O. sphegodes, syn. *O. aranifera* (Early spider orchid). Deciduous, terrestrial orchid. **H** 4–18in (10–45cm). In spring–summer bears spikes of flowers, ¹/₂in (1cm) long, that vary from green to yellow and have spider-like, blackish-brown marks on lips. Leaves are oval to lance-shaped and 1¹/₂–3in (4–8cm) long. Z7–9 H9–7.

O. tenthredinifera (Sawfly orchid), illus. p.466. Deciduous, terrestrial orchid. **H** 6–22in (15–55cm). In spring has spikes of flowers, ¹/₂in (1cm) long, in colors of white to pink, or blue and green, with violet or bluish lip edged with pale green. Has basal rosette of oval to oblong leaves, 2–3¹/₂in (5–9cm) long. Z7–9 H9–7.

O. vernixia. See *O. speculum.*

Ophthalmophyllum herri. See *Conophytum longum.*
Ophthalmophyllum longum. See *Conophytum longum.*
Ophthalmophyllum villetii. See *Conophytum concordans.*

OPLISMENUS
GRAMINEAE/POACEAE

See also GRASSES, BAMBOOS, RUSHES and SEDGES.

O. africanus, syn. *O. hirtellus* (Basket grass). **'Variegatus'** illus. p.469.

O. hirtellus. See *O. africanus.*

OPLOPANAX
ARALIACEAE

Genus of deciduous, summer-flowering shrubs, grown for their habit, fruits and spiny foliage. Young growth may be damaged by late frosts. Prefers partial shade and moist soil. Propagate by seed in fall or by root cuttings in late winter.

O. horridus (Devil's club). Deciduous, spreading, open, sparsely branched shrub. **H** and **S** 6ft (2m). Prickly stems bear large, oval, 7–9-lobed, toothed, mid-green leaves. Bears dense umbels of small, star-shaped, greenish-white flowers from mid- to late summer, followed by spherical, red fruits. Z7–9 H9–7.

OPUNTIA
CACTACEAE

Genus of perennial cacti, ranging from small, alpine, groundcover plants to large, evergreen, tropical trees, with at times insignificant glochids—short, soft, barbed spines produced on areoles. Mature plants carry masses of short-spined, pear-shaped, green, yellow, red or purple fruits (prickly pears), edible in some species. Hardy species must be kept dry during winter in order to survive low temperatures. Needs sun and well-drained soil. Water container specimens when in full growth. Propagate by seed or stem cuttings in spring or summer. Some species can spread and

become invasive. Contact with the bristles causes intense irritation to skin, and they are difficult to remove.

O. brasiliensis, syn. *Brasiliopuntia brasiliensis.* Treelike, perennial cactus. **H** 18ft (5.5m), **S** 10ft (3m). Cylindrical, green stem bears bright green branches of flattened, oval, spiny segments. Sheds 2–3-year-old side branches. Masses of shallowly saucer-shaped, yellow flowers, 1¹/₂in (4cm) across, are produced in spring–summer, on plants more than 2ft (60cm) tall, and are followed by small, yellow fruits. Z11–12 H12–9.

O. cylindrica, syn. *Austrocylindropuntia cylindrica.* Bushy, perennial cactus. **H** 12–20ft (4–6m), **S** 3ft (1m). Cylindrical stems bear short-lived, cylindrical, dark green leaves on new growth. Areoles may lack spines or each produce 2 or 3 barbed ones. Shallowly saucer-shaped, pink-red flowers are produced in spring–summer, on plants more than 6ft (2m) tall, and are followed by greenish-yellow fruits. Z11–12 H12–9.

O. erinacea. See *O. polyacantha.*

O. ficus-indica (Indian fig, Prickly pear). Bushy to treelike, perennial cactus. **H** and **S** 15ft (5m). Bears flattened, oblong, spineless, blue-green stem segments. In spring–summer has masses of shallowly saucer-shaped, yellow flowers, 4in (10cm) across, followed by edible, purple fruits. Z11–12 H12–9.

O. humifusa, illus. p.494.

O. microdasys (Bunny ears). Bushy, perennial cactus. **H** and **S** 2ft (60cm). Has flattened, oval, green stem segments that develop brown marks in low temperatures. Bears spineless areoles, with white, yellow, brown or red glochids, closely set in diagonal rows. Masses of funnel-shaped, yellow flowers, 2in (5cm) across, are borne in summer on plants more than 6in (15cm) tall, and are followed by small, dark red fruits. Z11–12 H12–9. **var. albispina** illus. p.483. illus. p.483.

O. polyacantha, syn. *O. erinacea,* illus. p.481.

O. robusta, illus. p.488.

O. tunicata, syn. *Cylindropuntia tunicata,* illus. p.496.

O. verschaffeltii, syn. *Austrocylindropuntia verschaffeltii,* illus. p.486.

ORBEA
ASCLEPIADACEAE/APOCYNACEAE

Genus of clump-forming, perennial succulents with erect, 4-angled stems. Stem edges are often indented and may produce small leaves that drop after only a few weeks. Needs sun or partial shade and well-drained soil. Propagate by seed or stem cuttings in spring or summer.

O. variegata, syn. *Stapelia variegata,* illus. p.488.

ORCHIDS
ORCHIDACEAE

Family of perennials, some of which also produce evergreen or semievergreen, grown for their unusual flowers. These consist of 3 outer sepals and 3 inner petals, the lowest of which, known as the lip, is usually enlarged and different from the others in shape, markings and color. There are about 750 genera and 22,500 species, together

with an even greater number of hybrids, bred partly for their vigor and ease of care. They are divided into epiphytic and terrestrial plants. (The spread of an orchid is indefinite.)

Epiphytic orchids

Epiphytes have more flamboyant flowers than terrestrial orchids and are more commonly grown. In the wild, they grow on tree branches or rocks (lithophytes), obtaining nourishment through clinging roots and moisture through aerial roots. Most consist of a horizontal rhizome, from which arise vertical, water-storing, often swollen stems known as pseudobulbs. Flowers and foliage are produced from the newest pseudobulbs. Other epiphytes consist of a continuously growing upright rhizome; on these, flower spikes appear in the axils of leaves growing from the rhizome. In temperate climates, epiphytes need to be grown under glass.

Cultivation of epiphytes

For cultivation purposes, epiphytes, which are all tender (they cannot withstand freezing temperatures), may be divided into three groups: cool-greenhouse types, which require min. 50°F (10°C) and max. 75°F (24°C); intermediate-greenhouse types, needing a range of 55–80°F (13–27°C); and warm-greenhouse types, requiring 65–80°F (18–27°C). In summer, temperatures need to be controlled by shading the glass and by ventilation. Cool-greenhouse orchids may be placed outdoors in summer; this improves flowering. Other types may also be grown outdoors if the air temperature remains within these ranges.

The amount of light required in summer is given in individual plant entries. All epiphytic orchids, however, need to be kept out of direct sun in summer to avoid scorching, and require full light in winter.

Epiphytic orchids, whether grown indoors or outside, require a special soil-free compost obtained from an orchid nursery or made by mixing 2 parts fibrous material (such as bark chippings and/or peat) with 1 part porous material (such as moss and/or expanded clay pellets). Most epiphytes may be grown in pots, although some may be successfully cultivated in a hanging basket or on a slab of bark (with moss around their roots) suspended in the greenhouse.

In summer, water plants freely and spray regularly. Those suspended on bark slabs need a constantly moist atmosphere. In winter, water moderately and, if plants are in growth, spray occasionally. Some orchids rest in winter and require scarcely any water or none at all. Orchids benefit from weak foliar feeds; apply as for watering. Repot plants every other year, in spring; if they are about to flower, repot after flowering.

Terrestrial orchids

Terrestrial orchids, some of which also produce pseudobulbs, grow in soil or leaf mold, sustaining themselves in the normal way through roots or tubers. Some may be grown in borders, but many in temperate climates need to be cultivated in pots and protected under glass in winter.

Cultivation of terrestrial orchids

Terrestrial orchids are hardy to tender, min.

O

65°F (18°C). *Cypripedium* species may be grown outdoors in any area, preferably in neutral to acid soil, but cannot withstand severe frost, if frozen solid in pots or without snow cover, or tolerate very wet soil in winter. Other terrestrial orchids, except in very mild areas, are best grown in pots; use the same compost as for epiphytes but add 1 part grit to 2 parts compost. Place pots outdoors in a peat bed or in a glasshouse in the growing season. Keep dry when dormant. Under glass, light requirements, watering, feeding and repotting are as for epiphytes.

Orchid propagation

Orchids with pseudobulbs may be increased by removing and replanting old, leafless pseudobulbs when repotting in spring. Take care to retain at least 4 pseudobulbs on the parent plant. Some genera that may be propagated in this way are: *Ada*, x *Aliceara*, *Anguloa*, *Bletilla*, *Brassavola* (large plants only and retaining at least 6 pseudobulbs on the parent), x *Brassocattleya*, *Bulbophyllum*, *Calanthe*, *Cattleya*, *Coelogyne*, *Cymbidium*, *Dendrobium*, *Dendrochilum*, *Encyclia*, *Gomesa*, *Gongora*, *Laelia*, *Lycaste*, *Maxillariella*, *Miltonia*, *Miltoniopsis*, *Oncidium*, *Phaius*, *Pleione*, *Stanhopea* and *Zygopetalum*.

Some orchids without pseudobulbs produce new growth from the base. When a plant has 6 new growths, divide it in spring into 2 and repot both portions. Propagate *Disa*, *Paphiopedilum* and *Phragmipedium* in this way. Large specimens of *Eria* and *Masdevallia* may be divided in spring, leaving 4–6 stems on each portion.

Propagation of *Phalaenopsis* is by stem cuttings taken soon after flowering. *Vanda* may be increased by removing the top half of the stem once it has produced aerial roots and leaves; new growths will develop from the leafless base. With both these methods, achieving success is difficult and not recommended for the beginner.

Propagate terrestrial orchids with tubers by division of the tubers. Genera that may be increased in this way are: *Cypripedium* (in spring), *Dactylorhiza* (spring), *Ophrys* (fall), *Serapias* (fall) and *Spiranthes* (spring). *Calypso* is rarely propagated successfully in cultivation. *Angraecum* should not be propagated in cultivation, because the parent plant is easily endangered. Propagate *Ponerorchis* by small tubers that form around the base of the stem, when repotting tubers before growth commences in early spring. Seedlings may appear in the compost around the parent plant.

The most easily increased orchids are *Cymbidium*. Propagation of *Epidendrum* may be extremely difficult; see genus for specific details.

Orchids are illustrated on pp.466–67. See also *Ada*, x *Aliceara*, *Anacamptis*, *Angraecum*, *Anguloa*, *Bletilla*, *Brasiliorchid*, *Brassavola*, x *Brassocattleya*, *Bulbophyllum*, *Calanthe*, *Calypso*, *Cattleya*, x *Cattlianthe*, *Coelogyne*, *Cymbidium*, *Cypripedium*, *Dactylorhiza*, *Dendrobium*, *Dendrochilum*, *Disa*, *Encyclia*, *Epidendrum*, *Eria*, *Gomesa*, *Gongora*, *Guarianthe*, *Habenaria*, *Laelia*, *Lycaste*, *Masdevallia*, *Maxillariella*, *Miltonia*, *Miltoniopsis*, *Oncidium*, x *Oncidopsis*, x *Oncostele*, *Ophrys*, *Paphiopedilum*, *Phaius*,

Phalaenopsis, *Phragmipedium*, *Pleione*, *Ponerorchis*, *Psychopsis*, x *Rhyncattleanthe*, x *Rhycholaeliocattleya*, *Rhynochostele*, *Rossioglossum*, *Serapias*, *Specklinia*, *Spiranthes*, *Stanhopea*, *Vanda* and *Zygopetalum*.

Orchis elata. See *Dactylorhiza elata*.
Orchis maderensis. See *Dactylorhiza foliosa*.
Orchis morio. See *Anacamptis morio*.

OREOCEREUS
CACTACEAE

Genus of mainly columnar, perennial cacti with thick, cylindrical, much-ribbed stems with spines, usually branching from the base, and, in some species, covered in long hairs. Solitary, tubular-funnel-shaped flowers are produced near stem tips during the day in summer. Requires full sun and very well-drained, slightly alkaline soil. Water well in spring-summer, much less so in fall-winter. Propagate by seed in spring or summer.
O. aurantiacus. See *Matucana aurantiaca*.
O. celsianus, syn. *Cleistocactus celsianus*, illus. p.493.
O. trollii, syn. *Cleistocactus trollii*. Slow-growing, columnar, perennial cactus. **H** 28in (70cm), **S** 4in (10cm). Cylindrical, green stem, 3–4in (7–10cm), with thick, golden spines, is almost hidden by long, wispy, hairlike, white spines. Has pink flowers, 4in (10cm) long, with recurved tips, in summer on fully mature plants.

OREOPTERIS
THELYPTERIDACEAE

Genus of deciduous ferns, spreading via underground rhizomes to form colonies. Some species can be invasive. Needs sun or partial shade and moist or very moist soil. Remove fading fronds regularly. Propagate by division in spring.
O. limbosperma, syn. *Thelypteris oreopteris* (Mountain buckler fern, Mountain fern, Mountain wood fern). Deciduous fern. **H** 2–3ft (60cm–1m), **S** 1ft (30cm). Has mainly lance-shaped, much-divided fronds, with oblong to lance-shaped, mid-green pinnae. Z12–15 H12–10.

ORIGANUM
Marjoram, Oregano
LABIATAE/LAMIACEAE

Genus of deciduous subshrubs and perennials, sometimes with overwintering leaf rosettes. Some species are grown as culinary herbs, others for their clusters of tubular, usually pink flowers. Most species have arching, prostrate stems and are useful for trailing over rocks, banks and walls. Prefers sun and well-drained, alkaline soil. Propagate by division in spring, by cuttings of non-flowering shoots in early summer or by seed in fall or spring.
O. amanum. Deciduous, rounded, compact subshrub. **H** and **S** 6–8in (15–20cm). Open funnel-shaped, pale pink or white flowers are borne all summer above small, heart-shaped, pale green leaves. Makes a good alpine house plant; dislikes a damp atmosphere. Z5–8 H8–5.
O. dictamnus (Dittany of Crete, Hop marjoram). Prostrate perennial. **H** 5–6in

(12–15cm), **S** 16in (40cm). Arching stems are clothed in rounded, aromatic, hairy, gray-white leaves. Has pendent heads of open funnel-shaped, purplish-pink flowers in summer. Z8–11 H12–8.
O. 'Kent Beauty', illus. p.339.
O. laevigatum, illus. p.340.
O. rotundifolium. Deciduous, prostrate subshrub. **H** 9–12in (23–30cm), **S** 12in (30cm). In summer bears whorls of pendent, funnel-shaped, pale pink flowers, surrounded by yellow-green bracts. Has small, rounded, mid-green leaves. Z7–9 H9–7.
O. vulgare (Oregano). Mat-forming, woody-based perennial. **H** and **S** 18in (45cm). Has oval, aromatic, dark green leaves, above which branched, wiry stems bear clusters of tiny, tubular, 2-lipped, mauve flowers in summer. Z4–9 H10–2.
'Aureum', illus. p.274.

ORNITHOGALUM
Star-of-Bethlehem
HYACINTHACEAE/ASPARAGACEAE

Genus of bulbs, grown for their mostly star-shaped, white flowers, usually backed with green. Needs sun or partial shade and well-drained soil. Lift and dry tender species for winter, if grown outside in summer, and replant in spring. Propagate by seed or offsets, in fall for spring-flowering plants, in spring for summer-flowering ones. ① Handle carefully as all parts may cause severe discomfort if ingested; the sap may irritate skin.
O. arabicum, illus. p.408.
O. balansae, syn. *O. oligophyllum* of gardens, illus. p.414.
O. lanceolatum, illus. p.415.
O. magnum, illus. p.382.
O. montanum, illus. p.415.
O. narbonense, illus. p.408.
O. nutans, illus. p.399. Spring-flowering bulb. **H** 6–14in (15–35cm), **S** 3–4in (8–10cm). Has cluster of linear, channeled, semierect, basal leaves. Stem bears spike of pendent, bell-shaped, translucent, white flowers, ¾–1¼in (2–3cm) long, with pale green outsides. Prefers partial shade.
O. oligophyllum of gardens. See *O. balansae*.
O. saundersiae (Giant chincherinchee). Summer-flowering bulb. **H** to 3ft (1m), **S** 6–8in (15–20cm). Produces basal cluster of strap- or lance-shaped, semierect leaves. Stem bears flat-topped head of erect, flattish, white or cream flowers, each with blackish-green ovary forming dark eye. Z7–10 H10–7.
O. thyrsoides, illus. p.408.
O. umbellatum, illus. p.416. Spring-flowering bulb. **H** 4–12in (10–30cm), **S** 4–6in (10–15cm). Linear, channeled, semierect, green leaves each have white line on upper surface. Bears loose, flat-topped head of star-shaped, white flowers, backed with green.

Orobus vernus. See *Lathyrus vernus*.

ORONTIUM
Golden club
ARACEAE

Genus of one species of deciduous, perennial, deep-water plant, grown for its floating foliage and flower spikes. Needs full sun. Remove faded flower

spikes. Propagate by seed when fresh, in mid-summer.
O. aquaticum, illus. p.444.

OROSTACHYS
CRASSULACEAE

Genus of short-lived, basal-rosetted, perennial succulents, grown for their very fleshy, sword-shaped leaves. Produces flowers 3 years from sowing seed, then dies. Requires sun and well-drained soil. Propagate by seed or division in spring or summer.
O. chanetii. Basal-rosetted, perennial succulent. **H** 1½in (4cm), **S** 3in (8cm). Bears gray-green leaves that are shorter in rosette center. Flower stem produces dense, tapering spike of star-shaped, white or pink flowers, ½–¾in (1–2cm) across, in spring–summer. Z13–15 H12–1.

OROYA
CACTACEAE

Genus of spherical, perennial cacti. Inner flower petals form a tube and outer ones open fully. Needs sun and well-drained soil. Propagate by seed in spring or summer.
O. neoperuviana. See *O. peruviana*.
O. peruviana, syn. *O. neoperuviana*, illus. p.486.

Orphanidesia gaultherioides. See *Epigaea gaultherioides*.

ORTHROSANTHUS
IRIDACEAE

Genus of perennials with short, woody rhizomes, grown for their flowers. Prefers sun and well-drained soil. Propagate by division or seed in spring.
O. chimboracensis. Tufted, rhizomatous perennial. **H** 2ft (60cm) in flower, **S** 6in (15cm). Has very narrow, grasslike, ribbed, stiff leaves, to 18in (45cm) long, with finely toothed margins. In summer produces clusters of short-lived, long-stalked, shallowly bowl-shaped, lavender-blue flowers, each enclosed in 2 leaflike bracts. Z10–11 H12–1.

ORYCHOPHRAGMUS
CRUCIFERAE/BRASSICACEAE

Genus of late spring- to summer-flowering annuals. Needs sun and fertile, well-drained soil. Propagate by seed in spring.
O. violaceus. Moderately fast-growing, upright annual or biennial. **H** 12–24in (30–60cm), **S** 12in (30cm). Has branching flower stems and pointed, oval, pale green leaves. Heads of 4-petaled, purple-blue flowers are produced in spring. Z10–13 H8–1.

OSBECKIA
MELASTOMATACEAE

Genus of evergreen, summer-flowering perennials, subshrubs and shrubs, grown for their flowers and foliage. Needs full light or partial shade and rich, well-drained soil. Water container specimens freely when in full growth, moderately at other times. Cut back flowered stems by at least half in early spring to maintain vigor and to produce large flower trusses. Propagate

647

by seed in spring or by greenwood cuttings in summer.

O. stellata. Evergreen, rounded, stiff-stemmed shrub. **H** and **S** 3–6ft (1–2m). Has narrowly oval, hairy, prominently veined leaves. Bears terminal clusters of 4-petaled, rose-purple flowers in late summer. Z14–15 H12–10.

OSCULARIA
AIZOCEACE

Genus of spreading, sometimes erect, subshrubby perennial succulents, grown for their daisylike, white to pink flowers, and usually angular, fleshy, grayish-green leaves. Becomes woody with age. Makes good summer bedding or pot plants. Requires full sun and very well-drained soil. Propagate by seed or stem cuttings in spring or fall.

O. deltoides, syn. *Lampranthus deltoides,* illus. p.485.

OSMANTHUS
OLEACEAE

Genus of evergreen shrubs and trees, grown for their foliage and small, fragrant flowers. *O.* x *burkwoodii* and *O. heterophyllus* may be used for hedging. Needs sun or partial shade and fertile, well-drained soil. Restrict growth by cutting back after flowering; trim hedges in mid-summer. Propagate by semiripe cuttings in summer.

O. armatus. Evergreen, bushy, dense shrub. **H** and **S** 12ft (4m). Large, oblong, dark green leaves are rigid and sharply toothed. Has tubular, 4-lobed, white flowers in fall, followed by egg-shaped, dark violet fruits. Z8–9 H9–8.

O. x burkwoodii, syn. x *Osmarea burkwoodii,* illus. p.110.

O. decorus, syn. *Phillyrea decora.* Evergreen, upright, rounded, dense shrub. **H** 10ft (3m), **S** 15ft (5m). Has large, oblong, glossy, dark green leaves. Bears tubular, 4-lobed, white flowers in mid-spring, followed by egg-shaped, blackish-purple fruits. Z6–9 H9–6.

O. delavayi, syn. *Siphonosmanthus delavayi,* illus. p.110.

O. forrestii. See *O. yunnanensis.*

O. fragrans (Fragrant olive, Sweet olive). Evergreen, upright shrub or tree. **H** and **S** 20ft (6m). Very fragrant, tubular, 4-lobed, white flowers are borne amid oblong, glossy, dark green leaves, from early to late summer, followed by ovoid, blue-black fruits. Is suitable only for a very mild area. Z8–11 H12–8. **f. aurantiacus** has orange flowers. Z7–10 H10–7.

O. heterophyllus (False holly). **'Aureomarginatus',** illus. p.119. **'Gulftide'** is an evergreen, bushy, dense shrub. **H** 8ft (2.5m), **S** 10ft (3m). Holly-shaped, sharply toothed, glossy, dark green leaves set off tubular, 4-lobed, white flowers in fall.

O. yunnanensis, syn. *O. forrestii.* Evergreen, treelike, upright, then spreading shrub. **H** and **S** 30ft (10m). Has large, oblong, glossy, bright green leaves, bronze when young. Produces tubular, 4-lobed, creamy-white flowers in clusters in late winter or early spring. Z8–9 H9–8.

x Osmarea burkwoodii. See *Osmanthus Osmanthus* x *burkwoodii.*
Osmaronia. See *Oemleria.*

OSMUNDA
OSMUNDACEAE

Genus of deciduous ferns. Requires shade, except for *O. regalis,* which also tolerates sun. *O. cinnamomea* and *O. claytoniana* need moist soil; *O. regalis* prefers very wet conditions. Remove fading fronds regularly. Propagate by division in fall or winter or by spores as soon as ripe.

O. cinnamomea (Cinnamon fern). Deciduous fern. **H** 3ft (1m). **S** 18in (45cm). Outer, lance-shaped, divided, pale green sterile fronds, with deeply cut pinnae, surround brown fertile fronds, all arising from a fibrous rootstock. Z4–8 H8–1.

O. claytoniana (Interrupted fern). Deciduous fern. **H** 2ft (60cm). **S** 1ft (30cm). Has lance-shaped, pale green fronds, divided into oblong, blunt pinnae; outer sterile fronds are larger than fertile ones at center of plant. Z2–10 H9–1.

O. regalis, illus. p.443.

OSTEOMELES
ROSACEAE

Genus of evergreen, summer-flowering shrubs, grown for their habit, foliage and flowers. In most areas, plant against a south- or west-facing wall. Requires sun and fertile, well-drained soil. Propagate by semiripe cuttings in summer.

O. schweriniae, illus. p.129.

OSTEOSPERMUM
COMPOSITAE/ASTERACEAE

Genus of evergreen, semiwoody perennials. Does best in warm areas. Requires sun and well-drained soil. Propagate by cuttings of non-flowering shoots in mid-summer.

O. barberae of gardens. See *O. jucundum.*

O. 'Blue Streak', syn. *O. ecklonis* 'Blue Streak'. Evergreen, upright perennial. **H** and **S** 18in (45cm). In summer–fall, daisylike flower heads, with dark slate-blue centers and white ray florets, blue on reverse, are borne above lance-shaped, gray-green leaves. Z10–11 H6–1.

O. 'Buttermilk', illus. p.319.

O. 'Cannington Roy'. Evergreen, clump-forming, prostrate perennial. **H** 12in (30cm), **S** 18in (45cm). Large, daisylike, pink flower heads, with darker eyes, are borne profusely in summer–fall. Leaves are linear and gray. Z10–11 H6–1.

O. Cape Daisy Series NASINGA PURPLE ('Aksullo'), illus. p.311.

O. ecklonis. Evergreen, upright or somewhat straggling perennial. **H** and **S** 18in (45cm). In summer–fall, daisylike, white flower heads, with dark blue centers, are borne singly above lance-shaped, gray-green leaves. Z10–11 H6–1. **'Blue Streak'.** See *O.* 'Blue Streak'.

O. jucundum, syn. *O. barberae, Dimorphotheca barberae,* illus. p.265.

O. 'Nairobi Purple'. Evergreen, semi-prostrate perennial. **H** 12in (30cm), **S** 12–18in (30–45cm). Bears daisylike, velvety, deep purple-red flower heads, with darker streaks on outside of ray petals, in summer. Has fresh green, lance-shaped leaves. Will not flower freely in rich soils. Z10–11 H6–1.

O. Sunny Series 'Sunny Marina', illus. p.301.

O. 'Whirlygig', illus. p.298.

OSTROWSKIA
Giant bellflower
CAMPANULACEAE

Genus of one species of summer-flowering perennial. Prefers a warm, sunny situation and rich, moist but well-drained soil. May be difficult to grow because it requires a resting period after flowering, so cover with a frame until late fall to keep dry. Propagate by seed in fall or spring.

O. magnifica. Erect perennial. **H** 5ft (1.5m), **S** 1¹/₂ft (45cm). From early to mid-summer produces very large, bell-shaped flowers of light blue-purple, veined with darker purple. Produces whorls of oval, blue-gray leaves. Z7–8 H8–7.

OSTRYA
CORYLACEAE/BETULACEAE

Genus of deciduous trees, grown for their foliage, catkins and fruits. Needs sun or partial shade and fertile, well-drained soil. Propagate by seed in fall.

O. carpinifolia (European hop hornbeam). Deciduous, rounded tree. **H** and **S** 50ft (15m). Has gray bark and oval, glossy, dark green leaves that turn yellow in fall. Yellow catkins in mid-spring are followed by hop-like, greenish-white fruit clusters that become turn in fall. Z6–9 H9–6.

O. virginiana, illus. p.72.

OTHONNA
SYN. OTHONNOPSIS
COMPOSITAE/ASTERACEAE

Genus of evergreen shrubs, grown for their daisylike flower heads in summer. Needs sun and well-drained soil. Propagate by softwood cuttings in early summer.

O. cheirifolia, illus. p.344.

Othonnopsis. See *Othonna.*

OURISIA
SCROPHULARIACEAE/PLANTAGINACEAE

Genus of evergreen perennials with creeping rootstocks. Is suitable for peat beds and walls. Needs partial shade and moist, peaty soil. Propagate by division or seed in spring.

O. caespitosa, illus. p.360.

O. coccinea, illus. p.269.

O. 'Loch Ewe'. Vigorous, evergreen, rosetted perennial. **H** and **S** 12in (30cm). Prostrate stems have heart-shaped, leathery, mid-green leaves. Produces dense spikes of outward-facing, tubular, salmon-pink flowers in late spring and early summer. Z7–8 H8–7.

O. macrocarpa. Vigorous, evergreen, prostrate perennial. **H** 24in (60cm), **S** 8in (20cm). Has rosettes of heart-shaped, leathery, dark green leaves. Produces spikes of open cup-shaped, yellow-centered, white flowers in late spring. Z7–9 H9–7.

O. magellanica. See *O. ruellioides.*

O. microphylla, illus. p.362.

O. ruellioides, syn. *O. magellanica.* Evergreen, straggling perennial. **H** 1¹/₂in (4cm), **S** to 6in (15cm). In summer produces tubular, scarlet flowers above broadly heart-shaped leaves. Z7–9 H9–7.

OXALIS
Shamrock, Sorrel
OXALIDACEAE

Genus of tuberous, rhizomatous or fibrous-rooted perennials and semievergreen subshrubs, grown for their colorful flowers, which in bud are rolled like an umbrella, and their often ornamental leaves. Leaves are mostly less than ³/₄in (2cm) across and are divided into 3 or more leaflets. Some species may be invasive; smaller species and cultivars are suitable for rock gardens. Needs full sun or partial shade and well-drained soil. Propagate by division in fall or early spring.

O. acetosella (Wood sorrel). Creeping, spring-flowering, rhizomatous perennial. **H** 2in (5cm), **S** 12–18in (30–45cm). Forms mats of clover-like, 3-lobed leaves. Delicate stems bear cup-shaped, white flowers, ¹/₂in (1cm) across, with 5 purple-veined petals. Prefers partial shade. Z3–8 H8–1. **var. purpurascens.** See *O. acetosella* var. *subpurpurascens.* **var. subpurpurascens,** syn. *O. acetosella* var. *purpurascens,* illus. p.352.

O. adenophylla, illus. p.352.

O. bowiei, syn. *O. purpurata* var. *bowiei.* Spring- to summer-flowering, tuberous perennial. **H** 12in (30cm), **S** 6in (15cm). Has long-stalked, clover-like, 3-lobed leaves. Stems each produce loose head of 3–10 widely funnel-shaped, pinkish-purple flowers, 1¹/₄–1¹/₂in (3–4cm) across. Needs a sheltered, sunny site. Z8–10 H10–8.

O. chrysantha. Creeping, fibrous-rooted perennial. **H** 1¹/₂–2in (4–5cm), **S** 6–12in (15–30cm). Forms mats of clover-like, 3-lobed leaves. Stems each produce funnel-shaped, bright yellow flower, ³/₄–1¹/₄in (2–3cm) across, in summer. Requires a sheltered position. Z8–10 H10–8.

O. deppei. See *O. tetraphylla.*

O. depressa, syn. *O. inops,* illus. p.364.

O. enneaphylla. Tuft-forming, rhizomatous perennial. **H** 2–3in (5–7cm), **S** 3–4in (8–10cm). Gray-green leaves are divided into narrowly oblong to oval leaflets. In summer, stems bear widely funnel-shaped, lilac-pink or white flowers, 1¹/₄–1¹/₂in (3–4cm) wide. Z5–9 H9–5.

O. hedysaroides. Semievergreen, bushy subshrub. **H** 3ft (1m), **S** 1–1¹/₂ft (30–45cm). Stems have clover-like, green leaves with 3 elliptical leaflets, the central leaflet on a stalk. Leaf axils bear clusters of widely funnel-shaped, yellow flowers, ³/₄–1¹/₄in (2–3cm) across, in spring–summer. Z9–10 H10–9.

O. hirta. Late summer-flowering, tuberous perennial. **H** 12in (30cm), **S** 4–6in (10–15cm). Stem produces scattered leaves, with 3 narrowly lance-shaped leaflets. Leaf axils each produce solitary, widely funnel-shaped, rose-purple flower, ³/₄–1¹/₄in (2–3cm) wide, with yellow center. Z9–10 H10–9.

O. inops. See *O. depressa.*

O. 'Ione Hecker'. Tuft-forming, rhizomatous perennial. **H** 2in (5cm), **S** 2–3in (5–8cm). Gray leaves are divided into narrowly oblong, wavy leaflets. In summer bears funnel-shaped, pale purple-blue flowers, 1¹/₂in (4cm) across, with darker veins. Z8–9 H9–8.

O. laciniata. Tuft-forming, rhizomatous perennial. **H** 2in (5cm), **S** 2–3in (5–8cm). Has blue-gray leaves divided into narrowly

O

oblong, crinkly-edged leaflets. In summer bears widely funnel-shaped, steel-blue flowers, $1\frac{1}{2}$in (4cm) across, with darker veins. Z8–9 H9–8.

O. perdicaria, illus. p.371.

O. purpurata* var. *bowiei. See *O. bowiei*.

O. spiralis* subsp. *vulcanicola, syn. *O. vulcanicola*. Evergreen subshrub. **H** and **S** 12in (30cm). Succulent red stems bear clover-like, 3-lobed leaves in shades of reddish-yellow to dark or mid-green. Widely funnel-shaped, yellow flowers, $\frac{5}{8}$in (1.5cm) across, are borne in clusters from spring to fall. Is often used in summer bedding or in a hanging basket.

O. tetraphylla, syn. *O. deppei*, illus. p.338.

O. vulcanicola. See *O. spiralis* subsp. *vulcanicola*.

OXYDENDRUM

ERICACEAE

Genus of one species of deciduous tree, grown for its flowers and fall color. Needs an open position in sun or partial shade and moist, acid soil. Propagate by softwood cuttings in summer or by seed in fall.

O. arboreum, illus. p.76.

Oxypetalum caeruleum. See *Tweedia caerulea*.

OZOTHAMNUS

COMPOSITAE/ASTERACEAE

Genus of evergreen, summer-flowering shrubs, grown for their foliage and small, densely clustered flower heads. Requires full sun and well-drained soil. Propagate by semiripe cuttings in summer.

O. coralloides, syn. *Helichrysum coralloides*, illus. p.347.

O. ledifolius, syn. *Helichrysum ledifolium*, illus. p.151.

O. rosmarinifolius, syn. *Helichrysum rosmarinifolium*. Evergreen, upright, dense shrub. **H** 6–10ft (2–3m), **S** 5ft (1.5m). Has rosemary-like, linear, dark green leaves, woolly beneath, the margins curved under. Clusters of fragrant, white flower heads are produced in early summer. Z8–9 H9–8.

O. selago, syn. *Helichrysum selago*, illus. p.347.

P

PACHYCEREUS

CACTACEAE

Genus of slow-growing, columnar, perennial cacti, branching with age. The funnel-shaped flowers are unlikely to appear in cultivation as they are produced only on plants over 10ft (3m) high. Requires sun and well-drained soil. Propagate by seed in spring or summer.

P. marginatus, syn. *Lemaireocereus marginatus, Marginatocereus marginatus, Stenocereus marginatus*, illus. p.494.

P. pecten-aboriginum (Hairbrush cactus). Columnar, perennial cactus. **H** 35ft (11m), **S** 10ft (3m). Dark green stems bear 9–11 deep ribs. Each areole has 8 radial spines, $\frac{1}{2}$in (1cm) long, and longer central spines. Red-based, dark brown spines fade to gray. Z13–15 H12–10.

P. pringlei, illus. p.483.

P. schottii, syn. *Lophocereus schottii*, illus. p.493. **'Monstrosus'** is a columnar, perennial cactus. **H** 22ft (7m), **S** 6ft (2m). Irregular, olive- to dark green stems have 4–15 ribs and no spines. Has funnel-shaped, pink flowers, $1\frac{1}{4}$in (3cm) wide, at night in summer. Z13–15 H12–10.

PACHYPHRAGMA

CRUCIFERAE/BRASSICACEAE

Genus of perennials with rosettes of basal leaves, often grown as groundcover under shrubs. Needs sun or partial shade and moist soil. Propagate by division or stem cuttings in late spring, or by seed in fall.

P. macrophyllum, syn. *Thlaspi macrophyllum*, illus. p.255.

PACHYPHYTUM

CRASSULACEAE

Genus of rosetted, perennial succulents, closely related to *Echeveria*, with which it hybridizes. Needs sun and well-drained soil. Propagate by seed in spring or by leaf or stem cuttings in spring or summer.

P. compactum, illus. p.491.

P. oviferum, illus. p.490.

PACHYPODIUM

APOCYNACEAE

Genus of bushy or treelike, perennial succulents, mostly with swollen stems, closely related to *Adenium*, except that most species have spines. Requires full sun and very well-drained soil. May be very difficult to grow. Propagate by seed in spring or summer.

P. lamerei, illus. p.494.

P. succulentum. Treelike, perennial succulent. **H** 2ft (60cm), **S** 1ft (30cm). Swollen trunk, 6in (15cm) across, has narrow, vertical, green to gray-brown stems. Trumpet-shaped, pink-crimson flowers, $\frac{3}{4}$in (2cm) across, are borne near stem tips in summer. Z14–15 H12–10.

PACHYSANDRA

BUXACEAE

Genus of evergreen, creeping perennials and subshrubs, grown for their tufted foliage. Is useful for groundcover. Tolerates dense shade and grows in any but very dry soil. Propagate by division in spring.

P. axillaris. Evergreen, mat-forming subshrub. **H** 8in (20cm), **S** 10in (25cm). Stems are each crowned by 3–6 oval, toothed, leathery leaves. Produces small, white flowers in erect spikes in late spring.

P. terminalis, illus. p.375. **'Variegata'** is an evergreen, creeping perennial. **H** 4in (10cm), **S** 8in (20cm). Diamond-shaped, cream-variegated leaves are clustered at stem tips. In early summer bears spikes of tiny, white flowers, sometimes flushed purple.

PACHYSTACHYS

ACANTHACEAE

Genus of evergreen perennials and shrubs, grown for their flowers. Needs partial shade and fertile, well-drained soil. Water container plants freely when in full growth, moderately at other times. Cut back flowered stems in late winter to maintain a bushy habit. Propagate by greenwood cuttings in early summer. Whitefly and red spider mite may cause problems.

P. cardinalis. See *P. coccinea*.

P. coccinea, syn. *P. cardinalis, Jacobinia coccinea, Justicia coccinea* (Cardinal's guard). Evergreen, erect, robust shrub. **H** 4–6ft (1.2–2m), **S** 2–3ft (60cm–1m) to flower well. Leaves are oval and deep green. Has tubular, bright red flowers in tight, green-bracted spikes, 6in (15cm) long, in winter. Z13–15 H12–10.

P. lutea, illus. p.459.

Pachystima. See *Paxistima*.

x PACHYVERIA

CRASSULACEAE

Hybrid genus (*Echeveria* x *Pachyphytum*) of clump-forming, rosetted, perennial succulents, sometimes almost stemless. Requires full sun or partial shade and very well-drained soil. Propagate by leaf or stem cuttings in spring or summer.

x *P. glauca*, illus. p.490.

PAEONIA

Peony

PAEONIACEAE

Genus of late spring-flowering perennials and deciduous shrubs ("tree peonies"), grown for their bold foliage, showy blooms and, in some species, colorful seed pods. Young growth (especially on tree peonies) may be damaged by late spring frosts. Prefers sun (but tolerates partial shade) and rich, well-drained soil. Tall and very large-flowered cultivars need support. Propagate all species by seed in fall (may take up to 3 years to germinate), tuberous species by root cuttings in winter, tree peonies by semiripe cuttings in late summer or by grafting in winter. Perennials may also be propagated by division in fall or early spring. Is prone to peony wilt. ① All parts can cause mild stomach upset if ingested. See also feature panel pp.228–9.

Flower forms

Unless stated otherwise, peonies described below flower between late spring and early to mid-summer and have large, alternate leaves divided into oval to lance-shaped or linear leaflets. Flowers are single, semidouble, double or anemone-form.

Single—flowers are mostly cup-shaped, with 1 or 2 rows of large, often lightly ruffled, incurving petals and a conspicuous central boss of stamens.

Semidouble—flowers are similar to single ones, but have 2 or 3 rows of petals.

Double—flowers are rounded, usually composed of 1 or 2 outer rows of large, often lightly ruffled, incurving petals, the remaining petals being smaller, usually becoming more densely arranged and diminishing in size toward the center. Stamens are few, inconspicuous or absent.

Anemone-form (Imperial or Japanese)—flowers usually have 1 or 2 rows of broad, incurving, outer petals; the center of the flower is often filled entirely with numerous densely arranged, sometimes deeply cut, narrow petaloids derived from stamens.

P. 'Alice Harding'. Clump-forming perennial. **H** and **S** to 3ft (1m). Bears very large, fragrant, double, creamy-white flowers. Z3–8 H8–1.

P. 'America', illus. p.229. Clump-forming perennial. **H** and **S** to 3ft (1m). Has large, single flowers with very broad, crimson petals, lightly ruffled at edges. Z3–8 H8–1.

P. 'Argosy'. Deciduous, upright shrub (tree peony). **H** and **S** to 5ft (1.5m). Large, single, lemon-yellow flowers have crimson-purple blotch at base. Is hard to propagate. Z3–8 H8–1.

P. arietina. See *P. mascula* subsp. *arietina*.

P. 'Auguste Dessert'. Clump-forming perennial. **H** and **S** to 30in (75cm). Has masses of fragrant, semidouble flowers; carmine petals are tinged salmon-pink and have slightly ruffled, silvery-white edges. Foliage provides rich fall color. Z3–8 H8–1.

P. 'Avant Garde'. Clump-forming perennial. **H** and **S** to 3ft (1m). Has luxuriant foliage. Medium-sized to large, fragrant, single flowers are pale rose-pink with darker veins and bright golden anthers that have yellow-red filaments. Flowers are borne on stiff, straight stems in mid-spring and are ideal for cutting. Z3–8 H8–1.

P. 'Ballerina'. Clump-forming perennial. **H** and **S** 3ft (1m). Fragrant, double flowers are soft blush-pink, tinged lilac at first, later fading to white. Outer rows of petals are loosely arranged, very broad and incurving; inner petals are also incurving, but more densely arranged, narrower, more uneven in size and often have slightly ruffled margins. Foliage provides fall color. Z3–8 H8–1.

P. 'Baroness Schroeder'. Vigorous, clump-forming perennial. **H** and **S** to 3ft (1m). Is very free-flowering with large, fragrant, globe-shaped, double flowers, tinged with pale flesh-pink on opening but fading to almost pure white. Produces several rows of nearly flat, outer petals; inner petals are incurving, ruffled and very tightly arranged. Is one of the best peonies for cutting. Z3–8 H8–1.

P. 'Barrymore'. Clump-forming perennial. **H** and **S** to 34in (85cm). Has very large, anemone-form flowers with broad, outer petals that are palest blush-pink on

P

649

opening, later white. Clear pale golden-yellow petaloids are very narrow, relatively short and are neatly and densely arranged. Z3–8 H8–1.

***P.* 'Bartzella',** illus. p.229. Clump-forming, free-flowering hybrid between an herbaceous perennial and a tree peony. **H** and **S** 3ft (90cm). In early summer bears large, scented, double, lemon-yellow flowers, marked with red.

***P.* 'Bowl of Beauty',** illus. p.228. Clump-forming perennial. **H** and **S** to 3ft (1m). Has very large, anemone-form flowers with pale carmine-pink, outer petals and numerous narrow, densely arranged, ivory-white petaloids. Z3–8 H8–1.

***P.* 'Buckeye Belle',** illus. p.229. Clump-forming perennial. **H** and **S** 3ft (90cm). Has red-tinged, mid-green leaves and semidouble, dark red flowers with a mass of central, golden staminodes. Z3–8 H8–1.

***P.* 'Callie's Memory'.** Clump-forming, free-flowering hybrid between an herbaceous perennial and a tree peony. **H** 24–28in (60–80cm), **S** 24in (60cm). Produces large, scented, double, dark-centered, cream flowers marked red-pink at the edges and base.

P. cambessedesii (Majorcan peony), illus. p.228. Clump-forming perennial. **H** and **S** 18in (45cm). Has dark green leaves with veins, stalks and under-surfaces suffused purple-red. Single, deep rose-pink flowers are borne in mid-spring. Z3–8 H8–1.

***P.* 'Cheddar Cheese'.** Clump-forming perennial. **H** and **S** to 3ft (1m). Produces well-formed, large, double flowers in mid-summer. Neatly and densely arranged, slightly ruffled, ivory-white petals, the inner ones incurving, are interspersed with shorter, yellow petals. Z3–8 H8–1.

P

***P.* 'Cheddar Gold',** illus. p.228. Clump-forming perennial, **H** and **S** 28–32in (70–80cm). Bronze or reddish-brown stems bear dark green leaves divided into 9 lance-shaped leaflets. In late spring or early summer produces strongly scented flowers, with rounded, white petals surrounding central boss of golden staminodes.

***P.* 'Chocolate Soldier'.** Clump-forming perennial. **H** and **S** to 3ft (1m). Has mid- to dark green leaves that are often tinged bronze-red when young. Semidouble, purple-red flowers, borne in early summer, have yellow-mottled centers. Z3–8 H8–1.

***P.* 'Claire de Lune',** illus. p.229. Clump-forming perennial. **H** and **S** 28–32in (70–80cm). In mid-spring, single, pale yellow flowers, each with central boss of golden staminodes, are borne in pairs. Z3–8 H8–1.

***P.* 'Colonel Heneage'.** Clump-forming perennial of upright habit. **H** and **S** to 34in (85cm). Has masses of anemone-form flowers with both outer petals and inner petaloids of dark rose-crimson. Z3–8 H8–1.

***P.* 'Coral Charm',** illus. p.228. Clump-forming perennial. **H** and **S** 28in (70cm). Bears semidouble, peach-pink flowers opening from darker buds. Z3–8 H8–1.

***P.* 'Coral Fay'.** Clump-forming perennial forming a rather spreading dome. **H** and **S** 32–36in (80–90cm). Semidouble, pink-tinged, rich crimson flowers are paler toward petal bases; stamens are golden-yellow.

P. corallina. See *P. mascula* subsp. *mascula*.

***P.* 'Cora Louise'.** Clump-forming, free-flowering hybrid between an herbaceous perennial and a tree peony. **H** 24–32in (60–80cm), **S** 24in (60cm). Bears large, scented, semidouble, white flowers; each petal has purplish blotch at base.

***P.* 'Cornelia Shaylor'.** Erect, clump-forming perennial. **H** and **S** to 34in (85cm). Fragrant, double flowers, flushed rose-pink on opening and fading to blush-white, are borne freely from early to mid-summer. Ruffled petals are neatly and densely arranged. Z3–8 H8–1.

***P.* 'Dayspring'.** Clump-forming perennial. **H** and **S** to 28in (70cm). Has an abundance of fragrant, single, clear pink flowers borne in trusses. Z3–8 H8–1.

P. decora. See *P. peregrina.*

***P.* 'Defender'.** Vigorous, clump-forming perennial. **H** and **S** to 3ft (1m). Single, satiny, crimson flowers, to 6in (15cm) across, with central boss of golden anthers, are borne on strong stems. Z3–8 H8–1.

P. delavayi, illus. p.136. **var. *angustiloba*** is a deciduous, upright, open, suckering shrub or subshrub (tree peony). **H** to 3ft (1m), **S** 4ft (1.2m). Leaves are divided into pointed, oval leaflets, often with reddish stalks. Produces small, bowl-shaped, red, red-purple, yellow, orange or white flowers, 2–21⁄2in (5–6cm) across, with conspicuous, leafy bracts beneath, in late spring. **var. *angustiloba* f. *alba*,** syn. *P. potaninii* f. *alba* has white flowers. **var. *angustiloba* f. *angustifolia*,** syn. *P. potaninii* produces dark red, red or reddish-purple flowers. **var. *angustiloba* f. *trollioides*,** syn. *P. potaninii* var. *trollioides, P. trollioides* has yellow or orange flowers. **var. *delavayi* f. *delavayi*** has dark red to purplish flowers. **var. *delavayi* f. *lutea*,** syn. *P. lutea* has orange, yellow or greenish-yellow flowers, sometimes red at the bases or on the petal margins. **var. *ludlowii*.** See *P. ludlowii.*

***P.* 'Dresden'.** Robust, clump-forming perennial. **H** and **S** to 34in (85cm). Has single, ivory-white flowers tinged soft blush-rose-pink. Foliage provides fall color. Z3–8 H8–1. ***P.* 'Duchesse de Nemours',** syn. *P.* 'Mrs. Gwyn Lewis'. Vigorous, clump-forming perennial. **H** and **S** to 28in (70cm). Produces masses of richly fragrant, double flowers with very large, incurving, outer petals, tinged palest green at first, soon fading to pure white; inner petals with irregular margins are densely arranged toward center and are creamy-yellow at base. Z3–8 H8–1.

***P.* 'Early Windflower'.** Clump-forming perennial. **H** 28in (70cm), **S** 20in (50cm). Has bronze-tinged, mid-green leaves. Produces pendent, cup-shaped, single, pure white flowers.

P. emodi (Himalayan peony), illus. p.228. Clump-forming perennial. **H** to 4ft (1.2m), **S** to 3ft (1m). Glossy, green foliage is topped by tall stems bearing several large, fragrant, single, pure white flowers, with golden-yellow anthers. Z6–8 H8–6.

***P.* 'Evening World'.** Clump-forming perennial. **H** and **S** to 3ft (1m). Has abundant, large, anemone-form flowers with soft blush-pink, outer petals and very tightly arranged, pale flesh-pink petaloids. Z3–8 H8–1.

***P.* 'Félix Crousse',** syn. *P.* 'Victor Hugo', illus. p.229. Vigorous, clump-forming perennial. **H** and **S** to 30in (75cm). Bears a profusion of fragrant, double, rich carmine-pink flowers, with darker red centers. Petals are ruffled, very numerous and tightly arranged, with edges sometimes tipped silvery-white. Z3–8 H8–1.

***P.* 'Festiva Maxima',** illus. p.228. Clump-forming perennial. **H** and **S** to 3ft (1m). Has dense, spreading foliage and huge, fragrant, double flowers borne on strong stems. Rather loosely arranged petals are large with irregular margins; outer petals are pure white, inner ones each have crimson, basal blotch. Z3–8 H8–1.

***P.* 'Flamingo'.** Clump-forming perennial. **H** and **S** to 34in (85cm). Double flowers are large and clear pale salmon-pink. Foliage provides fall color. Z3–8 H8–1.

***P.* 'Garden Treasure',** illus. p.229. Clump-forming, free-flowering hybrid between an herbaceous perennial and a tree peony. **H** and **S** 28–32in (70–80cm). Has large, semidouble, bright yellow flowers.

***P.* 'Globe of Light'.** Clump-forming perennial. **H** and **S** to 3ft (1m). Has large, fragrant, anemone-form flowers. Outer petals are pure rose-pink, petaloids clear golden-yellow. Z3–8 H8–1.

***P.* 'Heirloom'.** Compact, clump-forming perennial. **H** and **S** to 28in (70cm). Bears masses of large, fragrant, double, pale lilac-pink flowers. Z3–8 H8–1.

***P.* 'Instituteur Doriat'.** Clump-forming perennial. **H** and **S** to 3ft (1m). Has abundant, large, anemone-form flowers, with reddish-carmine, outer petals and densely arranged, relatively broad petaloids, paler and more pink than outer petals, with ruffled, silvery-white margins. Foliage provides fall color. Z3–8 H8–1.

***P.* 'Jan van Leeuwen',** illus. p.228. Clump-forming perennial, **H** 36in (90cm), **S** 28in (70cm). Bronze or reddish-brown stems bear dark green leaves divided into leaflets. In late spring or early summer produces scented, white, bowl-shaped flowers, with large, floppy petals and yellow staminodes.

P. japonica, illus. p.228. Compact, clump-forming perennial. **H** 12–16in (30–40cm), **S** 8in (20cm). In early spring produces pink-tinged stems bearing soft green leaves with 7–9 rounded leaflets. Produces short-lived, cup-shaped, single, white flowers; after flowering, leaves continue to develop and turn to green. Z3–8 H8–1.

***P.* 'Kelway's Fairy Queen',** illus. p.228. Compact, clump-forming perennial. **H** and **S** 28–32in (70–80cm). Bronze-brown stems bear dark green leaves divided into lance-shaped leaflets. In late spring to early summer bears bowl-shaped, semidouble, soft pink flowers, with deeper outer petals and golden staminodes.

***P.* 'Kelway's Gorgeous',** illus. p.229. Clump-forming perennial. **H** and **S** to 34in (85cm). Single, intense clear carmine flowers, with a hint of salmon-pink, are borne very freely. Z3–8 H8–1.

***P.* 'Kelway's Majestic'.** Clump-forming perennial. **H** and **S** to 3ft (1m). Freely borne, large, fragrant, anemone-form flowers have bright cherry rose-pink, outer petals and lilac-pink petaloids flecked with silver or pale gold. Z3–8 H8–1.

***P.* 'Kelway's Supreme'.** Clump-forming perennial. **H** and **S** to 3ft (1m). Has large, strongly fragrant, double flowers, produced over a long period, sometimes borne in clusters on well-established plants. Petals are broad, incurving, soft blush-pink, fading to milk-white. Single or semidouble axillary flowers are often produced. Foliage provides fall color. Z3–8 H8–1.

***P.* 'Knighthood',** illus. p.229. Clump-forming perennial. **H** and **S** to 30in (75cm). Double flowers have densely arranged, rather narrow, ruffled petals of unusually rich burgundy-red. Z3–8 H8–1.

***P.* 'Krinkled White'.** Robust, clump-forming perennial. **H** and **S** to 32in (80cm). Large, bowl-shaped, single, milk-white flowers are sometimes flushed palest pink. Petals are large with ruffled margins. Z3–8 H8–1.

***P.* 'L'Espérance',** syn. *P.* x *lemoinei* 'L'Espérance', illus. p.229. Deciduous, upright shrub (tree peony). **H** and **S** to 5ft (1.5m). Has very large, single, primrose-yellow flowers with carmine blotch at base of each petal. Z3–8 H8–1.

P. lactiflora (Common garden peony). Variable, clump-forming perennial. **H** 28–48in (70–120cm), **S** 28–39in (70–100cm). Bronze or reddish-brown stems bear dark green leaves divided into 9 lance-shaped leaflets. In late spring or early summer, 1–3 scented, bowl-shaped, white flowers are borne on each stem. Is more often represented in garden by named selections, most of which are hybrids. Z3–8 H8–1.

***P.* 'Lady Alexandra Duff',** illus. p.228. Clump-forming perennial. **H** and **S** 36in (90cm). Bronze or reddish-brown stems bear dark green leaves divided into leaflets. In late spring or early summer produces large, scented, double flowers, with soft pink outer petals and smaller, white inner ones. Flowers fade white in sun. Z3–8 H8–1.

***P.* 'Laura Dessert',** illus. p.229. Clump-forming perennial. **H** and **S** to 30in (75cm). Produces fragrant, double flowers with creamy blush-white, outer petals. Densely arranged, incurving, inner petals are flushed rich lemon-yellow, and their margins are sometimes deeply cut. Z3–8 H8–1.

P.* x *lemoinei (*P. suffruticosa* and *P. lutea*). Variable, deciduous, upright, open shrub. **H** 6ft (2m) or more, **S** 3ft (1m). Bears bold, mid-green leaves divided into pointed leaflets. In early summer produces large, bowl-shaped, often double flowers in a range of colors, notably yellow. Z3–8 H8–1. **'High Noon'** (illus. p.229), **H** and **S** 4½ft (1.3m), has semidouble, bright yellow flowers, often marked with crimson toward center. Z3–8 H8–1. **'L'Espérance'.** See *P.* 'L'Espérance'.

P. lobata. See *P. peregrina.*

P. ludlowii, syn. *P. delavayi* var. *ludlowii, P. lutea* var. *ludlowii*, illus. p.229. Deciduous, upright, slightly suckering shrub. **H** to 11ft (3.5m), **S** to 5ft (1.5m). Leaves are divided into sharply pointed, bright green leaflets. Produces large, bright yellow flowers, to 5in (12cm) across, in late spring. Z3–8 H8–1.

P. lutea. See *P. delavayi* var. *delavayi* f. *lutea*. **var. *ludlowii*.** See *P. ludlowii.*

***P.* 'Madame Louis Henri'.** Deciduous, upright shrub (tree peony). **H** and **S** to 5ft (1.5m). Has loosely semidouble, whitish-yellow flowers with large, incurving, outer petals very heavily suffused with rusty-red. Smaller, often darker, inner petals each have basal, dull red blotch. Z3–8 H8–1.

P. 'Magic Orb', illus. p.229. Clump-forming perennial. **H** and **S** to 3ft (1m). Bears masses of large, strongly fragrant, double flowers, each with several outer whorls of fairly broad, ruffled, intense cherry-pink petals and center of densely arranged, smaller, incurving petals. Outermost rows of central petals are blush-white, heavily shaded with mid-rose-carmine; the innermost petals are mostly creamy-white. Foliage provides fall color. Z3–8 H8–1.
***P. mascula* subsp. *arietina*,** syn. *P. arietina* Tuberous perennial. **H** and **S** to 30in (75cm). Foliage is hairy underneath and dark green; stems are dark red. Has single, reddish-pink flowers. Seed capsules with 2–5 boat-shaped sections split to reveal purplish-black seeds. Z3–8 H8–1. **subsp. *mascula*,** syn. *P. corallina*, **H** and **S** to 3ft (1m), is clump-forming and has hairless leaflets. Produces purple- or carmine-red, occasionally pink or white flowers, with bosses of golden-yellow anthers borne on purple filaments.
***P. mlokosewitschii*,** illus. p.227.
P. 'Mother of Pearl'. Clump-forming perennial. **H** to 30in (75cm), **S** to 24in (60cm). Has grayish-green leaves and single, dog rose-pink flowers. Z3–8 H8–1.
P. 'Mrs. Gwyn Lewis'. See *P.* 'Duchesse de Nemours'.
***P. obovata* var. *alba*,** illus. p.228. Clump-forming perennial. **H** and **S** 28–36in (70–90cm). Has erect stems and large, deep green leaves, each with 9 uneven, broadly elliptic leaflets, pale gray-green and slightly hairy beneath. Bears single, cup-shaped, white flowers, with purple filaments. Z3–8 H8–1.
P. officinalis (Common peony). Clump-forming, tuberous perennial. **H** and **S** to 24in (60cm). This single, red apothecaries' peony has long been in cultivation, but is seldom seen today, having been superseded by larger, often double-flowered hybrids, such as the following. Z3–8 H8–1. **'Alba Plena',** **H** and **S** to 30in (75cm), has double, white flowers that are sometimes tinged with pink. **'China Rose',** **H** and **S** to 18in (45cm), has dark green foliage and single flowers, with incurving, clear dark salmon-rose petals and orange-yellow anthers. **'Crimson Globe',** **H** and **S** 28–34in (70–85cm), produces single, garnet-red flowers, with golden-yellow stamens. **'Rubra Plena'** (illus. p.229), **H** and **S** to 30in (75cm), is long-lived and has leaves divided into broadly oval leaflets, and double, vivid pinkish-crimson flowers, with ruffled petals.
P. 'Paul M. Wild', illus. p.229. Clump-forming perennial. **H** and **S** 36in (90cm). Bronze-brown stems bear dark green leaves divided into 9 lance-shaped leaflets. In late spring or early summer produces large, fully double, bowl-shaped, ruby-red flowers.
***P. peregrina*,** syn. *P. decora, P. lobata*. Clump-forming, tuberous perennial. **H** and **S** to 3ft (1m). Bears bowl-shaped, single, ruby-red flowers. Z3–8 H8–1. **'Otto Froebel'** (illus. p.229) has glossy, bright green leaves and bears large, single, vermilion flowers, tinged with salmon-rose.
P. 'Pillow Talk', illus. p.228. Clump-forming perennial. **H** and **S** 28–32in (70–80cm). Bronze or reddish-stems bear dark green leaves divided into leaflets. Between late spring and early summer bears double, soft pastel-pink flowers, slightly richer at petal tips. Z3–8 H8–1.
***P. potaninii*.** See *P. delavayi* var. *angustiloba* f. *angustifolia*. **f. *alba*.** See *P. delavayi* var. *angustiloba* f. *alba*. **var. *trollioides*.** See *P. delavayi* var. *angustiloba* f. *trollioides*.
P. 'Président Poincaré'. Clump-forming perennial. **H** and **S** to 3ft (1m). Fragrant, double, clear rich ruby-crimson flowers are borne very freely. Foliage provides fall color. Z3–8 H8–1.
P. 'Red Charm'. Clump-forming perennial with rather spreading dome. **H** and **S** 32in (80cm). Bears large, double, rich red flowers. Is good for cut flowers.
***P. rockii*,** syn. *P. suffruticosa* subsp. *rockii*. Deciduous, upright shrub. **H** and **S** to 7ft (2.2m). Produces large, spreading, semidouble, white flowers; inner petals each have basal, dark maroon blotch. Is difficult to propagate. Z3–8 H8–1.
P. 'Sarah Bernhardt', illus. p.228. Vigorous, erect, clump-forming perennial. **H** and **S** to 3ft (1m). Bears masses of huge, fragrant, fully double flowers, with large, ruffled, slightly dull rose-pink petals fading to silvery blush-white at margins. Z3–8 H8–1.
P. 'Shirley Temple', illus. p.228. Clump-forming perennial. **H** and **S** to 34in (85cm). Profuse, soft rose-pink flowers, fading to palest buff-white, are fully double, with broad petals arranged in whorls; innermost petals are smaller and more loosely packed. Z3–8 H8–1.
P. 'Silver Flare'. Clump-forming perennial. **H** and **S** to 3ft (1m). Stems are flushed dull reddish-brown. Produces masses of fragrant, single flowers, with rather long, slender, rich carmine-pink petals, each feathering to silvery-white edge. Foliage provides fall color. Z3–8 H8–1.
P. 'Sir Edward Elgar'. Clump-forming perennial. **H** and **S** to 30in (75cm). Has masses of single, chocolate-brown-tinged, rich crimson flowers, with bosses of loosely arranged, clear lemon-yellow anthers. Foliage provides fall color. Z3–8 H8–1.
***P. x smouthii*.** Clump-forming perennial. **H** and **S** to 24in (60cm). Produces masses of fragrant, single, glistening, dark crimson flowers, with yellow stamens, although both flowers and foliage may vary in color. Z3–8 H8–1.
P. 'Souvenir de Maxime Cornu'. Deciduous, upright shrub (tree peony). **H** and **S** to 5ft (1.5m). Large, richly fragrant flowers are fully double with warm golden-yellow petals densely arranged toward center; ruffled margins are dull reddish-orange. Z3–8 H8–1.
P. suffruticosa (Moutan). Deciduous, upright shrub (tree peony). **H** and **S** to 7ft (2.2m). Bears variable, large, cup-shaped flowers, single or semidouble, with incurving, rose-pink or white petals, each sometimes with usually chocolate-maroon, basal blotch. Has given rise to many cultivars with semidouble and double flowers. Z5–8 H8–5. **'Cardinal Vaughan'** (illus. p.229) has semidouble, ruby-purple flowers. **'Duchess of Marlborough',** **H** and **S** 5ft (1.5m) or more, produces semidouble, soft, warm pink flowers, with feathery petals. Z3–8 H8–1. **'Godaishu'** ('Large Globe') bears semi- or fully double, white flowers, with yellow centers, amid light green leaves that are fringed and twisted. **'Hakuo-jisi'** (illus. p.228), **H** and **S** 5ft (1.5m) or more, is strong growing and bears large, double, white flowers in early summer; petals are finely marked with purple at base. **'Hana-daijin'** ('Magnificent Flower'), **H** and **S** 6ft (2m) or more, is a vigorous cultivar that bears masses of double, purple flowers. Z3–8 H8–1. **'Hana-kisoi'** ('Floral Rivalry'; illus. p.228) has double, pale cerise-pink flowers. **'Kamada-nishiki'** ('Kamada Brocade'), **H** and **S** to 4ft (1.2m), produces large, double flowers, to 8in (20cm) across, that are lilac-pink striped white at petal margins. Z3–8 H8–1. **'Quing Long Wo Mo Chi',** **H** and **S** 10ft (3m), has large, scented, semidouble, dark purple flowers, with petals marked green toward base. Z3–8 H8–1. **'Reine Elizabeth',** **H** and **S** to 6ft (2m), has large, fully double flowers with broad, salmon-pink petals, flushed with bright copper-red and lightly ruffled at margins. Z3–8 H8–1. **'Renkaku'** ('Flight of Cranes'), **H** and **S** to 3ft (1m), bears double flowers, each with broad, incurving, slightly ruffled, ivory-white petals, loosely arranged in 3 or more whorls, that surround large boss of long, golden-yellow anthers. Z3–8 H8–1. **'Rimpo'** (illus. p.229), **H** and **S** 5ft (1.5m) or more, has large, scented, semidouble, dark mauve-purple flowers with ruffled petals. **subsp. *rockii*.** See *P. rockii*. **'Tama-fuyo'** ('Jewel in the Lotus') is vigorous and freely produces double, pink flowers earlier than most other cultivars. Z3–8 H8–1. **'Wu Long Peng Sheng',** **H** and **S** 10ft (3m), has scented, rounded, double, magenta-red flowers, with golden staminodes. Z3–8 H8–1. **'Yachiyo-tsubaki'** (illus. p.228), **H** and **S** 5ft (1.5m) or more, produces masses of semidouble, clear pink flowers.
P. tenuifolia (Fernleaf poppy). Clump-forming perennial. **H** and **S** to 18in (45cm). Has single, dark crimson flowers, with golden-yellow anthers. Deep green leaves, pale and gray-green beneath, are finely divided into pointed, linear segments. Z3–8 H8–1.
P. 'Thunderbolt', illus. p.229. Clump-forming perennial. **H** 3½ft (1.1m), **S** 28–32in (70–80cm). In mid-spring has masses of slightly pendent, single, deep red flowers, often streaked dark purple.
***P. trollioides*.** See *P. delavayi* var. *angustiloba* f. *trollioides*.
***P. veitchii*,** illus. p.229. Clump-forming perennial. **H** and **S** to 30in (75cm). In early summer produces nodding, cup-shaped, single, purple-pink flowers. Glossy, bright green leaves are divided into oblong to elliptic leaflets. Z3–8 H8–1.
P. 'Victor Hugo'. See *P.* 'Félix Crousse'.
P. 'White Wings', illus. p.228. Clump-forming perennial. **H** and **S** to 34in (85cm). In mid-summer produces masses of large, fragrant, single flowers, with broad, white petals, sometimes tinged sulfur-yellow, that are each slightly ruffled at tip. Glossy, dark green leaves provide fall color. Z3–8 H8–1.
P. 'Whitleyi Major', illus. p.228. Clump-forming perennial. **H** to 3ft (1m), **S** to 2ft (60cm). Large, single, ivory-white flowers have satin sheen and central bosses of clear yellow anthers. Foliage and stems are flushed rich reddish-brown. Z3–8 H8–1.
***P. wittmanniana*.** Clump-forming perennial. **H** and **S** to 3ft (1m). Has large, single, pale primrose-yellow flowers, each with large, central boss of yellow anthers on purple-red filaments. Leaves are divided into broadly oval leaflets, shiny dark green above, paler beneath. Z3–8 H8–1.

PALIURUS

RHAMNACEAE

Genus of deciduous, spiny, summer-flowering shrubs and trees, grown for their foliage and flowers. *P. spina-christi* is also grown for its religious association, reputedly being the plant from which Christ's crown of thorns was made. Requires full sun and well-drained soil. Propagate by softwood cuttings in summer or by seed in fall.
***P. spina-christi*,** illus. p.116.

PAMIANTHE

AMARYLLIDACEAE

Genus of one species of evergreen, spring-flowering bulb, grown for its large, strongly fragrant, showy flowers. Needs partial shade and rich, well-drained soil. Feed with high-potash liquid fertilizer in summer. Reduce watering in winter but do not allow to dry out. Propagate by seed in spring or by offsets in late winter.
***P. peruviana*,** illus. p.399.

PANCRATIUM

Sea lily

AMARYLLIDACEAE

Genus of bulbs, grown for their large, fragrant, daffodil-like flowers in summer. Needs sun and well-drained soil that is warm and dry in summer when bulbs are dormant. Plant at least 6in (15cm) deep. Feed with a high-potash liquid fertilizer every 2 weeks from fall to spring. Propagate by seed in fall or by offsets in early fall.
***P. illyricum*,** illus. p.408.
P. maritimum (Sea daffodil). Late summer-flowering bulb. **H** 18in (45cm), **S** 10–12in (25–30cm). Has strap-shaped, erect, grayish-green, basal leaves. Produces head of 5–12 white flowers, each with large, deep cup in center and 6 spreading petals. Is shy-flowering in cultivation. Z8–11 H12–8.

PANDANUS

Screw pine

PANDANACEAE

Genus of evergreen trees, shrubs and scramblers, grown for their foliage and overall appearance. Flowers and fruits appear only on large, mature specimens. Needs full light or partial shade and fertile, well-drained soil. Water container plants freely when in full growth, moderately at other times. Propagate by seed or suckers in spring or by cuttings of lateral shoots in summer. Red spider mite may be troublesome.
P. odoratissimus of gardens. See *P. tectorius*.
***P. tectorius*,** syn. *P. odoratissimus* (Thatch screw pine). Evergreen, rounded tree. **H** to 20ft (6m), **S** 10ft (3m) or more. Has rosettes of strap-shaped, deep green leaves, 3–5ft (1–1.5m) long, with spiny margins and spiny midrib beneath. Small flowers, the males in clusters, each with a lance-shaped,

white bract, are borne mainly in summer. Fruits are like round pineapples. Z14–15 H12–10. **'Veitchii'**, syn. *P. veitchii*, illus. p.454.

P. veitchii. See *P. tectorius* 'Veitchii'.

PANDOREA
BIGNONIACEAE

Genus of evergreen, woody-stemmed, twining climbers, grown for their flowers and leaves. Needs sun and well-drained soil. Prune after flowering to restrain growth. Propagate by seed in spring or by stem cuttings or layering in summer.

P. jasminoides, syn. *Bignonia jasminoides*, illus. p.459.

P. lindleyana. See *Clytostoma callistegioides*.

P. pandorana, syn. *Tecoma australis*, *Bignonia pandorana* (Wonga wonga vine). Fast-growing, evergreen, woody-stemmed, twining climber. **H** 20ft (6m) or more. Leaves have 3–9 scalloped leaflets. Bears small, funnel-shaped, cream flowers, streaked and often spotted with red, brown or purple, in clusters in summer. H12–8.

P. ricasoliana. See *Podranea ricasoliana*.

PANICUM
GRAMINEAE/POACEAE

See also GRASSES, BAMBOOS, RUSHES, and SEDGES.

P. capillare (Witch grass). Tuft-forming, annual grass. **H** 2–3ft (60cm–1m), **S** 1ft (30cm). Has broad leaves and hairy stems. Top half of each stem bears a dense panicle of numerous, minute, greenish-brown spikelets on delicate stalks in summer. H12–1.

P. virgatum 'Northwind', illus. p.289.

PAPAVER
Poppy
PAPAVERACEAE

Genus of annuals, biennials and perennials, some of which are semievergreen, grown for their cup-shaped flowers. Needs sun or partial shade and prefers moist but well-drained soil. Propagate by seed in fall or spring, *P. orientale* and its cultivars by root cuttings in winter. Self-seeds readily.

P. alpinum subsp. burseri. See *P. burseri*.

P. atlanticum. Clump-forming, short-lived perennial. **H** and **S** 4in (10cm). Has oval, toothed, hairy leaves and, in summer, single, dull orange flowers. Is good for a rock garden. Z5–7 H7–4.

P. burseri, syn. *P. alpinum* subsp. *burseri*. Semievergreen, tuft-forming, short-lived perennial, best treated as an annual or biennial. **H** 6–8in (15–20cm), **S** 4in (10cm). Has finely cut, gray leaves. Produces single, white flowers in summer. Is suitable for a rock garden, wall or bank. Z5–8 H8–5.

P. commutatum, syn. *P. commutatum* 'Ladybird'. Fast-growing, erect, branching annual. **H** and **S** 18in (45cm). Has elliptic, deeply lobed, mid-green leaves and, in summer, single, red flowers, each with black blotch in center. H8–1. **'Ladybird'**. See *P. commutatum*.

P. croceum, syn. *P. nudicaule* (Arctic poppy, Iceland poppy). Tuft-forming perennial. **H** to 12in (30cm), **S** 4in (10cm). Hairy stems each produce solitary,

fragrant, single, white-and-yellow flower, sometimes marked green outside, in summer. Many color forms have been selected. Leaves are oval, toothed and soft green. Needs partial shade. Is good for a rock garden. Z2–7 H9–2.

P. fauriei, syn. *P. miyabeanum* of gardens, illus. p.373.

P. 'Fireball', illus. p.238. Tuft-forming perennial, spreading by stolons. **H** 14in (35cm), **S** 12–24in (30–60cm). Has elliptical, lobed, toothed, hairy, mid-green leaves. In early summer, upright, rather wiry stems produce large, solitary, double, bright tangerine-orange flowers. Z4–9 H9–1.

P. 'Medallion', illus. p.238. Tuft-forming perennial, spreading by stolons. **H** 34in (85cm), **S** 28–39in (70–100cm). Has elliptical, lobed, toothed, hairy, mid-green leaves. In early and late summer, numerous upright, sturdy stems bear large, solitary, pinkish-purple flowers that last for several days.

P. miyabeanum of gardens. See *P. fauriei*.

P. nudicaule of gardens. See *P. croceum*.

P. orientale (Oriental poppy). Rosetted perennial. **H** 3ft (1m), **S** 1–3ft (30cm–1m). Single, brilliant vermilion flowers, with dark blotches at bases of petals, are borne in early summer. Has broadly lance-shaped, toothed or cut, rough, mid-green leaves. Flowering stems need support. Z3–9 H9–1. **'Allegro'**, syn. *P. orientale* 'Allegro Viva', **H** 24–30in (60–75cm), has bright scarlet flowers. **'Allegro Viva'**. See *P. orientale* 'Allegro'. **'Beauty of Livermere'**, illus. p.235. **'Black and White'** (illus. p.238) is vigorous and has large, white flowers. **var. bracteatum** (illus. p.238), **H** 4ft (1.2m), is a robust, vigorous perennial with ruff of bract-like leaves held below large, deeply cupped, blood-red flowers, with black, basal blotches. **'Cedric Morris'**, **H** 28in (70cm), produces pastel grayish-pink flowers. **'Choir Boy'** (illus. p.238) is variable, compact and bears ruffled, white flowers marked at base with 4 black blotches. **'Graue Witwe'** has ruffled, gray-white flowers. **'Indian Chief'** has deep mahogany-red flowers. **'Karine'** (illus. p.238) has bowl-shaped, soft pale pink flowers marked with dark red blotches. **'Kleine Tänzerin'** bears abundant, ruffled, dark pink flowers. **'Lauren's Lilac'** has soft lilac-mauve flowers. **'May Queen'** bears double, orange flowers. **'Mrs. Perry'** has large, salmon-pink flowers. **'Patty's Plum'** (illus. p.238) produces rich muddy-purple flowers that fade as they age. **'Perry's White'**, **H** 32in (80cm), has satiny, white flowers with purple centers. **'Prinzessin Victoria Louise'** has large, salmon-pink flowers. **'Turkish Delight'** (illus. p.238) bears unblotched, bright salmon-pink flowers. **'Watermelon'** has flowers of vivid watermelon-pink.

P. rhoeas (Corn poppy, Field poppy, Flanders poppy). **Shirley Group** (double) is a fast-growing, slender, erect annual. **H** 24in (60cm), **S** 12in (30cm). Has lobed, light green leaves. In summer produces rounded, often cup-shaped, double flowers, in shades of red, pink or white, including bicolors; (single) illus. p.310. H11–1.

P. somniferum (Opium poppy). Fast-growing, upright annual. **H** 30in (75cm), **S** 12in (30cm). Has oblong, lobed, light grayish-green leaves. Large, single flowers,

to 4in (10cm) wide, in shades of red, pink, purple or white, are produced in summer. Z3–8 H8–1. Several double-flowered forms are available, including **Carnation-flowered Series**, with fringed flowers in mixed colors; **Paeoniiflorum Group**, illus. p.303. **'Pink Beauty'**, which has salmon-pink flowers; and **'White Cloud'**, which produces large, white flowers.

PAPHIOPEDILUM
Slipper orchid
ORCHIDACEAE

⚠ Contact with foliage may aggravate skin allergies. See also ORCHIDS.

P. appletonianum. Evergreen, terrestrial orchid. **H** 3in (8cm). In spring, green flowers, 2$\frac{1}{2}$in (6cm) across and each with pouched, brownish lip and pink-flushed petals, are borne singly on tall, slender stems. Has oval, mottled leaves, 4in (10cm) long. Needs shade in summer. Z12–15 H12–6.

P. armeniacum, illus. p.467. Evergreen, terrestrial orchid. **H** 20in (50cm), **S** 10in (25cm). In spring, pouch-lipped, bright yellow flowers, 2$\frac{1}{2}$–4$\frac{1}{2}$in (6–11cm) across, with red lines in centers, are borne singly on tall stem. Strap-shaped leaves, 2$\frac{1}{2}$–16in (6–15cm) long, marbled light and dark green above, purple spotted beneath, are borne from creeping rhizome. Needs shade in summer.

P. bellatulum, illus. p.467. Evergreen, terrestrial orchid. **H** 2in (5cm). Bears solitary, almost stemless, rounded, pouch-lipped, white flowers, 3in (8cm) across, spotted with dark maroon, in spring. Oval, marbled leaves are 3in (8cm) long. Needs shade in summer. H11–6.

P. Buckhurst gx 'Mont Millais', illus. p.467. Evergreen, terrestrial orchid. **H** 4in (10cm). Solitary, rounded, yellow-and-white flowers, to 5in (12cm) across, lined and spotted with red, are produced in winter. Has oval leaves, 4in (10cm) long. Requires shade in summer. H11–6.

P. callosum. Evergreen, terrestrial orchid. **H** 3in (8cm). Purple- and green-veined, white flowers, 3in (8cm) across, are borne on tall stems in spring–summer. Has oval, mottled leaves, 4in (10cm) long. Needs shade in summer. Z12–15 H12–6.

P. fairrieanum, illus. p.467. Evergreen, terrestrial orchid. **H** 3in (8cm). Solitary, rich purple- and green-veined flowers, 2in (5cm) across, with curved petals and orange-brown pouches, are borne in fall. Oval leaves are 3in (8cm) long. Needs shade in summer. H11–6.

P. Freckles gx, illus. p.466. Evergreen, terrestrial orchid. **H** 4in (10cm). Solitary, rounded, reddish-brown-spotted and pouched, white flowers, 4in (10cm) across, are produced in winter. Has oval leaves, 4in (10cm) long. Needs shade in summer. H11–6.

P. haynaldianum. Evergreen, terrestrial orchid. **H** 5in (12cm). In summer, long-petaled, brown-marked, green-, pink-and-white flowers, to 6in (15cm) across, are produced singly. Has oval leaves, 8–9in (20–23cm) long. Requires shade in summer. Z12–15 H12–6.

P. Lyric gx 'Glendora', illus. p.467. Evergreen, terrestrial orchid. **H** 4in (10cm). Solitary, rounded, glossy, white-red-and-green flowers, 4in (10cm) across, are

produced in winter. Has oval leaves, 6in (15cm) long. Needs shade in summer. H11–6.

P. Maudiae gx, illus. p.467. Evergreen, terrestrial orchid. **H** 4in (10cm). Solitary, clear apple-green or deep reddish-purple flowers, 4in (10cm) across, appear on long stems in spring or early summer. Has oval, mottled leaves, 4in (10cm) long. Requires shade in summer. H11–6.

P. niveum. Evergreen, terrestrial orchid. **H** 2in (5cm). Solitary, white flowers, 1$\frac{1}{2}$in (4cm) across, are produced mainly in spring. Oval, marbled leaves are 3in (8cm) long. Needs shade in summer. Z12–15 H12–6.

P. rothschildianum, illus. p.467. Evergreen, clump-forming, terrestrial orchid. **H** and **S** 20in (50cm). Spikes of 2–6 pouch-lipped, creamy-yellow flowers, with maroon stripes, mahogany pouch and elongated petals, to 5$\frac{1}{2}$in (14cm) long, are produced in summer. Has strap-shaped, mid-green leaves, to 24in (60cm) long. Needs shade in summer. H11–1.

P. sukhakulii. Evergreen, terrestrial orchid. **H** 3in (8cm). In spring–summer, solitary, purple-pouched, black-spotted, green flowers, 3in (8cm) across, are borne on tall stems. Has oval, mottled leaves, 4in (10cm) long. Needs shade in summer. Z12–15 H12–6.

P. venustum. Evergreen, terrestrial orchid. **H** 4in (10cm). Solitary, variably colored flowers, 2$\frac{1}{2}$in (6cm) across, ranging from pink to orange with green veins and darker spots, are borne in fall. Has oval, mottled leaves, 4in (10cm) long. Needs shade in summer. Z12–15 H12–6.

PARADISEA
Paradise lily, St. Bruno's lily
LILIACEAE/ASPARAGACEAE

Genus of perennials, grown for their flowers and foliage. Requires sun and fertile, well-drained soil. Propagate by division in spring or by seed in fall. After division may not flower for a season.

P. liliastrum (St. Bruno's lily). Clump-forming, fleshy-rooted perennial. **H** 12–24in (30–60cm), **S** 12in (30cm). Slender stems, bearing racemes of saucer-shaped, white flowers in early summer, arise above broad, grasslike, grayish-green leaves. Z7–9 H9–7.

PARAHEBE
SCROPHULARIACEAE/PLANTAGINACEAE

Genus of evergreen or semievergreen, summer-flowering perennials, subshrubs and shrubs, similar to *Hebe* and *Veronica*. Is suitable for rock gardens. Needs sun and well-drained, peaty, sandy soil. Propagate by semiripe cuttings in early summer.

P. catarractae, illus. p.342.

P. lyallii. Semievergreen, prostrate shrub. **H** 6in (15cm), **S** 8–10in (20–25cm). Has oval, toothed, leathery leaves. In early summer, erect stems bear loose sprays of flattish, pink-veined, white flowers. Z8–9 H9–8.

P. perfoliata, syn. *Veronica perfoliata*, illus. p.271.

PARAQUILEGIA
RANUNCULACEAE

Genus of tufted perennials, grown for their cup-shaped flowers and fernlike foliage. Is difficult to cultivate and flower successfully. Prefers dry winters and cool climates. Is

P

good in alpine houses and troughs. Needs sun and gritty, well-drained, alkaline soil. Propagate by seed in fall.

P. anemonoides, syn. *P. grandiflora*, illus. p.350.

P. grandiflora. See *P. anemonoides*.

PARASERIANTHES
LEGUMINOSAE/MIMOSACEAE

Genus of deciduous or semievergreen trees, grown for their feathery foliage and unusual flower heads, composed of numerous stamens and resembling bottlebrushes. Do not plant out until late spring. Needs full sun and well-drained soil. Propagate by seed in spring.

P. lophantha, syn. *Albizia distachya*, *Albizia lophantha*, illus. p.89.

PARIS
LILIACEAE/MELANTHIACEAE

Genus of summer-flowering, rhizomatous perennials. Flowers are followed by fleshy fruits with black or red seeds. Requires full or partial shade and rich soil. Propagate by division in spring or by seed in fall. ⊕ The seeds may cause mild stomach upset if ingested.

P. polyphylla, syn. *Daiswa polyphylla*. Erect, rhizomatous perennial. **H** 2–3ft (60cm–1m), **S** to 1ft (30cm). In early summer, at tips of slender stems, produces unusual flowers consisting of ruff of green sepals, with another ruff of greenish-yellow petals, marked with crimson above, crowned by violet-purple stigma. Leaves, borne in whorls at stem tips, are lance-shaped to oval and mid-green. Z5–8 H8–5.

PARKINSONIA
LEGUMINOSAE/CAESALPINIACEAE

Genus of evergreen, spring-flowering shrubs and trees, grown for their flowers and overall appearance. Needs full sun, a dry atmosphere and fertile, well-drained soil. Water container specimens moderately when in full growth, sparingly at other times. Pruning is tolerated, but spoils the natural habit. Propagate by seed in spring.

P. aculeata (Jerusalem thorn). Evergreen, feathery shrub or tree with spiny, green stem. **H** and **S** 10–20ft (3–6m) or more. Long, linear leaves have winged midribs bearing tiny, elliptic, short-lived leaflets. Produces fragrant, 5-petaled, yellow flowers in arching racemes in spring. Z11–12 H12–10.

PARNASSIA
Bog star, Grass of Parnassus
PARNASSIACEAE/CELASTRACEAE

Genus of rosetted, mainly summer-flowering perennials, grown for their saucer-shaped flowers. Is good for rock gardens. Needs sun and wet soil. Propagate by seed in fall.

P. palustris, illus. p.336.

PAROCHETUS
LEGUMINOSAE/PAPILIONACEAE

Genus of trailing, evergreen perennials. Grows best in alpine houses. Needs partial shade and gritty, moist soil. Propagate by division of rooted runners year-round.

P. communis, illus. p.370.

PARODIA
CACTACEAE

Genus of rounded, perennial cacti with tubercles arranged in ribs that often spiral around green stems. Crown forms woolly buds, then funnel-shaped flowers. Requires full sun or partial shade and very well-drained soil. Water very lightly in winter; tends to lose roots during a long period of drought. Propagate by seed in spring or summer.

P. chrysacanthion, illus. p.496.

P. concinna, syn. *Notocactus apricus*. Flattened spherical, perennial cactus. **H** 3in (7cm), **S** 4in (10cm). Much-ribbed, pale green stem is densely covered with short, soft, golden-brown spines. In summer, crown produces flattish, glossy, bright yellow flowers, 3in (8cm) across, with purple stigmas. Prefers partial shade. Z13–15 H12–1.

P. erinacea, syn. *Wigginsia vorwerkiana*. Slow-growing, flattened spherical, perennial cactus. **H** 3in (8cm), **S** 3½in (9cm). Glossy stem, with up to 20 wartlike ribs, has yellow-white spines and bears yellow flowers in summer. Z13–15 H12–10.

P. haselbergii (Scarlet ball cactus). **subsp. graessneri** is a slow-growing, flattened spherical, perennial cactus. **H** 4in (10cm), **S** 10in (25cm). Bristly, golden spines cover much-ribbed, green stem. Slightly sunken crown bears funnel-shaped, glossy, greenish-yellow flowers, with yellow stigmas, in early spring. Prefers partial shade. **subsp. haselbergii**, syn. *Notocactus haselbergii*, illus. p.487.

P. leninghausii, syn. *Notocactus leninghausii*. Clump-forming, perennial cactus. **H** 3ft (1m), **S** 1ft (30cm). Woolly crown always slopes toward sun. In summer, on plants more than 4in (10cm) tall, yellow blooms open flat. Z13–15 H12–10.

P. mammulosa, syn. *Notocactus mammulosus*. Spherical, perennial cactus. **H** and **S** 4in (10cm). Green stem has about 20 ribs and straight, stiff, yellow-brown to white spines. Woolly crown produces masses of golden flowers in summer. Z13–15 H12–10.

P. microsperma, syn. *P. sanguiniflora*, illus. p.487.

P. mueller-melchersii, syn. *P. rutilans*, *Notocactus rutilans*, illus. p.486.

P. nivosa, illus. p.487.

P. ottonis, syn. *Notocactus ottonis*. Variable, spherical, perennial cactus. **H** and **S** 4in (10cm). Pale to dark green stem has 8–12 rounded ribs bearing stiff, golden radial spines and longer, soft, red central spines. In summer, crown bears flattish, glossy, golden flowers, with purple stigmas. Offsets freely from stolons. Prefers sun. Z13–15 H12–1.

P. rutilans. See *P. mueller-melchersii*.

P. sanguiniflora. See *P. microsperma*.

P. scopa, syn. *Notocactus scopa* (Silver ball cactus). Spherical to columnar, perennial cactus. **H** 10in (25cm), **S** 6in (15cm). Stem, with 30–35 ribs, is densely covered with white radial spines and longer, red central spines, 3 or 4 per areole. Crown bears funnel-shaped, glossy, yellow flowers, with purple stigmas, in summer. Prefers a sunny position. Z13–15 H12–1.

PARONYCHIA
Whitlow-wort
ILLECEBRACEAE/CARYOPHYLLACEAE

Genus of evergreen perennials, grown for their loose mats of prostrate stems. Is useful for rock gardens and walls. Needs sun and well-drained soil. Propagate by division in spring.

P. capitata (Nailwort, Willow wort). Vigorous, evergreen, mat-forming perennial. **H** ½in (1cm), **S** 16in (40cm). Silvery leaves are small and oval. In summer produces inconspicuous flowers surrounded by papery bracts. Makes good groundcover. Z8–10 H10–8.

P. kapela **subsp. serpyllifolia**, illus. p.375.

PARROTIA
HAMAMELIDACEAE

Genus of one species of deciduous tree, grown for its flowers and fall color. Flower buds may be killed by hard frosts. Requires full sun and prefers fertile, moist but well-drained soil. Is lime-tolerant, but usually colors best in acidic soil. Propagate by softwood cuttings in summer or by seed in fall.

P. persica, illus. p.77.

PARROTIOPSIS
HAMAMELIDACEAE

Genus of one species of deciduous tree or shrub, grown for its ornamental, dense flower heads surrounded by conspicuous bracts. Needs sun or partial and any fertile, well-drained soil except very shallow soil over chalk. Propagate by softwood cuttings in summer or by seed in fall.

P. jacquemontiana. Deciduous, shrubby or upright tree. **H** 20ft (6m), **S** 12ft (4m). Has witch-hazel-like, dark green leaves that turn yellow in fall. From mid- to late spring and in summer bears clusters of minute flowers, with tufts of yellow stamens, surrounded by white bracts. Z6–9 H9–6.

PARTHENOCISSUS
VITACEAE

Genus of deciduous, woody-stemmed, tendril climbers, grown for their leaves, which often turn beautiful colors in fall. Broad tips of tendrils have sucker-like pads that cling to supports. Has insignificant, greenish flowers in summer. Will quickly cover a north- or east-facing wall or fence and may be grown up a large tree. Needs full or partial shade and well-drained soil. Propagate by softwood or greenwood cuttings in summer or by hardwood cuttings in early spring. ⊕ The berries may cause mild stomach upset if ingested.

P. henryana, syn. *Vitis henryana*. Deciduous, tendril climber with 4-angled, woody stems. **H** to 30ft (10m) or more. Leaves have 3–5 oval, toothed, velvety, deep green or bronze leaflets, 1½–5in (4–13cm) long, with white or pinkish veins. Small, dark blue berries are produced in fall. Leaf color is best with a north or east aspect. Z8–9 H9–1.

P. quinquefolia, syn. *Vitis quinquefolia* (Virginia creeper). Deciduous, woody-stemmed, tendril climber. **H** 50ft (15m) or more. Leaves have 5 oval, toothed, dull

green leaflets, paler beneath, that turn crimson in fall. Blue-black berries are produced in fall. Is ideal for covering a high wall or building. Z7–9 H9–1.

P. striata. See *Cissus striata*.

P. thomsonii. See *Cayratia thomsonii*.

P. tricuspidata, illus. p.209. **'Lowii'**, illus. p.209. **'Veitchii'**, syn. *Ampelopsis veitchii*, illus. p.210.

PASSIFLORA
Granadilla, Passion flower
PASSIFLORACEAE

Genus of evergreen or semievergreen, woody-stemmed, tendril climbers, grown for their unusual flowers, each one with a central corona of filaments. Produces egg-shaped to rounded, fleshy, edible fruits that mature to orange or yellow in fall. Needs sun or partial shade and fertile, well-drained soil. Water freely in full growth, less at other times. Stems need support. Thin out and spur back crowded growth in spring. Propagate by seed in spring or by semiripe cuttings in summer.

P. x allardii, syn. *P. 'Allardii'*. Strong-growing, evergreen, woody-stemmed, tendril climber. **H** 22–30ft (7–10m). Has 3-lobed leaves. Pink-tinged, white flowers, 3–4in (7–10cm) wide, with purple-banded crowns, are produced in summer–fall. Z7–9 H9–7.

P. 'Allardii'. See *P. x allardii*.

P. antioquiensis, syn. *Tacsonia van-volxemii* (Red banana passionflower). Fast-growing, evergreen, woody-stemmed, tendril climber. **H** 15ft (5m) or more. Has downy leaves, with 3 deep lobes. Bears long-tubed, rose-red flowers, 4–5in (10–12cm) across, with purplish-blue centers, in summer–fall. Z12–15 H12–10.

P. caerulea, illus. p.204. **'Constance Elliot'** is a fast-growing, evergreen or semievergreen, woody-stemmed, tendril climber. **H** 30ft (10m) or more. Has rich green leaves. In summer–fall produces bowl-shaped, fragrant, white flowers, with pale blue or white filaments. Z6–9 H9–6.

P. x caeruleoracemosa. See *P. x violacea*.

P. x caponii 'John Innes'. Strong-growing, evergreen, woody-stemmed, tendril climber. **H** 25ft (8m). Has 3-lobed leaves and bowl-shaped, nodding, white flowers, flushed claret-purple, with purple-banded, white crowns, in summer–fall. Z13–15 H12–10.

P. coccinea, illus. p.462.

P. x exoniensis. Fast-growing, evergreen, woody-stemmed, tendril climber. **H** 25ft (8m) or more. Leaves have 3 deep lobes and are softly downy. Rose-pink flowers, 3in (8cm) across, with purplish-blue crowns, are produced in summer–fall. Z13–15 H12–10.

P. manicata (Red passionflower). Fast-growing, evergreen, woody-stemmed, tendril climber. **H** 10–15ft (3–5m). Has slender, angular stems and 3-lobed leaves. Red flowers, with deep purple and white crowns, are borne in summer–fall. Z12–15 H12–10.

P. mollissima, syn. *Tacsonia mollissima*. Fast-growing, evergreen, woody-stemmed, tendril climber. **H** 15ft (5m) or more. Softly downy leaves have 3 deep lobes. Long-tubed, pink flowers, to 3in (8cm) wide, with purplish-blue crown, are borne in summer–fall.

P. quadrangularis, illus. p.462.
P. racemosa (Red passionflower). Fast-growing, evergreen, tendril climber with slender, woody stems. **H** 15ft (5m). Has wavy, leathery leaves with 3 deep lobes. In summer–fall bears terminal racemes of pendent, crimson flowers, 3–4in (8–10cm) across, with white- and purple-banded crowns. Z13–15 H12–10.
P. sanguinea. See *P. vitifolia*.
P. x violacea, syn. *P. x caeruleoracemosa*. Vigorous, evergreen, woody-stemmed, tendril climber. **H** 30ft (10m). Has 3-lobed leaves. Purple flowers, 3in (8cm) across, are produced in summer–fall. Z12–15 H12–10.
P. vitifolia, syn. *P. sanguinea*. Evergreen, woody-stemmed, tendril climber; slender stems have fine, brown hairs. **H** to 15ft (5m). Has 3-lobed, lustrous leaves. In summer–fall bears bright scarlet flowers, 5in (13cm) wide, with short crown, banded red, yellow, and white. Z10–11 H12–10.

PATERSONIA
IRIDACEAE
Genus of evergreen, clump-forming, spring- and early summer-flowering, rhizomatous perennials. Needs full sun and light, well-drained soil. Leave undisturbed once planted. Propagate by seed in fall.
P. umbrosa. Evergreen, clump-forming, spring- and early summer-flowering rhizomatous perennial. **H** 12–18in (30–45cm), **S** 12–24in (30–60cm). Has erect, basal leaves and tough flower stems bearing a succession of iris-like, purple-blue flowers, 1¼–1½in (3–4cm) across. Z11–15 H12–6.

PATRINIA
VALERIANACEAE/CAPRIFOLIACEAE
Genus of perennials, with neat clumps, grown for their flowers. Is suitable for rock gardens and peat beds. Needs partial shade and moist soil. Propagate by division in spring or by seed in fall. Self-seeds freely.
P. triloba, illus. p.275.

PAULOWNIA
SCROPHULARIACEAE/PAULOWNIACEAE
Genus of deciduous trees, grown for their large leaves and foxglove-like flowers, borne before the foliage emerges. Flower buds and young growth of small plants may be damaged by very hard frosts. Requires full sun and fertile, moist but well-drained soil. Propagate by seed in fall or spring or by root cuttings in winter.
P. fortunei. Deciduous, spreading tree. **H** and **S** 25ft (8m). Has large, oval, mid-green leaves. In late spring bears large, fragrant flowers, purple-spotted and white inside, pale purple outside. Z5–8 H8–4.
P. imperialis. See *P. tomentosa*.
P. tomentosa, syn. *P. imperialis*, illus. p.72.

PAVONIA
MALVACEAE
Genus of evergreen, mainly summer-flowering perennials and shrubs, grown usually for their flowers. Needs full light or partial shade and rich, well-drained soil. Water freely in full growth, moderately at other times. Leggy stems may be cut back hard in spring. Propagate

by seed in spring or by greenwood cuttings in summer. Whitefly and red spider mite may be troublesome.
P. hastata. Evergreen, erect shrub. **H** 6–10ft (2–3m), **S** 3–6ft (1–2m). Has lance-shaped to oval, mid-green leaves, with 2 basal lobes. Funnel-shaped, pale red to white flowers, with darker basal spotting, are produced in summer.

PAXISTIMA
SYN. PACHYSTIMA
CELASTRACEAE
Genus of evergreen, spreading shrubs and subshrubs, grown for their foliage. Is suitable for groundcover. Needs sun or partial shade and rich, moist but well-drained soil. Propagate by division in spring or by semiripe cuttings in summer.
P. canbyi (Cliff green, Ratstripper). Evergreen, spreading subshrub. **H** 6–12in (15–30cm), **S** 8in (20cm). Leaves are linear or oblong. Short, pendent spikes of tiny, greenish-white flowers are produced in summer. Z3–7 H7–1.

Pedilanthus tithymaloides. See *Euphorbia tithymaloides*.

PELARGONIUM
Geranium
GERANIACEAE
Genus of mainly summer-flowering perennials, most of which are evergreen, often cultivated as annuals. Is grown for its colorful flowers and is useful in pots or as bedding plants; in warm conditions, flowers are borne almost continuously. A sunny site with 12 hours of daylight is required for good flowering. Prefers well-drained, neutral to alkaline soil. Dislikes very hot, humid conditions. Dead-head frequently and fertilize regularly if grown in containers; do not overwater. Plants may be kept through winter in the greenhouse by cutting back in fall–winter to 5in (12cm) and repotting. Propagate by softwood cuttings from spring to fall. ① Contact with the foliage may occasionally aggravate skin allergies.

Pelargoniums may be divided into six groups; all flower in summer–fall unless stated otherwise. See also feature panel p.309.
Angel—plants with rounded, sometimes scented, usually mid-green leaves, and clusters of small, single flowers of the regal type.
Ivy-leaved—trailing, evergreen plants, ideal for hanging baskets, with lobed, sometimes pointed, stiff, fleshy, usually mid-green leaves and flowers similar to those of zonal pelargoniums.
Regal—shrubby, evergreen plants with rounded, sometimes lobed or partially toothed, mid-green leaves and clusters of single, rarely double, broadly trumpet-shaped, exotic-colored flowers that are prone to weather damage in the open.
Scented-leaved and species—evergreen plants with small, single, often irregularly star-shaped flowers; scented-leaved forms are grown for their fragrance.
Unique—Tall-growing, evergreen subshrubs with rounded or lobed, sometimes incised, mid-green leaves, often with a pungent scent when crushed. Produces clusters of single, trumpet-

shaped, brightly colored flowers of the regal type, which appear continuously through the season.
Zonal—succulent-stemmed, evergreen plants with rounded, leaves, distinctively marked with a darker "zone," and single (5-petaled), semidouble or fully double flowers. Zonal pelargoniums can be separated into the following groups: cactus-flowered; double- and semidouble-flowered; fancy-leaved; Formosum hybrids; Rosebud; Single-flowered; and Stellar.

P. acetosum. Species pelargonium. **H** 20–24in (50–60cm), **S** 8–10in (20–25cm). Stems are succulent with fleshy, gray-green leaves that are often margined red. Bears single, salmon-pink flowers. Is good as a pot plant in a greenhouse. Z12–15 H12–1.
P. 'Alberta', illus. p.309. Evergreen, single-flowered zonal pelargonium. **H** 18in (45cm), **S** 12in (30cm). Bears clusters of small, crimson-and-white flowers. Is best grown as a bedding plant. H11–1.
P. AMETHYST ('Fisdel'). Evergreen, trailing ivy-leaved pelargonium. **H** and **S** to 5ft (1.5m). Leaves are fleshy with pointed lobes. Bears fully double, light mauve-purple flowers. Z12–15 H12–1.
P. Antik Series. Vigorous, evergreen, single-flowered zonal pelargonium grown as a climber or, with pinching, as groundcover. **H** and **S** 36–48in (90–120cm). Has rounded, lobed, plain green leaves and large clusters of flowers in orange, pink, violet, salmon, or scarlet. **ANTIK SALMON ('Tiksal')**, illus. p.309, bears salmon-pink flowers. H11–1.
P. 'Apple Blossom Rosebud'. Evergreen, rosebud zonal pelargonium. **H** 12in (30cm), **S** 9in (23cm). Fully double, pinkish-white flowers, margined with red, look like miniature rosebuds. Z12–15 H12–1.
P. 'Autumn Festival'. Evergreen, bushy regal pelargonium. **H** and **S** 12in (30cm). Salmon-pink flowers have pronounced, white throats. Z12–15 H12–1.
P. 'Bird Dancer'. Dwarf, stellar zonal pelargonium. **H** 6–8in (15–20cm), **S** 5–6in (12–15cm). Has clusters of single flowers, with pale pink lower petals and salmon-pink upper petals. H11–1.
P. BLUE WONDER ('Pacbla'), illus. p.309. Evergreen, semidouble-flowered zonal pelargonium. **H** 12in (30cm), **S** 16in (40cm). Has rounded, lobed, plain green leaves and large clusters of vivid rich lilac flowers (not blue). H11–1.
P. 'Bredon'. Strong-growing, evergreen regal pelargonium. **H** 18in (45cm), **S** to 12in (30cm). Bears large, maroon flowers. Z12–15 H12–1.
P. 'Brookside Primrose', illus. p.309. Dwarf, fancy-leaved zonal pelargonium. **H** 4–5in (10–12cm), **S** 3–4in (7–10cm). Bears double, pale pink flowers. Leaves have butterfly mark in center of each leaf. Is good as a pot plant or for bedding. H11–1.
P. Bulls Eye Series. Evergreen, single-flowered zonal pelargonium. **H** 13–15in (33–38cm), **S** 11–13in (28–33cm). Has rounded, lobed, chocolate-brown leaves with green edges. Produces large clusters of flowers in shades of red, pink, or a mixture. Propagate by seed. **'Bulls Eye Salmon'** (illus. p.309) has salmon-pink flowers. H11–1.
P. 'Butterfly Lorelei'. Fancy-leaved zonal pelargonium. **H** 10–12in (25–30cm), **S** 6–8in

(15–20cm). Has butterfly-shaped leaves and double, pale salmon-pink flowers. Is suitable as a container plant in a greenhouse. Z12–15 H12–1.
P. 'Caligula'. Evergreen, miniature, semidouble-flowered zonal pelargonium. **H** 6–8in (15–20cm), **S** 4in (10cm). Has small, crimson flowers and tiny, dark green leaves. Is suitable for a windowsill. H11–1.
P. 'Capen'. Bushy, semidouble-flowered zonal pelargonium. **H** 15–18in (38–45cm), **S** 6–8in (15–20cm). Bears semidouble, coral-pink flowers. Is good as a container plant. Z12–15 H12–1.
P. capitatum. Evergreen, scented-leaved pelargonium. **H** 12–24in (30–60cm), **S** 12in (30cm). Has mauve flowers and irregularly 3-lobed leaves that smell faintly of roses. Is mainly used to produce geranium oil for perfume industry, but may be grown as a container plant. Z12–15 H12–1.
P. carnosum. Deciduous, shrubby pelargonium (unclassified), with thick, succulent stems and woody, swollen, tuber-like rootstock. **H** and **S** 12in (30cm). Has long, gray-green leaves with triangular, deeply lobed leaflets. Produces branched, umbel-like flower heads with white or greenish-yellow flowers, the upper petals streaked red and shorter than green sepals. Z12–15 H12–1.
P. 'Cherry Blossom'. Vigorous, evergreen, single-flowered zonal pelargonium. **H** and **S** to 18in (45cm). Mauve-pink flowers have white centers. Z12–15 H12–1.
P. 'Chew Magna'. Evergreen regal pelargonium. **H** 12–18in (30–45cm), **S** to 12in (30cm). Each petal of pale pink flowers has wine-red blaze. Z12–15 H12–1.
P. 'Clorinda', illus. p.309. Vigorous, scented-leaved pelargonium. **H** 18–20in (45–50cm), **S** 8–10in (20–25cm). Leaves smell of cedar and are 3-lobed. Bears large, single, rose-pink flowers. Is suitable for a greenhouse or patio. H11–1.
P. 'Coddenham'. Miniature, double-flowered zonal pelargonium. **H** 4–5in (10–12cm), **S** 3–4in (7–10cm). Produces clusters of orange-red flowers.
P. crispum 'Variegatum'. Evergreen, upright, scented-leaved pelargonium. **H** to 3ft (1m), **S** 1–1½ft (30–45cm). Has gold-variegated leaves that tend to turn creamy-white in winter. Produces small, pale lilac flowers. Z12–15 H12–1.
P. 'Dale Queen'. Evergreen, bushy, single-flowered zonal pelargonium. **H** 9–12in (23–30cm), **S** 9in (23cm). Flowers are delicate salmon-pink. Is particularly suitable for a pot. Z12–15 H12–1.
P. Decora Series. Evergreen, trailing ivy-leaved pelargonium. **H** 6–8in (15–20cm), **S** to 4ft (1.2m). Bears fresh green leaves without dark zone, and narrow-petaled flowers in red, lilac, or shades of pink. **'Decora Dark Pink'** (illus. p.309) is dark rose-pink. H11–1.
P. 'Dolly Varden'. Evergreen, fancy-leaved zonal pelargonium. **H** 12in (30cm), **S** 9in (23cm). Green leaves have purple-brown, white and crimson markings. Single, scarlet flowers are insignificant. Z12–15 H12–1.
P. 'Emma Hössle'. See *P. 'Frau Emma Hössle'*.
P. 'Evka', illus. p.309. Evergreen, trailing, bushy ivy-leaved pelargonium. **H** 6in (15cm), **S** 18in (45cm). Has pale green

P

leaves edged in creamy-white. Bears clusters of small, single, deep rose-red flowers. H11–1.

P. 'Fair Ellen'. Compact scented-leaved pelargonium. **H** and **S** 12in (30cm). Has dark green leaves and pale pink flowers marked with red. Z12–15 H12–1.

P. Fireworks Series. Bushy, compact evergreen perennial. **H** 8–10in (20–25cm), **S** 6–8in (15–20cm). Has shallowly 5-lobed, aromatic, matt, dark green leaves, with lobes suffused purplish-green. From spring to early fall produces upright, dense clusters of red, white, pink or bicolored flowers, with 5 sharply pointed lobes. **Fireworks Scarlet ('Fiwoscarl')**, illus. p.309, has bright scarlet flowers. H11–1.

P. 'Flower of Spring' (Silver-leaved geranium). Vigorous, evergreen, fancy-leaved zonal pelargonium. **H** 24in (60cm), **S** 12in (30cm). Has green-and-white leaves and single, red flowers. Z12–15 H12–1.

P. x fragrans. See P. 'Fragrans'.

P. 'Fragrans', syn. P. x fragrans, P. Fragrans Group. Evergreen, very bushy, scented-leaved pelargonium. **H** and **S** 12in (30cm). Rounded, shallowly lobed, gray-green leaves smell strongly of pine. Bears small, white flowers. Z12–15 H12–1.

P. 'Fraiche Beauté', syn. P. 'Fraicher Beauty', illus. p.309. Evergreen, double-flowered zonal pelargonium. **H** 12in (30cm), **S** 9in (23cm). Perfectly formed, white flowers have thin, red edge to each petal. Is excellent as a pot plant. H11–1.

P. 'Fraicher Beauty'. See P. 'Fraiche Beauté'.

P. 'Francis Parrett'. Evergreen, short-jointed, double-flowered zonal pelargonium. **H** 6–8in (15–20cm), **S** 4in (10cm). Bears purplish-mauve flowers and small, green leaves. Is good for a windowsill. Z12–15 H12–1.

P. 'Frau Emma Hössle', syn. P. 'Emma Hössle'. Evergreen, dwarf, double-flowered zonal pelargonium. **H** 8–10in (20–25cm), **S** 6in (15cm). Bears large, mauve-pink flowers. Is useful for a windowbox. Z12–15 H12–1.

P. 'Friesdorf'. Evergreen, fancy-leaved zonal pelargonium. **H** 10in (25cm), **S** 6in (15cm). Has dark green leaves and narrow-petaled, single, orange-scarlet flowers. Is good for a windowbox or planted in a large group. Z12–15 H12–1.

P. 'Golden Lilac Mist'. Bushy, fancy-leaved zonal pelargonium. **H** 10–12in (25–30cm), **S** 6–8in (15–20cm). Golden-yellow leaves are marked with bronze. Bears double, lavender-pink flowers. Is a good window-box plant. Z12–15 H12–1.

P. 'Gustav Emich'. Vigorous, evergreen, semidouble-flowered zonal pelargonium. **H** and **S** to 24in (60cm). Semidouble flowers are vivid scarlet. Z12–15 H12–1.

P. 'Happy Thought', illus. p.307.

P. Horizon Devas Series. Evergreen, single-flowered zonal pelargonium. **H** and **S** 12–18in (30–45cm). Has rounded, lobed, often bronze-zoned, mid-green leaves and large, domed heads of flowers with speckled or picotee pattern, or a combination of the two. Propagate by seed. **'Horizon Deva Orange Ice'** (illus. p.309) is white with an orange picotee and veining and orange on reverse. H11–1. **'Horizon Deva Raspberry Ripple'** (illus. p.309) is white with rich pattern of deep red speckles and occasional streaks. H11–1.

P. 'Irene'. Evergreen, semidouble-flowered zonal pelargonium. **H** 18in (45cm), **S** 9–12in (23–30cm). Bears large, light crimson blooms. Z12–15 H12–1.

P. 'Ivalo'. Evergreen, bushy, short-jointed, semidouble-flowered zonal pelargonium. **H** 9–12in (23–30cm), **S** 9in (23cm). Large, semidouble flowers are pale pink with crimson-dotted, white centers. Z12–15 H12–1.

P. 'Lachsball'. Vigorous, semidouble-flowered zonal pelargonium. **H** 18–20in (45–50cm), **S** 6–8in (15–20cm). Bears salmon-pink flowers with scarlet eye. Is good for summer bedding. Z12–15 H12–1.

P. 'Lachskönigin', illus. p.309. Evergreen, trailing, brittle-jointed pelargonium. **H** and **S** to 24in (60cm). Has fleshy leaves, with pointed lobes, and semidouble, deep rose-pink flowers. Is suitable for a hanging basket or windowbox. H11–1.

P. 'Lady Plymouth', illus. p.309. Scented-leaved pelargonium. **H** 12–16in (30–40cm), **S** 6–8in (15–20cm). Has eucalyptus-scented, silver-margined, mid-green leaves and clusters of lavender-pink flowers. H11–1.

P. 'L'Elégante'. Evergreen, trailing ivy-leaved pelargonium. **H** and **S** to 24in (60cm). Foliage is variegated with creamy-white margins, sometimes turning pink at edges. Semidouble flowers are pale mauve. Is best grown in a hanging basket. Z12–15 H12–1.

P. 'Lesley Judd'. Vigorous, evergreen, bushy regal pelargonium. **H** 12–18in (30–45cm), **S** to 12in (30cm). Flowers are soft salmon-pink with red central blotch. Pinch out growing tips before flowering, to control shape. Z12–15 H12–1.

P. 'Mabel Grey'. Evergreen, scented-leaved pelargonium. **H** 18–24in (45–60cm), **S** 12–18in (30–45cm). Has diamond-shaped, rough-textured, toothed, strongly lemon-scented leaves, with 5–7 pointed lobes, and mauve flowers. Z12–15 H12–1.

P. 'Madame Fournier'. Evergreen, short-jointed, single-flowered zonal pelargonium. **H** 6–8in (15–20cm), **S** 4in (10cm). Small, scarlet flowers contrast well with almost black leaves. Is useful for a pot or as a summer bedding plant. Z12–15 H12–1.

P. 'Manx Maid'. Evergreen regal pelargonium. **H** 12–15in (30–38cm), **S** 10in (25cm). Flowers and leaves are small for regal type. Pink flowers are veined and blotched with burgundy. Z12–15 H12–1.

P. 'Mauritania'. Evergreen, single-flowered zonal pelargonium. **H** 12in (30cm), **S** 9in (23cm). White flowers are ringed toward centers with pale salmon-pink. Z12–15 H12–1.

P. Maverick Series. Evergreen, single-flowered zonal pelargonium. **H** and **S** 12–18in (30–45cm). Has rounded, lobed, mainly bronze-zoned, mid-green leaves. Produces large, domed heads of flowers in reds, pinks, a bicolor or white. Propagate by seed. **'Maverick Star'** (illus. p.309) is blushed white with deep rose-pink eyes. H11–1.

P. 'Mini Cascade'. Evergreen, trailing, short-jointed, ivy-leaved pelargonium. **H** and **S** 12–18in (30–45cm). Bears many single, red flowers. Regular dead-heading is essential for continuous display. Z12–15 H12–1.

P. 'Mr. Everaarts'. Bushy, dwarf, double-flowered zonal pelargonium. **H** 6–8in (15–

20cm), **S** 4–5in (10–12cm). Bears bright pink flowers. Is good in a windowbox. Z12–15 H12–1.

P. 'Mr. Henry Cox', syn. P. 'Mrs. Henry Cox'. Evergreen, fancy-leaved zonal pelargonium. **H** 12in (30cm), **S** 6in (15cm). Mid-green leaves are marked with red, yellow and purple-brown. Flowers are single and pink. Z12–15 H12–1.

P. 'Mrs. Henry Cox'. See P. 'Mr. Henry Cox'.

P. 'Mrs. Pollock'. Evergreen, single-flowered zonal pelargonium. **H** 12in (30cm), **S** 6in (15cm). Each golden leaf has gray-green butterfly mark in center, with bronze zone running through it. Bears small, orange-red flowers. Z12–15 H12–1.

P. 'Mrs. Quilter'. Evergreen, fancy-leaved zonal pelargonium. **H** 12in (30cm), **S** 9in (23cm). Has yellow leaves with wide, chestnut-brown zones and single, pink flowers. Z12–15 H12–1.

P. Multibloom Series. Seed-raised, single-flowered zonal pelargonium. **H** 10–12in (25–30cm), **S** 12in (30cm). Abundant flowers in shades of white, pink, and red, some with white eyes, are borne in clusters. Is early-flowering and continues over a long period. Is tolerant of wet conditions. Z12–15 H12–1.

P. 'Orange Ricard'. Vigorous, robust, evergreen, semidouble-flowered zonal pelargonium. **H** 18–24in (45–60cm), **S** 12in (30cm). Has masses of large, orange blooms. Z12–15 H12–1.

P. 'Paton's Unique'. Vigorous unique pelargonium with pungent-smelling leaves. **H** 15–18in (38–45cm), **S** 6–8in (15–20cm). Flowers are single, red or pale pink, with small, white eye. Z12–15 H12–1.

P. peltatum. Evergreen, trailing, brittle-jointed pelargonium from which ivy-leaved cultivars have been derived. **H** and **S** to 5ft (1.5m). Has fleshy leaves, with pointed lobes. Produces single, mauve or white flowers. Cultivars are suitable for hanging baskets and windowboxes. Z12–15 H12–1.

P. 'Polka'. Vigorous unique pelargonium. **H** 18–20in (45–50cm), **S** 8–10in (20–25cm). Flowers are semidouble. Upper petals are orange-red, blotched, and feathered deep purple; lower ones are salmon-orange. Z12–15 H12–1.

P. 'Prince of Orange'. Scented-leaved pelargonium. **H** 10–12in (25–30cm), **S** 6–8in (15–20cm). Small, rounded leaves smell of orange. Bears single, mauve flowers. Is good as a pot plant indoors. Z12–15 H12–1.

P. 'Purple Emperor'. Evergreen regal pelargonium. **H** 18in (45cm), **S** 12in (30cm). Pink-mauve flowers have deeper, central coloration. Flowers well into fall. Z12–15 H12–1.

P. 'Purple Unique'. Vigorous, evergreen, upright, shrubby unique pelargonium. **H** and **S** 3ft (1m) or more. Rounded, large-lobed leaves are very aromatic. Has single, open trumpet-shaped, light purple flowers. Does well when trained against a sunny wall. Z12–15 H12–1.

P. Regalia Series. Evergreen, bushy, single-flowered regal pelargonium. **H** and **S** 12–15in (30–38cm). Has clusters of prolific flowers in pink, deep purple, red, lilac or salmon, all with darker marks in throats. **'Regalia Chocolate'** (illus. p.309) is crimson with deep purplish-red marks. H11–1.

P. 'Rica'. Bushy, single-flowered zonal pelargonium. **H** 12–15in (30–38cm), **S** 6–8in (15–20cm). Flowers are deep rose-pink, with large, white eye. Is good in a windowbox or as a greenhouse container plant. Z12–15 H12–1.

P. 'Robe'. Vigorous, semidouble-flowered zonal pelargonium. **H** 15–18in (38–45cm), **S** 6–8in (15–20cm). Bears cerise-crimson flowers. Is suitable as a container plant in a greenhouse, or as a bedding plant, and is good for exhibition. Z12–15 H12–1.

P. 'Rollisson's Unique'. Evergreen, shrubby unique pelargonium. **H** 24in (60cm) or more, **S** 12in (30cm). Has oval, notched, pungent leaves and small, single, open trumpet-shaped, wine-red flowers, with purple veins. Z12–15 H12–1.

P. 'Rouletta'. Vigorous, evergreen, trailing ivy-leaved pelargonium. **H** and **S** 2–3ft (60cm–1m). Bears semidouble, red-and-white flowers. To control shape, pinch out growing tips regularly. Z12–15 H12–1.

P. 'Royal Oak'. Evergreen, bushy, compact scented-leaved pelargonium. **H** 15in (38cm), **S** 12in (30cm). Oaklike, slightly sticky, dark green leaves have spicy fragrance and central, brown markings. Flowers are small and mauve-pink. Z12–15 H12–1.

P. 'Schöne Helena'. Evergreen, semidouble-flowered zonal pelargonium. **H** 12–18in (30–45cm), **S** 9in (23cm). Produces masses of large, salmon-pink flowers. Z12–15 H12–1.

P. 'Splendide'. Slow-growing, short-branching pelargonium. **H** 10–12in (25–30cm), **S** 6–8in (15–20cm). Butterfly-shaped flowers are borne singly or in clusters. Dark red upper petals have black spot at base; lower petals are white, sometimes stained red.

P. Sprinter Series. Group of slow-growing, evergreen, branching, bushy, single-flowered zonal pelargoniums, grown as annuals. **H** and **S** 12–24in (30–60cm). Has rounded, lobed, light to mid-green leaves. Bears large, domed flower heads in shades of red. Is very free-flowering. Z12–15 H12–1.

P. 'Tavira'. Evergreen, trailing, brittle-jointed pelargonium. **H** and **S** 12–16in (30–40cm). Has fleshy leaves, with pointed lobes, and single, soft cerise-red flowers. Is suitable for growing in a hanging basket or windowbox. Z12–15 H12–1.

P. 'The Boar'. Evergreen, trailing pelargonium. **H** and **S** to 24in (60cm). Has 5-lobed, notched, mid-green leaves with dark brown center. Produces long-stemmed, single, salmon-pink flowers. Is useful for a hanging basket. Z12–15 H12–1.

P. 'Timothy Clifford'. Evergreen, short-jointed, semidouble-flowered zonal pelargonium. **H** 6–8in (15–20cm), **S** 4in (10cm). Has dark green leaves and fully double, salmon-pink flowers. Is suitable for a windowsill. Z12–15 H12–1.

P. 'Tip Top Duet', illus. p.309. Evergreen, bushy, free-branching regal pelargonium. **H** 12–15in (30–38cm), **S** 10in (25cm). Leaves and blooms are small for regal type. Bears pink-veined, white flowers; uppermost petals have dark burgundy blotches. H11–1.

P. tomentosum (Peppermint geranium). Evergreen, bushy scented-leaved pelargonium. **H** 12–24in (30–60cm), **S** 36in (1m). Large, rounded, shallowly lobed, velvety, gray-green leaves have strong peppermint aroma. Bears clusters of small, white flowers. Pinch out growing tips, to control spread. Dislikes full sun. Z12–15 H12–1.

P. Video Series. Group of slow-growing, evergreen, branching, bushy single-flowered zonal pelargoniums, grown as annuals. **H** and **S** 12–24in (30–60cm). Has rounded, lobed, bronze-zoned, deep green leaves and large, domed, single flower heads in white and shades of pink or red. Z12–15 H12–1.

P. 'Voodoo', illus. p.309. Unique pelargonium. **H** 20–24in (50–60cm), **S** 8–10in (20–25cm). Flowers are single and pale burgundy with purple-black blaze on each petal. Is suitable as a greenhouse container plant. H11–1.

PELIOSANTHES

CONVALLARIACEAE/ASPARAGACEAE

Genus of evergreen, rhizomatous perennials, grown for their foliage and delicate flowers. Needs partial or full shade and fertile, moist but well-drained, acidic soil. Propagate by divisions of the rhizome in spring or by seed in fall.

P. arisanensis, illus. p.472.

PELLAEA

ADIANTACEAE/PTERIDACEAE

Genus of deciduous, semievergreen or evergreen ferns. Needs partial shade and moist but well-drained, gritty soil. Remove fading fronds regularly. Propagate by spores in summer.

P. atropurpurea (Purple rock brake, Purple-stemmed cliff brake). Semievergreen or evergreen fern. **H** and **S** 12in (30cm). Small, narrowly lance-shaped, divided fronds have oblong, blunt pinnae and are dark green with purplish tinge. Z8–10 H10–8.

P. rotundifolia (Button fern). Evergreen fern. **H** and **S** 6in (15cm). Small, narrowly lance-shaped, divided fronds are dark green and have rounded pinnae. Z8–10 H10–8.

Pellionia daveauana. See *Elatostema repens.*
Pellionia repens. See *Elatostema repens.*

PELTANDRA

Arrow arum

ARACEAE

Genus of deciduous, perennial, marginal water plants, grown for their white flower spathes. Needs full sun and wet soil. Propagate by division of the rhizome when dormant or by seed in spring.

P. undulata. See *P. virginica.*
P. virginica, syn. *P. undulata,* illus. p.443.

Peltiphyllum. See *Darmera.*

PENNISETUM

GRAMINEAE/POACEAE

See also GRASSES, BAMBOOS, RUSHES and SEDGES.

P. alopecuroides, syn. *P. compressum* (Fountain grass). Tuft-forming, herbaceous, perennial grass. **H** 3ft (1m), **S** 1½ft (45cm). Has narrow, mid-green leaves; leaf sheaths have hairy tip. In late summer bears arching, cylindrical panicles, with purple bristles, that last well into winter. Z6–9 H9–6.

P. compressum. See *P. alopecuroides.*
P. 'Fairy Tails' (Fairy Tails). Clump-forming, herebaceous, perennial grass. **H** 4ft (1.2m), **S** 24in (60cm). Has long, bottlebrush-like panicles of beige spikelets, with pinkish bristles, borne in late summer above slender, arching green leaves.
P. glaucum 'Purple Majesty', illus. p.311.
P. longistylum. See *P. villosum.*
P. ruepellii. See *P. setaceum.*
P. setaceum, syn. *P. ruepellii* (Fountain grass). Tuft-forming, herbaceous, perennial grass. **H** 3ft (1m), **S** 1½ft (45cm). Has very rough, mid-green leaves and stems. In summer bears dense, cylindrical panicles of copper-red spikelets, with bearded bristles, that last well into winter. Z8–11 H12–8.
'Rubrum', illus. p.312.
P. villosum, syn. *P. longistylum,* illus. p.286.

PENSTEMON

SCROPHULARIACEAE/PLANTAGINACEAE

Genus of annuals, perennials, subshrubs and shrubs, most of which are semievergreen or evergreen. Prefers full sun and fertile, well-drained soil. Propagate species by seed in fall or spring or by softwood or semiripe cuttings of non-flowering shoots in mid-summer, cultivars by cuttings only. See also feature panel pp.236-7.

P. 'Alice Hindley', illus. p.236. Large-leaved, semievergreen perennial. **H** 36in (90cm), **S** 18in (45cm). Bears tubular to bell-shaped, pale lilac-blue flowers, white inside, tinged mauve-pink outside, from mid-summer to early or mid-fall. Leaves are linear to lance-shaped and mid-green. Z7–10 H10–7.

P. 'Andenken an Friedrich Hahn', syn. *P. 'Garnet',* illus. p.237. Vigorous, semievergreen, bushy perennial. **H** 2–2½ft (60–75cm), **S** 2ft (60cm). Bears sprays of tubular, deep wine-red flowers from mid-summer to fall. Has narrow, fresh green leaves. Z7–10 H10–7.

P. 'Apple Blossom', illus. p.236. Semievergreen, bushy perennial. **H** and **S** 24in (60cm). Bears sprays of small, tubular, pale pink flowers from mid-summer onward above narrow, fresh green leaves. Z7–10 H10–7.

P. 'Barbara Barker'. See *P. 'Beech Park'.*
P. barbatus, syn. *Chelone barbata* (Beardlip penstemon), illus. p.237. Semievergreen, rosette-forming perennial. **H** 3ft (1m), **S** 1ft (30cm). From mid-summer to early fall bears racemes of slightly nodding, tubular, 2-lipped, rose-red flowers. Flower stems arise from rosettes of oblong to oval, mid-green leaves. Z4–9 H9–2.

P. 'Beech Park', syn. *P. 'Barbara Barker',* illus. p.236. Semievergreen perennial. **H** and **S** 24in (60cm). Bears bright pink and white flowers. Leaves are linear and light green. Z7–11 H12–3.

P. 'Blackbird'. Vigorous, semievergreen perennial. **H** 4ft (1.2m), **S** 18in (45cm). Produces willowy, purplish-red stems clothed in long, lance-shaped, dark green leaves and racemes of deep red-purple flowers, with throats densely streaked deep red, from mid-summer to fall.

P. Burford Seedling. See *P. 'Burgundy'.*
P. 'Burford White'. See *P. 'White Bedder'.*

P. 'Burgundy', syn. *P. Burford Seedling,* illus. p.237. Robust, semievergreen perennial. **H** 4ft (1.2m), **S** 2ft (60cm). Produces purplish-red flowers, with white throats streaked dark red. Leaves are linear and light green. Z7–11 H11–3.

P. campanulatus, syn. *P. pulchellus.* Semievergreen, upright perennial. **H** 12–24in (30–60cm), **S** 12in (30cm). Long racemes of bell-shaped, dark purple, violet or, occasionally, white flowers are borne in early summer above lance-shaped, toothed, mid-green leaves. Z7–10 H12–3.

P. 'Candy Pink'. See *P. 'Old Candy Pink'.*
P. cardwellii. Spreading, sometimes stem-rooting, evergreen subshrub. **H** and **S** 12–20in (30–50cm). In early summer produces raceme-like panicles of slender, tubular to funnel-shaped, deep purple flowers. Leaves are elliptic, finely toothed and mid-green. Z6–9 H9–6.

P. 'Cherry' of gardens. See *P. 'Cherry Ripe'.*
P. 'Cherry Ripe', syn. *P. 'Cherry',* illus. p.237. Semievergreen perennial. **H** 3½ft (1.1m), **S** 1½–2ft (45–60cm). Has lance-shaped, mid-green leaves. From mid-summer to fall produces an abundance of deep rose-red flowers, with golden sheen and white throats, streaked deep red.

P. 'Chester Scarlet', illus. p.237. Semievergreen perennial. **H** and **S** 36in (90cm). Large, bright red flowers are borne above narrowly lance-shaped, light green leaves. Z7–10 H10–7.

P. confertus. Semievergreen, neat, clump-forming perennial. **H** 18in (45cm), **S** 12in (30cm). Bears spikes of tubular, creamy-yellow flowers above long, lance-shaped, mid-green leaves in early summer. Z7–10 H10–7.

P. 'Connie's Pink'. Semievergreen, erect, much-branched perennial. **H** 4ft (1.2m), **S** 2ft (60cm). Has slender, bright rose-pink flowers, with deep pink corolla lobes and red-pencilled, white throats, from early summer to fall. Pale green leaves are lance-shaped to oval.

P. 'Countess of Dalkeith'. Semievergreen, erect perennial. **H** 3ft (1m), **S** 2ft (60cm). Produces large, deep purple flowers, with pure white throat. Leaves are linear and light green. Z7–10 H10–7.

P. davidsonii. Evergreen, prostrate shrub. **H** 3in (8cm) or occasionally more, **S** 6in (15cm) or more. In late spring and early summer, funnel-shaped, violet to ruby-red flowers, with protruding lips, develop from leaf axils. Leaves are small, oval or rounded and leathery. Trim after flowering. Z5–9 H9–5. **var. menziesii,** syn. *P. menziesii,* **H** 2in (5cm), **S** 8in (20cm), produces lavender-blue flowers and rounded, toothed leaves. Z6–9 H9–6.

P. diffusus. See *P. serrulatus.*
P. digitalis 'Husker Red', illus. p.236. Vigorous, semievergreen or deciduous, basal-rosetted perennial. **H** 20–30in (50–75cm), **S** 12in (30cm). Has stems often marked reddish-purple bearing inversely lance-shaped, entire or sparsely toothed, mid-green leaves that are maroon-red when young. Produces panicles of tubular to bell-shaped, pink-tinted, white flowers, with purple lines inside, in summer. Z3–8 H8–1.

P. 'Ellenbank Amethyst'. Bushy, semievergreen perennial. **H** 36in (90cm), **S** 18in (45cm). Has lance-shaped, mid-green

leaves. In summer bears racemes of large, tubular, soft purple flowers, with white throat, edged with vivid rosy-purple.

P. 'Evelyn', illus. p.233.
P. 'Firebird'. See *P. 'Schoenholzeri'.*
P. 'Flamingo', illus. p.236. Semievergreen, open, much-branched perennial. **H** 36–38in (90–95cm), **S** 24in (60cm). From summer to fall produces white-throated, deep purplish-pink flowers, the white extending onto corolla lobes, with a few darker, reddish-pink pencillings on lower lobes. Leaves are mid-green, lance-shaped to oval.

P. fruticosus (Shrubby penstemon). Evergreen, upright, woody-based subshrub. **H** and **S** 6–12in (15–30cm). Has lance-shaped to oval, toothed leaves and, in early summer, funnel-shaped, lipped, lavender-blue flowers. Is suitable for a rock garden. Trim back after flowering. Z4–9 H9–1. **var. scouleri,** syn. *P. scouleri* has pale to deep purple flowers. **var. scouleri f. albus,** syn. *P. scouleri f. albus* (illus. p.236) has white flowers.

P. 'Garnet'. See *P. 'Andenken an Friedrich Hahn'.*
P. 'Geoff Hamilton'. Vigorous, semievergreen perennial. **H** 30in (75cm), **S** 24in (60cm). Has lance-shaped to oval, mid-green leaves. Produces large, open, purple flowers, with white throats and white-flecked lobes, from early summer to fall.

P. 'George Home'. Narrow-leaved perennial. **H** 30in (75cm), **S** 18in (45cm). Produces small, tubular to bell-shaped, wine-red flowers, with white throats, the white extending over lips, from mid-summer to early or mid-fall.

P. glaber, illus. p.237. Evergreen, variable subshrub. **H** and **S** 20–30in (50–75cm). In summer produces clusters of snapdragon-like, sky-blue to indigo flowers, with maroon pencilings in white or pale blue throats. Lance-shaped to inversely oval leaves are mid-green. Requires a sunny, dry site.

P. hartwegii. Semievergreen, erect perennial. **H** 24in (60cm) or more, **S** 12in (30cm). Bears sprays of slightly pendent, tubular to bell-shaped, scarlet flowers from mid- to late summer. Lance-shaped leaves are mid-green. Z4–9 H9–1.

P. heterophyllus (Foothill penstemon). Evergreen subshrub. **H** and **S** 12–20in (30–50cm). In summer produces racemes of tubular to funnel-shaped, pinkish-blue flowers, with blue or lilac lobes. Leaves are linear to lance-shaped, entire and mid-green or bluish-green. Z7–10 H10–7. **'Heavenly Blue'** (illus. p.237), **H** 2ft (60cm), **S** 1ft (30cm), produces tubular, mauve-tinged, blue flowers from mid-summer until first frosts. **'True Blue'** has pale green leaves and pure blue flowers, borne on short sideshoots. Trim back after flowering. Is suitable for a rock garden.

P. 'Hidcote Pink', illus. p.236. Narrow-leaved perennial. **H** 24–30in (60–75cm), **S** 18in (45cm). Produces small, tubular, pale pink flowers, with spreading lobes marked with crimson lines inside, from mid-summer to early or mid-fall.

P. hirsutus. Short-lived, evergreen, open subshrub. **H** 2–3ft (60cm–1m), **S** 1–2ft (30–60cm). In summer produces hairy, tubular, lipped, purple- or blue-flushed, white flowers. Leaves are oval and dark green. Is suitable for a rock garden. Z3–9 H9–1. **var. pygmaeus**, illus. p.361.

P. 'Hopleys Variegated', illus. p.237. Large-leaved, semievergreen perennial. **H** 36in (90cm), **S** 18in (45cm). Is a sport of *P.* 'Alice Hindley' with yellow-speckled leaves.

P. isophyllus, illus. p.153.

P. 'Kilimanjaro'. Vigorous, semievergreen perennial. **H** 32in (80cm), **S** 24in (60cm). Has long, lance-shaped, mid-green leaves. From summer to fall produces long racemes of purplish-pink flowers, with white throats.

P. 'King George V', illus. p.237. Narrow-leaved perennial. **H** 24in (60cm), **S** 18in (45cm). Bears small, tubular to bell-shaped, bright deep scarlet flowers, with white throats, from mid-summer to early or mid-fall.

P. kunthii, illus. p.236. Variable, woody-based, willowy perennial. **H** 3–4ft (90cm–1.2m), **S** 2ft (60cm). Has lance-shaped, toothed, mid-green leaves. From mid-summer to late fall produces many-flowered racemes of red to maroon-red flowers, with white streaks in throats. Requires a sunny, dry site.

P. 'Madame Golding'. Strong-growing, semievergreen perennial. **H** 30in (75cm), **S** 16–18in (40–45cm). Is similar to *P.* 'Old Candy Pink', but has paler pink flowers.

P. 'Margery Fish', illus. p.236. Almost mat-forming, woody-based perennial. **H** and **S** 20in (50cm). Has narrow, shiny, mid-green leaves. Produces dense spikes of pale blue to violet-mauve flowers, with white penciling in throats, in summer–fall.

P. 'Maurice Gibbs'. Semievergreen perennial. **H** 3ft (90cm), **S** 2ft (60cm). Bears claret-red flowers, with white throats. Has lance-shaped, light green leaves. Z9–11 H12–3.

P. menziesii. See *P. davidsonii* var. *menziesii*.

P. 'Modesty'. Strong-growing, semievergreen, erect perennial. **H** 3ft (90cm), **S** 1½ft (45cm). Has lance-shaped, glossy, olive-green leaves. Produces bright red-pink flowers, with white throats sparsely penciled purplish-red, in summer–fall.

P. 'Mother of Pearl', illus. p.236. Narrow-leaved perennial. **H** to 30in (75cm), **S** 18in (45cm). Has small, tubular to bell-shaped, pearl-mauve flowers, tinted pink and white, with white throats and red lines, from mid-summer to early or mid-fall.

P. newberryi (Mountain pride). Evergreen, mat-forming shrub. **H** 6–8in (15–20cm), **S** 12in (30cm). Branches are covered in small, oval, leathery, dark green leaves. Bears short sprays of tubular, lipped, deep rose-pink flowers in early summer. Trim back after flowering. Is good for a rock garden. Z7–10 H10–7. **f. humilior**, illus. p.340.

P. 'Old Candy Pink', syn. *P.* 'Candy Pink'. Strong-growing, semievergreen perennial. **H** 30in (75cm), **S** 16–18in (40–45cm). Has lance-shaped, mid-green leaves. Produces bright crimson flowers, with darker crimson lines in white throats and small, rounded, white patches at base of each lobe, from early summer to mid-fall.

P. 'Osprey', illus. p.236. Vigorous, semievergreen, open-branched perennial. **H** 3½ft (1.1m), **S** 2ft (60cm). Has lance-shaped to oval, mid-green leaves. Produces

creamy-white flowers, with spreading, purplish-pink lobes and white throats, in summer–fall. As flowers age the pink coloration deepens and extends into flower tubes.

P. 'Papal Purple', illus. p.237. Semievergreen, mound-forming perennial. **H** 20in (50cm), **S** 14in (35cm). Has narrowly lance-shaped, mid-green leaves. In summer bears small, rather rounded, white-throated, lilac-purple flowers.

P. 'Penbow'. Semievergreen, bushy, rather upright perennial. **H** 36in (90cm), **S** 16in (40cm). Has narrowly lance-shaped, blue-green leaves. From mid-summer to fall bears slender racemes of small, tubular, bright azure-blue flowers.

P. 'Pennington Gem'. Vigorous, semievergreen perennial. **H** 3ft (1m), **S** 18in (45cm). Bears sprays of tubular, pink flowers from mid-summer to fall. Leaves are narrow and fresh green. Z6–9 H9–6.

P. 'Pensham Just Jayne', illus. p.237. Robust, semievergreen, bushy perennial. **H** 3–4ft (90cm–1.2m), **S** 2ft (60cm). Has lance-shaped to oval, deep green leaves. Produces rich deep cerise-pink flowers, with faintly white-lined, magenta throats, from early summer to fall.

P. 'Pensham Petticoat'. Semievergreen, bushy perennial. **H** 24in (60cm), **S** 14in (35cm). Has lance-shaped, mid-green leaves. In summer produces racemes of large, tubular, rather frilly-looking, white flowers, edged with rose-pink.

P. 'Pershore Fanfare'. Vigorous, semievergreen perennial. **H** 36in (90cm), **S** 18in (45cm). Has lance-shaped, mid-green leaves. In summer bears racemes of large, tubular, lavender-blue flowers, with white throat striped in darker purple.

P. pinifolius, illus. p.340. **'Mersea Yellow'** is an evergreen, bushy subshrub, **H** 4–8in (10–20cm), **S** 10in (25cm). Branched stems are clothed in fine, dark green leaves. In summer, very narrow, tubular, bright deep yellow flowers are borne in loose, terminal spikes.

P. 'Port Wine', illus. p.237. Vigorous, semievergreen, upright perennial. **H** 3ft (1m), **S** 2ft (60cm). Has lance-shaped to oval, mid- to dark green leaves. Produces deep claret to deep purple flowers, with white throats heavily penciled deep claret, from early summer to fall.

P. procerus. Semievergreen, upright perennial. **H** 20in (50cm), **S** 8in (20cm). Leaves are oblong to lance-shaped. Produces slim spikes of funnel-shaped, blue-purple flowers in summer. Is suitable for a rock garden. Z4–10 H10–1.

P. pulchellus. See *P. campanulatus*.

P. 'Raven', illus. p.237. Strong-growing, semievergreen, erect perennial. **H** 3½ft (1.1m), **S** 2ft (60cm). Has lance-shaped to oval, mid- to dark green leaves. Dark purple-red flowers, with white throats penciled faint, dark red in tubes, coalescing into patches of blackish-purple-red at lobe bases, are produced freely in summer–fall.

P. 'Red Emperor'. Robust, semievergreen, erect perennial. **H** 3ft (90cm), **S** 18–20in (45–50cm). Has lance-shaped to oval, mid-green leaves and vivid, bright scarlet flowers, with golden sheen and white throats streaked and suffused red, in summer–fall.

P. 'Rich Ruby'. Strong-growing, semievergreen, erect perennial. **H** 32–39in

(80–100cm), **S** 24in (60cm). Red-purple stems bear lance-shaped to oval, dark green leaves. In summer–fall produces large, rich, dark red-purple blooms, with white throats heavily streaked and suffused dark red, coalescing into dark brown-purple patch at mouth of each flower tube.

P. 'Royal White'. See *P.* 'White Bedder'.

P. 'Rubicundus', illus. p.237. Semievergreen, erect perennial. **H** 4ft (1.2m), **S** 2ft (60cm). Bears very large, bright red flowers, with white throat. Leaves are linear and light green. Z6–9 H9–6.

P. rupicola (Rock penstemon). Evergreen, prostrate shrub. **H** 2in (5cm), **S** 6in (15cm). Has rounded to oval, fleshy, blue-gray leaves and, in summer, variable, funnel-shaped, pale to deep pink flowers. Is best grown in a rock garden. Z4–9 H9–1.

P. 'Russian River', illus. p.237. Vigorous, semievergreen, sturdy, erect perennial. **H** 28in (70cm), **S** 16in (40cm). Purplish stems bear lance-shaped, mid-green leaves. In summer produces racemes of tubular, plum-purple flowers, with lavender-purple throat lined with darker markings.

P. 'Schoenholzeri', syn. *P.* 'Firebird', illus. p.237. Vigorous, semievergreen, upright perennial. **H** 3ft (1m), **S** 1–1½ft (30–45cm). Produces racemes of trumpet-shaped, brilliant scarlet flowers from mid-summer to fall. Lance-shaped to narrowly oval leaves are mid-green. Z6–9 H9–6.

P. scouleri. See *P. fruticosus* var. *scouleri*. **f. albus**. See *P. fruticosus* var. *scouleri* f. *albus*.

P. serrulatus, syn. *P. diffusus*, illus. p.341.

P. 'Six Hills'. Evergreen, prostrate shrub. **H** 2in (5cm), **S** 6in (15cm). Has rounded, fleshy, gray-green leaves. In summer bears funnel-shaped, cool lilac flowers at stem tips. Is suitable for a rock garden. Z4–10 H10–1.

P. 'Snow Storm'. See *P.* 'White Bedder'.

P. 'Sour Grapes', illus. p.237. Semievergreen perennial. **H** 36in (90cm), **S** 24in (60cm). Light green leaves are narrowly lance-shaped. Bears deep purple-blue flowers suffused violet. Z7–10 H10–7.

P. 'Southgate Gem'. Vigorous, semievergreen perennial. **H** 30in (75cm), **S** 18in (45cm). Has lance-shaped, dark green leaves. Produces an abundance of bright rose-red flowers, with white throats sparsely penciled crimson, in summer–fall.

P. 'Stapleford Gem', illus. p.236. Semievergreen, large-leaved perennial. **H** to 24in (60cm), **S** 18in (45cm). Bears large, tubular to bell-shaped, lilac-purple flowers from mid-summer to early or mid-fall; upper lips are pale pink-lilac; lower lips and throats are white with purple lines. Leaves are linear to lance-shaped and mid-green. Z6–9 H9–6.

P. 'Stromboli', illus. p.236. Vigorous, semievergreen perennial. **H** 2–3ft (60–90cm), **S** 1½–2ft (45–60cm). Produces pale creamy-white flowers, with purplish-pink lobes and faintly purple-pink-streaked, white throats, in summer–fall. Mid-green leaves are lance-shaped to oval.

P. 'The Juggler', illus. p.236. Semievergreen, erect perennial. **H** 3½ft (110cm), **S** 1½–2ft (45–60cm). Produces white-throated, magenta flowers in summer–fall.

P. 'Torquay Gem'. Semievergreen, woody-based perennial. **H** 2ft (60cm), **S** 12–16in (30–40cm). Has long, lance-

shaped, light green leaves. Produces deep rose-red flowers, with a few carmine lines in white throats, in summer–fall.

P. whippleanus (Whipple's penstemon), illus. p.237. Semievergreen, erect, basal-rosetted perennial. **H** 2ft (60cm), **S** 1ft (30cm). Has rounded basal leaves and slender stems bearing lance-shaped, glossy, pale green leaves. In summer, pendent, tubular, dark purple flowers, with cream-marked throats, are borne in clusters around raceme. Z3–8 H8–1.

P. 'White Bedder', syn. *P.* 'Burford White', *P.* 'Royal White', *P.* 'Snow Storm', illus. p.236. Semievergreen, free-flowering perennial. **H** 28in (70cm), **S** 24in (60cm). Has white flowers with dark anthers, and linear, fresh green leaves. Z7–10 H10–7.

PENTACHONDRA
EPACRIDACEAE

Genus of evergreen, spreading shrubs, grown for their heather-like leaves. Needs sun and moist, gritty, peaty soil. Is difficult to grow, especially in hot, dry areas. Propagate by rooted offsets in spring, by semiripe cuttings in summer or by seed in fall.

P. pumila. Evergreen, mat-forming, dense shrub. **H** 1¼–4in (3–10cm), **S** 8in (20cm) or more. Has oblong to narrowly oval, purplish-green leaves. Small, tubular, white flowers, with reflexed lobes, in early summer, are followed, though rarely in cultivation, by small, spherical, orange fruits. Z7–10 H10–7.

Pentapterygium. See *Agapetes*.

PENTAS
RUBIACEAE

Genus of mainly evergreen perennials and shrubs, grown for their flowers. Needs full light or partial shade and fertile, well-drained soil. Water freely when in full growth, moderately at other times. May be hard-pruned in winter. Propagate by softwood cuttings in summer or by seed in spring. Is prone to whitefly.

P. carnea. See *P. lanceolata*.

P. lanceolata, syn. *P. carnea*, illus. p.300.

PEPEROMIA
PIPERACEAE

Genus of annuals and evergreen perennials, grown for their foliage. Needs full light or partial shade, ideally in a peat-based medium. Do not overwater. Propagate by division, by seed or by leaf or stem cuttings in spring or summer.

P. argyreia, syn. *P. sandersii* (Watermelon peperomia). Evergreen, bushy, compact perennial. **H** and **S** 8in (20cm). Has red-stalked, oval, fleshy, dark green leaves, to 4in (10cm) or more long, striped with broad bands of silver. Flowers are insignificant. Z14–15 H12–10.

P. caperata, illus. p.465.

P. clusiifolia (Red-edge peperomia). Evergreen perennial with branching, sometimes prostrate, reddish-green stems. **H** to 8in (20cm), **S** 10in (25cm). Narrowly oval, fleshy, dark green leaves, 3–6in (8–15cm) long, have red edges. Flowers are insignificant. Z14–15 H12–10. **'Variegata'** has cream-variegated, mid-green leaves, with red margins.

P. glabella, illus. p.474.

P. griseoargentea, syn. *P. hederifolia* (Ivy-leaf peperomia). Evergreen, bushy perennial. H to 6in (15cm), S 8in (20cm). Oval, fleshy leaves, 2in (5cm) or more long, have heart-shaped base, quilted green surface and silvery sheen. Flowers are insignificant. Z14–15 H12–10.

P. hederifolia. See *P. griseoargentea*.

P. magnoliifolia. See *P. obtusifolia*.

P. marmorata, illus. p.474.

P. metallica (Red tree). Evergreen perennial with erect, branching, reddish-green stems. H and S to 6in (15cm). Narrowly oval, dark green leaves, to 1in (2.5cm) long, have metallic sheen and wide, pale midribs above, reddish-green veins below. Flowers are insignificant. Z14–15 H12–10.

P. nummulariifolia. See *P. rotundifolia*.

P. obtusifolia, syn. *P. magnoliifolia* (Baby rubber plant, Pepper face). Evergreen perennial. H and S 10in (25cm). Has leathery, dull green leaves. Bears spikes of white flowers, generally in late summer. Z14–15 H12–10. **'Green and Gold'** has green leaves with golden-yellow margins. **'Variegata'**, illus. p.474.

P. rotundifolia, syn. *P. nummulariifolia* (Yerba linda). Evergreen, creeping perennial. H 2–3in (5–8cm), S 12in (30cm) or more. Very slender stems produce tiny, rounded, fleshy, bright green leaves, ½in (1cm) wide. Flowers are insignificant. Is useful for a hanging basket. Z14–15 H12–10.

P. rubella. Evergreen perennial with erect, branching, red stems. H and S 6in (15cm). Narrowly oval, fleshy, dark green leaves, ½in (1cm) long, crimson below, are in whorls of 4. Flowers are insignificant. Z14–15 H12–10.

P. sandersii. See *P. argyreia*.

P. scandens (False philodendron). Evergreen, climbing or trailing perennial with pinkish-green stems. H and S to 3ft (1m). Oval, pointed, fleshy leaves, to 2in (5cm) or more long, are waxy and bright green. Flowers are insignificant. Z14–15 H12–10.

PERESKIA

CACTACEAE

Genus of deciduous cacti, some of which are climbing, with fleshy leaves and woody, green, then brown stems. Is considered the most primitive genus of the Cactaceae, producing true leaves unlike most members of the family. Needs sun and well-drained soil. Water moderately in summer. Propagate by stem cuttings in spring or summer.

P. aculeata, illus. p.479. **var. godseffiana.** See *P. aculeata* 'Godseffiana'. **'Godseffiana'**, syn. *P. aculeata* var. *godseffiana* is a fast-growing, deciduous, erect, then climbing cactus. H to 30ft (10m), S 15ft (5m). Broadly oval, slightly fleshy, orange-brown leaves, 3½in (9cm) long, usually purplish beneath, mature to glossy green. Short flower stems, bearing roselike, single, orange-centered, cream flowers, 2in (5cm) across, are produced in fall only on plants more than 3ft (1m) high. Cut back hard to main stems in fall. Z12–15 H12–10.

P. grandifolia, syn. *Rhodocactus grandifolius*, illus. p.485.

PERICALLIS

COMPOSITAE/ASTERACEAE

Genus of perennials and subshrubs, sometimes grown as annuals, especially for their daisylike flower heads. Requires sun or partial shade and fertile, well-drained soil. Propagate by seed from spring to mid-summer.

P. x hybrida, syn. *Cineraria cruentus*, *Cineraria x hybridus*, *Senecio x hybridus* (Florists' cineraria). Slow-growing, evergreen, mound- or dome-shaped perennial. H 18–24in (45–60cm), S 10–24in (25–60cm). Has oval, serrated, mid- to deep green leaves. Large, daisylike, single, semidouble or double flower heads, in shades of blue, red, pink or white, sometimes bicolored, are produced in winter or spring. Cultivars are grown as biennials. Z12–13 H7–1. **'Brilliant'** has large flower heads in mixture of white, blue, deep red, copper and rose-pink, and bicolors. **'Royalty'** is late-flowering, with flower heads in sky-blue, cherry-red, lilac with white eye, and bicolors. **'Spring Glory'** has flowers in mixture of colors in spring. **'Star Wars'**, H 6in (15cm), S 8in (20cm), is compact, with flower heads in mixture of white, blue, rose-pink, carmine-red and purple; is ideal for a small container. **P. Senetti Series Senetti Blue Bicolor ('Sunseneribuba')**, illus. p.314.

PERILLA

LABIATAE/LAMIACEAE

Genus of annuals, grown for their foliage. Needs sun and fertile, well-drained soil. Pinch out growing tips of young plants to encourage a bushy habit. Propagate by seed sown under glass in early spring.

P. frutescens (Shiso). Moderately fast-growing, upright, bushy annual. H 24in (60cm), S 12in (30cm). Has oval, toothed, aromatic, reddish-purple leaves. In summer produces spikes of very small, tubular, white flowers. H12–1.

P. 'Magilla Vanilla', illus. p.318.

PERIPLOCA

ASCLEPIADACEAE/APOCYNACEAE

Genus of deciduous or evergreen, twining climbers, grown for their leaves. Stems exude milky juice if cut. Needs sun and well-drained soil. Propagate by seed in spring or by semiripe cuttings in summer. ① The fruits and sap may cause stomach upset if ingested.

P. graeca (Silk vine). Deciduous, twining climber. H to 28ft (9m). Oval, glossy leaves are 1–2in (2.5–5cm) long. In summer has clusters of 8–12 greenish-yellow flowers, purplish-brown inside, with 5 lobes. Scent of flowers is thought by some to be unpleasant. Pairs of narrowly cylindrical seed pods, 5in (12cm) long, contain winged, tufted seeds. Z6–8 H8–6.

PERISTROPHE

ACANTHACEAE

Genus of mainly evergreen perennials and subshrubs, grown usually for their flowers. Needs sun or partial shade and well-drained soil. Do not over-water plants in winter. Propagate by stem cuttings in spring or summer.

P. angustifolia. See *P. hyssopifolia*.

P. hyssopifolia, syn. *P. angustifolia*. Evergreen, bushy perennial. H to 2ft (60cm), S 3–4ft (1–1.2m). Broadly lance-shaped leaves, 3in (8cm) long, have long-pointed tips. Small clusters of tubular, deep rose-pink flowers are borne in winter. **'Aureovariegata'**, illus. p.476.

Pernettya mucronata. See *Gaultheria mucronata*.

Pernettya prostrata. See *Gaultheria myrsinoides*.

Pernettya pumila. See *Gaultheria pumila*.
Pernettya tasmanica. See *Gaultheria tasmanica*.

PEROVSKIA

LABIATAE/LAMIACEAE

Genus of deciduous subshrubs, grown for their aromatic, gray-green foliage and blue flowers. Requires full sun and very well-drained soil. Cut plants back hard, almost to base, in spring, as new growth starts. Propagate by softwood cuttings in late spring.

P. atriplicifolia (Russian sage). Deciduous, upright subshrub. H 4ft (1.2m), S 3ft (1m). Gray-white stems bear narrowly oval, coarsely toothed leaves. Produces 2-lipped, violet-blue flowers in long, slender spikes, from late summer to mid-fall. Z6–9 H9–6.

P. 'Blue Spire', illus. p.159.

P. 'Hybrida'. Deciduous, upright subshrub. H 3ft (1m), S 2½ft (75cm). Has oval, deeply lobed and toothed leaves and, from late summer to mid-fall, tall spires of 2-lipped, deep lavender-blue flowers. Z6–9 H9–6.

PERSICARIA

Fleeceflower, Knotweed

POLYGONACEAE

Genus of annuals, sometimes invasive perennials and rarely evergreen, semievergreen or deciduous subshrubs, grown for their fall leaf color. Has spikes or panicles of small, usually long-lasting, white, pink or red flowers. Needs sun or partial shade and moist soil. Propagate by seed in spring, divide perennials in spring or fall. ① Contact with all parts may irritate skin; the sap may cause mild stomach upset if ingested.

P. affinis, syn. *Polygonum affine* (Himalayan knotweed). Evergreen, mat-forming perennial. H 6–12in (15–30cm), S 12in (30cm) or more. Sturdy stems bear small, lance-shaped, glossy, green leaves that turn red-bronze in winter. From mid-summer to mid-fall produces dense spikes of small, funnel-shaped, rose-red flowers, fading to pale pink. Is good on a bank or in a rock garden. Z3–8 H8–1. **'Darjeeling Red'**, H 8–10in (20–25cm), has long spikes of deep red flowers. **'Donald Lowndes'**, illus. p.365. **'Superba'** (illus. p.234) is vigorous and has pale pink flowers, becoming deep pinkish-red, with red calyces; leaves turn rich brown in fall.

P. amplexicaulis, syn. *Polygonum amplexicaule* (Bistort, Mountain fleece). Clump-forming, leafy perennial. H and S 4ft (1.2m). Bears profuse spikes of small, rich red flowers in summer–fall. Has oval to heart-shaped, mid-green leaves. Z3–8 H8–1. **'Alba'**, H 36in (90cm), S 48in (120cm), has showy spikes of white flowers. **'Firetail'** (illus. p.234). H to 3–4ft

(1–1.2m), S to 24in (60cm), bears slender spikes of bright red flowers above heart-shaped leaves in summer–fall. **Taurus ('Blotau')**, H to 32in (80cm), S to 36in (100cm), bears bright crimson-red flowers; is reputed to be less spreading than many other selections.

P. bistorta, syn. *Polygonum bistorta* (Bistort, Snakeweed). **'Superba'** (illus. p.234) is a vigorous, clump-forming perennial. H 24–40in (60–75cm), S to 24in (60cm). Produces spikes of soft pink flowers above oval leaves in summer. Z4–8 H8–1.

P. campanulata, syn. *Polygonum campanulatum*, illus. p.234. Compact, mat-forming perennial. H and S 3ft (1m). Bears branching heads of bell-shaped, pink or white flowers from mid-summer to early fall. Has oval leaves, brown-felted beneath. Z5–8 H8–5. **'Rosenrot'** (illus. p.234), H 4ft (1.2m), S 3ft (1m), has reddish-pink flowers in summer.

P. capitata, syn. *Polygonum capitatum*. Compact, spreading perennial. H 2in (5cm), S 6–8in (15–20cm). Small, oval leaves are green with darker marks. Small, spherical heads of pink flowers are borne in summer. Is suitable for a rock garden or bank. Z8–9 H9–8.

P. macrophylla, syn. *P. sphaerostachya*, *Polygonum macrophyllum*, *Polygonum sphaerostachyum*, illus. p.265.

P. microcephala. Spreading, leafy, rhizomatous perennial. H to 2ft (60cm), S 3ft (1m) or more. Has lance-shaped, reddish-green leaves, with darker zonal markings. Branching stems bear small, rounded heads of minute, white flowers in summer. **'Red Dragon'** (illus. p.234), H 28in (70cm), has deep red leaves, marked with silvery chevron. Leaves develop greenish tints as they age.

P. milletii, syn. *Polygonum milletii*. Compact perennial. H and S 24in (60cm). Produces slender spikes of rich crimson flowers from mid-summer to early fall. Narrowly lance-shaped leaves are mid-green. Z5–8 H8–5.

P. polymorpha, illus. p.234. Clump-forming, leafy perennial. H and S 6ft (2m) or more. Sturdy, branching stems bear large, elliptic-lance-shaped, mid-green leaves. In mid-summer produces frothy, terminal heads of tiny, long-lasting, creamy-white flowers.

P. sphaerostachya. See *P. macrophylla*.

P. vacciniifolia, syn. *Polygonum vacciniifolium*, illus. p.373.

P. virginiana. Rather variable, clump-forming perennial. H to 4ft (1.2m), S to 2ft (60cm). Oval, pale green leaves have brownish-mauve blotches, brightest in spring. In late summer produces spikes of insignificant, green flowers. Z5–9 H9–5. **'Batwings'**, H and S to 32in (80cm), has narrowly oval leaves with dark red chevron mark. **'Lance Corporal'** (illus. p.234), H and S to 32in (80cm), has a rich brown chevron mark on each leaf. **'Painter's Palette'**, syn. *Tovara virginiana* 'Painter's Palette', *Polygonum virginianum* 'Painter's Palette' (illus. p.234) has green leaves with central, brown zones, ivory-yellow splashes and stripes and an overall deep pink tinge. Seldom flowers in cultivation.

P

PETASITES
Butterbur, Sweet coltsfoot
COMPOSITAE/ASTERACEAE

Genus of invasive perennials, grown for their usually large leaves and useful as groundcover. Needs partial or full shade and prefers moist but well-drained soil. Propagate by division in spring or fall.

P. fragrans (Winter heliotrope). Spreading, invasive perennial. **H** 9–12in (23–30cm), **S** 4ft (1.2m). Has rounded to heart-shaped, dark green leaves. Small, vanilla-scented, daisylike, pinkish-white flower heads are produced in late winter before foliage. Z7–9 H9–7.

P. japonicus (Fuki). Spreading, invasive perennial. **H** 2ft (60cm), **S** 5ft (1.5m). In early spring produces dense cones of small, daisylike, yellowish-white flowers before large, light green leaves emerge. Z5–9 H9–5.

PETCHOA
SOLANACEAE

Hybrid genus (*Calibrachoa* x *Petunia*) of trailing, evergreen perennials, grown as annuals for their colorful flowers. Is suitable for hanging baskets and containers. Needs sun and moist but well-drained soil. Propagate by cuttings.

P. Supercal Series SUPERCAL NEON ROSE **('Kakegawa S89')**, illus. p.303.

PETREA
VERBENACEAE

Genus of evergreen shrubs and woody-stemmed, twining climbers, grown for their flowers. Needs full light and fertile, well-drained soil. Water regularly when in full growth, less at other times. Provide support. Thin out and spur back crowded growth in spring. Propagate by semiripe cuttings in summer. Mealy bug and whitefly may cause problems.

P. volubilis, illus. p.463.

PETROCOSMEA
GESNERIACEAE

Genus of evergreen, rhizomatous perennials. Needs partial shade and well-drained, peaty soil. Propagate by seed in early spring or by leaf cuttings in early summer.

P. kerrii, illus. p.361.

Petrophyton. See *Petrophytum*.

PETROPHYTUM
SYN. PETROPHYTON
Rock spirea
ROSACEAE

Genus of evergreen, summer-flowering shrubs, grown for their spikes of small, fluffy flowers. Is good for growing on tufa or in alpine houses. Needs sun and gritty, well-drained, alkaline soil. May be difficult to grow. Propagate by softwood or semiripe cuttings in summer or by seed in fall. Aphids and red spider mite may be troublesome in hot weather.

P. caespitosum. Evergreen, mat-forming shrub. **H** 2–3in (5–8cm), **S** 4–6in (10–15cm). Has clusters of small, spoon-shaped, silky-hairy, bluish-green leaves. Flower stems,

---

¾in (2cm) long, bear conical spike of small, fluffy, white flowers, with prominent stamens, in summer. Z6–9 H9–6.

P. hendersonii. Evergreen, mound-forming shrub. **H** 2–4in (5–10cm), **S** 4–6in (10–15cm). Has branched stems covered in hairy, rounded, blue-green leaves. Conical spikes of small, cup-shaped, fluffy, white to creamy flowers are produced on stems, 1in (2.5cm) long, in summer. Z6–9 H9–6.

PETRORHAGIA
CARYOPHYLLACEAE

Genus of annuals and perennials, grown for their flowers. Is suitable for rock gardens and banks. Prefers sun and well-drained, sandy soil. Propagate by seed in fall. Self-seeds readily.

P. saxifraga, syn. *Tunica saxifraga*, illus. p.361. **'Rosette'** is a mat-forming perennial. **H** 4in (10cm), **S** 6in (15cm). Has tufts of grasslike leaves. In summer, slender stems bear a profusion of cup-shaped, double, white to pale pink flowers, sometimes veined deeper pink.

PETTERIA
LEGUMINOSAE/PAPILIONACEAE

Genus of one species of deciduous shrub, grown for its flowers. Is related to *Laburnum*, differing in its erect racemes. Requires full sun and fertile, well-drained soil. Propagate by softwood cuttings in summer or by seed in fall. ① The seeds may cause stomach upset if ingested.

P. ramentacea (Dalmatian laburnum). Deciduous, upright shrub. **H** 6ft (2m), **S** 3ft (1m). Has dense, upright spikes of fragrant, laburnum-like, yellow flowers in late spring and early summer. Mid-green leaves have 3 oval leaflets.

PETUNIA
SOLANACEAE

Genus of annuals and perennials, wholly grown as annuals, with showy, colorful flowers. Needs a sunny, sheltered position and fertile, well-drained soil. Deadhead regularly. Propagate by seed sown under glass in fall or mid-spring. May suffer from viruses, including cucumber mosaic and tomato spotted wilt.

The many cultivars that have been produced are moderately fast-growing, branching, bushy plants, H 6–12in (15–30cm), S 12in (30cm), with oval, mid- to deep green leaves, usually 2–5in (5–12cm) long. In summer–fall, they produce flared, trumpet-shaped, single or double flowers in a wide range of colors (available in mixtures or singly), including blue, violet, purple, red, pink and white. Some have dark veining, central white stars, halos (throats in contrasting colors), or picotee margins. Petunias are generally hardy in Z11 H12–1.

The cultivars are divided into 2 groups, Grandiflora and Multiflora petunias.

Grandiflora petunias have very large flowers, 3–4in (8–10cm) wide, but they are easily damaged by rain and are best grown in sheltered hanging baskets and pots.

Multiflora petunias are bushier than the Grandiflora petunias, and produce smaller flowers, 2in (5cm) wide, in greater quantity. They tend to be more resistant to rain damage, and are excellent for summer bedding or for a mixed border.

P. Aladdin Series. Grandiflora petunia. **H** to 12in (30cm), **S** 12–36in (30–90cm). Has flowers in a range of colors, including strong shades of red and salmon-pink. Z9–11 H12–1.

P. Carpet Series. Multiflora petunia. **H** 8–10in (20–25cm), **S** 12–36in (30–90cm). Bears flowers in color range that includes strong reds and oranges. Z8–11 H12–1.

P. Cascade Series. Grandiflora petunia. **H** 8–12in (20–30cm), **S** 12–36in (30–90cm). Trailing stems produce flowers in wide range of colors.

P. 'Cherry Tart'. Multiflora petunia. **H** 6–12in (5–30cm), **S** 12–24in (30–60cm). Bears double, deep pink-and-white flowers.

P. 'Colour Parade'. Grandiflora petunia. **H** 8–12in (20–30cm), **S** 12–36in (30–90cm). Has wide color range of flowers with ruffled petals.

P. Daddy Series. Grandiflora petunia. **H** 14in (35cm), **S** 12–36in (30–90cm). Bear large, heavily veined flowers in pastel to deep pink, salmon-pink, purple or lavender-blue. **Daddy Series 'Sugar Daddy'**, illus. p.312.

P. Flash Series. Compact, Grandiflora petunia. **H** 9–16in (23–40cm), **S** 12–36in (30–90cm). Produce flowers in range of bright colors, including bicolors.

P. 'Gypsy'. Multiflora petunia. **H** 6–12in (5–30cm), **S** 12–24in (30–60cm). Has salmon-red flowers.

P. Jamboree Series. Multiflora petunia. **H** 6–12in (15–30cm), **S** 12–36in (30–90cm). Produce pendulous stems bearing flowers in range of colors.

P. 'Keiyeul'. See *P.* Surfinia Series SURFINIA LIME.

P. 'Kerpril'. See *P.* Tumbelina Series PRISCILLA.

P. 'Magic Cherry'. Compact, Grandiflora petunia. **H** 8–12in (20–30cm), **S** 12–24in (30–60cm). Has cherry-red flowers.

P. 'Mirage Velvet'. Multiflora petunia, illus. p.308.

P. Pearl Series. Dwarf, Multiflora petunia. **H** 6–8in (15–20cm), **S** 8–20in (20–50cm). Bear small flowers in wide range of colors.

P. Picotee Series. Grandiflora petunia. **H** 6–12in (15–30cm), **S** 12in (30cm). Have flared, somewhat trumpet-shaped, red flowers, edged with white. Z9–11 H12–1.

P. Picotee Ruffled Series. Multiflora petunia. **H** 6–12in (15–30cm), **S** 12–36in (30–90cm). Bear ruffled flowers, edged with white, in range of colors.

P. Plum Crazy Series. Multiflora petunia. **H** 6–8in (15–20cm), **S** 12–36in (30–90cm). Produce flowers with contrasting veins and throats. Colors available include white, with yellow throat and veins, and shades of violet, pink and magenta, all with darker throats and veins.

P. Primetime Series. Multiflora petunia. **H** to 14in (35cm), **S** 12–36in (30–90cm). Bear flowers in very wide range of colors, including white, blue, pink or red, some with dark veins or central stars, or picotee margin. Z9–11 H12–1.

P. 'Razzle Dazzle'. Grandiflora petunia. **H** 8–12in (20–30cm), **S** 12–36in (30–90cm). Has flowers in various colors, striped with white.

P. Recoverer Series. Grandiflora petunia. **H** 6–12in (15–30cm), **S** 12in (30cm). Have large, flared, trumpet-shaped, white flowers. Z9–11 H12–1.

P. 'Red Satin'. Multiflora petunia. **H** 6–12in (5–30cm), **S** 12–24in (30–60cm). Has brilliant scarlet flowers.

P. Resisto Series. Multiflora petunia. **H** 6–12in (15–30cm), **S** 12in (30cm). Have intense blue and rose-pink flowers. Z9–11 H12–1.

P. 'Sunsolos'. See *P.* Surfinia Series SURFINIA BLUE VEIN.

P. Surfinia Series SURFINIA BLUE VEIN **('Sunsolos')** illus. p.311. **Surfinia Series** SURFINIA LIME **('Keiyeul')**, illus. p.316. **'Surfinia Purple'** is a vigorous Grandiflora petunia. **H** 9–16in (23–40cm), **S** 12–36in (30–90cm). Bears masses of magenta flowers with purple veining. Has good wet-weather tolerance.

P. Tumbelina Series PRISCILLA **('Kerpril')**, illus. p.311.

P. WonderWave Series 'Wave Purple'. Very vigorous, trailing or spreading Multiflora petunia. **H** 4–6in (10–15cm), **S** 3ft (1m). Has prolific, single, vibrant magenta flowers.

PHACELIA
HYDROPHYLLACEAE/BORAGINACEAE

Genus of annuals, biennials and perennials. Needs sun and fertile, well-drained soil. Tall species may need support. Propagate by seed in spring or early fall. ① Contact with foliage may aggravate skin allergies.

P. campanularia, illus. p.314.

P. tanacetifolia (Fiddleneck). Moderately fast-growing, upright annual. **H** 24in (60cm) or more, **S** 12in (30cm). Has feathery, deep green leaves. In summer bears spikes of bell-shaped, lavender-blue flowers. Z5–10 H9–1.

PHAEDRANASSA
Queen lily
AMARYLLIDACEAE

Genus of bulbs, grown for their tubular, often pendent flowers. Needs full sun or partial shade and fairly rich, well-drained soil. Feed with high-potash fertilizer in summer. Reduce watering in winter. Propagate by seed or offsets in spring.

P. carmioli, illus. p.410.

Phaedranthus buccinatorius. See *Distictis buccinatoria*.

Phaiophleps biflora. See *Olsynium biflorum*.

PHAIUS
ORCHIDACEAE

See also ORCHIDS.

P. tankervilleae (Nun orchid), illus. p.467. Semievergreen, terrestrial orchid. **H** 30in (75cm). Tall spikes of flowers, 3½in (9cm) across, brown within, silvery-gray outside and with long, red-marked, pink lips, are produced in early summer. Has broadly oval, ribbed leaves, 24in (60cm) long. Provide partial shade in summer. H11–6.

PHALAENOPSIS
Moth orchid
ORCHIDACEAE

See also ORCHIDS.

P. Allegria. Evergreen, epiphytic orchid for a warm greenhouse. **H** 6in (15cm). Produces sprays of white flowers, to 5in (12cm) across; flowering season varies. Broadly oval, fleshy

P

659

leaves are 6in (15cm) long. Needs shade in summer. Z14–15 H12–6.

P. cornu-cervi. Evergreen, epiphytic orchid for a warm greenhouse. **H** 6in (15cm). Yellowish-green flowers, 2in (5cm) across, with brown marks, are borne successively, either singly or in pairs, in summer. Has broadly oval leaves, 4in (10cm) long. Needs shade in summer. Z14–15 H12–6.

P. Lady Pink Lips gx, illus. p.466. Evergreen, epiphytic orchid for a warm greenhouse. **H** 6in (15cm). Tall, pendent spikes of pink flowers, 3¹/₂in (9cm) across, are borne at varying times of year. Broadly oval leaves are 4in (10cm) long. Requires shade in summer. Z14–15 H12–6.

P. Lundy gx, illus. p.467. Evergreen, epiphytic orchid for a warm greenhouse. **H** 6in (15cm). Has sprays of red-striped, yellow flowers, 3in (8cm) across; flowering season varies. Broadly oval leaves are 9in (23cm) long. Needs shade in summer. Z14–15 H12–6.

PHALARIS
GRAMINEAE/POACEAE

See also GRASSES, BAMBOOS RUSHES and SEDGES.

P. arundinacea var. picta, syn. *P. arundinacea* 'Picta' (Gardeners' garters). Evergreen, spreading, perennial grass. **H** 3ft (1m), **S** indefinite. Has broad, white-striped leaves and produces narrow panicles of spikelets in summer. Z4–9 H9–1.
'Picta'. See *P. arundinacea* var. *picta*.

Phanerophlebia fortunei. See *Cyrtomium fortunei*.
Phaseolus caracalla. See *Vigna caracalla*.
Phedimus aizoon. See *Sedum aizoon*.
Phedimus kamtschaticus. See *Sedum kamtschaticum*.
Phedimus spurius. See *Sedum spurium*.

PHEGOPTERIS
Beech fern
THELYPTERIDACEAE

Genus of deciduous ferns. Grow in partial shade and rich, moist but well-drained soil. Propagate by division in spring or by spores in summer.

P. connectilis, syn. *Thelypteris phegopteris* (Narrow beech fern). Deciduous fern. **H** 9in (23cm), **S** 12in (30cm). Broadly lance-shaped, mid-green fronds, each consisting of tiny, triangular pinnae on wiry stalks, arise from creeping rootstock. Is useful for groundcover. Z4–6 H6–1.

PHELLODENDRON
Cork tree
RUTACEAE

Genus of deciduous trees, grown for their foliage, which colors well in fall. Male and female flowers are produced on different plants. Young growth is susceptible to damage by late frosts. Needs full sun and fertile, well-drained soil. Does best in hot summers. Propagate by softwood cuttings in summer, by seed in fall or by root cuttings in late winter.

P. amurense (Amur cork tree). Deciduous, spreading tree. **H** 40ft (12m), **S** 50ft (15m). Has corky, dark bark when old. Aromatic, glossy, dark green leaves, with 5–11 oblong leaflets, turn yellow in fall. Tiny, green

flowers, in early summer, are followed by small, rounded, black fruits. Z4–7 H8–5.
P. chinense, illus. p.75.

Phemeranthus sediformis. See *Talinum okanoganense*.

PHILADELPHUS
Mock orange
HYDRANGEACEAE/PHILADELPHACEAE

Genus of deciduous, mainly summer-flowering shrubs, grown for their usually fragrant flowers. Needs sun and fertile, well-drained soil. After flowering, cut some older shoots back to young growths, leaving young shoots to flower the following year. Propagate by softwood cuttings in summer. May become infested with aphids.

P. 'Beauclerk', illus. p.127.
P. 'Belle Etoile', illus. p.128.
P. 'Boule d'Argent', illus. p.128.
P. coronarius (Mock orange). **'Aureus'** is a deciduous, upright shrub. **H** 8ft (2.5m), **S** 5ft (1.5m). Clusters of very fragrant, 4-petaled, creamy-white flowers are produced in late spring and early summer. Oval, golden-yellow, young leaves turn yellow-green in summer. Protect from full sun. Z4–7 H7–1. **'Variegatus',** illus. p.131.
P. 'Dame Blanche', illus. p.129.
P. delavayi. Deciduous, upright shrub. **H** 10ft (3m), **S** 8ft (2.5m). Dense clusters of very fragrant, 4-petaled, white flowers, with sometimes purple-flushed, green sepals, open from early to mid-summer. Leaves are dark green, oval and toothed. Z6–9 H9–6. **f. melanocalyx,** syn. *P. purpurascens*, illus. p.131.
P. 'Lemoinei', syn. *P. x lemoinei*, illus. p.129.
P. magdalenae. Deciduous, bushy shrub. **H** and **S** 12ft (4m). Bark peels on older shoots. Narrowly oval, dark green leaves set off fragrant, 4-petaled, white flowers in late spring and early summer. Z6–8 H8–6.
P. 'Manteau d'Hermine', illus. p.149.
P. purpurascens. See *P. delavayi* f. *melanocalyx*.
P. 'Sybille'. Deciduous, arching shrub. **H** 4ft (1.2m), **S** 6ft (2m). Bears masses of fragrant, 4-petaled, white flowers, with central, pink stain, in early and mid-summer. Leaves are mid-green and oval. Z5–8 H8–5.
P. 'Virginal'. Vigorous, deciduous, upright shrub. **H** 10ft (3m), **S** 8ft (2.5m). Has oval, dark green leaves. Produces masses of large, very fragrant, double or semidouble, pure white flowers in loose racemes from early to mid-summer. Z5–8 H8–5.

x PHILAGERIA
LILIACEAE/PHILESIACEAE

Hybrid genus (*Philesia* x *Lapageria*) of one evergreen, scrambling or twining shrub. Needs partial shade and well-drained, preferably acidic soil. Propagate by layering in late summer or fall.

x P. veitchii. Evergreen, scrambling or twining shrub. **H** 10–12ft (3–4m). Has oblong, slightly toothed leaves. Nodding, tubular, rose-pink flowers are produced in leaf axils in summer. Z11–13 H12–10.

PHILESIA
LILIACEAE/PHILESIACEAE

Genus of one species of evergreen shrub, grown for its showy flowers. Thrives only in mild, moist areas. Needs partial shade

and rich, moist, acidic soil. Apply an annual dressing of leaf mold. Propagate by semiripe cuttings in summer or by suckers in fall.

P. magellanica. Evergreen, erect shrub. **H** 3ft (90cm), **S** 6ft (2m). Bears trumpet-shaped, waxy, crimson-pink flowers, in leaf axils, from mid-summer to late fall. Narrowly oblong, dark green leaves are bluish-white beneath. Z7–8 H8–7.

PHILLYREA
OLEACEAE

Genus of evergreen shrubs and trees, with inconspicuous flowers, grown for their foliage. Prefers full sun and fertile, well-drained soil. To restrict growth, cut back in spring. Propagate by semiripe cuttings in summer.

P. angustifolia. Evergreen, bushy, dense shrub. **H** and **S** 10ft (3m). Leaves are narrowly oblong and dark green. Small, fragrant, 4-lobed, greenish-white flowers, in late spring and early summer, are followed by spherical, blue-black fruits. Z7–9 H9–7.
P. decora. See *Osmanthus decorus*.
P. latifolia. Evergreen, rounded shrub or tree. **H** and **S** 25ft (8m). Has oval, glossy, dark green leaves. Bears tiny, fragrant, 4-lobed, greenish-white flowers, from late spring to early summer, followed by spherical, blue-black fruits. Z7–9 H9–7.

PHILODENDRON
ARACEAE

Genus of evergreen shrubs and woody-based root climbers, grown for their leaves. Intermittently bears insignificant flowers. Needs partial shade and rich, well-drained soil. Water moderately, sparingly in cold weather. Provide support. Young stem tips may be removed to promote branching. Propagate by leaf-bud or stem-tip cuttings in summer. ⓘ All parts may cause severe discomfort if ingested; contact with sap may irritate skin.

P. auritum of gardens. See *Syngonium auritum*.
P. bipinnatifidum, syn. *P. selloum*, illus. p.458.
P. 'Burgundy'. Slow-growing, evergreen, woody-based, root climber. **H** 6ft (2m) or more. Has narrowly oblong, red-flushed, deep green leaves, to 12in (30cm) long, wine-red beneath. Z14–15 H12–1.
P. cordatum. See *P. hederaceum*.
P. domesticum, syn. *P. hastatum* (Elephant's ear). Fairly slow-growing, evergreen, woody-based, root climber. **H** 6–10ft (2–3m). Lustrous, bright green leaves, 12–16in (30–40cm) long, are arrow-shaped on young plants and later have prominent, basal lobes. Z14–15 H12–1.
P. erubescens (Blushing philodendron, Red-leaf philodendron). Evergreen, erect, woody-based, root climber. **H** to 10ft (3m). Oval to triangular leaves, 6–10in (15–25cm) long, have long, red stalks and are dark green with lustrous, coppery flush. Z14–15 H12–1.
P. hastatum of gardens. See *P. domesticum*.
P. hederaceum, syn. *P. cordatum* (Heart leaf). Moderately vigorous, evergreen, woody-based, root climber. **H** 10ft (3m) or more. Has heart-shaped, lustrous, rich

green leaves, to 18in (45cm) long.
P. laciniatum. See *P. pedatum*.
P. melanochrysum (Black gold philodendron, Velour philodendron). Robust, fairly slow-growing, evergreen, woody-based, root climber. **H** 10ft (3m) or more. Heart-shaped leaves, to 30in (75cm) long, are lustrous, deep olive-green with coppery sheen and pale veins. Z14–15 H12–10.
P. pedatum, syn. *P. laciniatum*. Slow-growing, evergreen, woody-based, root climber. **H** 6–10ft (2–3m). Has oval, glossy, deep green leaves, 12–32in (30–80cm) long, with 5 or 7 prominent lobes. Z14–15 H12–1.
P. sagittatum. See *P. sagittifolium*.
P. sagittifolium, syn. *P. sagittatum*. Slow-growing, evergreen, woody-based, root climber. **H** 6–10ft (2–3m). Oval, glossy, bright green leaves, with basal lobes, are up to 16–24in (40–60cm) long. Z14–15 H12–1.
P. scandens, illus. p.463.
P. selloum. See *P. bipinnatifidum*.
P. trifoliatum. See *Syngonium auritum*.

PHLEBODIUM
POLYPODIACEAE

Genus of evergreen or semievergreen ferns. Needs full light or partial shade and rich, moist but well-drained soil. Remove fading fronds regularly. Propagate by division in spring or by spores in summer.

P. aureum, syn. *Polypodium aureum*, illus. p.478. **'Mandaianum',** illus. p.479.

PHLOMIS
LABIATAE/LAMIACEAE

Genus of evergreen, summer-flowering shrubs and perennials, grown for their conspicuous, hooded flowers, which are borne in dense whorls, and for their foliage. Prefers full sun and well-drained soil. Propagate by seed in fall, shrubs by softwood cuttings in summer, perennials by division in spring.

P. cashmeriana. Evergreen, upright shrub. **H** 24in (60cm), **S** 18in (45cm). Produces masses of 2-lipped, pale lilac flowers in summer. Narrowly oval, mid-green leaves have woolly, white undersides. Z8–9 H9–8.
P. chrysophylla (Goldleaf Jerusalem sage). Evergreen, rounded, stiffly branched shrub. **H** and **S** 3ft (1m). Bears 2-lipped, golden-yellow flowers in early summer. Oval leaves are gray-green when young, becoming golden-green. Z9–10 H10–9.
P. fruticosa, illus. p.160.
P. italica, illus. p.152.
P. longifolia var. bailanica. Evergreen, bushy shrub. **H** 4ft (1.2m), **S** 3ft (1m). Leaves are oblong to heart-shaped, deeply veined and bright green. Has 2-lipped, deep yellow flowers from early to mid-summer. Z8–9 H9–8.
P. russeliana, illus. p.243.

PHLOX
POLEMONIACEAE

Genus of mainly late spring- or summer-flowering annuals and perennials, some of which are semievergreen or evergreen, grown for their terminal panicles or profusion of brightly colored flowers. Prefers sun or partial shade and fertile, moist but well-drained soil; some species

P

prefer acidic soil; in light, dry soils is better grown in partial shade. Trim back rock garden species after flowering. Propagate rock garden species and hybrids by cuttings from non-flowering shoots in spring or summer; species by seed in fall or spring; *P. maculata, P. paniculata* and their cultivars also by division in early spring or by root cuttings in winter; and annuals by seed in spring. *P. maculata, P. paniculata* and their cultivars are susceptible to eelworm. See also feature panel p.240.

P. adsurgens. Evergreen, mat-forming, prostrate perennial. **H** 4in (10cm), **S** 12in (30cm). Woody-based stems are clothed in oval, light to mid-green leaves. In summer produces terminal clusters of short-stemmed, saucer-shaped, purple, pink or white flowers, with overlapping petals. Is good for a rock garden or peat bed. Prefers partial shade and gritty, peaty, acidic soil. Z4–8 H8–1. **'Wagon Wheel',** illus. p.363.

***P. amoena* 'Variegata'.** See *P. x procumbens* 'Variegata'.

P. bifida, illus. p.366.

P. caespitosa. Evergreen, mound-forming, compact perennial. **H** 3in (8cm), **S** 5in (12cm). Leaves are narrow and needlelike. Solitary, almost stemless, saucer-shaped, lilac or white flowers are borne in summer. Is suitable for a rock garden or trough. Needs sun and very well-drained soil. Z4–8 H8–1.

***P.* 'Camla',** illus. p.365.

***P.* 'Chattahoochee'.** See *P. divaricata* subsp. *laphamii*'Chattahoochee'.

P. divaricata (Blue phlox, Wild sweet William, Woodland phlox). Semievergreen, creeping perennial. **H** 12in more (30cm) or more, **S** 8in (20cm). In early summer, upright stems bear saucer-shaped, lavender-blue flowers in loose clusters. Leaves are oval. Is suitable for a rock garden or peat bed. Prefers partial shade and moist but well-drained, peaty soil. Z4–8 H8–1. **subsp. *laphamii*,** illus. p.341. **subsp. *laphamii* 'Chattahoochee',** syn. *P.* 'Chattahoochee', illus. p.341.

***P. douglasii.* 'Boothman's Variety',** illus. p.366. **'Crackerjack',** illus. p.365. **'May Snow'** is an evergreen, mound-forming perennial. **H** 3in (8cm), **S** 8in (20cm). Has lance-shaped, mid-green leaves. Masses of saucer-shaped, white flowers are borne in early summer. Is suitable for a rock garden, wall or bank. Vigorous, compact **'Red Admiral',** **H** 6in (5cm), has crimson flowers.

P. drummondii (Annual phlox). **Beauty Series** is a group of moderately fast-growing, compact, upright annuals. **H** 6in (15cm), **S** 4in (10cm). Has lance-shaped, pale green leaves. From summer to early fall produces heads of star-shaped flowers in many colors, including red, pink, blue, purple and white. **Buttons Series, H** and **S** 6–10in (15–25cm), has flowers in range of colors from deep red to pink and white. H12–1. **'Carnival'** has larger flowers with contrasting centers. **'Chanal',** illus. p.305. **'Petticoat'** has bicolored flowers. **'Sternenzauber',** syn. *P. drummondii* 'Twinkle' has star-shaped flowers in bright mixture of colors, some with contrasting centers. **'Twinkle'.** See *P. drummondii* 'Sternenzauber'.

***P.* 'Emerald Cushion',** illus. p.367.

P. hoodii. Evergreen, compact, prostrate perennial. **H** 2in (5cm), **S** 4in (10cm). Solitary, flat, white flowers are borne in early summer above fine, needlelike, hairy leaves. Is suitable for a rock garden. Needs sun and very well-drained soil.

P. maculata (Meadow phlox, Wild sweet William). Erect perennial. **H** 3ft (1m), **S** 1½ft (45cm). In summer produces cylindrical panicles of tubular, 5-lobed, mauve-pink flowers above oval, mid-green leaves. Z5–8 H8–1. **'Alpha'** has rose-pink flowers. **'Omega'** has white flowers, each with lilac eye.

P. paniculata (Garden phlox). Upright perennial, seldom grown, as is replaced in gardens by its more colorful cultivars. **H** 4ft (1.2m), **S** 2ft (60cm). Tubular, 5-lobed flowers are borne in conical heads above oval, mid-green leaves in late summer. Z4–8 H8–1. **'Aida'** is purple-red, each flower with purple eye. Flowers of **'Amethyst'** (illus. p.240) are pale lilac with paler-edged petals. **'Balmoral'** has large, rosy-mauve flowers. **'Brigadier'** (illus. p.240) has deep orange-red flowers. **'Bright Eyes'** has pale pink flowers, each with red eye. **'Eva Cullum'** (illus. p.240) has clear pink flowers with magenta eyes. **'Eventide'** produces lavender-blue flowers. **'Fujiyama'.** See *P. paniculata* 'Mount Fuji'. Flowers of **'Graf Zeppelin'** are white with red centers. **'Hampton Court'** (illus. p.240) has mauve-blue flowers and dark green foliage. **'Harlequin'** has reddish-purple flowers. Leaves are variegated ivory-white. **'Junior Bouquet'** has deep pink flowers with prominent, white eye. **'Le Mahdi'** has deep purple flowers. **'Mia Ruys'** (illus. p.240), **H** 18in (45cm), has large, white flowers, **'Mother of Pearl'** has white flowers tinted pink. **'Mount Fuji',** syn. *P. paniculata* 'Fujiyama', illus. p.230. **'Norah Leigh'** (illus. p.240) has pale lilac flowers and ivory-variegated leaves. **'Prince of Orange',** illus. p.235. **'Russian Violet'** is of open habit and has pale lilac-blue flowers. Flowers of **'Sandringham'** have widely spaced petals and are pink with darker centers. **'Sir John Falstaff'** has large, deep salmon flowers, each with a cherry-red eye. **'White Admiral'** bears pure white flowers. Those of **'Windsor'** (illus. p.240) are carmine-rose with red eyes.

***P. x procumbens* 'Millstream'.** Evergreen, prostrate perennial. **H** to 6in (15cm), **S** 12in (30cm). Has narrowly oval, glossy, green leaves. In early summer bears small, saucer-shaped, white-eyed, deep lavender-pink flowers. Is suitable for a rock garden. Z3–8 H8–1. **'Variegata',** syn. *P. amoena* 'Variegata', **H** 1in (2.5cm), **S** 10in (25cm), has white-margined leaves and bright cerise-pink flowers.

P. stolonifera (Creeping phlox). Evergreen, prostrate, spreading perennial. **H** 4–6in (10–15cm), **S** 12in (30cm) or more. Has small, saucer-shaped, pale blue flowers in early summer. Leaves are oblong to oval. Prefers moist, peaty, acidic soil. Is good for a peat bed or rock garden. Z4–8 H8–1. **'Ariane',** illus. p.359. **'Blue Ridge'** has masses of lavender-blue flowers.

P. subulata (Creeping phlox, Moss phlox). Evergreen, mound-forming perennial. **H** 4in (10cm), **S** 8in (20cm). Bears fine, needlelike leaves. Masses of star-shaped, white, pink or mauve flowers are produced in early summer. Is good for a sunny rock garden. Z3–8 H8–1. **'Marjorie',** illus. p.365.

PHOENIX

PALMAE/ARECACEAE

Genus of evergreen palms, grown for their overall appearance and their edible fruits. Prefers full light and fertile, well-drained soil. Water container specimens moderately, less during winter. Propagate by seed in spring at not less than 75°F (24°C). Red spider mite may be a nuisance.

P. canariensis (Canary Island date palm). Evergreen, upright palm with a robust trunk. **H** 60ft (18m) or more, **S** 30ft (10m) or more. Feather-shaped, arching leaves, to 15ft (5m) long, are divided into narrowly lance-shaped, leathery, bright green leaflets. Bears large, pendent clusters of tiny, yellowish-brown flowers that on mature specimens are followed by shortly oblong, yellow to red fruits in fall–winter. Z11–12 H12–10.

P. roebelenii (Miniature date palm, Pygmy date palm). Evergreen palm with slender trunk. **H** 6–12ft (2–4m), **S** 3–6ft (1–2m). Has feather-shaped, arching, glossy, dark green leaves, 3–4ft (1–1.2m) long, and, in summer, large panicles of tiny, yellow flowers. Egg-shaped, black fruits are borne in pendent clusters, 18in (45cm) long, in fall. Z11–12 H12–10.

PHORMIUM

AGAVACEAE/HEMEROCALLIDACEAE

Genus of evergreen perennials, grown for their bold, sword-shaped leaves. Requires sun and moist but well-drained soil. Propagate by division or seed in spring.

***P.* 'Bronze Baby'.** Evergreen, upright perennial. **H** and **S** 18–24in (45–60cm). Has tufts of bold, stiff, pointed, wine-red leaves. Panicles of reddish flowers are occasionally produced on purplish stems in summer. Z9–11 H12–6.

P. colensoi. See *P. cookianum.*

P. cookianum, syn. *P. colensoi* (Mountain flax). Evergreen, upright perennial. **H** 3–6ft (1–2m), **S** 1ft (30cm). Has tufts of sword-shaped, dark green leaves. Panicles of tubular, pale yellowish-green flowers are borne in summer. Z9–11 H12–1. **'Black Adder'** has burgundy-black leaves. **subsp. *hookeri* 'Tricolor'** has leaves striped vertically with red, yellow and green. **'Variegatum'** has cream-striped leaves.

***P.* 'Dazzler',** illus. p.216.

P. tenax (New Zealand flax). Evergreen, upright perennial. **H** 10ft (3m), **S** 3–6ft (1–2m). Has tufts of sword-shaped, stiff, dark green leaves. Panicles of tubular, dull red flowers are produced on short, slightly glaucous green stems in summer. Thrives by the sea. Z9–11 H12–6. **'Aurora'** has leaves vertically striped with red, bronze, salmon-pink and yellow. **Purpureum Group, H** 6–8ft (2–2.5m), **S** 3ft (1m), has rich reddish-purple to dark copper leaves. Z9–11 H11–2. **'Veitchianum',** syn. *P. tenax* 'Veitchii' bears broad, creamy-white-striped leaves. **'Veitchii'.** See *P. tenax* 'Veitchianum'.

PHOTINIA

SYN. STRANVAESIA

ROSACEAE

Genus of evergreen or deciduous shrubs and trees, with small, white flowers, grown for their foliage and, in the case of deciduous species, for their fall color and fruits. Protect evergreen species from strong, cold winds. Requires sun or partial shade and fertile, well-drained soil; some species prefer acidic soil. Propagate evergreen and deciduous species by semiripe cuttings in summer, deciduous species also by seed in fall.

P. arbutifolia. See *Heteromeles salicifolia.*

P. davidiana, illus. p.90.

***P.* x *fraseri*.** Group of evergreen, hybrid shrubs. **H** and **S** 15ft (5m). Have oblong, dark green leaves. Young growths are attractive over a long period. Has good resistance to damage by late frosts. Z8–9 H9–8. **'Birmingham'** has heads of small, white flowers in late spring. **'Red Robin',** illus. p.111.

P. nussia. Evergreen, spreading tree. **H** and **S** 20ft (6m). Produces oblong, leathery, glossy, dark green leaves and saucer-shaped, 5-petaled, white flowers in mid-summer, followed by rounded, orange-red fruits. Z9–10 H10–9.

P. serratifolia, syn. *P. serrulata*, illus. p.111.

P. serrulata. See *P. serratifolia.*

P. villosa (Oriental photinia). Deciduous, upright shrub or spreading tree. **H** and **S** 15ft (5m). Oval, dark green leaves, bronze-margined when young, become brilliant orange-red in fall. Clusters of 5-petaled flowers, produced in late spring, are followed by spherical, red fruits. Prefers acidic soil. Z4–9 H9–1.

PHRAGMIPEDIUM

ORCHIDACEAE

See also ORCHIDS.

P. besseae (illus. p.467). Evergreen, terrestrial orchid for an intermediate greenhouse. **H** 3ft (1m). Pouch-lipped, bright scarlet red, orange-red or yellow flowers are borne in upright racemes in spring. Has strap-shaped leaves. Needs shade in summer. H11–1.

P. caudatum. Evergreen, epiphytic orchid for an intermediate greenhouse. **H** 24in (60cm). In summer produces sprays of flowers with light green and tan sepals and pouches and drooping, ribbon-like, yellow and brownish-crimson petals. Has narrowly oval leaves. Needs shade in summer. Z14–15 H12–10.

PHUOPSIS

RUBIACEAE

Genus of one species of mat-forming, summer-flowering perennial, grown for its small, pungent, tubular flowers. Is good for groundcover, especially on banks and in rock gardens. Needs sun and well-drained soil. Propagate by division in spring, by semiripe cuttings in summer or by seed in fall.

P. stylosa, syn. *Crucianella stylosa*, illus. p.338.

PHYGELIUS

SCROPHULARIACEAE

Genus of evergreen or semievergreen shrubs and subshrubs, grown for their showy, tubular flowers. Grows best if planted in a sheltered position; will attain a considerably greater height when grown against a south- or west-facing wall. Needs sun and fertile, well-drained but not too dry soil. Cut back to just above ground level in spring, or, if plants have woody bases, prune to live wood. Propagate by softwood cuttings in summer.

P. aequalis, illus. p.156. **'Yellow Trumpet'**, illus. p.160.
P. capensis (Cape figwort, Cape fuchsia). Evergreen or semievergreen, upright subshrub. **H** 5ft (1.5m), **S** 6ft (2m). Has tubular, curved, bright orange-red flowers, with red mouth and yellow throat, from mid-summer to early fall, in tall, slender spires amid triangular, dark green leaves. Z8–9 H9–8.
P. x rectus 'Winchester Fanfare'. Evergreen or semievergreen, upright subshrub. **H** 5ft (1.5m), **S** 6ft (2m). Has triangular, dark green leaves. Pendulous, tubular, dusky, reddish-pink flowers, with scarlet lobes and yellow throat, are borne from mid-summer to early fall. Z8–9 H9–8.

Phyllanthus nivosus. See *Breynia disticha.*

x PHYLLIOPSIS
ERICACEAE

Hybrid genus (*Phyllodoce* x *Kalmiopsis*) of one species of evergreen shrub, grown for its flowers. Is suitable for peat beds and rock gardens. Needs partial shade and peaty, acidic soil. Trim back after flowering to maintain a compact habit. Propagate by semiripe cuttings in late summer.

x P. hillieri 'Pinocchio'. Evergreen, upright shrub. **H** 8in (20cm), **S** 10in (25cm). Branched stems bear thin, oval leaves. Long, open clusters of bell-shaped, very deep pink flowers are produced in spring and intermittently thereafter. Z4–8 H8–1.

Phyllitis scolopendrium. See *Asplenium scolopendrium.*

PHYLLOCLADUS
Celery pine
PHYLLOCLADACEAE/PODOCARPACEAE

See also CONIFERS.
P. aspleniifolius (Tasman celery pine). Slow-growing, upright conifer. **H** 15–30ft (5–10m), **S** 10–15ft (3–5m). Instead of true leaves has flattened, leaflike shoots known as phylloclades; these are dull dark green and resemble celery leaves in outline. Produces inedible, white-coated nuts, with fleshy, red bases.
P. trichomanoides, illus. p.101.

PHYLLODOCE
ERICACEAE

Genus of evergreen shrubs, grown for their heather-like leaves and flowers. Needs partial shade and moist, peaty, acidic soil. Propagate by semiripe cuttings in late summer or by seed in spring.

P. caerulea, syn. *P. taxifolia*, illus. p.334.
P. empetriformis, illus. p.334.
P. x intermedia. 'Fred Stoker' is an evergreen, upright shrub. **H** and **S** 9in (23cm). Has narrow, glossy, green leaves. From late spring to early summer produces terminal clusters of pitcher-shaped, bright reddish-purple flowers on slender, red stalks. Z3–7 H7–1. **'Drummondii'**, illus. p.333.
P. nipponica. Evergreen, upright shrub. **H** 4–8in (10–20cm), **S** 4–6in (10–15cm). Freely branched stems bear fine, linear

leaves and, in late spring and summer, stalked, bell-shaped, white flowers from tips. Z3–7 H7–1.
P. taxifolia. See *P. caerulea.*

PHYLLOSTACHYS
GRAMINEAE/POACEAE

See also GRASSES, BAMBOOS, RUSHES and SEDGES.
P. aurea, illus. p.288.
P. aureosulcata (Yellow-groove bamboo). Evergreen, clump-forming bamboo. **H** 20–25ft (6–8m), **S** indefinite. Rough, brownish-green stems have striped sheaths and yellow grooves. Mid-green leaves are up to 6in (15cm) long; flowers are unimportant as they are so rarely produced. Z3–11 H12–3.
P. bambusoides, illus. p.287.
P. flexuosa (Zigzag bamboo). Evergreen, clump-forming bamboo. **H** 20–25ft (6–8m), **S** indefinite. Has slender, markedly zigzag stems that turn black with age. Leaf sheaths have no bristles. Leaves stay fresh green all winter. Z6–11 H11–1.
P. 'Henonis'. See *P. nigra* f. *henonis.*
P. nigra, illus. p.286. **f. henonis**, syn. *P.* 'Henonis' illus. p.287.
P. viridiglaucescens, illus. p.287.
P. vivax f. aureocaulis, illus. p.289.

x PHYLLOTHAMNUS
ERICACEAE

Hybrid genus (*Phyllodoce* x *Rhodothamnus*) of one species of evergreen shrub, grown for its foliage and flowers. Is good for peat beds and rock gardens. Needs a sheltered, partially shaded site and moist, acidic soil. Propagate by semiripe cuttings in late summer.

x P. erectus. Evergreen, upright shrub. **H** and **S** 6in (15cm). Has small, linear, glossy, deep green leaves. Clusters of slender-stalked, bell-shaped, soft rose-pink flowers are produced in late spring and early summer. Z6–8 H8–6.

PHYSALIS
Ground cherry
SOLANACEAE

Genus of summer-flowering perennials and annuals, grown mainly for their lantern-like calyces and fruits, produced in fall. Needs sun or partial shade and well-drained soil. Propagate by division or softwood cuttings in spring, annuals by seed in spring or fall.
① All parts of *P. alkekengi*, except the fully ripe fruit, may cause mild stomach upset if ingested; contact with foliage may irritate skin.
P. alkekengi (Chinese lantern, Japanese lantern). Spreading perennial, grown as an annual. **H** 18in (45cm), **S** 24in (60cm). Inconspicuous, nodding, star-shaped, white flowers in summer are followed by rounded, bright orange-red fruits, surrounded by inflated, orange calyces. Leaves are mid-green and oval. Z3–9 H8–1.

PHYSOCARPUS
ROSACEAE

Genus of deciduous, mainly summer-flowering shrubs, grown for their foliage and flowers. Requires sun and fertile, not too dry soil. Prefers acidic soil and does not

grow well on shallow, chalky soil. Thin established plants occasionally by cutting some older shoots back to ground level after flowering. Propagate by softwood cuttings in summer.
P. opulifolius (Ninebark). Deciduous, arching, dense shrub. **H** 10ft (3m), **S** 15ft (5m). Has peeling bark and broadly oval, toothed and lobed, mid-green leaves. Bears clusters of tiny, at times pink-tinged, white flowers in early summer. Z3–7 H7–1.
'Dart's Gold', illus. p.159.

PHYSOPLEXIS
CAMPANULACEAE

Genus of one species of tufted perennial, grown for its flowers. Is good grown on tufa, in rock gardens, troughs and alpine houses. Needs sun and very well-drained, alkaline soil, but should face away from midday sun. Keep fairly dry in winter. Propagate by seed in fall or by softwood cuttings in early summer. Is susceptible to slug damage.
P. comosa, syn. *Phyteuma comosum*, illus. p.366.

PHYSOSTEGIA
Obedient plant
LABIATAE/LAMIACEAE

Genus of summer- to early fall-flowering perennials. Needs sun and fertile, moist but well-drained soil. Propagate by division in spring.
P. virginiana (False dragonhead, Obedient plant). Erect perennial. **H** 3ft (1m), **S** 2ft (60cm). In late summer produces spikes of hooded, 2-lipped, rose-purple flowers, with hinged stalks that allow flowers to remain in position once moved. Has lance-shaped, toothed, mid-green leaves. Z4–8 H8–1. **subsp. speciosa 'Variegata'.** See *P. virginiana* 'Variegata'. **'Summer Snow'** has pure white flowers. **'Variegata'**, syn. *P. virginiana* subsp. *speciosa* 'Variegata', illus. p.233. **'Vivid'**, illus. p.280.

PHYTEUMA
CAMPANULACEAE

Genus of early- to mid-summer-flowering perennials that are useful for rock gardens. Needs sun and well-drained soil. Propagate by seed in fall.
P. comosum. See *Physoplexis comosa.*
P. scheuchzeri, illus. p.342.

PHYTOLACCA
Pokeweed
PHYTOLACCACEAE

Genus of perennials and evergreen shrubs and trees, grown for their overall appearance and decorative but poisonous fruits. Needs sun or partial shade and fertile, moist soil. Propagate by seed in fall or spring. ① All parts may cause severe discomfort if ingested; the fruit of *P. americana* may be lethal if eaten. Contact with the sap may irritate skin.
P. americana, syn. *P. decandra* (Pigeon berry, Pokeweed, Red ink plant). Upright, spreading perennial. **H** and **S** 4–5ft (1.2–1.5m). Oval to lance-shaped, mid-green leaves are tinged purple in fall. Shallowly cup-shaped, sometimes pink-

flushed, white-and-green flowers, borne in terminal racemes in summer, are followed by poisonous, rounded, fleshy, blackish-purple berries. Z5–9 H9–5.
P. clavigera. See *P. polyandra.*
P. decandra. See *P. americana.*
P. polyandra, syn. *P. clavigera.* Sturdy, upright perennial. **H** and **S** 4ft (1.2m). Has brilliant crimson stems and oval to lance-shaped, mid-green leaves that turn yellow in fall. In summer bears clusters of shallowly cup-shaped, pink flowers, followed by poisonous, blackish-purple berries. Z5–9 H9–5.

PICEA
Spruce
PINACEAE

Genus of conifers with needlelike leaves set on a pronounced peg on the shoots and arranged spirally. Cones are pendulous and ripen in their first fall; scales are woody and flexible. See also CONIFERS.
P. abies, illus. p.98. Z3–8 H8–1.
'Clanbrassiliana' is a slow-growing, rounded and spreading conifer. **H** 15ft (5m), **S** 10–15ft (3–5m). Has needlelike, dark green leaves and bears pendulous cones. **'Gregoryana'**, **H** and **S** 2ft (60cm), is slow-growing, with a dense, globose form. **'Inversa'**, **H** 15–30ft (5–10m), **S** 6ft (2m), has an erect leader, but pendent side branches. **'Little Gem'**, **H** and **S** 12–20in (30–50cm), has nest-shaped, central depression caused by spreading branches. **'Nidiformis'**, **H** 3ft (1m), **S** 3–6ft (1–2m), is a slow-growing, bushy shrub with a hollow "nest" in center. **'Ohlendorffii'** (illus. p.105), **H** and **S** 3ft (1m), is slow-growing, initially rounded, becoming conical with age. **'Reflexa'**, **H** 1ft (30cm), **S** 15ft (5m), is prostrate and ground-hugging, but may be trained up a stake, to form a mound of weeping foliage.
P. breweriana, illus. p.99.
P. engelmannii, illus. p.99.
P. glauca (White spruce). Narrowly conical conifer. **H** 30–50ft (10–15m), **S** 12–15ft (4–5m). Glaucous shoots produce blue-green leaves. Ovoid, light brown cones fall after ripening. Z2–7 H7–2. **var. albertiana 'Conica'**, syn. *P. glauca* 'Albertiana Conica', **H** 6–15ft (2–5m), **S** 3–6ft (1–2m), is of neat, pyramidal habit and slow-growing, with longer leaves and smaller cones. Z2–6 H6–1. **'Albertiana Conica'.** See *P. glauca* var. *albertiana* 'Conica'. **'Coerulea'**, illus. p.99. **'Echiniformis'**, **H** 20in (50cm), **S** 36in (90c), is a dwarf, flat-topped, rounded form.
P. likiangensis, illus. p.100.
P. mariana (Black spruce). Conical conifer, whose lowest branches often layer naturally, forming ring of stems around parent plant. **H** 30–50ft (10–15m), **S** 10ft (3m). Leaves are bluish-green or bluish-white. Oval cones are dark gray-brown. Z3–6 H6–1. **'Doumetii'**, illus. p.103. **'Nana'**, **H** 20in (50cm), **S** 20–32in (50–80cm), is a neat shrub with blue-gray foliage. Z2–6 H6–1.
P. x mariorika 'Gnom', syn. *P. omorika* 'Gnom'. Shrublike conifer. **H** to 5ft (1.5m), **S** 3–6ft (1–2m). Has pendent branches arching at tips. Dark green leaves are white beneath. Z5–8 H8–5.
P. morrisonicola, illus. p.101.
P. omorika, illus. p.98. **'Gnom'.** See *P. x mariorika* 'Gnom'. **'Nana'** is a slow-growing, rounded or oval conifer. **H** and

P

S 3ft (1m). Branches are pendulous and arch out at tips. Has dark green leaves that are white below. Violet-purple cones age to glossy brown. Z3–7 H7–1.

P. orientalis (Caucasian spruce, Oriental spruce). Columnar, dense conifer. **H** 70ft (20m), **S** 15ft (5m). Has glossy, deep green leaves and ovoid to conical, dark purple cones ripening to brown, the males brick-red in spring. Z5–8 H8–5. **'Aurea'** has golden, young foliage in spring, later turning green. **'Skylands'**, illus. p.99.

P. pungens (Colorado spruce). Columnar conifer. **H** 50ft (15m), **S** 15ft (5m). Has scaly, gray bark and very sharp, sturdy, grayish-green or bright blue leaves. Cylindrical, light brown cones have papery scales. Z3–8 H8–1. **'Globosa'** (illus. p.105) is a slow-growing, rounded form of dense habit and glaucous-blue leaves. Z2–8 H8–1. **'Hoopsii'**, **H** 30–50ft (10–15m), has silvery-blue foliage. **'Koster'**, illus. p.99. **'Montgomery'**, **H** and **S** 3ft (1m), is dwarf, compact, spreading or conical, with gray-blue leaves.

P. sitchensis (Sitka spruce). Very vigorous, broadly conical conifer. **H** 100–160ft (30–50m) in damp locations, 50–70ft (15–20m) in dry situations, **S** 20–30ft (6–10m). Develops bark scales on old trees. Has prickly, bright deep green leaves and cylindrical, papery, pale brown or whitish cones. Is good on an exposed site or one with poor soil. Z7–8 H8–7.

P. smithiana (Himalayan spruce). Slow-growing conifer, conical when young, columnar with horizontal branches and weeping shoots when mature. **H** 80–100ft (25–30m), **S** 20ft (6m). Has dark green leaves and cylindrical, bright brown cones. Z7–8 H8–1.

PICRASMA

SIMAROUBACEAE

Genus of deciduous trees, grown for their brilliant fall color. Produces insignificant flowers in late spring. Requires sun or partial shade and fertile, well-drained soil. Propagate by seed in fall.

P. ailanthoides. See *P. quassioides*.

P. quassioides, syn. *P. ailanthoides*, illus. p.92.

PIERIS

ERICACEAE

Genus of evergreen shrubs, grown for their foliage and small, profuse, urn-shaped flowers. Needs a sheltered site in sun or partial shade and moist, peaty, acidic soil. *P. floribunda*, however, grows well in any acidic soil. Young shoots are sometimes frost-killed in spring and should be cut back as soon as possible. Dead-heading after flowering improves growth. Propagate by soft-tip or semiripe cuttings in summer. ① Leaves may cause severe discomfort if ingested.

P. 'Bert Chandler'. Evergreen, bushy shrub. **H** 6ft (2m), **S** 5ft (1.5m). Lance-shaped leaves are bright pink when young, becoming creamy-yellow, then white and finally dark green. Produces white flowers only very rarely. Likes an open position. Z7–9 H9–7.

P. floribunda, illus. p.120.

P. 'Forest Flame'. Evergreen, upright shrub. **H** 12ft (4m), **S** 6ft (2m). Narrowly

oval, glossy leaves are brilliant red when young, then turn pink, cream and finally dark green. White flowers are borne with young leaves from mid- to late spring. Z6–9 H9–6.

P. formosa. Evergreen, bushy, dense shrub. **H** and **S** 12ft (4m). Large, oblong, glossy, dark green leaves are bronze when young. Bears large clusters of white flowers from mid- to late spring. Z7–9 H9–7. **var. forrestii 'Wakehurst'**, illus. p.137. **'Henry Price'** has deep-veined leaves, which are bronze-red when young.

P. japonica, illus. p.110. **'Daisen'** is an evergreen, rounded, dense shrub. **H** and **S** 10ft (3m). Oval, bronze leaves mature to glossy, dark green. Bears drooping clusters of red-budded, deep pink flowers in spring. Z6–8 H8–6. **'Dorothy Wyckoff'** has deep crimson buds, opening to pink flowers; foliage is bronze in winter. Z6–8 H8–4. Young foliage of **'Mountain Fire'** is brilliant red. Z5–9 H9–1. **'Scarlett O'Hara'**, illus. p.120. The leaves of **Taiwanensis Group**, syn. *P. taiwanensis*, **S** 15ft (5m), are narrow, and bronze-red when young. Bears clusters of white flowers in early and mid-spring. Z3–6 H6–1. Slow-growing **'Variegata'** has small leaves, edged with white. Z6–8 H8–4.

P. nana, syn. *Arcterica nana*. Evergreen, prostrate shrub. **H** 1–2in (2.5–5cm), **S** 4–6in (10–15cm). Has tiny, oval, leathery, dark green leaves, usually in whorls of 3, on fine stems that root readily. In early spring bears small, terminal clusters of white flowers, with green or red calyces. Is excellent for binding a peat wall or in a rock garden. Z3–6 H6–1.

P. taiwanensis. See *P. japonica* Taiwanensis Group.

PILEA

URTICACEAE

Genus of bushy or trailing annuals and evergreen perennials, grown for their ornamental foliage. Needs partial or full shade and well-drained soil. Keep out of drafts and do not over-water in winter. Pinch out tips in growing season to avoid straggly plants. Propagate perennials by stem cuttings in spring or summer, annuals by seed in spring or fall. Red spider mite may be a problem.

P. cadierei, illus. p.465.

P. involucrata, syn. *P. mollis* (Friendship plant, Panamiga). Evergreen, bushy perennial. **H** 6in (15cm), **S** 12in (30cm). Oval to rounded, corrugated, bronze leaves, to 2in (5cm) long, are reddish-green below; leaves are green when grown in shade. Z14–15 H12–1.

P. mollis. See *P. involucrata*.

P. nummulariifolia, illus. p.474.

PILEOSTEGIA

HYDRANGEACEAE

Genus of evergreen, woody-stemmed root climbers. Tolerates sun and shade and needs well-drained soil; is therefore useful for planting against a north wall. Prune in spring, if required. Propagate by semiripe cuttings in summer.

P. viburnoides, syn. *Schizophragma viburnoides*, illus. p.196.

PILOSOCEREUS

CACTACEAE

Genus of columnar, summer-flowering, perennial cacti with wool-like spines in flowering zones at crowns. Some species are included in *Cephalocereus*. Needs full sun and very well-drained soil. Propagate by seed or stem cuttings in spring or summer.

P. leucocephalus, syn. *P. palmeri*, illus. p.483.

P. palmeri. See *P. leucocephalus*.

PIMELEA

THYMELAEACEAE

Genus of evergreen shrubs, grown for their flowers and overall appearance. Needs full sun and well-drained, neutral to acidic soil. Water container plants moderately, less when temperatures are low. Needs good winter light and ventilation in northern temperate greenhouses. Propagate by seed in spring or by semiripe cuttings in late summer.

P. ferruginea, illus. p.454.

PINELLIA

ARACEAE

Genus of summer-flowering, tuberous perennials, grown for their slender, hood-like, green spathes, each enclosing and concealing a pencil-shaped spadix. Needs partial shade or sun and rich soil. Water well in spring–summer. Is dormant in winter. Propagate by offsets in early spring or by bulbils borne in leaf axils in late summer.

P. ternata. Summer-flowering, tuberous perennial. **H** 6–10in (15–25cm), **S** 4–6in (10–15cm). Has erect stems crowned by oval, flat, 3-parted leaves. Leafless stem bears tubular, green spathe, 2–2¹/₂in (5–6cm) long, with hood at tip. Z6–9 H9–6.

PINGUICULA

Butterwort

LENTIBULARIACEAE

Genus of summer-flowering perennials with sticky leaves that trap insects and digest them for food. Is useful in pots under glass among plants at risk from aphids. Needs sun and wet soil. Propagate by division in early spring or by seed in spring.

P. caudata. See *P. moranensis* var. *caudata*.

P. grandiflora, illus. p.368.

P. moranensis var. caudata, syn. *P. caudata*. Basal-rosetted perennial. **H** 5–6in (12–15cm), **S** 2in (5cm). Leaves are narrowly oval and dull green with inrolled, purplish margins. In summer, 5-petaled, deep carmine flowers are produced on long stems. Z13–15 H12–10.

PINUS

Pine

PINACEAE

Genus of small to large conifers with spirally arranged leaves in bundles, usually of 2, 3 or 5 needles. Cones ripen over 2 years and are small in the first year. See also CONIFERS.

P. aristata, illus. p.103.

P. armandii (Armand pine). Conical, open

conifer. **H** 30–50ft (10–15m), **S** 15–25ft (5–8m). Has pendent, glaucous blue leaves and conical, green cones ripening to brown. Z6–8 H8–6.

P. ayacahuite, illus. p.95.

P. banksiana, illus. p.102.

P. bungeana (Lacebark pine), illus. p.78. Slow-growing, bushy conifer. **H** 30–50ft (10–15m), **S** 15–20ft (5–6m). Has gray-green bark that flakes to reveal creamy-yellow patches, darkening to red or purple. Leaves are dark green. Z4–7 H7–1.

P. cembra, illus. p.101.

P. cembroides, illus. p.103.

P. chylla. See *P. wallichiana*.

P. contorta, illus. p.102. **var. latifolia**, illus. p.101. **'Spaan's Dwarf'** is a conical, open, dwarf conifer with short, stiffly erect shoots. **H** and **S** 30in (75cm). Has bright green leaves in 2s and conical to ovoid cones. Z6–8 H8–6.

P. coulteri, illus. p.96.

P. densiflora (Japanese red pine). Flat-topped conifer. **H** 50ft (15m), **S** 15–22ft (5–7m). Has scaling, reddish-brown bark, bright green leaves and conical, yellow or pale brown cones. Z4–7 H7–1. **'Alice Verkade'**, **H** and **S** 30in (75cm), is a rounded form and has fresh green leaves. **'Tagyosho'.** See *P. densiflora* 'Umbraculifera'. **'Umbraculifera'**, syn. *P. densiflora* 'Tagyosho', **H** 12ft (4m), **S** 20ft (6m), is a slow-growing, rounded or umbrella-shaped form.

P. excelsa. See *P. wallichiana*.

P. griffithii. See *P. wallichiana*.

P. halepensis, illus. p.102.

P. heldreichii, syn. *P. heldreichii* var. *leucodermis*, *P. leucodermis*, illus. p.98. **'Compact Gem'**, syn. *P. heldreichii* var. *leucodermis* 'Compact Gem' is a broadly conical, dense, dwarf conifer. **H** and **S** 10–12in (25–30cm). Has very dark green leaves in 2s. Grows only 1in (2.5cm) a year. Z6–8 H8–6. **var. leucodermis.** See *P. heldreichii*. **var. leucodermis 'Compact Gem'.** See *P. heldreichii* 'Compact Gem'. **var. leucodermis 'Schmidtii'.** See *P. heldreichii* 'Smidtii'. **'Smidtii'**, syn. *P. heldreichii* var. *leucodermis* 'Schmidtii' (illus. p.105) is a dwarf form, with an ovoid habit and sharp, dark green leaves.

P. x holfordiana, illus. p.95.

P. insignis. See *P. radiata*.

P. jeffreyi, illus. p.97.

P. leucodermis. See *P. heldreichii*.

P. mugo (Mountain pine, Mugo pine). Spreading, shrubby conifer. **H** 10–15ft (3–5m), **S** 15–25ft (5–8m). Has bright to dark green leaves in 2s and ovoid, brown cones. Z3–7 H7–1. **'Gnom'**, **H** and **S** to 6ft (2m), and **'Mops'** (illus. p.105), **H** 3ft (1m), **S** 6ft (2m), are rounded cultivars.

P. muricata, illus. p.97.

P. nigra (Austrian pine, European black pine). Upright, later spreading conifer. **H** to 100ft (30m), **S** 20-25ft (6–8m). Has dark green leaves in 2s and ovoid, yellow-brown cones. Is generally grown in one of the following forms. Z5–8 H8–4. **'Hornibrookiana'**, **H** 5–6ft (1.5–2m), **S** 6ft (2m), is shrubby with sturdy, spreading or erect branches. **subsp. laricio**, syn. *P. nigra* var. *maritima* (Corsican pine) is fast-growing and narrowly conical with an open crown; bears gray-green leaves and ovoid to conical, yellow- or pale gray-brown cones. **var. maritima** see *P. nigra*

subsp. *laricio*. **subsp. *nigra***, illus. p.98.
P. parviflora, illus. p.99. **'Adcock's Dwarf'** is a slow-growing, rounded, dense, dwarf conifer. **H** 6–10ft (2–3m), **S** 5–6ft (1.5–2m). Bears gray-green leaves in 5s and ovoid cones.
P. patula, illus. p.97.
P. peuce, illus. p.95.
P. pinaster, illus. p.97.
P. pinea, illus. p.104.
P. ponderosa, illus. p.97.
P. pumila (Dwarf Siberian pine). Spreading, shrubby conifer. **H** 6–10ft (2–3m), **S** 10–15ft (3–5m). Has bright blue-green leaves in 5s. Ovoid cones are violet-purple, ripening to red-brown or yellow-brown, the males bright red-purple in spring. Z3–6 H7–1. **'Globe'**, **H** and **S** 1¹/₂–3ft (50cm–1m), has a rounded habit and blue foliage.
P. radiata, syn. *P. insignis*, illus. p.98.
P. rigida, illus. p.100.
P. strobus, illus. p.96. **'Radiata'** is a rounded, dwarf conifer with an open, sparse, whorled crown. **H** 3–6ft (1–2m), **S** 6–10ft (2–3m). Gray bark is smooth at first, later fissured. Bears gray-green leaves in 5s and cylindrical cones.
P. sylvestris (Scots pine), illus. p.78. Conifer, upright and with whorled branches when young, that develops a spreading, rounded crown with age. **H** 50–80ft (15–25m), **S** 25–30ft (8–10m). Bark is flaking and red-brown on upper trunk, fissured and purple-gray at base. Has blue-green leaves in 2s and conical, green cones that ripen to pale gray- or red-brown. Z3–7 H7–1. **'Aurea'**, illus. p.104. **'Beuvronensis'**, **H** and **S** 3ft (1m), is a rounded shrub. Z2–7 H7–1. **'Doone Valley'**, **H** and **S** 3ft (1m), is an upright, irregularly shaped shrub. Z2–7 H7–1. **'Fastigiata'**, syn. *P. sylvestris* f. *fastigiata*, **H** to 25ft (8m), **S** 3ft (1–3m), has a narrow, obelisk habit; suffers wind damage in an exposed site. Z2–7 H7–1. **'Gold Coin'**, **H** and **S** 6ft (2m), is a dwarf version of *P.s.* 'Aurea'. **'Nana'** of gardens. See *P. sylvestris* 'Watereri'. **'Watereri'**, syn. *P. sylvestris* 'Nana', **H** and **S** 20in (50cm), has a very dense habit and widely spaced leaves. Z2–7 H7–1.
P. thunbergii, illus. p.100.
P. virginiana (Scrub pine, Virginia pine). Conifer of untidy habit. **H** 40ft (12m), **S** 25ft (8m). Gray- to yellow-green leaves are in 2s. Young shoots have pinkish-white bloom. Bears oblong to conical, red-brown cones. Z3–7 H7–1.
P. wallichiana, syn. *P. chylla*, *P. excelsa*, *P. griffithii*, illus. p.97.

PIPTANTHUS

LEGUMINOSAE/PAPILIONACEAE

Genus of deciduous or semievergreen shrubs, grown for their foliage and flowers. In cold areas, needs the protection of a south- or west-facing wall. Requires sun and fertile, well-drained soil. In spring, cut some older shoots back to ground level and prune any frost-damaged growths back to healthy wood. Propagate by seed in fall.
P. laburnifolius. See *P. nepalensis*.
P. nepalensis, syn. *P. laburnifolius*, illus. p.206.

PISONIA

NYCTAGINACEAE

Genus of evergreen shrubs and trees, grown for their foliage and overall appearance. Needs full light or partial shade and rich, well-drained soil. Water container specimens freely when in full growth, moderately at other times. Pruning is tolerated, if required. Propagate by seed in spring or by semiripe cuttings in summer.
P. brunoniana. See *P. umbellifera*.
P. umbellifera, syn. *P. brunoniana*, *Heimerliodendron brunonianum* (Bird-catcher tree, Parapara). Evergreen, rounded shrub or tree. **H** and **S** 10–20ft (3–6m). Bears oval, leathery, lustrous leaves. In spring produces clusters of tiny, green or pink flowers, followed by 5-winged, sticky, brownish fruits. Z13–15 H12–10.

PISTACIA

Pistachio

ANACARDIACEAE

Genus of evergreen or deciduous trees, grown for their foliage and overall appearance. Requires full light and well-drained, even dry soil. Water container plants moderately when in full growth, sparingly at other times. Pruning is tolerated, if necessary. Propagate by seed in spring or by semiripe cuttings in summer.
P. lentiscus (Mastic tree). Evergreen, irregularly rounded shrub or tree. **H** 15ft (5m), **S** to 10ft (3m). Leaves are divided into 2–5 pairs of oval, leathery, glossy leaflets. Axillary clusters of insignificant flowers, from spring to early summer, are followed by globose, red then black fruits in fall. Z9–11 H12–9.
P. terebinthus (Cyprus turpentine, Terebinth tree). Deciduous, rounded to ovoid tree. **H** 20–28ft (6–9m), **S** 10–20ft (3–6m). Leaves have 5–9 oval, usually lustrous, rich green leaflets. Axillary clusters of small flowers, in spring and early summer, are followed by tiny, globular to ovoid, red then purple-brown fruits in fall. Z9–10 H12–9.

PISTIA

Shell flower, Water lettuce

ARACEAE

Genus of one species of deciduous, perennial, floating water plant, grown for its foliage. In water above 66–70°F (19–21°C) is evergreen. Is suitable for tropical aquariums and frost-free ponds. Needs sun or partial shade. Remove fading foliage and thin plants out as necessary. Propagate by separating plantlets in summer.
P. stratiotes, illus. p.442.

PITCAIRNIA

BROMELIACEAE

Genus of evergreen, rosette-forming perennials, grown for their overall appearance. Needs partial shade and well-drained soil. Water moderately during growing season, sparingly at other times. Propagate by offsets or division in spring.

P. andreana. Evergreen, clump-forming, basal-rosetted perennial. **H** 8in (20cm), **S** 12in (30cm) or more. Loose rosettes comprise narrowly lance-shaped, strongly arching, green leaves, gray-scaled beneath. Racemes of tubular, orange-and-red flowers are borne in summer.
P. heterophylla. Evergreen, basal-rosetted perennial with swollen, much-branched rhizomes. **H** 4in (10cm) or more, **S** to 12in (30cm). Outer leaves resemble barbed spines, inner leaves are strap-shaped, low-arching and green, with downy, white undersides. Produces almost stemless spikes of tubular, bright red or rarely white flowers in summer. Z13–15 H12–1.

PITTOSPORUM

PITTOSPORACEAE

Genus of evergreen trees and shrubs, grown for their ornamental foliage and fragrant flowers. Does best in mild areas; in cold regions, grow against a south- or west-facing wall. *P. crassifolium* and *P. ralphii* make wind-resistant hedges in mild, coastal areas; like forms with variegated or purple leaves, prefer sun. Others will grow in sun or partial shade. All need well-drained soil. Propagate *P. dallii* by budding in summer, other species by seed in fall or spring or by semiripe cuttings in summer, selected forms by semiripe cuttings only in summer.
P. crassifolium (Karo). Evergreen, bushy-headed, dense tree or shrub. **H** 15ft (5m), **S** 10ft (3m). Has oblong, dark green leaves, gray-felted beneath. Clusters of small, fragrant, star-shaped, dark reddish-purple flowers are borne in spring. Z9–11 H12–10.
P. dallii, illus. p.119.
P. eugenioides (Lemonwood, Tarata). Evergreen, columnar tree. **H** 30ft (10m), **S** 15ft (5m). Narrowly oval, wavy-edged leaves are glossy, dark green. Honey-scented, star-shaped, pale yellow flowers are produced in spring. Z9–11 H12–10. **'Variegatum'**, illus. p.93.
P. 'Garnettii', illus. p.119.
P. ralphii. Evergreen, bushy-headed tree or shrub. **H** 12ft (4m), **S** 10ft (3m). Large leaves are oblong, leathery and gray-green, very hairy beneath. Produces small, fragrant, star-shaped, dark red flowers in spring. Z9–10 H10–9.
P. tenuifolium, illus. p.120. **'Margaret Turnbull'** is an evergreen, compact shrub. **H** 6ft (1.8m), **S** 3ft (1m). Has oval, wavy-edged, dark green leaves centrally splashed golden-yellow. Bears star-shaped, honey-scented, purple flowers in late spring. Z9–10 H10–9. **'Tom Thumb'**, illus. p.164.
P. tobira (Japanese mock orange). Evergreen, bushy-headed, dense tree or shrub. **H** 20ft (6m), **S** 12ft (4m). Has oblong to oval, glossy, dark green leaves. Very fragrant, star-shaped, white flowers, borne in late spring, later become creamy-yellow. Z9–10 H10–9.
P. undulatum (Australian mock orange, Cheesewood). Evergreen, broadly conical tree. **H** 40ft (12m), **S** 25ft (8m). Has long, narrowly oval, pointed, wavy-edged, dark green leaves. Fragrant, star-shaped, white flowers are borne in late spring and early summer, followed by rounded, orange fruits. Z9–10 H10–9.

PITYROGRAMMA

PTERIDACEAE/ADIANTACEAE

Genus of semievergreen or evergreen ferns, suitable for hanging baskets. Needs partial shade and rich, moist but well-drained soil. Remove fading fronds regularly. Water carefully to avoid spoiling farina on fronds. Propagate by spores in late summer.
P. triangularis (Goldback fern). Semievergreen or evergreen fern. **H** and **S** 18in (45cm). Has broadly triangular, delicately divided, mid-green fronds with orange or creamy-white farina. Z10–11 H12–9.

Plagiorhegma dubia. See *Jeffersonia dubia*.

PLANTAGO

Plantain

PLANTAGINACEAE

Genus of summer-flowering annuals, biennials and evergreen perennials and shrubs. Many species are weeds, but a few are grown for their foliage and architectural value. Needs full sun and well-drained soil. Water container plants moderately, sparingly in winter. Propagate by seed or division in spring.
P. nivalis, illus. p.376.

PLATANUS

Plane, Sycamore

PLATANACEAE

Genus of deciduous trees, grown for their habit, foliage and flaking bark. Flowers are inconspicuous. Spherical fruit clusters hang from shoots in fall. Needs full sun and deep, fertile, well-drained soil. Propagate species by seed in fall, *P. x hispanica* by hardwood cuttings in early winter. All except *P. orientalis* are susceptible to the fungal disease plane anthracnose. ① Contact with the basal tufts of hair on the fruits may irritate the skin and respiratory system.
P. x acerifolia. See *P. x hispanica*.
P. x hispanica, syn. *P. x acerifolia*, illus. p.63. **'Suttneri'** is a vigorous, deciduous, spreading tree. **H** 70ft (20m), **S** 50ft (15m). Has flaking bark and large, palmate, 5-lobed, sharply toothed, bright green leaves that are blotched with creamy-white. Z5–8 H8–5.
P. orientalis, illus. p.63.

PLATYCARYA

JUGLANDACEAE

Genus of one species of deciduous tree, grown for its foliage and catkins. Requires full sun and fertile, well-drained soil. Propagate by seed in fall.
P. strobilacea. Deciduous, spreading tree. **H** and **S** 30ft (10m). Has ashlike, bright green leaves with 5–15 leaflets. Upright, green catkins are borne from mid- to late summer; males are slender and cylindrical, often drooping at tips, females are cone-like, become brown and persist through winter. Z6–9 H9–6.

PLATYCERIUM

Staghorn fern

POLYPODIACEAE

Genus of evergreen, epiphytic ferns, best grown in hanging baskets or fastened to and suspended from pieces of wood.

Produces 2 kinds of fronds: permanent, broad, sterile "nest leaves" forming the main part of the plant; and strap-shaped, usually partly bifurcated, arching fertile fronds. Prefers warm, humid conditions in partial shade and needs fibrous, peaty growing medium with hardly any soil. Propagate by detaching buds in spring or summer or by spores in summer or early fall.

P. alcicorne of gardens. See *P. bifurcatum*.
P. bifurcatum, syn. *P. alcicorne*, illus. p.479.

PLATYCLADUS

CUPRESSACEAE

See also CONIFERS. ① Contact with the foliage may aggravate skin allergies.

P. orientalis, syn. *Biota orientalis*, *Thuja orientalis* (Biota, Chinese arbor-vitae, Chinese thuja). Conifer with an irregularly rounded crown. **H** 30–50ft (10–15m), **S** 15ft (5m). Has fibrous bark and flattened, vertical sprays of scalelike, scentless, dark green leaves. Egg-shaped cones are glaucous gray. **'Aurea Nana'** (illus. p.105), **H** and **S** 2ft (60cm), is a dwarf cultivar with yellow-green foliage that turns bronze in winter. Z6–9 H9–6. **'Semperaurea'**, **H** 10ft (3m), **S** 6ft (2m), is compact, with golden leaves.

PLATYCODON

Balloon flower

CAMPANULACEAE

Genus of one species of perennial, grown for its flowers in summer. Needs sun and light, sandy soil. Propagate by basal cuttings of non-flowering shoots in summer, with a bit of root attached, or by seed in fall.

P. grandiflorus, illus. p.269. **var. mariesii**, syn. *P. grandiflorus* 'Mariesii' is a clump-forming perennial. **H** and **S** 12–18in (30–45cm). In mid-summer produces solitary, terminal, large, balloon-like flower buds opening to bell-shaped, blue or purplish-blue flowers. Has oval, sharply toothed, bluish-green leaves. Z3–8 H8–1.
'Mariesii'. See *P. grandiflorus* var. *mariesii*.

PLATYSTEMON

Creamcups

PAPAVERACEAE

Genus of one species of summer-flowering annual. Needs sun and fertile, well-drained soil. Propagate by seed in spring or early fall.

P. californicus, illus. p.321.

PLECTRANTHUS

LABIATAE/LAMIACEAE

Genus of evergreen, trailing or bushy perennials, grown for their foliage. Needs partial shade or full light and moist soil. Cut back stem tips in growing season if plants become too straggly. Propagate by stem cuttings or division in spring or summer.

P. australis of gardens. See *P. verticillatus*.
P. coleoides 'Variegatus' of gardens. See *P. madagascariensis* 'Variegated Mintleaf'.
P. forsteri 'Marginatus', illus. p.298.
P. fructicosus 'James', illus. p.454.

P. madagascariensis (Mintleaf). Creeping perennial. **H** 12in (30cm), **S** indefinite. Has rounded, scalloped, fleshy leaves. Bears 2-lipped, lavender-blue or white flowers, often dotted with red. H12–1. **'Variegated Mintleaf',** syn. *P. coleoides* 'Variegatus' has variegated, white leaves.
P. oertendahlii (Candle plant). Evergreen, prostrate perennial. **H** to 6in (15cm), **S** indefinite. Rounded, scalloped, dark green leaves are reddish-green below, with white veins above. Has racemes of tubular, white or pale mauve flowers at irregular intervals throughout year. Z11–12 H12–1.
P. scutellarioides. See *Solenostemon scutellarioides*.
P. thyrsoideus, syn. *Coleus thyrsoideus*. Fast-growing, bushy perennial, often grown as an annual. **H** to 3ft (1m), **S** 2ft (60cm). Has heart-shaped, toothed, mid-green leaves. Produces spikes of tubular, bright blue flowers at various times of year. Z11–12 H12–1.
P. verticillatus, syn. *P. australis*. Evergreen, trailing perennial with square stems. **H** to 6in (15cm), **S** indefinite. Has rounded, waxy, glossy, green leaves, with scalloped edges. Racemes of tubular, white or pale mauve flowers are produced intermittently through year. H12–1.

PLEIOBLASTUS

GRAMINEAE/POACEAE

See also GRASSES, BAMBOOS, RUSHES and SEDGES.

P. variegatus, syn. *Arundinaria fortunei*, *Arundinaria variegata*, illus. p.284.
P. viridistriatus, syn. *Arundinaria auricoma*, illus. p.289.

PLEIONE

ORCHIDACEAE

See also ORCHIDS.

P. bulbocodioides, illus. p.466. Deciduous, terrestrial orchid. **H** 8in (20cm). In spring, usually before solitary leaf is produced, bears pink, rose or magenta flowers, 2–5in (5–12cm) across, with darker purple marks on lips. Leaf is narrowly lance-shaped, 5½in (14cm) long. Is often difficult to flower: regular feeding helps to increase pseudobulbs to flowering size. Z9–10 H10–9.
P. x confusa. Deciduous, terrestrial orchid. **H** 6in (15cm). Solitary, canary-yellow flowers, 2–3in (5–8cm) across, with brown or purple blotches on lips, are borne in spring, before foliage. Has lance-shaped leaves, 4–7in (10–18cm) long. Does best in an alpine house. Needs partial shade. Z9–10 H12–10.
P. hookeriana. Deciduous, terrestrial orchid. **H** 3–6in (8–15cm). Solitary, lilac-pink, rose or white flowers, 2–3in (5–7cm) across, with brown- or purplish-spotted lip, are borne in spring, at same time as lance-shaped leaves, 2–8in (5–20cm) long. Z9–10 H12–10.
P. humilis. Deciduous, terrestrial orchid. **H** 2–3in (5–8cm). In winter, before foliage appears, white flowers, 3–3½in (7–9cm) across, with crimson-spotted lip, are borne singly or in pairs. Lance-shaped leaves are 7–10in (18–25cm) long. Z9–10 H12–10.
P. praecox. Deciduous, terrestrial orchid. **H** 3–5in (8–13cm). White to pinkish-purple or lilac-purple flowers, to 3in (8cm) across,

with violet marks, are produced in pairs in fall, after foliage. Has oblong to lance-shaped leaves, 6–10in (15–25cm) long. Z9–10 H12–10.

PLEIOSPILOS

Living granite

AIZOACEAE

Genus of clump-forming, perennial succulents, grown for their flowers and almost stemless rosettes bearing up to 4 pairs of fleshy, erect leaves, like pieces of granite, each with a flat upper surface and each pair united at the base. Flowers are daisylike. Individual species are very similar, and many are difficult to identify. Needs sun and well-drained soil. Propagate by seed or division in spring or summer.

P. bolusii, illus. p.495.
P. compactus, illus. p.495.

PLUMBAGO

Leadwort

PLUMBAGINACEAE

Genus of annuals, evergreen or semievergreen shrubs, perennials and woody-stemmed, scrambling climbers, grown for their primrose-shaped flowers. Grow in full light or partial shade and fertile, well-drained soil. Water regularly when in full growth, less at other times. Tie stems to supports. Thin out or spur back all previous year's growth in early spring. Propagate by semiripe cuttings in summer. Whitefly may be a problem.

P. auriculata, syn. *P. capensis*, illus. p.205.
P. capensis. See *P. auriculata*.
P. indica, syn. *P. rosea* (Scarlet leadwort). Evergreen or semievergreen, spreading shrub or semi-climber. **H** 6ft (2m), **S** 3–6ft (1–2m). Leaves are oval to elliptic and mid-green. Has terminal racemes of primrose-shaped, red or pink flowers, 1in (2.5cm) long, produced in summer (if hard-pruned annually in spring) or from late winter onward (if left unpruned and trained as a climber). Z12–15 H12–1.
P. rosea. See *P. indica*.

PLUMERIA

Frangipani, Pagoda tree, West Indian jasmine

APOCYNACEAE

Genus of mainly deciduous, fleshy-branched shrubs and trees, grown for their flowers in summer–fall. Requires full sun and well-drained soil. Water container specimens moderately while in growth, keep dry in winter when leafless. Stem tips may be cut out to induce branching. Propagate by seed or leafless stem-tip cuttings in late spring. Red spider mite may be a nuisance. ① The milky sap may cause mild stomach upset if ingested.

P. acuminata. See *P. rubra* f. *acutifolia*.
P. acutifolia. See *P. rubra* f. *acutifolia*.
P. alba (West Indian jasmine). Deciduous, rounded, sparingly branched tree. **H** to 20ft (6m), **S** to 12ft (4m). Has lance-shaped and slender-pointed leaves, to 12in (30cm) long. Terminal clusters of fragrant, yellow-eyed, white flowers, with 5 spreading petals and tubular base, are produced in summer. Z11–12 H12–10.

P. rubra, illus. p.453. **f. acutifolia**, syn. *P. acuminata*, *P. acutifolia* is a deciduous, spreading, sparsely branched tree or shrub. **H** and **S** 12ft (4m) or more. Produces fragrant, yellow-centered, white flowers, with 5 spreading petals, in summer–fall. Has lance-shaped to oval leaves, 8–12in (20–30cm) long.

PODALYRIA

LEGUMINOSAE/PAPILIONACEAE

Genus of evergreen, mainly summer-flowering shrubs, grown for their flowers and overall appearance. Requires full light and fertile, well-drained soil. Water container plants moderately when in full growth, less at other times. Prune, if necessary, after flowering. Propagate by seed in spring or by semiripe cuttings in summer.

P. sericea. Vigorous, evergreen, rounded shrub. **H** and **S** 4–10ft (1.2–3m). Has oval, downy, mid-green leaves and sweet pealike, pink flowers, 1¼–1½in (3–4cm) wide, in summer.

PODOCARPUS

PODOCARPACEAE

See also CONIFERS.

P. alpinus (Tasmanian podocarp). Rounded, spreading, shrubby conifer. **H** 6ft (2m), **S** 10–15ft (3–5m). Has linear, dull green leaves and rounded, egg-shaped, fleshy, bright red fruits. Z7–10 H10–7.
P. andinus. See *Prumnopitys andina*.
P. macrophyllus (Buddhist pine, Kusamaki, Southern yew). Erect conifer. **H** 30ft (10m), **S** 10–15ft (3–5m). Long, linear leaves are bright green above, glaucous beneath. May be grown as a shrub, **H** and **S** 3–6ft (1–2m), and planted in a tub in hot climates. Z7–11 H12–7.
P. nivalis (Alpine totara), illus. p.105. Rounded, spreading, shrubby conifer. **H** 6ft (2m), **S** 10–15ft (3–5m). Is very similar to *P. alpinus*, but leaves longer, broader, more rigid leaves. Z7–9 H11–7.
P. salignus, illus. p.100.

PODOPHYLLUM

Mayapple

BERBERIDACEAE

Genus of spring-flowering, rhizomatous perennials. Young leaves may be damaged by frost. Prefers partial shade and moist, peaty soil. Propagate by division in spring or by seed in fall. ① All parts of the plants are highly toxic if ingested.

P. emodii. See *Sinopodophyllum hexandrum*.
P. hexandrum. See *Sinopodophyllum hexandrum*.
P. peltatum (American mandrake, Mayapple). Vigorous, spreading, rhizomatous perennial. **H** 12–18in (30–45cm), **S** 12in (30cm). Palmate, sometimes brown-mottled, light green leaves, with 3–5 deep lobes, push up through soil, looking like closed umbrellas, and are followed, in spring, by nodding, cup-shaped, white flowers. Produces large, fleshy, plumlike, glossy, deep rose-pink fruits in fall. Z3–9 H8–2.

PODRANEA

BIGNONIACEAE

Genus of evergreen, twining climbers, grown for their foxglove-like flowers. Needs full light and fertile, well-drained soil. Water regularly, less in cold weather. Provide support. Thin out crowded growth in winter or early spring. Propagate by seed in spring or by semiripe cuttings in summer.

P. ricasoliana, syn. *Pandorea ricasoliana*, *Tecoma ricasoliana*. Fast-growing, evergreen, twining climber. **H** 12ft (4m) or more. Has leaves divided into 7 or 9 lance-shaped to oval, wavy, deep green leaflets. Bears loose clusters of fragrant, pink flowers, with darker veins, from spring to fall.

Poinciana gilliesii. See *Caesalpinia gilliesii*.
Poinciana pulcherrima. See *Caesalpinia pulcherrima*.

POLEMONIUM

Jacob's ladder

POLEMONIACEAE

Genus of late spring- or summer-flowering annuals and perennials, some perennials tending to be short-lived. Prefers sun and fertile, well-drained soil. Propagate by division in spring or by seed in fall.

P. caeruleum, illus. p.270. Brise d'Anjou ('Blanjou') illus. p.270.
P. carneum, illus. p.269.
P. foliosissimum (Leafy Jacob's ladder). Vigorous, clump-forming perennial. **H** 30in (75cm), **S** 24in (60cm). Terminal clusters of cup-shaped, lilac flowers, with yellow stamens, are borne in summer above oblong to lance-shaped, mid-green leaves, divided into numerous, small leaflets. Z4–8 H8–1. **var. flavum** produces yellow flowers shaded orange-red outside.
P. pulcherrimum (Skunkleaf Jacob's ladder). Vigorous, summer-flowering perennial. **H** 20in (50cm), **S** 12in (30cm). Has bright green leaves divided into leaflets and tubular, purple-blue flowers, with yellow or white throats. Z4–8 H8–1.

POLIANTHES

AGAVACEAE/ASPARAGACEAE

Genus of tuberous perennials, grown for their fragrant flowers in summer. Needs a sheltered site in full sun and well-drained soil. Water well in spring–summer; feed liquid fertilizer every 2 weeks when in growth. Dry off after leaves die down in winter. Propagate by seed or offsets in spring.

P. geminiflora, syn. *Agave duplicata*, *Bravoa geminiflora*, illus. p.413.
P. tuberosa, syn. *Agave polianthes* (Tuberose). Summer-flowering, tuberous perennial. **H** 24–36in (60–90cm), **S** 4–6in (10–15cm). Has basal cluster of strap-shaped, erect leaves; flower stem also bears leaves on lower part. Produces spike of funnel-shaped, single, white flowers, with 6 spreading petals. A double form is also available. Z7–11 H11–7. **'The Pearl'**, illus. p.385.

POLIOTHYRSIS

FLACOURTIACEAE/SALICACEAE

Genus of one species of deciduous tree, grown for its foliage and flowers. Needs sun or partial shade and fertile, well-drained soil. Propagate by softwood cuttings in summer.

P. sinensis. Deciduous, spreading tree. **H** 30ft (10m), **S** 20ft (6m). Bears long, oval, sharply toothed, glossy, dark green leaves, with wine-red stalks. Fragrant, star-shaped, white, later yellow flowers are produced in late summer and early fall. Z7–9 H9–7.

POLYGALA

Milkwort, Seneca, Snakeroot

POLYGALACEAE

Genus of annuals, evergreen perennials, shrubs and trees, grown mainly for their pealike flowers. Needs full light or partial shade and moist but very well-drained soil. Water container specimens freely when in full growth, moderately at other times. Lanky stems may be cut back hard in late winter. Propagate by seed in spring or by semiripe cuttings in late summer. Is susceptible to whitefly.

P. calcarea, illus. p.370. **'Bulley's Form'** is an evergreen, prostrate perennial. **H** 1in (2.5cm), **S** 3–4in (8–10cm). Has rosettes of small, narrowly oval leaves. Bears loose heads of deep blue flowers in late spring and early summer. Prefers rich soil. Z7–9 H9–7. **'Lillet'**, illus. p.369.
P. chamaebuxus, illus. p.371. **var. grandiflora**, syn. *P. chamaebuxus* var. *purpurea*, *P. chamaebuxus* var. *rhodoptera*, illus. p.354. **var. purpurea**. See *P. chamaebuxus* var. *grandiflora*. **var. rhodoptera**. See *P. chamaebuxus* var. *grandiflora*.
P. x dalmaisiana, syn. *P. myrtifolia* var. *grandiflora*, illus. p.457.
P. myrtifolia var. grandiflora of gardens. See *P. x dalmaisiana*.
P. vayredae. Evergreen, mat-forming shrub. **H** 2–4in (5–10cm), **S** 8–12in (20–30cm). Slender, prostrate stems bear small, linear leaves. Pealike, reddish-purple flowers, with yellow lip, are produced in late spring and early summer. Is suitable for a rock garden or alpine house. Z7–9 H9–7.

POLYGONATUM

Solomon's seal

LILIACEAE/ASPARAGACEAE

Genus of spring- or early summer-flowering, rhizomatous perennials. Requires full or partial shade and fertile, well-drained soil. Propagate by division in early spring or by seed in fall. Sawfly caterpillar is a common pest. ① All parts may cause mild stomach upset if ingested.

P. biflorum, syn. *P. canaliculatum*, *P. commutatum*, *P. giganteum* (Small Solomon's seal). Arching, rhizomatous perennial. **H** 5ft (1.5m) or more, **S** 2ft (60cm). Bears oval to oblong, mid-green leaves. Pendent clusters of bell-shaped, white flowers are borne in leaf axils in late spring. Z3–7 H9–1.
P. canaliculatum. See *P. biflorum*.
P. commutatum. See *P. biflorum*.
P. giganteum. See *P. biflorum*.
P. hirtum, syn. *P. latifolium*. Upright, then arching, rhizomatous perennial. **H** 3ft (1m),

S 1ft (30cm). Clusters of 2–5 drooping, tubular, green-tipped, white flowers are produced in late spring. Undersides of stems, leaf stalks and oval to lance-shaped, mid-green leaves are hairy. Z5–8 H8–5.
P. hookeri, illus. p.353.
P. x hybridum, illus. p.223.
P. latifolium. See *P. hirtum*.
P. multiflorum. Arching, leafy perennial with fleshy rhizomes. **H** 3ft (1m), **S** 1ft (30cm). Bears clusters of 2–6 pendent, tubular, green-tipped, white flowers in late spring, followed by spherical, black fruit. Has oval to lance-shaped, mid-green leaves. Z4–8 H8–1. **'Flore Pleno'** has double flowers that look like ballet dancers' skirts. **'Striatum'**, syn. *P. multiflorum* 'Variegatum', **H** 2ft (60cm), has leaves with creamy-white stripes. **'Variegatum'**. See *P. multiflorum* 'Striatum'.
P. odoratum (Fragrant Solomon's seal). Arching, rhizomatous perennial. **H** 24in (60cm), **S** 12in (30cm). Produces pairs of fragrant, tubular to bell-shaped, green-tipped, white flowers in late spring. Oval to lance-shaped leaves are mid-green. Z3–8 H9–1.
P. verticillatum (Whorled Solomon's seal). Upright, rhizomatous perennial. **H** 4ft (1.2m), **S** 1½ft (45cm). Bears whorls of stalkless, lance-shaped, mid-green leaves. In early summer produces narrowly bell-shaped, greenish-white flowers. Z5–8 H8–5.

Polygonum affine. See *Persicaria affinis*.
Polygonum amplexicaule. See *Persicaria amplexicaulis*.
Polygonum aubertii. See *Fallopia aubertii*.
Polygonum baldschuanicum. See *Fallopia baldschuanica*.
Polygonum bistorta. See *Persicaria bistorta*.
Polygonum campanulatum. See *Persicaria campanulata*.
Polygonum capitatum. See *Persicaria capitata*.
Polygonum macrophyllum. See *Persicaria macrophylla*.
Polygonum milletii. See *Persicaria milletii*.
Polygonum sphaerostachyum. See *Persicaria macrophylla*.
Polygonum vacciniifolium. See *Persicaria vacciniifolia*.
Polygonum virginianum 'Painter's Palette'. See *Persicaria virginiana* 'Painter's Palette'.

POLYPODIUM

POLYPODIACEAE

Genus of deciduous, semievergreen or evergreen ferns, grown for their sculptural fronds. Needs partial shade and fibrous, moist but well-drained soil. Propagate by division in spring or by spores in late summer.

P. aureum. See *Phlebodium aureum*.
P. australe. See *P. cambricum*.
P. cambricum, syn. *P. australe*, *P. vulgare* subsp. *serratum*. Deciduous, creeping fern. **H** 6–24in (15–60cm), **S** indefinite. Has broadly lance-shaped to broadly triangular-ovate, divided, mid-green fronds, with linear or oblong pinnae that often have toothed margins. New fronds are produced in late summer and die back by early

summer. Sori are conspicuously yellow in winter. Z6–8 H8–6. **'Richard Kayse'**, illus. p.293.
P. glycyrrhiza (Licorice fern). Terrestrial, deciduous fern. **H** and **S** 18in (45cm). Has oblong–triangular to narrowly oval, divided, mid-green fronds, with lance-shaped to oblong pinnae that arise from licorice-scented rootstock. Z4–9 H9–1.
P. interjectum 'Cornubiense', syn. *P. vulgare* 'Cornubiense', illus. p.291.
P. vulgare, illus. p.291. **'Cornubiense'**. See *P. interjectum* 'Cornubiense'. **'Cristatum'** is an evergreen, creeping fern. **H** and **S** 10–12in (25–30cm) Narrowly lance-shaped, divided, mid-green fronds, with semi-pendulous, terminal crests, grow from creeping rhizomes covered with copper-brown scales. **subsp. serratum**. See *P. cambricum*.

POLYSCIAS

ARALIACEAE

Genus of evergreen trees and shrubs, grown for their foliage. Sometimes has insignificant flowers in summer, but only on large, mature specimens. Needs partial shade and rich, well-drained soil. Water container plants freely when in full growth, moderately at other times. Straggly stems may be cut out in spring. Propagate by seed in spring or by stem-tip or leafless stem-section cuttings in summer. Red spider mite may be troublesome.

P. filicifolia, illus. p.458. **'Marginata'** is an evergreen, erect, sparsely branched shrub. **H** 6ft (2m) or more, **S** 3ft (1m) or more. Leaves, 1ft (30cm) long, are divided into many small, oval to lance-shaped, toothed, bright green leaflets, with white edges. Z14–15 H12–1.
P. guilfoylei (Coffee tree, Geranium aralia). Slow-growing, evergreen, rounded tree. **H** 10–25ft (3–8m), **S** to 6ft (2m) or more. Leaves, 10–16in (25–40cm) long, are divided into oval to rounded, toothed, deep green leaflets. Z14–15 H12–1. **'Victoriae'**, illus. p.458.

POLYSPORA

SYN. GORDONIA

THEACEAE

Genus of evergreen shrubs and trees, grown for their flowers and overall appearance. Prefers sun or partial shade and rich, acidic soil. Water potted plants moderately, less in winter. Propagate by semiripe cuttings in late summer or by seed when ripe, in fall, or in spring.

P. axillaris. Evergreen, bushy shrub or tree. **H** and **S** 10–15ft (3–5m), sometimes much more. Has lance-shaped, leathery, glossy leaves, each with a blunt tip, and bears, from fall to spring, saucer-shaped, white flowers.
P. lasianthus. Evergreen, upright tree. **H** to 70ft (20m), **S** to 30ft (10m). Lance-shaped to elliptic leaves are shallowly serrated. Has fragrant, saucer- to bowl-shaped, white flowers in summer. Needs sub-tropical summer warmth to grow and flower well.

Polystichium aculeatum 'Pulcherrimum'. See *Polystichum setiferum* 'Pulcherrimum Bevis'.

P

POLYSTICHUM

DRYOPTERIDACEAE

Genus of evergreen, semievergreen or deciduous ferns. Prefers partial shade and moist but well-drained soil enriched with fibrous organic matter. Remove faded fronds regularly. Propagate species by division in spring or by spores in summer, selected forms by division in spring.

P. acrostichoides (Christmas fern). Evergreen fern. **H** 24in (60cm), **S** 18in (45cm). Slender, lance-shaped, deep green fronds have small, holly-like pinnae. Is excellent for cut flowers. Z3–8 H8–1.

P. aculeatum (Hard shield fern, Prickly shield fern). Semievergreen fern. **H** 24in (60cm), **S** 30in (75cm). Broadly lance-shaped, yellowish-green, then deep green fronds, with oblong to oval, spiny-edged, glossy pinnae, are produced on stems often covered in brown scales. Z3–8 H8–1.

P. braunii. Evergreen or semievergreen fern. **H** and **S** 18–30in (45–75cm). Produces rosette of spreading to arching, lance-shaped, divided, dark green fronds. Young fronds are densely covered with orange-brown scales when unfurling in spring. Z3–8 H8–1.

P. munitum, illus. p.293.

P. polyblepharum (Japanese tassel fern). Evergreen fern. **H** 24–32in (60–80cm), **S** 36in (90cm).Produces "shuttlecocks" of spreading, lance-shaped, divided, shiny, dark green fronds, covered with golden hairs when they unfurl. Pinnae lobes are oblong-ovate and have spiny-toothed margins. Z6–8 H8–5.

P. rigens. Evergreen fern. **H** 16in (40cm), **S** 24in (60cm). Has "shuttlecocks" of narrowly ovate-oblong, divided, leathery, harsh-textured, dull green fronds. Broad, lance-shaped pinnae are divided into ovate, spiny-toothed lobes. Fronds are yellowish-green in spring. Z6–9 H9–6.

P. setiferum (Hedge fern). Z6–9 H9–6. **Divisilobum Group**, syn. *P. setiferum* 'Divisilobum', illus. p.291. **'Divisilobum'.** See *P. setiferum* Divisilobum Group. **Plumosodivisilobum Group**, illus. p.291. **'Pulcherrimum Bevis'**, syn. *Polystichium aculeatum* 'Pulcherrimum', illus. p.290. **P. tsussimense**, illus. p.292.

PONCIRUS

RUTACEAE

Genus of one species of very spiny, deciduous shrub or small tree, grown for its foliage, showy flowers and orange-like fruits. Is very effective as a protective hedge. Needs sun and fertile, well-drained soil. Cut out dead wood in spring, and trim hedges in early summer. Propagate by semiripe cuttings in summer or by seed when ripe, in fall.

P. trifoliata (Japanese bitter orange), illus. p.142. Deciduous, bushy shrub or tree. **H** and **S** 15ft (5m). Sturdy, spiny, green shoots bear dark green leaves, divided into 3 oval leaflets. Has fragrant, white flowers, with 4 or 5 large petals, in late spring and often again in fall. Rounded fruits are $^3/_4$–1$^1/_4$in (2–3cm) wide. Z5–9 H9–5.

PONERORCHIS

ORCHIDACEAE

See also ORCHIDS.

P. graminifolia. Deciduous, terrestrial orchid for an alpine greenhouse. **H** 6in (15cm), **S** 4in (10cm). Terminal racemes of variable 2–15 flowers, with 3-lobed lips and pronounced spurs, are borne in late spring and summer in shades of pink, purple and white. Has 2–4 narrowly linear leaves, to 6in (15cm) long.

PONTEDERIA

Pickerel weed

PONTEDERIACEAE

Genus of deciduous, perennial, marginal water plants, grown for their foliage and flower spikes. Needs full sun and up to 9in (23cm) depth of water. Remove fading flowers regularly. Propagate in spring by division or seed.

P. cordata, illus. p.441.

POPULUS

Aspen, Cottonwood, Poplar

SALICACEAE

Genus of deciduous trees, grown for their habit, foliage and very quick growth. Has catkins in late winter or spring. Female trees produce copious amounts of fluffy, white seeds. Prefers full sun and needs deep, fertile, moist but well-drained soil; resents dry soil, apart from *P. alba*, which thrives in coastal gardens. Extensive root systems can undermine foundations and so make poplars unsuitable for planting close to buildings, particularly on clay soil. Propagate by hardwood cuttings in winter. Is susceptible to bacterial canker and fungal diseases.

P. alba, illus. p.60. Is much confused with the commoner *P.* x *canescens*. Z4–9 H9–1. **f. pyramidalis**, syn. *P. alba* 'Pyramidalis' is a vigorous, deciduous, upright tree. **H** 70ft (20m), **S** 15ft (5m). Broadly oval, wavy-margined or lobed, dark green leaves, white beneath, turn yellow in fall. **'Raket'**, syn. *P. alba* 'Rocket', S25ft (8m), is narrowly conical. **'Richardii'**, **H** 50ft (15m), **S** 40ft (12m), has leaves golden-yellow above. **'Rocket'.** See *P. alba* 'Raket'.

P. balsamifera (Balsam poplar, Tacamahac). Fast-growing, deciduous, upright tree. **H** 100ft (30m), **S** 25ft (8m). Oval, glossy, dark green leaves, whitish beneath, have strong fragrance of balsam when young. Z5–9 H9–5.

P. x **berolinensis** (Berlin poplar). Deciduous, columnar tree. **H** 80ft (25m), **S** 25ft (8m). Has broadly oval, bright green leaves, white beneath. Z2–8 H8–1.

P. x **canadensis** (Canadian poplar). Z5–9 H9–5. **'Eugenei'** is a deciduous, columnar tree. **H** 100ft (30m), **S** 40ft (12m). Has broadly oval, bronze, young leaves, maturing to dark green, and red catkins in spring. **'Robusta'**, illus. p.62. **'Serotina de Selys'**, syn. *P.* x canadensis 'Serotina Erecta', illus. p.61. **'Serotina Erecta'.** See *P.* x canadensis 'Serotina de Selys'.

P. x **candicans** of gardens. See *P.* x jackii.

P. x **canescens**, illus. p.60.

P. deltoides (Cottonwood, Eastern cottonwood, Necklace poplar). Very fast-growing, deciduous, spreading tree.

H 100ft (30m), **S** 70ft (20m). Has lush growth of broadly oval, glossy, bright green leaves. Z3–9 H9–1.

P. gileadensis. See *P.* x jackii.

P. x **jackii**, syn. *P.* x candicans, *P. gileadensis* (Balm of Gilead). Very fast-growing, deciduous, conical tree. **H** 80ft (25m), **S** 30ft (10m). Oval leaves are dark green and, when young, balsam-scented. Is very susceptible to canker. Z4–9 H9–1. **'Aurora'**, **H** 50ft (15m) or more, **S** 20ft (6m), has leaves that are heavily but irregularly blotched with creamy-white.

P. lasiocarpa (Chinese necklace poplar). Very fast-growing, deciduous, spreading tree. **H** 50ft (15m), **S** 40ft (12m). Has sturdy shoots and very large, heart-shaped, mid-green leaves with red veins, on long, red stalks. Bears sturdy, drooping, yellow catkins in spring. Z6–9 H9–6.

P. maximowiczii, illus. p.61.

P. nigra (Black poplar). Fast-growing, deciduous, spreading tree. **H** 80ft (25m), **S** 70ft (20m). Has dark bark. Diamond-shaped, bronze young leaves turn bright green, then yellow in fall. Male trees bear red catkins in mid-spring. Z3–9 H9–1. **'Italica'**, illus. p.63.

P. szechuanica. Very fast-growing, deciduous, conical tree. **H** 80ft (25m), **S** 30ft (10m). Has flaking, pinkish-gray bark and large, heart-shaped, dark green leaves. Z4–9 H9–1.

P. tremula (European aspen). Vigorous, deciduous, spreading tree. **H** 50ft (15m), **S** 30ft (10m). Rounded leaves are bronze-red when young, gray-green when mature, and yellow in fall. Flattened stalks make foliage tremble and rattle in wind. Z2–8 H8–1. **'Erecta'**, **S** 15ft (5m), has an upright habit. **'Pendula'**, illus. p.74.

P. tremuloides (Quaking aspen). Very fast-growing, deciduous, spreading tree. **H** 50ft (15m) or more, **S** 30ft (10m). Has rounded, finely toothed, glossy, dark green leaves that flutter in the wind and turn yellow in fall. Z1–8 H8–1.

P. trichocarpa (Black cottonwood, Western balsam poplar). Very fast-growing, deciduous, conical tree. **H** 100ft (30m) or more, **S** 30ft (10m). Bears dense growth of oval, glossy, dark green leaves with green-veined, white undersides, strongly balsam-scented when young. Foliage turns yellow in fall. Z4–9 H9–1.

PORANA

CONVOLVULACEAE

Genus of evergreen or deciduous, twining climbers, grown for their flowers. Needs full light and fertile, moist but well-drained soil. Water freely in full growth, sparingly in cold weather. Stems require support. Thin out evergreen species and cut back deciduous ones to just above ground level in late winter or early spring. Propagate by basal, softwood cuttings in late spring or early summer or by seed in spring.

P. paniculata (Snow in the jungle, White corallita). Vigorous, evergreen, twining climber. **H** 20–30ft (6–10m). Large, loose panicles of small, elder-scented, trumpet-shaped, white flowers are produced from late summer to mid-winter. Leaves are heart-shaped. Z13–15 H12–1.

PORTULACA

Purslane, Rose moss

PORTULACACEAE

Genus of fleshy annuals and perennials, grown for their showy, cup-shaped flowers, which open in sun and close in shade. Needs full light and well-drained soil. Propagate by seed sown under glass in early spring or outdoors in late spring. Is prone to attack by aphids.

P. grandiflora (Moss rose, Rose moss, Sun plant). Slow-growing, partially prostrate annual. **H** 6–8in (15–20cm), **S** 6in (15cm). Has lance-shaped, succulent, bright green leaves. In summer and early fall bears shallowly bowl-shaped flowers, 1in (2.5cm) wide, with conspicuous stamens, in shades of yellow, red, orange, pink or white. Z9–11 H12–1. **Minilaca Hybrids** are compact and have double flowers. **Sundance Hybrids** are semi-trailing and have semidouble or double flowers, 2in (5cm) wide, in broad range of colors. **Sundial Series** have double flowers in broad color range. Are bred for longer flowering in poor conditions and cooler climates. **Sundial Series 'Mango'**, illus. p.324.

PORTULACARIA

PORTULACACEAE/DIDIEREACEAE

Genus of one species of evergreen or semievergreen, succulent-leaved shrub, grown for its foliage. Needs full sun and well-drained soil. Water container plants moderately when in full growth, sparingly at other times. Propagate by semiripe cuttings in summer.

P. afra, illus. p.457. **'Foliisvariegatus'**, syn. *P. afra* 'Variegatus' is an evergreen or semievergreen, erect shrub with more or less horizontal branches. **H** and **S** 6–10ft (2–3m). Has oval to rounded, fleshy, cream-edged, bright green leaves. From late spring to summer bears tiny, star-shaped, pale pink flowers in small clusters. Z13–15 H12–10. **'Variegatus'.** See *P. afra* 'Foliisvariegatus'.

POTAMOGETON

POTAMOGETONACEAE

Genus of deciduous, perennial, submerged water plants, grown for their foliage. Is suitable for cold-water ponds and aquariums. Prefers sun. Remove fading foliage and thin plants as necessary. Propagate by stem cuttings in spring or summer.

P. crispus, illus. p.442.

P. pectinatus (Fennel-leaved pondweed). Deciduous, perennial, submerged water plant. S10ft (3m). Has very narrow, linear, green to brownish-green leaves, and produces inconspicuous flowers in summer. Is suitable for a medium to large pond.

POTENTILLA

Cinquefoil

ROSACEAE

Genus of perennials and deciduous shrubs, grown for their clusters of small, flattish to saucer-shaped flowers and for their foliage. Tall species—particularly the shrubs—are useful in borders. Dwarf potentillas are

good for rock gardens. Prefers full sun, but flower color is better on orange-, red- and pink-flowered cultivars if they are shaded from hottest sun. Needs well-drained soil. Propagate perennial species by seed in fall or by division in spring or fall, and selected forms by division only in spring or fall; shrubby species may be raised by seed in fall or by softwood or greenwood cuttings in summer, and selected forms by softwood or greenwood cuttings in summer.
***P.* 'Abbotswood'.** See *P. fruticosa* 'Abbotswood'.
P. alba, illus. p.359.
P. arbuscula. See *P. fruticosa* var. *arbuscula.*
***P.* 'Arc-en-ciel',** illus. p.268.
P. argyrophylla. See *P. atrosanguinea* var. *argyrophylla.*
P. atrosanguinea, illus. p.269. **var. *argyrophylla,*** syn. *P. argyrophylla* is a clump-forming perennial. **H** 18in (45cm), **S** 24in (60cm). Saucer-shaped, yellow or yellow-orange flowers are produced in profusion from early to late summer above strawberry-like, silvery leaves.
P. aurea, illus. p.372.
***P.* 'Beesii'.** See *P. fruticosa* 'Beesii'.
P. crantzii (Alpine cinquefoil). Upright perennial with thick, woody rootstock. **H** and **S** 4–8in (10–20cm). Produces wedge-shaped, 5-lobed leaves and, in spring, flattish, orange-centered, yellow flowers. Is good in a rock garden. Z5–8 H8–5.
P. davurica* var. *mandschurica of gardens. See *P. fruticosa* 'Manchu'.
***P.* 'Daydawn'.** See *P. fruticosa* 'Daydawn'.
***P.* 'Elizabeth'.** See *P. fruticosa* 'Elizabeth'.
P. eriocarpa, illus. p.372.
***P.* 'Etna'.** Clump-forming perennial. **H** 30in (75cm), **S** 18in (45cm). In mid-summer produces saucer-shaped, maroon flowers above strawberry-like, dark green leaves. Z5–8 H8–5.
P. fruticosa (Shrubby cinquefoil). Deciduous, bushy, dense shrub. **H** 3ft (1m), **S** 5ft (1.5m). From late spring to late summer produces saucer-shaped, bright yellow flowers. Dark green leaves are divided into 5 narrowly oblong leaflets. Z3–7 H7–1. **'Abbotswood',** syn. *P.* 'Abbotswood', illus. p.149. **var. *arbuscula,*** syn. *P. arbuscula,* S4ft (1.2m), bears golden-yellow flowers amid gray-green to silver-gray leaves. **'Beesii',** syn. *P.* 'Beesii', *P.* 'Nana Argentea', **H** 30in (75cm), **S** 3ft (1m), is slow-growing and compact. Has golden-yellow flowers and silver leaves. **'Daydawn',** syn. *P.* 'Daydawn', illus. p.162. **'Elizabeth',** syn. *P.* 'Elizabeth', illus. p.160. **'Farrer's White',** illus. p.149. **'Friedrichsenii',** illus. p.160. **'Gold Drop',** syn. *P. parvifolia* 'Gold Drop', **H** and **S** 4ft (1.2m), bears a mass of golden-yellow flowers amid bright green leaves. Z2–7 H7–1. **'Goldfinger',** syn. *P.* 'Goldfinger' bears large, rich yellow flowers in profusion. **'Jackman's Variety',** syn. *P.* 'Jackman's Variety', **H** 4ft (1.2m), has large, bright yellow flowers. **'Maanelys',** syn. *P.* 'Maanelys', *P.* 'Manelys', *P.* 'Moonlight', **H** 4ft (1.2m), **S** 6ft (2m), has soft yellow flowers and gray-green foliage. **'Manchu',** syn. *P. davurica* var. *mandschurica, P.* 'Manchu' has pure white flowers and silvery-gray leaves. **'Red Ace',** syn. *P.* 'Red Ace', illus. p.156. **'Royal Flush',** syn. *P.* 'Royal Flush', **H** 18in (45cm), **S** 30in (75cm), produces mid-green leaves and sometimes semidouble, yellow-stamened, rich pink flowers, fading to white in full sun. **'Sunset',** syn. *P.* 'Sunset', illus. p.162. **'Tangerine',** syn. *P.* 'Tangerine', **H** 4ft (1.2m), bears yellow flowers, flushed with pale orange-red, amid mid-green leaves. **'Vilmoriniana',** syn. *P.* 'Vilmoriniana', illus. p.159.
***P.* 'Gibson's Scarlet'.** Clump-forming perennial. **H** and **S** 18in (45cm). Bears saucer-shaped, brilliant scarlet flowers from mid- to late summer. Dark green leaves are strawberry-like. Z5–8 H8–5.
***P.* 'Gloire de Nancy',** syn. *P.* 'Glory of Nancy'. Clump-forming perennial. **H** and **S** 18in (45cm). Very large, saucer-shaped, semidouble, orange and coppery-red flowers are produced throughout summer. Has strawberry-like, dark green leaves. Z5–8 H8–5.
***P.* 'Glory of Nancy'.** See *P.* 'Gloire de Nancy'.
***P.* 'Goldfinger'.** See *P. fruticosa* 'Goldfinger'.
***P.* 'Jackman's Variety'.** See *P. fruticosa* 'Jackman's Variety'.
***P.* 'Maanelys'.** See *P. fruticosa* 'Maanelys'.
***P.* 'Manchu'.** See *P. fruticosa* 'Manchu'.
***P.* 'Manelys'.** See *P. fruticosa* 'Maanelys'.
P. megalantha, illus. p.276.
***P.* 'Monsieur Rouillard'.** Clump-forming perennial. **H** and **S** 18in (45cm). Bears saucer-shaped, double, blood-red flowers in summer above strawberry-like, dark green leaves. Z5–8 H8–5.
***P.* 'Moonlight'.** See *P. fruticosa* 'Maanelys'.
***P.* 'Nana Argentea'.** See *P. fruticosa* 'Beesii'.
***P. nepalensis* 'Miss Willmott',** illus. p.265.
P. nitida. Dense, mat-forming perennial. **H** 1–2in (2.5–5cm), **S** 8in (20cm). Has rounded, 3-lobed, silver leaves. Flower stems each bear 1–2 rose-pink flowers, with dark centers, in early summer. Is often shy-flowering. Is suitable for a rock garden or trough.
***P. parvifolia* 'Gold Drop'.** See *P. fruticosa* 'Gold Drop'.
P. recta. Clump-forming, hairy perennial. **H** 24in (60cm), **S** 18in (45cm). From early to late summer bears pale yellow flowers. Gray-green to mid-green leaves are divided into 3 toothed leaflets. Z4–8 H8–1. **'Macrantha'.** See *P. recta* 'Warrenii'. **'Warrenii',** syn. *P. recta* 'Macrantha' has rich, golden-yellow flowers throughout summer.
***P.* 'Red Ace'.** See *P. fruticosa* 'Red Ace'.
***P.* 'Royal Flush'.** See *P. fruticosa* 'Royal Flush'.
***P.* 'Sunset'.** See *P. fruticosa* 'Sunset'.
***P.* 'Tangerine'.** See *P. fruticosa* 'Tangerine'.
P. x tonguei. Mat-forming perennial. **H** 2in (5cm), **S** 10in (25cm). Has rounded, 3–5 lobed, green leaves. Prostrate branches bear flattish, orange-yellow flowers, with red centers, in summer. Is good for a rock garden. Z5–10 H8–3.
***P.* 'Vilmoriniana'.** See *P. fruticosa* 'Vilmoriniana'.
***P.* 'William Rollison'.** Clump-forming perennial. **H** and **S** 18in (45cm). From mid- to late summer bears saucer-shaped, semidouble, scarlet-suffused, deep orange flowers, with yellow centers. Has dark green leaves. Z4–7 H7–1.
***P.* 'Yellow Queen'.** Clump-forming perennial. **H** to 24in (60cm) or more, **S** 18in (45cm). Has strawberry-like, dark green leaves. Produces bright yellow flowers in mid-summer. Z5–8 H8–5.

Pothos. See *Epipremnum.*
x *Potinara* Cherub gx 'Spring Daffodil'. See x *Rhyncattleanthe* Cherub gx 'Spring Daffodil'.
Pratia angulata. See *Lobelia angulata.*
Pratia penduncultata. See *Lobelia pedunculata.*

PRIMULA

Primrose

PRIMULACEAE

Genus of mainly herbaceous perennials, some woody-based and evergreen. All have leaves in basal rosettes and tubular, bell- or primrose-shaped flowers. In some primulas, the flower stems, leaves, sepals and, occasionally, sections of the petals are covered with a waxy powder known as farina. There are primulas suitable for almost every type of site: the border, scree garden, rock garden, peat garden, bog garden, pond margin, greenhouse and alpine house. Some may be difficult to grow as they dislike winter damp or summer heat. Repot pot-grown plants annually. Tidy up fading foliage and deadhead as flowering ceases. Propagate species by seed when fresh or in spring, selected forms when dormant, by division in fall–spring or by root cuttings in winter, auricula primulas by offsets in early spring or early fall. Border cultivars may be prone to slug damage in damp places and to attack by root aphids when grown in very dry conditions or in pots. Primulas are divided into many different horticultural groups, of which the following are in common use. See also feature panel pp.258–9.

Auricula primulas
These are evergreen primulas, derived from hybrids between *P. auricula* and *P. hirsuta,* producing flat, smooth flowers carried in an umbel on a stem above the foliage. There are 3 main subgroups: alpine, show and border.
Alpine Auricula Group. In these, the color of the flower center is strikingly different from that of the petals. They may be either light-centered (white or pale in the center) or gold-centered (yellow or gold in the center). There is no meal or "farina" on either leaves or flowers. Grow in an alpine house or rock garden.
Show Auricula Group has flowers with a distinct circle of white meal or "paste" in the center. Some are self-colored, with one color, which may be red, yellow, blue or violet, from the central paste to the petal margins; edged cultivars have a black ring surrounding the central paste, feathering out to an often green, gray or white margin; in fancy cultivars, the paste is surrounded by a color other than black, with a green, gray or white margin. Show Auriculas have white farina on their foliage (except those with green-edged flowers), on their flower eyes and, sometimes, on their petal margins. Grow under glass to protect flowers from rain.
Border Auricula Group has generally robust, garden Auricula primulas, which are often very fragrant. Some have farina on flower stems and leaves. Grow in a mixed or herbaceous border.

Candelabra primulas
These are robust, herbaceous perennials with tubular, flat-faced flowers borne in tiered whorls up tall, sturdy stems. Some are deciduous, dying back to basal buds; others are semievergreen, dying back to reduced rosettes. Grow in moist shade or woodland, especially by streams.

Primrose-Polyanthus primulas
A diverse group of evergreen, semievergreen or deciduous perennial hybrids, derived from *P. vulgaris,* crossed with *P. veris, P. juliae* and other species. They are divided into two main groups.
Primrose Group Most produce solitary flowers among the leaves. Are mainly grown as herbaceous perennials, flowering in spring, or as biennial greenhouse container plants flowering in winter-spring.
Polyanthus Group Produce flowers in long-stalked umbels. Usually grown as biennials for bedding, sown in summer to flower in winter and the following spring, or under glass as winter- and spring-flowering container plants.

Cultivation
Primulas have varying cultivation requirements. For ease of reference, these have been grouped as follows:
1—Full sun or partial shade, in moist, but well-drained, rich soil.
2—Partial shade, in deep, rich, moist, neutral to acidic soil.
3—Deep or partial shade, in peaty, gritty, moist but very well-drained, acidic soil. Protect from excessive winter wet.
4—Under glass in an alpine house or frame. Avoid wetting foliage of mealy species and hybrids.
5—Full sun with some midday shade, or partial shade, in rich, moist but well-drained, gritty, slightly alkaline soil.
6—In a cool or temperate greenhouse, or as a houseplant, in bright, filtered light.

***P.* 'Adrian'.** Alpine Auricula primula. **H** and **S** 4in (10cm). Produces flat, light to dark blue flowers, with light centers and paler margins, from mid- to late spring. Leaves are oval to rounded and mid-green. Is useful for exhibition. Cultivation group 1 or 4. Z4–8 H8–1.
P. allionii, illus. p.257. Rosette-forming, evergreen perennial. **H** 3–4in (7–10cm), **S** 8in (20cm). Better grown in an alpine house. Tubular, rose, mauve or white flowers cover a tight cushion of oval, mid-green leaves in spring. Cultivation group 4. Z4–8 H8–1.
P. alpicola, illus. p.259. Compact, rosette-forming perennial. **H** 20in (50cm), **S** 12in (30cm). Produces terminal clusters of pendent, bell-shaped, yellow to white or purple flowers, on slender stems, in early summer. Mid-green leaves are oval to lance-shaped. Cultivation group 2. Z4–8 H8–1. **var. *alpicola,*** syn. *P. alpicola* var. *luna* has soft sulfur-yellow flowers. **var. *luna.*** See *P. alpicola* var. *alpicola.*
P. aurantiaca. Small, rosette-forming Candelabra primula. **H** 12in (30cm), **S** 16in (40cm). Tubular, reddish-orange flowers are borne in early summer. Has long, broadly oval to lance-shaped, coarse, mid-green leaves. Cultivation group 2. Z5–8 H8–1.
P. aureata, illus. p.259. Rosette-forming, evergreen perennial. **H** 6in (15cm), **S** 8in (20cm). Bears small umbels of flat, cream to

yellow flowers in spring. In summer, oval, toothed, mid-green leaves have purple-red midribs; in winter, leaves form tight buds covered with whitish farina. Cultivation group 3 or 4. Z4–8 H8–1.

P. auricula. Rosette-forming, evergreen, sometimes white-mealy perennial. **H** 8in (20cm), **S** 10in (25cm). Bears fragrant, flat, yellow flowers, in large umbels, in spring. Oval, soft, pale green to gray-green leaves are densely covered with white farina. Cultivation group 1, 4 or 5. Z3–8 H8–1.

P. Barnhaven Blues Group, illus. p.258. Vigorous, rosette-forming, evergreen or semievergreen, Primrose Group primula. **H** and **S** 6–8in (15–20cm). Flat flowers in a range of mainly dark blue shades, all with small, yellow eyes, are borne singly on reddish stems in spring. Have long, oval, slightly purple-tinted, green leaves. Cultivation group 1 or 2.

P. beesiana, syn. *P. bulleyana* subsp. *beesiana,* illus. p.258. Rosette-forming, deciduous or semievergreen, Candelabra primula. **H** and **S** 2ft (60cm). In summer, sturdy, white-mealy stems bear whorls of tubular, yellow-eyed, reddish-pink flowers. Has inversely lance-shaped to oval, toothed, mid-green leaves, with red midribs. Cultivation group 2. Z5–8 H8–5.

P. Belarina Series. Vigorous, rosette-forming, evergreen or semievergreen, Primrose Group primula. **H** 6in (15cm), **S** 9in (23cm). Have oval to lance-shaped, dark green leaves. In late winter and spring produce flat, fully double flowers, with slightly ruffled petals. Cultivation group 1 or 2. **'Belarina Cobalt Blue'** (illus. p.258) has very dark green leaves and vivid deep blue flowers. **BELARINA PINK ICE ('Kerbelpice'),** illus. p.303.

P. bhutanica 'Sherriff's Variety', syn. *P. whitei* 'Sherriff's Variety'. Rosette-forming perennial. **H** 6in (15cm), **S** 8in (20cm). Often short-lived. In spring produces neat umbels of tubular, pale ice-blue to sky-blue flowers, with strongly-toothed petals and greenish-yellow eye surrounded by broad, white zone, close to oval to lance-shaped, crinkled, mid-green leaves. Cultivation group 3.

P. 'Blairside Yellow', illus. p.259. Compact, border Auricula primula. **H** 4in (10cm), **S** 8in (20cm). In early spring, bell-shaped, golden-yellow flowers nestle in rosette of tiny, rounded to oval, pale green leaves. Cultivation group 2 or 5. Z4–8 H8–1.

P. 'Blossom'. Vigorous, alpine Auricula primula. **H** and **S** 4in (10cm). Flat, deep crimson to bright red flowers, with golden centers, are borne profusely in spring. Has oval, dark green leaves. Is suitable for exhibition. Cultivation group 1 or 4. Z4–8 H8–1.

P. bulleyana, illus. p.259. Rosette-forming, semievergreen, Candelabra primula. **H** and **S** 24in (60cm). Tubular, deep orange flowers are produced in early summer. Leaves are oval to lance-shaped, toothed and dark green. Cultivation group 2. Z5–8 H8–5. **subsp. beesiana.** See *P. beesiana.*

P. Charisma Series. Rosette-forming, semievergreen or evergreen, Primrose Group primulas, usually grown as biennials. **H** and **S** 8in (20cm). Have inversely oval, wrinkled, dark green leaves. In spring produce tubular flowers in

variety of different colors or self-colored. Cultivation group 1, 2, or 6. **'Charisma Blue'** (illus. p.258) has yellow-eyed, blue to purple-blue flowers. **'Charisma Red'** (illus. p.257) has pink to red flowers, with yellow centers.

P. chionantha subsp. melanops, syn. *P. melanops.* Rosette-forming perennial. **H** 14in (35cm), **S** 20in (50cm). In summer has umbels of pendent, narrowly funnel-shaped, deep violet-purple flowers, with black eyes, above long, strap-shaped, mid-green leaves. Cultivation group 2 or 4. Z4–8 H8–1.

P. 'Chloë'. Green-edged, show Auricula primula. **H** and **S** 4in (10cm). In late spring produces flat, dark-green-edged flowers with black body color and brilliant white paste centers. Oval leaves are dark green and have no farina. Is good for exhibition. Cultivation group 4. Z5–8 H8–5.

P. chungensis, illus. p.259. Vigorous, rosette-forming Candelabra primula. **H** 32in (80cm), **S** 24in (60cm). In summer bears tiered whorls of tubular, orange flowers among oval to lance-shaped, mid-green leaves. Cultivation group 2. Z5–8 H8–5.

P. clarkei. Small, rosette-forming perennial. **H** 3in (7cm), **S** 6in (15cm). In spring has flat, rose-pink flowers, with yellow eyes, just above clump of rounded to oval, pale green leaves. Cultivation group 2 or 4. Divide in late winter. Z6–8 H8–6.

P. clusiana. Small, rosette-forming, evergreen perennial. **H** 3in (8cm), **S** 6in (15cm). In spring bears umbels of tubular, rose-pink flowers, with white eyes. Leaves are oval, glossy and mid-green. Cultivation group 4 or 5. Z5–8 H8–5.

P. 'Craddock White'. Rosette-forming, deciduous or semievergreen, Primrose Group primula. **H** to 5in (12cm), **S** 10in (25cm). Fragrant, upward-facing, flat, white flowers, with yellow eyes, are borne in spring just above long, oval, red-veined, dark green leaves. Cultivation group 1 or 2. Z4–8 H8–1.

P. Crescendo Series, illus. p.258. Rosette-forming, evergreen or semievergreen, Polyanthus Group primula, usually grown as biennials. **H** and **S** 8in (20cm). Have inversely oval, wrinkled, dark green leaves. In spring produce umbels of flat, yellow-centered flowers. Cultivation group 1 or 2. Z5–7 H7–5. **'Crescendo Bright Red'** (illus. p.258) has bright scarlet flowers. **'Crescendo Pink and Rose Shades'** (illus. p.257) produces flowers in shades of rich purplish-pink.

P. 'David Green'. Rosette-forming, Primrose Group primula. **H** 4in (10cm), **S** 6–8in (15–20cm). In spring produces flat, bright crimson-purple flowers amid oval, coarse, mid-green leaves. Cultivation group 1 or 2.

P. 'Dawn Ansell', illus. p.257. Vigorous, evergreen or semievergreen, Primrose Group primula. **H** 8in (20cm), **S** 12in (30cm). Has oval to lance-shaped, slightly toothed, fresh green leaves. In spring produces double, white flowers set in an enlarged, leafy green calyx. Cultivation group 2.

P. denticulata (Drumstick primula). Robust, rosette-forming perennial. **H** and **S** 18in (45cm). From early to mid-spring, dense, rounded heads of flat, lilac, purple, or pink flowers are borne on tops of sturdy

stems. Mid-green leaves are broadly lance-shaped and toothed. Cultivation group 1 or 2. Z2–8 H8–1. **var. alba** (illus. p.257) has white flowers.

P. 'Don Keefe', illus. p.258. Vigorous, rosette-forming, evergreen or semievergreen, Polyanthus Group primula. **H** and **S** 8in (20cm). Reddish stems bear umbels of flat, slightly wavy, soft orange-red flowers, with tiny yellow eyes, in spring. Has long, oval, dark green leaves. Cultivation group 2.

P. 'Dreamer'. Rosette-forming, Primrose Group primula. **H** 3–4in (8–10cm), **S** 6–8in (15–20cm). Has oval leaves and, in spring, bears flat flowers in cream, apricot, pink or rose-pink; all bicolors have darker eyes and yellow centers. Cultivation group 2.

P. edgeworthii. See *P. nana.*

P. elatior (Oxlip), illus. p.259. Variable, rosette-forming, evergreen or semievergreen perennial. **H** 12in (30cm), **S** 10in (25cm). Has umbels of small, fragrant, tubular, yellow flowers, in spring, held above neat, oval to lance-shaped, toothed, mid-green leaves. Cultivation group 1 or 2. Z4–8 H8–1.

P. 'Elizabeth Killelay', illus. p.258. Vigorous, rosette-forming, evergreen or semievergreen, Polyanthus Group primula. **H** and **S** 8in (20cm). Small, fragrant, double, maroon flowers, with creamy edge to each petal and yellow eye, are borne in umbels on reddish stems in spring. Has long, oval, dark green leaves. Cultivation group 2.

P. 'E.R. Janes'. Vigorous, rosette-forming, semievergreen, Primrose Group primula. **H** 4–6in (10–15cm), **S** 12–16in (30–40cm). Flat, pale rose-pink flowers, flushed with orange, are borne in spring amid broadly oval, toothed, mid-green leaves. Cultivation group 1 or 2. Z5–8 H8–5.

P. farinosa (Bird's-eye primrose). Rosette-forming perennial. **H** and **S** 10in (25cm). In spring, umbels of tubular, lilac-pink, occasionally white, flowers are borne on short, sturdy stems. Oval, toothed, mid-green leaves are densely covered with white farina. Cultivation group 2 or 4. Z4–8 H8–1.

P. flaccida, syn. *P. nutans* of gardens. Lax, rosette-forming, short-lived perennial. **H** 20in (50cm), **S** 12in (30cm). In early summer, each sturdy stem produces conical head of pendent, bell-shaped, lavender or violet flowers above narrowly oval, pale to mid-green leaves. Cultivation group 3 or 4. Z4–8 H8–1.

P. florindae, illus. p.445.

P. forrestii, illus. p.259. Rosette-forming, evergreen perennial. **H** 24in (60cm), **S** 18in (45cm). Dense umbels of flat, yellow flowers, with orange eyes, are borne in late spring or early summer. Has oval, toothed, dark green leaves. Cultivation group 4 or 5. Z6–8 H8–6.

P. 'Fransisca', illus. p.259. Vigorous, rosette-forming, evergreen or semievergreen, Polyanthus Group primula. **H** and **S** 8in (20cm) In spring has umbels of large, flat, slightly ruffled, pale green flowers, with large, star-shaped, yellow eye marked with 5 slender, orange streaks. Cultivation group 2.

P. frondosa, illus. p.257. Compact, rosette-forming perennial. **H** 6in (15cm), **S** 10in (25cm). In spring bears umbels of flat, yellow-eyed, lilac-rose to reddish-purple flowers, on short stems, above oval, mid-green leaves, densely covered with

white farina. Cultivation group 2 or 4. Z4–8 H8–1.

P. 'Garryarde Guinevere'. See *P.* 'Guinevere'.

P. Gold-laced Group, illus. p.259. Erect, semievergreen or evergreen, Polyanthus Group primulas. **H** 10in (25cm), **S** 12in (30cm). Produce flat flowers, in variety of colors, with gold-laced margins, from mid- to late spring. Leaves are oval and mid-green, sometimes tinged red. Raise annually by seed. Cultivation group 2 or 4. Z5–8 H8–4.

P. gracilipes. Rosette-forming, evergreen or semievergreen perennial. **H** 4in (1cm), **S** 8in (20cm). Solitary, tubular, purplish-pink flowers, with greenish-yellow eyes, are borne in spring or early summer among oval, wavy, toothed, mid-green leaves. Cultivation group 3 or 4. Z5–8 H8–5.

P. Grand Burgundy Series. Rosette-forming, semievergreen or evergreen, Polyanthus Group primula. **H** and **S** 6–8in (15–20cm). Have inversely oval, wrinkled, mid- to dark green leaves. In spring produce umbels of tubular, yellow-eyed flowers in variety of colors. Cultivation group 1, 2 or 6.

P. 'Guinevere', syn. *P.* 'Garryarde Guinevere', illus. p.257. Vigorous, rosette-forming, evergreen, Polyanthus Group primula. **H** 5in (12cm), **S** 10in (25cm). Flat, purplish-pink flowers, with yellow eyes, are produced in spring among oval, toothed, bronze-green leaves. Cultivation group 2.

P. 'Harlow Carr'. Rosette-forming, Alpine Auricula primula. **H** 4–6in (10–5cm), **S** 6–8in (15–20cm). In spring produces flat, white flowers, on short stems, above oval, soft, mid-green leaves. Cultivation group 1 or 4. Z3–8 H8–1.

P. helodoxa. See *P. prolifera.*

P. hirsuta, syn. *P. rubra.* Rosette-forming, evergreen perennial. **H** 4in (10cm), **S** 10in (25cm). Produces small umbels of flat, rose or lilac flowers in spring. Has small, rounded to oval, sticky, mid-green leaves. Cultivation group 1, 2, or 4. Z3–8 H8–1.

P. Husky Series. Rosette-forming, evergreen or semievergreen, Primrose Group primula, usually grown as a biennial. **H** and **S** 8in (20cm). Has inversely oval, wrinkled, dark green leaves. In late winter and spring produces flat, brightly yellow-eyed flowers in 8 colors. Cultivation group 1 or 2. **[white],** illus. p.257.

P. 'Inverewe', illus. p.258. Vigorous, rosette-forming, semievergreen, Candelabra primula. **H** 30in (75cm), **S** 24in (60cm). Tubular, bright orange-red flowers are produced in summer on stems coated with white farina. Has oval to lance-shaped, toothed, coarse, mid-green leaves. Cultivation group 2. Z4–8 H8–1.

P. ioessa. Rosette-forming perennial. **H** and **S** 12in (30cm). Clustered heads of funnel-shaped, pink or pinkish-mauve, or sometimes white, flowers are borne in spring or early summer above oval to lance-shaped, toothed, mid-green leaves. Cultivation group 2, 3 or 4. Z5–8 H8–5.

P. 'Janet'. Vigorous, rosette-forming, alpine Auricula. **H** 6–8in (15–20cm), **S** 6in (15cm). In spring, clusters of outward-facing, flat, purplish-pink flowers are produced above oval to rounded, soft, mid-green leaves. Cultivation group 1 or 4. Propagate by offsets after flowering. Z3–8 H8–1.

P. 'Janie Hill'. Rosette-forming, alpine Auricula. **H** 4in (10cm), **S** 6in (15cm). Flat, dark to golden-brown flowers, with golden centers, are produced in mid- to late spring. Has oval, mid-green leaves. Is useful for exhibition. Cultivation group 4 or 5. Z3–8 H8–1.

P. japonica (Japanese primrose). Robust, rosette-forming, Candelabra primula. **H** and **S** 18in (45cm). In early summer produces tubular, deep red flowers, on sturdy stems, above oval to lance-shaped, toothed, coarse, pale green leaves. Cultivation group 2. Z4–8 H8–1. **'Miller's Crimson'**, illus. p.257. Has intense crimson flowers. Z4–8 H8–1. **'Postford White'**, illus. p.257. Bears white flowers. Z4–8 H8–1.

P. Joker Series. Compact, rosette-forming, evergreen or semievergreen perennial. **H** 3–4in (8–10cm), **S** 10in (25cm). Have short-stemmed, inversely lance-shaped to oval, mid-green leaves. In spring produce tubular flowers, in range of colors, including bicolors, with yellow or creamy-yellow eyes. Are also available in selected color variants. Z6–8 H8–6. **'Cherry'** has mid-pink petals with crimson bases. **'Red and Gold'** has golden-yellow flowers with wide, red margins.

P. kewensis, illus. p.259. Rosette-forming, evergreen perennial. **H** 18in (45cm), **S** 8in (20cm). Produces whorls of fragrant, tubular, bright yellow flowers in early spring. Oval to spoon-shaped, toothed, mid-green leaves are sparsely covered with white farina. Cultivation group 6. Z9–11 H6–1.

P. 'Lady Greer', illus. p.257. Semi-creeping, rosette-forming, semievergreen, Polyanthus Group primula. **H** and **S** 4–6in (10–15cm). Has umbels of fragrant, funnel-shaped, creamy-yellow flowers in spring. Small, bright green leaves are produced close to ground. Cultivation group 2. Z3–8 H8–1.

P. 'Linda Pope', syn. *P. marginata* 'Linda Pope'. Vigorous, rosette-forming, evergreen or semievergreen perennial derived from *P. marginata*. **H** 6in (15cm), **S** 12in (30cm). In spring bears flat, mauve-blue flowers, on short stems, above oval, toothed, mid-green leaves covered with white farina. Cultivation group 4 or 5. Z4–8 H8–1.

P. malacoides (Fairy primrose). Erect, rosette-forming, evergreen perennial, usually grown as an annual. **H** 12–18in (30–45cm), **S** 8in (20cm). In winter–spring, small, flat, single or double, pale lilac-purple, reddish-pink and white flowers are borne in whorls of decreasing size up slender, softly hairy stems. Leaves are oval, slightly frilly-margined, softly downy and pale green. Cultivation group 6. Z8–10 H10–8.

P. 'Margaret Martin', illus. p.259. Rosette-forming, show Auricula primula. **H** 4in (10cm), **S** 6in (15cm). Bears flat, gray-edged flowers, with black body color and white centers, in mid- to late spring. Has spoon-shaped, gray-green leaves covered with white farina. Is excellent for exhibition. Cultivation group 4. Z4–8 H8–1.

P. marginata. Rosette-forming, evergreen or semievergreen perennial. **H** 6in (15cm), **S** 12in (30cm). In spring, clusters of funnel-shaped, blue-lilac flowers are produced above oval, toothed, mid-green leaves densely covered with white farina. Cultivation group 4 or 5. Z3–8 H8–1. **'Prichard's Variety'** has lilac-purple flowers with white eyes.

P. marginata 'Linda Pope'. See *P.* 'Linda Pope'.

P. 'Mark', illus. p.258. Vigorous, alpine Auricula primula. **H** and **S** 4in (10cm). Produces flat, pink flowers, with light yellow centers, in spring. Has oval, vibrant green leaves. Is good for exhibition. Cultivation group 4. Z4–8 H8–1.

P. 'Matthew Yates', illus. p.258. Vigorous, double auricula. **H** and **S** 5in (12cm). Produces fully double, very dark blackish-red flowers, in tight trusses, in spring. Leaves are inversely oval and mid-green with some farina. Is good for exhibition. Cultivation group 1 or 4.

P. melanops. See *P. chionantha* subsp. *melanops*.

P. 'Miss Indigo', syn. *P. vulgaris* 'Miss Indigo', illus. p.258. Vigorous, rosette-forming, evergreen or semievergreen perennial. **H** 8in (20cm), **S** 14in (35cm). Has oval to lance-shaped, toothed, bright green leaves. In spring produces flat, double, deep rich purple flowers, with creamy-white tips. Cultivation group 2. Z4–8 H8–1.

P. modesta. Rosette-forming perennial. **H** and **S** 8in (20cm). Dense heads of small, tubular, pinkish-purple flowers, on short stems, are produced in spring. Rounded to oval, mid-green leaves are covered with yellow farina. Cultivation group 1 or 4. Z4–8 H8–1. **var. fauriae**, **H** and **S** 2in (5cm), produces yellow-eyed, pinkish-purple flowers and leaves covered with white farina.

P. 'Moonstone'. Rosette-forming, Border Auricula primula. **H** 5in (12cm), **S** 6in (15cm). Rounded, double, whitish- or greenish-yellow flowers are produced in profusion in spring. Leaves are oval and mid-green. Preferably, grow under glass. Cultivation group 4 or 5. Z4–8 H8–1.

P. 'Mrs. J.H. Wilson', syn. *P. x pubescens* 'Mrs. J.H. Wilson'. Rosette-forming, Alpine Auricula primula. **H** and **S** 4–6in (10–15cm). Bears small umbels of flat, white-centered, purple flowers in spring. Oval leaves are grayish-green. Cultivation group 1 or 4. Z4–8 H8–1.

P. nana, syn. *P. edgeworthii*. Rosette-forming perennial. **H** 4in (10cm), **S** 6in (15cm). Solitary, flat, pale mauve flowers, with white eyes, are produced among oval, toothed, pale green leaves in spring. Cultivation group 3 or 4. Z4–8 H8–1.

P. nutans of gardens. See *P. flaccida*.

P. obconica. Erect, rosette-forming, evergreen perennial, usually grown as an annual. **H** 9–16in (23–40cm), **S** 10in (25cm). Flat, purple, lilac or white flowers, with yellow eyes, are borne in dense umbels in winter–spring. Leaves are oval, toothed, hairy and pale green. Cultivation group 6. Z10–12 H6–1.

P. 'Orb'. Neat, Show Auricula primula. **H** and **S** 4in (10cm). Flat, dark-green-edged flowers, with black body color and central zone of white paste, are produced from mid- to late spring. Has spoon-shaped, dark green leaves without farina. Is good for exhibition. Cultivation group 4.

P. Pacific Series. Rosette-forming, Polyanthus Group primulas, normally grown as biennials. **H** and **S** 8–9in (20–22cm); dwarf: **H** and **S** 4–6in (10–15cm). Have lance-shaped leaves. Heads of large, fragrant, flat flowers, in shades of blue, yellow, red, pink or white, are produced in spring. Cultivation group 1, 2, 4, or 6.

P. palinuri, illus. p.259. Rosette-forming, evergreen perennial. **H** and **S** 12in (30cm). One-sided clusters of semi-pendent, narrowly funnel-shaped, yellow flowers, on thick stems, are produced in early summer. Has rounded to oval, lightly toothed, thick-textured, powdered, green leaves. Cultivation group 1 or 4; requires full sun. Z6–8 H8–1.

P. petiolaris. Rosette-forming, evergreen perennial. **H** 4in (10cm), **S** 8in (20cm). Solitary, tubular, purplish-pink flowers, with toothed petals, are borne in spring. Has small, oval, toothed, mid-green leaves. Cultivation group 3 or 4. Z4–8 H8–1.

P. poissonii. Rosette-forming, evergreen perennial. **H** 18–20in (45–50cm), **S** 8–10in (20–25cm). Has long, inversely lance-shaped, dark green leaves. Produces 4–5 whorls of tubular, plum-purple flowers, with golden eyes, in early and mid-summer. Cultivation Group 3.

P. polyneura, illus. p.258. Rosette-forming perennial. **H** and **S** 18in (45cm). Dense heads of tubular, pale rose, rich rose or purple-rose flowers are produced in late spring or early summer. Rounded to oval, shallowly lobed, downy, soft leaves are mid-green. Cultivation group 2. Z3–8 H8–1.

P. prolifera, syn. *P. helodoxa*, illus. p.445.

P. x pubescens 'Mrs. J.H. Wilson'. See *P.* 'Mrs. J.H. Wilson'.

P. pulverulenta, illus. p.258. Rosette-forming, Candelabra primula. **H** 36in (90cm), **S** 24in (60cm). In early summer bears tubular, deep red flowers, with purple-red eyes, on stems covered with white farina. Has broadly lance-shaped, toothed, coarse, mid-green leaves. Cultivation group 2. Z4–8 H8–1. **'Bartley'** has pink flowers.

P. reidii. Robust, rosette-forming perennial. **H** 2–6in (5–15cm), **S** 4–6in (10–15cm). Produces dense clusters of bell-shaped, pure white flowers, on slender stems, in early summer. Has oval, hairy, pale green leaves. Cultivation group 3 or 4. Z5–8 H8–5. **var. williamsii** is more robust and has purplish-blue to pale blue flowers.

P. rosea. Rosette-forming perennial. **H** and **S** 8in (20cm). In early spring bears small clusters of flat, glowing rose-pink flowers, on short stems, among oval to lance-shaped, mid-green leaves, often bronze-flushed when young. Cultivation group 2. Z3–8 H8–1.

P. 'Royal Velvet'. Vigorous, rosette-forming, Border Auricula primula. **H** and **S** 6–8in (15–20cm). Flat, velvety, blue-tinged, maroon flowers, with frilled petals and large, creamy-yellow centers, are produced in spring. Has large, spoon-shaped, pale green leaves. Cultivation group 2 or 5.

P. rubra. See *P. hirsuta*.

P. x scapeosa. Vigorous, rosette-forming perennial. **H** 4in (10cm), **S** 10in (25cm). Clusters of outward-facing, flat, mauve-pink flowers, in early spring, are initially hidden by broadly oval, sharply toothed, mid-green leaves covered at first with slight farina; later, flower stem elongates above leaves. Cultivation group 3 or 4. Z2–8 H8–1.

P. secundiflora. Rosette-forming, evergreen or semievergreen perennial. **H** 24–36in (60–90cm), **S** 24in (60cm). Has clusters of pendent, funnel-shaped, reddish-purple flowers, in summer, above lance-shaped, toothed leaves. Cultivation group 2. Z4–8 H8–1.

P. sieboldii, illus. p.258. Rosette-forming perennial. **H** 12in (30cm), **S** 18in (45cm). Umbels of flat, white, pink or purple flowers, with white eyes, are borne above oval, round-toothed, downy, soft, pale green leaves in early summer. Cultivation group 2. Z4–8 H8–1. **'Geisha Girl'** (illus. p.257) bears large, pink flowers, with deeply cut petals. **'Sumina'** bears large, wisteria-blue flowers. **'Wine Lady'** has white flowers, strongly suffused with purplish-red.

P. sikkimensis (Himalayan cowslip), illus. p.259. Rosette-forming perennial. **H** 24–36in (60–90cm), **S** 24in (60cm). Pendent clusters of funnel-shaped, yellow flowers are borne in summer. Has rounded to oval, toothed, pale green leaves. Cultivation group 2. Z4–8 H8–1.

P. sinensis. Erect, rosette-forming, evergreen perennial. **H** and **S** 6–8in (15–20cm). Flat, purple, purple-rose, pink or white flowers, with yellow eyes, are produced in neat whorls in winter–spring. Leaves are oval, toothed, hairy and mid-green. Cultivation group 6. Z7–8 H8–7.

P. sonchifolia. Rosette-forming perennial. **H** 2in (5cm), **S** 12in (30cm). Produces dense umbels of tubular, blue-purple flowers, with white eyes and yellow margins, in spring. Leaves are oval to lance-shaped, toothed and mid-green. Cultivation group 3 or 4. Z5–8 H8–5.

P. Super Giants Series. Rosette-forming Polyanthus Group primulas, usually grown as biennials. **H** and **S** 6–8in (15–20cm). Produce large, fragrant, flat flowers, in wide range of colors, in spring. Cultivation group 1 or 2. Z6–8 H8–1.

P. 'Tawny Port'. Very dwarf, rosette-forming, evergreen or semievergreen, Polyanthus Group primula. **H** 4–6in (10–15cm), **S** 6–8in (15–20cm). Bears flat, port-wine-colored flowers, on short stems, in spring. Rounded to oval, toothed leaves are reddish-green. Cultivation group 1, 2, or 4. Z3–8 H8–1.

P. 'Trouble', illus. p.259. Vigorous, double auricula. **H** and **S** 5in (12cm). Leaves are broad, inversely oval, mid-green and irregularly toothed. Produces fully double flowers, a blend of yellow and pink, resulting in pale coffee-colored blooms borne in tight trusses in spring. Cultivation group 1 or 4.

P. veris, illus. p.263. **'Katy McSparron'** (illus. p.259) is a rosette-forming, evergreen or semievergreen perennial. **H** and **S** 10in (25cm). Bears tight clusters of fragrant, tubular, fully double, yellow flowers, with enlarged, grayish calyx, in spring. Leaves are oval to lance-shaped, toothed and mid-green. Cultivation group 1 or 2.

P. verticillata, illus. p.259. Rosette-forming perennial. **H** 8–10in (20–25cm), **S** 6–8in (15–20cm). Fragrant, bell-shaped, yellow flowers are borne in whorls in spring. Has oval, toothed, mid-green leaves. Cultivation group 4 or 6. Z3–8 H8–1.

P. vialii, illus. p.257. Rosette-forming, often short-lived perennial. **H** 12–24in (30–60cm), **S** 12in (30cm). Dense, conical spikes of tubular, bluish-purple and red flowers are produced in late spring. Has lance-shaped, toothed, soft, mid-green leaves. Cultivation group 1 or 2. Z5–8 H8–5.

P. vulgaris (Primrose), illus. p.259. Rosette-forming, evergreen or semievergreen perennial. **H** 8in (20cm), **S** 14in (35cm). Solitary, flat, soft yellow flowers, with darker eyes, are borne among oval to lance-shaped, toothed, bright green leaves in spring. Cultivation group 2. Z4–8 H8–1. **'Alba Plena'** (illus. p.257) has double, white flowers. **'Gigha White'** is very floriferous and has yellow-eyed, white flowers. **'Lilacina Plena'** is vigorous and free-flowering, with fully double, lilac-purple flowers. **'Miss Indigo'**. See *P.* 'Miss Indigo'. **subsp. sibthorpii** (illus. p.258) has pink or purplish-pink flowers.

P. Wanda Supreme Series. Evergreen or semievergreen perennials. **H** 3–4in (8–10cm), **S** 6in (15cm). Have inversely lance-shaped to oval, bronze to dark green foliage. From winter to mid-spring produce flowers in different shades of blue, yellow, purple, burgundy, red, rose and pink bicolors. Cultivation group 1 or 2. Z5–8 H8–5.

P. warshenewskiana. Rosette-forming perennial. **H** 3in (7cm), **S** 6in (15cm). Tiny, flat, white-eyed, bright pink flowers are borne just above spoon-shaped, dark green leaves in early spring. Cultivation group 2 or 4. Divide clumps regularly in late winter before flowering. Z4–8 H8–1.

P. whitei 'Sherriff's Variety'. See *P. bhutanica* 'Sherriff's Variety'.

P. 'Woodland Walk', illus. p.257. Rosette-forming, evergreen or semievergreen, Primrose Group primula. **H** and **S** 8in (20cm). Has inversely oval, wrinkled, bronze-tinted, dark green leaves. In late winter and spring, flat flowers, with heart-shaped petals, are borne on single stems and range in color from faintly pink-tinted white to vivid pink, each petal edged with darker pink. Cultivation group 2.

P. 'Yellow Dream'. Rosette-forming, Polyanthus Group primula. **H** and **S** 6–9in (15–23cm). Has ovate, toothed leaves. Produces large, fragrant, bright yellow flower heads, with slightly darker yellow centers, in late winter and spring.

PRINSEPIA

ROSACEAE

Genus of deciduous, usually spiny, spring- and early summer-flowering shrubs, grown for their habit, flowers and fruits. Does well against a south- or west-facing wall. Needs sun and any not too dry soil. Propagate by softwood cuttings in summer or by seed in fall.

P. uniflora, illus. p.129.

PROBOSCIDEA

Unicorn plant

MARTYNIACEAE/PEDALIACEAE

Genus of annuals and perennials. Needs a sunny, sheltered position and fertile, well-drained soil. Propagate by seed sown under glass in early spring.

P. fragrans. Moderately fast-growing, upright annual. **H** 24in (60cm), **S** 12in (30cm). Has rounded, serrated or lobed leaves. Fragrant, bell-shaped, crimson-purple flowers, in summer–fall, are

followed by rounded, horned, brown fruits, 3–4in (8–10cm) long, which, if gathered young, may be pickled and e aten. Z8–9 H9–7.

P. jussieui. See *P. louisianica*.

P. louisianica, syn. *P. jussieui*, *P. proboscidea*, *Martynia louisianica* (Common devil's claw, Common unicorn plant, Ram's horn). Erect to spreading annual. **H** 18in (45cm), **S** 36in (90cm). Has rounded to ovate, unlobed leaves. In summer bears funnel-shaped, fragrant, reddish-purple to purple flowers, followed by narrow, crested fruit, to 2¹⁄₂in (6cm) long, with beaklike projections. Z7–9 H9–7.

P. proboscidea. See *P. louisianica*.

Prometheum sempervivoides. See *Sedum sempervivoides*.

PROSTANTHERA

Mint bush

LABIATAE/LAMIACEAE

Genus of evergreen shrubs, grown for their flowers and mint-scented foliage. Requires full light or partial shade and fertile, well-drained soil. Water container specimens freely when in full growth, moderately at other times. Leggy stems may be cut back after flowering. Propagate by seed in spring or by semiripe cuttings in late summer.

P. cuneata, illus. p.197.

P. lasianthos. Evergreen, erect shrub. **H** and **S** to 6ft (2m). Has lance-shaped, aromatic, mid-green leaves. In spring produces masses of branched, terminal panicles of 2-lipped, purple-tinted, white or cream flowers.

P. melissifolia. Evergreen, erect shrub. **H** and **S** 6ft (2m). Has ovate to elliptic, very aromatic, mid-green leaves. In summer produces terminal racemes of 2-lipped, bright lilac, purple or pink flowers.

P. ovalifolia, illus. p.457.

P. rotundifolia, illus. p.138. **'Rosea'**, illus. p.192.

PROTEA

PROTEACEAE

Genus of evergreen shrubs and trees, grown mainly for their colorfully bracted flower heads. Is difficult to grow. Requires full light and well-drained, neutral to acidic soil, low in phosphates and nitrates. Water container specimens moderately, less when not in full growth. Plants under glass must have plenty of ventilation throughout the year. Prune, if necessary, in early spring. Propagate by seed in spring or by semiripe cuttings in summer.

P. barbigera. See *P. magnifica*.

P. cynaroides, illus. p.454.

P. magnifica, syn. *P. barbigera* (Woolly-bearded protea). Evergreen, rounded to spreading shrub. **H** and **S** 3ft (1m). Has oblong to elliptic, leathery, mid- to grayish-green leaves. Spherical flower heads, 6–8in (15–20cm) wide, with petal-like, pink, red, yellow or white bracts, are borne in spring–summer. Z9–10 H10–9.

P. mellifera. See *P. repens*.

P. neriifolia, illus. p.454.

P. repens, syn. *P. mellifera* (Honey flower, Sugarbush). Evergreen, ovoid to rounded shrub. **H** and **S** 6–10ft (2–3m). Mid-green leaves are narrowly oblong to elliptic and tinted blue-gray. In spring–summer

produces cup-shaped flower heads, 5in (13cm) long, with petal-like, pink, red or white bracts. Z9–10 H10–9.

PRUMNOPITYS

PODOCARPACEAE

See also CONIFERS.

P. andina, syn. *Podocarpus andinus* (Plum yew). Conifer with domed crown on several stems. **H** 50ft (15m), **S** 25ft (8m). Has smooth, gray-brown bark, needlelike, flattened, bluish-green leaves and edible, yellowish-white fruits like small plums. Z8–10 H10–8.

PRUNELLA

Selfheal

LABIATAE/LAMIACEAE

Genus of semievergreen perennials with spreading mats of leaves from which arise short, stubby flower spikes in mid-summer. Is suitable for rock gardens. Needs sun or partial shade and moist but well-drained soil. Propagate by division in spring.

P. grandiflora, syn. *P. x webbiana*, illus. p.368. **'Loveliness'** is a semievergreen, basal-rosetted, groundcover perennial. **H** 4–6in (10–15cm), **S** 12in (30cm). Bears whorls of pale purple flowers in terminal spikes on leafy stems in summer. May be invasive; cut old flower stems before they seed. Z5–8 H8–5. **'Pink Loveliness'** bears soft pink flowers in terminal spikes in summer. Makes good groundcover, but may be invasive. Cut off old flower stems before they produce seed. Z5–8 H8–5. **'White Loveliness'** has white flowers. Z5–8 H8–5.

P. x webbiana. See *P. grandiflora*.

PRUNUS

Almond, Cherry, Cherry laurel, Nectarine, Peach, Plum

ROSACEAE

Genus of deciduous or evergreen shrubs and trees. The trees are grown mainly for their single (5-petaled) to double flowers and fall color; the shrubs for their fall color, bark, flowers or fruits. All have oval to oblong leaves. Evergreen species need sun or partial shade; deciduous species prefer full sun. All may be grown in any but waterlogged soil. Trim deciduous hedges after flowering, evergreen ones in early or mid-spring. Propagate deciduous species by seed in fall, deciduous hybrids and selected forms by softwood cuttings in summer, evergreens by semiripe cuttings in summer. Birds may eat flower buds and foliage may be attacked by aphids, caterpillars and the fungal disease silver leaf. Flowering cherries are prone to a fungus that causes "witches' brooms" (abnormal, crowded shoots). Certain *Prunus* species and cultivars, notably cultivars of the almond (*P. dulcis*) and the peach (*P. persica*), are grown for their edible fruits. ① Leaves and fruits of most other species may cause severe discomfort if ingested.

P. 'Accolade', illus. p.83.

P. 'Amanogawa'. Deciduous, upright tree. **H** 30ft (10m), **S** 12ft (4m). Bears fragrant, semidouble, pale pink flowers in late spring. Oblong to oval, taper-pointed, dark green leaves turn orange and red in fall. Z6–8 H8–6.

P. amygdalopersica. See *P.* x *persicoides*.

P. avium, illus. p.67. **'Plena'**, illus. p.71.

P. x blireana. Deciduous, spreading shrub or small tree. **H** and **S** 12ft (4m). Bears double, pink flowers in mid-spring and has oval, purple leaves. Z5–8 H8–5.

P. campanulata (Bell-flowered cherry, Taiwan cherry). Deciduous, spreading tree. **H** and **S** 25ft (8m). Shallowly bell-shaped, deep rose-red flowers are produced from early to mid-spring, before or with oval, taper-pointed, dark green leaves. Fruits are small, rounded and reddish. Z7–8 H8–7.

P. cerasifera (Cherry plum, Myrobalan). Z4–8 H8–1. **'Nigra'**, illus. p.86. **'Pissardii'** is a deciduous, round-headed tree. **H** and **S** 30ft (10m). Small, 5-petaled, pale pink flowers open from early to mid-spring and are often followed by edible, plumlike, red fruits. Has oval, red, young leaves turning deeper red, then purple. Is suitable for hedging.

P. 'Cheal's Weeping'. See *P.* 'Kiku-shidare-zakura'.

P. x cistena, illus. p.146.

P. davidiana (David's peach). Deciduous, spreading tree. **H** and **S** 25ft (8m). Saucer-shaped, 5-petaled, white or pale pink flowers are borne on slender shoots in late winter and early spring, but are susceptible to late frosts. Leaves are narrowly oval and dark green. Fruits are rounded and reddish. Z4–8 H8–1.

P. dulcis (Common almond). **'Roseoplena'** is a deciduous, spreading tree. **H** and **S** 25ft (8m). Bears double, pink flowers in late winter and early spring, before oblong, pointed, toothed, dark green leaves. Z5–8 H8–5.

P. glandulosa. **'Alba Plena'**, illus. p.145. **'Rosea Plena'.** See *P. glandulosa* 'Sinensis'. Z5–8 H8–3. **'Sinensis'**, syn. *P. glandulosa* 'Rosea Plena' is a deciduous, rounded, open shrub. **H** and **S** 5ft (1.5m). Produces double, bright rose-pink flowers in late spring and oval, mid-green leaves. Flowers best when grown against a south- or west-facing wall. Cut back young shoots to within a few buds of old wood after flowering. Z5–8 H8–3.

P. 'Hally Jolivette'. Deciduous, rounded, compact tree. **H** and **S** 15ft (5m). Double, white flowers open from pink buds in late spring. Leaves are oval and dark green. Z6–8 H8–3.

P. x hillieri 'Spire'. See *P.* 'Spire'.

P. 'Hokusai', syn. *P.* 'Uzuzakura', illus. p.82.

P. incisa, illus. p.81. **'February Pink'** is a deciduous, spreading tree. **H** and **S** 25ft (8m). Oval, sharply toothed, dark green leaves are reddish when young, orange-red in fall. In mild, winter periods bears 5-petaled, pale pink flowers. Has tiny, rounded, reddish fruits. Z6–8 H8–6.

P. jamasakura, syn. *P. serrulata* var. *spontanea*, illus. p.71.

P. 'Kanzan', illus. p.72.

P. 'Kiku-shidare-zakura', syn. *P.* 'Cheal's Weeping', illus. p.83.

P. 'Kursar'. Deciduous, spreading tree. **H** and **S** 25ft (8m). Bears masses of small, 5-petaled, deep pink flowers in early spring. Oval, dark green leaves turn brilliant orange in fall. Z6–8 H8–6.

P. laurocerasus (Cherry laurel, English laurel). Evergreen, dense, bushy shrub becoming spreading and open. **H** 20ft (6m), **S** 30ft (10m). Has large, oblong, glossy,

bright green leaves. Long spikes of small, single, white flowers, from mid- to late spring, are followed by cherry-shaped, red then black fruits. Restrict growth by cutting back hard in spring. Z6–9 H9–6. **'Otto Luyken'**, illus. p.145. **'Schipkaensis'**, **H** 6ft (2m), **S** 10ft (3m), has a spreading habit, narrow leaves and freely borne flowers in upright spikes. **'Zabeliana'**, illus. p.145.
P. lusitanica (Laurel, Portugal laurel). Evergreen, bushy, dense shrub or spreading tree. **H** and **S** 20–30ft (6–10m). Reddish-purple shoots bear oval, glossy, dark green leaves. Slender spikes of small, fragrant, 5-petaled, white flowers, in early summer, are followed by egg-shaped, fleshy, deep purple fruits. Restrict growth by pruning hard in spring. Z7–9 H9–4. **subsp. azorica**, illus. p.119. **'Variegata'**, illus. p.119.
P. maackii (Amur cherry). Deciduous, spreading tree. **H** 30ft (10m). **S** 25ft (8m). Has peeling, yellowish-brown bark. Produces spikes of small, white flowers in mid-spring. Pointed, dark green leaves turn yellow in fall. Z3–7 H7–1.
P. mahaleb, illus. p.71.
P. **'Mount Fuji'**. See *P.* 'Shirotae'.
P. mume (Japanese apricot). **'Beni-chidori'**, syn. *P. mume* 'Beni-shidon', illus. p.123. **'Beni-shidon'**. See *P. mume* 'Beni-chidori'. **'Omoi-no-mama'**, syn. *P. mume* 'Omoi-no-wac' is a deciduous, spreading shrub. **H** and **S** 8ft (2.5m). Has fragrant, semidouble, occasionally single, pink-flushed, white flowers wreathing young growths in early spring, before broadly oval, toothed leaves emerge. Sometimes produces edible, apricot-like, yellow fruits. Z6–8 H8–6. **'Pendula'**, **H** and **S** 20ft (6m), has weeping branches and pink flowers. **'Omoi-no-wac'**. See *P. mume* 'Omoi-no-mama'.
P. **'Okame'**. Deciduous, bushy-headed tree. **H** 30ft (10m), **S** 25ft (8m). Bears masses of 5-petaled, carmine-pink flowers in early spring. Oval, sharply toothed, dark green leaves turn orange-red in fall. Z5–8 H8–5.
P. padus (European bird cherry). Deciduous, spreading tree, conical when young. **H** 50ft (15m), **S** 30ft (10m). Bears fragrant, white flowers in pendent spikes in late spring, followed by small, black fruits. Dark green leaves turn yellow in fall. Z4–8 H8–1. **'Colorata'**, illus. p.72. **'Grandiflora'**. See *P. padus* 'Watereri'. **'Plena'** has double, pink flowers and oval, reddish-purple young leaves that mature to dark green and then turn to red or yellow in fall. **'Watereri'**, syn. *P. padus* 'Grandiflora', illus. p.71. bears long racemes of flowers from mid- to late spring.
P. **'Pandora'**, illus. p.82.
P. pendula **'Pendula Rubra'**. See *P.* x *subhirtella* 'Pendula Rubra'. **'Stellata'**, syn. *P.* 'Pink Star', *P.* x *subhirtella* 'Stellata', illus. p.83.
P. pensylvanica (Pin cherry). Deciduous, spreading tree. **H** 50ft (15m), **S** 30ft (10m). Has peeling, red-banded bark and oval, taper-pointed, bright green leaves. Produces clusters of small, star-shaped, 5-petaled, white flowers from mid- to late spring, followed by small, pea-shaped, red fruits. Z6–8 H8–6.
P. persica (Peach). Z4–8 H8–1. **'Clara Meyer'** is a deciduous, spreading tree. **H** 15ft (5m) **S** 20ft (6m). Bears double, bright pink flowers in mid-spring. Has

slender, lance-shaped, bright green leaves. Is susceptible to the fungal disease peach leaf curl. **'Prince Charming'**, illus. p.83.
P. x *persicoides*, syn. *P. amygdalopersica*. Z6–8 H8–6. **'Pollardii'** is a deciduous, spreading tree. **H** and **S** 22ft (7m). Large, 5-petaled, bright pink flowers are borne from early to mid-spring, before oval, glossy, mid-green leaves emerge. Green then brown fruits are like almonds in shape and taste.
P. **'Pink Perfection'**, illus. p.83.
P. **'Pink Shell'**, illus. p.84.
P. **'Pink Star'**. See *P. pendula* 'Stellata'.
P. sargentii, illus. p.77.
P. serotina, illus. p.66.
P. serrula, illus. p.78. Deciduous, round-headed tree. **H** and **S** 30ft (10m). Has gleaming, coppery-red bark that peels. In late spring bears small, 5-petaled, white flowers amid oval, tapering, toothed, dark green leaves that turn yellow in fall. Fruits are tiny, rounded and reddish-brown. Z6–8 H8–6.
P. serrulata var. spontanea. See *P. jamasakura*.
P. **'Shimidsu'**. See *P.* 'Shogetsu'.
P. **'Shirofugen'**, illus. p.83.
P. **'Shirotae'**, syn. *P.* 'Mount Fuji'. illus. p.82.
P. **'Shogetsu'**, syn. *P.* 'Shimidsu', illus. p.81.
P. spinosa (Blackthorn, Sloe). **'Purpurea'**, illus. p.115.
P. **'Spire'**, syn. *P.* x *hillieri* 'Spire', illus. p.82.
P. x *subhirtella* (Higan cherry, Rosebud cherry). Deciduous, spreading tree. **H** and **S** 25ft (8m). From early to mid-spring, a profusion of small, 5-petaled, pale pink flowers are produced before oval, taper-pointed, dark green leaves, which turn yellow in fall. Has small, rounded, reddish-brown fruits. Z6–8 H8–6. **'Autumnalis'** has semidouble, white flowers, pink in bud, in mild periods in winter. **'Pendula Rubra'**, syn. *P. pendula* 'Pendula Rubra', illus. p.83. **'Stellata'**. See *P. pendula* 'Stellata'.
P. **'Taihaku'**, illus. p.82.
P. tenella, illus. p.146. **'Fire Hill'** is a deciduous, bushy shrub with upright, then spreading branches. **H** and **S** 6ft (2m). Narrowly oval, glossy, dark green leaves are foil for small, almond-like, single, very deep pink flowers borne profusely from mid- to late spring, followed by small, almond-like fruits. Z6–8 H8–6.
P. tomentosa (Manchu cherry, Nanking cherry). Deciduous, bushy, dense shrub. **H** 5ft (1.5m), **S** 6ft (2m). Has small, 5-petaled, pale pink flowers, from early to mid-spring, before oval, downy, dark green leaves emerge. Fruits are spherical and bright red. Thrives in hot summers. Z2–7 H7–1.
P. **'Trailblazer'**. Deciduous, spreading tree. **H** and **S** 15ft (5m). Bears 5-petaled, white flowers, from early to mid-spring, sometimes followed by edible, plumlike, red fruits. Oval, light green, young leaves mature to deep red-purple. Z6–8 H8–6.
P. triloba **'Multiplex'**. Deciduous, bushy, spreading tree or shrub. **H** and **S** 12ft (4m). Double, pink flowers are borne in mid-spring. Has oval, dark green leaves, often 3-lobed, that turn yellow in fall. Does best against a sunny wall. Cut back young shoots to within a few buds of old wood after flowering. Z6–8 H8–6.
P. **'Ukon'**, illus. p.82.
P. **'Uzuzakura'**. See *P.* 'Hokusai'.
P. virginiana (Choke cherry, Virginian

bird cherry). Z3–8 H8–1. **'Schubert'** is a deciduous, conical tree. **H** 30ft (10m), **S** 25ft (8m). Produces dense spikes of small, star-shaped, white flowers, from mid- to late spring, followed by dark purple-red fruits. Has oval, pale green, young leaves, turning deep reddish-purple in summer.
P. **'Yae-murasaki'**, illus. p.82.
P. x *yedoensis*, illus. p.82.

PSEUDERANTHEMUM

ACANTHACEAE

Genus of evergreen perennials and shrubs, grown mainly for their foliage. Requires partial shade and fertile, well-drained soil. Water container plants freely when in full growth, moderately at other times. Tip-prune young plants to promote a bushy habit. Cut leggy plants back hard in spring. Propagate by greenwood cuttings in spring or summer. Whitefly may sometimes be troublesome.
P. atropurpureum, syn. *Eranthemum atropurpureum*. Evergreen, erect shrub. **H** 3–4ft (1–1.2m), **S** 1–2ft (30–60cm). Has oval, strongly purple-flushed leaves and, mainly in summer, short spikes of tubular, purple-marked, white flowers. Z13–15 H12–1.

PSEUDOCYDONIA

ROSACEAE

Genus of one species of deciduous or semievergreen, spring-flowering tree, grown for its bark, flowers and fruits. It is best grown against a south- or west-facing wall. Requires full sun and well-drained soil. Does well only in hot summers. Propagate by seed in fall.
P. sinensis, syn. *Cydonia sinensis*. Deciduous or semievergreen, spreading tree. **H** and **S** 20ft (6m). Has flaking bark. Shallowly cup-shaped, pink flowers, borne from mid- to late spring, are followed after hot summers by large, egg-shaped, yellow fruits. Oval, finely toothed leaves are dark green. Z6–8 H8–4.

Pseudofumaria alba. See *Corydalis ochroleuca* of gardens.
Pseudofumaria lutea. See *Corydalis lutea*.
Pseudofumaria ochroleuca. See *Corydalis ochroleuca* of gardens.

PSEUDOGYNOXYS

COMPOSITAE/ASTERACEAE

Genus of evergreen shrubs and woody-stemmed, twining climbers, grown for their large, daisylike, yellow and orange flowers. Needs sun and well-drained soil. Propagate by semiripe cuttings or layering in summer or by seed in fall. ① All parts may cause severe discomfort if ingested.
P. chenopodioides, syn. *Senecio confusus* (Mexican flame vine). Evergreen, woody-stemmed, twining climber. **H** to 10ft (3m) or more. Bears clusters of daisylike, orange-yellow flower heads, aging to orange-red, mainly in summer. Z13–15 H12–10.

PSEUDOLARIX

PINACEAE

See also CONIFERS.
P. amabilis, syn. *P. kaempferi*, illus. p.102.
P. kaempferi. See *P. amabilis*.

Pseudolobivia aurea. See *Echinopsis aurea*.
Pseudomuscari azureum. See *Muscari azureum*.

PSEUDOPANAX

SYN. NEOPANAX

ARALIACEAE

Genus of evergreen trees and shrubs, grown for their unusual foliage and fruits. Is excellent for landscaping and may also be grown in large containers. Insignificant flowers are produced in summer. Needs sun or partial shade and fertile, well-drained soil. Propagate by semiripe cuttings in summer or by seed in fall or spring.
P. crassifolius (Lancewood). Evergreen tree, unbranched for many years, then becoming round-headed. **H** 20ft (6m), **S** 6ft (2m). Dark green leaves are very variable in shape on young trees, but eventually become long, narrow, rigid and downward-pointing on older specimens. Female plants bear small, rounded, black fruits. Z8–10 H10–8.
P. ferox, illus. p.88.

PSEUDOSASA

GRAMINEAE/POACEAE

See also GRASSES, BAMBOOS, RUSHES and SEDGES.
P. japonica, syn. *Arundinaria japonica*, illus. p.287.

PSEUDOTSUGA

PINACEAE

See also CONIFERS.
P. douglasii. See *P. menziesii*.
P. menziesii, syn. *P. douglasii*, *P. taxifolia* (Douglas fir). Fast-growing, conical conifer. **H** 80ft (25m), **S** 25–40ft (8–12m). Has thick, corky, fissured, gray-brown bark. Spirally arranged, aromatic, needlelike, slightly flattened leaves, which develop from sharply pointed buds, are dark green with white bands beneath. Elliptic cones, 3–4in (8–10cm) long, with projecting bracts, are dull brown. Z5–7 H7–5. **'Fletcheri'**, **H** 10ft (3m), **S** 6–10ft (2–3m), makes a flat-topped shrub. **'Fretsii'**, **H** 20ft (6m) or more, **S** 10–12ft (3–4m), is slow-growing, with very short, dull green leaves. **var. glauca**, illus. p.96. **'Oudemansii'** is very slow-growing, with ascending branches and short, glossy leaves, dark green all over.
P. taxifolia. See *P. menziesii*.

PSEUDOWINTERA

WINTERACEAE

Genus of evergreen shrubs and trees, grown for their foliage. Needs sun or partial shade and rich, moist but well-drained soil, ideally neutral to acidic. Water container plants freely when in full growth, only moderately at other times. Pruning is tolerated, if needed. Propagate by semiripe cuttings in summer or by seed when ripe, in fall, or in spring.
P. axillaris, syn. *Drimys axillaris* (Heropito, Pepper-tree). Evergreen, rounded shrub or tree. **H** and **S** 10–25ft (3–8m). Has oval, lustrous, mid-green

leaves, blue-gray beneath. Tiny, star-shaped, greenish-yellow flowers, in spring–summer, are followed by bright red fruits. Z9–10 H10–9.

P. colorata, syn. *Drimys colorata*. Evergreen, bushy, spreading shrub. **H** 3ft (1m), **S** 5ft (1.5m). Has oval, leathery, pale yellow-green leaves, blotched with pink and narrowly edged with deep red-purple; undersides are bluish-white. Clusters of 2–5 small, star-shaped, greenish-yellow flowers are borne in mid-spring. Provide shelter in all but the mildest areas. Z9–10 H10–9.

PSYCHOPSIS
Butterfly orchid
ORCHIDACEAE

See also ORCHIDS.

P. papilio, syn. *Oncidium papilio* (Butterfly orchid), illus. p.467. Evergreen, epiphytic orchid for a warm greenhouse. **H** 6in (15cm). In summer, solitary, rich yellow-marked, orange-brown flowers, 3in (8cm) long, are borne in succession on tops of stems. Has oval, semi-rigid, mottled leaves, 4–6in (10–15cm) long. Needs good light in summer. H11–6.

PSYLLIOSTACHYS
Statice
PLUMBAGINACEAE

Genus of annuals, perennials and evergreen subshrubs, grown for cut flowers and for drying. Is suitable for coastal areas. Grow in sun and fertile, well-drained soil. If required for drying, cut flowers before they are fully open. Cut down dead stems of perennials in fall. Propagate by seed sown under glass in early spring, perennials and subshrubs also by softwood cuttings in spring. Botrytis and powdery mildew may be troublesome.

P. suworowii, syn. *Limonium suworowii*, *Statice suworowii*. Fairly slow-growing, erect, branching annual. **H** 18in (45cm), **S** 12in (30cm). Has lance-shaped leaves. Bears branching spikes of small, tubular, pink to purple flowers in summer and early fall. H12–6.

PTELEA
RUTACEAE

Genus of deciduous trees and shrubs, grown for their foliage and fruits. Needs sun and fertile soil. Propagate species by softwood cuttings in summer or by seed in fall, selected forms by softwood cuttings only in summer.

P. trifoliata (Hop tree, Stinking ash). Deciduous, bushy, spreading tree or shrub. **H** and **S** 22ft (7m). Produces aromatic, dark green leaves divided into 3 narrowly oval leaflets. Clusters of small, star-shaped, green flowers, from early to mid-summer, are followed by clusters of winged, pale green fruits. Z5–9 H9–5. **'Aurea'**, illus. p.138.

PTERIS
Brake, Table fern
PTERIDACEAE/ADIANTACEAE

Genus of deciduous, semievergreen or evergreen ferns. Needs partial or full shade and moist, peaty soil. Remove faded fronds

regularly. Propagate by division in spring or by spores in summer.

P. cretica (Cretan brake). Evergreen or semievergreen fern. **H** 18in (45cm), **S** 12in (30cm). Produces triangular to broadly oval, divided, pale green fronds that have finger-like pinnae. Z12–15 H12–10.
'Albolineata', syn. *P. cretica* var. *albolineata* has pale green fronds centrally variegated with creamy-white. **'Mayi'**, **H** 12in (30cm), has crested frond tips.
'Wimsettii', illus. p.478. is compact, with the margins of pinnae deeply and irregularly lobed.
P. cretica var. **albolineata**. See *P. cretica* 'Albolineata'.
P. ensiformis (Sword brake). Deciduous or semievergreen fern. **H** 12in (30cm), **S** 9in (23cm). Dark green fronds, often grayish-white around midribs, are coarsely divided into finger-shaped pinnae. Z10–11 H12–10.
'Arguta', **H** 18in (45cm), has deeper green fronds with central, silver-white marks.

PTEROCARYA
Wingnut
JUGLANDACEAE

Genus of deciduous trees, grown for their foliage and catkins. Needs full sun and deep, moist but well-drained soil. Remove suckers regularly. Propagate by softwood cuttings in summer, by suckers in fall or by seed, when ripe, in fall.

P. fraxinifolia (Caucasian wingnut). Deciduous, spreading tree. **H** 80ft (25m), **S** 70ft (20m). Large, ashlike, glossy, dark green leaves turn yellow in fall. Long, green catkins are borne in summer, the females developing winged, green then brown fruits. Z6–9 H9–6.
P. x rehderiana, illus. p.65.
P. stenoptera (Chinese wingnut). Deciduous, spreading tree. **H** 70ft (20m), **S** 50ft (15m). Ashlike, bright green leaves, with winged stalk, turn yellow in fall. Produces long, green catkins in summer; females develop winged, pink-tinged, green fruits. Z7–9 H9–7.

PTEROCELTIS
ULMACEAE

Genus of one species of deciduous tree, with inconspicuous flowers in summer, grown for its foliage and fruits. Needs full sun and well-drained soil. Does best in hot summers. Propagate by seed in fall.

P. tatarinowii. Deciduous, spreading tree with arching branches. **H** 40ft (12m), **S** 30ft (10m). Has peeling, gray bark and oval, dark green leaves, to 4in (10cm) long, with toothed margins. In fall bears small, spherical, green fruits, with broad, circular wing.

PTEROCEPHALUS
DIPSACACEAE/CAPRIFOLIACEAE

Genus of compact, summer-flowering annuals, perennials and semievergreen subshrubs, grown for their scabious-like flower heads and feathery seed heads. Is useful for rock gardens. Requires sun and well-drained soil. Propagate by softwood or semiripe cuttings in summer or by seed in fall. Self-seeds moderately.
P. parnassi. See *P. perennis*.
P. perennis, syn. *P. parnassi*, illus. p.364.

PTEROSTYRAX
STYRACACEAE

Genus of deciduous trees and shrubs, grown for their foliage and fragrant flowers. Requires sun or partial shade and deep, well-drained, neutral to acid soil. Propagate by softwood or semiripe cuttings in summer or by seed in fall.
P. hispida, illus. p.73.

Ptilotrichum spinosum. See *Alyssum spinosum*.

PUERARIA
LEGUMINOSAE/PAPILIONACEAE

Genus of deciduous, woody-stemmed or herbaceous, twining climbers. Needs full sun and well-drained soil. Propagate by seed in spring.
P. hirsuta. See *P. lobata*.
P. lobata, syn. *P. hirsuta*, *P. montana* var. *lobata*, *P. thunbergiana* (Japanese arrowroot). Deciduous, woody-stemmed, twining climber with hairy stems. **H** to 15ft (5m), or to 100ft (30m) in the wild. Leaves have 3 broadly oval leaflets. In summer produces racemes, to 12in (30cm) long, of small, scented, sweet-pea-like, reddish-purple flowers, followed by long, slender, hairy pods, 2¹⁄₂–3in (6–8cm) long. In cold areas is best grown as an annual. Z7–9 H9–3.
P. montana var. **lobata**. See *P. lobata*.
P. thunbergiana. See *P. lobata*.

PULMONARIA
Lungwort
BORAGINACEAE

Genus of mainly spring-flowering perennials, some of which are semievergreen with small, overwintering rosettes of leaves. Prefers full or partial shade and moist but well-drained soil. Propagate by division in spring or fall.
P. angustifolia (Blue cowslip, Blue lungwort). Clump-forming, usually deciduous perennial. **H** 9in (23cm), **S** 8–12in (20–30cm) or more. Has lance-shaped, unspotted, mid-green leaves, 16in (40cm) long. In early spring produces heads of tubular, 5-lobed, borage-like, sometimes pink-tinged, deep blue flowers. Z2–7 H8–1. **'Azurea'**, **H** and **S** 12in (30cm), has dark green leaves and produces pinkish buds that open to rich gentian-blue flowers.
P. 'Beth's Pink'. Semievergreen, clump-forming perennial. **H** 10in (25cm), **S** 20in (50cm). Has oval to lance-shaped, hairy, dark green leaves spotted with silvery-white. In early and mid-spring bears heads of tubular, 5-lobed, borage-like, purplish-pink flowers. Z5–8 H8–5.
P. 'Blue Ensign'. Semievergreen, clump-forming perennial. **H** 10in (25cm), **S** 20in (50cm). Has broadly oval, hairy, dark green leaves. In early and mid-spring produces heads of tubular, 5-lobed, borage-like, rich blue flowers. Z5–8 H8–5.
P. 'Cotton Cool'. Semievergreen, clump-forming perennial. **H** 12in (30cm), **S** 20in (50cm). Has narrowly elliptic, hairy, dark green leaves marked almost entirely with silver. In early and mid-spring bears heads of tubular, 5-lobed, borage-like, pink and blue flowers.

P. 'Excalibur', illus. p.261. Vigorous, semievergreen, clump-forming perennial. **H** 12in (30cm), **S** 20in (50cm). Has narrowly lance-shaped, hairy, silver leaves, with narrow, green edge. In early and mid-spring, heads of tubular, 5-lobed, borage-like, light blue flowers open from pink buds. Z4–8 H8–1.
P. 'Glacier'. Semievergreen, clump-forming perennial. **H** 8–12in (20–30cm), **S** 20in (50cm). Has broadly oval, hairy, mid-green leaves spotted with silver. In early and mid-spring produces heads of tubular, 5-lobed, borage-like, pale blue and pale pink flowers.
P. 'Ice Ballet'. Vigorous, semievergreen, clump-forming perennial. **H** 12in (30cm), **S** 20in (50cm). Has broadly oval, hairy, mildew-resistant, mid-green leaves well spotted with silver. In early and mid-spring bears heads of large, tubular, 5-lobed, borage-like, pure white flowers.
P. 'Lewis Palmer', illus. p.261. Vigorous, semievergreen, clump-forming perennial. **H** 14in (35cm), **S** 20in (50cm). Has oval, hairy, silver-spotted, mid-green leaves. In early and mid-spring, heads of tubular, 5-lobed, borage-like, clear blue flowers open from pinkish buds. Z5–8 H8–5.
P. longifolia (Longleaf lungwort). Clump-forming, deciduous perennial. **H** 12in (30cm), **S** 18in (45cm). Bears very narrowly lance-shaped, dark green leaves spotted with silvery-white. Heads of tubular, 5-lobed, borage-like, vivid blue flowers are produced in late spring. Z3–8 H8–4.
'Bertram Anderson' has long leaves especially well spotted with silver and bears brighter blue flowers.
P. 'Margery Fish', illus. p.261. Semievergreen, clump-forming perennial. **H** 12in (30cm), **S** 20in (50cm). Has narrowly lance-shaped, hairy, mid-green leaves marked heavily with silver. In early spring, heads of tubular, 5-lobed, borage-like, pink flowers gradually turn to blue as they age. Z6–8 H8–6.
P. 'Mary Mottram', illus. p.261. Vigorous, semievergreen, clump-forming perennial. **H** 14in (35cm), **S** 20in (50cm). Has oval, hairy leaves marked heavily with silver with narrow, green margin. In early spring bears heads of large, tubular, 5-lobed, borage-like, pink and violet flowers.
P. 'Mawson's Blue', illus. p.261. Semievergreen, clump-forming perennial. **H** 8–12in (20–30cm), **S** 20in (50cm). Has oval, hairy, mid-green leaves, bronze tinged when young. In early spring, heads of tubular, 5-lobed, borage-like, azure-blue flowers are often produced before leaves fully develop. Z5–8 H8–5.
P. officinalis 'Sissinghurst White', syn. *P. saccharata* 'Sissinghurst White', illus. p.254.
P. Opal ('Ocupol'), illus. p.261. Semievergreen, clump-forming perennial. **H** 10in (25cm), **S** 20in (50cm). Has oval, hairy, silver-spotted, mid-green leaves. In spring, heads of tubular, 5-lobed, borage-like, glowing, pale blue flowers open from pink buds.
P. rubra (Red lungwort), illus. p.261. Semievergreen, clump-forming perennial. **H** 12in (30cm), **S** 24in (60cm). Has oval, velvety, mid-green leaves. Heads of tubular,

P

673

5-lobed, borage-like, brick-red flowers are borne from late winter to early spring. Z5–8 H8–3. **'David Ward'** (illus. p.261) has narrow, white-edged, soft green leaves and pale red flowers. Needs a sheltered spot.

P. saccharata (Bethlehem sage). Semievergreen, clump-forming perennial. **H** 12in (30cm). **S** 24in (60cm). Long, elliptic leaves are variably spotted with creamy-white. In spring bears funnel-shaped flowers, opening pink and turning to blue. Z4–8 H8–1. **'Leopard'** has silver-spotted, dark green leaves and reddish-pink flowers that fade to lilac. **'Mrs. Moon'** bears leaves spotted liberally with silver and heads of pinkish-mauve flowers. **'Sissinghurst White'**. See *P. officinalis* 'Sissinghurst White'.

P. 'Weetwood Blue'. Usually semievergreen, clump-forming perennial. **H** 8in (20cm). **S** 20in (50cm). Has lance-shaped, hairy, green leaves occasionally spotted with white. In spring bears heads of tubular, 5-lobed, borage-like, clear blue flowers that darken as they age.

PULSATILLA

RANUNCULACEAE

Genus of perennials, some of which are evergreen, grown for their large, feathery leaves, upright or pendent, bell- or cup-shaped flowers, covered in fine hairs, and feathery seed heads. Has fibrous, woody rootstocks. Leaves increase in size after flowering time. Is suitable for large rock gardens. Needs full sun and rich, well-drained soil. Resents disturbance to roots. Propagate by root cuttings in winter or by seed when fresh. ① All parts of the plant may cause mild stomach upset if ingested, and, in rare instances, contact with the sap may irritate skin.

P. alpina, illus. p.332. **subsp. apiifolia**, syn. *P. alpina* subsp. *sulphurea* is a clump-forming perennial. **H** 6–12in (15–30cm). **S** to 4in (10cm). Has feathery, soft green leaves. Bears upright, bell-shaped, soft pale yellow flowers in spring, followed by feathery, silvery seed heads. **subsp. sulphurea**. See *P. alpina* subsp. *apiifolia*.

P. halleri, illus. p.334. **subsp. grandis**, syn. *P. vulgaris* subsp. *grandis* is a clump-forming perennial. **H** and **S** 6–9in (15–23cm). In spring, before feathery, light green leaves emerge, bears large, upright, shallowly bell-shaped, lavender-blue flowers, with bright yellow centers. Flower stems rapidly elongate as the feathery, silvery seed heads mature.

P. occidentalis. Clump-forming perennial. **H** 8in (20cm). **S** 6in (15cm). In late spring to early summer, solitary, nodding buds develop into erect, goblet-shaped, white flowers, stained blue-violet at base outside and sometimes flushed pink, followed by feathery, silvery seed heads. Bears feathery leaves. Is extremely difficult to grow and flower well at low altitudes. Z5–7 H7–5.

P. vernalis, illus. p.349.

P. vulgaris, illus. p.334. **subsp. grandis**. See *P. halleri* subsp. *grandis*.

PUNICA

Pomegranate

LYTHRACEAE/PUNICACEAE

Genus of deciduous, summer-flowering shrubs and trees, grown for their bright red flowers and yellow to orange-red fruits,

which ripen and become edible only in warm climates. Needs a sheltered, sunny position and well-drained soil. Propagate by seed in spring or by semiripe cuttings in summer.

P. granatum (Pomegranate). Deciduous, rounded shrub or tree. **H** and **S** 6–25ft (2–8m). Has narrowly oblong leaves and, in summer, funnel-shaped, bright red flowers, with crumpled petals. Fruits are spherical and deep yellow to orange. May be grown in a southern or eastern aspect, either free-standing or, in frost-prone climates, against a wall. Z7–10 H12–1. **var. nana**, illus. p.340.

PUSCHKINIA

LILIACEAE/ASPARAGACEAE

Genus of dwarf, *Scilla*-like bulbs, grown for their early spring flowers. Needs sun or partial shade and rich soil that has grit or sand added to ensure good drainage. Plant in fall. Dies down in summer. Propagate by offsets in late summer or by seed in fall.

P. libanotica. See *P. scilloides* var. *libanotica*.

P. scilloides var. libanotica, syn. *P. libanotica*, illus. p.421. **var. libanotica** **'Alba'**, illus. p.415.

PUYA

BROMELIACEAE

Genus of evergreen, rosette-forming perennials and shrubs, grown for their overall appearance. Requires full light and well-drained soil. Water moderately in growing season, sparingly at other times. Propagate by seed or offsets in spring.

P. alpestris. Evergreen perennial with sturdy, branched, prostrate stems. **H** to 6ft (2m). **S** 10ft (3m). Linear, tapering, arching, bright green leaves are fleshy, with hooked, spiny teeth along edges and dense, white scales beneath. Tubular, deep metallic-blue flowers, aging to purple-red, are borne in stiff, erect panicles in early summer. Z9–15 H12–1.

P. chilensis, illus. p.471. Evergreen, upright perennial with short, woody stem. **H** and **S** to 6ft (2m). Stem is crowned by dense rosette of linear, tapering, arching, fleshy, gray-green leaves, with margins of hooked, spiny teeth. Bears tubular, metallic- or greenish-yellow flowers, in erect, branched panicles, in summer. Z9–11 H11–1.

PYCNOSTACHYS

LABIATAE/LAMIACEAE

Genus of bushy perennials, grown for their whorled clusters of flowers. Needs bright light and fertile, well-drained soil. Propagate by stem cuttings in early summer.

P. dawei, illus. p.473.

P. urticifolia. Strong-growing, erect perennial with square stems. **H** 3–6ft (1–2m), **S** 8–24in (20–60cm). Has oval, toothed, hairy, mid-green leaves. Bears whorls of small, tubular, bright blue flowers, in racemes, in winter. Z13–15 H12–1.

PYRACANTHA

Firethorn

ROSACEAE

Genus of evergreen, spiny, summer-flowering shrubs, grown for their foliage, flowers and fruits. Requires a sheltered site

in sun or partial shade and fertile soil. To produce a compact habit on a plant grown against a wall, train and cut back long shoots after flowering. Propagate by semiripe cuttings in summer. Is susceptible to scab and fireblight. ① The seeds may cause mild stomach upset if ingested.

P. angustifolia. Evergreen, bushy, dense shrub. **H** and **S** 10ft (3m). Has narrowly oblong leaves, dark green above, gray beneath. Bears clusters of small, 5-petaled, white flowers in early summer, followed by spherical, orange-yellow fruits in fall. Z4–8 H12–1.

P. atalantioides. Vigorous, evergreen shrub, part upright, part arching. **H** 15ft (5m), **S** 12ft (4m). Leaves are glossy and dark green. Large clusters of small, 5-petaled, white flowers, in early summer, are followed by spherical, red fruits in early fall. Z6–9 H9–6. **'Aurea'**, illus. p.118.

P. coccinea (Scarlet firethorn). Evergreen, dense, bushy shrub. **H** and **S** 12ft (4m). Dense clusters of small, 5-petaled, white flowers are produced amid oval, dark green leaves in early summer and are followed by spherical, bright red fruits. Z6–9 H9–6. **'Lalandei'** has larger leaves and larger, orange-red fruits.

P. 'Golden Charmer', illus. p.141.

P. 'Golden Dome', illus. p.144.

P. 'Mohave', illus. p.209.

P. 'Orange Glow'. Evergreen, upright, dense shrub. **H** 15ft (5m), **S** 10ft (3m). Has oblong, glossy, dark green leaves. Clusters of small, 5-petaled, white flowers, in early summer, are followed by spherical, orange fruits. Z7–9 H9–7.

P. rogersiana. Evergreen, upright then arching shrub. **H** and **S** 10ft (3m). Leaves are narrowly oblong, glossy and bright green. Produces clusters of small, 5-petaled, white flowers, in early summer, followed by spherical, orange-red or yellow fruits. Z8–9 H9–6.

P. 'Waterer's Orange'. See *P. x watereri*.

P. x watereri, syn. *P.* 'Waterer's Orange', illus. p.128.

Pyrethropsis hosmariense. See *Rhodanthemum hosmariense*.

Pyrethrum 'Brenda'. See *Tanacetum coccineum* 'Brenda'.

Pyrethrum coccineum. See *Tanacetum coccineum*.

Pyrethrum parthenium. See *Tanacetum parthenium*.

Pyrethrum roseum. See *Tanacetum coccineum*.

PYROLA

Shinleaf, Wintergreen

PYROLACEAE/ERICACEAE

Genus of evergreen, spreading, spring- and summer-flowering perennials. Is suitable for light woodlands. Needs partial shade, cool conditions and well-drained, peaty, acidic soil. Resents disturbance. Propagate by seed in fall or spring or by division in spring.

P. asarifolia. Evergreen, rosette-forming perennial. **H** 6–10in (15–25cm), **S** 6in (15cm) or more. Has kidney-shaped, leathery, glossy, light green leaves. Bears tubular, pale to deep pink flowers in spring. Z5–8 H8–5.

P. rotundifolia (Round-leaved wintergreen, Wild lily-of-the-valley). Creeping, evergreen, rosette-forming

perennial. **H** 9in (23cm), **S** 12in (30cm). Produces rounded, leathery, glossy, mid-green leaves and, in late spring and early summer, sprays of fragrant, white flowers that resemble lily-of-the-valley. Z5–8 H8–5.

PYROSTEGIA

BIGNONIACEAE

Genus of evergreen, woody-stemmed, tendril climbers, grown for their flowers. Needs full light and fertile, well-drained soil. Water regularly, less in winter. Provide support. Thin stems after flowering. Propagate by semiripe cuttings or layering in summer.

P. ignea. See *P. venusta*.

P. venusta, syn. *P. ignea*, illus. p.464.

PYRUS

Pear

ROSACEAE

Genus of deciduous, spring-flowering trees, grown for their habit, foliage, flowers and edible fruits (pears). Prefers full sun and needs well-drained soil. Propagate species by seed in fall, cultivars by budding in summer or by grafting in winter. Many species are susceptible to fireblight and scab and, in North America, pear decline.

P. amygdaliformis. Deciduous, spreading tree. **H** 30ft (10m), **S** 25ft (8m). Lance-shaped leaves are gray when young, maturing to glossy, dark green. Clusters of 5-petaled, white flowers, in mid-spring, are followed by small, brownish fruits. Z7–9 H9–7.

P. calleryana (Callery pear). Deciduous, broadly conical tree. **H** and **S** to 50ft (15m). Oval, glossy, dark green leaves often turn red in fall. Bears 5-petaled, white flowers, from mid- to late spring, followed by small, brownish fruits. Z5–8 H8–3. **'Bradford'**, S30ft (10m), is resistant to fireblight. **'Chanticleer'**, illus. p.71.

P. communis (Common pear). Z5–9 H9–5. **'Beech Hill'** is a deciduous, narrowly conical tree. **H** 30ft (10m), **S** 22ft (7m). Oval, glossy, dark green leaves often turn orange and red in fall. From mid- to late spring bears 5-petaled, white flowers as leaves emerge, followed by small, brownish fruits.

P. elaeagrifolia. Deciduous, spreading, thorny tree. **H** and **S** 25ft (8m). Has lance-shaped, gray-green leaves. Produces loose clusters of 5-petaled, creamy-white flowers, in mid-spring, followed by small, pear-shaped, brownish fruits. Z5–9 H9–5.

P. salicifolia (Willow-leaved pear). Deciduous, mound-shaped tree with slightly drooping branches. **H** 15–25ft (5–8m), **S** 12ft (4m). White flowers, with 5 petals, are borne as lance-shaped, gray leaves emerge in mid-spring. Fruits are small and brownish. Z5–9 H9–5. **'Pendula'**, illus. p.88.

QR

Quamoclit coccinea. See *Ipomoea coccinea.*
Quamoclit lobata. See *Ipomoea lobata.*
Quamoclit pennata. See *Ipomoea quamoclit.*

QUERCUS
Oak
FAGACEAE

Genus of deciduous or evergreen trees and shrubs, grown for their habit, foliage and, in some deciduous species, fall color. Produces insignificant flowers from late spring to early summer, followed by egg-shaped to rounded, brownish fruits (acorns). Needs sun or partial shade and deep, well-drained soil; except where stated otherwise, will tolerate limestone. Propagate species by seed in fall, selected forms and hybrids by grafting in late winter. May be affected, though not usually seriously, by mildew and various galls, and in North America by oak wilt.

Q. acutissima (Sawtooth oak). Deciduous, round-headed tree. **H** and **S** 50ft (15m). Has sweet-chestnut-like, glossy, dark green leaves, edged with bristle-tipped teeth, that last until late in year. Z5–8 H8–3.
Q. aegilops. See *Q. ithaburensis* subsp. *macrolepis.*
Q. agrifolia, illus. p.80.
Q. alba, illus. p.66.
Q. aliena (Oriental white oak). Deciduous, spreading tree. **H** 50ft (15m), **S** 40ft (12m). Has large, oblong, prominently toothed, glossy, dark green leaves. Z6–9 H9–6.
Q. alnifolia (Golden oak of Cyprus). Evergreen, spreading tree. **H** 20ft (6m), **S** 15ft (5m). Rounded, leathery leaves are glossy, dark green above, with mustard-yellow or greenish-yellow felt beneath.
Q. canariensis, illus. p.62.
Q. castaneifolia, illus. p.64.
Q. cerris (Turkey oak). Fast-growing, deciduous, spreading tree of stately habit. **H** 100ft (30m), **S** 80ft (25m). Oblong, glossy, dark green leaves are deeply lobed. Thrives on shallow, chalky soil. Z7–9 H9–7. **'Argenteovariegata',** illus. p.73.
Q. coccifera (Kermes oak). Evergreen, bushy, compact tree or shrub. **H** and **S** 15ft (5m). Holly-like leaves are glossy, dark green and rigid, with spiny margins. Z7–9 H9–7.
Q. coccinea, illus. p.65. **'Splendens'** is a deciduous, round-headed tree. **H** 70ft (20m), **S** 50ft (15m). Oblong, glossy, mid-green leaves, with deep, toothlike lobes, turn deep scarlet in fall. Prefers acidic soil. Z5–9 H9–5.
Q. dentata (Daimyo oak). Deciduous, spreading, sturdy-branched tree of rugged habit. **H** 50ft (15m), **S** 30ft (10m). Has oval, lobed, dark green leaves, 12in (30cm) or more long. Prefers acidic soil. Z6–8 H8–6.
Q. ellipsoidalis, illus. p.65.
Q. frainetto, illus. p.64.
Q. garryana, illus. p.74.
Q. x heterophylla, illus. p.77.
Q. x hispanica 'Lucombeana', syn. *Q. x lucombeana* 'William Lucombe', illus. p.68.
Q. ilex (Holly oak, Holm oak). Evergreen, round-headed tree. **H** 80ft (25m), **S** 70ft (20m). Glossy, dark green leaves are silvery-gray when young and very variably shaped, but are most often oval. Thrives on shallow chalk and is excellent for an exposed, coastal position. Z4–8 H9–2.
Q. imbricaria (Shingle oak). Deciduous, spreading tree. **H** 70ft (20m), **S** 50ft (15m). Produces long, narrow leaves that are yellowish when young, dark green in summer and yellowish-brown in fall. Z5–8 H8–4.
Q. ithaburensis subsp. macrolepis, syn. *Q. aegilops, Q. macrolepis,* illus. p.75.
Q. laurifolia, illus. p.64.
Q. x lucombeana 'William Lucombe'. See *Q. x hispanica* 'Lucombeana'.
Q. macranthera, illus. p.61.
Q. macrocarpa, illus. p.75.
Q. macrolepis. See *Q. ithaburensis* subsp. *macrolepis.*
Q. marilandica, illus. p.75.
Q. mongolica subsp. crispula var. grosseserrata. Deciduous, spreading tree. **H** 70ft (20m), **S** 50ft (15m). Has large, oblong, lobed, dark green leaves, with prominent, triangular teeth.
Q. muehlenbergii, illus. p.62.
Q. myrsinifolia, illus. p.80.
Q. nigra, illus. p.63.
Q. palustris, illus. p.66.
Q. petraea (Durmast oak). Deciduous, spreading tree. **H** 100ft (30m), **S** 80ft (25m). Has oblong, lobed, leathery, dark green leaves, with yellow stalks. Z5–8 H8–5.
'Columna', illus. p.63.
Q. phellos, illus. p.67.
Q. pontica (Armenian oak). Deciduous, sometimes shrubby tree with upright, sturdy branches and broadly oval head. **H** 20ft (6m), **S** 15ft (5m). Large, oval, toothed, glossy, bright green leaves turn yellow in fall.
Q. robur (English oak, Pedunculate oak). Deciduous, spreading, rugged tree. **H** and **S** 80ft (25m). Bears oblong, wavy, lobed, dark green leaves. Z5–8 H8–3.
'Concordia', **H** 30ft (10m), is slow-growing and has golden-yellow, young leaves that become yellowish-green in mid-summer.
f. fastigiata, illus. p.62.
Q. rubra, illus. p.65. **'Aurea',** illus. p.72.
Q. suber (Cork oak), illus. p.78. Evergreen, round-headed tree. **H** and **S** 70ft (20m). Has thick, corky bark. Oval, leathery leaves are glossy, dark green above and grayish beneath. Z7–9 H9–7.
Q. x turneri, illus. p.68.
Q. velutina (Black oak). Fast-growing, deciduous, spreading tree. **H** 100ft (30m), **S** 80ft (25m). Large, oblong, lobed, glossy, dark green leaves turn reddish-brown in fall. Z4–8 H8–1.

QUISQUALIS
COMBRETACEAE

Genus of evergreen or deciduous, scandent shrubs and twining climbers, grown for their flowers. Needs full light or partial shade and rich, moist but well-drained soil. Water freely when in full growth, less in cold weather. Stems need support. Thin out crowded growth in spring. Propagate by seed in spring or by semiripe cuttings in summer.

Q. indica, syn. *Combretum indicum,* illus. p.462.

RAMONDA
GESNERIACEAE

Genus of evergreen perennials, grown for their rosettes of rounded, crinkled, hairy leaves and for their flowers. Is useful for rock gardens and peat walls. Prefers partial shade and moist soil. Water plants well if they curl in a dry spell. Propagate by rooting offsets in early summer or by leaf cuttings or seed in early fall.

R. myconi, syn. *R. pyrenaica,* illus. p.369.
R. nathaliae. Evergreen, basal-rosetted perennial. **H** and **S** 4in (10cm). Has small, pale green leaves. In late spring and early summer bears umbels of small, outward-facing, flattish, white or lavender flowers, with yellow anthers. Z6–7 H7–6.
R. pyrenaica. See *R. myconi.*
R. serbica. Evergreen, basal-rosetted perennial. **H** and **S** 4in (10cm). Is similar to *R. nathaliae,* but has cup-shaped, lilac-blue flowers and dark violet-blue anthers. May be difficult to grow. Z6–7 H7–6.

RANUNCULUS
Buttercup, Crowfoot
RANUNCULACEAE

Genus of annuals, aquatics and perennials, some of which are evergreen or semievergreen, grown mainly for their flowers. Many species grow from a thickened rootstock or a cluster of tubers. Some are invasive. Aquatic species are seldom cultivated. Needs sun or partial shade and moist but well-drained soil. Propagate by seed when fresh or by division in spring or fall. ① Contact with the sap may irritate skin.

R. aconitifolius, illus. p.223. **'Flore Pleno',** illus. p.230.
R. acris (Tall buttercup). **'Flore Pleno',** illus. p.276.
R. alpestris, illus. p.349.
R. amplexicaulis. Upright perennial. **H** 10in (25cm), **S** 4in (10cm). Has narrowly oval, blue-gray leaves. In early summer produces clusters of shallowly cup-shaped, white flowers, with yellow anthers. Needs rich soil. Z4–8 H8–1.
R. aquatilis (Water crowfoot). Aquatic annual or usually evergreen perennial. **H** 1/2in (1cm), **S** indefinite. Submerged, branched, slender stems bear dark green leaves, with many threadlike segments; floating leaves are kidney-shaped to rounded, deeply divided into 3–7 lobes. In mid-summer produces solitary, bowl- or saucer-shaped, white-based, yellow flowers, on water surface. Z5–8 H8–5.
R. asiaticus, illus. p.410. **var. flavus,** illus. p.412.
R. bulbosus 'Speciosus Plenus' of gardens. See *R. constantinopolitanus* 'Plenus'.
R. bullatus. Clump-forming perennial with thick, fibrous roots. **H** 2–3in (5–8cm), **S** 3–4in (8–10cm). Has fragrant, shallowly cup-shaped, bright yellow flowers in fall. Oblong to oval, puckered, dark green leaves have sharply toothed tips. Is suitable for an alpine house or rock garden. Z7–9 H9–7.
R. calandrinioides, illus. p.346.
R. constantinopolitanus 'Plenus', syn. *R. bulbosus* 'Speciosus Plenus', *R. gouanii* 'Plenus', *R. speciosus* 'Plenus', illus. p.275.
R. crenatus. Semievergreen, rosetted perennial with thick, fibrous roots. **H** and

S 4in (10cm). Produces rounded, toothed, green leaves and, in summer, short stems bearing 1 or 2 shallowly cup-shaped, white flowers just above foliage. May also be propagated by removing a flower stem at its first joint in summer; rosettes will form and may then be rooted. Rarely sets seed in cultivation. Is suitable for an alpine house or rock garden. Z5–7 H7–5.
R. ficaria, syn. *Ficaria verna* (Lesser celandine). Z4–8 H8–1. **var. albus,** syn. *R. ficaria* 'Albus' illus. p.349. **var. aurantiacus,** syn. *R. ficaria* 'Aurantiacus', illus. p.359. **'Brazen Hussy'** is a mat-forming, tuberous perennial. **H** 2in (5cm), **S** to 8in (20cm). Has heart-shaped, purple-bronze leaves. Shallowly cup-shaped, glossy, sulfur-yellow flowers, with bronze undersides, are produced in early spring. Dies down in late spring. May spread rapidly. Is good for a wild garden. **var. flore-pleno.** See *R. ficaria* Flore Pleno Group. **Flore Pleno Group,** syn. *R. ficaria* 'Flore Pleno', *R. ficaria* var. *flore-pleno,* illus. p.357.
R. glacialis. Hummock-forming perennial with fibrous roots. **H** 2–10in (5–25cm), **S** 2in (5cm) or more. Bears rounded, deeply lobed, glossy, dark green leaves. In late spring and early summer produces clusters of shallowly cup-shaped, white or pink flowers. Is very difficult to grow at low altitudes. Is suitable for a screen or alpine house. Prefers rich, moist, acid soil that is drier in winter. Slugs may be troublesome. Z3–5 H5–1.
R. gouanii 'Plenus'. See *R. constantinopolitanus* 'Plenus'.
R. gramineus, illus. p.345.
R. lingua, illus. p.444. **'Grandiflorus'** is a deciduous, perennial, marginal water plant. **H** 3ft (1m), **S** 1ft (30cm). Has sturdy, pinkish-green stems, lance-shaped, glaucous leaves and, in late spring, racemes of large, saucer-shaped, yellow flowers. Z4–9 H9–1.
R. lyallii (Giant buttercup, Mount Cook lily). Evergreen, sturdy, upright, tufted perennial. **H** and **S** 12in (30cm) or more. Has rounded, leathery, dark green leaves. In summer bears panicles of large, shallowly cup-shaped, white flowers. Is very difficult to flower in hot, dry climates. Is suitable for an alpine house. Rarely sets seed in cultivation. Z4–9 H9–1.
R. montanus 'Molten Gold'. Clump-forming, compact perennial. **H** 6in (15cm), **S** 4in (10cm). Leaves are rounded and 3-lobed. Flower stems produce solitary, shallowly cup-shaped, shiny, bright golden-yellow flower in early summer. Is useful for a sunny rock garden. Z5–8 H8–5.
R. speciosus 'Plenus'. See *R. constantinopolitanus* 'Plenus'.

RANZANIA
BERBERIDACEAE

Genus of one species of perennial, grown for its unusual appearance as well as its flowers. Is ideal for woodland gardens. Prefers full or partial shade and rich, moist soil. Propagate by division in spring or by seed in fall.

R. japonica. Upright perennial. **H** 18in (45cm), **S** 12in (30cm). Produces 3-parted, fresh green leaves and, in early summer, small clusters of nodding, shallowly cup-shaped, pale mauve flowers. Z4–8 H8–1.

RAOULIA
COMPOSITAE/ASTERACEAE

Genus of evergreen, mat-forming perennials, grown for their foliage. Some species are suitable for alpine houses, others for rock gardens. Needs sun or partial shade and moist but well-drained, gritty, peaty soil. Propagate by seed when fresh or by division in spring.

R. australis, illus. p.376.
R. eximia (Vegetable sheep). Evergreen, cushion-forming perennial. **H** 1in (2.5cm), **S** 2in (5cm). Has oblong to oval, overlapping, woolly, gray leaves. In late spring-summer bears small, rounded heads of yellowish-white flowers. Is suitable for an alpine house. Prefers partial shade. Z7–8 H8–7.
R. haastii, illus. p.376.
R. hookeri var. albosericea, illus. p.374.
R. leontopodium. See *Leucogenes leontopodium*.

RAVENALA
Traveler's tree
STRELITZIACEAE

Genus of one species of evergreen, palm-like tree, grown for its foliage and overall appearance. Is related to *Strelitzia*. Requires full light and rich, well-drained soil. Water container specimens freely in summer, less in winter or when temperatures are low. Propagate by seed in spring. Red spider mite may be troublesome.

R. madagascariensis. Evergreen, upright, fan-shaped tree. **H** and **S** to 30ft (10m). Has banana-like, long-stalked leaves, 10–20ft (3–6m) long, with expanded stalk bases. Groups of boat-shaped spathes, with 6-parted, white flowers, are produced from leaf axils in summer. Z11 H12–1.

REBUTIA
CACTACEAE

Genus of mostly clump-forming, spherical to columnar, perennial cacti, grown for their flowers, which are produced in profusion from plant bases, usually 2–3 years after raising from seed. Much-ribbed, tuberculate, green stems have short spines. A few species are sometimes included in *Aylostera*. Requires sun or partial shade and well-drained soil. Propagate by seed in spring or summer.

R. arenacea, syn. *Sulcorebutia arenacea*, illus. p.496.
R. aureiflora. See *R. einsteinii* subsp. *aureiflora*.
R. 'Carnival', illus. p.483.
R. deminuta, syn. *R. spegazziniana*, illus. p.486.
R. einsteinii subsp. aureiflora, syn. *R. aureiflora*. Clump-forming, perennial cactus. **H** 4in (10cm), **S** 8in (20cm). Dark green stem, often tinged violet-red, has stiff, radial spines and longer, soft, central spines. Bears masses of yellow, violet or red flowers in late spring.
R. fiebrigii, syn. *R. muscula*, illus. p.496.
R. 'Jenny', illus. p.484.
R. krainziana. See *R. minuscula*.
R. marsoneri. See *R. minuscula*.
R. minuscula, syn. *R. krainziana*, *R. marsoneri*, *R. senilis*, *R. violaciflora*, illus. p.486.

R. muscula. See *R. fiebrigii*.
R. neocumingii, syn. *Weingartia neocumingii*. Spherical, perennial cactus. **H** and **S** 4in (10cm). Stem is tuberculate and green. Areoles bear dense clusters of yellow spines, some thicker than others, and cup-shaped, dark yellow flowers in spring. Z12–15 H12–10.
R. pygmaea, syn. *Lobivia pygmaea*. Clump-forming, columnar, perennial cactus. **H** 2in (5cm), **S** 4in (10cm). Very short, comb-like spines are pressed against gray- to purple-green stem. Trumpet-shaped, pink to salmon or rose-purple flowers are borne in spring. Prefers a sunny position. Z12–15 H12–10.
R. rauschii. See *R. steinmannii*.
R. senilis. See *R. minuscula*.
R. spegazziniana. See *R. deminuta*.
R. steinbachii subsp. tiraquensis, syn. *R. tiraquensis*, *Sulcorebutia tiraquensis*, illus. p.487.
R. steinmannii, syn. *R. rauschii*, *Sulcorebutia rauschii*. Flattened spherical, perennial cactus. **H** 2in (5cm), **S** 4in (10cm). Gray-green stem bears very short, comb-like, golden or black spines. Bears flattish, deep purple flowers in spring. Grows better when grafted.
R. tiraquensis. See *R. steinbachii* subsp. *tiraquensis*.
R. violaciflora. See *R. minuscula*.

REHDERODENDRON
STYRACACEAE

Genus of deciduous, spring-flowering trees, grown for their flowers and fruits. Needs sun or partial shade, some shelter and fertile, moist but well-drained, acid soil. Propagate by semiripe cuttings in summer or by seed in fall.

R. macrocarpum. Deciduous, spreading tree. **H** 30ft (10m), **S** 22ft (7m). Young shoots are red. Pendent clusters of lemon-scented, cup-shaped, pink-tinged, white flowers are borne amid oblong, taper-pointed, red-stalked, glossy, dark green leaves in late spring. Bears cylindrical, woody, red then brown fruits in fall. Z8–10 H10–8.

REHMANNIA
SCROPHULARIACEAE/PLANTAGINACEAE

Genus of spring- and summer-flowering perennials. Needs sun and well-drained soil. Propagate by seed in fall or spring or by root cuttings in winter.

R. angulata of gardens. See *R. elata*.
R. elata, syn. *R. angulata* of gardens, illus. p.234.
R. glutinosa. Rosette-forming perennial. **H** 12in (30cm), **S** 10in (25cm). Bears tubular, purple-veined, pink, red-brown or yellow flowers, on leafy shoots in late spring and early summer. Has lance-shaped to oval, toothed, hairy, light green leaves. Z9–11 H12–9.

REINWARDTIA
LINACEAE

Genus of evergreen subshrubs, grown for their flowers. Needs full light or partial shade and fertile, well-drained soil. Water freely when in growth, moderately at other times. Tip prune young plants to promote branching; cut back hard after flowering. Propagate by softwood cuttings annually

in late spring. Red spider mite may cause problems.

R. indica, syn. *R. trigyna*, illus. p.459.
R. trigyna. See *R. indica*.

RESEDA
Mignonette
RESEDACEAE

Genus of annuals and biennials, grown for their flowers, which attract bees and are suitable for cutting. Needs sun and fertile, well-drained soil. Deadhead regularly to ensure a prolonged flowering period. Propagate by seed in spring or early fall.

R. odorata, illus. p.300.

RETAMA
LEGUMINOSAE/PAPILIONACEAE

Genus of deciduous shrubs grown for their willowy, dark green or silky gray stems and pealike, white or yellow flowers. Needs full sun, sharply drained soil and a sheltered site against a south- or west-facing wall. Propagate from seed in a cold frame or under glass or by semiripe cuttings in summer.

R. monosperma, syn. *Genista monosperma*. Deciduous, almost leafless, graceful, arching shrub. **H** to 12ft (4m), **S** 5ft (1.5m). Slender, silky-gray shoots bear clusters of small, very fragrant, white flowers in early spring. Has a few linear leaves, which soon fall. Grow against a south- or west-facing wall. Z9–10 H10–1.

RHAMNUS
RHAMNACEAE

Genus of deciduous or evergreen shrubs and trees, with inconspicuous flowers, grown mainly for their foliage and fruits. Requires sun or partial shade and fertile soil. Propagate deciduous species by seed in fall, evergreen species by semiripe cuttings in summer. ① All parts may cause severe discomfort if ingested.

R. alaternus (Italian buckthorn). Z7–9 H9–7. **'Argenteovariegata'** is an evergreen, bushy shrub. **H** and **S** 10ft (3m). Has oval, leathery, glossy, gray-green leaves margined creamy-white. Tiny, yellowish-green flowers, produced from early to mid-summer, are followed by spherical, red then black fruits.
R. imeretina. Deciduous, spreading, open shrub. **H** 10ft (3m), **S** 15ft (5m). Sturdy shoots bear large, broadly oblong, prominently veined, dark green leaves that turn bronze-purple in fall. Small, green flowers are borne in summer. Z6–8 H8–6.

RHAPHIOLEPIS
ROSACEAE

Genus of evergreen shrubs, grown for their flowers and foliage. In most areas, does best against a sheltered wall. Needs sun and fertile, well-drained soil. Propagate by semiripe cuttings in late summer.

R. x delacourii 'Coates' Crimson'. Evergreen, rounded shrub. **H** 6ft (2m), **S** 8ft (2.5m). Clusters of fragrant, star-shaped, deep pink flowers, produced in spring or summer, are set off by oval, leathery, dark green leaves. Z8–10 H10–8.
R. indica (Indian hawthorn). Evergreen, bushy shrub. **H** 5ft (1.5m), **S** 6ft (2m).

Clusters of fragrant, star-shaped, pink-flushed, white flowers are borne in spring or early summer amid narrowly lance-shaped, glossy, dark green leaves. Z8–11 H9–3.
R. japonica. See *R. umbellata*.
R. ovata. See *R. umbellata*.
R. umbellata, syn. *R. japonica*, *R. ovata*, illus. p.150.

RHAPIS
Lady palm
PALMAE/ARECACEAE

Genus of evergreen fan palms, grown for their foliage and overall appearance. May have tiny, yellow flowers in summer. Needs partial shade and rich, well-drained soil. Water container specimens freely when in growth, moderately at other times. Propagate by seed, suckers or division in spring. Is susceptible to red spider mite.

R. excelsa, syn. *R. flabelliformis*, illus. p.458.
R. flabelliformis. See *R. excelsa*.

Rhazya orientalis. See *Amsonia orientalis*.

RHEUM
Rhubarb
POLYGONACEAE

Genus of perennials, grown for their foliage and overall appearance. Includes the edible rhubarb and various ornamental plants. Some species are extremely large and require plenty of space. Prefers sun or partial shade and deep, rich, well-drained soil. Propagate by division in spring or by seed in fall. ① Leaves may cause severe discomfort if ingested.

R. nobile. Clump-forming perennial. **H** 5ft (15m), **S** 3ft (1m). Has oblong to oval, leathery, basal, mid-green leaves, 2ft (60cm) long. In late summer produces long stems and conical spikes of large, overlapping, pale cream bracts that hide insignificant flowers. Z6–9 H9–6.
R. palmatum (Chinese rhubarb). Clump-forming perennial. **H** and **S** 6ft (2m). Has rounded, 5-lobed, mid-green leaves, 2–2½ft (60–75cm) long. In early summer produces broad panicles of small, creamy-white flowers. Z5–9 H9–5. **'Atrosanguineum'**, illus. p.439.

Rhipsalidopsis gaertneri. See *Hatiora gaertneri*.
Rhipsalidopsis rosea. See *Hatiora rosea*.

RHIPSALIS
CACTACEAE

Genus of epiphytic, perennial cacti with usually pendent, variously formed stems. Flowers are followed by spherical, translucent berries. Needs partial shade and rich, well-drained soil. Prefers 80% relative humidity—higher than for most cacti. Give only occasional, very light watering in winter. Propagate by seed or stem cuttings in spring or summer.

R. capilliformis. See *R. teres*.
R. cereuscula, illus. p.483.
R. clavata. See *R. gaertneri*.
R. crispata. Bushy, then pendent, perennial cactus. **H** 3ft (1m), **S** indefinite. Has leaflike, elliptic to oblong, pale green stem segments with undulating edges that

produce short, funnel-shaped, cream or pale yellow flowers, to ½in (1cm) across, with recurved tips, in winter–spring, followed by white berries. Z13–15 H12–10.

R. floccosa, illus. p.493.

R. gaertneri, syn. *R. clavata, Hatiora clavata.* Pendent, perennial cactus. **H** 2ft (60cm), **S** 3ft (1m). Multi-branched, cylindrical, dark green stems widen towards tips. Masses of terminal, bell-shaped, white flowers, ⅝in (1.5cm) wide, are produced in late winter and early spring on plants more than 1ft (30cm) high.

R. paradoxa (Chain cactus). Bushy, then pendent, perennial cactus. **H** 3ft (1m), **S** indefinite. Triangular, green stems have segments alternately set at different angles. Short, funnel-shaped, white flowers, ¾in (2cm) across, with recurved tips, in winter–spring, are followed by red berries. Z13–15 H12–10.

R. salicornioides. See *Hatiora salicornioides.*

R. teres, syn. *R. capilliformis.* Pendent, perennial cactus. **H** 3ft (1m), **S** 20in (50cm). Has freely branching, cylindrical, green stems and, in winter–spring, short, funnel-shaped, white flowers, to ½in (1cm) wide, with recurved tips, followed by white berries.

R. warmingiana. See *Lepismium warmingianum.*

RHODANTHE
SYN. ACROCLINIUM
Strawflower
COMPOSITAE/ASTERACEAE

Genus of drought-tolerant annuals, perennials and subshrubs, grown for their daisylike, papery flower heads, which are excellent for cutting and drying. Needs sun and poor, very well-drained soil. Propagate by seed in mid-spring. Aphids may cause problems.

R. chlorocephala subsp. rosea, syn. *Acroclinium roseum, Helipterum roseum,* illus. p.303.

R. manglesii, syn. *Helipterum manglesii* (Swan River everlasting). Moderately fast-growing, erect annual. **H** 12in (30cm), **S** 6in (15cm). Has pointed, oval, grayish-green leaves and daisylike, papery, red, pink or white flower heads, in summer and early fall. Z11 H9–1.

RHODANTHEMUM
COMPOSITAE/ASTERACEAE

Genus of mat-forming, often rhizomatous perennials and subshrubs, grown for their solitary, large, daisylike, white flower heads, surrounded by prominent, usually green bracts. Needs full sun and moderately fertile, very well-drained soil. Propagate by seed in spring or by softwood cuttings in summer.

R. hosmariense, syn. *Chrysanthemum hosmariense, Pyrethropsis hosmariense,* illus. p.332.

RHODIOLA
CRASSULACEAE

Genus of perennials, some dioecious, with thick, fleshy rhizomes producing scaly, brown basal leaves and stiffly erect stems that bear triangular-oval to lance-shaped, fleshy, gray-green leaves. Star-shaped

flowers have prominent stamens, and may be unisexual or bisexual. Needs full sun and moderately fertile soil. Propagate by seed in spring or fall, by division of rhizomes in spring or early summer or by leaf cuttings in summer.

R. heterodonta, syn. *Sedum heterodontum, Sedum rosea var. heterodontum,* illus. p.268.

R. rosea, syn. *Sedum rosea* (Roseroot). Clump-forming perennial. **H** and **S** 12in (30cm). Stems are clothed with oval to inversely lance-shaped, toothed, fleshy, glaucous leaves. In late spring or early summer, pink buds on dense, terminal heads open to small, star-shaped, greenish-, yellowish- or purplish-white flowers. Z4–8 H8–1.

Rhodocactus grandifolius. See *Pereskia grandifolia.*

RHODOCHITON
SCROPHULARIACEAE/PLANTAGINACEAE

Genus of one species of evergreen, leaf-stalk climber, grown for its unusual flowers. Does best when grown as an annual. May be planted against a fence or trellis or be used as groundcover. Needs sun and well-drained soil. Propagate by seed in early spring.

R. atrosanguineus, syn. *R. volubilis,* illus. p.203.

R. volubilis. See *R. atrosanguineus.*

RHODODENDRON
ERICACEAE

Genus of evergreen, semievergreen or deciduous shrubs, ranging from a dwarf habit to a treelike stature, grown mainly for beauty of flower. Most prefer dappled shade, but a considerable number tolerates full sun, especially in cool climates. Needs neutral to acid soil—ideally, rich and well-drained. Shallow planting is essential, as plants are surface-rooting. Deadhead spent flowers, wherever practical, to encourage energy into growth rather than seed production. Propagate by layering or semiripe cuttings in late summer. Yellowing leaves are usually caused by poor drainage, excessively deep planting or lime in soil. Weevils and powdery mildew may also cause problems. ① The nectar of some rhododendron flowers may cause severe discomfort if ingested. See also feature panel pp.124–125.

Rhododendrons and azaleas
The genus *Rhododendron* includes not only evergreen, large-leaved and frequently large-flowered species and hybrids, but also dwarf, smaller-leaved shrubs, both evergreen and deciduous, with few-flowered clusters of usually small blooms. "Azalea" is the common name given to the deciduous species and hybrids, as well as to a group of compact, evergreen shrubs derived mainly from Japanese species. They are valued for their mass of small colorful blooms produced in late spring. Many of the evergreen azaleas (sometimes known as Belgian azaleas) may also be grown as houseplants. Botanically, however, all are classified as *Rhododendron.* The flowers are usually single, but may be semidouble or double, including hose-in-hose (one flower tube

inside the other). Unless otherwise stated below, flowers are single and leaves mid- to dark green and oval.

R. aberconwayi. Evergreen, distinctly erect rhododendron. **H** to 8ft (2.5m). **S** 4ft (1.2m). Has small, broadly lance-shaped, rigid, deep green leaves. Bears saucer-shaped, white flowers in late spring.

R. albrechtii. Deciduous, upright, bushy azalea. **H** to 10ft (3m), **S** 6ft (2m). Has spoon-shaped leaves, clustered at branch tips, and, in spring, loose clusters of 3–5 bell-shaped, green-spotted, purple or pink flowers. Z6–8 H8–6.

R. 'Alison Johnstone'. Evergreen, bushy, compact rhododendron. **H** and **S** 6ft (2m). Produces masses of bell-shaped, peach-pink flowers in spring. Has waxy, gray-green leaves. Z7–9 H9–7.

R. 'Angelo'. Evergreen, bushy rhododendron. **H** and **S** to 12ft (4m). Has bold foliage and large, fragrant, bell-shaped, white flowers in mid-summer. Is good in light woodland. Z7–9 H9–7.

R. arboreum (Tree rhododendron), illus. p.125. Evergreen, treelike rhododendron. **H** to 40ft (12m), **S** 10ft (3m). Undersides of broadly lance-shaped leaves are silver, fawn or cinnamon. In spring has dense clusters of bell-shaped flowers in colors ranging from red (most tender form) through pink to white. Z7–9 H9–7.

R. argyrophyllum. Evergreen, spreading rhododendron. **H** and **S** to 15ft (5m). Oblong leaves are silvery-white on undersides. Loose bunches of bell-shaped, rich pink flowers, sometimes with deeper colored spots, are borne in spring. Is ideal in light woodland. Z7–9 H9–7.

R. arizelum. See *R. rex* subsp. *arizelum.*

R. 'Ascot Brilliant'. Evergreen, bushy rhododendron. **H** and **S** 10ft (3m). Leaves are broadly oval. In spring produces loose bunches of funnel-shaped, waxy, rose-red flowers, with darker edges. Z8–10 H10–7.

R. augustinii, illus. p.125. Evergreen, bushy rhododendron. **H** and **S** to 12ft (4m). Has lance-shaped to oblong, light green leaves and, in spring, bears masses of multi-stemmed, widely funnel-shaped, pale to deep blue or lavender flowers. Z6–9 H9–6.

R. auriculatum. Evergreen, bushy, widely branching rhododendron. **H** and **S** to 20ft (6m). Has large, oblong, hairy leaves with distinct, earlike lobes at base. In late summer bears loose bunches of 7–15 large, heavily scented, tubular to funnel-shaped, white flowers. Is best in light woodland. Z6–11 H12–6.

R. 'Azor'. Evergreen, upright rhododendron. **H** and **S** to 12ft (4m). Leaves are broadly oval. Produces large, fragrant, funnel-shaped, salmon-pink flowers in mid-summer.

R. 'Azuma-kagami'. Evergreen, compact azalea. **H** and **S** 4ft (1.2m). Bears many small, hose-in-hose, deep pink flowers in mid-spring. Is best in partial shade. Z7–9 H9–7.

R. barbatum. Evergreen, upright rhododendron. **H** and **S** to 30ft (10m). Has lance-shaped, dark green leaves covered with bristles, on stems; bark is plum-colored and peeling. Bears tight bunches of tubular to bell-shaped, bright scarlet flowers in early spring.

R. 'Beauty of Littleworth'. Evergreen, open, shrubby rhododendron. **H** and **S**

12ft (4m). In late spring bears huge, conical bunches of scented, funnel-shaped, crimson-spotted, white flowers. Z7–9 H9–7.

R. 'Beefeater'. Evergreen, bushy rhododendron. **H** and **S** to 8ft (2.5m). Leaves are broadly lance-shaped. Produces flat-topped bunches of bell-shaped, scarlet flowers in late spring and early summer.

R. 'Blaauw's Pink', illus. p.125. Evergreen, compact azalea. **H** and **S** 5ft (1.5m). Bears masses of funnel-shaped, salmon-pink flowers, with paler blush, in late spring.

R. 'Blue Danube', illus. p.125. Evergreen, upright azalea. **H** 6ft (2m), **S** 5ft (1.5m). Produces bell-shaped, vivid violet-blue flowers in spring. Z6–9 H9–6.

R. 'Blue Diamond'. Evergreen, upright rhododendron. **H** and **S** to 5ft (1.5m). Small, neat leaves contrast with funnel-shaped, bright blue flowers borne in mid- to late spring. Prefers full sun. Z6–9 H9–1.

R. 'Blue Peter'. Evergreen, bushy rhododendron. **H** and **S** to 12ft (4m). In early summer produces bold, open funnel-shaped, 2-tone lavender-purple flowers, with frilled petal margins. Z6–9 H9–6.

R. calendulaceum (Flame azalea). Deciduous, bushy azalea. **H** and **S** 6–10ft (2–3m). In early summer bears funnel-shaped, scarlet or orange flowers in bunches of 5–7. Z5–8 H9–4.

R. calophytum, illus. p.124. Evergreen, widely-branched rhododendron. **H** and **S** to 20ft (6m). Produces large, lance-shaped leaves and, in early spring, huge bunches of bell-shaped, white or pale pink flowers, with crimson spots. Z6–9 H9–6.

R. calostrotum. Evergreen, compact rhododendron. **H** and **S** to 3ft (1m). Has blue-green leaves and, in late spring, saucer-shaped, purple or scarlet flowers in clusters of 2–5. Z7–9 H9–7.

R. 'Catawbiense Album'. Evergreen, rounded rhododendron. **H** and **S** to 10ft (3m). Bears glossy leaves and, in early summer, dense, rounded bunches of bell-shaped, white flowers. Z4–8 H8–1.

R. 'Catawbiense Boursault'. Evergreen, rounded rhododendron. **H** and **S** to 10ft (3m). Has glossy leaves. Dense, rounded bunches of bell-shaped, lilac-purple flowers are borne in early summer. Z4–8 H8–1.

R. x cilpinense. See *R.* 'Cilpinense'.

R. 'Cilpinense', syn. *R.* x *cilpinense.* Semievergreen, compact rhododendron. **H** and **S** to 5ft (1.5m). Leaves are dark green and glossy. Bears masses of large, bell-shaped, blush-pink flowers, flushed deeper in bud, in early spring. Flowers are vulnerable to frost damage. Z8–9 H9–8.

R. cinnabarinum, illus. p.125. Evergreen, upright rhododendron. **H** and **S** 5–12ft (1.5–4m). Has blue-green leaves with small scales. Narrowly tubular, waxy, orange to red flowers are borne in loose, drooping bunches in late spring. Z8–9 H9–8. **subsp. xanthocodon,** syn. *R. xanthocodon* has aromatic, mid-green leaves, which are blue-green when young, and yellow flowers in late spring.

R. 'Coccineum Speciosum'. Deciduous, bushy azalea. **H** and **S** 5–8ft (1.5–2.5m). Produces open funnel-shaped, brilliant rich orange-red flowers in early summer. Broadly lance-shaped, dark green leaves turn yellow or orange in fall Z9–10 H10–9.

R. 'Corneille'. Deciduous, bushy azalea. **H** and **S** 5–8ft (1.5–2.5m). In early summer

Q
R

produces fragrant, honeysuckle-like, cream flowers, flushed pink outside. Has colorful fall foliage. Z5–8 H8–5.

***R.* 'Crest',** syn. *R.* 'Hawk Crest'. Evergreen rhododendron of open habit. **H** and **S** 5–12ft (1.5–4m). Has broadly lance-shaped leaves. Bell-shaped flowers are borne in loose, flat-topped bunches, and are apricot in bud, opening to clear sulfur-yellow in late spring. Z7–9 H9–7.

R. cubittii. Evergreen rhododendron now included in *R. veitchianum*. **H** 5ft (1.5m), **S** to 3ft (1m). Has purple-brown young shoots and oblong to elliptic, leathery, sparsely scaly, mid- to dark green leaves. In mid- and late spring bears funnel-shaped, white to pale pink flowers, with brownish or yellow-orange markings. Z8–10 H9–7.

***R.* 'Cunningham's White'.** Evergreen, compact rhododendron. **H** 8ft (2.5m), **S** 6ft (2m). In spring produces open trusses of funnel-shaped, pale lilac flowers, which fade to white, speckled with purple and yellow. Z6–8 H8–1.

***R.* 'Curlew',** illus. p.125. Evergreen rhododendron of compact, spreading habit. **H** and **S** 1ft (30cm). Produces dull green leaves and, in late spring, relatively large, open funnel-shaped, yellow flowers. Z7–9 H9–7.

***R.* 'Cynthia'.** Vigorous, evergreen, dome-shaped rhododendron. **H** and **S** to 20ft (6m). Bears conical bunches of bell-shaped, magenta-purple flowers, marked blackish-red within, in late spring. Thrives in sun and shade. Z6–9 H9–6.

R. dauricum. Evergreen, upright rhododendron. **H** and **S** to 5ft (1.5m). Produces funnel-shaped, vivid purple flowers in loose clusters throughout winter. Dark green leaves turn purple-brown in frosty conditions. Z4–8 H8–1.

R. davidsonianum. Deciduous, upright rhododendron. **H** 5–12ft (1.5–4m). Aromatic leaves are lance-shaped to oblong. In late spring has clusters of funnel-shaped flowers, ranging from pale pink to mid-lilac-mauve. Z7–9 H9–7.

***R.* 'Daviesii',** illus. p.125. Deciduous, upright azalea. **H** and **S** 6ft (2m). Fragrant, funnel-shaped, white flowers, with yellow flare, are borne in spring. Z5–8 H8–5.

R. decorum, illus. p.124. Evergreen, bushy rhododendron. **H** and **S** 12ft (4m). Oblong to lance-shaped leaves are mid-green above, paler beneath. Large, fragrant, funnel-shaped, white or shell-pink flowers, green- or pink-spotted within, are produced in early summer. Z7–9 H9–7.

R. degronianum* var. *heptamerum, syn. *R. metternichii*. Evergreen, upright rhododendron. **H** and **S** 5–12ft (1.5–4m). Has oblong leaves, glossy and green above, reddish-brown-felted beneath. Bell-shaped, rose-red flowers, borne in spring, are in rounded bunches of 10–15, often subtly spotted within. Z5–7 H7–5.

R. discolor. See *R. fortunei* subsp. *discolor*.

***R.* 'Doncaster'.** Evergreen, compact rhododendron. **H** and **S** 6–8ft (2–2.5m). Has leathery, glossy leaves and, in late spring, funnel-shaped, dark red flowers in dense bunches. Z5–8 H8–5.

***R.* 'Dopey'.** Evergreen, compact rhododendron. **H** and **S** 5ft (1.5m). In spring has bell-shaped, flame-orange flowers in rounded trusses. Z7–9 H9–7.

***R.* 'Dora Amateis'.** Evergreen, compact rhododendron. **H** and **S** 2ft (60cm). Leaves are slender, glossy and pointed. Masses of broadly funnel-shaped, white flowers, tinged with pink and marked with green, are borne in late spring. Is sun tolerant. Z5–8 H8–1.

***R.* 'Elizabeth'.** Evergreen, dome-shaped rhododendron. **H** and **S** to 5ft (1.5m). Leaves are oblong. Has large, trumpet-shaped, brilliant red flowers in late spring. Is good in sun and partial shade. Z7–9 H9–7.

***R.* 'Elizabeth Lockhart'.** Evergreen, dome-shaped rhododendron. **H** and **S** 2ft (60cm). Produces shiny, purple-green leaves that become darker in winter. Bell-shaped, deep pink flowers are borne in spring. Z7–9 H9–7.

***R.* 'English Roseum'.** Vigorous, evergreen, bushy rhododendron. **H** and **S** 8ft (to 2.5m). Dark green leaves are paler beneath. Bears compact bunches of funnel-shaped, lilac-rose flowers in late spring.

***R.* 'Fabia'.** Evergreen, dome-shaped rhododendron. **H** and **S** 6ft (2m). Leaves are lance-shaped. Loose, flat trusses of funnel-shaped, orange-tinted, scarlet flowers are borne in early summer. Z8–9 H9–8.

R. falconeri, illus. p.124. Multi-stemmed, evergreen rhododendron. **H** to 40ft (12m), **S** 15ft (5m). Has flaking, red-brown bark and broadly elliptic to oval, dark green leaves, brown-felted beneath. In mid-spring produces widely bell-shaped, fleshy, creamy-white or yellow flowers, sometimes pink-tinged, often with purple marks inside. Z8–9 H9–8.

***R.* 'Fastuosum Flore Pleno',** illus. p.125. Evergreen, dome-shaped rhododendron. **H** and **S** 5–12ft (1.5–4m). In early summer bears loose bunches of funnel-shaped, double, rich mauve flowers, with red-brown marks and wavy margins. Z5–8 H8–5.

***R.* 'Fireball'.** Evergreen, compact rhododendron. **H** and **S** 6ft (2m). Has rounded trusses of bell-shaped, vivid scarlet flowers in early spring. Z5–9 H9–3.

***R.* 'Firefly'.** See *R.* 'Hexe'.

R. fortunei* subsp. *discolor, syn. *R. discolor*. Evergreen, treelike rhododendron. **H** and **S** to 25ft (8m). Leaves are oblong to oval. Bears fragrant, funnel-shaped, pink flowers in mid-summer. Is ideal in light woodland. Z5–9 H9–5.

***R.* 'Fragrantissimum',** illus. p.124. Lax, evergreen rhododendron. **H** and **S** 6ft (2m). Nutmeg-scented, broadly funnel-shaped, sometimes pink-flushed, white flowers, with yellow throats, are borne in mid-spring. Leaves are hairy. Z9–10 H10–9.

***R.* 'Freya'.** Deciduous azalea of compact, shrubby habit. **H** and **S** 5ft (1.5m). Fragrant, funnel-shaped, pink-flushed, orange-salmon flowers are produced from late spring to early summer. Z5–8 H8–5.

***R.* 'Frome'.** Deciduous azalea of shrubby habit. **H** and **S** to 5ft (1.5m). In spring bears trumpet-shaped, saffron-yellow flowers, overlaid red in throats; petals are frilled and wavy-margined. Z5–8 H8–5.

R. fulvum, illus. p.125. Evergreen, bushy rhododendron. **H** and **S** 5–12ft (1.5–4m). Oblong to oval, glossy, deep green leaves are brown-felted beneath. In early spring has loose bunches of bell-shaped, red-blotched, pink flowers, which fade to white. Z7–9 H9–7.

***R.* 'George Reynolds'.** Deciduous, bushy azalea. **H** and **S** to 6ft (2m). Large, funnel-shaped, yellow flowers, flushed pink in bud, are borne with or before leaves in spring. Z5–8 H8–5.

***R.* 'Gibraltar',** illus. p.125. Deciduous, bushy azalea. **H** 5ft (1.5m), **S** 3ft (1m). In spring produces tubular, flame-red flowers, which are deep orange in bud. Z5–8 H8–5.

***R.* 'Gloria Mundi'.** Deciduous, twiggy azalea. **H** and **S** to 6ft (2m). Produces fragrant, honeysuckle-like, yellow-flared, orange flowers, with frilled margins, in early summer. Z5–8 H8–5.

***R.* 'Glory of Littleworth'.** Evergreen or semievergreen, bushy hybrid between a rhododendron and an azalea. **H** and **S** 5ft (1.5m). Compact bunches of fragrant, bell-shaped, orange-marked, creamy-white flowers are borne abundantly in late spring and early summer. Is not easy to cultivate. Z7–9 H9–7.

***R.* 'Gold Crown'.** See *R.* 'Goldkrone'.

***R.* 'Golden Torch',** illus. p.124. Evergreen, compact rhododendron. **H** and **S** 3ft (1m). In spring has bell-shaped, pink-budded, pale yellow flowers. Z7–9 H9–7.

***R.* 'Goldkrone',** syn. *R.* 'Gold Crown', illus. p.125. Compact, evergreen shrub. **H** and **S** 5ft (1.5m). Funnel- to bell-shaped, bright golden-yellow flowers, delicately spotted ruby-red inside, are borne in succession in mid-spring. Z6–9 H9–6.

***R.* 'Gomer Waterer',** illus. p.124. Evergreen, compact rhododendron. **H** and **S** 5–12ft (1.5–4m). Leaves are curved back at margins. Bell-shaped flowers, borne in dense bunches in early summer, are white, flushed mauve, with mustard, basal blotch. Likes sun and partial shade. Z5–8 H8–1.

***R.* 'Grace Seabrook',** illus. p.125. Evergreen, upright rhododendron. **H** and **S** 6ft (2m). Leaves are pointed. In spring bears funnel-shaped, deep red flowers, which are paler towards edges.

R. griffithianum. Evergreen, upright rhododendron with peeling, red bark. **H** 20ft (to 6m), **S** 10ft (3m). Bears loose trusses of fragrant, bell-shaped, white flowers in spring. Has large, elliptic, glabrous leaves. Z7–9 H9–7.

***R.* 'Hatsugiri'.** Evergreen, compact azalea. **H** and **S** 2ft (60cm). Has masses of small, funnel-shaped, bright crimson-purple flowers in spring. Flowers very reliably. Z6–9 H9–6.

***R.* 'Hawk Crest'.** See *R.* 'Crest'.

***R.* 'Hexe',** syn. *R.* 'Firefly'. Evergreen azalea of neat habit. **H** and **S** 2ft (60cm). Has numerous relatively large, hose-in-hose, glowing, crimson flowers in spring. Z7–9 H9–7.

***R.* 'Hinode-giri'.** Evergreen, compact azalea. **H** and **S** 5ft (1.5m). Bears masses of small, funnel-shaped, bright crimson flowers in late spring. Likes sun and partial shade. Z6–9 H9–6.

***R.* 'Hinomayo'.** Evergreen, compact azalea. **H** and **S** 5ft (1.5m). Masses of small, funnel-shaped, clear pink flowers are produced in spring. Likes sun and light shade. Z7–9 H9–7.

R. hippophaeoides. Evergreen, erect rhododendron. **H** and **S** 5ft (1.5m). Narrowly lance-shaped, aromatic leaves are gray-green. Has small, funnel-shaped, lavender or lilac flowers in spring. Tolerates wet, but not stagnant, soil. Z5–8 H8–5.

***R.* 'Homebush'.** Deciduous, compact azalea. **H** and **S** 5ft (1.5m). In late spring bears tight, rounded heads of trumpet-shaped, semidouble, rose-purple flowers, with paler shading. Z5–8 H8–5.

***R.* 'Hotei',** illus. p.125. Evergreen, compact rhododendron. **H** and **S** 5–8ft (1.5–2.5m). Large, funnel-shaped, deep yellow flowers are freely produced in late spring. Z7–9 H9–7.

***R.* 'Humming Bird'.** Evergreen, dome-shaped rhododendron of neat, compact habit. **H** and **S** to 5ft (1.5m). From mid- to late spring has bell-shaped, rose-pink flowers, in loose, nodding bunches, above rounded, glossy leaves. Z7–9 H9–7.

***R.* 'Hydon Hunter'.** Evergreen rhododendron of neat habit. **H** and **S** to 5ft (1.5m). In late spring or early summer has masses of large, narrowly bell-shaped, red-rimmed flowers, paler towards center and orange-spotted within. Z7–9 H9–7.

R. impeditum. Slow-growing, evergreen rhododendron. **H** and **S** to 2ft (60cm). Aromatic leaves are gray-green. Funnel-shaped, purplish-blue flowers are borne in spring. Is ideal in a rock garden. Z5–8 H8–1.

***R.* 'Irohayama'.** Evergreen, compact azalea. **H** and **S** to 5ft (1.5m). Has abundant, small, funnel-shaped, white flowers, with pale lavender margins and faint, brown eyes, in spring. Does well in partial shade. Z7–9 H9–7.

***R.* 'Jalisco'.** Deciduous, open, bushy rhododendron. **H** and **S** 5–12ft (1.5–4m). Bears bunches of narrowly bell-shaped, straw-colored flowers, tinted orange-rose at tips, in early summer.

***R.* 'Jeanette'.** Semievergreen, upright azalea. **H** and **S** 5–6ft (1.5–2m). Has funnel-shaped, vivid phlox-pink, dark blotched flowers, in spring. Is good in partial shade and full sun.

***R.* 'John Cairns'.** Evergreen, upright, compact azalea. **H** and **S** 5–6ft (1.5–2m). Bears abundant funnel-shaped, orange-red flowers in spring. Grows reliably in sun and partial shade. Z6–9 H9–6.

R. kaempferi (Torch azalea). Semievergreen, erect, loosely branched azalea. **H** and **S** 5–8ft (1.5–2.5m). Leaves are lance-shaped. Has masses of funnel-shaped, orange or red flowers in late spring and early summer. Z6–9 H9–6.

***R.* 'Kilimanjaro'.** Evergreen, bushy rhododendron. **H** and **S** 5–12ft (1.5–4m). Bears broadly lance-shaped leaves. Produces large, rounded bunches of funnel- to bell-shaped, wavy-edged, maroon-red flowers, spotted chocolate within, in late spring and early summer. Z7–9 H9–7.

***R.* 'Kirin'.** Evergreen, compact azalea. **H** and **S** to 5ft (1.5m). In spring has numerous hose-in-hose flowers that are deep rose, shaded delicate silvery-rose. Looks best in partial shade. Z7–9 H9–7.

R. kiusianum (Kyushu azalea). Semievergreen azalea of compact habit. **H** and **S** to 2ft (60cm). Leaves are narrowly oval. Produces clusters of 2–5 funnel-shaped flowers, usually lilac-rose or mauve-purple, in late spring. Prefers full sun. Z7–9 H9–7.

***R.* 'Lady Alice Fitzwilliam'.** Evergreen, bushy rhododendron. **H** and **S** 5–12ft (1.5–4m). Leaves are glossy, dark green.

Loose bunches of heavily scented, broadly funnel-shaped, white flowers, flushed pale pink, are produced in mid- to late spring. Grow against a south-or west-facing wall.

***R.* 'Lady Clementine Mitford'.** Evergreen, rounded, dense rhododendron. **H** and **S** 12ft (4m). Has broadly oval, glossy, dark green leaves that are silvery when young and, in late spring and early summer, bold bunches of tubular- to bell-shaped flowers, peach-pink fading to white in center, with V-shaped, pink, green and brown marks within. Z7–9 H9–7.

***R.* 'Lady Rosebery'.** Evergreen, stiffly branched rhododendron. **H** and **S** 5–12ft (1.5–4m). Bears clusters of drooping, narrowly bell-shaped, waxy, deep pink flowers, which are paler towards petal margins, in late spring. Is ideal for woodland margin.

***R. laetum*.** Evergreen, erect rhododendron. **H** and **S** 5ft (1.5m). Elliptic to broadly elliptic, glossy, dark green leaves have tiny, white scales beneath. In spring, red flower stalks bear funnel-shaped, golden-yellow flowers, later suffused orange-red. Z7–9 H9–7.

***R.* 'Lem's Cameo'.** Evergreen, rounded, bushy rhododendron. **H** and **S** 5–8ft (1.5–2.5m). Leaves are rounded. In spring has large-domed bunches of open funnel-shaped, pale peach flowers, deep pink in bud, shaded to pink at margins, with basal, deep rose-colored blotches. Z7–9 H9–7.

***R. leucaspis*.** Densely branched, evergreen rhododendron. **H** 3ft (1m), **S** 5ft (1.5m). Has broadly elliptic, dark green leaves, bristly above, scaly and yellowish-green beneath. In early spring bears saucer-shaped, white flowers, with chocolate-brown anthers. Z8–9 H9–7.

***R.* 'Loderi King George',** illus. p.124. Large, evergreen rhododendron of open habit. **H** and **S** 12ft (4m). Has large leaves. In late spring and early summer, pale pink buds open to huge trusses of fragrant, funnel-shaped, pure white flowers, with subtle green marks in throats. Z7–9 H9–7.

***R. lutescens*.** Semievergreen, upright rhododendron. **H** and **S** 5–10ft (1.5–3m). Has oval to lance-shaped leaves that are bronze-red when young. In early spring bears funnel-shaped, primrose-yellow flowers. Is effective in light woodland. Z7–9 H9–7.

R. luteum (Pontic azalea), illus. p.125. Open deciduous azalea. **H** and **S** 5–8ft (1.5–2.5m). Mid-green leaves are oblong to lance-shaped. Has very fragrant, funnel-shaped, bold yellow flowers in spring. Fall foliage is rich and colorful. Z7–9 H9–7.

***R. maccabeanum*.** Evergreen, treelike rhododendron. **H** and **S** to 45ft (13.5m). Has bold, broadly oval leaves, dark green above, gray-felted beneath, and, in early spring, large bunches of bell-shaped, yellow flowers, blotched purple within. Z8–11 H11–10.

***R. mallotum*.** Evergreen, upright, open rhododendron, occasionally treelike. **H** and **S** to 12ft (4m). Oblong to oval leaves are deep green above, red-brown-felted beneath. Showy, tubular, crimson flowers in loose bunches are borne in early spring.

***R.* 'May Day'.** Evergreen, spreading rhododendron. **H** and **S** to 5ft (1.5m). Leaves are fresh green above, whitish-felted beneath. Has masses of loose bunches of long-lasting, funnel-shaped, scarlet flowers in late spring; petal-like calyces match flower color. Z7–9 H9–7.

***R.* 'Medway'.** Deciduous, bushy, open azalea. **H** and **S** 5–8ft (1.5–2.5m). In late spring has large, trumpet-shaped, pale pink flowers, with darker margins and orange-flashed throats; petal margins are frilled. Z5–8 H8–5.

***R. metternichii*.** See *R. degronianum* var. *heptamerum*.

***R.* 'Moonshine Crescent'.** Evergreen, rounded to upright rhododendron. **H** 6–8ft (2–2.5m), **S** 6ft (2m). In late spring produces compact trusses of bell-shaped, yellow flowers. Leaves are oblong to oval and dark green. Z6–8 H8–6.

***R.* 'Mother's Day',** illus. p.125. Evergreen, compact azalea. **H** and **S** 3ft (1m). Has funnel-shaped, bright red flowers in spring.

***R. moupinense*.** Evergreen, rounded, compact rhododendron. **H** and **S** to 5ft (1.5m). Produces funnel-shaped, pink flowers, in loose bunches, in late winter and early spring. Leaves are glossy, dark green above, paler beneath. Is best grown in a sheltered situation to reduce risk of frosted flowers. Z7–9 H9–7.

***R.* 'Mrs. G.W. Leak'.** Evergreen, upright, compact rhododendron. **H** and **S** 12ft (4m). In late spring bears compact, conical bunches of funnel-shaped, pink flowers, with black-brown and crimson marks within. Z7–9 H9–7.

***R. nakaharae*.** Evergreen, mound-forming azalea. **H** and **S** 2ft (60cm). Shoots and oblong to oval leaves are densely hairy. Funnel-shaped, dark brick-red flowers are borne in small clusters in mid-summer. Is ideal for a rock garden. Z5–8 H8–5.

***R.* 'Nancy Waterer'.** Deciduous, twiggy azalea. **H** and **S** 5–8ft (1.5–2.5m). Has large, long-tubed and honeysuckle-like, brilliant golden-yellow flowers in early summer. Is good in partial shade and full sun. Z5–8 H8–5.

***R.* 'Narcissiflorum'.** Vigorous, deciduous, compact azalea. **H** and **S** 5–8ft (1.5–2.5m). Sweetly scented, hose-in-hose, pale yellow flowers, darker outside and in center, are borne in late spring or early summer. Fall foliage is bronze. Z5–8 H8–5.

***R. niveum*,** illus. p.125. Evergreen, shrubby rhododendron. **H** 16ft (5m), **S** 10ft (3m). Narrowly oval to lance-shaped, dark green leaves are white felted when young and brown felted beneath when mature. Bell-shaped, plum-purple flowers, in compact, rounded heads, are borne in spring.

***R.* Nobleanum Group.** Evergreen, upright shrub or treelike rhododendron. **H** and **S** to 15ft (5m). Bears large, compact bunches of broadly funnel-shaped, rose-red, pink or white flowers in winter or early spring. Will flower for long periods in mild weather. Is best in a sheltered position. Z7–9 H9–7.

***R.* 'Norma'.** Vigorous, deciduous, compact azalea. **H** and **S** to 5ft (1.5m). Bears masses of hose-in-hose, rose-red flowers, with salmon glow, in spring. Grows well in sun and partial shade. Z6–9 H9–6.

***R.* 'Nova Zembla'.** Vigorous, evergreen, upright rhododendron. **H** and **S** 5–12ft (1.5–4m). Has funnel-shaped, dark red flowers, in closely set bunches, from late spring to early summer. Z5–8 H8–1.

R. occidentale (Western azalea). Bushy, deciduous, azalea. **H** and **S** 5–8ft (1.5–2.5m). Glossy, mid-green leaves turn yellow or orange in fall. Bears fragrant, funnel-shaped, white or pale pink flowers, with yellow-orange, basal blotch, from early to mid-summer. Z7–9 H9–7.

***R.* 'Olive'.** Upright, evergreen rhododendron. **H** 4ft (1.2m), **S** 3ft (1m). Small, oval to elliptic, mid-green leaves are paler green beneath. Has funnel-shaped, mauve-pink flowers, with darker spots inside, in early spring. Z6–9 H9–6.

***R. orbiculare*,** illus. p.124. Evergreen rhododendron of compact habit. **H** and **S** to 10ft (3m). Has rounded, bright green leaves and bell-shaped, rose-pink flowers, in loose bunches, in late spring. Z7–9 H9–7.

***R. oreotrephes*.** Deciduous, upright shrub or treelike rhododendron. **H** and **S** to 15ft (5m). Has scaly, gray-green leaves. In spring bears loose bunches of 3–10 broadly funnel-shaped flowers, usually mauve or purple, but variable, often with crimson spots. Z7–9 H9–7.

***R. pachysanthum*,** illus. p.124. Evergreen, compact, rounded rhododendron. **H** and **S** 6ft (2m). New shoots and oblong leaves, with pointed tips, are covered in fawn felt. Trusses of open bell-shaped, white to pale pink flowers, sometimes with purple flecks, are borne in mid- and late spring. Z7–9 H9–7.

***R.* 'Palestrina'.** Evergreen or semievergreen, compact, free-flowering azalea. **H** and **S** to 4ft (1.2m). Has large, open funnel-shaped, white flowers, with faint, green marks, in late spring. Grows well in partial shade. Z5–8 H8–3.

***R.* 'Patty Bee',** illus. p.125. Evergreen, compact rhododendron. **H** and **S** 3ft (1m). Produces trusses of funnel-shaped, lemon-colored flowers in spring. Z5–9 H9–6.

***R.* 'Percy Wiseman',** illus. p.122.

***R.* 'Peter John Mezitt',** syn. *R.* 'P.J. Mezitt'. Evergreen, compact rhododendron. **H** and **S** to 5ft (1.5m). Aromatic leaves are small, dark green in summer, bronze-purple in winter. Bears frost-resistant, funnel-shaped, lavender-pink flowers in early spring. Is good in full sun. Z4–8 H8–1.

***R.* 'P.J. Mezitt'.** See *R.* 'Peter John Mezitt'.

***R.* 'Pink Pearl',** illus. p.125. Vigorous, evergreen, upright, open rhododendron. **H** and **S** 12ft (4m) or more. Bears tall bunches of open funnel-shaped, pink flowers in late spring. Z7–9 H9–7.

***R.* 'Polar Bear',** illus. p.124. Vigorous, multi-stemmed, evergreen rhododendron. **H** 15ft (5m), **S** 12ft (4m). In late summer bears strongly scented, tubular to funnel-shaped, white flowers, with light brown-flecked, pale green throats. Z7–9 H9–7.

***R. praecox*,** illus. p.125. Partially deciduous, compact rhododendron. **H** 5ft (1.5m), **S** 3ft (1m). Funnel-shaped, rose-purple flowers, in 2s and 3s, are borne at ends of shoots in late winter and early spring. Elliptic leaves are aromatic when bruised. Z6–8 H8–6.

***R.* 'Ptarmigan'.** Evergreen, spreading rhododendron that forms compact mound. **H** to 1ft (30cm), **S** 2½ft (75cm) or more. Funnel-shaped, pure white flowers are borne in early spring. Prefers full sun. Z7–9 H9–7.

***R.* 'Purple Splendour',** illus. p.125. Evergreen, bushy rhododendron. **H** and **S** to 10ft (3m). Has bunches of open funnel-shaped, rich royal-purple flowers, with black marks in throats, in late spring or early summer. Z6–9 H9–6.

***R.* 'Queen Elizabeth II'.** Evergreen, bushy rhododendron. **H** and **S** 5–12ft (1.5–4m). Bears funnel-shaped, greenish-yellow flowers in loose bunches in late spring. Leaves are narrowly oval or lance-shaped, glossy and mid-green above, paler beneath. Z7–9 H9–7.

***R.* 'Queen of Hearts'.** Evergreen, open rhododendron. **H** and **S** 5–12ft (1.5–4m). Has masses of domed bunches of funnel-shaped, deep crimson flowers, black-speckled within, in mid-spring.

***R. quinquefolium*,** illus. p.124. Deciduous, bushy shrub. **H** 10–13ft (3-4m), **S** 10ft (3m). Has obovate to diamond-shaped, mid-green leaves in whorls of 4 or 5 at shoot ends. Leaves have reddish edges when young and color well in fall. In mid- and late spring bears small clusters of pendent, saucer-shaped, green-spotted, white flowers.

***R. racemosum*.** Evergreen, upright, stiffly branched rhododendron. **H** and **S** to 8ft (2.5m). Has clusters of widely funnel-shaped, bright pink flowers borne along the stems in spring. Small, aromatic, broadly oval leaves are dull green above, gray-green below. Z6–9 H9–6.

R. rex*.** Vigorous, evergreen, upright shrub or treelike rhododendron. **H** and **S** 12ft (4m) or more. Leaves are pale buff-felted beneath. Pink or white flowers have crimson blotch and spotted throat. Z8–10 H10–8. **subsp. *arizelum*,** syn. *R. arizelum*, **H** and **S** 25ft (8m), has inversely oval leaves and usually yellow, sometimes pink, rarely white flowers, with crimson marks in throats. **subsp. *fictolacteum (illus. p.124), **H** to 45ft (13.5m), has large leaves, green above, brown-felted beneath. Bears bunches of bell-shaped, white flowers in spring, with maroon blotch and often spotted throat.

***R.* 'Romany Chai'.** Vigorous, evergreen rhododendron, open when young, becoming denser with age. **H** and **S** 5–12ft (1.5–4m). Has dark green, bronze-tinged foliage. In early summer produces large, compact bunches of broadly funnel-shaped, rich brown-red flowers, with maroon, basal blotch. Is suitable for light woodland.

***R.* 'Roseum Elegans'.** Vigorous, evergreen, rounded rhododendron. **H** and **S** 8ft (2.5m) or more. Foliage is bold and glossy, deep green. In early summer bears rounded bunches of broadly funnel-shaped, reddish-purple flowers, marked with yellow-brown. Z5–9 H9–4.

***R.* 'Roza Stevenson'.** Vigorous, evergreen, upright rhododendron of open habit. **H** and **S** 5–12ft (1.5–4m). Produces masses of fine, loose bunches of saucer-shaped, lemon flowers from mid- to late spring. Is excellent in partial shade. Z7–9 H9–7.

***R. rubiginosum*.** Vigorous, evergreen, upright, well-branched rhododendron. **H** 20ft (6m), **S** 8ft (2.5m). Aromatic leaves are lance-shaped, dull green above, reddish-brown beneath. Has funnel-shaped, lilac-purple flowers in loose bunches in mid-spring.

R. schlippenbachii (Royal azalea). Deciduous, rounded, open azalea. **H** and **S** 8ft (2.5m). Spoon-shaped leaves are in whorls at branch ends. Bears loose bunches of 3–6 saucer-shaped, pink flowers in mid-spring. Is suitable for light woodland. Z5–8 H8–5.

R. 'Seta', illus. p.125. Evergreen, erect rhododendron. **H** 5ft (1.5m), **S** 3–5ft (1–1.5m). In early spring bears loose bunches of tubular, vivid pink-and-white-striped flowers, fading to white at bases. Z7–9 H9–7.

R. 'Seven Stars'. Vigorous, evergreen, upright, dense rhododendron. **H** and **S** 6–10ft (2–3m). Has yellowish-green foliage and, in spring, masses of bunches of large, bell-shaped, wavy-margined, white flowers, flushed with apple-blossom pink, pink in bud. Z7–9 H9–7.

R. sinogrande, illus. p.124. Evergreen, bushy rhododendron. **H** and **S** 30ft (10m). Has very large, oblong to lance-shaped, glossy, dark green leaves, silver- to buff-felted beneath. In mid- and late spring bears widely bell-shaped, pale yellow to creamy-white flowers, marked crimson inside. Z8–10 H10–8.

R. 'Snowdrift'. Deciduous, bushy azalea. **H** and **S** to 8ft (2.5m). Bears bunches of large, slender-tubed flowers in spring before leaves are produced. White flowers have yellow marks that deepen to orange. Z6–8 H8–6.

R. souliei. Evergreen, open rhododendron. **H** and **S** 5–12ft (1.5–4m). Has rounded leaves and, in late spring, saucer-shaped, soft pink flowers. Grows best in areas of low rainfall. Z7–9 H9–7.

R. 'Spek's Orange'. Deciduous, bushy azalea. **H** and **S** to 8ft (2.5m). In late spring bears bold bunches of large, slender-tubed, bright reddish-orange flowers, with greenish marks within. Z5–8 H8–5.

R. 'Strawberry Ice'. Deciduous, bushy azalea. **H** and **S** 5–8ft (1.5–2.5m). In late spring, deep pink buds open into trumpet-shaped, flesh-pink flowers, with deep yellow-marked throats and mottled deeper pink petal margins Z4–8 H8–1.

R. 'Surprise'. Evergreen, dense azalea. **H** and **S** to 5ft (1.5m). Has abundant, small, funnel-shaped, light orange-red flowers in mid-spring. Looks effective when mass planted and is ideal in partial shade and full sun. Z7–9 H9–7.

R. 'Susan'. Close-growing, evergreen rhododendron. **H** and **S** 5–12ft (1.5–4m). Foliage is glossy, dark green. In spring bears large bunches of open funnel-shaped flowers in 2 shades of blue-mauve, spotted purple within. Z6–9 H9–6.

R. sutchuenense. Evergreen, spreading shrub or treelike rhododendron. **H** and **S** to 16ft (5m). Has large leaves and, in early spring, large bunches of broadly funnel-shaped, pink flowers, spotted deeper within. Is suitable for light woodland. Z6–9 H9–6.

R. 'Temple Belle'. Evergreen rhododendron of neat, compact habit. **H** and **S** 5–8ft (1.5–2.5m). Loose bunches of bell-shaped, clear pink flowers are produced in spring. Rounded leaves are dark green above, gray-green beneath. Z8–9 H9–8.

R. thomsonii. Evergreen, rounded rhododendron of open habit. **H** and **S** to 18ft (5.5m). Leaves are waxy, dark green above, whiter beneath. Peeling, fawn-colored bark contrasts well with bell-shaped, waxy, red flowers in spring. Z8–12 H12–10.

R. 'Vuyk's Scarlet'. Evergreen, compact azalea. **H** and **S** to 2ft (60cm). In spring bears masses of relatively large, open funnel-shaped, brilliant red flowers, with wavy petals, which completely cover glossy foliage. Z6–9 H9–5.

R. wardii. Evergreen, compact rhododendron. **H** and **S** 5–12ft (1.5–4m). Leaves are rounded. In late spring bears loose bunches of saucer-shaped, clear yellow flowers, with crimson, basal blotches. Z7–9 H9–7.

R. williamsianum, illus. p.124. Evergreen rhododendron of compact, spreading habit. **H** and **S** 5ft (1.5m). Young leaves are bronze, maturing to mid-green. Has loosely clustered, bell-shaped, pink flowers in spring. Is ideal for a small garden. Z7–9 H9–7.

R. 'Woodcock'. Evergreen, compact, spreading rhododendron. **H** and **S** 5–8ft (1.5–2.5m). Has semi-glossy, dark green leaves and, in spring, masses of loose bunches of funnel-shaped, rose-red flowers. Z7–9 H9–7.

R. xanthocodon. See *R. cinnabarium* subsp. *xanthocodon*.

R. yakushimanum, illus. p.124. Evergreen, dome-shaped rhododendron of neat, compact habit. **H** 3ft (1m), **S** 5ft (1.5m). Leaves are broadly oval, silvery at first, maturing to deepest green, and brown-felted beneath. In late spring has open funnel-shaped, pink flowers, green flecked within, that fade to near white. Z5–9 H9–5.

R. 'Yellow Hammer', illus. p.126.
R. yunnanense. Semievergreen, open rhododendron. **H** and **S** 5–12ft (1.5–4m). Has aromatic, gray-green leaves and masses of butterfly-like, pale pink or white flowers, with blotched throats, in spring. Z6–9 H9–6.

RHODOHYPOXIS

HYPOXIDACEAE

Genus of dwarf, spring- to summer-flowering, tuberous perennials, grown for their pink, red or white flowers, each comprising 6 petals that meet at the center, so the flower has no eye. Needs full sun and sandy, peaty soil. Water freely when in growth. Propagate in spring by seed or offsets.

R. 'Albrighton', illus. p.365.
R. baurii. Spring- and early summer-flowering, tuberous perennial. **H** 2–4in (5–10cm), **S** 1–2in (2.5–5cm). Has erect, basal tuft of narrowly lance-shaped, hairy leaves. Bears succession of erect, flattish, white, pale pink or red flowers, on slender stems. Z9–10 H10–9. **var. platypetala** has larger, white or very pale pink flowers.

R. 'Douglas'. Spring- and early summer-flowering, tuberous perennial. **H** 2–4in (5–10cm), **S** 1–2in (2.5–5cm). Has erect, basal tuft of narrowly lance-shaped, hairy leaves. Bears succession of solitary, upright, flattish, rich deep red flowers, on slender stems. Z9–10 H 10–9.

R. 'Margaret Rose', illus. p.362.

RHODOLEIA

HAMAMELIDACEAE

Genus of evergreen, mainly spring-flowering trees, grown for their foliage and flowers. Needs full light or partial shade and rich, well-drained, neutral to acid soil. Water container specimens freely when in full growth, sparingly at other times. Tolerates pruning, if necessary. Propagate by semiripe cuttings in summer or by seed when ripe, in fall, or in spring.

R. championii. Evergreen, bushy tree. **H** and **S** 12–25ft (4–8m). Elliptic to oval, bright green leaves, to 3½in (9cm) long, are borne near shoot tips. Clusters of tiny flowers, surrounded by petal-like, pink bracts, are produced in spring. Z11 H12–10.

RHODOPHIALA

AMARYLLIDACEAE

Genus of bulbs, grown for their large, funnel-shaped flowers. Needs full sun or partial shade and well-drained soil. Keep dormant bulbs dry in winter. Propagate by seed in spring or by offsets in spring (summer-flowering species).

R. advena, syn. *Hippeastrum advenum*, illus. p.410.

RHODOTHAMNUS

ERICACEAE

Genus of one species of evergreen, semi-prostrate, open shrub, grown for its flowers. Is suitable for rock gardens and peat beds. Needs sun and rich, well-drained, acid soil. Propagate by seed in spring or by semiripe cuttings in summer.

R. chamaecistus, illus. p.338.

RHODOTYPOS

ROSACEAE

Genus of one species of deciduous shrub, grown for its flowers. Needs sun or partial shade and fertile, moist but well-drained soil. After flowering, on established plants, cut back some older shoots. Propagate by softwood cuttings in summer or by seed in fall.

R. kerrioides. See *R. scandens*.
R. scandens, syn. *R. kerrioides*, illus. p.149.

Rhoeo discolor. See *Tradescantia spathacea*.
Rhoeo spathacea. See *Tradescantia spathacea*.

RHOICISSUS

VITACEAE

Genus of evergreen, tendril climbers, grown for their foliage. Bears inconspicuous flowers intermittently. Needs sun and fertile, moist but well-drained soil. Water regularly, less in cold weather. Provide support. Remove crowded stems when necessary or in early spring. Propagate by seed in spring or by semiripe cuttings in summer.

R. capensis (Cape grape). Vigorous, evergreen, tendril climber. **H** and **S** to 15ft (5m). Rounded, toothed, lustrous, mid- to deep green leaves, to 8in (20cm) wide, have

deeply rounded, heart-shaped bases. Z11 H12–10.

R. rhombifolia. See *Cissus rhombifolia*.
R. rhomboidea. See *Cissus rhombifolia*.

RHOMBOPHYLLUM

AIZOACEAE

Genus of mat-forming, perennial succulents with dense, basal rosettes of linear or semicylindrical leaves, each expanded towards middle or tip; leaf tip is reflexed or incurved. Needs sun and very well-drained soil. Propagate by seed or stem cuttings in spring or summer.

R. rhomboideum, illus. p.494.

RHUS

Sumac

ANACARDIACEAE

Genus of deciduous trees, shrubs and scrambling climbers, grown for their divided, ashlike foliage, fall color and, in some species, showy fruit clusters. Requires sun and well-drained soil. Propagate by semiripe cuttings in summer, by seed in fall or by root cuttings in winter. May be attacked by coral spot fungus.

① All parts of *R. verniciflua* are highly toxic if ingested; contact with its foliage, and that of a number of related species, including *R. succedanea*, may aggravate skin allergies.

R. aromatica (Fragrant sumac). Deciduous, bushy shrub. **H** 3ft (1m), **S** 5ft (1.5m). Deep green leaves, divided into 3 oval leaflets, turn orange or reddish-purple in fall. Tiny, yellow flowers are borne in mid-spring, before foliage, followed by spherical, red fruits. Z2–8 H8–1.

R. copallina (Dwarf sumac, Shining sumac). Deciduous, upright shrub. **H** and **S** 3–5ft (1–1.5m) or more. Glossy, dark green leaves, divided into numerous lance-shaped leaflets, turn red-purple in fall. Minute, greenish-yellow flowers, borne in dense clusters from mid- to late summer, are followed by narrowly egg-shaped, bright red fruits. Z5–9 H9–4.

R. cotinoides. See *Cotinus obovatus*.
R. cotinus. See *Cotinus coggygria*.
R. glabra, illus. p.140.
R. hirta. See *R. typhina*. **'Laciniata'**. See *R. typhina* 'Dissecta'.
R. potaninii. Deciduous, round-headed tree. **H** 40ft (12m), **S** 25ft (8m). Large, dark green leaves, with usually 7–11 oval leaflets, turn red in fall. In summer produces dense clusters of tiny, yellow-green flowers. Female flower clusters are followed by tiny, spherical, black or brownish fruits. Z5–9 H9–5.

R. succedanea, syn. *Toxicodendron succedaneum* (Wax tree). Deciduous, spreading tree. **H** and **S** 30ft (10m). Large, glossy, dark green leaves, divided into 9–15 oval leaflets, turn red in fall. Has dense clusters of tiny, yellow-green flowers in summer. Female flowers are followed by tiny, spherical, black or brownish fruits. Z5–8 H8–5.

R. trichocarpa, illus. p.90.
R. typhina, syn. *R. hirta* (Staghorn sumac, Velvet sumac). Deciduous, spreading, suckering, open shrub or tree. **H** 15ft (5m), **S** 20ft (6m). Velvety shoots are clothed in dark green leaves divided into oblong

leaflets. Produces minute, greenish-white flowers from mid- to late summer. Leaves become brilliant orange-red in fall, accompanying clusters of spherical, deep red fruits on female plants. Z3–8 H8–1. **'Dissecta'**, syn. *R. hirta* 'Laciniata', *R. typhina* 'Laciniata' illus. p.117. **'Laciniata'** of gardens. See *R. typhina* 'Dissecta'.
R. verniciflua, syn. *Toxicodendron vernicifluum* (Varnish tree). Deciduous, spreading tree. **H** 50ft (15m), **S** 30ft (10m). Large, glossy, bright green leaves, divided into 7–13 oval leaflets, redden in fall. Bears dense clusters of tiny, yellow-green flowers in summer, followed by berry-like, brownish-yellow fruits. ① Contact with the sap may severely irritate the skin. Z6–9 H9–6.

x RHYNCATTLEANTHE

ORCHIDACEAE

See also ORCHIDS.
x R. Cherub gx 'Spring Daffodil', syn. x *Potinara* Cherub gx 'Spring Daffodil'. Evergreen, epiphytic orchid for an intermediate greenhouse. **H** 6in (15cm). Sprays of yellow flowers, 2in (5cm) across, are produced in spring. Broadly oval, rigid leaves are 4in (10cm) long. Needs good light in summer.

Rhynchelytrum repens. See *Melinis repens*.
Rhynchelytrum roseum. See *Melinis repens*.

x RHYNCHOLAELIOCATTLEYA

ORCHIDACEAE

See also ORCHIDS.
x R. Hetherington Horace gx 'Coronation', syn. x *Brassolaeliocattleya* Hetherington Horace gx 'Coronation'. Evergreen, epiphytic orchid for an intermediate greenhouse. **H** 18in (45cm). Bears stiff, oval leaves, 4–6in (10–15cm) long, and fragrant, light pink flowers, 4in (10cm) across, with deep pink-yellow lips, up to 4 to a stem, mainly in spring. Provide good light in summer.
x R. Mount Adams gx, syn. x *Brassocattleya* Mount Adams gx, illus. p.466. Evergreen, epiphytic orchid for an intermediate greenhouse. **H** 18in (45cm). Intermittently produces lavender-pink flowers, to 6in (15cm) across, with darker lip marked yellow and red, up to 4 per stem. Has oval, stiff leaves, 4–6in (10–15cm) long. Needs good light in summer.
x R. St. Helier gx, syn. x *Brassolaeliocattleya* St. Helier gx. Evergreen, epiphytic orchid for an intermediate greenhouse. **H** 18in (45cm). Produces oval, stiff leaves, 4–6in (10–15cm) long. Pinkish-purple flowers, to 4in (10cm) across, with yellow-marked, rich red lips, are borne 1–4 to a stem, mainly in spring. Grow in good light in summer.

RHYNCHOSPORA

CYPERACEAE

See also GRASSES, BAMBOOS, RUSHES and SEDGES.
R. colorata, syn. *Dichromena colorata*, illus. p.437.

RHYNCHOSTELE

ORCHIDACEAE

See also ORCHIDS.
R. bictoniensis, syn. *Lemboglossum bictoniense, Odontoglossum bictoniense*. Evergreen, epiphytic orchid for a cool greenhouse. **H** 9in (23cm). Olive-green flowers, 1½in (4cm) across, barred with dark brown and sometimes pink-flushed, white lip, are produced in spikes in late summer. Has narrowly oval leaves, 4–6in (10–15cm) long. Requires shade in summer.
R. cervantesii, syn. *Lemboglossum cervantesii, Odontoglossum cervantesii*. Evergreen, epiphytic orchid for a cool greenhouse. **H** 3in (8cm). In winter produces sprays of papery, white flowers, 1in (2.5cm) across, with cobweb-like, light brown marks. Has narrowly oval leaves, 4–6in (10–15cm) long. Grow in shade in summer.
R. cordatum, syn. *Lemboglossum cordatum, Odontoglossum cordatum*. Evergreen, epiphytic orchid for a cool greenhouse. **H** 5in (12cm). Sprays of brown-marked, corn-yellow flowers, 1in (2.5cm) across, are produced in spring. Leaves are narrowly oval and 4–6in (10–15cm) long. Provide shade in summer and keep very dry in winter.
R. rossii, syn. *Lemboglossum rossii, Odontoglossum rossii*, illus. p.466. Evergreen, epiphytic orchid for a cool greenhouse. **H** 3in (8cm). In fall–winter, white to mushroom-pink flowers, 1in (2.5cm) across, speckled beige-brown, are borne in spikes. Narrowly oval leaves are 4–6in (10–15cm) long. Needs shade in summer.

RIBES

Flowering currant

GROSSULARIACEAE

Genus of deciduous or evergreen, mainly spring-flowering shrubs, grown for their edible fruits (currants and gooseberries) or their flowers. Needs full sun and well-drained, fertile soil, but *R. laurifolium* tolerates shade. After flowering, cut out some older shoots and, in winter or early spring, prune straggly, old plants hard. Propagate deciduous species by hardwood cuttings in winter, evergreens by semiripe cuttings in summer. Aphids attack young foliage.
R. aureum of gardens. See *R. odoratum*.
R. laurifolium, illus. p.165.
R. odoratum, syn. *R. aureum* (Buffalo currant, Clove currant). Deciduous, upright shrub. **H** and **S** 6ft (2m). Clusters of fragrant, tubular, golden-yellow flowers are borne from mid- to late spring, followed by rounded, purple fruits. Rounded, 3-lobed, bright green leaves turn red and purple in fall. Z5–8 H8–5.
R. sanguineum (Flowering currant). **'Brocklebankii'** is a deciduous, spreading shrub. **H** and **S** 4ft (1.2m). Has aromatic, pale yellow leaves. Pendent clusters of small, pale pink flowers, in spring, are followed by white-bloomed, black fruits. Z6–8 H8–6. **'Edward VII'**, illus. p.146. **'Pulborough Scarlet'**, illus. p.123. **'Tydeman's White'**, **H** and **S** 8ft (2.5m), has pure white flowers.
R. speciosum, illus. p.193.

RICHEA

ERICACEAE/EPACRIDACEAE

Genus of evergreen, summer-flowering shrubs, grown for their foliage and densely clustered flowers. Needs sun or partial shade and moist, peaty, neutral to acid soil. Propagate by semiripe cuttings in summer or by seed in fall.
R. scoparia. Evergreen, upright shrub. **H** and **S** 6ft (2m). Shoots are covered with narrowly lance-shaped, sharp-pointed, dark green leaves. Bears dense, upright spikes of small, egg-shaped, pink, white, orange or maroon flowers in early summer. Z9–10 H10–9.

RICINUS

EUPHORBIACEAE

Genus of one species of fast-growing, evergreen, treelike shrub, grown for its foliage. In cool climates, is grown as an annual. Needs sun and fertile to rich, well-drained soil. May require support in exposed areas. Propagate by seed sown under glass in early spring. ① All parts of *R. communis*, particularly the seeds, are highly toxic if ingested; contact with the foliage may aggravate skin allergies.
R. communis, illus. p.318. **'Impala'**, illus. p.308.

ROBINIA

LEGUMINOSAE/PAPILIONACEAE

Genus of deciduous, mainly summer-flowering trees and shrubs, grown for their foliage and clusters of pealike flowers. Is useful for poor, dry soil. Needs sun and any but waterlogged soil. Branches are brittle and may be damaged by strong winds. Propagate by seed or suckers in fall or by root cuttings in winter. ① All parts may cause severe discomfort if ingested.
R. x ambigua 'Decaisneana'. Deciduous, spreading tree. **H** 50ft (15m), **S** 30ft (10m). Dark green leaves are divided into numerous oval leaflets. Long, hanging clusters of pealike, pink flowers are borne in early summer. Z4–11 H12–1.
R. hispida, illus. p.133. **var. kelseyi**, syn. *R. kelseyi* (Allegheny moss locust) is a deciduous, spreading, open shrub. **H** 8ft (2.5m), **S** 12ft (4m). Clusters of pealike, rose-pink flowers, in late spring or early summer, are followed by pendent, red seed pods. Dark green leaves are divided into 9 or 11 oval leaflets.
R. kelseyi. See *R. hispida* var. *kelseyi*.
R. pseudoacacia (Black locust). Fast-growing, deciduous, spreading tree. **H** 80ft (25m), **S** 50ft (15m). Dark green leaves are divided into 11–23 oval leaflets. Has dense, drooping clusters of fragrant, pealike, white flowers in late spring and early summer. Z4–9 H9–3. **'Frisia'**, illus. p.76. **'Umbraculifera'**, **H** and **S** 20ft (6m), rarely produces rounded, dense flower head. Z4–9 H9–1.
R. x slavinii 'Hilleri', illus. p.86.

Rochea coccinea. See *Crassula coccinea.*

RODGERSIA

SAXIFRAGACEAE

Genus of summer-flowering, rhizomatous perennials. Is ideal for pond sides. Needs shelter from strong winds, which may damage foliage. Requires sun or partial shade and moist soil. Propagate by division in spring or by seed in fall.
R. aesculifolia, illus. p.437.
R. pinnata 'Fireworks' Clump-forming, rhizomatous perennial. **H** 3ft (1m), **S** 2ft (60cm). Has large creeping root and large, pinnate, red-tinged, mid-green leaves divided into narrowly oval leaflets. In summer produces much-branched, loose panicles of small, star-shaped, pink-red flowers. **'Superba'**, **H** 3–4ft (1–1.2m), **S** 2½ft (75cm), has bronze-tinged, emerald-green leaves and bright pink flowers. Z3–7 H7–1.
R. podophylla, illus. p.436.
R. sambucifolia, illus. p.437.
R. tabularis. See *Astilboides tabularis.*

ROMNEYA

Matilija poppy, Tree poppy

PAPAVERACEAE

Genus of summer-flowering, woody-based perennials and deciduous subshrubs. Requires a warm, sunny position and deep, well-drained soil. Is difficult to establish, resents being moved and, in very cold areas, roots may need protection in winter. Once established, may spread rapidly. Propagate by softwood cuttings of basal shoots in early spring, by seed in fall (transplanting seedlings without disturbing rootballs) or by root cuttings in winter.
R. coulteri, illus. p.216.
R. 'White Cloud'. Vigorous, bushy, woody-based perennial. **H** and **S** 3ft (1m). Throughout summer produces large, slightly fragrant, shallowly cup-shaped, white flowers, with prominent golden stamens. Leaves are oval, deeply lobed and gray. Z8–10 H9–2.

ROMULEA

IRIDACEAE

Genus of crocus-like corms, grown for their funnel-shaped flowers. Needs full light and well-drained, sandy soil. Water freely in growing period. Most species die down in summer and then need warmth and dryness. *R. macowanii*, however, is dormant in winter. Propagate by seed in fall, or in spring for *R. macowanii*.
R. bulbocodioides of gardens. See *R. flava*.
R. bulbocodium, illus. p.419.
R. flava, syn. *R. bulbocodioides*. Early spring-flowering corm. **H** to 4in (10cm), **S** 1–2in (2.5–5cm). Has threadlike, erect, basal leaf and 1–5 upright, widely funnel-shaped, usually yellow flowers, ¾–1½in (2–4cm) across, with deeper yellow centers. Z9–10 H10–9.
R. longituba. See *R. macowanii* var. *alticola*.
R. macowanii var. alticola, syn. *R. longituba*. Summer-flowering corm. **H** and **S** ½–¾in (1–2cm). Leaves are threadlike, erect and basal. Produces 1–3 upright, yellow flowers, 1¼in (3cm) across with long tube pushing upward to become wide funnel shape. Z8–10 H10–8.
R. sabulosa. Early spring-flowering corm. **H** 2–6in (5–15cm), **S** 1–2in (2.5–5cm). Forms

threadlike, erect, basal leaves. Stems bear 1–4 upward-facing, funnel-shaped, black-centered, bright red flowers that open flattish, to 1½–2in (4–5cm) across, in sun. Z9–10 H10–9.

RONDELETIA

RUBIACEAE

Genus of evergreen, mainly summer-flowering trees and shrubs, grown mainly for their flowers. Requires full light or partial shade and fertile, well-drained soil. Water container specimens freely when in full growth, moderately at other times. Stems may be shortened in early spring if necessary. Propagate by seed in spring or by semiripe cuttings in summer.

R. amoena. Evergreen, rounded shrub. **H** and **S** 6–12ft (2–4m). Oval, dark green leaves are brown hairy beneath. Produces dense clusters of tubular, 4- or 5-lobed, pink flowers in summer. Z11 H12–10.

Rooksbya euphorbioides. See *Neobuxbaumia euphorbioides.*

ROSA

Rose

ROSACEAE

Genus of deciduous or semievergreen, open shrubs and scrambling climbers, grown for their profusion of flowers, often fragrant, and sometimes for their fruits (rose hips). Leaves are divided into usually 5 or 7 oval leaflets, with rounded or pointed tips, that are sometimes toothed. Stems usually bear thorns, or prickles. Most of the bush and climbing roses grow well in Z5–9 H9–5 (unless otherwise stated) but are often grown in colder zones and protected for the winter by mounding, deep planting, or burying. Prefers an open, sunny site and requires fertile, moist but well-drained soil. Avoid planting in an area where roses have been grown in recent years, as problems due to harmful organisms may occur: either exchange the soil, which may be used satisfactorily elsewhere, or choose another site for the new rose. To obtain blooms of high quality, feed in late winter or early spring with a balanced fertilizer and apply a mulch. In spring and summer, feed regularly at 3-weekly intervals. Remove spent flower heads from plants that are "remontant" ("rising up again"; other terms used are repeat- or perpetual-flowering). May be trimmed for tidiness in early winter. To improve health, flower quality and shape of bush, prune in the dormant season or, preferably, in early spring, before young shoots develop from dormant growth buds: remove dead, damaged and dying wood; lightly trim Old Garden and Groundcover roses (see below); remove two-thirds of previous summer's growth of Modern bush, including miniature, roses. Correct treatment of Modern shrub and climbing roses, ramblers and Species roses depends on the individual cultivar, but in general they should be pruned only lightly. Propagate by budding in summer or by hardwood cuttings in fall. All roses are prone to attack by various pests and diseases, including aphids, blackspot, powdery mildew, rust and sawfly.
Rose species and cultivars are often

regarded as 2 separate groups. Cultivars are farther divided into Old Garden and Modern roses. Each group comprises different types, based, it is claimed, on the functional qualities of each plant, such as whether it is repeat-flowering, rather than on any historical, botanical or genetical relationships. Flowers occur in a variety of forms (illustrated and described on p.172). and are single (4–7 petals), semidouble (8–20 petals), double (20–30 petals) or fully double (over 30 petals). Many modern rose cultivars are sold under names other than the registered Plant Breeder's Rights (PBR) names; where this is the case, the plant is listed under its trade name, with the PBR name in brackets afterwards. Roses are illustrated on pp.172–187.

Species roses

Species, or wild, roses (including those interspecific hybrids that share most of the characteristics of their parent species) are either shrubs or climbers, mostly bearing single, 5-petaled, often fragrant flowers in summer, usually in one flush on short shoots from second-year wood; the flowers are followed by red or black hips in fall.

Old Garden roses

This category is so large that it is divided into two groups. Roses in Group A are mostly of European origin, while those in Group B are hybrids between Oriental and European roses.

Group A
Alba—large, freely branching shrubs with only a few prickles on the stems. They bear clusters of 5–7 semi- to fully double, scented flowers in mid-summer, on shoots from second-year wood. Have abundant, grayish-green leaves. Most are good for borders and as hedges or as specimen plants.
Centifolia (or **Provence**)—lax, thorny shrubs that produce often scented, double to fully double flowers, borne singly or in 3s, in summer, on shoots from second-year wood. Leaves are matt, dark green. Are suitable for borders.
Damask—open shrubs with prickly stems and downy leaves. They produce often very fragrant, semi- to fully double flowers, borne singly or in loose clusters of 5–7 mainly in summer, on shoots from second-year wood; a few also flower on new wood in fall. Are suitable for borders or training against a support.
Gallica—shrubs of fairly dense, free-branching habit, with usually thorny stems, and mostly dull, dark green leaves. Produce mostly scented, single to fully double, richly colored flowers, often in clusters of 3, in summer on shoots from second-year wood. Are suitable for borders and as hedging.
Moss—often lax shrubs with a furry, mosslike growth on stems and calyces. Leaves are usually dark green. Usually fragrant, semi- to fully double flowers, often in clusters of 3 or more, are borne on very thorny shoots from second-year wood in summer. Are suitable for beds and borders.
Scots (or **Scotch**)—suckering shrubs, selections or hybrids of *R. spinosissima*, of low, spreading, rarely upright habit, with prickly stems and dark green leaves. Occasionally scented, single to double

flowers are solitary or borne in clusters of 3 or more, on short stems from second-year wood, usually in early summer. Are suitable for beds and borders.
Sweet Briar—vigorous, free-branching shrubs with usually thorny stems and sweetly scented, dark green leaves. In summer, they bear usually scented, single to double flowers, singly or in clusters of up to 7, on short shoots from second-year wood. Use as hedges, as specimen plants and in large borders.

Group B
Bourbon—large, open, repeat-flowering shrubs and climbing roses, often with long, smooth or prickly stems, which may be trained to climb. They have often glossy leaves and numerous scented, double or fully double flowers, borne commonly in 3s, in flushes in summer and usually fall. Flowers are borne on short shoots from second-year wood and on new wood. Are suitable for borders and for training over fences, walls and pillars.
Boursault—climbing roses with long, arching, usually smooth stems and dark green leaves. They bear slightly scented, semidouble or double flowers, singly or in clusters of 3, in early summer, on short shoots from second-year wood. Are suitable for sheltered walls and fences.
China—spindly, repeat-flowering shrubs with mostly smooth stems, bearing only a few reddish-brown prickles, and glossy leaves. They produce sometimes scented, single to fully double flowers, singly or in clusters of 3–13, in flushes in summer–fall. Flowers appear on short shoots from second-year wood and on new wood. Need a sheltered site. Are suitable for borders and walls.
Hybrid Musk—vigorous, repeat-flowering shrubs with prickly stems and abundant foliage. They produce mainly double blooms, often very fragrant, either singly or in clusters of 2–7 or more, in flushes from mid-summer to fall. Are good for shrub borders, and can be trained on walls.
Hybrid Perpetual—free-branching, repeat-flowering shrubs with upright, prickly growth and dark green leaves. They bear often scented, fully double flowers, held singly or in 3s, in flushes in summer–fall on shoots from second-year wood and on new wood. Are suitable for beds and borders.
Noisette—repeat-flowering climbing roses that bear clusters of 3–15 semidouble to fully double flowers, with a slight spicy fragrance, in flushes in summer–fall. Flowers are borne on shoots from second-year wood, occasionally on new wood. Have generally smooth stems and glossy leaves. Are suitable for sheltered, south- or west-facing walls.
Portland (or **Damask Portland**)—upright, compact, repeat-flowering shrubs with thorny stems and usually dark green leaves. They produce usually scented, semi- to fully double flowers, held singly or in 3s, in flushes in summer–fall, mainly on shoots from second-year wood. Are suitable for beds and borders.
Sempervirens—vigorous, semievergreen climbing or rambler roses with shiny, light green leaves. Arching, thorny stems bear clusters of 3–15 unscented, semi- to fully double flowers in summer, on short stems

from second-year wood. Are ideal for naturalizing or for growing on fences and pergolas.
Tea—repeat-flowering shrubs and climbing roses with smooth to thorny stems, sometimes bearing a few large, red prickles, and glossy, light or sometimes dark green leaves. They produce spicy-scented, slender-stemmed, semi- to fully double flowers, borne singly or in 3s, in flushes in summer–fall, on shoots from second-year wood and on new wood. Need a sheltered site. Are suitable for beds and borders and trained against walls.

Modern roses

Climber—often vigorous climbing roses with thorny, arching, stiff stems and usually dense, glossy, mid- to dark green foliage. They bear generally scented flowers in a variety of forms, singly or in clusters of 3–7 or more. Some bloom in summer only, on short shoots from second-year wood; many are repeat-flowering and also flower on new wood. Train against walls, fences or use to cover garden structures.
Climbing Miniature—repeat-flowering, climbing roses with restrained, sparsely thorny growth. Clusters of 3–9 tiny, rarely scented, single to fully double flowers are borne in flushes in summer–fall, on shoots from second-year wood and on new wood. Grow against low walls, fences and pillars.
Floribunda (or **Cluster-flowered bush**)—repeat-flowering, free-branching shrubs of upright or bushy habit, usually with prickly stems and glossy, dark green leaves. Sometimes scented, single to double flowers are usually in clusters of 3–25, rarely solitary, and are borne continuously in summer–fall on shoots from second-year wood and on new wood. Are excellent for borders and as hedges.
Groundcover—trailing and spreading roses, mostly with prickly stems, producing often glossy leaves. They bear clusters of numerous, sometimes scented, single to fully double flowers; some flower in summer only, on short shoots from second-year wood; others are repeat-flowering, and also flower on new wood. Many bear flowers all along the stems. Are ideal for beds, banks and containers, and for trailing over walls.
Hybrid Tea (or **Large-flowered bush**)—repeat-flowering, free-branching shrubs of upright or bushy habit, with usually thorny stems and glossy or matt, mid- to dark green leaves. Large, often scented, usually double flowers are borne singly or in 3s in flushes in summer–fall on shoots from second-year wood and on new wood. Use in formal borders, as hedges and for cut flowers.
Miniature—repeat-flowering shrubs with very compact, rarely spreading, sparsely thorny, short growth. Sprays of 3–11 tiny, rarely scented, single to fully double flowers are borne in flushes in summer–fall on very short shoots from second-year wood and on new wood. Have tiny leaves. Are suitable for edging paths and driveways, and for rock gardens, raised beds and container growing.
Patio (or **Dwarf cluster-flowered bush**)—repeat-flowering shrubs with compact growth, sometimes prickly stems, and usually glossy leaves. They bear clusters of 3–11 usually unscented, single

Q
R

to double flowers in flushes in summer–fall, on shoots from second-year wood and on new wood. Are ideal for beds, borders and as hedges and for growing in containers.

Polyantha—compact, repeat-flowering shrubs with sparsely thorny stems and glossy leaves. Sprays of many small, rarely scented, single to double flowers are borne in summer–fall on shoots from second-year wood and on new wood. Are suitable for beds and borders, as hedges and for containers.

Rambler—a diverse group of vigorous roses with long, arching, thorny stems and dense, usually glossy foliage. They have clusters of 3–21 sometimes scented, single to fully double flowers, mainly in summer, on short shoots from second-year wood and on new wood. Train over walls, fences, pergolas and into trees.

Rugosa—hardy shrubs with tough, wrinkled, usually bright green leaves and prickly stems. Most bear scented, single or semidouble flowers, in clusters of 3–11, in summer–fall, on short shoots from second-year wood. They are often followed by tomato-like, usually red hips. Use as hedges, for beds and borders and as specimen plants.

Shrub—roses in this diverse group are usually larger than bush roses (a general term used to describe Floribundas, Hybrid Teas, Miniatures, Patio roses and occasionally Groundcover roses). They often have thorny stems and bear usually scented, semidouble to double flowers in few- to many-flowered clusters, sometimes singly, in summer–fall. Some bloom in summer only from second-year wood; most are repeat-flowerers and also flower on new wood. Use as hedges, in beds and borders and as specimen plants.

***R.* 'Aimèe Vibert'**, syn. *R.* 'Bouquet de la Mariée'. Noisette rose with smooth stems. **H** 15ft (5m), **S** 10ft (3m). Bears lightly scented, cupped, fully double, blush-pink to white flowers, 3in (8cm) across, in summer–fall. Leaves are glossy, dark green. May be grown as a shrub. Z6–9 H9–6.

***R.* Alan Titchmarsh ('Ausjive').** Bushy Shrub rose with good disease resistance and matt foliage. **H** 5½ft (1.6m), **S** 4ft (1.2m). Produces sweetly scented, rosette, double, deep pink flowers, 5in (12cm) across, with lighter pink outer petals, in summer and again in fall. Z5–9 H9–5.

***R.* x *alba* 'Semiplena'.** See *R.* 'Alba Semiplena'.

***R.* 'Alba Semiplena'**, syn. *R.* x *alba* 'Semiplena'. Vigorous, bushy Alba rose. **H** 6ft (2m), **S** 5ft (1.5m). Bears sweetly scented, flat, semidouble, white flowers, 3in (8cm) across, in mid-summer. Leaves are grayish-green. Is suitable for a hedge. Z3–9 H9–1.

***R.* 'Albéric Barbier'**, illus. p.184.

***R.* 'Albertine'**, illus. p.185.

***R.* Alec's Red ('Cored')**, illus. p.181.

***R.* Alexander ('Harlex')**, syn. *R.* 'Alexandra', illus. p.180.

***R.* 'Alexandra'.** See *R.* Alexander ('Harlex').

***R.* 'Alfred de Dalmas'** of gardens. See *R.* 'Mousseline'.

***R.* Alibaba ('Chewalibaba')**, illus. p.187.

***R.* Alissar Princess of Phonecia ('Harsidon')**, illus. p.174.

***R.* 'Alister Stella Gray'**, syn. *R.* 'Golden Rambler'. Noisette rose with long, vigorous, upright stems. **H** 15ft (5m), **S** 10ft (3m). Bears clusters of musk-scented, quartered, fully double, yolk-yellow flowers, 2½in (6cm) across, in summer–fall. Has glossy, mid-green leaves. Z6–9 H9–6.

***R.* 'Aloha'**, illus. p.185.

***R.* 'Alpine Sunset'.** Compact Hybrid Tea rose with moderate disease resistance. **H** and **S** 2ft (60cm). Fragrant, rounded, fully double, peach-yellow flowers, 8in (20cm) across, are produced on short stems in summer and again in fall. Has large, semi-glossy leaves. May die back in hard winters. Z5–9 H9–5.

***R.* Amber Queen ('Harroony').** Spreading, cluster-flowered bush rose with good disease resistance and repeat-flowering in summer–fall. **H** and **S** 20in (50cm). Amber flowers are fragrant, rounded and fully double, 3in (8cm) across. Has abundant, reddish foliage. Z5–9 H9–5.

***R.* 'American Pillar'.** Vigorous Rambler of lax growth. **H** to 15ft (5m), **S** 12ft (4m). Large clusters of cupped, single, carmine-red flowers, with white eyes, are borne freely in mid-summer. Leathery foliage is glossy, mid-green. Z5–9 H9–5.

***R.* 'Amruda'.** See *R.* Red Ace.

***R.* 'Andeli'.** See *R.* Double Delight.

***R.* Angela Rippon ('Ocaru').** Miniature rose with good disease resistance. **H** 18in (45cm), **S** 12in (30cm). Produces slightly scented, urn-shaped, fully double, salmon-pink flowers, 1½in (4cm) across, in summer and again in fall. Has many small, dark green leaves. Z5–9 H9–5.

***R.* 'Angelita'.** See *R.* Snowball ('Macangeli').

***R.* Anisley Dickson ('Dickimono')**, syn. *R.* 'Dicky'. Vigorous Floribunda rose with good disease resistance. **H** 3ft (1m), **S** 2½ft (75cm). Produces large clusters of slightly scented, pointed, double, salmon-pink flowers 3in (8cm) across, in summer and again in fall. Z5–9 H9–5.

***R.* Anna Ford ('Harpiccolo')**, illus. p.180.

***R.* Anne Harkness ('Harkaramel').** Upright Floribunda rose with good disease resistance. **H** 4ft (1.2m), **S** 2ft (60cm). Slightly scented, urn-shaped, amber flowers, 3in (8cm) across, are borne in sprays of many blooms in summer and again in fall. Z5–9 H9–5.

***R.* Aphrodite ('Tanetidor')**, illus. p.178.

***R.* 'Apothecary's Rose'.** See *R. gallica* var. *officinalis*.

***R.* 'Arthur Bell'**, illus. p.182.

***R.* 'Assemblage des Beautès'**, syn. *R.* 'Rouge Eblouissante'. Upright, dense Gallica rose. **H** 4ft (1.2m), **S** 3ft (1m). In summer bears faintly scented, rounded, fully double, green-eyed, cerise to crimson-purple flowers, 3in (8cm) across. Has rich green leaves. Z6–10 H10–1.

***R.* 'Ausmary'.** See *R.* Mary Rose.

***R.* 'Ausmas'.** See *R.* Graham Thomas.

***R.* 'Austance'.** See *R.* Constance Spry.

***R.* 'Baby Carnival'.** See *R.* Baby Masquerade ('Tanba').

***R.* Baby Masquerade ('Tanba')**, syn. *R.* 'Baby Carnival'. Dense Miniature rose with good disease resistance. **H** and **S** 16in (40cm), more if not pruned. Bears clusters of rosette, double, yellow-pink flowers, 1in (2.5cm) across, in summer and again in fall. Has plentiful, leathery leaves. Z5–9 H9–5.

R. banksiae, syn. *R. banksiae* var. *normalis* (Lady Banks' rose). Climbing Species rose with good disease resistance. **H** and **S** 30ft (10m). Dense clusters of fragrant, flat, single, white flowers, 1in (2.5cm) across, are borne on thornless, light green stems in a single flush in summer. Leaves are small and pale green. Is uncommon in cultivation. Z8–9 H9–8. **'Lutea'** has scentless, rosette, fully double, yellow flowers, ¾in (2cm) across. Needs a sunny, sheltered wall and pruning of spent wood only. **var. *normalis*.** See *R. banksiae*.

***R.* 'Beauty of Glazenwood'.** See *R.* x *odorata* 'Pseudindica'.

***R.* 'Belle Courtisanne'.** See *R.* 'Königin von Dänemark'.

***R.* 'Belle de Crècy'.** Gallica rose of rather lax growth, few thorns and moderate disease resistance. **H** 4ft (1.2m), **S** 3ft (1m). In a single flush in summer produces rosette, fully double, pink flowers, 3in (8cm) across, with green eyes and spicy fragrance. Z3–9 H9–1.

***R.* 'Belle de Londres'.** See *R.* 'Compassion'.

***R.* Belmonte ('Harpearl')**, illus. p.179.

***R.* Benjamin Britten ('Ausencart')**, illus. p.175.

***R.* 'Bizarre Triomphant'.** See *R.* 'Charles de Mills'.

***R.* 'Blanche Moreau'.** Moss rose of rather lax growth. **H** 5ft (1.5m), **S** 4ft (1.2m). Fragrant, cupped, fully double, white flowers, 4in (10cm) across, with brownish "mossing", are borne in summer. Has dull green leaves. Z8–9 H9–1.

***R.* 'Blessings'.** Upright Hybrid Tea rose with moderate disease resistance. **H** 3ft (1m), **S** 2½ft (75cm). Slightly scented, urn-shaped, fully double, salmon-pink flowers are borne singly or in clusters in summer and again in fall. Has large, dark leaves. Z5–9 H9–5.

***R.* Blue Moon ('Tannacht')**, syn. *R.* 'Mainzer Fastnacht', *R.* 'Sissi'. Hybrid Tea rose of open habit. **H** 3ft (1m), **S** 2ft (60cm). Sweetly scented, pointed, fully double, lilac flowers, 4in (10cm) across, are borne in summer–fall. Leaves are large and dark green. Z5–9 H9–5.

***R.* 'Bluenette'.** See *R.* Blue Peter ('Ruiblun').

***R.* Blue Peter ('Ruiblun')**, syn. *R.* 'Bluenette'. Miniature rose of neat habit. **H** 14in (35cm), **S** 12in (30cm). Slightly scented, cupped, double, purple flowers, 2in (5cm) across, are produced in summer–fall. Leaves are small and plentiful.

***R.* 'Blue Rambler'.** See *R.* 'Veilchenblau'.

***R.* 'Blush Noisette'.** See *R.* 'Noisette Carnée'.

***R.* 'Blush Rambler'.** Vigorous Rambler. **H** 10ft (3m), **S** 12ft (4m). Clusters of delicately fragrant, cupped, semidouble, light pink flowers, 1½in (4cm) across, are borne in summer. Has an abundance of glossy leaves. Is a particularly good scrambler for an arch, pergola or tree. Z5–9 H9–5.

***R.* 'Bobbie James'.** Rampant Rambler. **H** to 30ft (10m), **S** 20ft (6m). Large clusters of cupped, semidouble, scented, creamy-white flowers, 2in (5cm) across, are produced in summer. Glossy leaves are reddish-green when young, mid-green when mature.

***R.* 'Bonica '82'.** See *R.* Bonica ('Meidomonac').

***R.* Bonica ('Meidomonac')**, syn. *R.* 'Bonica '82'. Vigorous, spreading shrub rose with very good disease resistance and repeat-flowering in summer–fall. **H** 3ft (1m), **S** 3½ft (1.1m). Bears large sprays of slightly fragrant, cupped, fully double, rose-pink flowers, 3in (7cm) across. Foliage is glossy and plentiful. Z4–9 H9–1.

***R.* 'Boule de Neige'.** Upright Bourbon rose with arching stems and very good disease resistance. **H** 5ft (1.5m), **S** 4ft (1.2m). Very fragrant, cupped to rosette, fully double, white flowers, 3in (8cm) across, sometimes tinged pink, are produced in summer–fall. Leaves are glossy and dark green. Z6–9 H9–6.

***R.* 'Bouquet de la Mariée'.** See *R.* 'Aimèe Vibert'.

***R.* 'Brass Ring'.** See *R.* Peek-A-Boo ('Dicgrow').

***R.* Breath of Life ('Harquanne').** Stiff, upright Climber with moderate disease resistance. **H** 9ft (2.8m), **S** 7ft (2.2m). Slightly scented, rounded, fully double, pinkish-apricot flowers, 4in (10cm) across, are borne in summer and again in fall. Leaves are semi-glossy. Z5–9 H9–5.

***R.* Bridge of Sighs ('Harglow')**, illus. p.187.

***R.* Bright Smile ('Dicdance').** Bushy Floribunda rose with good disease resistance and repeat-flowering in summer–fall. **H** and **S** 18in (45cm). Bears clusters of slightly scented, flat, semidouble, yellow flowers, 3in (8cm) across. Has glossy, bright green leaves. Z5–9 H9–5.

***R.* 'Buff Beauty'**, illus. p.177.

***R.* Burgundy Ice ('Prose')**, illus. p.181.

***R. californica*.** Shrubby Species rose. **H** 7ft (2.2m), **S** 6ft (2m). Fragrant, flat, single, lilac-pink flowers, 1½in (4cm) across, are borne freely in mid-summer, sparsely in fall. Has small dull green leaves. Z6–9 H9–6. **'Plena'.** See *R. nutkana* 'Plena'.

***R.* 'Canary Bird'.** See *R. xanthina* 'Canary Bird'.

***R.* 'Candide'.** See R. Goldstar.

***R.* 'Capitaine John Ingram'.** Vigorous, bushy Moss rose. **H** and **S** 4ft (1.2m). In summer bears fragrant, cupped, fully double, rich maroon-crimson flowers, 3in (8cm) across; petals are paler on reverses. Foliage is dark green. Z4–9 H9–1.

***R.* 'Cardinal de Richelieu'**, illus. p.175.

***R.* Cardinal Hume ('Harregale')**, illus. p.175.

***R.* Carris ('Harmanna')**, illus. p.180.

***R.* Casino ('Macca')**, syn. *R.* 'Gerbe d'Or'. Upright, free-branching Climber with moderate disease resistance. **H** 10ft (3m), **S** 7ft (2.2m). Slightly scented, rounded, double, yellow flowers, 3½in (9cm) across, are borne in summer and again in fall. Sparse, dark green leaves are produced on stiffly arching stems. Z5–9 H9–5.

***R.* 'Cécile Brünner'**, illus. p.186.

***R.* 'Céleste'**, syn. *R.* 'Celestial', illus. p.173.

***R.* 'Celestial'.** See *R.* 'Céleste'.

R.* x *centifolia (Cabbage rose, Provence rose). **'Cristata'**, syn. *R.* 'Chapeau de Napoléon', *R.* 'Cristata' (Crested moss) Bushy, lanky Centifolia rose. **H** 5ft (1.5m), **S** 4ft (1.2m). In summer, very fragrant, cupped, fully double, pink flowers, 3½in (9cm) across, with tufted sepals, are borne on nodding stems amid dull green foliage. May be grown on a support. **'Muscova'** (Common moss, Old pink moss) is a vigorous, lax Moss rose with dense moss on stems and calyces. Bears rounded to

cupped, mossed, pink flowers, 8cm (3in) across. Leaves are matt, dull green.
R. 'Cerise Bouquet'. Very vigorous Shrub rose of arching habit. **H** and **S** to 11ft (3.5m). Produces masses of flat, semidouble, cherry-red flowers, 2½in (6cm) across, in summer. Leaves are small and grayish-green. Z5–9 H9–5.
R. Champagne Cocktail ('Horflash'). Upright Floribunda rose with very good disease resistance. **H** 3ft (1m), **S** 2ft (60cm). Fragrant, cupped, double, yellow-pink flowers, 3½in (9cm) across, opening wide are borne in summer and again in fall. Z5–9 H9–5.
R. Champagne Moments ('Korvanaber'), illus. p.177.
R. Chandos Beauty ('Harmisty'), illus. p.178.
R. 'Chapeau de Napoléon'. See *R.* x *centifolia* 'Cristata'.
R. 'Chaplin's Pink Companion', illus. p.185.
R. Charles Darwin ('Auspeet'). Bushy shrub rose with very good disease resistance and glossy, light green foliage. **H** 6ft (1.8m), **S** 4ft (1.2m). Quartered-rosette, fully double, golden-yellow flowers, 4in (10cm) across, with occasional pink flush on outer petals, are borne in summer and again in fall. Z5–9 H9–5.
R. 'Charles de Mills', syn. *R.* 'Bizarre Triomphant'. Upright, arching Gallica rose with fairly smooth stems. **H** 4ft (1.2m), **S** 3ft (1m). Very fragrant, quartered-rosette, fully double, crimson-purple flowers, 4in (10cm) across, are borne in summer. Leaves are plentiful and mid-green. May be grown on a support. Z3–9 H9–1.
R. 'Chewarvel'. See *R.* Laura Ford.
R. *chinensis* var. *minima*. See *R.* 'Rouletii'. **'Mutabilis'.** See *R.* x *odorata* 'Mutabilis'.
R. City of London ('Harukfore'). Rounded Floribunda rose. **H** 3ft (1m), **S** 2½ft (75cm). In summer–fall bears dainty sprays of sweet-smelling, urn-shaped, double, blush-pink flowers, 3in (8cm) across, amid bright green foliage. Z5–9 H9–5.
R. 'Climbing Lady Hillingdon'. Stiff climbing Tea rose. **H** 12ft (4m), **S** 6ft (2m). Has dark green leaves on reddish-green stems. Bears spice-scented, pointed, double, apricot-yellow flowers, 4in (10cm) across, in summer–fall. Is best in a sheltered site. Z6–9 H9–6.
R. 'Climbing Mrs. Sam McGredy'. Vigorous, stiff, branching Climber. **H** and **S** 10ft (3m). Leaves are glossy, rich reddish-green. Bears faintly fragrant, large, urn-shaped, fully double, coppery salmon-pink flowers, 4½in (11cm) across, in summer and again, sparsely, in fall. Z4–9 H9–4.
R. Colibre '79 ('Meidanover'). Upright, rather open Miniature rose with good disease resistance. **H** 15in (38cm), **S** 10in (25cm). Urn-shaped, double, red-veined, orange flowers, 1½in (4cm) across, are borne in summer and again in fall. Z5–9 H9–5.
R. 'Commandant Beaurepaire', syn. *R.* 'Panachée d'Angers'. Vigorous, spreading Bourbon rose. **H** and **S** 4ft (1.2m). Fragrant, cupped, double, blush-pink flowers, 4in (10cm) across, splashed with mauve, purple, crimson and scarlet, are borne in summer–fall. Light green leaflets have wavy margins. Z6–9 H9–1.
R. 'Compassion', syn. *R.* 'Belle de Londres', illus. p.185.
R. 'Complicata', illus. p.174.
R. 'Comte de Chambord' of gardens. See *R.* 'Madame Knorr'.
R. Congratulations ('Korlift'), syn. *R.* 'Sylvia'. Upright, vigorous Hybrid Tea rose. **H** 4ft (1.2m), **S** 3ft (1m). Produces neat, urn-shaped, fully double, deep rose-pink flowers, 4½in (11cm) across, on long stems in summer–fall. Leaves are large and dark green. Makes a tall hedge. Z5–9 H9–5.
R. 'Conrad Ferdinand Meyer'. Vigorous, arching shrub rose with good disease resistance. **H** 8ft (2.5m), **S** 4ft (1.2m). Cupped, fully double, pink flowers, 3in (7cm) across, are richly fragrant and borne freely in a single flush in summer. Foliage is leathery and prone to rust. Z4–9 H9–1.
R. Constance Spry ('Austance'), illus. p.174.
R. Crazy for You ('Wekroalt'), illus. p.179.
R. 'Cristata'. See *R.* x *centifolia* 'Cristata'.
R. 'Cuisse de Nymphe'. See *R.* 'Great Maiden's Blush'.
R. Dancing Queen ('Fryfestoon'), illus. p.186.
R. 'Danse du Feu', syn. *R.* 'Spectacular'. Vigorous, stiffly branched Climber with moderate disease resistance. **H** and **S** 8ft (2.5m). Slightly scented, rounded, double, scarlet flowers, 3in (8cm) across, are borne in summer and again in fall. Has abundant, glossy foliage. Z5–9 H9–5.
R. Darcey Bussell ('Ausdecorum'). Compact Shrub rose with good disease resistance and matt, mid-green leaves. **H** 4ft (1.2m), **S** 3ft (1m). Fragrant, quartered-rosette, fully double, crimson flowers, 4in (10cm) across, aging to purple shades, are produced in summer and again in fall. Z5–9 H9–5.
R. Darling Flame ('Meilucca'). Well-branched Miniature rose. **H** 16in (40cm), **S** 12in (30cm). Leaves are glossy and dark green. Urn-shaped, double, orange-red flowers, 1½in (4cm) across, are borne freely in summer–fall. Z5–9 H9–5.
R. 'Dicdance'. See *R.* Bright Smile.
R. 'Dicdivine'. See *R.* Pot O' Gold.
R. 'Dicgrow'. See *R.* Peek-A-Boo.
R. 'Dicjana'. See *R.* Elina.
R. 'Dicjem'. See *R.* Freedom.
R. 'Dicjubell'. See *R.* Lovely Lady.
R. 'Dickimono'. See *R.* Anisley Dickson.
R. 'Dicky'. See *R.* Anisley Dickson ('Dickimono').
R. 'Diclulu'. See *R.* Gentle Touch.
R. 'Dicmagic'. See *R.* Sweet Magic.
R. 'Doris Tysterman'. Vigorous, upright Hybrid Tea rose with moderate disease resistance. **H** 4ft (1.2m), **S** 2½ft (75cm). Slightly scented, pointed, fully double, orange-red flowers, 4in (10cm) across, are borne in summer and again in fall. Leaves are large, glossy and dark green. Z5–9 H9–5.
R. 'Dortmund', illus. p.186.
R. Double Delight ('Andeli'), illus. p.180.
R. 'Double Velvet'. See *R.* 'Tuscany Superb'.
R. 'Doux Parfum'. See *R.* L'aimant ('Harzola').
R. Drummer Boy ('Harvacity'). Dwarf Floribunda rose of bushy, spreading habit. **H** and **S** 20in (50cm). In summer–fall bears faintly scented, cupped, double, bright crimson flowers, 2in (5cm) across, in dense sprays. Has abundant, small, dark green leaves. Makes a good, low hedge.
R. Dublin Bay ('Macdub'), illus. p.186.
R. 'Duchesse d'Istrie'. See *R.* 'William Lobb'.
R. 'Duftzauber '84'. See *R.* Royal William ('Korzaun').
R. 'Du Maître d'Ecole'. Bushy, spreading Gallica rose. **H** 4ft (1.2m), **S** 3ft (1m). Bears fragrant, quartered-rosette, fully double, carmine to light pink flowers, 4in (10cm) across, in summer. Foliage is dull green.
R. 'Dupontii', syn. *R. moschata* var. *nivea*, illus. p.173.
R. 'Easlea's Golden Rambler'. Vigorous, arching Rambler. **H** 15ft (5m), **S** 10ft (3m). Scented, cupped, fully double, yellow flowers, 4in (10cm) across and flecked with red, are produced, usually in clusters, in summer. Has plentiful, leathery foliage.
R. 'Easter Morn'. See *R.* 'Easter Morning'.
R. 'Easter Morning', syn. *R.* 'Easter Morn'. Upright Miniature rose. **H** 16in (40cm), **S** 10in (25cm). In summer–fall, faintly fragrant, urn-shaped, fully double, ivory-white flowers, 1¼in (3cm) across, are borne freely amid glossy, dark green leaves.
R. Easy does it ('Harpagent'), illus. p.183.
R. Easy Going ('Harglow'), illus. p.182.
R. *ecae*. Erect, wiry Species rose with very good disease resistance. **H** 5ft (1.5m), **S** 4ft (1.2m). Cupped, single, bright yellow flowers, ¾in (2cm) across, with light musky scent, are borne close to reddish stems in a single flush in summer. Foliage is fernlike. Needs shelter. Z7–9 H9–7.
R. *eglanteria*. See *R. rubiginosa*.
R. Elina ('Dicjana'), syn. *R.* 'Peaudouce'. Vigorous, shrubby Hybrid Tea rose. **H** 3½ft (1.1m), **S** 2½ft (75cm). Lightly scented, rounded, fully double, ivory-white flowers, 6in (15cm) across, with lemon-yellow centers, are borne freely in summer–fall. Has abundant, reddish foliage. Z4–11 H12–1.
R. 'Elizabeth Harkness'. Neat, upright Hybrid Tea rose with moderate disease resistance. **H** 32in (80cm), **S** 24in (60cm). Fragrant, pointed, fully double, buff-tinted, pale creamy-pink flowers, 5in (12cm) across, are borne in summer and again in fall. Has abundant, dark green foliage. Z5–9 H9–5.
R. 'Emily Gray', illus. p.187.
R. 'Empereur du Maroc'. Compact, shrubby Hybrid Perpetual rose with good disease resistance. **H** 4ft (1.2m), **S** 3ft (1m). Fragrant, quartered-rosette, fully double, rich purplish-crimson flowers, 3in (8cm) across, are borne freely in a single flush in summer. Z5–9 H9–5.
R. Escapade ('Harpade'). Dense Floribunda rose with good disease resistance. **H** 30in (75cm), **S** 24in (60cm). Fragrant, cupped, semidouble, rose-violet flowers, 3in (8cm) across, with white eyes, are borne in sprays in summer and again in fall. Foliage is light green and glossy. Z5–9 H9–5.
R. Evelyn ('Aussaucer'), illus. p.177.
R. 'Fantin-Latour', illus. p.173.
R. Fascination ('Poulmax'), syn. *R.* 'Fredensborg'. Vigorous Floribunda rose. **H** 3ft (1m), **S** 2ft (60cm). In summer–fall bears fragrant, rounded, double, shrimp-pink flowers amid dark green, glossy foliage. Is good for a bed or hedge. Z4–11 H12–1.
R. 'Felicia', illus. p.173.
R. 'Félicité Parmentier'. Vigorous, compact, upright Alba rose. **H** 4ft (1.2m), **S** 3ft (1m). Fragrant, cupped to flat, fully double, pale flesh-pink flowers, 2½in (6cm) across, are borne in mid-summer. Has abundant, grayish-green leaves. Makes a good hedge. Z3–9 H9–3.
R. 'Félicité Perpétue', illus. p.184.
R. Felicity Kendal ('Lanken'). Sturdy, well-branched Hybrid Tea rose. **H** 3½ft (1.1m), **S** 2½ft (75cm). Lightly fragrant, rounded, fully double, bright red flowers, 4½in (11cm) across, are produced among a mass of dark green foliage in summer–fall.
R. 'Fellemberg', syn. *R.* 'Fellenberg'. Vigorous, shrubby Noisette rose. **H** 8ft (2.5m), **S** 4ft (1.2m). Leaves are purplish-green. Clusters of faintly scented, rounded to cupped, fully double flowers, 2in (5cm) across, in shades of light crimson, are borne in summer–fall. Prune to grow as a bedding rose or support as a climber.
R. 'Fellenberg'. See *R.* 'Fellemberg'.
R. Fellowship ('Harwelcome'), illus. p.183.
R. *filipes* 'Kiftsgate', illus. p.184.
R. 'Fire Princess'. Upright Miniature rose with good disease rsistance. **H** 18in (45cm), **S** 12in (30cm). Bears sprays of rosette, fully double, scarlet flowers, 1½in (4cm) across, in summer and again in fall. Has small, glossy leaves. Z5–9 H9–5.
R. Flower Carpet ('Noatraum'), illus. p.179.
R. *foetida* 'Persiana', syn. *R.* 'Persian Yellow'. Upright, arching Species rose with moderate disease resistance. **H** and **S** 5ft (1.5m). Cupped, double, yellow flowers, 1in (2.5cm) across, are produced in a single flush in summer. Glossy leaves are prone to blackspot. Prune spent branches only. Shelter from cold winds. Z3–9 H9–1.
R. 'Fortune's Double Yellow'. See *R.* x *odorata* 'Pseudindica'.
R. Fragrant Cloud ('Tanellis'). Bushy, dense Hybrid Tea rose. **H** 30in (75cm), **S** 24in (60cm). Very fragrant, rounded, double, dusky-scarlet flowers, 5in (12cm) across, are borne freely in summer–fall. Has plentiful, dark green foliage. Z4–11 H12–1.
R. 'Fragrant Delight'. Bushy Floribunda rose of uneven habit. **H** 3ft (1m), **S** 2½ft (75cm). Clusters of fragrant, urn-shaped, double, salmon-pink flowers, 3in (8cm) across, are borne freely in summer–fall amid abundant, reddish-green foliage. Z5–9 H9–5.
R. 'François Juranville'. Vigorous, arching Rambler. **H** 20ft (6m), **S** 15ft (5m). Bears clusters of apple-scented, rosette, fully double, rosy-salmon-pink flowers, 3in (8cm) across, in summer. Produces a mass of glossy leaves. Is prone to mildew in a dry site. Z5–9 H9–5.
R. 'Fredensborg'. See *R.* Fascination ('Poulmax').
R. Freedom ('Dicjem'), illus. p.182.
R. 'Friesia'. See *R.* 'Korresia'.
R. 'Frühlingsmorgen', syn. *R.* 'Spring Morning'. Open, free-branching Shrub rose. **H** 6ft (2m), **S** 5ft (1.5m). Foliage is grayish-green. In late spring, hay-scented,

Q
R

cupped, single, pink flowers, 5in (12cm) across, with primrose center and reddish stamens, are produced. Z4–9 H9–4.
***R.* 'Fryminicot'.** See *R.* SWEET DREAM.
***R. gallica* var. *officinalis*,** syn. *R.* 'Apothecary's Rose', *R. officinalis* (Apothecary's rose, Crimson damask rose, Provins rose, Red rose of Lancaster). Bushy Species rose of neat habit. **H** to 32in (80cm), **S** 36in (1m). In summer bears flat, semidouble, pinkish-red flowers, 3in (8cm) across, with moderate scent. Z3–9 H9–1. **'Versicolor'**, illus. p.174.
***R.* GARDENERS GLORY ('Chewability'),** illus. p.187.
***R.* 'Gaumo'.** See *R.* ROSE GAUJARD.
***R.* GENTLE TOUCH ('Diclulu').** Upright, dwarf Floribunda rose. **H** 20in (50cm), **S** 12in (30cm). Bears sprays of faintly scented, urn-shaped, semidouble, pale salmon-pink flowers, 2in (5cm) across, in summer–fall. Leaves are small and dark green. Is good as a low hedge. Z5–9 H9–5.
***R.* GEOFF HAMILTON ('Ausham').** Bushy Shrub rose with good disease resistance and most flowers produced near top of bush. **H** 5½ft (1.6m), **S** 3ft (1m). Rounded buds open to sweetly scented, quartered-rosette, double, light rose-pink flowers, 4in (10cm) across, intensifying to rose-pink in centers, in summer and again in fall. Z5–9 H9–5.
***R.* GEORGE BEST ('Dichimanher'),** illus. p.181.
***R.* 'Geranium'.** See *R. moyesii* 'Geranium'.
***R.* 'Gerbe d'Or'.** See *R.* CASINO ('Macca').
***R.* GERTRUDE JEKYLL ('Ausbord'),** illus. p.175.
***R.* 'Gioia'.** See *R.* PEACE ('Madame A. Meilland').
***R.* 'Gipsy Boy'.** See *R.* 'Zigeunerknabe'.
***R.* GLAMIS CASTLE ('Auslevel').** Compact Shrub rose with good disease resistance and glossy, mid-green leaves. **H** 5ft (1.5m), **S** 4ft (1.2m). Produces fragrant, quartered-rosette, fully double, cream-centered, white flowers, 4in (10cm) across, in summer and again in fall. Z5–9 H9–5.
***R. glauca*,** syn. *R. rubrifolia*, illus. p.176. Vigorous, arching Species rose with very good disease resistance. **H** 6ft (2m), **S** 5ft (1.5m). Flat, single, pale-centered, cerise-pink flowers, 1½in (4cm) across, with gold stamens, in a single flush in summer, are followed by red hips in fall. Has grayish-purple leaves and red stems. Z2–8 H8–1.
***R.* 'Glenfiddich'.** Upright Floribunda rose with moderate disease resistance. **H** 30in (75cm), **S** 24in (60cm). Fragrant, urn-shaped, double, amber-yellow flowers, 4in (10cm) across, are borne singly or in clusters in summer and again in fall. Z5–9 H9–5.
***R.* 'Gloire de Dijon',** illus. p.184.
***R.* 'Gloire des Mousseux'.** Vigorous, bushy Moss rose. **H** 4ft (1.2m), **S** 3ft (1m). Has plentiful, light green foliage. In summer bears fragrant, cupped, fully double flowers, 6in (15cm) across. These are bright pink, paling to blush-pink, with light green "mossing". Z5–9 H9–1.
***R.* 'Gloria Dei'.** See *R.* PEACE ('Madame A. Meilland').
***R.* GOLDEN BEAUTY ('Korberbeni'),** illus. p.182.
***R.* GOLDEN CELEBRATION ('Ausgold').** Bushy Shrub rose with good disease resistance and glossy, mid-green leaves. **H** 5ft (1.5m), **S** 4ft (1.2m). In summer and again in fall, abundant, plump, rounded buds open to slightly scented, rosette, fully double, golden-yellow flowers, 5in (12cm) across, taking on pink hues as they age. Z5–9 H9–5.
***R.* GOLDEN MEMORIES ('Korholesea'),** illus. p.182.
***R.* GOLDEN PENNY ('Rugul'),** syn. *R.* 'Guletta', *R.* 'Tapis Jaune'. Compact, dense Patio rose with moderate disease resistance. **H** 12in (30cm), **S** 16in (40cm). Cupped to flat, double, yellow flowers, 2in (5cm) across, are borne in summer and again in fall. Has rich green leaves. Z5–9 H9–5.
***R.* 'Golden Rambler'.** See *R.* 'Alister Stella Gray'.
***R.* 'Golden Showers'.** Stiff, upright Climber with moderate disease resistance. **H** 6ft (2m), **S** 7ft (2.2m) or more. In summer and again in fall produces many slightly scented, pointed, double, yellow flowers, 4in (10cm) across, that open flat. May be pruned to grow as a shrub. Z5–9 H9–5.
***R.* 'Golden Sunblaze'.** See *R.* 'Rise 'n' Shine'.
***R.* 'Golden Wings'.** Bushy, spreading Shrub rose. **H** 3½ft (1.1m), **S** 4½ft (1.35m). Bears fragrant, cupped, single, pale yellow flowers, 5in (12cm) across, amid light green foliage, in summer–fall. Is good for a hedge. Z4–9 H9–1.
***R.* 'Goldfinch'.** Vigorous, arching Rambler. **H** 9ft (2.7m), **S** 6ft (2m). In summer produces lightly scented, rosette, double, yolk-yellow flowers, 1½in (4cm) across, that fade to white. Has plentiful, bright light green leaves. Z5–9 H9–5.
***R.* 'Gold of Ophir'.** See *R.* x *odorata* 'Pseudindica'.
***R.* 'Goldsmith'.** See *R.* SIMBA ('Korbelma').
***R.* GOLDSTAR ('Candide').** Neat, upright Hybrid Tea rose. **H** 3ft (1m), **S** 2ft (60cm). Amid glossy, dark green leaves, lightly scented, urn-shaped, fully double, yellow flowers, 3in (8cm) across, are borne in summer–fall. Z5–9 H9–5.
***R.* GORDON'S COLLEGE ('Cocjabby'),** illus. p.179.
***R.* GRAHAM THOMAS ('Ausmas'),** illus. p.176.
***R.* 'Grandpa Dickson',** syn. *R.* 'Irish Gold'. Neat, upright Hybrid Tea rose with moderate disease resistance. **H** 32in (80cm), **S** 24in (60cm). Bears many pointed, fully double, light yellow flowers, 7in (18cm) across, in summer and again in fall. Has sparse, glossy, pale green leaves. Z5–9 H9–5.
***R.* 'Great Maiden's Blush',** syn. *R.* 'Cuisse de Nymphe', *R.* 'La Séduisante', illus. p.173.
***R.* GROUSE ('Korimro').** Trailing Groundcover rose with good disease resistance. **H** 1½ft (45cm), **S** 10ft (3m). Slightly fragrant, flat, single, blush-pink flowers, 1½in (4cm) across, are borne close to stems in a single flush in summer. Has abundant, glossy foliage. Z5–9 H9–6.
***R.* 'Guinée',** illus. p.186.
***R.* 'Guletta'.** See *R.* GOLDEN PENNY ('Rugul').
***R.* GUY SAVOY ('Delstrimen'),** illus. p.181.
***R.* GUY'S GOLD ('Harmatch'),** illus. p.182.
***R.* HANDEL ('Macha').** Stiff, upright Climber with moderate disease resistance. **H** 10ft (3m), **S** 7ft (2.2m). Slightly scented, urn-shaped, double, cream flowers, 3in (8cm) across, edged with pinkish-red, are borne in clusters in summer and again in fall. Has glossy, dark green leaves. Z5–9 H9–5.
***R.* HANNAH GORDON ('Korweiso').** Bushy, open Floribunda rose. **H** 30in (75cm), **S** 2ft (60cm). Sprays of slightly fragrant, cupped, double, blush-pink flowers, 3in (8cm) across, margined with reddish-pink, are produced in summer–fall. Leaves are dark green. Z4–11 H12–1.
***R.* 'Harbabble'.** See *R.* SUNSET BOULEVARD.
***R.* 'Hardinkum'.** See *R.* PRINCESS OF WALES.
***R.* 'Hardwell'.** See *R.* PENNY LANE.
***R.* 'Harkaramel'.** See *R.* ANNE HARKNESS.
***R.* 'Harkuly'.** See *R.* MARGARET MERRIL.
***R.* 'Harlex'.** See *R.* ALEXANDER.
***R.* 'Harmantelle'.** See *R.* MOUNTABATTEN.
***R.* 'Harpade'.** See *R.* ESCAPADE.
***R.* 'Harpiccolo'.** See *R.* ANNA FORD.
***R.* 'Harquanne'.** See *R.* BREATH OF LIFE.
***R.* 'Harqueterwife'.** See *R.* PAUL SHIRVILLE.
***R.* 'Harregale'.** See *R.* CARDINAL HUME.
***R.* 'Harroony'.** See *R.* AMBER QUEEN.
***R.* 'Harrowbond'.** See *R.* ROSEMARY HARKNESS.
***R.* 'Harsherry'.** See *R.* SHEILA'S PERFUME.
***R.* 'Harukfore'.** See *R.* CITY OF LONDON.
***R.* 'Harvacity'.** See *R.* DRUMMER BOY.
***R.* 'Harwanna'.** See *R.* JACQUELINE DU PRE.
***R.* 'Harwanted'.** See *R.* MANY HAPPY RETURNS.
***R.* 'Haryup'.** See *R.* HIGH HOPES.
***R.* 'Harzola'.** See *R.* L'AIMANT.
***R.* 'Heartthrob'.** See *R.* PAUL SHIRVILLE ('Harqueterwife').
***R.* 'Heideröslein'.** See *R.* 'Nozomi'.
***R.* 'Henri Martin',** illus. p.175.
***R.* HERTFORDSHIRE ('Kortenay').** Free-flowering Groundcover rose of compact, uneven, spiky habit. **H** 18in (45cm), **S** 3ft (1m). Has dense, bright green leaves and flat, single, carmine-pink flowers, 1¾in (4.5cm) across, with paler pink centers, in large clusters on short stems, in summer–fall. Z5–9 H9–5.
***R.* HIGH HOPES ('Haryup'),** illus. p.185.
***R.* 'Honorine de Brabant'.** Vigorous, bushy, sprawling Bourbon rose. **H** and **S** 6ft (2m). Fragrant, quartered, double flowers, 4in (10cm) across, lilac-pink, marked with light purple and crimson, are produced in summer–fall. Has plentiful, light green foliage. Z5–9 H9–5.
***R.* 'Horflash'.** See *R.* CHAMPAGNE COCKTAIL.
***R.* HOT COCOA ('Wekpaltlez').** Upright Floribunda rose with good disease resistance and repeat-flowering in summer–fall. **H** 3ft (1m), **S** 32in (80cm). Produces semi-glossy, dark green leaves and cupped, double flowers, 3in (7cm) across, in burnt-orange, tending towards brown, lighter in centers with hint of tangerine. H5–9 H9–5.
***R.* 'Hula Girl'.** Wide, bushy Miniature rose with moderate disease resistance. **H** 18in (45cm), **S** 16in (40cm). Urn-shaped, fully double, salmon-orange flowers, 1in (2.5cm) across, are produced freely in summer and again in fall. Has glossy, dark green leaves. Z5–9 H9–5.
***R.* ICEBERG ('Korbin'),** syn. *R.* 'Schneewittchen', illus. p.177.
***R.* 'Iced Ginger'.** Upright Floribunda rose with moderate disease resistance. **H** 36in (90cm), **S** 28in (70cm). Pointed, fully double, buff to copper-pink flowers, 4½in (11cm) across, are borne singly or in clusters in summer and again in fall. Has sparse, reddish-green foliage. Z5–9 H9–5.
***R.* INGRID BERGMAN ('Poulman').** Upright, branching Hybrid Tea rose. **H** 30in (75cm), **S** 24in (60cm). Bears slightly scented, urn-shaped, double, dark red flowers, 4½in (11cm) across, in summer–fall. Has leathery, semi-glossy, dark green foliage. Z5–9 H9–5.
***R.* 'Interall'.** See *R.* ROSY CUSHION.
***R.* INVINCIBLE ('Runatru').** Upright Floribunda rose. **H** 3ft (1m), **S** 2ft (60cm). Faintly scented, cupped, fully double, bright crimson flowers, 3½in (9cm) across, are produced in open clusters in summer–fall. Leaves are semi-glossy.
***R.* 'Irish Gold'.** See *R.* 'Grandpa Dickson'.
***R.* ISN'T SHE LOVELY ('Diciluvit'),** illus. p.177.
***R.* 'Ispahan',** syn. *R.* 'Pompon des Princes', *R.* 'Rose d'Isfahan'. Vigorous, bushy, dense Damask rose. **H** 5ft (1.5m), **S** 4ft (1.2m). Produces fragrant, cupped, double, clear pink flowers, 3in (8cm) across, amid grayish-green foliage in summer–fall. Z4–9 H9–1.
***R.* JACQUELINE DU PRE ('Harwanna'),** illus. p.172.
***R.* JOIE DE VIVRE ('Korfloci 01'),** illus. p.179.
***R.* JULIA CHILD ('Wekvossutono'),** illus. p.182.
***R.* 'Julia's Rose'.** Spindly, branching Hybrid Tea rose. **H** 30in (75cm), **S** 18in (45cm). In summer–fall produces faintly scented, urn-shaped, double, brownish-pink to buff flowers, 4in (10cm) across. Foliage is reddish-green. Is good for cut flowers. Z5–9 H9–1.
***R.* 'Just Joey',** illus. p.183.
***R.* 'Kathleen Harrop'.** Arching, lax Bourbon rose. **H** 8ft (2.5m), **S** 6ft (2m). Fragrant, double, cupped, pale pink flowers, 3in (8cm) across, are borne in summer–fall. Plentiful, dark green foliage is susceptible to mildew. May be grown as a climber or hedge. Z6–9 H9–6.
***R.* KEEPSAKE ('Kormalda').** Neat, bushy Hybrid Tea rose with good disease resistance. **H** 30in (75cm), **S** 24in (60cm). Scented, rounded, fully double, pink flowers, 5in (12cm) across, are freely produced in summer and again in fall. Foliage is plentiful and glossy. Z5–9 H9–5.
***R.* KENT ('Poulcov'),** illus. p.177.
***R.* 'Königin von Dänemark',** syn. *R.* 'Belle Courtisanne'. Vigorous, rather open Alba rose with good disease resistance. **H** 5ft (1.5m), **S** 4ft (1.2m). Scented, quartered-rosette, fully double, warm-pink flowers, 3in (8cm) across, with green button eyes, are produced in a single flush in summer. Z3–9 H9–1.
***R.* 'Korbelma'.** See *R.* SIMBA.
***R.* 'Korbin'.** See *R.* ICEBERG.
***R.* 'Korblue'.** See *R.* SHOCKING BLUE.
***R.* 'Korgund'.** See *R.* LOVING MEMORY.
***R.* 'Korimro'.** See *R.* GROUSE.
***R.* 'Korlift'.** See *R.* CONGRATULATIONS.
***R.* 'Kormalda'.** See *R.* *Keepsake*.
***R.* 'Korpeahn'.** See *R.* The Times Rose.
***R.* 'Korresia',** syn. *R.* 'Friesia'. Bushy, upright Floribunda rose with moderate disease resistance. **H** 30in (75cm), **S** 24in (60cm). Bears open sprays of strongly scented, urn-shaped, double flowers, 3in (8cm) across, with wavy, yellow petals, in summer and again in fall. Z5–9 H9–5.
***R.* 'Kortenay'.** See *R.* HERTFORDSHIRE.
***R.* 'Korweiso'.** See *R.* HANNAH GORDON.
***R.* 'Korzaun'.** See *R.* ROYAL WILLIAM.

R. L'Aimant ('Harzola'), syn. *R.* 'Doux Parfum'. Vigorous Floribunda rose. H 3ft (1m), S 2¹/₂ft (75cm). Strongly fragrant, cupped, fully double, pink blooms, 3¹/₂in (9cm) across, are produced in summer–fall on dark-foliaged plants. Is good as a bedding plant or as cut flowers.

R. 'Lady Waterlow'. Stiff Climbing Hybrid Tea rose. H 12ft (4m), S 6ft (2m). Bears scented, pointed to cupped, double, light pink shaded, salmon flowers, 5in (12cm) across, mainly in summer, but some may also appear in fall. Leaves are mid-green.

R. Lancashire ('Korstesgli'), illus. p.181.

R. 'Lanken'. See *R.* Felicity Kendal.

R. 'La Séduisante'. See *R.* 'Great Maiden's Blush'.

R. La Sévillana ('Meigekanu'). Dense, bushy Groundcover rose. H 2¹/₂ft (75cm). S 3ft (1m). Clusters of faintly scented, cupped, double, bright red flowers, 3in (8cm) across, are borne freely in summer–fall. Produces masses of dark green leaves. Is suitable for growing as a hedge or groundcover. Z6–9 H9–5.

R. Laura Ford ('Chewarvel'), illus. p.187.

R. L.D. Braithwaite ('Auscrim'). Lax, open Shrub rose with moderate disease resistance and dull, mid-green leaves. H 6ft (1.8m), S 4ft (1.2m). Scented, quartered-rosette, fully double, deep crimson flowers, 5in (12cm) across, fading to lighter crimson, are produced sparingly in summer and again in fall. Z5–9 H9–5.

R. 'Leggab'. See *R.* Pearl Drift.

R. 'Legnews'. See *R.* News.

R. 'Lenip'. See *R.* Pascali.

R. Light Fantastic ('Dicgottago'). Compact, bushy Floribunda rose with good disease resistance and repeat-flowering in summer–fall. H and S 2¹/₂ft (75cm). Produces clusters of up to 9 rosette, double, lemon-yellow flowers, 2in (5cm) across. Has glossy, light green leaves.

R. Little Rambler ('Chewramb'). Climber with very good disease resistance and repeat-flowering in summer–fall. H 5ft (1.5m), S 4ft (1.2m). Produces small, glossy, light green leaves and tight clusters of moderately scented, cupped, semidouble, rose-pink flowers, 2in (5cm) across, fading to pale pink with lilac hue.

R. 'Louise Odier', syn. *R.* 'Madame de Stella'. Upright Bourbon rose. H 6ft (2m), S 4ft (1.2m). Has light grayish-green foliage and fragrant, cupped, fully double, warm rose-pink flowers, 5in (12cm) across, borne in summer–fall. Z3–9 H9–1.

R. Lovely Lady ('Dicjubell'). Dense, rounded Hybrid Tea rose with moderate disease resistance. H 32in (80cm), S 28in (70cm). Slightly scented, pointed, fully double, rose-pink flowers, 4in (10cm) across, are produced freely in summer and again in fall. Z5–9 H9–5.

R. Loving Memory ('Korgund'), illus. p.181.

R. Lucky! ('Frylucy'). Upright Floribunda rose with very good disease resistance and repeat-flowering in summer–fall. H 3ft (1m), S 2¹/₂ft (75cm). Cupped, double flowers, 3in (7cm) across, deep rose-pink in bud, open lighter. Has matt dark green leaves.

R. 'Macangeli'. See *R.* Snowball.

R. 'Macar'. See *R.* Piccadilly.

R. 'Macca'. See *R.* Casino.

R. 'Maccarpe'. See *R.* Snow Carpet.

R. 'Macdub'. See *R.* Dublin Bay.

R. 'Macha'. See *R.* Handel.

R. 'Macmi'. See *R.* Mischief.

R. 'Macrexy'. See *R.* Sexy Rexy.

R. macrophylla. Vigorous Species rose. H 12ft (4m), S 10ft (3m). Bears moderately fragrant, flat, single, red flowers, 2in (5cm) across, in summer, followed by flask-shaped, red hips. Has red stems and large, mid-green leaves. Z5–9 H9–1.

R. 'Mactru'. See *R.* Trumpeter.

R. 'Madame Alfred Carrière', illus. p.184.

R. 'Madame A. Meilland'. See *R.* Peace.

R. 'Madame de Stella'. See *R.* 'Louise Odier'.

R. 'Madame Ernest Calvat'. Vigorous, arching Bourbon rose. H 6–10ft (2–3m), S 6ft (2m). Fragrant, cupped to quartered-rosette, fully double, rose-pink flowers, 6in (15cm) across, are borne freely in summer–fall. Has plentiful, large leaves. Z6–9 H9–1.

R. 'Madame Grégoire Staechelin', syn. *R.* 'Spanish Beauty', illus. p.185.

R. 'Madame Hardy', illus. p.172.

R. 'Madame Hébert'. See *R.* 'Président de Sèze'.

R. 'Madame Isaac Pereire', illus. p.174.

R. 'Madame Knorr', syn. *R.* 'Comte de Chambord'. Vigorous, erect Portland rose. H 4ft (1.2m), S 3ft (1m). In summer–fall, fragrant, quartered-rosette, fully double, lilac-tinted, pink flowers, 4in (10cm) across, are produced amid plentiful, light green foliage. Is suitable for a hedge. Z5–9 H9–5.

R. 'Madame Pierre Oger'. Lax Bourbon rose. H 6ft (2m), S 4ft (1.2m). In summer–fall, slender stems bear sweetly scented, cupped or bowl-shaped, double, pink flowers, 3in (8cm) across, with rose-lilac tints. Has light green leaves. Grows well on a pillar. Z6–9.

R. Maid of Honour ('Jacwhink'), illus. p.178.

R. 'Maigold', illus. p.187.

R. 'Mainzer Fastnacht'. See *R.* Blue Moon ('Tannacht').

R. Many Happy Returns ('Harwanted'), illus. p.178.

R. 'Maréchal Davoust'. Vigorous, bushy Moss rose. H 5ft (1.5m), S 4ft (1.2m). In summer bears moderately fragrant, cupped, fully double, deep reddish-pink to purple flowers, 4in (10cm) across, with green eye and brownish "mossing". Leaves are dull green and lance-shaped. Z5–9 H9–1.

R. 'Maréchal Niel'. Vigorous, spreading Noisette or climbing Hybrid Tea rose. H 10ft (3m), S 6ft (2m). Drooping stems bear rich green foliage and moderately scented, pointed, fully double, clear yellow flowers, 4in (10cm) across, in summer–fall. Z7–9 H9–7.

R. Margaret Merril ('Harkuly'), illus. p.177.

R. 'Marguerite Hilling', syn. *R.* 'Pink Nevada', illus. p.173.

R. Mary Rose ('Ausmary'). Bushy, spreading Shrub rose. H and S 4ft (1.2m). Produces moderately fragrant, cupped, fully double, rose-pink flowers, 3in (9cm) across, in summer–fall. Has plentiful leaves. Z6–9 H9–6.

R. 'Meidanover'. See *R.* Colibre '79.

R. 'Meidomonac'. See *R.* Bonica.

R. 'Meigekanu'. See *R.* La Sévillana.

R. 'Meijikitar'. See *R.* Orange Sunblaze.

R. 'Meilucca'. See *R.* Darling Flame.

R. Meredith ('Wekmeredoc'), illus. p.179.

R. 'Mermaid', illus. p.187.

R. 'Mignon'. See *R.* 'Cécile Brünner'.

R. Mischief ('Macmi'). Upright Hybrid Tea rose. H 3ft (1m), S 2ft (60cm). Moderately fragrant, urn-shaped, double, salmon-pink flowers, 4in (10cm) across, are borne freely in summer–fall. Leaves are plentiful but prone to rust. Z5–9 H9–5.

R. Molineux ('Ausmol'). Compact Shrub rose with very good disease resistance and shiny, mid-green foliage. H 5ft (1.5m). S 4ft (1.2m). Slightly scented, rosette, canary-yellow flowers, 4in (10cm) across, with slightly paler outer petals, are produced in summer and again in fall. Z5–9 H9–5.

R. 'Morning Jewel'. Free-branching Climber. H 8ft (2.5m), S 7ft (2.2m). Has plentiful, glossy foliage and cupped, double, bright pink flowers, 3¹/₂in (9cm) across, freely borne, usually in clusters, in summer–fall. May be pruned to a shrub. Z5–9 H9–1.

R. 'Morsherry'. See *R.* Sheri Anne.

R. moschata var. nivea. See *R.* 'Dupontii'.

R. Mountbatten ('Harmantelle'), illus. p.182.

R. 'Mousseline', syn. *R.* 'Alfred de Dalmas'. Bushy Moss rose with twiggy growth. H and S 3ft (1m). Mainly in summer bears scented, cupped, fully double, blush-pink flowers, 3in (8cm) across, with little "mossing". Has matt green leaves. Z6–9 H9–1.

R. moyesii. Vigorous, arching Species rose. H 12ft (4m), S 10ft (3m). In summer, faintly scented, flat, single, dusky-scarlet flowers, 2in (5cm) across, with yellow stamens, are borne close to branches. Produces long, red hips in fall. Sparse, small, dark green leaves are divided into 7–13 leaflets. Z4–9 H9–3. 'Geranium', syn. *R.* 'Geranium' (illus. p.176), H 10ft (3m), S 8ft (2.5m), has large, red hips. Z6–9 H9–1.

R. 'Mrs. John Laing', illus. p.174.

R. multibracteata, illus. p.176. Rounded, bushy Species rose with good disease resistance. H 6ft (2m), S 5ft (1.5m). Thin stems have abundant, small, gray-green leaves. Slightly scented, flat, single, pink flowers, 2in (5cm) across, with hint of lilac, and many bracts on stem behind each flower, are borne in a single flush in summer and are followed by small, rounded hips in fall–winter. Z7–9 H9–7.

R. 'National Trust'. Compact Hybrid Tea rose. H 30in (75cm), S 24in (60cm). Slightly scented, urn-shaped, fully double, scarlet-crimson flowers, 4in (10cm) across, are borne freely in summer–fall. Produces plentiful, dark green foliage. Makes a good, low hedge. Z5–9 H9–5.

R. 'Nevada', illus. p.173.

R. 'New Dawn', illus. p.185.

R. News ('Legnews'). Upright Floribunda rose. H 24in (60cm), S 20in (50cm). Has dark green leaves and, in summer–fall, clusters of slightly fragrant, cupped, wide-opening, double, bright reddish-purple flowers, 3in (8cm) across. Z5–9 H9–5.

R. 'Niphetos'. Branching, climbing Hybrid Tea rose. H 10ft (3m), S 6ft (2m). Long, pointed buds, on nodding stems, open to rounded, double, white flowers, 5in (12cm) across, mainly in summer, a few later. Pale green leaves are pointed.

R. 'Noisette Carnée', syn. *R.* 'Blush Noisette'. Noisette rose of branching habit and lax growth. H 6–12ft (2–4m), S 6–8ft (2–2.5m). In summer–fall, smooth stems bear clusters of spice-scented, cupped, double, blush-pink flowers, 1¹/₂in (4cm) across. Has matt foliage. May be grown as a shrub. Z6–9.

R. Nostalgia ('Taneiglat'), illus. p.179.

R. 'Nozomi', syn. *R.* 'Heideröslein'. Creeping, Groundcover rose with good disease resistance. H 1¹/₂ft (45cm), S 4ft (1.2m). Bears slightly scented, flat, single, blush-pink and white flowers, 1in (2.5cm) across, close to stems in a single flush in summer. Has small, dark green leaves. Is suitable for a container. Z5–9 H9–5.

R. 'Nuits de Young', syn. *R.* 'Old Black'. Erect Moss rose with wiry stems. H 4ft (1.2m), S 3ft (1m). In summer has slightly scented, double, flat, dark maroon-purple flowers, 2in (5cm) across, with brownish "mossing". Leaves are small and dark green. Z4–9 H9–1.

R. nutkana 'Plena', syn. *R.* californica 'Plena'. Robust Species rose. H to 10ft (3m), S 6ft (2m). Fragrant, cupped, semidouble, pink flowers, 1¹/₂in (4cm) across, are borne singly in summer. Has toothed, mid-green leaves. Z3–9 H9–1.

R. 'Ocaru'. See *R.* Angela Rippon.

R. x odorata 'Mutabilis', syn. *R.* chinensis 'Mutabilis' illus. p.174. 'Pallida', illus. p.174. 'Pseudindica', syn. *R.* 'Beauty of Glazenwood', *R.* 'Fortune's Double Yellow', *R.* 'Gold of Ophir', *R.* 'San Rafael Rose' is a lax Climber of restrained growth. H 8ft (2.5m), S 5ft (1.5m). In summer bears small clusters of scented, pointed to cupped, semidouble, copper-suffused, yellow flowers, 2in (5cm) across. Leaves are glossy, light green. Prune very lightly. Z8–9 H9–8.

R. officinalis. See *R.* gallica var. officinalis.

R. 'Old Black'. See *R.* 'Nuits de Young'.

R. 'Omar Khayyám'. Dense, prickly Damask rose. H and S 3ft (1m). Fragrant, quartered-rosette, fully double, light pink flowers, 3in (8cm) across, are borne amid downy, grayish foliage in summer. Z5–9 H9–1.

R. omeiensis f. pteracantha. See *R.* sericea subsp. omeiensis f. pteracantha.

R. 'Opa Potschke'. See *R.* 'Precious Platinum'.

R. 'Ophelia'. Upright, open Hybrid Tea rose. H 3ft (1m), S 2ft (60cm). In summer–fall produces sweetly fragrant, urn-shaped, double, creamy-blush-pink flowers, 4in (10cm) across, singly or in clusters. Dark green foliage is sparse. Z5–9 H9–5.

R. Orange Sunblaze ('Meijikitar'), syn. *R.* 'Sunblaze'. Compact Miniature rose with moderate disease resistance. H and S 12in (30cm). Rosette, fully double, bright orange-red flowers, 1¹/₂in (4cm) across, are freely produced in summer and again in fall. Has plentiful, dark green leaves. Z5–9 H9–5.

R. 'Panachée d'Angers'. See *R.* 'Commandant Beaurepaire'.

R. Pascali ('Lenip'). Upright Hybrid Tea rose. H 3ft (1m), S 2ft (60cm). Bears faintly scented, neat, urn-shaped, fully double, white flowers, 3¹/₂in (9cm) across, in summer–fall. Has deep green leaves. Z4–11 H12–1.

R. Pat Austin ('Ausmum'). Bushy Shrub rose with very good disease resistance and matt, mid-green leaves. **H** 4ft (1.2m), **S** 3ft (1m). In summer and again in fall, cupped, fully double, rich orange flowers, with some red veining on petals, fade to peach. Z5–9 H9–5.

***R.* 'Paul's Himalayan Musk'.** Very vigorous Rambler. **H** and **S** 30ft (10m). Large clusters of slightly fragrant, rosette, double, blush-pink flowers, 1½in (4cm) across, are freely borne in late summer. Has thorny, trailing shoots and drooping leaves. Is suitable for growing up a tree or in a wild garden. Z6–9 H9–6.

***R.* Paul Shirville ('Harqueterwife'),** syn. *R.* 'Heartthrob', illus. p.178.

***R.* 'Paul's Lemon Pillar',** illus. p.184.

***R.* 'Paul Transon'.** Vigorous, rather lax Rambler. **H** 12ft (4m), **S** 5ft (1.5m). In summer has slightly fragrant, flat, double, faintly coppery, salmon-pink flowers, 3in (8cm) across, with pleated petals. Plentiful foliage is glossy, dark green. Z5–9 H9–1.

***R.* Peace ('Madame A. Meilland'),** syn. *R.* 'Gioia', *R.* 'Gloria Dei', illus. p.182.

***R.* Pearl Drift ('Leggab').** Bushy, spreading Shrub roses with good disease resistance. **H** 3ft (1m), **S** 4ft (1.2m). Produces clusters of lightly scented, cupped, double, blush-pink flowers, 4in (10cm) across, in summer and again in fall. Leaves are plentiful and glossy. Z5–9 H9–5.

***R.* 'Peaudouce'.** See *R.* Elina ('Dicjana').

***R.* Peek-a-boo ('Dicgrow'),** syn. *R.* 'Brass Ring'. Dense, cushion-forming Patio rose with moderate disease resistance. **H** and **S** 18in (45cm). Produces sprays of urn-shaped, double, apricot-pink flowers, 1½in (4cm) across, in summer and again in fall. Leaves are narrow and dark green. Z5–9 H9–5.

***R.* 'Penelope',** illus. p.172.

***R.* Penny Lane ('Hardwell'),** illus. p.186.

***R.* 'Perle d'Or'.** China rose that forms a twiggy, leafy, small shrub. **H** 2½ft (75cm), **S** 2ft (60cm). Slightly scented, urn-shaped, fully double, honey-pink flowers, 1½in (4cm) across, are borne in summer–fall. Leaves have pointed, glossy leaflets. Z4–11 H12–1.

***R.* 'Persian Yellow'.** See *R. foetida* 'Persiana'.

***R.* Piccadilly ('Macar').** Vigorous, bushy Hybrid Tea rose with moderate disease resistance. **H** 3ft (1m), **S** 2ft (60cm). Pointed, double, red and yellow flowers, 5in (12cm) across, are produced singly or in clusters in summer and again in fall. Abundant foliage is reddish-green and glossy. Z5–9 H9–5.

***R. pimpinellifolia*.** See *R. spinosissima*.

***R.* Pink Bells ('Poulbells').** Very dense, spreading Groundcover rose with good disease resistance. **H** 2½ft (75cm), **S** 4ft (1.2m). Produces clusters of many pompon, fully double, pink flowers, 1in (2.5cm) across, in summer and again in fall. Has abundant, small, dark green leaves. Z5–9 H9–5.

***R.* 'Pink Grootendorst'.** Upright, bushy Shrub rose with very good disease resistance. **H** 6ft (2m), **S** 5ft (1.5m). Sprays of rosette, double flowers, 2in (5cm) across, with toothed, clear pink petals, are borne in summer and again in fall. Z3–9 H9–1.

***R.* 'Pink Nevada'.** See *R.* 'Marguerite Hilling'.

***R.* 'Pink Parfait'.** Bushy Floribunda rose. **H** 2½ft (75cm), **S** 2ft (60cm). In summer–fall, slightly fragrant, urn-shaped, double flowers, 3½in (9cm) across, in shades of light pink, are produced freely. Has plentiful foliage. Z4–11 H12–4.

***R.* Pink Perfection ('Korpauvio'),** illus. p.180.

***R.* 'Pink Perpétué'.** Stiffly branched Climber with moderate disease resistance. **H** 9ft (2.8m), **S** 8ft (2.5m). Produces clusters of slightly scented, cupped to rosette, double, deep pink flowers, 3in (8cm) across, in summer and again in fall. Leathery foliage is plentiful. May be pruned to grow as a shrub. Z5–9 H9–5.

***R.* 'Pompon de Paris'.** See *R.* 'Rouletii'.

***R.* 'Pompon des Princes'.** See *R.* 'Ispahan'.

***R.* Pot o' Gold ('Dicdivine').** Hybrid Tea rose with neat, even growth and moderate disease resistance. **H** 30in (75cm), **S** 24in (60cm). Fragrant, rounded, fully double, golden-yellow flowers, 3½in (9cm) across, are produced singly or in wide sprays in summer and again in fall. Z5–9 H9–5.

***R.* 'Poulbells'.** See *R.* Pink Bells.

***R.* 'Poulcov'.** See *R.* Kent.

***R.* 'Poulman'.** See *R.* Ingrid Bergman.

***R.* 'Poulmax'.** See *R.* Fascination.

***R.* 'Poumidor'.** See *R.* Troika.

***R.* 'Precious Platinum',** syn. *R.* 'Opa Potschke'. Vigorous Hybrid Tea rose with moderate disease resistance. **H** 3ft (1m), **S** 2ft (60cm). Bears slightly scented, rounded, fully double, deep crimson-scarlet flowers, 4in (10cm) across, in summer and again in fall. Foliage is abundant and glossy. Z5–9 H9–5.

***R.* 'Président de Sèze',** syn. *R.* 'Madame Hébert'. Vigorous, rather open Gallica rose. **H** and **S** 4ft (1.2m). Bears fragrant, quartered-rosette, fully double, magenta-pink to pale lilac-pink flowers, 4in (10cm) across, in summer. Z3–9 H9–1.

R. primula (Incense rose). Lax, arching Species rose with very good disease resistance. **H** and **S** 6ft (2m). Produces scented, cupped, primrose-yellow flowers, 1½in (4cm) across, in a single flush in summer. Foliage is plentiful, aromatic and fernlike. May die back in hard winters. Z5–9 H9–5.

***R.* Princess of Wales ('Hardinkum').** Vigorous, compact Floribunda rose. **H** 30in (75cm), **S** 24in (60cm). Tight clusters of scented, rounded, fully double, paper-white blooms, 3½in (9cm) across, nestle among crisp, dark leaves in summer–fall. Is good for a bed or as hedging. Z4–9 H9–4.

***R.* 'Queen Elizabeth',** syn. *R.* 'The Queen Elizabeth', illus. p.178.

***R.* 'Queen of the Violets'.** See *R.* 'Reine des Violettes'.

***R.* Rachel ('Tangust'),** illus. p.183.

***R.* 'Rambling Rector',** illus. p.184.

***R.* 'Ramona',** syn. *R.* 'Red Cherokee'. Rather stiff, open Climber. **H** 9ft (2.7m), **S** 10ft (3m). Fragrant, flat, single, carmine-red flowers, 4in (10cm) across, with grayish-red undersides and gold stamens, are produced mainly in summer. Has sparse foliage. Does best against a warm wall. Z7–9 H9–1.

***R.* Red Ace ('Amruda').** Compact Miniature rose with good disease resistance. **H** 14in (35cm), **S** 12in (30cm). Slightly scented, rosette, double, dark red flowers, 1½in (4cm) across, are borne in summer and again in fall. Z5–9 H9–5.

***R.* 'Red Cherokee'.** See *R.* 'Ramona'.

***R.* Red Finesse ('Korvillade'),** illus. p.181.

***R.* 'Reine des Violettes',** syn. *R.* 'Queen of the Violets'. Spreading, vigorous Hybrid Perpetual rose. **H** and **S** 6ft (2m). Has grayish-toned leaves and fragrant, quartered-rosette, fully double, violet to purple flowers, 3in (8cm) across, in summer–fall. May be grown on a support. Z5–9 H9–5.

***R.* 'Reine Victoria',** illus. p.173.

***R.* Remember Me ('Cocdestin'),** illus. p.183.

***R.* Remembrance ('Harxampton'),** illus. p.181.

***R.* Rhapsody in Blue ('Frantasia'),** illus. p.175.

***R.* 'Rise 'n' Shine',** syn. *R.* 'Golden Sunblaze'. Bushy, upright Miniature rose with moderate disease resistance. **H** 16in (40cm), **S** 10in (25cm). Bears rosette, fully double, yellow flowers, 1in (2.5cm) across, in summer and again in fall. Foliage is dark green. Z5–9 H9–5.

***R.* 'Rose d'Isfahan'.** See *R.* 'Ispahan'.

***R.* Rose Gaujard ('Gaumo').** Upright, strong Hybrid Tea rose. **H** 3½ft (1.1m), **S** 2½ft (75cm). Has plentiful, glossy foliage. Bears slightly scented, urn-shaped, double, cherry-red and blush-pink flowers, 4in (10cm) across, freely in summer–fall.

***R.* Rosemary Harkness ('Harrowbond').** Vigorous Hybrid tea rose with moderate disease resistance. **H** 3ft (1m), **S** 2½ft (75cm). Bears strongly scented, pointed, double flowers, 4in (10cm) across, in salmon-pink and orange, singly or in clusters in summer and again in fall. Has abundant, glossy leaves. Z5–9 H9–5.

***R.* 'Roseraie de l'Haÿ',** illus. p.175.

***R.* Rosy Cushion ('Interall').** Dense, spreading Shrub rose with very good disease resistance and repeat-flowering in summer–fall. **H** 3ft (1m), **S** 4ft (1.2m). Clusters of slightly scented, cupped, semidouble flowers, 2½in (6cm) across, are pink with ivory centers. Has plentiful, glossy, dark green leaves. Z5–9 H9–5.

***R.* 'Rosy Mantle'.** Stiff, open-branched Climber with good disease resistance. **H** 8ft (2.5m), **S** 6ft (2m). Very fragrant, pointed, fully double, rose-pink flowers, 4in (10cm) across, are borne in summer and again in fall. Dark green foliage is rather sparse. Z5–9 H9–5.

***R.* 'Rouge Eblouissante'.** See *R.* 'Assemblage des Beautès'.

***R.* 'Rouletii',** syn. *R. chinensis* var. *minima*, *R.* 'Pompon de Paris'. Compact Miniature rose with thin stems. **H** and **S** 8in (20cm). Has mid-green leaves divided into many lance-shaped leaflets. Freely produces cupped, double, deep pink flowers, ¾in (2cm) across, in summer–fall. Z5–9 H9–5.

R. roxburghii (Burr rose, Chestnut rose, Chinquapin rose), illus. p.176. Compact, bushy Species rose with good disease resistance. **H** and **S** 4ft (1.2m). Has flaky bark and light to mid-green leaves, often with up to 15 leaflets that look as if they are almost arranged on the plant. In a single flush in summer produces flat, double, pink flowers, 2in (5cm) across, followed by spiked hips, which remain green and fall in late summer. Z6–9 H9–5.

***R.* 'Royal Dane'.** See *R.* Troika ('Poumidor').

***R.* Royal William ('Korzaun'),** syn. *R.* 'Duftzauber '84', illus. p.180.

***R. rubiginosa*,** syn. *R. eglanteria* (Eglantine rose, Sweet briar), illus. p.176. Vigorous, arching, thorny Species rose with very good disease resistance. **H** and **S** 8ft (2.4m). Has apple-scented foliage. Bears cupped, single, pink flowers, 1in (2.5cm) across, in a single flush in summer and red hips in fall. Z4–9 H9–1.

***R. rubrifolia*.** See *R. glauca*.

***R.* Ruby Anniversary ('Harbonny').** Bushy Patio rose with good disease resistance and repeat-flowering in summer–fall. **H** 28in (70cm), **S** 20in (50cm). Produces highly glossy, dark green leaves and large, wide clusters of cupped, double, ruby-red flowers, 2in (5cm) across.

R. rugosa (Hedgehog rose, Japanese rose, Ramanas rose, Sea tomato), illus. p.176. Vigorous, dense Species rose with very good disease resistance. **H** and **S** 3–6ft (1–2m). Has wrinkled leaves and large, red hips. Bears cupped, single, white or purplish-red flowers, 3½in (9cm) across, in a single flush in summer. Z2–9 H9–1. **var. *alba*** has white flowers opening from pale pink buds.

***R.* 'Rugul'.** See *R.* Golden Penny.

***R.* 'Ruiblun'.** See *R.* Blue Peter.

***R.* 'Runatru'.** See *R.* Invincible.

***R.* 'Saint Nicholas'.** Vigorous, erect Damask rose. **H** and **S** 4ft (1.2m). In summer bears lightly scented, cupped, semidouble, rose-pink flowers, 5in (12cm) across, with golden stamens, followed by red hips in fall. Has plentiful, dark green foliage. Z6–9 H9–1.

***R.* 'Sally Holmes',** illus. p.173.

***R.* 'Sander's White Rambler'.** Vigorous Rambler of lax growth. **H** 10ft (3m), **S** 8ft (2.5m). Fragrant, rosette, fully double, white flowers, 2in (5cm) across, are borne in clusters in late summer. Small, glossy leaves are plentiful. Z5–9 H9–5.

***R.* 'San Rafael Rose'.** See *R.* x *odorata* 'Pseudindica'.

***R.* Savoy Hotel ('Harvintage'),** illus. p.178.

***R.* Scepter'd Isle ('Ausland').** Bushy Shrub rose with good disease resistance and dark green foliage. **H** 5ft (1.5m), **S** 3ft (1m). In summer and again in fall produces scented, cupped, fully double, rose-pink flowers, 4in (10cm) across, eventually opening to show yellow stamens. Z5–9 H9–5.

***R.* 'Schneewittchen'.** See *R.* Iceberg ('Korbin').

***R.* 'Schoolgirl'.** Stiff, rather lanky, large-flowered Climber. **H** 9ft (2.7m), **S** 7ft (2.2m). Large, deep green leaves set off moderately fragrant, rounded, fully double, apricot-orange flowers, 4in (10cm) across, borne in summer–fall. Z5–9 H9–5.

***R. sericea* subsp. *omeiensis* f. *pteracantha*,** syn. *R. omeiensis* f. *pteracantha* (Winged thorn rose), illus. p.176. Stiff, upright, vigorous Species rose. **H** 8ft (2.5m), **S** 7ft (2.2m). Has small, fernlike, light green leaves and large, red thorns on young stems. In summer, solitary, flat, white flowers, 1–2½in (2.5–6cm) across, are borne briefly along stems. Z6–9 H9–5.

***R.* Sexy Rexy ('Macrexy').** Compact, bushy Floribunda rose with moderate disease resistance. **H** and **S** 2ft (60cm). Bears clusters of slightly scented, cupped, camellia-like, fully double, pink flowers, 3in (8cm) across, in summer and again in fall. Leaves are dark green. Z6–9 H9–5.

***R.* Sheila's Perfume ('Harsherry').** Upright Floribunda rose. **H** 2½ft (75cm),

S 2ft (60cm). Has glossy, reddish foliage. Fragrant, urn-shaped, double, red-and-yellow flowers, 3^1/2in (9cm) across, are produced singly or in clusters in summer–fall. Z5–9 H9–5.

R. Sheri Anne ('Morsherry'). Upright Miniature rose with moderate disease resistance. **H** 18in (45cm), **S** 12in (30cm). Produces slightly scented, rosette, double, light red flowers, 1in (2.5cm) across, in summer and again in fall. Has leathery, glossy leaves. Z5–9 H9–5.

R. Shocking Blue ('Korblue'). Bushy Floribunda rose. **H** 2^1/2ft (75cm), **S** 2ft (60cm). In summer–fall bears fragrant, pointed, well-formed, fully double, purple flowers, 4in (10cm) across, singly or in clusters. Foliage is dark green. Z5–9 H9–5.

R. Silver Anniversary ('Poulari'), illus. p.177.

R. 'Silver Jubilee'. Dense, upright Hybrid Tea rose with good disease resistance. **H** 3^1/2ft (1.1m), **S** 2^1/2ft (75cm). Bears slightly scented, pointed, fully double, soft salmon-pink flowers, 5in (12cm) across, very freely in summer and again in fall. Foliage is abundant and glossy. Z5–9 H9–5.

R. Simba ('Korbelma'), syn. *R.* 'Goldsmith'. Upright Hybrid Tea rose with moderate disease resistance. **H** 30in (75cm), **S** 24in (60cm). Slightly scented, urn-shaped, fully double, yellow flowers, 3^1/2in (9cm) across, are borne freely in summer and again in fall. Leaves are large and dark green. Z5–9 H9–5.

R. Simply Sally ('Harpaint'), illus. p.180.

R. Simply the Best ('Macamster'), illus. p.183.

R. 'Sissi'. See *R.* Blue Moon ('Tannacht').

R. Snowball ('Macangeli'), syn. *R.* 'Angelita'. Compact, creeping Miniature rose with moderate disease resistance. **H** 8in (20cm), **S** 12in (30cm). Pompon, fully double, white flowers, 1in (2.5cm) across, are borne in summer and again in fall. Leaves are small, glossy and plentiful. Z5–9 H9–5.

R. Snow Carpet ('Maccarpe'). Prostrate, creeping Miniature rose. **H** 6in (15cm), **S** 20in (50cm). Has many small glossy leaves and pompon, fully double, white flowers, 1^1/2in (3cm) across, in summer, a few in fall. Makes good, compact groundcover. Z5–9 H9–5.

R. 'Southampton', syn. *R.* 'Susan Ann', illus. p.183.

R. 'Souvenir d'Alphonse Lavallée'. Vigorous, sprawling Hybrid Perpetual rose. **H** 7ft (2.2m), **S** 6ft (2m). Fragrant, cupped, double, burgundy-red to maroon-purple flowers, 4in (10cm) across, are borne in summer–fall. Leaves are small and mid-green. Is best grown on a light support. Z6–9 H9–6.

R. 'Souvenir de la Malmaison'. Dense, spreading Bourbon rose. **H** and **S** 5ft (1.5m). Bears spice-scented, quartered-rosette, fully double, blush-pink to white flowers, 5in (12cm) across, in summer–fall. Rain spoils flowers. Has large, dark green leaves. Z6–9 H9–6.

R. 'Spanish Beauty'. See *R.* 'Madame Grégoire Staechelin'.

R. 'Spectacular'. See *R.* 'Danse du Feu'.

R. spinosissima, syn. *R.* pimpinellifolia (Burnet rose, Scotch rose, Scots rose). 'Plena' is a dense, spreading, prickly Species rose with good disease resistance.

H 3ft (1m), **S** 4ft (1.2m). Bears cupped, double, creamy-white flowers, 1^1/2in (4cm) across, in a single flush in summer. Has small, fernlike, dark green leaves and blackish hips. Z3–9 H9–1.

R. 'Spring Morning'. See *R.* 'Frühlingsmorgen'.

R. 'Stacey Sue'. Spreading Miniature rose with good disease resistance. **H** and **S** 15in (38cm). Slightly scented, rosette, fully double, pink flowers, 1in (2.5cm) across, are produced freely in summer and again in fall. Has plentiful, dark green leaves. Z5–9 H9–5.

R. Strawberry Hill ('Ausrimini'), illus. p.174.

R. Summer Song ('Austango'), illus. p.177.

R. Summer Wine ('Korizont'), illus. p.187.

R. 'Sunblaze'. See *R.* Orange Sunblaze ('Meijikitar').

R. Sunset Boulevard ('Harbabble'). Upright Floribunda rose. **H** 3ft (1m), **S** 2ft (60cm). Bears open sprays of lightly scented, pointed to cupped, double, salmon-pink flowers, 3^1/2in (9cm) across, in summer–fall on glossy-foliaged plants. Is excellent in a bed or for cut flowers.

R. Super Trooper ('Fryleyeca'), illus. p.183.

R. 'Susan Ann'. See *R.* 'Southampton'.

R. Susan Daniel ('Harlibra'), illus. p.178.

R. Sweet Dream ('Fryminicot'), illus. p.179.

R. Sweet Magic ('Dicmagic'), illus. p.183.

R. 'Sylvia'. See *R.* Congratulations ('Korlift').

R. 'Sympathie', illus. p.186.

R. 'Tanba'. See *R.* Baby Masquerade.

R. 'Tanellis'. See *R.* Fragrant Cloud.

R. 'Tanky'. See *R.* Whisky Mac.

R. 'Tannacht'. See *R.* Blue Moon.

R. 'Tapis d'Orient'. See *R.* 'Yesterday'.

R. 'Tapis Jaune'. See *R.* Golden Penny ('Rugul').

R. Teasing Georgia ('Ausbaker'), illus. p.176.

R. Tess of the d'Urbervilles ('Ausmove'). Slightly lax, arching shrub rose with good disease resistance and repeat-flowering in summer–fall. **H** 6ft (1.8m), **S** 5ft (1.5m). Scented, quartered-rosette, red flowers, 5in (12cm) across, fade with sun and age to pink-red. Foliage is mid-green. Z5–9 H9–5.

R. 'The Fairy', illus. p.178.

R. The Pilgrim ('Auswalker'), illus. p.176.

R. The Prince's Trust ('Harholding'), illus. p.186.

R. 'The Queen Elizabeth'. See *R.* 'Queen Elizabeth'.

R. The Times Rose ('Korpeahn'), illus. p.180.

R. 'Tour de Malakoff'. Provence rose of open habit and good disease resistance. **H** 6ft (2m), **S** 5ft (1.5m). In a single flush in summer produces scented, rosette, double, violet-veined, magenta flowers, 5in (12cm) across, fading to grayish-purple. Z4–9 H9–1.

R. 'Tricolore de Flandre'. Vigorous, upright Gallica rose. **H** and **S** 3ft (1m). Fragrant, pompon, fully double, blush-pink flowers, 2^1/2in (6cm) across, striped with pink and purple, are borne in summer. Has dull green leaves. Z3–9 H9–1.

R. Troika ('Poumidor'), syn. *R.* 'Royal Dane'. Vigorous, dense Hybrid Tea rose with moderate disease resistance. **H** 3ft (1m),

S 2^1/2ft (75cm). Fragrant, pointed, double, pink-tinged, orange-red flowers, 6in (15cm) across, are produced in summer and again in fall. Has semi-glossy leaves. Z5–9 H9–5.

R. Trumpeter ('Mactru'). Neat, bushy Floribunda rose with moderate disease resistance. **H** 24in (60cm), **S** 20in (50cm). Produces many cupped, fully double, bright red flowers, 2^1/2in (6cm) across, in summer and again in fall. Leaves are deep green and semi-glossy. Z5–9 H9–5.

R. 'Tuscany Superb', syn. *R.* 'Double Velvet'. Vigorous, upright Gallica rose. **H** 3^1/2ft (1.1m), **S** 3ft (1m). In summer produces, slightly scented, cupped to flat, double flowers, 2in (5cm) across, deep crimson-maroon, aging to purple, with gold stamens. Leaves are dark green. Z3–9 H9–1.

R. 'Variegata di Bologna'. Upright, arching Bourbon rose. **H** 6ft (2m), **S** 4^1/2ft (1.4m). Has small leaves and, in summer–fall, fragrant, quartered-rosette, fully double flowers, 3in (8cm) across, blush-pink, striped with rose-purple. Needs fertile soil and is prone to blackspot. Z6–9 H9–6.

R. 'Veilchenblau', syn. *R.* 'Blue Rambler', illus. p.185.

R. Warm Wishes ('Fryxotic'), illus. p.179.

R. 'Wedding Day'. Rampant Rambler. **H** 25ft (8m), **S** 12ft (4m). Produces large clusters of fruity-scented, flat, single, creamy-white flowers, 1in (2.5cm) across, that mature to blush-pink, in late summer. Is suitable for growing up a tree or in a wild garden. Z5–9 H9–1.

R. 'Wee Jock' ('Cocabest'). Dense, bushy Patio rose with good disease resistance. **H** and **S** 18in (45cm). Bears rosette, fully double, crimson flowers, 1^1/2in (4cm) across, in summer and again in fall. Plentiful leaves are small and dark green. Z5–9 H9–5.

R. 'Wekmeredoc'. See *R.* Meredith.

R. 'Wekvossutono'. See *R.* Julia Child.

R. Whisky Mac ('Tanky'). Neat, upright Hybrid Tea rose. **H** 2^1/2ft (75cm), **S** 2ft (60cm). Fragrant, rounded, fully double, amber flowers, 3^1/2in (9cm) across, are borne freely in summer–fall. Reddish foliage is prone to mildew. May die back in a hard winter. Z5–9 H9–5.

R. 'White Cockade'. Slow-growing, bushy, upright Climber. **H** 6–10ft (2–3m), **S** 5ft (1.5m). Bears slightly fragrant, rounded, well-formed, fully double, white flowers, 3^1/2in (9cm) across, in summer–fall. May be pruned and grown as a shrub. Z5–9 H9–5.

R. White Gold ('Cocquiriam'). Vigorous Floribunda rose with very good disease resistance. **H** 4ft (1.2m), **S** 3ft (1m). Has semi-glossy, dark green leaves. Dense clusters of strongly scented, rounded, fully double, off-white flowers, 3in (7cm) across, with creamy-white centers, are produced in summer and again in fall.

R. White Star ('Harquill'), illus. p.184.

R. Wild Rover ('Dichirap'). Upright Floribunda rose with good disease resistance and repeat-flowering in summer–fall. **H** 3ft (1m), **S** 2^1/2ft (75cm). Produces clusters of 5 or more lightly scented, flat, semidouble, rich purple flowers, 3in (7cm) across, with yellow stamens. Has matt, mid-green leaves.

R. 'William Lobb', syn. *R.* 'Duchesse d'Istrie', illus. p.175.

R. William Shakespeare 2000 ('Ausromeo'). Bushy Shrub rose with good disease resistance and matt, dark green leaves. **H** 5ft (1.5m), **S** 3ft (1m). Strongly scented, quartered-rosette, fully double, crimson flowers, 4in (10cm) across, with slightly pink outer petals, are produced in summer and again in fall. Z5–9 H9–5.

R. Winchester Cathedral ('Auscat'). Bushy Shrub rose with good disease resistance and dark green leaves. **H** 4ft (1.2m), **S** 3ft (1m). Myrrh-scented, rosette, double, white flowers, 4in (10cm) across, with light pink blushes when young, are produced in summer and again in fall. Z5–9 H9–5.

R. Wisley 2008 ('Ausbreeze'). Bushy Shrub rose with very good disease resistance and dull, mid-green leaves. **H** 4ft (1.2m), **S** 3ft (1m). Sweetly scented, quartered-rosette, fully double, light rose-pink flowers open from plump, rounded buds in summer and again in fall. Z5–9 H9–5.

R. xanthina 'Canary Bird', syn. *R.* 'Canary Bird'. Vigorous, dense, arching Species hybrid with very good disease resistance. **H** and **S** 7ft (2.1m). Cupped, single, yellow flowers, 2in (5cm) across, with musky scent, are produced in a single flush in summer. Has small, fernlike leaves. May die back in hard winters. Z5–9 H9–5.

R. 'Yesterday', syn. *R.* 'Tapis d'Orient'. Bushy, arching Polyantha rose. **H** and **S** 30in (75cm), or more if lightly pruned. Fragrant, rosette, semidouble, lilac-pink flowers, 1in (2.5cm) across, are borne, mainly in clusters, from summer through to early winter. Produces small, dark green leaves. Makes a good hedge. Z5–9 H9–5.

R. 'Yvonne Rabier'. Dense, bushy Polyantha rose. **H** 18in (45cm), **S** 16in (40cm). Plentiful leaves are bright green. Bears moderately scented, rounded, double, creamy-white flowers, 2in (5cm) across, in summer–fall. Z5–9 H9–5.

R. 'Zéphirine Drouhin', illus. p.185.

R. 'Zigeunerknabe', syn. *R.* 'Gipsy Boy'. Vigorous, thorny Bourbon rose of lanky habit. **H** and **S** 6ft (2m). Faintly scented, cupped to flat, double, purplish-crimson flowers, 3in (8cm) across, are borne in summer. Leaves are dark green. Z6–9 H9–6.

ROSCOEA

ZINGIBERACEAE

Genus of late summer- and early fall-flowering, tuberous perennials, related to ginger, grown for their orchid-like flowers. Each flower has a hooded, upper petal, a wide-lobed, lower lip and 2 narrower petals. Is suitable for open borders, rock gardens and woodland gardens. Needs sun or partial shade and cool, well-drained rich soil that must be kept moist in summer. Dies down in winter, when a top-dressing of leaf mold or well-rotted compost is beneficial. Propagate by division in spring or by seed, exposed to frost for best germination, in fall or winter.

R. alpina. Herbaceous, creeping, tuberous perennial. **H** and **S** 8in (20cm). Has 1–5 deep purple, pink or white flowers, borne in succession at the top of leafy shoot, in summer. Produces 1–2 rather short, lance-shaped, mid-green leaves at flowering time, increasing to 5–6 leaves, to 10in (25cm) long. Requires a shady site. Z6–9 H9–6.

R. auriculata, illus. p.411.

R. australis. Summer-flowering, tuberous perennial. **H** 10–16in (25–40cm), **S** 10in (25cm). Has 2–7 broadly lance-shaped, glossy, dark green leaves, arranged in opposite pairs, forming a pseudostem bearing 1–2 purple or white flowers, with shallowly lobed lips. Is intolerant of winter wet so is better in a cold frame. Is sometimes confused with *R. tibetica*. Z6–9 H9–6.

R. cautleyoides, illus. p.424.

R. humeana, illus. p.423.

R. procera. See *R. purpurea*.

R. purpurea, syn. *R. procera*. Summer-flowering, tuberous perennial. **H** 8–12in (20–30cm), **S** 6–8in (15–20cm). Lance-shaped, erect leaves are long-pointed and wrap around each other at base to form false stem. Produces long-tubed, purple flowers. Z6–9 H9–6.

R. scillifolia, illus. p.477. Upright, tuberous perennial. **H** 2–12in (5–30cm), **S** 4–10in (10–25cm). Small, purple-black or light pink flowers are produced in summer–fall above narrowly lance-shaped to linear, mid-green leaves. Z8–9 H9–8.

R. tibetica. Rosette-forming, tuberous perennial. **H** 2–8in (5–20cm), **S** 4–12in (10–30cm). Has broadly lance-shaped, pleated, mid-green leaves. In summer produces purple, pink or white flowers, with deeply lobed lips, at top of stem. Z6–9 H9–6.

Rosmarinifolius lavandulaceus of gardens. See *Rosmarinus officinalis* 'Prostratus'.

ROSMARINUS
Rosemary

LABIATAE/LAMIACEAE

Genus of evergreen shrubs, grown for their flowers and aromatic foliage, which can be used as a culinary herb. At limits of hardiness grow against a south- or west-facing wall. Requires sun and well-drained soil. Cut back frost-damaged plants to healthy wood in spring; straggly, old plants may be cut back hard at same time. Trim hedges after flowering. Propagate by semiripe cuttings in summer.

R. officinalis, illus. p.157. **'Miss Jessopp's Upright'** is an evergreen, compact, upright shrub. **H** and **S** 6ft (2m). From mid- to late spring and sometimes again in fall bears small, 2-lipped, blue flowers amid narrowly oblong, aromatic, dark green leaves. Is good when grown for hedging. Z7–11 H12–1. **'Prostratus'**, syn. *Rosmarinifolius lavandulaceus*, **H** 6in (15cm), is prostrate and among the least hardy forms. Z8–11 H12–1. **'Severn Sea'**, **H** 3ft (1m), has an arching habit, and produces bright blue flowers. Z8–11 H12–1.

ROSSIOGLOSSUM

ORCHIDACEAE

See also ORCHIDS.

R. grande, syn. *Odontoglossum grande* (Clown orchid, Tiger orchid), illus. p.467. Evergreen, epiphytic orchid for a cool greenhouse. **H** 6in (15cm). Spikes of rich yellow flowers, to 6in (15cm) across, heavily marked with chestnut-brown, are produced

in fall. Has broadly oval, stiff leaves, 6in (15cm) long. Provide shade in summer and keep very dry in winter. Z14–15 H12–6.

ROTHMANNIA

RUBIACEAE

Genus of evergreen, summer-flowering shrubs and trees, grown for their flowers. Is related to *Gardenia*. Needs full light or partial shade and rich, well-drained, neutral to acid soil. Water container plants freely when in full growth, moderately at other times. Propagate by seed in spring or by semiripe cuttings in summer.

R. capensis, syn. *Gardenia capensis*, *Gardenia rothmannia* (Candlewood). Evergreen, ovoid shrub or tree. **H** 20ft (6m) or more, **S** 10ft (3m) or more. Leaves are oval, lustrous and rich green. Has fragrant, tubular flowers, with 5 arching, white to creamy-yellow petal lobes and purple-dotted throats, in summer. Z13–15 H12–10.

ROYSTONEA
Royal palm

PALMAE/ARECACEAE

Genus of evergreen palms, grown for their majestic appearance. Produces racemes of insignificant flowers in summer. Needs full light or partial shade and fertile, moist but well-drained soil. Water container plants freely when in full growth, less at other times, especially when temperatures are low. Propagate by seed in spring at not less than 81°F (27°C). Red spider mite may be a problem.

R. regia. Evergreen palm with an upright stem, sometimes thickened about the middle. **H** 70ft (20m) or more, **S** to 20ft (6m). Leaves are feather-shaped, 10ft (3m) long, upright at first, then becoming arching and pendent, and are divided into narrowly oblong, leathery, bright green leaflets. Z11–12 H12–10.

RUBUS

ROSACEAE

Genus of deciduous, semievergreen or evergreen shrubs and woody-stemmed, scrambling climbers. Some species are cultivated solely for their edible fruits, which include raspberries and blackberries. Those described here are grown mainly for their foliage, flowers or ornamental, often prickly stems, though some may also bear edible fruits. Deciduous species grown for their winter stems prefer full sun; other deciduous species need sun or partial shade; evergreens and semievergreens tolerate sun or shade. All *Rubus* require fertile, well-drained soil. Cut old stems of *R. biflorus*, *R. cockburnianus* and *R. thibetanus* to ground after fruiting. Propagate by seed or cuttings (semiripe for evergreens, softwood or hardwood for deciduous species) in summer or winter, *R. odoratus* by division in spring and *R.* 'Benenden' and *R. ulmifolius* 'Bellidiflorus' by layering in spring.

R. 'Benenden', syn. *R.* 'Tridel', illus. p.128.

R. biflorus, illus. p.143.

R. cockburnianus (Ghost bramble). Deciduous, arching shrub. **H** and **S** 8ft (2.5m). Prickly shoots are brilliant blue-white in winter. Dark green leaves, white beneath, are usually divided into 9 oval leaflets. Bears

panicles of 5-petaled, purple flowers in early summer, followed by unpalatable, spherical, black fruits. Z6–8 H8–6.

R. henryi var. bambusarum. Fast-growing, vigorous, evergreen, woody-stemmed, scrambling climber. **H** to 20ft (6m). Leaves are divided into 3 broadly oval leaflets, white-felted beneath. Tiny, pink flowers are borne in small clusters in summer. Z5–9 H9–5.

R. odoratus (Flowering raspberry, Thimbleberry). Vigorous, deciduous, upright, thicket-forming shrub. **H** and **S** 8ft (2.5m). Thornless, peeling shoots bear large, velvety, dark green leaves, with 5 broadly triangular lobes. Large, fragrant, 5-petaled, rose-pink flowers are produced from early summer to early fall, and are sometimes followed by unpalatable, flattened, red fruits. Z3–7 H7–1.

R. thibetanus, illus. p.143.

R. tricolor. Evergreen shrub with both prostrate and arching shoots covered in red bristles. **H** 2ft (60cm), **S** 6ft (2m). Oval, toothed, glossy, dark green leaves set off cup-shaped, 5-petaled, white flowers borne in mid-summer. Has edible, raspberry-like, red fruits. Makes good groundcover. Z7–9 H9–7.

R. 'Tridel'. See *R.* 'Benenden'.

R. ulmifolius 'Bellidiflorus'. Vigorous, deciduous or semievergreen, arching shrub. **H** 8ft (2.5m), **S** 12ft (4m). Prickly stems bear dark green leaves, divided into 3 or 5 oval leaflets, and, in mid- to late summer, large panicles of daisylike, double, pink flowers. Z6–9 H9–6.

RUDBECKIA
Coneflower

COMPOSITAE/ASTERACEAE

Genus of annuals, biennials and perennials, grown for their flowers. Needs sun or partial shade and well-drained or moist soil. Propagate by division in spring or by seed in fall or spring.

R. fulgida (Black-eyed Susan). Z4–9 H9–1. **var. deamii** (illus. p.251) is an erect perennial. **H** 3ft (1m), **S** 2ft (60cm) or more. In late summer and fall produces daisylike, yellow flower heads, with central, black cones. Has narrowly lance-shaped, mid-green leaves. Prefers moist soil. **var. speciosa** (illus. p.251) has elliptic to lance-shaped, almost sickle-shaped basal leaves and coarsely toothed stem leaves. **var. sullivantii 'Goldsturm'** (illus. p.251), **H** 30in (75cm), **S** 12in (30cm) or more, has golden-yellow flower heads.

R. 'Goldquelle'. See *R. laciniata* 'Goldquelle'.

R. hirta (Black-eyed Susan, Gloriosa daisy). Moderately fast-growing, upright, branching, short-lived perennial, grown as an annual. **H** 1–3ft (30cm–1m), **S** 1–1½ft (30–45cm). Has lance-shaped, mid-green leaves and, in summer–fall, large, daisylike, deep yellow flower heads, with conical, purple centers. Needs sun and well-drained soil. Z3–7 H7–1. **Becky Mixed**, **H** 10in (25cm), have yellow, dark red or reddish brown flowers. **'Goldilocks'**, illus. p.325. **'Irish Eyes'**, **H** to 2½ft (75cm), has yellow flower heads, with olive-green centers. **'Marmalade'**, illus. p.323. **'Rustic Dwarfs'**, **H** to 24in (60cm), bears yellow, mahogany or bronze flower heads. **'Toto Gold'**, illus. p.320.

R. laciniata (Coneflower). **'Golden Glow'** Erect perennial. **H** 6–7ft (2–2.2m), **S** 2–3ft (60cm–1m). Bears daisylike, double, golden-yellow flower heads, with green centers, in late summer and fall. Mid-green leaves are divided into lance-shaped leaflets, themselves farther cut. Prefers well-drained soil. Z3–9 H9–1. **'Goldquelle'**, syn. *R.* 'Goldquelle', illus. p.222. **'Herbstsonne'** (illus. p.251) has single, bright yellow flower heads. Z3–9 H9–1.

R. maxima, illus. p.251. Clump-forming perennial. **H** 6ft (2m) or more, **S** 2ft (60cm). Has broadly spoon-shaped, waxy, blue-green, basal leaves. In summer, sturdy stems bear solitary, daisylike flower heads with slender, reflexed, yellow ray florets and large, central, black cones. Z4–8 H8–1.

R. occidentalis. Clump-forming perennial. **H** 24–72in (60–180cm), **S** 18in (45cm) or more. Has oval, mid-green, basal leaves. In summer, erect, leafy, occasionally branched stems bear daisylike flower heads with large, central, brownish-black cone surrounded by short, pointed, green bracts; they have no true ray florets ("petals"). Z3–10 H9–1. **'Green Wizard'** (illus. p.251), **H** 5ft (1.5m), has a more even height range.

R. purpurea. See *Echinacea purpurea*.

R. triloba (Brown-eyed Susan), illus. p.251. Short-lived, upright, clump-forming perennial. **H** 32in (80cm), **S** 16in (40cm). Has 3-lobed, hairy, mid- to pale green, basal leaves. From late summer until fall frosts, leafy stems bear masses of daisylike, bright yellow flower heads with central, blackish-brown cones. Self-seeds freely. Z3–11 H12–1.

RUELLIA

ACANTHACEAE

Genus of perennials and evergreen subshrubs and shrubs, grown for their showy flowers. Needs a humid atmosphere, partial shade and moist but well-drained soil. Propagate by stem cuttings or seed, if available, in spring.

R. amoena. See *R. graecizans*.

R. devosiana, illus. p.465.

R. graecizans, syn. *R. amoena*. Evergreen, bushy subshrub with wide-spreading stems. **H** and **S** 24in (60cm) or more. Has oval, pointed leaves. Intermittently bears clusters of small, tubular, scarlet flowers on stalks to 4in (10cm) long. Z14–15 H12–10.

R. makoyana (Monkey plant, Trailing velvet plant). Hairy, spreading perennial. **H** to 2ft (60cm), **S** 1½ft (45cm). Has oval, silver-veined, purple leaves, dark purple beneath. In summer bears solitary, funnel-shaped, carmine-pink flowers from leaf axils. Z4–5 H12–10.

RUSCHIA

AIZOACEAE

Genus of mostly small, tufted, perennial succulents and evergreen shrubs with leaves united up to one-third of their lengths around stems or with very short sheaths. Needs sun and well-drained soil. Propagate by seed or stem cuttings in spring or summer.

R. acuminata. Evergreen, erect, succulent shrub. **H** 8in (20cm), **S** 20in (50cm). Has woody stems as well as non-woody, bluish-

Q
R

689

green stems with darker dots. Produces solid, 3-angled leaves, 1¼in (3cm) long, with blunt keel and short sheather. Daisylike, white to pale pink flowers, 1¼in (3cm) across, are produced in summer. Z13–15 H12–10.

R. crassa. Evergreen, erect, succulent shrub. **H** and **S** 20in (50cm). Bears solid, 3-angled, bluish-green leaves, ¾in (2cm) long, with short, white hairs; the undersides are keeled and have single tooth. Has daisylike, white flowers, 1in (2.5cm) across, in summer. Z13–15 H12–10.

R. macowanii. Erect, then spreading, perennial succulent. **H** 6in (15cm), **S** 3ft (1m). Has solid, slightly keeled, 3-angled, bluish-green leaves, to 1¼in (3cm) long. In summer bears masses of daisylike, bright pink flowers, 1¼in (3cm) across, with darker stripes. Z13–15 H12–10.

RUSCUS

LILIACEAE/RUSCACEAE

Genus of evergreen, clump-forming, spring-flowering shrubs, grown for their foliage and fruits. The apparent leaves are actually flattened shoots, on which flowers and fruits are borne. Usually, separate male and female plants are required for fruiting. Is particularly useful for dry, shady sites. Tolerates sun, full or partial shade and any soil other than waterlogged. Cut back dead shoots to base in spring. Propagate by division in spring. ⚠ The berries of *R. aculeatus* may cause mild stomach upset if ingested.

R. aculeatus, illus. p.167.
R. hypoglossum, illus. p.167.

RUSSELIA

SCROPHULARIACEAE

Genus of evergreen shrubs and subshrubs, grown for their showy flowers. Needs sun or partial shade and rich, light, well-drained soil. Propagate by stem cuttings or division in spring.

R. equisetiformis, syn. *R. juncea,* illus. p.470.
R. juncea. See *R. equisetiformis.*

RUTA

RUTACEAE

Genus of evergreen, summer-flowering subshrubs, with deeply divided, aromatic leaves, grown for their foliage and flowers and used as a medicinal herb. Requires sun and well-drained soil. Cut back to old wood in spring to keep compact. Propagate by semiripe cuttings in summer. ⚠ All parts may cause severe discomfort if eaten; the foliage may cause photodermatitis on contact.

R. graveolens (Common rue). **'Jackman's Blue',** illus. p.159.

S

SABAL

PALMAE/ARECACEAE

Genus of evergreen fan palms, grown for their foliage and overall appearance. Prefers full sun and fertile, well-drained soil. Water moderately when in full growth, less at other times. Propagate by seed in spring. Red spider mite may be troublesome.

S. minor, illus. p.457.

SAGINA

CARYOPHYLLACEAE

Genus of mat-forming annuals and evergreen perennials, grown for their foliage. Is suitable for banks and in paving. Some species may be very invasive. Prefers sun and gritty, moist soil; dislikes hot, dry conditions. Propagate by division in spring, by seed in fall or, for *S. boydii,* by tip cuttings in summer. Aphids and red spider mite may cause problems.

S. boydii, syn. *S. procumbens* 'Boydii', illus. p.376.
S. procumbens 'Boydii'. See *S. boydii.*

SAGITTARIA

Arrowhead

ALISMATACEAE

Genus of deciduous, perennial, submerged and marginal water plants, grown for their foliage and flowers. Some species are suitable for pools, others for aquariums. All require full sun. Remove fading foliage as necessary. Propagate by division in spring or summer or by breaking off turions in spring.

S. graminea 'Crushed Ice'. Deciduous, perennial, marginal water plant or bog plant. **H** 9in (23cm), **S** 6in (15cm). Has linear, pointed leaves marbled cream and green. Bears 3-petaled, white flowers from early to mid-summer.

S. japonica. See *S. sagittifolia* 'Flore Pleno'.
S. latifolia, illus. p.434.
S. sagittifolia (Japanese arrowhead). Deciduous, perennial, marginal water plant. **H** 18in (45cm), **S** 12in (30cm). Upright, mid-green leaves are acutely arrow-shaped. In summer produces 3-petaled, white flowers, with dark purple centers. May be grown in up to 9in (23cm) depth of water. Z5–11 H12–13. **'Flore Pleno',** syn. *S. japonica* (Japanese arrowhead) has double flowers.

SAINTPAULIA

African violet

GESNERIACEAE

Genus of evergreen, rosette-forming perennials, grown for their showy flowers. Needs a constant temperature, a humid atmosphere, partial shade and fertile soil. Propagate by leaf cuttings in summer. Whitefly and mealy bug may cause problems with indoor plants.

African violet cultivars
There are over 2, 000 cultivars, mainly derived from *S. ionantha,* with star- or bell-

shaped, white, pink, red, blue, violet, bi- or multi-colored flowers, borne throughout the year. They may be single, semidouble or fully double. Petal edges may be ruffled, rounded, frilled or fringed. The broadly ovate to oval leaves are usually mid- or dark green, and may be feathered, flecked or variegated white, pink or cream. See also feature panel p.472.Cultivars are divided into 5 groups, according to rosette size. The measurement given below is the diameter of the rosette; the spread of each cultivar is the same as this: Micro-miniature—less than 8cm (3in); Miniature—8–16cm (3–6in); miniature—16–21cm (6–8in); Standard—21–40cm (8–16in); Large—over 40cm (16in).

S. 'Bright Eyes', illus. p.472. Standard Group. **H** to 6in (15cm). Has dark green leaves and single, deep violet-blue flowers with yellow centers. H12–10.
S. 'Chantabent'. Semi-miniature Group. **H** 4–6in (10–15cm). Has dark green leaves, with deep red undersides, and bears large, single, violet-blue flowers. H12–10.
S. 'Colorado', illus. p.469.
S. 'Delft'. Standard Group. **H** to 6in (15cm). Leaves are dark green, and flowers are semidouble and violet-blue. H12–10.
S. 'Dorothy'. Standard Group. **H** to 6in (15cm). Has long-stalked, light green leaves, and bears large, single, rich pink flowers with frilled, white margins. H12–10.
S. 'Falling Raindrops', illus. p.472. Standard Group with trailing habit. **H** 4–6in (10–15cm). Has mid-green leaves and single, violet-blue flowers. H12–10.
S. 'Garden News', illus. p.472. Standard Group. **H** to 6in (15cm). Has bright green leaves and double, pure white flowers. H12–10.
S. 'Ice Maiden', illus. p.472. Standard Group. **H** to 6in (15cm). Bears single, white flowers with purple-blue markings. H12–10.
S. 'Ionantha'. Evergreen, stemless, rosette-forming perennial, often forming clumps. **H** to 4in (10cm), **S** 10in (25cm). Almost rounded, scalloped, long-stalked, fleshy, usually hairy leaves, to 3in (8cm) long, are mid-green above and often reddish-green below. Loose clusters of 2–8 tubular, 5-lobed, violet-blue flowers, to 1in (2.5cm) across, are produced on stems held above leaves and appear year-round. H12–10.
S. 'Pip Squeek', illus. p.472. Micro-miniature Group. **H** to 3in (8cm). Produces dark green leaves and bell-shaped, pale pink flowers. H12–10.
S. 'Porcelain', illus. p.472. Standard Group. **H** to 6in (15cm). Bears semidouble, white flowers with purple-blue edges. H12–10.
S. 'Powder Keg', illus. p.472. Large Group. **H** 4–6in (10–15cm). Bears dark green leaves and semidouble, deep red flowers, with white margins to petals. H12–10.
S. 'Rainbow's Limelight'. Standard Group. **H** 4–6in (10–15cm). Has mid-green leaves and single, lime-green and yellow flowers.
S. 'Rococo Anna', syn. *S.* 'Rococo Pink'. Standard Group. **H** to 6in (15cm). Bears double, iridescent pink flowers. H12–10.
S. 'Rococo Pink'. See *S.* 'Rococo Anna'.

S. 'Starry Trail', illus. p.472. Standard Group. **H** to 6in (15cm). Has dark green leaves and narrow-petaled, semidouble to double, white flowers, sometimes flushed pale pink. H12–10.
S. 'Zoja', illus. p.472. Standard Group. **H** to 6in (15cm). Produces large, single to semidouble, purple-blue flowers, with bold white line at petal margins. H12–10.

SALIX

Willow

SALICACEAE

Genus of deciduous trees and shrubs, grown for their habit, foliage, catkins and, in some cases, colorful winter shoots. Male catkins are more striking than female; each plant usually bears catkins of only one sex. Most prefer full sun. Most species grow well in any but very dry soil; *S. caprea, S. purpurea* and their variants also thrive in dry soil. Plants grown for their colorful winter shoots should be cut back hard in early spring, every 1–3 years. Propagate by semiripe cuttings in summer or by hardwood cuttings in winter. Fungal diseases may cause canker, particularly in *S. babylonica* and *S.* x *sepulcralis* var. *chrysocoma.* Willows may become infested with such pests as caterpillars, aphids and gall mites.

S. aegyptiaca (Musk willow). Vigorous, deciduous, bushy shrub or tree. **H** 12ft (4m), **S** 15ft (5m). Gray catkins that mature to yellow are produced on bare, sturdy shoots in late winter or early spring, before large, narrowly oval, deep green leaves. Z5–8 H8–5.
S. alba (White willow). Z4–9 H9–1.
f. argentea. See *S. alba* var. *sericea.*
'Britzensis'. See *S. alba* var. *vitellina* 'Britzensis'. **var. caerulea** (Cricket-bat willow) is a very fast-growing, deciduous, conical tree with upright branches. **H** 80ft (25m), **S** 30ft (10m). Has long, narrowly lance-shaped, deep bluish-green leaves and, in early spring, small, pendent, yellowish-green catkins. **'Chermesina'.** See *S. alba* var. *vitellina* 'Chermesina'. **var. sericea,** syn. *S. alba* f. *argentea, S. alba* 'Sericea' (Silver willow), **H** 50ft (15m), **S** 25ft (8m), is a spreading tree that is conical when young and has bright silvery-gray leaves. **'Sericea'.** See *S. alba* var. *sericea.* **'Tristis',** syn. *S. vitellina* 'Pendula' has a more weeping habit and produces only female catkins. **'Tristis'** of gardens. See *S.* x *sepulcralis* var. *chrysocoma.* **var. vitellina,** illus. p.69. **var. vitellina 'Britzensis',** syn. *S. alba* 'Britzensis' has green leaves and bright orange-red, young shoots and is usually cut back to near ground level to provide winter color. **var. vitellina 'Chermesina',** syn. *S. alba* 'Chermesina' has carmine-red, young winter shoots.
S. apoda, illus. p.356.
S. arbuscula (Mountain willow). Deciduous, spreading shrub. **H** and **S** 2ft (60cm) or more. In spring, dark brown stems produce narrowly oval, toothed leaves and white-haired, sometimes red-tinged, yellow catkins. Is suitable for a rock garden. Z3–9 H9–1.
S. babylonica (Weeping willow). Deciduous, weeping tree with slender, pendent shoots that reach almost to the ground. **H** and **S** 40ft (12m). Bears narrowly

lance-shaped, long-pointed leaves. Has yellowish-green catkins in early spring. Is susceptible to canker and has been largely replaced in cultivation by *S.* x *sepulcralis* var. *chrysocoma*. Z6–9 H9–1. **var. *pekinensis* 'Tortuosa',** syn. *S. matsudana* 'Tortuosa', illus. p.80.
S. bockii. Deciduous, bushy shrub. **H** and **S** 8ft (2.5m). Has slender, upright, gray-hairy shoots and oblong, glossy, bright green leaves, with silky-hairy undersides. Usually female in cultivation; bears green catkins in early and mid-fall. Z4–7 H7–1.
***S.* x *boydii*,** illus. p.347.
S. caprea (French pussy willow, Goat willow). Deciduous, bushy shrub or tree. **H** 30ft (10m), **S** 25ft (8m). Oval leaves are dark green above, gray beneath. Catkins are borne in spring before foliage emerges: females are silky and gray, males are gray with yellow anthers. Z6–8 H8–6. **'Kilmarnock',** **H** 5–6ft (1.5–2m), **S** 6ft (2m), is dense-headed and weeping. From early to mid- spring produces gray catkins that later become yellow.
S. chrysocoma. See *S.* x *sepulcralis* var. *chrysocoma*.
***S. daphnoides*,** illus. p.69.
S. elaeagnos (Rosemary willow). Deciduous, upright, dense shrub. **H** 10ft (3m), **S** 15ft (5m). In spring, long shoots bear slender, yellow catkins as leaves emerge. These are narrowly oblong and dark green, with white undersides, and turn yellow in fall. Z4–7 H7–1.
***S. exigua*,** illus. p.112.
***S. fargesii*,** syn. *S. moupinensis*. Deciduous, upright, open shrub. **H** and **S** 10ft (3m). Has purplish-red winter shoots and buds. Slender, erect, green catkins are produced in spring, at same time as bold, oblong, glossy, dark green leaves. Z5–8 H8–5.
S. fragilis (Crack willow). Deciduous tree with broad, bushy head. **H** 50ft (15m), **S** 40–50ft (12–15m). Has long, narrow, pointed, glossy, bright green leaves. Catkins, borne in early spring, are yellow on male plants, green on females. Z4–7 H7–1.
S. gracilistyla. Deciduous, bushy shrub. **H** 10ft (3m), **S** 12ft (4m). Large, silky, gray catkins with red then bright yellow anthers, from early to mid-spring, are followed by lance-shaped, silky, gray, young leaves that mature to bright, glossy green. Z5–8 H8–5. **'Melanostachys',** syn. *S.* 'Melanostachys' (Black willow) bears almost black catkins, with red anthers, in early spring, before bright green leaves emerge.
***S. hastata* 'Wehrhahnii',** illus. p.145.
***S. helvetica*,** illus. p.335.
S. herbacea (Dwarf willow, Least willow). Deciduous, creeping shrub. **H** 1in (2.5cm), **S** 8in (20cm) or more. Has small, rounded to oval leaves. In spring produces small, yellow or yellowish-green catkins. Is good for a rock garden. Needs moist soil.
S. irrorata. Deciduous, upright shrub. **H** 10ft (3m), **S** 15ft (5m). Purple, young shoots are white-bloomed in winter. Catkins with red then yellow anthers are produced from early to mid-spring, before narrowly oblong, glossy, bright green leaves emerge. Z5–9 H9–5.
***S. lanata*,** illus. p.147. **'Stuartii'.** See *S.* 'Stuartii'.
S. lindleyana. Deciduous, creeping, mat-forming shrub with long, creeping stems. **H** 3/4–1 1/4in (2–3cm), **S** 16in (40cm) or more. Small, narrowly oval to linear, pale green leaves are densely set on short branchlets that produce brownish-pink catkins in spring. Is suitable for a rock garden or bank. Needs partial shade and damp soil. Is often confused with the very similar *S. furcata* (syn. *S. fruticulosa*, *S. hylematica*), which is more lax, with spreading, sometimes erect stems. Z7–8 H8–7.
S. magnifica. Deciduous, upright shrub. **H** 15ft (5m), **S** 10ft (3m). Produces very long, slender, green catkins, on sturdy, red shoots, in spring, at same time as large, magnolialike, blue-green leaves emerge. Z7–8 H8–7.
***S. matsudana* 'Tortuosa'.** See *S. babylonica* var. *pekinensis* 'Tortuosa'.
***S.* 'Melanostachys'.** See *S. gracilistyla* 'Melanostachys'.
S. moupinensis of gardens**.** See *S. fargesii*.
S. pentandra (Bay willow, Laurel willow). Deciduous, large shrub, then small tree with broad, bushy head. **H** and **S** 30ft (10m). Oval, glossy, dark green leaves are blue-white beneath. Catkins—males bright yellow, females gray-green—are produced in early summer, when tree is in full leaf. Z5–9 H9–1.
S. purpurea (Purple osier). Deciduous, bushy, spreading shrub. **H** and **S** 15ft (5m). Gray, male catkins, with yellow anthers, and insignificant, female catkins are both borne on slender, often purple shoots in spring, before narrowly oblong, deep green leaves emerge. Z4–7 H7–1. **'Nana',** **H** and **S** 5ft (1.5m), is dense, with silver-gray leaves; is good as a hedge.
***S. repens*,** illus. p.147.
***S. reticulata*,** illus. p.357.
***S.* x *rubens* 'Basfordiana'.** Deciduous, spreading tree. **H** 50ft (15m), **S** 30ft (10m). Has bright orange-yellow, young shoots in winter and long, narrow leaves, gray-green when young, becoming glossy, bright green in summer. Yellowish-green catkins are borne in early spring. Z5–7 H7–5.
***S. sachalinensis* 'Sekka'.** See *S. undensis* 'Sekka'.
***S.* x *sepulcralis* var. *chrysocoma*,** syn. *S. alba* 'Tristis', *S. chrysocoma*, illus. p.69.
***S.* 'Stuartii',** syn. *S. lanata* 'Stuartii'. Slow-growing, deciduous, spreading shrub. **H** 3ft (1m), **S** 6ft (2m). Has yellow winter shoots. Sturdy, gray-green catkins open from orange buds in spring, as oval, woolly, gray leaves emerge. Z5–9 H9–5.
***S. undensis* 'Sekka',** syn. *S. sachalinensis* 'Sekka'. Deciduous, spreading shrub. **H** 15ft (5m), **S** 30ft (10m). Has flattened shoots that are red in winter and lance-shaped, glossy, bright green leaves. Silver catkins are produced in early spring. Z4–7 H7–1.
***S. vitellina* 'Pendula'.** See *S. alba* 'Tristis'.

SALPIGLOSSIS

SOLANACEAE

Genus of annuals and biennials. Usually only annuals are cultivated, either for color in borders or as greenhouse plants. Needs sun and rich, well-drained soil. Stems need support. Deadhead regularly. Propagate by seed sown under glass in early spring, or in early fall for winter flowering indoors. Aphids may be troublesome.
***S. sinuata* Bolero Hybrids** Group of moderately fast-growing, branching, upright annuals. **H** 2ft (60cm), **S** 1ft (30cm). Has lance-shaped, pale green leaves. Outward-facing, widely flared, trumpet-shaped, conspicuously veined flowers, 2in (5cm) across, are produced in summer and early fall. Is available in mixture of rich colors. **Casino Series** are available in red, blue, purple, yellow or orange flowers. **'Friendship'** has upward-facing flowers in a range of colors.

SALVIA

Sage

LABIATAE/LAMIACEAE

Genus of annuals, biennials, perennials and evergreen or semievergreen shrubs and subshrubs, grown for their tubular, 2-lipped, often brightly colored flowers and aromatic foliage. Leaves of some species may be used for flavoring foods. Needs sun and fertile, well-drained soil. Propagate perennials by division in spring, perennials, shrubs and subshrubs by softwood cuttings in mid-summer, half-hardy annuals by seed sown under glass in early spring and fully-hardy species by seed sown outdoors in mid-spring.
***S. argentea*,** illus. p.250. Rosette-forming, short-lived perennial. **H** 36in (90cm), **S** 24in (60cm). Has ovate to elliptic, toothed, silvery-woolly leaves. From mid- to late summer bears many-branched, terminal panicles of white flowers, sometimes pink-flushed. Z5–8 H8–5.
S. blepharophylla. Spreading, rhizomatous perennial. **H** and **S** 18in (45cm). Has oval, glossy, dark green leaves and slender racemes of bright red flowers, with maroon calyces, in summer–fall. Z8–10 H10–8.
S. bulleyana. Rosette-forming perennial. **H** and **S** 24in (60cm). Racemes of nettlelike, yellow flowers, with maroon lips, are borne in summer above basal mass of broadly oval, coarse, prominently veined, dark green leaves. Z7–9 H9–7.
S. discolor. Semievergreen, compact subshrub. **H** and **S** to 3ft (1m). Ovate, silvery-green leaves and stems are covered in woolly, white hairs. Has terminal racemes of purple flowers, sometimes almost black, from late summer to early fall. Z9–11 H12–3.
***S. elegans* 'Scarlet Pineapple'** (Pineapple sage). Clump-forming, woody-based perennial. **H** and **S** 3ft (1m). Hairy stems bear heart-shaped, downy, glaucous leaves, which are pineapple scented when bruised. Bears loose panicles of large, crimson-pink flowers in winter–spring.
S. farinacea.* f. *alba Moderately fast-growing, upright perennial, grown as an annual. **H** 3ft (1m), **S** 1ft (30cm). Has lance-shaped, mid-green leaves. Spikes of white flowers are produced in summer. **'Strata',** illus. p.314. **'Victoria',** illus. p.312. Dwarf forms are also available.
S. forsskaolii. Basal clump-forming perennial. **H** and **S** 20in (50cm). Ovate, toothed, hairy, mid-green leaves mature to dark green by summer. In summer produces sparse whorls of violet-blue flowers, with white and yellow markings on lower lips.
***S. fulgens*,** illus. p.156.
***S. glutinosa*,** illus. p.250. Clump-forming, sticky-hairy perennial. **H** and **S** 36in (90cm). Branched or unbranched stems bear heart-shaped, toothed, mid-green leaves. From mid-summer to mid-fall produces loose, terminal racemes of softly hairy, maroon-spotted, pale yellow flowers, with red-brown marks on lower lips. Z7–9 H9–7.
S. grahamii. See *S. microphylla* var. *microphylla*.
S. greggii. Evergreen, erect subshrub. **H** to 3ft (1m), **S** to 2ft (60cm). Leaves are narrowly oblong and matt, deep green. Has terminal racemes of bright red-purple flowers in fall. Z7–9 H9–4. **'Devon Cream'.** See *S. greggii* 'Sungold'. **'Icing Sugar'** (illus. p.155) has deep purplish-pink flowers, with frosted pink lower lips. **'Sungold',** syn. *S. greggii* 'Devon Cream' has warm yellow flowers.
S. guaranitica. Deciduous, upright subshrub. **H** 8ft (2.5m), **S** 3ft (90cm). Branched, dark green stems bear ovate, hairy, wrinkled, mid-green leaves. Deep blue flowers, with purple calyces, are produced in terminal and axillary spikes from late summer to fall. Z7–10 H11–8. **'Black and Blue'** (illus. p.250) has rich blue flowers, with dark purple-blue calyces. Z7–10 H12–8. **'Blue Enigma'** Clump-forming perennial. **H** and **S** 3ft (1m). Has long racemes of small, slightly fragrant, pale blue flowers, with green calyces, in summer–fall.
S. haematodes. See *S. pratensis* Haematodes Group.
S. horminum. See *S. viridis*.
S. involucrata. Bushy, woody-based perennial. **H** 2–2 1/2ft (60–75cm) or more, **S** 3ft (1m). Has oval, mid-green leaves and, in late summer and fall, racemes of large, rose-crimson flowers. Z11–15 H12–10. **'Bethellii',** illus. p.221.
S.* x *jamensis (*S. microphylla* x *S. greggii*). Very variable, evergreen, bushy shrub. **H** 3ft (1m), **S** 2–2 1/2ft (60–75cm). Has ovate to elliptic, toothed, mid-green leaves. In summer–fall produces terminal racemes of 2-lipped flowers, varying in color from red to rose-pink, salmon-pink and orange to creamy-yellow. **'Hot Lips'** (illus. p.155) has white upper flower lips and vivid red lower lips but may also produce pure white or pure red flowers. Z9–10 H10–9. **'James Compton'** bears deep crimson flowers. **'La Luna'** (illus. p.155) has creamy-yellow flowers with reddish-brown hairs on upper lips. Z9–10 H10–9. **'Maraschino'** (illus. p.155) has cherry-red flowers. Z9–10 H10–9. **'Pat Vlasto'** bears pink-suffused, orange flowers. **'Raspberry Royale'** produces bright raspberry-red flowers. **'Red Velvet'** (illus. p.155) has velvety, red flowers, with dark calyces. Z9–10 H10–9. **'Sierra San Antonio'** (illus. p.155) bears peach-rose flowers, with yellow lower lips. Z9–10 H10–9.
S. jurisicii. Rosette-forming perennial. **H** 18in (45cm), **S** 12in (30cm). Stems are clothed with mid-green leaves, divided into 4–6 pairs of linear leaflets. In early summer produces racemes of inverted, violet-blue flowers. Z6–9 H9–6.
S. lavandulifolia (Spanish sage). Prostrate, woody-based perennial. **H** and **S** 12in (30cm). Has narrowly oblong, downy, aromatic, gray-green leaves. Spikelike racemes of violet to lavender-blue flowers are borne from late spring to early summer. Z5–9 H9–5.
S. leucantha (Mexican bush sage). Evergreen, erect, well-branched shrub. **H** and **S** to 2ft (60cm) or more. Narrowly lance-shaped, finely wrinkled leaves are deep green above, white-downy beneath.

S

In summer–fall produces terminal spikes of hairy, white flowers, from woolly, violet calyces. Z9–11 H12–4.

S. microphylla. 'Cerro Potosi' (illus. p.155) is an evergreen, erect, well-branched shrub. **H** and **S** 3–4ft (1–1.2m). Has oval to elliptic, mid- to deep green leaves. Racemes of magenta flowers, aging to purple and with purple-tinted calyces, are produced in late summer and fall. Z12–15 H12–10. **'Kew Red'** (illus. p.155) has large, almost glabrous leaves and large, vivid red flowers. Z12–15 H12–10. **'La Foux'** (illus. p.155) is similar to *S.m.* 'Kew Red', but is more intense in color and has purplish-black calyces. Z12–15 H12–10. **var. microphylla**, syn. *S. grahamii*, *S. neurepia*, illus. p.156. **'Newby Hall'** (illus. p.155) has pale to mid-green leaves and bright red flowers. Z12–15 H12–10. **'Pink Blush'** (illus. p.155) bears reddish-pink flowers. Z12–15 H12–10.

S. nemorosa, syn. *S. virgata* var. *nemerosa*. Neat, clump-forming perennial. **H** 36in (90cm), **S** 18in (45cm). Has narrowly oval, rough, mid-green leaves and, in summer, branching racemes densely set with violet-blue flowers. Z5–9 H9–5. **'Amethyst'** (illus. p.250) has violet flowers, with purple calyces and bracts. **'Caradonna'** (illus. p.250), **H** 12in (30cm), has blackish-purple stems and bracts and bright purple flowers. **'East Friesland'**. See *S. nemorosa* 'Ostfriesland' **'Lubecca'** (illus. p.250), **H** 18in (45cm), has pinkish-purple bracts and deep blue flowers. **'Ostfriesland'**, syn. *S. nemorosa* 'East Friesland' (illus. p.250), **H** 2½ft (75cm), is smaller.

S. neurepia. See *S. microphylla* var. *microphylla*.

S. officinalis (Common sage), illus. p.155. Evergreen or semievergreen, bushy shrub. **H** and **S** 20in (30cm). Lance-shaped, downy, aromatic, gray-green leaves are used as a culinary and medicinal herb. Lax racemes of purple-blue flowers are produced in summer. Z5–8 H8–5. **'Alba'**. See *S. officinalis* 'Albiflora'. **'Albiflora'**, syn. *S. officinalis* 'Alba', **H** 2ft (60cm), **S** 3ft (1m), has white flowers. **'Berggarten'** (illus. p.155), **H** 16in (40cm), has a spreading habit and round-tipped, silvery-gray leaves. **'Icterina'** (illus. p.155) has gray-green leaves variegated with pale green and yellow. Occasionally bears small spikes of purplish flowers. **'Purpurascens'** (illus. p.155), **H** 2ft (60cm), **S** 3ft (1m), has purple-flushed leaves when young. Z4–10 H10–1. **'Tricolor'** (illus. p.155) has very aromatic, cream-margined, gray-green leaves; young leaves are flushed pinkish-purple. Z7–8 H8–1.

S. patens, illus. p.250. Erect, tuberous perennial often grown as an annual. **H** 18–24in (45–60cm), **S** 18in (45cm). Branching stems bear ovate to triangular, mid-green leaves, spear-shaped at base. From mid-summer to mid-fall produces terminal racemes of widely 2-lipped, deep to pale blue or white flowers. Z8–9 H9–8. **'Cambridge Blue'** has pale blue flowers. **S. pratensis**. Clump-forming, woody-based perennial. **H** 3ft (90cm), **S** 1ft (30cm). Has ovate, wrinkled, toothed, mid-green, basal leaves. Erect, usually branched, terminal spikes of violet, blue, pink or white flowers are borne in summer. Z7–10 H10–7. **Haematodes Group**, syn. *S. haematodes*,

S18in (45cm), have wavy-edged, rough, dark green leaves and lavender-blue flowers. **'Indigo'** (illus. p.250) bears dark blue flowers. Z3–9 H9–1. **'Pink Delight'** (illus. p.250) produces mid- to deep pink flowers. Z3–9 H9–1. **'Swan Lake'** (illus. p.250) has pure white flowers. Z3–9 H9–1. **S. sclarea** var. **turkestanica**, illus. p.313. **S. splendens**. Slow-growing, bushy perennial or evergreen subshrub, grown as an annual. **H** to 12in (30cm), **S** 8–12in (20–30cm). Has oval, toothed, fresh green leaves, and dense racemes of scarlet flowers in summer and early fall. Z11–12 H12–1. **'Blaze of Fire'** has brilliant scarlet flowers. **Cleopatra Series** are available in mixed or single colors including salmon-pink and deep violet-purple flowers. Z11–13 H12–1. **'Rambo'**, **H** to 24in (60cm), is very tall, vigorous, and bushy, with dark green leaves and scarlet flowers. **'Red Riches'**, syn. *S. splendens* 'Ryco', S12–16in (30–40cm), has dark green leaves and scarlet flowers. **'Scarlet King'** has bright scarlet flowers in dense, terminal spikes in early summer. Z11 H11–10. **Sizzler Series 'Sizzler Salmon Bicolour'** has dense racemes of salmon-tinted, white flowers, with rich salmon calyces. **Vista Series**, illus. p.308. **'Ryco'**. See *S. splendens* 'Red Riches'. **S. x superba**. Clump-forming, erect, branched perennial. **H** 24–36in (60–90cm), **S** 18–24in (45–60cm). Leaves are lance-shaped to oblong, scalloped and mid-green, slightly hairy beneath. Slender, terminal racemes of bright violet or purple flowers are produced from mid-summer to early fall. Z5–9 H9–5.

S. x sylvestris. Clump-forming, erect, branched perennial. **H** 32in (80cm), **S** 12in (30cm). Has lance-shaped to oblong, scalloped, softly hairy, mid-green leaves. Dense, terminal racemes of pinkish-violet flowers are produced from early to mid-summer. Z5–9 H9–4. **'Blauhügel'** (illus. p.250), **H** 18in (45cm), has mid-blue flowers and purple bracts. Z5–9 H9–4. **'Mainacht'**, syn. *S. x sylvestris* 'May Night' (illus. p.250), **H** 36in (90cm), **S** 18in (45cm), has violet-blue flowers in late spring and summer. **'May Night'**. See *S. x sylvestris* 'Mainacht'. **S. uliginosa** (Bog sage), illus. p.250. Upright, branching perennial. **H** 6ft (2m), **S** 18in (45cm). Has oblong to lance-shaped, deeply toothed, mid-green leaves and, in fall, long racemes with whorls of bright blue flowers. Prefers moist soil. Z8–11 H12–7. **S. verticillata**. Erect perennial. **H** 36in (90cm), **S** 18in (45cm). Has ovate to elliptic, deeply toothed, dark green leaves, with large terminal lobes. Produces branched racemes with whorls of lilac to violet-blue, occasionally white, flowers in summer. **'Purple Rain'** (illus. p.250) produces red-purple stems and flowers. Z6–8 H8–6. **S. virgata** var. **nemerosa**. See *S. nemorosa*.

S. viridis, syn. *S. horminum*. Moderately fast-growing, upright, branching annual. **H** 18in (45cm), **S** 8in (20cm). Has oval leaves. Pink to pale purple flowers, enclosed by dark-veined, violet bracts, are borne in spikes at tops of stems in summer and early fall. H9–1. **'Bouquet'**, syn. *S. viridis* 'Monarch Bouquet' has blue, rose-pink, white, deep carmine-pink or purple bracts; also available as single colors. Z11–15 H12–10. Bracts of **Claryssa**

Series are in wide range of brilliant colors, including white, pink, purple and blue. **'Monarch Bouquet'**. See *S. viridis* 'Bouquet'. **'Oxford Blue'**, **H** 12in (30cm), has violet-blue bracts.

SALVINIA
SALVINIACEAE

Genus of deciduous, perennial, floating water ferns, evergreen in tropical conditions and aquariums. Prefers full light and warm water. Remove fading foliage, and thin plants when crowded. Propagate by division in summer.

S. auriculata. Deciduous, spreading, perennial, floating water plant, evergreen in tropical conditions. **S** indefinite. Has rounded, pale to mid-green leaves, sometimes suffused purplish-brown, in pairs on branching stems. Z14–15 H12–1. **S. natans**. Deciduous, perennial, floating water plant. **S** indefinite. Oval, elongated, mid-green leaves are borne on branching stems. Tolerates colder conditions than other species and is often used in a cold-water aquarium.

SAMBUCUS
Elder
CAPRIFOLIACEAE

Genus of perennials, deciduous shrubs and trees, grown for their foliage, flowers and fruits. Needs sun and fertile, moist soil. For best foliage effect, cut all shoots to ground in winter or prune out old shoots and reduce length of young shoots by half. Propagate species by softwood cuttings in summer, by seed in fall or by hardwood cuttings in winter, some forms by cuttings only. ⚠ All parts may cause severe discomfort if ingested, although fruits are safe when cooked; contact with leaves may irritate skin.

S. canadensis, syn. *S. nigra* subsp. *canadensis* (American elder, Black elder). Z4–9 H9–1. **'Aurea'** is a deciduous, upright shrub. **H** and **S** 12ft (4m). Has large, golden-yellow leaves, divided into usually 7 oblong leaflets. In mid-summer bears large, domed heads of small, star-shaped, creamy-white flowers, followed by spherical, red fruits. **S. nigra** (Elderberry, European elder, European red elder). Z6–8 Z6–8. **'Aurea'** (Golden elder) is a deciduous, bushy shrub. **H** and **S** 20ft (6m). Has sturdy, corky shoots and golden-yellow leaves divided into usually 5 oval leaflets. Flattened heads of fragrant, star-shaped, creamy-white flowers, in early summer, are followed by spherical, black fruits. **subsp. canadensis**. See *S. canadensis*. Dark green foliage of **f. porphyrophylla 'Guincho Purple'** matures to deep blackish-purple. Bears purple-stalked flowers, pink in bud and opening to white within, pink outside. Z6–8 H8–6. **S. racemosa** (Red-berried elder). Deciduous, bushy shrub. **H** and **S** 10ft (3m). Mid-green leaves are divided into usually 5 oval leaflets. Star-shaped, creamy-yellow flowers, borne in dense, conical clusters in mid-spring, are followed by spherical, red fruits. Z3–7 H7–1. **'Plumosa'** has leaves with finely cut leaflets. **'Plumosa Aurea'**, illus. p.139.

SANCHEZIA
ACANTHACEAE

Genus of evergreen, mainly summer-flowering perennials, shrubs and scrambling climbers, grown for their flowers and foliage. Requires full light or partial shade and fertile, well-drained soil. Water container plants freely when in full growth, less at other times. Tip prune young plants to promote branching. Propagate by greenwood cuttings in spring or summer. Is prone to whitefly and soft scale.

S. nobilis of gardens. See *S. speciosa*. **S. speciosa**, syn. *S. nobilis*. Evergreen, erect, soft-stemmed shrub. **H** 4–7ft (1.2–2.2m), **S** 3–5ft (90–150cm). Glossy leaves have yellow- or white-banded main veins. Tubular, yellow flowers are produced in axils of red bracts, in summer. Z14–15 H12–10.

SANDERSONIA
LILIACEAE/COLCHICACEAE

Genus of one species of deciduous, tuberous climber, grown for its urn-shaped flowers in summer. Needs a sheltered, sunny site and well-drained soil. Support with sticks or canes. Lift tubers for winter. Propagate in spring by seed or by naturally divided tubers.

S. aurantiaca, illus. p.413.

SANGUINARIA
PAPAVERACEAE

Genus of one species of spring-flowering, rhizomatous perennial. Needs sun or partial shade and rich, moist but well-drained soil. Propagate by division of rhizomes in summer or by seed in fall.

S. canadensis, illus. p.348. **f. multiplex 'Plena'**, syn. *S. canadensis* 'Flore Pleno' is a clump-forming, rhizomatous perennial. **H** 6in (15cm), **S** 12–18in (30–45cm). Has fleshy, underground stems that exude red sap when cut. Short-lived, rounded, fully double, white flowers, in spring, are followed by large, rounded to heart-shaped, scalloped, gray-green leaves, with glaucous undersides. **'Flore Pleno'**. See *S. canadensis* f. *multiplex* 'Plena'. Z3–9 H9–1.

SANGUISORBA
Burnet
ROSACEAE

Genus of perennials, grown for their bottlebrushlike flower spikes. Requires sun and moist soil. Propagate by division in spring or by seed in fall.

S. canadensis, illus. p.437. **S. obtusa**. Clump-forming perennial. **H** 3–4ft (1–1.2m), **S** 2ft (60cm). Arching stems bear spikes of rose-crimson flowers in mid-summer. Pairs of oval leaflets are pale green above, blue-green beneath. Z4–8 H8–3. **S. officinalis** (Greater burnet). Z4–7 H8–3. **'Rubra'** is a clump-forming perennial. **H** 4ft (1.2m), **S** 2ft (60cm). Produces small spikes of red-brown flowers in late summer. Mid-green leaves are divided into oval leaflets. Z3–8 H8–1. **S. tenuifolia 'Alba'**, illus. p.216.

SANSEVIERIA

AGAVACEAE/DRACAENACEAE

Genus of evergreen, rhizomatous perennials, grown for their rosettes of stiff, fleshy leaves. Needs sun and tolerates most soil conditions if not over-watered. Propagate by leaf cuttings or division in summer.

S. cylindrica. Evergreen, stemless, rhizomatous perennial. **H** 1½–4ft (45cm–1.2m), **S** 4in (10cm). Has rosette of 3–4 cylindrical, erect, stiff, fleshy, dark green leaves, to 4ft (1.2m) long, with paler horizontal bands. Racemes of small, tubular, 6-lobed, pink or white flowers are occasionally produced. Z12–15 H12–1.

S. trifasciata (Mother-in-law's tongue, Snake plant). Evergreen, stemless, rhizomatous perennial. **H** 1½–4ft (45cm–1.2m), **S** 4in (10cm). Has rosette of about 5 lance-shaped, pointed, erect, stiff, fleshy leaves, to 4ft (1.2m) long, banded horizontally with pale green and yellow. Occasionally produces racemes of tubular, 6-lobed, green flowers. Z14–15 H12–1. **'Golden Hahnii'**, illus. p.476. **'Hahnii'**, illus. p.475. **'Laurentii'**, illus. p.476.

SANTOLINA

COMPOSITAE/ASTERACEAE

Genus of evergreen, summer-flowering shrubs, grown for their aromatic foliage and their buttonlike flower heads. Needs sun and not too rich, well-drained soil. Cut off old flower heads and reduce long shoots in fall. Cut straggly plants back hard each spring. Propagate by semiripe cuttings in summer.

S. chamaecyparissus, syn. *S. incana* (Lavender cotton). Evergreen, rounded, dense shrub. **H** 2½ft (75cm), **S** 3ft (1m). Shoots are covered with woolly, white growth, and narrowly oblong, finely toothed leaves are also white. Bright yellow flower heads are borne in mid- and late summer.

S. incana. See *S. chamaecyparissus.*

S. neapolitana. See *S. pinnata* subsp. *neapolitana.*

S. pinnata. Evergreen shrub mainly grown as Z9–11 H12–9. **subsp. neapolitana,** syn. *S. neapolitana,* which is of rounded and bushy habit. **H** 2½ft (75cm), **S** 3ft (1m). Slender flower stems bear head of lemon-yellow flowers in mid-summer, amid feathery, deeply cut, gray-green leaves. **subsp. neapolitana 'Sulphurea',** illus. p.159.

S. rosmarinifolia, syn. *S. virens.* Evergreen, bushy, dense shrub. **H** 2ft (60cm), **S** 3ft (1m). Has finely cut, bright green leaves. Slender stem produces head of bright yellow flowers in mid-summer. Z6–9 H9–6. **'Primrose Gem'** has pale yellow flower heads.

S. virens. See *S. rosmarinifolia.*

SANVITALIA

COMPOSITAE/ASTERACEAE

Genus of perennials and annuals. Needs sun and fertile, well-drained soil. Propagate by seed in spring or early fall.

S. procumbens, illus. p.320. **'Mandarin Orange',** illus. p.324.

SAPIUM

EUPHORBIACEAE

Genus of evergreen trees, grown for their ornamental appearance. Prefers full light and fertile, well-drained soil. Water container plants freely when in full growth, less at other times. Pruning is tolerated, if necessary. Propagate by seed in spring or by semiripe cuttings in summer. ① All parts may cause severe discomfort if ingested; contact with their poisonous, milky sap may irritate skin.

S. sebiferum (Chinese tallow tree, Vegetable tallow tree). Fast-growing, evergreen, erect to spreading tree. **H** to 25ft (8m), **S** 12ft (4m) or more. Rhombic to oval, mid-green leaves turn red with age. Clusters of tiny, greenish-yellow flowers develop into rounded, black fruits covered by layer of white wax. Z8–10 H10–8.

SAPONARIA

Soapwort

CARYOPHYLLACEAE

Genus of summer-flowering annuals and perennials, grown for their flowers. Is good for rock gardens, screes and banks. Needs sun and well-drained soil. Propagate by seed in spring or fall or by softwood cuttings in early summer.

S. 'Bressingham', syn. *S.* 'Bressingham Hybrid'. Loose, mat-forming perennial. **H** 3in (8cm), **S** 4in (10cm). Has small, narrowly oval leaves. Flattish, deep vibrant pink flowers are borne in clustered heads in summer. Is good for a trough. Z4–8 H8–1.

S. 'Bressingham Hybrid'. See *S.* 'Bressingham'.

S. caespitosa, illus. p.364.

S. ocymoides, illus. p.364.

S. officinalis 'Rubra Plena'. Upright perennial. **H** to 3ft (1m), **S** 1ft (30cm). Has oval, rough, mid-green leaves on erect stems. Clusters of ragged, double, red flowers are produced on upper part of flower stems in summer. Z3–9 H9–1.

S. x olivana, illus. p.362.

SARCOCAPNOS

PAPAVERACEAE/FUMARIACEAE

Genus of spring-flowering perennials. Is useful for rock gardens. Prefers sun and well-drained, alkaline soil. Propagate by seed in spring.

S. enneaphylla. Loose, upright perennial. **H** and **S** 6in (15cm). Slender, much-branched stems bear small, divided, glaucous green leaves with oval to rounded segments. In spring, small, spurred, yellowish-white flowers, tipped with purple, are produced in short racemes. Protect from winter wet. Z6–8 H8–6.

SARCOCOCCA

Christmas box, Sweet box

BUXACEAE

Genus of evergreen shrubs, grown for their foliage, fragrant, winter flowers and spherical fruits. Flowers are tiny—the only conspicuous part being the anthers. Is useful for cutting in winter. Prefers deep or partial shade and fertile, not too dry soil. Propagate by semiripe cuttings in summer or by seed in fall.

S. confusa, illus. p.142. Evergreen, bushy, dense shrub. **H** and **S** 3ft (1m). Leaves are small, oval, taper-pointed, glossy and dark green. Has tiny, white flowers, in winter, followed by black fruits. Z6–9 H9–6.

S. hookeriana. Evergreen, upright, dense, suckering shrub. **H** 5ft (1.5m), **S** 6ft (2m). Forms clumps of narrowly oblong, pointed, dark green leaves. Tiny, white flowers are produced in leaf axils in winter. Fruits are black. Z6–9 H9–6. **var. digyna,** illus. p.164. **var. digyna 'Purple Stem'** has young shoots flushed dark purple-pink, and pink-tinged flowers. **var. humilis.** See *S. humilis.*

S. humilis, syn. *S. hookeriana* var. *humilis,* illus. p.164.

S. ruscifolia. Evergreen, upright, arching shrub. **H** and **S** 3ft (1m). Has oval, glossy, dark green leaves and, in winter, creamy-white flowers, followed by red fruits. Z8–9 H9–7. **var. chinensis** has narrower leaves.

SARMIENTA

GESNERIACEAE

Genus of one species of evergreen, woody-stemmed, scrambling or trailing perennial. Is suitable for hanging baskets. Needs partial shade and rich soil that does not dry out. Propagate by seed in spring or by stem cuttings in summer or fall.

S. repens, syn. *S. scandens.* Evergreen, slender-stemmed, scrambling perennial. **H** and **S** 2ft (60cm) or more. Tips of oval leaves have 3–5 teeth. In summer produces small, tubular, coral-pink flowers, narrowed at the base and towards mouth, which has 5 deeper pink lobes.

S. scandens. See *S. repens.*

SARRACENIA

Pitcher plant

SARRACENIACEAE

Genus of insectivorous perennials, some of which are evergreen, with pitchers formed from modified leaves with hooded tops. Needs sun or partial shade and rich, moist but very well-drained, acid soil. Keep very wet, except in winter, when drier conditions are needed. Propagate by seed in spring.

S. flava, illus. p.445.

S. purpurea, illus. p.439.

SASA

GRAMINEAE/POACEAE

See also GRASSES, BAMBOOS, RUSHES and SEDGES.

S. albomarginata. See *S. veitchii.*

S. palmata. Evergreen, spreading bamboo. **H** 6ft (2m), **S** indefinite. Produces broadly elliptic, rich green leaves, to 16in (40cm) long. Hollow, purple-streaked stems have one branch at each node. Flower spikes are unimportant. Z7–11 H12–7.

S. veitchii, syn. *S. albomarginata,* illus. p.284.

SASSAFRAS

LAURACEAE

Genus of deciduous trees, with inconspicuous flowers, grown for their aromatic foliage. Needs sun or partial shade and deep, fertile, well-drained, preferably acid soil. Propagate by seed or suckers in fall or by root cuttings in winter.

S. albidum, illus. p.64.

SATUREJA

LABIATAE/LAMIACEAE

Genus of summer-flowering annuals, semievergreen perennials and subshrubs, grown for their flowers and highly aromatic leaves. Is useful for rock gardens and dry banks. Needs sun and well-drained soil. Propagate by seed in winter or spring or by softwood cuttings in summer.

S. montana (Winter savory). Semievergreen, upright perennial or subshrub. **H** 12in (30cm), **S** 8in (20cm) or more. Leaves are linear to oval, aromatic and green or grayish-green. Produces loose whorls of tubular, 2-lipped, lavender flowers in summer. Z5–8 H12–1. **'Prostrate White',** **H** 3–6in (7–15cm), has a prostrate habit and bears white flowers.

SAUROMATUM

ARACEAE

Genus of spring-flowering, tuberous perennials, grown for their tubular spathes that expand into waved, twisted blades. Tubers will flower without soil or moisture, and before leaves appear. Needs a sheltered, partially shaded position and rich, well-drained soil. Water well in summer. Dry off or lift when dormant in winter. Propagate by offsets in spring.

S. guttatum. See *S. venosum.*

S. venosum, syn. *S. guttatum,* illus. p.403.

SAURURUS

SAURURACEAE

Genus of deciduous, perennial, bog and marginal water plants, grown for their foliage. Prefers full sun, but tolerates some shade. Remove faded leaves and divide plants as required to maintain vigor. Propagate by division in spring.

S. cernuus, illus. p.435.

SAXEGOTHAEA

PODOCARPACEAE

See also CONIFERS.

S. conspicua (Prince Albert's yew). Conifer that is conical to bushy in mild areas, more bushy in cold districts. **H** 15–50ft (5–15m), **S** 12–15ft (4–5m). Needlelike, flattened, dark green leaves are produced in whorls at ends of shoots. Bears globose, fleshy, glaucous green cones. Z8–10 H10–8.

SAXIFRAGA

Saxifrage

SAXIFRAGACEAE

Genus of often rosetted perennials, most of which are evergreen or semievergreen, grown for their flowers and foliage. Is excellent in rock gardens, raised beds and alpine houses. Propagate by seed in fall or by rooted offsets in winter. For cultivation, saxifrages may be grouped as follows:
1—Needs moist soil and protection from midday sun.
2—Needs partial shade and well-drained soil. Is good among rocks and screes.
3—Thrives in well-drained rock pockets, troughs, alpine-house pans etc, shaded from midday sun. Must never be dry at roots. Most form tight cushions and flower in early spring, flower stems being barely visible above leaves.

4—Needs full sun and well-drained, alkaline soil. Suits rock pockets. Most have hard leaves encrusted in lime.
S. aizoides. Evergreen perennial forming a loose mat. **H** 6in (15cm), **S** 12in (30cm) or more. Has small, narrowly oval, fleshy, shiny, green leaves and, in spring–summer, terminal racemes of star-shaped, bright yellow or orange flowers, often spotted red, on hairy stems. Cultivation group 1. Z1–6 H6–1.
S. aizoon. See *S. paniculata.*
S. x anglica 'Cranbourne', syn. *S.* 'Cranbourne'. Evergreen, cushion-forming perennial. **H** and **S** 5in (12cm). In early spring produces solitary, cup-shaped, bright purplish-lilac flowers on short stems just above tight rosettes of linear, green leaves. Flower stems are longer if plant is grown in an alpine house. Cultivation group 3. Z7–9 H9–7.
S. x apiculata 'Gregor Mendel', syn. *S.* 'Gregor Mendel', illus. p.357; cultivation group 2.
S. 'Arco'. See *S.* x *arco-valleyi* 'Arco'.
S. x arco-valleyi 'Arco', syn. *S.* 'Arco'. Evergreen perennial forming a tight cushion. **H** and **S** 4in (10cm). In early spring produces upturned, cup-shaped to flattish, pale lilac flowers almost resting on tight rosettes of oblong to linear leaves. Cultivation group 3. Z6–8 H8–6.
S. 'Bob Hawkins'. Evergreen perennial with a loose rosette of leaves. **H** 1–2in (2.5–5cm), **S** 6in (15cm). Bears small, upturned, rounded, greenish-white flowers in summer on upright stems. Oval, green leaves are white-splashed. Cultivation group 1. Z6–8 H8–6.
S. x boydii 'Hindhead Seedling', illus. p.356; cultivation group 2.
S. 'Brookside'. See *S. burseriana* 'Brookside'.
S. brunoniana. See *S. brunonis.*
S. brunonis, syn. *S. brunoniana.* Semievergreen, rosetted perennial. **H** 4in (10cm), **S** 8in (20cm). Small, soft green rosettes of lance-shaped, rigid leaves produce masses of long, threadlike, red runners. Many of the rosettes die down to large terminal buds in winter. Short racemes of 5-petaled, spreading, pale yellow flowers are produced in late spring and summer. Is difficult to grow; cultivation group 1. Z6–8 H8–6.
S. burseriana, illus. p.348. Cultivation group 3. Z6–8 H8–6. **'Brookside',** syn. *S.* 'Brookside' is a slow-growing, evergreen perennial forming a hard cushion. **H** 1–2in (2.5–5cm), **S** to 4in (10cm). Has broadly linear, spiky, gray-green leaves. In early spring bears upturned, rounded, shallowly cup-shaped, bright yellow flowers on short, red stems. Flowers of **'Crenata',** syn. *S.* 'Crenata' have fringed, white petals and red sepals. **'Gloria',** syn. *S.* 'Gloria' has dark reddish-brown stems, bearing 1 or 2 flowers, with red sepals and white petals, in late spring.
S. callosa, syn. *S. linguata,* illus. p.337; cultivation group 4.
S. cochlearis. Evergreen, rosetted perennial. **H** 8in (20cm), **S** 10in (25cm). Has spoon-shaped, green leaves with white-encrusted edges. Produces loose panicles of rounded, white flowers, often with red-spotted petals, in early summer. Cultivation group 4. Z7–8 H8–7. **'Minor',** **H** and **S** 5in (12cm), has smaller leaf rosettes and loose panicles of red-spotted, white flowers on red stems. Is ideal for a trough.
S. cortusifolia var. fortunei. See *S. fortunei.*
S. cotyledon. Evergreen perennial. **H** and **S** to 12in (30cm). Has large rosettes of oblong to inversely lance-shaped, pale green leaves, which die after flowering. In late spring and early summer produces arching, conical panicles of cup-shaped, white flowers, sometimes strongly marked red internally. Cultivation group 2. Z4–6 H6–1.
S. 'Cranbourne'. See *S.* x *anglica* 'Cranbourne'.
S. 'Crenata'. See *S. burseriana* 'Crenata'.
S. cuneifolia, illus. p.337. Cultivation group 1.
S. x elisabethae, syn. *S.* 'Elisabethae', illus. p.357. Cultivation group 2.
S. exarata subsp. moschata. Evergreen perennial forming a loose to tight hummock. **H** and **S** 4in (10cm). Rosettes comprise small, lance-shaped, sometimes 3-toothed, green leaves. Bears 2–5 star-shaped, creamy-white or dull yellow flowers, on slender stems, in summer. Cultivation group 1. Z5–7 H7–5. **subsp. moschata 'Cloth of Gold',** illus. p.377.
S. federici-augusti subsp. grisebachii 'Wisley Variety', syn. *S. grisebachii* 'Wisley Variety', illus. p.353. Cultivation group 4.
S. ferdinandi-coburgi. Evergreen, cushion-forming perennial. **H** and **S** 6in (15cm). Forms rosettes of linear, spiny, glaucous green leaves and, in early spring, bears racemes of open cup-shaped, rich yellow flowers on red-tinged stems. Cultivation group 3. Z6–8 H8–6.
S. fortunei, syn. *S. cortusifolia* var. *fortunei.* Semievergreen or herbaceous, clump-forming perennial. **H** and **S** 12in (30cm). Has rounded, 5- or 7-lobed, fleshy, green or brownish-green leaves, red beneath. In fall produces panicles of tiny, mothlike, white flowers, with 4 equal-sized petals and 1 elongated petal, on upright stems. Propagate by division in spring. Cultivation group 1. Z6–8 H8–6. **'Rubrifolia'** has dark red flower stems and dark reddish-green leaves, beetroot-red beneath.
S. x geum. Evergreen, mat-forming perennial. **H** 6–8in (15–20cm), **S** 12in (30cm). Has shallow-rooted rosettes of spoon-shaped, hairy leaves. In summer, star-shaped, pink-spotted, white flowers, deep pink in bud, are borne on loose panicles on slender stems. Cultivation group 1. Z6–8 H8–6.
S. 'Gloria'. See *S. burseriana* 'Gloria'.
S. granulata, illus. p.332; cultivation group 1. **'Plena'** is a clump-forming perennial. **H** 9–15in (23–38cm), **S** to 6in (15cm) or more. Kidney-shaped, glossy, pale to mid-green leaves die down soon after flowering. Has loose panicle of large, rounded, double, white flowers in late spring or early summer. Bulbils or resting buds form at base of foliage.
S. 'Gregor Mendel'. See *S.* x *apiculata* 'Gregor Mendel'.
S. grisebachii 'Wisley Variety'. See *S. federici-augusti* subsp. *grisebachii* 'Wisley Variety'.
S. hirsuta. Evergreen, mound-forming perennial. **H** 6–8in (15–20cm), **S** 8in (20cm). Has rosettes of rounded, hairy leaves. Bears loose panicles of tiny, star-shaped, white flowers, often yellow-spotted at petal bases, in late spring and early summer. Cultivation group 1. Z2–6 H6–1.
S. x irvingii 'Jenkinsiae', syn. *S.* 'Jenkinsiae', illus. p.350. Cultivation group 3. **'Walter Irving',** is a very slow-growing, evergreen, hard-domed perennial. **H** 3/4in (2cm), **S** 3in (8cm). Bears minute leaves in rosettes. Stemless, cup-shaped, lilac-pink flowers are borne in early spring.
S. 'Jenkinsiae'. See *S.* x *irvingii* 'Jenkinsiae'.
S. linguata. See *S. callosa.*
S. longifolia. Rosetted perennial. **H** 24in (60cm), **S** 8–10in (20–25cm). Has long, narrow, lime-encrusted leaves. After 3–4 years develops long, arching, conical to cylindrical panicles bearing numerous rounded, 5-petaled, white flowers in late spring and summer. Rosettes die after flowering, and no daughter rosettes are formed, so propagate by seed in spring or fall. In cultivation, hybridizes readily with other related species. Cultivation group 4. Z6–7 H7–6.
S. oppositifolia, illus. p.353; cultivation group 1. **'Ruth Draper'** is an evergreen, loose mat-forming perennial. **H** 1–2in (2.5–5cm), **S** 6in (15cm). Has small, opposite, oblong to oval, white-flecked, dark green leaves closely set along prostrate stems. Large, cup-shaped, deep purple-pink flowers are borne in early spring just above foliage. Prefers peaty soil.
S. paniculata, syn. *S. aizoon.* Evergreen, tightly rosetted perennial. **H** 6–12in (15–30cm), **S** 8in (20cm). In summer produces loose panicles of rounded, usually white flowers, with or without purplish-red spots, on upright stems above rosettes of oblong to oval, lime-encrusted leaves. Is very variable in size. Pale yellow or pale pink forms also occur. Cultivation group 4. Z2–6 H6–1.
S. x primulaize, syn. *S.* 'Primulaize'. Evergreen, loosely rosetted perennial. **H** and **S** 6in (15cm). In summer, branched flower stems produce star-shaped, salmon-pink flowers. Leaves are tiny, narrowly oval, slightly indented and fleshy. Cultivation group 1. Z6–7 H7–6.
S. sancta, illus. p.358. Cultivation group 2.
S. sarmentosa. See *S. stolonifera.*
S. scardica, illus. p.348. Cultivation group 3.
S. sempervivum, illus. p.353. Cultivation group 3.
S. 'Southside Seedling', illus. p.338. Cultivation group 4.
S. stolonifera, syn. *S. sarmentosa* (Mother of thousands). Evergreen, prostrate perennial with runners. **H** 6in (15cm) or more, **S** 12in (30cm) or more. Has large, rounded, shallowly lobed, hairy, silver-veined, olive-green leaves, reddish-purple beneath. Loose panicles of tiny, mothlike, white flowers, with 4 equal-sized petals and 1 elongated petal, are borne in summer on slender, upright stems. Makes good groundcover. Cultivation group 1. Z7–9 H9–5. **'Tricolor',** syn. *S.* 'Tricolor' (Strawberry geranium) has green-and-red leaves with silver marks. Cultivation group 1.
S. stribrnyi, illus. p.354. Cultivation group 3.
S. 'Tricolor'. See *S. stolonifera* 'Tricolor'.
S. 'Tumbling Waters', illus. p.333. Cultivation group 4.
S. x urbium (London pride). Evergreen, rosetted, spreading perennial. **H** 12in (30cm), **S** indefinite. Has spoon-shaped, toothed, leathery, green leaves. Flower stems bear tiny, star-shaped, at times pink-flushed, white flowers, with red spots, in summer. Is useful as groundcover. Cultivation group 1. Z6–7 H7–6.
S. 'Valerie Finnis'. Evergreen, hard cushion-forming perennial. **H** and **S** 4in (10cm). Short, red stems bear upturned, cup-shaped, sulfur-yellow flowers above tight rosettes of oval, green leaves in spring. Cultivation group 3. Z7–10 H10–7.

SCABIOSA
Scabious

DIPSACACEAE

Genus of annuals and perennials, some of which are evergreen, grown for their flower heads, which are good for cutting. Prefers sun and fertile, well-drained, alkaline soil. Propagate annuals by seed in spring, perennials by cuttings of young, basal growths in summer, by seed in fall or by division in early spring.
S. arvensis. See *Knautia arvensis.*
S. atropurpurea (Pincushion flower, Sweet scabious). Moderately fast-growing, upright, bushy annual. **H** to 3ft (1m), **S** 8–12in (20–30cm). Has lance-shaped, lobed, mid-green leaves. Domed heads of scented, pincushionlike, deep crimson flower heads are produced on wiry stems in summer and early fall. Tall forms, 3ft (1m), and dwarf, **H** 18in (45cm), are available with flower heads in shades of blue, purple, red, pink or white. Z4–11 H8–3.
S. caucasica 'Floral Queen' is a clump-forming perennial. **H** and **S** 24in (60cm). Large, frilled, violet-blue flower heads, with pincushionlike centers, are produced throughout summer. Light green leaves are lance-shaped at base of plant and segmented on stems. **'Clive Greaves',** illus. p.271. **'Miss Willmott'** has creamy-white flowers.
S. columbaria var. ochroleuca. See *S. ochroleuca.*
S. graminifolia. Evergreen, clump-forming perennial, often with woody base. **H** and **S** 6–10in (15–25cm). Has tufts of narrow, grasslike, pointed, silver-haired leaves. In summer produces stiff stems with spherical, bluish-violet to lilac flower heads like pincushions. Resents disturbance. Is suitable for a rock garden. Z5–7 H7–5.
S. lucida, illus. p.341.
S. ochroleuca, syn. *S. columbaria* var. *ochroleuca.* Clump-forming perennial. **H** and **S** 3ft (1m). In late summer, branching stems bear many frilled, sulfur-yellow flower heads, with pincushionlike centers. Has narrowly oval, toothed, gray-green leaves. Z4–9 H9–1.
S. rumelica. See *Knautia macedonica.*

SCADOXUS

AMARYLLIDACEAE

Genus of bulbs, grown for their dense, mainly spherical, umbels of red flowers. Requires partial shade and rich, well-drained soil. Reduce watering in winter, when not in active growth. Propagate by seed or offsets in spring.
S. multiflorus, syn. *Haemanthus multiflorus.* Summer-flowering bulb. **H** to

28in (70cm), **S** 12–18in (30–45cm). Has broadly lance-shaped, semierect, basal leaves. Produces spherical umbel of up to 200 narrow-petaled flowers. Z14–15 H12–10. **subsp. katherinae,** syn. *Haemanthus katherinae*, illus. p.386.
S. puniceus, syn. *Haemanthus magnificus, Haemanthus natalensis, Haemanthus puniceus* (Giant stove bush). Spring- and summer-flowering bulb. **H** 12–16in (30–40cm), **S** 12–18in (30–45cm). Has elliptic, semierect leaves in basal cluster. Leaf bases are joined, forming a false stem. Flower stem bears up to 100 tubular, orange-red flowers in conical umbel surrounded by whorl of red bracts. Z13–15 H12–1.

SCAEVOLA
GOODENIACEAE

Genus of short-lived, mainly evergreen perennials but also scrambling climbers, shrubs and small trees, grown for summer display, usually in containers. Needs sun or partial shade and moist but well-drained, fertile soil. Propagate by softwood cuttings in late spring or summer.
S. aemula 'Little Wonder'. Evergreen, trailing, bushy perennial, grown as an annual. **H** 12in (30cm), **S** 16in (40cm). Has spoon-shaped, rich green leaves. In summer produces 5-lobed, blue flowers, with yellow ring round white throat.

SCHEFFLERA
SYN. BRASSAIA, HEPTAPLEURUM
ARALIACEAE

Genus of evergreen shrubs and trees, grown mainly for their foliage. Needs full light or partial shade and fertile, moist but well-drained soil. Water container specimens freely when in full growth, moderately at other times. Pruning is tolerated, if needed. Propagate by air-layering in spring, by semiripe cuttings in summer or by seed as soon as ripe, in late summer.
S. actinophylla, illus. p.452.
S. arboricola. Evergreen, erect, well-branched shrub or tree. **H** 6–15ft (2–5m), **S** 3–10ft (1–3m). Leaves are divided into 7–16 oval, stalked, glossy, deep green leaflets. Mature plants bear small, spherical heads of tiny, green flowers in spring–summer. Z11–12 H12–1.
S. digitata. Evergreen, rounded to ovoid shrub or bushy tree. **H** and **S** 10–25ft (3–8m). Leaves are hand-shaped, divided into 5–10 oval, glossy, rich green leaflets. Has tiny, greenish flowers in large, terminal panicles, in spring, followed by tiny, globular, dark violet fruits in fall. Z11–12 H12–1.
S. elegantissima, syn. *Aralia elegantissima, Dizygotheca elegantissima*, illus. p.457.

SCHIMA
THEACEAE

Genus of one species of very variable, evergreen tree or shrub, grown for its foliage and flowers. Is related to *Camellia*. Prefers sun or partial shade and rich, well-drained, neutral to acid soil. Water container plants freely in full growth, moderately at other times. Pruning is tolerated, if necessary. Propagate by seed as soon as ripe or by semiripe cuttings in summer.

S. wallichii. Robust, evergreen, ovoid tree or shrub. **H** 80–100ft (25–30m), **S** 40ft (12m) or more. Elliptic to oblong, red-veined, dark green leaves are 4–7in (10–18cm) long, red-flushed beneath. In late summer has solitary, fragrant, cup-shaped, white flowers, 1¹/₂in (4cm) wide, red-flushed in bud. Z9–10 H10–9.

SCHINUS
ANACARDIACEAE

Genus of evergreen shrubs and trees, grown mainly for their foliage and for shade. Needs full light and well-drained soil. Water container specimens moderately when in growth, hardly at all in winter. Propagate by seed in spring or by semiripe cuttings in summer.
S. molle (Pepper tree, Peruvian mastic tree). Fast-growing, evergreen, weeping tree. **H** and **S** to 25ft (8m). Fernlike leaves are divided into many narrowly lance-shaped, glossy, rich green leaflets. Has open clusters of tiny, yellow flowers, from late winter to summer, followed by pea-sized, pink-red fruits. Z8–11 H12–8.
S. terebinthifolius. Evergreen shrub or tree, usually of bushy, spreading habit. **H** 10ft (3m) or more, **S** 6–10ft (2–3m) or more. Leaves have 3–13 oval, mid- to deep green leaflets. Tiny, white flowers, borne in clusters in summer–fall, are followed by pea-sized, red fruits, but only if plants of both sexes are grown close together. Z9–11 H12–9.

SCHISANDRA
SCHISANDRACEAE

Genus of deciduous, woody-stemmed, twining climbers. Separate male and female plants are required in order to obtain fruits. Is useful for growing against shady walls and training up pillars and fences. Needs sun or partial shade and rich, well-drained soil. Propagate by greenwood or semiripe cuttings in summer.
S. grandiflora var. rubrifolia of gardens. See *S. rubriflora*.
S. henryi. Deciduous, woody-stemmed, twining climber. **H** 10–12ft (3–4m). Stems are angled and winged when young. Glossy, green leaves are oval or heart-shaped. Small, cup-shaped, white flowers are produced in spring. Pendent spikes, 2–3in (5–7cm) long, of spherical, fleshy, red fruits are borne in late summer on female plants. Z7–9 H9–7.
S. rubriflora, syn. *S. grandiflora var. rubrifolia*, illus. p.202.

SCHIZANTHUS
Butterfly flower, Poor man's orchid
SOLANACEAE

Genus of annuals, grown for their showy flowers. Makes excellent pot plants. Needs a sunny, sheltered position and fertile, well-drained soil. Pinch out growing tips of young plants to ensure a bushy habit. Propagate by seed sown under glass in early spring for summer–fall flowers and in late summer for plants to flower in pots in late winter or spring. Is prone to damage by aphids.
S. 'Dwarf Bouquet', illus. p.304.

S. pinnatus. Moderately fast-growing, upright, bushy annual. **H** 1–4ft (30cm–1.2m), **S** 1ft (30cm). Has feathery, light green leaves. In summer–fall bears rounded, lobed, multicolored flowers in shades of pink, purple, white or yellow. Z12–15 H8–1.
S. 'Star Parade'. Compact annual with pyramidal habit. **H** 8–10in (20–25cm), **S** 9–12in (23–30cm). Has almost fernlike, light green leaves. From spring to fall bears tubular then flared, 2-lipped, white, yellow, pink, purple or red flowers. Z12–15 H8–1.

Schizocentron elegans. See *Heterocentron elegans.*

SCHIZOPETALON
CRUCIFERAE/BRASSICACEAE

Genus of slender-stemmed, hairy annuals. Needs sun and fertile, well-drained soil. Propagate by seed sown under glass in spring.
S. walkeri. Moderately fast-growing, upright, slightly branching annual. **H** 18in (45cm), **S** 8in (20cm). Has deeply divided, mid-green leaves and, in summer, almond-scented, white flowers with deeply cut and fringed petals. H8–1.

SCHIZOPHRAGMA
HYDRANGEACEAE

Genus of deciduous, woody-stemmed, root climbers, useful for training up large trees. Flowers best in sun, but will grow against a north-facing wall. Needs well-drained soil. Tie young plants to supports. Propagate by seed in spring or by greenwood or semiripe cuttings in summer.
S. hydrangeoides, illus. p.197. **'Roseum'** is a deciduous, woody-stemmed, root climber. **H** to 40ft (12m). Has broadly oval leaves. Small, white or creamy-white flowers, in flat heads, 8–10in (20–25cm) across, are produced on pendent side-branches in summer; these are surrounded by marginal, sterile flowers, with bractlike, pink-flushed, pale yellow sepals. Z6–9 H9–6.
S. integrifolium, illus. p.197.
S. viburnoides. See *Pileostegia viburnoides.*

SCHIZOSTYLIS
IRIDACEAE

Genus of rhizomatous perennials, grown for their flowers, which are excellent for cutting. Requires sun and fertile, moist soil. Propagate by division in spring.
S. coccinea, syn. *Hesperantha coccinea.* Z7–9 H9–7. **'Grandiflora'.** See *S. coccinea* 'Major'. **'Major',** syn. *S. coccinea* 'Grandiflora', illus. p.279. **'Mrs. Hegarty'** is a vigorous, clump-forming, rhizomatous perennial. **H** 24in (60cm), **S** 9–12in (23–30cm). In mid-fall produces spikes of shallowly cup-shaped, pale pink flowers above tufts of grasslike, mid-green leaves. **'Sunrise',** illus. p.278. **'Viscountess Byng'** has pink flowers that last until late fall.

SCHLUMBERGERA
CACTACEAE

Genus of bushy, perennial cacti with erect, then pendent stems and flattened, oblong stem segments with indented notches at margins—like teeth in some species. Stem tips produce flowers with prominent

stigmas and stamens and with petals of different lengths set in 2 rows. In the wild, frequently grows over mossy rocks, rooting at ends of stem segments. Requires partial shade and rich, well-drained soil. Propagate by stem cuttings in spring or early summer.
S. 'Bristol Beauty', illus. p.488.
S. x buckleyi (Christmas cactus). Erect, then pendent, perennial cactus. **H** 6in (15cm), **S** 3ft (1m). Has glossy, green stem segments and produces red-violet flowers in mid-winter. Z11–12 H12–1.
S. 'Gold Charm', illus. p.486.
S. truncata, syn. *Zygocactus truncatus*, illus. p.487.
S. 'Wintermärchen'. Erect, then pendent, perennial cactus. **H** 6in (15cm), **S** 12in (30cm). Has glossy, green stem segments. In early fall bears white flowers that become pink-and-white in winter. Z13–15 H12–10.
S. 'Zara'. Erect, then pendent, perennial cactus. **H** 6in (15cm), **S** 12in (30cm). Has glossy, green stem segments. Deep orange-red flowers are produced in early fall and winter. Z13–15 H12–10.

SCHOENOPLECTUS
CYPERACEAE

See also GRASSES, BAMBOOS, RUSHES and SEDGES.
S. lacustris subsp. tabernaemontani 'Zebrinus', syn. *Scirpus lacustris var. tabernaemontani* 'Zebrinus', *Scirpus tabernaemontani* 'Zebrinus', illus. p.436.

SCHWANTESIA
AIZOACEAE

Genus of cushion-forming, perennial succulents, grown for their stemless rosettes of unequal-sized pairs of keeled leaves and daisylike, yellow flowers. Needs full sun and well-drained soil. Propagate by seed or stem cuttings in spring or summer.
S. ruedebuschii, illus. p.491.

SCIADOPITYS
SCIADOPITYACEAE

See also CONIFERS.
S. verticillata, illus. p.101.

SCILLA
LILIACEAE/HYACINTHACEAE

Genus of mainly spring- and summer-flowering bulbs, with leaves in basal clusters, grown for their spikes of small, often blue flowers. Needs an open site, sun or partial shade and well-drained soil. Propagate by division in late summer or by seed in fall.
S. adlamii. See *Ledebouria cooperi.*
S. bifolia. Early spring-flowering bulb. **H** 2–6in (5–15cm), **S** 1–2in (2.5–5cm). Has 2 narrowly strap-shaped, semierect, basal leaves that widen towards tips. Stem bears one-sided spike of up to 20 star-shaped, purple-blue, pink or white flowers. Z3–8 H8–1.
S. campanulata. See *Hyacinthoides x massartiana.*
S. chinensis. See *S. scilloides.*
S. cooperi. See *Ledebouria cooperi.*
S. hispanica. See *Hyacinthoides x massartiana.*
S. italica. See *Hyacinthoides italica.*

S

695

S. japonica. See *S. scilloides*.

S. litardierei, syn. *S. pratensis*. Clump-forming, early summer-flowering bulb. **H** 4–10in (10–25cm), **S** 2–3in (5–8cm). Produces up to 5 narrowly strap-shaped, semierect, basal leaves. Stem bears dense spike of flat, star-shaped, violet flowers. Z6–9 H9–6.

S. mischtschenkoana, syn. *S. tubergeniana*, *S.* 'Tubergeniana', illus. p.420.

S. non-scripta. See *Hyacinthoides non-scripta*.

S. nutans. See *Hyacinthoides non-scripta*.

S. peruviana, illus. p.423.

S. pratensis. See *S. litardierei*.

S. scilloides, syn. *S. chinensis*, *S. japonica*, illus. p.413.

S. siberica (Siberian squill, Spring squill). Z5–8 H8–5. 'Alba', illus. p.416. 'Atrocoerulea', illus. p.420.

S. socialis. See *Ledebouria socialis*.

S. tubergeniana. See *S. mischtschenkoana*.

S. 'Tubergeniana'. See *S. mischtschenkoana*.

S. violacea. See *Ledebouria socialis*.

SCINDAPSUS

ARACEAE

Genus of evergreen climbers, closely related to *Epipremnum* and grown for their pointed-tipped leaves. Is good as houseplants. Requires partial shade and fertile, moist but well-drained soil. Water well in growing season, sparingly at other times. Propagate by stem-tip cuttings in summer or by layering in spring and summer.

S. aureus 'Marble Queen'. See *Epipremnum aureum* 'Marble Queen'.

S. pictus 'Argyraeus', syn. *Epipremnum pictum* 'Argyraeum' (Silver vine). Slow-growing, evergreen, woody-stemmed, root climber. **H** 6–10ft (2–3m) or more. Heart-shaped leaves are dark green with silver markings.

SCIRPOIDES

CYPERACEAE

See also GRASSES, BAMBOOS, RUSHES and SEDGES.

S. holoschoenus, syn. *Scirpus holoschoenus* (Round-headed club-rush). Z6–9 H9–6. 'Variegatus' is an evergreen, tuft-forming, perennial rush. **H** 3ft (1m), **S** 1¹/₂ft (45cm). Rounded, leafless, green stems are striped horizontally with cream and bear long-stalked, dense, spherical heads of egg-shaped, awned, brown spikelets, from mid-summer to early fall.

Scirpus holoschoenus. See *Scirpoides holoschoenus*.

Scirpus lacustris var. tabernaemontani 'Zebrinus'. See *Schoenoplectus lacustris* subsp. *tabernaemontani* 'Zebrinus'.

Scirpus setaceus. See *Isolepis setaceus*.

Scirpus tabernaemontani 'Zebrinus'. See *Schoenoplectus lacustris* subsp. *tabernaemontani* 'Zebrinus'.

SCLEROCACTUS

CACTACEAE

Genus of perennial cacti, grown for their depressed-spherical to club-shaped or columnar stems, each with a long, fleshy tap root and deeply notched or warty ribs. Needs full sun with some midday shade and very well-drained soil. Propagate by seed in spring.

S. scheeri, syn. *Ancistrocactus megarhizus*, *Ancistrocactus scheeri*, *Echinocactus scheeri*, illus. p.495.

S. uncinatus, syn. *Ancistrocactus uncinatus*, *Echinocactus uncinatus*, *Glandulicactus uncinatus*, *Hamatocactus uncinatus*. Globose to columnar, perennial cactus. **H** 8in (20cm), **S** 4in (10cm). Stem is blue-green. Areoles produce 1–4 very long, hooked, reddish spines and 15–18 straight ones. Has cup-shaped, brown-green or reddish flowers, ³/₄in (2cm) across, in spring. Z13–15 H12–10.

SCOLIOPUS

LILIACEAE/TRILLIACEAE

Genus of spring-flowering perennials, grown for their neat habit and curious flowers, which arise directly from buds on the rootstock early in the season. Is suitable for alpine houses, rock gardens and peat beds. Requires sun or partial shade and moist but well-drained soil. Propagate by seed when fresh, in summer or fall.

S. bigelovii. See *S. bigelowii*.

S. bigelowii, syn. *S. bigelovii*, illus. p.349.

Scolopendrium vulgare. See *Asplenium scolopendrium*.

SCOPOLIA

SOLANACEAE

Genus of spring-flowering perennials. Prefers shade and fertile, very well-drained soil. Propagate by division in spring or by seed in fall. ① All parts are highly toxic if ingested.

S. carniolica, illus. p.260.

SCROPHULARIA

Figwort

SCROPHULARIACEAE

Genus of perennials and subshrubs, some of which are semievergreen or evergreen. Most species are weeds, but some are grown for their variegated foliage. Prefers partial shade and moist soil. Propagate by division in spring or by softwood cuttings in summer.

S. aquatica 'Variegata'. See *S. auriculata* 'Variegata'.

S. auriculata 'Variegata', syn. *S. aquatica* 'Variegata' (Water figwort). Evergreen, clump-forming perennial. **H** 24in (60cm), **S** 12in (30cm) or more. Has oval, toothed, dark green leaves with cream marks. Remove spikes of insignificant summer flowers. Z5–9 H9–5.

SCUTELLARIA

Skullcap

LABIATAE/LAMIACEAE

Genus of rhizomatous perennials, grown for their summer flowers. Needs sun and well-drained soil. Propagate by softwood cuttings in summer or by seed in fall.

S. indica. Upright, rhizomatous perennial. **H** 6–12in (15–30cm), **S** 4in (10cm) or more. Leaves are oval, toothed and hairy. Has dense racemes of long-tubed, 2-lipped, slate-blue, occasionally white flowers in summer. Is suitable for a rock garden. Z6–8 H8–6.

S. orientalis, illus. p.372.

S. scordiifolia. Mat-forming, rhizomatous perennial. **H** and **S** 6in (15cm) or more. Bears narrowly oval, wrinkled leaves. In summer–fall has racemes of tubular, hooded, purple flowers, with white-streaked lips. Propagate by division in spring. Z5–8 H8–5.

SEDUM

Stonecrop

CRASSULACEAE

Genus of often fleshy or succulent annuals, evergreen biennials, mostly evergreen or semievergreen perennials and evergreen shrubs and subshrubs, suitable for rock gardens and borders. Needs sun and prefers fertile, well-drained soil. Propagate perennials, subshrubs and shrubs by division or by softwood cuttings of non-flowering shoots from spring to mid-summer or by seed in fall or spring, annuals and biennials by seed, sown under glass in early spring or outdoors in mid-spring. ① All parts may cause mild stomach upset if ingested; contact with the sap may irritate skin.

S. acre, illus. p.371. 'Aureum', illus. p.371.

S. aizoon, syn. *Phedimus aizoon*. Evergreen, erect perennial. **H** and **S** 18in (45cm). Mid-green leaves are oblong to lance-shaped, fleshy and toothed. In summer bears flat heads of star-shaped, yellow flowers. Z3–8 H8–1. 'Aurantiacum' (illus. p.279) has rounded heads of dark yellow flowers followed by red seed capsules.

S. anacampseros, syn. *Hylotelephium anacampseros*. Semievergreen, trailing perennial with overwintering foliage rosettes. **H** 4in (10cm), **S** 10in (25cm) or more. Prostrate, loosely rosetted, brown stems bear oblong to oval, fleshy, glaucous green leaves. Has dense, sub-globose, terminal heads of small, cup-shaped, purplish-pink flowers in summer.

S. 'Bertram Anderson'. Clump-forming perennial. **H** 8in (20cm), **S** 12in (30cm). Has prostrate stems bearing rounded, toothed, fleshy, dusky-purple leaves. In late summer bears rounded, flattened, terminal heads of star-shaped, dark pink flowers.

S. caeruleum, illus. p.315.

S. cauticola, syn. *Hylotelephium cauticola*. Trailing, shallow-rooted perennial with stolons. **H** 2in (5cm), **S** 8in (20cm). Has oval to oblong, stalked, fleshy, blue-green leaves on procumbent, purplish-red stems. Bears leafy, branched, flattish heads of star-shaped, pale purplish-pink flowers in early fall. Cut back old stems in winter.

S. erythrostictum. Clump-forming perennial. **H** 16–24in (40–60cm), **S** 16in (40cm). Unbranched stems bear oval, toothed, fleshy, gray-green leaves. In late summer produces domed, terminal heads of star-shaped, pink and white flowers, with leafy bracts. Z6–9 H9–6. 'Frosty Morn' has variegated, narrowly spoon-shaped leaves, edged with white. Flower heads in late summer also display variegation. 'Mediovariegatum' (illus. p.279) bears yellow-green leaves with central, creamy-white mark.

S. ewersii, syn. *Hylotelephium ewersii*. Trailing perennial. **H** 2in (5cm), **S** 6in (15cm). Is similar to *S. cauticola*, but has more rounded, stem-clasping leaves, often tinted red, and dense, rounded flower heads. Z5–9 H9–5.

S. 'Herbstfreude'. Clump-forming perennial. **H** 24in (60cm), **S** 20in (50cm). Has oval, toothed, fleshy, gray-green leaves on sturdy, erect stems. In late summer and fall bears broad, flattened, terminal heads of small, star-shaped, brick-red flowers that fade to brown.

S. heterodontum. See *Rhodiola heterodonta*.

S. kamtschaticum, syn. *Phedimus kamtschaticus*. Semievergreen, prostrate perennial with overwintering foliage rosettes. **H** 2–3in (5–8cm), **S** 8in (20cm). Bears narrowly oval, toothed, fleshy, mid-green leaves. Spreading, terminal clusters of star-shaped, orange-flushed, yellow flowers are produced in summer–fall. Z3–8 H8–1. 'Variegatum', illus. p.377.

S. lydium, illus. p.374.

S. 'Matrona', illus. p.279. Clump-forming perennial. **H** 24in (60cm), **S** 20in (50cm). Has oval, toothed, fleshy, purple-flushed, brown-green leaves on erect, dark purple stems. In late summer bears flattened, terminal heads of small, star-shaped, pink flowers. Z3–8 H9–1.

S. morganianum (Burro's tail). Evergreen, prostrate, succulent perennial. **H** 12in (30cm) or more, **S** indefinite. Stems are clothed in oblong to lance-shaped, almost cylindrical, fleshy, waxy, white leaves. Has terminal clusters of star-shaped, rose-pink flowers in summer. Z11–12 H12–1.

S. obtusatum, illus. p.374.

S. palmeri. Evergreen, clump-forming perennial. **H** 8in (20cm), **S** 12in (30cm). Bears sprays of star-shaped, yellow or orange flowers in early summer above oblong-oval to spoon-shaped, fleshy, gray-green leaves.

S. populifolium, syn. *Hylotelephium populifolium*. Semievergreen, bushy perennial. **H** 12–18in (30–45cm), **S** 12in (30cm). Terminal clusters of hawthorn-scented, star-shaped, pale pink or white flowers are borne in late summer. Has broadly oval, irregularly toothed, fleshy, mid-green leaves. Z6–9 H9–6.

S. 'Red Cauli', illus. p.279. Clump-forming, compact perennial. **H** 12–16in (30–40cm), **S** 12in (30cm). Has oval, toothed, fleshy, gray-purple leaves on erect stems. In summer bears cauliflowerlike, domed, terminal heads of star-shaped, rich red flowers.

S. reflexum. See *S. rupestre*.

S. rosea. See *Rhodiola rosea*. **var. heterodontum.** See *Rhodiola heterodonta*.

S. 'Ruby Glow', illus. p.279. Clump-forming, deciduous perennial with prostrate stems. **H** 8in (20cm), **S** 16in (40cm). Has elliptic, toothed, fleshy, gray-purple leaves. In late summer bears loose terminal heads of star-shaped, pink and ruby-red flowers. Z5–9 H9–1.

S. rupestre, syn. *S. reflexum*, illus. p.345.

S. sempervivoides, syn. *Prometheum sempervivoides*. Evergreen, basal-rosetted biennial. **H** 3–4in (8–10cm), **S** 2in (5cm). Has oval to strap-shaped, leathery, glaucous green leaves marked red-purple. Bears domed heads of star-shaped,

scarlet flowers in summer. Dislikes winter wet. Is good in an alpine house. Z9–10 H10–9.
S. sieboldii, syn. *Hylotelephium sieboldii.* Z6–9 H9–6.
'Mediovariegatum', syn. *S. sieboldii* 'Variegatum' is an evergreen, spreading, tuberous perennial with long, tapering tap roots. **H** 4in (10cm), **S** 8in (20cm) or more. Rounded, fleshy, blue-green leaves, splashed cream and occasionally red-edged, are in whorls of 3. Bears open, terminal heads of star-shaped, pink flowers in late summer. Is good in an alpine house. **'Variegatum'.** See *S. sieboldii* 'Mediovariegatum'.
S. spathulifolium, illus. p.374. **'Cape Blanco',** syn. *S. spathulifolium* 'Cappa Blanca', illus. p.375. **'Cappa Blanca'.** See *S. spathulifolium* 'Cape Blanco'.
S. spectabile, syn. *Hylotelephium spectabile* (Everlasting, Showy stonecrop). Clump-forming perennial. **H** and **S** 18in (45cm). Has oval, indented, fleshy, gray-green leaves, above which flat heads of small, star-shaped, pink flowers are borne in late summer. Flowers are attractive to butterflies. Z4–9 H9–1. **'Brilliant',** illus. p.278. **'Iceberg'** (illus. p.279) has pale green leaves and heads of greenish-white flowers that develop pink tinges with age. **'Stardust'** produces flower heads that may be white or pink on the same plant.
S. spurium, syn. *Phedimus spurius.* Semievergreen, mat-forming, creeping perennial. **H** 4in (10cm) or more, **S** indefinite. Oblong to oval, toothed leaves are borne along hairy stems. Large, slightly rounded heads of small, star-shaped flowers are borne in summer. Flower color varies from deep purple to white. Z4–9 H9–1.
S. 'Stewed Rhubarb Mountain'. Clump-forming, compact perennial. **H** and **S** 12in (30cm). Has oval, toothed, fleshy, pinkish-green leaves on erect stems. In late summer bears rounded, terminal heads of star-shaped, pale green, pale pink and darker pink flowers.
S. tatarinowii, syn. *Hylotelephium tatarinowii.* Arching, spreading, tuberous perennial. **H** 4in (10cm), **S** 8in (20cm). Rounded, terminal heads of star-shaped, pink-flushed, white flowers are produced in late summer above small, oval, toothed, green leaves borne along purplish stems. Is suitable for an alpine house.
S. telephium. Rather variable, clump-forming perennial, sometimes with rather open, lax habit. **H** 24–28in (60–70cm), **S** 20in (50cm). Erect stems bear oval, fleshy, blue-green leaves that are often toothed. In late summer–fall bears domed, branched terminal heads of star-shaped, reddish- or purplish-pink flowers. Z4–9 H9–1. **Atropurpureum Group** have red stems bearing dark red leaves with pink flowers. **'Gooseberry Fool'** (illus. p.279), **H** 20in (50cm), **S** 12in (30cm), bears red-flushed, greenish-gray leaves and domed heads of green and white flowers. **'Purple Emperor'** (illus. p.279), **H** 20in (50cm), **S** 12in (30cm), is neat and compact, with dark purple leaves and pinkish-red flowers.
'Strawberries and Cream' (illus. p.279), **H** and **S** 20–24in (50–60cm), has

purple stems, toothed, green-purple leaves and pinkish-green flowers opening from dark pink buds.

SELAGINELLA
SELAGINELLACEAE

Genus of evergreen, mosslike perennials, grown for their foliage. Prefers partial shade and needs moist but well-drained, peaty soil. Remove faded foliage regularly. Propagate from pieces with roots attached that have been broken off plant year-round.
S. kraussiana, illus. p.478. **'Aurea'** is an evergreen, mosslike perennial. **H** ¹/₂in (1cm), **S** indefinite. Spreading, filigreed, bright yellowish-green fronds are much-branched, denser towards growing tips and easily root on soil surface. Z6–9 H12–1. **'Variegata'** has foliage splashed with creamy-yellow. Z6–9 H12–1.
S. lepidophylla (Resurrection plant, Rose of Jericho). Evergreen, mosslike perennial. **H** and **S** 4in (10cm). Bluntly rounded, emerald-green fronds, aging red-brown or gray-green, are produced in dense tufts. On drying, fronds curl inwards into a tight ball; they unfold when placed in water. Z8–10 H10–8.
S. martensii, illus. p.478.

SELENICEREUS
CACTACEAE

Genus of summer-flowering, perennial cacti with climbing, 4–10-ribbed, green stems, to ³/₄in (2cm) across. Nocturnal, funnel-shaped flowers eventually open flat. Needs sun or partial shade and rich, well-drained soil. Propagate by seed or stem cuttings in spring or summer.
S. grandiflorus, illus. p.479.

SELINUM
UMBELLIFERAE/APIACEAE

Genus of summer-flowering perennials, suitable for informal gardens and backs of borders. Prefers sun and well-drained soil. Once established, roots resent disturbance. Propagate by seed when fresh, in summer or fall.
S. wallichianum, illus. p.230.

SEMELE
LILIACEAE/RUSCACEAE

Genus of one species of evergreen, twining climber. Male and female flowers are produced on the same plant. Needs partial shade and prefers rich, well-drained soil. Propagate by division or seed in spring.
S. androgyna. Evergreen climber, twining in upper part, branched and bearing oval cladodes, 2–4in (5–10cm) long. **H** to 22ft (7m). Star-shaped, cream flowers are produced in notches on cladode margins, in early summer, followed by orange-red berries. Z9–10 H10–9.

SEMIAQUILEGIA
RANUNCULACEAE

Genus of perennials, grown for their flowers. These differ from those of *Aquilegia,* with which it is sometimes included, by having no spurs. Is good for

rock gardens. Requires sun and moist but well-drained soil. Propagate by seed in fall.
S. ecalcarata, illus. p.341.

SEMIARUNDINARIA
GRAMINEAE/POACEAE

See also GRASSES, BAMBOOS, RUSHES and SEDGES.
S. fastuosa, syn. *Arundinaria fastuosa,* illus. p.287.

SEMPERVIVUM
Houseleek
CRASSULACEAE

Genus of evergreen perennials that spread by short stolons and are grown for their symmetrical rosettes of oval to strap-shaped, pointed, fleshy leaves. Makes ground-hugging mats, suitable for rock gardens, screes, walls, banks and alpine houses. Flowers are star-shaped with 8–16 spreading petals. Needs sun and gritty soil. Takes several years to reach flowering size. Rosettes die after flowering but leave numerous offsets. Propagate by offsets in summer.
S. arachnoideum (Cobweb houseleek), illus. p.377. Evergreen, mat-forming perennial. **H** 2–5in (5–12cm), **S** 4in (10cm) or more. Rosettes of oval, fleshy leaves with red tips are covered in web of white hairs. Bears loose clusters of star-shaped, rose-red flowers in summer. Z5–8 H8–5.
S. 'Blood Tip', illus. p.377. Evergreen, basal-rosetted, mat-forming succulent. **H** to 4in (10cm), **S** to 12in (30cm). Has thick, green leaves strongly suffused purple-red with deeper red, bristly tips. Z6–9 H9–6.
S. calcareum, illus. p.377. Variable, evergreen, mat-forming, basal-rosetted perennial. **H** 2–3in (5–7cm), **S** 8–10in (20–25cm). Has bluish-green leaves with dark reddish-brown tips. Erect stems bear terminal clusters of star-shaped, red-based, creamy-white flowers in summer. Is excellent in a trough or on a dry wall. Z6–9 H9–6. **'Extra'** (illus. p.377) has intense, dark leaf tips.
S. ciliosum, illus. p.375.
S. 'Commander Hay'. Evergreen, basal-rosetted perennial. **H** 6in (15cm), **S** to 12in (30cm). Has inversely lance-shaped, glossy, dark red leaves, with mid-green tips. Terminal clusters of dull greenish-red flowers are produced in summer. Z7–10 H10–7.
S. 'Gallivarda', illus. p.377. Evergreen, mat-forming, basal-rosetted perennial. **H** 2–3in (5–8cm), **S** 8–10in (20–25cm). Red leaves turn to orange-red in summer, then to purplish-red. Z5–8 H8–5.
S. giuseppii, illus. p.377. Vigorous, evergreen, prostrate perennial. **H** in flower3–4in (8–10cm), **S** 4in (10cm). Leaves are hairy, especially in spring, and have dark spots at tips. Produces terminal clusters of star-shaped, deep pink or red flowers in summer. Z7–9 H9–7.
S. globiferum subsp. globiferum. See *Jovibarba sobolifera.* **subsp. hirtum.** See *Jovibarba hirta.*
S. grandiflorum. Evergreen, basal-rosetted perennial. **H** 4in (10cm), **S** to 8in (20cm). Variable, densely haired, red-tinted, dark green rosettes exude goatlike smell when crushed. Produces loose, terminal clusters of yellow-green flowers,

stained purple in centers, on long flower stems in summer. Prefers rich, acid soil. Z6–9 H9–6.
S. 'Gulle Dame', illus. p.377. Evergreen, mat-forming, basal-rosetted perennial. **H** 2–3in (5–8cm), **S** 8–10in (20–25cm). Has dark red leaves with long, white hairs, in spring and summer, gradually changing to green in winter.
S. 'Kappa', illus. p.377. Evergreen, mat-forming, basal-rosetted perennial. **H** 2–3in (5–8cm), **S** 6–8in (15–20cm). Deep purple-red leaves are covered in cobwebs of white hairs.
S. montanum, illus. p.377. Evergreen, mat-forming perennial. **H** 3–6in (10–15cm), **S** 4in (10cm). Has dark green rosettes of fleshy, hairy leaves. Star-shaped, wine-red flowers are borne in terminal clusters in summer. Is a variable plant that hybridizes freely. Z5–8 H8–5.
S. 'Rosie', illus. p.377. Evergreen, mat-forming, open-rosetted perennial. **H** 2–3in (5–8cm), **S** 8–10in (20–25cm). Green-flushed, purple-red leaves have short, marginal hairs. Z4–9 H9–3.
S. tectorum (Hens and chicks, Roof houseleek), illus. p.377. Vigorous, evergreen perennial. **H** 4–6in (10–15cm), **S** to 8in (20cm). Has purple-tipped, blue-green leaves, sometimes suffused deep red. In summer produces clusters of star-shaped, reddish-purple flowers. Z4–8 H8–1.

SENECIO
COMPOSITAE/ASTERACEAE

Genus of annuals, succulent and non-succulent perennials and evergreen shrubs, subshrubs and twining climbers, grown for their foliage and usually daisylike flower heads. Some shrubby species are now referred to the genus *Brachyglottis.* Shrubs are excellent for coastal gardens. Most prefer full sun and well-drained soil (although *S. articulatus* and *S. rowleyanus* tolerate partial shade and need very well-drained soil). Propagate shrubs and climbers by semiripe cuttings in summer, annuals by seed in spring, perennials by division in spring, *S. articulatus* and *S. rowleyanus* by seed or stem cuttings in spring or summer. ① All parts may cause severe discomfort if ingested.
S. articulatus, syn. *Kleinia articulata* (Candle plant). Deciduous, spreading, perennial succulent. **H** 2ft (60cm), **S** indefinite. Branching, gray-marked, blue stems have weak joints. Bears rounded to oval, 3–5-lobed, gray leaves and flattish heads of small, cup-shaped, yellow flowers from spring to fall. Offsets freely from stolons. Z13–15 H12–10. **'Variegatus',** illus. p.486.
S. cineraria, syn. *S. maritimus.* Moderately fast-growing, evergreen, bushy subshrub, often grown as an annual. **H** and **S** 1ft (30cm). Has long, oval, very deeply lobed, hairy, silvery-gray leaves. Rounded, yellow flower heads are produced in summer, but are best removed. Z8–11 H12–1. **'Cirrus'** has elliptic, finely toothed or lobed, silvery-green to white leaves. **'Silver Dust',** illus. p.315.
S. compactus. See *Brachyglottis compacta.*
S. confusus. See *Pseudogynoxys chenopodioides.*
S. Dunedin Hybrids. See *Brachyglottis* Dunedin Group.

S

S. elegans. Moderately fast-growing, upright annual. **H** 18in (45cm), **S** 6in (15cm). Has oval, deeply lobed, deep green leaves. Daisylike, purple flower heads are produced in summer. H8–1.

S. grandifolius, syn. *Telanthophora grandiflora.* Evergreen, erect, robust-stemmed shrub. **H** 10–15ft (3–5m), **S** 6–10ft (2–3m). Has oval, toothed, boldly veined leaves, rich green above, red-brown-haired beneath. Bears terminal clusters of small, daisylike, yellow flower heads in winter–spring. Z12–15 H12–1.

S. greyi of gardens. See *Brachyglottis* Dunedin Group.

S. x hybridus. See *Pericallis x hybrida.*

S. laxifolius. See *Brachyglottis laxifolia.*

S. laxifolius of gardens. See *Brachyglottis* Dunedin Group.

S. macroglossus (Cape ivy, Natal ivy). Evergreen, woody-stemmed, twining climber. **H** 10ft (3m). Leaves are sharply triangular, fleshy-textured and glossy. Loose clusters of daisylike, white flower heads, with yellow centers, are borne mainly in winter. Z12–15 H12–10.

'Variegatus', illus. p.464.

S. maritimus. See *S. cineraria.*

S. mikanioides, syn. *Delairea odorata* (German ivy, Parlor ivy). Evergreen, semiwoody, twining climber. **H** 6–10ft (2–3m). Has fleshy leaves with 5–7 broad, pointed, radiating lobes. Mature plants produce large clusters of small, yellow flower heads in fall–winter. Z12–15 H12–1.

S. monroi. See *Brachyglottis monroi.*

S. przewalskii. See *Ligularia przewalskii.*

S. pulcher, illus. p.278.

S. reinholdii. See *Brachyglottis rotundifolia.*

S. rotundifolius. See *Brachyglottis rotundifolia.*

S. rowleyanus, syn. *Kleinia rowleyana,* illus. p.481.

S. smithii. Bushy perennial. **H** 3–4ft (1–1.2m), **S** 2½–3ft (75cm–1m). Woolly stems are clothed with long, oval, toothed, leathery, dark green leaves. Daisylike, white flower heads, with yellow centers, are borne in terminal clusters in early summer. Likes boggy conditions. Z6–8 H8–6.

S. tamoides. Evergreen, woody-stemmed, twining climber. **H** 15ft (5m) or more. Has ivy-shaped, light green leaves. In fall–winter bears daisylike, yellow flower heads with only a few ray petals. Z6–8 H8–6.

SENNA

LEGUMINOSAE/CAESALPINIACEAE

Genus of evergreen trees, shrubs and perennials, grown for their pealike flowers. Requires full sun and moist but well-drained soil. Propagate by seed in spring or by semiripe cuttings in summer, divide perennials in spring.

S. artemisioides, syn. *Cassia artemisioides* (Silver cassia). Evergreen, erect to spreading, wiry shrub. **H** and **S** 3–6ft (1–2m). Leaves are divided into 6–8 linear leaflets covered with silky, white down. Axillary spikes of cup-shaped, yellow flowers are produced from winter to early summer.

S. corymbosa, syn. *Cassia corymbosa,* illus. p.459.

S. didymobotrya, syn. *Cassia didymobotrya,* illus. p.459.

S. x floribunda, syn. *Cassia corymbosa* var. *plurijuga, Cassia x floribunda.* Vigorous, evergreen or deciduous, rounded shrub with robust stems. **H** and **S** 5–6ft (1.5–2m). Bright green leaves are divided into 4–6 oval leaflets. Has very large clusters of bowl-shaped, rich yellow flowers in late summer.

S. siamea, syn. *Cassia siamea.* Fast-growing, evergreen, rounded tree. **H** and **S** 25–30ft (8–10m) or more. Leaves are divided into 7–12 pairs of elliptic leaflets. Large terminal panicles of small, cup-shaped, bright yellow flowers are borne in spring, followed by flat, dark brown pods. Z10–11 H12–10.

SEQUOIA

TAXODIACEAE

See also CONIFERS.

S. sempervirens, illus. p.97.

SEQUOIADENDRON

TAXODIACEAE

See also CONIFERS.

S. giganteum, illus. p.98. **'Pendulum'** is a weeping conifer. **H** 30ft (10m), **S** 6ft (2m) or more. Bark is thick, soft, fibrous and red-brown. Has spiralled, needlelike, incurved, gray-green leaves that darken and become glossy.

SERAPIAS

ORCHIDACEAE

See also ORCHIDS.

S. cordigera. Deciduous, terrestrial orchid. **H** 16in (40cm). Spikes of reddish or dark purple flowers, 1½in (4cm) long, are borne in spring. Has lance-shaped, red-spotted leaves, 6in (15cm) long. Needs partial shade.

SERENOA

PALMAE/ARECACEAE

Genus of one species of evergreen fan palm, grown for its foliage. Requires full light or partial shade and well-drained soil. Water container plants moderately in growing season, less at other times. Propagate by seed or suckers in spring. Red spider mite may be troublesome.

S. repens (Saw palmetto, Scrub palmetto). Evergreen, rhizomatous fan palm, usually stemless. **H** 2–3ft (60cm–1m), **S** 6ft (2m) or more. Palmate, gray to blue-green leaves are divided into 6–20 strap-shaped lobes. Clusters of tiny, fragrant, cream flowers are hidden among leaves in summer, and are followed by egg-shaped, purple-black fruits. Z9–11 H12–9.

SERISSA

RUBIACEAE

Genus of one species of evergreen shrub, grown for its overall appearance. Needs sun or partial shade and fertile, well-drained soil. Water container specimens moderately, less when not in growth. May be trimmed after flowering. Propagate by semiripe cuttings in summer.

S. foetida. See *S. japonica.*

S. japonica, syn. *S. foetida.* Evergreen, spreading to rounded, freely branching shrub. **H** to 2ft (60cm), **S** 2–3ft (60cm–1m). Has tiny, oval, lustrous, deep green leaves. Small, funnel-shaped, 4- or 5-lobed, white flowers are borne from spring to fall. Z11–15 H12–10.

SERRATULA

COMPOSITAE/ASTERACEAE

Genus of perennials, grown for their thistlelike flower heads. Requires sun and well-drained soil. Propagate by seed or division in spring.

S. seoanei, syn. *S. shawii.* Upright, compact perennial. **H** 9in (23cm), **S** 5–6in (12–15cm). Stems bear feathery, finely cut leaves and, in fall, terminal panicles of small, thistlelike, purple flower heads. Is useful in a rock garden.

S. shawii. See *S. seoanei.*

SESLERIA

GRAMINEAE/POACEAE

See also GRASSES, BAMBOOS, RUSHES and SEDGES.

S. heufleriana (Balkan moor grass). Evergreen, tuft-forming, perennial grass. **H** 20in (50cm), **S** 12–18in (30–45cm). Bears rich green leaves, glaucous beneath and, in spring, compact panicles of purple spikelets. Z5–8 H8–5.

SETARIA

GRAMINEAE/POACEAE

See also GRASSES, BAMBOOS, RUSHES and SEDGES.

S. italica (Foxtail millet, Italian millet). Moderately fast-growing, annual grass with sturdy stems. **H** 5ft (1.5m), **S** to 3ft (1m). Has lance-shaped, mid-green leaves, to 1½ft (45cm) long, and loose panicles of white, cream, yellow, red, brown or black flowers in summer–fall. Z9–10 H10–9.

S. macrostachya, illus. p.318.

Setcreasea purpurea. See *Tradescantia pallida* 'Purpurea'.

SHEPHERDIA

ELAEAGNACEAE

Genus of deciduous or evergreen shrubs, grown for their foliage and fruits. Separate male and female plants are needed in order to obtain fruits. Requires sun and well-drained soil. Propagate by softwood cuttings in summer or by seed in fall.

S. argentea (Silver buffalo berry). Deciduous, bushy, often treelike shrub. **H** and **S** 12ft (4m). Bears tiny, inconspicuous, yellow flowers amid oblong, silvery-gray leaves in spring, followed by small, egg-shaped, bright red fruits. Z3–6 H6–1.

SHIBATAEA

GRAMINEAE/POACEAE

See also GRASSES, BAMBOOS, RUSHES and SEDGES.

S. kumasasa, illus. p.287.

SHORTIA

DIAPENSIACEAE

Genus of evergreen, spring-flowering perennials, grown for their leaves that often turn red in fall–winter. Buds may be frosted in areas without snow cover. Is difficult to grow in hot, dry climates. Needs full or partial shade and well-drained, peaty, sandy, acid soil. Propagate by runners in summer or by seed when available.

S. galacifolia, illus. p.349.

S. soldanelloides, illus. p.352. **var. ilicifolia** is an evergreen, mat-forming perennial. **H** 2–4in (5–10cm), **S** 4–6in (10–15cm). Has rounded, toothed leaves. In late spring each flower stem bears 4–6 small, pendent, bell-shaped flowers, with fringed edges and rose-pink centers shading to white. Flowers of **var. magna** are rose-pink throughout.

S. uniflora 'Grandiflora'. Vigorous, evergreen, mat-forming perennial with a few rooted runners. **H** 3in (8cm), **S** 8in (20cm). Leaves are rounded, toothed, leathery and glossy. Flower stems bear cup-shaped, white-pink flowers, with serrated petals, in spring. Z5–8 H8–5.

SIBIRAEA

ROSACEAE

Genus of deciduous shrubs, grown for their foliage and flowers. Needs sun and well-drained soil. Prune out old or weak shoots to base after flowering. Propagate by softwood cuttings in summer.

S. altaiensis. See *S. laevigata.*

S. laevigata, syn. *S. altaiensis.* Deciduous, spreading, open shrub. **H** 3ft (1m), **S** 5ft (1.5m). Has narrowly oblong, blue-green leaves and, in late spring and early summer, dense, terminal clusters of tiny, star-shaped, white flowers. Z6–8 H8–6.

SIDALCEA

MALVACEAE

Genus of summer-flowering perennials, grown for their hollyhocklike flowers. Needs sun and well-drained soil. Propagate by division in spring.

S. 'Loveliness'. Upright perennial. **H** 3ft (1m), **S** 1½ft (45cm). Has buttercuplike, divided leaves with narrowly oblong segments. In summer bears racemes of shallowly cup-shaped, shell-pink flowers. Z9–10 H10–9.

S. 'Oberon', illus. p.233.

S. 'Puck'. Upright perennial. **H** 2ft (60cm), **S** 1½ft (45cm). Has buttercuplike, divided leaves with narrowly oblong segments. In summer bears racemes of shallowly cup-shaped, deep pink flowers. Z6–8 H8–6.

S. 'Sussex Beauty'. Upright perennial. **H** 4ft (1.2m), **S** 1½ft (45cm). Has buttercuplike, divided leaves, with narrowly oblong segments, and, in summer, shallowly cup-shaped, deep rose-pink flowers. Z6–8 H8–6.

SIDERITIS

LABIATAE/LAMIACEAE

Genus of evergreen perennials, subshrubs and shrubs, grown mainly for their foliage. Needs full light and well-drained soil. Water container plants moderately, less when temperatures are low. Remove spent flower spikes after flowering. Propagate by seed in spring or by semiripe cuttings in summer.

S. candicans. Evergreen, erect, well-branched shrub. **H** to 2½ft (75cm), **S** to 2ft (60cm). Lance-shaped to narrowly oval or triangular leaves bear dense, white wool. Produces leafy, terminal spikes of tubular, pale yellow- and-light-brown or orange-red flowers in summer. Z9–10 H10–9.

SILENE
Campion, Catchfly
CARYOPHYLLACEAE

Genus of annuals and perennials, some of which are evergreen, grown for their mass of 5-petaled flowers. Needs sun and fertile, well-drained soil. Propagate by softwood cuttings in spring or by seed in spring or early fall.

S. acaulis, illus. p.352.
S. alpestris, syn. *Heliosperma alpestre*, illus. p.359.
S. armeria 'Electra'. Moderately fast-growing, erect annual. **H** 12in (30cm), **S** 6in (15cm). Has oval, grayish-green leaves. Heads of 5-petaled, bright rose-pink flowers are produced in summer and early fall. H8–1.
S. coeli-rosa, syn. *Agrostemma coeli-rosa*, *Lychnis coeli-rosa*, *Viscaria elegans*, illus. p.303.
S. elisabethae. Basal-rosetted perennial. **H** 4in (10cm), **S** 8in (20cm). Has rosettes of strap-shaped, mid-green leaves. In summer, stems bear large, often solitary, deep rose-red flowers with green centers and long-clawed petals. Is suitable for a rock garden. Z7–9 H9–7.
S. hookeri. Short-lived, trailing, prostrate, late summer-deciduous perennial with long, slender tap root. **H** 2in (5cm), **S** 8in (20cm). Slender stems bear oval, gray leaves and, in late summer, soft pink, salmon or orange flowers, deeply cleft to base. Z5–8 H8–5.
S. maritima 'Flore Pleno'. See *S. uniflora* 'Robin Whitebreast'.
S. pendula (Nodding catchfly). Moderately fast-growing, bushy annual. **H** and **S** 6–8in (15–20cm). Has oval, hairy, mid-green leaves and, in summer and early fall, clusters of light pink flowers.
S. schafta, illus. p.346.
S. uniflora 'Robin Whitebreast', syn.*S. maritima* 'Flore Pleno', *S. uniflora* 'Flore Pleno', *S. vulgaris* subsp. *maritima* 'Flore Pleno'. Lax perennial with deep, wandering roots. **H** and **S** 8in (20cm). Bears lance-shaped, gray-green leaves. Bears pomponlike, double, white flowers, on branched stems, in summer. Z3–7 H7–1.
S. vulgaris subsp. **maritima 'Flore Pleno'**. See *S. uniflora* 'Robin Whitebreast'.

SILPHIUM
COMPOSITAE/ASTERACEAE

Genus of fairly coarse, summer-flowering perennials. Needs sun or partial shade and moist but well-drained soil. Propagate by division in spring or by seed when fresh, in fall.

S. laciniatum (Compass plant, Pilot plant, Polar plant). Clump-forming perennial. **H** 6ft (2m), **S** 2ft (60cm). Mid-green leaves, divided into opposite pairs of oblong to lance-shaped leaflets, face north and south wherever the plant is grown, hence the common name. Large clusters of slightly pendent, daisylike, yellow flower heads are borne in late summer. Z5–9 H9–5.

SILYBUM
COMPOSITAE/ASTERACEAE

Genus of thistlelike biennials, grown for their foliage. Needs sun and well-drained soil. Propagate by seed in late spring or early summer. Is prone to slug and snail damage.

S. marianum, illus. p.304.

Sinarundinaria jaunsarensis. See *Yushania anceps*.
Sinarundinaria murieliae. See *Fargesia murieliae*.
Sinarundinaria nitida. See *Fargesia nitida*.

SINNINGIA
GESNERIACEAE

Genus of usually summer-flowering, tuberous perennials and deciduous subshrubs, grown for their showy flowers. Prefers a humid atmosphere, partial shade and moist but not waterlogged, peaty soil. When leaves die down after flowering, allow tubers to dry out; then store in a frost-free area. Propagate in spring by seed or in late spring or summer by stem cuttings or by dividing tubers into sections, each with a young shoot.
S. barbata. Bushy, tuberous perennial with square, red stems. **H** and **S** 2ft (60cm) or more long. Broadly lance-shaped, glossy, mid-green leaves, to 6in (15cm) long, are reddish-green beneath. In summer has 5-lobed, pouched, white flowers. Z14–15 H12–10.
S. concinna. Rosetted perennial with very small tubers. **H** and **S** to 6in (15cm). Oval to rounded, scalloped, velvety, red-veined, mid-green leaves, $^3/_4$in (2cm) long, are red below. Trumpet-shaped, bicolored, purple and white or yellowish-white flowers, are borne in summer. Z14–15 H12–10.
S. 'Etoile du Feu'. Short-stemmed, rosetted, tuberous perennial. **H** 12in (30cm), **S** 16in (40cm) or more. Has oval, velvety leaves, 8–9$^1/_2$in (20–24cm) long. Upright, trumpet-shaped, carmine-red flowers are produced in summer. Z14–15 H12–10.
S. 'Mont Blanc'. Short-stemmed, rosetted, tuberous perennial. **H** 12in (30cm), **S** 16in (40cm) or more. Oval, velvety, mid-green leaves are 8–9$^1/_2$in (20–24cm) long. In summer has upright, trumpet-shaped, pure white flowers. Z14–15 H12–10.
S. 'Red Flicker'. Short-stemmed, tuberous perennial. **H** to 12in (30cm), **S** 18in (45cm). Has rosettes of oval, velvety leaves, to 8in (20cm) long. Fleshy, nodding, funnel-shaped, pinkish-red flowers, pouched on lower sides, are borne in summer. Z14–15 H12–10.
S. speciosa, syn. *Gloxinia speciosa* (Florists' gloxinia). Short-stemmed, rosetted, tuberous perennial. **H** and **S** to 1ft (30cm). Oval, velvety, green leaves are 8in (20cm) long. Nodding, funnel-shaped, fleshy, violet, red or white flowers, with pouches on lower sides, are produced in summer. Is a parent of many named hybrids, of which a selection is included above and below.
S. 'Switzerland', illus. p.470.
S. 'Waterloo'. Short-stemmed, rosetted, tuberous perennial. **H** 12in (30cm), **S** 16in

(40cm) or more. Has oval, velvety leaves, 8–9$^1/_2$in (20–24cm) long. Upright, trumpet-shaped, bright scarlet flowers are produced in summer. Z14–15 H12–10.

SINOFRANCHETIA
LARDIZABALACEAE

Genus of one species of deciduous, twining climber, grown mainly for its foliage. Is suitable for covering buildings and growing up large trees. Separate male and female plants are required in order to obtain fruits. Needs partial shade and well-drained soil. Propagate by semiripe cuttings in summer.
S. chinensis. Deciduous, twining climber. **H** to 50ft (15m). Mid- to dark green leaves are divided into 3 oblong to oval leaflets, 2–6in (5–15cm) long. In late spring has small, dull white flowers in pendent racemes, to 4in (10cm) long. Pale purple berries, containing many seeds, follow in summer. Z7–10 H10–7.

SINOJACKIA
STYRACACEAE

Genus of deciduous shrubs and trees, grown for their flowers. Requires a sheltered position in sun or partial shade and fertile, rich, moist, acid soil. Propagate by softwood cuttings in summer.
S. rehderiana. Deciduous, bushy shrub or spreading tree. **H** and **S** 20ft (6m). Nodding, saucer-shaped, white flowers, with yellow anthers, are produced in late spring and early summer. Oval leaves are dark green and glossy. Z6–10 H10–6.

SINOPODOPHYLLUM
BERBERIDACEAE

Genus of one species of spring-flowering, rhizomatous perennial, grown for its flowers, often marbled foliage and large, red fruit. Requires partial shade and rich, moist soil. Propagate in fall by division of the rhizome or by seed. ① All parts are toxic if eaten.
S. hexandrum, syn. *Podophyllum emodii*, *Podophyllum hexandrum*, illus. p.255.

SINOWILSONIA
HAMAMELIDACEAE

Genus of one species of deciduous tree, grown for its foliage and catkins. Requires sun or partial shade and fertile, moist but well-drained soil. Propagate by seed in fall.
S. henryi. Deciduous, spreading, sometimes shrubby tree. **H** and **S** 25ft (8m). Has oval, toothed, glossy, bright green leaves, and long, pendent, green catkins in late spring. Z6–9 H9–6.

Siphonosmanthus delavayi. See *Osmanthus delavayi*.

SISYRINCHIUM
IRIDACEAE

Genus of annuals and perennials, some of which are semievergreen. Prefers sun and well-drained or moist soil. Propagate by division in early spring or by seed in spring or fall.
S. angustifolium. See *S. graminoides*.
S. bellum of gardens. See *S. idahoense*.
S. californicum (Golden-eyed grass).

Semievergreen, upright perennial. **H** 12–24in (30–60cm), **S** 12in (30cm). Has grasslike tufts of light green, basal leaves. In spring–summer produces flattish, bright yellow flowers, with slightly darker veins, on winged stems. Outer leaves may die off and turn black in fall. Dwarf forms are known as *S. brachypus*. Prefers moist soil. Z8–9 H9–7.
S. douglasi. See *Olsynium douglasii*.
S. 'E.K. Balls', illus. p.342.
S. graminoides, syn. *S. angustifolium*. Semievergreen, erect perennial. **H** to 12in (30cm), **S** 3in (8cm). Has tufts of grasslike leaves. Small, irislike, pale to dark purplish-blue flowers, with yellow bases, are borne in terminal clusters in late spring and early summer. Z5–8 H8–5.
S. grandiflorum. See *Olsynium douglasii*.
S. idahoense, syn. *S. bellum*, illus. p.369.
S. odoratissimum. See *Olsynium biflorum*.
S. palmifolium. Semievergreen, upright perennial. **H** 18in (45cm), **S** 12in (30cm). Produces a fan of narrowly sword-shaped, mid-green leaves. In summer bears dense spikes of widely funnel-shaped, golden-yellow flowers.
S. striatum, illus. p.274. **'Aunt May'**, syn. *S. striatum* 'Variegatum' is a semievergreen, upright perennial. **H** 18–24in (45–60cm), **S** 12in (30cm). Produces tufts of long, narrow, cream-striped, grayish-green leaves. Slender spikes of trumpet-shaped, purple-striped, straw-yellow flowers are borne in summer. **'Variegatum'**. See *S. striatum* 'Aunt May'.

SKIMMIA
RUTACEAE

Genus of evergreen shrubs and trees, grown for their spring flowers, their aromatic foliage and their fruits. Except with *S. japonica* subsp. *reevesiana*, separate male and female plants are needed in order to obtain fruits. Requires shade or partial shade and fertile, moist soil. Poor soil or too much sun may cause chlorosis. Propagate by semiripe cuttings in late summer or by seed in fall. ① The fruits may cause mild stomach upset if ingested.
S. anquetilia. Evergreen, bushy, open shrub. **H** 4ft (1.2m), **S** 6ft (2m). Produces small clusters of tiny, yellow flowers, from mid- to late spring, followed by spherical, scarlet fruits. Leaves are oblong to oval, pointed, strongly aromatic and dark green. Z7–9 H9–7.
S. x formannii of gardens. See *S. japonica* 'Veitchii'.
S. japonica, illus. p.164. **'Fructo Albo'**, illus. p.163. subsp. **reevesiana 'Robert Fortune'**, syn. *S. reevesiana*, illus. p.164. **'Rubella'**, illus. p.164. **'Veitchii'**, syn. *S. x formannii* is a vigorous, evergreen, upright, dense, female shrub. **H** and **S** 5ft (1.5m). Broadly oval leaves are rich green. In mid- and late spring bears dense clusters of small, star-shaped, white flowers, followed by large, spherical, bright red fruits.
S. reevesiana. See *S. japonica* subsp. *reevesiana* 'Robert Fortune'.

SMILACINA
LILIACEAE/CONVALLARIACEAE

Genus of perennials, grown for their graceful appearance. Prefers partial shade and rich, moist, neutral to acid soil.

Propagate by division in spring or by seed in fall.
S. racemosa, syn. *Maianthemum racemosum*, illus. p.223.

SMILAX
LILIACEAE/SMILACACEAE

Genus of deciduous or evergreen, woody-stemmed or herbaceous, scrambling climbers with tubers or rhizomes. Separate male and female plants are required in order to obtain fruits. Needs sun or partial shade and well-drained soil. Propagate by division or seed in spring or by semiripe cuttings in summer.
S. china. Deciduous, woody-based, scrambling climber with straggling, sometimes spiny stems. **H** to 15ft (5m). Leaves are broadly oval to rounded. Umbels of yellow-green flowers are produced in spring; tiny, red berries develop in fall. Z7–10 H10–7.

SMITHIANTHA
GESNERIACEAE

Genus of bushy, erect perennials with tuberlike rhizomes, grown for their flowers and foliage. Needs bright light (but not direct sun) and rich, well-drained soil. Reduce watering after flowering and water sparingly in winter. Propagate by division of rhizomes in early spring.
S. cinnabarina. Robust, erect, rhizomatous perennial. **H** and **S** to 2ft (60cm). Broadly oval to almost rounded, toothed leaves, to 6in (15cm) long, are dark green with dark red hairs. Bell-shaped, orange-red flowers, lined with pale yellow, are produced in summer–fall. Z14–15 H12–10.
S. 'Orange King', illus. p.471.
S. zebrina. Bushy, rhizomatous perennial with velvety-haired stems. **H** and **S** to 3ft (1m). Oval, toothed, hairy leaves, to 7in (18cm) long, are deep green marked with reddish-brown. In summer produces tubular flowers, scarlet above, yellow below, spotted red inside and with orange-yellow lobes. Z14–15 H12–10.

SMYRNIUM
UMBELLIFERAE/APIACEAE

Genus of biennials, grown for their flowers. Needs sun and fertile, well-drained soil. Propagate by seed in fall or spring.
S. perfoliatum, illus. p.321.

SOLANDRA
SOLANACEAE

Genus of evergreen, woody-stemmed, scrambling climbers, grown for their large, trumpet-shaped flowers. Needs full light and fertile, well-drained soil. Water freely when in full growth, sparingly in cold weather. Tie to supports. Thin out crowded stems after flowering. Propagate by semiripe cuttings in summer.
S. grandiflora of gardens. See *S. maxima*.
S. maxima, syn. *S. grandiflora*, illus. p.464.

SOLANUM
SOLANACEAE

Genus of annuals, perennials (some of which are evergreen) and evergreen, semievergreen or deciduous subshrubs,

shrubs (occasionally scandent) and woody-stemmed, scrambling or leaf-stalk climbers, grown for their flowers and ornamental fruits. Requires full sun and fertile, well-drained soil. Water regularly but sparingly in winter. Support scrambling climbers. Thin out and spur back crowded growth of climbers in spring. Propagate by seed in spring or by semiripe cuttings in summer. Red spider mite, whitefly and aphids may cause problems. ① All parts of most species, especially the fruits of *S. capsicastrum* and *S. pseudocapsicum*, can cause severe discomfort if ingested.
S. betaceum, syn. *Cyphomandra betacea, Cyphomandra crassicaulis*, illus. p.456.
S. capsicastrum (False Jerusalem cherry, Winter cherry). Fairly slow-growing, evergreen, bushy subshrub, grown as an annual. **H** and **S** 1–1½ft (30–45cm). Has lance-shaped, deep green leaves. In summer bears small, star-shaped, white flowers, followed by egg-shaped, pointed, orange-red or scarlet fruits, which are at their best in winter. Z13–15 H12–10.
S. crispum 'Glasnevin', illus. p.204.
S. jasminoides. See *S. laxum*.
S. laxum, syn. *S. jasminoides* (Potato vine). Semievergreen, woody-stemmed, scrambling climber. **H** to 20ft (6m). Oval to lance-shaped leaves may be lobed or have leaflets at base. Small, 5-petaled, pale gray-blue flowers are produced in summer–fall, followed by tiny, purple berries. **'Album',** illus. p.195.
S. pseudocapsicum (Christmas cherry, Jerusalem cherry, Winter cherry). Fairly slow-growing, evergreen, bushy shrub, usually grown as an annual. **H** and **S** to 4ft (1.2m). Has oval or lance-shaped, bright green leaves. Small, star-shaped, white flowers, in summer, are followed by spherical, scarlet fruits. Has several smaller selections. Z11–12 H12–6. **'Balloon',** illus. p.327. **'Fancy', H** 1ft (30cm), has scarlet fruits. Z12–14 H12–1. **'Joker'** has yellow fruit turning orange and red. Z12–14 H12–1. **'Red Giant',** illus. p.327. **'Snowfire', H** 1ft (30cm), has white fruits that later turn red. Z12–14 H12–1.
S. rantonnei. See *Lycianthes rantonnetii*.
S. rantonnetii. See *Lycianthes rantonnetii*.
S. seaforthianum, illus. p.463.
S. wendlandii, illus. p.463.

SOLDANELLA
Snowbell
PRIMULACEAE

Genus of evergreen perennials, grown for their early spring flowers. Is good for rock gardens, troughs and alpine houses. Flower buds are set in fall and may be destroyed by frost if there is no snow cover. Requires partial shade and rich, well-drained, peaty soil. Propagate by seed in spring or by division in late summer. Slugs may attack flower buds.
S. alpina, illus. p.354.
S. minima (Least snowbell). Evergreen, clump-forming, prostrate perennial. **H** 1in (2.5cm), **S** 4in (10cm). Has rounded, glossy, mid-green leaves. In early spring produces solitary, almost stemless, bell-shaped, pale lavender-blue or white flowers, with fringed mouths. Z4–7 H7–1.

S. montana. Evergreen, mound-forming perennial. **H** 4in (10cm), **S** 6in (15cm). In early spring, tall flower stems bear long, pendent, bell-shaped, lavender-blue flowers, with fringed mouths. Leaves are rounded and leathery. Z4–7 H7–1.
S. villosa, illus. p.354.

SOLEIROLIA
Baby's tears, Mind-your-own-business, Mother of thousands
URTICACEAE

Genus of one species of usually evergreen, prostrate perennial that forms a dense carpet of foliage. Tolerates sun or shade, and prefers moist soil. Propagate by division from spring to mid-summer.
S. soleirolii, syn. *Helxine soleirolii*, illus. p.283.

SOLENOSTEMON
LABIATAE/LAMIACEAE

Genus of evergreen, bushy, subshrubby perennials, grown for their colorful leaves and flowers. Makes excellent pot plants. Needs shelter, sun or partial shade and fertile, well-drained soil. Water freely in summer, much less at other times. Pinch out growing shoots of young plants to encourage a bushy habit. Propagate by seed sown under glass in spring or by softwood cuttings in spring or summer. Mealy bugs and whitefly may cause problems.
S. 'Chocolate Mint', illus. p.311.
S. scutellarioides, syn. *Coleus blumei* var. *verschaffeltii, Plectranthus scutellarioides*. Fast-growing, bushy perennial, grown as an annual. **H** to 18in (45cm), **S** 12in (30cm) or more. Leaves are mixture of colors, including pink, red, green or yellow. Flower spikes should be removed. Z11 H11–1. **'Brightness'** has rust-red leaves, edged with green. Z13–15 H12–1. **'Fashion Parade'** has multicolored, toothed leaves of various shapes, from oval and unlobed to deeply lobed. Z11–12 H12–1. **'Inky Fingers',** illus. p.311. **Kong Series 'Kong Scarlet',** illus. p.310. **'Scarlet Poncho', H** 12in (30cm), has a pendulous habit and oval, toothed, bright red leaves. Z11–12 H12–1. **Wizard Series, H** 12in (30cm), produces oval, toothed leaves in very wide range of leaf colors. Z11–12 H12–1.

SOLIDAGO
Golden rod
COMPOSITAE/ASTERACEAE

Genus of summer- and fall-flowering perennials, some species of which are vigorous, coarse plants that tend to crowd out others in borders. Most tolerate sun or shade and well-drained soil. Propagate by division in spring. Occasionally self-seeds.
S. 'Goldenmosa', illus. p.251.
S. 'Golden Wings'. Upright perennial. **H** 5ft (1.5m), **S** 3ft (1m). Bears large, feathery panicles of small, bright yellow flower heads in early fall. Has lance-shaped, toothed, hairy, mid-green leaves. Z5–9 H9–5.
S. 'Laurin'. Compact perennial. **H** 24–30in (60–75cm), **S** 18in (45cm). Has mid-green leaves. Bears spikes of deep yellow flowers in late summer. Z5–8 H8–5.

S. x luteus, syn. x *Solidaster hybridus*, x *Solidaster luteus*, illus. p.275. **subsp. alpestris.** See *S. virgaurea* subsp. *minuta*.
S. virgaurea subsp. minuta, syn. *S. virgaurea* subsp. *alpestris*. Mound-forming perennial. **H** and **S** 4in (10cm). Has small, lance-shaped, green leaves and, in fall, neat spikes of small, yellow flower heads. Is suitable for a rock garden, trough or alpine house. Needs shade and moist soil. Z5–9 H9–5.

x Solidaster hybridus. See *Solidago* Solidago x luteus.
x Solidaster luteus. See *Solidago* Solidago x luteus.

SOLLYA
Bluebell creeper
PITTOSPORACEAE

Genus of evergreen, woody-based, twining climbers, grown for their bell-shaped, usually blue flowers. Needs sun and well-drained soil. Propagate by seed in spring or by softwood or greenwood cuttings in summer.
S. heterophylla, illus. p.194.

SONERILA
MELASTOMATACEAE

Genus of evergreen, bushy perennials and shrubs, grown for their foliage and flowers. Prefers a humid atmosphere, partial shade and peaty soil. Propagate by tip cuttings in spring.
S. margaritacea. Evergreen, bushy, semiprostrate perennial. **H** and **S** 8–10in (20–25cm). Red stems produce oval, dark green leaves, 2–3in (5–8cm) long, reddish below, silver-patterned above. Has racemes of 3-petaled, rose-pink flowers in summer. Z15 H12–10. **'Argentea'** has more silvery-gray leaves, with green veins. **'Hendersonii'** is more compact and has white-spotted leaves.

SOPHORA
Kowhai
LEGUMINOSAE/PAPILIONACEAE

Genus of deciduous or semievergreen trees and shrubs, grown for their habit, foliage and flowers. Requires full sun and fertile, well-drained soil; *S. microphylla* and *S. tetraptera* usually need to be grown against a south- or west-facing wall. Propagate by seed in fall, semievergreens also by cuttings in summer.
S. davidii, syn. *S. viciifolia*, illus. p.138.
S. japonica (Japanese pagoda tree). Deciduous, spreading tree. **H** and **S** 70ft (20m). Dark green leaves are divided into 9–15 oval leaflets. On mature trees, long clusters of pealike, creamy-white flowers are produced in late summer and early fall. Thrives in hot summers. Z5–9 H9–1. **'Pendula', H** and **S** 10ft (3m), has long, hanging shoots clothed with dark green leaves. Z5–9 H9–5. **'Violacea',** illus. p.67.
S. microphylla, syn. *Edwardsia microphylla*. Semievergreen, spreading tree. **H** and **S** 25ft (8m). Dark green leaves are divided into numerous tiny, oblong leaflets. Produces clusters of pealike, deep yellow flowers in late spring. Z8–10 H10–8.
S. tetraptera, illus. p.84.
S. viciifolia. See *S. davidii*.

S

x SOPHROLAELIOCATTLEYA

ORCHIDACEAE

See also ORCHIDS.
x *S.* Hazel Boyd gx 'Apricot Glow'. See x *Cattlianthe* Hazel Boyd gx 'Apricot Glow'.
x *S.* Trizac gx 'Purple Emperor', syn. x *S.* Trizac gx 'Purple Emperor'. Evergreen, epiphytic orchid for an intermediate greenhouse. **H** 4in (10cm). In spring bears crimson-lipped, pinkish-purple flowers, 2½in (6cm) across, in small heads. Has oval, rigid leaves, 4in (10cm) long. Needs good light in summer. Z14–15 H12–10.

SORBARIA

ROSACEAE

Genus of deciduous, summer-flowering shrubs, grown for their foliage and large panicles of small, white flowers. Prefers sun and deep, fertile, moist soil. In winter, cut out some older stems on mature plants and prune back remaining shoots to growing points. Remove suckers at base to prevent *Sorbaria* spreading too widely. Propagate by softwood cuttings in summer, by division in fall or by root cuttings in late winter.
S. aitchisonii. See *S. tomentosa* var. *angustifolia*.
S. arborea. See *S. kirilowii*.
S. kirilowii, syn. *S. arborea, Spiraea arborea*. Vigorous, deciduous, arching shrub. **H** and **S** 20ft (6m). Leaves are divided into 13–17 lance-shaped, taper-pointed, deep green leaflets. Nodding panicles of star-shaped, white flowers are produced in mid- and late summer. Z5–9 H9–5.
S. sorbifolia, syn. *Spiraea sorbifolia*, illus. p.128.
***S. tomentosa* var. *angustifolia*,** syn. *S. aitchisonii, Spiraea aitchisonii*. Deciduous, arching shrub. **H** and **S** 10ft (3m). Shoots are red when young. Leaves are divided into 11–23 narrowly lance-shaped, taper-pointed, dark green leaflets. Upright panicles of star-shaped, white flowers are produced from mid- to late summer. Z8–11 H12–8.

SORBUS

ROSACEAE

Genus of deciduous trees and shrubs, grown for their foliage, small, 5-petaled flowers, colorful fruits and, in some species, fall color. Leaves may be whole or divided into leaflets. Needs sun or partial shade and fertile, moist but well-drained soil. Species with leaves composed of leaflets do not grow well in very dry soil. Propagate by softwood cuttings or budding in summer, by seed in fall or by grafting in winter. Is susceptible to fireblight. ① Raw fruit may cause mild stomach upset if ingested.
S. alnifolia (Korean mountain ash). Deciduous, conical, then spreading tree. **H** 50ft (15m), **S** 25ft (8m). Oval, toothed, bright green leaves turn orange and red in fall. Produces small, white flowers in late spring, followed by egg-shaped, orange-red fruits. Z3–6 H8–1.
S. americana (American mountain ash, Dogberry). Deciduous, round-headed tree. **H** 30ft (10m), **S** 22ft (7m). Light green leaves, divided into 11–17 narrowly oval leaflets, usually color well in fall. Bears small, white flowers in early summer, followed by rounded, bright red fruits, ripening in early fall. Z3–8 H8–1.
S. aria (Whitebeam). Deciduous, spreading tree. **H** 50ft (15m), **S** 30ft (10m). Oval, toothed leaves are silvery-gray when young, maturing to dark green above, white-felted beneath. Clusters of small, white flowers in late spring are followed by rounded, brown-speckled, deep red fruits. Z4–5 H8–6. **'Chrysophylla'**, **H** 30ft (10m), **S** 22ft (7m), bears golden-yellow, young leaves. Z4–7 H7–1. **'Decaisneana'.** See *S. aria* 'Majestica'.**'Lutescens'** (illus. p.91) has orange-red fruits. **'Majestica'**, syn. *S. aria* 'Decaisneana' has larger leaves, white-haired when young, and larger fruits. Z4–7 H7–1.
S. aucuparia (European mountain ash, Rowan), illus. p.91. Deciduous, spreading tree. **H** 50ft (15m), **S** 22ft (7m). Leaves are divided into mid-green leaflets that turn red or yellow in fall. Bears white flowers in spring and red fruits in fall. Z4–7 H7–1. **'Fastigiata'**, syn. *S. scopulina*, **H** 25ft (8m), **S** 15ft (5m), is a conical tree with upright branches and dark green leaves. **'Fructu Luteo'**, **S** 25ft (8m), a spreading tree. Leaves are divided into 13–15 narrowly oval, mid-green leaflets that turn yellow or red in fall. Bears orange-yellow fruits. **'Rossica'.** See *S. aucuparia* 'Rossica Major'.Fruits of **'Rossica Major'**, syn. *S. aucuparia* 'Rossica' are large and deep red. **'Sheerwater Seedling'**, **S** 12ft (4m), has a narrow, upright habit.
S. cashmiriana, illus. p.91. Deciduous, spreading tree. **H** 25ft (8m), **S** 22ft (7m). Has leaves divided into 6–9 pairs of rich green leaflets. Pink-flushed, white flowers in early summer are followed by large, white fruits in fall. Z5–7 H7–5.
S. commixta, syn. *S. discolor*, illus. p.91. Vigorous, deciduous, spreading tree. **H** 30ft (10m), **S** 22ft (7m). Leaves are divided into 6–8 pairs of glossy, deep green leaflets that turn orange and red in fall. White flowers in spring are followed by bright red fruits. Z6–8 H8–6. **'Embley'**, **H** 40ft (12m), **S** 28ft (9m), has steeply ascending branches, bright red leaves, divided into 13–17 leaflets, in late fall, and fruits profusely.
S. cuspidata. See *S. vestita*.
S. decora. Deciduous, spreading, sometimes shrubby tree. **H** 30ft (10m), **S** 25ft (8m). Leaves are divided into oblong, blue-green leaflets. Small, white flowers in late spring are followed by rounded, orange-red fruits. Z3–8 H8–1.
S. discolor of gardens. See *S. commixta*.
S. esserteauana, illus. p.91. Deciduous, spreading tree. **H** and **S** 30ft (10m). Dark green leaves, divided into broadly oblong leaflets, redden in fall. Has small, white flowers, in late spring, followed by large clusters of rounded, bright red, sometimes orange-yellow fruits. Z6–8 H8–6.
S. forrestii, illus. p.91. Deciduous, spreading tree. **H** 20ft (6m), **S** 13ft (4m). Bluish-green leaves are divided into 15–19 oval to elliptic, toothed leaflets. Corymbs of creamy-white flowers, in spring, are followed by small, spherical, fleshy, white fruits, tinted crimson at bases. Z6–8 H8–6.
S. hupehensis (Hubei mountain ash). Deciduous, spreading tree. **H** 40ft (12m), **S** 25ft (8m). Leaves are divided into 9–17 oblong, blue-green leaflets that turn orange-red in late fall. Small, white flowers, in late spring, are followed by clusters of rounded, pink-tinged, white fruits. Z3–8 H8–1. **var. *obtusa*** has heavy trusses of rose-pink fruits. **'Rosea'.** See *S. pseudohupehensis*.
***S. hybrida* 'Gibbsii'.** Deciduous, compact tree. **H** to 22ft (7m), **S** 13ft (4m). Broadly ovate, mid-green leaves, with gray undersides, are more deeply lobed towards bases. Produces large clusters of cream flowers in spring, followed by bright red fruits.
S. insignis. Deciduous, spreading tree. **H** 25ft (8m), **S** 20ft (6m). Leaves are divided into usually 9–21 large, oblong, glossy, dark green leaflets. Large clusters of small, creamy-white flowers, in late spring, are followed by rounded, pink fruits that become white in winter. Z8–10 H10–8.
S. intermedia (Swedish whitebeam), illus. p.91. Deciduous, broad-headed, dense tree. **H** and **S** 40ft (12m). Has broadly oval, deeply lobed, dark green leaves. Clusters of small, white flowers, in late spring, are followed by rounded, red fruits. Z5–8 H8–3.
***S.* 'Joseph Rock'.** Deciduous, upright tree. **H** 30ft (10m), **S** 22ft (7m). Bright green leaves, divided into up to 21 leaflets, turn orange, red and purple in fall. White flowers, in late spring, are followed by large clusters of small, yellow berries in late summer–fall. Z7–8 H8–7.
***S.* x *kewensis*,** syn. *S. pohuashanensis*, illus. p.91. Deciduous, spreading tree. **H** 30ft (10m), **S** 25ft (8m). Dark green leaves are divided into 11–15 oblong leaflets. Has small, white flowers in late spring, followed by dense clusters of rounded, red fruits. Z6–8 H8–6.
S. latifolia. Deciduous, spreading tree. **H** 40ft (12m), **S** 30ft (10m). Has peeling bark and broadly oval, sharply lobed, glossy, dark green leaves. Small, white flowers, in late spring, are followed by rounded, brownish-red fruits. Z6–8 H8–5.
S. megalocarpa, illus. p.91. Deciduous, spreading tree with sturdy branches. **H** to 22ft (7m), **S** 13ft (4m). Has oval, coarsely toothed, dark green leaves. Corymbs of pungent, creamy-white flowers in spring are followed by speckled-brown fruits. Z6–8 H8–6.
***S.* 'Mitchellii'.** See *S. thibetica* 'John Mitchell'.
S. pohuashanensis of gardens. See *S.* x *kewensis*.
S. prattii. Deciduous, spreading tree. **H** and **S** 20ft (6m). Dark green leaves are divided into 21–9 oblong, sharply toothed leaflets. Produces small, white flowers in late spring, followed by rounded, white fruits. Z6–8 H8–6.
S. pseudohupehensis, syn. *S. hupehensis* 'Rosea', illus. p.73.
S. reducta, illus. p.346.
S. sargentiana (Sargent's rowan), illus. p.91. Deciduous, sparsely branched, spreading tree. **H** and **S** 20ft (6m). Has sturdy shoots and large, mid-green leaves, divided into 7–11 oblong leaflets, that turn brilliant red in fall. Small, white flowers in late spring are followed by rounded, red fruits. Z5–7 H7–5.
S. scalaris, illus. p.91. Deciduous, spreading tree. **H** and **S** 30ft (10m). Leaves are divided into 21–33 narrowly oblong, glossy, deep green leaflets and become deep red and purple in fall. Produces small, white flowers in late spring, followed by rounded, red fruits in large, dense clusters. Z6–8 H8–6.
S. scopulina of gardens. See *S. aucuparia* 'Fastigiata'.
S. thibetica. Deciduous, conical tree. **H** 70ft (20m), **S** 50ft (15m). Large, broadly oval, dark green leaves are silvery-white when young and remain so on undersides. Clusters of small, white flowers, in late spring, are followed by rounded, brown fruits. Z5–7 H7–5. **'John Mitchell'**, syn. *S.* 'Mitchellii' (illus. p.91) has white flowers in spring and brown fruits in late summer.
***S.* x *thuringiaca*.** Deciduous, broadly conical, compact tree. **H** 40ft (12m), **S** 25ft (8m). Oval, dark green leaves are deeply lobed and have 3 pairs of basal leaflets. Small, white flowers, in late spring, are followed by rounded, bright red fruits. Z5–8 H8–5. **'Fastigiata'** has upright branches and a broad, oval, dense crown. **'Scarlet King'** produces bright scarlet-red fruits in larger trusses and has large leaves bearing up to 6 pairs of leaflets.
S. vestita, syn. *S. cuspidata*. Deciduous, broadly conical tree. **H** to 80ft (25m), **S** 30ft (10m). Has very large, veined, gray-green leaves, white-haired when young. Clusters of pink-stamened, white flowers, in late spring or early summer, are followed by rounded, russet or yellowish-red fruits. Z6–8 H8–6.
S. vilmorinii, illus. p.91. Deciduous, spreading, arching tree. **H** and **S** 15ft (5m). Leaves divided into 9–14 pairs of dark green leaflets turn to orange- or bronze-red in fall. Has white flowers in late spring and small, rounded, deep pink fruits in fall. Z6–8 H8–6.
***S.* 'Wilfred Fox'.** Deciduous tree, upright when young, later with dense, oval head. **H** 50ft (15m), **S** 30ft (10m). Has broadly oval, glossy, dark green leaves and small, white flowers in late spring, followed by rounded, orange-brown fruits. Z5–7 H7–5.

SPARAXIS

Harlequin flower

IRIDACEAE

Genus of spring- and early summer-flowering corms, grown for their very gaudy flowers. Needs sun and well-drained soil. Plant in fall. Dry off corms after flowering. Propagate by offsets in late summer or by seed in fall.
S. elegans, syn. *Streptanthera cuprea, Streptanthera elegans*. Spring-flowering corm. **H** 4–10in (10–25cm), **S** 3–5in (8–12cm). Has lance-shaped leaves in erect, basal fan. Stem produces loose spike of 1–5 flattish, orange or white flowers, 1¼–1½in (3–4cm) wide, with yellow center surrounded by purple-black band. Z10–11 H12–10.
***S. fragrans* subsp. *grandiflora*,** syn. *S. grandiflora*. Spring-flowering corm. **H** 6–16in (15–40cm), **S** 3–5in (8–12cm). Has sword-shaped leaves in erect, basal fan. Stem bears loose spike of up to 5 flattish, yellow-tubed, deep purple flowers, 1½ -2in (4–5cm) across. Z10–11 H12–10.
S. grandiflora. See *S. fragrans* subsp. *grandiflora*.
S. tricolor, illus. p.418.

SPARGANIUM

Bur reed

SPARGANIACEAE/TYPHACEAE

Genus of deciduous or semievergreen, perennial, marginal water plants, grown for their foliage. Prefers sun or partial

shade and cold water. Remove faded foliage and cut plants back regularly to control growth. Propagate by seed or division in spring.
S. erectum, syn. *S. ramosum*, illus. p.442.
S. minimum. See *S. natans*.
S. natans, syn. *S. minimum*. Vigorous, deciduous or semievergreen, perennial, marginal water plant. **H** 1–3ft (30cm–1m), **S** 1ft (30cm). Mid-green leaves are grasslike, some erect, some floating. In summer has insignificant, brownish-green flowers, in the form of burs. Z5–9 H9–1.
S. ramosum. See *S. erectum*.

Sparmannia. See *Sparrmannia*.

SPARRMANNIA
SYN. SPARMANNIA
TILIACEAE/SPARRMANNIACEAE

Genus of evergreen trees and shrubs, grown for their flowers and foliage. Prefers full light and fertile, well-drained soil. Water freely when in full growth, moderately at other times. Flowered stems may be cut back after flowering to promote a more compact habit. Propagate by greenwood cuttings in late spring.
S. africana, illus. p.453.

SPARTINA
GRAMINEAE/POACEAE

See also GRASSES, BAMBOOS, RUSHES and SEDGES.
S. pectinata 'Aureomarginata', syn. *S. pectinata* 'Aureovariegata', illus. p.289.
'Aureovariegata'. See *S. pectinata* 'Aureomarginata'.

SPARTIUM
LEGUMINOSAE/PAPILIONACEAE

Genus of one species of deciduous, almost leafless shrub, grown for its green shoots and showy flowers. Needs sun and not too rich, well-drained soil. To maintain a compact habit, trim in early spring. Propagate by seed in fall.
S. junceum, illus. p.140.

SPATHIPHYLLUM
ARACEAE

Genus of evergreen perennials, with rhizomes, grown for their foliage and flowers. Prefers a humid atmosphere, partial shade and rich, moist soil. Propagate by division in spring or summer.
(!) All parts of the plants may cause mild stomach upset if ingested, and contact with the sap may irritate skin.
S. 'Clevelandii'. See *S. wallisii* 'Clevelandii'.
S. floribundum. Evergreen, tufted, short-stemmed perennial. **H** and **S** to 1ft (30cm). Has clusters of lance-shaped, long-pointed, long-stalked, glossy, dark green leaves, to 6in (15cm) long. Intermittently bears narrowly oval, white spathes, to 3in (8cm) long, enclosing green-and-white spadix. Z14–15 H12–1.
S. 'Mauna Loa', illus. p.468.
S. wallisii, illus. p.468. **'Clevelandii'**, syn. *S.* 'Clevelandii' is an evergreen, tufted perennial. **H** and **S** to 2ft (60cm). Has broadly lance-shaped, semierect, glossy, mid-green leaves, 1ft (30cm) or more long. Intermittently bears

oval, white spathes, 6in (15cm) long with central, green line, that surround fragrant, white spadix.

SPATHODEA
BIGNONIACEAE

Genus of evergreen trees, grown for their flowers, mainly from fall to spring, and for their overall appearance. Container-grown and immature plants seldom bear flowers. Needs full light and fertile, moist but well-drained soil. Propagate by seed in spring or by semiripe cuttings in summer.
S. campanulata, illus. p.453.

SPHAERALCEA
MALVACEAE

Genus of perennials and deciduous subshrubs, evergreen in warm climates. Requires sun and fertile, well-drained soil. Propagate by seed or division in spring or by softwood cuttings in mid-summer.
S. ambigua, illus. p.246.
S. munroana. Branching, woody-based perennial. **H** and **S** 18in (45cm). Solitary, broadly funnel-shaped, brilliant coral-pink flowers are borne in leaf axils from summer until first frosts. Has oval, round-toothed, hairy, mid-green leaves. Z4–10 H12–8.

Spiloxene capensis. See *Hypoxis capensis*.

SPIRAEA
ROSACEAE

Genus of deciduous or semievergreen shrubs, grown for their mass of small flowers and, in some species, their foliage. Requires sun and fertile, well-drained but not over-dry soil. On species and cultivars that flower on the current year's growth—*S. x billiardii, S. douglasii* and *S. japonica* and its cultivars—cut back young stems and remove very old ones in early spring. On species that flower on old wood, cut out older shoots in early spring, leaving young shoots to flower that year. Propagate *S. douglasii* by division from late fall to early spring, other species and cultivars by softwood cuttings in summer.
S. aitchisonii. See *Sorbaria tomentosa* var. *angustifolia*.
S. arborea. See *Sorbaria kirilowii*.
S. 'Arguta' (Bridal wreath, Foam of May). Deciduous, arching, dense shrub. **H** and **S** 8ft (2.5m). Produces clusters of 5-petaled, white flowers from mid- to late spring. Leaves are narrowly oblong and bright green. Z5–8 H8–5.
S. aruncus. See *Aruncus dioicus*.
S. x billiardii. Deciduous, upright, dense shrub. **H** and **S** 8ft (2.5m). Has oval, finely toothed, dark green leaves and dense panicles of 5-petaled, pink flowers in summer. Z4–8 H8–1. **'Triumphans'** has large, broadly conical panicles of bright purplish-pink flowers.
S. canescens, illus. p.128.
S. douglasii. Vigorous, deciduous, upright shrub. **H** and **S** 6ft (2m). Dense, narrow panicles of 5-petaled, purplish-pink flowers are borne from early to mid-summer among oblong, mid-green leaves, with gray-white undersides. Z5–8 H8–5. Leaves of **subsp. menziesii**, **H** 3ft (1m), are green on both sides.

S. japonica 'Anthony Waterer', illus. p.154. **'Goldflame'**, illus. p.156. **'Little Princess'**, illus. p.153.
S. nipponica. Deciduous, arching shrub. **H** and **S** 8ft (2.5m). Bears dense clusters of 5-petaled, white flowers in early summer. Sturdy, red shoots bear small, rounded, dark green leaves. Z4–8 H8–1. **'Halward's Silver'**, **H** and **S** 3ft (1m), is slow-growing, very dense and flowers profusely. **'Snowmound'**, syn. *S. nipponica* var. *tosaensis*, illus. p.131. **var. tosaensis** of gardens. See *S. nipponica* 'Snowmound'.
S. prunifolia. Deciduous, arching shrub. **H** and **S** 6ft (2m). In mid- and late spring has clusters of rosettelike, double, white flowers amid rounded to oblong, bright green leaves, coloring to bronze-yellow in fall. Z5–8 H8–5.
S. 'Snow White', syn. *S. trichocarpa* 'Snow White'. Deciduous, arching shrub. **H** and **S** 6ft (2m). Leaves are oblong and mid-green. Dense clusters of 5-petaled, white flowers are borne in late spring and early summer. Z5–8 H8–5.
S. sorbifolia. See *Sorbaria sorbifolia*.
S. thunbergii. Deciduous or semievergreen, arching, dense shrub. **H** 5ft (1.5m), **S** 6ft (2m). Small clusters of 5-petaled, white flowers are borne from early to mid-spring. Has narrowly oblong, pale green leaves. Z5–8 H8–5.
S. trichocarpa 'Snow White'. See *S.* 'Snow White'.
S. trilobata. Deciduous, arching shrub. **H** 3ft (1m), **S** 5ft (1.5m). In early summer bears 5-petaled, white flowers in clusters along slender shoots. Has rounded, shallowly lobed, toothed, blue-green leaves. Z3–7 H7–1.
S. ulmaria. See *Filipendula ulmaria*.
S. x vanhouttei, illus. p.145.
S. veitchii. Vigorous, deciduous, upright shrub. **H** and **S** 10ft (3m). Has arching, red branches and oblong, dark green leaves. Produces heads of 5-petaled, white flowers from early to mid-summer. Z4–7 H7–1.

SPIRANTHES
ORCHIDACEAE

See also ORCHIDS.
S. cernua, illus. p.466. Deciduous, terrestrial orchid. **H** 20in (50cm). Spikes of delicate, white flowers, $\frac{1}{2}$in (1cm) long, with pale yellow centers, are produced in fall. Has narrowly lance-shaped leaves, 2–5in (5–12cm) long. Requires partial shade in summer. Z4–8 H8–4.

SPREKELIA
AMARYLLIDACEAE

Genus of one species of bulb, grown for its showy, red flowers in spring. Needs an open, sunny site and well-drained soil. Keep dry in winter; start into growth by watering in spring. Propagate by offsets in early fall.
S. formosissima, illus. p.402.

STACHYS
LABIATAE/LAMIACEAE

Genus of late spring- or summer-flowering perennials, shrubs and subshrubs, some of which are evergreen. Species mentioned below prefer an open, sunny position; others are woodland plants and grow better in partial shade.

Needs well-drained soil, tolerating even poor soil. Propagate by division in spring.
S. byzantina, syn. *S. lanata, S. olympica*, illus. p.274. **'Primrose Heron'**, illus. p.275. **'Silver Carpet'** is an evergreen, mat-forming perennial. **H** 6in (15cm), **S** 24in (60cm). Has oval, woolly, gray leaves. Rarely produces flowers. Makes an excellent front-of-border or groundcover plant.
S. coccinea. Clump-forming perennial. **H** 24in (60cm), **S** 18in (45cm). Has oval, mid-green leaves, with pronounced network of veins. From early to late summer, spikes of small, hooded, bright scarlet flowers, protruding from purple calyces, arise from leaf axils. Z4–8 H8–1.
S. lanata. See *S. byzantina*.
S. macrantha. Clump-forming perennial. **H** and **S** 12in (30cm). Has heart-shaped, crinkled, round-toothed, soft green leaves. Whorls of large, hooded, rose-purple flowers are produced in summer. Z7–9 H9–7. **'Superba'**, illus. p.270.
S. officinalis, syn. *Betonica officinalis* (Bishop's wort, Wood betony). Mat-forming perennial. **H** 18–24in (45–60cm), **S** 12–18in (30–45cm). Produces whorls of hooded, tubular, purple, pink or white flowers on sturdy stems, arising, in summer, from mats of oval to oblong, round-toothed, mid-green leaves. Z5–8 H8–4. **'Hummelo'**, illus. p.268. **'Rosea'** has flowers of clearer pink.
S. olympica. See *S. byzantina*.

STACHYURUS
STACHYURACEAE

Genus of deciduous shrubs, grown for their flowers, which are borne before the leaves. Flower spikes, formed in fall, are harmed by hard frosts. Requires sun or partial shade and fertile, moist but well-drained, not too heavy soil, preferably peaty and acid. Propagate by softwood cuttings in summer.
S. chinensis. Deciduous, spreading, open shrub. **H** 6ft (2m), **S** 12ft (4m). Pendent spikes of small, bell-shaped, pale yellow flowers are produced in late winter and early spring. Leaves are oval and deep green. Z8–9 H9–8.
S. praecox, illus. p.144. **'Magpie'** is a deciduous, spreading, open shrub, less vigorous than the species. **H** 5ft (1.5m), **S** 6ft (2m). Has arching, red-purple shoots and oval, tapered, gray-green leaves, edged with creamy-white. Bell-shaped, pale yellow flowers are borne in late winter and early spring. Z7–9 H9–7.

STANHOPEA
ORCHIDACEAE

See also ORCHIDS.
S. tigrina. Evergreen, epiphytic orchid for a cool greenhouse. **H** 9in (23cm). Pendent spikes of fragrant, waxy, rich yellow and maroon flowers, 6in (15cm) across, with red-spotted, white lips, are produced in summer. Has broadly oval, ribbed leaves, 1ft (30cm) long. Is best grown in a hanging, slatted basket. Needs partial shade in summer. Z13–15 H12–10.

STAPELIA

ASCLEPIADACEAE

Genus of clump-forming, perennial succulents with erect, 4-angled stems. Stem edges are often indented and may bear small leaves that drop after only a few weeks. Flowers are often foul-smelling. Requires sun or partial shade and moderately fertile, well-drained, gritty soil. Propagate by seed or stem cuttings in spring or summer.

S. europaea. See *Caralluma europaea*.
S. flavirostris. See *S. grandiflora*.
S. gigantea, illus. p.496.
S. grandiflora, syn. *S. flavirostris*, illus. p.488.
S. variegata. See *Orbea variegata*.

STAPHYLEA

Bladder nut

STAPHYLEACEAE

Genus of deciduous, spring-flowering shrubs and trees, grown for their flowers and bladderlike fruits. Requires sun or partial shade and fertile, moist soil. Propagate species by softwood or greenwood cuttings in summer or by seed in fall, selected forms by softwood or greenwood cuttings in summer.

S. colchica. Deciduous, upright shrub. **H** and **S** 11ft (3.5m). Erect panicles of bell-shaped, white flowers are borne in late spring and are followed by inflated, greenish-white fruits. Bright green leaves are divided into 3–5 oval leaflets. Z6–9 H9–6.
S. holocarpa 'Rosea', illus. p.111.
S. pinnata, illus. p.110.

Statice suworowii. See *Psylliostachys suworowii*.

STAUNTONIA

LARDIZABALACEAE

Genus of evergreen, woody-stemmed, twining climbers. Separate male and female plants are required in order to obtain fruits. Needs sun or partial shade and well-drained soil. Propagate by seed in spring or by stem cuttings in summer or fall.

S. hexaphylla, illus. p.192.

STENANTHIUM

LILIACEAE/MELANTHIACEAE

Genus of summer-flowering bulbs, grown for their flowers. Needs sun and well-drained soil. In cool areas, plant in a warm, sheltered site in light soil that does not dry out excessively. Propagate by seed in fall or by division in spring.

S. gramineum. Summer-flowering bulb. **H** to 5ft (1.5m), **S** 1¹⁄₂–2ft (45–60cm). Has long, narrowly strap-shaped, semierect, basal leaves. Stem produces dense, branched, often arching spike of fragrant, star-shaped, white or green flowers, ¹⁄₂–⁵⁄₈in (1–1.5cm) across. Z7–9 H9–7.

STENOCACTUS

syn. ECHINOFOSSULOCACTUS

CACTACEAE

Genus of spherical, perennial cacti with spiny, green stems that have very narrow, wavy ribs. Needs sun and well-drained soil. Water well in growing season, much less when dormant in winter as it may rot off.

Propagate by seed in spring or summer.
S. coptonogonus, illus. p.487.
S. crispatus, syn. *Echinofossulatus lamellosus*. Spherical, perennial cactus. **H** and **S** 3in (8cm). Green stem has 30–35 ribs. Funnel-shaped, flesh-colored or red flowers, ¹⁄₂–1¹⁄₄in (1–3cm) across, are produced from crown in spring. Has flattened upper radial spines, shorter, more rounded lower ones and longer, rounded central spines with darker tips. Z12–15 H12–1.
S. lamellosus. See *S. obvallatus*.
S. obvallatus, syn. *S. lamellosus*, *Echinofossulatus pentacanthus*, *Echinofossulatus violaciflora*, illus. p.484.

STENOCARPUS

PROTEACEAE

Genus of evergreen, summer- and fall-flowering trees, grown for their flowers and foliage. Needs full light and fertile, well-drained soil. Water container plants moderately, less in winter. Pruning is rarely necessary. Propagate by seed in spring or by semiripe cuttings in summer.

S. sinuatus (Firewheel tree). Slow-growing, evergreen, upright tree. **H** 40ft (12m) or more, **S** 15ft (5m). Has lustrous, deep green leaves, 5–10in (12–25cm) long, lance-shaped and entire or with pairs of oblong lobes. Bottle-shaped, bright scarlet flowers, clustered like spokes of a wheel, are produced from late summer to fall. Z11 H12–10.

STENOCEREUS

CACTACEAE

Genus of treelike or shrubby, perennial cacti with prominently ribbed stems often densely spined. Needs full sun and very well-drained soil. Propagate by seed in spring or by stem cuttings in summer.
S. marginatus. See *Pachycereus marginatus*.
S. thurberi, syn. *Lemaireocereus thurberi*. Columnar, perennial cactus, branching from low down. **H** to 22ft (7m), **S** 3ft (1m). Has 5–6-ribbed, glossy, dark green stems with very short-spined areoles set in close rows down each rib. Produces funnel-shaped, purple or pink flowers, with red sepals, in summer. Z14–15 H12–10.

Stenolobium stans. See *Tecoma stans*.

STENOMESSON

AMARYLLIDACEAE

Genus of bulbs, grown for their long, often pendent, tubular flowers. Needs an open, sunny situation and well-drained soil. Propagate by offsets in fall.
S. miniatum, syn. *Urceolina peruviana*, illus. p.407.
S. variegatum, illus. p.407.

STENOTAPHRUM

GRAMINEAE/POACEAE

See also GRASSES, BAMBOOS, RUSHES and SEDGES.
S. secundatum (Buffalo grass, St. Augustine grass). **'Variegatum'** is an evergreen, spreading, rhizomatous, perennial grass. **H** 6in (15cm), **S** indefinite. Cream-striped, mid-green leaves last well into winter. In summer has erect racemes of brownish-green spikelets. In warm climates is used for a lawn. Z9–11 H12–9.

STEPHANANDRA

ROSACEAE

Genus of deciduous, summer-flowering shrubs, grown for their habit, foliage, fall color and winter shoots. Needs sun or partial shade and fertile, not too dry soil. On established plants, cut out some older shoots after flowering. Propagate by softwood cuttings in summer or by division in fall.

S. incisa. Deciduous, arching shrub. **H** 5ft (1.5m), **S** 10ft (3m). Oval, deeply lobed and toothed, bright green leaves turn orange-yellow in fall and stems become rich brown in winter. Produces crowded panicles of tiny, star-shaped, greenish-white flowers in early summer. Z3–8 H8–4. **'Crispa', H** 2ft (60cm), has wavy-edged and more deeply lobed leaves.
S. tanakae, illus. p.132.

STEPHANOTIS

ASCLEPIADACEAE

Genus of evergreen, woody-stemmed, twining climbers, grown for their scented, waxy flowers. Needs partial shade and rich, well-drained soil. Water moderately, less in cold weather. Provide stems with support. Shorten over-long or crowded stems in spring. Propagate by seed in spring or by semiripe cuttings in summer.

S. floribunda, illus. p.460.

Sterculia acerifolia. See *Brachychiton acerifolius*.
Sterculia diversifolia. See *Brachychiton populneus*.
Sterculia x platanifolia. See *Firmiana simplex*.

STERNBERGIA

AMARYLLIDACEAE

Genus of spring- or fall-flowering bulbs, grown for their large, crocuslike flowers. Needs full sun and well-drained, heavy or light soil that dries out in summer, when bulbs die down and need warmth and dryness. Leave undisturbed to form clumps. Propagate by division in spring or fall.

S. candida, illus. p.415.
S. clusiana. Fall-flowering bulb. **H** to ³⁄₄in (2cm), **S** 3–4in (8–10cm). Strap-shaped, semierect, grayish-green, basal leaves, often twisted lengthways, are produced after flowering. Stems bear erect, goblet-shaped, yellow or greenish-yellow flowers, 1¹⁄₂–3in (4–8cm) long. Z7–10 H10–7.
S. lutea. Fall-flowering bulb. **H** 1–6in (2.5–15cm), **S** 3–4in (8–10cm). Strap-shaped, semierect, deep green, basal leaves are produced at same time as funnel-shaped, bright yellow flower, 1–2¹⁄₂in (2.5–6cm) long, on leafless stem. Z7–9 H9–6.
S. sicula. Fall-flowering bulb. **H** 1–3in (2.5–7cm), **S** 2–3in (5–8cm). Narrowly strap-shaped, semierect, deep green, basal leaves, with central, paler green stripe, are produced at same time as flowers. Each stem bears funnel-shaped, bright yellow flower, ³⁄₄–1¹⁄₂in (2–4cm) long. Z6–9 H9–6.

STETSONIA

CACTACEAE

Genus of one species of treelike, perennial cactus with a sturdy trunk. Nocturnal, funnel-shaped flowers are 6in (15cm) long. Needs sun and well-drained soil. Propagate by seed in spring or summer.

S. coryne. Treelike, perennial cactus. **H** 25ft (8m), **S** 12ft (4m). Has short, swollen trunk bearing 8- or 9-ribbed, blue-green stems. Black spines fade with age to white with black tips. Funnel-shaped, white flowers are produced at night in summer. Z13–15 H12–10.

STEWARTIA

syn. STUARTIA

THEACEAE

Genus of deciduous trees and shrubs, grown for their flowers, fall color and usually peeling bark. Needs shelter from strong winds, a sunny position, but preferably with roots in shade, and fertile, moist but well-drained, neutral to acid soil. Resents being transplanted. Propagate by softwood cuttings in summer or by seed in fall.

S. malacodendron. Deciduous, spreading tree or shrub. **H** 12ft (4m), **S** 10ft (3m). Roselike, purple-stamened, white flowers, sometimes purple-streaked, are borne in mid-summer amid oval, dark green leaves. Z7–9 H9–6.
S. monadelpha, illus. p.76.
S. pseudocamellia, illus. p.78. Deciduous, spreading tree. **H** 70ft (20m), **S** 25ft (8m). Has ornamental, peeling bark and bears roselike, white flowers in mid-summer. Oval, mid-green leaves turn orange and red in fall. Z5–8 H8–4.
S. sinensis. Deciduous, spreading tree. **H** 40ft (12m), **S** 22ft (7m). Has peeling bark and oval, bright green leaves that turn brilliant red in fall. Fragrant, roselike, white flowers are produced in mid-summer. Z5–8 H8–5.

STIGMAPHYLLON

MALPIGHIACEAE

Genus of evergreen, woody-stemmed, twining climbers, grown for their flowers. Needs partial shade and fertile, well-drained soil. Water freely when in full growth, less in low temperatures. Provide stems with support. Thin out crowded stems in spring. Propagate by semiripe cuttings in summer.

S. ciliatum, illus. p.464.

STIPA

GRAMINEAE/POACEAE

See also GRASSES, BAMBOOS, RUSHES and SEDGES.
S. arundinacea. See *S. lessoniana*.
S. calamagrostis, syn. *Achnatherum calamagrostis*, illus. p.286.
S. gigantea, illus. p.287.
S. lessoniana, syn. *S. arundinacea*, *Anemanthele lessoniana*, illus. p.289.
S. tenuissima, illus. p.288.

S

703

STOKESIA

COMPOSITAE/ASTERACEAE

Genus of one species of evergreen, summer-flowering perennial. Requires sun or partial shade and fertile, well-drained soil. Propagate by division in spring or by seed in fall.

S. laevis, illus. p.269. **'Blue Star'** is an evergreen, basal-rosetted perennial. **H** and **S** 12–18in (30–45cm). Bears cornflowerlike, deep blue flower heads singly at stem tips in summer. Has narrowly lance-shaped, dark green leaves.

STOMATIUM

AIZOACEAE

Genus of mat-forming, perennial succulents with short stems, each bearing 4–6 pairs of solid, 3-angled or semicylindrical leaves, often with toothed edges and incurved tips. Needs sun and well-drained soil. Propagate by seed or stem cuttings in spring or summer.

S. agninum. Mat-forming, perennial succulent. **H** 2in (5cm), **S** 3ft (1m) or more. Has solid, 3-angled or semicylindrical, soft gray-green leaves, $1\frac{1}{2}$–2in (4–5cm) long, often without teeth. In summer, fragrant, daisylike, yellow flowers, $\frac{3}{4}$–2in (2–5cm) across, open in evening. Z13–15 H12–10.
S. patulum. Mat-forming, perennial succulent. **H** $1\frac{1}{4}$in (3cm), **S** 3ft (1m). Has semicylindrical, gray-green leaves, $\frac{3}{4}$in (2cm) long, with rough dots and 2–9 teethlike tubercles on upper surface. Bears fragrant, daisylike, pale yellow flowers, $\frac{3}{4}$in (2cm) across, in evening in summer. Z13–15 H12–10.

Strangweja spicata. See *Bellevalia hyacinthoides.*
Stranvaesia. See *Photinia.*

STRATIOTES

HYDROCHARITACEAE

Genus of semievergreen, perennial, submerged, free-floating water plants, grown for their foliage. Requires sun. Grows in any depth of cool water. Thin plants as required. Propagate by separating young plants from runners in summer.
S. aloides, illus. p.435.

STRELITZIA

Bird-of-paradise flower

MUSACEAE/STRELITZIACEAE

Genus of large, evergreen, tufted, clump-forming, palmlike perennials, grown for their showy flowers. Grow in bright light shaded from direct sun and fertile, well-drained soil. Reduce watering in low temperatures. Propagate by seed or division of suckers in spring.
S. nicolai. Evergreen, palmlike perennial with a sturdy trunk. **H** 25ft (8m), **S** 15ft (5m). Has oblong leaves, 5ft (1.5m) or more long, on very long stalks and intermittently bears beaklike, white and pale blue flowers in boat-shaped, dark purple bracts. Z12–15 H12–10.
S. reginae, illus. p.476.

Streptanthera cuprea. See *Sparaxis elegans.*
Streptanthera elegans. See *Sparaxis elegans.*

STREPTOCARPUS

GESNERIACEAE

Genus of perennials, some of which are evergreen, with showy flowers. Needs a humid atmosphere, bright light away from direct sunlight and rich, moist soil. Avoid wetting leaves when watering; water less during cold periods. Propagate by seed in spring, by division after flowering, bushy species by tip cuttings in spring or summer, stemless species by leaf cuttings in spring or summer.

S. 'Amanda', illus. p.473.
S. caulescens. Erect perennial. **H** and **S** 18in (45cm) or more. Has small, narrow to oval, fleshy, dark green leaves. Stalked clusters of small, tubular, violet-striped, violet or white flowers are produced in leaf axils intermittently. Z14–15 H12–10.
S. 'Constant Nymph'. Evergreen, stemless, rosetted perennial. **H** 10in (25cm), **S** 20in (50cm). Has strap-shaped, wrinkled leaves. Funnel-shaped, purplish-blue flowers, darker veined and yellow-throated, are intermittently produced in small clusters. Z13–15 H12–10.
S. 'Crystal Ice', illus. p.465.
S. kentaniensis. Stemless perennial. **H** 10in (25cm), **S** 8in (20cm). Has loose whorls of narrowly lance-shaped, wrinkled, semierect, hairy, dark green leaves, with prominent mid-vein. Clusters of 2–5 small, white flowers, with radiating, violet vein pattern, are borne mainly in winter but can appear all year long under ideal conditions.
S. 'Nicola', illus. p.469.
S. rexii. Stemless, rosetted perennial. **H** to 10in (25cm), **S** to 20in (50cm). Has strap-shaped, wrinkled, green leaves. Stems bear loose clusters of funnel-shaped, pale blue or mauve flowers, with darker lines, intermittently at any time of year. Z13–15 H12–10.
S. saxorum, illus. p.310.

STREPTOSOLEN

SOLANACEAE

Genus of one species of evergreen or semievergreen, loosely scrambling shrub, grown for its flowers. Requires full sun and rich, well-drained soil. Water freely when in full growth, less at other times. After flowering or in spring, remove flowered shoots and tie in new growths. Propagate by softwood or semiripe cuttings in summer.
S. jamesonii, illus. p.464.

STROBILANTHES

ACANTHACEAE

Genus of perennials and evergreen subshrubs, grown for their flowers. Needs partial shade and fertile, well-drained soil. Propagate by seed, basal stem cuttings or division in spring.
S. atropurpureus, illus. p.250.
S. dyerianus, illus. p.311.

STROMANTHE

MARANTACEAE

Genus of evergreen, creeping perennials, grown mainly for their foliage. Prefers high humidity, sun or partial shade and fertile, moist but well-drained soil. Use soft water if possible and do not allow to dry out completely. Propagate by division in spring.
S. sanguinea. Strong-growing, evergreen, creeping perennial. **H** and **S** to 5ft (1.5m). Lance-shaped leaves, to 18in (45cm) long, are glossy, green above with paler midribs, reddish beneath. Bears panicles of small, 3-petaled, white flowers in axils of showy, bright red bracts, usually in spring but also in summer–fall. Z13–15 H12–10.

STROMBOCACTUS

CACTACEAE

Genus of extremely slow-growing, hemispherical to cylindrical, perennial cacti. Takes 5 years from seed to reach $\frac{1}{2}$in (1cm) high. Funnel-shaped flowers are $1\frac{1}{2}$in (4cm) across. Needs sun and very well-drained soil. Susceptible to over-watering. Propagate by seed in spring or summer.
S. disciformis, illus. p.481.

STRONGYLODON

LEGUMINOSAE/PAPILIONACEAE

Genus of evergreen, woody-stemmed, twining climbers, grown for their large, clawlike flowers. Needs partial shade and rich, moist but well-drained soil. Water freely when in full growth, less at other times. Provide support. If necessary, thin crowded stems in spring. Propagate by seed or stem cuttings in summer or by layering in spring.
S. macrobotrys (Emerald creeper, Jade vine). Fast-growing, evergreen, woody-stemmed, twining climber. **H** to 70ft (20m). Leaves are divided into 3 oval, glossy leaflets. Has clawlike, luminous, blue-green flowers in long, pendent spikes in winter–spring. Z15 H12–10.

Stuartia. See *Stewartia.*

STYLIDIUM

STYLIDIACEAE

Genus of perennials with grasslike leaves, grown for their unusual flowers that have fused, "triggered" stamens adapted for pollination by insects. Needs bright light and fertile soil. Propagate by seed in spring.
S. graminifolium (Trigger plant). Rosetted perennial. **H** and **S** to 6in (15cm) or more. Grasslike, stiff, dark green leaves, with toothed margins, rise from ground level. Bears tiny, pale pinkish-mauve flowers in narrow spikes, 12in (30cm) or more long, in summer. Z13–15 H12–10.

STYLOPHORUM

PAPAVERACEAE

Genus of spring-flowering perennials with large, deeply lobed leaves, nearly all as basal rosettes. Needs partial shade and rich, moist, peaty soil. Propagate by division in spring or by seed in fall.
S. diphyllum. Rosetted perennial. **H** and **S** to 12in (30cm) or more. Has large, lobed, hairy leaves. Bears open cup-shaped, golden-yellow flowers in spring on upright, branched stems. Prefers rich, woodland conditions. Z5–8 H8–1.

STYRAX

STYRACACEAE

Genus of deciduous, summer-flowering trees and shrubs, grown for their foliage and flowers. Prefers a sheltered position in sun or partial shade and moist, neutral to acid soil. Propagate by softwood cuttings in summer or by seed in fall.
S. japonicus, illus. p.72.
S. obassia (Fragrant snowbell). Deciduous, spreading tree. **H** 40ft (12m), **S** 22ft (7m). Bears long, spreading clusters of fragrant, bell- to funnel-shaped, white flowers in early summer. Has rounded, dark green leaves, blue-gray beneath, turning yellow in fall. Z6–8 H8–6.
S. officinalis, illus. p.112.
S. wilsonii, illus. p.129.

Sulcorebutia arenacea. See *Rebutia arenacea.*
Sulcorebutia rauschii. See *Rebutia steinmannii.*
Sulcorebutia tiraquensis. See *Rebutia steinbachii* subsp. *tiraquensis.*

SUTERA

SCROPHULARIACEAE

Genus of annuals, evergreen, creeping perennials and evergreen shrubs and subshrubs, grown for their showy but small, flowers. Is suitable for hanging baskets and containers. Needs full sun and fertile, moist but well-drained soil. Propagate in spring by seed or division or in spring–summer by stem-tip cuttings.
S. cordata Snowstorm Series Giant Snowflake ('Danova906'), illus. p.298.
S. grandiflora. See *Jamesbrittenia grandiflora.*
S. 'Snowflake'. Freely branching, trailing perennial. **H** 4in (10cm), **S** 8in (20cm) or more. Heart-shaped, hairy leaves are $\frac{1}{2}$in (1cm) wide. Has 5-lobed, white flowers, $\frac{3}{4}$in (2cm) wide, with yellow stamens, borne towards shoot tips.

SUTHERLANDIA

LEGUMINOSAE/PAPILIONACEAE

Genus of evergreen shrubs, grown for their flowers and fruits. Requires full light and fertile, well-drained soil. Water container specimens freely when in full growth, moderately at other times. Remove old, twiggy stems at ground level in late winter. Propagate by seed in spring. Red spider mite may be troublesome.
S. frutescens, illus. p.456.

SWAINSONA

LEGUMINOSAE/PAPILIONACEAE

Genus of annuals, evergreen perennials, subshrubs and shrubs, grown for their flowers. Needs full light or partial shade and rich, well-drained soil. Water freely when in growth, moderately at other times. Propagate by seed in spring or by semiripe cuttings in summer.
S. galegifolia (Darling pea, Swan flower). Evergreen, sprawling subshrub. **H** 2–4ft (60cm–1.2m), **S** 1–2ft (30–60cm). Leaves are divided into 11–25 narrowly oval, mid- to deep green leaflets. Bears pealike, red, pink, purple, blue or yellow flowers in late spring and summer. Remove old, flowered shoots in late winter. Z13–15 H12–10.

SYAGRUS
Queen palm
PALMAE/ARECACEAE

Genus of one species of evergreen palm, grown for its majestic appearance. Requires full light or partial shade and rich, well-drained soil. Water container specimens moderately, less when temperatures are low. Propagate by seed in spring at not less than 75°F (24°C). Red spider mite may be a nuisance.

S. romanzoffiana, syn. *Arecastrum romanzoffianum* (Queen palm). Sturdy, evergreen palm. **H** to 70ft (20m), **S** 20–30ft (6–10m). Has feather-shaped leaves divided into lustrous, green leaflets. Mature trees bear clusters of yellow flowers in summer. Z15 H12–11.

SYCOPSIS
HAMAMELIDACEAE

Genus of evergreen trees and shrubs, grown for their foliage and flowers. Needs a sheltered position in sun or partial shade and fertile, not too dry, peaty soil. Propagate by semiripe cuttings in summer.

S. sinensis. Evergreen, upright shrub. **H** 15ft (5m), **S** 12ft (4m). Leaves are oval, glossy and dark green. Flowers lack petals but have showy, dense clusters of red-tinged, yellow anthers in late winter or early spring. Z11 H12–10.

SYMPHORICARPOS
CAPRIFOLIACEAE

Genus of deciduous shrubs, with inconspicuous, bell-shaped flowers, grown mainly for their clusters of showy, long-persistent fruits. Requires sun or partial shade and fertile soil. Propagate by softwood cuttings in summer or by division in fall. ① The fruits may cause mild stomach upset if ingested; contact with them may irritate skin.

S. albus (Snowberry). Z3–7 H7–1. **var. laevigatus** (illus. p.142) is a vigorous, deciduous, dense shrub, part upright, part arching. **H** and **S** 6ft (2m). Pink flowers, in summer, are followed by large, marblelike, white fruits. Rounded leaves are dark green.

S. x chenaultii 'Hancock'. Deciduous, procumbent, dense shrub. **H** 3ft (1m), **S** 10ft (3m). Has oval, bronze leaves maturing to bright green. White flowers are produced from early to mid-summer. Small, spherical, deep lilac-pink fruits are sparsely borne. Makes excellent groundcover. Z4–7 H7–1.

S. orbiculatus (Coralberry, Indian currant). Deciduous, bushy, dense shrub. **H** and **S** 6ft (2m). Has white or pink flowers in late summer and early fall, followed by spherical, deep purplish-red fruits. Oval leaves are dark green. Does best after a hot summer. Z2–7 H7–1. **'Foliis Variegatis'**, syn. *S. orbiculatus* 'Variegatus', illus. p.160. **'Variegatus'.** See *S. orbiculatus* 'Foliis Variegatis'.

Symphyandra armena. See *Campanula armena.*
Symphyandra pendula. See *Campanula pendula.*
Symphyandra wanneri. See *Campanula wanneri.*

SYMPHYTUM
Comfrey
BORAGINACEAE

Genus of vigorous, coarse perennials, most suitable for wild gardens. Prefers sun or partial shade and moist soil. Propagate by division in spring or by seed in fall, named cultivars by division only. Usually self-seeds. ① The roots and leaves may cause severe discomfort if ingested; contact with foliage may irritate skin.

S. caucasicum, illus. p.227.
S. 'Goldsmith', syn. *S. ibericum* 'Jubilee'. Clump-forming perennial. **H** and **S** 12in (30cm). Has ovate, hairy, dark green leaves with gold and cream markings. Bears pale blue flowers, tinged cream or pink, in spring. Z5–9 H9–5.
S. grandiflorum of gardens. See *S. ibericum.*
S. 'Hidcote Blue'. Clump-forming perennial. **H** 20in (50cm), **S** 24in (60cm). Is similar to *S. ibericum*, but has pale blue flowers. Z4–7.
S. ibericum, syn. *S. grandiflorum*. Clump-forming perennial. **H** 10in (25cm), **S** 24in (60cm). Has lance-shaped, hairy, rich green leaves. Bears one-sided racemes of tubular, creamy flowers in spring. Makes good groundcover. Z3–9 H9–1.
S. ibericum 'Jubilee'. See *S.* 'Goldsmith'.
S. x uplandicum (Russian comfrey). **'Variegatum'**, illus. p.227.

SYMPLOCOS
SYMPLOCACEAE

Genus of evergreen or deciduous trees and shrubs, of which only the species described below is in general cultivation, being grown for its flowers and fruits. Fruits are most prolific when several plants are grown together. Needs full sun and fertile, moist but well-drained soil. Propagate by seed in fall.

S. paniculata (Sapphireberry, Chinese lilac), illus. p.142. Deciduous, bushy shrub or small tree. **H** and **S** 15ft (5m). Has oval, dark green leaves. Panicles of small, fragrant, star-shaped, white flowers, in late spring and early summer, are followed by small, metallic-blue fruits. Z5–8 H8–4.

Synadenium compactum var. rubrum. See *Euphorbia bicompacta var. rubra.*
Synadenium grantii 'Rubrum' of gardens. See *Euphorbia bicompacta var. rubra.*

SYNGONIUM
ARACEAE

Genus of evergreen, woody-stemmed, root climbers, grown for their ornamental foliage. Flowers are seldom produced in cultivation. Needs partial shade and rich, well-drained soil. Water moderately, less in low temperatures. Provide support, ideally with moss poles. Remove young stem tips to promote branching. Propagate by leaf-bud or stem-tip cuttings in summer. ① All parts may cause mild stomach upset if ingested; contact with the sap may irritate skin.

S. auritum, syn. *Philodendron auritum, Philodendron trifoliatum* (Five fingers). Fairly slow-growing, evergreen, woody-stemmed, root climber. **H** 3–6ft (1–2m). Has glossy, rich green leaves divided into 3, sometimes 5, oval leaflets, the central one the largest. Z14–15 H12–10.
S. erythrophyllum. Slow-growing, evergreen, root climber with slender, woody stems. **H** 3ft (1m) or more. Young plants have arrowhead-shaped leaves, flushed purple beneath. Leaves on mature plants have 3 lobes or leaflets and thicker, longer stems. Z14–15 H12–10.
S. hoffmannii. Moderately vigorous, evergreen, woody-stemmed, root climber. **H** 6–10ft (2–3m). Young plants have arrowhead-shaped leaves; mature ones have leaves divided into 3 gray-green leaflets, with silvery-white veins. Z14–15 H12–10.
S. podophyllum, syn. *Nephthytis triphylla*, illus. p.463. **'Trileaf Wonder'**, illus. p.460.

SYNNOTIA
IRIDACEAE

Genus of spring-flowering corms, with fans of lance-shaped leaves, grown for their loose spikes of flowers, each with 6 unequal petals, hooded like a small gladiolus. Needs sun and well-drained soil. Plant in fall. Dry off after flowering. Propagate by seed or offsets in fall.

S. variegata. Spring-flowering corm. **H** 4–14in (10–35cm), **S** 3–4in (8–10cm). Produces erect leaves in basal fan. Long-tubed flowers have upright, purple, upper petals and narrower, pale yellowish-purple, lower ones curving downwards. Z9–10 H10–9. **var. metelerkampiae** produces smaller flowers.

SYNTHYRIS
SCROPHULARIACEAE

Genus of evergreen or deciduous, spring-flowering perennials with gently spreading, rhizomatous rootstocks. Is useful for rock gardens and peat beds. Prefers partial shade and moist soil. Propagate in late spring by seed or division.

S. missurica var. stellata. See *S. stellata.*
S. reniformis. Evergreen, clump-forming perennial. **H** 3–4in (8–10cm), **S** 6in (15cm). Has kidney-shaped to rounded, toothed, dark green leaves and, in spring, short, dense racemes of small, bell-shaped, blue flowers. Z7–9 H9–7.
S. stellata, syn. *S. missurica* var. *stellata*, illus. p.355.

SYRINGA
Lilac
OLEACEAE

Genus of deciduous shrubs and trees, grown for their dense panicles of small, tubular flowers, usually extremely fragrant. Needs sun and deep, fertile, well-drained, preferably alkaline soil. Obtain plants on their own roots, since grafted plants usually sucker freely. Remove flower heads from newly planted lilacs, and dead-head for first few years. Cut out weak shoots in winter and, to maintain shape, prune after flowering. Straggly, old plants may be cut back hard in winter, but the next season's flowers will then be lost. Propagate by softwood cuttings in summer. Leaf miners, leaf spot and lilac blight may be troublesome. See also feature panel p.115.

S. 'Belle de Nancy'. See *S. vulgaris* 'Belle de Nancy'.
S. 'Bellicent'. See *S. x josiflexa* 'Bellicent'.
S. 'Blue Hyacinth'. See *S. x hyacinthiflora* 'Blue Hyacinth'.
S. 'Charles Joly'. See *S. vulgaris* 'Charles Joly'.
S. x chinensis (Rouen lilac). Deciduous, arching shrub. **H** and **S** 12ft (4m). Bears large, arching panicles of fragrant, tubular, single, lilac-purple flowers in late spring. Oval leaves are dark green. Z3–8 H8–1. **'Alba'** has white flowers.
S. 'Clarke's Giant'. See *S. x hyacinthiflora* 'Clarke's Giant'.
S. 'Congo'. See *S. vulgaris* 'Congo'.
S. 'Cora Brandt'. See *S. x hyacinthiflora* 'Cora Brandt'.
S. 'Decaisne'. See *S. vulgaris* 'Decaisne'.
S. emodi (Himalayan lilac). Vigorous, deciduous, upright shrub. **H** 15ft (5m), **S** 12ft (4m). Bears unpleasantly scented, tubular, single, very pale lilac flowers, in large, upright panicles, in early summer. Has large, oval, dark green leaves. Z7–8 H8–7.
S. 'Esther Staley'. See *S. x hyacinthiflora* 'Esther Staley'.
S. 'Fountain'. Vigorous, deciduous, arching, open shrub. **H** 12ft (4m), **S** 15ft (5m). Large, nodding panicles of fragrant, tubular, single, deep pink flowers are produced above large, oval, dark green leaves in early summer. Z7–8 H8–7.
S. x hyacinthiflora 'Blue Hyacinth', syn. *S.* 'Blue Hyacinth' Deciduous, bushy shrub, upright when young, later spreading. **H** and **S** 10ft (3m). Bears large, loose panicles of fragrant, single, pale lilac-blue flowers from mid-spring to early summer. Has broadly heart-shaped, mid-green leaves. Z3–7 H7–1. **'Clarke's Giant'**, syn. *S.* 'Clarke's Giant', **H** and **S** 15ft (5m), has lavender flowers, mauve-pink within, opening from mauve-pink buds from mid-to late spring. Has dark green leaves. **'Cora Brandt'**, syn. *S.* 'Cora Brandt' produces double, white flowers in large open panicles. **'Esther Staley'**, syn. *S.* 'Esther Staley' is vigorous, with broadly conical panicles of red buds opening to lilac-pink flowers.
S. 'Isabella'. See *S. x prestoniae* 'Isabella'.
S. 'Jan van Tol'. See *S. vulgaris* 'Jan van Tol'.
S. x josiflexa 'Bellicent', syn. *S.* 'Bellicent'. Deciduous, upright, then arching shrub. **H** 12ft (4m), **S** 15ft (5m). Large panicles of fragrant, tubular, single, clear pink flowers are borne above oval, dark green leaves in late spring and early summer.
S. 'Katherine Havemeyer'. See *S. vulgaris* 'Katherine Havemeyer'.
S. komarowii subsp. reflexa, illus. p.115. Vigorous, upright shrub. **H** and **S** 13ft (4m). Sturdy stems bear elliptic–oblong, dark green leaves. Rich purple-pink flowers are borne in slender, nodding panicles in late spring and early summer. Z6–7 H7–6.
S. 'Madame Antoine Buchner'. See *S. vulgaris* 'Madame Antoine Buchner'.
S. 'Madame F. Morel'. See *S. vulgaris* 'Madame F. Morel'.
S. 'Madame Florent Stepman'. See *S. vulgaris* 'Madame Florent Stepman'.
S. 'Madame Lemoine'. See *S. vulgaris* 'Madame Lemoine'.
S. 'Maréchal Foch'. See *S. vulgaris*

S

'Maréchal Foch'.

S. 'Masséna'. See *S. vulgaris* 'Masséna'.

S. 'Maud Notcutt'. See *S. vulgaris* 'Maud Notcutt'.

S. meyeri 'Palibin', syn. *S. palibiniana, S. velutina,* illus. p.115. Slow-growing, deciduous, bushy, dense shrub. **H** 5–6ft (1.5–2m), **S** 5ft (1.5m). Has small, oval, deep green leaves. Produces dense panicles of fragrant, tubular, single, lilac-pink flowers in late spring and early summer. Z4–7 H7–1.

S. 'Michel Buchner'. See *S. vulgaris* 'Michel Buchner'.

S. microphylla. See *S. pubescens* subsp. *microphylla.*

S. 'Monge'. See *S. vulgaris* 'Monge'.

S. 'Mrs. Edward Harding'. See *S. vulgaris* 'Mrs. Edward Harding'.

S. palibiniana of gardens. See *S. meyeri* 'Palibin'.

S. 'Paul Thirion'. See *S. vulgaris* 'Paul Thirion'.

S. x persica (Persian lilac), illus. p.115. Deciduous, bushy, dense shrub. **H** and **S** 6ft (2m). Produces small, dense panicles of fragrant, tubular, purple flowers in late spring. Leaves are narrow, pointed and dark green. Z3–7 H7–1. **'Alba'** (illus. p.115) has white flowers.

S. 'Président Grévy'. See *S. vulgaris* 'Président Grévy'.

S. x prestoniae 'Isabella', syn. *S.* 'Isabella'. Vigorous, deciduous, upright shrub. **H** and **S** 12ft (4m). Has large, nodding panicles of fragrant, tubular, single, lilac-purple flowers, almost white within, in early summer, and large, oval, dark green leaves.

S. 'Primrose'. See *S. vulgaris* 'Primrose'.

S. pubescens subsp. microphylla, syn. *S. microphylla.* Deciduous, bushy shrub. **H** and **S** 6ft (2m). Small panicles of very fragrant, tubular, single, pink flowers are borne in early summer, and often again in fall, amid oval, mid-green leaves. **'Superba'** (illus. p.115) has rose-pink flowers. After initial flowering, it blooms irregularly until fall. **subsp. patula 'Miss Kim'** (illus. p.115) bears purple flowers maturing to bluish-white.

S. reticulata. Deciduous, broadly conical tree or shrub. **H** 30ft (10m), **S** 20ft (6m). Large panicles of fragrant, tubular, single, creamy-white flowers are borne above oval, taper-pointed, bright green leaves from early to mid-summer. Z3–8 H8–3.

S. 'Souvenir de Louis Späth'. See *S. vulgaris* 'Andenken an Ludwig Späth'.

S. velutina of gardens. See *S. meyeri* 'Palibin'.

S. vulgaris. Z3–8 H8–3. **'Andenken an Ludwig Späth',** syn. *S.* 'Souvenir de Louis Späth' (illus. p.115) is a deciduous, upright, then spreading shrub. **H** and **S** 15ft (5m). Long, slender panicles of fragrant, tubular, single, deep purplish-red flowers are borne profusely above heart-shaped, dark green leaves in late spring. Z4–8 H8–1. **'Belle de Nancy',** syn. *S.* 'Belle de Nancy' has large, dense panicles of double, mauve-pink flowers opening from purple-red buds. Z4–8 H8–1. **'Charles Joly',** syn. *S.* 'Charles Joly', **H** and **S** 10ft (3m), bears deep purple-red flowers from mid-spring to early summer. Z4–8 H8–1. **'Congo',** syn. *S.* 'Congo' bears large panicles of single, deep lilac-purple flowers, purplish-red in bud, in spring. Z4–8 H8–1. **'Decaisne',** syn. *S.* 'Decaisne' is compact, with masses of single, dark blue flowers that are shaded purple, and mid-green leaves. Z4–8 H8–1. **'Firmament'** (illus. p.115) bears masses of lilac-blue flowers in mid-spring. Z4–8 H8–1. **'Jan van Tol',** syn. *S.* 'Jan van Tol' bears long, semipendent panicles of single, narrow-petaled, pure white flowers. Z4–8 H8–1. **'Katherine Havemeyer',** syn. *S.* 'Katherine Havemeyer' (illus. p.115) has double, lavender-purple, then lavender-pink flowers in dense, conical panicles. Z4–8 H8–1. **'Madame Antoine Buchner',** syn. *S.* 'Madame Antoine Buchner' bears long, narrow panicles of deep purple-red buds, which open to double, pinkish-mauve flowers, fading with age. Z4–8 H8–1. **'Madame Florent Stepman',** syn. *S.* 'Madame Florent Stepman', illus. p.113. **'Madame F. Morel',** syn. *S.* 'Madame F. Morel' produces large panicles of single, light violet-purple flowers that are purple in bud. Z4–8 H8–1. **'Madame Lemoine',** syn. *S.* 'Madame Lemoine' (illus. p.115) bears compact panicles of large, double, white flowers. Z4–8 H8–1. **'Maréchal Foch',** syn. *S.* 'Maréchal Foch' has broad, open panicles of very large, single, carmine-pink flowers. Z4–8 H8–1. **'Masséna',** syn. *S.* 'Masséna' bears loose panicles of large, deep red-purple flowers. Z4–8 H8–1. **'Maud Notcutt',** syn. *S.* 'Maud Notcutt' produces large panicles of single, pure white flowers. Z4–8 H8–1. **'Michel Buchner',** syn. *S.* 'Michel Buchner' has large panicles of double, pink-lilac flowers, with white eyes. Z4–8 H8–1. **'Monge',** syn. *S.* 'Monge' produces masses of very large, single, deep purple-red flowers. Z4–8 H8–1. **'Mrs. Edward Harding',** syn. *S.* 'Mrs. Edward Harding' has large panicles of double or semidouble, purple-red flowers that fade to pink. Z4–8 H8–1. **'Paul Thirion',** syn. *S.* 'Paul Thirion' produces double lilac-pink flowers that open from deep purple-red buds. Z4–8 H8–1. **'Président Grévy',** syn. *S.* 'Président Grévy' bears very large panicles of double, lilac-blue flowers that open from red-violet buds. Z4–8 H8–1. **'Primrose',** syn. *S.* 'Primrose' has small, dense panicles of pale yellow flowers. Z4–8 H8–1.

S. yunnanensis. Deciduous, upright shrub. **H** 10ft (3m), **S** to 10ft (3m). In early summer, large, oval, pointed, dark green leaves set off slender panicles of 4-petaled, pale pink or white flowers. Z6–7 H7–6.

SYZYGIUM

MYRTACEAE

Genus of evergreen shrubs and trees, grown for their overall appearance. Prefers full light and fertile, well-drained soil. Water container plants freely when in full growth, moderately at other times. Is very tolerant of pruning, but is best grown naturally. Propagate by seed in spring or by semiripe cuttings in summer.

S. paniculatum, syn. *Eugenia australis, Eugenia paniculata,* illus. p.450.

T

TABEBUIA

BIGNONIACEAE

Genus of deciduous or evergreen, mainly spring-flowering trees, grown for their flowers and for shade. Requires full light and fertile, well-drained but not dry soil. Pot-grown plants are unlikely to flower. Pruning, other than shaping while young in fall, is not needed. Propagate by seed or air-layering in spring or by semiripe cuttings in summer.

T. chrysotricha, illus. p.452.

T. donnell-smithii. See *Cybistax donnell-smithii.*

T. pentaphylla of gardens. See *T. rosea.*

T. rosea, syn. *T. pentaphylla* (Pink trumpet tree). Fast-growing, evergreen, rounded tree, deciduous in cool climates. **H** and **S** 50ft (15m) or more. Leaves are divided into 5 oval leaflets. Produces trumpet-shaped, rose- to lavender-pink or white flowers, with yellow throats, in terminal clusters in spring. Z14–15 H12–10.

TACCA

TACCACEAE/DIOSCOREACEAE

Genus of perennials with rhizomes, grown for their curious flowers. Needs a fairly humid atmosphere, partial shade and peaty soil. Water sparingly during resting period in winter. Propagate by division or seed, if available, in spring.

T. chantrieri (Bat flower, Cat's whiskers, Devil flower). Clump-forming, rhizomatous perennial. **H** and **S** 12in (30cm). Narrowly oblong, stalked, arching leaves are 18in (45cm) or more long. In summer produces flower umbels with green or purplish bracts on stems to 24in (60cm) long. Individual flowers are nodding, bell-shaped, 6-petaled and green, turning purple with long, pendent, maroon to purple threads. Z14–15 H12–10.

T. leontopetaloides (East Indian arrowroot, South Sea arrowroot). Clump-forming, rhizomatous perennial. **H** and **S** 1$\frac{1}{2}$ft (45cm). Long-stalked, green leaves, to 3ft (1m) long, are deeply 3-lobed, each lobe also divided. In summer, stems to 3ft (1m) long bear flower umbels of 4–12 purple or brown bracts and 20–40 small, 6-petaled, yellow or purplish-green flowers, with long, purple to brown threads. Rhizomes yield edible starch. Z14–15 H12–10.

Tacitus bellus. See *Graptopetalum bellum.*

Tacsonia mollissima. See *Passiflora mollissima.*

Tacsonia van-volxemii. See *Passiflora antioquiensis.*

TAGETES

Marigold

COMPOSITAE/ASTERACEAE

Genus of annuals that flower continuously throughout summer and until the fall frosts. Is useful as bedding plants and for edging. Needs sun and fertile, well-drained soil. Deadhead to ensure a long flowering period. Propagate by seed sown under glass in mid-spring. Is prone to slugs, snails and botrytis. The African marigolds are excellent for formal bedding, whereas the French, Afro-French and Signet marigolds are more suitable for the edge of a mixed border. All are good in containers and provide long-lasting cut flowers. ☺ Contact with the foliage may aggravate skin allergies. Four main hybrid groups are grown.

African marigolds (African Group) Compact annuals, derived from *T. erecta,* with angular, hairless stems and pinnate, sparsely glandular leaves, 2–4in (5–10cm) long, each with 11–17 narrowly lance-shaped, pointed, sharply toothed leaflets, to 2in (5cm) long. Large, densely double, pompon-like, terminal flower heads, usually to 5in (12cm) across, each with 5–8 or more ray-florets and numerous orange to yellow disc-florets, are produced from late spring to fall. **S** to 18in (45cm).

French marigolds (French Group) Compact annuals, derived from *T. patula,* with hairless, purple-tinged stems and pinnate leaves, to 4in (10cm) long, with lance-shaped to narrowly lance-shaped, toothed leaflets, to 1¼in (3cm) long. Solitary, usually double flower heads, typically to 2in (5cm) across, with few to many red-brown, yellow, orange or parti-colored ray-florets and usually several disc-florets, are borne singly or in cyme-like inflorescences from late spring to fall. **S** to 12in (30cm).

Afro-French marigolds (Afro-French Group) Bushy annuals, derived from crosses of *T. erecta* and *T. patula,* with angular to rounded stems, branched and sometimes stained purple, and pinnate leaves, 2–5in (5–13cm) long, with lance-shaped leaflets, to 2in (5cm) long. Numerous small, single or double, yellow or orange flower heads, usually 1–2½in (2.5–6cm) across, often marked red-brown, are borne singly or in cyme-like inflorescences from late spring to fall. **S** 12–16in (30–40cm).

Signet marigolds (Signet Group) Upright annuals, derived from *T. tenuifolia,* with cylindrical, simple or many-branched stems and pinnate leaves, 2–5in (5–13cm) long, with narrowly lance-shaped, toothed leaflets, to 3⁄4in (2cm) long. Many single flower heads, usually to 1in (2.5cm) across, with yellow or orange florets (few ray-florets and several disc-florets), are borne in cyme-like inflorescences from late spring to fall. **S** to 16in (40cm).

T. Antigua Series. Compact African marigolds. **H** to 12in (30cm). Bear orange, lemon-yellow, golden-yellow or primrose-yellow flower heads from late spring to early fall. H12–1.

T. Beaux Series. Afro-French marigolds. **H** 14in (35cm). Bear double flower heads of rich golden-yellow, orange with red splash, or copper-red, from late spring to early fall. H12–1.

T. Bonanza Series. French marigolds. **H** 12in (30cm). In summer have double flowers in deep orange-mahogany with gold margins, golden orange-mahogany or orange-yellow-mahogany. H12–1.

T. Boy Series. Compact French marigolds. **H** 8–12in (20–30cm). Have divided, mid-green leaves. Produce double, crested flower heads in shades of orange, yellow, gold, mahogany-red, and yellow with mahogany-brown centers from late spring to summer. H12–1. [Orange], illus. p.324.

T. 'Cinnabar', illus. p.308.

T. Disco Series. French marigolds. H 8–10in (20–25cm). Single, weather-resistant flower heads in range of colors, including yellow, golden-yellow with mahogany markings, golden-red and red-orange, are borne from late spring to early fall. H12–1.

T. erecta (African marigold). Fast-growing, upright, bushy annual. H 1–3ft (30cm–1m), S 1–1½ft (30–45cm). Has very deeply divided, aromatic, glossy, deep green leaves. Daisylike, double flower heads are produced in summer and early fall. H12–1.

T. Gem Series. Signet marigolds. H to 9in (23cm). Produce flower heads in lemon-yellow, deep orange, or bright orange with darker markings. H12–1. **'Lemon Gem'** has lemon-yellow flower heads.
'Tangerine Gem', illus. p.326.

T. Gold Coins Series, illus. p.320.

T. 'Honeycomb'. French marigold. H 10in (25cm). Produces crested, double, yellow- and reddish-orange flower heads. H12–1.

T. Lady Series. African marigolds. H 16–18in (40–45cm). Produce orange, primrose-yellow, yellow or golden-yellow flower heads from late spring to early fall. H12–1.

T. Marvel Series. Compact African marigolds. H 18in (45cm). Produce densely double flower heads in gold, orange, yellow, lemon-yellow, or in formula mixture of colors, from late spring to early fall. H12–1.

T. Mischief Series. French marigolds. H to 12in (30cm) or more. Have single flower heads in mahogany-red, yellow or golden-yellow, with some bicolors, from late spring to early fall. H12–1.

T. 'Naughty Marietta', illus. p.322.

T. patula (French marigold). Fast-growing, bushy annual. H and S to 1ft (30cm). Has deeply divided, aromatic, deep green leaves. Single or carnation-like, double flower heads, in shades of yellow, orange, red or mahogany, are borne in summer and early fall. H12–1.

T. Safari Series 'Safari Tangerine'. French marigold. H 8–10in (20–25cm). Has double, broad-petaled, rich tangerine-orange flower heads from late spring to early fall. H12–1.

T. 'Vanilla'. African marigold. H to 14in (35cm). Has creamy-white flower heads from late spring to early fall. H12–1.

T. Voyager Series. Compact African marigolds. H 12–14in (30–35cm). Large, yellow or orange flower heads are borne from late spring to early fall. H12–1.

T. Zenith Series. Afro-French marigolds. H 12in (30cm). Have flower heads in yellow, golden-yellow, lemon-yellow, red or orange, from late spring to early fall. H12–1.

Talbotia elegans. See *Vellozia elegans*.

TALINUM
Fameflower

PORTULACACEAE

Genus of summer-flowering perennials, some of which are evergreen, grown for their flowers and succulent foliage. Is useful for rock gardens, troughs and alpine houses and as pot plants. Needs sun and

---

well-drained, not too dry, gritty soil. Propagate by seed in fall.

T. okanoganense, syn. *T. sediforme, Phemeranthus sediformis.* Cushion- or mat-forming, prostrate perennial. H to 1½in (4cm), S to 4in (10cm). Succulent stems produce tufts of cylindrical, succulent, grayish-green leaves. Tiny, cup-shaped, white flowers are borne in summer. Is excellent for a trough or alpine house. Z6–8 H8–6.

T. sediforme. See *T. okanoganense*.

TAMARINDUS

LEGUMINOSAE/CAESALPINIACEAE

Genus of one species of evergreen tree, grown for its edible fruits and overall appearance as well as for shade. Needs full light and well-drained soil. Propagate by seed or air-layering in spring.

T. indica (Tamarind). Slow-growing, evergreen, rounded tree. H and S to 80ft (25m). Leaves are divided into 10–15 pairs of oblong to elliptic, bright green leaflets. Produces profuse racemes of asymmetric, 5-petaled, red-veined, pale yellow flowers, in summer, followed by long, brownish pods containing edible but acidic pulp. Z5–9 H9–5.

TAMARIX
Tamarisk

TAMARICACEAE

Genus of deciduous or evergreen shrubs and trees, grown for their foliage, habit and abundant racemes of small flowers. In mild areas, is very wind-resistant and thrives in exposed, coastal positions, making excellent hedges. Requires sun and fertile, well-drained soil. Restrict growth by cutting back in spring; trim hedges at the same time. Propagate by semiripe cuttings in summer or by hardwood cuttings in winter.

T. gallica. Deciduous, spreading shrub or tree. H 12ft (4m), S 20ft (6m). Purple, young shoots are clothed with tiny, scalelike, blue-gray leaves. Star-shaped, pink flowers are borne in slender racemes in summer. Z6–10 H10–5.

T. pentandra. See *T. ramosissima*.
T. ramosissima, syn. *T. pentandra*, illus. p.114.

TANACETUM

COMPOSITAE/ASTERACEAE

Genus of perennials, some of which are evergreen, often with aromatic foliage, grown for their daisylike flower heads. Needs sun and fertile, well-drained soil. Propagate by division in spring. *T. parthenium* self-seeds freely. ① Contact with the foliage may aggravate skin allergies.

T. argenteum, syn. *Achillea argentea*, illus. p.346.

T. coccineum, syn. *Chrysanthemum coccineum, Pyrethrum coccineum, Pyrethrum roseum* (Painted daisy, Pyrethrum). Z5–9 H9–5. **'Brenda'**, syn. *Pyrethrum* 'Brenda' is an erect perennial, H 24in (60cm), S 18in (45cm) or more. Has somewhat aromatic, feathery leaves. Single, magenta-pink flower heads are borne in late spring and early summer. **'Eileen May Robinson'**, illus. p.232. **'James Kelway'** has deep crimson flower heads aging to pink.

T. densum subsp. amani, syn. *Chrysanthemum densum*, illus. p.347.

T. haradjanii, syn. *Chrysanthemum haradjanii*. Evergreen, mat-forming, woody-based perennial with a taproot. H and S 9–15in (23–38cm). Has broadly lance-shaped, much-divided, silvery-gray leaves and, in summer, terminal clusters of bright yellow flower heads. Is useful for a rock garden or an alpine house. Z7–10 H10–5.

T. parthenium, syn. *Chrysanthemum parthenium, Pyrethrum parthenium*, illus. p.300. **'Aureum'** is a short-lived, bushy perennial, grown as an annual. H and S 8–18in (20–45cm). Has oval, lobed, aromatic, green-gold leaves and, in summer and early fall, white flower heads.

TANAKAEA
Japanese foam flower

SAXIFRAGACEAE

Genus of one species of evergreen, spreading perennial, grown for its foliage and flowers. Is suitable for rock gardens and peat beds. Needs partial shade and well-drained, peaty, sandy soil. Propagate by runners in spring.

T. radicans. Evergreen, dense, basal-rosetted perennial. H 2½–3in (6–8cm), S 8in (20cm). Has narrowly oval to heart-shaped, leathery, mid- to dark green leaves. Bears small panicles of tiny, outward-facing, star-shaped, white flowers in late spring. Z6–8 H8–6.

TAPEINOCHILOS

COSTACEAE/ZINGIBERACEAE

Genus of mostly evergreen perennials, grown for their colorful, leaflike bracts. Needs high humidity, partial shade and rich soil. Is not easy to grow successfully in pots. Propagate by division in spring. Red spider mite may be a problem with container-grown plants.

T. ananassae. Evergreen, tufted perennial. H to 6ft (2m), S 2½ft (75cm). Non-flowering stems are erect and unbranched, with narrowly oval, long-pointed leaves, to 6in (15cm) long. Flowering stems are leafless, 3ft (1m) or more long, and, in summer, bear ovoid, dense spikes, 6in (15cm) or more long, of small, tubular, yellow flowers. Showy, recurved, hard, scarlet bracts enclose and almost hide flowers. Z15 H12–10.

TAXODIUM

TAXODIACEAE

See also CONIFERS.
T. distichum, illus. p.99.

TAXUS
Yew

TAXACEAE

① All parts (but not the seed coating) are highly toxic if ingested. See also CONIFERS.

T. baccata (English yew). Slow-growing conifer with a broadly conical, later dome-shaped crown. H 30–50ft (10–15m), S 15–30ft (5–10m). Needlelike, flattened leaves are dark green. Female plants bear cup-shaped, fleshy, bright red fruits; only the red part, not the seed, is edible. Will

---

regrow if cut back. The following forms are H 20–30ft (6–10m), S 15–25ft (5–8m) unless otherwise stated. Z7–8 H8–7.

'Adpressa' is a shrubby, female form with short, broad leaves. **'Aurea'**. See *T. baccata* Aurea Group. **Aurea Group,** syn. *T. baccata* 'Aurea' have golden-yellow foliage. **'Dovastoniana'** is spreading, with weeping branchlets. **'Dovastonii Aurea'** (illus. p.105) is similar to *T.b.* 'Dovastoniana', but has golden shoots and yellow-margined leaves. **'Fastigiata'**, illus. p.101. **'Fastigiata Aurea'** is similar to *T.b.* 'Fastigiata', but has gold-variegated leaves. **'Lutea'**, illus. p.102. **'Repandens'**, H 2ft (60cm), S 15ft (5m), is a spreading form. **'Semperaurea'**, H 10ft (3m), S 15ft (5m), has ascending branches with dense, golden foliage.

T. cuspidata, illus. p.104. **'Aurescens'** is a spreading, bushy, dwarf conifer. H 1ft (30cm), S 3ft (1m). Is hardier than *T. baccata* forms. Needlelike, flattened leaves are deep golden-yellow in their first year and mature to dark green. Z4–7 H7–1. **'Capitata'**, H 30ft (10m), S 6ft (2m), is upright in habit. Z5–7 H7–5. **'Densa'**, H 4ft (1.2m), S 20ft (6m), is a female form with short, erect shoots. Z5–7 H7–5.

T. x media. Dense conifer that is very variably shaped. H and S 10–20ft (3–6m). Has needlelike, flattened leaves, spreading either side of olive-green shoots. Leaves are stiff, broad and widen abruptly at base. Fruits are similar to those of *T. baccata*. Z5–7 H7–5.
'Brownii', H 8ft (2.5m), S 11ft (3.5m), is a dense, globose form with dark green foliage. **'Densiformis'**, H 6–10ft (2–3m), is dense and rounded, with masses of shoots that have bright green leaves. **'Hicksii'**, H to 20ft (6m), is columnar and has ascending branches. Male and female forms exist. **'Hillii'**, H and S 10ft (3m), is a broadly conical to rounded, dense bush with glossy, green leaves. **'Wardii'**, H 6ft (2m), S 20ft (6m), is a flat, globose, female form.

TECOMA
syn. TECOMARIA

BIGNONIACEAE

Genus of mainly evergreen shrubs and trees, grown for their flowers from spring to fall. Prefers full light and moist but well-drained soil. Water container specimens moderately, hardly at all in winter. May be pruned annually after flowering to maintain as a shrub. Propagate by seed in spring or by semiripe cuttings in summer. Red spider mite may be troublesome.

T. australis. See *Pandorea pandorana*.
T. capensis, syn. *Bignonia capensis, Tecomaria capensis* (Cape honeysuckle). Evergreen, scrambling climber, shrublike when young. H 6–10ft (2–3m). Leaves are divided into 5–9 rounded, toothed, glossy, dark green leaflets. Tubular, orange-red flowers are borne in short spikes mainly in spring–summer. Z12–15 H12–10. **'Aurea'**, illus. p.464.
T. grandiflora. See *Campsis grandiflora*.
T. ricasoliana. See *Podranea ricasoliana*.
T. stans, syn. *Bignonia stans, Stenolobium stans*, illus. p.452.

TECOMANTHE

BIGNONIACEAE

Genus of evergreen, twining climbers, grown for their flowers. Needs partial shade and rich, well-drained soil. Water freely when in full growth, less at other times. Provide stems with support. If necessary, thin out crowded stems in spring. Propagate by seed in spring or by semiripe cuttings in summer.

T. speciosa. Strong-growing, evergreen, twining climber. **H** to 30ft (10m) or more. Has leaves divided into 3 or 5 oval leaflets. Bears dense clusters of foxglove-like, fleshy-textured, green-tinged, cream flowers in fall. Z14–15 H12–10.

Tecomaria capensis. See *Tecoma capensis*.
Tecomaria. See *Tecoma*.

TECOPHILAEA

LILIACEAE/TECOPHILAEACEAE

Genus of spring-flowering corms, rare in cultivation and extinct in the wild, grown for their crocus-like, brilliantly colored flowers. Because of rarity usually grown in a cold greenhouse or cold frame. Requires sun and well-drained soil. Water in winter and spring. Keep corms dry, but not sunbaked, from early summer to fall, then replant. Propagate in fall by seed or offsets.

T. cyanocrocus, illus. p.420.
'Leichtlinii'. See *T. cyanocrocus* var. *leichtlinii*. **var. leichtlinii,** syn. *T. cyanocrocus* 'Leichtlinii', illus. p.420.

Telanthophora grandiflora. See *Senecio grandifolius*.

TELEKIA

COMPOSITAE/ASTERACEAE

Genus of summer-flowering perennials, grown for their bold foliage and large flower heads. Needs partial shade and moist soil. Propagate by division in spring or by seed in fall.

T. speciosa, syn. *Buphthalmum speciosum*. Upright, spreading perennial. **H** 4–5ft (1.2–1.5m), **S** 3–4ft (1–1.2m). Mid-green leaves are heart-shaped at base of plant, oval on stems. In late summer, branched stems bear large, daisylike, rich golden-yellow flower heads. Is ideal for a pool side or woodland. Z5–8 H8–5.

TELLIMA

Fringe cups

SAXIFRAGACEAE

Genus of one species of semievergreen, late spring-flowering perennial. Makes good groundcover and is ideal for cool, semi-shaded woodland gardens and beneath shrubs in sunny borders. Prefers partial shade and moist but well-drained soil. Propagate by division in spring or by seed in fall.

T. grandiflora. Semievergreen, clump-forming perennial. **H** and **S** 24in (60cm). Has heart-shaped, toothed, hairy, purple-tinted, bright green leaves. Bears racemes of small, bell-shaped, fringed, cream flowers, well above foliage, in late spring. Z4–8 H8–1. **Rubra Group,** syn. *T.*

grandiflora 'Purpurea', *T. grandiflora* 'Rubra Group', illus. p.279. **'Purpurea'.** See *T. grandiflora* Rubra Group.

TELOPEA

Waratah

PROTEACEAE

Genus of evergreen trees and shrubs, grown mainly for their flower heads. Requires full sun or partial shade and rich, moist but well-drained, neutral to acidic soil. Water container plants freely when in full growth, moderately at other times. Propagate by seed in spring or by layering in winter.

T. speciosissima, illus. p.137.
T. truncata, illus. p.123.

TEMPLETONIA

LEGUMINOSAE/PAPILIONACEAE

Genus of evergreen shrubs, grown for their flowers. Prefers full light and well-drained, alkaline soil. Water container specimens moderately, less in winter. Propagate by seed in spring or by semiripe cuttings in summer.

T. retusa (Cockies' tongues, Coral bush, Flamebush). Evergreen, erect, irregularly branched shrub. **H** 6ft (2m), **S** 3–5ft (1–1.5m). Has oval to elliptic, leathery, bluish-green leaves. Pealike, red flowers, sometimes pink or cream, are produced in spring–summer. Z14–15 H12–10.

TERMINALIA

COMBRETACEAE

Genus of evergreen trees and shrubs, grown for their overall appearance, edible seeds (nuts) and for shade. Requires full light and well-drained soil. Water container specimens moderately, scarcely at all when temperatures are low. Propagate by seed in spring.

T. catappa (Indian almond). Evergreen, rounded tree. **H** and **S** 50ft (15m) or more. Has broadly oval, lustrous, green leaves at stem tips. Small, greenish-white flowers, in spring, are followed by flattened ovoid, keeled, green to red fruits, each with edible seed. Z14–15 H12–10.

TERNSTROEMIA

THEACEAE

Genus of evergreen trees and shrubs, grown for their overall appearance. Requires full sun or partial shade and rich, well-drained, neutral to acidic soil. Water container specimens copiously when in full growth, moderately at other times. Propagate by seed when ripe or in spring or by semiripe cuttings in late summer.

T. gymnanthera, syn. *T. japonica*. Evergreen, rounded, dense shrub. **H** and **S** 6ft (2m). Oval leaves are lustrous, mid- to deep green. In summer, solitary, pendent, 5-petaled, white flowers are borne from leaf axils. Pea-sized, berry-like, bright red fruits develop in fall. Z8–10 H10–8. Leaves of **'Variegata'** are white-bordered with pink tinge.
T. japonica. See *T. gymnanthera*.

Testudinaria elephantipes. See *Dioscorea elephantipes*.

TETRACENTRON

TETRACENTRACEAE

Genus of one species of deciduous tree, grown for its foliage and catkins. Needs sun or partial shade and fertile, well-drained soil. Propagate by seed in fall.

T. sinense. Deciduous, spreading tree. **H** and **S** 30ft (10m) or more. Bears oval, finely toothed, dark green leaves and long, slender, yellow catkins in early summer. Z6–8 H8–6.

TETRADIUM

SYN. EUODIA, EVODIA

Bee tree

RUTACEAE

Genus of deciduous trees, grown for their foliage, late flowers and fruits. Needs full sun and fertile, well-drained soil. Propagate by softwood cuttings in summer, by seed in fall or by root cuttings in late winter.

T. daniellii, syn. *Euodia hupehensis*. Deciduous, spreading tree. **H** and **S** 50ft (15m). Ashlike, dark green leaves, divided into 5–11 oval to oblong leaflets, turn yellow in fall. Has small, fragrant, 5-petaled, white flower clusters in early fall, followed by beaked, red fruits. Z5–8 H8–5.

TETRANEMA

SCROPHULARIACEAE

Genus of shrubby, evergreen perennials, grown for their trumpet-shaped flowers in summer. Needs partial shade and well-drained soil; avoid waterlogging and a humid atmosphere. Propagate by division or seed, if available, in spring.

T. mexicanum. See *T. roseum*.
T. roseum, syn. *T. mexicanum*, illus. p.472.

TETRAPANAX

ARALIACEAE

Genus of one species of evergreen, summer- to fall-flowering shrub, grown for its foliage. Requires full sun or partial shade and rich, moist but well-drained soil. Water container specimens freely, less in winter. Leggy stems may be cut back to near ground level in winter. Propagate by suckers or seed in early spring. Severe frosts can cause stems to die back but will regrow in spring.

T. papyrifer, syn. *Fatsia papyrifera*, illus. p.120.

TETRASTIGMA

VITACEAE

Genus of evergreen, woody-stemmed, tendril climbers, grown for their foliage. Needs partial shade and fertile, well-drained soil. Water freely while in growth, less in low temperatures. Support stems and cut out crowded stems in spring. Propagate by layering in spring or by semiripe cuttings in summer.

T. voinierianum, syn. *Cissus voinieriana*, illus. p.463.

TEUCRIUM

LABIATAE/LAMIACEAE

Genus of evergreen or deciduous shrubs, subshrubs and perennials, grown for their flowers, foliage (sometimes aromatic) or habit. Needs full sun and well-drained soil.

Propagate shrubs and subshrubs by softwood or semiripe cuttings in summer, perennials by seed or division in spring.

T. aroanium. Evergreen, procumbent, much-branched subshrub. **H** 1in (2.5cm), **S** 4–6in (10–15cm). Has white-haired twigs and oblong to oval, slightly hairy leaves, which are densely hairy below. In summer produces whorls of small, tubular, 2-lipped, purple flowers. Is good for a trough. Z7–10 H10–7.
T. fruticans (Shrubby germander, Tree germander). Z8–9 H9–8. **'Azureum'** is an evergreen, arching shrub. **H** 6ft (2m), **S** 12ft (4m). Has oval, aromatic, gray-green leaves, white beneath. Bears tubular, 2-lipped, deep blue flowers, with prominent stamens, in summer. Cut out dead wood in spring.
T. polium, illus. p.366.

THALIA

MARANTACEAE

Genus of deciduous, perennial, marginal water plants, grown for their foliage and flowers. Needs an open, sunny position in up to 18in (45cm) depth of water. Some species tolerate cool water. Remove fading foliage regularly. Propagate in spring by division or seed.

T. dealbata. Deciduous, perennial, marginal water plant. **H** 5ft (1.5m), **S** 2ft (60cm). Oval, long-stalked, blue-green leaves have mealy, white covering. Spikes of narrowly tubular, violet flowers are borne in summer. Tolerates cool water. Z6–11 H12–6.
T. geniculata. Deciduous, perennial, marginal water plant. **H** 6ft (2m), **S** 2ft (60cm). Has oval, long-stalked, blue-green leaves and, in summer, spikes of narrowly tubular, violet flowers. Needs a warm pond. Z8–11 H12–7.

THALICTRUM

Meadow rue

RANUNCULACEAE

Genus of perennials, grown for their divided foliage and fluffy flower heads. Flowers lack petals, but each has prominent tufts of stamens and 4 or 5 sepals, which rapidly fall. Does well at edges of woodland gardens. Tall species and cultivars make excellent foils in borders for perennials with bolder leaves and flowers. Requires sun or partial shade and well-drained soil; some species prefer cool, moist conditions. Propagate by seed when fresh, in fall, or by division in spring.

T. angustifolium. See *T. lucidum*.
T. aquilegiifolium, illus. p.239. **'Thundercloud',** illus. p.233. **'White Cloud'** is a clump-forming perennial. **H** 3–4ft (1–1.2m), **S** 1ft (30cm). Has finely divided, grayish-green leaves. In summer produces terminal sprays of fluffy, white flowers. Z5–9 H9–5.
T. chelidonii. Clump-forming perennial. **H** 3–5ft (1–1.5m), **S** 2ft (60cm). Has finely divided, mid-green leaves and, in summer, produces panicles of fluffy, 4- or 5-sepaled, mauve flowers. Prefers cool soil that does not dry out. Z5–9 H9–5.
T. delavayi, syn. *T. dipterocarpum* (Yunnan meadow rue). Clump-forming perennial. **H** 5–6ft (1.5–2m), **S** 2ft (60cm).

T

Has divided, mid-green leaves. Bears large panicles of nodding, lilac flowers, with 4 or 5 sepals and prominent, yellow stamens, from mid- to late summer. Z4–7 H7–1. **'Hewitt's Double'**, illus. p.220.
T. diffusiflorum. Clump-forming perennial. H 3ft (1m), S 1–2ft (30–60cm). Has much-divided, mid-green, basal leaves. Slender stems produce large sprays of drooping, mauve flowers in summer. Prefers cool, moist soil. Z5–9 H9–5.
T. dipterocarpum of gardens. See **T. delavayi**.
T. 'Elin', illus. p.218.
T. flavum (Yellow meadow rue). Clump-forming perennial. H 4–5ft (1.2m–1.5m), S 2ft (60cm). Has much-divided, glaucous blue-green leaves. From mid- to late summer produces clusters of fluffy, pale yellow flowers on slender stems. Z3–10 H10–9. **'Illuminator'** is a pale yellow cultivar with bright green foliage.
T. kiusianum. Mat-forming perennial with short runners. H 3in (8cm), S 6in (15cm). Has small, fernlike, 3-lobed leaves and, throughout summer, loose clusters of tiny, purple flowers. Is excellent in a peat bed, rock garden, trough or alpine house. Is difficult to grow in hot, dry areas. Prefers shade and moist, sandy, peaty soil. Z4–8 H8–1.
T. lucidum, syn. T. angustifolium. Clump-forming perennial. H 3–4ft (1–1.2m), S 20in (50cm). Has glossy leaves divided into numerous leaflets. Sturdy stems bear loose panicles of fluffy, greenish-yellow flowers in summer. Z5–9 H9–5.
T. orientale. Spreading perennial with short runners. H 6in (15cm), S 8in (20cm). Leaves are fernlike with oval to rounded, lobed leaflets. Bears small, saucer-shaped, blue-mauve to violet flowers, with yellow stamens and large sepals, in late spring. Z5–9 H9–1.

THAMNOCALAMUS
POACEAE

See also GRASSES, BAMBOOS, RUSHES and SEDGES.
T. crassinodus 'Kew Beauty', illus. p.286.
T. falconeri. See Himalayacalamus falconeri.
T. murieliae. See Fargesia murieliae.
T. spathaceus of gardens. See Fargesia murieliae.

THELOCACTUS
CACTACEAE

Genus of spherical to columnar, perennial cacti with ribbed or tuberculate stems. Elongated areoles in crowns produce funnel-shaped flowers. Requires sun and well-drained soil. Propagate by seed in spring or summer.
T. bicolor, illus. p.484.
T. leucacanthus. Clump-forming, perennial cactus. H 4in (10cm), S 12in (30cm). Spherical to columnar, green stem has 8–13 tuberculate ribs. Areoles bear up to 20 short, golden spines and yellow flowers, 2in (5cm) across, in summer. Z12–15 H12–10.
T. macdowellii, syn. Echinomastus macdowellii. Spherical, perennial cactus. H and S 6in (15cm). Has tuberculate, dark green stem densely covered with

white spines. Violet-red flowers, 1½in (4cm) across, are produced in spring–summer. Z12–15 H12–10.
T. setispinus, syn. Ferocactus setispinus, illus. p.495.

THELYPTERIS
THELYPTERIDACEAE

Genus of deciduous ferns. Prefers sun or semi-shade and moist or very moist soil. Remove fading fronds regularly. Propagate by division in spring.
T. oreopteris. See Oreopteris limbosperma.
T. palustris, illus. p.291.
T. phegopteris. See Phegopteris connectilis.

THERMOPSIS
LEGUMINOSAE/PAPILIONACEAE

Genus of summer-flowering perennials. Prefers sun and rich, light soil. Propagate by division in spring or by seed in fall.
T. caroliniana. See T. villosa.
T. montana. See T. rhombifolia.
T. rhombifolia, syn. T. montana, illus. p.243.
T. villosa, syn. T. caroliniana. Straggling perennial. H 3ft (1m) or more, S 2ft (60cm). Bears racemes of pealike, yellow flowers in late summer. Glaucous leaves are divided into 3 oval leaflets. Z4–8 H9–1.

THESPESIA
MALVACEAE

Genus of evergreen perennials, shrubs and trees, grown for their flowers. Requires full light and well-drained soil. Water container plants freely when in full growth, less at other times. Prune in early spring to maintain as a shrub. Propagate by seed in spring or by semiripe cuttings in summer. Whitefly and red spider mite may be a nuisance.
T. populnea (Portia tree). Evergreen tree, bushy when young, thinning with age. H 40ft (12m) or more, S 10–20ft (3–6m). Leaves are heart-shaped. Intermittently, or all year round if warm enough, produces cup-shaped, maroon-eyed, yellow flowers that age to purple. Grows well by the sea. Z14–15 H12–10.

THEVETIA
APOCYNACEAE

Genus of evergreen shrubs and trees, grown for their flowers from winter to summer. Is related to Frangipani. Needs full light and well-drained soil. Water container specimens moderately, less in winter. Young stems may be tip-pruned in winter to promote branching. Propagate by seed in spring or by semiripe cuttings in summer. ① The seeds are highly toxic if ingested, and the milky sap that exudes from broken stems may irritate skin and cause severe discomfort if ingested.
T. neriifolia. See T. peruviana.
T. peruviana, syn. T. neriifolia (Yellow oleander). Evergreen, erect tree. H 6–25ft (2–8m), S 3–10ft (1–3m). Has narrowly lance-shaped, rich green leaves and funnel-shaped, yellow or orange-yellow flowers from winter to summer. Z14–15 H12–10.

THLADIANTHA
CUCURBITACEAE

Genus of herbaceous or deciduous, tendril climbers, grown for their bell-shaped, yellow flowers and oval to heart-shaped, mid-green leaves. Requires a sheltered position in full sun and fertile, well-drained soil. Propagate by seed in spring or by division in early spring.
T. dubia, illus. p.206.

THLASPI
CRUCIFERAE/BRASSICACEAE

Genus of annuals and perennials, some of which are evergreen, grown for their flowers. Small plants may flower themselves to death, so remove buds for 2 years, to encourage a large plant. Is difficult to grow at low altitudes and may require frequent renewal from seed. Is good for screes and troughs. Needs sun and moist but well-drained soil. Propagate by seed in fall.
T. alpestre of gardens. See T. alpinum.
T. alpinum, syn. T. alpestre (Alpine penny-cress). Evergreen, mat-forming perennial. H 2in (5cm), S 4in (10cm). Has small, oval, mid-green leaves. Produces racemes of small, 4-petaled, white flowers in spring. Z6–9 H9–6.
T. bulbosum. Clump-forming, tuberous perennial. H 3in (8cm), S 6–8in (15–20cm). Bears broadly oval, glaucous leaves and, in summer, racemes of 4-petaled, dark violet flowers. Is suitable for a rock garden. Z8–10 H10–8.
T. cepaeifolium subsp. rotundifolium, syn. T. rotundifolium, illus. p.352.
T. macrophyllum. See Pachyphragma macrophyllum.
T. rotundifolium. See T. cepaeifolium subsp. rotundifolium.

THUJA
Arborvitae
CUPRESSACEAE

① Contact with the foliage may aggravate skin allergies. See also CONIFERS.
T. koraiensis (Korean arborvitae). Upright conifer, sometimes sprawling and shrubby. H 10–30ft (3–10m), S 10–15ft (3–5m). Scalelike foliage is bright green or yellow-green above, glaucous silver beneath, and smells of almonds when crushed. ① Contact with the foliage may aggravate skin allergies. Z5–7 H7–5.
T. occidentalis (American arborvitae, Eastern arborvitae, White cedar). Slow-growing conifer with a narrow crown. H 50ft (15m), S 10–15ft (3–5m). Has orange-brown bark and flat sprays of scalelike, yellowish-green leaves, pale or grayish-green beneath, smelling of apples when crushed. Ovoid cones are yellow-green, ripening to brown. Z2–7 H7–1. **'Caespitosa'**, H 12in (30cm), S 16in (40cm), is a cushion-shaped, dwarf cultivar. **'Fastigiata'**, H to 50ft (15m), S to 15ft (5m), is broadly columnar, with erect, spreading branches and light green leaves. **'Filiformis'**, H 5ft (1.5m), S 5–6ft (1.5–2m), forms a mound with pendent, whiplike shoots. **'Hetz Midget'**, H and S 20in (50cm), growing only 1in (2.5cm) each year, is a globose, dwarf form with blue-green foliage. **'Holmstrup'**,

H 10–12ft (3–4m), S 3ft (1m), is slow-growing, dense and conical, with rich green foliage. **'Little Champion'**, H and S 20in (50cm) or more, is a globose, dwarf form, conical when young, with foliage turning brown in winter. **'Lutea Nana'**, H 6ft (2m), S 3–6ft (1–2m), is a dwarf form with golden-yellow foliage. **'Rheingold'**, H 10–12ft (3–4m), S 6–12ft (2–4m), is slow-growing, with golden-yellow foliage that becomes bronze in winter. **'Smaragd'**, H 6–8ft (2–2.5m), S 2–2½ft (60–75cm), is slow-growing and conical, with erect sprays of bright green leaves. **'Spiralis'**, H 30–50ft (10–15m), S 6–10ft (2–3m), has foliage in twisted, fernlike sprays. **'Woodwardii'**, H 8ft (2.5m), S to 15ft (5m), is very slow-growing and globose, with mid-green foliage.
T. orientalis. See Platycladus orientalis.
T. plicata (Western red cedar). Fast-growing, conical conifer that has great, curving branches low down. H 70–100ft (20–30m), S 15–25ft (5–8m), greater if lower branches self-layer. Has red-brown bark, scalelike, glossy, dark green leaves, which have pineapple aroma when crushed, and erect, ovoid, green cones, ripening to brown. Z6–8 H8–6. **'Atrovirens'** has darker green foliage. **'Aurea'** has golden-yellow foliage. **'Collyer's Gold'**, H to 6ft (2m), S 3ft (1m), is a dwarf form with yellow, young foliage turning light green. **'Cuprea'**, H 3ft (1m), S 2½–3ft (75cm–1m), is a conical shrub with copper- to bronze-yellow leaves. **'Hillieri'**, H and S to 3ft (1m), is a slow-growing, dense, rounded, dwarf shrub with mosslike, rich green foliage. **'Stoneham Gold'** (illus. p.105), H 3–6ft (1–2m), S 3ft (1m), is a conical, dwarf form with bright gold foliage. **'Zebrina'**, H 50ft (15m), has leaves banded with yellowish-white.

THUJOPSIS
CUPRESSACEAE

See also CONIFERS.
T. dolabrata (Hiba arborvitae). Conical or bushy conifer with a mass of stems. H 30–70ft (10–20m), S 25–30ft (8–10m). Produces heavy, flat sprays of scalelike leaves, glossy, bright green above, silvery-white beneath. Small, rounded cones are blue-gray. Z5–7 H7–5. **'Variegata'**, illus. p.104.

THUNBERGIA
ACANTHACEAE

Genus of annual or mainly evergreen, perennial, twining climbers, perennials and shrubs, grown for their flowers. Needs sun or partial shade and fertile, well-drained soil. Water freely when in growth, less at other times. Requires support. Thin out crowded stems in early spring. Propagate by seed in spring or from softwood or semiripe cuttings in summer.
T. alata, illus. p.207.
T. coccinea. Evergreen, woody-stemmed, perennial, twining climber with narrowly oval leaves. H 20ft (6m) or more. Pendent racemes of tubular, scarlet flowers are produced in winter–spring. Z14–15 H12–10.
T. gibsonii. See T. gregorii.
T. grandiflora (Blue trumpet vine, Sky vine). Evergreen, woody-stemmed,

perennial, twining climber. **H** 20–30ft (6–10m). Oval leaves have a few toothlike lobes. In summer has trumpet-shaped, pale to deep violet-blue flowers. Z14–15 H12–10.

T. gregorii, syn. *T. gibsonii*. Evergreen, woody-stemmed, twining climber, usually grown as an annual. **H** to 10ft (3m). Triangular to oval leaves have winged stalks. Glowing orange flowers are borne in summer. Z13–15 H12–10.

T. mysorensis, illus. p.464.

THYMUS
Thyme
LABIATAE/LAMIACEAE

Genus of evergreen, mat-forming and dome-shaped shrubs, subshrubs and woody-based perennials, grown for their aromatic leaves. Is useful for growing on banks and in rock gardens, troughs and paving. Commonly grown as a culinary herb, it is also suitable for containers. Requires sun and moist but well-drained soil. Propagate by seed in spring or by softwood or semiripe cuttings in summer.

T. azoricus. See *T. caespititius*.

T. 'Bressingham', illus. p.365.

T. caespititius, syn. *T. azoricus, T. cilicicus*, illus. p.366.

T. carnosus. Evergreen, spreading shrub. **H** and **S** 8in (20cm). Has tiny, narrowly oval, aromatic leaves. Erect flowering stems bear whorls of small, 2-lipped, white flowers in summer. Needs a sheltered position. Z5–9 H9–5.

T. cilicicus. See *T. caespititius*.

T. x citriodorus 'Silver Queen'. Evergreen, rounded shrub. **H** to 12in (30cm), **S** to 10in (25cm). Has narrowly oval-diamond-shaped to lance-shaped, more or less hairless, aromatic, silvery-green leaves, with creamy-white markings. In summer produces 2-lipped, pale lavender-pink flowers in terminal clusters. Z6–9 H9–6.

T. herba-barona (Caraway thyme, Herb baron). Evergreen subshrub. **H** in flower 2–4in (5–10cm), **S** to 8in (20cm). Forms a loose mat of tiny, caraway-scented, dark green leaves. In summer, small, lilac flowers are borne in terminal clusters. Z6–9 H9–6.

T. leucotrichus of gardens. See *T.* 'Peter Davis'.

T. micans. See *T. caespititius*.

T. 'Peter Davis', syn. *T. leucotrichus*, illus. p.367.

T. 'Porlock'. Evergreen, dome-shaped perennial. **H** 3in (8cm), **S** 8in (20cm). Thin stems are covered in small, rounded to oval, very aromatic, glossy, green leaves. In summer produces clusters of small, 2-lipped, pink flowers. Z4–8 H8–1.

T. pseudolanuginosus (Woolly thyme). Evergreen, prostrate shrub. **H** 1–2in (2.5–5cm), **S** 8in (20cm) or more. Has dense mats of very hairy stems bearing tiny, aromatic, gray leaves. Produces 2-lipped, pinkish-lilac flowers in leaf axils in summer. Z4–9 H9–1.

T. pulegioides 'Aureus'. Evergreen, spreading shrub. **H** 4in (10cm), **S** 4–10in (10–25cm). Tiny, rounded to oval, golden-yellow leaves are very fragrant when crushed. Produces terminal clusters of small, 2-lipped, lilac flowers in summer. Cut back in spring. Z4–8 H8–1.

T. serpyllum (Mother of thyme, Serpolet, Wild thyme). Evergreen, mat-forming subshrub. **H** 10in (25cm), **S** 18in (45cm). Finely hairy, trailing stems bear linear to elliptic to oval, mid-green leaves. Whorls of two-lipped, purple flowers are borne in summer. Z4–9 H9–1. **'Annie Hall'**, **H** 2in (5cm), **S** 8in (20cm), has pale purple-pink flowers and light green leaves. **'Elfin'**, **H** 2in (5cm), **S** 4in (10cm), produces emerald-green leaves in dense hummocks; occasionally bears purple flowers.

TIARELLA
Foam flower
SAXIFRAGACEAE

Genus of perennials, some of which are evergreen, that spread by runners. Is suitable as groundcover and for woodland gardens. Tolerates deep shade and prefers moist but well-drained soil. Propagate by division in spring.

T. cordifolia, illus. p.333. **var. collina**. See *T. wherryi*.

T. wherryi, syn. *T. cordifolia* var. *collina*. Slow-growing, clump-forming perennial. **H** 4in (10cm), **S** 6in (15cm). Triangular, lobed, hairy, pale green, basal leaves are stained dark red, with heart-shaped bases. Bears racemes of tiny, star-shaped, soft pink or white flowers from late spring to early summer. Z3–7 H7–1.

TIBOUCHINA
MELASTOMATACEAE

Genus of evergreen perennials, subshrubs, shrubs and scandent climbers, grown for their flowers and leaves. Prefers full sun and fertile, well-drained, neutral to acidic soil. Water container specimens freely when in full growth, moderately at other times. Cut back flowered stems, to 2 pairs of buds each, in spring. Tip-prune young plants to promote branching. Propagate by greenwood or semiripe cuttings in late spring or summer.

T. semidecandra of gardens. See *T. urvilleana*.

T. urvilleana, syn. *T. semidecandra*, illus. p.457.

TIGRIDIA
Peacock flower, Tiger flower
IRIDACEAE

Genus of summer-flowering bulbs, grown for their highly colorful but short-lived flowers, rather iris-like in shape, with 3 large, outer petals. Needs sun and well-drained soil, with ample water in summer. Plant in spring. Lift in fall; then partially dry bulbs and store in peat or sand at 46–54°F (8–12°C). Propagate by seed in spring.

T. pavonia, illus. p.413.

TILIA
Linden
TILIACEAE

Genus of deciduous trees, grown for their small, fragrant, cup-shaped flowers and stately habit. Flowers attract bees, but are toxic to them in some cases. Requires sun or partial shade and fertile, well-drained soil. Propagate species by seed in fall, selected forms and hybrids by grafting in

late summer. Except for *T. x euchlora*, trees are usually attacked by aphids, which cover growth and ground beneath with sticky honeydew. ① The nectar of *T.* 'Petiolaris' and *T. tomentosa* may be toxic, especially to bumblebees.

T. americana (American linden, Basswood). Deciduous, spreading tree. **H** 80ft (25m), **S** 40ft (12m). Has large, rounded, sharply toothed, glossy, dark green leaves. Small, yellowish-white flowers are borne in summer. Z2–8 H8–1.

T. cordata (Littleleaf linden). Deciduous, spreading tree. **H** 100ft (30m), **S** 40ft (12m). In mid-summer has small, glossy, dark green leaves and small, yellowish-white flowers. Z3–8 H8–1. **'Greenspire'**, **S** 25ft (8m), is very vigorous and pyramidal in habit, even when young. Z4–8 H8–1. **'Rancho'**, illus. p.75.

T. x euchlora (Crimean linden). Deciduous, spreading tree with lower branches that droop with age. **H** 70ft (20m), **S** 30ft (10m). Rounded, very glossy, deep green leaves turn yellow in fall. Bears small, yellowish-white flowers, toxic to bees, in summer. Is relatively pest-free. Z3–7 H7–1.

T. x europaea, syn. *T. x vulgaris* (European linden). Vigorous, deciduous, spreading tree. **H** 120ft (35m), **S** 50ft (15m). Trunk develops many burs. Has rounded, dark green leaves. Small, yellowish-white flowers that are toxic to bees are produced in summer. Periodically remove shoots from burrs at base. Z4–7 H7–1.

T. henryana. Deciduous, spreading tree. **H** and **S** 30ft (10m). Broadly heart-shaped, glossy, bright green leaves, fringed with long teeth, are often tinged red when young. Has masses of small, creamy-white flowers in fall. Z6–8 H8–6.

T. mongolica (Mongolian linden). Deciduous, spreading tree. **H** 50ft (15m), **S** 40ft (12m). Young shoots are red. Heart-shaped, coarsely toothed, glossy, dark green leaves turn yellow in fall. Small, yellowish-white flowers are borne in summer. Z3–7 H7–1.

T. oliveri, illus. p.63.

T. 'Petiolaris', syn. *T. petiolaris*, illus. p.64.

T. platyphyllos (Large-leaved linden). Deciduous, spreading tree. **H** 100ft (30m), **S** 70ft (20m). Has rounded, dark green leaves and small, dull yellowish-white flowers in mid-summer. Z2–6 H6–1. **'Prince's Street'** is upright, with bright red shoots in winter. Z5–8 H8–5. **'Rubra'**, illus. p.63.

T. tomentosa (European white linden, Silver linden). Deciduous, spreading tree. **H** 80ft (25m), **S** 70ft (20m). Leaves are large, rounded, sharply toothed, dark green above and white beneath. Very fragrant, small, dull white flowers, toxic to bees, are borne in late summer. Z6–9 H9–6.

T. x vulgaris. See *T. x europaea*.

TILLANDSIA
Air plant
BROMELIACEAE

Genus of evergreen, epiphytic perennials, often rosette-forming, some with branching stems and spirally arranged leaves, all grown for their flowers or overall appearance. Requires partial shade and a rooting medium of equal parts rich soil and either sphagnum moss or bark or plastic chips used for orchid culture. May also

be grown on slabs of bark or sections of trees. Using soft water, water moderately in summer, sparingly at other times; spray plants grown on bark or tree sections with water several times a week from mid-spring to mid-fall. Propagate by offsets or division during spring. See also feature panel p.471.

T. argentea, illus. p.471. Evergreen, basal-rosetted, epiphytic perennial. **H** and **S** 4–6in (10–15cm). Very narrow, almost threadlike leaves, covered with white scales, are produced in dense, near-spherical rosettes, with fleshy, bulblike bases. In summer, small, loose racemes of tubular, red flowers are produced. Z13–15 H12–1.

T. caput-medusae. Evergreen, basal-rosetted, epiphytic perennial. **H** and **S** 6in (15cm) or more. Linear, channeled, twisted and rolled, incurved leaves, covered in gray scales, develop in loose rosettes that have hollow, bulblike bases. In summer, spikes of tubular, violet-blue flowers are produced above foliage. Z13–15 H12–1.

T. cyanea. Evergreen, basal-rosetted, epiphytic perennial. **H** and **S** 10in (25cm). Forms dense rosettes of linear, pointed, channeled, arching, usually deep green leaves. In summer, broadly oval, bladelike spikes of pansy-shaped, deep purple-blue flowers, emerging from pink or red bracts, are produced among foliage. Z13–15 H12–1.

T. fasciculata (Wild pineapple). Evergreen, basal-rosetted, epiphytic perennial. **H** and **S** 12in (30cm) or more. Has dense rosettes of narrowly triangular, tapering, arching, mid-green leaves. In summer, flat spikes of tubular, purple-blue flowers emerge from red or reddish-yellow bracts, just above leaf tips. Bracts require strong light to develop reddish tones. Z13–15 H12–1.

T. ionantha (Sky plant). Evergreen, clump-forming, basal-rosetted, epiphytic perennial. **H** and **S** 5in (12cm). Linear, incurved, arching leaves, covered in gray scales, are produced in dense rosettes; inner leaves turn red at flowering time. Spikes of tubular, violet-blue flowers, emerging in summer from narrow, white bracts, are borne just above foliage. Z13–15 H12–1.

T. lindenii (Blue-flowered torch), illus. p.471. Evergreen, basal-rosetted, epiphytic perennial. **H** and **S** 16in (40cm). Linear, pointed, channeled, arching, mid-green leaves, with red-brown lines, form dense rosettes. In summer produces bladelike spikes of widely pansy-shaped, deep blue flowers, emerging from sometimes pink-tinted, green bracts, which are borne just above leaves. Z13–15 H12–1.

T. recurvata (Ball moss). Evergreen, basal-rosetted, epiphytic perennial. **H** and **S** 4–8in (10–20cm). Has long, loose, stem-like rosettes of linear, arching to recurved leaves, densely covered in silvery-gray scales. In summer produces short, dense spikes of small, tubular, pale blue or pale green flowers, which appear above leaves. Z13–15 H12–1.

T. stricta, illus. p.471. Evergreen, clump-forming, basal-rosetted, epiphytic perennial. **H** and **S** 8–12in (20–30cm). Narrowly triangular, tapering, arching, mid-green leaves, usually with gray scales, are produced in dense rosettes. Large, tubular, blue flowers emerge from drooping, conelike spikes of bright red bracts, usually in summer. Z13–15 H12–1.

T. usneoides (Spanish moss). Evergreen, pendent, epiphytic perennial. **H** 3ft (1m) or more, **S** 4–8in (10–20cm). Slender, branched, drooping stems bear linear, incurved leaves, densely covered in silvery-white scales. Inconspicuous, tubular, greenish-yellow or pale blue flowers, hidden among foliage, are produced in summer. Z9–15 H12–1.

TIPUANA
Tipu tree

LEGUMINOSAE/PAPILIONACEAE

Genus of one species of evergreen, spring-flowering tree, grown for its flowers and overall appearance when mature and for shade. In certain conditions, may be deciduous. Container-grown plants will not produce flowers. Requires full light and fertile, well-drained soil. Propagate by seed in spring.

T. speciosa. See *T. tipu*.
T. tipu, syn. *T. speciosa* (Brazilian rosewood, Pride of Bolivia, Tipu tree). Fast-growing, mainly evergreen, bushy tree. **H** 30ft (10m), **S** 25–30ft (8–10m). Leaves are divided into 11–25 oval leaflets. Produces pealike, orange-yellow flowers, 1¼in (3cm) wide, in spring, followed by short, woody, winged, brownish pods in fall–winter. Z13–15 H12–10.

TITANOPSIS

AIZOACEAE

Genus of basal-rosetted, perennial succulents eventually forming small, dense clumps. Produces fleshy, triangular leaves, narrow at stems and expanding to straight tips. Requires sun and well-drained soil. Propagate by seed in spring or summer.

T. calcarea, illus. p.496.
T. schwantesii (White jewel plant). Clump-forming, basal-rosetted, perennial succulent. **H** 1¼in (3cm), **S** 4in (10cm). Has triangular, gray-blue leaves, covered with small, wartlike, yellow-brown tubercles. Produces daisylike, light yellow flowers, ¾in (2cm) wide, in summer–fall. Z13–15 H12–10.

TITHONIA
Mexican sunflower

COMPOSITAE/ASTERACEAE

Genus of annuals. Needs sun and fertile, well-drained soil. Provide support and deadhead regularly. Propagate by seed sown under glass in late winter or early spring.

T. rotundifolia (Mexican sunflower). Z10–11 H12–1. **'Torch'**, illus. p.324.

TOLMIEA

SAXIFRAGACEAE

Genus of one species of perennial that is sometimes semievergreen and is grown as groundcover. Is suitable for cool woodland gardens. Needs partial or full shade and well-drained, neutral to acidic soil. Propagate by division in spring or by seed in fall.

T. menziesii (Piggyback plant, Thousand mothers, Youth-on-age). Mat-forming perennial, sometimes semievergreen. **H** 18–24in (45–60cm), **S** 12in (30cm) or more. Young plantlets develop where ivy-shaped, mid-green leaves join stem. Produces spikes of tiny, nodding, tubular to bell-shaped, green and chocolate-brown flowers in spring. Z6–9 H9–6.

TOLPIS

COMPOSITAE/ASTERACEAE

Genus of summer-flowering annuals and perennials. Needs sun and fertile, well-drained soil. Propagate by seed in spring.

T. barbata. Moderately fast-growing, upright, branching annual. **H** 1½–2ft (45–60cm), **S** 1ft (30cm). Has lance-shaped, toothed, mid-green leaves. Daisylike, bright yellow flower heads, 1in (2.5cm) or more wide, with maroon centers, are produced in summer. H9–1.

TOONA

MELIACEAE

Genus of deciduous trees, grown for their foliage, fall color and flowers. Prefers full sun and requires fertile, well-drained soil. Propagate by seed in fall or by root cuttings in winter.

T. sinensis, syn. *Cedrela sinensis*, illus. p.73.

TORENIA
Wishbone flower

SCROPHULARIACEAE

Genus of annuals and perennials. Is often grown as summer bedding. Needs a partially shaded, sheltered position and fertile, well-drained soil. Pinch out growing shoots of young plants to encourage a bushy habit. Propagate by seed sown under glass in early spring.

T. fournieri (Bluewings, Wishbone flower). Moderately fast-growing, erect, branching annual. **H** 12in (30cm), **S** 8in (20cm). Has toothed, light green leaves. Dark blue-purple flowers, paler and yellow within, are borne in summer and early fall. Z12–13 H6–1.
T. Moon Series Blue Moon ('Dantmoon'). Dense, trailing perennial, grown as an annual. **H** 6–8in (15–20cm), **S** 18in (45cm). Has oval, toothed, dark green leaves. In summer–fall bears tubular, flared, 2-tone blue flowers, with dark throats. Z10–11 H10–1.

TORREYA
Nutmeg yew

TAXACEAE

See also CONIFERS.
T. californica, illus. p.101.

Tovara virginiana 'Painter's Palette'. See *Persicaria virginiana* 'Painter's Palette'.

TOWNSENDIA

COMPOSITAE/ASTERACEAE

Genus of evergreen, short-lived perennials and biennials, grown for their daisylike flower. Is suitable for alpine houses as dislikes winter wet. Needs sun and moist soil. Propagate by seed in fall.

T. grandiflora, illus. p.369.
T. parryi. Evergreen, basal-rosetted, short-lived perennial. **H** 3–6in (7–15cm), **S** 2in (5cm). In late spring produces daisylike, lavender or violet-blue flower heads, with bright yellow centers, above spoon-shaped leaves. Z4–7 H7–1.

Toxicodendron succedaneum. See *Rhus succedanea*.
Toxicodendron vernicifluum. See *Rhus verniciflua*.

TRACHELIUM
SYN. DIOSPHAERA

CAMPANULACEAE

Genus of small perennials, useful for rock gardens and mixed borders. Some are good in alpine houses. Flowers of some species are ideal for cutting. Protect under cover in winter since they resent damp conditions. Needs a sunny, sheltered position and fertile, very well-drained soil; *T. asperuloides* prefers lime-rich soil. Propagate by seed in early or mid-spring or by softwood cuttings in spring.

T. asperuloides, syn. *Diosphaera asperuloides*, illus. p.369.
T. caeruleum, illus. p.313.

TRACHELOSPERMUM

APOCYNACEAE

Genus of evergreen, woody-stemmed, twining climbers with stems that exude milky sap when cut. Needs sun or partial shade and well-drained soil. Propagate by seed in spring, by layering in summer or by semiripe cuttings in late summer or fall.

T. asiaticum, illus. p.196.
T. jasminoides, illus. p.195.

TRACHYCARPUS

PALMAE/ARECACEAE

Genus of evergreen, summer-flowering palms, grown for their habit, foliage and flowers. Prefers a position sheltered from strong, cold winds, especially when young and requires full sun and fertile, well-drained soil. Propagate by seed in fall or spring.

T. fortunei, illus. p.80.

TRACHYMENE

UMBELLIFERAE/APIACEAE

Genus of summer-flowering annuals. Needs a sunny, sheltered position and fertile, well-drained soil. Support with sticks. Propagate by seed sown under glass in early spring.

T. coerulea, syn. *Didiscus coeruleus* (Blue lace flower). Moderately fast-growing, upright, branching annual. **H** 18in (45cm), **S** 8in (20cm). Has deeply divided, pale green leaves. Spherical heads, to 2in (5cm) wide, of tiny, blue flowers are produced in summer. Is excellent for cut flowers. H12–6.

TRADESCANTIA

COMMELINACEAE

Genus of perennials, some of which are evergreen, grown for their flowers or ornamental foliage. Hardy species are useful in shady gardens. Needs sun or partial shade and fertile, moist to dry soil. Cut back trailing species when they become straggly. Propagate hardy species by division or seed in fall or spring, frost-tender species by tip cuttings year-round. ⓘ Contact with the foliage may cause skin irritation.

T. albiflora. See *T. fluminensis*.
T. Andersoniana Group. 'J.C. Weguelin', syn. *T.* 'J.C. Weguelin' Clump-

forming perennial. **H** to 2ft (60cm), **S** 1½ft (45cm). Has narrowly lance-shaped, fleshy, green leaves, 6–12in (15–30cm) long. In summer produces clusters of 3-petaled, lavender-blue flowers, surrounded by 2 leaflike bracts. **'Osprey'**, syn. *T.* 'Osprey', illus. p.263. **'Purple Dome'**, syn. *T.* 'Purple Dome', illus. p.269.
T. blossfeldiana. See *T. cerinthoides*.
T. cerinthoides, syn. *T. blossfeldiana*. Evergreen, creeping perennial. **H** 2in (5cm), **S** indefinite. Narrowly oval, fleshy, stem-clasping leaves, to 4in (10cm) long, are glossy, dark green above, purple with long, white hairs below. Intermittently produces clusters of tiny, pink flowers, with white centers, surrounded by 2 leaflike bracts. Z14–15 H12–10. Leaves of **'Variegata'** have longitudinal, cream stripes.
T. fluminensis, syn. *T. albiflora* (Wandering Jew). Evergreen perennial with trailing, rooting stems. **H** 2in (5cm), **S** to 24in (60cm) or more. Oval, fleshy leaves, 1½in (4cm) long, that clasp the stem, are glossy and green above, sometimes tinged purple below. Intermittently has clusters of tiny, white flowers enclosed in 2 leaflike bracts. Z13–15 H12–1. **'Albovittata'**, illus. p.468. **'Variegata'** has irregularly striped creamy-white leaves. Z14–15 H12–1.
T. 'J.C. Weguelin'. See *T.* 'J.C. Weguelin' Andersoniana Group.
T. navicularis. See *Callisia navicularis*.
T. 'Osprey'. See *T.* 'Osprey' Andersoniana Group.
T. pallida 'Purpurea', syn. *T. pallida* 'Purple Heart', *Setcreasea purpurea*, illus. p.310. **'Purple Heart'.** See *T. pallida* 'Purpurea'.
T. pexata. See *T. sillamontana*.
T. 'Purple Dome'. See *T.* 'Purple Dome' Andersoniana Group.
T. purpusii. See *T. zebrina* 'Purpusii'.
T. sillamontana, syn. *T. pexata, T. velutina*, illus. p.469.
T. spathacea, syn. *Rhoeo discolor, Rhoeo spathacea* (Moses-in-the-cradle, Three-men-in-a-boat). Evergreen, clump-forming, rosetted perennial. **H** 20in (50cm), **S** 10in (25cm). Lance-shaped, fleshy leaves, to 12in (30cm) long, are green above, purple below. Bears tiny, white flowers, enclosed in boat-shaped, leaflike bracts, year-round. Z11–12 H12–1. **'Vittata'** has leaves striped longitudinally with pale yellow.
T. velutina. See *T. sillamontana*.
T. zebrina, syn. *Zebrina pendula*, illus. p.469. **'Purpusii'**, syn. *T. purpusii* is a strong-growing, evergreen, trailing or mat-forming perennial. **H** 4in (10cm), **S** indefinite. Has elliptic, purple-tinged, bluish-green leaves and tiny, shallowly cup-shaped, pink flowers. **'Quadricolor'** has leaves striped green, pink, red and white.

TRAPA
Water chestnut

TRAPACEAE/LYTHRACEAE

Genus of deciduous, perennial and annual, floating water plants, grown for their foliage and flowers. Requires sun. Propagate in spring from seed gathered in fall and stored frost-free, in water or damp sand.

T. natans, illus. p.442.

Trichocereus bridgesii. See *Echinopsis lageniformis*.

T

Trichocereus candicans. See *Echinopsis candicans.*

Trichocereus spachianus. See *Echinopsis spachiana.*

TRICHODIADEMA
AIZOACEAE

Genus of bushy, perennial succulents with woody or tuberous roots and cylindrical to semicylindrical leaves. Needs sun and well-drained soil. Propagate by seed or stem cuttings in spring or summer.

T. densum. Tufted, perennial succulent. **H** 4in (10cm), **S** 8in (20cm). Cylindrical, pale green leaves, $^1/_2$–$^3/_4$in (1–2cm) long, are tipped with clusters of white bristles. Roots and prostrate, green stem are both fleshy and form caudex. Stem tip bears daisylike, cerise-pink flower heads, $1^1/_4$in (3cm) across, in summer. Z13–15 H12–1.

T. mirabile, illus. p.481.

TRICHOSANTHES
CUCURBITACEAE

Genus of annual and evergreen, perennial, tendril climbers, grown for their fruits and overall appearance. Needs full sun or partial shade and rich soil. Water freely in growing season, less in cool weather. Provide support. Propagate by seed in spring at not less than 70°F (21°C).

T. anguina. See *T. cucumerina* var. *anguina.*

T. cucumerina* var. *anguina, syn. *T. anguina* (Serpent cucumber, Snake gourd). Erect to spreading, annual, tendril climber. **H** 10–15ft (3–5m). Has broadly oval to almost triangular, sometimes shallowly 3- to 5-lobed, mid- to pale green leaves. In summer produces 5-petaled, white flowers, with heavily fringed petals; females are solitary, the males in racemes. Cylindrical, green-and-white striped fruit, often twisted or coiled, ripens to dull orange. Z14–15 H12–10.

Trichosma suavis. See *Eria coronaria.*
Tricuspidaria lanceolata. See *Crinodendron hookerianum.*

TRICYRTIS
Toad lily
LILIACEAE/CONVALLARIACEAE

Genus of late summer- and fall-flowering, rhizomatous perennials. Needs partial shade and rich, moist soil. Propagate by division in spring or by seed in fall.

T. formosana, syn. *T. stolonifera,* illus. p.247.

T. hirta. Upright, rhizomatous perennial. **H** 1–3ft (30cm–1m), **S** 1$^1/_2$ft (45cm). In late summer and early fall, clusters of large, open bell-shaped, white-spotted, purple flowers are produced from axils of uppermost leaves. Narrowly oval, hairy, dark green leaves clasp stems. Z4–9 H9–1.
var. *alba,* illus. p.277.

T. macrantha. Upright, rhizomatous perennial. **H** and **S** 24in (60cm). In early fall has loose sheaves of open bell-shaped, deep primrose-yellow flowers, spotted light chocolate, at tips of arching stems. Small, oval leaves are dark green. Z8–9 H9–8.

T. stolonifera. See *T. formosana.*

TRIFOLIUM
Clover
LEGUMINOSAE/PAPILIONACEAE

Genus of annuals, biennials and perennials, some of which are semievergreen, grown for their rounded, usually 3-lobed leaves and heads of pealike flowers. Some species are useful in rock gardens or on banks, others in agriculture. Many are invasive. Needs sun and well-drained soil. Propagate by division in spring or by seed in fall. Self-seeds readily.

***T. repens* 'Purpurascens',** illus. p.375.

TRILLIUM
Trinity flower, Wakerobin, Wood lily
LILIACEAE/TRILLIACEAE

Genus of rhizomatous perennials with petals, sepals and leaves that are all borne in whorls of 3. Is excellent for woodland gardens, and also shaded borders and rockeries. Prefers partial shade and fertile, moist but well-drained, neutral to acidic soil. Propagate by division after foliage has died down in summer or by seed in fall.

T. cernuum (Nodding trillium). Clump-forming perennial. **H** 12–18in (30–45cm), **S** 12in (30cm). Has nodding, maroon-centered, white flowers borne in spring beneath luxuriant, 3-parted, mid-green leaves. Z3–7 H8–1.

T. chloropetalum, illus. p.255.
T. erectum, illus. p.260.
T. grandiflorum, illus. p.255. **'Flore Pleno'** is a clump-forming perennial. **H** 15in (38cm), **S** 12in (30cm). Large, solitary, double, pure white flowers, borne in spring, turn pink with age. Has large, broadly oval, dark green leaves.

T. nivale (Dwarf white wood lily, Snow trillium). Early spring-flowering, rhizomatous perennial. **H** 3in (7cm), **S** 4in (10cm). Whorls of 3 oval leaves are produced at same time as outward-facing, slightly nodding, white flowers, with 3 narrowly oval petals. Thrives in a trough or alpine house. Is difficult to grow. Z5–8 H8–5.

T. ovatum, illus. p.255.
T. rivale, illus. p.350.
T. sessile, illus. p.260.
T. undulatum (Painted trillium, Painted wood lily). Clump-forming perennial. **H** 4–8in (10–20cm), **S** 6–8in (15–20cm). Solitary, open funnel-shaped flowers, with red-edged, green sepals and 3 white or pink petals with carmine, basal stripe, are borne in spring, above broadly oval, blue-green, basal leaves. Z4–8 H8–1.

TRIPETALEIA
ERICACEAE

Genus of one species of deciduous shrub, grown for its flowers; is now often included in *Elliottia*. Needs partial shade and moist, peaty, neutral to acidic soil. Propagate by softwood cuttings in summer or by seed in fall.

T. paniculata, syn. *Elliottia paniculata.* Deciduous, upright shrub. **H** and **S** 5ft (1.5m). Bears upright panicles of pink-tinged, white flowers, with 3 (or 4 or 5) narrow petals, from mid-summer to early fall. Lance-shaped, dark green leaves persist well into fall. Z6–9 H9–6.

TRIPTERYGIUM
CELASTRACEAE

Genus of deciduous, twining or scrambling climbers, grown for their foliage and fruits. Needs sun or partial shade and fertile, well-drained soil. Water freely while in growth, less in low temperatures. Provide stems with support. Thin out crowded stems in winter or early spring. Propagate by seed when ripe or in spring or by semiripe cuttings in summer.

T. regelii. Deciduous, thin-stemmed, twining or scrambling climber. **H** 30ft (10m). Leaves are oval and usually rich green. In late summer produces clusters, 8–10in (20–25cm) long, of small, off-white flowers, followed by winged, green fruits. Z5–8 H8–5.

Tristania conferta. See *Lophostemon confertus.*

TRITELEIA
LILIACEAE/ALLIACEAE

Genus of late spring- and early summer-flowering corms with wiry stems carrying *Allium*-like umbels of funnel-shaped flowers. Long, narrow leaves usually die away by flowering time. Needs an open but sheltered, sunny situation and well-drained soil that dries out to some extent in summer. Dies down in mid- to late summer until spring; plant during dormancy in early fall. Propagate by seed or offsets in fall.

T. hyacinthina, syn. *Brodiaea hyacinthina, Brodiaea lactea,* illus. p.408.

T. ixioides, syn. *Brodiaea ixioides, Brodiaea lutea* (Pretty face). Early summer-flowering corm. **H** to 20in (50cm), **S** 3–4in (8–10cm). Bears semierect, basal leaves. Stem bears loose umbel, to 5in (12cm) across, of yellow flowers; petals have purple-stripe. Z7–13 H12–7. **'Starlight',** illus. p.407.

T. laxa, syn. *Brodiaea laxa,* illus. p.411. **'Koningin Fabiola',** syn. *Brodiaea laxa* 'Queen Fabiola', illus. p.411.

T. peduncularis, syn. *Brodiaea peduncularis.* Early summer-flowering corm. **H** 4–16in (10–40cm), **S** 4–6in (10–15cm). Bears semierect, basal leaves. Stem bears loose umbel, to 14in (35cm) across, of white flowers faintly tinged blue. Z7–13 H12–7.

TRITONIA
IRIDACEAE

Genus of corms, with sword-shaped, erect leaves, grown for their spikes of colorful flowers. Needs a sunny, sheltered site and well-drained soil. Plant corms in fall (*T. disticha* subsp. *rubrolucens* in spring). Dry off once leaves die back in summer (winter for *T. disticha* subsp. *rubrolucens*). Propagate by seed in fall or by offsets at replanting time.

T. crocata, syn. *T. hyalina.* Spring-flowering corm. **H** 6–14in (15–35cm), **S** 2–3in (5–8cm). Has erect, basal leaves. Each wiry stem bears loose spike of up to 10 widely cup-shaped, orange or pink flowers, 1$^1/_2$–2in (4–5cm) across, with transparent margins. Z8–10 H10–8.

T. disticha* subsp. *rubrolucens, syn. *T. rosea, T. rubrolucens,* illus. p.409.

T. hyalina. See *T. crocata.*
T. rosea. See *T. disticha* subsp. *rubrolucens.*
T. rubrolucens. See *T. disticha* subsp. *rubrolucens.*

TROCHOCARPA
EPACRIDACEAE

Genus of evergreen shrubs, grown for their nodding flower spikes. Requires sun and moist but well-drained, peaty, sandy soil. Propagate by semiripe cuttings in summer.

T. thymifolia. Slow-growing, evergreen, erect shrub. **H** 12in (30cm), **S** to 8in (20cm). Stems are covered in minute, thyme-like leaves. Produces spikes, 1$^1/_2$in (4cm) long, of tiny, bell-shaped, pink flowers in summer–fall. Is suitable for an alpine house. Z4–7 H7–1.

TROCHODENDRON
TROCHODENDRACEAE

Genus of one species of evergreen tree, grown for its foliage and flowers. Needs shelter from strong, cold winds. Requires sun or partial shade and moist but well-drained soil; dislikes very dry or very shallow, chalky soil. Propagate by semiripe cuttings in summer or by seed in fall.

T. aralioides, illus. p.79.

TROLLIUS
Globeflower
RANUNCULACEAE

Genus of spring- or summer-flowering perennials that thrive beside ponds and streams. Prefers sun or partial shade and moist soil. Propagate by division in early fall or by seed in summer or fall.

***T. x cultorum* 'Alabaster',** illus. p.436. **'Earliest of All'** is a clump-forming perennial. **H** 24in (60cm), **S** 18in (45cm). Solitary, globular, butter-yellow flowers are borne in spring, above rounded, deeply divided, mid-green leaves. **'Goldquelle'** has large, rich orange flowers. **'Orange Princess',** **H** 30in (75cm), bears orange-gold flowers.

T. europaeus, illus. p.445. **'Canary Bird'** is a clump-forming perennial. **H** 24in (60cm), **S** 18in (45cm). In spring bears globular, canary-yellow flowers above rounded, deeply divided, mid-green leaves.

T. pumilus, illus. p.358.

T. yunnanensis. Clump-forming perennial. **H** 24in (60cm), **S** 12in (30cm). Has broadly oval leaves, with 3–5 deep lobes. Buttercup-like, bright yellow flowers are produced in late spring or summer. Z5–8 H8–5.

TROPAEOLUM
TROPAEOLACEAE

Genus of annuals, perennials and herbaceous, twining climbers, grown for their brightly colored flowers. Most species prefer sun and well-drained soil. Propagate by seed, tubers or basal stem cuttings in spring. Aphids and caterpillars of cabbage white butterfly and its relatives may cause problems.

T. azureum. Herbaceous, leaf-stalk climber with small tubers. **H** to 4ft (1.2m). Leaves have 5 narrow lobes. Small, trumpet-shaped, short-spurred, purple-

T

blue flowers, ⁵⁄₈–³⁄₄in (1.5–2cm) wide, with notched petals, are produced in late summer. Z11 H12–1.

T. canariense. See *T. peregrinum*.

T. 'Empress of India'. Fast-growing, bushy annual. **H** 12in (23cm), **S** 18in (45cm). Has rounded, purple-green leaves. Trumpet-shaped, spurred, semidouble, rich scarlet flowers, 2in (5cm) wide, are borne from early summer to early fall. Z11 H12–1.

T. Gleam Series. Fast-growing, semi-trailing annuals. **H** 16in (40cm), **S** 24in (60cm). Have rounded, mid-green leaves. From early summer to early fall bear trumpet-shaped, spurred, semidouble flowers, 2in (5cm) wide, in single colors or in mixture that includes scarlet, yellow and orange and pastel shades. Z11 H12–1.

T. Jewel Series, illus. p.327.

T. majus (Indian cress, Nasturtium). Fast-growing, bushy annual. **H** 3–10ft (1–3m), **S** 5–15ft (1.5–5m). Has rounded to kidney-shaped, wavy-margined, pale green leaves. From summer to fall bears trumpet-shaped, long-spurred, red, orange or yellow flowers, 2–2¹⁄₂in (5–6cm) wide. Many cultivars often attributed to *T. majus*, and with similar characteristics to the species, are of hybrid origin, and are described in this book under their cultivar names. Z11 H12–1. **Alaska Series,** illus. p.323. **'Hermine Grashoff',** illus. p.307.

T. 'Peach Melba'. Fast-growing, bushy annual. **H** to 18in (45cm), **S** 12in (30cm). Bears rounded, mid-green leaves. Trumpet-shaped, spurred, scarlet-blotched, pale yellow flowers, 2in (5cm) wide, are produced from early summer to early fall. Z11 H12–1.

T. peregrinum, syn. *T. canariense* (Canary creeper). Herbaceous, leaf-stalk climber, best grown as an annual in cool areas. **H** to 6ft (2m). Gray-green leaves have 5 broad lobes. Small, bright yellow flowers, the 2 upper petals much larger and fringed, are borne from summer until first frosts. Z10–11 H12–1.

T. polyphyllum, illus. p.276.
T. speciosum, illus. p.202.
T. tricolor. See *T. tricolorum*.
T. tricolorum, syn. *T. tricolor*, illus. p.461.
T. tuberosum. Herbaceous, tuberous-rooted, leaf-stalk climber. **H** 6–10ft (2–3m). Grayish-green leaves have 3–5 lobes. From mid-summer to late fall produces cup-shaped, long-spurred, orange-yellow flowers, with orange-red sepals. Z8–15 H12–8. **var. lineamaculatum 'Ken Aslet',** illus. p.207.

T. Whirlybird Series. Fast-growing, bushy annuals. **H** 10in (25cm), **S** 14in (35cm). Have rounded, mid-green leaves. Trumpet-shaped, spurred, single to semidouble flowers, 2in (5cm) wide, are borne in mixture or in single colors from early summer to early fall. Z11 H12–1.

TSUGA
Hemlock
PINACEAE

See also CONIFERS.

T. canadensis, illus. p.102. Z4–8 H8–1. **'Aurea'** is a broadly conical conifer, often with several stems. **H** 15ft (5m) or more, **S** 6–10ft (2–3m). Shoots are pale gray with spirally-arranged, needlelike, flattened

leaves, golden-yellow when young, aging to green in second year; those along top are inverted to show silver bands. Has ovoid, light brown cones. **'Bennett', H** 3–6ft (1–2m), **S** 6ft (2m), is a compact, dwarf form with arching branches and nest-shaped, central depression. **'Pendula',** syn. *T. canadensis* f. *pendula*, **H** and **S** 10–15ft (3–5m), has weeping branches that may be trained to create a dome; if left to spread at ground level, **H** 20in (50cm), **S** 6–15ft (2–5m).

T. caroliniana (Carolina hemlock). Conifer with a conical or ovoid crown. **H** 30–50ft (10–15m), **S** 15–25ft (5–8m). Red-brown shoots produce spirally-set, needlelike, flattened, glossy, dark green leaves. Bears ovoid, green cones, ripening to brown. Z3–8 H7–3.

T. diversifolia (Northern Japanese hemlock). Conifer with a broad, dense crown. **H** 30–50ft (10–15m), **S** 25–40ft (8–12m). Has orange shoots and needlelike, flattened, glossy, deep green leaves, banded with white beneath, that are spirally set. Ovoid cones are dark brown. Z6–8 H8–6.

T. heterophylla (Western hemlock). Vigorous, conical conifer with drooping branchlets. **H** 70–100ft (20–30m), **S** 25–30ft (8–10m). Gray shoots bear spirally-set, needlelike, flattened, dark green leaves, with silvery bands beneath. Green cones ripen dark brown. Z6–8 H8–6.

T. mertensiana. Narrowly conical conifer with short, horizontal branches. **H** 25–50ft (8–15m), **S** 10–20ft (3–6m). Red-brown shoots bear needlelike, flattened, glaucous blue-green or gray-green leaves, spirally arranged. Cones are cylindrical and yellow-green to purple, ripening to dark brown. Z6–8 H8–6. **'Glauca',** illus. p.99.

T. sieboldii (Southern Japanese hemlock). Broadly conical conifer. **H** 50ft (15m), **S** 25–30ft (8–10m). Has glossy, buff shoots that bear needlelike, flattened, lustrous, dark green leaves, set spirally. Cones are ovoid and dark brown. Z6–8 H8–6.

TSUSIOPHYLLUM
ERICACEAE

Genus of one species of semievergreen shrub, grown for its flowers. Is similar to *Rhododendron* and is suitable for rock gardens and peat beds. Requires partial shade and well-drained, peaty, sandy soil. Propagate by softwood cuttings in spring or early summer or by seed in fall or spring.

T. tanakae. Semievergreen, spreading shrub. **H** 6in (15cm) or more, **S** 10in (25cm). Twiggy, branched stems bear tiny, narrowly oval, hairy leaves. In early summer produces small, tubular, white or pinkish-white flowers at stem tips. Z6–8 H8–6.

TUBERARIA
CISTACEAE

Genus of annuals, grown for their shallowly cup-shaped flowers. Requires sun and very well-drained soil. Propagate by seed in spring.

T. guttata, syn. *Helianthemum guttatum*. Moderately fast-growing, upright, branching annual. **H** and **S** 4–12in (10–30cm). Has lance-shaped, hairy,

mid-green leaves. In summer produces yellow flowers, sometimes red-spotted at base of petals, that look like small, single roses. H9–1.

TULBAGHIA
LILIACEAE/ALLIACEAE

Genus of clump-forming, mainly deciduous, sometimes semievergreen, rhizomatous or bulbous perennials. Needs full sun and well-drained soil. Propagate by division or seed in spring.

T. fragrans. See *T. simmleri*.
T. natalensis. Semievergreen, clump-forming perennial. **H** 5in (12cm), **S** 4in (10cm). In mid-summer, umbels of delicately fragrant, tubular, yellow-centered, white flowers, with spreading petal lobes, are produced above fine, grasslike, mid-green foliage. Z7–9 H9–7.
T. pulchella. See *T. simmleri*.
T. simmleri, syn. *T. fragrans*, *T. pulchella*, *T. simmieri*, illus. p.411.
T. violacea, illus. p.280.

TULIPA
Tulip
LILIACEAE

Genus of mainly spring-flowering bulbs, grown for their bright, upward-facing flowers. Each bulb produces a few linear to lance-shaped, green or gray-green leaves on the stem. Flowers bear 6 usually pointed petals (botanically known as perianth segments) and 6 stamens, singly, unless otherwise stated below. Each plant has a spread of up to 8in (20cm). Requires sun and well-drained soil and appreciates a summer baking; in cool, wet areas, bulbs may be lifted, when the leaves have died down, and stored in a dry place for replanting in fall. Propagate by division of bulbs in fall or, for species, by seed in spring or fall. ① If ingested, all parts may cause mild stomach upset, and contact with any part may aggravate skin allergies. See also feature panel pp.400–401. Horticulturally, tulips are grouped into the following divisions.

Single Early Group (Div.1)—has cup-shaped, single, white to dark purple flowers, to 3in (7cm) across, often margined, "flamed" or flecked with a contrasting color, from early to mid-spring. H 6–18in (15–45cm).

Double Early Group (Div.2)—has bowl-shaped, fully double, dark red to yellow or white flowers, to 3in (8cm) across, often margined or flecked with another color, borne in mid-spring. H 12–16in (30–40cm).

Triumph Group (Div.3)—sturdy stems bear cup-shaped, single flowers, to 2½in (6cm) across, in a range of colors and often margined or flecked with a contrasting color, in mid- and late spring. H 14–24in (35–60cm).

Darwin Hybrid Group (Div.4)—has egg-shaped, single flowers, to 3in (7cm) across, in a range of colors and usually flushed, "flamed" or margined with a different color and often with contrasting bases, from mid- to late spring. H 20–28in (50–70cm).

Single Late Group including Cottage and Darwin Hybrids (Div.5)—has cup- or goblet-shaped, single flowers,

sometimes several to a stem, in white to yellow, pink, red or almost black, often with contrasting margins, in late spring. H 18–30in (45–75cm).

Lily-flowered Group (Div.6)—strong stems bear goblet-shaped, single flowers, to 3in (8cm) across, with reflexed, pointed petal tips and sometimes margined, "flamed" or flushed with a contrasting color, in late spring. H 18–26in (45–65cm).

Fringed Group (Div.7)—flowers are similar to those in Div.6, but have fringed petals. H 14–26in (35–65cm).

Viridiflora Group (Div.8)—has cup- or almost closed bowl-shaped, single flowers, to 3in (8cm) across, sometimes entirely green, margined with another color, or white to yellow, red or purple, "flamed" or striped green, with contrasting centers, borne in late spring. H 16–22in (40–55cm).

Rembrandt Group (Div.9)—comprises mostly very old cultivars, similar to Div.6, but has colors "broken" into striped or feathered patterns owing to virus. Flowers in late spring. H 18–26in (45–65cm).

Parrot Group (Div.10)—has cup-shaped, single, white to pink or violet-blue flowers, to 4in (10cm) across, often unevenly striped with different colors, including green, borne in late spring. Petals are finely and irregularly cut. H 14–26in (35–65cm).

Double Late Group (peony-flowered) (Div.11)—has bowl-shaped, fully double flowers, to 5in (12cm) across, in white to purple, sometimes margined or "flamed" in a different color, borne in late spring. H 14–24in (35–60cm).

Kaufmanniana Group (Div.12)—comprises *T. kauffmanniana* and hybrids and has bowl-shaped, single flowers, 3–4in (8–10cm) across, frequently multicolored and usually with distinctively colored bases, in early or mid-spring. Leaves are sometimes marked bronze, red or purple. H 6–12in (15–30cm).

Fosteriana Group (Div.13)—comprises *T. fosteriana* and hybrids and has bowl-shaped, single flowers, to 5in (12cm) across, in white to yellow or dark red, often margined or "flamed" in another color and with contrasting bases, borne in mid-spring. Leaves are sometimes marked red-purple. H 8–26in (20–65cm).

Greigii Group (Div.14)—comprises *T. greigii* and hybrids and has bowl-shaped, single, yellow to red flowers, to 4in (10cm) across, sometimes "flamed" or margined in a different color and with contrasting bases, borne in early or mid-spring. Blue-green leaves are generally wavy-margined and always marked dark bluish-maroon. H 6–12in (15–30cm).

Miscellaneous Group (Div.15)—comprises all species and hybrids not included in other divisions. Flowers are produced from late winter to late spring.

T. 'Abu Hassan' Div.3, illus. p.401. Mid- to late spring-flowering bulb. **H** 20in (50cm). Produces cardinal-red flowers with pinkish-red stripes and yellow edges. Z3–8 H8–1.

T. acuminata (Horned tulip) Div.15, illus. p.401. Mid-spring-flowering bulb. **H** 12–18in (30–45cm). Flowers are 3–5in (7–13cm) long, with long-pointed, tapered, pale red or yellow petals, often tinged with red or green outside. Z3–8 H8–1.

***T.* 'Ad Rem'** Div.4. Mid- to late spring-flowering bulb. **H** 24in (60cm). Flowers are scarlet with black bases and yellow margins. Anthers are yellow. Z3–8 H8–1.
T. aitchisonii. See *T. clusiana.*
***T.* 'Albert Heijn'** Div.13, illus. p.400. Early spring-flowering bulb. **H** 14in (35cm). Bears deep rose-pink flowers with purple sheen and paler pink edges. Z3–8 H8–1.
***T.* 'Ancilla'** Div.12. Early spring-flowering bulb. **H** 6in (15cm). Flowers are pink and reddish outside, white inside, with central, red ring. Z3–8 H8–1.
***T.* 'Angélique'** Div.11. Late spring-flowering bulb. **H** 16in (40cm). Delicately scented, double, pale pink flowers deepen with age. Each petal has paler streaks and lighter margin. Is good for bedding. Z3–8 H8–1.
***T.* 'Apeldoorn's Elite'** Div.4, illus. p.401. Mid- to late spring-flowering bulb. **H** 24in (60cm). Has buttercup-yellow flowers feathered with cherry-red and with yellowish-green bases. Z3–8 H8–1.
***T.* 'Apricot Beauty'** Div.1. Early spring-flowering bulb. **H** 16in (40cm). Flowers salmon-pink faintly tinged red. Z3–8 H8–1.
***T.* 'Artist'** Div.8, illus. p.401. Late spring-flowering bulb. **H** 18in (45cm). Flowers are salmon-pink and purple outside, sometimes marked with green, and deep salmon-pink and green inside. Z3–8 H8–1.
***T.* 'Attila'** Div.3. Mid-spring-flowering bulb. **H** 16in (40cm). Strong stems bear long-lasting, pink flowers. Z3–8 H8–1.
T. aucheriana Div.15. Early spring-flowering bulb. **H** to 8in (20cm). Has gray-green leaves. Bears oval-petaled, yellow-centered, pink flowers, ¾–2in (2–5cm) long, tapered at base. Z3–8 H8–1.
T. australis. See *T. sylvestris.*
T. bakeri. See *T. saxatilis.*
***T.* 'Balalaika'** Div.5. Late spring-flowering bulb. **H** 20in (50cm). Bright red flowers have yellow bases and black stamens. Z3–8 H8–1.
***T.* 'Ballade'** Div.6, illus. p.400. Late spring-flowering bulb. **H** 20in (50cm). Reddish-magenta flowers, with white-margined, yellow bases, have long, white-margined petals. Z3–8 H8–1.
***T.* 'Ballerina'** Div.6, illus. p.401. Late spring-flowering bulb. **H** 24in (60cm). Produces lemon-yellow flowers, with flamelike, blood-red markings, orange-yellow veins near margins and star-shaped yellow bases. Inner surfaces are bright red, feathered marigold-orange, with pale golden-yellow anthers. Z3–8 H8–1.
T. batalinii Div.15. Early spring-flowering bulb. **H** 4–12in (10–30cm). Is often included under *T. linifolia.* Leaves are gray-green. Flowers, ¾–2½in (2–6cm) long, have broadly oval petals and are bowl-shaped at base. Pale yellow petals are darker yellow or brown at bases inside. Several cultivars are hybrids between *T. batalinii* and *T. linifolia.* Z3–8 H8–1. These include **'Apricot Jewel'** Div.15, with flowers that are orange-red outside, yellow inside; **'Bright Gem'** Div.15, which has yellow flowers flushed with orange; and **'Bronze Charm'** Div.15, which bears yellow flowers with bronze feathering.
***T.* 'Bellona'** Div.1, illus. p.401. Early spring-flowering bulb. **H** 12in (30cm). Fragrant flowers are deep golden-yellow. Is good for bedding and forcing. Z3–8 H8–1.
T. biflora, syn. *T. polychroma* Div.15. Early spring-flowering bulb. **H** 2–4in (5–10cm). Has gray-green leaves. Stem bears 1–5 fragrant, yellow-centered, white flowers, ⅝–1½in (1.5–3.5cm) long and tapered at bases. Narrowly oval petals are flushed outside with greenish-gray or greenish-pink. Is suitable for a rock garden. Z4–7 H7–1.
***T.* 'Bing Crosby'** Div.3. Mid- to late spring-flowering bulb. **H** 20in (50cm). Has scarlet flowers. Z3–8 H8–1.
***T.* 'Bird of Paradise'** Div.10, illus. p.400. Late spring-flowering bulb. **H** 18in (45cm). Produces orange-margined, cardinal-red flowers, with bright yellow bases. Anthers are purple. Z3–8 H8–1.
***T.* 'Black Hero'** Div.11, illus. p.401. Late spring-flowering bulb. **H** 24in (60cm). Flowers have maroon outer petals and darker, almost black edges and dark purple-black inner petals. Z3–8 H8–1.
***T.* 'Black Jewel'** Div.7. Late spring-flowering bulb. **H** 20in (50cm). Produces deep maroon-purple, almost black flowers with crystalline fringe very lightly marked with golden-yellow. Z3–8 H8–1.
***T.* 'Blue Parrot'** Div.10, illus. p.401. Late spring-flowering bulb. **H** 24in (60cm). Very large, bright violet flowers, sometimes bronze outside, are borne on strong stems. Z3–8 H8–1.
***T.* 'Burgundy Lace'** Div.7. Late spring-flowering bulb. **H** 24in (60cm). Flowers are wine-red with fringed margins. Z3–8 H8–1.
***T.* 'Candela'** Div.13, illus. p.401. Early to mid-spring-flowering bulb. **H** 12in (30cm). Large, long-lasting, yellow flowers have black anthers. Z3–8 H8–1.
***T.* 'Cape Cod'** Div.14. Mid- to late spring-flowering bulb. **H** 18in (45cm). Gray-green leaves have reddish stripes. Yellowish-bronze flowers have black-and-red bases; petals are margined yellow outside. Z3–8 H8–1.
***T.* 'Carnaval de Nice'** Div.11, illus. p.400. Late spring-flowering bulb. **H** 16in (40cm). Double, white flowers are feathered with deep red. Z3–8 H8–1.
***T.* 'China Pink'** Div.6, illus. p.400. Late spring-flowering bulb. **H** 22in (55cm). White-based, pink flowers have slightly reflexed petals. Z3–8 H8–1.
***T.* 'Chopin'** Div.12. Early spring-flowering bulb. **H** 8in (20cm). Has brown-mottled, gray-green leaves. Lemon-yellow flowers have black bases. Z3–8 H8–1.
T. chrysantha. See *T. clusiana* var. *chrysantha.*
***T.* 'Clara Butt'** Div.5. Late spring-flowering bulb. **H** 24in (60cm). Flowers are salmon-pink. Is good for bedding. Z3–8 H8–1.
T. clusiana, syn. *T. aitchisonii* (Lady tulip) Div.15. Mid-spring-flowering bulb. **H** to 12in (30cm). Has gray-green leaves. Each stem bears 1 or 2 flowers, ¾–2½in (2–6.5cm) long, that are bowl-shaped at base. Narrowly oval, white petals are purple or crimson at base inside, striped deep pink outside. Stamens are purple. Z3–8 H8–1. Flowers of **var. *chrysantha,*** syn. *T. chrysantha* Div.15 (illus. p.401) are yellow, flushed red or brown outside, with yellow stamens,. **var. *stellata*** Div.15 has white flowers with yellow bases and yellow stamens.
***T.* 'Couleur Cardinal'** Div.3. Mid-spring-flowering bulb. **H** 14in (35cm). Plum-purple flowers are dark crimson-scarlet inside. Z3–8 H8–1.
T. dasystemon of gardens**.** See *T. tarda.*
***T.* 'Dawnglow'** Div.4. Mid- to late-spring-flowering bulb. **H** 24in (60cm). Pale apricot flowers are flushed with deep pink outside and are deep yellow inside. Z3–8 H8–1.
***T.* 'Diana'** Div.1. Early spring-flowering bulb. **H** 11in (28cm). Large, pure white flowers are borne on strong stems. Z3–8 H8–1.
***T.* 'Dillenburg'** Div.5. Late spring-flowering bulb. **H** 26in (65cm). Flowers are brick-orange. Is good for bedding. Z3–8 H8–1.
***T.* 'Don Quichotte'** Div.3. Mid-spring-flowering bulb. **H** 16in (40cm). Purple-pink flowers are long-lasting. Z4–7 H7–1.
***T.* 'Dreamboat'** Div.14. Mid- to late spring-flowering bulb. **H** 10in (25cm). Produces gray-green leaves with brown stripes. Urn-shaped, red-tinged, amber-yellow flowers have greenish-bronze bases with red blotches. Z3–8 H8–1.
***T.* 'Dreaming Maid'** Div.3, illus. p.401. Mid- to late spring-flowering bulb. **H** 22in (55cm). Flowers have white-margined, violet petals. Z3–8 H8–1.
***T.* 'Dreamland'** Div.5, illus. p.400. Late spring-flowering bulb. **H** 24in (60cm). Flowers are red with white bases and yellow anthers. Z3–8 H8–1.
T. eichleri. See *T. undulatifolia.*
***T.* 'Esperanto'** Div.8, illus. p.400. Late spring-flowering bulb. **H** 12in (30cm). Produces flowers with rose-pink petals that fade to pale pink toward base, and green-feathered mid-veins. Has cream-edged, gray-green leaves. Z3–8 H8–1.
***T.* 'Estella Rijnveld'** Div.10, illus. p.400. Late spring-flowering bulb. **H** 24in (60cm). Large, red flowers are streaked with white and green. Z3–8 H8–1.
***T.* 'Fancy Frills'** Div.10. Late spring-flowering bulb. **H** 20in (50cm). Fringed, ivory-white petals are striped and margined pink outside; inside, base is rose-pink. Anthers are pale yellow. Z3–8 H8–1.
***T.* 'Flaming Parrot'** Div.10. Late-spring flowering bulb. **H** 22in (55cm). Deep yellow flowers, "flamed" dark red, have primrose-yellow bases. Insides are primrose-yellow with glowing, blood-red "flames." Anthers are purple-black. Z3–8 H8–1.
T. fosteriana Div.15. Early spring-flowering bulb. **H** 8–18in (20–45cm). Has a downy stem and gray-green leaves, downy above. Flowers, to 4in (10cm) long, are bowl-shaped at base with narrowly oval, bright red petals, and purplish-black center inside, ringed with yellow. Z3–8 H8–1.
***T.* 'Fringed Beauty'** Div.7. Early to mid-spring-flowering bulb. **H** 13in (32cm). Fringed petals are bright red with yellow margins. Is excellent for forcing. Z3–8 H8–1.
***T.* 'Fringed Elegance'** Div.7. Late spring-flowering bulb. **H** 20in (50cm). Produces pale yellow flowers dotted with pink outside; inside, bases have bronze-green blotches. Each petal has yellow fringe. Anthers are purple. Z3–8 H8–1.
***T.* 'Gala Beauty'** Div.9. Late spring-flowering bulb. **H** 24in (60cm). Yellow flowers are streaked with crimson. Z3–8 H8–1.
***T.* 'Garden Party'** Div.3. Mid- to late spring-flowering bulb. **H** 16–18in (40–45cm). Produces white flowers; petals are margined deep pink outside, and inside are streaked with deep pink. Z3–8 H8–1.
***T.* 'Giuseppe Verdi'** Div.12, illus. p.407.
***T.* 'Glück'** Div.12, illus. p.401. Early spring-flowering bulb. **H** 6in (15cm). Has reddish-brown-mottled, gray-green leaves. Petals are red outside, margined bright yellow, and yellow inside, with darker bases. Z3–8 H8–1.
***T.* 'Golden Apeldoorn'** Div.4, illus. p.401. Mid- to late spring-flowering bulb. **H** 20–24in (50–60cm). Golden-yellow flowers have black bases and stamens. Z3–8 H8–1.
***T.* 'Golden Artist'** Div.8. Late spring-flowering bulb. **H** 18in (45cm). Flowers are bright golden-yellow. Z3–8 H8–1.
***T.* 'Gordon Cooper'** Div. 4. Mid- to late spring-flowering bulb. **H** 24in (60cm). Petals are deep pink outside, margined red; and inside are red with blue-and-yellow bases. Has black anthers. Z3–8 H8–1.
***T.* 'Greenland'.** See *T.* 'Groenland'.
T. greigii Div.15. Early spring-flowering bulb. **H** 8–18in (20–45cm). Has downy stems. Leaves are streaked or mottled with red or purple. Cup-shaped flowers, 1¼–4in (3–10cm) long, with broadly oval, red or yellow petals, have yellow-ringed, black centers. Z3–8 H8–1.
***T.* 'Greuze'** Div.5. Late spring-flowering bulb. **H** 26in (65cm). Flowers are dark violet-purple. Is good for bedding. Z3–8 H8–1.
***T.* 'Groenland',** syn. *T.* 'Greenland' Div.8, illus. p.400. Late spring-flowering bulb. **H** 20in (50cm). Bears flowers with green petals that are margined rose-pink. Is a good bedding tulip. Z3–8 H8–1.
T. hageri Div.15. Mid-spring-flowering bulb. **H** 4–12in (10–30cm). Stem has 1–4 flowers, 1½–2½in (3–6cm) long, tapered at base and with oval, dull red petals tinged with green outside. Z3–8 H8–1.
***T.* 'Heart's Delight'** Div.12. Early spring-flowering bulb. **H** 8–10in (20–25cm). Has green leaves striped red-brown. Deep pinkish-red flowers, margined pale pink, have pale pink inside with red-blotched, yellow bases. Z3–8 H8–1.
***T.* 'Hollywood'** Div.8. Late spring-flowering bulb. **H** 12in (30cm). Red flowers, tinged and streaked with green, have yellow bases. Is good for bedding. Z3–8 H8–1.
T. humilis Div.15. Variable, early spring-flowering bulb, often considered to include *T. aucheriana, T. pulchella* and *T. violacea.* **H** to 8in (20cm). Has gray-green leaves. Stem bears usually 1, sometimes 2 or 3, pinkish-magenta flowers, ¾–2in (2–5cm) long, tapered at base and with yellow center inside. Petals are oval. Is suitable for a rock garden. Z3–8 H8–1.
***T.* 'Jack Laan'** Div.9. Late spring-flowering bulb. **H** 24in (60cm). Purple flowers are shaded with brown and feathered with white and yellow. Z3–8 H8–1.
***T.* 'Juan'** Div.13. Early to mid-spring-flowering bulb. **H** 14in (35cm). Flowers are deep orange overlaid with scarlet. Leaves are marked with reddish-brown. Z3–8 H8–1.
T. kaufmanniana (Water lily tulip) Div.15, illus. p.401. Early spring-flowering bulb. **H** 4–14in (10–35cm). Leaves are gray-green. Stem has 1–5 often scented flowers, 1½–4in (3–10cm) long and bowl-shaped at base. Narrowly oval petals are usually cream or

T

yellow, flushed with pink or gray-green outside; centers are often a different color. Pink, orange or red forms occasionally occur. Z3–8 H8–1.

T. 'Keizerskroon' Div.1. Early spring-flowering bulb. **H** 14in (35cm). Flowers have crimson-scarlet petals, with broad, bright yellow margins. Is a good, reliable bedding tulip. Z3–8 H8–1.

T. 'Kingsblood' Div.5. Late spring-flowering bulb. **H** 24in (60cm). Cherry-red flowers are margined scarlet. Z3–8 H8–1.

T. linifolia Div.15. Variable, early spring-flowering bulb, often considered to include *T. batalinii* and *T. maximowiczii*. **H** 4–12in (10–30cm). Has gray-green leaves. Red flowers, 3/4–2in (2–6cm) long, are bowl-shaped at base and, inside, have blackish-purple centers that are usually ringed with cream or yellow. Petals are broadly oval. Z3–8 H8–1.

T. 'Lustige Witwe', syn. *T.* 'Merry Widow' Div.3. Mid- to late spring-flowering bulb. Flowers have deep glowing red petals margined white. Z3–8 H8–1.

T. 'Madame Lefèber', syn. *T.* 'Red Emperor' Div.13, illus. p.401. Early to mid-spring-flowering bulb. **H** 14–16in (35–40cm). Produces very large, brilliant red flowers. Z3–8 H8–1.

T. 'Maja' Div.7, illus. p.401. Late spring-flowering bulb. **H** 20in (50cm). Has egg-shaped, pale yellow flowers, with fringed petals, that are bronze-yellow at base. Anthers are yellow. Z3–8 H8–1.

T. 'Margot Fonteyn' Div.3. Mid- to late spring-flowering bulb. **H** 16–18in (40–45cm). Yellow-margined, bright red flowers have yellow base inside. Anthers are black. Z3–8 H8–1.

T. marjolletii Div.15. Mid-spring-flowering bulb. **H** 16–20in (40–50cm). Produces flowers, 1 1/2–2 1/2in (4–6cm) long and bowl-shaped at base, with broadly oval, creamy-white petals, margined and marked deep pink. Z3–8 H8–1.

T. 'Maureen' Div.5. Late spring-flowering bulb. **H** 28in (70cm). Bears marble-white flowers. Z3–8 H8–1.

T. maximowiczii Div.15. Early spring-flowering bulb. **H** 4–12in (10–30cm). Has gray-green leaves. Bright red flowers, 3/4–2 1/2in (2–6cm) long, with broadly oval petals, have white-bordered, black centers and are bowl-shaped at base. Z3–8 H8–1.

T. 'Menton' Div.5, illus. p.401. Late spring-flowering bulb. **H** 24in (60cm). Flowers have light orange-margined, rose-pink petals with bright yellow and white bases. Anthers are yellow. Z3–8 H8–1.

T. 'Merry Widow'. See *T.* 'Lustige Witwe'.

T. 'Monte Carlo' Div.2. Early spring-flowering bulb. **H** 16in (40cm). Has double, bright yellow flowers with sparse, red streaks. Z3–8 H8–1.

T. 'Negrita' Div.3, illus. p.401. Mid- to late spring-flowering bulb. **H** 18in (45cm). Produces deep purple flowers with red-purple streaks. Z3–8 H8–1.

T. 'New Design' Div.3. Mid-spring-flowering bulb. **H** 16in (40cm). Flowers have yellow petals that fade to pinkish-white and are margined red outside and marked apricot inside. Leaves have pinkish-white margins. Z3–8 H8–1.

T. 'Orange Emperor' Div.13. Early to

mid-spring-flowering bulb. **H** 16in (40cm). Flowers are bright orange, with yellow base inside and have black anthers. Z3–8 H8–1.

T. 'Orange Triumph' Div.11. Late spring-flowering bulb. **H** 20in (50cm). Has double, soft orange-red flowers flushed with brown, and yellow margins. Z3–8 H8–1.

T. 'Oranje Nassau' Div.2. Early spring-flowering bulb. **H** 10–12in (25–30cm). Has double, blood-red flowers flushed fiery orange-red. Z3–8 H8–1.

T. 'Oratorio' Div.14. Mid- to late spring-flowering bulb. **H** 8in (20cm). Has brown-mottled, gray-green leaves. Broadly urn-shaped flowers are rose-pink outside, apricot-pink inside with black bases. Z3–8 H8–1.

T. orphanidea Div.15, illus. p.401. Mid-spring-flowering bulb. **H** 4–12in (10–30cm). Green leaves often have reddish margins. Stem has 1–4 flowers, 1 1/4–2 1/2in (3–6cm) long and tapered at base. Oval, orange-brown petals are tinged green outside and often purple. Z3–8 H8–1.

T. 'Page Polka' Div.3. Mid-spring-flowering bulb. Large, deep red flowers have white bases and are striped with white. Anthers are yellow. Z3–8 H8–1.

T. 'Palestrina' Div.5. Late spring-flowering bulb. **H** 18in (45cm). Petals of large, salmon-pink flowers are green outside. Z3–8 H8–1.

T. 'Peach Blossom' Div.2. Early spring-flowering bulb. **H** 10–12in (25–30cm). Produces double, silvery-pink flowers flushed with deep pink. Z3–8 H8–1.

T. 'Peer Gynt' Div.3. Mid- to late spring-flowering bulb. **H** 20in (50cm). Purple-margined, fuchsia-red flowers have white bases spotted with yellow. Anthers are purplish-gray. Z3–8 H8–1.

T. 'Plaisir' Div.14. Mid- to late spring-flowering bulb. **H** 6–8in (15–20cm). Has gray-green leaves mottled with red-brown. Bears broadly urn-shaped, pale yellow-margined, deep pinkish-red flowers, with black-and-yellow bases. Z3–8 H8–1.

T. polychroma. See *T. biflora*.

T. praestans. 'Fusilier' Div.15 Early spring-flowering bulb. **H** 4–18in (10–45cm). Has minutely downy stem and downy, gray-green leaves. Stem bears 3–5 flowers, 2 1/4–2 1/2in (5.5–6.5cm) long, with bowl-shaped bases. Oval petals are orange-scarlet. 'Unicum' Div.15 (illus. p.401) has leaves that are margined pale yellow. Yellow-based, bright red flowers have blue-black anthers. 'Van Tubergen's Variety' Div.15 produces 2–5 flowers, which are often yellow-based, per stem; increases very freely.

T. 'Prinses Irene' Div.1, illus. p.401. Early spring-flowering bulb. **H** 12–14in (30–35cm). Produces orange flowers streaked with purple. Z3–8 H8–1.

T. pulchella Div.15. Early spring-flowering bulb. **H** to 8in (20cm). Has gray-green leaves. Oval-petaled, purple flowers, 3/4–2in (2–5cm) long, are tapered at base and have yellow or bluish-black center inside. Is useful for a rock garden. Z3–8 H8–1.

T. 'Purissima', syn. *T.* 'White Emperor' Div.13, illus. p.400. Early to mid-spring-flowering bulb. **H** 14–16in (35–40cm). Flowers are pure white. Z3–8 H8–1.

T. 'Queen of Night' Div.5, illus. p.401. Late spring-flowering bulb. **H** 24in

(60cm). Has long-lasting, very dark maroon-black flowers on sturdy stems. Is the darkest of all tulips. Is useful for bedding. Z3–8 H8–1.

T. 'Queen of Sheba' Div.6. Late-spring-flowering bulb. **H** 24in (60cm). Bears orange-margined, glowing, brownish-red flowers. Z3–8 H8–1.

T. 'Red Emperor'. See *T.* 'Madame Lefèber'.

T. 'Red Parrot' Div.10. Late spring-flowering bulb. **H** 24in (60cm). Large, raspberry-red flowers are borne on strong stems. Z3–8 H8–1.

T. 'Red Riding Hood' Div.14, illus. p.401. Late spring-flowering bulb. **H** 8in (20cm). Has vivid, black-based, scarlet flowers amid spreading, dark green leaves mottled brownish-purple. Z3–8 H8–1.

T. saxatilis, syn. *T. bakeri* Div.15, illus. p.400. Early spring-flowering bulb. **H** 6–18in (15–45cm). Has glossy, mid-green leaves. Stem produces 1–4 scented flowers, 1 1/2–2 1/4in (4–5.5cm) long and tapered at base. Oval, pink to lilac petals are yellow at base inside. Z3–8 H8–1.

T. 'Shakespeare' Div.12. Early spring-flowering bulb. **H** 5–6in (12–15cm). Petals are deep red outside, margined salmon, and salmon inside, flushed red with yellow base. Z3–8 H8–1.

T. 'Shirley' Div.3, illus. p.400. Mid- to late spring-flowering bulb. **H** 20in (50cm). Bears ivory-white flowers with pinkish-purple petal edges and flecks. Z3–8 H8–1.

T. sprengeri Div.15, illus. p.401. Late spring- and early summer-flowering bulb. **H** 12–18in (30–45cm). Flowers are 1 3/4–2 1/2in (4.5–6.5cm) long and tapered at base. Bears narrowly oval, orange-red petals, the outer 3 with buff-yellow backs. Is latest-flowering tulip; increases rapidly. Z3–8 H8–1.

T. 'Spring Green' Div.8, illus. p.400. Late spring-flowering bulb. **H** 14–15in (35–38cm). Has white flowers feathered with green. Anthers are pale green. Z3–8 H8–1.

T. sylvestris, syn. *T. australis* Div.15, illus. p.401. Early spring-flowering bulb. **H** 4–18in (10–45cm). Yellow flowers, 1 1/2–2 3/4in (4–7cm) long, usually borne singly, are tapered at base. Narrowly oval petals are often tinged with green outside. Z3–8 H8–1.

T. tarda, syn. *T. dasystemon* Div.15. Early spring-flowering bulb. **H** to 6in (15cm). Has glossy, bright green leaves. Each stem bears 4–6 flowers, 1 1/4–1 1/2in (3–4cm) long, with tapered bases. Oval, white petals have yellow lower halves inside and are tinged with green and sometimes red outside. Is suitable for a rock garden or raised bed. Z3–8 H8–1.

T. 'Toronto' Div.14. Mid- to late spring-flowering bulb. **H** 12in (30cm). Has mottled leaves and 2 or 3 long-lasting flowers per stem. Open, broadly cup-shaped flowers have pointed, bright red petals with brownish-green-yellow base inside. Anthers are bronze. Z3–8 H8–1.

T. turkestanica Div.15, illus. p.400. Early spring-flowering bulb. **H** 4–12in (10–30cm). Has hairy stem and gray-green leaves. Stem bears up to 12 unpleasant-smelling flowers, 5/8–1 1/2in (1.5–3.5cm) long, with tapered bases. Oval, white petals are flushed green or pink outside; flowers have yellow or orange centers inside. Z3–8 H8–1.

T. 'Uncle Tom' Div.11, illus. p.401. Late spring-flowering bulb. **H** 20in (50cm). Double flowers are maroon-red. Z3–8 H8–1.

T. undulatifolia, syn. *T. eichleri* Div.15. Early to mid-spring-flowering bulb. **H** 6–20in (15–50cm). Has downy stem and gray-green leaves. Flowers, 1 1/4–3in (3–8cm) long, are bowl-shaped at base. Narrowly oval, red or orange-red petals have pale red or buff backs and yellow-bordered, dark green or black blotch at base inside. Z3–8 H8–1.

T. 'Union Jack' Div.5. Late spring-flowering bulb. **H** 24in (60cm). Ivory-white petals, marked with deep pinkish-red "flames," have blue-margined, white bases. Z3–8 H8–1.

T. urumiensis Div.15. Early spring-flowering bulb. **H** 4–8in (10–20cm). Stem is mostly below soil level. Leaves are green or grayish-green. Bears 1 or 2 flowers, 1 1/2in (4cm) long, with tapered bases. Narrowly oval, yellow petals are flushed mauve or red-brown outside. Is useful for a rock garden. Z4–7 H8–1.

T. violacea Div.15. Early spring-flowering bulb. **H** to 8in (20cm). Has gray-green leaves. Oval-petaled, violet-pink flowers, 3/4–2in (2–5cm) long, are tapered at base and have yellow or bluish-black centers inside. Is suitable for a rock garden or raised bed. Z3–8 H8–1.

T. 'West Point' Div.6. Late spring-flowering bulb. **H** 20in (50cm). Primrose-yellow flowers have long-pointed, recurved petals. Z4–7 H7–1.

T. 'White Dream' Div.3, illus. p.400. Mid- to late spring-flowering bulb. **H** 16–18in (40–45cm). Flowers are white with yellow anthers. Z3–8 H8–1.

T. 'White Emperor'. See *T.* 'Purissima'.

T. 'White Parrot' Div.10. Late spring-flowering bulb. **H** 22in (55cm). Large flowers have ruffled, white petals, flecked green near base. Is good for cut flowers. Z3–8 H8–1.

T. 'White Triumphator' Div.6, illus. p.400. Late spring-flowering bulb. **H** 26–28in (65–70cm). White flowers have reflexed petals. Z3–8 H8–1.

T. whittallii Div.15. Mid-spring-flowering bulb. **H** 12–14in (30–35cm). Stem produces 1–4 oval-petaled, bright brownish-orange flowers, 1 1/4–2 1/2in (3–6cm) long, with tapered bases. Z3–8 H8–1.

T. 'Yokohama' Div.1. Early to mid-spring-flowering bulb. **H** 14in (35cm). Pointed flowers are deep yellow. Z3–8 H8–1.

Tunica saxifraga. See *Petrorhagia saxifraga*.

TURRAEA

MELIACEAE

Genus of evergreen trees and shrubs, grown for their flowers and foliage. Prefers full sun and needs fertile, well-drained soil. Water freely when in growth, less at other times. Young plants may need growing point removed to promote branching. Prune after flowering if necessary. Propagate by seed in spring or by semiripe cuttings in summer.

T. obtusifolia. Evergreen, rounded, bushy, arching shrub. Has oval to lance-shaped leaves. Bears fragrant, white flowers from fall to spring, followed by orange-yellow fruits like tiny, peeled tangerines. Z10–11 H12–10.

TWEEDIA
ASCLEPIADACEAE

Genus of herbaceous, twining climbers; only one species is in general cultivation. In cool climates, may be grown as an annual. Requires sun and well-drained soil. Pinch out tips of shoots to encourage branching. Propagate by seed in spring.

T. caerulea, syn. *Oxypetalum caeruleum*. Herbaceous, twining climber with white-haired stems. **H** to 3ft (1m). Pink-flushed buds open, in summer and early fall, to reveal small, fleshy, pale blue flowers, maturing purple. Has green fruits, to 6in (15cm) long. Z12–15 H12–10.

TYLECODON
CRASSULACEAE

Genus of deciduous, bushy, winter-growing, succulent shrubs with very swollen stems. Requires sun and very well-drained soil. Propagate by seed or stem cuttings in summer. ① The leaves of *T. wallichii* are highly toxic if ingested.

T. paniculatus, syn. *Cotyledon paniculata* (Botterbom, Butter tree). Deciduous, bushy, succulent shrub. **H** and **S** 6ft (2m). Swollen stem and branches have papery, yellow coverings. Leaves are oblong to oval, fleshy and bright green. In summer, clusters of tubular, green-striped, red flowers are produced at stem tips. Z12–15 H12–10.

T. papillaris subsp. wallichii. See *T. wallichii*.

T. reticulatus, syn. *Cotyledon reticulata* (Barbed-wire plant). Deciduous, bushy, succulent shrub. **H** and **S** 1ft (30cm). Swollen branches bear cylindrical leaves in winter. Has tubular, green-yellow flowers, on woody stem, in fall. Z12–15 H12–10.

T. wallichii, syn. *T. papillaris subsp. wallichii, Cotyledon wallichii*. Deciduous, bushy, succulent shrub. **H** and **S** 1ft (30cm). Has cylindrical, grooved-topped, gray-green leaves at stem tips. After leaf fall, stems are neatly covered in raised leaf bases. Bears tubular, yellow-green flowers, ³⁄₄in (2cm) long, in fall. Z12–15 H12–10.

TYPHA
Cattail
TYPHACEAE

Genus of deciduous, perennial, marginal water plants, grown for their cylindrical seed heads. Tolerates sun and shade. Propagate in spring by seed or division. **T. latifolia,** illus. p.442. **'Variegata'** is a deciduous, perennial marginal water plant. **H** 3–4ft (90cm–1.2m), **S** indefinite. Strap-shaped, mid-green leaves have longitudinal, cream stripes. Spikes of beige flowers, in late summer, are followed by cylindrical, dark brown seed heads. Z2–11 H12–1.

T. minima, illus. p.443.

UVW

UGNI
MYRTACEAE

Genus of densely leafy, evergreen shrubs or trees. *U. molinae*, the only species usually cultivated, is grown for its foliage, flowers and fruit. Needs sun or partial shade and moist but well-drained soil. Propagate by semiripe cuttings in late summer.

U. molinae, syn. *Eugenia ugni, Myrtus ugni* (Chilean guava). Evergreen, upright, densely branched shrub. **H** 5ft (1.5m), **S** 3ft (1m). Glossy, dark green leaves are oval. Has fragrant, slightly nodding, cup-shaped, pink-tinted, white flowers in late spring, followed by aromatic, edible, spherical, dark red fruits. Is good for hedging in mild areas. Z9–10 H10–9.

ULEX
Furze, Gorse
LEGUMINOSAE/PAPILIONACEAE

Genus of leafless, or almost leafless, shrubs, grown for their spring flowers. Plants have year-round, green shoots and spines so appear to be evergreen. Needs full sun and prefers poor, well-drained, acidic soil. Trim each year after flowering to maintain compact habit. Straggly, old plants may be cut back hard in spring. Propagate by seed in fall. ① The seeds may cause mild stomach upset if ingested.

U. europaeus, illus. p.148. **'Flore Pleno'** is a leafless, or almost leafless, bushy shrub. **H** 3ft (1m), **S** 4ft (1.2m). In spring bears masses of fragrant, pealike, double, yellow flowers on leafless, dark green shoots. Z6–8 H8–6.

Ulma carpinifolia. See *Ulmus minor*.
Ulma 'Dicksonii'. See *Ulmus minor 'Dicksonii'*.
Ulma minor 'Sarniensis Aurea'. See *Ulmus minor 'Dicksonii'*.
Ulma 'Wheatleyi Aurea'. See *Ulmus minor 'Dicksonii'*.

ULMUS
Elm
ULMACEAE

Genus of deciduous or, rarely, semievergreen trees and shrubs, often large and stately, grown for their foliage and habit. Inconspicuous flowers appear in spring. Requires full sun and fertile, well-drained soil. Propagate by softwood cuttings in summer or by seed or suckers in fall. Is susceptible to Dutch elm disease, which is quickly fatal, although *U. parvifolia* and *U. pumila* appear more resistant than other species and hybrids.

U. americana (American elm). Deciduous, spreading tree. **H** and **S** 100ft (30m). Has gray bark and drooping branchlets. Large, oval, dark green leaves are sharply toothed and rough-textured. Z3–9 H9–1.

U. angustifolia. See *U. minor* subsp. *angustifolia*. **var. cornubiensis.** See *U. minor* 'Cornubiensis'.

U. 'Camperdownii'. See *U. glabra* 'Camperdownii'.

U. glabra (Dutch elm). Deciduous, spreading tree. **H** 100ft (30m), **S** 80ft (25m). Has broadly oval, toothed, very rough, dark green leaves, often slightly lobed at tips. From mid- to late spring bears clusters of winged, green fruits on bare branches. Z3–9 H8–2. **'Camperdownii',** syn. *U. 'Camperdownii'* illus. p.88. **'Exoniensis'** (Exeter elm) **H** 50ft (15m), **S** 15ft (5m), is narrow with upright branches when young, later becoming more spreading. Z5–7 H7–5.

U. x hollandica (Holland elm). Vigorous, deciduous tree with a short trunk and spreading to arching branches. **H** 100ft (30m), **S** 80ft (25m). Has oval, toothed, glossy, dark green leaves. Is very susceptible to Dutch elm disease. Z5–7 H7–5. **'Jacqueline Hillier', H** and **S** 6ft (2m), is slow-growing and suitable for hedging. Small leaves, rough-textured and sharply toothed, form 2 rows on each shoot; they persist into early winter. **'Vegeta'** (Huntingdon elm), **H** 120ft (35m), has upright central branches and pendent outer shoots. Broadly oval leaves turn yellow in fall.

U. minor, syn. *Ulma carpinifolia* (European field elm, Smooth-leaf elm). Deciduous, spreading tree with arching branches and pendent shoots. **H** 100ft (30m), **S** 70ft (20m). Small, oval, toothed, glossy, bright green leaves turn yellow in fall. Z5–8 H8–5. **subsp. angustifolia,** syn. *U. angustifolia* (Goodyer's elm) has a rounded canopy and elliptic to oval, double-toothed, mid- to dark green leaves, paler beneath. **'Cornubiensis',** syn. *U. angustifolia* var. *cornubiensis* (Cornish elm), **S** 50ft (15m), is conical when young and with a vase-shaped head when mature. **'Dicksonii',** syn. *Ulma 'Dicksonii', Ulma minor 'Sarniensis Aurea', Ulma 'Wheatleyi Aurea'* illus. p.76. **'Sarniensis'** (Jersey elm, Wheatley elm), **S** 30ft (10m), is a conical, dense tree with upright branches. Small, broadly oval leaves are mid-green.

U. parvifolia (Chinese elm, Lacebark elm). Deciduous or semievergreen, rounded tree. **H** and **S** 50ft (15m). Small, oval, glossy, dark green leaves last well into winter or, in mild areas, may persist until fresh growth appears. Z5–9 H9–5.

U. procera (English elm). Vigorous, deciduous, spreading tree with a bushy, dense, dome-shaped head. **H** 120ft (35m), **S** 50ft (15m). Broadly oval, toothed, rough, dark green leaves turn yellow in fall. Z5–8 H8–1.

U. pumila (Siberian elm). Deciduous, spreading, sometimes shrubby tree. **H** 50ft (15m), **S** 40ft (12m). Has oval, toothed, dark green leaves. Has some resistance to Dutch elm disease, but seedlings may be susceptible in hot summers. Z3–9 H9–1.

U. 'Wheatleyi Aurea'. See *U. minor* 'Dicksonii'.

UMBELLULARIA
LAURACEAE

Genus of evergreen, spring-flowering trees, grown for their aromatic foliage. Requires shelter from strong, cold winds when young. Needs sun and fertile, moist but well-drained soil. Propagate by seed in fall. ① The scent of crushed leaves may induce headaches and nausea.

U. californica, illus. p.69.

Urceolina peruviana. See *Stenomesson miniatum*.
Urginea maritima. See *Drimia maritima*.

URSINIA
COMPOSITAE/ASTERACEAE

Genus of annuals, evergreen perennials and subshrubs, grown mainly for their flower heads usually in summer, a few species for their foliage. Needs full light and well-drained soil. Water container plants moderately when in full growth, less at other times. Requires good ventilation if grown under glass. Propagate by seed or greenwood cuttings in spring. Aphids are sometimes troublesome.

U. anthemoides, illus. p.322.

U. chrysanthemoides. Evergreen, bushy perennial. **H** and **S** 2ft (60cm) or more. Has narrowly oval, feathery, strongly scented, green leaves. Bears small, long-stalked, daisylike, yellow flower heads, sometimes coppery below, in summer. Z13–15 H12–10.

U. sericea. Evergreen, bushy subshrub. **H** and **S** 10–18in (25–45cm). Leaves are cut into filigree of very slender, silver-haired segments. Daisylike, yellow flower heads are produced in summer. Is mainly grown for its foliage. Z13–15 H12–10.

UTRICULARIA
Bladderwort
LENTIBULARIACEAE

Genus of deciduous or evergreen, perennial, carnivorous water plants with bladder-like, modified leaves that trap and digest insects. Most species in cultivation are free-floating. Some species are suitable only for tropical aquariums; those grown in outdoor pools require full sun. Thin out plants that are overcrowded or become laden with algae. Propagate by division of floating foliage in spring or summer.

U. exoleta. See *U. gibba*.

U. gibba, syn. *U. exoleta*. Deciduous, perennial, free-floating water plant that is evergreen in very warm water. **S** 6in (15cm). Slender stems bear finely divided, mid-green leaves on which small bladders develop. Pouched, bright yellow flowers are produced in summer. Is suitable only for a tropical aquarium. Z12–15 H12–10.

U. vulgaris. Deciduous, perennial, free-floating water plant. **S** 12in (30cm). Much-divided, bronze-green leaves, studded with small bladders, are produced on slender stems. Bears pouched, bright yellow flowers in summer. May be grown in a pond or cold-water aquarium. Z12–15 H12–10.

UVULARIA
Merrybells
LILIACEAE/CONVALLARIACEAE

Genus of spring-flowering perennials that thrive in moist woodlands. Requires partial shade and prefers moist but well-drained, peaty soil. Propagate by division in early spring, before flowering.

U. grandiflora, illus. p.262.

U. perfoliata. Clump-forming perennial. **H** 18in (45cm), **S** 12in (30cm). In spring, clusters of pendent, bell-shaped, pale yellow flowers, with twisted petals, are produced on numerous slender stems above stem-clasping, narrowly oval, mid-green leaves. Z4–9 H9–1.

VACCINIUM

Blueberry, Cranberry, Huckleberry

ERICACEAE

Genus of deciduous or evergreen subshrubs, shrubs and trees, grown for their foliage, fall color (on deciduous species), flowers and fruits, which are often edible. Needs sun or partial shade and moist but well-drained, peaty or sandy, acidic soil. Propagate by semiripe cuttings in summer or by seed in fall.

V. angustifolium var. laevifolium, illus. p.163.
V. arctostaphylos (Caucasian whortleberry). Deciduous, upright shrub. **H** 10ft (3m), **S** 6ft (2m). Has red-brown young shoots and oval, dark green leaves that mature to red and purple in fall. Bell-shaped, white flowers, tinged with red, are produced in spreading racemes in early summer, followed by spherical, purplish-black fruits. Z6–8 H8–6.
V. corymbosum, illus. p.150. **'Pioneer'** illus. p.163.
V. glaucoalbum, illus. p.165.
V. myrtillus (Sourtop blueberry). Deciduous, usually prostrate shrub. **H** 6in (15cm) or more, **S** 12in (30cm) or more. Bears small, heart-shaped, leathery, bright green leaves. Pendent, bell-shaped, pale pink flowers, in early summer, are followed by edible, spherical, blue-black fruits. Z5–7 H7–5.
V. nummularia. Evergreen, prostrate shrub. **H** 4in (10cm), **S** 8in (20cm). Slender stems, covered in red-brown bristles, bear oval, wrinkled, bright green leaves, with red-brown bristles at margins. Small racemes of bell-shaped, white to deep pink flowers at stem tips in early summer are followed by small, spherical, black fruits. Is suitable for a rock garden or peat bed. Needs partial shade. May also be propagated by division in spring. Z7–9 H9–7.
V. parvifolium, illus. p.163.
V. vitis-idaea (Cowberry). Vigorous, evergreen, prostrate shrub, spreading by underground runners. **H** ¾–10in (2–25cm), **S** indefinite. Forms hummocks of oval, hard, leathery leaves. Bell-shaped, white to pink flowers are borne in nodding racemes from early summer to fall, followed by spherical, bright red fruits in fall–winter. May also be propagated by division in spring. Z2–6 H6–1. **subsp. minus,** syn. *V. vitis-idaea* 'Minus' illus. p.351. **'Minus'.** See *V. vitis-idaea* subsp. *minus*.

VALERIANA

Valerian

VALERIANACEAE

Genus of summer-flowering perennials that are suitable for growing in borders and rock gardens. Requires sun and well-drained soil. Propagate by division in fall, *V. officinalis* by seed in spring.
V. officinalis, illus. p.231.
V. phu 'Aurea', illus. p.262.

VALLEA

ELAEOCARPACEAE

Genus of one species of evergreen shrub, grown for its overall appearance. Prefers full sun and rich, well-drained soil. Water container plants freely in growing season,

moderately at other times. Untidy growth may be cut out in early spring. Propagate by seed in spring or by semiripe cuttings in summer. Red spider mite may be a nuisance.
V. stipularis. Evergreen, erect, then loose and spreading shrub. **H** and **S** 6–15ft (2–5m). Leaves are lance-shaped to rounded and lobed, deep green above, gray beneath. Small, cup-shaped flowers, with 5 deep pink petals that have 3 lobes, are borne in small, terminal and lateral clusters in spring–summer. Z9–10 H10–9.

VALLISNERIA

HYDROCHARITACEAE

Genus of evergreen, perennial, submerged water plants, grown for their foliage. Is suitable for ponds and aquariums. Requires sun or partial shade and deep, clear water. Remove fading foliage, and thin overcrowded plants as required. Propagate by division in spring or summer.
V. americana, syn. *V. gigantea*. Vigorous, evergreen, perennial, submerged water plant. **S** indefinite. Quickly grows to form colonies of long, strap-shaped, mid-green leaves. Produces insignificant, greenish flowers all year-round. Z4–11 H12–1.
V. gigantea. See *V. americana*.
V. spiralis (Eel grass, Tape grass). Vigorous, evergreen, perennial, submerged water plant. **S** indefinite. Forms a mass of long, strap-shaped, mid-green leaves, but on a smaller scale than *V. americana*. Insignificant, greenish flowers are borne year-round. Z4–11 H12–1.

Vallota speciosa. See *Cyrtanthus elatus*.

VANCOUVERIA

BERBERIDACEAE

Genus of perennials, some of which are evergreen, suitable for groundcover. Prefers partial shade and moist, peaty soil. Propagate by division in spring.
V. chrysantha. Evergreen, sprawling perennial. **H** 12in (30cm), **S** indefinite. Oval, dark green leaves borne on flower stems are divided into rounded diamond-shaped leaflets with thickened, undulating margins. Loose sprays of small, bell-shaped, yellow flowers are borne in spring. Z6–8 H8–6.
V. hexandra. Vigorous, spreading perennial. **H** 8in (20cm), **S** indefinite. Leathery leaves are divided into almost hexagonal leaflets. Bears open sprays of many tiny, white flowers in late spring and early summer. Makes good woodland groundcover. Z5–8 H8–5.

VANDA

ORCHIDACEAE

See also ORCHIDS.
V. Rothschildiana gx, illus. p.466. Evergreen, epiphytic orchid for a cool or intermediate greenhouse. **H** 24in (60cm). Sprays of dark-veined, violet-blue flowers, 4in (10cm) across, are borne twice a year in varying seasons. Has narrowly oval, rigid leaves, 4–5in (10–12cm) long. Grow in a hanging basket and provide good light in summer. Z15 H12–10.

VELLOZIA

VELLOZIACEAE

Genus of evergreen perennials and shrubs, grown for their showy flowers. Needs full sun and moderately fertile, very well-drained soil. Propagate by seed or division in spring.
V. elegans, syn. *Barbacenia elegans, Talbotia elegans*. Evergreen, mat-forming perennial with slightly woody stems. **H** to 6in (15cm), **S** 6–12in (15–30cm). Lance-shaped, leathery, dark green leaves, to 8in (20cm) long, have V-shaped keels. In late spring bears solitary, small, star-shaped, white flowers on slender stems above leaves. Z14–15 H12–10.

VELTHEIMIA

LILIACEAE/HYACINTHACEAE

Genus of winter-flowering bulbs, grown for their dense spikes of pendent, tubular flowers and rosettes of basal leaves. Needs full light, to keep foliage compact and to develop flower colors fully, and well-drained soil. Plant in fall with tips above soil surface. Reduce watering in summer. Propagate by seed or offsets in fall.
V. bracteata, syn. *V. capensis* of gardens, *V. undulata, V. viridifolia*, illus. p.414.
V. capensis, syn. *V. glauca, V. viridifolia* of gardens. Winter-flowering bulb. **H** 12–18in (30–45cm), **S** 8–12in (20–30cm). Has basal rosette of lance-shaped leaves, usually with very wavy edges. Stem produces dense spike of pink or red flowers, ¾–1½in (2–3cm) long. Z12–15 H12–10.
V. capensis of gardens. See *V. bracteata*.
V. glauca. See *V. capensis*.
V. undulata. See *V. bracteata*.
V. viridifolia. See *V. bracteata*.
V. viridifolia of gardens. See *V. capensis*.

x Venidioarctotis. See *Arctotis*.

VERATRUM

LILIACEAE/MELANTHIACEAE

Genus of perennials, with poisonous black rhizomes, ideal for woodland gardens. Requires partial shade and fertile, moist soil. Propagate by division or seed in fall. ① All parts are highly toxic if ingested. Contact with the foliage may irritate skin.
V. album (False hellebore, White hellebore). Clump-forming perennial. **H** 6ft (2m), **S** 2ft (60cm). Basal leaves are pleated, oval and dark green. Stems bear dense, terminal panicles of saucer-shaped, yellowish-white flowers in summer. H11–10.
V. nigrum, illus. p.216.

VERBASCUM

Mullein

SCROPHULARIACEAE

Genus of mainly summer-flowering perennials, some of which are semievergreen or evergreen, and evergreen biennials and shrubs. Prefers an open, sunny site and well-drained soil. Propagate species by seed in spring or late summer or by root cuttings in winter, selected forms by root cuttings only. Some species self-seed freely.

V. bombyciferum (Turkish mullein). Evergreen, erect biennial. **H** 4–6ft (1.2–2m), **S** 2ft (60cm). Oval leaves and stems are covered with silvery hairs. Produces upright racemes densely set with 5-lobed, yellow flowers in summer. Z5–9 H9–2.
V. chaixii (Nettle-leaved mullein). Erect perennial, covered with silvery hairs. **H** 3ft (1m), **S** 2ft (60cm). Has oval, toothed, rough, nettle-like leaves. Produces slender spires of 5-lobed, yellow, sometimes white flowers, with purple stamens, in summer. Z5–9 H9–5.
V. 'Cotswold Beauty', illus. p.246.
V. 'Cotswold Queen'. Short-lived, rosette-forming perennial. **H** 3–4ft (1–1.2m), **S** 1–2ft (30–60cm). Throughout summer, branched racemes of 5-lobed, apricot-buff flowers are borne on stems that arise from oval, mid-green leaves. Z5–9 H9–5.
V. densiflorum, syn. *V. thapsiforme*. Fairly slow-growing, semievergreen, rosette-forming, upright perennial. **H** 4–5ft (1.2–1.5m), **S** 2ft (60cm). Has large, oval, crinkled, hairy, mid-green leaves. Each hairy stem produces bold spike of flattish, 5-lobed, yellow flowers in summer. Z5–9 H9–5.
V. dumulosum, illus. p.345.
V. 'Gainsborough', illus. p.243.
V. 'Letitia', illus. p.343.
V. lychnitis (White mullein). Slow-growing, evergreen, upright, branching biennial. **H** 2–3ft (60cm–1m), **S** 2ft (60cm). Has lance-shaped, dark gray-green leaves. Flattish, 5-lobed, white flowers are borne on branching stems in summer. Z5–8 H8–5.
V. nigrum (Dark mullein). Semievergreen, clump-forming perennial. **H** 2–3ft (60cm–1m), **S** 2ft (60cm). Bears narrow spikes of small, 5-lobed, purple-centered, yellow flowers in summer–fall. Oblong, mid-green leaves are downy beneath. Z6–9 H9–6.
V. olympicum, illus. p.219.
V. 'Pink Domino'. Short-lived, rosette-forming perennial. **H** 4ft (1.2m), **S** 1–2ft (30–60cm). Produces branched racemes of 5-lobed, rose-pink flowers in summer above oval, mid-green leaves. Z5–9 H9–1.
V. thapsiforme. See *V. densiflorum*.

VERBENA

VERBENACEAE

Genus of summer- and fall-flowering biennials and perennials, some of which are semievergreen. Prefers sun and well-drained soil. Propagate by stem cuttings in late summer or fall or by seed in fall or spring.
V. alpina of gardens. See *Glandularia x maonettii*.
V. bonariensis, syn. *V. patagonica*, illus. p.221.
V. chamaedrifolia. See *Glandularia peruviana*.
V. chamaedrioides. See *Glandularia peruviana*.
V. x hortensis. See *Glandularia x hybrida*.
V. x hybrida. See *Glandularia x hybrida*.
V. patagonica. See *V. bonariensis*.
V. rigida, syn. *V. venosa*, illus. p.269.
V. 'Sissinghurst'. See *Glandularia* 'Sissinghurst'.
V. tenera var. maonettii. See *Glandularia x maonettii*.
V. venosa. See *V. rigida*.

U V W

VERONICA

Speedwell

SCROPHULARIACEAE

Genus of perennials and subshrubs, some of which are semievergreen or evergreen, grown for their usually blue flowers. Some need sun and well-drained soil, others prefer sun or partial shade and moist soil. Propagate by division in spring or fall, by softwood or semiripe cuttings in summer or by seed in fall.

V. austriaca. Mat-forming or upright perennial. **H** and **S** 10–20in (25–50cm). Leaves are very variable: from broadly oval to narrowly oblong, and from entire to deeply cut and fernlike. Short, dense or lax racemes of small, saucer-shaped, bright blue flowers are produced in early summer. Is suitable for a rock garden or a bank. Z4–8 H8–2. **subsp. *teucrium*,** syn. *V. teucrium* illus. p.343. **subsp. *teucrium* 'Kapitan',** syn. *V. prostrata* 'Kapitan' illus. p.343. **subsp. *teucrium* 'Royal Blue'** has deep royal-blue flowers.

V. beccabunga, illus. p.442.

V. cinerea. Spreading, much-branched, woody-based perennial. **H** 6in (15cm), **S** 12in (30cm). Has small, linear, occasionally oval, hairy, silvery-white leaves. Trailing flower stems bear saucer-shaped, deep blue to purple flowers, with white eyes, in early summer. Is suitable for a sunny rock garden. Z5–8 H8–5.

V. exaltata. See *V. longifolia.*

V. fruticans (Rock speedwell). Deciduous, upright to procumbent subshrub. **H** 6in (15cm), **S** 12in (30cm). Leaves are oval and green. Spikes of saucer-shaped, bright blue flowers, with red eyes, are borne in summer. Is suitable for a rock garden. Z5–8 H8–5.

V. gentianoides, illus. p.271.

V. incana. See *V. spicata* subsp. *incana.*

V. longifolia, syn. *V. exaltata.* Variable, upright perennial. **H** 3–4ft (1–1.2m), **S** 1ft (30cm) or more. In late summer and early fall, long, terminal racemes of star-shaped, lilac-blue flowers are borne on stems with whorls of narrowly oval to lance-shaped, toothed, mid-green leaves. Z4–8 H8–1.

V. pectinata. Dense, mat-forming perennial that is sometimes semierect. **H** and **S** 8in (20cm). Has small, narrowly oval, hairy leaves. Bears loose sprays of saucer-shaped, soft blue to blue-violet flowers in summer. Is good for a rock garden or a bank. Z2–7 H7–1. **'Rosea',** **H** 3in (8cm), has rose-lilac flowers. Z3–7 H7–1.

V. peduncularis, illus. p.271.

V. perfoliata. See *Parahebe perfoliata.*

V. prostrata, syn. *V. rupestris,* illus. p.343. **'Kapitan'.** See *V. austriaca* subsp. *teucrium* 'Kapitan'. **'Spode Blue'** is a dense, mat-forming perennial. **H** to 12in (30cm), **S** indefinite. Upright spikes of small, saucer-shaped, china-blue flowers are borne in early summer. Leaves are narrowly oval and toothed. **'Trehane'** illus. p.343.

V. rupestris. See *V. prostrata.*

V. spicata (Spiked speedwell). Clump-forming perennial. **H** 12–24in (30–60cm), **S** 18in (45cm). Spikes of small, star-shaped, bright blue flowers are borne in summer above narrowly oval, toothed, mid-green leaves. Z3–8 H8–1. **subsp. *incana*,** syn. *V. incana* illus. p.271. **'Romiley Purple'** illus. p.239.

V. teucrium. See *V. austriaca* subsp. *teucrium.*

V. virginica. See *Veronicastrum virginicum.* **f. *alba*.** See *Veronicastrum virginicum* f. *album.*

VERONICASTRUM

SCROPHULARIACEAE

Genus of evergreen perennials, grown for their pale blue flowers. Requires sun and moist soil. Propagate by division in spring or fall, by softwood or semiripe cuttings in summer or by seed in fall.

V. virginicum, syn. *Veronica virginica* (Culver's root). Upright perennial. **H** 4ft (1.2m), **S** 1½ft (45cm). In late summer, racemes of small, star-shaped, purple-blue or pink flowers crown stems clothed with whorls of narrowly lance-shaped, dark green leaves. Z3–8 H8–1. **f. *album*,** syn. *Veronica virginica* f. *alba* has small, white flowers, with pink-flushed bases and pink anthers. **'Fascination'** illus. p.220.

VESTIA

SOLANACEAE

Genus of one species of evergreen shrub, grown for its flowers and foliage. At the limits of hardiness is often cut to ground level and is best grown against a south-facing wall. Requires sun and well-drained soil. Propagate by semiripe cuttings in summer or by seed in fall or spring.

V. foetida, syn. *V. lycioides,* illus. p.194.

V. lycioides. See *V. foetida.*

VIBURNUM

CAPRIFOLIACEAE

Genus of deciduous, semievergreen or evergreen shrubs and trees, grown for their foliage, fall color (in many deciduous species), flowers and, often, fruits. Fruiting is generally most prolific when several plants of different clones are planted together. Needs sun or partial shade and deep, fertile, not too dry soil. To thin out overgrown plants, cut out some older shoots after flowering. Propagate by cuttings (softwood for deciduous species, semiripe for evergreens) in summer or by seed in fall. ⓘ The fruits of viburnums may cause mild stomach upset if ingested. See also feature panel p.142.

V. acerifolium, illus. p.151.

V. betulifolium, illus. p.142. Deciduous, upright, arching shrub. **H** and **S** 10ft (3m). Bright green leaves are slightly glossy beneath. Heads of small, tubular, white flowers, in early summer, are followed by profuse, nodding clusters of spherical, bright red fruits in fall–winter. Z5–8 H8–5.

V. bitchiuense, illus. p.122.

V. x bodnantense. Z7–8 H8–7. **'Dawn'** illus. p.143. **'Deben'** is a deciduous, upright shrub. **H** 10ft (3m), **S** 6ft (2m). Oval, toothed, dark green leaves are bronze when young. Clusters of fragrant, tubular, white flowers, tinted with pale pink, are borne during mild periods from late fall through to early spring.

V. x burkwoodii. Semievergreen, bushy, open shrub. **H** and **S** 8ft (2.5m). Rounded heads of fragrant, tubular, pink, then white flowers are borne amid oval, glossy, dark green leaves from mid- to late spring. Z5–8 H8–1. **'Anne Russell',** **H** and **S** 5ft (1.5m), is deciduous and has very fragrant, white flowers. Z4–8 H8–1. **'Park Farm Hybrid'** bears very fragrant, white flowers that are slightly pink in bud, and older leaves turn bright red in fall. Z4–8 H8–1.

V. x carlcephalum, illus. p.111.

V. carlesii, illus. p.146. **'Diana'** is a deciduous, bushy, dense shrub. **H** and **S** 6ft (2m). Broadly oval leaves are bronze when young and turn purple-red in fall. From mid- to late spring bears rounded heads of red buds that open to very fragrant, tubular, pink flowers fading to white.

V. cinnamomifolium. Evergreen, bushy or treelike shrub. **H** and **S** 15ft (5m). Large, oval leaves, with 3 prominent veins. Bears broad clusters of small, star-shaped, white flowers, in early summer, followed by egg-shaped, blue fruits. Z7–9 H9–7.

V. davidii, illus. p.165.

V. dilatatum (Arrow-wood). Deciduous, upright shrub. **H** 10ft (3m), **S** 6ft (2m). Oval, sharply toothed, dark green leaves sometimes redden in fall. Flat heads of small, star-shaped, white flowers, in late spring and early summer, are followed by egg-shaped, bright red fruits. Z5–8 H8–5. **'Catskill'** illus. p.130.

V. farreri, syn. *V. fragrans,* illus. p.143. **'Candidissimum'** is a deciduous, upright shrub. **H** 10ft (3m), **S** 6ft (2m). Oval, toothed, dark green leaves are pale green when young. Produces clusters of fragrant, tubular, pure white flowers in late fall and during mild periods in winter and early spring.

V. foetens, syn. *V. grandiflorum* f. *foetens,* illus. p.143.

V. fragrans. See *V. farreri.*

V. grandiflorum. Deciduous, upright, open shrub. **H** and **S** 6ft (2m). Stiff branches bear oblong, dark green leaves that become deep purple in fall. Dense clusters of fragrant, tubular, white-and-pink flowers open from deep pink buds from mid-winter to early spring. Z6–8 H8–6. **f. *foetens*.** See *V. foetens.*

V. x juddii, illus. p.146.

V. lantana (Wayfaring tree). Vigorous, deciduous, upright shrub. **H** 15ft (5m), **S** 12ft (4m). Has broadly oval, gray-green leaves that redden in fall. Flattened heads of small, tubular, 5-lobed, white flowers, in late spring and early summer, are followed by egg-shaped, red fruits that ripen to black. Z4–8 H8–1.

V. lentago (Nannyberry, Sheepberry). Vigorous, deciduous, upright shrub. **H** 12ft (4m), **S** 10ft (3m). Oval, glossy, dark green leaves turn red and purple in fall. Bears flattened heads of small, fragrant, star-shaped, white flowers, in late spring and early summer, followed by egg-shaped, blue-black fruits. Z2–8 H8–1.

V. odoratissimum (Sweet viburnum). Evergreen, bushy shrub. **H** and **S** 15ft (5m). Clusters of small, fragrant, star-shaped, white flowers, borne amid oval, leathery, glossy, dark green leaves in late spring, are followed by egg-shaped, red fruits that ripen to black. Z8–10 H10–7.

V. opulus (European cranberry bush, Guelder rose). Vigorous, deciduous, bushy shrub. **H** and **S** 12ft (4m). Bears broadly oval, lobed, deep green leaves that redden in fall and, in late spring and early summer, flattened, lacecap-like heads of tubular, white flowers. Produces large bunches of spherical, bright red fruits. Z3–8 H8–1. **'Compactum'** illus. p.162. **'Xanthocarpum'** has yellow fruits and mid-green leaves that turn yellow in fall.

V. plicatum (Japanese snowball bush). Deciduous, bushy, spreading shrub. **H** 10ft (3m), **S** 12ft (4m). Oval, toothed, deeply veined, dark green leaves turn reddish-purple in fall. Dense, rounded heads of large, sterile, saucer-shaped, white flowers are borne along branches in late spring and early summer. Z4–8 H8–1. **'Mariesii'.** See *V. plicatum* f. *tomentosum* 'Mariesii'. **'Nanum Semperflorens',** syn. *V. plicatum* 'Watanabe', *V. plicatum* 'Watenabei', *V. watenabei,* **H** 6ft (2m), **S** 5ft (1.5m), is slow-growing, conical and dense, and produces small flower heads from late spring until early fall. Z6–8 H8–6. **'Pink Beauty'** (illus. p.142) bears white flowers maturing to pink, and fruits freely. **f. *tomentosum*** (Doublefile viburnum) has tiered branches, flattish, lacecap-like flower heads and red fruits, ripening to black. Z5–8 H8–1. **f. *tomentosum* 'Mariesii',** syn. *V. plicatum* 'Mariesii', illus. p.110. **'Watanabe'.** See *V. plicatum* 'Nanum Semperflorens'. **'Watenabei'.** See *V. plicatum* 'Nanum Semperflorens'.

V. x pragense. See *V.* 'Pragense'.

V. 'Pragense', syn. *V.* x *pragense,* illus. p.131.

V. rhytidophyllum, illus. p.112.

V. sargentii (Sargent viburnum). Deciduous, bushy shrub. **H** and **S** 10ft (3m). Maple-like, mid-green leaves often turn yellow or red in fall. Broad, flattish, lace-cap-like heads of tubular, white flowers in late spring are followed by spherical, bright red fruits. Z4–7 H7–1. **'Onondaga',** S6ft (2m), has bronze-red, young leaves, becoming deep green, then bronze-red again in fall. Flower buds are pink.

V. sieboldii. Deciduous, rounded, dense shrub. **H** 12ft (4m), **S** 20ft (6m). Has large, oblong to oval, glossy, bright green leaves. Rounded heads of tubular, creamy-white flowers are borne in late spring, followed by egg-shaped, red-stalked, red fruits that ripen to black. Z5–8 H8–5.

V. tinus (Laurustinus). Evergreen, bushy, compact shrub. **H** and **S** 10ft (3m). Has oval, dark green leaves. Freely produced flat heads of small, white flowers open from pink buds in late winter and spring. Z8–10 H10–8. **'Eve Price'** illus. p.143. **'Gwenllian'** has flattened heads of small, star-shaped, pale pink flowers freely borne from deep pink buds amid oval, dark green leaves in winter–spring and followed by abundant, ovoid, blue fruits.

V. watenabei. See *V. plicatum* 'Nanum Semperflorens'.

VIGNA

LEGUMINOSAE/PAPILIONACEAE

Genus of evergreen, annual and perennial, erect or scrambling and twining climbers, grown mainly as crop plants for their leaves, pods and seeds. Provide full light and rich, well-drained soil. Water freely when in full growth, sparingly at other times. Stems require support. Thin crowded stems or cut back hard in spring. Propagate by seed in fall or spring.

V. caracalla, syn. *Phaseolus caracalla* (Snail flower). Fast-growing, evergreen, perennial, twining climber. **H** 10–15ft (3–5m). Leaves are divided into 3 oval leaflets. From summer to early fall produces pealike, purple-marked, cream flowers that turn orange-yellow. H12–10.

Villarsia nymphoides. See *Nymphoides peltata.*

VINCA
Periwinkle

APOCYNACEAE

Genus of evergreen, trailing subshrubs and perennials, grown for their foliage and flowers. Flowers are tubular with 5 spreading lobes. Is useful for groundcover in shade, but flowers more freely given some sun. Tolerates any soil that is not too dry. Propagate by semiripe cuttings in summer or by division from fall to spring. ⓘ All parts may cause mild stomach upset if ingested.
V. difformis. Evergreen, prostrate subshrub. **H** 12in (30cm), **S** indefinite. Slender, trailing stems bear oval, glossy, dark green leaves. Erect flower stems produce pale blue flowers in late fall and early winter. Z8–9 H9–8.
V. major (Blue buttons). Evergreen, prostrate, arching subshrub. **H** 18in (45cm), **S** indefinite. Leaves are broadly oval, glossy and dark green. Large, bright blue flowers are produced from late spring to early fall. Z7–9 H9–7. **subsp. *hirsuta*.** See *V. major* var. *oxyloba*. **var. *oxyloba*,** syn. *V. major* subsp. *hirsuta* has leaves, leaf stalks and calyces edged with long hairs. **'Variegata'** illus. p.164.
V. minor, illus. p.165. **'Alba Variegata'** is an evergreen, prostrate subshrub. **H** 6in (15cm), **S** indefinite. Forms extensive mats of small, oval, glossy, dark green leaves, edged with pale yellow, above which white flowers are borne from mid-spring to early summer, then intermittently into fall. **'Bowles' Blue'.** See *V. minor* 'La Grave'. **'Bowles' White'** bears large, white flowers that are pinkish-white in bud. **'Gertrude Jekyll'** is of dense growth and produces a profusion of small, white flowers. Flowers of **'La Grave',** syn. *V. minor* 'Bowles' Blue' are large and lavender-blue.
V. rosea. See *Catharanthus roseus.*

VIOLA
Pansy, Violet

VIOLACEAE

Genus of annuals, perennials, some of which are semievergreen, and deciduous subshrubs, grown for their 5-petaled flowers. Annuals are suitable as summer bedding, perennials and subshrubs are good in rock gardens, screes and alpine houses. Needs sun or partial shade and moist but well-drained soil unless otherwise stated; a few species prefer acidic soil. Propagate annuals by seed sown according to flowering season, perennials and subshrubs by softwood cuttings in spring unless otherwise stated, species also by seed in spring or fall.
V. aetolica, illus. p.359.
V. biflora (Twin-flowered violet). Creeping, rhizomatous perennial. **H** 2–6in (5–15cm), **S** 6in (15cm). Flat-faced, deep lemon-yellow flowers, veined dark brown, are borne singly or in pairs on upright stems in summer. Leaves are kidney-shaped and mid-green. Needs shade. May be propagated by division. Z4–8 H8–1.
V. 'Bowles's Black', syn. *V. tricolor* 'Bowles' Black', illus. p.355.
V. calcarata, illus. p.354.
V. cazorlensis. Tufted, woody-based perennial. **H** to 2in (5cm), **S** to 3in (8cm). Has small, linear to lance-shaped leaves. In late spring produces small, flat-faced, long-spurred, deep pink flowers, singly on short stems. Is suitable for an alpine house. Is difficult to grow. Z8–10 H10–8.
V. cenisia. Spreading perennial with runners. **H** 3in (7cm), **S** 4in (10cm). Small, flat-faced, bright violet flowers, with deep purple line radiating from center, are produced on very short stems in summer. Has deep taproot and tiny, heart-shaped or oblong, dark green leaves. Is suitable for a scree. Propagate by division in spring. Z8–10 H10–8.
V. cornuta (Horned violet). Rhizomatous perennial. **H** 5–8in (12–20cm), **S** 8in (20cm) or more. Has oval, toothed leaves and flat-faced, angular, spurred, pale to deep purplish-blue, occasionally white flowers in spring and much of summer. Z6–9 H9–1. **'Minor'** illus. p.356.
V. cucullata. See *V. obliqua.*
V. elatior. Upright, little-branched perennial. **H** 8–12in (20–30cm), **S** 6in (15cm). Leaves are broadly lance-shaped and toothed. Produces flat-faced, pale blue flowers, with white centers, in early summer. Prefers partial shade and moist soil. Propagate in spring by division. Z5–8 H8–5.
V. glabella (Stream violet). Clump-forming perennial with a scaly, horizontal rootstock. **H** 4in (10cm), **S** 8in (20cm). Produces flat-faced, bright yellow flowers, with purplish-veined lower petals, in late spring above heart-shaped, toothed, bright green leaves. Needs shade. Propagate by division in spring. Z5–8 H8–5.
V. gracilis. Mat-forming perennial. **H** 5in (12cm), **S** 6in (15cm) or more. Flat-faced, yellow-centered, violet-blue or sometimes yellow flowers are produced in summer. Has small, dissected leaves, with linear or oblong segments. Needs sun. Z5–8 H8–5.
V. 'Green Goddess', syn. *V. tricolor* 'Green Goddess', illus. p.318.
V. 'Haslemere'. See *V.* 'Nellie Britton'.
V. hederacea, syn. *V. reniforme, Erpetion reniforme* (Australian violet, Ivy-leaved violet, Trailing violet). Evergreen, creeping, mat-forming perennial. **H** 1–2in (2.5–5cm), **S** indefinite. Has tiny, rounded leaves and bears purple or white flowers, with squashed appearance, on short stems in summer. Is suitable for growing in an alpine house. Prefers partial shade. Propagate by division in spring. Z8–9 H9–8.
V. 'Huntercombe Purple', illus. p.368.
V. 'Irish Molly'. Evergreen, clump-forming, short-lived perennial. **H** 4in (10cm), **S** 6–8in (15–20cm). Has broadly oval, dissected leaves and, in summer, a succession of flat-faced, old-gold flowers, with brown centers. Flowers itself to death. Needs sun. Z5–7 H7–5.
V. 'Jackanapes', illus. p.359.
V. Joker Series, illus. p.312.
V. labradorica 'Purpurea'. See *V. riviniana* Purpurea Group.
V. lutea (Mountain pansy). Mat-forming, rhizomatous perennial. **H** 4in (10cm), **S** 6in (15cm). Has small, oval to lance-shaped leaves. Flat-faced, yellow, violet or bicolored flowers are produced in spring–summer. Z4–8 H8–1.
V. 'Nellie Britton', syn. *V.* 'Haslemere', illus. p.367.
V. obliqua, syn. *V. cucullata* (Marsh blue violet). Variable, spreading perennial with fleshy rhizomes. **H** 2in (5cm), **S** 4–6in (10–15cm). Has kidney-shaped, toothed, mid-green leaves. In late spring produces flat-faced, blue-violet, sometimes white or pale blue flowers. Propagate in spring. Z4–9 H9–7.
V. odorata (English violet, Garden violet, Sweet violet). Semievergreen, spreading, rhizomatous perennial. **H** 3in (7cm), **S** 6in (15cm) or more. Leaves are heart-shaped and toothed. Long stems bear solitary, fragrant, flat-faced, violet or white flower from late winter to early spring. Is useful in a wild garden. Self-seeds prolifically. May also be propagated by division. Z6–8 H8–6.
V. palmata. Spreading perennial. **H** 4in (10cm), **S** 6in (15cm). Has deeply dissected leaves. Short-stemmed, flat-faced, pale violet flowers are produced in late spring. Prefers dry, well-drained soil. Self-seeds readily. Z8–9 H9–8.
V. pedata, illus. p.355. **var. *bicolor*** is a clump-forming perennial with a thick rootstock. **H** 2in (5cm), **S** 3in (8cm). Solitary, flat-faced, velvety-purple or white flowers are borne on slender stems in late spring and early summer. Leaves are finely divided into 5–7 or more, narrow, toothed segments. Is suitable for an alpine house. May be difficult to grow; needs peaty, sandy soil.
V. reniforme. See *V. hederacea.*
***V. riviniana* Purpurea Group,** syn. *V. labradorica* 'Purpurea', *V. riviniana* 'Purpurea', illus. p.355.
V. 'Sunvioki'. See *V.* x *wittrockiana* Friolina Gold.
V. tricolor, illus. p.355. **'Bowles' Black'.** See *V.* 'Bowles's Black'.**'Green Goddess'.** See *V.* 'Green Goddess'.
V.* x *wittrockiana (Pansy). Group of slow- to moderately fast-growing, mainly bushy perennials, usually grown as annuals or biennials. **H** 6–8in (15–20cm), **S** 8in (20cm). Have oval, often serrated, mid-green leaves. Flattish, 5-petaled flowers, 1–4in (2.5–10cm) across, in very wide color range, are produced throughout summer or in winter–spring. Z6–9 H9–1. The following are among those available: **Angel Series 'Tiger Eye'** (spring-flowering), illus. p.323. **'Baby Lucia'** (summer-flowering) has small, deep blue flowers. **Clear Crystals Series** (summer-flowering) is in wide range of clear colors. Z8–11 H9–1. **'Clear Sky Primrose'** (winter- to spring-flowering) produces primrose-yellow flowers brushed in canary-yellow. Z4–8 H9–1. **Crystal Bowl Series** (summer-flowering) are in range of colors, including yellow. Z8–11 H9–1. **Floral Dance Series** (winter-flowering), illus. p.308 have wide range of colors, including white. Z8–11 H12–1. **Forerunner Series** (winter- to spring-flowering) bear medium-sized flowers in range of bright, single colors and bicolors. Z8–11 H12–1. **Friolina Gold ('Sunvioki')** (summer-flowering) has yellow flowers, with faintly streaked orange centers. Is ideal for a hanging basket. Z8–11 H9–1. **Imperial Series 'Imperial Frosty Rose',** illus. p.312. **Imperial Series 'Orange Prince'** (summer-flowering) has orange flowers with black blotches. Z8–11 H9–1. **Imperial Series 'Sky Blue'** (summer-flowering) has sky-blue flowers, with deeper-colored blotch. Z8–11 H9–1. **'Majestic Giants'** (summer-flowering) has large flowers in wide color range. Z8–11 H9–1. **Panola Series** (summer-flowering) produce large, bright yellow, black-centered flowers. Z8–11 H9–1. **Princess Series** (spring- to summer-flowering) are neat in habit, and produce small flowers in blue, cream, bicolored purple and white, dark purple or yellow. Z8–11 H9–1. **'Silver Princess'** (summer-flowering) has white flowers, each with a deep pink blotch. Z8–11 H9–1. **Sorbet Series** (winter- to spring-flowering) has small flowers, with or without whiskers, in more than 20 color combinations. Z8–11 H9–1. **'Sorbet Black Delight',** illus. p.312. **'Super Chalon Giants'** (summer- to autumn-flowering) have ruffled and waved, bicolored flowers. Z8–11 H9–1. **'True Blue'** (winter- to summer-flowering) bears large, clear sky-blue flowers with small, yellow eyes. Z4–8 H9–1. **Ultima Radiance Series** (winter- to spring-flowering) has large, neatly rounded flowers in up to 30 color combinations. Z8–11 H9–1, illus. p.313. **Ultima Series** (winter- to spring-flowering) have medium-sized flowers in very broad range of colors, including bicolors. Z8–11 H9–1. **Universal Series** (winter- to spring-flowering) produce flowers in an extensive range of separate colors as well as in mixture of colors. Z8–11 H9–1.

VIRGILIA

LEGUMINOSAE/PAPILIONACEAE

Genus of short-lived, evergreen shrubs and trees, grown for their flowers which are borne in spring and summer. Prefers full light and well-drained soil. Water container plants freely when in growth, less at other times. Propagate in spring by seed, ideally soaked in warm water for 24 hours before sowing.
V. capensis. See *V. oroboides.*
V. oroboides, syn. *V. capensis.* Fast-growing, evergreen, rounded shrub or tree. **H** and **S** 20–30ft (6–10m). Has leaves divided into 11–21 oblong leaflets. Racemes of fragrant, pealike, bright mauve-pink flowers, sometimes pink, crimson or white, are produced in late spring and summer, usually in great profusion. Z10–11 H12–10.

Viscaria alpina. See *Lychnis alpina.*
Viscaria elegans. See *Silene coeli-rosa.*

VITALIANA

PRIMULACEAE

Genus of one species of evergreen, spring-flowering perennial, grown for its flowers. Is often included in *Douglasia* and is useful for rock gardens, screes and alpine houses. Requires sun and moist but well-drained soil. Propagate by softwood cuttings in summer or by seed in fall.
V. primuliflora, syn. *Douglasia vitaliana*, illus. p.358.

VITEX

VERBENACEAE/LAMIACEAE

Genus of evergreen or deciduous trees and shrubs, grown for their flowers. At limits of hardiness grow against a south- or west-facing wall. Needs full sun and well-drained soil. Propagate by semiripe cuttings in summer or by seed in fall or spring.
V. agnus-castus (Chaste tree).

Deciduous, spreading, open, aromatic shrub. **H** and **S** 8ft (2.5m). Upright panicles of fragrant, tubular, violet-blue flowers are borne in early and mid-fall. Dark green leaves are divided into 5 or 7 long, narrowly lance-shaped leaflets. Z6–9 H9–6.

V. negundo (Chaste tree). Deciduous, bushy shrub. **H** and **S** 10ft (3m). Mid-green leaves are divided into 3–7 narrowly oval, sharply toothed leaflets. Has loose panicles of small, tubular, violet-blue flowers from late summer to early fall. Z6–9 H9–6.

VITIS
Grape
VITACEAE

Genus of deciduous, woody-stemmed, tendril climbers, grown for their foliage and fruits (grapes), which are produced in bunches. Prefers sun or partial shade and fertile, well-drained, chalky soil. Produces the best fruits and fall leaf color when planted in a warm situation. Propagate by hardwood cuttings in late fall.

V. aconitifolia. See *Ampelopsis aconitifolia.*

V. amurensis (Amur grape). Vigorous, deciduous, woody-stemmed, tendril climber. **H** 20ft (6m). Bears 3- or 5-lobed, dark green leaves, 5–12in (12–30cm) long, that mature to red and purple in fall. Has inconspicuous flowers, in summer, followed by tiny, black fruits. Z4–9 H9–1.

V. 'Brant', illus. p.208. Deciduous, woody-stemmed, tendril climber. **H** to 22ft (7m) or more. Lobed, toothed, bright green leaves, 10–22cm (4–9in) long, mature in fall to brown-red, except for veins. Has inconspicuous flowers, in summer, followed by green or purple fruits.

V. coignetiae, illus. p.209.

V. davidii. Deciduous, woody-stemmed, tendril climber. **H** to 25ft (8m) or more. Young stems are densely covered with short prickles. Heart-shaped, dark green leaves, 4–10in (10–25cm) long, are blue- or gray-green beneath, turning scarlet in fall. Insignificant, greenish flowers in summer are followed by small, black fruits. Z7–10 H10–7.

V. henryana. See *Parthenocissus henryana.*

V. heterophylla. See *Ampelopsis brevipedunculata* var. *maximowiczii.*

V. quinquefolia. See *Parthenocissus quinquefolia.*

V. striata. See *Cissus striata.*

V. vinifera (Grape vine). **'Purpurea'** illus. p.210.

VRIESEA
BROMELIACEAE

Genus of evergreen, rosette-forming, epiphytic perennials, grown for their flowers and overall appearance. Needs partial shade and a rooting medium of equal parts rich soil and either sphagnum moss or bark or plastic chips used for orchid culture. Using soft water, water moderately when in growth, sparingly at other times, and from mid-spring to mid-fall keep rosette centers filled with water. Propagate plants by offsets or seed in spring. See also feature panel p.471.

V. fenestralis. Evergreen, epiphytic perennial with dense, funnel-shaped

rosettes. **H** and **S** 12–16in (30–40cm). Pale green leaves, with dark lines and cross-bands, are very broadly strap-shaped and arching or rolled under at tips. In summer, flat racemes of tubular, yellowish-green flowers, with green bracts, are borne above the foliage. Z14–15 H12–10.

V. fosteriana. Evergreen, epiphytic perennial with dense, funnel-shaped rosettes. **H** and **S** 24in (60cm) or more. Has broadly strap-shaped, arching, yellowish- to deep green leaves, cross-banded with reddish-brown, particularly beneath. In summer–fall, flat spikes of tubular, pale yellow or greenish-yellow flowers, with brownish-red tips, are produced well above foliage. Z14–15 H12–10.

V. hieroglyphica. Evergreen, epiphytic perennial with dense, funnel-shaped rosettes. **H** and **S** 2–3ft (60cm–1m). Produces broadly strap-shaped, arching, yellowish-green leaves, cross-banded and checkered with dark brownish-green. In summer bears panicles of tubular, yellow flowers well above the leaves. Z11–12 H12–1.

V. platynema. Variable, evergreen, epiphytic perennial with dense, funnel-shaped rosettes. **H** and **S** 24in (60cm). Broadly strap-shaped, mid- to light green leaves, with purple tips, form dense rosettes. In summer, flat racemes of tubular, green-and-yellow flowers, with red or yellow bracts, are produced. Z14–15 H12–1.

V. psittacina. Evergreen, spreading, epiphytic perennial with dense, funnel-shaped rosettes. **H** and **S** 16–24in (40–60cm). Has strap-shaped, arching, pale green leaves. Flat spikes of tubular, yellow flowers, with green tips, emerging from red-and-yellow or red-and-green bracts, are borne above foliage in summer–fall. Z14–15 H12–1.

V. splendens (Flaming sword), illus. p.471. Evergreen, epiphytic perennial with dense, funnel-shaped rosettes. **H** and **S** 12in (30cm). Has strap-shaped, arching, olive-green leaves, with purple to reddish-brown cross-bands. Bears flat, sword-shaped racemes of tubular, yellow flowers, between bright red bracts, in summer–fall. Z14–15 H12–1.

x Vuylstekeara Cambria gx 'Lensing's Favorite'. See x *Oncidopsis* Cambria gx 'Lensing's Favorite'.

WACHENDORFIA
HAEMODORACEAE

Genus of summer-flowering perennials with deep roots, to guard against frost. Requires full sun and moist soil. Propagate by division in spring or by seed in fall or spring.

W. thyrsiflora. Clump-forming perennial. **H** 5–6ft (1.5–2m), **S** 1½ft (45cm). Shallowly cup-shaped, yellow to orange flowers are produced in dense panicles in early summer. Mid-green leaves are narrowly sword-shaped, pleated and rather coarse. Z9–10 H10–9.

WAHLENBERGIA
CAMPANULACEAE

Genus of summer-flowering annuals, biennials and short-lived perennials, grown for their bell-shaped flowers.

Is useful for alpine houses. Needs a sheltered site, partial shade and well-drained, peaty, sandy soil. Propagate by seed in fall.

W. albomarginata (New Zealand bluebell). Basal-rosetted, rhizomatous perennial. **H** and **S** 6in (15cm) or more. Slender stems bear solitary, bell-shaped, clear blue flower that opens flat in summer. Has narrowly elliptic to oval, mid-green leaves in tufts. Is good in a rock garden. Z6–7 H7–6.

W. congesta, syn. *W. saxicola* var. *congesta.* Mat-forming, creeping, rhizomatous perennial. **H** 3in (7cm), **S** 4in (10cm). Has small, rounded or spoon-shaped, mid-green leaves. In summer, solitary, bell-shaped, lavender-blue or white flowers are borne on wiry stems. Z8–10 H10–8.

W. saxicola var. **congesta.** See *W. congesta.*

W. serpyllifolia. See *Edraianthus serpyllifolius.*

WALDSTEINIA
ROSACEAE

Genus of semievergreen, creeping perennials with runners. Makes good groundcover. Needs sun and well-drained soil. Propagate by division in early spring.

W. ternata, syn. *W. trifolia,* illus. p.372.

W. trifolia. See *W. ternata.*

WASHINGTONIA
ARECACEAE/PALMAE

Genus of evergreen palms, grown for their stately appearance. Needs full sun and fertile, well-drained soil. Water container specimens freely in summer, moderately at other times. Remove skirt of persistent dead leaves regularly as they are a fire risk. Propagate by seed in spring at not less than 75°F (24°C). Red spider mite may be a nuisance.

W. filifera (Northern washingtonia). Fast-growing, evergreen palm. **H** and **S** to 80ft (25m). Has fan-shaped, long-stalked, gray-green leaves, each lobe with a filamentous tip. Long-stalked clusters of tiny, creamy-white flowers, in summer, are followed by berry-like, black fruits in winter. Z8–11 H12–8.

W. robusta, illus. p.451.

WATSONIA
IRIDACEAE

Genus of clump-forming corms, *Gladiolus*-like in overall appearance, although flowers are more tubular. Requires an open, sunny position and light, well-drained soil. Plant in fall, 4–6in (10–15cm) deep; protect with bracken, loose peat or similar during first winter, if frost is expected. Feed with slow-acting fertilizer, such as bonemeal, in summer. Corms are best left undisturbed to form clumps. Propagate by seed in fall.

W. beatricis. See *W. pillansii.*

W. borbonica, syn. *W. pyramidata,* illus. p.386.

W. fourcadei. Clump-forming, summer-flowering corm. **H** to 5ft (1.5m), **S** 1–1½ft (30–45cm). Sword-shaped, erect leaves are mostly basal. Has dense spike of tubular, 6-lobed, salmon-red flowers, 3–3½in (8–9cm) long. Z9–10 H10–9.

W. meriana, illus. p.385.

W. pillansii, syn. *W. beatricis,* illus. p.386.

W. pyramidata. See *W. borbonica.*

Wattakaka sinensis. See *Dregea sinensis.*

WEIGELA
CAPRIFOLIACEAE

Genus of deciduous shrubs, grown for their funnel-shaped flowers. Fully hardy. Prefers sun and fertile soil. To maintain vigor, prune out a few older branches to ground level, after flowering each year. Straggly, old plants may be pruned hard in spring (although this will lose one season's flowers). Propagate by softwood cuttings in summer.

W. 'Bristol Ruby'. Vigorous, deciduous, upright shrub. **H** 8ft (2.5m), **S** 6ft (2m). Deep red flowers open from darker buds amid oval, toothed, mid-green leaves in late spring and early summer. Z4–9 H9–4.

W. 'Candida'. Deciduous, bushy shrub. **H** and **S** 8ft (2.5m). Pure white flowers are produced in late spring and early summer. Leaves are oval, toothed and bright green. Z5–9 H9–5.

W. 'Eva Rathke'. Deciduous, upright, dense shrub. **H** and **S** 5ft (1.5m). Has oval, toothed, dark green leaves. Broad-mouthed, crimson flowers open from darker buds from late spring to early summer. Z5–9 H9–5.

W. florida. Deciduous, arching shrub. **H** and **S** 8ft (2.5m). Bears deep pink flowers, pale pink to white inside, in late spring and early summer. Oval, toothed leaves are mid-green. Z5–8 H8–4. **'Foliis Purpureis'** illus. p.153. **'Variegata'** illus. p.152.

W. 'Looymansii Aurea'. Weak-growing, deciduous, upright shrub. **H** 5ft (1.5m), **S** 3ft (1m). From late spring through to early summer produces pale pink flowers amid oval, toothed, golden-yellow leaves, with narrow red rims. Needs protection from hot afternoon sun. Z5–8 H7–4.

W. middendorffiana, illus. p.159.

W. praecox. Deciduous, upright shrub. **H** 8ft (2.5m), **S** 6ft (2m). Fragrant, pink flowers, marked inside with yellow, are produced in late spring. Leaves are bright green, oval and toothed. Z5–7 H7–4. **'Variegata'** has leaves with broad, creamy-white margins.

Weingartia neocumingii. See *Rebutia neocumingii.*

WEINMANNIA
CUNONIACEAE

Genus of evergreen trees and shrubs, grown for their foliage, flowers and overall appearance. Requires partial shade or full light and rich, well-drained but not dry soil, ideally neutral to acidic. Water container plants freely when in growth, moderately at other times. Pruning is tolerated if needed. Propagate by seed in spring or by semiripe cuttings in summer.

W. trichosperma. Evergreen, ovoid to round-headed tree. **H** 40ft (12m) or more, **S** 25–30ft (8–10m). Glossy, rich green leaves are divided into 9–19 oval, boldly toothed leaflets that are borne on winged midrib. Spikes of tiny, fragrant, white flowers, with pink stamens, are produced in early summer. Z8–10 H10–7.

WELDENIA
COMMELINACEAE

Genus of one species of summer-flowering, tuberous perennial, grown for its flowers. Is suitable for alpine houses. Needs sun and gritty, well-drained soil. Keep dry from fall until growth restarts in late winter. Propagate by root cuttings in winter or by division in early spring.
W. candida, illus. p.348.

WELWITSCHIA
WELWITSCHIACEAE

Genus of one species of evergreen, desert-growing perennial with a deep taproot. Has only 2 leaves, which lie on the ground and grow continuously from the base for up to 100 years. Requires sun and sharply drained soil. Needs desert conditions: may succeed in a mixture of stone chips and leaf mold, in a length of drainpipe to take its long taproot. Propagate by seed when ripe.
W. bainesii. See *W. mirabilis*.
W. mirabilis, syn. *W. bainesii*. Evergreen perennial with a short, woody trunk. **H** to 12in (30cm), **S** indefinite. Has 2 strap-shaped leaves, to 8ft (2.5m) long, with tips splitting to form many tendril-like strips. Bears small, reddish-brown cones. Z13–15 H12–10.

WESTRINGIA
LABIATAE/LAMIACEAE

Genus of evergreen shrubs, grown for their flowers and overall appearance. Requires full light and well-drained soil. Water container specimens moderately when in full growth, less at other times. Propagate by seed in spring or by semiripe cuttings in late summer.
W. fruticosa, syn. *Westringiana rosmariniformis*, illus. p.453.

Westringiana rosmariniformis. See *Westringia fruticosa*.

WIGANDIA
HYDROPHYLLACEAE

Genus of evergreen perennials and shrubs, grown for their flowers and foliage. Needs full light and moist but well-drained soil. Water container plants freely when in full growth, moderately at other times. Cut down flowered stems in spring to prevent plants from becoming straggly. Propagate by seed or softwood cuttings in spring. Whitefly is sometimes troublesome.
① Contact with foliage may aggravate skin allergies.
W. caracasana. Evergreen, erect, sparsely branched shrub. **H** 6–10ft (2–3m), **S** 3–6ft (1–2m). Produces oval, wavy-edged, toothed, deep green leaves, 18in (45cm) long and covered with white hairs beneath. Produces 5-petaled, violet-purple flowers, in large, terminal clusters, in spring–fall. Is often grown annually from seed for its leaves. Z13–15 H12–.

Wigginsia vorwerkiana. See *Parodia erinacea*.

Wilcoxia albiflora. See *Echinocereus leucanthus*.
Wilcoxia schmollii. See *Echinocereus schmollii*.
x Wilsonara Hambühren Stern gx 'Cheam'. See *Oncidium* Hambühren Stern gx 'Cheam'.
x Wilsonara Wigg's gx 'Kay'. See *Oncidium* Memoria Commander Wiggs gx 'Kay'.
Wintera aromatica. See *Drimys winteri*.

WISTERIA
LEGUMINOSAE/PAPILIONACEAE

Genus of deciduous, woody-stemmed, twining climbers, grown for their fragrant, pealike flowers in pendent racemes. Is suitable for walls and pergolas and for growing against buildings and trees. Needs sun and fertile, well-drained soil. Prune after flowering and again in late winter. Propagate by bench grafting in winter or by seed in fall or spring. Plants grown from seed may not flower for some years and often have poor flowers. ① All parts may cause severe discomfort if ingested. See also feature panel p.205.
W. brachybotrys (Silky wisteria). Deciduous, woody-stemmed, twining climber. **H** to 28ft (9m) or more. Softly hairy leaves are divided into 9–13 oval leaflets. Racemes, 4–6in (10–15cm) long, of scented, pealike, violet to white flowers, with yellow blotch at base of upper petal, are borne in early summer. Sometimes flowers again sparsely in fall. Z5–9 H9–5.
f. alba. See *W. brachybotrys* 'Shiro-kapitan'. **'Alba'**. See *W. brachybotrys* 'Shiro-kapitan'. **'Alba Plena'**. See *W. brachybotrys* 'Shiro-kapitan'. **'Murasaki-kapitan'**, syn. *W. venusta* f. *violacea*, *W. venusta* 'Violacea' has deep blue-violet flowers, with white, slightly yellow-tinged markings on standards. **f. plena**. See *W. brachybotrys* 'Shiro-kapitan'. **'Shiro-kapitan'**, syn. *W. brachybotrys* f. *alba*, *W. brachybotrys* 'Alba', *W. brachybotrys* 'Alba Plena', *W. brachybotrys* f. *plena*, *W. venusta*, *W. venusta* f. *alba*, *W. venusta* 'Alba', *W. venusta* 'Alba Plena', (illus. p.205) has white flowers with yellow stain at base of each standard. Occasionally bears double flowers. Z5–8 H8–5. **'White Silk'** (illus. p.205) is similar to *W.b.* 'Shiro-kapitan' but produces much longer racemes. Z5–8 H8–5.
W. chinensis. See *W. sinensis*.
W. floribunda (Japanese wisteria). Vigorous twining climber. **H** 28ft (9m) or more. Has pinnate leaves divided into 11–19 ovate to lance-shaped leaflets. In early summer, fragrant, pealike, blue to violet, pink or white flowers, are produced in pendent racemes, to 12in (30cm) or more long, the flowers opening gradually from bases to tips. Standards are marked with white and yellow. Flowers are often followed by beanlike, velvety green seed pods. Z5–9 H9–5. **'Alba'**, syn. *W. floribunda* 'Shiro Noda' illus. p.196. bears white flowers in racemes 24in (60cm) long. **'Black Dragon'**. See *W. floribunda* 'Yae-kokuryu'. **'Domino'** has light violet-blue flowers with light purple-blue standards, marked yellow at base, and darker purple-blue wing and keel petals, borne in spring and sometimes again in fall. Z5–9 H9–3.

'Hon-beni' (illus. p.205). See *W. floribunda* 'Rosea'. **'Lawrence'** has densely packed racemes of pale violet-blue flowers, with greenish-yellow bases on standards and darker blue-violet on keel and wing petals, borne in spring. Z5–9 H9–3. **'Macrobotrys'**. See *W. floribunda* 'Multijuga'. **'Multijuga'**, syn. *W. floribunda* 'Macrobotrys' has lilac-blue flowers in racemes 3–4ft (90–120cm) long. **'Rosea'**, syn. *W. floribunda* 'Hon-beni' (illus. p.205) has racemes, 12–16in (30–40cm) long, of dark purplish-pink flowers with yellow mark on standard bases. Z5–9 H9–3. **'Shiro Noda'**. See *W. floribunda* 'Alba'. **'Violacea Plena'** is similar to *W.f.* 'Yae-kokuryu', but has double, lavender-purple flowers and no dark purple-indigo central petals. **'Yae-kokuryu'**, syn. *W. floribunda* 'Black Dragon', *W. x formosa* 'Black Dragon', *W. x formosa* 'Double Black Dragon' (illus. p.205) has racemes, 14in (35cm) long, of slightly ragged, fully double, lilac-purple flowers, with dark purple-indigo centers. Z5–9 H9–3.
W. x formosa (*W. floribunda* x *W. sinensis*). Vigorous, twining climber. **H** 28ft (9m) or more. Has pinnate leaves divided into 9–15 broadly ovate to elliptic leaflets. Fragrant, pealike, violet-blue flowers, with white and yellow markings, are borne in pendent racemes, to 10in (25cm) long, in late spring and early summer, and are often followed by beanlike, velvety green seed pods. Z6–9 H9–6. **'Black Dragon'**. See *W. floribunda* 'Yae-kokuryu'. **'Double Black Dragon'**. See *W. floribunda* 'Yae-kokuryu'.
W. frutescens (American wisteria), illus p.205. Deciduous, woody-stemmed twining vine with pinnately compound leaves composed of 9–15 bright green, oblong to lance-shaped leaflets. **H** 25–30ft (8–10m). Fragrant, lilac to pale purple, pealike flowers bloom in drooping clusters during early summer after the foliage has emerged. In late summer, 3–4in (8–10cm) long, beanlike olive-green seedpods form; these hang on into winter before splitting and ejecting the seeds. Z5–9 H9–5. **'Amethyst Falls'**, (illus. p.205) has fragrant flowers with a bluish tint. **'Longwood Purple'** (illus. p.205) has flowers with a deeper purple color than the species. **'Nivea'** is a white-flowered selection.
W. macrostachya (Kentucky wisteria). Deciduous, woody-stemmed twining vine with pinnately compound leaves composed of 8 to 10 bright green, lance-shaped leaflets. **H** 15–25ft (4–8m). The fragrant, lilac purple flowers bloom in dense, drooping racemes in early- to mid-summer. Slightly twisted, olive green, beanlike seedpods develop in late summer and persist into winter. Z4–9 H9–4. **'Abbeville Blue'** has bluish purple flowers. **'Clara Mack'** has white flowers.
W. sinensis, syn. *W. chinensis* (Chinese wisteria). Vigorous, deciduous, woody-stemmed, twining climber. **H** to 100ft (30m). Has leaves divided into 11 leaflets. Fragrant, pealike, blue or pale violet flowers, in racemes 8–12in (20–30cm) long, in early summer, are followed by velvety seed pods. Z6–9 H9–6. **'Alba'** has strongly scented, white flowers. Z5–8 H8–5. **'Prolific'** (illus. p.205) bears masses of

single, lilac-blue to pale violet-blue flowers. Z5–8 H8–5.
W. venusta. See *W. brachybotrys* 'Shiro-kapitan'. **f. alba**. See *W. brachybotrys* 'Shiro-kapitan'. **'Alba'**. See *W. brachybotrys* 'Shiro-kapitan'. **'Alba Plena'**. See *W. brachybotrys* 'Shiro-kapitan'. **f. violacea**. See *W. brachybotrys* 'Murasaki-kapitan'. **'Violacea'**. See *W. brachybotrys* 'Murasaki-kapitan'.

WOLFFIA
LEMNACEAE

Genus of semievergreen, perennial, floating water plants, grown for their curiosity value as the smallest known flowering plants. Is ideal for cold-water aquariums. Needs a sunny position. Remove excess plantlets as required. Propagate by redistribution of plantlets as required.
W. arrhiza. Semievergreen, perennial, floating water plant. **S** indefinite. Leaves are rounded and mid-green. Insignificant, greenish flowers appear year-round. Z8–10 H10–8.

WOLLEMIA
ARAUCARIACEAE

Genus of conifers with narrowly oblong, pointed, needlelike, dark green leaves set opposite each other along shoot. See also CONIFERS.
W. nobilis, illus. p.96.

WOODSIA
DRYOPTERIDACEAE

Genus of deciduous ferns, suitable for rock gardens and alpine houses. Prefers partial shade and fertile, moist but very well-drained soil. May be difficult to cultivate: crowns of plants must sit above soil to avoid rotting. Propagate by division in early spring.
W. polystichoides (Holly-fern woodsia). Deciduous, tufted fern. **H** 4–12in (10–30cm), **S** 8–16in (20–40cm). In early spring has lance-shaped, divided, pale green fronds, to 14in (35cm) long, softly hairy on both surfaces and scaly beneath; each is divided into 15–30 pairs of narrowly sickle-shaped or oblong pinnae, with slightly toothed margins. May be damaged by late frosts. Z4–8 H8–1.

WOODWARDIA
Chain fern
BLECHNACEAE

Genus of evergreen or deciduous ferns. Prefers partial shade and fibrous, moist, peaty soil. Remove faded fronds regularly. Propagate by division in spring.
W. radicans (European chain fern). Vigorous, evergreen, spreading fern. **H** 4ft (1.2m), **S** 2ft (60cm). Large, broadly lance-shaped, coarsely divided, arching, mid-green fronds have narrowly oval pinnae. Z8–9 H9–8.
W. unigemmata (Asian chain fern). Evergreen, spreading fern. **H** 3ft (1m), **S** 10ft (3m). Is very similar to *W. radicans*, but new foliage emerges brilliant red and fades to brown and then green. Z8–9 H9–8.

WORSLEYA
Blue amaryllis
AMARYLLIDACEAE

Genus of one species of evergreen, winter-flowering bulb, with a neck up to 2½ft (75cm) high crowned by a tuft of leaves and a leafless flower stem. Needs full sun and moist but well-drained soil, or potting medium mixed with osmunda fiber, perlite or bark chips and some leaf mold. Soil should never dry out. Propagate by seed in spring.

W. procera. See *W. rayneri.*
W. rayneri, syn. *W. procera, Hippeastrum procerum.* Evergreen, winter-flowering bulb. **H** 3–4ft (1–1.2m), **S** 1½–2ft (45–60cm). Bears long, strap-shaped, strongly curved leaves and up to 14 funnel-shaped, lilac-blue flowers, 6in (15cm) long, with wavy-edged petals. Z14–15 H12–10.

WULFENIA
SCROPHULARIACEAE

Genus of evergreen, basal-rosetted perennials, suitable for alpine houses. Needs full sun and well-drained soil. Propagate by division in spring or by seed in fall.

W. amherstiana, illus. p.341.
W. carinthiaca. Evergreen, basal-rosetted perennial. **H** and **S** 10in (25cm). Has oblong to oval, toothed, dark green leaves, hairy beneath. Produces dense spike of small, tubular, violet-blue flowers in summer. Z5–9 H9–1.

U
V
W

XYZ

XANTHOCERAS
SAPINDACEAE

Genus of one species of deciduous, spring-to summer-flowering shrub or tree, grown for its foliage and flowers. Requires sun and fertile, well-drained soil. Does best in areas with hot summers. Propagate by seed in fall or by root cuttings or suckers in late winter. Is susceptible to coral spot fungus.
X. sorbifolium, illus. p.112.

XANTHOPHTHALMUM
COMPOSITAE/ASTERACEAE

Genus of annuals, grown for their daisy-like flower heads. Prefers full sun and well-drained soil. Propagate by seed in spring.
X. coronarium, syn. *Chrysanthemum coronarium.* Fast-growing, upright, branching annual. **H** 1–3ft (30cm–90cm), **S** 15in (38cm). Has feathery, divided, light green leaves. In summer bears single or semi-double, daisy-like, yellow or yellow-and-white flower heads, to 2in (5cm) across. H9–1.
X. segetum, syn. *Chrysanthemum segetum,* illus. p.322.

XANTHORHIZA
RANUNCULACEAE

Genus of one species of deciduous, spring-flowering shrub, grown for its leaves, clustered at the shoot tips, and star-shaped flowers. Needs full or partial shade and moist soil. Propagate by division in fall.
X. apiifolia. See *X. simplicissima.*
X. simplicissima, syn. *X. apiifolia* (Yellow-root). Deciduous, upright shrub that spreads by underground stems. **H** 2ft (60cm), **S** 5ft (1.5m). Bright green leaves, divided into usually 5 oval to lance-shaped, sharply toothed leaflets, turn bronze or purple in fall. Bears nodding panicles of tiny, star-shaped, purple flowers from early to mid-spring as foliage emerges. Z3–9 H9–1.

XANTHORRHOEA
Blackboy, Grass tree
XANTHORRHOEACEAE

Genus of evergreen, long-lived perennials, grown mainly as foliage plants. Needs full sun, well-drained soil and a fairly dry atmosphere. Propagate by basal offsets or seed in spring.
X. australis. Evergreen perennial with a sturdy, dark trunk. **H** 2–4ft (60cm–1.2m), **S** 4–5ft (1.2–1.5m). Very narrow, arching, flattened, silvery-green leaves, 2ft (60cm) or more long, spread from top of trunk. In summer may produce small, fragrant, 6-petaled, white flowers, in dense, candle-like spikes, 2ft (60cm) or more long, on stems of similar length. Z8–10 H11–7.

XANTHOSOMA
Yautia
ARACEAE

Genus of perennials, with underground tubers or thick stems above ground, grown mainly for their foliage. Many species are cultivated in the tropics for their edible tubers. Requires partial shade, rich, moist soil and a moist atmosphere at all times. Propagate by division year-round or by stem cuttings in spring or summer.
X. nigrum, syn. *X. violaceum.* Stemless perennial with large, underground tubers and leaves rising from ground level. **H** and **S** 4ft (1.2m). Purplish leaf stalks, 2ft (60cm) or more long, bear arrow-shaped, dark green leaf blades, 28in (70cm) long, with purple midribs and veins. Intermittently bears greenish-purple spathes, yellower within, surrounding brownish spadix. Z8–10 H11–1.
X. sagittifolium, illus. p.474.
X. violaceum. See *X. nigrum.*

XERANTHEMUM
COMPOSITAE/ASTERACEAE

Genus of summer-flowering annuals. Needs sun and fertile, very well-drained soil. Propagate by seed in spring.
X. annuum, illus. p.305.

XEROCHRYSUM
SYN. BRACHTEANTHA
COMPOSITAE/ASTERACEAE

Genus of herbaceous perennials and annuals, grown for their daisy-like flower heads with papery bracts. Stalkless, hairy leaves are borne on erect, branching stems. *X. bracteatum* is often grown for cutting and drying. Needs full sun and moderately fertile, moist but well-drained soil. Propagate by seed in spring.
X. bracteatum, syn. *Bracteantha bracteata* (Everlasting flower, Immortelle, Strawflower). Moderately fast-growing, upright, branching annual. **H** 4–39in (10–100cm), **S** 12in (30cm). Has broadly lance-shaped, gray-green leaves. From late spring to fall produces solitary, papery, daisy-like, bright white, yellow, pink or red flower heads. Z10–11 H12–3. **'Bright Bikini'**, **H** and **S** 12in (30cm), has mid-green leaves and large, double flower heads in many colors. **Monstrosum Series**, **H** 3ft (90cm), has large, fully double flower heads in pink, red, orange, yellow or white. Flowers dry well. **Sundaze Series** SUNDAZE GOLD **('Redbragol')** illus. p.320.

XERONEMA
AGAVACEAE/PHORMIACEAE

Genus of evergreen, robust, tufted perennials, with short, creeping rootstocks, grown for their flowers. Needs sun or partial shade and rich, well-drained soil. Propagate by seed or division in spring.
X. callistemon. Evergreen, iris-like, clump-forming perennial. **H** 2–3ft (60cm–1m), **S** indefinite. Erect, folded leaves, 2–3ft (60cm–1m) long, are very narrow and hard-textured. In summer, short-stalked, 6-petaled, red flowers, to 1¼in (3cm) wide, are borne on one-sided racemes, 6–12in (15–30cm) long. Z13–15 H12–10.

XEROPHYLLUM
LILIACEAE/MELANTHIACEAE

Genus of summer-flowering, rhizomatous perennials. Prefers full sun and moist, peaty soil. May be difficult to cultivate. Propagate by seed in fall.

X. tenax (Bear grass). Clump-forming perennial. **H** 3–4ft (1–1.2m), **S** 1–2ft (30–60cm). Star-shaped, white flowers, with violet anthers, are borne in dense, terminal racemes in summer. Has tufted, linear, rough-margined, mid-green, basal leaves, glaucous blue-green beneath. Z5–8 H8–5.

YUCCA
SYN. HESPEROYUCCA
AGAVACEAE

Genus of evergreen shrubs and trees, grown for the architectural value of their bold, sword-shaped, clustered leaves and showy panicles of usually white flowers. Makes fine container-grown plants. Requires full sun and well-drained soil. Water container specimens moderately when in growth, less at other times. Regularly remove spent flowering stems. Propagate frost-tender species in spring by seed or suckers, hardier species in spring by root cuttings or division.
Y. aloifolia (Dagger plant, Spanish bayonet). Slow-growing, evergreen shrub or small tree with few branches. **H** 25ft (8m), **S** 12–15ft (4–5m). Has sword-shaped, deep green leaves, and large panicles of purple-tinted, white flowers in summer–fall. Z12–15 H12–1.
Y. elephantipes 'Variegata'. Evergreen, upright shrub or tree. **H** to 30ft (10m), **S** 15–25ft (5–8m). Several to many sparsely branched trunks arise near ground level. Leaves are narrowly lance-shaped, leathery, light to mid-green and creamy-white at margins. On mature plants, hemispherical, white to cream flowers are borne in dense, erect panicles in summer–fall. Z11–12 H12–10.
Y. filamentosa (Adam's needle). Clump-forming, evergreen, basal-rosetted shrub. **H** 6ft (2m), **S** 5ft (1.5m). From mid- to late summer, tall panicles of pendulous, tulip-shaped, white flowers rise up through low-growing tufts of sword-shaped, deep green leaves, edged with white threads. Z4–11 H11–5.
Y. filifera 'Ivory'. See *Y. flaccida* 'Ivory'.
Y. flaccida 'Ivory', syn. *Y. filifera* 'Ivory', illus. p.151.
Y. gloriosa, illus. p.132. **'Nobilis'** is an evergreen shrub. **H** and **S** 6ft (2m). Stem is sturdy and usually unbranched, and crowned with large tuft of long, sword-shaped, sharply pointed, blue-green leaves, the outer ones semi-pendent. Pendulous, tulip-shaped, red-backed, white flowers are borne in long, erect panicles from mid-summer to early fall. Z7–10 H10–7.
Y. parviflora. See *Hesperaloe parviflora.*
Y. whipplei, illus. p.151.

YUSHANIA
Anceps bamboo
GRAMINEAE/POACEAE

See also GRASSES, BAMBOOS, RUSHES and SEDGES.
Y. anceps, syn. *Arundinaria anceps, Arundinaria jaunsarensis, Sinarundinaria jaunsarensis* (Anceps bamboo). Evergreen, rhizomatous, spreading bamboo. **H** 6–10ft (2–3m), **S** indefinite. Erect, later arching, shiny, dark green stems bear several branches at each node. Has narrowly lance-shaped, mid-green leaves, rounded at base, with purple-tinted stalks. Z8–13 H12–8. **'Pitt White',** illus. p.288.

ZALUZIANSKYA

SCROPHULARIACEAE

Genus of sticky, low-growing annuals and short-lived, evergreen perennials and sub-shrubs, grown for their spikes of fragrant, tubular flowers with spreading petals. Needs full sun and rich, moist but well-drained soil. Propagate by stem-tip cuttings in summer.

Z. ovata. Clump-forming, evergreen perennial. **H** to 10in (25cm), **S** to 24in (60cm). Branching, brittle stems bear ovate, toothed, sticky, gray-green leaves. Crimson-backed, white flowers are produced in summer. Z9–10 H10–9.

ZANTEDESCHIA

Calla lily

ARACEAE

Genus of summer-flowering, tuberous perennials, usually remaining evergreen in a warm climate, grown for their erect, funnel-shaped spathes and club-shaped spadix. Requires sun or partial shade and well-drained soil. Z. aethiopica will also grow in 6–12in (15–30cm) of water and therefore is suitable as a marginal water plant. Propagate by offsets in winter. ① All parts of the plant may cause mild stomach upset if ingested, and contact with the sap may irritate the skin.

Z. aethiopica. '**Crowborough**', illus. p.437. '**Green Goddess**', illus. p.408.
Z. albomaculata syn. *Z. melanoleuca* (Spotted calla). Summer-flowering, tuberous perennial. **H** 12–16in (30–40cm), **S** 12in (30cm). Bears arrow-shaped, semierect, mid-green, basal leaves, with transparent spots. Has yellow spadix inside white spathe, 5–8in (12–20cm) long, shading to green at base and with purple blotch inside. Z11–10 H12–7.
Z. 'Black-eyed Beauty'. Summer-flowering, tuberous perennial. **H** 12–16in (30–40cm), **S** 6in (15cm). Broadly heart-shaped, semierect, mid- to dark green, basal leaves are heavily white-spotted. Each flower stem has yellow spadix and cream spathe, 6in (15cm) long, with central, black mark in throat. Z8–10 H10–4.
Z. 'Black Magic'. Summer-flowering, tuberous perennial. **H** 30in (75cm), **S** 8in (20cm). Broadly heart-shaped, semierect, mid- to dark green, basal leaves are heavily mottled with white. Each flower stem produces golden-yellow spadix, surrounded by black-throated, yellow spathe, 6in (15cm) long. Z8–10 H10–4.
Z. 'Cameo', illus. p.395.
Z. elliottiana, illus. p.393.
Z. melanoleuca. See *Z. albomaculata*.
Z. rehmannii (Pink arum). Summer-flowering, tuberous perennial. **H** 16in (40cm), **S** 12in (30cm). Dark green, basal leaves are arrow-shaped and semierect. Each flower stem has yellow spadix, surrounded by reddish-pink spathe, 5in (12cm) long. Z8–10 H10–4.

ZANTHOXYLUM

RUTACEAE

Genus of deciduous or evergreen, spiny shrubs and trees, grown for their aromatic foliage, fruits and habit. Requires sun or partial shade and fertile soil. Propagate by

seed in fall or by root cuttings in late winter.
Z. piperitum (Japan pepper). Deciduous, bushy, spiny shrub or tree. **H** and **S** 8ft (2.5m). Has aromatic, glossy, dark green leaves divided into many oval, toothed leaflets. Tiny, greenish-yellow flowers in spring are followed by spherical, red fruits. Z6–9 H9–6.
Z. simulans, illus. p.141.

ZAUSCHNERIA

California fuchsia

ONAGRACEAE

Genus of sub-shrubby, evergreen, semi-evergreen or deciduous perennials, grown for their mass of flowers. Requires sun and well-drained soil. Propagate by seed or division in spring or by taking sideshoot cuttings in summer.

Z. californica, syn. *Epilobium californicum*. Evergreen or semi-evergreen, clump-forming, woody-based perennial. **H** and **S** 18in (45cm). Terminal clusters of tubular, bright scarlet flowers, on slender stems, are produced in late summer and early fall. Bears lance-shaped, rich green leaves. Z8–11 H12–8. **subsp. cana**, syn. *Z. cana, Epilobium canum*, **H** 12in (30cm), is deciduous and produces linear, gray leaves and fuchsia-like, brilliant scarlet flowers. **subsp. cana 'Dublin'.** See *Z. californica* 'Dublin'. '**Dublin**', syn. *Z. californica* subsp. *cana* 'Dublin', *Z. californica* 'Glasnevin' illus. p.340. '**Glasnevin**'. See *Z. californica* 'Dublin'.
Z. cana. See *Z. californica* subsp. *cana*.
Z. septentrionalis, syn. *Epilobium septentrionale*. Mat-forming, non-woody, deciduous perennial. **H** 4–8in (10–20cm), **S** to 8in (20cm). Terminal clusters of numerous, short-stalked, tubular, scarlet flowers are produced in late summer. Has oval to lance-shaped, gray to gray-green leaves. Z8–10 H10–7.

ZEA

GRAMINEAE/POACEAE

See also GRASSES, BAMBOOS, RUSHES and SEDGES.

Z. mays (Corn). Fairly fast-growing, upright annual. **H** to 12ft (4m), **S** 2ft (60cm). Has lance-shaped, arching, wavy leaves. In mid-summer produces tassel-like flower head followed by cylindrical seed head ("cob") of edible, fleshy, usually yellow kernels. H12–1. '**Gracillima Variegata**', **H** 3ft (90cm), **S** 1–1¹⁄₂ft (30–45cm), has leaves striped green and creamy. Silvery flower heads are followed by large, bright yellow seed heads (cobs). '**Harlequin**', **H** 3–6ft (1–2m), **S** 2ft (60cm) long, has leaves striped with green, red and white and bears yellow seed heads (cobs), with deep red kernels. '**Strawberry Corn**', **H** 4ft (1.2m), produces seed heads with small, yellow to burgundy-red kernels within yellow-green spathe-bracts.

Zebrina pendula. See *Tradescantia zebrina*.

ZELKOVA

ULMACEAE

Genus of deciduous trees, grown mainly for their foliage and habit. Is best when planted as a single specimen. Has insignificant flowers in spring. Prefers full

sun and requires deep, fertile, moist but well-drained soil. Propagate by seed in fall.
Z. abelicea, syn. *Z. cretica*. Deciduous, bushy-headed, spreading tree. **H** 15ft (5m), **S** 22ft (7m). Produces small, oval, dark green leaves that are prominently toothed. Z8–9 H9–8.
Z. carpinifolia, illus. p.64.
Z. cretica. See *Z. abelicea*.
Z. serrata, illus. p.67.

ZENOBIA

ERICACEAE

Genus of one species of deciduous or semievergreen, summer-flowering shrub, grown for its flowers. Requires partial shade and moist, acidic soil. Prune out older, weaker shoots after flowering to maintain vigor. Propagate by semi-ripe cuttings in summer.

Z. pulverulenta, illus. p.130.

ZEPHYRANTHES

Rain lily, Rainflower, Zephyr lily

AMARYLLIDACEAE

Genus of clump-forming bulbs, grown for their erect, crocus-like flower on each stem. Needs a sheltered, sunny site and open, moist but well-drained soil. Container-grown bulbs need a dryish, warm period after foliage dies down in summer, followed by copious amounts of water to stimulate flowering. Propagate by seed in fall or spring.

Z. atamasco (Atamasco lily). Clump-forming, early summer-flowering bulb. **H** 6–10in (15–25cm), **S** 3–4in (8–10cm). Basal leaves are very narrow, grass-like and semierect. Each stem produces solitary, widely funnel-shaped, purple-tinged, white flower, to 4in (10cm) wide, in spring or summer. Z7–10 H12–10.
Z. candida, illus. p.424.
Z. carinata, syn. *Z. grandiflora*, illus. p.413.
Z. citrina. Clump-forming, fall-flowering bulb. **H** 4–6in (10–15cm), **S** 2–3in (5–8cm). Has rush-like, erect, basal leaves. Stems produce funnel-shaped, bright yellow flowers, to 1¹⁄₂–2in (4–5cm) wide, in fall. Z7–10 H10–7.
Z. grandiflora of gardens. See *Z. carinata*.
Z. robusta. See *Habranthus robustus*.
Z. rosea. Fall-flowering bulb. **H** 8in (20cm), **S** 2in (5cm). Short-tubed, funnel-shaped, sugar-pink flowers, 1¹⁄₄in (3cm) long, are produced among narrowly linear, semierect, basal leaves. Z7–10 H12–10.

ZIGADENUS

LILIACEAE/MELANTHIACEAE

Genus of summer-flowering bulbs, grown for their spikes of star-shaped, 6-petaled flowers. Requires sun or partial shade and well-drained soil. Water copiously in spring and summer, less at other times. Remains dormant in winter. Propagate by division in early spring or by seed in fall or spring. ① All parts are highly toxic if ingested.
Z. elegans. Clump-forming, summer-flowering bulb. **H** 12–20in (30–50cm), **S** 4–6in (10–15cm). Bears long, narrow, semierect, gray-green, basal leaves. Each stem has spike of greenish-white flowers, ¹⁄₂in (1cm) wide, with yellowish-green nectaries. Z5–9 H9–5.

Z. fremontii (Star lily). Clump-forming, early summer-flowering bulb. **H** 12–20in (30–50cm), **S** 4–6in (10–15cm). Has long, strap-shaped, semierect, grayish-green, basal leaves. Stem produces spike of star-shaped, pale creamy-green flowers, ⁵⁄₈in (1.5cm) wide, with darker green nectaries on petal bases. Z8–9 H9–8.
Z. nuttallii. Clump-forming, summer-flowering bulb. **H** 12–24in (30–60cm), **S** 3in (8cm). Narrowly strap-shaped, semierect, basal leaves are mid- to dark green. Produces dense spikes of tiny, creamy-yellow flowers, 6–8mm (¹⁄₄–³⁄₈in) across. Z6–9 H9–6.

ZINGIBER

ZINGIBERACEAE

Genus of herbaceous or evergreen perennials, grown for their spicy rhizomes and flowers arranged in a pine-cone-shaped head, borne on separate stems to the leaves. Needs partial shade and rich, moist but well-drained soil. Propagate by division in spring.

Z. mioga. Herbaceous, clump-forming perennial. **H** 32in (80cm), **S** 20in (50cm). Short-stemmed spikes, 2–6in (5–15cm) long, of pale cream to yellow flowers, 2in (5cm) across, with reddish-purple bracts, are borne in late summer. Has tall, leafy pseudostems of narrowly lance-shaped, pale green leaves. Z7–10 H10–1.

ZINNIA

COMPOSITAE/ASTERACEAE

Genus of annuals, grown for their large, dahlia-like flower heads, which are excellent for cutting. Requires sun and fertile, well-drained soil. Remove dead flower heads regularly to promote flowering. Propagate by seed sown under glass in early spring.

Z. angustifolia '**Orange Star**'. See *Z. haageana* 'Orange Star'. '**Persian Carpet**'. See *Z. haageana* 'Persian Carpet'.
Z. elegans. Moderately fast-growing, upright, sturdy annual. **H** 2–2¹⁄₂ft (60–75cm), **S** 1ft (30cm). Bears oval to lance-shaped, pale or mid-green leaves. Daisy-like, purple flower heads, 2in (5cm) or more wide, are produced in summer and early fall. Hybrids of Z. elegans are available in various shades. H12–1. **Cactus-flowered Group**, **H** 24–36in (60–90cm), have large, semi-double flower heads, similar to those of cactus dahlias, with long, narrow, quilled petals, in broad range of colors. **Dreamland Series [Scarlet]** illus. p.306; **[Yellow]**, **H** and **S** 12in (30cm), have large, semidouble flower heads in summer and fall. '**Envy**' illus. p.316. **Hobgoblin Series**, **H** to 18in (45cm), produce sturdy plants, with small, single flower heads in broad range of colors. **Peter Pan Series**, **H** 8in (20cm), are dwarf, with double flower heads in wide range of colors. '**Red Sun**', **H** and **S** 12–16in (30–40cm), has semi- to fully double, deep bright red flower heads. **Short Stuff Series**, **H** 10in (25cm), are dwarf, with double flower heads in broad range of colors. **Small World Series**, **H** to 18in (45cm), are dwarf and have double flower heads in wide range of colors. '**State Fair**', **H** to 30in (75cm), is vigorous, and produces large, double flower heads in many colors.

Z. haageana 'Classic'. See *Z. haageana* 'Orange Star'. **'Orange Star',** syn. *Z. angustifolia* 'Orange Star', *Z. haageana* 'Classic', illus. p.325. **'Persian Carpet',** syn. *Z. angustifolia* 'Persian Carpet'. is a moderately fast-growing, upright, dwarf annual. **H** 15in (38cm), **S** 12in (30cm). Pale green leaves are lance-shaped and hairy. Small, weather-resistant, dahlia-like, double flower heads, 1in (2.5cm) or more wide, are produced in summer, in range of colors. H12–1.
Z. x marylandica Profusion Series 'Profusion Cherry', illus. p.307. **Zahara Series 'Zahara Starlight Rose',** illus. p.298.

ZIZANIA
Water oats, Wild rice

GRAMINEAE/POACEAE

See also GRASSES, BAMBOOS, RUSHES and SEDGES.
Z. aquatica (Annual wild rice, Canadian wild rice, Water rice). Annual, grass-like, marginal water plant. **H** 10ft (3m), **S** 18in (45cm). Has grasslike, mid-green leaves. In summer produces grasslike, pale green flowers, followed by edible rice-like seeds that attract waterfowl. Needs sun; is suitable for up to 9in (23cm) deep water. Propagate from seed stored damp and sown in spring. Z3–9 H9–1.

Zygocactus truncatus. See *Schlumbergera truncata.*

ZYGOPETALUM
Caper bean

ORCHIDACEAE

See also ORCHIDS.
Z. mackaii. See *Z. mackayi.*
Z. mackayi, syn. *Z. mackaii.* Evergreen, epiphytic orchid for a cool or intermediate greenhouse. **H** 12in (30cm). In fall produces long sprays of fragrant, brown-blotched, green flowers, 3in (8cm) across, with reddish-indigo veins and white lips. Narrowly oval, ribbed leaves are 12in (30cm) long. Requires partial shade in summer. Z12–14 H11–1.
Z. Perrenoudii gx, illus. p.466. Evergreen, epiphytic orchid for a cool or intermediate greenhouse. **H** 12in (30cm). Spikes of fragrant, violet-purple-lipped, dark brown flowers, 3in (8cm) across, are borne in winter. Has narrowly oval, ribbed leaves, 12in (30cm) long. Requires partial shade in summer. Z14–15 H12–6.

X
Y
Z

INDEX OF COMMON NAMES

A

727

D

P

S

S

GLOSSARY OF TERMS

Terms printed in italics refer to other glossary entries.

Acidic [of soil]. With a *pH* value of less than 7; see also *alkaline* and *neutral*.

Adventitious [of roots]. Arising directly from a stem or leaf.

Aerial root. See *root.*

Air-layering. A method of propagation by which a portion of stem is induced to root by enclosing it in a suitable medium, such as damp moss, and wrapping it with plastic; roots will form if the moss is kept moist.

Alkaline [of soil]. With a *pH* value of more than 7; some plants will not tolerate alkaline soils and must be grown in *neutral* or *acidic* soil.

Alpine house. An unheated greenhouse, used for the cultivation of mainly alpine and bulbous plants, that provides greater ventilation and usually more light than a conventional greenhouse.

Alternate [of leaves]. Borne singly at each *node*, on either side of a stem.

Annual. A plant that completes its life cycle, from germination through to flowering and seeding and then death, in one growing season.

Anther. The part of a stamen that produces pollen; it is usually borne on a filament.

Apex. The tip or growing point of an organ such as a leaf or shoot.

Areole. A modified, cushionlike *tubercle,* peculiar to the family Cactaceae, that bears hairs, spines, leaves, side-branches, or flowers.

Asclepiad. A member of the family Asclepiadaceae, e.g., *Asclepias, Hoya, Stephanotis.*

Auricle. An earlike lobe such as is sometimes found at the base of a leaf.

Awn. A stiff, bristlelike projection commonly found on grass seeds and *spikelets.*

Axil. The angle between a leaf and stem where an axillary bud develops.

Bedding plant. A plant that is mass-planted to provide a temporary display.

Biennial. A plant that flowers, seeds, and dies in the second season after germination, producing only stems, roots, and leaves in the first season.

Blade. The flattened and often broad part of a leaf.

Bloom. 1. A flower or blossom. 2. A fine, waxy, whitish or bluish-white coating on stems, leaves, or fruits.

Bog garden. An area where the soil is kept permanently damp but not waterlogged.

Bole. The trunk of a *tree* from ground level to the first major branch.

Bolt. To produce flowers and seed prematurely, particularly in the case of vegetables such as lettuce and beets.

Bonsai. A method of producing dwarf trees or shrubs by special techniques that include pruning roots, pinching out shoots, removing growth buds, and training branches and stems.

Bract. A modified leaf at the base of a flower or flower cluster. Bracts may resemble normal leaves or be reduced and scalelike in appearance; they are often large and brightly colored.

Bud. A rudimentary or condensed shoot containing embryonic leaves or flowers.

Bulb. A storage organ consisting mainly of fleshy scales and swollen, modified leaf-bases on a much reduced stem. Bulbs usually, but not always, grow underground.

Bulbil. A small, *bulblike* organ, often borne in a leaf *axil,* occasionally in a *flower head;* it may be used for propagation.

Bulblet. A small *bulb* produced at the base of a mature one.

Bur. 1. A prickly or spiny *fruit,* or aggregate of fruits. 2. A woody outgrowth on the stems of certain trees.

Cactus (pl. cacti). A member of the family Cactaceae, often *succulent* and spiny.

Calyx (pl. calyces). The outer part of a flower, usually small and green but sometimes showy and brightly colored, that encloses the petals in bud and is formed from the *sepals.*

Capsule. A dry *fruit* that splits open when ripe to release its seeds.

Carpel. The female portion of a flower, or part of it, consisting of an *ovary, stigma,* and *style.*

Catkin. A flower cluster, normally pendulous. Flowers lack petals, are often stalkless, surrounded by scalelike *bracts,* and are usually unisexual.

Caudex (pl. caudices). The stem base of a woody plant such as a *palm* or tree fern.

Cladode. A stem, often flattened, with the function and appearance of a leaf.

Claw. The narrow, basal portion of petals in some genera, e.g., *Dianthus.*

Climber. A plant that climbs using other plants or objects as a support: a **leaf-stalk** climber by coiling its leaf stalks around supports; a **root** climber by producing aerial, supporting roots; a **self-clinging** climber by means of suckering pads; a **tendril** climber by coiling its tendrils; a **twining** climber by coiling stems. **Scandent, scrambling,** and **trailing climbers** produce long stems that grow over plants or other supports; they attach themselves only loosely, if at all.

Clone. A group of genetically identical plants, propagated vegetatively.

Compound. Made up of several or many parts, e.g. a leaf divided into 2 or more *leaflets.*

Cone. The clustered flowers or woody, seed-bearing structures of a conifer.

Coppice. To cut back to near ground level each year in order to produce vigorous, ornamental shoots, as is usual with some *Cornus* and *Eucalyptus.*

Cordon. A trained plant restricted in growth to one main stem, occasionally 2–4 stems.

Corm. A *bulblike,* underground storage organ consisting mainly of a swollen stem base and often surrounded by a papery tunic.

Cormlet. A small *corm* arising at the base of a mature one.

Corolla. The part of a flower formed by the petals.

Corona (crown). A petal-like outgrowth sometimes borne on the *corolla,* e.g., the trumpet or cup of a *Narcissus.*

Corymb. A racemose flower cluster in which the inner flower stalks are shorter than the outer, resulting in a rounded or flat-topped head.

Cotyledon. See *seed leaf.*

Creeper. A plant that grows close to the ground, usually rooting as it spreads.

Crisped. Minutely wavy-edged.

Crown. 1. The part of the plant at or just below the soil surface from which new shoots are produced and to which they die back in fall. 2. The upper, branched part of a tree above the *bole.* 3. A *corona.*

Culm. The usually hollow stem of a grass or bamboo.

Cutting. A section of a plant that is removed and used for propagation. The various types of cutting are: **basal**—taken from the base of a plant (usually herbaceous) as it begins to produce growth in spring; **greenwood**—made from the tip of young growth; **hardwood**—mature wood taken at the end of the growing season; **leaf**—a detached leaf or part of a leaf; **root**—part of a semimature or mature root; **semiripe**—half-ripened wood taken during the growing season; **softwood**—young growth taken at the beginning of the growing season; **stem**—a greenwood, hardwood, semiripe, or softwood cutting; **tip**—a greenwood cutting.

Cyme. A flower cluster in which each growing point terminates in a flower.

Dead-head. To remove spent flower heads so as to promote further growth or flowering, prevent seeding, or improve appearance.

Deciduous. Losing its leaves annually at the end of the growing season; **semi-deciduous** plants lose only some leaves.

Decumbent. Growing close to the ground but ascending at the tips.

Dentate. With toothed margins.

Dieback. Death of the tips of shoots due to frost or disease.

Dioecious. Bearing male and female flowers on separate plants.

Disbud. To remove surplus buds to promote larger flowers or fruits.

Disk floret, disk flower. A small and often inconspicuous, usually tubular flower, one of many that comprise the central portion of a composite flower head such as a daisy.

Division. A method of propagation by which a clump is divided into several parts during dormancy.

Elliptic [of leaves]. Broadening in the center and narrowing toward each end.

Entire [of leaves]. With untoothed margins.

Epiphyte. A plant that grows on the surface of another without being parasitic.

Evergreen. Retaining its leaves at the end of the growing season although losing some older leaves regularly throughout the year; **semievergreen** plants retain only some leaves or lose older leaves only when the new growth is produced.

F1 hybrid. The first generation derived from crossing 2 distinct plants, usually when the parents are purebred lines and the offspring are vigorous. Seed from F1 hybrids does not come *true* to type.

Fall. An outer *perianth segment* of an iris, which projects outward or downward from the inner segments.

Fan palm. A *palm* with *palmate* rather than *pinnate* leaves.

Farina. A powdery, white, sometimes yellowish deposit naturally occurring on some leaves and flowers.

Fibrous root. A fine, young root, usually one of many.

Filament. The stalk of an *anther.*

Floret. A single flower in a head of many flowers.

Flower. The basic flower forms are: **single,** with one row of usually 4–6 petals; **semidouble,** with more petals, usually in 2 rows; **double,** with many petals in several rows and few or no stamens; **fully double,** usually rounded in shape, with densely packed petals and the stamens absent or obscured.

Flower head. A mass of small *flowers* or *florets* that together appear as one flower, e.g., a daisy.

Force. To induce artificially the early production of growth, flowers, or *fruits.*

Frond. The leaflike organ of a fern. Some ferns produce both barren and fertile fronds, the fertile fronds bearing *spores.*

Fruit. The structure in plants that bears one or more ripe seeds, e.g., a berry or nut.

Glabrous. Not hairy.

Glaucous. Bluish-white, bluish-green, or bluish-gray.

Globose. Spherical.

Glochid. One of the barbed bristles or hairs, usually small, borne on a cactus *areole.*

Grafting. A method of propagation by which an artificial union is made between different parts of individual plants; usually the *shoot* (scion) of one is grafted onto the *rootstock* (stock) of another.

Heel. The small portion of old wood that is retained at the base of a cutting when it is removed from the stem.

Herbaceous. Dying down at the end of the growing season.

Hose-in-hose [of flowers]. With one *corolla* borne inside another, forming a double or semidouble *flower.*

Inflorescence. A cluster of flowers with a distinct arrangement, e.g., *corymb, cyme, panicle, raceme, spike, umbel.*

Insectivorous plant. A plant that traps and digests insects and other small animals to supplement its nutrient intake.

Key. A winged seed like those produced by the sycamore maple (*Acer pseudoplatanus*).

Lateral. A side growth that arises from the side of a shoot or root.

Layering. A method of propagation by which a stem is induced to root by being pegged down into the soil while it is still attached to the parent plant. See also *air-layering.*

Leaflet. The subdivision of a compound leaf.

Lenticel. A small, usually corky area on a stem or other part of a plant, which acts as a breathing pore.

Lime. Compounds of calcium; the amount of lime in soil determines whether it is *alkaline, neutral,* or *acidic.*

Linear [of leaves]. Very narrow with parallel sides.

Lip. A lobe comprising 2 or more flat or sometimes pouched *perianth segments*.

Loam. Well-structured, fertile soil that is moisture-retentive but free-draining.

Marginal water plant. A plant that grows partially submerged in shallow water or in moist soil at the edge of a pond.

Midrib. The main, central vein of a leaf or the central stalk to which the *leaflets* of a *pinnate* leaf are attached.

Monocarpic. Flowering and fruiting only once before dying; such plants may take several years to reach flowering size.

Mulch. A layer of organic matter applied to the soil over or around a plant to conserve moisture, protect the roots from frost, reduce the growth of weeds, and enrich the soil.

Naturalize. To establish and grow as if in the wild.

Nectar. A sweet, sugary liquid secreted by the **nectary**—glandular tissue usually found in the flower but sometimes found on the leaves or stems.

Neutral [of soil]. With a *pH* value of 7, the point at which soil is neither *acidic* nor *alkaline*.

Node. The point on a stem from which a leaf or leaves arise.

Offset. A small plant that arises by natural vegetative reproduction, usually at the base of the mother plant.

Opposite [of leaves]. Borne 2 to each *node*, one opposite the other.

Ovary. The part of the female portion of the flower, containing embryonic seeds, that will eventually form the *fruit*.

Palm. An evergreen *tree* or *shrub*like plant, normally single-stemmed, with *palmate* or *pinnate* leaves usually in terminal rosettes; strictly a member of the family Palmae.

Palmate. Lobed in the fashion of a hand, with 5 lobes arising from the same point.

Pan. A shallow, free-draining pot in which alpine plants or bulbs are grown.

Panicle. A branched *raceme*.

Papilla (pl. papillae). A minute protuberance or glandlike structure.

Pealike [of flowers]. Of the same structure as a pea flower.

Peat bed. A specially constructed area, edged with peat blocks and containing moisture-retentive, acidic, peaty soil.

Pedicel. The stalk of an individual flower.

Peduncle. The stalk of a flower cluster.

Peltate [of leaves]. Shield-shaped, with the stalk inserted toward or at the center of the blade and not at the margin.

Perennial. Living for at least 3 seasons. In this book the term when used as a noun, and unless qualified, denotes an *herbaceous* perennial. A woody-based perennial dies down only partially, leaving a woody stem at the base.

Perianth. The outer parts of the flower comprising the *calyx* and the *corolla*. The term is often used when the calyx and the corolla are very similar in form.

Perianth segment. One portion of the *perianth*, resembling a *petal* and sometimes known as a *tepal*.

Petal. One portion of the often showy and colored part of the *corolla*. In some families, e.g., Liliaceae, the *perianth segments* are petal-like and referred to horticulturally as petals.

Petaloid. Like a petal.

Petiole. The stalk of a *leaf*.

pH. The scale by which the acidity or alkalinity of soil is measured. See also *acidic, alkaline, neutral*.

Phyllode. A flattened leaf stalk, which functions as and resembles a leaf.

Pinch out. To remove the growing tips of a plant to induce the production of side shoots.

Pinna (pl. pinnae). The primary division of a *pinnate* leaf. The fertile pinnae of ferns produce spores; vegetative pinnae do not.

Pinnate [of leaves]. Compound, with *leaflets* arranged on opposite sides of a central stalk.

Pistil. The female part of a flower comprising the *ovary, stigma,* and *style*.

Pollard [of a tree]. To cut back to its main branches in order to restrict growth.

Pollination. The transfer of pollen from the *anthers* to the *stigma* of the same or different flowers, resulting in fertilization of the embryonic seeds in the *ovary*.

Procumbent. Prostrate, creeping along the ground.

Raceme. An unbranched flower cluster with several or many stalked flowers borne singly along a main axis, the youngest at the apex.

Ray floret, ray flower. One of the flowers, usually with strap-shaped petals, that together form the outer ring of flowers in a composite *flower head* such as a daisy.

Ray petal. The petal or fused petals, often showy, of a ray *floret*.

Recurved. Curved backward.

Reflexed. Bent sharply backward.

Revert. To return to its original state, as when a plain green leaf is produced on a variegated plant.

Rhizome. An underground, creeping stem that acts as a storage organ and bears leafy shoots.

Root. The part of a plant, normally underground, that functions as anchorage and through which water and nutrients are absorbed. An **aerial root** emerges from the stem at some distance above the soil level.

Rootball. The roots and accompanying soil or compost visible when a plant is lifted.

Rootstock. A well-rooted plant onto which a scion is grafted; see *grafting*.

Rosette. A group of leaves radiating from approximately the same point, often borne at ground level at the base of a very short stem.

Runner. A horizontally spreading, usually slender stem that forms roots at each node; often confused with *stolon*.

Scale. 1. A reduced or modified leaf. 2. Part of a conifer cone.

Scandent. See *climber*.

Scarify. To scar the coat of a seed by abrasion in order to speed water intake and hence germination.

Scion. See *grafting*.

Scree. An area composed of a deep layer of stone chips mixed with a small amount of loam. It provides extremely sharp drainage for plants that resent moisture at their base.

Seed head. Any usually dry *fruit* that contains ripe seeds.

Seed leaf (cotyledon). The first leaf, pair of leaves, or occasionally group of leaves produced by a seed as it germinates. In some plants they remain below ground.

Self-seed. To produce seedlings around the parent plant.

Sepal. Part of a *calyx*, usually insignificant but sometimes showy.

Series. The name applied to a group of similar but not identical plants, usually annuals, linked by one or more common features.

Sessile. Without a stalk.

Sheath. A cylindrical structure that surrounds or encircles, partially or fully, another plant organ such as a stem.

Shoot. The aerial part of a plant that bears leaves. A **side shoot** arises from the side of a main shoot.

Shrub. A plant with *woody stems*, usually well-branched from or near the base.

Shy-flowering. Reluctant to flower; producing few flowers.

Simple [of leaves]. Not divided into leaflets.

Soft-stemmed. The opposite of *woody-stemmed*.

Spadix (pl. spadices). A *spike*like flower cluster that is usually fleshy and bears numerous small flowers. Spadices are characteristic of the family Araceae, e.g., *Arum*.

Spathe. A large *bract*, or sometimes 2, frequently colored and showy, that surrounds a *spadix* (as in *Arum*) or an individual flower bud (as in *Narcissus*).

Sphagnum. Mosses common to bogs; their moisture-retentive character makes them ideal components of some growing media. They are used particularly for orchid cultivation.

Spike. A racemose flower cluster with several or many unstalked flowers borne along a common axis.

Spikelet. 1. The flowering unit of grasses comprising one or several flowers with basal *bracts*. 2. A small *spike*, part of a branched flower cluster.

Spore. The minute reproductive structure of flowerless plants, e.g., ferns, fungi, and mosses.

Sporangium (pl. sporangia). A body that produces *spores*.

Sport. A mutation, caused by an accidental or induced change in the genetic makeup of a plant, which gives rise to a shoot with different characteristics from those of the parent plant.

Spur. 1. A hollow projection from a petal, often producing *nectar*. 2. A short stem bearing a group of flower buds such as is found on fruit trees.

Spur back. To cut back side shoots to within 2 or 3 buds of the main shoot.

Stamen. The *anther* and *filament*.

Standard. 1. A *tree* or *shrub* with a clear length of bare stem below the first branches. Certain shrubs, e.g., roses and fuchsias, may be trained to form standards. 2. One of the 3 inner and often erect *perianth segments* of the iris flower. 3. The larger, usually upright back petal of a flower in the family Leguminosae, e.g., *Lathyrus*.

Stapeliad. A member of the genus *Stapelia* and closely related genera of the family Asclepiadaceae.

Stem segment. A portion of a jointed stem between 2 *nodes*, most frequently occurring in cacti.

Sterile. Infertile, not bearing *spores*, pollen, seeds, etc.

Stigma. The part of the female portion of the flower, borne at the tip of the *style*, that receives pollen.

Stipule. A small scale, or leaflike appendage, usually one of a pair, mostly borne at a *node* or below a leaf stalk.

Stock. See *rootstock*.

Stolon. A horizontally spreading or arching stem, usually above ground, which roots at its tip to produce a new plant.

Stop. To remove certain growing points of a plant so as to control growth or the size and number of flowers.

Stratify. To break the dormancy of some seeds by exposing them to a period of cold.

Style. The part of the flower on which the *stigma* is borne.

Subglobose. Almost spherical.

Subshrub. A plant that is woody at the base although the terminal shoots die back in winter.

Succulent. A plant with thick, fleshy leaves and/or stems; in this book, it is evergreen unless otherwise stated.

Sucker. A shoot that arises from below ground level, directly from the *root* or *rootstock*.

Summer-deciduous. Losing its leaves naturally in summer.

Taproot. The main, downward-growing root of a plant; it is also applied generally to any strong, downward-growing root.

Tendril. A threadlike structure, used to provide support; see also *climber*.

Tooth. A small, marginal, often pointed lobe on a leaf, *calyx*, or *corolla*.

Tepal. See *perianth segment*.

Tree. A woody plant usually having a well-defined trunk or stem with a head of branches above.

Trifoliate. With 3 leaves; loosely, with 3 leaflets; **trifoliolate,** with 3 leaflets.

True [of seedlings]. Retaining the distinctive characteristics of the parent when raised from seed.

Truss. A compact cluster of flowers, often large and showy, e.g., those of pelargoniums and rhododendrons.

Tuber. A thickened, usually underground, storage organ derived from a stem or root.

Tubercle. A small, rounded protuberance; see also *areole*.

Turion. 1. A bud on a *rhizome*. 2. A fleshy, overwintering bud found on certain water plants.

Umbel. A usually flat-topped or rounded flower cluster in which the individual flower stalks arise from a central point. In a compound umbel, each primary stalk ends in an umbel.

Upright [of habit]. With vertical or semi-vertical main branches.

Water bud. See *turion*.

Whorl. The arrangement of 3 or more organs arising from the same point.

Winged [of seeds or fruits]. Having a marginal flange or membrane.

Woody-stemmed. With a stem composed of woody fibers and therefore persistent, as opposed to soft-stemmed and *herbaceous*. A **semiwoody stem** contains some softer tissue and may be only partially persistent.

x The sign used to denote a hybrid plant derived from the crossing of 2 or more botanically distinct plants.

+ The sign used to denote a graft hybrid; see *grafting*.

ACKNOWLEDGMENTS

Special thanks to **John R.L. Carter** for pictures of water plants; **Tony Russell** for his tree and shrub photography; **Dr Evelyn Stevens** for her help with *Meconopsis* entries and images, and also to **Julian Shaw** for additional help and support throughout the preparation of the 5th edition.

The publisher would like to thank the following for their kind permission to reproduce their photographs. Illustrations elsewhere in the book use the key: a-above; b-below/bottom; c-centre; f-far; l-left; r-right; t-top.

Every effort has been made to trace the copyright holders. Dorling Kindersley apologizes for unintentional ommissions, and would be pleased, if any such case should arise, to add an appropriate acknowledgment in future editions.

2 Corbis: Eric Crichton. **3 Getty Images:** Gyro Photography/amanaimages RF. **4 Getty Images:** Evan Sklar. **6 Corbis:** Radius Images. **12-13 GAP Photos:** Richard Bloom/Design: Adrian Bloom. **13 GAP Photos:** Jerry Harpur/ Design: Andy Sturgeon, RHS Chelsea Flower Show 2006 (tl). **Clive Nichols:** Pettifers Garden, Oxfordshire (ftr). **14 Marianne Majerus Garden Images:** Marianne Majerus. **15 Clive Nichols:** Lady Farm, Somerset: Designer, Judy Pearce (t). **Photolibrary:** Friedrich Strauss (b). **16 GAP Photos:** Marcus Harpur (t). **Getty Images:** John Glover (bc). **Clive Nichols:** Designer: Dominic Skinner (bl). **17 Marianne Majerus Garden Images:** Marianne Majerus/ Susanne Blair (t); Marianne Majerus/RHS Hyde Hall Garden (br). **18 Clive Nichols:** Design: Ivan Tucker (b). **Photolibrary:** Ellen Rooney (t). **19 Photolibrary:** Allan Mandell (tl). **20 Marianne Majerus Garden Images:** Marianne Majerus/ Hermannshof, Weinheim, Germany / Cassian Schmidt (b). **Clive Nichols:** Wollerton Old Hall, Shropshire (t). **21 GAP Photos:** Elke Borkowski (cra); Martin Hughes-Jones (br). **Marianne Majerus Garden Images:** Andrew Lawson/Piet Oudolf/Bury Court, Hants. (bl). **22 GAP Photos:** Designer: Marcus Barnett and Philip Nixon (bl); Location: The Summer Garden, Bressingham Gardens, Norfolk, UK (br). **Clive Nichols:** Pettifers Garden, Oxfordshire (cr); Winkworth Arboretum, Surrey (tr). **23 Clive Nichols:** (tr, cr, crb, br). **24 GAP Photos:** Matt Anker (tl); Jonathan Buckley, Design:Carol and Malcolm Skinner (br). **Marianne Majerus Garden Images:** Marianne Majerus (clb). **Clive Nichols:** (cl, bl). **25 GAP Photos:** (br); Friedrich Strauss (bc). **Marianne Majerus Garden Images:** Bennet Smith (bl). **32 GAP Photos:** S & O. **34 Alamy Images:** Arco Images GmbH (c). **GAP Photos:** John Glover (bl). **35 GAP Photos:** Dave Zubraski (br). **36 Alamy Images:** Florapix (br). **37 GAP Photos:** John Glover (br). **38-39 GAP Photos:** Jerry Harpur, Design: Naila Green. **39 Getty Images:** Martin Page (c). **40 GAP Photos:** Carole Drake (t). **Photolibrary:** Garden Pix LTD (b). **41 GAP Photos:** Adrian Bloom (tr); Neil Holmes (cr). **42 GAP Photos:** Neil Holmes (cl). **Garden World Images:** T Sims (cr). **43 Alamy Images:** John Glover (tc). **GAP Photos:** Nicola Browne, Design: Bernard Hicks (cr). **44 GAP Photos:** Carole Drake, Location: Sir Harold Hillier Gardens/Hampshire County Council (c); Howard Rice (bl). **45 Alamy Images:** Steffen Hauser / botanikfoto (ca); The Garden Picture Library (tc). **GAP Photos:** Elke Borkowski (br). **Garden World Images:** N+R Colborn (cra). **46 GAP Photos:** Martin Hughes-Jones (br). **47 Alamy Images:** Charles Stirling (cr). **49 GAP Photos:** Mark Bolton (cr). **50 Garden World Images:** L Thomas (fcrb). **Photolibrary:** Photos Lamontagne/ GPL (crb). **51 Alamy Images:** Christopher Burrows (br). **52 GAP Photos:** Mark Bolton (br). **Garden World Images:** MAP/Jean-Yves Grospas (crb). **53 GAP Photos:** Richard Bloom (br); Howard Rice (cra). **Garden World Images:** John Martin (c). **54 GAP Photos:** Richard Bloom (clb); Jonathan Need (cb). **55 GAP Photos:** Carole Drake, Design: Josse and Brian Emerson (tr); Howard Rice (br). **Getty Images:** Ron Evans (cb). **John McCormack:** (bc). **56-57 Clive Nichols. 57 Clive Nichols:** (ftl, tl, tr, ftr). **59 GAP Photos:** Elke Borkowski (tr). **60 Garden World Images:** MAP/Arnaud Descat: *Fraxinus excelsior* 'Jaspidea'. **Photolibrary:** Paroli Galperti: *Davidia involucrata* **61 Alamy:** K-Pix: *Fagus sylvatica* 'Riversii'. **Garden World Images:** Gilles Delacroix: *Fagus sylvatica* 'Rohanii' **62 Alamy:** blickwinkel: *Celtis australis*. **Getty:** DEA/D. Dagli Orti: *Juglans regia*. **Marianne Majerus Garden Images:** Marianne Majerus: *Quercus robur f. fastigiata* **63 Alamy:** CuboImages srl: *Platanus* x *hispanica*. **GAP Photos:** Martin Hughes-Jones: *Tilia platyphyllos* 'Rubra'. **Garden World Images:** W E Procter: *Platanus orientalis* **64 Alamy:** blickwinkel: *Fagus sylvatica* 'Aspleniifolia'. **Getty:** DEA/C. Sappa: *Zelkova carpinifolia*. **Photoshot:** Michael Warren: *Tilia* 'Petiolaris'. **Science Photo Library (SPL):** Vaughan Fleming: *Quercus frainetto* **65 Garden World Images:** *Pterocarya* x *rehderiana*. **Science Photo Library (SPL):** Bob Gibbons: *Quercus coccinea* **66 Alamy:** Holmes Garden Photos: *Acer rubrum*. **GAP Photos:** Heather Edwards: *Cercidiphyllum japonicum;* Martin Hughes-Jones: *Fraxinus angustifolia* 'Raywood'. **Garden World Images:** MAP/Frédéric Didillon: *Quercus palustris* **67 Alamy:** Bob Gibbons: *Prunus avium;* Steffen Hauser/botanikfoto: *Juglans ailantifolia var. cordiformis* **68 Alamy:** John Glover: *Quercus* x *turneri*. **Garden World Images:** Gilles Delacroix: *Eucalyptus johnstonii* **69 Alamy:** John Glover: *Salix daphnoides;* Martin Hughes-Jones: *Malus hupehensis*. **Frank Lane Picture Agency (FLPA):** Keith Rushforth: *Nothofagus menziesii*. **Science Photo Library (SPL):** John Stiles: *Nothofagus betuloides* **70 Alamy:** CuboImages srl: *Magnolia* 'Ann'; fotoFlora: *Magnolia campbellii subsp. mollicomata;* Andrea Jones: *Magnolia sprengeri var. diva, Magnolia* x *brooklynensis* 'Yellow Bird'; The Garden Picture Library: *Magnolia grandiflora* 'Exmouth'. **Corbis:** Mark Bolton: *Magnolia liliiflora* 'Nigra'; Clive Nichols: *Magnolia* 'Galaxy'. **Garden World Images:** Adrian James: *Magnolia* 'Butterflies'; J Lilly: *Magnolia wilsonii;* John Martin: *Magnolia* 'Pinkie'. **Getty:** Richard Bloom: *Magnolia* 'Black Tulip'. **Photolibrary:** Howard Rice: *Magnolia* 'Vulcan'; J S Sira: *Magnolia* x *loebneri* 'Leonard Messel', *Magnolia* x *soulangeana* 'Rustica Rubra' **71 Marianne Majerus Garden Images:** Marianne Majerus: *Halesia monticola* **72 Garden World Images:** Paul Lane: *Paulownia tomentosa;* John Martin: *Quercus rubra* 'Aurea'. **The Garden Collection:** Derek Harris: *Aesculus* x *neglecta* 'Erythroblastos' **73 A-Z Botanical Collection:** *Drimys winteri*. **Alamy:** CuboImages srl: *Quercus cerris* 'Argenteovariegata'. **Frank Lane Picture Agency (FLPA):** Keith Rushforth: *Toona sinensis*. **GAP Photos:** Dianna Jazwinski: *Eucryphia cordifolia*. **Photolibrary:** J S Sira: *Catalpa fargesii f. duclouxii*. **Science Photo Library (SPL):** Jim D Saul: *Acer pseudoplatanus* 'Simon Louis Frères' **74 Alamy:** blickwinkel: *Acer negundo* 'Variegatum'. **GardenPhotos.com:** judywhite: *Kalopanax septemlobus* **75 Frank Lane Picture Agency (FLPA):** Keith Rushforth: *Phellodendron chinense, Quercus marilandica*. **GardenPhotos.com:** judywhite: *Quercus ithaburensis subsp. macrolepis*. **Science Photo Library (SPL):** John Stiles: *Emmenopterys henryi* **76 Frank Lane Picture Agency (FLPA):** David Hosking: *Oxydendrum arboreum*. **Garden World Images:** John Swithinbank: *Acer henryi* **77 Alamy:** Andrea Jones: *Acer capillipes*. **Garden World Images:** *Nyssa sinensis*. **Marianne Majerus Garden Images:** Fiona Edmond: *Parrotia persica* **78 Alamy:** Mark Boulton: *Quercus suber;* John Glover: *Acer pensylvanicum* 'Erythrocladum', *Betula ermanii;* Brian Hoffman: *Acer griseum;* MBP-One: *Betula utilis var. jacquemontii* 'Grayswood Ghost'; Wildscape: *Acer grosseri*. **GAP Photos:** Fiona Lea: *Betula utilis var. jacquemontii* 'Jermyns'. **Garden World Images:** T Sims: *Acer palmatum* 'Sango-kaku'. **Getty:** Clive Nichols: *Pinus sylvestris*. **Photolibrary:** Richard Bloom: *Pinus bungeana;* Mark Bolton: *Stewartia pseudocamellia;* John Glover: *Prunus serrula;* Francois de Heel: *Acer davidii* **79 Frank Lane Picture Agency (FLPA):** Martin B Withers: *Fraxinus excelsior* 'Pendula'. **The Garden Collection:** Andrew Lawson: *Acer pensylvanicum* **80 Garden World Images:** John Swithinbank: *Trachycarpus fortunei* **81 Garden World Images:** *Aesculus californica* **83 Garden World Images:** Gilles Delacroix: *Prunus persica* 'Prince Charming' **84 Garden World Images:** *Laburnum* x *watereri* 'Vossii'. **Getty:** Geoff Kidd: *Malus floribunda* **85 Alamy:** fotoFlora: *Eucryphia glutinosa;* Martin Hughes-Jones: *Hoheria lyallii*. **GAP Photos:** Martin Hughes-Jones: *Hoheria angustifolia*. **Getty:** Scientifica: *Cornus kousa*. **Science Photo Library (SPL):** Adrian Thomas: *Eucryphia lucida* **87 Alamy:** Holmes Garden Photos: *Cornus mas;* Martin Hughes-Jones: *Cornus capitata, Cornus kousa* 'National'; John Martin: *Cornus kousa* 'Miss Satomi'; Organica: *Cornus kousa var. chinensis*. **GAP Photos:** Dave Bevan: *Cornus kousa var. chinensis* 'China Girl'; Dave Zubraski: *Cornus nuttallii* 'Monarch'. **Garden World Images:** G. Delacroix: *Cornus alternifolia;* Paul Lane: *Cornus florida* 'Cherokee Chief'; MAP/Arnaud Descat: *Cornus florida* 'Cherokee Princess'; MAP/ Nicole et Patrick Mioulane: *Cornus mas* 'Aureoelegantissima'; L Thomas: *Cornus florida* 'Rainbow' **88 Frank Lane Picture Agency (FLPA):** Keith Rushforth: *Ehretia dicksonii*. **Garden World Images:** *Ulmus glabra* 'Camperdownii' **89 Frank Lane Picture Agency (FLPA):** Ron Boardman, Life Science Image: *Koelreuteria paniculata*. **Garden World Images:** *Paraserianthes lophantha* **90 Alamy:** imagebroker: *Acer palmatum* 'Osakazuki' **91 Alamy:** Richard Becker: *Sorbus aucuparia;* blickwinkel: *Sorbus intermedia*. **GAP Photos:** Dave Bevan: *Sorbus* x *kewensis;* Sarah Cuttle: *Sorbus esserteauana;* Howard Rice: *Sorbus thibetica* 'John Mitchell'. **Photoshot:** Photos Horticultural: *Sorbus megalocarpa*. **Science Photo Library (SPL):** Malcolm Richards: *Sorbus forrestii* **92 Corbis:** Eric Crichton: *Malus* 'Golden Hornet'. **Garden World Images:** MAP/Arnaud Descat: *Acer laxiflorum* **93 GAP Photos:** Martin Hughes-Jones: *Pittosporum eugenioides* 'Variegatum'. **Garden World Images:** *Arbutus unedo* **94 Alamy:** Holmes Garden Photos: *Ilex aquifolium* 'Ferox Argentea'; Martin Hughes-Jones: *Ilex aquifolium* 'Madame Briot', *Ilex* x *altaclerensis* 'Belgica Aurea'; Plantography: *Ilex* x *altaclerensis* 'Camelliifolia'; The Garden Picture Library: *Ilex aquifolium* 'Bacciflava', *Ilex* x *altaclerensis* 'Golden King'. **Garden World Images:** Floramedia: *Ilex aquifolium* 'Silver Queen'; M Hughes-Jones: *Ilex aquifolium;* MAP/Arnaud Descat: *Ilex pernyi*. **Photolibrary:** Carole Drake: *Ilex crenata* 'Convexa' **95 Alamy:** Arco Images GmbH: *Abies procera* **96 Alamy:** WILDLIFE GmbH: *Wollemia nobilis*. **Garden World Images:** *Chamaecyparis lawsoniana* 'Intertexta'. **Photolibrary:** Leonie Lambert: *Cedrus deodara* **97 Garden World Images:** *Cedrus libani* **98 Alamy:** F Davis: *Araucaria araucana*. **Getty:** Tim Gainey: *Araucaria araucana* **99 GAP Photos:** Adrian Bloom, location: David Wards Garden, Leeds, Yorkshire: *Picea engelmannii*. **Garden World Images:** *Taxodium distichum*. **Photoshot:** *Tsuga mertensiana* 'Glauca'. **Savill Gardens:** *Picea glauca* 'Coerulea' **100 Alamy:** kpzfoto: *Juniperus chinensis* 'Keteleeri'. **GAP Photos:** FhF Greenmedia: *Picea likiangensis* **102 Photolibrary:** *Pinus contorta, Pseudolarix amabilis, Pseudolarix amabilis, Taxus baccata* 'Lutea'; Leonie Lambert: *Pseudolarix amabilis;* Fritz Polking: *Pinus contorta;* Howard Rice: *Taxus baccata* 'Lutea' **103 Garden World Images:** *Juniperus chinensis* 'Obelisk'. **Science Photo Library (SPL):** Chris Hellier: *Juniperus chinensis* 'Robust Green' **104 Alamy:** Martin Hughes-Jones: *Pinus sylvestris* 'Aurea'. **Frank Lane Picture Agency (FLPA):** R P Lawrence: *Taxus cuspidata*. **Garden World Images:** *Pinus pinea*. **Photolibrary:** Ron Evans: *Chamaecyparis obtusa* 'Crippsii' **105 Alamy:** CuboImages srl: *Podocarpus nivalis;* Martin Hughes-Jones: *Juniperus squamata* 'Blue Carpet'. **Corbis:** Patrick Johns: *Abies cephalonica* 'Meyer's Dwarf'. **GAP Photos:** Adrian Bloom: *Abies concolor* 'Compacta', *Pinus heldreichii* 'Smidtii', *Taxus baccata* 'Dovastonii Aurea'; J S Sira/Design: Collin Elliott: *Juniperus* x *pfitzeriana* 'Old Gold'. **Garden World Images:** *Chamaecyparis obtusa* 'Nana Gracilis', *Juniperus squamata* 'Holger', *Microbiota decussata, Platycladus orientalis* 'Aurea Nana', *Thuja plicata* 'Stoneham Gold'; R Coates: *Juniperus squamata* 'Holger'; G. Delacroix: *Microbiota decussata;* MAP/Nathalie Pasquel: *Chamaecyparis obtusa* 'Nana Gracilis', *Platycladus orientalis* 'Aurea Nana'. **GardenPhotos.com:** judywhite: *Chamaecyparis pisifera* 'Filifera Aurea', *Juniperus scopulorum* 'Skyrocket'. **Photolibrary:** Jerry Pavia: *Picea pungens*

'Globosa' **106-107 GAP Photos:** Richard Bloom. **107 GAP Photos:** Sharon Pearson (ftl). **Clive Nichols:** (tl) (ftr) (tr). **110 Garden World Images:** *Amelanchier lamarckii* **111 Garden World Images:** *Dipelta floribunda*. **Photolibrary:** Howard Rice: *Berberis valdiviana* **112 Alamy:** Holmes Garden Photos: *Salix exigua* **113 Garden World Images:** Martin Hughes-Jones: *Crinodendron patagua, Elaeagnus umbellata* **114 GAP Photos:** Christina Bollen: *Buddleja davidii* 'White Profusion'; FhF Greenmedia: *Buddleja salviifolia;* Lynn Keddie: *Buddleja* x *weyeriana* 'Moonlight'; Rob Whitworth: *Abutilon vitifolium* 'Veronica Tennant'. **Garden World Images:** D Brown: *Buddleja colvilei* 'Kewensis'; M Hughes-Jones: *Buddleja* 'Lochinch', *Buddleja davidii* 'Pink Delight', *Buddleja* x *weyeriana* 'Sungold'. **The Garden Collection:** Jonathan Buckley: *Buddleja* 'Lochinch', *Buddleja davidii* 'Black Knight'; Nicola Stocken Tomkins: *Buddleja davidii* 'Dartmoor' **115 Alamy:** Holmes Garden Photos: *Syringa vulgaris* 'Andenken an Ludwig Späth'. **Garden World Images:** G. Delacroix: *Syringa pubescens subsp. patula* 'Miss Kim'; M Hughes-Jones: *Syringa* x *persica;* MAP/Arnaud Descat: *Syringa komarowii subsp. reflexa, Syringa vulgaris* 'Firmament', *Syringa vulgaris* 'Katherine Havemeyer'. **Marianne Majerus Garden Images:** Marianne Majerus: *Syringa* x *persica* 'Alba' **116 Garden World Images:** Derek Gould: *Genista tenera* 'Golden Shower' **117 Garden World Images:** *Cotoneaster* 'Cornubia'. **John Glover:** *Cotinus* 'Flame' **118 Alamy:** John Glover: *Hamamelis* x *intermedia* 'Arnold Promise', *Hamamelis* x *intermedia* 'Barmstedt Gold', *Hamamelis* x *intermedia* 'Jelena'; MBP-Plants: *Hamamelis* x *intermedia* 'Pallida'. **GAP Photos:** Richard Bloom: *Hamamelis* x *intermedia* 'Jelena'. **Garden World Images:** Jacqui Dracup: *Hamamelis* x *intermedia* 'Robert'. **Marianne Majerus Garden Images:** Marianne Majerus: *Azara microphylla*. **Photolibrary:** Richard Bloom: *Hamamelis* x *intermedia* 'Primavera' **119 GAP Photos:** Geoff Kidd: *Pittosporum dallii*. **Garden World Images:** G Kidd: *Prunus lusitanica subsp. variegata;* Geoff Kidd: *Prunus lusitanica subsp. variegata* **120 Alamy:** Martin Hughes-Jones: *Camellia* 'Cornish Snow'. **GAP Photos:** Fiona Lea: *Camellia japonica* 'Hagoromo'. **Garden World Images:** *Camellia japonica* 'Alba Plena', *Camellia japonica* 'Nobilissima', *Tetrapanax papyrifer, Tetrapanax papyrifer;* MAP/A Descat/Collection Pepineiere Stervinou: *Camellia japonica* 'Nobilissima'; John Martin: *Camellia japonica* 'Alba Plena' **121 Alamy:** blickwinkel/Jagel: *Camellia* 'Spring Festival'; John Glover: *Camellia japonica* 'Lavinia Maggi'. **GAP Photos:** Richard Bloom: *Camellia* 'Inspiration'; Lynn Keddie: *Camellia* x *williamsii* 'J.C. Williams'; Geoff Kidd: *Camellia japonica* 'Brushfield's Yellow'; Howard Rice: *Camellia japonica* 'Tricolor'; S & O: *Camellia* x *williamsii* 'Jury's Yellow'; J S Sira: *Camellia japonica* 'Bob's Tinsie'. **Garden World Images:** G. Delacroix: *Camellia reticulata* 'Captain Rawes'; MAP/A Descat/Collection Pepineiere Stervinou: *Camellia* 'Black Lace', *Camellia* 'Freedom Bell'; T Sims: *Camellia japonica* 'Adolphe Audusson'. **Photolibrary:** Clive Nichols /GPL: *Camellia* x *williamsii* 'Debbie' **122 GAP Photos:** J S Sira: *Viburnum bitchiuense*. **Garden World Images:** *Choisya* 'Aztec Pearl', *Rhododendron* 'Percy Wiseman'; MAP/ Nicole et Patrick Mioulane: *Choisya* 'Aztec Pearl' **123 Alamy:** Auscape International Pty Ltd: *Telopea truncata;* John Glover: *Prunus mume* 'Beni-chidori'. **GAP Photos:** S & O: *Ribes sanguineum* 'Pulborough Scarlet'. **Garden World Images:** *Leptospermum scoparium* 'Red Damask' **124 GAP Photos:** Dave Bevan: *Rhododendron sinogrande*. **Garden World Images:** M Hughes-Jones: *Rhododendron* 'Gomer Waterer', *Rhododendron quinquefolium;* MAP/ Nathalie Pasquel: *Rhododendron* 'Golden Torch'; J Need: *Rhododendron calophytum*. **Photolibrary:** Georgianna Lane: *Rhododendron decorum;* Brigitte Thomas: *Rhododendron williamsianum*. **Photoshot:** Michael Warren: *Rhododendron decorum*. **Royal Horticultural Society (RHS):** Carol Sheppard: *Rhododendron pachysanthum* **125 Alamy:** Brian Hoffman: *Rhododendron arboreum;* Holmes Garden Photos: *Rhododendron praecox*. **GAP Photos:** Richard Bloom: *Rhododendron* 'Fastuosum Flore Pleno'; Christina Bollen: *Rhododendron niveum;* FhF Greenmedia: *Rhododendron cinnabarinum;* Neil Holmes: *Rhododendron* 'Blue Danube'. **Garden World Images:** G Delacroix: *Rhododendron* 'Blaauw's Pink', *Rhododendron* 'Purple Splendour'; M Hughes-Jones: *Rhododendron* 'Daviesii', *Rhododendron fulvum;* Christopher Lavis-Jones: *Rhododendron* 'Patty Bee'. **Photolibrary:** Georgianna Lane: *Rhododendron* 'Hotei'. **Royal Horticultural Society (RHS):** Rebecca Ross: *Rhododendron* 'Gibraltar' **126 Alamy:** Holmes Garden Photos: *Cornus sericea* 'Flaviramea'; J Need: *Cornus sericea* 'White Gold'; Plantography: *Cornus alba* 'Elegantissima'. **GAP Photos:** J S Sira: *Corylopsis pauciflora;* Jo Whitworth: *Cornus sericea* 'Kelseyi'. **Garden World Images:** Jacqui Dracup: *Edgeworthia chrysantha;* T Sims: *Cornus alba* 'Aurea', *Cornus sanguinea* 'Midwinter Fire' **127 GAP Photos:** Neil Holmes: *Forsythia* x *intermedia* 'Beatrix Farrand'. **Garden World Images:** *Deutzia scabra, Kerria japonica* 'Pleniflora', *Lindera benzoin;* Liz Cole: *Deutzia scabra*. **Photolibrary:** Mel Watson: *Philadelphus* 'Beauclerk' **129 Garden World Images:** Martin Hughes-Jones: *Clethra barbinervis* **130 Garden World Images:** Gilles Delacroix: *Leptospermum scoparium* 'Snow White'; Trevor Sims: *Colletia hystrix*. **P-Pod:** Tim Argles: *Olearia ilicifolia*. **Photoshot:** Photos Horticultural: *Zenobia pulverulenta*. **Science Photo Library (SPL):** Nick Wiseman: *Escallonia virgata* **132 Alamy:** Holmes Garden Photos: *Olearia macrodonta*. **GAP Photos:** Martin Hughes-Jones: *Hibiscus syriacus* 'Red Heart'; Mel Watson: *Aloysia triphylla* **133 Garden World Images:** *Robinia hispida* **134 Alamy:** Martin Hughes-Jones: *Hydrangea paniculata* 'Silver Dollar'; Andrea Jones: *Hydrangea paniculata* PINKY-WINKY. **GAP Photos:** Martin Hughes-Jones: *Hydrangea serrata* 'Diadem'; Rob Whitworth: *Hydrangea macrophylla* 'Madame Emile Mouillère'. **Garden World Images:** G. Delacroix: *Hydrangea arborescens* 'Annabelle', *Hydrangea quercifolia* 'Snowflake'. **Marianne Majerus Garden Images:** Marianne Majerus: *Hydrangea serrata* 'Kiyosumi'; Marianne Majerus/RHS Wisley Garden: *Hydrangea paniculata* 'Big Ben'. **Photolibrary:** Sunniva Harte: *Hydrangea heteromalla* 'Snowcap'; Marga Werner: *Hydrangea paniculata* 'Phantom'. **Science Photo Library (SPL):** A-Z Botanical Collection: *Hydrangea macrophylla* 'Générale Vicomtesse de Vibraye' **135 Alamy:** John glover: Hydrangea paniculata PINK DIAMOND; Holmes Garden Photos: *Hydrangea macrophylla* 'Ami Pasquier'; Andrea Jones: *Hydrangea paniculata* 'Dharuma'. **GAP Photos:** Martin Hughes-Jones: *Hydrangea paniculata* 'Limelight'. **Garden World Images:** R Coates: *Hydrangea macrophylla* 'Europa', *Hydrangea serrata* 'Grayswood'; Rita Coates: *Hydrangea aspera* 'Mauvette'; G. Delacroix: *Hydrangea macrophylla* 'Libelle', *Hydrangea macrophylla* 'Möwe'; Steffen Hauser: *Hydrangea aspera subsp. sargentiana;* K Howchin: *Hydrangea macrophylla* 'Ayesha' **136 Alamy:** The Garden Picture Library: *Paeonia delavayi*. **Garden World Images:** MAP/Nathalie Pasquel: *Erythrina* x *bidwillii* **137 Alamy:** Milestone Media: *Abutilon* 'Ashford Red'. **Garden World Images:** *Camellia japonica* 'Mathotiana' **138 Garden World Images:** *Ceanothus impressus*. **Photolibrary:** Sunniva Harte: *Iochroma australe* **140 Garden World Images:** *Euonymus europaeus* 'Red Cascade'. **The Garden Collection:** Andrew Lawson: *Rhus glabra* **141 GAP Photos:** David Dixon: *Berberis* x *carminea* 'Barbarossa'. **Garden World Images:** *Leonotis leonurus*. **Getty:** Rob Whitworth: *Disanthus cercidifolius* **142 Alamy:** CuboImages srl: *Cotoneaster conspicuus, Cotoneaster* x *watereri* 'John Waterer'; Steffen Hauser/botanikfoto: *Cotoneaster salicifolius;* Colin Underhill: *Euonymus hamiltonianus subsp. sieboldianus*. **Garden World Images:** S Hauser: *Daphne mezereum;* D Murphy: *Cotoneaster frigidus*. **Janet Johnson:** *Hippophae rhamnoides*. **Photolibrary:** Richard Bloom: *Cornus alba* 'Sibirica Variegata' **143 Alamy:** Steffen Hauser/ botanikfoto: *Viburnum farreri*. **Garden World Images:** *Nandina domestica* 'Fire Power', *Viburnum tinus* 'Eve Price'; Christopher Lavis-Jones: *Viburnum tinus* 'Eve Price'. **The Garden Collection:** Jonathan Buckley: *Viburnum foetens* **144 GAP Photos:** John Glover: *Fatsia japonica* 'Variegata'. **Getty:** Hemant Jariwala: *Mahonia japonica* **145 Alamy:** blickwinkel: *Buxus balearica*. **Garden World Images:** *Gaultheria* x *wisleyensis* 'Wisley Pearl', *Prunus laurocerasus* 'Zabeliana'; Trevor Sims: *Prunus laurocerasus* 'Zabeliana' **146 Alamy:** Holmes Garden Photos: *Ribes sanguineum* 'Edward VII'; Martin Hughes-Jones: *Chaenomeles speciosa* 'Snow' **148 Alamy:** Chris Howes/Wild Places Photography: *Ulex europaeus*. **The Garden Collection:** Derek Harris: *Choisya ternata* SUNDANCE **149 Garden World Images:** *Convolvulus cneorum,* x *Halimiocistus sahucii* **150 Garden World Images:** *Rhaphiolepis umbellata* **151 GAP Photos:** J S Sira: *Hebe recurva*. **Garden World Images:** Martin Hughes-Jones: *Ozothamnus ledifolius;* M Hughes-Jones: *Ozothamnus ledifolius*. **Science Photo Library (SPL):** Anthony Cooper: *Lomatia silaifolia* **152 GAP Photos:** Dianna Jazwinski: *Deutzia* 'Mont Rose' **154 Alamy:** Arco Images GmbH: *Fuchsia* 'Riccartonii'; John Glover: *Fuchsia magellanica;* Martin Hughes-Jones: *Escallonia* 'Donard Beauty'. **GAP Photos:** Dave Zubraski: *Fuchsia* 'Howlett's Hardy'. **Garden World Images:** T Sims: *Fuchsia* 'Corallina'. **Getty:** Dave Zubraski: *Fuchsia* 'Mrs Popple', *Fuchsia magellanica* 'Thompsonii'. **Marianne Majerus Garden Images:** Marianne Majerus: *Fuchsia magellanica var. gracilis*. **Science Photo Library (SPL):** Mike Danson: *Fuchsia* 'Madame Cornélissen' **155 Alamy:** Martin Hughes-Jones: *Salvia* x *jamensis* 'La Luna'; Plantography: *Salvia microphylla* 'La Foux', *Salvia* x *jamensis* 'Maraschino'. **GAP Photos:** Heather Edwards: *Salvia microphylla* 'Cerro Potosi'; FhF Greenmedia: *Salvia* x *jamensis* 'Red Velvet'; Marcus Harpur: *Salvia microphylla* 'Kew Red'. **Garden World Images:** N R Colborn: *Salvia* x *jamensis* 'Hot Lips'; G Delacroix: *Salvia* x *jamensis* 'Sierra San Antonio'; G. Delacroix: *Salvia officinalis* 'Berggarten'; L Thomas: *Salvia greggii* 'Icing Sugar'. **Getty:** *Salvia officinalis,* *Salvia officinalis* 'Purpurascens', *Salvia officinalis* 'Tricolor'; De Agostini: *Salvia officinalis;* Linda Lewis: *Salvia officinalis* 'Tricolor'. **Photolibrary:** Geoff Kidd: *Salvia microphylla* 'Newby Hall'; Juliette Wade: *Salvia microphylla* 'Pink Blush' **158 Alamy:** John Glover: *Lavandula* x *chaytorae* 'Sawyers'; Holmes Garden Photos: *Lavandula* 'Fathead', *Lavandula angustifolia* 'Miss Katherine'. **GAP Photos:** Elke Borkowski: *Lavandula pedunculata subsp. pedunculata* 'James Compton'; Suzie Gibbons: *Lavandula angustifolia* 'Wendy Carlile'; Dianna Jazwinski: *Lavandula angustifolia* 'Imperial Gem'; J S Sira: *Lavandula* 'Helmsdale', *Lavandula angustifolia* 'Loddon Blue', *Lavandula stoechas f. rosea* 'Kew Red'. **Garden World Images:** G. Delacroix: *Lavandula lanata;* C Fairweather: Lavandula angustifolia LITTLE LOTTIE, *Lavandula stoechas* 'Snowman'; MAP/N Pasquel: *Lavandula angustifolia* 'Little Lady'; T Sims: *Lavandula angustifolia* 'Hidcote'; L Thomas: *Lavandula* 'Regal Splendour', *Lavandula* 'Willow Vale'. **Photolibrary:** Chris L Jones: *Lavandula* x *intermedia* 'Alba' **159 Alamy:** Martin Hughes-Jones: *Ceanothus thyrsiflorus var. repens*. **Garden World Images:** *Ceratostigma willmottianum* **160 Garden World Images:** Gilles Delacroix: *Symphoricarpos orbiculatus* 'Foliis Variegatis' **161 GAP Photos:** Martin Hughes-Jones: *Hypericum* x *inodorum* 'Elstead'; J S Sira: *Halimium lasianthum subsp. formosum*. **Garden World Images:** *Coriaria terminalis var. xanthocarpa, Hypericum kouytchense* **162 Garden World Images:** *Berberis* 'Rubrostilla', *Cytisus scoparius f. andreanus*. **Photolibrary:** Mark Bolton: *Cuphea cyanea;* Mark Turner/GPL: *Myrica gale* **163 GAP Photos:** Adrian Bloom: *Fothergilla gardenii*. **The Garden Collection:** Jonathan Buckley: *Lonicera* x *purpusii* **164 Alamy:** Plantography: *Pittosporum tenuifolium* 'Tom Thumb' **165 GAP Photos:** Friedrich Strauss: *Artemisia abrotanum* Artemisia abrotanum. **Garden World Images:** *Hebe cupressoides* **166 Alamy:** J S Sira/ GPL: *Erica carnea* 'Challenger'; Arco Images GmbH: *Erica vagans* 'St Keverne'; John Glover: *Calluna vulgaris* 'Annemarie', *Calluna vulgaris* 'Peter Sparkes', *Calluna vulgaris* 'Wickwar Flame'; Martin Hughes-Jones: *Erica carnea* 'Ann Sparkes'; Piotr & Irena Kolasa: *Calluna vulgaris* 'Dark Star'. **GAP Photos:** Mark Bolton: *Erica* x *darleyensis* 'Arthur Johnson'; Geoff Kidd: *Erica* x *darleyensis* 'Furzey'. **Garden World Images:** I Anderson: *Erica erigena* 'Irish Dusk'; G. Delacroix: *Erica erigena f. alba* 'Brian Proudley'; T Jennings: *Erica vagans* 'Birch Glow'; M Hughes-Jones: *Erica carnea* 'Golden Starlet'; MAP/N Pasquel: *Erica vagans* 'Mrs D. F. Maxwell'. **GardenPhotos.com:** Judy White: *Calluna vulgaris* 'Beoley Gold' **167 GAP Photos:** Geoff Kidd: *Ruscus aculeatus* Ruscus aculeatus. **Garden World Images:** Trevor Sims: *Leucothöe fontanesiana* 'Rainbow' **168 GAP Photos:** Geoff Kidd. **168 Garden World Images:** Trevor Sims. **169 GAP Photos:** Mark Anker (ftr); FhF Greenmedia (ftl); Leigh Clapp (tr). **176 Alamy:** John Glover: *R. moyesii* 'Geranium'; Holmes Garden Photos: *R. sericia subsp. omeiensis f. ptenracantha*. **GAP Photos:** Jonathan Need: *R. roxburghii*. **Garden World Images:** MAP/Jean-Yves Grospas: *R. rubiginosa;* Trevor Sims: *R. multibracteata*.

ACKNOWLEDGMENTS

Getty: Rob Whitworth: *R. rugosa*. **Marianne Majerus Garden Images:** Marianne Majerus: *R. glauca* **177 Alamy:** Martin Hughes-Jones: *R.* 'Buff Beauty'. **GAP Photos:** Michael Howes: *R.* EVELYN; Rob Whitworth: *R.* KENT. **Photoshot:** Photos Horticultural: *R.* SILVER ANNIVERSARY. **Roses UK:** *R.* ISN'T SHE LOVELY **178 Alamy:** Natural Garden Images: *R.* . MANY HAPPY RETURNS. **GAP Photos:** FhF Greenmedia: *R.* SUSAN DANIEL. **Photolibrary:** Leonie Lambert: *R.* SAVOY HOTEL **179 Alamy:** Roger Cope: *R.* NOSTALGIA. **C & K Jones:** *R.* CHRIS BEARDSHAW. **David Austin Roses:** *R.* BRAVEHEART. **Garden World Images:** Gilles Delacroix: *R.* FLOWER CARPET **181 Garden World Images:** MAP/Nicole et Patrick Mioulane: *R.* GUY SAVOY. **Photoshot:** Michael Warren: *R.* LANCASHIRE **182 Garden World Images:** G Delacroix: *R.* ABSOLUTELY FABULOUS; Christopher Lavis-Jones: *R.* 'Arthur Bell'; Jenny Lilly: *R.* GOLDEN BEAUTY. **The Garden Collection:** Derek Harris: *R.* GUY'S GOLD **183 GAP Photos:** Howard Rice: *R.* SIMPLY THE BEST. **Harkness Roses, roses.co.uk:** *R.* EASY DOES IT. **Roses UK:** *R.* SUPER TROOPER **184 Botanical Garden Collection:** *R. filipes* 'Kiftsgate'. **Garden World Images:** *R.* 'Félicité Perpétue' **185 Garden World Images:** *R.* 'Veilchenblau' **186 GAP Photos:** Howard Rice: *R.* 'Cécile Brünner'. **Garden World Images:** *R.* 'Guinée' **187 Chris Warner:** *R.* GARDENERS GLORY. **GAP Photos:** Maxine Adcock: *R.* SUMMER WINE; Visions Premium: *R.* BRIDGE OF SIGHS. **Garden World Images:** *R.* 'Mermaid'. **Roses UK:** *R.* ALIBABA **189 GAP Photos:** Andrea Jones (tl); Jerry Harpur (ftl); Marcus Harpur (ftr). **190 GAP Photos:** John Glover (bl). **191 GAP Photos:** Maddie Thornhill (tr). **192 Alamy:** Holmes Garden Photos: *Prostanthera rotundifolia* 'Rosea'; Martin Hughes-Jones: *Acradenia frankliniae;* JTB Photo Communications, Inc.: *Stauntonia hexaphylla*. **Garden Picture Library:** *Ercilla volubilis*. **Garden World Images:** Trevor Sims: *Holboellia latifolia*. **Photos Horticultural:** *Decumaria sinensis* **193 Alamy:** John Glover: *Jasminum beesianum*. **Garden World Images:** *Campsis radicans* 'Indian Summer', *Clianthus puniceus, Mitraria coccinea, Ribes speciosum;* MAP/Arnaud Descat: *Mitraria coccinea;* Trevor Sims: *Campsis radicans* 'Indian Summer', *Ribes speciosum* **194 GAP Photos:** Martin Hughes-Jones: *Sollya heterophylla*. **Garden World Images:** Lee Thomas: *Humulus lupulus* 'Aureus'. **Photolibrary:** Mark Bolton: *Ceanothus arboreus* 'Trewithen Blue'; Philippe Bonduel: *Eriobotrya japonica* **195 GAP Photos:** John Glover: *Ampelopsis brevipedunculata var. maximowiczii* 'Elegans'. **Garden World Images:** *Araujia sericifera, Hydrangea petiolaris, Jasminum mesnyi;* Geoff Kidd: *Araujia sericifera;* Trevor Sims: *Hydrangea petiolaris* **196 Garden World Images:** Trevor Sims: *Hydrangea seemannii;* Lee Thomas: *Jasminum officinale f. affine*. **Science Photo Library (SPL):** Bob Gibbons: *Hydrangea serratifolia*. **The Garden Collection:** Andrew Lawson: *Trachelospermum asiaticum* **197 Alamy:** Holmes Garden Photos: *Prostanthera cuneata*. **GAP Photos:** Geoff Kidd: *Drimys lanceolata*. **Garden World Images:** *Anredera cordifolia, Schizophragma hydrangeoides;* Gilles Delacroix: *Schizophragma hydrangeoides*. **Photolibrary:** Howard Rice: *Dregea sinensis* **198 GAP Photos:** Fiona Lea: *Clematis* 'Avalanche'; J S Sira: *Clematis cartmannii* 'Joe'. **Garden World Images:** MAP/A Descat: *Clematis fasciculiflora;* T Sims: *Clematis* 'Andromeda'; Trevor Sims: *Clematis* 'Andromeda'; Lee Thomas: *Clematis* 'Avalanche', *Clematis* 'Early Sensation', *Clematis* ARCTIC QUEEN, *Clematis cartmannii* 'Joe'. **Photolibrary:** Ron Evans: *Clematis montana;* Abbe Green-Armytage: *Clematis* 'Guernsey Cream'. **Photoshot:** Photos Horticultural: *Clematis* 'Bella' **199 Alamy:** Roger Cope: *Clematis* PINK CHAMPAGNE. **GAP Photos:** Martin Hughes-Jones: *Clematis* 'Barbara Jackman'. **Garden World Images:** R Coates: *Clematis* 'Jacqueline du Pré'; A Graham: *Clematis* 'Barbara Jackman'; C Lavis-Jones: *Clematis* 'Barbara Dibley', *Clematis* 'Barbara Dibley'; B Stojanovic: *Clematis* 'Corona'. **Marianne Majerus Garden Images:** Marianne Majerus, RHS Wisley Garden: *Clematis cirrhosa*. **Photolibrary:** Howard Rice: *Clematis* 'Jan Lindmark', *Clematis montana var. rubens*. **Raymond Evison:** *Clematis* BLUE MOON, *Clematis* CHANTILLY, *Clematis florida* PISTACHIO, *Clematis* VIENNETTA **200 Alamy:** CuboImages srl: *Clematis* 'Perle d'Azur'; John Glover: *Clematis* 'Abundance'. **GAP Photos:** Mark Bolton: *Clematis* 'Silver Moon'. **Garden World Images:** Floramedia: *Clematis* 'Columella', *Clematis* 'Frankie'; Martin Hughes-Jones: *Clematis* 'Frances Rivis'; C Lavis-Jones: *Clematis* 'Westerplatte'; MAP/A Descat: *Clematis* 'Black Prince'; MAP/N Pasquel: *Clematis* 'Abundance', *Clematis* 'Betty Corning'. **Raymond Evison:** *Clematis* AVANT-GARDE, *Clematis* BOURBON, *Clematis* ROSEMOOR, *Clematis* VINO. **The Garden Collection:** Torie Chugg: *Clematis* 'Betty Corning' **201 Alamy:** Niall McDiarmid: *Bomarea edulis*. **Garden World Images:** *Lathyrus odoratus* 'Lady Diana'. **Photolibrary:** Anne Green-Armytage: *Jasminum* x *stephanense*. **Photos Horticultural:** *Lathyrus odoratus* 'Charles Unwin', *Lathyrus odoratus* 'Mrs Bernard Jones' **202 Garden World Images:** *Ipomoea lobata*. **Getty:** Ron Evans: *Lapageria rosea;* Leroy Simon: *Ipomoea quamoclit*. **Paul Beard Photo Agency:** *Lathyrus odoratus* 'Barry Dare' **203 Alamy:** Holmes Garden Photos: *Callistemon subulatus;* Martin Hughes-Jones: *Desfontainia spinosa*. **GAP Photos:** Martin Hughes-Jones: *Grevillea rosmarinifolia*. **Garden World Images:** *Callistemon citrinus* 'Splendens', *Cestrum* 'Newellii'; Trevor Sims: *Cestrum* 'Newellii'. **Getty:** *Abutilon megapotamicum*. **Photolibrary:** J S Sira: *Campsis grandiflora* **204 GAP Photos:** Geoff Kidd: *Aconitum hemsleyanum;* J S Sira: *Ipomoea hederacea*. **Garden World Images:** *Akebia trifoliata, Cobaea scandens;* Trevor Sims: *Akebia trifoliata*. **Marianne Majerus Garden Images:** Andrew Lawson: *Passiflora caerulea* **205 Alamy Images:** Frank Paul: *Wisteria frutescens* 'Amethyst Falls'. **Frank Lane Picture Agency (FLPA):** Brian Davis: *Wisteria brachybotrys* 'White Silk'. **GAP Photos:** Richard Bloom: *Ceanothus* 'Puget Blue'; Neil Holmes: *Plumbago auriculata;* Martin Hughes-Jones: *Wisteria frutescens* 'Longwood Purple'. **Garden World Images:** MAP/Arnaud Descat: *Wisteria floribunda* 'Yae Kokoryu'; John Martin: *Wisteria sinensis* 'Prolific'. **Photolibrary:** Jerry Pavia: *Wisteria frutescens;* Mark Turner: *Wisteria floribunda* 'Hon-Beni'. **Royal Horticultural Society (RHS):** Graham Titchmarsh: *Ceanothus* 'Burkwoodii' **206 GAP Photos:** John Glover: *Fremontodendron* 'California Glory'; Martin Hughes-Jones: *Campsis radicans f. flava;* Geoff Kidd: *Hypericum* 'Rowallane'; Howard Rice: *Jasminum humile* 'Revolutum'. **Garden World Images:** *Piptanthus nepalensis* **207 Alamy:** Martin Hughes-Jones: *Lonicera periclymenum* 'Red Gables'. **GAP Photos:** Howard Rice: *Lonicera etrusca* 'Michael Rosse'. **Garden World Images:** MAP/Arnaud Descat: *Lonicera henryi*. **Photolibrary:** Kate Boykin: *Lonicera sempervirens;* Howard Rice: *Lonicera etrusca* 'Superba' **208 Alamy:** Charles Stirling: *Cotoneaster horizontalis*. **Garden World Images:** *Jasminum polyanthum, Vitis* 'Brant'; Lee Thomas: *Vitis* 'Brant'. **Marianne Majerus Garden Images:** Marianne Majerus: *Campsis* x *tagliabuana* 'Madame Galen'. **Photolibrary:** Howard Rice: *Campsis radicans* 'Flamenco' **209 Photolibrary:** Gert Tabak: *Celastrus orbiculatus* 'Diana' **210 Alamy:** Andrea Jones: *Ampelopsis megalophylla* **211 Alamy:** John Glover: *Acacia dealbata*. **Garden World Images:** Martin Hughes-Jones: *Garrya elliptica* 'James Roof' **212-213 GAP Photos:** Elke Borkowski. **213 GAP Photos:** Lynn Keddie (tl); Clive Nichols (tr); Howard Rice (ftl); Visions (ftr). **214 GAP Photos:** Richard Bloom (crb); Howard Rice (bl). **215 GAP Photos:** John Glover (bc/metal spirals). **216 GAP Photos:** Geoff Kidd: *Impatiens tinctoria;* Rob Whitworth: *Sanguisorba tenuifolia* 'Alba'. **Garden World Images:** Derek Gould: *Artemisia lactiflora* **217 GAP Photos:** Mark Bolton: *Delphinium* 'Red Caroline'. **Photolibrary:** Paroli Galperti: *Delphinium* 'Cliveden Beauty'; J S Sira/GPL: *Delphinium* 'Elizabeth Cook' **218 Alamy:** John Glover: *Meconopsis paniculata*. **Dr Evelyn Stevens:** *Meconopsis grandis, Meconopsis* 'Jimmy Bayne', *Meconopsis* 'Marit', *Meconopsis baileyi* 'Alba', *Meconopsis* x *cookei* 'Old Rose'; Plant Heritage National Plant Collection: *Meconopsis* 'Marit', *Meconopsis baileyi* 'Alba', *Meconopsis* x *cookei* 'Old Rose'. **GAP Photos:** Leigh Clapp: *Meconopsis* 'Lingholm'; Fiona Lea: *Galega* x *hartlandii* 'Lady Wilson'; Howard Rice: *Meconopsis* 'Slieve Donard'. **Garden World Images:** Martin Hughes-Jones: *Thalictrum* 'Elin'. **Photolibrary:** Howard Rice: *Meconopsis* 'Crewdson Hybrid' **219 Alamy:** Florapix: *Ligularia* 'The Rocket'; John Glover: *Musa basjoo, Musa basjoo*. **Photoshot:** Photos Horticultural: *Acanthus mollis* 'Hollard's Gold' **220 Alamy:** Jim Allan: *Thalictrum delavayi* 'Hewitt's Double'. **Eric Crichton Photos:** *Anemone* x *hybrida* 'Honorine Jobert'. **GAP Photos:** Victoria Firmston: *Veronicastrum virginicum* 'Fascination'. **Marianne Majerus Garden Images:** Marianne Majerus: *Hedychium* x *moorei* 'Tara'. **Photoshot:** Photos Horticultural: *Eremurus* x *isabellinus* 'Cleopatra' **221 Alamy:** WILDLIFE GmbH: *Echinacea paradoxa*. **GAP Photos:** Visions: *Eupatorium maculatum* 'Riesenschirm'. **Garden World Images:** *Echinacea* 'Harvest Moon', *Echinacea purpurea* 'Coconut Lime', *Echinacea purpurea* 'Doubledecker', *Echinacea purpurea* 'Fragrant Angel', *Echinacea purpurea* 'Sundown', *Salvia involucrata* 'Bethellii'; G Delacroix: *Echinacea* 'Harvest Moon'; G. Delacroix: *Echinacea purpurea* 'Coconut Lime', *Echinacea purpurea* 'Fragrant Angel', *Echinacea purpurea* 'Sundown'; J Spears: *Echinacea purpurea* 'Doubledecker'. **Photolibrary:** Cubo Images: *Echinacea purpurea* 'Magnus'; Antonio Molero: *Echinacea angustifolia;* J S Sira: *Echinacea purpurea* 'Razzmatazz' **222 Alamy:** Steffen Hauser/botanikfoto: *Helianthus salicifolius*. **GAP Photos:** J S Sira: *Anemone hupehensis* 'Bowles's Pink'. **Garden World Images:** L Thomas: *Anemone hupehensis* 'Praecox', *Anemone* x *hybrida* 'Robustissima'. **Photolibrary:** Paroli Galperti: *Anemone* x *hybrida* 'Whirlwind'; J S Sira: *Anemone hupehensis var. japonica* 'Pamina'; Richard Surman: *Anemone* x *hybrida* 'Konigin Charlotte'; Mark Turner: *Anemone* x *hybrida* 'September Charm'. **Royal Horticultural Society (RHS):** *Anemone hupehensis var. japonica* 'Bressingham Glow'. **The Garden Collection:** Andrew Lawson: *Helianthus* 'Lemon Queen' **223 Alamy:** Zena Elea: *Diascia personata*. **Garden World Images:** *Aquilegia vulgaris var. stellata* 'Black Barlow' **224 Alamy:** John Glover: *Iris* 'Deep Black'. **British Iris Society:** *Iris japonica*. **GAP Photos:** Mark Bolton: *Iris* x *robusta* 'Gerald Darby'; Jonathan Buckley: *Iris* 'Green Spot'. **Garden World Images:** *Iris hoogiana*. **Picturesmiths Ltd.:** *Iris* 'English Cottage', *Iris* 'Frost and Flame', *Iris ensata* 'Moonlight Waves', *Iris germanica* 'Florentina', *Iris orientalis, Iris sanguinea* 'Snow Queen' **225 Alamy:** John Glover: *Iris sibirica* 'Shirley Pope'; Holmes Garden Photos: *Iris* 'Berlin Tiger'. **GAP Photos:** Richard Bloom: *Iris foetidissima;* S & O: *Iris* 'Holden Clough'. **Garden World Images:** *Iris winogradowii*. **Photolibrary:** Chris Burrows/GPL: *Iris sibirica* 'Papillon'. **Picturesmiths Ltd.:** *Iris* 'Kent Pride', *Iris* 'Perry's Blue', *Iris* 'Tropic Night', *Iris sibirica* 'Soft Blue' **226 Andrew Lawson Digital:** *Aquilegia viridiflora*. **Andrew Lawson Photography:** *Aquilegia longissima*. **Anne Green-Armytage:** *Aquilegia vulgaris* 'William Guiness'. **Garden World Images:** *Aquilegia* 'Dragonfly', *Aquilegia* 'Hensol Harebell', *Aquilegia coerulea, Aquilegia flabellata var. pumila, Aquilegia Songbird Series* 'Bunting', *Aquilegia triternata;* Brian Gadsby: *Aquilegia triternata;* S Hauser: *Aquilegia coerulea;* MAP/A Descat: *Aquilegia Songbird Series* 'Bunting'; T Schilling: *Aquilegia* 'Hensol Harebell'; Darren Warner: *Aquilegia* 'Dragonfly'. **John Glover:** *Aquilegia canadensis*. **Photolibrary:** Tracey Rich: *Aquilegia* 'Nora Barlow'. **Thompson & Morgan:** *Aquilegia chrysantha* **227 Garden World Images:** *Doronicum columnae* 'Miss Mason' **228 GAP Photos:** S & O: *Paeonia suffruticosa* 'Hakuo-jisi'; Rob Whitworth: *Paeonia* 'Coral Charm', *Paeonia* 'Kelway's Fairy Queen'. **Garden World Images:** *Paeonia* 'Cheddar Gold', *Paeonia* 'Festiva Maxima', *Paeonia* 'Jan van Leeuwen', *Paeonia obovata var. alba;* S Chesterman: *Paeonia* 'Cheddar Gold'; C Harris: *Paeonia* 'Jan van Leeuwen'; T Jennings: *Paeonia* 'Festiva Maxima'. **Marianne Majerus Garden Images:** Marianne Majerus: *Paeonia suffruticosa* 'Yachiyo-tsubaki'; Marianne Majerus/The Manor, Hemingford Grey: *Paeonia* 'Lady Alexandra Duff'. **Photolibrary:** Martin Page: *Paeonia* 'Pillow Talk' **229 Alamy:** Ros Drinkwater: *Paeonia* x *lemoinei* 'High Noon'. **Collection & Photo Riviere (France, 26 Drôme):** *Paeonia* x *lemoinei* 'L'Espérance'. **GAP Photos:** Visions: *Paeonia* 'Félix Crousse'; Rob Whitworth: *Paeonia suffruticosa* 'Rimpo'. **Garden World Images:** G Delacroix: *Paeonia* 'Thunderbolt'; L Thomas: *Paeonia* 'Paul M. Wild'. **Getty:** Martin Page: *Paeonia* 'Bartzella', *Paeonia* 'Garden Treasure'. **Marianne Majerus Garden Images:** Marianne Majerus: *Paeonia* 'Claire de Lune'. **Photolibrary:** Martin Page: *Paeonia* 'Buckeye Belle' **230 GAP Photos:** Suzie Gibbons: *Selinum wallichianum*. **Garden World Images:** Gilles Delacroix: *Leucanthemum* x *superbum* 'Aglaia' **231 GAP Photos:** Jo Whitworth: *Anaphalis triplinervis* 'Sommerschnee'; Rob Whitworth: *Gaura lindheimeri*. **Garden World Images:** Lee Thomas: *Leucanthemum* x *superbum* 'Sonnenschein' **232 Alamy:** CuboImages srl: *Astilbe* 'Europa'; John Glover: *Astilbe* 'Amethyst'; Steffen Hauser/botanikfoto:

Astilbe 'Granat'; Martin Hughes-Jones: *Astilbe* 'Europa'. **Garden World Images:** G Delacroix: *Astilbe* 'Deutschland'; M Thornhill: *Astilbe* x *crispa* 'Perkeo' **233 Marianne Majerus Garden Images:** Marianne Majerus: *Thalictrum aquilegiifolium* 'Thundercloud' **234 GAP Photos:** Richard Bloom: *Persicaria campanulata* 'Rosenrot'. **Garden World Images:** *Persicaria* 'Red Dragon', *Persicaria virginiana* 'Lance Corporal', *Persicaria virginiana* 'Painter's Palette', *Rehmannia elata;* M Hughes-Jones: *Persicaria* 'Red Dragon'; T Sims: *Persicaria virginiana* 'Lance Corporal', *Persicaria virginiana* 'Painter's Palette'. **Getty:** Dave Zubraski: *Persicaria affinis* 'Superba'. **Photolibrary:** Carole Drake/ GPL: *Persicaria polymorpha* **235 GAP Photos:** J S Sira: *Hemerocallis* 'Red Precious'. **Garden World Images:** *Lychnis chalcedonica, Lychnis chalcedonica, Phlox paniculata* 'Prince of Orange'; Rodger Tamblyn: *Lychnis chalcedonica, Lychnis chalcedonica* **236 Photolibrary:** J S Sira: *Penstemon* 'The Juggler' **237 bloompictures:** *Penstemon* 'Chester Scarlet', *Penstemon* 'King George V'. **Garden World Images:** *Penstemon* 'Cherry Ripe', *Penstemon* 'Papal Purple', *Penstemon* 'Russian River'; G. Delacroix: *Penstemon* 'Cherry Ripe'; Derek Gould: *Penstemon* 'Russian River'. **Marianne Majerus Garden Images:** Marianne Majerus/ Little Llanavon, Herefordshire: *Penstemon heterophyllus* 'Heavenly Blue'. **Photolibrary:** Chris Burrows: *Penstemon whippleanus* **238 Alamy:** Holmes Garden Photos: *Astrantia major* 'Ruby Wedding'; Martin Hughes-Jones: *Papaver* 'Fireball'; Wildscape: *Papaver orientale* 'Black and White'. **GAP Photos:** J S Sira: *Filipendula purpurea*. **Garden World Images:** M Hughes-Jones: *Papaver orientale* 'Karine'; MAP/A Descat: *Papaver* 'Patty's Plum'; L Thomas: *Papaver* 'Medallion'. **Marianne Majerus Garden Images:** Marianne Majerus, Bankton Cottage, Sussex: *Geranium palmatum*. **Photolibrary:** Chris Burrows/GPL: *Papaver orientale* 'Choir Boy'; John Glover: *Papaver orientale* 'Turkish Delight'; Hermant Jariwala/GPL: *Papaver orientale var. bracteatum* **239 Alamy:** blickwinkel: *Linaria triornithophora, Linaria triornithophora;* WILDLIFE GmbH: *Monarda fistulosa, Monarda fistulosa* **240 Alamy:** Shorelark Nigel Downer: *Eryngium alpinum*. **GAP Photos:** Mark Bolton: *Nepeta* 'Six Hills Giant'. **Garden World Images:** *Agapanthus inapertus subsp. pendulus* 'Graskop', *Phlox paniculata* 'Windsor'; Martin Hughes-Jones: *Agapanthus inapertus subsp. pendulus* 'Graskop'. **John Glover:** *Phlox paniculata* 'Hampton Court'. **Science Photo Library (SPL):** A-Z Botanical Collection: *Phlox paniculata* 'Amethyst' **241 Alamy:** Holmes Garden Photos: *Campanula persicifolia* 'Chettle Charm'; imagebroker: *Echinops bannaticus* 'Taplow Blue'. **GAP Photos:** Jonathan Buckley: *Agapanthus* 'Purple Cloud'; Clive Nichols: *Agapanthus* 'Northern Star'. **Garden World Images:** G Delacroix: *Campanula takesimana;* M Hughes-Jones: *Campanula lactiflora* 'Prichard's Variety'; P Smith: *Campanula punctata* 'Cherry Bells'; L Thomas: *Campanula trachelium* 'Bernice'; Lee Thomas: *Aconitum* 'Stainless Steel' **242 Alamy:** Holmes Garden Photos: *Astelia chathamica*. **GAP Photos:** Jonathan Buckley: *Astelia chathamica*. **Garden World Images:** Gilles Delacroix: *Artemisia* 'Powis Castle'. **Marianne Majerus Garden Images:** Marianne Majerus, The Old Vicarage, East Ruston: *Mathiasella bupleuroides* 'Green Dream' **243 GAP Photos:** Flora Press: *Gentiana lutea;* Martin Hughes-Jones: *Berkheya macrocephala*. **GardenPhotos.com:** Judy White: *Phlomis russeliana* **244 bloompictures:** *Hemerocallis* 'Cherry Cheeks'. **GAP Photos:** Clive Nichols: *Hemerocallis* 'Pardon Me'. **Garden Picture Library:** J S Sira: *Hemerocallis* 'Neyron Rose'. **Garden World Images:** *Hemerocallis* 'Canadian Border Patrol', *Hemerocallis* 'Luxury Lace', *Hemerocallis* 'Prairie Blue Eyes'; G Delacroix: *Hemerocallis* 'Luxury Lace'; L Thomas: *Hemerocallis* 'Canadian Border Patrol'. **The Garden Collection:** Derek Harris: *Hemerocallis* 'Stoke Poges' **245 bloompictures:** *Hemerocallis* 'Cream Drop'. **GAP Photos:** Adrian Bloom: *Hemerocallis* 'Whichford'; Martin Hughes-Jones: *Hemerocallis* 'Cathy's Sunset'. **Garden Picture Library:** M Bolton: *Hemerocallis dumortieri;* C Burrows: *Hemerocallis* 'Little Wine Cup'. **Garden World Images:** G Delacroix: *Hemerocallis* 'Green Flutter'; G Harper: *Hemerocallis* 'Lemon Bells'; T Jennings: *Hemerocallis* 'Chicago Sunrise'. **Peter Stiles Photography:** *Hemerocallis* 'Cartwheels'. **The Garden Collection:** Andrew Lawson: *Hemerocallis* 'Bonanza'; Nicola Stocken Tomkins: *Hemerocallis* 'Black Magic' **246 Alamy:** Holmes Garden Photos: *Euphorbia griffithii* 'Fireglow'. **Garden World Images:** Martin Hughes-Jones: *Verbascum* 'Cotswold Beauty' **247 Alamy:** Holmes Garden Photos: *Achillea ptarmica* 'The Pearl'. **GAP Photos:** Lynn Keddie: *Achillea* 'Belle Epoque'; J S Sira: *Achillea* 'Christine's Pink'. **Garden World Images:** A Biddle: *Achillea* 'Lachsschönheit'; N R Colborn: *Achillea* 'Heidi'; G. Delacroix: *Achillea millefolium* 'Red Velvet'; D Rose: *Achillea millefolium* 'Kelwayi'; L Thomas: *Achillea* 'Terracotta'. **Getty:** Martin Page: *Achillea filipendulina* 'Parker's Variety' **248 Alamy:** Steffen Hauser/botanikfoto: *Helenium* 'Feuersiegel'; Martin Hughes-Jones: *Helenium* 'Potter's Wheel'; Leonie Lambert: *Lobelia cardinalis* 'Queen Victoria', *Lobelia cardinalis* 'Queen Victoria'. **Garden World Images:** G. Delacroix: *Helenium* 'Waltraut'; G Harper: *Helenium* 'Indianersommer'; M Hughes-Jones: *Helenium* 'Double Trouble', *Helenium* 'Red Army', *Helenium* 'Rubinzwerg'. **Photolibrary:** Neil Holmes: *Helenium* 'Butterpat' **249 Alamy:** John Martin: *Aster* 'Photograph'. **Garden World Images:** G. Delacroix: *Aster* x *frikartii* 'Wunder von Stäfa'; MAP/A Descat: *Aster novae-angliae* 'Rosa Sieger'; T Sims: *Aster novi-belgii* 'Carnival'. **GardenPhotos.com:** Graham Rice: *Aster* 'Sunhelene'. **Getty:** Rob Whitworth: *Aster novi-belgii* 'Chequers'. **Photolibrary:** Mark Bolton: *Aster* 'Little Carlow', *Aster novae-angliae* 'Violetta'; Sunniva Harte: *Aster* 'Coombe Fishacre'; Stephen Henderson: *Aster divaricatus* **250 Alamy:** Carole Drake: *Salvia glutinosa*. **GAP Photos:** Richard Bloom: *Salvia nemorosa* 'Ostfriesland'; Jonathan Buckley: *Salvia guaranitica* 'Black and Blue'; Heather Edwards: *Salvia patens;* John Glover: *Salvia verticillata* 'Purple Rain'; Marcus Harpur: *Salvia nemorosa* 'Lubecca'; Neil Holmes: *Salvia* x *sylvestris* 'Blauhügel'. **Garden World Images:** Gilles Delacroix: *Salvia argentea, Salvia nemorosa* 'Caradonna', *Salvia pratensis* 'Indigo', *Salvia pratensis* 'Swan Lake'; Martin Hughes-Jones: *Salvia pratensis* 'Pink Delight'. **Marianne Majerus Garden Images:** Marianne Majerus: *Salvia nemorosa* 'Amethyst'. **Photolibrary:** Ron Evans: *Salvia* x *sylvestris* 'Mainacht' **251 Alamy:** blickwinkel: *Rudbeckia fulgida var. speciosa;* Organica: *Rudbeckia triloba;* The Garden Picture Library: *Rudbeckia occidentalis* 'Green Wizard'. **GAP Photos:** Richard Bloom: *Rudbeckia maxima;* Marcus Harpur: *Kirengeshoma palmata, Kirengeshoma palmata*. **Garden World Images:** *Rudbeckia fulgida var. deamii, Rudbeckia laciniata* 'Herbstsonne'; John Martin: *Rudbeckia fulgida var. deamii*. **Photolibrary:** Brian Carter: *Solidago* 'Goldenmosa' **252 Garden World Images:** M Hughes-Jones: *Chrysanthemum* 'Innocence'; J Need: *Chrysanthemum* 'Chesapeake'. **GardenPhotos.com:** Graham Rice: *Chrysanthemum* 'Emperor of China', *Chrysanthemum* 'Nell Gwynn', *Chrysanthemum* 'Purleigh White'. **Royal Horticultural Society (RHS):** Ali Cundy: *Chrysanthemum* 'Aunt Millicent', *Chrysanthemum* 'Spartan Seagull' **253 Alamy:** Martin Hughes-Jones: *Chrysanthemum* 'Duchess of Edinburgh'. **GAP Photos:** Richard Bloom: *Chrysanthemum* 'Cottage Apricot'; Howard Rice: *Chrysanthemum* 'Mary Stoker'. **Garden World Images:** *Chrysanthemum* 'Apollo', *Chrysanthemum* 'Doctor Tom Parr', *Chrysanthemum* 'Nantyderry Sunshine', *Chrysanthemum* 'Ruby Mound', *Chrysanthemum* 'Tapestry Rose'; R Coates: *Chrysanthemum* 'Ruby Mound'; R Ditchfield: *Chrysanthemum* 'Doctor Tom Parr'; G Harper: *Chrysanthemum* 'Nantyderry Sunshine'; MAP/A Kubacsi: *Chrysanthemum* 'Apollo'. **GardenPhotos.com:** Graham Rice: *Chrysanthemum* 'Bronze Elegance', *Chrysanthemum* 'Grandchild', *Chrysanthemum* 'Perry's Peach', *Chrysanthemum* 'Sea Urchin'. **John McCormack:** *Chrysanthemum* 'Chelsea Physic Garden'. **Marianne Majerus Garden Images:** Marianne Majerus/ NCCPG National Plant Collection: *Chrysanthemum* 'Mrs Jessie Cooper', *Chrysanthemum* 'Paul Boissier', *Chrysanthemum* 'Rumpelstilzchen'. **Photoshot:** Photos Horticultural: *Chrysanthemum* 'Anastasia'. **Royal Horticultural Society (RHS):** Ali Cundy: *Chrysanthemum* 'Carmine Blush' **254 GAP Photos:** FhF Greenmedia: *Kniphofia* 'Atlanta'. **Garden World Images:** *Kniphofia* 'Green Jade', *Kniphofia* 'Prince Igor', *Kniphofia* 'Royal Standard', *Kniphofia* 'Toffee Nosed', *Kniphofia* 'Wrexham Buttercup', *Kniphofia caulescens, Kniphofia thomsonii* var. *snowdenii;* G Delacroix: *Kniphofia* 'Royal Standard'; D Gould: *Kniphofia* 'Prince Igor'; M Hughes-Jones: *Kniphofia* 'Wrexham Buttercup'; MAP/N Pasquel: *Kniphofia* 'Green Jade'; T Sandell: *Kniphofia* 'Toffee Nosed'. **Getty:** Martin Page: *Kniphofia* 'Wrexham Buttercup'. **Photolibrary:** Chris Burrows/GPL: *Kniphofia* 'Bees' Sunset'; Howard Rice/ GPL: *Kniphofia rooperi* **255 Alamy:** Steffen Hauser/botanikfoto: *Convallaria majalis*. **Garden World Images:** *Sinopodophyllum hexandrum*. **Marianne Majerus Garden Images:** Marianne Majerus: *Helleborus* x *ericsmithii* 'Bob's Best' **256 Alamy:** GardenPhotos.com: *Cypripedium* Ulla Silkens gx; Martin Hughes-Jones: *Geranium macrorrhizum* 'Ingwersen's Variety'. **GAP Photos:** FhF Greenmedia: *Helleborus* x *ericsmithii* IVORY PRINCE; Andrea Jones: *Chrysosplenium macrophyllum;* Gerald Majumdar: *Geranium macrorrhizum* 'Ingwersen's Variety'. **Marianne Majerus Garden Images:** Marianne Majerus/Emile Becker: *Helleborus thibetanus*. **Photolibrary:** Clive Nichols: *Bergenia* 'Beethoven' **257 Alamy:** John Glover: *Primula* 'Guinevere', *Primula* 'Woodland Walk'; June Green: *Primula Husky Series [white]*. **GAP Photos:** J S Sira: *Primula sieboldii* 'Geisha Girl'. **Garden World Images:** *Primula* 'Dawn Ansell', *Primula* 'Lady Greer', *Primula vialii;* T Sims: *Primula* 'Lady Greer'; D Wildridge: *Primula* 'Dawn Ansell'. **Science Photo Library (SPL):** Bjanka Kadic: *Primula Crescendo Series* 'Crescendo Pink and Rose Shades' **258 Alamy:** John Glover: *Primula* 'Elizabeth Killelay'. **GAP Photos:** Visions: *Primula* 'Don Keefe'. **Garden World Images:** *Primula* 'Belarina Cobalt Blue', *Primula* 'Mark'; L Thomas: *Primula* 'Belarina Cobalt Blue'. **Photolibrary:** Sunniva Harte: *Primula Crescendo Series* 'Crescendo Bright Red' **259 Garden World Images:** M Hughes-Jones: *Primula* 'Fransisca'. **Photolibrary:** Sunniva Harte: *Primula veris* 'Katy McSparron'. **Picturesmiths Ltd:** R. Smith: *Primula* 'Trouble' **260 Alamy:** Karen Appleyard: *Helleborus purpurascens;* Florapix: *Lathyrus vernus, Lathyrus vernus*. **Garden World Images:** *Glaucidium palmatum, Lathraea clandestina, Lathraea clandestina;* Dr Alan Beaumont: *Lathraea clandestina, Lathraea clandestina*. **The Garden Collection:** Nicola Stocken Tomkins: *Epimedium epsteinii* **261 Alamy:** Martin Hughes-Jones: *Brunnera macrophylla* 'Jack Frost'. **GAP Photos:** Carole Drake, courtesy The Sir Harold Hillier Gardens/Hampshire County Council: *Pulmonaria* 'Lewis Palmer'; Heather Edwards: *Pulmonaria* 'Mawson's Blue'. **Garden World Images:** G Delacroix: *Pulmonaria* 'Margery Fish'; G. Delacroix: *Pulmonaria* 'Excalibur'; MAP/A Descat: *Pulmonaria* 'Mary Mottram'; L Thomas: *Pulmonaria OPAL* Pulmonaria OPAL. **Getty:** Martin Page: *Mertensia virginica, Mertensia virginica*. **Photolibrary:** John Glover / GPL: *Pulmonaria rubra* 'David Ward'; Howard Rice/GPL: *Pulmonaria rubra* **262 GAP Photos:** Richard Bloom: *Helleborus argutifolius* 'Silver Lace'; Martin Hughes-Jones: *Euphorbia amygdaloides var. robbiae*. **Garden World Images:** F Davis: *Helleborus argutifolius* 'Pacific Frost'. **Photolibrary:** Howard Rice: *Valeriana phu* 'Aurea' **263 Alamy:** The Garden Picture Library: *Doronicum orientale* 'Magnificum'. **Garden World Images:** *Epimedium* 'Amber Queen', *Leucanthemum* x *superbum* 'Esther Read'; N R Colborn: *Epimedium* 'Amber Queen' **264 Photolibrary:** Joshua McCullough: *Deinanthe bifida*. **Photos Horticultural:** *Diplarrhena moraea* **265 Eric Crichton Photos:** *Osteospermum jucundum*. **Photolibrary:** Rex Butcher: *Dactylorhiza foliosa*. **Science Photo Library (SPL):** A-Z Botanical Collection: *Lychnis viscaria* 'Splendens Plena' **266 Alamy:** The Garden Picture Library: *Dianthus* 'Inchmery'. **Garden World Images:** T Sims: *Dianthus* 'Cranmere Pool'; L Thomas: *Dianthus* 'Devon Dove', *Dianthus* CANDY FLOSS, *Dianthus* LADY MADONNA. **GardenPhotos.com:** Graham Rice: *Dianthus* 'Brilliant Star', *Dianthus* 'Evening Star'. **Royal Horticultural Society (RHS):** Sue Drew: *Dianthus* 'Coquette', *Dianthus* 'Milky Way' **267 Alamy:** Christopher Burrows: *Dianthus superbus* 'Crimsonia'; Glenn Harper: *Dianthus* 'Neon Star'. **Allwoods Nursery:** *Dianthus* 'Tayside Red'. **Garden World Images:** *Dianthus* 'Devon Wizard', *Dianthus* 'Fusilier', *Dianthus* 'Lily the Pink', *Dianthus* 'Monica Wyatt', *Dianthus* 'Moulin Rouge', *Dianthus* 'Passion', *Dianthus* 'Pixie Star', *Dianthus* 'Rose de Mai', *Dianthus* 'Tickled Pink', *Dianthus* 'Valda Wyatt', *Dianthus* FEUREHEXE, *Dianthus* STARLIGHT; R Coates: *Dianthus* 'Monica Wyatt'; G Delacroix: G Harper: *Dianthus* 'Moulin Rouge'; T Sims: *Dianthus* 'Rose de Mai'; L Thomas: *Dianthus* 'Fusilier', *Dianthus* 'Lily the Pink', *Dianthus* 'Passion', *Dianthus* 'Pixie Star', *Dianthus* 'Tickled Pink', *Dianthus* 'Valda Wyatt',

GardenPhotos.com: Graham Rice: *Dianthus* 'India Star'. **Marianne Majerus Garden Images:** Marianne Majerus: *Dianthus* 'Queen of Sheba'. **Royal Horticultural Society (RHS):** Sue Drew: *Dianthus* 'Prado Mint' **268 Alamy:** Christopher Burrows: *Potentilla* 'Arc-en-ciel'; CuboImages srl: *Stachys officinalis* 'Hummelo'. **Bleddyn Wynn Jones:** *Crusea coccinea*. **Photolibrary:** Richard Bloom: *Geum* 'Bell Bank'. **Photoshot:** Photos Horticultural: *Coreopsis* 'Limerock Ruby' **269 GAP Photos:** Jonathan Buckley: *Berkheya purpurea*. **Garden World Images:** Tony Schilling: *Ourisia coccinea* **270 Alamy:** Hillhead: *Geranium* 'Johnson's Blue' **271 Alamy:** CuboImages srl: *Geranium* ROZANNE; Martin Hughes-Jones: *Amsonia orientalis*. **Garden World Images:** *Myosotidium hortensia* **272 Alamy:** Ros Drinkwater: *Hosta* 'Invincible'; Holmes Garden Photos: *Hosta* 'June'. **GAP Photos:** Dave Bevan: *Hosta* 'Gold Edger'; Clive Nichols: *Hosta* 'Night Before Christmas'. **Garden World Images:** L Thomas: *Hosta* 'Minuteman'. **GardenPhotos.com:** judywhite: *Hosta* 'Cherry Berry' **273 GAP Photos:** Howard Rice: *Hosta* 'Brim Cup'; Jo Whitworth: *Hosta lancifolia*. **Garden World Images:** G Delacroix: *Hosta* 'Fragrant Bouquet'; Ellen McKnight: *Hosta* 'Sagae'. **Photoshot:** Photos Horticultural: *Hosta* 'Hydon Sunset', *Hosta* 'Remember Me', *Hosta* 'Revolution'. **The Garden Collection:** Torie Chugg: *Hosta* 'Tattoo' **274 Alamy:** John Glover: *Mentha suaveolens* 'Variegata', *Mentha suaveolens* 'Variegata'. **GAP Photos:** Neil Holmes: *Artemisia ludoviciana* 'Valerie Finnis'. **Garden World Images:** *Hosta tokudama f. aureonebulosa* **275 Alamy:** blickwinkel: *Alchemilla conjuncta*. **Photolibrary:** Howard Rice: *Stachys byzantina* 'Primrose Heron', *Stachys byzantina* 'Primrose Heron'. **Rosemary Kautzky:** photographersdirect.com: *Calanthe striata* **276 Alamy:** Holmes Garden Photos: *Tropaeolum polyphyllum* **277 Alamy:** Holmes Garden Photos: *Hieracium lanatum*. **GAP Photos:** Visions: *Gaillardia* 'Oranges and Lemons'. **Garden World Images:** Richard Shiell: *Libertia ixioides* 'Goldfinger' **278 Alamy:** The Garden Picture Library: *Astrantia maxima*. **GAP Photos:** J S Sira: *Astrantia major* 'Roma'. **John Fielding:** *Begonia taliensis*. **Marianne Majerus Garden Images:** Marianne Majerus: *Begonia grandis subsp. evansiana* **279 GAP Photos:** Paul Debois: *Sedum telephium* 'Strawberries and Cream'. **Garden World Images:** N Appleby: *Sedum* 'Matrona'; L Every: *Sedum telephium* 'Purple Emperor'; D Gould: *Sedum spectabile* 'Iceberg'; G Harper: *Sedum telephium* 'Gooseberry Fool'; L Thomas: *Sedum erythrostictum* 'Mediovariegatum'. **Marianne Majerus Garden Images:** Marianne Majerus: *Sedum* 'Red Cauli'. **Photolibrary:** Mark Bolton: *Sedum* 'Ruby Glow' **280 Alamy:** John Glover: *Heuchera* 'Plum Pudding', *Heuchera* 'Plum Pudding'. **GAP Photos:** Martin Hughes-Jones: *Agastache* 'Black Adder', *Geranium* 'Orion'. **Garden World Images:** *Bergenia purpurascens, Tulbaghia violacea;* Gilles Delacroix: *Bergenia purpurascens* **281 GAP Photos:** FhF Greenmedia: *Helleborus niger* 'HGC Joseph Lemper'; John Glover: *Helleborus* x *hybridus Harvington hybrids* [single, white]; Marcus Harpur: *Helleborus* x *hybridus Bradfield hybrids* [double, apricot with spots]; Howard Rice: *Helleborus* x *hybridus* [single, apricot]. **Garden World Images:** L Thomas: *Helleborus niger* 'Potter's Wheel', *Helleborus* x *nigercors*. **GardenPhotos.com:** Graham Rice: *Helleborus* x *hybridus* [single, white with spots]. **Getty:** Richard Bloom: *Helleborus* x *hybridus* [double, slate]; Jonathan Buckley: *Helleborus* x *hybridus Ashwood Garden hybrids* [double, black]; Dave Zubraski: *Helleborus* x *hybridus* [single, yellow with spots]. **Marianne Majerus Garden Images:** Marianne Majerus/The Old Rectory, Sudborough: *Helleborus* x *hybridus* [single, yellow]. **Peter Stiles Photography:** *Helleborus* x *hybridus* [single, red]. **Photolibrary:** Clive Nichols /GPL: *Helleborus* x *hybridus Harvington hybrids* [double, apricot]; Garden Pix Ltd/ GPL: *Helleborus* x *hybridus Ashwood Garden hybrids* [double, pink]; Anne Green-Armytage/GPL: *Helleborus* x *hybridus* [double, white]; Howard Rice: *Helleborus* x *hybridus* [single, green]; Howard Rice/GPL: *Helleborus* x *hybridus* [double, plum]. **The Garden Collection:** Nicola Stocken Tomkins: *Helleborus* x *hybridus* [double, white with spots] **282 GAP Photos:** BBC Magazines Ltd: *Heuchera* 'Black Beauty'; Jonathan Buckley: *Heuchera* 'Silver Scrolls'; Lynn Keddie: *Heuchera* 'Peppermint Spice'; Visions Premium: *Heuchera* 'Ginger Ale'; Rob Whitworth: *Heuchera* 'Ebony and Ivory', *Heuchera* 'Southern Comfort'. **Garden World Images:** Rita Coates: *Heuchera* 'Midnight Rose'; G Delacroix: *Heuchera* 'Purple Petticoats', *Heuchera sanguinea var. pulchra* 'Snow Storm', *Heucherella tiarelloides* 'Stoplight'; G. Delacroix: *Heuchera* 'Lime Rickey'; Richard Shiell: *Heuchera* 'Amber Waves'; L Thomas: *Heuchera* 'Beauty Colour', *Heuchera* 'Blackbird', *Heuchera* 'Can-can', *Heuchera* 'Georgia Peach', *Heuchera* 'Green Spice', *Heuchera* 'Peach Flambé', *Heuchera* 'Tiramisu', *Heuchera* CRÈME BRÛLÉE, *Heucherella tiarelloides* 'Kimono'; D Wildridge: *Heuchera* 'Pewter Moon'. **GardenPhotos.com:** Graham Rice: *Heuchera* 'Cinnabar Silver'. **Getty:** Jo Whitworth: *Heuchera* 'Chocolate Ruffles' **283 Alamy:** John Glover: *Helleborus foetidus Wester Flisk Group*. **GAP Photos:** Geoff Kidd: *Ophiopogon japonicus;* Howard Rice: *Helleborus odorus;* J S Sira: *Helleborus cyclophyllus*. **Garden World Images:** Gilles Delacroix: *Dianella caerulea* CASSA BLUE. **Marianne Majerus Garden Images:** Marianne Majerus/Harveys Garden Plants: *Helleborus* x *sternii* 'Boughton Beauty' **284 GAP Photos:** Mark Bolton: *Cortaderia richardii*. **Garden World Images:** Gilles Delacroix: *Calamagrostis brachytricha* **285 Alamy:** The Garden Picture Library: *Miscanthus sinensis* 'Yakushima Dwarf'. **GAP Photos:** Adrian Bloom: *Miscanthus sinensis var. condensatus* 'Cosmopolitan'; Ron Evans: *Chionochloa rubra;* Jo Whitworth, location: Knoll Gardens: *Eragrostis curvula* 'Totnes Burgandy'. **Garden World Images:** Martin Hughes-Jones: *Molinia caerulea subsp. caerulea* 'Heidebraut'. **Photolibrary:** Jerry Pavia: *Elegia capensis* **286 GAP Photos:** Carole Drake, courtesy The Sir Harold Hillier Gardens/Hampshire County Council: *Thamnocalamus crassinodus* 'Kew Beauty'. **GardenPhotos.com:** judywhite: *Miscanthus sinensis* 'Gracillimus'. **Getty:** Richard Bloom: *Miscanthus sinensis* 'Flamingo'; Rob Whitworth: *Stipa calamagrostis*. **Photolibrary:** Stephen Henderson: *Molinia caerulea subsp. arundinacea* 'Transparent' **287 Alamy:** Holmes Garden Photos: *Chimonobambusa timidissinoda*. **GAP Photos:** Howard Rice: *Ampelodesmos mauritanica* **288 Alamy:** Holmes Garden Photos: *Yushania anceps* 'Pitt White'. **GAP Photos:** BBC Magazines Ltd: *Phyllostachys aurea*. **Photoshot:** Photos Horticultural: *Luzula sylvatica* 'Hohe Tatra' **289 Photolibrary:** Adrian Bloom: *Panicum virgatum* 'Northwind'. **The Garden Collection:** Andrew Lawson: *Phyllostachys vivax f. aureocaulis* **290 Alamy:** Debbie Monique Jolliff: *Athyrium niponicum var. pictum* 'Burgandy Lace'. **Garden World Images:** Lee Thomas: *Athyrium* 'Ghost' **292 Eric Crichton Photos:** *Adiantum venustum*. **Garden World Images:** Lee Thomas: *Polystichum tsussimense*. **The Garden Collection:** Andrew Lawson: *Blechnum chilense* **293 Alamy:** Dave Gowan: *Polystichum munitum;* John Swithinbank: *Dryopteris erythrosora*. **The Garden Collection:** Torie Chugg: *Polypodium cambricum* 'Richard Kayse' **294-295 GAP Photos:** Elke Borkowski. **295 GAP Photos:** Lee Avison (ftr); John Glover (ftl); Sharon Pearson (tl); Dave Zubraski (tr). **296 GAP Photos:** Charles Hawes (t); Martin Hughes-Jones (b). **298 Garden World Images:** Anthony Baggett: *Dahlia Gallery Series* 'Gallery Art Fair'; Dr Alan Beaumont: *Dahlia Gallery Series* 'Gallery Art Fair'; G Delacroix: *Euphorbia hypericifolia* DIAMOND FROST, *Lobularia maritima* 'Snow Crystals', *Sutera cordata* Snowstorm Series GIANT SNOWFLAKE; Gilles Delacroix: *Euphorbia hypericifolia* DIAMOND FROST, *Lobularia maritima* 'Snow Crystals', *Sutera cordata* Snowstorm Series GIANT SNOWFLAKE; R Shiell: *Zinnia* x *marylandica Zahara Series* 'Zahara Starlight Rose'; Richard Shiell: *Zinnia* x *marylandica Zahara Series* 'Zahara Starlight Rose' **299 Garden World Images:** *Euphorbia marginata, Eustoma grandiflorum, Nicotiana* x *sanderae* 'Saratoga Series' [white] **300 Alamy:** Martin Hughes-Jones: *Argyranthemum* 'Summer Melody'. **Garden World Images:** *Catharanthus roseus* Boa Series 'Boa Peach', *Martynia annua;* R Shiell: *Calibrachoa* Caberet Series LIGHT PINK, *Catharanthus roseus Boa Series* 'Boa Peach'; Richard Shiell: *Calibrachoa* Calibrachoa Caberet Series LIGHT PINK, *Catharanthus roseus Boa Series* 'Boa Peach'. **Photolibrary:** Chris Burrows: *Brachyscome* 'Strawberry Mousse'; Chris Burrows/GPL: *Brachyscome* 'Strawberry Mousse' **301 Garden World Images:** N R Colborn: *Diascia* LITTLE DANCER; G Delacroix: *Lantana camara* Lucky Series LUCKY HONEY BLUSH; Trevor Sims: *Lathyrus odoratus* Cupid Series 'Cupid Pink'; L Thomas: *Nemesia* AMELIE, *Osteospermum* Sunny Series 'Sunny Marina'. **The Garden Collection:** Liz Eddison: *Gaura lindheimeri* 'Rosyjane' **302 Garden World Images:** *Fuchsia* 'Dollar Prinzessin', *Fuchsia* 'Nellie Nuttall', *Fuchsia* 'Sunray', *Fuchsia triphylla* 'Firecracker', *Fuchsia Windchimes Series* 'Windchimes Pink and White'; G. Delacroix: *Fuchsia Windchimes Series* 'Windchimes Pink and White'; MAP/N Pasquel: *Fuchsia triphylla* 'Firecracker'; P Smith: *Fuchsia* 'Sunray'. **Marianne Majerus Garden Images:** Simon Meaker: *Fuchsia California Dreamers Series* 'Snowburner'. **Young Plants Limited:** *Fuchsia* 'Joanna Lumley', *Fuchsia Mojo* 'Beebop', *Fuchsia Shadowdancer* PEGGY; Proven Winners: Chris Wright Photography: *Fuchsia* 'Joanna Lumley' **303 GAP Photos:** Geoff Kidd: *Primula* Belarina Series BELARINA PINK ICE. **Garden World Images:** MAP/N Pasquel: *Antirrhinum* Luminaire Series LUMINAIRE HOT PINK; MAP/ Nathalie Pasquel: *Antirrhinum* Luminaire Series LUMINAIRE HOT PINK; R Shiell: *Petchoa* Supercal Series SUPERCAL NEON ROSE; Lee Thomas: *Glandularia* x *hybrida* Aztec Magic Series AZTEC DARK PINK MAGIC. **Unwins Seeds Ltd:** *Gomphrena globosa* **304 Garden World Images:** *Lobularia maritima* 'Rosie O'Day', *Schizanthus* 'Dwarf Bouquet' [mixed]. **Unwins Seeds Ltd:** *Iberis umbellata* Fairy Series **305 Andrew Lawson Photography:** *Clarkia amoena* 'Sybil Sherwood'. **Garden World Images:** *Nicotiana* x *sanderae* Saratoga Series [deep rose] **306 Andrew Lawson Photography:** T Chugg: *Zinnia elegans* Dreamland Series [scarlet]. **GAP Photos:** Rob Whitworth: *Antirrhinum majus* 'Black Prince'. **Garden World Images:** G Delacroix: *Calibrachoa* Million Bells Series MILLION BELLS CHERRY PINK; Simon Keeble: *Brassica Northern Lights Series;* Richard Shiell: *Catharanthus roseus* Cobra Series 'Cobra Burgundy'; L Thomas: *Cuphea* x *purpurea* 'Firecracker', *Dahlia* HAPPY SINGLE ROMEO; **Thompson & Morgan:** *Cosmos atrosanguineus* CHOCAMOCHA **307 Garden World Images:** Eric Crichton: *Nemesia strumosa Carnival Series;* Dan Sams: *Impatiens Expo Series* 'Expo Pink'; Richard Shiell: *Glandularia* x *hybrida* Corsage Series 'Corsage Red'; Trevor Sims: *Tropaeolum majus* 'Hermine Grashoff'. **Photolibrary:** J S Sira: *Zinnia* x *marylandica* Profusion Series 'Profusion Cherry'. **Thompson & Morgan:** *Impatiens walleriana* MASQUERADE **308 Garden World Images:** *Salvia splendens Vista Series [red], Tagetes* 'Cinnabar'. **Photoshot:** *Alonsoa warscewiczii*. **Unwins Seeds Ltd:** *Petunia* 'Mirage Velvet' **309 Chris Burrows:** *Pelargonium Horizon Deva Series* 'Horizon Deva Raspberry Ripple'. **GAP Photos:** Friedrich Strauss: *Pelargonium* Antik Series ANTIK SALMON; Graham Strong: *Pelargonium* Maverick Series 'Maverick Star'. **Garden World Images:** R Coates: *Pelargonium* Regalia Series 'Regalia Chocolate'; J Spears: *Pelargonium* BLUE WONDER; L Thomas: *Pelargonium Bulls Eye Series* 'Bulls Eye Salmon', *Pelargonium* Fireworks Series FIREWORKS SCARLET. **Photolibrary:** Chris Burrows/GPL: *Pelargonium* Decora Series 'Decora Dark Pink', *Pelargonium* Horizon Deva Series 'Horizon Deva Orange Ice'; Andrew Lord/GPL: *Pelargonium* 'Evka' **310 Alamy:** WILDLIFE GmbH: *Heliotropium arborescens*. **Garden World Images:** MAP/N Pasquel: *Solenostemon scutellarioides Kong Series* 'Kong Scarlet'; **311 GAP Photos:** Christina Bollen: *Lobelia erinus* Waterfall Series 'Waterfall Light Lavender'; J S Sira: *Petunia* Petunia Surfinia Series SURFINIA BLUE VEIN, *Solenostemon scutellarioides* 'Inky Fingers'. **Garden World Images:** G Delacroix: *Ipomoea batatas* 'Blackie', *Osteospermum* Cape Daisy Series NASINGA PURPLE, *Solenostemon* 'Chocolate Mint'; Steffen Hauser: *Pennisetum glaucum* 'Purple Majesty'; T Sims: *Dahlia* HAPPY SINGLE WINK; L Thomas: *Angelonia angustifolia AngelMist Series* 'AngelMist Lavender Stripe', *Petunia* Tumbelina Series PRISCILLA. **Photolibrary:** Photos Lamontagne/GPL: *Alternanthera dentata* 'Purple Knight'. **The Garden Collection:** Liz Eddison: *Strobilanthes dyerinanus* **312 GAP Photos:** Friedrich Strauss: *Viola* x *wittrockiana* Sorbet Series 'Sorbet Black Delight'. **Garden Picture Library:** *Cerinthe major* 'Purpurascens'. **Garden World Images:** *Nierembergia linariifolia* 'Purple Robe', Gilles Delacroix: *Glandularia* x *hybrida* Aztec Magic Series AZTEC SILVER MAGIC, *Pennisetum setaceum* 'Rubrum'. **Suttons Seeds:** *Viola* x *wittrockiana Imperial Series* 'Imperial Frosty Rose' **313 GAP Photos:** Marcus Harpur: *Myosotis Sylva Series*. **Garden World Images:** *Campanula medium* 'Bells of Holland', *Salvia sclarea var. turkestanica , Trachelium caeruleum*, Gilles Delacroix: *Viola* x *wittrockiana*

Ultima Radiance Series [deep blue]; Trevor Sims: *Salvia sclarea* var. *turkestanica*. **Thompson & Morgan:** *Isotoma Avant-Garde Series* **314 Alamy:** Anna Yu: *Salvia farinacea* 'Strata'. **Garden World Images:** Lee Thomas: *Lobelia erinus Waterfall Series* 'Waterfall Blue', *Pericallis* Senetti Series SENETTI BLUE BICOLOR **315 Alpine Garden Society:** *Cynoglossum amabile* 'Firmament'. **Garden World Images:** *Commelina coelestis, Myosotis sylvatica* 'Blue Ball' **316 Alamy:** Christopher Burrows: *Petunia* Surfinia Series SURFINIA LIME. **Garden World Images:** Gilles Delacroix: *Zinnia elegans* 'Envy' **317 Alamy:** WILDLIFE GmbH: *Begonia* x *tuberhybrida Mocha Series* [Scarlet]. **Garden World Images:** G. Delacroix: *Begonia* 'Dragon Wing Red', *Begonia* 'Ikon White Blush'; R Shiell: *Begonia Illumination Series* 'Illumination Salmon Pink', *Begonia* x *tuberhybrida Non Stop Series [White]*. **The Garden Collection:** Liz Eddison: *Begonia boliviensis* 'Bonfire' **318 Garden World Images:** MAP/Nathalie Pasquel: *Perilla* 'Magilla Vanilla'; MAP/Nicole et Patrick Mioulane: *Ipomoea batatus* 'Margarita'. **Photolibrary:** Chris Burrows: *Viola* 'Green Goddess'; Stephen Henderson: *Setaria macrostachya* **319 Eric Crichton Photos:** *Argyranthemum* 'Jamaica Primrose'. **Garden World Images:** *Brugmansia* x *candida* 'Grand Marnier', Gilles Delacroix: *Antirrhinum majus Liberty Classic Series* 'Liberty Yellow'; Lee Thomas: *Duranta erecta* 'Gold Edge'. **Photolibrary:** Photos Lamontagne/GPL: *Argyranthemum* BUTTERFLY, *Bidens* 'Gold Star' **320 GAP Photos:** Friedrich Strauss: *Nemesia Sunsatia Series SUNSATIA MANGO*. **Garden World Images:** *Antirrhinum majus* Chimes Series [yellow]. **Photolibrary:** Photos Lamontagne/GPL: *xerochrysum bracteatum* Sundaze Series SUNDAZE GOLD. **Thompson & Morgan:** *Rudbeckia hirta* 'Toto Gold' **321 Photos Horticultural:** *Calendula officinalis* 'Daisy May'. **Thompson & Morgan:** *Platystemon californicus* **322 GAP Photos:** Paul Debois: *Mimulus Magic Series* 'Magic Yellow Blotch' **323 Alamy:** CuboImages srl: *Gazania Daybreak Series* 'Daybreak Bright Yellow'. **Garden World Images:** Trevor Sims: *Carthamus tinctorius*. **Photolibrary:** Michael Davis: *Viola* x *wittrockiana Angel Series* 'Tiger Eye'; J S Sira: *Lysimachia congestiflora* 'Outback Sunset' **324 Alamy:** Kevin Wheal Commercial: *Gazania Kiss Series* 'Kiss Orange Flame'. **Garden World Images:** *Erysimum* x *allionii* 'Orange Bedder', Gilles Delacroix: *Portulaca* Sundial Series 'Mango' **325 GAP Photos:** Friedrich Strauss: *Impatiens* Sunpatiens Series SUNPATIENS COMPACT ORANGE. **Garden World Images:** *Calendula officinalis Fiesta Gitana Group*, Richard Shiell: *Impatiens* Fusion Series FUSION PEACH FROST **326 Garden World Images:** *Calendula officinalis* 'Geisha Girl', *Coreopsis* 'Rum Punch'; Lee Thomas: *Coreopsis* 'Rum Punch' **327 Eric Crichton Photos:** *Gaillardia pulchella* 'Lollipops'. **Garden World Images:** *Solanum pseudocapsicum* 'Red Giant'. **Photolibrary:** Photos Lamontagne/GPL: *Dahlia Dahlietta Surprise Kelly*. **Plant Pictures World Wide:** *Eschscholzia californica Thai Silk Series* **328-329 GAP Photos:** Christina Bollen. **329 GAP Photos:** Lee Avison (tl). **330 GAP Photos:** Elke Borkowski (r). **332 Alamy:** WILDLIFE GmbH: *Pulsatilla alpina*. **GAP Photos:** John Glover: *Cassiope tetragona* **333 Garden World Images:** *Saxifraga* 'Tumbling Waters'. **Photolibrary:** Mark Turner: *Dodecatheon hendersonii*. **The Garden Collection:** Andrew Lawson: *Dodecatheon meadia f. album, Jeffersonia diphylla* **334 Alpine Garden Society:** *Aquilegia alpina, Daphne* x *hendersonii* 'Blackthorn Rose', *Phyllodoce empetriformis*. **Garden World Images:** *Omphalodes verna*. **Photolibrary:** Harald Lange: *Pulsatilla halleri* **335 Eric Crichton Photos:** *Aurinia saxatilis* 'Variegata'. **Garden World Images:** *Chiastophyllum oppositifolium*. **Photolibrary:** Howard Rice: *Corydalis cheilanthifolia* **336 Alamy:** AP: *Armeria pseudarmeria* **337 Clive Nichols:** *Saxifraga callosa*. **Garden World Images:** *Hebe vernicosa;* Derek Gould: *Diascia* ICE CRACKER **338 Garden World Images:** *Rhodothamnus chamaecistus*. **The Garden Collection:** Torie Chugg: *Oxalis tetraphylla* **339 Alpine Garden Society:** *Dianthus carthusianorum*. **Garden World Images:** Martin Hughes-Jones: *Crassula sarcocaulis* **340 The Garden Collection:** Andrew Lawson: *Origanum laevigatum* **342 Alamy:** Martin Hughes-Jones: *Phyteuma scheuchzeri*. **Alpine Garden Society:** *Lithodora oleifolia*. **Garden World Images:** *Convolvulus sabatius* **343 Eric Crichton Photos:** *Hypericum olympicum f. uniflorum* 'Citrinum', *Lithodora diffusa* 'Heavenly Blue' **345 Alamy:** National Geographic Image Collection: *Ononis natrix*. **Eric Crichton Photos:** *Helianthemum* 'Ben More' **346 Alamy:** Steffen Hauser/botanikfoto: *Ceratostigma plumbaginoides*. **Garden World Images:** *Gaultheria cuneata, Ranunculus calandrinioides*. **Photolibrary:** DEA: *Sorbus reducta* **347 Alpine Garden Society:** *Androsace vandellii*. **Garden World Images:** *Hebe cupressoides* 'Boughton Dome' **348 Photolibrary:** Rex Butcher: *Weldenia candida* **349 Garden World Images:** Gilles Delacroix: *Leptinella atrata subsp. luteola* **350 Alpine Garden Society:** *Paraquilegia anemonoides* **351 Garden World Images:** *Daphne arbuscula, Epigaea gaultherioides* **352 Garden World Images:** *Arabis alpina subsp. caucasica* 'Douler Angevine', *Silene acaulis;* Dave Bevan: *Arabis alpina subsp. caucasica* 'Douler Angevine' **354 Garden World Images:** Lee Thomas: *Aubrieta* 'Greencourt Purple'. **Photos Horticultural:** *Soldanella villosa* **355 Alpine Garden Society:** *Jancaea heldreichii*. **Spectrum Photofile:** *Aubrieta* 'Purple Charm' **356 Alamy:** blickwinkel: *Mertensia maritima*. **Garden World Images:** Martin Hughes-Jones: *Viola cornuta* 'Minor' **357 GAP Photos:** Juliette Wade: *Ranunculus ficaria Flore Pleno Group*. **Garden World Images:** *Draba longisiliqua, Draba rigida, Saxifraga* x *elizabethae* **358 Garden World Images:** *Erysimum helveticum* **359 Garden World Images:** *Viola aetolica* **360 Alpine Garden Society:** *Lewisia rediviva* [white form] **361 Eric Crichton Photos:** *Carlina acaulis*. **Garden World Images:** *Alstroemeria hookeri* **362 Alpine Garden Society:** *Convolvulus althaeoides* **363 Garden World Images:** *Dianthus pavonius* **364 Alamy:** Bob Gibbons: *Pterocephalus perennis*. **Alpine Garden Society:** *Dianthus alpinus*. **Eric Crichton Photos:** *Dianthus* 'Annabelle' **365 Alpine Garden Society:** *Lewisia rediviva [pink form]* **367 Garden World Images:** *Viola* 'Nellie Britton' **368 Alamy:** Brian & Sophia Fuller: *Pinguicula grandiflora*. **Alpine Garden Society:** *Aquilegia jonesii*. **Eric Crichton Photos:** *Edraianthus pumilio* **369 Eric Crichton Photos:** *Globularia cordifolia*. **GAP Photos:** Neil Holmes: *Polygala calcarea* 'Lillet'. **Garden World Images:** *Cyananthus microphyllus, Townsendia grandiflora* **370 GAP Photos:** Michael Howes: *Gentiana* 'Inverleith', *Gentiana* 'Shot Silk'. **Garden World Images:** *Gentiana sino-ornata;* Jenny Lilly: *Gentiana* 'Soutra'; Lee Thomas: *Gentiana* 'Blue Silk'. **Marianne Majerus Garden Images:** Marianne Majerus: *Gentiana* 'Ettrick', *Gentiana* 'Eugen's Allerbester'. **Muriel Hodgeman:** *Eritrichium nanum*. **Photolibrary:** Sunniva Harte: *Parochetus communis*. **The Garden Collection:** Jonathan Buckley: *Gentiana* 'Strathmore' **371 Garden World Images:** Dave Bevan: *Gunnera magellanica* **373 Eric Crichton Photos:** *Gaultheria procumbens*. **Garden World Images:** *Hippocrepis comosa, Nertera granadensis* **375 Alamy:** Steffen Hauser/ botanikfoto: *Paronychia kapela* subsp. *serpyllifolia;* Organica: *Arabis procurrens* 'Variegata'. **Garden World Images:** *Arctostaphylos uva-ursi* 'Point Reyes' **376 Alpine Garden Society:** *Arctostaphylos uva-ursi* **377 Fernwood Nursery:** *Sempervivum* 'Blood Tip', *Sempervivum* 'Gallivarda', *Sempervivum* 'Gulle Dame', *Sempervivum* 'Kappa', *Sempervivum* 'Rosie', *Sempervivum calcareum* 'Extra'. **Photolibrary:** Frederic Didillon: *Sempervivum calcareum* **378-379 GAP Photos:** Richard Bloom. **379 GAP Photos:** Carole Drake (ftl); Dianna Jazwinski (tl); Clive Nichols (ftr). **380 Corbis:** Clive Nichols (bl). **GAP Photos:** (fcla); FhF Greenmedia (fcl); Virginia Grey (cl); Geoff Kidd (cla). **Getty Images:** Wally Eberhart (bl/tuber). **Marianne Majerus Garden Images:** Marianne Majerus, Goodnestone Park Gardens (br). **382 Alamy:** MBP-Plants: *Fritillaria imperialis* 'Lutea'. **Eric Crichton Photos:** *Fritillaria persica*. **GAP Photos:** Sabina Ruber: *Fritillaria persica* 'Ivory Bells'. **Getty:** Ron Evans: *Allium aflatunense*. **Photolibrary:** Chris Burrows: *Ornithogalum magnum* **383 Alamy:** Michel Foret: *Fritillaria recurva;* Jacky Parker: *Gladiolus murielae* **384 Alamy:** CuboImages srl: *Gladiolus* 'Wine and Roses'. **GAP Photos:** John Glover: *Gladiolus* 'White Prosperity'; Martin Hughes-Jones: *Gladiolus* 'Impressive'; Visions: *Gladiolus* 'Blue Frost', *Gladiolus* 'Columbine', *Gladiolus* 'Her Majesty', *Gladiolus* 'Morning Gold', *Gladiolus* 'Nova Lux', *Gladiolus* 'Nymph', *Gladiolus* 'Oscar', *Gladiolus* 'Purple Flora', *Gladiolus* 'Velvet Eyes'. **Garden World Images:** *Gladiolus* 'Green Woodpecker'. **Getty:** Gerald Majumdar: *Gladiolus* 'Stella'. **Photoshot:** Photos Horticultural: *Gladiolus* 'Sancerre' **385 Alamy:** The National Trust Photolibrary: *Cardiocrinum giganteum*. **GAP Photos:** Carole Drake: *Allium* 'Mount Everest'. **Garden World Images:** *Watsonia meriana;* John Martin: *Allium* 'Mount Everest'. **Marianne Majerus Garden Images:** Marianne Majerus, Rita Streitz: *Polianthes tuberosa* 'The Pearl' **386 Garden World Images:** *Notholirion campanulatum, Watsonia borbonica* **387 Alamy:** Holmes Garden Photos: *Alstroemeria* 'Blushing Bride'. **GAP Photos:** Howard Rice: *Alstroemeria* 'Apollo', *Alstroemeria* 'Moulin Rouge', *Alstroemeria* 'Serenade'; Visions: *Alstroemeria* 'Inca Ice', *Alstroemeria* 'Inca Tropic', *Alstroemeria* 'Tara'. **Garden World Images:** G Harper: *Alstroemeria* 'Friendship'; J Lloyd: *Alstroemeria psittacina;* MAP/A Descat: *Alstroemeria aurea* 'Orange King'; L Thomas: *Alstroemeria* PRINCESS ARIANE, *Alstroemeria* PRINCESS JULIETA. **Science Photo Library (SPL):** Neil Joy: *Alstroemeria* 'Red Beauty'. **Viv Marsh:** *Alstroemeria* 'Elvira' **388 Alamy:** Gig Binder: *Lilium* 'White Heaven'. **Andrew Lawson Photography:** *Lilium* 'Arena', *Lilium* 'Sterling Star'. **Garden World Images:** *Lilium* 'Altari', *Lilium* 'Black Magic', *Lilium* 'Olivia'; G Delacroix: *Lilium* 'Altari'. **Photolibrary:** James Guilliam/ GPL: *Lilium TRIUMPHATOR* Lilium TRIUMPHATOR. **Science Photo Library (SPL):** Ian Gowland: *Lilium* 'Lady Alice'. **The Garden Collection:** Derek Harris: *Lilium* 'Nymph' **389 Alamy:** Chris Burrows/GPL: *Lilium cernuum;* Brian Hoffman: *Lilium* 'Elodie'; The Garden Picture Library: *Lilium cernuum*. **Andrew Lawson Photography:** *Lilium lankongense*. **GAP Photos:** Paul Debois: *Lilium* 'Tiger Woods'; Clive Nichols: *Lilium* 'Miss Lucy'; Visions: *Lilium* 'Star Fighter', *Lilium* 'Sweet Lord'. **Garden World Images:** G. Delacroix: *Lilium* 'Tom Pouce'; N Johnson: *Lilium* 'Netty's Pride'. **GardenPhotos.com:** Graham Rice: *Lilium* 'Sumatra'. **Jerry Harpur:** Cherry Williams: *Lilium* 'Rosita'. **Photolibrary:** Sarah Cuttle/ GPL: *Lilium* 'Black Out' **390 Andrew Lawson Photography:** *Lilium regale* 'Royal Gold', *Lilium rosthornii*. **Garden Library:** *Lilium* 'Roma'. **Garden World Images:** *Lilium* 'Bright Star', G Delacroix: *Lilium* 'Conca d'Or'; Floramedia: *Lilium* 'Boogie Woogie'; John Swithinbank: *Lilium leichtlinii*. **Jerry Harpur:** *Lilium* 'Limelight'. **Photolibrary:** Richard Bloom/GPL: *Lilium Citronella Group* **391 Alamy:** Martin Hughes-Jones: *Lilium* African Queen Group. **Andrew Lawson Photography:** *Lilium* 'Crimson Pixie', *Lilium* 'Karen North', *Lilium pomponium*. **GAP Photos:** Graham Strong: *Lilium* 'Orange Electric'. **Garden Library:** *Lilium* 'Gran Paradiso', *Lilium* 'Red Carpet'. **Picturesmiths Ltd.:** *Lilium* 'Grand Cru' **392 GAP Photos:** Clive Nichols: *Allium atropurpureum;* Clive Nichols, Design: Angel Collins: *Allium* 'Gladiator'. **Photolibrary:** Suzie Gibbons: *Allium* 'Globemaster' **393 Garden World Images:** *Lilium Golden Splendor Group* **394 Alamy:** John Henwood: *Canna* 'Brillant'. **GAP Photos:** Richard Bloom: *Canna* 'Lucifer', *Canna* 'Lucifer'; Sarah Cuttle: *Canna* 'Richard Wallace'; Neil Holmes: *Canna* 'Picasso'. **Garden World Images:** Anthony Baggett: *Canna* 'Louis Cottin', *Canna* x *ehemanii;* Eric Crichton: *Canna* 'Striata'; G. Delacroix: *Canna* 'Ambassadour'. **Marianne Majerus Garden Images:** Marianne Majerus: *Canna* 'Stuttgart'. **Photolibrary:** Mark Bolton: *Canna* 'Durban'; Mark Bolton/ GPL: *Canna* 'Durban'; David Cavagnaro: *Canna* 'Konigin Charlotte', *Canna* 'Konigin Charlotte'. **Reedy Meadow Nursery:** *Canna* 'Wyoming', *Canna* 'Wyoming' **395 Garden World Images:** *Amaryllis belladonna* 'Hathor', *Canna iridiflora, Gladiolus papilio, Zantedeschia* 'Cameo'; Liz Cole: *Zantedeschia* 'Cameo' **396 Alamy:** Holmes Garden Photos: *Dahlia* 'White Moonlight'. **Aylett Nurseries:** *Dahlia* 'White Ballet'. **GAP Photos:** Lucy Griffiths: *Dahlia* 'Eveline'. **Garden World Images:** T Sandell: *Dahlia* 'Café au Lait'. **Peter Stiles Photography:** *Dahlia* 'B. J. Beauty' **397 Alamy:** John Maud: *Dahlia* 'Tiptoe'. **GAP Photos:** Jonathan Buckley: *Dahlia* 'Bishop of Auckland'; Clive Nichols: *Dahlia* 'Carolina Moon'; J S Sira: *Dahlia* 'Gerrie Hoek'; Visions: *Dahlia* 'Karma Choc', *Dahlia* 'Natal', *Dahlia* 'Sorbet'; Visions/Elburg Botanic Media: *Dahlia* 'New Dimension'. **GardenPhotos.com:** Graham Rice: *Dahlia* 'Gallery Art Nouveau'. **Photolibrary:** Ron Evans: *Dahlia* 'Franz Kafka'; Michael Howes: *Dahlia* 'Cornel'; Ellen Rooney: *Dahlia* 'Ruskin Charlotte' **398 Alamy:** RDE Flora: *Dahlia* 'Ellen Huston'. **Eric Crichton Photos:** *Dahlia* 'Comet'. **GAP Photos:** Graham Rice: *Dahlia* 'Happy Single First Love'. **Garden World Images:** T Jennings: *Dahlia* 'Bishop of York'. **P-Pod:** *Dahlia* 'Moonglow'. **Photolibrary:** Richard Surman: *Dahlia* 'Alva's Supreme' **399 Garden World Images:** *Pamianthe peruviana*. **Getty:**

ACKNOWLEDGMENTS

Clive Nichols: *Ornithogalum nutans.* **Trecanna Nursery:** *Bellevalia romana* **400 Alamy:** John Glover: *Tulipa* 'Shirley'. **Eric Crichton Photos:** *Tulipa* 'Purissima'. **GAP Photos:** Visions: *Tulipa* 'Esperanto'. **Garden World Images:** Nathalie Pasquel: *Tulipa* 'Albert Heijn' **401 Alamy:** West Country Images: *Tulipa* 'Ballerina'. **GAP Photos:** Clive Nichols: *Tulipa* 'Abu Hassan'; Visions: *Tulipa* 'Black Hero', *Tulipa* 'Negrita' **403 Alamy:** Organica: *Ixiolirion tataricum*. **GAP Photos:** Clive Nichols: *Anemone coronaria De Caen Group* 'Mister Fokker'; Visions: *Hyacinthus orientalis* 'Blue Jacket' **404 GAP Photos:** Richard Bloom: *Narcissus* 'Fragrant Breeze'. **Photoshot:** Photos Horticultural: *Narcissus* 'Mount Hood' **405 GAP Photos:** Rob Whitworth: *Narcissus* 'Sir Winston Churchill'. **Garden World Images:** Martin Hughes-Jones: *Narcissus* 'Jenny' **407 Alamy:** CuboImages srl: *Ferraria crispa.* **GAP Photos:** J S Sira: *Triteleia ixioides* 'Starlight' **408 Alamy:** Hideo Kurihara: *Habenaria radiata.* **Eric Crichton Photos:** *Ornithogalum thyrsoides.* **Garden World Images:** *Ornithogalum arabicum* **409 Alamy:** Christopher Burrows: *Calochortus superbus;* Plantography: *Eucomis pallidiflora;* The Garden Picture Library: *Tritonia disticha subsp. rubrolucens.* **GAP Photos:** Jonathan Buckley: *Allium schubertii.* **The Garden Collection:** Jonathan Buckley: *Allium neapolitanum Cowanii Group* **410 GAP Photos:** Martin Hughes-Jones: *Crocosmia* 'Severn Sunrise'; Visions Premium: *Crocosmia* 'Honey Angels'. **Marianne Majerus Garden Images:** Andrew Lawson: *Crocosmia* 'Star of the East'; Marianne Majerus: *Crocosmia* 'George Davison'. **Photolibrary:** Mark Bolton: *Crocosmia* 'Solfatare' **411 GAP Photos:** Richard Bloom: *Camassia quamash;* J S Sira: *Roscoea auriculata, Triteleia laxa* 'Koningin Fabiola'. **Photolibrary:** Michele Lamontagne: *Tulbaghia simmleri* **412 GAP Photos:** J S Sira: *Ismene* x *spofforthiae* 'Sulphur Queen'. **Garden World Images:** *Arisaema griffithii, Eucomis bicolor, Ranunculus asiaticus var. flavus* **413 Alamy:** Emmanuel Lattes: *Tigridia pavonia.* **Photos Horticultural:** *Nerine* 'Orion' **414 Garden World Images:** *Eucharis amazonica, Ornithogalum balansae* **415 Alamy:** Jacquie Green: *Hyacinthus orientalis* 'White Pearl'. **International Flower Bulb Centre:** *Iris* 'Natascha'. **Photolibrary:** Howard Rice: *Muscari botryoides* 'Album' **416 Alamy:** Elizabeth Whiting & Associates: *Allium acuminatum;* WoodyStock: *Ornithogalum umbellatum.* **GAP Photos:** John Glover: *Scilla siberica* 'Alba'. **Garden World Images:** *Anemone tschaernjaewii* **417 Alamy:** idp crocus collection: *Crocus chrysanthus* 'Zwanenberg Bronze'. **Garden World Images:** *Crocus* 'Blue Bird', *Crocus* 'Cream Beauty', *Crocus* 'Eyecatcher', *Crocus speciosus* 'Conqueror'. **Pat Brindley:** *Crocus vernus* 'Remembrance'. **Photolibrary:** Howard Rice: *Crocus goulimyi;* Francesca York: *Crocus vernus* 'Queen of the Blues' **418 Alamy:** Bob Gibbons: *Babiana rubrocyanea;* J Marshall - Tribaleye Images: *Sparaxis tricolor.* **GAP Photos:** Visions: *Iris* 'Pixie' **420 Garden World Images:** *Tecophilaea cyanocrocus var. leichtlinii* **421 Alamy:** Holmes Garden Photos: *Puschkinia scilloides var. libanotica.* **Garden World Images:** *Crocus* 'Blue Pearl', *Hyacinthella leucophaea* **422 Garden World Images:** *Allium narcissiflorum, Cyclamen purpurascens, Dipcadi serotinum* **423 Garden World Images:** *Scilla peruviana.* **Photolibrary:** Chris Burrows: *Anomatheca laxa* **424 Alamy:** Neil Overy: *Acis autumnalis.* **Garden World Images:** *Chlidanthus fragrans* **425 Garden World Images:** *Cyclamen graecum* **426 Garden World Images:** *Colchicum autumnale, Cyclamen rohlfsianum* **427 GAP Photos:** Mark Bolton: *Galanthus* 'Hill Poë' **428 GAP Photos:** Richard Bloom: *Cyclamen coum Pewter Group* 'Maurice Dryden'. **Garden World Images:** *Galanthus nivalis* 'Sandersii'. **Getty:** Garden Picture/Photolibrary: *Galanthus woronowii* **429 Garden World Images:** *Lachenalia aloides* 'Nelsonii', *Lachenalia aloides var. quadricolor* **430-431 GAP Photos:** Fiona Lea. **431 GAP Photos:** Pernilla Bergdahl (tl); Jo Whitworth (tr); Mark Bolton (ftr); S&O (ftl). **432 GAP Photos:** (cra). **435 Garden World Images:** *Caltha leptosepala, Hottonia palustris.* **Science Photo Library (SPL):** *Aponogeton distachyos, Stratiotes aloides* **436 GardenPhotos.com:** judywhite: *Filipendula ulmaria* **437 GAP Photos:** Frederic Didillon: *Rodgersia sambucifolia* **438 Corbis:** Markus Botzek: *Nelumbo nucifera.* **Garden World Images:** G. Delacroix: *Filipendula rubra;* M Hughes-Jones: *Cardamine pratensis* Cardamine pratensis. **Photoshot:** Dave Watts: *Cardamine raphanifolia* **439 GardenPhotos.com:** judywhite: *Geum coccineum, Lobelia cardinalis.* **Getty:** John & Barbara Gerlach: *Sarracenia purpurea* Sarracenia purpurea. **Photolibrary:** Claire Takacs: *Iris fulva* **440 Eric Crichton Photos:** *Nymphaea* 'James Brydon' **441 Corbis:** Fred Hirschmann/Science Faction: *Iris setosa.* **Frank Lane Picture Agency (FLPA):** Winfried Wisniewski: *Iris sibirica.* **Garden World Images:** M Hughes-Jones: *Iris ensata.* **GardenPhotos.com:** judywhite: *Myosotis scorpioides* 'Mermaid'. **Photoshot:** Michael Warren: *Lobelia siphilitica.* **Science Photo Library (SPL):** *Pontederia cordata.* **The Garden Collection:** Liz Eddison: *Mimulus ringens* **442 Biophoto Associates:** *Potamogeton crispus.* **Garden World Images:** *Sparganium erectum.* **Photolibrary:** Ulrich Niehoff: *Iris versicolor* **443 Photolibrary:** Fredrik Ehrenstrom: *Myriophyllum verticillatum.* **Photoshot:** Michael Warren: *Peltandra virginica* **444 Alamy:** Arco Images GmbH: *Nymphoides peltata* **445 Frank Lane Picture Agency (FLPA):** Michael Durham: *Mimulus* x *hybrida.* **GAP Photos:** Richard Bloom: *Ligularia* 'Britt Marie Crawford' **446-447 GAP Photos:** Martin Hughes-Jones. **447 GAP Photos:** Lee Avison (tl); Frederic Didillon (ftr); John Glover (ftl); Jo Whitworth (tr). **448 Alamy Images:** Douglas Peebles Photography (bl). **GAP Photos:** Jerry Harpur (r); Visions (cl). **450 Garden World Images:** *Bauhinia variegata, Chorisia speciosa.* **Photolibrary:** Gerry Whitmore: *Brachychiton acerifolius* **451 GAP Photos:** Trevor Nicholson Christie: *Jacaranda mimosifolia* **452 Garden World Images:** *Ficus benghalensis* **453 Garden World Images:** *Sparrmannia africana, Spathodea campanulata.* **Photolibrary:** Ed Reschke: *Calliandra eriophylla* **454 P-Pod:** *Plectranthus fructicosus* 'James' **455 Garden World Images:** *Epacris impressa, Medinilla magnifica;* Sam Tran: *Medinilla magnifica* **456 Garden World Images:** Gilles Delacroix: *Ixora coccinea* **457 Garden World Images:** *Polygala* x *dalmaisiana, Tibouchina urvilleana* **459 Garden World Images:** *Senna corymbosa, Senna didymobotrya* **460 Garden World Images:** *Lophospermum erubescens* **461 Alamy:** The Garden Picture Library: *Mandevilla* x *amabilis* 'Alice du Pont'. **GAP Photos:** Jerry Harpur: *Clytostoma callistegioides.* **Photos Horticultural:** *Agapetes variegata var. macrantha* **462 Eric Crichton Photos:** *Passiflora quadrangularis.* **Garden Picture Library:** *Hardenbergia violacea* 'Happy Wanderer'. **Garden World Images:** *Aristolochia littoralis* **464 Garden World Images:** *Streptosolen jamesonii* **465 Alamy:** blickwinkel: *Episcia dianthiflora.* **Photolibrary:** Chris Burrows: *Streptocarpus* 'Crystal Ice' **467 Alamy:** CuboImages srl: *Paphiopedilum armeniacum.* **Garden World Images:** MAP/Arnaud Descat: *Phragmipedium besseae.* **Photolibrary:** Paroli Galperti: *Paphiopedilum rothschildianum* **469 GAP Photos:** J S Sira: *Tradescantia zebrina.* **Garden World Images:** *Achimenes* 'Little Beauty' **470 Garden World Images:** *Russelia equisetiformis, Sinningia* 'Switzerland'; Gilles Delacroix: *Russelia equisetiformis* **471 Alamy:** CuboImages srl: *Episcia cupreata* **472 Bleddyn Wynn Jones:** *Peliosanthes arisanensis.* **Dibleys Nurseries:** *Saintpaulia* 'Falling Raindrops', *Saintpaulia* 'Powder Keg'. **Garden World Images:** *Browallia speciosa* **473 Alamy:** Steffen Hauser/ botanikfoto: *Hemigraphis repanda.* **GAP Photos:** Lynn Keddie: *Streptocarpus* 'Amanda' **474 Photolibrary:** Georgianna Lane: *Asparagus densiflorus* **476 Garden World Images:** *Impatiens repens* **477 Alamy:** Christopher Burrows: *Roscoea scillifolia;* Tim Gainey: *Costus speciosus;* Inga Spence: *Curcuma petiola.* **Bleddyn Wynn Jones:** *Hedychium stenopetalum.* **Dave Skinner:** *Alpinia hainanensis, Cornukaempferia aurantiflora* 'Jungle Gold', *Curcuma zedoaria, Hedychium thyrsiforme.* **GAP Photos:** Martin Hughes-Jones: *Hedychium yunnanense.* **Marianne Majerus Garden Images:** Marianne Majerus: *Hedychium maximum* **478 Garden World Images:** *Aeschynanthus speciosus* **482 Alamy:** John Glover: *Agave americana* 'Marginata'. **Roy Mottram:** *Agave macroacantha, Agave parrasana, Agave polianthiflora, Agave potatorum* **483 Garden World Images:** J Lilly: *Rebutia* 'Carnival' **484 Roy Mottram:** *Rebutia* 'Jenny' **485 Alamy:** GFC Collection: *Frithia pulchra* **486 Photolibrary:** Harald Lange: *Adenium obesum* **488 Garden World Images:** *Schlumbergera* 'Bristol Beauty' **490 Garden World Images:** *Kalanchoe tomentosa* **493 Roy Mottram:** *Aloe hemmingii* **494 Alamy:** shapencolour: *Mammillaria elongata* **496 Alamy:** John Glover: *Kalanchoe delagoensis.*

All other images © Dorling Kindersley
www.dkimages.com

The publishers would like to thank all those who generously assisted the photographers and provided plants for photography, in particular the curators, directors and staff of the following organizations and those private individuals listed below. Special thanks are due to those at the Royal Botanic Gardens, Kew, and the Royal Horticultural Society's Garden, Wisley, for their invaluable assistance and support.

African Violet Centre, Terrington St Clement, Norfolk; Ken Akers, Great Saling, Essex; Jacques Amand Ltd, Clamphill, Middx; Anmore Exotics, Havant, Hants; David Austin Roses, Albrighton, Shrops; Avon Bulbs, Bradford-on-Avon, Wilts; Ayletts Nurseries, St Albans, Herts; Steven Bailey Ltd, Sway, Hants; Bill Baker, Tidmarsh, Berks; Batsford Arboretum, Moreton-in-Marsh, Glos; Booker Seeds, Sleaford, Lincs; Rupert Bowlby, Reigate, Surrey; Bressingham Gardens, Diss, Norfolk; Roy Brooks, Newent, Glos; British Orchid Growers' Association; Broadleigh Gardens, Somerset; Burford House Gardens, Tenbury Wells, Shrops; Cambridge Bulbs, Newton, Cambs; Nola Carr, Sydney, Australia; Beth Chatto Gardens, Colchester, Essex; Chelsea Physic Garden, London; Colegrave Seeds, Banbury, Oxon; County Park Nurseries, Hornchurch, Essex; Jill Cowley, Chelmsford, Essex; Mrs Anne Dexter, Oxford; Edrom Nurseries, Coldingham, Berwicks; Dr Jack Elliott, Ashford, Kent; Joe Elliott, Broadwell, Glos; Erdigg (National Trust), Clwyd, Wales; Fibrex Nurseries, Pebworth, Warwicks; Fisk's Clematis Nursery, Westleton, Suffolk; Mr & Mrs Thomas Gibson, Westwell, Oxon; Glasgow Botanic Garden, Glasgow; 'Glazenwood', Braintree, Essex. R. Harkness & Co. Ltd, Hitchin, Herts; Harry Hay, Lower Kingswood, Surrey; Hazeldene Nurseries, East Farleigh, Kent; Hidcote Manor (National Trust), Chipping Camden, Glos; Hillier Gardens and Arboretum, Romsey, Hants; Hillier Nurseries (Winchester) Ltd, Romsey, Hants; Holly Gate Cactus Nursery, Ashington, Sussex; Hopleys Plants, Much Hadham, Herts; Huntingdon Botanical Gardens, San Marino, California; W.E.Th. Ingwersen Ltd, East Grinstead, Sussex; the late Clive Innes; Kelways Nurseries, Langport, Somerset; Kiftsgate Court Gardens, Chipping Camden, Glos; Lechlade Fuchsia Centre, Lechlade, Glos; The Living Desert, Palm Desert, California; Robin Loder, Leonardslee, Sussex; Los Angeles State and County Arboreta and Botanical Gardens, Los Angeles, California; Lotusland Foundation, Santa Barbara, California; McBeans Orchids, Lewes, Sussex; Merrist Wood Agricultural College, Worplesdon, Surrey; Mrs J.F. Phillips, Westwell, Oxon; Mr & Mrs Richard Purdon, Ramsden, Oxon; Ramparts Nurseries, Colchester, Essex; Ratcliffe Orchids, Didcot, Oxon; Mrs Joyce Robinson, Denmans, Fontwell, Sussex; Peter Q. Rose, Castle Cary, Somerset; Royal Botanic Garden, Edinburgh; Royal Botanic Gardens, Kew, Surrey; Royal Botanic Gardens, Sydney, Australia; Royal National Rose Society, St Albans, Herts; Royal Horticultural Society's Garden, Wisley, Surrey. Santa Barbara Botanic Garden, Santa Barbara, California; Savill Garden, Windsor, Berks; Mr & Mrs K. Schoenenberger, Shipton-under-Wychwood, Oxon; Mrs Martin Simmons, Burghclere, Berks; Dr James Smart, Barnstaple, Devon; Arthur Smith, Wigston, Leics; P.J. Smith, Ashington, Sussex; Springfields Gardens, Spalding, Lincs; Staite & Sons, Evesham, Worcs; Stapeley Water Gardens, Nantwich, Cheshire; Strybing Arboreta Society of Golden Gate Park, San Francisco, California; David Stuart, Dunbar, East Lothian; Suffolk Herbs, Sudbury, Suffolk; University Botanic Garden, Cambridge; University of British Columbia Botanical Garden, Vancouver; University of California Arboretum, Davis, California; University of California Arboretum, Santa Cruz, California; University of California Botanical Garden, Berkeley, California; University of California Botanical Gardens, Los Angeles, California; University of Reading Botanic Garden, Reading, Berks; Unwins Seeds Ltd, Histon, Cambridge; Jack Vass, Haywards Heath, Sussex; Rosemary Verey, Barnsley, Glos; Vesutor Air Plants, Ashington, Sussex; Wakehurst Place (Royal Botanic Gardens, Kew), Ardingly, Sussex; Primrose Warburg, Oxford; Waterperry Gardens, Wheatley, Oxon; Westonbirt Arboretum, Westonbirt, Glos; Woolman's Nurseries, Dorridge, West Midlands; Wyld Court Orchids, Newbury, Berks; Eric Young Orchid Foundation, Jersey, Channel Islands.

Dorling Kindersley would also like to thank the following for their help with the third North American edition: Malavika Talukder, Eman Chowdhary, Pakshalika Jayaprakash, Sreshtha Bhattacharya, Kanarindhana Kathirvel, Roma Malik, Antara Moitra, Neha Pande, Rupa Rao, Neha Ruth Samuel, Himanshi Sharma, Janashree Singha.

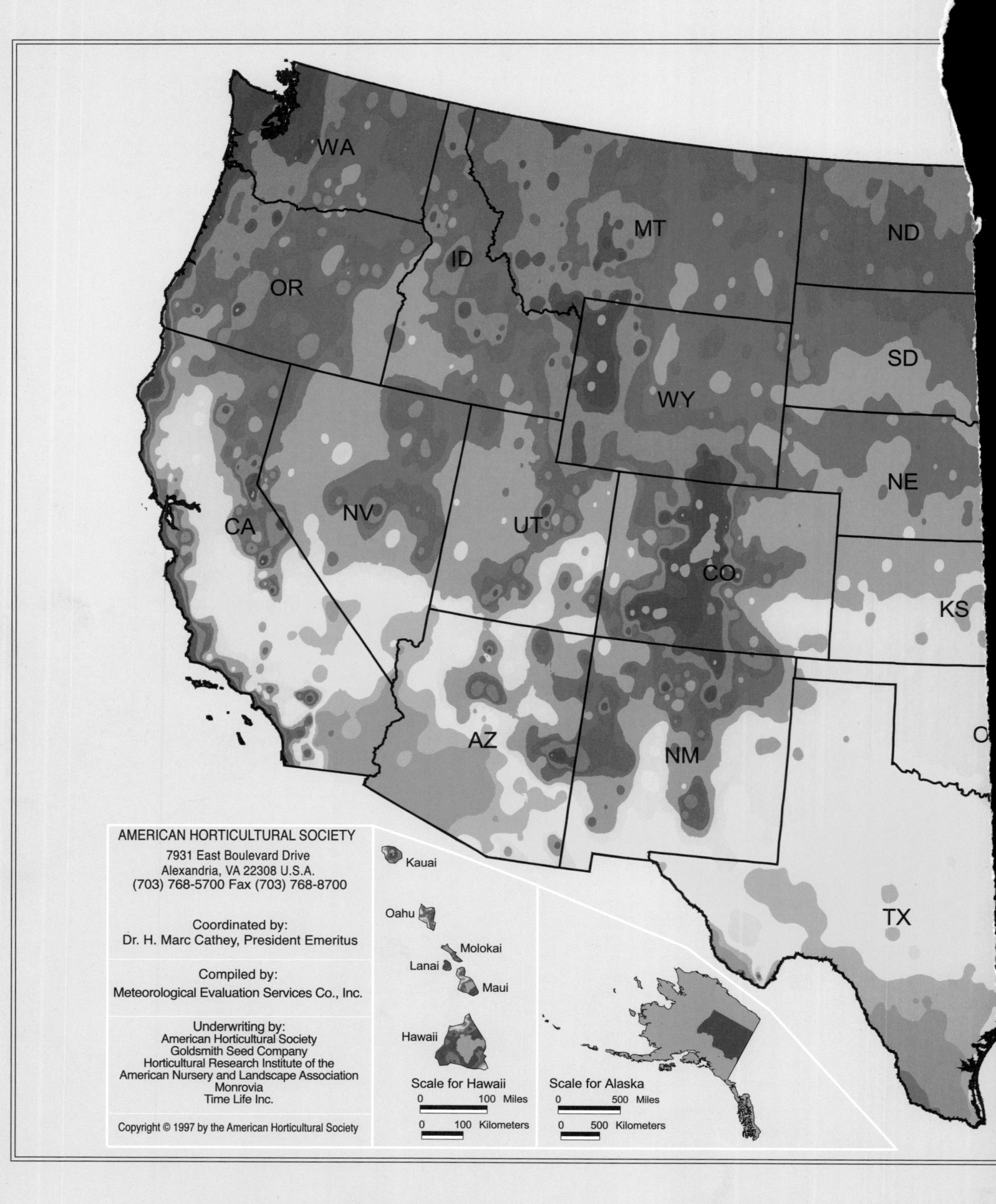

WA

OR

ID

MT

ND

SD

WY

NV

UT

CA

CO

NE

KS

AZ

NM

TX

O

AMERICAN HORTICULTURAL SOCIETY

7931 East Boulevard Drive
Alexandria, VA 22308 U.S.A.
(703) 768-5700 Fax (703) 768-8700

Coordinated by:
Dr. H. Marc Cathey, President Emeritus

Compiled by:
Meteorological Evaluation Services Co., Inc.

Underwriting by:
American Horticultural Society
Goldsmith Seed Company
Horticultural Research Institute of the
American Nursery and Landscape Association
Monrovia
Time Life Inc.

Copyright © 1997 by the American Horticultural Society

Kauai

Oahu

Molokai

Lanai

Maui

Hawaii

Scale for Hawaii

0   100   Miles

0   100   Kilometers

Scale for Alaska

0   500   Miles

0   500   Kilometers